VOLUME 17

Languages

IVES GODDARD

Volume Editor

SMITHSONIAN INSTITUTION

WASHINGTON

1996

For sale by the Superintendent of Documents,
U.S. Government Printing Office, Washington, D.C. 20402.

Library of Congress Cataloging in Publication Data

Handbook of North American Indians.

   Bibliography.
   Includes index.
   CONTENTS:

v. 17. Languages.

   1. Indians of North America.
I. Sturtevant, William C.

E77.H25   970´.004´97   77–17162

Languages Volume Planning Committee

Ives Goddard, Volume Editor

William C. Sturtevant, General Editor

Marianne Mithun, Associate Volume Editor

Mary Haas

Michael Silverstein

Contents

Technical Alphabet

Consonants

		bilabial	labiodental	dental	alveolar	alveopalatal	velar	back velar	glottal
stop	vl	*p*		*t*	*t*		*k*	*q*	*ʔ*
	vd	*b*		*d*	*d*		*g*	*ġ*	
affricate	vl			*θ̂*	*c*	*č*			
	vd			*δ̂*	*ʒ*	*ǰ*			
fricative	vl	*φ*	*f*	*θ*	*s*	*š*	*x*	*x̣*	*h*
	vd	*β*	*v*	*δ*	*z*	*ž*	*γ*	*γ̇*	
nasal	vl	*M*			*N*		*Ṇ*		
	vd	*m*			*n*			*ŋ*	
lateral	vl				*ł*				
	vd				*l*				
semivowel	vl	*W*					*Y*		
	vd	*w*					*y*		

vl = voiceless; vd = voiced

Other symbols include: λ (voiced lateral affricate), ƛ (voiceless lateral affricate), ʕ (voiced pharyngeal fricative), ħ (voiceless pharyngeal fricative), *r* (medial flap, trill, or retroflex approximant). Where in contrast, *r* is a flap and *R* is a continuant.

Vowels

	front	central	back
high	*i (ü)*	*ɨ*	*u (ɨ)*
	ɪ		*ʊ*
mid	*e (ö)*	*ə*	*o*
	ɛ		*ɔ*
		ʌ	
low	*æ*	*a*	*a*

Unparenthesized vowels are unrounded if front or central, and rounded if back; *ü* and *ö* are rounded; *ɨ* is unrounded. The special symbols for lax vowels (*ɪ, ʊ, ɛ, ɔ*) are generally used only where it is necessary to differentiate between tense and lax high or mid vowels. *i* and *a* are used for both central and back vowels, as the two values seldom contrast in a given language.

Modifications indicated for consonants are: glottalization (*ɨ, ḱ,* etc.), fronting (*ç, ʒ̂, x̣, γ̂,* etc.), retroflexion (*ţ*), palatalization (*tʸ, kʸ, nʸ, lʸ*), labialization (*kʷ*), aspiration (*tʰ*), length (*t·*). For vowels: length (*a·*), three-mora length (*a:*), nasalization (*ą*), voicelessness (*A*). The commonest prosodic markings are, for stress: *á* (primary) and *à* (secondary), and for pitch: *á* (high), *à* (low), *â* (falling), and *ǎ* (rising); however, the details of prosodic systems and the uses of accents differ widely from language to language.

For a comparison of phonetic alphabets, see "Introduction," table 4, this volume.

Nontechnical Equivalents

Correct pronunciation, as with any foreign language, requires extensive training and practice, but simplified (incorrect) pronunciations may be obtained by ignoring the diacritics and reading the vowels as in Italian or Spanish and the consonants as in English. For a closer approximation to the pronunciation or to rewrite into a nontechnical transcription the substitutions indicated in the following table may be made.

technical	nontechnical	technical	nontechnical	technical	nontechnical
æ	ae	*M*	mh	*Y*	yh
β	bh	*N*	nh	*ž*	zh
c	ts		ng	*ʒ*	dz
č	ch	*Ṇ*	ngh	*ǰ*	j
δ	dh	*ɔ*	o	*ʔ*	'
ɛ	e	*θ*	th	*ḱ, ṗ, ɨ,* etc.	k', p', t', etc.
γ	gh	*φ*	ph	*a·, e·, k·, s·,* etc.	aa, ee, kk, ss, etc.
ł	lh	*š*	sh	*ą, ę,* etc.	an, en, etc.
λ	dl	*W*	wh	*kʸ, tʸ,* etc.	ky, ty, etc.
ƛ	tlh	*x*	kh	*kʷ*	kw

Transliteration of Russian Cyrillic

А	а	a		І	і [a]	ī		С	с	s		Ъ	ъ [b]	″
Б	б	b		И	й	ĭ		Т	т	t		Ы	ы	y
В	в	v		К	к	k		У	у	u		Ь	ь	′
Г	г	g		Л	л	l		Ф	ф	f		Ѣ	ѣ [a]	i͡e
Д	д	d		М	м	m		Х	х	kh		Э	э	ė
Е	е	e		Н	н	n		Ц	ц	t͡s		Ю	ю	i͡u
Ё	ё	ë		О	о	o		Ч	ч	ch		Я	я	i͡a
Ж	ж	zh		П	п	p		Ш	ш	sh		Ѳ	ѳ [a]	ḟ
З	з	z		Р	р	r		Щ	щ	shch		Ѵ	ѵ [a]	ẏ
И	и	i												

[a]Not in the alphabet adopted in 1918.
[b]Disregarded in final position.

The Library of Congress transliteration of Russian Cyrillic script displayed here has been used in the titles of items in the bibliography and for some names without established spellings in English. The older alphabet has been followed when the sources use it.

Credits and Captions

Credit lines give the source of the illustrations. The numbers that follow are the manuscript or negative numbers of that repository. When the photographer mentioned in the caption is the source of the print reproduced, no credit line appears. "After" means that the *Handbook* illustrators have redrawn, rearranged, or abstracted the illustration from the one in the cited source. All maps and drawings not otherwise credited are by the *Handbook* illustrators. The following abbreviations are used in the credit lines:

Amer.	American
Anthr.	Anthropology, Anthropological
Arch.	Archives
Assoc.	Association
BAE	Bureau of American Ethnology
Co.	County
Coll.	Collection(s)
Dept.	Department
Div.	Division
fol.	folio
Hist.	History
Histl.	Historical
Ind.	Indian
Inst.	Institute
Lib.	Library
Ms.	Manuscript
Mus.	Museum
NAA	National Anthropological Archives
Nat.	Natural
Natl.	National
neg.	Negative
NOAA	National Oceanic and Atmospheric Administration
Prov.	Provincial
Res.	Reservation, Reserve
Soc.	Society
U.	University

Preface

This is the tenth volume to be published of a 20-volume set planned to give an encyclopedic summary of what is known about the prehistory, history, and cultures of the aboriginal peoples of North America who lived north of the urban civilizations of central Mexico. The titles of all the volumes in the series, and their dates of publication, appear on p. *i* here.

This volume is a basic reference work on the Native languages of the continent (north of Middle America), their characteristics and uses, their historical relationships, and the history of research on these languages. Grammatical sketches provide more details on 12 languages, a representative selection from the several hundred Native languages of North America.

Volumes 5-15 of the *Handbook* cover aboriginal cultures and their histories in each of the culture areas of North America (mapped in those volumes). Each of those volumes also includes chapters on the languages of that area, while the chapter describing each culture includes a note on the writing system(s) employed for the relevant language.

Other volumes in the *Handbook* are, like this one, continental in scope. Thus volume 2 contains detailed accounts of the different kinds of Native communities in the late twentieth century and describes their relations with one another and with the surrounding non-Indian societies. Volume 3 gives the environmental and biological backgrounds within which the Native societies developed, summarizes the early and late human biology or physical anthropology of Indians and Eskimos, and surveys the earliest prehistoric cultures. Volume 4 contains details on the history of the relations between Native American and Euro-American societies. Volume 16 is a continent-wide survey of technology and the visual arts. Volumes 18 and 19 are a biographical dictionary. Volume 20 contains an index to the whole series and includes a list of errata found in all preceding volumes.

The first handbook covering these topics was issued by the Smithsonian Institution in two volumes in 1907-1910, entitled *Handbook of American Indians North of Mexico* (Hodge 1907-1910). Subsequent handbooks covered South America in seven volumes (Steward 1946-1959) and Middle America in 16 volumes (Wauchope 1964-1976). By 1965 it was evident that the earlier handbook on North America was badly out of date. An entirely new up-to-date reference encyclopedia on North American Indians was clearly needed. Preliminary discussions on the feasibility of such a work began in what was then the Smithsonian's Office of Anthropology. In the early years, the content and production of all volumes of the *Handbook* were planned, as indicated in the detailed history of the whole *Handbook* given in volume 1. By 1970 an editor for each volume was selected, with Ives Goddard (then on the staff of the Department of Linguistics, Harvard University) assuming the editorship of *Languages*.

The initial planning committee for this volume consisted of Goddard, Mary Haas, and Michael Silverstein. They met in Chicago in November 1970 to prepare a preliminary outline with suggested authors. Twelve chapters on general topics and 14 grammatical sketches were proposed. The Volume Editor began inviting contributors in February 1971, sending each a paragraph outlining the scope of the assigned chapter and a "Guide for Contributors" prepared by the General Editor (which described the general aims and methods of the *Handbook* and the editorial conventions). The first draft manuscript was received in the General Editor's office on May 3, 1972. Over the next few years the outline was somewhat revised, and a few more draft chapters were received. The publication schedule for the whole *Handbook* was then revised, and editorial attention turned to other volumes, which have since been published.

In April 1991 intensive work to complete the *Languages* volume began. Marianne Mithun was invited to join the Planning Committee as associate volume editor and to provide two important new chapters. The outline was revised and improved, although most of the general articles cover the same topics and are written by the same authors as proposed in 1970. Of the 12 grammatical sketches in this volume, five are as originally proposed while seven are of other languages. New manuscripts were received after 1991, and all the chapters then on hand were significantly revised and updated, sometimes with the aid of newly appointed co-authors. As they were received, and especially after 1991, the chapters were reviewed by the Volume

Editor and outside specialists, and usually by committee members Silverstein or Mithun. Extensive changes often resulted.

One manuscript, by a deceased author, was accepted by the Volume Editor on March 20, 1974. The first editorial acceptance of the other final manuscripts was on May 21, 1993, and the last on December 12, 1995. Edited manuscripts were sent from the Washington office for the authors' final approval between January 13, 1995, and March 11, 1996. These dates for all chapters are given in the list of Contributors. Late dates may reflect late invitations as well as late submissions.

Bibliography

All references cited by contributors have been unified in a single list at the end of the volume. Citations within the text, by author, date, and often page, identify the works in this unified list. Wherever possible the *Handbook* Acting Bibliographer, Cesare Marino, has resolved conflicts between citations of different editions, corrected inaccuracies and omissions, and checked direct quotations against the originals. The bibliographic information has been verified by examination of the original work or from standard reliable library catalogs (especially the National Union Catalog, the published catalog of the Harvard Peabody Museum Library, and the OCLC/PRISM on-line catalog). The unified bibliography lists all and only the sources cited in the text of the volume, except personal communications. In the text, "personal communications" to an author are distinguished from personal "communications to editors."

Illustrations

Authors were requested in early 1994 to suggest appropriate illustrations for their chapters. Many responded with excellent suggestions. Locating these and additional photographs and drawings was the responsibility of the Illustrations Researcher, Joanna Cohan Scherer. Maps for some grammatical sketches were drawn by the *Handbook* Cartographer, Terence Arundel, using information from the chapter manuscripts, from the authors, and from other sources. Maps for the chapter "Language and the Culture History of North America" were prepared by Daniel G. Cole, of the Smithsonian Automatic Data Processing office, and by Marcia Bakry, Scientific Illustrator. The large color map was produced by the Maryland Cartographic Division of GeoSystems from data provided by the Volume Editor. Ackoff digitally prepared the charts and diagrams, was responsible for the layout and design of the illustrations, and served as liaison for many of the cartographic services. Captions for illustrations were usually composed by Scherer and Ackoff, and for maps by Arundel. All illustrations, including maps, and all captions, have been approved and sometimes revised by the Volume Editor, the authors of the chapters in which they appear, and the General Editor.

Acknowledgements

During the first few years of this project, the *Handbook* editorial staff in Washington worked on materials for all volumes of the series. Since intensive preparation of this volume began in 1994, especially important contributions were provided by the Editorial Liaison, Paula Cardwell; the Production Manager and Manuscript Editor, Diane Della-Loggia; the Bibliographer, Lorraine H. Jacoby (until 1995); the Researcher and Acting Bibliographer (1995-), Cesare Marino; the Scientific Illustrator, Karen B. Ackoff; the Cartographer, Terence Arundel (1993-1995); the Illustrations Researcher, Joanna Cohan Scherer; the Administrative Specialist, Melvina Jackson; and the Managing Editor, Karla Billups (through 1995). Patricia O. Afable and Peter Yiotis served as bibliographic assistants during the later stages of volume preparation. Valuable technical support was provided to the Acting Bibliographer by Phillip L. Thomas and Lyn Donaldson. Hazel Bobb provided additional typing. The Illustrations Researcher was assisted by Mercy McDonald, Michelle Aasrud, Jennifer Crane, and Joella Wilson as interns while the Scientific Illustrator was assisted with some production by Alexia S. Scott. The index was compiled by Winfield Swanson.

The special linguistic characters appearing in this volume were created by Typo-Repro Service, Inc. of Atlanta using Macromedia Fontographer®.

Beginning in July 1995, Carolyn Rose served as advisor to the editorial staff in addition to her other duties as Deputy Chairman of the Department of Anthropology, National Museum of Natural History.

The Volume Editor would like to thank Patricia O. Afable for research assistance from 1991 to 1995. For reading manuscripts and advice and information on linguistic, historical, and archeological matters, he thanks Robin Beck, Ian W. Brown, Don Burgess, Catherine A. Callaghan, Lyle Campbell, Barry Carlson, Billy L. Cypress, John Dedrick, Scott DeLancey, Rebecca Dobkins, Raymond Fogelson, Michael Fortescue, Patricia Galloway, Victor Golla, David J. Hally, Tammy Hannibal, Paul Hernandez,

Thom Hess, Leanne Hinton, Charles Hudson, Dell H. Hymes, Anna Jacobson, Steven Jacobson, Lawrence Kaplan, Duane H. King, M. Dale Kinkade, Fujiko Kitagawa, Peter J. Knapp, Vernon James Knight, Jr., John Koontz, Michael E. Krauss, Igor Krupnik, Margaret Langdon, Jeffrey Leer, Wayne Leman, Floyd G. Lounsbury, Liana Lupas, Jack Martin, John E. McLaughlin, Sally McLendon, Lynette Renee Melnar, William Merrill, Karin Michelson, Jerald T. Milanich, John D. Nichols, Lynn Nichols, Robert L. Oswalt, Douglas Parks, David Pentland, Thomas Perrin, William Poser, J.V. Powell, Robert L. Rankin, Willem de Reuse, Richard Rhodes, Keren Rice, Bruce Rigsby, David Shaul, William F. Shipley, Shirley K. Silver, Michael Silverstein, Marvin Smith, Dean Snow, Ron Stoltzfus, William C. Sturtevant, Wayne Suttles, Marie Lucie Tarpent, Sandra A. Thompson, H. Trawick Ward, Gregory A. Waselkov, Laurel Watkins, Jim Watters, Anthony C. Woodbury, and John E. Worth.

The following contributors to the volume would like particularly to acknowledge the support of various individuals (in addition to those persons whose contributions are identified in appropriate sections of the text), scholarly institutions, and organizations that helped to make their research possible. Patricia O. Afable thanks Haruo Aoki, Jeffrey Leer, James Kari, Knut Bergsland, Willem de Reuse, Robert Rankin, and John Ritter. Marianne Mithun thanks Irvine Davis, Michael Fortescue, M. Dale Kinkade, Robert Rankin, Keren Rice, Laurel Watkins, and Anthony Woodbury. Osahito Miyaoka thanks Michael E. Krauss, Irene Reed, Anthony C. Woodbury, Steven Jacobson, Jeffrey Leer, and Emiko Hayatsu; the Department of Linguistics, University of Alaska (1967-1969); the Institute of Social, Economic, and Government Research (1968-1969); the Alaska Native Language Center (1973); the Yupik Language Center (1977-1984); and the Japanese Ministry of Education (Monbusho) International Scientific Research Program (1967, 1980, 1982, 1988-1990, 1992). Victor Golla thanks the Survey of California and Other Indian Languages, University of California, Berkeley; and the Hupa Language Program. H.C. Wolfart thanks the University of Manitoba Research Board; the Social Sciences and Humanities Research Council of Canada; the American Philosophical Society; the National Science Foundation; the Studienstiftung des deutschen Volkes; and the Wenner-Gren Foundation. Charlotte Reinholtz thanks the University of Manitoba Research Board; and the Social Sciences and Humanities Research Council of Canada. Sally McLendon thanks the Survey of California and Other Indian Languages, University of California, Berkeley (1959-1964); the Guggenheim Foundation; the National Institute of Mental Health; the National Endowment for the Humanities; and the City University of New York. Wallace L. Chafe thanks Floyd G. Lounsbury and Marianne Mithun. Laurence C. Thompson, M. Terry Thompson, and Steven M. Egesdal thank Aert H. Kuipers, Michael Silverstein, Wayne Suttles, and M. Dale Kinkade; the National Science Foundation; the National Endowment for the Humanities; the Guggenheim Foundation; the Whatcom Museum, Bellingham, Washington; the University of Hawaii; and the Royal British Columbia Museum.

Acknowledgement is due to the Department of Anthropology, National Museum of Natural History, Smithsonian Institution (and to its other curatorial staff), for releasing Sturtevant and Goddard from part of their curatorial and research responsibilities so that they could devote time to editing the *Handbook*.

Preparation and publication of this volume have been supported by federal appropriations made to the Smithsonian Institution.

May 13, 1996   William C. Sturtevant
                                             Ives Goddard

Introduction

IVES GODDARD

This volume surveys the native languages of North America, those spoken by American Indians, Eskimos, and Aleuts. It contains 15 chapters on general topics and 12 grammatical sketches of individual languages.

The term North America is used in the *Handbook of North American Indians* in its anthropological sense, referring to the peoples north of the urban civilizations in central Mexico. The Native peoples of Middle America are surveyed in the *Handbook of Middle American Indians* (Wauchope 1964-1976). As an exception to this repartition, the peoples of Baja California, which are treated in the *Handbook of Middle American Indians*, are not covered in the *Handbook of North American Indians*. Despite this general exclusion of these peoples, because the languages of Baja California have generally figured in classifications of North American languages they are discussed in this volume.

The native languages of North America do not belong to a single family or conform to a single uniform type. For the consideration of general questions in linguistic theory regarding the nature of human language and its varieties, the North American languages take their places among the languages of the rest of the world. In fact these languages are extraordinarily diverse, and concomitantly they attest some types of linguistic organization that are rare elsewhere and whose study has greatly enriched the understanding of the basic principles of language.

In spite of this diversity several factors make it reasonable to treat these languages in a single volume. They are the languages of the peoples of North America, forming the linguistic component of the cultures treated in the *Handbook*. They share similar recent histories, circumstances, and histories of study. And they have faced similar fates as they pass out of use with accelerating speed.

Coverage of Topics

The general topics selected for treatment are those with a substantive linguistic or ethnographic content, or both, that were judged most likely to be of wide interest. Additional chapters on more restricted linguistic topics or with some linguistic content appear in other volumes of the *Handbook*. In particular, each of the areal volumes (5-15) contains one or more general chapters on the languages spoken in the culture area covered in the volume. The ethnographic chapters include orthographic footnotes giving information on the sound system of each language and how it is transcribed. Individual words in native languages may be located by consulting the volume indexes under "Indian words" or "Eskimo and Indian words."

Grammatical Sketches

The languages described in the 12 grammatical sketches were selected to provide a diversity of language types and geographical coverage. No judgments about relative prominence or historical significance were involved. The authors of these sketches use various styles of presentation, sometimes extremely detailed and technical, sometimes less compact and perhaps more accessible to a general readership. In all cases it should be borne in mind that every language is inherently highly complex and to learn anything substantive about it requires a certain amount of intellectual effort. Readers may find that working through one or more of these sketches taking notes will be the most rewarding way to approach them.

Although some attempt was made to standardize aspects of the presentation of the linguistic materials, complete uniformity has not been imposed. For typographical reasons the editors encouraged the use of linear glossing after examples wherever possible, but interlinear glossing, which is easier to follow in more complex cases, has been used in some sketches. The grammatical abbreviations used are listed in table 1, but the particular application of the terms is partly dependent on the specific definitions the terms have in the grammatical terminologies for the individual languages. Abstract phonological representations give the elements making up a word in the abstract shapes they are analyzed to have as separate entities, before the application of phonological rules that adjust these shapes to their particular environment. In most cases these are presented as underlying forms and enclosed in vertical bars (|...|), but in Seneca they are reconstructions (or virtual reconstructions) of Proto–Northern

Table 1. Abbreviations of Grammatical Terms

1, 1st	first person	hab	habitual	pat	patient
1A	first person agent	hort	hortative	perf	perfective
1P	first person patient	hrsy	hearsay evidential	perl	perlative
2, 2d	second person	imm	immediate	pf	perfective
2A	second person agent	imp, imve	imperative	pl	plural, pluralizer
3, 3d	third person	impf, impv	imperfective	poss	possessive, possessor
3R	reflexive third person	inc, incl	inclusive	possib	possibility
A	adverbial-prefix slot	incept	inceptive	pP	nonsingular patient
abl	ablative	inch/inst	inchoative-instrumental	ppf	present perfect
abm	ablative-modalis	incr	stem increment	PR	pronoun
abs	absolutive	ind, indic	indicative	pret	preterit
act	active	indep	independent	priv	privative
ag, agt	agent	instr	instrument, instrumental	prob	probability
ag	agentive (Sahaptin)	inter	interrogative	prox	proximate
all	allative	intr, intrans	intransitive	pst	past
ben, benef	benefactive	inv	inverse	pun, punc	punctual
C	consonant	IPC	indeclinable particle	Q	question
caus	causative	IPV	indeclinable preverb	quan	quantity
ch	changed	iter	iterative	quot	quotative
cj	conjunct	iv	intransitive verb	rec	reciprocal
coin	coincident	loc	locative	red, redup	reduplication
coll	collective	ma	masculine agent	ref, refl, reflex	reflexive
com	comitative	masc	masculine	rel	relational (Cree)
cond	conditional	mid	middle	rel	relative (Yupik, Sahaptin)
connec	connective	mom	momentaneous	S	subject
cont	continuative	mp	masculine patient	S	subject nominal (Sahaptin)
coref	coreference	MpA	masculine plural agent	sbj	subjunctive
csl	cislocative	MpP	masculine plural patient	semel	semelfactive
dat	dative	n, N	noun	sg	singular
del	delayed	NA	animate noun (Cree)	sns	simple noun suffix
desid	desiderative	NA	neuter agent (Seneca)	spec	specific
dim	diminutive	NDA	dependent animate noun	sr	switch reference
dir	direct (Cree)	NDI	dependent inanimate noun	stat	stative
dir	directional (Eastern Pomo)	neg	negative	subj	subject
dir	directive (Seneca)	neut	neuter	subjunc	subjunctive
dir	directive object (Sahaptin)	NI	inanimate noun	subord	subordinate (Shoshone)
dis, dist, distr	distributive	nom	nominalizer (Sahaptin)	subord	subordinative (Yupik)
dist	distal (Bella Coola)	nom	nominative (Sahaptin)	temp	temporal
du	dual, dualic	NP	neuter patient	tloc	translocative
dur	durative	nprox	nonproximal	top	topic
emph	emphatic	O	object	tr, tran	transitive
equal	equalis	O	object nominal (Sahaptin)	trl	translocative
erg	ergative	O	object-marker slot (Hupa)	trns	transitivizer
evid	evidential	O	obviative (Fox)	tv	transitive verb
ex, exc, excl	exclusive	obj	object, objective	V	verb
extent	extentive	obv	obviative	V	vowel
fac	factual	opt	optative	VAI	animate intransitive verb
fp	feminine patient	p	particle	VII	inanimate intransitive verb
fut	future	P	proximate (Fox)	voc	vocative
gen	genitive	pA	plural agent	VTA	transitive animate verb
ger	gerund, gerundive	part	participle, participial	VTI	transitive inanimate verb

NOTES: The abbreviations generally appear without periods in interlinear and formulaic glosses.

For the specific use of the abbreviations and the terminology they represent, which may differ depending on the language, see the explanations in the grammatical sketches.

2

Iroquoian and are given with the conventional asterisk used to mark reconstructed forms. The sketches have detailed tables of contents that can be used as an index to the treatment of topics.

Each sketch is accompanied by a selected vocabulary. These have purposely not been restricted to a single uniform list of words but reflect the particularities of the individual languages and of their speakers' aboriginal and contemporary ways of life. A quick comparison of a few selected words from these vocabularies will make clear the diversity of these languages.

Survival and Extinction

In 1995 there were approximately 209 native North American languages still spoken, perhaps roughly half the number that existed five hundred years earlier. This number is misleading, though, because many of these were spoken by only a handful of elderly speakers, and only 46 were spoken by children (table 2). In other words, nearly 80 percent of the extant native languages of North America were no longer spoken by children and were facing effective extinction within a single lifetime or, in most cases, much sooner. This represents a tremendous loss to the cultural richness and distinctness of the native communities. Because of the diversity and, in some cases, the uncommon nature of the structural patterns of these languages, their precipitous extinction also represents a great potential setback to the development of general theoretical accounts of human language, especially since many of their most unusual and thus most significant features are still incompletely described and imperfectly understood.

Table 2. Status of the Native Languages of North America in 1995

1. *Languages still spoken by significant numbers of children* (46): Alabama, Attikamek, Bearlake, Beaver, Cahitan, Central Alaskan Yupik, Central Siberian Yupik, Central Southern Ojibwa, Cherokee, Chipewyan, Choctaw, Dogrib, East Cree, East Greenlandic, Eastern Canadian Inuit, Eastern Swampy Cree, Guarijío, Hare, Hitchiti, Hopi, Jemez, Kickapoo, Lower Piman, Montagnais, Naskapi, Navajo, Northern Tepehuan, Pame, Plains Cree, Rio Grande Keresan, Saulteaux, Seri, Severn Ojibwa, Sioux, Slavey, Southern Tepehuan, Taos, Tarahumara, Upland Yuman, Upper Piman, Western Apache, Western Canadian Inuit, Western Swampy Cree, West Greenlandic, Woods Cree, Zuni.

2. *Languages spoken by adults but by no or very few children* (91): Acoma-Laguna, Ahtna, Aleut, Arapaho, Arikara, Assiniboine, Babine, Bella Coola, Blackfoot, Caddo, Carrier, Cayuga, Cheyenne, Chickasaw, Chilcotin, Coast Tsimshian, Cocopa, Columbian, Comanche, Comox, Creek, Crow, Eastern Ojibwa, Haida, Haisla, Halkomelem, Heiltsuk-Oowekyala, Hidatsa, Hupa, Ingalik, Jicarilla, Kalispel, Kaska, Kiowa, Koasati (?), Kootenai, Koyukon, Kumeyaay, Kutchin, Kwakiutl, Lillooet, Lower Tanana, Luiseño, Makah, Maliseet-Passamaquoddy, Maricopa, Micmac, Mescalero-Chiricahua, Mitchif, Mohave, Mohawk, Mountain, Nass-Gitksan, Naukanski Yupik, Nez Perce, Nitinaht, Nootka, North Alaskan Inupiaq, Northern Algonquin, Northern Paiute–Bannock, Northern Tutchone, Okanagan, Oneida, Onondaga, Ottawa, Pacific Yupik, Paipai, Picuris, Quechan, Sahaptin, Sauk-Fox, Sekani, Seneca, Seward Peninsula Inupiaq, Shawnee, Shoshone, Shuswap, Southern Tiwa, Southern Tutchone, Stoney, Tahltan, Tanacross, Tanaina, Tewa, Thompson, Tipai, Tlingit, Upper Kuskokwim, Upper Tanana, Ute, Winnebago.

3. *Languages spoken by only a few of the oldest people* (72): Achumawi, Atsugewi, Cahuilla, Central Pomo, Central Sierra Miwok, Chiwere, Clallam, Coeur d'Alene, Copper Island Aleut Creole, Cowlitz, Cupeño, Eastern Abenaki, Eastern Pomo, Eyak, Gashowu, Gros Ventre, Han, Holikachuk, Ipai, Karok, Kashaya, Kawaiisu, Kiksht, Kiliwa, Kings River, Kiowa Apache, Klamath, Konkow, Lake Miwok, Lower Chehalis, Lushootseed, Maidu, Mandan, Menominee, Mono, Munsee Delaware, Nisenan, Northeastern Pomo, Northern Pomo, Northern Sierra Miwok, Northern Straits, Omaha-Ponca, Osage, Panamint, Patwin, Pawnee, Plains Miwok, Potawatomi, Quileute, Quinault, Sarcee, Sechelt, Serrano, Sirenikski, Southeastern Pomo, Southern Pomo, Southern Sierra Miwok, Squamish, Tolowa, Tubatulabal, Tule-Kaweah, Tuscarora, Unami Delaware, Upper Chehalis, Valley Yokuts, Wappo, Washoe, Western Abenaki, Wichita, Wintu-Nomlaki, Yuchi, Yurok.

4. *Extinct languages* (120): Adai, Alsea, Antoniano, Apalachee, Aranama, Awaswas, Barbareño, Bay Miwok, Beothuk, Besawunena, Biloxi, Borjeño, Buena Vista, Cadegomeño, Cahto, Calusa, Carolina Algonquian, Catawba, Cathlamet, Cayuse, Central Kalapuyan, Chalon, Chemakum, Chimariko, Chitimacha, Chochenyo, Coahuilteco, Coast Miwok, Comecrudo, Cotoname, Eastern Atakapa, Eel River, Esselen, Etchemin, Eudeve, Gabrielino, Galice-Applegate, Garza, Guaicura, Hanis, Huron, Ignacieño, Ineseño, Island Chumash, Kansa, Karankawa, Karkin, Kitanemuk, Kitsai, Konomihu, Kwalhioqua-Clatskanie, Laimón, Lipan, Laurentian, Loup, Lower Chinook, Mahican, Mamulique, Maratino, Massachusett-Narragansett, Mattole, Miami-Illinois, Migueleño, Miluk, Mohegan-Pequot, Molala, Monqui-Didiu, Mutsun, Nanticoke-Conoy, Naolan, Natchez, Nawathinehena, New River Shasta, Nicola, Nooksack, Nottoway, Obispeño, Ofo, Okwanuchu, Old Algonquin, Ópata, Palewyami, Pentlatch, Piro, Purisimeño, Quapaw, Quinigua, Quiripi-Unquachog, Ramaytush, Rumsen, Shasta, Siuslaw, Solano, Susquehannock, Tagish, Takelma, Tamyen, Tataviam, Tawasa, Tillamook, Timucua, Tonkawa, Tsetsaut, Tualatin-Yamhill, Tubar, Tunica, Tutelo, Tututni, Twana, Upper Umpqua, Ventureño, Virginia Algonquian, Western Atakapa, Wiyot, Woccon, Yana, Yaquina, Yatasi, Yoncalla, Yuki, and an unknown number of others.

SOURCES: Krauss (1991; Michael Krauss, personal communication 1995), Hinton and Montijo (1994), Grimes (1992).

NOTE: The judgments reflected in this table are subjective and to some extent based on variable criteria, but in general errors are most likely to be on the side of optimism. Languages spoken by children as their native language from birth in at least one community are included in the first category. Languages for which there was not known to be a single person with complete native knowledge in 1995 are in the fourth category, excluding languages for which there are no data.

Classification

Corresponding to their structural variety, the languages of North America are genetically diverse as well. Attempts to classify them into groups of related languages are surveyed in the chapter "The Classification of the Native Languages of North America." A conservative consensus classification based on studies available in 1995 as evaluated by the volume editor is given in table 3 and on the volume map. The sequence in which the families are listed follows as much as possible the sequence of the areal volumes of the *Handbook* and of the chapters within those volumes.

This classification omits proposals for deeper, more inclusive groupings that had not achieved general acceptance among specialists. It also does not give in every case the full detail of the subclassification of languages within families, which is often subject to revision and disagreement. In fact, in some cases specialists debate even the possibility of subclassification. For the Athapaskan branch of Nadene the subclassification given follows one prepared by Keren Rice (communication to editors 1995), but other Athapaskan specialists argue that the overlapping distribution of numerous diagnostic features over the continuum formed by these languages precludes meaningful subclassification into a tree with discrete branches (vol. 6:68). Similar problems are found in other language families.

Names of Languages

A number of languages have been referred to by more than one name or name variant. The choice of the name

---

Table 3. Consensus Classification of the Native Languages of North America

1) ESKIMO-ALEUT
  ESKIMOAN
    SIRENIKSKI-YUPIK
      Sirenikski
      Naukanski Yupik
      Central Siberian Yupik
      Central Alaskan Yupik (Egegik, General Central
        Yupik, Hooper Bay–Chevak, Nunivak, and
        Norton Sound)
      Pacific Yupik (Alutiiq)(Chugach and Koniag)
    INUIT-INUPIAQ
      Seward Peninsula Inupiaq (Bering Strait and
        Qawiaraq)
      North Alaskan Inupiaq (Malimiut and North Slope)
      Western Canadian Inuit (Siglit, Copper, Caribou,
        and Netsilik)
      Eastern Canadian Inuit (Aivilik, South Baffin,
        Tarramiut, North Baffin–Iglulik, Itivimmiut, and
        Labrador)
      West Greenlandic (Standard West Greenlandic and
        Polar Eskimo)
      East Greenlandic
    ALEUT
      Aleut (Western and Eastern)
      Copper Island Aleut Creole
2) ALGIC
  ALGONQUIAN
    Blackfoot
    CREE-MONTAGNAIS
      CREE
        Plains Cree
        Mitchif
        Woods Cree
        Western Swampy Cree
        Eastern Swampy Cree (Eastern Swampy and
         Moose)
        Attikamek

      MONTAGNAIS-NASKAPI
        East Cree (Northern and Southern)
        Naskapi (Fort Chimo and Davis Inlet)
        Montagnais (Pointe Bleue, Escoumains,
         Bersimis, Moisie, and Lower North Shore)
    ARAPAHOAN
      ARAPAHO-GROS VENTRE
        Gros Ventre (Atsina)
        Besawunena
        Arapaho
      Nawathinehena
    Cheyenne
    Menominee
    OJIBWAYAN
      NORTHERN OJIBWA
        Severn Ojibwa
        Northern Algonquin
      SOUTHERN OJIBWA
        Saulteaux
        Central Southern Ojibwa
        Eastern Ojibwa
        Old Algonquin
        Ottawa
        Potawatomi
    SAUK-FOX-KICKAPOO
      Sauk-Fox (Sauk and Mesquakie)
      Kickapoo
    Shawnee
    Miami-Illinois
    EASTERN ALGONQUIAN
      Micmac
      ABENAKIAN
        Maliseet-Passamaquoddy
        Eastern Abenaki (Penobscot, Caniba,
         Arosaguntacook, and Pigwacket)
        Western Abenaki
      Etchemin

SOUTHERN NEW ENGLAND
  Massachusett-Narragansett
  Loup
  Mohegan-Pequot (Mohegan, Pequot, Niantic, and
    Montauk)
  Quiripi-Unquachog
DELAWARAN
  Mahican (Stockbridge and Moravian)
  Munsee Delaware (Munsee and Wappinger)
  Unami Delaware (Northern Unami, Southern
    Unami, and Unalachtigo)
  Nanticoke-Conoy (Nanticoke-Piscataway)
  Virginia Algonquian
  Carolina Algonquian
RITWAN
  Wiyot
  Yurok
3) NADENE
  Tlingit
  ATHAPASKAN-EYAK
    Eyak
    ATHAPASKAN
      SOUTHERN ALASKA
        Ahtna (Lower, Central, Western, and Mentasta)
        Tanaina (Upper Inlet, Lower Inlet, Outer Inlet,
          Lake Iliamna, and Inland)
      CENTRAL ALASKA-YUKON
        KOYUKON-INGALIK
          Ingalik (Yukon and Kuskokwim)
          Holikachuk (Upper Innoko)
          Koyukon (Lower, Central, and Upper)
        TANANA-TUTCHONE
          Upper Kuskokwim (Kolchan)
          TANANA
            Lower Tanana (Minto-Nenana, Chena, and
              Salcha-Goodpaster)
            Tanacross (Healy Lake–Mansfield Lake
              and Tetlin)
            Upper Tanana
          TUTCHONE
            Northern Tutchone
            Southern Tutchone
        KUTCHIN-HAN
          Kutchin (Eastern and Western)
          Han (Eagle and Dawson)
      NORTHWESTERN CANADA
        CORDILLERA
          CENTRAL CORDILLERA
            Tagish
            Tahltan
            Kaska
          SOUTHEASTERN CORDILLERA
            Sekani
            Beaver
        MACKENZIE
          SLAVEY-HARE
            Slavey (Slave)
            Mountain

           Bearlake
           Hare
          Dogrib
         Chipewyan
      CENTRAL BRITISH COLUMBIA
        BABINE-CARRIER
          Babine (Bulkley River [Witsuwit'en] and
            Babine)
          Carrier (Central, Stoney Creek–Prince
            George, and Southern)
        Chilcotin
        Nicola (?)
      Tsetsaut
      Sarcee
      PACIFIC COAST ATHAPASKAN
        Kwalhioqua-Clatskanie (Kwalhioqua [Willapa
          and Suwal] and Clatskanie)
        OREGON ATHAPASKAN
          Upper Umpqua
          Tututni (Tututni–Chasta Costa and Coquille)
          Galice-Applegate
          Tolowa (Chetco and Tolowa)
        CALIFORNIA ATHAPASKAN
          Hupa (Hupa and Chilula-Whilkut)
          Mattole (Mattole and Bear River)
          Eel River (Nongatl, Lassik, Sinkyone, and
           Wailaki)
          Cahto
      APACHEAN
        WESTERN APACHEAN
          Navajo
          Western Apache (Tonto, Cibecue, San Carlos,
           and White Mountain)
          Mescalero-Chiricahua
        EASTERN APACHEAN
          Jicarilla
          Lipan
          Kiowa Apache
4) Haida (Northern [Masset and Alaskan] and Southern
    [Skidegate and Kunghit])
5) WAKASHAN
  KWAKIUTLAN (NORTHERN WAKASHAN)
    Haisla
    Heiltsuk-Oowekyala (Haihais–Bella Bella and
      Oowekeeno)
    Kwakiutl (Kwak'wala)
  NOOTKAN (SOUTHERN WAKASHAN)
    Nootka
    Nitinaht
    Makah
6) CHIMAKUAN
  Chemakum
  Quileute
7) SALISHAN
  Bella Coola
  CENTRAL SALISH
    Comox (Sliammon and Island Comox)
    Pentlatch

Sechelt
Squamish
Halkomelem (Cowichan, Musqueam, and Chilliwack)
Nooksack
Northern Straits (Saanich, Sooke, Songhees, Samish, Lummi, and Semiahmoo)
Clallam
Lushootseed (Northern Lushootseed [Skagit, Sauk-Suiattle, Snohomish, Skykomish] and Southern Lushootseed [Snoqualmie, Duwamish, Puyallup, Nisqually, Sahewamish])
Twana
TSAMOSAN
Quinault
Lower Chehalis
Upper Chehalis (Satsop, Oakville Chehalis, and Tenino Chehalis)
Cowlitz
Tillamook
INTERIOR SALISH
Lillooet
Thompson
Shuswap (Western and Eastern)
Okanagan (Northern Okanagan, Lakes, Colville, Sanpoil-Nespelem, Southern Okanagan, and Methow)
Kalispel (Flathead, Kalispel, and Spokane)
Coeur d'Alene
Columbian (Sinkayuse, Wenatchee, and Chelan)
Proposed Penutian Superfamily (families 8-18):
8) TSIMSHIANIC
Coast Tsimshian (Coast and Southern Tsimshian)
Nass-Gitksan (Nisgha and Gitksan)
9) CHINOOKAN
Lower Chinook
UPPER CHINOOK
Cathlamet
Kiksht (Multnomah-Clackamas and Cascades-Wasco-Wishram)
10) ALSEAN
Alsea
Yaquina
11) Siuslaw (Siuslaw and Lower Umpqua)
12) COOSAN
Hanis
Miluk
13) TAKELMAN
Takelma
KALAPUYAN
Tualatin-Yamhill
Central Kalapuyan (Santiam, Mary's River, and others)
Yoncalla
14) WINTUAN
Wintu-Nomlaki
Patwin (Hill Patwin, River Patwin, and Southern Patwin)
15) MAIDUAN
Maidu
Konkow

Nisenan
16) UTIAN
MIWOKAN
WESTERN MIWOK
Coast Miwok (Bodega and Marin)
Lake Miwok
EASTERN MIWOK
Bay Miwok (Saclan)
Plains Miwok
Northern Sierra Miwok
Central Sierra Miwok
Southern Sierra Miwok
COSTANOAN
NORTHERN COSTANOAN
Karkin
Ramaytush (San Francisco)
Chochenyo (San José)
Tamyen (Santa Clara)
Awaswas (Santa Cruz)
Chalon (Soledad)
SOUTHERN COSTANOAN
Mutsun (San Juan Bautista)
Rumsen (Monterey)
17) YOKUTSAN
Palewyami (Poso Creek)
Buena Vista (Tulamni and Hometwoli)
Tule-Kaweah (Wikchamni and Yawdanchi)
Kings River (Chukaymina, Michahay, Ayticha, and Choynimni)
Gashowu
Valley Yokuts (Southern Valley Yokuts [Wechihit, Nutunutu-Tachi, Chunut, Wo'lasi-Choynok, Koyeti-Yawelmani], Northern Valley Yokuts [Nopchinchi, Merced, Chawchila, Chukchansi, Kechayi-Dumna], Far Northern Valley Yokuts [Yachikumne (Chulamni), Lower San Joaquin, and Lakisamni-Tawalimni])
18) PLATEAU PENUTIAN
Klamath (Klamath and Modoc)
SAHAPTIAN
Sahaptin (Northwest Sahaptin [Klikitat, Yakima, Taitnapam, Mishalpam, Pshwanwapam], Northeast Sahaptin [Walla Walla, Lower Snake, Wanapam, Palouse], and Columbia River Sahaptin [Tygh Valley, Tenino, Celilo, John Day, Rock Creek, Umatilla])
Nez Perce
Molala
Proposed Hokan Superfamily (families 19-28):
19) Karok
20) Chimariko
21) SHASTAN
Shasta
New River Shasta
Okwanuchu
Konomihu
22) PALAIHNIHAN
Achumawi

Atsugewi
23) POMOAN
   Northeastern Pomo
   Southeastern Pomo
   Eastern Pomo
   Northern Pomo
   Central Pomo
   Southern Pomo
   Kashaya (Southwestern Pomo)
24) Yana (Northern Yana, Central Yana, and Yahi)
25) SALINAN
   Antoniano
   Migueleño
26) COCHIMÍ-YUMAN
   YUMAN
      PAI
         Paipai
         Upland Yuman (Havasupai, Walapai, and Yavapai)
      RIVER
         Mohave
         Quechan
         Maricopa (Maricopa, Kavelchadom, and Halchidhoma)
      DELTA-CALIFORNIA
         DIEGUEÑO
            Ipai (Northern Diegueño)
            Kumeyaay (Southern Diegueño)
            Tipai (Mexican Diegueño)
         Cocopa (Cocopa, Halyikwamai, and Kahwan)
      Kiliwa
   COCHIMÍ
      Borjeño
      Ignacieño
      Cadegomeño
      Laimón
      Monqui-Didiu
27) Seri
28) Washoe
29) YUKIAN
   Yuki (Yuki, Coast Yuki, and Huchnom)
   Wappo
30) Esselen
31) CHUMASHAN
   Obispeño
   Purisimeño
   Ineseño
   Barbareño
   Ventureño
   Island Chumash (Cruzeño)
32) UTO-AZTECAN[a]
   NUMIC
      WESTERN NUMIC
         Mono (Monache [Northfork, Wobonuch, Entimbich, Waksachi, and others] and Owens Valley Paiute)
         Northern Paiute–Bannock
      CENTRAL NUMIC
         Panamint
         Shoshone (Western, Northern, and Eastern)
         Comanche

SOUTHERN NUMIC
         Kawaiisu
         Ute (Chemehuevi, Southern Paiute, and Ute)
   Tubatulabal
   TAKIC
      SERRANO-GABRIELINO
         Serrano (Serrano and Vanyume)
         Kitanemuk
         Gabrielino (Gabrielino and Fernandeño)
      CUPAN
         Cahuilla
         Cupeño
         Luiseño (Luiseño and Juaneño)
      Tataviam (?)
   Hopi
   TEPIMAN
      Upper Piman (Pima, Papago [Tohono O'odham], and Névome)
      Lower Piman (Mountain Piman) (Yepachi and Yécora-Maycoba)
      Northern Tepehuan
      Southern Tepehuan (Southern Tepehuan and Tepecano)
   TARACAHITAN
      TARAHUMARAN
         Tarahumara (Western, Ariseachi, Summit, Northern, Central, and Southern)
         Guarijío (Upland and Lowland)
      OPATAN
         Ópata
         Eudeve
      Cahitan (Yaqui and Mayo)
   Tubar
33) KIOWA-TANOAN
   Kiowa
   Jemez (Jemez and Pecos)
   TIWA
      NORTHERN TIWA
         Taos
         Picuris
      Southern Tiwa (Isleta and Sandia)
   Tewa (Rio Grande Tewa [San Juan, Santa Clara, San Ildefonso, Pojoaque, Nambe, and Tesuque] and Tano [Arizona Tewa])
   Piro
34) KERESAN
   Acoma-Laguna (Western Keresan)
   Rio Grande Keresan (Eastern Keresan) (Zia, Santa Ana, San Felipe, Santo Domingo, Cochiti)
35) Zuni
36) Guaicura
37) OTOMANGUEAN[b]
   OTOMIAN
      Pame
38) Coahuilteco
39) COMECRUDAN
   Comecrudo
   Mamulique
   Garza
40) Cotoname

Table 3. Consensus Classification of the Native Languages of North America (continued)

41) Aranama (Aranama-Tamique)
42) Solano
43) Maratino
44) Quinigua
45) Naolan
46) Karankawa
47) Kootenai
48) Cayuse
49) SIOUAN-CATAWBA
 SIOUAN
  MISSOURI RIVER
   Hidatsa
   Crow
  Mandan
  MISSISSIPPI VALLEY
   DAKOTAN
    Sioux (Santee-Sisseton, Yankton-Yanktonai, and
     Teton [Lakhota])
    Assiniboine
    Stoney
   DHEGIHA
    Omaha-Ponca
    Osage
    Kansa
    Quapaw
   CHIWERE-WINNEBAGO
    Chiwere (Otoe, Missouri, and Iowa)
    Winnebago
  OHIO VALLEY (SOUTHEASTERN)
   Ofo
   Biloxi
   Tutelo (Tutelo, Saponi, and Occaneechi)
 CATAWBAN
  Catawba
  Woccon
50) Tonkawa
51) CADDOAN
 NORTHERN CADDOAN
  Arikara
  Pawnee (South Band and Skiri)
  Kitsai
  Wichita

 SOUTHERN CADDOAN
  Caddo
  Yatasi (?)
52) Adai
53) ATAKAPAN
  Western Atakapa (Western Atakapa and Akokisa)
  Eastern Atakapa
54) Chitimacha
55) Tunica
56) MUSKOGEAN
 WESTERN MUSKOGEAN
  Choctaw
  Chickasaw
 CENTRAL MUSKOGEAN
  Hitchiti (Hitchiti and Mikasuki)
  Apalachee
  Alabama
  Koasati
 Creek (Creek and Seminole)
57) Natchez
58) Yuchi
59) TIMUCUAN
 Timucua
 Tawasa
60) Calusa
61) IROQUOIAN
 NORTHERN IROQUOIAN
  Tuscarora
  Nottoway
  Huron (Huron and Wyandot)
  Laurentian (Saint Lawrence Iroquoian)
  Seneca
  Cayuga
  Onondaga
  Susquehannock
  Mohawk
  Oneida
 Cherokee (Southern Iroquoian)
62) Beothuk

SOURCE: "The Classification of the Native Languages of North America," this vol., and references cited there.

NOTES: Language names are in normal type, with synonyms or component dialects given in parentheses. Names of families that contain more than one language are in all capital letters, and those of subfamilies and other intermediate branches are in small capitals. The indentations are determined by the degree of ramification in the subclassification of the families and are not commensurate in time-depth or extent of similarity. One version of the proposed Penutian and Hokan superfamilies is indicated; other proposed deeper groupings are omitted. Some details of subclassification within families are not given. It has not been possible to apply a uniform set of criteria for evaluating whether similar forms of speech are languages or dialects; in some cases the degree of social or political distinctness has been a factor in the decision. Dialects are not indicated for some languages that have dialectal differentiation but for which the demarcation and nomenclature of the dialects has not been established (for California, see vol. 8:89-90). Only languages for which data are known are included.

Queries indicate uncertain placement within families.

[a]Two additional branches of Uto-Aztecan, Corachol (Cora and Huichol) and Aztecan (Nahuatl-Pipil and Pochutec), are outside ethnographic North America.

[b]The other Otomanguean languages are outside ethnographic North America.

to be used for such languages in this volume has depended on the consideration of a number of factors, including consistency with other *Handbook* volumes, appropriateness as a name in English, general and local usage, and the preference of the speakers of the language. Since these criteria conflict in many cases, the names chosen for use here are unavoidably sometimes ones that not everyone would prefer. The desire for consistency has meant that *Handbook* usage has generally been conservative in retaining older designations and spellings in the face of new forms proposed during the period when the different volumes have been appearing. The criterion of suitability as a name in English has tended to disfavor names written in practical orthographies that are simply respellings of familiar names, or that would present typographical problems in ordinary English media, or whose pronunciation as a term in standard nonspecialist English is not established and ostensibly difficult. Also, names of languages that differ from the designations of their speakers have generally been avoided as violating the usual English pattern according to which a language name is identical to the corresponding ethnic adjectival or attributive form. Specific names and their variants and synonyms are often discussed in the synonymy sections of the appropriate chapters in the areal volumes of the *Handbook*.

Mapping of Language Locations

The volume map (in pocket) aims to place the consensus classification on a mapping of the languages at the approximate time of first European contact. Because first contact occurred at widely different times in different areas of the continent, the map incorporates chronological skewing. Since some languages had disappeared or relocated before others were first documented, this skewing is unavoidable if the classification is to appear on a single map. The time periods represented on the map range from the midsixteenth century to the nineteenth century, and in some details to the twentieth century.

The locations of the languages on the map generally follow those given for the corresponding ethnic groups in the areal volumes, particularly as summarized on the individual volume maps. These maps include many compromises, and the present volume map is not intended to specify the exact territories used or claimed by the speakers of the languages. It is intended only to give a reasonable idea of the locations and distributions of the languages at the time of the earliest available usable and appropriate information.

The earliest locations on the map are those in the areas of earliest European contact, beginning in the sixteenth century on the lower Saint Lawrence River and in parts of the Southeast and Southwest. Otherwise the Northeast and the Southeast are shown as they were in the seventeenth century, and the more westerly parts of the continent generally reflect the earliest reliable information in the nineteenth century. Some details in the mapping in northern Mexico reflect twentieth-century information, in cases where the inferences to be drawn about earlier language distribution are uncertain. The languages in the Southwest are mapped in their ancient and continuing twentieth-century locations in the case of most of the Pueblos, otherwise in their earlier ranges, with Piro, Tano (Southern Tewa), and the unknown language of the Ubates being placed where they were before the Pueblo Revolt in 1680 (vol. 9:238–239). The languages of Chukotka, Alaska, the western Canadian arctic, and Greenland are mapped as of approximately 1825, following Burch (1983, 1994; vol. 5:248, 6:285, 557; Ernest S. Burch, Jr., communication to editors 1996; Igor Krupnik, communication to editors 1996), an earlier period than that depicted on the volume and language maps in volumes 5:*ix*, 50 and 6:*ix*, 70–71. The locations shown for these languages have remained generally the same through the twentieth century, though there have been some significant localized population shifts.

In the interior of the Northeast and in parts of the Southeast language shifts and major changes in the locations of languages during the historic period and a lack of early linguistic data account for the extensive blank areas on the map. The blank areas in northern Mexico generally reflect the lack of documentation as the result of early extinction. There were people in most of these areas, but there is no information on their languages, or at least not enough to permit them to be mapped with sufficient certainty. The area shown as blank in the Ohio Valley was depopulated as a consequence of intertribal conflicts in the protohistoric period of the seventeenth century and was later inhabited by peoples who came from outside the area and hence are shown elsewhere on the map. The western part of this area may have had no permanent inhabitants after depopulation in the late prehistoric period (Williams 1990). The Shawnee and the Yuchi were in this region, but their exact locations are unknown and the positions shown for them on the map are convenient guesses; the Shawnee found in Ohio in the historic period had returned there from the refuge areas to which they had dispersed. The Ofo, another refuge group from the Ohio Valley, are mapped in the location where they were found, under the name Monsoupelea, in 1673 (Swanton 1923, 1943; Rankin 1979). Unclassified enclaves could have been added in a few other places on the map to represent undocumented languages whose status and identity are uncertain, such as those of the Ha'anahawunena, an Arapaho band, and of the Tchiwak, a tribe on the high plains in the early nineteenth century.

The Southeast presents the greatest challenges for a map of this kind. Three hundred years of historical information beginning with the Spanish explorers of the early sixteenth century and supported by archeological studies document widespread political and demographic changes including extensive movements of peoples during this period (Hudson and Tesser 1994; M.T. Smith 1987; Hally 1994; Worth 1993, 1995). From the perspective of later information, the Southeast east of the Mississippi appears to be dominated by speakers of Muskogean, Catawban, and Timucuan languages, but there are many difficulties encountered in trying to project linguistic identifications onto the map of earliest locations. There is evidence throughout the historic period of widespread multilingualism and the use of regional lingua francas. Speakers of Muskogean languages expanded their influence over groups that spoke other languages, and Creek and Choctaw in particular displaced the languages of other groups that were absorbed into the Creek and Choctaw confederacies. Mobilian, a form of Choctaw, perhaps pidginized, was spoken widely among non-Muskogean peoples. Catawba was used as a lingua franca by the speakers of numerous distinct languages who ended up in the Carolina Piedmont in the eighteenth century. As a consequence, evidence for the use of one of these languages in a given location in the early period does not guarantee or even necessarily strongly indicate that the local population as a whole did not speak a different language of its own. Accordingly the map restricts these known languages to the locations that their most likely original core speakers are assumed to have inhabited in the earliest historical period. A certain amount could be said about language use in the areas left blank, but the available information and the conclusions of varying degrees of certainty that might be drawn from it cannot readily be represented on a general map. One area known to have been a largely unpopulated buffer zone in the sixteenth century is the Savannah River valley and the interior of western South Carolina. Biloxi is shown in the area where the Biloxi are first reported in 1699, reflecting a later situation than most of the rest of the Southeast. Earlier it must have been spoken somewhere else, presumably referred to by another, as yet unidentified name. The information locating Choctaw in the adjacent Mobile Delta area is also from the same, later period.

In the case of languages for which no reliable data are known, their names (generally the same as the corresponding group names) are placed in parentheses. These are languages that are mentioned in the historical literature as distinct but for which there are either no data or only extremely scanty data of uncertain attribution or validity. If these languages can be classified with some degree of confidence on the basis of nonlinguistic information they are indicated as members of the family they are taken to belong to. In other cases they are left unclassified. There may have been additional undocumented languages in some poorly known areas, for example those assigned to Nanticoke-Conoy and Virginia Algonquian. For the assignment to Uto-Aztecan of Mexican languages for which there are few or no data, Miller (1983; vol. 10:122) has been followed.

Orthography

In order to present Native American languages with the same degree of authority and respect that would be demanded for any language it is necessary to transcribe them accurately, spelling their distinctive sounds in a consistent and fully explicit way. This entails developing for each language a writing system in which there is only one way to write each type of sound that can potentially distinguish words, and in which each such sound is written differently from every other in the language. These distinctive sounds of a language are its phonemes, and such a writing system is a phonemic system. Since phonemes are defined for individual languages each phonemic system is unique, but it is convenient to symbolize the phonemes of different languages in consistent ways, writing similar sounds in all languages with similar letters and symbols as much as possible. This is the goal of phonetic alphabets, which in principle provide a distinct way to write every sound of every language.

Over the years a number of phonetic alphabets have been particularly significant in the study of the native languages of North America. These are given in a comparative table together with the *Handbook* technical alphabet, presented on page *x* of volumes 5-15, and the International Phonetic Alphabet (IPA) (table 4). The aim in the *Handbook* has been to use the *Handbook* technical alphabet as much as possible in the phonemic transcription of languages, with the standard values defined for the technical alphabet providing the specification of the phonetics. Deviations and special uses are explained in the orthographic footnotes, which list the phonemes for each language or refer to where they are described. Where there are established practical alphabets these are described separately.

Despite the existence of standard phonetic alphabets, it should be recognized that there is always a tension between the desire to use a writing system that is as nearly as possible uniform for all languages and the desire to use a writing system adapted to the peculiarities of each language and the preferences of its speakers. This tension inevitably leads to inconsistencies, and indeed phonetic alphabets have generally been promoted only as ideal systems that explicitly allow exceptions and simplifications where warranted by the facts of a particular language.

One type of exception to uniformity in the use of phonetic symbols is inherent in the nature of phonemic systems. A phonetic alphabet like the IPA can in principle aim for the ideal of having a separate symbol for every potentially distinctive sound, but a phonemic alphabet must by definition conform to the peculiarities of the specific language for which it is developed. A phoneme in one particular language often comprises two or more distinct phonetic sounds, each of which may be contrastive and hence belong to separate phonemes in some other language or languages. Sometimes the different phonetic sounds making up a phoneme vary freely, but usually they each occur in different phonetic environments, which may then be said to condition the different sounds. In such cases, the representation of the phoneme in all its occurrences by a single symbol will necessarily violate the goal of writing each physically different sound with a separate symbol. For example the sound spelled with ⟨t⟩ in the English word *stick,* which would be written in a phonetic alphabet as [t], differs from the sound spelled with ⟨t⟩ in *tick,* which includes a following aspiration and would be written phonetically as [tʰ]. The distinct phonetic sounds [t] and [tʰ] are part of the same English phoneme /t/, and in a phonemic transcription they are written with the same phonemic symbol ⟨t⟩. Following the usual practice, the simpler symbol is chosen to represent the phoneme. Since phonemic symbols are used in different ways in different languages, an integral part of the presentation of any phonemic system is the specification of how the phonemes are pronounced in the particular language. In the present case the English phoneme /t/ can be described as ordinarily aspirated (phonetic [tʰ]), but unaspirated (phonetic [t]) after /s/. (Additional conditioned pronunciations of /t/ can be specified for other environments.) English speakers are typically unaware of the distinction between the aspirated and unaspirated pronunciations of their phoneme /t/ and may even deny it, though the physical contrast can easily be observed when a tissue is held near the mouth while pronouncing words that illustrate the contrast, such as *stick* and *tick.* This tendency of the speakers of a language to perceive its phonemes as invariant units is the phenomenon sometimes referred to as the psychological reality of the phoneme. (Note the standard linguistic use of different kinds of brackets: ⟨...⟩ for letters, /.../ for phonemes, and [...] for phonetic symbols.)

A second major source of exceptions to the ideal of the uniform use of symbols in phonemic transcriptions is the desire to simplify the writing of each language as much as possible, as in the use of the letter ⟨t⟩ to write the English phoneme that includes both [t] and [tʰ]. Simple symbols, such as the letters of the familiar alphabet, are usually preferred to complex ones. In the writing of native North American languages this tendency toward the use of simple symbols has been accelerated by the development of practical orthographies, which have been influenced by the desire to use only the letters and symbols found on standard typewriters and keyboards and, in some cases, by the desire to use letters in their familiar English values.

The effect of practical considerations on the development of writing systems is illustrated by the long-established Navajo practical orthography, which, as an exception to the usual practice, is used to write Navajo words in the *Handbook* (vol. 10:489). Navajo has the sounds [t] and [tʰ] roughly as in English, but in Navajo these are contrasting phonemes /t/ and /tʰ/; on the other hand, Navajo has no /d/ phoneme. In Navajo orthography the two available and convenient letters ⟨t⟩ and ⟨d⟩ are redefined to write the two contrasting sounds, ⟨t⟩ being used to write the Navajo phoneme /tʰ/, and ⟨d⟩ being used to write the phoneme /t/. This same convention is followed in the phonemic transcription of all Athapaskan languages in the *Handbook.* Another type of external influence on orthographic choices is illustrated by Seneca. In the transcription of the Northern Iroquoian languages described and used in volume 15, Seneca and the other languages are written in a technical phonemic transcription. In that transcription, Seneca has a phoneme /t/, which is pronounced [t], [tʰ], or [d] depending on the environment; it may occur in the sequence /th/ (pronounced as separate sounds, roughly as in English *meathook).* In contrast, in the "Sketch of Seneca, an Iroquoian Language" (this vol.) ⟨t⟩ and ⟨d⟩ are written depending on their pronunciation, with ⟨t⟩ being written for the /th/ of the technical transcription (to be interpreted as having the aspirated [tʰ] value of English /t/). This newer writing system reflects the perception of bilingual native speakers and their desire to write Seneca sounds the way they are used to writing the English sounds that they perceive to be the same. In fact, for at least some of these speakers the phonemic system of Seneca appears to have been restructured, presumably under the influence of English, and what was the two-phoneme sequence /th/ for earlier speakers has become the unit phoneme /tʰ/. The transcription used in "Sketch of Lakhota, a Siouan Language" adopts some conventions from practical orthographies, writing, for example, ⟨th⟩ for /tʰ/, ⟨tʼ⟩ for /t̓/, ⟨ȟ⟩ for /x/, and ⟨ǧ⟩ for /γ/.

Ordinarily words and sentences written with phonetic symbols do not use capital letters to indicate proper names or the beginning of sentences. When a capital letter is used it has a particular phonetic value different from that of the corresponding lower-case letter, specifically the voiceless counterpart of resonants and vowels. In practical alphabets, on the other hand,

Table 4. Comparison of Phonetic Alphabets

Handbook	Pickering	Cass	Hale	Lepsius	Whitney I	Whitney II	Powell
Stops							
(voiceless)							
p	p	p	p	p	p	p	p
t	t	t	t	t	t	t	t
ḱ[2]				ḱ			
k	k	k	k	k	k	k	k
q				q			
q̓[3]				;			
ʼ				ʼ			
(voiced)							
b	b	b	b	b	b	b	b
d	d	d	d	d	d	d	d
gʸ				ǵ			
g	g	g	g	g	g	g	g
ġ							
Affricates							
(voiceless)							
θ̂							
c	ts, tz[5]	ts, tz[5]		ts, ṭ			
č	tsh	tsh	tç	tš, ṭ; č[6]	ch	c, ch, tsh	tc
λ			tχl				
(voiced)							
δ̂							
ʒ	ds, dz[5]	ds, dz[5]		dz, ḍ			
ǯ	dj, dsh, dzh	dg	dj	dž, ḍ; ǰ[6]	j	j	dj
λ							
Fricatives							
(voiceless)							
φ					ph		
f	f	f	f	f	f	f	f
θ	th	(th)[7]	ϑ	θ, θʼ	th	th	ç
s	s	s	s	s	s	s	s
š	sh		ç	š	sh	sh	c
x	kh	kh	χ	χ, χ̇	kh	kh	q
ẋ			q[9]			qh[10]	
h	h	h	h	h	h	h	h
ḥ				ḥ́			
(voiced)							
β						bh	
v	v	v	v	v	v	v	v
δ	dh	dh	δ	θʼ, δ	dh	dh	¢
z	z	z	z	z	z	z	z
ž	zh	zh	j	ž	zh	zh	j
γ	gh	gh	γ	χ̇, γ	gh	gh	x
γ̇							
Nasals							
(voiceless)							
M							
N							
Ŋ							
(voiced)							
m	m	m	m	m	m	m	m
n	n	n	n	n	n	n	n
n		ng	ŋ	ṅ	ñ	ñ	ñ
ŋ̇							

12

	Boas	AAA	Americanists	IPA	

Stops

(voiceless)

	Boas	AAA	Americanists	IPA
p	p	p		p
t	t	t		t^l
$k^\backslash$	k	ky	k^y	c
k	k	k		k
q	q	q, ḵ		q
$\c{c}$				$\c{c}$
$\textrm{ʔ}$	ε	'	ꞏ, ʔ	ʔ

(voiced)

	Boas	AAA	Americanists	IPA
b	b	b		b
d	d	d		d^l
$g^\backslash$		gy	g^y	ɟ
g	g	g		g
$\dot{g}$	g̣[4]	g̣		G

Affricates

(voiceless)

	Boas	AAA	Americanists	IPA
$\hat{\theta}$		tθ		
c		ts	c	ts
$\check{c}$		tc	č	tʃ, c
λ	L	tł, tʟ	λ	tḷ̊

(voiced)

	Boas	AAA	Americanists	IPA
$\hat{\delta}$		dʊ̃		
$\textrm{ʒ}$		dz	ʒ	dz
$\check{\textrm{ʒ}}$		dj	ǯ	dʒ, ɟ
λ	ʟ̣	dl	λ	dl

Fricatives

(voiceless)

	Boas	AAA	Americanists	IPA
ϕ		f		Φ
f	f	f		f
θ	ȼ[8]	θ		θ
s	s	s		s
$\check{s}$	c	c		ʃ
x	x̣	x		x
$\dot{x}$	x	x̣		χ
h	h	h,		h
$\d{h}$				ħ

(voiced)

	Boas	AAA	Americanists	IPA
β		v		β
v	v	v		v
δ	ç[8]	ʊ̃		ð
z	z	z		z
$\check{z}$	j	j		ʒ
γ	γ	γ		ɣ
$\dot{\gamma}$	γ	γ̣		ʁ

Nasals

(voiceless)

	Boas	AAA	Americanists	IPA
M	m̥	M		m̥, hm
N	n̥	N		n̥, hn
N	ñ̥	Ñ		ŋ̥, hŋ

(voiced)

	Boas	AAA	Americanists	IPA
m	m	m		m
n	n	n		n
ŋ	ñ	ñ	ŋ[11]	ŋ
$\dot{\textrm{ŋ}}$	ṇ̃	ṇ̃		N

Table 4. Comparison of Phonetic Alphabets (continued)

Handbook	Pickering	Cass	Hale	Lepsius	Whitney I	Whitney II	Powell
Semivowels							
(voiceless)							
W							
Y							
(voiced)							
w	w	w	w	w	w	w	w
y	y	y	y	y	y	y	y
Laterals							
(voiceless)							
ł					kl, tkl, tlk[12]		
(voiced)							
l	l	l	l	l	l	l	l
Tap, trill, retroflex approximant							
r	r	r, r̈	r	r, ṙ[13]	r	r, rh[13]	r, ɹ[13]
Vowels							
(front)							
i	i	ee	i, ī	ī	i, ī	i, ī	ĭ
ɪ	i	i	i, ĭ	ĭ	i, ĭ	i, ĭ	i
e	e	aa	e, ē	ẹ̄	e, ē	e, ē	ĕ
ɛ	e	e	e, ĕ	ĕ	e, ĕ	e, ĕ	e
æ		a	a, ă	ĕ̱	a̱	ä	ä
(back)							
u	u	oo	u, ū	ū	u, ū	u, ū	u
ʊ	u	oe	u, ŭ	ŭ	u, ŭ	u, ŭ	ŭ
o	o	oa	o, ō	ọ̄	o, ō	o, ō	o
ŏ		o	o, ŏ	ŏ	o, ŏ	o, ŏ	ŏ
ɔ	aw	au	ɒ	ŏ̱, ō̱	â	â	â
a	a	ar	a, ā	ā̱	a, ā	a, ā	a
(central unrounded)							
ɨ							
ə				ə̥			
ʌ	o, o	u	ʊ, ŭ	ọ̱̆	u̱	û	û
a				ă̱	a, ă	a, ă	
(front rounded)							
ü				ū̱, ŭ̱		ü	ü
ö				ọ̱, ọ̱			û
Aspiration							
pʰ, tʰ				ph, p˙		p˙, t˙	p˙, t˙
Glottalization							
ṗ, ṫ, k̇							b', k'
Labialization							
kʷ							
Length							
aˑ, tˑ; aː[16]	ā			ā	ā[17]	ā	([18])
Nasalization							
ą	ą			ã	aⁿ	aⁿ	aⁿ
Palatalization							
nʸ, lʸ	ly, li; ny, ni			ń, l´		ny, ly	ny, ly
Retroflexion							
ṭ, ç				ṭ, ṇ, ṣ̌			
Voicelessness							
A, N							

	Boas	AAA	Americanists	IPA
Semivowels				
(voiceless)				
W				ʍ
Y				y̥
(voiced)				
w	w	w		w
y	y	y		j
Laterals				
(voiceless)				
ł	ł	ł, L		ł
(voiced)				
l	l	l		l
Retroflex approximant				
r	r	r, ɾ[13]		r, ɹ,[14] ʀ[13]
Vowels				
(front)				
i	i	i, ī		i
ɪ		ɪ, i̯		ɪ, I
e	e	e, ē		e
ɛ		ɛ, e		ɛ
æ		ä, ă		æ
(back)				
u	u	u, ū		u
U		ʊ, u		ɷ, U
o	o	o, ō		o
ŏ		ɔ, o		o, ɔ
ɔ	â	ω		ɔ
a	a	a		a (front)
(nonfront unrounded)				
ɨ		ï		ɨ, ɯ
ə	E	ə		ə
ʌ		α, ȧ		ʌ
a				ɑ (back)
(front rounded)				
ü	ü	ü		y
ö	ö	ö		ø
Aspiration				
	pʿ	pʿ, pʰ		pʿ, pʰ
Glottalization				
	p!	p'	p'	p'
Labialization				
		kw, k_w	pʷ	kw; kʷ[15]
Length				
		ā[18]	aˑ, a:[16]	a:
Nasalization				
	aⁿ	ą, ę		ã, ẽ
Palatalization				
		ny, n_y	pʸ	ɲ, nj[19]; tʲ[15]
Retroflexion				
				(²⁰)
Voicelessness				
		N, R		ɽ

Table 4. Comparison of Phonetic Alphabets (continued)

SOURCES: Pickering (1820), Cass (1821-1821a), Hale (1846), Lepsius (1855, 1863), Whitney I: William Dwight Whitney in Gibbs (1861), Whitney II: Powell (1877), Powell (1880), Boas (1911), AAA: Boas et al. (1916), Americanists: Herzog et al. (1934), International Phonetic Association (1949, 1989).

NOTES: This table compares how most of the significant sounds used in North American languages are written in several important phonetic alphabets. It is not a complete summary of these alphabets and in particular is not intended to include all notations for non-contrastive phonetic detail. The individual symbols are named and discussed by Pullum and Ladusaw (1986).

The early alphabets generally do not distinguish clearly between vowel tensing (raising) and vowel length. In these cases the comparative table equates tense with long vowels, and lax with short.

Pickering (1820:14) suggested printing a small letter over a vowel to indicate a change in height or rounding.

Lepsius (1855:44) treats affricates as consonant clusters but also provides unit symbols that can be used if an affricate results historically from a single sound or is represented by a single alphabetical sign. Boas (1911) and the AAA committee (Boas et al. 1916:6) regarded affricates as sequences of stops and spirants. The IPA writes affricates as digraphs but provides for indicating that they are units.

Powell (1880:15, 16) recommended the use of inverted letters for unusual sounds not covered by his orthography; in handwriting the letters to be inverted were indicated by an ⟨x⟩ written underneath.

[1] Lepsius (1855) provides for distinguishing between dentals ⟨t, d, n⟩ and alveolars ⟨t̠ d̠ n̠⟩.

[2] Voiceless fronted velar stop.

[3] When ⟨ˁ⟩ is used for a pharyngeal resonant (as in Thompson), ⟨ˁ̓⟩ is used for the pharyngeal stop.

[4] Misprinted ⟨g⟩ in the table but used in the sketches (Boas 1911:23, 429).

[5] Pickering and Cass do not clearly distinguish between [c] and [ʒ].

[6] The symbols following the semicolon are introduced in Lepsius (1863:10, 77).

[7] Wrongly exemplified by English *there*.

[8] Probably ⟨ç⟩ and ⟨¢⟩ were reversed in Boas's (1911:23) table, since elsewhere he used ⟨¢⟩ for the voiced fricative (Boas and Swanton 1911:881, 883), agreeing with Powell (1880).

[9] "A very harsh guttural, pronounced deep in the throat" (Hale 1846:ix).

[10] ⟨qh⟩ appears in the table but is misprinted ⟨gh⟩ in the text (Powell 1877:5-6).

[11] The use of Greek eta in the value [ŋ] is not a misprint, as Pullum and Ladusaw (1986:104) believed; this symbol was subsequently used in C.F. Voegelin's (1935:60) Tubatulabal grammar.

[12] For "the clucks occurring in Chinook, &c., ... according to their analysis" (Whitney in Gibbs 1861:19).

[13] Uvular trill.

[14] Retroflex approximant; several *r*-forms are provided for in the IPA, with the proviso that ⟨r⟩ can be substituted if there is no contrast.

[15] Superscripts introduced in International Phonetic Association (1989).

[16] Extra long.

[17] Whitney (in Gibbs 1861:18) suggested writing a syllable separately if its vowel was long, and joining it to the next syllable if the vowel was short.

[18] Powell (1880:15) and the AAA committee (Boas et al. 1916:7) proposed to mark expressive vowel length with +.

[19] A palatalized consonant may be marked in the IPA by a superior dot, a left hook attached beneath, a digraph with ⟨j⟩, or in some cases a special unitary symbol.

[20] The IPA uses special unitary symbols for retroflex consonants.

---

as in the transcriptions of Navajo and Lakhota, capitalization is used as in English. In addition, in the citation of Lakhota forms, word-final capital ⟨A⟩ and ⟨A̧⟩ are used as diacritics to mark classes of words that show certain patterns of vowel alternation. Thus in Lakhota words capital ⟨A⟩ has two values, neither of which is the standard value of ⟨A⟩ in the *Handbook* technical alphabet.

As far as possible, words in a given language are cited in the same transcription throughout the *Handbook*. Despite this ideal, it has not been practicable to obtain normalized phonemicizations of all the examples cited in this volume, and some appear as they are in the sources, or with only partial normalization.

The Description of the Native Languages of North America Before Boas

IVES GODDARD

From the time of first European contact to the emergence of modern, scientific linguistics at the end of the nineteenth century, the native languages of North America were described by numerous observers with a variety of backgrounds and interests. These early descriptions, sometimes unfairly denigrated as merely prescientific, preserve important information on many languages and dialects. A number of them show deep insights into the workings of the languages and lay the foundation for later studies.

From the beginning visitors who came into contact with American Indians recorded individual words and word lists. All early recorders struggled with the problem of writing unfamiliar sounds with the imprecise alphabets of standard European languages. This problem of phonetic accuracy remained until a comprehensive scientific understanding of phonetics emerged, beginning in the last third of the nineteenth century. Before there was a general science of phonetics, students of language had no way of accurately describing and hence understanding how sounds were produced by the organs of speech, and hence even when an observer learned to recognize a new sound there was no way of defining a new phonetic symbol for it or of otherwise communicating clearly to others the nature of the sound. There was thus little effective cumulative knowledge about the sounds used in the languages of the world. This situation did not change until after European and American scholars studied the linguistic treatises of ancient India and learned from them how to describe the production of various kinds of sounds. A pioneer in this work was William Dwight Whitney (1862; Silverstein 1971:215-248), who showed that the ancient Hindu grammarians had a better understanding of phonetics than the best European phoneticians of the mid-nineteenth century. It was several decades after Whitney's (1862) paper before scholars understood how all the sounds to be found in Native American languages were produced and could be written, and even then many who wrote down these languages proved unable to apply this knowledge consistently and recorded them imperfectly. Imperfect phonetic recordings were more than a minor blemish or inconvenience; they obscured the correct shape of words and elements and thus made it impossible to give accurate accounts of morphology (word formation and inflection). Early grammars thus often used the descriptive technique of presenting grammar by citing the varying shapes of whole words, without detailed analysis of all the constituent parts.

The earliest recordings of New World vocabulary by Europeans were the individual words noted by Christopher Columbus in his journal of 1492-1493 (Tuttle 1976:596), setting aside the four putative Eskimo names in *Erik the Red's Saga* (G. Jones 1964:186; Thalbitzer 1913). In the early sixteenth century Spanish expeditions to the Southeast recorded some ethnic, local, and personal names, which have been used to postulate routes of exploration and language distributions (Swanton 1939: 47-61; Booker, Hudson, and Rankin 1992). Fewer than a dozen words of Calusa are preserved in the 1575 account of Escalante Fontaneda (1944), who had been a captive in south Florida. The earliest systematically collected linguistic data from North America were in the vocabularies of Saint Lawrence Iroquoian published in 1545 that had been recorded from Indians captured by Jacques Cartier in 1534 and 1535 (Biggar 1924:57, 63, 80-81, 241-246; vol. 15:335). Barbeau (1949:226-228, 1961: 220-222) conjectured that the words were taken down in France by François Rabelais. They come from a population that had disappeared by the time of French settlement on the Saint Lawrence in the seventeenth century and appear to be from several distinct Northern Iroquoian languages (Mithun 1982a). The earliest known description of a North American language was a grammar of Guale written by the Spanish Jesuit missionary Domingo Agustín Váez after 1565; but all trace of it has been lost, and the identity of this language, spoken on the coast of Georgia, remains uncertain (Rogel 1861; Swanton 1946:135-136; Lanning 1935: 11; Sturtevant 1994). A vocabulary of a language spoken on the sea islands in the same area, unidentified but presumably Guale, was collected by René Laudonnière in 1562 but never published (Laudonnière 1853:29; Brinton 1870:303). A few words recorded on the California coast by Francis Drake in 1579 can be identified as Coast Miwok (Heizer 1947, 1974).

The first known systematic record of an Algonquian language was made by Thomas Harriot, a member of Walter Raleigh's 1585-1586 English colony in North Carolina. His general account contains a number of words of Carolina Algonquian, mostly botanical terms, in addition to place- and personal names (Harriot 1588, 1972; Quinn 1955:35-40, 314-387; Hakluyt 1965:748-760), and he also contributed the names of birds and fishes to John White's drawings (Swanton 1934; Hulton and Quinn 1964). James A. Geary conveniently gathered the corpus of 82 words (in Quinn 1955:884-900), but his analyses are not reliable; an additional two-word phrase is in Quinn (1970:273). Harriot had an uncertain amount of other materials on Carolina Algonquian, perhaps including a dictionary, but these have not survived. He developed a phonetic alphabet to write the Indian language, though known examples contain no Indian words (Quinn 1955:389; Salmon 1992). Tantalizingly he describes two of his vowel symbols as found only in Indian words and having values that could only be given orally. The only other record of Carolina Algonquian is a small early eighteenth-century word list by John Lawson (1709:225-230; Pollard 1894:14), the surveyor-general of North Carolina, who called it Pampticough (the place-name that is now Pamlico). The earliest recording of any Algonquian was a three- or four-word phrase of uncertain analysis and meaning shouted by some Micmacs to members of Cartier's 1534 expedition (Bigger 1924:50).

The first information on an Eskimoan language was a vocabulary of 17 words recorded by Christopher Hall on Martin Frobisher's expedition of 1576 to Baffin Island and published by Richard Hakluyt (1589:622, 1599-1600, 2:32, 1965:622; Stefánsson and McCaskill 1938, 1:154, 2:233-236; Dorais 1993:37-41). A 40-word vocabulary included in the account of John Davis's second voyage of 1586 presents considerably more problems of interpretation (Hakluyt 1589:783, 1965:783, 967; Dorais 1993:37-41).

Seventeenth Century

In the seventeenth century increased contacts and European settlements along the East coast led to a great increase in the amount of linguistic material obtained. The earliest surviving grammar written of any language of North America was a description of Timucua by Francisco Pareja, a Spanish Franciscan missionary who arrived in Florida in 1595 (Milanich and Sturtevant 1972:6-20). Printing was begun in Mexico in 1614 but not completed, and the work was unknown until the 1880s (Pareja 1886). The writing system devised by Pareja included some deviations from Spanish conventions designed to make the pronunciation more self-evident (Granberry 1956:103-104, 1990, 1993). Many Timucuas, both men and women, learned to read and write using Pareja's books, and at least two official letters in Timucua survive. Pareja also composed a bilingual Spanish and Timucua catechism and confessional,

the earliest known examples of connected text in a native North American language. Pareja's successor, Gregorio de Movilla, produced additional religious translations in Timucua.

Native literacy in Apalachee, which must reflect at least some study of the language by the Spanish missionaries, is attested by an Apalachee letter sent to the king of Spain in 1688 (Buckingham Smith 1860; Kimball 1987, 1988). The orthography writes preconsonantal /h/ with ⟨h⟩ and indicates /ł/ as ⟨lz⟩.

The most extensive record from the Virginia colony was the word list of Virginia Algonquian compiled by William Strachey from his own knowledge and other sources. It survives in two slightly differing copies (Wright and Freund 1953:174-207), whose philological problems have been addressed by Geary (in Wright and Freund 1953:208-214), Harrington (1955), and Siebert (1975), and totals about 800 discrete entries. Capt. John Smith's vocabulary of 65 words published in 1612 includes also 11 sentences (Barbour 1969:331-334, 1972), but these are actually in a form of pidgin, which lacks the inflections and syntactic complexities of a true Algonquian language. Some fragmentary notations dating from a slightly later time and perhaps of a different dialect are also known (Barbour 1976).

The English Jesuit Andrew White worked with Piscataway and Patuxent Indians in Maryland and wrote a grammar, vocabulary, and catechism for Piscataway (Conoy) after 1634 (Pilling 1891:525-526). All that is known to survive of this work is a copy White made of some of his translated Roman Catholic prayers on the endpapers of a priests' handbook (White 1640; Barringer et al. 1976; vol. 15:73). These show some pidgin features as well as rudimentary Algonquian inflectional morphology. A number of unsuccessful attempts have been made to locate White's Piscataway catechism in the Jesuit archives in Rome (Kenny 1961:31-33).

The pidgin Algonquian in the materials of John Smith and Andrew White has parallels along the East coast. In several areas pidginized forms of the local Algonquian language came into use between Indians and Europeans, and it was sometimes these that were recorded rather than the authentic local languages (Goddard 1977:41). The best attested of these pidgins is Pidgin Delaware, the language represented in all putative documentations of the Delaware language from New Sweden to New Netherland before the work of the Moravian missionaries in the eighteenth century (Goddard 1995, 1996). Pidgin Delaware was best documented by a vocabulary and a translation of the Lutheran catechism by the Swedish missionary Johannes Campanius, who served in New Sweden from 1642 to 1648 (Campanius 1696, 1937, 1938). Although providing no information on the inflections and syntax of true Delaware, Campanius's word list affords a good documentation of basic vocabulary, especially concrete nouns. Campanius was able to achieve a level of phonetic accuracy in the recording of Delaware long vowels and consonants that was not equaled until the twentieth century owing to the established use of doubled letters to indicate similar sounds in Swedish orthography. Other sources of Pidgin Delaware were a word list from the Delaware River (De Laet 1633:75, 1909:58-60), a 1681 New Jersey trader's vocabulary called "The Indian Interpreter" (Anonymous 1684; Nelson 1894:133-139; Prince 1912; Thomason 1980), a few lines of dialogue and some numbers given by a settler in a description of New Jersey (Thomas 1698, 1:47, 2:7-13, 1848), a few words included in a 1683 letter by William Penn, the proprietor of the Pennsylvania colony (Penn 1912; Myers 1937:26-28), and other, scattered attestations. The writers on Pidgin Delaware give no indication that they knew that it was substantially different from the real Delaware language, though other contemporary observers were well aware of this fact (Jonas Michaëlius in Jameson 1909:128).

Another substantial body of Pidgin Algonquian from the East coast is in the Quiripi Catechism written by Abraham Pierson, who was minister of the church in Branford, Connecticut (1658, 1873). Although this uses some correct inflectional forms, such as simple plurals, the words are strung together in unidiomatic constructions. James Noyes collected a vocabulary of Pequot near Stonington, Connecticut, after 1669 (Levine and Bonvillain 1980:52-53).

The closely similar Narragansett and Massachusett languages of southeastern New England were well documented in the seventeenth century. William Wood of Lynn, Massachusetts, appended a vocabulary of 275 Massachusett words to his 1634 report on the colony (Wood 1977:117-124; Aubin 1978). Roger Williams, a minister and trader and the founder of the settlement of Providence, published a topically arranged vocabulary and phrase book of Narragansett, which described many aspects of Indian life and provided extensive basic and culturally important vocabulary (Williams 1643, 1936; Goddard 1981). Williams wrote his book from memory during a sea voyage from New Amsterdam to England to obtain a charter for the colonies of Providence Plantations and Rhode Island, in order not to forget the language during his absence. He shows an extensive knowledge of vocabulary and a fair control of the basic grammar, but his idiomatic usage breaks down outside the commonest everyday expressions, as when he tries to write dialogues on Christian doctrine.

The Congregationalist minister John Eliot began the study of Massachusett about 1643 as part of a missionary effort and completed a translation of the whole Bible in 1663, working with Job Nesutan and other native speakers. He wrote a grammatical sketch that surveyed the sounds, major grammatical categories, and derivational processes of the language and gave extensive verbal paradigms, which he learned by systematic elicitation (Eliot 1666, 1822, 1822a). Eliot, who had acquired at Jesus College, Cambridge, the best linguistic training available in England at the time, clearly recognized the differences between Massachusett and the familiar languages of the Old World and presented an analysis of its grammar on its own terms. His Massachusett alphabet provided for all the phonemes of the language, though with some redundancy and inconsistency; it included a special o-o digraph (⟨ꝏ⟩) for the sound [ū] (distinguished from the disyllabic sequence ⟨oo⟩) and used the circumflex accent (⟨ô⟩) to indicate the unique nasalized vowel [ą]. His translation is highly accurate in its use of the complex inflections of Massachusett, though generally following his English model too literally. He also produced a catechism, a logic primer, a translation of the Book of Genesis with interlinear English, and translations of religious materials (Eliot 1655, 1669, 1672; Eames 1890; Pilling 1891:127-184; Miner 1974).

The documentation of the languages of New England had actually begun before settlement, the earliest being a vocabulary taken down on the Saint George River of Maine in 1605 by James Rosier and first published in 1625 (Quinn and Quinn 1983:310-311). Although clearly Eastern Algonquian, the specific language represented is uncertain. Some words are unidentified, and those that are dialectally distinctive in some cases match Eastern Abenaki and in other cases Maliseet-Passamaquoddy (Siebert 1943:506).

It is possible that Rosier's word list is of the extinct coastal language called Etchemin ("Etechemin") by Marc Lescarbot in 1609 and described as spoken between the Kennebec and Saint John rivers (Lescarbot 1907-1914, 2:277, 3:114; vol. 15:70-71). Lescarbot recorded only the numbers from 'one' to 'ten', probably on the Saint John or the Saint Croix River in 1607, but these are enough to document the existence of an Eastern Algonquian language different from any known later.

Lescarbot also published a Micmac vocabulary of 99 entries in 1611 (Lescarbot 1907-1914, 3:117-120, 366-367). This contains some words from the Basque-Micmac pidgin used on the North Atlantic coast (Bakker 1989), and the numbers 'one' to 'ten' that he published as Micmac ("Souriquois"), first in 1609, are actually Maliseet-Passamaquoddy.

Most of the early linguistic work in New France was by Jesuit and Recollect missionaries (Hanzeli 1969). Much of the surviving work from the early period remained in manuscript in the 1990s, and the detailed history of the working out of the analysis of Algonquian grammar remained untraced. The linguistic historian's task is complicated by the missionaries' practice of copying manuscripts as a way of learning Indian languages and acquiring personal reference works, the result being that the writer of a surviving manuscript is often not the primary author of its contents. The French work on Algonquian languages must be seen as a cumulative endeavor, ultimately extending over three centuries, with later authors drawing on the work of a long line of major and minor predecessors.

The first printed record of Montagnais was a translation of several prayers by the Jesuit Énemond Massé (Champlain 1632:16-20). Paul Le Jeune described some of the features of Montagnais for a general audience in 1634, emphasizing and illustrating the richness of vocabulary and the agreement of verbs with various categories of objects (JR 7:20-33; Cowan 1983). He noted the existence of the two Algonquian genders, which he called animate and inanimate, and observed that the animate includes some things that have no souls, as apples and tobacco. Le Jeune translated some prayers into Montagnais and compiled a preliminary or partial dictionary, which is lost (JR 5:174-175, 188-189, 7:152-156; Cooter and Simard in Silvy 1974:xii-xiii). The work of Le Jeune, François de Crespieul, and others presumably underlies the two Montagnais dictionaries that do survive from the seventeenth century to document the collective scholarship of the Jesuit linguists, a fuller one by Bonaventure Fabvre (1970) and an abridged and somewhat more standardized one by Antoine Silvy (1974).

The most extensive linguistic documentation by the French was of Algonquin (the dialect of the Ottawa River valley as spoken in the missions along the Saint Lawrence) and Ottawa (of the missions on the upper Great Lakes). The Algonquin studied in the early period was a variety of Eastern Ojibwa sometimes called Old Algonquin, which went out of use by the middle of the nineteenth century and is distinct from the dialects called Algonquin in the twentieth century (Cuoq 1872; vol. 6:56-58; vol. 15:792).

The early French missionary linguists recognized that the French and Latin alphabets were inadequate for noting all the distinctions in sounds that they encountered in the Indian languages, but although they developed some innovative transcriptional conventions, they never completely solved the problem of accurate transcription. In Algonquin they had no consistent way to distinguish long from short vowels, or fortis stops (geminate or preaspirated) from lenis. In rare cases a contrast of vowel length having a grammatical function was marked with an ad hoc notation, such as by distinguishing *a* and *a·* as ⟨a⟩ and ⟨á⟩, ⟨ă⟩ and ⟨á⟩ (or ⟨à⟩), or even ⟨e⟩ and ⟨a⟩ (Hanzeli 1969:75, 108-109). The Greek omicron-upsilon diagraph ⟨ȣ⟩ was generally adopted as a substitute for French ⟨ou⟩ after being introduced by Jean de Brébœuf for Huron in 1636 (Hanzeli 1969:73), but it was used indiscriminately in three phonemic values, *o*, *o·*, and *w*.

The progress in acquiring and recording knowledge of Algonquin grammatical distinctions is evident in a series

of manuscripts from the 1660s (Hanzeli 1969:67-124). What is probably the earliest comprehensive grammatical sketch of Algonquin is in a manuscript of about 1662, one of three descriptions by an anonymous writer (Hanzeli 1969:84-85, 103-116). The major grammatical categories found generally in Algonquian languages are distinguished and extensive paradigms of nominal and verbal inflections are provided. The description is consistently focused on the particular features of Algonquin grammar, sometimes presented on their own terms with innovative terminology and sometimes presented contrastively, with reference to categories and constructions that would have been familiar in French or Latin. The three orders of verbal inflection were distinguished and labeled, along with their submodes and tenses. The distinction between inclusive and exclusive first-person plural was consistently noted. Some of the major derivational categories were also surveyed. Although paradigms are favored for presenting the inflections for subject, object, and nominal possessor, morphological analysis is also given and some complex endings are presented as built up incrementally with distinct elements.

A quite full understanding of Algonquian grammatical categories and inflectional processes is attested by the Algonquin grammar written by Louis Nicolas about 1672-1674 (Hanzeli 1969:69, 117-121; Daviault 1987, 1988; Sioui 1979; Gagnon 1979). Other significant surviving French works on Ojibwa dialects from the seventeenth century include grammatical notes on Ottawa by Louis André and Algonquin and Ottawa dictionaries, the earliest from 1661 and 1662 (Hanzeli 1969:122-124, 126-127). Little of this linguistic work was published, but an Algonquin letter from an Indian neophyte to a French benefactor was included in the Jesuit *Relation* for 1642-1643 by Barthélemy Vimont (JR 24:38-42; Cowan 1991).

The French Jesuit linguists used their understanding of Algonquin grammar to help them learn and analyze other Algonquian languages. The study of Eastern Abenaki presumably began with the visits of Gabriel Druillettes to the Kennebec villages in the period 1646-1652, and subsequently work was done in the refugee missions on the Saint Lawrence. Sébastien Râle began his dictionary at Saint-François de Sales mission, at the falls of the Chaudiere River, in 1691 and later corrected and augmented it in Norridgewock village (Râle 1833). He recorded the Caniba dialect of the Kennebec Valley, particularly in his later entries, and apparently also some information on other, more westerly dialects (Siebert 1980:116-124). His transcriptional system, though somewhat redundant and inconsistent, permitted all the phonemic distinctions of the language to be noted, as well as most combinations, except for the pitch accent; it probably derived at least in part from Râle's predecessor and contemporary Jacques Bigot. Râle wrote the single nasalized vowel *ą* (corresponding to Penobscot α) as

⟨añ⟩, innovated the use of subscript ⟨ȣ⟩ to indicate non-syllabic *w* in environments where it might be wrongly read as *o*, added diacritics to differentiate prevocalic ⟨kȣ⟩ (*kʷ*) from ⟨kȣ̈⟩ (*kəw*), and used the Greek rough breathing ⟨'⟩ to indicate *h* before a consonant. The dictionary, a cumulative notebook rather than a finished work, shows evidence of special attention being given to the elicitation of irregular and unusual forms.

Jacques Gravier, who arrived at the Illinois missions in 1689, had the reputation among his contemporaries of having first analyzed the grammar of the Illinois language (JR 66:244-246). His Illinois-French dictionary survives in manuscript (Hanzeli 1969:126). A supposedly earlier work on Illinois, a manuscript prayer book that Claude Allouez is said to have prepared for Jacques Marquette in 1668 (Neilson 1908), is of uncertain date and authorship. It appears to be in the handwriting of Sébastien Râle, presumably composed during his stay in the Illinois mission in 1691-1693, in which case the translations are probably Gravier's.

Work on Micmac was begun by the Jesuits Pierre Biard and Énemond Massé, who arrived in Port Poyal in 1611 and began a short-lived mission. The language was also studied by the Recollect Chrétien Le Clercq beginning in 1675, but no definite traces of seventeenth-century linguistic work on Micmac are known, except for a few words and phrases and perhaps some religious translations, whose dating and ascription are uncertain (Pilling 1891:359).

There does not seem to have been much if any influence between the seventeenth-century linguists working on Algonquian languages in different areas. The only known case of contact was the visit of Druillettes to Eliot in 1650, during which the two men are known to have discussed Algonquian grammar (JR 36:90; Powicke 1931:55). It is possible that Eliot learned from Druillettes the terms animate and inanimate that he used for the two Algonquian genders, as the French equivalents had been earlier used by Le Jeune (JR 7:22-23; Eliot 1666:9).

French missionaries also began the study of Northern Iroquoian languages in the seventeenth century (Barbeau 1949; Hanzeli 1969). The first studies were done by Recollects working on Huron after 1615, beginning with a Huron dictionary undertaken by Joseph le Caron in 1616 but now lost (Le Clercq 1881, 1:249; Pilling 1888:106). The only work of the Recollects that survives is a dictionary and phrase book by Gabriel Sagard-Théodat (1632, 1865), which may incorporate the earlier work of others. Beginning in 1625 the Jesuits displaced the Recollects, working first in the Huron villages on Georgian Bay and after the Huron diaspora in mission villages at Lorette and elsewhere. Jean de Brébœuf published a Huron catechism in 1630 and a general description of the language in the 1636 *Relation*, commenting on the basic morphological patterns and grammatical categories of the language (JR 10:116-122). Jérôme Lalemant included a Huron prayer with interlinear translation in the *Relation* for 1640-1641 (JR 21:250-264). A Huron dictionary ascribed to Brébeuf survives, and a late copy of a grammar ascribed to Pierre-Joseph-Marie Chaumonot (1920; Lagarde 1980). A few other early Huron linguistic manuscripts are known that are of less certain attribution, and many have been lost (Hanzeli 1969:22, 127-128).

In addition to the omicron-upsilon diagraph ⟨ȣ⟩ for *w* and *o*, the Jesuits introduced the use of a Greek iota subscript before vowels to indicate a sound in Huron corresponding to the *k* of related languages; this may have been pronounced [y], as in later Wyandot, or as a voiced velar fricative [γ].

The earliest published record of Mohawk was in a 1624 Dutch publication that gave the numbers from 'one' to 'ten' and some month names (Jameson 1909:73). A Mohawk vocabulary of 192 entries was recorded by Harmen Meyndertsz van den Bogaert, surgeon of Fort Orange (Albany), in a journal written during a journey into the Iroquois country in 1634 (Van den Bogaert 1988:51-65). Scattered Mohawk words and phrases appeared in other early Dutch publications (Jameson 1909). The Swedish Lutheran missionary Johannes Campanius obtained a brief Susquehannock vocabulary in the 1640s, the only record of the language (Campanius 1696:157-160). The recordings are accurate enough to permit the position of Susquehannock within Northern Iroquoian to be determined (Mithun 1981).

French work on the languages of the League of the Iroquois began with Onondaga, a manuscript Huron and Onondaga dictionary being perhaps the oldest to survive (Hanzeli 1969:23-24, 128). Attribution of this and other surviving manuscripts is uncertain, but among them are a 1668 essay on Mohawk verbal inflection by Jacques Frémin and a Mohawk dictionary by Jacques Bruyas (1863; K. Michelson 1981; Dinneen 1990). Bruyas's dictionary is based on a sophisticated analysis of inflectional and derivational classes and is presented according to root words, the analytical starting points for sets of forms taken to be derivationally related, which are grouped into five conjugations and alphabetized by the first letter following the prefix complex.

The first information on Greenlandic Eskimo was a 106-word vocabulary recorded by Adam Olearius from Greenlanders who had been taken to Denmark in 1654 (Olearius 1656, 1659, 1:133-134). A 250-word vocabulary was collected by Caspar Bartholinus (Bartholinus 1675, 2:71-77).

Eighteenth Century

The eighteenth century saw the continuation of work on Algonquian and Iroquoian languages and the beginnings of work in many new areas of North America.

• ALGONQUIAN Although most of the work on Algonquin remained in manuscript, Louis-Armand de Lom d'Arce, Baron de Lahontan, published a small French-Algonquin dictionary, including an attempt at a partial paradigm of a transitive animate verb, which was widely copied and referred to throughout the century (Lahontan 1703:195-217; Gille 1939; Wolfart 1988, 1989b).

Among the French Sulpician missionaries at the Lake of Two Mountains, Jean-Claude Mathevet, who served there from 1746 to 1781, had the reputation of knowing Algonquin the best (Cuoq 1894:173). He also worked on Eastern Abenaki and Mohawk, and he made the only known record of the central Connecticut River valley language the French called Loup, a compilation of vocabulary notes (Day 1975). He wrote an Algonquin-French dictionary about 1750 and hymns, prayers, and sermons in Algonquin and Eastern Abenaki, as well as a catechism, an Old Testament history, and a life of Christ in Algonquin (Cuoq 1894:172-173; Pilling 1891:345-346, 373-374; Hanzeli 1969:70, 127). Although none of his work was published in his lifetime, his linguistic writings were used by later French missionary linguists and his religious writings were published in the nineteenth century. An Algonquin dictionary and a phrase book were compiled by Vincent-Fleuri Guichart de Kersident, who served at Lake of Two Mountains after 1754 (Pilling 1891:216; Hanzeli 1969:127). He also learned Mohawk and composed extensive religious writings in both languages. Pierre du Jaunay compiled a manuscript French-Ottawa dictionary at Michilimackinac between 1740 and 1748 (Cuoq 1886:38; Pilling 1891:260; Hanzeli 1969:127).

An important source for Illinois is the large French-Illinois dictionary by Jean-Baptiste Le Boullenger, compiled after 1716, which includes also religious texts and two pages of verbal paradigms (Hanzeli 1969:126).

A Montagnais dictionary of 1726 by Pierre Laure survives only in an incomplete copy made in 1823 (Laure 1988; Cooter 1989). Other writings of his are known, but his grammar is lost (Pilling 1891:298). Jean-Baptiste de La Brosse drew upon manuscripts by Laure and Silvy to produce Montagnais linguistic and religious materials, including a primer and a catechism published in 1767 (fig. 1), a Montagnais-Latin dictionary completed in 1775, a Montagnais grammar dated 1768, and a Latin-Montagnais dictionary dated 1772 (Hébert 1979; Cooter and Hébert in Laure 1988:xv, xxv; Pilling 1891:281-282; Barbeau 1957:230).

Râle's dictionary of Eastern Abenaki was seized with the rest of his papers by English troops in an attack on Norridgewock village in 1722, but other manuscript dictionaries of the language were produced in

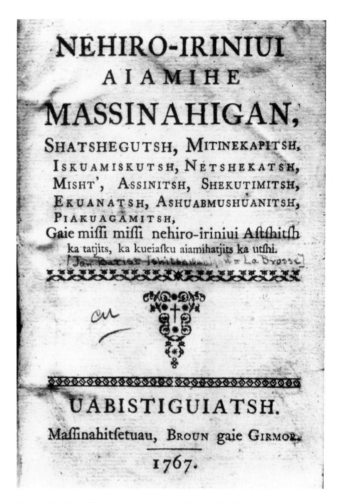

Smithsonian, Natl. Mus. of the Amer. Ind.: Gaines 1929:139.
Fig. 1. Montagnais primer and catechism published by La Brosse (1767), title page.

the eighteenth century. A French-Abenaki dictionary was completed in 1715 by Joseph Aubery, who worked at the Saint Francis mission from 1709 to 1755 (Aubery 1715). A second, Abenaki-French dictionary, a polished, analytical work containing much ethnographic detail, was ascribed to Aubery by Gill (1886:11) but was earlier taken as the work of Jacques-François Le Sueur (Aubery 1715a; Maurault 1866:503-504; Pilling 1891:312). It documents the Arosaguntacook dialect, spoken on the Androscoggin River, and contains also a few words in two other dialects apparently spoken to the west and south (Seeber 1986). From various manuscript sources La Brosse (1760) also compiled an Eastern Abenaki dictionary (Hanzeli 1969:126; Hébert 1979).

Pierre-Antoine Maillard, a missionary and church official in Acadia (Nova Scotia) from 1738 to 1768, wrote the first grammar of Micmac (Maillard 1864; Hewson 1994). In addition, he produced a large number of religious writings in the language.

The earliest substantial documentation of Cree was a dictionary of 600 expressions in Woods Cree compiled in the first two decades of the eighteenth century by

Henry Kelsey, a major figure in the Hudson Bay fur trade (Wolfart and Pentland 1979).

Following Eliot, a number of other Congregationalist ministers learned Massachusett and became involved in the production of religious literature in the language, prominent among them being members of the Cotton family of Plymouth and the Mayhew family of Martha's Vineyard (Pilling 1891). Native literacy became widespread in the praying towns of the eighteenth century (Goddard and Bragdon 1988). Josiah Cotton compiled a Massachusett vocabulary about 1707-1708 in which he employed additional diacritics in an attempt to clarify the values of vowels that were ambiguous in Eliot's system (Cotton 1829, 1830). Experience Mayhew, of the fourth generation of the family, grew up as a native speaker of Massachusett as well as English (Goddard and Bragdon 1988:716). In collaboration with John Nesnumun, a bilingual Massachusett from the mainland, he began a revision of Eliot's translation of the Bible, producing the Psalms and the Gospel of John (Mayhew 1709). This translation employs a somewhat regularized and more consistent version of Eliot's orthography and introduces many revisions of detail, in part reflecting dialectal differences. Regrettably the only linguistic writing by Mayhew, who did not have a college degree, is a few remarks on miscellaneous topics in a 1722 letter (Mayhew 1885). Mayhew also used his improved Massachusett orthography to record the Lord's Prayer in Pequot in 1721, providing the most accurate transcription of that language (Trumbull 1873:34-36).

German-speaking Moravians of the United Brethren began their mission among the Delawares and Mahicans in 1740. Johann Jacob Schmick, an East Prussian who worked among Mahican converts at the Gnadenhütten missions in Pennsylvania, compiled a dictionary between 1753 and 1767 that is the most extensive record of the language (Masthay 1991). In adapting the German alphabet to the writing of Mahican, the Moravians sometimes used diacritics to mark stress and vowel length. There was some literacy in this orthography among the Mahican converts (Masthay 1980:27-28). More extensive linguistic work was done with the Delawares, especially on the Northern Unami dialect that predominated in most Moravian mission villages. David Zeisberger compiled a Delaware primer, the first school book used in the state of Ohio, later extensively revised (Zeisberger 1776, 1806). He also wrote religious translations and a grammar that was published posthumously (Zeisberger 1821, 1827). He compiled a dictionary of English to German, Onondaga, and Delaware, which includes forms from various dialects of Unami and from Munsee, as well as shorter vocabularies (Zeisberger 1887, 1887a).

The work of English missionaries on Mahican began with the arrival of John Sergeant in Stockbridge, Massachusetts, in 1735. Many converts became literate in the English-based orthography that was developed, and some wrote religious translations and vocabularies (Quinney 1795; Holmes 1804). Perhaps the most significant grammar of a North American language published in the eighteenth century was a sketch of Mahican by Jonathan Edwards, Jr., who as the son of a missionary grew up at Stockbridge with a native speaker's command of the language (Edwards 1788). Edwards laid out concisely a number of the significant grammatical categories of the language, and although his presentation was occasionally contrastive he made it clear that Mahican had functionally equivalent devices in cases where it lacked the formal equivalent of some aspects of the grammars of familiar European languages.

A number of significant vocabularies of Algonquian languages were collected in the eighteenth century. Ezra Stiles, the president of Yale College, recorded word lists of Pequot in 1762 and "Narragansett" (probably Eastern Niantic as spoken among the remnant Narragansetts) in 1769 (Cowan 1973, 1973a). Thomas Jefferson took down a vocabulary of Unquachog at the Poosepatuck settlement on Long Island in 1791 and one of Unami in New Jersey in 1792 (Boyd 1982, 20:467-470; Levine and Bonvillain 1980:137-141). Nanticoke vocabularies were obtained on the Choptank River in Maryland by William Vans Murray, a local lawyer and politician, and from refugees among the Iroquois by the English-born Moravian missionary John Gottlieb Ernestus Heckewelder (Speck 1927; Pentland 1979:277-320). James Isham compiled an extensive list of words and phrases in Woods Cree in 1743 (Isham 1949:3-34, 38-41, 47-64), as well as a shorter vocabulary of Assiniboine (Isham 1949:42-47) and the numbers from 'one' to 'ten' in Cree, Saulteaux, Blackfoot, Crow, Mohawk, Assiniboine, and Chipewyan (Isham 1949:34-37). Edward Umfreville, a trader for the Hudson's Bay Company and later the North West Company, published parallel 44-word vocabularies of Cree, Assiniboine, Gros Ventre, Blackfoot, and Sarcee (1790:facing 202, 1954; Pentland 1976).

• IROQUOIAN   The culmination of the Jesuits' work on Huron was the compendious and insightful synthesis by the Belgian Pierre Potier, based on his own studies and manuscript writings by Étienne de Carheil and Joseph Chaumonot. Working in the Wyandot mission near Detroit, he completed his grammar in 1745 and his dictionary in 1751 (Potier 1920; Hanzeli 1969:26; Barbeau 1949:230). Guichart de Kersident compiled a Mohawk dictionary, and François-Auguste Magnon de Terlaye completed an Onondaga dictionary and studied Seneca (Hanzeli 1969:29-30, 128).

The first publication in a language of the Five Nations Iroquois, a book of religious questions and answers in Mohawk, Latin, English, and Dutch, appeared in 1707 (fig. 2) (Anonymous 1707). It probably derives from materials prepared by Bernardus

23

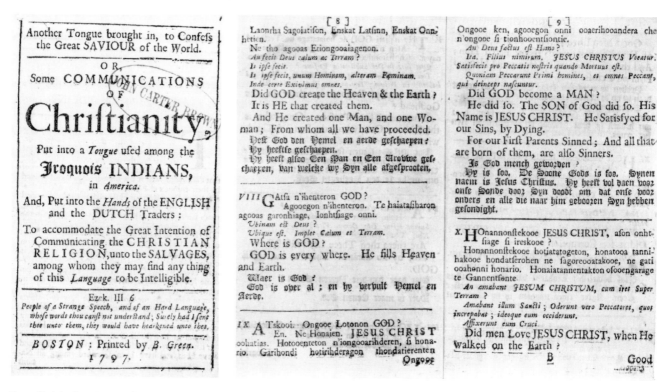

Fig. 2. A book of Christian doctrine in Mohawk, probably written by Bernardus Freeman, title page and pp. 8 and 9 (Anonymous 1707).

Freeman, a Dutch Reformed minister in Schenectady at the beginning of the eighteenth century who translated prayers into Mohawk and assisted English missionaries (Trumbull in Pilling 1888:5). A Mohawk prayer book credited to Lawrence Claesse, who had learned the language as a captive and later served as an interpreter, also probably owed something to materials from Freeman (Claesse 1715; Beauchamp 1881:416-417; Humphreys in Pilling 1888:65). The Dutch background of these early works accounts for the presence of some Dutch features in the transcriptions of Mohawk used then and later by the English, such as the use of ⟨gh⟩ for *h* before consonants and word-finally. An abridged reprint of the 1715 edition appeared in 1763 (Pilling 1888:126), followed by a series of revisions (Andrews, Barclay, and Ogilvie 1769; Claus 1780, 1787). By the 1760s literacy was widespread among the Mohawks (Beauchamp 1881:417). The 1780 reprint was supervised by Col. Daniel Claus, who had spoken Mohawk since childhood, and for the first time used accents to indicate the placement of stress. Paulus Sahonwádi, a Mohawk clerk and schoolmaster, assisted in the correction of proofs (Pilling 1888:15, 46-47). The 1787 reprint also included a translation of the Gospel of Mark by the Mohawk chief Joseph Brant (Thayendanegea).

Among the Moravian missionaries, Johann Christoph Pyrlaeus wrote grammatical studies of Mohawk as well as religious translations, recorded some Oneida, and compiled an Onondaga dictionary (Pyrlaeus 1745-1751, 1745-1751a, 1745-1751b, 1745-1751c), and Zeisberger wrote an Onondaga grammar and dictionary and included Onondaga in his four-language dictionary (Zeisberger 1776a, 1887, 1888).

John Lawson (1709:225-230) collected the earliest vocabulary of Tuscarora.

• ESKIMO-ALEUT The systematic study of West Greenlandic began with the arrival in Greenland of the Danish Lutheran missionary Hans Poulsen Egede in 1721 (R. Petersen in vol. 5:640). He published brief remarks on the language and began the task of religious translation (H. Egede 1729, 1741). His son, Poul Hansen Egede, who learned to speak Greenlandic as a teenager, continued his father's work and wrote the first grammar and dictionary of any Eskimoan language (P. Egede 1750, 1760). The Egedes introduced the orthographic practice of writing Eskimo /γ/ with ⟨g⟩ and /ɣ̇/ with ⟨r⟩, using these letters in values approximating ones they had in Danish. Some early letters attest to native Greenlandic literacy (Cranz 1765:1076-1100). Subsequently, Otto Fabricius, who worked as a missionary in Greenland from 1768 to 1773, translated religious materials into Greenlandic and produced a grammar and a dictionary, building on Poul Egede's work (Fabricius 1791, 1801, 1804). Other information on Eskimoan in the eighteenth century was provided by Johann Anderson from Greenland (1746:285-325), Arthur Dobbs (1744:203-205) from Hudson Bay,

William Anderson and Alexander Walker from Prince William Sound (Cook and King 1784, 2:374-376, 3:554-555; Walker 1982:156-160, 270-271), and James King from Norton Sound (Cook and King 1784, 3:554-555; Jacobson 1984:frontispiece, 1).

The first vocabulary of Aleut was taken down by P.S. Pallas in Irkutsk, and there was a scattering of other records made toward the end of the century (Bergsland 1959:6).

• SOUTHEASTERN LANGUAGES Lutheran Salzburger emigrants who arrived in Georgia in 1734 transcribed Creek and Yuchi words using Greek letters (Sturtevant 1994). Moravians in their short-lived mission near Savannah from 1735 to 1740 also used an orthography for Creek based on Greek and compiled a vocabulary of the language (Anonymous 1740). John Lawson (1709:225-230) collected the only known vocabulary of Woccon. The first published information on Catawba was a vocabulary of 31 words obtained by Benjamin Smith Barton from Catawba visitors to Philadelphia (Barton 1798).

• SIOUAN John Fontaine, an Irishman of French Huguenot origin, recorded 46 words, phrases, and sentences of a language he called "Saponey" at Fort Christanna, Virginia, in 1716. Most of the vocabulary documents a language very similar to Tutelo, perhaps indeed the Saponi language, which was said to be very close to Occaneechi and Tutelo, but since the numbers are Algonquian and Iroquoian the vocabulary may represent specifically the use of Occaneechi as a trade language in the area (Alexander 1971; Goddard 1972; Beverley 1947:191). Jonathan Carver, a militia officer from Connecticut who traveled far into the interior of the continent in 1766-1768, published the first data on Sioux, a short vocabulary of Santee together with a song (Carver 1778:433-441; DeMallie 1976:210-221).

• COAHUILTECO The Spanish Franciscan missionary Bartolomé García compiled a bilingual Coahuilteco and Spanish confessional for use in the San Antonio and Rio Grande missions (García 1760; "Sketch of Coahuilteco, a Language Isolate of Texas," this vol.). Drawing on and perfecting a tradition of linguistic work on the language, he arrived at an extremely accurate orthography that marked vowel length with accents and indicated glottalized consonants with an apostrophe, and he produced what appears to be a highly accurate and idiomatic text that also reflects considerable ethnographic sensitivity. The transcriptions of Coahuilteco are the earliest to mark glottalization for any language in North America, but in the absence of any general theory of articulatory phonetics this achievement had no impact on other linguists.

• ATHAPASKAN The earliest vocabulary of an Athapaskan language was one containing about 280 Chipewyan words and phrases collected by Edward Thompson, a ship's surgeon, in 1742 (Dobbs 1744:206-211; vol. 6:80). Isham (1949:183-191) compiled a vocabulary of the same language the next year, and Alexander Mackenzie collected a Chipewyan vocabulary in 1789 (Mackenzie 1801:cxxix-cxxxii, 1760:156-159) as well as one of Carrier ("Nagailer") in 1793 (Mackenzie 1801:257-258, 1970:322). The earliest material recorded from an Alaskan Athapaskan language consists of the Tanaina numerals, recorded in 1778 by William Anderson on Capt. James Cook's third voyage and included with Pacific Yupik (Alutiiq) words in a Prince William Sound vocabulary (Cook and King 1784, 2:375-376; Krauss 1964:127).

• NORTHWEST COAST LANGUAGES The first Tlingit vocabulary, 28 numerals and 5 nouns, was collected in Lituya Bay in 1786 by Robert de Paul, Chevalier de Lamanon, a geologist on the voyage of Jean François Galaup, comte de Lapérouse (Lapérouse 1797:210-213). Similar small word lists from Norfolk Sound, Portlock Harbor, and Sitka were published in the following years in accounts of other voyages (Krauss and McGary 1980:150). A Yakutat vocabulary of some 150 items, including 25 numerals, was compiled by members of the Alessandro Malaspina expedition in 1791 (Malaspina 1885:349-351).

Seafarers putting in at Cumshewa on the Queen Charlotte Islands in 1791 collected the earliest Haida vocabularies (Hoskins 1941:236-237; Krauss and McGary 1980:79; vol. 7:98).

The first recordings of Salishan languages were Alexander Mackenzie's short vocabularies of Shuswap ("Atnah") and Bella Coola ("Friendly Village") collected in 1793 (Mackenzie 1801:257-258, 376, 1970:322, 394).

On Capt. Cook's third voyage in 1778, William Anderson compiled an extensive vocabulary of Nootka (Cook and King 1784, 2:335-336, 3:542-548; Beaglehole 1967, 3:323-330), and David Samwell recorded a shorter one (Beaglehole 1967, 3:1104). Anderson's vocabulary was widely used by visitors to the Northwest Coast in the years after its 1784 publication, contributing to the rise of the Nootka traders' jargon that was later lexically expanded to become Chinook Jargon (Hale 1846:635-636; Howay 1942; Sturtevant 1948, 1981; Samarin 1986; cf. Kaufman 1971:275; Hymes 1980; Thomason 1983; Thomason and Kaufman 1988:176-177, 182-183, 257-258). Alexander Walker collected an extensive Nootka vocabulary in 1786, but it was not published contemporaneously (Walker 1982:91-104, 277-303). Vocabularies of Makah and Nootka were obtained on the 1792 expedition of Juan Francisco de la Bodega y Quadra, the Nootka being compiled by the Mexican botanist José Mariano Moziño Suárez de Figueroa (Espinosa y Tello 1802:41-42, 178-184; Moziño 1913:ci-cvii, 83-100, 1970:xiii-xiv, 99-110). Other early Nootka vocabularies are listed by M. Dale Kinkade (vol. 7:98).

• CALIFORNIA LANGUAGES The earliest systematic linguistic data from California were brief vocabularies of Rumsen (Costanoan) and Esselen collected in 1786 by Lamanon (Lapérouse 1797, 2:291-292). Vocabularies of Esselen and Rumsen were also obtained by Dionisio Alcalá Galiano on his 1792 expedition (Espinosa y Tello 1802:172-173; Beeler 1978), together with an Esselen catechism, probably from Fermín Francisco de Lasuén (Shaul 1995).

• MEXICAN LANGUAGES Grammars of several of the Uto-Aztecan languages of northern Mexico appeared in the eighteenth century (Bright 1967): one of Cáhita, an early form of Mayo, ascribed to Tommaso Basilio (1737, 1890), and ones of Ópata (Lombardo 1702), Lower Piman (Buckingham T. Smith 1862), and Tepehuan (Rinaldini 1743). The Lower Piman grammar and a vocabulary of the same language apparently by the same author may have been written by the Jesuit Baltasar de Loaysa in the 1660s, relying in part on earlier work by Francisco Oliñano (Pennington 1979, 2:xxi). An anonymous description of Eudeve surviving in two manuscript versions incorporates earlier work dating to the seventeenth century (Pennington 1981; Shaul 1991). A sketch of Guaicura was published (Baegert 1772). A grammatical study of the Otomanguean language Pame is found in an eighteenth-century manuscript (Valle 1892; Schuller 1925).

• SURVEYS Toward the end of the eighteenth century systematic attempts at bringing together information on native North American languages began, generally as a way of exploring their historical relations and origins. Primary sources became more apt to contain vocabularies of several languages, as in the case of Umfreville (1790:facing 202, 1954), and significant secondary compilations by armchair scholars began to be undertaken. Benjamin Smith Barton compiled vocabularies of many languages from printed and manuscript sources and directly from speakers (Barton 1797). Additional languages are represented in his second edition (Barton 1798), though the Quapaw vocabulary claimed for his source by Pilling (1887a:4) consists of a single word from Jean-Bernard Bossu (1962:60) that seems actually to be Natchez (Crawford 1975:90).

Nineteenth Century

In the nineteenth century linguistics (at first called philology) emerged as a distinct field of inquiry aimed at discovering the general principles of all human language and their manifestations in the variety of actual speech. Data from North American languages figured in general discussions of the nature of language, and compilations became more comprehensive. The number of vocabularies collected increased rapidly as more and more explorers and travelers visited all parts of the continent, and in fact for many languages vocabularies were the only documentation available before the twentieth century. Grammatical descriptions and more substantial lexical studies were for the most part produced only for languages spoken in areas where there had been extensive contact with Europeans, especially missionaries, and thus languages in certain major language families tended to be much better described than others that were spoken in regions where contact was later.

A major attempt to gather information on these languages was carried on for years by Thomas Jefferson before and during his terms as president, 1801-1809. He obtained vocabularies by correspondence and fieldwork, and most importantly from Meriwether Lewis and William Clark, who had collected linguistic information on their overland expedition to the Pacific, 1803-1806. Although almost all of Jefferson's linguistic materials were destroyed by a thief (Jackson 1978, 2:465, 633), his systematic attempt to collect comparable linguistic data using a standardized questionnaire set a pattern that was followed with successive improvements throughout the century. John Pickering, a Boston lawyer and student of languages, devised a standardization of the alphabet to be used for writing Indian languages (Pickering 1820). Lewis Cass included a phonetic alphabet of his own (fig. 3) in a circular questionnaire he prepared, while governor of the Territory of Michigan, for gathering ethnographic and linguistic data on the Indians of the Midwest (Cass 1821, 1821a, 1823; E.W. Voegelin 1939:xix-xx; Kinietz 1946:15-17). A series of reports compiled for Cass between 1823 and 1825 by C.C. Trowbridge includes substantial linguistic information on Unami, Menominee, Miami, Kickapoo, Ojibwa, Shawnee, Dakota, and Winnebago. Commissioner of Indian Affairs Thomas L. McKenney circulated a vocabulary schedule with grammatical inquiries that was drawn up by Albert Gallatin (U.S. Department of War 1825-1826), and Henry Rowe Schoolcraft used a schedule to obtain a number of vocabularies, which he published (Schoolcraft 1851-1857; Nichols 1954). The Smithsonian Institution issued a guide for descriptive fieldwork, covering concisely all fields of anthropology, which included a vocabulary list and a simple phonetic alphabet that was devised by William Dwight Whitney (Gibbs 1861, 1863a, 1865; Golla 1992). This phonetic alphabet was expanded by Whitney for John Wesley Powell's *Introduction to the Study of Indian Languages*, which included extensive vocabulary schedules (Powell 1877), and then thoroughly revised by Powell in the second edition (Powell 1880).

Besides that of Schoolcraft, the major published compendia of data in the nineteenth century were by Lorenzo Hervás y Panduro (1800-1805), J.C. Adelung and J.S. Vater (1806-1817, 3, part 3), Gallatin (1836, 1848), Johann Carl Eduard Buschmann (1856, 1857,

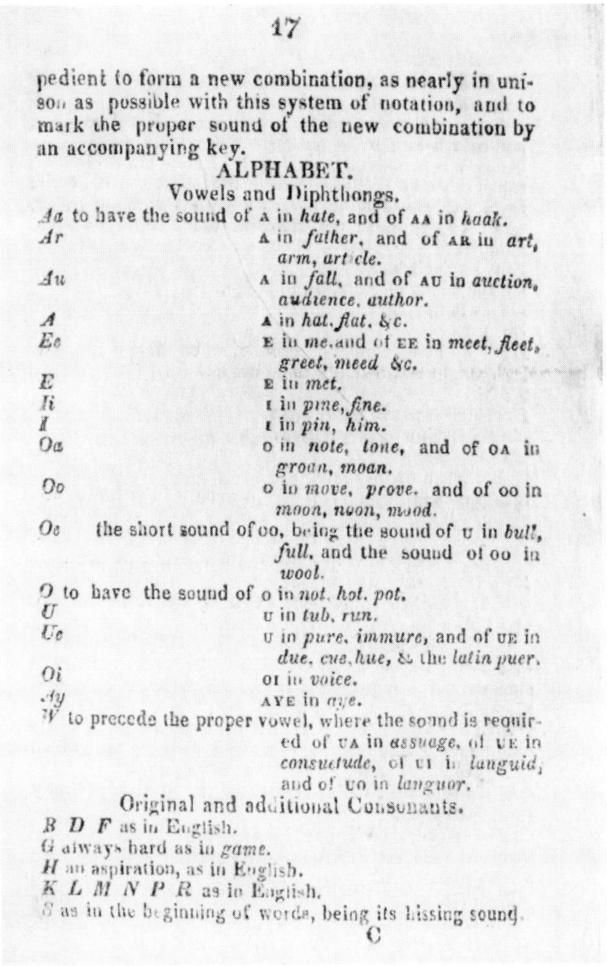

17

pedient to form a new combination, as nearly in uni-
son as possible with this system of notation, and to
mark the proper sound of the new combination by
an accompanying key.

ALPHABET.
Vowels and Diphthongs.

Aa to have the sound of A in *hate*, and of AA in *haak*.

Ar   A in *father*, and of AR in *art*,
arm, *article*.

Au   A in *fall*, and of AU in *auction*,
audience, *author*.

A   A in *hat*, *flat*, &c.

Ee   E in *me*, and of EE in *meet*, *fleet*,
greet, *meed* &c.

E   E in *met*.

Ii   I in *pine*, *fine*.

I   I in *pin*, *him*.

Oa   o in *note*, *tone*, and of OA in
groan, *moan*.

Oo   o in *move*, *prove*, and of oo in
moon, *noon*, *mood*.

Oe   the short sound of oo, being the sound of U in *bull*,
full, and the sound of oo in
wool.

O to have the sound of o in *not*, *hot*, *pot*.

U   U in *tub*, *run*.

Ue   u in *pure*, *immure*, and of UE in
due, *cue*, *hue*, & the *latin puer*.

Oi   OI in *voice*.

Ay   AYE in *aye*.

W to precede the proper vowel, where the sound is required of UA in *assuage*, of UE in
consuetude, of UI in *languid*,
and of UO in *languor*.

Original and additional Consonants.

B D F as in English.

G always hard as in *game*.

H an aspiration, as in English.

K L M N P R as in English.

S as in the beginning of words, being its hissing sound.

C

Fig. 3. Lewis Cass's phonetic alphabet, included in a linguistic
supplement to his ethnographic questionnaire (Cass 1821, 1821a).
These were reprinted as Cass (1823), which was used by C.C.
Trowbridge and other early investigators.

1859); for Plains languages Thomas Say, a naturalist
on Major Stephen H. Long's expedition (James 1823,
2:lxx-lxxxv), Alexander Philipp Maximilian, Prince of
Wied (Maximilian 1839-1841, 2:455-653, 1906, 3:199-
312), and Ferdinand Vandeveer Hayden, a surgeon,
naturalist, and geologist on various western surveys
(Hayden 1862); for the southern Plains, the Southwest,
and southern California Lt. Amiel Weeks Whipple,
who commanded the 1853-1854 Pacific Railroad
Survey (Whipple, Ewbank, and Turner 1855:81-85;
Whipple 1941); for the Northwest Coast and the
Plateau William Fraser Tolmie and George Mercer
Dawson (Scouler 1841; Tolmie and Dawson 1884),
Horatio Hale (1846), George Gibbs (1877), an early
Oregon settler, and the naturalist William Healy Dall
(1877); for California John Wesley Powell of the U.S.
Geographical and Geological Survey of the Rocky
Mountain Region (in Powers 1877); and for southern
California and the Southwest Lt. George M. Wheeler of

the U.S. Army Corps of Engineers, who also worked
for the Survey (Wheeler 1879:399-485). Collections
that were part of discussions of linguistic classification
are surveyed in "The Classification of the Native
Languages of North America," this volume. Staff
workers and associates of the Bureau of Ethnology
(later Bureau of American Ethnology) of the
Smithsonian Institution, founded in 1879 under
Powell's direction, collected vast amounts of linguistic
material on field trips and from Indian visitors to
Washington, most of which remains in manuscript
(National Anthropological Archives 1975; Glenn 1992;
Hinsley 1981). Some early manuscripts are in the
American Philosophical Society in Philadelphia
(Freeman 1966; Kendall 1982), the Newberry Library
in Chicago (Butler 1937:186-213), and the Bancroft
Library in Berkeley (Morgan and Hammond 1963).
Published and manuscript works from this and previous
centuries were comprehensively surveyed by James C.
Pilling for nine of the larger families: Algonquian
(Pilling 1891), Athapaskan (Pilling 1892), Chinookan
and Chinook Jargon (Pilling 1893), Eskimo-Aleut
(Pilling 1887), Iroquoian (Pilling 1888), Muskogean
(Pilling 1889), Salishan (Pilling 1893a), Siouan
(Pilling 1887a), and Wakashan (Pilling 1894). For languages outside these families early sources can be
found in Pilling's (1885) *Proof-sheets*. Pilling's bibliographies include translations and other often obscure
religious publications by missionaries, which became
extremely numerous in the nineteenth century. Also
useful for early materials are linguistic bibliographies
for Alaska Indian languages (Krauss and McGary
1980), Athapaskan (Parr 1974), California (Bright
1982), and the Southeast (Booker 1991). Some of the
sections in Sebeok (1973, 2), provide extensive bibliographic listings and discussions of early sources.

• ALGONQUIAN Work on Algonquian languages by
francophone missionary linguists in the nineteenth century produced several significant studies. Georges
Antoine Belcourt published a grammar of the Saulteaux
variety of Ojibwa (Belcourt 1839) and wrote a dictionary, and Albert Lacombe compiled an extensive dictionary and grammar of Plains Cree (Lacombe 1874)
and later worked on Blackfoot. The crowning achievement of the French missionary tradition of Algonquian
linguistic studies was the work of the Sulpician Jean-
André Cuoq, who wrote a dictionary and grammar of
Algonquin based on the dialect of the Lake of Two
Mountains mission (Cuoq 1886, 1891-1893), which was
in fact historically Nipissing and not the descendant of
Old Algonquin (Cuoq 1872). Earlier Cuoq had written
two monographs on the grammatical categories of
Algonquin and Mohawk, one an attack on the thesis of
the Semiticist Ernest Renan that American Indian languages were inferior (Cuoq 1864, 1870) and one a more
general survey (Cuoq 1866). Cuoq's work rested on that

of his predecessors, especially the lexicographical compilations of Jean-Baptiste Thavenet (Cuoq 1886:128; Laurencich-Minelli 1990:28), but he made a number of advances. He was, for example, the first to make a principled distinction between stem-forming elements that occurred word-initially (later called initials) and those that only occurred after an initial element (medials and finals), and he coined the term obviative (French *obviatif*) for the distinctive secondary third person of Algonquian. Georges Lemoine wrote a dictionary and grammar of Montagnais based on the Escoumains dialect (Lemoine 1901) and a French-Algonquin dictionary that supplements Cuoq's (Lemoine 1912).

Tangential to the francophone Algonquianist tradition was the work of the Slovenian Roman Catholic missionary Friderik Baraga, who began his studies with Ottawa and later wrote a grammar and dictionary of Southwestern Ojibwa (Baraga 1850, 1853, 1878, 1878-1880; Šmitek 1993). The first publication in Ottawa was either the catechism and primer of Auguste Dejean, a Roman Catholic missionary at Arbre Croche, Michigan, or a similar book of about the same data by the Congregationalist Isaac Van Tassel then in Ohio (Dejean 1830; Pilling 1891:106, 503; McMurtrie 1931:165-166). Anglophone studies of Cree suffered from the lack of an accepted standard orthography, generally using an English-based system with the somewhat inconsistent addition of diacritics, as in the dictionary of Plains Cree by Edward Arthur Watkins (1865) and the grammar of Moose Cree by John Horden (1881). Joseph Howse, a Hudson's Bay Company employee, wrote a grammar of the Woods Cree dialect that was substantially independent of the missionary tradition and contained a number of original insights into Algonquian grammar (Howse 1884). He included comparative examples of Ojibwa forms taken from the translation of the Gospel of John by John Jones and Peter Jones (Jones and Jones 1831), Methodist religious teachers of part Mississauga Ojibwa origin. The Anglican missionary James Hunter (1875) published a discussion of the grammar of Plains Cree with an extensive compilation of verbal paradigms. He and his second wife, Jean, who spoke Cree natively, had earlier produced a series of translations of scripture and other religious texts. The Cree syllabary developed by the Methodist missionary James Evans in 1841 provided for an accurate phonemic transcription of Cree (Nichols 1984), but it was only used for religious translations, not for linguistic works. An extensive verbal paradigm of Southwestern Ojibwa and other

miscellaneous data published by Schoolcraft (1851-1857, 5:297-388, 593-620) were widely referred to.

Heckewelder (1819:450-464) wrote on the Northern Unami dialect of Delaware and engaged in a published correspondence with Peter Stephen Duponceau on a range of descriptive and theoretical questions regarding American Indian languages (Heckewelder and Duponceau 1819). Heckewelder's work was critically reviewed by Lewis Cass on the basis of information that C.C. Trowbridge had obtained on the Southern Unami dialect (Cass 1826), though the criticisms in part reflect confusion over differences of dialect and orthography. Duponceau's studies of Delaware and Onondaga based on the work of the Moravian missionaries led to his formulation of the concept of polysynthesis, which he proposed as a fundamental and distinctive characteristic of American Indian languages (Duponceau 1838). Duponceau's essay was the most important contribution to linguistic theory to come out of American Indian studies before the twentieth century, and the implications of his claim were still being explored and debated in the 1990s (Smith 1983; Robins 1987). A compilation of Delaware words by Christian Frederick Dencke, principally Northern Unami from Zeisberger's (1776, 1806) *Spelling-Book*, was edited by Daniel Garrison Brinton, a Philadelphia doctor and scholar, with the assistance of Albert Seqaqkind Anthony, a native speaker of Munsee from Six Nations Reserve, Ontario, where he served as an Anglican missionary (Brinton and Anthony 1889).

Among the Western Abenakis of Saint Francis, Quebec, a native literacy and grammatical tradition developed exemplified by the work of Pierre Paul Osunkherhine (Wzokhilain 1830) and Joseph Laurent (1884), whose transcriptions were close to phonemic. Osunkherhine adopted an underlined ⟨o⟩ to write the single nasalized vowel pronounced [ɔ] and [ʌ] and wrote /ə/ distinctively as ⟨e⟩ and ⟨ŭ⟩.

The Baptist missionary Jotham Meeker, who ran the Baptist Mission Press successively at Shawanoe, Stockbridge, and Ottawa, Kansas, from 1834 to 1854, developed a series of consistent but somewhat idiosyncratic orthographies for several languages, printing works by himself and other Baptist, Methodist, and Presbyterian missionaries in the Algonquian languages Delaware (Unami), Ottawa, Potawatomi, Shawnee, and Wea, as well as in Choctaw, Creek, Iowa, Kansa, Otoe, and Osage (figs. 4-6) (Pilling 1891:352-356; McMurtrie and Allen 1930; "Native Writing Systems," this vol.).

Fig. 4. Delaware and Shawnee publications from Jotham Meeker's Shawanoe Baptist Mission Press, on the site of the town of Shawnee, later incorporated into Greater Kansas City, Kansas. top, Delaware primer, title page and p. 12 (Blanchard 1834), with a vocabulary of 1- and 2-syllable words and short dialogues for practice in reading and writing. This was the first book printed in Indian Territory. bottom, Shawnee reader, title page and p. 9 (Lykins 1834), with the beginning of the story of Lazarus being raised from the dead.

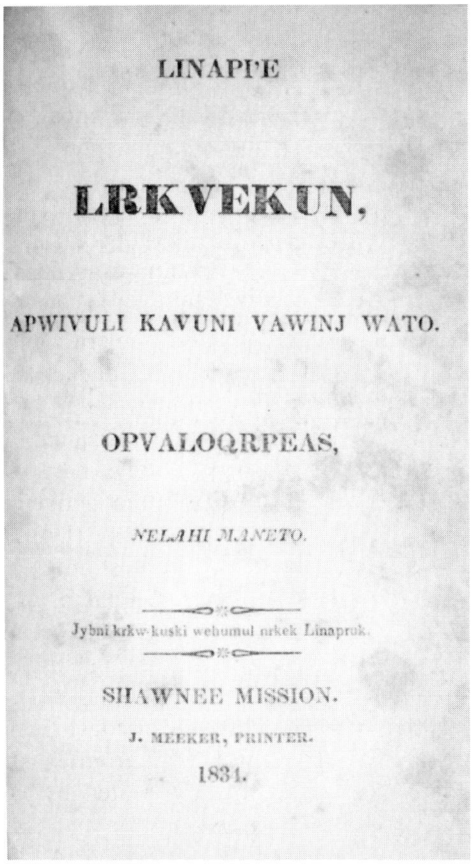

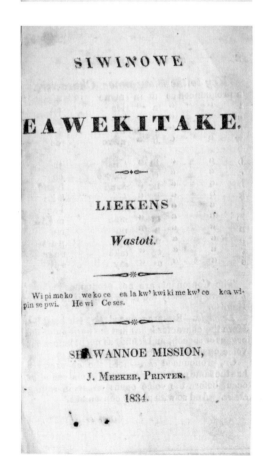

Top-left page

LINAPI'E

LRKVEKUN,

APWIVULI KAVUNI VAWINJ WATO.

OPVALOQRPEAS,

NELAHI MANETO.

Jybni krkw-kuski wehumul nrkek Linapruk.

SHAWNEE MISSION.

J. MEEKER, PRINTER.

1834.

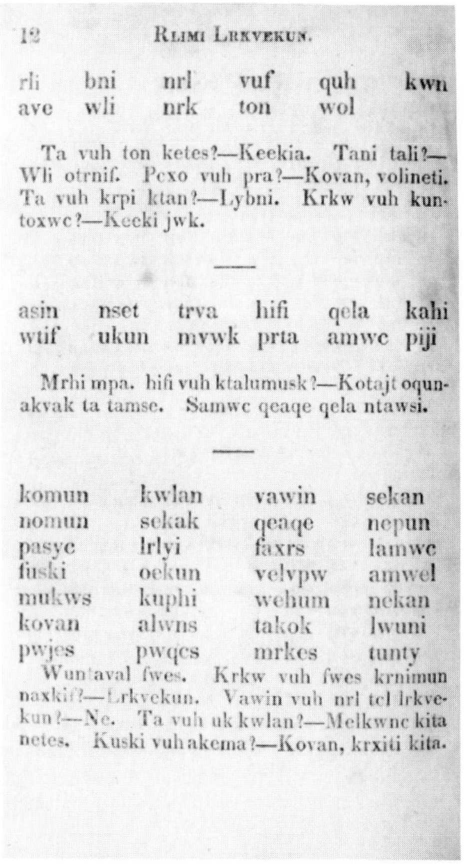

Top-right page

rli   bni   nrl   vuf   quh   kwn
ave   wli   nrk   ton   wol

Ta vuh ton ketes?—Keekia. Tani tali?—
Wli otrnif. Pcxo vuh pra?—Kovan, volineti.
Ta vuh krpi ktan?—Lybni. Krkw vuh kun-
toxwc?—Keeki jwk.

—

asin   nset   trva   hifi   qela   kahi
wtif   ukun   mvwk   prta   amwc   piji

Mrhi mpa. hifi vuh ktalumusk?—Kotajt oqun-
akvak ta tamse. Samwc qeaqe qela ntawsi.

—

komun   kwlan   vawin   sekan
nomun   sekak   qeaqe   nepun
pasyc   lrlyi   faxrs   lamwc
fuski   oekun   velvpw   amwel
mukws   kuphi   wehum   nekan
kovan   alwns   takok   lwuni
pwjes   pwqcs   mrkes   tunty

Wuntaval fwes. Krkw vuh fwes krnimun
naxkif?—Lrkvekun. Vawin vuh nrl tcl lrkvekun?—Ne. Ta vuh uk kwlan?—Melkwnc kita
netes. Kuski vuh akema?—Kovan, krxiti kita.

Bottom-left page

SIWINOWE

EAWEKITAKE.

LIEKENS

Wastoti.

Wi pi me ko we ko ce ea la kw' kwi ki me kw' ce   kea wi-
pin se pwi.   He wi Ce ses.

SHAWANNOE MISSION,

J. MEEKER, PRINTER.

1834.

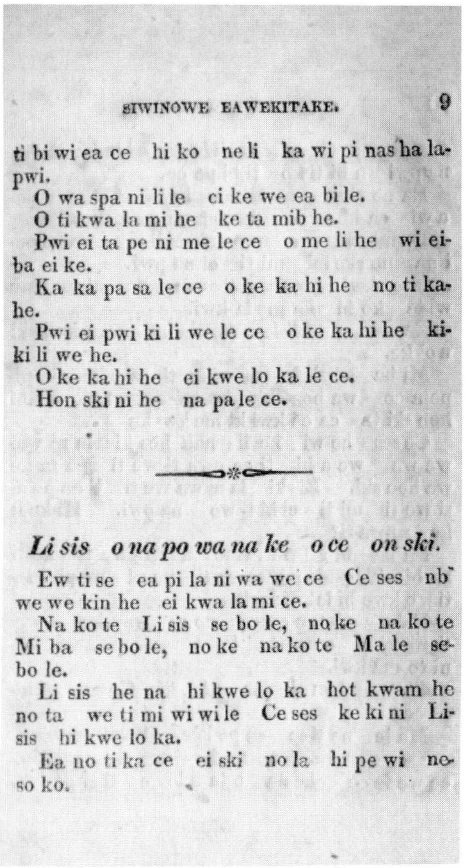

Bottom-right page

ti bi wi ea ce   hi ko   ne li   ka wi pi nas ha la-
pwi.
    O wa spa ni li le   ci ke we ea bi le.
    O ti kwa la mi he   ke ta mib he.
    Pwi ei ta pe ni me le ce   o me li he   wi ei-
ba ei ke.
    Ka ka pa sa le ce   o ke ka hi he   no ti ka-
he.
    Pwi ei pwi ki li we le ce   o ke ka hi he   ki-
ki li we he.
    O ke ka hi he   ei kwe lo ka le ce.
    Hon ski ni he   na pa le ce.

—

Li sis o na po wa na ke o ce on ski.

Ew ti se   ea pi la ni wa we ce Ce ses nb'
we we kin he   ei kwa la mi ce.
    Na ko te Li sis se bo le, no ke   na ko te
Mi ba se bo le, no ke na ko te Ma le se-
bo le.
    Li sis he na hi kwe lo ka hot kwam he
no ta we ti mi wi wi le Ce ses ke ki ni Li-
sis hi kwe lo ka.
    Ea no ti ka ce ei ski no la hi pe wi no-
so ko.

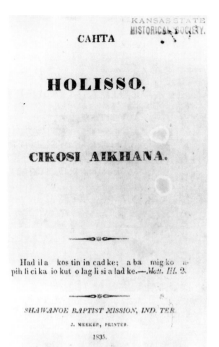

CAHTA

HOLISSO.

CIKOSI AIKHANA.

Had ila kostin in cadke; aba migko a-
pih li ci ka io kut o lag li si a lad ke.—*Matt. III. 3.*

SHAWANOE BAPTIST MISSION, IND. TER.

J. MEEKER, PRINTER.

1835.

9

A ba Pig ke io kut na na mo ma ho-
ka pi sa po la ho ke.
A ba Pig ke io ka ki pi so kia pi pig-
sa bi ka ca tok o ke
A ba Pig ke o kut na na mo ma pim-
ag da ka pi ma tok o ke
A ba Pig ke ia i kan ca hi ma ki iw il-
lah na hi tok o ke.

Ala ut tak di
Foh kol ut nar re
Ha do kut o fo
Tan ci og com pa
Tan ci a hok ci
Pok po ag dan nih
Co ka ag ta ki iw
Wa kut ik sa nio ho ke

La pid ut o la
Ian ha iut di pa
Bad po iog ho io
I ti a bad li
Ti ak og di mih
Wak ag io re
Wa kut ag ia ho ke
Lad pa hog mar re

Ag pi ni o kut tod bit ta ha.
Oti od ta hog i mal i ka mo.
Hi na ia muk od ig co ka o na.
Ha tak i li mo ma kut ta na hi o-
ke.
Im pat i sa fo ka a la la hi.
Bad po ut ta le ka lo i od to ba.
Lo ak ak ki iw hok ma pi lad pa hi-
ki iw.
Ka ta hog id pi sa to kog?

11

Ho li so hut ri la fat ta ha.
Ci ho a ho kut pia pi la ca tok o ke.
A ba Pig ke Ci ho a ho kut a cok-
ma fi na ho ke.
Ci ho a ho kut na na ok log ha i-
ma ia ho ke.
Ci ho a ho kut na na a iag ri bi e ka
hog pim a pi sa ho ke.
Na na hod Ci ho a hok a ik bi tok-
ke iw ho ke.
Ci sus Klaist o kut Ci ho a o di
io ke.
Ci sus Klaist pig hol lo fih na ho-
ke.
Ci sus Klaist o kut ha tak il ba da
io ka ig hol lo fi nah ho ke.
Ci sus Klaist ak ke iwk ma, pi ok-
ca ia hi ma ke iw ho ke.
Nak ni ho ci fo kut Al um ut tok-
o ke.
Al um ak od ha tak in tigk ba tok-
o ke.
If ak od o ho io mo ma ka ig tik ba
fih na hut tok o ke.
Na hol lo a to pas ka ia sa pi ta tok.
Ag bad po ut a im pa no tak a i tog-
la.
Ho lis so no ta i to la kak og i di.

Kansas State Histl. Soc., Topeka.

Fig. 5. Choctaw primer, title page and pp. 9 and 11 (Birch 1835). The title ⟨CAHTA HOLISSO, CIKOSI AIKHANA.⟩ can be translated 'Choctaw book, to learn from quickly'. Made up of short religious and other phrases, the primer was designed to illustrate written Choctaw for the beginner. The spellings show many archaisms that differ from the Choctaw of the 1990s. The first sentence on p. 9 is 'God our Father sees everything', and the first on p. 11 is 'The paper is torn' (Pamela Munro and Catherine Willmond, communication to editors 1995).

Silas Tertius Rand, a Baptist missionary in Nova Scotia, after experimenting with the use of special characters, developed an English-based orthography for Micmac in which he produced numerous religious translations, in addition to writing a primer of topically arranged vocabulary and expressions and a dictionary (Rand 1875, 1888). Though he somewhat overdifferentiated vowel quality, he accurately noted distinctive contrasts of vowel length. Joseph Barratt, a Connecticut doctor, wrote a brief introduction to Passamaquoddy vocabulary and grammar (Barratt 1851). An important record of Miami was made by the French count and traveler Constantine-François Volney (1803, 2:525-532). A grammar and dictionary of Blackfoot was written by John William Tims (1889) of the Church Missionary Society, and another grammar of the language was compiled by C.M. Lanning (1882) on the basis of materials prepared by Joseph Kipp and W.S. Gladston, Jr. Two Italian Jesuits, Peter Paul Prando and Joseph Damiani, also worked on Blackfoot and produced hymns and devotional texts in the language (Schoenberg 1957:22-23, 33; Pilling 1891:406).

• IROQUOIAN Jean-André Cuoq discussed topics in Mohawk grammar extensively in his general works (Cuoq 1864, 1866, 1870) and published a Mohawk dictionary (fig. 7) (Cuoq 1882) based on a manuscript dictionary and grammar by Joseph Marcoux, a secular priest and missionary. Missionary translations into Mohawk in the English orthography included a Gospel of John by John Norton, a Scot who claimed to be half-Cherokee and learned to speak Mohawk (Norton 1804, 1970; Fogelson 1978), and an Anglican Book of Common Prayer by the Canadian missionary Abraham Nelles and John Hill, Jr., a Mohawk catechist at Six Nations Reserve (Nelles and Hill 1842). The English orthography was used in native-written Mohawk and Onondaga texts of the traditional Condolence Council used by ceremonial practitioners at Six Nations Reserve and Onondaga (Hale 1883). Eleazer Williams, a Caughnawaga Mohawk catechist and minister in American Congregationalist and Episcopal missions, used the French orthography for Mohawk in a primer and an Episcopal prayer book, among other publications (Williams 1813, 1853). Asher Wright, a missionary on the Buffalo Creek Reservation and, after its removal, at Cattaraugus, developed an alphabet for writing Seneca and published numerous works, including a primer and a spelling book containing word lists and grammatical information (Wright 1836, 1842; Fenton 1956:575). Earlier publications in Seneca by other missionaries, dating from 1818, included spelling books, hymns, and scriptural translations in different orthographies; and at least two similar publications in Tuscarora are known from this period. Schoolcraft (1846, 1847) compiled vocabularies of Tuscarora (collected by William Chew), Mohawk and Cayuga (collected by Adam Elliot),

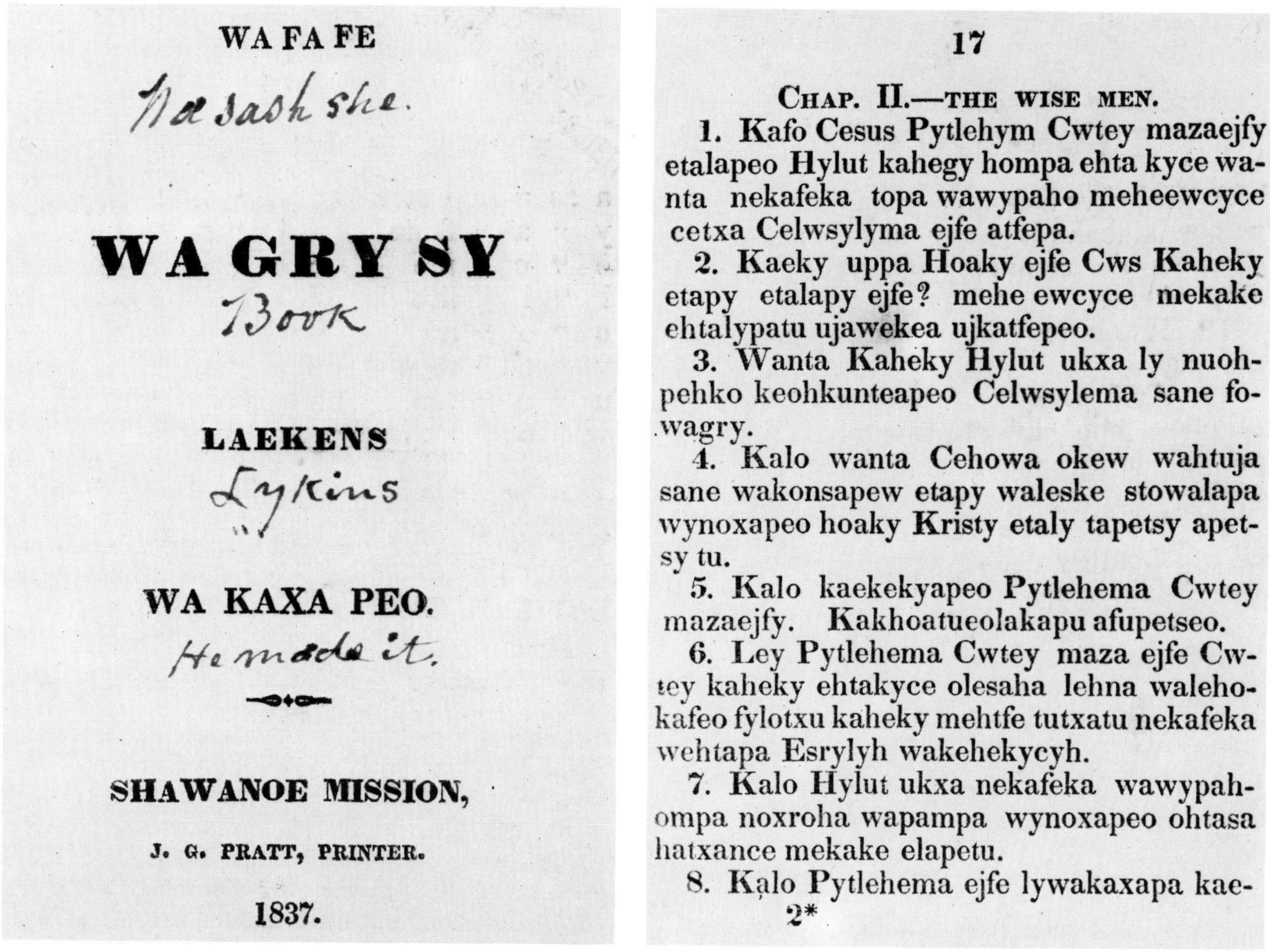

WA FA FE

Naɟaɟhɟhe.

WA GRY SY

Book

LAEKENS

Lykins

WA KAXA PEO.

He made it.

——◆◆◆◆——

SHAWANOE MISSION,

J. G. PRATT, PRINTER.

1837.

17

CHAP. II.—THE WISE MEN.

1. Kafo Cesus Pytlehym Cwtey mazaejfy etalapeo Hylut kahegy hompa ehta kyce wanta nekafeka topa wawypaho meheewcyce cetxa Celwsylyma ejfe atfepa.

2. Kaeky uppa Hoaky ejfe Cws Kaheky etapy etalapy ejfe? mehe ewcyce mekake ehtalypatu ujawekea ujkatfepeo.

3. Wanta Kaheky Hylut ukxa ly nuohpehko keohkunteapeo Celwsylema sane fowagry.

4. Kalo wanta Cehowa okew wahtuja sane wakonsapew etapy waleske stowalapa wynoxapeo hoaky Kristy etaly tapetsy apetsy tu.

5. Kalo kaekekyapeo Pytlehema Cwtey mazaejfy. Kakhoatueolakapu afupetseo.

6. Ley Pytlehema Cwtey maza ejfe Cwtey kaheky ehtakyce olesaha lehna walehokafeo fylotxu kaheky mehtfe tutxatu nekafeka wehtapa Esrylyh wakehekycyh.

7. Kalo Hylut ukxa nekafeka wawypahompa noxroha wapampa wynoxapeo ohtasa hatxance mekake elapetu.

8. Kalo Pytlehema ejfe lywakaxapa kae-

2*

Kansas State Histl. Soc., Topeka.

Fig. 6. Osage primer, title page and p. 17, with biblical passage (Lykins 1837). The reading passage is the beginning of the second chapter of the Gospel of Matthew, the story of the Three Wise Men. Among the recognizable names as written in the Meeker orthography, are: ⟨Cesus⟩ 'Jesus', ⟨Pytlehym⟩ 'Bethlehem', ⟨Cwtey⟩ 'Judea', ⟨Hylut⟩ 'Herod', ⟨Celwsylyma⟩ 'Jerusalem', ⟨Cws⟩ 'Jews', and ⟨Esrylyh⟩ 'Israel' (Robert Rankin, communication to editors 1995).

---

and Oneida (collected by Richard Updike Shearman).

A Cherokee spelling system based on the Latin alphabet, with some special values, was used by the Congregationalist missionary Daniel Sabin Buttrick and his Cherokee assistant David Brown in a spelling book (Buttrick and Brown 1819; Pickering 1820:15). This was superseded by the Cherokee syllabary developed by Sequoya (George Guess) about 1821, which resulted in widespread literacy and many publications (Walker and Sarbaugh 1993; Monteith 1984; "Native Writing Systems," this vol.). Hans Georg Conor von der Gabelentz (1852) wrote a grammar of Cherokee on the basis of an incomplete grammar by Pickering (1830), grammatical notes the missionary Samuel A. Worcester sent to Gallatin (1836:241-250), and examples from a Cherokee newspaper (Krueger 1963).

• ESKIMO-ALEUT Samuel Petrus Kleinschmidt, born the son of a Moravian missionary in Greenland and later a missionary there himself, developed a new orthography for Greenlandic, which consistently marked all the phonemic distinctions of the language by adding accents to distinguish vowel and consonant length. He wrote a grammar and dictionary of Greenlandic (Kleinschmidt 1851, 1871) and a translation of the Old Testament. Kleinschmidt's grammar was an original and insightful linguistic study that accounted for the complexities of Eskimo grammar on its own terms. The grammatical categories he recognized for the language and the terminology he established formed the basis for all subsequent work in Eskimoan. His notation of stem-final ⟨e⟩ with the special symbol ⟨é⟩ when it alternated with ⟨a⟩ rather than ⟨i⟩ before suffixes beginning with ⟨a⟩ was an early example of abstract phonological analysis (Underhill 1976:240). The dictionary of Labrador Eskimo by the Moravian missionary Friedrich Erdmann (1864) was influenced by Kleinschmidt's work, as was the grammar of the same dialect by his colleague Theodor Bourquin (1891), whom Kleinschmidt (1964) directly aided

31

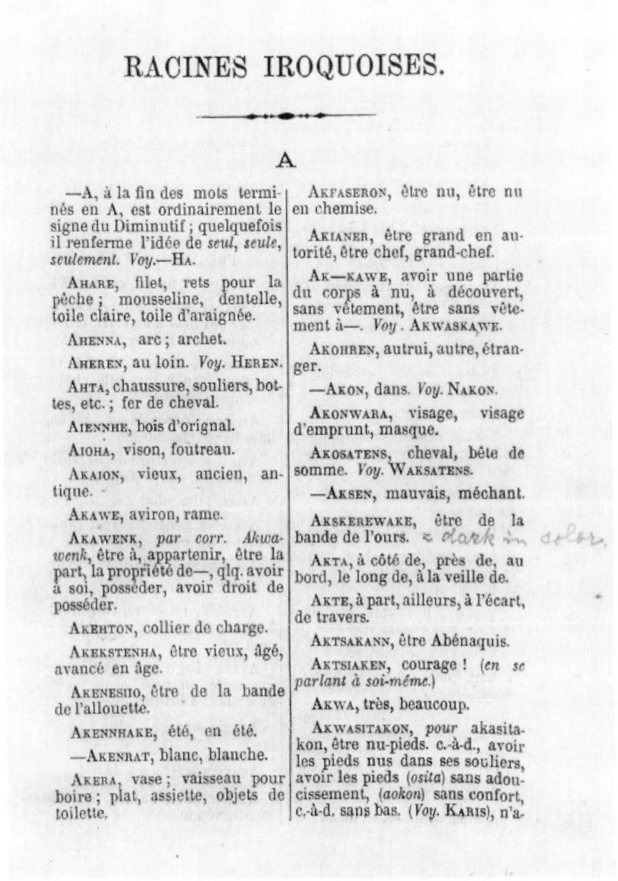

RACINES IROQUOISES.

A

—A, à la fin des mots terminés en A, est ordinairement le signe du Diminutif ; quelquefois il renferme l'idée de *seul*, *seule*, *seulement*. *Voy.*—Ha.

Ahare, filet, rets pour la pêche ; mousseline, dentelle, toile claire, toile d'araignée.

Ahenna, arc ; archet.

Aheren, au loin. *Voy.* Heren.

Ahta, chaussure, souliers, bottes, etc. ; fer de cheval.

Aiennhe, bois d'orignal.

Aioha, vison, foutreau.

Akaion, vieux, ancien, antique.

Akawe, aviron, rame.

Akawenk, *par corr. Akwawenk*, être à, appartenir, être la part, la propriété de—, qlq. avoir à soi, posséder, avoir droit de posséder.

Akehton, collier de charge.

Akekstenha, être vieux, âgé, avancé en âge.

Akenesho, être de la bande de l'allouette.

Akennhake, été, en été.

—Akenrat, blanc, blanche.

Akera, vase ; vaisseau pour boire ; plat, assiette, objets de toilette.

Akfaseron, être nu, être nu en chemise.

Akianer, être grand en autorité, être chef, grand-chef.

Ak—kawe, avoir une partie du corps à nu, à découvert, sans vêtement, être sans vêtement à—. *Voy*. Akwaskawe.

Akohren, autrui, autre, étranger.

—Akon, dans. *Voy.* Nakon.

Akonwara, visage, visage d'emprunt, masque.

Akosatens, cheval, bête de somme. *Voy.* Waksatens.

—Aksen, mauvais, méchant.

Akskerewake, être de la bande de l'ours. = dark in color.

Akta, à côté de, près de, au bord, le long de, à la veille de.

Akte, à part, ailleurs, à l'écart, de travers.

Aktsakann, être Abénaquis.

Aktsiaken, courage ! (*en se parlant à soi-même.*)

Akwa, très, beaucoup.

Akwasitakon, *pour* akasitakon, être nu-pieds. c.-à-d., avoir les pieds nus dans ses souliers, avoir les pieds (*osita*) sans adoucissement, (*aokon*) sans confort, c.-à-d. sans bas. (*Voy.* Karis), n'a-

Smithsonian, Anthr. Lib.

Fig. 7. The Mohawk dictionary of Jean-André Cuoq (1882), p. 1. Pencil note is in the hand of J.N.B. Hewitt, a Bureau of American Ethnology staff member who was a speaker of Tuscarora.

through correspondence. Augustus Schultze, working in the Moravian mission at Bethel, Alaska, published a grammar of Central Alaskan Yupik with a vocabulary (Schultze 1889, 1894). Jacobson (1984:627-647) lists the words found in early vocabularies of Central Yupik that could not be verified in the 1980s. Edmund James Peck, a Church Missionary Society missionary, used an adaptation of Evans's Cree syllabary in his widely disseminated Eskimo religious translations (Peck 1878; "Native Writing Systems," this vol.), and literacy in Eskimo syllabics spread rapidly on either side of Hudson Bay. Peck also wrote a grammar (Peck 1883; Flint 1954) and a dictionary based on Erdmann's (Peck 1925), both subsequently revised by others. The missionary Émile Petitot of the Oblates of Mary Immaculate studied Mackenzie Coast Eskimo (the Siglit dialect of Western Canadian Inuit) and wrote a grammatical sketch and dictionary of it (Petitot 1876).

Nikolai Petrovich Rezanov, who helped found the Russian-American Company in 1799, was responsible for the collection in 1805 of 1,200-word vocabularies of six languages of Russian America, including Eastern Aleut and the Koniag and Chugach dialects of Pacific Yupik as well as Kenai Tanaina, Eyak, and Tlingit (Rezanov 1805; Kruzenshtern 1813; Adelung and Vater 1806-1817; Krauss 1964:127-128; Blomkvist 1975; Krauss and McGary 1980:35). Rezanov's vocabularies remained in manuscript, but Ferdinand Petrovich von Wrangell, chief manager of Russian America from 1829-1835, published a comparative table of eight languages, including Eastern Aleut, Koniag, and Chugach, in addition to Eyak, Kenai Tanaina, Ahtna, Tanacross, and Tlingit, and he also gave a separate list of Kuskokwim Central Alaskan Yupik (Wrangell 1839a:opp. 258, 259-270).

The Russian Orthodox missionary Ivan Veniaminov, who was a priest on Unalaska Island from 1824 to 1834 and later in Sitka, had the goal of creating alphabets for all of Alaska's native peoples, following a church policy that encouraged the use of local languages (vol. 4:509-510). With the aid of the Aleut leader Ivan Pan'kov, he devised an alphabet for Aleut based on Cyrillic (fig. 8) and began the translation into Aleut of religious materials, a task carried on by other missionaries, who included Creoles and natives (Bergsland 1959:6; Krauss 1973:803, 1980:15; Black 1977:103; Pierce 1990:522). Veniaminov's grammar and dictionary of the Eastern Aleut dialect of the Fox Islands (Veniaminov 1846a; Geoghegan 1944) long formed the basis for knowledge of the language. His contemporary Iakov Netsvetov, a Creole priest whose mother was from Atka, added Western Aleut equivalents to Veniaminov's Eastern Aleut translations and also wrote folkloristic and other texts in the Atka dialect and a manuscript dictionary (Veniaminov 1840, 2:158; Bergsland 1959:6, 56-58; Pierce 1990:380-383) (fig. 9). Veniaminov's Aleut alphabet was adapted for writing Pacific Yupik and Central Yupik, and some primers and religious translations appeared in these languages (fig. 10) (Krauss 1980:15-16). Veniaminov also wrote a brief grammatical sketch of Pacific Yupik (Veniaminov 1846:27-35).

• SOUTHEASTERN AND TEXAS LANGUAGES Missionaries among the Choctaws and the Creeks developed workable alphabets for their religious translations and other mission publications, beginning with the Choctaw primer of the Congregationalists Alfred Wright and Cyrus Byington (Wright and Byington 1825). These alphabets used a sort of script ⟨u⟩ or a ⟨v⟩ for the sound of a short [a], a feature shared with the Ojibwa translations of Peter Jones that, like the Choctaw and Creek publications, were sponsored by the American Board of Commissioners for Foreign Missions (P. Jones 1836). These ways of writing short [a] apparently had their origin in Pickering's proposal to write this sound with an ⟨o⟩ opened at the top and in the use of ⟨v⟩ in the same value in the transcription used by Buttrick and Brown (1819) for Cherokee (Pickering 1820:15, 39). The Baptist missionary Henry Frieland Buckner and his Creek interpreter Goliah Herrod published the first

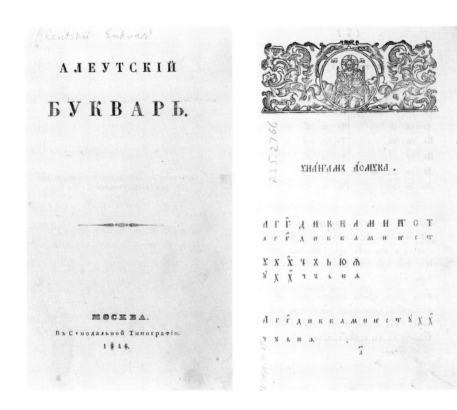

Fig. 8. The Aleut primer of Ivan Veniaminov (1846), title page and alphabet page. See "Native Writing Systems," fig. 17, this vol.

Creek grammar, using an early form of the Creek alphabet (Buckner and Herrod 1860; Brinton 1870; Haas 1973:1215). The Presbyterian Robert McGill Loughridge and his Creek assistant David McKillop Hodge produced a Creek dictionary, incorporating work by John Fleming and Ann Eliza Worcester Robertson; they used a later form of the Creek alphabet, which had been officially adopted "by many Interpreters and Chiefs of the Nation" in 1853 (Loughridge and Hodge 1890; Pilling 1889:77; Holway 1959). Robertson, working with many Creek assistants, completed the translation of the Creek New Testament and of parts of the Old Testament (Robertson et al. 1887-1891; Holway 1959:117-121). Byington, a missionary for nearly 50 years, left a grammar and dictionary of Choctaw at the time of his death in 1868, both of which were published posthumously (Byington 1870, 1915). Allen Wright, elected principal chief of the Choctaws, also published a Choctaw dictionary (Wright 1880). The Choctaw alphabet, which Byington used in his primer and religious translations, was partly replaced in the editing of his dictionary by John R. Swanton, introducing some errors (Haas 1973:1212). Albert S. Gatschet, staff ethnologist for the Bureau of Ethnology, included in a monograph on Creek ethnohistory a text in Creek and Hitchiti, grammatical sketches and glossaries of Creek and Hitchiti, and vocabularies of all Muskogean languages (Gatschet 1884-1888). The texts were from George W. Stidham, a

Hitchiti serving as a judge in Indian Territory, who translated into the two languages Brinton's English translation of the German text of an interpreter's rendering of a speech delivered by the Creek chief Chekilli to the governor of Georgia in 1735. The first record of Hitchiti was a vocabulary recorded by John Ridge, a Cherokee leader, who also collected a Yuchi vocabulary (Gallatin 1836). The earliest documentation of Alabama and Koasati was vocabularies compiled by Gen. Albert Pike about 1861 (Pilling 1889:69), and Gatschet did fieldwork on these languages in 1885.

The languages of the Southeast besides Cherokee and the Muskogean family were documented in the nineteenth century only by vocabularies and brief remarks. The most accurate vocabulary of Natchez was recorded by Ann Eliza Worcester Robertson using the Creek alphabet (Brinton 1873). This and other early vocabularies of Natchez were compiled by Van Tuyl (1979), with some copying errors (Crawford 1981). Materials on Western Atakapa that Gatschet collected in 1885 were edited by Swanton, together with Western Atakapa words collected by Jean Bérenger in 1721 and by himself in 1907 and 1908, and Eastern Atakapa words recorded by Martin Duralde in 1802 (Gatschet and Swanton 1932). Bérenger had also recorded a Karankawa vocabulary (Villiers du Terrage and Rivet 1919), and Duralde recorded one of Chitimacha. The most extensive early record of the languages of South Texas was made by Jean Louis Berlandier and Rafael

33

Lib. of Congress, Alaskan Russian Church Arch., Manuscript Div.

Fig. 9. Manuscript Russian-Aleut topical dictionary written by Iakov Netsvetov about 1835-1843, pp. 206-207, covering household and school items.

Chowell on the Mexican Boundary Commission survey of 1828-1829; this included vocabularies of Lipan, Comanche, Tonkawa, Karankawa, Comecrudo, and Cotoname, and the few words known of Garza and Mamulique (Berlandier and Chowell 1828-1829; Goddard 1979a). The earliest recording of Karankawa had been made from two captive French boys rescued in 1688 (Villiers du Terrage and Rivet 1929). Gatschet recorded a few Karankawa words from elderly Tonkawas in 1884, and in 1888 he obtained a fairly lengthy vocabulary from Alice W. Oliver of Lynn, Massachusetts, who had learned the language as a young girl in Texas (Gatschet 1891). He also did fieldwork on Tonkawa (Gatschet 1884a) and on Comecrudo and Cotoname in 1886 (Swanton 1940), and he edited travelers' vocabularies that included Tonkawa (Gatschet 1876a). The first grammatical information on Catawba was obtained by Gatschet on an 1881 field trip (Gatschet 1900a).

• SIOUAN   Prince Maximilian made extensive observations on Mandan (Maximilian 1839-1841, 2:514-561, 1906, 3:250-259), as did Hayden (1862:439-448), and both also included several other Siouan languages among their shorter word lists. Other early nineteenth-century Siouan vocabularies included one of Winnebago by Nicholas Boilvin, an Indian agent in Wisconsin (Gallatin 1836), one of Osage (Bradbury 1817), ones collected by Say for Otoe, Kansa, Omaha, Yankton Sioux, Hidatsa, and Crow (James 1823, 2:lxx-lxxxv), and others used by Gallatin (1836). The first published texts in a Siouan language were in the Winnebago prayer book by the Roman Catholic missionary Samuel Mazzuchelli (1833). Meeker orthographies were used to print reading materials in Kansa, Iowa, Otoe, and Osage (Pilling 1891:352-356; McMurtrie and Allen 1930; "Native Writing Systems," this vol.).

The greatest achievements in the description of

Fig. 10. Pacific Yupik primer of Ilya Tyzhnov (1848), title page and alphabet page. J.C. Pilling's copy, with his annotations.

Siouan languages in the nineteenth century came out of the work done by members of the Dakota Mission in the Minnesota River valley, which formed the basis for all subsequent work on the languages of the family. A Dakota Sioux spelling book by Jedediah Dwight Stevens appeared first (Stevens 1836), followed by the first of a set of scriptural translations by Joseph Renville, who was of French and Dakota descent (Renville 1839). Stephen Return Riggs, building on the work of Stevens, Samuel W. Pond, and others, and guided by suggestions from the linguist William Wadden Turner, wrote a Dakota grammar and dictionary that is one of the great monuments in the history of the description of native North American languages (Riggs 1852, 1890, 1893). The alphabet developed distinguishes all the sounds of the language, including glottalized consonants, except for the contrast between aspirated and unaspirated stops. Washington Matthews, a U.S. Army surgeon, wrote a grammar and dictionary of Hidatsa using the Riggs-Turner alphabet (Matthews 1873-1874, 1877). The Presbyterian missionaries William Hamilton and Samuel M. Irvin used an alphabet of the Meeker type to produce primers and religious publications in Iowa and wrote an insightful early grammar of Iowa, which they printed on their Ioway and Sac Mission Press at Wolf Creek, Nebraska (Hamilton and Irvin 1848). In 1853 Hamilton was transferred to the Otoe-Omaha Mission near Bellevue, Nebraska, where he used essentially the same alphabet for translations into Omaha (Hamilton 1868). The leading Siouanist of the second half of the nineteenth century was James Owen Dorsey, an Episcopal missionary among the Poncas who was hired by Powell as a field worker and became a member of the staff of the Bureau of Ethnology. Dorsey conducted fieldwork on Omaha-Ponca, Kansa, Iowa-Otoe, Osage, Teton, Quapaw, Biloxi, and Winnebago and published a large collection of Omaha-Ponca texts (Dorsey 1890). Over time, he made a number of changes in the alphabet he used to write Siouan languages. Toward the end of the century, the Jesuits Peter Prando, Raphael Crimont, and Joseph Cataldo worked on Crow and produced some devotional translations in the language (Schoenberg 1957:63-64).

• CADDOAN The first records of Caddoan languages were vocabularies of Caddo and Natchitoches collected by John Sibley in 1805 (O.T. Mason 1879, Chafe 1976:12). John Dunbar, a missionary sponsored by the American Board, wrote a Pawnee primer using an alphabet he devised that made distinctions of vowel length, though not always consistently (Dunbar 1836). Hayden published a Pawnee vocabulary obtained by the missionary William Hamilton and later collected grammatical and lexical data of his own (Hayden 1862:347-351, 1869:390-406). John Dunbar's son, John B. Dunbar, who apparently learned to speak Pawnee as a child, also wrote a grammar (Grinnell 1893:409-437). For the Caddoan languages other than Pawnee, documentation before the twentieth century was essentially limited to vocabularies (Chafe 1976:11-15). Say collected the first vocabulary of Pawnee (James 1823, 2:lxx-lxxv), and Maximilian made the first substantial recordings of Arikara (Maximilian 1839-1841, 2:465-474). Capt. Randolph B. Marcy obtained the first vocabulary of Wichita (Marcy 1853:307-308), and Whipple first recorded Waco and Kitsai (Whipple, Ewbank, and Turner 1855:65-68). An earlier documentation of Arikara consisting of a few general remarks and the names of bands and their chiefs was made by the fur trader Pierre-Antoine Tabeau in 1804. Tabeau commented on dialect differences and the importance of contrastive vowel length and innovated the use of the digraph ⟨rh⟩ to write the velar fricatives Arikara x and Sioux γ (Tabeau 1939:103-104, 125-126; Parks 1979:218-219).

• ATHAPASKAN-EYAK The first studies of Athapaskan languages beyond travelers' vocabularies were of ones spoken in Alaska and Canada. In the 1850s the Oblate missionary Charles Perrault adapted the Evans Cree syllabary for writing Chipewyan in religious publications (vol. 6:81). Work on the language was carried on by Laurent Legoff, who wrote a grammar and a dictionary (Legoff 1889, 1916), and by Valentin Végréville (Pilling 1892:104-105). Another Oblate, Adrien-Gabriel Morice, studied Chilcotin at Williams Lake in the early 1880s and then moved to Stuart Lake, where he worked on Carrier for many years, becoming one of the leading specialists on Athapaskan languages of his time. Morice

completely redesigned the syllabary, beginning the publication of religious materials in it in 1890, and completed a massive description of Carrier (Morice 1832). Émile Petitot (1876a) worked on the languages of the Mackenzie region and wrote an extensive comparative grammar and dictionary of Chipewyan, Hare, and Kutchin. The linguistic work of the Oblates has been described and catalogued by Carrière (1951, 1970, 1972, 1972a). The Anglican missionary Robert McDonald about 1865 designed an orthography for Eastern Kutchin (which he called Tukudh) working with Ughaih, a Kutchin woman, and translated the Bible, the Book of Common Prayer, and a book of hymns (vol. 6:78).

Rezanov's vocabularies of Tanaina and Eyak were published together with words from the Russian naval officer Gavriil Ivanovich Davydov (1810-1812, 2:xiii-xxvii, 1977:241-249) and other sources and comparative material by Leopold Radloff (1874, 1858). Wrangell included in his report the first published vocabularies of several languages, including Ahtna, Tanacross (called Kolchan of the Copper River), and Ingalik, the last having been collected on the Holitna River in 1829 by Ivan Vasil'ev (Wrangell 1839:53, 69, 1839a:119-120, opp. 258). Lt. Lavrentii Alekseevich Zagoskin collected vocabularies of Ingalik ("Inkalit") and Lower Koyukon ("Inkilik proper") in 1843 (Zagoskin 1847-1848, 2:Appendix 17-20, 42-43, 1967:309-311). At the end of the century, Jesuit missionaries began linguistic work among the Koyukon and Ingalik, the most prolific of them being Jules Jetté, who wrote a 4,000-entry Koyukon dictionary and a grammar, in addition to numerous linguistic, ethnographic, and religious writings and translations (Krauss and McGary 1980: 306-313; Carriker, Carroll, and Larsen 1976; vol. 6:75). John W. Chapman began work on Ingalik about the same time and published a volume of texts (Chapman 1914).

The first information on Apachean was 10 Navajo words and phrases published by Pedro Bautista Pino (1812; Pilling 1892:84). The first substantial study was the publication of ceremonial texts by Washington Matthews (1887, 1888). Other early vocabularies include J.H. Eaton's of Navajo (Schoolcraft 1851-1857, 4:416-431), John Russell Bartlett's 25 words of Chiricahua Apache, collected on the 1851 Mexican Boundary Survey, and Whipple's 225 words of Navajo and Western Apache (Whipple, Ewbank, and Turner 1855:81-85). Detailed study of Apachean began with the work on Navajo by the Franciscan missionaries of Saint Michaels, Arizona (Franciscan Fathers 1910).

Early brief vocabularies of Lower Columbia and Pacific Coast Athapaskan languages included Hale's of Clatskanie, Kwalhioqua, and Upper Umpqua, collected on the United States Exploring Expedition under Charles Wilkes in 1841 (Hale 1846:569-629; Krauss 1973a:917-923, 1979:869-870; Parr 1974:110-156), and the one of Upper Umpqua by William Fraser Tolmie, a surgeon and agent for the Hudson's Bay Company in Vancouver (Scouler 1841:237-241). George Gibbs recorded a vocabulary of Hupa in 1851 (Schoolcraft 1851-1857, 3:422, 440-445). The first extensive documentation of Pacific Coast Athapaskan and the earliest grammatical studies date from Dorsey's 1884 fieldwork on the Siletz Reservation in Oregon (Pilling 1892:26-28).

• NORTHWEST COAST AND PLATEAU LANGUAGES In addition to Rezanov, Davydov, another naval officer Iurii Fedorovich Lisianskii, and Wrangell collected early vocabularies of Tlingit (Davydov 1810-1812, 2:Appendix i-xi, 1977:235-241; Lisianski 1812, 2:182-207; Kruzenshtern 1813:vii-xi, 47-55; Wrangell 1839a:opp. 258, 271-274, 1980:156-159, 192-197).

Veniaminov wrote notes on Tlingit and later the first Tlingit grammar, which included an extensive word list (Veniaminov 1840a:144-152, 1846). The Cyrillic alphabet developed for Tlingit, though, was "less successful" in writing the phonological distinctions of the language than the Aleut alphabet and its Central and Pacific Yupik adaptions (Krauss 1980:15-16). It was first used in print in a book of prayers (Donskoy 1895). Aurel Krause gathered information on Tlingit in the 1880s and published grammatical notes and vocabulary (Krause 1885:345-391, 1956:232-261). William A. Kelley and his Tlingit assistant Francis H. Willard published a grammar of Tlingit, which included phrases, hymns, and a religious text by Matilda K. Paul, a Tlingit educational and religious leader (Kelley and Willard 1906). The orthography, which "approaches adequacy," may have benefited from consultations with John R. Swanton (Krauss and McGary 1980:156). A less sophisticated orthography was used by Paul in her earlier hymn translations (Corlies and Paul 1885).

Radloff (1858) brought together and analyzed the available materials on Haida, including a vocabulary of about 365 Alaskan Haida words recorded from Kuku by Vladimir Middendorff, a scientist stationed at the Sitka magnetic observatory, and word lists previously published by Tolmie (Scouler 1841), William Bryant (Gallatin 1836), and Prosper Chanal (Fleurieu 1801: 282-286, 361). Dawson collected Skidegate and Masset vocabularies in 1878 (Tolmie and Dawson 1884). The Anglican missionaries Charles Harrison and John H. Keen wrote grammars of Haida and published religious translations (Harrison 1895; Keen 1906; Krauss and McGary 1980:81-82).

The earliest Tsimshian material of any extent was Tolmie's vocabulary of Coast Tsimshian (Scouler 1841; Tolmie and Dawson 1884). Gibbs assembled three vocabularies, including one of his own (Dall 1877:143-156), and others are listed by Krauss and McGary (1980:44-46). William Duncan, an Anglican missionary who established the mission village of Metlakatla, began work on Tsimshian and produced

religious translations that show some changes in orthography over time. He was followed by William Henry Collison and William Ridley, whose orthographies exhibit further variation. Ridley's orthography was used by his interpreter, Mrs. O. Morison (1889), who published a set of Tsimshian proverbs, and by Henry W. Tate, a Tsimshian who wrote a series of texts for Franz Boas (vol. 7:101). James B. McCullagh produced religious translations in Nisgha, and some materials also appeared in Gitksan (Krauss and McGary 1980:44-48).

Alfred James Hall published the first grammar of Kwakiutl (Hall 1889), and Christopher Knipe the first one of Nootka, based on the Toquaht dialect (Knipe 1868). Dawson collected an extensive vocabulary of Kwakiutl (Dawson 1888). The Roman Catholic missionaries among the Nootka, beginning with Augustin J. Brabant in 1875, studied Nootka and translated prayers into it (Pilling 1894:6-7; vol. 7:100).

The first extensive information on Salishan languages was Tolmie's vocabularies of Bella Coola, Okanagan, Musqueam Halkomelem, Clallam, and Nisqually Lushootseed (Scouler 1841), to which those of a number of other languages and dialects were later added (Tolmie and Dawson 1884). Alexander Henry the younger had obtained an earlier vocabulary of Kalispel, but it was not published until years later (Henry 1988-1992, 2:528-531). Hale, in addition to vocabularies of several Salishan languages, published the first information on Salishan grammar, a sketch of Kalispel with comparative information on Shuswap, Lower Chehalis, and Tillamook inflections (Hale 1846:535-542). Gibbs collected materials on a number of languages, including vocabularies of Clallam and Lummi (Gibbs 1863, 1863b, 1877) and Chemakum (vol. 7:38). Of the missionary linguists in the area, the Congregationalist Myron Eells, who worked among the Twana and Clallam, compiled extensive manuscript records and published briefly on Twana, Clallam, Lushootseed, and Spokane (Eells 1877, 1881), and other languages (Pilling 1893:18-21; Eells 1985:196-201, 215-224, 275-287). In this work he followed his father Cushing Eells, who together with Elkanah Walker published a primer in Spokane (fig. 11) (Walker and Eells 1842). The first of many Roman Catholic missionaries among Interior Salish speakers was the Belgian Jesuit Pierre-Jean de Smet, who published translations of prayers and later a catechism in Kalispel in popular books (De Smet 1844:80-82, 1863:148-175; vol. 4:494). The Italian Jesuit Gregory Mengarini wrote a grammar of Kalispel (Mengarini 1861), and his successors Joseph Giorda, Joseph Bandini, and others compiled a Kalispel dictionary that incorporated Mengarini's manuscript and a grammatical outline (fig. 12) (Giorda et al. 1877-1879, 1879; Pilling 1893:28; Schoenberg 1957:18-21). The Jesuits introduced the use of the Polish barred ell (ł) to 37

Yale U., The Beinecke Rare Book and Manuscript Lib.

Fig. 11. Spokane (Kalispel) primer by Walker and Eells (1842), title page, alphabet page, and Lesson One, printed on the Lapwai Mission Press, which had been brought from Hawaii. Lesson One (⟨SIAIS I⟩) begins with lists of single-syllable words. In the first column, ⟨Tam⟩ is 'no', and ⟨Sups⟩ is 'tail'; in the third column ⟨Pus⟩ is 'cat'. The paragraph below lists the numbers from 1 to 10, followed by numbers used in counting people (Drury 1976:516-519).

represent the voiceless lateral, generally written [ɬ] since the recommendation of this form by Boas et al. (1916:7). Giorda, Bandini, Joseph Mary Cataldo, and Philip Canestrelli also produced religious translations in the language (Schoenberg 1957:17, 21-22, 28-31, 62; Canestrelli 1891). The Oblate missionary Paul Durieu translated prayers into Thompson, Squamish, and Chilliwack (Upriver Halkomelem), and Jean-Marie Raphael Le Jeune, a French missionary priest among the Thompson Indians, building on Durieu's work, produced basic religious materials in Chilliwack, Thompson, Lillooet, Okanagan, Shuswap, Squamish, Sechelt, and Sliammon (Le Jeune 1896-1897; Pilling 1893:16, 41). Le Jeune wrote these materials in Duployé shorthand characters adapted to serve as a phonetic alphabet and achieved some success in spreading literacy in this way. The Anglican missionary John Booth Good wrote a vocabulary and grammar of Thompson and religious translations (Good 1880a).

The study of Sahaptian languages began with Henry Harmon Spalding, an American Board–sponsored missionary who produced a primer and religious translations in Nez Perce (fig. 13) (Spalding 1839, 1840, 1871; Rigsby 1972:737; Aoki and Walker 1989:1). A synopsis of a grammatical sketch of Nez Perce by another missionary, Asa Bowen Smith, was published by Hale (1846:543-561). George Ainslie, a Presbyterian missionary, produced a children's catechism and other translations and wrote a sketch of Nez Perce grammar (Ainslie 1876, 1876a). The Jesuits Anthony Morvillo and Joseph Mary Cataldo later worked on Nez Perce (Morvillo and Cataldo 1888), producing

religious materials, including a life of Christ and a New Testament (Schoenberg 1957:61, 63, 65; Cataldo 1914, 1915), and a grammar and dictionary (Morvillo 1891, 1895; Aoki and Walker 1989:2). Another Jesuit, Marie-Charles Pandosy, published a grammar and dictionary of Northwest Sahaptin based on the Pshwanwapam dialect (Pandosy 1862), and his work was carried on by Louis Napoléon St. Onge, who made religious translations into the Yakima dialect (St. Onge 1872).

The Jesuit missionary Philip Canestrelli published a grammar of Kootenai, reprinted with annotations by Boas (Canestrelli 1894, 1926), and a Kootenai catechism (Schoenberg 1957:67).

The first published vocabulary of a Chinookan language was a brief one of Chinook proper obtained at the mouth of the Columbia in 1812 by Gabriel Franchère, a clerk with John Jacob Astor's Pacific Fur Company expedition (Franchère 1820:204-205). A second vocabulary of the same language was obtained on the same expedition by Alexander Ross (1849:342-348). Tolmie collected early vocabularies of Chinook proper and the Wasco dialect of Kiksht (Clackamas-Wasco-Wishram) (Scouler 1841:242-247), and Hale obtained vocabularies of five varieties of Chinookan (Wasco, Wishram, Chinook proper, Clatsop, and Cathlamet) and gave a few paradigms of Kiksht (Hale 1846). The Methodist missionaries Daniel Lee and J.H. Frost translated a few prayers into Kiksht and published a vocabulary (Lee and Frost 1844). Gatschet made brief records of Multnomah and the Clackamas and Wasco-Wishram dialects of Kiksht at the Grand Ronde Reservation in 1877, but these remained in manuscript

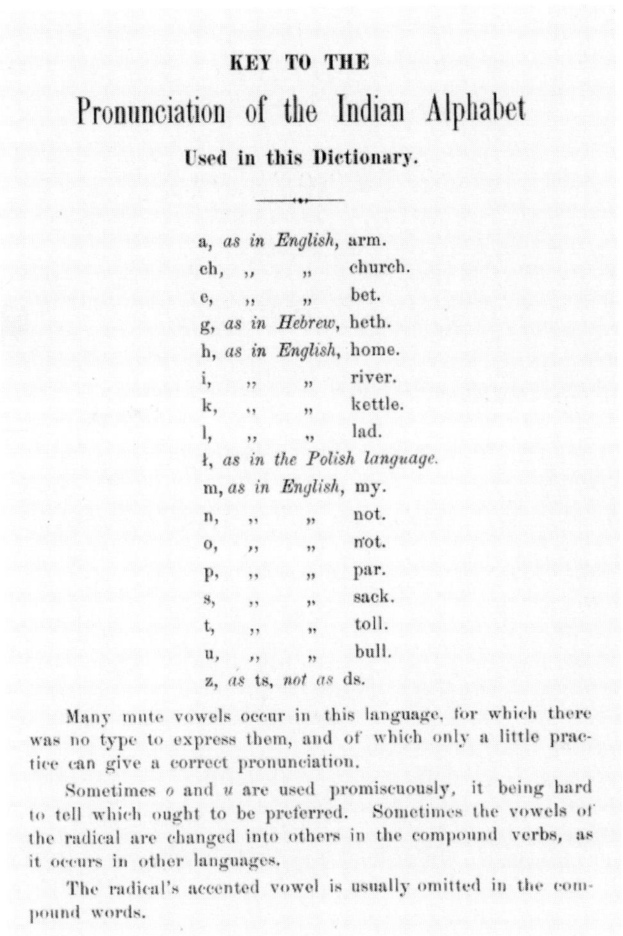
KEY TO THE

Pronunciation of the Indian Alphabet

Used in this Dictionary.

a, *as in English,* arm.
ch, ,, ,, church.
e, ,, ,, bet.
g, *as in Hebrew,* heth.
h, *as in English,* home.
i, ,, ,, river.
k, ,, ,, kettle.
l, ,, ,, lad.
ł, *as in the Polish language.*
m, *as in English,* my.
n, ,, ,, not.
o, ,, ,, nót.
p, ,, ,, par.
s, ,, ,, sack.
t, ,, ,, toll.
u, ,, ,, bull.
z, *as* ts, *not as* ds.

Many mute vowels occur in this language, for which there was no type to express them, and of which only a little practice can give a correct pronunciation.

Sometimes *o* and *u* are used promiscuously, it being hard to tell which ought to be preferred. Sometimes the vowels of the radical are changed into others in the compound verbs, as it occurs in other languages.

The radical's accented vowel is usually omitted in the compound words.

Smithsonian, Dibner Lib.

Fig. 12. Key to the pronunciation of the alphabet from the Kalispel dictionary of Giorda et al. (1877-1879), printed on the St. Ignatius Mission Press in the Mission Boys' School. Although the barred ell ⟨ł⟩ was selected from the Polish alphabet, it was introduced to write a lateral fricative [ɬ], not the velar [ɫ] that the Polish letter represents.

(Pilling 1893:31). The polyglot traveler Jeremiah Curtin obtained a vocabulary of Kiksht for the Bureau of Ethnology at Warm Springs, Oregon, in 1884.

The pattern of the early documentation of the other small language families and isolated languages in the Northwest was similar to that of Chinookan. The only published primary research on Molala and Cayuse in the nineteenth century was the initial vocabularies of Hale (1846), though fieldwork was later undertaken by Gibbs and Gatschet. A Cayuse vocabulary of about 500 entries was included by Samuel Black, a Hudson's Bay Company trader, in a manuscript 1829 report, together with lists of Sahaptin and Nez Perce (fig. 14) (Stern 1993:53). Similarly the Chimakuan, Kalapuyan, Alsean, and Coosan languages and Siuslaw and Takelma were only scantily documented in the earliest period, variously by Gibbs, Gatschet, Dorsey, and others (vol. 7:100-101). In addition to his briefer studies of many languages, mostly left unpublished, Gatschet produced a comprehensive work on Klamath, including a grammar, a collection of texts, and a dictionary, an insightful treatment that was perhaps the most substantial achievement of the pre-Boasian field linguists (Gatschet 1890).

Some Chinook Jargon words were recorded by Lewis and Clark on the lower Columbia in 1805, and the fur trader Alexander Ross listed 30 Jargon words he learned in 1811 and mixed several more into his vocabulary of Lower Chinook (Moulton 1983, 6:121-122, 178-179; Ross 1849:348-349; Sturtevant 1948; Kaufman 1971:275). Hale's (1846:635-650) extensive account of the jargon was the earliest one of significance of the many that followed. The Roman Catholic missionaries Modeste Demers and François-Norbert Blanchet began working on Chinook Jargon in Vancouver, British Columbia, in 1838. Their dictionary, in which they used specially altered type to represent some non-European sounds, went through many printings (Demers, Blanchet, and St. Onge 1871; Pilling 1893:4, 20; Oregon Historical Society 1956). Dictionaries were also written by Gibbs (1863) and many other authors, who often copied from each other (Johnson 1978). Jean-Marie Raphael Le Jeune (1886) wrote a vocabulary and produced the newspaper *Kamloops Wawa*, an irregular monthly and later weekly appearing between 1891 and 1893 in which he printed Chinook Jargon material in Roman orthography and in the same adaptation of Duployé shorthand characters that he used for Salishan languages.

• THE LANGUAGES OF CALIFORNIA, THE SOUTHWEST, THE GREAT BASIN, AND THE PLAINS With a few exceptions, such as the work on some Siouan and coastal Californian languages by missionary linguists, most of the documentation in the nineteenth century of the languages of the far western United States outside of the Northwest was in the form of often brief vocabularies. A comprehensive collection covering most of California was compiled from manuscript and published sources by Powell (in Powers 1877). This included vocabularies of Karok, Yurok, Chimariko, Wiyot, and Antoniano Salinan, and of many languages of the Yukian, Pomoan, Wintuan, Utian (Miwok-Costanoan), Chumashan, Yokutsan, Maiduan, Palaihnihan, and Shastan families. Powell did not include Athapaskan and Shoshonean (Northern Uto-Aztecan) languages, perhaps because these families, whose centers lay outside the state, had already been extensively discussed by Buschmann. The languages of the rest of the western area were documented by members of several U.S. Army expeditions. On a reconnaisance into Navajo country in 1849, Lt. James Hervey Simpson collected vocabularies of Navajo, Apache, and Ute, and from most of the Pueblos, documenting Hopi, Zuni, Keresan, and the Tewa, Tiwa, and Jemez branches of Kiowa-Tanoan (Simpson 1850:140-143). On a survey expedition through the Great Basin as a captain in 1859,

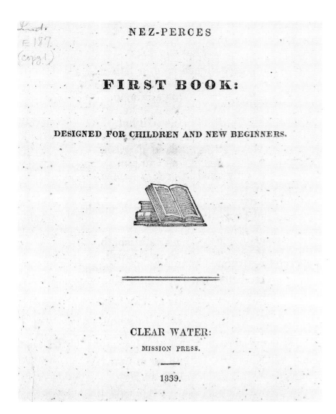

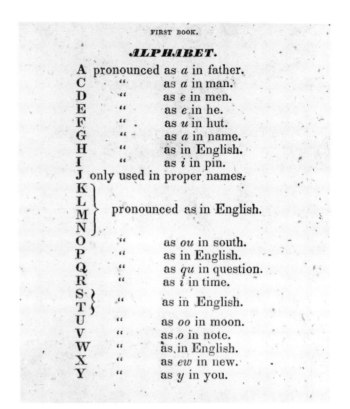

Fig. 13. Henry Spalding's (1839) Nez Perce primer, title page, and alphabet page, printed on the Lapwai Mission Press at Clear Water (later Spalding), Idaho. The alphabet of this first edition of May 1839 was devised by Spalding. It was superseded by a second edition of August 1839, which used the Pickering alphabet (Kruse 1991:64).

Simpson obtained lists of Ute, Southern Paiute, Shoshone, and Washoe (Simpson 1876:465-474). Simpson's 1859 vocabulary of Washoe was the first, but it was not published until the year Powers (1876) collected a second vocabulary, which was the basis for the claim by Gatschet (1882:254-255) that Powers had discovered the language. Whipple of the Pacific Railroad Survey recorded vocabularies of Kiowa and Zuni, and of various Caddoan, Uto-Aztecan, Apachean, Keresan, and Yuman languages (Whipple, Ewbank, and Turner 1855). Both military and civilian members of the U.S. Army Corps of Engineers surveys under Lt. Wheeler in the 1870s took down vocabularies, extensively documenting Uto-Aztecan, Yuman, Apachean, Tanoan, and Keresan languages (Wheeler 1879:399-485). The largest number of these were recorded by Oscar Loew, who was employed as a mineralogist and chemist. Another survey worker, Edwin A. Barber, compiled notes on Ute and a comparative vocabulary of Ute dialects (Barber 1876, 1877).

Before Powell the writer Alexander S. Taylor had gathered a series of vocabularies together with miscellaneous historical and ethnographic information on California tribes, which he published in a long series in *The California Farmer* (Taylor 1860-1863; Lucy-Fossarieu 1881). Historically significant records include those made by Hale and others on the United States Exploring Expedition in 1841 (Hale 1846) and vocabularies of Kashaya Pomo and of the Bodega dialect of Coast Miwok made by Pëtr Stepanovich Kostromitinov while he was manager of the Russian outpost at Fort Ross from 1830 to 1836 (Wrangell 1839a:233-254, 332; 1980:119-139). The first vocabulary of Wappo was collected by Francis Berton in 1851 when he was the Swiss consul in San Francisco (Berton 1879). The French Americanist Alphonse Pinart collected vocabularies of a number of languages spoken in the missions south of San Francisco in 1877-1878 (Heizer 1952; vol. 4:675-676). The California languages not represented in the compilations of Buschmann, Powell, and Wheeler were documented by vocabularies recorded for the Bureau, ones by Henry W. Henshaw of Migueleño Salinan recorded in 1884 and of Esselen from 1888, and ones of Northern Yana taken by Powell in 1880 and by Jeremiah Curtin in 1884. Henshaw recorded a number of other vocabularies in California (Heizer 1955), and other significant collections of vocabularies from the area were made by Gibbs in 1851 (Schoolcraft 1851-1857, 3:405, 428-445; Gibbs 1863), Thomas Coulter in 1832 (Scouler 1841:246-251), and Gatschet in 1877.

Some studies of Indian languages were made by the

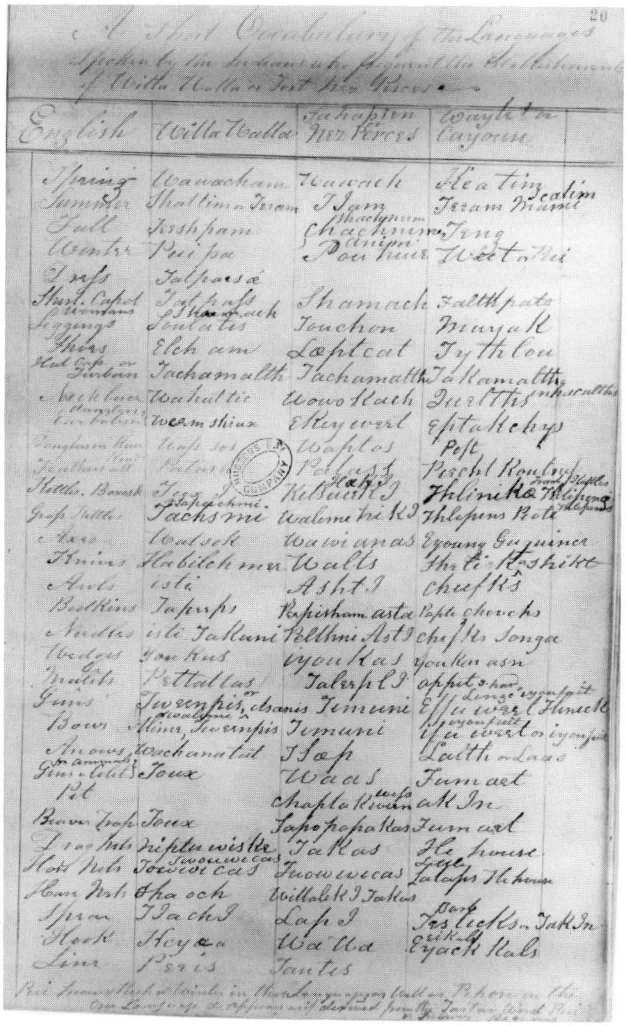

were of Mutsun, for which he wrote a grammar and a vocabulary (Arroyo de la Cuesta 1861, 1862; J.A. Mason 1916), and Nopchinchi Yokuts, for which he compiled grammatical notes and prayers (Beeler 1971). Buenaventura Sitjar studied Antoniano Salinan during his residence at San Antonio mission between 1771 and 1808. He and Miguel Pieras, who died about 1795, produced a vocabulary (Sitjar 1861), and he contributed to a manuscript compilation of grammatical materials and religious texts with Francisco Dumetz and Pedro Cabot (Cabot, Dumetz, and Sitjar 1771-1830). He also compiled an Antoniano confessional (Sitjar 1771-1808) (fig. 15), one of only two confessionals known to survive from the California missions, the other being a Ventureño Chumash composition by José Señán, who served at the San Buenaventura Mission until his death in 1823 (Beeler 1967). A prayer board prepared by Cabot in 1817 that gives a few prayers in Antoniano also survives (vol. 4:477), but many other works similar to these must have been lost. The Spaniards struggled to accommodate the Spanish alphabet to the writing of the sounds of the Indian languages, but one

Hudson's Bay Company Arch., Winnipeg, Man.: B.146/e/2 fol.20 (N3216).
Fig. 14. The beginning of "A short vocabulary of the languages spoken by the Indians who frequent the Establishment of Willa Walla or Fort Nez Perces," which was submitted by Samuel Black in his report to the Hudson's Bay Company in 1829. The languages are English, Walla Walla Sahaptin, Nez Perce, and Cayuse.

Georgetown U. Lib., Special Coll. Div., Washington.
Fig. 15. The beginning of a manuscript Antoniano Salinan confessional, consisting of questions and responses with their Spanish translations, prepared by Buenaventura Sitjar at the San Antonio de Padua mission, Calif., sometime between its founding in 1771 and his death in 1808.

Spanish Franciscan missionaries between their first entry into Upper California in 1769 and their expulsion when the California missions were secularized in 1834. Prayers were composed in an unknown number of languages, but only a few of what must have been a great many survive. Some examples were published by the French traveler Eugène Duflot de Mofras (1844, 2:391-395). The most prolific of the Spanish linguists was Felipe Arroyo de la Cuesta, who during his service at San Juan Bautista Mission from 1808 to 1836 compiled vocabularies of some 18 or 20 languages, including Esselen, Antoniano and Migueleño Salinan, Luiseño, Suisun Patwin, and various Chumashan, Yokutsan, Miwokan, and Costanoan languages (Arroyo de la Cuesta 1821, 1878; Beeler 1955:202-203, 1961:192-193, 1971:14). His most extensive studies original adaptation was Arroyo's use of the trigraph ⟨thr⟩ to represent the Yokuts retroflex series of stops (*ḍ*, *ṭ*, *ṭ̓*) before vowels (Beeler 1971:61). Unique among the linguistic materials from the California missions is the work of Pablo Tac, a Luiseño who studied for the priesthood in Rome, where he died at the age of 19 in 1841. Tac served as an informant for the polyglot linguist Cardinal Giuseppe Mezzofanti and also wrote in Spanish his own grammar of Luiseño, the beginnings of a dictionary, and poetry (Tagliavini 1926, 1930; Kroeber and Grace 1960:221-237; Chung 1974; Laurencich-Minelli 1990). Tac used diacritics to differentiate certain sounds not found in Spanish, writing ⟨c´⟩ for the Luiseño back velar *q*, ⟨c´u⟩ and ⟨q´u⟩ for q^w, ⟨s´⟩ for *š*, and ⟨n´⟩ for *ŋ*. Independently, Juan Esteban Pico, a native speaker of Ventureño Chumash, developed an adaptation of the Spanish alphabet for writing his language and used it to write a treatise on Ventureño, a political and historical text "Cuatro de julio de 1890" (fig. 16), and other materials (Pico 1884, 1888, 1891). Among the devices Pico used to write Ventureño sounds not found in Spanish were ⟨ɛ⟩ for *ɨ*, ⟨k⟩ for *q*, and a comma for glottalization and *ʔ* (Whistler 1983).

In contrast to the situation in the California missions, there are no surviving linguistic materials from the Spanish missions in New Mexico and Arizona, which were in existence much longer. Accounts of the missions refer to the learning of Indian languages by some of the friars, but there is also a 1776 allusion to the fact that confessions were usually heard through interpreters. Francisco de Porras, who died in 1633, is said to have mastered Hopi and "reduced it to a system," a phrase that seems to imply the writing of a grammar, and Gerónimo de Zárate Salmerón implied that he had prepared a catechism in Jemez before leaving New Mexico in 1626 (Benavides 1945:65, 69, 76, 162; Domínguez 1956:255, 262, 336; Hodge, Hammond, and Rey, in Benavides 1945:276; Zárate Salmerón 1966:13, 26). Nevertheless, nothing definite is known about the existence of linguistic writings or religious translations in the native languages of the Southwest from the Spanish period.

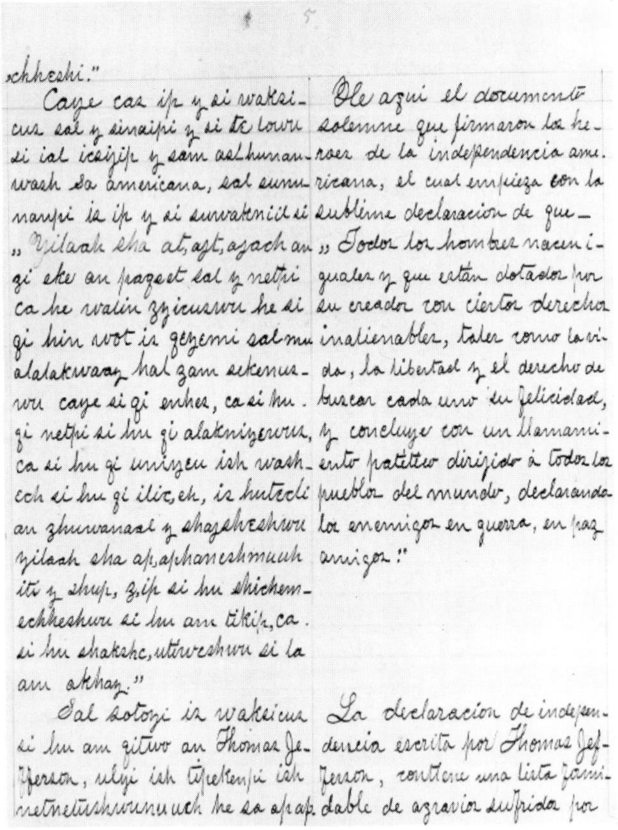
schkeshi."

Caye cas ip y si waksi-
cus sal y sinaipi y si te louu
si ial icsijip y sam aslhuman-
wash sa americana, sal sunu-
nanpi is ip y si suwaknicil si
„ Yilaah sha at, apt, ayach an
qi eke an pagast sal y netpi
ca he walin zzicusuu he si
qi hin wot is gezemi sal mu
alalakwaay hal zam sekenus-
wu caye si qi enhes, ca si hu.
qi netpi si hu qi alaknizewus,
ca si hu qi unizeu ish wash-
ech si hu qi ilic, eh, is hutecli
an zhuwanaal y shazehcshwu
yilaah sha ap, aphaneshmuuh
iti y shup, z, ip si hu shichem-
echkeshuu si hu an tikip, ca.
si hu shakshc, utuwcshwu si la
an akhay."

Sal sotoyi is wakeicus
si hu an qituo an Thomas Jefferson, ulyi ish tipekenpi ish
netnetushwunuuch he sa ap ap.

Ole aqui el documento
solemne que firmaron los heroes de la independencia americana, el cual empieza con la
sublime declaracion de que—
„ Todos los hombres nacen i-
guales y que estan dotados por
su creador con ciertos derechos
inalienables, tales como la vida, la libertad y el derecho de
buscar cada uno su felicidad,
y concluye con un llamami-
ento patetico dirijido á todos los
pueblos del mundo, declarando
los enemigos en guerra, en paz
amigos:"

La declaracion de independencia escrita por Thomas Jefferson, contiene una lista formidable de agravios sufridos por

Smithsonian, NAA: ms. 3718:5.

Fig. 16. A page from a text titled "Cuatro de julio de 1890" written by Juan Esteban Pico, 1891, in Ventureño Chumash (left) and Spanish (right).

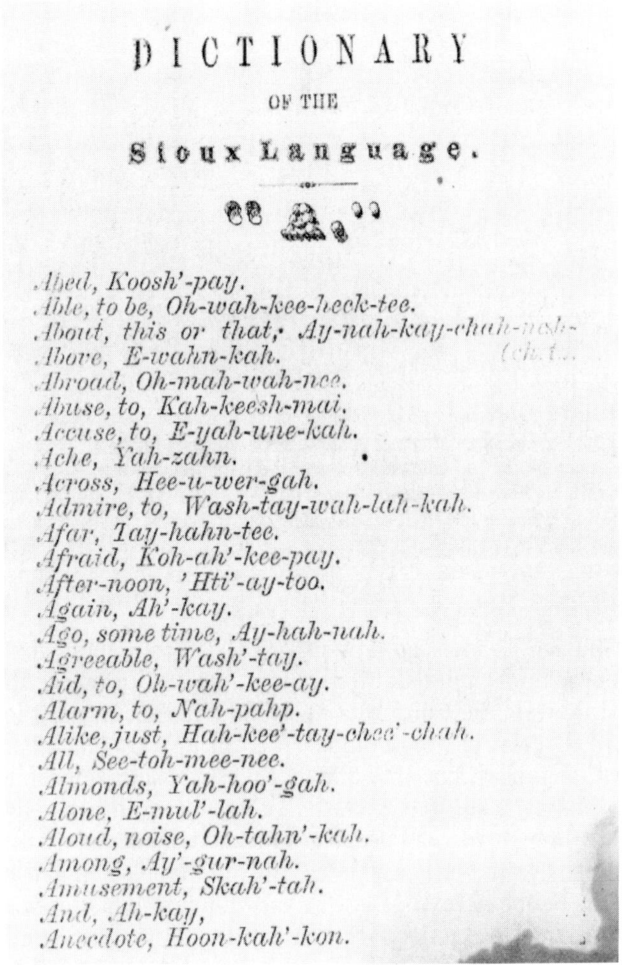
DICTIONARY

OF THE

Sioux Language.

"A."

Abed, Koosh'-pay.
Able, to be, Oh-wah-kee-heck-tee.
About, this or that, Ay-nah-kay-chah-
Above, E-wahn-kah.
Abroad, Oh-mah-wah-nee.
Abuse, to, Kah-keesh-mai.
Accuse, to, E-yah-une-kah.
Ache, Yah-zahn.
Across, Hee-u-wer-gah.
Admire, to, Wash-tay-wah-lah-kah.
Afar, Tay-hahn-tee.
Afraid, Koh-ah'-kee-pay.
After-noon, 'Hti'-ay-too.
Again, Ah'-kay.
Ago, some time, Ay-hah-nah.
Agreeable, Wash'-tay.
Aid, to, Oh-wah'-kee-ay.
Alarm, to, Nah-pahp.
Alike, just, Hah-kee'-tay-chee'-chah.
All, See-toh-mee-nee.
Almonds, Yah-hoo'-gah.
Alone, E-mul'-lah.
Aloud, noise, Oh-tahn'-kah.
Among, Ay'-gur-nah.
Amusement, Skah'-tah.
And, Ah-kay,
Anecdote, Hoon-kah'-kon.

Yale U., The Beinecke Rare Book and Manuscript Lib.

Fig. 17. The beginning of the *Dictionary of the Sioux Language* (Hyer and Starring 1866). The authors, U.S. Army lieutenants on the Wyoming frontier, compiled the dictionary with the aid of Charles Guerreu, an Indian interpreter, and printed it at Fort Laramie.

The Description of the Native Languages of North America: Boas and After

MARIANNE MITHUN

The study of North American Indian languages has evolved over the twentieth century as more has become known about each language, as more has been understood about language in general, and as linguistic theory and technology have developed. Yet even over the course of its evolution, the field has been characterized by a remarkable coherence, attributable in part to the subject matter, in part to the nature of the scholarly community.

Nearly all the languages are destined to disappear by the middle of the twenty-first century (see "Introduction," table 2, this vol.), which has made basic documentation a priority. Most have been recorded by at best a handful of scholars, usually in settings of special cultural richness. Accordingly, researchers have not generally restricted their interests to a single feature of language structure, but have rather, by choice and necessity, been concerned with all aspects of a language and its relation to its cultural context. Many scholars have worked with multiple languages and even multiple families. These experiences have tended to add diachronic and typological perspectives to their work.

There has also been a remarkable continuity of community over the years, a community that began largely with Franz Boas and his students, then expanded to include their students, then students of those students. Members of this last generation now have students of their own who are engaged in fieldwork and meet regularly to exchange ideas. Discussions of the contributions of these scholars and the evolution of the field can be found in a number of surveys, among them Andrews et al. (1943), Kroeber et al. (1943), and Dürr, Kasten, and Renner (1992) on Boas; papers in Koerner (1984) and in Cowan, Foster, and Koerner (1986), and Darnell (1990) on Sapir; papers in Hockett (1970), in Hall and Koerner (1987) and Hall (1990) on Bloomfield; Haas (1976a) on all three scholars; Hymes and Fought (1981) on American structuralism in linguistics, and Murray (1994) on the social history of North American linguistic traditions.

It would be impossible within the space of one chapter to chronicle all or even the most significant individual contributions made to the description of North American Indian languages during the twentieth century. Researchers have worked with over 230 languages, producing substantial grammars, dictionaries, and text collections, as well as thousands of articles describing specific aspects of structure and use. Discussion of these works and full bibliographical references can be found in "Sources," this volume, and Mithun (1997).

Franz Boas and the Boasians

The direction of twentieth-century research was set by Franz Boas (vol. 4:623-624), both intellectually and practically. His approach to the languages took a clear turn from the nineteenth-century emphasis on the simple collection of vocabulary for purposes of genetic classification. His interests lay in the grammatical categories that reflect cognitive categories, in the role of grammar in its textual context, and in the place of language in its cultural context.

Born in Westphalia, Prussia, in 1858, Boas was trained in physics, mathematics, and geography at the universities of Heidelberg, Bonn, and Kiel. His 1881 dissertation was in the field of physics (Contributions to the Perception of the Color of Water). His scientific training left him with a standard of rigor that is evident throughout his work, but also with an appreciation of the fundamental differences between the physical and social sciences.

His first field experience was in Baffinland, Canada, in 1883-1884, where he traveled widely by dog sled in the company of Inuits (vol. 5:10). His observations were published in reports on the geography of the area and the ethnology of the Baffinland Eskimo. On his return to Germany he joined the Museum für Völkerkunde, Berlin, then received his Habilitation at the University of Berlin. In 1885 a group of Bella Coola Salish people traveled to Berlin as part of an exhibition (vol. 7:76), and Boas spent the year working with them and with related museum collections. The study resulted in publications on language and culture and stimulated a lifelong interest in the Northwest Coast (vol. 7:74-77). Field trips led to professional contacts and positions in America, first as assistant editor of *Science* (1887-1888), next as a faculty member at Clark University, Worcester, Massachusetts (1888-1892, then as chief assistant in the Department of Anthropology at the World's Columbian Exposition, Chicago (1892-1984) and as curator of anthropology at the Field Museum that grew out of the exposition, then as curator of ethnology and somatology at the American Museum of Natural History in New York. In 1899 he became professor of anthropology at Columbia University, New York, where he remained until his death in 1942.

The Boasian Tradition in Linguistics

Boas documented an extraordinary number and variety of North American languages, some in considerable depth, among them various Eskimoan languages, Coast Tsimshian, Kwakiutl (Kwak'wala), Nootka, Bella Bella, Heiltsuk, Chemakum, Upper Chehalis, Lower Chehalis, Kootenai, Chinookan (Lower Chinook, Cathlamet), Chinook Jargon, Keresan (Laguna, Cochiti, Santo Domingo), and Sioux (Lakhota, Dakota), in addition to briefer work with many others, including Masset Haida, Tlingit, Nisgha, Makah, some Athapaskan languages (Nicola, Tsetsaut), a number of Salishan languages (Comox, Pentlatch, Sechelt, Squamish, Cowichan Halkomelem, Songhees, Tillamook, Lillooet, Thompson, Okanagan), Isleta, Zuni, and Oneida. He left over 700 publications on a wide range of topics, including insightful language descriptions, such as his sketches of Tsimshian (1911a), Kwakiutl (1911b), and Chinook (1911c), and his full grammars of Lakhota (Boas and Deloria 1941), and Kwakiutl (1947). The grammars were based on language in use, with examples drawn from the connected speech of texts. He published ethnographically important text collections as well: material from Lower Chinook (1894a), Cathlamet (1901), Tsimshian (1902, 1912), Bella Bella (1928, 1932), Kwakiutl (Boas and Hunt 1902-1905, 1906; Boas 1910, 1935-1943), and other languages. Beyond his contributions to the documentation of the languages, Boas established the patterns and practices that most work on North American languages was to follow throughout the twentieth century. He provided models implicitly by example in his own work, and explicitly in classic writings such as his introduction to the *Handbook of American Indian Languages* (1911), his editorial statement in the inaugural issue of the *International Journal of American Linguistics* (*IJAL*) (1917), and his chapter on language in *General Anthropology* (1938).

The first languages Boas encountered differ strikingly from most Indo-European languages in the functions and forms of their grammatical categories. Both Eskimoan languages and Kwakiutl, for example, have grammaticized elaborate spatial distinctions that could not fail to impress a geographer. Both contain hundreds of suffixes expressing concepts that could be conveyed only by full words or phrases in German or English. It is easy to see how field experiences with languages such as these would stimulate an interest in the cultural

and cognitive differences they encode. Boas emphasized (1911-1941, 1:63) the relationship between linguistics and ethnology: "If ethnology is understood as the science dealing with the mental phenomena of the life of the peoples of the world, human language, one of the most important manifestations of mental life, would seem to belong naturally to the field of work of ethnology." He also pointed to the special value of language for understanding cognition. "The great advantage that linguistics offers in this respect is the fact that, on the whole, the categories which are formed always remain unconscious, and that for this reason the processes which lead to their formation can be followed without the misleading and disturbing factors of secondary explanations, which are so common in ethnology, so much so that they generally obscure the real history of the development of ideas entirely" (Boas 1911-1941, 1:70-71).

Boas was keenly aware of the ways in which languages can differ. In his landmark paper "On Alternating Sounds" he pointed out that different principles for classifying speech sounds across languages result in different perceptions of them (Boas 1889). He recognized the cultural implications of differences in vocabulary: in the distinctions revealed by elaborate repertoires of specialized terms as well as the abstractions encoded by general terms: "On the whole the degree of specialization will depend upon cultural interests. Categories that are culturally unessential will not be found; those culturally important will be detailed.... In regard to all these matters language is exceedingly plastic and follows the demands of culture.... The vocabulary develops in conformity with the expanding or changing activities" (Boas 1938:1941). His sensitivity to differences was one of his most important contributions to the field: a desire to understand individual language structures in their own terms. He cautioned students and researchers against being blinded by premature assumptions. Because of this sensitivity it has sometimes been mistakenly assumed that he felt that languages vary in all ways without limit and are thus incommensurable. On the contrary, the general plan he set forth for grammatical sketches provides a clear framework for the analysis and description of languages of quite diverse types, on all levels of structure. The goal of the (1911) *Handbook* was to provide a basis for comparison, for discovering deeper truths about the nature of language and cognition.

> It seems well worth while to subject the whole range of linguistic concepts to a searching analysis, and to seek in the peculiarities of the grouping of ideas in different languages an important characteristic in the history of the mental development of the various branches of mankind. From this point of view, the occurrence of the most fundamental grammatical concepts in all languages must be considered as proof of the unity of fundamental psychological processes (Boas 1911-1941, 1:71).

Discussions of the plan can be found in Voegelin (1952) and Stocking (1974).

Boas devoted relatively little attention to historical linguistics. Unlike Edward Sapir and Leonard Bloomfield, he had not spent his early years practicing Indo-European philology and the comparative method. He had, however, developed high standards of rigor. Since the clearer genetic relationships among North American languages had already been established by the 1891 classification of John Wesley Powell, further diachronic research could be directed only to more remote relationships, where degrees of certainty are necessarily smaller. The longer two languages have been separated, the fewer the remaining common inheritances and the more difficult they are to identify. At greater time-depths it becomes increasingly difficult to distinguish cognates from chance resemblances or loans. Boas was more aware than most of the pervasive effects of language contact on both vocabulary and grammatical structure. He had an impressive knowledge of linguistic areas, geographic areas over which linguistic features are shared by neighboring but genetically unrelated languages. The value he placed on rigor lessened the appeal of work in a domain where rigor was difficult to achieve. Yet he was by no means ahistorical in his outlook. He often pointed in his writings to the dynamic character of language as an explanation of the kinds of structures that appear synchronically.

Boas's Institutional Contributions

Boas was a driving force behind research and publication throughout his career. During his 10 years as curator at the American Museum of Natural History, he instigated an impressive amount of field research, including the Jesup North Pacific Expedition to British Columbia, Washington, Oregon, and California. He was a major figure in the reorganization of the *American Anthropologist,* the journal of the American Anthropological Association. As honorary philologist of the Bureau of American Ethnology, he assembled grammars and texts for the *Handbook of American Indian Languages,* which covered 20 distinct language families, each represented by one, or in a few cases more than one, language (Boas 1911-1941). He was responsible for the publication of additional textual material in the *Publications of the American Ethnological Society* and the *Columbia University Contributions to Anthropology.* Beginning in 1925, he chaired the Committee on Research in American Native Languages of the American Council of Learned Societies, with Edward Sapir and Leonard Bloomfield as comembers. Although the Council offered researchers only field expenses, under its auspices a substantial body of material was collected

from 70 different languages during the 1920s and into the 1930s.

As more researchers were sent to the field, it became clear that greater standardization of phonetic transcription for American languages would be helpful. In 1912 Boas established a committee of the American Anthropological Association for this purpose, with himself as chair and Pliny Earle Goddard, Edward Sapir, Alfred L. Kroeber, and John Peabody Harrington as members. Harrington was later removed because he was not a member of the Association. Their report (Boas, Goddard, Sapir, and Kroeber 1916) presented two systems—a simpler one for the recording and publication of large bodies of texts, and a more detailed, comprehensive one, with additional symbols, for descriptions of the precise phonetic character of the sounds (see "Introduction," table 4, this vol.).

One of Boas's most influential projects was the founding in 1917 of the *International Journal of American Linguistics,* a journal devoted to research on American Indian languages. His editorial statement in the inaugural issue shows remarkable vision, detailing the wide range of topics needing attention. All have in fact been foci of inquiry throughout the twentieth century. He placed priority on basic grammatical and textual documentation. Although his own text collections are magnificent, he was keenly aware of the difficulty of capturing the complexity of connected speech: "The slowness of dictation that is necessary for recording texts makes it difficult for the narrator to employ that freedom of diction that belongs to the well-told tale, and consequently an unnatural simplicity of syntax prevails in most of the dictated texts" (Boas 1917:1). As a measure against this problem, he urged the teaching of writing to speakers of the languages, so that they could produce texts of more refined style at their leisure. He took seriously collaboration with speakers themselves, among them George Hunt, Kwakiutl (vol. 4:551; vol. 7:103; Berman 1994), and Ella Deloria (Lakhota).

He urged the collection of material on a variety of topics, in a variety of genres, and the examination of individual variation, special speech styles, and poetry. He appreciated the central role of conversation, a direction of research that has been pursued with the aid of tape recorders: "The available material gives a one-sided presentation of linguistic data, because we have hardly any records of daily occurrences, everyday conversation, descriptions of industries, customs, and the like" (Boas 1917:2).

Despite his own concentration on synchronic description, he encouraged work on language change and classification but laid special emphasis on understanding the effects of language contact, particularly the precise ways in which phonological and morphological traits may be borrowed.

Boas's Students

Throughout his time at Columbia, Boas offered a course in American Indian linguistics, and much of what is known of many languages comes from the students he sent to the field. He was a member of an anthropology department, and not all his students specialized in linguistics, but even those who were primarily ethnologists did fieldwork in the Boasian tradition, with an emphasis on understanding a language as a system in its own terms, in its cultural and linguistic context. They learned to analyze languages on the basis of the connected speech of texts. This practice has resulted in grammatical sketches and text collections that provide a continuing basis for new discoveries and understanding of the languages.

Boas's students include the majority of figures in American Indian linguistics of the early twentieth century. Their work spans a wide variety of languages and language families. In 1892 at Clark University he awarded the first American doctorate in anthropology to Alexander Chamberlain, who worked with Micmac, Mohawk, Kootenai, Ojibwa, and Ute. Boas's first Columbia doctoral student, Alfred L. Kroeber (fig. 1), received his degree in 1901 and established the anthropology department and museum at the University of California in Berkeley, where he set about documenting California languages and cultures as thoroughly as possible (vol. 8:8–15; Gibson and Rowe 1961). Though Kroeber's focus on remote genetic relationships led him to concentrate on vocabulary, and phonetic accuracy was not his strength, much of what is known of now vanished California languages is due to him. He worked intensively with Yurok, Yuki, Yokuts, and Mohave, in addition to briefer contact with the Algic Arapaho, Gros Ventre, Nawathinehena, and Wiyot; the Uto-Aztecan Bannock, Shoshone, Uintah Ute, Northern Paiute, Tubatulabal, Cahuilla, Chemehuevi, Cupeño, Fernandeño, Gabrielino, Hopi, Kawaiisu, Kitanemuk, Luiseño, Mono, Panamint, and Serrano; the Maiduan Nisenan; the Yuman Diegueño; the Athapaskan Hupa, Cahto, and Lassik; Southern and Northern Sierra Miwok and Rumsen; Barbareño Chumash; Migueleño Salinan; Shasta; Yana; Esselen; Karok; Eastern Pomo; Wappo and Yuki; Patwin and Wintu; Washoe; and Zuni. Kroeber was also instrumental in encouraging work on California languages by others, and saw that vocabularies, grammatical descriptions, and texts were published in the *University of California Publications in American Archaeology and Ethnology,* a series he inaugurated in 1903 and that ran until 1964.

Other Boas students similarly left their mark on the field, ultimately documenting a tremendous array of

left, State Histl. Soc. of Wis., Madison; right, Smithsonian, NAA: Ms. 2560-A,10:32.

Fig. 1. Alfred L. Kroeber (b. 1876, d. 1960). left, At the Laboratory School of Anthropology, Santa Fe, New Mexico, summer 1929. Kroeber was one of the group leaders that season (Zumwalt 1992:14). right, First 2 pages of a comparative vocabulary of Arapahoan languages collected by Kroeber among the Southern Arapaho in the first year of his fieldwork, 1899. The two languages, Nawathinehena and Besawunena, fell into disuse after the separate bands that spoke them were absorbed into the Arapaho in the 19th century. These vocabularies, the only known records of these extinct varieties of speech, were published in part (Kroeber 1916:75-76).

languages. Among them are John Swanton (vol. 4:688; Steward 1960) (Skidegate and Masset Haida, Tlingit, Lakhota, Ofo, Chitimacha, Tunica), Leo Frachtenberg (Hanis Coos; Lower Umpqua; Siuslaw; Alsea; Molala; various Salishan languages; Yamhill, Mary's River, Tualatin, and Yoncalla Kalapuya; Tututni and Galice Athapaskan; Quileute; Tutelo), Robert Lowie (vol. 4:661; Lowie, Lowie, and Richardson 1958) (Crow, Hidatsa, Mandan, Assiniboine, Stoney, Blackfoot, Kiowa, Bannock, Washoe), Paul Radin (Winnebago, Wappo, Wiyot, Wintu, Patwin), Roland Dixon (vol. 8:11-13) (Maidu, Chimariko, Shasta, Achumawi, Atsugewi), T.T. Waterman (Yurok, Diegueño, Yana), Melville Jacobs (vol. 7:102) (Sahaptin; Clackamas Chinook; Hanis and Miluk Coos; Tillamook; Alsea; Cayuse; Galice Athapaskan; Santiam, Tualatin, and Yoncalla Kalapuya; Lummi; Molala; Alsea; Chinook Jargon), Manuel Andrade (Quileute), Ruth Bunzel (Zuni), Gladys Reichard (Wiyot, Coeur d'Alene, Navajo), William Jones (Ojibwa, Fox, Sauk, Kickapoo), Hermann Haeberlin (Lushootseed, Shuswap), Alexander Goldenweiser (Onondaga, Cayuga), May Edel (Tillamook), Frank Speck (vol. 15:12) (Penobscot, Eastern Abenaki, Western Abenaki, Mohegan, Unami, Munsee, Montagnais, Catawba, Tutelo, in addition to brief work with many others), Archie Phinney (Nez Perce), Alexander Lesser (Kitsai), Gene Weltfish (Pawnee), Edward Kennard (Hopi, Mandan), Amelia Susman (Tsimshian, Winnebago), and Edward Sapir.

Edward Sapir and the Sapirians

The second major figure in twentieth-century research was Edward Sapir. His intellectual brilliance, his general approach to language, and his insightful documentation and analysis of a variety of languages still serve as an inspiration to those working with languages of North America and elsewhere. His genius as a teacher has also shaped the field.

Born in Pomerania, Prussia, in 1884, Sapir arrived in the United States with his parents at the age of five. As an undergraduate at Columbia University, he majored in Germanic philology but enrolled in a two-year graduate seminar on American Indian linguistics with Boas. After receiving his bachelor's degree in 1904 and his master's in 1905, he began doctoral work at Columbia, concentrating on linguistics with additional courses in anthropology and Indo-European languages. He spent the summer of 1905 in Washington State on the Yakima Reservation working on Wishram, a Chinookan language related to the Lower Chinookan and Cathlamet that Boas had recorded. Material collected on this trip appears in Boas's (1911c) Chinook sketch in the *Handbook*. The following year he worked

with Takelma, a language of southwestern Oregon. The resulting grammar, a model of insight, was submitted in 1907 as his doctoral dissertation and published in the second volume of the *Handbook* (Sapir 1922).

Invited to California by Kroeber as a research assistant in Anthropology during 1907-1908, Sapir began work with Yana and other California languages. From 1908 to 1910 he served as an instructor at the University of Pennsylvania, Philadelphia. There he worked with Tony Tillohash (vol. 11:102), a Kaibab Southern Paiute speaker from Arizona, recording extensive texts, songs, and supplementary grammatical material. Within about four months he collected the material for another landmark work, the volumes of Southern Paiute grammar, dictionary, and texts completed in 1917 but not published until later (Sapir 1930-1931). In 1910, he went to Ottawa as chief of the new Division of Anthropology of the Geological Survey of Canada, where he remained for 15 years (Preston 1980). During that time he began research on languages of western Canada. In his work with Nootka of Vancouver Island, a Wakashan language related to the Kwakiutl studied so intensively by Boas, he collaborated closely with Alex Thomas, the grandson of his first Nootka consultant, and taught him to write his language. During the same period, Sapir worked with Athapaskan languages, an interest first discovered when he had encountered Chasta Costa Tututni in Oregon in 1906, and one that he pursued throughout his lifetime.

Despite the opportunities it offered for fieldwork, the museum position brought a certain intellectual isolation, and Sapir gladly accepted a position as professor of anthropology and linguistics at the University of Chicago in 1925 (vol. 9:18). Here he attracted enthusiastic students, a number of whom were to become important figures themselves in American Indian linguistics. During the Chicago years he was able to continue fieldwork, particularly with the Athapaskan languages Hupa and Navajo. In 1931 he accepted a position at Yale as Sterling Professor of Linguistics and Anthropology, where he remained until his death in 1939.

Sapir's Legacy

Like Boas, Sapir left a mark on American linguistics. His documentation of languages was masterful. He had a keen ear and followed the Boasian tradition of describing languages in their own terms on the basis of connected speech. He left substantial records of a number of languages, among them Wishram Chinook, Takelma, Yana (including Yahi), Nootka, Sarcee, Kutchin, Hupa, Navajo and Southern Paiute, as well as notes on many more, including Munsee Delaware, Eastern Abenaki, Maliseet, Micmac, Montagnais, East

Cree, Eastern Ojibwa, Mohawk, Seneca, Tutelo, Hopi, Alsea, Achumawi, Chasta Costa Tututni, Chimariko, Yurok, Thompson, Comox, Coast Tsimshian, Chilkat Tlingit, Ingalik, and Haida. In addition to his grammars of Takelma and Southern Paiute, he published collections of texts in Takelma (1909), Yana (1910), Nootka (1939 with Swadesh), and Navajo (1942), and hundreds of articles on American Indian languages (Bright 1990a; Golla 1991). His linguistic interests were wide ranging, taking in all levels of grammatical structure from phonetics through phonology, morphology, and syntax, as well as typology, genetic classification, historical reconstruction (especially Uto-Aztecan and Athapaskan), language contact, and special speech registers such as baby language (motherese), poetic language, and ritual language. His scholarly interests ranged beyond linguistics as well, notably to culture and personality (Mandelbaum 1949; Newman 1951).

Sapir's deeper thinking in linguistics, like that of Boas, emerged in large part from his concentrated experience with the languages themselves. An important way in which he extended the work of Boas was in his recognition of the importance of pattern. As early as 1889 Boas had pointed out that human beings perceive the sounds of new languages in terms of the categories of the languages they already speak. In his famous article "Sound Patterns in Language" (1925a), Sapir took up this observation and carried it further, proposing that the "fundamental sounds" of a language are subject to two kinds of variation: that due to simple variation on the part of individuals, and that dependent on phonetic context. This was of course the phonemic principle. "Individual variations and such conditional variations as we have discussed once cleared out of the way, we arrive at the genuine pattern of speech sounds ... it almost goes without saying that two languages, A and B, may have identical sounds but utterly distinct phonetic patterns; or they may have mutually incompatible phonetic systems, from the articulatory and acoustic standpoint, but identical or similar patterns" (Sapir 1925a:42).

Sapir's experiences in teaching Tony Tillohash and Alex Thomas (vol. 7:103) to write their languages alerted him to the "psychological reality" of these phonological categories, the "fundamental sounds" or phonemes (Sapir 1933). His recognition of phonological patterning, parallel to similar work in Europe but apparently conceived of independently, had a major effect on North American linguistics. It became the foundation of structuralist linguistics during the first half of the century, when theories of phonological and morphological structure were carefully worked out. It also revolutionized the collection and analysis of data. Once procedures were developed for the establishment of phonemic systems, the analysis of morphological systems became more straightforward. Both

advances streamlined the comparison of languages for establishing genetic relations and reconstructing proto-languages.

Perhaps more than Boas, Sapir was conscious of the diachronic dimension of language, of the fact that language structure is the product of constant evolution over time. His descriptions of languages contain references to diachronic processes. Synchronic alternations are often presented in dynamic or processual terms as well, and frequent reference is made to use, as in his discussion of Chasta Costa indefinite futures. "Futures . . . are explicitly rendered by suffixing -t'e to present (generally indefinite) forms; but simple indefinite forms, particularly with adverbs pointing to future time, may often be used as futures in contrast to definite present forms" (Sapir 1914:327).

Sapir pointed out that the diachronic evolution of language is the result of individual variation in speech but is not random. In his book *Language* (Sapir 1921c) he introduced the concept of "drift," the notion that certain structural characteristics of a language may predispose it to change in a specific direction. Sapir's historical interest led to some of his more controversial work on possible deeper genetic relationships than those established with the Powell classification. The work emerged in part from of an interest in typology, in discovering patterns of structural similarities and differences among languages. Influenced by the work of Kroeber and Dixon in California, Sapir began to wonder whether the structural similarities he saw among supposedly unrelated languages might be evidence of more remote genetic relationships among the families to which they belonged. The result was a classification of the 58 Powell language families of North America into six superstocks. The proposals were first presented in a lecture at the University of Chicago in 1920, then published in *Science* in 1921, and finally published in slightly revised form in the *Encyclopedia Britannica* in 1929 (Sapir in Bright 1990:81-92; "The Classification of the Native Languages of North America," this vol.). Although some of the proposed superstocks, such as Hokan-Siouan, were abandoned early, others, such as the enlarged Penutian, stimulated intensive comparative work.

Inspired by the variety of structures he discovered in the languages he worked with, Sapir (1921c:16) continued Boas's interest in the complex relations between language and thought: "We see this complex process of the interaction of language and thought actually taking place under our eyes. The instrument makes possible the product, the product refines the instrument."

Sapir's Students

All who remember Sapir cite his brilliance as a speaker and teacher. (Some tributes can be seen in Cowan,

Foster, and Koerner 1986; see also Darnell 1990). His brilliance and clarity of expression can still be appreciated in his writing. Sapir had a shorter teaching career than Boas, since he spent 15 years in museum work and died at the age of 55. Nonetheless, he inspired a strong core of students who in turn passed on their fervor to students of their own.

At Chicago Sapir attracted a talented group of graduate students, among them Morris Swadesh, Stanley S. Newman, Fang-Kuei Li, Mary Haas, Harry Hoijer, Walter Dyk, and Carl Voegelin. Other scholars came to Chicago to sit in on his lectures, among them Ruth Bunzel, who worked with Zuni, and Father Berard Haile, who worked with Navajo (vol. 4:647-648). When Sapir moved to Yale University, the core of graduate students moved with him. Several more began their work at Yale, among them Benjamin L. Whorf and Charles F. Hockett. George L. Trager, who already had a degree in Romance and Slavic from Columbia, joined the group in 1936. Sapir also reached a number of other students, among them Kenneth Pike, by teaching an introductory class and a course on field methods at the 1937 Linguistic Institute at Ann Arbor.

Inspired by his courses in Primitive Languages and Comparative Problems in Primitive Languages at Yale, students set out to document languages and to unravel deeper genetic relationships, although by this time Sapir's own interests had moved beyond classification. Swadesh left notes on a large array of North American languages (particularly Chitimacha, Cayuse, Nitinaht, and Nootka, as well as Catawba, Koasati, Central Alaskan Yupik, Menominee, Mahican, Sahaptin, Nez Perce, Makah, and others). He also pursued remote relationships actively. Newman's grammar of Yokuts has been cited as "the fullest example of Sapir's mature linguistic methods" (Harris 1944:198), and his work with Zuni, Bella Coola, and the reconstruction of Salish is also admired. Li worked with Mattole, Wailaki, Sarcee, Hare, Chipewyan, and Eyak. Haas worked with Nitinaht, Tunica, Natchez, Atakapa, Creek and other Muskogean languages, and explored remote relations (see Haas 1978). Whorf, an inspector for the Hartford Fire Insurance Company, did not finish a degree but did do considerable work with Hopi and comparative Uto-Aztecan and is well known for his discussions of the relation between language and thought (Whorf 1956). Hoijer worked with Tonkawa and Athapaskan languages, especially Navajo and Chiricahua and Mescalero Apache. Voegelin worked with Shawnee, Delaware, Tubatulabal, Hopi, and other languages. Hockett's (1939) dissertation on Potawatomi was completed after Sapir's death, with Leonard Bloomfield as outside examiner.

As Sapir and his students refined methods of phonemic and morphophonemic analysis, they came to feel that transcription should reflect the analysis. They sent a draft of orthographic recommendations to Boas for publication in *IJAL* proposing that each unit phoneme be represented by a unitary symbol and that certain Americanist symbols be changed to correspond to international linguistic usage. Boas rejected the draft on the grounds that phonemic transcription would result in the loss of too much information. The recommendations were published in the *American Anthropologist* over the names of George Herzog, Stanley Newman, Edward Sapir, Mary Haas Swadesh, Morris Swadesh, and Charles F. Voegelin (1934) (see "Introduction," table 4, this vol.).

For some time, Sapir had planned a volume of grammatical sketches in honor of Boas, but he died before the collection was assembled. His students and other associates carried out the plan, and the volume, *Linguistic Structures of Native America,* appeared in 1946, edited by Hoijer. It contains tight-knit sketches of South Greenlandic by Swadesh, Chiricahua Apache and Tonkawa by Hoijer, Proto-Central Algonquian by Bloomfield, Unami Delaware by Voegelin, Hopi and Milpa Alta Aztec by Whorf, Taos by Trager, Yokuts by Newman, Quechan by Halpern, Chitimacha by Swadesh, Tunica by Haas, and Chipewyan by Li. The dedicatory preface, written by Leonard Bloomfield in 1944, closes with the words "In our work we have thought of Franz Boas, the pioneer and master in the study of American languages and the teacher, in one or another sense, of us all" (Hoijer 1946:5; Bloomfield 1972).

Leonard Bloomfield and the Bloomfieldians

A third major figure in American linguistics of the first half of the twentieth century is Leonard Bloomfield (Hall and Koerner 1987). His own primary contributions to North American Indian linguistics were his work with Menominee, Cree, and Ojibwa, and the application of the comparative method to the reconstruction of what he at first referred to as Primitive Central Algonquian and later concluded was effectively equivalent to Proto-Algonquian, based on these languages and Fox (Bloomfield 1925a, 1946). Detailed discussions of his Algonquian work are in Hockett (1948) and Goddard (1987, 1994a). He also played an important role in shaping the discipline.

Bloomfield was born in Chicago in 1887 to German-speaking Austrian immigrants and spent his childhood in Wisconsin. After completing an undergraduate degree at Harvard in 1906, he began graduate work at the University of Wisconsin, Madison, in German and Germanic philology, with courses in Bulgarian, Lithuanian, Russian, and Sanskrit. He continued work in these areas at the University of Chicago, writing a dissertation, "A Semasiologic Differentiation in Germanic Secondary Ablaut" in 1909. His early academic *49* positions were in German, at the University of Cincinnati (1909-1910) and at the University of Illinois, Urbana (1910-1921). By 1913 he had completed his first book, *An Introduction to the Study of Language* (1914). The year 1913-1914 was spent in Göttingen and Leipzig, amidst Neogrammarians August Leskien, Karl Brugmann, and Jakob Wackernagel. Their insistence on the regularity of sound change instilled in him a vision of an absolutely rigorous science of language.

While at the University of Illinois, Bloomfield began to move beyond Indo-European studies. In 1917 his *Tagálog Texts with Grammatical Analysis* appeared, based on the speech of Antonio Viola Santiago, a student at Illinois. The work follows Boasian principles, with detailed analyses of phonetics, morphology, and syntax based on dictated textual material. In 1920 he began fieldwork on his first Algonquian language, Menominee, in Wisconsin.

From 1921 to 1927 he held a position as professor of German and linguistics at Ohio State University, Columbus. During this time he undertook fieldwork with Plains Cree in Saskatchewan and Swampy Cree in Manitoba. A friendship established at Ohio State with the behaviorist psychologist Albert Paul Weiss was to shape his subsequent thinking. In 1927 he moved to Chicago as chair of Germanic philology. His textbook *Language,* a major revision of his earlier book, appeared in 1933. In 1940 he accepted a Sterling Professorship of Germanic Languages at Yale, where he remained until his death in 1949.

Bloomfieldian Linguistics

Bloomfield, like Boas and Sapir, was concerned that the languages indigenous to North America be recorded as fully as possible before they disappeared. He produced substantial documentation of several Algonquian languages, including a Cree grammatical sketch (1928), texts (1930, 1934) and word list (1984); a Menominee grammar (1962), texts (1928a), and word list (1975); and a grammatical sketch of an Ottawa dialect of Southern Ojibwa with texts and word list (1957), as well as numerous articles on specific topics (Hockett and Hall 1987). Goddard (1987:180) remarks that "Bloomfield's achievement, in the strength of the American linguistic tradition, was to bring explicitness and orderliness to the description of Algonquian inflectional and derivational morphology. The framework that he set up has formed the basis for all useful work on Algonquian since." Bloomfield accorded full respect to spoken language and went further to address the problem of selecting a single variety of speech as representative of community norms (Bloomfield 1927). His work on comparative Algonquian demonstrated that the comparative method developed for Indo-European

languages could be applied as rigorously and successfully to unwritten languages as to those with written records.

Like Boas and Sapir, Bloomfield was dedicated to a systematic approach to understanding language structure. He was perhaps the most concerned of the three with terminological and methodological precision, as can be seen in "A Set of Postulates for the Science of Language" (1926), modeled on "One Set of Postulates for a Behaviorist Psychology" of his Ohio State colleague Weiss (1925). In the interest of rigor, he felt it necessary to define the field of linguistics more narrowly than had Boas or Sapir.

> Discussion of the fundamentals of our science seems to consist one half of obvious truisms, and one half of metaphysics; this is characteristic of matters which form no real part of a subject: they should properly be disposed of by merely naming certain concepts as belonging to the domain of other sciences.
>
> Thus, the physiologic and acoustic description of acts of speech belongs to other sciences than ours. The existence and interaction of social groups held together by language is granted by psychology and anthropology (Bloomfield 1926:153-154).

This strong distinction between linguistics and psychology had not been present in his early work. Earlier in his career Bloomfield had followed the mentalist thinking of the time, appealing freely to the mind, to introspection, and to "speech feeling": "It is remarkable and perhaps characteristic of the progress of investigation into the more habitual and socialized of our mental processes, that linguistic theory is by no means clear as to the nature of subject and predicate in language, in spite of the fact that our speech-feeling seems to distinguish quite clearly between predicating and non-predicating utterances" (Bloomfield 1917a:13). His later work, by contrast, shows a strong shift to behaviorism ("objectism," "materialism," or "mechanism"). Influenced by Weiss, he rejected as unscientific attempts to understand linguistic structure through hypothesized mental phenomena; science should be based only on that which is directly observable. "The danger here lies in mentalistic views of psychology, which may tempt the observer to appeal to purely spiritual standards instead of reporting the facts. To say, for instance, that combinations of words which are 'felt to be' compounds have only a single high stress (e.g. *blackbird* as opposed to *black bird*), is to tell exactly nothing, since we have no way of determining what the speakers may 'feel'" (Bloomfield 1933:38). His commitment to mechanism had a substantial effect on the subsequent development of the discipline.

Bloomfield's Institutional Contributions

Bloomfield strove to create a more scientific linguistics both ideologically in his writings and institutionally, with his participation in the founding of the Linguistic Society of America in 1924, its journal *Language,* and its summer Linguistic Institute.

50

He did not train many graduate students for work with North American languages, but he did have a strong influence on colleagues and other followers. While at Chicago, he met regularly with Voegelin and Hoijer. His book *Language* served as the basic textbook in the field for generations of linguists. He animated the large and active Yale Linguistics Club during his years of teaching there. After Sapir became ill, Bloomfield took over the introductory course at the 1938 Linguistic Institute in Ann Arbor, a course attended by nearly all students at the Institute. He also conducted a field methods class with an Ottawa speaker. It was there that he became acquainted with Hockett. He appeared at subsequent Institutes, where other Americanists began to gather as well, and taught again at the 1941 Institute at Chapel Hill, giving an introductory course and another course in field methods. His courses and those given by other Americanists at the Institutes heightened the visibility of American Indian languages within the field of linguistics.

The Bloomfieldians

Bloomfield's followers shared his concern for formal rigor and carried it further than he had himself, striving to develop a fully explicit formal model of language. Basic field research on North American languages continued much as before in the Boasian tradition, with the collection of texts, the compilation of grammars and dictionaries, and the application of the comparative method, but certain differences began to appear in the presentation of analyses.

Where Sapir and his students had drawn freely on processual metaphors for the description of interacting components of language structure, an approach also used by Bloomfield in his paper on "Menomini Morphophonemics" (1939), such "item and process" models were rejected by Neo-Bloomfieldians as mentalistic and therefore unscientific. They were replaced by "item and arrangement" models, considered freer of potential teleological implications. Earlier descriptions were recast in the new framework and published as "structural restatements," the first of which appeared in Harris's (1944) review of Newman's Yokuts grammar.

> Another term that is disappearing today, no doubt under the influence of Bloomfield's Language, is "process." There is involved here a method, not merely a term. Newman uses "process" to indicate a relation between two forms one of which may be viewed as consisting of the other plus some change or addition. Thus, the addition of suffixes to a base is a process, as is the assimilation of a pre-glottal-stop vowel to the quality of the vowel after the glottal stop..., and the changing of vowels in the base when suffixes are added. All such cases can be viewed differently, without bringing in the time or motion analogy implicit in "process." Instead of talking about the word 'cumoꞏ-'uy *that which was devoured* and 'cumaꞏ-'an (*he*) *is devouring* as the resultants of adding the suffix 'uy and 'an to the base *'coꞏmu, we can say that the two words contain each the

morpheme 'coꞏmu and respectively the suffixes 'uy and 'an, each suffix containing a vowel change. We now have not a process from base to word via suffixation, but an inventory of the elements (morphemes) present in two utterances. We can then rearrange this inventory by listing all the utterances in which a given morpheme occurs (Harris 1944:203-204).

The increasing attention to formal models of presentation can be seen throughout American linguistics of the time. It persists in some quarters in the 1900s.

University-Sponsored Research

Inspired by the vision of Boas, his students and their students instilled similar ideals and enthusiasm in students of their own. At Berkeley, Boas's student Kroeber supervised few graduate students in linguistics, but one he did train was Lucy S. Freeland, who worked extensively with California languages, particularly Central, Northern, and Southern Sierra Miwok, Lake Miwok, Eastern Pomo, Nisenan, and Atsugewi. J. Alden Mason, who had begun his study of linguistics with Sapir at Pennsylvania, continued as a graduate student with Kroeber, recording Salinan and Slavey (vol. 6:21). Dorothy Demetracopoulou Lee, who was primarily interested in relations between language and culture, worked for three summers with Wintu speakers. Abraham Halpern began studying with Kroeber at Berkeley but was soon sent to work with Hoijer at Chicago. Early in his career as an academic and after his retirement from government service, Halpern recorded considerable material from Pomoan and Yuman languages. Another Berkeley student, William W. Elmendorf, pursued ethnographic and linguistic work with Twana, developing a lifelong interest in Salishan (Twana, Columbian, Spokane) and other North American languages.

Melville Jacobs took a position at the University of Washington in the department of anthropology, where T.T. Waterman had been teaching, and during the period 1928-1939 recorded extensive material from the remaining languages of Oregon, among them Alsea, Cayuse, Molala, Sahaptin, Hanis and Miluk Coos, Kalapuyan (Tualatin, Santiam, and Yoncalla), Clackamas Chinook, Chinook Jargon, and various Athapaskan languages (Galice, Euchre Creek, Chetco, Coquille, Upper Umpqua). His transcription was highly accurate, and, in the Boasian tradition, he collected texts whenever possible. The texts in turn served as the basis for his grammatical descriptions (for a partial bibliography see vol. 7:694-695).

Morris Swadesh (Hymes 1983:273-330) had relatively little opportunity to train students in the United States, ultimately settling in Mexico, but during his two years at the University of Wisconsin he engaged Floyd G. Lounsbury to collaborate on a Works Progress

Administration project teaching Oneida speakers to write. Lounsbury subsequently wrote an important dissertation on Oneida (1949) and trained his own students in Iroquoian at Yale: Wallace Chafe (Seneca, Onondaga), William Cook (Cherokee), Hanni Woodbury (Onondaga), Marianne Mithun (Tuscarora, Mohawk, Cayuga), and Clifford Abbott (Oneida).

Stanley Newman, who had begun studying with Sapir at Chicago and followed him to Yale, took a position as linguist in the anthropology department at the University of New Mexico, Albuquerque. There he continued his Yokuts and Salish projects and began work with Zuni. George L. Trager, who had done fieldwork at Taos Pueblo (F.H. Trager 1971) taught at Buffalo and then Southern Methodist University, Dallas, where he trained Tanoanists Randall Speirs (Rio Grande Tewa), William Leap (Isleta), and Elizabeth Brandt (Sandia).

Fang-Kuei Li went to China to work on Chinese dialectology and minority languages and Thai, but he returned to America to teach at Harvard, Yale, and the University of Washington, Seattle. In 1957 he was joined by Laurence Thompson, who had been trained in Slavic at Yale. Thompson and his wife M. Terry Thompson began work with Salish languages of the region (Thompson, Clallam, Tillamook, Nooksack, Lushootseed, Lummi), and a circle of Salishanists formed around them. They trained a number of students in Northwest languages, first at the University of Washington and then at the University of Hawaii after their move there in 1966. Among the doctoral students they supervised were Thom Hess on Lushootseed, Barry Carlson on Spokane, James Gibson on Shuswap, Anthony Mattina on Colville-Okanagan, Jay Powell on Quileute, Timothy Montler on Saanich, and Steven Egesdal on Thompson. In 1966 Lawrence and Terry Thompson inaugurated the Salish Conference, which has continued annually, and in 1973 they established the Jacobs Research Funds to support fieldwork on Northwest Coast languages, named for Melville and Elizabeth Jacobs.

Harry Hoijer, who had studied Navajo as a student of Sapir, taught anthropological linguistics at the University of Chicago and then joined the anthropology department at the University of California at Los Angeles. He became a central figure in Athapaskan studies, working with Navajo and other Apachean languages, as well as with the last speakers of Tonkawa (Bright 1964). His student William Bittle worked with Kiowa Apache. Charles Hockett, who had completed his dissertation on Potawatomi in 1939, joined the anthropology department at Cornell University, Ithaca, New York, where he continued work in Algonquian and theoretical linguistics.

Carl Voegelin had begun work with Kroeber and Lowie at Berkeley before moving first to Chicago and then on to Yale to continue with Sapir. He had also had good opportunities for discussion with Bloomfield, with whom he shared a house at several Linguistic Institutes (fig. 2). Voegelin did his dissertation on Tubatulabal (1935) and later worked on Algonquian languages (Shawnee, Unami Delaware, Blackfoot), before going back to Uto-Aztecan for extended studies of Hopi. He accepted a position at Indiana University in Bloomington, where he built a strong anthropology department with a focus on North American Indian anthropological linguistics. In 1944 he revived the *International Journal of American Linguistics* and edited it through 1980. He trained a number of important scholars in the Bloomington department and at the field school he established in Flagstaff, Arizona. One of these students was Florence M. Robinett, who arrived in 1951. She worked with Carl on his Shawnee material and in 1954 completed a dissertation on Hidatsa. The same year she married Voegelin, and a lifelong collaboration began, with annual trips to the field station and work on a variety of topics and languages, especially Hopi (C.F. Voegelin and F.M. Voegelin 1957). Florence Voegelin became the first director of the Archives of Languages of the World established in Bloomington in 1954 and continued her work with it until 1986. She initiated a new journal, *Anthropological Linguistics,* and served as its editor from 1959 to 1987. Another of the Indiana students was Dell H. Hymes, who worked with Boas's Cathlamet Chinook material for his (1955) dissertation and carried out fieldwork with Wasco Chinook speakers. Hymes has continued to be an important figure in linguistics and anthropology, at Harvard, then Berkeley, the University of Pennsylvania, and finally at the University of Virginia, Charlottesville, laying the foundation for a number of lines of inquiry, especially in the areas of language, culture, and society; ethnopoetics; and text analysis. A third Indiana student, Kenneth L. Hale, completed his dissertation on Papago (Tohono O'odham) in 1959 and joined the faculty at the Massachusetts Institute of Technology, Cambridge. Throughout his career he worked with a wide range of languages, including from North America also Navajo, Lower Piman, Hopi, Jemez, Tewa, Micmac, Tahltan, and Winnebago. M. Dale Kinkade completed his dissertation on Upper Chehalis at Indiana in 1963, then accepted positions first at the University of Kansas then the University of British Columbia, Vancouver. He became a major figure in North American Indian linguistics, languages of the Northwest, and especially Salishan languages, supervising a number of students and advising many others.

The Voegelins played an important role in perpetuating the community of scholars working with North American languages. At the 1964 Linguistic Institute at Bloomington a group was gathered to assess the status

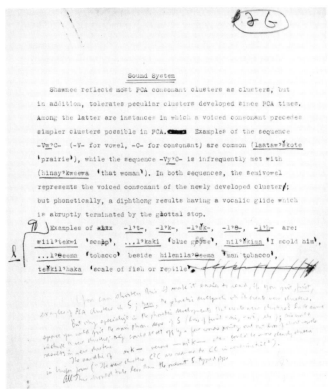

left, Amer. Ind. Research Inst., Bloomington; right, Amer. Philosophical Soc., Philadelphia: Ms. coll. No. 68, Series III-B.

Fig. 2. left, Carl Voegelin (center); Margaret Haven, Hidatsa (left); and Henrietta Pretty On Top, Crow (right), at the Linguistic Institute, Indiana University, 1953. Voegelin was the director of the Institute, Haven was one of the native speakers working with Florence Voegelin, and Pretty On Top was working with Dorothea Kaschube on Crow. right, Page from C.F. Voegelin's unpublished manuscript "Basic Shawnee," describing consonant clusters, with handwritten comments by Leonard Bloomfield suggesting revisions.

of genetic classification, the first general appraisal since Sapir's grand scheme. The group met again at the December 1964 meeting of the American Anthropological Association, and the results were published as commentary on a map issued in 1966. These meetings began an important tradition for scholars, the Conference on American Indian Languages (CAIL), held at the annual meeting of the American Anthropological Association. Organized unofficially by Carl Voegelin every year until 1980, it continued after his retirement to serve as a lively forum for papers on all aspects of languages indigenous to the Americas. When a more formal organization became necessary, it was this group that in December 1981 formed the Society for the Study of the Indigenous Languages of the Americas (SSILA), the primary scholarly society of those working with American languages.

A major arena of research on North American languages was created by Sapir's student Mary Haas at Berkeley. After World War II, a group of Berkeley linguists had formed a committee for a doctoral program in linguistics, although there was as yet no department. Murray Emeneau, a specialist in Indic languages who had also worked with Sapir, collaborated with Haas in securing funding for the Survey of California Indian Languages (later called Survey of California and Other Indian Languages). In 1953 the Department of Linguistics was established. Haas trained dozens of students, who, supported by the Survey, produced in-depth documentation of languages all over California and beyond. The materials resulting from their work permitted further exploration of genetic and areal relationships. Wallace Chafe came from the Bureau of American Ethnology to the department in 1962, adding to its strength in North American languages. The first Berkeley graduate student to be sponsored by the Survey was William L. Bright, who completed his dissertation on Karok in 1957. This work was the beginning of an extraordinarily productive career. Bright joined the Department of Anthropology at the University of California at Los Angeles, where he continued work with California languages and others, pioneered work in areal contact, variation, and oral literature, edited the journal *Language* from 1966 to 1987 and the journal *Language in Society* from 1993, and trained students of his own.

Other Berkeley students who have done fieldwork with North American languages include Sylvia Broadbent (Southern Sierra Miwok), Karl Teeter (Wiyot, Maliseet-Passamaquoddy), Sydney Lamb

53

(Monache), William Shipley (Maidu), M.A.R. Barker (Klamath), Catherine Callaghan (Northern Sierra Miwok, Plains Miwok, Lake Miwok, Bodega Miwok), James Crawford (Cocopa), Robert Oswalt (Kashaya Pomo, Southern Pomo, Central Pomo), Harvey Pitkin (Wintu), William Jacobsen (Washoe, Makah, Nootka), Sally McLendon (Eastern Pomo), Thomas Collord (Chukchansi Yokuts), Margaret Langdon (Mesa Grande Diegueño), Haruo Aoki (Nez Perce), Shirley Silver (Shasta), Jesse Sawyer (Wappo), Robert Hollow (Mandan), Wick Miller (Acoma, Western Shoshone), Allan Taylor (Blackfoot, Lakhota, Gros Ventre), Victor Golla (Hupa, Tututni, Tagish), Russell Ultan (Konkow), Julius Moshinsky (Southeastern Pomo), Leonard Talmy (Atsugewi), Jean-Pierre Bélan (Attikamek), Douglas Parks (Pawnee, Arikara, Sioux, Shawnee), David Rood (Wichita, Lakhota), Brent Galloway (Halkomelem, Nooksak, Samish, Cahuilla), Bruce Pearson (Delaware), Ken Whistler (Northern Patwin), Geoffrey Gamble (Wikchamni Yokuts), Anthony Woodbury (Central Alaskan Yupik), Jon Dayley (Panamint), Alice Schlichter Shepherd (Wintu, Yuki), Mary Catherine O'Connor (Northern Pomo), Amy Dahlstrom (Cree, Fox), Alan Shaterian (Yavapai), Monica Macaulay (Karok), David J. Costa (Shawnee), and Lawrence Morgan (Kootenai). Much of this work has been published in the *University of California Publications in Linguistics* series.

Many of the Berkeley-trained linguists have taken positions in anthropology or linguistics departments to train students of their own. David Rood, who joined Allan Taylor in the linguistics department of the University of Colorado in Boulder, assumed the editorship of the *International Journal of American Linguistics* in 1981. Wick Miller, who joined the department of anthropology at the University of Utah, was instrumental in the founding of SSILA. Victor Golla, first a member of the anthropology department at George Washington University, Washington, and then at Humboldt State University, California, became the secretary-treasurer of SSILA, producing a remarkable newsletter documenting developments in the discipline such as publications, meetings, events, developments in computer technology, and potential topics of discussion for future conferences.

Another important center of research, the Alaska Native Language Center, was established by Michael E. Krauss at the University of Alaska in Fairbanks. When he accepted a position at the University of Alaska in 1960, Krauss undertook intensive work with the native languages of Alaska. With the help of native speakers, he began teaching Central Alaskan Yupik in the classroom. In 1972 funding for the Center was appropriated by the Alaska state legislature, and since that time a staff of linguists and speakers has been documenting the languages with

texts, grammars, and dictionaries and developing orthographies and curriculum materials for use in schools ("Native Writing Systems," this vol.). Staff linguists have included Jeff Leer, Steven Jacobson, Lawrence Kaplan, James Kari, Chad Thompson, John Ritter, Irene Reed, and Native language specialists Eliza Jones (Koyukon), Ruth Ridley (Han), Katherine Peter (Kutchin), Paschal Afcan (Central Alaskan Yupik), and Edna MacLean (Inupiaq), among many others. Krauss has remained indefatigable in his efforts on behalf of the languages of Alaska and of endangered languages everywhere.

Not all documentation of North American languages has been done by North Americans. Scholars have come from abroad, some, like Fang-Kuei Li, for graduate training that led to an interest in the languages, others as established professionals. Considerable work has been done by Europeans on Eskimo-Aleut languages. William Thalbitzer of the University of Copenhagen, originally trained in Indo-European philology, became a fluent speaker of East Greenlandic and published extensively on the language (vol. 5:9, 799). He also served as associate editor of *IJAL* from 1917 until his death in 1958. Christian Schultz-Lorentzen, another Dane, produced a dictionary (1927) and lucid grammar (1945) of West Greenlandic. Louis L. Hammerich, also of the University of Copenhagen, did extensive work on Eskimoan languages, including a dialect survey of Western Eskimo (1958). Jørgen Rischel, of the University of Copenhagen, has similarly contributed to the documentation of Greenlandic and served on the editorial board of *IJAL*. Michael Fortescue, head of the Institute of Eskimology in Copenhagen, continued work on Greenlandic and other Eskimo languages. A major figure in both Eskimo and Aleut studies throughout the second half of the twentieth century is Knut Bergsland, of the University of Oslo. Substantial material has been published by Russians, in particular G.A. Menovshchikov, E.S. Rubtsova, Nikolai Vakhtin, and Evgeniy Golovko on Siberian languages. Full descriptions of these traditions appear in Krauss (1973). Osahito Miyaoka, a Japanese scholar, began work with Central Alaskan Yupik with the Alaska Native Language Center. After his return to Japan he continued his Yupik research and began training new generations of graduate students for fieldwork with Northwest Coast languages, first at Hokkaido University and then at Kyoto University.

Several Europeans worked with other North American languages and served on the editorial board of *IJAL*. C.C. Uhlenbeck, of the University of Leiden in the Netherlands, was originally trained in Dutch and Indo-European philology but developed an early interest in American languages and spent the summers of 1910 and 1911 among the Blackfeet, eventually publishing texts (1911), two vocabularies (1930, 1934, both with

R.H. van Gulik), and a grammar (1938). Hans Vogt, of the University of Oslo, had been trained in classical languages in Oslo, studied at the Sorbonne with Meillet, and worked with South Caucasian languages in Tbilisi. He received his doctorate in Oslo in 1936 then spent a year studying at Yale with Sapir. After 11 weeks of fieldwork among the Kalispel in 1937, he wrote a grammar that is still admired by Salishanists (Vogt 1940). Hansjakob Seiler, of the University of Cologne, worked with Cahuilla, producing a grammar, texts, and several articles (vol. 8:760).

Hans Jørgen Uldall, a Dane who had studied at the University of Copenhagen with Otto Jespersen and then at University College London with Daniel Jones, responded to a call from the Committee on Research in American Native Languages and worked with Nisenan (Maidu) and Achumawi during the 1920s and 1930s, as well as teaching phonetics to students at Berkeley. The German Günter Wagner spent five months in 1928 and 1929 working with Yuchi speakers in Oklahoma under the sponsorship of the American Council of Learned Societies, producing a grammatical sketch for the *Handbook* (Wagner 1933), and a text collection for Boas's *American Ethnological Society* series (Wagner 1931). The Swede Sven Liljeblad, an ethnologist at Lund and Uppsala universities with field experience in Lapland, went to Berkeley in 1939 to study under Kroeber and Lowie, and did extensive fieldwork on Shoshone and Bannock (Northern Paiute) (vol. 11:102). R.H. Robins, trained by J.R. Firth in London, carried out fieldwork on Yurok in 1951 under the auspices of the Survey of California Indian Languages. His grammar, texts, and lexicon appeared in the *University of California Publications in Linguistics* series in 1958. Aert Kuipers, of the University of Leiden, published a grammar, texts, and numerous articles on Squamish and trained several doctoral students in Salishan languages.

Museum-Sponsored Research

Substantial documentation of North American Indian languages has been accomplished over the twentieth century under the auspices of museums. Boas himself was associated with museums throughout a good part of his career. The Jesup North Pacific Expedition, which he directed from 1897 to 1903, was sponsored by the American Museum of Natural History, New York. In addition to ethnological, archeological, and physical anthropological work, it permitted the collection of linguistic data by Boas himself (Bella Coola, Kwakiutl), by his Columbia colleague Livingston Farrand (Quinault, Tututni, Bella Bella, Quileute, Alsea), and by his student John Swanton (Haida,

Tlingit). The Bureau of American Ethnology supported the fieldwork of the graduate students Boas was training at Columbia, beginning with Swanton, who joined the Bureau in 1900. Leo Frachtenberg, also a student of Boas, worked for the Bureau from 1909 to 1917. Also at the Bureau during this period were Truman Michelson ("Discourse," fig. 3, this vol.) and John Napoleon Brinton Hewitt (fig. 3). Michelson, originally trained in Indo-European, concentrated on Algonquian languages, particularly Menominee, Fox, Ojibwa, Blackfoot, Kickapoo, and Cree. Hewitt, of Tuscarora descent, had learned Tuscarora at the age of 11 from friends at school. He began working for the Bureau in 1880 documenting Iroquoian languages and at his death in 1939 left extensive lexical and textual material, in Tuscarora as well as Mohawk, Onondaga, and Seneca. Bureau ethnologists like WJ McGee also recorded vocabularies (vol. 9:16). Roland B. Dixon, another Boas student, worked under the auspices of the American Museum of Natural History. Although primarily an ethnographer, he also recorded languages, particularly Maidu and Chimariko (vol. 8:730).

Sapir similarly spent a good part of his career in museum work in Ottawa from 1910 to 1925. Also at the museum in Ottawa was C. Marius Barbeau, a Canadian trained in Britain. Barbeau was primarily an ethnographer, but he recorded Tsimshian, Carrier, and Wyandot, as well as other Iroquoian languages. J. Alden Mason, trained by Sapir and Kroeber, also went into museum work. As a student at the University of Pennsylvania, Mason had accompanied Sapir to Utah in 1909 to work with Ute. After Sapir left for Ottawa, Mason completed his degree at the University of California at Berkeley with work on Salinan published in 1918. He then accepted museum positions first at the Field Museum, Chicago, then the American Museum of Natural History, and ultimately the University Museum at the University of Pennsylvania.

The most extensive documentation of North American languages ever accomplished by a single individual was also done under the auspices of a museum. The colorful but secretive John Peabody Harrington (fig. 4) (vol. 8:10-11), who had taken a Berkeley summer school course from Kroeber while a student at Stanford, was employed by the Bureau of American Ethnology from 1915 to 1954. Harrington roamed the country, concentrating on the West and particularly California where linguistic diversity was the greatest, recording material from nearly 100 languages. He had an unusually fine ear and a passion for accuracy. Analysis was of secondary interest to him, so more time was spent on basic documentation, which ranged from rehearings of earlier vocabularies, place-names, ethnobotanical terms, and other vocabulary, through grammar and texts where possible. He recorded hundreds of texts from Barbareño Chumash

Smithsonian, NAA: left, Portraits 39-D; right, Ms. 16.

Fig. 3. John Napoleon Brinton Hewitt (b. 1859, d. 1937). left, Possibly by De Lancey Gill, Bureau of American Ethnology photographer, about 1890s. right, Page of a cosmological myth dictated to Hewitt in the Munsee language in 1896 by John Armstrong, a resident of the Cattaraugus Reservation, who was of Seneca and Munsee descent. Armstrong also dictated to Hewitt a longer version of the same myth in Seneca (Hewitt 1903:137, 221-254; Goddard 1979b:8).

alone. In addition, he made or had made sound recordings on wax cylinders and aluminum disks. Little of his linguistic work was published while he was alive. He concealed his itineraries and the names of his consultants from everyone, including the Bureau, and stored his field notes in various locations throughout the country. Fortunately most have been returned to the Smithsonian, and nearly a million manuscript pages have been made available on microfilm (Mills, Brickfield, and Mills 1981-1991). They are serving as a valuable resource for descendants of the people he worked with and for linguists, ethnologists, and ethnohistorians. A community of those working with the Harrington materials has formed and meets regularly to share the results of research and answers to the puzzles pervading the manuscripts of this enigmatic but passionate scholar.

Museum-sponsored research has continued since Harrington's time. In the Department of Anthropology of the Smithsonian Institution, the descendant of the Bureau, Algonquianist Ives Goddard has continued work with Unami, Munsee, and Fox speakers and with

Fox and Massachusett manuscript collections. As ethnologists at the Canadian National Museum of Man in Ottawa (later called the Canadian Museum of Civilization and moved to Hull, Quebec), Gordon Day recorded Western Abenaki, Michael Foster carried out extensive work with speakers of Cayuga, and Albert D. DeBlois has worked on Micmac.

Native Speaker Researchers

Throughout the twentieth century there have been native speakers of North American languages who have worked to preserve their mother tongues. Some have become academics themselves, pursuing advanced degrees in linguistics and anthropology; some have worked in collaboration with linguists, and some have worked independently.

A number of these researchers have been part of the Boas and Sapir traditions. George Hunt, a Tlingit who also spoke Kwakiutl, learned to write the language from Boas and composed tens of thousands of pages in

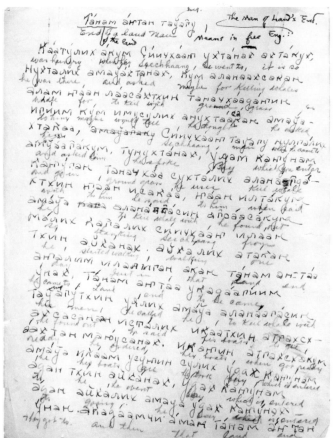

Smithsonian, NAA: left, 81-13606; right, The Papers of John P. Harrington, reel 6.
Fig. 4. John Peabody Harrington (b. 1884, d. 1961). left, With one of his main assistants and collaborators, Father Makary A. Baranoff, St. Paul I., Alaska, 1941. right, Aleut story "The Man of Land's End," written for Harrington in the Aleut Cyrillic alphabet by Ivan Alexis Yatchmeneff, with his own interlinear English translation, St. Paul I., Alaska, about 1941. The notation at top right is by Harrington.

it with interlinear translations, which he sent to Boas. This material comprises the bulk of the 11 volumes of Kwakiutl ethnographic and folkloric texts published by Boas (Berman 1994). Henry W. Tate, a Coast Tsimshian speaker, learned a missionary orthography and sent texts to Boas as well (Maud 1993). William Jones, a Fox speaker, completed a dissertation on word formation under Boas in 1904 and compiled a Fox grammatical sketch (1911) as well as texts in Fox (1907) and Ojibwa (1917-1919). Archie Phinney, a Nez Perce speaker who had worked with Boas, recorded extensive texts from his mother (1934). Ella Deloria, a Lakhota speaker, collaborated with Boas on an important grammar and published texts in addition to other writings (see J. Murray 1974; Rice 1992, 1993). Francis La Flesche (fig. 5), an Omaha speaker, was an employee of the Bureau and published a dictionary and texts in Osage (Liberty 1978). Alex Thomas, a Nootka speaker, learned to write his language in 1914 from Sapir. Over a number of years he prepared texts and sent them to Sapir; he continued transcribing texts into his 70s, collaborating also with Eugene Arima. Lawrence Nicodemus, a Coeur d'Alene speaker,

worked both with linguists and independently for many years, beginning by collaborating with Gladys Reichard and spending 1935 and 1936 at Columbia; he published a grammar and dictionary with sound cassettes (Nicodemus 1975). William Morgan, a Navajo speaker, collaborated for over a half-century with Robert Young to produce extensive materials on his language (vol. 10:667).

Particularly as Native communities have become aware of the threat of language loss, more speakers have undertaken linguistic work and have produced important documentation of their languages. Among the many speaker-scholars who have produced materials since 1970 are Josephine Stands in Timber Glenmore (Cheyenne), Norma Jean Russell (Blackfoot), Bernard Francis (Micmac), David Francis (Passamaquoddy), Freda Ahenakew (Cree), Ernest McGregor (Ojibwa), Durbin Feeling (Cherokee), Esther Blueye (Seneca), Reginald Henry (Cayuga and Onondaga), Alberta Austin (Seneca) ("Sketch of Seneca, an Iroquoian Language," fig. 4, this vol.), Josie White Eagle (Winnebago), Parker MacKenzie (Kiowa); LaVerne Masayevsa Jeanne (Hopi), Ofelia

57

left, Harvard U., Peabody Mus., Cambridge, Mass.: N961; right, Smithsonian, NAA:3861.
Fig. 5. Francis La Flesche (b. 1857, d. 1932). left, Demonstrating the position assumed in throwing the stick in the Omaha game of *wahí gasnugiðe* 'bone slide'. The player throws the sticks so they skim or slide along the level ground or the ice; the one who threw them the farthest won all the sticks (Fletcher and La Flesche 1911:364). Photographed at the Peabody Museum, Harvard, about 1900. right, Facing pages in a notebook written by La Flesche in which the rectos and versos make up discrete manuscripts treating different languages. Here the left page has part of a list of Omaha kinship terms while the right page is part of a listing of Osage song names.

Zepeda (Papago), Lucille Watahomigie (Walapai), Vi Hilbert (Lushootseed), Mandy Jimmie (Thompson), Arnold Guerin (Musqueam and Cowichan Halkomelem), Desmond Peters (Lillooet), Larry Pierre (Okanagan), Tillie George (Colville-Okanagan), Bernice Touchie (Nitinaht), Gordon Robertson (Haisla), Alice Neundorf (Navajo), Elavina Tsosie Perkins (Navajo), Mary Ann Willie (Navajo), Merton Sandoval (Jicarilla), Eliza Jones (Koyukon), Nora Dauenhauer (Tlingit), Erma Lawrence (Haida), Moses Dirks (Aleut), Isabella Avtonova (Naukanski), Vera Oovi Kaneshire (Central Siberian Yupik), Linda Womkon Badten (Central Siberian Yupik), Marie Oovi (Central Siberian Yupik), Roger Silook (Central Siberian Yupik), Willis Wallunga (Central Siberian Yupik), Anders Appassingok (Central Siberian Yupik), Adelinda Womkon (Central Siberian Yupik), Darlene Orr (Central Alaskan Yupik, Siberian Yupik), Elsie Mather (Central Alaskan Yupik) ("Sketch of Central Alaskan Yupik, an Eskimoan Language," figs. 3-4, this vol.), Marie Blanchette (Central Alaskan Yupik), Anna Jacobson (Central Alaskan Yupik), Edna Ahgeak MacLean (Inupiaq), Leona Okakok (Inupiaq), Jana Harcharek (Inupiaq), Ruth Samson (Inupiaq), Taamusi Qumaq (Inuit), Mark Kalluak (Inuit), Robert Petersen (West Greenlandic), Brigitte Jacobsen (West Greenlandic), Lise Lennert Olsen (West Greenlandic), and Rose Jeddore (Labrador Inuit).

Missionary Contributions

Throughout the twentieth century, contributions to North American linguistics have continued to come from missionaries living in Native communities. Their extended contact with the languages, in many cases coupled with training in basic techniques of linguistic analysis, has resulted in much fine work, not only the creation of orthographies and liturgical and pedagogical materials, but also extensive basic documentation of the languages.

Particularly in northern areas, priests of several Roman Catholic orders have produced grammars, dictionaries, and texts. Father Adrien-Gabriel Morice left considerable documentation on Carrier, Chipewyan, Slavey, and Hare, as well as notes on Beaver, Kutchin, and Dogrib (see Carrière 1972; and vol. 6:780-781). Father Berard Haile spent much of his life among the Navajo and left extensive materials, both published (D. Powell 1961), and unpublished (Phyllis Ball 1984). Father Augustin J. Brabant prepared a grammar and dictionary of Nootka (vol. 7:660), Father Edouard Gouy a Slavey dictionary and grammatical sketch (Freeman 1966:365), Father Lucien Schneider considerable material on Inuit (vol. 5:794), and Father Pacifique (1939) extensive lessons in Micmac (Hewson and Francis 1990). Moravian missionaries had established a post at Bethel, Alaska, in 1885, and several produced Central Alaskan Yupik materials, in particular

Ferdinand Drebert and John Hinz (Henkelman and Vitt 1985). Moravian missionaries also settled among the Labrador Eskimo and produced materials in their language, particularly the Reverends Walter Perrett and William F. Peacock. A Mennonite minister, Rodolphe C. Petter, published a Cheyenne grammar (1907, 1952) and dictionary (1915). Detailed discussion of missionary work among Eskimo-Aleut and Athapaskan peoples can be found in Krauss (1973).

The Summer Institute of Linguistics (SIL) was formally incorporated in 1935 after two summer training camps for prospective Bible translators. Participants worked first in Mexico, learning to analyze the structures of indigenous languages and translate the Bible into them. In 1944 the work was extended to the United States. A leading figure in the organization from the outset has been Kenneth Pike, who attended the Linguistic Institute at Ann Arbor in 1937 in order to study with Sapir. In addition to liturgical and pedagogical materials, SIL members have produced important documentation of North American languages. Among these are volumes on Comanche by Elliott Canonge, on Santa Ana Keresan by Irvine Davis, on Papago and Pima by Dean and Lucille Saxton, on Tlingit by Constance Naish and Gillian Story, on Blackfoot by Donald Frantz, on Cheyenne by Wayne Leman, on Central Carrier by Richard Walker, on Chipewyan by Bud Elford and Marjorie Elford, and on Naskapi by Bill Jancewicz. Significant contributions have also been made to the study of Inupiaq, Central Alaskan Yupik, Upper Kuskokwim, Koyukon, Kutchin, Upper Tanana, Babine, Sekani, Chilcotin, Beaver, Slavey, Dogrib, Stoney, Ojibwa, Algonquin, East Cree, Kickapoo, Crow, Northern Paiute, Ute, Jemez, Southern Tiwa, Northern Tiwa, and Tewa (Summer Institute of Linguistics 1992).

Some researchers first discovered an interest in North American languages while serving as missionaries, then pursued this interest in graduate studies in linguistics. Pliny Earle Goddard left missionary work to study for a doctorate in linguistics at Berkeley under the German-trained Hellenist Benjamin Ide Wheeler, then became assistant in anthropology in 1901 with the establishment of the department and museum of anthropology there under Kroeber. During his career he carried out fieldwork particularly with Pacific Athapaskan languages and cultures, publishing extensively on Hupa, Lassik, Cahto, Chilula, Wailaki, Galice, Tolowa, and other languages (vol. 8:736-737; see also Freeman 1966). He also served as coeditor of *IJAL* until his death in 1929. A number of other missionaries and researchers supported by missions have also taken advanced degrees, some remaining in their mission roles, others entering academia.

Independent Researchers

Not all documentation of the languages has been accomplished under institutional sponsorship. James Teit went to the Northwest from Scotland at the age of 19 as an apprentice storekeeper. He learned to speak Thompson Salish as well as some Shuswap, Lillooet, Kaska, and Tahltan. Boas, who met him in 1894, was highly impressed with his knowledge of the languages and the cultures of the area and supported him in collecting more information and publishing it. Teit left much important material, including the results of a dialect survey he conducted in British Columbia, Washington, and Montana (vol. 7:733). Charles Hill-Tout, an Englishman who arrived in British Columbia as a teacher, recorded texts in a number of Salishan languages (vol. 7:689; Maud 1978). C. Hart Merriam (vol. 8:10, 751-752) collected extensive vocabularies over the first half of the twentieth century, particularly on the languages of the West. Supported by a private bequest, he canvassed California and recorded dozens of languages, some of which are known chiefly through his notes, but he was unfortunately untrained in linguistics and reluctant to publish his material. It remains in manuscript form in the Department of Anthropology at the University of California, Berkeley. Philip Stedman Sparkman, a storekeeper near Rincón in southern California, worked on Luiseño with speaker Silvestre Gamez. When Kroeber visited him in 1904, he urged him to publish his work. Sparkman published a grammar in 1905 and continued to collect material until his death in 1907 (vol. 8:762). In 1960, all the Sparkman material was organized, edited, and published by Kroeber and George Grace.

Jaime de Angulo, a physician and amateur anthropologist, married Kroeber's student Lucy Freeland and joined her in documenting California languages, among them Achumawi, Karok, Yamhill Kalapuya, Patwin, Konomihu, Shasta (vol. 8:721-722), and Taos. Frank T. Siebert, a physician, worked extensively with several languages, particularly Eastern Abenaki (Penobscot) and Catawba (vol. 15:137, 873; Booker 1991:174-175). Robert Young was a self-trained linguist who first learned to speak Navajo in 1937 from his co-worker William Morgan. The pair developed an orthography and, during the 1940s and 1950s, began producing grammatical, lexical, and textual materials while employed by the Bureau of Indian Affairs (vol. 10:666-667, 838-839). Their work may be the most extensive record of any North American language.

Lines of Research, 1970s-1990s

During the last quarter of the twentieth century, research on North American languages increased, as did communication among researchers. Basic documentation continued to be a priority. since the languages were then disappearing more rapidly than before. Most researchers felt that they could not afford to focus solely on issues of the day; a foundation had to be laid for the investigation of questions yet to be formulated. The Boasian and Sapirian emphasis on the collection of connected speech in its cultural context continued to be valued for this reason.

At the same time, as more became known about the basic structures of the individual languages, and as linguistic theory developed, it became possible to describe more accurately and comprehensively the phonological, grammatical, and discourse structures observed. Tape recorders and computer software were used to document and analyze the intonation and prosody of natural speech. Grammatical categories and structures that are particularly well developed in certain North American languages were explored more closely, such as obviation, logophoricity, noun incorporation, switch reference, ergativity, inverse marking, irrealis modality, and evidentiality. Connected speech could be captured with audio and video recordings, particularly conversation. These and other developments were making possible the examination of larger structures in discourse. At the same time there was an increasing interest in the description of extinct languages and earlier forms of extant languages on the basis of written documents using the techniques of philological analysis.

Discussions of genetic relationships and reconstruction continued throughout the twentieth century, as more data became available for comparison and grammatical structures became better understood. All degrees of relationship were explored, from close ones like those among Arapahoan or Creek dialects, to mid-level ones such as Aleut-Eskimo, to more remote hypotheses, such as Haida-Tlingit-Eyak-Athapaskan, Siouan-Caddoan-Iroquoian, Hokan, and Penutian.

The effects of contact have always been of interest, both among North American languages and between American and European languages. Earlier work focused on vocabulary: loanwords as well as the extension of native linguistic resources for introduced items. Such studies can reveal who was in contact with whom and much about the nature of the contact and the level of bilingualism. They can also teach about the structure of languages, by displaying the ways in which foreign forms are adjusted to fit into the borrowing language. Later studies examined the effects of contact on higher levels of structure, especially grammatical and discourse patterns, and the complex social aspects of contact, including constructive uses of bilingualism. An ultimate result of language contact, obsolescence, has also been examined more closely. Linguists and Native communities alike want to know how the structure of a language is affected as it is spoken by fewer and fewer persons in ever more limited settings.

Throughout the twentieth century there was interest in special speech styles and registers. Beginning with Chamberlain's descriptions of baby talk (motherese) and Sapir's abnormal types of speech in Nootka (special forms that imply something about the status, sex, age, or other characteristics of the speaker, addressee, or person spoken of), there have been discussions of baby talk, men's and women's language, and forms of respect, such as "mother-in-law language." Special genres are highly developed in many cultures, including myths, songs, poetry, and ritual language. Only since the general availability of the tape recorder has it become possible to examine conversation, one of the richest and most complex genres of all.

The community of North Americanists was strong and active in the 1990s. Members of SSILA gathered every winter at the annual meeting of the American Anthropological Society or the Linguistic Society of America (LSA), and every other summer at the LSA Linguistic Institute. The plenary presentation of papers and discussion preserves an awareness of typological, areal, and possible genetic relations among the languages. Researchers remain linked by a common journal, *IJAL,* and the SSILA newsletter. In addition to this larger community, groups of scholars interested in individual language families or areas met regularly as well.

Fieldwork with speakers of Algonquian languages expanded considerably after the work of Bloomfield and Hockett. Scholars interested in the language, culture, and prehistory of speakers of Algonquian languages met every fall at the Algonquian Conference. Those who have been particularly active throughout this time include (in approximate chronological order) Karl Teeter (Maliseet-Passamaquoddy), Gordon Day (Western Abenaki), Frank Siebert (Eastern Abenaki), Allan Taylor (Blackfoot, Gros Ventre), Paul Voorhis (Kickapoo, Fox, Ojibwa, Cree), Ives Goddard (Unami, Munsee, Massachusett, Fox), H. Christoph Wolfart (Cree, Ojibwa), Zdeněk Salzmann (Arapaho), Wayne Leman (Cheyenne), Donald Frantz (Blackfoot), Albert D. DeBlois (Micmac), Evelyn Todd (Ojibwa), Alan Ford (Montagnais), Glyne Piggott (Ojibwa), Marguerite MacKenzie (Cree, Montagnais), Sandra Clarke (Montagnais), José Mailhot (Montagnais), Louis-Phillippe Vaillancourt (Montagnais), Bruce Pearson (Unami), Watson Williams (Micmac), George Aubin (Ojibwa), John Hewson (Micmac), Deborah James (Cree), David Pentland (Cree), Lynn Drapeau (Montagnais), Pierre Martin (Montagnais), Richard Rhodes (Ojibwa), John Nichols (Ojibwa, Cree, Potawatomi), Alana Johns (Ojibwa), Robert Papen (Mitchif), John O'Meara (Munsee), Paul Proulx (Micmac), Amy Dahlstrom (Cree, Fox), David Sherwood (Maliseet), Lásló Szabó (Maliseet), Robert Leavitt (Passamaquoddy), Philip LeSourd (Passamaquoddy), Donna Starks (Cree), Lisa Valentine

(Ojibwa), Danielle Cyr (Montagnais), J. Randolph Valentine (Ojibwa), David J. Costa (Illinois), and Charlotte Reinholtz (Cree). The newsletter *Algonquian and Iroquoian Linguistics* is published quarterly by John Nichols from the University of Manitoba, Winnipeg.

Work with speakers of Iroquoian languages developed initially under the guidance of Floyd Lounsbury at Yale. Linguists gathered every fall with ethnologists, ethnohistorians, and archeologists at the Conference on Iroquois Research. Those working with Iroquoian speakers included Lounsbury (Oneida), Wallace Chafe (Seneca, Onondaga), Michael Foster (Cayuga), Hanni Woodbury (Onondaga), Marianne Mithun (Tuscarora, Mohawk, Cayuga, Seneca), Clifford Abbott (Oneida), Nancy Bonvillain (Mohawk), Karin Michelson (Oneida, Mohawk), Blair Rudes (Tuscarora), and Janine Scancarelli (Cherokee).

Muskogean linguistics has developed in several quarters, particularly under Robert Rankin at the University of Kansas, Lawrence, and Pamela Munro at the University of California at Los Angeles. Scholars working actively with speakers during this period in addition to Rankin (Creek, Choctaw) and Munro (Choctaw, Chickasaw, Seminole Creek), included Dale Nicklas (Choctaw), Sylvia Boynton (Mikasuki), Karen Lupardus (Alabama), Mary Derrick-Mescua (Mikasuki), Michele Nathan (Seminole Creek), Emmanuel Drechsel (Mobilian Jargon), Karen Booker (Creek, Choctaw, Mikasuki), Geoffrey Kimball (Koasati), Charles Ulrich (Choctaw), Aaron Broadwell (Choctaw), Philip Davis (Alabama), Donald Hardy (Creek), Heather Hardy (Alabama), Timothy Montler (Alabama), Jack Martin (Creek, Mikasuki), Patricia Kwachka (Choctaw), and Robert Williams (Choctaw).

Researchers specializing in Siouan and Caddoan languages joined forces to meet together annually. Those who have been particularly active in work with Siouan languages during this period include Allan Taylor (Lakhota), Robert Hollow (Mandan), David Rood (Lakhota), Richard Carter (Lakhota, Mandan), Robert Rankin (Quapaw, Kansa), Patricia Shaw (Lakhota, Dakota, Stoney, Assiniboine), Jimm Good Tracks (Chiwere), Wesley Jones (Hidatsa), Randolph Graczyk (Crow), John Koontz (Omaha), Catherine Rudin (Omaha), Louanna Furbee (Chiwere), Jill Hopkins (Chiwere), Lori Stanley (Chiwere), Sara Sistrunk (Lakhota), Mauricio Mixco (Mandan), and Kathleen Shea (Ponca). All materials ever collected on Siouan languages were assembled in the Siouan Languages Archive in Boulder at the University of Colorado as a basis for the reconstruction of Proto-Siouan. Researchers working with Caddoan speakers were Wallace Chafe (Caddo), David Rood (Wichita), Douglas Parks (Pawnee, Arikara), and Lynette Melnar (Caddo).

Those working with Kiowa-Tanoan languages and Keresan also met together. Active in the field during this period were Laurel Watkins (Kiowa, Jemez), Paul Kroskrity (Arizona Tewa), Randall and Ann Speirs (Rio Grande Tewa), Amy Zaharlick (Picuris), Robert Sprott (Jemez), Donna Gardiner and Barbara Allen (Isleta). Those working with speakers of Keresan dialects include Irvine Davis (Santa Ana), Wick Miller (Acoma), and Hilaire Valiquette (Laguna, Cochiti).

Every summer the Friends of Uto-Aztecan assembled to share their work. Those working actively with speakers in the last quarter of the twentieth century included Carl and Florence Voegelin (Hopi), Wick Miller (Shoshone, Comanche, Kawaiisu, and others), Jane Hill (Cupeño, Papago), Kenneth Hill (Serrano, Hopi), Dean and Lucille Saxton (Papago, Pima), Ken Hale (Papago), Talmy Givón (Ute), Pamela Munro (Luiseño, Chemehuevi, Hopi, Kawaiisu, Tubatulabal, Pima), Susan Steele (Luiseño), Brent Galloway (Cupeño), Michael Nichols (Northern Paiute), Paul Kroskrity (Monache), Kay Fowler (Northern Paiute), Margaret Press (Chemehuevi), John Dayley (Shoshone), LaVerne Jeanne (Hopi), Maurice Zigmond (Kawaiisu), Curtis Booth (Kawaiisu), Ekkehart Malotki (Hopi), Ofelia Zepeda (Papago), Pamela Bunte (Southern Paiute), Robert Franklin (Southern Paiute), David Shaul (Hopi), John McLaughlin (Panamint, Comanche), Evan Norris (Owens Valley Paiute), Chris Loether (Monache), Jim Armagost (Comanche), and Jean Charney (Comanche).

Scholars working with languages of the West gathered each summer at the Hokan-Penutian conference, where a number of language families were represented. Genetic relationships among the families were not assumed to be established, but the joint gathering permitted continued investigation into certain possibilities and into language contact. Researchers working with speakers of Yuman languages included Margaret Langdon (Diegueño, Cocopa), who trained a number of Yumanists at the University of California at San Diego, Pam Munro (Mohave, Tolkapaya Yavapai, Maricopa), James Crawford (Cocopa), Leanne Hinton (Havasupai, Diegueño), Mauricio Mixco (Kiliwa), Akira Yamamoto (Havasupai, Walapai), Martha Kendall (Yavapai), Heather Hardy (Tolkapaya Yavapai), Lucille Watahomigie (Walapai), Lynn Gordon (Maricopa), and Amy Miller (Jamul Diegueño). William Jacobsen continued his work with Washoe. Research with Pomoan speakers was continued by Robert Oswalt (Kashaya, Southern Pomo, Central Pomo), Sally McLendon (Eastern Pomo), Mary Catherine O'Connor (Northern Pomo), and Marianne Mithun (Central Pomo). William Bright continued work with Karok, joined by Monica Macaulay and Julian Lang. Work with the last speakers of Yuki was done by Jesse Sawyer, and of Wappo by Jesse Sawyer, Charles Li, and Sandra Thompson. Work with Yokuts speakers was carried out by Geoffrey Gamble (Wikchamni), Howard Berman (Chukchansi), and Susan Britsch (Tachi). Extensive research on Miwok languages has been done by Catherine Callaghan throughout the period, and Suzanne Wash did fieldwork as well. William Shipley continued work with Maiduan. For Wintuan, work was done by Harvey Pitkin (Wintu), Ken Whistler (Northern Patwin), and Alice Schlichter Shepherd (Wintu). Documentation of Sahaptian languages was done by Haruo Aoki, Bruce Rigsby, Virginia Hymes, and Noel Rude.

Researchers interested in Northwest Coast languages met every summer at the Salish Conference. Several language families were usually represented: Wakashan, Chimakuan, Kootenai, Tsimshian, and Salish. Those active in work with speakers of Wakashan languages included William Jacobsen (Nootka, Makah), Emmon Bach (Haisla), Neville Lincoln (Haisla, Kwakiutl), John Rath (Haisla, Heiltsuk-Oowekyala), Evelyn Windsor (Haisla, Heiltsuk-Oowekyala), Steven Anderson (Kwakiutl), Bob Levine (Kwakiutl), Suzanne Rose (Nootka), Barry Carlson (Nitinaht), Thom Hess (Nitinaht), Ann Renker (Makah), Jay Powell (Nootka, Kwakiutl), and Toshihide Nakayama (Nootka). Jay Powell also worked with Quileute speakers. Kootenai was documented extensively by Lawrence Morgan and Steven Egesdal. Those working with speakers of Tsimshianic languages included Bruce Rigsby, John Dunn, Jean Mulder, and Marie-Lucie Tarpent.

A lively group of Salishanists grew up around Laurence Thompson and Dale Kinkade, many of whom continued to be active fieldworkers. In addition to Thompson (Thompson, Clallam, Tillamook, Nooksack, Lushootseed, Lummi), and Kinkade (Upper Chehalis, Columbian, Cowlitz, Thompson, Lower Chehalis, Twana), these included Aert Kuipers (Squamish, Shuswap), Thom Hess (Lushootseed, Saanich, Sliammon), Barry Carlson (Spokane), Philip Davis (Bella Coola), Ross Saunders (Bella Coola), Richard Demers (Lummi), Thomas Hukari (Cowichan Halkomelem), Tony Mattina (Colville-Okanagan, Flathead), Jay Powell (Musqueam Halkomelem, Shuswap), Brent Galloway (Chilliwack Halkomelem, Nooksak, Samish), Randy Bouchard and Dorothy Kennedy (Lillooet, Squamish, Okanagan, Sechelt), Toby Langen (Lushootseed), David Rozen (Cowichan Halkomelem), Donna Gerdts (Halkomelem), John Davis (Sliammon), Dawn Bates (Spokane, Lushootseed), Hank Nater (Bella Coola), Nile Thompson (Twana, Skokomish), Timothy Montler (Saanich, Clallam), Vi Hilbert (Lushootseed), Dwight Gardiner (Shuswap), Gary Palmer (Shuswap, Coeur d'Alene), Marianne Boelscher-Ignace (Shuswap), Mandy Jimmie (Thompson), Ewa Czaykowska-Higgins (Columbian),

Jan van Eijk (Lillooet), Sarah Thomason (Flathead), Ivy Doak (Coeur d'Alene), Steven Egesdal (Thompson, Clallam, Spokane, Flathead), Paul Kroeber (Sliammon, Thompson), Eloise Jelinek (Lummi, Straits), Henry Davis (Lillooet), Andie Palmer (Lushootseed, Shuswap), Nicola Bessel (Interior Salish), Susan Blake (Sliammon, Lillooet), Honoré Watanabe (Sliammon), Patricia Shaw (Lillooet), Peter Jacobs (Squamish), Nancy Mattina (Okanagan), Taylor Roberts (Lillooet), Elizabeth Currie (Lillooet), Hamida Demirdache (Lillooet), and Lisa Matthewson (Lillooet).

Athapaskanists met annually in the summer as well. In part because this family contains more languages than any other in North America, in part because some of the languages, particularly Navajo, have comparatively large numbers of speakers, the Athapaskanists constituted one of the larger groups of North Americanists. Those most active documenting languages during this period included Robert Young (Navajo), William Morgan (Navajo), Kenneth Hale (Navajo, Tahltan), Constance Naish (Beaver, Dogrib, Carrier, Babine [Witsu Wit'en]), Gillian Story (Beaver, Dogrib, Carrier, Babine), Michael Krauss (all Alaskan Athapaskan, Eyak), Victor Golla (Hupa, Tututni, Tagish), Jeff Leer (Tlingit, Kutchin, Tanana, Upper Tanana, Sarcee), Phil Howard (Slavey), Ray Collins (Upper Kuskokwim), Robert Howren (Dogrib), Paul Platero (Navajo), Keith Basso (Western Apache), Muriel Saville-Troike (Navajo), Gary Witherspoon (Navajo), Martha Austin (Navajo), Irvy Goossen (Navajo), Alan Wilson (Navajo), Frank Hardy (Navajo, Jicarilla, Western Apache), Eung-Do Cook (Sarcee, Tahltan, Chilcotin, Babine, Carrier, Chipewyan), Eliza Jones (Koyukon), Jim Kari (Navajo, Ahtna, Tanana, Tanaina, Ingalik, Holikachuk, Babine, Upper Tanana), Alice Neundorf (Navajo), John Ritter (Han, Kutchin, Northern Tutchone, Southern Tutchone, Tagish, Kaska, Tahltan), Ellavina Perkins (Navajo), Chad Thompson (Koyukon, Hupa), Scott Rushforth (Hare, Bearlake, Mescalero), Ronald Scollon (Chipewyan, Tanacross), Keren Rice (Slavey, Hare), Jim Seaberg (Tolowa), Leslie Saxon (Dogrib), Lynda Ackroyd (Dogrib), Melissa Axelrod (Koyukon), Sally Midgette (Navajo), Sharon Hargus (Sekani, Babine, Ingalik), Pat Moore (Kaska), Clay Slate (Navajo), Susan Foster-Cohen (Navajo), Aryeh Faltz (Navajo), Patricia Shaw (Tahltan), Mary Ann Willie (Navajo), Eloise Jelinek (Navajo), Tiina Randoja (Sekani), Loren Bommelyn (Tolowa), David Dinwoodie (Chilcotin), Siri Tuttle (Salcha Lower Tanana, Upper Tanana), Willem de Reuse (Apache dialects), Nobukatsu Minoura (Upper Tanana), William Poser (Carrier), Alice Taff (Ingalik), and Dagmar Jung (Jicarilla Apache). Tlingit scholars in particular have worked intensively with speakers: Constance Naish, Gillian Story, Jeff Leer, Nora Marks Dauenhauer, and Richard Dauenhauer. Work with

Haida has been done by Robert Levine, Jeff Leer, Erma Laurence, Carol Eastman, Elizabeth Edwards, John Enrico, and Hirofume Hori.

Intensive work with speakers of Eskimo-Aleut languages continued. In part because of the large number of communities speaking varieties of the languages, there was a comparatively large group of active researchers, a number of them also speakers. Linguists and anthropologists gathered at the Inuit Studies Conference, and there is an interdisciplinary journal *Inuit Studies*. Among those who have documented the languages since the 1970s were G.A. Menovshchikov (Naukanski, Chaplinski Central Siberian Yupik, Sirenikski, Big Diomede Inupiaq), Knut Bergsland (Aleut, Nunamiut Inupiaq, West Greenlandic), Michael Krauss (all Alaskan Eskimo, Siberian Yupik), Irene Reed (Central Alaskan Yupik, Alutiiq), Frederik Nielsen (Greenlandic), Christian Berthelsen (Greenlandic), Mark Kalluak (Inuit), Louis-Jacques Dorais (Inuit, East Greenlandic), Osahito Miyaoka (Central Alaskan Yupik), Robert Petersen (West Greenlandic), Steven Jacobson (Central Alaskan Yupik, Siberian Yupik), Mick Mallon (Inuit), Pierre and Bernadette Robbe (East Greenlandic), Inge Kleivan (Greenlandic), Adelinda Womkon Badten (Central Siberian Yupik), James Nageak (Inupiaq), Jørgen Rischel (West Greenlandic), Moses Dirks (Aleut), Edna Ahgeak MacLean (Inupiaq), Leona Okakok (Inupiaq), Lawrence Smith (Inuit), Jeff Leer (Alutiiq, Inupiaq), Willis Wallunga (Central Siberian Yupik), Anders Appassingok (Central Siberian Yupik), Vera Oovi Kaneshiro (Central Siberian Yupik), Lawrence Kaplan (Inupiaq), Jana Harcharek (Inupiaq), Ruth Samson (Inupiaq), Wolf Seiler (Inupiaq), Nikolai Vakhtin (Aleut, Central Siberian Yupik, Sirenikski), Roger Silook (Central Siberian Yupik), Henrik Aagesen (West Greenlandic), Taamusi Qumaq (Inuit), Rose Jeddore (Labrador Inuit), Chet Creider (Inuit), Betty Harnum (Inuit), Minouru Oshima (Aleut), Anthony Woodbury (Central Alaskan Yupik), Michael Fortescue (Inuit-Inupiaq, Polar Eskimo, Greenlandic), Jerrold Sadock (West Greenlandic, Inuit), Ronald Lowe (Inuit), Susan Sammons (Inuit), Isabella Avtonova (Naukanski), Evgeniy Golovko (Commander Island Aleut, Naukanski), Phyllis Morrow (Central Alaskan Yupik), Willem de Reuse (Central Siberian Yupik), Darlene Pungowiyi Orr (Central Siberian Yupik, Sirenikski), Martha Crago (Inuit), Philippe Mennecier (East Greenlandic), Jean Briggs (Inuit), Niels Grann (East Greenlandic), Lars Kristoffersen (West Greenlandic), Per and Karen Langgaard (West Greenlandic), and Birgitte Jacobson (West Greenlandic, Polar Eskimo).

Language and the Culture History of North America

MICHAEL K. FOSTER

Language as an Instrument of Prehistory

The methods of comparative and historical linguistics are used to establish genetic relationships among languages, reconstruct hypothetical parent forms (protolanguages), and separate borrowed from inherited features. When the primary interest is the history of the languages themselves, the term linguistic prehistory is used (Haas 1969, 1976). Because languages are not spoken in a vacuum, but by human beings living in particular places at particular times, they reflect the social and cultural conditions of their speakers (Sapir 1912, 1916, 1949:432-433; Watkins 1971:1498). Words whose form and meaning have been reconstructed at the level of a protolanguage may contain clues about the economy, social organization, religious life, and environment of the speakers of the protolanguage, while the distribution of a language family on the map may, when the divisions internal to it have been properly determined, point to a homeland and indicate the direction of later spreads from it. Similarly, patterns of linguistic borrowing can shed light on the nature of prehistoric contacts. The term paleolinguistics (or linguistic archeology) has been used for the various concerns, assumptions, and methods by which language serves as an instrument of prehistory (Sapir 1916; Saussure 1959:224; Swadesh 1952, 1959a; Lounsbury 1968:182-183). For the distribution of the languages and language families in North America, see "Introduction" and the pocket map, this volume. See also "The Classification of the Native Languages of North America," this volume.

In spite of the strong stance in twentieth-century American anthropology toward treating race, language, and culture as independent variables (Sapir 1921c:213-214), historical linguistics has in fact long acted as a handmaiden to archeology, and to a lesser extent physical anthropology, in confronting problems of North American prehistory. In the absence of written records for all but the most recent centuries, it has been regarded as useful to consider all the inferential techniques available to deal with the many millennia of pre-European occupation. It is true that unless an artifact contains linguistic inscriptions, as in the case of the Mayan stelae, identifying a prehistoric assemblage by language remains a matter of sophisticated guesswork, fraught with interpretive difficulties (Kroeber 1955:104; cf. Hughes 1992). At the same time, linguistics and archeology can, when certain precautions are observed, lend perspective to each other's findings and compensate for each other's weaknesses (Eggan 1952:37; Ehret 1976). A major strength of archeology is the variety of means it has for assigning dates, or ranges of dates, to artifacts and whole cultures; but archeology is constrained in terms of the inferences that can be made about non-material aspects of prehistoric cultures, and here linguistic evidence is often useful for filling in the gaps. For its part, historical linguistics has means for determining the relative order of prehistoric events, such as deciding on the order of splits within a family tree, but it lacks accurate methods for assigning dates to such events. Here, the archeologist's methods and evidence may bring precision to the linguist's inferences.

Kinds of Linguistic Evidence Used for Culture-Historic Inference

Language Distribution and the Center of Gravity Principle

Assuming that change in language proceeds at a more or less even rate over time, the deepest splits within a family reflect the greatest age, and the location of these splits on the map points to the area where the protolanguage began to diversify (Sapir 1916, 1949: 452-455; cf. Swadesh 1964:548). Shallower splits are also significant: when these are placed in relation to the deeper splits it may be possible to infer the directions in which a language family spread as it continued to diversify. It is important not to confuse a family's center of gravity as determined by its internal divisions with the family's geographic center, which may fall in a different location. Thus, the geographic center of Salishan is found within the western part of the Plateau—roughly the region where Okanagan and Thompson were spoken aboriginally—but the deepest splits within Salishan occur on the coast, and it is there rather than on the Plateau that the Salishan homeland must be assumed to lie. Failure to understand the difference between a family's center of gravity and its geographic center has sometimes led to misinterpretations of North American linguistic prehistory.

The center of gravity principle can provide valuable clues about linguistic prehistory, but it must contend with certain limitations. First, although linguistic relationships are often represented in the form of branching tree diagrams, the actual histories of languages are usually far more complex than such schemata imply. The so-called chain model may better represent the history of a language family in a given case (Bloomfield 1933:310-319; Swadesh 1959, 1964:546; Lounsbury 1968:179-182; Krauss 1976a:311-312; Miller 1984), but such a model does away with the hierarchy of internal divisions upon which the center of gravity principle operates. Second, it should be possible theoretically to extend the center of gravity principle to groupings beyond the family level such as stocks and "phyla," and this has been done in a number of cases, in order, for example, to infer the relative age of early migrations to the Americas (C.F. Voegelin 1945, 1958). But unlike family-level groupings, only a few of the proposals for higher-order relationships are well supported, and culture-historical inferences based on such relationships must be regarded as speculative. Third, the area implied by the center of gravity principle as a homeland may or may not be suitable for human habitation at the appropriate time level. Thus, Death Valley emerges as a plausible homeland for the Numic branch of Uto-Aztecan (Lamb 1958:98) only if the area was more hospitable for human occupancy 2,000-3,000 years ago than it is today. In general, linguistic diversity is a function not only of time but also of environmental factors (cf. Jett 1977:73-75). Finally, although the linguistic homeland concept may be useful for addressing issues such as whether the Salishans originated on the Northwest Coast or in the interior, the areas designated as protolanguage homelands must be assumed in most cases to be far more restricted geographically than the areas occupied by the descendant languages, a situation that arises through processes of language extinction and replacement. As a consequence, large sections of the continent, which often contain hundreds of prehistoric sites, are unaccounted for linguistically and are therefore beyond the scope of paleolinguistics (Lamb 1964a; cf. Kinkade and Powell 1976:93, fig. 5).

Lexicostatistics and Glottochronology

The term glottochronology refers to a mathematical method for calculating the dates of splits within a language grouping (Hymes 1960:4; C.F. Voegelin 1962:147; Swadesh 1964a:289); in many respects it is simply a more precise formulation of the center of gravity principle (Swadesh 1952:454). To the extent that glottochronology draws upon statistical procedures, it may be seen as a type of lexicostatistics, and the two terms are often used interchangeably. But lexicostatistics is a broader field and includes other statistical approaches, such as comparative lexicostatistics, whose purpose is to classify languages (Dyen 1962, 1962a, 1964, 1965, 1975; Miller 1984). As a generalization, it may be said that lexicostatistical procedures yield measures of distance among genetically related languages, whereas glottochronological procedures purport to translate measures of relative distance into actual dates. Such dates should include error ranges at specified confidence levels, although frequently they do not, leaving the false impression that a pair of languages began to diverge from each other in a particular year.

Glottochronology was developed by Morris Swadesh and his coworkers in the 1950s. Its key assumption is that words belonging to a language's so-called basic vocabulary—that segment of the general vocabulary relating to categories of human experience presumed to be universal and therefore most resistant to borrowing—are replaced at a constant rate as the language evolves over time. The constant, expressed as a percentage of loss (or retention) in basic vocabulary per unit of time, usually the century, was discovered empirically by studying replacement rates in a variety of Old World languages with documented histories. These rates were found to cluster within a sufficiently narrow mathematical range to suggest that the replacement rate was a "near universal" in the world's languages. It was this feature that made glottochronology an immediate success in North America, since it provided a way of dating splits within language families lacking records for all but the most recent centuries.

The principal assumptions of glottochronology—that the meanings of basic vocabulary items are universal, that basic vocabulary undergoes replacement at a constant rate and is unaffected by factors such as word taboo and contact between languages, and that change in vocabulary is a measure of change in language generally—have all been called into question and vigorously debated. This has resulted in a number of improvements to the method, particularly with regard to the mathematical formulas used in determining time-depths. On balance, glottochronology has had about as many supporters as detractors over the years (Embleton 1986:45-59). Despite the controversy surrounding the method, glottochronological dates are still routinely cited in discussions of North American prehistory, even as the writers sound warnings about the method's lack of reliability.

The Analyzability of Words

Words that are analyzable into segments (e.g., *railroad*), are normally of more recent coinage than those that are unanalyzable, and this provides a means for establishing the relative age not only of the words but also of the cultural concepts expressed by them (Sapir 1916, 1949:434-439; cf. Chafe 1964a, Goss 1968; Jacobsen 1968:49). The analyzability criterion applies especially well in languages belonging to the Athapaskan and Iroquoian families, which treat new concepts, such as those arising in the contact situation, by drawing on their own powers of derivation, rather than by adopting foreign terms outright. Allowance must be made for the effects of borrowing and word taboo when the analyzability criterion is applied. Borrowings may or may not be analyzable in the donor language, but they are rarely analyzable in the borrowing language. By their opacity, borrowed words give an impression of age, whereas in fact they may be recent additions to a language. Word taboo produces nearly the opposite effect: the replacement of old unanalyzable terms by freshly coined descriptive ones. The new words give a spurious impression of recency to the concept involved. The problems introduced by borrowing and word taboo are easier to control when the analyzability criterion is applied to vocabulary sets rather than to single words.

Reconstructed Vocabulary

In contrast to the basic vocabulary used in glottochronology, which is somewhat inaccurately said to be "culture free," other sectors of vocabulary act as a kind of mirror to culture. Since this is true at any stage of a language's development, the reconstruction of protovocabularies can shed light on the society, culture, and physical surroundings of the proto-speech community (Sapir 1912, 1916, 1936, 1949:432,449-450; Thieme 1964; Gamkrelidze and Ivanov 1990). From the reconstruction of proto-kinship terminologies, for instance, it may be possible to infer rules of marriage, descent, and residence in the ancestral community (Matthews 1959; Hockett 1964; Dyen and Aberle 1974; Walker 1975; Aberle 1984). The reconstruction of terms in a protolanguage for a practice such as agriculture provides prima facie evidence for the presence at that level of the practice itself (Law 1961; Joël 1978). Although the absence of reconstructible terms in a protolanguage for a cultural complex like agriculture does not rule out the existence of the complex at that level, a strong case exists for its absence, especially when the languages descending from the protolanguage are found to have developed separate vocabularies for it (Mithun 1984b; Rankin 1992a). Vocabulary reconstruction has also been used to place the homeland of a protolanguage, thus providing an independent check on hypotheses based on the center of gravity principle. If the prehistoric ranges of plants and animals for which prototerms exist are plotted on the map, the area delimited by the greatest number of overlapping ranges points to a probable homeland for the proto-speech community (Siebert 1967; Fowler 1972, 1983; Whistler 1977, 1988).

The use of reconstructed vocabulary as the basis for culture-historic inference, which is sometimes referred to as the *Wörter-und-Sachen* technique ('words and things'), is the most precise of the various lines of evidence here reviewed, although it is perhaps the most challenging from a technical point of view. For instance, it is often difficult, particularly in the case of plant and animal terms, to establish precise denotata for cognates in the daughter languages (Fowler 1972:107). Moreover, even when precise denotata have been established, the meanings may be quite divergent in the daughter languages, and there must be a reasoned basis for selecting a particular meaning for the reconstructed protoform (Thieme 1964). Such divergences in meaning can prove useful, since they may reveal semantic shifts that shed significant light on prehistory. From the fact that the Proto-Algonquian word for 'woodland caribou' shifted in some Eastern Algonquian languages to 'deer', one may safely conclude that speakers of the Eastern languages moved south of the range of the caribou at some point (Siebert 1967:23-25, 37). Another challenge lies in trying to determine the ranges of species at the time-depth represented by the protolanguage; these ranges may be quite different from the modern ones. This can prove daunting in the face of incomplete palynological and other prehistoric biological data (Friedrich 1970). Finally, it should be noted that it is possible to draw spurious conclusions about the protoculture using entirely correct methods of linguistic reconstruction, as shown, for instance, by the fact that respectable protoforms for 'gun' and 'whiskey' can be reconstructed in Proto-Algonquian, although these items were not acquired by Algonquian peoples until after contact (Bloomfield 1946:106-107; cf. Hockett 1948:127-128.) This problem can usually be overcome by selecting unanalyzable rather than analyzable terms for reconstruction.

Evidence of Borrowing

Borrowed elements in a language provide prima facie evidence of contacts among peoples, and the type of borrowing may reveal a good deal about the cultural and social relationships among the groups involved (Sapir 1921c: 205-220, 1916, 1949:458-459; Sherzer and Bauman 1972). The borrowing of a few vocabulary items implies a situation of casual contact, such as might arise through intermittent trade. At the other extreme, extensive diffusion not only of vocabulary but also of phonological and grammatical features implies a stable enough contact situation over time for bilingualism to develop. Retention of borrowed elements may even reveal a situation where one language has wholly replaced another, with traces of the earlier language turning up as "substrate" features in the surviving language (Hinton 1991). Language spread without a significant movement of people is seemingly a rare phenomenon in North America, but it is by no means unheard of. It tends to arise in situations of multiple language use where a prestige form replaces a nonvalued form among bilingual speakers (Sapir 1916, 1949:453; Jacobs 1937; Lamb 1964a:459-461; Whistler 1979:24; Krauss 1980:9; vol 6:61; Fredrickson 1984:495).

Linguistic diffusion has the advantage over cultural diffusion that the direction of borrowing can be determined more easily in the former case (Sapir 1916, 1949:445). Linguistic diffusion provides clues about the movement of artifacts and ideas named in borrowed terms. Borrowed terms can also shed light on the relative priority of groups in an area. One line of evidence comes from place-names: if a group has borrowed place-names from another, the borrowers are assumed to be later comers. A familiar example is the ubiquitous occurrence of aboriginal place-names in North American English. Another line of evidence comes from borrowed terms for plants and animals: a group adopting terms from another for species indigenous to an area is likely to have arrived later. Finally, patterns of borrowing may reveal contacts that occurred at the protolanguage stage and that may thus shed light on the early locations and movements of peoples (M.J.P. Nichols 1981).

The Scale of Paleolinguistic Applications

The question arises as to how far back in time the various lines of linguistic evidence can be carried for purposes of culture-historic inference. Certain practical considerations limit the range to about six millennia. This ceiling is in part set by glottochronology, whose upper range of applicability is 5,000 years. But even more, it is determined by the status of classificatory and protolanguage reconstruction work in North America: the consensus among linguists in the late twentieth century was that in the majority of cases relationships could be spoken of with confidence only up to the family level, and in a very few cases, to the stock level (Haas 1969; Campbell and Mithun 1979a).

Nevertheless, classificatory schemes depicting higher-order groupings have been used extensively in interpretations of North American prehistory. The most influential of the grand reductionist schemes in the twentieth century was Edward Sapir's (1921b, 1929) continental classification (fig. 1). Sapir grouped all of the families of North America and Mexico into six all-embracing phyla and drew certain culture-historic conclusions from their distributions (Foster 1988). The Sapir classification stimulated a great deal of historical

research on aboriginal languages and underwent substantial revision (fig. 2) (C.F. Voegelin 1941c; C.F. Voegelin and E.W. Voegelin 1944; C.F. Voegelin and F.M. Voegelin 1964, 1965, 1966, 1977). Most of Sapir's phylum proposals were eventually discarded, and a certain caution then set in. By the 1970s a very conservative "splitter's" classification had emerged (Campbell and Mithun 1979a; cf. Coe, Snow, and Benson 1986:42-45; "Introduction," table 3, this vol.).

A few linguists have worked in the reductionist tradition of Sapir, notably Joseph Greenberg, whose hemispheric classification is even more radical than Sapir's (Greenberg 1960, 1979, 1987; cf. Ruhlen 1987, 1989, 1991). In this scheme, all the aboriginal languages of the Americas are subsumed under just three headings: Eskimo-Aleut, Na-Dene, and "Amerind." The first grouping was established before Sapir's time and has been accepted by the majority of linguists; the second (with the controversial inclusion of Haida) was proposed by Sapir and was accepted in 1995 by few besides Greenberg and his associates. Amerind involves an entirely different order of magnitude from the first two groupings: it consists of all the remaining aboriginal languages of the western hemisphere grouped into 11 branches, which themselves comprise vast superstocks (Greenberg 1987:387, map). The Greenberg classification has attracted a good deal of attention in fields outside of linguistics that are concerned with the problem of the peopling of the Americas (Turner 1983, 1986; Greenberg, Turner, and Zegura 1985, 1986; cf. Greenberg 1989). It has also entered a broader arena of debate over human evolution and the evolution of human language (Cavalli-Sforza et al. 1988; Lewin 1988; Ross 1991; R. Wright 1991).

Serious substantive and methodological questions have been raised about Greenberg's approach, and these, too, have had reverberations beyond linguistics (Chafe 1987; Goddard 1987a, 1990b; Campbell 1988, 1991, 1995; Golla 1988; Jacobsen 1988, 1988a, 1995; O'Grady et al. 1989; Bateman et al. 1990, 1990a; Goddard and Campbell 1994; Rankin 1992a; Cann 1995). Even if an entity like Amerind is someday shown to have a historical basis, the time for it to have reached the present state of diversity of the languages it putatively comprises greatly exceeds even the earliest archeological dates for the peopling of the Americas (Johanna Nichols 1990, 1995). Since the Greenberg classification is far from having been validated on linguistic grounds, any use of it for culture-historic inference must be regarded as premature.

Linguistic distributions have figured in one other approach to the prehistory of North America, which takes as its point of departure the high concentration of aboriginal languages on the Pacific coast. Two-thirds of the families and isolates of North America fall within an area west of the Rocky Mountains, about

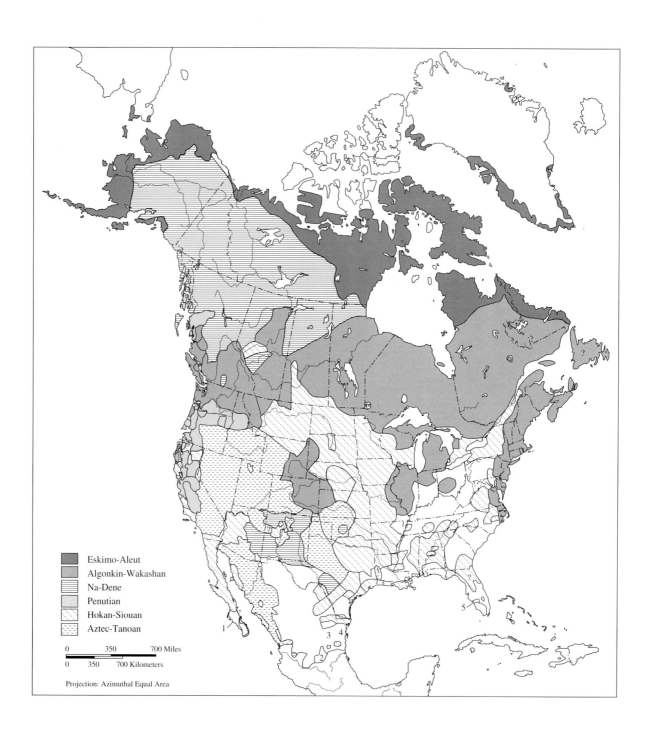

Fig. 1. Sapir's (1929) classification mapped on the language locations of the volume map (in pocket). See "The Classification of the Native Languages of North America," table 5, this vol. Included on the map are five linguistic stocks that Sapir mentioned but did not include in his North American classification: 1, Waicuri; 2, Otomian; 3, Janambre; 4, Olive; 5, Arawak. The first four of these, in northern Mexico, were outside North America as Sapir defined it, and the "Arawak colony of Florida" he considered a diffusion ultimately from South America. Janambre, Olive, and the unnamed language of the Florida colony of putatively Arawakan-speaking Indians from Cuba became extinct without being documented. The speakers of Olive were said to have been immigrants within the historical period from somewhere along the Gulf Coast (Thomas 1902:44). It is not known whether Janambre and Olive have any relationship to Naolan and Maratino. The question marks indicate three languages whose classification was queried by Sapir. The Sapir classification was published on a different base map by C.F. Voegelin and E.W. Voegelin (1944).

FOSTER

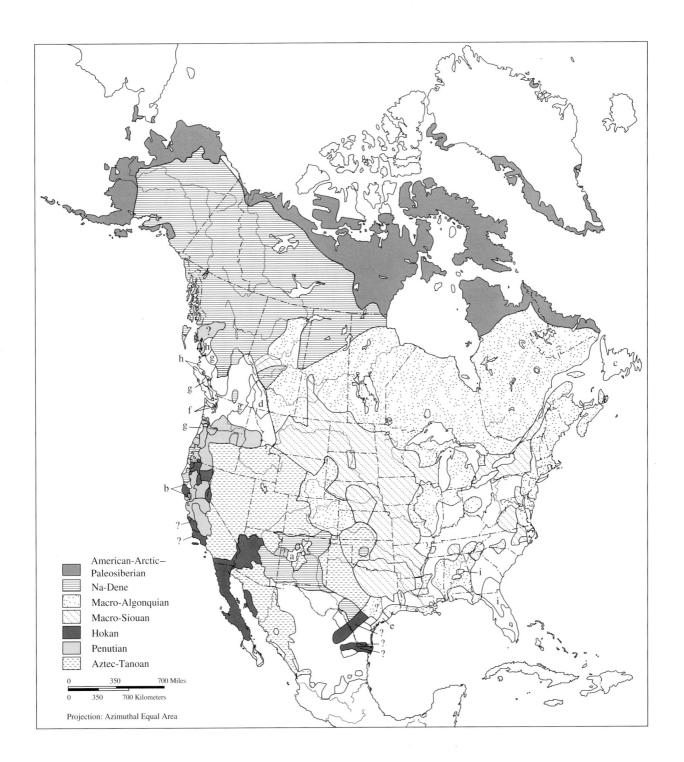

Fig. 2. Consensus Classification of 1964 (C.F. Voegelin and F.M. Voegelin 1965) mapped on the language locations of the volume map (in pocket). See "The Classification of the Native Languages of North America," table 6, this vol. This classification includes 7 phyla and 9 "isolates and families with undetermined phylum affiliations north of Mexico." The American Arctic–Paleosiberian Phylum also includes the Chukchi-Kamchatkan language family. The isolates and unaffiliated families are: a, Keres; b, Yuki, c, Beothuk; d, Kootenai; e, Karankawa; f, Chimakuan; g, Salish, h, Wakashan; i, Timucua. The isolated languages of northern Mexico were not included, being outside North America as politically defined. The question marks indicate languages and small families classified "dubiously" or "with reservations." A revised version of this classification, including Mexican and Central American languages, appeared on a different base map as C.F. Voegelin and F.M. Voegelin (1966).

69

one-quarter of the total land mass; and one-half fall within the Pacific strip alone, about one-tenth of the total land mass (Jacobsen 1989a). One suggestion is that a string of coastal refugia beyond the reach of the Pleistocene glaciers may have provided the principal route by which people entered the New World, rather than, as traditionally held, the so-called ice-free corridor in the interior (Fladmark 1975, 1978, 1979, 1983, 1986, 1990). The density of language families and isolates along the Pacific coast has been offered as prima facie support for this idea (Gruhn 1988, 1994, 1995). A related hypothesis has the glaciers forming barriers to the inland settlement of North America, with groups such as the Proto–Eskimo-Aleuts, Proto–Na-Deneans, and Proto-Algonquians skirting south around them 18,000 years ago, and then moving into the deglaciated zones following recession of the ice around 10,000 years ago (Rogers 1985, 1985a, 1986, 1987).

The linguistic components of the coastal entry and glacial barrier hypotheses have been called into question. The relationship between linguistic diversity and age applies only to groupings of genetically related languages: the mere fact that a large number of languages are spoken within an area is not in itself proof of great age. Adopting a world perspective, coastal areas have often served as the end points of migrations—as reservoirs of colonizers at the peripheries of expansion zones; in some cases they may even be younger than core areas (Jacobsen 1989a; Johanna Nichols 1990). In terms of strategies of adaptation, coastal areas offer rich natural resources and provide self-sufficiency for small groups. With regard to the glacial barrier hypothesis, if colonizers did enter North America during the Wisconsinan glaciation, which seems likely, they could not literally have been Proto-Algonquians, Proto–Na-Deneans or Proto–Eskimo-Aleuts, since these speech communities existed at time-depths that are only a fraction of the 18,000 years since the Wisconsinan maximum. Indeed, a number of languages could easily have come and gone in the areas in question in the intervening time (Meltzer 1989; Goddard and Campbell 1994). Nevertheless, for certain stocks, such as Nadene (Athapaskan-Eyak–Tlingit, excluding Haida) and Algic, and certain families, such as Salishan, Chinookan, and Sahaptian, a reasonable case can be made on the basis of the center of gravity principle for a movement of peoples inland from coastal staging areas, and such movements lend support to the coastal entry route hypothesis (Jacobsen 1989a).

With continued classificatory and reconstructive work, it may be possible eventually to understand genetic linguistic relationships before 4000 B.C., but genetic relationships may not even be detectable beyond 10,000 years B.C., using known linguistic methods (Johanna Nichols 1995). In view of the fact that some archeologists see the peopling of the Americas as

beginning more than twice that number of years ago (Gruhn 1988:84ff.; Bahn 1991), such methods are of little use, although statistical approaches to estimating time-depth based on typological comparisons and the distribution of linguistic diversity on a world scale appear promising (Johanna Nichols 1990, 1995).

Eskimo-Aleut

The Eskimo-Aleut family consists of at least seven languages, distributed in predominantly coastal Arctic locations from Siberia to Alaska and across northern Canada to Greenland (vol. 5:49-56). The Aleut branch consists of a single language spoken in two main dialects (excluding the postcontact Copper Island Creole); it probably once included other languages lost to history. The Eskimoan branch divides into two subgroups: Sirenikski-Yupik (Western Eskimo) and Inuit-Inupiaq (Eastern Eskimo). The four Yupik languages are seen as forming a chain on the two sides of Bering Strait (vol. 5:53-56), rather than distinct Siberian and Alaskan subgroups, as once held (Hammerich 1958). Although the Inuit-Inupiaq subbranch is less diverse than the Yupik subbranch, the claim that a single language is spoken all the way from Northern Alaska to Greenland (Rasmussen 1927:x) understates the diversity of this vast dialect area.

The classification of Eskimo-Aleut has generated a great deal of interest in the fields of Arctic archeology and physical anthropology. This arises from the fact that the Eskimos and Aleuts have long been thought to form a unified racial, cultural, and linguistic grouping that is distinct from all Indian groupings (Sapir 1911a:790, 1916, 1949:398, 1921c:215; C.F. Voegelin 1958:47; Driver 1961:577, 1975:102; McGhee 1976:64; Laughlin 1963a:641, 1975:515; Spuhler 1979:161-163); however, this view has been challenged (Hrdlička 1945; Szathmary and Ossenberg 1978; vol. 5:70-71; Ossenberg 1994). If the variables of race, culture, and language, which are usually regarded as independent, are seen to overlap to a significant degree, then the findings of one discipline are likely to be used to fill in gaps, or even guide research, in another.

Another factor that has influenced discussions of Eskimo-Aleut prehistory is the family's location in the extreme north and northwest of the continent astride the Bering Strait. This has suggested to many that Eskimo-Aleut must represent the last major aboriginal migration to North America (Sapir 1916, 1949:455; C.F. Voegelin 1945; Swadesh 1954; Cressman et al. 1960:74; Greenberg 1987:334). It has also fostered a view of Eskimo-Aleut as the New World family most likely to have Old World relatives. One proposal has linked Eskimo-Aleut with some segment of the controversial "Ural-Altaic" phylum, particularly Uralic

(Bergsland 1958, 1959a), although a link with Tungusic, Korean, and Japanese—a grouping favored over Altaic, which formerly included Tungusic (Bateman et al. 1990:4)—has also been argued, along with an elaborate paleolinguistic hypothesis of Eskimo-Aleut origins in Asia (Fortescue 1981). A second proposal has linked Eskimo-Aleut with Indo-European, although diffusion is generally preferred over shared genetic ancestry as an explanation for the similarities found (reviewed by Krauss 1976:230). A third proposal has linked Eskimo-Aleut with Chukotko-Kamchatkan (also called Chukotan or Luoravetlan), distributed in eastern Siberia from the Chukchi to the Kamchatka peninsulas (Swadesh 1962; Hamp 1976). None of these proposals can be regarded as proven, although the first holds more promise for some (vol. 5:62), and the third for others (Krauss 1976:231, 1988:148). The link with Chukotko-Kamchatkan (Luoravetlan) has aroused the most interest among Arctic archeologists. Given the uncertain status of the Asian groupings, these proposals are not necessarily mutually exclusive.

The Linguistic Evidence

The principal lines of linguistic evidence used for culture-historical inference in the Arctic have been the center of gravity principle and glottochronology. Although comparative Eskimo-Aleut had advanced considerably in the late twentieth century (Bergsland 1986, 1989), little attempt had been made to infer the location of the Proto–Eskimo-Aleut homeland or the nature of Proto–Eskimo-Aleut society and culture from reconstructed vocabulary: such studies would undoubtedly shed light on the relative age of Eskimo and Aleut coastal adaptations as well as on the acquisition and spread of important marker technologies and tools such as pottery making, the harpoon, and the bow and arrow. Inferences of earlier contacts based on borrowed vocabulary would also be of interest, but such studies as have been made are for the most part confined to the postcontact period (Hammerich 1953, 1954; Worth 1960, 1963; A. Taylor 1962; Heinrich 1971), for which extensive ethnohistorical documentation exists. Nevertheless, the presence of borrowed Pacific Yupik marine terms in Tanaina, the only Alaskan Athapaskan speech community with direct access to the sea, implies that Eskimos may have occupied the lower Cook Inlet before the Tanaina did (Kari 1988). For earlier periods, around A.D. 1, the apparent absence of loanwords between Proto-Eskimoan and Proto-Athapaskan implies a lack of contact (Krauss 1979:804-805, 1980:5). Contact at this stage would presumably have resulted in Athapaskan loans turning up in the more peripheral dialects of Inuit-Inupiaq, or Eskimoan loans turning

up in southern Athapaskan languages like Navajo and Apache. The fact that they do not lends support to the idea of a western Alaska homeland for Proto-Eskimoan and, at some geographic remove, an interior homeland for Proto-Athapaskan.

• THE CENTER OF GRAVITY PRINCIPLE The prevailing view of Eskimo origins in the nineteenth century, with some adherents in the early twentieth, placed them in the central interior Arctic, whence ancestral Eskimos migrated to coastal locations both east and west (Boas 1888; J. Murdoch 1888; Birket-Smith 1929; Kroeber 1939:20-22; Collins 1951). Once it was appreciated that the deepest cleavage in Eskimo-Aleut lay in southwestern Alaska, a strong argument existed for an Alaska—indeed, a western Alaska—homeland (Sapir 1949:457-458). The first detailed evidence for the split between Sirenikski-Yupik and Inuit-Inupiaq came later (Hammerich 1936; Swadesh 1951a). By the late 1950s the basic divisions within Sirenikski-Yupik were understood, and the boundary separating the two branches of Eskimoan in the twentieth century was determined to be at Unalakleet on Norton Sound (Hammerich 1958). North and east of this point Inuit-Inupiaq had all the earmarks of a typical "migratory colonial language" (Hammerich 1960:86). The resource-rich district around Iliamna Lake at the base of the Alaska Peninsula was proposed as a promising homeland area for Eskimo-Aleut, and one to which archeologists should direct their efforts (Hammerich 1958a:643, 1960; cf. Hammerich 1976:45).

Linguistic research has confirmed a western Alaska homeland for Eskimo-Aleut, although this has been broadened from a more narrowly southwestern area to include the Bering Sea coast generally (Krauss 1979: 805, 1980:7-9). In this view, the historical boundary between the Eskimoan and Aleut branches does not so much mark the location of the Eskimo-Aleut homeland as the extent of a later spread south of Proto-Eskimoan from the Bering Strait area, with the loss or absorption of intermediate languages that once belonged to the Eskimo-Aleut continuum. The distribution of Eskimo-Aleut on the map can thus be taken as supporting either a south-to-north spread of Proto-Eskimoan (Iliamna Lake or Alaska Peninsula homeland) or a north-to-south spread (Bering Strait homeland).

• GLOTTOCHRONOLOGY Eskimo-Aleut, along with Athapaskan and Salishan, was one of the language families centrally involved in the development of lexicostatistics and glottochronology. One consequence of this was that the family early became embroiled in a debate over the universality of the retention rate used to calculate divergence times. The possibility that the process of word tabooing could result in higher loss rates in basic vocabulary had already been raised for Salishan (Elmendorf 1951; Swadesh 1952:459). The most fully documented case in North America involved

East Greenlandic Eskimo, which showed divergence times of 1,200-1,700 years from West Greenlandic, whereas it was known that the two speech communities had been separated for only a few centuries (Bergsland 1958a; Bergsland and Vogt 1962). The distortion resulted from the fact that personal names in Greenlandic Eskimo are often based on morphemes denoting types of persons and body part terms, categories that make up a third of the 100-item basic vocabulary list. A taboo against using the names of the dead thus effectively removes stems for common words too, resulting in an unusually high loss rate in basic vocabulary. Although the notion of a universal retention rate was defended on statistical and other grounds (Hymes 1960:9, 1962a, 1964; Swadesh 1962a), the East Greenlandic case, when combined with European cases used to argue the complementary point that languages can also have especially low loss rates in basic vocabulary owing to such factors as conservative literary traditions (Bergsland and Vogt 1962), was decisive for many in exposing the fundamental weaknesses of glottochronology. But despite the issues raised by the East Greenlandic case, glottochronological dates continue to be cited in the Arctic literature in support of particular prehistoric hypotheses.

Another consequence of the involvement of Eskimo-Aleut in the development of glottochronology was that divergence times for the family fluctuated considerably as the method itself underwent revision and improvement: the dates proposed for the divergence of Eskimo and Aleut during the method's first decade ranged between 4000 and 1000 B.C. while those for Sirenikski-Yupik and Inuit-Inupiaq ranged between A.D. 1 and 1000 (table 1). These fluctuations presented a special challenge to archeologists.

The date of 2000 B.C. for Eskimo-Aleut comfortably accommodated the earliest radiocarbon date of 1000 B.C. then obtained from the Chaluka site on Umnak Island in the Aleutian Islands. Assuming a southwestern Alaska homeland for Eskimo-Aleut, the date allowed for 1,000 years of common development on the mainland before Proto-Aleuts moved into the Aleutians (Laughlin and Marsh 1951). When the glottochronological date was reduced to 1000 B.C. the exact match with the Chaluka radiocarbon date was heralded as a vindication for interdisciplinary approaches to Arctic prehistory (Collins 1954), and the implied shift in the point of Eskimo-Aleut dispersion from the mainland to the Aleutians passed without comment. The reduction of the Sirenikski-Yupik–Inuit-Inupiaq split to A.D. 1000 was greeted with particular enthusiasm, because the date coincided with the eastward expansion of the Thule culture, which was generally recognized as being directly ancestral to that of the modern Eskimos.

Table 1. Eskimo-Aleut Divergence Times Estimated by Glottochronology

Source	Eskimo and Aleut	Sirenikski-Yupik and Inuit-Inupiaq
Swadesh 1951a	—	A.D. 1-500[a]
Marsh and Swadesh 1951	2000 B.C.[b]	—
Swadesh 1952, 1954	1000 B.C.[c]	A.D. 1000[c]
Swadesh 1958	2600 B.C.[d]	A.D. 600[d]
Bergsland 1958a	2500 B.C.[e]	—
	4000 B.C.[f]	—

[a]Estimated on analogy to English and German, which share a similar percentage of cognates. Basic vocabulary list not standardized.

[b]Retention rate based on retention rate between Old and Modern English. Basic vocabulary list not standardized.

[c]Retention rate set at 81 ± 2% per millennium at the .9 confidence level, based on average of control cases as determined by Lees (1953). Basic vocabulary list first set at 215 items, but then standardized to 200 items.

[d]Following improvements in glottochronological method (Swadesh 1955), basic vocabulary list reduced to 100 most "stable" items, and cognate retention rate recomputed to 86% per millennium to counteract the effect of increased persistence of items in the shorter list.

[e]Based on the elimination of 13 questionable items from Swadesh's list of Eskimo-Aleut cognates (Swadesh 1954:362; Bergsland 1958a:656) and the 81 ± 2% retention rate.

[f]Same basis as in e but with the 86% retention rate.

Language and Arctic Prehistory

At the time that the glottochronological dates for Eskimo-Aleut were first announced, the prehistory of Alaska was confined to 3,000 years, but within a few years substantially earlier radiocarbon dates were obtained. First came the discovery of a core and blade assemblage on Anangula Island, just offshore from Umnak Island, which yielded dates of 6000 B.C. or earlier (Laughlin 1963, 1963a). Chaluka and other sites were linked, to the satisfaction of some, in a broad developmental sequence culminating in the historic Aleut (Laughlin and Aigner 1975; cf. vol. 5:123-124). Then, so-called Paleo-Arctic assemblages, with roots ultimately in Asia and dating to as early as 9000 B.C., were discovered along some of the river systems of western Alaska (Anderson 1968, 1970, 1970a; vol. 5:72-73, 81-82; Powers and Hoffecker 1989). The artifacts sufficiently resembled those at Anangula for that site to be considered a variant of the Paleo-Arctic tradition. Because of the presumed continuity of the Aleutian tradition from Paleo-Arctic times to the historic period, there was a tendency to place the cultural ancestor of the Eskimos and Aleuts at the Paleo-Arctic level.

One theory had groups of Eskimo-Aleut–speaking Paleo-Arctic Mongoloids migrating out of Asia more than 10,000 years ago and taking up positions along the southern coastline of the Bering land bridge before its flooding: those reaching the lower Kuskokwim River area and farther north became Eskimos, while those reaching Umnak Island at the southern end of the land bridge became Aleuts (Laughlin 1963a, 1975). On the linguistic side, the Eskimo-Aleut glottochronological dates had to be set aside as too shallow; support for the theory was sought, instead, in the hypothesis of distant genetic relationship involving Chukotko-Kamchatkan in Siberia. A variant of the theory had Paleo-Arctic Eskimo-Aleuts present on the Alaska Peninsula around 7500 B.C., those colonizing the Aleutian Islands evolving into Aleuts and those colonizing the Pacific coast and Kodiak Island evolving into Eskimos, who later moved north (McGhee 1976, 1988; Clark 1979).

Establishing cultural continuity on mainland Alaska for the Eskimoan branch from Paleo-Arctic times to the historic period has proven far more challenging than establishing such a continuity in the Aleutian Islands. Eskimoan development has been traced back with some confidence to the Norton tradition, a maritime culture that flourished after 1000 B.C. and that is found at sites from the Alaska Peninsula to just beyond the Canadian border (Dumond 1975:168, 1987a:103-118; vol. 5:76-77, 87-88, 99-101). The archeology has suggested to some that the carriers of the Norton tradition may have come from South Alaska and have then moved north along the coastline (McGhee 1976:73-74, 1978:76-77, 1988). The distribution and age of Norton make it a plausible culture to associate with Proto-Eskimoan. Between A.D. 1 and 500 Norton-type cultures in northwestern Alaska and eastern Siberia received an infusion of cultural traits from farther west in Asia. The result was a Siberian-based cultural florescence, designated by the terms Okvik, Old Bering Sea, Punuk, and Birnirk, which culminated in the highly successful maritime hunting culture of the historic Eskimos (Collins 1960:135-136; McGhee 1978:77-82, 1988:374-375; vol. 5:77, 90-92; Dumond 1987a:128-150). Then, around A.D. 1000, during the Birnirk phase, northern Alaska became the staging area for the Thule expansion, which carried early Eskimo culture and the Inuit-Inupiaq language across Canada to Greenland. The timing of the Thule expansion and its distribution from northern Alaska to Greenland clearly place it at a stage following the separation of Sirenikski-Yupik and Inuit-Inupiaq.

While the last 3,000 years of Eskimo development seem secure, there is still a vast gap in time between the Norton stage and the Paleo-Arctic stage presumed to represent the common ancestor to Eskimo-Aleut. The picture is further complicated by the fact that for the period between 4000 and 2000 B.C., the fringes of western Alaska were dominated by the Northern Archaic tradition, a primarily interior adaptation with links to the south (vol. 5:73-74) that is generally thought to represent an Indian incursion (Dumond 1977:155, McGhee 1988:372). An attempt was made to bridge the time gap and bypass the complications raised by the spread of the Northern Archaic by using linguistic distributions as a guide to interpreting Alaskan prehistory (Dumond 1965, 1969, 1977). The Arctic Small Tool tradition, which spread to North America from Asia about 2000 B.C. (Irving 1962, 1969-1970; cf. Collins 1962, 1964; Laughlin 1963a:639), had a distribution roughly matching that of the Eskimoan branch languages but excluding the Aleut branch. The Arctic Small Tool tradition preceded the Norton tradition by a millennium and was thought by many to be ancestral to it. It was hypothesized that carriers of the Arctic Small Tool tradition, who were culturally and linguistically Eskimo, had not developed in Alaska at all, but had arrived independently of the Aleuts. The Eskimo-Aleut split must then have occurred in Siberia in Paleo-Arctic times, with one group of ancestral speakers arriving on the Alaska Peninsula around 7000 B.C., moving thence to the eastern Aleutians, and another group remaining behind to develop into Proto-Eskimos, who arrived in Alaska five millennia later. It was noted that the implied divergence times for both Eskimo-Aleut and Sirenikski-Yupik–Inuit-Inupiaq were way out of line with the glottochronological dates for these separations, although Bergsland's date of 4000 B.C. for the deepest split was seen as being within reasonable range (Dumond 1965:1252).

The hypothesis of the separation of Eskimos and Aleuts in Asia in Paleo-Arctic times and their independent migrations to the New World has not stood up under scrutiny. It suffers from the extreme view it takes of the period of Eskimo-Aleut divergence (cf. vol. 5:78; Dumond 1987:35,47). The relationship between the Eskimoan and Aleut branches has been compared to that between the Germanic and Balto-Slavic branches of Indo-European (Michael Krauss, personal communication, cited in Dumond 1987:35)—nothing approaching the 10,000 or more years the model implies. In addition, the evidence linking the Arctic Small Tool tradition with later cultural horizons in Alaska is open to interpretation, although in the eastern Arctic it has been firmly established as the precursor to the Dorset culture. The Arctic Small Tool tradition probably represents a separate migration of Arctic Mongoloids, who may or may not have spoken a language related to Eskimo-Aleut.

Two views of Eskimo-Aleut origins have emerged in the late twentieth century. In one, Eskimo-Aleut speakers are seen as having arrived in the eastern Aleutians by 6000 B.C. and having later spread to the South Alaska coast. From there, after 1000 B.C., carriers of the Norton tradition, who are taken to be Proto-Eskimos, began moving north along the Alaska coast, while Proto-Aleuts continued to develop in the Aleutian Islands (McGhee l976, 1978, 1988). The main difficulties with this model are the great age it accords Eskimo-Aleut and the tenuousness of the links between the Norton tradition found north of the Alaska Peninsula and contemporaneous cultures in South Alaska (Clark 1982). The second view, which takes as a point of departure the estimates of linguistic age based on glottochronology and analogies to Old World families, greatly reduces the time frame for the development of Eskimo-Aleut in the New World to the period 2500-500 B.C. (Bergsland 1986:68-69, 1989:72-70; Dumond 1987, 1987a). Anangula is thus removed from the direct line of Eskimo-Aleut ancestry, and the search continues for a "composite" culture on the Alaska Peninsula that can serve as a plausible ancestor for the Aleutian midden tradition (2000 B.C.) and the Norton tradition (1000 B.C.), two cultural manifestations that resemble each other closely enough to suggest the likelihood of a common source despite the difference in their ages.

Athapaskan-Eyak

One branch of Athapaskan-Eyak consists of a single language found in a restricted area along the Gulf of Alaska; the other is a ramified branch of over 30 languages spread discontinuously over large portions of western North America. Although Eyak has been known since the 1930s (Birket-Smith and De Laguna 1938), its relationship to Athapaskan was established only in the 1950s and 1960s (Krauss 1964, 1965, 1965a; Victor Golla, personal communication 1993). Lexicostatistical measures showed it to be no more closely related to its immediate Athapaskan neighbor Ahtna than to Navajo in the Southwest (Krauss 1976a:330). Much of the classificatory work on the family and the culture-historical inferences drawn from it were conducted before the link with Eyak was known, and the single term Athapaskan occurs most frequently in the literature. Another development that occurred before Eyak was formally linked to Athapaskan was the proposal of a deeper genetic relationship between Athapaskan, Tlingit, and Haida (Sapir's Na-Dene hypothesis), and this added to speculation about Athapaskan origins and for a while had considerable impact on Alaskan archeology.

The Athapaskan branch proper comprises three geographic groupings that fall within four culture areas: indeed, Athapaskan has long served as a favorite example of the anthropological dictum that linguistic and cultural groupings need not coincide (Sapir 1921c:213-214). The northern Athapaskan languages are spoken throughout the western Subarctic and on the northern Plains (vol. 5:67-85; Krauss 1982a). Despite efforts

beginning in the 1930s to provide a coherent classification of northern Athapaskan, early attempts ended up merely being lists of low-level groupings often referred to as "divisions" (Osgood 1936; C.F. Voegelin 1941c:19-20; Hoijer 1946:11, 1963). The present view is that northern Athapaskan comprises a vast dialect-and-language complex consisting of up to 30 separate languages; some scholars consider any attempt to represent this complex in the form of a branching tree diagram to be misleading (Krauss 1976a:323ff., 1979:847-849), while others think that meaningful subgroups can be suggested ("Introduction," table 3, this vol.). The Apachean (or Southern Athapaskan) languages, spoken in the Southwest and southern Plains, appear to comprise a dialect complex in which anywhere from two (Hoijer 1971a) to seven (vol. 10:393-400) languages have been counted. Of these, Kiowa Apache is generally considered the most divergent. A third grouping, Pacific Coast Athapaskan, consists of from four (Krauss 1976a:304, 1979:871; Whistler 1979:14) to eight languages (vol. 5:67) in northwestern California and southwestern Oregon and an additional language on the lower Columbia River. The central historical problem in Athapaskan paleolinguistic studies has been to explain the far-flung distribution of the languages falling within the Athapaskan branch.

The Northern Origin of the Athapaskans

The center of gravity principle and reconstructed vocabulary both figured in early demonstrations of the northern provenience of the Athapaskan branch, and both are classic illustrations of paleolinguistic method. In the first, it was argued that because the divergence among various "divisions" of northern Athapaskan was greater than the divergence between those divisions and the languages belonging to the other two branches, the "historical centre of gravity" for the family must lie in the north (Sapir 1916, 1949:457). Subsequent comparative and lexicostatistical studies have confirmed that the northern Athapaskan languages are more diverse than the other two groupings and have shown that Pacific Coast Athapaskan is more diverse than Apachean (Hoijer 1956a; Hymes 1957). It is generally agreed that the Athapaskan homeland lay in interior Alaska and perhaps parts of northwestern Canada, with incursions first into California and Oregon and later into the Southwest (Krauss 1976a:284, 1979:805, 860, 1980:11-12; vol. 5:67-68). According to one theory, the breakup of Athapaskan may have been triggered by a devastating volcanic eruption in the eastern Saint Elias Mountains, followed by a massive eastward-spreading ash fall in the southern Yukon during the middle of the first millennium A.D. (Workman 1974: 253-256, 1979:352). While this claim has not been substantiated archeologically, it finds support in northern

Athapaskan oral traditions (Moodie, Catchpole, and Abel 1992). A late eastward expansion of northern Athapaskan languages toward Hudson Bay is suggested by the lower linguistic diversity of the Chipewyan area. With the discovery of Eyak the case for northern provenience was further strengthened, since the deepest cleavage within the family now occurred in the lower Copper River area of southern Alaska. As a coastal language, Eyak may represent an early movement of Proto–Athapaskan-Eyak speakers out of the interior. The lack of Proto–Eskimo-Aleut loanwords in Apachean and of Proto–Athapaskan-Eyak loanwords in the more easterly Eskimo languages implies absence of contact between the Athapaskans and the coastally oriented Eskimos during their early histories (Krauss 1979:804-806, 1980:5-6).

The second demonstration of the northern provenience of Athapaskan, also by Sapir (1936), was based on reconstructed vocabulary, or, more precisely, on changes in the meanings of key cultural terms in Navajo. The Navajo word for 'gourd', for example, is traceable to a Proto-Athapaskan noun stem meaning 'animal's horn', which evolved first into 'horn ladle' and then into 'gourd ladle' in early Apachean, and finally into 'gourd' (*Cucurbita*) in Navajo. Similarly, the Navajo term 'seed lies' (following broadcasting) is an extension of an earlier term reconstructible as 'it lies like flakes of snow'; and a Navajo ritual expression for 'sleeplessness' includes a verb traceable to a Proto-Athapaskan stem meaning 'travel by canoe'. These and other semantic shifts are more easily interpreted as coming about as a result of speakers' making linguistic adjustments as they moved from the northern boreal forest to the Southwest than the reverse.

Attempts to tie the Pacific Coast languages in with particular segments of the northern Athapaskan complex have not proven very successful, although certain features suggest a link with Tahltan rather than Chilcotin, the southernmost member of the northern group (Krauss 1976a:304-305). Two alternative routes south have been proposed, one across the Columbia River basin through central Oregon to the river systems of northern California (Jacobs 1937:67), and the other along the eastern side of the Coast Ranges (Cressman 1977:93-94; Whistler 1977:171, 1979:24; Fredrickson 1984:484). Neither route has been substantiated archeologically, but the Coast Ranges route has the advantage that it offers immigrants from the western Subarctic a higher degree of environmental continuity. It has been suggested that speakers of Athapaskan languages may have arrived in northwestern California around A.D. 1300 or perhaps a few centuries earlier, the more southern groups eventually expanding up the Eel River at the expense of Yukian-speaking groups (Whistler 1977, 1979; Victor Golla, personal communication 1993). This would make the Athapaskans the latest aboriginal arrivals in prehistoric California (vol. 8:82). However, the archeology of northwestern California is sketchy, and only the early presence of the Tolowa along the California-Oregon border seems adequately supported (Fredrickson 1984:501; Moratto 1984:565, 570).

Apachean forms a shallower and more clearly defined subgroup than Pacific Coast Athapaskan. Glottochronology indicates a divergence from the northern languages around A.D. 1000 (Hoijer 1956a). Proto-Apacheans probably did not reach the Southwest much earlier than A.D. 1400 (vol. 10:385), and some would argue not until a century later (vol. 9:162). The archeology of the early Apacheans is meager; assemblages such as the Dismal River aspect, which are known to be associated with them, postdate contacts with Spanish explorers. The question of the route by which the Apacheans reached the Southwest thus remains open. Some have argued for an intermontane route through the Plateau and Great Basin, with groups like the Kiowa Apache and Lipan later moving onto the Plains (cf. vol. 10:382-385). Others favor a route through the Plains along the east side of the Rocky Mountains, with a late incursion by Navajos and other western Apachean groups into the Southwest culture area (D. Gunnerson 1956; J. Gunnerson and D. Gunnerson 1971; vol. 9:163; vol. 10:393). Although Apachean appears to have the closest ties with Sarcee in the north, this does not necessarily support a Plains route, since the Sarcee themselves only recently moved onto the Plains from the Subarctic (vol. 5:69). Ecological arguments have been advanced for both routes: a fairly high degree of continuity between the northern Athapaskan area and the Plateau in the first case, and a southward drift by nomadic hunters in pursuit of the bison in the second (D. Gunnerson 1972). A third possibility is that the original Apachean community may have split in the north, with the ancestors of the Kiowa Apache taking the Plains route and the remaining groups taking a route through the Plateau and Great Basin (Wilmeth 1979), a view that is consistent with the linguistic separation of Kiowa Apache from the other Apachean groups (Hoijer 1971a). However, until the archeology of groups like the Navajo is better understood, the question of routes cannot be satisfactorily resolved (vol. 10:489).

Lexicostatistics and Glottochronology

Experiments with Athapaskan glottochronology confirmed the existence of the three principal subbranches and reinforced the idea that Pacific Coast Athapaskan had separated earlier from the northern languages than Apachean had (Hoijer 1956a). The first time-depths arrived at for the three branches were regarded as too shallow (Kroeber 1959:241; Hymes 1960:22), and recalculations resulted in somewhat earlier dates without altering the basic picture of subgrouping or relative separation times (Hymes 1957).

Navajo was the focus of a study that challenged the notion that the items in the basic vocabulary list could be translated unambiguously into all languages (Hoijer 1956). Another study compared subgroupings of Athapaskan as determined by lexicostatistics and by the comparative method, the resulting discrepancies being attributed to the greater susceptibility of lexicostatistics to the distorting effects of borrowing (Hoijer 1962). The most perplexing discrepancy between the two methods was the different subgroupings they yielded for Apachean. The traditional subgrouping, based on a comparative study of stem-initial consonants, indicated a division into a Western Group (Navajo, San Carlos, Chiricahua, and Mescalero) and an Eastern Group (Jicarilla, Lipan, and Kiowa Apache) (Hoijer 1938). From this it was inferred that Proto-Apacheans came to the Southwest as a single group and then split into the two subgroups that subsequently diversified. The conclusion drawn from the lexicostatistic application, on the other hand, was that there were only two languages, Kiowa Apache and all the rest, which formed a dialect complex. Although this conclusion has been criticized as representing a too radical foreshortening of time-depth (cf. Krauss 1976a:332), the notion that Kiowa Apache stands apart from the remaining languages has gained some acceptance and suggests that the Kiowa Apache may have arrived separately from the other Apacheans in the Southwest and perhaps at a later time (Hoijer 1971a; cf. Hollow and Parks 1980:72).

The earliest divergence times obtained for Athapaskan as a whole ranged between 1,300 and 1,500 years ago (Hoijer 1956a; Swadesh 1958). Improved data, refinements in glottochronological method, and repeated experimentation resulted in deeper divergence times: 2,400 ± 500 years ago for Athapaskan alone, and 3,400 ± 500 years ago for Athapaskan-Eyak (Krauss 1965a:185; cf. Krauss 1979:846). These dates suggest that Proto–Athapaskan-Eyaks could have inhabited interior Alaska and the Yukon between three and four millennia ago and that ancestral Eyaks may have split off from the parent community around three millennia ago and moved to the coast.

The Na-Dene Hypothesis, Glottochronology, and Northwestern Prehistory

Although speculation about a genetic relationship among Athapaskan, Tlingit, and Haida dates to the early nineteenth century (Krauss 1964:128), an attempted demonstration of the relationship based on comparative phonological, lexical, and particularly

morphological evidence came only in the twentieth (Sapir 1915b; cf. Sapir 1925:491-492). The hypothesis had two immediate consequences for Alaskan prehistory: it gave additional weight to the idea that the Athapaskans originated in the north, and it provided the basis for inferring a coastal homeland—specifically on the Alaska panhandle—for the presumed common ancestor of the three groups, since it was here that the deepest cleavages in Na-Dene were found (Sapir 1915b:558, 1916, 1949:457; cf. Greenberg, Turner, and Zegura 1985:34). Athapaskan was seen as a "specialized interior offshoot" and Haida a "specialized island offshoot" from the common coastal ancestor.

Sapir's Na-Dene hypothesis was greeted initially with some skepticism (P.E. Goddard 1920; Boas 1920, 1929), but by the 1950s it had gained acceptance among the majority of linguists (Hoijer 1941:4-6, 1954:6; Swadesh 1951, 1952:453, 1954; Newman 1954:633; Hymes 1955a, 1956; Haas 1964:495; C.F. Voegelin and F.M. Voegelin 1965:127-128). Its acceptance in other fields was encouraged by the publication of two wall maps of North American language groupings (C.F. Voegelin and E.W. Voegelin 1944; C.F. Voegelin and F.M. Voegelin 1966; cf. Carlson 1983:86) (figs. 1-2). From the beginning, Haida was understood to be the most divergent member of Na-Dene, and most of the discussion revolved around the relationship between Athapaskan and Tlingit. Although these two were shown to have a number of structural similarities, it proved difficult to find cognate stems on which sound correspondences could be based, particularly when Eyak was included, and this stymied comparative work for a time (Krauss 1964, 1965, 1965a, 1969, 1976a:336-343; but cf. Pinnow 1964a, 1968, 1977). Despite these difficulties, glottochronological applications were made to Na-Dene, both with and without Haida. The wide fluctuations in divergence times that resulted reflected the poor quality of the source data as well as revisions to glottochronological method taking place in the 1950s (table 1, notes). The earliest studies proposed a minimum time-depth for Athapaskan and Tlingit of 2,000 years (Swadesh 1951, 1952:453, 1954), but this figure was revised to 5,000 years (Swadesh 1959b) after the first figure was recognized as being improbably low (Kroeber 1955:92-93; Eggan 1958:648-649). Taking the Athapaskan-Eyak divergence time of 3,400 ± 500 years into account, a 5,000-year divergence time for Athapaskan-Eyak and Tlingit was considered likely, although the problem of establishing cognates in stem lexicons and other uncertainties precluded drawing more than tentative conclusions (Krauss 1976a:333).

In the 1970s linguists became skeptical about Na-Dene as a genetic grouping (Krauss 1979:841-842; Thompson 1979:752). Following a thorough review of the evidence and arguments, Haida was removed from the grouping and returned to the status of an isolate (Levine 1979). Although Na-Dene in its classic form has had later defenders (notably Greenberg 1987), the consensus among linguists in the 1990s was that a convincing case had not been made. A genetic link between Athapaskan-Eyak and Tlingit, on the other hand, appeared likely (Krauss 1979:890; vol. 5:67), and the name Nadene was retained for this smaller grouping (here labeled with Sapir's alternate spelling without the hyphen).

The use of Sapir's Na-Dene hypothesis in other fields of prehistory has not kept pace with its changing fortunes in linguistics. Even after serious doubts had been raised about its validity as a genetic grouping, it was being used along with other controversial superstocks as the basis for plotting the distributions of genetic and other physical traits in native populations (Spuhler 1979; Ubelaker and Jantz 1986). Na-Dene was also used to give ethnolinguistic identity to a population cluster (the "Greater Northwest Coast Indians") defined on grounds of dental morphology, although the linguistic and dental distributions did not match at all closely (Turner 1983, 1986; cf. Szathmary 1986:490). Later, dental evidence was combined with linguistic and—more tentatively—genetic evidence, to argue that Na-Dene constituted one of the three founding aboriginal migratory movements to the New World (Greenberg, Turner, and Zegura 1985, 1986; Greenberg 1987). All these correlations are flawed to the extent that Na-Dene as a linguistic grouping is unproven, and the linguistic and biological connotations of the term remain as discrepant as they are.

Within archeology, the distribution of Na-Dene on the map suggested to some prehistorians that speakers of ancestral Na-Dene could have been carriers of the microblade technologies found at sites in interior Alaska as early as 9000 B.C. and in western Canada and Washington state by 4500 B.C. (Borden 1970, 1979:970; cf. Clark in vol. 6:107-129 on the distribution and composition of microblade sites). In one interpretation, it was hypothesized that the microblade carriers were still undifferentiated Na-Deneans who, after reaching the southern limit of their expansion, came in contact with people who made side-notched blades; after adding this new technology to their tool kit the Proto–Na-Deneans then spread back to the north, splitting into the major subbranches along the way (Dumond 1969). The south-to-north spread was inferable both from the fact that the mixed assemblages appeared to represent progressively later stages toward the north and from the fact that the deepest cleavages within Na-Dene occurred in the southern part of the area. In a more general version of this hypothesis, four "basal" archeological cultures were correlated with language phyla of the 1964 Consensus Classification as shown on the C.F. Voegelin and F.M. Voegelin (1966)

map (fig. 2), the microblade tradition being assigned to Na-Dene purely on distributional grounds (Carlson 1979, 1983; vol. 7:60-69).

It has been suggested that Athapaskan-Eyak and Tlingit may corrrelate with the Interior and Coastal variants of the microblade tradition (vol. 5:67). The archeological relationship between the Interior and Coastal microblade subtraditions is not well understood, and both have roots that reach back so far before the hypothetical date of 3000 B.C. for the Athapaskan-Eyak–Tlingit split that the correlation seems dubious (vol. 7:68; cf. vol. 6:110; Wright, Prest, and Vincent 1987; Donald Clark, personal communication 1992).

Proto-Athapaskan Kinship and Society

Athapaskan, before it was connected with Eyak, became the focus of a debate over methods of reconstructing prehistoric kinship systems and the inferences that can be drawn from them. It was early suggested that the kinship systems found among Apachean groups in the Southwest could be classified into two principal types, the "Chiricahua" (a bifurcate collateral system with Hawaiian cousin terms) and the "Jicarilla" (a bifurcate merging system with Iroquois cousin terms), and that the prototype for both of these was a system like the Chiricahua (Opler 1936). This view was criticized for ignoring the linguistic facts and making unwarranted historical claims about the prototypical system, which linguistic reconstruction showed to be more like that of the Navajo, classified as Jicarilla in type (Kroeber 1937). The linguistic approach was thought to be superior, because it traced the actual histories of the terms comprising the systems, whereas the typological approach was not regarded as a strictly historical process at all (Kroeber 1937:607).

This early exchange defined the poles of a debate that unfolded between those who argued that prehistoric kinship systems could be reconstructed solely by comparing kin categories and piecing together their logical antecedents (Murdock 1949, 1955; White 1957) and those who argued that linguistic reconstruction was the primary, if not exclusive, means of recovering such systems (Hoijer 1956b; Hymes and Driver 1958; Dyen and Aberle 1974; cf. Hockett 1977). Neither of the approaches led to consistent conclusions about the nature of the Proto-Athapaskan kinship system or its social correlates. The supposition that the system had Hawaiian cousin terms, for instance, from which bilateral descent might reasonably be inferred, had supporters from both camps (Murdock 1949; Hoijer 1956b), as did the supposition that Proto-Athapaskan (or earlier Na-Dene) had Iroquoian cousin terms, from which some form of unilineal descent might be inferred (Murdock 1955; Dyen and Aberle 1974). And whereas the method of lexical reconstruction led in one case to the conclusion that, of the Apachean systems, the Navajo most closely resembled the Proto-Athapaskan system (Kroeber 1937), in another it led to the conclusion that the Eastern Apachean and Kiowa Apache systems were closer to the protosystem, from which the inference was drawn that the eastern groups had arrived in the Southwest later and perhaps by a route different from that of the Western Apacheans (Hoijer 1956b).

The most exhaustive review of the subject, which was based primarily on lexical reconstruction (Dyen and Aberle 1974; cf. Aberle 1974, 1984; Hockett 1977; Wurm 1977; Campbell 1976), concluded that the Proto-Athapaskan system had Iroquois cousin terms and bifurcate aunt and uncle terms, although whether collateral or partially merging could not be determined. A statistical comparison based on 250 societies indicated that such a system reliably predicted unilineal or double unilineal descent and unilocal residence. However, the longstanding issues of whether Proto-Athapaskan descent was matrilineal or patrilineal, and whether Proto-Athapaskan residence was matrilocal or patrilocal, could not be conclusively resolved, although the authors suggested that the most parsimonious explanation for the variety of descent and residence rules found among contemporary Athapaskan groups was that the Proto-Athapaskans were matrilineal and matrilocal, with various groups later shifting to bilateral or even patrilineal descent after coming in contact with surrounding peoples (Dyen and Aberle 1974:428; cf. Hockett 1977: 89-90).

Salishan

The 23 languages of the Salishan family once occupied a nearly continuous area from southern British Columbia, Washington State, and northern Oregon to Idaho and western Montana. The languages of the coastal area comprise four branches: a large Central Salish group; Tsamosan (or Olympic) in western Washington; Tillamook, an outlier in northwestern Oregon; and Bella Coola, an outlier in British Columbia. The precise subgrouping of the main body of the coastal languages has been a matter of continuing debate. The Interior languages, on the other hand, were early recognized as forming a distinct subgroup.

The earliest attempts to classify the Salishan languages were motivated primarily by the need to determine family affiliations in a heterogeneous linguistic region: they did not go beyond grouping dialects into languages (Powell 1891:104-105; Boas 1894; C.F. Voegelin 1941c; C.F. Voegelin and E.W. Voegelin 1944). Interest in a more comprehensive classification was stimulated by two developments: the careful mapping of sound correspondences among the approximately three dozen known Salishan dialects (Boas and Haeberlin 1927; Boas 1928a), and the reduction of these to a more tractable list of some 16 languages, based on fieldworkers' judgments with regard to mutual intelligibility (C.F. Voegelin 1941c:18-19). Despite these efforts, isoglosses for a number of the sound shifts were found to cut across language lines, and this raised the possibility of prehistoric contacts among groups that in some cases were now geographically separated (Swadesh 1949, 1952a). The early injection of the contact factor into discussions of Salishan linguistic prehistory influenced the direction of later research. At the same time, a question was raised about the reliability of mutual intelligibility tests as a basis for classifying languages. It was suggested that comparative studies of vocabulary might yield a more accurate picture of relationship (Swadesh 1950:162-163), and with this the idea of lexicostatistics was born.

Lexicostatistics and Glottochronology

Salishan contributed significantly to the theory and practice of glottochronology and lexicostatistics. The first comprehensive classification of the Salishan languages was also the first published application of lexicostatistics to an American Indian language family (Swadesh 1950; cf. Swadesh 1952:454). The tables of cognate percentages used to classify Salishan suggested an early separation of Bella Coola from the main group and a later split between the Interior and the Coast languages. The most important finding for prehistory was that the Coast division was considerably more diverse than the Interior division. According to the center of gravity principle, this implied that the Salishan homeland lay on the coast, specifically in an area extending from the lower Fraser Valley somewhat to the northwest. The Interior languages were taken as representing a later expansion across the Pacific Ranges (Swadesh 1950:166-167, 1952:461; cf. Kroeber 1955:98-101). These findings were ignored by archeologists at the time, because they were incompatible with the current theory that the Salishans had originated in the interior.

The tables of cognate percentages in the 1950 study were at first used for purely lexicostatistical purposes to establish relative distances among the languages and to provide a classification. Following the standardization of the basic vocabulary list to 200 items and the setting of the retention rate at 81 ± 2% per millennium, time-depths were announced of 1400 to 1500 B.C. for the Interior division, 2600 B.C. for the Coast division, and 3500 B.C. for the family as a whole (Swadesh 1952:461, 1953:41ff., 1954:362). The last figure was corrected to 2900 B.C. (Swadesh 1958:673), after the basic vocabulary list and the replacement rate were revised (Swadesh 1955).

The effects of intrafamily contact on vocabulary replacement rates were first investigated in Salishan applications. Another concern that emerged in the early Salishan applications was the effect of word taboo on replacement rates, an issue that later gained prominence in Eskimo-Aleut lexicostatistics as well. The distorting effects of intrafamily contact and word taboo on replacement rates were viewed as complementary processes: contact presumably slowed the replacement rate, leading to an underestimation of time-depth, whereas word tabooing presumably accelerated the replacement rate, leading to an overestimation of time-depth. It was suggested that the greater diversity of the coastal Salishan languages compared with the interior group might be due at least in part to the tabooing of names of higher-status males on the coast (Elmendorf 1951). Morphemes in common words that appeared in these names, or that were phonetically similar to them, came under the scope of the taboo, and this contributed to an accelerated replacement rate in basic vocabulary. Against this, it was argued that word tabooing was not an extraneous factor but one of several factors contributing to the basic replacement rate, and one that was balanced by the retarding effects of intrafamily contact (Swadesh 1952:459; Hymes 1960). In the long run, studies tended to show that accelerated replacement rates due to word tabooing could not be dismissed so easily, at least in the case of the coastal Salishan languages (Elmendorf 1962, 1970), and Eskimo-Aleut (Bergsland and Vogt 1962).

The effects of intrafamily contact on replacement rates in both cultural and basic vocabulary were tested in studies of Salishan dialects (Elmendorf and Suttles 1960; Elmendorf 1962a; cf. Elmendorf 1973). Salishan was also featured in several general studies, where an effort was made to develop methods for compensating for the effects of borrowing and word taboo (Dyen 1962, 1963; Elmendorf 1969; Jorgensen 1969). This research resulted in revisions to the 1950 Salishan classification (Dyen 1962; Elmendorf 1962b, 1969). A debate over the methods used for grouping languages by lexicostatistics led to still other subgrouping proposals (Kronenfeld and Thomas 1983; Weller and Buchholtz 1986), which demonstrated that the same body of data— Swadesh's cognate percentage tables from 1950—could lead to alternative subgroupings if different clustering methods were used. More recent consensus classifications of Salishan, which are said to be based on other than lexicostatistical principles, match the 1950 classification and its revisions in the main (Thompson 1979:693; vol 7:34-35; cf. vol. 7:105).

The Mosan Hypothesis

The possibility of a genetic relationship among the Salishan, Wakashan, and Chimakuan families was the subject of speculation around the turn of the twentieth century (Powell 1891:104; Boas 1894:346; Sapir 1916, 1949:458). The proposed grouping, dubbed Mosan (Frachtenberg 1920), was carried as an intermediate phylum in Sapir's (1929) continental classification. Lexical, grammatical, and phonological evidence was provided later (Swadesh 1949, 1953, 1953a). The hypothesis received cautious acceptance in some quarters (Kroeber 1955:97-98; Haas 1960:980), and glottochronological methods were applied to arrive at a time-depth of 6600 B.C. for the grouping (Swadesh 1954:362), but others rejected it outright (Kuipers 1967-1969, 1:401-405; Klokeid 1969), or at least regarded it as unproven (Suttles and Elmendorf 1963:47). Mosan is no longer seen as credible, although a remote link between the Chimakuan and Wakashan families alone is considered possible by some (J.V. Powell 1993; cf. Thompson 1976:380, 1979:748-751; Jacobsen 1979b:796-797). An even broader grouping in the Sapir classification, "Algonkin-Wakashan," linked Mosan with Algic, Kootenai, and Beothuk, but this has been rejected by nearly all linguists and has had little impact on North American archeology.

Archeological Perspectives on Prehistory

The combination of great linguistic diversity and spotty archeological work on the Northwest Coast led early researchers to conclude that the cultural substratum for the area was an "Eskimoid" one, linked ultimately to developments in Asia and oriented to the sea, while the Northwest Coast cultures known in historic times were viewed as adaptations made by successive waves of immigrants from the interior—an interpretation that has been dubbed the "recent emergence" theory (Suttles 1987, 1987a:265-266; cf. Adams, Van Gerven, and Levy 1978:489; vol. 7:107-108). Of the later groups, the Wakashans, whose material culture most strongly resembled the original Eskimoid one, were thought to be the earliest arrivals from the interior, and these were followed in turn by Salishans, Chimakuans, and Chinookans (Borden 1950, 1951, 1954, 1954a, 1975, 1979; Drucker 1955:195-208, 1955a, 1965).

Migration-and-replacement models dominated archeological thinking about Northwest Coast origins until the mid-1950s, when radiocarbon dating began to reveal dramatically older ages for coastal sites. From an estimated time-depth of less than a millennium, archeologists had, by the mid-1970s, come up with dates of 6000-7000 B.C. for coastal sites, with still earlier dates on the Alaska panhandle (Suttles 1987a:267-270; vol. 7:109-110). While some archeologists continued to work within the framework of interior origins, a consensus emerged that the distinctive culture of the Northwest Coast had recognizable coastal roots extending back at least 5,000 years (MacDonald 1969;

Inglis and MacDonald 1975; Fladmark 1975). Moreover, salmon fishing, the primary subsistence adaptation on the coast, could be dated to as early as 5500 B.C. at some sites, and there was evidence of a movement of people into the interior as the migratory ranges of the fish themselves gradually shifted up the inland waterways (vol. 7:66, 109).

As the emphasis in archeology shifted from recent emergence to in situ models, the number of lithic traditions regarded as basal for the larger Northwest increased from one—the Eskimoid—to four (vol. 7:110-115). These traditions, which were dated to around 8000 B.C., were speculatively aligned with four linguistic phyla of the 1964 Consensus Classification (Carlson 1979, 1983; vol. 7:60-69). Two of the traditions were seen as southward-spreading cultures, linked primarily to the coast: the Microblade tradition, which was associated with Na-Dene, and the Pebble Tool tradition, which was associated with Salishan and perhaps Wakashan. A partial version of the Mosan hypothesis was invoked in the case of the Pebble Tool tradition, because the distribution of the linguistic grouping fitted the distribution of Pebble Tool sites quite closely (Carlson 1983:96). Since the Mosan hypothesis never gained general acceptance among linguists, its association with a specific archeological tradition is unwarranted. In addition, the dates of the Pebble Tool tradition place it beyond the time-depth of any established North American linguistic grouping. Finally, as a general rule, the distribution of contemporary languages on a map can only be taken as reflecting the most recent period of a family's history; the distribution of a family's protolanguage would undoubtedly have been very different, and probably far more restricted in space. In effect, for any early archeological tradition with a broad distribution of sites, much of the area would be linguistically unaccounted for (Lamb 1964a).

Linguistic Perspectives on Prehistory

Since the publication of Swadesh's lexicostatistical classification of Salishan (Swadesh 1950), linguists have tended to place the family's homeland west of the Coast Mountains between the Strait of Georgia and Puget Sound. The presence of Salishan languages outside this area is assumed to represent later expansions to the north, the south, and eastward into the Plateau (although some have argued in the case of Bella Coola that it may simply have been cut off from an originally more extended speech chain by a transverse movement of Wakashan or Athapaskan speakers). However, these ideas were overlooked by Northwest Coast archeologists, who only abandoned the recent emergence theory when archeological data began to contradict it, and some not even then (Wayne Suttles, personal communication 1987).

The inference of a coastal homeland for Salishan was based on the center of gravity principle, which contributed to the development known as Migration Theory. The purpose of Migration Theory was to introduce greater rigor into the procedures used for inferring centers of population dispersal and directions of migration from language distributions (Dyen 1956), and Salishan served as the basis of an early application (Diebold 1960). Although Migration Theory proved useful in determining the dispersal points for some other language families, in the case of Salishan it did not significantly advance understanding of the homeland problem, since the coast and interior languages were treated as forming a continuous chain without taking the varying diversity within the chain into account. It was thus concluded that the family's homeland could lie anywhere within the area of the chain as a whole, with only the areas of the two outliers excluded (Diebold 1960:10). Nor did a second conclusion—that the separation of Bella Coola and Tillamook from the main group could have resulted either from migrations or from intrusions across the original dialect chain by non-Salishan groups—shed much light on Salishan prehistory.

A significant advance on the homeland problem came when specialists determined that the family consisted of two chains, one oriented north-south and comprising the Coast branches (with Bella Coola and Tillamook regarded as outliers) and the other oriented northwest-southeast and comprising the Interior branch (Suttles and Elmendorf 1963). Combining the fact that the two chains adjoined in the Fraser drainage (cf. Elmendorf 1965:75; Suttles 1987a:277) with the fact that the coastal chain was considerably more ramified than the interior chain led to the hypothesis that Salishan diversification had begun on the western side of the Pacific Ranges, perhaps in the Fraser delta but extending as far south as Puget Sound, with expansions into the Plateau, British Columbia, and Washington and Oregon (Suttles and Elmendorf 1963:45). Within the coastal chain, Tillamook was closer to Twana on the Hood Canal than to the intervening Tsamosan group, implying that Tsamosan represented a later incursion across a continuum that embraced the Tillamook and Tsamosan areas (Suttles and Elmendorf 1963:44-47). Within the Interior chain the greatest diversity occurred at the northwest end, so that the inferred direction of expansion was toward the southeast (Elmendorf 1965). Subsequent statements of the Salishan homeland and migrations based on language have deviated little from this model, except that the earliest split within Proto-Salishan is now seen as involving Bella Coola rather than the Interior group (Suttles and Elmendorf 1963:45; Jorgensen 1969:23, 105; Kinkade and Powell 1976:91-92, Thompson 1979:693-695; Suttles 1987:259-260; vol. 7:47; cf. Swadesh 1950:167, fig. 2).

That the Proto-Salishan homeland lay along the coast rather than in the interior receives additional support from studies of reconstructed cultural vocabulary. Salishan presents a particularly ripe field for such an approach because it is distributed across two ecological zones, and the flora and fauna of these zones vary considerably. Of the 140 plant and animal terms that have been reconstructed for Proto-Salishan so far, around two dozen apply to species that occur exclusively on the coast, such as various clams and cockles, the barnacle, and certain fern and berry species; the homeland thus must have included access to tideflats (Kinkade 1989). Since some of the species denoted by Proto-Salishan terms do not occur north of Vancouver or on Vancouver Island, it is possible to narrow the homeland even further to the area lying between the Fraser and Skagit rivers and the Coast Mountains. In view of the likelihood of a coastal homeland for Proto-Salishan, it is noteworthy that Bella Coola has borrowed extensively from the cultural vocabulary of the neighboring Wakashan language Heiltsuk (Bella Bella), with nearly half the terms relating to the sea (Newman 1974). This implies temporal priority of the Bella Bella in the region and raises the possibility that the Bella Coola may have been oriented more toward an inland environment at an earlier stage.

Summing up, in the late twentieth century it appeared that Salishan archeology and linguistics were converging around the idea of a coastal homeland, which acted as a staging area for expansions north and south, and east into the Plateau.

Other Northwestern Families

At the height of the reductionist trend in American Indian linguistic classification, all the families of the Northwest Coast and Plateau culture areas were grouped into one of three phyla: Na-Dene, Algonkin-Wakashan, and Penutian (Sapir 1929). The partial or complete dismantling of Na-Dene and Algonkin-Wakashan has left a number of families and single languages without clear affiliations. Although Na-Dene figured prominently in speculation regarding the prehistory of the Northwest, neither Tlingit nor Haida as a separate language has received much attention from this point of view (cf. Krauss 1976a:317-319, 1979:838-842). In the case of Tlingit, there is greater dialectal diversity in the south than in the north, and this implies a spread of the language to the north and west at the expense of Eyak, a process that continued well into the historic period (Krauss 1980:13). With regard to Sapir's Algonkin-Wakashan, one effect of the phylum's being discredited is that Kootenai has been left as a language isolate on the Plateau. If Kootenai turns out to be related to Salishan, as some think it is,

it may prove ultimately to have roots on the coast, (Jacobsen 1989a), but in the absence of firm proof of such a relationship, a move of ancestral Kootenai speakers across the Rocky Mountains from the east must be seen as equally feasible (Kinkade and Powell 1976:92).

Wakashan

The Wakashan area covers much of the British Columbia coast and across the Strait of Juan de Fuca to the Olympic Peninsula in Washington State. Wakashan figured in some of the earliest experiments in glottochronology (Swadesh 1952:454). A time-depth of 2,900 years was calculated for the family using the 200-word list and the $81 \pm 2\%$ retention rate (Swadesh 1954:362), but this figure was found to be too low, since it did not take into account the effects of prolonged intrafamily contact. When an algorithm was used to calculate time-depth that incorporated a variable borrowing rate, the estimated divergence time for the family jumped to 5,500 years ago (Embleton 1985, 1986).

During the first half of the twentieth century when theories of Northwest Coast culture origins were dominated by the idea of "recent emergence," the Wakashans were thought to be the earliest arrivals from the interior, since their material culture resembled the "Eskimoid" cultural substrate more than the cultures of other coastal peoples did. The shift in archeology from recent migration theories to in situ explanations of coastal origins, and the dismantling of the Mosan grouping, resulted in a shift in interest to the prehistory of Wakashan itself. The deepest cleavage within the family, that between the Kwakiutlan and Nootkan branches, occurs toward the north end of Vancouver Island; the homeland for the family is thus more likely to be located there than on the mainland (Suttles and Elmendorf 1963:47; Kinkade and Powell 1976:92; Jacobsen 1979a:766). Another line of evidence lends indirect support to this inference, or at least to the likelihood that Wakashan speakers preceded Salishan speakers to Vancouver Island. A number of reconstructed Proto-Salishan plant and animal terms denote species that do not occur on Vancouver Island (Kinkade 1989), and this implies that the Salishan homeland was not located on the island and that the presence of Salishan languages there represents a later spread.

For subsequent phases of Wakashan prehistory, Nootka dialect intergrading on the west coast of Vancouver Island implies movement of Proto-Nootkan speakers south along the coast and across the Strait of Juan de Fuca to Cape Flattery, probably not reaching the cape until 1,000 years ago, while Proto-Kwakiutlan speakers expanded northward to the mainland and up the coast, at the expense of Salishan-speaking peoples (vol. 7:47; Kinkade and Powell 1976:94-98). The northward expansion must have occurred before the Salishan-speaking Bella Coola reached their present location, since the Bella Coola borrowed a number of terms relating to the sea from the Heiltsuk (Newman 1974). The displacement or absorption of Comox people by Kwakiutl speakers between Kelsey Bay and Campbell River on the east coast of Vancouver Island is suggested by the borrowing of Salishan place-names by the Kwakiutl in the Johnstone Strait area (Taylor and Duff 1956; vol. 7:36).

Chimakuan

Chimakuan consists of two languages located on the Olympic Peninsula in Washington: Quileute on the western coast and Chemakum at the eastern end of the strait of Juan de Fuca. A glottochronological time-depth of 2,100 years was calculated for the family (Swadesh 1954:362), and this has not been subsequently revised. The most likely place of origin of the Chimukuans is the northern Olympic Peninsula, perhaps somewhat inland (Kinkade and Powell 1976:95). The Quileute may have moved west to the coast from a more central position (vol. 7:48). If so, this must have occurred before the arrival of the Wakashan-speaking Makah at Cape Flattery, because the Makah borrowed at least eight place-names from Chimakuan (although not necessarily from Quileute), and this implies prior occupation of the cape by Chimakuans, who may have been the so-called Ozette people of Cape Alava (Kinkade and Powell 1976:94ff.). On the other hand, Quileute borrowed terms from Makah for sea mammal hunting and fishing (Jacobsen 1976a), which supports the view that the Makah brought whaling to the Washington coast where it was adopted by the Chimakuans (vol. 7:420). At a still later time, Salishan-speaking Clallams presumably crossed the Strait of Juan de Fuca, effectively separating the two Chimakuan speech communities (Farrand 1907; Kinkade and Powell 1976:97; Jacobsen 1979b: 792; vol. 7:48).

Northern Penutians

Penutianists are generally optimistic that many of the ties that have been proposed between California Penutian and various families in Oregon, Washington, and British Columbia will eventually be established. At the same time, the specific subgrouping proposals for the northern Penutian languages made by Sapir (1929) have not held up. In particular, neither the Oregon Penutian branch, consisting of Takelman, Coosan, Siuslaw, and Alsean, nor the Plateau Penutian branch, consisting of Sahaptian, Molala-Cayuse, and Klamath,

is seen as well motivated (though there is more support for Plateau Penutian with Cayuse excluded). If anything, there may be closer ties between certain members across these branches, or between them and the languages belonging to Sapir's California Penutian (Wintuan, Maiduan, Utian, and Yokutsan), than among the members of the branches as defined by Sapir (Rigsby 1966, 1969; Shipley 1966; Silverstein 1979:678-680; DeLancey, Genetti, and Rude 1988).

The likelihood that the northern languages are indeed Penutian leads to speaking of the "Northern Penutians" with some confidence; the uncertainty that surrounds many details of Penutian classification makes it prudent to treat the northern families and languages separately from the California group. For several of these, only brief speculative remarks are possible with regard to linguistic prehistory. Hence, Coosan, Siuslaw, and Alsean, once linked as a subbranch of Sapir's "Oregon Penutian" but now regarded as separate languages with only general Penutian affiliation, are said to have been spoken by "essentially inland peoples," who migrated independently to the Oregon coast (vol. 7:45). It can at least be said of Takelman, the other subbranch of Sapir's Oregon Penutian, which consists of the three Kalapuyan languages and Takelma, that it forms a low-level genetic subgrouping (Shipley 1969). A movement of early Takelman speakers from north to south is inferable from the fact that there is greater diversity in the Kalapuyan area in the middle and upper Willamette valley than in the Takelma area in the Rogue valley to the south (vol. 7:47). Membership of the Sahaptian family in "Plateau Penutian," another branch of Sapir's Penutian, has been challenged on several fronts—not least that it may prove ultimately to be more closely linked with certain Penutian languages of western Oregon than with any of the Plateau Penutian languages (Silverstein 1979:679-680). Such ties would be deeper and older than those binding the Sahaptian languages into a single family, and a general west to east spread would then be inferable. Sahaptian consists of two languages, Sahaptin and Nez Perce, spoken in the middle Columbia and Snake river watersheds as far east as Idaho. While there appears to be greater dialect diversity in Sahaptin than in Nez Perce, this could be due as much to recent dialect leveling in Nez Perce following forced relocation as to greater time-depth in the Sahaptin area (Haruo Aoki, personal communication 1992).

It has been suggested that the Chinookan homeland may originally have been located somewhat inland in northwestern Oregon, perhaps around the confluence of the Willamette and Columbia rivers; from there speakers moved down the Columbia to the Pacific littoral (vol. 7:45-46). A later reverse spread up the Columbia can be inferred on both distributional and grammatical grounds. The deepest division within the family is that between Lower Chinook, consisting of a single language (Chinook proper) spoken around the mouth of the Columbia, and Upper Chinook, a dialect chain comprising two or three languages spread along the Columbia to just beyond The Dalles (vol. 7:533). The center of gravity principle implies a movement of Chinookans upriver. The direction of the spread is also inferable from developments in Chinookan tense-aspect systems and from other grammatical and lexical features (Silverstein 1974; cf. Sherzer and Bauman 1972:136). The tense-aspect systems found in Upper Chinook dialects are built up successively from the simpler systems downriver: the simplest system of all occurs in Lower Chinook. It is clear that the upriver systems developed out of a downriver base rather than the reverse, and this is taken as implying a linguistic spread upriver. The timing of the spread has not been determined, but it seems likely that it occurred after ancestral speakers of Tillamook (Salishan) had moved south across the Columbia River to the Oregon coast (Suttles and Elmendorf 1963:48). In any event, Chinookan was influenced by Salishan before it had begun significantly to diversify and spread upriver, since borrowed coastal Salishan features such as grammatical gender are found throughout the family rather than exclusively in Lower Chinook.

The most problematic of the Northwestern families claimed to be affiliated with Penutian is Tsimshianic, a family lying along the northern coast of British Columbia and somewhat inland (Silverstein 1979:680-681). It consists of two major dialect clusters, one comprising the Nass (or Nisgha) and Gitksan dialects (together also called Interior Tsimshian) found on the Nass and upper Skeena rivers, and the other comprising Coast Tsimshian found on the lower Skeena and south to Milbanke Sound (vol. 7:267-268). It has been suggested that Coast Tsimshian consists of two languages, Coast Tsimshian and Southern Tsimshian or Klemtu (Dunn 1979). The Tsimshianic homeland probably lay on the coast rather than in the interior: instead of ancestral Tsimshians coming down the Nass and Skeena rivers to the coast, as argued by proponents of the "recent emergence" theory of coastal origins, the rivers may well have served as conduits from the coast into the interior. Tsimshianic is more diverse on the coast than up the river systems, and patterns of borrowing suggest a later rather than an earlier adaptation to the environment of the interior (Rigsby 1981; Rigsby and Kari 1987; cf. Sherzer and Bauman 1972:142-143). Thus, Gitksan has borrowed words for inland fauna such as 'beaver kit', 'caribou', 'moose', 'moose calf', 'mountain sheep', 'Dolly Varden trout', and several varieties of whitefish from the Babine-speakers who inhabited the interior west of the Gitksan.

Yukian

Yukian is a family isolate consisting of two languages spoken in different areas in northwestern California (Shipley 1976:447-448, vol. 8:87, 249-255, 256-263). The three closely related dialects of Yuki were spoken in the upper drainage of the Eel River and a section of the adjacent coast (Elmendorf 1968). Wappo was spoken in four dialects in the Napa Valley to the south, separated from Yuki by Pomoan, Lake Miwok, and Hill Patwin. A fifth Wappo dialect called Clear Lake (or Lile'ek) formed an enclave west of Clear Lake. There are probably no surviving speakers of any of the Yukian languages (Elmendorf 1981).

Yuki and Wappo are quite divergent grammatically and lexically. One authority has even expressed doubts as to whether they are genetically related; such similarities as are found are said to result from the diffusion of areal features (Sawyer 1964, 1965, 1980; cf. Elmendorf 1968:5-6; Shipley 1976:447, vol. 8:87). The two areas where Yukian is spoken are also quite different culturally, and the speakers apparently belonged to distinct physical types (vol. 8:258; Gifford 1926a). This could mean that the people called Wappo were originally non-Yukian but shifted to Yukian as a result of intensive contact and bilingualism (vol. 8:258). If the languages are related, as the majority believes (cf. Whistler 1978:27; Elmendorf 1981a), the split between them must nevertheless be quite old. The glottochronological date of 2,500 to 3,000 years ago for the split (Elmendorf 1968) seems underestimated.

Efforts to link Yukian with other language families have not been very convincing. Sapir (1921b, 1929) placed Yukian broadly within his Hokan-Siouan phylum, without indicating close affiliations; but he did not present any evidence, and Hokan-Siouan has since been discredited. Others have suggested affiliation more narrowly with Hokan (Swadesh 1954; Gursky 1965; Oswalt 1978) or Siouan-Yuchi (Elmendorf 1963, 1964). Links have also been suggested with Penutian (Shipley 1957; Wenger 1973) and the "Gulf" grouping (Haas 1954; Swadesh 1954:324; Greenberg 1987:144, 336). The last, like the Siouan-Yuchi proposal, would imply a migration from the Mississippi valley or the Southeast. Of the various proposals, the suggestion of a link between Yukian and Siouan-Yuchi is perhaps the most promising (Shipley 1976:448; vol. 8:87).

Linguistic and archeological evidence has been interpreted as meaning that ancestral Yukians were the earliest inhabitants of California, even antedating Hokan-speaking groups (vol. 8:82; Fredrickson 1984:473, 495; Moratto 1984:536, 544). Their territory is hypothesized once to have extended all the way from the Klamath Mountains bordering Karok territory in the north to the San Francisco Bay area in the south (Elmendorf 1981a; Moratto 1984:545, fig. 11.4).

Lengthy Yukian occupation of the Eel River drainage is suggested by an unbroken archeological sequence spanning virtually the whole Archaic period (about 8,000 years); the only interruption to the sequence occurred when Athapaskan-speaking groups arrived in the lower drainage about 600 years ago (Fredrickson 1984:495). Some would even extend the Yukian presence in northwestern California into the Paleo-Indian period, identifying the so-called Post Pattern, a manifestation of the Western Fluted Point tradition dating to about 9000-10,000 B.C. as "Pre–Proto-Yukian" (Fredrickson 1984:485, 497, 523-524; Whistler 1988:84). The Western Fluted Point tradition has also been associated with "Pre–Proto-Hokan" to the south and east (Moratto 1984:543-544). Clearly, at this time-depth archeological-linguistic correlations are tenuous in the extreme.

As to the cause of the separation between the two Yukian groups, one possibility, which has received little support, is that ancestral Yuki and Wappo entered northwestern California as already distinct communities that settled in different locations (cf. Whistler 1988: n. 18). Another view favors a southward migration of ancestral Wappo speakers from a Proto-Yukian homeland in the Eel River drainage. Wappo is seen as the more likely candidate for a migration because it has been extensively influenced by surrounding languages (vol. 8:258). A third possibility, which has attracted the largest following among archeologists, is that a Proto-Yukian continuum was forced apart by Pomoan expansions from the Clear Lake area, the presumed Proto-Pomoan homeland (Oswalt 1964a:420; Moratto 1984; Whistler 1988). Assuming that the original Yukian territory extended along the coast as far as the north Bay area, the Proto-Pomoan expansion from Clear Lake to the middle Russian River valley before 4,000 years ago would have isolated the speech community ancestral to Wappo. The Proto-Pomoan expansion has been correlated with the spread of the Late Borax Lake Pattern. Around 3,500 years ago Proto-Miwokans, associated with the Berkeley Pattern, expanded north and west from the Delta, displacing the Proto-Wappo community to the north (Moratto 1984:278-281, 555). Prior occupancy of the north Bay area by the Wappo is implied linguistically by the fact that the terms for some Coast Range species such as the redwood and black oak were borrowed by the Western Miwok from the Wappo (Levy 1978). Then, about A.D. 500, the Wappo were pushed into the Napa valley by an expansion of Western–branch Pomoans down the Russian River, a shift possibly signaled archeologically by the spread of the Saint Helena aspect of the Augustine Pattern in the Napa valley (Moratto 1984:566; Whistler 1988:86).

A relatively late incursion of Athapaskans on former Yukian territory is suggested by shallow glottochronological dates, a tendency in California

Athapaskan languages to favor analyzable over unanalyzable terms for local plant and animal species, and the likelihood of a shift from Yukian to Athapaskan languages among the Cahto and Wailaki (Whistler 1979; cf. Moratto 1984:541, 570-571). The archeological picture for the Athapaskan arrival is not so clear, since both the Athapaskan and Yukian peoples of the Eel River area had a similar material culture known as the Shasta aspect of the Augustine Pattern, which lasted into the historic period (Fredrickson 1984: 495-496, 525).

Hokan

Hokan is a loose collection of more than a dozen geographically dispersed families and isolates falling mainly within California but spilling over into Nevada, Arizona, and northwestern Mexico, with outliers sometimes also claimed in southern Mexico and Honduras; it is best considered a hypothetical stock whose members are only remotely related, if at all (Haas 1963, 1964a; Jacobsen 1966:121-126, 1976, 1979, 1986; Langdon 1974, 1979; Bright 1976:363; Shipley 1976:440-446; vol. 8:85-87). The "core" Hokan group consists of at least the Pomoan, Palaihnihan, Shastan, Salinan, and Cochimí-Yuman families, and the isolates Karok, Chimariko, Yana, Washoe, and Seri; the Chumashan family and the isolate Esselen were also included by Sapir and others.

Following the formulation of the Hokan hypothesis (Dixon 1905; Dixon and Kroeber 1912, 1913, 1919; Kroeber 1915; Sapir 1917), certain languages of eastern Texas and the lower Rio Grande were linked to California Hokan to form the "Hokan-Coahuiltecan" (or "Hokaltecan") grouping (Swanton 1915; Sapir 1920, 1920a, 1921), and this was subsumed, along with Yukian and several families of eastern North America, in Sapir's vast "Hokan-Siouan" phylum (Sapir 1921b, 1925:525-527, 1929). Evidence for Hokan-Siouan was never published, and it has generally been viewed as untenable by linguists and culture historians. Hokan-Coahuiltecan, on the other hand, gained qualified support for a period of time (Hoijer 1941, 1954:5-6; Haas 1954; Swadesh 1954:362, 1967:289; Bright 1955; Kroeber 1955; Gursky 1964, 1966a; C.F. Voegelin and F.M. Voegelin 1965:141-142, 1966; Langdon 1974), even becoming the focus of several glottochronological studies, which yielded time-depths of 2500-3500 B.C. (Greenberg and Swadesh 1953; Swadesh 1954, 1967a:100; Kroeber 1955; Bright 1956; cf. Jacobsen 1966:123-124, 1986:37-38). However, the scantily documented Coahuiltecan languages (Coahuilteco, Comecrudan, and Cotoname) probably belonged to or constituted separate families rather than forming a genetic grouping, and neither they nor the languages of east Texas (Tonkawa and Karankawa) are relatable to the Hokan languages of California on the basis of the available evidence (Goddard 1979a; cf. Jacobsen 1986:37).

Before their demise, Hokan-Siouan and particularly Hokan-Coahuiltecan had at least some impact on interpretations of Southwestern prehistory. Thus, following the publication of the C.F. Voegelin and E.W. Voegelin (1944) wall map, which grouped aboriginal languages according to Sapir's (1929) continental classification (fig. 1), it seemed straightforward to conclude that Hokan-Siouan was the most diverse and most dispersed of the superstocks and therefore constituted the oldest grouping in North America (C.F. Voegelin 1945, 1958; cf. Hoijer 1958; Newman 1959; Jacobsen 1989a:12). However, the Hokan-Siouan hypothesis exerted little influence on North American archeology (Foster 1988), and by the mid-1950s the principal segments of the grouping had been recast along other lines. These adjustments were reflected in the Consensus Classification of 1964, appearing on the influential C.F. Voegelin and F.M. Voegelin (1966) map of aboriginal language phyla, which dispensed with Hokan-Siouan but preserved Hokan-Coahuiltecan (fig. 2).

It was Sapir himself who drew the inference from the distribution of Hokan and Coahuiltecan that they must once have formed a continuum across the Southwest that was disrupted first by a migration of Uto-Aztecans from the south and later by a migration of Athapaskans from the north (Sapir 1916, 1949:457, 1917a:450, 1920:290, 1921:72). Although this model was based on linguistic distributions without reference to archeology, it was later easily accommodated to archeological speculation, when radiocarbon dating revealed that the so-called Desert (or Western Archaic) culture of the Great Basin, rather than being a recent development, actually spanned a history of 10 millennia or more (Jennings and Norbeck 1955; Jennings 1964; cf. vol. 11:21). It was hypothesized that the earliest carriers of the Desert culture were bands of Proto-Hokaltecans occupying the Great Basin and the Gulf Coast, and that the Hokaltecan continuum was disrupted by waves of Uto-Aztecan "highlanders" arriving from the north, instead of, as Sapir thought, from the south (W. Taylor 1961; cf. Swadesh 1964:553-554; Hopkins 1965). The main complication to this scenario was that the archeologists failed to identify any significant discontinuities in the Desert culture sequence that could be linked to an invasive migration. The proposal was defended on the grounds that the extreme conditions of the arid Southwest would probably cause any group arriving there to quickly adopt a similar lifeway, and this would be reflected in a similar material culture (W. Taylor 1961:73-74). This claim made the replacement hypothesis virtually impossible to test archeologically, and the

doctrine of cultural uniformity in the Great Basin has been seriously challenged (Bettinger and Baumhoff 1982:498).

The discrediting of Hokan-Coahuiltecan as a genetic grouping to some extent undermined the notion that Hokan-speaking peoples were the earliest inhabitants in the greater Southwest, but in spite of this, similar inferences were made about core Hokan and its neighbors within the geographically more restricted context of California. The map showed that central California and the San Francisco Bay area were dominated by a block of Penutian languages; Hokan, on the other hand, was distributed in what were sometimes referred to as "islands" around the peripheries of the state. On the assumption that Proto-Hokan and Proto-Penutian once represented unified speech communities that entered California as single migrations, the discontinuous configuration of Hokan implied that it had undergone dispersal at the hand of later-arriving Penutians. In one scenario, what was called an "old Washo-Pomo-Yana continuum" in northern California was disrupted by Proto-Penutians moving southward from an Oregon homeland (Sapir 1921:72, 1921a). In another, the separation of the northern Hokan groups was said to be the result of an expansion of Penutians up the Central Valley, while the separation of Yuman from the coastal Hokan languages was the result of a westward movement of "Shoshoneans" from the Great Basin (Kroeber 1923). The idea that the distribution of Hokan could be explained as the result of disruptive Penutian migrations has been dubbed the "Hokan-Penutian model" (Whistler 1978:112-115, 1979:15-16); it usually includes provision for the later entry of Athapaskan and Algic groups in northwestern California, which further affected the distribution of Hokan.

The Hokan-Penutian model has exerted a considerable influence on interpretations of California prehistory over time (Kroeber 1955:101-103; W. Taylor 1961; Baumhoff and Olmsted 1963, 1964; Miller 1966:92; Kinkade and Powell 1976:90; Cressman 1977:101; vol. 8:81-82; Jacobsen 1979:547; M.J.P. Nichols 1981:7; Raven 1984:460; Moratto 1984:539). From the 1940s to the early 1970s California archeology was dominated by the Central California Taxonomic System (Lillard, Heizer, and Fenenga 1939; Beardsley 1954; cf. Fredrickson 1974:41), which was at first limited to prehistoric sequences in the Delta and San Francisco Bay areas but was later extended to ever larger portions of central California. In this system, the "Early Horizon" was correlated with Hokan, the "Middle Horizon" with an initial Penutian expansion, and the "Late Horizon" with the spread of Miwok (Whistler 1978:116-117, 1988; vol. 8:37-57; Moratto 1984:178-216, 237-238). The Central California Taxonomic System was superseded by the so-called "pattern" approach to California archeology

(Fredrickson 1974, 1984), but even then, Hokan, along with Yukian, were touted as prime candidates for early occupation of the state (Whistler 1977:169; Fredrickson 1984:495; Moratto 1984:536). The argument was again primarily linguistic: great age was assumed in the case of Yukian because of its lack of known affiliations, and in the case of Hokan because of its discontinuous distribution and the obviously distant links among its branches.

In a purely speculative vein, it has been hypothesized by archeologists that the earliest occupants of California were carriers of the Western Fluted Point tradition (10,000-9000 B.C.): those in the central, eastern, and southern part of the state were identified as "Pre–Proto-Hokan," while those in the northwestern part of the state were identified as "Pre–Proto-Yukian," with perhaps some ancestral Hokan communities present too (Moratto 1984:79-88, 543-545, fig. 11.4). The succeeding Pluvial Lakes tradition (9000-5000 B.C.) was correlated with Proto-Hokan proper (Cressman 1977; Moratto 1984:90-103). The best case for the linkage between Hokan and these early cultures can perhaps be made in the southern coast region, where the archeological sequence terminating in ethnographic groups like the Yuman and Chumash can be interpreted as involving at least 8,000 years of in situ development (Moratto 1984:158-165, 544, 551).

About 7,000-8,000 years ago, as the hot dry conditions of the Altithermal succeeded the cool moist conditions of the Anathermal during which the Pluvial Lakes tradition had thrived, Proto-Hokan speakers may have begun spreading up the Central Valley into northern California, bringing the "millingstone cultures" with them (Whistler 1988:84; cf. Fredrickson 1984:509-510). Between 4000 and 2000 B.C. Hokan was diversifying into the protolanguages of the families known in historic times, and Uto-Aztecan and Penutian (Proto-Utian) speakers were entering California from the Colorado and Columbia plateaus respectively, separating the already linguistically distinct Hokan speech communities (Moratto 1984: 547-552).

Cochimí-Yuman

A case can be made for long in situ development of Hokan peoples in the southern coastal region of California, a sequence uninterrupted until the arrival around 1000 B.C. of Takic branch Uto-Aztecans in the Los Angeles Basin (Kowta 1969:50; Moratto 1984:560; cf. Kroeber 1925:578-579). Although it is tempting on geographic grounds to see this incursion as causing a separation of the Proto-Chumash from the Proto–Cochimí-Yumans, Chumashan shows almost no linguistic affinity with Cochimí-Yuman, and indeed is one of the most problematic putative members of the

Hokan grouping (Margaret Langdon, personal communication 1993). The effects of the Takic incursion can be detected in the influence that Yuman languages exerted on the phonological systems of the Cupan languages (Luiseño and Cahuilla-Cupeño) of the Takic branch that border Yuman just to the north. It is hypothesized that the territory occupied by the Cupan languages was once Yuman, and that intertribal marriage and periods of conquest led to a situation of bilingualism, with Yuman populations in the border area eventually switching to Luiseño and Cahuilla-Cupeño, which were much affected phonologically in the process (Hinton 1991).

The Yuman segment of the Cochimí-Yuman family comprises eight or 10 languages falling into four branches (vol. 10:4-12; "Introduction," table 3, this vol.). Three of the branches are coordinate, but the fourth, consisting of the single language Kiliwa, is quite divergent from the rest. The deepest split within Yuman thus occurs in northern Baja California, implying a homeland generally in the southern part of the area occupied by the family (vol. 9:174). This is consonant with the location of the Cochimí segment of the family in central Baja California. The distribution of the eastern Yuman branches in relation to Californian and Sonoran Uto-Aztecan is suggestive of an eastward Yuman expansion across formerly Uto-Aztecan territory (Miller 1966:91). The languages making up the Pai branch have a discontinuous distribution: Upland Yuman is spoken by Walapai, Havasupai, and Yavapai peoples in western Arizona, while Paipai is spoken in northern Baja California. The two languages are separated by the Delta-California and River branches located along the United States–Mexican border and the Colorado River (vol. 10:8).

Two hypotheses have been advanced to explain the distribution of the Pai branch. The first is that Yuman at one time formed a dialect complex, with the dialects situated along the Colorado River undergoing rapid change as a result of contact with outside peoples; these dialects developed into the separate River and Delta-California languages, while the more conservative dialects belonging to the Pai group retained a number of original features in common (Kroeber 1943; Joël 1964). The second hypothesis is that the Paipai are simply a group of Upland Yuman (Yavapai) speakers who migrated from Arizona to northern Baja California in relatively recent times (Winter 1967). The second view has been criticized on the grounds that Paipai is not intelligible with Yavapai, and archeological evidence for a Paipai migration is lacking (vol. 10:8). In fact, neither the in situ nor the migration hypothesis is particularly well supported on linguistic grounds, and the matter remains unresolved (Langdon 1974:76).

A study of reconstructed Yuman vocabulary concludes that the Yuman segment of the family at least has occupied either its present area, or one with a similar environment, from Proto-Yuman times on, and that the Proto-Yumans practiced shamanism and depended on both agriculture and hunting-and-gathering for subsistence (Law 1961). Although the study yields some curious anomalies, for example, providing evidence of protoforms for 'corn', 'beans', and 'squash', but not for 'flour', 'cornmeal', or 'bean flour', its conclusions have generally been corroborated by other lines of evidence (Langdon 1974:75-76, Margaret Landgon personal communication 1993). Another study confirmed the Proto-Yuman status of the word for 'corn' (which was shown to derive from 'seed') and 'squash' but raised the possibility that the word for 'beans' might be an early borrowing from Uto-Aztecan, possibly Hopi (Joël 1978).

Palaihnihan

A model of Palaihnihan prehistory was developed by combining the findings of archeology and glottochronology (Baumhoff and Olmsted 1963, 1964). On the archeological side, the sequence at the Lorenzen site in northeastern California indicated continuous occupation for three or four millennia, and this matched quite closely the minimum glottochronological divergence time obtained for Achumawi and Atsugewi of 1500-1100 B.C. The older material at the Lorenzen site resembled that classed as the "Early Horizon" in the Central California Taxonomic System: it was concluded that the Palaihnihans were Hokan groups driven out of the Central Valley by an expansion of Penutians who were represented in the archeological record as the "Middle Horizon." The people settling north of the Pit River became the Achumawi, and those south of the river became the Atsugewi. The Baumhoff-Olmsted model of Palaihnihan development in the Pit River area is still regarded by archeologists as a productive working hypothesis (Raven 1984:459-460); indeed, Palaihnihan could represent the last stage of lengthy in situ development of Proto-Hokan peoples present in northern California for 8,000 years or more (Moratto 1984:543-546).

Pomoan

The Pomoan family consists of seven languages in west-central California. The deepest splits within the family are those represented by Southeastern Pomo and Eastern Pomo, which adjoin in the Clear Lake area. Four of the five remaining languages are found in the Russian River drainage and make up a single branch called Western (or Russian River) Pomo. The position of the geographically separate Northeastern Pomo within the family is uncertain (Halpern 1964; Oswalt 1964a, 1976; McLendon 1973; vol. 8:274-275). The

center of gravity principle implies a Proto-Pomoan homeland in the vicinity of Clear Lake, with a spread westward to the Russian River valley (Halpern 1964:91; Oswalt 1964a:419; Whistler 1988:86; cf. Basgall 1982). The westward expansion of the Pomoans was undoubtedly the cause of the division of the Yukian languages into Yuki and Wappo. An alternative hypothesis places the Proto-Pomoan homeland in the Russian River valley, with an eastward spread of "Lake Pomo" to the Clear Lake area, which then diversified into Southeastern Pomo and Eastern Pomo (Webb 1971; cf. Kroeber 1925:227; Levy 1978). This view has won few adherents.

From an extensive reconstructed Proto-Pomoan lexicon containing many cultural terms, it is possible to conclude that the Proto-Pomoans were hunter-gatherers who had long occupied an environment similar to that of the ethnographic Pomoans (McLendon 1973:61-63). Since the Russian River valley and Clear Lake are separated by barely 15 air miles, and the flora and fauna of the two areas are very similar, reconstructed species terms are for the most part of little help in settling the issue of the Pomoan homeland, except to rule out a coastal orientation (Levy 1978, 1979:7-8). Nevertheless, a watershed boundary separates Clear Lake from the Russian River, and there are some differences in the ranges of fish species in the two areas: Proto-Pomoan terms can be reconstructed for the blackfish and the Sacramento perch, which occur in Clear Lake but are absent natively from the Russian River, and this provides at least a small bit of lexical support for the Clear Lake homeland hypothesis (Whistler 1988). Since the terms for these fish types are attested in Southeastern Pomo and Eastern Pomo, the conclusion that Proto-Pomoan terms exist for them depends on the presumption that these languages represent the deepest splits within the family.

Assuming a Clear Lake homeland, the Pomoans may have arisen from Hokan antecedents who were responsible for bringing the "millingstone cultures" to northern California between 5500 and 5000 B.C. The crystallization of Pomoan and its spread to the middle Russian River valley may correlate with the spread of the Late Borax Lake Pattern around 3000 B.C.; and the later movements involving the spread of the western Pomoan languages through the Russian River valley can also be detected in the archeological record (Whistler 1988:84-86; Fredrickson 1984:497-500, 509-511).

Penutian

The term Penutian has one narrow and several broad senses (Shipley 1976:433-440; vol. 8:82-85; Silverstein 1979), all of which have had some impact on culture-historical interpretations in the far west. In the narrow sense, equivalent to California Penutian, the term applies to a grouping proposed early in the twentieth century by Dixon and Kroeber (1912, 1913, 1919) consisting of five contiguous families in central California: Wintuan, Maiduan, Yokutsan, Costanoan, and Miwokan—the last two later joined under the heading Utian (cf. Kroeber 1910:259-260, 1911: 306-307; Callaghan 1967, 1990:16; Silverstein 1979: 676). Although some Penutianists regard California Penutian as an unverified hypothesis (vol. 8:81; Shipley 1988), many have accepted it as a valid stock grouping, based on extensive comparative work (Shafer 1947, 1952; Pitkin and Shipley 1958; Callaghan 1958; Broadbent and Pitkin 1964; Silverstein 1972, 1975, 1979; cf. Shipley 1966:489, note 2).

Soon after the California Penutian "kernel" was formulated, more distant links were suggested with families and isolates outside California (Sapir 1949:453, 1921a, 1921b; Frachtenberg 1918:177). What was referred to as "Sapir's Penutian" eventually consisted of California Penutian, two intermediate-level stocks (Oregon Penutian and Plateau Penutian), Chinookan, Tsimshianic, and an outlying Mexican branch (Sapir 1929, 1949:172). The North American parts of the proposal have received a good deal of support (Swadesh 1954; Hymes 1957, 1964, 1964a, 1964b; Shipley 1966, 1970, 1976:433-440; vol. 8:84-85; C.F. Voegelin and F.M. Voegelin 1965:143-144, 1966; Thompson 1976:367-377; vol. 7:45), although it is probably best considered a series of "interlocking hypotheses" on which considerable progress has been made short of establishment (Silverstein 1979:650). Moreover, while Penutianists are optimistic that most of the putatively included families north of California will eventually be shown to have affiliations with California Penutian, they are skeptical about the specific way Sapir classified them (reviewed by Silverstein 1979).

Both California Penutian and Sapir's Penutian contributed to the formulation of the so-called Hokan-Penutian model, the former by providing underpinnings to the idea that Hokan groups had been dispersed to the peripheries of the state by Penutians expanding through the Sacramento valley (Kroeber 1923), and the latter by implying a northern homeland for the Penutians, whose migrations south caused Hokan groups in northern California to separate into "islands" (Sapir 1921:72). Two groupings, which were even broader than the one envisaged by Sapir, were suggested later. The first, "Macro-Penutian," linked Sapir's Penutian with the speculative Aztec-Tanoan stock, Mayan, and other Mexican families. The second, "Penutioid," was similar to Macro-Penutian in some respects but added other Latin American families and excluded Aztec-Tanoan (Swadesh 1956). Neither of these proposals ever received more than impressionistic support, and neither gained a following among linguists (cf. Shipley 1976:433-435). Nevertheless, both exerted some influence on archeological interpretations in western North America.

In a sweeping synthesis of prehistory spanning more than 10,000 years and covering most of the continent west of the Rocky Mountains, ancestral Macro-Penutians (the putative ancestors of the Penutians and the Uto-Aztecans) were seen as spreading south from the mountainous terrain north of the Great Basin, some of them moving east into Oregon and eventually south into California to become Penutians, while others continued down the cordillera to become Uto-Aztecans (the people who displaced the "Hokaltecans" in the Great Basin) and the Penutian-speaking groups of Latin America (W. Taylor 1961; cf. Hopkins 1965). In a later synthesis, Macro-Penutian was correlated with the Stemmed Point tradition (9000-7000 B.C.), representing Paleo-Indian big game hunters, one of four basal cultures posited for western North America (Carlson 1979, 1983). When it emerged that Macro-Penutian was not a valid genetic grouping, the Stemmed Point tradition was limited to only segments of Sapir's Penutian, such as Sahaptian and Chinookan (vol. 7:62). But correlations at such time-depths are highly speculative and usually raise more questions than they resolve. The Stemmed Point tradition, for instance, is regarded as an expression of the Western Pluvial Lakes tradition (Carlson 1983:83), which is more often associated with Hokan than Penutian (Moratto 1984:90-103). Moreover, the Stemmed Point tradition is thought to have spread from the Plains west to the Columbia River and its tributaries, but the linguistic picture implies a spread in the opposite direction, since there is greater diversity among the Penutian languages in western Oregon than on the Plateau.

Although attempts to link archeological assemblages with constructs like Macro-Penutian and Penutioid were doomed to fail, the idea that the Penutians came from Oregon or the northern Great Basin has served as a cornerstone of Penutian origin hypotheses ever since Sapir extended the stock outside California. The assumption underlying earlier hypotheses was that the Proto-Penutians migrated as a single speech community to central California, whence they diversified and spread out in several directions: up and down the Central Valley, and east and west into the Coast Ranges and Sierra Nevada foothills (Sapir 1916, 1921:72, 1949:459-460; Kroeber 1923:131-132). The main support for the single-migration hypothesis is the fact that the California Penutian branches form a contiguous block in the central part of the state: such a configuration, particularly when compared with Hokan, suggests in situ development and diversification from a single center, perhaps in the Delta area, although doubts have

88

been expressed that this "overflowed region of sloughs and tule swamps" would have made a suitable homeland (Kroeber 1925:348-349).

The tendency in later hypotheses has been to posit separate entries at different times and possibly from different locations by groups constituting the California branches (Whistler 1977:160). The arguments are again linguistically based. First, although the four branches of the California kernel are indeed contiguous, it has proven extremely challenging to demonstrate relationships among them. A theory of multiple entry would remove some of the mystery surrounding the California configuration, since under such a model Proto-Penutian would have undergone diversification outside the state at least to the level of the intermediate protolanguages representing the separate branches, and these would have developed in isolation during the period of migration until they again came in contact in central California. There is especially convincing linguistic support for the separate entry of Wintuan. Second, areal features implying periods of early contact among Penutian, Uto-Aztecan, and Hokan groups can be more easily explained under a hypothesis of multiple Penutian entry (M.J.P. Nichols 1981). Finally, the notion of multiple entry fits the California archeological picture considerably better than the idea of a single entry. The culture-historical sequence that follows must nevertheless be regarded as highly speculative.

Two extra-California homeland areas have been suggested for Proto-Penutian: the northern Willamette valley in western Oregon (vol. 7:45), and a larger area to the east comprising parts of the Columbia Plateau and the northwestern Great Basin (Moratto 1984:544-546, fig. 11.4). A third possibility is that both areas were involved (Whistler 1977). In favor of the Willamette valley location is the fact that the area of greatest diversity for the languages claimed to have Penutian affiliation occurs between the Coast Ranges and the Cascade Range in Oregon: there the Chinookan and Plateau Penutian families adjoin the Kalapuyan branch of Takelman, with the Alsean and Coosan families and the Siuslaw language lying on the coast just to the west and Takelma a short distance to the south. The center of gravity principle thus supports a homeland in the western part of the area. The argument for a Columbia Plateau–northwestern Great Basin homeland location is primarily archeological: the so-called Windmiller Pattern, which is associated with the entry of Proto-Utian in the Delta area of California, appears to have links around 2700 B.C. with both the "Altithermal" cultures of the Columbia Plateau and the Lovelock culture at Lovelock Cave in northwestern Nevada (Moratto 1984:552). The third scenario has the breakup of Penutian occurring somewhere in the Plateau–Great Basin area, but with Proto-Wintuan, and

perhaps Proto-Maiduan, becoming established in western Oregon before spreading south into California (Whistler 1977).

The consensus under the multiple-entry hypothesis is that the first Penutian group to enter California was the Proto-Utians, who are associated with the Windmiller Pattern, a riverine and wetland adaptation that developed along the lower Sacramento river around 2500 B.C. with links to the northeast (summarized by Whistler 1979:166-172; Moratto 1984:201-207, 552-553). The date of the Windmiller Pattern is close to the maximum glottochronological divergence time of 2900 B.C. calculated for Utian (Swadesh 1958:672). Around 2000 B.C. some of the Proto-Utians began moving westward toward the San Francisco Bay area, presumably occupied by Yukian groups to the north and pre-Esselen (Hokan) groups to the south. Contact between Proto-Utians and the prior inhabitants is reflected archeologically in the emergence of the Berkeley Pattern (Fredrickson 1974; Moratto 1984:207-211, 277-281, fig. 6.16). Over the next two millennia Utians fully occupied the area around San Francisco Bay and as far south as Monterey Bay.

North of Carquinez Strait, Proto–Western-Miwok speakers spread into Marin County at the expense of Yukians, a development that gave rise to Coast Miwok. The borrowing of several terms for shellfish species by Coast Miwok from Pomoan and Wappo and of the term for redwood from Wappo implies prior occupancy by Pomoan and Wappo and provides prima facie evidence of an interior homeland for the Miwokans (Levy 1978, 1979:8, 15-16). A careful plotting of the distributions of plant terms reconstructible at the Proto-Miwokan level points to the Sierra Nevada foothills as the most likely homeland for this branch of Utian (Callaghan 1982). By 500 B.C. the presence of the Houx aspect of the Berkeley Pattern at Clear Lake may represent the arrival of ancestral Lake Miwok from the southeast (Fredrickson 1984:499, 508, 511; Whistler 1988:85). The spread of the Berkeley Pattern to the east about A.D. 1, on the other hand, probably represents an expansion of Sierra Miwok peoples farther into the foothills from the homeland region (vol. 8:399-400; Moratto 1984:560-562; cf. Dixon and Kroeber 1919:102).

Developments south of Carquinez Strait involve the rise of the Costanoan branch of Utian, which spread southward from the San Francisco Bay area to a point somewhat below Monterey Bay (Moratto 1984:279). It has been suggested that much of this region was once under Esselen control (Beeler 1977:44), and that the Esselen, or their Hokan forebears, were the carriers of the Sur Pattern culture. Around 500 B.C. this was replaced by the Monterey Pattern culture, which may represent the arrival of the Costanoans (Breschini and Haversat 1980; Moratto 1984:246-247). On the linguistic side, the notion that the Costanoans came to the coast relatively late from the interior is supported by the number of terms for interior species reconstructible at the Proto-Costanoan level; that a displacement of Esselen people was involved is implied by the borrowing of terms for coastal species such as the shark, the whale, the sea otter, and the pelican from Esselen into Costanoan (Levy 1978, 1979).

It has been argued on grounds of lower glottochronological divergence time, shallower internal diversity, and greater geographic compactness, that ancestral Yokutsan speakers are likely to have entered California after the Utians, perhaps around 1500 B.C. They, too, may have come first to the Delta–northern San Joaquin valley region and then, between 1000 and 500 B.C., spread south of the Miwokans along the Sierra Nevada foothills and finally into the southern San Joaquin valley (Whistler 1977:170; Levy 1978; vol. 8:398-413; Moratto 1984:554-555). That the foothills were settled before the southern valley is implied by the fact that terms for foothills species such as digger pine, buckeye, interior live oak, and black oak can be reconstructed in Proto-Yokutsan and the fact that the foothills are linguistically more diverse than the valley (Levy 1978:4-5, 1979:8; Whistler 1984). There is archeological evidence that, following the abrupt onset of drying climatic conditions around A.D. 500, the Yokutsans underwent a period of depopulation that resulted in a contraction of their territory, but that following an improvement of climatic conditions about A.D. 1400 they again expanded throughout the San Joaquin valley, establishing themselves in their ethnographic position (Levy 1979:22; Moratto 1984:563-564, 571-572). The glottochronological shallowness of the numerous dialects of Valley Yokuts reflects that expansion, masking the earlier period when Yokutsan speakers also occupied the valley.

Opinion varies as to whether Proto-Maiduans or Proto-Wintuans were the next group to enter California (cf. Whistler 1977:171). If, as some have argued, the Maiduans were the carriers of the Martis complex (2000 B.C.–A.D. 1) found in the Lake Tahoe area (cf. Moratto 1984:294-303), their entry could rival that of the Yokutsans in date. The archeological picture is better known after A.D. 1, and this is a good deal closer to the glottochronological divergence time of A.D. 500 calculated for Proto-Maiduan (Levy 1979), as well as being more in accord with patterns of "irregularity, innovation, and borrowing" in Maiduan that imply a relatively late entry from outside California (Kenneth Whistler in Moratto 1984:562). After A.D. 1 the Maiduans expanded east, west, and south through the northern Sierra Nevada at the expense of the Washoe and Yana; and after A.D. 1300, the Nisenan pushed still farther south, putting pressure on the Sierra Miwok (Levy 1979:17; Moratto 1984:562, 571).

Of the four California Penutian families, Wintuan is the most likely to have originated in interior northwestern California or southwestern Oregon. The chief argument favoring this location over the Columbia Plateau or the northern Great Basin comes from reconstructed Proto-Wintuan plant and animal terms. Proto-Wintuan terms for species such as the king snake, the salmon, the black oak, the white alder, the sugar pine, one kind of wild tobacco, and a few others limit the homeland to the cismontane area from northern California to southwestern Oregon (Whistler 1977). This is only slightly south of the Willamette valley, inferred as the Penutian homeland on the basis of the center of gravity principle. Ancestral Wintuans may have reached the upper Sacramento valley between A.D. 1 and 500 (Moratto 1984:562). This development may be signaled archeologically by the onset of the Augustine Pattern, which represents a fusion of older Berkeley Pattern elements with new traits, some, such as the bow and arrow, being imported from the north possibly as a result of contacts with Algic peoples (Whistler 1977:170-171; Moratto 1984:211-214, 282-283, 562-563; cf. Hughes 1992:324). Between about A.D. 500 and 700 the Patwin may have reached the southern Sacramento Valley, followed by a movement of Hill Patwin west into Pomo territory (Whistler 1988:86; Moratto 1984:571). The relatively recent arrival of the Patwin in the southern Sacramento valley is inferred from the fact that they borrowed a number of terms for species endemic to central California from Miwokan (Whistler 1977). Terms for six species are crucial to the argument: digger pine, pine nut, live oak, incense cedar, manzanita, and buckeye. A northern, possibly non-California, homeland for Wintuan is thus implied by two complementary sets of data, one indicating that Proto-Wintuan had plant and animal terms for species with ranges extending from cismontane California into southwestern Oregon, and the other indicating that the names for a number of important plants in the heart of the Patwin area in central California are borrowings. Following the Patwin expansions, Wintu speakers in the north pushed into the Trinity River system at the expense of the Chimariko around A.D. 1000 (Whistler 1977:171), a development that may be marked archeologically by the spread of the Shasta aspect of the Augustine Pattern, and linguistically by the presence of a number of borrowed Chimariko place-names in Wintu (Bauman 1980a).

Uto-Aztecan

Uto-Aztecan is one of the best-studied language stocks in North America (Haas 1976:42) and has provided something of a model for the way in which language

90

can serve the ends of culture history. Classification work on this far-flung stock comprising over 30 languages dates to the middle and late nineteenth century (Buschmann 1859; Brinton 1891; cf. Lamb 1964:111-120), and the stock enjoys the distinction of being the first in the Americas to which the comparative method was comprehensively applied, resulting in a reconstruction of the Proto–Uto-Aztecan sound system (Sapir 1913-1914; cf. Newman 1954:630). Early workers divided the Uto-Aztecans into three branches, mainly on the basis of geography: (1) "Shoshonean," centered in the American Southwest and consisting of the Numic and Takic subgroups, and the Hopi and Tubatulabal languages; (2) "Sonoran," centered in northwestern Mexico and consisting of the Tepiman, Taracahitan, and Corachol subgroups; and (3) the Aztecan grouping of closely related languages distributed in southern Mexico and elsewhere in Central America (Brinton 1891; Sapir 1913-1914, 1929, 1949; Kroeber 1907, 1934; Mason 1936). This is referred to in the literature as the family-tree model of Uto-Aztecan relationships.

The unity of Shoshonean and Sonoran as subgroupings eventually came under fire (Whorf 1935, 1935a; Kroeber 1934); and in the 1950s, as glottochronology began to have an impact on linguistic classifications, a different picture of Uto-Aztecan relationships emerged, in which the stock was divided into eight or nine distinct branches that were seen as descendants of original Uto-Aztecan dialects forming a long chain in the Southwest and parts of Mexico (Swadesh 1954-1955, 1964). The chain model to a certain extent supplanted the family-tree model (Lamb 1958:95, 1964; Miller 1964, 1966, 1967, 1984; vol. 10:117-119; Miller, Tanner, and Foley 1971), although the family-tree model continued to have some adherents (K. Hale 1958, 1964; C.F. Voegelin, F.M. Voegelin, and K. Hale 1962). The possibility that high-level divisions exist within Uto-Aztecan later resurfaced in the claim that the stock initially split into Proto–Northern Uto-Aztecan (equivalent to Shoshonean) and Proto–Southern Uto-Aztecan (comprising Sonoran and Aztecan) (Heath 1977, 1978; Campbell and Langacker 1978; cf. Fowler 1983:234-242). One classification, which represents something of a compromise between the family-tree and chain models, lists five coequal branches: Numic, Tubatulabal, Takic, Hopi, and far-flung Southern Uto-Aztecan, the last comprising all the former Sonoran and Aztecan languages in a new arrangement of subgroups (Miller 1984:21, table 9; cf. Cortina-Borja and Valiñas 1989). The four American branches are not grouped as Northern Uto-Aztecan, although the evidence continues to mount that such a subgrouping is justified (Manaster Ramer 1992). If, however, the splits within the northern group are as deep separately as the whole of Southern Uto-Aztecan,

the stock's center of gravity would lie in a region embracing southeastern California, Arizona, and the northwestern part of the Mexican state of Sonora, but not extending very far south of this. This region is shared with the Yuman and Apachean languages, so that any hypothesis that posits a Uto-Aztecan homeland there must take into account the presence of the other language groupings as well.

Higher-Level Groupings and Prehistory

More distant genetic links have been proposed for Uto-Aztecan, and these have figured in various ways in interpretations of Southwestern prehistory. The first was Sapir's Aztec-Tanoan proposal, which linked Uto-Aztecan and Kiowa-Tanoan (Sapir 1921b); Zuni was later tentatively included (Sapir 1929, 1949:173). A cautiously favorable consensus emerged about Aztec-Tanoan after fairly extensive evidence was published, although Zuni was usually excluded from the discussions (Whorf and Trager 1937; C.F. Voegelin and E.W. Voegelin 1944; Trager 1951, 1967:338; Newman 1954:630; Miller 1959, 1966:79; Lamb 1959:45, 1964:109; C.F. Voegelin and F.M. Voegelin 1965:144, 1966; K. Hale 1967; Davis 1979:408-413, 1989; vol. 9:171). Aztec-Tanoan was seen as opening "a perspective of vast ethnological and historical interest" (Whorf and Trager 1937:610), but the response to it was actually rather muted. One speculative scheme had Proto–Aztec-Tanoans arriving in the Southwest from an unspecified northern location, some pushing on to Mexico, and others tarrying in the Southwest to participate in the Pre-Pueblo and Pueblo cultural sequences beginning a few centuries before the Christian era (Trager 1951). Another drew on the Aztec-Tanoan grouping to explain the distribution of Pueblo peoples in the northern Rio Grande area (Wendorf and Reed 1955).

The second, more far-reaching proposal, "Macro-Penutian," has had a greater impact on interpretations of Southwestern prehistory, although it was never supported by published evidence. Macro-Penutian included California Penutian and its northern congeners, Aztec-Tanoan (with Zuni), Mayan, and still other Latin American families (Whorf 1935a:608; cf. Mason 1940; Trager 1945:188). It attracted the attention of linguists mainly to the extent that it once figured in a specific sequence by which founding peoples were said to have reached North America (C.F. Voegelin 1958:55), and that it appeared (with Aztec-Tanoan listed separately) on the C.F. Voegelin and F.M Voegelin (1966) wall map of aboriginal languages (cf. C.F. Voegelin and F.M. Voegelin 1965:126–127). Macro-Penutian has generally been treated with a large measure of skepticism by linguists (Newman 1954:630; Lamb 1964:125; Miller 1966:88; Shipley 1976:433-435; Campbell 1979:964; Campbell and Mithun 1979a:

38). Nevertheless, outside linguistic circles, Macro-Penutian has exerted a certain amount of influence, particularly in efforts to identify early populations and their movements in the Plateau and Southwest.

In one interpretation, Macro-Penutian was correlated with the Stemmed Point tradition representing big game hunters in western North America between 9000 and 7000 B.C. (Carlson 1979, 1983; vol. 7:60-69). Such a correlation must be discounted on the basis of what is known of the linguistic relationships involved. In another interpretation, the Great Basin was said to be occupied around 8000 B.C. by Hokan-Coahuiltecan bands bearing the Desert culture; somewhere north of the Great Basin, the Proto–Macro-Penutian speech community divided into Penutian proper, which spread to Oregon and later to California, and Uto-Aztecan, which spread through the Great Basin (W. Taylor 1961; cf. Euler 1964:380; Hopkins 1965). From there some ancestral Uto-Aztecans continued south to Mexico, while others were left along the way in the Great Basin and the southern California deserts—the ancestral Tubatulabal, Takic, Numic, and Hopi speakers, who ended up in a cul-de-sac in southeastern California. Several difficulties attend this interpretation. First and most obviously, neither Macro-Penutian nor Hokan-Coahuiltecan is well supported as a valid linguistic subgrouping. Second, the Desert culture sequence in the Great Basin lacks a clear discontinuity at the appropriate time-depth that can be associated with the putative Uto-Aztecan incursion. Third, and perhaps most germane, the notion of Uto-Aztecans moving southwest across the Great Basin and "piling up" in the vicinity of the California-Nevada-Arizona border runs counter to the linguistic facts, which reveal the border area to be far more diverse and therefore older than the Great Basin proper.

A variant of the northern Uto-Aztecan origin hypothesis took greater cognizance of the linguistic facts (Hopkins 1965). This version also assumed the validity of Macro-Penutian, but it had a more plausible explanation for the developments in the Great Basin. As the arid conditions of the Altithermal reached a peak around 5000 B.C. Uto-Aztecans started south from the Plateau, skirting around the inhospitable Great Basin: one group proceeded along the western slopes of the Rocky Mountains and continued on to Mexico, while the other group moved along the eastern slopes of the Sierra Nevada to southeastern California, whence Numic-speaking groups fanned out into the Great Basin after climatic conditions had ameliorated. Although this scenario is flawed to the extent that it rests on Macro-Penutian, it is more in keeping with later Uto-Aztecan homeland hypotheses in its suggestion of a California connection for Uto-Aztecan and in its treatment of the Numic spread.

The Proto–Uto-Aztecan Homeland and Culture

The tendency has been to place the Uto-Aztecan homeland in the American Southwest, usually within an area between southeastern California, central Arizona, and northwestern Mexico. The time-depth of the stock has been calculated at around 3000 B.C. (Swadesh 1954:362, 1954-1955, 1958, 1963, 1964:550-551, 1967a:98; K. Hale 1958, 1959; vol. 9:171). The choice of a specific homeland location depends on the approach taken. To those who espouse the chain model of Uto-Aztecan (the view that the stock consists of eight or nine coequal branches) the Arizona-Sonora border area seems a logical choice, since this is where five of the branches converge; expansion to the northwest and south would have occurred from there (Lamb 1958:99; Miller 1966:90; Swadesh 1964:550-553; Cressman 1977:98; vol. 9:174-177). If, on the other hand, the Mexican families and isolates form a single branch that is coequal with the Tubatulabal, Takic, Numic, and Hopi branches separately, as proposed in Miller's (1984) Uto-Aztecan classification, the homeland is nudged somewhat to the northwest where three of the northern branches adjoin. The position of Hopi would reflect a later migration to the east (Miller 1966:93-94; vol. 10:123; vol. 9:233; Fowler 1972:110-111; Jacobsen 1989a:6). A link between Uto-Aztecan and Kiowa-Tanoan could be taken as implying a homeland more toward the eastern end of the area.

The reconstruction of Proto–Uto-Aztecan cultural vocabulary has provided another avenue for locating the homeland. In one such approach it was claimed that terms for pine, juniper, oak, reed or cane (*Phragmites communis*), prickly pear cactus, and bear grass were sufficiently widely distributed in the stock to be considered retentions from the Proto–Uto-Aztecan level (though the supporting etymologies were not published). Since these plants occur in intermediate altitude zones in the Southwest, the homeland most likely fell in the region between the upper Gila River drainage and the northern Sierra Madre in Mexico (Romney 1957). A later study was able to confirm solid Proto–Uto-Aztecan etymologies for only about half the terms: 'pine', 'reed or cane', and 'prickly pear cactus' (Miller 1966:97), thereby weakening the case for a Gila drainage–Sierra Madre homeland. Another study based on nine assured and 18 likely reconstructed Proto–Uto-Aztecan plant and animal terms concludes that the homeland occurred in a "mixed woodland/grassland setting, in proximity to montane forests," a large region in the Southwest extending from southeastern California across Arizona and into northwestern Mexico (Fowler 1983:230-235, map 3). The region was occupied historically by Uto-Aztecan languages, but excludes most of the Numic area, hence ruling out a homeland in the Great Basin itself as some have argued

(Goss 1977), or in the central and southern parts of Mexico.

While the proposed Uto-Aztecan homeland is located to the north of the inferred Yuman homeland in northern Baja California and the lower Colorado River, it intersects the northeastern salient of Yuman comprising the Pai branch. This distribution could have been achieved by the Uto-Aztecans' making a flanking movement around Pai branch Yumans already in place, but a more likely scenario involves a Pai migration across Uto-Aztecan territory (Miller 1966:90-91, 1984:19; vol. 9:175-176; Fowler 1983:242). Given the relatively shallow time-depth of Yuman of about two millennia, this thrust must have occurred after Southern Uto-Aztecan separated from the northern branches, which were already differentiated among themselves; the territory could even have been abandoned by Uto-Aztecans expanding away from their homeland area before the Pai people moved in. The presence of Athapaskan-speaking peoples such as the Western Apacheans in the region between Uto-Aztecan groups somewhat to the east belongs to considerably later history, since the Apacheans arrived in the Southwest only around A.D. 1400-1500.

Although several lines of evidence point to a Proto–Uto-Aztecan homeland in the southern Southwest, patterns of borrowing between Uto-Aztecan, apparently at the Proto–Uto-Aztecan stage, and the ancestors of several California families have generated the more radical proposal that the Uto-Aztecans may have originated in northern California and southern Oregon (M.J.P. Nichols 1981). In the so-called Old California Uto-Aztecan hypothesis, Proto-Yukian, Proto–Northern Hokan, Proto-Pomoan and, before their spread south, Proto-Utian and Proto-Maiduan, received an influx of lexical items and some grammatical features from Uto-Aztecan; this occurred before the separation of Southern Uto-Aztecan from the main stock. At a later stage, following the Southern Uto-Aztecan split, Esselen, Yokutsan, Plains Miwok, Sierra Miwok, and Chumashan in central and southwestern California also borrowed lexical items. The pattern of borrowing in space and time suggests a gradual movement of Uto-Aztecan speakers from north to south, with the degree of influence on surrounding languages being commensurate with changes taking place within Uto-Aztecan itself.

The Old California Uto-Aztecan hypothesis revives the idea of northern Uto-Aztecan origins, but based on more convincing evidence of early contacts rather than on inferences stemming from the Macro-Penutian concept. How these findings can be reconciled with the equally plausible evidence supporting a Southwest homeland remains to be resolved. Among the outstanding issues is where to place the parent speech community at the time when Southern Uto-Aztecan split off from the main stock. If Northern Uto-Aztecan turns out to have the same status as a major branch that Southern Uto-Aztecan has, the split could have occurred in central California, whence Southern Uto-Aztecan began its spread toward Mexico, while Northern Uto-Aztecan spread to southeastern California, where it subsequently divided into the Numic, Tubatulabal, Takic, and Hopi branches. If the Uto-Aztecan homeland falls in the Southwest rather than northern or central California, it may be associated with components of the Pinto period (Western Archaic) hunting-and-gathering cultures, which developed between 5000 and 2000 B.C. as a response to the arid conditions of the Altithermal in the region between the southern Sierra Nevada, the Mojave Desert, and northern Arizona. Such an association assumes later Uto-Aztecan expansions westward as the stock underwent diversification during the Gypsum period (2000 B.C.-A.D. 500) and the Saratoga Springs period (A.D. 500-1200) (Moratto 1984:551, 559, 567; cf. Warren 1984:410-430; vol. 11:183-193).

The roots of Uto-Aztecan culture appear to lie in the preagricultural Archaic period. Nevertheless, it has been claimed that the Proto–Uto-Aztecans were agricultural on the grounds that prototerms could be reconstructed for 'planting stick', 'mano', 'metate', 'corn' (two words), and 'planted field' (Romney 1957:38). The majority of Uto-Aztecanists dispute this claim, which was made without the publication of the linguistic evidence (Miller 1966:100-101; vol. 10:123-124; Swadesh 1964:552-553; Campbell and Langacker 1978:262-279; Fowler 1972:111, 1983). While there may be plausible etymologies for 'planting stick' and 'metate', the artifacts themselves could belong to the preagricultural period: 'planting stick' could represent a semantic shift for an implement that once meant 'digging stick', and the metate was used to grind seeds as well as corn. Moreover, the possibility of borrowing from a non–Uto-Aztecan language cannot be ruled out in the case of the crucial words for 'corn'. The word for 'beans', which was not included in the original list, is clearly a borrowing, and no data are provided in the later lists for the term 'planted field'. There is also negative evidence for the lack of agriculture in Proto–Uto-Aztecan times: the absence of any terms suggesting "village life or barter" (Swadesh 1964:552).

Prehistory of the Northern Uto-Aztecan Branches

Two of the northern branches, Numic and Takic, are familylike clusters; the remaining two branches, Hopi and Tubatulabal, are single languages. Hopi probably originated from farther west, closer to the center of gravity for the northern branches. If, as has been argued on phonological grounds, Hopi is somewhat closer to Takic than to the other branches, it might have come from even farther west, perhaps between the Virgin and Colorado rivers (Miller 1966:94; Fowler 1972:110-111). The lack of a cognate term for 'corn' in Sonoran and Hopi suggests that the Hopi may not have been farmers before they arrived in northeastern Arizona (Miller 1966:100). Tubatulabal is both geographically and linguistically intermediate between Numic and Takic and has most likely been developing in situ since its branches began to diverge (vol. 10:123; Miller 1984:13-16). By 1200 B.C. Tubatulabal can be distinguished archeologically from Numic (Moratto 1984:559). At the time that Uto-Aztecan was diversifying into branches, Takic probably occupied a more restricted area in the southern Sierra Nevada, with no access to the sea (Kroeber 1925:578-579; M.J.P. Nichols 1981:9). The archeological picture suggests that around 1000 B.C. Takic-speaking peoples expanded west to the southern California coast (Kowta 1969:50; Cressman 1977:99; Moratto 1984:560). That the branch later expanded to the south, cutting into Yuman territory, is inferable from contact relations between Yuman and the Cupan subbranch of Takic (Hinton 1991). Further support for a move by Takic speakers from a Sierran location south into the Mojave Desert comes from a list of desert plant terms uniquely reconstructible in Proto-Takic (Fowler 1983:244-245).

The northern Uto-Aztecan branch that has received the greatest amount of attention from a paleolinguistic point of view is Numic, which occupies a vast region encompassing nearly all of the Great Basin, with an extension (Comanche) in the Plains (vol. 11:98-106). Although Numic was known to consist of three subdivisions (Kroeber 1907, 1925:577), Western, Central, and Southern Numic, the linguistic makeup of these subdivisions and their implications for culture history were not well understood until Lamb (1958) pointed out that each subdivision consisted of essentially two languages, one occupying a small territory toward the southwestern corner of the family and adjoining Tubatulabal or Takic in California, and the other showing only shallow dialect variation and occupying a large segment of the Great Basin to the north and east (cf. vol. 11:99); he considered Comanche a dialect of Shoshone. Applying the center of gravity principle, Lamb (1958:98) concluded that the Numic homeland lay "somewhere around Death Valley," and that the languages had fanned outward from this point into the Great Basin. Since divergence times among the various northern Uto-Aztecan languages had already been determined (Swadesh 1954-1955), it was possible to assign approximate dates to these events: by about 2000 B.C. Numic had become distinct from the other northern Uto-Aztecan branches; by about A.D. 1 Numic was breaking up into subdivisions; and after A.D. 1000, the languages in the separate subdivisions were spreading rapidly through the Great Basin. Comanche, a

Central Numic language closely related to Shoshone, reached the central Plains in the eighteenth century after the Comanches acquired the horse and then moved south.

The picture of graded Numic linguistic diversity provided by Lamb has been upheld (Miller 1966, 1970; vol. 11:98-106; Miller, Tanner, and Foley 1971; Goss 1965, 1968), and the majority of linguists agree with Lamb's inferences about the Numic homeland and spread (C.F. Voegelin 1958:49; Swadesh 1964:550; Hopkins 1965; Miller 1966; Jacobsen 1966a, 1968, 1989a; Fowler 1972, 1983:242-244; vol. 9:174; vol. 10:113-114). Reconstructed Proto-Numic plant and animal terms reinforce these conclusions and imply a homeland habitat of diverse elevation, in or near "cold" desert zones, with access to substantial water resources (Fowler 1972). The southern Sierra Nevada and the White Mountains of Arizona both fit this description, but reconstructed terms for 'oak' and 'piñon' make the former location more likely. Other clues that the Numic arrival in the northern Great Basin was relatively recent are provided by the analyzability criterion applied to place-names and by the evidence of borrowing from Sahaptian (vol. 11:103-104). For Southern Numic, most Ute, Southern Paiute, and Chemehuevi place-names are fully analyzable, implying relatively recent occupancy of the southern Great Basin (Goss 1968:32-33). For Central Numic, place-names tend to be unanalyzable in Panamint but fully analyzable in Shoshone; the same situation obtains in Western Numic with respect to Mono and Northern Paiute; this matches the southwest-to-northeast language-and-dialect gradation found in these subdivisions. As between the two subdivisions, the Bannock dialect of Northern Paiute borrowed most of its place-names from Shoshone, implying that Bannock speakers arrived after Shoshone speakers in northern Nevada. Both Northern Paiute and Shoshone have borrowed terms for fish species found in southern Idaho from Nez Perce, which suggests a later arrival in the area by the Numic speakers (vol. 11:103). Finally, the recency of Comanche in the southern Plains is supported by its having a number of analyzable compounds as names for animals indigenous to the area (Casagrande 1954-1955:25).

The Lamb hypothesis has exerted considerable influence on Southwest archeology, although sometimes in unforeseen ways. It was used, along with glottochronological figures for the breakup of the Numic subdivisions, to argue for continuity between the prehistoric Anasazi Pueblo or Pueblo-like cultures in southern Nevada and Utah and historic Numic groups, who were said to have given up agriculture and to have reverted to a hunting-and-gathering existence (J. Gunnerson 1962). But the assumption that the Numic peoples had once been agricultural was based on dubious linguistic claims (Romney 1957), and the proposed

Numic homeland in the area defined by the Virgin River Anasazi branch in northern Arizona and southern Utah does not fit the picture of graded Numic diversity or the evidence of reconstructed plant and animal vocabulary. The in situ hypothesis is not well supported on archeological grounds either: a discontinuity in the late twelfth century between the Pueblo and Desert cultures is more amenable to a hypothesis of replacement than a hypothesis of rapid change involving a "regression" in subsistence methods. The consensus is that Southern Paiute peoples spread to the Virgin River and Sevier-Fremont region from the southwest, either replacing the Pueblo agriculturalists (Schroeder 1963; Euler 1964; Hopkins 1965:57-58; cf. Warren 1984:424-430), or occupying territory earlier abandoned by them (Goss 1965, 1968). Turning to the Western and Central subdivisions, support for the Numic spread comes from the distribution of arrow points, pottery types, rock art, and stratigraphic disconformities (Madsen 1975; G. Wright 1978; Moratto 1984: 567-570). As to the mechanism impelling Numic groups into the Great Basin, it has been suggested that their food-processing strategies gave them a selective advantage over the groups they displaced (Bettinger and Baumhoff 1982; Moratto 1984:567-570; cf. Shaul 1986; T. Jackson 1989:361).

Kiowa-Tanoan, Keresan, and Zuni

The Kiowa-Tanoan family and the isolates Keresan and Zuni comprise the core of the Pueblo cultural area in the Southwest (vol. 9:224-235). The Hopi, who belong to the area culturally, are included within the Uto-Aztecan section for linguistic reasons, while the Kiowa, who are a Plains people, are included here because of their linguistic connection with the Tanoans.

Given that the Southwest of the last two millennia is one of the most closely described and dated regions in North America, one might expect the task of correlating archeological and linguistic distributions to be a straightforward matter, but this is far from the case. On the archeological side, the wholesale abandonment of Pueblo sites in the late thirteenth century and the scattering of the inhabitants to a variety of locations (Snow 1976a:148-152; vol. 9:128-130, 147-151) have complicated the task of tying ethnographic peoples to specific archeological sites. Moreover, pottery styles have played a significant role in differentiating archeological traditions in the Southwest, and whether a single artifact category can be meaningfully correlated with language is, to say the least, untested (Ford, Schroeder, and Peckham 1972: 37; vol. 9:147). On the linguistic side and despite past speculation, Kiowa-Tanoan, Keresan, and Zuni are considered to be genetically

unrelated, and only Kiowa-Tanoan has a possible affiliation outside the area (with Uto-Aztecan). Any attempt to infer an earlier location for Keresan and Zuni, such as that they or their antecedents originated on the Pacific Coast (Rogers 1985a; Jacobsen 1989a), must be held in abeyance until convincing links are established with families elsewhere. The concentration of three unrelated and probably unaffiliated groupings within a small geographic region raises especially challenging problems for both linguistic and cultural prehistory. Despite this, or because of it, there has been no dearth of speculation regarding the linguistic identity of the prehistoric Pueblos (for reviews see Wendorf 1954:219-222; Wendorf and Reed 1955:158-165; cf. Davis 1959:81-83; Trager 1967:347-348).

Kiowa-Tanoan

Tanoan was recognized as a family over 100 years ago (Davis 1979; vol. 9:170-177), and Harrington (1910a) recognized a tripartite division into Tiwa, Tewa, and "Towa" (Jemez) branches and also proposed the link with Kiowa (Harrington 1910). Tiwa had long been known to consist of two geographically separated branches, which comprise three distinct languages: Taos and Picuris, forming Northern Tiwa, and Southern Tiwa (Sandia and Isleta dialects) (Trager 1967). The extinct and poorly documented Piro language may belong to the Tiwa branch or be a separate branch altogether (Davis 1959:76, 1979:403). Jemez is a single language spoken at Jemez Pueblo west of the Rio Grande; an extinct dialect was once also spoken along the Pecos River to the east. Tewa is the language of a cluster of Pueblo communities located on the northern Rio Grande, with a postcontact outlier in Arizona. There was a tendency initially to reserve judgment on whether Tanoan and Kiowa were related (Newman 1954), but later work has confirmed the proposal (Miller 1959; Trager and Trager 1959; K. Hale 1962, 1967; cf. Davis 1979:401; vol. 9:171). As for remoter connections, the linking of Kiowa-Tanoan with Uto-Aztecan in the Aztec-Tanoan superstock has won at least qualified acceptance, although with Zuni usually omitted. Such a link raises the possibility that ancestral Kiowa-Tanoans may have originated in southern Arizona or southeastern California (cf. Davis 1959:82).

Two contrasting models of relationship were proposed for Kiowa-Tanoan, and this tended to undercut the usefulness of linguistic findings for culture-historical inference. The first was a family-tree model, which used lexicostatistics to establish relative distances among the languages (Davis 1959). It was claimed that Tiwa and Tewa were more closely related to each other than either was to Jemez, and that Kiowa was even more divergent. Later phonological and grammatical evidence tended to bear these conclusions out, although Jemez and Kiowa were said on these grounds to be equally divergent from Tiwa and Tewa (Trager 1967). These studies announced widely divergent time-depth estimates for the family, ranging from 2000 B.C. to A.D. 1 for Proto–Kiowa-Tanoan, with similarly discrepant figures for later splits. The differences in dating present a significant problem, since the earlier figure places Proto–Kiowa-Tanoan well back in the Archaic period, while the later figure places it at the point where the agricultural traditions in the Southwest were beginning to emerge. Another review attributed a time-depth of 3,000 years (maximum) to the family as a whole, and hence dates of about 500 B.C. for the Jemez split, A.D. 200 for the Tewa split, and A.D. 1400 for the separation of Northern and Southern Tiwa (vol. 9:171). These figures imply that Kiowa split from Tanoan before the emergence of agriculture in Basketmaker II times. The second model of Kiowa-Tanoan relationship, based on unpublished lexical, grammatical, and phonological evidence, rejects Tanoan as a subgroup and postulates four coequal branches for the family, which presumably underwent nearly simultaneous separation from the Proto–Kiowa-Tanoan base (Ford, Schroeder, and Peckham 1972:34). No time-depth figure for the separation was provided. The two models are evidently irreconcilable and have different implications with regard to the movement of prehistoric Tanoans.

Because of the location of the historic Tanoans, Tanoan is usually associated with the Anasazi tradition, although a similar claim has been made for Uto-Aztecan, Keresan, and Zuni (Davis 1979:414-416; vol. 9:177; cf. Trager 1951:342-343; Coe, Snow, and Benson 1986:69, map). It has also been argued that Tanoan roots are to be found in the Mogollon tradition lying to the south (Ellis 1967). The agricultural Anasazi, whose culture spread through a large area surrounding the Four Corners after A.D. 1 and developed into one of the great Pueblo traditions until their centers were abandoned around A.D. 1300, shared a number of traits with the Mogollon people, but they also had many distinctive features (Snow 1976a:110-152; vol. 9:108-130, 131-151). One suggestion is that Tanoan-speaking Anasazi originated in the San Juan valley, expanding into the Colorado River region (Reed 1949; Ford, Schroeder, and Peckham 1972; vol. 9:233; cf. Davis 1979:414-415). Assuming that Kiowa separated from Tanoan before A.D. 1, the Kiowas are less likely to have been an Anasazi group that reverted to an Archaic lifeway after migrating to the Plains than a group that never underwent the Anasazi transformation in the first place (vol. 9:175). In fact, Kiowa historic traditions tell of origins far to the north, at the headwaters of the Missouri River in western Montana, and of a migration to the southern Plains in the eighteenth century (Mooney 1898:153, 1907a:699;

Harrington 1910; cf. K. Hale 1962:1; vol. 9:162). The original Kiowa-Tanoan split could still have occurred in the south in pre-Anasazi times, with ancestral Kiowas moving first to the north and then returning to the southern Plains in historic times (Kinkade and Powell 1976:90), although there is no archeological support for such a hypothesis, and the linguistic evidence is inconclusive.

The discontinuous distribution of Tiwa suggests two possibilities (Davis 1959:81): either or both of the branches could have ended up in their present locations as the result of a migration (Wendorf 1954:222; cf. Wendorf and Reed 1955:162); or Tiwa could have formed an early continuum that was bisected by migrating Tewa (Reed 1949; cf. Ford, Schroeder, and Peckham 1972:30). The second hypothesis assumes long Tiwa occupation in the area, although it does not accord very well with the family-tree model of Kiowa-Tanoan. On the other hand, the suggestion that some Tiwas migrated north during the so-called Classical or Pueblo IV period (A.D. 1300-1600)—perhaps around Tewas already in place—fits the divergence time of 600 years for Northern and Southern Tiwa quite closely (Wendorf 1954; Davis 1959:81). Should Piro prove to be a Tiwa language, its location south of Southern Tiwa would provide additional linguistic support for a more southerly dispersal point for the branch: Piro has a divergence time of about 1,200 years from the Tiwa languages. The Tewa and Jemez separations may relate to developments occurring at the headwaters of the San Juan River about A.D. 1 (Davis 1979:414-415). So far, linguistics has shed little light on the movements of the early Tanoans.

Keresan

Keresan consists of seven dialects that cluster in two locations, which can be considered to delimit two languages. The western dialects of Acoma and Laguna are spoken on the Rio San Jose, while the eastern dialects of Zia, Santa Ana, San Felipe, Santo Domingo, and Cochiti are spoken along the Rio Grande and the Jemez River (vol. 9:173, 225; Davis 1959:77-79, 1979:407-408). Cognate counts yield a time-depth of only 500 years for Keresan, but this must be treated as a minimum figure, due to the long history of contact among Keresan-speaking groups, the effects of which would be to slow basic vocabulary replacement. Although distant links for Keresan have been suggested variously with Aztec-Tanoan, Zuni, the now discredited Hokan-Siouan, and Macro-Siouan or some segment of it (Swadesh 1967:292; Rood 1973a; Davis 1974; Greenberg 1987:162), none of these is particularly convincing, although the possibility of a link with Uto-Aztecan is said to hold some promise (Davis 1979:411).

There is little doubt that the Keresans, like their Tanoan neighbors, participated in the Anasazi tradition, particularly its later stages (vol. 9:177), but their earlier history remains problematic. One archeologically based hypothesis traces them back into the Desert Archaic, specifically to the San Jose variant of the Oshara tradition (after 3000 B.C.), and to a movement of Mogollon peoples into the Anasazi area from the south (Ellis 1967:37; vol. 9:39, 439). Another hypothesis places Keresan origins in the north—the upper San Juan River and its tributaries—with a later expansion southeastward to the western Rio Grande drainage, either displacing or mingling with Tanoans already there (Wendorf 1954:219; Wendorf and Reed 1955; Davis 1959:83; Ford, Schroeder, and Peckham 1972). The complexity of the problem is reflected in the fact that the San Juan valley has also been claimed for the Tanoans (cf. vol. 9:177). Archeology has not been able to resolve whether Keresan or Tanoan speakers were the first to occupy the upper Rio Grande valley.

Zuni

At various times, Zuni has been linked with Keresan, Aztec-Tanoan, Penutian, and Macro-Penutian (cf. Davis 1979:410-411; vol. 9:173). Of these, only a link with California Penutian is at all promising (Newman 1964; Trager 1967:339; Hamp 1975; Shipley 1976:439). Such a link raises the possibility of a migration of ancestral Zunis from the far west (cf. Trager 1967:347; vol. 9:175), but the evidence is still too slim to draw definite conclusions. Moreover, even if there is a link it would be at such a remote time-depth as to make it difficult, if not impossible, to correlate it meaningfully with the archeological traditions of the Southwest.

Algic

The term Algic is used for a genetic grouping that includes two languages in northwestern California, Yurok and Wiyot, and the geographically far-flung Algonquian family, which consists of three dozen or more languages (Teeter 1964a, 1965, 1967:4; vol. 8:87). There is some evidence that Yurok and Wiyot may form a subgrouping in opposition to Algonquian (Berman 1982, 1984, 1990a), but a more conservative view is that the California languages comprise independent branches coequal with the entire Algonquian family (Whistler 1979:13; Proulx 1984:166). The first detailed evidence supporting Algic was presented early in the twentieth century (Sapir 1913a). Despite some initial skepticism (Michelson 1914, 1915; cf. Sapir 1915, 1923a), the proposal was generally well received (Dixon and Kroeber 1913, 1919; Kroeber 1917a), although it only began to attract close attention in the

1950s (Haas 1958, 1960:977-980, 1966, 1969:66-70, 1976:27). Later work demonstrated the validity of the grouping (Teeter 1964, 1964a, 1964b, 1974; Goddard 1975, 1986; Proulx 1984a, 1985; Berman 1982, 1984, 1990; Goddard 1990c:108-109; Campbell and Mithun 1979a:40).

It has been said that the linking of Algonquian with two affiliates in California raises far-reaching questions for the prehistory of North America (Sapir 1913a:646; Goddard 1975:249), but a fully satisfactory explanation of the distribution of Algic has yet to be offered (cf. Kinkade and Powell 1976:88). The tendency has been to integrate the prehistory of Wiyot and Yurok with developments in northern California, and to treat Algonquian prehistory as a separate problem. In a purely speculative vein, if Wiyot and Yurok comprise branches coequal with Algonquian, the sheer number of Algonquian languages known in historic times carries no more weight in placing the Algic homeland than the separate California languages. The homeland could have been in the far west, with early Proto-Algonquians moving east and then diversifying and spreading through much of central and eastern North America (cf. Proulx 1982:191; Fiedel 1987:7, 1991:26; Jacobsen 1989a:5-6; Berman 1982:419). Or, the homeland could have been in the east—perhaps in the Great Lakes region—with the Wiyot and Yurok migrating westward at an early time and losing their "eastern Algonkin culture" along the way (Kroeber 1923:132). But some intermediate location—present-day southern Alberta or northern Idaho—would be just as feasible, with the Wiyot and Yurok moving southwestward to the Pacific Coast, and the pre–Proto-Algonquians moving to the east, where they underwent diversification and spreads (Whistler 1979:16-17, 24; Denny 1991a; Fredrickson 1984:483; Moratto 1984:543). The distribution of the Algic branches does not in itself provide a clear choice among these alternatives. The reconstruction of Proto-Algic cultural vocabulary might shed light on the question, but a lack of convincing cognates among the three branches for cultural and natural history items stymies this approach (Whistler 1979:20; Goddard 1986:196-197).

Distant Links

Two hypotheses of distant relationship involving Algic have been suggested; these imply rather different views of prehistory. The first proposal is Sapir's (1921b, 1949:172) vast "Algonkin-Wakashan" phylum, which linked Beothuk with Algic, and both of these with Kootenai and Mosan. Although Algonkin-Wakashan would certainly have opened up interesting perspectives on North American prehistory if it had been convincingly demonstrated, the only links in this vast chain to survive subsequent scrutiny were those binding the

Algic languages together. In fact, Algonkin-Wakashan had very little impact on North American archeology (Foster 1988), and it served the ends of culture history only to the extent of being compared with Sapir's other phylum groupings in a now outdated hypothetical sequence of New World migrations (C.F. Voegelin 1945, 1958:56; Cressman et al. 1960:74; cf. Suttles 1987a:277).

The second hypothesis, "Macro-Algonquian," involved a radically different alignment for Algic. Instead of links with the Pacific Northwest, it tied Algic to the "Gulf" languages of the Southeast and Texas and Tonkawa (Haas 1958a, 1959, 1960: 983-987). The Gulf grouping, which itself is controversial, included Muskogean, Natchez, Tunica, Chitimacha, and Atakapan. Macro-Algonquian was publicized on the C.F. Voegelin and F.M. Voegelin (1966) wall map of aboriginal language phyla (fig. 2) and has had at least some impact on archeology. One suggestion is that the carriers of the Archaic cultures of eastern North America were speakers of Proto–Macro-Algonquian (Willey 1958); those who moved into the Northeast became speakers of Algonquian proper (Tuck 1975, 1977; Snow 1976a:34, 1980:28; Lathrap and Troike 1988). Another suggestion is that the carriers of the much earlier Fluted Point tradition were Proto–Macro-Algonquian speakers (Carlson 1983:86). The first proposal is more appealing in terms of geographic distribution and the time-depth attributed to Macro-Algonquian, which was around 5,000 years (Haas 1969:62, table XII). But both proposals are flawed to the extent that Macro-Algonquian remains unproven; most linguists in fact reject Macro-Algonquian (Goddard 1979:106; Campbell and Mithun 1979a:38; Jacobsen 1989a:13).

Algic and California Prehistory

Wiyot is hypothesized to have arrived in northwestern California around A.D. 900, and Yurok around A.D. 1100 (Whistler 1977:168-170, 1979:23-24). Since the time-depth of Algic must exceed the three-millennium maximum estimated for Proto-Algonquian, northwestern California is ruled out as a homeland for Proto-Algic. One suggestion is that the ancestors of the Wiyot and Yurok originated in the lower Columbia River valley, moving up the Willamette, across the Umpqua and Rogue river drainages, and down the Klamath River to the coast (Whistler 1977:170; cf. Kroeber 1923:132).

The Wiyot and Yurok incursions have been correlated archeologically with the emergence of the Gunther Pattern, a riverine and coastal adaptation that developed in northwestern California around A.D. 1000 (Whistler 1979:23; Fredrickson 1984:484-491, 525; Moratto 1984:564-566). If the correlation stands, then

Algic peoples brought the bow and arrow, a new form of harpoon, gravepit burning, and a number of other material traits to northern California, influencing prior inhabitants like the Karok, as well as the later-arriving Athapaskans, with their specialized technology (Whistler 1977:170). Many strikingly similar artifact types are found north of California along the middle Columbia River (Moratto 1984:565, table 11.3), and this raises the possibility of a homeland in this area for Wiyot and Yurok, with perhaps separate migrations south by way of the Deschutes River in central Oregon (Whistler 1979:24). A middle Columbia River homeland for Wiyot and Yurok is most consistent with the idea of an intermediate homeland location for Proto-Algic.

Algonquian

Speculation as to the homeland and culture history of Algonquian proper has been closely tied to the classification of the family: as classifications have changed, so have ideas about Algonquian prehistory. The earliest classification (Michelson 1912) provided a breakdown into four branches, the first three being the Plains languages (Blackfoot, Cheyenne, and Arapaho), and the fourth being a large subgrouping, "Eastern-Central," which included all the remaining languages. With regard to linguistic prehistory, the family's center of gravity was drawn toward the west, because the Plains languages were considered to be more divergent among themselves and in relation to Eastern-Central than the members of that group were among themselves (Sapir 1916, 1949:453-456). Indeed, Algonquian was one of three type cases used by Sapir to illustrate the point that a family's linguistic center should be carefully distinguished from its geographic center, which for Algonquian lay in the Great Lakes area. It seemed to follow from the divergent position of the Plains languages that ancestral Algonquians had made a "general movement" from west to east.

The Michelson classification was rendered obsolete by the work of Leonard Bloomfield (1925, 1946), which provided solid underpinnings to comparative Algonquian. Bloomfield's reconstructions of the Proto-Algonquian sound system and morphology were based on only the four best-documented languages: Fox, Plains Cree, Menominee, and Southern Ojibwa. But as comparative Algonquian was subsequently enriched by work on the Plains and Eastern languages, only minor emendations to Bloomfield's reconstructions were found to be necessary: all the languages (with the possible exception of Blackfoot) were shown to fit the basic scheme quite comfortably, despite some strikingly aberrant developments in the phonologies of the Plains languages (Siebert 1941; Voegelin 1944:57; C.F. Voegelin and E.W. Voegelin 1946:189-192; Goddard 1967, 1967a, 1974a, 1979; Pentland 1979a:

41). The view that Bloomfield's reconstructions applied strictly to a subset of the languages and should properly be labeled "Proto–Central Algonquian" (Hockett 1948:130, 1957, 1964) was abandoned (Hockett 1966:59; Teeter 1967:2; Goddard 1979:95). The picture that emerged was thus not of Proto-Algonquian breaking up into an "Eastern-Central" group on the one hand, and the branches ancestral to the Plains languages on the other, but of the protolanguage diversifying into 11 independent languages that developed into the dialect groups known under the names Blackfoot, Cheyenne, Arapahoan, Cree-Montagnais, Ojibwa, Potawatomi, Menominee, Sauk-Fox-Kickapoo, Miami-Illinois, Shawnee, and an ancestor of the Eastern languages (Proto–Eastern Algonquian), the last eventually spreading from the Gaspé Peninsula south along the Eastern seaboard as far as North Carolina (vol. 15:586; Goddard 1979:94-95). An important consequence of the discovery that the Plains languages were only superficially divergent from the remaining stock was that the family's center of gravity had to be shifted from the west to the Great Lakes region.

Other than the likelihood that Ojibwa and Potawatomi may have descended from an intermediate ancestor (vol. 15:585-586), the only clear instance of a subgrouping within Algonquian is that involving the Eastern languages (Goddard 1965, 1967, 1967a, 1974a, 1979:96-102; vol. 15:70-77). The remaining nine or 10 branches are seen as coequal. Although the Proto–Eastern Algonquian hypothesis has been criticized (Pentland 1979a; Proulx 1980:12-14, 1980a, 1984a), the effect of the debate in the long run has been to place it on even firmer ground (Goddard 1979c, 1980, 1981a, 1983; cf. Rhodes 1990:1). A proposal that Menominee forms a genetic subgrouping with Eastern Algonquian (Proulx 1980), on the other hand, has not stood up (Goddard 1981a), although the possibility of recontacts between Menominee and some of the Eastern languages following the initial breakup of Proto- Algonquian cannot be ruled out (Proulx 1984a). Moreover, some of the non-Eastern languages may form intermediate subgroups (Rhodes 1990) or constitute dialect areas reflecting chronological layers (Goddard 1994).

The idea of a Great Lakes homeland, which is implied by the present Algonquian family tree, receives additional support from a study of reconstructed Proto-Algonquian plant and animal terms (Siebert 1967; cf. Walker 1975). From a total of 53 terms for which it is possible to determine Proto-Algonquian etyma, some 20 refer to species whose ranges overlap in southern Ontario between Georgian Bay, Lake Ontario, and the middle Ottawa River (Siebert 1967:35, map 10); the Proto-Algonquian homeland is presumed to fall within this mixed forest zone at around 1200 B.C. An expansion outward from the focal area about 900

B.C. is detectable from certain semantic shifts: thus, as speakers moved east and south beyond the range of the caribou, they transferred the Proto-Algonquian term for 'caribou' to the deer, while in the west, ancestral Arapahoan speakers transferred the same Proto-Algonquian term to the bighorn sheep when they moved onto the Plains.

The reconstruction of natural history terms provides a strong basis for inferring the location of a linguistic homeland. The main difficulty in the present case is that the area defined as the Proto-Algonquian homeland overlaps to a considerable extent the part of southern Ontario that archeologists have assigned to the development of Iroquoians (J. Wright 1966, 1972, 1984). This difficulty can largely be overcome if the number of prototerms used for setting the boundaries of the Algonquian homeland is limited to just those denoting species with the most sharply defined ranges, a total of five tree and six animal terms (Snow 1976, 1977:108). This approach yields a homeland of increased size—defined most succinctly by the overlapping distributions of the beech and tamarack—including the Great Lakes lowlands east of Lake Superior, the Saint Lawrence valley, New England, and Maritime Canada. Since it is likely that this region was not continuously occupied but rather served as a vast hunting and trapping zone for nomadic bands, the presence of Iroquoians in southern Ontario through much of the period of Algonquian development does not prove fatal to the Great Lakes homeland hypothesis.

Estimates of Proto-Algonquian time-depth range from 1000 B.C. to A.D. 500, based on glottochronology and analogies to families of comparable diversity (Kroeber 1959:260; Haas 1966:103, 1969:66; Siebert 1967:35; Voorhis 1978). Allowing for 2,000 years of internal divergence within Eastern Algonquian (vol. 15:70), a figure of 1000-500 B.C. would be a reasonable estimate for the age of Proto-Algonquian (vol. 15:586). Attempts to establish archeological correlates for Proto-Algonquian at the appropriate time-depth and with the appropriate geographic distribution have met with only limited success. Two problems impede progress in this area. First, there is the longstanding difficulty of sorting out which of the prehistoric cultures in the Northeast properly belong to the Algonquian line of development and which to the Iroquoian line. Some have argued, for instance, that the carriers of the Point Peninsula culture of the Woodland period were Proto-Algonquians (Walker 1975; Fiedel 1987, 1990, 1991); a variant of this hypothesis aligns the Laurentian Archaic precursors of Point Peninsula with Proto-Algonquian (Seeber 1982). But Point Peninsula and presumably its immediate antecedents are more often included in the Iroquoian line of development.

A second problem involves the dating of Proto-Algonquian and the archeological record. As long as a relationship was thought to exist between Algonquian and the "Gulf" languages of the Southeast, a perspective of sufficient age was opened up to accommodate Algonquian within the Late Archaic period (4000-1500 B.C.) in eastern North America (Snow 1976b:34-36). The persistence of the Archaic lifeway over thousands of years in the Northeast, and its culmination for parts of the eastern Subarctic in the ethnographic Algonquian cultures, have fostered the idea of long in situ development of Algonquian-speaking peoples in the Northeast, as opposed to the previous theories of a late Woodland migration (Snow 1977:109, 1980; vol. 15:34, 60; Tuck 1975, 1977; J. Wright 1972; cf. sequence of maps in J. Wright 1987, 1987a, 1987b). The dating of Proto-Algonquian at around three millennia nevertheless again raises the possibility of migration, unless, as does not seem very likely, the family spread through its historic territory by some process of language shift (Denny 1989, 1991, 1991a). If a movement of people was involved in the spread of Algonquian around 3,000 years ago, there should be a clearer indication of this movement in the archeological record than has been detected.

The situation involving Eastern Algonquian is nearly as equivocal. Some archeologists see the split between the Eastern languages and the remaining members of the family as resulting from an intrusion of Iroquoian speakers originating somewhere in the Southeast and driving a "wedge" across the Algonquian speech area (Snow 1977:109-110, 1980:27, 258, 1984, 1992; Seeber 1982:141; Fiedel 1987:4, 1990:223, 1991:20; Lathrap and Troike 1988:15). The presence of Iroquoian languages in the Southeast is often cited in support of this view. On the Algonquian side, it has been argued by a critic of the Eastern Algonquian concept that even if such an entity once existed, it was soon submerged during an extended period of trade and recontact that allowed for the diffusion of many features; and it was this reconstituted Algonquian speech area that was split apart by Iroquoians around A.D. 500 (Proulx 1980, 1982). Against the Iroquoian "wedge" hypothesis, it should be noted, first, that many Northeastern archeologists favor long in situ development of the Iroquois in New York State and adjacent southern Ontario, extending to at least 1000 B.C. and perhaps well into the Laurentian Archaic period (J. Wright 1972, 1984). Iroquoian linguists also tend to favor an Iroquoian homeland in the New York–Pennsylvania– northeastern Ohio area over one in the southern Appalachians, where the Southern Iroquoian branch (Cherokee) is found (vol. 15:336). Third, and perhaps most telling, Eastern Algonquian languages show a "distinctness and internal cohesion" as a group that makes it unlikely that their geographic separation from the remaining languages was the result of an Iroquoian intrusion; more likely, speakers of Proto–Eastern Algonquian moved east and south around already entrenched Northern Iroquoians, taking up various positions in the Maritimes and along the Eastern seaboard over time (vol. 15:586-587). This view is supported by glottochronological figures and at least one interpretation of New England and Maritimes archeology (Luckenbach, Clark, and Levy 1987; cf. Fiedel 1990).

Proto-Algonquian Kinship and Society

Reconstruction of Proto-Algonquian kinship terms shows that the Proto-Algonquians equated certain categories of kin, in particular: father's sister with mother-in-law, brother's son (woman speaking) or sister's son (man speaking) with son-in-law, and cross-cousin with brother- or sister-in-law. A preference for cross-cousin marriage has been inferred from these equations (Hockett 1964). Other equations allow for further refinements: the Proto-Algonquians probably preferred matrilateral cross-cousin marriage (unions between a man and a woman classed as the man's mother's brother's daughter), and patrilocal residence. Although it is generally agreed that the Proto-Algonquians practiced cross-cousin marriage, the narrowing of the rule to matrilaterality has been rejected by some in favor of a bilateral rule (Hickerson 1967; Aberle 1974:73-74; Walker 1975; Wheeler 1982). It has also been argued from nonlexical approaches to the reconstruction of proto-kinship systems that the Proto-Algonquians had a bilateral rule of descent, rather than matrilineality or patrilineality (Aberle 1974:73-74, 1984:133-134).

Siouan-Catawba

The history of Siouan-Catawba comparative studies dates to the first half of the nineteenth century (reviewed by Swanton 1936; Crawford 1975a:49-59; Chafe 1976; Rood 1979; Hollow and Parks 1980). The earliest classification (Gallatin 1836, 1848) recognized only a block of western Siouan languages and Winnebago. By the late nineteenth and early twentieth centuries this arrangement had been fleshed out by the addition of several geographically peripheral languages: Tutelo (or "Virginia Siouan") in 1870 (H. Hale 1883b; cf. Swanton 1936:371, 381; Sapir 1913; Frachtenberg 1913; Sturtevant 1958; Gruber 1967:15), Catawba (or "Carolina Siouan") in the early 1880s (Swanton 1936:371, 373), and Biloxi and Ofo in 1886 and 1908 respectively (Dorsey 1894a; Dorsey and Swanton 1912; Swanton 1923:34, 1936:373, 381; Siebert 1945, 1945a; Haas 1968, 1969b).

These developments led to the first modern classification of the Siouan-Catawba family (Swanton 1923).

In this scheme, Catawba was placed within Siouan in a subgroup of its own, with Woccon "left out of consideration" (cf. Siebert 1945:100-101): it was said to be no more closely related to Tutelo, its immediate neighbor in the east, than to the rest of the family. For its part, Tutelo was placed in a subgroup with geographically distant Dakota and Hidatsa, along with the southern outliers Biloxi and Ofo. It was claimed that Biloxi and Ofo were more closely related to each other and to Dakota than to Quapaw, their nearest Siouan neighbor to the north. Chiwere and Dhegiha formed separate subgroups, and Mandan was left unplaced. The importance of Swanton's classification lay in demonstrating the complexity of the relationships among the Siouan-Catawba languages and the way the relationships cut across geographic lines. Swanton drew on the new classification and ethnohistorical research to formulate the hypothesis that the Siouan-Catawba peoples had originated in the Ohio valley (Swanton 1936). The Tutelos went to Virginia from there, perhaps by way of the Kanawha River, while the Catawbas had presumably arrived in the Carolinas at a much earlier time. These inferences mark the beginning of a debate over the location of the Siouan-Catawba homeland, which remains unresolved.

Later work confirmed the closeness of Biloxi and Ofo in the south (C.F. Voegelin 1939) and Crow and Hidatsa in the west (C.F. Voegelin 1941a, 1941b), but a review of the evidence underlying Swanton's classification led C.F. Voegelin (1941a, 1941b) to propose a considerably revised four-branch scheme: Eastern, consisting of Catawba alone; Ohio Valley, consisting of Ofo, Biloxi, and Tutelo; Missouri River, consisting of Hidatsa and Crow; and Mississippi Valley, the most far-flung branch, consisting of Chiwere and Winnebago, with Dhegiha, Mandan, and Dakota included provisionally. The treatment of Catawba as the most divergent Siouan language followed Swanton, and subsequent work supported this finding (Siebert 1945, 1945a; Sturtevant 1958; Carter 1980). On the other hand, the placing of Crow and Hidatsa in a branch separate from Dakota was new, as was the grouping of Ofo, Biloxi, and Tutelo in the Ohio Valley branch. But Voegelin subsumed Chiwere and Dhegiha, which were once seen as separate branches, under the single Mississippi Valley subgrouping. He embraced Swanton's idea of an Ohio valley homeland from which the Tutelo had migrated east; to this he added the inference that the Ofo and Biloxi had migrated from the Ohio valley to the south (C.F. Voegelin 1941b:247). With regard to Missouri River Siouan, he suggested that Crow speakers had probably split off from the Proto–Crow-Hidatsa speech community on the upper Missouri River and moved west, rather than the Hidatsa going east from a western location (C.F. Voegelin 1941b:249; cf. C.F. Voegelin 1958:48-49).

The Voegelin classification has become the standard for comparative work in Siouan-Catawba (Haas 1968; Chafe 1976:41; cf. A. Taylor 1976:288; Carter 1980:180; Hollow and Parks 1980:76; Rankin 1985). Among other things, the branch designations Missouri River, Mississippi Valley, and Ohio Valley (sometimes called Southeastern) are still in common use, although the precise makeup of the branches has changed over time. An assessment of the Voegelin classification (Rood 1979:243-250) underscores the tenuousness of the evidence supporting the Ohio Valley and Mississippi Valley subgroups; indeed, only Missouri River is said to be adequately supported. Other approaches to Siouan-Catawba classification, which conclude that the family consists of six or seven coequal branches (Wolff 1950-1951; Matthews 1958), have attracted few adherents (cf. Rood 1979:250-251) and have had virtually no impact on interpretations of Siouan-Catawba prehistory.

Glottochronology and Lexicostatistics

Siouan-Catawba has been the subject of a number of glottochronological studies (Swadesh 1967a; Voorhis 1978; Matthews 1979; Hollow and Parks 1980; Grimm 1985, 1987; cf. Springer and Witkowski 1983). These have yielded a disconcertingly wide range of time-depth estimates for all but the most recent splits in the family. Thus, the Siouan-Catawban split could fall anywhere between 6000 and 1100 B.C.; the breakup of Proto-Siouan has been dated to between 1700 and 100 B.C.; and the breakup of Mississippi Valley Siouan has been dated to between 400 B.C. and A.D. 900. The spread in the figures results from using sources of varying quality, from experimenting with different retention rates, from disagreements among researchers about cognacy, and from various other factors (cf. Grimm 1987). The problems are exemplified in a series of studies limited to the split between just Crow and Hidatsa, which have yielded figures ranging from A.D. 1 to 1400 (Pierce 1954; Headley 1971; Matthews 1979; Hollow and Parks 1980; Grimm 1985, 1987). The variability in the time-depth estimates must obviously be taken into account in any attempt to correlate Siouan-Catawba linguistic prehistory with archeology.

As something of a corrective to the problem of variable glottochronological figures, impressionistic time-depths based on analogies to Indo-European family relationships with established chronologies have been offered (Rankin 1988:647, 1992a). These suggest that the Siouan-Catawban split was on the order of 2000 B.C., while the breakup of Siouan itself was about 1000 B.C., and the Mississippi Valley separation was between 500 B.C. and A.D. 1000. A novel, if untested, approach to the problem of Siouan chronology assigns dates to Siouan linguistic prehistory according to when different cultigens reached the Mississippi valley and adjacent areas (Rankin 1992a). On the basis of there being at least one cucurbit term in Proto-Siouan, the protolanguage probably did not greatly antedate 1000 B.C., when gourds appeared in the archeological record. On the other hand, the absence of prototerms for corn implies that Proto-Siouan had ceased to be a single speech community before A.D. 200, when corn appeared in the area. On the Mississippi Valley level, Dhegiha and Chiwere-Winnebago must have separated from each other, and presumably from Dakotan, before A.D. 600-1000 when corn had risen in importance in the region, since they developed separate terminologies for this cultigen. The figures obtained by this method agree substantially with those based on the Indo-European analogies and fall in the middle range of the glottochronological estimates. A reasonable estimate for the time-depth of Proto-Siouan would be 1000 B.C.

Finally, it should be noted that two independently conducted lexicostatistical classifications of Siouan (Headley 1971; Grimm 1985) arrived at similar subgrouping schemes, bearing out the Voegelin classification in the main. However, both placed Mandan with Crow and Hidatsa rather than with Mississippi Valley or in a separate branch, as is more often done (cf. Wolff 1950-1951; Matthews 1958, 1970, 1979; Chafe 1976:42; Rood 1978; Robert Rankin, personal communication 1993).

Proposed Affiliations of Siouan-Catawba

The "Hokan-Siouan" phylum in Sapir's (1921b, 1929) continental classification raised a number of possibilities of remote relationships for Siouan-Catawba. Of these, only a few of the lower-level linkages have survived subsequent scrutiny. The superstock itself has been universally abandoned and has never had more than a minor impact on speculation about North American prehistory. Thus, although the possibility of a link between Siouan-Catawba and the Yukian family of California (Elmendorf 1963, 1964) raises interesting questions about the prehistory of North America similar to those raised by the Algic grouping, it would be fruitless to pursue these until the relationship has been placed on a surer footing. The same can be said of the "Eastern group" in Sapir's scheme, which linked Siouan-Catawba and the "Gulf" languages of the Southeast (Haas 1951, 1952).

Within the "Eastern group," the proposed close link between Siouan-Catawba and the Yuchi language of eastern Tennessee has turned out to be quite promising. While some of the evidence first brought forward to support what was called Siouan-Yuchi (Haas 1951, 1964, 1969:90-92; Elmendorf 1964) could involve borrowing as a source of the resemblances (Crawford

1979:340-343), later work gave the proposal a more solid basis (Rudes 1974, 1987; Carter 1980), although dissenting voices are still heard (Ballard 1978; Campbell and Mithun 1979a:41; Hollow and Parks 1980:81; Rankin 1988:645). In addition, Sapir's scheme suggests a close relationship between Iroquoian and Caddoan, and this has also received support (Rudes 1974, 1982; Chafe 1976:47-52, 1977a; Wallace Chafe, personal communication 1992).

The possibility that Siouan-Catawba, Iroquoian, and Caddoan are all distantly related is implicit in Sapir's classification, and a substantial amount of evidence has accumulated in favor of this so-called Macro-Siouan hypothesis (Allen 1931; Chafe 1964, 1976, 1977; Rudes 1974, 1982; Carter 1980:180-182; cf. C.F. Voegelin and F.M. Voegelin 1965:129, 1966). Although a case has been made for Macro-Siouan, it is less compelling than, say, the case for Algic (cf. Ballard 1978; Campbell and Mithun 1979a:41; Hollow and Parks 1980:80-81; Rankin 1981:174-176, 1988:645, personal communication 1993). The discussion of Macro-Siouan relationships has evolved from a simple three-branch model to a model that sets Siouan-Yuchi against Iroquoian-Caddoan.

On a purely speculative level, the deepest splits within the proposed Siouan-Yuchi subgrouping lie in the east: Yuchi in eastern Tennessee and Catawba in the Carolinas. According to the center of gravity principle, this draws the Siouan-Catawba homeland toward the Southeast. Turning to the other main proposed grouping, Iroquoian-Caddoan, the deepest split within Caddoan occurs in eastern Texas between Wichita and Caddo, and the deepest split within Iroquoian lies between Cherokee in the southern Appalachians and Tuscarora in the Coastal Plain of North Carolina and Virginia. The Southeast thus also emerges as a possible location for the Proto–Iroquoian-Caddoan homeland, although a separation of more than 600 miles between the families prevents specifying the location more narrowly. If, however, the aligning of Yuchi with Siouan-Catawba, on the one hand, and Iroquoian with Caddoan, on the other, is valid, then the deepest splits within Macro-Siouan as a whole would occur in the vicinity of the old Eastern Cherokee homeland along the Tennessee–North Carolina border, for it is there that Yuchi, Cherokee, and Catawba are neighbors. This area, perhaps extending somewhat to the west, would constitute a plausible Proto–Macro-Siouan homeland, with later spreads to the southwest (Proto-Caddoan), the west (Proto-Siouan) and the northeast (Proto-Iroquoian) (Blair Rudes, personal communication 1987).

Linguistics and Archeology

If Macro-Siouan and its divisions are eventually established at the same level of confidence as Algic,

Proto–Macro-Siouan would represent a speech community that existed at least as early as 2000 B.C. and more likely by 4000 B.C. This places the protospeech community well within the Archaic period in the Eastern Woodlands, but beyond that nothing can be said about possible archeological correlates for this grouping, or even the putative Siouan-Yuchi grouping. Hypotheses of Siouan-Catawba origins have been confined to Proto–Siouan-Catawba, or the proposed subbranches of the family. Of course the homeland postulated for Proto–Macro-Siouan need not coincide with the homeland postulated for Proto–Siouan-Catawba, since two entirely different stages of development are involved. While a Macro-Siouan homeland in the Southeast is compatible with the linguistic facts, the distribution of the Siouan-Catawba languages neither supports nor invalidates such a location. At the level of the deepest split within Siouan-Catawba that—between Catawban (Catawba-Woccon) and the remaining languages—neither a more easterly nor a more westerly homeland can be ruled out. The sheer number of Siouan languages located along the western watershed of the Mississippi River does not tip the scales toward a western location, because at the time of the earliest split the ancestor of these languages would have constituted a relatively undifferentiated dialect cluster, and this would have been on a par linguistically with a similarly undifferentiated Proto-Catawban.

Swanton (1923, 1936) and C.F. Voegelin (1941b) both favored an Ohio valley homeland for the Siouan-Catawba peoples. From there, expansions were postulated first to South Carolina (Catawban), then to Virginia (Tutelo), and much later to Mississippi and Alabama (Ofo and Biloxi). The remainder of the family presumably spread west and ultimately northwest, a process that continued into the historic period with the cultural transformations brought on by acquiring the horse. The Ohio valley homeland hypothesis came under attack on both ethnohistorical and archeological grounds (Griffin 1942, 1943), and a debate ensued that has not been resolved (cf. Griffin 1960:812-816; Headley 1971:29-31, 72-75). One reason for doubting the Ohio valley location is that the middle Ohio valley was dominated during much of the past millennium by the Mississippian-influenced Fort Ancient culture, which is usually associated with Algonquian-speaking groups, particularly the Shawnee (Snow 1976a:78; Springer and Witkowski 1983:79).

The main alternative to the Ohio valley hypothesis is a proposal that places the Siouan-Catawba homeland in the Mississippi valley. Little attempt has been made to find archeological correlates in this area for the earliest phase of Siouan-Catawba development involving the separation of Catawban. Nor have specific correlates been suggested for Proto-Siouan. Time-depth estimates for the breakup of Proto-Siouan range

between 1700 and 100 B.C. placing this event at the level of the Adena-Hopewell cultures or earlier, although archeological speculation about Siouan origins has not been extended to this level. Rather, attempts to link archeological complexes with Siouan linguistic prehistory begin with the more northerly variants of the Mississippi or "Temple Mound" tradition (Griffin 1964:248-249), which followed the Adena-Hopewell after about A.D. 1200.

The first suggestion made along these lines was that the carriers of the Oneota culture, a variant of the Middle Mississippian found in Wisconsin, southeastern Minnesota, and Iowa, may have been the ancestors of the Chiwere-Winnebago (Griffin 1937). This correlation was cited in C.F. Voegelin's (1941b:249) classification and became the subject of commentary and refinement (Griffin 1960, 1964:251; Wedel 1964:211-212; Headley 1971:70-72; Jennings 1974:273-275; Snow 1976a:78; Rankin 1988:644). Oneota was originally seen as being later than, and deriving from, the Middle Mississippian tradition, but archeologists now see the two traditions as developing in situ from Woodland antecedents (Gibbon 1983; Brown 1983; Springer and Witkowski 1983). This view presupposes that much of the middle and upper Mississippi valley was occupied by Siouan speakers and that Mississippi Valley Siouan had divided into its major branches by the time the Oneota and Middle Mississippian traditions had emerged. In general, Chiwere-Winnebago is thought to equate with Oneota, Dhegiha with the Middle Mississippian, and Dakotan with non-Mississippian Woodland manifestations to the northwest (Brown 1983:109).

One lingering problem concerns the southern extent of Mississippi Valley Siouan. Archeologically, Quapaw appears to belong with Biloxi and Ofo (Griffin 1960:813), but linguistically it clearly belongs in the Dhegiha subgroup, not to the Ohio Valley subgroup (Rankin 1985, 1988). Mississippi Valley Siouan thus probably extended nearly to the Arkansas-Louisiana border. Except for the Ofo and Biloxi enclaves, which could represent late migrations, Siouan is unlikely to have spread south of this point: the Caddoan Mississippian tradition to the southwest is associated with Caddoan, while the Plaquemine and South Appalachian Mississippian traditions to the south and southeast are associated with Muskogean and other Southeast language families (cf. Snow 1976a:74-75; Coe, Snow, and Benson 1986:54, map).

Proto-Siouan Kinship and Society

The variety of kinship systems and rules of descent found among historic Siouan peoples presents a challenge to those attempting to reconstruct Proto-Siouan kinship and society. One approach has been to compare whole systems and to determine according to some more or less explicit principle which type is earlier. Lesser (1930) noted that three different systems were found in the family and that these correlated with different rules of descent and marriage: the Dakota type with bilaterality and an absence of sibs and exogamy, the Omaha type with patrilineality and exogamous moieties, and the Crow type with matrilineality and exogamous clan groups. On the assumption that simpler systems evolve into more complex systems over time, Lesser concluded that the Dakota type was historically prior to the Crow and Omaha types and that the Proto-Siouans thus lacked unilineal descent and clan-based exogamy. Another approach bases inferences about protosystems on lexical reconstruction, by applying the comparative method to kinship terms. The advantages of this approach over the nonlinguistic approach taken by Lesser and others have been extensively discussed with regard especially to Proto-Athapaskan kinship and society. For Siouan, the lexical reconstruction method yielded an Omaha-type system for the protolanguage (Matthews 1959), and from this it was concluded that the Proto-Siouan people had a patrilineal rule of descent. Still a third possibility, that Proto-Siouan had a matrilineal descent rule, was later suggested in a different kind of nonlinguistic approach, in which the prototype was assumed to be the system or rule that involved the least number of intermediate developmental stages to produce the historically attested types (Aberle 1974, 1984). The only descent rule not considered likely in any of these approaches was double descent.

A review of the Proto-Siouan kinship question cautiously sides with Lesser that the system was probably bilateral and lacked an explicit marriage "prescription" (Barnes 1984:232). There is no necessary or causal relationship between Crow and Omaha systems and particular rules of descent (Lounsbury 1964), although statistically Omaha systems tend to correlate with patrilineality and Crow systems with matrilineality (Murdock 1949:239-241, 245-246; Aberle 1974:72). In sum, despite fairly extensive attempts to reconstruct Proto-Siouan kinship and society, the results remain inconclusive.

Caddoan

Although the languages recognized as making up the Caddoan family were documented during the first half of the nineteenth century, it was only in the 1880s that Caddo, the most divergent language, was decisively linked with Pawnee-Arikara, Kitsai, and Wichita (A. Taylor 1963). The first modern classification divided the family into two branches consisting of Caddo, on the one hand, and the remaining languages, making up

what is now called Northern Caddoan, on the other (Lesser and Weltfish 1932). The poorly documented Adai language has sometimes been classified as Caddoan (cf. A. Taylor 1963:57). Dialect variation was described for several of the languages: in the case of Pawnee, it was claimed that the South Band and Skiri dialects were mutually intelligible, whereas Arikara was sufficiently divergent to be classed as a separate language. The Lesser-Weltfish classification has been largely upheld (A. Taylor 1963a; Chafe 1979; cf. Chafe 1976:11, 16; Hollow and Parks 1980:75-77).

A glottochronological time-depth of 1500-1300 B.C. has been suggested for Caddoan (Swadesh 1958:673, 1967a:90). Time-depth estimates for the Northern Caddoan branch fall within the range of A.D. 1-100, although the originators of the study caution that these may be too early (Hollow and Parks 1980:80, table 4). Within Northern Caddoan, Wichita is the most divergent language. Glottochronological figures and other information imply that Kitsai is closer to Pawnee than to Wichita (Hollow and Parks 1980:77; cf. Lesser and Weltfish 1932:1). Following the separation of Caddo from Northern Caddoan, presumably Wichita was the next language to separate and then Kitsai, with Pawnee undergoing a late diversification.

Linguistic Prehistory

At the time of White contact, Caddoan groups were distributed discontinuously through portions of the western watershed of the Mississippi River from Louisiana to South Dakota (Chafe 1976:11-16, 1979:213). Caddo bands occupied the Red River and adjoining areas in western Louisiana, southwestern Arkansas, and eastern Texas. During the early contact period, the Wichita were located in central Kansas; they later moved south as far as the Brazos River in Texas under pressure from the Osage and other groups (Mooney 1910). By the nineteenth century, they were the next group to the west of the Caddo in the middle Red River drainage. Whites first contacted Kitsai speakers in northeastern Texas, but the Kitsai may have been located earlier in Oklahoma. The Pawnee were located in eastern Nebraska. Farthest to the north were the Arikara, cut off from the South Band and Skiri groups by Siouans. During the historic period they moved up the Missouri River from South Dakota to North Dakota.

The Caddoan languages formed an intergrading language-and-dialect complex, with the deepest splits in the south and the shallowest splits in the north, a situation that implies a southern homeland with a later northward spread (cf. Kinkade and Powell 1976:88). Such a hypothesis remains to be tested with studies of reconstructed cultural vocabulary: if offshoots of ancestral Caddoans migrated north and west from, say, the lower Red River area, these movements should have left some traces in terms of patterns of borrowing and semantic shift as new groups and new environmental conditions were encountered.

Caddoan has been linked with the Iroquoian family and, at a remoter level, with Siouan and Yuchi in the hypothetical superstock Macro-Siouan.

Linguistics and Archeology

The area suggested by the center of gravity principle as the Proto-Caddoan homeland overlaps closely with the manifestation of the Mississippian tradition known as the Caddoan Mississippian, which emerged between A.D. 500 and 1000 (Sears 1964; Snow 1976a:67-78). Caddoan Mississippian sites cluster along the lower Red River in Arkansas and Louisiana, with a scattering of other sites in eastern Oklahoma (Coe, Snow, and Benson 1986:54, map). It is generally thought that Caddoan Mississippian peoples spoke Caddoan languages (Snow 1976a:75). Even if the glottochronological time-depths for Caddoan are overestimates, Caddo very likely had separated from Northern Caddoan by the time the Caddoan Mississippian tradition had emerged. The archeological correlates of Proto-Caddoan undoubtedly lie in the Late Archaic or Early Woodland period.

Iroquoian

At the time of White contact, Iroquoian-speaking peoples occupied three distinct zones: the Saint Lawrence Lowlands, part of the coastal plain of North Carolina and Virginia, and a section of the southern Appalachians, extending from western Virginia along the Tennessee–North Carolina border to northern Georgia. The Saint Lawrence Lowlands include the Saint Lawrence valley, southern Ontario, upper New York State, and the Susquehanna valley in Pennsylvania (vol. 15:2). Laurentian (Saint Lawrence Iroquoian) has the distinction of being the first language in North America to be recorded by Europeans. It is known from two mid-sixteenth century word lists totaling just over 200 items (Biggar 1924; Hoffman 1961; cf. Chafe 1976:17-18). The best-documented of the languages north of the lower Great Lakes is Huron (Chafe 1976:18-19; R. Wright 1978; Mithun 1979:166-169, 1985; Lagarde 1980). West of the Huron were the Petun, whose speech was closely related to Huron and may have been that of the refugee group known as the Wyandot (vol. 15:334; Mithun 1979:142). Farther west and south were the Neutrals, the Wenros, the Eries, and still other groups whose languages are virtually unknown but identifiable as Iroquoian from a few place- and tribal names appearing on early maps and in missionary accounts (Fenton 1940; R. Wright 1974,

1978, 1978a). The best-known and studied of the Saint Lawrence Lowlands languages are those of the Five Nations Iroquois—the Mohawk, Oneida, Onondaga, Cayuga, and Seneca (Chafe 1973a, 1976; vol 15:334-343; Mithun 1979). South of the Five Nations in the Susquehanna valley were the Susquehannocks, whose language is known from a single word list of some 80 items (Campanius 1696; Holm 1834; cf. Mithun 1979:160, 1981).

The Iroquoian-speaking peoples of the Virginia–North Carolina coastal plain originally included the Tuscarora, the Nottoway, and the Meherrin (vol. 15:282-289). The Tuscarora language was extensively documented from speakers among the Five Nations Iroquois (Williams 1976; Rudes 1976, 1987a; Rudes and Crouse 1987). Although the documentation of extinct Nottoway is slim, it appears to be a distinct language closely related to Tuscarora (Rudes 1976, 1981a; Mithun 1979:164-166). Meherrin, also extinct, is known from only one or two place-names, which show it to be Iroquoian and perhaps related to Tuscarora (Mithun 1979:139; Rudes 1981). The Iroquoian-speaking people of the southern Appalachian region were the Cherokees. Although some Cherokees remained in the 1990s in the eastern homeland area, the majority lived in Oklahoma (Chafe 1976:25-27). There is some dialectal divergence between and within the two communities (Gilbert 1943:178-182; King 1975).

The principal linguistic division within Iroquoian is that between Southern Iroquoian, consisting only of Cherokee, and Northern Iroquoian, consisting of all the other languages. The possibility of a relationship between Cherokee and the northern languages was raised in the late eighteenth century (Barton 1797), but it was not until the late nineteenth that the relationship was placed on a firm footing (H. Hale 1883a:26-28; Gatschet 1886; Hewitt 1887). Impressionistically, the divergence between Northern and Southern Iroquoian is probably somewhat greater than that between any of the languages of the Germanic or the Romance families, but not so great as that between languages belonging to the separate branches of Indo-European (vol. 15: 334). A glottochronological estimate of 1800-1500 B.C. for the Northern-Southern split was determined using the Swadesh 200-word test list and a retention rate that took into account the greater resistance to replacement of test list items over time (Lounsbury 1961).

Although the Tuscarora and their congeners were located closer to the Cherokees in the south than to the Saint Lawrence Lowlands groups before their eighteenth-century migration north, their languages clearly belong to the Northern Iroquoian branch, of which they are nevertheless the most divergent members. A comparison of Tuscarora with three Five Nations languages indicates a separation time of 400 B.C.-A.D. 100

105

(Lounsbury 1961). The time-depth for the Five Nations languages proper has been estimated at between A.D. 500 and 800. The relative linguistic distances between Northern and Southern Iroquoian, and between Tuscarora and the Five Nations group, have been borne out in other statistical and nonstatistical studies (Hickerson, Turner, and Hickerson 1952; Hoffman 1959; Blin-Lagarde 1972; cf. vol. 15:335).

Subgrouping within Northern Iroquoian at levels shallower than the Tuscarora split is more problematic. To be sure, the Five Nations had formed a close political alliance, but their languages cannot be assumed to constitute an exclusive subgroup. Even from the limited evidence available, Susquehannock appears to be fairly close to Onondaga and therefore probably belongs to the Five Nations group (vol. 15:336) while Cayuga, which was once seen as a mere offshoot of its neighbor Seneca (Fenton 1940:224), may actually have undergone a lengthy early period of separation from the core Northern group, only later assuming its place among the Five Nations languages after coming in contact with Seneca and Onondaga (Chafe and Foster 1981; compare Niemczycki 1984:76-77 on possible archeological correlates).

It has been suggested that the Ontario Iroquoian languages may have constituted a subgroup, which has been called Huronian (vol. 15:335; cf. R. Wright 1978:149). If this is eventually substantiated, it would represent a later split than that involving Tuscarora-Nottoway, but earlier than the diversification of Five Nations and Susquehannock. The evidence supporting an exclusive Huronian branch is slim, and the question is complicated by the fact that Ontario refugees who were taken in by the League Iroquois following the termination of hostilities in the mid-seventeenth century apparently introduced several phonological innovations among them (Mithun 1985). Finally, just where Laurentian fits into the Northern Iroquoian picture has not been determined, although it is no longer seen as simply a dialect of Huron or one of the Five Nations languages (Chafe 1962a; vol. 15:335; Mithun 1982a). In sum, while there is general agreement regarding the split between Northern and Southern Iroquoian, and within Northern Iroquoian between Tuscarora-Nottoway and the remaining languages, the makeup of lower-level groupings is a matter of continuing discussion. This should be kept in mind when interpreting Iroquoian family-tree diagrams (e.g., vol. 15:336; Mithun 1984b:264).

Origins: Linguistic Perspectives

Assuming the validity of the assertion that a linguistic homeland is likely to fall within an area where at least one of the contemporary members of a family is found (Dyen 1956:617-618), the presence of Iroquoian-speaking peoples in the Northeast and the Southeast raises the question of which of these two areas represents a more plausible Proto-Iroquoian homeland.

Probably a majority of Iroquoian linguists favors a northern over a southern homeland (Foster 1987). Three arguments have been advanced to support the northern hypothesis. The first is based on the claim—where a family has a discontinuous distribution—that the language or subbranch whose sound system adheres most closely to the reconstructed prototype is more likely to occupy the homeland area than the language or subbranch whose sound system has departed significantly from the ancestral prototype (vol. 15:336). Since the Northern Iroquoian languages are the closest to Proto-Iroquoian in their phonologies, and Cherokee is the most divergent, the Saint Lawrence Lowlands are seen as the more likely homeland, at least within the last four or five millennia. The second argument is external to Iroquoian. Although a linguistic map of eastern North America can certainly be interpreted as implying that Iroquoians drove a "wedge" across the Algonquian speech area, separating the eastern languages from the main group to the west (Fenton 1940:164; Snow 1977:109; Fiedel 1991:20), such a view does not mesh very well with the linguistic facts for Algonquian (vol. 15:586-587). If Iroquoian had cut across a chain of already differentiated Algonquian languages, the eastern Algonquian languages should show patterns of innovation in common with their western and northern relatives for all but the most recent period. But in fact the languages of the Eastern seaboard represent a distinct subbranch (Eastern Algonquian) and as a group show unique patterns of innovation that in many cases are old. Such a situation is more compatible with a migration, not of Iroquoians, but of speakers of a relatively undifferentiated Proto–Eastern Algonquian east and south around Iroquoians already in place. It follows from this that since Eastern Algonquian is estimated to extend back to A.D. 1 (vol. 15:70), Northern Iroquoian languages would have been in the Northeast at least since then. The third argument favoring a northern homeland is based on Sapir's principle that unanalyzable words tend to be older than analyzable ones (Sapir 1916, 1949:434-441). When the principle was applied to two Seneca cultural complexes, stems associated with shamanism were found to be mostly unanalyzable, whereas stems associated with calendrical ceremonialism were found to be mostly analyzable, and this implies that shamanism was the older cultural complex (Chafe 1964a; cf. Tooker 1960:69-71). It was once suggested that horticultural Iroquoians had moved into the Northeast in Late Woodland times, acquiring a thin overlay of boreal forest traits like shamanism from their Algonquian neighbors (Fenton 1940:164); however, the Seneca, at least, appear to have been deeply rooted in an ancient cultural pattern of the Northeast, and horticulture, associated with calendrical ceremonialism, seems to have been the more recent acquisition. The analyzability criterion does not, of course, provide time-depth estimates in years, but it can provide significant leads in terms of relative chronology.

The principal support for a southern homeland for Proto-Iroquoian comes from an application of the center of gravity principle: the deepest division within the family is found in North Carolina, with the split between Cherokee and Tuscarora-Nottoway. At the time of contact much of the intervening region was occupied by Catawban groups, but the two Iroquoian-speaking areas were separated by only 200-300 air miles. Secondary support for a southern homeland comes from the possibility that Macro-Siouan, a putative deeper-level grouping consisting of Siouan-Yuchi and Iroquoian-Caddoan, may have had a Southeast—perhaps a southern Appalachian—homeland. The argument is similar to one used by Sapir to support a northern homeland for Athapaskan: not only were the deepest splits within Athapaskan found in the western Subarctic rather than on the Pacific Coast or in the Southwest, but still deeper splits involving the so-called Na-Dene grouping, consisting of Athapaskan, Tlingit, and Haida, were also found in the north, and this was said to "clinch" the matter of northern provenience (Sapir 1915b:558, 1916, 1949:456-457). Although the possibility of a Southeast homeland for Macro-Siouan lends support to the argument for a Proto-Iroquoian homeland in the Southeast, it by no means clinches it. Proto–Macro-Siouan represents a hypothetical grouping that, if it existed at all, existed long before the emergence of Proto-Iroquoian (perhaps two millennia before Northern and Southern Iroquoian began to separate), and the emergence could well have taken place in an entirely different location. Nevertheless, the location of Cherokee in the heart of the hypothesized Macro-Siouan homeland lends some weight to the idea of a southern homeland for Iroquoian.

Very different prehistoric sequences are of course implied by the northern and southern hypotheses. The northern hypothesis favors occupation of the Saint Lawrence Lowlands by Proto-Iroquoians, with a migration south of Proto–Southern Iroquoians sometime after 1500 B.C., and of Proto-Tuscaroras sometime after A.D. 100 (Lounsbury 1961; vol. 15:336). The southern hypothesis, on the other hand, favors development of Proto-Iroquoian in the Southeast, with the separation of Northern and Southern Iroquoian occurring in the area. The movement of Iroquoian groups north would presumably have occurred only after the Tuscarora split. In this scenario, ancestral Tuscaroras were left behind in the vicinity of the early Cherokee, while the ancestors of the Five Nations and Ontario Iroquoians migrated north, their languages continuing to diversify as they went.

Two lines of linguistic evidence could help to resolve the Iroquoian homeland issue. One of these has shown a promising start; the other is virtually untried. The most direct way to link Proto-Iroquoian with a particular environmental region would be to plot the distributions of plant and animal species and other natural phenomena for which terms can be reconstructed in the protolanguage. The region of greatest overlap for such distributions would then approximately delimit the homeland. A first step has been made by dividing Iroquoian cultural vocabulary sets into terms that can be reconstructed at the Proto-Iroquoian level, the Proto–Northern Iroquoian level, and at shallower levels within Northern Iroquoian (Mithun 1984b). An important, if expected, finding is that no horticultural terms can be reconstructed at the Proto-Iroquoian level; indeed, most reconstruct unambiguously only at the Proto–Five Nations level. Horticulture must thus have been acquired by Iroquoians after the separation of the Northern and Southern Iroquoian branches, and most likely after Tuscarora-Nottoway had separated from the remaining Northern group. Although the study identifies a number of plant and animal terms at the Proto-Iroquoian and Proto–Northern Iroquoian levels, it does not take the next step of plotting the distributions of the species themselves at the appropriate time levels. However, there is at least a hint of a northward movement of Iroquoians in the build-up of conifer terms over time: no terms for conifers can be reconstructed at the Proto-Iroquoian level; one ('pine') reconstructs at the Proto–Northern Iroquoian level, and two or three ('hemlock', 'balsam fir', and possibly 'tamarack') reconstruct at the Proto–Five Nations level. The presence of terms for 'balsam fir' and 'tamarack', especially, implies a late movement of Iroquoian speakers into the mixed forest zone of the Northeast.

The second line of evidence that could help to resolve the homeland issue relates to patterns of borrowing. Such patterns have proven useful, particularly in the far West, in determining the relative priority of groups in an area. Latecomers are more likely to borrow cultural terms and place-names from earlier inhabitants than the reverse. In the postcontact period, the borrowing of many Northern Iroquoian place-names into English in central and upper New York State (Beauchamp 1907a; Lounsbury 1960) clearly indicates prior occupation by Iroquoian-speaking groups. Applying such reasoning to the prehistoric period, if Iroquoians had arrived in the Northeast relatively late, and well after the Algonquians, they might be expected to borrow terms, or—more likely, given Iroquoian word structure—to form loan translations from Algonquian languages for the features they encountered in their new environment. They might also be expected to borrow some place-names. However, there appear to be only slight influences between Algonquian and Iroquoian languages (cf. vol. 15:76-77, 587), despite documented instances of bilingualism, such as that involving the Huron and their trading partners (Trigger 1976:65, 355), which would be expected to promote borrowing. The lack of mutual influence has been attributed to various ecological, social, and political factors peculiar to the East, and particularly the Northeast, which set this region off against areas like the Northwest Coast, where languages from unrelated families have exerted strong influences on one another (Sherzer 1976:153-154). More extensive borrowing has been reported in the Southeast, such as that involving the Creek and Cherokee (Haas 1961), although the evidence has not been published. In general, the question of cross-family borrowing in the Eastern Woodlands has received very little attention.

Origins: Archeological and Ethnological Perspectives

Influenced by national trends within the disciplines, Iroquoian studies have been subject to swings between migrationist and in situ explanations of Iroquoian origins. The earliest theories, which were migrationist, argued for a Saint Lawrence homeland, from which speakers moved south and southwest (summarized by Trigger 1970:10-16). Linguistic evidence was brought in to bolster such theories (H. Hale 1883a; cf. Powell 1891:77). A popular theory, the first to be archeologically based, located ancestral Iroquoians in the middle Mississippi valley, whence separate expansions took place up the Ohio River (Parker 1916; cf. H.M. Lloyd in Morgan 1901, 2:188). In this view, Iroquoians brought horticulture and a number of other cultural traits to the Saint Lawrence Lowlands around A.D. 1400, absorbing or replacing the previous occupants who were assumed to be Algonquians (Parker 1922). On the ethnological side, the apparently "intrusive" cultural position of the Iroquois in the Northeast was noted early in the twentieth century (Boas 1910a; Sapir 1911a, 1916, 1949:424). This idea was developed in great detail three decades later, with the Southeast, rather than the Mississippi valley, serving as the presumed source for many defining Iroquoian cultural traits (Fenton 1940).

Continuing archeological work failed to locate a convincing source or routes of entry for the Northern Iroquoian cultural complex outside the Saint Lawrence Lowlands (Kraus 1944:311; Griffin 1944), and this marked the beginning of a fundamental shift in thinking about Iroquoian origins. With the discovery that Iroquoian ceramic styles could he traced through more than two millennia of continuous development within the historic Iroquoian area, the in situ hypothesis of Iroquoian origins was born (MacNeish 1952; cf. Ritchie 1961; J. Wright 1966:5-8). It has been supported by a data base broadened to include other artifact classes as well as settlement and subsistence patterns, burial practices, and the like (see J. Wright 1984:283 for a review of key sources).

Most archeologists favor the idea that ancestral Iroquoians have been in the Saint Lawrence Lowlands since well before the arrival of corn horticulture about A.D. 500-1000. This would mean that horticulture arrived by trade and diffusion, probably from Hopewell sources to the southwest, and not as the result of an in-migration by horticultural peoples who displaced earlier Archaic hunter-gatherers. Some archeologists trace in situ Iroquoian occupation to the earliest phases of the Woodland period around 1000 B.C. Others carry in situ Iroquoian development well back into the Archaic period, perhaps 3000-2000 B.C. (J. Wright 1972, 1984, 1987, 1987a, 1987b; Tuck 1977). From a linguistic point of view, the people involved would have to be pre-Iroquoian speakers, but they could have spoken languages in the ancestral Iroquoian line. The in situ hypothesis is compatible with the linguistic arguments supporting a long period of development in New York State and north-central Pennsylvania, with incursions taking place first to the south and then north into Ontario and the Saint Lawrence valley (vol. 15:336).

The most serious problem with the in situ theory is the lack of convincing archeological evidence for a southward movement of Proto–Southern Iroquoians out of the Saint Lawrence Lowlands when the earliest linguistic split occurred around 2000-1500 B.C. (Snow 1984:247). Further, the in situ hypothesis is open to certain theoretical and procedural criticisms (Trigger 1970:26-35).

The question of continuities and discontinuities in the archeological record has been much debated by Northeastern archeologists. Those who favor migration and replacement hypotheses naturally focus on the discontinuities, even though periods of lengthy in situ development before and after such breaks are acknowledged (cf. Snow 1984:243). Two suggestions have been made in this regard, one of which posits a relatively early entry point for the Iroquoians and the other a relatively recent entry point. In the first proposal, Iroquoians are said to have entered New York from the south during the so-called Frost Island phase, between the end of the Late Archaic period about 1700 B.C. and the beginning of the Woodland period about 1200 B.C. (Snow 1977, 1980:251-259, 1984). Although this hypothesis provided a chronological framework that correlated quite well with the glottochronological time-depth estimate for Proto-Iroquoian, it came under fire on archeological grounds and was abandoned (J. Wright 1984:294-297; Fiedel 1987:4, 1991:25).

In another replacement hypothesis, Iroquoian entry was correlated with the Owasco and Glen Meyer cultures, which emerged in New York and Ontario respectively around A.D. 900 (Snow 1995). In this scenario, not only the cultures of the Late Archaic period but also those assigned to the Early and Middle Woodland periods belonged to the previous occupants, presumably Algonquians (cf. Fiedel 1987). The late northward movement of Iroquoians into New York and Ontario was traced to cultural developments that began in the Susquehanna valley in central Pennsylvania around A.D. 800. This is far too late to involve Proto-Iroquoian speakers: it would have to involve Northern-branch Iroquoians at a stage when already distinct Five Nations and Huronian sub-branches were diversifying into the languages of the historic period. The notion of an Owasco–Glen Meyer Iroquoian entry fits better with the hypothesis of an Iroquoian homeland in the Southeast, which sees the split involving the Tuscarora as taking place by A.D. 100 and speakers of the remaining Northern languages starting north sometime after that date and then settling in the Susquehanna valley for a period of time. By A.D. 800, speakers of partially differentiated Five Nations and Huronian branch languages were spreading into central New York and southern Ontario. It must be stressed, though, that the parts of this hypothesis involving an early movement of Northern Iroquoians into the Susquehanna valley have yet to be substantiated archeologically.

Reasonable cases can be made on archeological and linguistic grounds for both a northern and a southern Iroquoian homeland. What is at issue is not so much whether the homeland was in the Northeast or the Southeast but at what time and by what route Iroquoian-speaking peoples arrived in their historic seats both north and south. In the late twentieth century that issue was far from settled.

Languages of the Southeast

The Southeast, like the south Texas and Rio Grande area, was once a region of great linguistic diversity (Swanton 1946:240; Crawford 1975a:1; Haas 1979:299; Goddard 1979a:355). Records exist of numerous tribes in both regions whose languages were lost in the early contact period. Many of the languages spoken by Southeastern peoples must have belonged to family groupings, but the bulk of those that survived to be documented are isolates or small isolated families without wider family affiliations. These include Tunica, Natchez, and Chitimacha in the lower Mississippi valley; Atakapan along the Texas and Louisiana coasts; and Timucuan and Calusa in Florida. All these except Calusa have at least moderately extensive documentation (Crawford 1975a; Haas 1976, 1979).

The one family in the early contact period that was located entirely within the Southeast was Muskogean: at one time it dominated much of the region from South Carolina to the Mississippi River. When discussions of Southeastern prehistory refer to language at all, it is usually to Muskogean alone or to one of the languages or outside families speculatively linked to it. For the most part, the language isolates have been ignored in such discussions: by their very nature as unaffiliated "orphans," they provide little perspective on the past (Haas 1969:60-61, 1979:317). Muskogean consists of four languages or closely related language pairs—Choctaw-Chickasaw, Alabama-Koasati, Hitchiti-Mikasuki, and Creek-Seminole—and the long-extinct Apalachee language of northern Florida.

The Muskogean languages are closely related, representing around 2,000 years of divergence time (Haas 1969:66). Two classifications of the family have been proposed, and these have different implications for prehistory. The first, and best-known, classification defines a Western Division, consisting of only Choctaw and Chickasaw, and an Eastern Division, consisting of the three remaining languages or language pairs arranged as coequal subbranches (Haas 1941, 1946a, 1947, 1949, 1950, 1969, 1976, 1979; cf. Crawford 1975; Pulte 1975).

The second classification (Munro 1987) is almost the mirror image of the first: the first split involves the separation of Northern Muskogean, consisting of Creek-Seminole alone, from Southern Muskogean, consisting of all the remaining languages. Within Southern Muskogean, Hitchiti-Mikasuki splits from a subbranch called Southwestern, which then divides into Alabama-Koasati and Choctaw-Chickasaw. Apalachee is linked most closely to Alabama-Koasati.

In the Haas classification, the deepest split within the family separates Choctaw and Chickasaw from the remaining languages along a line that runs through western Alabama. In the Munro classification, the deepest split separates Creek-Seminole from the remaining languages in Georgia, with shallower splits grading from east to west; the split separating Choctaw-Chickasaw from Alabama-Koasati is the shallowest of all. If one applies the center of gravity principle, the Haas classification implies a Muskogean spread to the east from the Mississippi-Alabama area, while the Munro classification implies a spread to the west from central Georgia.

Proposed Muskogean Affiliations

As a result of work conducted by John R. Swanton in the early twentieth century, relationships were proposed among Tunica, Chitimacha, and Atakapan, and between Muskogean and Natchez (cf. Haas 1958a:240, 1979:313). Swanton's "Tunican" grouping and his "Natchez-Muskogean" were carried as branches of the Hokan-Siouan superstock in Sapir's (1929) continental classification. Haas brought together the four isolates from the region and Muskogean in a grouping she called "Gulf" (Haas 1951, 1952, 1954, 1956; cf. Haas 1958a). An impressionistic time-depth of 1000 B.C. was later assigned to this grouping (Haas 1969:62, table XII).

The Gulf grouping had certain implications for prehistory. The Tunica, Natchez, and Chitimacha were located in the lower Mississippi valley, and the Atakapans were located along the Texas-Louisiana coast. If all the branches of Gulf, including Muskogean, were coequal, as they were usually portrayed, then the deepest splits within the grouping should lie in the lower Mississippi valley, and this area would be the logical choice for the Gulf homeland (Eggan 1952:43, Kinkade and Powell 1976:92). The subsequent spread of the Muskogean languages to the east, implied by the Haas classification, would be consistent with such a location. A considerable amount of evidence has been assembled in support of the Gulf hypothesis, and many consider it a promising, if not a fully proven grouping (cf. Haas 1979:318; Greenberg 1987:144), but others find the evidence unconvincing (Campbell and Mithun 1979a:40).

An even more far-reaching relationship was proposed between the Gulf grouping and Algic (Haas 1958a; cf. Haas 1960:983-987). "Algonkian-Gulf" was regarded at the time as a bold departure, since it involved a fundamental realignment of superstocks within the Sapir classification (Sapir 1921b, 1929). After Tonkawa was linked with Algic (Haas 1959), the larger grouping became known as "Macro-Algonquian." The significance of Macro-Algonquian for the prehistory of Eastern America lies in the extent of its geographic spread (Haas 1958a:236, fig. 1; C.F. Voegelin and F.M. Voegelin 1966). However, both Algonkian-Gulf and Macro-Algonquian have been treated with considerable skepticism (cf. Goddard 1979:106; Campbell and Mithun 1979a:38, Jacobsen 1989a:13).

Linguistics and Archeology

The only genetic grouping that can be considered adequately demonstrated in the Southeast is Muskogean. This effectively limits any attempt to correlate language and archeology in the region to the last 2,000 years, although many sites attest to the presence of much earlier populations.

There is some consensus among archeologists that just as Siouan-speaking groups were probably responsible for the development of the Middle Mississippian tradition and its more northern variants, so Muskogeans were responsible for the spread of the more southerly variants of the tradition in the Southeast (Eggan 1952:43; Spencer and Jennings 1965:405; Willey 1966:294; Snow 1976a:78). On purely linguistic grounds, it has even been argued that Muskogeans—specifically speakers of Choctaw and Chickasaw—may have been fundamentally involved in the development of the Middle Mississippian tradition, since the western Muskogean languages have more ramified vocabularies for the kinds of religious, social, and political institutions and subsistence patterns practiced by Mississippian peoples than the Siouan languages have (Mochon 1972; cf. Springer and Witkowski 1983:79). In any case, after about A.D. 1000 the variant of the Mississippian in South Carolina and Georgia termed the South Appalachian is thought to have evolved into the culture of the historic Creeks as well as certain non-Muskogean groups (Willey 1966:300-309; Snow 1976a:78-79; Coe, Snow, and Benson 1986:54, map). During the same period, the variant of the Mississippian known as the Plaquemine is seen as evolving into the culture of the historic Natchez and perhaps some western Muskogean groups (Eggan 1952:44; Sears 1964:284; Snow 1976a:74).

The archeology of the Southeastern sites indicates discontinuities in the central part of the region between the Mississippian tradition and the Woodland cultures that preceded it; by contrast, there is greater continuity between these earlier cultures and the late prehistoric cultures at the peripheries of the region. The overall situation suggests that the Mississippian tradition spread to the Southeast from the Mississippi valley by an "aggressive" migration, and that the previous occupants were either absorbed or fled to the peripheries where they continued a pre-Mississippian lifeway (Eggan 1952:43-44). The Haas classification of Muskogean is compatible with this interpretation, but not the Munro classification, which implies a movement from east to west.

Borrowing

CATHERINE A. CALLAGHAN AND GEOFFREY GAMBLE

Borrowing is one of the most complex problems facing students of Native American languages, who cannot consult many centuries of written records as can their European counterparts. Yet it is a problem that must be tackled if the linguistic history of North America is to be recovered, especially in light of the mass comparisons among Indian languages proposed by Greenberg (1987), since the results of diffusion among these languages can potentially be mistaken for the residue of deep genetic relationship.

Lexical Borrowing

The simplest type of borrowing is lexical. The most familiar examples are loanwords from Algonquian into American English (vol. 6:153), such as *squash* (shortened from an earlier English form *isquoutersquash* borrowed from Narragansett ⟨askútasquash⟩, *skunk*, earlier also *squnck*, from an unrecorded Massachusett word, *tomahawk* from Virginia Algonquian ⟨tamahaac⟩, and *Mississippi* from Illinois ⟨missisipioui⟩ (⟨missi⟩ 'big' + ⟨sipioui⟩ 'river') (Morris 1973; Ives Goddard, personal communication 1995). *Squaw* from Massachusett ⟨squa⟩ 'younger woman' has acquired the specialized meaning of 'Indian woman' and is now considered derogatory. These words illustrate the commonest semantic areas of borrowing from the older language of an area into an intrusive dominant language—namely, local plant and animal terms, place-names, and names for aboriginal people or their cultural items. Cutler (1994) is a popular account of Indian, Eskimo, and Aleut loanwords in current American English; the most extensive technical information on these loans is in the second edition of *The Random House Dictionary* (Flexner 1987). Brown (1994) studied lexical acculturation in 196 American Indian languages.

Loans from European Languages

There are many instances of borrowing from European languages into Native American languages. An example of direct borrowing is Nez Perce *lapatá·t* 'potato' from the Canadian French phrase *la patate* 'the potato' (Aoki 1971:1). Here, of course, there is no question as to the direction of borrowing. The potato is an introduced item, and the French definite article *la* is appended to the Nez Perce form, marking it etymologically as a borrowed noun phrase rather than a single word. Besides English and French, European languages that were sources of loanwords include Spanish, Russian (Jacobson 1984:678-685; Bergsland 1994:657-662), and Dutch (Goddard 1974b; Swiggers 1985).

Compounds and Semantic Extensions

Cultural items of European provenience were often designated by compounds or semantic extensions of native terms rather than loanwords. Examples of compounding include the famous Algonquian words for 'whiskey', such as Cree *iskote·wa·poy* from *iskote·w* 'fire' plus *-a·poy* 'water, liquid' (Bloomfield 1946: 107). Hopi *tá·wa* now means 'clock' and 'watch' in addition to 'sun, day, today', an example of semantic extension (Voegelin and Voegelin 1957:14, 24).

Sometimes the structure of the recipient language dictated the choice. According to Sapir (1921c:209), "The Athapaskan languages of America are spoken by peoples that have had astonishingly varied cultural contacts, yet nowhere do we find that an Athapaskan dialect has borrowed at all freely from a neighboring language. These languages have always found it easier to create new words by compounding afresh elements ready to hand." Structurally, the Athapaskan languages are polysynthetic, replete with morphemes composed of one, two, or three phonemes, and endowed with active processes of word formation. Consider Navajo *ch'il łigaii* 'cabbage, lettuce, cauliflower, lit. white plant', from *ch'il* 'plant' and *łigai* 'white' plus *-ii* 'the one'. But Navajo words such as *bilasáana* 'apple' from Spanish *mansana* 'apple' and *béégashii* 'cow, cattle' from Zuni *wa·kaši* from Spanish *vacas* 'cows' indicate more openness to loanwords, at least in recent times (Hoijer 1974:102, 103, 254, 255, 280). Kari (1977) lists possible instances of stem diffusion between two Athapaskan languages, Tanaina and Ahtna.

Role of Contact Situation

In some instances, the incentive for lexical borrowing was partly determined by the contact situation. Dozier (1956) contrasts the Yaqui Indians of Sonora with the

Tewa Indians of New Mexico. The Yaqui were missionized by the Jesuits, who entered the area without military escort, learned the native language, and were protective of the Indians and relatively tolerant toward indigenous cultures and ceremonies. As a result, Yaqui culture became hybridized in little more than a century. The Yaqui language reflects this state of affairs and readily incorporates Spanish loanwords. New coinages and loan translations are rare and the former usually include borrowings, such as *liosnooka* 'to pray' from Spanish *Dios* 'God' and Yaqui *nooka* 'speak'.

By contrast, the Spaniards established themselves as the oppressors among the Rio Grande Pueblos. Missionary activity was conducted by the Franciscans with military support. They did not learn the native languages, and they attempted to suppress all customs they considered pagan. Consequently, the Pueblo cultures did not undergo syncretism. The Indians became outwardly Roman Catholic and continued their native religious practices in secret.

In like manner, the Spanish language had little influence on Tewa, a Pueblo language, leaving its phonemic, morphological, and syntactic patterns largely untouched, even after most speakers had become bilingual. Borrowing from Spanish was mostly restricted to nouns designating introduced items of Spanish or Mexican origin. Examples are *besero* 'calf' from Spanish *becerro* 'calf' and *serêˀsa* 'cherry' from Spanish *cereza* 'cherry'.

These words exhibit nonnative phonological patterns and are easily recognized as such by Tewa speakers, who often avoid them in favor of native locutions, especially to preserve secrecy in the presence of Spanish-speaking outsiders. An example is *púˑpíˀ* 'beet' from *púˑ* 'root, base, buttocks' plus *píˀ* 'red'. Tewa *dìˑ* 'chicken', a term that originally referred to any fowl, is now restricted to domesticated chickens. The small number of Spanish loanwords form a separate system like other introduced Spanish cultural elements. In contrast, Tewa shows much less resistance to loanwords from English, especially among younger people; and the attitude toward Anglo-Americans is correspondingly more tolerant.

Exactly the reverse situation obtained in northern California, where over 100 years of contact resulted in very few loanwords from English into any indigenous language, regardless of its structural type (Bright 1960:233-234). By contrast, the languages of southern and central California borrowed extensively from Spanish, and Kashaya acquired at least 12 loanwords from Russian during only 29 years of contact at Fort Ross (Oswalt 1958). Resistance to English loanwords coincided with far crueler treatment on the part of the Anglo-American than either the Russian or the Spaniard.

Instances of semantic extension or composition involving native elements were especially common when the borrowed item, or at least awareness of it, spread faster than large-scale colonial contact. The earliest Lake Miwok term for 'horse' was recorded as ⟨ōpōīnī⟩ (Barrett 1908:74), which can be phonemicized as *ˀópˑoy-ni* 'what one rides on' from *ˀópˑoy* 'to go around, ride' plus *-ni* 'instrumental agentive'. This construction was soon replaced by *káway* from Spanish *caballo* 'horse', probably a back formation from the objective case, *kawáˑyu-c*, reinterpreted as *kawáˑy-uc* (as if from |káway-uc|).

Elsewhere, words for 'horse' were often based on 'dog', 'deer', or 'elk' (Bright 1960:216-17), such as Wintu ⟨bo-hí-neh su-hoh⟩ 'big dog' (cited from Powers 1877:524) and Northeastern Pomo *bŏˀŏ̌-kʰá*, originally 'elk', judging from Barrett's (1908:62) recording of ⟨bōō-ka⟩ as 'elk'. Extension sometimes resulted in a shift in the central meaning of the word. Barrett (1908:71) gives Lake Miwok ⟨kōnō⟩ as the word for 'bow', but now it most commonly means 'gun'. *hintíˑl kóˑno* 'old-time gun' specifically refers to 'bow'.

Lexical borrowings from European languages are sometimes hard to trace. Contact is usually through speakers of a nonstandard dialect. Lake Miwok *lóˑho* 'lazy' is from colloquial Spanish *flojo* rather than common dictionary Spanish *perezoso* (Callaghan 1965:80). In the case of animals, the source may be a calling term, as in Munsee *kóˑškoˑš* 'pig', probably from the Dutch-Flemish hog call [kuš-kuš-kuš] (Goddard 1974:155). Sometimes the foreign source is obscured by a radical shift in meaning, such as Lake Miwok *hintíˑl*, an adjective meaning 'old-time, Indian' from Spanish *gentil* 'pagan', presumably a term used by the Spaniards to refer to unbaptized Indians.

Words were often borrowed through other Indian languages rather than directly, as in the case of Navajo *béégashii* 'cow, cattle' from Zuni *waˑkaši* from Spanish *vacas* 'cows'. The widespread occurrence of similar forms of this word, from Gros Ventre *wóˑkoč* in the north to Cora *waˑkasi* 'cows' in the south, makes the exact route of diffusion uncertain to some extent.

Diffusion Chains and Phonological Markers

Some loanwords are phonologically aberrant. Lake Miwok *f* is found only in exclamations and loanwords from Spanish, such as *fíˑnu* 'fine (not coarse)' from Spanish *fino* 'fine'; note word-initial *sk*, as in *skóˑwa* 'broom' from Spanish *escoba* 'broom', even though initial *sk* does not occur in Spanish either. Words may be borrowed first with naturalized phonology, and later adjusted to match the source more closely as more speakers master the foreign sounds. Munsee borrowed English *fair* as *péˑliˑn* 'the fair is on' and *farmer* as *páˑməl*, later replacing these with *féˑliˑn* and *fáˑməl* (Ives Goddard, personal communication 1995).

Shipley (1962) has shown how phonologically aberrant features in Spanish loanwords can be used to chart chains of diffusion in central California, as in Nisenan [ʔoˑdo], Konkow [ʔodo], and Maidu ʔódo, all originally from Spanish *oro* 'gold'. Shipley's article illustrates the value of loanwords in tracking the spread of introduced items and practices.

Occasionally, an aberrant feature marks a class of loanwords. McLendon (1969) observed that practically all Eastern Pomo and Wappo words of Spanish origin end in ʔ, which is not an automatic feature either of Spanish or of the Indian languages. Influence from another language is suspected. The best candidates are the nearby Miwok languages. In Lake Miwok, and probably also Coast Miwok, final juncture is often marked by glottal stricture. In Plains and Sierra Miwok (and probably Bay Miwok), the nominative case is -ʔ after vowels. Eastern Pomo and Wappo Indians may have first encountered Spanish loanwords from Miwok Indians, either at the San Rafael Arcángel and San Francisco de Solano missions or on expeditions. Once final ʔ was perceived as a marker for such words, it would spread by analogy to additional Spanish loanwords.

Although loanwords from European languages are most commonly nouns, other items were also borrowed. Even in Tewa, two of the loanwords are conjunctions, *si* 'if' from Spanish *si* 'if' and *pòkeʰ* 'because' from Spanish *porque* 'because', although both can be expressed by Tewa equivalents (Dozier 1956:155).

Yaqui has borrowed a number of verbs and adjectives from Spanish, as well as the above two conjunctions (Spicer 1943:412). Examples are *pásiyalóa* 'to make a visit' from Spanish *pasear* 'to make a visit' and *líhto* 'ready' from Spanish *listo* 'ready'. Verbal expressions are regularly incorporated into Yaqui by means of the suffix *-oa*, after which they may be inflected by means of the Yaqui verbal suffixes, demonstrating the degree to which Spanish loanwords have been integrated into the Yaqui system.

Influence on Syntax

Spanish has affected Yaqui syntactic patterns as well. Lindenfeld (1971) describes new Spanish-influenced comparative constructions (2) that exist side by side with a presumably older Yaqui construction (1):

  (1) *hu oʔóo (čéʔa) húme haamúčim beppá bweʔú.*
  (2) *hu oʔóo (čéʔa) bweʔú ke húme haamúčim beppá,*
or   *hu oʔóo čéʔa bweʔú ke húme haamúčim.*
    'Este hombre es más grande que estas mujeres.'
    'This man is bigger than these women.'
    (*čéʔa* 'more', *bweʔú* 'big', *beppá* 'over, on top of', *ke* < Spanish *que* 'than'.)

After comparing the native Yaqui constructions with the ones influenced by Spanish, Lindenfeld (1971:

9-10) schematizes the probable development of the latter from the former:

    Yaqui NP$_1$ + *čéʔa* + NP$_2$ + *beppá* + Adj. →
    Spanish-influenced Yaqui
      NP$_1$ (+ *čéʔa*) + Adj. + *ke* + NP$_2$ + *beppá* ~
      NP$_1$ + *čéʔa* + Adj. + *ke* + NP$_2$.

There is also an incipient Spanish-influenced comparison of equality (i.e., 'as big as') incorporating *ke* < Spanish *que* along with a similar Yaqui construction, although usage here does not seem to correlate with the degree of bilingualism; in fact, the Spanish comparison of equality *tan...como* makes no use of *que*.

So far, Yaqui speakers have resisted Spanish influence in comparisons of inferiority (e.g., Spanish *menos...que* 'less than'), probably because Yaqui expresses this relationship by other means (but see Dedrick 1977 for a critical analysis of Lindenfeld's claims). In Yaqui, there is apparently resistance to Spanish-influenced syntactic restructuring beyond a certain point, despite the fact that at least two-thirds of the Yaqui speakers appear to be bilingual to a degree.

Mixed Language

One of the most bizarre instances of language contamination resulted in a truly mixed language, Mitchif or Métis (vol. 6:54; Bakker 1992, 1994). This variety of Cree, spoken in the Canadian Prairie provinces and North Dakota, consists largely of Cree verbs, personal pronouns, postpositions, question words, and demonstratives plus French nouns, adjectives, articles, and numerals. It preserves the morphological complexities of both source languages, including gender distinctions, article usage, and verb morphology. An example sentence is: *Le petit garçon puis la petite fille ki·wa·pame·wak un cheval.* 'The little boy and the little girl saw a horse.'

The above categories are generally used as in the source languages, and even the French and Cree phonological systems are preserved without interference, despite the fact that most Mitchif speakers are not fluent in both languages. Mitchif represents the opposite of a jargon or a pidgin-based creole, since the language underwent an increase rather than a reduction in morphological complexity during its formation.

Mitchif arose around 1800 in the central Canadian provinces as the result of intermarriage between French fur traders and Cree-speaking women who were often the daughters of their Indian trading partners. Mitchif speakers rapidly attained identity as a new ethnic group, the Métis, even to the point of resisting the arrival of new European settlers from 1812 onward.

Mixed languages come into being as a result of what Bakker (1992) calls 'language intertwining'. Most share their lexicons with one language and their grammatical systems with another. Some mixed languages start as secret languages of nomadic or semi-nomadic bilinguals, in which case the grammatical system of the local language is combined with the lexicon of an imported language. Other such languages arise in bilingual groups that stress their new ethnic identity by mixing their languages. Typically, the fathers and mothers of the first generation speak different languages, and the resulting speech combines the lexicon of the fathers' language with the grammatical system of the mothers' language.

Bakker argues that Mitchif is a deviant instance of this phenomenon. Cree nouns are relatively simple, but the polysynthetic Cree verb is composed entirely of bound morphemes whose boundaries are often blurred; consequently, it can be considered part of the Cree grammatical system. Cree nominal affixes are attached to French noun stems, as predicted by Bakker's model.

Aboriginal Patterns of Borrowing and Their Consequences

The problem of borrowing between Indian languages is extremely complex, since written records prior to contact do not exist for the languages north of Mesoamerica, and the direction of borrowing is often difficult to determine. Haas (1969:79) is one of the few who have tackled this problem systematically. Her general guidelines are worth citing in full:

(1) The phonological evidence must be taken into account. (If the presumed loan has *l* in A and *n* in B, the DL [donor language] is A if A has both *l* and *n* and B has only *n* in their respective phonemic inventories.)

(2) The morphological evidence must be taken into account. (If the word has an etymology in A but not in B, then A is the DL.)

(3) If both A and B have several congeners, the DL is likely to be the one whose congeners also have the term. (But if the term is widely used in both families, then the DL may be a third language, or the borrowing may even have taken place between the protolanguages; in this case the true origin may be difficult to determine.)

(4) If A has congeners and B has none, A is likely to be the DL if the term is widespread in the family, particularly if the regular sound correspondences which should pertain in the circumstances actually do pertain.

An important point is that loanwords cannot be detected apart from morphological analysis of relevant items and identification of cognates in genetically related languages. It goes without saying that the reverse is also true; it is impossible to establish genetic families and reconstruct protolanguages without separating loan words from cognates.

Applying her own principles, Haas (1969:81) concludes that Biloxi (Siouan) borrowed ⟨tcuwa´hana´⟩ (presumably phonemic *čuwahna*) 'cedar' from a Muskogean form like *čuwahla* 'cedar' (found with minor differences in Choctaw, Alabama, and Koasati), since the Muskogean languages have both *l* and *n* as phonemes, but Biloxi has only *n*. Cherokee (Iroquoian) *kahlkwo·ki* 'seven', which does not resemble anything in other Iroquoian languages, is apparently a loan from neighboring Creek (Muskogean) *kulapâ·kin* 'seven', which has an etymology (< *kul-* 'two' + *apâ·kin* 'added on').

Phonological Restructuring

Massive borrowing can lead to the restructuring of the phonemic system of the recipient language, as in the case of Lake Miwok (Callaghan 1964, 1987). Speakers of Patwin, Wappo, Lake Miwok, and the Pomoan languages enjoyed common access to Clear Lake, California. Although they spoke highly divergent tongues, their cultures were nearly identical. They attended each other's festivals, and intermarriage and multilingualism were of frequent occurrence. All the languages were structurally receptive to loanwords.

Wappo, Patwin, and the Pomoan languages shared glottalized affricates and multiple series of stops, including glottalized stops. Patwin also had three laterals, *l*, *ł*, and *λ̇*. Phonologically, Lake Miwok most clearly resembled Patwin in having four series of stops (voiced, voiceless, aspirated, and glottalized), glottalized affricates, and the above three laterals. Proto-Miwok had a single series of stops, one affricate (**č*), and one lateral (**l*) (Callaghan 1972), as did all the daughter Miwok languages including Bodega Miwok, which was closely related to Lake Miwok. Moreover, Lake Miwok "aberrant" phonemes (those that do not reconstruct to Proto-Miwok) occur in stems, but not in productive affixes except for reduplicative affixes and free variants of the objective case.

Callaghan's (1964) study of Lake Miwok stems containing aberrant phonemes revealed that about 30 percent closely resembled corresponding words in nearby languages. Usually, these words did not have Miwok cognates and consequently were probable loanwords from the languages in question, most commonly from neighboring Cache Creek Patwin.

An example is Lake Miwok *k̓úpum* 'finger', which does not resemble a corresponding word in any other Miwok language. In fact, Lake Miwok is the only member of the family having a specific word for 'finger' as distinct from 'hand'. Bodega Miwok *ʔúk·uh* designates both, while its Lake Miwok cognate *ʔúk·u* (< Proto-Miwok **ʔek·us*) now means only 'hand'. Instead, Lake Miwok *k̓úpum* 'finger' is most certainly borrowed from neighboring Cache Creek Patwin, in which *kupum* means 'finger' and there is a separate word *čem*, meaning 'hand'. To clinch matters, the word for 'finger' in other dialects of Patwin is *k̓upum* or *čopom*, which gives Cache Creek Patwin cognates within Patwin (see Haas's principle [3]).

Another example is Lake Miwok *?upúṣmin* 'hell-diver or grebe'. Whistler (1978a:54) gives Cache Creek Patwin *hupusmen* as 'grebe', where *hupu* means 'to dive', *-s* is a neutral unmarked tense suffix, and *-men* is a noun-deriving suffix. The Cache Creek Patwin word is polymorphemic, yielding evidence that the direction of borrowing is from that language into Lake Miwok (Haas's principle [2]).

There are at least four dozen probable loanwords from Patwin into Lake Miwok, more than from all the other nearby languages put together, and they involve body parts, brightly feathered birds, basketry terms, and verbs of operation such as 'split', 'peel', and 'knock on'. The Patwin in the Cache Creek and Long Valley areas were cut off by a long canyon and secondary mountain range from the rest of the Patwin territory. Consequently, they had much closer intercourse with the Miwok and Pomo of Clear Lake (Kroeber 1925:357).

Both Kroeber (1925:364-390) and Johnson (in vol. 8:353-354) emphasized the elaboration of cults and rituals among the Patwin. All these facts are consistent with a view of the Patwin as a source of culture, ceremony, and technology. The result was a flood of loanwords.

Aberrant phonemes are also found in some Lake Miwok words with Miwok etymologies (Callaghan 1987). The most probable explanation for this phenomenon is "naturalization" of these phonemes. Once they had been incorporated into the Lake Miwok system through massive borrowing of words from neighboring languages, they participated in regular sound change, analogy, onomatopoeia, and sound symbolism.

Specifically, pre–Lake Miwok **p* > Lake Miwok *ṗ* ~ *p* before *óc*. Hence Proto–Western Miwok **póc·iṣ* 'woman' > Lake Miwok *póc·i* ~ *póc·i* 'woman' (**-ṣ* > **-h* > *-Ø* in nouns of this canon).

Glottalization also became associated with small, quick, often semiaccidental action, as in Lake Miwok *c̓ít-ak* 'to wink' < Proto-Miwok **čit...* 'wink'. Note also *kič̓-n·i* 'index finger: pointer', a reduced grade of *kí·ci* 'to point' plus *-n·i* 'instrumental agentive'. Here, the underlying verb lacks glottalization. This phenomenon has spread to at least one loanword, *k̓učí·ya* ~ *kučí·ya* 'butcher knife' < Spanish *cuchilla* 'kitchen knife'.

In like manner, *b* became associated with words meaning 'bubble', such as *bók-bok-oṣi* 'to boil, bubble' < Proto-Miwok **pok-*.

Loanwords and Prehistory

Borrowing between Lake Miwok and Patwin was by no means a one-way operation, as the following sets illustrate. Wintu, the language of the northwestern Sacramento Valley, is related to Patwin.

English	Lake Miwok	Proto-Miwok	Patwin	Wintu
pine nuts	ṣának	*san(·)ak	sanak	cati
manzanita berries	?éy·e	*?ey·e ~ *?e·ye	?e·ye, ?e·ya	pʰa(·)y, pʰuṭi
buckeye	?ú·nu	*?u·nu	?u·nu, ?u·no	yonot

The Lake Miwok word for each of these important fruits derives from Proto-Miwok, while the Wintu evidence (cited from Pitkin 1985) indicates that the corresponding Patwin word cannot be traced to Proto-Wintuan (see Haas's principle [3]). Consequently, Patwin probably borrowed these words from a Miwokan language, not necessarily Lake Miwok. In the case of 'manzanita berries', it was more likely an Eastern Miwok language, judging by Plains Miwok and Northern Sierra Miwok *?e·ye* 'manzanita berries'.

Whistler (1977) has collected many such sets, several of which designate plants peculiar to the oak woodland and chaparral in and near the great Central Valley of California, the current homeland of the Wintu, Patwin, and Miwok Indians. These facts suggest that Proto-Wintuan speakers came from a different environment, and that the Patwin were recent arrivals to the southwestern Sacramento Valley and adjacent foothills, probably encountering Miwok speakers who formed a band connecting Eastern and Western Miwok areas.

The newly arrived high-prestige group, the Patwin, borrowed terms for local flora from the earlier inhabitants, much as European settlers on the east coast borrowed Algonquian words. Patwin also served as the donor language for loanwords in all categories. The degree to which groups of Patwin speakers moved into new areas, as opposed to there being a simple language shift on the part of aboriginal Miwok speakers, cannot be determined. The extent of "Patwinization" of Lake Miwok suggests that speakers might have shifted languages at some point in the future if there had been no European contact.

Whistler (1977) cites animal and plant names that can be reconstructed to Proto-Wintuan, including **?iw* 'acorn' (generic), **yiwit* 'acorn soup or mush', **pene(·)l* 'California black oak acorn', **qalaw* 'white alder', **sumu* 'sugar pine', **?eli* '*Brodiaea pulchella*', **handVp-* 'kingsnake', and **nur* ~ **hur* 'salmon'. The existence of acorn-related terms in this list suggests that Proto-Wintuan speakers had an acorn complex and access to oak trees. The combined range of the other terms is confined to California and southern Oregon, particularly interior northwest California and southwest Oregon, which qualifies as the most probable homeland of Proto-Wintuan. This example illustrates how an analysis of cognates and loanwords can dovetail to describe prehistory.

Loanwords between currently noncontiguous areas may argue for prehistoric contact, but extreme caution must be exercised here. Troike (1961) presents evidence that Coahuilteco *cikʷaˑs* 'six' was a borrowing from Nahuatl *cikʷaseˑ(n)* 'six'. The territories of the two languages were hundreds of miles apart; however, the borrowing was postcontact. During the missionization period in northern Mexico, Spanish friars often brought with them groups of Christian Tlaxcalans from central Mexico, who spoke a dialect of Nahuatl.

Diffusion Areas

The spread of areal features across linguistic boundaries is a common phenomenon. Jacobs (1954) notes that the languages of the Pacific Northwest from the Rogue River, Oregon, up to and including Tlingit share numerous phonological features, although they are genetically affiliated with several different families. These features include multiple laterals, also a mid-palatal and velar series as well as rounded velar phonemes, or more specifically:

g	*gʷ*	*g̓*	*g̓ʷ*
k	*kʷ*	*q*	*qʷ*
k̓	*k̓ʷ*	*q̓*	*q̓ʷ*
x	*xʷ*	*x̣*	*x̣ʷ*

The cause of this diffusion area is unclear. Trade, intermarriage, and the existence of the Chinook Jargon (if it was precontact) may have facilitated dissemination. Pinnow (1968) cites instances of probable reshaping of animal terms used by Tlingit, Eyak, Haida, and Athapaskan traders in order to maintain mutual intelligibility. Jacobs (1954:54) points out that the meticulous reconstruction of protolanguages and the investigation of intercommunity relationships are both needed to address these questions.

Sound Symbolism

Sound symbolism may play a role in diffusion areas, but in this case, it is difficult to distinguish diffusion from recurrent universal tendencies. Haas (1970) describes similar diminutive and augmentative consonantal changes in the languages of northwestern California. Nichols (1971:828) notes the "hardness shifts" that often accompany diminutive symbolism in western North America, that is, *s* > *c* or *č*, *ł* > *λ*, lenis stop, > fortis, stop > ejective, and sonorant > glottalized. Note also the possible diminutive symbolism of glottalization in Lake Miwok.

Borrowing of Categories

Instances of category borrowing, and even more so the direction in which the borrowing took place, are difficult to determine in most cases because of the dearth of historical grammars and dictionaries.

Kari (1977) lists common features of Tanaina and Ahtna that are not shared by other Athapaskan languages. The majority of these are stems or phonological features, but he includes a stem suffix -*x* used in the customary of stative verbs such as Tanaina *ašdu-x* and Ahtna *esdaa-x* 'I customarily stay, sit'. Kari cannot determine the direction of borrowing with certainty, but he notes that the Ahtna tend to be socially dominant.

Haas (1969:93-94) notes that the Athapaskan languages have a mixed system of classificatory verbs. One is a set of neuter verbs subclassified on the basis of the subject, such as 'a living being lies', 'a round object lies'. The other is a set of active verbs subclassified by the object, such as 'to pick up a round object'. She notes similar systems in Takelma and Klamath, and she speculates that these similarities are due to diffusion.

Conclusion

In-depth study of individual native American languages is necessary to separate loanwords from cognates and resemblant forms arising from onomatopoeia and universal tendencies. The paucity of borrowing studies, especially between indigenous languages, results in part from the second-class status often accorded to loans, as things that must be "weeded out" in the search for cognates (Haas 1969:80). Borrowed items are not weeds. They are coequal with cognates in uncovering prehistory.

Dynamics of Linguistic Contact

MICHAEL SILVERSTEIN

In the documented period of the gradual penetration of North America by speakers of nonaboriginal languages there have been profound changes in the speech communities of the continent. The repertoire of languages and varieties known and used in communication, the sociocultural status of these languages and varieties, and the political and economic conditions of those who use them have all been affected.

The earliest records by newcomers who were in communicative contact with indigenous groups vary considerably by date of first contact in the different regions of North America. These records are highly biased by coeval European cultural views of language in a period in which Europeans' own languages had just been emerging as standardized, written vehicles and communicative emblems of crowns, of nation-states, and of aggressive colonial enterprises (Anderson 1991). Sometimes they represent most directly European views of colonizable and colonized "primitive" peoples as humans and as political groups, for example, seeing American peoples as having no discernible "language" at all, or as communicating more with manual signals than with verbal language. Over time the historical material increases in density and amount, of course, and eventually is coeval with observational records of ethnologists, linguists, and other investigators of the period from the late nineteenth century to the present. These records, too, require special interpretive strategies to be useful in conjunction with other materials to differentiate perduring and transformed linguistic and cultural situations.

The overall picture starts from a situation in which newcomers are concerned to establish practical communication with North American peoples for specific purposes. They attempt to discern the limits of various languages and language families, which can guide them in judging the importance of acquiring (learning) one or another language spoken by the peoples they have encountered in an area or region. They observe various situations of bi- or multilingualism, particularly asymmetric ones in which, over a whole region that comprises multiple sociopolitical groups identifiable by distinct primary languages, a uniform secondary language is widely known and used as a lingua franca in intergroup communication. They frequently record their astonishment at the prior familiarity of local people with words or expressions of European languages, bespeaking some inferable earlier direct contact with speakers of European languages or some regional indigenous transmission of these forms once they were introduced. The communicating presence of ever more powerful newcomers seems inevitably to rearrange the communicative economies of whole regions. Such presence has again and again stimulated the rapid emergence of new lingua francas in the form of jargons, and of pidginized forms of languages (or even stable pidgin languages). This history of contact-driven reorganization of linguistic communities has also ultimately transformed some lingua francas into neoindigenous languages, "creolized" languages or creoles, at the same time as it has contributed to the shift of linguistic competence of indigenous peoples from precontact American languages to both local and more widespread variants of Euro-American languages.

From the initial conditions as attested, the dynamics of linguistic situations develop as a function of the sometimes abrupt, sometimes protracted, shifts in the sociopolitical relations of indigenous peoples one with another and each with the heterophone newcomers. Ships, missions, forts, trading posts, rancherias and colonies of agriculturalists, later towns and cities of settlers, residential schools, and governmental institutions at several levels, have obtruded on the communicative horizon of indigenous peoples. These all constitute at one or another time new and distinctive sites of interaction, the communicative dimensions of which seem to have transformed linguistic communities. In both the United States and Canada there emerged policies of setting aside reservations or reserves that as frequently as not amalgamated populations of speakers of very different primary languages. Until the 1960s, the main trajectory of formal schooling for indigenous peoples in North America, both religious and secular, has focused on the medium of languages of European origin. As indigenous linguistic communities have been administratively and otherwise forced into the mold of stratified deethnicization comparable to immigrant groups, one predictable result has been loss of communicative competence in indigenous "heritage" languages concurrent with—and in the particular circumstances perhaps a price of—increasing competence in Euro-American languages. Efforts on the part of indigenous linguistic communities to cope with, and to transform, these circumstances have taken place within a shifting political field of issues of the relation of societal and other forms of institutional governance to cultural diversity. Within the professional field of linguistics, the issue had developed around a discourse of linguistic and cultural "endangerment" by the mid-to-late 1980s, as seen in discussions of "endangered languages" (Robins and Uhlenbeck 1991; K. Hale et al. 1992; Ladefoged 1992; Dorian 1993), parallel to issues of threatened biodiversity.

The Situation Perceived at European Contact

All the initial encounters between Europeans and Indians were carried on either by the use of signs or by interpreters from some group with whom both newly met parties shared a means of communication. The standard form of sign language as practiced on the Great Plains (see "Nonspeech Communication Systems," this vol.; Taylor 1981:187-195 and references there) was only gradually learned by Europeans, much after the first contact with most groups. The first communication with signs was ad hoc. The use of interpreters, on the other hand, gives evidence of the presence or absence among distinct political groups of precontact languages that served them as lingua francas throughout some region.

From the earlier sources, the fact that contiguous groups frequently had members who understood the neighboring language was at least as important as the reported vast geographical extension of dialectally related forms of speech. The Spanish expeditions under Juan Bautista de Anza, for example, traveled extensively from among the Pimas to the Gila and Colorado River peoples and thence into California in 1771-1776. Among them, Father Francisco Garcés spoke Pima, and he depended on Pimas resident among the Quechan to converse with the Quechan (Bolton 1930, 2:67, 73, 322, 4:90-91); in turn, they depended on Quechans resident among the Cocopa-speaking groups to converse with them (Coues 1990, 1:173, 185). On the other hand, they discovered that the language of the Maricopas they met was the same as Quechan, though these groups were politically independent (Bolton 1930, 2:122-123, 266; Coues 1900, 1:116). Similarly, among the "Tushepaws" (Flathead) in 1805, Meriwether Lewis and William Clark held a conversation by means of

a boy a snake (Soshonee) by birth who had been taken prisoner by some northern band retaken by the Tushepaws whose language he had acquired. I spoke in English to Labieche ... — he translated it to Chaboneau in French — he to his wife [Sacagawea] in Minnetarée [Hidatsa] — she in Shoshoné to the boy — the boy in Tushepaw to that nation (Nicholas Biddle transcription of Clark recollection in Jackson 1962:519).

Numerous such examples can be found (Garcés in Coues 1900, 1:275; Mackenzie in Lamb 1970:319; Lewis and Clark in Thwaites 1904-1905, 2:362; 3:193; Henry in Coues 1897, 1:269; Parker 1838:289-290; Demers in Landerholm 1956:11-12). This chain interpretation depends on the fortuitous circumstance of having someone present in one group who speaks the language of another.

Such reports are evidence of the lack of a lingua franca used among all the groups involved. If only a few people—slaves, prisoners, married outsiders—can understand the neighboring languages, then it implies that the groups do not share a language, in the sense of general mutual intelligibility, and also that no regular general contact takes place that would lead to the development of a lingua franca.

General contact involves a socially recognized contact community with a sizable number of members of the groups participating. Apparently intergroup diplomacy did not usually form the basis of a contact community on the Plains. Alexander Henry reports, for example, that in 1806 the Pawnee delegation to the Mandan villages used sign language principally (a few in each group understanding spoken language), that the Hidatsa brought their own interpreter with them, and that the Mandan-Hidatsa delegation to the Cheyenne camp could not understand a word of that language (Coues 1897, 1:335, 377). Similarly, Bradbury in 1810 notes that an Arikara man served as interpreter when some Cheyenne messengers arrived among them (Thwaites 1904-1907, 5:139).

Rather, contact communities of the kind that lead to general knowledge of a lingua franca are associated with constant, perhaps to a certain extent sedentary, interaction. From the earliest documents, it seems that several such lingua francas were in existence among Indian groups. Clearly, the fur trade may have influenced the wide extension of some of these languages. Groups with whom the Europeans dealt in turn acted as agents for or as tribute-collectors from more remote and weaker groups, for example, the Chinooks who tried preventing the other groups about Astoria from trading directly, and the Crees who dominated some of the Chipewyan-speaking groups in the Athabasca Department. The dialect or language of those closest to the Europeans acquired a certain importance, since the traders usually attempted to learn some form of it, or some pidgin or jargon directly related to it.

French observers, for example, report uniformly from the seventeenth century that there are two basic "languages" in New France, Algonquin and Huron, each with a vast geographical extension, but Algonquin especially so because "commonly the *Iroquese* make use of [Algonquin] in their Harangues and Councils, when they enter upon a Negotiation with the *French* or *English*" (Lahontan in Thwaites 1905, 2:746-747).

They correctly perceived the relationship of the languages spoken by all the groups, though they had no means of interpreting the data scientifically and named the entire family from the language spoken closest to their own settlement. But it is not certain what should be made of their claims about being able to speak "Algonquin" for hundreds of leagues in every direction (Jérôme Lalemant in JR 20:41; Charlevoix 1744, 3:183, 185, 189). Le Jeune notes in 1633 that the interpreter to the Algonquins is well understood among the Montagnais (JR 5:232); Lahontan (in Thwaites 1905, 2:734) notes that "all the languages of *Canada*, excepting the *Huron* and those which retain to it, come as near to the *Algonkine* as the *Italian* to the *Spanish*: and 'tis for this reason that . . . so many different Nations affect to speak it with all manner of nicety." This means either that a dialect chain existed, quite plausible on the basis of later, accurate evidence; that this "Algonquin," or Eastern Ojibwa in Rhodes's (1982:6) identification for the nineteenth century, was indeed a lingua franca east of Georgian Bay; or, that the French spoke a form so pidginized that it was equally intelligible (or unintelligible) to most of the Indians in the eastern cluster of Central Algonquian languages.

A similar situation is claimed for "Huron" among the Iroquoian languages; "whoever knows Huron, understands them all" (Charlevoix 1744, 3:189). Vast geographical extension of intelligibility is again described (JR 42:221, 67:145, 68:279). Lahontan (in Thwaites 1905, 2:733) explains that it "is understood by the Iroquese, for the difference betwixt the *Huron* and the *Iroquese* Language is not greater than that between the *Norman* and the *French*."

In these cases, French-speaking interpreters probably did speak some generalized, or pidginized form of the languages, while the Indians perhaps had knowledge of the dialects of closely related groups. It is curious that the only explicit statements of intelligibility of a speaker involve Europeans and Indians. In such a case, it would be going too far to attribute lingua franca status to Algonquin and Huron among the Indian groups themselves, before the arrival of the French.

Whatever was the situation in the region first colonized, it appears that in the eighteenth and nineteenth centuries Southwestern Ojibwa or "Chippewa" (also called Saulteaux or Algonquin, though identified as the language of the "Chippeways") was spoken widely as a second language by all the Indian groups about the western Great Lakes area (Long in Thwaites 1904-1907, 2:28, 61; Pike in Jackson 1966, 1:62, 210, 217). Menominee bilingualism in Ojibwa may go back farther, since Allouez (JR 44:235) paid them a visit in 1670, and addressed them in "Algonquin": "I had difficulty in understanding them, but in time made the discovery that their language is Algonquin, though much corrupted. They succeeded in understanding me better

than I understood them." Since Allouez spoke what the French intended as Algonquin, it is reasonable to conclude that they understood him through knowledge of Ojibwa, though whether Eastern Ojibwa or not is impossible to determine. By the nineteenth century, Rhodes (1982:4-5) infers, the region between Eastern and Western Ojibwa—between Lake Michigan and Lake Ontario, roughly—was the region of a distinct lingua franca, Ottawa (also called "Chippewa" by many speakers), while north of the Great Lakes, Cree predominated in this function.

In the early eighteenth century, Beverley (1722:161) observed of the Virginia Indians:

> Their Languages differ very much, as antiently in the several parts of Britain; so that Nations at a moderate distance do not understand one another. However, they have a sort of general Language, like what *Lahontan* calls the *Algonkine*, which is understood by the chief Men of many Nations, as *Latin* is in the most parts of Europe and *Lingua Franca* quite thro' the Levant.
>
> The general Language here us'd, is said to be that of the *Occaneeches*, tho' they have been but a small Nation, ever since those parts were known to the English: but in what this Language may differ from that of the *Algonkines*, I am not able to determine.

It is possible, as Goddard (1972:220) notes, that a 1716 vocabulary (Alexander 1971) labeled "Sapoiney" is actually a vocabulary of this lingua franca. The words are mainly Siouan, akin to Tutelo, except the numerals, which are principally Algonquian, with one or two from Iroquoian. Though this would tend to belie Beverley's identification of the lingua franca as Occaneechi pure and simple, it does give evidence of some mixed vocabulary in use at the time. Observe also that Beverley states that this Occaneechi lingua franca was the religious language of all the Algonquian tribes in the area.

As the fur trade spread to the western part of Canada, the extension of two other languages is noted. One, Cree, already a lingua franca among indigenous peoples north of the Great Lakes, seems to have been somewhat pidginized as a lingua franca on the Canadian plains. Mackenzie (1970:149, 240), speaking of the late eighteenth century, says that the Chipewyans who traded at the Hudson's Bay Company "have a smattering of the Knisteneaux [Cree] tongue, in which they carry on their dealings with us." He also reported that by 1793, sizable bands of eastern Beavers spoke it. Similarly, Alexander Henry in 1810 mentioned that at Rocky Mountain House among the Piegans, Cree was "the only tongue in vogue here, of which I understand a little" (Coues 1897, 2:648). Of the Sarcees, he remarked: "Most of them have a smattering of the Cree language, which they display in clamorous and discordant strains, without rule or reason. Their own language is so difficult to acquire that none of our people have ever learned it" (Coues 1897, 2:737). The fur trade must have been an important factor in the spread of this "smattering" of Cree, a pidginized form of Cree no doubt, among other groups of primary Athapaskan-dialect speech.

In contrast, the reported widespread use of "Chipewyan" must be understood as due to dialect linkages of the northern Athapaskan languages that permitted partial intelligibility. Traveling with Chipewyans who traded at Hudson Bay, Hearne (1795:124) in 1771 found that the "Copper Indians" (Yellowknife) north of the Great Slave Lake "are in reality the same people in every respect [as the Chipewyans], and their language differs not so much as the dialects of some of the nearest counties in England do from each other." Similarly, Mackenzie (1970:182, 211) traveling in 1789 with a party under The English Chief (a Chipewyan who spoke Cree, by the way), reported a high degree of understanding between them and Slaveys and Dogribs (but not Hares). Traveling to the Pacific in 1793, he reports that his eastern Beaver interpreters "understood very little" of the speech of the Slouacuss-Dinais (Tluskez Village, a Carrier settlement), which is difficult to understand unless there was a fade-out of intelligibility among dialects, some people actually controlling more than one. Mackenzie (1970:192, 194, 207) clearly reported mutual intelligibility between Chipewyan and Dogrib, as between Dogrib and the speech of the Upper Porcupine River Kutchin, but only possible one-way intelligibility between the first and the last. Nevertheless, he observed that "a Chepewyan, from which tribe they have all sprung, might leave Churchill River, and proceeding in every direction to the North-West . . . without knowing any language except his own, would understand them all" (Mackenzie 1970:398). This passed into the general knowledge that Whites maintained about these Athapaskan peoples, reduced to terms of "the same language" (Wilkes 1845, 4:451; Demers in Landerholm 1956:158). Jenness (1932:20) repeats the same information, that Chipewyans of Great Slave Lake can "readily converse" with Carriers of British Columbia. This should not obscure the fact that important linguistic differences existed among these groups, making complete intelligibility doubtful.

In the nineteenth century, there may have emerged from this situation quasiconventionalized yet regionally differentiated "jargon" forms of communication, Slavey Jargon (Broken Slavey) and Jargon Kutchin (Loucheux), in the Mackenzie and Yukon River regions (see Bakker 1994a:28-29).

The early French travelers who descended the Mississippi found that Illinois (that is, Peoria) served "about a hundred leagues down the river" from its junction with the Illinois River (Membré in Shea 1982:184). This was because they found interpreters among all the groups they passed, down to the Arkansas River, where the Quapaws resided (Marquette in French 1850, 2:288, 294, 295; Claude Delisle's copy of Henri Joutel's journal in Margry 1876-1886, 3:475-476, 483; Pénigaut in Margry 1876-1886, 5:409). But what is interesting is Joutel's report that among both the Quapaw and the Cahinnio (Caddo Confederacy), he heard some words of the language of the north, which must mean some type of Algonquian, in particular ⟨Nicana⟩ (representing approximately [nikana]) 'my brother'; perhaps ⟨Panchougua⟩ ([pą̄sugwa]) 'chief' is to be included, though not identifiably Algonquian in ultimate etymology (Margry 1876-1886, 3:412, 434).

This would tend to indicate that the Algonquian languages of the tributaries of the Mississippi were dominant at least to the extent of having widespread scattered knowledge, and having been the source of loanwords as far south as the Siouans and Caddoans of the Mississippi. Delisle says that René-Robert Cavelier, sieur de La Salle learned 'my brother' from Shawnees, and Joutel says that it is common "among all the nations higher up the river." This argues strongly against any form of Mobilian Jargon having been the dominant lingua franca on this part of the Mississippi and may explain why there are so many words from Algonquian that made their way into Mobilian, after the French settled in Lower Louisiana.

Many of the northern Athapaskan groups seem to have had some familiarity with a pidginized form of Eskimo from a very early date. Mackenzie reported in 1789 that his Kutchin guides to the Arctic "took much Pains to show us that [they] knew the Eskmeaux [and] their Customs," making fun of them and pronouncing words (Mackenzie 1970:194). Similarly, Stefánsson (1909:219-220) reports that the Kutchin then spoke a Pidgin Eskimo with the Eskimo, significantly richer in preserving Eskimo structure than the pidgin used between the Europeans and Eskimos. For example, they preserved the Eskimo conjugational -q on forms and Eskimo word order. Jenness (1932:117), apparently mistaking this pidgin for real Eskimo, states that the Kutchin generally knew Eskimo "from time immemorial." This pidgin seems to have existed before the Europeans encountered these groups.

For other areas, there are only vague or negative reports on contact communication and intelligibility over wide geographical areas. Creek was no doubt widely spoken by member groups of the Creek Confederacy; James Oglethorpe wrote in 1734 (Jones 1966:515) of the Indians of present Georgia:

As for their Language they have two kinds, One which is a vulgar Dialect, different in each Town, the other a general Language common to the Creek Nations the Chactaws and the Blew Mouths, which if thoroughly searched into would (I believe) be found to be the radical Language of all America.

Similarly Francis Le Jau wrote from South Carolina in 1708-1710 about the lingua franca status of

Algonquian languages to the north, related to the local Shawnee, and of Creek in the southern realms (Klingberg 1956:19, 41, 49, 57, 68, 73). This use of Creek continued into later times, and as Creek-speaking sociopolitical groups absorbed other groups, these groups learned Creek as a secondary language at least (Adair 1775: 267; Bartram 1792:461-463; Gatschet 1884-1888, 1:90; Woodward 1859:41). In fact, with the exception of the Yuchis, "the other little tribes . . . all dwindled away [as distinct political units] and lost their language" by this process of absorption (Woodward 1859:29).

Finally, in the Northwest, it would appear from later accounts that Haida was used as a secondary contact language; Scouler (1905:182) reported in 1825 that the language of the Nisgha (Tsimshianic) "is a dialect of that spoken on Q. Charlotte's Island."

For the most part, the other groups on the continent were principally monolingual, with occasional members of the group who could serve as interpreters where necessary. The Europeans made great use of the lingua francas they perceived, probably helping to extend them more widely as knowledge of them became an even more valuable cultural possession with which to engage new sociopolitical groups. But there arose many pidgins and jargons serving as well as lingua francas, a function of economic and political and cultural contact between indigenous and nonindigenous people. Furthermore, the indigenous groups began to acquire competence in the European languages. The early literature of contact often mentions "wise chiefs" who sent a son to learn a colonial or missionary language of the Europeans, in some cases apparently following an indigenous pattern of training interpreters among political elites. As indigenous peoples were eventually channeled into Euro-American educational institutions, such sparse and elite multilingualism was transformed into the widespread loss of any indigenous linguistic competence in a heritage language, quite common in North America in the 1990s. The situation thus changes dramatically with European settlement as a permanent presence among the Indian groups.

Indian-European Contact Jargons and Pidgins

One of the clear traces of the transformation of American speech communities is the emergence of forms of communication in situations of trade and European settlement. There are clear recordings of such lingua francas from many parts of the continent, each seeming to have its peak period of usage at some point between first contact across the divide of language communities and the present time. Of course, there are different historical circumstances in the constitution of each of these new contact communities:

some emerge from the communicative situation of maritime trade, some from the establishment of permanent inland fur-trading posts central to an area of great multilingualism, and some from communicative patterns associable with colonial agricultural settlement. Yet in each of the attested cases, these originally simple forms of communication emerge in the context of social relations across what otherwise would be a linguistic divide.

In such contact situations in North America, forms of speech have been recorded that are, at least in their early phases of development, structurally (in sound system and grammar) and lexically (in conventional words and expressions) "simplified" when compared with records of the regularly used languages of any of the participating peoples. In contact communities, moreover, the etymological sources of lexical forms are frequently multiple, though at any historical period there is sometimes a preponderant lexifier language, that is, a language that has preponderantly contributed the conventionally used elementary forms for words and expressions.

Some of the attested communicative systems are of the jargon type. Speakers must have used a special contact set of formally invariant words and expressions according to a rudimentary combinatorics. Such a system can function communicatively, one might plausibly hypothesize, only insofar as it relies on something cognitively or communicatively "universal" and on the context-specificity (including accompanying gesture communication) of usage. Several of the attested systems seem to be pidginized forms of particular languages, in particular pidginized versions of indigenous American languages that emerged in the process of interpreters' and others' attempts at mastery; they also show characteristic structural and lexical reduction or simplification.

Such jargons and pidginized forms seem to have become the conventional means of communication in several contact communities, ultimately being used by speakers of many other languages as well as of the one originally pidginized or constituting the preponderant lexifier. At such a point of conventionality, this form of communication is labeled a pidgin language, or simply pidgin. A pidgin language generally constitutes a conventionalized structural and lexical system that anyone operating in a contact community will normatively master or seek to master, in addition to some primary language or languages. In some sedentary forms of social organization where a pidgin is central to the contact communicative regime, such as permanent multi-ethnic settlements, there is some suggestion of creolization of such contact systems, that is, their functional change into primary languages of a linguistic community, creole languages or creoles, mastered in the expected course of first language acquisition by members of a new linguistic community for whom it is a first tongue.

The recordings in the very early literature of trade and exploration suggest that a number of the Europeans who claimed to speak one or more of the Indian languages actually spoke a pidginized variety. The difficulties of recording in an alphabet ill-adapted for these languages cannot explain all the grammatical simplification and misrepresentation of inflections found in these records. Yet the intention of many of these documents appears to have been the representation of the "Indian" language as spoken. Thus, the number of jargon and pidgin situations must have been much higher than the few remains of direct evidence of such lingua francas would at first indicate.

Souriquois Jargon

Marc Lescarbot (1612, 3:693-694) mentions the existence of a medium of communication between the French colonists at Fort Royal (later Port Royal) and the Micmacs who lived there, based upon his observations during 1606 and 1607. He said that the Indians spoke their own language among themselves, but to communicate with the French, they used a language "which is more familiar to us," though the Indians explicitly disclaimed any intention of learning French; it is just by "long frequentation that one cannot but retain some words" (Lescarbot 1612, 3:695). There were then three languages in use in the colony—French, Micmac, and this jargon. Bakker (1989:129) demonstrates the close fit between a number of lexical items in this Souriquois Jargon and Basque, a language of a sizable component of European fishermen and sailors along the eastern coast of North America.

Some of the words of this jargon that appear to be from Basque are: ⟨kessona⟩ 'man' (cf. Basque *gizona*); ⟨atouray⟩ 'shirt' (cf. Basque *atorra*); ⟨Souriquois⟩ 'Micmac' (Basque *zurikoa* 'that of the Whites'); ⟨Capitaina⟩ 'captain, chief'; ⟨Normandia⟩ 'Norman'; ⟨Basquoa⟩ 'Basque'; ⟨Tabaguia⟩ 'banquet' (cf. Basque *tapaki(a)* 'blanket, covering; shelter'); ⟨Chabaia⟩ 'Indian' (cf. Basque *xabaia* /šabaia/ 'savage'). An element *-a* appears in these forms that seems etymologically to be the Basque determiner *-a*. Presumably the French used this means of communication as well as the Micmacs. Lescarbot (1612, 3:694) remarked of the Indians that "they pronounce the rest of the French language better than our Gascons . . .," which suggests that many of the vocabulary items of this contact medium were largely common to French, Basque, and other relevant European languages, so the specific source is difficult to determine (e.g., for Souriquois Jargon ⟨echpada⟩ 'sword' cf. Basque *ezpata*, Gascon and Spanish *espada*, French *espadon*).

Montagnais Jargon

A contact medium between the French and the Montagnais at Tadoussac on the Saint Lawrence River is mentioned by Paul Le Jeune (JR 5:112-115), writing from Quebec in 1633. Le Jeune calls this contact medium a "jargon" (French *baragouin*) used by the French and Montagnais both, who each thought the contact medium was the primary language of the other group in the contact community. Le Jeune had had his first introduction to "Montagnais," which he was endeavoring to learn, the previous year, and many words of this jargon were taught to him that he only later discovered to be part of the contact language.

The examples given of this jargon show that neither French nor Montagnais is the source of a good portion of the vocabulary, as Le Jeune himself notes in passing. Some lexical items are ultimately Basque, as Bakker (1989:135) demonstrates in the case of ⟨ania⟩ 'brother' ("mon frere"), used by both French and Montagnais (clearly from Basque *anaia* 'brother'). Similarly, Montagnais Jargon ⟨sagamo⟩ 'chief' is not a Montagnais word in origin; it is from some Eastern Algonquian language (cf. Trumbull 1903:144) such as Eastern Abenaki or perhaps seventeenth-century Micmac. The Montagnais word is *ocima·w*, which Le Jeune himself gives as ⟨oukhimau⟩. "There are many others like this," observes Le Jeune.

This indicates that it was probably the French and other Europeans who brought these non-Montagnais-derived Montagnais Jargon vocabulary items with them from the more easterly settlements, and used them in communicating with the Montagnais at Quebec and elsewhere. These indigenous people, too, would use Montagnais Jargon items for contact communication with the French, so that such jargonized contact media, which combined elements from many languages implicated in a varied interlocking chain of contact communities, are seen particularly to be ready means of mediated transfer of words even from one indigenous linguistic community to another. Perhaps this is why Le Jeune makes a point of saying that the French "think they are speaking Indian" and the Indians think they are speaking French, though both are really speaking a third thing, a substantially Basque-lexified contact jargon that spread westward from the easternmost mainland coast between the late sixteenth and mid-seventeenth centuries, with two centers of attestation, among the Micmacs and among the Montagnais.

Pidgin Delaware

The exigencies of dealing with the Delaware-speaking Indians among whom were founded the Middle Atlantic European colonies gave rise to a pidginized form of one of the local Delaware languages, Unami, that seems to have become a pidgin language of interpreters and others, such as missionaries, in this multilingual contact community of speakers of indigenous Munsee and Unami (in both Northern and Southern dialects) and colonial Dutch, Swedish, and English (Goddard 1995). There are scattered citations of words and phrases from this pidgin in various seventeenth-century sources, gathered and extensively annotated by Goddard (1996); the largest bodies of material are found in Johannes Campanius's (1696) mid-seventeenth-century vocabulary and catechism, in Thomas's (1698) account of Pennsylvania and West New Jersey, and in an anonymous list entitled "The Indian Interpreter" filed with a 1684 deed of Salem County, New Jersey (edited, with errors, in Prince 1912). It is clear from the remarks of Thomas, and from the title of the anonymous list, that these writings represent the attempt of secular as well as missionary Europeans to record the language in use between them and the Indians, which several of the writers thought was what the Indians spoke. For example, Thomas (1698:47) observed: "Their *Language* is Lofty and Elegant, but not Copious; *One* Word serveth in the stead of *Three*, imperfect and ungrammatical, which defects are supply'd by the Understanding of the Hearers." One observer, Jonas Michaëlius (in Jameson 1909:128) noted already in 1628 that the Indians consciously simplified their language for use with the colonists, speaking something else among themselves.

Here, too, the contact language, Pidgin Delaware, seems to have emerged quite rapidly in a specific place, and to have spread over a wide territory, incorporating traces of varied linguistic contact. As Goddard (1996) deduces, the pidginized form of Unami recorded first in de Laet (1633) must have arisen as a communication medium along the Delaware River around Burlington Island (below present-day Trenton) between the time of colonization in 1624 and the removal of all colonists to Manhattan Island (in Munsee-speaking territory) completed by October 1628. From the earliest period the Delaware Indians on this part of the Delaware River were trading as middlemen between the Virginia Indians and the Dutch on "Monadas" (Manhattan) (Beverley 1722:67, 1947:77).

Pidgin Delaware was also later used in dealing with local Indians by the English colonists, after they took over the Dutch colonies of New Amsterdam and (East) New Jersey in 1664, as is shown by the fact that the glosses of the 1684 "The Indian Interpreter" are in English. English colonists also transformed the lexicon of Pidgin Delaware with several indigenous-derived words that come from southern New England Algonquian languages, rather than from either Unami or Munsee, bespeaking their transmission in a southwestward direction. These include ⟨papouse⟩ 'suckling child' and ⟨squaw⟩ 'wife' (from Narraganset ⟨papoòs⟩

'child' and Massachusett ⟨squa⟩ 'younger woman'). The Delaware form of the word for 'woman' (e.g., Unami *xkwé·*) shows up in "The Indian Interpreter" pidgin ⟨aquittit⟩ 'little girl' formed with diminutive suffix ⟨-tit⟩ (Unami *-t·ət*), though Thomas renders ⟨squatid⟩, using the New England stem and the Delaware diminutive (see also Goddard 1996). The English no doubt transplanted these words to the later colonies on the middle Atlantic, just as the French transplanted words from the languages of Acadia to Quebec and the interior of New France.

By the late seventeenth century, then, the contact community, apparently centered on those who interpreted for some specific reasons, had widened to include primary speakers of at least Delaware, Dutch, German, Swedish, and English, and had a geographical spread at least from New York to Pennsylvania, centering on the Delaware River valley. The Delaware Indians started their gradual move west in the early eighteenth century, and the use of Pidgin Delaware in the middle Atlantic states probably ceased about this time. Goddard (1996) notes that a southern Unami vocabulary recorded in western Pennsylvania in 1785, after one stage of migration of Delaware people, contains Pidgin forms. It did not survive in anyone's memory long enough for there to be modern recordings of it.

The items reported in the specimens are associated with contact functions such as trade, getting information about people, Christian ministry, and concluding formal (treaty) arrangements. All of the vocabulary shows considerable reshaping in sound system in the items from Delaware and from other sources. The European speakers on their part were accommodating to the Indian sound system, as much as they were distorting it in their production of the predominantly Delaware vocabulary. For the most part, the complex morphological structure of Delaware words is eliminated from the Pidgin Delaware forms, and segments of the Delaware forms are preserved, centering of course on stressed or prominent syllabic stretches, with no regard to their status as fragments of well-formed words in the Delaware grammatical system. These word fragments, which have become independent words of the pidgin, are used in phrases without any declensional apparatus of Delaware nouns or conjugational apparatus of Delaware verbs. Note how sometimes the very syntactic category of a word is transformed in Pidgin Delaware usage, as for example the inflected verb in Unami *kə́ntka·n* 'one dances', which gave rise to Pidgin ⟨chíntika⟩ 'holy; prayer', used adjectivally and nominally (Goddard 1996).

For example, Goddard (1971:16) recorded in the 1960s a Delaware sentence that must have been the formulaic source in the seventeenth century for David de Vries's Pidgin Delaware expression

⟨rancontyn marenit⟩ 'make peace': the grammatically formed expression is *kəmanni·tó·ne·n=č ktə́li-=č -ɔ·wəlankuntí·ne·n* 'we (incl.) will make lasting peace together'. The *=č* is the future enclitic; prefix *kə-* (or *kt-*) together with suffix *-ne·n* expresses the first-person inclusive 'we'; *-əli-* on the second word is a complementizer. Of what is left, Pidgin Delaware ⟨rancontyn⟩ comes from the fragment *-lankunti·n-* (with *l* from earlier *r*), which includes the first consonant of the Delaware inflectional ending, while ⟨marenit⟩ corresponds to Unami *manni·t-*, which is from earlier **marəni·t-* (Goddard 1996:n. 119).

No functioning Unami grammatical structure seems to remain in Pidgin Delaware phrases and sentences. Etymologically, there are remnants of productive Unami grammatical processes represented in the pidginized word fragments, but these do not clearly have comparable identities in any Pidgin Delaware grammar. The grammar that is imposed onto the invariant, uninflected Delaware forms is reminiscent in some instances of phrase construction in the grammar of one or another of the European languages, for example, the invariant Pidgin Delaware words put into phrases that resemble parts of English sentences. Thomas (1698:9) shows by parallel-column treatment a virtual word-by-word translatability of Pidgin Delaware sentences and English sentences:

⟨Nee   hatah   huska   wees   youse   og   huska
'I   have   very   fat   meat   and very
chetena   chase   og   huska   orit   chekenip.⟩
strong   skins   and   very   good   turkeys.'

Each word of the Pidgin Delaware form corresponds to one word of the English. Tenses, singular or plural, and similar grammatical categories obligatory in either Unami or in English are not expressed in the Pidgin Delaware form.

Apalachee-Spanish

Before 1710 (the land grant having been made in 1705) Apalachee Indians went from Spanish settlements in Florida to live close to the French at Fort Mobile (Margry 1876-1886, 5:487). They had all become Roman Catholics and "sang their psalms in Latin, as is done in France." However, their everyday language was apparently Apalachee "mixed up with the language of the Spaniards and that of the Alabamas." This seems to indicate that during the years before 1710, there had arisen a jargon of some kind in the western Florida region, used by the Spaniards with Indians in the area, both Apalachees and Alabamas. That this jargon was apparently transplanted to Mobile is of importance for the later attestations of Mobilian Jargon. The population of Apalachees obviously became integrated into the contact community about Mobile after their resettlement; it is possible that the linguistic reflexes of the earlier Spanish-Apalachee contact medium are found in later recordings of Mobilian.

Mobilian Jargon or Pidgin Muskogean

What is referred to as Mobilian (by the French) or "the vulgar language" or "Choctaw (or Chickasaw) (trade) language" (by the English) or "yama" (by 20th-century Indians who remember some) likely originated in a pidginized form of a Western Muskogean language of the Choctaw type (if not a dialect of Choctaw itself) used in the early French-Indian contact community established through European colonization of the lower Mississippi region.

Some interpretive literature (Gatschet 1884-1888, 1892; Swanton 1911:7-39; Drechsel 1983, 1984) posits the existence of such a Mobilian Jargon in pre-French times; frequently this presumption is integral to an ethnological argument (Swanton 1911:22) and hence leads to circularity in establishing linguistic relationships. However, there is no direct attestation of the existence of Mobilian until six years after the commencement of the French colonization by Pierre Le Moyne d'Iberville in the Mobile and Mississippi River area. Iberville records in 1699 (Margry 1876-1886, 4:184) that the Houma, Bayogoula, Natchez, Taensa, Koroa, Chickasaw, Quinipissa, Washa, Chitimacha, and Yakna-Chitto "speak the same language" and can communicate with the Biloxi and Pascagoula peoples. Following this, in 1700 Iberville records that his brother, Jean-Baptiste Le Moyne, sieur de Bienville, is beginning to get along in Houma, Bayogoula, Chickasaw, Acolapissa, and three other languages "which are really the same—differ but little" (Margry 1876-1886, 4:412). Among the Natchez, whose "language is different from that of the Houmas," they found one person who could speak with Bienville. If the similarity of language referred to in this citation is an indication of the existence of Mobilian Jargon, then it had clearly not yet reached the Natchez as a functioning member group of a contact community. On the other hand, the languages mentioned in Iberville's 1700 list were probably all members of the Muskogean family. When the typical early attitudes toward the constitution of "languages" and their variant "dialects" are considered this is more likely a statement that all these groups formed a Muskogean dialect area of the Choctaw-Chickasaw type and that there was emerging some degree of French competence in using a contact version that crystallized as Mobilian.

The linguistic evidence points to the following situation. On the eastern side of the Mississippi, there was a very large dialect area of indigenous groups, dominated in population by Muskogean speech of the

Choctaw-Chickasaw type. Some speakers of a few groups of basically distinct speech, such as the Biloxi (Siouan) and Natchez, probably employed Muskogean as a local lingua franca by virtue of being completely surrounded by Muskogean languages. Thus André-Joseph Pénigaut (1953:24; Margry 1876-1886, 5:394) speaks of a Biloxi guide he met in the company of the French in 1700, who could converse with the Bayogoulas, clearly remarkable enough to be noted, as was the one person among the Natchez in 1700 who could converse with Bienville. The French left records of their discovery of dialectal (historical family) relationship among the Muskogean languages of the area. Thus Iberville in 1702 wrote that the Tohomé of the Tombigbee River "speak the language of the Bayogoulas; at any rate there is little difference" (Margry 1876-1886, 4:514). In the same year, Iberville sent a young boy who had mastered Houma, "which is nearly the same as Chickasaw," to learn Chickasaw proper (Margry 1876-1886, 4:521).

It is first in Pénigaut's (1953:81; Margry 1876-1886, 5:442) account of events of 1704 that a linguistic entity called "Mobilian" made its appearance. He wrote that during the five years he had been in Louisiana, he learned the indigenous languages "fairly well," especially Mobilian, the principal one, "which is understood among all the tribes" ("et qu'on entend par toutes les nations"). While it is clear from his descriptions of 1698 (Pénigaut 1953:12; Margry 1876-1886, 5:384) that he did not then understand any of the languages of the area, "Mobilian" early emerges as the French name for whatever pidgin they spoke everywhere with the Indians of the area, whose primary languages were dialects of Muskogean, predominantly those close to Choctaw-Chickasaw. (It was, no doubt, the later political and economic importance of the Chickasaw that led to Chickasaw Trade Language being synonymous with Mobilian by mid-eighteenth century.)

Among dialect groups whose primary languages are so close, there is little reason for significant pidginization to take place in achieving some common form of speech to serve in contact functions. Once the French were on the scene, there was ample reason for general use of a pidginized form that no doubt the French were using as the common medium of contact, intending to speak the Indian languages. At a slightly later time (having arrived in the area in 1718), Le Page du Pratz (1758, 2:218-219, 226, 242, 3:89) attributed use of Mobilian also to the Taensa, Choctaw, Chakchiuma, Ofo, Taposa, Natchitoches, Caddo, and Yazoo peoples, and in general to "all the peoples who are in the area of the Chickasaw" who "speak the Chickasaw language, though somewhat corrupted."

Mobilian spread, though apparently slowly, to a very extensive area during the eighteenth century. In 1708, Pénigaut (1953:126; Margry 1876-1886, 5:480) relates,

two French hunters used Mobilian to communicate with Alabamas near Pensacola Bay—speakers of another Muskogean language—who had taken them prisoner. He also claimed that he was the only person on a 1714 expedition who could communicate, presumably using Mobilian, somewhere on the Mississippi north of the Natchez (Margry 1876-1886, 5:514). Le Page du Pratz (1758, 1:113) says that at the conclusion of the Chitimacha War of 1718, Bienville directly addressed this group in Mobilian. The Chitimacha, then, were part of the Mobilian contact community at this time. And he claims that on his first going to the Natchez, among whom he spent several years trading, his first transaction in buying property was conducted "by means of an interpreter" (Le Page du Pratz 1758, 1:126), though

> the majority of the Natchez also spoke the common language [Mobilian] well, and I knew it so as to be able to make myself understood for the purposes of the necessities of life and for the purposes of trade; but I wanted also to learn the language of this people, to be able to speak to the women who do not speak the common language and who frequently brought us many things necessary for subsistence, and I was very pleased to be able to question them and answer them . . . (Le Page du Pratz 1758, 2:321).

Observe the gendered distinction of communicative competence implied.

By 1752, the use of Mobilian Jargon was apparently common as far north in the Mississippi River basin as the Wabash River. Mobilian Jargon was employed between Indian and Black and between Indian and French (Pease and Jenison 1940:756, 759). The Englishman John Adair, who claimed to speak "the Chickasaw language" (probably Mobilian Jargon), reported that the Creeks who spoke "the Muskolge dialect" could not understand him, nor he them (Adair 1775:274). Indeed, it is clear (Haas 1941:42-43, 45-46; Gatschet 1884-1888, 1:53) that Creek and Choctaw-Chickasaw are not mutually intelligible languages. Hence a pidgin based on Choctaw-Chickasaw would not, on the face of it, be intelligible to Creek speakers, without special learning of it. Therefore, it seems that the Creek did not participate in this contact community centered around the French at the time of Adair's activity in the region.

Referring to the region to the west of the Mississippi in the early nineteenth century Woodward (1859:79) notes that Mobilian, under that name, is the "trading language" of "almost all the tribes that have inhabited the country" in northeastern Texas. This fits with the evidence of John Sibley, who, reporting from Natchitoches in 1805, claimed that the Biloxi, Apalachee, Alabama, Pakana (of the Creek Confederacy), Tunica, Pascagoula, Taensa, and Choctaw spoke Mobilian, specifically excluding the groups of the Caddo Confederacy, the Comanches,

Karankawa, Atakapa, Opelousa, and Quapaw (Sibley 1832:721-725). Brackenridge (1814:82), at approximately the same time, gave a shorter list but did not contradict this.

The general use of Mobilian Jargon by groups with whom the Indians interacted is attested from the eighteenth century, then. Adair (1775:285) observed that "the French at Mobile, and some at New Orleans could speak the Choctah language extremely well," presumably meaning Mobilian, though he claimed that what he himself spoke was Chickasaw. In a letter dated 1802, from New Orleans, Duralde (1802:2) spoke of the difficulty of collecting vocabularies of the primary Indian languages of the region: "These peoples communicating with the whites only by means of the common Mobilian language, no one takes the interest to know the original ones." Black slaves were apparently kept by both Indians and French for employment as interpreters, using Mobilian Jargon. Adair (1775:327) spoke of communication by means of slaves of the French who spoke to Chickasaw couriers of the English. Similarly, Woodward (1859:108) noted of slaves of the Indians that "not one in fifty but speaks the English as well as the Indian language. Nearly all of them, at some time or other, are used as interpreters." As late as 1971, Crawford (1978:61) found an old man of French parentage who, in his youth in Elton, Louisiana, in the late nineteenth or early twentieth century spoke Mobilian with the Indians living there.

Crawford (1972:1-3; 1978:60-62) and Drechsel (1979, 1986:4-5) also located other very old people in southern Louisiana and eastern Texas who remembered a few words and phrases of "the old language" that seems to be the remnant of Mobilian Jargon. The Indian informants called this language *yamá* rather than Mobilian, and included people of Koasati, Alabama, and Choctaw descent. This would indicate that the general use of Mobilian continued in the western part of its extension well up to the late nineteenth century at least. Crawford's salvage documentation (in 1970-1971) of approximately 200 words and phrases and Drechsel's work beginning in 1976 constitute the only modern recordings and transcriptions of forms. Swanton (1911:32) had published nine words, which he identified principally as Mobilian, secured from two brothers of Biloxi-Pascagoula parents.

Mobilian shows the characteristic pidgin features of severe reduction in morphological complexity of words, with inflected forms of Muskogean languages sometimes deriving as simple and invariant vocabulary items. Thus note Alabama *am-okla* 'my friend' or Choctaw *am-oklah* 'my people' and Mobilian [mogula] 'friend'; Choctaw *ịki* 'his father' versus Mobilian [inkɛ] 'father', used with independent pronoun possessors: [šnu inkɛ] 'your father'. Mobilian also had a drastically reduced syntax when compared with Choctaw or

other Muskogean languages. Le Page du Pratz (1758, 2:323) asserts that rather than give rules of grammar, Mobilian "is learned better by use"; since he contrasts this with Natchez (in both its forms), he probably means that by comparison with any of the other languages he knew, Mobilian Jargon showed a bare constituent form, probably heavily dependent on context for understanding. Writing about the *yamá* of Crawford's survivors, Haas (1975:259) points out that the personal prefixes expressing verbal subject or object and those expected as possessors of nouns in Muskogean are replaced by independent pronoun forms, [ino] or [inu] 'I', [isnu] or [išnu] 'you', etc. The salvage data are only of minimally simple syntactic constructions, highly repetitive of syntactic type.

This lingua franca, like others, must always have varied somewhat depending on the primary languages of its speakers. In its salvage period, Crawford remarks on the differences in pronunciation of Mobilian between the speakers of Indian languages and the man of French parentage. Such variety may well have been general in the contact community, as indeed the very early Le Page du Pratz (1758, 3:6) attestation of the Mobilian of primary Natchez speakers would indicate: the imperative ⟨chpénélé⟩ 'sit down' seems to contain a prefix [š-] for second person, and a stem [binili] (cf. Choctaw *-biniˑli*), with a richer, more Muskogean and Natchez form of prefixal inflection than is elsewhere attested for Mobilian, in which Crawford (1978:92) records [išno binilliˑ], with invariant (unaffixed) form.

Phonologically, too, there has been a drastic reshaping of many of the Muskogean vocabulary items in the Mobilian Jargon forms. For example, since all the Indian languages of the area (except Biloxi and Ofo) include the voiceless lateral *ł* (see Haas 1969:34, 91; Swanton 1924:49; Haas 1956:61), and even the Siouan-language speakers seem to have been somewhat bilingual in Muskogean, it was speakers' accommodation to the contact situation that shows why items such as Mobilian [tašlapi] 'five' (Choctaw *tałapi*, Alabama *táłłâˑpi*), and Mobilian [šlašu] 'fish' (Choctaw *nani*, Alabama *łało*) should eliminate this sound in favor of a more European-sounding cluster [šl]. Perhaps revealingly, it is just this cluster that appears in one of the alternative names for the Natchez (Iberville in Swanton 1911:25), in which the French were attempting to represent the *ł* of Natchez. On the basis of seeking the most plausible Muskogean or other source for each Mobilian Jargon word, it appears that only about 12 words out of about 150 different lexical simplexes in Crawford's vocabulary come from Alabama-Koasati, while the rest from Muskogean sources come from Choctaw in one or another of its variant dialects (see Crawford 1978:76-80; cf. Haas 1975, and also Munro 1984; Drechsel 1987). The vexed question of Mobilian words of possible Algonquian-language provenience is discussed by Crawford (1978:63-75) and Drechsel (1985, 1993).

Chinook Jargon

Sometimes confusingly called "Chinook" (like the indigenous language family name of its principal early lexifier), Chinook Jargon (or The Jargon, The Oregon Trade Language, or Chinook Wawa) is the best documented contact language in North America; by the late nineteenth and early twentieth century at least one newspaper, the *Kamloops Wawa* (which used an adaptation of French shorthand) (fig. 1) and numerous bilingual lexicons and phrase books were being printed and popularly distributed as aids to communication in the greater Northwest. Reasonably fluent speaking competence survived here and there to nearly 1990 (Zenk 1984; Hymes and Zenk 1987:447-449).

As with Mobilian, some writers speculatively project Chinook Jargon back as the regional lingua franca in prehistoric times (Chamberlain 1907:274; E.H.

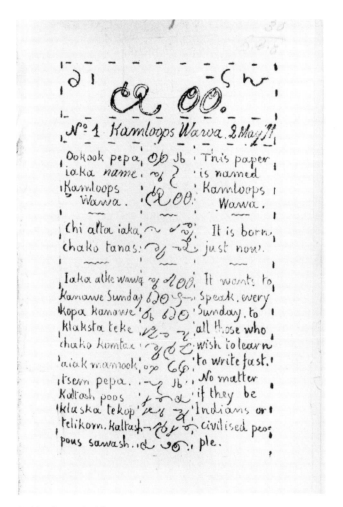

Smithsonian, Anthr. Lib.

Fig. 1. Front page of Jean-Marie Le Jeune's *Kamloops Wawa*, No. 1, 1891.

Thomas 1927:379-381, 1935:18-35; Ray 1938:36; Hymes 1980; Thomason 1983). With this have been linked spurious ethnological reconstructions, such as direct Nootkan-Chinookan trade. However, there are reasonably unambiguous records of the stages leading up to its constitution as the pidgin of a geographically locatable contact community, 1778-1835, and its far-flung spread through the region of European settlement, 1835 to about 1860, a wealth of material from its later stage as vigorous interethnic medium, 1860-1905, and finally attestations of its decline thereafter to memorialized retention in the mid-to-late twentieth century. In part, this abundance of material is due to the fact that it was used very widely during a comparatively late historical period when people wrote and published more extensively on practical knowledge for settlers and travelers (see S.V. Johnson 1978 on dictionaries); in part this is due to the greater number of such literate speakers in the contact community and the increasingly wistful and humorous affection of non-Indian people for "Chinook."

A major lexifier component of earliest Chinook Jargon, indicated by the centrality of the items contributed, derived from the Nootka dialect spoken about Nootka Sound on the west coast of Vancouver Island. This was the earliest center of fur-trade activity in the Pacific Northwest outside the sphere of Russian hegemony. The crew members of the first ship definitely recorded (1774) at Nootka Sound (Hope Bay), the Spanish *Santiago*, communicated with the inhabitants entirely by signs (Howay 1943:32). From March 30, 1778, when Capt. James Cook anchored there, come the first recordings of two words that eventually found their way into Chinook Jargon (Beaglehole 1967, 3, pt. 2:1394): ⟨Tike'mily⟩ "some tool made of iron" which one of the Nootka asked for; "to the man . . . was given some Medals and beads, he took them very thankfully; he often repeated the word *Macook*; he threw into the Ship in return some dried herrings." The first is recorded by Cook in his vocabulary taken by the ship's surgeon of the *Resolution*, William Anderson (Beaglehole 1967, 3, pt. 1:323-330), as ⟨Sēē kemāīle⟩ 'hatchet, nail, any sort of iron or white metal' (cf. Nootka čiˑskmin 'scrape-rattle'; Sapir and Swadesh 1939:282). This was obviously an extension of the Nootka meaning to cover new, shiny, scraping tools that the Europeans were starting to trade. The second term is also recorded as ⟨Ma'cook⟩ 'to exchange or barter' (cf. Nootka maˑkok 'trading, buying, selling'; Sapir and Swadesh 1939:264). Though Cook spent considerable time at Nootka, he confesses "we had learnt little more of their language than to ask the names of things and the two simple words yes and no" (Beaglehole 1967, 3, pt. 1:322-323).

Cook's vocabulary, published shortly after the completion of the voyage, and no doubt others like it, *127* published and unpublished, became the basis for a jargonized Nootka that ship-based fur traders of the late eighteenth century employed to make themselves understood, not only at Nootka but also elsewhere on the Northwest Coast (a view articulated in Sturtevant 1948; cf. Samarin 1986, 1988, 1992:3-6). There are explicit statements to this effect, for example, Barkley of the *Imperial Eagle* (Lamb 1942:55), and many, many reports of whether or not the indigenous peoples all along the coast from California northward understood or spoke languages like Nootka (see Cook in Beaglehole 1967, 3, pt. 1:351, 371; Vancouver 1801, 2:24, 50, 64, 70, 83, 4:4-5, 27). Broughton (Vancouver 1801, 3:96, 103, 138), exploring the lower Columbia River in October 1792, reported that "not a single word could be understood" of whatever the Chinookans they encountered there were speaking.

From such continuing jargon-mediated interactions with the Europeans and their various ship-based crews of Hawaiians and others from various places along trade routes, the local coastal and insular inhabitants were picking up some of this vocabulary, along with terms from English, Spanish, and whatever else was used.

The earliest definite evidence of the arrival in the south of the Nootkan-centered contact jargon occurs in the journals of Lewis and Clark. When they approached the mouth of the Columbia River, they reported of the Clatsops and Chinooks various knowledge of words and phrases of English (Thwaites 1904-1907, 3:200, 205, 276, 305-306, 4:200, 327, 344, 7:187), including *musket, powder, shot, knife, file, damned rascal, son of a bitch, heave the lead*, "and many blackguard phrases," and the names of 13 regular traders who visited them. While Lewis and Clark clearly expressed their own lack of knowledge about Clatsop (Thwaites 1904-1907, 3:360, 4:74), what they considered to be Clatsop is shown by Clark's observation on 10 December, 1805, that they "said in their own language" ⟨Clouch Musket, wake, com ma-tax Musket⟩ 'good musket, do not understand this kind of musket' (Thwaites 1904-1907, 3:276; Moulton 1983-, 6:121). All the words in this utterance, except *musket*, are Nootkan-derived contact vocabulary: [ƛuš] (European pronunciation [klowš] or [kluˑš]) from Nootka *ƛoł* 'pretty, good, correct, satisfactory, well, clean'); [wek] (Nootka *wik* 'not, nothing'); [kəm(a)təks] (Nootka *kamat-* 'known, definite' + *'-aˑḥ* 'irrealis' [Sapir and Swadesh 1939:310, 259, 284, 241]). In particular, the first word could only have come from the speech of Europeans and not by direct borrowing from Nootka, since the sound systems of both indigenous languages allow words of similar shape. Nootkan- and English-derived vocabulary entered the core of the contact medium at the mouth of the Columbia, and from this medium, "some of which we had learnt from them

during the winter" (Thwaites 1904-1907, 4:267), Lewis and Clark made comparisons with other Chinookan dialects upriver on their return trip.

With the establishment of Astoria by the Pacific Fur Company (1811-1813) the communication between Indians and Whites became regular. Both of the participant-chroniclers Gabriel Franchère and Alexander Ross claim to have spoken Chinook (Thwaites 1904-1907, 6:301-302, 389, 7:94-95). Franchère may have actually spoken Chinook Jargon, but Ross clearly perceived that

> Besides the [Chinookan] language, there is another lingo, or rather mixed dialect, spoken by the Chinook and other neighboring tribes; which is generally used in their intercourse with the whites. It is much more easily learned, and the pronunciation more agreeable to the ear than the other, as will appear from the annexed specimen (Thwaites 1904-1907, 7:328).

Gradually Chinook Jargon extended its area of use from the region of the lower Columbia (Fort Astoria to Fort Vancouver), so that Indian peoples farther afield acquired it as a medium of mobilization into regional trade with Europeans and others, and regional outsiders traveling in knew to secure some knowledge of it. By 1835, for example, Rev. Samuel Parker, on missionary reconnaissance, got to The Dalles, and "encamped with Captain Wyeth, and obtained from him a short vocabulary of the Chenook language, to enable me to do common business with the Indians residing along the lower part of this river"; the vocabulary is Chinook Jargon (Parker 1838:336-338). However, his attempts to employ it with the Sahaptins above Celilo, and with the Nez Perces along the Kooskooskie, were to no avail; he had to fall back on signs (Parker 1838:269, 278).

During the years following 1835, the missionaries of both Protestant and Roman Catholic churches were quick to seize on the availability of Chinook Jargon for purposes of proselytizing. Since the majority of them began their work in Oregon Territory by way of Fort Vancouver, at the time the headquarters of the Hudson's Bay Company, they were first exposed to Chinook Jargon as the language of contact with the Indians and others residing in and about the Fort (Roth 1992). Father Blanchet of the Quebec mission summarized the first perception of many, on his arrival (Landerholm 1956:19):

> The real language of the Chinooks is of almost insurmountable difficulty and is entirely different from that of the neighboring tribes. But they understand a jargon by means of which the whites generally can make themselves understood by the Indians frequenting Fort Vancouver. This jargon, composed of 350 to 400 words borrowed from different languages and distorted in pronunciation, is of so easy a study that, three months after the arrival of the missionaries, one of them, Mr. Demers, possessed it sufficiently well to be able to explain the catechism and give instruction to the catechumens without having to force himself to write what he had to tell them. A large number of the natives of the Cascades, as well as part of the Klickitats, understanding the jargon, regularly attend catechism and evening prayer, which are observed every day at Vancouver.

It seems that Chinook Jargon as a contact medium was functionally linked to the acceptance of the presence of Whites, conversion to trade with them, and of the mission influences in religion. By 1861, missionaries in British Columbia had started to compose their material in Chinook Jargon, taking it as far inland as the Thompson (J.B. Good in R.L. Reid 1942:5), and onto Vancouver Island, starting from the Songhees by 1860. The presence of the military to enforce Euro-American and Euro-Canadian settlement at this time added yet another group of Whites with whom contact was carried on in this fashion. Gen. Philip Sheridan, stationed at Vancouver, at Grand Ronde, and at Siletz, spoke it fluently (M.C. George 1914:67).

Chinook Jargon then, by about 1860, was the approved lingua franca for the Whites, and clearly accepted as such by acculturating Indians, over a vast area in the Pacific Northwest. It is clear that there was a movement of the boundaries of the contact community northward. From 1891 to 1905 Father Jean-Marie Le Jeune published the Chinook Jargon newspaper, the *Kamloops Wawa* (Chinook Jargon [wawa] 'word, speech; talk, speak, say, etc.'). Pilling (1893:vii) reported that Chinook Jargon was used as far north as southern Alaska.

By the beginning of the twentieth century, under pressure from English, which was being forced on Indian populations in boarding schools, preferred use of Chinook Jargon was severely on the decline, particularly in the southern portion of its range, within the United States. By 1912, it was spoken of in terms of memory at Grand Ronde (M.C. George 1914:69), and from numerous anecdotes of this period (Fee 1941:184) it appears that the Indian population considered communication in Chinook Jargon, as opposed to English, a badge of inferiority. Curiously, Leechman (1926:534) reports that about 1925,

> Nearly all the old people understand it well and the basket-sellers on the streets of Vancouver, Victoria or Seattle are highly delighted when spoken to by a white man in Chinook. Few white men speak it now except those living in the more remote parts of the coast and interior. Many of the Chinese understand it well, and it is not unusual to see an old Chinese talking it rapidly and easily to an Indian in almost "pure" jargon.

Jacobs (1936) could still get fluent text dictations in the late 1920s from speakers whose primary languages were Clackamas Chinook, Santiam Kalapuya, Saanich (Northern Straits), and Snoqualmie (Lushootseed) Salish, and Coquille (Tututni) Athapaskan. As late as 1995, people were found in Washington and Oregon who spoke Chinook Jargon in their youth.

Chinook Jargon served as a mechanism for the learning of English by the Indian population. The later recordings of Jargon are far higher in percentage of English-based words than the earlier ones (see Chamberlain 1907:275 for table; see Jacobs 1936 for exemplification of later texts). As the period of use came to a close, the syntax of Jargon became more and more heavily influenced by the English model. Myron Eells (1894:311), son of a missionary and himself one, who spoke Chinook Jargon from his boyhood in the mid-nineteenth century, stated that:

> There is no settled authority in regard to the order of the words. They are generally placed in much the same order as they are in the language which the speaker has been accustomed to use. An English-speaking person will place them in much the same order as in English, though there are a number of phrases of which this is not true; for instance, *halo nika kumtuks* (not I understand) is much more common than *nika halo kumtuks*. . . . An Indian who has learned somewhat the English order will arrange the words in much the same way; but if he is an old Indian, or one who knows but little about English, he will arrange them much as he is accustomed to do in his native language, which is very different from the English. As the tendency, however, is not for the whites to learn the native languages, but for the Indians to learn English, so the tendency is toward the English order of the words.

As English became ascendant as the lingua franca in the area (Jacobs 1932:27) by the beginning of the twentieth century, Chinook Jargon probably became a functional calque of pidginized forms of English, a more "Indian" version, as it were.

Though the percentages change through time, at all periods Chinook Jargon had a core vocabulary composed of words etymologically Nootka, French, Lower Chinook, English, and in perhaps a few cases Salish. The total composition of the vocabulary varied geographically, since there were groups in different areas of the contact community that had different primary languages and local pidginized forms, which became later lexifiers. (The Nootka-derived vocabulary is in general quite stable, as it was the earliest layer of contact vocabulary in the formation of Chinook Jargon, giving it a distinctive character even with respect to real Chinookan languages.) Chamberlain (1891:261) reports for example that the Chinook Jargon of western British Columbia included several words derived ultimately from Algonquian languages: ⟨mitas⟩ 'leggings', ⟨totoosh⟩ 'breasts, udders, milk', ⟨kinni-kinnik⟩ 'tobacco', ⟨lepishemo⟩ 'bed', and ⟨pāpūs⟩ 'infant'. The first three are found in most Jargon recorded; in contrast the Washington-Oregon area at that time used ⟨bed⟩ 'bed'; ⟨tenas⟩, ⟨dunas⟩, etc. 'infant' (from Nootka *tana* 'child'; one of the first set of contact vocabulary), and ⟨bacca⟩, ⟨kinootl⟩, ⟨kinoos⟩ 'tobacco' (Shaw 1909 for example). These Algonquian words came into Chinook Jargon through French or English, except perhaps ⟨totoosh⟩, which may have come through Mitchif. They indicate that Canadian members of the early Northwest contact community must have served as carriers of these words into new contact communities, much as had been the case in the Northeast. Chinook Jargon served also as a medium of loans into Indian languages and regional English of the twentieth century, and every lexicon of these shows numerous examples.

129

The form of connected Chinook Jargon speech shows complete elimination of any morphological variation in words, and complete absence of regular derivational patterns, other than those of compounding of stems, as in [kinčawč man] 'Englishman' (<*King George* + *man*), either of which can occur alone (i.e., there are no truly "bound" forms of completely grammatical value so characteristic of the morphologically complex languages of the Northwest Coast). The phrasal structure of Chinook Jargon utterances is thus completely linear, that is, there are no significant discontinuities in grammatical units such as abound in all the relevant primary languages. This applies as well to the sentence-level units, which are always in full form, never reduced like clauses of complex sentences in the various primary languages; they are strung along sequentially, one after another. For example, the following from a primary speaker of Snoqualmie (Salishan) dictated to Jacobs (1936:24; ⟨c⟩ = [š]):

⟨wɛ´l, u´kuk-tə´nəs-mɛ·´n ya´kə-łɛ·´dwa.
wɛ´l, tə´nəs-mɛ·´n ya´kə i´skəm u·´lali,
ya´kə ma´kmak u·´lali,
pɨ-ya´kə-i´skəm u·´lali,
pɨ-ya´kə-ma·´c kupa-ya´kə-bɛ·´skət.⟩

'Well, that little-man (= boy) he went.
Well, (the) little-man he got (= picked) berries,
he ate (the) berries,
then he got (more) berries,
then he put (them) into his basket.

Pidgin Eskimo

In the northern reaches of Alaska and adjacent Canada, there are reports of two forms of pidgin. One, lexified principally by Canadian Inuit, seems to have been used between Inuits and ship-based others, as well as with local government officialdom. The other, somewhat richer in preserving Eskimo structure as well as lexicon, seems to have been used with various Athapaskan-speaking Indian people, principally the Kutchin to the south who traded regularly at the Mackenzie River delta. Apparently originating long ago, both forms survived into the early twentieth century (Stefánsson 1909, 1913, 1921).

The first pidgin was clearly the conventionalized interethnic form of communication by that time (Stefánsson 1909:217). Stefánsson (1921:104) indicated that the Royal Canadian Mounted Police in 1913, "like all the police inspectors before," used Pidgin Eskimo. And a purportedly bilingual "English-Eskimo and Eskimo-English" vocabulary (Wells and Kelly 1890) (fig. 2) based on the usage of a ship's interpreter for the U.S. Navy in the late nineteenth century, actually documents this language—apparently taken for Canadian Inuit itself. The Mackenzie River Eskimo population that interacted both with the ships' crews

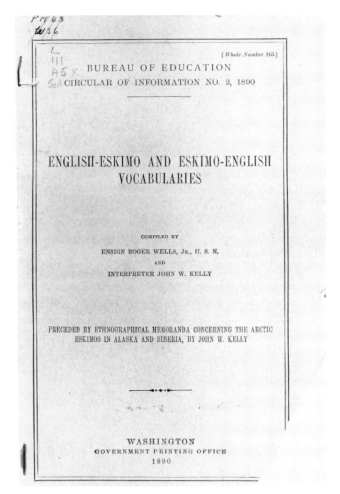

Smithsonian, Anthr. Lib.
Fig. 2. Cover of *English-Eskimo and Eskimo-English Vocabularies* by Wells and Kelly (1890).

and with the neighboring Athapaskan groups, such as the Kutchin, controlled the two pidginized forms, of differential richness, as well as their primary language (Stefánsson 1909:218-219).

The Athapaskans speak languages that share certain properties of sound system and of syntactic rules with Eskimo, and the common basis of speech differs less from Eskimo itself than does the more radically pidginized form used with Whites. "It has probably more than twice as extensive a vocabulary as the ships' variety and is so different from it that some white men who know the ships' jargon have employed as interpreters Loucheux Indians [Kutchins] under the impression that the Indians spoke real Eskimo" (Stefánsson 1909:219). He further observes the characteristic differences in pronunciation that come from the sound systems of speakers of various primary languages: "in the mouths of Norwegians, Germans, Kanakas [Hawaiians], and Cape Verde islanders [on ships] the words assume varied forms" (Stefánsson 1909:218).

Eskimoan languages have a morphology rich and complicated in derivational suffixation, giving rise to elaborate word-stems. They also use a large paradigm of inflectional suffixes on both nouns and verbs to cross-reference words in the sentence one to another. The ships' pidgin eliminates all this, and preserves single, invariant stems, as expected, frequently derived from complex items of Inuit-Inupiaq: [átka] 'name' derived from Inupiaq or Western Canadian Inuit *atqa* 'his name', rather than *atiq* 'name'; [iluáne] 'inside' (preposition) derived from *il'uani* or *iluani* 'inside of it', the locative case of *il'ua* (*ilua*) 'its inside' (Webster and Zibell 1970:135; Lawrence A. Kaplan, communication to editors 1995).

The inflectional categories of Canadian Inuit proper include singular, dual and plural numbers, numerous aspect and mood distinctions, two syntactic case forms (absolute and relative) of nouns and pronominal elements, and numerous postpositions for locatives. All these are eliminated from Pidgin Eskimo. The pronominal affixes for person, as, for example, possessives, are replaced by phrases: [awóŋa kámmĭk] 'my boot(s)' instead of Inupiaq *kamiŋa* 'my boot', *kammaka* 'my boots'. The words of this pidgin likewise become transformed in their grammatical functions, for example, the exclamation *a·riɣa·* 'fine! excellent!' becoming the adjective, verb, etc. [àdĭgá] '(be) fine', *quaq* 'raw frozen meat or fish' (noun) becoming the general descriptive [kwak] 'frozen'. The numerals are simplified, so that in pidginized form 'six' through 'nine' recapitulate the preceding series with 'six' being 'five' + 'one', and so forth.

From Stefánsson's recordings of Pidgin Eskimo, it appears that some of the specifically Inuit features of word order and phrase construction are retained. Thus the basic subject-object-verb constituent order, with subordinate clauses of purpose, intent, complementation, and so forth preceding the main verb of the sentence, seems to be the general outline, though there are many variations, particularly the placement of the subject after the main verb. Thus: [awoŋa iglupʌk ĕlĕkta] 'I'm going (or, I went) to Fort McPherson' (I big-house go); [innuk ababa tusara awoŋa] 'I know that a man is talking', 'I hear a man talking' (man talk understand/know I); [iglupʌk elekta ilipsi, iglupʌk kammik kečem, awoŋa pišuktu] 'When you go to Fort McPherson, get some Indian moccasins for me' (big-house go you, big-house shoes get; I want). (The source of [kečem] 'get' is English *catch 'em*.)

Trader Navajo

Among the people operating trading posts on and around the Navajo Reservation, Oswald Werner (1963) documented an asymmetrically used and pidginized form of Navajo. The primary language of the traders is English, and that of the customers is Navajo, the Navajo then noted for their stipulative monolingualism.

Hence the traders, to varying degrees, attempted to acquire some working form of Navajo that would suffice for these limited contact functions, in which "a few key phrases, questions and responses which the trader needs to understand in order to run a successful business" (Werner 1963:145) formed the core. The resulting pidginized form of Navajo has been called Trader Navajo by Werner, following William Y. Adams. All the reliable information on this pidgin derives from Werner's copious documentation of the speech of four such traders.

In general, the traders did not understand most Navajo used about them, and certainly their own speech productions were on circumscribed topics. The Navajos gave back their own primary language in transactions; they did not explicitly acknowledge the existence of this pidginized form as a separate entity, nor did they have a name for it (Werner 1963:137-138, 145, 146). The traders did not interact with each other by means of this pidgin but used it only in the contact situation. They reached varying degrees of approximation to Navajo proper, some knowing virtually nothing except that *hot dish of banana* meant 'what are you doing?' (Navajo *ha'át'ííshą' baa nan(i)ná*) or that *chee* meant 'red' (Navajo *łichíí'*) (Werner 1963:143; Willem de Reuse, communication to editors 1995). Others were more proficient up to the level of Navajo syntactic constituent order, for example Trader Navajo *dííyéé diné' 'éé 'áádoole 'éé nayishni, dááchi* (this Navajo he things them he.sells maybe), intending target Navajo proper *ńléi diné 'eii t'áadoo-le'é nayiiłniih, daats'í* 'perhaps that Navajo over there is selling those things' (yonder Navajo those things he.is.selling perhaps). Two of the four traders studied by Werner seem to have reached a degree of proficiency that enabled them to be understood in all common interactions, with a Navajo-derived vocabulary of approximately 500 items, approximately 12 sentence-frame types, and a morphology radically reduced to virtual simple stem forms, or related sets of suppletive forms. Under these best-achieved conditions, there were only about four or five misunderstandings noted per 100 recorded conversation segments (Werner 1963:135-136).

Though they did not communicate with each other, these four traders showed remarkable likeness in their pidginized forms at all levels, from phonology through syntax. Their competence was such that the better speakers elaborated on what the poorer speakers controlled, so that there was a core of pidginized Navajo language competence that was common. This cannot be attributed in this case to the existence of a contact community but must be referred to explanation on the basis of structural universals in language (see Silverstein 1972a) and principles of metalinguistic awareness in relation to translation equivalence between the two primary languages.

Learning of Colonial Languages by Indigenous Peoples

The principal colonial languages during the period of European presence in North America have been French, Spanish, Russian, and English. (For Souriquois Jargon and Pidgin Delaware, Basque and Dutch have also played major roles.) In areas where one linguistic group of colonizers held sway over an extended period of time, their language generally emerged as the contact medium used among the indigenous groups and the newcomers, and frequently also the lingua franca among indigenous groups, particularly as indigenous peoples were brought together in new social arrangements—trading-post camps, missions, rancherias, reservations, boarding schools—that were instrumental in processes of colonization. As the case of Trader Navajo shows, only the very restricted functions of commercial transactions at trading posts were still in the 1960s assumed by pidginized forms of Indian languages themselves.

Even lacking precise recordings in all cases, it is fair to assume that at some point in the process of colonialism, the Indians spoke pidginized versions of the colonizers' languages. There are, for example, numerous attestations of a sort of "broken English" that are reported in historical documents from an early period of New England colonization; these indications probably mean that there was a significantly pidginized form that was spoken by some Indians. Of course, by the mid-twentieth century, English in both national standard form and regionally recognized varieties had become a primary language among many reservation groups within the United States and the anglophone areas of Canada. Particularly for people under the age of 50 in every group in which linguistic fieldwork has been conducted since the mid-twentieth century, it is at least a strong secondary (official or principal contact) language. Some of the history of colonization-induced bilingualism and language shift can be discerned in the record for each of the major European languages.

French

In the early seventeenth century, Lescarbot (1612, 3:695) noted that the Micmacs of whom he wrote were unwilling to learn French, "which nevertheless is a very necessary thing." These negative statements about the Indians of eastern Canada persisted during the seventeenth century, though asserting not so much lack of competence in some form of French as lack of desire to use it. Certainly the Roman Catholic missionaries attempted to convert the Indians by the medium of the several primary languages. Lahontan, writing at the end of the seventeenth century, found it unusual enough to comment on an "Iroquois" man who "had a smattering

of the *French* tongue" (Thwaites 1905, 1:75). He also noted that the Indians do not "care to speak *French*, unless they are persuaded that the force of their Words will be perfectly understood." However, they do so "for some cases of necessity, when they are in company with the *Coureurs de Bois* that do not understand their language." He must have meant a form of French significantly affected by at least phonological interference from Iroquoian, since he insisted (Thwaites 1905, 2:747) that

> 'tis impossible for . . . them to learn French well. I have spent four days in trying to make the *Hurons* pronounce the Labial Letters, but could not accomplish it; nay, I am of the Opinion that in ten years time they would not learn to pronounce these Words, *Bon, Fils, Monsieur, Pontchartrain*: For instead of *Bon* they'd say *Ouon* [wǫ]; instead of *Fils, Rils* [ris]; instead of *Monsieur, Caounsieur* [kaüsyö]; and in the room of *Pontchartrain, Conchartrain* [kǫšartræ].

(See also Elliott 1886:166-169.) Seventeenth-century attestations about Huron people mostly refer to women who learned French as girls at Quebec (JR 41:231, 44:263, 49:129, 131). In 1776 Thomas Morris (Thwaites 1904-1907, 1:320) recounted having met a Huron man from the Jesuits' mission at Lorette, Quebec, a "Christian Savage, who spoke French fluently."

Certainly by the mid-eighteenth century, the French language was a major presence in North America, not only in Canada but also in Louisiana and in the Old Northwest. This led to some command of the language wherever exploration and fur trading was carried on, activities that depended on French-speaking personnel across much of the continent. Indeed, a large number of traders and early settlers who actually lived among Indian peoples all across the continent were French-Canadian men and their male descendants, marrying and having families with Indian women and themselves bilingual to a certain extent. This is consistent with numerous reports of some knowledge of French among the Plains groups around the Missouri River (Pike [1806] in Jackson 1966, 1:306; Brackenridge [1811] in Thwaites 1904-1907, 6:44-45; Frémont [1842] 1845:11). And it is central to understanding why Charles Wilkes, among others, discovered that French was the preponderant European language of the Vancouver and Okanagan trading posts of the Hudson's Bay Company, "as it is at all the other posts of the Company" among the "lower ranks" of trappers and traders and their children of mixed parentage, as well as associated full-blood Indian children (Wilkes 1845, 4:329, 332, 433; cf. Palmer in Thwaites 1904-1907, 30:180 on parallels in the Willamette Valley).

Such patterns of settlement and cross-linguistic intermarriage are consistent, furthermore, with the rise of the "mixed" structural system of Mitchif (French Cree), which marks the emergence of a distinct linguistic community norm different from both Plains Cree and local varieties of Canadian French (Bakker 1992, 1994; vol. 6:56, 370-371). First called to attention in its structural detail in Rhodes (1977), Mitchif is

a mixture of French and Cree in which the noun phrase, including articles and some adjectival modification, is French and maintains such characteristics as French gender distinctions as well as French phonological and morphophonemic patterns. Verbs come from Plains Cree, with a quite full representation of the complicated patterns of that language, although some speakers simplify at some points in favor of an increased dependence on prepositional patterns from French. A significant detail is that the animate-inanimate gender distinction of Cree is maintained in verbs, as well as a full set of demonstrative pronouns from Cree, so that nominals are marked for both the French and Cree gender systems. Syntax is heavily based on Cree patterns, but again with varying degrees of influence from French (Crawford 1983:48-49).

(There are also many English nouns used in contemporary attestations; Papen 1987:250.)

As of the 1990s, Mitchif was spoken as an "insider's language" (Rhodes 1986:289) in Métis communities (people with mixed French-Canadian and Cree ancestry) that are found "in and around the Turtle Mountain Reservation in north-central North Dakota as well as in a number of Métis communities in Manitoba and Saskatchewan" (Papen 1987:247) and elsewhere. Important documentation has come, for example, from Belcourt, North Dakota (Turtle Mountain Reservation); from San Clara, Boggy Creek, and Camperville (Pine Creek Reserve), Manitoba; from Saint Lazare, Manitoba; and Buffalo Narrows and probably Lac La Biche, Alberta (Crawford 1983; Rhodes 1982; Douaud 1985). The ethnohistorical implications of Mitchif, in relation to the history of contact communities and of regional indigenous lingua francas such as Cree and Ojibwa, remain to be worked out in detail. Intriguing for this history is a report (Drapeau 1992) of "a strikingly similar . . . situation observed in the speech of fluent bilingual speakers in some Montagnais communities in Northern Québec" involving French noun phrases or prepositional phrases in "otherwise perfectly grammatical Montagnais [syntactic constructions]."

In the region of the French settlements in lower Louisiana, Pénigaut reports having attempted in 1706 to teach some girls from among the Acolapissa to speak French, but with poor phonetic results (Margry 1876-1886, 5:469-470), while in 1727 the chief of one of the Tunica settlements could "speak a little French" (JR 67:309). Adair (1775:301) was not surprised at having been addressed by a Choctaw in French, and at the time of the Louisiana Purchase (1805), Sibley (1832:724-725), reporting from the region of Natchitoches, noted general French bilingualism (apparently productive control) for the Natchitoches, Apalachee, Alabama, Opelousa, Pascagoula, and Taensa peoples.

Spanish

The areas in which Spanish has played a large role in linguistic contact and shift are Florida, the Southwest, and California; at least partial Indian bilingualism in Spanish seems to have characterized these regions from an early period of contact.

From the time of Hernando De Soto's sixteenth-century expedition through the Southeast, the conquerors insisted on Spanish as the principal contact medium. Elvas (Rye 1851:42) says about slave laborers secured from the Apalachee by De Soto that "in a very short space they understood the language of the Christians." The expedition picked up such servants all along the way, and by the time the Spaniards left Minoya, on the Mississippi, in 1543, they left there "five hundred men and women, among whom were many boies and girls, which spake and understood the Spanish tongue" (Rye 1851:149). That they understood Spanish is fairly certain; the type of Spanish they spoke is unknown. Yet, from the later attestation by the French of the Spanish pidgin or jargon spoken by the Apalachee from Pensacola, it may well have been a contact language of that nature. In 1791, Bartram (1792:184) reported from Cuscowilla concerning the Lower Creeks and Seminoles that "most of them speak and understand Spanish."

After the conquest of Mexico, the Spaniards pushed out to colonize in several directions. At the beginning of the seventeenth century, with an insecure military domination, missionary activity was under way among the Sonoran Yaqui (Spicer 1961:32) and all along the Rio Grande Pueblos (Dozier 1961:121, 141), among speakers of Keresan and Kiowa-Tanoan languages. There were later expeditions and trading as far as the Caddoans of the Hasinai Confederacy in northeast Texas among whom Joutel reported various phrases and words of Spanish (⟨Vene a qua, seignore⟩, ⟨capita⟩, ⟨cahouaille⟩ for *caballo*) as early as 1687 (Margry 1876-1886, 3:308, 353); but he reported that his own Spanish-Italian jargon was not understood (Margry 1876-1886, 3:339). The Spaniards sent missionaries to the Hasinai in 1690, and by 1712 Pénigaut reported among them a baptized woman with whom Louis Juchereau de Saint-Denis could converse (Margry 1876-1886, 5:500). But the Spanish would never have hegemony in this region, nor would the Spanish language be important in linguistic contact in the Mississippi-Missouri river regions. Rather, the language became an important lingua franca during the seventeenth century only in the Southwest, as for example along the Rio Grande, and it served as both spoken and written vehicle for the missionary work of conversion to Roman Catholicism among many groups (Spicer 1961:64).

In the eighteenth century the Spaniards began to colonize Alta California, north of the present United

States–Mexican border, founding first the Mission of San Diego de Alcalá in 1769. The numerous expeditions from Mexico of soldiers and priests in the early 1770s left records of little or no Spanish among the groups along the lower Gila and Colorado rivers, or in the rest of southern California, except for those at the missions. Among the Quechan in 1774 Capt. Juan Bautista de Anza's expedition typically taught the people to salute *Ave Maria, Viva Dios y el Rey* (Bolton 1930, 2:72), but principally they depended on chains of interpreters, Pima-Spanish bilinguals at one end (Bolton 1930, 2:377, 4:38, 83-84) or merely signs (Bolton 1930, 2:59, 344, 417-418). In 1775, setting out from Tubac, they took along three interpreters, of Quechan, Kahwan ("Cajuenche"), and Halchidhoma (Bolton 1930, 4:23).

Only at the missions were the Indians speaking Spanish. In 1776, Father Pedro Font already noted the facility in Castillian of the Indians at San Gabriel (Takic), San Luis Obispo (Chumashan); San Antonio (Salinan); and La Soledad (Costanoan) (Bolton 1930, 4:181, 454, 280, 288). There the use of Spanish exclusively, or Spanish and "the vernacular" was the policy. Indeed, in 1776 Father Garcés met an apparently escaped or emissary Yokuts man on the White River of Arizona who spoke to him in Spanish (Coues 1900, 1:287). In 1792 and 1793 George Vancouver (1801, 3:7, 4:326-327) was able to communicate in Spanish with Indians at San Francisco and to the south, though in the Santa Barbara Channel this was not so. At Bodega Bay the party noted a highly pidginized Spanish spoken by the Indians, probably Miwoks (Vancouver 1801, 4:301).

By the middle of the nineteenth century, the predominantly coastal missions had been disbanded, and a great number of indigenous peoples captured into their system had been decimated. There were, by this time, many American settlers in the interior of California, particularly in northern and central parts of the region. It is interesting that Charles Wilkes (1845, 5:191) in 1842 observed only the "chief" of the Indians working for John A. Sutter on the Sacramento River to speak "a little Spanish." Similarly, when John C. Frémont descended the American River in 1844 to within 10 miles of the Sacramento, he found in "a large Indian village, where the people looked clean, and wore cotton shifts and various other articles of dress . . . one who spoke a little indifferent Spanish" with whom he conversed until a "well-dressed Indian . . . made his salutations in very well spoken Spanish" (Frémont 1845:245). Former Mission Indians, many of whom returned to their inland homelands, spoke Spanish, and they differentiated themselves as *mansitos* ('tame ones') from the other indigenous people (Frémont 1845:252, 254, 260). Mid-nineteenth century, then, marks a turning point in the influence of Spanish as a contact language for indigenous peoples in the United States, its utility declining particularly in the northern half of California.

It is thus only in the Southwest that Spanish continued to be a functioning second language of importance well into the twentieth century. Though Zebulon Pike in 1807 observed many people at Santo Domingo (Keresan) "who do not yet speak good Spanish" (Jackson 1966, 1:398), by the period of 1938-1940, Spencer (1947:132) reported that most Keresans were bilingual in their local Keresan dialect and New Mexican Spanish. At that time Trager (1939:51) likewise reported that at Taos those over 50 years of age were Taos-Spanish bilinguals, and only younger people controlled much English. All along the Rio Grande, at mid-twentieth century, Dozier (1961:120-121) reported a lingua franca function of Spanish (by then alternating with English). At this period, among groups such as the Yaqui, there was overwhelming bilingualism (see Spicer 1943:413; estimated at over two-thirds by Lindenfeld 1971:11); Spanish tended to be the language of home, Yaqui the ceremonial language (Spicer 1961:81-82, 84). In other words, throughout this whole region within the borders of the United States, Spanish has only gradually been succeeded by English in the second half of the twentieth century as the most important second language of wider communication.

The brief contact of the Spaniards and the Nootka apparently resulted in only fleeting acquisition of some Spanish by several Indians (Wilson 1970:84-85). It left no traces in Nootka.

A mixed language incorporating Spanish and Nahuatl elements was spoken in the late nineteenth century in Saltillo, Coahuila, by about 200 people out of a community numbering about 1,000 descended from Tlaxcalans brought to northeastern Mexico by the Spaniards in the colonial period (Gatschet 1887:413). Not enough of this form of speech is known to permit it to be typologized.

Russian

Though exploration had begun at least a century before, the colonization by Russia of extensive tracts along the southern coast of Alaska began soon after the middle of the eighteenth century. In April and May 1794, Vancouver stopped at various points along there, such as Cook Inlet, where he must have encountered Tanaina Athapaskans, as well as (probably) Pacific Yupik Eskimos. He reported that the people spoke Russian, which none of his crew understood (Vancouver 1801, 5:171-172, 220, 264), so it is difficult to determine the degree of their command of the language. Vancouver (1801, 5:344-345) observed of the Russians that "in all their establishments the children of the natives are taken at an early age to apartments provided on purpose, where they are maintained and educated in the Russian language . . . ." It was during the late eighteenth century that missionaries of the Russian Orthodox church started proselytizing among the inhabitants of Alaska. The church influence was strongest in the western portion of the colony, and the link between this religion and the Russian language was such that in 1952 Bergsland (1959:16) found that the older men among the Aleuts of Atka still had some active knowledge of Russian. But Russian ceased to be of use for official purposes in Alaska with the transfer to the United States by purchase in 1867. It is not clear what was the residual knowledge among groups such as the Tlingit and Yupik farther east, but clearly by the beginning of the twentieth century, the contact language was English, as is evidenced by Drucker's (1958:141) report on Alaska Native Brotherhood organizations. Even among the Aleuts, English was in the 1990s the important second language, or the primary one. However, Russian has left a profound influence in the lexicon of Aleut and other languages of this region (see Hammerich 1953, 1954; Brenckle 1975). There are even Russian loans in the coastal languages of northwestern California, in the region of the old Fort Ross.

English

Knowledge of some English is reported in the Virginia colony as early as the Jamestown settlement, Pocahontas by tradition having become a speaker (Beverley 1722:28). The Indian servants in the colony also seem to have spoken English with their employers by the 1620s (Beverley 1722:40). In the New England colonies, English also was being mastered by the early 1640s so that John Eliot could employ as interpreter a Long Island Indian, Cockenoe, who read and wrote English. By 1653, Harvard College undertook to educate the Indians of the area in English, Latin, and Greek, John Sassamon being the first such student in that year. There were thus people among several New England Algonquian groups who were literate in English by the time of King Philip's War, and there are preserved some of the documents that they wrote in an English not too far from the educated standard (Meserve 1956:266, 272-273, 269-270; Kittredge 1904:333-378; see also Bailey 1991:62-78).

Of course, there is a difference between actual fluent speaking of (and perhaps literacy in) English and being able to control a few jargonized words and phrases, or speaking in an essentially pidginized form of the target language, as was widely the case with non-Indians learning indigenous languages (Read 1941; Leechman and Hall 1955; Miller 1967; Goddard 1977, 1978; Flanigan 1984). During the next two centuries, the majority of reports of English usage among indigenous peoples indicate a progression of the level of competence among primary indigenous-language speakers, at the same time as a broadening sociological penetration of knowledge of English, in both regional vernacular (Honigmann 1949:137-138 on Kaska English) and more standard forms (Leap 1993). Indeed, early on in each of the regions of North America, there are reports of English words and phrases for objects and phases of trade, for greetings, and so forth, jargonized markers of limited contact; but relative fluency is reported very rarely.

Characteristically such fluency is attributed to chiefly people or people important as intermediaries with non-Indians. Thus Samuel Hearne (1795:52-53) reports on a Chipewyan chief Motanabbee who, having lived near Fort Prince of Wales had "acquired several words of English" as well as Chipewyan and Cree and was a very influential person. At the same period, a part-Creek, part-Choctaw chief at Mobile spoke, read, and wrote English very well (Bartram 1792:504). In 1795 the brother of the Nootka chief wiˈkinaniš spoke "a little English, and on every subject we discoursed on, was very ready to understand, and expressed himself in such a manner as to be easily understood by us" (Charles Bishop in Roe 1967:105). By the mid-nineteenth century, the Walla Walla chief Peupeumoxmox 'Yellow Serpent' specifically sent one of his sons to be educated in English by the Methodist missionaries on the Willamette (Palmer in Thwaites 1904-1907, 30:229). That such acquisition was reinforced as advantageous from the Euro-American perspective becomes clear from Gibbs's description of a Neah Bay Makah man called Flattery Jack (d. 1852 or 1853), who had been recognized as "chief" by the Whites precisely "from his speaking a little English and his greater familiarity with the traders" (Gibbs 1877:174; see also Townsend in Thwaites 1904-1907, 21:341).

But these cases seem to be unusual within their respective groups for the time period at which they are reported. For those groups that survived as indigenous linguistic communities, the more general knowledge of English as a language functioning in a secondary, and increasingly primary, communicative role seems to be a late nineteenth- or early twentieth-century phenomenon. This transformation followed upon schooling associated with resettlement of indigenous people on reservations—from the 1880s, boarding school education (Coleman 1993:108-108, 131, 140, 151-155)—and the increasingly pervasive demands of dealing at some length with an English-speaking bureaucracy and world of commerce.

Yet there are numerous reports of groups in which English did not make decisive inroads even into the twentieth century. For example, among the Fox people of Iowa in the 1930s, more than one-third of the population did not speak any English, though everyone spoke Fox (Joffe 1940:294); this seems to have been in spite of a lengthy history of contact with both French- and English-speaking colonial powers. The Southern Utes, similarly, in 1935 showed only six English speakers out of 450 people (Opler 1940:187), perhaps the result of lack of contact.

In general, at this period before the Second World War, the functioning linguistic competence among groups showed a stratification by age, with the oldest members controlling only indigenous languages (and perhaps another colonial language). The middle cohort under about 50 years old added English to their repertoire and perhaps lacked productive competence in the older colonial language. The youngest cohort, including then very young adults, were bilingual in the primary language and English, and in general were on a course toward primary use of English rather than the indigenous language. This was apparently true of groups with the following primary indigenous languages: Yaqui (Spicer 1961:72); Taos (Trager 1939:51); Pima (Herzog 1941:71, 72), where an older colonial language was Spanish; to some extent Navajo (Vogt 1961:324); Kwakiutl (Codere 1961:506); Wisconsin Oneida (Swadesh 1941:61), with no eldest-cohort other colonial language; Mandan (Kennard 1936:2; Bruner 1961:261-262, 267), where the pre-English bilingualism was in another Indian language, Hidatsa, with the speakers of which the Mandan intermarried upon tribal consolidation, leading to the virtual extinction of Mandan. An interesting inverse case is reported by Mead (1932:126-127) for the Omaha of the late 1920s, where knowledge of English was progressively weaker for the younger people she interviewed, perhaps indicating an increase in group isolation.

Since the Second World War, there has been extensive, and in many places, total, replacement of indigenous languages by English, notwithstanding increased sensitivity to heritage languages as important aspects of group culture. A locally particular mix of demographic and economic factors almost everywhere has shifted the functional significance of use of indigenous languages and English. The indigenous languages thus survive in public as a ceremonial or religious medium, as was already reported to be the case among the Yaqui in the 1950s (Spicer 1961:82). Given a strong re-ethnicization trend in the 1960s and 1970s (see Fishman et al. 1985; Fishman 1991:187-229), the situation in many communities was in unstable flux as efforts were made to define and implement, for example, through schools, some achievable community knowledge of heritage languages in the hope of maintaining some normative functions for them in the face of actual primary English-language competence.

Overview of General Characteristics

MARIANNE MITHUN

The several hundred languages indigenous to North America show tremendous diversity in their structures. This fact is not surprising, since they represent so many genetically distinct language families and are spoken over such a wide area. No characteristics are both universal and unique to the continent. Nevertheless, certain features quite unlike those familiar from the languages of Europe and Asia are well developed and pervasive (see Boas 1911).

Sounds

For the most part, vowel systems in North American languages are relatively simple, but consonant systems vary considerably. Most languages of eastern North America have small consonant inventories. Mistassini Cree, an Algonquian language of Quebec, contains the 10 consonants *p, t, k, č, š, h, m, n, w,* and *y* (Rogers 1960:90-91). Mohawk, an Iroquoian language of Ontario, Quebec, and New York State, also contains 10: *t, k, s, c, h, ʔ, n, r, w,* and *y*.* By contrast, many languages west of the Rockies show large inventories. Central Pomo, a Pomoan language of Northern California, contains 30 consonants: *p, pʰ, ṗ, b, t, tʰ, ṭ, ṭ, tʰ, ṭ, d, č, čʰ, č̣, k, kʰ, k̓, q, qʰ, q̓, ʔ, s, c̣, š, h, m, n, l, w,* and *y*. Heiltsuk, a Wakashan language of British Columbia, contains over 40: *p, pʰ, ṗ, t, tʰ, ṭ, c, cʰ, c̣, λ, λ̓, ƛ̓, kʸ, kˣʸ, k̓ʸ, kʷ, kˣʷ, k̓ʷ, q, qˣ, q̓, qʷ, qˣʷ, q̓ʷ, s, ł, xʸ, xʷ, x̣, x̣ʷ, m, ṃ, n, ṇ, l, ḷ, y, ẏ, w, ẇ, h,* and *ʔ* (Rath 1981).

Certain distinctions are especially common in North America. Ejectives (glottalized obstruents) such as *ṗ, ṭ, c̣, č̣, k̓,* and *q̓,* appear in many families, among them Siouan, Yuchi, Caddoan, Coahuilteco, Kiowa-Tanoan, Keresan, Athapaskan, Chumashan, Salinan, Yokutsan, Maiduan, Wappo, Pomoan, Yuki, Wintuan, Washoe, Yana, Chimariko, Shastan, Klamath, Takelman, Coosan, Siuslaw, Chinookan, Sahaptian, Chimakuan, Salishan, Wakashan, Tsimshian, Tlingit, and Haida. The distribution of ejectives is partially areal. The Yurok language of California, for example, contains

ejectives like its neighbors, although its genetic relatives, Wiyot and the Algonquian languages spoken in the Plains and the East, lack them. Clicks (suction stops) have not been documented.

Many languages, especially in the West, distinguish velars (e.g., *k, x*) from back velars or uvulars (e.g., *q, x̣*). Among these are the Chumashan languages, some Pomoan languages, Wintuan, Chimariko, Achumawi and Atsugewi, Alsean, Chinookan, Sahaptian, Chimakuan, Wakashan, Salishan, some Athapaskan languages, Tlingit, Tsimshian, Haida, and Eskimo-Aleut languages. Labio-velars (e.g., *k* with lip rounding: *kʷ*) appear over a large area, in Iroquoian, Yuchi, Natchez, Tonkawa, Coahuilteco, Zuni, Uto-Aztecan, Yuman, Alsean, Chimakuan, Salishan, Wakashan, Tlingit, and elsewhere. In some California languages there is a distinction between front and back *t*. Their positions range from dental (made with the tongue against the teeth as in Spanish or French), through alveolar (made with the tongue tip behind the teeth as in English), and postalveolar, to retroflex (made with the underside of the tongue tip). Distinctions between front and back *t* are found in the Yuman languages Diegueño, Cocopa, and Quechan (Yuma), Salinan, the Pomoan languages, Wappo, Yuki, and most Utian languages (Langdon and Silver 1984). A number of languages contain multiple laterals. In addition to plain *l,* one or more fricative or affricate laterals (*ł, λ, λ̣, λ̓*) appear in Muskogean, Zuni, Tonkawa, Alsean, Chinookan, Sahaptin, Chimakuan, Salishan, Wakashan, Athapaskan, and Tlingit. Pharyngeals have developed in northern Haida and several Salishan and Wakashan languages.

A few usually common sounds are conspicuously absent from particular languages. Languages of the Iroquoian and Athapaskan families, the Salishan language Tillamook, and Tlingit generally lack labial stops (*p, b*) apart from borrowed words and onomatopoeic or expressive vocabulary. Several other languages lack nasals (*m* and *n*); in the Wakashan languages Nitinaht and Makah, the Chimakuan language Quileute, and the Salishan languages Lushootseed and Twana, all spoken in adjacent areas of the Northwest Coast, original nasals have shifted to voiced stops *b* and *d*.

Syllable structure in some languages is relatively simple. The Mistassini verb *e·če·wi·nipa·ya·n* 'as I will

---

*Material cited from Mohawk, Central Pomo, Santee, and Cayuga comes from Mithun's work with speakers of these languages, whose names are given with the examples.

want to sleep' has syllables *e·.če·.wi·.ni.pa·.ya·n* (MacKenzie 1971:54). Syllable structures in a number of languages can be quite complex, beginning and ending with elaborate clusters of consonants. The Cathlamet Chinook word *ktkkála* 'fliers' begins with four consonants; the word *ítpckt* 'he came up' ends with five consonants (Hymes 1955:61, 66). It is not always clear just how a syllable should be defined, since in some languages, certain consonants can function as the nuclei of syllables; Nater (1984:5) cites the word *čłpxʷłtłpłskʷċ* 'then he had had in his possession a bunchberry plant' from Bella Coola, a Salishan language of British Columbia.

Languages with distinctive tone patterns are distributed over the continent. Among them are Cheyenne, Arapaho, Mohawk, Oneida, Cherokee, Caddo, Arikara, Crow, Mandan, Keres, the Kiowa-Tanoan languages, some Athapaskan languages, Karok, Achumawi, and Heiltsuk. In some of these languages, every syllable carries a distinctive tone that is memorized as a part of the word. In Kiowa, a Kiowa-Tanoan language of Oklahoma, for example, each syllable shows high (´), falling (ˆ), or low (ˋ) tone: *kʰɔybátô·léɔ·ìɔy* 'bat'. A change in tone can alter the meaning of the word just like a change in consonant or vowel: *pʰą́y* 'dust, dirt', *pʰą̂y* 'tie' (Watkins 1984:23, 29).

Some systems are of a type often referred to as pitch accent, whereby distinctive tone appears on only one syllable of the word, often the stressed syllable. In Mohawk, for example, stress usually falls on the next to the last syllable of the word. The stressed syllable has either high tone or falling tone: *oká·raʔ* 'story', *okâ·raʔ* 'eye'. Distinctive pitch patterns in a number of North American languages have developed relatively recently from syllable-final laryngeals ʔ and sometimes *h*.

Processes of vowel harmony appear in some languages. Wikchamni Yokuts of central California (Gamble 1978:14-15) contains high vowels *i, i̇, u,* and low vowels *a, o,* all long and short. In any verb root, all vowels match: *ṗiṅi* 'to sting', *tiʔis* 'to make', *hutu* 'to know', *tawatʰ* 'to run', *ṭoyox* 'to doctor'. If a stem containing high vowels is followed by a suffix with high vowels, the suffix vowels shift to match the last vowel of the stem. The shape of the aorist (nonfuture) suffix thus varies: *piṅ-ši* 'stung', *tiʔis-ši* 'made', *hut-šu* 'knew'. If a stem with low vowels is followed by a suffix with low vowels, the suffix vowels also shift to match the last vowel of the stem. The shape of the dubitative thus varies as well: *tawtʰ-at* '<u>might</u> run', *ṭoyx-ot* '<u>might</u> doctor'. If the suffix vowels are not of the same height as the stem, they do not shift to match: *tʰan-ši* 'went' (low-high), *huky-at* 'might mix' (high-low).

Some languages exhibit a kind of sound symbolism, whereby systematic alternations among certain consonants or vowels are associated with particular shifts in

meaning. The semantic effect is often related to size or intensity. Gamble (1975:308) cites sets of Koyeti Yokuts words with *n/t/c* alternations recorded by John Peabody Harrington: *no·ṅoʔ* 'man', *no·ṭoʔ* 'boy', *no·ċoʔ* 'handsome man'; *ga·ʔiṅaʔ* 'woman', *ga·ʔiṭaʔ* 'girl', *ga·ʔiċaʔ* 'pretty woman'. Boas and Deloria (1933:112-113) provide sets of verbs from Lakhota, a Siouan language of South Dakota, showing alternations of fricatives *s/š/x* or *z/ž/ɣ*: -*slí* 'water or a thin liquid is being squeezed out', -*šlí* 'thick semiliquid matter is being squeezed out', *xlí* 'it is muddy material'; *zí* 'it is yellow', *ží* 'it is tawny', *ɣí* 'it is brown'; -*ptuza* 'it is bent forward', -*ptuža* 'small pieces are cracked off an object without being broken off', -*ptuɣa* 'small pieces are cracked off an object so that they fall off'. Such symbolism appears pervasively in languages of the West, particularly California and the Northwest Coast. A general description is in Johanna Nichols (1971).

Kinds of Words

Words in European languages have traditionally been classified into parts of speech, usually nouns, verbs, adjectives, adverbs, prepositions or postpositions, and others. These lexical classes do have counterparts in some North American languages, but not all. Many languages have no distinguishable adjective category. Instead of adjectives ('the tall man ...'), nouns might be used ('the man, the tall one, ...') or descriptive verbs ('the man, he is tall, ...'). Instead of adverbs, ('she walked slowly'), separate verbs might be used ('she walked, she was slow') or prefixes and suffixes on the verb. Languages of the Wakashan, Salishan, and Chemakuan families of the Northwest have prompted important discussions about even the universality of nouns and verbs (Sapir 1921c:141-143; Sapir and Swadesh 1939:235-236; Swadesh 1939:78-79; Jacobsen 1979c; Kinkade 1983; van Ejik and Hess 1986; as well as "Sketch of Thompson, a Salishan Language," this vol.).

The lack of correspondence between word classes is related in part to a striking structural characteristic of many North American languages, termed polysynthesis. Their words tend to consist of many meaningful parts (morphemes). The Mohawk word below, for example, is not unusual. The first line shows the word as pronounced, the second its morphemes, the third the meaning of each morpheme, and the fourth the meaning of the word as a whole.

Mohawk (Mae Montour, personal communication 1975)
   sahu̜wanhotú̜kwahseʔ
   |s-a-hu̜wa-nho-tu̜-kw-ahs-eʔ|
   again-PAST-she/him-door-close-un-for-PERFECTIVE
   'She opened the door for him again.'

One might wonder why such an utterance is considered a single word. For Mohawk, the answer is clear. The first and most important indication is that Mohawk speakers know it is a single word, whether or not they have ever written their language, whether or not they have ever given the question any thought. A second is that speakers seldom pause in the middle of words, including words like this, although of course they might pause between words. (Similarly, English speakers rarely say *the re ... freshments* although they might say *the ... refreshments*.) A third is that a word cannot be interrupted by other words. A fourth is that the components of the word are not generally recognizable to speakers in isolation. A Mohawk speaker would no more identify the meaning of the first sound *s* out of context than an English speaker would identify the meaning of the sound *s* pronounced alone (the singular marker of *walks*). A fifth is that the relative order of morphemes within words is invariant, although the relative order of words within sentences is quite variable. If the position of any morpheme in the word above were altered, the entire word would be undecipherable. (Similarly, English *scape* would never be identified by English speakers as the plural of *cape* with just an alteration in morpheme order.) A sixth is the fact that many Mohawk morphemes have different forms when they appear at the beginning of a word than when they appear in the middle. The pronoun *-hṵwa-* 'she—him', for example, has the form *rṵwa-* at the beginning of a word. Finally, major Mohawk words are pronounced with one primary stress, one syllable that is more prominent than the others. The word above has primary stress on *-tṵ́-*. Criteria similar to many of these distinguish words in other languages across the continent.

The propensity for complex words raises several issues for the identification of parts of speech within languages. Should single morphemes be classified, like the Mohawk roots *-nho-* 'door' and *-tṵ-* 'close' above, or whole words, like *sahṵwanhotṵ́kwahseʔ* 'she opened the door for him again'? Some languages show a strong distinction between kinds of roots. In Mohawk, noun roots and verb roots appear with completely different sets of affixes (prefixes and suffixes). In other languages, some or all roots behave both as nouns and as verbs, much as in English *a stone* and *to stone*. In Acoma Keresan of New Mexico, some roots appear only with nominal affixes and name entities, some roots appear only with verbal affixes and describe events or states, and some roots appear with either (Miller 1965:146-147). The root *-ʔá·ṁa* means 'house' as a noun and 'dwell' as a verb. Coahuilteco and Central Alaskan Yupik contain similar ambivalent roots.

Even if whole words are classified rather than roots, classification could be based on various criteria. Words have been classified in at least three ways: on the basis of their internal structure (morphology), their meaning (semantics), and their syntactic use. Nouns might be defined morphologically as those words that can appear with plural marking, for example (*teacher-s, purse-s*), and verbs as those that can appear with tense marking (*walk-ed, like-d*). Alternatively, nouns could be defined semantically as those words that are the names of persons or objects (*teacher, purse*), and verbs as those that describe actions (*walk*). Finally, nouns could be defined syntactically as those words that function as subjects, direct objects, or objects of prepositions (*The teacher liked my purse*), and verbs as those words that function as predicates (*I walked*). In some languages, the three criteria generally yield the same categories; but in others, they do not.

In Mohawk, words fall into three distinct classes on the basis of their internal structure: nouns, verbs, and particles. Basic nouns contain only a prefix indicating the gender of the referent, the noun root, and a noun suffix: *ka-hná·t-aʔ* NEUTER-purse-NOUN.SUFFIX = 'purse'. Possession may be shown by a pronominal prefix referring to the possessor: *ak-hná·t-aʔ* my-purse-NOUN.SUFFIX = 'my purse'. A few other suffixes may appear as well. Mohawk verbs, like 'she opened the door for him again' above, show quite different internal structures. They can be extremely complex, with not only tense and aspect markers (past and perfective above), but also a pronominal prefix referring to the agent or patient of the event, or both ('she—him' above), various adverbial markers like the repetitive ('again') and reversive ('un-') above, markers of negation, direction of action, reflexive action, causation, and many more. They many even contain noun roots within them, like *-nho-* 'door'. Particles have no internal structure at all: *áhsṵ* 'three', *yáh* 'no', *tsi* 'as'.

A classification of Mohawk words based on meaning would sometimes yield the same categories as one based on internal morphological structure, but not always. Mohawk nouns are in fact always the names of entities, usually persons or objects, like *kahná·taʔ* 'purse'. Mohawk verbs often do describe actions. Yet many verbs are used to name entities. The word below has the internal structure of a verb, but a meaning more typical of nouns in other languages.

> *yṵterihwayṵstáhkhwaʔ*
> |yṵ-te-rihw-yṵ-hst-áhkw-haʔ|
> one-self-word-know-cause-use.for-habitually
> 'one uses it to cause oneself to know words' = 'school'

Syntactically, Mohawk nouns function as nominals in sentences, again as would be expected, identifying entities that would be subjects or objects in English. Verbs can function syntactically as predicates in sentences. They can also function as subjects, objects, or even adverbials. The sentence below comes from a tale in which a boy and his younger brother became lost. Four of the words have the internal structure of verbs (all but the particles *ne* 'the' and *kʌʔk* 'a bit'). Yet syntactically, the first is a predicate ('noticed'), the second identifies the subject ('the older one'), the third is an adverbial ('a short distance away'), and the fourth identifies the direct object ('light').

Mohawk (Rita Phillips, personal communication 1975)

VERB		VERB		VERB
waháttokeʔ	*ne*	*thakowá·nʌ*	*kʌʔk*	*niyó·reʔ*
he noticed it	the	he is larger	a bit	it is so far

VERB

tkaháhseroteʔ.

a light stands there

'A short distance away the older one noticed a light.'

As can be seen from the examples here, Mohawk verbs contain pronominal prefixes referring to their agents or patients, or both. For this reason they can and often do stand alone as fully grammatical sentences in themselves. Verbs like *sahʉwanhotúkwahseʔ* 'she opened the door for him again' and *waháttokeʔ* 'he noticed it' are grammatically complete. The three common criteria for establishing word classes—internal morphological structure, meaning, and syntactic use—thus do not yield the same categorizations in Mohawk.

Similar complexities are associated with definitions of the parts of speech in many languages. Because of the pervasiveness of polysynthesis in North America, lexical categories have often been defined in terms of the internal structure of the words, or morphology. For some languages, only two categories are distinguished: inflected words (those with prefixes or suffixes, or both) and uninflected words. For many others, three categories are distinguished: nouns, verbs, and particles, as in Mohawk. In still others, additional categories are recognized. In any case, the languages of North America provide good evidence that parts of speech, and the appropriate criteria for distinguishing them, are not equivalent cross-linguistically.

The Meaningful Pieces of Words

Morphemes, the meaningful components of words, are of three main kinds: roots, affixes, and clitics. Roots generally convey the principal meaning of words, like English *purse* in the noun <u>purse</u>-*s* and *walk* in the verb <u>walk</u>-*ed*, or Mohawk -*hnat*- 'purse' in *akhná·taʔ* 'my <u>purse</u>' and -*tok*- 'notice' in *waháttokeʔ* 'he <u>noticed</u> it'. Affixes usually modify or qualify the meanings of roots in some way, like the English plural suffix -*s* or the Mohawk possessive prefix *ak*- 'my'.

Clitics sound much like affixes in that they are pronounced as part of a larger word; however, they differ in their grammatical patterns. Affixes combine structurally with words of a particular class, such as nouns

or verbs; for example, the English plural suffix -*s* is attached to nouns: *[teacher]-<u>s</u>*. Clitics, by contrast, combine structurally with whole phrases or clauses; the English possessive clitic =*s* is attached to whole noun phrases: *[teacher]=<u>s</u> purse*, *[the man I go out with]=<u>s</u> mother*. Clitics appear at the edges of words, outside of affixes. Those that appear at the beginning of words, before prefixes, are termed proclitics; those that appear at the end, like the English possessive, are enclitics.

A distinction is sometimes drawn between derivation and inflection. Derivational affixes are used to create new words, words that would be listed as separate entries in a dictionary. The English -*ment* of *refreshment* is considered derivational. It creates nouns from verbs. One would expect to find *refresh* and *refreshment* listed as separate entries in a dictionary. Inflectional affixes do not create new words but systematically specify obligatory distinctions, like the English plural -*s*. One would not expect to find a separate dictionary entry for the term *refreshments*; *refreshment* and *refreshments* would be considered singular and plural forms of the same word. The term 'stem' is applied to both roots and roots with derivational affixes. English *purse*, *walk*, *fresh*, *refresh*, and *refreshment* are all stems. Inflectional affixes are added to stems: *purse-s*, *refreshment-s*, *walk-ed*, *refresh-ed*.

Root-Affix Combinations and the Distribution of Meaning

For the most part, the distribution of concepts between roots and affixes is comparable across languages. The meanings of most Mohawk roots are similar in kind to the meanings of English roots: -*nho*- 'door', -*hnat*- 'purse', -*khw*- 'meal', -*tʉ*- 'close', -*k*- 'eat', -*t*- 'stand'. Of course the meanings of individual roots do not always have perfect counterparts in other languages. Young and Morgan (1992:828) list 11 different roots in Navajo, an Athapaskan language of Arizona and New Mexico, that appear in verbs translated 'to handle'. Handling a solid, roundish, compact object, such as an apple, barrel, inflated balloon, basket, chair, chunk of cheese, hat, boot, or glove, is expressed by a verb built on the root -*ʔá*. Handling a slender, flexible object, such as a strip of bacon, uninflated balloon, belt, cornhusk, flower, blade of grass, or a pair of objects such as gloves or boots, is expressed by a verb built on a completely different root, -*lá*. Handling a thin, stiff object, such as an antler, arrow, banana, flat basket, string bean, bow, or broom is expressed by a verb built on the root -*tá*. Handling a flat, flexible object, such as an empty bag, blanket, coat, cobweb, dollar bill, newspaper, or quiver is expressed by a verb built on the root -*łtsooz*. Handling an animate object, such as a baby, a fly, a kitten, a snake, or a man (alive or dead), is expressed by a verb built on the root -*łtí*. Handling a mushy object, such as butter, melted cheese, cornmeal mush, scrambled egg, a gob of grease or ice cream, mud, pitch, or mashed potato, is expressed by a verb built on the root -tłééʔ. Handling multiple separable objects, such as acorns, beads, beans, or dishes is expressed by a verb built on the root -nil. Handling profuse, multiple objects is expressed by a verb built on the root -jaaʔ. Handling noncompact matter, such as a wad of down, horsetail, tangled pile of intestine, shredded lettuce, moss, snarled wad of thread or string, bunched up towel, or loose wool, is expressed by a verb built on the root -tjool. Handling an open container, such as acorns in a basket, ashes, beer in a mug or open bottle, or an ice cream cone, is expressed by a verb built on the root -ką́. Finally, handling a load or large, bulky object, such as a big bag, bed, rolled blanket, Christmas tree, firewood, or a man on a stretcher, is expressed by a verb based on the root -yį́. The different roots represent distinct concepts; the kind of action involved in handling a baby is quite different from that involved in handling a dollar bill or a mug of beer. At the same time, each of these roots forms the basis of other Navajo verbs translated variously as 'pick up', 'carry', 'haul', 'set down', and 'put'. The motions involved in picking up, carrying, and setting down a baby are expressed as having more in common than the motions involved in carrying a baby and carrying a man on a stretcher. Such distinctions are particularly well developed in Navajo, but similar lexical differences appear in many other North American languages.

The distribution of meaning between roots and affixes is not always what might be expected on the basis of European languages. The verbs below are from Nez Perce, a Sahaptian language of Idaho. Each contains a prefix before the root. In 'I hug' and 'I am walking', the distribution of meanings between the prefixes and roots is not surprising.

Nez Perce (Aoki 1970:82, 87, 1994:208, 343, 826, 1064)
waqalpísa (prefix waqa- 'in arms', root -lpí- 'seize')
'I hug'

ʔipsqíkeʔykse (prefix ʔipsqí- 'on foot', root -keʔy-
'I am walking'   'move')

Sometimes meaning conveyed by a root in English is expressed with an affix in Nez Perce and vice versa. In the verbs below, the galloping is expressed with a prefix. The roots express general motion and direction.

Nez Perce (Aoki 1970:83, 88, 1994:209, 297, 598, 1162)
hiqqúkeʔykse (prefix qqú- 'galloping', root -keʔy-
'he is galloping'   'move')

hiqqoláhsaya (prefix qqo- 'galloping', root -láhsa-
'she galloped up'   'up')

It is clear that the morpheme 'galloping' is a prefix because, like other adverbial prefixes in the language

(with meanings like 'underneath', 'at night', 'with teeth', 'backwards'), it cannot form the basis of a verb on its own. It must be followed by a verb root. A similar system is discussed in "Sketch of Sahaptin, a Sahaptian Language," this volume.

Stem Combinations: Compounding and Incorporation

Speakers of many languages form new words by combining roots, stems, or words with each other to form compounds, like English *doghouse* or *lawnmower*. Compounds can be interesting for the record they provide of the kinds of concepts speakers have felt a need to name, often in recent times, and of the features of these concepts they have found most salient, the terms in which they have chosen to describe them.

In many languages, compound nouns are formed by combining one noun with another (N + N > N). Watkins (1984) provides examples from Kiowa. The noun hɔ̀·+tʰɔ̀· 'ax' consists of the noun roots 'metal' and 'club'. The noun tɔ̀+á 'earring' consists of the noun roots 'ear' and 'stick'. Compound nouns may also be formed by combining a noun with a verb (N + V > N). The Kiowa noun zòn+tʰâ·pé 'squirrel' contains the noun 'pine' and the verb 'pick up'. The noun tʰɔ̀+tɔ̀·dé 'faucet' contains the noun 'water' and the verb 'flow'. The noun tò·+hî· 'tepee' consists of the noun 'house' and the verb 'be real'. The noun kɔ́á·l+sá 'broken dishes' consists of the noun 'dish' and the verb 'shatter'.

In some languages, compound verbs may be formed by combining one verb with another (V + V > V). The Kiowa verb pɔ̀·+kʰôy 'lead back' is composed of the verbs 'bring' and 'return'. The verb dè̀·+kʰáy+kɔ̀· 'lie stretched out sleeping' consists of the verbs 'sleep', 'stretch', and 'be lying'.

Compound verbs are also formed in some languages by combining a noun with a verb (N + V > V or V + N > V). Compounding of this type, termed noun incorporation, is especially well developed in a number of North American languages (see the grammatical sketches of Seneca, Shoshone, Zuni, Wichita, Lakhota, and Cree, this vol.). It is used by speakers in several ways (Mithun 1984).

Some noun incorporation is simply a basic word-building device, used to create new verbs for recognizable, nameworthy actions. The Kiowa verb stem dɔ̀m+sá· 'to plow' consists of the noun 'earth' and the verb 'shatter'. The verb stem dɔ̀m+kû· 'to hoe' consists of the noun 'earth' and the verb 'hit'. The verb stem á·+tʰà· 'to saw' consists of the noun root 'wood' and the verb root 'cut'. The resulting verb stems serve as the basis of full verb words. The word ètápèbà 'we went deerhunting' consists of the parts è-táp-è̀-bà 'we-deer-hunt-go.PERFECTIVE'. The word bécáthè·dè 'open the door' consists of the parts bé-cát-hèdè 'you/it-door remove.

141

Noun incorporation can allow speakers to shape the way in which information is presented. If one says in English 'my head hurts', the grammatical subject of the sentence is the head. Yet when a person's head hurts, speakers are usually more concerned about the owner of the head than the head itself. If the noun 'head' is incorporated, it no longer functions as a subject or core argument; it simply describes the kind of ache. The Kiowa verb à́lt^họ́k^họ̀pd^{ɔ̀}· '<u>I</u> have a headache' consists of à-ɔ́lt^họ́-k^họ̀p-d^{ɔ̀}· 'I-head-hurt-be'. With incorporation, the only core argument of the clause, represented in the pronominal prefix, is the speaker ('I'), not the head.

In some languages, noun incorporation is used pervasively for stylistic purposes. Separate nouns are typically used when the speaker wishes to direct special attention to a person or object, as when it is first introduced or when it represents important information, perhaps a focus of contrast. Once the person or object has become an established part of the scene, the noun may be backgrounded by incorporation. An example of such noun incorporation can be seen in the passage below from Arikara, a Caddoan language of North Dakota. When a son first asks for a hoop, he uses a separate noun to focus on the hoop. When he mentions it again in the following line, the noun is incorporated into the verb.

Arikara (Alfred Morsette in Parks 1991, 1:136)

atí^ʔAx	šku·súxto^ʔ	ta·wirás
Father	make it for me	<u>hoop</u>

'Father, make a hoop for me!'

tátska^ʔ	a·to·sta·wiráhNA
I want	that I <u>hoop</u> have

'I want to have a hoop.'

Grammatical Categories

Languages can differ in interesting ways in the meanings that become encoded in grammatical categories, the semantic distinctions speakers routinely and automatically indicate with prefixes and suffixes. In the many polysynthetic languages of North America, particularly elaborate sets of categories have been grammaticized. Some are typical of languages all over the world, such as causatives (English *moist-<u>en</u>* '<u>cause</u> to be moist'). Others are more unusual.

Languages can also differ in the choices they offer speakers. What is obligatorily specified in one language may be optional in the next. English speakers, for example, must distinguish masculine, feminine, and neuter gender, singular and plural number, and past, present, and future tense, if they are to speak grammatically for very long. Speakers of many North American languages need not specify gender, number, or tense at all,

although they can when they wish; however, their languages may require them to specify other distinctions.

Finally, languages can differ in where in their grammatical structure particular distinctions are expressed. In European languages, number (singular versus plural) is typically expressed on nouns and tense on verbs. In many North American languages, number is typically expressed on verbs but less often on nouns. In some, tense can be indicated on nouns. Such differences can subtly affect the kinds of distinctions encoded in the grammar.

Gender

In many of the world's languages, nouns or noun phrases carry indications of grammatical gender. Gender may be indicated by endings of nouns (Russian consonant-final masculines, *a*-final feminines, *o*-final neuters), by articles (French masculine *le*, feminine *la*), and by pronouns (English masculine *he*, feminine *she*, neuter *it*). In some languages, gender classifications are for the most part semantically motivated: male persons and animals are grammatically masculine; female persons and animals are grammatically feminine; all else is grammatically neuter. In other languages, there is more semantic arbitrariness: the grammatical gender of each noun is learned by rote. A large proportion of North American languages show no grammatical gender at all, but various kinds of gender systems have developed in some language families.

Some systems oppose animates and inanimates. In Southern Tiwa, a Tanoan language of New Mexico, animate nouns are marked with a suffix *-de*, while inanimate nouns carry no gender suffix. Brandt (1970:109), describing the Sandia dialect, reports that anything capable of independent motion is classified as animate: *sɔ́ani-<u>de</u>* 'man', *tùmubíli-<u>de</u>* 'automobile', *kəá^ʔì-<u>de</u>* 'bear', *wa^ʔí-<u>de</u>* 'wind', *kànkáruwi-<u>de</u>* 'wagon', *šíwi-<u>de</u>* 'eagle'. The nouns *nakáyu* 'tortilla', *làlúna* 'blue jeans', and *pién* 'mountain' are inanimate. Animate nouns have plural forms but inanimate nouns do not. Animate-inanimate gender systems are especially well developed in the Algonquian languages (see the grammatical sketch of Cree, this vol.).

Some North American languages do exhibit sex-based gender distinctions. In Tunica, a language of the Southeast, all nouns are classified as either masculine or feminine (Haas 1946). The distinction is marked in noun suffixes, independent personal pronouns, possessive pronominal prefixes on nouns, and pronominal prefixes on verbs. Gender is distinguished for both second-person 'you' and third persons 'he' versus 'she'. Neither gender form is derived from the other.

Tunica nouns or pronouns referring to male persons or animals are generally masculine: *ta·čɔha-<u>ku</u>* 'chief-MAS-CULINE'. Those referring to female persons or animals are feminine: *ta´nisara-h̆či* 'girl-FEMININE'. Most count nouns for inanimates are masculine (*ta´šihkali-ku* 'rock-MASCULINE'), although there are a few inexplicable exceptions (*ta´ri-h̆či* 'house-FEMININE'). Mass nouns are grammatically feminine: *ta´wiši-h̆či* 'water-FEMININE'. Gender distinctions are maintained in basic singular, dual, and plural, but collective animates are grammatically masculine: *ta´čahta-ku* 'Choctaw-MASCULINE', 'the Choctaw'.

Some impersonal verbs in Tunica are inflected only for third-person feminine singular subject: *ti´hikati´sihkŭn, pi´ratĭhc* 'when it (feminine) got to be seven years' = 'seven years later', *siho´t²ɔkɛ´nì* 'one (feminine) has finished them off' = 'they have become extinct'. Haas (1946:356) reports that weather verbs such as 'to rain', 'to snow', and 'to hail' appear with masculine subject pronouns, because in Tunica mythology the Thunder Being, who is thought to control this type of weather, is personified as a man: *sa´č²uhkí* 'he has rained'.

Quileute shows a different binary gender distinction. Demonstratives, independent pronouns, and pronominal suffixes carry a distinction between feminine and nonfeminine gender (Andrade 1933). Feminine forms refer to all female persons and animals, and nonfeminine to all other entities. The classification can be seen in articles, which distinguish gender, case, and definiteness. Among the subjects in a passage from a tale told by Seíxtis (Andrade 1933:279-282) are the feminines *yik á²čit.ĭ* 'the chief's wife', *yik likà·ċo²* 'the married woman', *yik káč.toĭ* 'the mother', *yik hadós·toĭ* 'the older sister', and *yik k̆adé²eĭoĭ* 'the younger sister', as well as the nonfeminines *yix á²čit* 'the chief', *yix ĭé²k̆a²à·* 'the tribe' and *yix λoĭoĭoót* 'the star'. Among the definite nonsubjects in the same passages are the feminines *ki² yalôlat* 'the wife', *ki² ha·dósya²ák* 'the older sister of hers', and *ki² k̆adé²ya²ák* 'the younger sister of hers', as well as the nonfeminines *xe² hé·ĭit* 'the husband', *xe² ĭé²k̆a²à·* 'the tribe', *xe² λoĭoĭoót* 'the star', *xe ičá·ĭát* 'the destination', and *xe² óq̇oce·šé·ĭilít* 'the place chosen'.

The Chinookan languages of the Columbia River area in Washington and Oregon show three gender categories, distinguished in pronominal prefixes on verbs and nouns, and in demonstratives. Boas (1911c:597-605) describes the gender categories of Lower Chinook. Gender classification of nouns referring to persons is straightforward. Masculine and feminine prefixes appear on nouns referring to male and female persons respectively: *í-pλ²au* 'widower', *ú-pλ²au* 'widow'; *i-láitix* 'male slave', *u-láitix* 'female slave'. The neuter gender can be used for indefinite persons or those of unknown or unspecified gender: *ĭ-kánax* 'a chief'. Similar prefixes appear on verbs with the meanings 'he', 'she', and 'someone': *n-í-tṗ* 'he came in (to)', *al-ú-mqta* 'she will die', *a-ĭ-úpa* 'it, someone goes out'. Gender classification of nouns referring to nonhumans is less straightforward. All genders appear. Boas hypothesized that large animals tend to be classified as masculine ('bear', 'squirrel', 'owl') but small animals as feminine ('beetle', 'chipmunk', 'woodpecker'). A size distinction appears with a few other pairs: *í-pqunx* 'large round spruce-root basket', *ú-pqunx* 'small round spruce-root basket'. Nouns expressing qualities tend to be masculine ('sharpness', 'diligence', 'cold'), as well as verbal nouns corresponding to past passive participles ('what is eaten'). Hymes (1955:142) points out that in fact little regularity appears in the nonhuman classification in Chinookan languages overall, but modern speakers of Wasco-Wishram, an Upper Chinook language, use the prefixes productively to introduce special distinctions of gender or size.

The Northern Iroquoian languages have also developed three gender categories in third-person pronominal prefixes on verbs and nouns: masculine, feminine-indefinite, and neuter-zoic ("Sketch of Seneca, an Iroquoian Language", this vol.). In Mohawk, Oneida, and Onondaga, the masculine is used for male persons and personified animals or characters (Mohawk *wahahnekí´ra²* 'he drank it'). The feminine-indefinite, which developed historically from an indefinite pronoun meaning 'one, someone, people', is still used for persons of unspecified sex, but it is also used for some female persons (*wa²ehnekí´ra²* 'someone or she drank it'). The neuter-zoic is used for objects and animals as well as for some female persons (*wa²kahnekí´ra²* 'it or she drank it'). Speakers thus have a choice of gender category when referring to women. Factors that enter into the choice include the dignity, size, gracefulness, and age of the referent, as well as her relationship to the speaker (Abbott 1984).

Sex-based grammatical distinctions appear in other areas of the grammars of some languages. In Mandan, speech addressed to men is distinguished from that to women by suffixes on verbs. Hollow (1970:456) reports that the indicative verb suffix "-o²š is used in addressing men, male animals, mixed groups, tobacco plants, rocks, and the Deity, whereas -o²re ... is used in addressing women, female animals and all plants except tobacco." The interrogative suffixes *-o²ša* and *-o²rą*, and the imperative suffixes *-ta* and *-ną*, show similar distributions. In other Siouan languages, speech by men is often distinguished from that by women. Martha St. John (personal communication 1983), a Santee speaker, notes that she would respond to a question with the feminine declarative marker: *hé bdatké=ye* '(Yes,) I drank that', while a man would respond with a masculine declarative: *hé bdatké=do*. In commands, she would use a feminine imperative marker; she would tell her grandson *hé čʰụšní=ye* 'Don't do that!' where a man would say *hé čʰụšní=wo*.

Shape and Position

In some languages, entities are classified in terms of their shape or position. Many languages encode such features lexically with different existential verbs. Compact objects appear with verbs for 'sit', tall ones 'stand', and elongated ones, those with a greater horizontal dimension, 'lie'. In Tunica, for example, humans and four-legged animals may appear with all three existential verbs: *-ná* 'sit', *-kali̱_rá* 'stand', *-rá* 'lie'.

Tunica (Haas 1941a:110-111)

taˊsăku, ʔuná	'There <u>is</u> the dog (in a sitting position).'
taˊsăku, ka'lʔurá	'There <u>is</u> the dog (in a standing position).'
taˊsăku, ʔurá	'There <u>is</u> the dog (in a lying position).'

Small, dumpy animals always appear with 'sit', and elongated animals with 'lie'.

tuˊrunatʔěku, ʔuná	'There <u>is</u> the bullfrog ('The bullfrog is sitting.')
teˊhkunăku, ʔuná	'There <u>is</u> the mosquito (sitting).'
taˊninĭku, ʔuná	'There <u>is</u> the fish (lying).'
tɔˊmahkăku, ʔuná	'There <u>is</u> the alligator (lying).'

Inanimate objects are classified according to their characteristic position.

ʔeˊkša ka'lʔurá	'There <u>is</u> a pine tree (standing).'
ha'lʔukin ʔaraˊnì	'There <u>was</u> a town.' ('A town was lying.')

Abstract nouns are classified as horizontal.

> *hiˊnahkŭn, laˊhon saˊhkŭn, ʔará, haˊtikán.*
> 'Now there <u>is</u> one morning (lying) again (left for you to do it).'

Shape and position are also encoded in the grammatical categories of some languages. In Yuchi, a language of Oklahoma, nouns are classified into animate and inanimate classes by suffixed articles (Wagner 1933:320-322). Animate nouns, identified by the suffix *-nɔ*, are further classified by internal suffixes into those referring to members of the Yuchi tribe versus all others, including other human beings, animals, and a few mythological beings such as the Sun and the Moon: *gɔnɨɛ-nɔ́* 'the (Yuchi) man', *gɔnɨɛ-wɔ-nɔ́* 'the man (a White man, Indian of another tribe, Black man)', *táɫa-wɔ-nɔ* 'the wolf'. Among those referring to members of the Yuchi tribe, certain kinship relations are specified: *cowatné-sɛ-nɔ* 'my (man's) sister'.

Nouns referring to inanimate objects are also further classified by their suffixed articles. There are three categories: *-fa* 'objects with a prevailingly vertical dimension, such as standing poles, trees, high mountains, tall houses' (*yá-fa* 'the tree', *yu-fa* 'the house'); *-ʔɛ* 'objects with a prevailingly horizontal dimension, such as lakes, streams, roads, fields, logs lying on the ground' (*ya-ʔɛ* 'the log', *sa-ʔɛ́* 'the field'); and *-ʒi* 'objects of a roundish shape or of a dimension that is indifferent to the ideas of vertical and horizontal, such as rocks, bushy trees, chairs, etc.' (*tí-ʒi* 'the rock', *yastadɛḱɔ́-ʒi* 'the chair') (Wagner 1933:221). Abstract nouns appear in all three categories.

The same classificatory suffixes appear with demonstratives: *né-nɔ gɔnɨɛ-nɔ* 'this (Yuchi) man', *né-sɛ-nɔ sanɨɛ-sɛ-nɔ* 'this girl (referring to a man's sister, etc.)', *né-fa yá-fa* 'this tree', *né-ʔɛ sá-ʔɛ* 'this field', *nɛ-ʒi dí-ʒi* 'this rock'. The distinctions between animates and inanimates, Yuchi and non-Yuchi, and degrees of kinship are marked on the pronominal prefixes as well.

Languages in the Dhegiha branch of the Siouan family—Omaha-Ponca, Kansa, Osage, and Quapaw—have also developed sets of definite article suffixes on nouns. The articles distinguish animacy, number, shape or position, and movement. Boas and Swanton (1911:939-941) list the Ponca definite articles. Articles for inanimate objects include *kʰe* for horizontal objects, *tʰe* standing objects and collectives, *ðą* rounded objects, *ge* scattered objects. Articles for animate agents include *akʰá* for singular animates at rest and *amá* for singular animates in motion or plurals. Articles for animate patients include *tʰą* for standing singulars, *ði* for moving singulars, *ma* for moving plurals, *ðikʰé* for sitting singulars, and *ðąkʰá* for sitting plurals. The use of the articles can be seen in the lines below from a narrative told by Nudą́axa, in which the hero, named Rabbit, is first characterized as a singular animate agent at rest with the article *akʰá*. The Pawnees are marked as plural sitting patients by *ðąkʰá*. In the second line, the sun is marked as an inanimate rounded object with the article *ðą*.

Ponca (Dorsey 1890:379)

maščįge akʰá	*pádi ðąkʰá*	*wéðai tʰe.*	
Rabbit <u>the</u>	Pawnee <u>the</u>	found them	

'Maščįge (the Rabbit) detected the Pawnees.

mį́ ðą	*hídexči*	*tʰédi, ...*
sun <u>the</u>	at the very bottom	when

When the sun was at the very bottom of the sky, ...'

Size

Many languages contain one or more augmentative or diminutive affixes indicating size. In some languages, such affixes appear with the nouns they qualify, as in Natchez, a language last spoken in Oklahoma (Mary

Haas, personal communication 1983 from work with Watt Sam, 1936). The derived nouns may have specialized meanings.

Natchez (Mary Haas, personal communication 1983)

		DIMINUTIVE	AUGMENTATIVE
ʔen	'fish'	ʔen-i·nuh	ʔen-ši·l
		'minnow'	'whale'
ʔaštip	'old woman'	ʔastip-i·nuh	
		'little old woman'	
ʔu·	'road'	ʔu·y-i·nuh	
		'trail, path'	
ʔi·tihi-	'doorway'	ʔi·tih-i·nuh	
		'window'	
popkeh	'beans'	popke-·nuh	
		'peas'	

Natchez, like some other languages, also contains diminutive affixes on verbs. Diminutive verbs can imply a small motion or a small participant, usually intransitive subject or transitive object.

		DIMINUTIVES	
heci-ʔiš	'sit, live'	he-ti-ci-ʔiš	'little one to sit, live'
hapiti-ʔiš	'go around'	hetpi-ti-ʔiš	'little one to go around'
heyahku-ʔiš	'find one'	he-li-yahku-ʔiš	'find a little one'
wehhelahci-ʔiš	'gather one'	wehhe-li-lahci-ʔiš	'gather little ones'

Person

The category of person traditionally refers to distinctions among the speaker (first person 'I', 'we'), the addressee (second person 'you'), and others (third person 'he', 'she', 'it', 'they'). Person distinctions appear most often in pronouns. In North American languages, they are often expressed in pronominal affixes on verbs and nouns. Person distinctions can be seen in the pronominal suffixes on the verbs and the possessive prefixes on the nouns below from Koasati, a Muskogean language of Louisiana.

Koasati (Kimball 1991:65, 434)

	VERBS		NOUNS	
1	ča-lhó·s	'I forget'	ča-halkí	'my wife'
2	či-lhó·s	'you forget'	či-halkí	'your wife'
3	ilhó·s	'(he, she) forgets'	halkí	'(his) wife'

In many pronominal systems, as here, there is no overt form for third person. Third persons are the participants usually identified by full noun phrases.

In addition to these three basic categories of person, several other categories have been grammaticized in various North American languages.

• INCLUSIVE AND EXCLUSIVE   A distinction common in North American languages, though by no means unique

to them, is that between inclusive and exclusive first persons. Both categories refer to the speaker plus one or more other people: 'we', 'us', 'our'. Inclusive forms include the addressee(s): 'you and I' or 'we and you'. Exclusive forms exclude the addressee(s): 'he, she, or they and I'. A good discussion of the distinction and the ways in which it can arise is in Jacobsen (1980).

Often the inclusive pronoun patterns as a separate basic category of person, alongside of first-, second-, and third-person singular. Such patterning can be seen in Southern Sierra Miwok, an Utian language of California. In Miwok, subjects and objects are specified by pronominal suffixes on verbs: čili·li·si· 'you're weaving' (Broadbent 1964:48). Among several series of pronominal suffixes are these subject suffixes.

Southern Sierra Miwok (Broadbent 1964:43)

SINGULAR		PLURAL	
-ma·	'I'	-mah·i·	'we' (he, she, or they and I)
-ti·	'you sg. and I'	-tič·i·	'we' (you pl. and I)
-si·	'you sg.'	-toksu·	'you pl.'
-·	'he, she, it'	-p·u·	'they'

The exclusive pronoun -mah·i· 'we (he, she, or they and I)' is formally the plural of the first person -ma· 'I'. The inclusive -ti· 'you sg. and I' patterns as a singular even though it refers to a group of two, the speaker and the hearer. The inclusive plural -tič·i· 'you pl. and I' refers to that group plus at least one other. Similar patterning can be seen in Lakhota.

• INDEFINITE   Some languages contain a special pronominal category for indefinite or unspecified referents. The Caddoan languages contain no basic third-person pronominal prefixes, but they do contain a set of prefixes translated 'one', 'someone'. The examples below are from Caddo, a language of Oklahoma.

Caddo (Chafe 1976:66)

|či-yibahwnah| → čí·báwnah	'I saw (it)'
|yahʔ-yibahwnah| → dâyybáwnah	'you saw (it)'
|yibahwnah| → dibáwnah	'(he, she) saw (it)'
|yi-yibahwnah| → dí·báwnah	'one saw (it)'

The indefinite pronoun is used to represent a person the speaker has no interest in identifying, perhaps because the identity is irrelevant or unknown. It might be used where English speakers would use a passive, as in: 'he's been fired' ('someone has fired him').

The Caddo indefinite category is used for other functions as well (Chafe 1992). In narrative, it can serve to keep reference straight. The central protagonist is typically introduced with a noun phrase, accompanied by verbs like the third one above without a pronominal prefix, then not overtly reidentified until there is some change of scene or participants. Secondary characters may also be introduced by a noun phrase and then referred to by the indefinite or defocusing pronoun in verbs like the fourth one above. The alternation between verbs with no pronoun, which describe actions of the hero, and verbs with the defocusing pronoun, which describe actions of others, serves to keep reference clear. Such alternation can be seen in the passages from a Caddo narrative below. The animals had held a council about the drought. It was decided that each would go out to look for water. When the turtle goes out, he is introduced with a noun phrase and a verb with no pronominal prefix.

Caddo (Sadie Bedoka Weller in Chafe 1977:28)
 bah?nah ná cah čáyáh, háhiyah kúkidah.
 It is said that Mr. Turtle went by the creek

The turtle finds a log and gets stuck. The verb again contains no pronoun.

 nátti? bah?nah dikahí·yah.
 There it is said got stuck

He gives a shout and the others rush over, stepping on him. At this point the other animals, secondary characters, are represented by the indefinite or defocusing pronominal prefix on the verb 'step on'.

 bah?nah nátti? di·niwsakáh ná nabít
 It is said there <u>one</u> stepped on him those others
 kahánná·bah.
 it was them

A second use of the Caddo indefinite pronouns is in the coining of names for objects, persons, or actions: |nak-yi-ka-dís| → *nakikadis* 'that with which <u>one</u> washes' = 'soap'; |nayt-ya-?i-yán-hah| → *naytda·yánhah* 'he catches <u>people</u>' = 'policeman'; |kak-yi-ka-dís| → *kakikadis* '(for <u>one</u>) to wash'.

A third use is in talk to or about an in-law; the verb |dikat-yi-?a?nih-hah| → *dikadi·nihah* 'what is <u>one</u> doing' could be used either to or about an in-law, 'What are you doing?' or 'What is he or she doing?'.

Finally, the indefinite or defocusing pronominal category has come to be used in Caddo with a dual or plural marker for inclusive first person: |yi-wiht-yi-bahw-nah| → <u>*díwísbáwnah*</u> 'we (you and I, dual) saw it', |yi-yi-wa-bahw-nah| → <u>*dí·wabáwnah*</u> 'we (you pl. and I) saw it'.

A number of other languages, including some in the Athapaskan family, show similar extensions of indefinite or defocused person categories.

• OBVIATION Among the grammatical devices that differentiate third persons is obviation, first recognized in languages of the Algonquian family. These systems contain two third-person categories, the first termed proximate, the second obviative. Goddard (1990) provides a good description of the distinction in Fox, an Algonquian language in Iowa. If there is only one third person under discussion, it is classified as proximate. If multiple third persons are involved, the one most central to the discussion is categorized as proximate, and all others as obviative. The proximate participant is the one from whose point of view events are presented. If only one participant is human, that one is proximate. In the passage below a woman and her son have become lost. The abbreviation P stands for proximate, O for obviative. Here the woman is proximate, the husband obviative.

Fox (Alfred Kiyana in Goddard 1990:320; Ives Goddard, personal communication 1993)
 we·či·či=ke·hi e·h=kehči-natone·hoči.
 where P came from=and P was greatly searched for
 'And where she (P) had come from a great search was made for her (P).

 ona·pe·mani apina=meko e·h=mahkate·wi·niči.
 P's husband-O even=EMPH O fasted
 Her (P) husband (O) even fasted.'

Goddard notes that the point of view may be shifted, with a change in categorization of the participant. The next sentence in the narrative shows such a shift from the woman, now obviative, to the husband, now proximate.

Fox (Goddard 1990:320)
 o·ni=·'pi we·wi·wita, "nahi´,
 then=HEARSAY O's husband-P well!
 'And then, it is said, her (O) husband (P) was told, "Well,

 wa·pake ki·h=ne·wa·wa ki·wa," e·h=ineči.
 tomorrow you will see P your wife-P P was told
 tomorrow you will see your wife." '

(Within the quotation there is only one third person, the wife, so she must be categorized as proximate. This categorization does not correlate with that outside of the quotation, where the husband is proximate.)

Of course the proximate-obviative distinction makes it easier for the audience to keep track of the identity of participants. In addition, the selection of the proximate participant and shifts to a new proximate play important roles in structuring discourse. As Goddard (1990) points out, for example, shifts often function as scene or episode delimiters.

Number

In most European languages, number distinctions, usually singular versus plural, are obligatorily specified with every count noun. In a substantial proportion of North American languages, nouns do not carry obligatory number markers. The same noun can refer to one individual or many.

Sometimes number is expressed lexically. In some languages, only a few nouns, usually those referring to certain human beings, have plural counterparts. The plural nouns that exist may not be derived from the singulars in a regular way. Silver (1966) reports that in

Shasta, a language of northern California, nouns do not distinguish singular from plural number, but some nouns have special paucal counterparts to refer to just a few: *súk·ax* 'boy(s)', *ʔéʷarár* 'a few boys'; *kíyaxáʔ* 'girl(s)', *yač·ápxa·* 'a few girls'.

Number is sometimes expressed as part of the meaning of the verb root. In many languages, one verb root is used to describe a particular action involving an individual, while a completely different root is used for a similar action by or toward a group. In Shasta, a verb based on the root *-at·i-* is used if one person walks alone, but a verb based on a different root, *-eʔ·i-*, is used for a group walking together. The root *-is·a·-* is used if a person sits alone, but the root *-ará·-* is used if several sit together. The root *-epxù-* describes the action of going out alone to camp, but the root *-axisu-* describes going out to camp together (Silver 1966:110-111). Walking alone and walking in a group are considered sufficiently different concepts to be given different labels, as are sitting alone and sitting in company, or camping alone and together.

Many languages contain optional grammatical devices for indicating number. In languages of the Chumashan family, spoken along the central California coast, basic nouns do not distinguish number; the noun *šik*, for example, is translatable as either 'louse' or 'lice'. Plurality may be indicated if desired by reduplication. Part or all of the noun is repeated. The Barbareño Chumash material cited here comes from notebooks kept by the last speaker of the language, Mary Yee, as she worked with John Peabody Harrington.

Barbareño Chumash (Yee 1956)

šik	'louse'	*šikšik*	(pl.)
kop	'toad'	*kopkop*	(pl.)
pulaḱaḱ	'redheaded woodpecker'	*pulpulaḱaḱ*	(pl.)
čikiy	'snake'	*čikčikiy*	(pl.)

Reduplication appears more often in verbs to pluralize some aspect of the action, yielding an iterative (action composed of repeated small actions), a distributive (action here and there), or a progressive (ongoing action). (In the examples below, the initial *s-* is the third-person subject 'he, she, or it'.)

s-pí·ṅan	'it (the ball) bounced'
s-piṅá·ṅan	'it is bouncing'
s-wotolḱoy	'he circled around'
s-wotwotolḱoy	'he keeps going around in circles'
s-niw	'he danced'
s-niwniẇ	'he is dancing'

Different verb stems show different patterns of reduplication; in many, the initial syllable is repeated, in some, a medial syllable, in others, the final syllable, and in still others, several syllables.

s-qonqoṅ	'he or she laughed and laughed'
k-ḱewḱé·wey	'I scalloped the edge'
s-am-kačtantaṅiw	'they (indefinite) cut it into small pieces'
k-ipá·ṗač	'I applauded'
s-iy-pilpilikumlili	'they (pl.) keep arriving one by one'
s-ututikwititin	'it (the buggy) goes bouncing up and down'

Reduplication is used for similar functions in many other languages.

Number is distinguished systematically in Chumashan, as in many North American languages, in the pronominal affixes on verbs. Singular, dual, and plural are obligatorily specified with the Barbareño pronominal prefixes.

k-ʔip	*k-is-ʔip*	*k-iy-ʔip*
'I said'	'we <u>two</u> said'	'we <u>all</u> said'
p-ʔip	*p-is-ʔip*	*p-iy-ʔip*
'you said'	'you <u>two</u> said'	'you <u>all</u> said'
s-ʔip	*s-is-ʔip*	*s-iy-ʔip*
'he, she said'	'they <u>two</u> said'	'they <u>all</u> said'

Number markers in many languages distinguish more than simple singular and plural. As seen above, basic Shasta nouns are not marked for singular and plural, although there are some special paucal forms for referring to 'a few'. Shasta nouns may carry a collective suffix if the speaker wishes to specify reference to an unindividuated group portrayed as a unit (Silver 1966:100-104, 108-113, 116, 165).

Shasta (Silver 1966)

súk·ax	'boy(s)'	*súk·ax-yá·war*	'a <u>group</u> of boys'
kíyaxáʔ	'girl(s)'	*kíyaxá-yá·war*	'a <u>group</u> of girls'
ʔís	'Indian(s)'	*ʔís-<u>yá·war</u>*	'a <u>group</u> of Indians'

Various number distinctions can also be made in verbs. Collective suffixes indicate action undertaken by a group together or action directed toward a group as a whole.

kwam·arimpá·ʔ	'they two (people) are having a fight'
ḱwám·ariw-e·ḱ-e	'they two (<u>groups</u>) were fighting'
kwím·ákwa·yanta·ʔ	'I told him'
kwim·ákway-a·k-enta·ʔ	'I told <u>them</u> (together)'

A distributive suffix indicates multiple distinct, individuated actions, perhaps distributed over significantly different individuals, places, or times.

yumpihé·wima	'a few of us (paucal) swam downstream'
yumpihé·w-iru·ma	'we swam downstream (<u>one by one</u>)'
ḱwá·yakn-iru-k	'they passed by (<u>one by one</u>)'

The verbal number markers are generally not agreement markers comparable to those of European languages. They quantify actions, not participants, although they may imply the involvement of multiple participants. Collective verbs in Shasta may be used with or without collective nouns, depending on what the speaker chooses to specify.

ʔís	kwehétaṗ·ik	'An Indian is gambling.'
ʔís	kwehétaṗ·e·ke̱ʔ	'Indians are gambling together.'
ʔís-yá·war	kwehétaṗ·e·ke̱ʔ	'Indians (a group) are gambling together.'

Collective and distributive markers may even cooccur within a verb, quantifying different aspects of the event.

ḱwíricw-e·ḵ-eʔ	'He worked' (lit. 'reached upward coll.')
ḱwíricw-e·k-e̱·k-eʔ	'They (coll.) worked (reached up) (coll.)'
kw-i·p̱·-irut-e·ḵ-eʔ	'he is leading them (coll.) around (coll.)'
ḱw-í·p̱·-irut-e·ḵ-e̱·k-eʔ	'they (coll.) led them (coll.) around (coll.)'
ḱw-í·p̱·-irut-e·ḵ-ir-a·ʔ	'they (coll.) led them (coll.) around (distr.)'

Nominal number marking and verbal number marking have similar but not necessarily equivalent semantic effects. Nominal number markers quantify participants, while verbal number markers often quantify some aspect of events. Of course one may imply the other. A plural noun like 'strawberries' in 'I picked strawberries' can imply multiple pluckings, and a collective verb like 'work as a group' can imply multiple workers. The nominal and verbal markers are not simply arbitrary formal altnernatives; what one may specify, the other may only imply.

The Roles of Primary Participants: Core Case

The roles of the primary or core participants in events are indicated in various ways in languages. In English, subjects and direct objects are differentiated primarily by word order (subject-verb-object) and by the shapes of pronouns (*I* versus *me*). In Russian and Latin, subject and object roles are indicated by nominative and accusative case suffixes on nouns and distinct pronouns. In German, they are indicated by the form of determiners and pronouns. Similar variety and more can be found among North American languages. Both the kind of marking and the case categories distinguished vary from language to language.

• NOMINATIVE-ACCUSATIVE SYSTEMS Languages of the Utian family of California indicate core case in ways similar to that of Russian or Latin, with suffixes on nouns. Okrand (1977:144-161) describes the case system of Mutsun, a language of the Costanoan branch of Utian formerly spoken around Mission San Juan Bautista south of San Francisco. As in many languages, subjects (nominative case) carry no suffixes.

Mutsun (Okrand 1977)
po·kon   kan-ʔissu(-Ø)
swells up   my-hand
'My hand is getting swollen.'

Objects are marked by an accusative case suffix -se.

ka·n   ṭa·kampi   to·ṭe-se
I   bring   meat-ACCUSATIVE
'I bring meat.'

In a large number of North American languages, the roles of the central participants are indicated by pronominal affixes on verbs. In the Chumashan languages, nouns carry no case marking; instead, subjects are specified by pronominal prefixes on the verb, and objects by pronominal suffixes.

Barbareño Chumash (Yee 1956)
k-ʔip	s-ʔip-it
'I said, spoke'	'he, she told me'
p-ʔip	s-ʔip-in
'you said, spoke'	'he, she told you'
s-ʔip	s-ʔip-it
'he, she said, spoke'	'he, she told him, her'

(Additional prefixes and suffixes indicate dual and plural subjects and objects.)

Because the verbs contain pronouns, they can constitute full grammatical sentences in themselves. Of course nouns may appear in sentences as well; however, Chumashan nouns, unlike those in Mutsun, carry no case markers. In the Barbareño Chumash sentence below, the subject is ʔašḱáʔ 'coyote'.

hika   s-ʔip   hi   ʔašḱáʔ
and then 3.SG-speak the   coyote
'And then Coyote spoke.'

When 'coyote' is the object of a sentence, the noun has the same form.

ču   k-uxnik-us   hi   ʔašḱáʔ
so that 1.SG-escape-3.SG the   coyote
'[How should I act] so that I may escape Coyote?'

It is the pronouns on the verb that mark case roles. It is clear that Coyote is the subject of the first sentence from the third-person singular subject pronoun prefix s- 'he' on the verb 'speak'. Coyote is identified as the object of the second sentence by the third-person singular object pronoun suffix -us 'him' on the verb 'escape'. If roles were reversed, and Coyote were escaping from me, only the verb would need to change: s-uxnik-it: 'he-escape-me'.

• AGENT-PATIENT SYSTEMS Not all languages identify the roles of major participants in terms of subject and object categories. An alternative kind of case organization, particularly common among the polysynthetic languages of North America, categorizes major participants in terms of their semantic roles as agents or patients (Mithun 1991). Agent-patient case organization can be seen in the Muskogean languages, Iroquoian languages, Caddoan languages, Siouan languages, Pomoan languages, Yuchi, Tunica, Keresan, Yuki, and Haida, among others (see the grammatical sketches of Seneca, Wichita, Lakhota, and Eastern Pomo, this vol.).

The pronominal affixes in Koasati follow an agent-patient pattern. One set of pronominal affixes represents agents, those participants who control actions, while another set represents patients, those not in control.

Koasati (Kimball 1991:58–70)

Agents	Patients
ó·ta-<u>l</u>	ča-ikní-h<u>ọ</u>
'<u>I</u> arrive there'	'<u>I</u>'m fat'
yiťápli-<u>l</u>	ča-tám
'<u>I</u> tear it down'	'<u>I</u> fall down'
wilaplí·či-<u>l</u>	ča-moklí·č
'<u>I</u> plow'	'<u>I</u> feel a throbbing'
í·si-<u>l</u>	ča-bàn
'<u>I</u> take one thing'	'<u>I</u> want, need (it)'
í·mo-<u>l</u>	ča-lhó·s
'<u>I</u> gather'	'<u>I</u> forget, <u>I</u>'m lost in the woods'

Transitivity has no effect on case marking. Agents of intransitive events like 'arrive' are expressed with the same form as agents of transitives like 'tear down'. Patients of intransitive states like 'fat' and intransitive events like 'fall down' are expressed with the same pronouns as those of transitive events like 'want' or 'burn'. The first sentence below is intransitive, the second transitive. (Third persons are not represented by affixes in Koasati.)

Koasati (Kimball 1991:251)

ča-libátli-t
1.SG.PATIENT-burn-PAST
'<u>I</u> got burned.'

nihahčí íkbak ča-libátli-t
grease hot 1.SG.PATIENT-burn-PAST
'The hot greased burned <u>me</u>.'

The agent and patient case categories are not equivalent to subjects and objects. The patient pronoun *ča-* above, for example, is translated with the English subject pronoun 'I' in the first sentence but with the object pronoun 'me' in the second.

In many languages with agent-patient case systems, speakers have no choice of case with a particular verb.

Some verbs always appear with agent-case pronouns, while others always appear with patient-case pronouns, regardless of the precise degree of control involved in the particular situation under discussion. In other languages, among them Koasati, some verbs may appear with either case, depending upon the amount of control involved.

Koasati (Kimball 1991:252)

Agent case	Patient case
nó·či-<u>li</u>-t	ča-nó·či-t
sleep-<u>1.SG.AGENT</u>.PAST	1.SG.PATIENT-sleep-PAST
'<u>I</u> slept'	'<u>I</u> fell asleep'
afá·ka-<u>li</u>-t	ča-afá·ka-t
laugh-<u>1</u>.SG.AGENT-PAST	1.SG.PATIENT-sleep-PAST
'<u>I</u> laughed'	'<u>I</u> burst out laughing'
nìhli-<u>l</u>	ča-nìhl
nod-<u>1</u>.SG.AGENT	1.SG.PATIENT-nod
'<u>I</u> nod'	'<u>I</u> am nodding off'

• ERGATIVE-ABSOLUTIVE SYSTEMS The core participants in an event may be categorized in a third way. Ergative-absolutive case marking is somewhat less common in North America than in some other parts of the world, but it does occur, notably in the Chinookan, Eskimoan and Tsimshianic languages, among others. Mulder (1988) describes case marking in Coast Tsimshianic a language spoken along the northern coast of British Columbia. The patterning of pronominal enclitics can be seen below. Absolutives, expressed by enclitics after the verb complex, represent the most immediately involved participant. This one usually corresponds to the single core participant of an intransitive verb (here 'run' and 'be alive') or the patient of a transitive (here 'find').

Coast Tsimshian (Mulder 1988:129, 54, 57)

la   dm   ba·=<u>yu</u>.
about FUTURE run=<u>1</u>.ABSOLUTIVE
'<u>I</u>'m about to run.'

la   wila   didu·ls=<u>u</u>
PAST be   alive=<u>1</u>.ABSOLUTIVE
'<u>I</u>'m still alive.'

ada   wil   m=way=<u>u</u>
and   then   2.ERGATIVE=find=<u>1</u>.ABSOLUTIVE
'And then you found <u>me</u>.' (Boas 1911a:384)

Ergatives, expressed by proclitics before the verbal complex, usually correspond to the agents of transitive verbs.

<u>n</u>=dm   man-gad=n.
<u>1</u>.ERGATIVE=FUTURE up-take=2.ABSOLUTIVE
'<u>I</u> will take you up.'

A comparison of the sentences above shows that the absolutive and ergative categories do not correspond to the subject and object categories of languages like

English. Some absolutives are translated with English subjects (I'm about to run'), some with English objects ('And then you found me'). Ergatives are usually translated with English subjects ('I will take you up'), but so are many absolutives ('I'm alive'). The absolutive and ergative categories do not correspond to the agent and patient categories of languages like Koasati, either. Some absolutives would be agents in such a system (I'm about to run'), others patients ('And then you found me'). Most ergatives would be agents, but some would be patients in many systems ('I want it.')

The Tsimshian case system, like many ergative systems, is complex, involving further distinctions of present versus absent participants, common versus proper nouns, and tense, aspect, and mode.

• DIRECT-INVERSE SYSTEMS In some languages, pronominal affixes referring to core participants do not carry indications of case themselves. They specify only person and number. Case is carried by another affix within the verb. Systems of this type, called inverse, are well known among languages of the Algonquian family and several others. The pattern is illustrated here with examples from Blackfoot, an Algonquian language of Montana and Alberta (see also the grammatical sketch of Cree, this vol.). A comparison of the verbs below shows that the shape of the pronominal affixes remains the same whatever the case.

Blackfoot (Frantz 1991:15)

Intransitive Agents

nit-á·kahkayi	'I'm going home'
kit-á·kahkayi	'you're going home'
á·kahkayi-wa	'he or she's going home'

Intransitive Patients

nit-áyo?ka	'I'm sleeping'
kit-áyo?ka	'you're sleeping'
áyo?ka·-wa	'he or she's sleeping'

Transitives

nit-sikákomimm-a-wa	'I love him or her'
kit-sikákomimm-a-wa	'you love him or her'
nit-sikákomimm-ok-a	'he or she loves me'
kit-sikákomimm-ok-a	'he or she loves you'

First-person singular has the form *nit-* whether it is an intransitive subject ('I'm going home') a transitive subject ('I love him or her'), or a direct object ('he or she loves me'), whether it is an agent ('I'm going home'; 'I love him or her'), or a patient ('I'm sleeping', 'he or she loves me'). Similarly, second-person singular 'you' remains *kit-*, and third person remains *-(w)a*. Yet 'I love him or her' is not the same as 'he or she loves me'. The difference is indicated by a suffix preceding the third-person pronominal suffix.

Transitive clauses in which a first or second person acts on a third ('I love him or her', 'you love him or her') are termed 'direct' and are marked with a direct

suffix (*-a-* above). Those in which a third person acts on a first or second ('he or she loves me', 'he or she loves you') are termed 'inverse' and are marked with an inverse suffix (*-ok-* above). In fact, direct constructions are somewhat more common in natural speech than inverse. Speakers tend to present events from their own point of view or that of their audience rather than of some other person. Second persons acting on first ('you love me') are classified in Blackfoot as direct, and first acting on second ('I love you') as inverse. Proximate third persons acting on obviatives ('he or she loves the other') are direct, while obviatives acting on proximates ('the other loves him or her') are inverse. There is thus a person hierarchy in Blackfoot:

2 (you) > 1 (I, we) > proximate (he, she, they) > obviative (other)

• MULTIPLE CORE CASE MARKING In some languages, core case roles are indicated only by case suffixes on noun phrases. In others, core case roles are indicated only on pronominal affixes in verbs. In some languages, case is marked on both nominals and predicates.

In such languages, both systems of case marking may follow the same pattern. In Coast Tsimshian both pronominal clitics on verbs and case enclitics with noun phrases follow an ergative-absolutive pattern. In other languages, different kinds of systems appear in different parts of the grammar. In Koasati pronominal affixes on verbs follow an agent-patient pattern, but case suffixes on nouns follow a nominative-accusative pattern: subjects are marked with the suffix *-k*, and objects with the suffix *-n*.

Possession

Possessive relationships are indicated in many European languages by a genitive case marker or preposition on the noun phrase representing the possessor: *[the whale's] bone*, or *the bone [of the whale]*. In most North American languages, possessors are marked on the noun referring to the possession.

Barbareño Chumash (Yee 1956)

he?	*s-sapiyiẃil*	*paxa·t*
this	its-bone	whale
'the whale's bone'		

The possessive affixes often resemble some of the pronominal affixes on verbs. In Chumashan, they match the pronominal prefixes referring to subjects. Chumashan possessed nouns usually appear with a demonstrative indicating the location of the object: *he?* 'this (near the speaker)', *ho?* 'that (removed from the speaker)', or *hu* 'that (not visible, remote in time or space)'.

Barbareño Chumash (Yee 1956)

he? k-pu	*he? k-?aġkaẏ*
'my hand'	'my trap'

he? p̲-pu	*he? p̲-?aq̇kaẏ*
'your hand'	'your trap'
ho? s̲-pu	*ho? s̲-?aq̇kaẏ*
'his, her hand'	'his, her trap'

In Eskimoan the ergative case is used for possessors.

A common distinction made in possessive constructions is that of 'inalienable' or 'inseparable' possession versus 'alienable' or 'separable' possession. Inalienable possessions normally exist only in relation to their possessors or even constitute a part of them. Typical inalienable possessions are body parts and kinsmen. Alienable possessions, by contrast, are separable from their possessors: they may exist independently and may be acquired or lost. Most material possessions fall into this category.

The distinction is expressed in a variety of ways. In some languages, inalienable possessors are indicated by pronominal affixes, while alienable possessors are indicated by independent pronouns. In Haida, for example, a language of Alaska and British Columbia, terms for body parts and kinsmen are never used without indication of a possessor. The possessor is specified with a possessive prefix: *dáŋ-aw* 'my-mother' (inalienable). Nouns for other entities may appear alone or with a separate possessive pronoun: *ɬuwá·y* 'boat', *dáŋgya· ɬuwá·y* 'my boat' (alienable) (Leer in Lawrence 1977:65).

In other languages, alienable and inalienable possessors are expressed by two different sets of pronominal affixes. In Tunica, inalienable possession is expressed with the same pronominal prefixes used for patients on verbs: *?ó·siku* 'his father'; *?ó·rusa* 'he knows'. Alienable possession is expressed with the pronominal prefixes used for agents on verbs: *?uhk-?íyut?eku* 'his hog'; *?éh-?uhk-i* 'he kicked' (Haas 1941a:37, 61, 38). Iroquoian languages show the opposite pairing: inalienable possession is indicated with agent pronominal prefixes, and alienable possession with patient pronominal prefixes.

Interestingly, inalienable and alienable categories are not identical from one language to the next. In languages of the Yuman family, only inalienable possession is expressed by pronominal prefixes on nouns. Amy W. Miller (1990:96) reports that in Jamul Diegueño, a Yuman language of Southern California, inalienable possessions include body parts; the nouns 'language', 'name', 'tribe, last name', and 'behalf'; only one kinship term, 'daughter'; and some articles of clothing: 'skirt', 'pants', 'eyeglasses', but not 'watch', 'jacket', 'hat', or 'shirt'. Gordon (1986:32-33) reports that in Maricopa, a Yuman language of Arizona, basic inalienables include primarily body parts, kinsmen, and clothing, such as 'shirt', 'hat', 'dress'. Some alienables can be converted to inalienables with a prefix -*ny*-, including 'man' > 'husband' and 'dog' >

'pet', 'house', and 'money'. In Papago (O'odham), a Uto-Aztecan language of Arizona, inalienable possessions include body parts, clothing, kin, tools (scissors, pot, bottle, basket, plate, pocket knife, shovel), and stirrups, saddles, houses, and cars (Zepeda 1983:80). In a number of languages, kinship relations are not expressed as either inalienable or alienable possession, but as a third kind of relationship (e.g., Seneca and Lakhota).

Some languages distinguish actions directed at one's own possessions versus those directed at the possessions of another. In Siouan languages, a middle voice prefix adds the meaning 'one's own' with transitive verbs.

Mandan (Kennard 1936:38; Hollow 1970:448)

níta-mìti-s	*kí-hata?*
your-village-the	own-look.at-MASC.IMP
'Look at your village'	

ki-rú-še-?š
own-by.hand-grasp-INDIC
'He picks up his own.'

The Roles of Other Participants: Obliques and Applicatives

The roles of other persons and objects involved in events as beneficiaries, companions, instruments, and locations are indicated in many European languages by case suffixes or prepositions on noun phrases (*to my mother*, *with my friend*, *at the store*). Similar constructions can be found in some North American languages. In addition to the nominative and accusative forms, Mutsun shows various oblique case suffixes on nominals (Okrand 1977):

ka·n	*wattin*	*me·s-tuk*
I	go	you-COMITATIVE
'I'm going with you.'		

waray	*tippe-sum*
cut!	knife-INSTRUMENTAL
'Cut it with a knife!'	

?urkan-tak	*wak*	*hutahne*
mortar-LOCATIVE	it	is ground up
'It is ground up in the mortar.'		

kalleh-tak	*ka·n*	*wattin*
sea-LOCATIVE	I	go
'I am going to the sea.'		

wa·te-ka	*?irek-tak-tum*
come-I	rock-LOCATIVE-ABLATIVE
'I come from the rock.'	

In many North American languages, such relationships are marked in the verb.

• DATIVES AND BENEFICIARIES Instead of dative case suffixes or prepositions on noun phrases (*I wrote to my mother, I made a kite for my nephew*), many North American languages contain special derived verbs for events directed to or done for someone. The grammatical object, patient, or absolutive of these benefactive verbs is the beneficiary. In Natchez, the benefactive suffix *-ši* adds the meaning 'to', 'for':

Mary Haas, personal communication (1983)

ha·wici-ʔiš	*ha·wici-ši-ʔiš*
'to tell'	'to tell to'
hapopay-ʔiš	*hapopay-ši-ʔiš*
'to carry'	'to carry around for'
ha-ʔiš	*hay-ši-ʔiš*
'to take'	'to take to, for'

• COMPANIONS   Instead of comitative case suffixes or prepositions on noun phrases ('I went <u>with</u> my friend'), some North American languages contain comitative verbal affixes that can be used to derive verbs describing actions done in the company of another, usually a person but sometimes an animal or even an object. The grammatical object, patient, or absolutive argument of the derived verb is usually the companion. An example of a comitative suffix is *-i·l* 'with' in Wintu.

Wintu (Pitkin 1984:109)

ča·wu	*ča·wuw-il*
'sing!'	'sing <u>with</u> them!'
wačạ	*wačuw-il*
'to cry in sympathy'	'to cry <u>with</u> someone'

Other Wintu verbs with comitative suffixes include *noy-i·l* 'to laugh <u>with</u> someone', *suk-i·l* 'to own', literally 'to be standing <u>with</u> particular ones', *čup-i·l* 'to wade <u>with</u> someone'.

• INSTRUMENTS   Instead of instrumental case suffixes or prepositions on noun phrases (*I cut it with a knife*) some North American languages contain verbal affixes used to derive verbs for actions with an instrument. The instrument assumes the role of grammatical object, patient, or absolutive. The Yuchi instrumental prefix is *hi-* 'with'.

Yuchi (Wagner (1933:357)

yǫtí	*hí-do-k̓ǫ*
knife	<u>with</u>-I-do
'I make it with a knife.'	

di-kéha	*hí-do-k̓ǫ*
my-teeth	<u>with</u>-I-do
'I do it with my teeth.'	

• LOCATIONS   Instead of locative case suffixes or prepositions with noun phrases (<u>on</u> *the table*, <u>into</u> *the house*), some North American languages contain verbal affixes signaling locative relationships. In Yuchi, verbal prefixes are used to derive verb stems describing motion in a specific location or direction.

Yuchi (Wagner 1933:359-360)

tǫpahošdú	*tí-hǫʔǫžinfwa*
gourd shell	<u>in</u>-she.had.put.(them)
'She had put them in a gourd shell.'	

nɛhìtabá	*pʰó-wɛʔǫ́*
your wings	<u>under</u>-put us
'Put us under your wings.'	

• OBLIQUE CASE MARKERS VERSUS APPLICATIVES   Benefactive, comitative, instrumental, and locative affixes within verbs, like those described above, are sometimes termed applicatives. Their functions are similar to those of dative, comitative, instrumental, and locative case markers on nouns, but they are not precisely equivalent. A benefactive verb does imply the involvement of a beneficiary, and a comitative verb the involvement of a companion. But nominal case markers portray relationships as attributes of the participants ('for my sister', 'with a friend', 'with a stick', 'to the bank'). Applicatives derive terms for kinds of activities that are more specific than those designated by the root alone ('tell-to', 'sing-with', 'make-with', 'put-in').

In some languages, applicatives may be highly productive, and in others less so, but they do not normally show the same ubiquitousness as inflectional case suffixes on nouns. Not all verb roots in a language will normally have benefactive forms, only certain ones that describe activities conventionally done for someone's benefit. The existence of a benefactive verb meaning 'cook-for' is common, but languages seldom contain a benefactive verb meaning 'walk-for'. The existence of a comitative verb 'walk-in.the.company.of' is common, but not 'cook-in.the.company.of'.

Applicatives have a grammatical effect that can be useful for discourse purposes. They alter the argument structure of verbs, casting a beneficiary, companion, instrument, or location as a core participant (object, patient, or absolutive). The grammatical object of the Natchez verb 'tell-to' is the person told rather than the tale, the grammatical object of the Wintu verb 'sing-with' is another singer rather than the song. Applicatives thus play a role in determining which participants will be cast as core grammatical arguments.

Adverbial Qualification

Many notions typically expressed by separate adverbs or adverbial phrases in most languages are marked by verbal affixes in some of the more polysynthetic languages of North America. Some of the most common adverbial categories that have been grammaticized are those relating to general location or direction and manner or medium.

• DIRECTION   Direction and location are indicated by verbal affixes in many North American languages. Some languages mark a basic two-way distinction:

'hither' or 'here' versus 'thither' or 'there' (e.g., Seneca and Sahaptin). The difference between verbs meaning 'come' and 'go', 'bring' and 'take', or 'throw here' and 'throw away' may be signaled entirely by the directional affix rather than the root.

A number of languages, many in northern California, contain more elaborate sets of directional affixes. Talmy (1972:40-41) describes the directional suffixes of Atsugewi, a Palaihnihan language. In addition to the general suffixes -ik· 'hither' and -im 'thither', there are many more specific directional suffixes. Among these are -iċt 'into a liquid', -cis 'into a fire', -isp-u· (with -im or -ik·) 'into an aggregate (bushes, a crowd, a ribcage)', -wam 'down into a gravitic container (basket, cupped hand, pocket, depression in the ground, lake basin)', -wamm 'horizontally into an areal enclosure (corral, field, area occupied by a pool of water)', ipsn" (with -im or -ik·) 'horizontally into a "volumar" enclosure (house, oven, crevice, deer's stomach)', -tip (with -im or -ik·) 'down into a large volumar enclosure in the ground (cellar, pit for trapping deer)', -ikn (with -im or -ik·) 'over the rim into a volumar enclosure (gopher hole, mouth)', -iќs" (with -im or -ík·) 'into a corner (between wall and floor, between two walls and the floor)', -miċ 'down onto the surface of or into the substance of the ground', -cis" (with -im or -ik·) 'down onto the upper surface of or into the substance of a solid resting on the ground (top of a tree stump)', and -iќs 'horizontally onto the lateral surface or into the substance of a solid resting on the ground (the side of a tree trunk)'.

Atsugewi (Talmy 1972:436)
sċwisɫaq́íќsa
|sʔw-ci-sɫaq́-iќs|
I/it-cause.with.hands-icky.material.move-horizontally.onto.the.lateral.surface.of.a.solid
'I patted some mud against the wall.'

sṁa·sɫaq́ípsnu
|sʔw-ma-sɫaq́-ipsn"-im|
I/it-cause.with.feet-icky.material.move-into.a.volumar.enclosure-thither
'I tracked the house up (with manure I stepped in there).'

• MANNER AND MEDIUM Languages in a number of North American families, among them Siouan, Uto-Aztecan (all Numic, some Tepiman), Chumashan, Pomoan, Washoe, Palaihnihan, Shastan, Haida, and others, contain sets of affixes that indicate kinds of motion ('by thrusting'), involvement of a kind of instrument ('by heat'), or a kind of medium ('involving water', 'involving the feet'). The affixes often add causative meaning as well.

Such affixes have traditionally been called instrumentals (see the grammatical sketches of Eastern Pomo, Shoshone, and Lakhota, this vol.). Their range

of functions can be seen in some verbal prefixes in Ineseño Chumash, spoken near the central coast of California.

Ineseño Chumash (Applegate 1972:345-353)
api-	aputi-
'of, with fire'	'of liquid in motion'
ax-	aqta-
'with the mouth'	'in, of the air'
aqul-	ašni-
'of, with a long thin object'	'with the feet'
maq-	maqili-
'of, with a line or rope'	'of a line, linear order'
naq-	pal-
'with the body'	'of, with pliable object'
pil-	qil-
'through the air'	'in, of water'
tak-	taya-
'with the hand'	'of rain'
waš-	ꞌyuq-
'with the hand'	'of the legs'

Some of their uses can be seen in the verbs below. A particular prefix does not necessarily indicate the same kind of involvement in each context. Sometimes it may indicate an instrument, sometimes a medium. Sometimes it may include causation, sometimes not.

Ineseño Chumash (Applegate (1972:345-353)
api-pleʔ	api-qen
by.fire-perish	by.fire-disappear
'to be scorched, burned up'	'to be burned entirely up'
ax-tap	ax-klaʔ
with.mouth-enter	with.mouth-crack
'to put into the mouth'	'to shell acorns with the teeth'

Affixes of this type may be highly productive, as in many Siouan languages, or less so, as in the Chumashan languages, but they are derivational, combining with specific roots to form new lexical items that are subsequently learned, understood, and used as conceptually unitary stems.

Time: Tense and Aspect

Tense markers such as past, present, and future specify the time at which an event occurs with respect to the time of speaking or some other point of reference. A few North American languages have elaborate tense distinctions. Washoe, a language centered around Lake Tahoe in Nevada and adjacent California, contains a rich set of tense suffixes described in detail in Jacobsen (1964:589, 631-653). Several degrees of past time are distinguished. The recent past suffix -leg "places the time of an event at an earlier point on the same day or during the preceding night." The intermediate past -ayʔ

"indicates a time in the past earlier than the same day but not in the extremely distant past." The pluperfect *-áẏiʔ* "places the event prior to that of another event in the past." The remembered past *-gul* indicates "a time in the distant past but still within the lifetime of the speaker." The distant past *-lul* places it "in the distant past before the lifetime of the speaker." Several degrees of futurity are also distinguished. The suffix *-hi* can indicate immediate futurity. The near future *-áša ʔ* 'extends from the immediate future to a time perhaps an hour or so later," implying at least a short interval before the event. The intermediate future *-tiʔ* marks an event that "is expected to take place in the future, not immediately but after the lapse of a short interval of time." The distant future *-gab* "indicates an event further in the future than the one indicated by the intermediate future suffix." A rare suffix *-elem* can precede the intermediate past, the distant past, or the distant future, to indicate an even more remote time.

By contrast, a significant number of languages do not distinguish past from present tense at all, although of course it is always possible to specify the time of occurrence with additional words like 'today' or 'long ago'. Another kind of temporal distinction is often well developed: aspect. Aspectual distinctions describe the internal temporal consistency of events or states, often distinguishing reference to an event as a whole, including its inception and completion, from reference to some portion of the event. English 'I ate', 'I was eating', and 'I used to eat' are all past tense, but they differ in aspect. 'I ate' represents a single whole event, complete with beginning and end, and no expressed internal structure. 'I was eating' captures a portion of the activity with an indication of its ongoing character. 'I used to eat' indicates a series of recurring actions. Aspectual categories differ considerably from one language to the next in both nature and number.

Acoma contains little overt indication of tense, but verbal suffixes distinguish several aspects (Miller 1965:125-132). There are continuatives (*suẏàiça·-ta* 'I am weeding'), repetitives (*kà·ča-sə* 'it keeps on raining'), a habitual (*kuẇâuša·ie·ʔe·-ẓáie·ʔe·se* 'they would go after meat'), an inceptive (*sîuiu·ním-ièa·tya* 'I started to remember things'), and a completive, that emphasizes that the action is finished (*šíwà·kučá-ṅi* 'I have it hidden').

In all languages, tense and aspect markers appear more commonly with verbs than with nouns, due to the dynamic character of events. Actions, expressed by verbs, typically show change over time, while entities, identified by nouns, show more stability. Still, in some North American languages temporal distinctions can be marked on nouns as well. Many languages contain a decessive or defunctive, indicating that the referent of the noun is no longer alive. Jacobsen (1964:482-483) notes that the Washoe defunctive, as in *iánuy-uṅil*

'deceased person, dead people', can have the added force of profanity: *géwey-uṅil* 'dead coyote, damn coyote'. Washoe also contains a noun suffix with the meaning 'discarded': *mókgoy-áyʔ* 'old shoe', *bumé·liʔ-áyʔ* 'ex-husband', *démluy-áyʔ* 'food-old' = 'garbage' (1964:484). Boas (1911b:486) provides examples from Kwakiutl (Kwak'wala), a Wakashan language of British Columbia, of past and future tense with nouns: *hayóˑtẇ- uł* 'former rival', *xwáˑḱuna-ƛ* 'a future canoe'. Liljeblad (cited in Jacobsen 1979c:149), reports that in Northern Paiute, a Uto-Aztecan language spoken in Idaho, Oregon, Nevada, and California, the same past participle marker that appears with verbs occurs with nouns: *níˑ múʔasu adimá=pi* 'I already it-taste= PAST.PARTICIPLE' = 'I have already tasted it'; *nobí=pi* 'house=PAST.PARTICIPLE' = 'ruins of a house'.

Modality

Many of the modal distinctions familiar from European languages, such as imperative, interrogative, conditional, optative, and subjunctive appear in North America. There is a comparable range of variation: some languages show only a few basic categories; others show more elaborate systems. Several modality distinctions of special interest have been grammaticized in certain languages, among them realis-irrealis and evidentiality.

A good example of the realis-irrealis distinction comes from Caddo. Caddo verbs contain pronominal prefixes referring to their agents or patients, or both. There are two full sets of pronominal prefixes, one realis, the other irrealis. The only formal difference between the two utterances below is the choice of first-person agent pronoun, but one is interpreted as a statement, the other a question.

Caddo (Chafe 1976:66)

Realis	Irrealis
cíˑbáwnah	*iáybáwnah*
|ci-yibahw-nah|	|ta-yibahw-nah|
1.AGT.REALIS-see-PAST	1.AGT.IRREALIS-see-PAST
'I saw it.'	'Did I see it?'

The realis pronouns appear in utterances that the speaker expects to be real or realized. These include positive declarative statements ('I saw it'), futures (*cíˑbáwʔaʔ* 'I will look at it'), positive imperatives, and question-word questions. In a question-word question like *dikadàyybáwnah* 'What did you (realis) see?', the speaker assumes that you did see something. The irrealis pronouns appear in yes-no questions ('Did I see it?'), negations (*kúyiábay* 'I don't see it'), conditions (*híiáybah* 'if I see it'), simulations (*dúyiáybah* 'as if I saw it'), prohibitions, obligations, and surprises.

A number of languages have developed elaborate evidential systems that specify the source and degree of certainty of statements made. Jacobsen (1986a) provides a survey of evidential systems with good examples from Makah, a Wakashan language of the Washington coast. In Makah, direct experience is usually unmarked (*wiki·ċaχaw* 'It's bad weather', *ċa·ʔu·qił* 'He's drunk'). Evidential suffixes mark inference from physical evidence (*wiki·ċaχakpi·d* 'It looks like bad weather'), from hearing (*wiki·ċaχakq̇adʔi* 'It sounds like bad weather'), quotations or hearsay (*wiki·ċaχakwa·d* 'I'm told there's bad weather'), physical evidence such as debris (*ċa·ʔu·qiłpi·dił* 'They must have been drunk'), visual evidence of the second person (*ċa·ʔuqiłq̇adʔic* 'It looks like you're drunk'), uncertain visual evidence (*ċa·ʔu·qiłcaqiłit* 'It looks like they're drunk'), and logical inference from unspecified evidence (*ċa·ʔu·qiłχa·tš* 'They might be drunk').

Simple Clause Structure and Word Order

Partly due to the high degree of polysynthesis of so many North American languages, their clauses often consist of relatively few words. In many languages, a single verb can serve as a sentence in itself, perhaps accompanied by various evidential and discourse particles. A verb may contain pronouns referring to its primary participants, perhaps an incorporated noun, and affixes indicating an instrument, a location, or direction, manner, and more. Clauses with two major constituents, a predicate and one other element such as a noun phrase or separate adverbial, are also common. Clauses with two or more full noun phrases are rarer.

All possible basic word orders of subject, object, and verb, or their syntactic equivalents (S, O, and V), can be found on the continent. A major proportion of the languages show basic verb-final, actually predicate-final, order (see the grammatical sketches of Eastern Pomo, Shoshone, Zuni, Lakhota, Coahuilteco, this vol.). These examples are from Laguna Keresan, of New Mexico.

Laguna (Valiquette 1990:124, 684, 685)

S			V
srpíkà	*k̇ʰánâ·ya*	*ái ʔ*	*ċaʔâuʔu*
Woodpecker	his mother	there	they two lived

'Woodpecker and his mother lived there.'

	O	V
šé·	*ẇáišťʰá·ni*	*čʰáyâuʔu* ...
then	bowl	she picked up

'Then she picked up a bowl ...'

S	O	V
srpíkà	*k̇ʰánâ·ya*	*čŭ·pe*
Woodpecker	his mother	he told her

'Woodpecker told his mother.'

A number of languages are predicate-initial, particularly in the Northwest (see "Sketch of Thompson, a Salishan Language," this vol.). These examples are from Nootka, a Wakashan language of Vancouver Island in British Columbia.

Kyuquot Nootka (Rose 1981:163, 38)

V	S
ṅiλk̇ʷaqšaʔλ	*λaʔuk̇ʷath̩*
fight-MOMENTANEOUS-TENSE	Clayoquot

'The Clayoquots were up in arms.'

V	O
hini·pšaʔλał	*qaẏuk̇ʷth̩*
there-obtain-MOMENTANEOUS-TENSE-PL	Kyuquot

'They reached Kyuquot.'

V	S	O
cas-ša-·ʔλ-na-qu·-č	*ʕini·-λ-k̇ʷ-q-s*	*muwič*
chase-MOM-TENSE-PAST-COND-INFERENTIAL	dog-POSS-SUBJ-1	deer

'My dog used to chase deer'.

The rigidity of basic word order varies from one language to the next. In some, like Lakhota, departure from the basic order is rare and highly marked pragmatically, while in others, like the Pomoan languages, word order is manipulated extensively for stylistic purposes.

Verbs in a number of languages contain pronominal affixes referring to their core participants: subjects and objects, ergatives and absolutives, agents and patients. The grammaticization of full sets of pronominal affixes, in three persons, can have important consequences for syntactic structure. Verbs with pronominal affixes can constitute grammatically complete clauses in themselves. Noun phrases that appear with such verbs may not bear precisely the same kinds of grammatical relations to them as subjects and objects do in languages like English. The noun phrases may function as appositives to the pronominal affixes within the verb, rather than filling core syntactic roles on their own; they may be syntactic adjuncts to the nuclear clause contained within the verb, instead of obligatory constituents of the nuclear clause. In such languages, word order may not be based on syntactic roles like subject and object, since those grammatical relations are already specified within the verb. Words may be ordered instead according to their importance to the discourse, with the most newsworthy elements appearing early in the clause, followed by words carrying successively less novel and crucial information (Mithun 1993, 1995).

Word order patterns based on pragmatic information are of course best seen by examining passages larger than a sentence. An idea of the patterns can be seen by comparing the sentences below from Cayuga, an

Iroquoian language of Ontario. When a customer in a hardware store asked for a hammer, the noun 'hammer', the most important element of the message, appeared first. The verb 'I'm seeking it', more predictable, followed.

Cayuga (Reginald Henry, personal communication 1980)

katšihwáʔ	kIhsaˑs.
hammer	I'm seeking (it)

'I'm looking for a hammer.'

After the salesman had shown him several hammers, he chose one and asked its price. Here, the verb 'it costs' appears early, the main point of the utterance, while the noun 'hammer' appears last, as established information.

toˑ	tiʔ	nikaˑnǫ́ˑʔ	nę̇ˑkyę́	katšihwaʔʔ
how	then	so it costs	this	hammer

'How much is this hammer?'

A hostess mentioned that there were some potatoes in a dish and asked her grumpy guest whether he liked them. He replied:

neˑʔ tshǫ́ˑ	neˑʔ	oaʔwistáʔ	thę̇ʔ	níˑʔ	tʔekeˑs
it is only	the peel		not I	not I like (them)

'It's just the peelings that I don't like.'

kwiskwís	kyę̇ˑʔ	hnéˑʔ	tshǫ́ˑ	kaˑtíˑs
pig	just	CONTR	only	they eat (them)
	neʔ	oáʔwista?.		
	the	peel		

'Only pigs eat the peelings.'

In the first line, 'just the peelings' appears first, a new entity and a focus of contrast. The verb of disliking, not unexpected given the question, appears last. In the second line, the first element is 'pigs', the only new entity and again a focus of contrast. The verb 'they eat them' is new but not unexpected, given the discussion. 'The peelings', just mentioned, is last.

Clause Combining

Patterns of clause combination, or the construction of compound and complex sentences, vary in intricacy across North America. In some languages, there is relatively little formal indication of syntactic links among related clauses. In the Iroquoian languages, every verb constitutes a complete, finite clause that can stand alone. Links between clauses may or may not be specified by particles. Intonation provides a sufficient indication of their relationships. Each of the Cayuga sentences below contains two clauses. In the first, the subject 'it' of 'it is dangerous' is the clause 'he would go after wood'. In the second, the object 'it' of 'I noticed it' is the clause 'it is dull'.

Cayuga (Reginald Henry, personal communication 1980)

aˑyę́	kiʔ	kyę́ˑʔ	ohtrǫ́ht	aˑhayę́takoʔ.
seemingly	just		it is	he would go
			dangerous	after wood

'It seems to be dangerous to go after wood.'

aˑyę́ˑʔtshǫ́ˑ	waʔhé	akęnIhnaˑtóˑk	teyokhyuʔktáʔo.
seemingly only	now	I noticed (it)	it is dull seems

'I just now noticed that they (my scissors) seem to be dull.'

Other languages show strong formal distinctions between independent and dependent clauses. Yawelmani Yokuts, a language of California, contains eight different gerundial suffixes that mark verbs as subordinate (Newman 1944:134-142). Gerundials contain no subjects of their own; their agents are either interpreted as the same as that of the main clause or expressed in the possessive case. Gerundials may have their own objects, however. There are consequent gerundials (ʔaˑx-*mi* naʔtanhin 'hav*ing* stayed overnight, I went'), contemporaneous gerundials (dub-ʔ*uṅay* ṭaw tanhin 'lead*ing* (him) by the hand, (he) went'), resultative gerundials (lihimhin naʔx̣at-e·ni 'I ran *to* eat'), passive gerundials (ʔutuy-*tun* naʔbaṭinhin 'be*ing* pushed, I fell down'), nondirective gerundials (piċiw-*taw* nin cawhin 'at my catch*ing* (him), (he, another) shouted'), precative gerundials (taxin-ʔ*as* ʔamin '*let* him come'), and multiplicative gerundials (bǫ̇ṅy-i*l̤* cawhin '*twice* (he) shouted'), from *bǫnǫy 'make two'). Languages of the Algonquian family also show strong differences in the inflection of verbs used in independent clauses and those used in subordinate (conjunct) clauses.

Many languages subordinate clauses by nominalizing them. In English, instead of 'I sing and that disturbs her' one can say 'My singing disturbs her'. Yawelmani shows similar constructions. Like gerundials, nominalizations do not appear with grammatical subjects, but an agent may be cast as a possessor. Nominalized clauses bear case suffixes like nouns. The nominal x̣at 'food', 'eating', in the sentence below is based on the verb x̣ata 'eat'.

Yawelmani Yokuts (Newman 1944:143)

ṣi̇lhin	naʔ	ʔamin	x̣at-a.
saw	I	his	eating-ACCUSATIVE

'I saw his food' or
'I saw his eating' = 'I saw him eating.'

A number of North American languages exhibit clause-combining markers sometimes referred to as switch reference (as in Eastern Pomo and Shoshone). Among the Yuman languages of California, Arizona, and Mexico, dependent clauses contain one of two suffixes. In Maricopa, the suffix -k appears on dependent clauses that share the subject of the main clause, while the suffix -m appears on dependent clauses with a distinct subject.

Maricopa (Gordon 1983:83)

n'a-n'-yu·-<u>k</u>   ʔayu·   ʔ-rav-k
when-1/2-see-<u>SAME</u>   something   1-hurt-ASPECT
'When I saw you, I was sick.'

n'a-n'-yu·-<u>m</u>   ʔayu·   ʔ-rav-k
when-3/1-see-   something   1-hurt-ASPECT
   <u>DIFFERENT</u>
'When he saw me, I was sick.'

Further discussion of such systems is in Jacobsen (1967), where the terminology was first introduced; see also Jacobsen (1983), other papers in Haiman and Munro (1983), and papers in *International Journal of American Linguistics* 1993 (vol. 59, no. 2).

The Development and Legacy of Grammatical Categories

The languages of North America present considerable diversity in all areas of their structures. A striking feature of many is their polysynthesis, their propensity for long, complex words. Many languages contain large sets of affixes and correspondingly rich repertoires of grammatical categories.

The grammatical categories that have developed are not entirely random; they are in large part the products of use, typically over long periods of time. The arrays of grammatical categories in a language can mirror distinctions that speakers of that language have expressed especially often. When the historical origins of affixes in the world's languages are known (attested or reconstructed), they are most often traceable ultimately to full words, words that appeared particularly frequently in collocations with other words. With use, those phrases became reanalyzed as compounds, single words with a single primary stress. Morphemes that occurred frequently in speech as components of many different compounds then took on lives of their own, as productive affixes. (More detailed discussions of the development of affixes from full words can be found in Meillet 1912; Heine and Reh 1984; Heine, Claudi, and Hünnemeyer 1991; and Hopper and Traugott 1993, among many others.) The difference between obligatory and optional affixes in languages is also in large part the result of use. Grammatical markers typically originate as optional, used only when the speaker wishes to specify a certain distinction, perhaps because it is particularly pertinent at that point. Plural markers still have that status in a number of North American languages, used only when number is particularly significant. Sometimes a marker comes to be used in more and more of the contexts in which it is applicable; speakers could, for example, specify plurality more and

more often when referring to multiple entities. At a certain point, addressees begin to assume that if the plural marker is not used, the entity referred to must not be plural. Its absence becomes meaningful. At this point, the marker changes from being optional to obligatory.

Most documentation of the development of grammatical categories comes from Indo-European languages, because of their long literary traditions. Attestation of North American languages does not begin to approach the antiquity of that of Indo-European languages, but lexical sources of some affixes are still perceptible. As described above, a number of languages contain prefixes that systematically specify the means or manner of action. Instrumental prefixes of this type can be seen in the Tümpisa Panamint verbs below, based on the verb *kaʔah* 'break (of flexible object)'. As Dayley (1989:93-101) points out, the sources of many can be traced to nouns or verbs in Proto–Uto-Aztecan.

		Proto–Uto-Aztecan	
<u>kuk</u>-kaʔah	'break from heat'	*kuh	'fire'
<u>kik</u>-kaʔah	'bite in two'	*kiʔi	'bite'
<u>pik</u>-kaʔah	'break with the butt'	*pih	'back'
<u>sik</u>-kaʔah	'break from cold'	*sip	'cold'
<u>cak</u>-kaʔah	'break by pulling apart'	*caʔi	'grasp' (N)

Additional instrumental prefixes appear with other verb roots.

<u>ma</u>-sutuhi	'rub with hand'	*ma·	'hand'
<u>pa</u>-aka	'give drink to'	*pa·	'water'
<u>su</u>-wa	'feel, want, think'	*su·na	'heart'
<u>ta</u>-suʔikuttih	'kick'	*tannah	'foot'

Counterparts of many of the grammatical markers in North American languages can of course be found in languages throughout the world, such as causatives and reflexives. Such categories generally represent distinctions fundamental to the human condition. A few of the grammatical markers of North American languages can be seen to reflect the natural environment in which the language evolved. Haida contains some directional suffixes that might appear in a language spoken anywhere. Leer (in Lawrence 1977:115) contrasts the verbs *qʰá·* 'walk, go, come', *qʰa-ċá·* 'enter, go or come <u>inside</u>', *qʰá·-kał* 'exit, go or come <u>outside</u>', *qʰá·-skyaˑŋ* 'go or come <u>into the next room</u>', and *qʰá·-ʔuŋkwaˑŋ* 'walk <u>around</u>'. It also contains some suffixes that are more specific: *qʰa-łeˑł* 'descend, go or come <u>down</u>, get <u>out</u> (of a boat)', *qʰá·-λiˑ* 'get <u>in</u> (a boat)', *qʰa-kał* 'go or come <u>up in woods</u>', *qʰa-sʔá·* 'go or come <u>down to beach</u>, <u>out to sea</u>'. The majority of grammatical categories in languages are of course not directly relatable to the physical environment. They represent alternative ways of categorizing human experience that have evolved over millennia of language use.

157

Native Writing Systems

WILLARD B. WALKER

Native literacy is something of a rarity among American Indians. It is often associated with dispersed monolingual communities that have adopted some form of it to maintain contact between widely separated kinsmen. Native literacy may decline in such groups if the dispersed population is reunited, if it remains separated for more than a generation or so, if it learns to communicate with a written form of some Euro-American language, or if it gets access to some other means of communication, such as the telephone. Native literacy is also often found in communities with strong political, religious, or other cultural institutions and may continue to flourish in such restricted contexts even after passing out of use in others, as when it becomes an integral component of religious practices.

In secular contexts, native literacy is overshadowed by literacy in whatever Euro-American language is prevalent in the area. In sacred contexts it may play a restricted role but tends to be overshadowed by the oral tradition, which has always been much valued and elaborated in Indian communities. Even Sequoya, the famed inventor of the Cherokee syllabary, seems never to have allowed his hard-won literacy to diminish his talents as an orator (Walker 1984); and the dominance of the oral tradition over literacy, even in ritual contexts, is typical, if not universal, in Indian religious practice. Native religious information is never put in writing in the Pueblos of the Southwest (Brandt 1980:134) or in many other Indian communities. Where written or printed Christian liturgical texts are used, as among Algonquian-speaking groups in central Canada and the Northeast, the texts are often not so much graphic representations of spoken texts as mnemonic devices that stimulate the recitation of memorized material (Walker 1984). Many speakers of American Indian languages are integrated into White social, economic, and educational structures and institutions that rely on literacy in a Euro-American language; but they are expected, when in their home communities, to participate in an oral tradition in which literacy, native or otherwise, either plays no role or is restricted to specific contexts.

This chapter surveys significant examples of past and present writing systems used by speakers of native North American languages, both those introduced by others and those devised or substantially modified by native speakers. Further information on this topic is in "The Description of the Native Languages of North America Before Boas," this volume. Technical alphabets are summarized in "Introduction," table 4, this volume. See also the orthographic footnotes in the ethnographic chapters in volumes 5-15.

Massachusett

Massachusett is an extinct Eastern Algonquian language that was spoken in eastern Massachusetts until sometime in the nineteenth century. It was the language of the Massachusetts, Nausets, and Pokanokets (or Wampanoags) who, when the first English colonists arrived, inhabited the coast from the Merrimac River, north of Boston, to Narragansett Bay, including Cape Cod, Martha's Vineyard, Nantucket, and the Elizabeth Islands (vol. 15:161). Documents written by native speakers at different locations in this area show that Massachusett was a single language, varying from one locality to another as would be expected. The native literacy associated with this language has been described by Goddard and Bragdon (1988), who reproduced, transcribed, translated, and analyzed over 150 native documents that represent "one of the earliest instances of widespread vernacular literacy in native North America," a literacy that was not only early, but "pervasive and enduring" (Goddard and Bragdon 1988:1, 18). The surviving texts were written from the 1660s until the 1750s. They were produced by native preachers, town officials, and ordinary members of their self-governing, Christian Indian communities, the "praying towns" that were established before and after the publication of John Eliot's (1663) translation of the Bible into Massachusett. Prior to King Philip's War, 1675-1676, there were 14 such towns in the Massachusetts Bay Colony and 14 more in Plymouth Colony. Only four survived the war in the Bay Colony, but many persisted on Cape Cod and the islands. By 1698 there were over 50 Christian Indian communities, each with a native minister or elder and usually a teacher who taught reading and writing to both children and adults. In the same year a committee appointed by a missionary group reported that "each native community had a number of literate members, and that many more were being instructed" (Goddard and Bragdon 1988:14). By the mid-1700s all the towns had come under the control of White guardians; church attendance had declined; and, although Massachusett was still widely spoken, native literacy soon ceased to be viable.

The Massachusett speakers who produced the earliest native documents learned John Eliot's orthography from Eliot himself or from one of his associates. Later writers often learned literacy from Indians or were self-taught. Much of the surviving native literature was produced by officials of the Indian towns and relates to local government, for example, records of town meetings, petitions, and arrest warrants (vol. 15:179). Other documents relate to private ownership and inheritance of property: deeds, wills, depositions, and powers-of-attorney. Still others are native ministers' records of marriages and the posting of banns. There are also notes by anonymous writers in the margins of published texts, as in copies of Eliot's Bible.

Writers varied as to their expertise in Eliot's orthography. Some show, by their spelling and choice of words, traces of dialects that differed from the mainland (Natick) dialect that Eliot used in his translation. The mainland dialect became the written standard, and its forms replaced other dialectal variants in some later documents from Cape Cod and the islands (Goddard and Bragdon 1988:19).

The native documents often include direct quotations, often statements made years earlier, but remembered verbatim by people giving testimony at a later date. This suggests that the acquisition of literacy by Massachusett speakers did not weaken their ability to remember statements made long before, a talent that is often associated with nonliterate societies. The earliest documents may have served more as mnemonic aids than as "independent forms of communication" (Goddard and Bragdon 1988:19), as when the records of town meetings systematically omit information that would be known to the townspeople and hence not necessary to write down. This suggests that Massachusett speakers, when they first accepted literacy, may have perceived it, not as a medium distinct from oral communication, but as a device for extending speech in time and space without supplanting the role of oratory. Many documents use formulaic phrases that are clearly derived from a much older oral tradition (Goddard and Bragdon 1988:22).

A striking feature of Massachusett literacy is the fact that fully literate Indians often had someone else write their depositions or other legal documents and that they often testified to the validity of their statements by making a mark, which might or might not be accompanied by their signature. Indeed, the signatures on petitions are often written, not by the petitioners themselves, but by the person who wrote the petition (Goddard and Bragdon 1988:22). This seems consistent with the notion that writing was adopted not to supplant but to extend and elaborate speech.

It is worth noting that Massachusett literacy was the product of communities committed to the worship of God, that it was disseminated through and by these religious communities, and that it declined only after the collapse of the native church organizations.

Massachusett had 12 consonants (Goddard and Bragdon 1988:474-482): five obstruents, which Eliot wrote ⟨p⟩, ⟨t⟩, ⟨te⟩ (probably a palatal stop /tʸ/), ⟨ch⟩, and ⟨k⟩; three voiceless continuants, which he wrote ⟨s⟩, ⟨sh⟩, and ⟨h⟩; and four voiced continuants, which he wrote ⟨m⟩, ⟨n⟩, ⟨w⟩, and ⟨y⟩.

Because his native language was English, Eliot heard Massachusett /p/ sometimes as voiceless [p], sometimes as voiced [b], and sometimes as a combination of the two. Accordingly he wrote /p/ as ⟨p⟩, ⟨b⟩, ⟨pb⟩, or (since English spelling conventions provide for geminate consonants in some cases) ⟨pp⟩ or ⟨bb⟩. Likewise he wrote /t/, /tʸ/, /ch/, /k/, and occasionally /s/ inconsistently in analogous ways: for example /t/ as ⟨t⟩, ⟨d⟩, ⟨tt⟩, ⟨td⟩, and ⟨dd⟩. The native writers saw all these variant spellings, but, since they made no distinction as to voicing in the spoken language, they tended either to use voiced and voiceless symbols interchangeably or to write the obstruents consistently, some favoring ⟨p⟩, for example, others ⟨b⟩.

There were six Massachusett vowels, two short and four long. The short vowels were /a/ and /ə/. Eliot wrote /a/ as ⟨a⟩ or ⟨o⟩, and /ə/ usually as ⟨u⟩, but as ⟨i⟩ or ⟨e⟩ in certain contexts. The long vowels were probably /iˑ/, /aˑ/, /ą̄ˑ/, and /uˑ/. Eliot wrote them in most cases as ⟨e⟩ or ⟨ee⟩; ⟨a⟩, ⟨o⟩, ⟨á⟩, or ⟨ó⟩; ⟨o⟩, ⟨ô⟩, ⟨om⟩, or ⟨on⟩, or with similar modifications of ⟨a⟩ or ⟨u⟩; and ⟨oo⟩ (a digraph that he invented) respectively (Goddard and Bragdon 1988:475).

Figure 1 is a petition written at Gay Head, on Martha's Vineyard, by Zachary Hossueit, the native minister of the Gay Head Congregational Church and also town clerk and justice of the peace (Goddard and Bragdon 1988:xxi). It can be dated to the third quarter of the eighteenth century.

Mahican

Mahican was written in English-based orthographies in the Stockbridge, Massachusetts, mission and in a German orthography in the Moravian missions. A word list and Lord's Prayer in Stockbridge Mahican were published by Jonathan Edwards, Jr. (1788), who became fluent in the language after moving to Stockbridge, at the age of six, in 1751-1752. Two

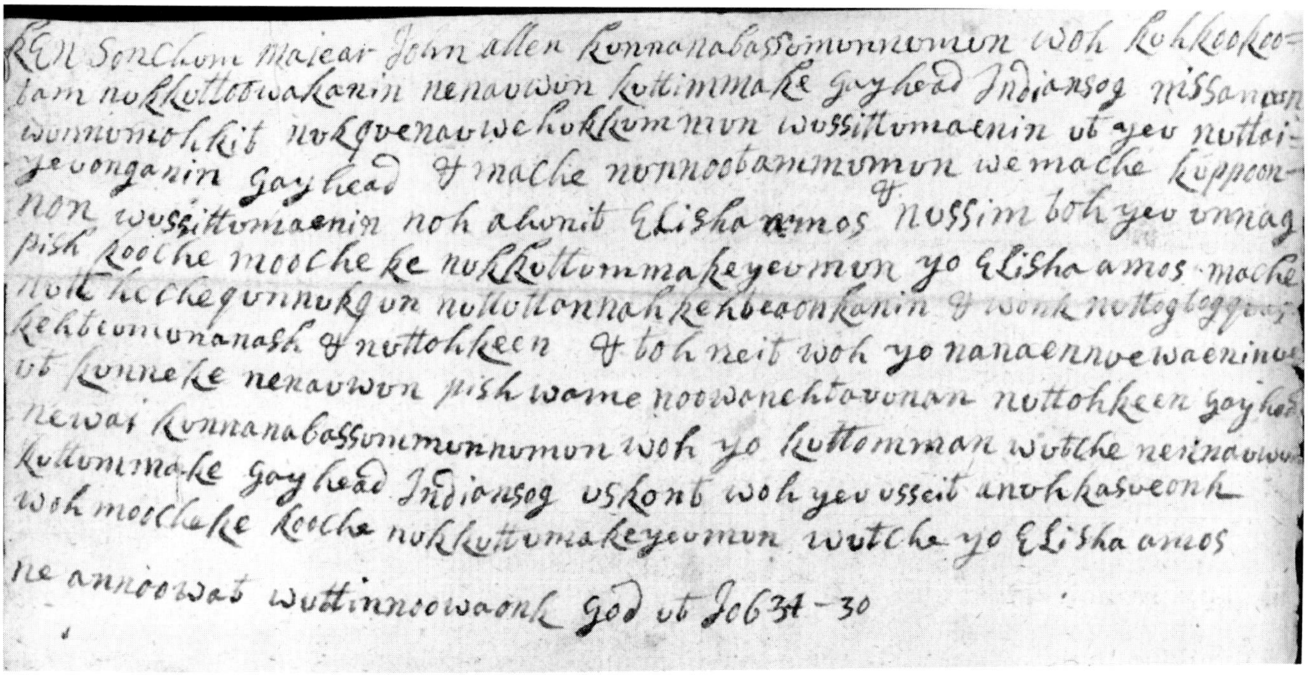
Ken Sonchem Maiear John allen kunnanabassumunnumun woh kohkookoo-
tam nukkuttoowakanin nenawun kuttimmake gayhead Indiansog nissanwun
wunnumohkit nukquenawwehokkommun wussittumaenin ut yeu nuttoi-
yeuonganin gayhead & mache nunnootammumun wemache kuppoon-
non wussittumaenin noh ahwonit Elisha amos & nussim boh yeu unnag
pish kooche mooche ke nukkuttummakeyeumun yo Elisha amos mache
noh necheqvnnukgun nuttuttonnahkehbeaonkanin & wonk nuttoggogq
kehteumonanash & nuttohkeen & toh neit woh yo nanaennoewaeninw
ut kunneke nenawun pish wame noowonehtouonan nuttohkeen gayhead
newaj kunnanabassumunnumun woh yo kuttummau wutche nenawun
kuttummake gayhead Indiansog uskont woh yeu usseit anohkasueonk
woh moochake kooche nukkuttumakeyeumun wutche yo Elisha amos
ne annoowat wuttinnoowaonk God ut Job 34-30

Mass. Histl. Soc., Boston.

Fig. 1. Petition written in Massachusett by Zachary Hossueit and sent by the Indians of Gay Head to the Commissioners of the New England Company. The petitioners objected to the appointment of Elisha Amos as a local magistrate and closed by citing Job 34:30: "let not the hypocrite rule" (Goddard and Bragdon 1988:224-225).

native residents of Stockbridge, John Quinney and Hendrick Aupaumut, translated *The Assembly's Shorter Catechism* into Mahican (Quinney 1795; Quinney and Aupaumut 1818) (fig. 2). Electa F. Jones (1854:120) mentions that Aupaumut "sent a speech," presumably written in Mahican, to his people at New Stockbridge, New York, inviting them to follow him to the White River in Indiana, where some of them joined him in 1818. Abiel Holmes (1804: 26-27) published a Mahican text comprising 80 words and phrases that had been written out by John Konkapot, Jr., "a young and intelligent Indian of the Stockbridge tribe." The orthography was that "adopted by the present secretary of the Grand Council of the tribe (who was educated at Dartmouth College) in their public records" (Holmes 1804:25). A Mahican translation of the 19th Psalm "done at the Cornwall School [in Connecticut], under the superintendance of Rev. John Sergeant, Missionary" (son of the earlier John Sergeant) is included in Morse (1822:359-360).

A letter and hymn translations by Jonas attest to Mahican literacy in the Moravian orthography (Masthay 1980:23, 27-28). The last Mahican text was recorded with an English translation at Red Springs, Wisconsin, by J. F. Estes, "an educated Dakota Indian . . . in the Dakota system of orthography" and may be found, together with a key to this orthography, in Prince (1905).

Delaware

Moravian missionaries among the Delaware developed an orthography for the Northern Unami dialect based on the German alphabet in the mid-eighteenth century. Literacy in this dialect was maintained in the Moravian mission at Moraviantown, Ontario, even when the predominant language spoken there shifted to Munsee. In the 1880s, the Moraviantown band chief was apparently literate only in Northern Unami, although a native speaker of Munsee, as shown by a letter he wrote for Daniel G. Brinton (fig. 3). Other Delawares in Canada became literate in Munsee using the English orthography of the Methodist and Anglican missionaries.

A text written in an English-based Munsee orthography and English by Nelles Montour of Six Nations Reserve, Ontario, was edited by Prince (1902:23-34). Prince (1902:21) observed that "Like all Indian scribes, . . . Chief Montour writes syllabically, separating the syllables of his texts and not the words, a process which makes a correct edition of his Mss. extremely difficult." Literacy in these two orthographies waned in the twentieth century in Canada, except for some passive ability to use hymnbooks and prayer books, but Goddard (1973:736) reported that "people living today can recall members of their parents' generation sending and receiving letters written in Delaware." Some Delawares in the main body of the tribe in Kansas and

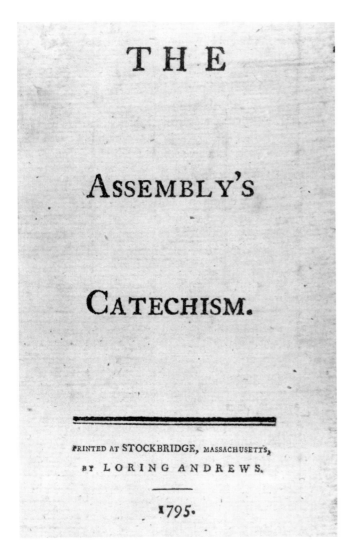

THE

ASSEMBLY'S

CATECHISM.

PRINTED AT STOCKBRIDGE, MASSACHUSETTS,
BY LORING ANDREWS.

1795.

THE

Affembly's Shorter Catechifm,

Qchemoentuewaunkun. KAUQUI nhaun unnᴏwwaunmawu nooh autennawufeet ?

Aukhchewch. Nook autennawufeet nhaun unnowwaux-maumuk, aunch aum maunioothpehhaut Pohtommauwau-fun, don wauwumwekihnaut honmewch.

Q. Kauqui Pohtommawwaus kmeenkonuh kavkuhkhum-mauquuq wauch aum wauwehtiyuq aunhqueh aum man moothpehhauyuq, don wauwuwwekihnauyuq ?

A. Nik wtauptoonnauwauhun Pohtommowwaus au-tennaukhautheek, neh mkhowoi wonk wfkoi nauktuhhau-fetup wfohekun, neh nun nquehcheh kaukuhkhummau-quq aunqueh aum maunoothpehhauyuq, don wauwau-wekehnauyuq.

Q. Kauquikuh neh wfoowhekun nhaun unneh kkuh-kotom ?

A. Nik wfoowhekun nhaun unneh kkuhkotom taun aum aunhqueh wnithtummuk nuh wcheh Pohtommau-waus, don aunch dootmauquq.

Q. Tauneek wtennoiyen nuh Pohtommawwaus ?

A. Nuk Pohtommuwwaus pauqueweh wchechukkoow nanowoiyo ; ftuh eyuhquauyoweh, don ftuh pepeenweh-nauweh neh aunnawufeet, wfaukhkunnuhkauwaukun, oneiwaukun, don onaumauwaukun.

Q. Kaukhoowwuk aut Pohtommuwwaufuk ?

Mass. Histl. Soc., Boston.
Fig. 2. Title page and first printed page of John Quinney's (1795) Mahican translation of the 1648 Shorter Catechism of the Westminster Assembly. It begins with the question and answer: "What is the chief end of man?" "Man's chief end is to glorify God and to enjoy Him forever." The English-based orthography is a modification of one introduced by John Sergeant in the 1740s.

later Oklahoma became literate in the orthography introduced by Jotham Meeker and Ira D. Blanchard, described below.

Micmac, Maliseet-Passamaquoddy, and Western Abenaki

In the traditional account of Micmac literacy obtained by Philip K. Bock the Micmacs are said to have

> secretly developed a nearly phonemic orthography using the Latin alphabet, probably in the late 18th or early 19th century. Finding this in wide use, Father Pacifique modified it somewhat and used it in translating the Scriptures, in encouraging literacy, and in publishing for 17 years the newspaper *The Micmac Messenger* in the native language. The traditional orthography, Pacifique's version of it, and combinations of the two were still in use among some older Micmacs into the 1970s (vol. 15:109).

In the last decades of the twentieth century several competing modified versions of the Pacifique orthography were developed. An earlier writing system, the Micmac "hieroglyphs," had been developed by Father Chrétien Le Clercq in the seventeenth century and carried on by Pierre-Antoine Maillard (see "Nonspeech Communication Systems," fig. 4, this vol.).

Several Maliseet-Passamaquoddy readers were produced in 1973 by the Wabnaki Bilingual Education Program of Indian Township, Maine, in an orthography based on Teeter (1971) (fig. 4). The Pleasant Point Bilingual program in Perry, Maine, also produced a number of Maliseet-Passamaquoddy instructional publications and bilingual texts (Leavitt and Francis 1986; Anonymous 1986). The wampum records of Lewis Mitchell, based on Prince (1921), were edited, retranslated, annotated, and transcribed

161

I, GOTTLIEB TOBIAS,

Nanne ni ngutschi nachguttemin, jun awen eet ma elekhigetup.
Woak alende nenostamen woak alende taku eli wtallichsin ele-
wondasik wiwonalatokowo pachsi wonamii lichsu woak pachsi pilli
lichsoagan. Taku ni nenostamowin. Lamoe nemochomsinga
achpami eet newinachke woak chash tichi kachtin nbibindameneb
nin lichsoagan. Mauchso lenno woak mauchso chauchshissis woak
juque mauchso chauchshissis achpo pomauchsu igabtshi lue wi-
wonallatokowo won bambil alachshe. Woak lue lamoe ni enda.
Mimensiane ntelsitam alowi ayachichson won elhagewit woak
ehelop ne likhiqui. Gichgi wonami lichso shuk tatcamse woak
gichgi minsiwi lichso.

TRANSLATION.

Then I will try to answer this (which) some one at some time
wrote. And some I understand, and some not, because his language
is called Wonalatoko, half Unami and half another language. I
do not understand it. Long ago my grandfather about 48 years
ago I heard it that language. One man and one old woman and
now another old woman here lives yet who uses this Wonalatoko
language just like this book and she said, I of old time when I was
a child heard more difficult dialect than the present, and many at
that time partly Unami he speak, but sometimes also partly
Minsi he speak.

Smithsonian, Anthr. Lib.: Brinton 1885:88.

Fig. 3. Text written in Northern Unami in the Moravian
missionaries' German-based orthography and in English by
Gottlieb Tobias of Moraviantown, Ont.

in the Teeter orthography by Leavitt and Francis
(1990).

It is said that native literacy in Western Abenaki
was formally taught for perhaps a century at the
Odanak settlement in Saint Francis, Quebec. Several
books by literate speakers of this language have
appeared (Masta 1932; Laurent 1884; Wzokhilain
1830, 1830a, 1832, 1844). There are slight differences
in the orthographies of these authors. The nasal vowel
ǫ ([ʌ], [ɔ]), which Day (1964:374) transcribed ⟨ɔ̃⟩, is
written ⟨o⟩ and ⟨o'⟩ by Wzokhilain (Pierre Paul
Osunkherhine) as in his name; as ⟨ô⟩ by Laurent, as in
the Western Abenaki form of his surname, ⟨Lolô⟩; and
as ⟨8⟩ by Masta.

Northern Iroquoian

The Northern Iroquoian languages have been written
in the roman alphabet from the time of Jacques
Cartier's first voyage in 1534 to the late twentieth
century, when books and public notices in these languages were still to be seen on the New York reservations and Ontario reserves and in other Iroquois
communities (vol. 4:458). In particular, Roman
Catholic Mohawks came to use an orthography
developed by French missionaries and codified in

the writings of Jean-André Cuoq. This writes most
segmental phonemes phonemically but does not mark
stress, falling tone, vowel length, postvocalic /h/
when not before a vowel (except occasionally), or /ʔ/,
and it is not completely successful in distinguishing
the nasalized vowels (ǫ [u̧] and ę [ʌ]) from sequences
with /n/. While Cuoq followed standard French practice in writing ⟨n⟩ to mark the preceding vowel as
nasalized, where this spelling would be ambiguous he
distinguished nasalized vowels from sequences of
vowel plus nasal consonant by writing the nasalized
vowels as ⟨oñ⟩ and ⟨eñ⟩ and the sequences as ⟨onn⟩
and ⟨enn⟩. Later he proposed writing the nasalized
vowels as ⟨on'⟩ and ⟨en'⟩ (Cuoq 1882:vi-vii) and
sometimes used ⟨onh⟩ and ⟨enh⟩ for these sounds.
(Asher Wright (1842, 1872) indicated nasalization in
his Seneca orthography with underlined vowels.)
Cuoq (1882:vi, 203) also adopted from English the
use of ⟨w⟩ to write /w/, abandoning his earlier use of
⟨8⟩, a substitution for the omicron-upsilon digraph ⟨ȣ⟩
that had been used by the French missionaries since
the seventeenth century. Cuoq explicitly rejected both
the syllabic orthography and Kauder's Micmac hieroglyphs in favor of the roman alphabet (Cuoq 1869:22,
1882:vii-viii, 203).

The title page of an eighteenth-century Mohawk
publication using an orthography derived from English
and Dutch is reproduced in figure 5.

Cherokee

The Cherokee syllabary was invented in 1819 or
shortly thereafter by Sequoya (George Gist), a monolingual and formerly illiterate Cherokee. The syllabary
was widely used by Cherokees as early as the 1820s
(vol. 4:44, 46) and remained in use in many Cherokee
communities in the 1990s, both in Oklahoma and North
Carolina (Walker 1969, 1975; Walker and Sarbaugh
1993; White 1962; Chafe 1973; Monteith 1984;
Scancarelli 1996).

Figure 6 gives the 85 characters of the syllabary,
with their phonemic values, as arranged by Worcester
(1828) and as presented in most Cherokee language
publications. The same characters appear in figure 7,
which shows the syllabary in the order used by
Sequoya prior to 1828. The characters are syllabic
except for the one that represents /s/ ([s] in
Oklahoma, [š] in the major North Carolina dialect).
Six characters represent the six vowels of Cherokee,
/a, e, i, o, u, ə /, often with a preceding glottal stop,
which is not otherwise indicated. The remaining 78
characters represent syllables composed of a consonant or consonant cluster plus a vowel, although one,
the character in the eighth row resembling a capital
G, is no longer used, and literate Cherokees either do

Wen ketowi mace posonutehket, tomkote
wen topaskula nemotahkapicihi towihtikonok,
wecihc wen wewitomosat. Kcuwi tepi
tomosak nemotahkapicik tan keti olkiqahk
ktoposonut. Yut ewikhasik posonut, akim
qotinsk nemotahkapicik etolowehkuhucik.
Qenoq nehtaw aqamkiqahk posonut,
aqameluk op nemotahkapicik ewehkuhucik.

Tomkote wen nanuhu nemotahkapicihi
elewolacihi, apc wen nanuhu uskitewolan.

Wen toke wiqnan apsatokosossilicil naka
wen wiwniyan nihikehs. Wen toke
topaskutun wiponut. Ska tepkiqonunuhk,
on wen tatli wiwniyan tohki tepkiqahk.

On wen toke kipikpenomon, naka
towihtikon sitopitun.

4

Fig. 4. Page 4 of instructions in Passamaquoddy for making a basket. Irene Newell Dana (b. 1913) demonstrates the process in a booklet titled *Eli Posonutekhotimok* 'How Baskets are Made' (Wabnaki Bilingual Education Program 1973). The page begins: 'Anyone who wants to start making a basket. . . .'

not know or do not agree on its former phonetic value.

Some of Sequoya's characters may have been borrowed from Greek or Cyrillic; others seem to have no precedent in other writing systems. Several closely resemble printed roman capital letters, although their phonetic values differ greatly from those of their roman counterparts, a fact that indicates that Sequoya was in no sense literate in any European language when he devised the syllabary.

In developing the syllabary Sequoya added characters from time to time and, at least once, deleted characters, perhaps as a result of his collaboration with Ahyokeh, his six-year-old daughter (Walker 1984a). Sequoya also experimented with different forms of his characters, some of which he expressly intended as forms to be cast in type. Several twentieth-century writers have stated that the forms of the syllabics used in printed Cherokee were designed by Samuel Worcester or some other White missionary (A.G. Kilpatrick and J. Kilpatrick 1966:8; J. Kilpatrick and A. G. Kilpatrick 1968:31-32, note 11; Traveller Bird 1971:84; Walker 1981:147-149, 1985:610). But the testimony of several of Sequoya's contemporaries, the evidence of a syllabary sent by Charles Renatus Hicks to Thomas L. McKenney in 1825, and documents written by Sequoya himself indicate that alterations in the forms of the syllabic characters are all attributable to Sequoya (Walker and Sarbaugh 1993). The dissemination of the syllabary was the result of Cherokee initiative as well; for correspondence in syllabics was reported by missionaries as being widespread in both the east and the west in the 1820s, at a time when White missionaries and government officials were still

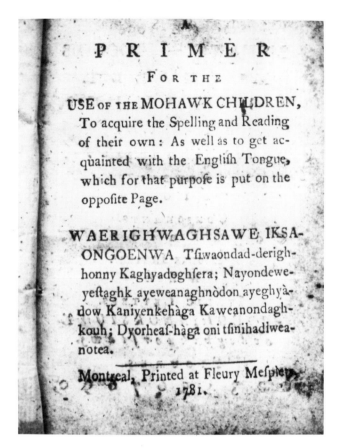

Smithsonian, Natl. Mus. of the Amer. Ind.: Gaines 1929:144.

Fig. 5. The title page of a Mohawk primer (Claus 1781). According to Pilling (1888:139) the only known copy is in the British Museum. The frontispiece from the 1786 edition is reproduced in vol. 4:285.

attempting to impose a roman alphabet on the Cherokees.

The only change in the syllabary that is clearly attributable to Whites was reported in Worcester (1828a), an account of the syllabary that appeared in the first issue of the *Cherokee Phoenix* on February 21, 1828. Here Worcester reported the deletion of one redundant character, making the new total 85, and offered his own innovation, a "systematic" arrangement of the characters based on the order of recitation of the English alphabet. This "systematic" arrangement has been reproduced in the various editions of the *Cherokee New Testament* (American Bible Society 1860) and elsewhere, and has become familiar to all Christian Cherokees, if not all Cherokee speakers. However, a syllabary written by Will West Long of Big Cove, North Carolina, in 1947 (Chiltoskey 1972), preserves essentially the sequence of Sequoya's linear syllabary. Long's characters are arranged in columns, like Worcester's; but if one reads the columns from top to bottom, beginning at the left, the resulting sequence is virtually identical to Sequoya's. Thus, Worcester's "systematic" arrangement, the only feature of the syllabary that

cannot be attributed to the Cherokees, had not replaced Sequoya's sequence for all Cherokees even in the mid-twentieth century.

The forms of the printed characters, the number of characters, and, for most Cherokees, their order of recitation and arrangement on the page have, since 1828, been remarkably stable. Only one minor change has occurred: the character representing /to/ and /tho/ appeared consistently as Λ in all publications of the Cherokee National Press through May 31, 1834, when the last issue of the *Cherokee Phoenix* was printed at New Echota in the Old Nation. It was inverted, as V, in the first edition of the *Cherokee Almanac* printed in 1836 at Union, Indian Territory (Bass 1936:213), and has remained so ever since.

Written Cherokee departs somewhat from the printed model and varies somewhat with locality, the expertise of the writer, and the degree of formality of the occasion. According to Anna and Jack Kilpatrick (1966:8), the syllabic characters in nineteenth-century manuscripts from Oklahoma are more like printed characters than those in nineteenth-century North Carolina manuscripts. However, Eastern texts from the twentieth century are sometimes as faithful to the printed standard as texts written in Oklahoma. An alternative form of the character Ᏼ /kwa, khwa/ that was sometimes used in Delaware County, Oklahoma, in the 1960s was Ᏼ, a departure from the printed standard that probably has no parallel in North Carolina. And some of the features that distinguish eastern manuscripts from printed texts can be found also in Oklahoma. Thus the Long syllabary of 1947 includes a very standard Ᏼ on page 53, but two deviant forms in the fragment of a dictionary on page 52. These variant forms occur also in manuscripts from Oklahoma.

Variations in written Cherokee, whether regional, temporal, or contextual, should not be overemphasized. Written Cherokee differs from the printed standard only superficially, and far less than cursive English differs from printed English (fig. 8).

Cherokee is written in accordance with certain spelling conventions that must be learned in addition to the 85 characters and their phonetic values. Words consisting of sequences of alternating consonants and vowels are, of course, written with sequences of characters representing the appropriate consonant-vowel syllables. The writing system does not distinguish certain phonemically distinct consonants and clusters. Thus /l/ and /hl/, /k/ and /kh/, /w/ and /hw/, /y/ and /hy/, and /ts/ and /tsh/ are not distinguished in written texts; /n/ and /hn/ and /tl/ and /thl/ are distinguished only in the context of a following /a/; and /t/ and /th/ are distinguished only in the context of a following /a/, /e/, or /i/. Moreover, pitch, stress, vowel length, and nasalization are not marked. For all these reasons, the written forms of

Ꭰ /a, ʔa/	Ꭱ /e, ʔe/	Ꭲ /i,ʔi/	Ꭳ /o, ʔo/	Ꭴ /u, ʔu/	Ꭵ /ə̨, ʔə̨/
Ꭶ /ka/	Ꭸ /ke, khe/	Ꭹ /ki, khi/	Ꭺ /ko, kho/	Ꭻ /ku, khu/	Ꭼ /kə̨, khə̨/
Ꭷ /kha/					
Ꭽ /ha/	Ꭾ /he/	Ꭿ /hi/	Ꮀ /ho/	Ꮁ /hu/	Ꮂ /hə̨/
Ꮃ /la, hla/	Ꮄ /le, hle/	Ꮅ /li, hli/	Ꮆ /lo, hlo/	Ꮇ /lu, hlu/	Ꮈ /lə̨, hlə̨/
Ꮉ /ma/	Ꮊ /me/	Ꮋ /mi/	Ꮌ /mo/	Ꮍ /mu/	
Ꮎ /na/	Ꮑ /ne, hne/	Ꮒ /ni, hni/	Ꮓ /no, hno/	Ꮔ /nu, hnu/	Ꮕ /nə̨, hnə̨/
Ꮏ /hna/	Ꮐ (not used)				
Ꮖ /kwa, khwa/	Ꮗ /kwe, khwe/	Ꮘ /kwi, khwi/	Ꮙ /kwo, khwo/	Ꮚ /kwu, khwu/	Ꮛ /kwə̨, khwə̨/
Ꮝ /s/					
Ꮜ /sa/	Ꮞ /se/	Ꮟ /si/	Ꮠ /so/	Ꮡ /su/	Ꮢ /sə̨/
Ꮣ /ta/	Ꮥ /te/	Ꮧ /ti/	Ꮩ /to, tho/	Ꮪ /tu, thu/	Ꮫ /tə̨, thə̨/
Ꮤ /tha/	Ꮦ /the/	Ꮨ /thi/			
Ꮬ /tla/	Ꮮ /tle, thle/	Ꮯ /tli, thli/	Ꮰ /tlo, thlo/	Ꮱ /tlu, thlu/	Ꮲ /tlə̨, thlə̨/
Ꮭ /thla/					
Ꮳ /tsa, tsha/	Ꮴ /tse, tshe/	Ꮵ /tsi, tshi/	Ꮶ /tso, tsho/	Ꮷ /tsu, tshu/	Ꮸ /tsə̨, tshə̨/
Ꮹ /wa, hwa/	Ꮺ /we, hwe/	Ꮻ /wi, hwi/	Ꮼ /wo, hwo/	Ꮽ /wu, hwu/	Ꮾ /wə̨, hwə̨/
Ꮿ /ya, hya/	Ᏸ /ye, hye/	Ᏹ /yi, hyi/	Ᏺ /yo, hyo/	Ᏻ /yu, hyu/	Ᏼ /yə̨, hyə̨/

Fig. 6. Sequoya's Cherokee syllabary in Worcester's "systematic" arrangement with corresponding phonemic transcriptions. The character representing /kwo, khwo/ is used by some writers to represent /kwu, khwu/. Vowels may be long or short, and the syllabic characters may also represent consonants alone before other consonants. This chart was generated on a computer using a PostScript™ font for the Macintosh platform digitized by Al Webster, Project Studio, Okla., 1992.

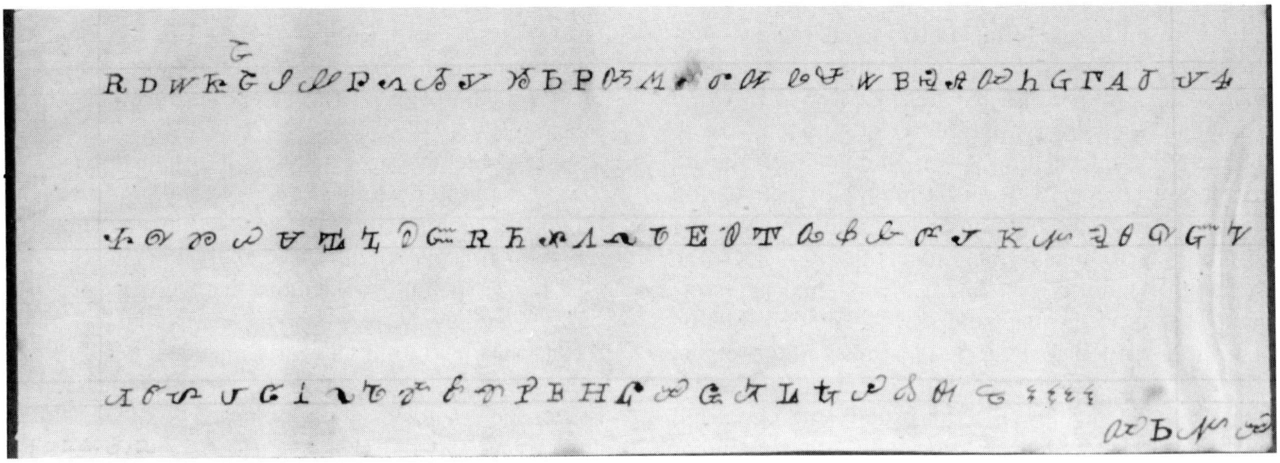

Thomas Gilcrease Inst. of Amer. Hist. and Art, Tulsa, Okla.

Fig. 7. The Cherokee syllabary written out by Sequoya for John Howard Payne, a lobbyist for the Cherokees. It is signed at the lower right, 1839.

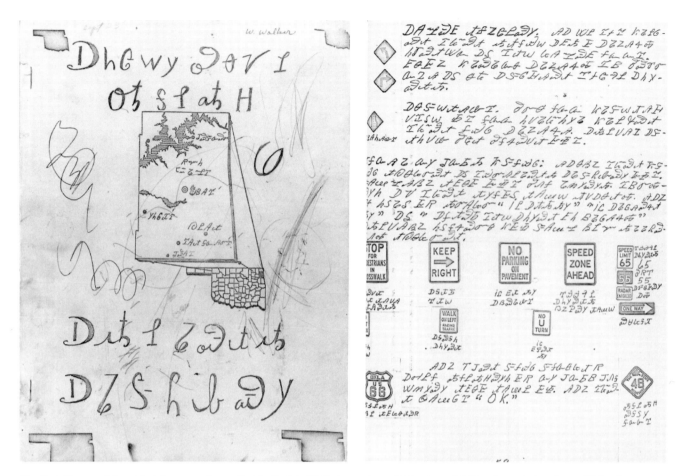

Fig. 8. A 71-page drivers' training manual compiled in the late 1960s in cursive syllabics to assist Cherokee speakers in qualifying for Oklahoma state drivers' licenses (Anonymous 1969). left, Cover with a map of Delaware County, Okla., giving prominence to the town of Jay; right, p. 59 with various speed and directional signs.

Cherokee words are more likely to be ambiguous than are their spoken forms.

The spelling of complex consonant clusters presents difficulties to both readers and writers. Clusters whose first component is /s/ are written with the character representing /s/ followed by the character representing the appropriate consonant plus vowel. Other clusters not provided for by the syllabary are written as though their two contiguous components were divided by an intervening vowel, and which of the six vowels must be indicated is a matter of convention not determined by phonological criteria. Thus the word *tshkwísti* 'many (inanimate things)' is written as though its initial consonant cluster had an intervening /i/ between /tsh/ and /kwi/. To identify this word in a written text the reader must interpret the first character as representing a consonant, rather than a consonant plus /i/ as is usually the case, and must interpret it as representing /tsh/ rather than /ts/. While these ambiguities in the writing system present obstacles to literacy and may account for the fact that some fluent speakers of the language fail to become literate despite years of exposure to and instruction in the syllabary, the spelling conventions of Cherokee are fewer and less complex than those of English and are probably much easier for fluent Cherokee speakers to acquire than are the spelling and reading conventions of English for English-speaking Americans. For more information on the relationship between Cherokee writing and Cherokee speech, see Scancarelli (1992).

Most contemporary Cherokees use the *Cherokee New Testament* (American Bible Society 1860) as the standard for correct spelling (fig. 9). However, literate members of the non-Christian Nighthawk communities in Oklahoma tend to use spelling conventions that were not preserved in the *Cherokee New Testament*. The Nighthawk manuscripts thus tend to reflect early nineteenth-century conventions more than do those of Christian writers. Prevocalic /s/, for example, is usually spelled with the appropriate syllabic character for /s/ plus a vowel by Christian Cherokees, but Nighthawks, like Sequoya himself, use the character for /s/ by itself followed by the appropriate syllabic character for /s/ plus a vowel.

166

Keetoowah Language Lesson #15

by Clara Proctor

ᏏᏲ! Happy 4th of July! Hope you get a chance to attend some of the celebrations in your area. If all goes well, we will be at Jay's Huckleberry Festival. There will be many activities: arts & crafts, quilt show, 3 on 3 basketball, Old-Timers Baseball, Giggers' Light Parade and live music. The highlight will be a fireworks display Monday, July 4th at 10 p.m. at the J.B. Earp Football Field.

This month's lesson includes a short article written in the Syllabary about the 4th of July. Hope you enjoy it. Stay "cool."

Set #48--Jay's Huckleberry Festival--July 2-4

Ka-ye-gwo-ni nv-gi-ne-i	I-tse-sv-i!	dla-gv
July 4th	(You all) go!	Jay

Ka-wa-ya di-ge-li-s-gi do-dv-ni-gi.
They will eat huckleberry pies. (r.o.)

Dla-gv-ke he-ga? — di-ta-s-gi-s-d
Are you going to Jay? — Fireworks

Tsu-wo-du tsu-no-tlv-nv <u>di-hya-tl-di</u> da-ni-n-de-ge-s-di.
They will be selling beautiful <u>necklaces</u> they made.
(r.o.)

ta-l di-ga-wa-ti a-ki-lv-do-di
bicycle (lit.: "two-wheeled vehicle to ride on")

Da-ni-hno-gi-s-ge-s-di. — A-na-l-s-gi-s-ge-s-di.
(They) will be singing. — They will be dancing.

<u>So-gwi-li</u> tsu-na-la-su-lo u-n-de-ge-s-di.
They will be throwing <u>horseshoes.</u> (r.o.)

A-n-da-nv-hnv-s-gv-ke da-ga-hi-ga-to-s-ta-n?
Are you going to watch the <u>parade</u>? (r.o.)
(lit.: "lining up;" it can also mean "graduation")

U-ni-go-di <u>yv-wi</u> a-ne-do-he-s-di.
There will be lots of <u>people.</u>

<u>I-hna-na</u> wi-da-ge-do-li.
I will go <u>there.</u> (r.o.)

Set #49--Questions

Ha-la-<u>yv</u> a-ne-ga?	Ha-<u>dlv</u> wa-ne-do-ha?
<u>When</u> are they going	<u>Where</u> are they? (refers to people)

ᎤᏁᎳᏅᎯ ᎤᏰᎾᏘ

(Cherokee syllabary article about the 4th of July)

Set #49--Questions (Continued)

Do-hv u-s-di ta-dv-ne-li?	Ha-<u>dlv</u> a-ne-ga?
What are you going to do?	<u>Where</u> are they going?
Ha-la yu-wa-hni-lv <u>no-wu</u>?	Ga-hv-yu-s-di na <u>a-ge-hya</u>?
What time is it <u>no-wu</u>?	Who is that <u>woman</u>?
Do-hv?	Do-u-s-di?	Do-gi-u-s-t?
Why?	What (is it)?	What? ("Huh?")
<u>Ha-la-i-ga</u> di-tsa-tse-li?	Ga-hv hi-yo-ha?
<u>How many</u> are yours?	Who are you looking for?

Set #50--Blackberry Pickin'

<u>Ka-nu-ga-tli</u> u-ni-hya-lu-ga.	<u>V-da-li</u> na-v a-ne-na.
They went to look for <u>blackberries.</u>	They went close (to the) <u>pond.</u>
Ta-lu-gi-s-gi da-ni-hye-ha.	Do-dv-ni-ka-li-li.
They're carrying <u>pails.</u>	They will fill them up.
<u>Di-ni-yo-tli</u> da-n-ti-hne-ha.	<u>Ka-nu-ga-tli</u> u-ni-lv-k-di di-ni-yo-tli.
They have <u>children</u> with them.	Children like <u>blackberries.</u>
<u>U-di-tle-gv</u> a-ne-do-ha.	<u>v-tla</u> yu-da-wa-di-a lv-dlv-i.
(They're) in <u>a hot place.</u>	There is <u>no</u> shade anywhere.
U-go-di <u>a-ma</u> a-n-di-ta-s-ge-s-di.	<u>Gu-gu</u> a-ne-do-ho-i
They will drink lots of <u>water.</u>	There are <u>ticks</u> there.
Ka-nu-ga-tli do-da-tl-ta-ni <u>e-tlo-gi</u>.	Ka-nu-ga-tli a-na-de-so-hnv, <u>a-ma-yi</u> dv-ne-si.
<u>My aunt</u> will can black-berries.	After they pick blackberries, they're going to the <u>creek.</u>

REVIEW--Match the following Syllabary words with their English equivalents.

1.	ᎠᎮ	A. huckleberries
2.	ᏃᏩ	B. 4th of July
3.	ᎯᏛ	C. How many?
4.	ᎧᏄᎦ	D. It's hot.
5.	ᎯᎳᏫᎬ	E. necklace
6.	ᎤᏗᏝᎬ	F. Jay
7.	ᏓᎳᎦ	G. Where?
8.	ᎯᎳᏘᏍ?	H. now
9.	ᎤᏁᎳᏅᎯ ᎤᏰᎾᏘ	I. blackberries
10.	ᎠᏕᏍᏗ	J. When

Answers: 1.F, 2.H, 3.G, 4.I, 5.J, 6.D, 7.A, 8.C, 9.B, 10.E

Fig. 9. A Cherokee lesson from the July 1994 *UKB News,* p. 6, published by the United Keetoowah Band. This band refers to Cherokee as Keetoowah.

The Meeker Alphabets and Alford's Shawnee Orthography

Jotham Meeker spent most of the period 1827-1833 as a schoolteacher and missionary to the Potawatomis, Ottawas, and Chippewas (Ojibwas) at three mission stations in Michigan. In these years he learned something of all three languages and is said to have become fluent in Ottawa, a variety of Ojibwa that was the lingua franca for all three groups in the lower peninsula of Michigan in the 1830s (vol. 6:61). After learning the printer's trade and being transferred to Sault Sainte Marie in 1832, he began to devise an orthography for Ojibwa and successfully taught two Ojibwa boys to read "after a few days' instruction" (McMurtrie and Allen 1930:26). In 1833 he went to Indian Territory (now Kansas) and established the Shawanoe Mission Press, which over the next 20 years was to print over 50 books and pamphlets in various Indian languages, as well as the *Siwinowe Kesibwi* (*šaˑwanoˑwi-kiˑšaʔθwa* 'Shawnee Sun'), the first newspaper published entirely in an American Indian language in the United States (McCoy 1840:486; McMurtrie 1933). Publications included primers, portions of the Bible, and other works in Choctaw, Unami Delaware, Iowa, Kansa, Creek, Osage, Otoe, Ottawa, Potawatomi, Shawnee, and Wea (Miami). They were printed in Meeker's "new system of writing and reading," which "*wholly excludes spelling*" and "enables the learner to paint his thoughts on paper, with precision, as soon as he acquires a knowledge of a number of characters about equal to the English alphabet" (McCoy [1840] quoted in Pilling 1891:353).

It is not clear that many Indians learned to read the Meeker orthographies, although some learned "in a surprisingly short time" (McMurtrie and Allen 1930:26-27) and Chief Charles Journeycake of the Delawares is said to be the author of a hymnal in the Meeker-Blanchard Delaware orthography. Significantly, perhaps, some Indians who learned the Meeker orthographies from missionaries passed on their skills to other Indians who were not taught literacy directly by White missionaries (McCoy 1840:471-475; McMurtrie and Allen 1930:28). Regardless of how many Indians learned to read the Meeker orthographies, the Shawanoe Mission Press must have had a considerable impact, for its publications were frequently read aloud by missionaries to groups of Indians (McMurtrie and Allen 1930:29).

The Meeker orthographies make use of English (roman) letters; but the phonetic values assigned to some of these letters vary from one orthography to another. The letter ⟨b⟩ for example, represents a stop consonant /p/ ([b]) in Potawatomi, but a spirant /θ/ in Shawnee, and the sequence /yu/ or /yoˑ/ in Delaware. Details of the orthographies used for Potawatomi,

Ottawa, Delaware, and Shawnee are presented in table 1; the title pages of books printed by the Shawanoe Mission Press in Delaware, Shawnee, Choctaw, and Osage are reproduced in "The Description of the Native Languages of North America Before Boas," figures 4-6, this volume. Further information on Meeker's publications is in McMurtrie and Allen (1930) and Pilling (1891:351-356).

A writing system that superficially resembles the Shawnee alphabet used by Meeker's colleague Johnston Lykins (table 1) was used in the twentieth century by Thomas Wildcat Alford, a native speaker of Shawnee. Like some other Meeker orthographies, it assigns the letter ⟨r⟩ to a vowel. Unlike the Meeker orthographies, Alford rather consistently distinguished long from short vowels. "The long vowels are a, e, o and r; and the short are a, i, u and v" (Alford 1929:199). Alford's system, then, was phonemic with regard to the vowels, except that, following Lykins (1834), perhaps, Alford's letter ⟨a⟩ represented both /e/ and /eˑ/. The other long vowels /iˑ/, /oˑ/, and /aˑ/ were written ⟨e⟩, ⟨o⟩, and ⟨r⟩, respectively. The remaining short vowels /i/, /o/, and /a/ were written ⟨i⟩, ⟨u⟩, and ⟨v⟩, respectively. Although the letter ⟨a⟩ represented both long /eˑ/ and short /e/, Alford distinguished these vowels by writing the voiced and voiceless allophones of the stops, which occur predictably, according to his statement, before long and short vowels, respectively: "B is sounded same as in English, and is always followed by long vowels," whereas "P. . . is always followed by short vowels" (Alford 1929:199-200). Thus ⟨ba⟩, ⟨da⟩, and ⟨ja⟩ are spelled /peˑ/, /teˑ/, and /čeˑ/, respectively, while ⟨pa⟩, ⟨ta⟩, and ⟨ca⟩ are spelled /pe/, /te/, and /če/. The distinction was less consistently made after /k/ and /kw/ and could not be made after continuants. Lykins wrote only ⟨p⟩, ⟨t⟩, ⟨c⟩ and ⟨k⟩ for the stops but did not indicate vowel length at all. Alford wrote the eight other Shawnee consonants /m/, /n/, /l/, /w/, /y/, /θ/, /š/ ([š], [s]), /h/ ([ʔ], [h]) and the clusters /kw/ and /ks/ as ⟨m⟩, ⟨n⟩, ⟨l⟩, ⟨w⟩, ⟨y⟩ (⟨i⟩ before short vowels), ⟨f⟩, ⟨s⟩, ⟨h⟩, ⟨q⟩, and ⟨x⟩, respectively. Although this system seems to derive from Lykins (1834) or some other Shawnee alphabet in the Meeker tradition, it is significant that Alford's system was phonetically far more accurate than its predecessors and, indeed, might easily have been converted into a phonemic transcription.

The Great Lakes Algonquian Syllabary

Variants of a native writing system used by Fox (Mesquakie), Sauk, Kickapoo, Potawatomi, and formerly Ottawa speakers have been described by W. Jones (1906), Michelson (1927), Voorhis (1972), and Nichols (1974). Little is known of the origins of this orthography, a syllabary derived ultimately from the

Table 1. Phonemic Values of Letters in the Meeker Orthographies for Potawatomi, Ottawa, Delaware, and Shawnee

Letters	Potawatomi	Ottawa	Delaware	Shawnee
e	/i/	/i·/, /i/, /y/	/i·/, /i/	/i/, /i·/
o	/o/, /ə/, /w-/	/o·/, /o/	/o·/, /u/, /ɔ·/, /ɔ/	/o/, /o·/
a	/a/	/a·/, /a/	/a·/, /a/	/e/, /e·/
i	/ə/	/i/	/i/, /ə/	/a/, /a·/
u	/ə/, Ø	/a/	/ə/, /a/	
r	/e/	/e·/	/e·/, /e/	
w	/w/	/w/	/w/, /u/, /o·/, /ə/	/w/
y	/ay/		/ay/	
b	[b] (probably /mp/)		/yu/, /yo·/	/θ/
c			/e/, /ə/	/č/
h	/č/, /č·/	/č/, /č·/	/č/, /č·/	/h/ ([h])
l	/š/, /š·/	/š/, /š·/	/l/	/l/
j			/š/, /š·/	
v			/h/	
p	/p/, /p·/	/p/, /p·/	/p/, /p·/	/p/
t	/t/, /t·/	/t/, /t·/	/t/, /t·/	/t/
k	/k/, /k·/	/k/, /k·/	/k/, /k·/	/k/
s	/s/, /s·/	/s/, /s·/	/s/, /s·/	/š/ ([š], [s])
m	/m/	/m/	/m/	/m/
n	/n/	/n/	/n/	/n/
f		/nk/	/nk/	
d	[d] (probably /nt/)			
g	[g] (probably /nk/)			
q	/kw/, /k·w/		/kw/, /k·w/	
x			/x/, /x·/	
'	/ʔ/[a]			

SOURCE: Pilling 1891:354-355.

[a]Prevocalic "aspiration" is marked by a circumflex over the following vowel.

roman alphabet (Justeson and Stephens 1993:12-15). The earliest contemporary evidence of its existence is a report that native-language literacy was widespread among the Fox and the Sauk in 1880 (ARCIA 1880:97; Goddard 1988:195). Four years later its use was apparently spreading but still not universal (Fletcher 1890:299, 1890a:354). The Potawatomis may have acquired the syllabary at about the same time to judge from the claim of Joe Ellick, a Forest band Potawatomi of Soperton, Wisconsin, that he had devised it in about 1878 "so that absent members of the tribe could write home to their people" (H. Smith 1933:12). A much earlier use by the Ottawa would be indicated by the statement of Andrew J. Blackbird, an Ottawa of Arbre Croche, Michigan, that his father Mackadepenessy had introduced a "Paw-pa-pe-po" alphabet about 1827 (Blackbird 1887:31), but Blackbird does not use the syllabary himself, and there is no other evidence of its existence at such an early date. The spelling in Blackbird's (1887: 105-128, 1897:78-94) religious translations and notes on Ottawa grammar uses both French and English conventions.

The Great Lakes Algonquian syllabary is based on a European cursive form of the roman alphabet. A possible French source is indicated by the fact that the vowel letters have continental, rather than English, phonetic values and by the shapes of some of the letters. Although the orthography is essentially alphabetic, it is learned and taught as a syllabary. Syllables, but not letters, are named; and each syllable is written as a connected or closely adjacent sequence of letters representing a consonant or consonant sequence plus a vowel, or a vowel alone, and is divided by a space from the following syllable. In the 1990s the system was used in the Fox, Sauk, and Kickapoo communities and among the Potawatomis.

The Fox syllabary is illustrated in figure 10, based on manuscripts written by four writers in the 1910s. Long vowels are not distinguished from short and /h/ is not indicated, although intervocalic /h/ is usually implied by a sequence of two vowel letters. The syllable /a/ is written by some writers as a capital ⟨A⟩. Some writers position ⟨y⟩ above the line, while others write it with a descender below the line. Most consonants are written with the corresponding European cursive letters, but /p/, /š/, and /č/ are written with letters that resemble ⟨b⟩ or ⟨l⟩, ⟨d⟩, and ⟨tt⟩, respectively. The cluster /kw/ is represented by most writers with a form of ⟨g⟩, but others use what looks like ⟨qu⟩, or more recently ⟨kw⟩.

Kickapoo phonology differs from Fox chiefly in that *169*

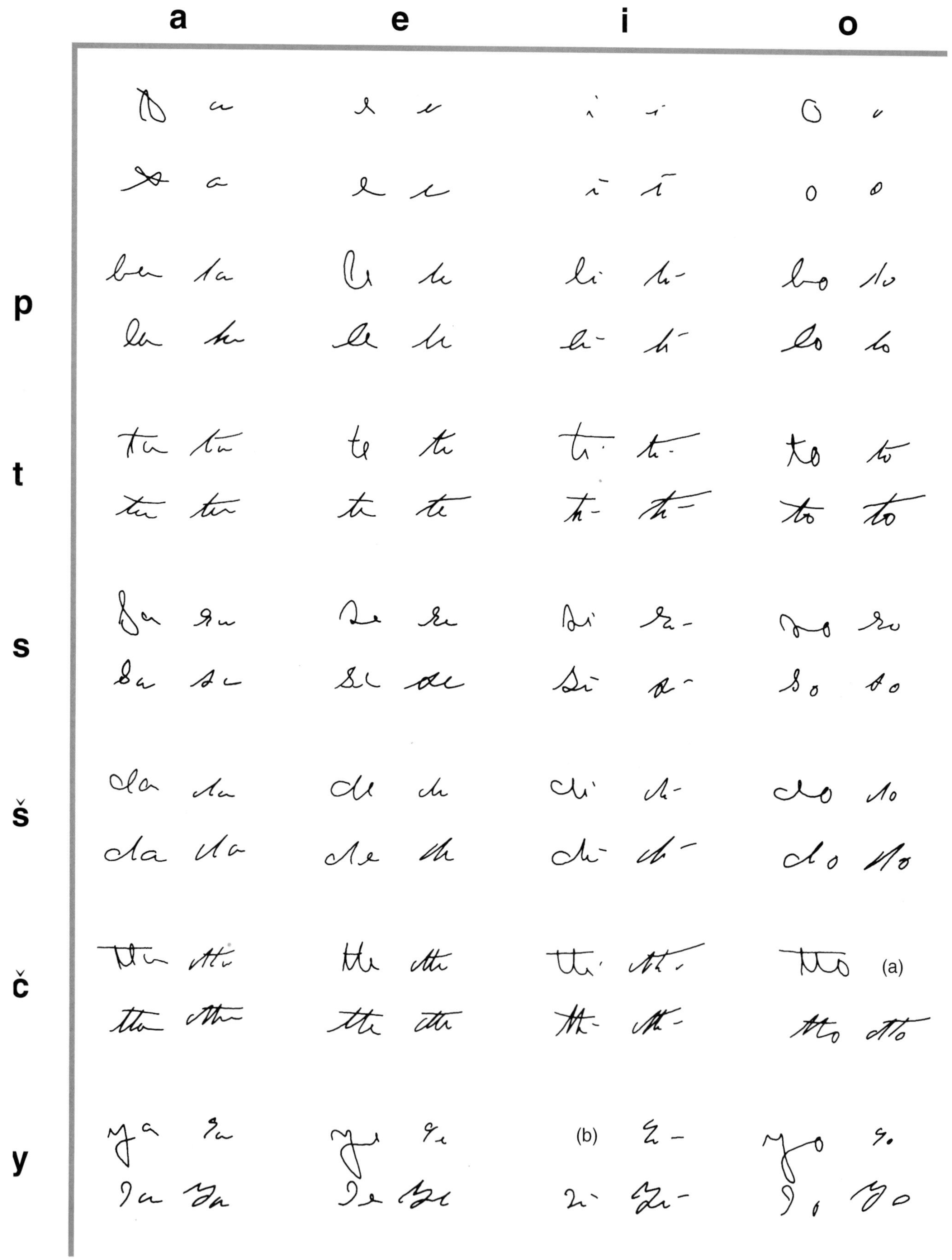
a e i o
p
t
s
š
č
(a)
y
(b)

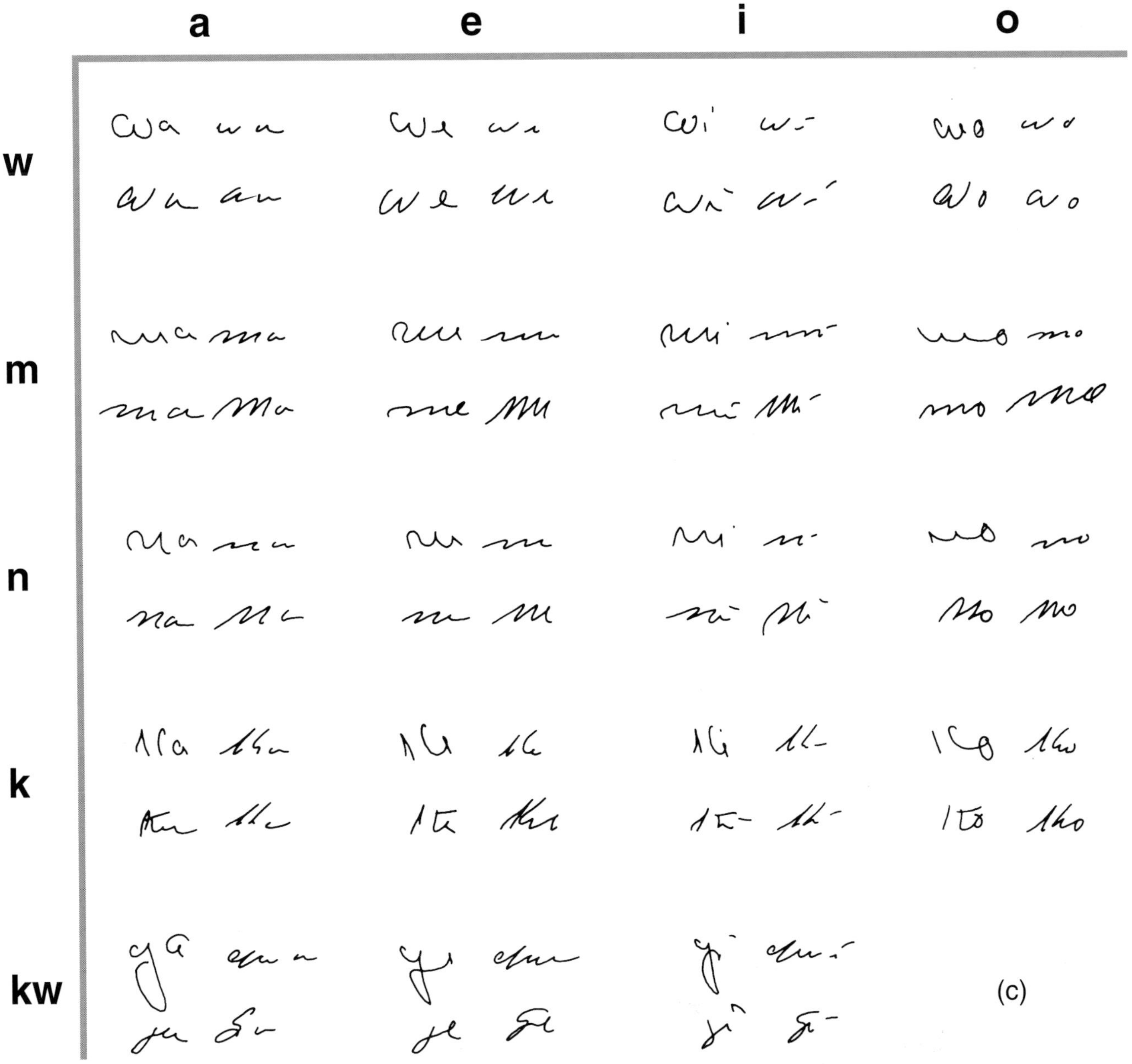

	a	**e**	**i**	**o**
w				
m				
n				
k				
kw				(c)

Notes: (a) No example found.

(b) ⟨yi⟩ does not write ⟨yi⟩, using ⟨ye⟩ instead.

(c) ⟨kwo⟩ occurs in syllabary matrices but is rare or absent in words; one example is known from Kiyana (perhaps a spelling error), but there are none from the other writers.

Smithsonian, NAA.

Fig. 10. The Fox (Mesquakie) syllabary (basic matrix). Each syllabic character indicates the combination of the consonant to the left of the row followed by the vowel at the top of the column (or, in the top row, the vowel by itself), with or without a preceding *h* and with either a long or short vowel (with some gaps). Hence the syllabic character ⟨a⟩ spells *a, a·, ha,* and *ha·,* and ⟨pa⟩ spells *pa, pa·, hpa,* and *hpa·.* The characters are illustrated by sets of four representative shapes from manuscripts written probably between 1912 and 1914 by four writers (clockwise from the top left in each set): Alfred Kiyana (b. 1877), Jim Peters (b. 1866), Charley H. Chuck (b. 1867), and Sakihtanohkweha (Mrs. Bill Leaf, b. 1875). There are additional matrices for syllables that have consonant combinations. To same scale but slightly reduced. Source for dates of birth: W. Jones (1939:121,123,127, 128).

pitch accent is phonemic and Kickapoo /θ/ and /s/ correspond to Fox /s/ and /š/, respectively. Accordingly, in the Kickapoo syllabary ⟨d⟩ represents /s/ and ⟨s⟩ represents /θ/. Also, capital ⟨A⟩ is not used for the syllable /a/. Otherwise it is identical to the Fox syllabary, although the Kickapoos living in Coahuila have acquired some Spanish spelling conventions, such as ⟨cu⟩ for /kw/ and ⟨ll⟩ for /y/.

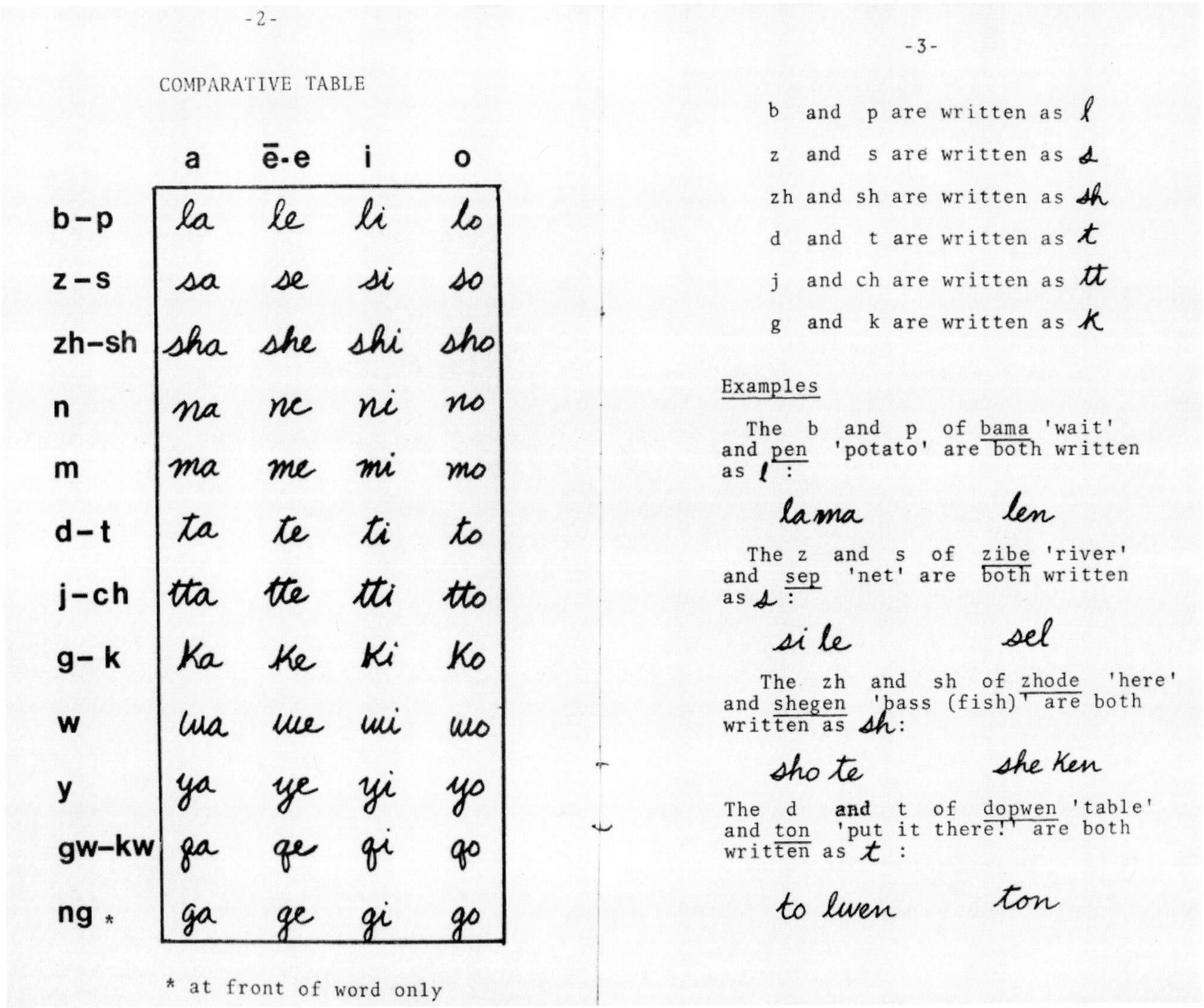

COMPARATIVE TABLE

	a	ē·e	i	o
b–p	*la*	*le*	*li*	*lo*
z–s	*sa*	*se*	*si*	*so*
zh–sh	*sha*	*she*	*shi*	*sho*
n	*na*	*ne*	*ni*	*no*
m	*ma*	*me*	*mi*	*mo*
d–t	*ta*	*te*	*ti*	*to*
j–ch	*tta*	*tte*	*tti*	*tto*
g–k	*Ka*	*Ke*	*Ki*	*Ko*
w	*wa*	*we*	*wi*	*wo*
y	*ya*	*ye*	*yi*	*yo*
gw–kw	*ga*	*ge*	*gi*	*go*
ng *	*ga*	*ge*	*gi*	*go*

* at front of word only

b and p are written as *l*

z and s are written as *s*

zh and sh are written as *sh*

d and t are written as *t*

j and ch are written as *tt*

g and k are written as *K*

Examples

The b and p of bama 'wait' and pen 'potato' are both written as *l* :

lama   *len*

The z and s of zibe 'river' and sep 'net' are both written as *s* :

si le   *sel*

The zh and sh of zhode 'here' and shegen 'bass (fish)' are both written as *sh*:

sho te   *she Ken*

The d and t of dopwen 'table' and ton 'put it there!' are both written as *t* :

to lwen   *ton*

Daniels and Daniels 1975a:2-3.

Fig. 11. The Potawatomi syllabary. These two pages explain the correspondences between the traditional syllabary and the phonemic practical orthography developed by the Wisconsin Native American Languages Project in 1974. In the practical orthography the letters ⟨b⟩, ⟨d⟩, ⟨j⟩, ⟨g⟩, ⟨'⟩, ⟨z⟩, ⟨zh⟩; ⟨p⟩, ⟨t⟩, ⟨ch⟩, ⟨k⟩, ⟨s⟩, ⟨sh⟩; ⟨e⟩, ⟨ē⟩ spell the phonemes *p, t, č, k, ʔ, s, š; pˑ, tˑ, cˑ, kˑ, sˑ, šˑ; ə, e*, respectively; the other letters spell phonemes written with the same respective letters.

Several other Fox orthographies have been reported, which make various substitutions for the consonant and vowel components of the syllables (W. Jones 1906:90-91; Michelson 1927). These variants were apparently used as secret writing and are not documented in manuscripts.

A page of a text illustrating the use of the Fox syllabary is in "Discourse," figure 3, this volume.

A chart of a twentieth-century Potawatomi version of the syllabary is reproduced in figure 11. Note that Potawatomi ⟨sh⟩ and ⟨q⟩ correspond to Fox ⟨d⟩ and ⟨g⟩. Cursive ⟨g⟩ appears in the Potawatomi orthography to represent word-initial /ng-/. Glottal stop (/ʔ/) is not indicated. A practical orthography developed for Potawatomi in 1974 made phonemic distinctions not indicated in the syllabary (fig. 12).

The Winnebago Syllabary

A version of the Great Lakes Algonquian syllabary, which must have been very similar to the later Fox syllabary, was learned by the Winnebagos in 1884. Some Winnebagos from Nebraska visited the Fox in Iowa, and one of them "acquired the alphabet, and became before long quite expert in its use, to his own amusement and that of his friends" (Fletcher 1890:299). Thus within a few weeks a writing system adapted to Fox, an Algonquian language, came to be used by the Siouan Winnebagos. "The knowledge spread rapidly among the Winnebagos of Nebraska, and also to that part of the tribe living in Wisconsin, so that at the present time the principal

WALKER

correspondence of the tribe takes place by means of these characters" (Fletcher 1890:299).

Winnebago literacy declined early in the twentieth century. Only a few people could read in 1912 (Radin 1954-1956, 1:21). Very few people in Wisconsin knew the syllabary in 1976, although Kenneth Miner (personal communication 1976) worked with one skilled writer.

According to Susman's (1943) phonemic analysis, spoken Winnebago has five oral vowels (*i, e, a, o, u*) and three nasalized vowels (*i̜, a̜, u̜*). Vowels are also phonemically either short or long and either stressed or unstressed. There are 20 consonants: six voiced stops and fricatives (*b, g, ǯ, z, ž, γ*); seven voiceless stops and fricatives (*p, t, k, č, s, š, x*); and seven resonants and glides (*m, n, w, r, y, h, ʔ*). There is a series of six glottalized consonants (*ṗ, k̇, č̇, ṡ, ṧ, ẋ*) (Radin 1949:6), interpreted as clusters of consonants plus /ʔ/ by Susman and effectively so treated by the native writing system.

In adapting the Fox orthography to their own language, the Winnebagos were faced with the problem of writing at least eight vowels (leaving aside the distinctions of length and stress) and 20 (or 26) consonants with an orthography that distinguished only four vowels and 10 consonants in Fox (Walker 1974). With regard to the vowels, their solution was to disregard the distinction between oral and nasalized vowels and also that between /o/ and /u/, as well as length and stress. Thus lower case cursive ⟨i⟩ represents /i, i̜/; ⟨e⟩ represents /e/; ⟨a⟩ represents /a/ and /a̜/; and ⟨o⟩ represents /o/, /u/, and /u̜/, all long or short. The voiced consonants that are paired with voiceless counterparts (*b, g, ǯ, z, ž, γ*) were written as cursive ⟨l⟩, ⟨k⟩, ⟨tt⟩, ⟨r⟩, ⟨d⟩, and ⟨x⟩, respectively. The letter resembling ⟨r⟩ corresponds to the ⟨s⟩ in the Fox syllabary, which also looks like an ⟨r⟩ in some Fox and Sauk hands; ⟨x⟩ is lacking in the Fox syllabary. Of the eight unpaired consonants, /m/, /n/, /w/, and /t/ are written, as in the Fox syllabary, with cursive ⟨m⟩, ⟨n⟩, ⟨w⟩, and ⟨t⟩, respectively. The consonant /r/ is written with a capital ⟨L⟩, and /y/ is written, as in Potawatomi and some Fox hands, with a cursive ⟨y⟩. The letter resembling a capital ⟨A⟩ in the Fox syllabary in older hands (spelling *a(·)* or *ha(·)*), appears in the Winnebago syllabary as the spelling of /h/ after vowels, but after one of the six letters that spell the paired consonants it marks the consonant as the voiceless member of the pair. Alternatively, voiceless /k/ is sometimes written with a special symbol resembling a capital ⟨K⟩. A consonant written without a linked vowel letter represents a consonant followed by an /a/-quality vowel. A glottalized consonant (or /Cʔ/ sequence) is indicated by a following ⟨a⟩ or a following sequence of two identical vowel letters. Initial glottal stop is not indicated.

The spelling conventions described above were used by Sam Blowsnake, whose version of the syllabary was well known to Paul Radin and Amelia Susman. Other writers used slightly different conventions. Kenneth Miner's consultant, in the 1970s, used the letter for /h/ to indicate that a preceding stop or affricate was voiceless but not to distinguish voiceless from voiced continuants. She wrote word-initial and postconsonantal /r/ as a capital ⟨L⟩, as did Blowsnake, but between vowels she wrote it as a cursive ⟨t⟩. Her spelling differed from Blowsnake's practice in several other particulars, which suggests that the spelling conventions used by nineteenth-century scribes may have varied also.

A sentence from a Winnebago syllabic text written by Sam Blowsnake illustrates the spelling conventions (Susman 1940):

⟨e tt ni ke Le de tto l A A Ke we A deke ny Le ra de⟩
ʔé·ža nigéreže žo·báha hakewehášge naíresʔáže
there somewhere.it.is four.times six.times.perhaps sleep.they
'Somewhere over there they sleep four or perhaps six times.'

The word *hakewehášge* could also be spelled ⟨A Ke we Ad ke⟩.

Cree-Montagnais and Ojibwa

Cree-Montagnais and Ojibwa are Algonquian language complexes spoken in some 200 communities—Cree-Montaignais across subarctic Canada from the Labrador coast to Alberta, Ojibwa in south-central Canada and the north-central United States (vol. 6:53-54). Cree-Montagnais comprises nine languages and Ojibwa seven, not all of which have names that identify them as varieties of Cree, Montagnais, or Ojibwa. Thus Attikamek (Tête de Boule), Mitchif, and Naskapi are varieties of Cree-Montagnais no less than the languages called East Cree, Plains Cree, and Woods Cree. Likewise, Algonquin, Saulteaux, and Ottawa are kinds of Ojibwa, no less than Central Southern Ojibwa, Eastern Ojibwa, and Severn Ojibwa. The lines between these languages and their dialects are complicated by the fact that there is a long history of bilingualism and bidialectalism among these peoples, often leading to the gradual replacement of one dialect (or language) by another in a given area.

Although the languages in each of these language complexes are similar, the discrepancies among them make it difficult to find an orthography that is acceptable to the speakers of all the languages in a given language complex. Also, resistance to standardized orthographies is stiffened by the fact that, while most Cree and Ojibwa speakers read English as a second, if not a first language, there are also Cree and Ojibwa communities that are literate in French, rather than

- 25 -

Lesson 8: ē

The letter **ē** stands for a sound

something like the e in the English

word mend. The sound of this letter

ē is different than the sound of

the letter **e** . Compare these

words:

migwen   (feather)

migwēn   (give it away!)

dēwē'gen   (a drum)

dēwē'gēn   (pound on it!)

The names of the objects below use

the letter **ē**. Write it in the blanks.

Be sure to make the mark on top of

it!

kw___   m__m__g___

Daniels and Daniels 1975:25.
Fig. 12. Lesson from a Potawatomi literacy primer explaining how to write the distinction between the vowels /e/ and /ə/. These vowels were both written as ⟨e⟩ in the traditional syllabary but were differentiated as ⟨ē⟩ and ⟨e⟩, respectively, in the practical orthography developed in 1974.

English. Thus Crees in the English-speaking area favor an English-based roman alphabet over a French-based one; but Attikamek (Cree) speakers and Algonquin (Ojibwa) speakers in southern Quebec do not share this preference. For a comparative table of roman orthographies used to write Ojibwa see volume 6:65.

Montagnais was probably the first variety of Cree-Montagnais to have a writing system. A Montagnais prayer book published by Rev. Jean Baptiste de La Brosse, perhaps the first book in a native language to be issued in Canada, was printed in 1767 ("The Description of the Native Languages of North America Before Boas," fig. 1, this vol.). La Brosse had 3,000 "books of alphabets" and 2,000 "books of prayers and catechism" printed in that year (Gaines 1929:142). La Brosse compiled the majority of the religious books that the Montagnais were using in the 1880s and translated considerable portions of the Bible into Montagnais (Taché 1884:116). Extensive native literacy in Montagnais resulted from La Brosse's efforts (Hébert 1979:424; Mailhot 1992).

By the late twentieth century the Montagnais in Quebec were using French loanwords and attending schools that complied with Quebec educational policies, whereas those in Labrador were using English loanwords and attending schools with quite different goals and orientations. For an account of the problems of maintaining a viable Montagnais literacy and establishing a standard orthography under such conditions see Mailhot (1985).

Many Cree communities, and many northern and western Ojibwa communities, are committed to the syllabic writing system developed by James Evans (b.1801, d. 1846), a Wesleyan Methodist missionary (Nichols 1996) (fig. 13). After first trying a roman orthography for Ojibwa (Evans 1837), Evans began experimenting with a writing system that used geometric shapes to represent syllables. As perfected in 1841 for writing Western Swampy Cree, this orthography used nine characters, each identified with a particular consonant or the absence of a consonant, in four different orientations, each associated with one of the four vowel qualities. Thus a given shape in a given orientation represented a particular vowel or consonant-vowel sequence. Diacritics were used to indicate /w/ and other additional features (Nichols 1984). Evans began printing Christian literature in Cree syllabics in 1840 at Rossville near Norway House, on Lake Winnipeg, at first using earlier versions of the syllabary. As superintendent of three other missionaries at widely separated posts in the Cree area, he subsequently disseminated syllabic literature and literacy through much of this region. His successor at Norway House, the Rev. William Mason, continued to print syllabic literature with the help of his wife Sophia, a native Cree speaker, publishing the entire Bible (fig. 14) (W. Mason 1861).

In the 1840s and 1850s syllabic literacy spread to most Cree and many Ojibwa communities. It was taught at mission schools and in hunting camps by Indian hunters. In the late twentieth century it was still widely used by the older generation (vol. 6:62). In the 1980s, in two Cree communities west of James Bay and two Ojibwa-speaking communities farther west, men over 45 and women over 30 were literate in syllabics, or in both syllabics and English. Men under 45 and women under 30 were literate in English, or in both English and syllabics. There was "nearly universal support for the script among Native people of all ages and a strong desire to maintain its use" (Bennett and Berry 1989:31).

Consonant	Vowels				Finals		
	e·	i, i·	o, o·	a, a·	West	East a-series	East i-series
none, h, ʔ	ᐁ	ᐃ	ᐅ	ᐊ	ᐦ	ᐦ	(ʔ) ᐃ
w (West)	ᐁᐧ	ᐃᐧ	ᐅᐧ	ᐊᐧ	ᐤ		
(East)	ᐌ	ᐎ	ᐒ	ᐗ		ᐤ	ᐤ or ·ᐃ
p	ᐯ	ᐱ	ᐳ	ᐸ	ᑊ	ᑉ	ᐱ
t	ᑌ	ᑎ	ᑐ	ᑕ	ᐟ	ᑦ	ᑎ
k	ᑫ	ᑭ	ᑯ	ᑲ	ᐠ	ᒃ	ᑭ
c	ᒉ	ᒋ	ᒍ	ᒐ	ᐨ	ᒡ	ᒋ
m	ᒣ	ᒥ	ᒧ	ᒪ	ᒼ	ᒻ	ᒥ
n	ᓀ	ᓂ	ᓄ	ᓇ	ᐣ	ᓐ	ᓂ
s	ᓭ	ᓯ	ᓱ	ᓴ	ᐢ	ᔅ	ᓯ
ŝ	ᔐ	ᔑ	ᔓ	ᔕ	ᐡ	ᔥ	ᔑ
y	ᔦ	ᔨ	ᔪ	ᔭ	•	ᔾ ᐤ	ᐃ
r (West)	ᕒᐁ	ᕒᐃ	ᕒᐅ	ᕒᐊ	ᕒ		
(East)	ᕃ	ᕆ	ᕈ	ᕋ		ᕐ	
l (West)	ᓬᐁ	ᓬᐃ	ᓬᐅ	ᓬᐊ	ᓬ		
(East)	ᓓ	ᓕ	ᓗ	ᓚ		ᓪ	
sk					ᔆ	ᔆ	
hk					ᕽ		

after Fiero 1985:98.

Fig. 13. The Cree syllabary, used to write some varieties of Cree-Montagnais and Ojibwa. A dot is placed above the appropriate syllabic character to indicate a distinctively long vowel (*i·*, *o·*, *a·*). The Western syllabary (also called the Plains Cree syllabary) is used in Eastern Swampy Cree communities from the Attawapiskat River north and west, and in communities speaking Western Swampy Cree, Plains Cree, Woods Cree, and Severn Ojibwa. This was the syllabary originated and used by James Evans. The Eastern (or Moose Cree) syllabary, which developed later, is used in Eastern Swampy Cree communities from the Albany River south (including the Moose Cree dialect) and in communities speaking East Cree and Central Southern Ojibwa (Northwestern and Central dialects).

The chart reproduced here is to some extent normative and especially intended for guidance in printed and keyboarded materials. There is a fair amount of subregional and individual variation in actual use, particularly in handwritten texts. For example, the Eastern Swampy Cree and Central Southern Ojibwa communities that use the Western syllabary for final consonants nevertheless write a preceding dot for /w/, as in the Eastern syllabary, and quite generally vowel length is not marked, or indicated only to avoid homographs.

This chart supersedes the one in vol. 6:63, which contains several errors.

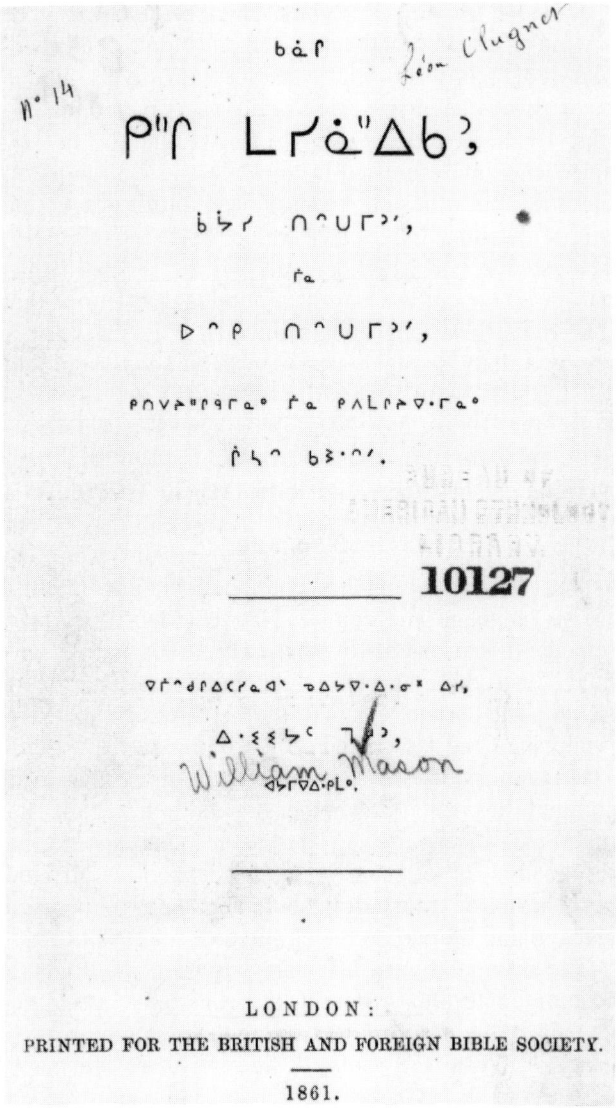

Smithsonian, Anthr. Lib.: W. Mason 1861.

Fig. 14. The title page of William Mason's Plains Cree Bible, printed in Western syllabics. Mason described the final revision of the translation as a collaborative effort of himself and his Cree wife, Sophia, while also acknowledging the assistance of Henry Steinhauer, an Ojibwa schoolmaster, and John Sinclair, a part-Cree interpreter (Pilling 1891:340). A revision of Mason's Bible was published in 1908 and has gone through many reprintings between then and 1983 (David H. Pentland, communication to editors 1995).

The transliteration of the syllabics on the title page is: ⟨kanāči kihči masināhikan, kāyāsi tistemint, mīna oski tistemint, kitipeyihčikeminaw mīna kipimāčiyiweminaw čīsas karyst. emīskočiitasinaak neiyawewinihk isi, willyam meson, ayamiewikimāw.⟩. In phonemic transcription this would be: *kana·či-kihči-masinahikan, kaya·si-tistemint, mi·na oski-tistemint, kitipe·yihčike·minaw mi·na kipima·čihiwe·minaw či·sas* [kráyst]. *e·=mi·škoči-itasinahahk ne·hiyawe·winihk isi,* [wílyəm méysən], *ayamihe·wikima·w.* 'The Holy Bible, Old Testament, and New Testament, of our Lord and Savior Jesus Christ. Translated into Cree by William Mason, minister.' The phonemicization of ⟨tistemint⟩ 'testament' is uncertain.

Syllabic literacy is a mark of ethnic identity. The script is identified with both sacred (vol. 6:61) and secular (vol. 6:64) activities, but not with myths, which have always been presented orally in native communities (Black-Rogers 1991:247). Native literacy is well entrenched and ramified in the Cree and Ojibwa communities, but it has not been allowed to infringe on the role of the story teller or the value of the spoken word. The esteem with which syllabic writing is regarded as part of native culture is reflected in local traditions that the syllabary was a gift made directly to the native people by a deity or other supernatural being (Bloomfield 1934:20-21; Bennett and Berry 1984:41).

By the 1950s most Cree-Montagnais and Ojibwa children were sent to boarding schools, where they were taught in either English or French. This led to a decline in native literacy and in fluency in the spoken languages among younger people, and this was perceived as threatening the continued viability of the native language and culture. Native groups sought to remedy this problem; by the early 1970s native language instruction was being integrated into school curricula. The Grand Council of the Crees of Quebec established the Cree Language Commission in 1990. The commission was authorized to survey the Cree communities, find out whether the children were learning Cree, discover who the people felt should be responsible for language maintenance, and identify the best means of transmitting both the spoken language and syllabic literacy to the children (Reid 1991).

The original Evans syllabary has been modified to accommodate the different varieties of Cree-Montagnais, many of which have more than the nine consonants of Western Swampy Cree, and there are many versions of the syllabary, which are only summarized in figure 13 (J.S. Murdoch 1981). Characters for /š/ (earlier used for Ojibwa), /l/, and /r/ were added in 1852 to write materials in the Moose dialect of Eastern Swampy Cree (Harper 1985:142, 153-155). Later, different characters for /l/ and /r/ were introduced for the more westerly varieties of Cree, chiefly to write foreign names, thus beginning the divergence between the western and eastern variants of the syllabary. The French Canadian Oblates of Mary Immaculate used the Western syllabary but with a third variety of characters for the /l/ and /r/ syllables (Thibault 1866; Lacombe 1886). The western and eastern syllabaries also differ in the position of the raised dot representing prevocalic /w/ and the symbols used to transcribe postvocalic consonants, referred to as "finals."

The Evans syllabary, and all subsequent variants of it, have one structural feature that can only have caused great difficulty for the many thousands of people who have struggled to become literate in Cree-Ojibwa syllabics. The characters are oriented not in accordance with any single pattern, but with two conflicting ones.

The characters for the vowels, /p/, /t/, or Eastern /r/ are oriented as follows: the /e/-column characters are rotated 180 degrees to form the /i/-column characters, which are rotated 90 degrees clockwise to form the /o/-column characters. And these are the mirror images of the corresponding /a/-column characters. A different set of relationships is found in the syllabics for /k/, /č/, /m/, /n/, /s/, /y/, and Eastern /l/. For these the /e/-column character is the mirror image of the /i/-column character, which is rotated 180 degrees to form the /o/-column character. And this is the mirror image of the /a/-column character. The mirror-image relationships between the characters in the /š/ row conform to this second pattern, but the /šo/ syllabic is the 90-degree rotation of the /še/ syllabic. Reading and writing Cree-Ojibwa syllabics, then, involves the identification of sounds with shapes that relate to one another in accordance with two contrasting patterns, or three patterns for the languages that have /š/.

Athapaskan

In the nineteenth century Robert McDonald, an Anglican Archdeacon at Peel River, designed an orthography for Kutchin and, with the help of a Kutchin woman named Ughaih, translated the entire Bible (McDonald 1886) (vol. 6:78), the Book of Common Prayer, and a selection of hymns into a standardized form of Eastern Kutchin that he called Tukudh (see Pilling 1892:57-60). In the 1970s McDonald's orthography was used for correspondence, and some older Han speakers also read the Tukudh Bible (vol. 6:506, 529).

A Kutchin revitalization movement took place around 1910. Its central figure, a former shaman named Albert Edward Tritt, preached the Christian gospel and taught McDonald's orthography (vol. 6:397). Kutchin was spoken by most children in each of several communities in 1980. A different orthography was designed for Western Kutchin by Richard Mueller of the Summer Institute of Linguistics in the 1960s, and a new Eastern Kutchin orthography was developed in the 1970s by the Department of Education, Yukon Territories.

Attempts were made in the nineteenth century to adapt Cree-Ojibwa syllabics to Athapaskan languages. William West Kirkby, an Anglican missionary who, early in his career, had adapted John Horden's Moose Cree hymnbook for use by the speakers of Western Swampy Cree at York Factory, published a Chipewyan "syllabarium" in 1881 (fig. 15). This orthography was evidently derived in part from the Cree syllabics used by the Oblates and differed in several respects from the Anglican syllabics. Kirkby's /l/ syllabics, for example, nearly match those of Thibault (1866) and Lacombe (1886) but are quite unlike the /l/ syllabics in Anglican orthographies.

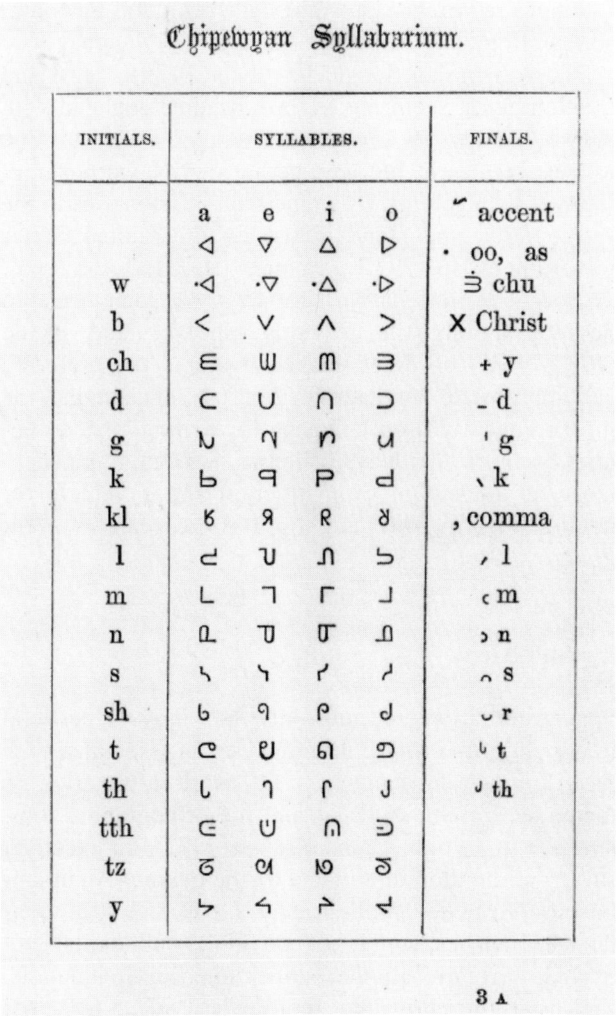
Chipewyan Syllabarium.
INITIALS.
SYLLABLES.
FINALS.
a e i o
accent
oo, as
chu
Christ
w
b
ch
d
g
k
kl
l
m
n
s
sh
t
th
tth
tz
y
y
d
g
k
comma
l
m
n
s
r
t
th
3 A

Smithsonian, Anthr. Lib.: Kirkby 1881.
Fig. 15. W.W. Kirkby's Chipewyan syllabary.

Kirkby's Chipewyan syllabics were read by Slavey speakers as well as by Chipewyans. Kari and Spolsky (1973:20) reported that a newspaper in Fort Simpson regularly published a page in the Slavey syllabary, and there was some letter writing in the Slavey syllabary.

Adapting the Cree-Ojibwa syllabary to Athapaskan languages is no easy task. Chipewyan, for example, has six vowels, so that one cannot specify each vowel, as in Cree, by selecting one of four orientations. Athapaskan languages also have many more consonants and consonant clusters than Cree. It is safe to say that no one would ever have suggested using syllabics for Athapaskan languages had it not been for the unparalleled prior success of the Cree syllabary. Nonetheless, both the Anglicans and the Roman Catholics wrote Chipewyan in syllabics and a native syllabic literacy took root. A letter written in syllabics in 1883 by two Chipewyan chiefs, Samuel Egon and Michel Deneyou, demonstrates the native use of the syllabary (vol. 6:81). Egon and Deneyou wrote the final /l/ in each of their Christian names with a small, raised ⟨s⟩, after the manner of the Oblate but not the Anglican, syllabaries.

In the mid-twentieth century roman orthography replaced syllabics for Chipewyan. Linguists associated with the Northern Canadian Evangelical Mission started a literacy program at Cold Lake, Alberta, and published a teaching grammar in the 1960s (vol. 6:81).

A completely reworked version of the Cree-Ojibwa syllabary was devised for Carrier by Adrien Gabriel Morice, a Roman Catholic priest in the Stuart Lake area of British Columbia. Morice (1889:166) reported that Indians were able to write and read the syllabary "after one or two weeks'. . . private instruction from others" (fig. 16).

Carrier prayer books, hymnbooks, and a newspaper were printed in the Morice syllabary. The prayer books were used at the Lejac Indian School at Fraser Lake, British Columbia, in the 1930s; copies were found in the possession of Babine speakers at Hagwilget by James Kari in 1973, but no one in the area was fully adept in the use of the syllabary. Only a few of the oldest speakers of Central Carrier could read the Carrier syllabary in the 1990s (William Poser, communication to editors 1995). Richard Walker of the Summer Institute of Linguistics found the Morice syllabary to be "19 letters short of a phonemic alphabet" (personal communication 1973) and devised a phonemic roman orthography for Carrier (R. Walker 1979; vol. 6:413), in which he and others have produced an English–Central Carrier dictionary, two primers, a grammatical sketch, and several readers. Bilingual literacy was being taught to 130 Central Carrier–speaking children by a native Carrier teacher at the Fort Saint James Roman Catholic school in the 1970s, and several of Walker's Carrier-speaking associates were literate in the phonemic orthography (fig. 17).

An enormous amount of literature in the Northern Athapaskan languages has been published in phonemic orthographies beginning in the 1960s by the Summer Institute of Linguistics, the Alaska Native Language Center of the University of Alaska, and the Alaska state-operated schools (see McGary 1979; Krauss and McGary 1980). These publications are in modified phonemic orthographies, which write some phonemes with digraphs. Thus ⟨ch⟩, for example, represents /č/ in Ingalik, Upper Kuskokwim, Kutchin, Tanacross, Tanaina, Lower Tanana, Upper Tanana (and also Haida and Tlingit). A few unit phonemes are written with trigraphs, as in the case of ⟨tth⟩, which appears in the Holikachuk, Ingalik, Kutchin, and Lower Tanana orthographies. Charts of the alphabets used for all these languages and for Ahtna and Koyukon may be found in the *Digest of Northern Learning Materials* (Anonymous 1974) distributed by the Alaska Native Language Center of the University of Alaska (and see the orthographic

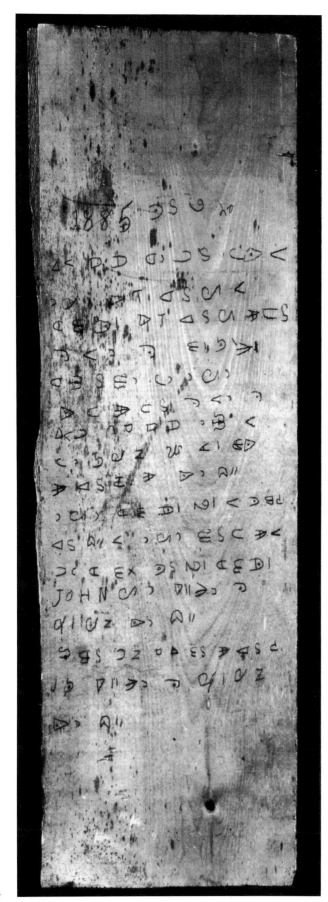

footnotes in vol. 6). This digest also contains an extensive bibliography of publications in these languages.

The Athapaskan languages of the Pacific coast and the Southwest seem not to have become engaged with native literacy to any great extent. Navajo has the longest history of literacy, perhaps. A Navajo orthography was developed by Franciscan missionaries in the early 1900s and standardized by the United States government in 1937 (Young 1977:460-465; vol. 10:666-667), but native literacy took some time to develop among the Navajos. Spolsky and Irvine (1982:74-75) observed that "Navajo is the preferred and appropriate language for oral use, and English the most frequently used language for writing." Nevertheless, by the 1990s Navajo literacy was gaining acceptance as a medium of instruction and a vehicle for cultural identity (McLaughlin 1992; Ciccarello 1984; Platero 1984).

Eskimo-Aleut

Space limitations permit only the most superficial treatment of the native writing systems associated with the Eskimo-Aleut languages. For more information on them, see volume 5:49-63 and the orthographic footnotes in that volume, and Krauss (1973), an excellent survey of the literature in and on the Eskimo-Aleut languages. Krauss's bibliography (1973:853-902) contains 855 entries, which include Soviet publications but exclude virtually all the publications in Greenlandic, said to number in the thousands (vol. 5:640-645; Berthelsen 1990, 1990a). See also McGary's (1979:62-145, 156-168) bibliography of educational publications for Eskimo-Aleut.

The West Greenlandic language is spoken by 91 percent of the inhabitants of Greenland and is supported by the schools, the mass media, the government, and by a viable and much diversified literature dating from the mid-seventeenth century (Krauss 1973:796, 842; R. Petersen 1990; Berthelsen 1990, 1990a; vol. 5:640-645). The writing system for most of this was based on a modification of Danish orthography made by Kleinschmidt (1851), which preserves morphophonemic distinctions that are no longer reflected in the surface phonology of the

Province of B.C., Heritage Properties Branch, Barkerville, B.C. (RG168-993.90.1).
Fig. 16. Graffiti in Carrier syllabics written on the wall of the Richfield, B.C., jail, dated 1885. One writer, signing himself John in Carrier and English, laments the evils of liquor, which has brought him a 3-month sentence for drunkenness. A second writer, Noolhi, complains that the jail is small (William Poser, communication to editors 1995). If the date is correct this would be the earliest example of written Carrier, predating Morice's first syllabic publications. The board with the graffiti was removed from the jail in 1914. Photograph by Lief Grandell, Barkerville, B.C., 1994.

178

left, The Children of Kingfisher Indian Day School 1970; right, Wilkinson and Martin 1976:46.

Fig. 17. Excerpts from 2 workbooks designed for use in schools with native literacy programs. left, 4 Cree words in syllabics, phonetic transcription, and English translation with associated drawings. A skidoo is a kind of snowmobile. From *Our Cree Dictionary* (The Children of Kingfisher Indian Day School 1970) made by grade school students at Kingfisher Lake, Ont., with the help of their teacher, R.V.F. Ryan, and Lydia Sakakeep. right, Carrier workbook (Wilkinson and Martin 1976). It has the readers fill in the missing letters in the blank in the top panel and choose the sentence in each of the righthand panels that best matches the illustration. (A similar page showing the use of ⟨sh⟩ in this orthography is in vol. 6:84.) Used by Carrier speakers in the Stuart Lake region of B.C., the orthography was developed by Richard Walker and David Wilkinson of the Summer Institute of Linguistics in the early 1970s.

spoken language and may have been archaic in Kleinschmidt's day. Krauss (1973:846) gives the example of ⟨-aigdl-⟩, ⟨-âvdl-⟩, ⟨-audtl-⟩, and other sequences, which are now all pronounced like ⟨-ādl-⟩ ([æ·ɬ]), and comments that "it is often difficult or impossible for the ordinary competent native speaker to figure out the underlying forms," which the spelling theoretically represents. Jonathan Petersen's (1968) monolingual Greenlandic dictionary provides a standard for spelling Greenlandic forms, but mounting pressure to revise the orthography, primarily by writing all long vowels and geminate consonants with double letters, culminated in an official spelling reform in 1972 (Krauss 1973:846-847; Grønlands Landsråds Forhandlinger. Efterårssamling 1972:210-228; vol. 5:595).

An orthography for the Labrador dialect of Eastern Canadian Inuit was developed in the eighteenth century by Moravian missionaries and later largely assimilated to the pre-1972 Greenlandic orthography. It preserves morphophonemic distinctions that are no longer made on the phonemic level of the spoken language. Although well established, it hampers written communication between the Labrador Eskimos and Eastern Canadian Inuit speakers in Quebec and the Central Arctic, who use two quite different orthographies, one an adaptation of the Cree syllabary and another based on the roman alphabet.

The Eskimo syllabary was devised by the Rev. E.A. Watkins and John Horden in 1865, on the basis of the syllabary Horden used for Moose Cree, which they had begun also using for the Inuit dialects of Arctic Quebec 10 years earlier (Harper 1985). It was widely disseminated by the scriptural translations and mission work of the Rev. Edmund J. Peck. In its original form (fig. 18) it failed to distinguish /q/ from /k/, /ŋ/ from /γ/ (both represented by the Cree /c/ characters), or any long vowels or geminate consonants from their simplex analogues. The four orientations of Cree characters were

	ā	e	o	u
	▽	△	▷	◁
p	∨	∧	>	<	‹
t	∪	∩	⟩	⊂	ᒡ
k	ᖴ	ρ	d	ᑫ	ᑊ
g	ᒉ	ᒋ	ᒍ	ᒡ	ᒻ
m	ᒲ	ᒥ	ᒧ	L	ᒼ
n	ᓄ	σ	ᓂ	ᓇ	ᓐ
s	ᔦ	ᔨ	ᔪ	ᔭ	ᔅ
l	ᕕ	ᕆ	ᕈ	ᕋ	ᕐ
y	ᓀ	ᕆ	ᕂ	ᕃ	
v	ᕝ	ᐱ	ᐳ	ᐸ	ᐯ
r	ᕗ	ᕿ	?	ᕐ	ᕚ

Butler and Tanner, The Selwood Printing Works, Frome, and London

Fig. 18. The traditional Eskimo syllabary as used in the publications of the Rev. Edmund J. Peck. The columns in Lewis's 1904 chart, reproduced here, are labeled with the vowels as spelled in the English-based roman orthography used by the Anglicans for Cree; their values in Inuit, from left to right, are: /ai/, /i/, /o/, and /a/. The smaller characters in the column at the right are for indicating syllable-final consonants, but they are omitted in most vernacular writing. The ⟨k⟩ characters were used for both /k/ and /q/, the ⟨g⟩ characters for /γ/ and /ŋ/, and the ⟨r⟩ characters for /ɣ̇/. West of Hudson Bay the ⟨r⟩ characters were not used (Thibert 1958:viii), the ⟨g⟩ characters being written also for /ɣ̇/.

preserved in the Eskimo syllabary but, as there are only three vowel phonemes in Canadian Inuit, the extra column of syllabics, corresponding to those with Cree /eˑ/, was used to represent syllables with the diphthong /ai/. Watkins and Horden introduced reduced forms of the /a/-column syllabics to indicate syllable-final (nonprevocalic) consonants, a convention Horden then adopted for writing Moose Cree (Murdoch 1981:35-36, 308; Harper 1985:151-152). (These finals are normally omitted in native manuscripts and vernacular printing.)

The fact that Eastern Canadian Inuit has no /š/ allowed Watkins and Horden to omit the /š/ row of syllabics, a happy circumstance since, as mentioned earlier, the orientations of /š/ syllabics do not conform to either of the patterns governing the other rows in the Moose Cree syllabary. Horden's /f/ character, used only in foreign words and names, was adopted in the Eskimo syllabary for the phoneme /v/.

Literacy in the Eskimo syllabary has long been widespread among Inuit speakers in all areas of Canada other than Labrador and the Mackenzie District (vol. 4:280; vol. 5:468, 494, 496, 674), although this literacy has never been supported by the schools (Krauss 1973:833). The Canadian government, the provincial government of Quebec, and church organizations, notably the Oblates of Mary Immaculate, have all published books and periodicals in the syllabary. In 1976 Inuit Tapirisat of Canada, the Canadian Inuit political and cultural umbrella organization, adopted a revised syllabary incorporating modified characters for writing syllables with /q/, /ŋ/, and /ɬ/ and the use of the superior dot to indicate long vowels, and eliminating the earlier /ai/ column (Dorais 1990:238-241; Nichols 1996:607). A standardized roman orthography was adopted at the same time. These "ITC" orthographies have been widely accepted, except in Labrador, with a few local demurrers on details (Dorais 1990:241-242). The ITC roman orthography grew out of one developed under the sponsorship of the Canadian government by G.R. Lefebvre (1957) and R.C. Gagné (1961). Gagné used as a point of departure his phonemic analysis of the Eastern Canadian Inuit dialect of Inukjuak (Port Harrison) on the east coast of Hudson Bay.

In Alaska the speakers of Inupiaq are committed to a phonemic roman orthography devised by Roy Ahmaogak and others in the 1940s and modified by Ahmaogak and Donald Webster in the 1960s. The Ahmaogak-Webster orthography, with the substitution of the letter ⟨q⟩ for ⟨k̇⟩, was accepted as the standard by a conference of Inupiaq representatives at Fairbanks in 1972 (Krauss 1973:831). Thus the Inuit-Inupiaq-speaking area stands divided into four orthographic areas: northern Alaska, Greenland, and Labrador, each with its respective roman orthography, and the rest of Canada, with an emergent roman orthography and (outside the Mackenzie region) syllabary, both showing some local variation.

Farther west, four more Eskimo-Aleut languages are spoken in North America: Central Siberian Yupik, on Saint Lawrence Island; Pacific Yupik, on the Alaska Peninsula and in Cook Inlet and Prince William Sound; Central Alaskan Yupik; and Aleut (vol. 5:50). For a brief description of Saint Lawrence Island Yupik phonology, an orthography and literature produced by the Alaska Native Language Center at the University of

Alaska in 1972 and thereafter, and the consequent spread of native literacy on the island, see Krauss (1973:820-821) and Anonymous (1974). Pacific Yupik is also represented in Krauss (1973:827-829) and McGary (1979:72-76, 157), which provide details of the phonology, of literacy, and of the literature in this language. The title page of Ilia Tyzhnov's Pacific Yupik primer of 1848, written in a Cyrillic orthography, is reproduced in "The Description of the Native Languages of North America Before Boas," figure 10, this volume.

Information on Central Alaskan Yupik phonology, orthography, literature, and literacy may be found in Krauss (1973:821-827), Anonymous (1974), McGary (1979: 77-98, 157-159), and "Sketch of Central Alaskan Yupik, an Eskimoan Language," this volume.

A syllabic orthography for Central Alaskan Yupik was devised by a speaker of the Kuskokwim dialect named Uyaquq ('Neck') shortly after 1900. Prior to that time he wrote the language with an ideographic system, apparently based on traditional pictographs, to which he began to add qualifying signs to generate words that his ideographs could not otherwise specify. The first eight pages of Uyaquq's notebook document a gradual shift from a purely ideographic system to a system in which some words are represented by ideographs for phonologically similar words but are further specified by additional symbols for syllables, most often in word-final position. A ninth page is blank; but the remainder of the notebook is in a completely syllabic orthography that became more and more consistent and refined through time. The earlier form of the orthography was adopted and used by two other men, Qavarliaq and Wassillie; and the fully developed syllabary was learned by several younger Yupik men and continued to be read as late as the mid-1980s (Henkelman and Vitt 1985:369). A second syllabic orthography, based on the same principles as Uyaquq's but with radically different symbols, was devised by Isaac (Qiatuaq) after a visit to Uyaquq's village during which he saw Uyaquq's manuscript while it was read to him. At least one other orthography, used by elderly women in the Kotzebue sound area, may be derived from an early version of Uyaquq's system (Schmitt 1951:172-177, table 5). For information on all these writing systems and their interrelationships, see Schmitt (1951) and references cited therein.

Uyaquq was exposed to English cursive writing through his second son, Hermann, who learned to write English at the Bethel Mission station, on the Kuskokwim River, sometime before his death in 1905-1906 at age 16. Hermann taught his father to write a few words, such as *Jesus,* in cursive English script, but Uyaquq did not learn the significance of individual letters. It is evident from his manuscript that he used words in English script to represent, not words in spoken English, but corresponding words in Yupik, since they appear together with symbols indicating Yupik inflectional suffixes (Schmitt 1951:105-106). Not knowing the English orthography, he invented his own; or, as he told Rev. John Hinz, "Because I was so stupid, God gave it to me" (Schmitt 1951:105). Qiatuaq also described his own orthography as a sudden gift of God (Schmitt 1951:163). Figure 19 consists of several passages showing the development of Uyaquq's writing style from pictographs to a syllabic system.

The first Central Alaskan Yupik novel, *Elnguq* by Anna W. Jacobson, was published in 1990.

Aleut was traditionally written in a modified Cyrillic orthography developed, with the help of Aleut coworkers, by Ivan Veniaminov, a Russian Orthodox priest who lived on Unalaska Island from 1824 to 1834 (Geoghegan 1944:91; Ransom 1946:49; Marsh and Swadesh 1951:211; vol. 4:507-510; "The Description of the Native Languages of North America Before Boas," fig. 9, this vol.). Some of the earliest literature printed in Aleut Cyrillic was translated by native Aleuts and Aleut-Russian Creoles, including Innokentii Shaiashnikov for Eastern Aleut and Iakov Netsvetov and Lavrentii Salamatov for the Western Aleut dialect of Atka. They "translated the Gospels and other religious material, and established the foundation for written literature in Aleut, in a Slavonic alphabet which they adapted very well to the needs of Aleut, including e.g. special symbols for the uvulars and voiceless continuants" (Krauss 1973:803).

Both Cyrillic and roman orthographies were used in Aleut native literacy programs begun in the 1970s. For a bibliography of Aleut educational materials see McGary (1979:62-71, 156). Figure 20 shows the Aleut phonemes as written in Knut Bergsland's roman orthography and in the Cyrillic alphabet developed by Veniaminov and his coworkers. The Cyrillic letter for /ŋ/ combines the Cyrillic letters corresponding to roman ⟨n⟩ and ⟨g⟩, and the letter for /q/ is the Cyrillic letter corresponding to roman ⟨k⟩ with an added stroke.

Ransom (1945) describes the history of native Aleut literacy, which dates from the 1820s and 1830s, when Veniaminov developed the Cyrillic orthography, produced a printed literature, and trained men as native "readers" to read sacred texts in church services. Prior to the acquisition of the Aleutian Islands by the United States, native literacy was taught in boys' schools associated with each of the Russian Orthodox churches in the islands. Thereafter, the orthography was used in both sacred and secular contexts, principally by men, who traditionally passed on this skill to their male *ana·qisan* 'younger friends and protegés'. After the end of the Russian period, native literacy was vigorously opposed and suppressed by church and federal authorities until the 1970s, by which time the number of native Aleut speakers had dropped "well below 1,000" and

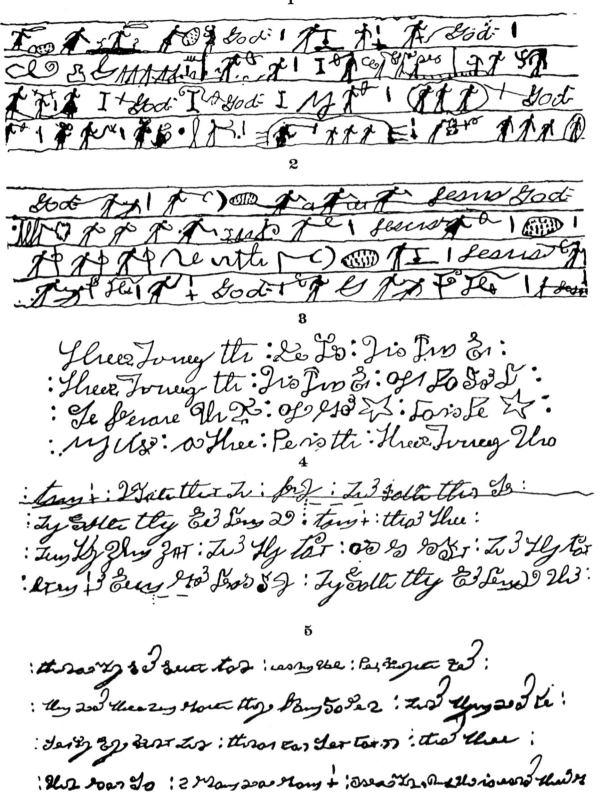

Henkelman and Vitt 1985:370.

Fig. 19. Examples of Uyaquq's writing showing the development from pictures to a syllabic system. Uyaquq (b. ca. 1860, d. 1924) was the son of an Alaskan Yupik shaman who converted to Christianity in the 19th century. Uyaquq also became a Christian and worked with Moravian missionaries as a preacher and missionary among his fellow Yupiks. He developed his writing system 1895-1905 to enhance his ability to teach Christianity to the native people in the Kuskokwim region (Henkelman and Vitt 1985:366-373).

CONSONANTS

p	t	č	k	q
p	t	ch	k	q
П	Т	Ч	К	К

v	δ	z	ɣ	ɣ̇
v	d	z	g	ĝ
В	Д	З	Г	Г

f		s	x	x̣
f		s	x	x̂
Ф		с	Х	Х

m	n		ŋ
m	n		ng
М	Н		Нг

M	N		Ŋ
hm	hn		hng
М̃	Н̃		Н̃г

l	r
l	r
Л	Р

ł
hl
Л

w	y
w	y
Ў	Ѧ ya(·), Ю yu(·); Ь (a)

W	Y	h
hw	hy	h
(b)	(b)	Ҁ

VOWELS

i	u	i·	u·
i	u	ii	uu
И	У	И́	У́

a		a·
a		aa
Ѧ		Ѧ́

Notes:

a) Soft sign.

b) Sometimes marked with the diacritic for *h* but not consistently distinguished from *w* and *y*.

Fig. 20. Aleut orthographies: phonemic (top row in each set), roman practical (middle row), and Aleut Cyrillic (bottom row). Not all phonemes (or letters) are used in all dialects. The Aleut Cyrillic orthography used in Russian Orthodox writings was based on the Slavonic forms of the Cyrillic alphabet (Russian *tserkovnaia pechat′* 'ecclesiastical letters') rather than the modern Russian forms *(grazhdanskaia pechat′* 'civil letters'). The Cyrillic letters reproduced here are from a late reprinting of Veniaminov and Netsvetov's *Rudiments of Christian Doctrine* (1893), except for those for the voiceless nasals; the letters for *M* and *N* are from Veniaminov's Aleut grammar (1846a:5), in which he used mostly Russian letter forms, and the one for *Ŋ*, which he does not list, is composed on their model. The diacritic used to indicate *h*, the voiceless resonants (*M, N, Ŋ, ł*), and the back-velar fricatives (*x, ɣ̇*) was originally in the shape of a smooth breathing ('), as seen here in the letters for the voiceless nasals, later like a rounded circumflex, and sometimes written as a macron, but as an indication of voicelessness it was often omitted. Atkan *z* was sometimes written as ⟨s⟩ or as ⟨s⟩ with a circumflex or other diacritic. The acute accent indicates vowel length, though not consistently, and also sometimes the nondistinctive stress. Under *y* the table gives the Slavonic vowels ⟨i͡a⟩ and ⟨i͡u⟩, used for the sequences ya(·) and yu(·) (with and without the acute accent to mark vowel length), and the soft sign, used in combination with these vowels after a consonant; these vowel letters were also commonly used for the plain vowels without *y* after ⟨l⟩ and ⟨s⟩. The voiced stops (*b* [sometimes spirantized], *d, g*), found in foreign names and loanwords, are written with the corresponding Cyrillic letters, with *d* and *g* thus spelled the same as δ and γ. The foreign vowels *e* and *o* are written as in Russian. The table does not cover some details of spelling and omits the Slavonic hard sign, a letter resembling a ⟨z⟩ written after every word-final consonant (vol. 5:161; Bergsland 1959:9, 1994:vxi-xvi). The roman practical and Cyrillic orthographies also include capital letters.

Fig. 21. Native writing programs in action. left, Rev. William J.R. James, Anglican missionary, conducting classes at Baker Lake, Chesterfield Inlet, N.W.T., for Caribou Eskimo children. He is using the Eskimo syllabary. Photograph by George Hunter, March 1946. right, Sam Hair, Cherokee, demonstrating the Cherokee writing system. Photographed at Wesleyan U., Middletown, Conn., 1967.

native literacy had been almost completely eradicated (Krauss 1973:803). Prior to the 1970s, there was no secular Aleut literature in print. As late as the 1930s there had been an extensive manuscript literature on secular topics (Ransom 1945:340), but most of this was destroyed during the Aleut relocations in World War II.

The Cyrillic Aleut orthography became the basis for a native semaphore system used between the two world wars ("Nonspeech Communication Systems," this vol.).

Luiseño

Despite the fact that it has never come into general use by Luiseño speakers, the orthography of Pablo Tac deserves mention. Tac (b. 1822, d. 1841), wrote several manuscripts, including a grammatical sketch and a fragment of a Luiseño-Spanish dictionary (Tac 1926; Tagliavini 1930; Kroeber and Grace 1960:214-215, 221-237). Tac's orthography was based on Spanish, the five vowels of Luiseño /a/, /e/, /i/, /o/, /u/ being represented as in Spanish. Doubled vowels were sometimes written to indicate vowel length, and doubled consonants seem to have been used to indicate that a preceding vowel was short and accented (Kroeber and Grace 1960:223-224). The Luiseño distinctions between /k/ and /q/, /s/ and /š/, and /n/ and /ŋ/, none of which is indicated in Spanish orthography, were neatly and efficiently preserved by Tac's device of writing a diacritic over ⟨c⟩ (before ⟨a⟩, ⟨o⟩, ⟨u⟩) and ⟨qu⟩ (before ⟨i⟩ or ⟨e⟩) to indicate the backed velar stop /q/, over ⟨s⟩ to indicate the backed fricative /š/, and over ⟨n⟩ to indicate the velar nasal /ŋ/, as distinct from /k/, /s/, and /n/, respectively.

Place-Names

PATRICIA O. AFABLE AND MADISON S. BEELER*

The native peoples of North America named their physical environment with a dense blanket of place-names. In some areas, where it has been possible to interview native speakers still living on their aboriginal lands, extensive lists of these names have been compiled, and much has been learned about the system of naming they reflect and the cultural knowledge they incorporate. In other areas, place-names of Indian origin may survive only as borrowed into English or another Euro-American language, and their original form and signification may be unknown or uncertain.

Where place-names can be accurately analyzed within their language of origin, they can throw light on the history, cultural attitudes, and values of the people that used them. Names of particular topographical features frequently survive their source language by centuries and may shed light on the existence and distribution of languages or dialects no longer spoken. In many parts of North America, toponyms of American Indian origin are often all that remain of a region's aboriginal languages and are an important part of local historical lore. Because the history of people's intimate relationships with their environment is often reflected in how they named their surroundings, political movements that seek to document land and other resource claims for native peoples, especially in the Arctic, Subarctic, Northwest, and Southwest regions, have utilized and supported place-name studies.

Place-names reflect and to an important extent constitute a detailed, encyclopedic knowledge of the environment, and they have much to tell about how native peoples perceive, communicate about, and make use of their surroundings. Place-names provide insight about what areas, points, land routes, and waterways native peoples considered significant and how they organized perceptions of their territory and space in general. They named prominent landmarks and places that were important for the plants, animals, and other resources found there. Other names indicate the sites of recurring activities or of singular events involving members of the community or supernatural figures. The clustering of toponyms in certain areas typically reflects the cultural importance of these areas, particularly for ritual and subsistence activities (figs. 1–2). The antiquity of names is associated with continued use of particular resources and offers information about the geographical extent and intensity of these activities.

Many writers have noted the highly descriptive nature of American Indian toponyms. Basso (1988:110) likens Cibecue Apache place-names to "mental pictures" that have great evocative power because of how their constituent parts point precisely to the features of the landscape that are being described. In his Aleut linguistic studies, Bergsland (1959:18-19, 1994:587-653) illustrates the high level of detail and discriminatory quality conveyed by place-names where the communication of highly specific knowledge about the environment is a prerequisite to human survival (fig. 3). The Aleut names that directly describe the nature of a place single out features such as darkness, landmarks, volcanic activity, currents, winds, and the quality of the shore and bottom, important considerations for landing skin boats. Sounds, such as echoes and the noise of tide rips, crucial factors in foggy weather, are described in place-names. Among names that refer to navigation and transportation, some indicate the possibility of landing on an island, or walking or carrying something across it. The large group of Aleut names that have ecological referents indicate especially the presence of objects necessary for work and subsistence (including water, flint, slate, land and sea plants, and all animals in the Arctic diet). Comparative names in Aleut point to resemblances of landscapes to parts of the human body, parts of the kayak, or to various implements. An equally comprehensive study, set in the contrasting environment of the Southwest, is Harrington's (1916) work on Tewa ethnogeography.

Studies of geographical knowledge also demonstrate the great extent of this expertise within certain communities and among certain individuals. The American Indians traveled over an extensive network of trails across the continent, for trade, visiting, and warfare; and they were knowledgeable about places far beyond their home regions (Bergsland 1959; Harrington 1916; Hunn 1994; Kari 1989, 1994). The most noted example of this ability was a Tanaina speaker of Upper Cook Inlet, Shem Pete, who was familiar with an area of approximately 13,000 square miles and listed 600

---

*The original version of this chapter submitted in 1974 by Beeler, who died in 1989, was corrected and revised by Afable, who added the section on sources.

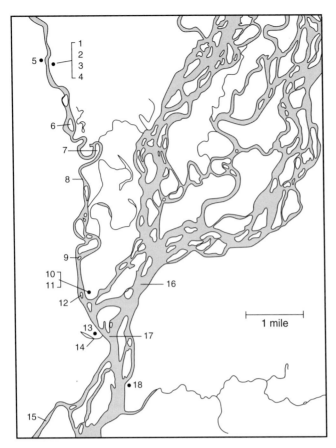

after Kari and Fall 1987:158.

Fig. 1. Density of Upper Inlet Tanaina place-names along a six-mile stretch of Kroto Creek and the area of its confluence with the Susitna River, Alaska. In addition to cemetery and settlement sites, place-names here derive from fishing, foraging, trapping, food-preparation activities, and the objects associated with them, including boats, caches, traps, fences, smokehouses, and charcoal. Kroto Village, the last Tanaina village on the Susitna River, was abandoned in the late 1930s. Sites on lower Kroto Creek: 1, *ƙiyɣ̓ayɣ̓akt* 'where fish is harvested'; 2, *nunucahdnulčet* 'where a fish fence was put across'; 3, *čaqenq̇akda* 'shabby smokehouse'; 4, *hčił nuɣiƙat* 'fish fence extends down' (1-4 were at a fish trap, fish camp, and old village location); 5, *cał dudidaht* (?) 'where coffins fall down', a cemetery site; 6, *tayin beq̇e tiytalyaši* 'fish trap floats upon it'; 7, *sdaƙdali* 'point that extends'; 8, *tuqentnu* 'clear water creek' or *dašq̇e betnu* 'on the bar creek', Kroto Creek (also called Deshka River); 9, *ƙčan beq̇e ʇełihi* (?) 'where grass is gathered'; 10, *ġis beq̇e ʇełihi* (?) 'where celery is gathered'; 11, *ƙɣučelyašt* 'butchering place'; 12, *ƙceł uq̇e ʇełihi* 'on it fish spreader sticks are gathered'; 13, *dašq̇e* 'on the bar', Kroto Village; 14, *ʇeł qelčentnu* 'fart smell creek'; 15, *beq̇e tačitqeyi q̇eɣci* 'slough where we sink into the water', Kroto Slough; 16, *susitnu* 'Susitna R.'; 17, *dašq̇e kaq̇* 'on the bar mouth', mouth of Kroto Creek; 18, *qektełčet* 'where fish swim over ripples', a boat-landing site. The locations of the queried names are approximate. Information obtained in the early 1980s by James Kari from Shem Pete and Katherine Nicolie (Kari and Fall 1987:153-169).

(1977:125-137). The distribution of toponyms, the analysis of their meanings, and the patterns of place-naming can contribute to the recovery of information on foraging, fishing, and hunting strategies and long-term land-use activities and on political organization, settlement boundaries, prehistoric travel and migration routes, and language contact (Bouchard and Kennedy 1979, 1984; Booker, Hudson, and Rankin 1992; Correll 1976; Ellanna and Balluta 1992; Gudgel-Holmes 1991; Hunn 1994; Kari 1989, 1989a; Kinkade 1967; Moore 1993; Ritter 1976a; Sapir 1907; vol. 11:103). Connections between toponymic density and distribution and demography and social differentiation are explored by Basso (1984a) and Hunn (1994).

Place-names also form a significant part of the oral traditions that are a major source of knowledge and instruction for members of the community. Geographic landmarks serve as mnemonic as well as symbolic devices in conversation and story-telling in many cultures (fig. 5). Historical tales, children's stories, myths, and invocations, important in many societies for teaching about the relationships of ancestors to the land and people, often contain specialized ritual knowledge about sacred sites and landscapes (vol. 11:407, 644, 645). A selection of studies devoted to the cognitive, metaphorical, and verbal artistic qualities of place-naming includes Arima (1976), Basso (1984, 1984a, 1988), Boas (1934), Farnell (1995), Haile and Oakes (1957), Hartley (1981), Kalifornsky (1977), Kari (1989), Kelley and Frances (1994), Momaday (1974), Palmer (1988), Parks and Wedel (1985), Reckord (1983), Rundstrom (1991, 1993), Yoke (1934-1937), and Young and Morgan (1954:10-17).

Studies of aboriginal place-names exist for only a few regions of North America and vary widely in coverage and quality. In general, studies for languages that have not been spoken for some years in their aboriginal areas have been possible only by using secondary sources, including dictionaries and textual and other linguistic studies that may not address the specific analytical problems presented by the names. As a consequence examples of reliably analyzed place-names are relatively scarce from the Northeast, Southeast, and Plains, although extensive studies are available for the history of the use of such place-names after being borrowed into English. In contrast, in other areas of the continent intensive fieldwork was done over the last two or three decades of the twentieth century with interested and knowledgeable native speakers, especially in the Arctic, Subarctic, and the Southwest, and reliably analyzed examples from these regions are plentiful. There is a comparable unevenness in the sources cited for the different parts of the continent, but a detailed evaluation of all the references mentioned has not been undertaken.

Tanaina names of places he knew in the region (Kari and Fall 1987). About 1,000 place-names, remembered by Tanaina speakers in the Kenai Peninsula, are collected by the native Tanaina writer Peter Kalifornsky

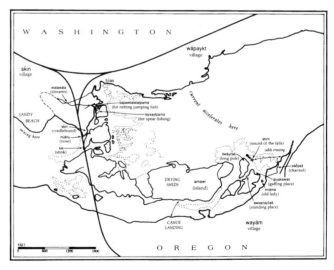

bottom left, Oreg. Histl. Soc., Portland: 25953; bottom right, Hunn 1991:173.

Fig. 2. Sahaptin names for Celilo Falls fishing sites on the Columbia River. There are 15 named fishing sites within a single square mile of the falls, an area where many Plateau tribes gathered to fish, primarily for salmon. The majority of names denote the type of fishing practice appropriate for each location, describe physical attributes of the places, including sound, smell, and rock shapes, or refer to mythological or ritual figures (Hunn 1991:172-173). top, View from the Oregon side looking toward Klickitat Hill in Washington state. At far left is Wishram Bridge, part of the Burlington Northern Railroad system. Photograph by Gladys Seufert, 1950-1956. bottom left, View of drying sheds and temporary dwellings along the Oregon river banks. Photographer and date not recorded. bottom right, Celilo Falls community and fishing sites of the 1930s, as remembered in 1987 by James Selam, a Columbia River Sahaptin; names of village sites are in larger type without glosses. The Celilo Falls area was flooded by the Dalles Dam in 1957.

187

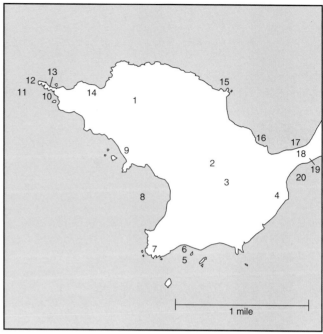

left, Dept. of Commerce, NOAA, Natl. Geodetic Survey, Silver Spring, Md.; right, after Bergsland 1994:636.

Fig. 3. Aleut place-names in the west end of Atka (*atχaχ*). left, The westernmost peninsula of Atka Island, Alaska, which except for the peak (*kiγun*) and the hill (*qaˑγa*) that dominate its landscape largely appears barren and featureless. Even so, Bergsland (1994:637) recorded a total of 20 place-names here, including 17 along its 6-mile coastline, denoting a former village, bights, lagoons, landing spots, and other points crucial to navigation. right, Key map of western Atka showing the locations of the named sites: 1, *kiˑγun* 'mountain', Cape Kigun; 2, *atχam aŋtaˑ* 'the end of Atka', a peninsula; 3, *qaˑγa* 'epithelium (of sea lion gut)', a hill with a speckled surface; 4, *atχam ača* 'mouth of Atka', a beach and ancient village; 5, *ŋam uŋluˑ* 'south pinnacle'; 6, *uŋim udaˑ* 'the bay of *uŋi-*'; 7, *ŋam hidaluˑ* 'south cape'; 8, *atχam aŋtan udaˑ* 'the bay of the end of Atka'; 9, *čuγaγliχ*, a rocky beach; 10, *uχtasuχ* 'as if lanced', a small lagoon under a rocky wall with a scarlike feature; 11, *txasis* 'tight —', Atka Pass, a passage known for tidal rips and strong currents; 12, *hadas*, a group of rocks; 13, *hadaŋin yaˑγa* 'the point of the *hadas*'; 14, *kmisχa(m)-tuγimaγa* 'the long beach of *kmisχa-*'; 15, *tuŋluqas*, group of two big and several small rocks; 16, *kasami(m)-čuγuˑ* 'eider duck sand', a bight; 17, *čuγuˑγiχ uγaluχ* 'northern spear', Kigun Bay; 18, *atχam ačan sisxi* 'the portage of *atχam ača*'; 19, *čalaˑluχ* 'place for getting ashore', a bight and a beach with big rocks; 20, *ŋuˑγiχ uγaluχ* 'southern spear', a bay. left, Photograph by Edwin D. Hawbecker, Sept. 1957.

Amer. Mus. of Nat. Hist., New York: 126209.

Fig. 4. The Old Village, Yakutat, Alaska. Its Tlingit name, *qaˑγacχaˑkʔaˑn*, was translated by one of John P. Harrington's informants as 'town between a person's thighs', a reference to its location between two long hills. In the historic period the town was renamed *qaˑχaśχaˑkʔaˑn* 'town between the ends of a person's mandible' because the original name came to have "a bad sound" (Jeff Leer, personal communication 1995). Photograph by George T. Emmons, 1915.

Natl. Park Service, Nez Perce Natl. Histl. Park, Spalding, Idaho.

Fig. 5. Monster's Heart, a topographical feature known to the Nez Perce as *tiṁné·pe* 'heart place', on the east bank of the Clearwater River, southeast of Kamiah, Idaho. It is one of a number of landmarks that the Nez Perce identify with various body parts of the Monster *ʔilcwé·wcix*. According to legend, Monster swallows up many animal beings and Coyote defeats him in a battle, cuts his body up, and throws the parts in different directions, liberating the captives. In Nez Perce tradition, the blood of the monster became the Nez Perce people (Aoki 1979:28-29). The site is now a part of Nez Perce Historical Park. Photographed about 1975.

Requirements for Place-Name Studies

At first glance, the vast documentation on American Indian place-names makes the task of choosing reliably interpreted examples for an onomastic study appear simple. However, much of this literature is of questionable validity because most writers on the subject have not been conversant with the languages involved. Many depended to a large extent upon local tradition and folklore for their explanations of a name's meanings. Typically in such work, poorly heard names that were imperfectly recorded in the first place are analyzed into smaller units, which are then compared with similar sequences in dictionaries. A conjectural meaning is then ascribed to the name on the basis of dictionary glosses obtained, without the use of a grammatical description of the language. This process has given rise to numerous highly conjectural and often fanciful etymologies, many of which have been copied over and over again in succeeding publications. Some examples of such faulty analysis are examined in Beeler (1954, 1957), Day (1977), Goddard (1977a), and Kenny (1956).

Through analyses of Mohawk place-names around Lake Champlain, Lounsbury (1960) demonstrates how the correctness of place-name interpretations may be judged and sets forth the standards for the etymological study of names. The ideal place-name analysis begins with knowledge of how a name was pronounced, what

the site was that it referred to, and what its meaning was. In order to ascertain the meaning of a name and that of its constituent parts, an adequate knowledge of the grammatical structure of the source language is necessary. Careful work with a knowledgeable native speaker is most desirable and, if this is not possible, names need to be reconstructed from the historical record and from a knowledge of the language of origin. Intensive and long-term collaboration with native speakers has been undertaken especially since the 1970s in research on Athapaskan and Eskimo-Aleut geographical names. The resulting voluminous literature has appeared in tandem with phonological and grammatical analyses, literacy texts, and literacy materials for the languages involved. Place-name studies in the rest of the continent have not been so fortunate in having widely traveled and interested native consultants for sources; and even the most painstaking work with historical, comparative linguistic, and grammatical tools has left many gaps.

A Classification of Place-Names

Place-name classifications are based on a variety of linguistic, semantic, motivational, or historical criteria (Holmer 1948; Stewart 1975:87). Here American Indian place-names are classified into four categories according to the types of meanings they employ, following a suggestion by Bright (1958:174-175) in his classification of Karok names: descriptive names, locational names, names referring to human activities, and names referring to history, mythology, or folklore.

Descriptive Names

By far the largest, the category of descriptive names has six subdivisions. The most important are: sites named from their physical configuration or appearance; sites named for associated vegetation; and sites named for animals, birds, insects, or fish, characterized by a permanent or seasonal (or single) occurrence there of members of the species named. Three other, smaller, subclasses are: sites named for parts of the human or animal body, or because of fancied resemblances to other objects; color names; and sound names.

Locational Names

A second large category of names implies a locational, orientational, or directional contrast, such as up versus down, this side versus the other side, upriver versus downriver, offshore versus onshore, or inland versus coastal. With few exceptions (for example, Bergsland 1959), the importance of cardinal directions in Euro-American naming patterns does not hold for American Indian place-names.

Names Referring to Human Activities Carried on at a Site

This category includes names whose meanings derive from frequent or seasonal events or the occurrence of man-made structures and culturally important objects other than flora and fauna.

Names Referring to History, Mythology, or Folklore

The meanings of toponyms of this type are often obscure and may be recoverable only from oral traditions and ethnohistorical materials. A striking example is *anatakaryásne*, the old Mohawk name for Washington, D.C., which translates as 'the place of the village destroyer' (Lounsbury 1960:26). Note also that the Euro-American practice of naming places after persons is not a common American Indian pattern (for exceptions, see Ritter 1976a; Boas 1934:21).

The Linguistic Form of Place-Names

In American Indian languages, the construction of geographical terms exhibits the same complexity as that found in the building of other words, phrases, or sentences. At the more elaborate end are phrases or whole sentences, such as occur in Western Apache, where verb stems are modified by series of affixes and noun stems (Basso 1988:111), or in Iroquoian languages, in which numerous place-names consist of nominalized verbs or verbs that incorporate noun stems and several classes of modifiers (Mithun 1984a:42). The simplest place-names are made up of a single unmodified noun, verb, or particle, such as Tanaina *nuti* 'saltwater', the name of Cook Inlet among Upper Inlet people, Washoe *dá?aw* 'lake' (Lake Tahoe, California-Nevada), or Klamath *blay* 'above' (Bligh, Oregon). In many languages, place-names have nouns, verbs, particles, affixes, or stems that express position, location, orientation, or direction. For example, in the Western Abenaki name for the Richelieu River, *bitawbágwizibó*, *bitaw-* is a general root meaning 'between'. Other devices having deictic function in the examples below are Western Apache *dah* 'above ground level', locative particles like Yurok *?o*, and locative affixes like Sahaptin *-as*, Eastern Ojibwa *-ink*, and Southern New England Algonquian *-ǝt* (as in the last part of *Connecticut*).

Many place-names include a component with a noun-like meaning that refers to the kind of topographical feature in focus. This may be a noun, which can occur as an independent word, or a component element used to form words but not used independently. In the Western Abenaki example cited above *-bagw* is a noun-forming component meaning 'body of water' and *zibo*

is the word for 'river'. Other generic terms for bodies of water, the most frequently named geographical features in North America, include: Ojibwa *si·pi* (as in *kič·či-si·pi* 'big river', the Mississippi), Choctaw *hača-* (as in Atchafalaya River, Louisiana), Teton Sioux (Lakhota) *mni-* as in *Mnĩšoše*, the Missouri River), Mohawk *-nyatar-* (as in *kanyatarakwá·rǫte*, Lake Champlain), Western Abenaki *-tegw* 'river' (as in *olategw*, Saint John River, Maine), a noun-final element used in addition to the independent noun *zibo*, and Ahtna *bene?* (as in *ʒen bene?*, Muskrat Lake, Alaska). Recurring names for land forms and other natural features are: Kwakiutl *-bi?* 'point', Tanaina *ken* 'ridge', Upper Inlet Tanaina *dɣelay* 'mountain', Navajo *dziɬ* 'mountain' and *tsé* 'rock', Aleut *gutix̣* 'sand bar, spit', and Ahtna *tayene?* 'straight stretch of river' and *-lu?* 'glacier'. Some treatments of linguistic and semantic aspects of place-name deixis and generics appear in Basso (1984a), Henry and Henry (1969), Jetté (1991), Kari (1985, 1987, 1989), Leer (1989) for Athapaskan languages; Boas (1934:14-22) for Kwakiutl; Day (1981), Hartley (1981), and Kenny (1961:11-14, 1976) for Algonquian languages; Farnell (1995) for Assiniboine; Bergsland (1959, 1994) for Aleut; Palmer (1988, 1990), Galloway (1993:561-568), and Galloway and Richardson (1983) for Salishan languages; Harrington (1916:70-93) for Tewa; Clark (1978) for Uto-Aztecan; and Waterman (1920:195-200) for Yurok.

Name clusters in a particular region sometimes result from the repetition of names that refer to fairly common physiographic phenomena. Alaska Athapaskan languages have many instances of these; the Susitna drainage in Alaska has Ahtna *nadiλi·s na?* 'flows-irregularly creek;' *nadiλi·s bene?* 'flows-irregularly lake;' and *nadiλi·s tayene?* 'flows-irregularly straight stretch (plain)' (Kari 1983:68).

Names also repeat across languages, especially for sites that are economically or culturally important to neighboring peoples. In the southern Yukon, many sites have both Tlingit and Tagish names with identical meanings, and these pairs of names are familiar to most of the population (Sidney 1980). Mount McKinley has two sets of names: one from peoples north or west of the Alaska range, who call it 'the high one'; and the other from peoples south of the range, who call it 'big mountain'. Given in the orthographies developed by the Alaska Native Language Center, Fairbanks, the first set is: Koyukon Deenalee, Holikachuk Denadhe, Lower Tanana Deenadhee, Upper Kuskokwim Denaze, Holikachuk Denadhe, Ingalik Dengadh or Dengadhiy; and the second set is: Upper Inlet Tanaina Dghelay Ka'a, Lower Inlet Tanaina Dghili Ka'a, and Ahtna Dghelaay Ce'e (Gudgel-Holmes 1991:76-77; Jetté 1991; Kari 1987a).

Finally, numerous examples show that the derivations of many ethnic, tribal, or other social group names parallel those of the names of the territories the groups occupy. Thus, Kari and Fall (1987:26-27) describe how most band names in the middle and upper Cook Inlet areas are based upon the place-names for major regions or waterways. Further illustrations may be found throughout Curtis (1907-1930, 3, 10, 12), and in Galloway (1993:649-650), Goddard (1984a), and Young and Morgan (1954).

Examples

The classification outlined above can be illustrated with examples drawn from a representative number of languages spoken in various parts of the United States and Canada. Examples in italics appear in the phonemic system used for each language in the *Handbook*, generally following the *Handbook* technical orthography; Navajo, Apache, and Sioux words are in practical orthographies used for those languages. Forms that could not be phonemicized appear in roman in the orthography of the original publication.

Descriptive Names

Names that describe physical features of the site include:

Western Abenaki: *olategw* 'good river', Saint John River, Maine (Day 1994:401).

Ahtna: *naci·łgosden* 'where snow avalanches', Mount Tiekel, lower Copper River region, Alaska (Kari 1983:4).

Western Apache: *Tsé Łigai Dah Sidil* 'white rocks live above in a compact cluster', hill in the Cibecue area, Arizona (Basso 1988:111).

Barbareño Chumash: *ʔalpinčéʔ* 'a thing that is split, or forked', a reference to acorns that split readily, a former village in the Santa Barbara area, California (Applegate 1974:197).

Hitchiti: *okifanô·ki* 'bubbling water', Okefenokee Swamp, Georgia and Florida (Read 1934:24; William C. Sturtevant and Billy L. Cypress, communication to editors 1995).

Eastern Canadian Inuit (Labrador): *nunainŋuaq* 'the image of no land', a long and straight bay on the northern Labrador coast, at Nain (Wheeler 1953:65; vol. 5:509).

Teton (Lakhota): *Mníšoše* 'turbid water', the Missouri River (Buechel 1970:339).

Menominee: *as wa·we·ya·hpetah* 'where there is a whirlpool', Appleton, Wisconsin (Bloomfield 1975:268).

Micmac: *kepe·k* 'narrows, strait', Halifax Harbor, Nova Scotia; also the source for the name of Quebec (Hewson 1981-1982:12; Martijn 1991).

Mohawk: *kanyatarakwá·rọteʔ* 'the bulge in the waterway', Lake Champlain, between New York and Vermont (Lounsbury 1960:39).

Navajo: *Tsé Bidádi'ní'ání* 'the plugged or sealed rock', Chetro Kettle, an Anasazi ruin in the Chaco Canyon, New Mexico, a reference to sealed niches in the kiva wall (Young and Morgan 1992:1078).

Sahaptin: *sḱin* 'cradleboard', the large Sahaptin village on the north bank of Celilo Falls, Washington, describing the shape of a prominent rock nearby (Hunn et al. 1990:94).

Seneca: *ohi·yoʔ* 'beautiful river', Allegheny-Ohio River (Chafe 1967:59; vol. 15:516).

Southern Paiute: *panákikippi* 'water tightened, spring in a tight place', Iron Springs, Utah (Sapir 1930-1931, 3:597).

Tunica: *táhtatʔɛ* 'great prairie', Mamou Prairie, Louisiana (Haas 1953:265).

Unami Delaware: *mehəməna·ɔnkéhəla·k* 'the one that flows with banks that continually cave off', Monongahela River (Ives Goddard, personal communication 1995).

Names that describe vegetation at the site include:

Western Abenaki: *zalọnaktegw* 'sumac cone river', Saranac River, New York (Day 1981:158).

Ahtna: *q̇ey ca·y beneʔ* 'dwarf birch lake', Hogan Hill lake, on the Gulkana River, Alaska (Kari 1983:50).

Coeur d'Alene: *hənċaq̇iłpenċ* 'firs on the mountainside', Spokane Bridge, Washington (Palmer 1990:275).

Fox: *šeka·ko·heki* 'at the wild onion (place)' (Ives Goddard, personal communication 1995); or Southern Ojibwa *šika·konk* 'at the skunk (place)' (Bloomfield 1957:261). Origin of the name of Chicago.

Kwakiutl: *cálxʷməȝis* 'crabapple trees on beach', a shore locality, Thompson Sound, British Columbia (Boas 1934: map 15, no. 31).

Lushootseed: *qʷqʷálb* 'where huckleberries are', a camping spot, Sinclair Inlet, Washington (Snyder 1968:132).

Menominee: *pawa·hekan* 'place for knocking down wild rice', Lake Poygan, Wisconsin (Bloomfield 1975:196).

Northern Tutchone: *inƛə́t čú* 'cranberry water (river)', river draining from Northern Lake into North Big Salmon River, southern Yukon (Tom 1988:14).

Sahaptin: *taⱦúsas* 'place of Indian hemp', lower Crab Creek area, Oregon (Hunn et al. 1990:94).

Yurok: *kwescin* 'strawberries', the sloping of a promontory, Patrick's Point, California (Waterman 1920:268).

Names referring to animals include:

Western Abenaki: *onegígwtegwíz* 'little river of otters', Little Otter Creek, Ferrisburg, New York (Day 1981:166).

Ahtna: *ȝen beneʔ* 'muskrat lake' Muskrat Lake, in the Chitina River region, Alaska (Kari 1983:8).

Ahtna: *saɣani naʔ* 'raven creek', stream above Horse

Creek on the Copper River, Alaska (Kari 1983:14).

Carrier: *calakoh* 'beaver-forepaw river', Mud River, British Columbia (Morice 1932, 1:59).

Coeur d'Alene: *hənčičilí* 'where there are muskrats', Benewah Bay, Idaho (Palmer 1990:275).

Teton Sioux (Lakhota): *pté-gli*ʔ*iyąka* 'buffaloes return running' (Boas 1934:20).

Ipai (Diegueño): *heťaw n·ewa·* 'rabbits' house', Los Conojes, California (Couro and Hutcheson 1973:21).

Eastern Canadian Inuit (Labrador): *kivalliq* 'place where ringed seals sleep on ice pans', point on north Labrador coast near Okak Bay (Wheeler 1953:51; vol. 5:509).

Kwakiutl: *ƛúbas* 'cormorant place', locality in British Columbia (Boas 1934, map 15, no. 139).

Menominee: *mahwɛ·w-se·pe·w* 'wolf river', Wolf River, Wisconsin (Bloomfield 1975:240).

Mohawk: *otskwaʔrhéhne* 'place of frogs', Frogtown, New York (Mithun 1934a:48).

Quileute: *ɬoqʷsá·tal* 'sea lion hunting place', Sea Lion Rock, La Push, Washington (Powell and Jensen 1976:64; Powell and Woodruff 1976:389, 490).

Southern Paiute: *patiyanukkinti* 'elk stream', Paria River, Utah (Sapir 1930-1931, 3:590).

Tagish: *ḱsambá·ʒéleʔ* 'ptarmigan mountain', Mount Lansdowne, southern Yukon (Sidney 1980:81).

Tanaina: *q̇in teƛi* 'exploded fish egg', hill west of Lime Village, Cook Inlet, Alaska (Kari 1989:143).

Tlingit: *x̌e·šawá· ša·yi* 'ptarmigan mountain', Mount Lansdowne, southern Yukon (Sidney 1980:81).

Upriver Halkomelem: *smə́məq̇ʷa* 'many little herons', Herrling Island, Fraser River, British Columbia (Galloway 1993:657).

Names describing body parts include:

Aleut: *kudutux̌* 'has big calf of leg', point on Atka Island, Aleutians (Bergsland 1959:27, 1994:246).

Barbareño Chumash: *šnoxš* 'it is (like) a nose', bluff near Maria Ignacia Creek, Santa Barbara region (Beeler 1954:272).

Carrier: *naḱal* 'dwarf vulva', named for large hole on the mountain top, Mount Pope, British Columbia (Morice 1932, 1:60).

Karok: *kitaxríhak* 'at a wing', site along Klamath River, California (Bright 1958:176).

Koyukon, Lower Tanana: *čeʒaye* '(moose) heart', Chitsia Mountain (Mooseheart Mountain) and Kantishna Hills, Alaska (Gudgel-Holmes 1991:57).

Kwakiutl: *aẇə́myiʔ* 'cheek', a steep bluff, Thompson Sound, British Columbia (Boas 1934:map 15, no. 11).

Nez Perce: *timné·pe* 'heart place'; *siɬé·x̌spe* 'liver place'; *qaháspa* 'breast place'. These are three landmarks in the Kamiah valley in Idaho, named after body parts of the Monster (Aoki 1979:13, 23-29, 1994:757) (fig. 5).

Tanaina: *ḱənuqaḱitnətant* 'where an animal is crouching', Peters Hills, Alaska (Kari and Fall 1987:146).

Ventureño Chumash: *kašoxšol kawi* 'deer's urine', a village near Ventura, California (Applegate 1974:195).

Names that refer to color include:

Choctaw: *oka losa* 'black water', Okaloosa, Louisiana (Read 1927:44).

Creek: *wi·lá·ni* 'yellow (or brown or green) water', interpretation of the name of Welawnee Creek, Alabama (Read 1937:77).

Kwakiutl: *məlís* 'white beach', beach site, Queen Charlotte Sound, British Columbia (Boas 1934:map 6, no. 70).

Lower Tanana: *toncux̌ no* 'yellow water creek', Creek on Kantishna River, Alaska (Gudgel-Holmes 1991:58).

Navajo: *Be'ek'id Halchíí'* 'red lake', Red Lake, Arizona, and Ganado Lake, Arizona (Young and Morgan 1980, 2:152; Jett 1970:175).

Ojibwa: *miskwa·kami·wi-sa·kaʔikani·nk* 'red lake', Red Lake Reservation, Minnesota (Nichols and Nyholm 1995:234).

Tanaina: *čatanalcəγ* 'yellow water flows out', creek into Susitna River known locally as "Shem Pete Slough," Alaska (Kari and Fall 1987:154).

Unami Delaware: *ɔ́pe·k sí·p·u* 'white river', White River, Indiana (Ives Goddard, personal communication 1995).

Yurok: *oʔʔso* 'red', a large hill, on the middle Klamath River, California (Waterman 1920:235).

Names that identify sounds include:

Ahtna: *nayʔƛi·sdiniʔa·den* 'where songs extend across', village site near Copper Center between Klutina and Tazlina Rivers, Alaska (Kari 1990:279).

Barbareño Chumash: *humaliwo* 'where it sounds continuously', village on the coast, west of Los Angeles; Malibu, California (Beeler 1957:237).

Kwakiutl: *dɔ́mliwas* 'place of rumbling noise', Baronet Passage, British Columbia (Boas 1934:map 15, no. 53).

Kwakiutl: *wáḱala* 'noise of river', many sites in British Columbia (Boas 1934:map 15, nos. 42, 84, 99).

Menominee: *sa·pi·wɛ·hekaneh* 'at calling distance in the woods', Sheboygan, Wisconsin (Bloomfield 1975:233).

Navajo: *Be'ek'id Di'nini* 'the lake that groans', Groaning Lake, Arizona (Young and Morgan 1980, 2:152).

Navajo: *Tséé'dóhdoon* 'inside the rock there is a rumbling noise', Taaiyalone Mountain, near Zuni Pueblo, New Mexico (Young and Morgan 1980, 2:732).

Tagish: *čʼoh desḱes ni* 'porcupine quill makes noise', site on east side of Marsh Lake, southern Yukon (Sidney 1980:10).

Yurok: *orä́ʔʔäm* 'sound of dancing, the drumming sound made by feet', a meadow along the lower

Klamath River, later a house name (Waterman 1920:242).

Yurok: o-tega´ 'where it thumps, a place where earth falls down in large chunks', site west of Klamath River, Humboldt County, California (Waterman 1920:261).

Locational, Directional, and Orientational Names

Western Abenaki: *bitawbágwi-zibó* 'between-lake (or double lake) river', the Richelieu River, Quebec, which drains Lake Champlain (Day 1981:149).

Western Abenaki: *tsitótegwihlá* 'the waterway continues', Ticonderoga, New York (Day 1981:168).

Coeur d'Alene: *hənčɛmcən* 'inner mouth, surface in the mouth', Saint Maries, Idaho (Palmer 1990:275).

Island Chumash: *nimatlala* 'center', the largest Chumash village on Santa Cruz Island (Applegate 1974:198).

Mohawk: *kahnawâ·ke* 'at the rapids', Caughnawaga, Quebec (vol. 15:479).

Mohawk: *skahnéhtati* 'beyond the pines', Albany, New York (Lounsbury 1960:26; vol. 15:466).

Mohawk: *tekotaró·ke* 'it is at the junction of two waterways', Ticonderoga, New York (Lounsbury 1960:49).

Quileute: *calilítqʷ* 'going over the hill', Bogachiel River, Washington (Powell and Jensen 1976:66; Powell and Woodruff 1976:444, 493).

Seneca: *tetyó·syo·ke̜·h* 'between the basswoods', Buffalo, New York (Chafe 1967:55).

Southern New England Algonquian: *kwənəhtəkwət* (recorded as Narragansett ⟨Quinníhticut⟩) 'on the long tidal river' (reflecting Proto–Eastern Algonquian *kwən-* 'long' + *-əhtəkw* 'tidal river' + *-ənk* 'locative', reshaped), Connecticut River, Connecticut (Ives Goddard, personal communication 1995; Trumbull 1881:60).

Tanaina: *duncix̧* 'toward the water', Iliamna Lake and Nondalton lowlands, Alaska (Kari and Kari 1982:24).

Tanaina: *tudačən* 'on water side', Coyote Lake, Alaska (Kari and Kari 1982:32).

Tanaina: *x̧i̧u bena* 'beneath (range) lake', Chelatna Lake, Alaska (Kari and Kari 1982:37).

Names Referring to Human Activities Carried on at a Site

Ahtna: *ćaqe· nanalye·sden* 'where the women are carried across', a fording place near rapids at upper Miles Lake, lower Copper River, Alaska (Kari 1983:3).

Ahtna: *ci̧s ɫeli·x̧den* 'where ocher is gathered', site on Matanuska River, Alaska (Kari 1990:7, 388).

Ahtna: *nekećalye·x̧den* 'where we turn around', Tahneta Pass, at the head of the Matanuska River, Alaska. People journeying from the Copper River to Cook Inlet down the Matanuska River would carry a handful of soil from their homes. When they reached the Pass, they turned and scattered the handful of soil and prayed for a safe journey. At this point, they had their last view of the Copper River country (Kari 1983:vii).

Aleut: *čunuɣusis* 'where one had to carry the boat overhead', low hill on Atka Island, "by the shortest way across the isthmus" (Bergsland 1959:27, 1994:155).

Lushootseed: *saxʷsaxʷáp* 'jumping down', a gambling and gaming place, where contests were held jumping off a rock, Sinclair Inlet, Puget Sound, Washington (Snyder 1968:132).

Navajo: *Tsék'i Na'asdzooí* 'rock upon which there is writing', Inscription Rock, El Morro, New Mexico (Young and Morgan 1980, 2:729).

Tagish: *edicʸa· ni* 'where one keeps oneself occupied', stream mouth near Little Atlin Lake, southern Yukon, Canada (Sidney 1980:39).

Tanaina: *čči̧hi kən* 'ridge where we cry', sloping ridge south of Mount Susitna, Alaska, so called because of emotional memories evoked by sweeping views of the surrounding Tanaina country from this height (Kari and Fall 1987:57).

Tewa: *tsimayó* 'good obsidian', a former pueblo in Chimayo, New Mexico (Harrington 1920:346).

Upriver Halkomelem: *sxʷhé·y* 'canoe-making place', Skway, British Columbia (Galloway 1993:651).

Ventureño Chumash: *weneṁu* 'sleeping place', where people from the Channel Islands who came to trade on the mainland spent the night on their way home, Hueneme, California (Applegate 1974:198; Beeler 1966:39).

Names Referring to History, Mythology, or Folklore

Western Abenaki: *Odzihózoiskwá* 'Odzihozo's wife', a rocky islet at one end of the canoe crossing between Shelburne Point and South Hero, New York. The Western Abenaki transformer, *Odzihózo*, is said to have created Lake Champlain and then changed himself into stone on another rocky islet (Rock Dunder) near Shelburne Point. Western Abenaki speakers left offerings of tobacco or pipes at these sites for a safe journey (Day 1981:157, 162).

Ahtna: *neceli²sy̧iɫdi²den* 'where someone shot someone in the rectum with an arrow', a point on the Copper River near the Chitina Fork (Kari 1983:11).

Ahtna: *say̧ani ga·y deɫu·le² nanelna²den* 'where raven forgot his rope', point on lower Copper River, Alaska (Kari 1989:143).

Aleut: *ta·muyas ya·ɣa* 'point of the magic puppets' Western Point, Kanaga Island, Aleutians. Supernaturals in the form of masked male or female puppets lived there and attacked people (Bergsland 1959:39, 1994:388).

Barbareño Chumash: *kumqaq̓* 'raven comes', Point Conception, California. A Chumash myth says that the soul passed this site on its way to the other world and that ravens of the other world came there and pecked out the eyes of the soul (Applegate 1974:200).

Teton Sioux (Lakhota): *thóka nuwéyapi* 'they made the enemies swim', Teton place-name (Boas 1934:21).

Diegueño (Ipai): *ča·wp nʸewa·* 'the place of Chaawp', a meteor or mythological spirit embodied in a fire ball, Chawp's Place, Black Canyon, California (Couro and Hutcheson 1973:13).

Kashaya Pomo: *čihtó·naw* 'bereaved', Walsh Landing, north of Fort Ross, California; after an incident in which a woman was killed here from a fall while trying to escape from Mexicans (vol. 8:279).

Karok: *ʔame·kyá·ra·m* 'salmon-making place', on Klamath River, California; a reference to the mythic origin of salmon (Bright 1957:317; incorrect in vol. 8:182).

Kwakiutl: *númasbiʔ* 'old-man (i.e., a sea monster) point'. Almost every dangerous point of land in Kwakiutl territory is named for the monster, called *númas* 'very old person', who is believed to dwell there (Boas 1934:14).

Kwakiutl: *yáłx̌ʷdəm̓a* 'where heads are hung on rock', a place where heads of slain enemies were hung on stakes or poles near Knight Inlet, British Columbia (Boas 1934:13, map 10, no. 15).

Lushootseed: *báysəx̌əb* 'to menstruate for the first time, girl at puberty', a camping place, where the large white rock represents a pubescent girl petrified by the transformer, Kitsap Peninsula, Washington (Snyder 1968:136).

Lushootseed: *x̌ililix̌* 'two groups fighting a battle', a site of a pile of rocks, Kitsap Peninsula, Washington. According to a myth, the rocks are warriors petrified by the transformer (Snyder 1968:131).

Tanaina: *qiči qinɣiłneqt* 'the old lady made it that far', a stream on the Chulitna River, Alaska. This is a reference to *čanqeł*, an extraordinary old woman from the Talkeetna River who is said to have camped in a cave along this stream (Kari and Fall 1987:175, 206-224).

Tanaina: *tununiłčulyutnu* 'river where people killed each other in water', Talachulitna River, Alaska (Kari and Fall 1987:120).

Names of Other Types

Some place-names do not fit into the classification used here, for example those based on the name of a tribe, like Unami Delaware *ka·nsiya·ʔi·sí·p·u* 'Kansa Indian river', Kaw River, Kansas (Ives Goddard, personal communication 1995). A name may have an obvious translation but still an uncertain interpretation. The Menominee name *sake·mɛ·watɛnoh* 'at mosquito hill', the name of New London, Wisconsin (Bloomfield 1975:229), appears to be descriptive, but in Fox the corresponding name *sakime·watenwi* 'mosquito hill' appears in a story, where it is explained as named after a man named *sakime·wa* 'mosquito' (Ives Goddard, personal communication 1995). Some names are partially or completely untranslatable, either because words or formative elements have gone out of use or because the name was originally borrowed from one Indian language into another. For example, the literal meaning of Fox *pi·kihtanwi* and Menominee *pe·keʔtanoh-se·pe·w* 'Missouri River' is not known, because although the element *-ihtanw* (*-eʔtanw*) clearly means 'stream, river' (and Menominee *se·pe·w* is 'river'), the initial element *pi·k-* (*pe·k-*) is not found in any other word in either language (Ives Goddard, personal communication 1995). The Munsee (Canadian Delaware) name for Six Nations Reserve is *šə̃wé·ka*, a borrowing probably from Seneca *swe·ge̱ʔ* (vol. 15:321). Place-names have also been borrowed from Euro-American languages. The Fox name for Saint Louis, Missouri, is *pe·ko·neki*, borrowed from *Pain Court* (pronounced [pɛ̃ kur]), literally 'short loaf', the French name for the trading center originally on the site, with the addition of the locative ending *-eki*. The important site of Rock Island is referred to in Fox, even in traditional historical accounts, as *nwa·hke·neneki*, a borrowing of the English name with *-eki* added (Ives Goddard, personal communication 1995). Archaic and borrowed names may be subject to reinterpretation and folk etymology; Fox speakers explain the meaning of the name of Saint Louis as 'at shallow-water' (Jones 1907:225), assuming a connection with the root *pe·kw-* 'dry' that is not supported by analysis.

Sources

Early Sources for Place-Names

Place-names in North American Indian languages were first recorded in the explorations of the sixteenth and early seventeenth centuries. Lists of local names in Algonquian and Iroquoian languages have been preserved from the first English and Portuguese explorations of the eastern seaboard. Micmac names of localities on the Atlantic coast of Cape Breton Island appeared on maps drawn in the 1550s by Diogo and Lopo Homem from information from Portuguese voyages three decades before (Ganong 1964:75-81; Hoffmann 1961:191). Accounts of Jacques Cartier's first two voyages, in 1534 and 1535-1536, introduced place-names from Northern Iroquoian languages of the Saint Lawrence valley, including names for settlements in present-day Quebec City and Montreal and the word from which the country name *Canada* derives (Biggar 1924:101-106, 196, 246; Ganong 1930:149; Robinson 1945; vol. 15:335). Place-names in the southernmost Eastern Algonquian languages were first recorded by John White and Thomas Harriot in the Roanoke Colony in the 1580s (Geary 1955:853-872) and then later by John Smith, in the early 1600s, in the Virginia Algonquian (Powhatan) language of the Chesapeake Bay area of Virginia (Barbour 1967, 1969, 1972). The records of the Spanish exploration of the Southeast in the sixteenth century have yielded locality names in Iroquoian, Muskogean, and Siouan languages and in Timucua and Yuchi; studies of these names are found in Swanton (1939, 1946), Hudson (1990), Hudson, DePratter, and Smith (1989), and Booker, Hudson, and Rankin (1992).

In addition to accounts of the first explorations, early sources of place-names in North America are maps made by American Indians or drawn by White explorers and traders on the basis of information directly supplied by American Indians. The few maps of this kind that survive not only display the great extent of the geographical knowledge of individual American Indians but also shed light on their contributions to the earliest cartographic descriptions of North America. Some of these maps indicate local group names as well and contribute to a reconstruction of the early history of settlement and of the economy in a particular region. The earliest maps of the Upper Great Lakes from the mid-seventeenth century were based ultimately on a Huron map drawn for or compiled by Paul Ragueneau in 1639 or 1640 (Goddard 1972a:123-126; Heidenreich 1988). The earliest record of Shawnee place-names appears on a map of the Ohio River drawn for René-Robert Cavelier, sieur de La Salle and incorporated into Franquelin's map of Louisiana (Franquelin 1684; Bauxar 1957). The maps drawn by the Blackfoot chief Ackomokki for Peter Fidler in 1801 were significant for their impact on the early exploration of the West (fig. 6).

Other early map sources that have been used in place-name studies in the Great Plains are J.C. Beltrami's (1962) map of his travels in 1823, showing the upper Mississippi, Saint Peters, and Red rivers, and indicating Siouan names for some rivers; and Joseph N. Nicollet's 1838 map of Yankton Sioux territory, incorporating Ojibwa and Sioux place-names from the upper Missouri River and modern South Dakota (Nicollet 1843; Howard 1972:289; Gasque and Van Balen 1989; Parks and Wedel 1985). Ojibwa place-names from about 1840 appear in the geologist Bela Hubbard's maps of the Lake Superior shoreline (Peters 1984).

Ferdinand Wrangell's map of 1839 (in Kari 1987b: 35), showing Tanaina and Ahtna place-names in the Cook Inlet region, supports the accounts of the vigorous trade conducted by speakers of these languages with Russian colonists. An early source of Tlingit and Kaska place-names is a map drawn in 1869 by the Tlingit leader Kohklux and his wives for the scientist George Davidson. The map shows a large portion of southeastern Alaska and the western part of the Yukon through which Kohklux traveled in 1852 on his way to destroy the Hudson's Bay Company post at Fort Selkirk (Cruikshank 1991:114-117; Davidson 1901). Examples of American Indian cartography in other regions and discussions of its principles appear in volume 6:62, 165; Beattie (1985-1986); Cumming, Hillier, Quinn, and Williams (1974:181, 206-207); Fletcher (1891); Lewis (1980, 1993); Luebke (1987); Moore (1993); Pentland (1975a); Ruggles (1991:63-67); Rundstrom (1991); Sølver (1957); Spink and Moodie (1972, 1976); Warkentin and Ruggles (1970); and Williams (1891).

Modern Studies

Most studies of native North American place-names concern those from Eskimo-Aleut languages; Algonquian and Iroquoian languages of the Northeast and Southeast; Athapaskan-Eyak languages of the Subarctic, the Northwest Coast, California, and the Southwest; Kiowa-Tanoan languages of the Southwest; Sahaptin and Salishan languages of the Northwest Coast and the Plateau; the Wakashan group in the Northwest Coast; and Chumashan, Pomoan, and Utian languages of California. Extensive gaps in place-name studies exist for the Southwest, Great Basin, Plains, and Southeast, particularly for geographical nomenclature in languages of the Caddoan, Kalapuyan, Keresan, Muskogean, Siouan, Tsimshian, Uto-Aztecan, Yukian, Yokutsan, and Yuman families. A large body of place-name literature exists in publications that are not widely accessible, including journals from local historical societies, newspapers, English and Geography Department master's theses, and manuscripts of travel journals. Useful regional linguistic bibliographies devoted to American Indians and incorporating some of this material are Booker (1991) for the Southeast, Bright (1982) for California, Krauss and McGary (1980) for Alaska, Pentland and Wolfart (1982) for Algonquian languages, and Read (1934a) for the Southeast. Comprehensive place-name bibliographies for the United States and Canada have appeared in *Names*, the journal of the American Name Society (M. Powell and S. Powell 1990; Sealock and M. Powell 1974, 1975, 1979; Sealock, Sealock, and M. Powell 1982; Sealock and Seely 1948, 1967; Seely and Sealock 1955, 1958, 1959, 1961, 1962, 1963, 1968, 1970, 1972). Other reference sources for American Indian place-name studies are the journals *Names in South Carolina* (Columbia), *Onomastica* (Toronto),

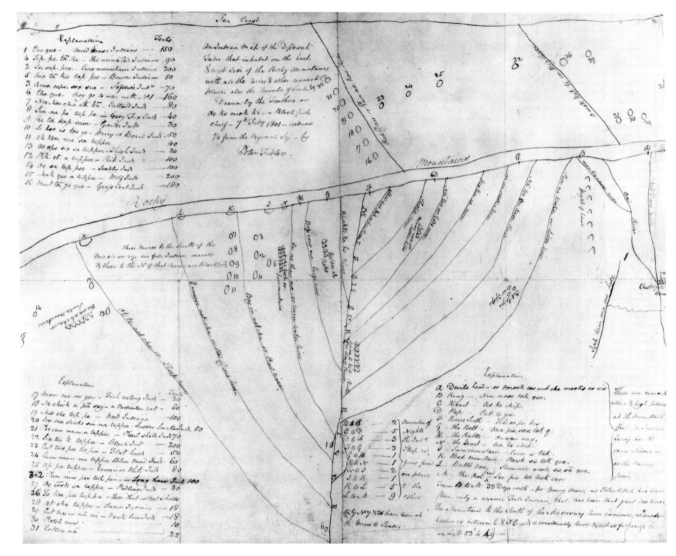

Hudson's Bay Company Arch., Prov. Arch. of Man., Winnipeg: Map coll., G. 1/25 (N4157).

Fig. 6. Map compiled by the Hudson's Bay Company cartographer Peter Fidler from two maps drawn for him by the Blackfoot chief Ackomokki (The Feathers) in 1801 at the newly founded settlement of Chesterfield House on the South Saskatchewan River. This map shows the Rocky Mountains (as a double line across the center of the map) and depicts, for the first time, the Snake and Columbia rivers to the west and 14 rivers that drain into the Missouri River to the east. The locations and names of 32 Indian groups and their relative population sizes (indicated by number of tepees), names of topographical features in the Rocky Mountains, and distances between landmarks, expressed in terms of the number of days' travel, are also indicated. Information from Ackomokki's maps was incorporated into the map of North America published by Aaron Arrowsmith in London in 1802 and was used in the planning of the Meriwether Lewis and William Clark expedition 4 years later (Moodie and Kaye 1977:11; Vollmar 1981:83-86; Ruggles 1991:60-63; Warhus 1993:19-20).

and *Western Folklore* (Los Angeles). Manuscript sources for the place-name studies of John Peabody Harrington, conducted in the first half of the twentieth century among a large number of western North American language groups, especially in California, the Great Basin, and the Southwest, are catalogued in Mills, Brickfield, and Mills (1981-1991).

A number of publications devoted to regional surveys of place-names of American Indian origin cut across geographical and linguistic classifications, and, because they are based on a wide range of published and unpublished sources, provide excellent bibliographies. Among

the most comprehensive are Huden (1962) for New England; Kenny (1961) for Maryland; Kuhm (1952) for Wisconsin; Read (1927) for Louisiana, Florida (1934), Alabama (1937, 1938), and Georgia (1949, 1950); Rydjord (1968) on Kansas, and Vogel on Illinois (1963), Iowa (1983), Michigan (1986), and Wisconsin (1991).

There are numerous other compendia based on county or state boundaries, which, while not devoted exclusively to names of American Indian origin, may be profitably consulted for their bibliographies. Barnes (1960) on Arizona; Becker (1964) on New Jersey;

Bright (1993a) on Colorado; Cassidy (1947) on Dane County, Wisconsin; Ehrensperger (1941) on South Dakota; Goff (1975) on Georgia; Gudde (1960, 1969) on California; Orth (1967) on Alaska; Ramsay, Read, and Leech (1934) on Missouri; and Upham (1969) on Minnesota are among these. Bright (1984) reviews some of these sources in relation to American Indian onomatological concerns. These compilations were written primarily with an interest in the historical circumstances surrounding the bestowal, usually by non-Indians, of names of geographical or political entities. Later works begin with compilations of names from topographical maps and gazetteers of the U.S. Board on Geographical Names or the reports of the Canadian Geographic Board. Some (for example, Ehrensperger 1941; Ramsay, Read, and Leech 1934) were spurred by an interest in dialectology and English onomastics. Biographical sketches of American Indians who have been immortalized in place-names are found in many of these studies. In Vogel's works, place-names of American Indian origin are taken to include French and English place-names that are assumed to be translations of American Indian expressions. For the most part, the etymologies given in these studies depend minimally on linguistic analysis and are based on dictionaries, popular tradition, and interviews with native speakers, with unevenly reliable results. Some linguistic studies of names of towns, states, and other political entities derived from American Indian languages may be found in Beeler (1954), Harrington (1920, 1944), Hinton (1994), Holmer (1967, 1969), and Kroeber (1916a).

• NORTHEAST The documentation of names in the Northeast has benefited from a sustained interest since the nineteenth century in the preservation of the linguistic record of its native languages. Systematic compilations of place-names, primarily from New England, have been produced from maps, land records, letters, manuscripts, newspapers, town histories, missionary notes, and other material in historical collections. Unfortunately, it has only rarely been possible to check with native speakers for the pronunciation and meanings of original forms; this and the lack of knowledge of the languages involved has diminished the reliability and research value of much of this material in the Northeast and elsewhere. Important exceptions, for their stress on the difficulties of reliably recording material and for furnishing careful documentation of the early spellings of place-names, are Eckstorm (1941), Ganong (1896, 1912-1916), Kenny (1961), and Trumbull (1870, 1881, 1974; see Goddard 1977a). Some compendia using published and unpublished material on Algonquian and Iroquoian languages from at least the nineteenth century are works by Beauchamp (1893, 1907a), Cassidy (1947), Donehoo (1928), Douglas-Lithgow (1909), Dunlap and Weslager (1950), Heckewelder (1834), Horsford (1886), Hubbard

(1884), Huden (1957, 1962), Kuhm (1952), Laurent (1884:205-222), Legler (1903), Lemoine (1901:279-281), Lindeström (1925:299-408), W. Moore (1930), Rand (1919), Ruttenber (1906), W.W. Tooker (1911), and Tyrrell (1915).

Some short studies devoted to place-names in individual Algonquian languages are available for Abenakian (Day 1975a, 1981, see also 1994; Gatschet 1897; and Vetromile 1866), Massachusett (Little 1984), Menominee (Skinner 1919a, 1921:379-390), Micmac (Hewson 1981-1982), Southern Ojibwa (Gilfillan 1887; Hartley 1980, 1981; Peters 1981, 1981a, 1984, 1985, 1986, 1994; Verwyst 1892, 1916), and Virginia Algonquian (Barbour 1967, 1969, 1972, 1979). Place-names in some Iroquoian languages are covered in the works of Chafe (1967, Seneca), Gordon (1984, Onondaga), Lounsbury (1960, Mohawk), Mithun (1984a, Mohawk), and Robinson (1945, Huron). Southern Ojibwa replaced Siouan languages in many of their former areas in the Northeast, and only a few Winnebago place-names from Wisconsin have been recorded (Kuhm 1952; Legler 1903).

• CALIFORNIA, SOUTHWEST, AND GREAT BASIN Following the examples of Boas (1901-1907, 1934) and Kroeber (1925, 1936) and their emphasis on the conceptual systems of cultures, field studies of western language groups in the first half of the twentieth century typically included detailed maps of tribal territories and discussed settlement patterns, cosmology, orientation, and the linguistic structure of place-names. Many of them contained a section on ethnogeography, based on interviews with the last remaining speakers of western languages. Some of this material is summarized in descriptions and maps of tribal territories of various California tribes in volume 8. In addition to Kroeber's work in California cited above, other systematic recordings of place-names across large western territories were made by John Peabody Harrington (see Mills, Brickfield, and Mills 1981-1991, 8; and vol. 8:738-739), Henry W. Henshaw and C. Hart Merriam (Heizer 1975; vol. 8:751-752), and John Wesley Powell (Fowler and Fowler 1971). Other extensive ethnogeographical studies in the West have been on Chumashan languages (Kroeber 1925; Beeler 1954; T. Hudson 1977; Heizer 1975; Applegate 1974), Karok (Bright 1957, 1958; Kroeber 1925, 1936), Pomoan languages (Barrett 1908; see also Kniffen 1939; Oswalt 1964; and O. Stewart 1943), Tewa (Harrington 1916), Wiyot (Loud 1918; Nomland and Kroeber 1936), and Yurok (Waterman 1920).

For other members of the proposed Penutian superfamily of languages, shorter place-name studies have been conducted on Miwokan languages, Nisenan, and Wintu-Nomlaki (Merriam 1976; Kroeber 1929; and Du Bois 1935 and Goldschmidt 1951, respectively). For the proposed Hokan superfamily, there are place-name studies for Achumawi, Chimariko, Wappo, Washoe (Kniffen 1928; Bauman 1980a; Driver 1936; and d'Azevedo 1956, respectively); for Salinan (R. Gibson 1985; Rivers and Jones 1993); and for two Yuman languages, Cocopa (Gifford 1933) and Walapai (Mekeel 1935). Couro and Hutcheson's (1973) dictionary may be consulted for Diegueño place-names.

Treatments of place-names in Uto-Aztecan languages may be found in the works of the following: Kroeber (1908a:34-35) for Cahuilla; Stephen (1936) for Hopi; O'Neil and Evans (1980) for Juaneño; Zigmond, Booth, and Munro (1991) for Kawaiisu; Gifford (1932) and Steward (1933) for Mono; E.W. Voegelin (1938) for Tubatulabal; Saxton, Saxton, and Enos (1983) and U.S. Office of Indian Affairs (1941) for Upper Piman; Chamberlin (1913) for Gosiute Western Shoshone; Fowler and Fowler's (1971) edition of Powell's manuscripts for Numic; and Kelly (1932, 1964) and Sapir (1930-1931, 3) for Ute and Southern Paiute.

In addition to Harrington's (1916) and Stephen's (1936) works on Tewa and Hopi, respectively, material for place-name studies in the Southwest has been most plentiful for the Apachean languages. These sources include dictionaries, large compilations of names, and studies of the symbolic and metaphorical importance of place-names: Basso (1984, 1984a, 1988), Franciscan Fathers (1910), Jett (1970), Van Valkenburgh (1941, 1974), Van Valkenburgh and Begay (1938), Wilson (1995), and Young and Morgan (1980, 1992). Kelley and Francis (1994) review a wide range of studies of Navajo culture and environment and include an extensive bibliography that contains place-name studies. Curtis's ethnological studies include lists of villages and other settlement sites for Hopi, Jemez, Laguna, Tewa, and Zuni (1907-1930, 12:223-224, 16:252, 16:258, 17:190, 17:195, respectively).

• NORTHWEST COAST AND PLATEAU Boas (1934, for Kwakiutl), de Laguna (1972, for Tlingit), Bouchard and Kennedy (1979, 1984, for Okanagan), and Waterman (1922, for Tlingit) provide the most extensive treatments of place-names and local geographical knowledge in the Northwest. Place-names in Salishan languages have also been treated for Upper Chehalis (Kinkade 1991a), Coeur d'Alene (Palmer 1988, 1990), Halkomelem (Galloway 1993:655-662 and map 2), Lillooet (Kennedy and Bouchard 1992; Tyhurst 1992), Lushootseed (Bates, Hess, and Hilbert 1994; Snyder 1968:130-136 and map; vol. 7:486), and Squamish (Kuipers 1967-1969, 2:32-39). Galloway's and Richardson's (1983) study of Noosack place-names incorporates George Gibbs's list from the 1857-1861 International Boundary Survey.

Sources for place-names in Sahaptian languages include a variety of texts, dictionaries, and ecological studies: Aoki (1979, 1994), Hunn (1991), Hunn et al.

(1990), Jacobs (1934-1937), Slickpoo and Walker (1973, 1), and Yoke (1934-1937). Place-names in two other languages of the Northwest are the subject of other studies: Barker (1963) and Spier (1930) for Klamath; and Powell et al. (1972) and Powell and Jensen (1976) for Quileute. Geographical knowledge in Tolowa and neighboring Athapaskan languages is discussed in Drucker (1937a).

• ARCTIC AND SUBARCTIC In contrast to much of North America, the work on geographical names in the Arctic and Subarctic undertaken in the final decades of the twentieth century was the result of intensive and long-term consultation and mapping with native speakers of different Alaska Athapaskan and Eskimo-Aleut languages who have lived and traveled widely in the areas under study. Starting with Bergsland's (1959, 1994) exemplary work on Aleut names in the 1950s and gaining in volume in the 1970s, this research has produced large compilations of place-names representing the collective knowledge of different communities about their territories and, in a few cases, the knowledge of exceptional individuals about a vast amount of territory (Gudgel-Holmes 1991; Kalifornsky 1977, 1991; Kari and Fall 1987; Kari and Kari 1982; Sidney 1980; Tom 1988). Among the results of this collaboration have been toponymic surveys and gazetteers, literacy materials, and oral historical accounts published under the auspices of the Alaska Native Language Center, the Yukon Native Language Center in Whitehorse, the Inuit Cultural Institute, the Canadian Department of Indian and Northern Affairs, and the Greenlandic Language Commission (Müller-Wille et al. 1987:1-8).

Franz Boas's (1885, 1888) work in Cumberland Sound and Baffin Island produced the first systematic exploration of geographical knowledge in the Arctic. In addition to Bergsland's (1959, 1994) works on Aleut, some important sources for place-names in Eskimo-Aleut languages are Freeman (1976) and Ray (1964, 1971) for the western Arctic; Burch (1994) for northwest Alaska; Müller-Wille et al. (1987) for Quebec and adjacent islands; Brice-Bennett (1977), MacMillan (1943), and Thalbitzer (1904a) for Greenland; and Wheeler (1953) for Labrador. See also volume 5:509 for Eastern Canadian Inuit names from along the Labrador coast; de Laguna (1972, 1:57-106) for some Eyak names; and Jacobson (1984:677) for a list of Central Alaskan Yupik toponyms.

In the last quarter of the twentieth century, place-name and ethnogeographical research among Athapaskan-Eyak and Tlingit speakers in Subarctic regions created a comprehensive collection of works that highlight the relationships of place-names to socio-economic activities, local history and folklore, and territorial and political organization. James Kari (1985, 1986, 1987, 1989, 1989a, and 1994) discusses these connections in considerable detail for the Cook Inlet area and beyond. The following sources cover most of the Athapaskan-Eyak languages of the Subarctic for which speakers have been available: Ahtna (Buck and Kari 1975; Kari 1983, 1990:85-86; Reckord 1983), Eyak (de Laguna 1972, 1; Krauss 1970), Kaska (Dawson 1888a; Moore 1993; Yukon Native Language Centre 1990), Koyukon (Gudgel-Holmes 1991; Jetté 1991; Jones 1986), Kutchin (Caulfield, Peter, and Alexander 1983; Ritter 1976a), Lower Tanana (Gudgel-Holmes 1991), Tagish (Sidney 1980), Tanaina (Ellanna and Balluta 1992; Kalifornsky 1991:338-353; Kari 1977a:127-130, 1987; P. Kari 1983; Kari and Kari 1982; Kari and Fall 1987), Tutchone (Ritter 1976, Tom 1988), and Upper Kuskokwim (Gudgel-Holmes 1991; Stokes 1985). Early work by Morice (1932, 1933) is the main source for Carrier place-names; later work is by the Carrier Linguistic Committee (1974). Tyrrell (1898) gives Chipewyan names from the northwest coast of Hudson Bay. Inland Tlingit place-names are given in Nyman and Leer (1993) and in Sidney (1980).

Place-names in far northern Algonquian languages may be found in the following: Bell (1891) and Tyrrell (1887 and 1915) for Cree and Northern Ojibwa; Lemoine (1901:279-281) for Montagnais. Other sources are Canada Board on Geographic Names (1928, 1933); Rayburn (1967, 1969); and White (1910).

• PLAINS An early source for Siouan place-names is the travel accounts of Giacomo Costantino Beltrami in 1823 on the Missouri River (Beltrami [1828] 1962). A small selection of sources devoted to place-names in Siouan languages of the Great Plains includes Boas (1934:21), Gasque and Van Balen (1989), Hamilton (1885), Tyrrell (1887), and Williamson (1885). Howard's (1972) collaboration with Ella Deloria included the checking of Sioux place-names on Nicollet's (1843) map. Assiniboine geographical names

and concepts receive considerable attention in Farnell's (1995) study of Plains sign language.

A few works provide toponyms in other Plains languages. Parks and Wedel (1985) focus on names, ritual functions, and mythological contexts of Pawnee sacred sites. Arikara and Pawnee site names also appear in Parks (1979) and Grinnell (1913). Cheyenne place-names may be found in Glenmore and Leman (1984:144) and Grinnell (1906). A few Caddoan names appear in Swanton (1942). Rydjord's (1968)'s compilation of American Indian place-names in Kansas remains the main reference for that region.

• SOUTHEAST The studies of place-names in the Southeast by Read (for example, 1927, 1934, 1934a, 1937, 1938, 1949, 1950) are valuable for their coverage of numerous historical sources. He identifies place-names of Muskogean origin (primarily Choctaw, Creek, Seminole, and Hitchiti) as well as some of Algonquian (Shawnee), Iroquoian (Cherokee), and Yuchi origins in Louisiana, Alabama, Florida, and Georgia. Read consulted available dictionaries of these languages as well as early maps and was aware of the linguistic construction of large numbers of toponyms. Gatschet (1884-1888, 1:121-151, 2:181-190) supplies a list of Creek settlement names from a variety of historical materials. Choctaw names are the subject of Halbert's (1898-1899, 1900, 1900a, 1902) studies; these appear in facsimile in Peterson (1985). An early source for Shawnee river names is Johnston (1849). Additional Southeastern place-names may be found in Bauxar (1957), Booker, Hudson, and Rankin (1992), Cushman (1899), Fairbanks (1974), Gannet (1902, 1905), Gatschet (1882a, 1901, 1902), Green and Millward (1971), Hudson (1990), Myer (1928), Pearson (1978), Swanton (1939, 1946), Verdery (1983), and Vickers (1983).

Personal Names

DAVID H. FRENCH AND KATHRINE S. FRENCH

Personal names are considered here to be those proper names that are applied to persons to identify, designate, differentiate, and often to classify them. There are important issues involved in defining proper names (including the subclass of personal names) outside the scope of this discussion; such issues have received the attention of philosophers, linguists, anthropologists, and others (Mill 1973; Frege 1952, 1952a; B. Russell 1940; Gardiner 1954; Hamp 1956; Searle 1958, 1967, 1969; Sørensen 1958, 1963; Hockett 1958; Quine 1960; Kuryłowicz 1966; Lévi-Strauss 1966; Weinreich 1966; Donnellan 1970; Jakobson 1971; Kripke 1972; Algeo 1973; Leach 1976:13, 20, 31; Lyons 1977; S. Bean 1980; Barnes 1980, 1982; Silverstein 1984).

Depending on context and speech intent, a name or names can single out a person as a unique individual and can be of significance to self-esteem, sense of identity, and aspirations. Names have a dual role, serving also as signs (or symbols) of social identities, relationships, categories, or positions and as vehicles for modes of social interaction. They "make statements," significant ones, both about persons and about groups. Personal names are thus referable (and relatable) to (1) the individual, the personal, the specific, the unique, or the temporary (events), or—depending on contexts—to (2) the generic, the sociocultural, the structural, or the timeless, or to both (van Gennep 1960:62; Fortes 1955:338; Firth 1956:6-9; Lévi-Strauss 1966:161-190; Goodenough 1965). The terms within each of these two sets can be related to each other, but they are not synonyms; the choice one makes among them in discussing personal names is—again—a question of context. Some distinctions between the sets are analogous to the contrast between behavior and culture and to the distinction between *parole* and *langue* made by Saussure (1959:7-15).

Included in the following discussion are many kinds of native North American names: secular, sacred, public, private, informal (or ordinary), and formal. Excluded are other terms of direct and indirect reference: kinship terms, pronouns, typical titles and other role and status terms, and purely descriptive words and phrases. (In many contexts, these have been used by speakers as preferred alternatives to names.)

Although regional consistencies in naming practices are evident, there are many discontinuities as well; no "name-areas" have been proposed. Also, linguistic and other cultural diversity was great enough that statements about the whole of North America risk being misleading or inaccurate. Nevertheless, a few limited generalizations can be made: in many societies, people could have multiple names, simultaneously or in sequence; frequently, there were explicit distinctions between nicknames and formal, validated names; quite often, there were restrictions on the uses of names. Almost everywhere, names were of considerable importance and were associated with a range of other social practices and institutions.

Types of Names

Gender-linked Names

Names could indicate the sex of the name-bearer. Often, there was simply a customary relationship between each sex and about half the available names. Where it was usual to name boys after male relatives and girls after female relatives, a distinction between the two sets of names was thereby maintained (Lantis [Nunivak Eskimo] 1946:236-237; French and French [Wasco] 1950-1992, [Warm Springs Sahaptin] 1949-1992; Gayton [Yokuts] 1945:413; Kroeber [Juaneño] 1925:646; F. Eggan [Cheyenne, Arapaho] 1955:63). Cheyenne berdaches (men who dressed as women and took women's roles) had two names, one male, one female (Grinnell 1923, 2:39-40). North Alaska Eskimos thought of particular names as belonging to men and others to women but often bestowed them without observing the distinction (Spencer 1959:290). Birket-Smith (1929:194, 282) reported that Caribou Eskimo children were dressed according to the gender implications, if any, of their names.

Among the Chiricahua Apaches, most names could be borne by either men or women; some could not, because the meanings included male or female denotations, as, for example, 'Thin Old Woman' (Opler 1941:429-430). Where names were "meaningful," that is, analyzable and at least partly translatable, certain subject matter seemed to enter more frequently into the names of one sex or the other. Spier thought, for example, that vegetation more often appeared as a meaningful element in Havasupai women's names and that hats, houses, and rocks were more characteristic of men's names (1928:305-306; cf. L.J. Bean [Cahuilla] 1972:142; Hearne [Chipewyan] 1968:93-94). At Jemez Pueblo, color terms in names retained customary associations with sex (blue with male, yellow with female); other sex-linked subject matter included: mountain, feather, eagle down (male, and flower, altar, bow (female) (Parsons 1925:31-32; cf. Stevenson [Zuni] 1915:86). Western Apaches thought that women's names should sound "soft and gentle," men's names "harsh and fierce" (Goodwin 1942:527; cf. Landes [Ojibwa] 1938:11-14).

The sex of the bearer of a name was sometimes indicated by conventionalized affixes. Western Apaches used the verb *hashkee* 'he is angry, brave, fierce' as a prefix with men's names (Goodwin 1942:522, 524). In the Unami Delaware language, separate sets of endings—the translations of which contribute little to the core meanings—distinguished men's names from those of women; for example, *-ú·x·we* 'walker' formed male names only (Goddard 1991:2-4; cf. Clifton [Potawatomi] 1977:109). Other examples of linguistic markers of gender could be given (M.R. Harrington [Delaware] 1913:213; C.F. Voegelin and E.W. Voegelin [Shawnee] 1935:618-619, 634; Chaput [Ojibwa] 1966:143; Kuipers [Squamish] 1967-1969, 2:40-41; Hill-Tout [Lillooet] 1905:151; Boas [Kwakiutl] 1932a:201; Sapir [Yana] 1922a:234; Driver [Wappo] 1936:205-207; C.F. Voegelin and F.M. Voegelin [Hopi] 1971:316-317).

Customary patterns of bestowing, assuming, and retaining names also differed for men and women in some societies, such as Creek (Speck 1907:116) and Omaha (Barnes 1984:112-115). Ceremonial recognition of girls' puberty did not often include the giving of names; Navajos (Witherspoon 1970:57-58) and the Arizona-Tewas (Dozier 1954:328) were exceptions. In North America, women frequently did not participate in the kinds of activities that provided occasions for new names for men (cf. Vickers [Choctaw] 1983:119). Only men among the Arizona-Tewas were initiated into a kiva group, receiving a new name (Dozier 1954:349). Seminole boys acquired ceremonial names as part of their introduction to adult male civic and military responsibilities (Toomey 1917:24-25; Spoehr 1942:89; Sturtevant 1960:508). Among the Mandans and Hidatsas, and among their Plains neighbors, a woman ordinarily retained throughout her life the name given her in childhood, whereas a young man, successful in a war party, received a new name commemorating his exploits (Bowers 1950:60, 1965:138, 219-220; Denig 1930:516-517; Lowie 1935:43). In contrast, if Dixon's (1905a:231) information was correct, the names of Maidu women may have been changed more often than those of men.

Age Distinctions

More or less formal distinctions between names used for infants and children and those of adults were common (Barnes [Omaha] 1984:105-110; Elmendorf and Kroeber [Twana] 1960:377; Goodwin [Western Apache] 1942:530-531). The ages at which infants received names and at which adult names superseded childhood names were not uniform. Furthermore, when multiple formal names were customary, they might or might not form a series associated with age-related statuses. In some instances, the association seems to have been only a very general rule. For instance, Blackfoot men, whose names as youths often ridiculed them, were given more dignified names later as they distinguished themselves (Wissler 1911:17). On the other hand, Utes ideally received new names at each of five transitions in life, such as becoming a parent (a "mother name" was *wisi-si?ipi* 'Yucca Blossom'; similarly, a "grandmother name" was *k*ʷ*anapi-mamaci* 'Sacred Eagle Woman'). Goss's (1973) analysis suggests that these names were selected according to syntactic and semantic rules in such a way as to form classes of names that are distinctive of sequenced stages of life.

Relationship Names, Including Teknonyms

One kind of naming that is widely distributed in the world is teknonymy, the use of a name based on the name of one's child, for example, "father of so-and-so." North American data suggest that teknonyms can be seen as one example of a larger category that might be called "relationship names." (An alternative, partially synonymous, term would be "kinship names.") Zuni adults were indeed known by their relationship to an offspring; lacking children, the relationship might be to a niece, nephew, or sibling (Kroeber 1917:72-73). Haidas also commonly used references to children, but married adults might instead be called "husband of so-and-so" or "wife of so-and-so," and there were other such uses of relationship names (Murdock 1934:372; cf. Garfield [Tsimshian] 1939:226). In addition to using teknonymy, Chiricahua Apaches identified young persons in terms of older relatives (Opler 1941:432). Many further examples of relationship names, mainly teknonyms, could be cited (Adair [Cherokee] 1930:199-200; Durlach [Tlingit, Haida] 1928:20, 173-177, 70-71, 79, 108; Elmendorf [Twana] 1946:432; Krause [Tlingit] 1956:152; Lowie [Hidatsa] 1917:34 and [Hopi] 1929:377-378; Morice [Sekani] 1933:645-646; Osgood [Kutchin] 1936a:140, 146, 150 and [Tanaina] 1937:161; Reichard [Navajo] 1928:100-101; Ross et al. [Kutchin] 1872:326; Steward [Owens Valley Paiute] 1933:293).

Interpretations of teknonymy have frequently associated the practice with the avoidance of "real" names.

Kroeber (1917:72) emphasized the intensely personal and religious meanings of names for the Zunis, and he suggested that because children had not yet entered fully into the religious life of the community, their names could be spoken more freely than those of adults (cf. Lantis [Nunivak Eskimo] 1946:238). Chiricahuas were explicit in accounting for their practice as one of the ways in which they avoided using personal names in inappropriate circumstances (Opler 1941:432). On the other hand, teknonymy was used at Cochiti Pueblo, even though there was no reluctance to use personal names (Lange 1953:682). In practice, teknonymy might serve to focus attention on a younger person, as when an older man's name was based on that of a son who was becoming prominent (Niblack [Tlingit, Tsimshian] 1890:371; Swanton [Muskogean] 1928b:698). Incidentally, Yavapais were said to use teknonymous expressions when they could not recall someone's name (Gifford 1936:305).

Titles and Name-titles

If English-language categories are used, titles seem to be easily distinguishable from personal names: the former imply social positions to which clusters of prerogatives and responsibilities are attached. Similarly, among many North American peoples, titles and names contrasted, and the use of either for reference or address depended on particular circumstances.

On the Northwest Coast, some names and titles merged. In households, lineages, or "tribes," a ranked series of names denoted ranked positions within the group. When an individual took a name, particularly one high in such a series, he assumed a social position and its associated obligations and benefits. Rules of succession and requirements for validation of what can thus be called name-titles differed among Tlingit, Haida, Tsimshian, Bella Coola, Kwakiutl, and Nootka communities, but the linkage of name and title appeared in all groups (Boas 1925:57, 1966:51-53; British Association for the Advancement of Science 1974:53-54, 102; Codere 1950:62-80; Drucker 1939: 62-63; de Laguna 1952:4-5; Emmons 1991; McIlwraith 1948:121-129, passim; Murdock 1936:8-10; Olson 1940:170-172, 177-179; 1954:229-231, passim; 1955: 326-328; Piddocke 1965:252; Rosmand and Rubel 1971:181-182, 195-196, passim, 1972:664-668; Vaughan 1984:64; Spier and Sapir [Wishram] 1930:259-260).

In the southeastern United States, certain names seem to have had properties shared with titles; these might also be called name-titles. Men acquired a series of names during their lives. These names were sometimes hereditary in kinship groups and were associated with ceremonial, civic, and military offices; the names entailed specific responsibilities and honors (Driver 1961:346-347; cf. Toomey 1917:24-25; Swanton 1928:100-102). Analogously, names and titles converged in chieftanship names among Iroquoian-speaking peoples of the Northeast (Beauchamp 1892:125-126, 1907; Quain 1937:258; Hewit 1910:921; Morgan 1901, 1:85, 2:238-239; Swanton 1910:17; Fenton 1936:6, 19-20; Tooker 1964:45, 1970:93, 96; Druke 1976:9-20).

Nicknames

Nicknames constitute an explicit category of subordinate names in English. Although categories precisely parallel to English usage do not necessarily exist in other languages, names that were alternatives to "real" names have been reported for most of North America (Driver 1961:469). Such names, for which the term "nicknames" will be used here, existed in addition to the "real" names (which could themselves be multiple). However, at least two subgroups of the Southern Paiute—San Juan and Kaibab—had only one category of names (Bunte and Franklin 1987:237-238). The patterns of acquisition and use were informal and resembled those of nicknames among other peoples.

Nicknames can be characterized (not defined) by the fact that they were given with little or no ceremony, that they were used in casual rather than in formal speech, and that their content—when they were translatable—often referred to personal characteristics (not necessarily of the person to whom they were applied) or to humorous, scandalous, or extraordinary events.

Nicknames could contrast with "real" names in style. The Twanas, for example, made a clear distinction: nicknames were translatable and descriptive; other names were not (Elmendorf and Kroeber 1960:377-378). For some groups, such as Plains Indians (Sapir 1924:118), contrasting styles were either not present or not consistent.

Contractions of "real" names forming sets of conventional nicknames (such as exist in many European languages) have not been reported for American Indians. Yet, contractions evidently could occur in the course of conversation (Matthews [Hidatsa] 1877, cited by Lowie 1917:51); they might in time become the usual form of a name (Garfield [Tsimshian] 1939:224; cf. Michelson [Fox] 1928:3, 1929:7; Weslager [Unami Delaware] 1971:280-281). Sets of customary nicknames (which were not contractions) did exist. Nicknames reported for the Pagago, for example, were descriptive terms used for persons who fit certain stereotypes. Thus anyone who talked all the time might be called 'Mockingbird' (Dolores 1936:45-46; cf. Parsons [Isleta Pueblo] 1932:217; Goodwin [Western Apache] 1942:526-527).

Characteristics of appearance or behavior have been widely reported as the subject matter of nicknames: *wi·htiko·w* 'cannibal monster' was applied to a hungry

202

Cree infant (Robert Brightman, personal communication 1980); an excitable Oklahoma Seminole child was called *tapó·ka* 'explosion' (Spoehr 1942:89; cf. I.T. Kelly [S. Paiute] 1932:161; Densmore [Chippewa] 1929:53). Also used as referents were events related to the experience of the recipient of the name, the name-giver, or a third party (Jenness [Copper Eskimo] 1922:167-168; Lantis [Nunivak Eskimo] 1946:237; Kuipers [Squamish] 1967-1969, 2:39, Sapir [Sarcee, Kutchin, Chippewa, Navajo] 1924:118; Cushing [Zuni] 1920:523-526; Dyk [Navajo] 1947:30, 176; Lowie [Crow] 1935:21; Bennett and Zingg [Tarahumara] 1935:223; Weslager [Unami Delaware] 1971:271, 275; Speck and Schaeffer [Catawba] 1942:572; Gilbert [Eastern Cherokee] 1955:300).

For relatives, Nunivak Eskimos used nicknames that were modifications of kin terms (cf. Weslager [Unami] 1971:274). Such nicknames were often initiated as "pet names" or names of endearment; however, once used, they might also come to be used by members of the family for whom the original kin term was inappropriate. For example, a woman's own children might call her by a term meaning 'little older sister', a nickname originally used for her by her parents and siblings. At least some of these nicknames became reciprocal: a child whose mother's brother called him 'little nephew' might be taught to use the same name for his uncle (Lantis 1946:237-239). Although the derivation of these nicknames was obvious to the Eskimos, the literal meaning was not necessarily salient in everyday usage, just as the nickname *Sonny* in American English need not denote or connote the relationship on which the term is based.

Nicknames were linked with kinship in a variety of ways; they occasionally have been alternates for European-style surnames (E.S. Rogers and M.B. Rogers [Weagamow Lake Ojibwa] 1978:329). Among the matrilineal Crows, nicknaming was a feature of the associations between a man and his father's clan (Lowie 1917:41-42). In some societies, joking relationships between relatives involved nicknaming (Skinner [Iowa] 1926:249; Goodwin [Western Apache] 1942:533; Gilbert [Eastern Cherokee] 1955:300; Drucker [Diegueño] 1937:50). In less structured ways, nicknames often offered opportunities not provided by formal names for inventiveness, play, humor, teasing, ridicule, aggression, intimacy, affection, and other dimensions of human interaction (see Burch [Interior North Alaska Eskimo] 1975:158).

The Giving and Taking of Names

Both the bestowing and the assuming of names occurred in North America. As might be expected, parents and other adults were responsible for most naming and nicknaming, although Lowie (1917:41-42) recorded an example of a Crow boy who exploited clan interrelationships by nicknaming an adult in order to obtain the customary return gift. Nicknaming probably occurred within young peer groups, but it has rarely been reported.

In some societies, people had a degree of control over their own names, including naming (or nicknaming) themselves. Southern Okanagan men might give themselves humorous and derogatory nicknames (M. Mandelbaum 1938:105); a Nootka with a conspicuous defect might give himself a special descriptive name (Lemert 1952:435; cf. Sapir 1915c:4-5); Mohave men assumed obscene nicknames to attract the attention of women (Kroeber 1925:749; cf. Forde [Quechan] 1931:149). On the other hand, a Kwakiutl who was the victim of an unflattering nickname could "pay" for it by sponsoring a potlatch and thus control it and prevent its further use (Olson 1954:226). Certain Apaches allowed an adult or a child who found a name unsatisfactory to refuse it or to ask to have it changed. Further, although a Western Apache could not create a new name for himself, he could take one already in existence or invented by someone else (Goodwin 1937:398, 1942:530-532).

On the Plains and in at least parts of the Northeast, men acquired new names based on their exploits in warfare and raiding, names that could be self-awarded as well as given by leaders or comrades (G. Dorsey and Murie [Pawnee] 1940:93; Skinner [Sauk] 1925:72; Wissler [Blackfoot] 1911:16). To be accepted, self-awarded names required consensus as to the merits of the deeds memorialized. The Pawnee required that names taken after the performance of an act that indicated "great ability or strength of character" be assumed openly, before people to whom the act was known (Fletcher 1899:86).

On the Northwest Coast, the exercise of rights to names was a central feature of an individual career. Henry W. Tate, a Tsimshian, wrote: "And when it [a child] grows up, it is named with another name; and when it is really full-grown, then it names itself with a great name" (Boas 1912:223; cf. Rosman and Rubel 1971; McIllwraith [Bella Coola] 1948, 1:272-273; de Laguna [Tlingit] 1952-4-5; Boas [Kwakiutl] 1925, 1935:184, 188-189; Spradley [Kwakiutl] 1969; Goldman [Kwakiutl] 1975:56-60; Jenness [Carrier] 1943:520-521).

Name-givers

The social identity of a name-giver was frequently a matter of considerable importance by virtue of: (1) being a member of a specific kinship group (Bowers [Mandan] 1950:59; Oberg [Tlingit] 1973:53, 95; Gilbert [Cherokee] 1955:300); (2) occupying a position of relative economic, religious, or political eminence (Goldfrank [Cochiti] 1927:77; Garfield [Tsimshian] 1939:221; Wallis and Wallis [Micmac] 1955:253); (3) having demonstrated qualities of character, achievement, long life, good health, or good fortune (Turney-High [Flathead] 1937:70; Wissler [Blackfoot] 1911:16-17; C.F. Voegelin and E.W. Voegelin [Shawnee] 1935:622; Hilger [Chippewa] 1944:238, 151:31-37; Goodwin [Western Apache] 1942:528; Foster [Huchnom] 1944:230); (4) having shown skill in creating names or in selecting "good" or "proper" names (McAllister [Kiowa Apache] 1955:139; Spencer [North Alaska Eskimo] 1959:289); or (5) possessing some supernatural authority (Jacobs [Coos] 1939:67; Jenness [Sekani] 1937:55; D.G. Mandelbaum [Plains Cree] 1940:241-242; Landes [Ojibwa] 1937:117-118; L. White [Acoma] 1932:133-134; R.M. Underhill [Papago] 1939:157; Mooney [Cherokee] 1900:2; Swanton [Caddo] 1942:160). Frequently, a name-giver had multiple attributes.

Rituals and Ceremonies

Very often, there was at least some ritual when names (except nicknames) were acquired, although a number of Eskimo and Numic speakers had little or none (Oswalt [North Alaska Eskimo] 1967:94; W.R. Miller [Shoshone] 1972:91-93; Bunte and Franklin [Southern Paiutes] 1987:237-238). The elaborateness of rituals was related to the degree of emphasis on ceremonialism in a society, to the social or religious importance of the type of name involved (Collins [Upper Skagit] 1974:221), or to the relative social position and wealth of family (St. Clair and Frachtenberg [Coos] 1909:26; Singh [Makah, Quileute, Quinault] 1966:115; Garfield [Tsimshian] 1939:221-222). Naming was sometimes one element in larger ceremonial complexes or events (Tooker [Iroquois] 1970a; Suttles [Coast Salish] 1958:500; K. French [Warm Springs Sahaptin] 1955:116; Murie [Pawnee] 1989:15, 152, 195).

A naming ceremony (fig. 1), whether simple or elaborate, achieved some degree of public recognition for a name; in fact, public validation was often the explicit ceremonial function (Fletcher [Pawnee] 1899:86) and might be symbolized by the distribution of gifts (B.J. Stern [Lummi] 1934:56; French and French [Warm Springs Sahaptin] 1949-1992, [Wasco] 1950-1992; Collins [Coast Salish] 1966:427; Skinner [Sioux] 1919:170). The "public" involved might be limited to the immediate family and close friends; it might represent larger kinship groups, or it might extend to the

community or the region. It might or might not include the supernatural world, as well as the human one. Differing audiences reflected differences in types of names; for example, household ceremonies were held for Tewa infant names, but moiety representatives were present when moiety names were given (Ortiz 1969:33-37). Moreover, the public appropriate for similar types of names was not necessarily the same from one society to another; clan-owned names were given to children in clan ceremonies by the Osages (La Flesche 1928:31, 33) but in community ceremonies by the Senecas (Barbeau 1913:459; cf. M.R. Harrington [Unami Delaware] 1913:213; Swanton [Creek] 1928:102).

So great is the diversity in naming ceremonies—diversity of personnel, action, and symbolism—that no attempt is made here to describe any rituals as such. Brief accounts are numerous, including many in sources cited here for other reasons. In addition, there exist a few extended accounts of naming ceremonies: La Flesche (1928) recorded two versions of Osage child-naming rites; Hilger (1944) described Chippewa child-naming in some detail; Voth (1905) provided an account of a Hopi naming ceremony (Beaglehole and Beaglehole 1935:35-37; Talayesva 1942:30-33), and Stevenson (1894:140-141) described a Zia Pueblo naming; Fletcher (1899, 1904) published accounts of a Pawnee ritual used when changing a man's name (although Weltfish 1965:481-482 has pointed out the weaknesses of the 1904 translation). In his life story, a Kiowa Apache recalled the ceremony at which he was named (Brant 1969:39-41). Ortiz (1969) described Tewa naming ceremonials in the context of the Tewa world view; Boas (1925:112-357) chronicled the life history of a Kwakiutl chief, including the acquisition of a series of names.

Sources of Names

The duality of names as relating to events and as reflecting cultural regularities is illustrated by the varying combinations of invented and traditional names that occurred in North America. Invented names were composed for a particular person at a particular time and, in native belief, were unique. Traditional names could involve more than just repeated names; there could be a (conceptually finite) reservoir of traditional personal designations. Many peoples used both styles of naming; "real" names were often, but not necessarily, traditional, while innovation was often associated with nicknames.

Fig. 1. A naming ceremony. top, Lizzie Harper giving an Otoe name to Austin DiPuma on the last day of the tribe's annual summer encampment. In the center is Mitzi Marlene White Feather Koch, grandmother of Austin DiPuma; holding the child is his mother, Tonya DiPuma (for a description of this ceremony see Schweitzer 1985). bottom, A feast following the naming for the relatives and friends who attended the ceremony. Photographs by Marjorie M. Schweitzer, Otoe-Missouria campground, near Red Rock, Okla., July 22, 1984.

PERSONAL NAMES

The Creation of Names

Despite any emphasis placed on the originality of names, their invention in any culture was patterned. They were shaped by purely linguistic rules (phonological and grammatical) and by conventions of appropriateness and style.

For example, names in some circumstances could be allusions to accomplishments of the person named (Crissey [Sioux] 1906:87-88; Hilger [Cheyenne] 1946:68 and [Arapaho] 1952:58-59); or, they could be allusions to events in the lives of name-givers (Sturtevant [Seminole] 1960:507; Lowie [Crow] 1935:42-43); both could be called event-names. The creation of a name was likely to be a serious undertaking, one that involved intellectual, as well as evaluative or aesthetic, criteria. The task of a Hopi woman in naming her brother's child was to produce a suitable name (in this case, choosing an old one or creating a new one) suggestive of the identity of the father's clan (C.F. Voegelin and F.M. Voegelin 1971:312, 316, passim; cf. Voth 1905, 1905a). Shawnee name-givers engaged in a night of contemplation, prayer, and perhaps dreaming, in order to find and interpret a good name (C.F. Voegelin and E.W. Voegelin 1935:622-623; cf. Jenness [Sarcee] 1938:18).

In some societies, it was considered essential to avoid any name that had been used before: this was one of the responsibilities of a Shawnee name-giver, and Cocopas went to great pains to avoid any repetition of men's names (W.H. Kelly 1942:683).

Nicknaming was almost always inventive, emphasizing the singularities of persons or relationships; nevertheless, under some circumstances nicknames could be inherited. A Tlingit child who was the reincarnation of a deceased person might be given not only that person's serious name or names but also his nickname (de Laguna 1972, 2:788; cf. also p. 784, on teknonymous names; and Garfield [Tsimshian] 1939:224, on acceptance of a nickname as a formal name by the person to whom it had been applied). In naming an Eskimo infant, the nickname of his namesake might be given (Spencer [North Alaska Eskimo] 1959:290; Jenness [Copper Eskimo] 1922:167). In such cases, the connotations of a name shifted from the individual and the temporary to the sociocultural and the timeless, and the name itself could become traditional.

Traditional Names

Names recurred—that is, they were traditional—among many North American peoples: for example, it was common in most Eskimo groups to name children after deceased persons, including relatives (Cranz 1767, 1:161; Hawkes 1916:112; Rasmussen 1929:172; Guemple 1972:3; Heinrick 1969:3-4; Spencer 1959:287; Damas 1972:48-49; Hughes 1958:1146; Bugge 1952:46). Elsewhere, similar practices were followed (Jacobs [Coos] 1939:67; Beals [Maidu] 1933:369; Wissler [Blackfoot] 1911:16-17; Speck [Yuchi] 1909:93-94).

Among other peoples, including Eskimos in the east central Artic, the name of a living person was given to a child (Guemple [Inuit of Quebec] 1972:3; F. Eggan [Cheyenne, Arapaho] 1955:63); sometimes the name was shared; sometimes the donor relinquished it and took a new name. Names of either living or deceased relatives were used by still other groups (Kroeber [Yokuts] 1906:142; Olson [Quinault] 1936:103; Collins [Upper Skagit] 1974:220-221; F. Eggan [Gros Ventre] 1955:63; Fenton [Seneca] 1936:20).

Sets of names, assigned to children by order of birth, were used more or less rigorously by some Siouan-speaking peoples. There were separate sets for boys and for girls, and each clan could have its own set (Fletcher [Sioux, Winnebago] 1905:426; Skinner [Iowa, Ponca] 1915:732-734, 799-800; J.O. Dorsey [Omaha] 1884:231-233, 237-251, 1886:394, 396; Barnes [Omaha] 1984:105-110; La Flesche [Osage] 1928:31). As a consequence of these and comparable

Smithsonian, NAA: 56,185.

Fig. 2. Pictographically rendered names of the heads of 84 families in the Oglala Sioux band led by Big-road. Big-road submitted the drawings to the United States Indian agent, James M. McLaughlin, after being taken to Standing Rock Agency, Dakota Terr., and required to give an account of his followers. "The translations of the names were made by the agency interpreter": No. 1. Big-road.
2. Bear-looking-behind. 3. Brings-back-plenty. 4. White buffalo. 5. The-real-hawk. 6. Shield-boy. 7. The-bear-stops. 8. Wears-the-feather.
9. Dog-eagle. 10. Red-horn-bull. 11. Low-dog. 12. Charging-hawk. 13. White-tail. 14. Blue-cloud (woman). 15. Shield. 16. Little-eagle.
17. Spotted-skunk. 18. White-bear. 19. White-hair. 20. His-fight. 21. Center-feather. 22. Kills-Crows (Indians). 23. The-bear-spares-him.
24. White-plume. 25. Fears-nothing. 26. Red crow. 27. The-last-bear. 28. Bird-man. 29. Horse-with-horns. 30. Fast-elk. 31. Chief-boy.
32. Spotted-elk. 33. Carries-the-badger. 34. Red-earth-woman. 35. Eagle-clothing. 36. Has-a-war-club. 37. Little-buffalo. 38. Has-a-point (weapon). 39. Returning scout. 40. Little-killer. 41. Whistler. 42. Tongue. 43. Black-elk. 44. Lone-woman. 45. Deaf-woman. 46. Long-dog.
47. Iron-hawk. 48. Pretty-weasel. 49. Short-buffalo. 50. Bull-with-bad-heart. 51. Four crows. 52. Tall-white-man. 53. Eagle-hawk.
54. Lone-man. 55. Causes-trouble-ahead. 56. Makes-dirt ("foul"). 57. Black-road. 58. Shot-close. 59. Iron-crow. 60. Running-horse.
61. Owns-an-animal-with-horns. 62. Blue-cloud-man. 63. Fingers. 64. Sacred-teeth. 65. Searching-cloud. 66. Female-elk-boy. 67. Little-owl.
68. Pretty-horse. 69. Running-eagle. 70. Makes-enemy. 71. Prairie-chicken. 72. Red-flute-woman. 73. Little-hawk. 74. Standing-buffalo.
75. Standing-bear. 76. Iron-white-man. 77. Bear-whirlwind. 78. Sacred-crow. 79. Blue-hawk. 80. Hard-to-kill. 81. Iron-boy. 82. Painted-rock.
83. Yellow-wolf. 84. Made-an-enemy (Mallery 1886:174-176).

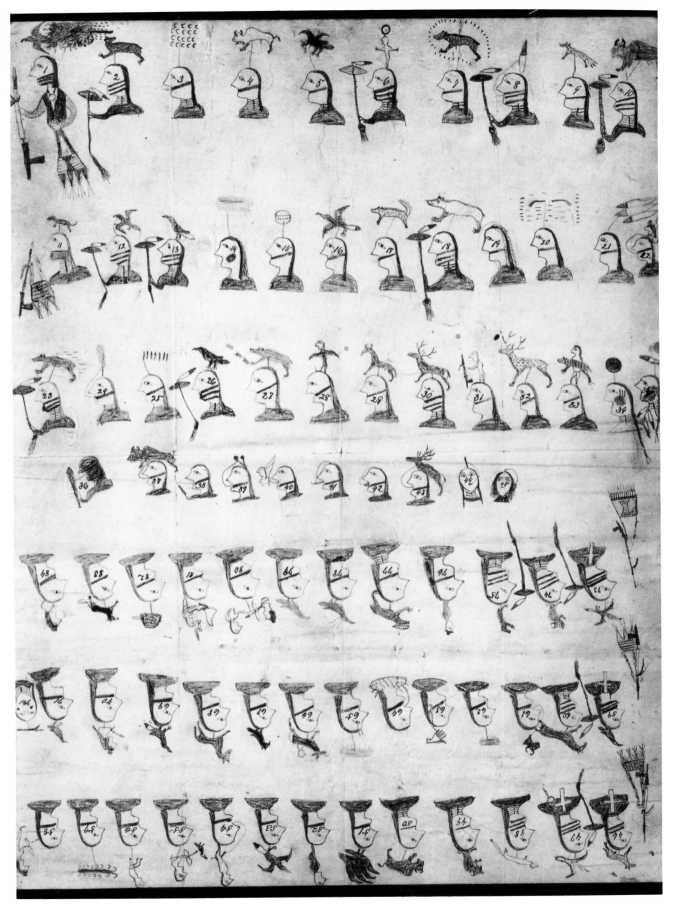

PERSONAL NAMES

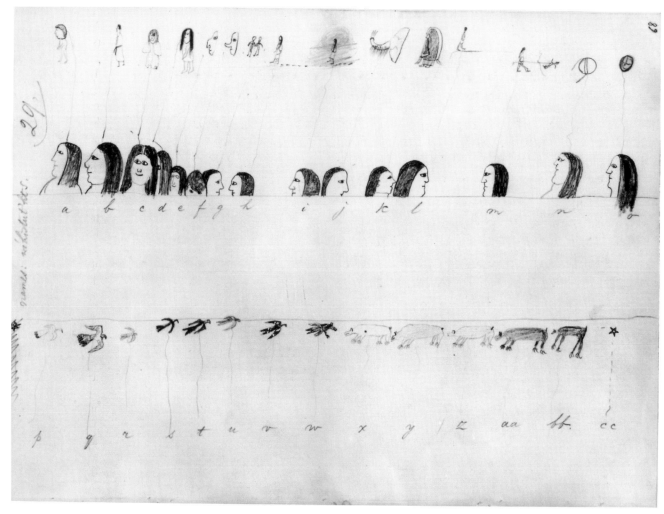

Fig. 3. Pictographic list of names of Northern Cheyenne men and women. Crayon drawings by Daniel Little Chief (*vóhpAhésO*) done in Washington, D.C., in 1891, with pencil key and annotations by Albert S. Gatschet of the Bureau of American Ethnology. The pictographs *a-o* are linked to largely stylized heads. A second version, in which the heads are almost completely uniform, is in the Smithsonian Institution, National Anthropological Archives, ms. 2016-a. The corresponding Cheyenne names listed by Gatschet from Little Chief, as phonemicized and glossed by Wayne Leman (communications to editors, 1995, 1996; Glenmore and Leman 1984), are as follows (uninterpretable words are in shallow-pointed brackets in Gatschet's transcription, with Little Chief's translations in double quotation marks): a, *maˀxEstséáhE* 'Big Head'; b, *aˀkótseehE* 'Cartridge Belt'; c, *maˀóˀkénéˀE* 'Red Blind Eye Woman'; d, *maˀovéséhE* 'Red Hair'; e, *vóoˀxénéhE* 'Roman Nose'; f, *káˀeēˀEsE* 'Pug Nose'; g, *héstahkE* 'Twin'; h, *ameóhtséˀE* 'Walking Woman'; i, *taaˀéveóhtséˀE* 'Nightwalks Woman'; j, *mámeˀšeāhtsE* 'Hairy Arm'; k, *maˀxekAsovááhE* 'Big Young Man'; l, *heˀámAhtamēhnEstsE* 'Highwalker'; m, *hóxovenaˀhānE* 'Kills Across'; n, *vóhpóóhévAtsE* 'Whiteshield'; o, *máˀxemE* 'Apple'; p, *netsE OhvóˀkomaestsE* 'White Eagle'; q, *netsE ⟨χü-immāsts⟩* "Spotted Eagle;" r, *maˀevèˀEsE* 'Redbird'; s, *moˀOhtáveaénohE* 'Black Hawk'; t, *heˀheēnO OhmoˀOhtávaestsE* 'Black Blackbird'; u, *heóveaénohE* 'Yellow Hawk'; v, *⟨χā´χki-amin⟩* "Spotted Bird;" w, *véˀkEséhenAhkohE* 'Bird Bear'; x, *vóhpenáhkohE* 'White Bear'; y, *náhkOxheóvaestsE* 'Yellow Bear'; z, *náhkOhmaˀaestsE* 'Red Bear'; aa, *moˀOhtáenáhkohE* 'Black Bear'; bb, *náhkOxháaˀého ́ oesE* 'High Bear'; cc, *hotòhkE* 'Star'.

practices, pools of traditional names existed, from which names for individuals were drawn. Such pools placed limits on choice; on the other hand, connections with ancestors and with social networks were maintained.

Collections of traditional names were not immune to change: names could be discarded, lost, or forgotten. For example, the personal characteristics of easterly Chinookans became associated with their names; a name with unfortunate associations was unlikely to be used again (Silverstein [Wasco, Cascades] 1966-1974,

1984; cf. Turquetil [Central Eskimo] 1929:60). Names must also have sometimes been forgotten if no suitable recipient was born within a reasonable time after a former holder died. Some Eskimo groups preserved names for a time by giving them to dogs until a human infant was born (Jenness [Copper Eskimo] 1922:167; Saladin d'Anglure [Inuit of Quebec] 1970:1015), but not Bering Strait Eskimo (Heinrich 1969:1-3).

Additions to pools of traditional names also occurred. Heinrich (1969:3-9) discusses several processes by which new names became traditional Bering

Strait Eskimo names. There, and elsewhere, for example, a nickname in one generation might become a formal name in a later generation. Names also were introduced through contact with other peoples: trading, travel, and intermarriage. The characteristics of any pool of names were influenced by the interplay between marriage patterns and the conventions of inheritance or transmission of names. In the case of stratified societies, differentials in the frequency of marriage with outsiders meant differences in the names available to persons of differing social positions. In addition, processes of linguistic change acted over time to modify collections of names, along with other aspects of vocabularies.

Knowledge of the distribution of traditional names within a region could provide useful indications of someone's provenience, ancestry, and family connections. Such was certainly the case in the Plateau, where every local group was the center of a network of relationships with other groups (Anastasio 1972), relationships that were reflected in some measure by the distribution of personal names (Teit 1930a:160; French and French 1949-1992). Bering Strait Eskimos made use of distributional features of names to place strangers in terms of their geographical origins, as well as to facilitate social and economic transactions (Heinrich 1969:10-11; cf. Collins [Coast Salish] 1966:430).

Supernatural Sources

Collective relationships with the supernatural world, sometimes expressed in myths, could provide explanations, sanctions, or contexts for names and naming behavior. For example, the Bella Coolas, and other Northwest Coast peoples, believed that many name prerogatives were acquired by their forebears in supernatural experiences (McIlwraith 1948, 1:121-123, 309-310, passim; Garfield [Tsimshian] 1939:224; Boas [Kwakiutl] 1921, 2:823-824). Ritual accounts of the origins of the names used by each Osage clan for children born into it were an important part of the naming ceremonies and the names could refer to ritual songs (La Flesche 1928:84, 1925:209). Winnebago clans had sets of names that were relatable to mythological origins of the clans (Radin 1915a:20-23).

Personal relationships with the supernatural world, for example, with guardian spirits, so characteristic of large parts of North America, could also be the source of human names. Often, a name was given or inspired by a guardian spirit (Boas [Kwakiutl] 1921, 2:945, 1966:135, and [Tsimshian] 1916:513; Barbeau [Interior Salish] 1913a:462; Turney-High [Flathead] 1937:71, and [Kootenai] 1941:115; M. Mandelbaum [Columbian Salish] 1938:105; Spinden [Nez Perce] 1908:247; Goodwin [White Mountain Apache] 1938:29, 31;

Lowie [Crow] 1935:65; J.O. Dorsey [Sioux] 1894:539-541; Braroe [Plains Cree] 1975:125-126; cf. Collins [Upper Skagit] 1974:220, who reports that people might use the name of their guardian spirit themselves or bestow it on a child to secure the child's protection). Names were also derived from dreams (Turner [Labrador Inuit] 1894:200; Lowie [Crow] 1935:43; Goodwin [Western Apache] 1942:527-528; Wissler [Blackfoot] 1911:17; Jenness [Sekani] 1937:55; Kohl [Ojibwa] 1956:273-274; Hallowell [Ojibwa] 1960:21-22; Beck [Maniwaki Algonquin] 1947:261; M.R. Harrington [Unami Delaware] 1913:213; Morice [Carrier] 1933:636). Indians on the Plains and in part of the Northeast used names that referred to sacred paraphernalia, in English often called "bundles," owned by the name-giver or a group to which he belonged (Skinner [Sauk] 1925:65; Bowers [Mandan] 1950:59, and [Hidatsa] 1965:76; Fletcher and La Flesche [Omaha] 1911:255).

The names of supernaturals or characters in myths seem rarely to have been used for humans except in enactments of mythological events (cf. Swanton [Haida] 1905:118; Parsons [Laguna Pueblo] 1923:191). Such names either constituted a separate set or were distinguished from human names (and ordinary vocabulary) by their linguistic form: for instance, *spílya* 'coyote' (the animal itself or a human nickname) versus *spilyái* 'Coyote' (a mythological personage) (French and French [Warm Springs Sahaptin] 1949-1992; cf. Jacobs [Northern Sahaptin] 1931:219-220; Aoki [Nez Perce] 1979:3-4).

Names and Souls

Some Eskimo peoples and Aleuts thought of names as souls, one of a number of kinds of souls. In general, a name and other personal attributes, such as character, wisdom, power, and skill, were thought of as bound together in a name-soul. In contrast to various other souls, a name-soul remained a part of human society beyond the lifetime of an individual human; it moved from a deceased person to an infant in a kind of reincarnation (Birket-Smith 1959:138, 153-154, 163; Wachtmeister 1956; Marsh [Eskimo-Aleut] 1954:23; Heinrich [Bering Strait Eskimo] 1969:4; Spencer [North Alaska Coast Eskimo] 1959:287-288; Stefánsson [Mackenzie Delta Eskimo] 1914:339, 357-358; Turquetil [Caribou Eskimo] 1926:421; Rasmussen [Netsilik] 1931:219-223, [Iglulik] 1929:58-59, 172, and [Polar Eskimo] 1908:116, Defour [Iglulik] 1975; Gessain [East Greenland Eskimo] 1967, 1980; Robbe [East Greenland Eskimo] 1981). It should be noted that such an association of names and souls was not made by all Eskimos (Oswalt 1967:194-195; Lantis [Nunivak Eskimo] 1946:237; Rainey [Tikiġaġmiut] 1947:271-272; Jenness [Copper Eskimo] 1922:168).

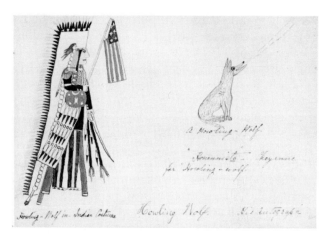

Southwest Mus., Los Angeles.

Fig. 4. Self-portrait of *ho?néohnéstoohE* or Howlingwolf, Southern Cheyenne. At left he portrays himself in traditional warrior headdress, breastplate, German silver gorget from his hair to his feet, breechcloth, holding a decorated shield but also wearing a U.S. military coat, holding a sword and carrying the American flag. To the right is his pictorial name sign with lines indicating howls from the wolf's mouth, described by the annotator as his autograph. Howling Wolf produced about 74 drawings of various subjects throughout his stay at the Fort Marion, Fla., prison (Szabo 1994). Pencil, crayon, ink, 1877.

Beliefs in souls and in reincarnation existed elsewhere in North America. Reincarnation was sometimes (Birket-Smith and de Laguna [Eyak] 1938:153; de Laguna [Tlingit] 1972, 2:785; Hallowell [Ojibwa] 1955:173), though not necessarily (Osgood [Kutchin] 1936a:140; Collins [Upper Skagit] 1974:221) marked by naming, but name-souls seem to have been distinctively Eskimo and Aleut.

Names and Social Systems

Descent Groups

Wherever in North America there was unilineal descent, significant linkages occurred, almost without exception, between descent groups and names. (A conspicuous exception was the Navajos; evidently, when they acquired matrilineal descent from Pueblo Indians—along with other cultural elements—some associated functions were not included.) Linkages were not limited to any single kind of relationship or to a single kind of group, such as clans, recruited by descent.

If a people was organized as two groups (moieties), these could be linked with names and with ceremonial functions associated with naming (Gifford [Miwok] 1916:146-148 ff.; Ortiz [Tewa] 1969:33-35; Skinner [Sauk] 1923:16-20, [Prairie Potawatomi] 1924:22-30; Hewitt [Creek] 1939:141). More frequently, sets of formal, traditional names were linked with less inclusive (patrilineal or matrilineal) groupings: phratries, clans (or sibs), and lineages (Tooker 1971:361-362; Olson 1933:357, 390; Lowie 1934:327-330; Speck 1907a:290). Sometimes the nature of these linkages was one of "ownership"; names, or rights to names, were property or valuable knowledge (Goldenweiser [Iroquois] 1912, 1914, 1914a; Powell [Wyandot] 1881:59-60; Swanton [Chickasaw] 1946:673; Radin [Winnebago] 1910:212-213, 1923:192-195; Skinner [Menominee] 1921:48-51; J.O. Dorsey [Omaha] 1884:227-251; Howard [Ponca] 1965:97; Whitman [Otoe] 1937:21-35; Goodwin [Western Apache] 1942:525, 529; Goldman [Kwakiutl] 1975:26-45; Oberg [Tlingit] 1934:151-152; McClellan [Tlingit] 1954:77; Sapir [Tsimshian] 1915:21-27; Emmons [Tahltan] 1911:103-104; Hughes [Saint Lawrence Island Eskimo] 1958:1146, 1960:266, 275).

Special kinds of relationships between descent groups and names included the use of a single name for all women in a clan among Yuman-speaking peoples of the Colorado River area (Gifford 1918:156-167; Kroeber 1922:289; Spier 1936:5, 18; Parsons 1937; Spier [Maricopa] 1933:187-188 and [Mohave] 1953:324; Kroeber [Mohave] 1902:278; Halpern [Quechan] 1942:438, 441; W.H. Kelly [Cocopa] 1942:683-684). In certain (matrilineal) groups, rights to give certain names were lodged in the recipient's father's clan (Lowie [Hidatsa] 1917:41-42; C.F. Voegelin and F. M. Voegelin [Hopi] 1970a:51; Spoehr [Seminole] 1941:15). Descent-linked names sometimes referred to symbols, to sacred events, or to myth personages important in the group's ritual or ideology (Swanton [Tlingit] 1908:421-423).

Among some peoples, names were controlled by families (Duff [Coast Salish] 1952:76; Colson [Makah] 1953:191; McKern [Patwin] 1922:241-242). Silverstein (1984) likened Chinookan naming to the display of valued family heirlooms. Groups without unilinear descent usually could exercise useful latitude in naming. Less often, there were explicit rules, such as for limited primogeniture (Rosman and Rubel [Kwakiutl, Nootka] 1971;113-114, 134-135).

Social stratification or class, when present, was significantly related to descent and alliance in North America; consequently, knowing that family members had certain names automatically provided information about their class membership.

Other Social Contexts and Systems

Among certain peoples, some names were linked with groupings that recruited membership by means other than descent. Bands that exploited hunting territories among northern Algonquians had what have been called patronyms or family names, used to indicate band membership (Speck 1915:301, 1915a:4, 1917:87-88, 1923:462, 466-467). Elsewhere, as among the Fox

FRENCH AND FRENCH

Indians and at Isleta Pueblo, names were based on membership in clanlike or moietylike groups that had means of recruitment in addition to considerations of descent (Tax 1955:263-264; W. Jones 1939:140; Parsons 1932:215, 261-262, 269). In some Pueblos, initiation into kivas, kachina societies, and curing groups included the bestowal of new names, although such names might not be used (Parsons 1939, 1:118, 142; see also Bunzel [Zuni] 1932a:541; L. White [Acoma Pueblo] 1943:319; Parsons [Jemez Pueblo] 1925:29; Dozier [Arizona Tewa] 1954:327, 349; Harvey [Lagunas at Isleta Pueblo] 1963:482).

Name-sharing was meaningful in many societies; whether accidental or intended, it might include expectations of special closeness or friendship (Ransom [Aleut] 1945:334-335; de Laguna [Tlingit] 1972, 2:783; Beals [Nisenan] 1933:369; F. Eggan [Cheyenne, Arapaho] 1955:63; Goodwin [Western Apache] 1942:526). Many Eskimos disapproved of marriage between namesakes (Stefánsson [Mackenzie Delta Eskimo] 1921:467); others regarded such unions as desirable (Hennigh [North Alaska Eskimo] 1972:90-91); both practices were explained by ties between namesakes. Broadly speaking, in the American Arctic, name-sharing was an important basis for extending and supplementing social relationships based on kinship. The western Eskimo practice of giving children multiple names taken from deceased persons provided the basis for extensive networks of linkages between individuals and families—networks useful in travel, trade, hunting, and other activities. More characteristic of eastern Eskimos was the bestowal of the name of a living person on a child, leading to economic and social exchanges between a restricted number of persons bearing the same name (see especially Guemple 1965, 1972a; Laughlin 1952:34; Saladin d'Anglure 1970).

Speech Behavior

Both the noncasual and the casual character of speech behavior involving personal names can be illustrated by the rules (explicit and implicit) governing their use and their avoidance.

Prescribed or Permitted Uses

The contexts in which names ought to be spoken were sometimes ceremonial: special sets of names were used during the North Alaska Messenger Feast (Spencer 1959:219, 290), the winter ceremonial season of the Kwakiutls (Boas 1897:418), and the Green Corn Dance of the Creeks (Swanton 1928a:614). All references to an individual in the Six Nations Iroquois Longhouse were by his Indian name (Shimony 1961:211). Names were used at initiations (Ellis [Jemez Pueblo]

1952:160-161), and the dead might be called by name at funerals or other rites (W. Jones [Fox] 1939:71-72; R. White [Luiseño] 1953:573-575).

Persons with a name and powers bestowed by a guardian spirit used such names only in appropriate ceremonial situations (Ray [Sanpoil, Nespelem] 1933:114; Boas [Tsimshian] 1916:513). Navajo personal names were used in the curing ceremonial known as Enemyway (Haile 1938:55-56). Names could be helpful in identifying the target of love magic (Swanton [Alabama] 1928a:635; Greenlee [Florida Seminole] 1944:324), or in witchcraft and to identify sorcerers (Wallace and Taylor [Hupa] 1950:188-193; Basso [Western Apache] 1969:35; Kluckhohn [Navajo] 1962:32, 136, 151; Parsons [Zuni] 1927:107; Mooney [Cherokee] 1891:343; Rasmussen [Caribou Eskimo] 1930:50).

Prescriptions for the appropriate use of names to express respect, courtesy, or consideration implied the possibility of misusing personal names deliberately to insult, to express hostility, or to provoke another. Navajos used nicknames in this way (Dyk 1947:216). Kaskas used relationship terms in ordinary speech, using names only in anger (Honigmann 1954:122). Kroeber (1925:179, 181) reported that Yukis named children after a slain enemy to insult him, and they assumed that anyone using the name of a dead person was motivated by hate (cf. Spier [Klamath] 1930:60; Aginsky [Miwok] 1943:448).

On the other hand, the use of a personal name in a plea for help often enhanced the likelihood of the request being granted. Chiricahuas, who regarded the improper use of a personal name as insulting, felt, in other circumstances, that "a man is willing to do anything if he calls him by name," for example, in asking for personal help or for volunteers for a war party (Opler 1941:430-432). In announcing a man's new name, a Blackfoot leader might say, "Now, if you wish this man to aid you, if you call upon him for help, etc., you must address him as —" (Wissler 1911:17). An Iroquois was most likely to receive assistance if he used the addressee's name in requesting it (Shimony 1961:212).

Among certain Eskimos, in contrast to the general North American pattern, strangers introduced themselves by name as part of the etiquette of greeting; names, sometimes combined with kinship terms, were the primary means of identifying people, and, in at least some cases, one did not refer to people except by names. Stories without the names of the principals were regarded as having little point. Good manners required that names be remembered, be applied accurately, and be pronounced correctly. Nicknames were properly used only between persons with close social ties (Spencer [North Alaska Eskimo] 1959:290; VanStone [Tikiġaġmiut Eskimo] 1962:82; Gubser

[Interior North Alaska Eskimo] 1965:5, 144, 206; Stefánsson [Copper Eskimo] 1914:234; Jenness [Copper Eskimo] 1922:168; Spier [Havasupai] 1929: 215; Gayton [Yokuts, Monache] 1948:234).

Tlingit kin terms could evoke sensitive matters of rivalry and comparative social position; high-ranking men, in particular, preferred to use personal names: "That's what names are for" (Durlach 1928:32-33, quoting a Tlingit).

"Taboos" on Names of the Dead

Some degree of sensitivity to the use of the name or names of dead persons was so common that its absence is noted only a few times in the ethnographic literature (Lowie [Hidatsa] 1917:50; Jenness [Copper Eskimo] 1922:168; Boas [for one Kwakiutl group, the Koskimo] 1932a:212; E.W. Voegelin [Tubatulabal] 1938:46; Honingmann [Eastern Swampy Cree] 1956:60).

For some native peoples, there are reports merely of reluctance to use the names of the dead (Spier [Havasupai] 1928:304-305; McKennan [Tanana] 1959:142, cf. 134). More commonly, definite restrictions (often called "taboos") existed: for some Northern Paiutes, the interdiction on a name was permanent (Stewart 1941:412); for the Carriers, use of a name was prohibited for a generation (Morice 1933:645; cf. Hill-Tout [Cowichan] 1907a:310). Maidus did not use a name for about a year (Krober 1925:403; cf. Hill-Tout [Lillooet] 1907:201); for Pawnees, restrictions lasted during mourning (G. Dorsey and Murie 1940:106); for the Bering Strait Eskimos (Heinrich 1969:4), interdiction lasted until the name was given to another person.

Respect and consideration for the bereaved and fear of the dead entered into native explanations of restrictions (Tooker [Huron] 1964:134; Essene [Pomoan] 1942:38; R.M. Underhill [Papago] 1953:193; Brant [Kiowa Apache] 1949:59; Opler [Chiricahua Apache] 1941:475-476; Gatschet [Tonkawa] 1891:133; Parsons [Pueblos] 1939, 1:69). Among some peoples, violations of restrictions on names were offenses serious enough to provoke fines or violent retaliation (Gunther [Clallam] 1927:250; Gatschet, Frachtenberg, and Jacobs [Kalapuyan] 1945:41-42, 198; Chase [Chasta Costa] 1869:431; Du Bois [Tolowa] 1932:252; E.W. Voegelin (various northeastern California groups] 1942:140-141; Bright [Karok] 1957:142-144, 1958: 177-178; Devereux [Mohave] 1951:108-109; Opler [Lipan Apache] 1945:127).

There were other consequences of prohibitions on names of the dead: Kiowa Apaches delayed giving formal names to children since, if a child died, the name had to be avoided (McAllister 1955:138; Loeb [Cahto] 1932:52). Elsewhere, a person who had the same name as that belonging to someone who died was expected to

avoid or change his own name as well (Nansen [East Greenland Eskimo] 1894:230; Eells [Coast Salish] 1889:656; Lopatin [Bella Bella] 1945:53; Downs [Washoe] 1966:44; Mekeel [Walapai] 1935:128-129; Essene [Pomoan] 1942:38; Tooker [Huron] 1964:134; Williams [Narragansett] 1973:248; Newcomb [Delaware] 1956a:34). Wishrams might change their names after a death in the family because the deceased had called them by those names (Spier and Sapir 1930:258; cf. W.H. Kelly [Cocopa] 1949:154). The death of a child whose name had been used for his parents (teknonymy) led to a change in their names, usually to that of the next oldest child (Swanton [Chickasaw] 1928c:187).

In some instances, after a death, lexemes in the ordinary vocabulary that were the same as, or similar to, the name of the deceased person, were also banned from ordinary use (Drucker [Nootka] 1951:148; Silverstein [Wishram] 1966-1974; P.E. Goddard [Hupa] 1903:73-74; Mooney [Kiowa] 1892:272, 1898:152; Opler [Mescalero Apache] 1946:457-458; Opler and Bittle [Kiowa Apache] 1961:386; Veniaminov in Geoghegan [Aleut] 1944:19). There have been attempts to evaluate the effects of this practice on lexical change (Kroeber [California] 1925:48-49; Elmendorf [Salishan] 1951, 1962, 1970; Swadesh 1952; cf. Perry 1983 on ethnographic reconstruction). Swanton (1905:118) reported that Haidas might make some phonological changes in a name when it was used after the death of its holder.

If proscribed names were to be used again, it was necessary for there to be ways to reinstate them. For many Eskimos, the act of naming a newborn child after a dead relative served to return the name to the domain of the living (Heinrich 1969:4; cf. Du Bois [Wintu] 1935:51, 67). Family-sponsored feasts marked the transfer of an ancestor's name to a living person in the Columbia Plateau (Ray [Sanpoil and Nespelem] 1933:114; J.R. Wallace [Warm Springs Sahaptin] 1954:52-55; cf. Drucker [Tolowa] 1937a:253). In societies in which names were a vehicle for the transmission of public duties or offices, more formal mechanisms existed; for example, the successor to a Nootka chief validated his assumption of the name by a potlatch (Drucker 1951:148-149); Hurons transferred a name in a community ceremony (Tooker 1964:44-46).

Proscriptions on Names of Living Persons

Restrictions on using the names of living persons also existed: sometimes in reference, frequently in address, and sometimes in both. Northern Paiutes were reported to be reluctant to give the names of other persons (Mayhew 1905:248); Pawnee names were not regarded as suitable for ordinary address; Omahas did not refer to other people by name in their presence, nor did they ask another person's name (Fletcher and La Flesche

1911:334, 335; McKinley 1971:418; cf. Kendall [Upland Yuman] 1980). Although a Blackfoot might speak his own name, it was considered rude to ask another's name; by so doing, a questioner would imply that the other person had no particular reputation (Wissler 1911:17-18). Derogatory nicknames were often avoided in the presence of the person so named (Morice [Carrier] 1933:638).

The avoidance of names frequently was an aspect of relationships of respect, distance, or formality—for example, with in-laws, spouses, or old people (Heinrich [North Alaska Eskimo] 1960:124; Lowie [Assiniboine] 1909:41, [Crow] 1912:213; Kohl [Ojibwa] 1956:275-276; Landes [Ojibwa] 1937:14, Bourke [Apache] 1892:462); frequently it was part of a general pattern of avoidance, such as of graves or of certain kin terms (Opler [Lipan Apache] 1945:126-127).

Nicknames, kinship terms, and descriptive words or phrases were widely used in circumstances in which Europeans would use formal personal names (cf. Trager [Picuris Pueblo] 1943:566). Moreover, proper usage varied with sex, age, and relationship (Loeb [Pomoan] 1926:257). For example, in addressing relatives, Quechan women used kinship terms, young men used names, and old men used either (Bee 1963:216; cf. Gifford [Kumeyaay Diegueño] 1931:62). Among the Nunivak Eskimos, a young man might be addressed by name by an old man whose name the former could not use in reference, much less in direct address (Lantis 1946:238; cf. Honigmann [Kaska] 1949:130-131). The Seminoles addressed children by the words for boy and girl or by their nicknames; adults were addressed by kinship terms (Spoehr 1942:89).

Indians in many parts of North America did not utter their own names or were reluctant to do so. Notable exceptions were the peoples of the eastern seaboard, the northern Plains, the Northwest Coast, and the Arctic coast. While restraints were not universal elsewhere, they have been widely reported (Nelson [Malimiut] 1899:289; Hilger [Chippewa] 1951:36-37; Honigmann [Kaska] 1954:157; Morice [Carrier] 1933:645; T. Kroeber [Yahi] 1969:127-128; Lowie (Shoshone] 1909a:211, 1924:272; Lumholtz [Tarahumara] 1902, 1:462; Powers [Maidu] 1877:315). These constraints have been variously associated with personal modesty (Kroeber [Mohave] 1925:749) and dignity (Kohl [Ojibwa] 1956:275) or with luck (F. Russell [Pima] 1908:188), sacredness, or supernatural power (Landes [Prairie Potawatomi] 1970:220-221). At least to some degree, these were indigenous explanations; they suggest the ways in which personal names were tied in with other aspects of native culture.

On another level of explanation, it would appear that where a formal name represented or was associated directly with the public position and reputation of its holder, it could be spoken by him (cf. Hymes [Wishram] 1966:141-149). Where names were related to personal safety, strength, skills, powers, or well-being, they were more likely to be used by the bearer only in special, sometimes highly restricted circumstances (Kluckhohn and Leighton [Navajo] 1962:114-115).

Some early European observers, who encountered resistance to the casual use of personal names, inferred that names were secret. A few instances of actual secrecy can be found: two Chugach Eskimos might share a secret nickname (Birket-Smith 1953:86; cf. Steward [Shoshone] 1943:354, 391); secret birth names, known only to the name-giver, the mother, and (eventually) the child, have been reported for some of the Muskogean-speaking peoples of the Southeast (Toomey 1917:25-26). Western Apaches tried to keep names from becoming known to rival groups who might use them for ridicule (Goodwin 1942:531). The use of false names to mislead strangers, rival groups, or malevolent supernatural forces also occasionally occurred (Spier [Havasupai] 1928:305; Hooper [Cahuilla] 1920:349-350; Strong [Cahuilla, Cupeño] 1929:78, 254-255; Heinrich [Bering Strait Eskimo] 1969:6; cf. Landes [Prairie Potawatomi] 1970:221). Anxieties about witchcraft led Navajos to suspect the motives of people who asked for the names of children (Sapir and Hoijer 1942:295; cf. L. White [Zia Pueblo] 1962:203); however, secrecy about names was far less important to Native Americans than was propriety (cf. L. White [Santa Ana Pueblo] 1942:165).

Language Analysis

Linguistic Features

Personal names are part of the lexical inventory of a language. While they may be words or phrases, they are also lexemes. Lexemes have been defined by Conklin (1962:121) as meaningful forms "whose signification cannot be inferred from a knowledge of anything else in the language"; see also Sturtevant (1964:106); Berlin, Breedlove, and Raven (1973:216-219); Agar (1974:10-12); Hockett 1956, 1958:311-313). As lexemes, personal names might be—but often are not—included in dictionaries (for dictionaries in which at least some personal names are included see Bright [Karok] 1957; Barker [Klamath] 1963a; Gatschet [Klamath] 1890; Hess [Lushootseed] 1976; Sapir and Swadesh [Yana] 1960; Shipley [Maidu] 1963; Uhlenbeck and van Gulik [Blackfoot] 1934; Riggs [Sioux] 1852).

Proper names exist in every language (Hockett 1966a:21-11), but "few languages, if any, seem to show consistent formal markers characterizing proper names" (Hamp 1959:57). The data have never been systematically assembled for North America as a whole, but distinctive attributes have been reported for personal names in some languages, for example, for Pawnee (Parks 1979a, 1980) and Arikara (Parks 1980). Furthermore, although personal names conform to the phonology of the language in which they are embedded, they may be analyzable in terms of semantics, syntax, or morphology (Goddard [Unami Delaware] 1991; Mithun [Mohawk] 1984a), or they may not.

To the extent that names were unanalyzable or untranslatable they might form a distinct segment of the vocabulary of a language (Lantis [Nunivak Eskimo] 1946:237; Spier and Sapir [Wishram] 1930:258; Sapir [Chinookan compared with Takelma] 1907:270; Douglas R. Parks [Caddo], personal communication 1991). Lower Chinook names received from guardian spirits were meaningful; ancestral names were not (Ray 1938:67). Certain indicators of gender could be specific to names. It has been reported that names with ordinary meanings might display slight phonological or syntactic differences from everyday vocabulary (Hill-Tout [Lillooet] 1905:154; Morice [Carrier] 1933:635; Bloomfield [Menominee] 1962:21-22). In the sign languages and pictographs of Plains Indians, various semiotic devices could be used to avoid ambiguity between personal names and ordinary words (Mallery 1881:365, 1886:169).

Meanings and Translations

Many names of Native North Americans not only designated persons but also "meant," or alluded to, to something else. Examples of such meanings or allusions are: (1) place of origin or birth (Boas [Kwakiutl] 1921, 1:653, 1932a:201; Elmendorf and Kroeber [Yurok] 1960:373-374; Waterman [Yurok] 1920:214-217; Heinrich [Bering Strait Eskimo] 1969:5; Stefánsson [Mackenzie Delta Eskimo and North Alaska Eskimo] 1914:346-347); (2) astronomical, climatic, and similar phenomena (Cooke [Iroquois] 1952:429-430; Morice [Carrier] 1933:633-634; Ortiz [Tewa] 1969:32-33; Dixon [Maidu] 1905a:231); (3) animals, plants, and other natural objects (or qualities) (Speck [Maliseet, Penobscot] 1917a:11-15; Stevenson [Zuni] 1915:86; Powers [Maidu] 1877:316; Stewart [Ute, Southern Paiute] 1942:307; Chamberlain [Kootenai] 1896:260; Ewers [Blackfoot] 1955:254-255; cf. J.O. Dorsey [Siouan] 1890a); and (4) characteristics of persons—and the events in their lives.

Such names have often been translated into English (as well as into Spanish, French, and differing Indian languages). English translations (discussed here because they were the most frequent) came to be used by both Indians and non-Indians; for various reasons they were rarely adequate substitutes for the original names.

Although there are some cases in which a name lexeme in a North American language can be directly matched with a name lexeme in English (the Karok man's name *či·pákpa·k* 'robin', Bright 1957:331, and the English name Robin), such close correspondence is rare. A good translation into English can be difficult (see Parks 1989:4), and the outcome is very often not an acceptable English name. Such translations are likely to seem overly long or complex, possibly exotic, perhaps peculiar, childish, or derogatory. Two examples can be given from Karok men's names: *ʔe·θʔakúnva·n* 'slug-hunter' (*ʔê·θ* 'slug', *ʔákunva* '(to) hunt', *-a·n* agentive, Bright 1957:117, 317, 332) and *ʔifuθkámʔi·pma* 'going backward', (*ʔífuθ* 'behind', *-kam* 'in the direction', *ʔi·pmu* '(to) go back', Bright 1957:79, 335-336, 347). Neither Slug-Hunter nor Going Backward is a satisfactory English name.

Misleading or faulty translations have occurred frequently, based on linguistic errors and on cultural misunderstandings. The name of an Oglala Sioux leader of the nineteenth century was commonly translated 'Young Man Afraid of His Horses' (fig. 5). Actually, he and his father shared a name that literally means 'his horses are feared or frightening', one explanation being that the original bearer had distinguished himself as so formidable a warrior that the very sight of his horses inspired fear in his enemies (Robinson 1910:1001; cf. Hyde 1937:67-68; 117-118; Humfreville 1903:137; Mallery 1886:136). Similarly, a Haida name, which appears in English as 'Unable-to-Buy', commemorated an occasion on which the bearer's rival was unable to buy a copper (Swanton 1910:18 cites this and comparable examples of misunderstandings).

Another difficulty encountered in translating personal names concerns those important dimensions of meanings that go beyond literal interpretations of lexemes (cf. Swanton [Choctaw] 1931:123-124), including reinterpretations (Sapir 1915d:27). Connotative dimensions may be personal, relating to self-identification and to private family traditions (Bertelson [Greenland Eskimo] 1918:278 ff.). They may also involve symbolic associations with leadership, power, prestige, wealth, religion, warfare, or kinship. It is clear that such considerations were very important in the selection of a particular name for a particular person and were likely to continue to be salient in at least some contexts throughout life. Connotations are distorted or lost when a name is translated. Inevitably, a translated name acquires new connotations that may be irrelevant, inappropriate, possibly elevating, often demeaning to the name holder (cf. Cook 1905; Fletcher 1905; Swanton 1910:16-18). Translated names have, for this reason, tended to become alternative names added to the name holder's repertoire, each name having its own use and context (cf. Daniels [Oglala Sioux] 1970:223-224).

Smithsonian, NAA: 3247-A.

Fig. 5. Young Man Afraid of His Horses *(Thašúka Khokhípapi)*. Photograph probably by George Trager, Pine Ridge Agency, S. Dak., 1891.

Adaptation and Borrowing

Native American names have also been adapted to European phonologies and orthographies and have survived as sets of "borrowed" lexemes. In Northern Mexico, as elsewhere, they persist as modern surnames. Spicer (personal communication 1975) described the situation among the Yaquis:

> Names of persóns in the Yaqui language have been combined for 350 years with Spanish Christian names, the Yaqui name being used as a surname. There are some four types of surname of this kind. One employs a relative suffix, as in *ka-heʔeme* (Spanish Cajeme) which means 'he-who-does-not-drink'; the -*ʔeme* suffix means 'he who', the *ka-* is the negative, the verb is *heʔe.* . . . A second and extremely common type employs the suffix -*mea*, which is an instrumental; examples are *huʔupaʔu-mea* 'with mesquite', *chai-mea* 'with a cry'. . . . A third type consists simply of a name for some object such as *wíikit* 'bird', *kúupis* 'lightning bugs', *máacil* 'scorpion', *wikoʔi* 'bow'; these serve as surnames in the same way as the other two types and do not seem to be nicknames. The fourth type is the nickname which sometimes replaces a surname; examples are *kuchu* 'fish', *táabu* 'cottontail', and many others.

Casagrande (1955:14-15) provides a number of pairs of Comanche and English versions of names, the English in use as surnames: *tasikwanaʔ* Tahsequaw; *monáʔsiʔ* Monoessy; *tanísutaiʔ* Tanishoti. Spier and Sapir (1930:260, 212) record *silátsi*, a Wishram man's name, and Siletsi, a surname of his lineal descendants (cf. Weeks [Yakima] 1971:252-253). In addition, the names of historically famous Indians have been "naturalized" in English: Sacagawea (incorrectly Sacajawea), Osceola, Tecumseh, and Deganawida are only a few of many (cf. Algeo 1973:60-63).

It should also be mentioned that linguistic modifications of European names occurred as they became items in native lexicons, such as in Woods Cree [misil] 'Michel', [pieðis] 'Pierre' + *is* (diminutive) (Robert Brightman, personal communication 1980); in Kootenai, *haˑléˑ* 'Harry', *nisapáł* 'Elizabeth' (Garvin 1947; see also Bright [Karok] 1957:278-281; Sapir and Swadesh [Nootka] 1939:245 ff.; Parsons [Zuni] 1923a, [Micmac] 1926:474, and [Caddo] 1941:26; Mooney [Cherokee] 1889; Casagrande [Comanche] 1954-1955(3):16; Chamberlin [Gosiute Shoshone] 1913:15; Bergsland [Aleut] 1959:17, 1994:579).

On a small scale, aboriginal North Americans have been a source of names for others. Although native systems of naming have had no impact on European cultural patterns, native names—most especially geographic names—have had salience for Whites, and they have acquired them in various ways since early periods of contact. Names of many sorts were involved, including translations of European names (e.g., French *Bellefeuille* to Nipissing *kwe·na·č ani·pi·šš* 'beautiful leaf', the name given to the missionary Charles-Louis DeBellefeuille; Chamberlain 1899:25). The bestowal of a name on a European could be associated with adoption or marriage into a group. It was often intended as a compliment or a gesture of appreciation or friendship and was so taken by the recipients (Fenton [Iroquois] 1965:254; Parker [Iroquois] 1968:14; Speck and Herzog [Tutelo] 1942:121; Parsons [San Juan Tewa] 1929:30). Indian names have continued to be symbols for Whites of a variety of relationships with Indians or to mark activities associated with Indian life as perceived by Whites, for instance, the use of "Indian" names by the Campfire Girls (see Smithsonian Institution. Bureau of American Ethnology 1926; Gulick 1961).

Persistence, Change, Revival

History

Before the coming of Europeans to North America, changes in naming customs occurred in response to contacts with other peoples, to evolving social arrangements, and to modifications in language (Callender [Central Algonquians] 1962). Borrowings are known to have occurred in pre- and postcontact times without direct European influence: names have moved across linguistic boundaries, for example, from Eyak to Tlingit (de Laguna 1972, 2:789-790), from Nez Perce to Salishan (Reichard 1933-1938:532), and among Pueblos (Parons 1923a:172; Bunzel 1933-1938:394). Also interior groups in western Canada developed systems of potlatch naming suggested by the customs of their coastal neighbors (Jenness [Sekani] 1937:55; Goldman [Carrier] 1940:338).

More than six Old World, mainly European, languages have contributed to both first names and surnames of Indians, Eskimos, and Aleuts. Among the sources are: (1) Danish, in Greenland (Rink 1877:230 ff.); (2) Russian, in the Aleutians (Geoghegan 1944:25, fn. 2; Bergsland 1959:17, 1994:579) and adjacent areas (Elliott [Pribilof Island Aleut] 1886:239; Oswalt [Kusquqvagmiut] 1973:173-174; Birket-Smith [Chugach Eskimo] 1953:1-6; L.F. Jones [Tlingit] 1914:37); (3) French, in eastern Canada, the northeastern United States (Parsons [Micmac] 1926:474), throughout the regions of the fur trade (Chaput [Upper Great Lakes Algonquians] 1966; Ritzenthaler [Southwestern Chippewa] 1945:175-176; Morice [Carrier] 1933:638),

and around the lower Mississippi and adjacent Gulf coast (Swanton [Houma] 1911:292); (4) Spanish, in northern Mexico and the southern United States from Texas to the Pacific (Dozier [Tewa] 1956:154-155; Gentry [Guarijío] 1963:123; Thord-Gray [Tarahumara] 1955:30; Reichard [Navajo] 1928:105-107; Herzog [Pima] 1941:69; Strong [Cahuilla] 1929:68, 181); and (5) English, over large parts of Canada and the United States, including Alaska. In some areas, English was the only source of non-Indian names; in others, it has been a second influence in regions first exposed to other languages, as, for example, the American Southwest (Bodine [Taos Pueblo] 1968) and Alaska (L.F. Jones 1914:37). In some places, (6) Dutch names have been acquired (Weslager 1959). Asiatic names occur; African names are a possibility, especially in the American South. It can be difficult, in certain areas, to decide which Native American or overseas language was the source of a surname (cf. Erickson [Maliseet] 1981).

The kinds of European names acquired by Native Americans were varied. Biblical names were common, provided by missionaries, and saints' names were customary as first names in areas of strong Roman Catholic and Russian Orthodox influence (Beals [Yaqui, Mayo] 1945:59; Hrdlička [Ópata] 1904:79; Parsons [Micmac] 1926:474; Bergsland [Aleut] 1959:17, 1994:579; Oswalt [Kusquqvagmiut] 1963a:30). The names of European explorers (Jenness [Copper Eskimo] 1922:167-168), captives (Hallowell [Wyandot] 1963:524), teachers, administrators, missionaries (D.B. Smith [Mississauga Ojibwa] 1975:171), army comrades (French and French [Warm Springs Sahaptin] 1949-1992), and settlers (Chase [Tillamook] 1869:429) were taken. For a time, numbers assigned by the United States Army were used by Apaches as "English" names (Goodwin and Kaut 1954:390; Granger 1961:33). Eventually, Native Americans came to have access to essentially the same pool of first names as their non-Indian neighbors (Casagrande 1954-1955, pt. 3:16-20) (fig. 6). On the other hand, surnames that differed from those of their neighbors (such as, French names from fur traders or translated names) have sometimes made possible the easy application of unfavorable stereotypes (Daniels [Oglala Sioux] 1970:210).

Representatives of religion and government (not infrequently combined in the same person), traders, settlers (Merrell [Catawba] 1989:126), employers (Braroe [Plains Cree] 1975:123; Jackson [Southwestern Chippewa] 1980:136; Ritzenthaler [Potawatomi] 1953:141-142), and teachers (Yava [Arizona Tewa] 1978:viii, 3), were all persistent agents of change (vol. 4:438). Many non-Indians, in addition to being baffled by unfamiliar phonologies, saw native names and naming systems as incompatible with the requirements of

Indian adaptation to Europe-derived governments, economies, and religions.

From very early postcontact times, the baptisms of infants and of converted adults were occasions on which Christian names were acquired by Native Americans (cf. Schwatka [Tarahumara] 1899:349-350; Ezell [Pima] 1961:82-85; King [Northern Athapaskan] 1967:8). Missionaries were sometimes systematic in assigning surnames, using approximations of native names, translations of native names, already acquired given names, and so forth (Fienup-Riordan [Nelson Island Eskimo] 1983:150; Oswalt [Kusquqvagmiut] 1963: 147; Catholic Church Records [Chinookans] 1972). In a few regions in North America, where European missionaries did not persist or were expelled, native versions of baptismal ceremonies, including and sometimes emphasizing the giving of names, survived for a time (Morice [Carrier, Babine] 1933:636-638; Goodwin and Kaut [Western Apache] 1954:395).

Administrative and legal considerations accompanying the extension of control by national governments stimulated efforts by secular authorities to assign European or Europeanized names to Native Americans. In particular, record-keeping in connection with the inheritance of property, for instance, land allotments, was felt to require a European-type "orderly" system for identifying persons and family relationships. Non-Indian fathers were one source of surnames (see Merrell [Catawba] 1989:126), but more important were official attempts to impose a patrilineal, binomial system. Accounts of these efforts (including the participation of a Dakota physician, Charles Eastman) have been provided by Eastman (1977:182-185), L.E. Underhill (1968), and Littlefield and Underhill (1971). Mutual misunderstandings inevitably accompanied the process; problems such as conflicts in patterns of land tenure (Service [Havasupai] 1947:360-366) and the reconciliation of matrilineal descent with European-type patronymics were intrinsically difficult (Spoehr [Oklahoma Seminole] 1942:89, 107; cf. Parsons [Jemez Pueblo 1925:30). The first name plus last name system itself was alien (even by 1992, middle names were rare among Indians). The history of Canadian surname adoption was analogous to that in the United States (cf. E.S. Rogers and J.H. Rogers [Mistassini Cree] 1963:18; E.S. Rogers and M.B. Rogers [Northern Ojibwa] 1978).

During the early twentieth century, some Indians, especially those who supported acculturation, regarded English names as one symbol of constructive relationships with Whites. Nevertheless, most retained Indian names and used them in appropriate contexts (Hertzberg 1971:31-58; Parker 1968).

The most severe challenges to the survival of native names came from those profound and irreversible changes in social and economic organization of native peoples that accompanied European political domination of the continent. Dispersal or decimation of populations, modifications of descent systems, atrophy of clans, suppression or dilution of religion, and economic impoverishment or— rarely—enrichment led to significant changes in naming practices. Patterns of control or ownership were distorted, lines of inheritance were confused, standards for validation were questioned, and names were simply forgotten. On the Northwest Coast, for example, new and disruptive possibilities for social mobility arose as a consequence of two developments: (1) high ranking name-titles became vacant as the population declined sharply; and (2) persons who had no inherited rights to traditional names acquired access to economic resources and the desire to use their wealth to improve their social position (Drucker 1939:63, 1955:128-129; cf. Adams [Gitksan] 1973; Blackman [Haida] 1973:50; Brink [Haida] 1974:169-170; Colson [Makah] 1953:209-212).

On the other hand, many names and much naming behavior have survived, including habits of usage (cf. Philips [Warm Springs Reservation] 1976; Gilbert [Eastern Cherokee] 1943:202, 251, 254; Stearns [Haida] 1977; Kenyon [Nootka] 1977). Native and European names have not, on the whole, been defined as mutually exclusive. Occasionally, renaming accompanied vigorous attempts to suppress all aspects of native culture and was actively resented and resisted (D. Eggan [Hopi] 1943:369). However, Native North Americans were not ordinarily much troubled by acquiring additional names (T. Stern [Klamath] 1966:52-54; Milan [North Alaska Coast Eskimo] 1964:59-60, 83-95). Not being sacred, European-type names were often not subject to the restrictions on use applied to native names (Hudson [Chumash] 1977:265); one result was that they could displace not native names but instead the alternative terminologies, such as kinship terms (Hilger [Chippewa] 1951:35 ff.; Spoehr [Oklahoma Seminole] 1942:105; Whitman [San Ildefonso Pueblo] 1940:453, F. Eggan [Picuris Pueblo] 1950:306).

Versions of aboriginal naming ceremonies, as well as names, have persisted in many areas (Dunning [Northern Ojibwa] 1959:99; Kinietz [Southwestern Chippewa] 1947:115-118; Dusenberry [Cree] 1962:90-91; K. French [Warm Springs Sahaptins] 1955:93, 115-117). Two systems often coexist: Native North American names are given in Native American ceremonies, and English names are given in Christian baptism or regularized by secular means (Whitman [San Ildefonso Pueblo] 1947:33-35; Lange [Cochiti Pueblo] 1959:402-405; Rohner [Kwakiutl] 1967:93). Mexican Kickapoos, descendants of nineteenth-century emigrants from the United States, have retained some traditional naming ceremonies (Ritzenthaler and Peterson 1956:47, 58; Latorre and Latorre 1976:278-

left page: bottom right, Gonzaga U. Folay Center Lib., Spokane, Wash.; right page: bottom, Haskell Indian Nations U., Lawrence, Kans.

Fig. 6. Names used by 20th-century Indians, combining given names that are mostly in general use with surnames of various origins. Team sports are an integrating force in American schools, and Native Americans are active participants in this arena. top left, Sho-Ban Chiefs basketball team of Sho-Ban Junior/Senior High School, Fort Hall, Idaho. front row, left to right: Conrad Benally, Lemhi Shoshone and Navajo; Kim Osborne, Northern Shoshone–Bannock; Deland Osborne, Northern Shoshone–Bannock. middle row: Kevin Yazzie, Northern Shoshone–Bannock and Navajo; Dusty Osborne, Northern Shoshone–Bannock and Yakima; Brandon Jim, Northern Shoshone–Bannock; Ryan Burnett, Eastern Shoshone and Arapaho; Ryan Pokibro, Northern Shoshone–Bannock and Ponca. back row: Ernest Todakozie, Navajo; Sam Matsaw, Northern Shoshone–Bannock; coach Michael Jordan, Colville Confederated Tribes, Moses Band; Shohn Dunn, Northern Shoshone–Bannock and Navajo; Benji Snipe, Northern Shoshone–Bannock; Levi Perdash, Northern Shoshone–Bannock; assistant coach Don Pine, Teton Sioux. Photograph by Delson Suppah, 1994. top right, Wyoming Indian High School Chiefs, Ethete, Wyo., versus Pine Bluffs High School, Pine Bluffs, Wyo., in the class 2-A basketball championships. Chiefs player #43 is Alfred Spoonhunter and player #31 is Darrell Bell (both Northern Arapahoe). Photograph by Tom Stromme, 1985. bottom left, St. Catherine Indian School girls varsity basketball team, Santa Fe, N. Mex. front row, left to right: Rochelle Nastascio, Zuni; Antoinette Toya, Jemez; Benelda Cohoe, Navajo; Monica Naranjo, San Ildefonso. middle row: Tarsicia Haskey, Navajo; Darrellene Clark, Navajo; Rebecca Sando, Jemez; Annette Waquie, Jemez. back row: Nichele Sando, Jemez; Sewa Quintero, Western Apache; Melanie Paytiamo, Acoma; Summer Escalanti, Mescalero Apache; coach Jose Aguilar, San Ildefonso. Photograph by Jennifer Reasoner, 1994-1995. bottom right, St. Francis Xavier's Mission, Mont., baseball team, about 1901. front row, left to right: John Sits Down Spotted, John (Tom) Little Owl, Gun Shows. middle row: Harry Beads, Frank He Does It, Sam Horn, Charley White Eagle. back row: Al Holds, Albert Iron, Paul Kills, Joseph Short Bull. All are from the Crow tribe.

Football teams. top, Eagles of St. Mary's Junior High School, Edmonton, Alta. All players are Blackfoot from Blood Reserve. front row, left to right: Curtis Rabbit, Ernest Black Rabbit, James Low Horn, Ivan Tallow, Dan or Duane Mistaken Chief, Kenneth Whiteman, L. Many Fingers, T. Yellow Old Woman, Dave Bullshields, A. Devine, John Chief Moon. back row: coach T. Duhaime, Jimmy Mills, Calvin Cross Child, Tom Healy, Calvin Chief Calf, Donald Big Swallow, Stan Eagle Bear, Delvin No Runner, Michael Fox, Dan Crazy Bull, Rex Plume, coach Don Behrens. Photograph by Jim Goodstriker, 1976. bottom, Fightin' Indians of Haskell Indian Nations U., Lawrence, Kans. front row, left to right: Shannon Dickey, Eastern Cherokee; Graham Snelding, Kaw-Kansa; Sonny Martin, Bad River Chippewa; Kevin Mann, Cherokee; Bobbie Williams, Absentee Shawnee; Dena Drye, Paiute; Buddie Hoodie, Shoshone; Michele Ferris, Choctaw; Rene Long, Eastern Cherokee; Josette Urich, Tesuque; Cheryl Mike, Navajo; Tess Long, Eastern Cherokee; Frank Curly, Navajo; Toby Gouge, Seminole-Creek; Steve Quetone, Kiowa; Harrison Watchman, Navajo. second row: Jud Earp, Cherokee; J.D. Richardson, Cherokee-Delaware; Ira Burnett, Cherokee; Baliente Herrera, Comanche; Charles T. Nez, Potawatomi; Steve Brown, Yuchi; Amari White, Seminole; Chiarpah Matheson, Coeur d'Alene; Michael Kelley, Choctaw; Darron Rhodd, Iowa-Otoe; Kelly England, Potawatomi; Henry Janes, Cherokee; Jason Branch, Navajo; Shawn Harrah, Pima; Jamie Earp, Cherokee. third row: Bryan Raymond, Cherokee; Delvin Bennett, Comanche; Robert Colbert, Creek-Seminole; Dominick Palone, Quechan; Kirk Blancett, Choctaw; Brent Raymond, Cherokee; Joseph Holford, Colville; Jim Pahcoddy, Comanche; Jeremiah Henley, Cherokee; Stoney Burris, Choctaw; Walt Davis, Choctaw; Jack Zachary, Nez Perce; Nial Long, Sioux; James Patterson, Cherokee; Nakoa Williams, Comanche; Jason French, Cherokee; Mike Running Crane, Blackfoot; coach Phil Homeratha, Otoe-Missouri; coach Todd Nugent, non-Indian; coach Richard Brewer, Sioux; head coach James Gary Tanner, Cherokee; coach Bryan Ishcomer, Choctaw; coach Mitch Gaffen, non-Indian; coach John Morris, Sauk-Fox; Aaron Mason, Cherokee; Tony Gibson, Shawnee–Sauk-Fox. Photograph by Anthony Schmidt, 1994.

281). Elsewhere in northern Mexico, non–Roman Catholic ceremonies have not been reported, although native language names have continued to be used (Beals [Cáhita] 1943:45; 1945:59; Johnson [Ópata] 1950:29; Spicer [Yaqui] 1961:21, 33, 34).

Functions and Significance

A single name might serve in a number of cultural contexts; often names were specific to particular contexts, and multiple names frequently existed. Name and context could be highly interactive. Similarly, on the Northwest Coast, the relationship between a name and its bearer was dynamic and reciprocal: the acquisition of a great name brought prestige to its holder, and, in turn, the reputation and value of a name rose and fell with the fortunes of its bearers (Boas [Tsimshian] 1916:497-498, 510; Suttles [Coast Salish] 1958:503). Names were rarely treated by observers as being "causal" (independent variables), but they have helped to label or map an individual's relationship with history, with the world, with society, with others, and with himself.

Names could embody parental aspirations and suggest future roles to children; subsequently, they could continue to signal responsibilities to the bearer. They could be used to express disapproval, ridicule, or mockery, as well as approbation (cf. Hymes 1961:64).

Names symbolized "personhood." Named, a child was a member of a social group (cf. La Flesche [Osage] 1921:50). Unnamed, he had fewer ties with the community into which he was born: for example, a child who had been named was less likely to be abandoned (Balikci [Netsilik Eskimo] 1967:619); burial practices were sometimes simpler for infants who died before they had been named (Bowers [Mandan] 1950:98). Conversely, giving resident outsiders local names made them more truly into persons with whom one could interact.

Names were not infrequently related to health and longevity. Cherokees sometimes named an unborn infant to facilitate an otherwise difficult birth (Mooney 1932:125); other groups might rename a child who failed to grow or who was sickly (Skinner [Menominee] 1913:36-38; Lowie [Hidatsa] 1917:50; Powers [Yuki] 1877:126). A change of name was often part of shamanistic curing (Ray [Modoc] 1963:103-104; Mooney [Cherokee] 1891:343; Mooney and Olbrechts 1932:63, 67-68; C.F. Voegelin and E.W. Voegelin [Shawnee] 1935:626-628; Balikci [Netsilik Eskimo] 1963:392; Landes [Prairie Potawatomi] 1970:203; McAllister [Kiowa Apache] 1955:139). People who had lived long and healthy lives might be preferred as namesakes or namegivers (Hilger [Chippewa] 1951:31, 37-38; cf. Kroeber [Gros Ventre] 1908:182).

Names seem, at least sometimes, to have represented the essence of a person. The belief that an individual has an essence is plausible in terms of certain European traditions; care should be taken not to exaggerate its prevalence among Indian and Arctic peoples. Nevertheless, names were clearly of great personal importance, often of significance in sacred and secular contexts involving personhood; use in some cases seems not merely to have identified but to have evoked their bearers. Among the Iroquois, the name of a sick person could be taken to a diagnostic or curing ceremony if the owner himself could not be present (Shimony 1961:211-212); the Tlingit belief in reincarnation (marked by identity of names, the equating of namesakes, and the use of the same basic stem in the expressions for 'to name' and 'to breathe') lies behind de Laguna's (1954:184) statements that Tlingit names "are thus an essential part of the self" (cf. Boas 1911:72; Benedict 1932:14). The relationships between names and souls that were held to exist by Bering Strait Eskimo also suggest that names participated in the essence of a person (Heinrich 1969:3-4). The phenomena just discussed are not identical, and some are not what European philosophers have meant by "essence."

Names have sometimes been seen as a part of a people's "oral literature [or oral history]" (Fortes 1955:339; Price and Price 1972:341). For Northern Yumans, Kendall (1980) treats names (noninherited) as "abbreviated texts," dealing with persons and social relations. Names were widely used to commemorate and record events, achievements, and relationships of importance. The creation of names had aesthetic aspects, and names (particularly nicknames) were not infrequently a vehicle for humor. Among many peoples, names were of sufficient importance to require specialists, individuals who were particularly gifted in composing, divining, selecting, or remembering them.

Sources

Although interest in names is longstanding, there have been few surveys or comparative studies. The questionnaire that Schoolcraft (1851-1857) sent to missionaries, Indian agents, and others included a request for information and examples of names; the results as published were not extensive. Hodge (1907-1910) incorporated many names of individuals with what was known about both the name and the person; in addition, Swanton (1910:16-18) contributed a short, general article on "Names and Naming." Curtis (1907-1930) collected information on names in many of the regions he visited. N. Miller (1927), Thurnwald (1927), Larock (1932), Pettitt (1946), Charles (1951), and Hultkrantz (1953) attempted general or comparative studies (focusing on or including North American data) with varying degrees of success. Data from the Human Relations Area Files were utilized in a world-wide cross-cultural study of naming practices and beliefs; seven North American cultures were included (Alford 1988).

In addition to general surveys, there have been productive explorations of relationships between names and naming and larger sociocultural or sociolinguistic systems. Among these are Barnes (1980), Bergsland (1994:579-585), Casagrande (1954-1955), Clifton (1977:106-111), Collins (1966), Damas (1972), Fienup-Riordan (1983:149-160), Friedrichs (1994), Garvin (1947), Goss (1973), Guemple (1965, 1972a), Heinrich (1963, 1969), Hymes (1966), Momaday (1976), Nuttall (1994), Silverstein (1984), C.F. Voegelin and E.W. Voegelin (1935), C.F. Voegelin and F.M. Voegelin (1970, 1970a), and Whiteley (1992). However specific the data in these works, the analyses have implications for comparative study.

Other sources include: biographies, historical works, travelers' accounts, church records, government publications and documents, and official and private archives (cf. Barnes 1984:xi-xii; Moore 1984:291-294; E.S. Rogers and M.B. Rogers 1978). Elsdon C. Smith (1952:135-139) and E.D. Lawson (1987:19-21, 29-31, 54) published personal name bibliographies with sections on American Indian names; in addition, from 1953 to 1976, the journal *Names* published an annual bibliography including items on native American names (E. Smith 1953-1976).

The Ethnography of Speaking

WICK R. MILLER

The ethnography of speaking—the study of language in its social and cultural context—is concerned with the nature of the speech community, function and use of language, speech styles, specialized vocabulary and the categories of people who use them, attitudes, what people believe about their own and other languages, and the place and function of bi- and multilingualism. It has been a focused field of study starting only in the second half of the twentieth century (Hymes 1962,1974; Gumperz 1962).

In earlier times, the ethnography of speaking tended to be slighted in the study of American Indian communities, with data often scattered and difficult to find. Linguists tended to concentrate narrowly on linguistic matters, especially if the language was in danger of becoming extinct. Ethnologists tended to ignore the topic because, if it dealt with language, many felt ill-equipped to deal with it if they lacked formal linguistic training. But happily there were a few anthropological linguists, most of them trained by Franz Boas, Edward Sapir, or Alfred L. Kroeber, who wrote on a number of topics dealing with the ethnography of speaking, though this term was not in use yet. Information can also be gleaned from introductions to and footnotes in grammars and text collections. Some ethnographies contain a fair bit of unsystematic material, but it is usually scattered and hard to find. Accounts of early travelers and missionaries sometimes include useful information.

The Speech Community

The speech community is a social rather than linguistic unit. Members of a speech community belong to the same social group and also share at least one variety of a language, along with rules or norms for its use. The community may be monolingual or multilingual. The size of the unit may vary, depending on the level of abtraction one is interested in, so that in one instance it may be a small face-to-face group, while in another instance it may be several such small groups, forming a larger community (Gumperz 1962:31; Hymes 1972:54, 1974:51). It is important to note that merely sharing the same language is not enough. The range of social and cultural variation in speech communities is exemplified by those in the Great Basin and the Pueblos.

Great Basin

The aboriginal inhabitants of the Great Basin spoke one of the Numic languages—Mono, Northern Paiute, Panamint, Shoshone, Kawaiisu, or Ute (including Southern Paiute and Chemehuevi dialects)—or Washoe, an unrelated Hokan language (W. Miller 1966, 1970, in vol. 11:98-106; Jacobsen 1986b).

The Basin people were nomadic hunters and gatherers, living in an area of low population density. In the spring and summer the group usually consisted of one or two related families. In the late summer or early fall, larger but more temporary groupings of 50 to 200 would form for one or two weeks for rabbit or antelope hunting. Winter would find a small number of families camped together in small villages. These larger fall gatherings and winter villages would have a "chief" with limited and temporary authority. Each family tried to follow the same annual circuit, but it was not always able to do so because of yearly variation in the availability of plants and animals. As a result, the composition of the fall and winter groups often varied from year to year.

It is not clear if there were permanent localized kin-based groups (Steward 1938; vol. 11:368-397, 466-498; Downs 1966). Likely such groups existed in some but not all parts of the Basin. But in either case, the shifting nomadic group produced an unbounded speech community. Each individual belonged to a network of kin-related folk, a network that had no sharp geographic boundaries. The largest permanent residential unit was the family, with larger groupings being temporary and often ephemeral.

As a consequence of the dislocations brought about by the arrival of Whites in the late nineteenth century, permanent settlements of Indians came into existence on a number of small scattered reservations and colonies (small settlements on the outskirts of major towns). Two important changes in the speech communities resulted. First, with permanent settlements, the speech communities were bounded. But the effects of this were minimized because there was a great deal of moving and visiting between the various communities.

Philbrook Mus. of Art, Tulsa, Okla.

Fig. 1. *Dakota Teaching*. In Native American societies instruction by older members of the family or group was often an important and valued source of linguistic socialization. Here an old man is depicted instructing children while seated on a hide outside a painted tepee. He wears a painted robe, holds an eagle feather, and has other items around him. The boy and girl on the left hold what appear to be eagle-bone whistles, while the child on the right holds a painted stick. Gouache painting by Oscar Howe, Yanktonai Sioux, 1951.

Second, English played an important role. In the 1990s almost everyone spoke at least some English, and there were few communities in which children were still learning the aboriginal language.

• SOCIALIZATION The child usually grew up in a small but heterogeneous group. Usually there was an aunt, grandparent, or some relative who came from a different area, who spoke another dialect or language, or who spoke the local language as a second language, and thus with an accent. A child, during the linguistically formative years, may have spent some time living with relatives in another area, with people who spoke a different language or dialect. This was the situation in the 1960s (W. Miller 1970), and early reports suggest that it was also the aboriginal pattern (Steward 1934; Hopkins 1883; Scott 1966). Reports from those who grew up around 1900 show that the child's playmates consisted mostly of his or her siblings.

• BILINGUALISM Considerable bilingualism was found in aboriginal times in the areas where two languages bordered each other. Bilingualism was facilitated by the close relationship of the Numic languages, a fact noted by the Numic speakers themselves. There was a strip, up to 100 miles wide, between the Shoshone and Northern Paiute, in which the whole population was bilingual (vol. 11:105). There was also a fair bit of bilingualism between the Washoe and Northern Paiute, and in the border area there were groups called "half Paiute" (Downs 1966:5). In such cases, language differences did not signal cultural differences and hence could not be used as symbols for cultural identity.

Native bilingualism persisted in the 1990s, especially between Shoshone and Northern Paiute, since there were a number of communities that included both groups. Trilingual individuals, who spoke Shoshone, Northern Paiute, and English, were not uncommon.

Passive bilingualism, the ability to understand but not speak a second language, was especially common between closely related languages. It was common in the 1990s in the Numic area and was probably also common in aboriginal times.

Because of accidents of personal history, some individuals were bidialectal. They may have grown up in more than one locality, their spouse might be from a different dialect area, they might move as adults (often moving to the spouse's community), or they might have traveled extensively. Extensive exposure does not guarantee bidialectalism, since a number of people thus exposed remained monodialectal. The ability to control more than one dialect was admired, but the inability to do so was not stigmatized.

Learning another dialect leads to three kinds of results: some individuals change dialects, losing their native dialect, others learn an additional dialect, keeping the two quite distinct, and still others end up with a mixture. All three, and with various gradations, are found in the Great Basin.

Bilingualism and bidialectalism were slightly more common among men than women, probably reflecting the fact that men were more apt to be well traveled.

• HIGHLY VALUED AND EXPRESSIVE SPEECH An oratorical style—in both the aboriginal language and English—was used in the 1990s by elders and, in the past, by chiefs in making announcements or preaching to a gathering such as a funeral (note that the Shoshone word for chief is *tekwahni* 'talker'). A chief was expected to be able to talk well, but with as much emphasis on being able to talk sense, give good advice, as on oratorical ability. The shaman, and his assistant or interpreter, also used a special valued style during shamanistic performances, and the negotiations in obtaining the services of a shaman may have also been in a special style.

Devices used in story telling include repetition and redundancy. In Shoshone and Southern Paiute, special suffixes are used in quoting Coyote (Sapir 1910a). There is a great deal of individual variation in the manner and delivery of the story. Listeners are expected to interact, usually by offering an occasional "yes" to show that attention is being maintained.

Songs are sharply differentiated from ordinary speech. Shoshone hand game songs are composed of meaningless words. But other songs—dance songs, shaman songs, and songs in stories—have words, and all are changed by certain phonological rules. Sapir (1910a) notes that certain phonological conventions are also used in rendering Southern Paiute songs. Swearing and slang have not been reported and may have been absent, though by the 1960s English was used for both (W. Miller 1970). Baby talk was weakly developed, with a specialized vocabulary being reported only among the Ute (J. Stewart 1960).

• ATTITUDES Good speech makers, good story tellers, good singers, and prolific song composers were admired. But since stylistic variation is not an area of cultural elaboration, the prevailing attitude toward language is somewhat casual. Learning another language or dialect is something one comes to do if one is exposed to it, and it is not thought of as especially difficult or eventful.

Language and dialect differences are seldom used as markers of cultural identity. There are some exceptions, for example, between the Ute and Southern Paiute, who speak different dialects of the same language, and for whom the dialect difference is the signal for ethnic identity. English is accorded greater prestige by some, though attitudes are variable. Other languages and dialects are accorded equal prestige. With some exceptions, the speech of others is not degraded; it is simply felt to be different and of equal validity (W. Miller 1970:32).

The Pueblos

The Pueblos consist of some 20 villages in northern New Mexico and Arizona, where nine languages are spoken: Hopi, Zuni, the two Keresan languages, and five Kiowa-Tanoan languages, Jemez, Tewa, and three in the Tiwa branch of the family. Some, like Zuni, are spoken at a single village, while others, such as Rio Grande Keresan, are spoken with dialectal variation at several villages. While there is cultural variation among the Pueblos Indians, it does not match the linguistic variation.

The Pueblo Indians have lived a similar way of life in settled farming villages for some 1,500 years. They are especially well known for their rich and highly developed ceremonial life. Each pueblo, consisting of a single village, or one central village with satellite villages, is a socially, politically, and ceremonially autonomous unit. Populations range from a few hundred to 4,000; in aboriginal times, the upper limit was probably much lower.

The Pueblos have maintained their social and cultural identity during 400 years of contact with Euro-American culture. But there have been social and cultural changes, instigated by the arrival of the Spaniards in the late sixteenth century, who especially affected the eastern Pueblos, and by the presence of Euro-Americans for over 100 years. In the 1990s, the native language was being passed on in some Pueblos and in some households, but English was increasingly becoming the child's first language (see Dozier 1970; Bauman 1980; Kroskrity 1993.)

• SOCIALIZATION The child grows up in a community that has well-delineated boundaries. In the past the child was probably little influenced by either Indians or non-Indians outside the Pueblo, but in the twentieth century outside events and institutions, such as the school, were of considerable importance.

The household includes more than the nuclear family, with many adults to provide a linguistic model. Older sisters typically spend a substantial part of their time as baby tenders, and they introduce the child early to well-developed play and peer groups (Dennis 1940).

Learning the various styles and levels of speech comes in late childhood, or early adulthood. Slang is picked up informally from peer group members (Newman 1955), but the more exalted levels come with more deliberate training. Thus a Hopi chief "will take his nephew out herding with him not only as shepherd or donkey boy but to teach him prayer-songs" (Stephen 1936:1i).

• BILINGUALISM Almost everyone was bilingual in English in the 1990s, largely because of the introduction of American schools. Spanish was still used, especially by older people, and by the Rio Grande Pueblos, who are located in an area that contains large numbers of native Spanish speakers.

The 600 or so Arizona Tewas present the most notable example of native bilingualism. They came from the Rio Grande Valley to the east, bringing their own language while fleeing the oppression of the Spaniards. They share First Mesa with the more numerous Hopi and speak both the Hopi and the Tewa languages (Dozier 1954:292).

Other examples of native bilingualism were less common, at least in part because of the availability of English as a lingua franca. It was more common in earlier times, but not so common as one might expect, considering the degree of linguistic diversity. Inter-Pueblo contacts among ceremonial leaders sometimes led to one or both leaders learning the other's language. Indian bilingualism was sometimes the result of one group moving to another Pueblo, usually during a time of distress, such as famine, and of intertribal marriages, which were not common. There are and were, of course, always individual exceptions of linguistic virtuosity. While bilingualism was not denigrated, neither was it highly valued (Kroskrity 1981, 1993; Leap 1973:277; Dozier 1954:297, 300; Stephen 1936:xxvii; White 1935:80). It does not appear that any Indian language ever served as a lingua franca (Voegelin, Voegelin, and Schutz 1967:430).

Some pueblos had an official interpreter, which might reflect the fact that native bilingualism was not common. A Zuni interpreter must know Zuni, English, and Spanish (Smith and Roberts 1954:27). The Hopis of First Mesa selected an Arizona Tewa, because of the Tewas' ability to speak several languages (Dozier 1954:291-292).

• HIGHLY VALUED AND EXPRESSIVE SPEECH Speech levels and styles are well defined and developed. The most important special style is ceremonial speech, present in all the Pueblos, and best described for Zuni (Newman 1955) and Keresan (White 1944). It is used in the kiva, the sacred ceremonial chamber, and on any other ceremonial or ritualistic occasions. Certain words are replaced by special "ceremonial words," words that

are often felt to be archaic. Other times metaphor is used, for example, Zuni takka 'frog' and its ceremonial equivalent woliye tinan kʔayapa, literally 'several-are-in-a-shallow-container they-sitting they-are- in-liquid' (Newman 1955:347). Not all words have a ceremonial equivalent. Words considered coarse, undignified, or ritually unpure are omitted in ceremonial speech, as are Spanish and English loanwords (Newman 1955; Trager 1944; Dockstader 1955).

Public functions call for oratory, which is well developed. The Tewa call speech-making tumahe, which Barbara Freire-Marreco describes as formulas that "are learned by heart, either by listening to more experienced speakers or by taking actual lessons from elder relatives and friends. . . . The conventional style approved was smooth, low-voiced, unemphatic: originality of form was to be avoided, and the object was to clothe originality of matter in traditional form, so as to be able to say of any proposal 'all this I heard from your fathers and uncles'" (Dozier 1958:272). Dozier (1958:272) suggests that the style reflected "reluctance to be assertive and conspicuous," which is typical of general Pueblo behavior (see Fox 1959:558-559 for a discussion of Cochiti oratorical style).

A speech type used by what have been called chanters, criers, or announcers is found mainly in the Western Pueblos. It is rigidly structured and especially well developed among the Hopi, where it is differentiated from both singing and speaking by a special term. The official crier or "speech chief" makes the official, public, and religious announcements. Anyone can make a secular announcement from the house top on personal matters, such as lost or stolen property, but it is common to ask a speech chief to do this. There is special training for the crier chief, the one who performs the religious (as opposed to the secular) chants (Dozier 1958:272; Black 1967; Voegelin and Euler 1957; Stephen 1936:941).

The language used in song differs from ordinary speech, at least in some cases, but there is no systematic discussion of this topic in the anthropological literature. Sacred songs at Cochiti seem to use ceremonial speech (Fox 1959:559). Songs are often borrowed, and Keresan seems to be a popular source (Stevenson 1904:183, 225, 424; Stephen 1936:137, 406).

Story telling, important for moral training, is a popular wintertime activity that takes place in the home. The genre has special linguistic markers that sharply differentiate it from ordinary speech. It is labeled by a special term (in Zuni telapnaawe), indicating that it is recognized as a special variety distinct from ordinary speech. Story tellers learn their art simply by listening, without undergoing any special training (Kroskrity 1985).

A baby talk vocabulary has been reported for Keresan (W. Miller 1965:112; Parsons 1923:168), and for Hopi

(Dennis 1940:35; Titiev 1946; C.F. Voegelin and F.M. Voegelin 1957:50), and it is likely a pan-Pueblo development. In Acoma, there are some 30 baby talk words, like 'mommy', 'bite', 'sleep', and 'kitty-cat', that replace the corresponding adult word. Adults claim the main reason for their use is their easier pronunciation, though an objective examination of the two sets of words does not always bear this out. Acoma baby *méuméu*, adult *mú·sa* 'cat'; baby *ʔáḱiʔáḱi*, adult *isḱa* 'drink' (W. Miller 1956-1959, 1965:112).

The vocabulary of men's and women's speech is differentiated for a few items in Hopi (Titiev 1946), Tewa (Kroskrity 1983), and Keresan (Sims and Valiquette 1990). While the number of sex-differentiated words is few, they are high-frequency words, so that the differences are salient.

Swearing has not been recorded, but slang has, at Zuni (Newman 1955), where it is used by teenagers and young adults. Older people view it as a worthless but harmless form of speech that the young will outgrow when they become mature.

Spanish and English function as additional styles for those that speak them. Lange (1959:19) notes that at Cochiti, where Spanish Americans live right in the pueblo, teenagers learn each other's language, and that Spanish is normally the appropriate language in dealing with Spanish Americans. English is, for example, the appropriate language for baseball (Fox 1959). At a few of the more highly acculturated Pueblos, and among families that live away from the Pueblo, English is used widely in a variety of contexts, especially by the young (Voegelin, Voegelin, and Schub 1967; Brandt 1970a; Leap 1973, 1974).

• ATTITUDES   The proper use of speech is highly valued. The ability to use the more elevated styles, especially the ceremonial language, is admired. Younger Zuni speakers admitted that they cannot explain all religious terms, but both young and old "can unhesitatingly identify particular words and phrases as belonging to the sacred, in contrast to the everyday, vocabulary" (Newman 1955:346). "To the native speaker of Zuni, the sacred vocabulary carried overtones of dignity and prestige" (Newman 1955:352).

Ethnocentrism was high, with each Pueblo feeling superior to its neighbors (Dozier 1970:209). When similarities of custom are noted, it is assumed that the neighboring Pueblos did the borrowing. These notions extend to language: Santo Domingo Indians "laugh at the way other Keresan Pueblos talk Keres" (White 1935:28-29). No single language or dialect is granted greater prestige. Thus, the conditions are met for language to serve as a symbol for self-identity and for identifying other groups.

Consistent with Pueblo ethnocentrism, bilingualism is neither highly valued nor widely practiced. The Arizona Tewa are, again, the exception, taking great pride in being completely bilingual in Hopi. According to a well-known traditional account, knowledge of Hopi is supposed to be open to the Tewa, but knowledge of Tewa, closed to the Hopi. Some Hopis do, in fact, know Tewa, particularly those married to Tewas, but such knowledge is usually concealed (Dozier 1954:292; Stephen 1936:556-557).

Small-Scale Societies

There is a myth about "primitive languages" that holds that such languages have a meager vocabulary, an ill-defined sound system, and a simple grammar that does not allow for the expression of complex or abstract thoughts. The myth has been exposed largely through the study of American Indian languages, with the first persuasive and influential attack coming from Boas (1911) in his Introduction to the *Handbook of American Indian Languages*. Here he laid out the general characteristics of Indian languages, which in turn proved to be the characteristics of language in general. Subsequent work with Indian languages, as well as with the languages of other small-scale societies, has simply added further support to Boas's thesis (A. Hill 1952; Strehlow 1947). One cannot predict the nature of the culture nor the complexity of the society of a people from the nature of the sound system or grammar of their language. Linguistic variation does not correspond to cultural or social variation in any straightforward way though there has been speculation that societal type can have some influence on the structural features of language (Swadesh 1971; Hymes 1961, 1974a). And societal type can clearly have an effect on semantic structure (Berlin 1972). There is also a relationship between societal type and culture and the nature of the speech community (Gumperz 1962; Hymes 1962, 1974, 1974a; Shener 1973:761).

Two general types of societies—large-scale states and small-scale societies—are defined primarily in terms of political and economic organization. States are characterized by a central government and by rank and stratification. A person is born into a particular class, with limited opportunity (until relatively recent times) of moving to another class. States often include a large population over an extended territory, with the state segmented into smaller, local political units. Such units often correspond to local communities that constitute local speech communities that are part of the larger speech community. States were represented in the Americas before European contact by Mesoamerican and Andean societies, but in North America only by the Natchez of the lower Mississippi and perhaps some of their neighbors. Reports on their precontact way of life were recorded but not in enough detail to reconstruct the nature of the Natchez speech community.

There are two types of small-scale societies, nomadic foraging societies and village societies. The former type sometimes had territorially based social units, with the political and economic unit often no larger than the family. Nomadic foraging societies were represented in the Great Basin, Subarctic, and Arctic. In village societies, the political unit was suprafamilial (namely the village), and leadership was more permanent. Village economy was often based on farming, as in the Pueblos and other Southwest groups, the Southeast, and many groups in the Northeast; but village societies were also represented in much of California and the Northwest Coast, where the economic base was formed by foraging and fishing, respectively. Rank and weak stratification were important in some areas, for example in northern California, Northwest Coast, and some areas in the Northeast and Southeast. But occupational stratification, typical of complex stratified states, was missing, so that, for example, all men in a Northwest Coast village were fisherman, all men in a Creek village were farmers, regardless of their rank.

• BOUNDARIES AND LINGUISTIC DIVERSITY   The speech communities of nomadic foraging societies typically lacked sharp boundaries, especially in those that lacked territorial-based social groups larger than the family. Instead, one found a network of relationships over a wide area. When two very different cultures and languages adjoined, there may have been a sharp boundary (such as the Northern Athapaskan and Eskimo), but it could be blurred with extended contact (as in the Washoe and Northern Paiute). The Great Basin case shows that language difference does not mean that there would necessarily be a difference in culture. There need not even be a sharp language boundary, as for the Northern Paiute and Shoshone, or the Cree and Ojibwa (Wolfart 1973a).

Village societies provided greater opportunity for sharp boundaries between speech communities than did nomadic foraging societies; however, the boundaries were not impermeable, since there was always a certain amount of contact between neighboring villages. Sometimes village speech communities were linked together into larger confederations. Examples in North America were the League of the Iroquois and the Creek Confederacy. Where there was linguistic diversity, there was the possibility of one language occupying a dominant position in the political life of the confederation. Several languages, all belonging to the Iroquoian family, were represented in the Iroquois League. The Creek Confederacy consisted of about 50 villages; most of the villages spoke one of several Muskogean languages, but Natchez, Yuchi, and Shawnee, which belonged to other language families, were also represented. Mohawk was the language of politics in the Iroquois League, while Creek served this role in the Creek Confederacy.

There is little chance for internal linguistic diversity within the social unit of a small-scale society, since it is a small, face-to-face community. Stratified societies, on the other hand, offer ample opportunity, both between the classes or castes, as well as between the local communities, since stratified states are often multilingual.

There is always some tendency for homogenization of the linguistic diversity within a stratified society, which can lead to sweeping language shift through replacive bilingualism. Language shift is found in small-scale societies, but unlike stratified societies, never on a sweeping scale involving large populations or large geographic areas.

While small-scale societies lack the internal linguistic diversity that is typical of many stratified societies, they offer a potential for greater overall diversity because they lack the homogenizing tendencies typical of stratified societies. Because village boundaries are usually sharper than between nomadic foragers, village societies offer the potential for greater linguistic diversity than do nomadic foraging societies. But additional factors play a role, so that village society does not guarantee linguistic diversity. History plays a part, but it is largely unknowable in preliterate society. The density, distribution, and stability of the population is important, which depends partly on societal level, and partly on the distribution and availability of the natural resources. California exhibits greater diversification of resources in a smaller area than any other place in North America, with a considerable variety of biotic resources often available within just a few square miles. Thus, small groups could be self-sufficient in settled villages that utilized resources from a small area. This, along with the fact that most California societies were well-bounded village societies, led to linguistic diversity that was not surpassed anywhere else in the world except perhaps in New Guinea.

Dialects are usually easier to delineate among villagers than nomadic foragers. For example, there are seven distinct dialects spoken in the seven Keresan Pueblos. There seems to have been a similar situation among the Yokutsan-speaking villages of California (Kroeber 1906a:657-658, 1925:474). Shoshone, on the other hand, has no sharply delineable dialects, even though the dialect diversity is at least as great, because the transitions are gradual (W. Miller 1970).

Cultural differences are always available as symbols of identity, and linguistic differences frequently serve as such. And they can be used also as symbols for group solidarity, but only if there are clear linguistic boundaries. The potential is greater, then, among villagers than among nomadic foragers. Language and dialect differences are more apt to be used as symbols of identity in areas of linguistic diversity, such as in the Pueblo area, especially in cases in which the languages are unique to a single community (for example, Zuni as opposed to Tewa), and where the linguistic differences are greater (for example, Hopi and Arizona Tewa as opposed to the Keresan dialects).

There is a difference in the sociolinguistic context of language socialization between nomadic foragers and villagers. The child in foraging groups is in contact with a smaller number of individuals, but because of fuzzier speech community boundaries these individuals display greater linguistic variation. Further, the peer group was smaller, sometimes consisted entirely of siblings, and sometimes was completely lacking.

• MISSING AND WEAKLY DEVELOPED FEATURES Missing from or only weakly developed in small-scale societies are: social dialects, prestige languages, lingua francas, societal bilingualism, honorifics, and writing.

Geographic dialects are the result of geographic isolation, while social dialects are the result of social isolation. (Sometimes distinct languages serve the same function as social dialects, such as the use of Aztec by the ruling class in the multilingual Aztec empire.) Since social isolation is associated with social class and stratified societies, social dialects are not found in small-scale societies.

The notion of a prestige language is sometimes found in small-scale societies, usually village societies where rank is present: thus the favored position of Creek in the Creek Confederacy, of Mohawk in the Iroquois League (Speck 1945:28), and of Hupa in northwestern California (Powers 1877:72-73). The notion of a prestige language reaches its most developed form in more complex societies such as those found in Mesoamerica and the Andes or in the standard languages of the modern world (see Garvin and Mathiot 1960; Haugen 1966:1-26).

There are two solutions to a situation in which speakers from diverse linguistic backgrounds interact. The first solution is more common in small-scale societies: individuals become bi- or multilingual, but there is no single language that is used by all. The second solution, societal multilingualism, is more common in stratified societies: a particular language, a lingua franca, is used by all. Trade is perhaps the most common context for which a lingua franca is used, but it is not the only one. Trade languages seem to be restricted to societies that have large-scale, institutionalized trade, with the marketplace and other such institutions being important, institutions that are the product of stratified societies. There are several examples of Indian languages or of pidginized varieties of Indian languages being used in trade with Europeans, such as Mobilian Jargon, a pidginized variety of Choctaw used in the lower Mississippi valley in the early eighteenth century, and Chinook Jargon, which emerged from a Nootka-based Jargon used in the fur trade in the Northwest. Although the opposite claim has sometimes

been made, these trade languages do not seem to be precontact development, but rather byproducts of European contact ("Dynamics of Linguistic Contact," this vol.)

The use of a prestige language in diplomacy, such as Creek and Mohawk, fits the definition of a lingua franca. But the use of diplomatic languages in North America never reached the scope found in stratified societies, such as Aztec in the Aztec Empire, Quechua in the Inca Empire, Akkadian in the Assyrian Empire, or French and English through out the world in the nineteenth and twentieth centuries. Thus lingua francas as languages of wider communication were found in North America, but in comparison to stratified societies they were weakly developed.

The use of a particular language in particular settings is closely related to societal multilingualism, a kind of multilingualism that is more common in stratified than small-scale societies.

The languages of some speech communities have special honorific forms for talking to special categories of people. Such specialized forms are found in some small-scale societies in North America, but complex elaborations, that sometimes reach the very core of the grammatical system, are found only in stratified societies (for example, Aztec, Javanese, and Japanese).

Writing was introduced, or its invention was stimulated, after contact but was missing in aboriginal times. Writing will seldom be found unless there is a need for the storage and transfer of information on a scale that cannot be handled by oral means, a condition not met in small-scale societies. The presence of writing makes it possible for oral tradition to become less elaborated and less important, particularly for those traditions important in the cultural transmission of information from one generation to the next.

Style

Certain participants, settings, or topics are associated with certain varieties of speech. These varieties are called styles. In choosing the proper style, speakers must control two sets of rules: the linguistic rules for marking the particular style, and rules of usage so that the appropriate style is used for the appropriate occasion.

A style may be marked in any of five ways: phonetically, grammatically, lexically (substitution of special vocabulary), by paralinguistic features, or by manner of organization and thematic content. These marking techniques can be used alone or in combination. Shoshone songs are marked by a phonetic rule that changes a geminated (double) stop to the corresponding nasal plus stop: *wekkumpiccih* 'buzzard' is changed in songs to *wenkumpincih*. Coyote speech in Shoshone myths is grammatically marked by randomly adding a special suffix -pai to one or more words in the sentence. Zuni ceremonial speech is lexically marked by changing certain words, as in the case of takka 'frog' being replaced by woliye tianan kʔayapa. Acoma baby talk is also lexically marked: mú·sa 'cat' becomes baby talk m̃éum̃éu. Paralinguistic features are those that overlay language, such as the palatalization that is almost universal in baby talk, or the special tone of voice that is typical of certain kinds of oratory or preaching; it is also illustrated by a characteristic tone of voice in the Hopi chants. Manner of organization and thematic content are illustrated by the rules for making a speech in Tewa, and by the rules for organizing a Hopi chant.

Speakers have names for some of the styles found in their speech community. Crumrine (1968) discusses the native names given to different styles in Mayo and Kroskrity (1993) for named styles in Arizona Tewa.

Soft speech is almost universal in American Indian speech communities, and outsiders sometimes mistakenly take it for lack of assertiveness. While widely noted by many researchers, it has seldom been reported in the literature. Similarly, the use of silence in Indian communities is often misinterpreted by outsiders since the rules for silence vary cross-culturally (Darnell 1970; Hymes 1966:134). Basso (1970) has discussed this topic for the Western Apache.

Participants and Stylistic Variation

A Pomo chief commented:

> My grandfather made a long speech in the sweathouse; he spoke for about twenty minutes; oh, how he could speak! the words just flowed and flowed, so easy, so smooth; he was a great speaker. Then he led me four times around the room. Then he said to the people, "This is the wampum with which we have taken care of our people; now we have given it to him as a sign that we resign our post to him." Then he told me to make a speech . . . That's how I was made a chief. I acted as chief for some years; I got used to making speeches (Loeb 1926:241).

This exemplifies the importance of the participant in the speech event and choice of style. It also illustrates the position of oratory in Pomo society, and it is typical of its position throughout North America. Another example, from an Apache speaker, shows what is expected of a skilled orator: "The leader has to be a good man, a good talker. . . He always has much to say. When anything is pending, he is asked about it, and he gives his opinion. What he says is respected, and his advice is usually followed" (Opler 1941:469; see Bowers 1950:34 for similar comments about Mandan chiefs). It should be noted that in most groups oratorical style could be used by any respected elder, not just chiefs (Crumrine 1968; Lumholtz 1902, 1:348; Lowie 1939:325).

In addition to participant, setting and topic are important for understanding the stylistic rules of usage, and again oratory provides a good example. Speeches are expected at certain events, for example at the potlatches in the Northwest Coast (vol. 7:731) (Sapir and Swadesh 1955), at Papago rituals (Underhill 1946:34), and Shoshone funerals. Location can play a part, so that, for example, an Apache leader was expected to deliver a speech from a hill or high place (Opler 1941:469). The topic usually concerned good behavior. Thus from the Washoe: "Behave well, do not fight, play! If you lose, do not get angry. Play ball; some win, others lose. Play the basket game. Shoot rabbits, eat them. Make soup and eat it. After a while, shoot deer" (Lowie 1939:303). The topic of speeches frequently catalogued what was considered good behavior, as among the Luiseño (Kroeber 1925:684-685), the Pomo (Kroeber 1925:252), the Havasupai (Smithson 1959:153; Spier 1928:261), the Tarahumara (Lumholtz 1902, 1:348-349; Bennett and Zingg 1935:331-332, 366), the Mayo (Crumrine 1968:21), and the Papago (Underhill 1946:34).

Styles must be learned, and in the case of oratory learning is conscious and deliberate. In the Northwest Coast, the training was formal and was usually provided by a father: "This training, plus, we may suppose, a certain native aptitude for the work, kept the speakership in certain families" (Drucker 1951:269). Training and practice is also important for an aspiring Iroquois speaker. While Iroquois rituals and speeches must be learned, they are believed to be learned automatically if the person has the gift (Foster 1971:97-102).

Some styles, like baby talk, are known to almost everyone, even children. But oratory, like the ceremonial style in Zuni, will be recognized by everyone, but not everyone will learn it. Those who control oratory and other highly valued styles are admired and gain prestige in the community. They must know how to use the style (marking rules) and when to use it (rules of usage).

Authority to speak could be delegated to a herald or speaker, as in the Northwest Coast (Drucker 1951:269; McIlwraith 1948, 2:68; Hymes 1966:136), the Southeast (Swanton 1928a:610; Speck 1909:82), the Plains (Lakota évapaha 'camp crier', Willem J. de Reuse, personal communication 1993), and other places (Barrett 1911:323; Fenton 1936:4; Powers 1877:139; Underhill 1939:70). The Fox had runners, called aška·pe·wa, who delivered messages (Michelson 1927a). So that the audience could hear and understand, a Northern Paiute "interpreter" repeated the words of the shaman, who often talked rapidly, or mumbled (Park 1934:104). Multilingual interpreters were used by some of the Pueblos; they were also used by the Iroquois (Foster 1971:29) .

229

Men's and Women's Speech

The distinction between men's and women's speech, which is found in all cultures, is sometimes formalized and clearly marked. One of the best-known examples, described by Haas (1944), was found in Koasati, a Muskogean language spoken in Louisiana. The men's form was made from the women's form by adding *-s* or replacing the last element with s:

Women's	Men's	
ką·	*ká·s*	'he is saying'
molhîl	*molhís*	'we are peeling it'
íˑp	*íˑps*	'he is eating it'

In the 1930s, when Haas studied this system, the women's forms were being replaced by the men's forms. The speech of the opposite sex was used in telling a story when quoting a person of the opposite sex. Formerly, parents of both sexes would correct children if they used the wrong form. Fragmentary evidence indicates that other Muskogean languages once had distinctions similar to those in Koasati.

Formalized differences between men's and women's speech are sometimes marked phonetically as in Koasati, or lexically, as in the Pueblo example. The Algonquian-speaking Gros Ventre of the Plains mark the difference phonetically (Flannery 1946). The Yana of California marked the difference phonetically (the women's form was derived from the men's by shortening it) and lexically (a few verb stems are altogether different for the sexes; Sapir 1929a). Among some Eskimos, the final stops (*p, t, k, q*) in men's speech were replaced by the corresponding nasals ([m, n, ŋ, ṅ]) in women's speech (Boas 1911:79); however, this gender distinction in Eskimo seems to have been lost (Kalmár 1979-15). Some Siouan groups differentiate sex forms, for example, the Biloxi (Haas 1944) and the Lakhota, who have two sets of forms for some of the grammatical enclitics. The resulting differences are slight, but the Lakhotas feel they are great (Allan R. Taylor, personal communication 1974).

In some speech communities, the rules of usage were sensitive to both speaker and hearer. For example, Yana men used the men's forms only in talking to men, but the women's forms in talking to women; women used the women's form in talking to either men or women. Among the Koasati, men always used the men's form, women the women's form, regardless of addressee.

Age Differences

All speech communities have rules of usage that concern age differences, so that younger people address elders with respect. Sometimes the rules of usage incorporate formalized markings. In the Pueblo of Sandia, linguistic changes have taken place, so that the older generation uses older linguistic forms, while the younger generation uses the newly introduced forms. These differences have taken on a social significance (Brandt 1970a). Among the Ute, there is a generational difference that is phonologically marked. It seems not to be the result of linguistic change, since age of both speaker and addressee must be considered in formulating the rules of usage (Goss 1974).

Honorifics or Respect Forms

All speech communities recognize that there are certain categories of people who deserve to be addressed in a respectful manner. Some languages have institutionalized the custom by having special respect forms or honorifics that are marked grammatically or lexically. Honorifics are sometimes also used when talking about such persons, or when talking about an exalted topic. In stratified societies, the use of honorifics is defined in terms of two dimensions, power and solidarity. The system is familiar to speakers of many European languages through the use of the so-called familiar versus polite forms of 'you'. In the power dimension, usage is nonreciprocal: the more powerful person (belonging to a higher class, older, or more respected) uses the familiar form, while the less powerful person responds with the polite form. In the solidarity dimension, usage is reciprocal, with friends exchanging the familiar form, strangers the polite form (Brown and Gilman 1958). Honorifics seem to be less common in small-scale societies, and further rules of usage differ. Usage is seldom nonreciprocal, probably because of the lack of a social class structure. Usage is sometimes defined in terms of friend versus stranger, but not commonly, probably because strangers in face-to-face communities are normally foreigners. Much more commonly, usage is defined in terms of sex and kinship, with cross-sex and in-law relations frequently receiving the honorific forms.

The plural was used in much of northern California in addressing, in particular, strangers and in-laws: the Cahto (P.E. Goddard 1909:143), the Monache (Kroeber 1925:588), the Yana (Sapir 1910:95, 101), and the Pomoans (Kroeber 1911:321). The Kashaya Pomo added the suffix *-ya?* to show respect, especially to in-laws (Robert L. Oswalt, personal communication 1974). The Sahaptin and Chinookan languages morphologically mark the forms used in addressing parents (Dell H. Hymes, personal communication 1974). The Navajo 4th person *-ji-* is used in addressing certain respected kin (Willem J. de Reuse, personal communication 1993). The Guarijío of northwest Mexico use grammatical markings in a complex system that involves pronouns and passive verbs in talking to certain categories of in-laws (W. Miller 1980). Early observers reported a difference of speech between the Natchez classes (Swanton 1928:128), differences that seemed to be lexically marked. Mary Haas (personal communication 1974) has recorded some Natchez forms that may be remnants of this system.

Contrasting with honorific or respect forms, the Haida of British Columbia used a suffix -Al in talking to a slave, or in a kindly manner to an equal; or in belittling oneself, out of courtesy (Swanton 1911b:254).

Highly Valued Speech

The effective use of highly valued speech styles is always admired and confers prestige. Some such styles are universal or nearly so, such as oratory, while others such as formal honorifics have a more limited distribution. Sometimes certain aspects of these styles are said to be archaic, which may sometimes be the case, while in other cases they may simply be uninterpretable because certain words were borrowed from a foreign dialect or language (as in the case considered earlier for songs in the Pueblo). (See Egesdal 1992:39-59, 75-83 for a discussion of foreign speech and archaisms in Thompson Salish.) Four widespread styles are oratory, ceremonial speech, prayer, and song.

Oratory

Oratory probably occurs in all speech communities. There is cross-cultural variation in how oratory articulates with other aspects of culture, in who uses it, and in how it is marked. Nevertheless, there are certain cross-cultural similarities. Lexical substitution, paralinguistic features, choice of thematic content, and manner of organization are the most common markers of this style.

Particularly common for lexical marking are metaphor and circumlocution. Coyote is the "woolly comrade" in a Papago speech (Underhill 1946:33). Some of the Delaware expressions have come into English usage: "To bury the hatchet," "You keep me in the dark," "You have spoken with your lips only, not from the heart," "Singing birds" (liars), "I will place you under my wings" (Heckewelder 1819:125-129). Metaphor was especially well developed in the Northwest Coast (Boas 1929a).

Paralinguistic features are probably universal to oratory, but the nature of such features is subject to cross-cultural variation. The Nootka of the Northwest Coast used a "laconic, somewhat explosive style" for formal addresses (Drucker 1951:269). Among the Sahaptins and Chinookans, a hired speaker at a ceremony would repeat the chief's words in a loud voice, with certain voice and intonational features added (French 1958:261). The oratorical style throughout California

was similar: an orator talked "just like a peanut vendor does now," according to one Tubatulabal (E. Voegelin 1938:58); the Patwin ritual orators used a "very high voice and jerky phrases" (Kroeber 1925:389); a Pomoan head chief shouted "in a peculiar jerky delivery, in detached statements, with endless repetitions" (Kroeber 1925:252); a Yokuts chief opened the mourning ceremony with a short speech "in extremely short, jerky sentences, with much repetition," such as: "The women—the women—the women—have the most—have the most—the most money—have the most money —the women—the women—have the most offerings—the most offerings—give the most—give the most—the women—the women—give the most" (Powers 1877:386-387). The Yuman-speaking Mohave and Quechan of Arizona were similar, using an "abrupt, staccato, forced delivery" (Spier 1933:168).

In preliterate speech communities, manner of organization is especially important, providing the speaker with a framework that serves some of the same functions as written notes do for a speakers in a literate speech community. In some groups, such as among the Iroquois, rules of composition are complex, and developed to a high art, so that considerable skill and training is needed (Foster 1971, 1974, 1974a). Beginnings and endings are particularly subject to convention. For example, an orator among the Plains Indians would start by listing his accomplishments, showing that he was a man whose opinion was worth considering (Bowers 1950:34).

The tradition of oratory continues in the modern context in public speaking in both native languages and English (figs. 2-3).

Ceremonial Speech

A special style for ceremonial speech, while perhaps not universal, is certainly very common. There is considerable cross-cultural variation in how well it is developed. It is always well developed in cultures in which ceremonialism is a focus of cultural interest, as among the Pueblos. Generally, the more highly developed the style, the more highly it is valued, and sometimes it is considered sacred. As with oratory, members of the speech community vary as to how effectively they use it, and it is a style that tends to be learned later in life.

Oratory and ceremonial speech have some similarities. They differ in usage in that oratory is almost always directed to other people, while ceremonial speech may be directed to other people or to supernaturals. While paralinguistic features and manner of organization are used in marking ceremonial speech, they are not so important as in oratory. Lexical choice is the most common technique used to mark ceremonial speech.

Fig. 2. Navajo Peter MacDonald (at the microphone) (vol. 10:639), a controversial figure (MacDonald and Schwarz 1993; Anonymous 1995) with a reputation as a spellbinding orator, testifying before the Senate Select Committee on Indian Affairs on the subject of the Navajo and Hopi relocation commission's report. left to right: Mae Horseson, Carl Beyal (interpreter), George Vlassis (general counsel, standing), Tribal Chairman MacDonald, Ated Tsotsie Yazzie, and June Benally were all witnesses for the Navajo Tribe. Photograph by Paul Natonabah (Navajo), Washington, D.C., May 1981.

Lexical changes include replacing certain profane words with a native word (often considered archaic), a foreign word, or a metaphorical phrase. Words considered too profane or sacrilegious are omitted. The Navajo system is typical. Some common unanalyzable words are replaced by an analyzable word or expression. 'American' (a Spanish loanword) becomes 'white-streak-under-grass', 'cattail' becomes 'many feathers', 'corn' becomes 'holy corn', 'cotton' becomes 'fluffed grass'. In other cases the common unanalyzable word is replaced by another unanalyzable word (Reichard 1950, 2:533-534; see also Kluckhohn and Leighton 1946:187).

Ceremonial speech is especially well developed in the Southwest. In addition to the Navajos and Pueblos, it has been reported and discussed for the Papago (Underhill 1946) and the Tarahumara (Bennett and Zingg 1935). It has been reported for several California groups: the Maidu (Powers 1877:307-310), the Pomo (Loeb 1926:343), and the Yurok (Kroeber 1960a:995-996); for the Mandan of the Plains (Bowers 1950:111, 135, 157); and for the Bella Coola (McIlwraith 1948, 1:576-577) and Kwakiutl (Boas 1897:346-353) of the Northwest Coast.

Prayer

Prayer may be a universal category, but there is considerable cross-cultural variation as to what constitutes a prayer and the role it plays in the culture. It is often in a special ceremonial style, set apart from other types of ceremonial speech. It is always highly structured, and sometimes a set, memorized piece. Special paralinguistic features are common. For example, the Delaware and Shawnee use a special sentence intonation, a flat monotone with a sharp drop at the end (Ives Goddard, personal communication 1975). Sometimes there are other markers, as in the use of the otherwise meaningless word *no·či* in Fox after almost every phrase (Michelson 1927a).

Some of the best descriptions of prayer are for Southwest groups: the Mayo (Crumrine 1968:24-26), the Tepecano (Mason 1918a), the Papago (Underhill 1946), and the Navajo (Reichard 1944:35-49, 1950; Matthews 1888). Sometimes there are two kinds of prayers, Christian (Roman Catholic) and native.

In contemporary life Indian languages are widely used for both Christian (fig. 4) and traditional (fig. 5) prayers.

MILLER

Fig. 3. Wade Hadley, president of the Rough Rock School Board Inc., speaking in Navajo at the dedication of the Rough Rock Demonstration School, Rough Rock, Ariz. left to right, seated behind the speaker: Emmett Bia, Sr., Navajo council delegate from Many Farms chapter, Ariz.; Jimmie C. Begay (partially obscured), executive director, Rough Rock School Board Inc.; unidentified non-Indian; Teddy McCurtain, Sr., member of the Rough Rock School Board Inc.; and in the foreground Mae Hatathlie, wife of the medicine man. The Rough Rock School program was a model that integrated the primary use of the Navajo language with English as a secondary language, and the study of Navajo culture, all under community control (vol. 10:660-667). Photograph by Robert Roessel, Jr., 1966.

Song

There is considerably more cross-cultural variation in the style used in songs than in the three styles just considered. There is variation in rules of usage, the role song plays in the culture, who knows how to sing or is allowed to sing, whether the songs are a set piece or vary with each performance, and whether the songs are worded, partially worded, or are without words. Often there are several different kinds of songs (fig. 6).

Certain songs are often part of a ceremony or a prayer. Such songs are sometimes said to be in an old or archaic language: the Mandan (Bowers 1950:111, 125, 157), the Pueblo (Laski 1958:119-120; Stevenson 1904), the Mayo (Crumrine 1968), the Tubatulabal (E.W. Voegelin 1938:58), the Maidu (Powers 1877: 307-310), the Delaware (C.F. Voegelin 1942), and the Teton Sioux (Densmore 1918).

Among the Yuman-speaking tribes in southern California and Arizona the myth is put to song. Among others, including the Great Basin people, songs are an integral part of the myth, with certain characters being identified by the song they sing (Sapir 1910a). Among the Central Siberian Yupik speakers, many myths and stories are identified by the song that occurs in them (Willem J. de Reuse, personal communication 1993).

Most groups also have more profane songs that occupy a less exalted cultural position, can be sung by all including children (though perhaps not as well as by adults), and can be sung on a wider set of occasions.   *233*

Fig. 4. Rev. Sydney Fort Chimo (East Main Cree), an Episcopal priest speaking to his East Main Cree congregation at Paint Hills, Que. Photograph by Ronald S. Fellows, March 1979.

Fig. 5. Joe Woodcock, Flathead, giving the prayer at the commencement of the Bitterroot ceremony feast. Woodcock was a principal singer of hymns in Flathead (Montana Salish) in the Roman Catholic church at St. Ignatius, Mont. Photograph by Dorothy M. Johnson, near town of Hot Springs, Flathead Reservation, Mont., 1962.

Hinton (1984) discusses such songs among the Havasupai of Arizona.

Some songs are individually owned, while others are open to anyone. For example, a Northern Paiute shaman's song is his private property, but any one may sing a round dance song (Park 1934).

Open sounds (such as low vowels, sonorants, voiced consonants) are more common in songs than more

Fig. 6. James Whiteplume (b. 1897, d. 1986), Northern Arapahoe, singing at the celebration of the first anniversary of the Morning Star Manor Nursing Home, where he resided. He was remembered for his singing at Sun Dances and powwows. The boy is not identified. Photograph by Dianna Troyer, Fort Washakie, Wyo., 1986.

closed sounds (such as high vowels, stops, voiceless consonants), at least in part because open sounds can more readily carry a pitch. There are two ways to achieve this: choose words that have more open sounds, and substitute more open sounds for closed sounds. Both techniques are discussed at length by Hinton (1984) for the Havasupai. The second technique has been noted for the Papago (Underhill 1946:36), Bella Coola (McIlwraith 1948, 2:268), Southern Paiute (Sapir 1910a), and Shoshone (Crum 1980).

Lexical marking is utilized in song, but it is less important than phonetic marking. Eskimo shaman songs, for example, make much use of metaphor, a technique that is typical of Eskimo ceremonial speech (Roberts and Jenness 1925:15). Songs may be partly or wholly in another language (Sapir 1910a; Stevenson 1904; Oswalt 1964:178; E.W. Voegelin 1938:58). Fox songs include word distortions, the omission of grammatical morphemes, and special vocabulary, often archaic (Goddard 1993).

234

Manner of organization and thematic content are important, a topic discussed by Hinton (1984) for the Havasupai, and Crum (1980) for Shoshone. Crum points out that almost all Shoshone round dance songs deal with themes from nature.

Other Special Styles

An aspect of culture that is the center of cultural focus is apt to be marked by a special highly valued speech style. It might be similar to other styles that are viewed as being culturally similar. For example, speech used by shamans often has its own well-marked style, a style that is often akin to ceremonial speech (see French 1958:259 concerning the Wasco and Wishram, and McIlwraith 1948; 1:576-577 concerning the Bella Coola). In some cases, shamans are said to have special linguistic skills, speaking the language of other peoples or even animals, or speaking a language known only to themselves (F. Johnson 1943:73; Laski 1958:119; L. Jones 1914 159; E.W. Voegelin 1938:58).

Another example can be found with the Plains Indians, for whom warfare was a topic of cultural focus. Most tribes had a society of warriors known as contraries or Crazy Dogs, who used a special style of speaking. Actions were done in reverse, and they talked crosswise, expressing the opposite of their real intentions (Lowie 1913:194, 1935:331; Steward 1931:202). The Navajo and Apache provide another example with "war path language," "war talk," or "not talking plainly." Lexical substitutions were made for certain animals and objects that warriors hoped to obtain when they entered the enemy's territory. On the homeward journey, the party lined up in a row facing the enemy's country, and sang a song at dawn. At a certain point in the song all turned toward home, and the restriction against "not talking plainly" was lifted (W. Hill 1936 12; Opler and Hoijer 1940; Reichard 1950, 1:269-270). One last example is a "salt language," used by Papago salt pilgrims, which was also lexically marked (Underhill 1946:33).

Expressive Speech

Expressive speech includes babytalk, slang, swearing, word taboo, speech play, and related phenomena. Such forms of speech are sometimes valued, but more often they are not. In fact, some varieties of expressive speech are viewed as being worthless, silly, or worse.

Baby Talk

Baby talk is a formalized, institutionalized type of speech that adults use in talking to young children, and which young children use (and must learn to use) in return. It often incorporates features that are common, or are believed to be common, in child language. It is not to be confused with child language, a simplified version that children use before they have mastered the full language.

Even the most proficient users of baby talk seldom take it seriously. It is viewed as being silly, not a topic worthy of serious discussion, and sometimes it is even denigrated (Gayton and Newman 1940). Adults sometimes believe that baby talk is easier for the child to learn than the adult language.

Baby talk is a common expressive style, but it is not universal. It is reported to be absent among the Hidatsa (Voegelin and Robinett 1954:69), the Gros Ventre (Flannery 1953:142-143), the Shoshone (W. Miller 1970:32), the Havasupai (Smithson 1959:40), and the Kaska (Darnell 1970:131). And where it does occur, it varies from being weakly to highly developed.

There are two very good descriptions of baby talk in North America, one by Crawford (1970, 1978a) for the Cocopa of the Lower Colorado River, the other by Casagrande (1948) for the Comanche of Oklahoma. Baby talk is also mentioned in Chamberlain (1890), Oswalt (1976a), and Sapir (1929).

Most baby talk systems are marked lexically, phonetically, grammatically, and paralinguistically. The lexical marking in Comanche is typical: a few dozen common objects and activities in the child's life have a special word that substitutes for the usual adult word. The baby talk word may or may not be similar to the adult word.

Phonetic markings typically substitute a sound that the adult perceives as "simpler" (English "wabbit" for "rabbit"), or make a simplification in the syllabic structure, by simplifying consonant clusters or omitting final consonants (English "tummy" for "stomach"). The rules for making such changes may be rather regular and uniform across speakers, or they may show considerable variation, depending on the particular baby talk system. Cocopa is unusual in that it utilizes a rather complex set of phonological rules in baby talk.

In terms of grammatical rules, the two most common are the use of the diminutive and reduplication. Both grammatical techniques are used in Comanche and Cocopa baby talk. Yokuts has a particular morphological construction that is found only in baby talk (Gayton and Newman 1940).

The paralinguistic features most commonly found in baby talk are palatalization and a high-pitched voice. Crawford and Casagrande provide some information on baby talk usage among the Cocopa and Comanche. Among the Cocopa, it is used more by women than by men, and it is used longer with girls than it is with boys.

Slang and Swearing

Most cultures have something that can be labeled slang and swearing, but it is difficult to provide satisfactory cross-cultural definitions. Slang is speech that is frivolous, rapidly changing, and common among adolescents and young adults. It is probably present in most speech communities, but it is absent in the Great Basin. Older adults usually view it as silly but harmless. Only Newman (1955) has discussed it for an American Indian community.

Swearing (or verbal abuse, or cursing, or the use of profanity) is a more difficult subject. It is sometimes reported absent in American Indian communities (Laski 1958:149; Ransom 1946:54), but such reports may hinge on the investigator's notion of swearing. It probably occurs in most, perhaps all, speech communities. It is often viewed as powerful malevolent speech. It will often include scatological or sexual reference, as among the Delaware, where such elements are incorporated into nouns and verbs: *húnti hú kpənš·e·t·iyéhəla!* 'Pretty soon you'll fall the hell off!', with *-š·e·tiye(·)-* 'anus' inserted between the initial and final elements of *kpəníhəla* 'you fall'; *mpas·alák·ay* 'the damned bus', from *mpás* 'bus' plus an element meaning 'penis' (Ives Goddard, personal communication 1975). Similar topics are used in swearing in Apache (Opler 1941:457) and Mohave (Devereux 1951).

Death, especially of a relative, is a frequent theme for verbal abuse in the Plains. In Blackfoot it is delivered in the third person: máipaxkòxsinisikàpokomipùminai 'his (meaning 'your') lice have a very bad-death-dirty taste' (Uhlenbeck and van Gulik 1934:303; Allan R. Taylor, personal communication 1975). Reference to death in swearing has also been reported for the Pomo (Robert L. Oswalt, personal communication 1975), Apache (Opler 1941:457), and Mohave (Devereux 1951).

A curse in Crow can be "You are a ghost," meaning you are practically invisible, crazy, and alone in the world; "You have no one to talk to," meaning all your relatives are gone, there is no one to support you, and hence cannot be of any account; "No one at all owns you," meaning you completely lack emotional ties, no one cares for you or feels for you; or a person can be likened to a lower animal (Lowie 1959:105). Verbal abuse has also been discussed for Chitimacha (Swadesh 1933:193), Yurok (Kroeber 1960a:997-998), and Tonkawa (Hoijer 1933:135).

Word Taboo

Name taboo is the practice of placing a restriction on the use of a dead person's name, and sometimes also on the use of similar sounding words. It is especially common in the Northwest Coast and adjacent areas (Kroeber 1925:181, 360, 469, 499, 749, and elsewhere),

and has been reported, though less commonly, in other parts of North America ("Personal Names," this vol.). Twana, a Southern Coast Salish language, provides an example. At death, a person's name immediately became taboo. At a following feast a word phonetically similar to the name was made taboo to the people in the village community, and replaced by a descriptive phrase; the taboo was lifted when the name was later given to a member of the deceased person's lineage. In the nineteenth century, for example, when a Duhlelap man named *x̣átwas* died, *x̣átx̣at* 'mallard duck' was replaced by *húbhubšəd* 'red foot', and when a Skokomish named *čatádad* died, *sčátas* 'rock' was replaced by *q̓ʷəl̓ílas* 'round object for cooking'. By the 1940s the word for 'mallard' had been permanently replaced by 'red foot', and only a few older people remembered the old word. The word for 'rock', however, came back into use after the taboo was lifted (Elmendorf 1951).

Animals that are considered physically or supernaturally dangerous are often accorded special linguistic treatment. Thus the Shoshone have special words for 'bear' during pine nut picking time, and for 'rattlesnake' when in areas apt to contain them (W. Miller 1965-1993).

Creeks who are bilingual in English tend to avoid Creek words that bear a phonetic resemblance to obscene or tabooed words in English. Thus *fákki* 'soil, earth' is avoided because it sounds like an English four-letter word (Haas 1951a). Choctaw speakers avoid /fakit/ [fʌkɪt] 'turkey' for the same reason (Willem J. de Reuse, personal communication 1993).

Northwest Coast

There is a particular kind of expressive speech that involves the diminutive, augmentative, sound symbolism, and other similar linguistic mechanisms. It has its focal point in the Northwest Coast and extends beyond this area in somewhat attenuated form, south into California, and east at least as far as Montana. The expressive system among the Nootka of Vancouver Island (Sapir (1915c), is used when talking to or about different kinds of people. It utilizes changes among the six sibilant consonants [s, š, c, č, c̓, č̓], with the addition of the the the diminutive suffix -ʔis and other suffixes, some of which are used only in this system. To show affection in talking to or about children, the diminutive suffix is used:

watširλaḥ 'I am going home.'

    (*wat* 'to return', *-šiλ* 'inceptive action',

    -ah 'first person present indicative').

watšiλʔisaḥ 'I am going home, little one.'

When talking to or about people with eye defects, the six sibilant consonants are changed to laterals (ł, λ, λ̓), and the diminutive suffix (changed to -ʔił by this rule) is added:

semi 'Sammy' (the English name given to a cross-eyed Nootka man)

łemiʔił 'little cross-eyed Sammy'

When talking to or about left-handed people, the meaningless element -*čḥ*- and the diminutive -*ʔis* are inserted after the first syllable:

yá·ƚʔaλma 'there now he is' (*yá·ƚ* 'be there'; -*ʔaλ* 'now'; -*ma* 'third person present indicative')

yá·ƚčḥʔičaλma 'there now the left-handed person is,' (-*ʔis* with the following |ʔ| changes to -*ʔič*)

There are also special ways of talking about fat or large people, unusually small people and birds, hunchbacks, lame people, circumcised males, greedy people, and cowards. If the characterization is unflattering, as most are, the form is used of a person, rather than to him, unless an insult is intended. A similar system of the neighboring Quileute (Frachtenberg 1920) has an additional form used by men in speaking directly to women, but used by women when speaking of a woman.

Mythological characters alter their speech by rules like those used in expressive speech. Thus, in Quileute, Raven's wife prefixes [c-] to words, and changes [b] to [m], and [d] and [l] to [n] (this is the only place nasals occur in Quileute speech; Frachtenberg 1920). Among the Thompson Salish of British Columbia, Coyote's speech is marked by the suffix -*olk̓* (Egesdal 1992:28). Similar changes are reported for Nootka (Sapir 1915c) and Chinookan (Hymes 1958). This trait is found in attenuated form further inland, so that in Shoshone and Southern Paiute Coyote has a special suffix that he adds to words while speaking (W. Miller 1972:26; Sapir 1910a). Some characters speak in another language, as Mouse, who speaks Colville in Columbian Salish, and Kootenai in Colville (M. Dale Kinkade, personal communication 1974; see also Egesdal 1992:39-59).

The system of expressive speech of the Northwest Coast has become enmeshed with a system of sound symbolism that is used for expressing the diminutive and augmentative. Many languages have a diminutive. Less common is the augmentative; its presence presupposes the diminutive (Haas 1972). The diminutive and augmentive forms can be used to indicate not only size but also a wide variety of things, including in particular one's psychological attitude toward the topic or person addressed. The diminutive is especially common in baby talk.

The diminutive and augmentative are most commonly marked by affixes, especially suffixes. However, there is a system of sound symbolism used by many languages in western North America in which consonant alternations, less commonly vowel alternations, are used in addition to or in place of the diminutive and augmentative affixes. For example, in Yurok *t* and *l* are replaced by *č* and *r* in the diminutive; in Wiyot, *t* is replaced by *c* in the diminutive, and by *č* in the augmentative (Haas 1972:149). Sound symbolism is especially common in the Northwest Coast, where it is utilized in expressive speech, and California; but it is also found sporadically eastward, especially in Siouan and Algonquian languages (Haas 1970; Johanna Nichols 1971; Harrington 1974:8-9).

Riddles, Puns, and Tongue-twisters

Speech play is not well represented in North America (Dundes 1967:57-58; Sapir 1932; Boas 1917; W. Hill 1943:27) but has been reported for Winnebago (Susman 1941), Eastern Shoshone (Shimkin 1947), Choctaw (Dundes 1964a), Gitksan (Rigsby 1970), Navajo (Sapir 1932; W. Hill 1943:18; Kluckhohn and Leighton 1946:187-188; Wilson and Dennison 1970), Pueblos (Parsons 1936), and Papago (Alvarez 1965).

Speakers of Salishan languages sometimes play around with words by adding inappropriate suffixes to give bizarre forms (M. Dale Kinkade, personal communication 1974). The Southern and Kashaya Pomo have taunts fitted to the song and rhythm of bird songs, so that, for example, the Southern Pomo taunt "The people from the south have shriveled testicles" is sung to the meadowlark song (Robert L. Oswalt, personal communication 1974). Speech surrogates occur sporadically ("Nonspeech Communication Systems," this vol.).

Word games and secret languages like Pig Latin, common throughout Eurasia (see, for example, Conklin 1959; Haas 1957), seem to be rare in North America. Willem J. de Reuse (personal communication 1993) has reported a variety for the Central Siberian Yupik on Saint Lawrence Island, which he thinks is due to Euro-American contact, in which the syllable /ləf/ is inserted in the middle of every vowel, so for example *nanuq* 'polar bear' becomes *naləfanuləfuq*. This form of speech play is the domain of high-school children. Marianne Mithun (personal communication 1994) has reported a similar word game for Central Pomo.

Attitudes and Beliefs about Language

The Navajo prays for the ability to speak well, just as he does for wealth and good health. He considers "His words are many, his speech is fluent" as high praise (Reichard 1945:156). All cultures value good speech, but how and to what degree is a matter of individual cultural taste.

Members of every speech community evaluate the speaking ability of others. A good speaker among the Iroquois (vol. 15:446) is said to have "gifts" that are judged by specific criteria: balance of content, memory, voice quality, ability to adapt to new situations, and discretion in personal reference (Foster 1971: 34-44, 1974). The Menominee distinguished good speakers from bad and were able to characterize those who spoke elevated, archaizing, barbarous, or elegant Menominee, or spoke it with racy idiom. They identified features that marked sentences, from their point of view, as good, correct, poetic, archaizing, illiterate, childish, and the like (Bloomfield 1927). Considerations of good and bad speech are also discussed for the Yokuts (Gayton and Newman 1940), Zuni (Newman 1955), Eastern Shoshone (Shimkin 1947), and Yurok (Kroeber 1960a; Buckley 1984).

Words are a source of power; language, a source of knowledge. A Navajo told Kluckhohn and Leighton (1946:187): "Some words attract good; others drive away evil. Certain words are dangerous—they may be uttered only by special persons under specially defined conditions. Hence there are specialized vocabularies known only to those who are trained in a craft or ceremonial skill. Young Navajos who have spent much time away at a boarding school or among whites will often complain of an uncle or grandfather, 'He uses hard words. I can't understand him'." The Navajos consider speech to be one of man's faculties. The word has existed from the beginning of time. Prayers and songs must be repeated exactly to maintain their potency (Reichard 1950, 1:267).

Among the Mayo, control of the sacred language is the key for tapping knowledge. But since there are more songs, prayers, myths, and other types of esoteric knowledge than one person can know, there are specialists (Crumrine 1968:29-30).

The Western Apache "speaking with names" provides a good example of the importance of appropriate usage. Advice or comfort is given obliquely by simply citing the place where a well-known incident took place. In discussing an incident in which a woman was thus counseled, a Western Apache speaker said that she was given "pictures to work on in her mind. We didn't speak too much to her. We didn't hold her down. That way she could travel in her mind. She could add on to them [i.e., the pictures] easily. . . We gave her clear pictures with placenames. So her mind went to those places, standing in front of them as our ancestors did long ago" (Basso 1988:108, 110). The place-names are complete sentences that frequently describe the place. Because of the polysynthetic nature of the language, such names are more compact than their English translation implies, for example, čiłdi·yé≈čo sika·d 'cluster of big walnut trees stands bushing out' (Basso 1984, 1988:125).

Words that name a speech act (such as speech, chant, slang, tongue twister), or way of speaking (such as whisper or lisp) indicate something about the cultural classification and what aspects of language are important. Some information is available on types of speech acts for the Mayo (Crumrine 1968); and on ways of speaking ('stammer', 'speaking brokenly',

'talks articulately') for the Yurok (Kroeber 1960a: 995), for the Western Apache (Basso 1984:33-35), and for the Arizona Tewa (Kroskrity 1993). It appears the topic is more elaborated in some speech communities than others. The Iroquois, for example, do not have a rich metalinguistics, nor is talk of talk a favorite topic (Foster 1971:44).

Language can serve as a symbol for cultural identity. A *yoreme* 'Mayo man' is usually defined as a man who speaks Mayo (Crumrine 1968:30). The Micmac see their language as the major cultural feature that sets off the group from Whites (Wallis and Wallis 1955:22). But language does not always serve this function, as in the Shoshone case (W. Miller 1970:33). If the number of speakers is small and the language uniquely defines a cultural group, like Zuni, there may also be the belief that the language is private property (in contrast to world languages like English or French, which are open for all to learn, and are spoken as the first or second language of people from widely different cultural backgrounds) and is uniquely suited for the transmission of that group's culture. An old Iroquois man expressed this when he admonished a teenager, who was teaching dancing to English-speaking Indian children: "What's the use of learning children how to dance until you've learned them to speak Indian?" (Foster 1971:44).

Dialect differences attract awareness. If a Navajo marries a woman from a different dialect area her relatives may tease him about his speech, but they do not feel he should modify it (Reichard 1945:159). Likewise, the Hopi (C.F. Voegelin 1959) and the Chippewa (Densmore 1929:11) expect a speaker to remain true to his native dialect, but it is not considered bad form for a Shoshone spouse or visitor to shift dialects, if he or she is capable of doing so (W. Miller 1970:31-33). In these cases, dialect differences are regarded as permissible, but such a view is not always present in the Pueblos (White 1935:28).

Dialect variation is normally continuous rather than discrete. The Tahltan and Kaska, Northern Athapaskans, know this. They know that a closer or more distant linguistic relationship corresponds to a closer or more distant geographic and social relationship (Teit 1956:43). More commonly, dialects are viewed as bounded, countable entities, as among the Pima and Papago (Saxton and Saxton 1969:183) and the Interior Salish (Ray 1933:10), who divide themselves into named dialects.

Native testimony on degree of linguistic distance is often influenced by social distance. Mohave and Kitanemuk, languages of Southern California belonging to different language families, have been reported by natives as being similar (Kroeber 1915a). Similarly, measured and claimed ability to understand different Iroquoian languages and dialects does not always match (Hickerson, Turner, and Hickerson 1952).

Speech communities vary in their awareness of dialect differences. The Hopis classify those that use /f/ in place of preconsonantal /p/ as *ef-taqa*, 'f (speaking) man' (C.F. Voegelin 1959). The Navajos refer to speakers that have a strongly articulated /x/ as *x daʔání* 'they say *x*', or speakers that use /z/ for /y/ as *zas daʔání* 'they say *zas*' (in place of *yas* 'snow') (Reichard 1945:159). Other times speakers are unable to pinpoint the dialect differences, as the Shoshone, who say "they speak slower," "they speak with a drawl," "their language has more swing to it," or the like (W. Miller 1965-1993).

A case of one-way intelligibility has been reported in northern California, which reflects social and attitudinal facts more than linguistic facts. It is claimed that the Atsugewis can understand the Achumawis, but not the reverse. The Atsugewi are a small group, who are surrounded by the more numerous Achumawi. It seems the Atsugewi have taken the trouble to learn Achumawi, but not the reverse (C.F. Voegelin 1946:101). Natives have minimized the linguistic differences (Kroeber 1925:28) because of close social relations, but the languages differ about as much as French and Spanish (de Angulo and Freeland 1930). One Achumawi stated: "I worked with some Hat Creeks [Atsugewi] on some [construction] jobs, and I always used to listen to them talk. But I never tried to speak it, because it seemed to me it was like stealing something of theirs. Some fellows they try to learn everybody's language, but not me. I just picked up a few words, like I did with Paiute when I worked with them. But I never did set my mind to it" (Olmsted 1954:183). Almost all Atsugewis have Achumawi relatives, but the reverse does not hold.

Language socialization practices reflect attitudes and beliefs about language. For example, the Hidatsa claim to use no baby talk, because, as one mother put it, "we want them to talk just like us, right from the start" (Voegelin and Robinett 1954:69). Instead, mothers say they talk more slowly and more clearly. But among the Comanche (Casagrande 1948), Hopi (Dennis 1940:35), and Acoma (W. Miller 1956-1959), baby talk is used because the adult speech is thought to be too difficult. If a child uses baby talk past about five, he is usually teased, though sometimes it is used with older children, as a display of affection (Casagrande 1948; Joseph, Spicer, and Chesky 1949:122; Crawford 1970).

The Mohave believe that a newborn baby has the ability to understand, even though it cannot speak (Devereux 1949). The Wishram believe a newborn speaks the language of dogs, coyotes, and guardian spirits (Hymes 1966:132-133). To guard against mutism, a Kaska mother wipes her index finger around the baby's mouth shortly after birth (Honigmann 1949:230). The Mohave also practice a variety of taboos (Devereux 1949). A child that is slow in learning to talk is fed hard-boiled meadowlark eggs among the Gros Ventre (Flannery 1953:142-143), and the tongue of a meadowlark among the Wishram (Dell Hymes, personal communication 1974).

There is a widespread belief that Indians can learn an Indian language much more easily than a non-Indian. For example, the Iroquois believe an Indian child will have an easy time learning Iroquois, even if he comes from an English-speaking home (Foster 1971:56). In a similar fashion, many Indians believe that it is more difficult for them to learn English than a non-Indian. A Shoshone once expressed surprise that her English did not improve after a blood transfusion from an English-speaking White person, the surprise also being predicated on the notion that there is a relationship between blood and race (W. Miller 1965-1993).

Multilingualism

The area of greatest multilingualism coincided with the area of greatest linguistic diversity, namely California. At time of European contact, there were some 60 to 80 languages (not counting distinct dialects, of which there were many more), in a population estimated to be 300,000, residing in perhaps 500 villages (Silver and Miller 1997: Chap. 9). Some of the best information for California is provided by Powers (1877), an early observer in the state. He noted that the Karok and Yurok usually learned each other's languages, but would often speak to each other in their own languages (1877:44); that in the Hupa area many Indians spoke five or more languages, always including Hupa, and generally English (1877:73); that along the border of Pomoan and Wailaki, nearly everyone understood both languages (1877:147); and that most of the Pomo knew more than one Pomoan language, with boys often being sent to neighboring villages to learn its language (1877:150). Powers (1877:198) also mentions a Wappo reputed to have known 14 Indian languages. The high incidence of multilingualism among the Yurok and their neighbors was the result of intertribal marriage. "Marrying close at home, on the other hand, was looked upon as evidence of sloth and lack of spirit" (Waterman 1920:224). Other references to California multilingualism are Barrett (1908:137), Gayton (1948:56), Kroeber (1925), and Gifford (1926:339).

Three interlinking patterns of social interaction fostered multilingualism: marriage alliances, ritual cooperation, and economic exchange. Rules of endogamy and other kinship restrictions were such that one often had to seek a spouse in a neighboring village, which, in linguistically diverse California, was often a village speaking another language. The elite, particularly in Northern California, preferred to marry within their own class. Since they were always a minority within their own village, it almost assured that their spouse would come from elsewhere. Headmen often would cement social, ritual, and political ties by marrying women from several different villages. There were several ritual complexes in native California that performed yearly rites that called for the cooperation of several villages, villages that normally encompassed several languages. Such religious gatherings were often the context for trading activities, as well. Trading also took place at trade feasts, occasions whose sole function was economic exchange in which several villages were involved.

The functions that different languages serve in the speech community allow the distinction between individual and societal multilingualism. In individual multilingualism, language choice is governed by what individuals happen to be present, rather than topic or setting; individual language repertoire is governed by the quirks of personal history (one parent may come from a different linguistic group, several childhood years may have been spent with relatives in a different linguistic group, or the like). In societal multilingualism, each language serves a particular function and is used in particular settings.

Examples of societal bilingualism in North America include the use of Creek and Mohawk as diplomatic languages (Speck 1945:28, Foster 1974), and Hupa in ritual settings (Powers 1877:73). But most North American cases of multilingualism, including the one just described for California, exemplify individual multilingualism. The two kinds of multilingualism could coexist, as for example in the Hupa case, and in the Creek Confederacy: intervillage marriages and other contacts led to individual multilingualism; but any man that aspired to political leadership had to know Creek, as well. Small-scale societies provide a much better milieu for a high level of individual multilingualism than do stratified societies, and in fact societal multilingualism in small-scale societies seems to be limited to those who have rank (Silver and Miller 1997: Chaps. 4 and 9).

Influencing the rate of multilingualism, in order of importance, were degree of linguistic diversity in the area, attitudes toward bilingualism, and utility. The areas of greatest linguistic diversity coincide with the areas of greatest bilingualism: California, the Northwest Coast (Jacobs 1937), and the Southeast. But as the Pueblo area illustrates, diversity does not guarantee multilingualism. Social and cultural forces help shape attitudes, for example, the marriage, ritual, and trading alliances in California provided a context in which multilingualism was valued, while the ethnocentrism in the Pueblo area provided the opposite context (see Dozier 1954:281, 297, 300; Fox 1968; Sherzer 1973: 786). Utility is seldom important in small-scale societies, and it is probably an important factor only in societal bilingualism.

Bilingualism, both individual and societal, can remain stable for centuries. In other cases, it is the first step on the road to language replacement. The most dramatic examples in history involve societal bilingualism in stratified societies, as when Latin swept through large portions of Europe, replacing local languages with what has become the Romance languages. Most examples of language shift are in areas where bilingualism is high: the Southeast, the Northwest Coast, and California (Boas 1891:584; Boas and Goddard 1924a:40; Gayton 1948:56; McClellan 1953:48; Powers 1877:87; Rigsby 1969: 73-75). Language shift in small-scale societies is usually limited to a few communities, and unlike stratified societies is never on a wide scale; one case involves Cree and Ojibwa (Wolfart 1973a). However, effects over time can be cumulative, as in the Northwest Coast (Jacobs 1937).

Modern Speech Communities

The Indian speech communities have become, in the late twentieth century, part of a larger one with the Indian languages being replaced by English. In some cases the replacing language was French (parts of Canada and Louisiana), Spanish (the Southwest and Southern California), or Russian (eastern Chukotka). Even in those few cases in which the native language was being transmitted to the next generation the European language played an important role in the speech community (fig. 7).

The modern communities have been restricted, and sometimes forcibly moved to a new location. Changes have taken place, some of which have been imposed, such as the forced use of English in boarding schools (Leibowitz 1971). Other changes are internal, brought about as a response to outside factors; for example, as the Peyote religion has spread, so has the use of English, since participants are often of a mixed tribal background (Stewart 1944:83). The native languages can no longer function as they once did. Some functions are lost, others are shifting or have shifted to English. New needs develop in the community that are sometimes served by the native language, but more often they are served by English.

Language Shift

Casagrande (1954-1955) described the Comanche speech community of the 1940s. He found those over 60 spoke little or no English, those under 30 little or no Comanche. In between was the bilingual generation, but with few of them being equally at home in both languages. Younger speakers spoke Comanche with an English accent, with simplification in the phonology,

left, Dept. of Ind. Affairs and Northern Development, Hull, Que.

Fig. 7. Tribal and intertribal meetings. In the 1990s such meetings were generally conducted in English, though opening prayers were typically given in Indian languages. left, Members of the Union of British Columbia Indian Chiefs reading responses to a position paper at their annual general assembly (left to right): Ron Seymour (Carrier), Forrest Walkem (Thompson), Herber Maitland (Haisla), George Manuel (Shuswap), Philip Paul (Halkomelem), Victor Adolph (Lillooet), and unidentified. Photograph by Andrews-Hunt, Williams Lake, B.C., 1974. right, Eastern Cherokee tribal council (left to right, seated around tables): Bailey Coleman, Jonathan Edd Taylor, Thomas Lambert, Eunise Ensley (assistant to English clerk), Winona Digh (clerk who transcribes the minutes into English), Robin Toineeta (standing and gesturing), Chairman Dan McCoy, Ammons Ratler, Maggie Wachacha (clerk who transcribes the minutes into Cherokee), Edmund Youngbird, Wilbur Sequoyah, and Roy French. Photograph by Mike Kelly, Eastern Cherokee Res. (Qualla Boundary), Cherokee, N.C., 1981.

Smithsonian, NAA: Honigman Coll., box 34.

Fig. 8. James Koe (b. 1905, d. 1980), Kutchin, broadcasting his Kutchin-language radio request program, "Yesterday Before," which aired on Saturday afternoons (Honigmann and Honigmann 1970:94). He worked for station CHAK (later the Canadian Broadcasting Corporation, Western Arctic service), providing news, traditional stories, Western music, and information. He also served as chief of Aklavik for 6 years. Photograph by John Honigmann, Inuvik, N.W.T., 1967.

morphology, and syntax. Often modern descriptive words were used in place of forgotten older words, and Comanche sentences often included English words and phrases. Settings in which Comanche was appropriate (traditional ceremonies, story telling) became less frequent, while settings in which English was appropriate (meetings with government officials, school) became more frequent. A half-century later, there were only 30 speakers and semispeakers (out of almost 10,000 enrolled Comanches), all over 70 (Jean Charney, personal communication 1992).

As in the Comanche case, new needs are usually served by the outside language. But sometimes, the aboriginal language is used in new settings, for example, the use of Cherokee and Cree (fig. 9) in writing, and the use of Navajo in some schools (vol. 10:667).

Casagrande's description of language shift among the Comanche is typical of many Indian communities, except that the description might be applied to a time period before or after the 1940s. Language shift has been observed for: Mohawk (Mithun and Chafe 1979), Athapaskan communities (Kari and Spolsky 1973), communities in Arizona (Voegelin, Voegelin, and Schutz 1967), Sandia Pueblo (Brandt 1970a), Tewa and Yaqui (Dozier 1956), Shoshone (W. Miller 1971), Arapaho (Gross 1951; Salzmann 1951), Delaware (Newcomb 1956a:115- 117), Omaha (Mead 1932, esp. p. 126), and Makah (Colson 1953, esp. pp. 54-55).

Language loss is seldom a sudden process. Children in those households that include a grandparent or other older relative frequently learn the language after language transmission has stopped in other families; language loss usually takes a full generation, sometimes much longer. There are frequently semispeakers whose command of the language is incomplete, and younger

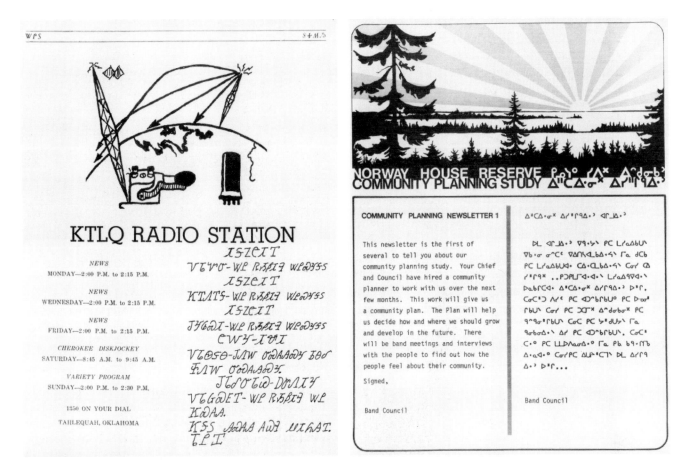

left, Willard Walker, Canaan, Me.

Fig. 9. Native writing in 20th-century usage. left, Radio program schedule from a bilingual Cherokee-English newsletter (Doublehead and Procter 1965:12). right, Bilingual newsletter in English and Western Swampy Cree, from Norway House Res., Man., dated May 1977 but distributed 1978 (David Pentland, communication to editors 1980).

individuals who understand the language and know several words and phrases.

The best study on phonological change is for Chipewyan and Sarcee (Cook 1989), and on grammatical change, for Cayuga (Mithun 1989). Ives Goddard (1988) has described the loss of the deliberate-style phonology among Mesquakies (Fox) born after 1910. Their use of only the casual-style phonology gives an incorrect impression of rapid language change.

When the native language goes, aspects of culture that are especially associated with language also go. Thus, no one becomes a shaman among the Washoe because knowledge of the language is a prerequisite (d'Azevedo et al. 1963:60).

Attitudes toward the Native and the Outside Language

The feeling people have in a language loss setting is captured by this remark of a Gros Ventre speaker: "That's a tough language you ran into, pardner . . . That's why we don't speak it ourselves; it's a hard language to learn. You can tell that—when we talk our own language, we have to think before we tell you" (Salzmann 1969:307). At the time Gros Ventre was remembered by only a few old people. Another comment, this time from an old Arapaho: "The youngsters speak a funny Arapaho; they don't use all the big words that we do and that our fathers did, and they take many short cuts. We can understand them all right, but it doesn't sound the way we would say it" (Salzmann 1951:100). Unfavorable comment on the speech of the younger generation has been noted for the Kwakiutl (Boas 1932b:90) and Makah (Colson 1953:54). A kind of Hopi interlarded with English words was referred to as "broken down Hopi" by one speaker (Voegelin 1959; see also Kennard 1963).

Casagrande (1954-1955, pt. 3:11) remarked: "Many of the younger Comanche feel that the speech of the older people is vulgar, an attitude that reflects the adoption by the Comanche of a White sense of propriety and prudishness, and there has been a direct extension of English word taboos to the native speech which is unashamed and forthright." Darnell (1974) discussed the attitudes held about Cree and English in a

242

changing community in which English was encroaching. Sometimes, as among the Shoshone (W. Miller 1972a:10), the native language is felt to be inferior to English.

The use of a native language has come to be a symbol of Indian identity, something that will separate Indians from their White neighbors. This topic is discussed for the Eastern Cherokee (Gulick 1958), Micmac (Wallis and Wallis 1955:22, 101), and Aleut (Geoghegan 1944:5). Some communities have formal programs in language instruction, not only to help preserve the language but also to provide instruction about it. One of the most successful, for Walapai, in Peach Springs, Arizona, was begun by Akira Yamamoto at the University of Kansas and later directed by people from within the community (Zepeda and Hill 1991:142-146). See also Mithun and Chafe (1979) for discussion of a Mohawk program.

Literate Speech Communities

While writing is never found in small-scale societies, it has come into use as Indian speech communities have become transformed and part of a larger society. In most cases English serves as the written language, but in a few cases writing in the native language serves (or served) important functions. Most often writing was developed by outsiders, but sometimes it was developed from within the community ("Native Writing Systems," this vol.).

Attitudes toward native literacy vary. Many Pueblo peoples are against it, but at least among the Hopi attitudes vary (Brandt 1981). Navajos' attitudes are positive (McLaughlin 1992). The Canadian Inuit feel that their Cree-derived syllabic writing system is more "Eskimo" than the roman alphabet (Basse and Jensen 1979; Dorais 1990). In some cases, as among the Lakhota, and the Micmac, competing writing systems produce conflicting attitudes (Willem J. de Reuse, personal communication 1993).

Indian English

There are certain characteristics that seem to be universal in the English used in Indian communities. At the turn of the twentieth century the Bureau of Indian Affairs operated a number of boarding schools that included students from a mixed linguistic background, and English had to be used as the lingua franca. It seems that the variety of English that came to be used was transmitted from one generation of students to the next (Spicer 1962:440; Leap 1974; Harvey 1974). Leap (1973, 1993) argues that some of the characteristics of Indian English come from native language interference. Rules of language usage also differ; Philips (1970, 1983) discusses this topic for the Warm Springs Reservation in Oregon, for both spoken and written English, and suggests that some of the differences reflect aboriginal practices.

Discourse

M. DALE KINKADE AND ANTHONY MATTINA

Background

Discourse, in its broadest sense, refers to any extended speech (and its representation) that stretches longer than a sentence. These stretches range from informal conversation to formal debate and discussion to speech making and to narrative performance. The focus here will be nearly exclusively on the last of these, for which there exists a vast and diverse quantity of data, both in terms of collections of native materials and of discussions and analyses of them. Most varieties of native discourse have been widely studied.

The linguistic discourse on discourse has deep roots, blossoming in the 1970s and 1980s with the publication of books and journals dedicated to that topic. Situating discourse in its psychosocial context, scholars have discussed questions that bear on discourse grammar, knowledge, and communication, and their acquisition. Under rubrics such as the ethnography of speaking, they have reported their findings on how information flows between members of the opposite sex, between client and professional, Anglo and Indian, lawyer and witness, parent and child. Attempts to identify differences between spoken and written language have been important byproducts of these studies (van Dijk 1985). Discourse studies in general since the 1970s have focused on the variety of activities just alluded to; most, if not all, reports on American Indian discourse that predate the 1970s focus on phenomena that can be subsumed under the rubrics of narrative and of ethnographic exposition. Although there has been a fair amount written on the analysis of conversation and other forms of dialogue, virtually none of it includes much native language material, and it does not conveniently come under the heading of discourse as it will be discussed here.

There are many sorts of narrative performance, some of the most obvious of which are sacred or ritual texts, myths and tales, historical narratives, speeches and exhortations, and poetry (including songs). Life histories (biographies and autobiographies) are yet another kind of narrative performance. All these kinds of performance were widely practiced in varying degrees (although formal poetry as such is probably infrequent) and are widely known around the world. In regard to American Indians, the greatest attention has been given to myths, tales, and sacred texts, although the boundaries and subdivisions of these genres are far from clear. Terminology is inconsistent and not necessarily comparable from one writer to another. Terms such as myth, sacred story, legend, narrative, tale, fable, and the like do not express precisely definable categories, although they are widely used as if they did. The eminent folklorist Stith Thompson (1929:xvii) felt that it is futile to attempt an exact definition of 'myth' as distinguished from 'tale'. He subsumes all these categories under 'folktales'; a useful overview of commonly encountered terms and their implications that can be included under this heading is Thompson (1946:7-10). In short, there is no consistent terminology in English for the types of discourse that Thompson included under 'folktale'. In part, this inconsistent usage reflects differences in the ways societies and languages categorize performative discourse, but it also masks comparability between groups that may actually be present. For example, what Ellis (1989:2), speaking of James Bay Cree, calls 'legendary tales' (referred to by others as 'sacred stories' and the like) may be comparable to, or a variety of, what Liljeblad (vol. 11:651-658), referring to the Great Basin, would call 'myths', rather than corresponding to Liljeblad's 'legends'; these seem to be more comparable to what Algonquianists call 'narratives' or 'tales' (and Ellis calls 'explanatory accounts' or 'action stories'; Ellis 1989:21-23). To compound problems with terminology even further, some writers avoid certain terms such as 'myth' because of perceived native sensibilities, although natives themselves may use terms like 'fairy tales' to refer to their folktales, a usage that may in turn offend nonnatives. Because of these problems, the use of these terms here will of necessity be inexact.

Terminology in the native languages, although of considerable interest for understanding native categorization, may also be inexact and is not necessarily comparable from one society to another. Nor should it be expected that native categories will correspond to English genres. Information on such terminology is limited and often filtered through Euro-American perspectives. Ellis (1989:2), based on categories named by or inferred from native terminology, classifies Western James Bay Cree discourse into two primary types, 'traditional discourse' and 'popular discourse'. The latter includes 'accounts of personal experiences or of events', 'reminiscences', 'descriptions', 'oratory', and 'correspondence' (with some question about the last two). The former includes discourse types more commonly associated with performative discourse. The basic contrasting types within this category are named: *a·talo·hka·na*, pl. (further subdivided by Ellis into legendary tales, heroic episodes, thematic episodes, and folktales), and *a·cimo·wina*, pl. (which can also apply to some types of popular discourse); songs constitute a third type. He notes that the distinctions among these literary types are "often internally and linguistically marked" (Ellis 1989:2).

Parks (1991, 3:49) provides another classification based on native perspective and terminology, this time for Arikara. He divides oral traditions into 'true stories' (unnamed) and 'tales' (*na·ʔi·káWIš*). The category 'true stories' includes far more than Euro-American society would consider "true"; it is divided into sacred stories (world origins, mythic dramas, visionary encounters, legends) and nonsacred stories (historical narratives and supernatural occurrences). Prayers and song texts are also considered to be 'true stories'. The category 'tales' includes trickster tales, animal tales, and adventure stories (Parks 1991, 3:49).

Both the Ellis (Cree) and Parks (Arikara) classifications are unusual in their detail. Neither, however, includes native names for more than two or three types of story. That, in fact, appears to be a widespread pattern, although the specific kinds of stories included in the two or three names a language has are not necessarily comparable. For example, Cahuilla (Uto-Aztecan) names *ʔáʔalxeʔat* 'myth' (note that the word means 'true story') and *selhiščeʔat* 'tale' (Seiler 1970:8); Osage has *óðake* 'story, legend, narrative, tradition' and *híko* 'fable, myth, a story not to be taken literally' (La Flesche 1932:60, 176); Squamish (Salish) has *sxʷəxʷiʔámʔ* 'nonrealistic story, myth' and *syə́c* 'realistic story' (Kuipers 1967-1969, 1:298, 300). In these cases, the status of songs in regard to these native classifications is not made clear.

Native narrative performances (and sometimes their types) are not always of indigenous origin; tales have been widely borrowed, both from native groups in North America and from European sources (particularly through English and French; see Mattina 1985 for such a tale adapted to Okanagan). There is even a type of discourse that might be called pseudo-narrative: speeches that have been concocted partly from native materials and largely from Euro-American ideas about what American Indians should have said (see, for example, Kaiser 1987; Hilbert 1991; and Gifford 1995, on Chief Seattle's "speeches").

Almost without exception, what fragmentary records are available of linguistic and discourse activities of American Indian groups have been prepared by outsiders: ethnographers, linguists, missionaries, journalists, traders, and travelers. The few extant fragments of native-recorded discourse activities have been prepared for an audience of outsiders, or at best, a mixed audience.

Examples of American Indian discourse have been collected since the earliest contacts with Europeans. Often these early samples were somewhat artificial, in that they were not in the native languages, but they nevertheless represent connected native speech. American Indian myths, folktales, and sacred or ritual texts have also been recorded for a long time, although often with little regard for either the native language or for structural or stylistic features found in the original narrations. Less frequently life histories, native speeches, and the like have been written down; however, these are almost exclusively in English, and sometimes with little regard for faithfulness to the originals.

Materials produced earlier than 1825 or so include little in the way of directly quoted material, and almost nothing in the native languages. However, they do contain valuable information on various discourse settings and dynamics of discourse. *The Jesuit Relations and Allied Documents* (JR 1896-1901), begun in 1632, and the records of other priests and missionaries have such information scattered through church reports. Analogously important are the journals, correspondence, and reports of explorers, travelers, and other missionaries, such as Ross (1849), de Smet (1843), and Cox ([1831] 1957). Many of these reports and narratives were reprinted in Thwaites's 38-volume series *Early Western Travels* (1904-1907). Other writings where one can find relevant ethnographic information that helps establish the setting of native discourse are in the works of two seventeenth-century missionaries, contemporaries who worked among the Algonquian natives of New England. In 1663 John Eliot published his translation of the Bible into Massachusett (vol. 4:287); he also wrote a Christian apologetic work *Indian Dialogues*, a condensed English paraphrase of conversations held by missionaries and unconverted Indians (Bowden and Ronda 1980). Roger Williams's writings comprise several volumes, including *A Key into the Language of America* (1643). Much information on early presentations of native oral literature in southern New England can be found in Simmons (1986). In the eighteenth century missionaries John Gottlieb Ernestus Heckewelder (1876, 1958) and David Zeisberger (1910, 1912; Olmstead 1991), who learned Onondaga, compiled reports. Reports of travelers are also numerous, for example, Maximilian (1843), Ross (1849), and J.W. Jones (1858-1859). Ross's writings are noteworthy for his relatively enlightened attitude toward the Indians; Jones's journal is an example of a brief manuscript (124 handwritten pages) that awaits study. All such materials, in fact, are in need of study and evaluation of the kind that one finds, for example, in Maud

(1982). Maud surveys the work of missionaries (among others), singling out that of Émile Petitot among the Mackenzie Eskimo and Kutchin and that of Adrien G. Morice among the Carrier.

The examples given here are meant to suggest that valuable contextual information is retrievable from these materials, and inferences about discourse can be made from this information. These early ethnographers also left reports scattered in their books of the native voices—or rather of what they heard as native voices—in the form of descriptions of circumstances where Indians spoke, held councils and meetings, greeted their visitors, or confronted them. William Clark, for example, reports that on September 4, 1805, having crossed the Bitterroot Mountains, he met a party of about 400 Flatheads, who "rec[ei]ved us friendly, threw white robes over our Sholders & Smoked in the pipes of peace, we Encamped with them & found them friendly. . . . The Chiefs harangued untill late at night, Smoked our pipe and appeared Satisfied. I was the first white man who ever wer on the waters of this river" (Moulton 1983-, 5:187). The journals of the expedition members do not say what the Flathead chiefs had to harangue about until late at night, but they record perceptions of the language as a "gugling kind of languaje Spoken much thro the Throught" (Moulton 1983-, 5:188), of the natives as "the likelyest and honestst Savages we have ever yet Seen" and speculations that perhaps they are "the welch Indians" (De Voto (1953:234). To study the provenance of the natives, Meriwether Lewis did take down "the names of everry thing in their Language" (De Voto 1953:234).

Alexander Ross spent 15 years among the tribes west of the Rocky Mountains (Ross 1849:21), including five among the Okanagan, before retiring to live in what is now Winnipeg. He married an Okanagan woman whom he called Sally and who bore him 13 children. Eventually he felt he knew enough about the natives to "take a cursory peep at the Indians of the interior; but more particuarly of the Oakinackens" (1849:272). In 1813, having arrived at the site where he would settle for the winter, he wrote, "I set to in earnest to learn the Indian language, and wrote vocabulary after vocabulary; and although the task was a hard one, I soon found, from my progress, that perseverance would overcome many difficulties" (1849:155). He came to understand some Okanagan, and learned to speak some too. He became accustomed to the sound of Okanagan, and admired it so much that he would say that "there is no bird nor beast of which they [the Okanagans] cannot imitate the voice so as to decoy it within their reach" (1849:283). His writings are peppered with reasonably transliterated Okanagan words and phrases, and accurately glossed kin terms: his Scomalt stands for *skʷúmalt* 'high-class maiden', Skyloo stands for *sqílxʷ* 'people, Indian', Sin-who-yelp-pe-took for

sənxʷyaʔɬpítkʷ 'Colville River'. While Ross shared in the perception of the Indians and their world as savage in opposition to the Whites and their world as civilized, he did not perceive a parallel opposition of primitive Indians and evolved Whites. His works, in sum, are a good early source of information pertinent to Okanagan discourse, like this relatively full report:

> . . . one of my men accosted the chief, calling him by name. The chief looked steadfastly at him, but made no reply. Being called again by name, he turned half round, and with a significant air, said, "You white people say you know all things; do you not then know that I have changed my name?" "No," said the man; "how could I know? for you change your names as often as the moon changes; but the whites, like the sun, never change." "And who made the moon?" said the Indian. "God, to be sure," rejoined the man. "And who made the sun?" continued the chief. "The same who made the moon," was the reply. "Then if God made us after the moon subject to change, and you after the sun unchangeable, why do you reproach us? In reproaching us, you reproach the master of life" (Ross 1849:306-307).

Not all early accounts of native discourse seem as balanced as Ross's. Ross Cox ([1831] 1957), another visitor to Okanagan country, reported stretches of speech that today appear like ludicrous imaginings, as when an Indian

> turning to his countrymen . . . continued, "Did I not tell you that the white men would not tell lies? You are fools, great fools, and have no patience. Let us now show our joy at meeting our friends; and to-morrow let all our hunters go into the plains, and up the hills, and kill birds and deer for the good white men." They then commenced dancing, jumping, and crying out in a most discordant manner,
>
> The good white men, the good white men,
>   Our hearts are glad for the good white men,
> The good white men, the good white men,
>   Dance and sing for the good white men.
>
> Then giving three cheers, something like the "Hip, hip, hurra!" of our domestic bacchanalians, they retired to the village (Cox 1957:183-184).

Cox reported a flowery style of Indian oratory, and this contrasts with another traveler, David Thompson, who wrote in the early nineteenth century: "The speeches of the Indians on both sides of the mountains are in plain language, sensible and to the purpose. They sometimes repeat a few sentences, two or three times; this is to impress on the hearers the object of the speech, but I never heard a speech in the florid, bombastic style I have often seen published as spoken to white men, and upon whom it was intended to have an effect" (D. Thompson 1971:249). An example from Thompson's journal is the (translated) quotation of a Lake chief who volunteered his services as guide. The occasion, in the spring of 1808, was the desertion of Thompson's previous guide and his search for another. The excerpt goes: "While I am alive, the white men who come to us with goods shall not perish in the mountains for want of a guide and a hunter; since your hearts [my fellow Lakes] are all weak, I will go with them" (D. Thompson 1971:252).

While Thompson's quoted speech may not always be a faithful translation of the original, his comments about the context of a speech event are informative. Indians greeted their visitors with speeches, as when Thompson, one of his men, and "an Indian lad" were approached by a Pend d'Oreille group. "As usual an old man made a short speech, and made a present . . ." (1971:261). In late June 1812, Thompson, navigating the Columbia downstream, passed the Spokane country where he sent for the "chiefs of the village to come and smoke." After a short welcoming speech and some peace smoking, "the chief made a long speech in a loud singing voice, and each sentence [was] responded to by the others by 'Oy Oy'" (D. Thompson 1971:292). The speech was then interpreted, at which Thompson reports that it "was thanks for our arrival, and hoping we would bring them guns, ammunition, axes, knives, awls, and not to forget steels and flints with many other articles; they were able and willing to hunt, and would be able to pay for everything they wanted . . . . The two Simpoil Indians were now called upon to tell them all the news they had collected; at the end of every three or four sentences, they stopped and the chief repeated the same aloud, so that all could hear, and was answered by 'Oy Oy'. We noticed that the news, whether good or bad, was pronounced in the same tone of voice" (D. Thompson 1971:292). Thompson's narrative shows also that the Indians knew more English and French than the Whites knew Indian and trade languages. As the party was about to leave Salish territory southwestward, "a fine-looking young man came to us and requested a passage in our canoe. . . . He remarked to us that the Simpoil Indians [Okanagan speakers] could not interpret for us much farther down the river, as the natives spoke a different language [of Sahaptian stock], which both he and his wife well understood" (D. Thompson 1971:294). Farther downstream, at the village of the Wow-thlar-lar, a chief invited Thompson to his house "built of logs" and kept talking "pointing out the arrangements of his house, and making use of as many English words as he had learned from the ships when trading with them, some of them not the best" (D. Thompson 1971:298).

While some authors made up Indian speeches, others were only confounded by what they heard. John W. Jones, who was forced to winter with the Kootenais, wrote in his journal that on December 23, 1858, his party joined their winter camp, where they observed their Christmas festivities. These included an orator who rushed "frantically in a semi-nudity state from the lodge into the open air," where he would deliver his oration into thin air until the cold drove him back inside (where the people were) to warm up; he repeated this practice through the night. Since Jones and his party understood none of what was said, all that is known of this particular oratory is its setting (J.W. Jones 1858-1859).

As Cox heard them sing the praise of the White fur traders, so the Jesuit Pierre Jean de Smet heard the Indians sing the praise of the priests. He recounts that on July 5, 1840,

about thirty of the principal chiefs of the Snake Indians invited me to a council. I explained to them the christian doctrine in a compendious manner—they were all very attentive—they then deliberated among themselves for about half an hour, and one of the chiefs, addressing me in the name of the others, said: "Black-gown, the words of thy mouth have found their way to our hearts; they never will be forgotten. Our country is open for thee; come to teach us what we have to do, to please the Great Spirit, and we will do according to thy words" (de Smet 1843:15).

Chittenden and Richardson, editors of the de Smet documents, add some fervor in their paraphrase of the events that followed de Smet's homily:

The savages paid the greatest attention, and appeared struck with wonder at the holy doctrine that I had been explaining to them. They then took counsel among themselves for the space of half an hour, when the spokesman, in the name of all the chiefs, addressed me in the following words: "Black-gown, your words have entered our hearts; they will never go out from them. We wish to know and practice the sublime law that you have just made known to us, in the name of the Great Spirit, whom we love. All our country is open to you, you need only choose to settle an establishment. We will all of us leave the plains and the forests, to come and put ourselves under your orders, about you" (Chittenden and Richardson 1905, 1:218).

The books discussed here are rich in contextual information, and poor in actual texts, many of which are, in any case, fabricated. These works are thus in complementary distribution with the bulk of the materials gathered under the auspices of the Smithsonian Institution, Bureau of American Ethnology, which have little or no contextual information. Collections that focus on narrative itself, and descriptive, analytical, and critical work based on texts extracted from their natural context, often reveal projections analogous to those of the early ethnographers.

Genuine, or more nearly genuine, examples of native narration can be found in Nabokov (1991). Here are assembled a variety of materials presenting Indian versions of, and views about, encounters with Europeans and Americans over 500 years. Many are verbatim excerpts from speeches, interviews, autobiographies, or letters; others are from traditional narratives and from Indian newspapers. Not all are translations; some of the excerpts (especially the later ones) were written by literate Indians in English, and these often retain stylistic traits of native narrative style.

In general, the narrative materials most commonly collected have been folktales, since these could easily be adapted to forms that were comprehensible to speakers of European languages. Until the mid-nineteenth century native folklore was rarely given serious scholarly attention or published with fidelity to the original native-language story. It was easy for anyone who could write to ask to have a story told; the story (whether working from notes or from memory) could then be molded into something like European folktales, usually modified considerably to suit European ideas, characters, and mores. The original native text was not considered important. Even missionaries who wrote down folktales often denigrated them, and taught their tellers that they were fairy tales (and they are frequently called that by natives today). The original Indian language was ignored completely (except for an occasional word or animal name), since it was the story itself that was considered important. Nor was thought given to the notion that any particular group might have a single large corpus of folktales; rather the casual collector was more interested in sampling one or several language groups and presenting those stories that appealed to the collector. Whatever interest or value these popular presentations may have (and they are often of interest and use both to scholars—for finding motifs and tale types, for example—and the general public), they cannot be considered truly representative of the narrative skill of native storytellers or of native literature.

Often these crude English-language collections are simply an attempt to present some of the folktales of Indians who lived in the collector's home area (Costello 1895; Palmer 1925), or are intended (however misguidedly) to preserve for the people themselves some of their literary heritage (Yanan 1971). Native peoples (including speakers) themselves sometimes published such collections (Mourning Dove 1933; Sampson 1938).

Even more common has been the publication in a local newspaper or magazine of an occasional Indian story as an example of native folklore (Sard-Khom 1906). Journalistic treatments of American Indian texts are found on occasion. In 1930 the Spokane newspaper *Washington Farmer* announced the publication of "A Series of New Stories a Thousand Years Old." The storyteller was Emily M. Phillips, granddaughter of Moses, chief of the Moses-Columbia people. The editor was Joe L. Ashlock, Phillips's journalism instructor. He promised that by means of these Indian stories readers would "glimpse a deep, inner pattern of human nature that is not of the paleface" (1930:3 [595]). Here is that version of the story of Chipmunk and his grandmother, a legend found throughout the Interior Salish.

Story of Chipmunk

Far off in the woods, away from any village, there lived little Chipmunk and his grandmother. They lived on the roots and camas that she dug and dried and the berries that she picked. Chipmunk was too small to hunt, so he played in the woods all day. One day, while roaming in the forest, he found some berries, the first berries of the season. He immediately went home and asked his grandmother for something to eat.

"Would you like some white camas?" she asked him.

"No-no-no," answered Chipmunk.

"Would you like some roots?" she asked again.

"No-no-no," answer [sic] Chipmunk.

She in turn named all the different kinds of food they had, but Chipmunk did not want any of them. He began to cry. His grandmother asked him then if he wanted berries, for she, too, had seen some already ripe.

"Yes-yes-yes," answer [sic] Chipmunk, starting to smile.

"Then take this little basket and pick 12 berries. Do not eat any until we have asked the blessing of the Great Spirit who has sent us the berries," she told him.

Chipmunk Goes Berrying

Chipmunk took the basket and ran out into the woods. He carefully counted and picked 12 nice, juicy-looking berries. In a few moments he was ready to start back. Being anxious to eat some of the berries, he started to run back just as fast as he could. He tripped over a log and down he went—his berries spilling and scattering in every direction. He began to pick them up. He found all but one of them. He looked and looked for it, but he could not find it. He began to cry, and as he put up his hand to wipe the tears from his eyes he saw the missing berry smashed on the palm of his hand. He was so happy that before he realized what he was doing he had put the berry in his mouth.

"M-m-m, how sweet and juicy it is," he said to himself. "I guess I'll go back and eat some more. My grandmother will not know it." He ate what was in the basket, then went back to the bush, where he ate some more. He ate all that he wanted. He climbed to the top of the bush where he swayed back and forth, singing a little song his grandmother had taught him. . .. (E.M Phillips 1930:9 [129]).

Treating Indian myths and legends as on a par with European folktales is widespread, and since the latter are commonly considered as most suitable for children (and are edited accordingly), so Indian stories have been widely adapted for children (Matson 1968, 1972). Many such collections have gained a modicum of popularity and influenced respected writers. Editing to make the stories suitable for children has resulted in even greater distortion and bowdlerization than in other popularizations; such bowdlerization was often self-imposed by narrators because of their own religious and moral indoctrination or desire not to offend the immediate audience. Somewhat more serious efforts at anthologizing American Indian folktales have both gleaned from these popularized collections and also gathered new materials directly (Clark 1953; Rustige 1988). Others base their popularized anthologies on more scholarly sources; for example, Erdoes and Ortiz (1984) make a serious attempt to recapture some of the original character of the stories presented. Such anthologies are always in English only, as is appropriate for their intended audience.

Serious scholarly collection of American Indian myths and folktales did not begin until the nineteenth century; interest in the American Indian remained intense throughout that century. For a quarter of a century through the 1850s, Henry Rowe Schoolcraft collected a large body of texts (in English), work that has been called a "landmark in the history of the recording of American Indian tales" (Thompson 1929:xv).

248

Schoolcraft edited the translations of his original materials at will, with a "sentimentality," said Thompson, that caused the general American public to identify Schoolcraft's idealizations with an American Indian norm. For an assessment of Schoolcraft's work, see Clements (1990).

Among the notable collectors who came after Schoolcraft are Hubert H. Bancroft, Andrew J. Blackbird, Daniel G. Brinton, Alexander F. Chamberlain, J.W. Chapman, Jeremiah Curtin, Charles Godfrey Leland, Silas T. Rand, Hinrich Johannes Rink, and Washington Matthews. Their work has been characterized as faithful and good, but too little intent on preserving variants and on capturing the narrator's style: "such embroidery as appears in the otherwise excellent volumes of Rink's Eskimo or Rand's Micmac tales seems to be in diction rather than in incident" (Thompson 1929:xvi).

Brinton's (1883) work included what is probably the earliest comprehensive survey of the extant native literary productions of the Americas. He edited a "Library of Aboriginal American Literature," giving the texts both in the original language and in translation; the series included Mohawk and Onondaga (Hale 1883), Maya (Brinton 1882), and Creek and Hitchiti texts (Gatschet 1884-1888). Brinton focused on productions that were transparently artistic, a focus predicated by his perception of an "oratorical [style that] was markedly different from the familiar or colloquial style" (Brinton 1883:44), a perception questioned by some later analysts but shared by others. Hymes (1987:17-20), for example, sees a uniform rhetorical organization of Chinookan and other North American Indian texts, whereas Mattina distinguishes storyteller Peter J. Seymour's artistic renditions of Okanagan *captíkʷɬ* ('myths, legends') from the run-of-the-mill production of other Interior Salish narrators (Mattina 1987a, 1994).

It was especially under the aegis of the Bureau of American Ethnology (founded in 1879) and Franz Boas (beginning in the 1890s) (vol. 4:623) that extensive and systematic text collection began. The establishment of the Bureau was an inevitable consequence of the curiosity about the aboriginal Americans, their languages, and their traditions. Much of American anthropology has been nearly isomorphic with the study of North American Indians, and one of its central concerns was the collection of texts in the native language, which Hymes characterizes as having followed from Boas's "powerful and instinctive urge to record all these forms of speech" (Boas 1939:105). James Owen Dorsey (fig. 1), who worked for John Wesley Powell at the Bureau, learned Ponca, and studied the Omaha and Osage. Jeremiah Curtin (fig. 2) also worked at times for the Bureau, collecting extensive mythological and linguistic material on several Oregon and northern

Smithsonian, NAA: Portrait 24C.
Fig. 1. James Owen Dorsey (b. 1848, d. 1895) (vol. 4:640). Photographed in 1875.

California groups (notably Wintu, Yana, Modoc, and Wasco) and on Seneca in the east. Frank Cushing, who also worked with Powell, is known principally for his ethnological work with the Zuni (vol. 9:14). He lived with them, learned their language, and was even initiated into Zuni society, becoming a member of their tribal council. Washington Matthews studied Hidatsa and in 1884 went to the Southwest where he studied Navajo and collected and translated traditional chants. James Mooney (vol. 4:669) collected Cherokee myths, wrote a calendar history of the Kiowa, and defended Native American Peyote religion; Jesse Walter Fewkes (vol. 9:7) made phonograph recordings of Zuni songs and wrote about the Hopi; and Alice Fletcher (vol. 4:61, 644) is best known for her work on the Omaha.

Not to be overlooked as writers and as collectors of folktales are native authors. Native-written texts of one sort or another have existed since colonial times, the earliest that are extant being seventeenth-century letters in Timucua and Apalachee (B. Smith 1860; Granberry 1993:xvi-xvii) and seventeenth- and eighteenth-century legal and religious records in Massachusett (Goddard and Bragdon 1988). The wide early literacy in Massachusett resulted from John Eliot's belief that "true conversion was not possible unless the Gospel was accessible to the Indians" (Goddard and Bragdon 1988:13). Among early native

Fig. 2. Jeremiah Curtin (b. 1835, d. 1906). Photographer and date not recorded.

authors were the Penobscot Joseph Nicolar, who wrote about native customs (1893), and Hendrick Aupaumut, a Stockbridge Mahican, who wrote a narrative of his 1792 peace mission to the midwestern tribes (1827) and a traditional history of the Mahicans (1854). Alphabets and syllabaries were developed for a number of North American languages, and these were used by native writers for many purposes ("Native Writing Systems," this vol.). In several areas, notably Cherokee, books and newspapers were regularly published in the native languages. Authors of texts in Fox wrote in a syllabary that had probably been developed for Potawatomi or Ojibwa; some of these texts have been retranscribed into phonetic form and published, then used for analysis. Thus Michelson (1921, 1925, 1925a, 1925b, 1925c) presents texts written in Fox by natives Alfred Kiyana (fig. 3), Sam Peters, and others; these, and other Fox manuscripts by Kiyana, are used in discussions of Fox by Goddard (1984, 1990, 1990a). Another collector of data was William Jones, one-quarter Mesquakie, who was raised among the Oklahoma Sac and Fox, and collected Fox, Kickapoo, and Ojibwa texts (Jones 1907, 1915, 1917-1919). Mary Lasley, who published several tales in English (1902), is identified as a Sauk, but the Indian-language version she gives of one story is in Iowa-Otoe (John E. Koontz, communication to editors 1995). A valuable source of information on writing by Native Americans is Wiget (1994); besides articles on 43 writers, the volume treats oral literature from regional perspectives and includes essays on various genres.

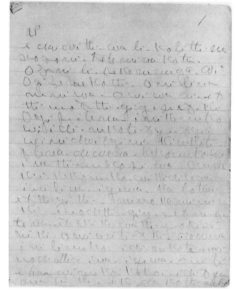

Fig. 3. left, Alfred Kiyana, Fox writer (b. 1877, d. 1918), and Truman Michelson (b. 1879, d. 1938). Photographed about 1912. right, Beginning of a 338-page Fox text written by Kiyana on the White Buffalo Dance, a ceremony of the Fox clan, in 1915. The narrow transliteration of the first sentence, which serves as a title, is: ⟨e da wi tti . wa li . ko li tti ne no so ni . ke te mi na ko ta .⟩. In phonemic transcription this is: e·šawiči wa·pi-kohpiči-nenoso·ni ke·temina·kota. 'What happened to the one blessed by the White Buffalo.'

Lewis Mitchell (fig. 4), a Passamaquoddy from Maine, wrote texts in English and in his native language, using an ad hoc alphabetic script; these were edited and published by Prince (1897), who also transcribed and published texts recorded on a phonograph by Newell S. Francis, Passamaquoddy (Prince 1899). Francis La Flesche ("The Description of the Native Languages of North America: Boas and After," fig. 5, this vol.), the Omaha with whom Alice Fletcher worked, went on to work for the Bureau and published texts of Osage ceremonies. J.N.B. Hewitt, a Tuscarora ("The Description of the Native Languages of North America: Boas and After," fig. 3, this vol.), also worked for the Bureau; he recorded native materials and collected texts in Tuscarora, Seneca, Onondaga, and Munsee. James R. Murie (fig. 5) was a mixed-blood Skiri Pawnee who assisted Fletcher in collecting ceremonial and other ethnographic material from the Pawnee and collaborated with George A. Dorsey in recording, transcribing, and translating large collections of Skiri Pawnee mythology, ceremonialism, and social life (Parks and DeMallie 1992:107-108; Murie 1981). George Sword (fig. 6) was an Oglala Sioux who wrote (in Teton [Lakhota]) ethnographic material and an autobiography under the aegis of James R. Walker, a medical doctor at Pine Ridge (Parks and DeMallie 1992:123-124). Yet another native hired by

Smithsonian, NAA: T-1672.

Fig. 5. James R. Murie (b. 1862, d. 1921) (right), Skiri Pawnee writer and ethnographic assistant *(saku·ru?tá·? 'Coming Sun')* with Emmet Pearson, Skiri Pawnee *(ri·sa·ru? rahísi·?u 'Prominent Chief')* (b. 1865, d. 1930). Photographed about 1910.

Smithsonian, NAA: 95-381.

Fig. 4. Lewis Mitchell (b. 1847, d. 1931), Passamaquoddy writer, holding splint baskets. Photographed in 1922.

the Bureau was George Bushotter (fig. 7), also a Teton speaker, who recorded myths and legends in his native language, and over a 6-month period provided James Owen Dorsey with 258 texts (DeMallie 1978:95). In 1912, at the behest of Paul Radin, Sam Blowsnake, using the syllabary of his native Winnebago, wrote down the Trickster myth from an older Winnebago (Radin 1956:111-112).

Boas taught George Hunt (vol. 4:551) (who was half Tongass Tlingit and married into Kwakiutl nobility; Berman 1991) to write Northern Wakashan and Henry W. Tate (a Tsimshian) to write Tsimshian, and Edward Sapir (vol. 9:18) taught Alex Thomas (vol. 7:103) to write in his native Nootka. All three then collected large quantities of texts in their native languages (Boas and Hunt 1902-1905, 1906; Boas 1912, 1916; Sapir and Swadesh 1939). Boas also brought Ella Deloria to New York to work with him and train students in her native Teton; she published texts in Teton and English which she had collected (Deloria 1932). Archie Phinney deserves the attention that Ralph Maud (1982) pays to him, and to the work of narration, transcription, and translation that he and Wayilatpu (Phinney's mother) did together (Phinney 1934, in Nez Perce and English). *251*

Fig. 6. George Sword, Oglala Sioux writer *(Miwákhą Yuhála* 'Sword Owner') (b. about 1847, d. 1910). He received this name, the name of one of his older brothers who had died, after returning from an expedition to Crazy Horse's camp in Montana in the winter of 1877. His earlier name was *Tok'ičhuwa,* interpreted as 'Enemy Bait' (Parks and DeMallie 1992). His uniform reflects the fact that he was captain of the Pine Ridge Reservation police. Photograph by John K. Hillers, Bureau of American Ethnology, Washington, D.C., 1891.

In a 1930 letter to Boas, Phinney wrote that he found in their collection "a more natural spirit, higher plot unity, and generally fuller elaboration of particular incidents" (Maud 1982:18).

Kaplan (1988) collected stories, oral history, and personal reminiscences in King Island Inupiaq that were collected, transcribed, and translated by native speakers; the Inupiaq and English versions are printed on facing pages. A similar collection of Central Alaskan Yupik lore was produced by the Lower Kuskokwim School District (Tennant and Bitar 1981). Cree writers have also produced a variety of texts in both syllabic and alphabetic scripts (often anecdotal stories and texts for teaching purposes). A few native writers have written European-style poetry in native languages, notably in Zepeda (1982) and Hinton and Watahomigie (1984; the series *Sun Tracks* has also published several works by native writers written only in English). Christian Indians have composed many hymns in Indian languages, for example in Cheyenne (Mennonite Indian Leaders Council 1982). The extensive literary output of Greenlandic speakers has been surveyed by the Greenlander Robert Petersen (vol. 5:640-645), and an anthology has been published by Fortescue (1990). A

Fig. 7. George Bushotter (b. 1864, d. 1892), Teton Sioux writer *(Othéĥi* 'Trouble'). He combined his earlier English name George Bush, with his Teton name, in the spelling Oteri, to make the surname Bushotter. He was the first Lakhota speaker to write an account of the customs and oral literature of his people in Sioux (DeMallie 1978:91-98). Photographed about 1888.

novel written in Central Alaskan Yupik has also been published (A. Jacobson 1990). A Quebec native has written in Montagnais a plea for Indian autonomy and cultural distinctness in the face of the inequities perpetrated by Euro-Canadian institutions (Kapesh 1976).

Many of the same scholars and Bureau employees who collected folktales also collected extensive ethnographic information. Their ethnographic reports need to be studied carefully for information on various types of discourse, as do the writings of amateur ethnographers who lived among the Indians. For example, Teit (1900:289) reports that among the Thompson, "orators possessed great influence and power, often swaying the mass of the people as they chose," and that Thompson chiefs were men "noted for wealth, wisdom, oratorical powers, or prowess in war." A person's well-spoken words were listened to: "the intercession of an orator or chief who favored peace would at times avert war" (1900:269); and even "a boy who was not bashful, but went up and met the flogger as he came into the house, made a speech to him, and, holding out his hands, blessed him, was generally exempt from the flogging" (1900:310). He also tells us that the most obscure language was that used by Indian doctors. He says that "when treating a sick person [the shaman] kept up his song which had been given to him by his guardian spirit, and sometimes he imitated the latter both by voice and gesture. At intervals he turned his song into a conversation with his spirit, which was rather unintelligible to the listeners" (1900:362). He reports that speeches were made at potlatches and at councils, where "such subjects as the organizing of war-expeditions, marriages, or other matters of public interest, were discussed, each man having a voice in the matter" (1900:289). At dances the chief would stand in the west, outside the circle of dancers, where he "made the principal speeches and prayers, kept time, and gave orders" and even "could prophesy, and used to tell about the future world" (1900:352).

Collections, usually handwritten from slow dictation by native story tellers, appeared in several government publication series and in museum and academic sources, and were often in both the native language and English. The most important of these series are *Bureau of American Ethnology Bulletins* and *Annual Reports, American Museum of Natural History Memoirs, Publications of the American Ethnological Society, Columbia University Contributions to Anthropology, University of Washington Publications in Anthropology, University of California Publications in American Archaeology and Ethnology, University of California Publications in Linguistics, Native American Texts Series,* and *American Tribal Religions* (all often in the native language as well as English), *Journal of American Folklore* and *Memoirs of the American Folklore Society* (mostly in English translation only). These remain outstanding sources of information on American Indian discourse, at least in terms of content; much stylistic data can also be recovered from them, although information on speech characteristics is usually lost, because suitable recording techniques were lacking at the time. Such collections were made throughout North America; extensive references can be found in Clements and Malpezzi (1984), Dundes (1976), and Walls (1987). Most collections were made at a time when skilled raconteurs were still alive; by the late twentieth century there were few speakers of American Indian languages left with comparable skills, and further collection of traditional tales became a salvage operation, rather than the comprehensive collection that was possible earlier. Nevertheless, text collections (with native language versions of the texts) from many parts of North America continued to appear, as in the *University of California Publications in Linguistics, Native American Text Series,* and *American Tribal Religions* series; examples of such

collections are those in Micmac (DeBlois 1991), Ojibwa (Kaye, Piggott, and Tokaichi 1971; Piggott and Kaye 1973; Nichols 1988; Kegg 1991); Cree (Wolfart 1988, in syllabics as well as alphabetic transcriptions); Cheyenne (Leman 1987), Arikara (Parks, 3:1991), and Hopi (Malotki 1978, 1985; Malotki and Lomatuway'ma 1984, 1987).

The quality of much of the folklore collected by professional ethnologists, linguists, native speakers, and the like, is often difficult to assess, especially by nonnatives. Nonspeaking specialists in a language may be able to make some evaluation of texts based on comparisons between texts narrated by different speakers, observations of certain stylistic features or complexities, or vocabulary selection, but even then expectations based on Euro-American literary traditions may color their judgments. Texts recorded from last speakers are sometimes of poorer quality than texts collected earlier, simply because these last speakers are more likely to have a more limited command of the language and all its nuances. The storytelling ability of a native speaker was not always of prime concern to the collector. For Boas and Sapir and their students, the goal was often to collect as many texts, in as many versions, and from as many speakers as possible, to obtain as large and comprehensive a corpus as could be made (especially for dying languages). These texts were themselves often used as the basis of grammars and dictionaries, which were then supplemented by direct elicitation. The text collection was widely considered by linguists to be one of the three components—texts, grammar, and dictionary—necessary for comprehensive documentation of a language. In contrast, ethnologists and folklorists might have different agendas, and they considered text collections as a goal in their own right.

Stith Thompson's work represents another landmark in the study of North American Indian narrative. Thompson's primary interest was in a world-wide survey of folklore aimed at an exhaustive index of motifs; therefore, he surveyed translations of narratives for their content and motifs, motifs being the segmental components, creatures, and concepts that make up a tale. Drawing on "by far the most extensive body of tales representative of any primitive people," Thompson (1929:vii) published a collection of tales arranged topically into mythological stories, trickster stories, stories of extraordinary but human deeds and events, and borrowed stories. He also mapped the distribution of motifs in North America. Although he did consider the various so-called culture areas of North America, Thompson (1929:xxii) concluded that continent-wide "likenesses" were more striking than "the differences in the various areas." Thompson (1946:295-363) also studied North American creation myths, trickster cycles, test and hero tales, journeys to the other world, animal wives and husbands, and miscellaneous tales as part of a world-wide survey of the folktale. Thompson (1955-1958) contains much bibliographic information.

An important contribution in the history of the methodology of text collection and study is by Garfield, who emphasized that "the responsibility of trained field workers is especially clear. Any data pertaining to the field situation are necessary" (1953:34). A complete (insofar as possible) record of the narrative is a prerequisite to any serious study: "As interests of scholars are focused on a greater [than theretofore recognized] variety of problems the responsibility of the recorder who furnishes the materials for studies also increases" (1953:25). Garfield allowed for the varied interests of students of texts, ranging from psychological content, to comparative and distributional surveys, to details of performance, and identified a growing interest in the "dynamics of myth making and in oral literature as it is integrated into specific cultures," adding that it is "in this field that folklorists are developing the greatest diversity of approaches in method

and aims" (1953:25). Postmodern thinkers can argue that the desire for a thorough and objective method of collection and the methods of presenting a narrative transcript have remained, as a matter of fact, no more and no less than the wishful thinking that they can only ever be: ethnographies are records in which recorder and recorded remain inextricably entangled each with the other, and texts are subject to as many analytical treatments as there are analysts. Analytical approaches have also remained varied, and that, too, was expected, although the scholarly climate since the 1950s has encouraged, at least in theory, the search for well-defined and appropriate (even if competing) models.

Inspired by analyses of the folktale by Propp (1958) and Wycoco (1951), Dundes (1964) theorized over American Indian texts with a structuralist approach loosely modeled after structural phonology, and aimed, as are all structural approaches, at discovering underlying patterns. In Dundes's view texts are sequences of paired motifemes such as Lack/Lack liquidated; Interdiction/Violation (and optionally Consequences/

Fig. 8. Horned serpent depicted in a struggle with its traditional enemies the Thunder-beings, who are often described as hurling lightning bolts. Variants of this motif were found over a wide area of North America, and the horned or plumed serpent was found as far south as Chile (Wissler 1922:212; Michelson 1930:54-55). Pen and ink drawing by the Cattaraugus Seneca artist Jesse J. Cornplanter, 1908.

254

Attempted escape from consequence). The manifestations themselves of motifemes (called allomotifs) are open-ended; these allomotifs are unconstrained by a required analog of motif similarity (as allophones of a phoneme share phonetic quality), so that, for example, hunger and celibacy can be allomotifs of the same motifeme, each a manifestation of Lack—of food, and of a mate, respectively. Dundes's work can be viewed as theoretical in the sense that he proposed a "model" of the American Indian tale, and, in this sense, his work may be deemed as reductionist as are the dramatic model of Jacobs and the verse model of Hymes, both discussed below. The interpretive approaches advocated by Jacobs and Dundes have not had a significant following. The presentational approach advocated by Hymes has roused conflicting reactions.

McClellan's (1970) monograph (in English) on the myth "The Girl Who Married the Bear" is important as Maud (1982:25) notes, because it treated the text as a piece of great artistic worth and because McClellan produced 11 versions of a single myth, with information about the circumstances of the tellings and about the narrators. Such contextual detail is usually missing from collections of texts.

Another genre of American Indian discourse that has received a great deal of attention is autobiography. Frederick (1989-1993) lists autobiographical writings divided by category. Here one finds listed well-known and diverse items such as *Son of Old Man Hat* (Dyk 1938), *The Surrounded* (McNickle 1936), *Crashing Thunder* (Radin 1920), *Storyteller* (Silko 1981), and critical works of Brumble (1981, 1988), Krupat (1985), and Swann and Krupat (1987), but not other important works such as *The People of Kauwerak* (Oquilluk 1973), *The Sun Came Down* (Bullchild 1985), and *Life Lived Like a Story* (Cruikshank 1990). Stating that "biography and autobiography are not indigenous Native American genres," Dauenhauer and Dauenhauer (1994:x) edited an anthology of Tlingit life stories, with a selection of native texts and their English translation appended.

Recording Techniques

Any recording of texts prior to the twentieth century was, of course, by hand. Popularizers were not concerned with the style of the original so were free to retell stories they heard, rather than record them verbatim. When scholars decided that they wanted truer records of the narrations, they had to come up with ways to write them down as they were being told. They did this by training narrators to recite slowly enough that their stories could be written down during the telling, or, in a few cases, by teaching native speakers to write their languages themselves. A few researchers

U. of Wyo., Amer. Heritage Center, Laramie.
Fig. 9. Plenty Coups (Crow) (b. about 1848, d. 1932), holding a copy of his book *American: The Life Story of a Great Indian*. Dictated to Frank B. Linderman, the book includes the dedication "I am glad I have told you these things, Sign-Talker. You have felt my heart, and I have felt yours. I know you will tell only what I have said, that your writing will be straight like your tongue, and I will sign your paper with my thumb so that your people and mine will know I have told you the things you have written down." Linderman said that Plenty Coups was "gifted with the power of impressive speech, and possessing a dignity of presence that readily won him any hearing..." (Linderman 1930:312).

tried using shorthand systems, but these were ill suited to the sound systems of American Indian languages and were more often used for ethnographic and miscellaneous notes.

The phonograph (patented in 1878) was first used to record American Indian speech in 1890, when Jesse Walter Fewkes by recording some songs and vocabulary "field-tested the device on an experimental visit to the Passamaquoddy Indians in Maine" (Brady et al. 1984-, 1:3) and recorded music of the Zuni Indians that summer (Brady et al. 1984-, 1:61). Because cylinders allowed only short recording times (3-4 minutes on a 4-inch cylinder, and up to 9 minutes on the 6-inch cylinder introduced in 1890; Brady 1985:27), they were awkward for recording myths and tales (although some were recorded, such as the Passamaquoddy tales in Prince 1899) and were more commonly used to record songs (fig. 10), including those occurring in stories. However, even songs might exceed the length of time a

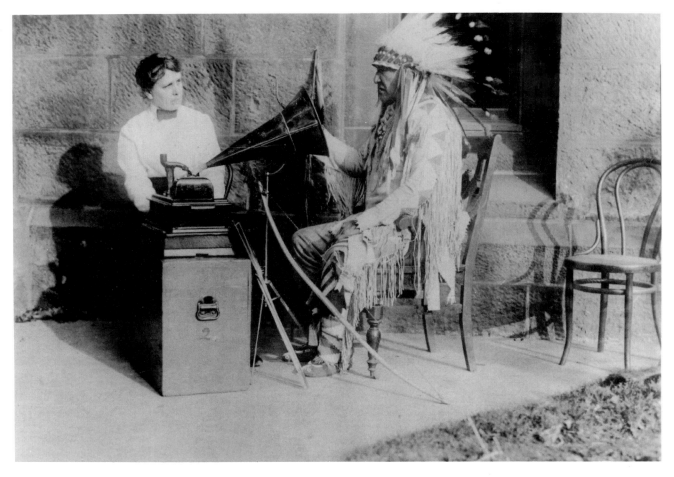

Smithsonian, NAA: 55,300.

Fig. 10. Frances Densmore with Mountain Chief (Blackfeet). He is recording a song that Gen. Hugh L. Scott had requested. According to a report of Densmore's fieldwork, the song was not transcribed, and the actual recording does not appear to have survived (Hunter 1943:9). The Edison phonograph being used recorded on 6-inch wax cylinders that ran for only 9 minutes. Photograph by Harris and Ewing, Washington, D.C., 1916.

cylinder (or early disk) could record, and then repetitions were often omitted or performances were interrupted, changing the apparent structure of the song (Vennum 1980:55-58). This recording equipment was inexpensive, and cylinders were used extensively until the early 1940s by many collectors. Thousands of cylinder recordings of Indian languages throughout North America can be found in various archives (Brady et al. 1984-; Gillis 1984; Keeling 1991; Seaburg 1982).

Although disk records were introduced in 1895 (Brady 1985:29), they were available only with prerecorded programs and only for playback. Transportable disk recorders did not become a reality until the 1930s, but these early models were extremely heavy, cumbersome, and expensive (vol. 7:102). Disks proved somewhat more suitable for recording narratives, although it was still often only songs that were recorded because not much more could be recorded on early disks than had been possible on cylinders. Disk technology developed, involving the use of pregrooved disks, aluminum disks (in the late 1930s), and acetate disks (also from the late 1930s). Magnetic recording devices were invented as early as 1899, and both tape and wire recorders were eventually developed; magnetic tapes for general use only became available in 1947. The sound quality of wire recordings tended to be poorer than that on other media and the wire was subject to breaking, and the era of wire recorders was brief. Tape recording quickly became the preferred method of recording linguistic material beginning in the mid-1940s because equipment was easily portable and tapes proved inexpensive and easy to use. Videotapes became available in the mid-1950s, although they have been used infrequently for recording American Indian myths and legends because until the mid-1970s this equipment was bulkier and more complicated to use than tape recorders, and because by this time there were far fewer competent story tellers available.

Of these various recording techniques, videotapes are among the best because they capture visual details of storytelling as well as the sound. Any disk or tape-recorded texts may include slips of the tongue or stumbling that makes them harder to transcribe; however, they do record the narrative at a natural speed. Transcriptions directly from dictation were possibly more accurate grammatically and allowed the narrator time to think about his presentation, but they must have been subject to distortion from the slower pace required to accommodate the writer. Vast quantities of recordings of all kinds were made in the nineteenth and twentieth centuries, although only limited amounts have been published.

Publication

When they were published, narrative texts have appeared in various formats. Until the 1960s it was taken for granted that Native American folktales were simply prose narratives, much like the most familiar European folklore, and they were so presented. If the presentation was for popular consumption, texts were severely edited to make them easier to read, eliminating most stylistic and ritual repetitions and anything that might be considered offensive or inappropriate for children and moral or religious sensibilities. Other stylistic features were also edited out if they did not accord with literary norms; thus, rhetorical lengthening, a common feature of narrative style everywhere, was nearly always left unnoted in published texts. Scholarly publications also assumed that the basic organization of folktales was prose. These publications usually left the text unchanged, presenting it exactly as told—except that until the middle of the twentieth century any sexual references might be translated into Latin.

The best way to publish texts is not easy to determine. Ideally texts should be presented in the original language as well as in translation. If the original language is given, a determination must be made as to how much additional information should be provided. Often a morpheme-by-morpheme translation is given, then a smooth translation of each sentence, all on succeeding lines. An example of this can be seen in a Bella Coola passage (Davis and Saunders 1980:35):

ks-is-kʷ-c̓   *łayx*   *ta-mila-s-tx̣*
pull-he/it-QUOT-PERF this.one NPROX-cane-his-DIST
He pulled his cane out.

The first line gives the Bella Coola, with morpheme divisions indicated by hyphens. The second line translates (glosses) each of these morphemes, often with an abbreviated grammatical label. The third line is a free translation of the whole sentence. A smoother translation of the entire text is then presented following the analyzed Bella Coola version.

If the language has complex modifications of words from underlying forms, it may be desirable to give an underlying representation of the native language material as well. Watkins (1984:246-257) does this for two Kiowa texts, presenting them in five parts: first the text in Kiowa, with each sentence numbered; then an English translation of the whole, keyed to the same numbers; then an underlying representation with morpheme divisions marked, and an interlinear gloss of each morpheme on the line below; and finally a separate section of grammatical notes. An even more elaborate presentation is given for the single Wichita text in Rood (1976:257-274). The text is given in five lines: the Wichita surface structure form, a free translation of each Wichita word, a morphological analysis of the sentence in which the morphemes are written in an abstract, so-called underlying form, a gloss for each morpheme, and a reference to the place in the preceding grammar where the morpheme is first introduced or discussed. The following is an example of this presentation, omitting footnote numbers and the fifth line, which is keyed to the grammar (Rood 1976:258):

4.a. *ka·kiya?*   *isí·?a!*
  b. Somebody   come!
  c. ka·   kiya?   i   s   uy   ?a
  d. indefinite person imperative 2nd person preverb come
                                subject

All this is followed by a free translation of the text. Such detailed information is primarily of scholarly interest and is usually given for only a few texts in a collection or for texts appended to grammars as illustrative material. Texts edited for a general audience or for use by native communities may include only the native text and a smooth translation, either on facing pages or on a split page (with one language on the top half, and the other language on the bottom), or the two versions may be given in separate sections of a volume (or in separate volumes if the collection is extensive enough to warrant it).

Publication of Native American texts is not exclusively in a printed medium. For a number of years Jerome Rosenberg and Dennis Tedlock co-edited *Alcheringa,* a now defunct journal dedicated to ethnopoetics, where the visual representation of artistic works (words, drawings, and photos) was sometimes accompanied by sound in the form of disk recordings, such as "Oratory in Three Languages" (Tedlock and Tedlock 1978). Occasionally notes with contextual detail and reading instructions were added, such as the following, which accompanied "A Prayer Over Dead Rabbits," translated by Dennis Tedlock and Joseph Peynetsa, from a tape-recorded performance in Zuni by Walter Sanchez: "This piece should be read aloud, with a short pause (about half-second) for each line change, a two-second pause for each double space, and extra stress for capitals. There should be no pauses within lines, even for punctuation . . ." (Tedlock and Peynetsa

1972:60). Some books of texts have been produced with accompanying cassettes, and in one well-known case a University of Arizona crew produced a series of documentaries for television entitled "Words and Place." Hopi and Apache story-telling and Navajo chanting are among the narrative performances videotaped.

Translation

Many published folktales were simply told in English, and these tales do retain many characteristics of the original languages (such as pattern numbers, original motifs, and native characters). However, in many other cases, the collector wanted to record the original language as well, either to ensure preservation of an original version of the text (which could be used for further study), or, as sometimes in the case of linguists, to provide an example of connected speech (as opposed to individual elicited and contextless sentences). Translations of American Indian folktales were often made by the narrators themselves, since collectors have rarely known the languages well enough for this task; native collectors could do their own translating, of course. It was also often necessary to use third parties as translators if the narrator and the transcriber did not share a language. Such intermediaries (who might even have had to work through a third language—one familiar to both him and the narrator or to both him and the transcriber) may not always have understood everything in the original or been able to convey it all in English, thus requiring considerable interpolation by the collector.

There are also numerous instances of translations of texts being based on a language other than the original one in which the story was told. When Franz Boas began his fieldwork in the Northwest in 1886, he nearly always had to work through the medium of Chinook Jargon. His earliest publications in German (Boas 1895) were translations from Chinook Jargon, which in turn were translations from various native languages (Kinkade 1992). Many of the English translations in Boas's earlier publications are almost certainly this sort of second-hand translation. There is no reason to believe that these translations of Boas are not reasonably accurate; however, greater attention should be given to the native-language version of such texts than is usually done. Other tales have come into English via translations from Spanish or French, where those were the dominant European languages in the areas where texts were collected.

Presenting any text in a language other than its original one creates difficulties and requires decisions about the goals of the translation and the audience it is to reach. (See Swann 1992, 1994 for essays dealing with various aspects of translating American Indian languages.) Translators (and editors) often modified native tales in many ways so that they would accommodate a style and format familiar to readers of tales of European origin. Expectations have changed over time; Clements (1992) and Krupat (1992) provide useful discussions of the translation of American Indian narrative from the late eighteenth to the late twentieth centuries. Clements (1992:43) believes that "translators who regarded American Indian oral literature as the product of savagism . . . probably produced more reliable texts than their more sympathetic contemporaries" in the nineteenth century. Some writers have not been concerned about possible literary value of native texts, and others have denied they have any: "The literary value of a great deal of primitive literature, whether myths or tales, is *nil*. That of much of the rest is apparent, in the raw form, only to connoisseurs, while those who undertake to retell some of it often achieve only emasculation" (La Farge 1959:7).

Remaining true to the general content of the original is not difficult as long as cultural concepts can be made clear. Krupat (1992:5) distinguishes between a literal and a literary translation, the former maintaining fidelity to the original, while the latter may be an artistic rendering. Examples of these two kinds of translation, both given by Schoolcraft for an Ojibwa song he recorded, are given in table 1. These different versions may serve different purposes, such as texts for scholarly study of form, style, and content, or as demonstrations of Native American "literature" to be compared with other literature. Tedlock (1983) compares the quality of various translations of Zuni narratives, and Huntsman does the same for several languages. The original and later versions of the first stanza of a Pawnee ceremony song discussed by Huntsman (1983:90-92) are given in table 2.

Translations are not actually either literal or literary; there is a continuum between the two poles. Translations in scholarly publications that include the original language are often less smooth, being fairly direct translations from the original language. The aim of the translations in these publications is to present the content, leaving style to be figured out from the original language. Interlinear translations are usually fairly literal, and most translations of texts collected for the Bureau of American Ethnology, such as Michelson's Fox texts, give literal translations. Translations of texts collected by Boas and his students were literal (although they might be annotated to provide information to make particular passages more readily understandable to a nonnative audience). In a discussion of Deloria's (1932) Sioux texts, Rice (1992a:278) points out some things that may be lost in a careful, literal translation; he notes the absence of "some of the techniques employed by the original narrator to convey

Table 1. Schoolcraft's "Chant to the Firefly," an Ojibwa Song

(Schoolcraft's 1845 orthography is preserved):

> Wau wau tay see!
> Wau wau tay see!
> E mow e shin
> Tshe bwau ne baun-e wee!
> Be eghaun—be eghaun—ewee!
> Wa Wau tay se!
> Wa wau tay see!
> Was sa koon ain je gun.
> Was sa koon ain je gun.

"Literal" translation, using a kind of highly exclamatory prose:

> Flitting-white-fire-insect! waving-white-fire-bug! give me light before I go to bed! give me light before I go to sleep. Come, little dancing white-fire-bug! Come, little flitting white-fire-beast! Light me with your bright white-flame-instrument—your little candle.

First four lines of the "literary" translation versified:

> Fire-fly, fire-fly! bright little thing,
> Light me to bed, and my song I will sing.
> Give me your light, as you fly o'er my head,
> That I may merrily go to my bed.

SOURCE: Krupat 1992:6–7; ultimately from Schoolcraft 1845:61.

NOTE: Nichols (1991) discusses the variants of this song and provides a phonemic transcription and corrected translation.

Table 2. "The Birth of Dawn," a Pawnee Ceremony Song

Pawnee original
> *HO-O-O!*
> *hatíraʔ sihwaˑtaʔ I;*
> *hatíraʔ sihwaˑtaʔ I;*
> *reˑsuˑruʔ tíʔaˑriʔ I;*
> *hatíraʔ sihwaˑtaʔ I.*
> (Fletcher 1904:123–124, phonemicized).

"Rhythmic rendition"
> Awake, Oh Mother, from sleep!
> Awake! The night is far spent;
> The signs of dawn are now seen
> In east, whence cometh new life.
> (Fletcher 1904:322).

Literary adaption
> Earth our mother, breathe forth life
>   all night sleeping
>   now awaking
>   in the east
>   now see the dawn
> (Brandon 1971:68).

Translation based on Fletcher's information and a Pawnee dictionary (Bevis 1974:696)
> Mother earth you arise now:
> Mother earth you arise now;
> Dawn is born now;
> Mother earth you arise now.

NOTE: In the Pawnee text vocables, which are not phonemicized, are in capital letters. The spoken-language equivalent is: *atíraʔ isihwaˑtaʔ. reˑsuˑruʔ tíʔaˑriʔ.* 'Mother, arise. It is becoming dawn.'

---

thematic emphasis," omission of many rhythmic repetitions, omission of stylistic details such as distinctions between informal and ceremonial language, and the omission of conventional narrative markers (such as reportative particles).

At the other extreme a literary translation may be little more than an equivalent in the target language of the original text, and there have been various approaches to creating these literary versions. Swann (1987) suggests that such translations might profitably be produced by collaboration between a native speaker or scholar of the language and a poet or other specialist in literary writing. This should, in his view, produce a text with recognizable literary qualities, but it would not necessarily reflect stylistic features of the original text. Rothenberg, who wishes both to translate poetry and to create poetry, speaks of his work as "partly assemblage, partly translation" (1992:65), thus justifying his departure from the literal meaning of the original. After examining the Navajo origin legend published in English by Matthews (1897:63–159), Zolbrod (1983:229–230) concludes that Matthews's version is an assemblage from different tellings and presents his own version, calling it a "revision" of the original. Speaking of his versions of Navajo legends, Zolbrod suggests that they "would stand as just one more performance—albeit written—of

a narrative cycle whose poetic strength resides in its elasticity" (1992:251), thus justifying whatever modifications he makes as being on a par with narrations of the same text by different native speakers.

These translators generally strive to reflect the original text, whether it be in its content or its style. Both literal and literary translations can be faithful and fair to the original version and can reflect different things about the skill of its narrator or writer. Efforts to encompass the content of the original while not distorting its form and style can result in excellent presentations that do credit to the original Indian storyteller; the Maidu texts translated by Shipley (1991) are a fine case in point.

Langen (1992:194) proposes a "list of qualities that any translator, past or present, might wish to be able to transfer from the source document . . . to the target document," although she acknowledges that inclusion of all these qualities in one translation is not likely. These qualities include style (diction and delivery of the storyteller, validation of the narrator, circumstances of the performance, language-specific features), content (the events of the story, its characters, setting, special vocabulary), form (order, pace, meter), literary history (how much the narrator contributes as contrasted with traditional elements that are expected to be present), reception (of the storyteller, the story itself, the activity of storytelling), and significance (reasons for telling the story, recognition of what the audience knows about the language and cultural context (Langen 1992:194-195). In an effort to retain some of the flavor of the translations given by his Okanagan assistants, Mattina (1987:137-142) uses what he calls "Red English," a distinctive dialect of English commonly heard from older Indians. This has the effect of giving a purposely exotic rendering and is intended to convey a positive view of differences of expression.

Some features of the original language may simply be lacking in the language into which a text is translated. Examples of this would be specific characteristics that are intended to typify a particular character (or animal), certain kinds of grammatical categories (such as special pronouns or demonstratives), or reportative particles or affixes (discussed further below). Such features may be compensated for in some way, thus possibly introducing distortions into the text, or they may be omitted from the translation, which may produce distortion of another sort. Omission of such features is not necessarily a defect, but may be necessary, given the intended purpose of a particular translation.

Translation of American Indian folktales has not been without its share of mistranslations and distortions, either deliberate or unintentional. Thus Tedlock (1983:59) criticizes Cushing's (1901) English renditions of Zuni folk tales on the grounds that he "embroidered" the tales "with devices, lines, and even whole passages which are clearly of his own invention," by inserting explanatory material not present in the original for the benefit of his readers, and for adding moralistic passages. Even when a collector and translator used an intermediary who knew both the original language and English, his translation might get modified to suit the understanding (or misunderstanding) of the collector. In at least one instance, Boas collected a text in Kwakiutl (in 1894), checked, and revised it later with native speakers (perhaps George Hunt or William Brotchie—although he may have concentrated on transcription rather than translation), but still seems to have misunderstood it and published a misleading translation (Berman 1992:125-162). In what is possibly a more extreme example of distortion, Nichols (1989) and Brightman (1989) cast suspicion on the authenticity of Howard Norman's "Wishing Bone Cycle" (1976, 1982), suggesting that his English texts are reworkings of English translations in other sources, and that his one Cree text (Huntsman 1983:94) may be an attempted "retranslation" by Norman from an English version. One of the best known such distortions is Longfellow's (1855) Song of Hiawatha, which is derived from confused accounts of Iroquois traditions published by Schoolcraft. Longfellow identifies the Onondaga (Iroquoian) figure with the Algonquian figure Nanabozho in his poem, which in turn is modeled on the Finnish epic *Kalevala* (vol. 15:422).

Structural Analysis

One may ask a number of questions about structure: Is a piece of narrative a self-contained structured entity? How much is context a determinant of structure? To what extent is structure an analyst's projection? In the end it is the complex of one's personal preferences that conspires to settle these questions, thus opening any and all analytical and descriptive approaches to criticism.

On the one hand, approaches that pay special attention to the context of narrative performances, such as the ethnography of speaking, stand to be accused of having "never had much in the way of theoretical content" (Turner 1987:100). On the other, approaches that focus on the text and its texture, especially when nonstandard orthographic practices are followed, are often seen as "narrowly linguistic, removed from cultural themes and values, and uninformed by personal and social dynamics. The result is inevitably the reification of the text and the context" (Turner 1987:101). Postmodern critics, too, speak of "the irony of representation, of that inescapable difference between appearance and reality." Expressing themselves in metaphors that are often religious, they point to "writing as the means that makes reality accessible only by occulting it in a simulacrum that substitutes itself for the reality it pretends to represent" (Tyler 1986:131). Proponents of receptionalist theory similarly object to the presentation of text as object, and insist that "the work and its parts" are "processes"; that "the phraseological unit consists . . . also and crucially of the informed but finally subjective response one makes to those [texts] in the larger context of the . . . reality of an oral tradition" (Foley 1986:203). Even so, it is a fact that a large part of the work being done on American Indian texts remains work that abstracts texts from their functional contexts and reifies texts in printed form.

Structure is the discovered shape and quality of discourse, the organization of its form, and the information to be conveyed. Structure indicates an "expression of affective meaning," indexes genre, regulates "dialogic interaction" (Woodbury 1985:153), and guides an audience in its (unconscious) evaluation of a performance. Dundes (1964) provided one of the early attempts to demonstrate how form (the use of content elements in a story and the relationships between them) is present in North American Indian folktales and how it may be structured. This quest to understand form and structure in discourse is discussed and developed further in the particular context of some Lushootseed tales by Langen (1986), and for Central Alaskan Yupik by Woodbury (1985).

Many things can be used to shape a text (whether oral or written): purely linguistic features (phonological, lexical, and grammatical), various rhetorical devices, or features of content or style (as defined and discussed below). Terminology used in discussions of these structural issues is not consistent from writer to writer, nor are the categories noted here necessarily discrete. Rather, different structural features interact in complex ways. Discussing textual organization in Central Alaskan Yupik, Woodbury (1985:172) observes that: "rhetorical structure organizes information in part within each component and in part through the interaction and juxtaposition of the components. Syntax, prosody, and particles are each capable of creating and interrelating functionally significant units. And syntax and prosody interact so that constituents can be prosodically isolated for prominence or marked as 'supplementary' with attenuated contours." Furthermore, different discourse genres commonly organize structural elements in different ways. In order to understand textual structure, it is necessary to look at each of these (and undoubtedly other) features and devices, see what sorts of units they suggest, and how they interact.

The phonological features most likely to be used in structuring a text are prosodic elements, especially intonation and pause. Other prosodic features (such as changes in pitch levels or the use of falsetto voice, the use of special voice qualities, loudness, and rhetorical lengthening) might also occasionally be used for structural purposes but are more commonly stylistic features. Generally absent in North America (except sometimes in songs) is the use of rhyme, alliteration, or rhythm for structural purposes. A number of studies of Native American discourse have examined the role of prosodic features, notably Tedlock (1972), Bright (1979), Kinkade (1987), McLendon (1982), and especially Woodbury (1985, 1987). Woodbury (1985:155) observes that the prosodic component is "pervasive and meaningful in discourse, operates both above and below the level of the sentence . . ., is formally distinguishable from syntax," and that "a range of other systems of formal features appear to pattern with the prosodic component." He has noted that clauses, sentences, and groups of each of these may have their own contours as expressed by intonation and pauses. These contours have been widely used to establish lines for presentational purposes.

Much has been made of the use of particular lexical items in the organization of discourse. Words that correspond to adverbs, conjunctions, and interjections are most likely to be used for this purpose, and when they are so used, they mostly introduce sentences or sections

of various sorts. Rhodes, in a careful study of Ojibwa discourse, identifies three kinds of usage of these particles. The first he labels "structural," which refers to "those things, either morphemes, words, or constructions, which serve to mark out where one is in the text, or at what level of prominence or focus a particular textual unit is, or where the points of transition are in the text structure" (Rhodes 1979:102); these points of transition may be marked by particles meaning things such as 'and, again' or 'once'. The second usage Rhodes calls "logical," that is, those things "which serve to indicate the logical relationships among the various clauses, sentences and even larger units" and which may be marked by words with meanings such as 'because', 'in vain', 'anyway', 'if', and the like. The third usage is labeled "interactive," and these phenomena "carry information regarding how the speaker feels about a particular textual unit or about how the speaker wants the hearer to feel about it" (1979:103). (Rhodes's interactive phenomena are often called evidential.) For each of these usages Rhodes identifies both particles and syntactic constructions as markers of that usage, reinforcing the observation made above about the interaction of structural features. The Ojibwa passage in table 3 (from an Ottawa speaker) shows how these particles can be used. The conjunction *keye·* 'and' or *mi·*, a predicative particle requiring subordination in what

Table 3. Excerpt from "Nenabush and the Partridges," an Ojibwa Folktale

ki·-ena· pitašš uwiti ka·-pi-uncipesot.	
uki·-wa·pema·n tašš wa·wa·ške·ššuwan ni·puwinit ekkita·kki.	
e·ka·c etašš uki·-uta·ppena·n umettikwa·pi·n,	
keye· kwa mi· ko ki·-pemwa·t,	
keye· kwa mi· ko ki·-mešwa·t,	5
keye· kwa mi· ko ki·-nessa·t.	
mi· tašš ekotekkoni·si·t uwiti ka·-pi-uncipesot.	
mi· tašš ki·-pekkona·t eniw wa·wa·ške·ššuwan.	
keye· kwa mi· ki·-menoswa·t.	
kekkina tašš ka·-menoswa·t	10
mi· peci·nak ki·-wi·ssenit.	
He looked toward the place from which he had tumbled.	
He saw a deer standing there at the top of the bluff.	
Slowly he picked up his bow.	
Then he shot at it,	
and then he hit it,	5
and then he killed it.	
Then he scrambled up the slope to where he had tumbled from.	
Then he skinned that deer.	
And then he roasted it.	
When he has roasted it all,	10
then at last he soon would eat.	

Source: Bloomfield 1957:220-222, from Andrew Medler.

Note: The reduced vowels found in the dialect of Ottawa recorded here are written *u* (representing /o/ and all short vowels before *w*) and *e* ([ə], representing /i/ and /a/ except before *w*).

follows, or both together, introduce 7 of the 11 lines. These particles do not usually occur in such a heavy concentration, but they lend striking organization when they do, as in the trio of lines 4-6 where only the verb root changes—'shoot', 'hit', 'kill'. These lines then have an echo three lines later, where the verb root is 'roast'. The particle *mi·* is one of those identified as marking points of transition (Rhodes 1979:102).

Some narrators in some languages use such particles even more systematically. Such usage can be seen in Kiksht, a Chinookan language, where long sequences of sentences begin with *aġa* 'now', *aġa kwápt* 'now then', or *aġa wîta* 'now again'. Hymes (1981) considers these connectives as demarcating a level he labels verses. In the passage in table 4 five verses in a row begin with *aġa* or *aġa kwápt*. The verses here are all short. This telling of the tale is itself quite short; one common way of lengthening a story is to add detail that might expand what are here analyzed as verses, to add whole verses, or to suggest reorganization of verses, stanzas, or other units. Only two of the verses have two lines, and in each case no special marking is used on the second line.

Wichita, a Caddoan language, makes frequent use of the conjunction *hiriwaʔ* 'and then' (Rood 1976). It is used less frequently and less systematically than the *aġa* of Kiksht, although its repetition can be striking where it does occur. As a conjunction, it normally occurs between two verbs, but it may also occur to connect sentences, and it is in this function that it is used in its first three occurrences in the passage in table 5. The last instance in this passage has the variant *híriwaʔ* linking two verbs, the second of which might be seen as a separate clause, hence a separate line of the text. Rood's translation, intended as a

Table 4. Excerpt from "The News About Coyote," a Kiksht Folktale

> *aġa kʷápt idwáča gačuxábu;—*
>   *náqi tíqíx gačtúx pu gaqawiqłáxit.*
> *aġa kʷápt dakdák gačíuxix idwáča.*
> *aġa kʷápt kánawi šan gaɬxlqłáxit,*
>   *qńgi nigíxatx iskúlia.*   5
> *aġa idwáča ničixádwaix.*
> *aġa kʷapt dakdák (n)itkšiqídamidaba idwáča.*

> Now then he locked up the news:—
>   he did not want it to be made known.
> Now then someone made the news loose.
> Now then everyone came to know
>   what Coyote did to himself.   5
> Now he had headed the news off.
> Now then they made the news break loose.

SOURCE: Hymes 1981:212-213, phonemicized, an edition of a text by Louis Simpson in Edward Sapir's 1905 field notebooks (cf. Sapir 1909a:30; Hymes 1981:136-137).

Table 5. Excerpt from "Turtle, Buffalo, and Coyote," a Wichita Folktale

> *hiriwaʔ na·hissah harah a·kikawa.*
> *hiriwaʔ nakhissah harah waʔ naka·ʔicakih*
> *a·kihiʔiyaskwa.*
> *hiriwaʔ nahité·tiskih*
> *nahiʔiyassissah,*   5
> *"haʔawíʔro·ʔ é·ka·ʔ hiriwaʔ."*
> *kiyakíʔctawi:ʔi híriwaʔ hako·citih.*

> So he (Turtle) went inside there.
> And while he was sitting inside,
> he went across the water.
> But when he came out onto the bank
> after crossing the water,   5
> "Okay, how?" (he wondered).
> It was hard for him then to get out.

SOURCE: Rood 1976:260-261, 1977:92, from Bertha Provost (line structure added and punctuation slightly modified); David S. Rood, communication to editors 1995.

smooth, easily readable one, translates *hiriwaʔ* differently each time it occurs here ('so', 'and', 'but') or leaves it untranslated. Although this practice is proper in providing good, high-style English, it does not reflect the actual structure inherent in the Wichita original.

One kind of interactive or evidential marker or particle is what is widely called a "quotative," or better, "reportative." These are often translated 'they say' or 'it is said'. In Cahto, an Athapaskan language of northern California, nearly every line ends with the reportative *yaʔni*. Only three clauses in the passage in table 6 lack a final reportative, and these are treated as components of multiclausal sentences having a single reportative at the end. In the last sentence here a word is added after the reportative, rather like an afterthought. Because reportatives do not translate well into English, they are commonly omitted entirely from smooth translations (they have been reintroduced in table 6 in brackets); thus an important structural marker may be completely absent in an English rendering of a text.

Even heavier line marking can be found. Tunica, a language isolate formerly spoken along the lower Mississippi River, uses both initial connectors and sentence-final reportatives. The sample in table 7 has both in every line. A few lines occur in the remainder of the text without the initial *hinya·tíhč*, usually either at the beginning of a significant block of material (stanza or scene?) or before quoted speech. A reportative occurs in every line of the text, either at the end or (in a very few cases) with a word or two of afterthought following. This heavy line marking, which is quite striking, suggests a very formal style for these narrations. Such intensive use of reportatives may even help to mark folktales or myths as a genre different from ordinary

Table 6. Excerpt from "The Man Eater," a Cahto Folktale

bet na[ˀ]təɣəƛon yaˀni
ƚeneˀ=haˀ nahneš ˀinče ˀonɣilaŋ yaˀni
sahdəŋ=haˀ čəgaƚ yaˀni
təbəƚ yiɣeƚ yaˀni
təč čəɣəƚtiƚ yaˀni   5
təbəƚ talon čəɣeƚ yaˀni
"šiyeˀ ˀinčeˀ," čin yaˀni
čəƚčəd yaˀni
nənčəstiŋ təbəƚ=biˀ no[ˀ]ƚtiŋ čətesɣiŋ yaˀni
čəŋ čiboš=ʒ wəyeh=tah wa[ˀ]ɣəɣəš   10
   təbəƚ nənčəƚɣaƚ wəčəŋˀah yaˀni
čəɣeƚ yaˀni yidag

They were setting snares for deer [they say].
All the people had gone after deer [they say].
She was walking alone [they say].
She was carrying a burden-basket [they say].
She was walking along with a cane [they say].   5
She was carrying a soft burden-basket [they say].
"My deer," she said [they say].
She caught him [they say].
She picked him up, put him in the basket, and carried
   him off [they say].
When she had to carry the basket under the branches of 10
   trees she whipped over her shoulder with her cane [they say].
She carried it along [they say], east up the hill.

SOURCE: P.E. Goddard (1909:179-180, 236), from Bill Ray, phonemicized by Victor Golla (communication to editors 1995); cf. K. Kroeber 1981:4-6.

NOTE: The phonemicization is based on internal and external evidence, including comparative data from other languages closely related to Cahto. The bracketed segments are absent from Goddard's text but restored by Golla; the presence of -ˀ-, the third-person human prefix, is not certain in all of the cases in which it has been restored.

Table 7. Excerpt from "The Origin of the Bean," a Tunica Folktale

ta´nisarăhč, sa´hkŭn, ˀuhta´kanˀa´kihč, ˀuhta´pˀɛkɛ´nì.
hinya´tíhč, ta´nahta ha´yihtăn, lɔ´tˀuwana´nì.
hinya´tíhč, ta´wišihč ˀasa´nì.
hinya´tíhč, ta´nahta ha´yihtˀu´nasăhč, ta´wišihč
   ˀunri´kita´pˀɛke´nì.
hinya´tíhč, tɔ´katɛ´kahăku, ˀu´wita wi´čˀuwa´nì,   5
   ta´nahta ha´yiht.
hinya´tíhč, ta´nisarăhč, ˀa´kˀamˀɛkɛ´nì.
hinya´tíhč, tɔ´katɛ´kahăku, ˀu´riš ˀa´mˀuhkɛ´nì.
hinya´tíhč, ˀu´kiku, ˀu´riš, ˀuhta´mˀuna´nì.
hinya´tíhč, se´hihtɛ´păn, ˀɔ´hɔyăhč, yu´katihpo´wan
   yakɔ´nì.
hinya´tíhč,, tihpo´wištukˀɔhɔ´nì.   10
hinya´tíhč, ˀu´riš ma´rˀuwa´nì.

The girl chased one (of them) and caught it [it is said].
[Now] the two (of them) were running toward the bank [it is
   said].
[Now] the waves were coming (toward them) [it is said].
[Now] when they came to the bank, the waves reached
   them and caught them [it is said].
[Now] then the orphan boy climbed up onto the bank   5
   alone [it is said].
[Now] the girl had gone down (into the water) and had
   disappeared [it is said].
[Now] the orphan boy went home [it is said].
[Now] he lived with his maternal uncle at (the latter's)
   home [it is said].
[Now] every morning he went (there) and tried to find his
   sister [it is said].
[Now] he could not find her [it is said].   10
[Now] he went back home [it is said].

SOURCE: Haas 1941a:135-143 from Sesostrie Youchigant. Translation of the initial connector and the reportative are in brackets.

---

narrative or other discourse inasmuch as it regularly distances the speaker from the time and content of the tale, which is likely to be believed to take place in a special myth time.

Rhodes and other writers have identified syntactic constructions as markers of organization in discourse. Rhodes, describing Ojibwa organization in terms of structural phenomena, finds that "the peak or climax of a text is often marked by the shortness of clauses as opposed to longer clauses with more embedded material in the buildup and post-peak" (1979:102), and that "constructions such as shifted word order, deictics . . ., and the use of plain conjuncts [which are normally subordinate] as independent verbs" (1979:103) mark logical usage. Others have observed that grammatical marking of person, tense, aspect, or mood, or the use of quotations within narrative may be manipulated in patterned ways and thus contribute to structure.

Particularly important is keeping track of the main topic of a given passage, whether it is subject or object

of the sentence. A number of grammatical devices have been noted as being used for this function, especially those that permit the labeling of a direct object as topic (since the usual expectation is that the subject will be topic): passive verbs, proximate-obviative distinctions, topical objects, word order changes, and the like. Passivization is one of the most widely used devices for switching the roles of subjects and objects so that an object can be in topic position. Also found in North America is the use of proximate-obviative distinctions on nouns and pronominal markers to distinguish between third persons; this marking can be maintained independently of designation as subject or object, allowing one to retain topicality relationships independently of syntactic roles. The use of this proximate-obviative contrast for topic maintenance is further supported (at least in Fox; Goddard 1990) by the use of two sets of demonstrative pronouns, a distal and an absentative, to relate back to preceding proximate and obviative referents (Goddard 1990:330). A distinction   *263* between proximate and obviative third persons is best known from Algonquian languages; but it or something similar is also found in Kootenai, Athapaskan languages, Eskimoan languages, and possibly in a few others. It has been extensively studied by Goddard (especially 1984, 1990) in Algonquian. The following Fox passage shows an alternation of use of proximate (marked P) and obviative (marked O) nouns and pronouns; they retain these statuses whichever is subject of its clause, thus keeping 'guests' as topic throughout.

> *o·ni wi·hkomečiki,*
> *mehteno·h=meko we·pi-kanakanawiničini*
>   *m[a]mi·ši·hahi,*
> *e·h=po·ni-nowi·wa·či.*
> *a·kwi=ke·hi=·pi ayi·ne·hka taši-kakano·neti·wa·čini.*
> *i·ni=meko, "o·=no·či," e·ničini=meko,*
> *e·h=po·ni-kanawiči owiye·ha.*

'Now as for the guests [P],
 whenever the attendants [O] merely start to give
   their speeches,
 they [P] stop going out.
 And they [P] do not keep on conversing.
 As soon as they [O] say, "o nochi,"
 anyone [P, hence of the guests] stops talking'
 (Goddard 1984:276).

The notion of "topical object," where a direct object suffix has a special shape when that object is the topic of the sentence, is explored by Kinkade (1990). In the Upper Chehalis sentence below, the final word ends in the third-person topical-object suffix -wali, showing that the subject of the first clause is still topic, even though 'he' is now designated as a direct object.

> *stálaqapitn tac yá·yṅs ƛa swins ʔit mát-<u>wali</u>.*
> he.calls.her the his.sister future her.being perfective
>   fetch-him
> 'He calls his sister to come fetch him.' (Kinkade
>   1990:344).

If a regular object suffix were used, the second clause would mean '(that) he will come fetch her'. Even the use or nonuse of overt nouns or noun phrases can indicate what is or is not a topic. For example, Fox may use an overt noun or noun phrase when there is a shift from one topic to another, where the earlier topic has been referred to by proximate subject affixes and the new topic is indicated by a proximate noun (Goddard 1990:339). The use of overt nouns is also important in Kiowa narratives; Watkins (1990:425) finds that "if there is a single topic or prominent character, the preference is to name that individual once early in the narrative or episode and not to repeat it," but if there are two characters, either of which may be topical and which interact directly, then definite nouns referring to both are more likely to occur.

A related grammatical category often used in organi-

zation of texts is switch-reference, first explicated by Jacobsen (1961, 1967; see also various essays in Haiman and Munro 1983). Although commonly used as a syntactic device for identifying continuity or discontinuity of subjects of sentences, it has also been shown to have an important role in linking and relating clauses both syntactically and semantically and in temporal sequencing of events (Dahlstrom 1982; Mithun 1993; Watkins 1993). Watkins (1993:149) also shows how switch-reference markers are used differently in various kinds of texts in Kiowa, with significantly greater frequency of use in traditional narratives than in, for example, letters written in Kiowa.

Another major class of features that are used to shape texts are various rhetorical devices. (These are also called literary or stylistic devices, although this use of "style" and "stylistics" is very different from the use of those terms below.) Terminology for referring to these rhetorical devices comes from studies of Western literature, and non-Western literature is not often described in these terms. Nevertheless, several studies have shown that these devices are important in the structure of folktales. Thus Woodbury (1985:173) discusses enjambment in Yupik Eskimo, and gives examples where "syntax, prosody, and particle placement conflict, creating marked, linguistically significant patterns of cohesion and disjunction." To illustrate this "conflict," he presents the same Yupik passage twice, first organized according to prosodic structure, then according to syntactic structure. He finds that "unexpected prosodic continuity signals cohesion of otherwise separate syntactic entities, while unexpected prosodic breaks signal disjunction in otherwise unitary syntactic constituents" (1985:174).

Goddard finds other rhetorical devices important in Algonquian languages. He discusses various kinds of repetition in Fox, especially chiasmus, where "corresponding elements in two parallel constructions appear in different orders" (1990a:160), and he finds similar constructions in Massachusett (Goddard and Bragdon 1988). In the following Fox passage, *wi·te·mekoči* '(that) they went with him' and *taswi* 'as many, so many' occur in different orders in the two clauses:

> *wi·te·mekoči taswi e·h=nahkohama·koči,*
> *taswi=meko wi·te·mekoči.*

'As many as went with him joined him in singing,
 everyone that went with him' (Goddard 1990a:160).

The repetition here is for emphasis, strengthened further by =meko (a marker of emphasis). Goddard also finds that more elaborate variation in order can occur, where more than two elements may be involved and one set may be elaborated more than the other. In an Upper Chehalis story a similar sequence of five events occurs before and after Bluejay's visit to the land of the dead. Kinkade (1987:295) notes that this "frame" structure "bears a striking resemblance to the 'ring composition' of Pindaric odes, in which the central third is framed by adjacent segments of the outer thirds." Woodbury (1985: 168) also finds examples of framing in Yupik Eskimo.

The unexpected can be used as a rhetorical device. Goddard (1990a:167) observes that "descriptive passages are so rare in Fox narratives that their appearance demands attention and explanation" and finds that they may serve as either transition to a character to whom focus is shifted or to focus the listener's attention on something that otherwise might not have seemed so important.

Yet another rhetorical device found widely in North American folktales is the use of parallelism. This can occur in many varieties, with the parallel repetitions being exactly the same or only lexically similar and the parallel structures being adjacent or not. In the following Fox example, the parallel lines are identical, although not adjacent:

o·ni·='pi e·h=naki·či.
'And then, it is said, he stopped.'
e·h=e·škamesiniči=meko okwisani.
'And his son got worse and worse.'
o·ni·='pi e·h=naki·či.
'And then, it is said, he stopped.'
na·hka=meko=wi·na okye·ni, "ayo·hi·'škwe
owihowi·kita·we," e·h=ikoči.
'And to him his mother said, "Say, let's live
here!"' (Goddard 1990a:160).

The two identical lines refer to different characters, first to the chief and his sick son, then to the hero, who has curative powers but is purposely staying elsewhere, and his mother; the repetition is a way of bringing the conflict between the two characters into relief while shifting from one to the other. On the other hand, in the following passage from Upper Chehalis, different words in identical constructions are used:

cílačs t máqʷm ƛala spanáqʷm,
'Five prairies for you to cross,
n ł míy łakʷxʷáws, šʔał tat ʔatəmš.
and you will just get back to your homeland.
. . .
cilčstálmaqʷm ƛala sitáqʷm,
Five prairies for you to cross,
n ł łakʷxʷáws čá· tala wíntn.
and you will get back where you live.' (Kinkade 1987:264, 274).

These two pairs of lines frame brief instructions on how to cross these prairies; the repetition emphasizes that there are five prairies that must be crossed successfully if Bluejay is to reach home. Langen (1989-1990) gives an extensive discussion of the use of parallelism in Lushootseed, showing how it is used at various levels to structure a folktale, including parallelism of lines, episodes, and ideas, as well as framing structures.

Presentational Format

Presentational practices have developed over many years throughout the world, with certain practices becoming standard in the various traditions. but without agreement on which practices are best for a given genre or in a particular locale. No Native American written forms were developed. Rather outsiders have, for their own reasons, used their own systems of transcription for Native American languages. To be sure, there have been serious proposals for certain standards in the report of discourse and performed speech, for example, Edwards (1992), but the history of transcription shows many practices. These have been surveyed in Luthin (1991).

All reports and transcripts of speech are imperfect records of the original (speech) events; there is always more that can be added. Personal interests shape the reports that are produced, and therefore these reports are only the reflection of the saliency that is found in or attributed to certain aspects of the speech event. American myths and tales have most commonly been presented as simple prose narratives, although Washington Matthews thought of Navajo songs and prayers within legends as verse and arranged them as such (Zolbrod 1983:226). Further organization into paragraphs was largely arbitrary, with breaks made between whatever the collector considered separate episodes; it must be recognized that any written representation of oral production will involve varying amounts of subjectivity on the part of the writer and analyst. Decisions about what kind of punctuation to use and where it goes, division into lines or sentences (or verses), and notation of prosodic features (such as intonation, volume, speed) all involve individual interpretations on what is important in the narrative performance and how best to portray it. However, the ultimate question is whether it is a necessary consequence of oral literature that all Native American texts be verse or any other specific format, or if these are reductionistic constructs.

It was not until the 1970s that scholars began to suggest that American Indian myths and tales could be presented in their entirety as something other than prose. Jacobs (1959:7) felt that treating Chinookan "literature as a kind of theater does better justice to its content, designs, and functions" than presenting it as a story or novel, and chose to emphasize "actors, acts, scenes, epilogues, and the like, rather than . . . plots, motifs, and episodes." This notion was extended by Tedlock, Hymes, and others, who detected even more structure and systematicity in myths and tales and determined that linguistic features could be used in deciding on presentational format.

One approach to the presentation of texts is that developed by Dennis Tedlock, who wished to represent the telling (or performance) on the printed page by recognizing the role of suprasegmental features (intonation, pause, rhetorical lengthening, loudness, use of falsetto voice) in the structure of narratives. Some of these features occur in all speech, including narration, oratory, and magic formulas, sometimes intentional, at other times accidental. Tedlock provides varying type size to represent different levels of loudness used by the narrator, line breaks and dots between lines to indicate pauses of different lengths, and dashes and repeated consonants or vowels to indicate rhetorical lengthening. He moves the type up or down within a line to represent intonation changes; he puts comments indicating, for example, tones of voice or audience responses in italics within parentheses, in addition to using other imaginative graphic devices. A text presented this way gives information to make it possible for readers to replicate (either mentally or aloud) the original telling of the story. Such an approach can provide information on cultural expectations about how myths should be presented. Unfortunately, this prosodic information is not available for texts written before adequate sound recording devices were available.

Others who have also taken pitch and other voice mannerisms in the native languages into account in their analyses of North American folktales are Woodbury (1985, 1987) for Central Alaskan Yupik, Bright (1979, 1982a) for Karok, McLendon (1982) for Eastern Pomo, and Kinkade (1984) for Upper Chehalis.

Hymes (1976) found that by arranging a text into lines some of the structure inherent in a text could be made more visually evident. The result was a kind of dramatic free verse (in the sense of not having meter or rhythm), where lines were arranged into successively larger units: verses, stanzas, scenes, and acts. This sort of verse is very different from rhymed or metrical poetry, or from song texts, which are indeed stylized and have structure of their own. The great amount of repetition in folklore makes considerable sense when organized this way. This format has been further developed (Hymes 1981), and its clearest explication is by V. Hymes (1987), who gives an analysis of a Warm Springs Sahaptin myth.

Analysis and organization within the framework suggested by Hymes has to do with the analyst's perception of plot development, interaction and movement of characters, perceived parallelisms, cultural salience, and the like. Because of this subjectivity, different analysts would not necessarily organize a text the same way, and the same analyst might perceive different structures at different times (as Hymes himself has done; Hymes 1981, 1992). Hymes has published this

sort of verse analysis of myths for a number of languages (Hymes 1981, 1987; samples are also given in vol. 7:597-600).

One concrete device that is used in the structuring of narratives is what has come to be called the pattern number of a society (Hymes 1992). All societies seem to favor certain numbers, considering them magical or simply using them in organizing the world around them. Western European society favors three, and European folklore is replete with sets of three—three persons, three tasks, three objects (Olrik 1965). American Indians most frequently use three or four as pattern numbers, and a few groups use five (particularly Chinookans and the Sahaptin along the lower Columbia River and several adjacent groups). Myth narrative can be seen as structured in units agreeing with these pattern numbers, with the units sometimes being grouped in sets of two or four and three or five. Different pattern numbers can be used within the same text, as when Tillamook or Tonkawa uses both fours and fives depending on whether men or women are involved, or by different narrators, as in Karok (Hymes 1992:97-98). Thus a tale may be seen as having three acts, acts may have three scenes, and so on, although such configurations are not necessarily linguistically marked; rather they may be subjective on the part of the analyst based on what are perceived to be coherent dramatic units.

In Upper Chehalis few myths were told without specific reference to the number five, and episodes (alternatively, scenes or stanzas) often occur in sets of five. Thus in the middle of the story "Daughters of Fire" (Kinkade 1983a), when Moon is being pursued by Fire, he runs successively to five natural objects in search of escape: Rock, Lake, Wind, Creek, and Trail. Only the last is able to save him. Each of the first four is given its own scene, and each scene (with slight variations) is divided into Moon's request for help and his rejection. Since Trail eventually saves him, this segment is much more elaborated. In "Bear and Bee" (Kinkade 1984), the use of fives is even more prominent. In this story Bear argues for darkness the entire winter so he can sleep, and Ant and Bee argue for daylight and short periods of darkness. The ensuing contest takes five nights (specifically counted), and each side sings one or two verses each night, each verse consisting of a line repeated five times. The result of all this is an enormous amount of repetition. Verse format gives a visual structure that helps to capture the oral effect of repetition, which would likely appear disruptive if presented as prose (even if just the songs were set as verses). The repetitions may also serve as a kind of refrain, and help the narrator count the number of times something is done in order to comply with the expected pattern number of the culture.

This pronounced use of a pattern number to delineate narrative structure in Upper Chehalis may be an extreme case, and it is not typical of most other Salishan languages. In Columbian (an Interior Salish language), for example, numbers almost never appear explicitly in texts, and when they do they are not used to structure the narrative the way they are in Upper Chehalis. Nevertheless, five is the pattern number in Columbian and does affect the organization of narratives in less concrete ways:

The difference between a prose and verse presentation can be seen by looking at a passage from a story about Chipmunk and Owl in Columbian Salish (table 8). This passage arguably constitutes the second scene

(in the sense of Hymes) of the story. Each printed line is a clause in Columbian. Many lines are a single word long; the heavy inflection used in this language often makes these words equivalent to whole sentences in English. Stanzas are printed flush left and verses are separated by blank lines. There is a certain amount of arbitrariness inherent in this sort of analysis, and other arrangements of the material are possible (for example, the second-person subject inflection in line 5 in the second verse and lines 6 and 7 in the third draw them together as opposed to lines 8 and 9, both with first-person plural inflection.)

Table 8. Excerpt from "Chipmunk and Owl," a Columbian Salish Folktale

Columbian		English	
"ʔíʿa, łíḷ,		"Oh, all right,	
yapkʷántxʷ ʔaci ẏẏámx̣ʷaʔ		you take along that little basket	
kʷaʔ kʷ xə́k̓m.		and you pick.	
xək̓mú		Pick	
kʷaʔ nasuʔ q̓ʷáčntxʷ.	5	until you fill it.	5
lút kasʔíłntxʷ		Don't eat it	
naʔ lckícxstxʷ,		until you get back,	
kʷaʔ nasuʔ k̓íʿʿʷntm;		and we will pray over it;	
kʷaʔ nasuʔ cmáʔ kt ʔíłntm."		and afterwards we will eat it."	
ʔíʿ yápkʷàs waʔ ʔałuni ẏẏámx̣ʷaʔ,	10	So he took along that little basket,	10
kʷaʔ náẇlx.		and he ran.	
ná···ẇlx,		He ran,	
ʔi tk̓íʿʿwlx k̓l syayaʔáłp,		and he climbed into the serviceberry bush,	
ʔi ʔicá xə́k̓m.		and then he picked.	
xək̓mú···	15	He picked	15
kʷaʔ q̓ʷq̓ʷáčt,		until it was almost full,	
waʔ ʔi lcwá···łk̓ʷp,		and he came back down,	
kʷaʔ ʔałi sʔacxʷúsəskaʔəxʷ.		and then he was in a rush to get back.	
ʔi txʷúsxnm		So he scurried along	
ʔíca łúcəc.	20	and he fell.	20
síxʷuxʷ waʔ ʔału . . .		They spilled, those . . .	
niʔtqáẇsc.		he smeared his hand in it.	
"ʔáʿni, kʷaʔ nasuʔ ʔakásn ʔaxá ʔani ʔinkálx."		"Oh, my! What will I do with my hand?"	
ʔáč̓ʔačxsc.		He lay there looking at it.	
ʔani kʷə́ṅ k̓aʔlá···	25	So then slowly	25
kʷaʔ łłáʿʿqʷs.		he licked at it.	
"ʔáni kʷə́ṅ q̓ʷáʿmqʷamt,		"Oh, my! It's really good,	
łə́x."		sweet."	
ʔíh łáʿʿqʷs		So he licked	
k̓ʷuʔłnús,	30	until it was all gone,	30
ʔìca ʔalnáẇlx.		and then he ran back.	
ná···ẇlx,		He ran,	
łtk̓íwlx,		(and) he climbed back up,	
ʔi cxək̓cíʿ···nm		and picked and ate	
húʿy kʷaʔ mq̓ánk.	35	until he was full.	35

SOURCE: 1969 narration by Margaret Piatote near Nespelem, Wash. Transcribed by Kinkade with the assistance of Mary Marchand.
NOTE: English punctuation is added; rhetorical lengthening is indicated by raised periods.

One of the features that stands out in this arrangement is the repetition of a word to begin a new verse: this can be seen moving from line 3 to line 4, from 11 to 12, from 14 to 15, and from 31 to 32. Lines are frequently marked by beginning with $k^wa\mathit{?}$ 'and'. Another feature is the use of a particle $\mathit{?}i$ or $\mathit{?}ih$ to begin stanzas (the occurrence in line 34 may indicate that this line should begin the following stanza, rather than a verse as here). Such use of markers for units larger than the line or verse seems to be relatively uncommon in North America. This particle (which is not used by all speakers of the language) has no independent meaning, and it tends not to be heard by native speakers unless their attention is called to it. In this story, it occurs consistently at the beginning of what can logically be called stanzas (23 or 24 of 31 stanzas begin this way). It is also sometimes used within verses for emphasis, although such usage shows no particular pattern. What are here given as verses can be seen through the English translation to be single episodes, and the stanzas as clusters of these episodes.

Projecting from transcriptional techniques, many scholars have come to think of American Indian narrative as verse, either as a reflection of its delivery, or as a representation of its rhetorical organization. It should be noted, before reviewing further the transcriptional and analytical preferences of scholars, that Hymes has conceded that "measured verse"—one of his posited basic structural units of American Indian narrative—may be restricted to (certain areas of) North America. Some practitioners have attempted to integrate the approaches of both Tedlock and Hymes when (and this might be the norm) the delivery does not match the perceived rhetorical organization of the narrative. McLendon (1982) and Woodbury (1985, 1987) have, in fact, attempted such syntheses, taking into account pause phrasing, prosodic phrasing, syntactic constituency, form-content parallelism, and adverbial-particle phrasing. But however each scholar ends up transcribing and formatting, it is easy to agree with Woodbury that "an astonishingly diverse range of linguistic phenomena underlie their similar-looking transcriptions" (Woodbury 1987:176), and this diversity is thereby obscured.

In the 1970s the presentation of texts in verse form gained popularity. Much of the justification is that for many the stories are more esthetically pleasing in such a format and that the reader becomes more aware of some of the structure of the narrations. For some, according to Hymes, "it slows the eye and hence feeds the mind" (McLendon 1982:287). An unrelated and unexpected early use of verse to represent native speech is found in Speare (1977), where much of the ordinary speech of an elderly Shuswap woman is presented as (English) verse. Some presentations utilize the full structural analysis promoted by Hymes (as in Kinkade 1987 for an Upper Chehalis story), some have published texts in lines and verses without electing to use a more detailed analysis (as in Bright 1979, 1980, 1982a for Karok, or Kroskrity 1985 for an Arizona Tewa story), and others have used a much freer line and verse structure. Krauss (1982), for example, explicitly states that the Eyak texts he recorded from Anna Nelson Harry are not, as he presents them, what is usually called poetry. Nevertheless, he begins a new line for every breath group or intonation contour and divides the text (admittedly inconsistently) into paragraphs according to pauses, tone changes, or conjunctions used as markers. The result, "gives some impression of the rhythm and style of Anna's storytelling, which is in fact a poetic art" (Krauss 1982:22). Woodbury (1984) presents (in less detail than in his later work) Central Alaskan Yupik stories from two different genres, both in verse format; he justifies and explicates his procedures, including notes on how he chose to translate the texts. Woodbury (1987) presents another Yupik story with much more structural detail, and he discusses how this can be justified by considering prosodic phrasing (intonation, rhythm, etc.), pause phrasing, syntactic constituency, and adverbial-particle phrasing. Dauenhauer and Dauenhauer give both Tlingit stories (1987) and oratory (1990) (in Tlingit and English) in a format using short lines split according to pauses and intonation. This is an attempt to reflect the rhythm and pace of the original narratives, and they state specifically that these renderings are not poems in any traditional sense (1987:8-9), although the result may be poetic.

Shipley gives only his English translations of a collection of Maidu myths. He justifies a presentation in verse as an attempt to reflect the beauty and style of the Maidu original; he strives for a translation "which would be as close as possible to the meaning of the Maidu but which, at the same time, would delight and satisfy an English ear. Just as with the Maidu, the English should be most effective when heard, not read silently. Thus the best analog in our English tradition is the theater—drama—and, to a lesser extent, poetry—not written prose" (Shipley 1991:178). In a similar vein, Bright (1993) gives a variety of Coyote stories (in English) from several languages. Wickwire, in Robinson (1989), also presents stories in English only, this time of Okanagan; however, her verse analysis is not based on an original Okanagan language version, as she collected the stories only in English. She felt that her narrator, Harry Robinson, was using Okanagan storytelling traditions in his English renditions. This suggests that many Native Americans may carry over traditions of storytelling from their native languages into English, a kind of translation of an original by the speaker himself instead of one provided by the non-native recorder.

Many have still preferred to publish texts as prose, giving various reasons for doing so. For example, Slavey texts have been presented as prose rather than verse because the "translators find that verse format imposes a very strong break on the flow of thought," and "they found that the reader might easily be induced to make longer pauses than exist in the original narration, a tendency that negates the purpose of using verse form to direct the reader toward a reading more faithful to the original performance" (Moore and Wheelock 1990:xxiv). Nevertheless, the editors note both pauses and repetitions of discourse markers and punctuate the texts so as to reflect both the structure and the performance of the narration. Similarly, Parks (1991) does not find a line-verse arrangement appropriate for his presentation of Arikara texts. He justifies his prose format on the grounds that these tellings were "not staged performances, since there was either no audience present . . . or it was at most a small, intimate one" and that nothing in the delivery style and arrangement of material "suggests a line-verse structure that would more accurately portray an underlying Arikara narrative form than what is achieved in prose" (Parks 1991, 3:60-61). He gives multiple presentations in both Arikara and English to provide accessibility to different audiences. Similar problems apply to the many cyclelike myth sets found all over North America (such as connected sets of Coyote stories or the Navajo creation story); no attempts at detailed verse analyses of any of these cycles had been published by the early 1990s.

Content and Style

Radin (1915:42) has commented that "only a few Indians in any tribe have the reputation of being excellent raconteurs. And it is a different kind of excellence with which each raconteur is credited." No one would contest the applicability of these remarks to any Western group. Contemporary workers report similar findings, yet presentations of texts often ignore matters of individual styles and focus instead on the discussion of traits that are assumed to be typical of the group.

Many features of both content and style have been identified for American Indian myths and tales. There is no general agreement on how content and style should be defined, or what matters should be subsumed under each; one of the fullest treatments of these subjects is Jacobs (1959), at least for Northwest myths and tales. (Jacobs 1964 provides a useful shorter treatment of how these topics can be identified and treated.) He recognizes several categories as features of content: tale types, plots, and motifs; social relationships; actor personalities; humor; cosmology and world view; religion; value ideals; and songs within texts (1964:328-332).

His list of stylistic categories is larger: linguistic features; recitalist-audience behavior; beginnings, pauses, continuations, and endings; pattern numbers; location expressions; time expressions; explanatory devices (such as geography and animal characteristics); plot devices (motifs); structuring of act, scene, or episode sequences; headings, titles, and manner of ready reference; descriptive inclusions and omissions; items of psychological commentary; speed of action; and vocal technique and mannerisms, repetition, rhythm, and intensity (Jacobs 1964:332-333).

These categories of content and style in Northwest myth suggested by Jacobs provide a useful framework for examining such features throughout North America. The strong concentration of Boas and his students (including Jacobs) on Northwest mythology has provided a huge corpus of myths from this region, and this corpus has been the subject of a large amount of analysis, perhaps more than for any other region of North America. Nevertheless, questions of content and style have not been neglected elsewhere. Liljeblad (vol. 11:641-659) treats them to a limited extent for the Great Basin, recognizing the use of metaphor and figurative speech, epigrammatic forms, and ritualistic aspects of performance as important features of style in the Great Basin, and a distinction between legends and myths along with the structure of songs as features of content. He also touches on several of the categories of content and style listed by Jacobs but does not attempt his sort of categorizations, and he emphasizes the tale types and motifs as categorized by Thompson (1955-1958) much more heavily than does Jacobs.

Jacobs based his analysis on his own large collections of myths and tales in Sahaptin, Upper Chinook, Kalapuyan languages, Hanis and Miluk Coos, Molala, and Chinook Jargon, as well as on his close familiarity with contemporary and earlier collections from elsewhere in the Northwest by Franz Boas, John R. Swanton, Manuel Andrade, Leo J. Frachtenberg, Hermann Haeberlin, Thelma Adamson, Erna Gunther, and others. Whether or not one agrees with his specific categories of content and style, they are useful for looking at folklore structure. Examples of many of his categories are not hard to find. Although Jacobs considered tale and motif types too broad categories, they have been widely recognized and catalogued; especially noteworthy is the work of Thompson (1955-1958), although his index needs updating to account for many motifs identifiable in North American folklore but not included in this monumental work. Examples of plot and tale types are creation myths (see Rooth 1957), Bungling Host, Earth Diver, Star Husband, Lodge-Boy and Thrown-Away (the last three discussed in detail by Reichard 1921), and Scabby Boy, all found among many groups. Well-known and widespread motifs are Youngest-Smartest,

Substituted Eyes, and Visit to the Land of the Dead (see Thompson 1929, 1946). Gayton (1935) compares areal affiliations of California tale types and motifs with other regions. Parks (1991) includes a rare attempt to trace parallels for the motifs and basic plots of his stories in a systematic way.

Social relationships found in folktales have to do with family relationships, social classes, community relationships, age classes, and ogres. In the Columbian Salish story (table 8), Chipmunk lives with his grandmother (who is Snowshoe Hare), reflecting a common practice throughout North America of a grandparent raising a child, or caring for the child while its parents are gathering or hunting. In this story, the grandmother teaches Chipmunk about praying over (first) foods, protects him from the Owl ogress, and brings him back to life after he has been eaten by Owl (whom they then kill together). Another widespread story tells of a granddaughter who marries a young man who appears so undesirable that the entire village abandons them; her grandmother leaves coals for them to keep a fire; the husband proves to be a great hunter and stores great stocks of food for his wife; he avenges his wife's abandonment by killing the villagers, but saving the grandmother (for a discussion of this "Cinderella" theme, see Randall 1949). This story gives instruction on proper familial and intravillage behavior. Also common are stories involving marital relationships; desertion of spouses; animal spouses; incest; sibling relationships; kidnapping; community relationships; roles of individuals of varying sex, age, or social rank; and the activities of shamans. Stories revolving around these relationships were instructive on proper and improper behavior. A special type of myth involving social relationships is found in the northern Northwest Coast area, where special tales are told of the origin of a specific family; such tales were used to validate the status of the family within the community and in relation to other families.

Actors in myths and tales do not reflect actual, historically known people. It is most widespread in North America that these actors are anthropomorphized faunal beings, although Bright (1993) shows how many of the traits often characteristic of the mythic Coyote also resemble the actual, biological coyote (such as wanderer, glutton, lecher, survivor), while others are more human (such as cheat, outlaw, pragmatist). These beings would often be assigned and stereotyped with particular human characteristics (not necessarily reflecting traits of the real animal or bird named) that would be constant from story to story. These personality characteristics (such as wisdom, cleverness, or good nature) are rarely expressed. Very widespread is the assignment of specific characters to the role of a culture hero, "who inhabits the earth throughout the myth age" preparing it for the needs of humans who are to come at a later time (Bierhorst 1985:15), and a trickster, who plays tricks on others, becomes the butt of his own and others' pranks, and does some adjusting of the world. A variant term applied to the culture hero is "transformer," although some (Bierhorst 1985:15) use this term for a protagonist whose activities are somewhat more limited than those of a culture hero often specifically involving the reshaping of the physical environment and creatures within it; "transformer" is commonly applied to characters in the folklore of the Northwest Coast and the Plateau. Often these roles are merged or divided in different ways; they are most commonly distinct on the Northwest Coast. There, for example, one finds Raven as transformer in the north (Goodchild 1991) (vol. 7:594) and Moon among several Coast Salish groups. Tricksters may be human or animal, or neither of these. In Winnebago, he is "primarily an inchoate being of undetermined proportions, a figure foreshadowing the shape of man" (Radin 1956:xxiv). The trickster in western Washington is commonly a humanlike character, such as *dúkwibəł* among the Lushootseed, *xʷənéxʷəne* among the Upper Chehalis, *mə́sp* among the Quinault, or *q̓ʷéˑti* among the Quileute. The Kiowa trickster, Saynday, was depicted by the artist Silverhorn in human form (fig. 11). Throughout much of the west, Coyote combines the roles of trickster and transformer. Other well-known culture heroes or trickster-heroes are Rabbit in the Southeast, Gluskap among northeastern Algonquian groups, Nanabozho among the Ojibwa, Wisakedjak among the West Main Cree of James Bay, and Spider among many central and northern Plains groups. Thompson (1929) is an important source of information about these characters; Bierhorst (1985) is also a useful overview.

It is common to find one major character, often an animal or a bird, who serves as the central figure in whole sets of tales. One of the most widespread of these is Coyote, trickster par excellence, who is popular throughout much of western North America (see for example Bright 1978, 1993). All the culture heroes, transformers, and tricksters named above typically have cycles devoted to them, as do Wolverine among the Northern Athapaskans and the Cree-Montagnais mythical hero Chahkabesh. There are also cycles for characters that are not culture heroes or tricksters, such as Mink among some Northwest Coast groups. Other animals or birds sometimes play various specialized roles: Mouse is a polyglot and translator on the Plateau, Mink is a notorious lecher on the Northwest Coast, Meadowlark is a wise advice-giver who helps others get out of trouble in the Northwest, Cottontail is a notorious rogue in the Great Basin; Raccoon is a practical joker, often cruel, in Fox; and Wolf is gluttonous but dimwitted (hence the butt of Raccoon's and other's pranks), also in Fox. Deer, dogs, and horses often appear simply

Smithsonian, NAA: 92-11395.

Fig. 11. Saynday *(séndé)*, the Kiowa trickster, captured by Sapoul *(sɔpʰól)*, the owllike mountain ogre, and put in a furry sack as depicted by Silverhorn. Saynday regains his freedom, by imitating the call of a "Cheet" bird (Greene 1993). The dash marks are used to represent footprints and the direction the actors are going. The Kiowa artist Silverhorn was the first to take the verbal stories of Saynday and put them into drawings. He produced hundreds of art works showing many facets of Kiowa life, including stories, warfare, religious ceremonies, and daily life, especially women's activities. Drawing by Silverhorn *(hɔ́·gù·)* in a target practice record book, about 1897.

as ordinary useful animals rather than myth figures but in other cases may be myth characters. Other nonhuman characters are common, sometimes as special kinds of ogres or as deformed individuals; thus one finds characters named, for example, Spear (Upper Chehalis, Adamson 1934:87-94, 227-230; Sahaptin, Jacobs 1934-1937, 1:148-153), Awl (Clackamas Chinook, Jacobs 1958-1959, 1:226-241; Keresan, Boas 1925a, 1:22-26), Flint (Boy) (Kalapuyan, Jacobs 1945:125-127; Clackamas Chinook, Jacobs 1958-1959, 1:166-179; Yana, Sapir 1910:216-221), Urine Boy (Adamson 1934:226), Boil (Sahaptin, Jacobs 1934-1937, 1:107; Upper Chehalis, Adamson 1934:131-132; Lushootseed, Hilbert 1985:15), Moon (Upper Chehalis, Adamson 1934:158-177; Lushootseed, Ballard 1929:69-80; Maidu, Shipley 1991:147-153), Thunder (Omaha-Ponca, Dorsey 1890:176-206; Maidu, Dixon 1912:140-173 and Shipley 1991:154-175; Lower Chehalis, Adamson 1934:315-324), Winds (Wishram Chinook, Sapir 1909a:102-105; Tillamook, E. Jacobs 1959:92-93, 123-147; Coast Tsimshian, Cove and MacDonald 1987:47-49), Fire (Upper Chehalis, Kinkade 1983a, Clackamas Chinook, Jacobs 1958-1959, 1:114-130).

Humor, which is pervasive in Native American tales, is used both to alleviate tension in serious myths and tales and purely for fun. It is often overtly sexual, as in the Wishram Chinookan myth in which Coyote commits fellatio on himself (Sapir 1909a:30-35; Hymes 1975, 1981:91-98; 212-214), or in several ribald Coast Salish stories in which Wren and his grandmother are involved in incest and other sexual escapades. In other stories Coyote does something foolish (like insulting Rock) and paying the consequences (he is pursued across the countryside by Rock). Humor was also expressed by vocal mannerisms; a figure might speak in a certain way that both characterized that actor and was considered humorous. Thus in Takelma, Grizzly Bear often prefixes *ɫʸ* (a voiceless palatalized lateral fricative) to words in his speech (Hymes 1979; Sapir 1909); in Nez Perce Bear slurs consonants into *l* and Skunk nasalizes in a high-pitched voice; in Quileute the trickster *q̓ʷéˑti* prefixes *sx-* to each word, and Raven prefixes *š-*; Chahkabesh and certain subhuman, devil-like creatures palatalize consonants in James Bay Cree (Ellis 1989:16; further examples can be found in Sapir's study of speech styles in Nootka; Sapir 1915c). *271*

Notions of world view were not necessarily elaborated in myths, although indications of how the universe was perceived are often reflected indirectly. Many groups have stories about how their individual world was made: a transformer may be depicted as creating specific local rivers, and he may stock rivers or lakes with fish and mountains with game; and a number of groups have specific creation myths. Rooth (1957) classifies North American creation myths into eight types: Earth Diver myths, World Parent myths, Emergence myths, Spider myths, Fighting or Robbery myths, Ymir myths, myths of Two Creators and their Contests, and Blind Brother myths. Respect for one's own people (kin or village or tribe) is often stressed. Tales frequently teach limits on hunting for and gathering food so as not to exhaust resources, and respect for foods is emphasized by telling about first-fruits ceremonies and proper disposal of remains. Myths and tales often reflect specifically the notions held about what happens to a person at death. It is not uncommon for there to be two or more locations for the dead; among the Upper Chehalis there were at least two—one for people who died of disease (from which a shaman might be able to bring the person back), and one for people who died by accident such as a fall or burning to death (from which recovery was not possible). It was also common to believe that there was a special land of the dead for babies.

Religious beliefs are often closely tied to people's world view, and for many groups do not represent a distinct category of content. The notion of one or more specific deities is by no means universal; such ideas, for example, were absent or weakly developed in the Northwest Coast. Elaborate religious ritual is well known for the Southwest, where specific rites are practiced for seasonal changes, first fruits, important events in the life of an individual, and for curing; these rituals are frequently motivated by myths and are important events within myths.

Values and moral precepts are commonly reflected in myths. Proper and improper behavior is specifically noted. Incest or adultery occur as a lesson that they should not be practiced in real life; generosity is extolled; chastity and fidelity in marriage are encouraged; hard work and bravery in battle are promoted. These are often emphasized by telling of a character who violates these values in an exaggerated way, and then showing the harm caused both to the violator and the people around him. Coyote's sexual extravagances and his tricks on others are held up to ridicule; Coyote himself is often the primary victim, and is either made to look a fool or dies as the result of his actions.

Songs are very commonly found in texts. They may occur as a series of nonsense syllables (or vocables; see Powers 1992 for an analysis of these in Lakhota), there

may be recognizable words, or the language in them may be archaic or disguised. Beside being sung or changed, they usually have structure different from the surrounding text. Their function within a myth can reflect the enactment of a ritual, they may be a shaman's curing song, an individual's spirit power song, or fun songs. The Upper Chehalis story of the contest on the relative length of day and night consists largely of a series of songs sung by Bear on the one hand and Ant and Bee on the other. Each song consists of a line repeated five times, and the ritual lasts for five days; because some songs are sung more than once, or one side may sing two songs at a session, there are 20 or more songs in the story. Examples of ceremonial songs and story songs found in Fox texts have been analyzed by Goddard (1993).

Although features of style are not always clearly distinct from features of content, the former often modify the latter in interesting ways. Thus passages in tales that explain a particular feature of an animal (a chipmunk's stripes, a bluejay's color, the length of a coyote's snout) or geography (why a falls blocks a river at a particular point, a peculiar rock formation) can be viewed as elements of style, while their aggregate may reflect part of a people's world view.

Specific linguistic devices are often used as stylistic features. Some of these can be manipulated by the narrator for specific effects, and others are devices used to characterize mythic narration. One might find archaic grammar or morphology, frequent use of otherwise infrequent grammatical features, special intonation patterns, or special idioms. Special speech habits used to characterize a certain actor in a story might violate patterns in the language; thus the ɫ̓ used in Takelma to characterize the speech of Grizzly Bear is not otherwise a phoneme in the language. In one of the Upper Chehalis stories about Wren, he inappropriately adds the lexical suffix for penis to several body-part terms ('stomach-penis', 'neck-penis') and to the name Raven in order to make fun of him. Characters in stories are often given special names or titles (honorifics). In Kalispel-Spokane (Salish), coyote the animal is snčlé ʔ, but Coyote the myth character is spílye ʔ; the proper name is borrowed from Sahaptin. A cluster of languages in northern California (as well as in some languages farther afield, such as Fox) marks some or all protagonists of myths with a special compound construction in which the second part is a way of indicating respect for the character; Coyote–Old Man, Bear–Old Lady, Deer–Young Lady, Grizzly Bear–Girl, Crane–Old [One], and the like in Eastern Pomo (where the second noun is called a 'personal noun'; McLendon 1975, 1977, 1978a), Patwin (Whistler 1977a, 1978a), Lake Miwok (Callaghan 1978), Wappo (Sawyer and Somersal 1977), Wailaki (Seaburg 1977), and Nisenan (Smith 1977).

Just as English-language folktales often begin with "once upon a time" and end with "they lived happily ever after," so Native American myths and tales often begin and end with stylized phrases. An Upper Chehalis story might begin ʔał tat ƛ́áqłnł 'a long time ago' and might end kʷalalí· šał tit tə́mš 'goodbye to the earth'; kʷalalí· tit cíłns ʔał panáxʷčł 'goodbye to the food from our house'; or, more simply, tu słíx̣uʔ 'that's all'. Wishram Chinook had a similar opening formula ġánġadix or ánġadix 'long ago', used for historical and quasi-historical narratives (Hymes 1981:128), but closings might consist of "a summary conclusion of the action in progress," an epilogue, and a formulaic ƙaní ƙaní 'story story' (Hymes 1981:322-323). Fox stories end with iˑni eˑhkwiči, or just eˑhkwiči, literally '(that's) how long he is', referring either to the story or to the main character. In the Northwest Coast audience response was usually expected during the narration of a story in the form of ʔáˑˑ, ʔéˑˑ, or ʔíˑˑ (literally 'yes'), uttered when the narrator paused; other responses were also used, such as həbúʔ in Lushootseed and similarly in Twana and hamúkʷiʔ or ososos among the Upper Chehalis, as indications that the listeners were awake and listening. Among the Coos, listeners would repeat each phrase after the narrator. Longer myths can be a sequence of episodes (which can also be told as independent stories) strung together; there are not necessarily formal breaks between these episodes, but transitions are often indicated by expressions such as 'he starts off; he doesn't go far and . . .', when a new episode begins.

Time, location, and aspects of nature and physical characteristics are often expressed only in general terms such as 'a long time', 'the next morning', 'upstream', 'in the village', 'along the trail', 'they lived there'. Passage of time is often indicated by stating that something happened a certain number of times or for a certain number of days, where the number specified is the pattern number of that culture; the implication in these cases is not a specific number of occurrences, but that the event occurred many times. The number specified is culturally determined, and allows patterned development of the text; the recurrences can be identical or each somewhat different, or some omitted, with the final one implying 'many times'. Thus when a child is said to live somewhere four years and then is an adult, magically rapid growth is not necessarily implied, only that enough time has passed for his growth (although actual rapid growth is itself a common motif). Other myths did require specific siting, especially if the story concerned or alluded to the creation or modification of a known geographical location. When the story is told of the Quileute trickster q̓ʷéˑti proceeding along the coast of what is now Washington putting people along the rivers and fish in those rivers, the rivers must be named (Andrade 1931).

When the people living along the Columbia River tell of Coyote going up that river leaving salmon in some tributaries but creating a barrier at those where the local tribe refuses him a wife, each stream is named. Among the Eastern Pomo, "all myths begin by describing the protagonists as living at a named real site, in order to orient the audience geographically" (McLendon 1977:162).

More casual references to locations and physical characteristics (particularly of animals) are specific. Such references are usually expressed as 'that's why X is the way it is' (see Waterman 1914 for a classic discussion of these explanatory devices). A specific rock may be called 'Coyote's Wife' because Coyote turned her to stone at that spot; Palouse Falls and other features of the Palouse River were formed when Beaver was being pursued by giants for oil from his tail (Palouse; Clark 1953:117-118); Coyote created the Big Dipper by stranding the five Wolf brothers and their dog in the sky with two Grizzly Bears who lived there (Wasco; Clark 1953:152-155). Chipmunk has stripes because Owl, chasing him, scratched his back as he ducked under a fence (Columbian Salish); Bobcat has a short tail with a black tip because one of the places he carried fire back home while he was fleeing an ogre was on the tip of his tail, and it burned short (Upper Chehalis); the sides of Muskrat's tail were cut off, making it slim, because he kept complaining about its width (James Bay Cree; Ellis 1989:25); Ant has a narrow waist because she kept tightening her belt during the contest with Bear over the length of a day (Upper Chehalis); Bullhead has a broad mouth because she fell on her face when she fell from the sky when the arrow chain broke on the descent from recovering fire (Columbian). Such explanatory items are usually not central to the story being told but interrupt the plot in part to break tension. Jacobs (1964:336) considered them as "stylistic punctuation" for this purpose.

Various vocal techniques and mannerisms also represent features of style. Some of these, such as pauses, variations in loudness, intonation patterns, whispering, and the like have been noted above in relation to the work of Woodbury, Bright, McLendon, Tedlock, and others. A possibly universal technique is the use of rhetorical lengthening of vowels, often in falsetto voice, to indicate duration of an event or distance. Several examples can be seen in the Columbian Chipmunk text (table 8).

Origin and Maintenance of Folktales

Folktales and myths occur worldwide, and many similar stories can be found in various parts of the world. Flood stories and creation or origin legends are nearly universal, Orpheus-like stories and tales about

Coyote was a very fast runner, but some of the people were fast runners too. They kept getting closer and closer . . . and Coyote ran faster and faster. He ran through a plum thicket, and down through a ravine, trying to lose the pursuers, but they kept close after him.

He ran through the forest, and out on the prairie, but all the people were still running after him, strung out with the fastest runners in the lead, and the slower ones panting along behind. But they never gave up.

❖ 67 ❖

Penney 1953:67.

Fig. 12. A traditional Cheyenne tale of Coyote (óʔkOhómE). As a result of a drought the food supply of the people was greatly reduced; a remaining small sack of corn was being guarded by Coyote, an honored and trusted chief. However, temptation overwhelmed him and he stole the sack, but not before Mouse hid in it and bit a hole through it, causing a trail of corn to fall. In his wild attempt to escape the enraged villagers, Coyote leaped into the sky. The sack empty, he had nothing for his theft. Afterward, when the Cheyenne saw the stars in the heavens known as the Milky Way, they would remember the story of the trusted chief named Coyote who became Coyote the thief. Drawn by Walter Richard West, about 1953.

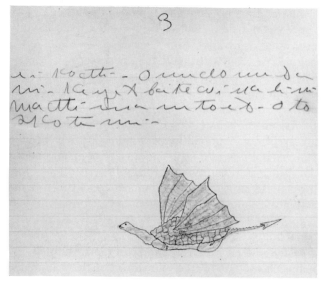

Smithsonian, NAA: top, ms. 2656:3; bottom, after Holmes 1886: fig. 412.
Fig. 13. Flying reptilians in mythology and art. top, Pencil drawing by Alfred Kiyana in the Fox text "The Man Who Was Blessed by the Evil Spirit Long Ago" of the Evil Spirit's friend, a flying snapping-turtle. bottom, Flying reptilian figure that appears on several Late Mississippian pots, A.D. 1200-1600, which is iconographically similar (Holmes 1886:401-402; Phillips, Ford, and Griffin 1951:fig. 111:g).

the theft of fire are very widespread. The question naturally arises whether these have spread from a single source or whether similar stories have developed spontaneously in several places. In the long run, the question of ultimate origin is unanswerable, although many have tried to find one. Some, particularly nineteenth-century scholars, wanted to find origins for all folklore in the great civilizations of the Near East or Mediterranean, assuming diffusion from there to the rest of the world. Others sought to find origins in "primitive" people's affinity with nature as providing a source for tales. Freudians sought to trace their origin, along with the source of dreams, to an expression of basic drives and conflicts. Related to this is the Jungian notion of the origin of folktales in dreams and the unconscious (for an application of this approach see Kimball 1989a). Yet others sought these origins in rites practiced by earlier peoples. None of these theories can be supported, and they have been generally discredited.

Rather than seek origins, many folklorists have sought to understand why similar myths and tales occur in different parts of the world. Folktales are unquestionably borrowed, being adapted to narrative and social patterns as they go. In his early work in North America, Franz Boas collected vast quantities of folklore. Besides simply wanting to preserve a record of this great folk literature, he hoped that themes found in myths would provide clues to how and from where myths were borrowed, and what this might tell about the migrations of peoples. Although the conclusions he reached have sometimes turned out to be incorrect (such as his belief that many Northwest Coast peoples, along with their myths, migrated to the coast from inland; Boas 1905:96-97), his work stimulated others to look for correlations in other parts of language and culture.

274

Nonspeech Communication Systems

ALLAN R. TAYLOR

Several nonspeech communication systems have been employed by North American Indians. The principal ones are sign language, distance signaling of various kinds, pictography or picture writing, and speech surrogates.

Sign Language

By far the most sophisticated of the nonspeech communication systems employed by North American natives is the Plains Indian sign language. The sign language is not a secondary system based on a particular language or languages, but an independently structured primary system for communicating ideas directly (West 1960, 1).

Origin

The circumstances of the origin of the sign language are unknown, although there is evidence of its existence prior to European contact (Wurtzburg and Campbell 1995). It may have originated in the communication needs of deaf individuals, or in the spontaneous signing of other particular contexts: war and hunting situations where silence was mandatory, face-to-face contacts between persons of different languages, or situations where distance prevented adequate verbal communication.

Trade may have been an important stimulus in the development of the sign language, and it was certainly an important factor in its diffusion after the rise of Plains horse nomadism.

There is some reason to believe that the sign language originated in the extreme southern fringe of the Plains, or on the Texas Gulf coast (Ives Goddard, personal communication 1970). The account of the Francisco Vásquez de Coronado expedition of 1541-1542 mentions communication with and between Texas natives by signs (Winship 1896:504, 527), and there is firm documentation for a fully developed sign language being in use in 1740 at the five San Antonio missions among the speakers of the numerous languages of south Texas (Santa Ana 1961:308). In contrast, La Vérendrye's (1927) account of his explorations on the Northern Plains (North and South Dakota) from July through September 1738 not only does not mention the sign language but also frequently records the difficulty of communicating with the natives without interpreters. Another report mentions the use of sign language among speakers of the large number of mutually unintelligible languages of eastern Texas in 1805 (Sibley 1832), a year when Meriwether Lewis and William Clark on the upper Missouri still made extensive use of interpreters, though sign language was by that time present in the area. Additional indications of southern origin are the well-documented northward spread of the sign language during the nineteenth and twentieth centuries and the fact that most of the groups on the Plains in the historical period are known to have been late arrivals from other areas. The spread of the sign language throughout the Plains and the Northern Plateau, which continued in the 1990s, probably dates from the 1740s.

Extent of Use

A 1956 survey revealed that sign use was not only still widespread in the Northern Plains of the United States but also had even spread well into British Columbia and the Canadian Plains (Alberta, Saskatchewan, Manitoba) where it was almost, or completely, unknown in the nineteenth century (West 1960, 2:62-68).

During the period when the sign language was the Plains lingua franca, not all tribes using the sign language were recognized as equally proficient. The Kiowas are frequently mentioned in the nineteenth century as excellent sign talkers, and this tribe was certainly a center of dissemination of sign use in the Southern Plains. The Comanches in the south, and Cheyennes and Arapahos in the Southern and Central Plains, were also highly regarded (Mallery 1881:318; Dodge 1882:385; Clark 1885:39; Critchley 1939:44).

Reliable nineteenth-century testimony on sign proficiency in the Northern Plains is lacking, but there can be no doubt that there were centers of dissemination of sign use there also. The Crows are credited with dissemination of sign language use into the Plateau, and the various Blackfoot-speaking tribes were intermediaries for the spread of sign language use farther north (see West 1960, 2:65-67).

In 1956, the Crows were regarded by other northern Indians as the most proficient sign users, with honors shared by northern Cheyennes and Blackfeet. Also generally proficient and avid sign users were the Assiniboines, Northern Arapahoes, and Crees. While not noted for sign use as tribes, excellent individual sign talkers were found also among the Nez Perces, Flatheads, Gros Ventres, Oglala Sioux, and Hidatsas. Sioux tribes other than the Oglalas were found to be rather undistinguished sign users (West 1960, 2:65).

Men appear to have always been the primary users of the sign language, but this is no doubt partly a function of the greater role men played in Plains Indian public life. However, women were not forbidden knowledge of the language, and their use of it is attested by both nineteenth and twentieth-century writers (Dodge 1882: 374-375; Mallery 1881:391; Clark 1885:407; West 1960, 2:78; Farnell 1990).

It is likely that deaf people have always used the sign language, a use that continued on Plains reservations in the late twentieth century.

Sign use was formerly not restricted to particular situations. Signing was of course usual when interlocutors had no language in common, but observers have frequently noted the use of signs between members of the same tribe, even between close friends or family members. It is clear that the sign language was, and is, regarded as an additional communications channel, in no way subordinated to the auditory (table 1) (Farnell 1990:10).

Where sign use was common in the late twentieth century as among the Crows, it was widely used for ordinary conversation (Raymond G. Gordon, personal communication 1972). Sign use also became a symbol of Indian identity, and formal signing was used at

Table 1. Correlation of Various Factors with Sign Use on the Northern Plains

Factor	Number of informants rated	Number of informants showing correlation	Percentage of total[a]
Fluency in sign language	111	97	87
Fluency in English	111	61	55
Knowledge of two or more Indian languages	111	20	18
Wide travel	111	47	42
Knowledge of sign language acquired away from home or from outside visitors	111	16	14
Deaf or in close contact with deaf person	111	21	18
Loss of hearing after learning sign language	111	7	6
Speech accompanying signs	122	53	43
Female informant	122	23	19
Informant under 60	122	28	23
Informant between 60 and 80	122	72	59
Informant over 80	122	22	18

SOURCE: West 1960, 2:62, 77

[a]Percentages have been recalculated for the entries where the test group was 111, due to unexplained arithmetic errors in West's tabulation.

ceremonials and powwows all over the Plains and other areas (fig. 1) (West 1960, 2:62,71; also Anonymous 1972; David S. Rood, personal communication 1972; and Farnell 1990:11-12).

Smithsonian, NAA: top, neg. no. 4A and 1A; center right: 91-8605; center left, Hamburgisches Mus. für Völkerkunde, Hamburg; bottom left, *Tundra Times,* Anchorage, Alaska.

Fig. 1. Sign communication. top, Tendoy (Lemhi Shoshone) (vol. 11:290–291), demonstrating signs, with the corresponding engravings from Garrick Mallery's (1881:458, 471) study. The sign on the left, used by the Shoshone and Bannock to denote the Kootenai people, was based on "their peculiar manner of holding the long bow horizontally in shooting" (Mallery 1881:471); the sign on the right, used by the Shoshone and Bannock to denote the Crow people, was an imitation of bird wings flapping. Mallery, a statistician and army officer working for the Smithsonian Bureau of Ethnology (Darnell 1969:3,131-132), used studio portraits of tribal delegates, made in Washington, D.C., as the basis for his illustrations, replacing Euro-American clothing with traditional Plains clothing such as this fringed buckskin shirt. Photograph by Charles M. Bell, Washington, 1880. center left, Max Bald Eagle (Oglala Sioux) on the right conversing with Narse (Arapaho), a visitor from the Wind River Reservation, Wyo. Although their spoken languages were completely different, the photographer reported that "they understood each other very easily and very quickly" (Hasberland 1986:141). Photograph by Frederick Weygold, Pine Ridge Reservation, S. Dak., 1909. center right, Gen. Hugh Scott watching Bitter-Root Jim (Flathead) telling a story in signs. Scott was a fluent sign talker and scholar of the sign language. He arranged a sign talking council at Browning, Mont., during which 14 members of as many different tribes were filmed telling stories and conversing in signs (Harrington 1938). Photographed in Browning, Mont., 1930. bottom left, Betty Thompson (Yakima), on the left, signing the Lord's Prayer, while Sally Hudson (Koyukon) recites it in Koyukon as the invocation for the Sixth Annual Conference of the North American Indian Women's Association. Photography by Lael Morgan, Cherokee, N.C., 1976. bottom right, Plains Sign Language being used in a conversation between members of the same tribe. Joseph Attocknie (Comanche) on the right is using the sign for 'horse' with his wife's grandfather, Oliver Pahopony (Comanche). Photograph by Thomas Kavanagh, Apache, Okla. 1985. Traditional storytelling events also remain important occasions for the use of the sign language (Farnell 1990,1995). (Caption based on information from Brenda Farnell, 1995.)

277

Nature of Signs

Sign systems and signs are of different types. Some signs are purely symbolic, in that the relation between the sign and its referent (what it denotes) is arbitrary and merely conventional. Other signs are iconic, that is, they bear some physical resemblance to whatever it is they refer to. An example of an arbitrary symbol is the use of a white flag to signal a surrender or truce. A familiar iconic sign is the extended left arm used to indicate an imminent left turn. Even iconic signs are to a degree conventional, since it is generally arbitrary which notional features of the referent are referred to, or which expressive signs are used in the representation.

Sign language, to a much greater degree than spoken language, can make effective use of iconicity, because it is easy to devise and use gestures that have iconic resemblance to their referents. This explains why individuals without a common verbal language universally resort to gestures, and why they often communicate so well in this fashion. And in fact the Plains sign language is overwhelmingly iconic, though this does not mean that convention has not been a significant factor in its evolution and use. On the contrary, many signs are purely conventional, while others that are basically iconic have to be understood in terms of culturally dictated conventions.

Mechanics of Sign Production

The production of signs can be described in terms that are often analogous to those used in the description of speech. In sign language articulation the analogue of the movable articulator in speech—the tongue and lips—is the hand or the hands. These may adopt several basic shapes—for example, open, clenched, one or more fingers extended with others closed, one or more fingers curved (West 1960, 1:42 and Mallery 1881:548 give sketches; see also Farnell 1990:xi-xiv).

No other part of the body is used as an articulator: even the rare full arm motions are accompanied by a distinctive hand gesture. Even signs for actions characteristic of the feet, such as walking and dancing, are made with the hand.

The hands may be used in a stationary position, moved up, down, forward, back, to the left, to the right, and, in concert, parallel to each other, or crossing over each other. Motion may be distinctively rapid and tense, slow and lax, or neither; distinctively far out from the body, close in, or neither; proceeding, again distinctively, in straight lines, through curves, in circles, trembling, or wagging from the wrist (West 1960, 1:42).

The analogue of the place of articulation in verbal speech (e.g., the palate, the upper teeth) is the point at which a gesture is made, or to which the hand moves during the gesture. West (1960, 1:20 f.) posits 40 of these, which he terms referents.

In most cases the place of articulation is a place on the signer's own body. Utilization of the back of the body as a place of articulation is rare, both due to its general inaccessibility to the articulator and to its invisibility to the interlocutor. When this part of the body is used, as in the sign for 'tail', the signer must turn so as to present his profile while signing. The place of articulation is often not actually touched; instead the hand is only brought into close proximity to the relevant body part. When the place of articulation is not a part of the body, it is somewhere in the space near the body, as in indicating a height in the sign for 'child'.

Signs are generally formed in a continuous flow, but sentences and longer segments of discourse may be set off by brief pauses, when the hands and arms are dropped to the speaker's sides or lap, or used for some other, nonsignaling purpose (West 1960, 1:53-55; Seton 1918:xlii-xliii).

A few examples of individual signs illustrate both the mechanics of the formation of signs and their conventional or iconic nature. The prose descriptions that follow are based on Clark (1885).

'Bad' (fig. 2). Conception: suddenly thrown away. Hold both closed hands, back up, in front of body, hands at same height and equidistant from body; move hands outward, downward, and simultaneously open them with a partial snap, terminating the movement with fingers extended and separated. This sign is frequently made with one hand only.

'Buffalo'. Conception: horns of buffalo. Bring hands, palms toward and close to sides of head, index fingers partially curved, others and thumbs closed; raise hands slightly and carry a little to the front.

'Dog' (fig. 2). Conception: dog drawing tepee poles. Bring right hand, back up, in front of and a little lower than left breast, first and second fingers extended, separated, and pointing to left; draw hand to right several inches, keeping index about parallel to front of body.

'Eat' (fig. 2). Bring tips of fingers of nearly compressed right hand, in front of, close to, and a little over

top, Tomkins 1926:10, 20, 22; center, after West 1960; bottom, Brenda Farnell, communication to editors 1995.
Fig. 2. Representations of Plains sign language. top, Iconic representations supplemented by verbal descriptions (Tomkins 1926; see also Mallery 1880; Seton 1918, Hadley 1893). Solid lines indicate the beginning position and dotted lines the end position of hand motion; arrows and other lines show the path of movement. center, Analysis into distinctive components of position and motion represented by arbitrary phonetic symbols and diacritics (West 1960). bottom, Representation using Labanotation, a movement script developed by Rudolph Laban (Farnell 1990). Graphic signs in Labanotation represent details of handshapes, movement paths, locations in space, and the body parts involved (Farnell 1994, 1995, 1995a; Brenda Farnell, communication to editors 1995).

Tomkins

BAD

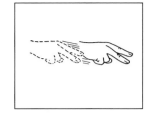
DOG

EAT

BAD (meaning: thrown away). Hold right fist near breast. Throw it out and down to right and while doing so open the hand.

DOG (meaning: wolf drawing tepee poles). Draw right hand across in front of body from left to right

EAT With nearly compressed right hand, pass tips of fingers in curve downward past mouth two or three times by wrist action.

West

ʔɛm̃ɛtɛ

BAD

ʔ	clench fist, palm active
ɛ	down
m	curved movement
~	from the wrist
ɛ	down
ɫ	half-spread extended fingers, cup palm strongly
ɛ	down

"Fist clenched, palm down, move hand in an arc with w[r]ist extension down fast; open and spread fingers, palm down" (West 1960:112).

cöno

DOG

c	extend second and third fingers, clench others
ö	left
n	straight movement
o	right

"Index and Mid-finger spread, extended to Left, move hand far to right" (West 1960:70).

ɫɔ·ƛ̃ɔɛ·

EAT

ɫ	all fingers pursed to a point, tips active
ɔ	toward referent
·	close to referent
ƛ	mouth as referent
m	curved motion
~	from the wrist
ɔ	toward referent
ɛ	down
·	short motion

(All fingers pursed to a point, tips near and toward mouth, move hand down in a short arc with wrist extension towards mouth.)

Farnell

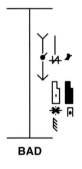
BAD

DOG

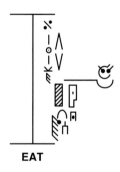
EAT

KEY TO SYMBOLS

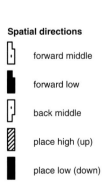

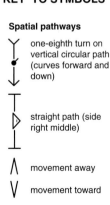

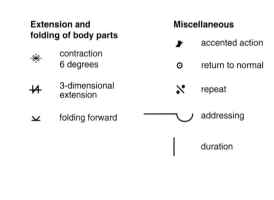

Body parts

	wrist (right)
	hand (right)
	index and second fingers
	thumb touching fingertips
	palm
	eyes

Spatial directions

	forward middle
	forward low
	back middle
	place high (up)
	place low (down)
	side left middle

Spatial pathways

Y	one-eighth turn on vertical circular path (curves forward and down)
T	straight path (side right middle)
Λ	movement away
V	movement toward

Extension and folding of body parts

※	contraction 6 degrees
	3-dimensional extension
	folding forward

Miscellaneous

	accented action
o	return to normal
	repeat
	addressing
	duration

279

mouth, back of hand to left and front, fingers pointing toward face and a little downward; by wrist action move hand downward, tips passing a little below and close to mouth. To represent eating rapidly, or eating a great deal, as at feasts, or many people eating, both hands are used, left being fixed similarly to right, hands passing round each other by rotary motion.

'Question'. Hold right hand, palm outward, well out in front of body, about height of shoulder, fingers and thumb extended, separated, and pointing upward. If addressee is close, turn hand slightly, by wrist action, two or three times, moving it also a trifle to right and left. If addressee is distant, hold hand higher, and move well to right and left.

'Trade' (also 'buy', 'sell'). The usual sign in the north is to bring both hands in front of body, index fingers extended, others and thumbs closed, back of right hand to right and front, back of left to left and front, right hand some inches higher than left, right index over left; lower right hand, crossing index fingers at right angles between first and second joints, side of right index resting on left.

In the south the more common gesture is to hold hands in front of shoulder, back of right to right, left to left, index fingers extended and pointing to front and upward, other fingers and thumb closed; move right hand to left and downward on curve, right hand passing above but close to left; terminate movement when wrists are crossed.

Language Structure

One of the major discoveries of West's (1960) study of the sign language is that it exhibits the same duality of patterning as spoken language. From around 80 mutually contrasting basic gestural units (kinemes) are built all the basic meaningful signs (sign morphemes). Typically, sign morphemes include three or four kinemes. Sign morphemes may be free—able to function alone as words—or bound—always used in conjunction with another sign or signs to constitute a word.

Almost all morphemes in the sign language have lexical rather than grammatical meaning. (Examples of English morphemes with lexical meaning are *tree* and *today*, with grammatical meaning, the *-ed* that indicates past tense with many verbs, and the *-s* that indicates plural number with most nouns.) Indeed, the only sign with pure grammatical meaning is the sign for 'question', which signals that the sentence that follows it is a question rather than a statement. Its meaning, according to context, is 'who', 'what', 'which', 'when', 'where', or 'why'.

Some lexical morphemes include obligatory repetition or features of sign execution that signal iteration, distribution, intensity of action, or other attendant circumstances—aspectual meanings that are often carried

in the grammatical apparatus of spoken languages. Other lexical morphemes can acquire similar aspectual meanings by the same kinds of variation on their normal execution, as in the case of 'eat' (fig. 2). Given the general character of the system, this should probably be regarded as a kind of lexical derivation (i.e., 'eat', 'gorge oneself', 'bolt down', etc.) rather than as a grammatical process.

Lexical means are also employed to express other grammarlike notions. Tense is indicated by separate words with temporal meaning such as 'now' or 'long ago'. Negation is expressed by a separate sign for 'no' immediately following the sign it negates. Commands may be expressed by the use of a sign such as 'push' added to the principal sign, or by nothing at all, the context alone supplying the meaning. Gender is sometimes expressed by different signs for male and female individuals, but sex difference may also be indicated by separate signs meaning 'male' and 'female'. Plural is expressed by the sign for 'all' added to other signs. Person is expressed by pointing; when someone not present is the subject, an appropriate noun must be used. Comparison is accomplished by the addition to the word compared of signs for 'big', 'little', or 'strong'. Possession is indicated by using the sign for 'possess' before the sign for the thing possessed.

Words in sign language consist of from one to several sign morphemes. When two or more sign morphemes function together as a word, it is highly characteristic that the first morpheme announces a topic, which is then followed by comments about the topic, which become progressively more specific and which eventually define it. Thus, "A is an X that has m" is a sufficient specification of A if A is the only X that has m (West 1960, 1:121). This is the same principle followed in the nomenclature system of scientific taxonomy. Some examples will make this clear (signs are represented by English words separated by +): 'Black person': 'Whiteman' + 'black'; 'sister-in-law': 'brother' + 'possess' + 'wife'; 'freeze': 'cold' + 'water' + 'hard'.

In the case of phrasal (compound) signs there is often some redundancy. A maximal example of this kind is the phrasal sign meaning 'skunk' (elements in the compound have been numbered for ease of reference): 1. 'small animal' + 2. 'plumed tail' + 3. 'striped back' + 4. 'stink, smell' + 5. 'bad' + 6. 'egg' + 7. 'smash'. 'Skunk' is also unambiguously indicated by the following portions of the above compound: 2; 1 + 3; 3 + 4; 2 + 4; 1 + 4 + 5; 2 + 4 + 5; 1 + 6 + 7; 2 + 6 + 7; 3 + 4 + 5; 3 + 6 + 7; 4 + 5 + 6 + 7 (West 1960, 1:121).

As can be seen from these examples, the order of constituents in a word is generally fixed. The order of words in the sentence, on the other hand, is fairly, though not totally, free. The rules, briefly stated, seem to be: topics precede qualifiers and complements (i.e., nouns precede modifiers and verbs); logical objects precede or follow their governing (verbal) sign, the exact position in each case possibly idiomatic; obligatorily the sign for 'question' begins an interrogative sentence, and the sign for 'no' directly follows the sign it modifies.

Two sentences will give an idea of sign syntax. 'It looks like rain today; we'll start our deer hunt tomorrow.' 'perhaps' + 'rain' + 'day' + 'now' + 'I' + 'all' + 'go' + 'tomorrow' + 'hunt' + 'deer'. 'Did you speak to me? Yes, I told you to follow me.' 'question' + 'you' + 'speak' + 'I'. 'yes' + 'I' + 'say' + 'you + 'follow' + 'I' (Tomkins 1929:95). See also Farnell (1990:200-251) for detailed grammatical analysis of a portion of a signed text.

Lexicon

The size of the lexicon of the sign language is as difficult to establish as that of a spoken language, and for the same reason: this area of any functioning language must be an open system, expandable at will to deal with newly arisen needs.

A count of the entries in a dictionary can give only a very rough idea of the size of the lexicon of a language, since there is no guarantee that the dictionary contains all, or even most, of the vocabulary in regular use.

The largest published sign vocabulary is that of Mallery (1880), which contains around 3,000 entries (fig. 1 top). That obtained by West (1960, 1:2) from his Arapaho informant numbered around 3,500. The Clark (1885) dictionary contains just short of 1,100 items, including nearly 100 personal and place-names. The Scott film dictionary contains around 1,200 items. Small collections are those of Seton (1918), Hadley (1893), Tomkins (1929), and Hofsinde (1956), which contain, respectively, around 700, 600, 500, and 400 words.

In seeking to interpret these figures, it is useful to know that around 750 signs are considered a minimum for communication by deaf Americans using the American Sign Language (Fant 1964). This suggests that the Clark and Scott collections represent—as their authors apparently intended—a minimum for effective communication in signs. The two larger collections, on the other hand, probably approach in size the upper limit of the working vocabulary of most sign users.

More significant than the size of the sign lexicon is its semantic adequacy. Obviously, not all topics can be discussed in the sign language with equal ease; West (1960) observed strong tendencies to include or exclude some semantic areas from spontaneous sign use.

Easily expressed were spatial relationships, physical activities, enumeration, specification, and comparison.

Animal names and descriptions of their characteristics and movements were abundantly represented in the texts. Personal and place-names were frequent. Humorous anecdotes were the favorite sort of story related in signs, a continuation of one of the principal nineteenth-century uses of the sign language (Dodge 1882:337).

Difficult to express were cause and effect statements, and emotive and evaluational terms were scanty. Plants and shrubs were little represented as named species, nor were there many terms for other natural categories.

Many changes in culture history are reflected in the sign lexicon; for example, the sign for 'dog' clearly reflects the prehorse period of Plains culture. Study of the obsolescence of some signs, and their replacement by others, would be as revealing of the dynamics of the sign language and of the cultures of its users as is the diachronic study of spoken languages.

Exact information is also needed on the extent of synonymy of generic (as opposed to definitional) signs. True synonymy seems to be rare. When different signs are said to have the same meaning, one is usually a regionalism, and most competent sign users recognize it as such (West 1960, 2:58).

Dialects

The fact of ready communication in signs between Indians from various parts of the trans-Mississippi region led most early observers to assume that the sign language was uniform throughout the West. But in the sense of a shared corpus of mutually intelligible signs, the sign language cannot be said to be uniform, as a comparison of published descriptions of signs will indicate.

In addition to the tribal and regional differences in lexicon that can be identified (for example, the sign for 'trade'), there exist many differences in body stance and technique of sign execution that are peculiar to particular tribes and to individual signers. These differences in vocabulary, formulation of signs, and speed of delivery are in every way analogous to dialectal and individual variation in spoken language.

The only delineation of sign language dialects that employed dialect distance testing was that of West (1960). Previous classifications had been based on informant testimony or on the intuition of the commentator (Clark 1885:13-14).

In testing for dialect distance, West asked his principal informant, an accomplished sign interpreter, to attempt to translate filmed sign language texts collected throughout the northern Plains. The amount of information transferred was assumed to be in direct proportion to dialect distance; low transfer of information was taken to indicate a distant dialect.

Based on these tests, West concluded that the northern Plains is divided sharply into two dialects: the "North Plains dialect," covering most of the area of the survey; and the "far northern" or "story-telling dialect," so named for the chief use of the sign language in that area, which is restricted to the far northern and northeastern fringe of the Plains in Alberta and Saskatchewan.

Most signs used in the North Plains dialect cluster around a norm that West (1960) terms the "Plains Standard"; this norm centers on the Crow and extends into the Plateau, northern Great Basin, and Northern Plains. The greatest variation away from the norm was encountered among the Sioux, the Oglala excepted.

West (1960, 2:65-69) assumes that a dialect highly similar to that of the Northern Plains is used in the Southern Plains, centering on the Kiowa or Comanche. Besides differences in vocabulary, speed of delivery contrasted in the two dialect areas. West (1960, 2:75-78) found a correlation between rapid delivery of signs, with dignified and restrained movement of the hands, and use of the Plains Standard, while slower execution of signs, with larger, freer movements, characterized informants from the far northern dialect and from along the eastern fringes of the Northern Plains.

Stylistic Differences

It is to be expected that signing techniques would differ from individual to individual. The same signer also varied his vocabulary and style from conversation to conversation in response to the proficiency and vocabulary of his interlocutor (Clark 1885:6; Mallery 1881:337). Dodge (1882:388) quite properly compared these differences to the differences in handwriting among Whites. Both abbreviation and calligraphic embellishment of signs are mentioned by numerous observers. For example, a sign in rapid conversation might differ as much from its formal version as a small "b" of a rapidly written document differs from the printed capital "B" (Dodge 1882:388).

The line between individual and regional styles is difficult to draw. For example, one manner of abbreviation was the restriction of signing to the right hand (Dodge 1882:389-390). This may be a regional feature: southern Indians tend to small movements, the use of single hand and finger positions, while northern Indians use the whole hand, two hands, and larger movements (Critchley 1939:43-44; see also Seton 1918:xxvi-xxvii).

Another characteristic of sign execution that has regional and personal variation is the accompaniment of signs by running speech or special facial expressions. (This use of speech is not to be confused with the accompaniment of some signs by onomatopoeic sounds intended to clarify the sign—as a characteristic bark with a sign for 'coyote' or 'fox'.)

Dodge reported that nineteenth-century Indians often accompanied signs by speech with the same meaning (Dodge 1882:384), and the accompaniment of signs by spoken language was a frequently encountered phenomenon in West's (1960) survey. Usually the commentary was in Indian languages, although some was in English. In some cases the speech paralleled the signs, in others it consisted of comments about what was being signed, and there were even cases when the speech and signs differed in content (West 1960, 2:76). In the late 1980s, Furbee (Bolen and Furbee 1991) found extensive use of signs by elderly Otoe-Missouria Indians while speaking English. The Otoe-Missouria, who now reside in Oklahoma, were never particularly proficient in sign use. The use of accompanying speech was especially common in the story-telling dialect. Many informants who maintained silence while signing indicated that they felt this was more proper and elegant (West 1960, 2:77).

Proven instances of the grammatical or syntactic influence of spoken languages on the structure of the sign language are rare, despite assertions to the contrary (Harrington 1938:28; Kroeber 1958:13). Possible instances are the use of the sign for 'possess' between the possessor sign and the possessed sign (see the example for 'sister-in-law'), which duplicates the stem and affix structure of possessed nouns in some Indian languages, for example, Siouan, and the placement of qualifier signs following the sign qualified, again suggestive of Siouan languages.

Spoken and sign lexicons do not exhibit the same degree of independence from mutual influence. Sign neologisms are sometimes sign translations of spoken words, so that sign talkers from different linguistic backgrounds would have different signs for some concepts (Clark 1885:58). Besides tending to create synonymous signs, this must have been a stimulus also to the creation of new spoken words, formed by back translation from signs. This process must be responsible in great measure for the high congruence of meaning in metaphorical terms and idioms found throughout the spoken languages of the Plains. Term after term is found to contain the same semantic elements in a number of different Plains languages, such as 'night sun' for moon, 'big horn' for Rocky Mountain sheep, 'flat water' for the Platte River.

Distance Signaling

None of the distance signaling systems used by American Indians approached the complexity or flexibility of the sign language. Generally speaking, distance signaling was capable of transmitting only limited kinds of information: meanings were either conventional, for example, announcing the presence of game or enemies, or else specific, assigned by prior agreement to particular signals.

Both audible and visual signals were used, and most were obsolete by the 1970s.

Audible signals were simple, limited for the most part to imitations of bird calls or animal cries. These signals were a widespread device for communication between scouts and their war parties or between members of war parties. Whistling was also used for attracting attention when stealth was not required (see, for example, Gatschet 1891:70; James 1830:90).

The kinds of visual signaling that could be used were largely dictated by terrain and visibility. Smoke and fire signals were used throughout the continent. The use of arm, body, blanket, and mirror signals was best in areas such as the Plains and Southwest, where wide visibility obtained.

Visual signaling was done whenever possible from prominent points, such as hills or headlands. Echoes of this use are still to be seen in place-names such as Signal Butte, Nebraska. Signaling from promontories not only ensured wide visibility but also signified that the act was intentional. Solitary Indians or small groups of Indians were always extremely careful otherwise to conceal their movements and fires from possible hostile view.

In smoke signaling a fire was fed with some poorly combustible fuel such as damp grass or green leaves and branches. By choice of fuel and manipulation of the smoke with a blanket, many different colors and shapes of smoke column could be produced. Gatschet (1891:70) reports the use of more than 20 different kinds of smoke signals by the Karankawa of Texas. Custer (1876:217-218) gives a detailed description of the mechanics of smoke signaling and indicates that such signals were visible on the Plains as far away as 50 miles.

Signaling by hand-held mirrors, though possible only in bright sunlight, was valued because of the speed and the great distance traversed by the flash. Mirror signals were used to attract attention, as in courtship, or for announcing approaching trouble or the discovery of game (Clark 1885:414). Dodge also indicates that movements of mounted (Sioux) warriors were sometimes directed by mirror signal (Dodge 1882:431).

Body signals used for long-distance communication employed gestures and bodily attitudes combined with different kinds and directions of gait. Usually the signaling was done by lookouts or scouts, although any person needing to communicate with others at a distance might do so on occasion.

Two types of body signal, sometimes combined, were used to indicate the discovery of enemies or game: the scout either either ran or rode in a circle, or

moved in a zigzag line. The rapidity of the motion indicated the importance and necessity for immediate action. Very fast motion called for desperate exertions (Clark 1885:411). The scout indicated "all is well" by coming into full view and remaining there for a time (Dodge 1882:432; Clark 1885:411).

Certain signs from the Plains sign language were also used in distance signaling. The motions were often rendered more conspicuous by holding a clearly visible object such as a blanket, shield, or lance. There were other "blanket signals" with no analogue in the sign language; one of these was described as follows (Clark 1885:412-413): "*To ask how many have been killed.* Make sign for 'question'; then grasp blanket with right hand, arm extended to full length, held in front of and nearly vertical from shoulder; then bend the body forward and swing blanket to front on the ground. In reply the number killed would be expressed by the number of times the blanket was swung forward on to the ground." (See, for example, Lowie 1935:227.)

Pictography

Widespread use was made in North America of physical representation of ideas. Representations ranged from largely sterotyped symbolization of things, such as totems or personal and tribal names (fig. 3), social position, or impending conflict, to productive representational systems by which almost any message could be conveyed. Only the last type, of which pictography is the most important, will be described.

Since pictographic representation is largely iconic, it is independent of particular languages. Any individual capable of recognizing the pictures (often reduced to bare essentials) can deduce the subject of the representation, although he may not be able to infer all the details, which often had to be supplied by the reader from his prior knowledge of the immediate context and the social system, customs, and traditions of the writer. It is for these reasons that ancient pictographs are largely undecipherable.

Many kinds of natural materials have served as the surface for inscription; smooth rock faces, the ground, snow, trees stripped of their bark, bark, smoothed wood, hide, bone, ivory, horn, shell, and paper are the most common. Pictures were scratched, engraved, burned, drawn, or painted on the surface, the method chosen depending on the nature of the writing surface, the availability of writing materials, and the preferences of the writer. Sometimes several techniques were used simultaneously. Direction of writing was not standard: it was in lines from either left or right, sometimes alternating, in clockwise or counterclockwise circles, or in spirals beginning at the center of the writing surface.

All picture writing, no matter how diverse, has two

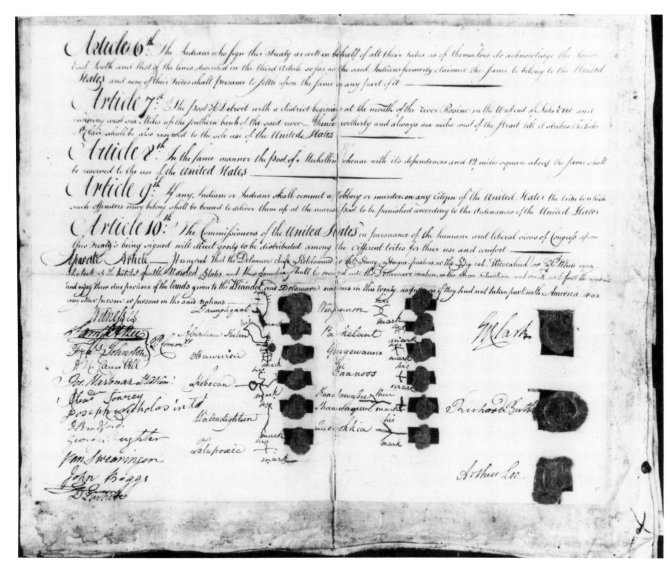

Natl. Arch.: RG 11, Indian Treaty No.10.

Fig. 3. Signature page of a treaty agreement between the Wyandot, Delaware, Chippewa, and Ottawa tribes, and the United States of America, Jan. 21,1785. Made at Fort McIntosh, downriver from Pittsburgh in the Northwest Terr., the treaty gave up lands that later became the state of Ohio; it required in part that hostages be given until the prisoners "white and black" (Kappler 1904-1941, 2:7) were restored, placed these groups under the protection of the United States, established boundary lines for a reserve for the said tribes, and set up a post at Detroit. It was signed with the pictographic marks of the head men, Daunghquat, Abraham Kuhn, Ottawerreri, Hobocan, Walendightun, Talapoxic, Wingenum, Packelant, Gingewanno, Waanoos, Konalawassee, Shawnaqum, and Quecookkia. United States representatives who signed were George Rogers Clark, Richard Butler, and Arthur Lee.

principal intents: to aid in the recollection of information, or to convey new information. Its function in the one case is mnemonic, in the other, notificational.

Mnemonic pictography was used chiefly for keeping records, generally as reminders for individual use. Originally these were largely religious and historical in nature, but after White contact commercial transactions were also so recorded. The use of mnemonic pictography in postcontact religions is known from the Micmac, for Roman Catholic texts (Ganong 1910:21-32), from the Central Alaskan Yupik, for Moravian religious texts ("Native Writing Systems," fig. 19, this

vol.), and from the Western Apache, for the prayers of the visionary Silas John Edwards (Basso and Anderson 1973; vol. 10:486-487).

The religious use of picture writing was to maintain the correct content and order of chants and spells (sometimes in archaic language), which were memorized. Carefully executed birchbark rolls were widely used for this purpose in northeastern North America; the texts were incised or painted on the bark (for a structural analysis and bibliography see Fulford 1989). Paper was used in the same way after contact (Hewitt and Fenton 1945:302).

The bark pieces varied in size from a few square inches for a charm record to a roll three or four feet wide and up to 15 feet long for a record of a complex ceremony (Kinietz 1939:39). In the texts, each phrase was represented by a single picture intended to recall that phrase to an instructed person as he proceeded through the ceremony. The individual picture was often meaningless outside its proper context, as was demonstrated by Mallery (1893:670) with Roman Catholic Micmacs trained to use a set of mnemonic "hieroglyphics" that had been standardized by missionaries. Informants could give words corresponding to particular pictures only by starting at the beginning of the prayer or hymn and proceeding to the picture for which a meaning was requested (fig. 4).

Figures 6-7 are examples of historical records (see also "Personal Names," figs. 2-3, this vol.). Such records were kept by all prominent Plains warriors. Originally they were painted in color on hide; after contact they were often done in pencil or watercolor on paper, for example, in bound ledger books. Tribal chronicles (often called "winter counts" after their Dakota name) were kept in the same way, with each year represented by one or two pictographs depicting

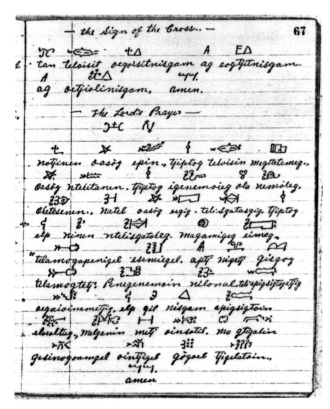

Smithsonian, NAA:ms. 4634:67.
Fig. 4. The Sign of the Cross and Lord's Prayer in Micmac hieroglyphics, copied from Kauder (1866), with an interlinear transcription in the Micmac practical orthography used in Roman Catholic publications. Copy made by Frank Navin (Micmac) in about 1943.

SONG FOR THE MEDICINE HUNTING, PARTICULARLY FOR BEAVERS.

Fɪɢ. 1.   2.   3.   4.

Fɪɢ. 1. Che-mahn-duk-kwa ne-muh-kwi-o-sa ne-ah-hah-wa, ne-an-hah-wa, ne-muh-kwi-o-sa, *he-ah-whe-he-ah!*

A bear, I walk like a bear myself; myself, I walk like a bear.

The medicine man here speaks in his disguise of a bear skin. Ne-muh-kwi-o-sa might be more literally translated " I walk a bear;" it is the compound of neen-muk-kwaw and pa-pah-mo-sa, or ba-bah-mo-sa. Che-mahn-duk is commonly used, in these songs, for a bear.

2. Ah-wes-sie hi-ah-wa-nah bah-twa-we-tahng-gah? Waw-wash-kesh e-wah bah-twa-we-tahng-gah.

A beast, what beast comes calling? It is a deer comes calling.

The word bah-twa-we-tahng-gah is expressive not only of the peculiar call of the male deer, at the rutting season, but also of the circumstance that the animal is approaching the speaker: were he going the other way, or even standing still, the word would be different.

3. O-num-mun-nah nin-go-che-we-nah. [Twice.]

This yellow ochre, I will try it.

This is the same, in all respects, as No. 18, in the preceding song to Na-na-bush.

4. Wun-ne ho-i-yahn, wun-ne ho-i-ah-na nah-we-he-a he-o-ge-mah-wah ka-be-waw-bum-me-kwain wun-ne-hoi-yah nah-we-ne-a.

I disguise myself to cheat you, so that only a chief, if he sees me, can know who I am.

The hunter, to deceive the animal he wishes to kill, puts on the dress of a white man, or assumes the appearance of some

Lib. of Congress: Tanner 1830:363.
Fig. 5. Pictographs used as mnemonics for an Ottawa hunting-medicine song. The pictographs were carved on a flat piece of wood, one for each of the 21 verses of the song, which was used especially for beavers. A bar after the ninth figure indicated the point when the dancing began. The corresponding verses and their translations were provided by John Tanner, who probably also copied the figures from the original. Tanner, a captive in a small band of Ottawa and Ojibwa hunters west of Lake Superior, about 1791-1820 (vol. 4:689), provided extensive examples and explanations of Indian pictographic writing from a native perspective.

memorable events that occurred during that year. Several Plains calendars of this kind are in existence; see Bad Heart Bull and Blish (1967), Wildhage (1988), and Feraca (1994) for samples and bibliographies. Petersen (1971) contains a useful dictionary of motifs and their connotations used by Arapaho, Cheyenne, and Kiowa pictographers during the third quarter of the nineteenth century.

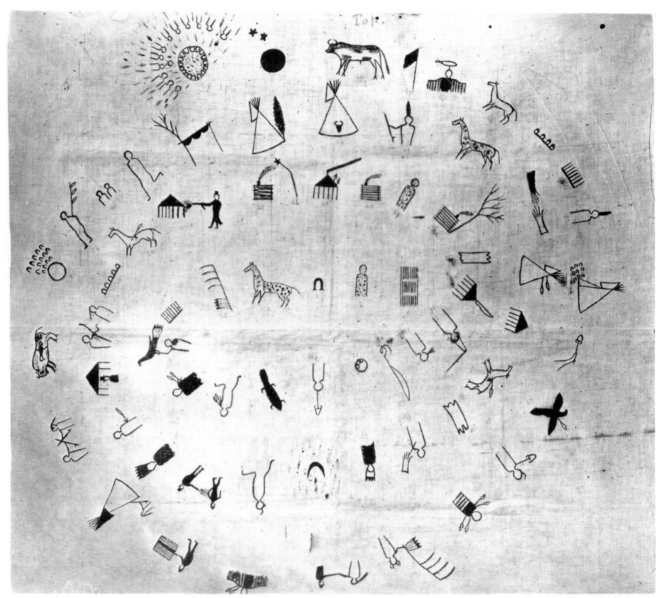

Fig. 6. Winter count of Lone Dog (Yanktonai Sioux) for 1800-1871. The original was a painted buffalo hide, which was probably buried with its owner (Raymond DeMallie, communication to editors 1995). The tracing was made about 1871 by Lt. H.T. Reed, U.S. Army, at Fort Sully and Fort Rice, Dak. Terr. (Mallery 1877: pl. 1, 3-23). The figures representing the years are in the form of a spiral running counterclockwise, the first year being at the inner point of the spiral. The first figure, 30 parallel black lines in 3 columns with the outer lines being joined, represents 30 Sioux who were killed in 1800-1801 by the Crow Indians. The next figure, with dotted head and body, represents the 1801-1802 smallpox epidemic. Next to this figure is a horseshoe, representing the period 1802-1803 when horses with iron shoes, which were previously unknown, were stolen from Whites. The next to last figure, a solid black circle and stars, represents a total eclipse of the sun in 1869. The final figure shows an attack on the Crow by the Teton Sioux in 1870-1871.

Figure 8 is a copy of a Passamaquoddy shop account made in Maine in 1888 (Mallery 1893:260). These records, kept by illiterate Indians, are of interest because of their mixture of aboriginal ideographic devices and symbols with numeric value, the idea for which was borrowed from Europeans.

Notificational pictographic texts were equivalent to letters; in aboriginal times they were left where the intended recipient would find them, or they were conveyed to him by a third person. In the early reservation period such messages, written on paper, were even sent through the U.S. mails (Mallery 1893:363). The usual message was a notice of a visit, of departure (with direction or destination indicated), of condition (starvation, illness), or of warning.

A concise description of the nature and use of such pictographic messages was given by Tanner (1830: 165):

Fig. 7. Ledger drawing by Howlingwolf (Cheyenne). One of 69 drawings known by this artist (Szabo 1989, 1994) it depicts a buffalo hunt, butchering of a buffalo, and an Indian man on a hill looking through binoculars. Pictographic conventions indicating movement are the W-shaped footprints for buffalo, the U-shaped footprints for horse, and the short lines for the men's footprints ("Discourse," fig. 11, this vol.). Pencil, crayon, and ink drawing done at Ft. Marion, Fla., 1876. (For the pictographic signature of Howlingwolf, see "Personal Names," fig. 4, this vol.)

As I was one morning passing one of our usual encamping places, I saw on shore a little stick standing in the bank, and attached to the top of it a piece of birch bark. On examination, I found the mark of a rattle snake with a knife, the handle touching the snake, and the point sticking into a bear, the head of the latter being down. Near the rattlesnake was the mark of a beaver, one of its dugs, it being a female, touching the snake. This was left for my information, and I learned from it that Wa-me-gon-a-biew, whose totem was She-she-gwah, the rattlesnake, had killed a man whose totem was Muk-kwah, the bear. The murderer could be no other than Wa-me-gon-a-biew, as it was specified that he was the son of a woman whose totem was the beaver, and this I knew could be no other than Net-no-kwa. As there were but few of the bear totem in our band, I was confident the man killed was a young man called Ke-zha-zhoons. That he was dead, and not wounded merely, was indicated by the drooping down of the head of the bear.

Figure 9 is a Mandan letter to a trader. This letter is of interest because it illustrates the (rare) graphic representation of a sign from the sign language.

By their very nature, pictographs share much with graphic art, and it is in this light that many surviving pictographs (especially on rock surfaces) are still appreciated even after their intent is lost.

Speech Surrogates

A speech surrogate is a signaling system in which individual structures of spoken language are themselves symbolized in some way. Most modern writing systems are speech surrogates, since individual morphemes, syllables, or sounds are represented by graphic symbols.

Whistle Speech

The only speech surrogate independently invented by North American natives is the "whistle speech" of the Mexican Kickapoo (Hurley 1968). Although living since the mid-nineteenth century in the Mexican state of Coahuila, these people are historically from the

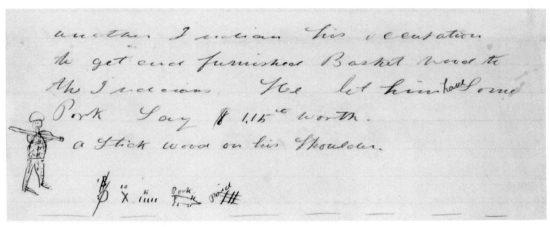

Fig. 8. Copy of pictographic entry in a shop account kept by an illiterate Passamaquoddy, sent to Charles G. Leland. The text reads: "another Indian his occupation to get and furnished basket wood to the Indians. He let him have some pork say $1.15 worth." The explanations "a stick wood on his shoulder," "1$," "10," "5," "pork," and "paid" were added by the copier, who was another Passamaquoddy. The Indian is identified by the stick of basket wood he carries. The value of the pork he was given on account is indicated by a ring with a line across it to denote $1.00, a cross to represent 10 cents, and 5 short vertical lines indicate an additional 5 cents, followed by the outline of a pig. The grid to the right denotes that the account is closed. Collected by Garrick Mallery in 1888.

Fig. 9. A Mandan letter to a trader (Maximilian 1839-1841:657). The cross at the center represents the sign-language sign for "trade" or "exchange." To the left of the cross are the objects offered for barter: a gun and 30 beaver pelts. To the right are the objects desired: a white (?) buffalo skin and the skins of a weasel and an otter. Collected by Prince Maximilian Wied-Neuwied about 1833-1834.

region just south of the Great Lakes.

Kickapoo whistle speech imitates certain characteristic features of the Kickapoo language in notes produced on the hands, which are cupped to form a chamber into which air is blown by placing the lips against the knuckles of the thumbs. Pitch is regulated by lifting the fingers of one hand from the back of the chamber. "Whistling" is thus a misnomer, since this is analogous to fluting in both production and sound. (See Ritzenthaler and Peterson 1956:61 for a photograph of a whistler.)

Whistling and fluting were widespread in North America as an adjunct to courtship, and Kickapoo whistle speech is clearly an outgrowth of this, made possible by the development in the Kickapoo language of sufficient prosodic contrasts.

Whistle speech is used almost exclusively in connection with courtship; both sexes use it, although it is usually males who compose whistled messages. Messages generally consist of standard phrases such as 'come on!' and 'what's keeping you?', but Ritzenthaler and Peterson (1954:1088) report that a full conversation can be conducted in whistle speech. One brief

study of Kickapoo whistle speech has been made by a professional linguist familiar with the Kickapoo language (Voorhis 1971).

A sentence in whistle speech consists of a sequence of notes of various lengths and pitches. If the shortest notes are said to have a length of one mora, then the six different notes encountered can be described as follows: one mora with high pitch, one mora with low pitch, two morae with high pitch, two morae with low pitch, two morae with falling pitch, and three morae with high pitch.

Notes within a word are separated by a brief silence with glottal closure or by one of several other apparently freely substitutable phenomena. Words are separated from each other by a longer silence. Voorhis (1971) transcribes whistle speech using an ⟨o⟩ for each mora of a note, a ⟨q⟩ for the transitional silence with glottal closure, an ⟨h⟩ for the silence without glottal closure, and a space for longer silence. The acute accent ⟨´⟩ is used to indicate a mora with high pitch, the grave accent ⟨`⟩, a mora with low pitch.

Notes of two morae with falling pitch are interpreted as a high followed by a low-pitched mora. An utterance final vowel is represented by a long, drawled óò, which may imitate the level or high falling pitch that occurs on the last vowel in an emphatic Kickapoo sentence.

Two examples of whistled and spoken Kickapoo follow, with accents indicating pitch changes added to the spoken forms (Voorhis 1971:239-340):

Whistled: óóqòhó óó qóqóóqòòqòò qóòhóò.
Spoken: *kéehtèná êena ketaahkwèehtai. kwéèse.*
'Are you really angry at me, darling?'

Whistled: óhóóhò hóóóqóhóóqó qòòqóhòòqóò.
Spoken: *ténaamì néiikamaaki pòohkámàaki.*
'My! I like to eat peaches!'

Aleut Semaphore

Another very different kind of speech surrogate is the wigwag semaphore of the Aleuts of Umnak, Alaska (fig. 10). The semaphore was invented by Afenogin Ermelov and others after a U.S. Coast Guard base was established on Unalaska Island during World War I (Ransom 1941; Laughlin 1980). Moreover, the wigwag would have been impossible if the Aleuts had not already possessed writing. The wigwag went out of use after two-way radios became common and has been obsolete since World War II.

The encoding system used by the Aleuts was quite different from that used in Euro-American semaphore, where the association of arm positions to letter values is conventional. In the Aleut semaphore the arm and body positions attempted to reproduce the shapes of the Cyrillic letters used in writing Aleut.

288

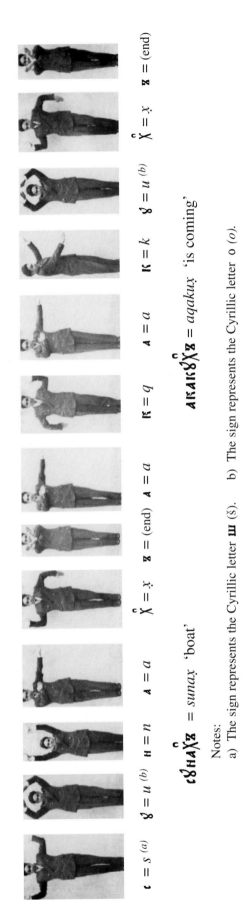

$t = s$ $^{(a)}$
$\underset{c}{\text{ʁ}} = u$ $^{(b)}$
$\text{н} = n$
$\text{а} = a$
$\underset{c}{\text{х}} = x$
$\text{ʁ} = $ (end)
$\text{а} = a$
$\text{а} = a$
$\text{ʁ} = q$
$\text{а} = a$
$\text{к} = k$
$\underset{c}{\text{ʁ}} = u$ $^{(b)}$
$\underset{c}{\text{х}} = x$
$\text{ʁ} = $ (end)

$\underset{c}{\text{г8на}}\underset{c}{\text{х}}\text{ʁ} = sunax\text{ }$ 'boat'

$\text{аʁак8}\underset{c}{\text{х}}\text{ʁ} = aqakux\text{ }$ 'is coming'

Notes:

a) The sign represents the Cyrillic letter щ (š).   b) The sign represents the Cyrillic letter o (o).

Fig. 10. Aleut semaphore message. The signs spell out the Eastern Aleut sentence *sunax aqakux* 'the boat is coming'. The end of each word is indicated by a sign based on the Cyrillic hard sign, made with several rapid passes of the hands back and forth before the chest. Ardelion Ermelov, photographed by Jay Ellis Ransom, Seattle, Wash., 1940.

Additional Illustrations

Illustrations of nonspeech communication may be found in other *Handbook* volumes:

Pictographic Signatures

White Swan's (Crow) painting of the Battle of the Little Bighorn with his pictographic signature (vol. 4:177).

Signatures of Delawares, Shawnees, and Iroquois on a treaty with the British (vol. 4:189).

Signatures of Ottawas, Wyandots, Chippewas, Munsee and Unami Delawares, Shawnees, and Potawatomis on a treaty with the U.S. (vol. 4:198).

Personal mark carved in a hunting lance shaft of a Bering Strait Eskimo (vol. 5:290-291).

Hopi petition with pictographic signatures (vol. 9:528).

Eastern Abenaki signature marks (vol. 15:144).

Signatures of Virginia Algonquians (vol. 15:245).

Signature of Seneca leader (vol. 15:356).

Signature marks of Iroquois (vol. 15:431).

Mnemonic Pictographs

Iroquois pictographs copied by the French (vol. 15:299).

Pictographs used to record Ojibwa Midewiwin songs (vol. 15:755).

Saulteaux birchbark scrolls used by a Mide priest for training (vol. 6:253).

Nisenan dunning sticks used as debt reminders (vol. 8:393).

Eastern Miwok invitation string with knots representing days before the event begins (vol. 8:410).

Pima calendar stick, which has symbols that represent years and events (vol. 10:157).

Potawatomi curer's stick with medicinal recipes (vol. 5:735).

Cane with representations of 50 Iroquois chiefs' titles (vol. 15:427).

Yupik Eskimo storyknife drawing (vol. 5:239).

Wampum

Iroquois wampum belts (vol. 15: 423, 429, 439, 474, 477).

The Classification of the Native Languages of North America

IVES GODDARD

From the time of first contact, European observers were aware that Native American languages were sometimes similar to each other and sometimes dissimilar. Out of such observations grew classifications of these languages into sets of related languages, or linguistic families. Through the years, with improved knowledge and techniques, these classifications have been broadened and putatively extended back more deeply in time and have become more complex in their internal subgrouping.

During the seventeenth and eighteenth centuries observations of language relationships were generally incidental to work on the study and description of specific languages. More comprehensive attempts at classification began toward the end of the eighteenth century and culminated in John Wesley Powell's (1891) classification, which recognized 58 distinct families. After Powell, efforts were made to group these families into larger units, with a wide range in the degree of acceptance of the proposed groupings. Work by historical linguists on the reconstructible histories of the families led to refinements in their internal subclassification and fuller, and in some cases quite detailed, accounts of the sequences of innovations that constitute their linguistic history.

Linguistic classification has always been based on similarities and dissimilarities in words and grammatical elements. At first, the accuracy of phonetic recording and grammatical analysis was often poor, and the observations of similarities between languages were unsystematic. Early writers often perceived multiple relationships or "affinities" between languages and sets of languages, a perception made possible both by the lack of any objective criteria for evaluating the relative significance of the observed similarities and by the common acceptance of the belief that languages were subject to changes caused by cultural factors and contact with other languages. This belief sometimes led to the conclusion that general features of grammar should be avoided as evidence for linguistic relationship, all the more so since such features were thought to be basically the same throughout the continent, though the existence of similarities in specific grammatical elements, if such could be found, was generally considered significant (Haas 1969). Observations of similarities became more reliable with the general improvement in phonetic recording and, concomitantly, grammatical analysis that began toward the end of the nineteenth century, and especially with the contemporaneous development of historical linguistics as a discipline. Historical linguistics furnished techniques for reconstructing rather than merely inferring linguistic history, and hence for distinguishing borrowed from inherited elements and for demonstrating that some similar features in languages were older than others and thus more likely to be shared inheritances from a common ancestor language.

A conservative consensus classification of the native languages of North America, based on studies available in 1995, is presented in the "Introduction" and on the volume map.

From the Beginnings to Powell

First Families

From the time of the first European knowledge of the languages of North America through the time of the appearance of the first comprehensive linguistic classification by Albert Gallatin (1836) (table 1), only a small number of families were recognized: (Central and Eastern) Algonquian, (Northern) Iroquoian, Eskimoan, Siouan, Catawban, Muskogean, and (northern) Athapaskan. Even these were incompletely known, and additional languages were linked with them in the following decades. A preliminary version of Gallatin's classification, now lost, had been sent to Alexander von Humboldt in 1823 and was used by Balbi (1826:279; Gallatin 1836:1); an early version was also printed for circulation with a War Department questionnaire (U.S. Department of War. Office of Indian Affairs 1826). Gallatin's most important predecessors were Barton (1797, 1798) and J.C. Adelung and J.S. Vater (1806-1817, 3, pt. 3); the basis for the classification by Constantine S. Rafinesque (1832-1833:6-8) is unknown, and it is generally considered to fall outside the scientific tradition. Gallatin (1848) issued a revised classification that incorporated the results of Horatio Hale's work on the Northwest Coast (table 2).

• ALGONQUIAN   From early in the seventeenth century the French in New France and the English in New

290

Table 1. Gallatin's First Classification

Gallatin's names	Handbook names
I. Eskimaux	Eskimoan
II. Kinai	Tanaina (Athapaskan)
III. Athapascas	Athapaskan (part)
IV. Algonkin-Lenape	Algonquian (part)
V. Iroquois	Northern Iroquoian
VI. Sioux	Siouan
VII. Catawbas (with Woccons, XIX)	Catawban
VIII. Cherokees	Southern Iroquoian
IX. Chahtas	Western Muskogean
X. Muskhogee	Eastern Muskogean
XI. Utchees	Yuchi
XII. Natches	Natchez
XIII. Adaize	Adai
XIV. Chetimachas	Chitimacha
XV. Attacapas	Atakapa
XVI. Caddoes	Southern Caddoan
XVII. Pawnees	Northern Caddoan
XVIII. Salish	Salishan (part)
XIX. Woccons (in Catawba family, VII)	(in Catawban)
XX. Fall Indians	Gros Ventre (Algonquian)
XXI. Black Feet	Blackfoot (Algonquian)
XXII. Shoshonees	Shoshone (Uto-Aztecan)
XXIII. Atnahs	Shuswap (Salishan)
XXIV. Straits of Fuca	Makah (Southern Wakashan)
XXV. Wakash	Nootka (Southern Wakashan)
XXVI. Salmon River	Bella Coola (Salishan)
XXVII. Koulischen	Tlingit
XXVIII. Chinooks	Chinookan
XXIX. Queen Charlotte's Island	Haida

SOURCE: "General Table of the Tribes, of which Vocabularies are Annexed" (Gallatin 1836:305-306).

Table 2. Gallatin's Second Classification

Gallatin's names	Handbook names
I. Eskimaux	Eskimoan
II. Kenai	Tanaina (Athapaskan)
III. Athapascas	Athapaskan
IV. Algonkins (includes Blackfeet and Shyennes)	Algonquian
V. Iroquois	Northern Iroquoian
VI. Sioux	Siouan
VII. Arrapahoes (and Atsinas or Gros-Ventres)	Arapaho (Algonquian)
VIII. Catawbas (includes Wookons)	Catawban
IX. Cherokees	Southern Iroquoian
X. Chocta-Muskhog (Floridian)	Muskogean
XI. Uchees	Yuchi
XII. Natchez	Natchez
XIII. Adaize (Adayes)	Adai
XIV. Chetimachas (Chetimaches)	Chitimacha
XV. Attacapas (Attakapas)	Atakapa
XVI. Caddos	Southern Caddoan
XVII. Pawnees	Northern Caddoan
XVIII. Koulischen	Tlingit
XIX. Skittagets (Skittagete)	Haida
XX. Naas (Naass)	Tsimshian
XXI. Wakash	Southern Wakashan
XXII. Kitunaha	Kootenai
XXIII. Tsihaili-Selish	Salishan
XXIV. Sahaptin	Sahaptian
XXV. Waiilatpu	Cayuse and Molala
XXVI. Tshinooks	Chinookan
XXVII. Kalapuya	Kalapuyan
XXVIII. Jacon	Alsean
XXIX. Lutuami	Klamath
XXX. Saste	Shasta
XXXI. Palainih	Palaihnihan
XXXII. Shoshonees	Shoshone (Uto-Aztecan)
Coco-Maricopas	Maricopa (Yuman)

Unclassified for lack of data	
Coosadas and Alibamous	Koasati and Alabama (Muskogean)
Kiaways	Kiowa (Kiowa-Tanoan)
Kaskaias	Kiowa Apache (Athapaskan)
Panis	Wichita (Caddoan)
Loucheux	Kutchin (Athapaskan)
Eutaws	Ute (Uto-Aztecan)
Cumanches	Comanche (Uto-Aztecan)
Apaches	Apache (Athapaskan)

SOURCE: "The Families of Languages as far as Ascertained" (Gallatin 1848:xcix-cix).

NOTE: Gallatin (1848:c) appended a disclaimer that "The languages of California have not been sufficiently investigated to arrange them according to families." The geographical labels of his table are here omitted, and variant spellings and statements of inclusion from his discussion are added, as is the listing of the Coco-Maricopas.

England recognized the relatedness of the Algonquian languages they came into contact with in their respective areas, and their distinctness from the Iroquoian languages. From at least the time of the visit of Gabriel Druillettes to John Eliot in 1650, French and English missionary linguists were aware of the close affinity of the Algonquian languages in the two areas (JR 36:90; Powicke 1931:55). As the French came in contact with other Central Algonquian languages around the upper Great Lakes, their close similarities and inclusion in the same group became evident. Louis-Armand de Lom d'Arce, baron de Lahontan (1703, 2:195), used the name *Algonkin* for this grouping, taken from the name of the Algonquin people of the Ottawa River valley, whose language was the one in the family that the French had studied the earliest and most intensively. The relationship of Central and Eastern Algonquian was explicitly recognized by Jonathan Edwards, Jr.

(1788:5-7), Adelung and Vater (1806-1817, 3, pt. 3:341-342), and Heckewelder (1819:106-112), who called the family Lenape, after the self-designation used by the Delaware. Gallatin (1836:21, 305-306) refers to this grouping as Algonkin-Lenape. He had vocabularies of Blackfoot and of Gros Ventre ("Fall Indians"), which he knew to be dialectally related to Arapaho, but did not recognize their Algonquian affinity (Gallatin 1836:132-133). On the basis of eight Cheyenne chief's names appearing in an 1825 treaty in Lakhota translation (Kappler 1904-1941, 2:232-234), Gallatin (1836:124, 379) listed a "doubtful" classification of Cheyenne as Siouan. In his later classification Gallatin (1848:xcix, civ, cvii, cx-cxii, cxiv-cxv) put Blackfoot and Cheyenne in Algonquian, but Arapaho was apparently first classified as Algonquian by Robert Gordon Latham (1856:62-64; 1860:315-316, 330-332) and Johann Carl Eduard Buschmann (1859:610-611). Henry Rowe Schoolcraft (1851-1857, 3:404) had asserted the affinity of Arapaho with Cheyenne in 1853.

- IROQUOIAN The relationship between Huron and the other Northern Iroquoian languages (those of the Iroquois, Erie, Susquehannock, and others) was obvious to the French from the time of first contact; it was noted in print in 1635 by Paul Le Jeune (JR 8:114-116). Lahontan (1703, 2:195) referred to this grouping, which constitutes Northern Iroquoian, as *Huron*, and Heckewelder (1819:105-106) and Gallatin (1836:69, 74, 305-306) called it Iroquois, extending the name used by the French for the confederacy of the Five Nations (later Six Nations). The connection between Northern Iroquoian and Cherokee (Southern Iroquoian) was first unambiguously suggested by Barton (1797:xlv, lxvii-lxviii; Gallatin 1836:91-93) but was not firmly established until Hale (1883a:26-28) and Albert Samuel Gatschet (1886) published comparisons of words and grammatical prefixes. In 1778, David Zeisberger had written that Cherokee was a mixture of other languages, including a little Shawnee and Iroquois and a great deal of Wyandot (Zeisberger 1910:142; cf. King 1977); the contemporary publication of this observation omits the qualification of differing proportions of admixture (Loskiel 1789:26). Similarly, Barton's observation is tempered by the fact that he also found affinities between Cherokee and Creek, Chickasaw, and Choctaw and between Muskogean and Northern Iroquoian languages (Barton 1797:lxviii, 1798:21-22) and, in fact, perceived widespread links among Indian languages and between them and languages in Asia.

- ESKIMO-ALEUT The Eskimoan languages are similar enough so that their relationship was obvious as soon as there was an opportunity to compare them. Gallatin (1836:9-13) understood the full extent of the family, including Siberian Yupik. The affinity between the lan-

guages of the Eskimos and the Aleuts was recognized in 1778 by Capt. James Cook (Cook and King 1784, 2:522, 3:554-555; Beaglehole 1967, 3:468), whose conclusions rested on observations that included a comparative vocabulary, though a skimpy one. Aleut was not covered by Gallatin, whose survey did not include the Aleutian Islands. Ferdinand Petrovich von Wrangell (1839:71-72, 1839a:122-124, 1970:15-16, 1980:62-63) conditionally accepted Cook's opinion that "the language of the Eskimos" was spoken on the Aleutian Islands, but he emphasized the differences between the languages (cf. Adelung and Vater 1806-1817, 3, pt. 3:458-460). By 1845 Latham (1860:272, 378) could state that the clear affinity between Eskimoan and Aleut had "long been recognised"; for Latham these were part of a larger grouping that also included Athapaskan, Eyak, and Tlingit. Veniaminov (1846a:27) noted the similarity in grammatical structure and divergence in lexicon of Eastern Aleut and its Eskimoan neighbor, Pacific Yupik. Buschmann (1859:697-702) argued against the relationship of Eskimoan and Aleut, but it was accepted by Berghaus (1852:53), though concededly on the evidence of grammatical structure rather than lexicon, and by Dall (1870:265; 1877:9). It appears to have become widely accepted without the publication of any but the slenderest supporting linguistic data. The few grammatical and lexical similarities between Eskimoan and Aleut that Rasmus Rask had noted in a manuscript of 1820 remained unpublished for a century (Thalbitzer 1921).

- SIOUAN AND CATAWBAN The relationship of the bulk of the Siouan languages was recognized by Gallatin (1836:120-128, 306), who referred to them as Sioux or "the Great Sioux Family." He grouped Catawba and Woccon together, without naming the unit they formed (Catawban), but he did not link these to Siouan (Gallatin 1836:87, 306; Adelung and Vater 1816, 3 pt. 3:308).

- MUSKOGEAN Gallatin (1836:101, 119, 306) stated that he thought the materials he had were sufficient to prove a common origin for Choctaw-Chickasaw and "Muskhogee" (Creek, to which he linked Hitchiti), referring to this grouping as Choctaw Muskhogee. An earlier observation by Barton (1797:lxviii) pointed to the same conclusion. Nevertheless, deferring to "received opinion," Gallatin listed these segments of Muskogean as two separate families. He also suspected that Alabama and Koasati belonged in the same family, though he lacked a vocabulary of either (Gallatin 1836:96). In his later classification Muskogean was given as a unit, with the name "Chocta-Muskhog," though in a list of families about which he conceded there could be some doubt (Gallatin 1848:c).

- ATHAPASKAN Following information and remarks from the explorers Alexander Mackenzie and John Franklin, Gallatin (1836:16-20) classed together the bulk of the Athapaskan languages of Canada under the name "Athapasca." This family was defined to include all the languages spoken from Hudson Bay to, and in some cases beyond, the Rocky Mountains that were south of the Eskimo and north of a line drawn westward from the mouth of the Churchill River, except for Kutchin, for which Mackenzie had no data. Gallatin (1836:14, 20) also recognized Tanaina ("Kinai") and Eyak ("Ugaljachmutzi") as a "a distinct family," and saw affinities between this and both Eskimoan and (Canadian) Athapaskan. Later Gallatin (1848:7) concluded that Tanaina and Eyak had "great affinity" with Athapaskan and some admixture of Eskimo. Hale added to the Athapaskan family the Kwalhioqua, Clatskanie, and Upper Umpqua languages, spoken in Washington and Oregon, using the name "Tahkali-Umkwa" for a western segment of the family that included them and Carrier (Hale 1846:202, 204). In reporting on Hale's work, Gallatin (1848:9, 77, 105) concurred and extended the name Athapasca to encompass these Northwest Coast languages.

Diversity Revealed

In the period between Gallatin and Powell scholars became aware of many previously unknown languages in the western parts of North America. Classification was to a large extent a matter of recognizing the distinctness of many individual languages and small contiguous groups of very similar languages. New languages were also added to already recognized families, and some additional widespread families were proposed. One active scholar in this work in the mid-nineteenth century was Latham (1860), who proposed affiliations as part of a broad typological and evolutionary hypothesis encompassing all the languages of the world. Although he was the first to publish a number of correct determinations or hypotheses of relationship, he also misclassified some languages and proposed deeper and multiple connections that were incorrect. For example, he wrote of Kootenai that "like all the languages of America, it has numerous miscellaneous affinities" (Latham 1862:396). Buschmann and Gatschet also often emphasized the multiple resemblances of languages. In surveying work of this kind inevitably more attention has tended to be paid to the suggestions that turned out to be correct than to those that never gained wider acceptance.

• NORTHWEST COAST The first major advance in this period was Horatio Hale's (1846) report of the results of his fieldwork with the United States Exploring Expedition, which Gallatin (1848) presented at length. Gallatin's 1848 classification superseded one he had included in an 1846 letter to the commissioner of Indian affairs that was published only later and imperfectly (Schoolcraft 1851-1857, 3:397-402). Hale furnished a nearly complete classification of the languages of the Northwest Coast and the Plateau, except for the northernmost part of the area. Within the area he covered Hale missed only Northern Wakashan and the Chimakuan family, for which he had no data. The non-Salishan character of Chemakum, at least, was noted by George Gibbs (1855:431) and by Myron Eells (1880:52), who reported the linguistic relationship and tradition of common origin of the Chemakum and Quileute. The two branches of the family are indicated with the joint name Chemakum on a later map compiled by Hale (1891).

• SALISHAN Hale (1846:205-212, 224) was the first to recognize the Salishan family, encompassing all branches including Bella Coola, for which he had Alexander Mackenzie's vocabulary from Burnt Bridge ("Friendly Village"; vol. 7:336). He omitted only the languages spoken inside Vancouver Island, along the straits of Georgia and Juan de Fuca, for which he had only vague reports (Hale 1846:220-221). Hale called the family "Tsihaili-Selish," combining names for the coastal Chehalis and interior Flatheads. He cited similarities among these languages in inflectional paradigms as well as in vocabulary as evidence for their relationship and formulated a few sound correspondences for Tillamook (Hale 1846:536-537). William Fraser Tolmie's vocabulary of Bella Coola ("Billechoola") (Scouler 1841) was put by Gallatin (1848:c, 77, 103) in his Naas family with Tsimshian and the Northern Wakashan language Heiltsuk, but Latham (1848:155, 1860:250) correctly identified it as the same language as that of Mackenzie's Friendly Village. Latham's (1848:157, 1856:71, 1860:252, 338-339) linking of Shuswap (the "Atnah" of Mackenzie) with Clallam (the "Noosdalum" of Tolmie [in Scouler 1841:242-247], a misprint for "Noosclalom" [Tolmie and Dawson 1884:12B]) and his inclusion in Salishan ("the Atna group") of these and Halkomelem (the "Kawitchen" of Scouler) filled in some of the gap left by Hale.

• SOUTHERN WAKASHAN Hale (1846:220) recognized that a vocabulary he had collected at Nahwitti on the northern end of Vancouver Island was "closely allied" with John R. Jewitt's vocabulary of Nootka, but although Nahwitti is in Kwakiutl territory the vocabulary he obtained there was in fact also Nootka. He was thus unaware of the distinctness of Northern Wakashan. From Jewitt's information it was known that Nootkan extended as far as the Makah on the south side of the Strait of Juan de Fuca. Hale suggested the name Nootka Family for this grouping, which he assumed covered all of Vancouver Island, but he did not include it on his map. Latham (1860:251-252, 340) grouped a number of Nootkan vocabularies as Wakash; some of these also were collected outside Nootkan territory and reflect the use of Nootka as a trade language.   *293*

• SAHAPTIAN, CHINOOKAN, AND KALAPUYAN Three other small families, each consisting of very similar, adjacent languages, were noted by Hale (1846:569). He called the Sahaptian family Sahaptin, his name for the Nez Perce, its other branch consisting of the varieties of the language later commonly called Sahaptin, Hale's Walawala (Hale 1846:212-214). He recognized the Chinookan family, which he called Tshinuk, uniting Lower Chinookan and Upper Chinookan (Hale 1846:214-215, 562). Hale also appears to have recognized the unity of the two northernmost Kalapuyan languages, Tualatin(-Yamhill) and Central Kalapuyan.

• SHOSHONEAN Although not included in his synoptic table, Hale's discussion shows that he recognized a relationship between the two major segments of what would later be called Shoshonean, the Numic and Takic languages (Hale 1846:218-219, 566-567, 569). He tempers this observation by asserting that although these languages showed "evident traces of connexion," this evidence probably would not "justify . . . classing them together as branches of the same family" (Hale 1846:219, 567). Latham (1860:303-304), referring to Gallatin's (1848:61-62) reprinting of Hale, agreed that there was "a *certain amount* of likeness" between the languages of the Takic branch and Shoshone.

• WAIILATPUAN Hale united the Cayuse and Molala languages under the label Waiilatpu, his name for the Cayuse (Hale 1846:214, 561, 569). He did not discuss the evidence for this relationship, though he did note that Cayuse and Nez Perce show resemblances in numerals and pronouns but not elsewhere and suggested that these might be due to borrowing.

Hale concluded that for several languages of the Northwest, the Plateau, and northern California the evidence he had did not permit them to be grouped with any others. These were Kootenai ("Kitunaha"), Yaquina ("Iakon"), Klamath ("Lutuami"), Shasta ("Saste"), and Achumawi ("Palaihnih") (Hale 1846:204-218, 569). Latham (1860:341-342) saw affinities among Klamath, Shasta, and Achumawi, and between these and Nez Perce, Cayuse, Shoshone, and Yaquina (all as documented by Hale's vocabularies).

Latham (1860:250-251, 339) recognized Tsimshian as distinct on the basis of a single vocabulary collected by Tolmie, and his location of Northern Wakashan ("Hailtsa") on northern Vancouver Island and the mainland to the north shows that he understood the extent of its inclusiveness. Tolmie and Dawson (1884:113B-114B, 116B-119B, map) clearly delimited these groupings, calling them Tshimsian and Kwakiool, respectively. Tolmie and Dawson also named as distinct Tlingit ("Thlinkit"), Haida, Athapaskan ("Tinnē"), Southern Wakashan ("Aht"), and Kootenai ("Kootenuha"); they differentiated five segments of Salishan without uniting them: Bella Coola ("Bilhoola"), northern Central Salish ("Kawitshin"), Lushootseed ("Niskwalli or Skwalliamish"), Tsamosan ("Tsheheilis"), and Interior Salish ("Selish"). They did not identify Chimakuan.

• CALIFORNIA AND THE SOUTHWEST After the annexation of Texas in 1845 and the Mexican Cession of 1848, materials on the languages of California and the Southwest became increasingly available. William W. Turner's classification of the vocabularies collected by Amiel W. Whipple on the Pacific Railroad Survey Expedition of 1853-1854 established the core of a number of families in the Southwest. He grouped the Northern Caddoan languages (represented by Pawnee, Arikara, and Wichita) under the name Pawnee, a relationship apparently previously known to Indian traders as it was mentioned by Josiah Gregg (1844, 2:251), though with no supporting data. Turner pointed tentatively to some "affinities" between Caddo (Southern Caddoan) and Northern Caddoan, but he was uncertain whether they indicated common origin or long contact; Latham (1856, 1860:367-368, 400) considered the relationship of these languages to be probable. Turner also put together the Keresan and Yuman languages for which he had vocabularies (Whipple, Ewbank, and Turner 1855:65-70, 86-90; 95-103). Turner was the first to establish the connection between the Apachean languages and the northern Athapaskan languages (Turner 1852; Whipple, Ewbank, and Turner 1855:81-85).

• NORTHERN CALIFORNIA The classification of the languages of California in the second half of the nineteenth century was largely a matter of pulling together vocabularies of neighboring and generally similar languages into small groupings and distinguishing them from one another. Important early work of this kind was done by Latham (1860) and Stephen Powers (1872, 1873-1874, 1877), and subsequently a large collection of vocabularies was assembled by Powell and published in a classificatory arrangement (in Powers 1877). Gatschet (1877) provided an early synthesis, based on the work of Gibbs, Latham, H.H. Bancroft, and Powers, but "frequently" corrected following unnamed "men of undoubted competency" (Gatschet 1877:153-154). He relied on Powers's (1872, 1873-1874) general articles in *The Overland Monthly* and published his paper before they appeared in revised form with Powell's collection of vocabularies (Powers 1877). Additions and further refinements were provided by Gatschet (1882).

The Athapaskan languages of California were recognized as such as their vocabularies became available, beginning with Hupa (Whipple, Ewbank, and Turner 1855:84-85; Latham 1860:314). Tolowa and Wailaki were added by Powers (1877:115-116), who also recognized the affinity with these of other small groups nearby. Latham (1860:342-343) had been unable to classify Tolowa, having only an imperfect vocabulary obtained from a Yurok (George Gibbs in Schoolcraft

GODDARD

1851-1857, 3:422). Gatschet (1877:163, 165) accepted the Athapaskan affiliation of Hupa and Wailaki, but demurred on the inclusion of Tolowa, as known from Gibbs's vocabulary, and of some of the small groups for which there was no linguistic data.

Latham (1860:343; 1862:410) recognized the affinity of Wiyot ("Weyot and Wishosk") with Yurok ("Weitspek"), revealed by similarities in body-part terms. These languages were then known from Gibbs's vocabularies in Schoolcraft (1851-1857, 3:434-445). Gatschet (1877:162-163) kept Wiyot and Yurok separate and even asserted that the words of "Weits-pek" (Gibbs's Yurok vocabulary from *wečpus* village) "totally disagree" with those of "Eurok" (Yurok, from Powers 1872, 3:530; cf. Powers 1877:44-45) and all other neighboring languages. Perhaps Gatschet was misled by Latham's (1860:344-345) mislabeling of a set of partly mistransliterated Kashaya ("Khwakhamaiu") words as "Weitspek," though the main list that Latham gives as "Weitspek" is clearly Yurok. Powell (in Powers 1877:460-473, 478-482) also kept Wiyot and Yurok separate.

Karok was set up to encompass vocabularies from several local bands, Gibbs's from the "Eh-nek . . . at the mouth of the Salmon, or Quoratem river" (Schoolcraft 1851-1857, 3:422), the only one known to Latham (1860:342), and four others (Powell in Powers 1877:447; Gatschet 1877:163).

The Pomoan languages were grouped together by Gibbs on the basis of native testimony and four vocabularies he collected (Schoolcraft 1851-1857, 3:108-110, 421-422, 428-439). Latham (1860:343-345) added Kostromitonov's Kashaya ("Khwakhamaiu") vocabulary (Wrangell 1839a:234-235) and tentatively suggested the name Mendocino for the family. Powell (in Powers 1877:491-517) published 10 vocabularies under the name Pomo, which Powers (1872, 6) had used (cf. Gatschet 1877:161-162).

Powers (1877:92; Powell in Powers 1877:474-477) speaks of the Chimariko and the Chimalakwe as sharing a distinct language, documented by a vocabulary; Gatschet (1882:255) credited him with discovering this language "entirely new to science."

Latham (1860:341-342) saw intersecting affinities among a number of the languages in the interior of Oregon and northern California first documented by Hale's (1846:569-629) vocabularies. These affinities linked Shasta, Palaihnihan, and Klamath, these three with Nez Perce (Sahaptian) and Cayuse (especially Klamath with Sahaptian), and the first group also with Shoshone and Yakonan. Later nineteenth-century classifications kept all these separate as small families or, in the case of Shoshone, as part of a larger grouping found mostly outside the area. Powers (1877:267, 274) gave the main divisions of the Pit River Indians, which included the Achumawi ("Achomâwi") and Atsugewi

("Pacamallies," "Pakamalli") branches of Palaihnihan (Gatschet 1877:164). The Shastan family was recognized as distinct on the basis of James Dwight Dana's vocabulary (Hale 1846:569-629), and the generally similar vocabularies published by Powell (in Powers 1877:243, 250, 607-613; Gatschet 1877:164).

The relationship of the Yukian languages was pointed out by Powers (1872, 5:306, 1877:197), who found lexical similarities linking Yuki, Huchnom, and Wappo; he recognized that the Yuki, Huchnom, and Coast Yuki spoke essentially the same language (Powers 1877:126). Powers called the family Yuki-Wappo, while Powell (in Powers 1877:483-489) applied the name Yuki to the family as a whole. Powers's (1872, 5) earlier name Yuka was used by Gatschet (1877:161).

The Wintuan family was proposed by Latham (1860:345-346), under the name Copeh, on the basis of vocabularies representing its three major components, Wintu, Nomlaki, and Patwin. Wintu was documented by a vocabulary from the upper Sacramento (Hale 1846:630; Gallatin 1848:122); Nomlaki by one from "near Mag Reading's," Maj. Pierson B. Reading's ranch at the junction of Cottonwood Creek and the Sacramento River (Schoolcraft 1851-1857, 4:414-415); and Patwin by one of "Copéh," the *ko·pe* tribelet on Putah Creek (Schoolcraft 1851-1857, 3:421, 428-434). Powers (1877:232) distinguished the Wintun (given as Win-tūn´ and Wintūn), comprising the Wintu and Nomlaki, from the Patwin (Pat-wīn´, Patwīn) but noted their relationship. Powell united these as the "Win-tūn´ Family" (in Powers 1877:518-534). Powers's (1873-1874, 12:530) earlier name Wintoon was used by Gatschet (1877:160-161) for the family.

Hale (1846:631-633) published without commentary a comparison of brief and imperfect vocabularies from three dialects of the Nisenan branch of Maiduan collected by Dana, "Pujūni," "Sekumne," and "Tsamak." Later writers accepted these as forming a separate family, Latham's (1860:346-347) Pujuni. Powers (1873-1874, 10:21, 1877:282-345, especially 313-314) separated the Maidu (Maidu and Konkow) and Nishinam (Nisenan) but observed that their dialects intergraded gradually and shared substantially the same numerals. Powers's (1873-1874) earlier form Meidoo was used by Gatschet (1877:159) for the family. Similarly, Powell united all branches under the label Mai´-du (in Powers 1877:586-600); he was the first writer to include a vocabulary of Maidu proper (Northeastern Maiduan).

Powers (1873-1874, 11:416, 1877:275-281) recognized Yana as distinct from other languages he knew about, calling the people Nozes or Noces (later Nozi); but Powell had no vocabulary, and the linguistic map in the volume assigns Yana territory to Maiduan. Gatschet (1877:160) tentatively assigned this group to Maiduan because of perceived similarities between their numerals, given by Powers (1873-1874, 11:417, 1877:277), and those of a Nisenan vocabulary. The distinctness of Yana was confirmed by vocabularies collected by Powell, in 1880, and Jeremiah Curtin, in 1884 (Powell 1891:135).

Washoe was first recognized as a separate family by Gatschet (1882:254-255) on the basis of a vocabulary collected by Powers in 1876 (Powers 1876). Its earlier classification as Shoshonean by Bancroft (1875-1876, 3:661; Gatschet 1877:155) does not seem to have been based on the examination of any data.

• CENTRAL CALIFORNIA   The sorting out of the linguistic families of the central California coast and contiguous inland areas first began to emerge in Latham's (1856, 1860:347-350) brief survey of a few early vocabularies. In the area where the Miwokan, Costanoan, Esselen, and Salinan languages were spoken he identified three linguistic groupings, which he called Moquelumne, Costano, and Salinas. Latham's Moquelumne comprised language samples referred to as Talatui (Plains Miwok), Tuolumne (Central Sierra Miwok), San Rafael (Coast Miwok), Tshokoyem (Coast Miwok), and Olamentke (Bodega dialect of Coast Miwok), and with less certainty Santa Clara (Tamyen Costanoan), Valle de los Tulares (Plains Miwok of the lower San Joaquin Valley), and Guiluco ("Guiloco"; probably Wappo). Latham's Costano was a "provisional division" set up as a rubric for the Indians living on San Francisco Bay, for which he had only a vocabulary of "Romonan" Costanoan (Schoolcraft 1851-1857, 2:506). Latham's (1860:350-351) "Salinas Group" included Ruslen (Rumsen Costanoan), Soledad (Chalon Costanoan), Eslen (Esselen), Carmel (Rumsen Costanoan), San Antonio (Salinan), San Miguel (Salinan), and possibly "Gioloco" (Guiluco). Latham did note similarities in some words among the languages of these three groupings, particularly among some of the languages that are in fact Costanoan, but he kept the groups separate, taking Costano to be "a transitional form of speech" between the languages spoken in various directions from San Francisco Bay.

Gatschet (1877:157-158) also noted similarities between Costanoan ("Mutsun") and Miwokan ("Chocuyem") languages (naming each group after one of its members), but although he thought that these groups "probably" went together, he considered the connection between the two a "supposition" that was not yet confirmed. At the same time he was uncertain where to draw the line between the two groups. He thought that Bodega Miwok and several other Coast Miwok varieties shared many words with both "Mutsun" and "Chocuyem" and called for grammatical information to settle the matter. Like Latham, he also failed to make a sharp distinction between Costanoan and Esselen and Salinan, including Esselen in "Mutsun"

and calling Chalon (La Soledad) Costanoan "largely intermixed with San Antonio [Salinan] elements." Powers (1877:346-347) used the name Miwok ("Mí'-wok") to include only the Plains and Sierra Miwok. This was his earlier Meewoc (Powers 1873-1874, 7; Gatschet 1877:159). Powers (1877:195) did not link these with the Coast Miwok, of whom he knew only that they spoke a language that was not Pomoan. Following Gatschet's qualified suggestion, Powell listed the Costanoan and Miwokan languages as members of a single family, which he called Mutsun (given as Mūt'-sūn) (in Powers 1877:535; Powell 1891:70). The correct demarcation between Miwokan and Costanoan was finally drawn by Curtin and confirmed by additional linguistic material collected by Henry W. Henshaw in 1888. Powell (1891:70) then separated the two groups into distinct families, overruling other staff members who argued in favor of their relationship (Gatschet 1888; Curtin 1888).

The mysterious Lord's Prayer in Guiluco, putatively a language spoken at the San Francisco Solano mission in the Sonoma Valley (Duflot de Mofras 1844, 2:391), which Latham thought might go in either his "Moquelumne" or his "Salinas" grouping, was conjecturally placed in Patwin by Gatschet (1877:161), under the name "Guilulos," and summarily declared to be Pomoan by Powell (1891:102). Apparently this linguistic sample received no further discussion in the literature, but it is most likely based on a form of Wappo, though with many unexplained features (Robert L. Oswalt, Marianne Mithun, and Sandra A. Thompson, personal communications 1993; Catherine A. Callaghan, personal communication 1994).

On the basis of two vocabularies, the Yokutsan languages were recognized as a separate group by Latham (1860:350), who called them the Mariposa languages. The extent of the family was described by Powers (1873-1874, 9, 1877:369-392) under the name Yocut (later Yokuts, "Yo'-kuts"), and Powell (in Powers 1877:570-585) added additional vocabularies. Gatschet (1877:158-159) used Yocut.

Chumashan was recognized by Latham (1860:351) under the name "Santa Barbara Group," which included Barbareno, Ineseño, and Obispeño Chumash. Powell (in Powers 1877:560-567) used the same name. Gatschet (1876:551-553, 1877:156-157; 1879:419) used the name Santa Barbara for a grouping whose core membership comprised Purisimeño, Ineseño, Barbareño, and Cruzeño Chumash, and which he suggested also possibly included Obispeño Chumash and Antoniano Salinan, which he described as showing "a pretty close relation" (Gatschet 1876:553).

The relationship of Antoniano and Migueleño Salinan was noted by Latham (1860:305-306). In a later study Salinan was subsumed by Latham (1860:350-351) in his "Salinas Group," which included

Esselen and some Costanoan languages in addition to the two Salinan languages. Antoniano Salinan, as documented by Sitjar (1861), was put with Chumashan by Gatschet (1876:553, 1877:156; 1879:419), but Powell (in Powers 1877:568) regarded the resemblances between these as too slight to posit a relationship. Vocabularies collected by Henshaw in 1884 confirmed the separateness of the Salinan family (Powell 1891:101).

Robert de Paul, Chevalier de Lamanon observed in 1786 that Esselen was distinct from all the other languages in the Monterey area (Lapérouse 1797, 2:291-292). Latham included it in his "Salinas Group," and Gatschet (1882:254) included it in "Mutsun" (Utian), in part relying on information from Felipe Arroyo de la Cuesta (1878) that Esselen was identical with the Huelel language of La Soledad, a mission where Chalon Costanoan was also spoken. Its distinctness was confirmed by additional data collected by Henshaw in 1888 (Henshaw 1890; Powell 1891:75-76).

Latham (1860:351-352, 392) pointed out the linguistic unity of Yuman, which he like Turner called Yuma. He saw evidence that the Cochimí languages Borjeño, Laimón, and Monqui also belonged in this group (Latham 1860:352-355, 393-394). Later, without citing any new evidence, he assigned all of Baja California to Yuman, including Guaicura (Waikuri), which he had earlier left separate, and Uchití (Hutchiti) and Pericú, for which there were no data (Latham 1862:426; cf. Latham 1860:353-356). The classification of Yuman was in some respects anticipated by Francisco Garcés (Coues 1900, 2:443-444) in an unpublished report of 1776, but Garcés did not explicitly distinguish the Yuman languages as a group separate from their neighbors. Garcés's listing was known to Gatschet (1877-1892, 1:388-389) from its incorporation in a manuscript report by José Cortez that was cited by Whipple, Ewbank, and Turner (1855:118-127).

• SOUTHWEST The principal linguistic divisions of the Southwest were recognized by the Spaniards, though their reports contain no linguistic data. For example, Alonso de Benavides (1916:13-30, 94-117; 1945:71) included a classification of the Pueblos into "nations," which he defined by their linguistic relationships, in his 1630 *Memorial*. He reported that the Pecos and Jemez Pueblos spoke one language, and he described the Northern Tiwa Pueblos of Taos and Picuris as being part of the Tiwa ("Téoas") nation. The Spaniards used the name Tiwa (Spanish *Tigua*) only for the Southern Tiwa pueblos of Isleta and Picuris, and in recognizing the affinity of the two branches of Tiwa, Benavides was extending his classification beyond that implied by the vernacular terminology in use at the time. In all, he distinguished the following linguistic groupings: Jemez and Pecos; Southern Tewa (Spanish *Tano*); Tompiro; Eastern Keresan (Spanish *Queres*);

Tiwa; Piro (or "Tihues"); Western Keresan (Acoma); Zuni; and Hopi (Harrington 1909:563; vol. 9:234-235). His omission of (Northern) Tewa (the later Rio Grande Tewa) was perhaps an oversight caused by his use of the name "Téoas" for Tiwa. The distinction Benavides made between the Tompiro and the Piro cannot be evaluated, as there is no linguistic material for the former and only very scanty material from the latter. The Tompiro and the Piro have been described as the eastern and western divisions of the Piro (Hodge in Bartlett 1909:426; Hodge 1907-1910, 2:261-262, 776-777); information from sixteenth-century reports hints at the possible relationships of these groups (vol. 9:236-242). The linguistic unity of Southern Tewa (Tano) and Northern Tewa was recognized by Vargas in 1692 (Espinosa 1940:76, 80; Reed 1943).

A detailed survey of the Pueblos in New Mexico by Francisco Atanasio Domínguez (1956), which appears in the journals of the Domínguez-Escalante expedition of 1776, includes the most systematic information up to that time on their linguistic affiliations. Domínguez distinguished the following linguistic groups: Tewa (*Tegua*), spoken by the (Northern) Tewa and the Southern Tewa (the Tanos of Galisteo Pueblo); Taos and Picuris (Northern Tiwa); Keresan (*Queres*), including the Rio Grande Keresans, Laguna, and Acoma; Zuni (*Zuñi*); Jemez and Pecos; Southern Tiwa (*Tigua*, at Sandia and Isleta); and Hopi (*Moqui*), mentioned as the language of a refugee group at Sandia. Domínguez (1956:207) also reported that the Northern and Southern Tiwa Pueblos spoke "substantially the same language."

Josiah Gregg's early report on the languages of the Pueblos showed only a partial and confused grasp of the diversity recognized by Domínguez, describing the Rio Grande groups as speaking "but three or four different languages" which might be distantly related: "Piro" (Tíwa), "Tegua" (Tewa), "Queres" (Keresan "and perhaps Sandía," also said to speak Tewa), and "Tagnos" (Pecos, Jemez, and Southern Tewa) (Gregg 1844, 1:269). In contrast, when Lt. James Hervey Simpson collected vocabularies of all the Pueblo languages in 1849, he correctly classified them into their lowest-level groupings: Hopi, Zuni, Keresan, and the Tewa, Tiwa, and Jemez branches of Tanoan (Simpson 1850:140-143, 1852:128-130, 1964:246-249). New Mexico governor William Carr Lane listed the Keresan, Tewa, and Tiwa Pueblos correctly in 1854, except for including Tesuque among the Tiwa, and distinguished these from Jemez-Pecos, Zuni, and Hopi (Schoolcraft 1851-1857, 5:689). Although Turner understood some aspects of the relationships of these languages, he called for more data, especially information on "grammatical structure," to permit their relationships to be ascertained (Whipple, Ewbank, and Turner 1855:93).

The unity of the Tanoan language family was determined by Gatschet, who initially referred to it simply as the "First family" of the four he identified in George M. Wheeler's Pueblo vocabularies (Gatschet in Wheeler 1875:180-187). In a compilation of vocabularies published in Germany, Gatschet (1876a:42) designated the family "die Pueblo-Sprachen im engern Sinne" ('Pueblo proper'). Later still, in a more comprehensive classification in English prepared in 1878 but not appearing until 1881, Gatschet referred to the family as the Rio Grande Pueblo stock (Gatschet 1879:415-417). He subdivided it as follows: Northern Tiwa ("Taos" including Picuris); Southern Tiwa ("Tanos," "Tagnos" [1876]; "Taño" [1878]); Tewa, including Arizona Tewa ("Tehua" [1876]; "Tewa" [1878]); Jemez, including Pecos ("Jemes" [1876]; "Jemez" [1878]); and Piro. He did not mention Piro in his 1876 publication but added it to the family in his 1878 paper on the evidence of a vocabulary collected by J.R. Bartlett (1909) from the emigrant Pueblo of Senecú, Chihuahua. In 1877 Gatschet went to work for John Wesley Powell as a philologist for the Geographical and Geological Survey of the Rocky Mountain Region, and Powell published the results of Gatschet's classification in an article on the identities of the Pueblos in *The Rocky Mountain Presbyterian* (Powell 1878); Powell, who used the name Taño for the family, did not subgroup the languages. Later Powell (1880a) proposed the name Téwan for the family, giving Gatschet's subclassification.

In the same comprehensive paper Gatschet (1879) recognized the linguistic unity of several other families, giving descriptions of the territories they occupied and, in most cases, detailed lists of the specific groups included. In some of these conclusions he followed other writers or independently reached the same results as earlier investigators whose work was unknown to him. The other families thus described were Athapaskan ("Tinné"), Uto-Aztecan, Yuman ("Yuma"), Keresan ("Kera"), Wintuan ("Wintun"), and Chumashan ("Santa Barbara"). Gatschet (1879:406) included in the territory of the Athapaskan speakers the mouth of the Copper River in Alaska. This might imply the inclusion of Eyak in the family, but he probably was referring to and mislocating Ahtna (cf. Latham 1860:270; Powell 1891:53). The Alaska Athapaskan languages had been added to the family by Buschmann (1855, 1856:250-253), a connection adumbrated by Gallatin (1848:7) for Tanaina, and Kutchin had been added by John Richardson (1851, 1:396-397; Buschmann 1856:163; Latham 1860:334, 385). Gatschet (1879:408-409) did not propose a name for Uto-Aztecan, which he described as comprising two divisions, Northern Uto-Aztecan ("Numa" or "Shoshoni") and Southern Uto-Aztecan (referred to collectively as "Nahuatl"). His enumeration of the languages included in these two divisions makes it clear

that they correspond to the northern and southern branches of Uto-Aztecan as later defined (Kaufman 1974a:73; Heath 1977:27, 1978:221-222, 1985). As evidence for the connection between the two divisions he cites similarities in "a number of radicals [i.e., basic word stems] which cannot simply be borrowed" as well as agreement in "grammatical affixes or formative elements." Gatschet (1877-1892, 1:386, 1879:413-414) subsumed in Yuman the core languages of the family and the languages of Baja California at least so far south as to include Cochimí, but although he thought Latham's (1862:426) inclusion of Guaicura plausible, he withheld final judgment because of the dearth of appropriate data. In 1883 he added Seri to the family, supporting a suggestion he credits to Wilhelm Herzog (Gatschet 1877-1892, 2:133-134). Gatschet (1879:417-418) followed Loew (1876) in recognizing that Keresan consisted of two branches, Eastern ("Quéres") on either side of the Rio Grande, and Western ("Sitsimé or Kawaíko"), at Laguna, Acoma, and their outliers. Gatschet's (1879:418) recognition of Wintuan follows Powers (1877:232). The listing of the components of Chumashan is left unclear by a statement that Antoniano Salinan and Obispeño Chumash "may possibly belong to this same family" (Gatschet 1879:419; cf. Gatschet 1876:553).

In addition to determining the major family groupings of the languages he examined, Gatschet noted vocabulary resemblances that cut across these groupings. These were ascribed to borrowing. For example, he gives lists of Jemez words that resemble words in Dakota (Eastern Sioux), the Takic branch of Uto-Aztecan, Zuni, and Kiowa (Gatschet 1875:183). Conversely, he observed that Kiowa showed similarities not only with the Tanoan languages, though mostly with different words in each, but also with Keresan, Zuni, and Hopi. He concluded that "the Kiowas are a medley of roving tribes and Pueblo Indians" (Gatschet 1875:184, 187, 1877:155), despite having once discussed them without comment among the Shoshoneans (Gatschet 1876a:31). Earlier Turner had observed Shoshonean "affinities" in Kiowa but concluded that they pointed to "long intercommunication" rather than genetic relationship (Whipple, Ewbank, and Turner 1855:80). Eventually Gatschet declared Kiowa to be independent of Shoshonean, though sharing some words with it (Gatschet 1879a:268).

• SOUTHEAST AND TEXAS With the exception of the Muskogean and Caddoan families, and the very small Catawban group, the languages of the Southeast and Texas were considered from the beginning to consist of a large number of distinct forms of speech spoken in many cases by very small groups. Observations of the extensive ethnic and linguistic diversity of the Indian groups were made for the Southeast east of the Mississippi in 1775 (Adair 1930), for Louisiana in 1805 (Sibley 1832), and for Texas in the eighteenth century (Goddard

1979a:355-356). Adair (1930:235-236) reported that the Catawba "nation" consisted of groups speaking 20 different "dialects"; it is clear that some of these groups spoke distinct non-Catawban languages. The Creek Confederacy also incorporated a number of groups speaking non-Muskogean languages (Adair 1930:274).

Sibley (1832) described many tribes in the Louisiana area as having distinct languages of their own. He named several that spoke Caddo or Wichita, described the Alabama and Koasati as speaking Creek and Choctaw, and referred to the Comanche, Plains Apache ("Cances"), Choctaw, and Quapaw, but besides these he mentioned 15 single, small groups and two pairs as speaking languages distinct from all others. These were the Adai, Akokisa, Apalachee, Bidai, Biloxi, Chatot, Eyeish, Kitsai, Maye, Opelousa, Pakana, Pascagoula, Taensa, Tonkawa, and Tunica, the Natchitoches and Yatasi, and the Atakapa and Karankawa. The language of the Washa was extinct, and no information was given about those of the Avoyel and Houma. Apparently by oversight he omitted the Chitimacha, and there would likely have been remnants in the area in 1805 of a few other groups mentioned in earlier historical sources, such as the Ofo (Swanton 1909) and the Koroa (Gatschet 1884-1888, 1:48). Gallatin (1836:115-118) commented on Sibley's list, and Latham (1860:366, 401-402) apparently knew it from secondary sources. Later information reduced only some of this diversity, showing Apalachee to be Muskogean (Gatschet 1884-1888, 1:74), Biloxi to be Siouan (Gatschet in Powell 1891:114; Swanton 1946:97), and Kitsai to be Caddoan (Whipple, Ewbank, and Turner 1855:65-70). Bidai, of which nine putative words were recorded, and Yatasi were eventually put in Caddoan, with little discussion. Of the rest, linguistic material exists only for Adai, Akokisa, Atakapa, Karankawa, Tonkawa, and Tunica, which Powell (1891) recognized as falling into five distinct families, with Akokisa and Atakapa being classified together as respectively the western and eastern branches of his Attacapan family. The Eyeish, Yatasi, and Natchitoches were politically allied with the Caddo Confederacy and have been placed in Southern Caddoan (Caddo) linguistically (Powell 1891:61), but Sibley explicitly stated that they spoke Caddo only as a second language and had two distinct languages of their own besides, one spoken by the Eyeish and one shared by the Yatasi and Natchitoches. Although Sibley's information that the Karankawa on the Texas coast spoke the same language as the Atakapa is wrong (it may reflect confusion with the Akokisa or bilingualism), his statements about the distinctions of language among the groups in Louisiana, a number of which had come from east of the Mississippi, seem largely reliable. Other groups east of the Mississippi recognized as speaking distinct languages that constituted separate families were the

Natchez, Yuchi, and Timucua (Gallatin 1836:95, 306; B. Smith 1858:1; Gatschet 1879b:77, 1887:413). Gatschet (1887:412) also recognized that many small historic groups on the Gulf Coast could not be classified owing to the lack of linguistic data.

Since no linguistic documentation was collected from many of the groups in Texas and the Southeast, and the documentation that existed in some cases was generally unavailable, their linguistic diversity has sometimes been unappreciated. One consequence of the absence of linguistic materials directly tied to most of the numerous distinct groups found historically in these areas has been that the linguistic classifications that have been proposed have relied heavily on inferences from cultural similarities and political associations. Since the political confederation of linguistically diverse peoples is known to have existed in these and other areas, and since population losses led to the widespread consolidation of many remnant peoples, such inferences are open to question. For example, the Pamunkey and Nansemond have been classified as Algonquian-speaking because of their membership in the Powhatan Confederacy, which was dominated by speakers of Virginia Algonquian (Powhatan), but the few words recorded from the remnants of these groups in the nineteenth century suggest the former presence of unclassifiable and otherwise unknown languages (vol. 15:74). Even if, as is certainly possible, these languages were not spoken by the seventeenth-century groups with the same names, a greater degree of earlier linguistic diversity than usually assumed is indicated. Many of the imputed linguistic categorizations in these areas require reexamination.

Powell's Classification

The publication of Powell's (1891) classification and map of the native languages of North America was a watershed event. This report, "Indian Linguistic Families of America North of Mexico," was issued in the Annual Report of the Bureau of Ethnology (later to be renamed the Bureau of American Ethnology) for the fiscal year 1885-1886 with a publication date of 1891, but it actually appeared in 1892 (Mason 1893a:480). A summary had been published in *Science* in February 1891, including a listing of all the linguistic families by the names Powell had established and their locations (Powell 1891a), and the map had been presented at the annual meeting of the American Association for the Advancement of Science in Washington in August 1891 (American Association for the Advancement of Science 1892:375; Mason 1893:435). Powell sought to classify all the languages for which data were available and to establish a nomenclature, based on principles of priority derived from systematic biology. He surveyed earlier work, and for each of the language families he recognized he gave an extensive summary of earlier classifications and names. A number of decisions regarding the distinctness or affinity of specific languages were based on fieldwork and analysis performed by members of the staff of the Bureau of Ethnology under Powell's direction. Powell particularly mentions Gatschet, Henshaw, and James Owen Dorsey in this regard, and the assistance of James C. Pilling in the compilation of bibliography. His statement that "for the classification itself . . . I am wholly responsible" (Powell 1891:142) must be understood in that context (Sturtevant 1959; Darnell 1969:83-95, 1971). Powell made the final decisions about which languages were to be grouped with which, in some cases choosing between or overruling conflicting recommendations of his staff; he established the principles of the nomenclatural system used; and he determined the application of these principles to specific cases and discussed his reasoning at length. At the same time, because Henshaw, who was put in charge of the classification and map by Powell, made many decisions regarding details, the classification has sometimes been considered to be largely his work (Powell 1888:xlv; Merriam 1904:913; Kroeber 1905:580, 1913:390, 1960:2-3; Davis 1915:77; Hodge and Merriam 1931:100, 103).

When Henshaw was formally put in charge of the project in 1885 he had a summary of the classification as it was at that date printed up for the use of Bureau collaborators (Smithsonian Institution. Bureau of [American] Ethnology 1885:1-2) (fig. 1). This gives 56 "Linguistic Families of the Indian Tribes North of Mexico." The families listed that were not in the final classification (Powell 1891) were: Catawban, Haeltzukan (Kwakiutlan), Taensan, and Unungunian (Aleut). Those in the final classification that were not listed in 1885 were: Beothukan, Chimarikan, Costanoan, Esselenian, Karankawan, and Tonikan. There were also some spelling changes and some name changes; the Ehnikan of 1885 became the Quoratean of 1891, Mendocinan became Kulanapan, and Nojan became Yanan.

Of the 58 families recognized by Powell (1891) (table 3), 26 were considered to be language isolates, single languages with no established relatives: Adaizan, Beothukan, Chimarikan, Chitimachan, Esselenian, Karankawan, Kiowan, Kitunahan, Koluschan, Kusan, Lutuamian, Natchesan, Palaihnihan, Quoratean, Sastean, Skittagetan, Takilman, Timuquanan, Tonikan, Tonkawan, Uchean, Washoan, Weitspekan, Wishoskan, Yanan, and Zuñian. Another four comprised, or were believed to comprise, a single pair of closely related languages: Attacapan, Chimakuan, Salinan, and Waiilatpuan. For these 30 families classification was a matter of recognizing their distinctness rather than finding evidence for internal relationships, and most of them had been so recognized before Powell's publica-

tion. The recognition of some of these resulted from Powell's studies of northern California vocabularies (in Powers 1877) or from fieldwork done for the Bureau that had already been reported in print, as in the case of Kusan and Takilman (Gatschet 1882:257-258), Tonikan (Gatschet 1887:412), and Karankawan, which was provisionally classified as distinct on the evidence of 25 words collected from Tonkawa speakers (Gatschet 1886a, 1887:414). Washoan had been set up by Gatschet (1882:255) on the basis of the vocabulary collected by Powers; Henshaw's 1883 fieldwork confirmed this (Powell 1887:xxx). Unpublished field investigations by Henshaw for the Bureau had established the independent status of Esselenian (in 1888), previously put in Costanoan (Gatschet 1878, 1882:254), and of Salinan (in 1884), whose status had been uncertain. Natchesan had been recognized by Gallatin (1836:95, 306), but the inclusion in the family of the politically related but linguistically undocumented Taensa was discussed at length to indicate acceptance of Brinton's (1885, 1885a, 1888) exposure of a purported Taensa grammar (Haumonte, Parisot, and Adam 1882) as a hoax (cf. Vinson 1886), despite Gatschet's (1888a, 1891) rebuttals. Powell did not mention Brinton's (1873) claim of a relationship between Natchesan and Muskhogean, which Brinton (1891:91) himself later seemed to withdraw. In some cases Bureau fieldwork had fleshed out knowledge of a previously recognized family, as with Gatschet's (1887:414) discovery of the Western Atakapa dialect. In the case of Chimarikan Powell apparently considered the evidence he had earlier cited for its distinctness (in Powers 1877:474-477; Gatschet 1882:255) to be insufficient until confirmed by additional field data collected for the Bureau by Curtin in 1889. The extinct and poorly documented Beothuk language was set up as a separate Beothukan family following the conclusion reached by Gatschet (1886b:423-428).

For another set of 21 families Powell accepted or confirmed classifications previously published, including those of his own for northern California (in Powers 1877); these were Algonquian, Athapascan, Caddoan, Chimmesyan, Chinookan, Copehan, Eskimauan, Iroquoian, Kalapooian, Keresan, Kulanapan, Mariposan, Muskhogean, Piman, Pujunan, Salishan, Shahaptian, Shoshonean, Tañoan, Yukian, and Yuman. Most of these corresponded exactly to the previously recognized families, though in some cases additional data permitted a more precise enumeration of the constituent languages. For example, Powell claimed a broader inclusion for the Kulanapan family because more constituent groups were named than in previous publications. Also, the first detailed account of the extent of Athapaskan in Oregon was given, based on fieldwork and analysis by Dorsey and Gatschet. Powell's Yuman was maximally inclusive, subsuming not only Cochimí but also Seri, following Gatschet

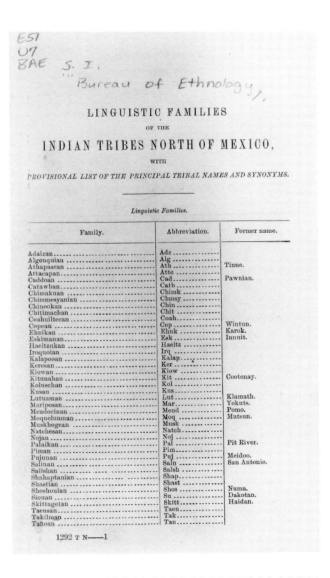

LINGUISTIC FAMILIES
OF THE
INDIAN TRIBES NORTH OF MEXICO,
WITH
PROVISIONAL LIST OF THE PRINCIPAL TRIBAL NAMES AND SYNONYMS.

Linguistic Families.

Family.	Abbreviation.	Former name.
Adaizan	Adz	
Algonquian	Alg	
Athapascan	Ath	Tinne.
Attacapan	Atta	
Caddoan	Cad	Pawnian.
Catawban	Catb	
Chimakuan	Chimk	
Chimmesyanian	Chmsy	
Chinookan	Chin	
Chitimachan	Chit	
Coahuiltecan	Coah	
Copean	Cop	Wintun.
Ehnikan	Ehnk	Karok.
Eskimauan	Esk	Innuit.
Haeltzukan	Haeltz	
Iroquoian	Irq	
Kalapooan	Kalap	
Keresan	Ker	
Kiowan	Kiow	
Kitunahan	Kit	Cootenay.
Koluschan	Kol	
Kusan	Kns	
Lutuaman	Lut	Klamath.
Mariposan	Mar	Yokuts.
Mendocinan	Mend	Pomo.
Moquelumnan	Moq	Mutsun.
Muskhogean	Musk	
Natchesan	Natch	
Nojan	Noj	
Palaikan	Pal	Pit River.
Piman	Pim	
Pujunan	Puj	Meidoo.
Salinan	Saln	San Antonio.
Salishan	Salsh	
Shahaptanian	Shap	
Shastian	Shast	
Shoshonian	Shos	Numa.
Siouan	Su	Dakotan.
Skittagetan	Skitt	Haidan.
Taensan	Taen	
Takilman	Tak	
Tañoan	Tan	

1292 T N——1

2   LINGUISTIC FAMILIES.

Linguistic Families—Continued.

Family.	Abbreviation.	Former name.
Tchumashan	Tchu	Santa Barbaran.
Timucuan	Timu	
Tonkawan	Tonk	
Uchean	Uch	
Unungunian	Unu	
Waiilatpuan	Wail	
Wakashan	Wak	Aht. Nootka.
Washoan	Wash	
Weitspekan	Weit	Yurok.
Wishoskan	Wish	
Yakonan	Yak	
Yukian	Yuk	
Yuman	Yum	
Zuñian	Zun	

Smithsonian, Anthr. Lib.

Fig. 1. *Linguistic Families of the Indian Tribes North of Mexico* . . . (Smithsonian Institution. Bureau of [American] Ethnology 1885), the first version of the Powell classification, privately circulated to collaborators.

(1877-1892, 2:133), and Guaicura and the undocumented languages of southernmost Baja California, following without discussion the suggestion of Latham (1862:426). The unity of Eskimauan (Eskimoan and Aleut) had been widely assumed (Dall 1870, 1877:9) but was at first not recognized by the Bureau (Smithsonian Institution. Bureau of [American] Ethnology 1885:1-2); it was later accepted, probably after Gatschet (1886c) argued for it, in time for Aleut to be included in the *Bibliography of the Eskimo Language* (Pilling 1887). Powell (1891:99, 109, 140), stressing his own acquaintance with Shoshonean languages, rejected the relationship of Shoshonean to Piman, and of these with the Mexican language Nahuatl (Aztec), which had been asserted by Gatschet (1877:155, 1879:408-409) and Brinton (1890:23).

It was for only seven families of an extent greater than one or two languages that Powell (1891) published new conclusions about distinctness or inclusiveness. The separateness of Chumashan proposed by Latham (1860:351) but somewhat obscured by Gatschet (1876: 553, 1877:156; 1879:419) was confirmed by vocabularies collected by Henshaw in 1884. Coahuiltecan was set up to embrace not only Coahuilteco, for which the latter name had been coined by Manuel Orozco y Berra (1864:309), but also Cotoname and Comecrudo, which Gatschet had documented with vocabularies collected in 1886, and a few group names for which there were no linguistic data. Gatschet (1887:411-412) reported a linguistic basis for grouping Comecrudo and Cotoname together, but evidence for Powell's Coahuiltecan family was never published. The extension of the name Coahuilteco to the Cotoname and Comecrudo apparently followed Orozco y Berra's map (cited by Powell 1891:68), on which the name Coahuilteco is extended eastward along the south bank of the Rio Grande, although Orozco y Berra (1864:292, 294, 296) himself classified the languages of that area as Tamaulipeco. Costanoan and Moquelumnan, which Powell (in Powers 1877:535) had united following Gatschet's (1877:157-158) suggestion, later argued for in detail (Gatschet 1888), were separated on the basis of an analysis by Curtin (1888) and further vocabularies collected by Henshaw in 1888. Siouan was expanded to encompass Catawban (Catawba and Woccon) on the basis of studies by Gatschet and Dorsey that followed up a suggestion by Morgan (1870:54; Siebert 1945:100-101); however, this expansion was decided on too late for Catawban references to be included in the *Bibliography of the Siouan Languages* (Pilling 1887). Alsean (Alsea and Yaquina) and Siuslaw (Siuslaw and Lower Umpqua), which Gatschet (1879c:167, 1882:256-257) had kept separate, were put together as Yakonan on the basis of fieldwork and studies by Dorsey. Wakashan, uniting Kwakiutlan (Northern Wakashan) and Nootkan (Southern Wakashan), was accepted as a unit following Boas's (1891:678-679) demonstration, made after his 1889

301

Table 3. Powell's Classification

Powell 1891	Powell 1915[a]	Boas 1911	Sapir 1929	Handbook names
Adaizan	(in Caddoan)	(in Caddoan)	(in Caddoan)	Adai
Algonquian	Algonquian	Algonquian	Algonkian	Algonquian
Athapascan	Athapascan	Athapascan	Athabaskan	Athapaskan
Attacapan	Attacapan	Atakapa	Atakapa	Atakapan
Beothukan	Beothukan	Beothuk	Beothuk	Beothuk
Caddoan	Caddoan[b]	Caddoan[b]	Caddoan[b]	Caddoan
Chimakuan	Chimakuan	Chemakum	Chimakuan	Chimakuan
Chimarikan	Chimarikan	Chimarico	Chimariko	Chimariko
Chimmesyan	Chimmesyan	Tsimshian	Tsimshian	Tsimshianic
Chinookan	Chinookan	Chinook	Chinook	Chinookan
Chitimachan	Chitimachan	Chitimacha	Chitimacha	Chitimacha
Chumashan	Chumashan	Chumashan	Chumash	Chumashan
Coahuiltecan	Coahuiltecan	Pakawan	Coahuiltecan	Coahuilteco, Comecrudan, Cotoname
Copehan	Copehan	Wintun	Wintun	Wintuan
Costanoan	Costanoan	Costanoan	Costanoan	Costanoan
Eskimauan	Eskimauan	Eskimo	Eskimoan	Eskimo-Aleut
Esselenian	Esselenian	Esselenian	Esselen	Esselen
Iroquoian	Iroquoian	Iroquoian	Iroquoian	Iroquoian
Kalapooian	Kalapooian	Kalapuya	Kalapuya	Kalapuyan
Karankawan	Karankawan	Karankawa	Karankawa	Karankawa
Keresan	Keresan	Keres	Keres	Keresan
Kiowan	Kiowan	Kiowa	Kiowa	Kiowa
Kitunahan	Kitunahan	Kutenai	Kootenay	Kootenai
Koluschan	Koluschan	Tlingit	Tlingit	Tlingit
Kulanapan	Kulanapan	Pomo	Pomo	Pomoan
Kusan	Kusan	Kus	Coos	Coosan
Lutuamian	Lutuamian	Klamath	Lutuami	Klamath
Mariposan	Mariposan	Yokuts	Yokuts	Yokutsan
Moquelumnan	Moquelumnan	Moquelumnan	Miwok	Miwokan
Muskhogean	Muskhogean[c]	Muskhogean[c]	Muskogian[c]	Muskogean
Natchesan	(in Muskhogean)	(in Muskhogean)	(in Muskogian)	Natchez
Palaihnihan	(in Shastan)	(in Shasta)	(in Shastan)	Palaihnihan
Piman	Piman	Pima	Piman (or Sonoran)	Uto-Aztecan (part)
Pujunan	Pujunan	Maidu	Maidu	Maiduan
Quoratean	Quoratean	Quoratean	Karok	Karok
Salinan	Salinan	Salinan	Salinan	Salinan
Salishan	Salishan	Salishan	Salishan	Salishan
Sastean	Shastan[d]	Shasta[d]	Shastan or Shasta-Achomawi[d]	Shastan
Shahaptian	Shahaptian	Sahaptin	Sahaptin	Sahaptian
Shoshonean	Shoshonean	Shoshonean	Shoshonean	Northern Uto-Aztecan
Siouan	Siouan	Siouan	Siouan	Siouan
Skittagetan	Skittagetan	Haida	Haida	Haida
Takilman	Takilman	Takelma	Takelma	Takelma
Tañoan	Tanoan	Tanoan	Tanoan	Tanoan
Timuquanan	Timuquan	Timuqua	Timuqua	Timucuan[e]
Tonikan	Tunican	Tunica	Tunica	Tunica
Tonkawan	Tonkawan	Tonkawa	Tonkawa	Tonkawa
Uchean	Uchean	Yuchi	Yuchi	Yuchi
Waiilatpuan	Waiilatpuan	Waiilatpuan[f]	Waiilatpuan	Cayuse, Molala
Wakashan	Wakashan	Wakashan	Wakashan	Wakashan
Washoan	Washoan	Washo	Washo	Washoe
Weitspekan	Weitspekan	Weitspekan	Yurok	Yurok
Wishoskan	Wishoskan	Wishosk[g]	Wiyot	Wiyot
Yakonan	Yakonan	Yakona	Yakonan, Siuslaw[h]	Alsean Siuslaw

Table 3. Powell's Classification (continued)

Powell 1891	Powell 1915[a]	Boas 1911	Sapir 1929	Handbook *names*
Yanan	Yanan	Yana	Yana	Yana
Yukian	Yukian	Yuki	Yuki	Yukian
Yuman	Yuman[i]	Yuma	Yuman,	Cochimí-Yuman,[e]
	and Serian		Waïcuri,[j]	Guaicura,
			Seri[j]	Seri
Zuñian	Zuñian	Zuñi	Zuñi	Zuni

SOURCES: Powell (1891), Powell (1915), Boas (1911:82-83), Sapir (1929:138-139, 1949:169-171).

NOTES:

[a]Also added to the map were Arawakan (in the West Indies, with an outlier in Florida) and (in eastern Siberia) Tungus and the "Americanoid" languages Yukaghir and an unnamed family comprising Chuckchi, Koryak, and Kamchadal; these are omitted from Boas's and Sapir's lists.

[b]Includes the Adaizan of Powell (1891).

[c]Includes the Natchesan of Powell (1891).

[d]Includes the Palaihnihan of Powell (1891).

[e]The original Powell (1891) family also included additional, undocumented languages.

[f]Misprinted as Waiilaptuan.

[g]Given as Wishok, probably following the misprinted Wishokan of the 1906 map (Powell 1906).

[h]Split by Frachtenberg (1914:4; P.E. Goddard 1914:563-564, 568) but not indicated as such on the 1915 map.

[i]Excludes Guaicura.

[j]Listed among the "Middle American" languages (Sapir 1929, 1949:176-177).

fieldwork on Nootka, which he reported to Henshaw and later sent to him in proof (Boas 1889a, 1890, 1890a). Hale (1891:554, map) accepted the family, referring to it as "the Kwakiutl-Nootka stock." The consolidation of what had been the separate Haeltzukan (Kwakiutlan) and Wakashan (Nootkan) families (Smithsonian Institution. Bureau of [American] Ethnology 1885:1-2) into a unified Wakashan was the last change in the classification before it went to press.

In addition to the detailed listing and discussion of the language families, Powell published his classification on a map that accompanied his report. Henshaw had exhibited and discussed a nearly final version before the Anthropological Society of Washington in January 1888 (fig. 2), and Powell had taken the opportunity of this first public presentation of the Bureau classification to recall the length and difficulty of the project and to acknowledge the many who had contributed to it (Henshaw 1888; Proudfit 1888). On the 1891 map (inserted in pocket) each of the 58 linguistic families was indicated with a distinctive (though not unique) color applied to an exclusive, separate area, or in some cases more than one noncontiguous area. A color, and hence a family, was assigned to every part of the whole of North America north of central Mexico, except for two areas in coastal North and South Carolina and the interior parts of Greenland, the islands of the Canadian Arctic, and northern Alaska. Such a map requires that decisions be made regarding the locations of Indian groups, most significantly decisions about the historical period to be depicted. Since in North America some

groups were displaced or extinct before others were first documented, the map necessarily incorporates the chronological skewing of the sources. Many compromises were consequently required in the mapping, including the incorporation of hypotheses about the linguistic affinities of the aboriginal inhabitants in some parts of the continent for which there were no linguistic data. The chief areas in which there were historically known but linguistically undocumented groups were the Ohio Valley, including the Monongahela and other tributaries, parts of the Southeast, especially the Atlantic and Gulf coasts and southern Florida, the lower Mississippi Valley, the entire Rio Grande Valley from central New Mexico to the Gulf, and parts of the Plains.

Brinton's (1891) classification has sometimes been described as a competing alternative to Powell's (Darnell 1971:90-95, 110, 1988:115-123). There are a number of differences between Powell's and Brinton's studies, notably the fact that Brinton included all of North and South America, and there was a rivalry between the two publications in that they raced each other into print. Powell seems to have won the race, on his terms, by getting the outline of his paper into *Science* (Powell 1891a) two weeks after Brinton's book was announced as in press but seven weeks before the first ads announcing its publication (Brinton 1891a:55, 182). Brinton (1891b) responded by attacking Powell's methodology and nomenclature. In spite of this jousting, though, Brinton's classification was in fact almost identical to Powell's for the languages both covered, for the good reason that

303

Brinton had made assiduous efforts to inform himself of the Bureau classification before it appeared. Henshaw had provided Brinton (1891:xii, 108-109) with the Bureau's names for all the families spoken in the Northwest Coast, Plateau, and California, had answered a series of questions from him about the Bureau's classification of several historically problematic languages, and had even lent him a draft copy of the map (Brinton 1890a, 1890b, 1890c, 1890d, 1890e, 1890f). Brinton's classification missed two late consolidations, that of Catawban with Siouan, which had not been published beforehand, and that of Haeltzukan and Wakashan, which was decided in late 1890, after the correspondence with Henshaw, and was in fact accepted by Brinton (1891:366) in an addendum on the basis of the same report by Boas that

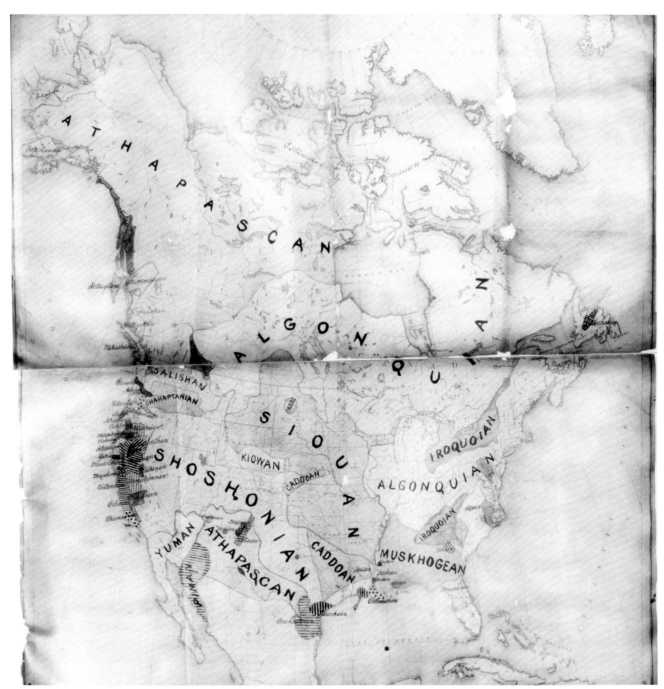

Smithsonian, NAA: Ms. 3969; Neg. 94-7558, 94-7560.

Fig. 2. Draft of Powell map of the language families of North America. This draft, probably originally compiled under the direction of Henry W. Henshaw about 1887, shows several changes made over the following years, including the removal of Taensan from the Gulf Coast and the consolidation of Catawban with Siouan. It must be closely similar, if not identical, to the map Henshaw exhibited in January 1888.

Hand-drawn colored draft, Bureau of [American] Ethnology, about 1887-1890.

had persuaded Powell. Maratino, listed by Brinton (1891:94) as a separate family in his North Atlantic geographical group, was not covered by Powell since it was spoken in Tamaulipas; Washoe was omitted by oversight. The only intentional, substantive difference in Brinton's classification was his acceptance of the consolidation of Shoshonean, Piman, and Nahuatl into a single family, for which he coined the name Uto-Aztecan (Brinton 1891:118). For this classification Brinton credited Buschmann (1859), as had Gatschet (1877:155, 1879:408-409), who concurred, and Powell (1891:99, 109, 140), who did not. As Brinton (1890:23) recognized, Buschmann had not himself argued that these languages were genetically related, being content to show that they at least showed evidence of linguistic contact, but Buschmann's readers have often concluded that genetic relationship was the only reasonable explanation for the extensive similarities he documented (Lamb 1964:114-115).

Revision of the Powell classification began as soon as it appeared. The Bureau itself issued a series of revisions of Powell's map that showed changes in the classification and in the locations or territorial extent of some groups. Because the maps were not accompanied by discussions of the revisions the reasons for the changes have to be inferred, though they tend to be obvious. The first revision of the map appeared in 1894 (Powell 1894) (fig. 4), prepared for inclusion in the report of the eleventh census (U.S. Bureau of the Census 1894:facing p. 36). This shows the deletion of Adaizan as a separate family and its inclusion in Caddoan, reflecting a conclusion that had been reached by Gatschet (1888b) and supported by J.O. Dorsey (1889) but that Powell (1891:46) had initially rejected on the grounds that not enough Adai material was available to establish the relationship. In fact, Adaizan had already been dropped from the initial synopsis of Powell's map by the time it appeared in the Smithsonian *Annual Report* (Mason 1893:448-450). There were thus 57 families on the 1894 map.

The 1894 map also had some changes in boundaries, most notably several that had been suggested by J.N.B. Hewitt (1891). These included extending Iroquoian eastward along the Saint Lawrence River, consolidating into one the two Iroquoian areas of coastal North Carolina, extending the eastern Siouan area out to the South Carolina coast where the 1891 map had left the languages unclassified, and adding Siouan along the Kentucky and Big Sandy rivers in the southern Ohio Valley. In consolidating the Tuscarora and Nottoway areas of North Carolina, the island of Siouan that marked the location of Woccon was obliterated; this was certainly an inadvertence rather than a reclassification, but it was not corrected

on the subsequent revisions of the map, despite the more accurate mapping of James Mooney (1894).

The Powell map was reissued again in 1906 (Powell 1906) (fig. 5) in advance of its publication in the first volume of Hodge (1907-1910). On this version there were once again 58 language families. One family was removed by the consolidation of Sastean and Palaihnihan into "Shastan," which followed a demonstration by Roland B. Dixon (1905) and had in fact been earlier argued for by Gatschet (1886c) but not accepted by Powell (1891:98). Dixon had called this grouping "Shasta-Achomawi." At the same time, Seri was separated from Yuman and set up as a separate family, Serian, and Arawakan was added in the previously unlabeled West Indies and in a small area in Florida between Fort Myers and Naples. Two formerly colored areas were left blank to indicate that the languages in them were considered unclassified. The southern end of Baja California, intended to correspond to the area in which Guaicura, Uchití, and Pericú were spoken, was removed from Yuman, and the southern half of Florida, the area of the Calusa, Ais, and Tequesta, was removed from Timuquanan. (The southern boundary of Yuman, as represented by Cochimí, was drawn incorrectly at about 28° north latitude instead of at 26°.) These six unclassified languages were essentially undocumented except for a brief grammatical sketch of Guaicura (Baegert 1773:175-194, 1952:94-104). The removal of the Baja California languages and Seri from Yuman followed the conclusions of Hewitt (1898:300*, 343*-344*), seconded by Gatschet (1900). Hewitt presented his arguments as a rebuttal of Brinton's (1891:113, 335) classification of Guaicura and Seri as Yuman without explicit reference to the Powell classification or to Gatschet's earlier opinion about Seri. The ethnohistorical evidence for the classification and location of the languages of Baja California has been reviewed in detail by Massey (1949). The removal of the southern Florida groups from Timuquanan was a reversion to the earlier opinion of Gatschet (1884-1888, 1:13, 15; Hodge 1907-1910, 1:195-196), which had been superseded by his subsequent declaration that their classification as Timuquanan was "very probable" (Gatschet 1887:413); Powell (1891:124) had accepted this classification on the basis of the concededly "slender evidence" of the shape of place-names. The small area of Arawakan added in Florida represents a community of Cuban origin encountered there in the sixteenth century (Escalante Fontaneda 1944:15; Mooney in Hodge 1907-1910, 1:74); it was classified as Arawakan because it was assumed that all of Cuba was Arawakan-speaking.

The 1906 map also showed a number of changes in the boundaries and locations of some families that did not involve reclassifications, and it added an inset of   *305*

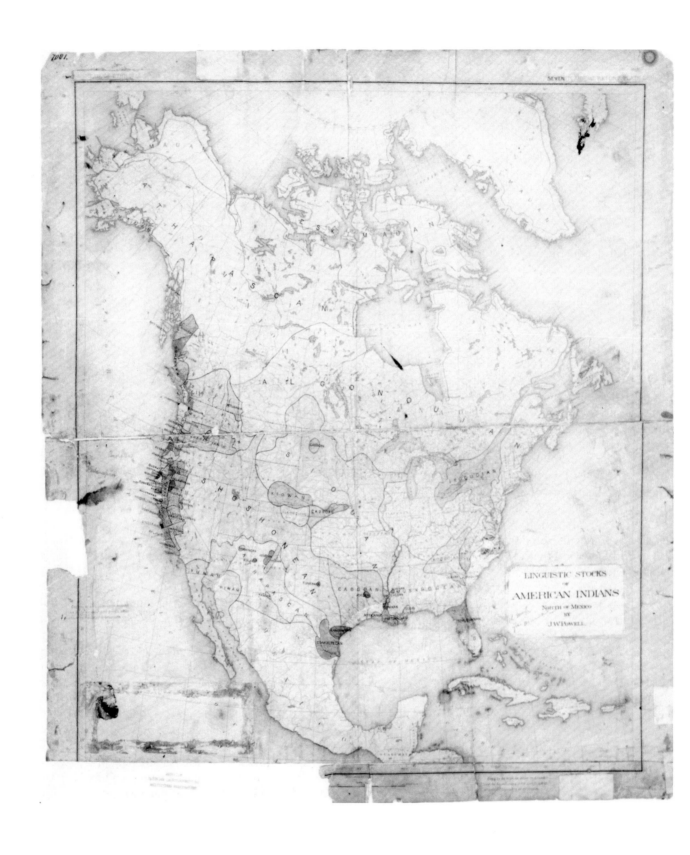

Fig. 3. Proof of the Powell map, "Linguistic Stocks of American Indians North of Mexico," about 1890, incorporating some of the final changes in the classification, nomenclature, and location. The names Kulanapan and Quoratean have been pasted in to replace Mendocinan and Ehnikan.

306

Fig. 4. The 1894 revision of the Powell map, *Map of Linguistic Stocks of American Indians chiefly within the present limits of the United States.*

THE CLASSIFICATION OF THE NATIVE LANGUAGES OF NORTH AMERICA

the languages of eastern Siberia. Algonquian was removed from Newfoundland, which was mostly assigned to Beothukan, with Eskimauan on the northern tip. An area corresponding to most of West Virginia and southwestern Pennsylvania was left blank. A small Tanoan area was added near the Hopi representing the Tano-speaking Arizona Tewa in their location after the Pueblo Revolt of 1680. A more extensive and definite southern extension of Piman was indicated. Tonkawan was placed at its earlier historical location near the Gulf Coast, next to expanded areas of Attacapan, Karankawan, and Coahuiltecan; these mappings may have followed research later published by Herbert E. Bolton (1914, 1:map).

The Powell map was again revised and reissued in 1915 (fig. 6), in advance of its publication in a census report (Powell 1915; U.S. Bureau of the Census 1915:facing p. 9). On this version Natchesan is no longer a separate family but has been merged with Muskhogean, following Swanton (1907) and the earlier view of Brinton (1873). There are thus 57 families. It is possible that some slight changes in the western end of the boundary between Caddoan and Attacapan were intended to indicate a reclassification of Bidai, which had been put in Caddoan by Gatschet (1891a:103) on the basis of extremely poor evidence. Bidai was not mentioned in Powell (1891), but the Bidai area was mapped as Caddoan. Later, ethnohistorical information discovered by Bolton (1914a:374) led to the reclassification of Bidai as Attacapan (Swanton 1911:36, 363). This information derives ultimately from a 1749 statement by Benito Fernández de Santa Ana that the Bidai, Deadoses, and Akokisa spoke the same language; the same connection is also supported by a Bidai tradition (Gatschet 1887a). Other shifts in boundaries did not reflect reclassifications. These included the correction of the southern boundary of Yuman (Cochimí-Yuman) in Baja California by shifting it to 26° north latitude, the expansion and consolidation of the Mariposan and Caddoan areas, the removal of Algonquian from the Savannah River, where it represented the temporary historical location of the Shawnee, and other, generally lesser changes.

Also generally included among the Bureau revisions of the Powell classification was Frachtenberg's resplitting of Yakonan into Yakonan (Alsean: Alsea and Yaquina) and Siuslaw (also referred to as Siuslawan, with dialects Siuslaw and Lower Umpqua), even though he also suggested the possibility that these two families might be ultimately related to each other and to Coosan (Frachtenberg 1914:4, 1917:437; P.E. Goddard 1914a:563-564, 568; Sapir 1929:139, 1949:171; Golla 1984:201). Recognition of this splitting would bring the total number of families in the final version of the Powell classification to 58, including Arawakan and Serian.

After Powell

The history of the classification of North American languages after Powell had several aspects: the renaming of recognized families, the consolidation or splitting of Powell's units, ethnohistorical research on the linguistic affinity of vanished groups, the subclassification of languages within families, the recognition as separate languages of what had been considered only dialects, and the working out of the actual linguistic history of families.

A trend to rename some of Powell's families was initiated by A.L. Kroeber (1905), who criticized the biological principle of nomenclatural priority as inappropriate for ethnology. As a consequence of this criticism the American Anthropological Association formed a Committee on Nomenclature of Indian Linguistic Families North of Mexico, chaired by F.W. Hodge. The committee recommended that names in widespread use be preferred to the unfamiliar and inappropriate names sometimes required by the principle of priority, and that Powell's family-name suffix-(i)an not be added to the recognized names of tribes or groups that themselves constituted the entire family (Hodge 1907; cf. Stocking 1974:475). These new principles and the committee's recommended names were reflected in the revised listings of Powell's families given by Boas (1911:78-79) and Sapir (1929:138-139, 1949:170-171) (table 3).

California

The more extensive consolidation of Powell's families began with reconsiderations of the diverse languages of California (Dixon and Kroeber 1919; Callaghan 1958; Shipley 1973, 1980; Langdon 1974; Jacobsen 1979; vol. 8:80-90). Dixon and Kroeber (1903) first attempted to classify the languages of California on the basis of the distribution of certain grammatical attributes, arguing that the extreme diversity of these languages made it difficult to classify them on the basis of lexicon. They grouped the California languages according to the presence or absence, or degree of elaboration, of selected typological features: pronominal affixes ("the incorporation into the verb of the pronoun, and at times even of the noun"); syntactic cases ("subjective, objective, and possessive"); adverbial cases ("such as locatives and instrumental"); noun pluralization; and "phonetics." They specifically stated that their classification was based on structural resemblances rather than genetic relationships.

This early typological approach was soon abandoned as evidence for genetic relationships began to accumulate, derived from new descriptive materials. Dixon and Kroeber (1903:3) already proposed the consolidation of Powell's Sastean (Shastan) and Palaihnihan, and of

GODDARD

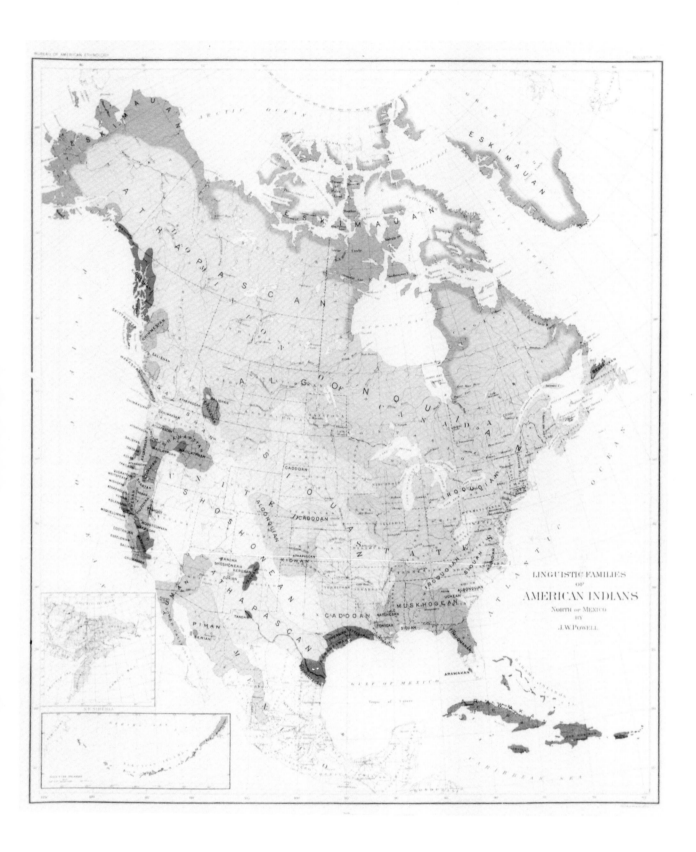

Fig. 5. The 1906 revision of the Powell map, *Linguistic Families of American Indians North of Mexico*, prepared by Bureau of American Ethnology staff after Powell's death.

Smithsonian, NAA: Ms. 3161; Neg. 94-7557.

Fig. 6. The 1915 revision of the Powell map, *Linguistic Families of American Indians North of Mexico,* prepared by Bureau of American Ethnology staff.

Moquelumnan (Miwokan) and Costanoan, groupings that Powell had rejected; the supporting data were given separately (Dixon 1905; Kroeber 1910:259-263). Later, Dixon (1910:335-339) presented evidence for a relationship between Chimarikan and Shastan-Palaihnihan. Then, almost simultaneously with the appearance of Kroeber's (1913) defense of the usefulness of a typological approach to classification and plea for recognition of the role of diffusion in grammar, Dixon and Kroeber (1912, 1913) announced a set of new genetic groupings of California languages in a note that appeared in both *Science* and the *American Anthropologist*. By the time the full presentation was made, the list of new groupings had expanded further (Dixon and Kroeber 1913a). The new units proposed by Dixon and Kroeber (1913a) were Penutian, Hokan, Iskoman, and Ritwan. Penutian comprised Miwok (Powell's Moquelumnan), Costanoan, Yokuts (Powell's Mariposan), Maidu (Powell's Pujunan), and Wintun (Powell's Copehan). Hokan included "Shasta" (Shastan-Palaihnihan), Chimariko (Powell's Chimarikan), Pomo (Pomoan; Powell's Kulanapan), Karok (Powell's Quoratean), Yana (Powell's Yanan), Yuman (Cochimí-Yuman), and Esselen (Powell's Esselenian). Iskoman united Salinan and Chumash (Chumashan), and Ritwan put together Wiyot (Powell's Wishoskan) and Yurok (Powell's Weitspekan). The possibility of connections between Hokan and Seri and Iskoman was also suggested. The evidence cited for these groupings was mostly short lists of basic vocabulary items, plus, for Penutian and Hokan, some general characteristics of grammatical typology and, for Penutian, the paradigms of the nominal cases. Later a much fuller survey of the evidence for Penutian was presented (Dixon and Kroeber 1919:55-102).

A series of studies soon added more languages and families to the Hokan set. Kroeber (1915) linked Seri and Tequistlatecan (Chontal de Oaxaca) to Yuman (represented by Mohave), supporting Brinton's (1891:109-113, 148, 335) claim that these languages were in his "Yuma stock" though not his equally confident inclusion of Guaicura; the proposed Yuman-Seri link had gone back to an early view of Gatschet, later rescinded (Gatschet 1877-1892, 2:133-134, 1900). Sapir (1917), in a study of the Hokan relationships of Yana, supported the previously less certain inclusion in the stock of the "Iskoman" languages, Salinan and Chumashan; earlier, Harrington (1913) had expressed the view that Yuman and Chumashan were related but published no evidence. Harrington (1917) announced the discovery of a link between Washoe and Chumashan, and independently Sapir (1917a, 1921) suggested that Washoe went in Hokan. The inclusion of Washoe was supported by comparisons drawn up by Dixon and Kroeber (1919:104-112), who also gave Sapir's evidence. They listed the consensus Hokan membership as:

Karok, Chimariko, Shastan (Shastan-Palaihnihan), Pomo, Yana, Washo, Esselen, Salinan, Chumash, Yuman (Cochimí-Yuman), Seri, and Tequistlatecan (Dixon and Kroeber 1919:112).

Sapir also linked to Hokan in a broader grouping two sets of languages far from California, "Coahuiltecan" (Sapir 1920) and Tlapanecan, also called Subtiaba-Tlapanec and Supanecan (Sapir 1925). Coahuiltecan comprised a set of languages spoken in southern Texas and the lower Rio Grande Valley that had been proposed as a genetic unit by Swanton (1915). These included not only Powell's Coahuiltecan family, but also his Karankawan, Tonkawan, and Attacapan, as well as the poorly known Maratino and the even more scrappily known Aranama and Solano. Sapir accepted Swanton's grouping but later suggested that Atakapa was not a core member but a possible "link between Coahuiltecan and the Tunica group" (Sapir 1921:72). In the end Sapir's (1925:525-526, 1929) Coahuiltecan was the Coahuiltecan of Swanton (1915:39) minus Atakapa. Tlapanecan consists of two languages of the Pacific coast, Tlapanec in Guerrero, Mexico, and Subtiaba in Nicaragua; Lehmann (1915, 1920) had shown their close relationship to each other and had found similarities with Washoe. Sapir (1925:525-526) called this broader grouping Hokan-Coahuiltecan.

Sapir was also finding relationships between Dixon and Kroeber's Penutian and languages beyond California, in this case to the north. As early as 1915 he already perceived the interconnection of most of what he later called Penutian in the broader sense, subsuming not only the five California language groups ("California Penutian"), but also Takelma (Powell's Takilman), Alsean (Frachtenberg's Yakonan), Siuslaw, Coosan (Powell's Kusan), Kalapuyan (Powell's Kalapooian), and Chinookan (these six constituting "Oregon Penutian"), and Tsimshian (Golla 1984:182-186, 202; Sapir 1921a). Frachtenberg (1918; Hodge 1921:25; Golla 1984:242) independently grouped together Takelma, Kalapuyan, and Chinookan, though he argued that, while their resemblances were too great to be explained away as due to chance or recent diffusion, they were not yet sufficient to prove genetic relationship; he also saw a possible relationship between Kalapuyan and Alsean, Siuslaw, and Coosan and found similarities between Kalapuyan and Klamath and Sahaptian as well.

Perhaps Sapir's most startling claim was his postulation of a link between Ritwan (Wiyot and Yurok) in California and the Algonquian family on the other side of the continent, a relationship vigorously disputed by Truman Michelson (Sapir 1913a, 1915, 1915a; Michelson 1914, 1915). Later Sapir (1923a) tried to support this connection further by a comparison of kinship terms. Because of the controversy, the relationship remained somewhat uncertain until later studies confirmed and expanded on Sapir's work (Haas 1958, 1966; Teeter 1964; Goddard 1975, 1986).

Other Areas

On the Northwest Coast as well, a typological classification led to the postulated consolidation of Powell families. Leaving aside Athapaskan and some small groups, Boas (1894) proposed grouping the languages of this area into four sets: Tlingit and Haida (Powell's Koluschan and Skittagetan); Tsimshian (Powell's Chimmesyan); Kwakiutl (Wakashan), Salish, and Chimakuan (represented by Chemakum); and Chinook. In an earlier listing of these potential stocks in a letter to Henshaw, Boas (1890b) put Athapaskan with Tlingit and Haida. He concluded that the structural resemblances of the languages in each set "could only be explained by the assumption of a common origin," despite the fact that the languages showed no appreciable similarities in vocabulary (Boas 1894:342, 346). Sapir (1915b) followed up on Boas's linking of Tlingit, Haida, and the Athapaskan languages, presenting evidence that they constituted a grouping he called Na-dene (and later Nadene). Swanton (1911:164, 1911a:209) had also noted morphological similarities among the three, as had some nineteenth-century Russian scholars whose work was generally ignored (Krauss 1964:127-128). Frachtenberg (1920a:295) supported the grouping of Wakashan, Salishan, and Chimakuan, coining the name Mosan for the hypothesized stock, and Sapir (1949a) had collected a small set of similar words in Salishan and Wakashan, mostly from Comox and Kwakiutl. There was little dissent from these proposals except, notably, from Boas himself (1920), who abandoned his earlier position and came to think diffusion was the best explanation for similarities like those among Athapaskan, Tlingit, and Haida. Similarly, P.E. Goddard (1920) objected that the lexical dissimilarity between Athapaskan and Tlingit ruled out a genetic connection and invoked borrowing as the explanation for what lexical resemblances there were.

There was also an emerging consensus that the Plateau languages that were not Salishan belonged together. Hewitt (1894) proposed linking together Sahaptian (Powell's Shahaptian), Waiilatpuan, and Klamath-Modoc (Powell's Lutuamian); his study was not published but his conclusions were reported by Powell (1897:1iii-liv, lxxxiv-lxxxv; Jacobs 1931:93). The Bureau accepted the new grouping for the classification of their linguistic manuscripts (under the name "Shahapwailutan") but did not incorporate it on the revisions of the Powell map. Hewitt's proposed classification recalled but did not refer to a guarded suggestion along the same lines by Gatschet (1890:lvi), as well as to some extent the earlier sug-

gestions by Hale (1846:214, 561, 569) and Latham (1860:341-342) about Plateau languages. Henshaw and Frachtenberg (1910) suggested that Sahaptian, Waiilatpuan, Shastan-Palaihnihan, and possibly Klamath-Modoc might be connected, and by 1917 Frachtenberg was claiming to Sapir that there was no doubt that Klamath-Modoc linked up with Sahaptian and Molala (Golla 1984:254).

Meanwhile, Sapir (1913-1914) published a definitive demonstration of the validity of Uto-Aztecan, uniting Powell's Shoshonean and Piman with Nahuatl. Except for its rejection by Powell, this family had been widely accepted, even within the Bureau. Swanton (1919) presented evidence for uniting Tunica, Chitimacha, and Atakapa (Powell's Tonikan, Chitimachan, and Attacapan), and Harrington (1910) showed the close relationship between Kiowa (Powell's Kiowan) and Tanoan.

Sapir's Classification

The revisions proposed for Powell's classification were recapitulated and extended even further by Sapir (1921b, 1925:525-526, 1929, 1949:169-175, 1990: 81-92; Golla 1984:449-457, 1986) in a classification that displaced Powell's as the framework for general discussions of the linguistic history of North America. Sapir actually presented three classifications: that of the revised Powell map of 1915, with the addition of Frachtenberg's splitting of Powell's Yakonan into Yakonan and Siuslaw and the replacement of some names (table 3); a list of proposed "reductions" of Powell families that he considered "either probable or very possible," almost all of which he or others had published in some form (table 4); and his own comprehensive "scheme . . . , suggestive but far from demonstrable in all its features at the present time" (Sapir 1929:139) (table 5) ("Language and the Culture History of North America," fig. 1, this vol.).

Although most of Sapir's intermediate-level "reductions" had received some public discussion, the evidence available to support them varied greatly. The most extensively documented was Uto-Aztecan, for which Sapir had published detailed information on comparative grammar and phonological history. He also had given a very extensive presentation of his ideas on Hokan and Penutian, including reconstructions. On the other extreme, there was no published evidence for Mosan or the interior Oregon group (table 4, e and j), and for the connection between Iroquoian and Caddoan there had not even been a public announcement. The only previous hint of the Iroquois-Caddoan link was Latham's (1846:44, 1860:290) assertion that Caddo had affinities with Iroquoian languages, Creek,

Catawba, and Pawnee. There had been no new discussion of Beothuk (Sapir 1921b). On two points he seemed to backtrack from earlier positions, presenting the connections between Algonquian and Wiyot-Yurok and between Haida and Athapaskan-Tlingit as less certain than the rest.

Sapir's comprehensive classification grouped all North American languages into six "major linguistic groups," later often referred to as superstocks or phyla. These were: Eskimo-Aleut, Algonkin-Wakashan, Nadene, Penutian, Hokan-Siouan, and Aztec-Tanoan. In his first presentation he expressed uncertainty about the classification of the Sahaptian-Waiilatpuan-Klamath grouping, Zuni, and Beothuk; later he put the first of these in the Penutian phylum, put Zuni in Aztec-Tanoan with a query, and put Beothuk in Algonkin-Wakashan, also with a query. The assignment of Timucua to Natchez-Muskogean in the Hokan-Siouan phylum was queried in both versions. Sapir thought of these superstocks as being each distinguished by a set of morphological characteristics, to some extent supported by lexical evidence. He stressed the tentative, heuristic nature of the classification. No evidence was ever published for major parts of it. After it appeared, work on classifying North American languages came almost to a standstill, except for some not published (Whorf 1935a:608; Trager 1945:188), and it was two decades before it served Sapir's intended purpose of being a framework subject to revision based on further investigation. The use of the Sapir classification on a widely used map of North American Indian languages (C.F. Voegelin and E.W. Voegelin 1944) gave it a pervasive and long-lasting influence in North American ethnology generally.

After Sapir

Work on classification after Sapir took several forms. Eventually proposals were made to modify Sapir's scheme, splitting and reassembling parts of it. At least as significant, though, was the consolidation of knowledge within accepted subunits, leading to refinements of subgrouping. An important part of this work involved reconstructing the linguistic histories of major families. Also, considerable effort was devoted to elucidating the status and internal composition of Hokan and Penutian, leading to the dismemberment of Sapir's Hokan-Siouan superstock and attempts to realign its constituent parts. Eventually two major conferences, held in 1964 and 1976, evaluated the status and degree of acceptance of this work.

• HOKAN As more accurate descriptive material became available the Hokan hypothesis was reexamined. The history of this work has been treated by Shipley (1973:1059-1065), Langdon (1974), and

Table 4. Sapir's Intermediate-Level Consolidations of Powell's Classification

a. Wiyot and Yurok, to which may have to be added Algonkian (of which Beothuk may be a very divergent member)

b. Iroquoian and Caddoan

c. Uto-Aztekan, consisting of Shoshonean, Piman and Nahuatl

d. Athabaskan and Tlingit, with Haida as a more distant relative

e. Mosan, consisting of Salish, Chimakuan, and Wakashan

f. Atakapa, Tunica, and Chitimacha

g. Coahuiltecan, Tonkawa, and Karankawa

h. Kiowa and Tanoan

i. Takelma, Kalapuya, and Coos-Siuslaw-Yakonan

j. Sahaptin, Waiilatpuan, and Lutuami

k. Hokan, consisting of Karok, Chimariko, Shastan, Yana, Pomo, Washo, Esselen, Yuman, Salinan, Chumash, and, in Mexico, Seri and Chontal

l. Penutian, consisting of Miwok-Costanoan, Yokuts, Maidu, and Wintun

SOURCE: Sapir (1929:139, 1949:171-172) gives these as "reductions" of the families in the revised Powell classification (table 3) that are "probable or very possible."

Jacobsen (1979). A number of studies compared pairs or small sets of languages and assembled lists of similar words. Bright (1954) compared Karok, Chimariko, and Shastan-Palaihnihan, which Sapir had grouped together as the subbranch "Northern Hokan (a);" Olmsted (1956, 1957, 1959) compared Shastan and Palaihnihan; and Silver (1964) Shasta and Karok. Other binary comparisons were made of Washoe and Karok (Jacobsen 1958), Yana and Karok (Haas 1964), Pomoan (represented by Eastern Pomo) and Yana, Sapir's "Northern Hokan (b) and (c)" (McLendon 1964), Chimariko and Yuman (James Crawford 1976), and Seri and Yuman (Judith Crawford 1976). Some of these included comparisons with additional languages. Haas (1963) examined a few words over the whole stock, building on Sapir's work to reconstruct a core of basic vocabulary with an outline of the phonological history thus implied. Gursky (1974) assembled extensive comparative lexical materials. Most of this work involved the comparison of lexical items accompanied by statements of phonological correspondences, while the morphological history was little investigated. The most extensive presentation of Hokan morphology had been given by Sapir (1925) in his article on Subtiaba, a study that was long considered definitive and an exemplary exposition of Sapir's method of discovering fossilized reflexes of earlier morphological patterns that demonstrated the links between distantly related languages. After the confirmation that Tlapanecan was, in fact, a member of the Otomanguean stock of Mesoamerica, as first suggested by Robert J. Weitlaner (Rensch 1977; Suárez 1979, 1980, 1983:2, 1986), the *313*

Table 5. Sapir's Classification

I. Eskimo-Aleut	(b) Yana
II. Algonkin-Wakashan	(c) Pomo
1. Algonkin-Ritwan	(2) Washo
(1) Algonkin	(3) Esselen-Yuman
(2) Beothuk (?)	(a) Esselen
(3) Ritwan	(b) Yuman
(a) Wiyot	(4) Salinan-Seri
(b) Yurok	(a) Salinan
2. Kootenay	(b) Chumash
3. Mosan (Wakashan-Salish)	(c) Seri
(1) Wakashan (Kwakiutl-Nootka)	(5) Tequistlatecan (Chontal)
(2) Chimakuan	B. Subtiaba-Tlappanec
(3) Salish	C. Coahuiltecan
III. Nadene	(1) Tonkawa
1. Haida	(2) Coahuilteco
2. Continental Nadene	(a) Coahuilteco proper
(1) Tlingit	(b) Cotoname
(2) Athabaskan	(c) Comecrudo
IV. Penutian	(3) Karankawa
1. California Penutian	2. Yuki
(1) Miwok-Costanoan	3. Keres
(2) Yokuts	4. Tunican
(3) Maidu	(1) Tunica-Atakapa
(4) Wintun	(2) Chitimacha
2. Oregon Penutian	5. Iroquois-Caddoan
(1) Takelma	(1) Iroquoian
(2) Coast Oregon Penutian	(2) Caddoan
(a) Coos	6. Eastern group
(b) Siuslaw	(1) Siouan-Yuchi
(c) Yakonan	(a) Siouan
(3) Kalapuya	(b) Yuchi
3. Chinook	(2) Natchez-Muskogian
4. Tsimshian	(a) Natchez
5. Plateau Penutian	(b) Muskogian
(1) Sahaptin	(c) Timucua (?)
(2) Waiilatpuan (Molala-Cayuse)	VI. Aztec-Tanoan
(3) Lutuami (Klamath-Modoc)	1. Uto-Aztekan
6. Mexican Penutian	(1) Nahuatl
(1) Mixe-Zoque	(2) Pima
(2) Huave	(3) Shoshonean
V. Hokan-Siouan	2. Tanoan-Kiowa
1. Hokan-Coahuiltecan	(1) Tanoan
A. Hokan	(2) Kiowa
(1) Northern Hokan	3. Zuñi (?)
(a) Karok, Chimariko, Shasta-Achomawi	

SOURCE: "Proposed Classification of American Indian Languages North of Mexico (and Certain Languages of Mexico and Central America)" (Sapir 1929:139, 1949:172-173).

speculative nature of Sapir's exposition of Hokan morphology and the need for a new synthesis became clear.

Overall evaluations of the Hokan hypothesis generally agreed that it merited further study, with varying degrees of confidence being expressed in the amount of promise it showed. For example, Campbell and Mithun (1979:43), stating a skeptical view, wrote that "the entire 'Hokan' complex . . . needs extensive reexamination and evaluation. As yet there has been no suffi-

cient demonstration that any two of the variously proposed branches are actually related genetically." In the same volume, Jacobsen (1979:570), whose detailed examinations of the evidence have taken a generally positive approach to the hypothesis, states: "The Hokan languages are extremely distantly related to each other, and the proof is really lacking that they are mutually more closely related than some might be to some other languages outside of the conventionally-recognized group. . . . Much of one's feeling that there may be a genuine relationship here is based on certain sets of basic words that run through many of the branches, many of which have been recognized from the earliest comparative works; . . .". Within the putative Hokan superstock as proposed by Sapir, the languages and families whose membership was the most in question, were (in addition to the reclassified Tlapanecan) Chumashan, Tequistlatec, and, because of the dearth of reliable data, Esselen (C.F. Voegelin and F.M. Voegelin 1965:142; Campbell 1979:965-967; cf. Waterhouse 1976). A proposed addition of Jicaque, a family of two languages spoken in Honduras (Greenberg and Swadesh 1953), was also considered an open question (Oltrogge 1977:40; Campbell 1979:965-967; Campbell and Oltrogge 1980). There was no evidence for subgrouping the branches that had won general acceptance. Kaufman (1989, 1989a) embarked on a comprehensive restudy of Hokan and reported initial positive results.

• PENUTIAN The reexamination of Sapir's Penutian led to new suggestions for subgrouping and a certain amount of work on the specifics of linguistic history (Hymes 1964a; Shipley 1973:1052-1059; Thompson 1973:987-997; Silverstein 1979). Work on reconstructing California Penutian as a separate unit, referred to as the "Penutian kernel" (Pitkin and Shipley 1958; Shipley 1973:1057), was succeeded by attempts to compare with this and with each other languages of Sapir's Oregon Penutian and Plateau Penutian. Shipley compared Kalapuyan with Takelma, providing evidence for a subgrouping of these languages as Takelman, a proposal that had first been made by Swadesh (1954a:327, 1956:21, 1965; Shipley 1970, 1969). Shipley (1966) and DeLancey (1987) compared Klamath with California Penutian, and Aoki (1963), Rude (1987), and DeLancey (1992) compared Klamath and Sahaptian. It remained unclear whether the results of these comparisons should be regarded as confirming Sapir's Penutian or as indicating the need to rearrange the membership in its major branches. Berman (1981:253-256, 1983) defended California Penutian by citing and reconstructing shared morphological elements. Rigsby (1966, 1969) re-examined the available, imperfect materials on Molala and Cayuse and concluded that they were probably not related on the family levels. His arguments have been generally accepted as refuting the validity of Powell's Waiilatpuan, which had been generally accepted since being proposed by Hale (1846). What resemblances there are between the languages may reflect areal relations, such as the borrowing that Hale conjectured, or a deeper genetic relationship in a putative grouping that also includes Sahaptian. Suggestions for possible arrangements of some of these languages were made by Silverstein (1979:679-680). Silverstein (1979:680) also

considered the inclusion of Chinookan in Penutian to be "probable" since its grammatical divergences from the other languages could be accounted for as innovations; he expressed the most reservations about Tsimshian, which "if related, is more problematic." Comparisons of Klamath, Sahaptian, and Tsimshian were published by DeLancey, Genetti, and Rude (1988).

As a sixth branch of Penutian Sapir had included the Mixe-Zoquean family and the Huave language, both spoken in Mexico. The idea for this extension of the superstock seems to have grown out of a suggestion made to Sapir by Dixon about Zoque (Freeland 1930; Shipley 1973:1052). Penutian connections for other Mexican languages have been suggested, beginning with Whorf (1935a; Mason 1940:58; Johnson 1940:104-110). None of these proposals has attracted the same degree of support as the rest of Sapir's Penutian, and there have been alternative suggestions (Campbell 1979:964). Apparent support for the distant relationship between California Penutian and Zuni suggested by Swadesh (1956), primarily in the form of lexical evidence and a discussion of structural similarities, is given by Newman (1964), but Newman is reported to have considered this paper a tongue-in-cheek effort to demonstrate the invalidity of the the the methodology used (Michael Silverstein, personal communication 1994). The five northernmost branches of Sapir's Penutian have continued to receive attention as promising candidates for inclusion in a single superstock, but without a comprehensive synthesis and evaluation of the supporting evidence.

• HOKAN-SIOUAN Sapir's largest and most diverse proposed superstock, Hokan-Siouan, has attracted the most criticism and undergone the most revision. Even some of the individual branches and subbranches of Hokan have been questioned as coherent entities. The credibility of the Hokan-Coahuiltecan branch suffered from the beginning from the fact that the Coahuiltecan component and even the segment of it that Sapir called Coahuilteco (Powell's Coahuiltecan) were in themselves questionable. Cyrus Thomas (1902:209, 215), a Bureau ethnologist, had pointed out early on that Powell's Coahuiltecan was "not to be taken as a true linguistic family or stock name" as it was based on a unit in the classification of Orozco y Berra (1864) that was merely geographical. His remarks in the Bureau classification of Mexican and Central American languages were more circumspect but still hinted at uncertainty about the inclusiveness of the Powell family, which he called Pakawan following an earlier usage of Gatschet's (Thomas 1911:38). Swanton (1940:144-145) himself expressed reservations about the higher-level Coahuiltecan while affirming belief in an ultimate relationship among the languages. In a generally positive examination of Sapir's Hokan-

Coahuiltecan (renamed Hokaltecan) Bright (1956:48) concluded that "Sapir's Coahuiltecan group must . . . be considered of doubtful validity." In the Consensus Classification of 1964, Sapir's Coahuiltecan was abandoned as a unit (splitting off Tonkawa and Karankawa), and Powell's Coahuiltecan was split into Comecrudan (Comecrudo and Cotoname) and Coahuiltecan (the Coahuilteco language) (C.F. Voegelin and F.M. Voegelin 1965:141, 142, 144). Goddard (1979a) pointed out the diversity and poor documentation of the languages involved and concluded that the number of family-level units subsumed in Powell's Coahuiltecan could not be reduced to less than three—Coahuilteco, Comecrudan (Comecrudo, Carrizo of Mamulique, and Garza), and Cotoname—with Solano and Aranama recognized as two additional if poorly known small families.

In a series of studies Mary R. Haas examined the possible relations of some of the components of Sapir's Hokan-Siouan among themselves as well as with some languages outside that stock. She proposed a grouping of languages called Gulf, which included Muskogean, Natchez, Tunica, Chitimacha, and Atakapan, and explored lexical similarities also between these and Siouan, Yuchi, and other languages (Haas 1941:55-56, 1951:71, 1952). Sapir had classified these languages as two of the branches of Hokan-Siouan. Haas (1956) presented analyzed lexical comparisons of Natchez and Muskogean to support the widely accepted relationship between these languages in what she called Natchez-Muskogean, equivalent to the Muskhogean of the 1915 Bureau map (Powell 1915). Later she concluded that a relatively closer relationship between Natchez and Muskogean within Gulf was not necessarily to be assumed (Haas 1969a:62, 1979:317-318). A major resorting of the components of Sapir's superstocks was implied when Haas (1958a) presented evidence for a linkage between the Algonquian family (in Sapir's Algonkin-Wakashan) and the Gulf languages (in Sapir's Hokan-Siouan). She went on to assemble comparative lexical data on Algonquian and Tonkawa (Haas 1959s 1967:316-317), Algonquian and Mosan, represented by Chemakum and Salishan languages (Haas 1960), Algonquian and Kootenai (Haas 1965), and Nadene and Siouan-Yuchi (Haas 1964). The significance of these and other observed similarities was left unclear, as Haas herself remarked; the proposed connections had come to link a broad subset of the languages of North America, cutting across recognized and proposed groupings in ways that were difficult to reconcile (Haas 1964a:84, 1967:318).

A different approach to the question of the relationships of Siouan is embodied in the Macro-Siouan hypothesis, which unites Siouan with Sapir's Iroquois-Caddoan (Allen 1931; Chafe 1964, 1976:43-53; Carter 1980:180-182). Although some comparisons made among these languages have been considered striking enough to merit further attention, the linkage has not been demonstrated (Rankin 1981:174-176).

Other attempts to confirm Sapir's Hokan-Siouan superstock included particular efforts on isolates outside of the Hokan and Coahuiltecan branches (Chafe 1976:53-54). Elmendorf (1963, 1964) compared words of Yukian and Yuchi with Siouan; these resemblances, as well as others found for Yuchi, remain inconclusive (Crawford 1979). Brinton and Gatschet both detected "affinities" between Timucua and Carib (Powell 1891:123), and similarities with Timucua have also been claimed for Muskogean, Gulf, Siouan, Arawakan, and Warao, a language of South America (Crawford 1979:336, 1988; Granberry 1993). Despite these efforts, the relationships of Timucua remain uncertain, beyond a second branch of the Timucuan family that appears to be attested by a 1707 vocabulary of Tawasa (Swanton 1929). Keresan was compared with Caddoan by Swadesh (1967), a suggestion cautiously supported by Rood (1973a) but seriously undermined by Hamp (in Rood 1973a) and Davis (1974). Davis (1979:412) later suggested looking for connections between Keresan and Uto-Aztecan.

• ALGONKIN-WAKASHAN In addition to Haas's comparisons of Algonquian with western members of Sapir's Algonkin-Wakashan superstock, there were examinations of smaller components within the superstock. The relationship of Algonquian to Wiyot and Yurok was confirmed on the basis of better data (Haas 1958, 1966; Teeter 1964; Goddard 1975, 1986). Swadesh (1949:167-171, 1953, 1953a) presented comparisons to support the validity of Mosan but later proposed splitting off Wakashan and aligning it more closely with Eskimo-Aleut and Asian languages (1962, 1964). The status of Mosan remained uncertain, possible genetic relationships being obscured by extensive borrowing among these groups (Thompson 1979:750-751; J.V. Powell 1993). Hewson (1968, 1971, 1978:138-146) brought together the lexical evidence on which any demonstration of a relationship between Beothuk and Algonquian would probably have to rest, but Goddard (1979:106-107) argued that it was unpersuasive. The only Powell-unit components of Sapir's Algonkin-Wakashan that were generally accepted as being related remained Algonquian and Ritwan (Wiyot and Yurok), referred to jointly as Algonquian-Ritwan or Algic.

• NADENE The major development in Sapir's proposed Nadene superstock was the rediscovery of Eyak in 1930. Data from studies of Eyak eventually undertaken in the 1950s and 1960s revealed that it was a sister language to Athapaskan, equally related to all languages of the family (Krauss 1964:128, 1965a, 1973a:932-934, 950; de Laguna in Cowan, Foster, and Koerner 1986:395-396). Under the name Ugalentzes or

Ugaljachmutzi the Eyak had been included in the Eskimauan family of Powell (1891:71), following the influential reports by Dall (1877:21) and by Petroff (1884:146), who described them as an Eskimoan group culturally assimilated to their Tlingit neighbors. At first Dall (1870:267-270, 1870a:401, 430, 548, 550) had classified an Eyak vocabulary from Wrangell labeled "Ugaléntsi" as "Tinneh" (Athapaskan) and a vocabulary from Gibbs labeled "Ugalákmut" as "Innuit" (Eskimoan), believing that these were two different groups. The vocabulary obtained from Gibbs was in fact an Eskimo vocabulary, similar to the Aglurmiut dialect of Central Alaskan Yupik, sent to him by Stepan Vasil'evich Voevodskii (1858), who had labeled it as being from near Mount Saint Elias (Miyaoka 1974; vol. 5:53). Later, correctly equating the names Ugaléntsi and Ugalákmut, but not noticing the mislabeling and discrepancy, Dall lumped these together as Eskimoan, an identification concurred with by Henshaw on the basis of the Voevodskii vocabulary. Previously, Eyak had been called a branch of Athapaskan by Buschmann (1855:233, 1856:253, 1859:686-689), a connection also suggested by Gallatin (1848:7); and others had grouped Eyak with Tlingit (Holmberg 1856) or had considered Athapaskan, Eyak, and Tlingit all to be related (Wrangell 1839:51-53; Radloff 1858).

The relationship between Tlingit and Athapaskan-Eyak was accepted on the basis of detailed similarities in grammatical subsystems but remained uncomplemented by extensive, close lexical matches supported by recurring sound correspondences of the sort that would ordinarily be expected between languages with such a degree of grammatical resemblance (Krauss 1973a:953-963, 1979:838; Leer 1990). The proposed link to Haida was clearly much more remote and generally considered undemonstrated (Krauss 1973a:956-962, 1979:838; Levine 1979; Leer 1990:73, 1991:162; Jacobsen 1993), though argued for by Hymes (1956), Pinnow (1985, 1985a, 1986, 1990), and Greenberg (1987:321-330). Thomason (1980a) presented methodological counterarguments to Hymes.

• AZTEC-TANOAN Evidence to support the relationship between Uto-Aztecan and Powell's Tanoan was presented by Whorf and Trager (1937). On the basis of a list of lexical comparisons they reconstructed an "Azteco-Tanoan" sound system and presented a table of sound correspondences. They felt at the time that the relationship between Kiowa and Tanoan that Sapir had accepted from Harrington was much more tenuous. Subsequently the close link between Kiowa and Tanoan was demonstrated (Miller 1959; Trager and Trager 1959; Hale 1962, 1967); it rests on both extensive sound correspondences and striking parallels in idiosyncratic morphological alternations. In fact, there is no clear indication that the Tanoan languages are more closely related among themselves than they are to

Kiowa (Davis 1979:401-403; vol. 9:171). In contrast, the proposed relationship between Uto-Aztecan and Tanoan has benefited from little additional work, and even some who have approached it with an essentially positive attitude consider it to be at best remote, perhaps only one of several comparably distant relationships of Uto-Aztecan (Davis 1979:408-409, 1989; Shaul 1985; vol. 9:171).

Despite the misgivings expressed by Leap (1971), Harrington's (1909) demonstration that Piro was a Tanoan language is generally accepted (Davis 1979: 403-404).

• CLASSIFICATION CONFERENCES In 1964 a conference called in Bloomington, Indiana, to solicit advice on the revision of the Voegelin map (C.F. Voegelin and E.W. Voegelin 1944) brought together most scholars then actively engaged in the historical study of North American languages. Although there were some differences of opinion, the views expressed were summarized in what has been called the Consensus Classification, which included annotations on points of uncertainty and disagreement (C.F. Voegelin and F.M. Voegelin 1965) (table 6) ("Language and the Culture History of North America," fig. 2, this vol.). These annotations were not included on the revised map (C.F. Voegelin and F.M. Voegelin 1966), which also suffers from a decision to omit all languages that happened to be extinct in 1965 unless they were isolates. In 1976 a conference was held in Oswego, New York, to consider critically the state of knowledge of the comparative and historical linguistics of North America, including Mesoamerica (Campbell and Mithun 1979). Campbell and Mithun (1979:39-46) summarized the results in a comprehensive classification that took a consistently cautious approach to undemonstrated claims of relationship (table 7).

Other presentations and discussions of classifications of the native languages of North America have included those of Voegelin (1941c), Hoijer (1946), Trager and Harben (1958), Lamb (1959), Pinnow (1964), and Gursky (1966).

• CONTINENT-WIDE HYPOTHESES Some writers have proposed much broader classificatory schemes than those generally accepted as plausibly demonstrated. These unite most of the languages of North America in a single genetic unit or divide all the languages of the New World into a small number of vast agglomerations as part of a reductionist classification of all the languages of the world (Radin 1919; Swadesh 1954a, 1967a:88-90, 1971:218; Greenberg 1987; Ruhlen 1991). Specialists in the historical analysis and classification of the languages of North America are in nearly unanimous agreement that these proposals lack merit.

The most thoroughly presented and discussed of these schemes is Greenberg's. Greenberg (1987:331) classifies all native languages of the New World into

317

three groups: Eskimo-Aleut, Na-Dene (including Haida), and Amerind. He divides the vast Amerind group into 11 subgroups, of which those with member languages in North America are: Almosan-Keresiouan, Penutian, Hokan, Central Amerind, and Chibchan-Paezan. Almosan-Keresiouan includes Sapir's Algonkin-Wakashan (Almosan) plus Caddoan, Iroquoian, Siouan-Yuchi, and Keresan (Keresiouan). Greenberg's Penutian is Sapir's Penutian, plus the Gulf languages, Yukian, Zuni, and Mayan and Totonac in Mexico. Hokan for Greenberg embraces Sapir's Hokan-Coahuiltecan plus Guaicura, Maratino, and Quinigua (in northern Mexico) and Jicaque (in Honduras) and Yurumanguí (in Columbia). Greenberg's Central Amerind covers Kiowa-Tanoan, Uto-Aztecan, and the Otomanguean family of Mexico and Central America (minus Tlapanecan). Chibchan-Paezan includes only Timucua in North America, the rest of this subgroup being found in Central America and northern South America. The extensive literature criticizing Greenberg's data, methodology, and classification, which gives further references, includes Campbell (1988), Goddard and Campbell (1994), Rankin (1992), Kimball (1992), Ringe (1992, 1993), and Poser (1993:221-222, 1993a).

• RELATIONS OUTSIDE THE AMERICAS A very large number of often contradictory hypotheses have been put forward about relationships between the native languages of the Americas and those of the rest of the world. Most of this literature is regarded by specialists as without merit. The only such hypothesis that has retained some degree of respectability is the proposed connection between Eskimo-Aleut and the Luoravetlan languages of extreme eastern Siberia, including Chukchi and its relatives (Swadesh 1962; Hamp 1976).

Subclassification and Reconstruction

Considerable progress was made toward the goal of reconstructing the detailed history of a number of language families, with concomitant refinements in the subclassification of the constituent languages. The standard procedure involved the use of the comparative method, a technique of linguistic triangulation "used to construct hypotheses about the undocumented history of related languages by systematically comparing their features" (Campbell and Goddard 1990:19). In the use of this method, when extensive comparison of two or more related languages shows that certain features in each regularly correspond, a hypothetical original form is reconstructed for the feature, together with the separate sequences of changes or unchanged stages needed to convert this reconstructed feature into the attested forms it has taken in the various languages. The systematic accumulation of these reconstructed features constitutes the hypothesized ancestral protolanguage of the language family. A set of shared innovations found only in some of the languages may support the postulation of a subgroup of languages within the family that descend from an intermediate protolanguage that had undergone these innovations.

• ALGONQUIAN The first detailed classification of the Algonquian languages was based on the occurrence of certain phonetic features and the pronominal inflection of verbs (Michelson 1912:226). Four major divisions were delimited: Blackfoot, Cheyenne, Arapaho, and Eastern-Central. The Central subdivision included Massachusett and Delaware as well as the languages of the Upper Great Lakes and the eastern Canadian Subarctic; the Eastern subdivision included only the languages of northern New England and the Maritimes. When Bloomfield (1925) reconstructed the sound system of Algonquian on the basis of what were at the time the four best attested languages—Fox, Cree, Menominee, and Ojibwa—he called the protolanguage Primitive Central Algonquian. Subsequently Michelson's (1935) work on Cheyenne and Arapaho, and C.F. Voegelin's (1941) and Siebert's (1941) on East Coast languages showed that Bloomfield's reconstruction was likely to be valid for the family as a whole, and when he published his sketch of Algonquian comparative grammar he referred to the protolanguage as Proto-Algonquian (Bloomfield 1946). Later work added many details including at least partial phonological histories of several individual languages (Goddard 1967a, 1979, 1979b, 1990c, 1994). The only major subgroup revealed by this work was Eastern Algonquian, comprising all the Algonquian languages of the Eastern Seaboard from Nova Scotia to northeastern North Carolina (vol. 15:70-77, 583-587; Goddard 1980, 1994:198-201). The status of Blackfoot, the most divergent Algonquian language, remained uncertain. Although Blackfoot reflexes can be traced for most Proto-Algonquian segments and clusters (Taylor 1960; Proulx 1989), no Algonquian source has been determined for many features of Blackfoot phonology (Goddard 1994:188). Blackfoot appears to be the earliest offshoot from the protolanguage, perhaps early enough to constitute a sister branch to the rest of the family.

Some progress was made reconstructing the history of Algic (Algonquian-Ritwan) (Berman 1982, 1990a; Proulx 1984, 1985; Goddard 1990c:108-111). Berman's work in particular provided concrete support for the long-suspected subgrouping of Wiyot and Yurok (as Ritwan) against Algonquian.

• ATHAPASKAN-EYAK Early work on the phonological history and classification of Athapaskan (Sapir 1914, 1931; Hoijer 1938, 1960, 1963, 1966) was superseded when materials from the northern languages with the most archaic phonologies were used (Krauss 1973a, 1986; Leer 1979; Krauss and Leer 1981; Cook and Rice 1989:6-14; vol. 6:67-85). A good understanding was

Table 6. Consensus Classification of 1964

I.	American Arctic–Paleosiberian Phylum		Vn	*Esselen language isolate[d]
	Ia Eskimo-Aleut language family		Vo	Jicaque language isolate
	IIa Chukchi-Kamchatkan[a] language family		Vp	Tlapanecan (Subtiaba-Tlapanec) language family
II.	Na-Dene Phylum		Vq	Tequistlatecan language family

I. American Arctic–Paleosiberian Phylum
  Ia   Eskimo-Aleut language family
  IIa Chukchi-Kamchatkan[a] language family
II. Na-Dene Phylum
  IIa Athapascan language family (includes Eyak)
  IIb Tlingit language isolate
  IIc Haida language isolate
III. Macro-Algonquian Phylum
  IIIa Algonquian language family[b]
  IIIb Yurok language isolate[b]
  IIIc Wiyot language isolate[b]
  IIId Muskogean language family
  IIIe Natchez language isolate
  IIIf *Atakapa
  IIIg Chitimacha language isolate
  IIIh Tunica language isolate
  IIIi *Tonkawa (dubiously classified)
IV. Macro-Siouan Phylum
  IVa Siouan language family
  IVb Catawba language isolate (part of or closely linked to Siouan)
  IVc Iroquoian language family
  IVd Caddoan language family
  IVe Yuchi language isolate
V. Hokan Phylum
  Va   Yuman language family[c]
  Vb   Seri language isolate
  Vc   Pomo language family
  Vd   Palaihnihan language family
  Ve   Shastan language family
  Vf   *Yanan language family
  Vg   Chimariko language isolate
  Vh   Washo language isolate
  Vi   *Salinan language family
  Vj   Karok language isolate
  Vk   *Chumashan language family[d]
  Vl   *Comecrudan language family[d]
  Vm   Coahuiltecan language isolate[d]
  Vn   *Esselen language isolate[d]
  Vo   Jicaque language isolate
  Vp   Tlapanecan (Subtiaba-Tlapanec) language family
  Vq   Tequistlatecan language family
VI. Penutian Phylum
  VIa Yokuts language family
  VIb Maidu language family
  VIc Wintun language family
  VId Miwok-Costanoan language family
  VIe Klamath-Modoc language isolate
  VIf Sahaptin–Nez Perce language family
  VIg *Cayuse language isolate
  VIh *Molale language isolate
  VIi Coos language family
  VIj Yakonan language family (or Alsea and Siuslaw–Lower Umpqua, two language isolates)
  VIk Takelma language isolate
  VII Kalapuya language family
  VIm Chinookan language family
  VIn Tsimshian language isolate[d]
  VIo Zuni language isolate[d]
VII. Aztec-Tanoan Phylum
  VIIa Kiowa-Tanoan language family
  VIIb Uto-Aztecan language family
VIII. Language Isolates and Families With Undetermined Phylum Affiliations North of Mexico
  VIIIa Keres language isolate
  VIIIb Yuki language family
  VIIIc *Beothuk language isolate
  VIIId Kutenai language isolate (with possible remote connections to Algonquian, Salish, and Wakashan)
  VIIIe Karankawa language isolate
  VIIIf Chimakuan language family
  VIIIg Salish language family (with possible affiliation to Algonquian)
  VIIIh Wakashan language family
  VIIIi *Timucua language isolate

SOURCE: "On-Going Revision of American Indian Language Classification" (C.F. Voegelin and F.M. Voegelin 1965:139-145).
NOTES:
  Also includes many notes on postulated "cognacy" and "interfamily connections" between components within phyla.
  * Indicated as extinct in 1964.
  [a]Misprinted as Chukchi-Kamchtkan.
  [b]In the "Algic affiliation."
  [c]Includes Cochimí.
  [d]With reservations on phylum affiliation.

---

achieved of the historical phonology of the family and its relation to Eyak, as well as of extensive segments of the morphology. The widespread overlapping distribution of most innovations has made subgrouping the languages controversial, except for the separate enclaves of Pacific Coast Athapaskan and Apachean (vol. 10:393-400). Oregon and California branches of Pacific Coast Athapaskan can be distinguished by divergent phonological innovations (Golla 1987).

• CADDOAN   The phonological inventory of Proto-Caddoan is generally well understood (Taylor 1963a; Chafe 1976:52, 1979:217-226). The family has two branches, Northern Caddoan, comprising the Pawnee, Arikara, Kitsai, and Wichita languages, and Southern Caddoan, consisting of the dialects of Caddo (Lesser and Weltfish 1932:2; Hollow and Parks 1980:77). The Pawnee language includes the South Band Pawnee and Skiri dialects, spoken by divisions of the Pawnee tribe. *319*

Table 7. Campbell and Mithun's Classification of 1979

1. Eskimo-Aleut	32. Subtiaba-Tlapanec family[h]
2. Nadene[a]	33. Tequistlatecan family[g]
-. Haida isolate[b]	34. Yokuts family
3. Algonquian-Ritwan	35. Maiduan family
4. Muskogean family	36. Wintuan family
5. Natchez isolate	37. Miwok family
6. Atakapa isolate[c]	38. Costanoan family
7. Chitimacha isolate	39. Klamath-Modoc isolate
8. Tunica isolate[c]	40. Sahaptian family
9. Tonkawa isolate	41. Cayuse isolate
10. Siouan family[d,e]	42. Molala isolate
11. Iroquoian family[e]	43. Coos family
12. Caddoan family[e]	44. Alsea isolate
13. Yuchi isolate[c]	45. Siuslaw–Lower Umpqua
14. Yuman family[f]	isolate
15. Seri isolate	46. Takelma isolate
16. Pomoan family[f]	47. Kalapuya family
17. Palaihnihan family	48. Chinookan family
18. Shastan family	49. Tsimshian isolate
19. Yanan family	50. Zuni isolate
20. Chimariko isolate	51. Kiowa-Tanoan family
21. Washo isolate	52. Uto-Aztecan family[i]
22. Salinan family	53. Keresan family[i]
23. Karok isolate	54. Yukian family
24. Chumashan family	55. Beothuk isolate
25. Cotoname isolate	56. Kutenai isolate[j]
26. Comecrudo isolate	57. Karankawa isolate
27. Coahuilteco isolate	58. Chimakuan family
28. Aranama-Tamique isolate	59. Salish family[j]
29. Solano isolate	60. Wakashan family
30. Esselen isolate	61. Timucua isolate
31. Jicaque family[g]	62. Adai

SOURCE: Campbell and Mithun (1979:39-46).

NOTES:

Includes discussions of proposed relationships in addition to those summarized in the following notes.

Numbers 14-23 "may be considered 'Core Hokan' languages"; the " 'Hokan' complex (14-33) needs extensive reexamination and evaluation."

Numbers 34-38 are "Core Penutian"; 34-50 "have variously been called Penutian."

[a]Nadene "includes the Athapaskan-Eyak family, to which Tlingit is perhaps distantly related."

[b]Discussed but by oversight not numbered.

[c]"Possible connections" among Yuchi, Atakapa, and Tunica have been suggested.

[d]Includes Catawba.

[e]There is "suggestive" evidence for a "distant" relationship among Siouan, Iroquoian, and Caddoan.

[f]There is a "promising relationship" between Yuman and Pomoan.

[g]Jicaque and Tequistlatecan are "probably related."

[h]The connection between Subtiaba-Tlapanec and Otomanguean appears "promising."

[i]"Possible connections" between Uto-Aztecan and Keresan have been suggested.

[j]There exist "possible connections" between Salish and Kutenai.

Parks (1979b-203; Hollow and Parks 1980:77) concluded that Kitsai was more closely related to Pawnee than to Wichita. There is evidence for additional extinct varieties of Arikara, Wichita, and Caddo (Parks 1979b:202-204), but there has been no comprehensive discussion of the fragmentary dialectal materials, such as the Yatasi vocabulary collected by Gatschet (1884:31-39). The diversity of the numerous political groups that came to be subsumed under the Caddo in particular has been stressed by ethnohistorians (Story 1978:50-51). As indicated also by Sibley's observations from the beginning of the nineteenth century, this diversity must correspond to an undetermined degree of linguistic diversity as well.

Adai has been accepted as probably or certainly Caddoan, but of uncertain classification within the family (Taylor 1963:57, 1963a:131; Chafe 1976:16). No comparative analysis of the fragmentary Adai materials has been published.

• CHUMASHAN There are three branches of Chumashan: Northern Chumash (comprising the Obispeño language), Central Chumash (Purisimeño, Ineseño, Barbareño, and Ventureño), and Island Chumash (Cruzeño) (vol. 8:86, 505). The comparative phonology is generally well understood, but there has been little published on it.

• ESKIMO-ALEUT Eskimoan is considered to be a family of eleven languages, with the greatest diversity in the western part of its territory and the greatest spread in the east (vol. 5:49-63). The five westernmost languages constitute the Sirenikski-Yupik (or Yupik) branch, a dialect chain extending across Bering Strait. Of these, Sirenikski, the most divergent, may form a branch separate from Yupik. The six easternmost languages comprise a long chain of partly intergrading dialects that make up the Inuit-Inupiaq branch and are similar enough to sometimes be considered to form only one or two languages. The phonology of Proto-Eskimoan is known in some detail, and a large comparative dictionary has been published (Fortescue, Jacobson, and Kaplan 1994). Detailed comparisons with Aleut have put the historical relationship between the two branches on a firm footing (Bergsland 1986).

• IROQUOIAN The Iroquoian family has two highly divergent branches, Southern Iroquoian, consisting of the single language Cherokee, and Northern Iroquoian, comprising 10 languages. The history of Northern Iroquoian can for the most part be understood as a series of splits (Mithun 1981:24), of which the deepest divided off Tuscarora and Nottoway. The next division separated Huron and Laurentian from each other and from the remainder. Next, Seneca, Onondaga, Susquehannock, and Mohawk-Oneida split up. And finally Mohawk and Oneida became differentiated from each other, though they remain very similar languages. In contrast, the history of Cayuga shows a series of divergent retentions and shared innovations that cannot be accounted for within this pattern of sharp splits. Chafe and Foster (1981) have proposed that Cayuga became separate early in the history of Northern Iroquoian, perhaps after undergoing some developments jointly with Tuscarora, and then was affected by three episodes of intermittent contact with the linguistic ancestors of the Senecas.

The phonological history of Northern Iroquoian is well understood, as is a great deal of its comparative morphology. The historical phonology is sketched in some detail by Mithun (1979), drawing in part on largely unpublished work by Floyd G. Lounsbury, Chafe, and Foster. Mithun (1981) and Rudes (1981a) show how Susquehannock and Nottoway, attested only by early vocabularies, can be derived from the proto-language. Comparisons with Cherokee have resulted in some reconstructed history at the Proto-Iroquoian level (vol. 15:338-343; Rudes 1995).

• KALAPUYAN Kalapuyan consists of three closely related languages. The comparative phonology was outlined by Shipley (1970), relying on somewhat problematical materials from Swadesh (1965). Berman's (1990) revision was based on greatly superior recordings and analysis.

• KERESAN The Keresan languages are very close to each other. They form a dialect continuum that has often been divided into Western Keresan (Acoma and Laguna) and Eastern Keresan, comprising the five Rio Grande languages, though this division is not particularly sharp (Davis 1979:407; vol. 9:173). The historical phonology has been outlined by Miller and Davis (1963).

• KIOWA-TANOAN Comparative Kiowa-Tanoan was put on a firm basis by the studies of Hale (1962, 1967), which Watkins (1978) and Davis (1989) supplement. Trager (1942) had described the historical phonology of the Tiwa branch. Some evidence has been claimed for subgrouping Tiwa and Tewa together (Trager 1967), the other main branches of the family being Kiowa and Jemez. Harrington considered the poorly documented Piro to be a subbranch of Tiwa, but Trager (1967) placed it as a separate branch of Tanoan, considering Harrington's evidence insufficient. The generally assumed close relationship between Pecos and Jemez rests on the testimony of observers whose knowledge of linguistic groupings has generally proved reliable (Benavides 1916:22, 103; Domínguez 1956:181, 214; Simpson 1852:22-23, 1964:22-23; William Carr Lane in Schoolcraft 1851-1857, 5:689). The branch putatively including these two languages was named Towa by Harrington (1909, 1910). Trager (1967) and Kenneth L. Hale (vol. 9:171) have questioned whether Pecos should be subgrouped with Jemez.

• MUSKOGEAN Comparative Muskogean studies effectively began with Haas's (1941) study of the phonology. Haas classified the family into Western Muskogean and Eastern Muskogean divisions, Western consisting solely of Choctaw-Chickasaw and Eastern including Hitchiti-Mikasuki, Alabama-Koasati, and Creek-Seminole. At the same time, she pointed out that diffusional influences had cut across these genetic divisions. Later Haas (1949) added Apalachee to Eastern Muskogean, presumptively as a member of the Alabama-Koasati subbranch, and she suggested that Hitchiti-Mikasuki was closer to this subbranch than to Creek-Seminole (Haas 1947:137). A more elaborate proposal addressed to the problem of overlapping innovations among the subbranches assumed a series of historical stages, each characterized by a different pattern of diffused changes (Haas 1979:302-307). A different evaluation of which innovations were shared and which diffused led Munro (1993:397) to propose a classification for the family in which the oldest split was between Northern Muskogean, consisting solely of Creek-Seminole, and Southern Muskogean, containing all the other languages. Martin (1994, 1994a) supported Munro's model with evidence from language contact and morphology. Booker (1993) compared the two classifications with respect to their implications for a number of innovations and concluded that the later Haas classification was to be preferred. She suggested that the subgroup within Eastern Muskogean that comprised Alabama-Koasati-Apalachee and Hitchiti-Mikasuki be called Central Muskogean. Kimball (1989) proposed Central Muskogean, comprising the same five languages, as a third major branch of the family and within it linked Apalachee most closely to Hitchiti-Mikasuki.

• POMOAN Considerable progress has been made in the systematic comparison of the Pomoan languages and in the reconstruction of their phonological history (Oswalt 1964a, 1964b, 1976; Halpern 1964; Grekoff 1964; McLendon 1973, 1976; Moshinsky 1976). Differing proposed subclassifications of the family are discussed by McLendon and Oswalt (vol. 8:275).

• SAHAPTIAN The two branches of Sahaptian, Sahaptin and Nez Perce, are very close. The Proto-Sahaptian sound system was reconstructed by Aoki (1962) and refined in later studies (Rigsby 1965; Rigsby and Silverstein 1969).

• SALISHAN In discussing Salishan sound changes, Boas and Haeberlin (1927) made a distinction between "coast dialects" and "interior dialects," but this subgrouping was not clearly supported by the phonological data discussed. For example, although the palatalization of *k* to *č* was found in most of the coast languages, each group had some languages with this innovation and some without it. Swadesh (1950:163-164), using lexicostatistics, classified the family into four divisions: Coast, Interior, Bella Coola (consisting of a single language), and Oregon (Tillamook and its dialect

Siletz). Later, on the basis of detailed comparative studies, Swadesh's Coast Division was split into Tsamosan (Quinault, Lower Chehalis, Upper Chehalis, and Cowlitz) and Central Salish, comprising all the coastal languages between Tsamosan and Bella Coola (Thompson 1979:693; vol. 7:33-35), a split that had been anticipated by Tolmie and Dawson (1884) and Boas and Haeberlin (1927:133). Of the five divisions thus recognized, the most divergent is Bella Coola, which may be set against the "Main Body" comprising all the rest (Thompson 1979:693). Central Salish and Tillamook exhibit shared features that suggest they might together form a single, geographically discontinuous division (Elmendorf 1962b).

The comparative phonology of Salishan has been investigated in detail (Thompson 1979:701-726; Kuipers 1981; Galloway 1988). The system of pronominal marking has also received extensive historical treatment and reconstruction (Newman 1976, 1979, 1979a, 1980). A number of other topics in comparative Salishan have been studied ("Languages," vol. 12).

• SIOUAN (SIOUAN-CATAWBA) The Siouan languages were classified by C.F. Voegelin (1941b) into four divisions: Eastern (Catawba), Ohio Valley (Ofo, Biloxi, Tutelo), Missouri River (Hidatsa, Crow), and Mississippi Valley (Iowa-Oto-Missouri, Winnebago, and possibly Dhegiha, Mandan, and Dakota). The term Ohio Valley Siouan was chosen in allusion to the supposed common homeland of the component languages of the division, and Haas's (1968:84) suggested substitute Southeastern Siouan has generally been used. Later classifications differ chiefly in recognizing a much greater split between Catawban (Catawba and Woccon) and the remainder, and in recognizing Mandan as a separate branch. Rankin calls the major divisions Catawban and Siouan ("Siouan Languages," vol. 13), while Carter (1980:181) labels them Eastern Siouan (comprising Catawba and Woccon) and Western Siouan. The components of Siouan proper (Carter's Western Siouan) are thus Missouri River (Hidatsa and Crow), Mandan, Mississippi Valley (Dakotan, Dhegiha, Chiwere, Winnebago), and Ohio Valley or Southeastern (Ofo, Biloxi, Tutelo). Rankin unites Mandan and Mississippi Valley into an intermediate subgroup called Central. The Dakotan subbranch includes all the dialects of Sioux, Assiniboine, and Stoney. Dhegiha includes Omaha-Ponca, Osage, Kansa, and Quapaw (Rankin 1988). Chiwere, consisting of the very similar Otoe, Missouri, and Iowa, is sometimes subgrouped with Winnebago.

It has been possible to classify several languages spoken in Virginia, West Virginia, and North Carolina as conclusively Siouan on the basis of fragmentary early data. These include Saponi, Occaneechi, and probably Moneton (Mooney 1894; Griffin 1943:32; Sturtevant 1958, Hoffman 1964:216-217; Alexander 1971; Goddard 1972). They are closely related to Tutelo, whose speakers migrated from the same area in the historical period.

Siouan comparative phonology was worked out by Wolff (1950-1951, 1952, 1952a) and further refined and explicated by Matthews (1958, 1970) and Rood (1979). The relationship between Siouan and Catawban was demonstrated by Siebert (1945) with Catawba lexical and grammatical materials and supported by Carter's (1980) study of Woccon vocabulary.

• TSIMSHIANIC Tsimshianic (or Tsimshian) consists of four quite similar forms of speech, Nisgha (Nass), Gitksan, Coast Tsimshian, and Southern Tsimshian (Klemtu). These can be grouped into two languages, Nass-Gitksan (Nisgha and Gitksan) and Coast Tsimshian, with Southern Tsimshian a divergent dialect of this (Marie-Lucie Tarpent, personal communication 1995; Dunn 1979), but they could also be considered four separate languages (Rigsby 1989: 245-247).

• UTIAN Extensive work on the comparative phonology and morphology of Utian (Miwok-Costanoan) has been done by Callaghan (1967, 1988).

• UTO-AZTECAN The Uto-Aztecan family has nine major branches: Numic, Tubatulabal, Takic, Hopi, Tepiman (Pima-Tepehuan), Taracahitan (Tarahumara-Guarijío, Ópata-Eudeve, Mayo-Yaqui), Tubar, Corachol (Cora-Huichol), and Aztecan (Lamb 1964; Steele 1979:449-450; vol. 10:121). Kaufman (1974, 1974a:73) puts Tubar in Taracahitan. There are also a number of extinct languages with poor or no documentation that are or may be Uto-Aztecan (vol. 10:122; Miller 1983). There is morphological evidence that supports the subgrouping of the first four branches as a separate Northern Uto-Aztecan division (corresponding to Powell's Shoshonean), the remainder forming Southern Uto-Aztecan (Heath 1977:27, 1978:221-222, 1985); this division of the family had been suggested by Gatschet (1879:408-409). Kaufman (1974, 1974a: 73) had used the same subgrouping without discussing the evidence for it. Miller (1984) argued that lexical similarities support Southern Uto-Aztecan as a unit though not a unified northern group, and Campbell and Langacker (1978:197, 269; Campbell 1979:908) also cite lexical evidence for Southern Uto-Aztecan.

Uto-Aztecan historical phonology has been worked out in some detail, and a large body of protoforms has been reconstructed (Voegelin, Voegelin, and Hale 1962; Miller 1967; Langacker 1970). Studies of comparative and historical morphology and syntax include Steele (1979), Langacker (1977, 1977a), and Heath's articles.

• WAKASHAN The Wakashan family has two branches, Kwakiutlan (Northern Wakashan) and Nootkan (Southern Wakashan), each comprising very similar languages. A phonological inventory for the protolanguage was given by Swadesh (1953:35), without discussion. An extensive comparative list of Kwakiutlan roots has been compiled by Lincoln and Rath (1980). Jacobsen (1969) treats a problem in comparative Nootkan phonology.

• YOKUTSAN On the basis of a comparative study of Yokutsan historical phonology and morphology Whistler and Golla (1986) classify the numerous distinct local varieties of Yokutsan speech. They distinguish three major branches, Poso Creek, Buena Vista, and Nim-Yokuts, the last two being subgrouped against the first. Nim-Yokuts is split into Tule-Kaweah and Northern Yokuts, and Northern Yokuts divides into Kings River, Gashowu, and Valley Yokuts, the last having numerous ramifications.

• YUKIAN Elmendorf (1968) has compiled comparative vocabularies for the four varieties of Yukian and tabulated assumed cognate sets. His data show that Yuki, Huchnom, and Coast Yuki are very closely related languages, which can be grouped as three languages of Northern Yukian or as three dialects of Yuki, and that the relationship of these to Wappo is quite remote. Although Elmendorf did not discuss sound correspondences, he argued that the apparent cognates and additional, unpublished structural evidence refuted Sawyer's (1964:167-168, 1965:vii) contention that Wappo might not be relatable to Northern Yukian.

• YUMAN (COCHIMÍ-YUMAN) The basic facts of the comparative phonology of Yuman are well understood (Langdon 1976; Langdon and Munro 1980; vol. 10:4-11). The family has four branches, Pai, River, Delta-California, and Kiliwa. There is also a more distant relationship to Cochimí, a small family of languages spoken in central Baja California (Troike 1976; Mixco 1978). This combined grouping, earlier called simply Yuman by Kroeber, Sapir, and others (table 3), is less ambiguously referred to as Cochimí-Yuman.

323

Sketches

Sketch of Central Alaskan Yupik, an Eskimoan Language

OSAHITO MIYAOKA

Central Alaskan Yupik is one of the five Yupik (Western Eskimo) languages, which together with the Inuit-Inupiaq (Eastern Eskimo) language constitute the Eskimo branch of the Eskimo-Aleut linguistic family. The other four Yupik languages are Alutiiq Alaskan Yupik, Central Siberian Yupik, Naukanski, and Sirenikski. See volume 5:49-63 for the classification, distribution, and prehistory of the family and Bergsland (1986) for Eskimo and Aleut historical linguistics. Central Alaskan Yupik, which is distributed south of Golovin and Elim (Norton Sound), on the Yukon (up to Holy Cross) and the Kuskokwim (up to Sleetmute), on Nunivak Island, down the coast to

Bristol Bay and the north coast of the Alaskan Peninsula, has five measurably diverged dialects with phonological and lexical variation: Norton Sound, Hooper Bay and Chevak, Nunivak, General Central Yupik (Yukon, Nelson Island, Kuskokwim, Bristol Bay, Nushagak River, and Lake Iliamna), and Egegik. There is evidence for at least one extinct dialect. Recorded from the Aglurmiut, it is apparently closest to the Nunivak dialect. Its location is uncertain.

This sketch is a description of General Central Yupik (fig. 1) with slightly heavier emphasis on the Yukon subdialect.

Central Alaskan Yupik exhibited the greatest vigor among the 20 Alaska Native languages in the 1990s, being spoken by a little more than 50 percent of the approximately 22,000 people in the traditional area and by perhaps a few thousand in urban areas in 1990. Most of them spoke Yupik and English with differing competency. The few Yupik monolinguals were mainly children before school age and the oldest people, including more women than men. Bilingual education started in 1970 for the first time in Alaska in the Central Yupik area (McGary 1979:77-98; Miyaoka 1980). See Krauss (1973, 1979, 1980, 1985) for details of the language situation and of linguistic work; Jacobsen (1995) provides a practical grammar of Central Alaskan Yupik.

Information on the Yukon subdialect was provided by, among others, Paschal L. Afcan (originally from Akulurak) (fig. 2), and information on the Kuskokwim subdialect by Elsie Mather (from Kwigillingok) (figs. 3-4) and Marie Meade (from Nupapitchuk).

Fig. 2. Paschal Afcan (b. 1938). He is standing in front of a display of Yupik language textbooks developed at the Eskimo Language Workshop, University of Alaska, Fairbanks. One of several native speakers who made an early contribution to material development for Yupik bilingual education, he was Miyaoka's first consultant, working with him from 1967 to 1969. Photograph by Osahito Miyaoka, Fairbanks, 1973.

1. MORPHOLOGY AND SYNTAX

1.1. MORPHOLOGY

Yupik is an almost exclusively suffixing language. As many suffixes may occur in a single (morphological) word, it is in structure a polysynthetic language in which a word may be the functional equivalent of a sentence embodying a number of more or less concrete ideas that in most languages would be rendered by independent words. A Yupik word is not merely a "static" construct but may approach a "dynamic" sentence in microcosm, which each speaker builds up to a certain extent on each occasion.

Yupik words are classified according to whether they inflect (i.e., take endings to indicate certain grammatical functions) or not: inflecting and noninflecting words. The noninflecting words, comprising particles and enclitics (which are most of the monosyllabic noninflecting words), are adverbial, modal, conjunctive, or

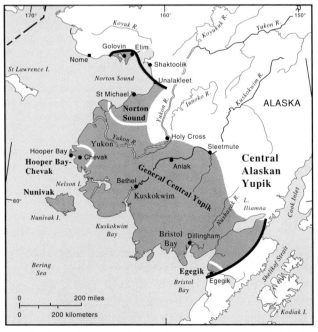

Fig. 1. Distribution of Central Alaskan Yupik language and dialects.

Fig. 3. Elsie Mather (b. 1936), an authority on Yupik language and culture. She started working with Miyaoka in 1977. Photographed at the Institute of Eskimology, University of Copenhagen, 1986.

interjectional in function. Inflecting words, which are verbs and nominals, consist of a single base followed by two kinds of suffixes, postbases and an ending, in that order. The base carries the "basic meaning" of the word (except for a very few bases with the most neutral meanings like |pi-| 'thing; to do'). The postbase generally elaborates the meaning or changes the grammatical function of the base, composing together with it a secondarily derived or expanded base. The ending expresses the grammatical relationship of number, person, case, and mood. Postbases are derivational suffixes, and endings, which form a closed class, are inflectional. Though postbases are much more limited in number than bases, the derivational processes represented by them constitute a highly developed and productive system in Yupik. The endings on inflecting words are combinations of two or three morphemes, which may be either phonologically fused together or more or less transparently segmentable. However, endings as well as expanded bases are given as a unit without indicating internal morpheme boundaries (+ or −; see 2.2.), unless this information is necessary for correct phonological derivation. Endings behave in some ways differently from postbases, and the bracket ([) is used to signal the start of an ending; an ending of the shape |+∅| will not be indicated in phonological representations. Other conventions are given in table 1.

The base, whether expanded or not, of an inflecting word is either nominal or verbal in function, though a small number of bases are both. The subscript ₙ or ᵥ may be used to indicate the functional class of a base. A postbase may also be defined in terms of the function of the base (or postbase) to which it is attached and the function of the resulting expanded base. Except for a few postbases relevant to particles, they fall into four functional classes: nominal-elaborating postbases (indicated by subscript ₙₙ), which are added to nominal bases to form nominal expanded bases; nominalizing postbases (ᵥₙ), which nominalize verb bases; verb-elaborating postbases (ᵥᵥ), which are added to verb bases to form verbal expanded bases; and verbalizing postbases (ₙᵥ), which verbalize nominal bases. The first two classes are nominal postbases, and the other two verbal. Some verb-elaborating postbases are adverbial and others syntactical.

The function of the adjective of other languages is taken care of by verbs (predicative), nominal-elaborating postbases, and certain nominals (attributive), while that of adverbs is taken care of by verb-elaborating postbases and noninflecting words.

Bases (and postbases), except some demonstrative bases, end in a vowel, apical stop (|t| or |c|), or velar (|γ|, |γ̇|, |x|, |x̣|, or |q|). The final |q| occurs after a full vowel (i.e., any vowel except |ə|) in nominal bases (or postbases) and a few mood markers. No nominal base (or postbase) ends in |c|. The shortest bases are monosyllabic, having the shapes CV, (C)VC, or (C)VCC. When cited in isolation, morphemes that do not occur word-finally end with a hyphen, and suffixes begin with a plus or minus sign (2.2.). Examples of bases are: |yuγ-|ₙ 'person', |aŋut-|ₙ 'man (male)', |pi-|ₙ,ᵥ 'thing; to do', |mikə-|ᵥ 'to be small', |inaγ̇c-|ᵥ 'to lie down'. Examples of postbases (with the number under which they

Table 1. Abbreviations

abm.	ablative-modalis
abs.	absolutive
all.	allative
connec.	connective
equal.	equalis
ind.	indicative
inter.	interrogative
intrans.	intransitive
loc.	locative
opt.	optative
part.	participle or participial
perl.	perlative
pl.	plural
refl.	reflexive
rel.	relative
sg.	singular
subord.	subordinative
tran.	transitive
1	first person
2	second person
3	third person
3R	reflexive third person (e.g., 2 pl.: intransitive verb with a second-person plural subject, 1sg.—3sg.: transitive verb with a first-person singular subject and third-person singular object; 2 dual—pl.: plural noun with a second-person dual possessor)

Qanrucit Taringnaurutait

Aperyarat ayuqenrilata taikaniumalriit ilait ukut iliitnek
canimegteggun igangqertut, kingunrata una nallunailkutaqluku.

C = Canineq
Q = Qaluyaat
KS = Kusquqvak
KP = Kuigpak
N = Nunivaaq
NC = Naparyaarmiut-Cev'aq

---

ac'eciyaraq

- Elrimi wall'u merr'ami qaqiarrluku aturiqengyaraq tuqullrem atranek (atkugluku, qasper-
luku, pilugirluku ilaitni-llu aliumaterluku);
aturiqengyaraq kassuusngualriignek mikel-
nguugnek Nakaciruami; aturiqengyaraq nasqunek
Kuigpagmi Kevgim nalliini

akngirqun

- Elrim kenkataa tuqulleq elriutetukii/
ac'etetukii

alailutet

- napalriit tuqullret nallunailkutait/
umyuaqutait

allungak /
qantam allungii

- qantam muragam terr'a (c.f. PERNEQ)

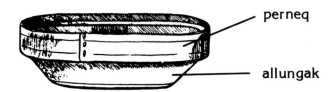

perneq

allungak

aluuyaq

- qantaq murak takluni

Smithsonian, Anthr. Lib.

328   Fig. 4. Elsie Mather's 1985 book titled *Cauyarnariuq* ('It is Time for Drumming'). left, P. 153; right, translation of the same page.

MIYAOKA

Explanation for the Words

Some of the words which are explained because they are different [depending on the dialects] have one of the [capital] letters beside them, making it clear where the words come from.

C	= Canineq:	Lower Coast
Q	= Qaluyaat:	Nelson Island
KS	= Kusquqvak:	Kuskokwim River
KP	= Kuigpak:	Yukon River
N	= Nunivaaq:	Nunivak Island
NC	= Naparyaarmiut-Cev' aq:	Hooper Bay and Chevak

---

ac' eciyaraq - custom of completely dressing the namesake of a dead person at the Memorial Feast [Elriq or Merr' aq] (putting on him/her a parka, a cloth parka cover, a skin boot, and sometimes mitten as well); custom of dressing the two 'married' children at the Would-be Bladder Beast [Nakaciruaq]; custom of dressing the 'head person' at the time of the Messenger Feast [Kevgiq] in the Yukon.

akngirqun - a dead person who is very dear to one who does the Memorial Feast (or does the dressing) for him/her.

alailutet - the [grave] posts that are to tell (or remember) the dead persons

allungak /
qantam allungii - the bottom part of a wooden bowl (cf. perneq bent part)

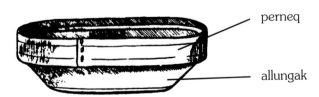

perneq

allungak

aluuyaq - a long [oval] wooden bowl

are given in section 8) are: 6 $|+k*aq-|_{NN}$ 'future', 30 $|-n\dot{\gamma}-|_{VN}$ 'more', 57 $|+la\dot{\gamma}-|_{VV}$ 'usually', 78 $|+tait-|_{NV}$ 'there to be no'.

What determines whether an expanded base is nominal or verbal is the function of the rightmost postbase, the one immediately preceding the ending. A verb base (with no postbase) or any expanded base in which the rightmost postbase is verbal (class $_{VV}$ or $_{NV}$) combines with inflectional categories such as mood and person. The word thus formed is a verb. Thus in $|qayaq_N+pa\gamma_{NN}$-li_{NV}-$qa\dot{\gamma}_{VV}+sqə_{VV}+zaaqə_{VV}$-$\dot{t}\dot{\gamma}u_{VV}[+\gamma*aqa|$ *qayaxpali·qaasqəssaaqəłxua·qa* 'I asked him to make a big kayak (but he has not yet made it)' the noun base $|qayaq-|_N$ is expanded by six postbases (1, 87, 50, 35, 64, and 53) of different functional classes. The completely expanded base is verbal and followed by the verbal ending $|+\gamma*aqa|$ 'ind. 1sg.—3sg.' (from two morphemes $|+\gamma*aq-|$ and $|-ka|$). A nominal base (with no postbase) or an expanded base in which the rightmost postbase is nominal (class $_{NN}$ or $_{VN}$) combines with inflectional categories such as case, number, and person, thus constituting a nominal: $|qayaq_N+pa\gamma_{NN}$-$li_{NV}+za\dot{\gamma}aq_{VN}[-ka|$ *qayaxpali·ya\dot{\gamma}a·qa* 'the way I make a big kayak', which is nominal with three postbases (1, 87, and 26) and the noun ending $|-ka|$ 'abs. 1sg.—sg.'.

A word as a morphological unit may be uttered by itself or together with one or more enclitics or nonenclitic words. Such a sequence bounded by pauses is a phonological phrase or prosodic domain. The left boundary of an enclitic and a nonenclitic word inside a phonological phrase may be marked respectively by the double hyphen (=) and the number sign (#), and the pause or the boundary of a phonological phrase by space or the doubled number sign (##). Each of these is a major boundary: ##nunaka=lu=\gammauq## *nuna·ka=łu·=xuq* 'also my land, they say', ##nunaka#tamana## *nuna·ka(t)#tama·na* 'that (extended) land of mine'.

Morphological processes such as compounding, prefixation, reduplication, infixation, and internal modification are not used, with a few exceptions. The only productive process is suffixation, by means of which Yupik attains one of the highest degrees of synthesis among known languages. Suffixation is accompanied by a variety of phonological (i.e., morphophonemic) adjustments outlined in section 3.

1.2. SYNTAX

As many grammatical relations are taken care of by the inflectional systems of mood, case, person and number reference, the word order in a sentence is far from rigid. Apart from exclamatory and interjectional expressions as well as nominals in some contexts, the presence of a verb to express the main predication is obligatory in full sentences.

An intransitive (i.e., intransitively inflected) verb has one core nominal argument, or simply core nominal, involved in it, and a transitive (i.e., transitively

inflected) verb has two. A core nominal is indexed on the verb ending but may not necessarily be overtly expressed by a nominal. If expressed, the core nominal is cross-referenced with the verb ending and is assigned a syntactic case according to the ergative pattern for a third-person referent and the neutral pattern for a non–third person referent. The core nominal for an intransitive verb to which the absolutive case is assigned is the subject of the verb. The core nominals for a transitive verb to which the relative and the absolutive cases are assigned are respectively the subject and the object. The subject is the nominal characterized by, among other things, the reflexive third person that refers back to it. A typical sentence obligatorily consists of a verb and one or two core nominals. A noncore nominal, not indexed on a verb ending, occurs in an adverbial case and is an (adverbial or adnominal) adjunct if not interjectional. A complex sentence consists of a main clause (with a verb in an independent mood) and a dependent clause (with a verb in a dependent mood). A compound sentence consists of two or more main clauses. A syntactic verb-elaborating postbase adds or removes one of the nominals of the verb. As the maximum number of core nominals indexed on a verb ending is two, nominal reduction has to occur if the nominals involved in the expanded verb exceed that number. A complex verb is one in which another verb is embedded.

Perhaps no language exceeds Yupik in the degree of functionality of its internal syntax. Unlike most polysynthetic languages the morphological structure of a Yupik word cannot simply be defined in terms of more or less fixed suffix positions (or slots) each filled with an appropriate suffix, particularly since: one and the same postbase can occur more than once in a word; nominalizations and verbalizations can occur serially and repeatedly; and a complex verb can be further expanded by one or more elaborating postbases and a nominalizing postbase of its own, and by one or more additional complex-verb–forming postbases (6.3.4.).

PHONOLOGY

2. PHONOLOGICAL ESSENTIALS

2.1. REPRESENTATIONS

The symbols used in phonological representations, enclosed between vertical bars ($|$ $|$), are given in tables 2 and 3.

By application of the phonological Rules P1 through P24 in 3., phonemic representations are derived from the phonological ones. These are written in italics and are used in citing actual Yupik forms. The "phonemic" level, as distinct from the phonological and the phonetic, is characterized by surface contrast: see P22. The phonemic symbols for vowels are the same as used in phonological representations (table 2), while

Table 2. Phonological and Phonemic Vowels

	front	*central*	*back*	
high	*i*	*ə*	*u*	
low		*a*		voiced

accent: acute (´), grave (`) on the vowel
lengthening: raised dot (·) after the vowel

Table 3. Phonological Consonants

	labial	*apical*		*velar*		
		dental	*alveo-palatal*	*front*	*back*	
stop	p	t	c	k	q	voiceless
fricative	f	ł	s	x	x̣	
	v	l	z	γ	γ̇	voiced
approximant	w		y			voiced
nasal	m	n		ŋ		

the consonantal phonemic symbols are summarized in table 4. Rules P12 and P13 account for the additional symbols, labial-velar fricatives, and voiceless nasals (see table 5, no. 16 also).

A full vowel may be lengthened, and any consonant can be geminated (Rule P22). A geminated consonant has a syllable boundary in the middle of the maintained articulation. In phonemic representations a lengthened vowel and a geminated consonant are indicated respectively by a postponed raised dot (·) and by doubling the consonant. On the phonemic level no more than two consonants or two vowels may occur in sequence, and consonant clusters are confined to word-medial position (except on loanwords) and cannot consist of two apical stops.

2.2. SUFFIX TYPES
Suffixation of postbases and endings results in a number of complex adjustments in the phonological segments that are brought into contact in the process. Since these adjustments are not completely predictable from the phonological shape of the elements involved, different suffix types must be distinguished according to the pattern of phonological adjustments they induce. The most important distinction is that between deleting suffixes and retaining suffixes. Deleting suffixes written with a preceding minus sign (as in |-put| 'abs.

1pl.—pl.') delete the final velar fricative of a preceding base or postbase, while retaining suffixes written with a preceding plus sign (as in |+put| 'abs. 1pl.—sg.') do not. Thus |acaγ[-put| 'our aunts' becomes |aca-put| (phonemically *aca·put*), with deletion of the |γ| of the base, while the deletion does not occur in |acaγ[+put| 'our aunt' (*acaxput*, in which |γ| has become *x* by another rule). This deletion (Rule P8) should apply to the phonological representation derived by Rules P1–P7, though these happen not to be relevant in this case. One class of suffixes has the subscript 1 (one) after the boundary, as in 98 |+₁paa|, 74 |+₁ŋ*at-|, and 20 |+₁uciq-|, which show special treatments of preceding apical stops, namely deletion and fricativization, as exemplified in Rule P2i. The subscript is given in phonological representations only in those contexts where relevant, that is, if the preceding base or postbase has final apical stop. Some suffix-initial velars, written with an asterisk as in 6 |+k*aq-|, 74 |+₁ŋ*at-|, 38 |+γ*i-|, and 65 |+₁γ̇*i-| behave in several respects differently from nonasterisked velars: see Rules P3ii-iii, P5i, P6, P9, and P10 for details.

3. PHONOLOGICAL RULES
Phonological representations consisting of the symbols so far introduced are converted to phonemic ones by the set of phonological Rules P1 through P24, which are postlexical. A rule applies rightward from the left (P5i, P9, P22). If more than one rule is relevant to a representation, the rules apply in numerical order. The rules given here handle only the adjustments of a more or less generalizable character and are not free from exceptions. Adjustments unique to specific bases or suffixes are mentioned as each case comes up, either in the body of the sketch or in table 5, and these lexical adjustments should be applied before the postlexical rules in 3. unless otherwise indicated. Stages in the phonological derivation are linked by the conventional arrow (>), to be read 'becomes'.

Rule P1 Accentuation on (C)VC bases. A monosyllabic base of the shape (C)VC is accentuated and is marked by a grave accent (cf. P22), for example, |yuγ-piγ| > |yùγ-piγ| *yuppik* 'Eskimo', |iŋ+u[+mi| > |ìŋ+u[+mi| *iŋŋumi* 'in the one over there', |mic-łγu[+γ*uq| > |mìc-łγu[+γ*uq| *mittałxuuq* 'he landed'.

Table 4. Phonemic Consonants

	labial	*apical*		*velar*		*labial-velar*		
		dental	*alveo-palatal*	*front*	*back*	*front*	*back*	
stop	*p*	*t*	*c*	*k*	*q*			voiceless
fricative	*f*	*ł*	*s*	*x*	*x̣*	*xʷ*	*x̣ʷ*	
	v	*l*	*z*	*γ*	*γ̇*	*γʷ*	*γ̇ʷ*	voiced
approximant	*w*		*y*					
nasal	*M*	*N*		*N̦*				voiceless
	m	*n*		*ŋ*				voiced

gemination: doubling of the consonant

Table 5. Special Conditions on Phonological Rules

1. Final apical deletion (P2i) applies also before some suffixes that do not begin with nonvelar stop: 10 |-ˌłuɣ-|, 28 |+ˌnɣ́-|, 30 |-ˌłɣ́-|, and the negative subordinative marker |-ˌna-| (6.2.6.). Only the postvocalic apical is fricativized before the connective marker |+ˌŋ*inaɣ́-| (6.2.5.8.) and the postbases 25 |+ˌviɣ-|, 66 |+ˌmi-|, 73 |+ˌŋ*ait-|, and 74 |+ˌŋ*at-|. An apical, if preceded by a fricative, is deleted before 19 |+ˌut-|, 20 |+ˌuciq-|, 31 |+ˌuc-| instead of being fricativized.

2. Initial |p| of a retaining suffix is fricativized to *v* intervocalically. Fricativization of |p| occurs also after an apical consonant if the |p| is followed by |ə|, and after |cic| in the case of 98 |+ˌpaa|, which in turn fricativizes the final |c| into *z* instead of deleting it by P2i.

3. Insertion of ə (P6) between two morpheme-final consonants also occurs before some suffixes beginning with a vowel: |+u-| (for nonabsolutive singular pronominal demonstrative bases, e.g., |akm+u[+mi| *akmumi* 'in the one across there', 7.4.3.1. (cf. P22ii-c) but |akm+a[+ni| *akMani* 'across there', 7.4.3.2.) and |+a-| (as in |nutɣ+a[+ɣ*uq| *nutɣauq* 'he is shooting').

4. P7i is blocked in the '2dual—3sg.' interrogative and optative endings. P7ii is blocked (a) after a noun-base-final ə before the postbases 60 |+zuumiit-|, 61 |+zuuma-|, 62 |+zuɣ-| (e.g., |nəqə+zuɣ[+tuq| *nəqyuxtuq* 'he wants fish') or (b) when ə separates two identical consonants (e.g., |kuvə+viɣ| *kuvəvvik* 'place for spilling'). P7ii applies also before the deleting postbase 36 |-zu-| and 59 |-zuit-|, the deleting suffixes in tables 10, 12, 13, which begin with a nasal plus vowel, and (optionally) |-ˌki-| (6.2.4.).

5. P8 tends to be blocked before a prevocalic velar stop, if the final velar is voiceless (e.g., |uivənqəx[-ku+ni| *uivənqəxkuni* 'if it is round') or is a back velar preceded by |ɣa| or |ɣa| in certain morphemes. These morphemes have the following phonological peculiarities. P19 is also blocked. After P22 the |ɣa| or |ɣa| is deleted before a major boundary or (though optionally with some morphemes) before a consonant. The deletion of |ɣa| is accompanied by assimilation of a following back velar to a front one: |tuɣkaɣaɣ́[-ka| *tuxkaɣaˑqa* or *tuxkaxqa* 'my ivory', |qulŋunɣitaɣaɣ́| *qulŋunɣitaˑx* 'nine', |piyuɣ[+ɣ*aq-ka| *piyuˑɣaqa* or *piyuˑxqa* 'I want to get it'. See the postbase 15 |-ɣuɣluɣ́-| for a similar syllable contraction.

6. P9 is blocked for |ŋ*| (cf. note to table 7) and the initial velar of the postbases 14 |+ɣ́*uɣaɣ́-| and 65 |+ˌɣ́*i-|.

7. Accentuation of P10 is blocked before the second-person optative marker |+ɣ*i-| and the postbase 44 |+ɣ*uɣaɣ́-|.

8. Devoicing (P13) and consonant cluster breaking by ə insertion (P17i) are blocked in loanwords and onomatopoeic words. Devoicing may occur also after accentuation (P22) in the Kuskokwim subdialect (as seen in *naxkina*, 6.2.4.).

9. Another type of |t| affrication occurs after P22 among younger speakers in particular: |t| becomes *c* before ə followed by geminated *s* or *c*: |kəxut-cuaɣaɣ́| *kəxuˑcəccuax* 'small tooth'.

10. A base-final apical and the initial |l| of the following mood markers are reduced to *t* after P1: optative |+li-| and |+la-| (including 1sg. |+lii| and 1dual |+luɣ|) and subordinative |+lu-|.

11. Base-final |t| becomes *c* before the |i| of the postbase 38 |+ɣ*i-| and 42 |+ima-| and before those postbases beginning with |li| (see table 5, no. 15) if the |l| and its preceding vowel are deleted.

12. ɣ́ is inserted before (i) the postbase 1 |+paɣ-| after noun-base-final vowel, (ii) the postbase 10 |+ˌłuɣ-| after noun-base-final |ə|, and (iii) the postbases 25 |+ˌviɣ-|, 60 |+zuumiit-|, 61 |+zuuma-|, 62 |+zuɣ-|, and 74 |+ˌŋ*at-| after noun-base-final |t|, with P7ii being blocked in the final ə.

13. Postbase-initial |u| (19 |+ˌut-|, 20 |+ˌuciq-|, 31 |+ˌuc-|, 42 |+uma-|) is deleted after a base-final full vowel.

14. The |s| of the postbases beginning with |s| plus apical stop (24 |+st-|, 34 |+sci(u)ɣ́-|, 55 |+sciiɣat-|) is deleted after a base-final velar.

15. Deleting suffixes beginning with |li| (87 |-li-|, 88 and 89 |-liqə-|, 90 |-liɣ́-|) may optionally drop the |l| together with a preceding vowel. See table 5, no. 11 also.

16. The *u* of certain nouns with the sequence *qu* or *ku* (e.g. |atəkuɣ-| 'parka' and body- or plant-part words that end in *quq*) optionally becomes a voiceless vowel with velar friction, if it is immediately followed by a vowel: |atəkuɣ[+ŋa| > *atkua* [atku̥ˑa] 'his parka', |uyaquq[+ŋa| > *uyaˑqua* [uya·qo̥ˑa] (or even > *uyaqxʷa*) 'his neck'.

17. Stative verbs that end in |cic| show fluctuation between final |c| and |t| as shown in the variation *ipəxcəcan ~ ipəxcəlan* (causal connec. 3sg.) 'because it is sharp', *kawixcəskan ~ kawixcəłkan* (conditional connec. 3sg.) 'if it is red', and *manixcəsŊatuq ~ manixcəłŋatuq* (with 74 |+ˌŋ*at-|) 'it seems to be smooth'.

See Rule P10 also.

Rule P2 Apical adjustment. (i) Before a suffix with the subscript 1 an apical is generally deleted if the suffix begins with nonvelar stop (|p, t, c|), but otherwise the final |t| and |c| are fricativized to *l* and *z* respectively: |niic[+ˌtuq| > |nii[+tuq| *niituq* 'he hears', |taic[+ˌk*i| > |taiz[+k*i| *taiski* '(you sg.) bring them along!', |pinɣit[+ˌɣu| > |pinɣil[+ɣu| *pinɣilɣu* '(you sg.) don't do it!', |taic[+ˌɣu| > |taiz[+ɣu| *taizɣu* '(you sg.) bring it along!'. See table 5, no. 1. (ii) Morpheme-final |c| becomes *t*: |ikiɣ́c+laɣ́[+ˌtuq| > |ikiɣ́t+laɣ́[+ˌtuq| > *ikixtəłaxtuq* 'it (usually) opens'. (iii) A |ə| is inserted

after a base or postbase that ends in |t| (but see table 5, no. 10): |ikiɣ́t+laɣ́[+ˌtuq| > |ikiɣ́tə+laɣ́[+ˌtuq| (just above), |kəxut[+pəci| > |kəxutə[+vəci| (table 5, no. 2) *kəxuˑtəfci* 'of your(pl.) teeth', |cavə+ut| > |cavə+utə| *cavun* 'oar'.

Rule P3 Velar adjustments. (i) Morpheme-final |q| is fricativized to ɣ́ except that it is deleted before a retaining suffix that consists of a single consonant or begins with a consonant cluster, or before an ending in table 6 that begins with CV or before 16 |+miu-| or 91 |+mət-|: |aŋyaq+paɣ| > |aŋyaɣ́+paɣ| *aŋyaxpak* 'big boat', |aŋyaq[+nka| > *aŋyanka* 'my boats'. (ii) Initial nonasterisked velar nasal of a retaining suffix is deleted after a velar: |atɣ́[+ŋa| > |atɣ́[+a| *atχa* 'his name'. (iii) Suffix-initial nonasterisked velar stop or fricative (except the dual |ɣ|) is assimilated to final velar as to whether it is front or back: |əlaɣ-qataɣ́[+tut| > |əlaɣ-kataɣ́ [+tut| *əla·kataχtut* 'they are about to dig', |amaɣ́[+ɣu| > |amaɣ́[+ɣ̇u| *ama·χu* '(you sg.) backpack it!' (table 7 note).

Rule P4 Suffix-initial adjustment. A |ə| is added to the beginning of a retaining suffix (but after the plus sign) that consists of a single consonant or begins with a consonant cluster (except the noun endings |+tɣun| and |+ttun| in table 6) if a consonant precedes: |acaɣ[+ɣ+mta| > |acaɣ[+əɣ+əmta| *acciiɣəmta* 'of our aunts (dual)'.

Rule P5 Central vowel adjustments. (i) Both of two single central vowels (|a| or |ə|) that flank a nonasterisked

front velar nonstop next to a boundary become *i*: |tumə[+ŋa| > |tumi[+ŋi| *tummii* 'his footprint', |acaɣ[+əɣ+əmta| > |aciɣ[+iɣ+əmta| P4. (ii) A nominal-base-final |ə| becomes *a* before |ŋi|: |tumə[+ŋi| > |tuma[+ŋi| *tummai* 'his footprints'.

Rule P6 Final cluster breaking. A |ə| is inserted between two contiguous base-final or postbase-final consonants if followed by a consonant (except an asterisked velar fricative) or a major boundary or if preceded by a third consonant: In the last case the |ə| insertion may alternatively occur before the two final consonants: |nutɣ+zuɣ[+tut| > |nutəɣ+zuɣ[+tut| *nutəɣɣuxtut* 'they want to shoot'. |nutɣ-lɣ| > |nutəɣ-ləɣ| *nutlək* 'one with a gun', |atɣ́=lu| > |atəɣ́=lu| *atəq·łu* 'also the name'; |aɣ́vinlɣ[+n| > |aɣ́vinləɣ[+ən| *aɣ́vinləɣən* or |aɣ́vinəlɣ[+ən| *aɣ́vinəlɣən* 'six' (cf. P4), |azvɣ́+ŋu[+ɣ*ut| > |azvəɣ́+u[+ɣ*ut| *azvəɣ́ɣ́uut* or |azəvɣ́+u[+ɣ*ut| *azəvɣ́uut* 'they are walruses' (cf. P3ii). See table 5, no. 3.

Rule P7 |ə| deletion. (i) A |ə| followed by CV within a suffix is deleted if the deletion does not violate the consonant cluster limitation (2.1.): |kəxutə[+vəci| > |kəxutə[+vci| (P2iii). (ii) Morpheme-final |ə| is deleted before a retaining suffix that begins with V or CV (where C is voiced): |kəxut[+pət| > |kəxutə[+vət| > |kəxut[+vət| *kəxutfət* 'of your(sg.) teeth' (cf. table 5, no. 2 and P2iii), |nəɣ́ə[+ɣ*ut| > |nəɣ́[+ɣ*ut| *nəɣ́ɣ́ut* 'they eat'. See table 5, no. 4.

Rule P8 Final velar deletion. A final velar is deleted

Table 6. Endings for Unpossessed Nouns

Case	Singular	Plural	Dual
Absolutive (+∅)	+∅	+t	+ɣ
Relative (+m)	+m	+t	+ɣ
Locative (+ni)	+mi	+ni	+ɣni
Allative (+nun)	+mun	+nun	+ɣnun
Ablative-modalis (+nəɣ)	+məɣ	+nəɣ	+ɣnəɣ
Perlative (+kun)	+kun	+tɣun	+ɣkun
Equalis (+tun)	+tun	+ttun	+ɣtun

NOTES: See P3i for deletion of morpheme-final |q| before an ending. The forms in this table are phonological representations.

Table 7. Optative Endings

			Intransitive	Transitive								
				Object								
				Third			First			Second		
				sg.	pl.	dual	sg.	pl.	dual	sg.	pl.	dual
S u b j e c t	Third	sg.	+∅	+ɣu	+ki	+kəɣ	+ŋa	+kut	+kuɣ	+tən	+ci	+təɣ
		pl.	+li-	+t	+tɣu	+tki	+tkəɣ	+tŋa	+tkut	+tkuɣ	+tɣən	+tci	+ttəɣ
		dual		+ɣ	+ɣnəɣu	+ɣnəki	+ɣnəkəɣ	+ɣtəɣŋa	+ɣt+kut	+ɣt+kuɣ	+ɣt+ɣən	+ɣtci	+ɣttəɣ
	First	sg.	+la-	(+lii)	+ku	+ki	+kəɣ				+(m)kən	+mci	+mtəɣ
		pl.		(+lta)	+ut	-put	+ɣput				+mt+ɣən	+mtci	+mttəɣ
		dual		(+luɣ)	+uɣ	-puɣ	+ɣpuɣ				+məɣtən	+məɣci	+məɣtəɣ
	Second	sg.	+ɣ*i-	+a +ˌtən +ˌu +∅	+ˌɣu	+ˌk*i	+ˌk*əɣ	+ˌŋ*a	+ˌk*ut	+ˌk*uɣ			
		pl.	~	+ˌci	+ˌci+ɣu	+ˌciki	+ˌcikəɣ	+ˌci+ŋa	+ˌcikut	+ˌcikuɣ			
		dual	+na-	+ˌtəɣ	+ˌtəɣu	+ˌtəki	+ˌtəkəɣ	+ˌtəɣŋa	+ˌtəɣkut	+ˌtəɣkuɣ			

NOTES: For the intransitive first person the endings with the mood and person markers fused are given in parentheses.

The |+ɣ*i-| for second-person subject endings only occurs after bases that end in a double vowel or |ə|, and even there it is not obligatory except before person markers of '2sg.' and '2sg.—3sg.'

Of the variants for '2sg.', |+ˌtən| occurs after final |c|, |+ˌu| after |t|, |+a| after other consonant bases, |+∅| after vowel bases.

The initial |ɣ| of '2sg.—3sg.' ending and a base-final velar fricative are reduced to a voiceless fricative after P3iii.

See table 5, no. 4 for the '2dual—3sg.' ending.

See table 5, no. 10 for the |l| of the mood markers |+li-| and |+la-|.

The '1pl.—3sg.' and '1dual—3sg.' are |+ɣ́put| and |+ɣ́puɣ| respectively for some speakers.

P9 applies to the |ŋ*| of '2sg.—1sg.' in spite of table 5, no. 6, if the mood marker |+ɣ*i-| or the aspectual marker |-ˌki-| occurs before the person marker.

The forms in this table are phonological representations.

333

before a deleting suffix: |əlaɣ-kataɣ́[+tut| > |əla-kataɣ́[+tut| (P3iii), |yùɣ-pix| > |yù-pix| (P1). See table 5, no. 5.

Rule P9 Intervocalic velar deletion. A single voiced velar next to a morpheme boundary is deleted if between two single vowels the first of which is a full vowel. This applies from the leftmost boundary in a word toward the right: |tuma[+ŋi| > |tuma[+i| (P5ii), |aciɣ[+iɣ+əmta| > |aci[+iɣ+əmta| (P5i), |kiu[+ɣ*aq+ŋa| > |kiu[+ɣa+a| *kiuɣaa* 'he answers her' (cf. P3i, ii), |mikəlŋuɣ́+ŋu[+ɣ*uq-ŋa| > |mikəlŋu+u[+ɣ*u-a| *mikəlŋuuɣua* 'I am a child' (cf. P3i, ii, P8). See table 5, no. 6.

Rule P10 Asterisked velar fricative deletion. An asterisked velar fricative is deleted after a consonant, with the same accentuation as P1 if the base takes the shape of (C)VC: |amaɣ́[+ɣ*aq+ŋa| > |amaɣ́[+a+a| *ama·ɣaa* 'he backpacks it' (cf. P3ii, iii, P9) |nəɣ́[+ɣ*ut| > |nəɣ́[+ut| (P7) |maniɣ+ɣ́*i[+ɣ*ut| > |maniɣ+i[+ut| *mani·ɣiut* 'they become smooth' (cf. P9). See table 5, no. 7.

Rule P11 |ci| plus apical adjustment. An |i| becomes |ə| between |c| and a non–word-final apical, with the apical being devoiced (see P13iii) if the |ci| is base-initial or in a base-final or postbase-final |cic|, in the interrogative marker |+ᵢci| (table 8), or in the second-person plural marker |+pəci| in connective mood and adverbial case endings (tables 9-10): |cila| > |cəła| *cəła* 'world', |ayaɣ+cic[+ᵢɣu| > |ayaɣ+cəs[+ɣu| *ayaxcəsxu* '(you—sg.) let it go!' (P2i), |ayaɣ[+cinuɣ| > |ayaɣ[+cəNuk| *ayaxcəNuk* 'we(dual) leave (inter.)' (cf. P13i, P19).

Rule P12 Labial-velar fricativization. The approximant |w| becomes a labial-velar fricative ɣʷ unless between vowels: |aw+na| > |aɣʷ+na| *aɣʷna* 'the one over there', |aw+u[+m| > |àw+u[+m| > |àɣʷ+u[+m| *aɣʷɣʷum*

'of the one over there' (cf. Pl) (cp. |awa[+ni| *awa·ni* 'over there'), |wa[+ni| > |ɣʷa[+ni| *xʷani* (see P13 for symbol xʷ). This applies also after gemination by P22: |tawaam| > taɣʷɣʷaam 'but'. See 15 |-ɣuɣ́luɣ́-| for the labial-velar ɣ́ʷ due to syllable contraction.

Rule P13 Devoicing. The voiceless nasals are represented by capital letters (*M*, *N*, and *Ŋ*), and the voiceless labial-velar fricative by xʷ. (i) Fricatives are devoiced when next to a major boundary or a voiceless consonant: |ɣʷa[+ni| > |xʷa[+ni| (P12), |atəɣ́=lu| > |atəx=łu| (P6), |aŋyaɣ́+paɣ| > |aŋyax+pax| (P3i), |kəxut[+vət| > |kəxut[+fət| (P7ii). (ii) Nasals are devoiced after stop and optionally after voiceless fricative, unless across a major boundary: |pi+st+ŋu[+ɣ*ut| > |pist+Ŋu[+ut| *pistəŊŊuut* 'they are servants' (lit. 'doers') (cf. P2iii, P7ii, P9), |azəmc+ni[+ɣ*aq+ŋa| > |azəmt+Ni[+a| *azəmNia* 'he says she cracked it in half' (cf. P2ii,iii, P3i,ii, P7ii, P9 and note to table 11). (iii) Fricative devoicing occurs also across an intervening |ə| particularly when |tə| is followed by the participial |-lɣ́iaq-| (6.2.2., 7.4.4.; see P11): |mic[+lɣia| > |mìtə[-łɣ̣ia| *mittəłxia* '(it) landing' (cf. P1, P2ii,iii). See table 5, no. 8.

Rule P14 |t| affrication. (i) A |t| and |s| across a suffix boundary become *c*: |nałunɣ́it+zuɣ[+tut| > |nałunɣ́icux[+tut| *nałunɣicuxtut* 'they want to know' (cf. P2iii, P7ii, P13i). (ii) A |t| becomes *c* before |ə| followed by preconsonantal |s|: |tuquc+sqə[+ɣ*ut| > |tuqutə+sq[+ut| > |tuqucə+sq[+ut| > *tuqu·cəsqut* 'they ask themselves to be killed' (cf. P2ii,iii, P7ii, P10). See P17iii and table 5, no. 9.

Rule P15 |t| deletion. Postconsonantal |t| is deleted before a nasal (except a nonasterisked velar): |azəmt+Ni[+a| > |azəm+Ni[+a| (P13ii), |ciniɣ́c+mi[+ɣ*ut| > |cəNixt+Mi[+ut| > |cəNix+Mi[+ut| *cəNixMiut* 'they

Table 8. Interrogative Endings

			Intransitive		Transitive								
					Object								
					Third			First			Second		
					sg.	pl.	dual	sg.	pl.	dual	sg.	pl.	dual
S	Third	sg.	+ᵢta-	+Ø	+ɣu	+ki	+kəɣ	+ŋa	+kut	+kuɣ	+tən	+ci	+təɣ
u		pl.	~	+t	+tɣu	+tki	+tkəɣ	+tŋa	+tkut	+tkuɣ	+tɣən	+tci	+ttəɣ
b		dual	+ɣ*a-	+ɣ	+ɣnəɣu	+ɣnəki	+ɣnəkəɣ	+ɣŋa	+ɣkut	+ɣt+kuɣ	+ɣt+ɣən	+ɣtci	+ɣttəɣ
j	First	sg.		+ŋa							+kən		
e		pl.	+ᵢci-	+ta									
c		dual		+nuɣ									
t	Second	sg.		+t	+ɣu	+ki	+kəɣ	+ŋa	+kut	+kuɣ			
		pl.		+ci	+ci+ɣu	+ciki	+cikəɣ	+ci+ŋa	+cikut	+cikuɣ			
		dual		+təɣ	+təɣu	+təki	+təkəɣ	+təɣŋa	+təɣkut	+təɣkuɣ			

NOTES: The initial |c| of the first- and second-person marker is fricativized to *z* after a vowel if the subject is singular and, though with some fluctuation, after bases that end in a stop plus |ə| if the subject is nonsingular.

See table 5, no. 4 for the '2dual—3sg.' ending.

See P11 for the mood marker |+ᵢci-|.

The first-person subject intransitive forms may be used for the first-person subject and the third-person object (with no distinction in number) transitive.

334   The forms in this table are phonological representations.

also visit' (cf. P2ii,iii, P7ii, P9, P11), |ənə[-məɣtni| > |ən[-məxNi| ənəmməxNi 'in their own house' (cf. table 5, no. 4, P13i,ii, P17ii).

Rule P16 |ə| assimilation. A |ə| assimilates to preceding full vowel: |mikəlŋuɣ́[+t| > |mikəlŋuɣ́[+ət| > |mikəlŋu[+ət| mikəlŋuut 'children' (cf. P4, P9).

Rule P17 |ə| insertion. A |ə| is inserted to break consonant clusters: (i) at a morpheme boundary in three-consonant clusters in order to meet the cluster limitation (2.1.) (see table 5, no. 8), |pist+Ņu[+ut| > |pistə+Ņu[+ut| (P13ii) |nəɣ́ə[+ŋ*a-mt+ɣu| nəɣ́ŋamtəxu 'as we ate it' (cf. P7ii, P13i); (ii) between the two consonants of a word-initial sequence |əCC| (except in a verb base having the shape |əCə-|) with the second consonant next to a boundary, |ətɣ́[+ŋa| > |ətəx̣[+a| ətəx̣x̣a 'his anus' (cf. P3ii, P13i); (iii) between |t| and an apical stop, with |t| being affricated, |qayaq[+ŋattun| > |qaya[+acətun| qayyaacətun 'like their kayak' (cf. P3i,ii, P9), see P14.

Rule P18 |a| raising. An |a| becomes ə in the sequence |qa| plus back velar fricative if the syllable is next to a boundary: |amaɣ́-qaɣ́[+ɣu| > |ama-qəɣ́[+ɣu| ama·qəx̣u '(you—sg.) please backpack it!' (cf. P8, note to table 7).

Rule P19 Word-final velar adjustment. Before a major boundary a velar fricative becomes a stop: |cali+viɣ| > |cali+vik| cali·wik 'place to work' (cf. P13i), |atəx̣=łu| > |atəq=łu| (P13i). See table 5, no. 5.

Rule P20 Word-final |ə| adjustment. Before a major boundary a |ə| becomes a except that postvocalic |tə| becomes n: |ənə| > |əna| əna 'house', |cali+st| > |cali+sta| calista (cf. P2iii) 'worker', |cavə+utə| > |cav+un| (P2iii, P7ii).

Rule P21 |v| and |z| adjustment. (i) A single |v| becomes w between full vowels unless it is base-final: |cali+vik| > |cali+wik| (P19) (cp. |cav+un| P20). (ii) Prevocalic single |z| next to a boundary becomes y unless

it is ending-initial: |nutəɣ+zuɣ[+tut| > |nutəɣ+yux[+tut| (P6, P13i) (cp. |pi[+cit| > |pi[+zit| pizit '(you—sg.) do (inter.)', cf. note to table 8), |pəkəc+ˌut| > |pəkəy+ut| pəkyun 'Monday, thing to move with' (cf. (P2i, P20) (cp. |kic+ˌut| kizzun 'sinker', cf. P1, P2i, P20).

Rule P22 Accentuation. Accentuation, which operates on a phonological phrase, is realized in quantity change (vowel lengthening and consonant gemination), pitch, stress, and tempo. Accentuation and its various phonetic realizations, which act to signal the different major boundaries, are governed by a foot-structuring principle that eliminates some types of foot in favor of others (Miyaoka 1971). Although accentuation is generally predictable, as is quantity to the same extent, some phonologically unpredictable but lexically conditioned changes (gemination, syllable contraction, etc.) produce surface contrasts between a single and a lengthened vowel and between a single and a geminated consonant. Hence quantity is indicated in phonemic representations.

Two kinds of accent are distinguished: rhythmical accent marked by acute accent (´) and regressive accent marked by grave (`): see P1 and P10 as well. A full vowel in a rhythmically accentuated open syllable is lengthened, while a rhythmically accentuated open syllable with ə or a regressively accentuated open syllable (with any vowel) becomes a closed syllable with its immediately following syllable-initial consonant becoming geminated. See 4. for stress and pitch. Syllable boundaries, indicated in this section by periods without following space, occur before an intervocalic single consonant, between two vowels, and between two consonants (geminates as well as clusters). The following rules, (i) through (iv), apply iteratively from the initial syllable of a phonological phrase to the end:

Table 9. Connective Mood Person Markers

			Intran-sitive	Transitive													
				Object													
				Third			First			Second			Reflexive		
				sg.	pl.	dual	sg.	pl.	dual	sg.	pl.	dual	sg.	pl.	dual
S u b j e c t	Third	sg.	+ŋan	+ŋaku	+ŋaki	+ŋakəy	+ŋaŋa	+ŋakut	+ŋakuɣ	+ŋatən	+ŋaci	+ŋatəy	+ŋani	+ŋatəŋ	+ŋatəy
		pl.	+ŋata	+ŋatyu	+ŋatki	+ŋatkəy	+ŋatŋa	+ŋatkut	+ŋatkuɣ	+ŋatyən	+ŋatci	+ŋattəy	+ŋatni	+ŋattəŋ	+ŋattəy
		dual	+ŋaɣnəy	+ŋaɣku	+ŋaɣki	+ŋaɣkəy	+ŋaɣŋa	+ŋaɣkut	+ŋaɣkuɣ	+ŋaɣtən	+ŋaɣci	+ŋaɣtəy	+ŋaɣni	+ŋaɣtəŋ	+ŋaɣtəy
	First	sg.	+ma	-mku	-mki	-mkəy				-mkən	-mci	-mtəy	-mni	-mtəŋ	-mtəy
		pl.	-mta	-mt+yu	-mt+ki	-mt+kəy				-mt+yən	-mtci	-mttəy	-mt+ni	-mttəŋ	-mttəy
		dual	+məynuɣ	+məynəyu	+məynəki	+məynəkəy				+məynəyən	+məyci	+məytəy	+məyni	+məytəŋ	+məytəy
	Second	sg.	+pət	+pəyu	+pəki	+pəkəy	+pəŋa	+pəkut	+pəkuɣ				+pəni	+pətəŋ	+pəkəy
		pl.	+pəci	+pəci+yu	+pəcikəy	+pəcikəy	+pəci+ŋa	+pəcikut	+pəcikuɣ				+pəcini	+pəcitəŋ	+pəcitəy
		dual	+pətəy	+pətəyu	+pətəyki	+pətəykəy	+pətəyŋa	+pətəykut	+pətəykuɣ				+pətəyni	+pətəytəŋ	+pətəykəy
	Refl. third	sg.	+mi	+mi+yu	+miki	+mikəy	+mi+ŋa	+mikut	+mikuɣ	+mitən	+mici	+mitəy			
		pl.	+məŋ	+məyt+yu	+məyt+ki	+məyt+kəy	+məyt+ŋa	+məyt+kut	+məyt+kuɣ	+məyt+yən	+məytci	+məyttəy			
		dual	+məy	+məynəyu	+məynəki	+məynəkəy	+məynəŋa	+məynəkut	+məynəkuɣ	+məynəyən	+məynəci	+məynətəy			

NOTES: Initial |m| of reflexive third-person subject marker is replaced with n after the mood marker |+ˌku-|. Table 5, no. 2 applies to all second-person subject forms. P15 is blocked in '1pl.—3Rsg.' and '3Rpl.—1sg.' endings.

See P11 for the second-person plural marker |+pəci-|.

The forms in this table are phonological representations.

Table 10. Adverbial Case Endings for Possessed Nouns

Possessor		Singular	Plural	Dual
Third	singular		+ŋani	+ŋini	+ɣkəni
			+ŋakun	+ŋikun	+ɣkənkun
			+ŋatun	+ŋitun	+ɣkətun
	plural		+ŋatni	+ŋitni	+ɣkətni
			+ŋatɣun	+ŋitɣun	+ɣkətɣun
			+ŋattun	+ŋittun	+ɣkəttun
	dual		+ŋaɣni	-kəɣni	+ɣkəɣni
			+ŋaɣkun	-kənkun	+ɣkənkun
			+ŋaɣtun	-kətun	+ɣkətun
First	singular		-mni	+ɣ+mni
			-mkun	+ɣ+mkun
			-mtun	+ɣ+mtun
	plural		-mt+ni	+ɣ+mt+ni
			-mt+ɣun	+ɣ+mt+ɣun
			-mttun	+ɣ+mttun
	dual		-məɣni	+ɣməɣni
			-məɣnəɣun	+ɣməɣnəɣun
			-məɣ(t)tun	+ɣməɣtun
Second	singular		+pəni	+ɣpəni
			+pəɣun	+ɣpəɣun
			+pətun	+ɣpətun
	plural		+pəcini	+ɣpəcini
			+pəcitɣun	+ɣpəcitɣun
			+pəcitun	+ɣpəcitun
	dual		+pətəɣni	+ɣpətəɣni
			+pətəɣnəɣun	+ɣpətəɣnəɣun
			+pətəɣtun	+ɣpətəɣtun
Reflexive third	singular		-mini	+ɣmini
			-mikun	+ɣmikun
			-mitun	+ɣmitun
	plural		-məɣt+ni	+ɣməɣt+ni
			-məɣt+ɣun	+ɣməɣt+ɣun
			-məɣ(t)tun	+ɣməɣ(t)tun
	dual		-məɣni	+ɣməɣni
			-məɣnəɣun	+ɣməɣnəɣun
			-məɣtun	+ɣməɣtun

NOTES: Each column gives the locative (marked by |ni|), perlative (|kun|), and equalis (|tun|) forms. The allative and ablative-modalis forms are obtained by replacing the final |i| of the locative form with |un| and |əɣ| respectively.

See table 5, no. 4 for deleting suffixes that begin with a nasal plus vowel. See P11 for the 2d-person pl. marker |+pəci|.

Table 5, no. 2, applies to all retaining suffixes beginning with |pV|.

P15 is blocked in the locative, allative, and ablative-modalis '1pl.—sg./pl.' and '1pl.—dual' endings.

The forms in this table are phonological representations.

(i) Rhythmical accent. Starting from a word-initial syllable that is accentuated if it is a closed syllable or unaccented if it is an open syllable, accents fall rhythmically on every two syllables: |aŋyaq-li-qataɣ̇[+tut| > |aŋ.ya.li.qa.taɣ̇.tut| (cf. P3, P8, P13) > áŋ.ya.lí·.qa.táx.tut 'they are about to make a boat', |qayaq-li-qataɣ̇[+tut| > |qa.ya.li.qa.taɣ̇.tut| (cf. P3, P8, P13) > qa.yá·.li.qá·.tax.tút > qa.yá·.li.qá·.tax.tut (cf. iii) 'they are about to make a kayak', |qayaq+paɣ[+mi=mi| > |qa.yax.paɣ.mi=mi| (cf. P3, P13) > qa.yáx.paɣ.mí·=mi 'how about in the big kayak?', |tuntuvaɣ+taŋqəx+zuɣnaɣ̇qə[+ɣ*uq=ɫu=ɣuq| > |tun.tu.wax.taŋ.qəx.suɣ.nax.quq=ɫu=xuq| (cf. P3, P7, P10, P13, P19, P21) > tún.tu.wáx.taŋ.qə̀x.suɣ.náx.quq=ɫú·=xuq 'also they say there seems to be a moose', |ə.tə.xa| (P17) ə.tə́x.xa.

(ii) Regressive accent. (ii-a) If the rhythmical accent is due to fall on the first vowel of a vowel cluster or a double vowel, the accent regresses onto the preceding syllable. This rule is blocked before a major boundary inside a phonological phrase: |cali+ɣ*aq[+m| > |ca.li.am| (cf. P3, P9) > ca.lí.am > càl.li.am (cf. i,iii) 'of the work' (cp. |cali=am| > ca.lí·=am 'get to work (hurry up)!'); |pis.tə.Ņú.ut| (P17) > pís.tə.Ņú.ut > pís.tə̀Ņ.Ņu.ut (cf. i,iii). (ii-b) If the rhythmical accent is due to fall on an open syllable immediately preceded by a closed syllable, the accent regresses onto the closed one. This rule is blocked before a major boundary: |qayaq+paɣ[+mini| > |qa.yax.paɣ.mi.ni| > qa.yáx.paɣ.mí.ni. > qa.yáx.pàɣ.mi.ni (i,iii) 'in his own big kayak' (cf. qa.yáx.paɣ.mí·=mi above), |aŋyaq+paɣ-li+zuɣŋa+zuɣnaɣ̇qə[+ɣ*ua| > |aŋ.yax.pa.li.yuɣ.ŋa.yuɣ.nax.qu.a| (cf. P3, P7, P8, P10, P13, P21) > áŋ.yàx.pa.lí·.yùɣ.ŋa.yúɣ.nàx.qu.a (cf. i,ii-a,iii) 'I seem able to make a big boat'. (ii-c) If the rhythmical accent is due to fall on an open syllable with |ə| that is preceded by another open syllable CV, the |ə| is syncopated, unless the consonants flanking the |ə| are identical ones (including quasi-identical |c| and |t|, or |q| and |x|) or unless the immediately preceding syllable consists of a word-initial |ə|: |kəmɣ[-ni| > |kə.mə.ni| (cf. P6, P8) > kə̀m.ni (cf. i) 'his own flesh' (cp. |kəmɣ[-mi| > |kə.mə.mi| (cf. P6, P8) > kə.mə́m.mi (cf. i) 'of his own flesh' and |əmɣ̇[-ni| > |ə.mə.ni| (cf. P6, P8) > ə.mə́n.ni (cf. i) 'his own water'), |aŋyaq+paɣ-ŋə-ciqə[+ɣ*uq| > |aŋ.yax.pa.ŋə.ci.quq| (cf. P3, P7, P8, P10, P13, P19) > áŋ.yàx.pa.ŋə́.ci.quq > áŋ.yàx.pàŋ.ci.quq (cf. i, ii-b, iii) 'he will get a big boat' (cf. |anyaq-piɣ-ŋə-ciqə[+ɣ*uq| > |aŋ.ya.pi.ŋə.ci.quq| (cf. P3, P7, P10, P19) > áŋ.ya.pí·.ŋə.cí·.quq (cf. i) 'he will get a genuine boat'.

(iii) Deaccentuation. If rhythmical accent is due to fall on a word-final syllable, it is deaccentuated before #(#): nu.tə́ɣ.yux.tut (P6) > nu.tə́ɣ.yux.tút (cf. i) > nu.tə́ɣ.yux.tut. A result of deaccentuation is an accentless disyllabic word whose first syllable is open and an accentless disyllabic hypermeter at the end of polysyllabic words: nu.tək 'gun' (cf. i).

(iv) Preboundary regressive accent. (iv-a) A syllable preceding a nonenclitic boundary receives regressive

Table 11. Indicative Endings

			Intransitive			Transitive — Object								
						Third			**First**			**Second**		
						sg.	pl.	dual	sg.	pl.	dual	sg.	pl.	dual
S	Third	sg.		+Ø		+ηa	+ηi	+γ	+ηaηa	+ηakut	+ηakuγ	+ηatən	+ηaci	+ηatəγ
u		pl.		+t		+ηat	+ηit	+γkət	+ηatηa	+ηitkut	+ηitkuγ	+ηatγən	+ηitci	+ηit(t)əγ
b		dual		+γ		+ηaγ	-kəγ	+γkəγ	+ηaγ(nə)ηa	+ηaγ(t+)kut	+ηaγ(t+)kuγ	+ηaytən	+ηayci	+ηaytəγ
j	First	sg.	+$_1$tuq-	-ηa		-ka	+nka	+γka				-mkən	-mci	-mtəγ
e		pl.	~	-kut	+γ*aq-	+put	-put	+γput				-mt+γən	-mtci	-mttəγ
c		dual	+γ*uq-	-kuγ		+puγ	-puγ	+γpuγ				-məytən	-məyci	-məytəγ
t	Second	sg.		-tən		+n	-tən	+γkən	+pəηa	+pəkut	+pəkuγ			
		pl.		-ci		+ci	-ci	+γci	+pəci+ηa	+pəcikut	+pəcikuγ			
		dual		-təγ		+təγ	-təγ	+γtəγ	+pətəγ(nə)ηa	+pətəγkut	+pətəγkuγ			

NOTES: In the sequence |CV₁[γaγ̇V₂| (< |CV₁[+γaq+ηV₂|, cf. P3i, ii), which results from suffixing third-person subject transitive endings with initial |η| to bases that end in a single full vowel the |aγ̇| is deleted. However, the |γ̇V₂| is deleted instead in '3pl.—1pl.', '3pl.—2pl.', and '3pl.—2dual' endings.

The second-person subject and the first-person object forms have the initial |-və| instead of |+pə| for some Kuskokwim speakers.

A |t| becomes c before an apical stop.

The forms in this table are phonological representations.

accent: |aηyaq[-ka#qaa| > |aη.ya.qa#qaa| (cf. P3, P8) > áη.ya.qà(q)#qaa (cf. i,iii) 'my boat?' (cp. |aηyaq[-ka=lu| > |aη.ya.qa=łu| [cf. P3, P8, P13] > áη.ya.qá·=łu [cf. i] 'my boat also'); nuna[-ka-lu#tanəm| (cf. P13) > nu.ná·.ka=łù(t)#ta.nəm (cf. i,iii) 'my land too! (annoyed)' (cp. |nuna[-ka=lu-γuq| > nu.ná·.ka=łú·=xuq 'my land too, they say'). (iv-b) A syllable preceding an enclitic boundary, if the postboundary segment is vocalic, receives regressive accent, replacing the rhythmical accent (if any) on the preboundary syllable: |nutγ=am| > |nu.tək=am| (cf. P6, P13, P19) > nu.tək=(k)am (cf. i) 'again the gun'; |ca.lis.ta=am| > ca.lís.tà·=am (cf. i) 'again the worker' (in this case the regressive accent lengthens the preboundary vowel because there is no consonant to be geminated next to the boundary).

Rule P23 Vowel cluster adjustments. (i) The second vowel of a double vowel is shortened: |isχat-kə[+γ*aa=lu| > ísχàtkaá·=łu (cf. P2, P7, P10, P13, P22i,ii-c,ii-b) 'it is his bag', cp. |isχat[-ka=lu| > ísχatká·=łu (cf. P2, P13, P22i,ii-c) 'my bag'; see 4. for the difference between kaá and ká·. (ii) Word-initial ia· and ua· become ya· and wa· respectively: |ua[+ni| > wa·ni (cf. P22i) 'down there'. (iii) Though with considerable fluctuation, accent in clusters ai· and au· (and also ui· and iu· for some speakers) tends to shift from the second vowel to the first, and the second vowel is shortened: |tau[+na| táuna (cf. P22i) 'that one'.

Rule P24 Boundary-related blockings (optional). Besides the obligatory blocking of P22ii-a, ii-b before a major boundary, some rules connected with a major boundary may optionally be blocked inside a phonological phrase, with the boundary behaving somewhat like |+|: |kuiγ=mi| > kuik=mi (cf. P13, P19) or kuiγmi (with P13, P19 blocked) 'how about the river?'; |nutγ=am| > nutək=(k)am (P22) or nutəγγam (with P13, P19 blocked); |əłpəc=kiq| > əłpət=kiq (cf. P2ii) or əłpəskiq (as if from |əłpəc+$_1$kiq|, cf. P2i, P13) 'I wonder, you...'; |kuiγ#un'a| > kuik#unna (cf. P13, P19) or kuiγunna (with P13, P19 blocked) 'the river down there'.

4. PHONETIC DETAILS

Phonetic details of each phonemic symbol (tables 2, 4) are further specified.

a is fronted, i.e., [æ] (with less pharyngeal tension than in English cat), after i; low back, i.e., [ɑ] (as in French cas), next to back velar or in lengthened form; otherwise low central (lower than English cut): azəmNia [azímNiæ] (P13), əla·kataχtut [əlá·katáχtut] (P3). i and u are high front and high back respectively (as in English lick and look), but lowered, that is, [e] (as in English bed) and [o] (as in German Gott) respectively, next to back velar: amik [amik] 'door', amiq [ameq] 'skin'; ukuk [ukuk] 'these(dual)', uquq [oqoq] 'oil'. i is markedly low, i.e., [ɛ], between back velar and a: mittəłxia [míttəłχɛæ] (P13). See table 5, no. 16 for the velarized voiceless variant of u. ə is central and somewhat close to [ɨ] (as in rapid colloquial American English But..., but..., but...! or Just a minute!), but lowered, that is, [ə] (like the unstressed vowel in English about) next to back velar, and is devoiced ([ɨ̥] or [ə̥]) if not next to a voiced sound. Initial ə may be preceded by glottal stop, especially when followed by geminated stop, and is usually not pronounced or barely heard when followed by single consonant: unəq [unəq] 'armpit', cəła [cíła] (P11), əqquq [ʔə̥qqoq] 'it shrinks', əna [(i)na] (P20). The variant of a vowel next to back velar may be accompanied by slight pharyngeal tension.

A short and a lengthened vowel contrast: uγiχtuq 'it beaches' (|uγiγ[+tuq|) versus uγi·χtuq 'it beaches suddenly' (|uγiγaγ[+tuq|, cf. table 5, no. 5). A vowel cluster or a double vowel is phonetically a single syllable.

An accented vowel tends to carry greater prominence with duration, pitch, and stress combined than an unaccented one: *akkia·ni* [àk.kiǽ·.ni] 'across it'; *isχatkaa꞊łu* [ís.χɑt.kɑá.łu] versus *isχatka·=łu* [ís.χɑt.kɑ́·.łu] (P23); *attauciq* [àt.táu.čeq] 'one'. Vowels across = or # belong to two syllables: *cali·=am* [čɑ.lí·.am] versus *calliam* [čàl.liæm] (P22). The hiatus may be emphasized by glottal stop especially if a double vowel or a vowel cluster comes next to the boundary: *qayyaa#aatama* [qɑ̀y.yɑáʔɑɑ́.ta.ma] 'my father's kayak'.

Stops are lenis with unaspirated quality. Thus *p* of *pin* 'your(sg.) thing' is more like the *p* of English *spin* than that of *pin*. *k* and *q* (and their corresponding fricatives for that matter) are functionally distinct (as in many Northwest American Indian languages): *aŋyak* [áŋyak] 'two boats' versus *aŋyaq* [áŋyɑq] 'boat'. *c* is an affricate [č] (like English *ch*) or before *ə* [c] (like the *ts* of English *tsetse*: *ciun* [čiun] 'ear', *cətuk* [cɨ̥tuk] 'fingernail'.

The fricatives *v* and *f* are like English (as *vast* and *fast*): *cavun* [čavun] (P2), *aftaa* [áftɑɑ] 'he divides it'. *l* is a lateral with the tongue blade more evenly elevated than English *l* (which is pronounced with a "sagging" tongue), and its corresponding voiceless *ł* has some friction like Welsh *ll* but is not aspirated: *calliuq* [čàllioq] 'he is working' versus *całłiuq* [čàłłioq] 'he may be doing something'. *z* and *s* are like English (as *zip* and *sip*): *pizit* [pizit] (P21), *ciisiq* [čiíseq] 'worm'. They are contextually labialized: *təŋsuun* [tíŋsʷuun] 'airplane'. *γ* is a voiced fricative similar to the Spanish intervocalic *g* (as in *lago*), while *γ̇* resembles the fricative nontrilled variant of French "r grasseyé"; correspondingly, *x* is like the German "ach-laut," and *x̣* resembles the *r* in French *quatre*: *əγnəq* [íγnəq] 'juice' versus *əγ̇nəq* [ə́γ̇nəq] 'day', *əxNəq* [íxN̥əq] 'throwing away' versus *əx̣Nəq* [ə́x̣N̥əq] 'dawning'. *γʷ* and its corresponding *xʷ* are front labial-velar fricatives (*γ* and *x* pronounced with lip rounding): *aγʷna* [áγʷna] (P12), *xʷani* [xʷani] (P12). The back labial-velar fricatives *γ̇ʷ* and *x̣ʷ* are marginal sounds (see 15 |-γ̇uγ̇luγ̇-| and table 5, no. 16). *w* and *y*, which are approximants at the positions of *u* and *i*, are glides: *awa·ni* [awá·ni] (P12), *qayaq* [qɑyɑq] 'kayak'.

The nasals *m*, *n*, and *ŋ* are voiced as in English *sum*, *sun*, and *sung*, and *M*, *N*, and *N̦* are their voiceless counterparts: *azəmnia* [azímniæ] 'he says it cracked in half' versus *azəmNia* [azímN̥iæ] (P13), *aŋyanka* [áŋyanka] (P3) with no nasal neutralization (like Russian *bánk* 'bank' with dental *n*, but unlike English *bank*.)

Single and geminated consonants contrast, with geminates straddling the syllable boundary: *taquq* [ta.qoq] 'braid' versus *taqquq* [táq.qoq] 'he finishes'. (In the Hooper Bay and Chevak dialect geminated consonants and like-consonant clusters contrast: *annuq* 'he goes out' versus *an⁽ə⁾nanγix̣tuq* 'he no longer

goes out', which has the *n* released in the first syllable: P22ii-c.)

The allocation of prominence in a phonological phrase varies greatly as it is a function of expressive, discourse, and other factors; but at least in a neutral utterance (such as in citation), the last accented syllable in the phrase tends to carry the greatest prominence. The pitch is lowest at the end of the first accented syllable of a word, then rising steadily toward the end of the word. It falls most markedly at the end of the last accented syllable of a whole phonological phrase. The end of a phonological phrase is also signaled by the slowing tempo: *qayáxpàγmini* (P22), *qayáxpaγmí·=mi* (P22), *imú·mì(q)#qázγiŋqətútx̣àtni qázγimi#uítauγ̇atútx̣uúŋa* 'in those old days when they had men's houses, I used to stay in one of them'. The degree of pitch fall is assumedly correlated with the syntactic constituency of the words involved (Woodbury 1989).

5. ORTHOGRAPHY

The practical orthography developed by the Eskimo Language Workshop at the University of Alaska has been employed in Central Alaskan Yupik villages since 1970, when bilingual education was inaugurated. In this sketch the Yupik orthography is given in the selected vocabulary section.

The Yupik orthography is fundamentally based on the phonological level on which accentuation Rule P22 is to apply. The following letters and digraphs are employed in the orthography: ⟨a, c, e, g, gg, i, k, l, ll, m, n, ng, p, q, r, rr, s, ss, t, u, v, vv, w, y⟩. The use of some symbols differs from the phonemic transcription. Orthographic ⟨e⟩ and ⟨ng⟩ correspond to phonemic *ə* and *ŋ* respectively: (orthographic) ⟨tengmiaq⟩ (phonemic) *təŋmiaq* 'goose'. Orthographic ⟨w⟩ represents only prevocalic *xʷ*, while the phonemic *γʷ* and preconsonantal *xʷ* are both represented by ligatured ⟨u͡g⟩ and the phonemic *v* and *w* both by ⟨v⟩: ⟨wani⟩ *xʷani* (P12), ⟨au͡gna⟩ *aγʷna* (P12), ⟨calivik⟩ *cali·wik*, ⟨cavun⟩ *cavun* (P2). Double fricatives in the orthography (⟨vv, ll, ss, gg, and rr⟩) are voiceless (phonemic *f, ł, s, x, and x̣* respectively): ⟨amarru⟩ *ama·x̣u* (P3). Single fricatives in the orthography (⟨v, l, s, g, and r⟩) are voiceless at the beginning or end of a word, next to a stop, or after a double fricative, but otherwise voiced (phonemic *v, l, z, γ and γ̇*): ⟨kuicuar⟩ *kuicuax̣* 'rivulet', ⟨nutegyugtut⟩ *nutəγyuxtut* (P6), ⟨qemaggvik⟩ *qəmaxfik* 'bag', ⟨arvinlegen⟩ *aγ̇vinləγən* (P6), ⟨ner' llinia⟩ *nəγ̇łinnia* '(I see) he has eaten it'. A nasal in the orthography is voiceless after a stop (and optionally after a double fricative): ⟨ukna⟩ *ukNa* 'the one coming', ⟨errneq⟩ *əx̣Nəq* (4.). The orthography does not represent vowel lengthening and consonant gemination of the type formulated in P22, but it indicates gemination of the other types by an apostrophe after the consonant: ⟨ner'ut⟩ *nəγ̇γ̇ut* (P7). An apostrophe is also used in the orthography to indicate word-final truncation (e.g., ⟨qaill'⟩ *qaił(un)* 'how?') or deviation from the general accentuation pattern (P22) due to syllable contraction (see table 5, no. 5) (e.g., ⟨angertu'rtuq⟩ *aŋə́xtúxtuq* 'he keeps saying yes' versus ⟨angerturtuq⟩ *aŋə́xtuxtuq* 'he is chewing gum', ⟨qulngunrita'ar⟩ *qúlŋùnɣita·x* 'nine'), to distinguish [nɣ] from [ŋ] (e.g., ⟨un'gani⟩ *unɣani* 'downriver' versus ⟨ungani⟩ *uŋa·ni* 'his own beard'), and to show that a fricative or a nasal is not devoiced in spite of its environment (e.g., ⟨nut'lek⟩ *nutłək* (P6), ⟨'lagiq⟩ *laɣiq* [table 5, no. 8] 'goose', ⟨up'nerkaq⟩ *upnəxkaq* 'spring'). In the orthography a hyphen is used to mark enclitics instead of ꞊ (e.g., ⟨una-llu⟩ *una·꞊łu* 'this one also') and to distinguish a native element from a nonnative one in a word ⟨town-ami⟩ 'in town'). A bar (−) on a nasal shows that the nasal is voiceless even if it does not follow a voiceless consonant ⟨asemn̄ia⟩ *azəmNia* [P9]). Punctuation is the same as in English. See Miyaoka and Mather (1979) for orthographic details.

GRAMMAR

6. VERBS

The categories for which verbs are inflected are person and number of core nominal arguments and mood. Derivation of syntactically different kinds of verbs is correlated with the case marking of the core nominals involved.

Tense-aspect specification is made by some postbases such as 53 |-łɣu-|ᵥᵥ and 46 |+₁ciqə-|ᵥᵥ: |kiu-łɣu[+*ɣuq| *kiułxuuq* 'he answered' and |kiu+ciqə[+*ɣuq| *kiuciquq* 'he will answer' versus |kiu[+*ɣuq| *kiuɣuq* 'he answers'. Isolated Yupik verbs with no tense-aspect specifications are here glossed by the English present tense, though they are actually either perfective ('he has (just) answered') or progressive ('he is answering'). Negation is indicated in verbs by the postbase 70 |-nɣit-|ᵥᵥ, |+₁pəkə-|ᵥᵥ (6.2.6.), or other postbases with negative connotation (47, 55, 59, 60, 73, 78, 92): |kiu-nɣit[+*ɣuq| *kiunɣituq* 'he does not answer', |kiu+pəkə[-na-ni| *kiufkəna·ni* '(he) not answering'.

Members of Yupik speech communities are highly sensitive to indirectness in expression and to interpersonal attitude as to who is spoken to or about. Indirect expression is not so much something like a special polite form to be used in certain situations as a very normal and common way of speaking in almost any situation irrespective of whom, when, or where a person is speaking. Making a definite statement concerning personal feelings or future events would not be well received. Attitudinal distinctions are made minimally among positive (elevating, respectful, or desirable), negative (deprecating, derogatory, or condescending), neutral, and endearing. This sensitivity is particularly reflected in the careful choice by the speaker of a verb mood (6.2.2., 6.2.3.), an enclitic (|꞊kin|, |꞊kiq|, |꞊ɣuq|),

and the postbase (e.g., 5, 7, 15, 50, 64, 67) to be used in a verb or a nominal, combined with the frequent use of certain set words. An expression heedless of these distinctions (nuances, subtleties, etc.) would sound very blunt or inappropriate.

6.1. PERSON (SUBJECT AND OBJECT)

The person category distinguishes first, second, third, and reflexive third person. The reflexive third person refers back to the subject of the main clause, and, accordingly, only dependent moods (6.2.5. and 6.2.6.) are inflected for this category: see 7.3. and 7.4.2. also. See 6.3.1. and 7.4.2. for the type of reflexivity where two core nominals (agent and patient) are coreferent.

Verbs are either intransitive—mononominal with the subject person indexed—or transitive—binominal with both the subject and the object indexed—although the subordinative indexes only one nominal even if two core nominals are involved. The subject and object markers in a verb ending make cross-reference to corresponding overtly expressed nominals and agree with them in number. However, when the subject or object of a transitive verb is overtly expressed by a nominal, a singular verb form is often used instead of the plural or dual form appropriate to the subject or object, or a plural form instead of the dual: *yuut taŋəxŋakut* (connec. 3sg.—1pl.) *anəłxuukut* 'because the people saw us, we went out' (cf. *taŋəxŋatkut* 3pl.—1pl.), *kipu·takək* (indic. 3dual—3pl.) *aŋyak* 'they(dual) buy the boats (dual)' (cf. *kipu·taxkək* 3dual—3dual).

It is to be noted (i) that most person markers on verbs (tables 7-9, 11) occur as the absolutive or relative possessive-pronominal endings on nouns (tables 12-13) as well, (ii) that the indicative transitive endings with the object in the third person (table 11) are almost perfectly identical with the possessed absolutive endings for the third person (table 12), and (iii) that the connective mood markers (table 9) are based on the relative endings (table 13) (hence the occasional use of the term relative mood for the connective).

One set of markers (verbal person markers) occurs only on verbs, except for the second person, and marks only intransitive subjects or transitive objects but not transitive subjects. These are 1sg. |+ŋa|, 1pl. |+kut|~|+ta|, 1dual |+kuɣ|~|+nuɣ|; 2sg. |+t(ən)|~|+kən|(|+ɣən|), 2pl. |+ci|, 2dual |+təɣ|; 3sg. |+ku|(|+ɣu|), 3pl. |+ki|, 3dual |+kəɣ|.

The marking of the persons follows the ergative pattern in the subordinative mood and the accusative pattern in the connective mood. The other moods in the first- and second-person singular and the indicative and participial moods in the first person dual and plural follow the ergative pattern but otherwise follow the accusative or the neutral pattern.

6.2. MOOD

There are six moods of two subtypes, the independent moods (indicative, participial, interrogative, and

339

Table 12. Absolutive Endings for Possessed Nouns

Possessor		Singular	Plural	Dual
Third	singular	+ŋa	+ŋi	+γ
	plural	+ŋat	+ŋit	+γkət
	dual	+ŋaγ	-kəγ	+γkəγ
First	singular	-ka	+nka	+γka
	plural	+put	-put	+γput
	dual	+puγ	-puγ	+γpuγ
Second	singular	+n	-tən	+γkən
	plural	+ci	-ci	+γci
	dual	+təγ	-təγ	+γtəγ
Reflexive third	singular		-ni	+γni
	plural	+təŋ	-təŋ	+γtəŋ
	dual	+təγ	-təγ	+γtəγ

NOTES: See table 5, no. 4, for deleting suffixes that begin with a nasal plus vowel; table 5, no. 2, applies to all retaining suffixes beginning with |pV|.

The forms in this table are phonological representations.

Table 13. Relative Endings for Possessed Nouns

Possessor		Singular	Plural	Dual
Third	singular	+ŋan	+ŋin	+γkən
	plural	+ŋata	+ŋita	+γkəta
	dual	+ŋaγnəγ	-kənka	+γkənka
First	singular		-ma	+γma
	plural		-mta	+γ+mta
	dual		-məγnuγ	+γməγnuγ
Second	singular		+pət	+γpət
	plural		+pəci	+γpəci
	dual		+pətəγ	+γpətəγ
Reflexive third	singular		-mi	+γmi
	plural		-məŋ	+γməŋ
	dual		-məγ	+γməγ

NOTES: See table 5, no. 4 for deleting suffixes that begin with a nasal plus vowel; table 5, no. 2, applies to all retaining suffixes beginning with |pV|.

The forms in this table are phonological representations.

optative) and the dependent moods (connective and subordinative). The independent moods are used only as main-clause predicates, while the dependent moods typically occur in clauses subordinate to independent verbs but are also used independently in a number of constructions. Some enclitics and verb-elaborating postbases select a certain mood.

6.2.1. INDICATIVE MOOD

The indicative mood makes a straight statement of an event or state. In the indicative the intransitive endings, indexing the subject person, have the mood marker |+₁tuq-| (after a consonant) ~|+γ*uq-| (after a vowel), and the transitive endings, indexing both subject and object, have |+γ*aq-| (table 11): *ila·kaqa aŋun* 'the man is my relative' (|ila-kə[+γ*aq-ka| 'I have him as (83 |-kə-|) a relative (|ila-|))', *taŋuxxaanka ayałxuut* 'my boys went away' (|ayaγ-łγu[+γ*uq+t| 'they went away'), *cə̥Nixciiqaaŋa ata·ku* 'he will visit me this evening'.

6.2.2. PARTICIPIAL MOOD

A participle expresses a potential predication, which becomes an actual predication with a more or less expressive force particularly with the addition of one of certain noninflecting words: a response in dialogues very often uses |=wa|(~|#wa|, 9.2.). If nonpredicative, a participle is nominal (7.4.4.). The participial marker |-lγiaq-| (cf. P13iii)~|+₁ŋuγ̇-| (after |t|) for the intransitive forms and |-₁kə-| for the transitive, is followed by the same person markers as in the indicative (table 11) except that |p| becomes *v* after the transitive |-₁kə-| (table 5, no. 2): 3sg. |-lγia|~|+₁ŋuγ̇|, 3pl. |-lγiit|~|+₁ŋuut|, 1sg. |-lγiaŋa|~|+₁ŋua|, 2pl. |-lγiaci|~|+₁ŋuci|; 3sg.—3sg. |-₁kii|, 1pl.—3sg. |-₁kvut|. Examples are: *atsanək=xʷa nəγ̇əlγ̇ia* (3sg.) 'he is eating berries' (more indirect than the indicative *atsanək nəγ̇γ̇uq*), *atsat=xʷa nəγ̇kai* (3sg.—3pl.) 'he is eating the berries', *tuaxpiaq nunnailŋutən* 'it seems you (sg.) have no place (to stay)' (|nuna+ŋit[+₁ŋuγ̇-tən| 2sg.), *akłəŋ pitaqłua nəγ̇ŋaiłkəfcia* 'poor guys, you (pl.) won't catch and eat me' (*pitaqłua* subord. 1sg., |nəγ̇ə+ŋ*ait[-₁kə+vci+ŋa| 2pl.—1sg.). A participial verb can take the place of an interrogative verb (6.2.3.): *qaku ima aya·katalγ̇ia·kut* 'when are we leaving (again, as I forgot)?'

6.2.3. INTERROGATIVE MOOD

An interrogative verb is used in information-asking questions, which require the use of an interrogative (7.4.6.) typically at the beginning of a sentence. This mood is not used in yes-or-no questions with |#qaa| (9.1.). The interrogative mood has different markers depending upon the subject, |+₁ta-| (after a consonant) ~|+γ*a-| (after a vowel) for third person and |+₁ci-| for first and second person (table 8). Examples are: *qaŋvaq nullian taŋəłxuzziu* 'when did you (sg.) see your (sg.) wife?' (|taŋx-łγu[+ci+γu| 2sg.—3sg.), *qaku nəγ̇ciqsəta* 'when will we eat?', *kittuuzit* 'who are you (sg.)?' (|kitu+ŋu[+₁ci+t| 2sg.), *ciin aptatNa nakən təki·təłxułəmnək* 'why are they asking me where I came from?' (|apəc[+₁ta+tŋa| 3pl.—1sg.), *qafcinək imaγ̇miutaxtəłxuat* 'how many minks did they catch?' (80 |+c-|). Addition of an enclitic as in *kina·=kiq* or *kina·=xuq taiγa* 'who is coming?' makes the question indirect. An interrogative verb expanded by the postbase 1 |+paγ-| (table 5, no. 2), or 43 |+₁pakaγ̇-| (table 5, no. 2), if used without an interrogative word, has an exclamatory force: *nacan asixpaxta* 'how nice your (sg.) hat is!'

6.2.4. OPTATIVE MOOD

The optative mood expresses the speaker's wish or request that an event or a state occur. As in the interrogative mood, the optative mood has different markers depending upon the subject, |+li-| for third person, |+la-| for first person, and |+γ*i-| for second person (table 5, nos. 7 and 10; table 7). The first- and third-person optatives may merely express the speaker's wish or may ask for permission or consent from the person spoken to: *taili* 'may he come (now)!', *iẏnia·tən ciumək nəẏlit* 'may your (sg.) children eat first?'; *malixłamtək* 'may I go with you (dual)?', *tua·vət aẏu·laiẏəłta* 'let us stop down there!' The second person expresses command, instruction, or prohibition to the person spoken to: *kuicua·ẏaam akkia·nun ama·qəxcikut* '(you pl.) please carry us over to the other side of the small river!' (more indirect and polite than *amaxcikut* without 50 |-qaẏ-|), *xʷani aqumyanẏilu* '(you sg.) don't be sitting here!' (|+γa-|ᵥᵥ 'continuously'). See 9.2. for the enclitics |=tuq| and |=kin| that select this mood. An optative form with the aspectual postbase |-ₗki-|ᵥᵥ (table 5, no. 4), which immediately precedes the ending, expresses a wish for accomplishment of an event or a state in the future, possibly with the connotation of a long and expectant wait: *taikili* 'may he come (in the future)!', *aqsilu·tən nəẏkina* '(you sg.) eat hearty!' (*aqsilu·tən* subord. 2sg. 'being full', |+na+Ø| special 2sg. optative ending after the postbase |-ₗki-|; *nəxkina* in the Kuskokwim dialect). The postbases |+zaqu-|ᵥᵥ and |+piiqə-|ᵥᵥ (table 5, no. 2), followed by |+na-| (cf. 6.2.6.) plus a second-person-subject optative ending (but 2sg. |+naγ|, 2sg.—3sg. |+naku|), express prohibition of a future and a continuative action respectively: *nəẏyaqu·nacciu* '(you pl.) don't eat it (in the future)!', *nəẏviiqNak* '(you sg.) don't be eating, stop eating!'. The postbase |-ₗki-| may also occur as a statement in the past context (with narrative force): *nəẏkilliu xʷanixpak naŋluki* 'he now ate all of them' (*naŋluki* subord. 3pl. 'using them up').

6.2.5. CONNECTIVE MOOD

A connective verb typically occurs in syntactic dependence upon another verb, and expresses cause, time, concession, condition, or the like, depending upon the connective-mood marker that stands before the person marker (table 9). The connective markers are (1) causal |+ₗŋ*a-| 'because, when', (2) contingent |+γ*aqa-| 'whenever', (3) precessive |+ₗpailγ-| (table 5, no. 2) 'before', (4) concessive |-ₗŋẏaẏ-| 'although', (5) conditional |-ₗku-| (table 5, no. 5) 'if', and (6) indirective |+zua-|. The final vowel of (1), (2), (5), and (6) is deleted together with the initial |ŋ| of third-person subject markers.

6.2.5.1.

A causal connective verb marked by |+ₗŋ*a-| ~ |+ₗŋa-| (with much fluctuation in the apical adjustment of P2i)

expresses an event or a state causing that of the main-clause verb. Examples are: *cikiẏŋamki* (1sg.—3pl.) *quyyaut* 'because I gave presents to them, they (others) are glad', *cikiẏŋamtən* (1sg.—3Rpl.) *quyyaut* 'because I gave presents to them, they (themselves) are glad', *upnəxkauxcan* (3sg.) *cəła nəŋlaiẏutuq* 'since it is spring now, it is not cold any more'. A base-final or postbase-final *ŋə* is often dropped before the marker: *aŋəŋŋata~aŋŋata* 'because they are big' (|aŋə[+ŋa+ŋata| 3pl.).

6.2.5.2.

A contingent connective verb marked by |+γ*aqa-| (< |+γ*aẏ-qa-|) expresses a generic condition (with indefinite temporal reference) on the main-clause verb, which requires the postbase 57 |+laẏ-|ᵥᵥ, 76 |-tu-|ᵥᵥ, or 59 |-zuit-|ᵥᵥ. Examples are: *quya·laxtua taŋxaqamkən* 'I am happy whenever I see you (sg.)', *cikuq aaẏnaẏẏia·qan kuiẏmun atxaxcəccuitəłxuakut* 'whenever the ice becomes dangerous, he never lets us go down toward the river'.

6.2.5.3.

A precessive connective verb marked by |+ₗpailγ-| (table 5, no. 2) indicates the temporal precedence of what is expressed by the main-clause verb: *taizγu ikixpailəxpəγu* 'bring it to me before you (sg.) open it!', *aŋu·tət maqiłxuut nəẏvailəγmən* 'the men took a bath before they ate'.

6.2.5.4.

A concessive connective verb marked by |-ₗŋẏaẏ-| (fricativizing only |t|, but not |c|, and changing |ŋẏaẏC| into *ŋəẏC*, with regressive accent on preceding syllable if it is unaccented) expresses concession: *aptəŋẏamtəxu kiuyuitaakut* 'although we asked him, he never answered us', *cali·yuumiiłəŋŋəẏma caliŋnaqqua* 'even if I don't want to work, I'm trying to work'.

6.2.5.5.

A conditional connective verb is marked by |-ₗku-|, and the reflexive third-person markers have *n* instead of *m*. It has three functions. It may indicate a prior condition for what is expressed by the main-clause verb: *amik cikuskani* (3sg.—3Rsg.) *ikixcəsciiγacciiquq* 'if the door freezes (lit. if it [impersonal] freezes the door, cf. 6.3.1.), it will not open'. It may also indicate a counterfactual condition if used with a main verb containing the postbase |+zaẏ-|ᵥᵥ: *natułxunẏiłkumku tammaanətəłxən cəNixtəłxuya·ẏamkən* 'if I had known that you(sg.) were there (lit. your(sg.) being there, cf. 91 |+nət-|ₙᵥ and 7.4.5.4.), I would have visited you(sg.)'. Finally, it may also be used as an indirect way of expressing one's wish or request, if used independently in connection with |tawaam| 'only, but' or |=wa| (~|#wa|, 9.2.): *maqi·kuvət taγʷγʷaam* 'perhaps you(sg.) had better take a bath', *ankuma·=xʷa* 'perhaps I should go'.

6.2.5.6.

An indirective connective verb marked by |+zua-|, which only occurs independently but with the enclitic |=lu| or |=li|, is an indirect way of expressing one's wish or request (cf. 6.2.5.5.): *anyuama=łu* 'perhaps I should go', *nəqmək=łi taicuavŋa* 'perhaps you should bring me a fish' (|tai+c[+zua+vŋa| 2sg.—1sg.).

6.2.5.7.

The connective markers |-łẏ-| (6.2.5.7.) and |+ˌŋ*inanẏ-| (6.2.5.8.), which are contemporative, have the peculiarity (i) that the intransitive forms take the locative case endings for possessed nouns (table 10) as person markers and (ii) that the transitive forms take the person markers in table 9, with |ni| inserted after |mi| for the reflexive third-person singular subject markers.

A contemporative (1) connective verb form marked by |-łẏ-| 'when (in the past)' (cf. 23 |-łẏ-|ᵥₙ) expresses an event or a state at the same time as that of the main-clause verb. Examples are: *aataka nəẏəłxani* (3sg.) *ayałxuuŋa* 'when my father ate, I left', *aatama nəẏəłxaku* (3sg.—3sg.) *ayalxuuŋa* 'when my father ate it, I left', *aataka quyyauq nəẏłəẏminniu* (3Rsg.—3sg.) 'my father is happy when he is eating it'.

6.2.5.8.

A contemporative (2) connective verb form marked by |+ˌŋ*inanẏ-| 'while' (table 5, no. 1; cf. 71 |+ˌŋ*inaẏ-|ᵥᵥ and 29 |-nẏ-|ᵥₙ) expresses a continuative action or state during which the event of the main-clause verb occurs: *qannaataaŋa nəẏŋinaˑnəẏminniu* 'he is talking to me while he is eating it'.

6.2.5.9.

There is a special use (sometimes called an independent relative, cf. 6.1.) of the intransitive person markers:

A stative or collective verb base may occur with the intransitive endings without any intervening mood marker. The first or second person expresses the bodily posture or degree of collectivity ('all, together, alone') of the absolute nominal (intransitive subject or transitive object) of the sentence, the third person that of the object, and the reflexive third person that of the subject. Examples are: *nəẏəłxuuŋa naŋəẏma* 'I ate, (I) standing (|naŋẏ-|)', *innaan taẏənẏaiẏaqa* 'I took his picture while he is lying (|inaẏ-|)', *quuyuẏmi taŋvaẏẏaaŋa* '(he) smiling (|quuyuẏ-|), he looked at me'; *kiima calliuŋa* 'I am working, (I being) alone (|kii-|)', *nəqa tammaan nəẏẏaa* 'he eats the whole fish (|tama(łku)ẏ-| '(to be) whole, all, both') (cp. *nəqəm illii nəẏẏaa* 'he eats part of the fish'; see 7.1.), *nəqa iituumaan nəẏẏaa* 'he eats the fish including the eye' (|+tuuma-|ₙᵥ '(to do) together with'). Some of the collective bases can be nominal as well.

6.2.6. SUBORDINATIVE MOOD

A subordinative verb expresses an event concomitant with or accompanying what is expressed by the verb on which it depends. Used independently, the subordinative has the force of the indicative or of the optative (as a command). A closely connected sequence of events (with the same subject) is very often related by subordinative verbs (especially in the narrative style). In a subordinative verb the mood marker |+lu-| (table 5, no. 10)~|-ˌna-| (negative; table 5, no. 1) is followed by a verbal person marker (6.1.) except for the reflexive third person: 1sg. |+lua| (< |+lu+ŋa|), 3Rsg. |+luni|.

The peculiarity of a subordinative verb is (i) that, even if it is transitive, it indexes only one nominal, namely, the nominal that is to occur in the absolutive case if overtly expressed, and (ii) that its subject nominal is coreferential with the main-clause subject. Thus the reflexive third-person subordinative is intransitive and its ending indexes the subject, while the third person is transitive and its ending indexes the object. The first- and the second-person subordinative can be either intransitive or transitive. Examples are: *təkiˑtua piyyuaˑlua* (1sg.) 'I arrived, (I) walking', *pisuẏyuxtua malixłutən* (2sg.) 'I want to go hunting, (I) following you (sg.)', *taŋxaa qiaˑluni* (3Rsg.) 'he saw her, (he) crying', *taŋxaa qiafkaẏluku* (3sg.) 'he saw her crying,' lit. 'he saw her, (he) having her cry'. In the last sentence the causative postbase 33 |+vkaẏ-|(~|+ˌcic-|) is added to the mononominal base |qia-| 'to cry' (with neutralization of the causative connotation), making its unexpressed subject nominal coreferential with the main-clause subject and allowing the (noncoreferential) third person for which it is indexed to function as the notional subject by making it the ostensible object of the causative. Because the verb here is mononominal, the causative postbase could be deleted (*qiaˑluku*) without causing ambiguity. However, the deletion is not acceptable in the following example, where more than one nominal is involved in the verb base |nəẏə-| 'to eat': *taŋxaqa nəẏəfkaẏluku* 'I saw him eating,' lit. 'I saw him, (I) having him eat'. Additional examples: *taiłxuukut əlitNaluˑta* 'we came to learn' (|+na-|ᵥᵥ intention in subordinative forms), *tuquˑciqNiluˑku qanəxtuq* 'he says (he saying) she will die' (|tuqu-ciqə+ni[+luku| 3sg.), *tuquˑciqNiluˑni* (3Rsg.) *qanəxtuq* 'he says (he saying) he (himself) will die'. Independent uses: *aqumlutən* '(you sg.) sit down!', *tuaˑi=łu aatama taŋəxłuku tuntuq* 'and then my father saw the caribou' (note the relative 1sg.—sg. *aatama* in construction with the subordinative 3sg. *taŋəxłuku*). A reflexive third-person subordinative may be used as an adnominal adjunct: *imna uquˑẏiluˑni aŋun taŋəxtuaˑqa* 'I saw that fat man'.

The negative subordinative marker |-ˌna-| only occurs after (i) the specific postbase |+ˌpəkə-| (table 5, no. 2), which negates the preceding base instead of 70 |-nẏit-|

(6) (e.g., |ayaɣ+pəkə[-na-| 'not leaving') or (ii) a base or postbase that ends in |cic| or |t| (with a preceding |i| being replaced by *u*) (e.g., |kiiɣ́cic[-ˌna-| > |kiiɣ́cəNa-| 'being hot' (cf. P11), |canimət[-ˌna-| > |caniməna-| 'being near', |nutɣ+ŋit[-ˌna-| > |nutɣuna-| 'lacking a gun'). The negative |-ˌna-| is followed by the same verbal person markers as |+lu-|: 3Rsg. |-ˌnani|, 1sg. |-ˌnii| (< |-ˌna+ŋa|), but 2sg. |-ˌnaɣ| (instead of |-ˌnatən|). Examples are: *nutxunnii* (1sg.) *ayatxua·ma* (connec. 1sg.) *pitaxkak taukuk pisutxunɣitaxka* 'because I went without a gun, I did not hunt those kinds of game (dual)', *iqtufkəna·ci* '(you pl.) don't tell a lie!', *cukkaunaku* 'don't do it fast!'.

6.3. BASIC SENTENCE TYPES

6.3.1. VERB BASES AND CORE NOMINALS

Mononominal bases, in which only one nominal, S(ubject), is involved, occur with intransitive endings only: |tuqu-|: *tuqquuq* 'he dies', |mikə-|: *mikkuq* 'he is small', |atsaɣ́tuɣ́-|: *atsaxtuxtuq* 'he eats berries' (note that the base is mononominal since a nominal base (|atsaɣ́-| 'berry') verbalized by a verbalizing postbase (77 |+tuɣ́-| 'to eat') is syntactically not a nominal). However, mononominal bases of motion may occur with transitive endings having the location as the object: |atɣ́aɣ́-|: *atxaxtuq* 'he goes down', *iŋɣ́iq atxaɣ́ɣ́aa* 'he goes down the mountain'.

Binominal bases, in which two nominals, P(atient) and A(gent), are involved, occur either with intransitive or transitive endings. P is the recipient of a verbal event, while A, which presupposes P (but not vice versa), initiates the event toward P as the more active participant with higher control. The binominal bases fall into three groups, distinguished by the syntactic-semantic relationship between their intransitive and transitive forms. The agentive binominal bases, which generally describe events focusing on the process of the A's action, are semantically transitive even with intransitive inflection, in which case P is shunted (6.3.3.ii). The intransitive verbs are antipassive: |kiu-|: *kiuɣaa* 'he answers her', *kiuɣuq* 'he answers (someone)', |nəɣ́ə-|: *nəɣ́ɣ́aa* 'he eats it', *nəɣ́ɣ́uq* 'he eats (something)'. However, in tense-aspect specified contexts, the agentive binominal bases with intransitive inflection may be passive with the agent being deleted: *aku·taq akka nəɣ́ɣ́uq* 'the ice-cream has already been eaten', *ukut kali·kat taɣi·ŋəci·qut ata·ta* 'this book will be understood later on'; see also 42 |+uma-|~|+ima-|ᵥᵥ. The nonagentive binominal bases, which generally describe events focusing on the result of the A's action, are semantically transitive with transitive inflection: |atɣ-|: *atxaa* 'he tears it', |iiɣ́-|: *iiɣ́aa* 'he hides it', |əɣ́uɣ́-|: *əɣ́u·ɣaa* 'he washes it'. With intransitive inflection they are medio-passive, in which case A is deleted or the opposition between P and A is nullified (6.3.3.iii), or

reflexive: *atəxtuq* 'it is torn (passive); it tears (medial)', *iixtuq* 'it is hidden; it hides', *əɣ́uxtuq* 'he washes himself'. Some of the nonagentive binominal bases are impersonal: A for them is something impersonal (such as a natural phenomenon or process), which is usually not overtly expressed: |ciku-|: *cikkua* '(the cold) freezes it, i.e., it freezes'.

There are a few trinominal bases, in which three nominals, P₁, P₂, and A, are involved: |cikiɣ́-|: *ciki·ɣaa* 'he gives her (something)' (cp. |tunə-|: *tunnaa* 'he gives it [to someone]').

The syntactic verb-elaborating postbases (8.3.1.) change the number of nominals involved in verb bases by adding or removing one nominal: |tuqu-| 'to die': |tuquc-| 'to kill' with 32 |+c-| (which binominalizes a mononominal base by adding A and changing S into P), |tuqucəsciɣ́-| 'to get killed' with 34 |+sci(u)ɣ́-|; |nəɣ́ə-| 'to eat': |nəɣ́əsqə-| 'to ask—to eat' with 35 |+sqə-| (6.3.4.); |atɣ-| 'to tear': |atɣi-| 'to tear; to tear on (to the disadvantage of)' with 38 |+ɣ*i-| (6.3.2.).

6.3.2. HALF-TRANSITIVE AND ADVERSATIVE-BENEFACTIVE VERBS

Nonagentive binominal bases, if expanded by 38 |+ɣ*i| (table 5, no. 11) or (much less productive) 31 |+ˌuc-| or |-kənə-| (deleting final |tə| after P8), are semantically transitive with intransitive inflection, that is, antipassive. They are the so-called half-transitive verbs (Kleinschmidt 1851: 55-56). *atxiuq* 'he tears (something)', *iiɣ́iuq* 'he hides (something)', *ika·yuutuq* 'he is helping (someone)' (|ikayuɣ́+uc-|); *akNixkənuq* 'he hurts (someone)' (|akniɣ́c-kənə-|). Half-transitive verbs turn out to be a specialized subtype of experiencer verbs. Experiencer verbs with |+ɣ*i-| are generally adversative in connotation, implying an event or a process taking place in such a way that it affects E(xperiencer), participant distinct from P, usually disappointing, victimizing, or causing a loss to E. Experiencer verbs with |+ˌuc-| are benefactive. If a primary base is mononominal, the experiencer verb base with |+ɣ*i-| is binominal, involving S and E. It can thus inflect transitively: |kicci-| (< |kic+ɣ*i-|): *kiccia* 'it sinks on him', or intransitively, in which case S is shunted (6.3.3.[ii]): *kicciuq* '(something) sinks on him'. If a primary base is binominal, the experiencer verb base is trinominal, involving P, E, and A, the first of which is shunted so that it may occur with a transitive ending: |təɣlɣi-| (from |təɣlɣ-|) *təɣləɣɣia* 'he steals (something) from her', |iiɣ́i-| (from |iiɣ́-|) *iiɣ́ia* 'he hides (something) on, from her', |cikui-| (from |ciku-|) *cikkuiɣaa* '(the cold) freezes (something) on him, (something) freezes on him'. It can also inflect intransitively. If the primary base is agentive, E is shunted (in addition to P being shunted): *təɣləɣɣiuq* 'he steals (something) (on, from someone)'. If impersonal, A is deleted (in addition to P being shunted) '(something) freezes on him' (6.3.3.iii). 343

If nonagentive, the adversative relation between A and E (which remain after P shunting) is nullified or, rarely, A is deleted (cf. 6.3.1., 6.3.3.iii): *aⱡxiuq* 'he tears (something); (someone) tears (something) on him'. The first reading is that of a half-transitive verb, which is nothing but an intransitively inflected experiencer verb from a nonagentive base. Further examples: (half-transitive) *kuvviⱡxuuq qaⱡtami·nək* 'he spilled (|kuvə-|, |+γ*i-|) his own pail (*qaⱡtami·nək* abm. 3Rsg.—sg.) (accidentally)' (cp. *kuvvaa qaⱡtani* 'he spilled his own pail (*qaⱡtani* abs. 3Rsg.—sg.) (deliberately)'), *aqfatuq qaⱡtamək* 'he is fetching (|aqfa-|, |+₁uc-|) a pail'; (adversative-benefactive) *kuvviⱡxua·qa qaⱡtamək* 'I spilled a pail on him, his pail', *aqfattaa qaⱡtamək aŋun* 'he is fetching a pail for the man'.

6.3.3. SIMPLE SENTENCES AND CASE MARKING
A syntactic case—absolutive or relative—is primarily assigned to the nominals involved in verb bases in the hierarchical order of S/P > E > A. Case assignments as formulated in this section, 6.3.4. and 7.2.5.(2) will show that one nominal with the same semantic role, such as A, can occur in no less than five different cases—absolutive, relative, ablative-modalis, allative, and locative. (i) The absolutive case is assigned to the first nominal along the nominal hierarchy, and the relative case to the second if any: *nayiq kittuq* 'the seal (*nayiq* abs., S) sinks', *aŋu·təm nayiq nəγγaa* 'the man (*aŋu·təm* rel., A) eats the seal (P)', *aŋu·təm nayiq kiccia* 'the seal (S) sinks on the man (E)', *aγnam kuvyaq aⱡxaa* 'the woman (*aγnam* rel., A) tears the net (*kuvyaq* abs., P)'. If there are more nominals involved in a verb base than can be referred to in an ending (one for intransitive endings and two for transitive), they have to be reduced to that number. The reduction to one core nominal, intransitivization, is morphologically accompanied by removal of one nominal from indexing on the verb. (ii) Except for the cases in (iii), nominal reduction is made by shunting the nominal in the absolutive case into the ablative-modalis and by promoting the next higher nominal to the absolutive. A shunted nominal is not a core nominal but an adverbial adjunct: *aŋun nayiγmək nəγγuq* 'the man (*aŋun* abs.) eats a seal (*nayiγmək* abm.)', *aŋun nayiγmək kicciuq* 'a seal sinks on the man'; *aγnam aŋun kuvyamək aⱡxia* 'the woman tears a net (*kuvyamək* abm.) on the man (E)'. (iii) Reduction to one core nominal is made (iii-a) in the case of a nonagentive base or its derivative base by deleting A or by nullifying the opposition between the two core nominals involved (A and P or A and E): *kuvyaq atəxtuq* 'the net is torn' (deletion), 'the net tears' (nullification); *aŋun kuvyamək atxiuq* 'the net is torn on the man' (deletion), 'the man tears a net' (nullification—half-transitive, which is much more common); and (iii-b) in the case of an impersonal nonagentive base or its derivative base by deleting A;

nayiq cikkuuq 'the seal is frozen' (cp. *nayiq cikkua* 'the seal is frozen' lit. '[the cold] freezes the seal').

6.3.4. COMPLEX-VERB SENTENCES
The syntactic verb-elaborating postbases 33 |+₁cic-| ~|+vkaγ-|, 35 |+sqə-|, 37 |+zukə-|, and 39 |+ni-| expand a verb base by adding A into a complex verb, where the primary verb base belongs to the (morphologically as well) embedded structure and the postbase to the matrix. The derived complex verb is nonagentive. The case is assigned from within the embedded structure by the rules in 6.3.3. Nominal reduction may either be made by (ii) above or by (iv) shunting A of the embedded verb into the allative case and by promoting the next higher nominal: *aγnam aŋutMun nayiq nəγəsqaa* 'the woman tells (|+sqə-|) the man (*aŋutMun* all.) to eat the seal' versus *aγnam aŋun nayiγmək nəγəsqaa* 'the woman tells the man to eat a seal' (cp. *aŋu·təm nayiq nəγγaa* 'the man eats the seal' versus *aŋun nayiγmək nəγγuq* 'the man eats a seal', 6.3.3.), *aγnaq aŋutMək nəγəsqiuq* 'the woman asks (half-transitive |+γ*i-|) a man to eat (something); the woman asks (someone) to eat a man'.

Albeit to a limited extent, a complex verb can be nominalized or further expanded by one or more of its own elaborating postbases; *ayaγyukəⱡqa* 'the one I thought had left' (|+zukə-|, 23 |-ⱡγ-|), *pisuγniqatxuuq* 'he briefly (50 |-qaγ-|) mentioned (|+ni-|) that he went hunting'. Two or more complex-verb–forming postbases can occur in a word to bring forth a multilayer structure: *əγu·γinisqiu aŋutMun* 'ask (|+sqə-|, |+γ*i-| above) the man to say (|+ni-|) that she is washing dishes!'.

6.3.5. COMPLEX VERSUS COMPOUND SENTENCES
A verb with one or more of its own core nominals (and adjuncts) can be embedded into a sentence to form a complex sentence. The main clause has an independent mood verb, while the dependent clause has a dependent mood verb: *aγnat iqfaⱡxuut uitəŋ kuvyiita* 'the women were berry-picking (*iqfaⱡxuut* indic. 3pl.) because their own husbands (*uitəŋ* abs. 3Rpl.—pl.) were net-fishing (|kuvya[+ŋ*ata| connec. 3pl.)'. A compound sentence, on the other hand, consists of two clauses each having an independent mood verb, with a conjunctional word typically occurring between them. Various combinations of moods take place, but the second clause tends to have a participial or (independently used) subordinative verb: *aγnat iqfaⱡxuut uiŋit=xʷa* (abs. 3pl.—pl.) *kuvyalγiit* (part. 3pl.) or *aγnat iqfaⱡxuut uiŋit=ⱡu kuvyalu·təŋ* (subord. 3Rpl.) 'the women were berry-picking, and their husbands were net-fishing' (note the syntactic independence as shown by *uiŋit* with the third-person suffix instead of *uitəŋ* with the reflexive third-person suffix in the complex sentence above, which refers back to the main clause subject), *aγnat qama·ni taŋaⱡxuanka iqfaγlutəŋ* (subord. 3Rpl.) 'I saw the women up there, and they were berry-picking', cp.

aγnat qama·ni taŋətχuanka iqfaχcətu·ki 'I saw the women up there berry-picking' (*iqfaχcətu·ki* subord. 3pl. '[having] them berry-pick', cf. 6.2.6.).

7. NOMINALS

Nominals are inflected for case, number, and person. They fall into subclasses: nouns, which have full inflection, and numerals, pronouns, demonstratives, participles, deverbal nominals, and interrogatives, which have less inflection and highly limited expansion by postbases. (The morphological and syntactic peculiarities of those other than nouns will be dealt with in 7.4.). Some deverbal nominals (7.4.5.) function as nominal clauses and relative clauses. A nominal stands as the subject or object of a verb or as an adverbial or adnominal adjunct depending upon the case in which it occurs, but it is interjectional otherwise. Two or more (typically contiguous) nominals may constitute a nominal phase (appositive, coordinate, or adnominal relative, 7.5.), which functions syntactically as a single nominal. The language has neither gender (noun class) nor noun classification.

Every noun is obligatorily inflected for one of three numbers (7.1.) and one of seven cases (7.2.), and optionally inflected for the person of a possessor (7.3.). The number and case suffixes for unpossessed nouns are in table 6. The suffix complexes used on possessed nouns to index the number and case of the noun and the person of the possessor are in tables 10, 12-13.

7.1. NUMBER

The three numbers are singular, dual, and plural: *yuk* 'one person', *yuuk* 'two persons', *yuut* 'persons (more than two)'; *aŋyaqa* 'my boat' (see 7.3. for the possessor 'my'), *aŋyanka* 'my boats (more than two)'; *aanaxka* 'my mother and father (lit. my two mothers)', *maγʷluqətxiik* 'a grandmother and her grandchild (dual part. with |mauγluγ̇-| 'grandmother' and 83 |-kə-|) all in absolute case. A composite object may be expressed by a plural or dual noun, while the singular form, if used at all, refers to one part of that object: *akχət* (pl.) 'a ladder or ladders' versus *akəq* (sg.) 'rung', *qəŋaxka* (1sg.—dual) 'my nose', *tanγuxxaam ikamγ̇ak atu·γ̇ak* 'the boy is using the dog sled (*ikamγ̇ak* dual)'. The generic singular is used (*yuum umyuγγaa* 'the human mind') as is singular ('part of') for plural ('some of') in a certain category of nominals: *yuum illii* (abs. 3sg.—sg., |ila-|), *xʷatən ayu· quq* 'some people are like this', *pisuγ̇yaγ̇am illii natłua·qa* 'I don't know some of the hunting methods'.

7.2. CASE

The seven cases are absolute (called objective by some authors), relative (or subjective), ablative-modalis, allative (or terminalis), locative, perlative (or vialis), and equalis (similaris or conformative). The absolute and relative cases are mostly syntactic, and the others generally adverbial, though there are syntactically specified uses of some of these. See 6.3.3. and 6.3.4. for the syntactic case markings of nominals. All the adverbial cases except the equalis are locational, but their frame of reference may be either spatial or temporal.

7.2.1.

The absolutive case indicates the topic of predication. The subject of an intransitive verb and the object of a transitive verb, so long as they refer to the third person, occur in the absolutive form, agreeing with the verb in number (see 7.2.5.[2]): *aγ̇nak taiγuk* 'the two women (*aγ̇nak* abs. dual) (they) are coming (*taiγuk* ind. 3dual)', *aγ̇nat asi·kanka* 'I like (them) (*asi·kanka* ind. 1sg.—3pl.) the women (*aγ̇nat* abs. pl.)', *aγ̇naq ənəmmətuq* 'the woman (*aγ̇naq* abs. sg.) (she) is in the house (*ənəmmətuq* ind. 3sg., 91 |+mət-|)' (information on the location of the [already known] woman, who is the topic) (cp. *aγ̇naxtaŋqəxtuq ənəmmi* 'there is a woman [*aγ̇naxtaŋqəxtuq* ind. 3sg., 79 |+taŋqx-|] in the house [*ənəmmi* loc. sg.].'—information on the existence itself of a woman, who is not the topic).

The absolutive singular form of a noun for a period of time may be used as an adverbial adjunct referring to the most recent instance of the time denoted, while the locative form (7.2.5.(1)) expresses more general time: *unuk təki·tətχuut* 'they came last night (*unuk* abs. sg.)' (cp. *unuγmi təki·tətχuuq* 'he came at night (not in the daytime) (*unuγmi* loc. sg.)', *kiak* 'last summer' (cp. *kiaγmi* 'in summer').

A vocative form, characterized by a doubling of the last vowel of the absolutive form unless it is in a vowel cluster (*ii* in the case of |ə|), is used in addressing persons at some distance or in an exaggerated way: *aanaa xʷantua* 'mother, I'm here!', *qəŋaxpalliik* 'you (sg.), (one with; 13 |-lγ-|) big nose!', *tupaxci꞊am ukkuut* 'you (pl.) (here), wake up!' (see 7.4.3.1.). But in addressing persons near the speaker truncated forms are commonly used: *qimux* 'dog!' (cf. *qimuxta* 'dog'), *aŋał* 'Angalgaaq!' (person's name), *us* for *uzzuuq* (7.4.3.1.). See also 7.2.5.(2).

7.2.2.

The relative case marks a nominal that is in construction with another nominal (as "genitive") or with a transitive verb (as "ergative").

A relative nominal in construction with a nominal refers to a possessor as the adjunct, and the other nominal (referring to a possessed entity) as the head must be inflected with a third-person possessive-pronominal suffix ('his', 'their'—7.3.) agreeing in number with the relative nominal. The two nominals linked in this construction, which constitute an adnominal relative phrase (7.5.3.), tend to occur contiguously in a sentence, the adjunct usually preceding the head. The case of the head nominal is determined by the syntactic role of the phrase in the sentence. (As in English, the grammatical category of "possession" includes ownership, associational, and part-to-whole relations, kinship relationship, and the like.) Examples are: *aγ̇nam atχa* 'the woman's (*aγ̇nam* rel. sg.) (her) name (*atχa* abs. 3sg.—sg.)', *aatama atχi* 'my father's (*aatama* rel. 1sg.—sg.) (his) names (*atχi* abs. 3sg.—pl.)', *aγ̇nak attiiγ̇nək atχa* 'the name of the father (*attiiγ̇nək* rel. 3dual—sg.) of the two women (*aγ̇nak* rel. dual)'.

A relative nominal in construction with a transitive verb is the subject of the verb, which agrees with it in number: *aγ̇nam aataka taŋχaa* 'the woman sees (him) (*taŋχaa* ind. 3sg.—3sg.) my father (*aataka* abs. 1sg.—sg.)', *taqu·kat taŋətχuatŊa* 'the bears saw me', *akəχtəm iixka akŊiχtətəˑγ̇ak* 'the sun hurts my eyes (dual)'. Note the ambiguous type *aγ̇nam atχa asiˑkaa* 'he likes the woman's name' (taking the relative *aγ̇nam* to be in construction with *atχa*) or 'the woman likes his name' (taking *aγ̇nam* with *asiˑkaa*).

7.2.3.

The ablative-modalis, which represents the merging together in the history of Yupik of two cases, the ablative (or distantialis) and the modalis (or instrumental), is marked primarily by the regular Yupik reflex of the original modalis. It indicates: (1) starting point, cause, and other adjunct roles: *təŋmiaq nanvamək təŋŋuq* 'the goose flies off from the lake (*nanvamək* abm. sg.)', *yuuχtətχanək* 'since he was born' (cf. 6.2.5.7.), *camək qannaacətək* 'what are you (dual) talking about?'; (2) a shunted nominal to which the absolutive case would be assigned before shunting (6.3.3.[ii]); the nominal has an indefinite connotation in this construction: *aŋun taqu·kamək taŋəχtuq* 'the man sees a bear (*taqu·kamək* abm. sg.)' (cp. *aŋu·təm taqu·kaq taŋχaa* 'the man sees the bear [*taqu·kaq* abs. sg.]'), *iiγ̇iuq nəqMək* 'he hides (*iiγ̇iuq*, 6.3.2.) a fish' (cp. *iiγ̇aa nəqa* 'he hides the fish'), *piyu·təmnək kipu·yutətχua·ŋa* 'he bought me (benefactive 31 |+₁uc-|, 6.3.2.) what I wanted ("relativizing" 23 |-łγ̇-|, 7.4.5.1.)'; (3) a nominal shunted from an appositive (7.5.1.) or a coordinate (7.5.2.) phrase as the other nominal is expanded by the nominal-elaborating 13 |-lγ-|ₙₙ or a verbalizing postbase (e.g., 79 |+taŋqx-|ₙᵥ, 87 |-li-|ₙᵥ, 96 |-ŋ*ə-|ₙᵥ, 97 |-ŋqx-|ₙᵥ): *qatətχia·mək atkulək* 'the one in a white parka' (cf. *qatətχia atkuk* 'white parka'), *malγ̇uγnək acaŋqəχtua* 'I have two aunts' (cf. *malγ̇uk acciik* 'two aunts'); *nəqəχłuxtaŋqəχtuq kəməγ̇mək=łu* 'there is some dried fish and meat' (cf. *nəqəχłuk kəmək=łu* 'dried fish and meat'), *ənəlliuq qanikcamək* 'he is building a house out of snow' (cf. *əna qanikcaq* 'house made of snow').

7.2.4.

The allative case indicates: (1) Destination, direction, or ending point: *ayaγγyuxtua nanvam akkia·nun* 'I want to go to the other side (*akkia·nun* all. 3sg.—sg.) of the lake', *kali·kamun atqa alŋautaqa* 'I write my name on

the paper', *təki·tətχanun* 'until he came' (cf. 6.2.5.7.). (2) A shunted nominal to which the relative case would be assigned before shunting; see complex-verb forming postbases in 6.3.4. as well as nominalizing postbase 20 |+₁uciq-|: *aγ̇nam taqu·kamun nəqa nəγ̇əsqaa* 'the woman tells (35 |+sqə-|) the bear (*taqu·kamun* all. sg.) to eat the fish' (6.3.4.), *nəqa nəγ̇əsquq taqu·kamun* 'the fish wants itself to be eaten by the bear', *aγ̇nam nəγ̇əłχunnia nəqa taqu·kamun* 'the woman says (39 |+ni-|) that the bear ate the fish'; *natłuuŋa nəqa taqu·kamun nəγ̇əłχuccia·nək* 'I don't know whether the bear ate the fish' (*nəγ̇əłχuccia·nək* abm. 3sg.—sg. with |+₁uciq-|, 7.4.5.4.)

7.2.5.

The locative case expresses: (1) Location or time at which an event or a state takes place: *iŋγ̇ini pisuχtut* 'they are hunting in the mountains (*iŋγ̇ini* loc. pl.)', *aca·mi cannia·ni aqquiγuq* 'he is playing beside (*cannia·ni* loc. 3sg.—sg.) his (own) aunt (*aca·mi* rel. 3Rsg.—sg.)', *taumi əγ̇nəγ̇mi natMuχtətχuuq* 'he went somewhere on that day' (*taumi* 'that' in apposition with *əγ̇nəγ̇mi* 'day', 7.5.1.). (2) A nominal (except for a personal pronoun) referring to the first or second person that would occur in a syntactic case if it were the third person: *xʷaŋkuta·=łu aγ̇nani manaγ̇yaγ̇aqłuta iqa·łua·nək* 'and we (table 14) women (*aγ̇nani* loc. pl.) go ice-fishing for (|+zaγ̇-|ᵥᵥ 'to go for —ing', |+γ*aqə-|ᵥᵥ 'usually') cod', *əłpət taaŋiqsuilŋuγ̇mi asi·kamkən* 'I like you (sg.: table 14) (one) who does not drink (*taaŋiqsuilŋuγ̇mi* loc. sg. part.)' (cp. *əłii taaŋiqsuilŋuq asi·kaqa* 'I like him [table 14] [one] who does not drink [*taaŋiqsuilŋuq* abs. sg.]'), *suχtulγ̇iami uła·γaqa* 'I who am tall (loc. sg. part., |suγtu-| 'tall') went to him'. This locative use of a nominal referring to the second person can be vocative: *tanγauγ̇luγ̇ni nəppaunaci pisu·laχci* 'you boys (*tanγauγ̇luγ̇ni* loc. pl.), hunt (*pisu·laχci* opt. 2pl.) quietly (*nəppaunaci* subord. 2pl. 'being without noise')!' (3) The person or thing compared, with a verb base expanded by |-nγu-|~|-₁łγ̇u-|ᵥᵥ (cf. the postbases 30 and 94; table 5, no. 1): *qaya·qa asinγ̇uuq* (or *mikətχuuq*) *pivni* 'my kayak is better (or smaller) than yours (*pivni* loc. 2sg.—sg. 'your thing')'. (4) The person or thing exclaimed about, when an exclamatory verb with 98

Table 14. Personal Pronouns

		Singular	Plural	Dual
Third	absolutive	əłii	əłait	əłkəγ
	relative	əłiin	əłaita	əłkənka
First		wii~wiiŋa	waŋkuta	waŋkuγ
Second		əłpə	əłpəci	əłpətəγ
Reflexive third		əłmi	əłmən	əłməγ

NOTE: The forms in this table are phonological representations.

|+₁paa| (table 5, no. 2) occurs in connection with the enclitic |=li|: *cəta·mi=łi asixpaa* 'my, the weather is fine!'

7.2.6.

The perlative case indicates: (1) Location or time through or along which an event takes place: *kuixpiim cəNNiikun ayaxciqu·kuk* 'we (dual) will go along the bank (*cəNNiikun* perl. 3sg.—sg.) of the Yukon' (*kuixpiim* rel. sg., lit. 'big river'), *nəẏtəẏmən kiŋŋua·kun yuẏa·liyaẏlutən* 'after (*kiŋŋua·kun* perl. 3sg.—sg., lit. 'its back part') their meal (*nəẏtəẏmən* rel. 3Rpl.—sg.)', they go for (|-liyaẏ-|ᵥᵥ) dancing'. (2) A part of the whole that is affected or damaged: *iẏuvɣun#qaa qimuxtəm kəxətxua·tən* 'did the dog bite you (sg.) on your (sg.) leg (*iẏuvɣun* perl. 2sg.—sg.)?' (3) Instrument or means: *aŋyaməxtəxun unnua·qu təki·ciiqut* 'they will arrive in their (own) boats tomorrow'.

7.2.7.

The equalis case indicates: (1) an entity that is similar or in some way equivalent to another: *mikəlŋuq ata·mitun ayu·quq* 'the child looks like his (own) father (*ata·mitun* equal. 3Rsg.—sg.)', *nalliat kassat yuppixtun qantua* 'which one (7.4.6.) of the White men (*kassat* rel. pl.) speaks (like an) Eskimo?', *ukuk pilu·ɣuuk tunyuɣaxka qultun* 'I wish to sell this pair of boots for 10 dollars'. (2) Point of comparison with a verb base expanded by the postbase 45 |+ta-|ᵥᵥ: *una miktauq tautun* 'this is as small as that (*tautun* equal. sg.)'. (3) Manner and time with 20 |+₁uciq-|ᵥₙ: *niiyucimtun* 'as soon as I heard', *pita·cimtun* 'as hard as I can' (with 45 |+ta-|).

The equalis and the locative of comparison (7.2.5.(3)) may follow another adverbial case ending: *qilaɣmitun* 'as in heaven', *ənən maanimi kiixtunẏuuq* 'your (sg.) house is warmer than here (*maani* loc. 7.4.3.2.)'.

7.3. PERSON (POSSESSOR)

A noun may be inflected with a possessive-pronominal suffix indexing the person of a possessor: *aŋyaput* 'our boats (abs. 1pl.—pl.)', *panixtək* 'your (dual) daughter (abs. 2dual—sg.)'. The person category of possessor is the same as that for verbs. The reflexive third person refers back to the subject of a sentence: *pani·ni asi·kaa* 'he likes his (own) daughter (*pani·ni* abs. 3Rsg.—sg.). Unlike the situation with verbs, the person inflection for nouns is obligatory only in certain cases. A third-person suffix is obligatory as a cross-reference on the head nominal of an adnominal relative phrase: *aŋu·təm pannia* 'the man's (*aŋu·təm* rel. sg.) daughter (*pannia* abs. 3sg.—sg.)'; *aŋamta atxit* 'our uncle's (*aŋamta* rel. 1pl.—pl.) names (*atxit* abs. 3pl.—pl.)'. But the third-person suffix is also used without an adjunct nominal as the equivalent of 'his, its, their, etc.': *pannia asi·kaa* 'he likes his (another's) daughter', *natu·yaɣu·tanka atxit* 'I have forgotten their names'.

A few subclasses of nouns, taken as inalienable, are obligatorily inflected for person: (1) body part terms

(*camna ityaqa puvvuq* 'my foot down there is swollen'), (2) nouns of location or part-to-whole (*canimtəNi uitauq* 'he is beside us'), and (3) kinship terms (*aatan təki·tuq* 'your (sg.) father has arrived'). See 7.4.1. for numerals with person inflection.

7.4. SUBCLASSES OF NOMINALS

Subclasses other than nouns have their own morphological or syntactic peculiarities.

7.4.1. NUMERALS

There are separate numeral bases for the units 1 through 6, 10, 15, and 20 as listed in table 15. The lacunae are filled by expanding these bases (i.e., 7 and 8 by adding |+nlɣ-| to bases of 2 and 3, but 9, 14, and 19 by adding |+ŋunẏitaɣaẏ-| to bases of 10, 15, and 20 respectively) or by combining two or more numerals (i.e., 11 through 13 by 10 plus 1 through 3, 16 through 18 by 15 plus 1 through 3; 40, 60, 80, and 100 by 2, 3, 4, and 5 plus |ipiaq-| (from |ipiɣ-| 'limb') in the appropriate number: 30, 50, 70, and 90 by 20, 40, 60, and 80 plus 10; numbers within the decades by 20 plus 1, etc.) For 1,000 the Russian loanword |tiisitsaaq-| is used.

The absolutive ending is |+∅| for the bases 1, 15, 20, and those with |+ŋunẏitaɣaẏ-|, |+ɣ| for 2, and |+n| for the rest: *attauciq* 'one', *qulŋunẏita·x* 'nine', *malẏuk yuuk* 'two persons', *piŋa·yun təŋsuutət mittut* 'three airplanes have landed' (*piŋa·yun* in apposition with *təŋsuutət*). For the other cases the bases take the unpossessed noun endings (table 6) of the appropriate number: *attaucimi* 'in one', *kipu·tətxua malẏuxtun* 'he bought it for two dollars (*malẏuxtun* equal. dual)', *qulŋunẏita·ẏnək kaukan* 'at nine o'clock' (lit. 'when it strikes nine').

Numeral bases expanded by |-ẏqu-|ₙₙ with the ablative-modalis ending of the appropriate number function as numbers of repetition: *nunniinun ayatxuuŋa malẏuxquɣnək* 'I visited his village twice (*malẏuxquɣnək* abm. dual)'.

Except for |ciuqliq-| 'the first' (from |ciu-| 'front') and |tuŋliq-| 'the second' (from |tuŋə-| 'direction'), numeral bases with a third-person possessive-pronominal suffix function as ordinal number: *cəta·miit* '(their) fourth (3pl.—sg.)', *iẏnia·məɣnuk ciuqliat* 'the first of our (dual) children'.

7.4.2. PERSONAL PRONOUNS

Personal pronouns refer only to humans. Only the (non-reflexive) third-person pronouns distinguish absolutive and relative forms. The other pronouns have a single syntactic case, used in both functions. The first-person

Table 15. Numeral Bases

1	atauciq	4	citama	10	qulə
2	malẏu	5	tałima	15	akimiaq
3	piŋayu	6	aẏvinlɣ	20	yuinaẏ

NOTE: The forms in this table are phonological representations. *347* pronouns are possibly derived from the demonstrative base |u-| (cf. *xʷani* 'here') and show resemblance in formation to demonstrative pronouns. Adverbial case endings are suffixed to |waŋ-| (singular) or |waŋku-| (nonsingular) (*xʷaŋtun* 'like me', *xʷaŋkuɣnun* 'to us (dual)'). The variant |wiiŋa| is more emphatic than |wii|. The adverbial cases for the other persons are made by inflecting the base |əɬ(ə)-| like a possessed noun: *əɬminun* 'to himself', *əɬpətəɣnun* 'to you (dual)', *əɬɬaitxun* 'through them'.

Since personal pronominal reference is made to the subject, object, and possessor by endings, the use of personal pronouns is highly restricted. They are employed for the sake of focus, contrast, narrative or expressive effect, and enumeration, as well as where reference to a person cannot otherwise be made: *əɬɬaita pikkaat* 'it belongs to them', lit. 'they (*əɬɬaita* rel. pl.) have (83 |-kə-|_NV) it', *xʷiiŋa aataka kipuˑcestəNNuuq* 'my father is a storekeeper', *xʷiiŋa aataka aanakaˑ=ɬu təkiˑtəɬxuukut* 'I, my father, and my mother arrived', *əɬɬiini uitauŋa* 'I am staying with him (*əɬɬiini* loc. 3sg.)', *taŋəxtuq əɬminək* 'he sees himself (in the mirror)', *xʷaŋŋuuq* 'it's me', *caŋaˑtənɣittua əɬpət=(t)am* 'I am fine, and you (sg.)?', *aŋyani əɬpənun aqfaqqaasqaa* 'he wishes you (*əɬpənun* all. 2sg., 7.2.4.(2)) to go to get his (own) boat'.

The bases |ila-| 'part, relative' and |aipaq-| 'other (of two), partner', which are generally inflected for person, function like pronouns: *ilaˑci* 'one of you', *aɣnat illiita iɣniaˑqaa* 'he is the child of one of the women' (*aɣnat* 'women (rel. pl.)', *illiita* 'one of them (rel. 3pl.—sg.)', 83 |-kə-|_NV); *aŋyaɣma aipaak* 'one of my boats (dual)'. See 7.1. and 7.4.6. also.

7.4.3. DEMONSTRATIVES

Demonstrative bases may be semantically classified into three groups as in table 16. The important factors in locating an entity or referring to a location by means of a demonstrative are its expanse or motion and the areal segments of the speaker's surroundings in relation to some topographical feature like the river or the sea, toward which much of the life of the Yupik people is oriented. The areal segmentation is correlated with verbs (see 'to go' in 10.). The "extended" (E) demonstratives indicate a broad location (or temporal duration) or an entity, not narrowly localized, that is horizontally lengthy or moving. The "nonextended" demonstratives indicate a more specific location (or time) or an entity that is stationary (or moving within a confined area) and can be precisely located. The basic difference between the "near" nonextended (N) and the "far" nonextended (F) is a matter of distance and distinctness. An N demonstrative refers to an entity or a location that is relatively near, distinct, and visible, while an F demonstrative refers to an entity or a location, indistinct and typically invisible, that is more distant than a corresponding N one. All the demonstratives are deictic, except that |im-| refers to shared knowledge and that |tau-| and |tamat-| can be either deictic or anaphoric. The opposite of |uk-|, motion away from the speaker (or time just passed), can be expressed by |aw-|.

Demonstrative bases occur as pronominal or adverbial demonstratives. Expanded by verbalizing postbases, they occur in verbs as well. Nominal and verbal endings are suffixed to certain expanded bases.

7.4.3.1.

Pronominal demonstratives occur with an unpossessed noun ending (table 6). The bases have to be expanded by |+na-| to take an absolute singular ending, by |+u-| (~|∅| after |tau-|; table 5, no. 3) to take a nonabsolute singular ending or a verbal ending for singular subject, and by |+ku-| to take a nonsingular ending or a verbal ending for nonsingular subject: |u-|: abs. sg. *una* (< |u+na[+∅]|), loc. sg. *uumi*, perl. pl. *ukutxun*; |am-|: abs. sg. *amna*, equal. sg. *ammutun*, all. dual *amkuɣnun*. Most pronominal demonstratives have vocative forms. The singular is formed by adding |+zuuq| directly to the base, the nonsingular by doubling the last vowel of the absolute form (7.2.1.): |u-|: sg. *uzzuuq*, pl. *ukkuut*. The bases |kan-|, |mat-|, and |tamat-| have irregular forms, listed here in the order absolute singular form, vocative singular form (if used), nonabsolute singular base, and nonsingular base: *kanna*, *kaccuuq*, |kàtu-|, |kanku-|; *manna*, *maccuuq*, |màtu-|, |maku-|; *tamaˑna*, |tamatu-|, |tamaku-|. When a base ending in |k| is expanded by the nonsingular marker |+ku-|, the sequence |k+ku| becomes *kɣ+ku*: |ik-|: abs/rel. pl. *ikəxkut*. A limited number of postbases occur with an expanded pronominal demonstrative base: 4 |-cuaɣaɣ-|: *unaˑcuaˑx* abs. sg. 'this small one', *uucuaɣmi* loc. sg., *ukuˑcuaˑɣaat* abs/rel. pl.; 94 |+ŋu-|: *uuŋuuq* 'it is this one', *ukkuuɣut* 'they are these ones'.

Table 16. Demonstrative Bases

Extended (E)	Nonextended Far (F)	Near (N)	
mat-		u-	'here (near to first person)'
tamat-		tau-	'there (near to second person)'
	im-		'aforementioned or known'
	uk-		'approaching (space and time)'
aw-	am-	iŋ-	'over there'
aɣ-	akm-	ik-	'across there, on the opposite'
paw-	pam-	piŋ-	'back, up there, away from river'
paɣ-	pakm-	pik-	'up, above there'
un-	cam-	kan-	'down, below there, toward river'
unɣ-	cakm-	uɣ-	'out there, down river, toward exit'
qaw-	qam-	kiuɣ-	'inside, up river, inland'
qaɣ-	qakm-	kəx-	'outside (immediate vicinity)'

NOTE: The forms in this table are phonological representations.

A pronominal demonstrative stands by itself or in appositive phrases with another nominal (7.5.1.): *una cauγa* 'what is this (N)?', *manna ənəvvut nəŋłixtuq* 'this (E) house of ours is cold', *uumi cassami* 'at this hour', *mattumi iγaˑlumi* 'in this month', *unnumək nayiγmək pisuˑqataxtua* 'I am about to hunt that (E) seal (in horizontal motion) down yonder', *kanna aŋyaq kittəqaˑtaxtuq* 'that (N) boat down there is about to sink', *camna kuixpiim paiŋa qailixtuq* 'it is rough down there (F) at the mouth of the Yukon'. The vocative form is used for address: *tuppii=am uzzuuq* 'you (sg.) (here), wake up!' Examples of |aw-| versus |uk-|: *aγ"zuuq nəqsuqaˑtaxtutən#qaa* 'hey, you (sg.) (moving away), are you going fishing?', *atam ukNa aŋyaq aγγiixtətxia ucippakaˑpixtuni* 'look, here comes that boat with a big load!' |im-| refers to an entity only in consciousness, which has no connection with physical location (often implying that the speaker cannot recollect the name of the entity): *imna tuquˑłəq akx"auwaq tuunγalγuuq* 'that person who died yesterday was a shaman'. It may occur in apposition with a deictic demonstrative: *imna payna* 'that one back there (shared knowledge)'. In the Norton Sound dialect the prefix |ta-| (prevocalic)~|taz-|(preconsonantal) occurs with any demonstrative base instead of an appositive phrase with |im-|. The expanded base |ima-| occurs only as a particle without further suffixation or in the particle |tayima| 'somewhere, there (out of sight)'.

7.4.3.2.

Adverbial demonstratives have expanded bases with |+a-| (blocking the accentuation of P1): |ika-| from |ik-|. Specific changes involved in the formation of expanded bases are: |(C)aγaa-| from |(C)aγ-|, |kia-| from |kiuγ-|, |(ta)maa-| from |(ta)mat-|, |wa-| from |u-|, |tua-| from |tau-|. Adverbial demonstratives occur only in the adverbial cases, but the case markers that are suffixed to the expanded base are somewhat different from those in table 6: loc. |+ni|, all. |+vət|~|+tmun|, abm. |+kən|, perl. |+xun| (*uuxun* instead of **x"axun* from |wa-|), equal. |+tən| (occurring only with |wa-| and |tua-|). The allative |+vət| is more particular or definite than |+tmun|, but the bases |wa-|, |tua-|, and F demonstratives only take |+vət|: *piaˑni* 'back there' (cf. *piŋŋumi* 'in the one back there'), *maatMun* 'toward here, this area', *maavət ałaˑnəq itałxuuq* 'the stranger came in here', *payγaani iŋγim qaiŋani yuγmək taŋəłxuuq* 'he saw a man above there on top of the mountain'. The expanded adverbial demonstrative base followed by |=i| is interjectional, though in the case of F demonstratives the expanded base occurs without |=i| in this function and |waniwa| is used instead of **wa=i|: *taŋ maa=i aγγiixtətxia təŋsuun* 'look, here comes the plane!', *tuaˑ=i ayaγniiłta* 'there (now), let us begin!' The bases |wa-|, |maa-|, and |tua-| in particular occur in various particles (9.1.). The expanded bases followed by |+t-|

function as nouns of location and are inflected for person (which indicates the point of reference; 7.3.): |ikat-|: *ikaˑtii* 'area across it', *ikaˑtəmkun* '(through) across me'; |awat-|: *awaˑtəmtəNi caγaˑyiit amłəxtut* 'there are a lot of bears around us'. Some demonstratives do not make these nouns in |+t-| and are replaced in this function by nondemonstrative bases: |qulə-| 'upper part, 10' (for **|pikat-|), |kəlu-| 'farther up behind' (for **|piat-|), |kət-| 'area toward river' (for **|kanat-|). The expanded base may occur with a few postbases: *pikaˑnətuq* 'it is up there (91 |+nət-|_NV)'. See also 86 |+viγc-|~|+tmuγc-|_NV.

7.4.4. PARTICIPLES

The participial mood marker (6.2.2.) functions as a nominalizing postbase to form a nominal participle. The intransitive nominal participle (|-łγiaq-|) is not inflected for person: *nəγəlγia* 'one who is eating', *taquˑmalγiit* 'complete (lit. finished) things', *taquˑmanγilŋuut* 'incomplete things', *taŋəxkək aipaqəłxiik* '(you sg.) look at the married couple (dual)!', *nayixculγiaˑγuŋaˑtuq* 'maybe he is (one who is) going out seal hunting'; *atsat nəγkai* 'the berries (the ones) he is eating' (*nəγkai* abs. 3sg.—pl.)'. The intransitive marker followed by |-ni| may mean 'when(ever)': *naułuulγiani it(əγ)laxtuq* 'when (someone is) sick, he always comes in'.

7.4.5. DEVERBAL NOMINALS

Deverbal nominals, formed with the nominalizing postbases (8.2.), show different types of nominalization.

7.4.5.1.

A clause with one or more of its own core nominals is changed by 23 |-łγ-| into a nominal phrase of past connotation that functions as a relative clause with the absolutive nominal as head: *aŋun atsanək nəγłəq* 'the man who ate berries' (*aŋun* 'man' and *nəγłəq* 'one who ate (abs. sg.)' constituting an appositive phrase, 7.5.1.) from *aŋun atsanək nəγγuq* 'the man is eating berries'; *aŋuˑtəm atsat nəγəłxi* 'the berries which the man ate' (a combination of the appositive *atsat nəγəłxi* 'berries, ones he ate (abs. 3sg.—pl.)' and the adnominal relative (7.5.3.) *aŋuˑtəm nəγəłxi* 'ones the man ate') from *aŋuˑtəm atsat nəγγai* 'the man is eating the berries'.

7.4.5.2.

A patient nominal is formed with 27 |+γ*aq-| (perfective) or |-ˌkənaq-|. An inflection for person indicates the agent: *iqqaiγaq* 'washed clothing', *iqqaiγanka* (abs. 1sg.—pl.) 'ones I washed'; *aŋyaq atuˑqəŋŋaa* 'the boat he is using'.

7.4.5.3.

An agent nominal is formed with 24 |+st-|, which requires a nonagentive verb base to be expanded by 38 |+γ*i-| (see 6.3.2.). An inflection for person indicates the patient: *kəxəsta* 'biter, one who bites', *kəxəstii* 'his biter, one who bites him', *əliˑcaγista* 'teacher' (|əlicaγ-| 'to teach').

349

7.4.5.4.

A gerundive nominal is formed with postbases such as 29 |-nɣ́-|, 22 |-ɬɣ́-|, and 20 |+₁uciq-|. Gerundives with |-nɣ́-| have no person inflection: *əmənnəq unnuaˑkumi assiiɬkaqa* 'I don't like drinking in the morning'; *əməɬɬəq unnuaˑkumi assiiɬkaqa* 'I don't like to drink in the morning'; *ayuˑqucia* 'its (way of) resembling, condition', *qaiɬun ayuˑqucciitaqa* 'I don't know how it is' (92 |+ŋit-|ₙᵥ 'to lack').

7.4.6. INTERROGATIVES

An interrogative is required in information-asking questions with an interrogative verb or (occasionally) a participial or optative verb: see 6.2.3. for interrogative sentences. Interrogatives are a morphologically miscellaneous albeit functionally distinct class of words. Some of them do not inflect: |qaiɬun| 'how'. Others are inflecting words, though they do not all inflect in the same way. |ca-| 'what' takes the unpossessed noun endings: abs/rel. pl. *cat*, all. sg. *camun*, loc. sg. *cami* (also 'when [specifically], sometime'). The general interrogative for reason *ciin* 'why' comes from |ca-| 'to do what, something' (< |ca[+ŋan| connec. 3sg., cf. 6.2.5.1.), from which base a person-specific interrogative is formed as well: *caavət* 'why you (sg.)', *caamən* 'why they'. |qafci-| 'how many' inflects like a numeral base: abs. *qafcin*, abm. *qafcinək*. |naliɣ́-| 'which', the interrogative equivalent of |ila-| (7.4.2.), inflects the same way: *nalliat* abs. 3pl.—sg. (*kassat* rel. pl.) 'which one (of the White men)', *nalixpuk* 'which one of us (dual)'. |kit-| 'who' inflects like a pronominal demonstrative, but the absolute and relative singular are *kina* and *kia* respectively, and the expanded base for adverbial-case singular is |kitu-| and that for the nonsingular is |kinku-|: loc. sg. *kituˑmi*, all. pl. *kinkunun*; inter. 2sg. *kittuuzit* 'who are you (sg.)?', *kia pikkaanək* 'for whom (lit. for whose future belonging, cf. 6 |+k*aq-|)?' (as in response to *naaŋuaˑmək canaˑqataxtua* 'I am going to carve a toy'). |na-| 'where' inflects like an adverbial demonstrative: loc. *nani*, abm. *nakən*, perl. *naxxun*, all. *natMun* (not *navət*), *nattii* 'where in relation to it'. |qaŋvaq-| 'when (in the past)' and |qaku-| 'when (in the future)' inflect, but to a very limited extent.

Some interrogatives function like indefinite pronouns or adverbs when used with a noninterrogative verb: *kina taiɣuq* 'somebody is coming', *kituˑmək taŋəɬxunɣ́ituˑkut* 'we did not see anybody', *nəɣ́ŋatuq tayiˑma nani caxxiɬqumi* 'he may be eating now somewhere in the opening'.

7.5. NOMINAL PHRASES

Two or more nominals, which are typically contiguous, constitute a nominal phrase: appositive, coordinate, or adnominal relative.

7.5.1.

In appositive phrases the two or more nominals stand in apposition, agreeing in number and case: *piŋaˑyun təŋsuutət* 'three airplanes', *aŋuˑtəm aŋyaa nutaˑɣaq aŋŋuq* 'the man's new boat is big' (*nutaˑɣaq* 'new one' in apposition with the adnominal relative phrase *aŋuˑtəm aŋyaa* 'man's boat'), *iɣ́niaˑma azɣ́im* 'of my naughty child' (note the unpossessed *azɣ́im* 'naughty one').

7.5.2.

In coordinate phrases the two or more nominals in the same case are connected by a conjunctive particle or enclitic (such as |waɬɬu| 'or', |cali| 'and also', |=lu| 'and'): *aɣ́naq aŋuˑtək=ɬu* 'the woman and two men', *attauciq malɣ́uk xʷaɬɬu piŋaˑyun* 'one, two or three'.

7.5.3.

In adnominal relative phrases a relative nominal as the adjunct is in syntactic subordination to the head nominal (7.2.2.). An adnominal relative phrase can be an adjunct to another noun, constituting a higher adnominal phrase: *aŋuˑtəm pannian atxa* 'the name of the man's daughter' (*pannian* rel. 3sg.—sg.)' (cf. *aŋuˑtəm pannia*, 7.3.).

8. POSTBASES

It is postbases that make Yupik a somewhat unique polysynthetic language (see 1.2.). Not only are they outstandingly productive in derivation, but they also have important syntactic functions and are relevant to speech styles as well. Many postbases are lexical in that they are very concrete in content, but there are no lexical or nominal suffixes like those in the Wakashan, Chimakuan, and Salishan languages that seemingly function as core nominals inside a verb. Some postbases may occur more than once in a word. The number of postbases that occur in a word is potentially unlimited, though in natural speech it rarely exceeds half a dozen. By contrast with the wide freedom of the order of words within a sentence, the relative position of postbases within a word is semantically or functionally determined. In general a postbase immediately follows the base or expanded base to which it is directly related. Thus the order of postbases may affect the meaning: *ayaxciqNia* 'he said she would go' versus *ayaɣniciˑqaa* 'he will say she went' (both being indic. 3sg.—3sg.; 46 |+₁ciqə-|ᵥᵥ and 39 |+ni-|ᵥᵥ).

No postbase is known to be a reduced form of a once independent base. A few postbases show combination or fusion of a case marker with some derivational element: 16 |+miu-|ₙₙ, 86 |+viɣ́c-|ₙᵥ, 91 |+mət-|ₙᵥ. The postbase |-klaaɣc-|ᵥᵥ, ₙₙ 'o'clock' (from English) is an isolated example reminiscent of a Chinook Jargon word borrowed as a suffix in Quileute (Boas 1947: 225). In some cases an obsolete postbase may be detected in a number of bases of a particular semantic category, though their primary bases may not be deducible. Note, for example, the relative abundance of |-quq-| in body-part terms.

The following list, far from exhaustive, gives only the more productive postbases grouped by the functional classes (8.1.–8.4.). Productivity varies even among these. Some are combinable with any semantically appropriate base of a base class, while others are affiliated with bases or endings of a certain category. Those postbases that belong to two or more of the classes are listed only once. A few postbases outside the four classes are miscellaneous in function (8.5.).

8.1. Nominal-elaborating Postbases ($_{NN}$)
See also 21, 23, 25, 71, and 72.

1 |+paγ-|~|+$_1$vaγ-|(optionally after |t|)$_{NN, VN}$, |-paγ-|~ |-vaγ-|$_{VV, NV}$ (often disturbs accentuation) '(one with) big, all, during (the time); intensely' (ciutəxpak or ciulvak 'big ear', unuxpak 'all night, during the night'; pámyuxpak 'big tail', pamyúxpak 'you, big tail! (expressive)'; kəxpaγγaa 'it bit him hard'; nəγ́əppaxtuq 'he eats a lot').

2 |-piγ-| 'genuine' (atpia 'his real name', yuppik 'Eskimo').

3 |+taγ́-| 'pertaining to' (yuppixtaat 'Eskimo things').

4 |-cuaγ́aγ́-|$_{NN}$ (table 5, no. 5), |-cuaγ́-|$_{VV}$ 'small, little' (ənəccuax 'small house'; taicua·qaa '(you sg.) please come for a moment').

5 |-cuŋaq-|$_{NN}$, |-cuŋaγ́-|$_{VV}$ 'cute, dear' (nukkacu·ŋaq 'cute Nuk'aq'; aya·cuŋaxtuq 'he (dear) leaves').

6 |+k*aq-| 'future' (aŋyaxkaq 'material for a boat', uitavixkaq 'place where one will stay'), cf. 23 |-łγ́-| and 27 |+γ*aq-|.

7 |-kayaγ-|$_{NN, VV}$ 'respectful, big, great(ly)' (una·kayak 'this [respectful] one'; aya·kayaxtuq 'he [respectful] leaves').

8 |-qva-| 'advanced in direction or time' (unukfani 'late at night', ukaqfani 'very near', quləqfani 'far way up').

9 |-qliγ́-| 'one located in' (quləqłiq 'one on top', quləqłika·caax 'the highest one' with |-kacaaγ́aγ́-| 'very, most').

10 |-$_1$łuγ-| (table 5, nos. 1 and 12) 'bad, old, kind of' (cəła·łuk 'bad weather').

11 |-łyut-|$_{NN, VN}$ 'partner in' (atəłxutka 'my namesake'; ayałxutkaqa 'he is my traveling companion' with 83 |-kə-|).

12 |-xaγ́-| 'little bit of' (cuya·xaq 'a little tobacco').

13 |-lγ-| 'one having' (pupsulək 'crab, one with pincer', aγ́naq iγ́niaxpalək 'woman who has a big child', qaya·lək aŋyamək=łu 'one having a kayak and a boat', cf. 7.2.3.(3)).

14 |+γ́*uγaγ́-| (table 5, no. 6) 'multitude of' (aŋyaγu·γaat 'many boats').

15 |-γ́uγ́luγ́-|$_{NN, VV}$ (contracts |γuγ́| to ´γ́^{w} after an unaccented vowel but deletes the first |γ́| after an accented

vowel) 'poor, sorry' (áŋyáγ́^{w}luq 'boat (poor)', qaya·uγ́luq 'kayak (poor)', aca·γuγ́luq 'aunt (poor)' with no P9 deletion of |γ|; aya·γuγ́luxtuq 'he (poor) leaves').

16 |+miu-| (deletes final |q|, P3i) 'inhabitant of' (cəNaγ́miu 'coast dweller', cammiuŋuzit 'where are you (sg.) from?').

17 |+nku-| 'associate' (upsankuuγut 'they are Upsaq's family').

18 |+ŋut-| 'supply of' (muγ́γautəka 'my wood supply').

8.2. Nominalizing Postbases ($_{VN}$)
27 selects binominal bases, and 30 mononominal ones. 21 and 24 require a nonagentive base to be expanded by 38 |+γ*i-| (6.3.2.). See also 1, 11, 7.4.4. and 7.4.5. Some deverbal nominals are lexicalized nouns.

19 |+$_1$ut-| (table 5, nos. 1 and 13) 'means, time, cause' (cavun 'oar', naułuun 'illness', kizzuttiini 'when he was drowned').

20 |+$_1$uciq-| (table 5, nos. 1 and 13) gerundive nominal (7.4.5.4.) (yuucia 'his (way of) living', taktaccia 'its length' with 45 |+ta-|).

21 |+cuut-|~|+suut-|(after vowel)$_{VN, NN}$ 'instrument, means' (cali·suun 'tool', kəppissuun 'wedge'; iγ́a·luxcuun 'calendar').

22 |-łγ́-| gerundive nominal (7.4.5.4.) (tama·łəq 'being lost', tamałqa 'my being lost', ali·ŋuq aya·ləxkami·nək 'he is afraid to go' with 6 |+k*aq-|).

23 |-łγ́-|$_{VN, NN}$ relative clause (past) (7.4.5.1.); 'former' (tama·łəq 'one that was lost', tamałqa 'one I lost', tama·γ́iłəq 'one who lost something'; uiłxa 'her ex-husband').

24 |+st-| (table 5, no. 14) agent nominal (7.4.5.3.) (nəqsuxta 'fisherman' with 81 |+suγ́-|, kəxəstəłxa 'one who bit him' with 23 |-łγ́-|).

25 |+$_1$viγ-|$_{VN, NN}$ (postconsonantal |t| deletion of P15; table 5, nos. 1 and 12) 'place' (mizvik 'airport', qəmaxfik 'bag', quya·wikkaa 'he is thankful to him' with 83 |-kə-|; qimuxtəγ́vik 'kennel').

26 |+zaγaq-| 'way, device, method' (yuγ́aγ́yaγ́aq 'how to dance', qanəγ́yaγ́aq 'language, word, saying', itəγ́yaγ́aq 'entrance').

27 |+γ*aq-| patient nominal (perfective) (7.4.5.2.) (nəγ́γaq 'one that has been eaten', tuqu·tauγuq 'he was killed' with 94 |+ŋu-|, iqqai(γ́a)xkaq (table 5, no. 5) 'clothing to be washed' with 6 |+k*aq-|).

28 |+$_1$nγ́-| (table 5, no. 1) noun of result (qupNəq 'crack', kumlanəq 'frozen fish', ayaγnəq 'beginning').

29 |-nγ́-| gerundive nominal with no person inflection (7.4.5.4.) (nəγ́nəq 'eating', qupnəq 'splitting', aya·nəq 'going').

30 |-nγ́-|~|-$_1$łγ́-|(after apical; table 5, no. 1) 'more, most' (aŋyam anənγ́a 'one bigger than the boat', aŋənγ́at 'the biggest'; assiiłxa 'one worse than it'). With 94 |+ŋu-| following (7.2.5.(3)) (aŋənγ́uuq 'it is bigger'; ayaγyuumiiłxuuq 'he is more reluctant to go').

8.3. VERB-ELABORATING POSTBASES (_vv_)

Some postbases in this class have a syntactic function (8.3.1.), while others are adverbial (8.3.2.).

8.3.1.

Syntactic verb-elaborating postbases affect the nominals involved in verb bases, typically by expanding or reducing verb bases by one nominal (6.3.1. through 6.3.4.). 33, 35, 37, and 39 form complex-verb bases (6.3.4.). 34 selects binominal bases. Bases expanded by 34 or 36 are mononominal.

31 |+₁uc-| (table 5, nos. 1 and 13) (adds P or E, changing S of mononominal bases into A, and shunting P with binominal bases, cf. 6.3.2.) (*anuˑtaa* 'he takes her out (with him); he goes out for her', *assiutaaŋa* 'he is being nice toward me', *kipuˑyuttaa* 'he buys (something) for her', *kipuˑyutuk* 'they (dual) buy (something) for each other, for themselves', *aqfataa* 'he fetches (something) for her', *aqfatuq* 'he fetches [something]').

32 |+c-| (adds A, with S of mononominal bases becoming P, cf. 6.3.1.) (*qamtaa* 'he turns it [stove] down', *qamtuq* 'it is turned down [by someone]', cp. *qammuq* 'it dies down').

33 |+₁cic-|(cf. P11)~|+vkaẏ-|(after vowel) 'to cause, let, allow' (*tuquˑcəttaa* 'he lets [someone] kill it', *nəẏəfkaẏẏai* 'he lets them eat, feeds them'). See 6.2.6. for noncausative use.

34 |+sci(u)ẏ-| (deletes A; table 5, no. 14) 'to be —ed (to the subject's damage or disadvantage)' (*caẏaˑyaɣmun malixcəscitxuuq* 'he was followed by the bear', cf. 6.3.4.(iv)).

35 |+sqə-| (with P5i blocked before this postbase) 'to tell, ask, want' (*tuquˑcəsqaa* 'he asks [someone] to kill it; he asks her to kill [something]').

36 |-zu-| (deletes P; table 5, no. 4) 'to be skillful, tend' (*nutyuuq* 'he is good at shooting', *kəxsuuq* 'it tends to bite').

37 |+zukə-| 'to think' (*aŋyauyukaˑqa* 'I think it is a boat').

38 |+ɣ*i-| (half-transitivizes but adds E for experiencer verbs, 6.3.2.) (*navɣiuq* 'he breaks [something]; [something] breaks on him', *navɣiaŋa* 'he breaks [something] on me', cp. *navɣaa* 'he breaks it', *navəxtuq* 'it is broken').

39 |+ni-| 'to say' (*asiẏniaˑqa* 'I say it is good').

40 |+naẏi-| 'to be time to' (*nəẏnaẏẏiuq* 'it is time [for him] to eat' [the subject can also be P], *nəẏnaẏẏia* 'it is time for him to eat' [the subject and object can also be A and P]).

41 |+naẏqə-| (|ẏ| being deleted before |qC|) 'should' (*nəẏnaxqaqa* 'I must eat it', *nəẏnaxquq* 'he should eat, it can be eaten', *nəẏnaqłuni* '(he) should eat').

8.3.2.

Adverbial verb-elaborating postbases include ones expressing tense-aspect, modality, and evidentiality as

well as manner, degree, intensity, and so forth. 45 and 65 select mononominal bases. A base expanded by 45 is mononominal. See also 1, 4, 5, 7, 15, 76, and 96.

42 |+uma-| (table 5, no. 13)~|+ima-|(after apical; table 5, no. 11) 'to be in a state of —ing' (*nəẏuˑmauq* 'he is eating (a long time); it has been eaten', *ikixcimmauq* 'it is open').

43 |+₁pakaẏ-| (table 5, no. 2) 'so much, so long' (*ciin nəẏvakaxta* 'why is he eating so much?', *caliˑwakaxta* 'what is he doing all the time?', *nəŋłixpakalẏia* 'one making so much noise').

44 |+tuẏaẏ-| (after velar; table 5, no. 5)~|+₁quẏaẏ-| (after apical, which is deleted; table 5, no. 5) ~ |+ɣ*uẏaẏ-| (after vowel; table 5, nos. 5 and 7) 'to keep —ing' (*azzauxtúxtuq* 'he keeps (boat-)poling', *nəẏuˑẏałxuuq* 'he kept eating').

45 |+ta-| 'to that degree' (often in construction with an equalis noun as object of comparison (7.2.7.) and reduplicatable in a word) (*asixtaccia* 'its goodness, how it is good' with 20 |+₁uciq-|, *aŋtattauq* 'it is that big').

46 |+₁ciqə-| (P2i deletion being accompanied by doubling of |i|) 'will (future)' (*qaku təkiˑciiqa* 'when will he come?'—more blunt than 67 |+niaẏ-|, *nəẏciqaˑqa* 'I will eat it').

47 |-ksait-| 'not yet' (*təkiˑtəksaituq* 'he has not arrived yet', *taŋəqsaitaqa* 'I have not seen him since').

48 |-qapiyc-| (table 5, no. 5) 'very, at all, just' (*asiˑqapixtuq* or emphatic *asiqqapixtuq* 'it is very good', *taiqapixtua* 'I just came').

49 |-qataẏ-| (table 5, no. 5) 'about to' (*anqataxtuq* 'he is about to go out').

50 |-qaẏ-| (table 5, no. 5) 'briefly, merely' (giving indirectness to an optative verb) (*patuˑqəẏẏaa* 'he merely covers it ', *umkaxu* '[you sg.] please shut it!').

51 |-łi-| 'perhaps' (*nəẏyułłiutən* 'would you [sg.] like to eat?').

52 |-łini-| 'evidently, now I see' (*caniˑmətqapixtəłiˑniuq* 'I see it is very near').

53 |-łẏu-| 'did (past)' (*ayałxuuq* 'he left'), cf. 23 and 94.

54 |-siyaaẏ-| 'too' (*miksiyyaaxtuq* 'it is too small').

55 |+sciẏat-|_vv, nv_ (table 5, no. 14) 'cannot' (*calisciiẏatuq* 'he cannot work'; *atkuxciiẏatuq* 'he cannot put on a parka').

56 |-xaaẏ-| 'first' (often in subordinative or optative forms) (*qawaˑxaaẏluta* 'we first sleeping, after we sleep', *əməxxaaẏlii* 'let me drink first').

57 |+laẏ-|(Yukon)~|-laẏ-|(Kuskokwim) 'habitually' (*uilukun nəẏlaẏaˑqa* 'I [usually] eat it with a spoon'), cf. 6.2.5.2.

58 |-łŋu-| 'to be tired of —ing' (*nutəłŋuuq* 'he is tired of shooting [but still doing it]').

59 |-ẑuit-| 'never' (*kəxsuituq* 'it never bites').

60 |+zuumiit-|_vv, nv_ (table 5, nos. 4 and 12) 'to have no desire (to)' (*məluɣyuumiitua* 'I don't wish to smoke').

61 |+zuuma-|(Yukon)~|+zuɣŋa-|(Kuskokwim)ᵥᵥ,ₙᵥ (table 5, nos. 4 and 12) 'can' (*kipaχcuumauq* 'he can walk around', *atuɣ́yuɣŋaa* 'he can use it').

62 |+zuɣ-|ᵥᵥ,ₙᵥ (table 5, nos. 4 and 12) 'to want (to)' (*malixcuɣamkən* 'I want to go with you (sg.)'; *qimuxtəɣ́yuxtuq* 'he wants a dog').

63 |+zuɣnaɣ́qə-| 'probably' (*ayałχuyuɣnaχquq* 'I guess he left').

64 |+zaaqə-| 'supposedly, fruitlessly, to no avail' (often implying politeness) (*taiłχuyyaaquq* 'he was supposedly coming [but has not shown up yet]; he came [but not fulfilling his purpose]', *aku·taxtuɣ́yuɣyaaqua* 'I would like to eat ice-cream').

65 |+ᵢɣ́*i-| (changing |t| to *l* after single vowel; table 5, no. 6)~|+li-|(after |ə|) 'to become, make (more)' (*cuka·ɣia* 'he causes it to be fast', *ukaqsiɣɣiuq* 'it is becoming near', *aŋliuq* 'it is becoming big', *nəqNiɣ́ɣia* 'he, it is making it tasty').

66 |+ᵢmi-| (table 5, no. 1) 'also' (*nałunɣ́ilmiuq* 'he also knows').

67 |+niaɣ́-| future (*nəɣ́niaxtukut* 'we will eat [soon]', *qaku·=kiq təkitNiaχta?* 'when will he come?', cf. 46).

68 |+nauɣ́-| 'now, habitually' (*nəɣ́nauxtukut* 'we will eat (now)', *ayaɣnauxtuq yaaqfanun* 'he would go farther away').

69 |-nqiɣc-| 'again' (*atunqixtuq* 'he is singing again').

70 |-nɣ́it-| 'not' (*qawanɣ́ituq* 'he is not sleeping', *nałunɣ́itaqa* 'I know it'), cf. 29 and 92.

71 |+ᵢŋ*inaɣ́-|ᵥᵥ,ₙₙ 'only, just, for no particularly purpose; only, totality of' (*məluɣŋinaxtuq* 'he is just smoking'; *paiŋinaɣ́mun* 'only to the mouth'); cf. *yuinaq* '20'.

72 |+ŋuaɣ́-|ᵥᵥ,ₙₙ 'to pretend to; imitation of' (*qawa·ɣ́uaxtuq* 'he pretends to be asleep'; *kəxutNuaq* 'false tooth').

73 |+ᵢŋ*ait-| (table 5, no. 1) 'will not' (*kipuzŋaitaa* 'he will not buy it').

74 |+ᵢŋ*at-|ᵥᵥ,ₙᵥ (table 5, nos. 1 and 12) 'maybe; to look like' (*ayaxciqNatuq* 'maybe he will go'; *kuiɣŋatuq* 'it is like a river').

75 |-ŋnaqə-| 'to try to' (*qanəŋnaquq* 'he is trying to speak').

8.4. VERBALIZING POSTBASES (ₙᵥ)

Bases expanded by 83, 90, 92, 93, 95, and 96 are binominal; the others are typically mononominal. See 55, 60, 61, 62, and 74 as well.

76 |+tu-|ₙᵥ, |-tu-|ᵥᵥ 'to have much; regularly, to the fullest extent' (*aki·tuuq* 'it is expensive', *kii·χtuuq* 'it is (generally) warm'; *qantuuq* 'he can speak').

77 |+tuɣ́-| 'to eat, use' (*atsaχtuχtuq* 'he eats berries', *qayaχtuχtuq* 'he uses a kayak').

78 |+tait-| 'there to be no — in it (at the time)' (*əna yuxtaituq* 'there is nobody in the house'), cf. 92.

79 |+taŋx-| 'there to be — in it (at the time)' (*kuiɣmi* (loc.) or *kuik* (abs.) *nəqtaŋqəxtuq* 'there are fish in the river (now)'; cf. 7.2.3.(3)), cf. 97.

80 |+c-| 'to catch, go to' (*nəqtuq* 'he is catching fish', *kipuzvixtuq* 'he is going to the store').

81 |+cuɣ́-| (after velar)~|+suɣ́-| (after vowel) 'to hunt, seek for' (*nəqsuxtuq* 'he is fishing', with the base |nəqə-| 'fish').

82 |+k*it-| 'to have a little' (*imaχkituq* 'it has not much content, is a low tide').

83 |-kə-| 'to have — as' (*qaya·qaqa* 'it is my kayak', lit. 'I have it as a kayak', cf. 94; *kuvyam kizzutkaa* 'it is a net sinker', *aipaqu·kuk* 'we [dual] are partners').

84 |-kəɣc-| 'to have a good —' (*təpkəxtuq* 'it smells good').

85 |-qsiɣ-| (with adverbial demonstrative bases or location nouns) 'to be far in that direction' (*ukaqsixtuq* 'it is near by' with |uk+a-|; *aciqsixtuq* 'it is far down').

86 |+viɣ́c-|~|+tmuɣ́c-| 'to go to' (*maaviχtuq* 'he is coming here'), cf. allative adverbial demonstratives (7.4.3.2.).

87 |-li-| (table 5, no. 15) 'to make (for)' (*aŋy(all)iuq* 'he is making a boat').

88 |-liqə-| (table 5, no. 15) 'to be afflicted in' (*kəxu·ciquq* or *kəxu·təli·quq* 'he has a toothache', *taaŋiquq* 'he is drunk').

89 |-liqə-| (table 5, no. 15) 'to catch a lot of' (*nəqliquq* or *nəqi·quq* 'he gets a lot of fish').

90 |-liɣ́-| (table 5, no. 15) 'to supply with, have plenty of' (*patu·liɣ́ɣaa* 'he puts a cover on it', *təŋmi(a·l)ixtuq* 'it (area) has many geese').

91 |+mət-|~|+nət-| 'to be at' (*qaya·mətuq* 'it is in the kayak', *qayyaanətuq* 'it is in his kayak', *nanta* 'where is it?'; cf. *qaya·mi* loc. sg., *qayyaani* loc. 3sg.—sg., *nani* loc.).

92 |+ŋit-| 'to have no' (*əna yuituq* 'the house is unoccupied', *uiŋituq* 'she has no husband', *nanlucciitaqa* 'I don't know where it is' with 91 |+nət-| and 20 |+ᵢuciq-|).

93 |+ŋiɣ́-| 'to have — removed' (*pattuiɣ́aa* 'he removes its cover', *ammiixtuq* 'it has been skinned').

94 |+ŋu-| 'to be (copula)' (*qayyauɣuq* 'it is a kayak', cf. 83).

95 |+ŋuɣ́c-| 'to become, make' (*kia·ɣ́uxtuq* 'it became summer', *yuuxtuq* 'he is born', *picciuxłuku* 'making it come true').

96 |-ŋ*ə-|ₙᵥ,ᵥᵥ 'to acquire; to begin to' (*uiŋuq* 'she gets married'; *nəɣ́ŋaa* 'he is beginning to eat it').

97 |-ŋqx-| 'to have' (*ilaŋqəxtua amłəɣ́nək* 'I have a lot of relatives'; cf. 7.2.3.(3)).

8.5. MISCELLANEOUS POSTBASES

98 |+ᵢpaa| (table 5, no. 2) exclamatory particle from verb base (*assiipaa* 'how bad!', *aŋvaa* 'how big!'; cf. 7.2.5.(4)).

99 |-ku| 'in the future' (*unnua·qu* 'tomorrow', cp. *unnuaq* 'this morning', *xʷani·ku* 'soon', cp. *xʷani* 'now').

100 |-ẏ-| 'to say' (verbalizing any word class) (ata·kiiẏaaŋa 'he says to me "let me see (|ataki|)"' [with i repeated]).

9. Noninflecting Words

As opposed to nominals and verbs, which constitute the inflecting word classes, particles and enclitics are noninflecting. Enclitics are monosyllabic, but there are also a few monosyllabic particles. They are clearly distinguished from each other in phonological phrases, especially by accentuation (P22).

9.1. Particles

Many particles are not analyzable; however, some appear to be petrified remnants of originally inflected words, and others allow of some analysis. Some nominals, deprived of almost all inflection, are close to particles. Although quite restricted in derivation and devoid of inflection, particles are highly important in the actual functioning of the language and are accompanied by multifarious delicate nuances. They are wide-ranging in function but may be classified very broadly as: interjectionals, adverbials (including modals), conjunctives, and sentence words, although the distinctions are often elusive. Some of the more common particles are listed:

Interjectionals: |àcaca(ki)| 'how little, how few!', |ala=i| 'oh, my! (surprise or fright)', |am(pi)| 'hurry up!', |atam| 'look, listen! (calling attention)', |ìkiki(ka)| 'how big, fast, much!', |taŋ| 'look!' Examples in context: qamna kuiẏəm kaŋŋia ikkiki nəqliqa·pixtəłxuuq 'my, there were a lot of fish up there at the end of the river!', atam manna yuk aɣɣiixtəłxia 'see, the man is coming this way!', qaya·qa(t)#taŋ 'look, my kayak!'

Adverbials: |atata| 'later on', |caknẏ| 'very much', |cali| 'more, yet, again', |kəziaŋẏ| 'always', |əɣmian| 'immediately', |ikik(a)| 'possibly, I suppose so', |ilumun| 'indeed, really', |ima| 'I forgot, you remember', |nau=wa| 'where', |tayima| 'somewhere, there (out of sight)', |tuaẏ(piaq)| 'it seems (like)': ikik tayi·ma piłłiuq 'possibly he must be doing it now (not here)', yua·ẏun tama·na attaam atu·qəxu '(you sg.) please sing again that song (you are singing now)'.

Connectives: |maatən| 'when', |tawaam| 'but, instead, only', |tuału| 'and then', |wàłu| 'or': taɣʷɣʷaam təxənẏət kiiməŋ unəxtauciqsuɣnaxqut 'however, only the old folks will probably be left behind', tuału=xuq tauna nunnailŋuq qazɣim qukkaanun aqu·məłi·niluni 'and then, that man without a place to stay sat down in the middle of the men's house'.

Sentence words: |aaŋ| 'yes; you are welcome', |iiyi| 'yes', |naamiki(ka)| 'I don't know', |qaa| 'is that so?; (in phonological phrases) marker of yes-or-no question in which the interrogative mood is not used', |qaaŋ| 'no', |qàŋa| 'no (strong denial or prohibition)', |quyana| 'thank you': uitalaxtuci(q)#qaa maani 'do you (pl.) live here?', iiyi, uitalaxtukut maani 'yes, we live here'.

9.2. Enclitics

Enclitics cannot occur independently. They are appended to (morphologically complete) words of any class but generally to the first word of a sentence (except |=lu|). One enclitic may be followed by another. Some enclitics can be particles (characterized by #) as well: |=wa|~|#wa|. The enclitic boundary occurs in some particles and interjectional demonstratives (tai=tai 'come!', cama·=i 'hello', pika·=i 'up there!'). Enclitics have a very limited membership:

|=am| 'again as usual, characteristically' implies surprise, amusement, praise, or frustration: aanaka·=am manaẏyałi·niuq 'I see my mother went ice-fishing again'.

|=ɣəm| '(but) I thought that' implies contradiction to what someone said: aanaka·=xəm manaẏyatxuuq '(but) I thought my mother went ice-fishing'.

|=ɣuq| 'he says that; tell (him) that' indicates communication through an intermediary: aanaka·=łu·=xuẏ=(ẏ)am manaẏyatxuuq 'tell him that / he told me that my mother also went ice-fishing as usual', cf. P24; (son) aataka qanẏutqaqqiu ayaɣyuxtua·=xuq 'please tell my father I want to go', (mother) (qətunẏaan=xuq ayaɣyuɣyaaquq 'your (sg.) son says he wants to go', (father) ayaɣli=xuq piyu·kuni 'tell him he can go if he wants', (mother) pi(x)=xuq piyu·kuvət 'he says you can go if you want'. See 6.2.3. as to the use for indirectness.

|=kin|~|#kin(a)| 'I hope', similar to |=tuq| below: pikNa=łu·=kin or pikNa=łu(k)#kin(a) 'I hope that one up there', nəẏli(k)#kin 'I hope he eats' or (indirectly) 'I hope I eat'.

|=kiq| 'I wonder', selecting the interrogative mood, implies wonder, curiosity, or surprise: aanaka·=kiq qaku manaẏyaẏniaxta 'I wonder when my mother will go ice-fishing', qaiłun=kiq aŋtattaa 'I wonder how big it is'.

|=łam| 'I wish it otherwise': aanaka·=łam manaẏyanẏilŋuq (part. 3sg.) 'why didn't my mother go ice-fishing?'

|=li| '...! (exclamation)', used in connection with a verb base expanded by 98 |+ₗpaa| (table 5, no. 2) (and a locative nominal, 7.2.5.(4)): nəŋłixpaa=łi (mattumi ənəmtəNi) 'my, it (this house of ours) is cold!'

|=lu| 'and, also', appended to the last in a series, indicates coordination: aanaka·=łu manaẏyaxciqu·kuk 'my mother and I will go ice-fishing', aŋu·tət mikəlŋuut qimuxtət=łu taiɣut 'men, children, and dogs are coming'.

|=mi| 'as for, then how about' indicates the topic of an interrogation: aanaka·=mi qaku manaẏyaẏciqa 'then how about my mother, when will she go ice-fishing?'; a) caŋa·ta uin 'how is your (sg.) husband?', b) caŋa·tənẏituq uika 'my husband is fine', a) ila·tən=mi 'how about your relatives?'

|=tuq| 'I wish', selecting an optative verb, implies hope or wish: *aanaka·=tuq manaɣ̇yaɣ̇li* 'I wish my mother would go ice-fishing', *malixłamci·=tuq* 'I wish I could go with you (sg.)'.

|=wa|~|#wa|, often used in connection with a participial, interrogative, or optative verb, is presentational, implying response, agreement, or contrast: *aanaka(xʷ)#xʷa manaɣ̇yaxciqəlɣ̇ia* 'well, my mother will go ice-fishing' (can be a response to *kina·=kiq manaɣ̇yaɣ̇niaxta* 'I wonder who will go ice-fishing?'); *ciin ukNa taiɣa* 'why is he coming this way?', *ciin=xʷa taiɣa* 'yes, I too wonder (I don't know either) why he is coming this way'; *maatən itəxtua aanaxka aqumɣalu·tək, ikNa=xʷa ałqaqa* 'when I entered, my mother and father (cf. 7.1.) were sitting, while my elder sister was across there'.

10. SELECTED VOCABULARY

The number of primary bases is small (perhaps not exceeding 2,000 in the last analysis) and postbases are even more limited in number (perhaps not more than 400), but the flexible and extensive use of postbases for derivation permits the building up of a huge lexicon as well as of words with complex internal syntax.

The following list gives basic nominals, verbs, and particles that mainly have an unexpanded base from the point of view of the present-day language, although many of these were evidently secondary derivatives at one time. Also included are postbases with more concrete meanings. A full Yupik dictionary is Jacobson (1984); Fortescue, Jacobson, and Kaplan (1994) is a comparative Eskimo dictionary with Aleut cognates.

It will be clear that for nonnative concepts the language has been more apt to create new descriptive words out of the native lexical stock or to extend the meaning of native words than to borrow words. However, there is a considerable influx of Russian loanwords ('bread', 'Christmas', 'clock', 'kettle', 'store', 'table', 'tent') and a few from English ('bullet'). For detailed information on loanwords see Hammerich (1954) and Jacobson (1984: 678-689).

After the English gloss in each entry, the Yupik form is given in phonemic representation, sometimes followed by the phonological representation (|...|), and in the Yupik orthography (in parentheses). The forms given are 'abs. 3sg.—sg.' for typically possessed nouns (*illua* 'inside of it'), 'abs. sg.' for other nominals (*kuik* 'river'), 'ind. 3sg.' for mononominal verb bases (*mikkuq* 'it is small'), and 'ind. 3sg.—3sg.' for binominal verb bases (*asi·kaa* 'he likes it'), unless otherwise noted. Bases not (easily) predictable from the phonemic form are added in vertical bars. The nonagentive and impersonal bases are respectively marked by (NA) and (I) after the phonemic form, and the transitive forms not so marked are agentive.

across there *ikNa*, etc. 'the one across there' (table 16) (ikna)

again |=am|; 69 |-nqiɣc-|

airplane *təŋsuun* (lit. 'flying instrument') (tengssuun)

all *tamaq* 'all, whole' |tamaq-| (tamaq)

tamaɣ̇məŋ 'they all' (6.2.5.9.) (tamarmeng)

already *akka* 'already, long time ago' (ak'a)

also *cali* 'also, still' (cali); |=lu|; 66 |+ˌmi-|

although See 6.2.5.4.

always *kəzzia·nək* (kesianek)

amulet *iinɣ̇uq* 'amulet, pill, medicine' (iinruq)

and |=lu|

angry, to be *qənəxtuq* |qənɣ̇-| (qenertuq)

animal *uŋuŋsiq* |uŋuŋsiq-| (ungungssiq)

answer, to *kiuɣaa* |kiu-| (kiugaa)

any *piccia·tun* (piciatun)

arm *tałiq* |tałiq| (talliq)

unəq 'armpit' (uneq)

around *awa·tii* 'area around it' |awat-| (avatii)

arrow *pitəxcaun* (pitegcaun)

ash *aɣ̇aq* |aɣ̇aq-| (araq)

ask, to *aptaa* 'he questions him' |apəc-| (aptaa)

ask, to 35 |+sqə-| 'to ask, want, tell'

aunt *acak* (paternal) (acak)

annaana (maternal) |anaana-| (anaana)

back *tunuq* (anatomical or locational) |tunuq-| (tunuq)

kiŋŋua 'its back' |kiŋu-| (kingua)

back there *piŋna*, etc. 'the one back there' (pingna) (table 16)

bad, to be *assiituq* |asiit-| (assiituq)

bag *isχan* 'carrying bag' (issran)

qəmaxfik (qemaggvik)

bark *qəłta* 'bark, fish scale, scab' |qəlt-| (qelta)

bark, to *qilu·ɣaa* 'it barks at him' |qiluɣ-| (qilugaa)

bath *maqi* 'steambath' (maqi)

maqqiuq 'he takes a bath' (maqiuq)

be, to 79 |+taŋqx-| 'there to be'; 78 |+tait-| 'there to be no'; 91 |+mət-| 'be at'; 94 |+ŋu-| (copula)

bear *taqu·kaq* 'brown or grizzly bear' |taqukaq-| (taqukaq)

caɣ̇a·yak 'bear, monster' (carayak)

tanɣ̇əɣ̇li 'black bear' (tan'gerli)

bear, to *iγ́niuq* 'she gives birth' (irniuq)

   yuuxtuq 'he was born' |yuuγ́c-| (yuurtuq)

beard *uŋak* (ungak)

because See 6.2.5.1.

become, to 65 |+₁γ́*i-|ᵥᵥ; 95 |+ŋuγ́c-|ₙᵥ

bed *iŋləq* (ingleq)

before See 6.2.5.3.

begin to *ayaγniγ́γ́aa* 'he begins it' (ayagniraa);
   96 |-ŋ*ə-|

behind *kəllua* 'area behind it' |kəlu-| (kelua)

belly *aqsaquq* |aqsaquq-| (table 5, no. 16) (aqsaquq)

below *accia* 'area below it' |aci-| (acia)

berry *atsaq* |atsaq-| (atsaq),

   cuγ́aq 'blueberry', |cuγ́aq-| (curaq);

   iqfaγ́γ́ai 'she picks them (berries)' |iqvaγ́-|
   (iqvarai)

beside *cannia* 'area beside it' |cani-| (cania)

big, to be *aŋŋuq* (ang'uq)

   aŋliuq 'he grows' (angliuq)

big 1 |+paγ-|; *ikkiki* 'so big, much!' (ik'iki)

bind, to *nəmγ́aa* 'he binds, wraps it' (NA) (nemraa)

   nəməq 'binding material' |nəmγ́-| (nemeq)

bird *yaqu·lək* (lit. 'one with wings') (yaqulek)

   təŋmiaq 'bird, goose, duck' |təŋmiaq-| (tengmiaq)

bite, to *kexxaa* (NA) |kəxə-| (keggaa)

black, to be *tuŋŋuuq* (tunguuq)

blood *auk* (auk)

boat *aŋyaq* |aŋyaq-| (angyaq)

   qayaq 'kayak' |qayaq-| (qayaq)

body *təma* 'body, torso' |təmə-| (tema)

bone *ənəq* 'bone, seed' (eneq), pl. *ən γ́ət* |(n)ənγ́-|
   (enret) (cf. water |əmγ́-|)

boot *pilu·γuk, kamγuk* 'knee-high boot' (piluguk,
   kamguk)

bow *uγ́luvəq* 'bow for arrows' (urluveq)

bread *qaqquq* |qàquq-|, *kəli·paq* |kəlipaq-| (qaq'uq,
   kelipaq)

break, to *navγaa* (NA) |navγ-| (navgaa)

   azəmtaa 'he breaks it in two' (NA) |azəmc-|
   (asemtaa)

breast *əvzaik* (evsaik)

breathe, to *anəγ́yaaxtuq* |anəγ́yaaγ́-| (aneryaartuq)

bright, to be *tanqixcətuq* |tanqiγcic-| (tanqigcetuq)
   (table 5, no. 17)

356   bring, to *taitaa* |taic-| (taitaa)

itγ́uttaa 'he brings it in' |itγ́uc-| (it'rutaa)

brother *annaq* 'elder brother' |annaq-| (anngaq),

   uyu·γ́aq 'younger sibling' |uyuγ́aq-| (uyuraq)

bullet *puuliq* |puuliq-| (puuliq); see 'content'

burn, to *əkkuq* 'it burns, is on fire' (ek'uq);

   əka 'fire' |əkə-| (eka)

but *taγʷγʷaam* 'however, only' (tau͡gaam)

buttock *nułuq* |nułuγ́-| (nulluq)

buy, to *kipu·taa* |kipuc-| (kiputaa)

cache *mamtəγ́aq* |mamtəγ́aq-| (mamteraq)

can 61 |+zuuma-|; 55 |+sciiγat-| 'cannot'

car *akalγ́ia* (lit. 'rolling one') (akalria)

caribou *tuntuq* 'caribou, reindeer' |tuntuq-| (tuntuq)

catch 80 |+c-|; 89 |-liqə-| 'to catch a lot'

cat's craddle *aixaq* |aixaq-| (airraq)

chair *aqumłitaq* |aqumłitaq-| (aqumllitaq)

check, to *paqtaa* 'he checks it' |paqc-| (paqtaa)

chest *qatγak* (qat'gak)

chief See 'parent'.

child *iγ́niaq* 'offspring' |iγ́niaq-| (irniaq)

   mikəlŋuq (lit. 'small one') |mikəlŋuγ́-|
   (mikelnguq)

chin *tamluq* |tamluq-| (tamluq)

Christmas *alu·sistuaq* |alusistuaq-| (Alussistuaq)

church *aγa·yuvik* (lit. 'place for worshiping')
   (agayuvik)

clam *uiluq* 'clam, spoon' |uiluq-| (uiluq)

clean, to *caxi·γ́aa* (NA) |caxiγ́-| (carriraa)

clock *cassaq* |càsaq-| (cass'aq); |-klaagc-|ᵥᵥ,ₙₙ
   'o'clock'

close, to *palu·taa* (NA) |paluc-| (palutaa)

clothing *atu·γ́aq* |atuγ́aq-| (aturaq); see 'to use'

cloud *amiγ́luq* |amiγ́luq-| (amirluq)

cold, to be *kumlataa* 'the cold is affecting it', (I)
   |kumlac-| (kumlataa)

   kumlatuq 'it is frozen' (kumlatuq)

   nəŋłixtuq 'it (weather) is cold' |nəŋłiγ́-|
   (nengllirtuq)

   nəŋłiuγ́aa 'the cold is affecting him' (I)
   (nenglliuraa);

   nəŋłiuxtuq 'he is cold' (nenglliurtuq)

come, to *taiγuq* |tai-| (taiguq)

   aγγiixtuq 'he comes (from distance)' |aγγiiγ́c-|
   (agiirtuq)

   təki·taa 'he arrives at it' |təkic-| (tekitaa)

content *imaq* 'content, pus, bullet' |imaq-| (imaq)

cook, to *əɣɣaa* 'she cooks, boils it' |əɣa-| (egaa)

cough *quzəq* 'cough, cold' (quseq)

    quzəχtuq 'he coughs, has a cold' |quzɣ́-| (qusertuq)

count, to *naaqaa* 'he counts, reads it' (NA) |naaqə-| (naaqaa)

cousin *iluχ* 'man's male cross-cousin or friend' |iluɣ́aɣ́-| (ilur) (table 5, no. 5),

    ilu·ŋaq 'woman's female cross-cousin or friend' |iluŋaq-| (ilungaq); see also 'part'

cover, to *pattua* 'he covers, closes it' (NA) (patua)

    patu 'cover, lid' (patu)

cry, to *qia·ɣaa* 'he cries over him' (qiagaa)

    qia·ɣuq 'he cries' (qiaguq)

cut, to *kili·ɣaa* 'he cuts, wounds him' (NA) |kiliɣ́-| (kiliraa);

    kəppaa 'he cuts it off' (NA) |kəpə-| (kepaa)

dance, to *yuɣ́aχtuq* |yuɣ́aɣ́-| (yurartuq)

daughter *panik* (panik)

day *əɣ́nəq* (erneq); *əχNəq* 'dawning' (errneq)

deep, to be *əttuuq* (etuuq)

die, to *tuqquuq* (tuquuq)

dig, to *əla·ɣaa* |əlaɣ-| (elagaa)

dirty, to be *iqqauq* (iqauq);

    iqqaiɣ́aa 'he washes it' (NA) |iqaiɣ́-| (iqairaa)

divide, to *aftaa* 'he divides it' (NA) |avc-| (avtaa)

do, to *pia* 'he does to him, does it' (with meaning depending upon context or a succeeding postbase) (pia); see 'what' and 'thing'

dog *qimuχta* (lit. 'one who pulls') |qimuɣt-| (qimugta)

dollar See 'whole' and 'half'

door *am(mi)ik* (ami(i)k)

down *kəttii* 'area down toward the river or sea' |kətə-| (ketii)

down there *kanna*, etc. 'the one down there' (kan'a) (table 16)

drink, to See 'water'

dry, to *kinɣ́aa* 'he dries it' (NA) |kinɣ́-| (kinraa)

dull, to be *ipxia·tuq* 'it is not sharp' |ipxiat-| (ipgiatuq)

dust *iqaq* 'dirt, dust, grime' |iqaq-| (iqaq)

ear *ciun* (ciun)

eat, to *nəɣ́ɣ́aa* |nəɣ́ə-|; 77 |+tuɣ́-| (neraa)

edge See 'shore', 'face', and 'limit'

egg *pəksuq* |pəksuq-| (peksuq) ~*kaya·ŋuq* |kayaŋuq-| (kayanguq) 'bird's egg'

    imlauk 'roe' (imlauk)

electricity See 'thunder'

end *iqqua* 'its tip, other end' |iquɣ-| (iqua)

enjoy, to *aŋlanniuq* 'he is having fun' (anglaniuq)

Eskimo *yuppik* (lit. 'genuine person') (Yup'ik)

eye *ii* (ii)

face *kəxi·naq* 'face, knife edge' |kəxinaq-| (kegginaq)

fall *uksuaq* '(last) autumn' |uksuaq-| (uksuaq)

fall, to *ixtuq* |iɣc-| (igtuq)

far, to be *yaaqsixtuq* |yaaqsiɣ-| (yaaqsigtuq)

fast, to be *cukkauq* (cukauq)

fat *tunuq* 'back fat' |tunuq-| (tunuq); see 'oil'

father *aata* |a(a)ta-| (aata); see 'mother'

fear, to *ali·ŋuq* 'he is afraid' (alinguq)

feather *məłquq* 'feather, fur, hair' |məłquq-| (melquq) (table 5, no. 16)

feces *anaq* |anaq-| (anaq)

    anaχtuq 'he defecates' |anaɣ́-| (anartuq)

    anaɣ́vik 'toilet' (anarvik)

few, to be *ikxətuq* |ikxət-| (ikgetuq); see 'little'

fight, to *cału·ɣaa* |całuɣ-| (callugaa)

find, to *nala·qaa* (NA) |nalaqə-| (nalaqaa)

finger *yua·ɣaq* |yuaɣ́aq-| (yuaraq)

    cətuk 'fingernail' (cetuk)

finish, to *taqqaa* |taqə-| (taqaa)

    naŋŋaa (NA) |naŋə-| (nangaa)

fire *kənəq* 'fire, match' (keneq); see 'to burn'

first *ciumək* (ciumek)

    ciuqłiq 'first one' |ciuqliq-| (ciuqliq)

fish *nəqa* 'fish, food' |nəqə-| (neqa)

    kumlanəq 'frozen fish' (kumlaneq)

    nəqəχłuk 'dried fish' (neqerrluk)

fish, to See 'hook' and 'net'

float, to *puxtauq* (pugtauq)

flow, to *caɣ́vuq* (carvuq)

flower See 'to grow'

fly *ciivak* 'house fly' (ciivak)

fly, to *təŋŋuq* 'it flies, takes off' (teng'uq)

follow, to *malixtaa* 'he goes with him' (maligtaa)

food *nəqkaq* 'food (prepared), meal' |nəqkaq-| (neqkaq); see 'fish'

357

foot   *itɣaq* |itəɣaq-| (it'gaq)

footprint   *tuma* 'footprint, track' |tumə-| (tuma)

forget, to   *nału·yaɣu·taa* 'he forgets it' |nałuyaɣuc-| (nalluyagutaa)

fox   *kavviaq* '(red) fox' |kaviaɣ-| (kaviaq)

freeze, to   see 'cold' and 'ice'

friend   see 'cousin' and 'part'

front   *ciuŋa* 'its front area, boat's bow' (ciunga)

future   6 |+k*aq-|₍ₙₙ₎; see 'will'

get   *aqfaa* 'he gets it' |aqfa-| (aqvaa); 96 |-ŋ*ə-|

girl   *nazzauɣluq* |nazauɣluɣ-| (nasaurluq)

give, to   *tunnaa* 'he gives, exchanges, sells it' (NA) |tunə-| (tunaa)

   ciki·ɣaa 'he gives him (something)' |cikiɣ-| (cikiraa)

go, to   *qəɣaχtuq* 'he goes across' |qəɣaɣ-| (qerartuq)

   ayaχtuq 'he goes away' |ayaɣ-| (ayagtuq)

   atχaχtuq 'he goes down' |atɣaɣ-| (atrartuq)

   itəχtuq 'he goes in' |itɣ-| (itertuq)

   annuq 'he goes out' (an'uq)

   aɣɣuq 'he goes over' (ag'uq)

   anəlɣaχtuq 'he goes toward exit, downriver' |anəlɣaɣ-| (anelrartuq)

   mayuχtuq 'he goes up, climbs' |mayuɣ-| (mayurtuq)

   taɣɣuq 'he goes up from river' (tag'uq)

   itχaχtuq 'he goes upriver' |itɣaɣ-| (itrartuq)

god   *aɣa·yun* (agayun)

good, to be   *asiχtuq* |asiɣ-| (assirtuq)

goodbye   *piuɣaa* (to one person) (piuraa)

goose   *nəqłəq, laɣiq* |laɣiq-| (neqleq, 'lagiq); see 'bird'

grandchild   *tutχaχ* |tutχaɣaɣ-| (table 5, no. 5) (tutgar)

grandfather   *appa* |àpa-| (ap'a)

grandmother   *mauɣluq* |mauɣluɣ-| (maurluq)

grass   *canək* (canek)

grave   *quŋuq* 'grave, coffin' |quŋuq-| (qunguq)

green, to be   *cuŋaxcətuq* 'it is green' |cuŋaɣcic-| (cungagcetuq) (table 5, no. 17)

grow, to   *nauɣuq* 'it (plant) grows' (nauguq)

   naucəttaaq 'blossom, flower, plant' |naucitaaq-| (naucetaaq)

gun   *nutək* (nutek); *nutχaa* 'he shoots it' |nutɣ-| (nutgaa)

guts   *qiluq* |qiluq-| (qiluq)

habitually   68 |+nauɣ-|; 57 |+laɣ-|~|-laɣ-| 'usually'

hair   *nuyaq* 'hair on head' |nuyaq-| (nuyaq); see 'feather'

half   *avək* 'half, 50 cents' (avek)

   avɣaa 'he halves it' (NA) |avɣ-| (avgaa)

hand   *aixaq* 'hand, seal flipper' |aixaq-| (aiggaq)

hang, to   *aɣaχtaa* (NA) |aɣaɣc-| (agartaa)

hard, to be   *təxxuq* 'it is hard, not soft' (tegg'uq)

hare   *maqa·ɣuaq* |maqaɣuaq-| (maqaruaq)

harness   *anuk* 'harness on dogs' (anuk)

harpoon   *nanəxpak* '(sealing) harpoon' (nanerpak)

hat   *nacaq* 'hat, hood (parka)' |nacaq-| (nacaq)

have, to   97 |-ŋqx-|; 92 |+ŋit-| 'not to have'

he   *əłii*, etc. (table 14) (ellii)

head   *nasquq* |nasquq| (nasquq) ~*qami·quq* |qamiquq| (table 5, no. 16) (qamiquq)

hear, to   *niitaa* 'he hears it' |niic-| (niitaa)

heart   *iχcaquq* |iɣcaquq| (table 5, no. 16) (ircaquq)

heavy, to be   *uqa·maituq* 'it is heavy' |uqamait-| (uqamaituq)

hello   *xʷaqqaa* (waqaa), *cama·=i* (cama-i)

help, to   *ika·yuɣɣaa* 'he helps him' (NA) |ikayuɣ-| (ikayuraa)

here   *una*, etc. 'the one here' (table 16) (una)

herring   *iqa·łuaxpak* (iqalluarpak)

hide, to   *ii·ɣaa* 'he hides it' (NA) |iiɣ-| (iiraa)

hit, to   *kauɣaa* 'he strikes it' |kauɣ-| (kaugaa)

hole   *uki·nəq* (ukineq); *uki·taa* 'he makes a hole in it' (NA) |ukic-| (ukitaa)

hook   *manaq* 'fishhook' |manaq-| (manaq)

   manaχtuq 'she jigs with a hook and line' |manaɣ-| (manartuq)

hope |=kin|~|#kin(a)|; |=tuq| 'I hope'

hot, to be   *kiiχcətuq* 'it (weather) is hot' |kiiɣcic-| (table 5, no. 17) (kiircetuq)

   uuqNaxquq 'it (thing) is hot' (uuqnarquq)

house   *əna* |ənə-| (ena)

   qazɣiq 'men's house, community house' |qazɣiq-| (qasgiq)

how   *qaiłun* (7.4.6.) (qaillun)

how many   *qafcin* (7.4.6.) (qavcin)

hungry, to be   *kaixtuq* |kaiɣ-| (kaigtuq)

hunt, to   81 |+cuɣ-|

   pisuχta 'hunter' |pisuɣt-| (pissurta)

hurt, to   *akNiχtaa* 'he hurts him' (NA) |akŋiɣc-| (akngirtaa) husband   *ui* (ui)

I   *xʷii* |wii|, etc. (table 14) (wii)

ice   *ciku* (ciku)

   cikkua   '(the cold) freezes it' (I) (cikua)

   cikkuuq   'it freezes' (cikuuq)

ice cream   *akuˑtaq*   'Eskimo ice cream' |akutaq-| (akutaq)

if   see 6.2.5.5.

immediately   *əɣmian* (egmian)

Indian   *iŋqiliq* |iŋqiliq-| (ingqiliq)

in-law   *nəŋŋauk*   'sibling's husband' (nengauk)

   ukuˑx̣aq   'sibling's wife' |ukux̣aq-| (ukurraq)

   cakiˑẏaq   'spouse's sibling' |cakiẏaq-| (cakiraq)

   cakiq   'spouse's parent' |cakiq-| (cakiq)

insect   *ciisiq*   'insect, worm, snake' |ciisiq-| (ciissiq)

inside   *illua*   'inside of it' |ilu-| (ilua)

inside there   *kiuɣna*, etc.   'the one inside there' (table 16) (kiugna)

island   *qikəx̣taq* |qikəẏtaq-| (qikertaq)

ivory   *tuxkax̣*   'walrus tusk' |tuɣkaɣaẏ-| (tugkar) (table 5, no. 5)

juice   *əɣnəq* (egneq)

kettle   *cainik* (cainik)

kill, to   *tuquˑtaa* (NA) |tuquc-| (tuqutaa)

knee   *ciisquq* |ciisquq-| (table 5, no. 16) (ciisquq)

knife   *ulluaq*   'woman's knife' |uluaq-| (uluaq); see 'metal'

know, to   *nałunɣittaa*   'he knows (lit. is not ignorant of) it' |nałunɣit-| (nallunritaa)

labret   *tuutaq* |tuutaq-| (tuutaq)

ladder   *akx̣ət* (akret), plural of *akəq* 'rung' (akeq)

lake   *nanvaq* |nanvaq-| (nanvaq)

lamp   *naniq*   'lamp, light' |naniq-| (naniq)

land   *nuna*   'land, place, country, soil, settlement' |nuna-| (nuna)

land, to   *mittuq*   'it lands (from air)' |mic-| (mit'uq)

language   *qanəẏyaẏaq*   'language, word (lit. way of speaking)' |qanəẏyaẏaq-| (qaneryaraq)

laugh, to   *əŋəllax̣tuq* |əŋəlaẏ-| (engelartuq, ngel'artuq)

leaf   *cuyaq*   'leaf, tobacco leaf' |cuyaq-| (cuyaq)

learn, to   *əliˑtaa* |əlic-| (elitaa)

left   *caẏuˑmik*   'left hand' (carumik)

leg   *iẏuq* |iẏuq-| (iruq)

letter   See 'paper' and 'to write'

lie down, to   *inax̣tuq* |inaẏ+c-|; see 6.2.5.9. (inartuq)

life   *uŋuˑwa* (unguva)

   uŋuˑwauq   'he is alive' (unguvauq)

like, to   *asiˑkaa* (NA) |asikə-| (assikaa)

limit   *əŋəllii*   'its limit, border, edge' |əŋələ-| ((e)ngelii)

liquor   *taaŋaq* |taaŋaq-| (taangaq)

   taaŋiquq   'he is drunk' (taangiquq)

little   4 |-cuaɣaẏ-|; 12 |-x̣aẏ-|

   accaca   'so little, few!' (ac'aca)

liver   *təŋuk* (tenguk)

load   *uci*   'load on sled or boat' (uci)

   amaq   'backpack' |amaq-| (amaq)

   amaˑẏaa   'he backpacks it' |amaẏ-| (amaraa)

long, to be   *takkuq* (tak'uq)

lose, to   *tamaˑẏaa* (NA) |tamaẏ-| (tamaraa)

louse   *nəẏəsta*   (lit. 'eater') |nəẏəst-| (neresta)

love, to   *kənkaa* (NA) |kənkə-| (kenkaa)

make, to   87 |-li-|; see 'to work'

man   *aŋun*   'man (male)' (angun)

many   14 |+ẏ*uɣaẏ-|

   akkakiˑka   'so many!' (ak'akika)

many, to be   *amłəx̣tut* (3pl.)   'they are many' (amllertut)

   amłəẏət   'many (things)' |amłẏ-| (amlleret)

mark   *alŋaq* |alŋaq-| (alngaq) ~*iɣaq* |iɣaq-| (igaq) 'mark, symbol, letter'; see 'to write'

marry, to   *kassuutaa* (NA) |kasuuc-| (kassuutaa); *kassuutuk* 'they (dual) marry' (kassuutuk)

match   *spiickaaq* |spiickaaq-| (table 5, no. 8) (spiickaaq); see 'fire'

maybe   74 |+ˌŋ*at-| 'to seem to'

meet, to   *paix̣taa*   'he goes to meet him' |paiẏc-| (pairtaa)

mend, to   *kituxtaa*   'he fixes it' (NA) |kituɣc-| (kitugtaa)

messenger   *kəvɣaq*   'messenger, servant' |kəvɣaq-| (kevgaq)

metal   *cawik*   'metal, knife' (cavik)

middle   See 'waist'

mind   *umyu(ɣ)aq*   'mind, idea' |umyu(ɣ)aq-| (umyu(g)aq)

mink   *imaẏmiutaq* |imaẏmiutaq-| (imarmiutaq)

mitten   *alliiman* (aliiman)

money   See 'opposite' and 'whole'

moon   *iẏaˑluq*   'moon, month' |iẏaluq-| (iraluq)

moose   *tuntuwak* |tuntuvaɣ-| (tuntuvak)

more   *cali*   'more, yet, again' (cali); 30 |-nɣ́-|; |-nɣ́u-| (7.2.5.(3)).

morning   *unnuaq*   '(this) morning' (unuaq)

mosquito   *makuɣ̇yaq* |makuɣ̇yaq-| (makuryaq)

mother   *aana* |a(a)na| (aana); *aanaka* or *ana·ka* 'my mother' (aanaka, anaka); see 'father'

mountain   *iŋɣ́iq* |iŋɣ́iq-| (ingriq)

mouth   *qanəq* (anatomical) (qaneq,

   paiŋa   'its (nonanatomical) mouth, opening' (painga)

move, to   *pəktuq*   'he, it moves' |pəkəc-| (pektuq)

name   *atəq* |atɣ́-| (ateq);

   atəłxun   'namesake' (atellgun)

narrow, to be   *iqkituq* |iqəkit-| (iqkituq)

near, to be   *cani·mətuq* |canimət-| (canimetuq)

neck   *uya·quq* |uyaquq-| (table 5, no. 16) (uyaquq)

needle   *miŋqun* (mingqun)

nephew   *qaŋŋiaẋ*   'man's brother's child' |qaŋiaɣaɣ́-| (table 5, no. 5) (gangiar)

   uzɣuq   'man's sister's child' |uzɣuq-| (usguq)

   anɣaɣ́aq   'woman's brother's child' |anɣaɣ́aq-| (an'garaq)

   nuẋẋaq   'woman's sister's child |nùẋaq-| (nurr'aq)

net   *kuvyaq*   'fishnet' |kuvyaq-| (kuvyaq)

   kuvyauq   'he fishes by drift-netting' (kuvyauq)

new   *nuta·ɣ́aq*   'new, fresh thing' |nutaɣ́aq-| (nutaraq)

niece   see 'nephew'

night   *unuk*   '(last) night' (unuk)

no   *qaaŋ, qaŋŋa* (qaang, qang'a)

noise   *nəpa*   'noise, sound' |nəpə-| (nepa)

   nəpłiẋtuq   'he/it is noisy' |nəpliɣ́-| (neplirtuq)

   nəppaituq   'he/it is quiet' |nəpait-| (nepaituq)

north   *nəɣɣaq*   'north, northwind' (negeq)

nose   *qəŋaq* |qəŋaq-| (qengaq)

not   70 |-nɣ́it-|_{VV}; |+pəkə-| (6.2.6.); 92 |+ŋit-|_{NV} 'not to have'

now   *xʷattua*   'now, a short while ago' (watua)

number   See 7.4.1. and table 15.

oar   *cavun*   (lit. 'thing to row by') (cavun)

oil   *uquq*   '(seal) oil, fat' |uquq-| (uquq)

   uqu·ɣ́iuq   'he is fat' (uquriuq)

old   *akkałaq*   'old, stale thing' |àkałaq-| (ak'allaq)

360   one   *attauciq* (7.4.1. and table 15) (atauciq)

only   *kiima* 'I only', etc. |kii-| (6.2.5.9.) (kiima); 71 |+ŋ*inaɣ́-|; see 'but'

open, to   *ikiẋtaa* (NA) |ikiɣ́c-| (ikirtaa)

opening   *caẋiłquq*   'open area' |caẋiłquq-| (carrilquq); see 'mouth'

opposite   *akkia*   'its opposite, equivalent, money' |aki-| (akia)

or   *xʷałłu* (wall'u)

other   *aipaq*   'the other (of two), partner' |aipaq-| (aipaq)

   ała   'another, different one' |ała-| (alla)

out there   *uɣna*, etc.   'the one out there' (table 16) (ugna)

outside   *əla·tii*   'its (immediate) outside, exterior' |əlat-| (elatii)

outside there   *kəẋNa*, etc.   'the one (immediate) outside there' (table 16) (keggna)

over there   *iŋna*, etc.   'the one over there' (table 16) (ingna)

pants   *qəẋu·łiik* (dual) (qerrulliik)

paper   *kali·kaq*   'paper, letter' (kalikaq)

   kali·kat   'book(s)' (7.1.) (kalikat)

parent   *aŋa·yuqaq*   'parent, chief' |aŋayuqaɣ́-| (angayuqaq)

parka   *atkuk* (table 5, no. 16) (atkuk)

   qaspəq   'parka (covering)' (qaspeq)

part   *ila*   'part, one of, some of, relative, cousin, friend' |ila-| (7.4.2.) (ila)

partner   11 |-łɣut-|; see 'other', 'name'

past   23 |-łɣ́-|_{VN, NN}; 53 |-łɣ́u-|_{VV}

path   *tumyaɣ́aq*   'path, road' |tumyaɣ́aq-| (tumyaraq)

person   *yuk*   'person, owner, spirit' (yuk)

picture   *taɣ́ənɣaq*   'picture, image, shadow' |taɣ́ənɣaq-| (tarenraq)

place   *əna*   'house, place' |ənə-| (ena); 25 |+₁viɣ́-|

plate   *qantaq*   'plate, bowl' |qantaq-| (qantaq)

play, to   *aqquiɣuq* |aqui-| (aquiguq)

pot   *əɣan* (egan)

ptarmigan   *aqəzɣiq* |aqəzɣiq-|, *qaŋqiiq* |qaŋqiiq-| (aqesgiq, qangqiiq)

pull, to   *nuqtaa* |nuqəc-| (nuqtaa)

pus   See 'content'

push, to   *ciŋŋaa* |ciŋə-| (cingaa)

put away, to   *qəmaẋtaa* (NA) |qəmaɣc-| (qemagtaa)

put down, to   *əłłia* (NA) |əłi-| (ellia)

put on, to   *attaa*   'he dons it' |ac-| (ataa)

quiet, to be   see 'noise'

radio   *niicuɣnissuun*   (lit. 'instrument for listening') (niicugnissuun)

rain   *cəɬaˑɬuk*   'bad weather' |ciɬaɬuɣ-| (cellalluk)

cəɬaˑɬiɣtuq   'it is raining' |ciɬaɬiɣ-| (cellallirtuq)

raise, to   *maktaa* (NA) |makəc-| (maktaa)

raven   *tuluˑkaɣuk* (tulukaruk)

reach, to   see 'to come'

read, to   see 'to count'

real   2 |-piɣ-| 'real, genuine'

red, to be   *kawixcətuq* |kaviɣcic-| (table 5, no. 17) (kavircetuq)

relative   see 'part'

resemble, to   *ayuˑqaa* |ayuqə-| (ayuqaa)

return, to   *utəxtuq*   'he comes back' |utəɣc-| (utertuq)

right   *əɬɬuaq*   'correct one' |əɬuaq-| (elluaq)

right   *taɬixpik*   'right hand' (tallirpik)

river   *kuik* (kuik)

root   *aciɬquq* |aciɬquq-| (table 5, no. 16) (acilquq)

rope   *qiɬ̇xutaq* |qiɬ̇ɣutaq-| (qillrutaq)

rotten, to be   *aɣuˑmauq* (arumauq)

salmon   *taɣyaqfak*   'king salmon' (taryaqvak)

sayak   'silver salmon' (sayak)

salt   *taɣyuq* |taɣyuq-| (taryuq)

sand   *qaɣʷyaq* |qawyaq-| (qaũgyaq)

say   39 |+ni-|; |=ɣuq|

school   *əliˑcaɣvik*   (lit. 'place to learn') (elicarvik)

scratch   *cətuɣmiɣɣaa* |cətuɣmiɣ-| (cetugmigaa); see 'finger'

sea   *imaxpik* (imarpik)

seal   *makɬak*   'bearded seal' (maklak)

nayiq   'hair seal' |nayiɣ-| (nayiq)

isuˑɣiq   'spotted seal' |isuɣiq-| (issuriq)

search, to   *yuaˑɣaa*   'he looks for it' |yuaɣ-| (yuaraa)

see, to   *taŋxaa* |taŋx-| (tangrraa)

seed   see 'bone'

sell, to   see 'to give'

settlement   see 'land'

sew, to   *miŋqaa* |miŋqə-| (mingqaa)

shaman   *aŋaɬkuq* |aŋaɬkuq-| (angalkuq)

sharp, to be   *ipəx(cə)tuq* |ipɣ(cic)-| (table 5, no. 17) (ipeg(ce)tuq)

she   see 'he'

shoot, to   see 'gun'

shore   *cəNa*   'shore, edge' |cina-| (ceña)

short, to be   *naniˑtuq* |nanit-| (nanituq)

shoulder   *tuzək* |tuzɣ-| (tusek)

shrink, to   *əqquq* |əqə-| (eq'uq)

sick, to be   *naŋtəquq, nauɬuuɣuq*   'he is ill' (nangtequq, naulluuguq)

sinew   *yuaˑluq* |yualuq-| (yualuq)

sing, to   see 'to use'

sink, to   *kittuq* |kic-| (kit'uq)

sister   *aɬqaq*   'elder sister' |alqaq-| (alqaq)

uyuˑɣaq   'younger sibling' |uyuɣaɣ-| (uyuraq)

sit down, to   *aquˑmuq* (aqumuq)

aqumɣauq   'he is sitting' (aqumgauq)

skillful, to be   36 |-zu-|

skin   *amiq* |amiq-| (amiq)

sky   *qilak*   'sky, heaven, ceiling' (qilak)

sled   *ikamɣak* (dual) (ikamrak)

sleep   *qawaxtuq* |qavaɣ-| (qavartuq)

sleeve   *aliq* |aliɣ-| (aliq)

small   4 |-cuaɣaɣ-|

small, to be   *mikkuq* (mik'uq)

smell   *təpa* |təpə-| (tepa)   'smell, fermented salmon head'

smell, to   *naɣ̇ɣaa* |naɣ̇ə-| (naraa)

smoke   *puyuq* |puyuq-| (puyuq)

smoke, to   see 'to suck'

smooth, to be   *manix(cə)tuq* |maniɣ(cic)-| (table 5, no. 17) (manig(ce)tuq)

snow   *aqixtaq*   'snow (soft and melting)' |aqiɣtaq-| (aqigtaq)

qanikcaq   'snow on the ground' |qanikcaq-| (qanikcaq)

qanuk   'snowflake' (qanuk)

qanixtuq   'it is snowing' |qaniɣ-| (qanirtuq)

snowshoe   *taŋluq* |taŋluq-| (tangluq)

some(-thing, etc.)   See 7.4.6.

son   *qətunɣaq* |qətunɣaɣ-| (qetunraq)

song   *yuaˑɣun* (yuarun)

sorry, to be   *iluˑtəquq*   'he is sorry, sad' (ilutequq)

south   *uŋaˑlaq* |uŋalaq-| (ungalaq) 'south, southwind'

speak, to   *qanəxtuq*   'he speaks' |qanɣ-| (qanertuq)

qannaaɣuq   'he talks' |qanaa-| (qanaaguq)

spear   *panaq* |panaq-| (panaq)

spill, to   *kuvvaa* (NA) |kuvə-| (kuvaa)

spirit *anə́ɣnəq* 'spirit, breath' (anerneq)

  tuunɣaq 'familiar spirit' |tuunɣaq-| (tuunraq); see 'person' and 'world'

spit, to *qəci·ɣaa* 'he spits at it' |qəciɣ-| (qeciraa)

split, to *quppaa* (NA) |qupə-| (qupaa)

spring (time) *upnəx̣kaq* |upənəɣ́kaq-| (up'nerkaq)

squeeze, to *qəttaa* |qəc-| 'he hugs, squeezes it' (qetaa)

stab, to *kappaa* (NA) |kapə-| (kapaa)

stand, to *naŋəx̣tuq* |naŋɣ́+c-| (nangertuq); see 6.2.5.9.

star *aɣyaq* |aɣyaq-| (agyaq)

stay, to *uitauq* (uitauq)

steal, to *təɣləɣɣaa* |təɣlɣ-| (teglegaa)

stick *awa·yaq* 'branch, stick' |avayaq-| (avayaq)

stone *ciimaq* |ciimaq-| (ciimaq)

stop, to *aɣu·laix̣taa* 'he stops it' (NA) (arulairtaa)

store *kipuzvik* (lit. 'place to buy') (kipusvik)
  laafkaaq |laavkaaq-| ('laavkaaq)

story *qanəmciq* |qanəmciq-| (qanemciq)

  quli·ɣ́aq 'legend' |quliɣ́aq-| (quliraq)

straight, to be *nałqix(cə)tuq* |nalqiɣ(cic)-| (table 5, no. 17) (nalqig(ce)tuq)

stranger *ała·nəq* 'stranger, visitor' (allaneq)

strike, to *kauɣaa* |kauɣ-| (kaugaa)

strong, to be *kayyuuq* (kayuuq)

suck, to *məlu·ɣaa* 'he sucks, smokes it' |məluɣ-| (melugaa)

summer *kiak* '(last) summer' (kiak)

sun *akəx̣ta* |akəɣ́t-| (akerta)

surface *qaiŋa* 'its surface, top' (qainga)

swallow, to *iɣɣaa* |iɣə-| (igaa)

swell, to *puvvuq* 'it is swollen' (puv'uq)

swim, to *kuimuq* (kuimuq)

table *stuuluq* |stuuluq-| (table 5, no. 8) (stuuluq)

tail *pamyuq* |pamyuq-| (pamyuq)

take, to *təɣɣua* 'he takes (in hands)' (NA) (tegua)

take off, to *yuuɣaa* 'he removes it' (NA) |yuu-| (yuugaa)

teach, to *əli·caɣaa* (NA) |əlicaɣ́-| (elicaraa)
  ~*əlitNauɣ́aa* |əlitnauɣ́-| (elitnauraa)

tear, to *ałxaa* (NA) |ałɣ-| (allgaa)

tent *pəla·təkaq* |pəlatəkaq-| (pelatekaq)

thankful, to be *quyyauq* 'he is thankful, glad' (quyauq)

  quya·na 'thank you' (quyana)

362 that see 'there'

thaw, to *uɣuxtuq* 'it thaws, melts' |uɣuɣ-| (urugtuq)

there *tauna*, etc. 'the one there' (table 16) (tauna)

thick, to be *cannuuq* |cànu-| (canuuq)

thin, to be *canxətuq* |canxət-| (canggetuq)

thing *pi* 'thing, property' (pi); see 'to do'

think *umyuax̣təquq* (umyuartequq); 37 |+zukə-|

this see 'here'

throat *iɣyaɣ́aq* |iɣyaɣ́aq-| (igyaraq)

throw, to *əxtaa* |əɣc-| (egtaa)

thunder *kałuk* 'thunder, electricity' (kalluk)

  kałix̣tuq 'it is thundering' |kałiɣ́-| (kallirtuq)

tide *ula* 'high tide, flood' |ulə-| (ula)

  ulluq 'it floods, rises' (ul'uq)

tie, to *qiłəx̣taa* (NA) |qiłəɣ́c-| (qillertaa)

tired, to be *məɣ́nux̣tuq* 'he is exhausted' |məɣ́nuɣ́-| (mernurtuq)

  taqsuquq 'he is tired (physically)' (taqsuquq)

tired, of, to be 58 |-łŋu-| 'to be bored'

tobacco see 'leaf'

today *əɣ́nəx̣pak* 'today, all day' (ernerpak)

  əɣ́nəqu 'today (in the future)' (ernequ)

together |+tuuma-|_NV (6.2.5.9.) '(to act) with'

tomorrow *unnua·qu* (unuaqu)

tongue *uluq* |uluq-| (uluq)

tooth *kəxun* (keggun)

top *kaŋɣ́a* 'its top, peak' |kaŋɣ́-| (kangra)

toward *tuŋŋii* 'area toward it, its direction' |tuŋə-| (tungii)

trap *talu·yaq* 'fishtrap' |taluyaq-| (taluyaq)

tree *uqfiaq* 'tree, willow' (uqviaq)

  uqfiat (uqviat), 'forest'

  napa 'tree, spruce' |napa-| (napa)

try to, to 75 |-ŋnaqə-|

tundra *nuna·pik* (lit. 'real land') (nunapik)

turn over, to *mumix̣taa* 'he turns it over, translates it' (NA) (mumigtaa)

twist, to *qipaa* (NA) |qipə-| (qipaa)

uncle *attaata* (paternal) |ataata-| (ataata)

  aŋak (maternal) (angak)

up *qullii* 'its upper part' |qulə-| (qulii)

up there *pikNa*, etc. 'the one up or above there' (table 16) (pikna)

urine *təqquq* |tèquq-| (teq'uq)

  quxx̣uq 'he urinates' (qurr'uq)

use, to   atu·ẏaa   'he uses, sings, wears it' |atuẏ-| (aturaa); 77 |+tuẏ-|

very   cakNəq   'very much' (cakneq); 48 |-qapiγc-|

visit, to   cəNiẋtaa |ciniẏc-| (ceñirtaa)

voice   əẏi·na(q) |əẏina(q)-| (erina(q))

waist   qukaq   'waist, middle' |qukaq-| (qukaq)

wait, to   uta·qaa |utaqa-| (utaqaa)

wake up, to   tupaxtuq |tupaγ-| (tupagtuq)

walk, to   piɣyua·ɣuq |piyua-| (piyuaguq)

walrus   azvəq (asveq)

warm, to be   puqłaniẋtuq |puqłaniẏ-| (puqlanirtuq)

wash, to   əẏmiγγaa   'he washes him (face)' (NA) |əẏmiγ-| (ermigaa)

ə̇ẏu·ẏaa   'he washes it (dish, etc.)' (NA) |əẏuẏ-| (eruraa); see 'to be dirty'

water   əməq (meq)

əməẏẏaa   'he drinks it' |əmẏ-| (meraa)

wave   qaiq |qaiẏ-| (qaiq)

wear, to   see 'to use'

weather   see 'world' and 'rain'

weave, to   tupi·γaa |tupiγ-| (tupigaa)

wet, to   məci·ẏaa   'he gets it wet, soaks it' (NA) |məciẏ-| (meciraa)

whale   aẏvəq   'black whale or bowhead' (arveq)

cəttuaq   'white whale or beluga' |cituaq-| (cetuaq)

when   qaŋvaq   'when (in the past)' (qangvaq)

qaku   'when (in the future)' (qaku); see 6.2.5.7., 7.4.4., and 7.4.6.

whenever   see 6.2.5.2. and 7.4.4.

where   nani   'where, somewhere' (7.4.6.) (nani)

which   nalliat   'which one of them?' (7.4.6.) (naliat)

while   See 6.2.5.8.

white, to be   qatəẋtuq |qatẏ-| (qatertuq)

White man   kassaq |kàsaq-| (kass'aq)

who   kina   'who, someone' (7.4.6.) (kina)

whole   tama(łku)q   '(to be) all, whole, dollar' |tama(lku)q-| (tama(lku)q)

why   ciin (7.4.6.) (ciin)

wide, to be   iqtuuq (iqtuuq)

wife   nulliaq |nuli(ẏ)aq-| (nuliaq)

nuli·ẋa or nullia·ẏa 'his wife' (nulirra, nuliara)

will   46 |+₁ciqe-|ᵥᵥ; 67 |+niaẏ-|ᵥᵥ; 73 |+₁ŋ*ait-|ᵥᵥ 'will not'

wind   anu·qa |anuqə-| (anuqa);

anuqliẋtuq   'it is windy, blows' |anuqliẏ-| (anuqlirtuq)

window   əγa·ləq (egaleq)

wing   yaquq |yaquq-| (yaquq)

winter   uksuq   '(last) winter, year' |uksuq-| (uksuq)

wipe, to   pəẋi·ẏaa (NA) |pəẋiẏ-| (perriraa)

wish to, to   62 |+zuγ-|; 60 |+zuumiit-| 'not to wish'

with   13 |-lγ-| 'one having'

wolf   kəγlunəq (kegluneq)

wolverine   qafcik (qavcik)

woman   aẏnaq |aẏnaq-| (arnaq)

wonder |=kiq| 'I wonder'

wood   muẏak   '(fire)wood, log' (murak)

work, to   callia   'he makes (something) for him' (calia)

world   (c)əła   'world, outdoors, weather, spirit' |cila-| ~|əła-| ((c)ella)

wound   əkiq   'wound, cut' |əkiq-| (ekiq)

write, to   alŋaẏẏaa~iγa·ẏaa   'he writes to him' |alŋaẏ-| ~|iẏaẏ-| (alngaraa, igaraa); see 'mark'

wrong   iqłu   'wrong one' (iqlu)

iqłua   'he tells him a lie'

caŋa·tuq   'something is wrong with him/it' (cangatuq)

year   ałẋakuq   'year, age' |ałẋakuq-| (allrakuq); see 'winter'

yes   ii=i, aaŋ   'yes; you are welcome' (ii-i, aang)

aŋẏaa   'he says yes to him' |aŋẏ-| (angraa)

yesterday   akxʷauɣaq |akwauɣaq-| (akwaugaq)

you   əłpət   'you (sg.)', etc. (table 14) (elpet)

Sketch of Hupa, an Athapaskan Language

VICTOR GOLLA

1. THE HUPA LANGUAGE

The language described here was spoken in 1991 by fewer than 25 people (see Hinton and Montijo 1994:6-7 for comparative estimates). Nearly all of them lived on or near the Hoopa Valley Reservation, located on the Trinity River in northwestern California.

The ethnographic Hupa of Hoopa Valley (the *na·tinixʷe·*) were the most important Hupa-speaking group of the precontact period, but not the only one. The Chilula and Whilkut of the Redwood Creek region (the *xʷiyɫ̣qidxʷe·*) also spoke Hupa, although apparently with a few lexical and grammatical differences from Hoopa Valley speech (P.E. Goddard 1914).* So did the *ce·niŋxʷe·*, the so-called South Fork Hupas, who lived along the Trinity River and its South Fork for about 30 miles upstream from Hoopa Valley and whose territory also seems to have overlapped with that of the ethnographic Chimariko in

the Burnt Ranch and New River areas (Baumhoff 1958:209-215). Much farther south, in the drainages of the upper Mad, Van Duzen, and Eel rivers, there were a number of other California Athapaskan groups—the Sinkyone, Wailaki, Mattole, and Cahto, among others (Baumhoff 1958)—who spoke languages closely related to Hupa but probably not fully mutually intelligible with it. More distantly related linguistically were the Tolowa, Tututni, Galice, and other Athapaskan-

*P.E. Goddard (1914) distinguished the lower Redwood Creek people, the Chilula, from those of upper Redwood Creek, the Whilkut. Some such division probably existed, but the terms Goddard used are misleading. *xʷiyɫ̣qid* was the Hupa designation for the entire Redwood Creek region, more particularly the ridge to the east (the "Bald Hills") where most of the villages were located, and all Hupa-speaking people of the area were *xʷiyɫ̣qidxʷe·*. "Chilula" is a rendition of Yurok *culu-la* 'Bald Hills people' (Robins 1958:195), the Yurok equivalent of Hupa *xʷiyɫ̣qidxʷe·*. (See also Baumhoff 1958:201-203.)

speaking groups of the southwest Oregon coast and immediately adjacent interior valleys of the Rogue, Coquille, and Umpqua rivers. That Hupa speakers recognized their linguistic kinship to all other Hupas as well as to other Athapaskans is reflected in the term *diniŋʔxine·W* 'speaker(s) of Hupa or any similar dialect' and their application of it to the Tolowa (*yide*ʔ *diniŋʔxine·W* 'downstream Hupa speakers'). (Merriam's conflicting information that this term was confined to the Hupa or even to the Hupa of the upper half of the valley [Baumhoff 1958:209, 212], rests on a misunderstanding.)

During the 140 years since contact, the geographical and social complexities of the aboriginal speech community have been considerably restructured. After the establishment of a reservation in Hoopa Valley in 1864, many Hupa speakers residing outside the valley were resettled there, where they intermarried with the local population. After 1900, English began making considerable inroads.

As late as 1897, when Pliny Earle Goddard began his work, few Hupas were literate in English, and Hupa was the language of everyday life in the community. The success of English language education (a boarding school was established in Hoopa in 1893) rapidly changed this situation during the next two generations, and after 1930 very few Hupa children acquired Hupa as their first language. The youngest fluent speakers of Hupa were nearly 60 in 1992, and most were 70 or older. In the face of this relentless decline in the traditional speech community, the Hoopa Tribe made attempts to preserve and teach their traditional language. Since 1981 the Hupa Language Program has been compiling linguistic and cultural materials for pedagogical purposes. A "Master-Apprentice" program involving elderly Hupa speakers and younger tribal members was piloted in 1993 (Hinton and Montijo 1994:6-7). A practical writing system, based on the orthography used in this sketch, has been formally adopted by the Tribe, and several publications have appeared using it (cf. Golla 1985).

2. SCOPE AND SOURCES

This sketch of Hupa grammar gives the reader an overview of Hupa, and more generally Athapaskan, morphosyntax. To a great extent it is a condensation of Golla (1970). The theoretical idiom is American structuralist, to some extent Sapirian, and deeply influenced by the work of Harry Hoijer (1971). For later treatments of Athapaskan phonology and grammar, readers should consult Cook and Rice (1989), particularly their introductory essay.

The author's knowledge of the Hupa language comes from four principal sources: his own fieldwork and that of Edward Sapir, Pliny Earle Goddard, and Mary Woodward. Golla's observations were made at Hoopa

during a nine-month period in 1962-1964 and during various shorter stays thereafter. His primary sources during the earlier part of his work were Mr. and Mrs. Ned Jackson; Mrs. Jackson's older sister, Minnie Reeves; and Rudolph Socktish (fig. 1), the Hupa religious leader. Most of his work was supported by the Survey of California and Other Indian Languages, University of California, Berkeley, where a complete copy of all notes and tapes is archived. Since 1981 Golla has been a consultant to the Hupa Language Program, supported by the Hoopa Tribe, where he has had the opportunity to work with a number of fluent speakers of Hupa in the course of developing pedagogical materials.

Sapir collected Hupa material during the summer of 1927. This consists of 11 manuscript notebooks containing 76 narrative texts, as well as an extensive lexical and grammatical file. The texts, dictated by Sam Brown, Jake Hostler, Oscar Brown, John Shoemaker (fig. 2), Mary Marshall, and Emma Frank, are especially valuable for their cultural and literary content. Sapir's principal source and translator was Sam Brown. These notes and files are in the Franz Boas Collection, American Philosophical Society Library, Philadelphia.

Goddard, who was a missionary to the Hupas from 1897 to 1900, carried out the first scholarly studies of Hupa language and culture (P.E. Goddard 1903, 1904, 1905, 1907, 1911). Goddard's (relatively infrequent) phonetic lapses and his shaky control of Athapaskan grammar are more than compensated for by the richness of his documentation.

Woodward carried out linguistic fieldwork in Hoopa Valley in 1953 (Woodward 1964).

3. THE SOUND SYSTEM

The basic phonological segments of Hupa are six vowels and 27 consonants. Hupa syllables have no tonal distinctions.

Hoopa Tribal Mus., Hoopa, Calif.

Fig 1. Rudolph Socktish (b. 1903, d. 1982), hereditary leader of the White Deerskin and Jump Dances, preparing a deer hide for the White Deerskin Dance. Photographed about 1975.

3.1. VOWELS

The six basic vowels of Hupa are *i a o* (short) and *e· a·* *o·* (long). However, in surface phonology there are seven vowels, since after the application of the phonological rules (section 4), basic short *i* is represented by *e* before a laryngeal consonant, and by *i* elsewhere. Both short and long vowels form diphthongs with the voiced semivowels (*y* and *w*), and the laryngeal consonant (*h* and *ʔ*) occur as increments to the short vowels.

The following are the occurring syllable peaks of Hupa surface phonology (simple vowels, vowels with laryngeal increment, and diphthongs), with approximate phonetic values as indicated:

i [ɪ] : *mis* 'cliff, riverbank', *łiŋʔ* 'dog, pet', *Wimił* 'my belly'.

eh [ɛh] : *žeh* 'pitch', *łehxiž* 'little girl', *gʸehs* 'fall run of salmon'.

eʔ [ɛʔ] : *meʔ* 'inside it', *mikʸeʔdiŋ* 'mouth of a river', *yeʔċ* 'wart'.

iy [i·] : *łiy* 'bet, price', *diyWoʔ* 'something'.

iw [ɪ̯ᵁ] : *ʔa·wiliw* 'what is done, way of doing things', *xožiwʔ* 'his ear'.

a [ʌ] : *mintaŋ* '10', *ġaskʸoh* 'soaproot', *xoʔad* 'his wife'.

ah [ɑh] : *ʔah* 'cloud', *nahnin* 'two people', *ʔiłgʸahs* 'break it off!'.

aʔ [ɑʔ] : *xotaʔ* 'his father', *taʔna·n* 'water', *nałmaʔċ* 'coil it!'.

ay [ʌ̯ᶦ] : *dinday* 'bullet, arrowhead', *hay* 'the, that one', *dayd* 'what?'.

aw [ʌ̯ᵁ] : *daw* 'no!', *kʸite·ław* 'Indian doctor, shaman', *ʔa·čilaw* 'he did it'.

o [ᵁ] : *tos* 'hot water', *xosował* 'his throat', *xoŋ(w)ož* 'his older brother'.

NAA, Smithsonian.

Fig. 2. Principal dancers John Shoemaker (left, front) and Bill Little (right, front) together with other dancers, in the staging area before the White Deerskin Dance (*xay čidilye* 'winter dance'). They wear crowns of sea-lion tusks (*kʸiwoʔ* 'teeth') and carry large obsidian blades (*to·nehwa·n* '(dark) like water'), symbols of wealth. The other dancers hold poles on which are mounted the hides of albino deer (*kʸiłixan łiqay* 'white deer'). Photographed by A. W. Ericson, 8 miles from the Yurok town of Weitchpec, Hoopa Valley, Calif., before 1897.

oh [oh] : *ġaWkʸoh* 'redwood', *tohdit* 'you (pl.) go!', *xowatkʸohs* 'give him (the blanket)!'.

oʔ [oʔ] : *ǯeˑloʔ* 'storage basket', *toʔkʸoh* 'sturgeon', *kʸoʔċ* 'sinew'.

oy [ᴜˑ] : *kʸiʌoy* 'basketry, weaving'.

ow [oᴜ] : *ticow* 'blue, green'.

e [ɛˑ] : *čidilyeˑ* 'ceremonial dance', *Wiceˑʔ* 'my (man's) daughter', *neˑs* 'long'.

eˑy [ɛˑⁱ] : *ċeˑy* 'brush', *xoǯeˑyʔdiŋ* 'right in front of him'.

eˑw [ɛˑᴜ] : *meˑw* 'underneath it'.

aˑ [ɑˑ] : *Waˑ* 'sun, moon', *Winaˑʔ* 'my eyes', *xosaˑstaˑn* 'his tongue'.

aˑy [ɑˑⁱ] : *Wikʸaˑy* 'my (woman's) daughter's child', *daˑyWoʔ* 'somewhere'.

aˑw [aˑᴜ] : *kʸimaˑw* 'medicine', *Widaˑwʔ* 'my mustache, whiskers'.

oˑ [oˑ] : *toˑ* '(body of) water', *xoċoˑʔ* 'her breast, nipples', *noˑkʸineˑyoˑd* 'dog'.

oˑy [oˑⁱ] : *mittoˑy* 'bucket'.

oˑw [oˑᴜ] : *kʸitoˑw* 'paddle'.

When the syllable peak *iw* is immediately followed by a syllable beginning with *i* (but not *e*), the two syllables are often collapsed into a single syllable with the peak [uˑ]. Thus: *kʸiwinyaʔn* [kʸuˑnyaʔn] 'what is eaten; acorns'; *ʌiwiW* [ʌuˑW] 'rattlesnake'. In the present analysis, this optional contraction is not considered to be a regular phonological process and is not written.

3.2. CONSONANTS

The 27 basic consonants of Hupa can be divided into stops (*ʔ, d, gʸ, ġ, t, kʸ, ṭ, kʸ, q̇*), affricates (*ʒ, ǯ, c, čʷ, ċ, čʷ, ʌ*), fricatives and voiceless semivowels (*s, x, xʷ, t, W,* and *h*), voiced semivowels (*y, w*), and sonorants (*m, n, l*). The phonological rules generate one additional sonorant in surface phonology, the nasal *ŋ*. In addition, *b, š, g, k,* and *kʼ* occur in expressive words (see section 10.3.). Examples are:

ʔ : *ʔehs* 'weir, fish dam', *Waʔad* 'my wife', *Wilaʔ* 'my hand'.

d : *diniW* 'manzanita', *nandil* 'snow', *tid* 'smoke'.

gʸ : *gʸehskʸoh* 'elk', *digʸaŋ* 'here', *xoˑwiligʸ* 'story'.

ġ : *ġoˑ* 'worm', *xoġaˑġeʔ* 'his throat, tonsils', *yinaġ* 'upstream'.

t : *taˑq̇* 'three', *mitis* '(moving) over it'.

kʸ : *kʸaʔ* 'dress', *nikʸaˑw* 'it is big'.

ṭ : *ṭeʔ* 'blanket', *ʔaWteˑ* 'I am (so)', *Wimiṭ* 'my belly'.

kʸ : *kʸinaʔ* 'Yurok Indian', *mikʸoˑċeʔ* 'its sinew', *dinkʸ* 'four'.

q̇ : *q̇ad* 'enough', *diq̇aˑn* 'ridge', *toˑq̇* 'salmon, fish'.

ʒ : *ʒiwol* 'little ball', *xʷeˑʒeʔ* 'his penis', *kʸiwidiʒ* 'string, rope'.

ǯ : *ǯeˑnis* 'day', *Wiǯiwʔ* 'my ears', *kʸileˑxiǯ* 'young boy'.

c : *ce* 'stone', *kʸehtcaˑn* 'young woman'.

čʷ : *čʷiǯ* 'firewood', *čiscʷeʔn* 'he made it'.

ċ : *ċeˑy* 'brush', *Wiċeˑq̇* 'my navel', *tiċ* 'cane, walking stick'.

č : *čahl* 'frog', *dinčaˑd* 'it aches, hurts', *dič* 'valley quail'.

ʌ : *ʌoh* 'grass', *xoʌaʔ* 'his buttocks', *čitehsdeˑʌ* 'they went off'.

s : *saˑċ* 'bear', *xosiċ* 'his skin', *ġehs* 'fall run of salmon.'

x : *xoŋʔ* 'fire', *xoxeʔ* 'his foot', *nahx* 'two'.

xʷ : *xʷeˑdaʔay* 'his head', *daxʷeˑd* 'how?', *naˑtinixʷ* 'Hoopa Valley'.

t : *taʔ* 'one', *mintaŋ* '10', *mit* 'with it'.

W : *Waˑ* 'sun, moon', *niWoˑn* 'it is good', *q̇ayliW* 'willow'.

h : *hanʔ* 'river', *dahanʔdidaŋʔ* 'when (in the past)?', *xontah* 'house'.

y : *yaʔ* 'louse', *hayaˑt* 'and then...', *naˑnyay* 'rain'.

w : *witdaŋʔ* 'yesterday', *naʔway* 'he went around', *daw* 'no!'.

m : *mis* 'riverbank', *tismil* 'eagle', *kʸeˑnim* 'eight'.

n : *ninʔ* 'ground, earth', *Winaˑʔ* 'my eyes', *tin* 'road, trail'.

ŋ : *Wiŋ(w)oǯ* 'my older brother', *Wiŋ* 'song'.

l : *lah* 'seaweed', *nilaʔ* 'your hand', *meʔdil* 'boat, canoe.'

3.2.1. MANNERS OF ARTICULATION

ʔ, d, gʸ, and *ġ* are voiceless stops, unaspirated in initial and medial position, released with slight aspiration in final position.

t and *kʸ* are strongly aspirated voiceless stops.

ṭ, kʸ, and *q̇* are glottalized stops, somewhat weakly released in initial and medial position, where they are sometimes difficult to distinguish from the voiceless unaspirated stops *d, gʸ,* and *ġ,* but released with a more distinct ejective quality in final position. Final *q̇* is sometimes affricated, for example, *taˑq̇* [tʼɑˑq̇x] 'three'.

ʒ and *ǯ* are voiceless affricates, unaspirated in initial and medial position, released with slight aspiration in final position.

c and *čʷ* are strongly aspirated voiceless affricates.

ċ, č, and *ʌ* are glottalized affricates, somewhat weakly released in initial and medial position, where *ċ* and *č* are sometimes difficult to distinguish from the voiceless unaspirated affricates *ʒ* and *ǯ,* but released with a more distinct ejective quality in final position.

s, x, xʷ, t, and *h* are voiceless fricatives.

W is a voiceless semivowel.

y and *w* are voiced semivowels.

m, n, and *ŋ* are nasals. *m* is fully voiced in all positions. *n* is fully voiced in all positions except in final position after a voiceless fricative, where it is usually voiceless (*kʸinasn* [kʸinasN] 'Karok Indians'). *ŋ*, which does not occur initially, is fully voiced in medial position but partially devoiced in final position (*kiŋ* [k'iŋ˙] 'stick, tree').

l is a lateral sonorant, fully voiced in all positions.

3.2.2. POINTS OF ARTICULATION

m is a bilabial consonant.

d, ʒ, t, c, ṭ, ċ, and *n* are dental-alveolar consonants.

ǯ, čʷ, and *č̣* are alveopalatal consonants. *čʷ* is also strongly rounded and aspirated as [W].

gʸ, kʸ, and *k̇ʸ* are front velar consonants, articulated with a distinct palatal release, heard as a y-like on-glide in a following vowel.

ġ, x, xʷ, and *q̇* are back velar consonants. *xʷ* is also strongly rounded.

ʔ and *h* are laryngeal (glottal) consonants.

y is a palatal semivowel, phonetically equivalent to [i].

w and *W* are labiovelar semivowels, phonetically equivalent to [u].

4. PHONOLOGICAL RULES

The following rules of reduction and assimilation apply to all strings of basic phonological elements, regardless of their meaning or function. The rules are partially ordered.

Rule 1: Desyllabification of *i*.

When basic *i* occurs at the end of a word or phrase and is immediately preceded by either *a˙* or *o˙*, *i* is replaced by *y*. (The vowel is then shortened by Rule 4). Examples are:

> *na˙-ʔ-wa˙=i > naʔway* 'he (who) goes about'
> *ne˙-s-no˙=i > nehsnoy* '(what) stands in a line'.

Rule 2: Voicing.

Before word-final *i*, *h* and *ł* are replaced by *w* and *l* respectively (and *i* is then elided by Rule 5). Examples are:

> *ni-kʸa˙h=i > nikʸa˙w* '(what) is big'
> *ʔa-ł-k̇ʸoh=i > ʔałk̇ʸow* '(what) is of such a size'
> *ʔi-ʔi-lih=i > ʔeʔiliw* 'it always becomes'
> *ni-te˙ł=i > nite˙l* '(what) is wide or flat'.

Rule 3: Treatment of n.

(a) *n* is replaced by *ŋ*:
  (1) at the end of a word or phrase.
> *kʸin > kʸiŋ* 'stick, tree'
> *si-ta˙n > sitaŋ* 'a sticklike object lies'
  (2) when it occurs before *ʔ, y, W, w, gʸ, kʸ, k̇ʸ, x, ġ,* or *q̇*.
> *nin-ʔił > niŋʔił* '(animals) arrive swimming'
> *ł-n-Wiŋ > łiŋWiŋ* 'you are black, dark'
> *ni-čʷin ʔ > ničʷiŋʔ* 'it is bad'

The sequence *ŋw* is (optionally) further reduced to *ŋ*.

> *Wi-nwoǯ > Wiŋwoǯ (> Wiŋoǯ)* 'my older brother'
> *yih-či-win-we·n=i > yehčiwiŋwe·n*
>   *(> yehčiwiŋe·n)* 'he brought (the pack) in'

(b) The sequence *nʔi* at the end of a word or phrase is replaced by *ʔni* (which is reduced to *ʔn* by Rule 5).

> *kʸi-win-yanʔ=i > kʸiwinyaʔn* 'what one eats; acorns'
> *ni-čʷinʔ=i > ničʷeʔn* '(what) is bad'

(c) When *n* occurs before *l* or *m* it is elided.

> *si-n-linʔ > siliŋʔ* 'you became'
> *ya˙-ʔ-win-me·λ=i > yaʔwime·λ* 'he threw them in the air'

(d) When *n* occurs before *n*:
  (1) it is replaced by *y* if preceded by a basically long vowel.
> *Wi-čo˙-n-ne· > Wičoyne·* 'help me!'
> *mi-de·-n-nah > midiynah* 'touch it!'
  (2) it is elided if preceded by *i*, and *i* is secondarily lengthened to *e·*.
> *kʸi-n-niW > kʸe·niW* 'you hear about it'
> *na˙-ʔ-win-ne·ł > naʔwe·neł* 'he played'

Rule 4: Shortening of long vowels.

A long vowel (*e·, a·, o·*) is replaced by a short vowel (*i* for *e·*, *a* for *a·*, *o* for *o·*) in a closed syllable.

> *si-ta·n > sitaŋ* (see Rule 3) '(a sticklike object) lies'
> *na˙-ʔ-wa˙=i > na˙-ʔ-wa˙=y* (Rule 1) *> naʔway* 'he (who) goes around'
> *Wi-čo˙-n-ne· > Wi-čo˙-y-ne·* (Rule 3d) *> Wičoyne·* 'help me!'

Furthermore:

(1) if the syllable is closed by *s, W, ł, ʒ, ǯ,* or *gʸ*, the laryngeal increment *h* is inserted after the vowel.

> *ʔe·s > ʔehs* 'weir, fish dam'
> *kʸi-si-e·-ł-me·ǯ=te· > kʸisehłmehǯ=te·* 'he will boil it'
> *di-ł-čʷo·gʸ > diłčʷohgʸ* 'brush them away!'

(2) if the syllable is closed by any glottalized consonant, the laryngeal increment *ʔ* is inserted after the vowel.

> *ye·ċ > yeʔċ* 'wart'
> *či-nin-de·λ̇ > činindeʔλ̇* 'they arrived'
> *kʸi-win-k̇ʸe·ł=te· > kʸiwink̇ʸeʔł=te·* 'there will be a creaking noise'

(3) if the syllable is closed by *d*, the laryngeal increment *h* is inserted after the vowel and the *d* is elided.

> *ło·d > łoh* 'scab'
> *či-win-ce·d=te· > čiwinceh=te·* 'he will break wind'

Rule 5: Deletion of short vowels.

A short vowel is elided when it occurs:
(1) at the end of a word or phrase.
> *yi-daġ-i > yidaġ* 'uphill'
> *mahni > mahn* 'war party'
> *či-nin-de·λ̇-i > čininde·λ̇* 'they (who) arrived'
(2) before another vowel.
> *Wi-an-čʷin > Wančʷiŋ* 'my mother'
> *či-o·-ne· > čo·ne·* 'he thinks about it'

(3) between *y, w, m, n,* or *l* and a word-final *ʔ*.

mi-čʷaˑn-iʔ > *mičʷaˑnʔ* 'its excrement'

mi-ǯeˑh-iʔ > *mi-ǯeˑw-iʔ* (Rule 2) > *miǯeˑwʔ* 'its pitch'

When the consonant is preceded by a short vowel this rule is optional.

Wi-ǯiwiʔ > *Wiǯiwʔ* or *Wiǯiweʔ* 'my ears'

Wi-čʷeˑxinoʔ > *Wičʷeˑxiŋʔ* or *Wičʷeˑxinoʔ* 'my anus'

When the elided vowel is *o*, an immediately preceding *x* is replaced by *xʷ*.

ni-kʸaˑh-xo > *nikʸahxʷ* 'in a big way'

xo-an-čʷin > *xʷančʷiŋ* 'his mother'

Rule 6: Contraction of *wi*.
When preceded by a long vowel, and in a closed syllable, *wi* is elided.

yaˑ-win-xič > *yaˑŋxič* '(birds) flew up in the air'

naˑ-wi-n-daˑɫ > *naˑndaɫ* 'you go along back'

čeˑ-wi-d-meˑλ̣=i > *čeˑdmeˑλ̣* '(what) has been thrown out'

Rule 7: Lowering of *i*.
When *i* occurs before a laryngeal consonant, it is replaced by *e*.

si-linʔ=i > *si-liʔn* (Rules 3b and 5) > *sileʔn* 'it became'

ʔi-ʔi-ɫih=i > *ʔi-ʔi-liw* (Rules 2 and 5) > *ʔeʔiliw* 'it always becomes'

Elsewhere *i* is rewritten as *i*.

5. VERBS: MORPHOLOGY
A Hupa verb consists of a lexical morpheme, the stem, preceded by one or more prefixes. Prefixes can have inflectional, derivational, or lexical meaning.

Any lexical prefixes that may occur, together with the stem, constitute the theme of a verb, which is all that need be entered in a dictionary. A theme expresses a fundamental verbal idea (-$ɫ_1$-*cis* 'see', -*čʷeh* 'cry', ni_6-*kʸaˑh* 'be big')[†] and implies a certain pattern of inflection: the theme -$ɫ_1$-*cis*, for example, is inflected for subject, object, and mode ('a subject sees an object, doing this in some mode of action' would be a more accurate translation of the theme), while the theme ni_6-*kʸaˑh* is inflected only for subject ('a subject is big'). Patterns of inflection, and the types of theme that can be distinguished on this basis, are described in section 6.

In many verbs the inflectional pattern is not the one basically specified by the theme, but another (or one of several) that can be substituted for it, with a predictable change in meaning. For example, the theme ni_6-*kʸaˑh* 'be big', basically inflected only for subject, is found also in a variant inflectional pattern, with inflection for

mode, meaning 'grow big, come to be big'. Such secondary themes are usually marked by one or more theme derivational prefixes (7.1.).

Any prefix that is not thematic (part of the basic theme or a marker of a secondary theme), or inflectional, is a derivational prefix whose meaning extends or modifies that of the entire inflected theme.

In this section are described the constituent morphemes of verb forms, their basic meanings, phonetic shapes, and relative order. As a descriptive framework, 11 position classes of verb morphemes can be identified. These are classes of mutually exclusive morphemes (except for prefix position 7, where object and deictic subject markers can co-occur), ordinarily found in the following relative order (moving left, or backward, from the stem):

Prefix position 1: Classifier
Prefix position 2: Subject
Prefix position 3: Mode
Prefix position 4: Distributive
Prefix position 5: Adverbial
Prefix position 6: Thematic
Prefix position 7: Object or deictic subject
Prefix position 8: Plural
Prefix position 9: Iterative
Prefix position 10: Adverbial or thematic.

5.1. CLASSIFIERS
There are three basic classifiers, *ɫ-, di-,* and *l-*; two compound classifiers, *ɫdi-* and *ldi-*; and three prefixes of restricted occurrence that it is convenient to identify as classifiers (although they are formally and semantically connected with thematic prefixes of position 6, see section 5.6.): *n-, s-,* and *W-*. With the exception of the last three, classifiers normally serve as the markers of certain secondary themes or are used as partial markers of some inflectional and derivational categories (potential mode and iterative). However, there are numerous instances of basic themes that include a classifier that is not (at least in modern Hupa) a theme-derivational prefix: -$ɫ_1$-*yoˑɫ* 'blow' (active intransitive), ni_6-$ɫ_1$-*taˑn* 'be soft', and $taˑ_{10}$-di_1-*naˑn* 'drink'.

The phonetic form of a classifier is changed, or the classifier is lost, in certain situations. (These changes, and other phonological processes that are specific to individual morphemes, are not covered by the general phonological rules outlined in section 4.):

(1) *ɫ-* or *l-* is lost after W_2- 'first-person singular subject' and s_3- 'perfective mode': *noˑxoWtiW* 'I put him down' (< $noˑ_{10}$-xo_7-W_2-$ɫ_1$-*tiW*), *wiWdaɫ* 'I run along' (< wi_3-W_2-l_1-*daˑɫ*).

(2) *ɫ-* is replaced by *l-* after di_2- 'first-person plural subject' and in verbs inflected for reciprocal object (with $nɫi_7$-): *xodilcis* 'we see him' (< xo_7-di_2-$ɫ_1$-*cis*); *yaʔnɫinilʔiŋ* 'they look at each other' (< ya_8-$či_7$-$nɫi_7$-ni_6-$ɫ_1$-*ʔeˑn*).

[†] Themes are cited with their morphemes (separated by hyphens) in their basic forms, prior to the operation of phonological rules. Subscript numerals indicate the position classes of prefixes.

(3) *l*- is replaced by *ł*- after *oh$_2$*- 'second-person plural subject': *tohłtoŋ?* 'you (pl.) jump off!' (< *ti$_5$-oh$_2$-l$_1$-ton?*).

5.2. SUBJECT

Only first- and second-person subjects are indicated by prefixes of position class 2. The four subject markers that occur here are: *W*- 'first-person singular', *n*- 'second-person singular', *di*- 'first-person plural', and *oh*- 'second-person plural.' The difference in meaning between *n*- and *oh*- (both translating English 'you') is simply a difference in the number of persons being spoken to: *n*- is 'you (alone)' and *oh*- is 'you (two or more)'. There are no overtones of intimacy in *n*- nor of formality in *oh*-.

The phonetic form of a subject prefix undergoes the following special adjustments:

(1) *W*- 'first-person singular' is replaced by *e·*- when it comes between a marker of perfective mode (*win$_3$*-, *nin$_3$*-, *s$_3$*-, or *we·s$_3$*-) and *ł$_1$*- or a stem (in active verbs only). In perfective neuters *W$_2$*- is retained: *siWte·n* 'I am lying down', *s*-perfective neuter. If the perfective marker is *win$_3$*- (itself reduced to *wi*- in this situation) contractions occur with preceding elements: *Ci-wi$_3$-e$_2$*- > *Ce·*-, and *CV·-wi$_3$-e$_2$*- > *CV·y*-: *na·se·ya?* 'I have gone about' (< *na·$_{10}$-s$_3$-W$_2$-ya?*), *no·xonehłtiŋ* 'I have put him down' (< *no·$_{10}$-xo$_7$-nin$_3$-W$_2$-ł$_1$-te·n*), *ne·Wo?n* 'I have been good' (< *ni$_6$-wi$_3$-e$_2$-Won?* < *ni$_6$-win$_3$-W$_2$-Won?*), *ya·ytwa?ł* 'I threw it up into the air' (< *ya·$_{10}$-wi$_3$-e$_2$-ł$_1$-wa·ł* < *ya·$_{10}$- win$_3$-W$_2$-ł$_1$-wa·ł*).

(2) *n*- 'second-person singular' is lost before *ł$_1$*- (and also before *l$_1$*-, but this is by a regular phonological rule) and is replaced by *y*- when immediately followed by a stem with initial *n*. The sequence *Ci-y$_2$* contracts to *Ce·*-. Thus: *?iłč^{w}e·* 'make it!' (< *?i-n$_2$-ł$_1$-c^{w}e·*), *Wičoyne·* 'help me!' (< *Wi-čo$_{10}$-n$_2$-ne·*), *ne·nehs* 'you are tall' (< *ni$_6$-y$_2$-ne·s* < *ni$_6$-n$_2$-ne·s*).

(3) *di*- 'first-person plural' is replaced by *y*- when it is followed by *di$_1$*- or by the stem -*dił*/*de·ł* (in themes referring to the movement of several people or objects). *Ci-y$_2$*- contracts to *Ce·*-. Thus: *naydił* 'we go about' (< *na·$_{10}$-di$_2$-dił*), *se·diyaŋ* 'we are old' (< *si$_6$-y$_2$-di$_1$-ya·n* < *si$_6$-di$_2$-di$_1$-ya·n*).

(4) *oh*- 'second-person plural' is replaced by *h*- when preceded by a long vowel: *nahdil* 'you (pl.) are walking about' (< *na·$_{10}$-oh$_2$-dił*).

5.3. MODE

There are eight overt mode markers: *nin*-, *win*-, *s*-, and *we·s*- 'perfective'; *wi*- 'progressive'; *?i*- 'customary'; *o·*- 'optative'; and *ni*- 'potential'. A verb form with no overt mode marker, but with a theme requiring mode inflection, is considered to be marked for 'imperfective' mode. Verb forms with the imperfective (zero) mode marker, or with customary, optative, or potential markers, automatically add an initial "peg syllable" *?i*- when there is no preceding prefix: *?iW?ač* 'I sneeze'

(< [zero$_3$]-*W$_2$-?ač*), *?e?iWliž* 'I habitually urinate' (< *?i$_3$-W$_2$-liž*).

For the meanings of the various mode markers see the discussion of mode inflection in section 6.7. For correlated stem variation, see section 5.12.

The following phonetic adjustments occur:

(1) *nin*-, *win*-, *s*-, and *we·s*- 'perfective' are replaced by *ni*-, *wi*-, *si*-, and *we·si*-, respectively, when they are followed by any subject marker of position 2: *niWdahW* 'I arrived running' (< *nin$_3$-W$_2$-l$_1$-da·W*), *siWtiŋ* 'I am lying down' (< *s$_3$-W$_2$-te·n*).

(2) *nin*- 'perfective' is replaced by *n*- when immediately preceded by a prefix ending in a long vowel: *nonde?ʎ* 'they (animals) went no farther' (< *no·$_{10}$-nin$_3$-de·ʎ*).

(3) *s*- 'perfective' is replaced by *si*- when no prefix precedes it: *siliŋ?* 'it became' (< *s$_3$-lin?*; third-person general subject is marked by zero in this form).

(4) *win*- 'perfective' is replaced by *n*- when it is immediately preceded by *k'i$_7$*- 'third-person specific subject or object': *yehk'iŋyohW* '(water) surged in' (< *yih$_{10}$-k'i$_7$-win$_3$-yo·W*).

(5) *o·*- 'optative' is replaced by *?o·*- when immediately preceded by a prefix ending in a long vowel: *na·?o·ya?* 'let it move about!' (< *na·$_{10}$-o·$_3$-ya?*).

5.4. DISTRIBUTIVE

A derivational prefix, *ti*- 'distributive', can occur between adverbial prefixes of position 5 and mode markers of position 3, and it is therefore assigned to position class 4. The distributive marker adds the meaning 'here and there' or 'at several times or places' to the meaning of the inflected theme. It appears to be related to several other morphemes with initial *t*, in particular the adverbial prefix *ti$_5$*- 'off, along' and the future tense enclitic *=te·*. The central idea from which they all diverge is extension outward across space (or time). The stem of the theme *ni$_6$-te·ł* 'be wide, flat' is probably also connected.

ti- is replaced by *te·*- when it precedes *s$_3$*- 'perfective': *te·te·se·łeh* 'I have drawn marks here and there' (< *ti$_5$-ti$_4$-s$_3$-e·$_2$-łih*).

5.5. ADVERBIAL

There are four adverbial derivational prefixes that occur in position 5: *di*- 'starting off', *ti*- 'off, along' *ni*- 'approaching, arriving', and *si*-. The last occurs only in combination with prefixes of position 10; *di*- and *ni*- also occur in such combinations.

The form of a position 5 prefix is altered to *Ce·*- when it precedes (with or without intervening *ti$_4$*-) *s$_3$*- 'perfective': *ne·siŋyaŋ* 'you grew up' (< *ni$_5$-s$_3$-n$_2$-ya·n*).

5.6. THEMATIC

If a basic theme includes a prefixed element, this element will occur either in position 6 or in position 10. There are about 20 thematic prefixes that occur in position 6, falling into two groups on a semantic basis: class markers, recurring in several themes with similar meaning (though not productive of new forms); and pure thematic prefixes, restricted to occurrence in single themes. The class markers are:

ni-, referring to surface qualities other than color: *ni₆-te·ł* 'be broad, wide', *ni₆-ł₁-ca·y* 'be dry'.

ni-, referring to the mind, feelings, judgment: *ni₆-sin* 'think', *ni₆-l₁-g*ʸ*id* 'be afraid'.

łi-, referring to color and some other nontactile qualities: *łi₆-ġay* 'be white', *łi₆-xan* 'be sweet, good-tasting'.

di-, referring to noise: *di₆-ne·/ni?* 'make a noise'.

di-, referring to protrusion or thrusting: *0-e·₁₀-di₆-lih* '(a war party) attacks', *di₆-?a·* '(one object) extends out (from a fixed point)', *di₆-ʒid* 'be short'.

di- (together with *l₁-*), referring to a collection or group: *di₆-s₃-l₁-če·* '(several) stay, dwell', *di₆-l₁-č*ʷ*an?* '(several) congregate for a feast'.

di- (together with *n₁-*), referring to a strong or distasteful perception: *di₆-n₁-q̇oč̓* 'be sour, salty'.

xo-, referring to awareness, knowledge: *xo₆-niW* 'be awake', *xo₆-lig*ʸ 'tell, mention'.

si-, referring to (usually temporary) states of being: *si₆-q̇ač̓* 'be cold', *si₆-łik̓*ʸ 'be slim'.

In some instances basic thematic classifiers (including some occurrences of *ł₁-* and *l₁-* and probably all occurrences of *n₁-* and *s₁-*) function as class markers: *l₁-* refers to color in themes such as *di₆-l₁-ma·y* 'be gray' and *di₆-l₁-xiǯ* 'be spotted, speckled', while *s₁-* refers to a state of being in the themes *di₆-s₁-k̓e·n* 'be stiff' and *mi₆-s₁-ġiy?* 'be small'. In all such instances the class-marking classifier bears a phonetic resemblance to a class marker of position 6 (*l₁-* to *łi₆-*, *s₁* to *si₆-*, etc.), while the theme also includes another marker (sometimes another class marker, sometimes a pure thematic prefix) in position 6.

The following are examples of pure thematic prefixes in position 6: *ti-* in *ti₆-ma?* 'there is a famine', *ne·-* in *ne·₆-yo·d* 'chase', *xi-* in *xi₆-na·* 'be safe, alive', *ǯi-* in *ǯi₆-woł* 'be round'.

The short *i* of any prefix of position 6 is replaced by *e·* when the prefix precedes (with or without an intervening prefix) *s₃-* 'perfective mode'.

5.7. OBJECT OR DEICTIC SUBJECT

Transitive verbs are inflected for direct object, and all personal verbs are inflected for third-person (deictic) subject, by markers in position class 7. The forms are as follows: *Wi-* 'first-person singular object' *ni-* 'second-person singular object', *noh-* 'first- or second-person plural object', *xo-* 'third-person human object', *di-* (with preceding *?a·₁₀-*) 'reflexive object', *nłi-* 'reciprocal object', *k̓ʸidi-* 'passive object'; *yi-* 'third-person general subject', *či-* 'third-person human subject', *xo-* 'third-person place subject or object', and *k̓ʸi-* 'third-person specific subject or object'.

If the theme of a verb requires object inflection and there is no overt marker in position 7, or a marker that is ambiguously subject or object occurs (*xo-* 'third-person place' or *k̓ʸi-* 'third-person specific') and is construed as a subject, then the verb is considered to be inflected for 'third-person general object'.

The third-person subjects and objects are divided into deictic (that is, designating or pointing out) categories parallel to those in other Athapaskan languages (for the deictic pronouns of Navajo see Young and Morgan 1944:55). The general third person (*yi-* subject, zero object) is best translated by English 'it' and specifically does not refer to an (adult) man, though it may refer to a woman or child. Usually it refers (as a subject) to animals or the inanimate forces of nature, or (as an object) to the wide range of inanimate things that can be acted upon. The human person (*či-* subject, *xo-* object) refers to an (adult) human actor or person acted upon, translating most often as English 'he/she' or 'him/her'. The place third person (*xo-* subject or object) refers to a location, situation, or point in time—translating the 'it' of such sentences as 'it is nice today' or 'I like it here'. The specific third person (*k̓ʸi-* subject or object) refers to a particular entity, animate or inanimate, that is understood from context ('you know what') or not known ('something, I'm not sure what'). It frequently occurs as the third-person inflection of verb themes that specify actions approximately done by or to only one, or a small class of, things. Thus, the theme *-wa·s* 'shave, whittle' often takes *k̓ʸi-* object: *k̓ʸiWwahs* 'I'm whittling something (i.e., a stick, wood)'.

The relational objects (reflexive, reciprocal, and passive) are distinguished as follows:

(*?a·₁₀-*) *di-* 'reflexive object' indicates that the subject of the verb performs the action on itself. If the subject is plural the implication is that each subject acts on its own: *ye?a·na?diwiłk̓a?* 'she put on a dress', literally 'she dressed herself', from the theme *-ł₁-k̓a?* 'dress (someone)'; *?a·diwidiwahs* 'we shaved ourselves' (i.e., 'each of us shaved himself'), from the theme *-wa·s* 'shave, whittle'.

nłi- 'reciprocal object' is used only with plural subjects and indicates that each subject acts on the others: *yanłinil?iŋ* 'they (animals) all look at each other', from the theme *ne·₆-ł₁-?e·n* 'look at'. (Note that verbs inflected for reciprocal object change classifier *ł₁-* to *l₁-*.)

k̓ʸidi- 'passive object' indicates that the grammatical subject is to be construed as the object and that the action is performed by 'people' or 'someone': *k̓ʸide·yłdiŋ?* 'people fell in love with me, I was loved by people', from the theme *-ł₁-diŋ?* 'love (someone)'. The "agentive passive" of Navajo resembles this Hupa formation (Sapir and Hoijer 1967:93).

371

When an object marker and a deictic subject marker occur together in the same verb form they are ordered according to the following rule: *ni-* 'second-person singular object' and *noh-* 'first-person or second-person plural object', as well as the *n* of *nɬi-* 'reciprocal object', precede any marker of third-person subject; other object markers, including the *ɬi* of *nɬi-* 'reciprocal object', follow a third-person subject marker.

The following phonetic adjustments also occur:

(1) A prefix ending in a long vowel is replaced by a prefix with the corresponding short vowel if it occurs immediately preceding an object marker with initial *n* (*ni-* 'second-person singular', *noh-* 'first- or second-person plural', or *nɬi-* 'reciprocal') or the third-person general subject marker *yi-*. *yi-* in this position is usually (but not always) reduced to *y-*. Thus: *naniWcis=te·* 'I'll see you again' (< *na·$_{10}$-ni$_{7}$-W$_{2}$-ɬ$_{1}$-cis*; *=te·* is the future tense enclitic), *ʔa·yanohčilah* 'they treated us so' (< *ʔa·$_{10}$-ya$_{8}$-noh$_{7}$-či$_{7}$-lah*), *nayxeʔine·W* 'it always speaks again' (< *na·$_{9}$-yi$_{7}$-xi$_{6}$-ʔi$_{3}$-ne·W-i*).

(2) *nɬi-* 'reciprocal object' is reduced to *ɬi-* at the beginning of a word or if preceded by a prefix ending in *i*: *ɬine·dilʔiŋ* 'we look at each other', *čiɬinilʔiŋ* 'they (humans) look at each other' (from the theme *ne$_{6}$-ɬ$_{1}$-ʔe·n* 'look at').

(3) *či-* 'third-person human subject' is replaced by *ʔ-* if it is preceded by a prefix ending in a long vowel and followed by a consonant, and it is lost if it stands at the beginning of a word immediately before the object marker *k'i-* 'third-person specific' or *k'idi-* 'passive': *naʔdiɬ* 'they go about' (< *na·$_{10}$-či$_{7}$-diɬ*), *ya·k'itaʔah* 'they are singing' (< *ya·$_{8}$-či$_{7}$-k'i$_{7}$-ti$_{5}$-ʔah*), *k'itaʔah* 'he is singing' (< *či$_{7}$-k'i$_{7}$-ti$_{5}$-ʔah*). *či-* is optionally replaced by *ći-* before an immediately following *s*: *ćisda·* 'he stays there' (< *či$_{7}$-s$_{3}$-da·*).

(4) *yi-* 'third-person general subject' is lost in most (but not all) intransitive forms: *timiW* 'it (dog, child) swims off' (< (*yi$_{7}$)-ti$_{5}$-miW*), *saʔaŋ* '(a single object) lies' (< (*yi$_{7}$)-s$_{3}$-ʔa·n*); but note *yixinehW* 'it (animal, child) speaks' (*xinehW* does not occur). (It is possible that the intransitive themes that occur with an overt *yi$_{7}$-* are those whose meanings imply a human actor.)

5.8. *Plural*

Verbs inflected for any subject or object except first- and second-person singular can be marked, with the derivational prefix *ya·-* in position 8, for emphatic plurality. In intransitive verbs *ya·$_{8}$-* marks plurality of subject, and when the subject inflection is first- or second-person plural, or when the theme implies plural action, the force of *ya·$_{8}$-* is emphatic or inclusive: *činindeʔƛ* 'they arrived', but *ya·ʔnindeʔƛ* 'they all arrived, the whole group arrived' (from the theme A-*diɬ/de·ƛ* '(several) go somewhere'). In transitive verbs the reference of *ya·$_{8}$-* can be either to the plurality of the

subject or to that of the object, or sometimes both (no form has more than one *ya·$_{8}$-*).

5.9. *Iterative*

The iterative marker, *na·-*, occurs in position 9 and has the same form as a proclitic particle meaning 'again', 'another', or 'once more' that occurs with nouns and verb modifiers. In verbs the force of *na·$_{9}$-* is to indicate either the repetition of an action or the reversal of a motion. With certain types of theme, iterative derivation is marked also by a change in classifier (zero to *di$_{1}$-*, *ɬ$_{1}$-* to *ɬdi$_{1}$-*, *l$_{1}$-* to *ldi$_{1}$-*): *yehnaʔwindiya* 'he went back inside' (< A-*ya·W/ya·* '(one person) goes somewhere'), *naʔWiwiɬditehɬ* 'he was taking me along back' (< *wi$_{3}$-ɬ$_{1}$-te·ɬ* 'move (one person) along' [progressive neuter]).

5.10. *Adverbial or Thematic*

Preceding all other verb prefixes is a class (position 10) made up of approximately 30 adverbial derivational prefixes and a somewhat smaller number of thematic prefixes. A theme with a thematic prefix in position 10 (e.g., *če·$_{10}$-sid* 'awaken', *sah$_{10}$-din?* '[several] go off together') cannot ordinarily take an adverbial prefix in position 10.

Some position 10 prefixes (both adverbial and thematic) require object inflection, the same inflectional pattern used to mark the possessor of a noun: O-*wa·$_{10}$-* 'through (something)', O-*no·$_{10}$-* 'penetrating into (something)'; O-*čo·$_{10}$-* in the theme O-*čo·$_{10}$-ne·/ni?* 'help (someone)'. (Here, and throughout, O- indicates that an object marker is required.)

A number of the derivational prefixes of position 10 occur only in combination with a prefix of position 5. In these cases the combination of prefixes is the derivational morpheme: *na·$_{10}$-ni$_{5}$-* 'across the river', and *de·$_{10}$-di$_{5}$-* 'into the fire'.

Prefixes of position 10, both adverbial and thematic, are sometimes more complex than a single syllable. Beside the analyzable complexity of prefixes with object inflection, there is the unanalyzable complexity of such adverbial prefixes as *žiwa·$_{10}$-* '(splitting) apart, open' and *xiʔe·$_{10}$-* 'away, out of sight, passing into the distance' and of such thematic prefixes as those in the themes *k'a·da$_{10}$-ne·/ni?* 'gather acorns' and *k'iɬžixa·$_{10}$-ʔaW/ʔa·n* 'fight'.

Two phonetic adjustments involving prefixes of position 10 are to be noted:

(1) After a prefix of position 10 ending in *h* (e.g., *yih-* 'into the house') certain mode markers add the "peg syllable" *ʔi-*. In this position the final *h* of the position 10 prefix is lost: *yeʔiŋyahW* 'go in!' (< *yih$_{10}$-ʔi-n$_{2}$-ya·W*).

(2) A prefix of position 10 ending in *n* or *y* has the *n* or *y* placed after the iterative marker (*na·$_{9}$-*) or the plural marker (*ya·$_{8}$-*) if either or both of these should occur in the form: *niyaŋʔisdehƛ* 'they all started to

dance' (< nin_{10}-ya_8-$\check{c}i_7$-s_3-$de\cdot\lambda$; note that $\check{c}i_7$- must be reduced to ʔ- [section 5.7.] before the n of nin_{10}- is shifted to precede it).

5.11. SEMITRANSITIVE

Some verb themes are semitransitive. They have the grammatical properties of transitive themes, but instead of being marked for object with a simple marker in position 7 they include a thematic prefix, -$o\cdot$-, in position 10, before which come not only the object markers but nearly all the third-person subject markers of position 7: $no\cdot ya\cdot dil\check{c}id$ 'we all know you' (< ni_7-$o\cdot$-ya_8-di_2-l_1-$\check{c}id$) and $\check{c}iWo\cdot diwi\mathit{ł}yehW$ 'he whistled at me' (< $\check{c}i$-Wi_7-$o\cdot$-di_6-wi_3-$\mathit{ł}_1$-$ye\cdot W$). There is one exception to this general rule: when the object marker is k^yi- 'third-person specific' or k^yidi_7- 'passive', the third-person human subject (basically $\check{c}i_7$-) is marked by ʔ- and this marker occurs after -$o\cdot$-: $k^yoʔdiwi\mathit{ł}yehW$ 'he whistled at something' (< k^yi_7-$o\cdot$-$ʔ_7$-di_6-wi_3-$\mathit{ł}_1$-$ye\cdot W$).

5.12. STEM

All verb forms have a stem, which is always the last morpheme in the form. (The enclitic particles, such as =$te\cdot$ 'future tense', that can follow stems are to be considered separate words.) A verb theme inflected for mode often has different stem variants with different modes. In nearly all instances these variants are phonetically related and, to a considerable extent, predictable. The unpredictable stem variants are those associated with the imperfective and perfective modes. If a theme distinguishes imperfective and perfective stem variants, this information must be supplied in the dictionary entry: -$\mathit{ł}_1$-$\check{c}^we\cdot$/$\check{c}^win^{ʔ}$ 'make' and -$ʔat$/$ʔa\cdot\lambda$ 'chew' (the imperfective variant is given first). The stem variants used with the other four modes can be predicted from the imperfective variant as follows.

The customary stem variant is identical with the imperfective variant unless that ends in n or a vowel, in which case ʔ is added and a long stem vowel is replaced by its short counterpart. -$\mathit{ł}_1$-$\check{c}^we\cdot$/$\check{c}^win^{ʔ}$ has -$\check{c}^wi^{ʔ}$ in customary forms; -$wa\cdot n$ 'kill (several)' has -$wan^{ʔ}$.

The optative stem variant is identical with the customary variant.

The potential stem variant is the customary stem variant plus -ni: -$\mathit{ł}_1$-$\check{c}^we\cdot$/$\check{c}^win^{ʔ}$ has -$\check{c}^wi^{ʔ}ni$ in potential forms; -wiW/$we\cdot n$ has -$wiWni$.

The progressive stem variant is formed by adding -$i\mathit{ł}$ to the imperfective variant, except that: (1) only -$\mathit{ł}$ is added if the imperfective stem ends in a vowel; (2) -$ʔi\mathit{ł}$ is added if the imperfective stem ends in n; (3) if the imperfective stem has the form $CV\cdot h$ or CVh the progressive stem is $CV\cdot\mathit{t}$; (4) if the imperfective stem ends in d, d is replaced by t to make the progressive stem. For example, -$lo\cdot s$ 'lead, pull (with a rope)' has -$lo\cdot si\mathit{ł}$ in progressive forms, -$\mathit{ł}_1$-$\check{c}^we\cdot$/$\check{c}^win^{ʔ}$ has -$\check{c}^we\cdot\mathit{t}$, -$yan$/$yan^{ʔ}$ 'eat' has -$yan\cdot i\mathit{ł}$, -$\mathit{ł}_1$-tah 'move (something coiled or wrapped)' has -$ta\cdot\mathit{ł}$, and -$\mathit{ł}_1$-$na\cdot d$/$na\cdot\dot{t}$ 'lick' has -$na\cdot\mathit{ł}$.

The following examples will give an indication of the typical range of stem variation, as well as of the operation of the principles of stem formation described above:

(1) $ʔi\mathit{ł}g^yahs$ 'snap (the stick, twig)!' (imperfective); $siht g^yahs$ 'I have snapped it' (perfective); $ʔeʔiWg^ya\cdot s$ 'I am (the one who is) always snapping it' (customary, here in a noun phrase formed with -i, a common occurrence of a customary form); $\check{c}oht g^yahs$ 'let him snap it!' (optative); $ʔini\mathit{ł}dig^yahsn$ '(Look out!) You might snap it!' (potential); $\check{c}iwi\mathit{ł}g^ya\cdot si\mathit{ł}$ 'he keeps on snapping it' (progressive). Theme: -$\mathit{ł}_1$-$g^ya\cdot s$.

(2) $\check{c}i\eta Weh$ 'spit it out!' (imperfective); $\check{c}e\cdot ne\cdot We^{ʔ}\dot{q}$ 'I spat it out' (perfective); $\check{c}e\cdot ʔiWWeh$ 'I always spit it out' (customary); $\check{c}e\cdot\check{c}o\cdot Weh$ 'let him spit it out!' (optative); $\check{c}e\cdot\check{c}o\cdot Wehn$ '(Look out!) He might spit it out!' (potential); $\check{c}eʔiWe\cdot l$ 'he (is the one who) keeps on spitting' (progressive, here in a noun phrase). Theme: -Wih/$We\cdot\dot{q}$.

(3) $naWxa\cdot$ 'I'm carrying (a basketful of something) around' (imperfective); $na\cdot se\cdot xa^{ʔ}$ 'I have carried it around' (perfective); $na\cdot ʔiWxa\cdot$=$neʔin$ 'I used to carry it around' (customary, with the completed-past tense enclitic =$niʔini$), $na\cdot\check{c}o\cdot xa^{ʔ}$ 'let him carry it around' (optative); $na\cdot\check{c}o\cdot xa^{ʔ}n$ '(look out!) he might carry it around!' (potential); $naʔwixah\mathit{ł}$ 'he keeps on carrying it around' (progressive). Theme: $na\cdot_{10}$-$xa\cdot$/$xa^{ʔ}$.

(4) $Wiwa\eta xahW$ 'give (the basketful of something) to me!' (imperfective); $niwa\cdot ne\cdot xa\eta$ 'I've given it to you' (perfective); $xowa\cdot ʔaWxa\cdot W$ 'I'm (the one who is) always giving it to you' (customary, in a noun phrase); $Wiwa\cdot\check{c}o\cdot xahW$ 'let him give it to me!' (optative); $niwa\cdot Wdixah Wn$ '(Look out!) I might give it to you!' (potential); $niwa^{ʔ}wixa\cdot Wi\mathit{ł}$ 'he keeps on giving it to you' (progressive). Theme: -$xa\cdot W$/$xa\cdot n$.

(5) $ʔiW\check{c}^we\cdot$ 'I'm making it' (imperfective); $seht\check{c}^wi^{ʔ}$ 'I have made it' (perfective); $ʔeʔiW\check{c}^we^{ʔ}$ 'I always make it' (customary); $\check{c}oht\check{c}^we^{ʔ}$ 'let him make it!' (optative); $ʔiniWdi\check{c}^we^{ʔ}n$ '(Look out!) I might make it!' (potential); $wiW\check{c}^weh\mathit{ł}$ 'I keep on making it' (progressive). Theme: -$\mathit{ł}_1$-$\check{c}^we\cdot$/$\check{c}^win^{ʔ}$.

6. VERBS: INFLECTION

Hupa verbs can be inflected for three categories: subject, object, and mode. Verb themes may require all, some, or none of these, or in some cases may require only the partial paradigm of a category. The possibilities are:

Subject inflection: A personal theme can be inflected for all subjects; an impersonal theme cannot be inflected for subject. A singular theme cannot be inflected for plural subjects; a plural theme cannot be inflected for singular subjects.

Object inflection: A transitive theme can be inflected for all objects; an intransitive theme cannot be inflected for object. Semitransitive themes are transitive themes requiring a special form of inflection.

Modal inflection: An active theme can be inflected for all modes; a neuter theme cannot be inflected for mode.

6.1. PERSONAL THEMES

The majority of verb themes are personal and designate activities performed by people.

Personal verb themes are inflected for all persons, both singular and plural, and for all the varieties of third person. First- and second-person subjects are marked by prefixes of position 2 (W_2- 'first-person singular', n_2- 'second-person singular', di_2- 'first-person plural', oh_2- 'second-person plural'). Third-person subjects are marked by prefixes of position 7 (yi_7- 'third-person general', $\check{c}i_7$- 'third-person human', xo_7- 'third-person place', $k^{y}i_7$- 'third-person specific').

6.2. IMPERSONAL THEMES

Some verb themes are impersonal and designate an activity, state, or quality typical of a nonhuman entity. Impersonal themes always imply a third-person subject. In some themes a particular third-person subject is always marked, in others no subject marker occurs; but in either case, no variation in subject inflection is possible.

Impersonal themes requiring the constant marking of a particular third-person subject include:

(1) Themes with constant $k^{y}i_7$- 'third-person specific', such as $k^{y}i_7$-mo·W 'a blister forms' and $k^{y}i_7$-di_1-mad 'water boils'. A large number of such themes refer to noises: $k^{y}i_7$-sa·y 'something makes a rattling noise, there is rattling'; $k^{y}i_7$-$k^{y}e·\hat{t}$ 'there is creaking'.

(2) Themes with constant yi_7- 'third-person general', designating the movement of certain natural phenomena: yi_7-$\hat{t}_1$-xa·/xa·n 'dawn comes', yi_7-$\acute{c}an^?$ 'sound travels, there is a noise heard from somewhere', yi_7-$\hat{t}_1$-$k^{y}id$ 'smoke, clouds move'.

(3) Themes with constant xo_7- 'third-person place', again designating changes in nature, but with emphasis on whole situations: $\check{c}^wa·_{10}$-xo_7-$\hat{t}_1$-wiɬ/we·$\overset{.}{\lambda}$ 'night falls, darkness comes'; xo_7-$\hat{t}_1$-We·n/Win$^?$ 'snow melts, there is a thaw'.

Impersonal themes with no subject marker include:

(1) A few noun themes that can also occur as verb themes, such as -ɬo$^?$ 'laughter' or dah_{10}-to·$^?$ 'dew'. (Compare ɬo$^?$ Wiɬk^{y}id 'I smile' < 'laughter catches.me' and Wa· winɬo$^?$ 'I laughed' < 'for.me laughter.occurred'.)

(2) Stative neuter themes referring to inanimate entities: s_3-$^?a·n$ '(a single object) lies'; s_3-ta·n '(a sticklike object) lies'.

(3) A number of themes referring to qualities or activities appropriate only to nonhumans or physical objects: di_6-$\check{c}^wiɬ$ 'be sharp (as a knife)'; -$\hat{t}_1$-$di\overset{.}{\lambda}$ 'quake (as the ground in an earthquake)'.

It should be noted that "ungrammatical" use of subject inflection with impersonal themes is possible in expressive language. Highly colorful, even poetic, metaphors are possible: $^?$into· 'you (being fluid like water) move, slosh', $\check{c}iɬdi\overset{.}{\lambda}$ 'he (being solid like ground) quakes'. The stative neuter theme s_3-xa·n '(a filled container) lies' is used with subject inflection as a vulgarism: $\check{c}isxa\eta$ 'she (containerlike) lies (i.e., submitting to sexual intercourse)'.

6.3. SINGULAR AND PLURAL THEMES

A few verb themes are semantically restricted to only singular or only plural subject inflection. A singular theme cannot be inflected for first- or second-person plural subjects, and third-person subjects are always interpreted as singular: $nina_{10}$-di_1-$\dot{g}i^?$ '(one person) gets up'; s_3-te·n '(one person) lies'. A plural theme cannot be inflected for first- or second-person singular subjects, and third-person subjects are always interpreted as plural: -di_1-$g^{y}id$ '(several) run in a herd, stampede'; s_3-te·č '(several persons) lie'.

6.4. TRANSITIVE THEMES

Transitive themes designate actions that reach a specific goal, designated by markers of the object category.

The object classes, and their markers, are as follows: First- and second-person objects (Wi_7- 'first-person singular', ni_7- 'second-person singular', noh_7- 'first- or second-person plural'). Third-person objects (zero marker for 'third-person general', xo_7- 'third-person human', xo_7- 'third-person place', $k^{y}i_7$- 'third-person specific'). Relational objects ($^?a·_{10}$-di_7- 'reflective', $nɬi_7$- 'reciprocal', $k^{y}idi_7$- 'passive').

6.5. INTRANSITIVE THEMES

Intransitive themes refer to actions that have no goal or whose goal is one particular object. In the second case the theme requires a constant third-person specific object marker ($k^{y}i_7$-): $k^{y}i_7$-$\mathring{\lambda}o·/\lambda on^?$ 'weave (a basket)'; $k^{y}i_7$-liW/la· 'move (one's hand)'. Intransitive themes cannot be inflected for object.

6.6. SEMITRANSITIVE THEMES

Semitransitive themes are characterized by the prefix -o·-, before which occur the subject and object prefixes of position 7 (see section 5.11. for the morphological details). Otherwise, semitransitive themes are transitive themes, capable of being inflected for all types of object. The difference in meaning between transitive and semitransitive formations (which sometimes both occur with the same stem) appears to involve the degree of completion of the action described. In most transitive forms the action is indicated as being carried through to a goal (the direct object); in semitransitive forms there is an implication that the goal, while being aimed at or proceeded toward, is not quite reached. Note the parallel themes with the stems -$^?i\mathrecheck{з}$, -taɬ/ta·$\overset{.}{\lambda}$, and -$\check{c}^wid$:

-$^?i\check{з}$ 'hit' (transitive)

-o·-$^?i\check{з}$ 'shoot at, hit at (and perhaps miss)' (semitransitive)

-$\hat{t}_1$-taɬ/ta·$\overset{.}{\lambda}$ 'kick, hit by kicking' (transitive)

-o·-ł₁-tał/ta·ƛ 'kick at, aim at with one's foot' (semi-transitive)

-ł₁-čʷid 'push, move with one's hand' (transitive)

-o·-ł₁-čʷid 'reach for, point at' (semitransitive)

6.7. ACTIVE THEMES

An active theme is inflected for mode and designates an action, process, or motion that can be viewed from the various points of view designated by the six types of mode: imperfective (an ongoing or otherwise unspecified activity), perfective (the beginning or end of an activity, or an activity seen as an event in the past or future), progressive (a continuous or repeated activity), customary (a habitual activity, one characteristic of the person performing it), optative (an activity the speaker feels the subject of the verb should perform), and potential (an activity the speaker feels will likely occur—usually spoken with a note of warning). Mode inflection is marked by prefixes in position 3 and (to some extent) by changes in stem form. The mode prefixes are: zero marker for 'imperfective'; win₃-, nin₃-, s₃-, or we·s₃- 'perfective'; wi₃- 'progressive'; ʔi₃- 'customary'; o·₃- 'optative'; ni₃- 'potential' (5.3.).

Optative inflection is restricted to forms with third-person subjects (including impersonal verbs).

All potential forms are marked by the potential stem variant, but only in forms inflected for first- or second-person subjects is the potential mode prefix ni₃- used. In these forms there is also a change in classifier (position 1): zero is changed to di₁-, ł₁- to łdi₁-, and l₁- to ldi₁-. In forms inflected for third-person subject, potential mode is marked by the optative mode prefix (o·₃-) and no change takes place in the classifier.

The choice among the four perfective mode markers (win₃-, nin₃-, s₃-, and we·s₃-) is determined by the theme or its adverbial modification.

6.8. NEUTER THEMES

A neuter theme refers to an action, process, or motion seen in only one modal perspective. Every neuter theme requires a constant mode marker. Neuter themes fall into five types according to their constant mode markers:

(1) Imperfective neuter themes (with zero marker in position 3), designating qualities: li₆-xan 'be sweet, good-tasting'; ni₆-kʾa·h 'be big'.

(2) and (3) nin-perfective and win-perfective neuter themes (with nin₃- or win₃-), referring to extension: nin₃-ʔa· '(a single object) extends along', A-win₃-lin '(a stream) flows (somewhere)'.

(4) s-perfective neuter themes (with s₃-), referring to motionless states: s₃-te·n '(one person) (lies)'; s₃-l₁-q̇a·s '(several) lie thrown in a heap'.

(5) Progressive neuter themes (with wi₃-), referring to continuous states of activity: wi₃-l₁-da·ł '(one) keeps on running'.

7. VERBS: DERIVATION

The meaning of a verb theme may be changed or added to by several derivational processes:

(1) The theme itself may be altered in its inflectional requirements through processes of theme derivation.

(2) The inflected theme may be modified by one or a combination of adverbial prefixes.

(3) The action of the inflected theme may be marked as distributive, iterative, or plural by markers of these categories.

7.1. THEME SYSTEMS

Every Hupa verb theme belongs to one of four theme systems—description, motion, extension, or action—and is either a primary theme in one of these systems or a derived theme (Golla 1970:156-208; Kari 1979). If derived, it is the result of the application to a primary theme of one or more of the derivational processes described in section 7.2.

7.1.1.

Primary description themes are always imperfective neuter intransitive with the general meaning 'something manifests a quality' and are formally characterized by having a thematic prefix in position 6. Examples are łi₆-Win 'be black' and di₆-ʒid 'be short'.

7.1.2.

There are four types of primary motion themes: directional themes, nondirectional themes, progressive themes, and stative themes.

Primary directional motion themes are active, either transitive or intransitive, have the general meaning 'move somewhere', and must always have an adverbial modifier indicating the direction of movement (symbolized by A-, see section 7.3.). Examples are A-la·d 'float, drift (somewhere)' (active intransitive), and A-tiW/ta·n 'move (a sticklike object) (somewhere)' (active transitive).

Primary nondirectional motion themes are active, either transitive or intransitive, have the general meaning 'move about, in no particular direction', and must always have the nondirectional adverbial modifier na·₁₀- (s-pf.). Examples are: na·₁₀-dił/de·ƛ '(several) go about' (active intransitive) and na·₁₀-ʔa·/ʔaʔ 'move (one object) about' (active transitive).

Primary progressive motion themes are progressive neuter, either transitive or intransitive, have the general meaning 'move along continuously', and have the constant progressive mode marker wi₃-. Examples are: wi₃-l₁-da·ł '(one) keeps on running' (neuter intransitive), and wi₃-leł 'move (several objects or a rope) along continuously' (neuter transitive).

Primary stative motion themes are perfective neuter intransitive, have the general meaning 'lie motionless', and have the constant mode marker s₃-. Examples are: s₃-ʔa· '(a single object) lies motionless' and s₃-te·n '(one person) lies motionless, is lying down'.

A small set of primary intransitive and transitive directional motion themes, referring to the motion of specific categories of objects, have formal and semantic links to specific primary nondirectional motion themes, primary progressive motion themes, and (in the case of the transitives) primary stative motion themes. These theme sets are commonly referred to in Athapaskan grammar as classificatory verbs. In Hupa, there are 13 full sets of classificatory themes:

(1) one object (intransitive) (A-$ya\cdot$W/$ya\cdot$, na_{10}-$ya\cdot$/$ya\cdot$$\textglotstop$, wi_3-$ya\cdot\textbarl$)

(2) one object (transitive) (A-$\textglotstop aW$/$\textglotstop a\cdot n$, na_{10}-$\textglotstop a\cdot\textbarl$/$\textglotstop a\textglotstop$, wi_3-$\textglotstop a\textbarl$, s_3-$\textglotstop a\cdot n$)

(3) one person (transitive) (A-$\textbarl_1$-tiW/$te\cdot n$, na_{10}-$\textbarl_1$-$te\cdot$/$te\textglotstop$, wi_3-$\textbarl_1$-$te\cdot\textbarl$, s_3-$te\cdot n$ and s_3-$\textbarl_1$-$te\cdot n$)

(4) several objects, people (intransitive) (A-$di\textbarl$/$de\cdot\grave{\textbarl}$, na_{10}-$di\textbarl$/$de\cdot\grave{\textbarl}$, wi_3-$di\textbarl$)

(5) several animals (intransitive) (A-$\textglotstop aW$/$\textglotstop a\cdot\check{c}$, na_{10}-$\textglotstop aW$/$\textglotstop a\cdot\check{c}$, wi_3-$\textglotstop aWi\textbarl$)

(6) several objects or a rope (transitive) (A-liW/$la\cdot$, na_{10}-$le\cdot$/$le\textglotstop$, wi_3-$le\cdot\textbarl$, s_3-$la\cdot$)

(7) a load, pack (transitive) (A-wiW/$we\cdot n$, na_{10}-$we\cdot$/$we\textglotstop$, wi_3-$we\cdot\textbarl$, s_3-$we\cdot n$)

(8) a floating mass (intransitive) (A-xiW/$xe\cdot n$, na_{10}-$xe\cdot$/$xe\textglotstop$, wi_3-$xi\textbarl$)

(9) a filled receptacle (e.g., basket) (transitive) (A-$xa\cdot W$/$xa\cdot n$, na_{10}-$xa\cdot$/$xa\textglotstop$, wi_3-$xa\cdot\textbarl$, s_3-$xa\cdot n$)

(10) a stick or canoe (transitive) (A-tiW/$ta\cdot n$, na_{10}-tin/$tin\textglotstop$, wi_3-$ti\textbarl$, s_3-$ta\cdot n$)

(11) a fabric (transitive) (A-$\textbarl_1$-$k^y o\cdot s$, na_{10}-$\textbarl_1$-$k^y o\cdot s$, wi_3-$\textbarl_1$-$k^y o\cdot si\textbarl$, s_3-$\textbarl_1$-$k^y o\cdot s$)

(12) a granular mass, pile (transitive) (A-$\check{z}i\check{z}$, na_{10}-$\check{z}i\check{z}$, wi_3-$\check{z}i\check{z}i\textbarl$, s_3-$\check{z}i\check{z}$)

(13) a doughy mass (transitive) (A-$\textbarl ih$/$\textbarl i\dot{q}$, na_{10}-$\textbarl ih$/$\textbarl i\dot{q}$, wi_3-$\textbarl e\cdot\textbarl$, s_3-$\textbarl i\dot{q}$).

7.1.3.

Primary extension themes are perfective neuter intransitive, have the general meaning 'extend (in some direction)', and must always have an adverbial modifier indicating the direction of extension (symbolized by A-). The constant mode marker of primary extension themes varies with the adverbial modifier. Examples are: A-$\textglotstop a\cdot$ '(a single object) extends (somewhere)' and A-$\textbarl in$ '(a steam) flows (somewhere)'.

7.1.4.

Primary action themes are active, either transitive or intransitive, and have the general meaning 'perform an action'. Transitive action themes typically specify actions having to do with the preparation of things and physical intervention, for example: -$\textbarl_1$-$\check{c}^w e\cdot$/$\check{c}^w in\textglotstop$ 'make, create (something)', or si_6-$\textbarl_1$-$we\cdot$/$we\cdot n$ 'kill (something)'. Intransitive action themes typically specify bodily or natural activities that do not imply directional motion, for example: ti_5-$\check{c}id$ 'grow weak, tired' or -l_1-$di\grave{\textbarl}$ '(earth) shakes, quakes'.

7.2. THEME DERIVATION

Several processes of theme derivation can operate on primary themes in all four theme systems. In addition, a derived theme can be further derived. Thus, from a neuter intransitive theme that is a primary theme of the descriptive system, a derived active intransitive with "transitional" meaning can be derived. From this secondary active intransitive can be derived an active transitive theme with "causative" meaning. From this active transitive a derived neuter "passive" theme may be derived. The processes of theme derivation are intricate and in many instances lexicalized, and a comprehensive treatment is not possible here. The most commonly occurring theme derivations are the following:

(1) From all imperfective and perfective neuter themes a secondary active ("transitional") theme can be derived with the general meaning 'something gets to be (or stops being) in some state'. The transitional theme usually has the form of the primary neuter theme, lacking only a thematically specified mode marker. In the case of imperfective neuters with thematic prefixes in position 6, some of these are dropped in transitionals (ti_6-, si_6-, etc.) but others (ni_6-, di_6-, etc.) are retained. If the stem of the neuter theme ends in a vowel, n, or y, the transitional stem adds -$\textglotstop$, while in a very few instances an irregular change occurs. Examples of transitional formations are:

$\textbarl i_6$-coh 'be blue, green' (imperfective neuter) > -coh 'become blue, green' (transitional)

A-win_3-$\textglotstop a\cdot$ '(one thing) extends (somewhere)' (win- perfective neuter) > A-$\textglotstop a\textglotstop$ '(one thing) comes to extend (somewhere)' (transitional)

s_3-$\textglotstop a\cdot n$ '(one object) lies' (s-perfective neuter) > -$\textglotstop a\textglotstop$ '(one object) comes to be lying' (transitional, with irregular stem change).

(2) From most active transitive themes a secondary neuter transitive ("passive") theme and a secondary active intransitive ("reflexive") theme can be formed.

Passives have the general meaning 'something has been acted upon' and are impersonal (cannot be inflected for subject) and progressive neuter (require the constant mode marker wi_3-). They are formed from the primary transitive theme by a change in classifier (zero to di_1-, $\textbarl_1$- to l_1-). The stem of the passive theme is the perfective variant of the primary theme. Examples of passive formation are:

A-$\textbarl_1$-tiW/$te\cdot n$ 'move (one person) (somewhere)' (active transitive) > A-wi_3-l_1-$te\cdot n$ '(one person) has been moved (somewhere)' (passive)

-$\textbarl_1$-$ta\check{c}$ 'tattoo' (active transitive) > wi_3-l_1-$ta\check{c}$ '(something) has been tattooed' (passive).

Reflexives have the general meaning 'something acts on itself' and are formed by changing the classifier (from zero or $\textbarl_1$- to di_1-). The reflexive stem is the imperfective variant of the stem of the primary theme. In a number of instances reflexive derivations are used with idiomatic meaning. Examples of reflexive formation are:

-*wa·n* 'kill (several), break (a complex thing)' (active transitive) > -*di₁-wa·n* '(a complex thing) breaks' (e.g., an automobile breaks down) (reflexive)

A-*mił/me·ƛ* 'throw (several things) (somewhere)' (active transitive) > A-*di₁-mił* '(several things) throw themselves, fall' (reflexive)

A-*ł₁-ġe·d* 'shove (a stick) (somewhere)' (active transitive) > A-*di₁-ġe·d* '(a stick) shoves itself, propels itself; a canoe moves on the water' (reflexive).

(3) From an active intransitive theme that does not refer to directional motion a secondary active transitive ("causative") theme can be formed. Causatives may also be formed from intransitive transitionals and from reflexives. The basic meaning of a causative is 'something causes something to perform an action'. Causatives are formed by changing the classifier of the primary theme (from zero or *l₁*- to *ł₁*-, from *di₁*- to *łdi₁*-). Examples of causative formation are:

-*ya·d* 'get hurt, wounded' (active intransitive) > -*ł₁-ya·d* 'cause (someone) to get hurt, wounded' (causative)

-*di₁-ġoł* 'tumble, squirm' (active intransitive) > -*łdi₁-ġoł* 'cause (someone) to tumble, squirm' (causative)

A-*ʔaʔ* '(one thing) comes to extend (somewhere)' (transitional) > A-*ł₁-ʔaʔ* 'cause (one thing) to extend (somewhere)' (causative).

7.3. ADVERBIAL DERIVATION

Many themes have adverbially modified variants formed with the adverbial prefixes of positions 5 and 10 (5.5. and 5.10.). Some themes occur only with such modification (marked with A-). The meaning added to a theme by adverbial modification varies widely, ranging from the nearly pure relational (O-*e·₁₀*- 'to [something]') to the quite specific (*če·₁₀*- 'out of the house; down to the river'). To some extent the meaning of an adverbial modifier changes with the meaning of the theme it is attached to. Thus, O-*e·₁₀*- with themes referring to directional motion (such as A-*l₁-da·W* 'run [somewhere]') designates motion 'to something' in the sense of 'up to and coming to a halt resting against (it)', while with an imperfective neuter theme it specifies that the quality referred to by the theme is 'compared to' or 'like' something else. It is a fair generalization that adverbial modifiers are fundamentally relational in meaning. Many require a secondary object inflection.

In forming theme variants, adverbial prefixes function in one of two ways:

(1) as single modifying prefixes, either in position 5 or in position 10 (*ni₅*- 'arriving', *tih₁₀*- 'into the water')

(2) as a combination of prefixes, one in each position,

functioning as a single modifier (*de·₁₀-di₅*- 'into the fire', O-*na·₁₀-si₅*- 'in a circle around [something]'). No Hupa verb occurs with more than one adverbial modifier.

In an active verb with adverbial modification, the choice of the perfective mode marker (*win₃*-, *nin₃*-, *s₃*-)[‡] is determined by the modifier. All active verbs modified by *yih₁₀*- 'into the house, enclosure', for example, are inflected for perfective mode with *win₃*-, and all those modified by *ya·₁₀*- 'into bits, pieces' are inflected for perfective mode with *s₃*-. In a few cases the same prefix or prefix combination has different meanings correlated with different perfective marker specifications: *na·₁₀-ni₅*- (*nin*-pf.) 'across the river', but *na·₁₀-ni₅*- (*win*-pf.) 'with violent force.'

Adverbial modifiers may be divided into four groups:

(1) Directional and locational modifiers, used with active verbs of directional motion and with *win*-perfective neuters (both of these theme types occur only with adverbial modification), as well as with other themes.

(2) Nondirectional modifiers, used with a small number of themes referring to specific actions (but never with verbs of directional motion or *win*-perfective neuters).

(3) The modifiers *ʔa·₁₀*- 'in such a way' and O-*e·₁₀*- 'compared to (something)' used with imperfective neuter themes.

(4) The modifier *na·₁₀*- (*s*-pf.) used only with certain themes referring to continuous, nondirectional motion. In general, every directional motion theme has a parallel "continuative" theme: A-*ya·W/ya·* '(one person) goes (somewhere)' (directional motion), (*na·₁₀*-)*ya·/yaʔ* '(one person) goes about' (continuative).

7.4. DIRECTIONAL MODIFIERS

O-*e·₁₀*- (*nin*-pf.) 'up to (something), up against (something) in a position of rest'.

O-*e·₁₀*- (*win*-pf.) 'touching (something), moving up against (something)'.

O-*e·₁₀-si₅*- (*s*-pf.) 'up along (something)'. The reference is often to a mountain.

yih₁₀- (*win*-pf.) 'into the house, into an enclosure or container'.

ya·₁₀- (*win*-pf.) 'up into the air, skyward'.

ni₅- (*nin*-pf.) 'approaching, arriving'.

nin₁₀-si₅- (*s*-pf.) '(jumping) up and down'.

nina·₁₀- (*s*-pf.) 'rising up from lying down'.

na·₁₀- (*s*-pf.) 'turning over, rotating, going back.'

na·₁₀- (*win*-pf.) 'down from vertically above, down from being suspended'.

[‡]In the citation of adverbial modifiers, or of themes (modified or otherwise) that require inflection with a specific mode marker, the abbreviations *win*-pf., *nin*-pf., and *s*-pf. will be used for *win₃*-, *nin₃*-, and *s₃*- requirements, respectively. *we·s₃*- marks perfective mode only in a few classes of derived themes.

O-*na·₁₀-si·₅*- (*s*-pf.) 'around (something) in a circle'.

na·₁₀-ni₅- (*nin*-pf.) 'across the river'.

O-*no·₁₀*- (*win*-pf.) 'penetrating into (something)'.

no·₁₀- (*nin*-pf.) 'to a certain point, to completion; (put) down; (go) so far'.

di₅- (*win*-pf.) 'starting off; (pick) up'.

de·₁₀-di₅- (*win*.pf.) 'into the fire'.

O-*de·₁₀*- (*win*-pf.) 'closely past (something), touching'.

O-*da·₁₀*- (*nin*-pf.) 'to the door, entrance to (something)'.

dah₁₀-di₅- (*win*-pf.) 'drawing away; (move) away slowly and stealthily'.

ti₅- (*s*-pf.) 'starting off, moving along'.

tin₁₀- (*win*-pf.) 'lost, astray'.

tih₁₀- (*win*-pf.) 'into the water (to stay)'.

ta·₁₀- (*win*-pf.) 'into the water (and out again), moving through the water'.

ta·₁₀- (*s*-pf.) 'dispersing, moving away in different directions'.

tah₁₀- (*s*-pf.) 'out of the water, fire; out of an entanglement of any kind'.

tah₁₀-di₅- (*s*-pf.) 'out of the water'.

O-*sa·₁₀*- (*win*-pf.) 'into (someone's) mouth'.

cin₁₀-ti₅- (*s*-pf.) 'off to safety, (run) for one's life'.

O-*wa·₁₀*- (*nin*-pf.) 'through (something); (give) to (someone)'.

O-*way₁₀*- (*win*-pf.) 'missing (something), moving off beyond (something)'.

O-*wan₁₀-di₅*- (*win*-pf.) 'removing (something), getting off from (something)'.

xi·ʔe·₁₀- (*win*-pf.) 'away, out of sight, passing into the distance'.

xa·₁₀- (*win*-pf.) 'up from beneath; out of the ground'.

xa·₁₀-si₅- (*s*-pf.) 'up to the top (of a mountain, the riverbank)'.

xoda·₁₀- (*win*-pf.) 'downhill, downstream'.

xoh₁₀- (*win*-pf.) 'down to the base (of a mountain)'.

ǯe·₁₀- (*win*-pf.) 'splitting apart, moving in opposite directions'.

čʷinʔda·₁₀- (*win*-pf.) 'to ruination'.

če·₁₀- (*nin*-pf.) 'out of the house; out of an enclosure or container; down to the riverbank'.

O-*ḱʸa·₁₀*- (*nin*-pf.) 'separating from (something)'.

7.5. NONDIRECTIONAL MODIFIERS

O-*e·₁₀*- (*s*-pf.) 'firmly attached to (something)'. Found mainly with themes referring to tying or fastening.

ya·₁₀- (*s*-pf.) 'into bits, pieces'. Used with themes that imply cutting, tearing, or similar actions.

ni₅- (*win*-pf.) '(striking) once, suddenly'. Used only with transitive themes that describe striking blows or hurling things forcefully.

na·₁₀-di₅- (*s*-pf.) 'along in a line'. Used with transitive themes referring to cutting, pulling, or pouring.

cih₁₀- (*win*-pf.) 'peeling skin off'. Used with themes

referring to peeling, slipping, tearing, and similar actions.

ǯiwa·₁₀- (*s*-pf.) '(splitting) apart, open'. Used with themes that imply cutting, tearing, or cracking.

ḱʸe·₁₀- (or *q̇e·₁₀*-) (*win*-pf.) '(cutting) off, severing'. Used with transitive verbs of cutting.

7.6. OTHER DERIVATIONS

Themes (with or without adverbial modification) may be marked for the distributive, plural, or iterative categories.

Distributive ('here and there', 'at several times or places') is marked by the prefix *ti₄*-. An active theme marked for distributive action is inflected for perfective mode with *s₃*-, and this requirement takes precedence over the perfective mode marker requirements of an adverbial modifier in the same form. Active themes are not inflected for customary mode when marked for distributive. In forms also marked for plurality by *ya·₈*-, or with themes having inherently plural meaning, the distributive indicates action by the subjects in turn, one after another. Typical distributive forms are: *naʔditiɬwaɬ* 'he pours it into several containers' (< -*ɬ₁-waɬ/wa·ƛ* 'throw, pour') and *xa·yaʔsitiwiW* 'each one carries (a rock) up the hill' (< -*wiW/we·n* 'carry a pack, burden').

Plurality of subject or object is indicated or emphasized by the marker *ya·₈*-.

Iterative action ('again' or 'back') is marked by the prefix *na·₉*- and, with some themes, a change in classifier. Themes requiring a change in classifier (zero to *di₁*-, *ɬ₁*- to *ɬdi₁*-, *l₁*- to *ldi₁*-) include intransitive directional-motion themes and progressive neuters. With such themes the meaning of the iterative derivation is basically reversative: '(go and) come back, return'. Typical iterative forms are: *na·ḱʸida·yeʔ* '(the flower) blooms again' (< *ḱʸi₇-da·yiʔ* '(a flower) blooms'); *yehnaʔwindiya·* 'he went back inside the house' (< A-*ya·W/ya·* '(one person) moves (somewhere)', with change of classifier from zero to *di*-, as compared with *yehčiwinya·* 'he went inside the house').

8. NOUNS

There are two kinds of nouns. General nouns name things that are usually unpossessed (such as 'smoke') or can be unpossessed (such as 'house'). General nouns occur both with and without inflection for possessor. Possessed nouns are always inflected for possessor. They either name people or things constantly possessed by, or associated with, someone, such as body parts or kinsmen ('my hand', 'my father'), or else they specify directions, locations, or relations among things ('underneath me', 'concerning it'). In the second case the inflection for possessor is actually, in terms of meaning, a marking of relational object. Possessed nouns with such relational meanings are called locative nouns. Some of the adverbial derivational prefixes in verbs (prefixes of position 10) are closely related in meaning to locative nouns and require possessor (object) inflection.

8.1. POSSESSOR INFLECTION

Nouns are inflected for possessor by a set of nine prefixes. These mark persons or relationships among persons (e.g., reciprocity). First- and second-person plural, and all third-person, inflections can also be marked for (emphatic) plurality by the preceding prefix $ya\cdot$- (see $ya\cdot_8$- 'plural' in verbs, 5.8.).

The possessive prefixes are similar in form (but not identical) to the object markers in verbs. They include: Wi- 'first-person singular', ni- 'second-person singular', noh- 'first- or second-person plural', mi- 'third-person general', $yidi$- 'third-person special animate', xo- 'third-person human', k^yi- 'third-person specific', $\Omega a\cdot di$- 'reflexive', and $nił$- 'reciprocal'.

The general third-person possessor, mi-, is sometimes marked by zero. This is regularly the case when it functions as the object of a locative adverbial prefix with initial w: $wa\Omega xahW$ 'she gives (a spoonful) to it' ($< (mi)$-$wa\cdot_{10}$-$či_7$-$xa\cdot W$), $waywe\cdot ya\cdot$ 'I passed by it' ($< (mi)$-way_{10}-wi_3-$e\cdot_2$-$ya\cdot$).

The third-person special animate marker, $yidi$-, is rarely found, occurring mainly as the object of locative adverbial prefixes. It appears to refer to an animate but nonhuman object. Compare $yide\cdot lwe\Omega\lambda$ 'it camped for the night' ('it' being a mythical being) with $x^we\cdot lwe\Omega\lambda$ 'he camped for the night' (both $< O$-$e\cdot_{10}$-wi_3-l_1-$we\cdot\lambda$ 'night overtook (someone)').

The reflexive possessor, $\Omega a\cdot di$-, is usually translated 'one's own' or (as an object of a locative noun) 'one's self': $\Omega a\cdot dila\Omega$ 'one's own hand', $\Omega a\cdot diq̇id$ 'on top of oneself'.

The reciprocal possessor, $nił$-, is usually translated 'each other's' or 'each other'. Before a noun beginning with a vowel it is reduced to $ł$-, and before a noun beginning with $ł$ it is reduced to $łi$-. Elsewhere, $nił$- is sometimes replaced by $yił$- or $\Omega ił$-. Thus: $łi\Omega$ 'in each other', $łitiŋ$ 'each other's friend, friends to each other', $niłq̇id$ (or $\Omega iłq̇id$) 'on top of each other.'

8.2. GENERAL NOUNS

General nouns range in form from single morphemes to complex phrases. Simple, single-morpheme nouns typically refer to natural phenomena or animals (Ωah 'cloud', $k^yiŋ$ 'stick, tree', $sa\dot c$ 'bear'), although a few are names of large cultural products (Ωehs 'fish dam', tin 'trail'). Some nouns are reminiscent of verb forms but cannot be analyzed. Typical of these are $na\cdot k^yine\cdot$ 'mountain quail', $dina\Omega$ 'milkweed', and $ta\cdot k^yiW$ 'sweathouse'. The bulk of polysyllabic nouns, and probably the majority of all general nouns, are fully analyzable as noun phrases, formed from verbs and sentences by the enclitic phrase marker $=i$. Typical phrase nouns are $k^yiłixan$ 'deer' ($< k^yi_7$-$łi_6$-xan 'something is sweet, good-tasting' + $=i$); $k^yiłna\cdot dił$ 'wolf'

($< k^yi$-$ł$ 'with something' + $na\cdot_{10}$-$(yi_7$-$)dił$ 'they (animals) move about' + $=i$); $misinto\Omega xole\cdot n$ 'silverside salmon' ($< mi$-$sinto\Omega$ 'its grease' + $(yi_7$-$)xo_6$-$le\cdot n$ 'it is plentiful' + $=i$).

When inflected for possessor all general nouns assume a special possessed form, marked principally with the suffix $-i\Omega$ ($-\Omega$ when the noun ends in a vowel, as do all phrase nouns). The reference here is to the basic phonological shape of a noun, not to the form it assumes after the application of phonological rules. The phrase noun is marked by $=i$. Thus the possessed form of $k^yiłixan$ 'deer' is $(xo)k^yiłixan\Omega$ '(his) deer' $< xo$-k^yi-$łi$-xan=i=Ω.

A few other phonetic changes occur, but the only one that is regular and predictable is the replacement of initial $ł$ by l (this change resembles that governed by Rule 4, section 4): $łid$ 'smoke', $Wilide\Omega$ 'my smoke'.

8.3. POSSESSED NOUNS

Possessed nouns ordinarily are single morphemes; however, some are compounds ($xona\cdot łaŋ\Omega$ 'his eyelid' $<$ 'eye'+'leaf') and a few body-part terms, such as $xok^ya\eta\Omega ay$ 'his arm', are based on noun phrases. Possessed nouns are cited with third-person human possessor (xo-), or, where more semantically appropriate, with third-person general possessor (mi-). Note that xo- $> x^w$- before vowels (section 4, Rule 5).

Possessed nouns other than locative nouns fall into three general semantic subclasses, with few exceptions:

(1) Body-part terms. Nearly all names of parts of the human body, as well as parts of animals, fish, and plants, are possessed nouns. Typical are: $xomił$ 'his stomach, belly', $mide\Omega$ 'its horn', $miłaŋ$ 'its leaf', $xoda\cdot si\dot c$ 'his lip' ($<$ 'his mouth-skin'), $x^we\cdot da\Omega ay$ 'his head' ($<$ 'what extends out against him').

(2) Possessions. A few possessed nouns refer to objects or properties an individual possesses: $x^we\cdot y$ 'his belongings', $xo\cdot We\Omega$ 'his name' ($< xo$-$o\cdot Wi\Omega$), $xos\Omega a\cdot n\Omega$ 'his reputation' ($<$ 'his what-lies-there').

(3) Kinship terms. All kinship relationships are expressed by possessed nouns. A few are compounds but most are single morphemes: $x^wa\cdot d$ 'his older sister', $xota\Omega$ 'his father', $xoya\cdot če\Omega$ 'her daughter'.

8.4. LOCATIVE NOUNS

Possessed nouns referring to locations, directions, or relations among things are nearly all single morphemes. Typical are: $x^we\cdot w$ 'underneath him', $xoma\Omega n$ 'opposite him', $xone\cdot ž̇id$ 'in the middle of him', $xowaŋ$ 'concerning him, because of him', $xoq̇eh$ 'according to him, following after him'.

Some locative nouns are used without possessor inflection as enclitic to other nouns: $ninis\Omega a\cdot n$=$ne\cdot ž̇id$ 'middle of the world', $xoŋ\Omega$=$čiŋ\Omega$ 'toward the fire', $nista\cdot n$=$q̇eh$ 'along the log'. Formations with enclitic $=q̇id$ 'on top of' are particularly common: $ce\cdot q̇id$ 'on top of the rock', mis=$q̇id$ 'on top of the riverbank' (a

Hupa village). The locative noun *xoł* 'with him' has the variant =*hił* when enclitic: *xočʷoˑ=hił* 'with his grand-mother'.

Two enclitic locative nouns have taken on more general syntactic functions:

=*tah* 'among' is used with some verb modifiers (section 9.3.) to indicate qualification: *meˑlah=tah* 'just a few' (literally 'some-among'), *doˑ=tah* 'maybe, possibly' (literally 'not-among').

=*hił*, the enclitic form of 'with', is used to conjoin nouns: *xontehłtaw čahli=hił* 'Coyote and Frog'.

9. OTHER WORDS

Besides nouns and verbs, seven other types of word can be distinguished in normal Hupa sentences.

Substitutes are replacements for words and phrases, in part translating the pronouns of English. Sentence modifiers are words that stand in syntactic relationship to whole sentences, expressing the speaker's attitude or serving to connect one sentence with another. Verb modifiers are equivalent to English adverbs, modifying the meaning of verbs with specifications of time, place, manner, and the like. Directionals and numerals are special types of verb modifiers. Word modifiers are enclitic particles indicating tense and similar categories. Phrase markers are proclitic or enclitic particles signaling the beginning or end of noun phrases, adverbial phrases, and locative phrases.

9.1. SUBSTITUTES

There are two kinds of substitute words, independent pronouns (substituting for nouns and noun phrases) and general/interrogative substitutes (substituting for a wider range of words and phrases).

(1) Independent pronouns. These comprise a set of six words particularly resembling the object inflection of verbs or the possessor inflection of nouns: *Weˑ* 'I', *niŋ* 'you', *neheˑ* 'we', *nohn* 'you (pl.)', *xoŋ* 'he, she', *miŋ* 'it' (rare).

(2) General/interrogative substitutes. This is a set of 12 words, in six pairs. Each pair consists of a general substitute (formed with -*Woʔ*) and an interrogative substitute (formed with basic -*di*), substituting for a particular type of word or phrase:

Noun phrase substitute (general)
  dayWoʔ (or *diyWoʔ*) 'something'
  dayd (or *diyd*) 'what?'
Noun phrase substitute (human)
  daŋWoʔ 'someone'
  dand 'who?'
Locative phrase substitute
  daˑyWoʔ 'in some place, at some time'
  daˑyd 'where? when?'
Number substitute
  dantaŋWoʔ 'some number'
  dantand 'how many?'

Extent modifier substitute
  dahaŋWoʔ 'to some extent'
  dahanʔd 'how far? how much?'
Manner modifier substitute
  daxoˑʔ 'in some way'
  daxʷeˑd (or *xʷeˑd*) 'how?'

9.2. SENTENCE MODIFIERS

Sentence modifiers are words whose syntactic function is to modify a sentence as a whole. Two formal subclasses can be distinguished: attitude words, serving to interject the speaker's opinions or attitudes into the sentence (or, in quotations, the attitudes of the purported speaker); and connectives, which serve to introduce or join sentences, particularly in extended narratives.

There are 10 attitude words: *ʔisdoʔ* 'please!', *ʔaŋʔ* 'it is so!', *ʔaŋ* 'is it?' *ʔanaˑnʔ* 'it is not so, it is questionable', *ʔaW* 'I wonder!', *doʔoŋ* 'it is so! really! see!', *xoW* 'I guess, probably, maybe', *čin* 'so they say, I have heard it said', *gʸaʔ* 'lo and behold!', *kʸeh* 'let (such and such happen)!'. Combinations of attitude words are common: *činaˑŋʔ* 'they say it was so' (< *čin* + *ʔaŋʔ*); *gʸaʔaW* 'I wonder what in the world...' (< *gʸaʔ* + *ʔaW*).

Conversational speech tends to be loaded with attitude words. *ʔaŋ* 'is it?' is especially common, being the most frequent way of posing a question in Hupa. Some typical usages are:

deˑd=aˑŋʔ niskʸiŋ ʔaŋʔ ʔaŋ (this.one=it.is.so! fir.tree it.is.so! is.it?) 'Is this a fir tree?'

xoW diyWoʔ yiłkʸid (I.guess something caught.it) 'I guess something caught it' (speaking of a lost chicken)

niłʔiŋ deˑ gʸaʔ (look! here lo.and.behold!) 'Look at this here!'

Connectives are used much more frequently in the recitation of a narrative than they are in casual conversation, indicating that the formal sequencing of events that they describe is largely an artifact of narrative structure. A rough hierarchy of cohesion can be stated: *hiǯid* 'and...' is usually restricted to conjoining sentences that indicate two or more actions performed in close sequence.

xolaʔkʸinʔ čiłkʸid, hiǯid čisġid hay xokʸaˑŋʔay
She caught hold of his wrist and sawed off his arm.

xoq̇eh xodaʔanaˑW, hiǯid naʔameʔ
They follow him down to the river and swim.

hayaˑł or *hayahiǯid* 'and then...' (apparently used interchangeably, in different proportions by different speakers) are the commonest connectives and usually serve to mark the basic sequential units of a narrative.

hayaˑł činindeˑλ hay q̇ančiwiłčʷil. hayaˑł čahl yaʔxowiłdeʔn.

And then the young men arrived. And then they fell in love with Frog.

haya·ł ʔina·ʔasdiġeʔ hayo·w k̓iwaŋxoya·n. hayahiʒid te·na·ʔnilay. hayahiʒid hayo·w k̓iwaŋxoya·n dahʒił=q̓id k̓e·ʔesyay, hiʒid na·na·ʔwilay.

And then that old man got up. And then he built a fire. And then that old man went up on the storage platform and brought some things down.

hayahmił 'and then, thereupon...' (literally 'from there') is used less frequently, and more specifically to indicate a sequence (or repetition) of actions.

haya·ł ʔa·čondehsneʔ, "xʷe·di-gʸaʔaW-ʔaŋ ʔahdiyaw?" hayahmił ʔa·čondehsneʔ, "k̓eh wiWahł!"

And then he thought, "I wonder what it is that did that?" And thereupon he thought, "Let me go and see!"

mine·ʒixomił 'after a (long) while...' marks the beginning of a new episode in a narrative.

xoł na·ʔwiŋyaʔ. mine·ʒixomił xomiʒeʔe·dinʔ ya·xohsleʔ.
She married him. After a while they had children.

hayahdeʔʒ and *hayahdiŋ* (literally 'at that place') are rare in the speech of most modern speakers but are attested in older texts, where they seem to have the force of *haya·ł* or *hayahiʒid*.

9.3. VERB MODIFIERS

Verb modifiers range in formal complexity from single morphemes (*do·* 'not', *xoh* 'vainly, ineffectually') to forms that represent fossilizations of verbs and phrases, particularly locative phrases (*yiwidindeʔ* 'finally, at last', *ciʔehʒidiŋ* 'for a short while'). Verb modifiers typically refer to time (*ʒid* 'just now', *daʔn* 'in the past', *doŋq̓a·* 'beforehand', *sa·ʔa·* 'for a long time', *xiłeʔdaŋʔ* 'in the morning', *wilwiłdiŋ* 'in the evening', etc.), place (*de·* 'here', *hayah* 'there', *yo·w* 'right there (in view)'), extent or frequency (*ʔahłiŋ* 'all, completely', *łah* 'once', *ta·n* 'many; many times', *ceʔehʒidiŋ* 'for a short while, slightly'), and manner (*xoh* 'vainly, ineffectually', *xoʔʒ* 'really, well, in the true manner', *sa·k̓idiŋ* 'suddenly, with surprise'). A few verb modifiers have more abstract meaning: *do·* 'not' (used for general negation), *k̓iye·* 'again' (equivalent to, and often used with or in place of, iterative inflection in the verb).

9.4. DIRECTIONALS

The directional words are special verb modifiers used to define the direction or location of an action in terms of a set of directional coordinates. These coordinates refer to a stream and its direction of flow. The five basic directions are: *yinaġ* 'upstream', *yideʔ* 'downstream', *yidaġ* 'away from the stream, uphill', *yiceʔn* 'toward the stream, downhill', *yima·n* 'across the stream'. Where no other stream is specified by context, the Trinity River in Hoopa Valley is understood, and directions or locations are calculated from the speaker's standpoint. In other, specific, contexts the "stream" can be another river or creek, the ocean (which was traditionally considered a stream circling the world, with an opposite bank), a trail or a modern highway, or a line of any sort to which a direction of flow can be attributed.

A finer set of coordinates is achieved by compounding the basic directional words: *yideʔ* + *yidaġ* 'downstream and uphill'; *yideʔ* + *yima·n* 'downstream on this bank and (then) across the river'. Since the Trinity River flows through Hoopa Valley from the southeast to the northwest, the common Hupa translations for the English cardinal directions are usually as follows (they assume the speaker is on the east bank of the river): *yideʔ* + *yidaġ* 'north', *yinaġi* + *yidaġ* 'east', *yinaġi* + *yiceʔn* 'south', *yideʔ*+*yiceʔn* 'west'.

9.5. NUMERALS

Numerals are special verb modifiers, indicating the number of times an action is performed or the number of instances of an event. The basic count is to 10: *łaʔ* 'one', *nahx* 'two', *ta·q̓* 'three', *diŋk̓ʸ* 'four', *čʷolaʔ* 'five', *xosta·n* 'six', *xohk̓ʸid* 'seven', *k̓e·nim* 'eight', *miq̓osław* 'nine', *minłaŋ* '10'. Higher numbers (except for *dik̓ʸin* '100') are indicated by phrases. The decades ('20', '30', etc.) are formed from *minłaŋ* '10' preceded by a locative phrase (NUMERAL)=*din* '(so many) times' indicating the number of the decade: *nah=diŋ minłaŋ* (two.times 10) '20' (the numeral *nahx* has the special form *nah-* before an enclitic phrase marker); *ta·q̓i=diŋ minłaŋ* (three.times 10) '30'. Numerals within a decade are formed from the number of the decade followed by *mi-wah na·=*(NUMERAL) 'alongside-it again-(so much)': *minłaŋ miwah na·=łaʔ* (10 alongside.it again.one) '11'; *nah=diŋ minłaŋ miwah na·ta·q̓* (20 alongside.it again.three) '23'.

Special noun phrases are formed from numerals with the noun phrase marker =*ni* (9.7.), indicating numbers of people in a group. *łaʔ* 'one' and =*ni* combine as *łiwaŋ*, and *nahx* takes the form *nahni-* before =*ni*: *łiwaŋ* 'one person', *nahni=n* 'two people', *ta·q̓i=n* 'three people', *diŋk̓ʸi=n* 'four people'. (Note the reduction of =*ni* to =*n* by phonological Rule 5.)

9.6. WORD MODIFIERS

Word modifiers are proclitic or enclitic—that is, like prefixes or suffixes, they cannot be spoken independently of the forms to which they are attached. However, unlike prefixes or suffixes, word modifiers can be attached to more than one type of word. From the syntactic point of view they are best considered separate, but dependent, words (similar to English forms such as *the* and *a*). Word modifiers can be grouped into four categories on the basis of meaning: iterative, tense, evidential, and diminutive/augmentative.

There is one iterative proclitic, *na·=*[§]. In verbs, this marker is incorporated into the prefix system (*na·₉-*),

---

[§]When cited separately, proclitic and enclitic forms are given in basic form, before the application of phonological rules.

but it occurs widely elsewhere as a proclitic: *na·=ła?* 'again, once more' (< *ła?* 'one'), *na·=yide?* 'back downstream' (< *yide?* 'downstream'). The name for Hoopa Valley, *na·tinix*[w], is probably analyzable as *na·=tini-xo* (back/reversing trail place) 'where the trail turns, doubles back'. In all occurrences, *na·=* has the general meaning of repetition (of an action) or turning back (of a motion or direction).

There are four tense enclitics: *=te·* 'future', *=te·ł* 'future' (a variant of *=te·*), *=ni?ini* 'past, completed', and *=ni?* 'future obligation'. Although most often found with verbs, tense enclitics occur after many types of words. Examples are:

yisxande? no?k'iŋxa·n na·ntan?=te· (tomorrow the. Acorn.Feast they.will.have.it') 'They will have the Acorn Feast tomorrow.'

hay camehsλo·n me·y=te· (the woman her.future.possessions) 'what is going to belong to the woman'.

do·=tehł (not=it.will.be) 'it will (soon) be over'

wiWxosił=ne?in 'I used to cough at lot'

Wa?ad=ne?in 'my late wife, my former wife'

k'iŋyan=ne? 'you must eat, you will have to eat'

xa? g'a?=ne? 'goodbye!' (< *xa?* 'quickly' + *g'a?* 'lo and behold!' + *=ni?* 'future obligation')

There are two evidential enclitics, indicating the speaker's assessment of the source of his (or the subject of the sentence's) knowledge: *=e·* (or *=e·yi*) 'it is, was evident from seeing', *=čih* 'it is, was evident from hearing (or feeling or tasting)'. Typical usages are:

ġančiwilč[w]*il čisle?n=e·* (a.young.man he.had.become= one.could.see) '(it was evident that) he had become a young man'

me?dildiŋ   na·ya·?andeλ̇=e·y   (at.Matilton they.arrived.back=and.were.seen) 'they (were seen to) arrive back at Matilton'

do·=čeh łixaŋ (not=it.feels/tastes it.is.good-tasting) 'it doesn't taste sweet (to me)'

čisnah yehWisłoh-čeh (a.bee has.stung.me=I.feel) 'a bee has stung me (it feels like)'

The diminutive enclitic, *=ǯi*, and the augmentative enclitic, *=k'oh*, are found most often with nouns. They occur frequently in the names of plants and animals, designating 'big' and 'little' varieties (*ġaW* 'yew tree', *ġaW=k'oh* ' redwood tree').

9.7. PHRASE MARKERS

A Hupa sentence (exclusive of sentence modifiers) can consist simply of a verb form, but more often there is, besides the verb, one or more syntactic constituents expanding on the lexical, inflectional, or derivational constituents of the verb. These syntactic constituents are of three types: noun phrases, adverbial phrases, and locative phrases. Each of these can be single word. A noun phrase can be a single noun; an adverbial phrase can be a single verb modifier, numeral, or directional;

a locative phrase can be a single locative noun. But these phrases can also be complex, consisting of one or more words (not infrequently verbs) marked as a phrase of a specific sort by an enclitic phrase marker (in the case of noun phrases, also usually by a proclitic phrase marker).

Noun phrase markers. Complex noun phrases are marked often (but not always) with proclitic *hay* (best translated as English 'the'), written without a special boundary. They are always marked with one of four enclitic phrase markers: *=i* (marking general noun phrases), *=din* (marking locational noun phrases), and *=x*[w]*e* or *=ni* (marking noun phrases referring to groups of people). Typical formations are:

hay k'iλoy 'the one who weaves baskets' (< *hay-k'iλo·=i*)

hay We·lwe?λ̇=tehł=diŋ 'the place where I am going to camp overnight' (< *hay Wi-e·-l-we·λ̇=te·ł=din*; note the occurrence of the word modifier *=te·ł* 'future')

danłaŋWo?=n 'several people' (< *danłaŋWo?* 'some number' + *=ni*)

Adverbial phrase markers. Complex adverbial phrases are marked with one of eight enclitics: *=hid* 'at the time that...'; *=di?* 'if; when (in the future)'; *=dan?* 'after; when (in the past)'; *=xo* 'in (such and such) a manner'; *=ġi* 'in a way similar to...'; *=tah* 'additionally...'; *=hih* 'emphatically'. Typical formations are:

Wila? yehk'e·la·=hid 'as soon as I put my hand in'

?ayniwinse?n=de? 'if you want it'

simiWgiy?=daŋ? 'when I was small, a child'

diġa·n=ġid=x[w] '(being) on top of the ridge'

niWoŋ=x[w] 'in a good way'

k'ida·y?=ġ̇ 'like a flower'

k'iwiyal=tah 'as well as food'

hayi=heh (that even.considering/emphatically.so) 'nevertheless'

Locative phrase markers. Complex locative phrases are marked with one of three enclitics: *=mił* 'when; after; as a result of'; *=min* 'so that; having....as a purpose'; *=ma·ni* 'because; on account of'. Additionally, all noun phrases formed with the phrase marker *=din* can function as locative phrases. Typical formations are:

minłan=diŋ na·yisxa·ni=mił (10-times when.it.has. dawned) 'after 10 days'

?e?łe?=miŋ 'so that they may get cooked'

do· niWo·ni=ma·n 'because it isn't good'.

10. SENTENCE TYPES

There are three types of sentence: normal sentences, restricted sentences, and expressive sentences.

10.1. NORMAL SENTENCES

Most sentences in conversation and in narrative are normal sentences, consisting of a verb and (optionally) one or more expansion phrases. Normal sentences in long narratives are usually joined by connectives, and in conversational speech they usually include one or more sentence-modifying attitude words.

It is one of the most distinctive features of Hupa syntax that normal sentences of all formations may occur nominalized. If a sentence is nominalized, the main verb is made into a general noun phrase with the phrase marker =i:

xontahdiŋ naˀtehsdiya· 'he went back home' (plain)
xontahdiŋ naˀtehsdiyay 'he went back home' (nominalized) (< ...-ya·=i).
do· k̇inaWlahł 'I'm not dreaming' (plain)
do· k̇inaWla·l 'I'm not dreaming' (nominalized) (< ...-la·ł=i).

While nominalized sentences with verbs inflected for perfective mode are especially frequent, nominalized sentences occur with verbs inflected for all modes except optative (for optatives in sentences see 10.2.). Nominalized sentences are favored in narrative.

It is not clear what additional meaning is to be assigned nominalized, as opposed to plain, sentences. It appears to be a matter of concreteness or definiteness. P.E. Goddard (1905:37) describes the difference between what is here called a nominalized sentence and its plain counterpart, when the verb is inflected for perfective mode, as the difference between "past definite" and "present definite" tense. Similar structures occur in many Athapaskan languages, and the difference is often spoken of as one between "light" (plain) and "heavy" (nominalized) verb forms, or more particularly verb stems. The phenomenon is nowhere as pervasive as it is in Hupa, and in languages like Navajo it is possible to describe "light" and "heavy" stem forms as mode variants. If one follows Sapir (1923:136), all these formations go back to an old "relative" enclitic.

10.2. Restricted Sentences

The two types of restricted sentences, imperative sentences and prohibitive sentences, are used in special circumstances (as positive and negative commands, respectively). An imperative sentence, like a normal sentence, consists of a verb and (optional) expansion phrases, but the verb is limited in its inflection to optative mode (with third-person subjects) or imperfective mode (with first- and second-person subjects). Nominalized sentences may not be formed. A prohibitive sentence consists only of an adverbial phrase, marked by =hih, and containing (in the commonest form) a passive verb, nominalized, and modified by do· 'not'. Examples are:

k̇iŋyaŋ 'eat!'
saˀxa·W k̇oˀyaŋˀ 'let him eat acorn soup!'
do· k̇iŋya·ni·heh 'don't eat!'
do· k̇iwidyaˀni·=heh 'let there be no eating!'

10.3. Expressive Sentences

Expressive sentences are of two types: single expressive words that do not occur in normal sentences; and normal sentences, or sentence fragments (particularly nouns used vocatively), with an altered phonetic form.

Expressive words convey a wide range of feelings and attitudes that are cumbersome to state in normal sentences: ˀa·gʸe· 'I'm lonesome', maW 'it stinks!', čiyo·W 'oh my!'. Some expressive words have sounds other than those occurring in normal sentence words: ˀilaš 'nasty!', ˀižibeh 'I'm scared!'

Phonetically altered words and sentences are used in "affectionate" or "endearing" contexts (between parents and their children, for example). The phonetic changes in affectionate language may be compared to similar processes of "diminutive symbolism" in other northwest California languages (see Haas 1970). The patterns of phonetic alteration are as follows:

Normal sound	Replacement in affectionate forms
w	b
W	s (or š)
ž	ž
čʷ	c
č	ċ
gʸ	g (or ġ)
kʸ	k
k̇ʸ	k̇ (or q̇)

Five sounds are found only in affectionate forms or expressive words. b is a voiceless, unaspirated, bilabial stop [p], parallel to d, gʸ, and ġ, and similar to French p. š is a voiceless alveopalatal fricative, very similar to the sh of English ship. g, k, and k̇ are palatovelar stops, midway in point of closure between gʸ and ġ; g is voiceless and unaspirated [k], k is voiceless and aspirated (and is virtually identical to English c as in cat) [kʰ], and k̇ is glottalized [k̇].

Some typical affectionate forms are: ˀiska·y 'my (dear little) grandchild!' (cf. Wik̇a·y 'my grandchild'; the replacement of Wi- by ˀis- instead of si- is usual); ˀisca·nˀ 'my (dear little) excrement!' (cf. Wič̇ʷa·nˀ 'my excrement'; this particular form occurs in a story in which a mythological creature uses his excrement as a helper); tilsod 'slide down (dear one)!' (cf. tilWod 'slide down!'; this sentence was spoken by a mother to her child as he was about to slide down a hill).

11. Selected Vocabulary

11.1. Basic Nouns

The following list includes the most commonly occurring nouns referring to: natural features, animals and fish, plants (especially those used for food or medicine), body parts, kinship relations, neighboring tribes, elements of traditional culture, and a few items of modern life. Each is given in the phonetic form it has when spoken as an isolated word. Possessed nouns are given with the possessor inflection xo- 'his, hers, one's' in parentheses unless the noun refers to something that cannot be possessed by a human being, in which case mi- 'its' is used. Where the noun theme is a compound or based on a phrase, a translation (but not an analysis) of the underlying form is given.

acorns (general term) *k'iwinya?n* ('what one eats')

acorn soup *sa?xa·W* ('what one spoons into the mouth')

ankle *(xo)ġe·ǯiwol?*

arm *(xo)k'a·ŋ?ay* ('what extends away from one')

arrow *na·ce·s*

arrowhead, bullet *dinday*

ashes *xon?din* ('what is at the place of the fire')

baby *miǯe·?e·din* ('what is lacking a mind')

back *(xo)ŋk'in?* (small of the back)

backbone *(xʷ)e·n?ċiŋ?*

bark *(mi)la·dosče?* (heavy bark of conifers)
  sik'e·ċ (thin bark of oaks)

basket (burden) *ġay?timił*

basket (cradle) *xe·ġay?*

basket (eating) *xayċa?*

basket (storage) *ǯe·lo?*

basket-hat (worn by women) *ġosta·n*

beads *nahdiyaw* (money beads, dentalia)
  na?k'idilyay (necklace)

bear *sa·ċ* (common brown bear)
  mik'ow? (grizzly bear)

beard *(xo)da·w?*

beaver *č'a?*

beer *miwoW tina·W* ('the one whose foam rises')

belly *(xo)mił*

berries *?isġo·ċ* (specifically, blackberries)

bird (general term) *k'iya·W*

blanket *łe?, (xo)Włe?*

bluejay *k'isłay?č''iŋ*

Boat Dance *ta·?ałtal* ('where one dances into the water')

body *(xo)niste?* (material substance, as opposed to spirit)
  (xo)xa·ġe? (flesh, frame)

bone *(xo)ċin?* (also 'leg')

bow (bow and arrow) *ċiłtiŋ?*

bowl *xayċa?*

boy *xixiy* (baby boy)

k'ile·xiǯ (boy child, from infancy to about age 16)

ġančiwiłčwil (young man before marriage)

brain *(xo)ce·łiġe?*

breast *(xo)łahdiye?* (chest)
  (xo)ċo·? (woman's breasts, milk)
  (xo)ǯe·? (also 'heart, mind')

brother, friend *(xo)łiŋ*

brother (older) *(xo)ŋwoǯ* or *(xo)ŋoǯ*

brother (younger) *(xo)k'il*

brother's son *(xo)te·diłe?*

brother's wife *(xo)čičinay* (man's brother's wife, after death of brother; wife's sister, after death of wife)

brother-in-law *(xo)ġe·y*

brush *ce·y*

Brush Dance *xon?na?we·* ('[where] one carries fire around')

buttocks *(xo)ła?*

cane *tič*

canoe *me?dil* ('what they travel in')

cat *bo·seh*

cedar *čime·č''iŋ*

charcoal *łehW*

cheeks *(xo)se·tol?*

children *xixe·x* (boy children)

chin *(xo)we·da?*

cigarette *te·lma·s* ('what is rolled up')

clay *łehǯma·*

cloud *?ah*

coffee *ta?na·n łiWin* ('black water')

corpse *čind*

cough *xos*

cow *mičo? čiłtig'* ('the one whose udders one squeezes')

cowife *(xo)łinče?*

coyote *xontehłtaw* ('the one in the flats')

crane *xahslintaw* ('the one at the riffles')

crotch *(xo)ġasła·w?*

dance *čidilye·* (White Deerskin Dance, Jump Dance)

daughter *(xo)ce·?* (man's daughter),
  (xo)ya·če? (woman's daughter)

daughter-in-law *(xo)yaW?ad*

deer *k'iłixan* ('what is sweet, good-tasting')

dentalia *nahdiyaw*

dirt *čʷiŋ*

disease *kʸičind*

doctor *kʸima·w čiɬčʷe·* ('the one who makes medicine')

doctor (sucking) *kʸite·ɫaw*

dog *no·kʸine·yo·d* ('what barks at something')
  ɫiŋʔ (xo)liŋkʸeʔ (pet)

door *no·na·wice·* ('what is shoved back')

dress *kʼaʔ, (xo)kʼaʔ*

duck (general term) *na·ɫawe·*

eagle *tismil*

ear *(xo)ǯiwʔ*

earth *ninʔ* (ground)
  ninisʔa·n (world)

eel *ɫiwiWxa·n or ɫiWxa·n*

egg *(mi)we·Weʔ*

eggs (fish) *q̇oŋʔ*

elbow *(xo)ċič*

elderberry *ċiWiW* (elder sticks)

elk *gʸehs-kʸoh or mikʸiġoċeʔ*

excrement *čʷaŋʔ, (xo)čʷa·nʔ*

eye *(xo)na·ʔ*

eyebrow *(xo)na·do·seʔ*

eyelash, eyelid *(xo)na·ɫaŋʔ* ('eye-leaf')

face *(xo)niŋʔ*

fall (of year) *ɫaŋq̇*

falls *noleh* ('[fish] swim no farther')

fat *kʸiq̇ah, (xo)q̇ah*

father *(xo)taʔ*

father-in-law *(xo)Wanċeʔ*

father's brother *(xo)ta·y*

father's sister *(xʷ)a·dičʷiŋ*

father's father *(xo)maʔ or (xo)maʔačʷiŋ*

father's mother *(xo)čin*

feast *noʔkʸiŋxa·n* ('[where] one puts the basket down') (Acorn Feast, traditionally held in the fall)

feather *(mi)čileʔ* (also 'wing')

finger *(xo)la·ʔ* (also 'hand')

fir *niskʸiŋ* (Douglass fir, tall conifers generally)

fire *xoŋʔ*

firewood *čʷiǯ*

fish (general term) *ɫo·q̇* (also 'salmon')

fish dam, weir *ʔehs*

fish trap *no·lʔge·d*

fishing platform *dahkʼiwe·wita·n*

flower *kʼida·y*

Flower Dance *kʼinahɫdaŋ* (girls' puberty ceremony)

fog *misǯeh*

food *kʼiwiyal* ('what is eaten')

foot *(xo)xeʔ*

forearm *(xo)ċe·lʔ*

fox *mičʷa·nʔ taɫta·n* ('the one whose excrement is soft')

friend *(xo)ma·lyawʔ, (xo)ɫiŋ* (brother)

frog *čahl*

fur *(mi)waʔ*

gambling game *kʼin-na·way* ('[where] the stick goes about')

genitals *(xʷ)e·ʒeʔ* (male genitals, penis),
  (xo)co·lʔ (female genitals)

ghost *ċindin*

girl *ɫehxiǯ* (girl before age 10)
  do·kʼinahɫdaŋ (girl from age 10 to puberty)
  kʼehtca·n (unmarried girl after puberty)

God *yima·nti(ŋ)ʔwinyay* ('the one who went away across [the ocean]') (Indian God, culture hero)

grandchild *(xo)yal* (son's child)
  (xo)co·y (man's daughter's child)
  (xo)kʼa·y (woman's daughter's child)

grass *ɫoh*

grease *(mi)sintoʔ*

gums *(xo)niŋgʸiǯeʔ*

hair *(mi)waʔ* (animal's hair, fur)
  ciwaŋʔ, (xo)ciwaʔneʔ (head hair)
  (xo)ce·ɫiwaʔ (woman's long hair)

hand *(xo)laʔ*

hazel *kʼila·ǯondeʔ*

head *(xʷ)e·da·ʔay* ('what extends out against one')

heart *(xo)kʼansaʔa·n* ('what lies in the breast'),
  (xo)ǯeʔ (mind)

heel *(xo)xe·taʔɫ*

hip *(xo)ġe·čeʔ*

horn (of animal) *(mi)deʔ*

horse *ɫiŋʔ, (xo)liŋkʸeʔ* (dog, pet)

house *xontah, (xo)xontawʔ*

husband *(xo)xaŋʔ*

ice *niŋxostiŋ*

intestines, guts *(xo)če·kʸeʔ*

385

jaw (xo)we·ċiŋˀ

Jump Dance ya·xo·ˀaW ('[where] they dance')
  xay-čidilye· ('winter-dance')

Karok kʸinasn

Kick Dance čiłtał ('[where] one kicks')

knee (xo)ġoł

knife ce·łče̓ˀ or ce·lisče̓ˀ

lake miŋ̇q̇

language xine·W ('what is said')

leader niŋxaˀłe·n (rich man)

leaf (mi)łaŋˀ

leg (xo)činˀ (also 'bone')

lip (xo)we·siċ ('jaw-skin')

liver (xo)sił

log nista·n

Mad River Indians ta·kʸeˀxʷe·

madrone ˀisde·w

man (adult male) xoˀosday

man (human being) kʸiwiŋyaˀnya·n ('acorn eater')

manzanita diniW

maple kʸiłaŋˀ ('leaf')

meat (xo)ciŋˀ

medicine kʸima·w

mind (xo)ǯe·ˀ (also 'heart, breast')

money nahdiyaw (also 'dentalia, beads')

moon Wa· (also 'sun')

mother (xʷ)ančʷiŋ

mother's brother (xo)sˀ

mother's sister (xo)ŋ̇qayˀ

mother's father (xo)čʷiwe·

mother's mother (xo)čʷo

mother-in-law (xo)me·če·ˀčʷiŋ

mountain ninisˀa·n (earth, world)
  nanċiŋ (peak)
  diq̇a·n (ridge)

mouth (xo)daˀ, (xo)sah (back of mouth)

mud łehłe·łe·ˀ

name (xʷ)o·Weˀ

navel (xo)ċe·q̇

neck (xo)q̇os

nephew (xʷ)a·W (man's nephew)
  (xo)te·dilłeˀ (woman's nephew or niece)

nest (mi)łoh

net kʸixa·q̇ (lifting net, large A-frame net)

niece (xʷ)a·sče̓ˀ (man's niece)
  (xo)te·dilłeˀ (woman's niece, nephew)

night xiłeˀ

nose (xo)nčʷiW

oak kʸinehsła·n (tan oak)

ocean miwaŋ

old man kʸiwaŋxoya·n ('one who knows about things')

old person kʸisdiya·n

old woman do·kʸiwile·

pack, load xehł

pack strap ƛoħł

pain sinsiŋ (entity causing pain extracted by sucking doctor)

people kʸiwiŋyaˀnya·n ('acorn eaters')

pine miǯe·wˀxole·n ('what has lots of pitch') (sugar pine)
  dilčʷe·gʸ (ponderosa pine)

pipe (for smoking) kʸiŋˀa·gʸa·n

pitch ǯeh, (mi)ǯe·wˀ

plank, board łisč

pocket (xo)łah

porcupine kʸoh

puberty ceremony for girls kʸinahłdaŋ (Flower Dance)

rain na·nyay ('what goes down')

rattlesnake ƛiwiW, miłcahxosin ('the dangerous one')

redwood ġaWkʸoh ('yew-big')

rich niŋxaˀłe·n (rich man, leader)
  ˀaWxiče̓ˀ (rich woman)

river hanˀ

road tin (trail)

root xay (pine root, used in basketry)
  ġad (willow root)
  (mi)xa·če̓ˀ (stump)

rope kʸiwidiʒ, ƛoħł

sack tehmil

salmon (general term) ło·q̇

salmon (king) xalo·q̇eˀ (spring salmon, first run of king salmon);
  čʷalo·q̇eˀ (Chinook salmon, large spring king salmon);
  ġehs (fall salmon, second run of king salmon)

salt łehq̇onʒ

sap *kʸinsinto*ʔ ('tree-grease') (also 'sugar')

scar *Woɫ*

seed *(mi)na·*ʔ ('its eye') (large seed, pit)
 (mi)sa·y (small seeds)

shoulder *(xo)ġantaġ*

sinew *kʼyoʔċ*

sister *(xo)de·* (woman's sister)
 (xo)ɫtisčeʔ (man's sister)

sister (older) *(xʷ)a·d*

sister (younger) *(xo)dehǯ*

sister-in-law *(xo)we·* (woman's husband's sister)
 (xo)we·čeʔ (man's wife's sister)

skin *(xo)siċ.*

skull *(xo)ce·ġe·čeʔ*

smoke *ɫid*

snow *nandil* ('the ones that fall')

son *(xo)Wxiyʔ*

son-in-law *(xo)wanda·n*

song *Wiŋ*

spirit *(xo)na·ɫawʔ* ('what flies about') (one's soul)
 kʸixinay ('the ones who are alive') (supernatural beings)
 ta·n (deer spirits)
 kʼyiɫwe· ('what fights') (evil spirits causing sickness)

spoon *kʼyide·kʸiŋ* (elkhorn spoon used by men);
 xosiċmil (mussel-shell used as a spoon by women)

spring (of year) *daŋʔ*

star *ciŋʔ*

steelhead *misintoʔxole·n* ('the one with plenty of grease') (silverside, summer run of steelhead)
 xay na·dil ('the ones who move about in the winter') (winter run of steelhead)

stick *kʸiŋ*

stick game, shinny *kʸitiġiǯ* ('[where] one tosses with a stick')

stomach *(xo)miɫ*

stone *ce·*

string *ʔisdiʒ, ƛohɫ*

sturgeon *ɫoʔkʸoh* ('big salmon')

sugar *kʸinsintoʔ* ('tree-grease') (also 'sap')

summer *xonsiɫ*

sun *Wa·* (also 'moon')

sweathouse *ta·kʸiW*

tail *(mi)kʸeʔ*

testicles *(xo)čʷoq̇*

thigh *(xo)q̇ayʔ*

thing *diyWoʔ*

throat *(xo)sowoɫ*

tobacco *mindeʔiɫčʷe·*

Tolowa *yideʔdiniŋʔxine·W* 'those downstream who speak a Hupa-like language'
 dilwa·š (pejorative of *dilwa·W* 'babblers')

tongue *(xo)sa·sta·n* ('what lies in the mouth')

tooth *(xo)woʔ*

trail *tin*

trash *čid*

tree *kʸiŋ* (stick)
 nista·n (fallen tree, log)

trout *ɫoʔya·W* ('little salmon')

urine *(xo)liʒeʔ*

village *ɫe·ne·W* (neighbors) ('those who go about with each other')

war dance *kʼyiwice·*

war party *mahn*

wart *yeʔċ*

water *ta·ʔna·n* (drinking water) ('what is drunk')
 to· (body of water, ocean)
 tos or *tosiɫ* (warm water)

waterfall *noleh* ('[fish] swim no farther')

White man *yima·nʔdil, kʼiwaʔmiɫ* ('the one with fur'; the *k̓* indicates this to be an "expressive" form; see 10.3.)

widow *kʼyisdiya·nčʷiŋ*

wife *(xo)ʔad*

wife's sister *(xo)čičinay* (wife's sister, after death of wife; brother's wife, after death of brother)

willow *q̇ayliW*

winter *xay*

wing *(mi)čileʔ* (also 'feather')

witchcraft *kʼyidoŋxʷe·* (witchcraft poison; an "Indian Devil," one believed to practice witchcraft)

Wiyot (Mad River Indians) *ta·kʸeʔxʷe·*

wolf *kʼyiɫna·dil* ('[one of] those who go about with something')

woman *camehƛo·n* or *camehsƛo·n*

woods *tintah* (out in the woods, away from the valley) ('trails-among')

woodpecker *kʼyiɫdikʸikʸoh* ('the.one.that.pecks-big') (large red-headed woodpecker)

387

world   *ninisʔa·n*   (also 'earth, mountain')

wrist   *(xo)laʔkʸinʔ*   ('hand-base')

yew   *ġaW*

Yurok   *kʸinaʔ*

11.2. COMMON VERBS

The following themes are only a small sample of the Hupa verb vocabulary. While the selection is essentially arbitrary, an attempt has been made to include the themes most commonly met with in speech. For each theme, the basic structure is indicated in parentheses, together with its inflectional type. For that the following abbreviations are used: "impf. neut.," imperfective neuter; "s-pf. neut.," s-perfective neuter; "act. intr.," active intransitive; "act. tr.," active transitive.

afraid   (*ni₆-l₁-gʸid* impf. neut.)   *činilgʸid* 'he's afraid'

be (so)   (*ʔa·₁₀-ni₆-ɫe·* impf. neut.)   *xʷe·diq̇ ʔaʔanɫe·* 'how is he (feeling)?'

become   (*-lih/linʔ* act. intr.)   *čisleʔn* 'he (who) became'

big   (*ni₆-kʸa·h* impf. neut.)   *nikʸah* 'it is big'

black   (*ɫi₆-Win* impf. neut.)   *ɫiWiŋ* 'it is black'

blue, green (*ɫi₆-coh* impf. neut.)   *ɫicoh* 'it is blue, green'

cold   (*si₆-q̇ac̓* impf. neut.)   *xosq̇ac̓* '(the weather) is cold'

cook   (O-*e·₁₀-ɫ₁-na·/naʔ* act. intr.)   *kʸiɫna·* 'cook it!'
kʸeʔwiɫnaʔ 'she cooked it'

cut   (*-ɫas/ɫa·c̓* act. tr.)   *kʸinɫas* 'cut it!'
kʸisɫaʔc̓ 'he cut it'

dance   (*di₆-l₁-ye·/yiʔ* act. intr.)   *dilye·* 'dance!'
čidiwilyeʔ 'he danced' (reference here is specifically to the White Deerskin or Jump dances)

drink   (*ta·₁₀-di₁-na·n/nanʔ* act. intr.) *tandinaŋ* 'drink!'
taʔwinaŋʔ 'he drank'

eat   (*kʸi₇-ya·n/yanʔ* act. intr.)   *kʸinyaŋ* 'eat!'
kʸiwinyaŋʔ 'he ate'

go about (one)   ([*na₁₀*]-*ya·/yaʔ*; 3d-person forms: (*na₁₀*)- *wa·/yaʔ* act. intr.)   *nanya·* 'go about!'
naʔwa· 'he goes about'
na·ʔisyaʔ 'he went about'

go about (several)   ([*na₁₀*]-*diɫ/de·ƛ̇* act. intr.)   *nahdiɫ* '(you pl.) go about!'
na·ʔisdeʔƛ̇ 'they went about'

go somewhere (one)   (A-*ya·W/ya·*; 3d-person forms: A-*na·W/ya·* act. intr.)   *tinyahW* 'go away!'

čitinahW   'he goes away'

čitehsya·   'he went away'

go somewhere (several)   (A-*diɫ/de·ƛ̇* act. intr.)
tohdiɫ '(you pl.) go away!'
čitehsdeʔƛ̇ 'they went away'

good   (*ni₆-Wo·n* impf. neut.)   *niWoŋ* 'it is good'

hit with a stick   (*-l₁-waɫ/wa·ƛ̇* act. tr.)   *kʸiɫwaɫ* 'hit it with a stick, chop it!'
kʸiswaʔƛ̇ 'he hit it'

kill   (*si₆-ɫ₁-we·/we·n* act. tr.)   *xosiɫwe·* 'kill him!'
čixosehtwiŋ 'he killed him'

know   (*-o·-ɫ₁-c̓id* act. semitransitive)   *Woɫc̓id* 'you know me'
čixo·ɫc̓id 'he knew him'

lie motionless (one object)   (*s₃-ʔa·n* s-pf. neut.)
saʔa·n 'the thing lying there'

lie motionless (several objects)   (*s₃-la·* s-pf. neut.)
silay 'the things lying there'

long, tall   (*ni₆-ne·s* impf. neut.)   *niWnehs* 'I am tall'
ne·s 'the long thing'

love   (*-l₁-yoʔ* act. tr.)   *niWyoʔ* 'I love you'
čixowehsyoʔ 'he loved her'

make   (*-ɫ₁-c̓ʷe·/c̓ʷinʔ* act. tr.)   *ʔiɫc̓ʷe·* 'make it!'
čisc̓ʷinʔ 'he made it'

move (one object) about   ([*na·₁₀*]-*ʔa·/ʔaʔ* act. tr.)
naŋʔa 'carry it about!'
na·ʔasʔaʔ 'he carried it about'

move (one object) somewhere   (A-*ʔaW/ʔa·n* act. tr.)
yaŋʔaW 'pick it up!'
yaʔwiŋʔaŋ 'he picked it up'

move (several objects about)   ([*na·₁₀*]-*le·/liʔ* act. tr.)
nale· 'carry them about!'
na·se·leʔ 'I have carried them about'

move (several objects) somewhere   (A-*liW/la·* act. tr.)   *yaliW* 'pick them up!'
yaʔwila· 'he picked them up'

old   (*si₆-di₁-ya·n* impf. neut.)   *kʸisdiya·n* 'old person'

say   (*ʔa·₁₀-di₆-ne·* impf. neut.)   *ʔa·diWne·* 'I say'

see   (*-ɫ₁-cis/ca·n*)   *xoWcis* 'I see him'
čiɫcaŋ 'he found it' (*-ɫ₁-ca·n*, inflected as imperfective, is used as the perfective of *-ɫ₁-cis*)

shove (a stick) somewhere   (A-*ɫ₁-ġe·d* act. tr.)
yeʔiɫgeh 'shove it in!'
yehčiwiɫge·d 'something shoved in by someone' (this theme is often used to describe the moving of a boat)

sing (*ḱʸiₛ-ʔah* act. intr.) *na·ḱʸiŋʔah* 'sing!'

   na·ḱʸiwiŋʔaw 'he (is the one who) has sung'

sit, stay (one) (*s₃-da·* s-pf. neut.) *ċisda·* 'he stays there'

sit, stay (several) (*de·₆-s₃-l₁-ċe·* s-pf. neut.) *yaʔdehłċe·* 'they all stay there'

speak (*xi₆-ni₆-ye·W*; 3d-person forms: *xi₆-ne·W* act. intr.) *xininyehW* 'speak!'

   ċixe·nehw 'he spoke'

stand (one) (*s₃-ye·n* s-pf. neut.) *ċisyiŋ* 'he is standing'

stand (several) (*na·₁₀-de·₆-s₃-l₁-ya·* s-pf. neut.) *naʔdehłya·* 'they are standing'

step somewhere (A-*tał*/*ta·λ̇* act. intr.) *ċintał* 'step out!'

če ʔninta ʔλ̇ 'he stepped out'

sweet (*łi₆-xan* impf. neut.) *łixaŋ* 'it tastes sweet'

think about (-*o·-ni₆-di₆-ne·*/*ni ʔ* act. semitransitive) *Wonde·ne·* 'think about me!'

   čixondehsne ʔ 'he thought about him'

   ʔa·čondehsne ʔ 'he thought

throw (a bunch, armload) somewhere (A-*mił*/*me·λ̇* act. tr.) *de·dimił* 'throw them into the fire!'

   de ʔdiwime ʔλ̇ 'he 'threw them into the fire'

tie up (-*loy ʔ* act. tr.) *ʔiloy ʔ* 'tie it up!'

   ċisloy ʔ 'he tied it up'

white (*łi₆-ġay* impf. neut.) *łiġay* 'it is white'

wide, broad (*ni₆-te·ł* impf. neut.)

   niteł 'it is wide, broad'

Sketch of Cree, an Algonquian Language

H.C. WOLFART

1. INTRODUCTION

Cree is an Algonquian language spoken from the west coast of James Bay to the foot of the Rocky Mountains, including the boreal forest regions of northern Ontario and Manitoba as well as the prairies of Saskatchewan and Alberta. Cree speakers are estimated to number between 60,000 and 70,000 (Canada. Indian Affairs Branch 1970); of these, approximately 26,000 use the Plains Cree dialect.

In the absence of detailed dialect studies, a working classification of Cree dialects based on the varying reflexes of Proto-Algonquian *l has found general acceptance, along with such crude labels as Plains Cree, Swampy Cree, Woods Cree, and Moose Cree (Lacombe 1874:xv; Michelson 1939; Wolfart 1973, 1992:356-359; for the controversial question of the eastern delimitation of Cree proper cf. Pentland 1978; and MacKenzie 1980). The major varieties of Cree could be considered either highly divergent dialects (vol. 6:52-53) or closely similar languages showing considerable mutual intelligibility ("Introduction," table 3, this vol.).

None of the dialects thus identified is completely homogeneous. The *y*-dialect, for example, which is spoken across Alberta and the major part of Saskatchewan (and somewhat beyond the Plains as a geographical zone), includes several variants that differ from one another phonologically, morphologically, and lexically. Cree speakers are fully aware of the more obvious differences; central Alberta speakers, for instance, identify northern Alberta Crees (from the areas north of Edmonton) by their use of the plural suffix *-wa·w-* where all other Plains Cree speakers use *-ik-*: *e·-na·tahkwa·w, e·-na·tahkik* 'they fetch it'.

The variety of Cree represented here is the Plains Cree of central Alberta and Saskatchewan (Bloomfield 1930; Wolfart 1973, 1992:29-30, 377-380); all the sentences used in illustration are drawn from spontaneous discourse (with a few exceptions, mainly the demonstration sentences used in section 2, explicitly identified as such by a trailing asterisk).

The early literature about Cree is largely the work of missionaries, both Roman Catholic and Protestant. Many of their writings remain unpublished, but they are well represented by the dictionaries of Watkins (1865) and Faries (1938), the paradigm tables of Hunter (1875), and the dictionary and grammar published by Lacombe (1874). Fur trade journals contain a great deal of incidental information about the Cree language, most of it lexical (Wolfart and Pentland 1978; Wolfart 1988; Pentland 1991). The remarkable work of Howse (1844) is the earliest published grammar of Cree.

Later works include two general introductions (Wolfart and Carroll 1981; Ahenakew 1987) and, for dialects other than Plains Cree, the language-learning handbooks of Ellis (1983) and Voorhis et al. (1977); in addition, several substantial dictionaries have been completed for Montagnais (e.g., Drapeau 1991) and the "East Cree" of eastern James Bay (MacKenzie et al. 1987). For Cree proper, aside from specialized vocabularies (Atimoyoo et al. 1987; Leighton 1985, 1993), the exhaustive glossaries accompanying many of the text editions listed below are the most accessible and reliable sources for lexical data (but note also the references in Pentland and Wolfart 1982 and the running bibliography published in the quarterly newsletter *Algonquian and Iroquoian Linguistics*). The sound system remains the most neglected aspect of Cree, mainly discussed in the context of orthographic conventions (Bloomfield 1930, Introduction; Longacre 1957; Ellis 1973; Pentland 1977; Martin et al. 1978; Wolfart and Ahenakew 1987) and with two brief papers by Cook (1991) and Russell (1992) the only theoretical studies devoted to Cree phonology. Aspects of grammatical structure have increasingly received attention (Ellis 1971; Wolfart 1971, 1973, 1978, 1989, 1989a, 1991, 1992; D. James 1982, 1984, 1986, 1991, 1991a; Ahenakew and Wolfart 1983; Ahenakew 1987:140-159; Coté, Ratt, and

Klokeid 1987; Dahlstrom 1989, 1991; Ogg 1991; Russell 1991; Clarke, MacKenzie, and James 1993; Blain 1994; Reinholtz 1994; Reinholtz and Russell 1994).

Two volumes of Plains Cree texts were published by Bloomfield (1930, 1934), with the text editions of the past decade (Vandall and Douquette 1987; Beardy 1988; Ahenakew 1989; Ahenakew and Wolfart 1991; Nêhiyaw 1991; Bear et al. 1992; Whitecalf 1993; Ellis 1995) representing an expanding range of genres, topics, dialects, and editorial styles; in addition to their ethnological, historical, and literary aspects, texts constitute a basic source of data for linguistic analysis.

2. SENTENCES*

Cree is a highly inflected language with elaborate systems of concord and cross-reference. Many syntactic relations are specified within the noun and, especially, the verb. The order of words and larger constituents is comparatively free.

In a simple transitive sentence, the verb form indicates which of the two nouns is the subject, and which the object:[†]

awa·sisak	*nipahe·wak*	*si·si·pa.(*)*
child(3p)	kill-someone(s.o.)	duck(3´)
	(VTA 3p-(3´) INDEP)	

'The children killed some ducks.'

Cree verbs like *nipah-* 'kill s.o.' specify both the subject and the object. In *nipahe·wak* 'they killed the other(s)', the ending *-e·wak* (the internal structure of which is explicated in 4.1) and the absence of a personal prefix together mark a third-person subject that is animate plural, and a third-person object that is animate obviative; as for the nouns, *awa·sisak* 'children' includes a plural ending *-ak*, and *si·si·pa* 'duck(s)' is number-indifferent but the ending *-a* marks it as obviative (table 1). Abbreviations are given in table 2.

---

*This section was written in 1994 by Charlotte Reinholtz and H.C. Wolfart. The rest of this sketch was written by Wolfart in 1973 and, aside from minor corrections, appears in its original form.

[†]Example sentences that are not extracted from spontaneous texts are marked as demonstration examples by a trailing asterisk in parentheses. For all other abbreviations see tables 1, 2, 30, and 31.

The terms subject and object are used only in section 2; in order to avoid ambiguity in the labeling of inverse verb forms, the terms agent and patient are used in all remaining sections.

For transitive animate verbs (VTA), the notation 3-1 indicates a third-person agent and a first-person patient. In forms that involve third-person referents exclusively, the one that is not expressed morphologically is enclosed in parentheses: 3-(3´) or (3´)-3. For transitive inanimate verbs (VTI), only the agent is indicated.

When cited in isolation, verbs are generally inflected for a third-person agent; nouns and pronouns are given in the proximate singular. In the interlinear translations, only the verb stem (rather than the entire inflected form) is glossed.

Phonemic notation is indicated by italics, while forms in morphophonological representations are enclosed in vertical bars.

Table 1. Gender-Person-Obviation-Number Combinations

Gender	Person	Obviation	Number	Code
animate	indefinite		(sg./pl.)	indf
	first and second		pl.	21
	first		sg.	1
			pl.	1p
	second		sg.	2
			pl.	2p
	third	proximate	sg.	3
			pl.	3p
		obviative	(sg./pl.)	3´
inanimate		proximate	sg.	0
			pl.	0p
		obviative	sg.	0´
			pl.	0´p

Table 2. Codes and Abbreviations

Stem Classes	
VAI	verb animate intransitive
VII	verb inanimate intransitive
VTA	verb transitive animate
VTI	verb transitive inanimate
NA	noun animate
NI	noun inanimate
NDA	noun dependent animate
NDI	noun dependent inanimate
PR	pronoun
IPC	indeclinable particle
IPV	indeclinable preverb

Verb System	
DIR	direct
INV	inverse
PROX	proximate
OBV	obviative
INDEP	independent
INDIC	indicative
PRET	preterit
CJ	conjunct
SIMPLE	simple
CH	changed
SBJ	subjunctive
ITER	iterative
IMVE	imperative
IMM	immediate
DEL	delayed
REL	relational
DIM	diminutive
RED	reduplication

Other	
EMPH	emphatic
LOC	locative
VOC	vocative

2.1. SALIENT PROPERTIES

The remarkable freedom in the order of the major constituents of a sentence, such as the verb, the subject (agent) and the object (patient), is probably the most striking syntactic trait of Cree. Other salient features of the grammatical design of Cree are the fact that the subject and object need not be expressed by noun phrases and the comparatively free occurrence of discontinuous constituents. Languages that exhibit this cluster of properties are called non-configurational.

First, in a simple declarative sentence (which, for demonstration purposes, fully specifies who did what to whom), the verb and the subject and object nouns can occur in all six of the logically possible word orders, and all six are grammatical sentences without any difference in referential meaning:

'The children killed some ducks.'

SVO:	*awaˑsisak nipaheˑwak siˑsiˑpa.(*)*	[children killed ducks]
SOV:	*awaˑsisak siˑsiˑpa nipaheˑwak.(*)*	[children ducks killed]
VSO:	*nipaheˑwak awaˑsisak siˑsiˑpa.(*)*	[killed children ducks]
VOS:	*nipaheˑwak siˑsiˑpa awaˑsisak.(*)*	[killed ducks children]
OVS:	*siˑsiˑpa nipaheˑwak awaˑsisak.(*)*	[ducks killed children]
OSV:	*siˑsiˑpa awaˑsisak nipaheˑwak.(*)*	[ducks children killed]

Second, subject and object noun phrases may be freely omitted.

> *nipaheˑwak siˑsiˑpa.(*)*
> 'They killed some ducks.'

> *awaˑsisak nipaheˑwak.(*)*
> 'The children killed them.'

> *nipaheˑwak.(*)*
> 'They killed them.'

All three of these are full, normal sentences, as illustrated by these text examples:

> *mostoswa waˑpameˑw.*
> buffalo(3´) see-s.o.(VTA 3-(3´) INDEP)
> 'He saw the buffalo.'

> *noˑtokeˑsiw waˑpameˑw.*
> old-woman(3) see-s.o.(VTA 3-(3´) INDEP)
> 'The old woman saw him.'

> *waˑpameˑw.*
> see-s.o.(VTA 3-(3´) INDEP)
> 'He saw him.'

Third, constituents may be discontinuous. In the noun phrase *oˑhi siˑsiˑpa* 'these ducks', for example, the determiner *oˑhi* 'these' may be separated from the noun *siˑsiˑpa* 'ducks':

> *nipaheˑwak oˑhi siˑsiˑpa.(*)*
> 'They killed these ducks.'

o·hi nipahe·wak si·si·pa.(*)
'They killed these ducks.'

Text examples of discontinuous noun phrases will be found throughout this sketch.

Taken together, properties like free word order, free omission of subject and object noun phrases, and discontinuous constituents may make a non-configurational language like Cree look very different from configurational languages such as English or French.

2.2. GRAMMATICAL DISTINCTIONS

In keeping track of the grammatical relations within a sentence, Cree relies heavily on features such as gender (animate and inanimate, 3.1.), the existence of two third-person categories (obviation, 3.4.), and the distinct verbal forms that occur in main and subordinate clauses (inflectional orders, 4.1.2.).

Cree nouns fall into two grammatical genders, animate and inanimate. There is no overt marker for gender, but both nouns and verbs are morphologically sensitive to this distinction. For example, animate and inanimate nouns take different plural markers: animate *-ak*, in *awa·sis* 'child', *awa·sisak* 'children'; inanimate *-a*, in *maskisin* 'shoe,' *maskisina* 'shoes'.

In the verbal system, gender agreement is pervasive, and gender is a principal term of classification. Intransitive stems fall into two inflectional and derivational classes according to the gender of the subject; for example, with the animate noun *si·si·p* 'duck': *pahkisin si·si·p* 'the duck fell down'; and with the inanimate noun *maskisin* 'shoe': *pahkihtin maskisin* 'the shoe dropped'.

Verbs like *nipah-* 'kill s.o.', which specify both the subject and the object, fall into two inflectional and derivational classes according to the gender of the object; for example, with the same nouns: *niwa·pama·w si·si·p* 'I saw the duck', *niwa·pahte·n maskisin* 'I saw the shoe'.

Obviation distinguishes between two or more third-person referents, one of whom is, roughly speaking, in the foreground (proximate) while all others are relegated to the background (obviative). As the several word order examples with two animate noun phrases illustrate, proximate nouns are morphologically unmarked, while obviative nouns are marked by the suffix *-a*.

Main (matrix) clauses are distinct from subordinate clauses, which form part of a larger, containing sentence. All subordinate sentences have verb forms inflected according to the conjunct order paradigm; such verb forms are identified by a distinct set of suffixes, for example, *-a·cik* 'they(3p)—the other(s)(3´)' of *e·-nipaha·cik* 'that they (proximate) killed the other(s) (obviative)' and they often appear with one of a small set of preverbs, for example, the e·-preverb that primarily marks subordination:

nikiske·yihte·n	*awa·sisak*	*e·-nipaha·cik*
know-something(s.t.)	child(3p)	kill-s.o. (VTA
(VTI 1 INDEP)		3p-(3´) CJ)

si·si·pa.(*)
duck(3´)
'I know that the children have killed some ducks.'

Verb forms inflected according to the independent order paradigm are typically found in matrix clauses; such verb forms are identified by distinct prefix-suffix combinations, such as the *ni—e·n* of *nikiske·yihte·n* 'I know it'. In the above example, there is an independent order verb form in the main clause and a conjunct order verb form in the subordinate clause.

In some cases, though, a main clause may have a conjunct verb. In the following two examples, taken from a single text, the main verb is independent in the first (with the prefix-suffix combination *ni—n* marking the first person), and conjunct in the second (with the preverb *e·* identifying the clause as subordinate and the suffix *-ya·n* marking the first person):

nikiskisin	*ma·na*	*nima·ma·*
remember-(s.t./s.o.)	usually	my(1)-mom(3)
(VAI-T 1 INDEP)		

e·-wi·cihak...
help-s.o.(VTA 1-3 CJ)
'I remember helping my mom ...'

e·kiskisiya·n	*nima·ma·*	*e·-wi·cihak...*
remember-(s.t./s.o.)	my(1)-mom(3)	help-s.o.
(VAI-T 1 CJ)		(VTA 1-3 CJ)

'I remember helping my mom...'

2.3. BASIC SENTENCE TYPES

Cree sentences exhibit three major types of predicate: verbal, impersonal, and nominal.

First of all, sentences can be formed with verbs denoting a specific action or state:

niwi·-nipaha·w.
intend-to-kill-s.o.(VTA 1-3 INDEP)
'I am going to kill him.'

niwi·-nipa·n.
intend-to-sleep(VAI 1 INDEP)
'I am going to sleep.'

Second, there are impersonal verbs that cannot take a subject:

e·kw	*a·t-i·spatina·w.*
then	gradually-be-a-hill(VII 0 INDEP)

'And then slowly it became hilly.'

...kwayas	*kimiwan;*	*nisto-ki·sika·w*
properly	be-raining(VII 0 INDEP)	three-day(IPC)

e·-kimiwahk,...
be-raining(VII 0 CJ)
'...it rained hard; it rained for three days,...'

e·-ota·kosiniyik,...
be-evening(VII 0´ CJ)
'Toward nightfall,...'

piyisk   mitoni   ki·sika·yiw.
finally   really   be-day(VII 0´ INDEP)
'At last it was full daylight.'

..., e·kwa   ka·-piponiyik   ma·na, ...
then   be-winter(VII 0´ CJ)   usually
'..., then when it would get winter,...'

As the above examples show, impersonal verbs tend to express natural states such as weather, season and time of day, or terrain and general environment.

Third, nominal predicates occur in verbless sentences where one noun phrase predicates a property (including identity) of the other:

kimotisk   ana!
thief(3)   that(3)
'He was a thief!'

e·yako   pe·yak   a·cimo·win.
this-one(0)   one   narrative(0)
'This one is one narrative.'

Nominal predicates are especially common with existential interrogatives:

ta·niwa·   ni·wa?
where-is-3   my-wife(3)
'Where is my wife?'

Equational sentences tend to be emphatic even when they occur in isolation; but the emphasis is especially obvious in examples like the following, where the order of constituents is (chiastically) reversed:

namo·y a·na   ki·wa.   kisi·m   ana.
not   that(3) your(2) your(2)   that(3)
                -wife(3) -younger
                          -sister(3)
'She is not your wife. She is your sister.'

Note that predicate nominals are not morphologically marked, nor do equational sentences exhibit a copula.

2.4. Sentence Functions
In addition to differences given by the predicate, Cree sentences also vary depending on their overall grammatical function and status. The following remarks concentrate on three major types: relative clauses, questions, and negated clauses.

2.4.1. Relative Clauses
The preverb *ka·*, with the verb inflected according to the conjunct order paradigm, is the most prominent marker of relative clauses:

si·si·p   ka·-nipahak(*)
duck(3)   rel-kill-s.o.(VTA 1-3 CJ)
'the duck that I killed'

Except for the preverb *ka·*, the verb form in a relative clause is indistinguishable from that found in any other type of subordinate clause:

kikiskisin   si·si·p   e·-nipahak(*)
remember-(s.t./s.o.) duck(3) kill-s.o.(VTA 1-3 CJ)
    (VAI-T 2 INDEP)
'you remember that I killed a duck'

..., e·-mihta·tahk   e·-ki-nipaha·t   owi·kima·kana.
regret-s.t.   past-kill-s.o.   his(3)-
    (VTI 3 CJ)   (VTA 3-(3´) CJ)   spouse(3´)
'..., [with him] regretting that he had killed his wife.'

Relativization also provides a means of discriminating between genuine cleft constructions and focus constructions (both of which tend to be translated into English as cleft constructions). The preferred word order in Cree is one where focus material (new or contrastively emphasized) appears before the verbal complex:

si·si·p   ninipaha·w.(*)
duck(3)   kill-s.o.(VTA 1-3 INDEP)
'I killed a duck.'

Topic material (known or presupposed) appears after the verbal complex. Cleft constructions are readily recognizable by the presence of the preverb *ka·* and the use of the conjunct:

si·si·p   ka·-nipahak.(*)
duck(3)   kill-s.o.(VTA 1-3 CJ)
'It was a duck that I killed.'

The focus material need not be a noun phrase; in the following example it is a temporal phrase:

..., e·kw   a·n[i]   e·kwa   ka·-kimiwahk.
then   (EMPH)   then   be-raining(VII 0 CJ)
'..., and it was then that it rained.'

Both the following examples have the location of the event in focus position, but only the second one exhibits the cleft construction marked by the preverb *ka·* and the conjunct:

e·kota mihce·t ninipaha·wak   niskak
there many kill-s.o.(VTA 1-3p INDEP) goose(3p)
mi·na si·si·pak,...
and   duck(3p)
'Over there I have killed a lot of geese and ducks,...'

ha·, kisiwa·k o·ta ka·-nipahakik!
well close-by here kill-s.o.(VTA 1-3p CJ)
'Ho, it was right close by here that I killed them!'

Cleft constructions and relativization also play a role in content questions.

2.4.2. Questions
Content questions and yes-no questions differ dramatically in their syntactic structures.

2.4.2.1. Yes-no Questions
In yes-no questions the question marker *ci·* follows the first word of the clause, and the verb is most commonly in the independent form:

kikisiwahitin   *ci·?*
anger-s.o.(VTA 1-2 INDEP)   (question)
'Have I made you angry?'

However, yes-no questions are not restricted to independent verbs:

e·-wi·-nakasiye·k   *ci·?*
going-to-leave-s.o.(VTA 2p-1 CJ)   (question)
'Are you going to leave me?'

ke·ya·pic   *ci·*   *ma·n*   *e·-mo·nahaskwe·t*
still   (question)   usually   dig-seneca-root
                                      (VAI 3 CJ)
wiya?
he(EMPH)
'Does he still dig seneca-root?'

The question marker *ci·* also has the effect of throwing the constituent it follows into relief:

ki·stawa·w   *ci·*   *ma·na*
you(2p)(contrastive-EMPH)   (question)   usually
kiki·-ma·wasakona·wa·w   *o·hi...*
past-collect(it/her)(VAI-T 2p INDEP)   this(0p)
'Did you, too, use to collect them...'

kiki·-a·h-a·cimosta·kawina·wa·w
past-tell-s.o.-many-stories(VTA INDF-2p INDEP)
ci·   *ma·na, ki·stawa·w?*
(question)   usually   you(2p)(CONTRASTIVE-EMPH)
'Did you use to have stories told to you, you too?'

kiya   *ci·*   *ka·-ki·-pakastawe·hwat*
you(2)(EMPH)   (question)   past-throw-s.o.-into-
                                   water(VTA 2-3 CJ)
no·kima·mina·n.
our(1p)-chief(3)
'Was it you who threw our chief into the water?'

awa   *ci·*   *e·-mamisiyan?*
this(3)   (question)   rely-on-(s.t./s.o.)(VAI-T 2CJ)
'Is this the one on whom you rely?'

The following examples show the question marker *ci·* in postinitial position after the quantifier *kahkiyaw* 'all':

ne·ka·,   *kahkiyaw*   *ci·*
my-mother(VOC)   all   (question)
kita·pacihcikana?
your(2)-implements(0p)
'Mother, are all your implements gone?'

kahkiyaw ci·   *ki·kihk*
all   (question)   your(2)-house-LOC
e·-ki·-aya·wacik   *awa·sisak?*
past-have-s.o.(VTA 2-3p)   child(3p)
'Did you have all the children at your house?'

Indirect yes-no questions in Plains Cree use the conditional marker *ki·spin* 'if', which usually appears at the beginning of the subordinate clause:

e·kwa, mo·y ma·ka nikiskisin
then   not   but   remember-(s.t./s.o.)(VAI-T 1 INDEP)
ki·spin   *wi·hka·c*   *ka-ki·-ata·wa·ke·t, ...*
if   ever   future-able-sell(VAI 3 CJ)
'But then I cannot remember if she would ever have been able to make a sale,...'

...,mo·y   *kikiske·yihte·n*   *ki·spin*
not   know-s.t.(VTI 2 INDEP)   if
e·-na·pe·wit   *ahpo·*   *e·-iskwe·wit.*
be-male(VAI 3 CJ)   or   be-female(VAI 3 CJ)
'you cannot know whether it is a man or a woman.'

2.4.2.2. CONTENT QUESTIONS

In Cree content questions, the interrogative pronoun (or phrase) usually appears first, and the verb is normally in the conjunct form:

ta·nite·   *e·-wi·-itohte·yan?*
whither   going-to-go-there(VAI 2 CJ)
'Where are you going to go?'

ta·nisi   *ma·ka*   *e·-isi-wa·pamat?*
how   but   thus-see-s.o.(VTA 2-3 CJ)
'And how do you see him?'

ta·ne·hki   *k-o·h-ma·toyan?*
why   thence-cry(VAI 2 CJ)
'Why do you weep?'

ta·nim   *e·sa*   *kiya?*
which-one(0)   evidently   you(2)(EMPH)
'And which one are you?'

Indirect content questions use the same interrogative pronouns:

... mo·y nikiskisin   *ta·nis*
   not   remember-(s.t./s.o.)(VAI-T 1 INDEP)   how
e·-isiyi·hka·sot.
be-thus-named(VAI 3 CJ)
'...I do not remember what his name was.'

niki·-wa·pama·w   *ta·nisi*
past-see-s.o.(VTA 1-3 INDEP)   how
e·-to·tahk.
so-do-s.t.(VTI 3 CJ)
'I have seen what he did.'

kakwe·cima·hke·k   *ta·nitowihk*
ask-s.o.(VTA 2p-3 DEL IMVE)   in what place
e·-ohci-nipit.
thence-die(VAI 3 CJ)
'Ask her in what spot a wound would cause her death.'

In indirect questions, however, it is not uncommon for the interrogative to appear noninitially:

kakwe·cihke·mo·w,   *okosisa*
ask-people(VAI 3 INDEP)   his(3)-son(3´)
otihta·wa·wa   *ta·nit[e·]*
his(3)-fellow-parent-in-law(3´)   where

                                                         395

e·-aya·yit.
be-located(VAI 3′ CJ)
'He made inquiries as to where his son and his son's father-in-law were staying.'

In fact, not just the focused constituent (here the general singular *ne·hiyaw* 'the Cree'), but even the entire indirect question may be preposed:

ne·hiyaw   *ta·nisi*   *e·-isi-pima·tisit, ...,*
Cree-person(3)   how   thus-live(VAI 3 CJ)
kahkiyaw   *nikiske·yihte·n*
all   know-s.t.(VTI 1 INDEP)
'How the Cree lived, ..., all of this I know.'

2.4.3. NEGATED SENTENCES

There are two negative markers in Cree, *namo·ya* (or its variant *nama*) and *e·ka·* (or its variant *e·ka·ya*). Their distribution coincides by and large (and with exceptions too complex to be treated here) with the distinction between main and subordinate clauses: *namo·ya* is used in main clauses while *e·ka·* appears in subordinate clauses.

The variant *e·ka·ya* is the preferred negation marker in all imperative sentences:

nisi·mis,   *e·ka·ya*   *ma·to!*
my-younger-brother(VOC) not   cry(VAI 2 IMVE)
'Little brother, do not weep!'

e·ka·ya   *ki·we·ta·k!*
not   go-home(VAI 21 IMVE)
'Let us not go home!'

e·ka·ya   *ta·pwe·htawa·hkan!*
not   believe-s.o.(VTA 2-3 DEL IMVE)
'Do not henceforth pay any heed to him!'

The negator need not be in absolute-initial position:

kahkiyaw e·ka·ya awiyak   *nipahihk!*
all   not   someone kill-s.o.(VTA 2p-3 IMVE)
'Let none of you slay anyone!'

In main clauses, negation is normally marked by *namo·ya*:

namo·ya   *nikiske·yima·w.*
not   know-s.o.(VTA 1-3 INDEP)
'I do not know him.'

The negator *namo·ya* is not restricted to verbs in the independent order, as for example in:

mo·y nikiske·yihte·n   *ta·nis*
not   know-s.t.(VTI 1 INDEP) how
e·-isiyi·hka·te·k.
be-thus-named(VII 0 CJ)
'I do not know what it is called.'

It also occurs in declarative main clauses employing the conjunct order:

ma·ka mo·y e·-kiske·yihtama·n   *ta·nis*
but   not   know-s.t.(VTI 1 CJ)   how

e·-isiyi·hka·te·k.
be-thus-named(VII 0 CJ)
'But I do not know what it is called.'

Compare the similar sentence with a verb of the independent order:

ma·ka   *namo·ya*   *nikiske·yihte·n ...*
but   not   know-s.t.(VTI 1 INDEP)
'But I do not know it...'

Subordinate clauses are normally negated by *e·ka·*:

kiske·yihtam   *e·ka·*   *e·-pakitiniht...*
know-s.t.   not   release-s.o.
(VTE 3 INDEP)   (VTA INDF-3 CJ)
'He knew that he would not be freed...'

osa·m   *mistahi*   *kikitima·kisina·naw,*
excessively   greatly   be-poor(VAI 21 INDEP)
e·ka· awiyak   *e·-wa·hko·ma·yahk.*
not   someone(3)   have-s.o.-as-relative(VTA 21-3 CJ)
'We are altogether too poor, since we have nobody for a kinsman.'

..., *ca·pihcikanis*   *ohci*   *e·-tahkama·t*
lance(0)   with   stab-s.o.(VTA 3-(3′) CJ)
awa   *e·ka·*   *wi·hka·c*   *ka·-no·tinike·t*
this(3) not   ever   go-to-war(VAI 3)
oskini·kiw.
young-man(3)
'That youth who had never been to war pierced them with his lance'.

This also includes content questions:

ta·ne·hk *a·wa*   *e·ka·*   *ka·-wi·-mi·cisot,*
why   this(3) not   going-to-eat(VAI 3 CJ)
ne·ka·,   *kite·m?*
mother(VOC)   your(2)-dog(3)
'Why will not this creature eat, Mother, this dog of yours?'

The use of *e·ka·* is most prominent in the various types of modal clauses (4.1.2.):

— *e·ka·* *wanikiskisiya·ni,...*
not   forget-(s.t./s.o.)(VAI-T 1 CJ SUBJ)
'— if I do not forget it, ...'

— *e·ka·*   *wa·h-to·tama·ni, ...*
not   going-to-do-s.t.(VTI 1 CJ ITER)
'— every time I would not do it, ...'

...; kik-a·so·namawak
future-pass-(s.t.)-on-to-s.o.(VTA 1-3 CJ)
ni·c-a·yisiyiniw,   *..., e·ka·y*
fellow-human(3)   not
ka-wanisimikot   *wa·piskiwiya·sa.*
future-mislead-s.o.(VTA (3′)-3 CJ) Whiteman(3′)
'...; to pass it on to my fellow people, ... lest the Whiteman lead them astray.'

pikw   *a·nima e·ka· ka-pakici·yan,* ...
it-is-necessary that(0) not future-give-up(VAI 2 CJ)
'You must not give up on this, ...'

In all negated clauses, whether main or subordinate, the perfective is marked by the preverbs *o·h* or *ohci* 'thence' instead of the preverb *ki·*, which appears in non-negative clauses:

..., *kahkiyaw ki·kway niki·-pe·-wi·htama·kona·n.*
all   thing(0)   past-hither-tell-(s.t.-to)-
                      s.o.(VTA 3-1p INDEP)
'..., she has told us about everything'.

mo·y wi·hka·t no·hci-pe·-kiske·yihte·n, ...
not ever   past(NEG)-hither-know-s.t.(VTI 1 INDEP)
'I have never yet known it, ...'

a·, nama   ki·kway no·h-kiske·yihte·n, ...
well nothing(3) past(NEG)-know-s.t.(VTI 1 INDEP)
'Well, I had not known anything, ...'

e·kwa mo·y wi·hka·c e·-ohci-kosta·ciya·hk, ...
then not ever   past(NEG)-be-afraid(VAI 1p CJ)
'And we had never been afraid, ...'

..., *wiya·kana e·ka· e·-ohci-ihtakoki.*
vessel(0p)   not   past(NEG)-exist(VII 0p CJ)
'..., since there were then no pots.'

But note that *ki·* does co-occur with a negator in the exhortative construction with the preverb combination *ka-ki·*:

ki·kway e·ka· ka-ki·-to·tama·hk,
thing(0) not   FUTURE-PAST-do-s.t.(VTI 1p CJ)
kahkiyaw ki·kway niki·-pe·-wi·htama·kona·n.
all   thing(0)   PAST-hither-tell-(s.t.-to)-
                       s.o.(VTA 3-1p INDEP)
'The things we should not do, she has told us about all these.'

2.5. SENTENCES IN CONTEXT

In spontaneous discourse, it is relatively rare for both the subject and the object of a verb to be expressed by two full noun phrases; sentences like *The farmer killed the duckling.* are noteworthy even in English. The textual examples which follow illustrate the six major types of constituent order (2.1.) and also highlight some of the contextual and stylistic features exhibited by sentences with two full noun phrases.

SVO:
ta·pwe· awa   iskwe·w   pakamahwe·w
truly   this(3)   woman(3)   strike-s.o.
                             (VTA 3-(3´) INDEP)
e·sa   o·hi   wi·htikowa.
reportedly this(3´) windigo(3´)
'Truly the woman struck down that windigo.'

SOV:
ke·tahtawe· iskwe·w   awa   ona·pe·ma
presently   woman(3) this(3) her(3)-husband(3´)

mo·we·w.
eat-s.o.(VTA 3-(3´) INDEP)
'Then that woman ate her husband.'

VSO:
... *namo·ya wa·pame·w   awa*
not   see-s.o.(VTA 3-(3´) INDEP) this(3)
iskwe·w   ocawa·simisa ...
woman(3) her(3)-child(3´)
'... the woman did not see her children...'

VOS:
mistahi miywe·yime·w   o·hi
greatly like-s.o.(VTA 3-(3´) INDEP) this(3´)
oskini·kiskwe·wa   awa   no·toke·siw, ...
young-woman(3´) this(3) old-woman(3)
'The old woman became very fond of the young woman, ...'

OVS:
owi·ce·wa·kana   miskawe·w
his(3)-companion(3´)   find-s.o.(VTA 3-(3´) INDEP)
awa   ne·hiyaw.
this(3) Cree(3)
'The Cree found his comrades.'

OSV:
a·w, wa·poso-mi·cima·poy niya
oh   rabbit-soup(0)   I(EMPH)
e·-wi·-mi·ciya·n.
going-to-eat-(s.t.)(VTI 1 CJ)
'Well, as for me, I am going to eat rabbit soup.'

Examples of OSV order with two full nouns are exceedingly rare; the sentence cited above has the full (and fairly emphatic) personal pronoun *niya* 'I' rather than an ordinary noun functioning as one of the noun phrases. The general point can also be illustrated with sentences that omit one of the major constituents; most commonly, these are sentences without overt agent noun but with the object noun before the verb:

mostoswa   wa·pame·w.   (OV)
buffalo(3´) see-s.o.(VTA 3-(3´) INDEP)
'He saw the buffalo.'

In Cree, sentences with full parallel noun phrases are highly marked and tend to be used for special emphasis or for the purpose of a general declaration. In narrative texts, they may mark the opening or closing of a discourse unit (whether a paragraph, a section, or a whole text) and they also seem characteristic of a sharp shift (peripeteia) in a narrative.

The most common context for two full noun phrases to occur within a single clause is the possessive construction in which a possessed noun phrase (in the SOV example, *ona·pe·ma* 'her husband', marked for a third-person possessor by the personal prefix *o(t)-* 'his, her') is matched by another noun phrase (here *iskwe·w awa* 'this woman') identifying the possessor.

397

As these examples show, demonstratives like *awa* (proximate) 'this' and *o·hi* (proximate) 'this' are often used with one or both of the full noun phrases.

Note, finally, that the text examples cited in this section (2.5.) are restricted to verb forms in the independent order. When full nouns appear, they are often part of a much more complex noun phrase, which includes at least one participial verb form adding new information. By far the most common pattern is the omission of one of the nouns, with a full noun being used only to express new or contrastive information.

3. GRAMMATICAL CATEGORIES

The major grammatical categories of Cree—gender, number, person, and obviation—are manifested in the inflection of verbs, nouns, and pronouns and constitute the basis for concord and cross-reference. Because of their general nature, they are treated separately from the purely verbal categories of modality, transitivity, and direction and the nominal category of possession.

In many cases, these general categories are expressed by the same affixes in verbs, nouns, and pronouns; for a summary of "universal" affixes see section 4.

The major dimensions of contrast among the general categories are displayed in table 1. The table also defines the abbreviations for the gender-person-obviation-number combinations.

One of the salient features of the system is the simultaneous function of the third-person category in two dimensions: it not only contrasts with the other two person categories but also is the domain of the contrast of proximate and obviative.

Another aspect of the system is less well understood in its semantic implications: throughout the grammatical system of Cree, the inanimate proximate plural category (0p) and the animate obviative category (number-indifferent, 3´) show the same morphological manifestations.

This identity is found in the number-obviation paradigm of nouns as well as in the independent order paradigm of verbs, that is, the obviative forms of all verbs with an animate agent (VTA, VTI, VAI) and the plural forms of the inanimate-agent verbs (VII). In all these paradigms, the inanimate plural and the animate obviative are both marked by the ending -(w)a. That this is not simply an accident of phonological development is evident from the corresponding pronominal endings (-hi, -e·ha·), which show the same identity.

While the common semantic feature of these two categories is yet to be found, there are several contexts in which the nominal complement of a transitive verb is ambiguous or unspecific with respect to these categories. This is the case for both the verb and the entire nominal phrase in the following example:

nana·tohk o·hi ki·kwa·sa o·hi

various this(0p/3´) something(0p/3´) this(0p/3´)

e·-wiye·simikot.
trick-him(VTA (0p/3´)-3) CJ)
'... all these various little things used to trick him.'

3.1. GENDER

Cree distinguishes animate and inanimate gender. Unlike the Indo-European languages, for example, where the grammatical category of gender largely correlates with the physical category of sex, Cree gender corresponds to a considerable extent to a division of physical phenomena into those that have life and those that do not. In either case grammatical and physical categories correlate only in a very general way and their correspondence is by no means complete: the German neuter noun *das Weib* 'the woman' and the Cree animate noun *asiniy* 'stone' are only the most striking examples from a large set.

3.1.1. MANIFESTATIONS OF GENDER
Gender is one of the basic criteria for the inflectional and derivational classification of verbs. Transitive verbs largely come in pairs, differing as to the gender of the goal, for example, transitive animate (VTA) *otine·w* 'he takes him',[‡] transitive inanimate (VTI) *otinam* 'he takes it'. Intransitive stems differ by the gender of the actor: animate intransitive (VAI) *ohpikiw* 'he grows up', inanimate intransitive (VII) *ohpikin* 'it grows up'.

With few exceptions, noun stems belong to only one gender class. While certain general criteria for gender assignment are outlined below, these are by no means exhaustive and only a list can account for the gender of Cree nouns.

Nouns that denote humans, animals, spirits, and trees are animate—*kise·yiniw* 'old man', *wacask* 'muskrat', *manito·w* 'spirit', *sihta* 'spruce'. Extensions of these are also animate—*ayi·siyini·hka·n* 'effigy, doll' (literally 'surrogate human').

In addition, there are several more or less clearly defined semantic groupings of nouns that are also animate; some of these might be considered extensions of the major group. These are: animal hides and garments made from them (*mostoswaya·n* 'buffalo robe'), some body parts (*nitihtikos* 'my kidney') some phenomena of the natural environment (*ko·na* 'snow', *asiniy* 'rock, stone', *pi·sim* 'sun, moon'), some articles of personal or household use (*asa·m* 'snowshoe', *askihk* 'kettle'), items used in smoking (*ciste·ma·w* 'tobacco', *ospwa·kan* 'pipe'), certain plants and their products (*paka·n* 'nut', *pahkwe·sikan* 'bannock [fried bread]').

[‡]Cree does not distinguish in the 3d-person singular between 'he' and 'she'. In this sketch Cree third singulars referring to human beings are translated by convention with the English masculine singular pronouns ('he', 'him,' 'his'), but, where contextually appropriate, translations with feminine pronouns ('she', 'her') would be equally correct.

Among inanimate nouns, the most clearly defined group is that of abstract nouns derived from verbs, for instance, with the suffix *-win*: *ne·hiyawe·-* VAI 'speak Cree', *ne·hiyawe·win* 'Cree speech'; *mi·ci-* VAI 'eat (something)', *mi·ciwin* 'food'.

A few noun stems appear with both animate and inanimate endings and verb forms: *akohp* 'blanket'; in some cases, the animate and inanimate stems have different meanings: *mistik* NA 'tree', *mistik* NI 'stick'.

3.1.2. GENDER CHANGE

All reference to speaker and addressee is (semantically at least) animate. However, if otherwise inanimate nouns (or pronouns) function as complements of verbs of speaking, the conflict of semantic (animate) and morphological (inanimate) patterns results in a great deal of variation. Even the same narrator may use either gender in essentially the same context:

kahkiyaw ki·kway   *e·-ki·-waye·sihtahk*
every   something(0)   trick-s.t.-by-speech(VTI 3 CJ)
'everything he used to trick by speech'

kahkiyaw ki·kway
every   something(0)
e·-ki·-waye·sima·t
trick-s.o.-by-speech(VTA 3-(3´) CJ)
'everything he used to trick by speech'

While inanimate nouns may function like animate nouns syntactically, animate nouns do not, in a similar way, function like inanimate. It is this "absorptive" (Hockett 1966) nature of the animate gender (rather than the fact that it includes nouns whose denotata are "lifeless" from the English speaker's point of view) that seems to point to the animate gender as the more general of the two.

3.2. NUMBER

In the opposition of singular and plural, singular is the unmarked member. Beyond the morphological fact that a plural morpheme is added to singular forms (*si·si·p* |si·si·p-a| 'duck', *si·si·pak* |si·si·p-a-k| 'ducks'), the singular is used in statements of general application;

ayisk ki·-miywe·yihtam
(for   PAST(IPV)-be-glad-about-s.t.(VTI 3 INDEP)
ayi·siyiniw,   *e·-matotisicik,*
human-being(3)   have-a-steambath(VAI 3p CJ)
no·tokwe·siwak,   *kise·yiniwak.*
old-woman(3p)   old-man(3p)
'For people used to like it, to have a steambath, old women and old men.'

The number contrast is completely absent in several contexts, including most prominently the animate obviative forms of nouns and verbs: *osi·ma* 'his(3) younger brother/brothers(3´)', *apiyiwa* 'he(3´) sits, they(3´) sit'.

The verbal complement may be of either number when the participant is not expressed morphologically as part of the verb, as is the case in transitive inanimate (VTI) verbs: *miskam mistik* 'he found (VTI 3) a stick (NI 0)', *miskam mistikwa* 'he found (VTI 3) sticks (NI 0p)'. The number distinction is lacking in the indefinite possessor of nouns (4.2.1.) and in the indefinite actor forms of verbs (4.1.1.2.); the same holds for the inanimate actor of VTA verbs (4.1.4.2.).

Finally, in the you-and-me set of the transitive animate (VTA) paradigm, the second person is number-indifferent when cooccurring with the first-person plural (lp); the imperative, *ma·mitone·yimina·n* 'think of us (lp)', for instance, may be addressed to one or several persons.

3.3. PERSON

Distinctions of person are found in the actor and, within the transitive animate (VTA) paradigm, also in the goal of verbs. They further appear in the possession paradigm of nouns and in the personal pronoun set.

Inanimate intransitive (VII) verbs and the number-obviation paradigm of nouns and pronouns function as third persons in terms of cross-reference, with respect to their inflectional affixes, and most obviously in their participation in the obviation system (3.4.1.).

3.3.1. THE BASIC PERSONS

The person category of Cree has three basic members: the first (speaker) and second (addressee) persons, as direct participants in the speech act, constitute a subgroup vis-à-vis the third person (neither speaker nor addressee); the significance of this grouping (termed "local" by Hockett 1966) is evident in the morphological and semantic structure of the various verbal paradigms (table 3).

Table 3. Examples of Person-Number Combinations

Singular	*Plural*
Speaker (first person) *nima·ci·n* 'I hunt'	Speakers (may include third person but not addressee) *nima·ci·na·n* 'we (but not you) hunt'
	Speaker(s) *and* Addressee(s) (as well as any third person) *kima·ci·naw* 'we (you and I) hunt'
Addressee (second person) *kima·ci·n* 'you hunt'	Addressees (may include third person but not speaker) *kima·ci·na·wa·w* 'you (but not I) hunt'
Third person *ma·ci·w* 'he hunts'	Third persons (may include neither speaker nor addressee) *ma·ci·wak* 'they hunt'

The characteristically Algonquian distinction of two "third-person" referents is subordinate to the third person rather than coordinate with it; for a discussion of obviation see section 3.4.

The Cree person category is the domain of a fundamental order principle whose manifestations can be observed throughout the structure of the language: the second person ranks higher than the first, which in turn outranks the third.

This order principle is most obvious among the mutually exclusive personal prefixes that constitute a position class: in case of conflict (for instance in a transitive animate (VTA) verb that involves two participants), the more highly ranked person is expressed by the prefix, irrespective of its status as agent or patient. Thus, whenever a second person is involved, the prefix is *ki-*; if there is a first person (but no second), the prefix is *ni-*; and only if there are no first or second persons at all, can the third person be expressed by the prefix *o-* or by the absence of a prefix.

This ranking principle is also manifest in the fixed sequence of affixes in both verb and noun inflection: non-third markers always precede third-person markers, and among non-third markers, second-person markers precede first-person markers (4.1.4.).

3.3.2. OTHER PERSON CONFIGURATIONS

When the three basic person categories are pluralized, an additional combination emerges. The plurality that includes both speaker and addressee is traditionally known as the first-person inclusive plural (as opposed to the exclusive plural). In English and other Indo-European languages both these functions are served by the single first-person plural category reflected in 'we', and it is not surprising that the corresponding category in Cree (and many other non-European languages) has been identified as a first-person plural. However, the distribution of the personal prefixes, in accord with the order principle of 3.3.1., identifies this form as a second-person form primarily, 'you, including one or more of us' rather than 'we, including one or more of you'. Thus, in Cree the contrast of inclusive versus exclusive appears to function in the second-person plural rather than in the first. While this analysis may seem implausible from a typological perspective, it is supported by comparative evidence that shows that, unlike Cree, most Algonquian languages (Goddard 1967) have generalized one of the original suffixes so that the distinction of the two plurals involving the speaker rests entirely in the prefix.

Simple reflexives are formed derivationally: *nitasamison* 'I feed myself' (cf. the primary stem *asam-* VTA 'feed someone' and the derivational suffix *-iso-*). No forms appear to exist for the complex reflexivization that would involve a plural category with one of its constituent singular categories, as in 1-1p 'I feed us'.

3.4. *OBVIATION*

Contrasts of obviation in Cree function within the third-person category rather than on a par with the three basic persons. By identifying only one third-person referent in each contextual span as proximate and all others as obviative, the dimension of obviation marks a semantic system of focus in addition to the syntactic construction of cross-reference.

While the choice of focus clearly depends on the preceding sentences and on the structure of the discourse as a whole, the correlates of focus in terms of discourse analysis are not known in detail, and Bloomfield's (1962:38) statement is only an approximation: "The proximate third person represents the topic of discourse, the person nearest the speaker's point of view, or the person earlier spoken of and already known."

Contrasts of obviation are found in the inflection of verbs, in the possession paradigm of nouns, and in the number-obviation paradigm of animate nouns and pronouns.

Plains Cree (unlike more eastern Cree dialects) does not distinguish obviation in inanimate nouns; nevertheless, obviation is present covertly, as is shown by the verb with which the noun is in concord:

> *e·kosi osihta·w   e·-misa·yik   o·si.*
> thus   build(VAI 3 CJ) be-big(VII 0´) canoe(0)
> 'Thus he built a big canoe.'

3.4.1. FOCUS ASSIGNMENT

Where no determining context (e.g., a preceding sentence) exists, a single third person is proximate, for example, *mostoswak* in

> *mihce·t ninipahe·wak   mostoswak.*
> many   kill-s.o.(VTA 1-3p INDEP) buffalo(3p)
> 'I have killed many buffalo.'

If there are two (or more) third-person referents, only one may be proximate (*mistanask*) while all others are obviative (*mostoswa*):

> *mihcet nipahe·w   mistanask*
> many   kill-s.o.(VTA 3-(3´) INDEP) Badger(3)
> *mostoswa.*
> buffalo(3´)
> 'Badger has killed many buffalo.'

With three third-person referents, two of them obviative (*mostoswa* and *owi·kima·kana*):

> *aka·wa·tamawe·w   o·ma*
> desire(s.t./s.o.)-of-s.o.(VTA 3-(3´ INDEP) that
> *ka·-nipaha·yit   mostoswa owi·kima·kana.*
> kill-s.o.(VTA 3-(3´) CJ) buffalo(3´) his(3)-spouse(3´)
> 'He envied his wife the way she had killed the buffalo.'

The only exception to this rule occurs when two nouns are conjoined (in close parataxis):

e·-ki·-no·tinitocik,   *ayahciyiniwak*
fight-each-other(VAI 3p CJ) Blackfoot(3p)
e·kwa ne·hiyawak ...
and   Cree(3p)
'they used to fight one another, the Blackfoot and the Cree ...'

Cross-reference provides a syntactic constraint that makes focus fully predictable in one case: if a noun is inflected for a third-person possessor, the noun itself is obligatorily obviative:

... namo·ya wa·pame·w   *awa*
not   see-s.o.(VTA 3-(3´) INDEP) this(3)
iskwe·w   *ocawa·simisa ...*
woman(3)   her(3)-child(3´)
'... the woman did not see her children ...'

a·h, ni·so nipe·-tahkama·wak;
well two   come-stabbing-s.o.(VTA 1-3p INDEP)
ote·miwa·wa   *no·tinima·wa;*
their(3p)-horse(3´) take-s.o.(1-3´)
'Oh, two I stabbed on the way; I took their horses.'

Focus assignment is also largely expectable if a main clause involving a third person is modified by an inanimate clause indicating a state of the physical environment (climate, season, time of day, etc.):

e·-ota·kosiniyik   *iyikohk,*   *ki·we·w.*
be-evening(VII 0´ CJ) at-that-time go-home
                            (VAI 3 INDEP)
'When it was evening, she went home.'

3.4.2. FOCUS CHANGE

While the focus system permits two distinct third persons in Cree, it cannot distinguish between several obviative referents. (The distinction of two obviative categories in Cree [Bloomfield 1946:94; Hockett 1966; Ellis 1971], which would fit well with the historical evidence, does not appear to be justifiable synchronically [Wolfart 1973, 1978]). Disambiguation depends on the context, unless the span is ended and a new span, with new focus assignment, is begun. While focus changes are frequent and spans thus relatively brief, long spans do occur and at least one text (Bloomfield 1930:text 10) has been observed to have constant focus assignment throughout; that is, the entire text constitutes only one span.

Change of focus (‖) may be indicated, even within a sentence, by indexing a new referent as proximate:

ninayoma·w   *e·-sa·kihak,*
carry-s.o.(VTA 1-3 INDEP) love-s.o.(VTA 1-3 CJ)
‖ *nika·wiy*   *e·-ma·mitone·yimak*
   my-mother(3) think-about-s.o.(VTA 1-3 CJ)
e·-wi·-pe·tamawak.
want-to(IPV)-bring-(s.t./s.o.)-to-s.o.(VTA 1-3 CJ)
'I carried it(i.e. a kettle (3)) on my back, I prized it, ‖ I thought of my mother and wanted to bring it to her.'

Conversely, the same referent may be assigned to different focus categories:

e·kwa mi·na ma·na anihi
then   and   always that(3´)
k-a·cima·t   ‖   *kaya·s*
tell-about-s.o.(VTA 3-(3´) CJ)   long-ago
ka·-ki·-kimotit anihi   *so·niya·wa.*
steal(VAI 3 CJ)   that(3´)   money(3´)
'And then he told about that one ‖ who long ago stole that money.'

When several obviative referents occur within a single span, word order may provide some clues; however, in the main, the identification of referents in such a case rests on meaning and context:

..., pe·yak piko nipahe·yiwa
     one   only   kill-s.o.(VTA 3´-(3´) INDEP)
omisa   *wa·poswa.*
his(3)-older-sister(3´) rabbit(3´)
'..., his sister had killed but one rabbit.'

o·ki   *wiya oskini·kiwak kahkiyaw*
this(3p) EMPH youth(3p)   all
nipahe·yiwa   *ote·miwa·wa*
kill-s.o.(VTA 3´-(3´) INDEP) their(3p)horse(3´)
ayahciyiniwa.
Blackfoot(3´)
'As for these young men, the Blackfoot killed all their horses.'

3.4.3. THE MARKED STATUS OF THE OBVIATIVE

In the opposition of proximate and obviative, the obviative is the marked member.

In addition to strictly morphological evidence (the obviative consistently shows a morpheme added to the nonobviative form), the proximate is characterized as unmarked by its appearance in isolation (3.4.1.) and in contexts of neutralization. For instance, the personal pronouns *wiya* and *wi·sta* are used with both proximate and obviative referents. The most typical context of neutralization involves a verb with coordinate complements, one of which is proximate, the other obviative; the verb is then inflected for a nonobviative plural referent:

e·-kiske·yima·t,   *e·-no·hte·hkwasiyit,*
know-s.o.(VTA 3-(3´) CJ) be-sleepy(VAI 3´ CJ)
e·kwa kawisimo·wak.
then   go-to-bed(VAI 3p INDEP)
'When he knew the other to be sleepy, then they went to bed.'

Thus the nonobviative category, being unmarked, has a wide and a narrow function and meaning. The term "proximate" is used only of the narrow meaning, where it is opposed to "obviative." For the wide meaning, where the opposition of obviation is neutralized, the term "third person" is obviously appropriate. The   *401* present analysis in terms of marked and unmarked members of an opposition is in fact inherent in the system of abbreviations used by many Algonquianists. In practice, the traditional definitions of the abbreviations differ; 3 is normally used only in its narrow meaning, 'proximate'.

4. INFLECTION

Apart from the four personal prefixes, Cree inflection consists of suffixation exclusively.

The complexity of the affix combinations is the primary reason (confirmed by the evidence of word formation) for the typological characterization (cf. Sapir 1921c) of Cree as polysynthetic and fusional.

The fundamental order principle, which may be symbolized as $2\rightarrow1\rightarrow3$ (3.3.1.), operates not only among the personal prefixes that are members of one position class (paradigmatically) but also in the linear sequence of verbal and nominal affixes (syntagmatically). The linear order of the person affixes is fixed.

A significant proportion of Cree affixes occur in different modal categories and across paradigms and even word classes. The personal prefixes, the thematic obviative sign |eyi|, and the person and number markers of nouns and of the independent order of verbs are most prominent among these "universal" affixes.

The inflectional system of Cree is the result of extensive paradigmatic leveling (4.1.4.1.1.; Michelson 1912; Goddard 1967a; Wolfart 1973; Dahlstrom 1989). For example, the present similarity between the VAI and VTI paradigms fails to reflect substantial earlier differences, and it seems quite clear from the structure of the paradigms that the direction of development in the VTA paradigm is from generally opaque "fusional" to more transparent "agglutinative" forms (in the terminology of Sapir 1921c). In addition, there appears to be a development (for instance, in the emergence of forms based on the "inverse elements" |ek, ekawi, ekw, eko, eko·w|) from inflectional to derivational expression of certain semantic relations.

4.1. VERB INFLECTION

In addition to the general categories presented in section 3, the verb system exhibits modal categories, distinctions of transitivity, and a category of direction that, though superficially similar to voice in Indo-European, appears to be a distinctly Algonquian phenomenon.

4.1.1. TRANSITIVITY

The morphological structure of the Cree verbal system does not match the syntactic properties of individual forms in all cases; there are several points where the semantic categories distinguished in the inflectional paradigms do not have a one-to-one correspondence to the syntactic uses of the forms in context. For example, only one participant is morphologically expressed in third-person VTA verbs, but two function syntactically and referentially. As a consequence, the morphological classification of verbs, which is traditional in Algonquian linguistics, is insufficient with respect to the verbal system as a whole.

4.1.1.1. VERB TYPES

The basic verb types, as defined morphologically and by syntactic-semantic criteria, are summarized in table 4. No attempt is made to present a full classification in terms of syntactic function.

The four morphological classes are defined by the dimensions of transitivity and gender. Transitivity dominates since both transitive and intransitive stems largely come in derivational pairs differentiated by gender. Intransitive verbs differ by the gender of the agent while transitive verbs differ by the gender of the patient:

> intransitive, with inanimate agent (VII):
> *mihkwa·w* 'it is red'
> intransitive, with animate agent (VAI):
> *mihkosiw* 'he is red'
> transitive, with inanimate patient (VTI):
> *pakamaham* 'he strikes it'
> transitive, with animate patient (VTA):
> *pakamahwe·w* 'he strikes him'

This derivational pairing reflects the syntactic-semantic category of transitivity rather than the morphological class of the stem:

> *wanihta·w*   VAI-T   'he loses it'
> *wanihe·w*   VTA   'he loses him'

For a discussion of the so-called inanimate agent forms of VTA and VAI verbs, see section 4.142.

4.1.1.1.1.

Intransitive verbs involve only one referent, the agent; they neither express a patient morphologically nor do they occur with a patient complement of any kind.

VII-P:
> *ta·pwe·*   *miywa·siniyiwa*   *otayo·winisa.*
> truly   be-beautiful   her(3)-clothes(0p)
>   (VII 0´p INDEP)
> 'Truly, excellent were her clothes.'

There is only one verb type, the impersonal verbs (VII-N), that never occurs with an agent complement; however, the agent is expressed morphologically in the verb:

> *piyisk   mitoni ki·sika·yiw.*
> finally   really be-day(VII 0´ INDEP)
> 'At last it was full daylight.'

VAI-I:
> *apiw*   *e·kota*   *awa*   *oskini·kiw.*
> sit(VAI 3 INDEP)   there   this(3)   young-man(3)
> 'The youth sat down there.'

Table 4. Basic Verb Types

Basic Verb Type		Stem Class	Morphological Participants	Syntactic Referents	Example
VII-P	inanimate intransitive (personal)	VII	agent	agent	*misa·w* 'it is big'
VII-N	inanimate intransitive (non-personal)	VII	agent	[agent]	*ki·sika·w* 'it is day'
VAI-I	animate intransitive (intransitive)	VAI	agent	agent	*apiw* 'he sits'
VAI-T	animate intransitive (transitive)	VAI	agent	agent-patient	*kimotiw* 'he steals (s.t./s.o.)' *a·pacihta·w* 'he uses (s.t.)'
VAI-A	animate intransitive (ambivalent)	VAI	agent	agent-(patient)	*osi·misiw* 'he has (him as) younger sibling'
VTI-T	transitive inanimate (transitive)	VTI	agent	agent-patient [inanimate]	*wa·pahtam* 'he sees it'
VTI-I	transitive inanimate (intransitive)	VTI	agent	agent	*ma·ham* 'he canoes downriver'
VTA-1	transitive animate (single patient)	VTA	agent-patient[a]	agent-patient [animate]	*wa·pame·w* 'he sees him'
VTA-2	transitive animate (double patient)	VTA	agent-patient[a]	agent-patient (1) [animate]-patient (2) [unspecified]	*miye·w* 'he gives (s.t./s.o.) to him'

[a]Only one participant is morphologically expressed in third-person forms (cf. 4.1.4.).

VTI-I:

e·kosi   ma·hamwak, ...
thus   canoe-downriver(VTI 3p INDEP)
'Thus they went downstream, ...'

4.1.1.1.2.

Transitive verbs involve both an agent and a patient. Verbs of type VTI-T and VAI-T stems in -*hta·*- may occur only with an inanimate patient, and the patient's number and obviation are not expressed in the verb:

o·ma   a·pacihta·   ca·pihcikanis, ...
this(0) use-(s.t.)(VAI 2 IMVE) spear(0)
'Use this spear, ...'

wa·pahtam   e·kota nana·tohk mi·ciwina
see-s.t.(VTI 3 INDEP) there   all-kinds foodstuff(0p)
'There he saw all kinds of foods.'

The VAI-T type also includes a number of primary (and derivationally opaque) stems that occur with patients of either gender:

mi·na pa·skisikan me·kiw, ...
also gun(0)   give(s.t./s.o.)-out(VAI 3 INDEP)
'He also gave out a gun, ...'

ta·pwe· me·kiw   pe·yak misatimwa;
truly   give(s.t./s.o.)   one   horse(3´)
         -out(VAI 3 INDEP)
'Truly he gave out one horse;'

Note that the stem *me·ki*- is often used to refer to the giving of a woman in marriage (Wolfart 1992:393-395).

There is at least one verb type, VAI-A, which is ambivalent with respect to transitivity. Verbs of this type are typically derived from dependent noun stems (or possessed themes; 4.2.1.) and may function both intransitivity and transitively:

"ko·na·pe·min   ci·?"
have-(him-as)-a-husband(VAI 2 INDEP) (question)
'"Are you married?"'

"ko·na·pe·min e·wakw   a·na   oskini·kiw," ...
have-(him-as)- that-one(3) that(3) youth(3)
a-husband)
(VAI 2 INDEP)
' "You are consorting with that young man," ...'

Verbs of type VTA-1 mark both agent and patient morphologically (except in those forms that involve third-person referents only; 4.1.4.):

e·kota mihce·t ninipaha·wak
there   many   kill-s.o.(VTA 1-3p INDEP)
niskak   mi·na si·si·pak, ...
goose(3p) and   duck(3p)
'Over there I have killed a lot of geese and ducks, ...'

VTA-2 verbs involve a second patient in addition to the morphologically marked patient. This second patient is not marked morphologically and may be of any gender, number, or obviation status:

..., *pe·yakwasa·kay   mihkwe·kin*
one-coat's-worth   red-cloth(0)
kika-miyitin, ...
give-(s.t., s.o.)-to-s.o.(VTA 1-2) INDEP)
'..., I will give you one coat's worth of red flannel. ...'

nitawa·simisa ohcitaw
my-son(3´)   indeed
nimiya·w
give-(s.t., s.o.)-to-s.o.(VTA 1-3 INDEP)
wa·piski-wiya·s, ...
Whiteman(3)
'My son indeed I give to the White man, ...'

piyisk awa   aw   o·skini·kiw
finally this(3) this(3) young-man(3)
... *oste·sa   miyik   ospwa·kana, ...*
his(3)-older- give-(s.t., s.o.)-to   pipe(3´)
brother(3´)   -s.o.(VTA (3´)
                -3 INDEP)
'At last the youth ... was given a pipe by his elder brother, ...'

4.1.1.2. THE INDEFINITE AGENT

The indefinite agent (4.2.1.) is the only verbal category that does not participate in concord or complementation of any kind:

ki·yipa ma·na   picina·niwiw,
early   always move-camp(VAI INDF INDEP)
ki·kise·pa·   e·-wi·-picihk.
in-the-morning   intend(IPV)-move-camp
                    (VAI INDF CJ)
'We always move camp early, when we move camp in the morning.'

English translations of indefinite agent forms tend to be fairly free; a close translation of the preceding example would have to use circumlocutions such as 'camp is broken early', or 'breaking of camp takes place early'. Indefinite agent forms are often translated by English impersonal passives:

"..." *e·-itikawiya·n*
say-so-to-s.o.(VTA INDF-1 CJ)
    '"..." one calls me', or '"..." I am called'

... *e·-asamiht,   piyisk   tipiska·yiw.*
feed-s.o.   finally   be-night
(VTA INDF-3 CJ)   (VII 0´ INDEP)
'... as he was being served, night fell.'

404

As an inflectional category, the indefinite agent is asymmetrical; actions on general patients are expressed by secondary derivatives (5.3.3.3.). Its representation in the basic paradigms is incomplete, and the suppletive paradigms (4.1.4.2.) might well be treated as instances of secondary derivation.

4.1.1.3. THE RELATIONAL

Relational verb forms relate the action denoted by the stem to a person other than the agent in a way that is not specified; while some instances may be interpreted as benefactive, others are completely neutral. There is no concord of any kind.

Relational forms are based on VAI and VTI stems and constitute a marginal paradigm (4.1.4.2.).

kimiywe·yihtamwa·n   *k-e·si-ne·hiyawe·t.*
like-s.t.   thus(IPV)-speak-Cree
  (VTI 2 INDEP REL)   (VAI 3 CJ CH)
'Do you like (with respect to him) the way he talks Cree?'

Relational forms frequently occur with possessed nouns (a situation that has led some grammarians to confuse relational forms with those marking obviative participants):

..., *ki·spin ta-otinamwak*
      if   take-s.t.(VTI 1 CJ REL)
opi·kiskwe·winiwa·wa.
their(3p)-speech(0p)
'... if I had recorded (with relation to them) their speeches.'

The indefinite agent appears to be particularly frequent among relational forms:

e·-poyo·wiht   e·kwa,   kwiye·skimot ...
stop(VAI INDF   then   transform-oneself
  CJ REL)   (VAI 3 CJ CH)
'when it was time to stop (with relation to him), he transformed himself ...'

4.1.2. MODAL CATEGORIES

Plains Cree verbs are inflected in three orders: independent, conjunct, and imperative. The orders use different sets of affixes (although some subsets recur in more than one order).

The orders also differ in their syntactic function. Briefly, independent and imperative order forms occur as whole sentences:

nipimipahta·n.
run(VAI 1 INDEP)
'I was running.'

tapasi·k!
flee(VAI 2p IMVE)
'Flee!'

Conjunct forms tend to occur in dependent clauses:

ta·pwe· e·-ki·-mi·cisot kawisimo·w e·-nipa·t.
truly   past(IPV)-eat   lie-down   sleep
             (VAI 3 CJ)   (VAI 3 INDEP)   (VAI 3 CJ)
'Truly, when he had eaten, he lay down to sleep.'

Moreover, the three inflectional orders coincide only partially with the modal categories that may be observed in various types of clause linkage.

The discrepancies between inflectional orders and noninflectional modal categories are most sharply illuminated by the distribution of the negators. In the most common pattern, *namo·ya* with independent appears in a declarative clause and *e·ka·* with conjunct in a conditional clause:

cike·ma· namo·ya miywa·sin
evidently not   be-good(VII 0 INDEP)
e·ka· ta-a·kaya·si·mot   *ayisiyiniw.*
not   FUTURE-speak-English(VAI 3 CJ)   person(3)
'Of course it is not good if a person does not speak English.'

Both *namo·ya* and *e·ka·* occur with the conjunct; *namo·ya*, for example, in a declarative or narrative clause,

..., namo·ya e·-nihta·-a·kaya·si·moya·n, ...
      not   be-competent-speaking-English(VAI 1 CJ)
'..., I cannot speak English, ...'

and *e·ka·* in a causal clause,

..., e·ka· a·kaya·si·mowin   e·-aya·ya·n, ...
     not   English-language(0) have-(s.t.)(VAI 1 CJ)
'..., because I do not have fluency in English, ...'

e·ka· 'not' (or, more commonly, the variant *e·ka·ya*) is the only negator to occur with the imperative. With the conjunct, it is most prominent in causal and conditional clauses and also in purpose (avolitional, prohibitive) clauses:

..., e·ka· ka-wa·pamikoye·k.
      not   future-see-s.o.(VTA 3-2p CJ)
'..., lest she see you.'

In jussive clauses (4.1.2.4.), *e·ka·* also occurs with verb forms of the independent order.

namo·ya (also *nama*) 'not' primarily occurs in declarative and narrative clauses and with the independent:

... namo·ya nita·pacihta·n   anima, ...
     not   use-(s.t.)(VAI 1 INDEP) that(0)
'... I do not have the use of that, ...'

Many narrative and declarative clauses also exhibit *namo·ya* with the conjunct:

..., namo·y e·-nana·tawa·piyit.
      not   look-about(VAI 3' CJ)
'..., he [the other] was not looking about.'

..., mo·y wi·hka·t ka-ki·-pakitinama·n, ...
     not   ever   FUTURE-be-able-let-s.t.-go
                    (VTI 1 CJ)
'..., I will never be able to let it go, ...'

Within the orders there are further inflectional distinctions of mode. However, many of these modes are very poorly attested in contemporary Plains Cree, and the missionary sources, which offer a bewildering array of paradigms, are yet to be fully evaluated. Therefore, no attempt is made here to present a unified account of the interrelations of the verbal modes.

Dubitative forms, for example, occur in both the independent and conjunct order, but only a handful of forms have been recorded (4.2.3.3.; Wolfart 1973:44). In addition to doubt, the dubitative expresses expected but not fully certain facts:

..., ta·nite·   mi·na we·htina·hkwe· askihkwa.
     from-where also   take-s.o.-from-   pail(NA 3')
                       there(VTA 3-
                       (3') CJ DUB)
'I wonder where he got a pail.'

4.1.2.1.
The indicative is the primary mode of the independent order; it is used in independent sentences.

The three preterit modes, which are identified by their suffixes, are rare and incompletely attested (tables 5-6). Their semantic structure is only partially understood.

The h-preterit and ht-preterit are the only part of the entire verbal system to exhibit the third-person prefix *o-*. The h-preterit frequently denotes events that persist, while both the ht-preterit and the p-preterit seem to be used mostly of events that are completed. The p-preterit seems to be restricted to inanimate intransitive (VII) stems (and to VAI and VTA indefinite-agent forms, which pattern like VII stems; 4.1.4.2.). Examples are:

ma·ninakisk mihti   otawata·h.
then   wood(0)   haul(VAI 3 h-PRET)
'Then he kept hauling wood.' (informant's translation)

e·wakw a·wa otawa·sisiwihtay
that-one this be-a-child(VAI 3 HT-PRET)
wi·sahke·ca·hk.
Wisahkechahk(3)
'That boy was Wisahkechahk (the culture hero) in his childhood.'

aspin ni·mihitona·niwi·pan.
there dance(VAI INDF p-PRET)
'There had been dancing there.'

4.1.2.2.
The four modes of the conjunct order are characterized by two morphological criteria that intersect: initial change (a systematic modification of the first vowel of   *405*

Table 5. VTA h- and ht-preterit

		DIRECT				INVERSE	
		-3	-3p	-3′		3-	3p-
MIXED	1-	niwa·pama·h 'I saw him' |ne—a·-h| 1—dir-	niwa·pama·htayak 'I saw them' |ne—a·-htay-a-k| 1—dir- -3-p	niwa·pamima·h 'I saw him' |ne—em-a·-h| 1—obv-dir-	-1	niwa·pamikoh 'he saw me' |ne—ekw-[i]-h| 1—inv-	niwa·pamikohtayak 'they saw me' |ne—ekw-[i]-htay-a-k| 1—inv- -3-p
			niwa·pama·htay 'I saw him' |ne—a·-htay-a| 1—dir- -3				
	2-	kiwa·pama·h 'you saw him' |ke—a·-h| 2—dir-			-2	kiwa·pamikoh 'he saw you' |ke—ekw-[i]-h| 2—inv-	
					-21	kiwa·pamikohta·naw 'he saw us' |ke—ekw-[i]-htay-enaw-a| 2—inv- -21-3	
THIRD-PERSON	3-		owa·pama·h 'he saw (him)' |we—a·-h| 3—dir-		-3		owa·pamikoh '(he) saw him' |we—ekw-[i]-h| 3—inv-
	3p-		owa·pama·hta·wa·w 'they saw (him)' |we—a·-htay-ewa·w| 3—dir- -p				
YOU-AND-ME	2-	-1 kiwa·pamih 'you saw me' |ke—i-h| 2—dir-			-2	1- kiwa·pamitih 'I saw you' |ke—eti-h| 2—inv-	

NOTE: The forms of the ht-preterit are underlined.

the stem; 6.3.7.) and the suffix |ih|, which closes the construction.

The general meaning of these modes is indicated by the following glosses:

simple (no initial change, no |ih|)	'that it is ...'
changed (initial change, no |ih|):	'it being ...'
subjunctive (no initial change, |ih|)	'if it be ...'
iterative (initial change, |ih|)	'whenever it is ...'

There seems little justification for attempting a hierarchical ranking of these four modes; both defining criteria correlate with specific syntactic-semantic features, and it is no surprise that the iterative shares the salient characteristics of both: the occurrence in participial and narrative clauses typical of initial change, as well as the conditionality associated with |ih|.

The simple conjunct generally expresses subsequence or purpose; it most commonly occurs with the purposive preverb *kita, ta*:

kit-a·pacihta·t   *nika-miya·w.*
PURPOSIVE(IPV)-use   PURPOSIVE(IPV)
-(it)(VAI 3 CJ SIMPLE)   -give-(s.t.)-to-s.o.
   (VTA 1-3 INDEP)

'I will give him things to use.'

It is also governed by certain conjunctions, such as *nawac* 'it is better that', *maywe·s, pa·moye·s* 'before', or *ta·nika, pitane·* 'would that':

nawac sipwe·hte·yahk.
better   leave(VAI 21 CJ SIMPLE)
'we had better go away from here.'

ta·nika ki·h-wa·pama·yahkok.
I wish   see-s.o.(VTA 21-3p CJ SIMPLE)
'I wish we could have seen them.'

Table 6. VAI, VTI, and VII Preterit

		h-preterit	ht-preterit	p-preterit
VAI	1	*nitapih* 'I sat' |ne(t)—h| 1—		
	2	*kitapih* 'you sat' |ke(t)—h| 2—		
	21		*kitapihta·naw* 'we sat' |ke(t)—htay-enaw| 2— -21	
	2p		*kitapihta·wa·w* 'you sat' |ke(t)—htay-ewa·w| 2— -2p	
	3	*otapih* 'he sat' |we(t)—h| 3—	*otapihtay* 'he sat' |we(t)—htay| 3—	
	3p		*otapihta·wa·w* 'they sat' |we(t)—htay-ewa·w| 3— -p	
VTI	1	*nimiske·h* 'I found it' |ne—e·-h| 1—		
	2	*kimiske·h* 'you found it' |ke—e·-h| 2—		
	3	*omiske·h* 'he found it' |we—e·-h| 3—		
VII	0	*misa·h* 'it was big' |-h|		*misa·pan* 'it used to be big' |-Lpan|

The changed conjunct indicates subordination in an entirely neutral way. It is the most versatile of the conjunct modes and consequently the most widely used as well. Examples:

te·kohte·t   awa   kise·yiniw, ...
arrive(VAI 3 CJ CH) this(3) old-man(3)
apiyiwa   onaha·hkisi·ma.
sit(VAI 3′ INDEP) his(3)-nephew(NDA 3′)
'When the old man arrived, ... his nephew sat down.'

... papa·mita·cimo·w,   e·-nitonawa·t.
crawl-about   look-for-s.o.
  (VAI 3 INDEP INDIC)   (VTA 3-(3′) CJ CH)
'... he crawled about, looking for him.'
ha·, kiske·yihtam   e·-macihtwa·yit.
well know-s.t.(VTI 3 INDEP) be-evil(VAI 3′ CJ CH)
'Well, he knew that he (the other) was evil.'

ta·nisi e·-to·tahk.
how   do-s.t.(VTI 3 CJ CH)
'How does he do it?'

Initial change may operate on the first vowel of the verb stem, as in the first example above. More typically, it affects one of a small set of preverbs (5.4.), such as *ki·*, which appears as *ka·*. The most frequent preverb is *e·*, which does not affect the meaning of the verb and seems to serve only as a "vehicle" for initial change; its underlying, unchanged form does not occur in Cree.

The subjunctive mode expresses a condition:

ki·spin   nipahikawiya·ni, ...
if   kill-s.o.(VTA INDEF-1 CJ SBJ)
'if I am slain, ...'

The iterative mode denotes repeated events:

ki·tahtawe·   ma·na   se·pwe·hte·ci,
presently   always   leave(VAI 3 CJ ITER)
owi·kima·kana   wawe·siyiwa.
his(3)-wife(3´)   dress-up(VAI 3´ INDEP)
'Then presently, whenever he went away, his wife dressed up.'

Expressions of season often show the iterative: *niyi·piniyiki* 'in summer-time (obv.)', *pe·poniyiki* 'in winter-time, every winter (obv.)'.

4.1.2.3. MODES OF THE IMPERATIVE ORDER

Imperative forms are used for commands and exhortations. The immediate imperative is unmarked; while it expresses no particular time, it typically refers to the situation at hand:

kite·m   miyin.
your(2)-horse(3)   give-(s.t.)-to-s.o.
                    (VTA 2-1 IMVE IMM)
'Give me your horse.'

The delayed mode indicates that the command or exhortation is to be obeyed not immediately but at a later point in time. It is frequently found together with a conditional clause:

miskawa·ye·ko,   *nipaha·hke·k ...*
find-s.o.   kill-s.o.
(VTA 2p-3 CJ SBJ)   (VTA 2p-3 IMVE DEL)
'If you find him, kill him then ...'

4.1.2.4. NONINFLECTIONAL MODAL CATEGORIES

Not all modal distinctions are expressed inflectionally. For example, the preverb *kita, ta* with an independent order verb not only marks subsequence or purpose but also may express a mild command:

ha·w, ki·we·payi.   *e·wakonik*
well ride-back(VAI 2 IMVE)   that-one(3p)
aniki   ne·wo   anik   o·kima·wak , ...
that(3p)   four   that(3p) chief(3p)
kita-pe·-itohte·wak   *o·ta ...*
hither (IPV)-come(VAI 3p INDEP)   here
'Very well, ride back. Let those four chiefs come here ...'

This jussive category is overtly marked only in negative sentences. While future phrases show the negator *namo·ya*, the jussive is negated by *e·ka(ya)*:

namo·ya   ta-takosin.
not   arrive(VAI 3)
'He will not be coming.'

e·ka·ya   ma·ka   kotak   awiyak
not   but   other(3) someone(3)
kita-pe·-itohte·w;
hither(IPV)-come(VAI 3)
'But let no one else come here;'

Time relations are a major area of noninflectional modality. Temporal-aspectual reference in Cree remains poorly understood.

The verbal paradigms express time relations in only two places: in the preterit mode of the independent order (4.1.2.1.) and in the delayed mode of the imperative order (4.1.2.3.)

The expression of time relations is localized at a different point within the verbal complex, namely in the preverbs that follow the personal prefixes but are separated from the main stem by a phonological word boundary (cf. 5.4. and 6.1.2.2.)

For example, subsequence or future is indicated by *ka* and *kita, ta*:

ma·sko·c   ahpo·   kita-nipahe·w   wi·htiko·wa.
perhaps   even   kill-s.o.   Windigo (3´)
                    (VTA 3-(3´) INDEP)
'Perhaps he will even kill the Windigo.'

The past is marked by the preverbs *ki·₁* and *o·h, ohci*; in negative clauses the second is preferred. For example,

namo·ya   wa·pahtam   ita
not   see-s.t.(VTI 3 INDEP) where
e·-ki·-pimohte·yit;
PAST(IPV)-walk(VAI 3´ CJ)
'He could not see (the tracks) where the other had walked;'

ma·ka   namo·ya   wi·hka·c   a·ta
but   not   even   nevertheless
no·h-nayawapin.
run.out.of.breath (VAI 1 INDEP)
'But in spite of that I never ran out of breath.'

..., namo·y   o·hci-misikitiw   ma·ka
      not   be.big(VAI 3 INDEP)   but
ki·-okima·wiw   e·sa   mistahi.
be.chief(VAI 3 INDEP)   (EMPH)   much
'he was not a big man but he was a chief indeed.'

The examples reflect the primary meanings of the most common time-preverbs. But the system as such, and the interrelations of the various time references especially, are yet to be analyzed satisfactorily.

4.1.3. DIRECTION

The category of direction serves to specify agent and patient in transitive animate (VTA) verbs, as in

(1) *kiwa·pamin*
    see-him(VTA 2-1 INDEP)
    'you see me'

(2) *kiwa·pamitin*
    see-him(VTA 1-2 INDEP)
    'I see you'

Direct forms[§] involve actions

(a) from a second person onto a first person: *kitasamin* 'you feed me (2-1)';

(b) from a non-third person onto a third person: *nitasama·w* 'I feed him (1-3)';

(c) from a proximate third person onto an obviative third person: *asame·w* 'he feeds him (3-(3´))';

(d) from an obviative third person onto another: *asame·yiwa* 'he feeds him (3´-(3´))'.

The forms of the imperative order are all direct, either with a second person acting on a first person: *pe·hik* 'wait for me! (2p-1)'; or with a second person acting on a third person: *pe·hihk* 'wait for him! (2p-3)'.

Inverse forms are exactly symmetrical to the direct set (except for the imperative and the indefinite agent forms). The action is

(a) from a first person onto a second person: *kitasamitin* 'I feed you (1-2)';

(b) from a third onto a non-third person: *nitasamik* 'he feeds me (3-1)';

(c) from an obviative third person onto a proximate third person: *asamik* 'he feeds him ((3´)-3)';

(d) from another obviative onto an obviative third person: *asamikoyiwa* 'he feeds him ((3´)-3´)'.

For identically glossed pairs such as (c) *asame·w* and *asamik*, see 4.1.3.3.

The indefinite-agent forms (4.1.1.2) show the same structure as the direct forms, notably the direction marker |a·| in the independent order, for example, *wa·pama·w* 'he is seen'. Morphologically, they are agentless forms that only express the patient. (The indefinite-agent forms of the suppletive paradigm (4.1.4.2.) are based on a suffix |ekawi| whose relation to the inverse marker |ekw| remains to be clarified.)

[§]Bloomfield's terminology, which has found wide acceptance in later studies, is based on the actual morphological theme signs and restricts the terms direct and inverse to those forms that involve a third-person participant. Bloomfield's (1946:98-99) themes and their labels (1957:46) correspond to the analysis here as follows:

theme 1 (direct)	:	direct	[cases (b)-(d)]
theme 2 (inverse)	:	inverse	[cases (b)-(d)]
theme 3 (thou-me)	:	direct	[case (a)]
theme 4 (I-thee)	:	inverse	[case (a)].

4.1.3.1. MORPHOLOGICAL EXPRESSION

Direction is morphologically expressed by theme signs. In sentence (3), for example, the direct theme sign |a·| indicates the noun *atim* as patient, whereas the inverse theme sign |ekw| (appearing as *-iko*) marks the same noun as agent in (4).

(3) *nise·kiha·na·n   atim.* (*)
    scare-s.o.(1p-3) dog(3)
    'We scare the dog.'

(4) *nise·kihikona·n   atim.* (*)
    scare-s.o.(3-1p) dog(3)
    'The dog scares us.'

4.1.3.2. DIRECTION AND FOCUS

Where a third person interacts with a first or second person, direction is strictly a function of the extralinguistic situation; sentences (3) and (4) simply denote opposite events.

If both referents are third persons, the choice of direction may depend on previous focus assignment (3.4.1.):

(5) *[a·say mi·na kita·pamik;*
    again   and   look-at-s.o.(VTA (3´)-3)
    wi·sta   ka-kita·pame·w.]
    he-too(3)   look-at-s.o.(VTA 3-(3´))
    kinwe·sk   kita·pamik;
    long   look-at-s.o.(VTA (3´)-3)
    piyis   pi·htoke·yiwa.
    finally   enter(VAI 3´)
    '[Again he [the bear] looked at him; he, too, kept looking at him [the bear].] For a long time he [the bear] looked at him; at last he [the bear] came inside.'

The extreme case of direction being obligatorily determined is rare; it occurs only in cross-reference when a possessed noun acts on its possessor:

(6) *[ka·so·w   aw   o·skini·kiw.] namo·ya*
    hide(VAI 3) this(3) youth(3)   not
    wa·pamik   wi·timwa.
    see-s.o.(VTA (3´)-3) his(3)-sister-in-law(3´)
    '[This young man hid himself.] His sister-in-law did not see him.'

In general, the choice of direction is not predetermined, as it is in the above examples, and the interplay of direction and focus (obviation) gives rise to four possibilities; note that word order is irrelevant.

(7) *se·kihe·w   na·pe·w atimwa.(*)*
    scare-s.o.(3-(3´)) man(3) dog(3´)
    'Man scares dog.'

(8) *se·kihik   na·pe·wa atim.(*)*
    scare-s.o.((3´)-3) man(3´) dog(3)
    'Man scares dog.'

(9) *se·kihe·w   na·pe·wa atim.(*)*
    scare-s.o.(3-(3´)) man(3´) dog(3)
    'Dog scares man.'

409

(10) *se·kihik*　　　　　*na·pe·w atimwa.(*)*
　　scare-s.o.((3´)-3)　man(3)　dog(3´)
　　'Dog scares man.'

Sentences (7) and (8) are paraphrases of one another. They describe the same extralinguistic event but differ in both focus and direction: *se·kihe·w* (7) is direct, *se·kihik* (8) is inverse; in (7) *na·pae·w* 'man' is proximate and *atimwa* 'dog' is obviative, while in (8) *na·pe·wa* 'man' is obviative and *atim* 'dog' proximate. The same relation holds between sentences (9) and (10).

In any such pair the direct sentence, for instance (7), is the more neutral; the inverse sentence either indicates the persistence of an earlier focus assignment or expresses special emphasis.

In the remaining pairs, opposite events are described if two sentences differ in only one of the categories under discussion. Sentences (7) and (9) are identical with respect to direction (*se·kihe·w*) but differ in focus (*na·pe·w* vs. *na·pe·wa*, *atimwa* vs. *atim*). Sentences (7) and (10) on the other hand, while identical in focus, differ with respect to direction.

In spite of superficial similarities, direction in Cree is fundamentally different from voice in the Indo-European languages. While the Cree relation of direction functions between sentences that denote opposite events, such as (7) and (10), the English relation of voice exists between sentences that denote the same event, such as the glosses:

(7) 'Man scares dog.'
(8) 'Dog is scared by man.'

As a practical consequence, the voice of English glosses is irrelevant from a Cree point of view. Whether sentence (4) is glossed 'the dog scares us' or 'we are scared by the dog' has no bearing on the meaning of the Cree sentence.

4.1.3.3. MARKEDNESS

Within the category of direction, direct is the unmarked member. For example, isolated sentences that involve two unrelated third-person referents show the direct verb rather than the inverse; unless the choice is influenced by preceding syntactic context, sentence (7) is normal while sentence (8) provides special emphasis.

The morphology of the paradigms, and the highly productive theme sign |ekw| in particular, clearly shows inverse to be the marked member of the opposition.

The unmarked status of the direct member of the direct-inverse opposition finds strong support in the fundamental order principle that holds among the person categories of Cree (3.3.1.) and in turn emphasizes the generality of that phenomenon. The relative position of the person markers within a two-referent verb form is fixed. In the direct forms, the actual linear sequence (in time or "left-to-right") of the prefixes and

suffixes corresponds exactly to the priority of second over first, and of second or first over third. In the inverse forms, the actual linear sequence remains unchanged, but the reversal of the fundamental priority order is indicated by theme signs.

4.1.4. BASIC PARADIGMS

The paradigms in tables 7-12 are included as illustrations only; they are not intended as a formal set of rules. As a consequence, different alternants (rather than one highly abstract form) are cited for many morphemes (e.g., |e·kw ~ ye·kw| '2p'), and no zero morphemes are included.

The glosses are informal free translations that are included for readability alone. In the case of individual morphemes, glosses are omitted where they would have been too cumbersome to be helpful (cf. 4.1.4.1.2.) or where, as in the case of unsegmentable endings, they would simply repeat the information provided by row and column headings. Each form is fully characterized by its paradigmatic parameters.

Connective |i| is enclosed in square brackets; all morphophonological rules are presented in 6.3. Accidental lacunae are indicated by empty brackets.

There are 10 verbal suffix positions:
　　1, Thematic obviative sign |em|
　　2, Theme signs [VTA, VTI]
　　3, Thematic obviative sign |eyi|
　　4, Mode signs: h- and ht-preterit
　　5, Non–third person suffixes
　　6 and 7, Mode signs: p-preterit, dubitative
　　8, Third-person suffixes
　　9, Third-person plural and obviative suffixes
　　10, Mode signs: subjunctive and iterative.

4.1.4.1. The structure of the VTA paradigm.
The VTA paradigm as a whole falls into three parts, which are distinct in both semantic and morphological structure.

The mixed set consists of forms that involve both third-person and non-third person referents, for example, *niwa·pama·wak* 'I see them'. On morphological grounds, the indefinite-agent forms of the basic paradigms are included in this set. At least in the independent order, both referents are morphologically expressed, for example, in the preceding example by |ne| '1' and |wa-k| '3p'.

The third-person set consists of forms that are restricted to third-person referents exclusively. Morphologically, these forms differ from the mixed forms by expressing only one referent; the other is, in effect, left unspecified. Syntactically and referentially, the other referent is always an obviative third person.

In direct third-person forms, a constraint on the range of the morphologically unexpressed referent (the patient) is sometimes provided by the morpheme |em| which marks it as obviative (3.4.2.).

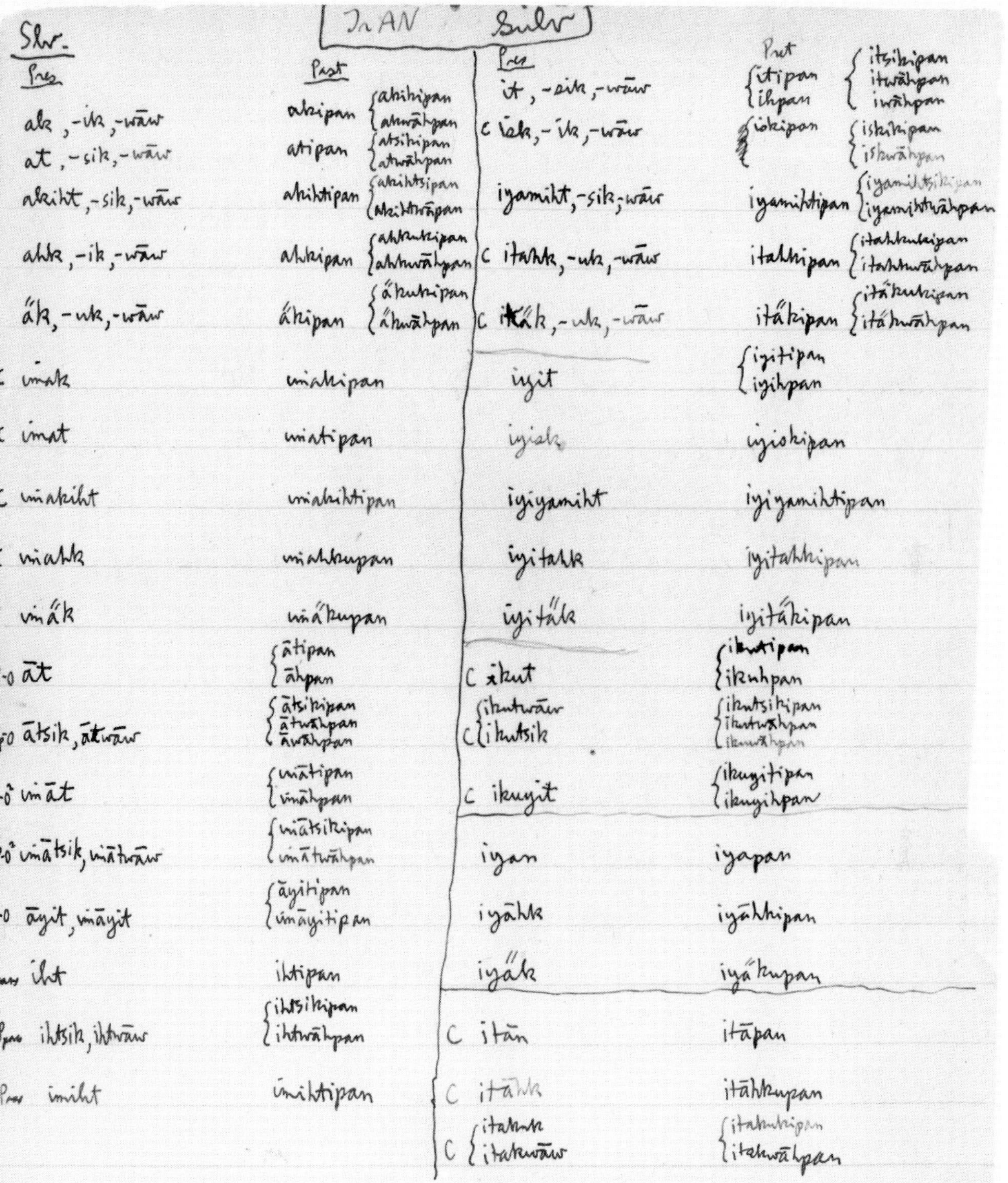

Tr AN Subv

Sbv.

Pres	Past	Pres	Pret
ak, -ik, -wāw	akipan {akikipan / akwāhpan}	it, -sik, -wāw	{itipan / ihpan} {itsikipan / itwāhpan / iwāhpan}
at, -sik, -wāw	atipan {atsikipan / atwāhpan}	C isk, -ik, -wāw	{iskipan} {iskikipan / iskwāhpan}
akiht, -sik, -wāw	akihtipan {akihtsipan / akihtwāhpan}	iyamiht, -sik, -wāw	iyamihtipan {iyamihtsikipan / iyamihtwāhpan}
ahk, -ik, -wāw	ahkipan {ahkukipan / ahkwāhpan}	C itahk, -uk, -wāw	itahkipan {itahkukipan / itahkwāhpan}
āk, -uk, -wāw	ākipan {ākukipan / ākwāhpan}	C itāk, -uk, -wāw	itākipan {itākukipan / itākwāhpan}
C imak	imakipan	iyit	{iyitipan / iyihpan}
C imat	imatipan	iyisk	iyiskipan
C imakiht	imakihtipan	iyiyamiht	iyiyamihtipan
C imahk	imahkupan	iyitahk	iyitahkipan
C imāk	imākupan	iyitāk	iyitākipan
3-0 āt	{ātipan / āhpan}	C ikut	{ikutipan / ikuhpan}
3p-0 ātsik, ātwāw	{ātsikipan / ātwāhpan / āwāhpan}	C {ikutwāw / ikutsik}	{ikutsikipan / ikutwāhpan / ikuwāhpan}
C 3-0' imāt	{imātipan / imāhpan}	C ikuyit	{ikuyitipan / ikuyihpan}
C 3p-0' imātsik, imātwāw	{imātsikipan / imātwāhpan}	iyan	iyapan
0-0 āyit, imāyit	{āyitipan / imāyitipan}	iyāhk	iyāhkipan
C 3pass iht	ihtipan	iyāk	iyākupan
C 3ppass ihtsik, ihtwāw	{ihtsikipan / ihtwāhpan}	C itān	itāpan
C 0pass imiht	imihtipan	C itāhk	itāhkupan
		C {itakuk / itakwāw}	{itakukipan / itakwāhpan}

Smithsonian, NAA: Bloomfield uncatalogued ms.

Fig. 1. Paradigms of transitive animate conjunct verb (here called subordinative - "sbv."), present and past (or preterit) tense. Published in facsimile in Bloomfield (1984, 2:314). Extracted by Leonard Bloomfield from Hunter (1875). Bloomfield did his fieldwork among the Plains Cree in 1925.

Table 7. VTA Independent Indicative

direct

		-3	-3p	-3´
MIXED	indf-	waˑpamaˑw 'one sees him' |-aˑ-wa| -dir-3	waˑpamaˑwak 'one sees them' |-aˑ-wa-k| -dir-3-p	waˑpamimaˑwa 'one sees him' |-em-aˑ-wa-h| -obv-dir-3-obv
	1-	niwaˑpamaˑw 'I see him' |ne—aˑ-wa| 1—dir-3	niwaˑpamaˑwak 'I see them' |ne—aˑ-wa-k| 1—dir-3-p	niwaˑpamimaˑwa 'I see him' |ne—em-aˑ-wa-h| 1—obv-dir-3-obv
	2-	kiwaˑpamaˑw 'you see him' |ke—aˑ-wa| 2—dir-3	kiwaˑpamaˑwak 'you see them' |ke—aˑ-wa-k| 2—dir-3-p	kiwaˑpamimaˑwa 'you see him' |ke—em-aˑ-wa-h| 2—obv-dir-3-obv
	1p-	niwaˑpamaˑnaˑn 'we see him' |ne—aˑ-enaˑn-a| 1—dir-1p-3	niwaˑpamaˑnaˑnak 'we see them' |ne—aˑ-enaˑn-a-k| 1—dir-1p-3-p	niwaˑpamimaˑnaˑna 'we see him' |ne—em-aˑ-enaˑn-a-h| 1—obv-dir-1p-3-obv
	21-	kiwaˑpamaˑnaw 'we see him' |ke—aˑ-enaw-a| 2—dir-21-3	kiwaˑpamaˑnawak 'we see them' |ke—aˑ-enaw-a-k| 2—dir-21-3-p	kiwaˑpamimaˑnawa 'we see him' |ke—em-aˑ-enaw-a-h| 2—obv-dir-21-3-obv
	2p-	kiwaˑpamaˑwaˑw 'you see him' |ke—aˑ-ewaˑw-a| 2—dir-2p-3	kiwaˑpamaˑwaˑwak 'you see them' |ke—aˑ-ewaˑw-a-k| 2—dir-2p-3-p	kiwaˑpamimaˑwaˑwa 'you see him' |ke—em-aˑ-ewaˑw-a-h| 2—obv-dir-2p-3-obv

		-3	-3´
THIRD-PERSON	3-	waˑpameˑw 'he sees (him)' |-eˑ-wa| -dir-3	waˑpamimeˑw 'he sees him' |-em-eˑ-wa| -obv-dir-3
	3p-	waˑpameˑwak 'they see (him)' |-eˑ-wa-k| -dir-3-p	waˑpamimeˑwak 'they see him' |-em-eˑ-wa-k| -obv-dir-3-p
	3´-	waˑpameˑyiwa 'he sees (him)' |-eˑ-eyi-wa-h| -dir-obv-3-obv	

		-1	-1p
YOU-AND-ME	2-	kiwaˑpamin 'you see me' |ke—i-n| 2—dir-1	kiwaˑpaminaˑn 'you see us' |ke—i-enaˑn| 2—dir-1p
	2p-	kiwaˑpaminaˑwaˑw 'you see me' |ke—i-naˑ-ewaˑw| 2—dir- -2p	kiwaˑpaminaˑn 'you see us' |ke—i-enaˑn| 2—dir-1p

Table 7. VTA Independent Indicative (continued)

inverse

		3-	3p-	3´-
MIXED	-1	niwa·pamik 'he sees me' |ne—ekw-a| 1—inv-3	niwa·pamikwak 'they see me' |ne—ekw-a-k| 1—inv-3-p	niwa·pamikoyiwa 'he sees me' |ne—ekw-eyi-wa-h| 1—inv-obv-3-obv
	-2	kiwa·pamik 'he sees you' |ke—ekw-a| 2—inv-3	kiwa·pamikwak 'they see you' |ke—ekw-a-k| 2—inv-3-p	kiwa·pamikoyiwa 'he sees you' |ke—ekw-eyi-wa-h| 2—inv-obv-3-obv
	-1p	niwa·pamikona·n 'he sees us' |ne—ekw-ena·n-a| 1—inv-1p-3	niwa·pamikona·nak 'they see us' |ne—ekw-ena·n-a-k| 1—inv-1p-3-p	niwa·pamikona·na 'he sees us' |ne—ekw-ena·n-a-h| 1—inv-1p-3-obv
	-21	kiwa·pamikonaw 'he sees us' |ke—ekw-enaw-a| 2—inv-21-3	kiwa·pamikonawak 'they see us' |ke—ekw-enaw-a-k| 2—inv-21-3-p	kiwa·pamikonawa 'he sees us' |ke—ekw-enaw-a-h| 2—inv-21-3-obv
	-2p	kiwa·pamikowa·w 'he sees you' |ke—ekw-ewa·w-a| 2—inv-2p-3	kiwa·pamikowa·wak 'they see you' |ke—ekw-ewa·w-a-k| 2—inv-2p-3-p	kiwa·pamikowa·wa 'he sees you' |ke—ekw-ewa·w-a-h| 2—inv-2p-3-obv
THIRD-PERSON	-3	wa·pamik '(he) sees him' |-ekw-a| -inv-3		
	-3p	wa·pamikwak '(he) sees them' |-ekw-a-k| -inv-3-p		
	3´-	wa·pamikoyiwa '(he) sees him' |-eke-eyi-wa-h| -dir-obv-3-obv		

		1-	1p-
YOU-AND-ME	-2	kiwa·pamitin 'I see you' |ke—eti-n| 2—inv-2	kiwa·pamitina·n 'we see you' |ke—eti-ena·n| 2—inv-1p
	-2p	kiwa·pamitina·wa·w 'I see you' |ke—eti-na·-ewa·w| 2—inv- -2p	kiwa·pamitina·n 'we see you' |ke—eti-ena·n| 2—inv-1p

413

Table 8. VTA Conjunct Simple and Changed

direct

		-3	-3p	-3′
MIXED	indf-	e·-wa·pamiht 'as one sees him' |-eht|	e·-wa·pamihcik 'as one sees them' |-eht-[i]-k| -p	e·-wa·pamimiht 'as one sees him' |-em-eht| -obv-
	1-	e·-wa·pamak 'as I see him' |-ak|	e·-wa·pamakik 'as I see them' |-ak-[i]-k| -p	e·-wa·pamimak 'as I see him' |-em-ak| -obv-
	2-	e·-wa·pamat 'as you see him' |-at|	e·-wa·pamacik 'as you see them' |-at-[i]-k| -p	e·-wa·pamimat 'as you see him' |-em-at| -obv-
	1p-	e·-wa·pama·ya·hk 'as we see him' |-a·-ya·hk| -dir-1p	e·-wa·pama·ya·hkik 'as we see them' |-a·-ya·hk-[i]-k| -dir-1p-p	e·-wa·pamima·ya·hk 'as we see him' |-em-a·-ya·hk| -obv-dir-1p
	21-	e·-wa·pama·yahk 'as we see him' |-a·-yahkw| -dir-21	e·-wa·pama·yahkok 'as we see them' |-a·-yahkw-[i]-k| -dir-21-p	e·-wa·pamima·yahk 'as we see him' |-em-a·-yahkw| -obv-dir-21
	2p-	e·-wa·pama·ye·k 'as you see him' |-a·-ye·kw| -dir-2p	e·-wa·pama·ye·kok 'as you see them' |-a·-ye·kw-[i]-k| -dir-2p-p	e·-wa·pamima·ye·k 'as you see him' |-em-a·-ye·kw| -obv-dir-2p

		-3		-3′
THIRD-PERSON	3-	e·-wa·pama·t 'as he sees (him)' |-a·-t| -dir-3		e·-wa·pamima·t 'as he sees him' |-em-a·-t| -obv-dir-3
	3p-	e·-wa·pama·cik 'as they see (him)' |-a·-t-[i]-k| -dir-3-p		e·-wa·pamima·cik 'as they see him' |-em-a·-t-[i]-k| -obv-dir-3-p
	3′-	e·-wa·pama·yit 'as he sees (him)' |-a·-eyi-t| -dir-obv-3		

		-1	-1p	
YOU-AND-ME	2-	e·-wa·pamiyan 'as you see me' |-i-yan| -dir-2	e·-wa·pamiya·hk 'as you see us' |-i-ya·hk| -dir-1p	
	2p-	e·-wa·pamiye·k 'as you see me' |-i-ye·kw| -dir-2p	e·-wa·pamiya·hk 'as you see us' |-i-ya·hk| -dir-1p	

NOTES: The preverb e· does not appear in the simple conjunct; the endings are identical.

The subjunctive and iterative modes show the plural marker \|wa·w\| instead of \|k\| and add \|ih\| (which palatalizes a preceding \|t\|) to the ending.

Table 8. VTA Conjunct Simple and Changed (continued)

inverse

		3-	3p-	3´-
MIXED	-1	*eˑ-waˑpamit* 'as he sees me' |-it|	*eˑ-waˑpamicik* 'as they see me' |-it-[i]-k| -p	*eˑ-waˑpamiyit* 'as he sees me' |-iy-it| -obv-
	-2	*eˑ-waˑpamisk* 'as he sees you' |-esk|	*eˑ-waˑpamiskik* 'as they see you' |-esk-[i]-k| -p	*eˑ-waˑpamiyisk* 'as he sees you' |-iy-esk| -obv-
	-1p	*eˑ-waˑpamikoyaˑhk* 'as he sees us' |-ekw-[i]-yaˑhk| -inv-1p	*eˑ-waˑpamikoyaˑhkik* 'as they see us' |-ekw-[i]-yaˑhk-[i]-k| -inv-1p-p	*eˑ-waˑpamikowaˑyaˑhk* 'as he sees us' |-ekow-aˑ-yaˑhk| -inv-[dir?]-1p
	-21	*eˑ-waˑpamikoyahk* 'as he sees us' |-ekw-[i]-yahkw| -inv-21	*eˑ-waˑpamikoyahkok* 'as they see us' |-ekw-[i]-yahkw-[i]-k| -inv-21-p	*eˑ-waˑpamikowaˑyahk* 'as he sees us' |-ekow-aˑ-yahkw| -inv-[dir?]-21
	-2p	*eˑ-waˑpamikoyeˑk* 'as he sees you' |-ekw-[i]-yeˑkw| -inv-2p	*eˑ-waˑpamikoyeˑkok* 'as they see you' |-ekw-[i]-yeˑkw-[i]-k| -inv-2p-p	*eˑ-waˑpamikowaˑyeˑk* 'as he sees you' |-ekow-aˑ-yeˑkw| -inv-[dir?]-2p
THIRD-PERSON	-3	*eˑ-waˑpamikot* 'as (he) sees him' |-ekw-[i]-t| -inv-3		
	-3p	*eˑ-waˑpamikocik* 'as (he) sees them' |-ekw-[i]-t-[i]-k| -inv-3-p		
	-3´	*eˑ-waˑpamikoyit* 'as (he) sees him' |-ekw-eyi-t| -inv-obv-3		

		1-	1p-	
YOU-AND-ME	-2	*eˑ-waˑpamitaˑn* 'as I see you' |-et-aˑn| -inv-1	*eˑ-waˑpamitaˑhk* 'as we see you' |-et-aˑhk| -inv-1p	
	-2p	*eˑ-waˑpamitakok* 'as I see you' |-et-akw-[i]-k| -inv-2-p	*eˑ-waˑpamitaˑhk* 'as we see you' |-et-aˑhk| -inv-1p	

Table 9. VTA Imperative

	you-and-me		mixed		
	-1	*-1p*	*-3*	*-3p*	*-3´*
			immediate		
2-	*wa·pamin*	*wa·pamina·n*	*wa·pam*	*wa·pam(ik)*	*wa·pamim*
	'see me'	'see us'	'see him'	'see them'	'see him'
	|-i-n|	|-i-ena·n|	|-i|	|-i-(k)|	|-em-i|
	-dir-1/2	-dir-1p		-(p)	-obv-
21-	—	—	*wa·pama·ta·n*	*wa·pama·ta·nik*	*wa·pamima·ta·n*
			'let's see him'	'let's see them'	'let's see him'
			|-a·-ta·n|	|-a·-ta·n-[i]-k|	|-em-a·-ta·n|
			-dir-	-dir- -p	-obv-dir-
2p-	*wa·pamik*	*wa·pamina·n*	*wa·pamihk*	*wa·pamihkok*	*wa·pamimihk*
	'see me'	'see us'	'see him'	'see them'	'see him'
	|-i-k|	|-i-ena·n|	|-ehkw|	|-ehkw-[i]-k|	|-em-ehkw|
	-dir-p	-dir-1p		-p	-obv-
			delayed		
2-	*wa·pami·hkan*	*wa·pami·hka·hk*	*wa·pama·hkan*	*wa·pama·hkanik*	*wa·pamima·hkan*
	'see me later'	'see us later'	'see him later'	'see them later'	'see him later'
	|-i-Lhk-an|	|-i-Lhk-a·hk|	|-a·-Lhk-an|	|-a·-Lhk-an-[i]-k|	|-em-a·-Lhk-an|
	-dir- -2	-dir- -1p	-dir- -2	-dir- -2-p	-obv-dir- -2
21-	—	—	*wa·pama·hkahk*	*wa·pama·hkahkik*	*wa·pamima·hkahk*
			'let's see him later'	'let's see them later'	'let's see him later'
			|-a·-Lhk-ahkw|	|-a·-Lhk-ahk(w)-[i]-k|	|-em-a·-Lhk-ahkw|
			-dir- -21	-dir- -21-p	-obv-dir- -21
2p-	*wa·pami·hke·k*	*wa·pami·hka·hk*	*wa·pama·hke·k*	*wa·pama·hke·kok*	*wa·pamima·hke·k*
	'see me later'	'see us later'	'see him later'	'see them later'	'see him later'
	|-i-Lhk-e·kw|	|-i-Lhk-a·hk|	|-a·-Lhk-e·kw|	|-a·-Lhk-e·kw-[i]-k|	|-em-a·-Lhk-e·kw|
	-dir- -2p	-dir- -1p	-dir- -2p	-dir- -2p-p	-obv-dir- -2p

The you-and-me set consists of forms that involve first and second persons exclusively. While some of these forms include markers for both referents (e.g., *ki—ina·n* '2-1p': \|ke\| '2', \|i\| 'direct', \|ena·n\| '1p'), the makeup of other forms is less obvious (Wolfart 1973:5.64).

All you-and-me forms neutralize the number distinction of the second person in the environment of the first-person plural;[||] they also pattern alike in expressing the "2p" referent in the 2p-and-1 forms and the "1p" referent in the 2(p)-and-1p forms.

4.1.4.1.1. Paradigm Leveling

At several points within the verbal paradigms one can observe relatively clear instances of paradigmatic reshaping. While this assertion is based primarily on internal evidence, it is supported by symptomatic differences between paradigms recorded at different places and times.

The mixed set of the conjunct order provides a major example. All endings with a plural non-third person participant (1p, 21, 2p) use the direction markers \|a·\| and \|ekw\| followed by the non-third person markers of the VAI paradigm. These forms constitute a major innovation over the paradigms of Hunter (1875[1862]) which show less segmentable endings; Lacombe (1874) cites both sets side by side. The emergence of more "agglutinative" forms appears to reflect a tendency toward more transparent structures. The Eastern Swampy Cree data of Ellis (1971) strikingly support this view since there the obviative marker of the direct subparadigms is extended to the inverse. In fact, a fully "regular" system has evolved in Eastern Swampy Cree, with both \|em\| and \|h\| marking the obviative throughout the conjunct order: *-imici* \|em-it-[i]-h\| (3´-1 CJ).

[||]In Ellis's (1971, 1983) Eastern Swampy Cree paradigms from the West Coast of James Bay, only the imperative order reflects the above pattern while the other orders show the opposite, neutralizing the number-distinction of the first person in the context of the second person.

Table 10. The VAI Paradigm

| | INDEPENDENT | CONJUNCT | | IMPERATIVE | |
	Indicative	Simple and changed	Subjunctive and iterative	Immediate	Delayed
indf		e·-apihk 'as one sits' |-hk|	apihki 'if one sits' |-hk-ih|		
1	nitapin 'I sit' |ne(t)—n|	e·-apiya·n 'as I sit' |-ya·n|	apiya·ni 'if I sit' |-ya·n-ih|		
2	kitapin 'you sit' |ke(t)—n|	e·-apiyan 'as you sit' |-yan|	apiyani 'if you sit' |-yan-ih|	api 'sit' |-h|	api·hkan 'sit later' |-Lhk-an|
1p	nitapina·n 'we sit' |ne(t)—ena·n|	e·-apiya·hk 'as we sit' |-ya·hk|	apiya·hki 'if we sit' |-ya·hk-ih|		
21	kitapina·naw 'we sit' |ke(t)—na·-enaw|	e·-apiyahk 'as we sit' |-yahkw|	apiyahko 'if we sit' |-yahkw-ih|	apita·n 'let's sit' |-ta·n|	api·hkahk 'let's sit later' |-Lhk-ahkw|
2p	kitapina·wa·w 'you sit' |ke(t)—na·-ewa·w|	e·-apiye·k 'as you sit' |-ye·kw|	apiye·ko 'if you sit' |-ye·kw-ih|	apik 'sit' |-k|	api·hke·k 'sit later' |-Lhk-e·kw|
3	apiw pimisin 'he sits/lies' |-wa|	e·-apit e·-pimisihk 'as he sits/lies' |-t/k|	apici pimisihki 'if he sits/lies' |-t/k-ih|		
3p	apiwak pimisinwak 'they sit/lie' |-wa-k|	e·-apicik e·-pimisihkik 'as they sit/lie' |-t/k-[i]-k|	apitwa·wi pimisihkwa·wi 'if they sit/lie' |-t/k-wa·w-ih|		
3´	apiyiwa 'he sits' |-eyi-wa-h|	e·-apiyit 'as he sits' |-eyi-t|	apiyici 'if he sits' |-eyi-t-ih|		

Transparency also appears to play a role in another problem involving |ekw| together with the y-alternants of the non-third person markers, for instance, |ya·hk ~ a·hk|. The y-alternants are morphophonologically regular after VAI long-vowel stems, and their occurrence throughout the VAI paradigm is clearly attributable to paradigmatic pattern pressure. The situation in the direct forms of the VTA paradigm is very similar, but no obvious motivation has been discovered for the inverse forms: whether the y-alternants provide the environment for the vocalization of the |w| of |ekw|, or whether an extended form |eko| conditions the occurrence of the y-alternants, remains an open question.

The forms for 3´-1p, 3´-21, and 3´-2p, finally, appear to consist of a derived stem in |ekow| followed by the direct theme sign and thus resemble the forms of the relational paradigm (4.1.4.2.). A specific motivation for the emergence of these remarkable forms has not been discovered, but the analysis finds some confirmation in Edwards's (1954) ending -ikowat for 3´-2.

4.1.4.1.2. Individual Problems

The following comments are intended to clarify questions that may arise from the paradigm tables.

The double role of |ewa·w|. The suffixes |ena·n, enaw, ewa·w| function both as non-third person markers (|ena·n| in the VTA imperative, which has no personal prefixes) and as mere plural markers for the personal prefixes. This second function is quite clear in the possession paradigm of nouns and especially in the preterit

Table 11. The VTI Paradigm

| | INDEPENDENT | CONJUNCT | | IMPERATIVE | |
	Indicative	Simple and changed	Subjunctive and iterative	Immediate	Delayed
indf-		e·-miskamihk 'as one finds it' |-am-ehk|	miskamihki 'if one finds it' |-am-ehk-ih|		
1	nimiske·n 'I find it' |ne—e·-n|	e·-miskama·n 'as I find it' |-am-a·n|	miskama·ni 'if I find it' |-am-a·n-ih|		
2	kimiske·n 'you find it' |ke—e·-n|	e·-miskaman 'as you find it' |-am-an|	miskamani 'if you find it' |-am-an-ih|	miska 'find it' |-a-h|	miskamo·hkan 'find it later' |-amw-[i]-Lhk-an|
1p	nimiske·na·n 'we find it' |ne—e·-ena·n|	e·-miskama·hk 'as we find it' |-am-a·hk|	miskama·hki 'if we find it' |-am-a·hk-ih|		
21	kimiske·(na·)naw 'we find it' |ke—e·-na·-enaw|	e·-miskamahk 'as we find it' |-am-ahkw|	miskamahko 'if we find it' |-am-ahkw-ih|	miske·ta·n 'let's find it' |-e·-ta·n|	miskamo·hkahk 'let's find it later' |-amw-[i]-Lhk-ahkw|
2p	kimiske·na·wa·w 'you find it' |ke—e·-na·-ewa·w|	e·-miskame·k 'as you find it' |-am-e·kw|	miskame·ko 'if we find it' |-am-e·kw-ih|	miskamok 'find it' |-amw-[i]-k|	miskamo·hke·k 'find it later' |-amw-[i]-Lhk-e·kw|
3	miskam 'he finds it' |-am-wa|	e·-miskahk 'as he finds it' |-am-k|	miskahki 'if he finds it' |-am-k-ih|		
3p	miskamwak 'they find it' |-am-wa-k|	e·-miskahkik 'as they find it' |-am-k-[i]-k|	miskahkwa·wi 'if they find it' |-am-k-wa·w-ih|		
3′	miskamiyiwa 'he finds it' |-am-eyi-wa-h|	e·-miskamiyit 'as he finds it' |-am-eyi-t|	miskamiyici 'if he finds it' |-am-eyi-t-ih|		

of verbs; preterit use provides the only context within the verbal system for the third-person prefix *o-* and its pluralization, |we—ewa·w|. (The relation of |ewa·w| to the third-person pluralizer of the conjunct order, |wa·w|, remains to be investigated.)

Forms without personal suffixes. The h-preterit is the only paradigm that does not show any person suffixes; thus it highlights the theme signs and the thematic suffixes |em| and |eyi|.

The inverse theme sign of the you-and-me set. |et| occurs in the conjunct, and |eti| in the independent order. The shape |eti| is indicated by the VTA 1-2 form of the h-preterit, |-eti-h|, where the theme sign is followed directly by the preterit suffix |h|.

Epenthetic *-na·-*. The 21 suffix of the VAI and VTI paradigms occurs both with and without an epenthetic

-*na·-*; the two forms appear to be in free variation (4.1.4.2.). The 2p suffix of the VAI and VTI paradigms, by contrast, is found only with *-na·-*, as *-na·wa·w*; note that this form also occurs in the you-and-me set of the VTA paradigm.

VTA imperative endings. The suffix |i| of the 2-3 form usually remains with stems that are monosyllabic and have a short vowel: *isi* 'tell him so' (6.35.). Otherwise it is apocopated.

For 2-3p, only the suffix |i| occurs in texts collected since 1967: *na·s* 'get them'; in Bloomfield's texts the ending |-i-k| is more frequent: *ntaw-asamik* 'go feed them'.

|a·hk| and |ahkw|. These suffixes, which mark 1p and 21 in the conjunct and delayed imperative, are subject to partial syncretism: both appear with and without the final |w|.

Table 12. The VII Paradigm

	INDEPENDENT Indicative	CONJUNCT Simple and changed	Subjunctive and iterative
0	misa·w miywa·sin 'it is big/good' |-wi|	e·-misa·k e·-miywa·sihk 'it being big/good' |-k|	misa·ki miywa·sihki 'if it is big/good' |-k-ih|
0p	misa·wa miywa·sinwa 'they are big/good' |-wah|	e·-misa·ki e·-miywa·sihki 'they being big/good' |-k-ih|	[ ]
0′	misa·yiw miywa·siniyiw 'it is big/good' |-eyi-wi|	e·-misa·yik e·-miywa·siniyik 'it being big/good' |-eyi-k|	misa·yiki miywa·siniyiki 'if it is big/good' |-eyi-k-ih|
0′p	misa·yiwa miywa·siniyiwa 'they are big/good' |-eyi-wah|	e·-misa·yiki e·miywa·siniyiki 'they being big/good' |-eyi-k-ih|	[ ]

The suffix |akw|. Occurring only in the 1-2p form of the VTA conjunct, |akw| appears to mark the second person; it is pluralized by |k| in the simple and changed modes and by |wa·w| in the subjunctive and iterative.

4.1.4.2. MARGINAL AND SUPPLETIVE PARADIGMS
A marginal paradigm diverges, however slightly, from one of the basic paradigms, while suppletive paradigms generally serve to fill gaps in the basic paradigms; both are formed by specific suffixes (table 13).

The boundaries delimiting marginal and suppletive paradigms from each other and from certain derivationally late derivatives are problematic. For example, the VAI and VTI indefinite-actor forms are morphologically indistinguishable from the basic VII paradigm; however, syntactically and semantically, they fill obvious gaps within their respective basic paradigms.

Relational themes are formed from VAI and VTI stems with the suffix |w| (which in the case of VTI stems is preceded by the theme sign |am(w)|). The function of relational forms is discussed in 4.1.1.3.

The conjunct suffixes clearly reflect the VTA endings, while those of the independent order resemble the VAI endings (table 14).

The diminutive suffix |esi| (note the corresponding nominal suffixes |es| and |esis|) in VAI and VTI verbs directly follows the stem (VAI) or theme sign (|a|, VTI) and precedes the usual VAI endings:

... si·pi·sis   o·ma   nica·sowahasin
   river(0 dim) this(0) cross-s.t.(VTI 1 INDEP DIM) ·
                  (|net-a·sowah-a-esi-n|)
'I crossed this little stream ...'

(In this example the palatalization of the |t| in the prefix |net| to c is an additional mark of the diminutive.) The same suffix has been observed to follow the theme sign in VTA stems, but the data do not suffice for a full statement.

The VTA inanimate-agent paradigm shows the inverse theme sign |ekw ~ eko| followed by the usual VAI endings; two of the independent third-person endings and all conjunct endings except for the singular mixed forms are identical with the corresponding VTA endings (table 14).

This paradigm thus provides important evidence for the postulated development of transparent (and, eventually, derivational) inverse forms (section 4); it also supports the hypothesis that the agent of third-person inverse forms (and perhaps of others as well) is unspecific (4.1.4.1.).

The VTA indefinite-agent paradigm (4.1.1.2.) is most typical of the suppletive type: while the indf-3 forms are part of the basic VTA paradigm, all others consist of a suffix |ekawi| followed by the usual VAI endings; for example,

nipi·htokwe·hikawina·n
take-s.o.-inside(VTA INDF-1p INDEP)
'we were taken inside'.

Regular indefinite-agent forms are found in the conjunct order of both VAI and VTI verbs. In the independent order, by contrast, this role is performed by forms based on the suffixes -(na·)niwan-, -(na·)niwin- or -(na·)niwi-, which are then inflected precisely like

419

Table 13. Summary of Marginal and Suppletive Paradigms

Paradigm	Stem	Suffix	Endings
Marginal			
Relational	VAI, VTI	|w|	VTA/VAI
Diminutive	VAI, VTA, VTI	|esi|	VAI
Inanimate agent	VTA	|ekw|~|eko|	VAI
Suppletive			
Indefinite agent	VTA	|ekawi|	VAI
Inanimate agent	VAI, VTI	|Lmakan|	VII
Indefinite agent	VAI, VTI	|(na·)niwan, (na·)niwin, (na·)niwi|	VII

Table 14. Relational and VTA Inanimate Agent Paradigms

Relational

	Independent		Conjunct
	indicative	*h-preterit*	
indf	-a·n	[ ]	-iht
1	ni—a·n	ni—a·h	-ak
2	ki—a·n	[ ]	-at
3	-e·w	[ ]	-a·t

VTA inanimate agent

	Independent	*Conjunct*
-1	ni—ikon	-ikoya·n
-2	ki—ikon	-ikoyan
-1p	[ ]	-ikoya·hk
-21	ki—ikona·naw	-ikoyahk
-2p	[ ]	-ikoye·k
-3	-iko·w, -ik	-ikot
-3p	-ikwak	[ ]
-3′	[ ]	[ ]

VII stems. Except for VAI stems in -*e·*- or -*a·*-, which show -*a·*- before the suffix in any case, all stems take the epenthetic -*na·*- (4.1.4.1.2.).

The VAI inanimate-agent forms are based on the suffix |Lmakan| and then inflected like VII n-stems.

4.2. NOUN INFLECTION

Nouns are inflected in two paradigms: the possession (PS) paradigm in the inner layer, and the number-obviation (NO) paradigm, which serves to mark concord, in the outer layer of inflection.

All affixes of the possession and number-obviation paradigms of nouns (with the exception of the prefix *mi*-) recur in the verbal paradigms.

4.2.1. POSSESSION

The possession paradigm provides cross-reference to a person other than that denoted by the noun itself.

When occurring with the possession paradigm, some stems form a special possessed theme by suffixing |em| directly to the stem; e.g. |si·si·p-| 'duck', |si·si·p-em|: *nisi·si·pim* 'my duck'.

Dependent noun stems are obligatorily inflected for possession. They mostly include kin terms and terms for body parts and a few personal possessions; there is no evidence for an alienable-inalienable dichotomy: for example, -*kosis*- 'son', -*i·w*- 'wife', -*to·te·m*- 'kinsman', -*sit*- 'foot', -*sikwanay*- 'tail' (of fish)', -*i·k*- 'dwelling', -*i·pisis*- 'arrow', |-*i·waθ*-| 'sacred pack', -*i·c*- (root) 'fellow'.

In some instances a dependent noun is paralleled by a nondependent noun of apparently identical denotation: -*te·m*- NDA 'dog, horse', *atimw*- NA 'dog', *mistatimw*- NA 'horse'. In these cases, the nondependent noun is not inflected for possession.

Dependent stems are bound and cannot occur without a personal prefix. If no specific possessor is involved, the "indefinite" prefix *mi*-, which is restricted to dependent stems, is used (4.1.1.2.):

e·koni   *miyawa*
that-one(0p)   (INDF POSS)-body(0p)
e·-nahasta·cik.
bury-(s.t.)(VAI 3p CJ)
'These bodies they buried.'

While *mi*- seems to be used primarily with human possessors, the third-person prefix *o*- ~ *w*- typically occurs in nouns denoting animal parts in the context of slaughtering:

asamin   *pe·yak osoy, ...*
feed-s.o.(VTA 2-1 IMVE) one   his(3)-tail(0)
'Give me one (beaver-) tail to eat, ...'

The form in *o*- also occurs as the base of further derivatives, for example the following from |-*te·h*-| 'heart': *ote·himin*- 'strawberry', *ote·hipakw*- 'cabbage'; -*te·m*- 'dog, horse': *ote·mi*- VAI 'have a dog, horse', *ote·mih*- VTA 'make him have a dog, horse':

wa·kayo·sa ote·miw   *iskwe·w.*
bear(3′)   have-a-dog/horse   woman (3)
         (VAI 3 INDEP)
'The woman had a bear for her beast of burden.'

Verbs of this type may even be derived from the possessed theme of nondependent stems: *na·pe·w* 'man',

-na·pe·m- 'husband': ona·pe·mi- VAI 'have (him for) a husband':

> namo·ya ona·pe·miwak.
> not   have-a-husband(VAI 3p INDEP)
> 'they do not have husbands.'

4.2.2. THE NUMBER-OBVIATION PARADIGM

The number-obviation paradigm is presented separately at the top of tables 15 and 16, and then in combination with the possession paradigm. The final vowel (-a, -i) of singular nouns appears only with monosyllabic noun stems (6.3.5.); *nisk-* NA 'goose': *niska; pihkw-* NI 'ashes': *pihko; -i·k-* NDI: *ni·ki* 'my dwelling'.

4.2.3. MINOR CATEGORIES

Possession alone of the nominal categories is closely tied to the general categories of gender, number, person, and obviation; the remaining categories are relatively isolated.

4.2.3.1. LOCATIVE

Nouns and particles alike are used as local complements and some particles even show the same locative suffix as nouns. When functioning as local complements, nouns do not express any distinctions of number or obviation; *nisit* 'my foot', *nisita* 'my feet', but *nistihk* 'on my foot, feet'. The obviation status of a possessor, on the other hand, is not affected: *ostikwa·nihk* 'on his (3) head', *ostikwa·niyihk* 'on his (3′) head'.

Nouns distinguish two types of locatives: the simple locative in |ehk| indicates location in the widest sense: within, upon, at, as in *wa·skahikanihk* 'in the house', *sa·kahikanihk* 'at the lake', *nistikwa·nihk* 'on my head'. The distributive locative, in |ena·hk|, is used only with nouns that denote humans or animals; it has not been recorded with possessed themes. The resulting forms mean 'in the land of such-and-such beings', 'at the place of such-and-such people', as in *sa·si·w-* 'Sarcee Indian': *sa·si·na·hk* 'at Sarcee Reserve', *mostosw-* 'buffalo': *mostosona·hk* 'in the buffalo country'.

4.2.3.2. VOCATIVE

The special address form or vocative functions outside the concord and person-obviation systems. However, it does show a number distinction: *nito·te·m* 'my fellow tribesman!', *nito·te·mitik* 'my fellow tribesmen!'.

With a limited number of stems (mainly kin terms), the vocative singular shows loss of final consonant, a suffix -*e·*, or both:

> |-moso·m-| NDA 'grandfather':   *nimoso·*
> |-ste·s-| NDA 'older brother':   *niste·se·*
> |-kosis-| NDA 'son':   *nikose·*

The plural suffix is |etik| throughout:

> |-si·m-| NDA 'younger sibling':   *nisi·mitik*
> |ne·hiyaw-| NA 'Cree':   *ne·hiya·tik*

Table 15. Animate Noun Inflection in Stems *si·si·p-* 'duck' and *-te·m-* 'horse, dog'

		Number-Obviation			Locative
		Proximate singular (3)	Proximate plural (3p)	Obviative (3′)	
		si·si·p |-a| 'duck'	*si·si·pak* |-a-k| 'ducks'	*si·si·pa* |-a-h| 'duck/ducks'	*si·si·pihk* |-ehk| 'in a duck'
		'___ horse'	'___ horses'	'___ horse/horses'	'on ___ horse'
1	'my ___'	*nite·m* |ne—a|	*nite·mak* |ne—a-k|	*nite·ma* |ne—a-h|	*nite·mihk* |ne—ehk|
2	'your ___'	*kite·m* |ke—a|	*kite·mak* |ke—a-k|	*kite·ma* |ke—a-h|	*kite·mihk* |ke—ehk|
1p	'our ___'	*nite·mina·n* |ne—ena·n-a|	*nite·mina·nak* |ne—-ena·n-a-k|	*nite·mina·na* |ne—ena·n-a-h|	*nite·mina·hk*
21	'your-and-my ___'	*kite·minaw* |ke—enaw-a|	*kite·minawak* |ke—enaw-a-k|	*kite·minawa* |ke—enaw-a-h|	*kite·mina·hk* |ke—enaw-ehk|
2p	'your ___'	*kite·miwa·w* |ke—ewa·w-a|	*kite·miwa·wak* |ke—ewa·w-a-k|	*kite·miwa·wa* |ke—ewa·w-a-h|	*kite·miwa·hk* |ke—ewa·w-ehk|
3	'his ___'	—	—	*ote·ma* |we—a-h|	*ote·mihk* |we—ehk|
3p	'their ___'	—	—	*ote·miwa·wa* |we—ewa·w-a-h|	*ote·miwa·hk* |we—ewa·w-ehk|
3′	'the other's ___'	—	—	*ote·miyiwa* |we—eyi-wa-h|	*ote·miyihk* |we—eyi-ehk|

(POSSESSION — left side label)

Table 16. Inanimate Noun Inflection in Stems *wiya·s-* 'meat' and *-spiton-* 'arm'

			Number-Obviation		Locative
			Proximate singular (0)	Proximate plural (0p)	
			wiya·s |-i| 'meat'	*wiya·sa* |-ah| 'pieces of meat'	*wiya·sihk* |-ehk| 'on the meat'
			'___ arm'	'___ arms'	'on ___ arm'
POSSESSION	indf	'an ___'	*mispiton* |me—i|	*mispitona* |me—ah|	*mispitonihk* |me—ehk|
	1	'my ___'	*nispiton* |ne—i|	*nispitona* |ne—ah|	*nispitonihk* |ne—ehk|
	2	'your ___'	*kispiton* |ke—i|	*kispitona* |ke—ah|	*kispitonihk* |ke—ehk|
	1p	'our ___'	*nispitonina·n* |ne—ena·n-i|	*nispitonina·na* |ne—ena·n-ah|	*nispitonina·hk*
	21	'your-and-my ___'	*kispitoninaw* |ke—enaw-i|	*kispitoninawa* |ke—enaw-ah|	*kispitonina·hk* |ke—enaw-ehk|
	2p	'your ___'	*kispitoniwa·w* |ke—ewa·w-i|	*kispitoniwa·wa* |ke—ewa·w-ah|	*kispitoniwa·hk* |ke—ewa·w-ehk|
	3	'his ___'	*ospiton* |we—i|	*ospitona* |we—ah|	*ospitonihk* |we—ehk|
	3p	'their ___'	*ospitoniwa·w* |we—ewa·w-i|	*ospitoniwa·wa* |we—ewa·w-ah|	*ospitoniwa·hk* |we—ewa·w-ehk|
	3´	'the other's ___'	*ospitoniyiw* |we—eyi-wi|	*ospitoniyiwa* |we—eyi-wah|	*ospitoniyihk* |we—eyi-ehk|

4.2.3.3. PRETERIT

Animate nouns, dependent or not, have a preterit form, which indicates that the noun's denotatum no longer exists. The suffix \|epan\| follows the possessed theme sign \|em\| but precedes the person suffixes of the possession paradigm: \|-moso·m-\| NDA 'grandfather': *nimoso·mipanina·nak* 'our late grandfathers'.

4.3. PRONOUN INFLECTION

The inflectional classification of pronouns coincides only partially with classifications based on syntactic and semantic criteria. Most of the pronominal stems also participate in a number of derivational processes (for examples see 5.3.3.2.).

In addition to the number-obviation paradigm of nouns, there are two specifically pronominal paradigms (I and II) and two isolated paradigms (table 17).

4.3.1. DEMONSTRATIVE PRONOUNS

The demonstrative pronouns *awa* 'this, *ana* 'that', and *naha* 'that yonder' constitute a semantic field whose internal structure remains to be explored more fully.

The delimiting demonstrative *e·wako* 'that one' also has the (interchangeable) variants *e·yako* and *e·ko*. This is the only nonverbal paradigm in Plains Cree that shows an inanimate obviative form, *e·wakoyiw*.

aya 'this one' occurs primarily as the final member of compounds, as in *osk-a·ya* 'a young one'. It is also very frequent as an articlelike hesitation signal:

o·k *a·yak* *no·tokwe·siwak*
this(3p) this-one(3p) old-woman(3p)
'these old women'.

4.3.2. INTERROGATIVE AND INDEFINITE PRONOUNS

The interrogative and indefinite pronouns show inflectional differences but also some overlap; the corresponding animate and inanimate stems are clearly built on the same root, even though their interrelations are not fully understood. The animate interrogative is *awi·na* 'who', and the animate indefinite *awiyak* 'someone'. The inanimate interrogative is *ki·kway* 'what', the inanimate indefinite *ki·kway* 'something'. The inanimate interrogative also has the qualitative meaning 'what kind'.

Both the animate and the inanimate stem also have a noninflectional function. When occurring with one of the demonstratives, of whatever inflection, the form *awi·na* expresses surprise:

awi·n *e·s* *o·hi* ...
(surprise) (EMPH) this(3´)
'What was this, ...'

422

Table 17. Pronouns

	Animate				Inanimate	
	Proximate singular (3)	Proximate plural (3p)	Obviative (3´)	Proximate singular (0)	Proximate plural (0p)	Obviative (0´)
Pronominal paradigm I	-a	-ki	-hi	-ma	-hi	
demonstrative 'this'	awa	o·ki	o·hi	o·ma	o·hi	
demonstrative 'that'	ana	aniki	anihi	anima	anihi	
demonstrative 'that yonder'	na·ha	ne·ki	ne·hi	ne·ma	ne·hi	
interrogative 'who'	awi·na	awi·niki	awi·nihi	—	—	
delimiting interrogative 'which one'	ta·ni	ta·niki	ta·nihi	ta·ni, ta·nima	ta·nihi	
Pronominal paradigm II	-a·	-e·hka·k	-e·ha·	-e·	-e·ha·	
existential interrogative 'where is he'	ta·niwa·	ta·niwe·hka·k	ta·niwe·ha·	ta·niwe·	ta·niwe·ha·	
existential demonstrative 'there he is'	e·wakwa·	[ ]	[ ]	e·wakwe·	[ ]	
Pronouns with noun endings	|-a|	|-a-k|	|-a-h|	|-i|	|-ah|	
interrogative 'what; what kind'	ki·kwaya	ki·kwayak	ki·kwaya	ki·kway, ki·kwayi	ki·kwaya	
indefinite 'something'	—	ki·kwayak	ki·kwaya	ki·kway, ki·kwayi	ki·kwaya	
weak demonstrative 'this one'	aya	ayak	aya	ayi	aya	
"nominal" 'another'	kotak	kotakak	kotaka	kotak	kotaka	
Isolated pronouns						
delimiting demonstrative 'that one'	e·wako	e·wakonik	e·wakoni	e·wako	e·wakoni	e·wakoyiw
indefinite 'someone'	awiyak	awiyak	awiya	—	—	

The preterital form *awi·nipan* (cf. 4.2.3.3.), which is not inflected for number-obviation, expresses surprise about a denotatum that no longer exists.

> *awi·nipan o·ma   mi·kiwa·hpis.*
> gone   this(0) wigwam(0)
> 'Gone was this wigwam.'

Together with the negator *nama*, *ki·kway* 'something' not only means 'nothing' but also closely parallels *awi·nipan*:

> *ma·k e·kwa, nama ki·kway   e·koni*
> but   then   not   something that-one(0p)

a·cimo·wina.
story(0p)
'But now there aren't any such stories.'

4.3.3. "EXISTENTIAL" PRONOUNS

The "existential" pronouns *ta·niwa·* 'where is he' and *e·wakwa·* 'there he is' are verb substitutes:

> *ta·niwe·ha·   kotaka   kitata·we·wina?*
> where-is-(0p) other(0p) your(2)-purchase(NI 0p)
> 'Where are your other groceries?'

Both are quite rare in texts; a third pronoun *o·ya·* 'that no longer here' requires further study before it can be assigned to this paradigm.

423

4.3.4. PERSONAL PRONOUNS

The personal pronouns are not inflected for number and obviation; however, as a set, they largely parallel the possession paradigm of nouns in the systematic use of personal prefixes and suffixes (table 18). (Note that *kiˑyaˑnaw* deviates from the general pattern by its long stem-final vowel.)

Both types of personal pronouns are emphatic; the affirmative pronouns are typically translated as (for *niˑsta*) 'I, too; I myself; I, by contrast.'

5. WORD FORMATION

The inflected words of Cree include verbs, nouns, and pronouns that are very similar to nouns inflectionally and syntactically. All uninflected words are subsumed under the term particle (or indeclinable).

5.1. PRIMARY STEM FORMATION

If all inflectional affixes are removed from a word, the remaining stem shows further internal structures; for example, *nimaˑkwahteˑn* 'I chew it' contains the stem *maˑkwaht-* VTI, which can be analyzed into a root *maˑkw-* 'press' and the final morpheme *-aht-* 'by mouth'. All Cree stems are treated as consisting of at least these two parts. (In certain cases, for instance, with unanalyzable noun stems such as *atimw-* 'dog, horse', it is convenient to posit a zero constituent.) A third constituent may optionally occur between them: *maˑkw-ahw-* VTA 'press him by tool' and *maˑkw-aˑskw-ahw-* VTA 'press him by tool as/with wood'. The three positions within a Cree stem are known as initial, medial, and final; the last two terms are also each used for the morpheme class whose members occur in the respective position.

The primary stems exemplified above are built on morphemes, including a root, which cannot occur by themselves (even if appropriate inflectional affixes were added). In addition, an entire stem may be combined with further derivational suffixes; for example, *maˑkwahcikeˑ-* |maˑkw-aht-[i]-keˑ| VAI 'chew (in general), chew things' where |keˑ| indicates the absence of a specific object. In a secondary stem the initial position is occupied by another stem (rather than by a root); as indicated in part A of figure 2, it is then followed optionally by a medial and obligatorily by a final.

Table 18. Personal Pronouns

		Simple -iˑya-	Affirmative -iˑsta-
1	'I'	*niˑya*	*niˑsta*
2	'you'	*kiˑya*	*kiˑsta*
1p	'we'	*niˑyanaˑn*	*niˑstanaˑn*
21	'you-and-me'	*kiˑyaˑnaw*	*kiˑstanaw*
2p	'you'	*kiˑyawaˑw*	*kiˑstawaˑw*
3	'he'	*wiˑya*	*wiˑsta*
3p	'they'	*wiˑyawaˑw*	*wiˑstawaˑw*

5.2. SECONDARY STEM FORMATION AND DEVERBAL SUFFIXES

The pattern of forming stems from other stem is extremely productive in Cree; as displayed in figure 3, nouns and verbs (including verbs of different stem classes) are freely derived from one another.

This "left-to-right" derivation is complemented by another, typically Algonquian, pattern that might be described as "vertical."

Many roots are paralleled by non-initial (or deverbal) alternants that occur as medials or finals; for example, consider the root *atimw-* 'dog, horse' (as in the identical noun stem) and the medial *-astimw-*, as in *kanawastimweˑ-* 'watch horses' (where it is followed by the VAI final *-eˑ-*) or in the noun stem *atimwastimw-* 'dog of a dog'. In many cases, the noninitial alternant lacks part of the initial alternant from which it is said to be derived; in *noˑtaˑposweˑ-* VAI 'hunt rabbits', for instance, the root is *noˑt-* 'pursue' and the medial is *-aˑposw-* 'rabbit'; compare the noun stem *waˑposw-* 'rabbit'. Note that the absence of morpheme-initial *w* is not a matter of phonological structure; contrast *apitwaˑwi* |api-t-waˑw-ih| 'if they sit'.

Not only roots but also entire stems may give rise to noninitial alternants (deverbal medials and finals). A deverbal final based on the stem *masinah-* VTI 'mark it, write it', for instance, occurs with the root *kiˑs-* 'complete' in *kiˑsasinaham* VTI 'he completes writing it'; a secondarily derived stem *masinahikeˑ-* VAI 'write things' is the basis of the deverbal final which follows the root *peˑt-* 'hither' in *peˑtasinahikeˑw* VAI 'he writes hither'.

The recursive nature of secondary ("left-to-right") derivation in combination with the free ("vertical") formation of deverbal medials and finals may be visualized as interlocking (see figure 2 where A is intended to symbolize the former, and B the latter). Together they account for much of the great productivity and complexity of Cree word formation (Wolfart 1980; Wolfart and Ahenakew 1987a).

5.3. ROOTS, MEDIALS, AND FINALS

All three morpheme classes have some members that occur in longer and shorter alternants. These alternations generally seem to depend on the morpheme's occurrence in specific words; the medial 'liquid', for example, has the shape *-ipeˑ-* in *naˑtipeˑw* VAI 'he fetches a liquid', but *-ipeˑk-* in *kisiˑpeˑkinam* VTI 'he washes it by hand'.

5.3.1. ROOTS

Many roots occur freely in primary verb, noun, and particle stems: *waˑp-* 'light, bright' in the verb *waˑpameˑw* VTA 'he sees him', the noun *waˑpastim* 'white horse or dog', or the particle *waˑpiski* 'white'.

5.3.2. MEDIALS

Medials are characterized primarily by the fact that they are not restricted to a particular stem class.

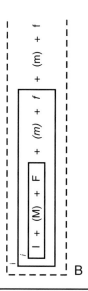

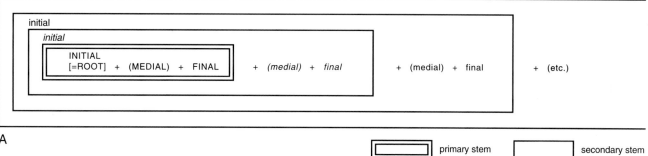

| INITIAL [=ROOT] + (MEDIAL) + FINAL | + (medial) + final | + (medial) + final | + (etc.) |

| | primary stem | | secondary stem |

Fig. 2. Stem formation. A = Concatenative ("left-to-right") derivation. B = Paradigmatic ("vertical") derivation.

-a·piski- 'stone, metal', for example, is found in the verb *kipa·piskaham* VTI 'he closes it with/as metal/stone', in the noun *ospwa·kana·pisk* 'pipestone', and in the indeclinable *pe·yakwa·pisk* 'one dollar' (cf. *ni·swa·pisk* 'two dollars').

Simple medials (i.e., those not paralleled by entire stems) in the main reflect two semantic areas: body parts and "classificatory" categories.

Many medials denoting body parts also occur in dependent nouns (4.2.1.): *-stikwa·n-*: *nistikwa·n* 'my head', *we·we·kistikwa·ne·w* VAI 'he has his head wrapped'; *-atay-*: *natay* 'my belly', *pikwa·taye·hwe·w* VTA 'he pierces s.o.'s belly by tool'. Others have not been observed in dependent nouns: *-iskw-* 'head': *sa·kiskwe·w* VAI 'he sticks his head out'; *-nisk-* 'arm': *isiniske·yiw* VAI 'he moves his arm thus'; *napate·nisk* 'with/at one arm'.

"Classificatory" medials indicate the characteristic features of a class of objects; these may apply to the agent, the patient, or neither (table 19).

5.3.3. FINALS
Finals determine the class of a stem, including the various stemclasses of verbs (4.1.1.1.). Many finals, such

as the animate intransitive verb final *-e·-*, seem to have no further meaning.

Some finals are specifically secondary, as the reciprocal |eto| in *no·tinito-* VAI 'fight one another' (cf. *no·tin-* VTA 'fight s.o.'). Others function in both primary and secondary word formation: the final *-h-* in *se·kihe·w* VTA 'he scares s.o.' and *ote·mihe·w* VTA 'he makes s.o. have a horse' (cf. *ote·mi-* VAI 'have a horse' and the dependent noun stem *-te·m-* 'horse').

5.3.3.1.
Productive noun finals are most clearly seen in secondary derivations. Table 20 includes at least one suffix that may be further analyzed: *-ihka·n* appears to consist of the suffix *-n* added to the animate intransitive verb final *-ihke·-/-ihka·-*, which forms verbs of making and arranging; in the absence of intermediate verb stems the suffix is considered a complex unit.

5.3.3.2.
By far the most common particle final is |i|, which leaves the meaning of the root unaffected. At the opposite extreme, finals like *-wa·w* '(so many) times' or *-ita* 'at a place' have a very concrete meaning (table 21).

425

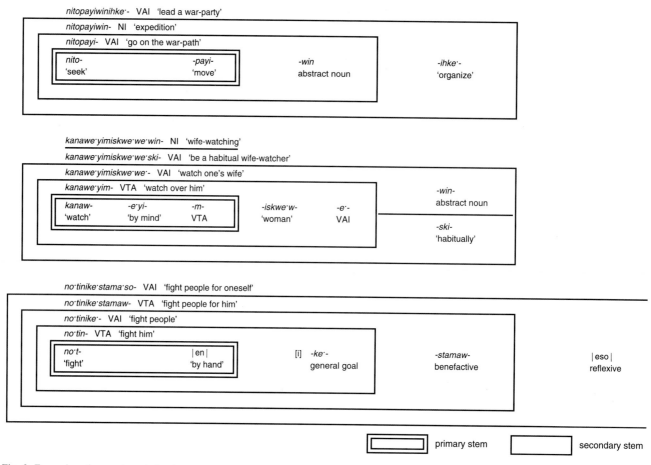

nitopayiwinihke·- VAI 'lead a war-party'

nitopayiwin- NI 'expedition'

nitopayi- VAI 'go on the war-path'

| *nito-* 'seek' | *-payi-* 'move' | *-win* abstract noun | *-ihke·-* 'organize' |

kanawe·yimiskwe·we·win- NI 'wife-watching'

kanawe·yimiskwe·we·ski- VAI 'be a habitual wife-watcher'

kanawe·yimiskwe·we·- VAI 'watch one's wife'

kanawe·yim- VTA 'watch over him'

| *kanaw-* 'watch' | *-e·yi-* 'by mind' | *-m-* VTA | *-iskwe·w-* 'woman' | *-e·-* VAI | *-win* abstract noun / *-ski-* 'habitually' |

no·tinike·stama·so- VAI 'fight people for oneself'

no·tinike·stamaw- VTA 'fight people for him'

no·tinike·- VAI 'fight people'

no·tin- VTA 'fight him'

| *no·t-* 'fight' | |en| 'by hand' | [i] *-ke·-* general goal | *-stamaw-* benefactive | |eso| reflexive |

primary stem   secondary stem

Fig. 3. Examples of secondary derivation.

Note that *-wa·w* and *-wayak* occur both as primary and secondary finals. The locative and temporal finals are paralleled by independent particles such as *ita* 'there', *ite·* 'hither', *isi* 'thus', *ispi·* 'then', *tahto* 'so many'. An almost complete set occurs with the delimiting interrogative *ta·n-* 'which one' and the corresponding demonstrative *e·kw-* 'that one' (cf. 4.3.1.) (table 22).

5.3.3.3.

Verb finals typically come in pairs according to the gender of the agent (in intransitive verbs) or the patient (in transitive verbs) (tables 23-24).

Transitive verb stems end in a single nonsyllabic or in a nonsyllabic preceded by *s* or *h*. Intransitive verb stems end in any vowel other than *a*, or in *n*. (For details and frequency figures see Wolfart 1973:5.5.)

5.4. COMPOUNDS

While functioning as words inflectionally, compounds are like phrases in having a phonological word boundary (indicated by a hyphen; 6.1.1.2.) between their members. In *nitis-a·pin* 'thus I sit', for example, the prefix *nit-* precedes the first member of the compound and the suffix *-n* follows the last. The word boundary

between the particle *isi* 'thus' and the verb stem *api-* 'sit', on the other hand, is marked by the external sandhi phenomena (6.2.2.) of loss of word-final *-i-* and lengthening of word-initial *-a-*. Contrast the unit word *itapiw* 'he sits thus', which shows the same root |eθ| 'thus' followed by the noninitial *-api-*. Where the phonological word boundary is less obvious, such as when a consonant is followed by a vowel, the distinction of compounds and unit words is frequently problematic.

Nominal and verbal compounds alike typically have a particle as their first member: *oski-mi·nisa* 'fresh berries'. Verb stems may be preceded by one or more preverb particles. Even though some preverbs (including all those of position 1) occur as preverbs only, they are treated as words with respect to external sandhi.

The three preverbs of position 1 are mutually exclusive (table 25); for further examples see 3.4.2., 4.1.2.2., 4.1.2.4. *e·* indicates subordination in an entirely neutral way; while *e·* and *ka·* show some overlap, *ka·* frequently occurs in relative clauses. *ka* and *kita* (*kita* optionally reduced to *ta*) mark subsequence; these three "future" preverbs are interchangeable in most contexts (except that only *ka* occurs with the personal prefixes *ni-* and *ki-*).

Table 19. "Classificatory" Medials

Medial	Gloss	Example
-a·skw-	'wood or solid of similar consistency'	kinwa·skosiw VAI 'he (tree) is long' ni·ma·skwe·w VAI 'he takes along (wooden) weapons'
-a·pisk-	'stone or solid of similar consistency'	mihkwa·piskiswe·w VAI 'he reddens him (stone) by heat' mo·hkoma·na·pisk NI 'knife-blade'
-e·kin-	'cloth or cloth-like, expanded object'	taswe·kinam VTI 'he spreads it out by hand' mihkwe·kin NI 'red cloth' masinahikane·kin NI 'paper'
-a·pe·k-	'rope, elongated object'	pakita·pe·kine·w VTA 'he lets him down by a rope' pima·pe·kisin VAI 'he (snake) lies extended'
-ipe·-	'liquid'	iskope·w VAI 'he is so deep in water' mo·nahipe·pitam VTI 'he digs a well' ki·skwe·pe·w VAI 'he is crazy from drink'

Table 20. Selected Noun Finals

Final	Gloss	Example Base	Derived Stem
-(w)aya·n	'hide, garment'	mostosw- NA 'buffalo'	mostoswaya·n 'buffalo robe'
-a·poy	'liquid, broth'	mihkw- NI 'blood'	mihkwa·poy 'blood soup'
		to·hto·s- NA 'breast'	to·hto·sa·poy 'milk'
[o(t)-] -w	[agent noun]	ma·ci- VAI 'hunt'	oma·ci·w 'hunter'
		a·hkosi- VAI 'be sick'	ota·hkosiw 'sick person, patient'
-win	[abstract noun]	a·cimo- VAI 'tell a story'	a·cimowin 'story'
		pima·tisi- VAI 'live'	pima·tisiwin 'life'
-kan	[instrument]	ci·kah- VTI 'chop it'	ci·kahikan 'axe'
		ma·mitone·yiht- VTI 'ponder it'	ma·mitone·yihcikan 'mind'
		pimiha·- VAI 'fly along'	pimiha·kan 'airplane'
-a·kan	[patient]	no·tin- VTA 'fight him'	no·tina·kan 'enemy'
		wi·kim- VTA 'live with him'	-wi·kima·kan 'spouse'
-ihka·n	[surrogate]	pi·simw- NA 'sun'	pi·simohka·n 'watch'
|ehka·n|		okima·w- NA 'chief, boss'	okima·hka·n 'elected or appointed chief'

Table 21. Selected Particle Finals

Final	Gloss	Example Base	Derived stem
|i|		oht- 'thence'	ohci 'thence, from'
		|eθ-| 'thus'	isi 'thus'
		kana·t- 'clean'	kana·ci 'clean'
-a·c		so·skw- 'smooth'	so·skwa·c 'smoothly, right away'
-taw		oht- 'thence'	ohcitaw 'on purpose, expressly'
-wa·w	'___ times'	mihce·t- 'many'	mihce·twa·w 'many times'
		tahtw- 'so many'	tahtwa·w 'so many times, every time'
		pe·yakw- 'one'	pe·yakwa·w 'one time, once'
-wayak	'in ___ ways/places'	mihce·t- 'many'	mihce·twayak 'in many ways/places'
		ta·nitahtw- 'how many'	ta·nitahtwayak 'in how many ways/places'
		ni·sw- 'two'	ni·swayak 'in two ways/places'
-ita	'at a place'	nikot- 'some, any'	nikotita 'just somewhere'
-ite·	'to a place'	a·stam- (toward speaker)	a·stamite· 'to the hither side'
		awas- (away from speaker)	awasite· 'to the further side'
-isi	'in a manner'	o·m- 'this'	o·misi 'this way', frequently accompanied by gestures

427

Table 22. Locative and Temporal Particle Finals with Pronominal Stems

	-ita 'at a place'	-ite· 'to a place'	-isi 'in a manner'	-ispi· 'at a time'	-tahto 'in such numbers'
o·- 'this'	o·ta 'here'	o·te· 'hither'			
an- 'that'	anita 'there'				
ne·- 'that yonder'		ne·te· 'yonder'			
ta·n- 'which one'	ta·nita 'where'	ta·nite· 'whither'	ta·nisi 'how'	ta·nispi· 'when'	ta·nitahto 'how much'
e·kw- 'that one'	e·kota '(just) there'	e·kote· '(just) thither'	e·kosi '(just) thus'	e·kospi· '(just) then'	

Table 23. Selected Intransitive Verb Finals

Final VAI	VII	Gloss	Example Base	VAI	VII
|esi|	-a·-	[verb]	kinw- [root] 'long'	kinosiw 'he is tall'	kinwa·w 'it is long'
	-an-	[verb]	kana·t- [root] 'clean'	kana·tisiw 'he is clean'	kana·tan 'it is clean'
-a·kosi-	-a·kwan-	["inverse"]	ite·yiht- VTI 'think so of it'	ite·yihta·kosiw 'he is thus thought of'	ite·yihta·kwan 'it is thus thought of'
-iko·wisi-		["inverse"]	ite·yim- VTA think so of him'	ite·yimiko·wisiw 'he is thus thought of by higher powers'	
-payi-	-payi-	'move'	oht- [root] 'thence'	ohcipayiw 'he moves from there'	ohcipayiw 'it moves from there'
			a·maciwe·- VAI 'go uphill'	a·maciwe·payiw 'he moves uphill'	
|ewi|	|ewi|	[verb of being]	mahi·hkan- NA 'wolf'	mahi·hkaniwiw 'he is a wolf'	
			ko·n- NA 'snow'		ko·niwiw 'it is snowy'
			ke·hte·- IPC 'old'	ke·hte·wiw 'he is old'	
			kisiwa·k- IPC 'near'		kisiwa·kiwiw 'it is near'
|i|		[verb of being, noun stems in -Vw-]	iskwe·w- NA 'woman'	iskwe·wiw 'she is a woman'	
[o(t)-] -i-		[possession]	mo·hkoma·n- NI 'knife'	omo·hkoma·niw 'he has a knife'	
			-kosis- NDA 'son'	okosisiw 'he has (him as) a son'	
|ehke·|		'arrange'	matotisa·n- NI 'sweat-lodge'	matotisa·nihke·w 'he makes a sweat-lodge'	
			nitopayiwin- NI 'war- party, raid'	nitopayiwinihke·w 'he arranges a war-party, organizes a raid'	
|ke·|		[general goal, VTI/VAI]	ma·kwaht- VTI 'chew it'	ma·kwahcike·w 'he chews, chews things'	
			me·tawe·- VAI 'play'	me·tawa·ke·w 'he plays with things'	
|eke·|		[general goal, VTA]	no·tin- VTA 'fight him'	no·tinike·w 'he fights with people'	
			te·pwe·stamaw- VTA 'act as announcer for him'	te·pwe·stama·ke·w 'he acts as announcer for people'	
|iwe·|		[general goal]	na·t- |na·θ-| VTA 'fetch him'	na·siwe·w 'he fetches people'	
|eto|		[reciprocal]	no·tin- VTA 'fight him'	no·tinito·wak 'they fight one another'	
|eso|		[reflexive]	asam- VTA 'feed him'	asamisow 'he feeds himself'	
|o|		["middle reflexive"]	a·cim- VTA 'tell of him'	a·cimow 'he tells of himself, narrates'	

The preverbs of position 2 constitute an open class of particles, several of which may occur in succession.

6. SOUNDS

The sounds of Cree are presented in terms of distinctive sounds or phonemes, the status and configuration of which are far from being fully understood. A summary of their phonetic manifestations is followed by a preliminary statement of their distribution and of prosodic phenomena. While surface variations and external sandhi are nonobligatory, they are important both to the analysis of Cree and for the practical problem of relating actual Cree utterances to the somewhat more abstract level of distinctive sounds. The rules of internal sandhi (morphophonological alternation rules), by contrast, are obligatory.

428

Table 24. Selected Transitive Verb Finals

Final VTA	VTI	Gloss	Example Base	VTA	VTI	Gloss
|en|	|en|	'by hand'	oht- [root] 'thence'	ohtine·w	ohtinam	'he takes him/it from there by hand'
			sa·m- [root] 'touch'	sa·mine·w	sa·minam	'he touches him/it by hand'
|eskaw|	|esk|	'by foot or body movement'	sa·m- [root] 'touch'	sa·miskawe·w	sa·miskam	'he touches him/it by foot'
|ehtaw|	|eht|	'by hearing'	nito- [root] 'seek'	nitohtawe·w	nitohtam	'he tries to hear him/it'
|naw|	|n|	'by vision'	|eθ| [root] 'thus'	isinawe·w	isinam	'he sees him/it thus'
-ahw-	-ah-	'by medium, tool'	sa·m- [root] 'touch'	sa·mahwe·w	sa·maham	'he touches him/it by tool'
			ki·sk- [root] 'sever'	ki·skahwe·w	ki·skaham	'he chops him/it through by tool'
-atahw-	-atah-	'by sticklike tool'	ki·sk- [root] 'sever'	ki·skatahwe·w	ki·skataham	'he chops him/it through by ax'
|esw|	|es|	'by cutting edge'	ki·sk- [root] 'sever'	ki·skiswe·w	ki·skisam	'he cuts him/it through'
|esw|	|es|	'by heat'	ki·s- [root] 'complete'	ki·siswe·w	ki·sisam	'he cooks him/it done'
-m-	-ht- |mt|	'by mouth, speech'	nito- [root] 'seek'	nitome·w		'he calls, invites him'
			ma·kw- [root] 'press'	ma·kwame·w	ma·kwahtam	'he chews him/it'
-e·yim-	-e·yiht-	'by mental action'	|eθ| [root] 'thus'	ite·yime·w	ite·yihtam	'he thinks so of him/it'
-h-	-hta- [VAI-T]	verb	ki·s- [root] 'complete'	ki·sihe·w	ki·sihta·w [VAI-T]	'he completes him/(it)'
			wan- [root] 'lose'	wanihe·w	wanihta·w [VAI-T]	'he loses him/(it)'
			mana·tisi- VAI 'act discreetly'	mana·tisihe·w 'he spares him'	mana·tisihta·w [VAI-T]	'he spares him, he is careful (of it)'
		causative	nikamo- VAI 'sing'	nikamohe·w		'he makes him sing'
-t- |θ|	-t- |t|	transitive verb	pi·kiskwe·- VAI 'speak'	pi·kiskwa·te·w	pi·kiskwa·tam	'he speaks to him/it'
|Lstaw|	|Lst|	transitive verb	nahapi- VAI 'sit down'	nahapi·stawe·w	nahapi·stam	'he sits down by him/it'
-totaw-	-tot-	transitive verb	sa·ke·we·- VAI 'come into view'	sa·ke·we·totawe·w	sa·ke·we·totam	'he comes into view of him/it'
-[am]aw-		benefactive	wi·ht- VTI 'tell it'	wi·htamawe·w		'he tells it to him'
-stamaw-		benefactive	pi·kiskwe·- VAI 'speak'	pi·kiskwe·stamawe·w		'he speaks for him'

Table 25. Selected Preverbs

Preverb	Gloss	Example
Position 1		
e·	subordinating	e·-apit, naki·yiwa. 'As he (3) sat down, the other (3´) stopped.'
ka·	subordinating	ki·tahtawe· ka·-wa·pama·t ayi·isiyiniwa. 'Suddenly [it was that] he saw people.'
		o·hi oskini·kiwa ka·-ki·-wa·pama·t 'that young man whom he had seen'
ka	future	nik-o·h-minahon kita-mi·cisoya·n. 'With these I will hunt to have something to eat.'
kita, ta		
Position 2		
ati	'progressively'	e·kosi po·siw, e-ati-nikamot. 'Then he embarked, beginning to sing.'
a·ta	'although'	e·-a·ta-nitonahk, nama ki·-miskam. 'Although she looked for it, she could not find it.'
ki·₁	'past'	e·-ki·-po·nahk, pimisin. 'Having made a fire, he lay down.'
ki·₂	'able to' [normally with negator or future preverb]	namo·ya nika-ki·-itwa·n. 'I cannot say.'
matwe·	'audibly'	pe·htamwak ... wi·htiko·wa e·-matwe·-ye·hye·yit. 'They heard the Windigo breathing loudly.'
me·kwa·	'while'	e·-me·kwa·-pimisihkik 'while they were lying down'
nihta·	'good at'	kinihta·-kakwe·-ci·sima·wa·w 'you are good at trying to deceive him by speech'
nitawi	'go to'	e·-pe·-na·nitaw-a·sama·t 'he kept going (reduplication -na·-) hither to feed him'
no·hte·	'want to'	nino·hte·-pi·htwa·n 'I want to smoke'
o·h, ohci	'thence, from, with'	acosis piko ki·-ohci-nipahe·wak 'with merely an arrow they killed them'
		e·koto·wahk nik-o·h-nipaha·wak 'with such I shall kill them'
	'remote past' [with negator]	nama ki·kway ohc-a·ya·wak iskote·w. '(Originally) they had no fire.'
pe·	'hither'	wa·hyaw e·-pe·-wa·paniyik 'as dawn appeared from afar'
wi·	'will, intend to'	e·-wi·-kakwe·-wa·pahtahk ki·kway 'when he was going to try to see something'

The phonological representation (italics) is identical to the orthography of Bloomfield's (1930, 1934) texts except for the purely mechanical substitution of o, $e\cdot$, c, and raised dot for Bloomfield's ⟨u⟩, ⟨ä⟩, and ⟨ts⟩, and macron. Morphophonological notation, with segments enclosed in vertical bars and the additional characters |e|, |θ|, and |L| (6.3.3.), is used only where it is immediately relevant to the discussion.

In Cree forms, leading or trailing hyphens indicate that the form cannot occur by itself; when forms are cited in morphophonological representation, leading or trailing hyphens are usually omitted. In phonological representation, a hyphen within a word marks it as compound.

6.1. DISTINCTIVE SOUNDS

6.1.1. SEGMENTAL UNITS

The segmental units of Cree are summarized in table 26.

p, t, and k are generally voiceless, lenis, and unaspirated. Considerable subdistinctive variation occurs within the stop series:

(a) Between two short vowels the stops are voiceless geminates (with an intervening syllable boundary); this is especially obvious when the following vowel is stressed: [attím] $atim$ 'dog, horse'.

(b) Between all other combinations of syllabics there appears to be free variation of voiced and voiceless stops; this is especially clearcut where the preceding vowel is long and in penultimate position;
[pʌkkáma·gʌn] $pakama\cdot kan$ 'club';
[ma·kʌ, ma·gʌ] $ma\cdot ka$ 'but';
[ŋke·twà·n, ŋge·twà·n] $nik\text{-}e\cdot twa\cdot n$ 'I will say so'.

(c) In word-final position, and possibly in environment (a) as well, stops with voiced onset and voiceless release appear to be in free variation with completely voiceless stops: [si·sí·bᵖ, si·sí·p] $si\cdot si\cdot p$ 'duck'.

(d) In word-initial position and in contiguity with a voiceless fricative, the stops are always voiceless. Under emphasis the stops may be fortis in any position and the resulting (nondistinctive) difference of lenis and fortis will sound quite similar to the (distinctive) voiced : voiceless difference of English.

s and c are voiceless; their articulation ranges, nondistinctively, from alveolar to alveopalatal. s shows considerable nondistinctive variation in length.

In the voiceless fricative h, glottal friction (or voicelessness) is accompanied by some oral friction, which in intervocalic position reflects the quality of the surrounding vowels: [kɪhíw] $kihiw$ 'eagle', [o·how] $o\cdot how$ 'owl'. Before a consonant, h is influenced by the preceding vowel only: [pɪhkúhk] $pihkohk$ 'in the ashes' vs. [ko·nihk] $ko\cdot nihk$ 'in the snow'; [ʌkúhp] $akohp$ 'blanket' and [sɪhkíhp] $sihkihp$ 'diver-duck'.

i tends to be realized as [i] before w and y, and as [ɪ] elsewhere.

o is lower high and strongly rounded.

For all other vowels, the "characteristic features"

Table 26. Summary of Segmental Units

Distinctive sound	Characteristic features	Approximate English counterpart
p	bilabial stop	s<u>p</u>ill
t	apico-alveolar stop	s<u>t</u>ill
c	alveolar-alveopalatal affricate	ha<u>ts</u>/mu<u>ch</u>
k	dorso-velar stop	s<u>k</u>ill
s	alveolar/alveopalatal fricative	<u>s</u>ea/<u>sh</u>e
h	glottal fricative	a<u>h</u>ead
m	bilabial nasal	<u>m</u>et
n	apico-alveolar nasal	<u>n</u>et
w	bilabial semivowel	<u>w</u>et
y	alveopalatal semivowel	<u>y</u>et
i	high front short vowel	h<u>i</u>t
a	low short vowel	c<u>u</u>p
o	high back short vowel	b<u>oo</u>k
$i\cdot$	high front long vowel	k<u>ee</u>n
$e\cdot$	low front long vowel	c<u>a</u>ne
$a\cdot$	low back long vowel	f<u>a</u>ther
$o\cdot$	high back long vowel	b<u>o</u>ne

given above closely reflect the phonetic manifestations. In the dialects of central Saskatchewan (Vandall and Douquette 1987; Whitecalf 1993), vowel length tends to be indeterminate before preaspirated stops: $okima(\cdot)hka\cdot n$ 'elected chief'; this phenomenon is not restricted to unstressed syllables. (Subdistinctive variations of vowel length and quality, especially with respect to position in the word, are discussed in some detail in Longacre 1957; 6.2.)

In some variants of Plains Cree, notably in the Saddle Lake area of east-central Alberta and in neighboring parts of Saskatchewan (Wolfart 1992:358, 377), the long front vowels $i\cdot$ and $e\cdot$ are not distinguished. (It is tempting to appeal to the simultaneous effects of pattern pressure—the asymmetry of the vowel system—and the small functional load of $e\cdot$ as determinants of an incipient merger.)

6.1.2. PROSODIC PHENOMENA

Neither intensity nor pitch appear to be phonologically distinctive in Plains Cree words; in the description of the placement of *stress* that term is used for what actually seems to be a combination of intensity and pitch. Intonation patterns that affect units larger than the word are yet to be investigated.

Phonologically, words are defined by bearing primary stress and by characteristic boundary phenomena (see 6.1.2.2.). With the exception of compound words (cf. 5.4.) and close-knit phrases (cf. 6.1.2.2.), these phonological criteria coincide with morphological criteria such as prefixation and suffixation and the syntactic criteria of mobility and isolability.

6.1.2.1. STRESS

The stress pattern of words seems to depend primarily on the number of syllables rather than on vowel length.

Disyllabic words are stressed on the last syllable: [ɪskwéˑw] *iskweˑw* 'woman', [mɪhtí] *mihti* 'piece of firewood'. However, note that disyllabic particles show a nondistinctive variation of ultimate and penultimate stress whose relation to sentence-level patterns remains to be studied: [maˑká, máˑka] *maˑka* 'but', [mahtí, máhtɪ] *mahti* 'let's see, come on'.

In words of three of more syllables, primary stress falls on the third syllable from the end. Secondary stress then falls on alternate syllables in either direction, reckoned from the antepenult: [néˑhiyàw] *neˑhiyaw* 'Cree Indian', [pàsʌkwàˑpɪsímowìn] *pasakwaˑpisimowin* 'Shut-Eye dance'. Note that the above rule holds for Plains Cree even where the penultima is long: [mítaˑtàht] *mitaˑtaht* '10', [úspwaˑgàn] *ospwaˑkan* 'pipe'.

6.1.2.2. BOUNDARIES

Word boundary may be marked by a gradual devoicing of a final vowel or by a voiceless on-glide in an initial vowel: [nɪskáh] *niska* 'goose', [háyapɪ] *ay-api* 'be seated'. These voiceless glides are not only nondistinctive but also completely optional.

Except perhaps statistically, the presence of |h| word-finally in the morphophonological representation appears to be irrelevant to the phonetic realization: [nɪté·, nɪté·h] *niteˑh* |neteˑh| 'my heart' (the *h* is written in accordance with the orthographical principles summarized in Wolfart and Ahenakew 1987:118-119, which are based on both phonological and morphological considerations; cf. *niteˑhinaˑna* 'our hearts'); [útɛˑmà, útɛˑmàh] *oteˑma* |oteˑmah| 'his dog, horse.'

Note that vowel coalescence under external sandhi (6.22.) may take place even where a word-final |h| is morphophonologically present; *míˑnis eˑ-kiˑ-kaˑh-kakwaˑhyakeˑyatiki* 'berries used to be varied and plentiful' (cf. |miˑnisah|); *opawáˑkan áˑna* 'that one's dream-spirit' (cf. |opawaˑkanah|). Note that the stress patterns reflect the full forms of the words (i.e., *míˑnisà, opawáˑkanà*); cf. also 6.222.

A glottal stop occurs in free variation with final devoicing in the three particles: [ę·haʔ] *eˑha* 'yes', [yoˑʔ, yoˑhoˑʔ] *yoˑ, yoˑhoˑ* '(exclamation of surprise)'.

Compound words are characterized by a phonological word boundary within a single inflectional unit: [niwíˑhátʊskàˑn] *niwiˑ-atoskaˑn* 'I am going to work'. (Contrast the situation in Menominee [Bloomfield 1962:20] where compounds are stressed like unit words.)

Words may enter into close-knit phrases that behave like unit words with respect to stress and word boundary. They consist typically of

(a) a verb or noun followed by a pronoun or particle: [kàˑtʊttáhkawà] *k-aˑtotahk awa* 'this one told about it' (cf. [káˑtʊtàhk awá]); [íˑncùaspàpʊwìnnsáwʊhcì] *iyinico-aspapiwinisa ohci* 'with an Indian saddle' (cf. íˑncùaspàpʊwínsà ʊhcí]);

(b) a verb or noun preceded by a pronoun: [awá mstìk] *awa mistik* 'this tree';

(c) pronouns and particles following one another: [eˑkwáhoˑmà] *eˑkwa oˑma* 'then this one'.

For the stress patterns that result under conditions of external sandhi see 6.2.2.2.

6.1.3. DISTRIBUTION

Vowels as a class may occur in any position in the word, but the long vowels *iˑ, eˑ*, and *oˑ* are quite rare in initial and final position, and *i* is infrequent in word-initial position. There are no vowel clusters.

The distribution of consonants and semivowels within the word and in relation to the vowels is summarized in table 27. The number sign (#) marks the word boundary, and parentheses indicate optional combinations. Note that only primary clusters are cited (as opposed to secondary clusters like *nt*, which arise from elision) and that recent loanwords, such as *anpweˑhta* 'Alberta' are excluded.

Although phonetically an affricate, *c* patterns with *p*, *t*, and *k* and is therefore included in the phonological class of stops.

h occurs before a consonant, between vowels, or followed by *w* and a vowel.

It is obvious from table 27 that the clusters of the word-final position differ from those of the word-medial one only by the absence of postconsonantal *w* in the former. This fact is particularly striking in the alternation of certain noun stems:

|mistikw-a| *mistik* 'tree', vs.
|mistikw-ak| *mistikwak* 'trees'.

On the morphophonological level, a very significant proportion of Cree words end in a vowel. If this pattern were to be extrapolated to all words (as appears to have been the case in Proto-Algonquian; Bloomfield

Table 27. Distribution of Consonants and Semivowels

# ___ V	V ___ V	V ___ #
p(w)	(h,s)p(w)	(h,s)p
t(w)	(h,s)t(w)	(h,s)t
c(w)	(h,s)c(w)	(h,s)c
k(w)	(h,s)k(w)	(h,s)k
	h(w)	
s	s(w)	s
m(w)	m(w)	m
n	n(w)	n
w	w	w
y	y(w)	y
	hy	

1946:92), a rather simple description of syllable structure might be achieved:

- (a) onset (optional):
    - (i) nonsyllabic, or
    - (ii) consonant followed by *w*;
- (b) peak (obligatory):
    - vowel;
- (c) *coda* (optional):
    - *s* or *h*.

There are no primary clusters of identical nonsyllabics, or of any fricative or semivowel followed by a fricative, nasal, or *y*.

In terms of this analysis, syllable and word structure in general might be represented as follows:

$$\text{syllable:} \quad \left(\left\{ \begin{matrix} \text{con } (w) \\ \text{semivowel} \end{matrix} \right\} \right) \; V \; \left(\left\{ \begin{matrix} s \\ h \end{matrix} \right\} \right)$$

$$\text{word:} \quad \# \left(\left\{ \begin{matrix} \text{con } (w) \\ \text{semivowel} \end{matrix} \right\} \right) V \left\{ \left\{ \begin{matrix} s \\ h \end{matrix} \right\} \text{con } (w) \atop \text{semivowel} \right\} V \; ... \; V \; \#.$$

6.2. NONDISTINCTIVE VARIATIONS

There is a wide variety of surface variations that center around a normal form. The normal form is found only in elevated or in especially slow, deliberate speech. For example, the normal form [kɪkánɪpáhɪtìn] *kika-nipahitin* 'I'll kill you' is under appropriate circumstances pronounced [kkàmpáyhtn̩].

6.2.1. SURFACE VARIATIONS

The most important areas of surface variation are the interrelated phenomena of stress, elision, and syllabicity and the realizations of *h*, *w*, and *y* in intervocalic position, e.g. [éˑnìpahísoyìt, énpáysoˑwìt] *e-nipahisoyit* 'the other is killing himself'; [n̩ttúhttáˑn] *nititohtaˑn* 'I take it there'; [askíˑyukì] *askiˑwiki* 'when it is a year, next year'; [apíw, apyú, apíǔ] *apiw* 'he is seated'.

Elision between homorganic consonants of short vowels, especially *i*, in unstressed syllables gives rise to secondary clusters: *nt* in *kon(i)ta* 'in vain, without reason', *nin(i)taweˑyihteˑn* 'I want (it)'.

Another common type of surface variation obscures the quantity and even the quality of vowels before homorganic semivowels;

iy ˜ iˑy	*e-teˑhtapiyaˑn* 'as I am mounted (on horseback)'
iˑy ˜ iy	*e-tapasiˑyaˑn* 'as I flee'
iw ˜ ow ˜ oˑw	*teˑhtapiw* 'he is mounted (on horseback)'
ow ˜ oˑw	*pimaˑmow* 'he flees along'
oˑw ˜ ow	*pasikoˑw* 'he arises from sitting'

For orthographic conventions intended to deal with this variation see Wolfart and Ahenakew (1987:115-120) and Wolfart (1992:351-352).

Phonological modifications that are a function of narrative style are termed rhetorical distortion. Vowels under rhetorical distortion are significantly longer than the corresponding long vowels; *i* and *iˑ* are in addition lowered to [eˑ].

Rhetorical distortion most frequently affects the first vowel of a sentence, for example, [aˑspín] *aspin* 'off, away' but is not restricted to that position, or even to the first vowel of a word, as in [mìtunéˑ, mèˑtuné] *mitoni* 'really', [èˑkusé] *eˑkosi* 'thus'. As the last two examples show, rhetorical distortion is frequently accompanied by an emphatic stress-intonation pattern. This emphatic pattern also occurs independently of vowel distortion: [nìpahéˑw] *nipahew* 'he surely killed him'.

In addition to the phonological phenomena of surface variation there exist a number of lexical doublets. Most striking are those that occur both with and without an initial consonant, for example, *saˑsay/aˑsay* 'already', *keˑyiweˑhk/eˑyiweˑhk* 'to a fair extent', *keˑyaˑpic/eˑyaˑpic* 'again', etc. While dialect and idiolect differentiation may play a role, some speakers use both forms interchangeably.

6.2.2. EXTERNAL SANDHI

External sandhi takes place between words as well as between the constituent members of compound words, that is, at all phonological word boundaries. It is distinct from the combination rules operating within the word (morphophonology or internal sandhi).

The rules of external combination are optional; their application correlates to some extent with style and speed of utterance. As with other types of surface variation, the more extreme modifications of external sandhi are avoided where they might impair the recognition of a form. Thus, instances of inflectional endings undergoing external sandhi are not uncommon (e.g., *ita waˑskahikan eˑ-asteˑki* 'where there are houses'; the stress, which in the full plural form *waˑskahikana* falls on the antepenult, remains on that syllable even when the final vowel takes part in contraction). Another example is: *maˑmaˑkwaht oˑma* 'chew this!' (cf. *maˑmaˑkwahta oˑma*). Nevertheless, inflectional endings seem more resistant to vowel coalescence than, for example, the final vowels of particles.

In addition, there is a fair amount of free variation; thus, within some texts there is an almost equal number of "deliberate" and "casual" transitions, often occurring side by side: *konit eˑ-taˑstakiskweˑyit eˑtokweˑ, konita eˑ-peˑhtaˑkosit*; 'Then up he raised his head, and then he made a big noise'.

Sequences of nonsyllabics or of nonsyllabics and vowels remain unmodified by external sandhi; thus, only sequences of word-final and word-initial vowels are affected. The two basic types of transition—with or without vowel coalescence—appear to occur in free variation.**

6.2.2.1. OPEN TRANSITION
Where both vowels are preserved, the word boundary may not be marked at all (hiatus), or it may be realized by the gradual devoicing of the word-final vowel, just as it would be before a nonsyllabic or in pausal position: [awáh ɪskwéˑw] *awa iskweˑw* 'this woman'.

If one of the vowels is a front vowel (*i, iˑ,* or *eˑ*), a transitional [y] may occur, as in [awáy ɪskwéˑw] *awa iskweˑw*. The transitional [h] or [y] may be part of the preceding or of the following syllable: [éˑḥ-ápɪcìk, éˑ-hápɪcìk] *eˑ-apicik* 'they are seated'. Where the second word begins in *i*, this *i* is frequently elided after a transitional glide: [éˑyɪtwéˑt, éˑytwéˑt] *eˑ-itweˑt* 'he is saying so'. If the preceding sequence of vowel and semivowel is homorganic, a single long vowel may result: [kíˑyɪtwéˑw, kíˑtwéˑw] *ki-itweˑw* 'he has said so'. If the word-final vowel is devoiced, the *i* may be elided and diphthongization of the preceding vowel takes place: [éˑhɪtwéˑt, éˑyhtwéˑt] *eˑ-itweˑt* 'he is saying so.' These variations exactly parallel surface variations, not described here, that occur within a word.

6.2.2.2. VOWEL COALESCENCE
Vowel coalescence under external sandhi may be informally summarized in a set of ordered rules as seen in table 28.

The vowel resulting from coalescence always carries the stress of the word-final vowel, and any preceding stress becomes secondary; [èˑyʊkw àˑcímoˑwìn] *eˑyako aˑcimowin* 'this story'. If the second word is disyllabic, its first syllable receives primary stress: [èˑyʊkw áˑwa] *eˑyakw aˑwa* 'this one'.

Rule 1: Word-final *o* is realized as *w* and the word-initial vowel, unless already long, is lengthened without any change in quality: [pɪkw íˑteˑ] *pikw iˑteˑ* 'everywhere' (cf. *piko, iteˑ*). (No evidence has been found for a parallel rule for *oˑ*, which very rarely occurs finally.)

Rule 2a: Where *a* or *aˑ* is followed by *i*, either *iˑ* or *eˑ* results; neither the conditioning factors nor the exact distribution of these variants has been established beyond the fact that preverbs ending in *a* or *aˑ* always yield *eˑ*: *nik-eˑtwaˑn* 'I'll say so' (cf. *nika, itweˑ-*); *k-eˑtweˑt* 'he is saying so' (cf. *kaˑ, itweˑ-*). Example of *iˑ*: *aw iˑskweˑw* 'this woman' (cf. *awa, iskweˑw*).

Rule 2b: *oˑh oˑteˑma* 'this horse of his' (cf. *oˑhi, oteˑma*); *nik-aˑpin* 'I'll sit down' (cf. *nika, api-*).

**There is at least one notable exception to this statement: the future markers *ka, kita, ta* do not take part in vowel coalescence in clauses involving doubt or an irrealis condition:
  taˑnis oˑma nika-itwaˑn 'how should I say this'.
Where the verb stem begins in a consonant, the hiatus is emphasized by strong devoicing of the final vowel (Wolfart 1989).

Long vowels in word-final position do not frequently show coalescence; moreover, word-final *iˑ* and *oˑ* are rare in any case. Examples: *k-iˑsi-nipahaci* 'once you have killed him' (cf. *kiˑ, isi*); *misiw iˑteˑ* 'all over, everywhere' (cf. *misiweˑ, iteˑ*).

Rule 3: Postconsonantal *w* that results from the application of Rules 1 or 2 is deleted obligatorily if it is followed by *oˑ*: *eˑyak oˑhci* 'from that same one' (cf. *eˑyako, ohci*).

6.3. MORPHOPHONOLOGY
The morphophonological rules that follow are based primarily on the alternations of inflectional affixes and stems.

The summary (table 29) includes only the more generally applicable rules; it also omits prefixation and initial change, which are discussed in 6.3.6. and 6.3.7. The hyphen (-) and the number sign (#) indicate morpheme and word boundary, respectively.

Rules 1 to 4 are rules of internal combination (internal sandhi). Rule 1, which also consists of ordered subrules, precedes all others. After the rules of internal combination have been applied, rules (R1) and (R2) yield the phonemic shapes.

6.3.1. CONSONANT SEQUENCES
When a morpheme-final |w| is followed by a morpheme-initial |w|, only one |w| remains: |waˑpam-aˑ-y-eˑkw-waˑw-h| *waˑpamaˑyeˑkwaˑwi* 'if you (pl.) see them'.

Table 28. External Sandhi: Vowel Coalescense Rules

(1)	*o* # V(ˑ)	→	*w* # Vˑ
(2a)	*a*(ˑ) # *i*	→	# *eˑ,* # *iˑ*
(2b)	V(ˑ)₁ # V(ˑ)₂	→	# Vˑ₂
(3)	C *w* # *o*(ˑ)	→	C # *oˑ*

Table 29. Summary of Major Morphophonological Rules

1	a	w-w	→	w
	b	(m,n)-(k,t)	→	h(k,t)
	c	C-C	→	C-iC
2		θ-(i,iˑ)	→	s(i,iˑ)
		t-(i,iˑ)	→	c(i,iˑ)
3		Vˑ-Vˑ	→	VˑyVˑ
		Vˑ₁-Vˑ₂	→	Vˑ₂
		Vˑ₁-Vˑ₂	→	Vˑ₁
		V₁-V₂	→	V₁
		V-L	→	Vˑ
4		Cw-iC, Cw-eC	→	CoC
		Vw-e, Vy-e	→	Vˑ
R1		V#	→	Ø#
		Cw#	→	C#
R2		θ	→	*t*
		e	→	*i*
		p, t, c, k, ...	→	*p, t, c, k, ...*

433

Before a morpheme-initial stop, a morpheme-final nasal is realized as |h|: |e·#kemiwan-k| *e·-kimiwahk* 'it is raining, |wa·pam-to-| *wa·pahto-* 'see each other'.

All other cases of a nonsyllabic followed by a consonant result in the insertion of a connective |i|: |e·#wa·pam-ak-k| *e·wa·pamakik* 'I am seeing them'.

6.3.2. PALATALIZATION

Before *i* (reflecting |i|) and *i·*, *t* (reflecting |θ|) alternates with *s*, and *t* (reflecting |t|) alternates with *c*; this is the major type of palatalization, called mutation. In spite of their parallel nature it is sometimes useful in Cree to separate the *t*/*c* alternation (or c-palatalization) from the *t*/*s* alternation (or s-palatalization). Note that neither *t* is affected by *i* (reflecting |e|):

ti		t-e	
ci		t-i	
ti		θ-e	
si		θ-i	

Examples:

	ke-na·θ-in		*kina·sin*	'you fetch me'
	ke-na·θ-etin		*kina·titin*	'I fetch you'
	ne-i·waθ-i		*ni·was*	'my sacred pack'
	ne-i·waθ-ah		*ni·wata*	'my sacred packs'
	e·#wa·pam-a·-t-k		*e·-wa·pama·cik*	'they are seeing the other'

There are, of course, individual exceptions to these palatalization rules: |ne-set-i| *nisit* 'my foot' (instead of the expected *nisic*).

Diminutives ending in |es, esis| show pervasive c-palatalization of all preceding *t*s; |ot-akohp-es| *ocakohpis* 'his little blanket'. Note that diminutive c-palatalization does not distinguish |t| and |θ|: |aθemw-esis| *acimosis* 'little dog'.

C-palatalization may be the only sign of diminutive formation; *yo·tin* 'it is windy', *yo·cin* 'it is a little windy'. The speech of Wisahkechahk, the culture hero, sometimes shows c-palatalization throughout, which Cree speakers say makes it "sound pitiful."

For the "compassionate" use (Nichols 1979) of pervasive palatalization, especially to *š* and *č*, see Wolfart (1992:378) and Pentland (1975).

Palatalization also plays an important part in word formation: |wi·ht-ika·θ-yo-w| *wi·hcika·so·w* 'he is named', |wi·ht-ika·θ-e-w| *wi·hcika·te·w* 'it is named'.

6.3.3. VOWEL COMBINATIONS

Long vowels are separated by |y|: |ki·sika·-a·pan| *ki·sika·ya·pan* 'it is daybreak'.

Before or after a long vowel, a short vowel disappears: |pemohte·-eyiwah| *pimohte·yiwa* 'the other walks'; |pi·htokwe·-akocin-w| *pi·htokwe·kocin* 'he comes flying inside'.

In a sequence of short vowels the second disappears: |pe·ho-eyiwah| *pe·hoyiwa* 'the other waits'.

A short vowel followed by the special symbol |L| results in a long vowel: |nipi-Lmakan-w| *nipi·makan* 'it dies'.

6.3.4. CONTRACTION

Interconsonantal |w-i| or |w-e| are realized as *o*:

| |ke-pakamahw-in| | *kipakamahon* | 'you hit me' |
| |ke-pakamahw-etin| | *kipakamahotin* | 'I hit you'. |

When a morpheme ending in a sequence of vowel and semivowel is followed by another beginning in |e|, the first vowel of the sequence is lengthened (unless it is already long) and the semivowel and |e| disappear; for example,

	mahke·siw-es		*mahke·si·s*	'little fox, coyote'
	k-i·k-enaw-ehk		*ki·kina·hk*	'our home'
	sa·si·w-ena·hk		*sa·si·na·hk*	'at Sarcee Reserve'
	ne-na·pe·w-em		*nina·pe·m*	'my husband'
	ispatina·w-es		*ispacina·s*	'little hill'
	asko·w-eto-wak		*asko·to·wak*	'they follow each other'
	n-atay-ehk		*nata·hk*	'on my belly'
	mi·cima·poy-ehk		*mi·cima·po·hk*	'in the soup, broth'

Contraction and palatalization permit the identification of *i* as |i| or |e|:

| |ke-wi·htamaw-etin| | *kiwi·htama·tin* | 'I tell you' |
| |ke-wi·htamaw-in| | *kiwi·htamawin* | 'you tell me'. |

See also Ahenakew and Wolfart (1991).

Contraction does not occur with monosyllabic stems: |mey-ek| *miyik* 'the other gives it to him'. In the area of derivation, the full range of applicability of the contraction rule remains to be determined.

6.3.5. PHONEMIC REALIZATION

The final short vowels of the morphophonological representation disappear in the phonemic realization: |si·si·p-a| *si·si·p* 'duck'. With monosyllabic stems, the final vowel remains: |eθ-i| *isi* 'tell him so!', |wa·w-i| *wa·wi* 'egg'; it is dropped in VTA imperatives with a long stem vowel, |na·θ-i| *na·s* 'bring him!'. (With respect to the final |i| of particles, this rule appears to be optional: *kwaya·c, kwaya·ci* 'ready'.)

Postconsonantal word-final |w| is dropped, including those that arise from loss of final vowel: |e·#api-yahkw| *e·-apiyahk* 'we are sitting', |aθemw-a| *atim* 'dog, horse' (cf. *atimwak* 'dogs, horses').

|θ| is realized as *t*, |e| as *i*, and |p, t, c, k, s, h, m, n, w, y, i, a, o, i·, e·, a·, o·| as *p, t, c, k, s, h, m, n, w, y, i, a, o, i·, e·, a·, o·*.

6.3.6. PREFIXATION

Before a vowel-initial stem, the personal prefixes |ke-|, |ne-|, |we-|, and |me-| take an epenthetic |t|, for example, |net-api-n| *nitapin* 'I sit'.

Instead of this |t|, the insertion of |h| or |w| has been observed in isolated instances: *nihaya·n* 'I have it', or *kiwa·tote·n* 'you tell it'.

Before dependent noun stems that begin in a vowel, the prefixes show the alternants |k-|, |n-|, |w-|, and |m-|, for example, *katay* 'your belly', *natay* 'my belly',

434

watay 'his belly'. Before dependent stems beginning in |o·|, the third-person prefix is realized as zero: *o·hkoma* 'his grandmother', cf. *no·hkom* 'my grandmother'.

Before stems beginning in |o| or |o·|, the regular pattern (epenthetic |t|) and the pattern found with dependent stems appear to be in free variation; note that |o| is lengthened in either case:

|net-okima·w-em-ena·n| *nito·kima·mina·n* 'our chief',
|n-okima·w-em-ena·n| *no·kima·mina·n* 'our chief'.

6.3.7. INITIAL CHANGE

In the changed and iterative modes of the conjunct order (4.1.2.2.), the first vowel of a stem or compound (5.4.) undergoes a systematic modification called initial change. C stands for any nonsyllabic, including none at all.

Ci/Ce·	*se·pwe·hte·ci*	'when he went out', cf. *sipwe·hte·-*
Ca/Ce·	*te·kohte·t*	'when he arrived', cf. *takohte·-*
Co/Cwe·	*we·htinahk*	'when he took it from there', cf. *ohtin-*
Ci·/Ca·	*wa·-ki·hce·kosi·ci*	'when she tried to climb up', cf. *wi·-ki·hce·kosi·-*[††]
Ci·/Ciyi·	*miyi·citwa·wi*	'when they had it to eat', cf. *mi·ci-*
Ce·/Ciye·	*piye·-takohte·ci*	'when he got hither', cf. *pe·-takohte·-*
Ca·/Ciya·	*wiya·pahtahki*	'when he sees it', cf. *wa·paht-*
Co·/Ciyo·	*ta·nisi tiyo·tahk*	'how did he do it', cf. *to·t-*

7. SELECTED VOCABULARY

all *kahkiyaw* IPC

almost *ke·ka·c* IPC

American *kihci-mo·hkoma·n* NA

and *mi·na* IPC

animal *pisiskiw* NA

arm *nispiton* NDI 'my arm'

arrive *takosin* VAI 'he arrives'

   takohte·w VAI 'he arrives walking'

   takopiciw VAI 'he arrives with his camp'

arrow *acosis* NI

ashes *pihko* NI 'ashes, dust'

ask *kakwe·cime·w* VTA 'he asks him'

aunt *nisikos* NDA 'my father's sister, mother's brother's wife, mother-in-law'

   nika·wi·s NDA 'my mother's sister, father's brother's wife' (Plains Cree only; cf. 'mother')

nito·sis NDA 'mother's sister, father's brother's wife' (Plains Cree and other Cree dialects)

automobile *se·hke·-pimipayi·s* NA

autumn *takwa·kin* VII 'it is autumn'

back *nispiskwan* NDI 'my back'

backbone *na·wikan* NDI 'my backbone'

bad *ma·ya·tan* VII 'it is bad'

badger *mistanask*, pl. *mistanaskwak* NA

bannock *pahkwe·sikan* NA 'bannock [fried bread]'

bead *mi·kisis* NA 'bead'

   pi·wa·piskominis NA 'metal bead'

bear *maskwa* NA

beaver *amisk*, pl. *amiskwak* NA

   amiskowiyiniw NA 'Beaver Indian'

believe *ta·pwe·htam* VTI 'he believes it'

belly *natay* NDI 'my belly'

berry *mi·nis* NI

   misa·skwato·min NI 'Saskatoon berry'

big *misa·w* VII 'it is big'

bird *pihye·si·s* NA

bite *tahkwahtam* VTI 'he bites it'

black *kaskite·siw* VAI 'he is black'

Blackfoot *kaskite·wayasit* NA

   ayahciyiniw NA 'stranger, enemy, Blackfoot'

blanket *akohp* NA, NI

blood *mihko* NI

   mihkowiyiniw NA 'Blood Indian'

blue *aski·htakwa·w* VII 'it is blue-green'

body *niyaw* NDI 'my body'

bone *niskan* NDI 'my bone'

boy *na·pe·sis* NA cf. 'man'

breathe *ye·hye·w* VAI 'he breathes'

brother *niste·s* NDA 'my older brother'

   oste·sima·w NA 'the eldest brother'

   nisi·m(is) NDA 'my younger sibling'

   osi·mima·w NA 'the youngest sibling'

   nitawe·ma·w NDA 'my sibling or parallel cousin of opposite sex'; for 'brother-in-law' see 'cousin'

buffalo *mostos*, pl. *mostoswak* NA

bullet *asiniy* NI

bundle *ni·was*, pl. *ni·wata* NDI 'my sacred bundle'

   mi·nisiwas, pl. *mi·nisiwata* NI 'berry bag'

burn *pasite·w* VII 'it burns'

bush *saka·w* NI 'bush, woods'

[††]For Plains Cree, the *i·/a·* alternation is attested only in the preverbs *ki·* and *wi·* (Wolfart 1973:appendix A7).

camp *matokahp* NI 'empty, abandoned campsite'

canoe *o·si* NI (Plains Cree only)

   ci·ma·n NI (Plains Cree and other Cree dialects)

   ma·ham VTI 'he canoes downriver'

   na·taham VTI 'he canoes upriver'

caribou *atihk*, pl. *atihkwak* NA

cent *pi·wa·piskos* NI 'wire, needle, cent'

chief *okima·w* NA 'chief, boss'

child *awa·sis* NA

coat *niskota·kay* NDI 'my coat, dress'

cold *kisina·w* VII 'it is cold weather'

count *akime·w* VTA 'he counts him'

   akihtam VTI 'he counts it'

cousin *ni·tim*, pl. *ni·timwak* NDA 'my cross-cousin of opposite sex, sibling-in-law'

   ni·cimos NDA 'my cross-cousin of opposite sex, my lover'

   ni·sta·w NDA 'my male cross-cousin, brother-in-law (male speaking)'

   nica·hkos NDA 'my female cross-cousin, sister-in-law (female speaking)'

   niciwa·m NDA 'my male parallel cousin, my friend (male speaking)'

crazy *mo·hcopiye·n* NA 'Crazy-Pierre (personal name)'

   mo·hco·hka·so·w VAI 'he pretends to be crazy'

Cree *ne·hiyaw* NA (Plains Cree only)

   ne·hiya·wiw VAI 'he is a Cree'

   ne·hiyawe·w VAI 'he speaks Cree'

   ne·hiyawe·win NI 'Cree matters, Cree expressions, the Cree language'

   paskwa·wiyiniw NA 'Plains Cree Indian'

   omaske·ko·w NA 'Swampy Cree Indian'

   saka·wiyiniw NA 'Bush Cree Indian'

Crow *ka·hka·kiwace·n* NA 'Crow Indian'

cut *manisam* VTI 'he cuts it'

dance *nipa·kwe·simo·w* VAI 'he dances the sun-dance' lit. 'thirst dance'

   pwa·tisimo·w VAI 'he dances the Sioux dance'

daughter *nita·nis* NDA 'my daughter'

dawn *wa·pan* VII 'it dawns'

day *ki·sika·w* VII 'it is day'

   ki·sika·w NI 'day'

die *nipiw* VAI 'he dies'

difficult *a·yiman* VII 'it is difficult'

dig *mo·naham* VTI 'he digs it/for it'

dog *atim*, pl. *atimwak* NA 'dog, horse'

acimosis NA 'dog'

nite·m NDA 'my dog, my horse'

wa·pastim, pl. *wa·pastimwak* NA 'white dog'

atimospikay NA 'Dogrib Indian'

drink *minihkwe·w* VAI 'he drinks'

dry *pa·hkwa·w* VII 'it is dry'

duck *si·si·p* NA 'duck'

   iyinisip NA 'mallard duck'

eagle *kihiw* NA

ear *nihtawakay* NDI 'my ear'

earth *askiy* NI 'land, country, earth; year'

eat *mi·ciso·w* VAI 'he eats'

   mi·ciw VAI 'he eats (it)'

egg *wa·wi* NI

eight *ayina·ne·w* IPC

elbow *nito·skwan* NDI 'my elbow'

eleven *pe·yakosa·p* IPC

enemy *no·tina·kan* NA 'adversary, enemy'

exist *ihta·w* VAI 'he exists'

   ihtakon VII 'it exists'

   namate·w VAI 'he does not exist'

eye *niski·sik*, pl. *niski·sikwa* NDI 'my eye'

face *nihkwa·kan* NDI 'my face'

fall *pahkisin* VAI 'he falls'

far *wa·hyaw* IPC

fat *pimiy* NI 'fat, grease'

father *no·hta·wiy* NDA 'my father'

   o·hta·wi·hka·win NA 'adopted father'; for 'father-in-law' see 'uncle'

fear *kostam* VTI 'he fears it'

feather *mi·kwan* NA

fellow *ni·ci-kise·yiniw* NDA 'my fellow-old-man'

   nikosa·k NDA 'my fellow-husband'

   ni·ci-nitopayima·kan NDA 'my fellow-member-of-a-war-party'

fight *no·tine·w* VTA 'he fights him'

fish *kinose·w* NA

fire *iskote·w* NI

fisher *oce·k* NA (animal)

five *niya·nan* IPC

flow *pimiciwan* VII 'it (river) flows along'

   kisiska·ciwan VII 'it (river) flows fast'

flower *wa·pakoni·w* NI

fly *pimiha·w* VAI 'he flies along'

foot *nisit* NDI 'my foot'

four *ne·wo* IPC

fox *mahke·si·s* NA 'fox, coyote'

freeze *kaskatin* VII 'it freezes up'

friend *nikwe·me·s* NDA 'my namesake, my friend', also 'cousin'

frog *ayi·kis* NA

fur *ata·wa·kan* NA 'fur, furred animal'

gaiter *nita·s* NDI 'my gaiter'; cf. 'trousers'

giant *mista·pe·w* NA

girl *iskwe·sis* NA cf. 'woman'

give *miye·w* VTA 'he gives (it/him) to him'

good *miywa·sin* VII 'it is good'

goose *niska* NA

grandchild *no·sisim* NDA 'my grandchild'

grandfather *nimoso·m* NDA 'my grandfather'

grandmother *no·hkom* NDA 'my grandmother'

grass *maskosiy* NI 'blade of grass'

Gros Ventre *pa·wistiko·yiniw* NA cf. 'rapids'

gull *kiya·sk,* pl. *kiya·skwak* NA

gun *pa·skisikan* NI

hand *nicihciy* NDI 'my hand, my finger'

head *nistikwa·n* NDI 'my head'

hear *pe·htawe·w* VTA 'he hears him'

heart *nite·h* NDI 'my heart'

heavy *kosikwan* VII 'it is heavy'

hill *ispatina·w* VII 'it is a steep hill'

hit *pakamahwe·w* VTA 'he hits him'

hold *tahkonam* VTI 'he holds it'

horse *mistatim,* pl. *mistatimwak* NA; cf. 'dog'
na·pe·stim, pl. *na·pe·stimwak* NA 'male horse, stallion'

house *ni·ki* NDI 'my home'
mi·kiwa·hp NI 'lodge, teepee'
wa·skahikan NI 'wooden cabin'

how *ta·nisi* IPC

hunt *ma·ci·w* VAI 'he hunts'

ice *miskwamiy* NA

if *ki·spin* IPC

Indian: for 'speak Indian' see under 'speak'

island *ministik,* pl. *ministikwa* NI

kettle *askihk,* pl. *askihkwak* NA 'kettle, pail'

kill *nipahe·w* VTA 'he kills him'

kinsman *nito·te·m* NDA 'my kinsman'

knife *mo·hkoma·n* NI

know *kiske·yime·w* VTA 'he knows him'
kiske·yihtam VTI 'he knows it'

lake *sa·kahikan* NI

laugh *pa·hpiw* VAI 'he laughs'
pa·hpihe·w VTA 'he makes him laugh'

leaf *ni·piy* NI

lie *pimisin* VAI 'he lies extended'

live *pima·tisiw* VAI 'he lives'

liver *niskon* NDI 'my liver'

long *kinwa·w* VII 'it is long'

look *wi·nina·kosiw* VAI 'he looks dirty'
kitima·kina·kosiw VAI 'he looks pitiable'

loon *ma·kwa* NA

louse *ihkwa* NA

lynx *pisiw* NA

maize *mahta·min* NA 'grain of maize, ear of maize'

man *ayi·siyiniw* NA 'man, human being, person'
na·pe·w NA 'man'; cf. *nina·pe·m* 'my husband'
oskini·kiw NA 'young man'
kise·yiniw NA 'old man'

many *mihce·t* IPC

measure *tipahikan* NI 'measure, yard, hour'

meat *wiya·s* NI
ka·hke·wak, pl. *ka·hke·wakwa* NI 'dried meat'

medicine *maskihkiy* NI 'medicine, herb'
maskihki·wiyiniw NA 'medicine-man, physician'
maskihki·wiskwe·w NA 'nurse'

metal *pi·wa·pisk,* pl. *pi·wa·piskwa* NI 'metal, iron'

money *so·niya·w* NA 'gold, money'

moose *mo·swa* NA

mother *nika·wiy* NDA 'my mother'
mana·cima·kan NA 'person to whom speech is avoided; mother-in-law (man speaking)'; for 'mother-in-law' see 'aunt'

mountain *waciy* NI 'hill, mountain'
asini·waciy NI 'the Rocky Mountains'

mouth *nito·n* NDI 'my mouth'

move *piciw* VAI 'he moves camp'
ma·hipiciw VAI 'he moves camp downriver'

muskrat *wacask,* pl. *wacaskwak* NA

name *wi·he·w* VTA 'he names him'
wi·ho·w VAI 'he names himself'
wi·ho·win NI 'name'

narrow *sa·kawa·sin* VII 'it is narrow'

near *ci·ki* IPC

nephew *nitihkwatim* NDA 'son of my sibling of opposite sex' *nito·sim* NDA 'child of my sibling of same sex'

niece *nistim* NDA 'daughter of my sibling of opposite sex'

night *tipiska·w* VII 'it is night'

   tipiska·w NI 'night'

nine *ke·ka·c-mita·taht* IPC

not *nama, namo·ya* IPC

nut *paka·n* NA

old *ke·hte·* IPC

   kaya·s IPC 'long ago, of old'

one *pe·yak* IPC

orphan *awahka·nisis* NA

other *kotak* PR

otter *nikik*, pl. *nikikwak* NA

owl *o·how* NA

paddle *apoy* NA

paper *masinahikan* NI 'paper, letter, book'

Piegan *pi·kanowiyiniw* NA

pipe *ospwa·kan* NA

play *me·tawe·w* VAI 'he plays'

pouch *ahpihcis* NA 'tobacco pouch, pouch'

prairie *paskwa·w* VII 'it is open prairie'

prairie-chicken *pihye·w* NA 'prairie-chicken, partridge'

   no·se·pihye·w NA 'prairie-hen, female partridge'

pull *manipitam* VTI 'he pulls it loose'

push *si·hkine·w* VTA 'he pushes him on'

rabbit *wa·pos*, pl. *wa·poswak* NA 'rabbit, hare'

rain *kimiwan* VII 'it rains'

rapids *pa·wistik*, pl. *pa·wistikwa* NI 'rapids, waterfall'

red *mihkwa·w* VII 'it is red'

rib *nispikay* NDI 'my rib'

river *si·piy* NI

road *me·skanaw* NI 'road, path'

rope *pi·sa·kana·piy* NI 'rawhide rope'

rosin *pikiw* NA 'rosin, gum'

run *pimipahta·w* VAI 'he runs along'

   na·tahipahta·w VAI 'he runs upriver'

sand *ye·kaw* NI

Sarcee *sa·si·w* NA

Saulteaux *nahkawiyiniw* NA

say *itwe·w* VAI 'he says so'

   ite·w VTA 'he says so to him'

see *wa·pame·w* VTA 'he sees him'

   wa·pahtam VTI 'he sees it'

seven *te·pakohp* IPC

sew *kaskikwa·tam* VTI 'he sews it'

sharp *ki·nika·w* VII 'it is sharp'

shoe *maskisin* NI 'moccasin, shoe'

short *cima·sin* VII 'it is short'

sing *nikamow* VAI 'he sings'

Sioux *pwa·t* NA

sister *nimis* NDA 'my older sister'

   omisima·w NA 'the eldest sister'; see also 'brother'; for 'sister-in-law' see 'cousin'

sit *apiw* VAI 'he sits'

six *nikotwa·sik* IPC

sky *ki·sik*, pl. *ki·sikwa* NI

Slavey *awahka·n* NA

sleep *nipa·w* VAI 'he sleeps'

small *apisa·sin* VII 'it is small'

smell *miya·htam* VTI 'he smells it'

smoke *pikihte·w* VII 'it smokes'

   pi·htwa·w VAI 'he smokes (tobacco)'

smooth *so·skwa·w* VII 'it is smooth'

snake *kine·pik*, pl. *kine·pikwak* NA

snow *ko·na* NA

snowshoe *asa·m* NA

some *a·tiht* IPC

soil *asiskiy* NI

son *nikosis* NDA 'my son'

   okosisi·hka·win NA 'adopted son'

   ninaha·hkisi·m NDA/NA 'my son-in-law'

soup *mi·cima·poy* NI

   mi·nisa·poy NI 'berry soup'

speak *ayahciyini·mow* VAI 'he speaks Blackfoot'

   ne·hiyawe·w VAI 'he speaks Cree'

   ne·hiyawimototawe·w VTA 'he speaks Cree to him'

   akaya·si·mow VAI 'he speaks English'

   we·mistiko·si·mow VAI 'he speaks French'

   nahkawe·w VAI 'he speaks Saulteaux'

   pwa·si·mow VAI 'he speaks Sioux'

   ta·pwe·w VAI 'he speaks the truth'

spirit *manitow* NA 'spirit, god'

   a·tayo·hkan NA 'spirit animal'

split *pasahike·w* VAI 'he splits things by tool'

spouse *wi·kima·kan* NA

squirrel *anikwaca·s* NA

stab *tahkame·w* VTA 'he stabs him'

stand *ni·pawiw* VAI 'he stands'

438

star *aca·hkos* NA

stick *mistik,* pl. *mistikwa* NI

stone *asiniy* NA

Stoney *opwa·si·mow* NA lit. 'Sioux speaker'

story *a·cimowin* NI 'story, narrative'

  a·tayo·hke·win NI 'sacred story'; cf. 'spirit'

straight *kwayask* IPC 'straight, proper'

stranger *pi·tosiyiniw* NA 'stranger, enemy'

summer *ni·pin* VII 'it is summer'

sun *pi·sim,* obv. *pi·simwa* NA

swamp *maske·k,* pl. *maske·kwa* NI

sweetgrass *wi·hkask,* pl. *wi·hkaskwa* NI

tail *nisoy* NDI 'my tail'

tea *maskihki·wa·poy* NI

ten *mita·taht* IPC

thick *kispaka·w* VII 'it is thick'

thin *papaka·w* VII 'it is thin'

think *ite·yime·w* VTA 'he thinks so of him'

three *nisto* IPC

throw *we·pinam* VTI 'he throws it away'

thunderbird *pihye·siw* NA

tie *sakahpite·w* VTA 'he ties him fast'

tobacco *ciste·ma·w* NA

town *o·te·naw* NI

tree *mistik,* pl. *mistikwak* NA

  sihta NA 'coniferous tree'

trousers *nita·s* NDA 'my trousers'; cf. 'gaiter'

truly *ta·pwe·* IPC 'truly, indeed'

turn *kwe·ski·w* VAI 'he turns'

twelve *ni·sosa·p* IPC

two *ni·so* IPC

uncle *nisis* NDA 'my mother's brother, father-in-law'

  no·hca·wi·s NDA 'my father's brother, mother's sister's husband' (Plains Cree only); cf. 'father'

  no·hkomis NDA 'my father's brother, mother's sister's husband' (Plains Cree and other Cree dialects)

walk *pimohte·w* VAI 'he walks along'

  ma·hohte·w VAI 'he walks downriver'

wash *ka·si·hwe·w* VTA 'he washes him, wipes him'

  kisi·pe·kinam VTI 'he washes it'

water *nipiy* NI

weasel *sihkos* NA

wet *sa·pope·w* VAI 'he is wet, drenched'

white *wa·piska·w* VII 'it is white'

  wa·piski-wiya·s NA 'White man'

  mo·niyaw NA 'White man, Canadian'

  we·mistiko·siw NA 'White man, Frenchman, Canadian'

wife *ni·wa* NDA 'my wife'

willow *ni·pisiy* NI

wind *yo·tin* VII 'it is wind'

windigo *wi·htikow* NA

winter *pipon* VII 'it is winter'

with *ohci* IPC (postposition)

woman *iskwe·w* NA 'woman'; cf. *nitiskwe·m* 'my wife'

  oskini·kiskwe·w NA 'young woman'

  no·tokwe·siw NA 'old woman'

yellow *osa·wa·w* VII 'it is yellow'

young *oski* IPC 'young, new'

Sketch of Lakhota, a Siouan Language

DAVID S. ROOD AND ALLAN R. TAYLOR

Lakhota is one dialect of a language widely spoken in the northern plains. It is not easy to find a universally acceptable designation for this language, given the fact that there is no unambiguous native name for it. Nineteenth and early twentieth-century scholars (Stephen R. Riggs, Franz Boas) used the term Dakota both for the language and for its eastern dialect. This is obviously awkward and liable to confusion. Here the designation *Sioux* is used for the language, reserving *Dakota* for the dialect. Many speakers of the language dislike the term *Sioux* because of its foreign origin (cp. Goddard 1984), its use primarily by non-Indians, and because some do not recognize that all the dialects represent the same language.

The Sioux language is the first or second language of about 10,000-12,000 people in the northern plains and contiguous areas of the United States and the Canadian prairie provinces. Some speakers of the language are to be found in other places in both countries as well, such as Los Angeles and Toronto. This is one of the largest surviving native language communities in North America.

Lakhota (Teton Sioux) is one of five closely related dialects. Parks (1990), based on extensive surveys of all the Sioux-speaking reservations and reserves in the late 1970s, identifies these as Santee-Sisseton, Teton, Yankton-Yanktonai, Assiniboine, and Stoney. The easternmost of these is Santee-Sisseton. Nineteenth-century scholars, following native usage, referred to this dialect as Dakota. The westernmost of the dialects, Teton, is designated by its native name, Lakhota or Lakota. Speakers of the Assiniboine and Stoney dialects call their language Nakoda. The remaining dialect, Yankton-Yanktonai, also located geographically between the Santee-Sisseton and Teton dialects, shows affinities with both Dakota and Nakoda, although speakers call their language Dakota.

Each of these dialects has reservation- or reserve-based subdialects, some quite different from the others. The subdialects of Teton Sioux oppose the southwest reservations (Pine Ridge and Rosebud) to those on the Missouri River (Cheyenne River, Lower Brule, Standing Rock). The populations on these reservations reflect earlier band divisions among the Teton Sioux, so the present linguistic differences quite likely reflect differences older than the reservation period, which dates only from the last third of the nineteenth century.

The Sioux language, in one or another of its dialects, but chiefly Dakota, has been written for over 150 years by missionaries, anthropologists, educators, and native speakers, using a variety of writing systems, all based on the Roman alphabet. Not surprisingly, there exists a sizable corpus of Sioux writings (see de Reuse 1987, 1990), some favoring a broad rendering of the sounds of the language, others a fairly narrow rendering. In most cases there is no indication with or in the document of the intended degree of phonological exactitude, although most are more broad than narrow.

1. PHONOLOGY

Table 1 gives the consonant phonemes of Sioux, and table 2, the vowels. The discussion that follows specifies the significant variants of these phonemes for the Teton dialect. Although the transcription is phonemic, it uses and adapts some conventions and diacritics from earlier practical orthographies and uses capitalization and punctuation in accordance with written English norms.

Table 1. Lakhota Consonants

		Labial	Dental	Palatal	Velar	Post Velar	Glottal
Obstruents							
stops	voiceless plain	*p*	*t*	*č*	*k*		*ʔ*
	voiceless aspirated	*ph*	*th*	*čh*	*kh*		
	voiceless glottalized	*pʔ*	*tʔ*	*čʔ*	*kʔ*		
	voiced	*b*			*g*		
fricatives	voiceless plain		*s*	*š*		*ȟ*	
	voiced		*z*	*ž*		*ǧ*	
Resonants							
nasals		*m*	*n*	*ň*			
lateral			*l*				
Glides		*w*		*y*			*h*

441

Table 2. Lakhota Vowels

	Front	Central	Back
high oral	*i*		*u*
nasal	*į*		*ų*
mid	*e*		*o*
low nasal		*ą*	
oral		*a*	

Stress and Pitch
　　　relative loudness, high pitch
　　Diacritics used in phonetic transcriptions:
　　　ˋ less loud than vowels stressed
　　　ˆ fading loudness, high falling pitch
　　　ˇ increasing loudness, high rising pitch

1.0. CONSONANTS

There are either 26 or 28 consonant phonemes in Lakhota, depending on how [b] and [g] are counted (1.1.3.).

1.1. STOPS

/p, t, k, ʔ/ are plain oral stops articulated at labial, dental, velar, and glottal positions. /č/ is a palatal affricate, but it patterns with the stops. The sounds represented by *p, t, k* can be compared with the English sounds represented by the letters *p, t,* and *c* in the words *spar, star,* and *scar.* English has no exact equivalent for the sound represented by Lakhota *č,* but the reader can easily create the sound by inventing an English word such as *schar,* pronounced to rhyme with *spar, star,* and *scar: ch* is here pronounced like Lakhota *č.* Lakhota words that contain these sounds are:

sápa	'black'
yúta	'to eat'
sáka	'dry'
hečá	'buzzard'.

/ʔ/ represents a soundless hiatus between other sounds: the hiatus occurs when the air stream is interrupted by tight closure of the glottis. The characteristic "sound" of this consonant is the sharp interruption of the air stream that occurs when the glottis is abruptly closed or an audible pop when the closure is released. An English example is the interjection *oh oh!* [óʔo] uttered by English speakers when they are confronted by something unexpected. Lakhota examples are:

| *aʔú* | 'to bring here' |
| *aʔí* | 'to take there'. |

1.1.1. ASPIRATED STOPS

The aspirated stops of Lakhota consist of a stop closure followed by a release accompanied by either glottal or velar friction. When the release has glottal friction, the sound is very much like the English aspirated stops found before stressed vowels as in the following English words: *pick, tick, chick,* and *kick.* Release with glottal friction occurs in Lakhota with *čh* and with other aspirated stops before the vowels /i u į/. Glottal friction is also sometimes heard before the vowel /ų/. Lakhota words in which the aspirated stops have glottal friction are the following:

phí	'liver'
thí	'to live'
čha	'so'
khí	'to reach home there'
phú	'rotten (wood)'
nuphį	'both'
phuté	'upper lip'.

Before other vowels except /e/ the aspiration is velar in release, rather than glottal. There are no English equivalents to the sound of the aspirated stops of this kind; they can be compared with the sound of the Navajo aspirated stops if these are known to the reader. Examples of velar release are the following:

[pxá]	'head'
[txápa]	'ball'
[kxáta]	'hot'
[txó]	'blue, green'
[kxá]	'to signify'
[txezí]	'stomach'
[otxúwahe]	'village'.

The distribution of the two kinds of release described above is not absolute: both kinds of release occur before the vowel /e/, and before this vowel, the distinction is phonemic in particular ideolects. It should be noted that all speakers agree on the nature of aspiration except before the vowel /e/ and that in these cases there is no variation: a speaker pronounces a given word with either one or the other kind of release quite consistently. The distinction is thus more lexical than phonological. Examples of this kind are:

[pheží, pxeží] 'grass'
[phehį́, pxehį́] 'hair of the head'.

Some speakers pronounce these words with glottal friction, others with velar friction, as indicated. Because the distinction between [h] and [x] is so nearly predictable and because speakers disagree about those places where it is not predictable, all aspirated stops are presented here as consonant plus /h/: *phá* 'head', *thápa* 'ball', *kháta* 'hot', etc.

1.1.2. GLOTTALIZED STOPS

The glottalized stops of Lakhota are ejectives; these sounds are not found in English or in any Western European languages. Ejective sounds are formed by the near simultaneous release of two closures, one in the mouth at the position of the stop, the other in the larynx at the glottis. Some compression of the air in the mouth occurs due to the double closure, and it is the release of this compressed air that gives the characteristic "crack" when the ejective is released. Lakhota words containing ejective stops are:

pʔó	'fog'
tʔá	'dead'
ičʔį́	'harness'
kʔú	'to give'.

1.1.3. VOICED STOPS

The phonemes /b/ and /g/ represent the same sounds as in English *bet* and *get*. They have a very restricted distribution in Lakhota, occurring only before sonorant consonants (l m n), the voiced glides (w y), and in various kinds of vowel-dropping situations (Section 4.3.1.2.) and reduplication (4.3.2.8.). Since /p/ and /k/ never occur in these positions, /b/ and /g/ are actually positional variants of the plain voiceless stops. There is nevertheless an extremely small number of words where the /b/ is not predictable, so it seems best to consider that sound marginally phonemic. Moreover, there is a long tradition of writing both *b* and *g* when they occur, despite their theoretical status, and that tradition is followed here.

When followed by a sonorant, the stop closure is released before the articulation of the sonorant is begun, giving a voiced, vowellike transition to the sonorant.

The first two of these examples sound very much like the English words *below* and (the first part of) *galore:*

bló	'potato'
gló	'to grunt'
tób	'four'
sabsápa	'severally black'
sabyá	'to blacken'
patḥág	'stopping, halting abruptly'
sagsáka	'dry'
nagwáka	'to kick out the foot'.

1.2.

Lakhota has a more extensive fricative system than does English, so some of the Lakhota fricatives have no English counterpart.

1.2.1. SIBILANTS

Lakhota /s z š ž/ are postdental and palatal in articulation; these sounds can be compared with the highly similar English sounds found in the words *seal, zeal, rasher,* and *azure.* Lakhota words that contain these sounds are:

Hásapa	'Black person'
máza	'metal'
maší	'he ordered me'
pheží	'grass'.

1.2.2. VELAR FRICATIVES

The Lakhota velar fricatives /ȟ, ǧ/ [x, γ] have no English equivalents, but they can be compared with sounds found in close relatives of English such as German and Spanish. /ȟ/ represents the final sound in the German word *Bach* or the initial sound in Spanish *jota.* Lakhota examples of this phoneme are:

ȟé	'mountain'
iȟá	'to laugh'
iȟʔé	'rock'.

The phoneme /ǧ/ has two positional variants, one an uvular tap, the other, a midvelar voiced fricative. The former sound occurs in Lakhota before the vowel /i/; an example is the word

ǧí	'yellow, brown'.

Compare this to the sound represented by *r* in the French word *Henri* when this name is pronounced very quickly. Examples of the other variant of /ǧ/ are the Lakhota words

ǧú	'burned'
káǧa	'to make'.

This sound is identical to Spanish *g* between vowels, as in the word *pagar* 'to pay'.

A lengthened form of the voiceless fricatives is found when these are initial before a stressed vowel. Examples of this lengthened fricative sound are:

sí	'foot'
šá	'red'
ȟóta	'gray'

1.3. SONORANTS

Lakhota /m n ň/ are respectively labial, dental, and velar in articulation. All have ready English equivalents: *him, sin,* and *sing.* A Lakhota example containing all three sounds is:

šųňmánitu	'coyote'.

For most speakers, Lakhota /l/ has a "clear" rather than a "dark" timbre. It is most like the "clear" *l* of Spanish or Italian *ala* 'wing' or French *elle* 'she'. It never sounds like English "dark" *l* after a vowel, e.g. *ball, well.* However, there are reports that some speakers have the same distribution of "clear" and "dark" *l* in Lakhota that they do in English. Lakhota examples of /l/ are:

lél	'here'
thaló	'meat'
Lakhóta	'Indian'.

1.4. GLIDES

The glides /w y h/ have more conditioned variants than any of the other consonant phonemes of Lakhota. This is probably due to the fact that their status as semivowels makes them highly sensitive to the vocalic environments in which they occur. /w y/ are voiced; /h/ is voiceless.

1.4.1.

/w y h/ are most clearly pronounced at the beginning of a word. Lakhota examples are:

wá	'snow'
yá	'to go'
há	'skin'.

443

Compare these with equivalent English sounds in the same position, as in the words *wet, yet,* and *hot.*

1.4.2.

When the glides come between vowels they are pronounced weakly, if at all. This is particularly the case with /w/ and /y/. Examples are the Lakhota words:

wayáwa	'he reads'
iyápi	'they say'
othų́wahe	'town'
yuwášte	'to make good'
hąhépi	'night'
čhąhápi	'sugar'.

1.4.3.

Before and between nasalized vowels all three Lakhota glides are pronounced with heavy nasalization. English equivalents for the nasalized glides are rare, although the sounds are easy to produce if the velic is open and air passes out of the nasal cavity during their articulation. Examples of nasalized /h/ do occur in English in the informal affirmative and negative particles *uh-huh* [ə̃hə̃́] 'yes' and *uh-uh* [(h)ə̃́ʔə̃] 'no'. Lakhota examples are:

wíyą	'woman'
chąhápi	'sugar'.

2. VOWELS

The vowel system of Lakhota has five oral vowels and three nasal vowels. They are typically rather short in duration. However, lengthened versions of all the vowels may occur lengthened due to contraction of identical vowels, and two additional long vowels having no short analogues result from the contraction of unlike vowels. Vowel contraction is described in sections 2.3. and 4.3.

2.1. ORAL VOWELS

The five oral vowels are very comparable in their typical value to the five "cardinal" vowels, for example, as these are realized in Spanish. All are "pure"; that is, there is no shift in articulators or articulatory position during their articulation. Pure cardinal vowels are difficult for English speakers to produce because precisely these vowels begin in English with a "pure" vowel and end with a glide pronounced in the same general area. This English glide is usually written with the mid-vowels /e/ and /o/ but not otherwise. Compare the following:

Lakhota	English
sí 'foot'	*see* (si + y-glide)
sú 'seed'	*sue* (su + w-glide)
blé 'lake'	*play* (ple + y-glide)
bló 'potato'	*below* (belo + w-glide).

The vowels /i/ and /u/ are front unrounded and back rounded, respectively. Compare their sounds to the same vowels in Spanish or Italian. Lakhota examples of these vowels are:

hí	'tooth'
hú	'leg'.

The vowels /e/ and /o/ are lower-mid; /e/ is front unrounded; /o/ is back rounded. There are no good phonetic analogues for these Lakhota vowels in English or other Western European languages. The sounds of these vowels are somewhat more open than the accepted pronunciation of the cardinal vowels *e* and *o*. Lakhota examples of these vowels are:

hé	'horn'
hó	'voice'.

The vowel /a/ is low and central, pronounced in Lakhota with its cardinal value: that is, it is pronounced with close to maximum opening. An adequate English analogue is the vowel in the first syllable of the word *father*. A Lakhota example is:

há	'skin'.

All Lakhota oral vowels are partially devoiced when they are stressed and in utterance-final position. This devoicing makes it sound like a final *h* follows the vowel. This is especially noticeable when words are pronounced very carefully, as in citation.

2.2. NASALIZED VOWELS

Nasalized counterparts exist for the two highest and the single lowest vowel: /į, ų, ą/. The nasalized vowels are phonetically lax. The sounds of these vowels are comparable to, but not identical with, certain English vowels followed in the same syllable by a nasal consonant. The sound of /į/ and /ą/ may be compared with the vowels in *sin* and *nun*. (Note that the comparison is to the sound of the vowel only, without the following nasal consonant.) American English has no equivalent for /ų/. Here are Lakhota examples of the nasalized vowels:

hį́	'hair'
hą́	'yes'
hų́ku	'his mother'.

While most Lakhota speakers agree as to which vowels are pronounced with nasalization, there are some vowels that are nasalized by some speakers, but not by others. Such cases no doubt represent doublets: both pronunciations are correct. (Compare this with a word such as *which* in English, where some speakers preaspirate and devoice the /w/, while others pronounce voiced /w/ alone.) Lakhota examples of such doublets are

ki, kį	'the'
náži, nážį	'to stand'.

2.2.1.

The vowels /i, u, a/ are always pronounced with some nasalization when they follow a nasal consonant. However, some speakers have a phonemic contrast between nasalized and nonnasalized vowels following nasal consonants. For these speakers, strong nasalization indicates that the vowel is phonemically nasalized, while weak nasalization indicates that the vowel is phonemically oral.

Speakers who have phonemic contrast after nasal consonants probably continue an earlier pattern in the language whereby there was full phonemic contrast in oral and nasal vowels after nasal consonants. That this is not an idiosyncratic feature of some persons' speech is shown by their agreement with speakers of other Sioux dialects such as Nakoda, where full contrast is found after nasal consonants. Some examples of contrasting nasality after nasalized consonants are:

mąká 'I sit'   versus   maká 'skunk'
gmúza 'slimy'   versus   gmúza 'closed, as the fist'
nįyá 'cause to live' versus niyá 'to breathe'.

At an abstract level, Patterson (1991) argues for three kinds of vowel nasalization in Lakhota: some vowels are [+nasal], some are [-nasal], and some are unmarked for this feature.

This chapter represents speech in which vowel nasalization is neutralized after nasal consonants, which appears to be the usage of the majority of Lakhota speakers. In this environment only oral vowels are written.

2.3. DIPHTHONGS AND CONTRACTED VOWELS
There is only one diphthong in Lakhota, the sequence /au/. This occurs in a single Lakhota word, one of whose functions is as a greeting to a man:

> *Hau!*   'greeting to an adult male'

The pronunciation of this word is identical to that of the English word *how*. This word may be a loan from a non-Siouan language.

While the case of diphthongs is quite simple in Lakhota, that of contracted vowels is not. Contracted vowels result from the conflation of syllables through the collapse of a syllable boundary or from the vocalization of consonantal elements followed by conflation with a preceding vowel. Contraction happens most often in rapid, colloquial speech, although there are a few examples where the contraction has become the standard form. A prominent example of this is the word [á·ta·] 'entirely', which must have an underlying form with normal short vowels. However, contemporary speakers cannot supply an underlying form for this word, which is unusual. Long contracted vowels of this sort are phonemic; and written double: /áataa/.

In almost all cases, the collapse of a syllable or word boundary results from the disappearance of a glide between vowels (section 1.4.2.). After the loss of the glide, the vowels in hiatus contract. The contracted vowel is nasalized if either of the uncontracted vowels was nasalized.

When the original vowels were of the same height, or if assimilation occurs before contraction, a simple long vowel results. Here are examples of this kind of contraction, with pitch marked as explained in section 3.2.:

[hă·pi] 'clothing', < *hayápi*
[mî·hakab] 'immediately after me' < *mí ihakab*
[kê·] 'he said that' < *kéye*
[û·kte] 'they will come' < *ú pi kte*
[ô·na] 'they wounded him and' < *ó pi na*
[chə̆̃·pi] 'sugar' < *chą-hápi* ('tree juice').

When the uncontracted vowels were of different heights or when feature contrasts exist between the vowels and the glide, the contracted vowel is qualitatively different from the uncontracted sequence. Here are Lakhota examples of the two vowels that result from this kind of contraction:

[iyæ̂·] < *iyáye* 'he left for there'
[wakhæ̂·ža] < *wakháyeža* or *wakháheža* 'child'
[mithɔ̂·] < *mitháwa* 'it is mine'
[ųyɔ̂·kte] < *ųyą́ pi kte* 'we will be going'

3. STRESS AND PITCH
Vowels in all languages are pronounced with some kind of accompanying melody (loudness, pitch). The word is the domain of stress in Lakhota. In Lakhota words the first (or only) stressed vowel has higher pitch and greater loudness than all other vowels in that word. Most of the time the stressed vowel is the second one in the word, but this is not always so. It is therefore necessary to write stress on every word. Compare the following Lakhota words from the same verbal paradigm:

> *iyáye*   'he set out to go there'
> *éyaye*   'they set out as a group to go there'.

A rare example with stress on other than the first or second syllable is *tuktená* 'which ones?'.

3.1. SECONDARY STRESS
There is usually only one stressed vowel in each word. Exceptions to this are compound words, which usually retain the stressed vowels of the originally separate words. In a compound word, therefore, there can be two or more stressed vowels; in such cases, the first stressed vowel has higher pitch and greater loudness than any subsequent stressed vowel. These two stress levels are referred to as primary and secondary stress, and when it is desirable to distinguish them the acute accent (´) can be used for primary stress and the grave accent (`) for secondary stress. Examples are:

> *mázaskà*   'money' (lit. 'white metal, silver')
> *šúkawakhà*   'horse' (lit. 'mystery dog').

Ordinarily this distinction is not marked, and the acute accent is used for both types of stress.

3.2. PITCH ON LONG VOWELS
Lakhota long vowels, which always result from vowel contraction, may be pronounced with rising or falling pitch, depending on the stress pattern of the original, uncontracted vowels. If the first uncontracted vowel had stress, the contracted sequence has higher pitch and greater loudness at the beginning of the contracted

sequence, with a fall in pitch and loudness as the sequence continues. If the uncontracted sequence had stress on the second vowel, then the contracted sequence shows a rise in pitch and loudness toward the end of the sequence. Compare the following examples, where a circumflex (^) marks a contracted vowel with the high point toward the beginning, and a wedge (ˇ) marks a contracted vowel with the high point toward the end of the sequence:

| [û·kte] | 'they will be coming' |
| [ǰ·phe] | 'I hit him'. |

In phonemic writing, long vowels are written as geminates, with the appropriate one stressed. For example, [î·] is /íi/ and [ǔ·] is /uú/.

4. THE PHONEMIC STRUCTURE OF WORDS

Lakhota phonemes are combined into words according to very regular rules, as is true of all languages. Some consonant and vowel sequences are exceedingly frequent, others are rare, and some theoretically possible combinations never occur.

4.1. SEGMENTAL SEQUENCES

Lakhota words in their basic form almost always end in a vowel. Of the consonants, only /l/ is at all frequent as the final sound in a word. Also occasionally found in word-final position are /b/, /g/, /m/, /n/, /s/, /š/, and /ȟ/. Of these, /n/ is most frequent.

Lakhota words begin, as a rule, with one or two consonants. Words written with an initial vowel are usually pronounced with a preceding [ʔ], although this sound may be omitted. Any vowel can follow any consonant except that nasalized vowels never follow /l/. In some dialects an /l/ following a nasalized vowel in the same syllable is replaced by /n/: *hehą́l* in these dialects is pronounced *hehą́n*. There are a number of restrictions on the makeup of consonant clusters; for example, there are no clusters with one fricative directly adjacent to another.

Within words, vowels and consonants almost always alternate, with each vowel separated by one, two, or (very rarely) three consonants.

There are nevertheless a few words in the language where vocalic prefixes are added to vowel-initial stems with no intervening consonant or consonantal element. Examples are:

naíčʔikeǧa	'to scratch oneself with the foot'
míoglasʔį	'mirror'
kaízu	'to pay off one's debts'
paóskiča	'to cram things into something'. (e.g., too many clothes into a washing machine)
paótkuǧa	'push, close, and lock with one motion, as a door with an automatic lock'
yuótkuǧa	'pull, close, and lock' (as above).

A similar phenomenon is more difficult to deal with, and speakers disagree about some of these examples. Vowels that are the same and that have no intervening consonant, especially /ii/, are frequently pronounced as a series of rearticulated vowels. Where one of the clustered vowels has stress, there is a rising (or falling) pitch on the phonetically lengthened vowel. Examples are:

lową́	'to sing'
ílową	'to sing about something'
íičʔilową	'to sing about oneself'
íiičʔilową	'to sing about one's impending death'
sabmíčʔiye	'I blackened myself, made myself black'
sabmíičʔiye	'I blackened myself because of some obligation or for some ceremonial purpose'.

Usually native speakers do not pronounce any of these vowel sequences with intervening glides or [ʔ], and they reject the insertion of such elements. It is unclear to what extent there may have been glide neutralization in such cases (see 4.3.1.3.) or whether a phonemic element was ever present between these vowels.

Refer to the sample vocabulary for examples of consonant and vowel sequences.

4.2. SYLLABIFICATION

The number of syllables per word is determined by the number of vowels present in the word: there is one syllable for each vowel. Taylor and Rood disagree about the accuracy of this statement for the identical adjacent vowels described just above: Taylor hears a simple long vowel in these contexts, while Rood believes that the vowels are separately rearticulated and thus constitute separate syllables. It is likely that speakers differ in the phonetic realization of these sequences.

The only other exception to this rule is the word *háu*, which includes the only diphthong known in the language. This word is a monosyllable.

Most syllables begin with one or two consonants and end, wherever possible, with a vowel:

[wa-yá-wa]	'he reads'
[la-kxó-ta]	'Indian'
[spa-yó-la]	'Mexican'
[o-í-yo-ki-phi]	'be happy'
[lél]	'here'
[nų́m]	'two'.

The syllable always ends in a vowel or a single consonant, but when two or more consonants come between vowels, it is not always easy to know whether the syllable boundary will come before all or between the first two.

If the consonants belong to the same morpheme (meaningful sequence of sounds), the syllable break comes before the consonants:

446

| [si-čá-mną] | 'it stinks' (cf. *mná* 'to stink') |
| [yu-ptá-ptą] | 'to rock back and forth with the hand' (cf. -ptą- 'unsteady, rocking'). |

But if the two consonants belong to different morphemes, the syllable boundary comes between the two:

| [nų́m-nų-pa] | 'two by two' (cf. *núpa* 'two') |
| [tób-to-pa] | 'four by four' (cf. *tópa* 'four'). |

Except before /m, n, l/, /b/ and /g/ occur only in morpheme-final position. Hence there will always be a syllable boundary after these sounds if any other consonant follows.

When three consonants are found between vowels within utterances, the consonant cluster is always divided by the syllable boundary, since such sequences are found only in compound words:

| [šųň-bló-ka] | 'male horse or dog'. |

4.3. PHONOLOGICAL CHANGES IN THE BASIC FORM OF WORDS

Pronunciation of isolated words is often different from the pronunciation of the same words in phonological contexts of larger size such as word compounds, phrases, or sentences. In some cases also the change of the grammatical form of a word can cause phonological changes in the word itself. In other words, the form of a word, or the forms of related words, are often affected by the presence of other linguistic elements.

4.3.1.

In all languages, rapid, colloquial speech often differs markedly from slow, careful speech. As a rule, rapid speech is a reduced form of slow speech. English examples of this are *spose* for 'suppose', *gotcha* for 'I've got you', and *gonna* for 'going to'.

There are many changes of this kind in colloquial Lakhota, and Lakhota speakers are themselves aware of the difference. Precise (unchanged) speech is called *yat?įsya-wóglakapi* 'firm or clear speech', while rapid, slurred speech is called *ikčéya-wóglakapi* 'ordinary or normal speech'.

4.3.1.1.

One of the most striking differences between precise and rapid speech is the replacement of the enclitic (suffixlike word; see 10.0.) *pi* in rapid speech by a vowel before the enclitics *kte, kį, kištó, na,* and possibly others. The vowel that replaces *pi* is determined by the height of the vowel that immediately precedes *pi*. If the vowel is high (/i/, /į/, /u/, /ų/), *pi* is replaced by /u/. If the vowel is mid or low (/e/, /o/, /a/, /ą/), *pi* is replaced by /o/. The replacing vowel is nasalized if the preceding vowel is nasalized. Here are some examples of this change:

Slow speech	Fast speech	Meaning
Hí pi kte.	[hí u kte]	'They will arrive here.'
Ú pi kte.	[û·kte]	'They will come.'
Čhį́ pi kte.	[čhį́ ų kte]	'They will want.'
Olé pi na	[olé o na]	'They looked for him and...'
Yatką́ pi na	[yatką́ o na]	'They drank it and...'
Oyúspa pi kištó.	[oyúspa o kštó]	'They caught him.'

4.3.1.2.

Also characteristic of rapid speech is the dropping of unstressed, word-final vowels. For example, in the enclitic *pi* /i/ is frequently lost when other enclitics follow. If a nasalized vowel precedes, and a fricative follows, /p/ is then changed to /m/:

Slow speech	Fast speech	Meaning
Awíčhayuštą pi šni.	[awíčhayuštą m šni]	'They aren't leaving them alone.'
Awíčhayuštą pi he?	[awíčhayuštą b he]	'Are they leaving them alone?'

/į/ in the article (8.3.1.) *kį* is also frequently dropped:

Slow speech	Fast speech	Meaning
hokšíla kį lé	[hokšíla g lé]	'this boy'

In these examples, note that *p* and *k* are voiced to *b* and *g* when they come to stand before a consonant. A similar process is described in 4.3.2.7. below.

Dropping of word-final vowels is particularly frequent when the following word begins with a vowel; note that such newly word-final /p/ and /t/ do not become /b/ or /l/. (The loss of /w/ is described in the next section.)

Slow speech	Fast speech	Meaning
Ağúyapi etą́ ophéthų wo!	[ağuáp et óphethų o]	'Buy some bread!'

4.3.1.3.

Another frequently encountered phenomenon is the dropping of glides and /ʔ/ when these phonemes are located between vowels. The vowels left without a separating consonant are sometimes then contracted into a single long vowel having some of the features of both original vowels (2.3.).

/w/ and /y/ are weakly pronounced, or dropped, when one of the neighboring vowels shares positional features with the glide: /u/, /ų/, or /o/ with /w/; /i/, /į/, or /e/ with /y/. An example of loss of /w/ is seen in the fast speech form given above for the (enclitic *wo*), pronounced [o]. An example of loss of /y/ is the word *áye* 'he took it', phonetically [áe].

Glides are also regularly dropped when the vowels on either side are /a/ or /ą/.

When glides are dropped from the sequences /aya/, /aye/, and /awa/ (/ą/ could appear instead of /a/ in any of these), the vowels usually further contract into a single long vowel. These resulting long vowels are [a·], [æ·], and [ɔ·], respectively, or if /ą/ is present, [ə·], [æ·], and [ɔ·].

447

The same vowels result from the dropping of /h/:

othúwahe → [ŏthúwæ·] 'town'
hąhépi → [hǽ·pi] 'night'
čhą-hápi → [chǽ·pi] 'sugar'

Situations also arise where a morpheme that ends in a vowel comes before one that begins with /ʔ/. Very often, both the vowel and the /ʔ/ are then dropped, and native speakers prefer the fast speech form as the citation form. When this rule will apply and when the underlying |Vʔ| sequence will be retained is not presently predictable. Examples of the loss are:

|ečháʔų| → *echú* 'he did it'
|thaʔóyąke| → *thóyąke* 'his agency'
|waʔíyatke| → *wíyatke* 'cup'
|ištáʔothó| → *ištóthò* 'he has a black eye'.

4.3.2.

Since a large part of the grammar of Lakhota concerns verbs, a number of phonological changes are restricted to, or at least most noticeable in, the verbal processes of the language. Some of them are productive (apply in all words); some are unproductive (apply in only some specific words).

4.3.2.1.

A frequently observed sound change is the shift of stress from one syllable to another. When prefixes are added to the basic form of a word, the stress is moved as far forward as is necessary to prevent it from standing on a syllable later than the second syllable of the new construction. Compare:

yuhá 'he has'   *ųyúha pi* 'we have'
wašté 'to be good'   *wayúwašte* 'to make things good'.

4.3.2.2.

Another very simple rule whose effect is most often seen in verb conjugation is the insertion of /ʔ/ whenever grammatical processes place an element beginning with a vowel immediately after a boundary between elements within the word. Examples are:

aʔí	'they arrived there' (*í* 'to reach a place away from here'; *a* 'collective plural')
iyéʔųyą pi	'we found him' (*iyéyA* 'to find'; *ų* 'we')
slolʔúyą pi	'we know him' (*slolyÁ* 'to know'; *ų* 'we')
thebʔúyą pi	'we ate it up' (*thebyÁ* 'to eat up'; *ų* 'we').

This inserted /ʔ/ can of course be dropped if it follows a vowel (4.3.1.3.).

4.3.2.3.

Still a third phonological change associated with verb conjugation is a phenomenon that can be called nasalization spread. When a nasalized and an oral vowel are separated by a glide it is quite usual for both of the vowels and the glide to be pronounced with nasalization; this does not happen if the spread is from left to right across the /y/ of a prefix (cf. Patterson 1991):

iyéʔųyą pi 'we found it',
   compare *iyéya pi* 'they found it'
wąyáke 'he saw it',
   compare *wąbláke* 'I saw it'
wąwáyąke 'he saw something',
   compare *waʔónaȟʔų* 'he' heard something'
ómakiyį kte 'it will help me',
   compare *ómakiye* 'it helped me'.

Compare these examples where there is no spread; here *-ya-* is a prefix:

ųyáȟtaka pi 'we bit him'
ųyákaǧa pi 'you made us'.

There seems to be some complex ordering between the nasal spread rule and the insertion of inflectional affixes, since the secondary nasalization of *-yą-* in 'to see' also occurs in *wąyéčhiyąka pi* 'you saw each other', but not in the simple *wąláke* 'you saw him'.

4.3.2.4.

When grammatical processes place /i/ (sometimes /e/) before *k* (whether plain, glottalized, or aspirated) plus a vowel (*khV*, *kʔV*, or *kV*), the *k* frequently becomes /č/, but not always. Compare *makʔú* 'he gave it to me', *čhičʔú* 'I gave it to you', *kú* 'he is coming home', *gličú* 'he reached home here', *ómakiye* 'he helped me', *óničiya he?* 'did he help you?' *kákẖiya* 'over yonder', and *héčhiya* 'over there'.

Exceptions to this rule are stative verbs, such as *okháyakA* 'to have things (such as leaves, burrs) stuck on' (*oníkhayake* 'you have things stuck on you'); adverbs; dependent verbs (verbs that require another verb in the same sentence) such as *kapí* 'be reluctant to'; and a few exceptional transitive verbs (cf. Boas and Deloria 1941:14). When a derivational prefix is added to a root and the resulting verb is stative (*katʔátʔA* 'to fall down by accident', from *tʔA* 'be dead'), the *k* does not change (*nikátʔatʔa* 'you fell down by accident'). But if the new verb is transitive, *k* changes to *č* providing that the pronominal prefix precedes the derivational one (*katʔátʔa* can also mean 'to knock someone out', and 'she knocked you out'* is *ničátʔatʔa*). If the pronoun precedes the root, *k* still does not change, even if the verb is transitive. Note *nikíza* 'you squeaked' and *naníkiza* 'he made you squeak by stepping on you'.

---

*In this sketch, Lakhota third-person singular pronouns referring to people are translated at random as either 'he' ('him', 'his') or 'she' ('her') when there is no determining context; either translation is correct.

4.3.2.5.

The affix (prefix or infix; see 9.3.1.) *ma-* 'I, me' loses its vowel when it is added to a stem that begins with /i/. Compare *mawášte* 'I am good', *mak[?]ú* 'he gave it to me' with *mitháwa* 'it is mine' *miglúkse* 'I cut myself', *mihákab* 'behind me.' Some verbal stems that have initial /i/ drop the /i/ when no affix precedes. 'It is his', for example, is *tháwa*. (Note that the position of stress on the old second syllable is evidence for the original presence of the initial /i/.)

4.3.2.6.

The final vowel of a large group of Lakhota verbs is subject to regular changes, depending on what follows the verb. A small number of enclitics also share this feature. For convenience of reference words with these vowel alternations are called "A-words," and such words are cited with a written final A or Ą. The form of words with these alternations is correct in each instance with a particular one of the alternating vowels. The vowels that alternate are /a/ or /ą/, /e/, and /į/ (for some speakers also /i/). When no element follows, /e/ is always found. When the enclitics *ktA* and *na* follow, the vowel is almost always /į/, but some speakers use /i/ before *na*, at least sometimes. Otherwise, either /a/ (/ą/) or /e/ is found, with each context calling for one or the other. Examples are *yatké* 'he drank it' and *t[?]é* 'he is dead'; *yatkį kte* 'he will drink it' and *t[?]į kte* 'he will die'; *yatką he* 'did he drink it?' and *t[?]á he* 'is he dead?'

Speakers do not always agree on which verbs show this kind of alternation, particularly when the verb in question is somewhat rare. For example, the verb *olúluta* 'be sweltering hot' is treated as nonalternating by some speakers but as alternating by others. The same thing is true for speakers of the other Dakota dialects. It appears that any verb that ends in *-a* in its basic form may be regarded by some as an alternating verb. Because of this, verb-final vowel alternation will probably become more widespread in the future and may possibly result eventually in a state where all historically *-a* verbs will become *-A* verbs.

The terminal vowel is lost entirely when verbs of this kind are reduplicated (4.3.2.8.) or incorporated as any but final member into a word compound. The consonant immediately before the dropped vowel may also change (4.3.2.7.). Examples are *sabsápA* 'black' (*sápA* 'to be black'), *yulphíčA* 'edible' (*yútA* 'to eat'), *čhebyÁ* 'to fatten' (*čhépA* 'to be fat'), and (*kaȟkhíyA*) 'to cause someone to make something' (*kágA* 'to make').

A number of nouns also lose their final vowel in the same kinds of constructions (though reduplicated nouns are rare): *nabkózA* 'to beckon' (*napé* 'hand'), *čheȟ[?]íkhą* 'bucket handle' (*čhéǧa* 'kettle'), *čhašthú* 'to make a name for oneself' (*čhažé* 'name').

Another kind of vowel loss is frequently seen in compounds also. When one member ending in a vowel stands before another that begins with a vowel, the first of the two vowels is ordinarily dropped. Examples are exceedingly numerous: *nab[?]ágle* 'to lay hands on' (*napé* 'hand', *aglé* 'to place on'), *itípakhįte* 'face towel' (*ité* 'face', *ipákhįta* 'to wipe with'; note that /t/ is not replaced by /l/—4.3.2.7.), *makhóȟloka* 'cave'(*makhá* 'earth', *oȟlóka* 'hole'), *kéyA* 'to say that' (*ká* 'that'; *eyÁ* 'to say'), and *wígločhethi* 'gas stove' (*wígli* 'oil', *očhéthi* 'stove').

4.3.2.7.

When vowel dropping (of any origin except possibly the fast speech phenomena illustrated in section 4.3.1.2.) places /p t č k/ in word-final position or at an internal boundary between linguistic elements, these become [b], [l], [l], [g], respectively. When a nasalized vowel precedes these sounds, they may further shift to a nasal consonant: [m], [n], [n], or [ň], respectively. Note that these shifts do not occur before vowels unless [[?]] is inserted to mark the boundary. Compare the examples in the preceding paragraph of *itípakihįte* versus *nab[?]ágle*. Examples of such consonant changes have already been seen. Further examples are *tób* 'four' (shortened from *tópa*) and *núm* 'two' (shortened from *núpa*); *khalyÁ* 'to heat' (cf. *khátA* 'to be hot') and *čhąnmášiče* 'I am sad' (shortened from *čhąté-mašíče*); *psípsil* 'skipping' (shortened from *psipsíčA*); *pathág* 'stopping short' (shortened from *patháka*) and *šųňwíyela* 'mare, bitch' (cf. *šúka* 'dog').

When the voiced fricatives /z ž ǧ/ come to stand at a boundary they are replaced by /s š ȟ/ respectively. Examples are *kóskoza* 'waving' (cf. *kózA* 'to wave'), *khušyÁ* 'to make nauseous' (cf. *khúžA* 'to be nauseous'), and *piȟyÁ* 'to boil' (cf. *píǧA* 'to be boiling').

4.3.2.8.

One of the most productive grammatical processes in Lakhota is reduplication, the repetition of a portion of a word. The repetition creates a new word whose basic meaning is similar to the unreduplicated form but whose grammatical meaning is different. The meaning of reduplication is variously plurality, repetition, distribution through space ("here and there"), or intensity. Although most words have just one correctly reduplicated form, the part to be repeated can be anywhere in the word. An example of full reduplication is *zizí* 'yellow'(cf. *zí* 'yellow'); an example with initial reduplication is *ȟolȟóta* 'gray' (cf. *ȟóta* 'gray'); with final reduplication *waštéšte* 'good' (inanimate plural; cf. *wašté* 'good'); with medial reduplication, *napčíyųňyųka* 'nine by nine' (cf. *napčíyųka* 'nine'). Note that consonant changes of the kind mentioned in 4.3.2.7. are very frequent in reduplication.

The part of a given word that is reduplicated can generally be predicted if enough is known about the etymology of the word: it is usually the last full syllable of the root. But this is nevertheless one of the more difficult parts of the grammar of Lakhota, even for native speakers. Refer to Carter (1974), Shaw (1980), and Patterson (1990:89-99) for details; Patterson reviews several other theoretical studies of Lakhota reduplication.

GRAMMAR

Lakhota sentences can be described as consisting of a series of optional and obligatory slots, each slot filled by a particular type of word or phrase. The maximum structure is

(interjection) (conjunction) (adverb(s))
(nominal) (nominal)(nominal)
(adverb(s)) verb (enclitic(s)) (conjunction)

(Parentheses imply optionality; (s) means there is no theoretical limit to the number of like elements that can occur in this position.)

Note that the only obligatory slot is that of the verb; every other position is optional.

Discussion of Lakhota grammar from the point of view of formal linguistic theory can be found in Van Valin (1985, 1987) and references there. Van Valin argues that a careful and accurate account of even the simplest Lakhota sentences requires major revisions in the Chomskyan models that dominated linguistic theory from the 1960s through the 1980s.

Discussion of Lakhota grammar will be organized around the sentence slots enumerated above; each slot, and its possible fillers, will be discussed in turn. Given first however, is a brief definition of the terms:

interjection: exclamation expressing surprise, hesitation, disgust, etc.
conjunction: connector, such as 'and,' 'but,' 'however,' 'furthermore.'
adverb: expression of time, place, manner (including instrument), or cause.
postposition: a word that relates a nominal to a verb; compare English prepositions. In Lakhota the relating word follows the element it governs.
nominal: a naming word or phrase: noun, pronoun, modified noun, or another element used as a noun.
verb: core word, predicator, word that says something about a nominal.
enclitic: almost a suffix, but actually a separate word; expresses tense, mood, aspect, and other similar grammatical notions.

The first two categories (interjections and conjunctions) are functionally distinct, but it is sometimes difficult to decide whether a particular "sentence launching word" belongs to one category rather than the other. Some of the words cited as examples in 5.0. or 6.0. might therefore be switched to the other category upon further investigation. However, it is certain that all words in either category will precede either adverbs or nominals.

5. INTERJECTIONS
Some examples of interjections include:

Ma líla olúluta. '<u>Gee</u>, it's hot (and humid).' (spoken by a woman)
Wą lé ąpétu kį líla kháte! '<u>Boy</u> but it's hot (and dry) today!' (spoken by a man)
Íska ⎫
⎬ 'Well...'; often used as a pause filler.
Eyá ⎭
Éyaš 'Well, but'

In the case of *íska*, the first vowel may be lengthened quite extensively for added effect:

įįįįįįįiska 'Weeeeeell'

There are no interjections equivalent to English profane or curse words.

See Buechel (1939: 126-127 and 266-267) for a list of interjections in use in the early twentieth century.

6. CONJUNCTIONS
Conjunctions connect two sentences, often showing something about the relationship between the sentences as well. They occur in two possible positions: in the second slot from the beginning or in the last slot in the sentence. The more common position is last in the sentence.

Several different Lakhota words translate the English word 'and'; but these words do not all mean the same thing in Lakhota. Examples are *na* or *nahą* 'and also'; *čha, čhąkhé* 'and so', *yúkhą* 'and then (rather unexpectedly)'. Other conjunctions include *éyaš* 'but', *na?íš* 'or', and *ho* (or *honá*) 'furthermore'.

Tákuni tokhų́k?ų pi šni éyaš, ųkóyuspa pi
nothing we.did pl. not <u>but</u> they.arrest.us pl.
'We didn't do anything, <u>but</u> they arrested us.'

Of course, conjunctions such as *na* or *na?íš* can join two of the parts of a sentence, such as nominals or verbs. In this case, they occur in the sentence position appropriate to the major part:

Čík?ala <u>na?íš</u> thąka čha yačhį́ he?
little <u>or</u> big a you.want question
'Do you want a little one <u>or</u> a big one?'

Some words that are conjunctions in English do not occur as such in Lakhota. The conjunction pair 'if...then', for example, is expressed in hypothetical sentences by simply nominalizing (see 8.5.) the *if* sentence and adding the *then* sentence:

<u>Máza-ska</u> <u>ųyúha</u> <u>pi</u> <u>kį,</u> iyéčhikiyąke wąží
<u>money</u> <u>we.have</u> <u>pl.</u> <u>the</u> car a
ophé?uthų pi kte
we-buy pl. potential
'If we had money, (then) we would buy a car.'

7. ADVERBS

Adverbs may occur either before or after the nominals of the sentence. In theory, there is no limit to their number, nor is there any preferred sequence or position for the various types: any number of adverbs may occur in any order in either place in the sentence.

Formally, adverbial expressions are of three possible types: words, phrases, or sentences.

7.1. SINGLE-WORD ADVERBS

Examples of single word adverbs:

ȟeyáta	'out in the country'
híȟạni	'this (past) morning'
ȟtáleȟạ	'yesterday'
áataa	'all; completely'
iníla	'quietly'
oȟ'ʔą́khoya	'quickly, without wasting time'
éna	'right there'
tạyą́	'well'.

Deictic adverbs are formed by adding a demonstrative (8.3.2.) to an adverb or a postposition (7.2.):

héna 'right there' *(hé, éna)*, *létu* 'here' *(lé, étu)*, *katą́* 'from yonder' *(ká, etą́hạ)*, *hél* 'there' *(hé, él)*.

Interrogative adverbs are also single words for the most part (note that all Lakhota interrogative words begin with *t-*):

tóhạ	'when?' (referring to a realized event)
tohą́l	'when?' (referring to an unrealized event)
tuktél	'where?'
tuktę́ él	'at which place?,' 'whereabouts?'
tókhiya	'where' (in or to what region)?'
tákuwe	'why?'
tókheškhe (tóškhe)	'how?'.

In some cases, one-word adverbs are words whose principal use is as some other part of speech. For example, *híȟạni* is a noun or verb meaning 'morning' or 'be morning'; *áataa* is a pronoun meaning 'all (of something)'; and *tạyą́* is a verb meaning 'to be well'.

Adverbs may be marked as intensive or repetitive by reduplication (4.3.2.8.) or by the addition of suffixlike particles such as *ȟča/ȟči* and *šna*:

Héktaktakiya wačhí.	'She kept dancing <u>backward</u>.'
Énagna hiyéye.	'They [inanimate] are lying <u>here and there</u>.'
Tạyé ȟči ečhú	'He did it <u>very well</u>.'
Éna šna yąké.	'He is <u>always there</u>.'

Buechel Mus., St. Francis, S. Dak.

Fig. 1. Rev. Eugene Buechel (b. 1874, d.1954) (right) and Red Feather. Buechel published numerous works in and about Lakhota, including a Bible history (1924), a prayer and hymn book (1927), and a grammar of Lakhota (1939). His 30,000 word and phrase cards were published as a Lakhota dictionary by Rev. Paul Manhart (1970). As a Jesuit, Buechel served at various times at both St. Francis Mission, 1902-1954, and Holy Rosary Mission, 1907-1929, S. Dak. He was called Black Eagle (*Wạblí Sápa*) by his parishioners. Red Feather, a Teton Sioux from either Rosebud or Pine Ridge, S. Dak., is listed in the dictionary as one of Buechel's consultants. Photographed about 1920s-1930s.

Hǫhépi iyóhila él　'Every night they would come
thiwáhepi kị ob　in with their families.'
thimá šna hiyú pi.

7.2. ADVERBIAL PHRASES

Adverbial phrases generally contain a nominal (8.0.), sometimes accompanied by a postposition. Other adverbs may also participate in addition to the nominal.

7.2.1.

In adverbial phrases of time, nominals are usually accompanied by the articles (8.3.1.) *kị* and *k'ų*. *kị* in such phrases marks the phrase as referring to 'hypothetical' (unrealized) time, while *k'ų* marks 'actual' (realized) time.

When the nominal expression does not include a postposition, its use is absolute (not grammatically marked):

Lé ǫpétu kị mǎȟpíyaya. 'It is cloudy today.'
Hǫhépi maǧážu. 'It rained last night.'

English analogs of these are seen in the sentences 'He came this morning', and 'It rained last night.'

Other examples of this kind are *hǐhąni kị* 'tomorrow', *hǫhépi kị* 'this evening'.

Nominals used absolutely as adverbs are often followed by a true adverb:

Okó　núpa k'ų　　héhą
week　two　the.past　then
'two weeks ago'

Wí　hináphe　šni　hą́ni
sun　come.out　not　not.then
'just before sunrise'.

Examples of postpositional phrases with temporal meaning are:

ȟta'íyokpaza óhakab
darkness　　after
'after dark'

ǫpétu　kị　hé　él
day　the　that　at
'on that day'

ǫpétu-wakhą́　núpa　okó
day-holy　　two　between
'between two Sundays'.

7.2.2.

Numerous postpositions are also used in adverbial phrases of place.

Mas'óphiye él ačhíphị　　kte
Store　　at　I.await.you　potential
'I'll wait for you at the store.'

Wačhípi　ektá　lá　pi　kta　he?
Dance　　to　you.go　pl.　potential　question
'Are you (pl.) going to go to the dance?'

Othų́wahe　etą́hą　wahí
town　　from　I.arrive
'I arrived from town.'

Thípi　kị　ókšą　énažị
house　the　around　they.stand
'They (collective) stood around the house.'

The line between adverbs and postpositions is sometimes difficult to draw, chiefly because the same words are often used both ways. English adverbs and prepositions show the same kind of interchangeability. 'Come on out from down in under there!' has six adverb/prepositions in this kind of ambiguous function. A Lakhota example is:

Owóte-thípi　　kị　wígli-o'ínažị　kị
eating.place-house　the　oil-stopping.place　the
hél　isákhib　hé.
there　beside　stand
'The cafe is there beside the gas station.'

In this example the adverb *isákhib* functions nearly as a postposition.

Very often, a noun will combine with a postposition to form a compound; the result is the conversion of a phrase into a single word adverb:

thimáhel	'in the house'
thí-mahél	'house'-'inside'
čhą'ákhotąhą	'across the woods'
čhą́-'akhótąhą	'tree'-'across'
thilázata	'behind the house'
thí-lazáta	'house'-'behind'

Most specific locational adverb/postpositions of place begin with *i:*

ilázata	'behind'
isákhib	'beside'
ihúkhuta	'below'
ihákab	'after'
ithókab	'in front of'.

For some of these there is a corresponding word without the *i*, which is only used as a postposition. For all of the *i-* adverbs there is an alternative form with stressed *i*, which marks the location as very close to or against the object:

ílazata	'right close behind'
ísakhib	'right next to'
íhukhuta	'just below'
íhakab	'right after (also refers to time)'
íthokab	'right before (also refers to time)'.

Both these sets of forms take personal object inflections (see 9.3.2.) when the object is an animate pronoun:

milázata	'behind me'
wičhíthokab	'in front of them'.

The stressed *í* appears as *íi* in inflected forms:

níisakhib   'very close to you'
ųkíihukhuta   'right below us'.

7.2.3.

Adverbs of manner are often single words formed from other classes of words. A frequently used formative of such adverbs is the suffix *-ya:*

wašíčųya   'in English' (*wašíču, wašíčų* 'White man')
šičáya   'badly' (*šíčA* 'be bad')
wakhą́ya   'mysteriously' (*wakhą́* 'wondrous, awesome').

Other suffixes are also used:

léchel   'thus, in this way' (*lé* 'this')
nah̃mála   'secretly' (*nah̃má* 'to hide')
mánikhel   'on foot' (*máni* 'to walk').

There are also postpositional phrases that express manner:

Wasnásnaheča	*chįčála*	*s'e*	*ipáh̃lala*
kingbird	offspring	like	in.a.row

yąká	*pi*
sit	pl.

'They are sitting in a row like young kingbirds.'

Chįčá	*pi*	*ob*	*hí*
offspring	pl.	with	come

'He came with their children.'

chąpágmiyąpi	*ogná*	*iyáye*
wagon	in	go

'He went in a wagon.'

7.2.4.

Instrument is sometimes expressed in the verbal prefix (see 9.2.1.). When a more specific instrumentality needs to be indicated, the postposition *ų* is used with an appropriate noun:

Iyéchįkiyąke	*ų*	*nat'é*
car	with	die.by.foot.action

'He was run over and killed by a car.'

Ağúyapi	*kį*	*ečéla*	*ų*	*wičháša*	*kį*	*ní*
bread	the	alone	with	man	the	live

pi	*šni*
pl.	not

'Men do not live by bread alone.'

7.3. ADVERBIAL CLAUSES

Sentences used as adverbs (adverbial clauses) are first nominalized; they are then the equivalent of a noun in absolute (see 7.2.1.) use. Following this nominal comes a time adverb or a postposition. (Compare this with the similar construction and use of phrases described in 7.2.)

Sentential time adverb:

Ȟ'okhá	*kį*	*hí*	*pi*	*k'ų*	*héhą,*
Singers	the	arrive	pl.	the.past	then

wachípi	*kį*	*iyáye.*
dance	the	start

'When the singers came, the dance began.'

Sentential place adverb:

Hé	*wą'ų́yąka*	*pi*	*okíhi*	*šni*	*wą*	*él*
He	he.see.us	pl.	he.be.able	not	a	to

iyáye.
he.go

'He went to (a place) where he could not see us.'

Sentential manner adverb:

Táku	*iyéya*	*okíhi*	*kį*	*hé*	*ų́*
What	he.find	he.be.able	the	that	with

chą́	*kį*	*kaksáksa.*
wood	the	he.chop

'He chopped the wood with whatever he could find.'

Buechel (1939 passim) contains a more complete description of adverbs than is presented here. Note that many of the words he calls 'adverbs' are called 'enclitics' in this sketch.

8. NOMINALS

There are from zero to three nominal expressions (apart from verbal affixes) in every Lakhota sentence. The three slots provided in the original sentence diagram serve three possible roles: subject, indirect object, direct object. If more than one nominal occurs in a sentence, the order will ordinarily be subject first, then either of the objects. For some speakers, there is no required order between direct and indirect objects; thus 'the men gave the boy to the bear' and 'the men gave the bear to the boy' are identical: *Wičháša kį hokšíla kį mathó kį k'ú pi* or *Wičháša kį mathó kį hokšíla kį k'ú pi.* Very rarely, however, does this cause any misunderstanding, since in most such sentences potential ambiguities are resolved by the meanings of the particular words. Other speakers insist that the order is subject–indirect object–direct object; for them, the two sentences above are not synonymous.

The presence of an indirect object is marked in the verb except for a handful of special verbs such as *k'ú* 'give', *lá* 'ask for' or *iyų́ğA* 'to ask someone something' (see 9.1.6. and 9.3.8.).

The grammatical roles of subject, object, or indirect object may be indicated by verbal affixes (prefixes or infixes; see 9.3.) instead of by overt nominals. If there are separate nominal expressions, they may be any of four types: pronouns, nouns, modified nouns, and sentences.

8.1. PRONOUNS

Independent pronouns are rarely used in ordinary Lakhota but are available for emphatic expressions or to serve as the objects of postpositions such as *kičhí* 'together with'. There are two sets. The first is simply emphatic; the second is used to contrast one referent with others.

453

Set 1:

miyé	'I'
ųkíye	'we'
niyé	'you'
iyé	'he, she, it, they'

Set 2:

míš	'I'
ųkįš	'we'
níš	'you'
įš	'he, she, it, they'

Examples of pronouns used as nominals:

Subject

<u>*Miyé*</u>, *wačhį šni.*	'<u>Me</u>, I don't want to.'
<u>*Míš*</u> *táku ophéwathų kta he?*	'And what shall <u>I</u> buy (now that the others have decided)?'

Object

Hená <u>*ųkíye*</u> *wą^ʔųyąka pi šni.*	'<u>As for us</u>, they didn't see us.'

Postpositional Object

Tuwá <u>*niyé*</u> *kičhí wačhí pi he?*	'Who danced with <u>you</u>?'

The two sets can be used together, for example, in the expression *míš-miyé kį* 'as for me; in my opinion; for my part'. Compare the expression *Nís ehą́* 'your turn', using the postposition *ehą́* 'at a time' with a contrastive pronoun.

8.2. NOUNS

Lakhota nouns are either simple or derived; derived nouns may be either compounds or affixed forms.

Examples of simple nouns include *čhą́* 'wood, tree'; *natá* 'head'; *šų́ka* 'dog', and *maȟpíya* 'cloud, sky'.

8.2.1.

Compound nouns consist of two (or more) nouns, or of a noun plus a verb. (De Reuse 1994 discusses the degree of "tightness" in noun-verb compounds.) The elements that enter into the compound may exist as independent words, or they may be compounding forms (essentially roots) that never appear in that form outside of compounds. Where all compounded elements occur alone as words, the compound is written with a hyphen between the elements. Where one or more of the compounded elements is in root form, the compound is written without separation of the constituent elements. Stresses after the first in any word should be read as secondary (see 3.1.).

In noun-noun compounds, the earlier element usually modifies the later. When non-nominal elements are present in the compound, these usually follow the nominal elements and modify them, but they precede in some cases.

Noun-noun compounds

1. Modifier-modified

wígli-o^ʔínažį	'gas station'
wígli	'grease'
o^ʔínažį	'stopping place'
čhą-hápi	'sugar'
čhą́	'tree'
hápi	'juice'
Khąǧí-wičháša	'Crow Indian'
khąǧí	'crow'
wičháša	'man'
mas^ʔóphiye	'store' (originally 'cash register')
máza	'metal'
ophíye	'box, storage place'

2. Modified-modifier

šųȟmánitu	'coyote'
šų́ka	'dog'
manítu	'wilderness, wild place'

Noun-verb compounds

pte-yúha	'rancher'
pté	'buffalo'
yuhá	'to have'
Mní-šoše	'Missouri River'
mní	'water'
šošé	'be turbid'
šųŋkhíyuȟa	'stud, stallion'
šų́ka	'dog, horse'
khiyúȟa	'to breed'
máza-ská	'money'
máza	'metal, iron'
ská	'be white'
šų́ka-wakhą́	'horse'
šų́ka	'dog'
wakhą́	'be awesome, be marvelous'
hąm^ʔíkčeka	'moccasin'
hápa	'shoe'
ikčéka	'be common'

Verb-noun compounds

tųwéya-wičháša	'scout'
tųwéyA	'to look around'
wičháša	'man'
wayáwa-thípi	'school'
wayáwa	'count things; read things'
thípi	'house'

Compounds of the verb-noun type may in reality be examples of noun + noun, if the first element is actually a nominalized verb (cf. *wayáwa wą* 'a student'). There are no known reliable criteria that can distinguish these possibilities.

Compounds that consist of more than two included elements also exist. These compounds have an internal hierarchy indicated by underlining in the examples:

Mni-<u>lúzahe</u>-othų́wahe
water-run.swiftly-town, <u>rapids</u> town
'Rapid City, South Dakota'

<u>*šųk^ʔáką*</u>-*yąkápi*
<u>horse/dog.on</u>-sit, <u>horseback</u> sit
'to ride horseback'

natá-yazápi-pheẑúta
head-ache-medicine
'aspirin'

šuň-sí-maza
dog/horse-foot-iron
'horseshoe'

máza-ská-zí
iron.be.white-be.yellow, silver-be.yellow
'gold'

8.2.2.

Nouns derived by affixation may have either prefixes or suffixes. Elements used as suffixes are usually identical to enclitics (10.). Prefixes tend to have fairly specific meanings, while the meanings of the suffixes are more general, though related to the meaning of the same element used as a verbal enclitic.

Some prefix examples:

o- 'place where'
  oʔínaẑi 'station' (cf. *ínaẑi* 'to stop')
  oyáke 'sitting place; agency' (cf. *yąkÁ* 'to sit')
  othí 'den' (cf. *thí* 'to dwell')
  ognáke 'container' (cf. *gnákA* 'to put away')
i- 'instrument for'
  waʔíyatke, wíyatke 'cup' (cf. *wayátkÁ* 'to drink things')
  waʔíkhalye, wíkhalye 'coffee pot' (cf. *wakhályA* 'to heat things')
  ičʔį 'harness' (cf. *kʔį* 'to pack on the back')
Some suffix examples:
  thípi 'house' (cf. *thí* 'to dwell')
  wakhályapi 'coffee' (cf. *wakhályA* 'to heat')
  yazápi 'pain' (cf. *yazá* 'to hurt or ache')
  waʔéčhučhuka 'jack-of-all-trades' (cf. *waʔéčhu* 'to do things')
  wamánusʔa 'thief' (cf. *wamánu* 'to steal things')

8.3. DETERMINERS

Determiners are a class of words that terminate nominal expressions. There are three kinds: articles, demonstratives, and quantifiers. Determiners occur in the order: (quantifier) (article) (demonstrative) (quantifier). Nominals may also appear without a determiner.

8.3.1. ARTICLES

Words that function as articles include *kį, kʔų, wą, wąẑí, wąẑíni, eyá, etá, etáni, tákuni, tuwéni, čha*.

The choice of the article depends on various features of the noun and of the sentence in which it occurs. The noun may be generic, that is, may refer to all or any of a class of objects, such as 'dogs', in 'dogs bark' or 'coffee' in 'coffee is brown.' Such nouns generally have no article in Lakhota no matter what the rest of the sentence may be. In addition, countable nouns used generically always take a plural verb:

Hé   wičháša kị   iyéčhįkiyąke   ophéthų.
That   man   the   <u>car</u>   buy
'That man buys <u>cars</u>.'

Igmúla sįté yukhą pi.
<u>cat</u>   tail have pl.
'<u>Cats</u> have tails.'

Hokšíla thąkthąka čhéya pi šni.
<u>boy</u>   big   cry   pl. not
'Big <u>boys</u> don't cry.'

Wakhályapi wačhį.
<u>coffee</u>   I.want
'I want <u>coffee</u>.'

A determiner is used in a generic construction when the construction could otherwise be understood as a word or phrase rather than as a sentence:

Lakhóta kį wačhí pi.	'<u>Indians</u> dance.'
cf. *Lakhóta-wačhípi*	'(an) Indian dance'
Thaspą kį šašá.	'<u>Apples</u> are red.'
cf. *thaspą šašá*	'red apples'

If a noun is not generic, it must be either definite or indefinite.

If the noun is definite, the article is either *kį* or *kʔų;* 'the' is the English equivalent of both of these. The difference between *kį* and *kʔų* seems to be that *kʔų* marks more emphatically definite nouns. Often, therefore, *kʔų* can be translated as 'the aforementioned', although this is usually abbreviated 'the.past' in glossing the examples:

Šúka kį   hél   yųké.
(dog the there lie)
'<u>The</u> dog is lying there.'

Šúka kʔų   thaló kį   thebyé.
(dog the.past meat the eat.up)
'<u>The aforementioned</u> dog ate up the meat.'
This example is from a traditional tale.

Recall that nominals in adverbial functions are nominalized by *kį* if the reference is to hypothetical time, but by *kʔų* if the reference is to real time. Sentences containing *kʔų* are always translated with the English past tense. This is evidently an attempt by Lakhota speakers to render the hyperreality of the Lakhota sentences with *kʔų*. In fact, at present *kį* is used regularly in real as well as hypothetical sentences. The difference between *kį* and *kʔų* may have been sharper at an earlier time, since different forms of the indefinite article are used in sentences with real versus hypothetical meaning.

All the other words listed above are indefinite articles. The choice of indefinite article is made on the basis of a number of covert classes to which nouns belong (table 3). These include mass form (that is, whether the object named by the noun can be counted, like houses, or not, like soup), human, and non-human. Moreover, there are different forms depending on whether the sentence in which they appear is negative

Table 3. Indefinite Articles

	Real	Hypothetical	Negative
Singular	*wą* 'a, an'	*wąží* 'a, an'	*wążíni* 'not...a, no, not any'
Plural			
Animate			
Human	*eyá* 'some'	*etą* 'some, any'	*tuwéni* 'no one, not..any'
Nonhuman	*eyá* 'some'	*etą* 'some, any'	*tákuni* 'no, not...any'
Inanimate	*eyá* 'some'	*etą* 'some, any'	*tákuni* 'no, not...any'
Noncountable	*eyá* 'some'	*etą* 'some, any'	*etąni* 'no, not...any'

NOTE: An older form of *eyá* in all its uses is *kʔeyá*. Some speakers still use this word.

or affirmative; and, if it is affirmative, whether it refers to real or to hypothetical things.

The following examples illustrate the use of the indefinite articles. Note that although nonhuman and inanimate plurals are marked in the same way, sentences with nouns from these categories differ because all animate (human and nonhuman) plural objects require *-wiča-* in the verb, and animate plural subjects require *pi*, while inanimates never occur with *-wiča-* or *pi* (see 9.3.2.-9.3.4.). In the examples below, then, the verbs used with 'houses' differ from those used with 'birds', even though the articles are the same:

Iyéčhįkįyąke wą ophéwathų.
'I bought a car.'
Iyéčhįkįyąke wąží ophéwathų kte.
'I'm going to buy a car.'
Iyéčhįkįyąke wąžíni ophéwathų šni.
'I didn't buy a car.'
Lakhota eyá hí pi.
'Some Indians have come.'
Lakhota etą hí pi he?
'Have any Indians come?'
Lakhota tuwéni hí pi šni.
'No Indians have come.'
Wakhąyeža eyá wąwíchablake.
'I saw some children.'
Zįtkála eyá wąwíchablake.
'I saw some birds.'
Čhą-thipi eyá wąbláke.
'I saw some houses.'
Wakhąyeža etą wąwíchalaka he?
'Did you see some/any children?'
Zįtkála etą wąwíchalaka he?
'Did you see some/any birds?'
Čhą-thipi etą wąláka he?
'Did you see some/any houses?'
Wakhąyeža tuwéni wąwíchablake šni.
'I didn't see any children.'
Zįtkála tákuni wąwíchablake šni.
'I didn't see some/any birds.'
Čhą-thipi tákuni wąláke šni he?
'Didn't you see any houses?'
Wahápi eyá očhéthi akąl hé.
'There's some soup on the stove.'

Wahápi etą yačhį he?
'Do you want some/any soup?'
Wahápi etąni yatké šni.
'He didn't eat (drink) any soup.'

A special construction exists to make a nominal emphatic (whether or not to call it "topicalized" depends on future studies of Lakhota discourse structure). This is often translated into English as 'It was a/the NOUN who/which VERB'. Emphatic nominals of this kind are marked by the article *čha*; if the noun is indefinite, no further determiner is used:

Hokšíla čha šųka-wakhą kį iwíčhaču pi.
'It was some boys who took the horses.'

If the emphatic nominal is also definite, the verb *é* 'be a certain one' precedes *čha*:

Hokšíla kį é pi čha šųka-wakhą kį iwíčhaču pi.
'It was the boys who took the horses.'

This use of *čha* is probably very closely related to the relative clause marker *čha* (8.4.2.3.).

8.3.2. DEMONSTRATIVES
Lakhota has three demonstrative roots: *lé* 'this,' *hé* 'that,' *ká* 'yonder.' Each of these can function in numerous ways: alone as a singular pronoun or as a noun modifier; with the suffix *-ná* as a plural pronoun or modifier (*lená* 'these', *hená* 'those', *kaná* 'the ones yonder'); or with the suffixes *-na* and *-ʔųs* (some speakers use *-yos*) as dual pronouns or modifiers (*henáʔųs, henáyos* 'those two'). Various adverbials are formed from demonstratives (7.1.).

Semantically, *hé* is the most neutral. Once a noun has been located, either by pointing or by description, in space or in the listener's mind, *hé* can then be used. Before that, *lé* or *ká* is usually used to demonstrate exactly what is meant, although *hé* may also be used while pointing.

Ká   šųka-wakhą kį   wąláka he?
that.(yonder) horse   the you.see question
Hé tuwá tháwa   he?
that who it.belong.to   question
'Do you see that horse? Who does he belong to?'

ROOD AND TAYLOR

When demonstratives are used as nominal markers, they are usually accompanied by an article. They indicate the number (singular, dual, or plural) of the noun: *hé wíyą kį* 'that woman', *hená²ųs wíyą kį* 'those two women', *hená wíyą kį* 'those women'. The demonstrative may either precede the noun or follow the article. If the demonstrative precedes the noun, an article must occur after the noun; if the demonstrative follows, the article may be omitted. By far the most common article used is *kį*, but expressions such as *hená wíyą eyá* 'these (indefinite) women' may be used, usually in relative clauses (see 8.4.3.).

The difference between singular and plural is always indicated when demonstratives are used with countable nouns. This differs from the use of *pi* and *wičha* to mark plural with verbs, since these verbal elements refer only to animate nouns (see 9.3.1.).

8.3.3. QUANTIFIERS

This class of words includes the numbers ('one' is the same as the singular indefinite article; table 3) *núpa* 'two', *yámni* 'three', *tópa* 'four', etc., a handful of indefinite numerals, such as *óta* 'many', *húh̃* 'some' (note: this is not the same 'some' as those translated by *eyá* or *etá*, see 8.3.1. and 8.3.4.), *čónala* 'few', *iyúha* 'all of a group' (distributive), *oyás²į* 'all of a group' (collective), and *áataa* 'all of a mass', and the interrogative words *tóna*, *tónakeča*, and *toháyą* 'how much? how many?'.

Many quantifiers may also function as stative verbs. Observe these examples:

Wičháša kį   óta   t²á pi.
man   the   many   die   pl.
'Many of the men died.'

Wičháša kį   óta   pi.
man   the   many   pl.
'There are many men.'

Wičháša kį   yámni iyéwičhaya pi.
man   the   three   find them   pl.
'They found three of the men.'

Wičháša kį   yámni pi.
man   the   three   pl.
'There are three men; the men are three.'

Quantifiers may occur with or without articles or demonstratives, and either before or after them, but the meanings differ depending on order:

wičháša óta	'many men'
wičháša hená óta	'many of those men'
wičháša óta hená	'those many men'
wičháša šakówį	'seven men'
wičháša kį yámni	'three of the men'
wičháša tópa kį	'the four men'.

8.3.4.
As can be seen from the examples, when used alone or before an article or a demonstrative, the quantifiers specify the size of the group. Used after the determiner, they indicate that the predicate refers to a specified part of the subject. The notion of partitive touched on here has complexities that call for further comment.

'Some' (= part of) is expressed in several different ways in Lakhota, depending on several factors: the nature of the whole, the nature of the part, and whether the part is positive, negative, or interrogative.

The whole may consist of separate, identifiable individuals (such as persons in a group), a single individual (for example, a watermelon), or an undifferentiated mass (flour). The whole may be either generic or specific. The part may be individuals, a portion of a single individual, or a portion of a mass.

Given these parameters, the choice of partitive marker is as given in table 4.

Examples
1. *Oyáte húh̃ wičhášiče.*   'Some people are evil.'
    Lakhóta tóna   'How many Indians do
    wąwíchalaka he?   you see?'
    H̃²okhá kį húh̃ hí pi.   'Some of the singers
                    have come.'

    H̃²okhá kį tóna hí   'How many of the
    pi he?   singers have cóme?'
    H̃²okhá kį wążíni   'None of the singers has
    hí (pi) šni.   come.'

2. *Špą̄-šni-yútapi hąké*   'We (habitually) eat
    ųyúta pi s²a.   some watermelon.'
    Špą̄-šni-yútapi toháyą   'How much watermelon
    yáta pi s²a he?   do you eat (habitually).'
    Aǧúyapi-skúyela kį   'We ate some of the
    hąké ųyúta pi.   cake.'
    Aǧúyapi-skúyela kį   'We didn't eat any of the
    hąkéni ųyúta pi.   cake.'
    Aǧúyapi-skúyela kį   'How much of the cake
    toháyą yáta pi he?   did you eat?'

Table 4. Lakhota Indefinite Partitive

	Affirmative	Negative[a]	Interrogative	Meaning
1.	*húh̃*	*wążíni*	*tóna* or *tónakeča*	Some individuals from a group of individuals
2.	*hąké*	*hąkéni*	*toháyą*	Some of a single individual
3.	*húh̃* or *etá*	*etáni*	*toháyą* or *tónakeča*	Some of an undifferentiated mass

[a]The notions generic and negative are incompatible. The negative partitive can thus be used only with specific reference.

457

3. *Phežúta hųħ phá.* 'Some medicine is bitter.'
Phežúta toháyą 'How much medicine
ničʔú he? did he give you?'
Ağúyapi-blú kį etá ų we. 'Use some of the flour.'
Ağúyapi-blú kį etáni 'She didn't use any of
ų šni. the flour.'
Ağúyapi-blú kį toháyą 'How much of the flour
nú he? did you use?'

8.3.5.

To summarize the discussion of determiners: the complete set of possible slots in the nominal composed of a noun and its determiners is as follows: (demonstrative) noun (quantifier) (article) (demonstrative) (quantifier).

8.4. MODIFIED NOUNS

8.4.1.

Possession is marked in one of three ways: by special affixes in the verb, by an appropriate modifying form of the stative verb *itháwa* 'belong to, own', or by special prefixes on the noun. Moreover, many (perhaps most) nouns, including some body parts such as *á* 'armpit' and *ablóhu* 'shoulder blade' cannot be formally marked for a possessor anywhere in the sentence. At present it appears impossible to predict whether a noun will be possessable or not, so this information must be part of each noun's dictionary entry. The marking of possession in the verb is discussed in 9.3.8.; the other expressions of possession will be described here.

If a noun can be possessed, the form of the possessive prefix differs depending on whether the noun is alienably or inalienably possessed. Alienably possessed nouns are things that can be acquired or given away; inalienably possessed nouns are understood as an inherent part of the owner's person; they include body parts, many relatives, and (formerly, at least) some essentially personal things such as tools, clothing, and pets. The prefixes are:

alienably possessed nouns		inalienably possessed nouns
mithá-	'my'	*ma-/mi-*
ųkítha-	'our'	*ųkí-*
nithá-	'your'	*ni-*
tha-	'his, hers'	Ø.

If the possessor is plural, *pi* follows the prefixed noun.

It is also possible to analyze the alienable prefixes as complex, consisting of a stem-derivational element *itha*, prefixed to the noun, to which stative verb affixes are then prefixed.

Because possessed nouns are always definite, a definite article almost always occurs with them. The only exceptions are in partitive usage, for example, *mithášųka wąží* 'one of my dogs', where a quantifier replaces the article. The choice between *ma-* and *mi-* is semantically determined in Oglala speech: *ma-* is used of concrete visible possessions, *mi-* of intangibles: *manáği kį* 'my shadow', *mináği kį* 'my spirit'. Speakers from other Lakhota-speaking groups differ as to their use of *ma-* and *mi-*.

Prefixation to show possession is not used with some possessable nouns. These are generally nouns that are not normally possessed, such as rocks or trees. For such nouns, the possessive construction uses the stative verb *itháwa*. *Itháwa* is nearly unique among stative verbs for two reasons. First, it carries possible double affixation (see 9.1.3.). Second, it occurs as a noun modifier in its inflected as well as uninflected forms.

The possessive construction with *itháwa* has the following structure:

noun + *itháwa* form + *kį*.

The *itháwa* form depends only on the possessor:

mitháwa	*ųkíthawa*	*ųkíthawa pi*
'my'	'belonging to you and me'	'our'
nitháwa		*nitháwa pi*
'your'		'your(pl.)'
tháwa		*tháwa pi*
'his, her'		'their'.

Examples:

Šúka-wakhá tháwa pi kį iyéwaye.
horse ___poss. pl.___ the I.find.it
'I found their horse.'

Phežúta nitháwa kį líla wašʔáke.
medicine ___you.sg..poss.___ the very be.strong
'Your medicine is very strong.'

The criteria for choosing between the *itháwa* construction and the prefixed forms are not well understood.

Kinship terms generally follow a separate paradigm. They are inalienably possessed, but they often take a suffix *-ku* when the possessor is a third person; moreover, many of the forms have separate roots for the various forms. Here, as samples, are paradigms for 'father' and 'mother':

até, atéwaye	'my father'	*iná, ináwaye*	'my mother'
niyáte	'your father'	*nihú*	'your mother'
atkúku	'his, her father'	*húku*	'his, her mother'
atéʔųyą pi	'our father'	*ináʔųyą pi*	'our mother'
niyáte pi	'your father'	*nihú pi*	'your mother'
atkúku pi	'their father'	*húku pi*	'their mother'

Buechel (1939:101-107) has extensive lists of paradigmatic forms for kin terms.

8.4.2.

There are no words in Lakhota strictly equivalent to English adjectives; nevertheless, Lakhota nouns can be modified. The modifiers are usually stative verbs (like *itháwa*), but the constructions used for modification differ for definite and indefinite noun phrases.

8.4.2.1. DEFINITE MODIFIED NOUN PHRASES

If a modified noun is definite (marked by *kį* or *kʔú*), it is usually possible to form a phrase with this structure:

noun + modifier + *kį*.

458

Examples are:

wičháša tháka ki (man + big + *ki*) 'the big man'
wakháyeža číkʔala ki (child + small + *ki*) 'the little
  child'
iȟʔé ská ki (rock + white + *ki*) 'the white rock'

If the noun is plural, the modifier is reduplicated:
(4.3.2.8.).

wakháyežą čigčíkʔala ki (child + small + *ki*) 'the little children'.

Phrases of this kind have a special intonation: only
the noun receives primary stress; the modifier receives
secondary stress (3.1.).

If the collocation of noun and modifier is very common, Lakhota speakers usually form a compound of the
two, rather than use the phrasal construction. Thus
šųwášte ki 'the good horse' is preferred over the possible, but unusual *šúka-wakhá wašté ki*.

8.4.2.2.

There are two constructions for modifying indefinite
nouns. The choice between the two is chiefly idiomatic.

The less frequent construction is exactly like the
construction used for modified definite nouns: noun +
modifier + article *(wą, eyá,* etc.) This construction is
used only when the modifier states an inherent quality
that is expectable for the given noun: 'a warm blanket'
or 'a tall tree' are examples of expectable inherent
qualities. Lakhota examples are:

thípi tháka wą   'a large house'
mní sní eyá   'some cold water'.

Such phrases are often replaced by compound nouns:
mni-sní eyá, šųwášte wą 'a good horse'.

If the modifier attributes to the noun a meaning that
is unusual or unexpected, another construction is used
instead: noun + indefinite article + modifier + *čha. Čha*
is sometimes omitted. The position of the indefinite
article immediately following the noun nevertheless
contrasts the present construction with the one last
described. Examples:

Šúka-wakhá wą hušté (čha) wabláke.
horse   a   limp   I-saw
'I saw a lame horse.' (Compare *Šųȟúšte wą*
wabláke. 'I saw a crippled horse.')

Zįtkála eyá thothó (čha) wawíčhablake.
bird   some blue/green I-see-them
'I saw some blue birds.'

Wįyą wą líla tháka (čha) amáphe.
woman a very big   hit-me
'A very big woman hit me.'

Mni-píǧa etá šíča (čha) ųyátką pi.
beer   indef.-art bad   we-drink pl.
'We drank some bad beer.'

The construction with *čha* may actually be used correctly for any indefinite modified noun, including collocations that are semantically expectable combinations.

Modified generic nouns follow the indefinite pattern
with *čha,* but without articles, of course:

Thaló aǧúyapi čha waȟtéwala šni.
meat burned   I.dislike
'I don't like burned meat.'

This leads naturally to a discussion of nouns that are
modified by more than a stative verb, that is, nouns
modified by a whole sentence. Sentence modifiers are
called relative clauses.

8.4.2.3.

A relative clause is a sentence that modifies a noun.
The noun being modified must also occur as part of the
modifying sentence. An English example would be
'They arrested the man who hit me.' In this sentence
'who hit me' modifies *man.* If this sentence were not
acting as a modifier, it could not have *who* as its subject. Instead, it would have to be 'A man hit me.' The
original sentence, then, contains two sentences, one
included in the other: *They arrested the man [a man hit
me].* English grammar requires that the modifying sentence follow the noun it modifies, and furthermore that
the noun in the modifying sentence be replaced by a
relative pronoun, in this case *who.* (*Which* and *that* are
also relative pronouns.)

In Lakhota relative clauses, the modifying sentence
comes before the noun it modifies; the noun in the main
sentence is then dropped, but the rest of the sentence
remains. To construct the Lakhota for the English
example above, begin with the modifying sentence (in
which the shared noun is always indefinite):

wičháša wą amáphe
man   a hit.me
'a man hit me'

Then add the main sentence:

wičháša ki oyúspa   pi
man   the arrest.him pl.
'They arrested the man.'

The result is:

Wičháša wą amáphe wičháša ki oyúspa pi.

Now drop the second *wičháša,* but keep its article:

Wičháša wą amáphe ki oyúspa pi. 'They arrested the
  man who hit me.'

Even if the noun in the modifying sentence is the
object of its sentence, it must come first in the complex
sentence. Hence *Wičháša wą hokšíla ki wąyáke ki* can
mean either 'the man who saw the boy' or 'the man
whom the boy saw'.

If the article in the second sentence is indefinite, it
changes to *čha:*

Wičháša wą amápha čha oyúspa pi. 'They arrested a
  man who hit me.'

The similarity between indefinite modified nouns and nouns modified by relative clauses should now be obvious:

> *Wičháša wą líla tȟáka čha oyúspa pi.* 'They arrested a very big man.'
> *Wičháša wą amápha čha oyúspa pi.* 'They arrested a man who hit me.'

Moreover, this construction is also reminiscent of the emphatic construction (8.3.1.):

> *Hokšíla čha owíčhayuspa pi.* 'It was boys whom they arrested.'
> *Hokšíla kị é pi čha owíčhayuspa pi.* 'It was the boys whom they arrested.'

A relative clause always comes first in a sentence, whether it modifies the subject or object; the resulting ambiguities are rarely a problem, since contexts or probabilities will clarify nearly anything.

Here are some more complex examples of relative clause constructions:

> *Hokšíla eyá šúka-wakhą iwíčhaču pi*
> boy   some horse   take.them pl.
> *kị čhąksá-yuhá kị owíčhayuspa pi.*
> the police   the arrest.them   pl.
> 'The police arrested the boys who took the horses.'

> *Šúka-wakhą eyá hokšíla kị iwíčhaču pi*
> horse   some boy   the take.them pl.
> *kị wičháša kị iyéwičhaya pi.*
> the man   the find.them   pl.
> 'The men found the horses the boys took.'

The two improbable sentences 'The boys who took the horses arrested the policemen' and 'The horses the boys took found the men' would be exactly like those two examples, but their improbable meanings would keep them from being understood in that way without elaborate explanatory context.

To summarize modified nominals, including those with relative clause modifiers:

(a) definite nominals: noun + modifier + $\left\{ \begin{matrix} kị \\ k^{\textipa{P}}ų \end{matrix} \right\}$

(b) indefinite nominals:
　1) semantically expectable collocations:
　　noun + modifier + article
　2) others:
　noun + article + $\left\{ \begin{matrix} \text{modifying word} \\ \text{modifying sentence} \end{matrix} \right\}$ + $\left\{ \begin{matrix} kị \\ k^{\textipa{P}}ų \\ čha \end{matrix} \right\}$

For a different approach to this and many other subordinate clause constructions, see Simons (1989).

8.5. Sentences as Nominals

Many verbs permit whole sentences to serve as their subjects or objects. English sentences used as nominals are marked in one of three ways: with *for...to*; with *that*; or with *'s...-ing*. Secondarily, *for*, *that*, *'s*, and *to* are sometimes omitted.

Observe these examples:

> It's time <u>for</u> him <u>to</u> take his medicine.
> I told him <u>to</u> come.
> She helped me (<u>to</u>) find the right page.
> I said (<u>that</u>) he should call me.
> The cat(<u>'s</u>) scratch<u>ing</u> (of) the couch annoys mother.

In Lakhota, too, sentences can serve as the subjects or objects of verbs. These sentences may be marked by *kị*, *k^{\textipa{P}}ų*, or by no article at all. If *kị* or *k^{\textipa{P}}ų* is used, a demonstrative (see 8.3.2.) may also be used. Usually the need for *kị* or *k^{\textipa{P}}ų* is determined by which main verb is used.

8.5.1.
The following verbs require a determiner on their complements: *slolyÁ* 'know', *iyókiphi* 'be happy that,' *šíčA* 'be bad that', *šičáya* 'be too bad that', *wašté* 'be good that', *waštélakA* 'like (it) that, *waȟtéla šni* 'dislike (it) that', *wąyákA* 'see that', *yawá* 'read that,' *naȟ^{\textipa{P}}ú* 'hear (something)' (note: not 'hear that') and *héčha* 'be necessary that ...right away'. Examples include:

> *Wąčhíyake kị lé wašté.*
> I.see.you   the this good
> 'It's good to see you.'

> *Kičhíwomayaglaka pi kị iyómakiphi.*
> you.discuss.with.me pl. the I.am.glad
> 'I'm glad you (pl.) discussed it with me.'

> *Mas^{\textipa{P}}óphiye ektá théhą ų pi šni kị wašté.*
> store   at   long stay pl. not the good.
> 'They better not stay at the store long.'

> *Agnes mni-píǧa yatké kị waȟtéwala šni.*
> Agnes beer   drink the I.like   not
> 'I don't like (for) Agnes to drink beer.'

The word *k^{\textipa{P}}ų* can substitute for *kị* under certain circumstances. *K^{\textipa{P}}ų* identifies a strongly asserted factual statement; it can only be used if the assertion is known to the speaker to have been an accomplished fact when the action described by the main verb began. Consequently it is never used with verbs expressing question, doubt, or value judgments.

8.5.2.
Verbs that require their complement sentence to be unmarked include *čhí* 'want', *eyÁ (kéyA)* 'say', *okíhi* 'be able to', *iyúkčą* 'to think, plan, expect', *onáȟ^{\textipa{P}}ų* 'to hear about', *kéya naȟ^{\textipa{P}}ú* 'to hear that...' and *okíyaka* 'to tell someone (that)'. Here are some examples:

> *Šúka-wakhą wąží ophéyathų yačhí he?*
> horse   one you.buy   you.want question
> 'Do you want to buy a horse?'

Šúka-wakhá wąží ophéthų onáyaȟʔų
horse   one   he.buy   you.hear.about
he?
question
'Did you hear about his buying a horse?'

Waná wachípi ektá ųkíyaya pi ųkókihi pi.
now   dance   to   we.leave pl. we.can pl.
'We can leave for the dance now.'

Ožážąglepi wąží bluǧą yachí   he?
window   a   I.open you.want question
'Do you want me to open a window?'

8.5.3.

A few verbs permit sentential complements that are like infinitive or participle constructions in English. An example of such an English sentence is *He told me to come*, in which the infinitive construction *me to come* represents a reduced sentence that is seen more clearly in *'He said that I should come.'*

In Lakhota constructions of this kind, the complement verb precedes the principal verb. If the complement verb is transitive it may have object affixes (9.3.2.), but otherwise it has no affixes. The principal verb has the expectable affixes (i.e., subject and/or object affixes). The close relationship between verbs in this construction may be shown in ways other than the unusual distribution of personal affixes. Stress patterns typical of compound words and phonological changes of the kind described in 4.3.2.6. and 4.3.2.7. are two such ways.

Examples of this kind of construction are as follows:

Wówapi kị   yawá maší.
book   the read me.he.commanded
'He told me to read the book.'

Owíchale   ómayakiya wachį́.
look.for.them   you.help.me I.want
'I want you to help me to look for them.' (This sentence contains two subordinate verbs, but only the first is of the type described here; cf. 8.5.2. for *chį́*.)

Nąhą́ȟčí   škal yúštą pi šni he?
yet   play finish pl. not question
'Haven't they finished playing yet?' (Note that *škal yúštą* is stressed like a compound.)

Two other uses for such reduced sentences are for purpose clauses with verbs of motion and for loosely joining sentences expressing sequential events, usually in stories. Here are examples:

Thaló ophéthų mní kte.
meat buy   I.go potential
'I'll go buy meat.'

Wichášą etą́ wąníyąg ú   pi kte.
man   some see.you come pl. potential
'Some men will come to see you.'

Tákuni isą́m tókhų šni, ųglíyachu   pi.
nothing more do   not we.come.home pl.
'Doing nothing more, we came home.'

In very colloquial speech, some verbal constructions of this kind may be reduced even further by completely omitting affixes from the first verb, and indicating all grammatical relations in the principal verb. If the principal verb is ordinarily intransitive, it nevertheless appears here with transitive affixes. Thus *Wichášą wą wąníyąg hí* 'A man came to see you' may become *Wichášą wą wąyą́g nihí*.

9. VERBS

Because it is the only obligatory element in the sentence, the verb is the most important kind of word in Lakhota. It is also the most complex. Analyzing verbs requires taking into account three different kinds of information: in what kinds of sentences a given verb may occur, what affixes or other markings a given verb may have, and how a verb may be expanded or changed in its basic meaning.

9.1. SENTENCE AND AFFIX TYPES

Part of the meaning of every Lakhota verb is a specification of the number of "participants" (the technical term is "arguments"), or things to which nominals or pronominal affixes can refer, in the event the verb describes. Simple sentences can, depending on the verbal category, imply zero, one, two, or three participants.

Verbs that imply one participant are in turn divided into two groups, depending somewhat on what they mean. If the verb describes an activity over which its participant has control, or which the participant can carry out willfully, it will select an affix from the set that marks the subject (technically, "agent") of a two-participant sentence. But if the situation described by the verb involves no will or control on the part of its participant, then that participant will be marked as if it were the object (technically: "patient") of a two-argument verb. These semantic definitions are not perfectly reliable, and occasionally a verb takes affixes that seem to belong logically to the other category. For example, *ní* 'to be alive, not dead' takes agent forms, while *kíza* 'squeak, as a mouse does' takes patient forms. See Legendre and Rood (1992) for a detailed discussion of these two classes.

Verbs thus fall into several classes according to their participant types: impersonal (no participants), stative (one objectlike participant), active intransitive (one subjectlike participant), transitive (two participants), and ditransitive (three participants). There is also a sixth class with very few members that takes two objectlike participants; this class is called "stative transitive." These verbs are so rare that "stative" will be used consistently for the one-participant statives in what follows, and "transitive" for "active transitive." *461*

9.1.1.

Impersonal verbs do not take any personal affixes. Most of them are limited semantically to expressions of natural states such as the weather or the time of day. Examples include:

Ąpétu kį lé osní.	'It's <u>cold</u> today.'
Mahél o'íyokpaze.	'It was very <u>dark</u> inside.'
Ičámna ȟče šni.	'It's not <u>snowing</u> much'
Hąhépi.	'<u>It is night</u>.'

There is also a small number of impersonal verbal expressions that refer to speaker-perceived states such as obligations, necessity, apparentness, and the like. Here are examples with the verbs *phíča, iyéčheča, s'eléčheča,* and *hécha:*

Ečhų phíča šni.
do   feasible not
'<u>It can</u> not <u>be</u> done, <u>it is</u> not <u>feasible</u>.'

Wičhįčala kį   khúža iyéčheča.
little.girl the sick   seem
'<u>It seems</u> that the little girl is sick.'

Šúka kį   thaló kį   yúte s'eléčheča.
dog   the   meat the   eat   seem
'<u>It seems</u> that the dog has eaten the meat.'

Phežúta   etą   iyáču   kte   hécha.
medicine   some you.take potential be.necessary
'You <u>must</u> take some medicine.'

These verbs can all be used with stative personal affixes, but with somewhat different meanings. For example, with personal affixes *hécha* means 'to be such a one' and *phíča* means 'to be glad'.

9.1.2.

Stative verbs ordinarily describe states or conditions. They are most reliably identified not by their meaning, but by the personal affixes they take. 'I' and 'you' with stative verbs are always expressed by *ma* and *ni* respectively. (Further details of affixation are given in 9.3.)

Examples of stative verbs are *khúžA* 'nauseated' (*makhúže* 'I am nauseated'), *í-puza* 'thirsty' (*í-mapúza* 'I am thirsty'), *wašté* 'good' (*niwášte* 'you are good'), and *zí* 'yellow; pale' (*nizí* 'you are pale').

Almost all nouns can also be used as stative verbs identifying the noun, although the verb *hécha* 'to be such a one' can also provide this meaning:

Wimáčhaša. ⎱	'I am a man.'
Wičháša hemácha. ⎰	
Nilákhota he? ⎱	'Are you an Indian?'
Lakhóta heníčha he? ⎰	
Hé čhą.	'That is a tree.'
Hená šúka pi.	'Those are dogs.'

9.1.3.

Stative transitive verbs (see 9.1.) permit two patients in their sentences. Most common among these is *itháwa*

'own' (see 8.4.1.), with which one can say *Nimíthawa* 'you are mine'. Other examples are *iyénimačheča* 'you look like me' and *iyónimakiphi* 'I find you congenial'. Additional examples are given in Boas and Deloria (1941:77).

9.1.4.

Active intransitive verbs are, like stative verbs, restricted to sentences with one participant; but these verbs take the affixes *wa* 'I' and *ya* 'you' (or variants thereof, see 9.3.), instead of *ma* and *ni*. Semantically, most of these verbs describe actions that the subject can perform. Examples include *hí* 'arrive' (*wahí* 'I have arrived'), *wačhí* 'dance' (*wawáčhi* 'I dance'), *okíhi* 'be able' (*oyákihi* 'you can'), and *nážį* 'stand' (*nayážį* 'you stand').

9.1.5.

Active transitive verbs require two participants in their sentences, an agent (subject) and a patient (object). Consequently they also permit two affixes to occur with them (inflectional details are given in 9.3.). Examples include *wąyákA* 'see', *aphÁ* 'hit', *slolyÁ* 'know', *iyéyA* 'find', and *kté* 'kill'.

Many Lakhota transitive verbs correspond to English verbs that are optionally transitive. For example, in English people say 'we are eating now' or 'we are eating meat'; the first sentence uses 'eat' intransitively, the second uses it transitively. Very few Lakhota verbs have this option. Two that do are *škátA* 'play' or 'play a game' and *hablé* 'dream' or 'dream about'. A Lakhota transitive verb that is used as an intransitive verb ordinarily requires the prefix *wa-*, which attributes an indefinite or implied object to the verb: *naȟ'ú* 'to hear', *wanáȟ'ų* 'to listen; to obey'; *manú* 'to steal an object', *wamánu* 'to steal things'. In some cases this *wa-* is concealed by sound changes: *yútA* 'to eat', but *wótA* 'to eat a meal'; *iwáyąkA* 'to examine, look at'; *wíwąyąkA* 'to examine things; to make a judgment.'

9.1.6.

Finally, there are a few Lakhota verbs that require three participants in their sentences. Verbs of this kind are *k'ú* 'to give something to someone' and *lá* 'to ask someone for something'.

Actually, most transitive and active and some stative verbs permit an indirect object (8.) in their sentence, but in this case the form of the verb itself is changed to show that a third participant has been added (9.3.8.).

9.2. VERBAL DERIVATION

9.2.1.

Lakhota speakers freely form compound verb stems for special meanings. Usually this is accomplished by prefixing a noun, an adverb, or another verb to the basic root. Thus from *wayáwa* 'to read; to attend school' and *glí* 'to arrive home, coming' is derived *wayáwa-glí* 'to have come home from school'; with *iglúštÁ* 'to finish for oneself' is formed *wayáwa-iglúštA* 'to have finished school', and so on. Some other examples include:

šuňʔákąyąkA (*šúka* 'horse', *aką́* 'on', *yąkÁ* 'sit') 'to ride horseback'

ločhí (*lo* 'food', not used as a free form today, and *čhí* 'want') 'to be hungry'

wakšíyužaža (*wakšíča* 'dishes', *yužáža* 'to wash') 'to wash dishes'

í-puza (*í* 'mouth', *púzA* 'be dry') 'to be thirsty'

In addition to these more or less obvious compounds, complex stems are often formed with prefixes. The first set of these prefixes sometimes, but not always, has adverbial meanings: *i-* 'with, instrumental', *o-* 'inside', *a-* 'on the surface of; because of', *khi-* 'at the middle'.

Examples of these prefixes are:

iyátkĄ (*yatkÁ* 'to drink') 'to drink with, to use for drinking'

othó (*thó* 'to be blue or green') 'to be bruised'

onáphA (*naphÁ* 'to run away, to flee') 'to flee into'

apáȟpa (*paȟpá* 'to push over') 'to push over onto'

aléžA (*léžA* 'to urinate') 'to urinate on'

ačhą́tešičA 'to be sad because of' (*čhątéšičA* 'to be sad')

khičáksA (*kaksÁ* 'sever by striking') 'to break in the middle by striking'

khiwápsakA (*wapsákA* 'to sever a string') 'to cut a string in two'

The meaning that has been added by the prefix is not always easy to specify. Compare, for example, *ománi* 'to travel' and *máni* 'to walk'; *ayúštĄ* 'to leave alone' and *yuštÁ* 'to finish'.

In a few cases, verbs exist only with the prefix; an equivalent form without the prefix cannot be found. An example of this is *alí* 'to climb on, to step on'.

Another set of prefixes has clear instrumental meaning. Seven of these are used very frequently; an eighth appears rarely. The instrumental prefixes often appear together with one of the adverbial prefixes just discussed.

In some cases the prefixes are added to verbs that are also used without the instrumental prefixes. In other cases (probably in most), an equivalent verb without the prefix is not used. The prefixes, with examples, are given beginning with the rather rare prefix *pu-*:

pu- 'by generalized pressure'
　puspÁ 'to glue, to seal'
　opúǧi 'to stuff soft material into an opening'
ka- 'by means of a blow'
　kačhéyA 'to cause to cry by striking'
　kabléčA 'to shatter by hitting'
　kaȟlókA 'to chop a hole in something'.

ka is also used in verbs that refer to action of wind, or other more or less spontaneous actions:

　kažó 'to fart'
　kaǧą́ 'to blow open'.

na- 'by foot action'
　natʔÁ 'to kill by stepping on'
　nabléčA 'to shatter something with the foot'
　naȟlókA 'to kick a hole in something'.

na- is used in verbs that refer to action accomplished by heat. It is also used when the action occurs by spontaneous inner force:

　našlí 'to ooze out'
　nagmú 'to curl up, to twist (drying material)'
　našá 'to blush'.

pa- 'by pushing or by pressure with the hands or the body'
　paʔíle 'to ignite by pushing, as a flashlight'
　pabléčA 'to shatter by sitting on'
　paȟlókA 'to pierce the ears'
wa- 'by cutting with a blade'
　wažáta 'to notch, to make forked by cutting or sawing'
　wabléčA 'to shatter by attempting to cut'
　waȟlókA 'to make a miscut while skinning'
wo- 'by piercing with a pointed object'
　woȟlá 'to make something sound (ring) by shooting it'
　wobléčA 'to break into pieces by striking with a pestle or by shooting'
　woȟlókA 'to punch or shoot a hole in'

wo- is also used in verbs that refer to action by blowing:

　woʔíle 'to make a fire blaze by blowing on it'.

ya- 'by means of the mouth or the teeth; by speaking'
　yaȟtákA 'to bite'
　yabléčA 'to shatter by biting'
　yaȟlókA 'to gnaw a hole'
　yašíčA 'to malign' ('bad mouth')
yu- 'by means of the hands'
　yuǧą́ 'to open up' (as a door or window)
　yubléčA 'to shatter with the hand'
　yuȟlókA 'to make a hole with the hand'

yu- is also used in verbs that have a general causative meaning (9.2.2.).

9.2.2.

The verbs that fit into the categories in 9.1. may either belong there inherently or be brought into that category by a derivational process. Thus, for instance, stative and intransitive verbs may be made transitive ('be sick' changes to 'make sick' or 'sing' changes to 'cause to sing' or 'let sing'). The indefinite object prefix *wa* (9.1.4.) could be listed here, too, as a device for changing transitive verbs into active intransitives.

9.2.2.1.

Lakhota stative and intransitive verbs are made transitive by means of a causative construction. Transitive verbs may also be made causative, in which case they become ditransitive verbs. There are three causative constructions:

1) Stative verbs that describe size or shape (so that the change being caused is one of degree, not of kind) and verbs of value judgment are made causative with the instrumental prefix *yu* (9.2.1.):

číkˀala 'small',	*yučíkˀala* 'reduce in size'
háska 'long',	*yuháska* 'lengthen'
tą́yą́ 'well',	*yutą́yą́* 'make right, fix up'
wašté 'good',	*yuwášte* 'improve, correct'.

2a) Stative verbs that refer to other kinds of conditions are made causative by using the suffixed auxiliary *-yA; -yA* is an active verb. Examples:

ǧú 'be burned',	*ǧuyÁ* 'to scorch'
sápA 'to be black',	*sabyÁ* 'to blacken'.

An interesting illustration of the meaning differences between (1) and (2a) is the root *ská* 'be white', which accepts both causatives: *yuská* means 'to clean; to make whiter', while *skayÁ* means 'to paint white; to whiten'.

Many of the verbs that take *-yÁ* for the general causative also take instrumental prefixes for special kinds of causative meaning; in these cases *-yA* is not used. Thus, from *khúžA* 'to be nauseated' can be derived *yukhúžA* 'to harass someone until he becomes sick' and *yakhúžA* 'to talk someone into being sick'.

2b) Active and transitive verbs may also be made causative with *-yA* if the causation was accidental or unintentional or indirect:

čhį́ 'want', *čhiyÁ* 'to cause to want' (for example, to cause someone to want food by eating in front of him)

maǧážu 'to rain', *maǧážuyA* 'to cause to rain' (for example, by doing something unusual; a lazy person suddenly beginning to work hard is said to make it rain)

yuhá 'to have', *yuháyA* 'to cause someone to have (perhaps by leaving it behind at his house)'

čhéyA 'to cry', *čhéyeyA* 'to cause to cry (by telling a sad story, perhaps)'.

Some verbs with the causative auxiliary *-yA* have no currently used non-causative. Such are *slolyÁ* 'to know' and *iyéyA* 'to find'.

3) When the causation is intentional, or when there is no desire to stop the action, active verbs are made causative by use of the active auxiliary verb *-khiyA*. English translations are more often 'let' than 'make':

čhéyekhiyA 'to let cry (without trying to stop)'
yuhákhiyA 'to let have (carry); to have carry'
ókiyekhiyA 'to let help'.

If a transitive verb is used with *-khiyA*, the main verb as well as the auxiliary may take affixes (the main verb takes object affixes only):

ómakiyečhíčhiyį kte
help.me.I.let.you potential
'I will let you help me'

óničiyewakhíye
help.you.I.let.him
'I let him help you'.

9.2.2.2.

Moving into the state designated by a stative verb is indicated in two different ways. Either *ki-* is prefixed to the verb, or the auxiliary verb *áyA* is used. Probably *áyA* is the verb 'to bring', since other verbs of bringing and taking also occasionally mean 'begin to', but in this construction it functions like a stative verb. In fact, although the meaning shift for this construction seems to be from stative to active intransitive, the formal affixation pattern for both the derived and underived constructions remains that of stative verbs. Examples are:

kiskúyA	'to become sweet'
čhépa áyA	'to get fat'.

In some cases a verb can be used with both, but with different meanings:

kithą́ka	'to grow old'
thą́ka áyA	'to get big'.

In most instances, *ki-* imparts a meaning of inevitable change into the state mentioned by the verb, change over which the referent has no control.

9.2.2.3.

There is no obvious formal process whereby active verbs may be shifted to the stative category. (In English this is done by the use of passive participles: break→be broken, find→be found, etc.) Such notions are expressed in Lakhota by using the third-person plural subject form (marked by *pi* after the verb) of an active transitive verb: 'they broke it', 'they found him', etc.

However, there is some syntactic evidence that *pi* in this construction is genuinely a passive marker rather than the subject pluralizer. With verbs like 'seem', most linguists agree that the subject of 'seem' and the subject of its complement have to be the same. Thus in 'She seemed to hit him' and 'She seemed to have been hit', "she" is the subject of both verbs in both sentences, even when, logically, "she" is the recipient or patient of the second one. If this is so, then in the Lakhota sentence *amápha pi sˀelémačheča* 'I seem to have been hit', *ma* rather than *pi* must represent the subject of *amápha pi*. Obviously, this analysis relies on a very specific notion of "subject." This notion has not yet been well explored for Lakhota.

9.3. VERB INFLECTION

Lakhota verbs may be inflected to indicate the person and number of subjects, direct objects, indirect objects, and possessors of objects. Inflection involves the addition of affixes to the verb. Note that "affix" is used here as a cover term for prefix, suffix, and infix; an infix is an element inserted into a stem. Many of the inflectional morphemes in Lakhota are either prefixed or infixed, depending on the verb. Sometimes the infixing is only apparent, as when the inflection follows a derivational prefix such as *na-* 'by means of the foot'. Thus a sequence like *na-wá-tʔe* 'I killed it with my foot' (from *natʔé* 'to die or kill by means of foot action') technically consists of two prefixes and a root. However, there are many cases where the inflectional morpheme is inserted into an otherwise (synchronically) unanalyzable stem, such as *máni* 'to walk' (*mawáni* 'I walk'), or *ophéthų* 'to buy' (*ophéwathų* 'I buy/bought it'), or *wičháša* 'man' (*wimáčhaša* 'I am a man'). In accord with Lakhota grammatical tradition and (most) native-speaker intuition, all the inserted inflectional elements are here called "infixes," and both these infixes and all the prefixes are called "affixes."

In addition to affixes, all verbal paradigms make use of the enclitic *pi* to mark a plural argument. An enclitic is like a suffix, except that it is a separate word.

The discussion of verb inflection can be divided into 10 subtopics: stative affixes, object affixes, active subject affixes, two-affix constructions, irregular paradigms, reflexives, reciprocal constructions, reflexive possessive, dative constructions, and benefactive constructions.

9.3.1.

The basic paradigm has positions for three persons and three numbers, although the dual is available only for the first-person inclusive subject ('you and I', but not 'he and I'). It is tempting to analyze the *ų(k)* without *pi* (the dual) as "inclusive singular" and thus make *pi* a consistent marker of the plural. This analysis must be rejected because *pi* is added to all objects (not stative subjects), both dual and plural, and *pi* neutralizes the inclusive/exclusive distinction.

In the third person, plural is marked for animate nouns only; inanimate plurals are marked by reduplication of the verb stem (see 4.3.2.8.). When the plural refers to human beings there is yet another distinction: distributive versus collective. "Distributive plurals" focus on plurality as a collection of separate individuals, while "collective plurals" focus on persons whose identities are fused into a group. An English noun with just these kinds of meanings is the word "family." When the verb used with *family* is singular (My family is waiting for me), the noun is collective in meaning. When the verb is plural (My family are all living in California now), the meaning is distributive. Many Lakhota verbs do not have collective forms; when such forms do not exist, the distributive plural forms are used instead. The collective sense is not necessarily lost in such cases, since a noun with collective meaning (or a quantifier such as *oyásʔį* 'all of a collective human group') may also be present in the sentence.

Here are the personal affixes used in the inflection of stative verbs.

Singular	Dual	Plural
1. *ma-*	*ų(k)-*	*ų(k)-...pi*
2. *ni-*		*ni-...pi*
3. *Ø-*		*Ø...pi* distributive
		wičha- collective

Ø means that there is no affix for that person.

ų(k) is written in this way to indicate that *ų* is used if any consonant but /ʔ/ follows the affix, while *ųk* appears if a vowel or /ʔ/ follows.

There are three patterns for the placement of these affixes in the verb: all affixes are prefixed; all affixes are infixed; *ų(k)* is prefixed and the others are infixed. Here are sample paradigms of each type:

hǫ́skA 'be long or tall' (prefix type)

Singular	Dual	Plural
1. *mahǫ́ske*	*ųhǫ́ske*	*ųhǫ́ska pi*
'I am tall'	'you and I are tall'	'we are tall'
2. *nihǫ́ske*		*nihǫ́ska pi*
'you are tall'		'you are tall'
3. *hǫ́ske*		*hǫ́ska pi*
'he is tall'		'they are tall' (distributive)
		wičháhǫske
		'they are tall' (collective)

í-puza 'be thirsty' (infix type)

Singular	Dual	Plural
1. *í-mapúza*	*í-ʔupúza*	*í-ʔupúza pi*
'I am thirsty'	'you and I are thirsty'	'we are thirsty'
2. *í-nipúza*		*i-nipúza pi*
'you are thirsty'		'you are thirsty'
3. *í-puza*		*í-puza pi*
'he is thirsty'		'they are thirsty'

ųspé 'to know how to' (mixed type)

Singular	Dual	Plural
1. *ųmáspe*	*ųkúspe*	*ųkúspe pi*
'I know how to'	'you and I know how to'	'we know how to'
2. *ųníspe*		*ųníspe pi*
'you know how to'		'you know how to'
3. *ųspé*		*ųspé pi*
'he knows how to'		'they know how to'

The stative paradigm is completely regular; there are no further subtypes within this conjugation. In particular, verbs such as *yąkÁ* 'to sit,' of which the first-person form is *mąké,* are not stative. See the description of active nasal stems in 9.3.3., and note that when an object affix appears on this verb in the construction described at the end of 8.5.3., the form is *mayą́ke.*

One further remark about the use of the stative verb inflection is in order. Stative verb affixes are regularly used to identify the possessor of an inalienably possessed noun (8.4.1.) that is the subject of a stative verb:

Natá   (kị)   mayáza̧.
head   the   I.hurt
'My head hurts.'

Napé   (kị)   mašpá̧.
hand   the   I.burn
'I burned my hand.'

Phehị̧   (kị)   nisábsapa.
hair   the   you.black
'You have black hair.'

9.3.2.
The paradigm for transitive objects (assuming a third-person singular subject) is almost like that for stative verb subjects, but there are two differences: first, there is no collective versus distributive distinction: the collective affix of the stative paradigm is used for all animate plural objects. Second, there is no separate form for the dual; *pi* is used with *ụ(k)* whenever it marks the object.

Here are the object affixes:

Singular		Plural
1. *ma*		*ụ(k)...pi*
2. *ni*		*ni...pi*
3. Ø		*wičha*

The placement of these affixes follows the same three patterns observed with the stative verbs: *ụ(k)* may be prefixed while the others are infixed, or all may follow the same pattern. Here are three paradigms:

khízA 'to attack; begin a fight with' (prefix type)

Singular	Plural
1. *makhíze*	*ụkhíza pi*
'he attacked me'	'he attacked us'
2. *ničhíze*	*ničhíza pi*
'he attacked you'	'he attacked you'
3. *khíze*	*wičhákhize*
'he attacked him'	'he attacked them'

slolyÁ (infix type)

Singular	Plural
1. *slolmáye*	*slolʔų́yą pi*
'he knows me'	'he knows us'
2. *slolníye*	*slolníyą pi*
'he knows you'	'he knows you'
3. *slolyé*	*slolwíčhaye*
'he knows him'	'he knows them'

aphÁ 'to hit' (mixed type)

Singular	Plural
1. *amáphe*	*ụkápha pi*
'he hit me'	'he hit us'
2. *aníphe*	*anípha pi*
'he hit you'	'he hit you'
3. *aphé*	*awíčhaphe*
'he hit him'	'he hit them'

9.3.3.
The active subject affixes come in three slightly different paradigms, all of which have the same positional arrangements (prefix, infix, mixed). The three paradigms differ only in the form of the affixes used for 'I' and 'you'. The remainder of the subject affixes are as in the stative paradigm except that motion verbs have *a* rather than *wicha* as the affix of the collective plural. Note that *ụ(k)* may mark either subject or object; its correct meaning has to be read from another affix or from the context. In y-stems, the *y-* changes to /l/ after first-person singular *b-* and disappears after *l-* in the second person. Actually, both y-stem and nasal-stem affixes are probably to be derived from the *wa-* and *ya-* of regular verbs by a series of phonological rules involving loss of the vowel of the affix and subsequent consonant assimilations. For detailed discussion, see Carter (1974:130-154) and Koontz (1983).

Here is a chart of the three sets of active subject affixes:

		1. Regular	2. Y-stem	3. Nasal Stem
Singular	1.	*wa*	*b*	*m*
	2.	*ya*	*l*	*n*
	3.	Ø	Ø	Ø
Dual	1.	*ụ(k)*	*ụ(k)*	*ụ(k)*
Plural	1.	*ụ(k)...pi*	*ụ(k)...pi*	*ụ(k)...pi*
	2.	*ya...pi*	*l...pi*	*n...pi*
Distributive	3.	Ø*...pi*	Ø*...pi*	Ø*...pi*
Collective		{ *a* / *wičha* }	{ *a* / *wičha* }	{ *a* / *wičha* }

The inflectional paradigm that is used for each active verb is partially predictable. For example, the affixes of paradigm 2 (y-stem) are used most often with verbs that have /y/ followed by an oral vowel at the point where the affix is added; the affixes of paradigm 3 (nasal stem) are used most often with verbs that have /y/ or /ʔ/ followed by a nasalized vowel at the point where the affix is added. There are a few exceptions to these general rules.

Given below are paradigms of verbs with active affixes. No attempt is made to illustrate the prefix-infix-mixed types, since the variations are exactly the same as for the stative or object affix paradigm types.

Examples of Paradigm 1 (regular)

hí 'arrive coming'

	Singular	Dual	Plural
1.	*wahí*	*ụhí*	*ụhí pi*
	'I came'	'you and I came'	'we came'
2.	*yahí*		*yahí pi*
	'you came'		'you came'
3.	*hí*		*hí pi*
	'he came'		'they came' (distributive)
			ahí
			'they came' (collective)

slolyÁ 'know' (looks like y-stem, inflected regularly)

Singular	Dual	Plural
1. *slolwáye*	*slol⁷úye*	*slol⁷úyą pi*
'I know him'	'you and I know him'	'we know him'
2. *slolyáye*		*slolyáya pi*
'you know him'		'you know him'
3. *slolyé*		*slolyá pi*
'he knows him'		'they know him'

⁷ú 'be (exist); stay'
(looks like nasal stem; inflected regularly)

Singular	Dual	Plural
1. *wa⁷ú*	*ųk⁷ú*	*ųk⁷ú pi*
'I am'	'you and I are'	'we are'
2. *ya⁷ú*		*ya⁷ú pi*
'you are'		'you are'
3. *ú*		*ú pi*
'he is'		'they are'

Examples of Paradigm 2 (y-stem)

yuhá 'have'

Singular	Dual	Plural
1. *bluhá*	*ųyúha*	*ųyúha pi*
'I have it'	'you and I have it'	'we have it'
2. *luhá*		*luhá pi*
'you have it'		'you have it'
3. *yuhá*		*yuhá pi*
'he has it'		'they have it'

wąyákA 'to see'
(looks like nasal stem; inflected like a y-stem)

Singular	Dual	Plural
1. *wąbláke*	*wą⁷úyąke*	*wą⁷úyąka pi*
'I saw him'	'you and I saw him'	'we saw him'
2. *wąláke*		*wąláka pi*
'you saw him'		'you saw him'
3. *wąyáke*		*wąyáka pi*
'he saw him'		'they saw him'

Note that /ą/ is changed to /a/ following /l/ in the 'I' and 'you' forms.

Examples of Paradigm 3 (nasal stem)

⁷ú 'to use; to wear'

Singular	Dual	Plural
1. *mú*	*ųk⁷ú*	*ųk⁷ú pi*
'I used it'	'you and I used it'	'we used it'
2. *nú*		*nú pi*
'you used it'		'you used it'
3. *ú*		*ú pi*
'he used it'		'they used it'

Note that some of the forms of this verb are identical to some forms of *⁷ú* 'exist'.

ečhá⁷ų 'to do'

Singular	Dual	Plural
1. *ečhámu*	*ečhúk⁷ų*	*ečhúk⁷ų pi*
'I did it'	'you and I did it'	'we did it'
2. *ečhánu*		*ečhánu pi*
'you did it'		'you did it'
3. *ečhú*		*ečhú pi*
'he did it'		'they did it'

Note that most forms of this verb have the loss of /a⁷/ described in 4.3.1.3.

yąkÁ 'to be seated'

Singular	Dual	Plural
1. *maké*	*ųyáke*	*ųyáka pi*
'I am seated'	'you and I are seated'	'we are seated'
2. *naké*		*naká pi*
'you are seated'		'you are seated'
3. *yąké*		*yąká pi*
'he is seated'		'they are seated' (distributive)
		wičháyąke
		'they are seated' (collective)

Verbs of motion utilize a collective prefix *a* different from that of other intransitive verbs. If the verb begins with *i*, the prefix *a* coalesces with the initial *i* of the stem to yield *é*:

áye 'they went (collective)'; compare *yá pi* 'they went (distributive)'

éyaye 'they (collective) started out, going'; compare *iyáya pi* (distributive)

énaži 'they (collective) went and stood'; compare *ináži pi* (distributive)

9.3.4.
Transitive verbs take two affixes whenever the subject and object are grammatical persons marked by affixes. The same is true of stative transitive verbs (9.1.3.). When two affixes are present, the usual order is first the object affix, then the subject affix. Another description of the order of sequence in the affixes would be (third person) (second person) (first person). This would eliminate rule 3 below, but not rule 1 in all cases. Similarly, describing the order as (third) (first) (second) would eliminate rule 1, but not rule 3. The object-subject description seems better, since there are other ways in which *ų(k)* is exceptional (e.g., prefixing to verbs where other affixes infix).

The combinations of affixes that appear are usually as given in the object and subject paradigms outlined in 9.3.2. and 9.3.3., but there are some additional complexities that cannot be predicted from a simple blending of the two sets. The complexities involve the affixes, some verb stems, and the enclitic pluralizer *pi*.

With respect to the affix combinations, the following rules apply:

1) *ų(k)* precedes all affixes but *wičha*
2) The combination of 'I' subject and 'you' object is represented in transitive verbs by a single affix: *čhi*.
3) In the stative transitive verbs, *ni* always precedes *ma*, regardless of the grammatical functions of the affixes. The meaning of verbal forms of this kind is therefore ambiguous.
4) y-stem or nasal stem transitive verbs with 'you' subject and 'me' or 'us' object have *yal* or *yan*, respectively, for 'you'.

Verbs that require *ų(k)* prefixed, but the others inserted, present a problem, since *ų(k)* must follow *wičha*, an inserted affix. In the speech of some persons this apparent contradiction is resolved by inserting both in the proper order, but repeating the entire verb stem after *ų(k)*. An example can be given using the verb *oyúspA* 'to arrest': *owíčhųkoyuspa pi* 'we arrested them'. Note that *wičha* is inserted after *o*, as required for this verb, and at the same time *ų(k)* precedes *o* as is also required by this particular verb. However, many persons simply insert both affixes, ignoring the apparent contradiction of not having *ų(k)* before *o*. In the speech of these persons, the correct form is *owíčhųyuspa pi*.

Pluralization can appear only once in each verbal form. Hence, either affix, or both simultaneously, may be pluralized by *pi*. Many verbal forms containing *pi* and affixes that may be either singular or plural are thus ambiguous, and only the context can indicate which participants are actually plural. For example *ųkóyuspa pi* can mean 'we arrested him', 'he arrested us', or 'they arrested us'. *iyéʔųyaya pi kte* can mean either 'you (sing.) will find us' or 'you (pl.) will find us'.

The combinations of affixes that occur in transitive verbs are shown in table 5.

9.3.5.
There are some verbs that have irregularities of one or another kind in their inflection. Among the most frequent are the verbs *eyÁ* 'to say' and its derivatives, the verb *yútA* 'to eat', and various motion verbs, especially *yÁ* and verbs based on it.

The transitive verb *eyÁ* 'to say' is conjugated as follows; note the stress shift in the third-person singular:

Singular	Dual	Plural
1. *ephé*	*ųkéye*	*ųkéya pi*
2. *ehé*		*ehá pi*
3. *éye*		*eyá pi*

A derivative of *eyÁ*, *eyáyalaka* 'to tell lies', is inflected doubly, with the same irregularities in both places: *epháphalaka*, etc.

468 The transitive verb *yútA* 'to eat' has these forms:

Singular	Dual	Plural
1. *wáte*	*ųyúte*	*ųyúta pi*
2. *yáte*		*yáta pi*
3. *yúte*		*yúta pi*

The verb *yÁ* 'to be going' normally conjugates according to active Paradigm 2 (9.3.3.): *blé, lé, yé, ųyé, ųyá pi, lá pi, yá pi*. However, whenever the syntax of the sentence demands that the final vowel be *į* (see 4.3.2.6.), the personal affixes are nasalized. Observe the difference between the second-person singular and plural forms of the potential paradigm: in the singular the vowel is *į*, but in the plural it is *a*:

Singular	Dual	Plural
1. *mní kte*	*ųyį́ kte*	*ųyą́ pi kte*
2. *ní kte*		*lá pi kte*
3. *yį́ kte*		*yá pi kte*

The verb *iyáyA* 'to set out' has two sets of subject affixes in the 'I' and 'you' forms: *ibláble, ilále, iyáye, ųkíyaye, ųkíyaya pi, ilála pi, iyáya pi*. When this verb is potential, the first affix is as just given, but the second is as in the potential inflection of *yÁ* alone: *iblámni kte, iláni kte*, but *ilála pi kte*. Many Oglalas in the 1990s prefer *iblábli̦ kte, iláli̦ kte*, even though this introduces an unexpected (and unparalleled) /l/ before a nasal vowel.

Another verb that has double inflection is *ʔíyąkA* 'to run':

	Singular	Dual	Plural
1.	*waʔį́mnake* 'I ran'	*ųkʔíyąke* 'you and I ran'	*ųkʔíyąka pi* 'we ran'
2.	*yaʔį́nake* 'you ran'		*yaʔį́naka pi* 'you all ran'
3.	*íyąke* 'he ran'		*íyąka pi* 'they ran'

Two other motion verbs have two different stem forms, one used when there is no personal affix, the other when there is a personal affix. The two are *khiglÁ* 'to set out to go home' and *gličú* 'to set out to come home'. This is the stem form for the third-person forms; the other stems are respectively -*khiyaglA* and -*gliyaču* (some speakers say -*gliyaku*). Compare the following:

Khiglé.	'He set out to go home.'
Wakhíyagle.	'I set out to go home.'
Gličú pi.	'They (distributive) set out to come home.'
Aglíyaču.	'They (collective) set out to come home.'

9.3.6.
Reflexive verbs are those in which the subject and the object refer to the same person: *I cut myself* is an English example.

Lakhota reflexive verbs have the affix *ičʔi* added to the transitive verb: *ičʔíkte* 'to kill oneself' (cf. *kté* 'to kill'), *óʔičʔičiyA* 'to help oneself' (cf. *ókiyA* 'to help').

Table 5. Affix Combinations in Active Transitive Verbs

Subject			Object			
	me	you sg.	him, her, it, them (inanimate)	us	you pl.	them (animate)
I	—	*čhi*	*Ø-wa* *Ø-b* *Ø-m*	—	*čhi...pi*	*wičha-wa* *wičha-b* *wičha-m*
you sg.	*ma-ya* *ma-yal* *ma-yan*	—	*Ø-ya* *Ø-l* *Ø-n*	*ų-ya...pi* *ų-yal...pi* *ų-yan*	—	*wičha-ya* *wičha-l* *wičha-n*
he, she, it	*ma-Ø*	*ni-Ø*	*Ø-Ø*	*ų(k)-Ø...pi*	*ni-Ø...pi*	*wičha-Ø*
we two	—	—	*ų(k)-Ø*	—	—	*wičha'?ų(k)*
we pl.	—	*ų-ni...pi*	*ų(k)-Ø...pi*	—	*ų-ni...pi*	*wičha'?ų(k)...pi*
you pl.	*ma-ya...pi* *ma-yal...pi* *ma-yan...pi*	—	*Ø-ya...pi* *Ø-l...pi* *Ø-n...pi*	*ų-ya...pi* *ų-yal...pi* *ų-yan...pi*	—	*wičha-ya...pi* *wičha-l...pi* *wičha-n...pi*
they animate	*ma-Ø...pi*	*ni-Ø...pi*	*Ø-Ø...pi*	*ų(k)-Ø...pi*	*ni-Ø...pi*	*wičha-Ø...pi*

NOTE: First-person *b-* and *m-* and second-person *(ya)l-* and *(ya)n-* occur with y-stem and nasal-stem verbs, respectively. See 9.3. for further explanation.

The personal affixes are those of the stative paradigm (9.3.1.). There are no collective plural reflexive forms. See Legendre and Rood (1992) for discussion of the abstract syntax of these forms.

Whenever *ič'i* precedes the instrumental prefixes *ya*, *yu*, *ka*, or *pa* (9.2.1.), the reflexive and instrumental affixes fuse to *igla*, *iglu*, *igla*, and *ikpa* respectively.

Here are sample paradigms of *ič'íkte* 'to kill oneself' and *iglúžaža* 'to wash oneself':

Singular	Dual	Plural
1. *mič'íkte* 'I kill myself'	*ųkíč'ikte* 'you and I kill ourselves'	*ųkíč'ikte pi* 'we kill ourselves'
2. *nič'íkte* 'you kill yourself'		*nič'íkte pi* 'you kill yourselves'
3. *ič'íkte* 'he kills himself'		*ičíkte pi* 'they kill themselves'
1. *miglúžaža* 'I washed myself'	*ųkíglužaža* 'you and I washed ourselves'	*ųkíglužaža pi* 'we washed ourselves'
2. *niglúžaža* 'you washed yourself'		*niglúžaža pi* 'you washed yourselves'
3. *iglúžaža* 'he washed himself'		*iglúžaža pi* 'they washed themselves'

There is a second reflexive paradigm (not well studied) in which the initial *i-* of the affix is doubled, without an inserted [?]. Its meaning is approximately that the action was not completely under the control of the subject. Compare: *namíč'iħtake* 'I kicked myself' with *namíič'iħtake* 'I could have kicked myself (for something I did)', or *sabmíč'iye* 'I blackened myself' with *sabmíič'iye* 'I blackened myself for a reason such as mourning.'

9.3.7.

The concept 'each other' is expressed by the affix -*kiči*- (or a variant of this affix) added to transitive verbs. Only dual and plural forms are used, of course. The reciprocal paradigm has these forms:

Dual	Plural
1. *ųkíči*	*ųkíči...pi*
2.	*yeči...pi*
3.	*kiči...pi*

Whenever these are attached to a stem beginning with *ki* or *khi*, that syllable of the verb stem is dropped. Examples of reciprocal verb forms are:

Wašté'ųkičhilake.	'You and I love each other.' (*waštélakA*)
Ųkíčhiza pi.	'We fought with each other.' (*khízA*)
Wąyéčhiyąka pi he?	'Did you see each other?' (*wąyákA*)
Ókičhiya pi.	'They helped each other.' (*ókiyA*)

See 4.3.2.3. for a comment on the nasalization of -*yą*- in 'see'.

9.3.8.

The next three sections of this sketch deal with very complex and highly idiosyncratic features of Lakhota verb inflection. It should be noted that this area of Lakhota grammar is not nearly so well explored as some other areas. Both the morphology and semantics of the paradigms to be discussed are unpredictable and often irregular, and they often vary from community to community and even from speaker to speaker within a community. It is very possible that many unexpected phenomena remain to be discovered here.

The semantic concepts expressed are: reflexive possession (the object of the verb belongs to the subject of the verb), dative (an indirect object, a person other than the subject and object of the verb is affected by the verbal action), and benefactive (one person performs the verbal action for another's benefit or in his place).

The morphological representations of these three are intertwined and often very confusing. The difficulty comes from two facts: the morphemes representing all three concepts have the basic form *ki*; and some instances of *ki* lose the /k/ or the /i/ in certain contexts, and some cause a following /k/ to change to /č/ while others do not. Part of the unpredictability appears to result from homonym avoidance: when words from two of the paradigms could be expected to be alike in form, one is often different through some kind of irregularity.

Carter (1974) is able to explain much, but not all, of this complexity by positing in some forms another morpheme with the shape *i*. This does not explain everything, and it is too abstract an argument for the description here.

When the /i/ of *ki* is lost before /y/, /k/, or /p/, the resulting clusters are, in the first two cases, /gl/, or in the third, /kp/; the specific places where this happens will be discussed below. When the /k/ is lost, the personal affixes coalesce with the remaining /i/ to give *we* 'I', *ye* 'you (agent)', *mi* 'me', *ni* 'you (patient)', and *či* 'I to/for you'. These coalesced affixes always take the stress·when they are the first element in the word.

9.3.8.1.
The fact that the object of the verb is possessed by the subject is shown in Lakhota by adding *ki* after the subject affix.

ki is reduced to /k/ alone before a y-stem verb (9.3.3.), and *ky* becomes /gl/. /i/ is also lost from *ki* before verbs beginning with /p/. When *ki* is used before the instrumental prefix *ka* (9.2.1.), the reflexive possessive affix and the instrumental prefix fuse to /gla/.

In the illustrative paradigms that follow, only the singular and dual forms are given. The corresponding plural words can be formed by adding *pi* to the second and third singular and the dual.

iyéyA 'to find'

This verb illustrates the behavior of the causative auxiliary (9.2.2.) -*yA*; before it the possessive *ki* loses neither *k* nor *i*.

Singular	Dual
1. *iyéwakiye*	*iyé²ųkiye*
'I found mine'	'you and I found ours'
2. *iyéyakiye*	
'you found yours'	
3. *iyékiye*	
'he found his own'	

kté 'to kill'

This verb follows the most regular rules: *ki* loses *k* after personal affixes.

Singular	Dual
1. *wékte*	*ųkíkte*
'I killed mine'	'you and I killed ours'
2. *yékte*	
'you killed yours'	
3. *kikté*	
'he killed his own'	

yuhá 'to have'

In this verb, *ki* is reduced to *k*, which fuses with *y* to form *gl*.

Singular	Dual
1. *waglúha*	*ųglúha*
'I have mine'	'you and I have ours'
2. *yaglúha*	
'you have yours'	
3. *gluhá*	
'he has his own'	

kabléča 'to shatter'

This verb works like *yuhá* but illustrates the *ka*- prefix.

Singular	Dual
1. *waglábleča*	*ųglábleča*
'I shattered mine'	'you and I shattered ours'
2. *yaglábleča*	
'you shattered yours'	
3. *glabléča*	
'he shattered his own'	

pazó 'show; point'

This verb is a verb with initial /p/.

Singular	Dual
1. *wakpázo*	*ųkpázo*
'I showed mine'	'you and I showed ours'
2. *yakpázo*	
'you showed yours'	
3. *kpazó*	
'he showed his own'	

ičú 'take'

This verb requires an extra *k* after the regular *ki*.

Singular	Dual
1. *iwékču*	*ųkíkikču*
'I took mine'	'you and I took ours'

2. *iyékču*
   'you took yours'
3. *ikíkču*
   'he took his own'

áyA 'to take along'

This verb illustrates the verbs of bringing and taking, which prefix *glo-* to form possessives; regular active affixes are then used:

Singular	Dual
1. *waglóʔaye*	*ųglóʔaye*
'I am taking mine along'	'you and I are taking ours along'
2. *yaglóʔaye*	
'you are taking yours along' ·	
3. *gloʔáye*	
'he is taking his along'	

There are other irregularities in the reflexive possessive that have not been illustrated. Some of these are described by Boas and Deloria (1941:86-102), but note that some of the details they give are not valid for Brule and Oglala speakers in the 1990s.

9.3.8.2.

The dative has one form but, from an English speaker's point of view, two meanings: the form can mean that the action was done to an object possessed by someone else ('I took his', 'he ate mine') or that it was done to or for someone else by accident or without his knowledge or permission. This second meaning is sometimes expressed by 'on' in colloquial English ('He ate it up on me'; or 'His wife emptied the bank account on him.'). Boas and Deloria (1941) and Carter (1974) refer to this as the 'first dative.'

The regular affix for these forms is again *ki*, but this *ki* never loses either the *k* or the *i*, nor does it cause a following *k* of the verb root to change to *č*, although *k*s in other prefixes do change.

In verbs of bringing and taking, *ka* is used instead of *ki*, and a *ki* (but an irregular one!) can then also be prefixed (see examples below). Before the causative *-yA*, *khi* is used instead of *ki*. In the sample paradigms that follow, only singular and dual forms are given. As usual, the plural forms differ only by the presence of *pi*.

ičú 'take'
This verb is regular; the affixes are inserted between *i* and *č*.

	mine / it on me	yours / it on you	his / it on him	ours / it on us	theirs / it on them
I	—	*ičíčiču*	*iwákiču*	—	*iwíčhawakiču*
you	*imáyakiču*	—	*iyákiču*	*ųkíyakiču pi*	*iwíčhayakiču*
he	*imákiču*	*iníčiču*	*ikíču*	*ųkíkiču pi*	*iwíčhakiču*
we	—	*ųkíničiču*	*ųkíčiču*	—	*iwíčhųkiču*

pazó 'show'
This verb is also regular; compare with the possessive paradigm above.

	mine / it to me	yours / it to you	his / it to him	ours / it to us	theirs / it to them
I	—	*čhičípazo*	*wakípazo*	—	*wičháwakipazo*
you	*mayákipazo*	—	*yakípazo*	*ųyákipazo pi*	*wičháyakipazo*
he	*makípazo*	*ničípazo*	*kipázo*	*ųkípazo pi*	*wičhákipazo*
we	—	*ųníčipazo*	*ųkípazo*	—	*wičhúkipazo*

ahí 'to arrive, bringing'
This illustrates the pattern common to all 'bring' and 'take' verbs.

	for me	for you	for him	for us	for them
I	—	*čhičáhi*	*wakáhi*	—	*wičháwakahi*
you	*mayákahi*	—	*yakáhi*	*ųyákahi pi*	*wičháyakahi*
he	*makáhi*	*ničáhi*	*kahí*	*ųkáhi pi*	*wičhákahi*
we	—	*ųníčahi*	*ųkáhi*	—	*wičhúkahi*

ahi 'to arrive, bringing'
This illustrates the alternate paradigm with *ki + ka*.

	for me	for you	for him	for us	for them
I	—	*čhíčaʔahi*	*wéčaʔahi*	—	*wičháwečaʔahi*
you	—	—	*yéčaʔahi*	—	*wičháyečaʔahi*
he	*míčaʔahi*	*níčaʔahi*	*kíčaʔahi*	*ųkíčaʔahi pi*	*wičhákičaʔahi*
we	—	*ųníčaʔahi*	*ųkíčaʔahi*	—	*wičhúkičaʔahi*

471

iyéyA 'to find'

This verb illustrates the dative of the causative; compare the possessive causative paradigm given above with the third-person object forms here.

	for me	for you	for him	for us	for them
I	—	*iyéčhičhiye*	*iyéwakhiye*	—	*iyéwičhawakhiye*
you	*iyémayakhiye*	—	*iyéyakhiye*	*iyéʔųyakhiya pi*	*iyéwičhayakhiye*
he	*iyémakhiye*	*iyéničhiye*	*iyékhiye*	*iyéʔųkhiya pi*	*iyéwičhakhiye*
we	—	*iyéʔųničhiye*	*iyéʔųkhiye*	—	*iyéwičhųkhiye*

9.3.8.3.

Benefactive verbal forms imply that the action was undertaken for someone purposefully and with his knowledge and permission. Boas and Deloria (1941) call this the 'second dative.' The regular benefactive has *ki* twice: the first behaves like the reflexive possessive (especially in that *k* is lost after 'I' and 'you' affixes), the second like the dative, except that when the first *ki* is actually present as the first syllable of the word, it is stressed. For example, note *kíčikte* 'He killed it for her'.

Note that in the forms for 'I—you' (*čhi*) and 'he—you' (*ni*) the difference between the dative and the benefactive is expressed solely by the stress position: *čhičíkte* 'I killed yours, I killed it on you' but *čhíčikte* 'I killed it for you'.

The benefactive affixes also occur regularly with intransitive and stative verbs. Observe *omíčimani* 'He travels for me' from *ománi* 'to travel', and *míčiskuye* 'mine is sweet; it's too sweet for me' from *skúyA* 'to be sweet'.

Before -*yA* (the causative auxiliary) *kiči* becomes *kičičhi*, and the first *k* disappears after 'I' and 'you' affixes. 'Bringing' and 'taking' verbs affix *kiči* to *ka* to give the meaning 'bring/take for someone with his permission'.

These forms are very regular (compared, at least, to the reflexive possessives and datives), so only three paradigms are given: a normal one, a 'bring' verb, and a causative.

yustą́ 'to finish'

	for me	for you	for him	for us	for them
I	—	*čhíčiyuštą*	*wéčiyuštą*	—	*wičháwečiyuštą*
you	*miyéčiluštą*	—	*yéčiyuštą*	*ųyéčiluštą pi*	*wičháyečiyuštą*
he	*míčiyuštą*	*níčiyuštą*	*kíčiyuštą*	*ųkíčiyuštą pi*	*wičhákičiyuštą*
we	—	*ųníčiyuštą*	*ųkíčiyuštą*	—	*wičhų́kičiyuštą*

aglí 'to arrive home, bringing'

	for me	for you	for him	for us	for them
I	—	*ačhíčičagli*	*awéčičagli*	—	*awíčhawečičagli*
you	*amíyečičagli*	—	*ayéčičagli*	*ųkáyečičagli pi*	*awíčhayečičagli*
he	*amíčičagli*	*aníčičagli*	*akíčičagli*	*ųkákičičagli pi*	*awíčhakičičagli*
we	—	*ųkáničičagli*	*ųkákičičagli*	—	*ųkáwičhųkičičagli*

iyéyA 'to find'

	for me	for you	for him	for us	for them
I	—	*iyéčhičičhiye*	*iyéwečičhiye*	—	*iyéwičhawečičhiye*
you	*iyémiyečičhiye*	—	*iyéyečičhiye*	*iyéʔųyečičhiya pi*	*iyéwičhayečičhiye*
he	*iyémičičhiye*	*iyéničičhiye*	*iyékičičhiye*	*iyéʔųkičičhiya pi*	*iyéwičhakičičhiye*
we	—	*iyéʔųničičhiye*	*iyéʔųkičičhiye*	*iyéʔųkičičhiye*	*iyéwičhųkičičhiye*

Some speakers can use a few verbs with both the benefactive and the possessive together, but in this case it is the beneficiary, not the object, that is owned. Thus *imíčigluha* 'she is keeping it for me and I belong to her (i.e., I am her relative)'; however, most verbs do not follow this pattern.

There are no reciprocal benefactives, but the reflexive can occur with the benefactives. For verbs that do not lose the *i* of *ki* when they form the possessive, and

for some others, there is no difference between the reflexive direct object form and the reflexive benefactive. Thus from *olé* 'to look for' comes *omíčʔile* 'I'm looking for myself' or 'I'm looking for it for myself'. But in most verbs where the *ki* of the possessive loses the *i*, the reflexive benefactive is formed by adding the reflexive (*ičʔi*, etc.) morpheme to the possessive verb form: *míčʔigluha* 'I am keeping it for myself', or *ųkíʔičʔikču héči* 'let's take it for ourselves (dual)'; but *iglúštą pi* 'they finished it for themselves' has no bene-factive morpheme at all.

Some speakers can inflect verbs for both direct and benefactive objects, but others reject these forms as meaningless. (Neither Buechel 1939 nor Boas and Deloria 1941 mention these paradigms.) The more complex pattern seems to begin with the benefactive form, into which are inserted the transitive affixes appropriate to the nonbenefactive verb. Thus, 'I'm looking for them for you' (verb stem *olé*) goes from *očhíčile* to *owíčhawačhičile*. Other speakers use a para-phrase: *owíčhale mayáši čha očhíčile* 'you told me to look for them so I'm looking for it for you'.

10. ENCLITICS

Except in those instances when a conjunction stands last in the sentence (section 6), postverbal elements belong to the class here called enclitics. These words express aspect, tense, modality, and, in one case, number.

In other descriptions of Lakhota, enclitics have been variously treated as suffixes, adverbs, or auxiliaries, and indeed the decision to treat the most common of them as enclitics rather than suffixes is based on semantics and on native-speaker intuition rather than on phonological criteria. Speakers recognize these words as independent, isolable, and as meaningful. But one-syllable enclitics are frequently not stressed, so they do sound as if they are suffixed to the verb.

There are several dozen of these words (Taylor 1974). Recall that vowel ablaut, in those elements that have final vowel ablaut, is determined by the following enclitic (4.2.6.).

There is a strict order in which enclitics occur, but the 12 position classes defined by this order have few definable semantic correlations. Table 6 includes the enclitics defined and discussed here; others would appear in position 12 on the chart and would have sim-ilar kinds of meanings. Determination of the exact meanings of the enclitics is difficult in some cases, par-ticularly those that express speaker attitude. While their general meaning is clear, individual meanings may vary from speaker to speaker and from situation to situation.

The enclitics are defined and discussed according to the position classes in table 6. Vowel ablaut specifica-tions refer to the effect that the particular enclitic has on a preceding A-final element (4.2.6.).

Some of the words described here are clearly a com-pound of two or more simple enclitics, but such com-pounds will be regarded as units in the discussion.

1. *hĄ;* a-ablaut. Judging from other Siouan languages and Sioux dialects, this is likely the stative verb 'be erect, be upright', but this verb is rare in Lakhota, and in any event semantically distant from the ele-ment here described as an enclitic. *hĄ* indicates that the verbal action or state was continuous at the time under consideration. Compare the following two sentences:
   Táku tókhanu hą he? 'What were you doing?'
   Táku tókhanu he? 'What did you do?'

2. *pi;* a-ablaut. *pi* marks animate plural subjects (9.3.) and pluralizes non–third-person objects (9.3.2.). Numerous examples have already been given.

3. *la;* e-ablaut. *la* denotes the speaker's affection or feeling of endearment with respect to other persons affected by the verbal action or state. The example of *la* is from a folktale:
   Misú, hé wóškatela kį ųspémakhiya pi la he! Míš-eyá waškáte la kte!
   'Little brothers, won't you please teach me that little game; I do so want to play it too!'

Table 6. Lakhota Enclitics

1	2	3	4	5	6	7	8	9	10	11	12	
hĄ	pi	la	kA	ktA	šni	s'a	yo, ye	séčA	kéyA	laȟ	hę	hųsé
							yethó, nithó, įthó	načhéčA	kéya pi	láȟčA	hųwó	čhé
							ye, na			láȟčakA	so, se	ní
											sél	šní
											s'elél	kįló
											yelakhá	ka
											héči	kačhá
											kį	škhÁ
											ye	tkhá
											yeló	
											kšt	
											kštó	
											k'ų	
											yewą, yemá	
											ȟčA	
											įčhéye	

473

4. *kA;* a-ablaut. *kA* attenuates the verbal meaning, 'rather' or 'somewhat' are good English translations of this enclitic:

> *Hé pte-blóka ki očhíšiča ke.*
> 'That bull is acting <u>kind of</u> mad.'

kA can also be used ironically:

> *Hé wašté ke yeló.*
> 'He certainly is a nice guy!' (Meaning: 'He is certainly <u>not</u> a nice person.')

5. *ktA; i-ablaut. ktA* marks a statement as not yet true at the time under discussion. It corresponds to the English future, subjunctive, or, in a sentence about the past, to the future anterior. *ktA* is never used in sentences that are commands.

> <u>*Mní*</u> *kte.* 'I <u>will</u> go.'
> *Yí* <u>*kta*</u> *ehátahaš šíči kte.* 'It <u>will</u> be bad if he <u>goes</u>.'
> *Yí* <u>*kta*</u> *kéye.* 'He said he <u>would</u> go.'

6. *šni;* e-ablaut. *šni* negates the verb with which it occurs.

> *Oyáte ki mní ki yatká pi okíhi pi šni.*
> 'The people could <u>not</u> drink the water.'

7. *s²a;* e-ablaut. *s²a* marks an oft-repeated action; it is frequently accompanied by the adverb *óhiniya* 'always'.

> *Lakhóta ki eháni zuyáya pi* <u>*s²a*</u>.
> 'The Indians <u>often used</u> to go on war parties.'

8. All these enclitics mark commands of various kinds. Several are used by only one sex and not by the other; this explains their rather large number.

Neutral commands are expressed by *yo* (men) and *ye* (women). (These become *wo* and *we* respectively when the immediately preceding word ends in /u/, /ų/, or /o/.) *yo* and *ye* have a-ablaut.

> *Ná khata eyá, wąží ičú* <u>*wo*</u>!
> 'Here are some plums, take one!'

Yethó (men) and *nithó* or *ithó* (women) indicate a familiar request; there is a connotation that the requested action will be of short duration and easy to accomplish. These enclitics call for i-ablaut.

> *Thóhiyąki* <u>*yethó*</u>. '<u>Just</u> wait a <u>minute</u>!'

The enclitics *ye* (men and women) and *na* (women) express a combined command-request. *ye* has i-ablaut, *na* has a-ablaut:

> *Ómakiyi* <u>*ye*</u>, *wanúni ye.* '<u>Please</u> help me, I'm lost!'
> *Mní húh mak²ú* <u>*na*</u>! '<u>Please</u> give me some water.'

Besides these command enclitics, some of the enclitics in position 12 are used in sentences that have the nature of both statements (or questions) and commands. These will be described together with the other enclitics in position 12.

9. *séčA,* e-ablaut; *načhéčA,* a-ablaut. These enclitics indicate that the statement is a conjecture by the speaker. Lakhota speakers translating into English sentences containing these enclitics ordinarily include expressions such as *probably, maybe, I guess, I suppose,* and the like.

> *Ektáwapha ki magážu kte séče.*
> 'It will <u>probably</u> rain later on today.'
> *Iyúha owíčhayuspa pi kta* <u>*načhéče*</u>.
> '<u>I suppose</u> they'll catch them all.'

10. *kéyA* and *kéya pi* are the third-person singular and plural respectively of the verb *kéyA* 'to say that'. Preceding A-words show a-ablaut. When used as enclitics, these words indicate that the speaker is quoting someone else. Such sentences always refer to events or states about which the speaker has no direct, personal knowledge. Hence, *kéyA* and *kéya pi* appear very frequently in historical narratives. The absence of *kéye* or *kéya pi* implies that the speaker has personal knowledge about the event or state he is reporting, unless the context is clearly one of reported information.

> *Čhąkhé thiblóku ki wagláka kéye.*
> 'And then she beheld her elder brother, <u>it is said</u>.'

11. Enclitics in this position all indicate that the speaker is not emotionally neutral to what he is reporting. Feelings indicated include mild yearning, mild discomfort, amusement, and probably others as well. *lah* is a sentence closing form, whereas *láhčA* and *láhčakA* can be followed by enclitics in position 12. Preceding A-words show e-ablaut.

> *Mni-píga wąží wačhí* <u>*lah*</u>!
> '<u>Gee</u>, I <u>sure</u> would like a beer!'
> *Wą líla olúluta lah*!
> '<u>Gosh</u> it <u>sure</u> is sultry! '
> *Iyáyekiya pi* <u>*láhčake*</u>!
> '<u>Boy</u>, did they <u>ever</u> take off!'

12. Several enclitics mark various kinds of questions. *he; hųwó;* a-ablaut. *he* marks a direct question. Although both men and women use *he*, men use *hųwó* (pronounced [h̃wó] in rapid speech) in relatively formal situations. Most questions, even those containing an interrogative word end in *he* or *hųwó.*

> *Tohál ya²ú kta* <u>*he*</u>? 'When will you come<u>?</u>'
> *Wašíču ki Pahá-sápa ki ičú pi šni* <u>*hųwó*</u>?
> 'Did not the White man take the Black Hills<u>?</u>'

so, se; e-ablaut. *So* (men) and *se* (women) mark a dubitative question. There is no presupposition that the person questioned knows the answer:

> *Tóškhe wašíčuya hé eyá pi* <u>*so*</u>?
> '<u>I wonder</u> how you say that in English<u>?</u>'

sél; a-ablaut. *sél* also marks a dubitative question, but it presupposes an affirmative reply:

> *Bébela ki waná yuhá pi* <u>*sél*</u>?
> '<u>I guess</u> they've had their baby by now, <u>huh</u>?'

s²elél; a-ablaut. *s²elél* marks a tag question.

474

Naháȟči wašʔáke šni sʔelél?
'He isn't very strong yet, is he?'

yelakhá; a-ablaut. *yelakhá* marks a sarcastic rhetorical question:

Čhįčá kį hé wakáštake yelakhá.
'Oh, so I'm the one who made the kid cry!'

Two enclitics from position class 12 are used to make deferential suggestions. They share the properties of a rhetorical question and a command.

héči; a-ablaut. *héči* is used when the speaker includes himself as a participant in the proposed action:

Waná ųyą́ pi héči.
'Let's go now!'
'Should we go now?'

Thaló etą́ awáʔu héči.
'Should I bring some meat?'
'How would it be if I brought some meat?'

kį; e-ablaut. *kį* is used when the speaker does not include himself:

Ogná bló etą́ ayáʔu kį.
'Maybe you could bring some potatoes.'
'Would you like to bring some potatoes?'

Several enclitics in position 12 are used to mark sentences that are assertions rather than simple statements. Sentences containing these enclitics often correspond to emphatic statements in English, but many Lakhota examples do not seem to be particularly emphatic. The assertion may be a (generally recognized) fact, or it may be a personal opinion.

ye; e-ablaut. *ye* marks the mild assertion of a generally recognized fact:

Osní ye, thimá glá pi yo!
'It's cold, go back inside!'

yeló (men), *yelé* (obsolescent, women) (*yeló* becomes *weló* when the immediately preceding vowel is /u/, /ų/ or /o/) and *kšt* (men), *kištó* (women; *kištó* is usually pronounced *kštó* in rapid speech) are comparable. *kšt* is stronger than *yeló; kištó* alone is used by most women to correspond to both *yeló* and *kšt* used by men. All require e-ablaut of a preceding A-word.

Há, henáʔųs čhebčhépa pi yeló.
'Yes, each of the two is fat.'

Aǧúyapi-blú etą́ wačhį́ kte kištó.
'I'll need some flour.'

Hi...yá, hé misų́kala kšt.
'No, he is too my younger brother!'

kʔų; e-ablaut. *kʔų* marks a strongly asserted fact; it is often used to make it clear that the reference is to past time or completed action. *kʔų* is pronounced [ų] in rapid speech.

Líla hú-mastáka čha héčhamu wačhį́ šni kʔų.
'I'm very tired and I do not want to do that!'

Hokšíla kį iyéya pi kʔų.
'The boys did leave.'

kį; e-ablaut. *kį* is also used to mark a strong assertion. It can have scolding or sarcastic overtones.

Tókša, ečhámu kte kį.
'Just a minute, I'll do it!'

kšt and *kištó* are probably built on this *kį.*

Asserted opinions are marked by several enclitics that vary from mild to very strong. *wą* (men) and *ma* (women) mark a mild opinion; *yewą́* and *yemá* are stronger. *wą* and *ma* require a-ablaut, *yewą́* and *yemá* require e-ablaut.

Wą hé heyé kʔų héčhetu séča wą.
'Hey, what he said there seems to be right, by gosh!'

Šíyi, kaʔíčhišniyą égnake yemá.
'Mercy me, he went and put it wrong!'

ȟčA; e-ablaut. *ȟčA* is widely used in Lakhota to strengthen the force of an accompanying word. It is thus much more free than most enclitics in terms of its sequential relations with other words. As a sentence-final enclitic, *ȟčA* marks an emphatic statement.

Compare these examples of the two related uses of *ȟčA* (word emphasizer versus sentence emphasizer):

Osní ȟče šni. 'It is not very cold.'
Osní šni ȟče. 'Heh! It's not really cold!'

įčhéye; e-ablaut. *įčhéye* asserts an opinion but presupposes that the interlocutor will agree:

Winóna šų́ka kį wókʔu šni įčhéye.
'Winona didn't feed the dog, right?'

Two (possibly archaic) enclitics mark assertions that the speaker believes to be true, but for which formal proof is lacking. These are *hųšé* and *čhé;* both require a-ablaut. The examples are from Buechel (1939).

Ehą́kʔų maȟpíyata Wakhą́-Thą́ka-thí kį lé thiyópa hųšé.
'Verily this is no other than the house of God and the gate of heaven!'

Táku wówaȟtani waníl tąyéȟči wóʔečhų ihų́nikiya pi kta čhé, eyápi čhé.
'I believe that they will finish everything blamelessly and well, as they say they will.'

ní; a-ablaut. A strong wish that something might come about is expressed by *ní:*

Hu-makáweǧe šni ní!
'I hope I don't break my leg!'

Wakhą́-Thą́ka ų́šimala ní!
'May God have mercy on me!'

Probably based on this *ni* is *šní* (note the stress), which expresses a similar strong desire. *šní* requires e-ablaut.

Hé šų́ka kį hé kté šní.
'I wish he would kill that dog!'
'He really ought to kill that dog!'

kįló; e-ablaut. a strong warning is expressed by *kįló:*

Niyáñ take kįló!
'Hey, watch out, he'll bite you!'

Two enclitics are used to mark emphatic negative sentences. These are *ka* and *kačhá*. Both require e-ablaut of preceding A-words.

Tasé héčhamu wačhį ka!
'Of course I do not want to do that!'
Wówaši-ečhú kačhá!
'He certainly does not work!'

kačhá usually has sarcastic or deprecating connotations. A better translation for the last example would be 'Don't tell me he works!'

škhÁ; a-ablaut. *škhÁ* is used to indicate that the statement is received knowledge, something about which the speaker has no direct, personal knowledge. As such, it appears frequently in historical and especially mythological narratives. Its meaning is 'purportedly, supposedly, allegedly'.

Iktómi kákhena tokhé ečháčha ománi-yá hạ škhé.
'Iktomi (Trickster) was walking around aimlessly over there (they say).'

tkhá; a-ablaut. *tkhá* is frequently shortened to *khá*. The enclitic appears to have several somewhat similar meanings, but the principal use is in conditional statements.

Máza-ská etạ awá²u kta tkhá.
'I should have brought some money.'
Čhạ wạ bluhá k²eš sịté-ñla kị wakát²a tkhá.
'If I had (had had) a stick I would kill (would have killed) the rattle snake.'
Lehạyela mat²á tkhá.
'I almost died.' ('I would have died if...')
Wičháñčala kị hé išnála thí hạ tkhá.
'That old man was living alone until recently.'

11. SELECTED VOCABULARY

The symbols A and Ạ at the ends of verbs in this list represent a vowel that changes, depending on grammatical context (4.3.2.6.).

airplane *kịyékhiyapi* 'they make them fly (in them)'

alive *ní*

animal *wamákhaškạškạ* 'those moving about on the earth'

ankle *iškáhu*

ant *thažúška*

antelope *thathókala* 'antelope; domestic goat'

anus *ųzé* 'anus; buttock'

apple *thaspạ*

Arapaho *Mañpíyathó* 'Blue-sky (Indian)' (This is apparently a reference to tattoos.)

Arikara *Paláni* 'Arikara, Ree'

476 arm *istó*

arrow *wahįkpe*

artichoke *phạǧí* (Jerusalem artichoke; domestic turnip)

ash tree *pséñtị*

ashes *čhañóta*

Assiniboine *Hóhe*

aunt *thụwí* 'father's sister' (The mother's sister is called 'mother'.)

aurora borealis *wanáǧiwačhípi* 'spirit dance'

automobile *iyéčhịkịyạke* 'runs by itself'

awl See needle

axe *nazúspe; ičákse* 'instrument for chopping'

baby *hokšícala*
  bébela (this is probably a loanword from French *bébé*)

back *hịyéte* 'upper back'
  čhuwí 'back below shoulder blades'

bacon *waší* 'bacon; animal fat'

bad *šíčA*

badger *ñoká*

ball *thápa*

bathe *nuwÁ* 'to swim, to bathe'

be *é* 'be a particular one (of animate things only)'; *hÁ* 'be upright (of inanimate things only)'; *héčha* 'be such a one, be of such a kind'; *hiyéyA* 'be located here and there (of inanimate things only)'; *ú* 'be, exist (of animate things only); be located somewhere (of all things)'; *yukhÁ* 'have, be (of intimate possessions only)'; *níčA* 'not to have, not to be (of intimate posessions only)'

beads *pšithó*

beadwork *wakšúpi* 'decoration'

beans *omníča*

bear *mathó*

beautiful See good

beaver *čhápa*

bed *oyúke*

bee *theñmúǧazizíla* 'little yellow banded fly'

beer *mnipíǧa*

bell *ñláñla*

belly *thezí*

bent *škópA*

big *thạka*

bighorn sheep See mountain sheep

bird *zịtkála*

bite *yañtákA*

bitter *phá*

black *sápA*

blackbird *wáȟpatháka*

Blackfeet Sioux *Sihásapa*

Black person *Hásapa* 'black skin'

blood *wé*

blue *thó* 'blue; green'

boil *píǧA* 'to be boiling'; *piȟyÁ* 'to cause to boil'

bone *hohú*

book *wówapi* 'book; letter; flag'

bow *itázipa*

boy *hokšíla*

brain *nasúla*

brave *ohítikA*

bread *aǧúyapi*

break *kawéǧA*

breast *azé* 'female breast'

breechcloth *čhegnáke* 'penis cover'

bring *ahí* 'to bring here'; *aʔú* 'to be bringing here'; *ahíyu* 'to leave to bring here'; *aglí* 'to bring home here'; *akú* 'to be bringing home here'; *aglíyaču* 'to leave to bring home here'

brother *čhiyé* 'older brother of a man'; *thibló* 'older brother of a woman'; *sukála* 'younger brother of man or woman'

brown *ǧí*

Brule Sioux *Sičháǧú* 'burned thigh'

buffalo cow *pté*

buffalo berry *maštíčaphuté* 'rabbit lip'

buffalo bull *thatháka*

bug *wablúška*

burn *ilé* burn, blaze up; *špá* 'to be burned, to be cooked (food), to be ripe (fruit)'

bush *hú*

butcher *phátA*

butterfly *kimímila*

buttock See anus

buy *ophéthu*

buzzard *hečá*

cactus *ukčéla*

cafe *owótethípi* 'eating house'

calf of leg *hučhóǧi*

carry on back *kʔí* 'carry; pack'

cat *igmúla*

catch *oyúspA*

chair *čhaʔákayakápi* 'wood to sit on'

cherry See chokecherry

chest *makhú*

Cheyenne *Šahíyela*

chicken *khokhéyaȟʔala; khokhóyaȟʔala* 'chicken, rooster'

chief *itháčha*

child *wakháyeža*

Chippewa see *Ojibwa*

chokecherry *čhaphá*

church *owáčhekiye* 'prayer places'; *thípiwakhá* 'holy house'

claw *šaké* 'claw (of animal or bird); fingernail (of human)'

cloth *mniȟúka*

cloud See sky

coat See shirt

coffee *wakhályapi*

cold *čhuwíta* 'to feel cold (internal sensation; used of animate things only)'; *sní* 'to feel cold (external sensation; used of inanimate things only)'; *osní* (used of atmosphere and weather)

come *glí* 'arrive at home here'; *gličú* 'leave for home here'; *hí* 'arrive here'; *hiyú* 'leave for here'; *kú* 'be on the way home here'; *ú* 'be on the way here'

converse *wóglakA* 'converse, talk'

cook *špayÁ* 'to cause to be burned; be cooked'; see burn

corn *wagmíza*

cottonwood *wáǧačhá* 'brittle wood'

count See read

cow *ptegléška, ptebléška* 'spotted buffalo'; *ptewániyapi* 'pet buffalo'

cowbird *wáȟpaȟóta*

coyote *šuŋmánitu* 'wilderness dog'; *mayásleča*

cradleboard *iyókʔipa*

crane *phehá*

crazy *witkó*

Cree *Šahíya*

creek *wakpála*

cricket *psipsíčala* 'little hopper'

crippled *hušté*

crow *khaǧí*

Crow *Khaǧíwičháša* 'Crow person'; *psáloka* (borrowed from Crow)

cry *čhéyA*

cup *wíyatke* 'instrument for drinking'

cut *waksáksA*

dance *wačhí* 'to dance'; *wačhípi* 'a dance'

day *ạpétu*

daughter *čhụkší*

deer *tháȟča*

die *tʔÁ* 'be dead'

digging stick *wíwopta* 'instrument for digging'

dish *wakšíča*

do *ečháʔụ, ečhú*

dog *šúka*

donkey *súsụla* 'donkey; mule'

door *thiyópa*

dragonfly *thuswéča*

dream *iháblA*

dress *čhuwígnaka* 'back cover'

dried meat *pápa*

drink *yatkÁ*

drum *čhácheǧa* 'wooden kettle'

dry *sáka*

duck *maǧá, maǧáksiča*

eagle *wạblí*

ear *núǧe* 'human ear'; *nakpá* 'animal ear'

earring *owị*

earth *makhá* 'earth, dirt'

east *wiyóhịyạpata* 'where the sun comes up'

eat *yútA*

eat up *thebyÁ*

egg *wítka* 'egg; testicle'

eight *šaglóǧạ*

elk *heȟáka* 'branched horns'

elm *pʔéčhạ*

enemy *thóka*

fall (season) *ptạyétu*

fall down *hịȟpáyA*

fat *čhépA* 'to be fat'; see also bacon

father *até* (term of address); *atéwaye kị* 'the one I have for father'

feather *wíyaka*

female *wíyela*

field See garden

fingernail See claw

fire *phéta*

478   firefly *ụzéblinkblink* 'blinking arse' (jocose)

fish *hoǧá*

five *záptạ*

flag *wówapi*

flea *psičála; hála*

flower *wanáȟča*

fly *theȟmúǧa, thoȟmúǧa, thaȟmúǧa* 'housefly; horsefly'; *kịyÁ* 'to fly'

fog *pʔó*

food *wóyute*

foot *sí*

forehead *ithúhu*

four *tópa, tób*

fox *thokhála, šụǧíla*

frog *gnašká*

gall bladder *phizí*

garden *wóžupi* 'garden, field'

gasoline See grease

gas station *wíglioʔínaži* 'gasoline stopping place'

girl *wičhíčala;* See also woman

give *kʔú*

give back *kičhú*

go *yÁ;* be on the way there; *glÁ* be on the way home there; *í* arrive there; *khí* arrive at home there; *iyáyA* leave for there; *khiglÁ* leave for home there

goat *tháȟča šúkala* 'dog deer'

good *wašté* 'good; beautiful'

goose *maǧášapa* 'dirty duck'

government (U.S.) *thụkášila* 'grandfather'

grandchild *thakóža*

grandfather *thụkášila*

grandmother *ụčí* (maternal), *khụší* (paternal)

grape *čhụwíyapehe* '(it) wraps around a tree'

grass *pheží*

grasshopper *gnugnúška; phežíhophop* 'grasshopper' (jocose) (note that /p/ is not replaced by /b/)

gray *ȟóta*

grease *wígli* 'grease; gasoline, oil'

green See blue

grind *yukpá*

Gros Ventre See Hidatsa

guts *šupé*

hail *wasú*

hair *phehí* 'head hair'

hairpipe breastplate *wawóslatawanápʔị* 'hairpipe necklace'

hand *napé*

hard *sutá*

hat *waphóštą*

have *yuhá* (used only of alienable things); see also be

hawk *chetą́*

head *natá, phá*

hear *naȟʔų́*

heart *chąté*

heavy *tké*

heron *hokhá*

Hidatsa *Ȟewáktokta* 'Hidatsa, Gros Ventre'

high *wąkátuya*

hill *pahá*

hit *aphÁ*

horns *hé*

horse *šųkawakhą́* 'wonderful dog'

    drafthorse *šųȟwówaši* 'working horse'

    mare *šųȟwíyela* 'female horse'

    saddle horse *šųkʔákąyąkapi* 'horse they sit on'

    stallion *šųkhíyuȟa* 'breeding horse'

hospital *okhúžethípi* 'sick house'

hot *khátA*

house *chą́thipi* 'wooden lodge'

Hunkpapa Sioux *Hų́kpapha* 'Hunkpapa, Standing Rock Sioux'

husband *hįgná*

ice *chághá*

Indian *Lakhota* 'Sioux Indian; American Indian'

iron see metal

jail *okáškethípi* 'detention house'

jerkey *wakáblapi* 'what has been pounded flat'

jump *psíčA*

June berry *wípazųtka, wípazųtką, wípazukha*

kettle *chéǧa*

kick *naȟtákA*

kidney *ažų́tka*

kill *kté*

knee *chąkpé*

knife *míla*

know *slolyÁ*

lake *blé*

land *makhóče*

laugh *iȟá* 'laugh; smile'

leaf *waȟpé*

leather *theȟpí*

left-handed *chatką́*

leg *hú*

legging *hųská*

lie (recline) *yųkÁ*

lie down *ȟpáyA*

light in weight *kapʔóžA*

lightning *wakį́yątųwápi* 'The Thunderers are blinking'

like *waštélakA* 'to like'; *sʔe* 'like, as, as though'

lip, lower *ihá*

    upper *phuté*

little *chíkʔala, chístila, chíschila*

live *thí*

liver *phí*

lizard *agléška*

lodge *thípi*

lodge cover *ákaȟpe*

lodge pole *thušú*

look for *olé*

louse *héya*

love *theȟíla*

Lower Brule Sioux *Khulwíchaša* 'Lower person'

lung *chaǧú*

magpie *halháta; ųkčékiȟa* 'buries his dung'

make *káǧA*

male *bloká*

man *wičháša*

    young man *khoškálaka*

    old man *wičháȟčala*

Mandan *Miwátani*

mare See horse

meadowlark *thašíyagnupá*

meat *thaló*

medicine *phežúta* 'herbal roots'

metal (iron) *máza*

Mexican *spayóla* (This is probably a loanword from French *espagnol*)

milk *asápi*

Milky Way *wanáǧithachą́ku* 'ghost road'

mink *íkhusą*

Minneconjou Sioux *Mnikhówožu* 'those who plant by water', *Mnikhówąžu* mirror *míyoglas'į*

moccasin *hąm'íkčeka* 'ordinary shoe'

money *mázaská* 'silver' 'white metal'

moon *wí* 'luminary'; *hąhépiwí* 'night luminary'

mosquito *čhaphúka*

mother *iná* (term of address); *ináwaye kį* 'the one I
  have for mother'

mountain *ȟé*

mountain lion *igmúthąka* 'big cat'

mountain sheep *héčhįškayapi* 'they make spoons
  from their horns'

mouse *ithúkala*

mouth *í*

movie *wówapiškąská* 'moving picture'

mule See donkey

muskrat *sįkphé, sįkphéla*

mustache *phutíhį* 'upper lip hair'

narrow *očík'a*

navel *čhekpá*

necklace *wanáp'į*

needle *thahíšpa* 'needle, awl'

new (young) *théča* 'new; young'

night *hąhépi*

nine *napčíyųka*

north *wazíyata*

northern lights See aurora borealis

nose *phasú*

nostril *phaȟláte*

Oglala Sioux *Oglála* 'Oglala Sioux, Pine Ridge
  Sioux'

oil See grease

Ojibwa *Ȟaȟáthųwą* 'those who live at the falls'

old *ká* 'old, worn out'

one *wáči* (used in counting); *wąží* (used in specifying an amount)

onion *pšį*

otter *ptą́*

owl *hįhą́*

pack *wak'į* 'backpack'

paint See write

pants See trousers

parfleche bag *wókpą*

pemmican *wasná*

penis *čhé; susú* 'testicle(s); male genitals'

people *oyáte* 'people; tribe'

pepper *yamnúmnuǧapi, yamnúmnužapi* (This term
  originally referred to the berries of the hackberry
  tree.)

picture *itówapi*

pig *khukhúše*

pigeon *wakįyela*

pine *wazí*

Pine Ridge Sioux See Oglala Sioux

pipe *čhąnúpa*

pipestem *čhąnúpasįté* 'pipe tail'

play *škátA*

plum *khą́ta*

porcupine *phahį́* 'sharp hair'

potato *bló*

prairie chicken *šiyó*

prairie dog *pispíza* 'squeaking, barking'

puppy *šųȟpála*

quillwork *wóska*

quilt *owįža*

rabbit *maštį́ča, maštį́čala*

racoon *wičhítegleǧa* 'striped face'

rain *maǧážu*

rainbow *wígmuke* 'snare, trap'

rattle *wagmúha*

rattlesnake *sįtéȟla* 'rattle tail'

rawhide *thahálo*

read *yawá* 'read; count'

red *šá*

relative *otákuye*

rib *thučhúhu*

rice *psį́*

rifle *mázawahką́* 'wonderful metal'

ripe See cook

river *makhízita*

root *húta*

rope *wíkhą*

Rosebud Sioux See Brule Sioux

run *íyąkA*

sack *wóžuha*

saddle *čhą́wak'į* 'wooden back rack'

salt *mniskúya* 'sweet water'

Sans Arc Sioux *Itázibčhó* 'those without bows'

Santee Sioux *Isą́yethi*

say *eyÁ*

480

school *owáyawa* 'reading place'

see *wayákA*

seven *šakówi*

sew *kayéǧA*

sharp (edge) *phé*

sharp (point) *phéstola*

shawl *šiná*

sheep *héčhiškayapi* 'they make spoons from their horns' 'bighorn sheep, mountain sheep'; *ptíčala* 'domestic sheep'

shield *waháčhaka*

shin *hubló*

shirt (coat) *ógle*

shoe *hápa*

shoot *khuté*

short *ptéčela*

Shoshone *Súsuni*

shoulder *abló*

sick *khúžA* 'to be nauseous'; *yazÁ* 'to hurt'

sinew *khá*

sing *lowá*

sister *thaké* 'older sister of a man'; *čhuwé* 'older sister of a woman'; *thakší* 'younger sister of a man'; *thaká* 'younger sister of a woman'

sit *yakÁ*

sit down *íyotakA*

six *šákpe*

skinny *thamáheča*

skunk *maká*

sky *maȟpíya* 'sky; cloud'

sleep *ištímA* 'to be asleep'

sleepy *ȟwá*

smoke *šóta*; *úpA* 'to smoke tobacco'

snake *zuzéča*

snow *wá* 'fallen snow'; *ičámna* 'falling snow'

socks *huyáku*

soda pop *kaphópapi* 'bursting, popping'

soft *phašpháža*

son *čhikší*

soup *wahápi*

south *itókağata*

speak *iyÁ*

spear *wahúkheza*

spider *iktó; iktómi*

spoon *čhiška*

spring (season) *wétu*

spring of water *wiwíla*

squash *wagmú* 'squash; gourd'

squirrel *zičá*

stand *ognáke* 'stand, chest'; *náži* 'be standing'

stand up *ínaži*

Standing Rock Sioux   See Hunkpapa Sioux

star *wičháȟpi*

stone *íya; iȟ'é*

store *mas'óphiye* 'cashbox'

stove *očhéthi*

sugar *čhahápi* 'tree juice'

summer *blokétu*

sun *wí* 'luminary'; *ápawí* 'day luminary'

sunflower *waȟčází* 'yellow flower'

swallow *ištáničatháka* 'cliff or barn swallow'; *napčÁ* 'to swallow; to internalize knowledge'

sweet *skúyA*

swim See bathe

table *wáglotapi*

tail *sité*

talk See converse

take *a'í* 'to take or convey there'; *akhí* 'to take or convey home there'; *áyA* 'to be taking or conveying there'; *aglÁ* 'to be taking or conveying home there'; *éyayA* 'to leave to take or convey there'; *akhíyaglA* 'to leave to take or convey home there'

take *ičú* 'take, get'

tall *háskA* 'tall; long'

tea *waȟpé* 'leaves'; *waȟpékhalyápi* 'leaf beverage'

telephone *mas'ápha*

ten *wikčémna*

tepee See lodge

testicle *itká*; see also egg

Teton Sioux *thíthuwa*

thick *šókA*

thigh (side) *sičhá*

    (front) *šúte*

thin *zizípa*

three *yámni*

throat *loté*

thunder *wakíyaȟothúpi* 'The Thunderers are calling'

tired *watúkha, hústakA*

tobacco *čhalí*

tomato   See wildrose

tongue   *čheží*

tooth   *hí*

travois   *čhuwíčʔipa*

tree   *čhą́* 'tree; wood'

tribe   See people

trousers   *ųzóǧi*

turkey   *waglékšą*

turnip   *thípsila* 'wild turnip'; see also artichoke

turtle   *khéya*

two   *núpa, núm*

Two-Kettle Sioux   *Oʔóhenúpa* 'those who boil meat twice'

uncle   *lekší* 'mother's brother' (The father's brother is called 'father'.)

use   *ų́* 'use; wear'

vegetation   *wóȟe* 'weeds'

vulva   *šą́*

wagon   *čhąpágmiyąpi* 'wood that is made to roll along'

walk   *máni*

warbonnet   *wapháha*

warclub   *íyąkapémnipi* 'stone club'

wash   *yužáža*

water   *mní*

watermelon   *špą́šniyutápi* 'they eat it raw'; *wagmúšpąšni* 'uncooked squash'

wear   See use

weasel   *ithų́kasą́, ithų́kasą́la*

weed   See vegetation

west   *wíyoȟpeyata* 'where the sun goes down'

wet   *spáyA*

whiskey   *mníwakhą́* 'wonderful water'

white   *są́* 'dull white'; *ská* 'clear white'

White man   *Wašíčų, Wašíču*

wide   *ópta*

wife   *thawíču*

wildrose   *ųžį́žįtka* 'rose hip; tomato'

willow   *čhąšáša* 'red stem dogwood'; *čhąwíwila* 'common willow'

wind   *thaté*

window   *ožą́žąglepi* 'frame to admit light'

wing   *ȟupáhu*

winter   *waníyetu*

woman   *wį́yą* 'woman'; *wikhóškalaka* 'young woman'; *winúȟčala* 'old woman'

wolf   *šųŋmánituthą́ka* 'big coyote'

wood   See tree

write   *owá* 'write; paint'

Yankton Sioux   *Ihą́gthųwą* 'those dwelling at the end'

yellow   *zí*

young   See new

Sketch of the Zuni Language

STANLEY NEWMAN

The Zuni language is spoken in western New Mexico in a pueblo with a population of about 8,000 in 1990 (Bureau of Indian Affairs 1991:table 3). Though English is commonly used, especially among the young people, in the 1990s Zuni was still the language of the home and continued to be the principal medium of communication in the pueblo (Edmund J. Ladd, communication to editors 1994).

The Zuni have been studied by anthropologists since the 1870s. The basic linguistics sources are Bunzel (1932, 1933, 1933-1938) and Newman (1958, 1965); these and other sources are cited by I. Davis (1979:398-399).

Compared to most languages, Zuni has a simple phonology. The inventory of phonemes consists of 16 consonants and 10 vowels. The heavy stress of the word falls regularly on the first syllable, that is, stress plays no functional role in the language. Words tend to be composed of single consonants followed by single vowels. Clusters of two consonants at the beginning or end of words, or as many as three consonants medially, are limited to only a few types of consonantal sequences. There are no vowel clusters.

Only a small number of phonemic shifts result from the influence of neighboring sounds. But changes conditioned by neighboring morphemes or words are more involved. Particularly complex are the various processes that give rise to short versus long forms of morphemes. Thus, word-final phonemes may be reduced or zeroed, depending upon the position of the word in the utterance. Some stems and affixes appear in forms of different length, the proper form being determined by the class of morphemes to which it is juxtaposed: *teyaʔu-*, *teyaˑ-*, and *tey-* are stems of *teyaʔu* 'to begin'; *-ʔan*, *-an*, *-n*, and *-Ø* are forms of one of the subordinating suffixes. A stem of several syllables may be abbreviated to the first syllable when it precedes other stems.

Zuni is primarily a suffixing language. Suffixes account for the inflections, that is, for the morphological processes that identify the word classes—the "parts of speech." The verb is marked inflectionally for tense, mode, or subordination, the noun for number, and the pronoun for number and case; the particle is uninflected. Only a single inflectional suffix, attached finally, can be added to a word. Most of the derivations are also expressed by suffixes, which precede the inflectional elements. Other affixing processes include some half-dozen prefixes and a few enclitics. Reduplication occurs, but it is limited to one of the 10 verb classes. Compounding is employed only in constructing nouns and particles; it is not a process for building verbs.

Among the word classes, the verb takes the heaviest morphological load. Its tense inflections include a suffix denoting the past as well as such tense-mode suffixes as the past conditional, the negative future, and the present or imperative. Two purely modal inflections—the hortatory and the permissive—comprise the category of mode. The subordinating suffixes, the most numerous of the inflections, express a variety of functions: one suffix, for example, indicates that the subordinate verb has the same subject as the following verb in the sentence, another that it has a different subject; another subordinating element forms modifiers that function like English adjectives or adverbs; and another refers to an event contemporaneous with that of the main verb. In addition to the inflections, most derivations of the verb are also expressed by suffixes; prefixation, reduplication, and suppletion (the complete replacement of a stem) play a minor role. The categories covered by derivations are those of voice (causative, reflexive), aspect (static, continuative), mode (indeterminate, negative), number (plural subject of transitive verb, plural subject of intransitive verb), and collectivity ('to be objects in a shallow container', 'to be objects growing together on the ground').

The noun has a simple inflectional system consisting of singular versus plural. The only derivational suffixes of the noun are those referring to various types of collectivity, and some of these suffixes the noun shares with the verb. In contrast to verbs, nouns can be formed by compounding.

Pronominal reference is expressed by independent words. The inflectional paradigm of the pronouns is built upon three stems, distinguishing first, second, and third persons. The pronouns are inflected for case (subject, object, possessive) as well as for number (singular, dual, plural). No derivational processes are associated with this class of words.

In many languages the particles—the uninflected words—consist of a small closed class of words belonging to a few functional types, such as conjunctions, relaters (such as 'in', 'at'), numerals, and exclamatives. But in Zuni they encompass a major portion of the vocabulary. Many of them are equivalent in meaning and syntactic function to English nouns and adjectives, as *tepi* 'bobcat' or *ʔančiʔmowa* 'dirty'. Since these uninflected words behave morphologically like *taˑp* 'and' or *ʔakka* 'in, with, because', they are classed as particles. Words of this class, although they do not participate in any inflections, undergo derivational processes. The particle-forming processes are few. Each of the derivational suffixes is limited to particles of a narrow semantic type: one suffix, for example, denotes familiarity and is added to some of the kinship terms; another is attached to tribal names to indicate behavior attributed to members of the tribe. In addition to suffixing, particles may also be derived by compounding.

In Zuni sentences the verb functions as the predicating element. A noun, pronoun, or particle may play the role of a substantive—that of denoting a subject or object. Word order is fairly free, but a few sequential patterns are invariable. The predicate verb always occurs finally in the simple sentence. In a complex sentence the independent predication—the main clause—appears last, with its verb placed at the end; each preceding dependent predication is also terminated by a verb, marked inflectionally by one of the subordinating suffixes. A typical Zuni sentence from one of the Coyote stories will illustrate some of the grammatical features of the language; each of the predications is translated separately.

tom tem leˑ hoł susk ʔaˑn-ap (just yet thus perhaps coyote go-subordinate)* 'after Coyote had gone just a little way'; *łapaˑ nišapak ʔaˑ-laʔhi-p* (flapping.noise mourning.dove plural.subject-fly-subordinate) 'when

*In order to facilitate the comprehension of examples, the following conventions are observed in illustrative sentences. In the Zuni sentence a hyphen separates the affix under scrutiny from the remainder of the stem. The literal translation follows the Zuni word order; each word or, in the hyphenated word, each morpheme is glossed by a single English word, wherever possible, or by a group of words separated by periods. This word-by-word rendition is followed by a free translation.

the mourning doves flew with a flapping noise'; *s yam tena·n ?okk?a-kka* (then his song-singular lose-past) 'he lost his song'.

In the first subordinate clause *susk*, a reduced form of *suski* 'Coyote', is a particle, uninflected like *tom* or *tem*; it is the subject of the subordinate verb *?a·nap*. In the second predication the prefix of the subordinate verb, which again appears last, indicates that the subject is plural, though *nišapak* 'mourning dove(s)' the particle subject, has no indication of number. The independent predication terminates the sentence with a verb containing a tense inflection; the object of the verb is an inflected noun, *tenan*, reduced from *tenanne* 'song'.

THE SYSTEM OF SOUNDS

1. PHONEMES

Zuni operates with 16 consonant and 10 vowel phonemes: *p, t, c, č, k, kʷ, ?, s, š, ł, h, m, n, l, w, y; i, i·, e, e·, a, a·, o, o·, u, u·*.[†] Stress is not phonemically significant: a heavy stress falls automatically on the first syllable of the word unit, and other syllables take a weaker level of stress.

1.1. STOPS AND AFFRICATES

Before vowels, *p, t,* and *?* are voiceless, lenis, and unaspirated; *k, kʷ, c,* and *č* are voiceless, fortis, and aspirated. Before consonants these sounds are unreleased.

p—bilabial stop, as in English *spin*, Spanish *padre*

t—interdental stop, as in Spanish *todo*

c—alveolar affricate, like the *ts* in English *hats*

č—alveopalatal affricate, like *ch* in English *church*

k—actualized in two positional variants: velar stop before *o* or *u*, as in English *cool*; palatal stop before *i, e,* or *a*, as in English *cute*

kʷ—labiovelar stop, as in English *quick*

?—glottal stop, as in English colloquial negation *uh-uh* or *mh-mh*

When any of these sounds (except *?*) is followed by *?*, a phonetically glottalized (ejective) consonant is produced: thus, the palatal release and the glottal release in *k?awe?* 'water' are approximately simultaneous, and this phonetic fusion takes place across word boundaries as well as within words.

1.2. SPIRANTS

Zuni spirants are always voiceless.

s—alveolar spirant, as in English *so*

š—alveopalatal spirant, as in English *show*

[†]The phonemic orthography used here is the same as that of Newman (1965). It differs from the practical orthography of the dictionary (Newman 1958), where ch, j, lh, q, sh, z, /, and (V)· referred, respectively, to the units symbolized by *č, h, ł, kʷ, š, c, ?,* and (V)· in this sketch.

In writing unassimilated or partly assimilated loanwords a few additional letters are used. In the loanwords *meliqa* 'White man' and *qapo* 'cowboy' *q* represents a velar stop (vol. 9:468), which contrasts with the regular palatalized variant [k̲] or Zuni *k* before *a* (see 1.1.). Technical discussions of the theoretical problems raised by the presence of this new sound sequence may be found in Michaels (1971).

ł—lateral spirant, which has no equivalent in English or in the more familiar European languages. It can be approximated by whispering a clear *l* sound and simultaneously producing friction by releasing an *h* over one side of the tongue.

h—actualized in two positional variants: glottal spirant before vowels, as in English *hot*; velar spirant elsewhere, like the Spanish *j* in *jota* or the German *ch* in *doch*

1.3. CONTINUANTS

The continuant sounds—*m, n, l, w, y*—are most commonly voiced; but they may be optionally unvoiced before *h* or *?*, either within words or across word boundaries.

m—bilabial nasal, as in English *man*

n—actualized in two positional variants: velar nasal before *k* or *kʷ*, as in English anchor; alveolar nasal elsewhere, as in English *none*

l—apical lateral, like the *l* in Spanish *lata*

w—rounded bilabial semivowel, as in English *will*

y—palatal semivowel, as in English *yard*

1.4. VOWELS

A fundamental distinction is made between short and long vowels, the long indicated by a raised period: *?a·k?oka* 'they cried' but *?ak?o·ka* 'he dug a hole'. Short vowels assume a slight increment of length when they occur in the initial open syllable of a word.

i—high front vowel, varying between close and open; most commonly actualized with the close quality of English *seat* but in weak-stressed syllables or in rapid speech taking on the open quality of English *sit*

i·—high front close vowel, as in English *see*

e, e·—mid-front vowels, varying between open and close; usually open, as in English *men* but occasionally pronounced like the close vowel of French *été*

a, a·—low central vowels, as in Spanish *casa*

o, o·—mid-back rounded vowels, varying between open and close; most frequently open, with the quality of the vowel in English *law* or French *botte* but sometimes like the close vowel in French *beau*

u—high back rounded vowel, varying between close and open; most commonly a close vowel, as in English *pool*, but occasionally actualized with the open quality of English *pull*

u·—high back rounded close vowel, as in English *rule*

2. PHONEMIC STRUCTURE OF SYLLABLES AND WORDS

In any sequence of phonemes, vowels always occur singly and are flanked either by consonants or word borders. Consonants appear singly or in clusters, depending upon the position of the cluster in the syllable and the position of the syllable in the word.

Syllabic structure is most conveniently described in terms of the initial borders, vowel nuclei, and final borders of syllables. All syllables must begin with at least one consonant. When the initial border of a syllable is a single consonant (CV, CVC, or CVCC), any consonant may fill this position. When the initial border is a cluster (CCV, CCVC, or CCVCC), this position is limited to *c?*, *č?*, *k?*, and *kʷ?*. Furthermore, *kʷ* and *kʷ?* are restricted in occurrence before vowels: they can precede *i*, *i·*, *e*, *e·*, *a*, *a·* but not *o*, *o·*, *u*, *u·*.

The single vowel that always forms the syllable nucleus may be long or short, and it may be preceded by one or two consonants. A short vowel may occur word-finally or be followed by one or two consonants. A long vowel may terminate the syllable or be followed by a single consonant; it may be followed by two consonants only if the second is a glottal stop.

When the final border of a syllable is a single consonant, it may be filled by any consonant. Similarly, any consonant may be the first member of a final cluster. Restrictions apply only to the second consonant of a final border and are contingent upon the character of the preceding consonant: if the first member of a final cluster is *c*, *č*, *kʷ*, or *l*, the following consonant must be an identical consonant or a glottal stop (e.g., *-cc* or *-c?*).

The structural minimum of the syllable, then, may be symbolized as CV. With (C) indicating an optional consonant and V· a long vowel, the syllabic types can be summarized as: (C)CV(C)(C), (C)CV·(C)(?).

The only syllables that may occur in any position within the word are those beginning in a single consonant and ending in a single consonant or a vowel. Syllables beginning with two consonants are limited to word-initial position, as in *k?okš?amme* 'it is not good'; however, the sole clusters found initially are *c?*, *č?*, *k?*, and *kʷ?*. When these clusters appear in the middle of words, they belong to two syllables, for in this position they are paralleled by other clusters that never occur initially and can be regarded only as ambisyllabic: thus, the *k?* in *ka·k?i* 'sometime' must be analyzed as belonging to two syllables because it is structurally equivalent to the strictly ambisyllabic clusters in *?eł?e* 'corpse', *he?šo* 'resin, rubber, chewing gum', or *?ikna?* 'like.'[‡]

As compared to syllables with two initial consonants, those ending in two consonants are somewhat less restricted in word position. They may occur medially before a glottal stop, as in *?apc?ika* 'he cut it', or in final position, as in *?ikʷ?ałt*, a reduced form of *?ikʷ?ałte* 'back'. A final -CC cluster is found only in reduced words (3.3.2.).

3. PHONEMIC CHANGES

Changes in sounds can best be considered in the context of sequences of phonemes, of morphemes, and of words.

3.1. PHONEME SEQUENCES

All changes in which one phoneme affects another are regressive; a phoneme can exert an influence only on a preceding phoneme.

The sole vowel change is the shortening of a fundamentally long vowel. Because a long vowel cannot occur before two consonants unless the second is a glottal stop, it is shortened when this constraint is violated through the operation of a morphological process: for example, the long vowel of the stem is maintained in *?aše·-?a* (-*?a* present tense) 'he is making it' but secondarily shortened in *?aše-kka* (-*kka* past tense) 'he was making it'.

Two consonants undergo change under the influence of following phonemes. The *l* can be followed only by the consonants *l* or *?*. When morphological process brings a consonant different from these after it, the *l* is replaced by *ł*: for example, *l* of the stem in *c?ililik?e·?a* 'he is making wheezing noises' is changed to *ł* in *c?iłc?inne* 'one who wheezes and coughs'.[§]

Of all consonants *kʷ* is the most restricted in its possibilities of occurrence. It may be followed only by *kʷ*, *?*, or an unrounded vowel. When these permitted environments are changed, the *kʷ* of the stem is replaced by *k*: the stem *kʷ* actualized in *?akʷa-Ø* (-Ø present tense) 'it is getting ripe' is replaced in *?ak-na-Ø* (-*na* static) 'it is ripe'. A similar change takes place before a back vowel, as in *?alek-u-nap-ka* (*?alekʷi* 'to be fried', -*u* causative, -*nap* plural subject, -*ka* past tense) 'they fried it'; and this change is effected even when a word boundary and *?* intervene, as in *?ehk ?ona* (*?ehkʷi* 'to be first', *?ona* agentive) 'the first one'.

3.2. MORPHEME SEQUENCES

More extensive than the changes of sounds conditioned by adjacent phonemes (3.1.) are those resulting from morphological constraints. There are three types of morphologically induced changes: abbreviation of a stem appearing in the first-position slot before other morphemes (3.2.1.); changes effected by affixes upon

[‡]The unique status of *c?*, *č?*, *k?*, and *kʷ?* in the structure of the syllable is also manifested on the morpheme level. These are the only glottal clusters found within unit morphemes; other clusters composed of consonant plus glottal stop are split by a morpheme border. All 4 glottal clusters occur initially in morphemes as well as in words; however, within morphemes, *kʷ?* is relatively rare and *č?* appears only initially in some half-dozen verb stems of a uniform semantic type, stems referring to liquidlike sounds. The distinctive syllabic and morphemic features of the 4 clusters invest them with a unitary character different from all other consonant clusters, suggesting that they may have been unit phonemes at an earlier time in the history of Zuni. The rarity of morpheme-internal *kʷ?* and *č?* further suggests a diminishing distribution for 2 of the 4 glottal clusters. Finally, their adaptation to a pattern prevailing at present in the language is revealed in their frequent word-medial occurrence where they behave like other glottal clusters in being split across morpheme borders; thus, the glottal stop belongs to the suffix (-*?an* locative) in *k?akʷ-?an* 'by the house' as in *?akl-?an* 'by the fire', although the *kʷ?* cluster can also occur morpheme-internally but the *kl?* cluster cannot.

[§]In one morpheme, -*la* 'objects in a shallow container', the *l* changes to *ł* even before *?*: the *l* of the morpheme in *mola·we?* 'spherical objects in shallow containers' is replaced in *moł?e* 'spherical objects in a shallow container.'

the initial and final phonemes of stems (3.2.2.-3.2.3.); and changes effected by stems upon the initial and final sounds of affixes (3.2.4.-3.2.5.).

3.2.1.

Stems containing more than one syllable are abbreviated to their initial CV or CCV before one of the suffixes (13.2.1.3.) and as first-position elements in compounds (11.3.3., 13.2.4.) and in constructions (11.2.3.): *pa-lokkʔa-·kʷe* 'Ramah Navajo' (*pa-* abbreviated from *paču* 'Navajo', *lokkʔa* 'to be gray', *-·kʷe* membership).

3.2.2.

The initial glottal stop of stems is deleted after certain prefixes. One of the plural prefixes (9.5.2.) appears as *ʔa·-* before stems beginning in a consonant other than *ʔ* but as *ʔa·w-* before stems that delete their initial *ʔ*: *ʔa·-šiwani* 'rain priests' (*šiwani* 'rain priest') but *ʔa·w-ikina* 'man's younger sisters' (*ʔikina* 'man's younger sister'). A few other prefixes follow this pattern, occurring in a vowel-ending form before stem consonants other than *ʔ* and in a consonant-ending form before stems with a deleted *ʔ* (see 9.1.1., 9.1.2., 9.4., 9.5.1.).

Prefixes with alternant forms of this type serve to maintain the structural requirement that prohibits the juxtaposition of vowels: that is, the final consonant in one of the prefix forms takes the place of the deleted stem *ʔ* in separating the prefix vowel from the stem vowel. This strategy of preserving structure is not automatic throughout the language, for other prefixes, such as *yu-* indeterminate (9.2.) and *ʔan-* indirective (9.3.), always appear with a final vowel or final consonant and do not produce any changes in stems.

3.2.3.

Another type of stem change—lengthening of the final vowel—is associated with certain suffixes; this influence is symbolized by a raised period preceding the suffix or by -(V)· if the suffix has no additional phonetic content. Thus, one of the suffixes having this vowel-lengthening effect is *-·weʔ* plural (11.2.2.), as in *šokʔo-·weʔ* 'spoons' (*šokʔo-nne* 'spoon'); another is the subordinating -(V)· (7.1.4.), as in *ʔota-· čuneka* 'he stopped dancing' (*ʔota* 'to dance').

3.2.4.

Affixes with differentiated forms are characteristic of Zuni morphology. But the patterns of affix alternants represent an intricately fragmented system, some of the alternants being distributed on a phonological, others on a morphological basis.

One of the phonologically conditioned affixes is the indirective (9.3.), which occurs as *ʔah-* before a stem beginning in *h*, *ʔal-* before *l*, *ʔam-* before *m* or *p*, *ʔaw-* before *w*, *ʔay-* before *y*, and *ʔan-* before all other stem-initial consonants. This is a unique pattern, in that no other affix in the language manifests such adaptive assimilation to the consonantism of the stem.

More common is the differentiation between affix forms added to a stem vowel and those attached to a stem consonant. Some prefixes delete the initial *ʔ* of stems (see 3.2.2.). These prefixes, at the same time, are conditioned by stems, for the vowel-beginning stems (whose initial *ʔ* has been deleted) select a consonant-ending form of the prefix, while stems with initial consonant take a vowel-ending form. A few suffixed elements follow the same phonological rationale, though these do not condition any changes in the stem: for example, the interrogative (14.4.) appears as *-ʔši* after stems ending in a vowel, *-ši* after stems with final consonant (see also 14.1., 14.2., 14.5.). The latter form (-CV after stem C, instead of -ʔCV), it should be noted, avoids a medial CʔC cluster of consonants, which is not permitted; in this cluster the syllable division would fall between C and ʔC, and a syllable-initial ʔC cannot occur (2.1.).

The plural suffix has distinctive forms based on the syllabicity of the stem, *-·weʔ* being added to polysyllabic stems, *-weʔ* to monosyllabic stems (11.2.2.). This phonological difference as well as that based on consonant versus vowel borders is observed by the continuative, which is actualized in three forms (8.4.2.): *-ye·* after monosyllabic stems, which always end in a vowel; *-y* after polysyllabic stems ending in *i*, *o*, or *u*; and *-e·* after polysyllabic stems ending in a consonant, these being derived from stems whose final *e* or *a* has been deleted.

3.2.5.

In contrast to the sparse and scattered distribution of affixes whose alternant forms are conditioned by a variety of phonological factors, the numerous affixes distributed in accordance with strictly morphological criteria are more representative of the prevailing affix patterns. All examples of this type are suffixes, whose alternant forms are distributed on the basis of verb-class categories. Some examples of these suffixes, grouped into sets, will serve to indicate the major patterns of alternants:

-ʔC, -CC, -C type: *-ʹka*, *-kka*, *-ka* past tense (7.2.1.); *-ʔšukʷa*, *-ššukʷa*, *-šukʷa* negative future tense or negative nonpast conditional (7.2.2.).

-CC, -C type: *-nna*, *-na* static (8.4.1.); *-ččo*, *-čo* repetitive (8.2.1.).

-ʔa, -a, -Ø type: *-ʔappa*, *-appa*, *-ppa* subordinate with subject different from that of the following verb (7.16.); *-ʔa*, *-a*, *-Ø* present tense or imperative (7.2.4.).

-ʔa, -a type: *-ʔamme*, *-amme* negative (8.1.2.): *-ʔan*, *-an* locative (14.1.).

These four types reflect two major patterns: -ʔC, -CC, -C (with its included set -CC, -C) and -ʔa, -a, -Ø (with its included set -ʔa, -a).

3.3. WORD SEQUENCES

In the context of discourse, words undergo reduction in their final phonemes. These changes affect words differentially in utterance-final and utterance-medial position.

3.3.1.

At the end of an utterance a short vowel may be unvoiced. This nonphonemic change is optional, but it occurs frequently in conversation and in dictated texts.

An utterance-final *n* or *ʔ* is invariably deleted: *ʔowannan ʔiˑyaʔsekʔa* 'mix it in the flour', but *ʔowanna* 'in the flour' as a separate utterance; *tešlanišši ʔ peka* 'he spoke fearfully', but *tešlanišši* 'fearfully' when pronounced in isolation.

3.3.2.

In words containing more than one syllable the final -V or -Vʔ is deleted before initial *h* or *ʔ* in the following word: the full form *kʷʔalaši* 'crow' occurs in isolation, but its final vowel is zeroed in *kʷʔalaš hatiyaˑka* 'Crow listened'; similarly, the full form *tešlanišši ʔ* appears in a reduced form in *tešlaniš ʔaˑwika* 'they arrived fearfully'.

Other types of utterance-medial reduction are encountered; but these are optional and seem to depend upon factors of speech style, such as the ages of the persons involved in speaking and the level of formality in the social situation. As noted above, a word appearing before an initial *h* or *ʔ* in the next word is especially vulnerable to reduction. In this environment the second consonant of a cluster, if it is a glottal stop or the second element of a geminate cluster, may be deleted as well as the following -V or -Vʔ: compare the full form of the noun in *kʔapʔe powaye* 'the bottle of liquid is standing' with the reduced form in *kʔap ʔimoʔka* 'there was a bottle of liquid'; compare *tešlanišši ʔ peka* 'he spoke fearfully' with *tešlaniš* (or *tešlanišš*) *ʔika* 'he arrived fearfully'. A postconsonantal continuant (*m, n, l, w, y*) before the deleted -V or -Vʔ is often unvoiced: the *n* of *hoʔnaʔ* 'us' is usually voiceless in a sentence such as *hoʔn ʔihakkʔakka* 'he asked us to do it'.

High-frequency morphemes tend to undergo the same types of reduction in any utterance-medial environment, not only before *h* or *ʔ*. These morphemes consist of frequently occurring particles and word-final suffixes, which normally appear within the body of an utterance. The following examples will serve to illustrate morphemes of this type in both their full and reduced forms: *si* > *s* 'and, then'; *laˑkʔi* > *laˑkʔ* or *laˑk* 'today, now'; -*nne* > -*nn* or -*n* singular; -*ʔappa, -appa, -ppa* > -*ʔap, -ap, -p* subordinate with subject different from that of the following verb.

The reduced word violates one constraint applying to unreduced forms: it may end in a -CC cluster, as illustrated above, whereas a final -CC is not permitted in the full form of a word (2.1.).

THE SYSTEM OF WORDS

4. PARTS OF SPEECH

4.1. FOUR WORD CLASSES

Word can be classified by their distinctive inflectional suffixes as verbs, nouns, or personal pronouns; particles are words that do not take inflections but may undergo derivational processes. Verbs are inflected for subordination, tense, and mode, nouns for number, and pronouns for number and case.

4.2. INFLECTIONS AND DERIVATIONS

An inflected form, to be a complete word, must end in one of the final suffixes that mark the word class, or part of speech, to which it belongs. An inflected word, then, consists minimally of a stem and its inflectional suffix, of which only one can occur; or the word may contain prefixes, all of which are derivational, and derivational suffixes preceding the final inflectional element. Thus, *kʔošo-ka* 'he washed it' (*kʔošo* 'to wash', -*ka* past) is a minimal inflected form; several derivational affixes are attached to the same verb in *ʔi-kʔošo-y-nap-ka* 'they were washing themselves' (*ʔi-* reflexive, -*y* continuative, -*nap* plural subject).

4.3. OVERLAPPING MEMBERSHIP AND CHANGES IN WORD CLASS

Each stem can be assigned to a single word class and subclass, with one exception. Some stems belonging to class 1 nouns have an overlapping membership with class 9 verbs: *ʔasi* is glossed as 'hand, to be a hand, to have a hand', for it takes noun as well as verb inflections, as in *ʔasi-nne* 'hand' (-*nne* singular) and *ʔasi-ye* 'it has a hand' (-*ye* present tense). But many class 9 verbs cannot add the noun inflections, and many class 1 nouns cannot participate in the verb formations. Apart from the few stems that belong to both noun class 1 and verb class 9, the word classes are kept sharply separated.

Furthermore, the morphological machinery for altering the class membership of words is rather sparse and unproductive. There are no processes for changing verbs to nouns. A few derivational suffixes of limited function convert verbs to particles, and a few semantically specialized suffixes give some nouns the dual membership in noun class 1 and verb class 9. Thus, -*kʔan* multiplicative forms particles from verbs as well as from other particles, as in *ʔemma-kʔan* 'many times' (*ʔemma* 'to increase'); -*ppo* '(to be) objects in a deep container' is added to nouns to form class 1 nouns and class 9 verbs, as in *heli-ppo-nne* 'can of paint, store paint' (*heli* 'paint, clay, mud', -*nne* singular) and *mo-ppo-pa* there are melons (or oranges, beads, etc.) in the box (or truck, hole, etc.)' (*mo* 'spherical object', -*pa* plural subject).

5. TYPES OF MORPHOLOGICAL PROCESSES

Stems may be modified by prefixation, suffixation, enclisis, suppletion, compounding, reduplication, and abbreviation.

5.1. PREFIXATION

Prefixation covers a relatively small area of the morphology as compared to suffixation. The half-dozen prefixes refer to the conceptual categories of voice (e.g., reciprocal, indirective), number (only the plural), aspect (only the inchoative), mode (only the indeterminate), and terrestrial (9.1.3.).

5.2. SUFFIXATION

Suffixation accounts for most of the formal machinery of word building. Inflections for all the word classes are formed solely by suffixes, and most of the derivations are expressed by suffixes as well. The inflectional categories are those of tense and tense-mode (e.g., past tense, present tense or imperative mode), pure mode (permissive, hortatory), subordination (e.g., contemporaneous, resultative), number in the noun (singular, plural) and in the pronoun (singular, dual, plural), and case in the pronoun (subject, object, and possessive). The derivational suffixes are more numerous, embracing the categories of voice (only the causative), aspect (e.g., continuative, static), mode (e.g., negative, indeterminate), mixed categories of aspect-voice or aspect-voice-mode (e.g., conversive causative punctiliar, conversive causative repetitive), number (only the plural subject of transitive verbs), and collectives ('[to be] objects growing together on the ground', '[to be] objects on the surface'). Various notions, which cannot be conveniently grouped into any of the more familiar categories, are expressed by a number of particle-forming suffixes (e.g., instrumental, ceremonial, familiar).

5.3. ENCLISIS

The language employs five enclitics (morphemes loosely attached to the end of the word). The interrogative -ʔši, -ši, for example, may be postposed to any word in the sentence. The few enclitics express a variety of concepts (such as locative, adversitive).

5.4. SUPPLETION

Suppletion—the complete replacement of a stem—is found with less than a dozen verbs. It duplicates the function denoted by one of the prefixes, that of indicating the plural subject of intransitive verbs or the plural object of transitives: ʔimo 'to be in a sitting position (sg. subj.)', tina 'to be in a sitting position (pl. subj.)'.

5.5. COMPOUNDING

A compound, like any other word unit in Zuni, is phonologically defined by having no more than one heavy stress, which falls on the initial syllable. Morphologically, the compound contains a first-position stem with a CV or CCV structure, which may be either a complete stem or an abbreviated form, plus another stem. Monosyllabic stems, fairly numerous in the language, are particularly productive as first-position elements in compounds: ha-ʔotta 'tumbleweed' (ha 'weed', ʔotta 'to be sharp'), mo-pinna-ka 'hail'

(mo 'spherical object', pinna 'to be windy', -ka instrumental). Longer stems are abbreviated to their initial CV or CCV: tu-mokʷkʷʔa 'stocking' (tu- < tukni 'toe', mokʷkʷʔa 'shoe'), pa-tuna 'Navajo One-Eye', nickname given to a Navajo man (pa- < pačų 'Navajo', tuna 'eye'). Compounds form nouns or particles, but no verbs. In noun compounds the first-position stem must be a noun, the second either a noun or a verb (11.3.3.). In particle compounds the first element may be either a particle or noun, the second a particle, noun, or verb (13.2.2.2.). True compounds are to be distinguished from syntactic constructions that may resemble them in some respects (see 11.2.3.). Zuni, like English, constructs word combinations with specialized, lexically unitary meanings, as he-ppo-ka wahta-nne 'wallet' (he 'coin, metal', -ppo '(to be) objects in a deep container', -ka instrumental, ẁahta 'bag', -nne singular).

5.6. REDUPLICATION

Reduplication has a limited range. It is employed only with one of the verb classes to express the mediopassive repetitive (10.1.1.) and semelfactive (10.1.2.).

5.7. ABBREVIATION

Abbreviation applies only to noun and particle stems. But it is used in a variety of combinations—in suffixed words containing a single stem, in compound words, and in syntactic construction (3.2.1.).

6. VERB CATEGORIES

6.1. CLASSES AND STEMS

Verbs are arranged in covert classes. The class membership of a verb, although not indicated by any explicit formal marking within the stem, is manifested by its distinctive behavior in stem formation and in suffix selection. Each verb appears in two stem forms that for convenience, are designated 'past' and 'present'. The past stem of all verbs not only adds the inflectional suffix of the past tense but also is used for other inflectional and derivational suffixes. Similarly, suffixes other than the present tense are attached to the present stem. Only suffixal morphemes participate in the system of verb stems; other types of morphemes, such as prefixes and reduplicatives, operate directly upon the base form of the verb.

Table 1 provides examples of the 10 verb classes. The base, which presents a single lexical shape for designating a given verb with its several stems, is the underlying form from which the stem can be constructed. For most verb classes, the base has the same shape as the full form of the present stem. There are two exceptions: in class 2 the baselike form appears in the past stem, and the final vowel of the base is deleted in the present stem; class 10 verbs, with their small number of suffixes all added to the past stem, lack a present stem. As shown in table 1, bases may be primary or secondary forms. The primary base is an unanalyzable

Table 1. Verb Classes: Bases and Stems

Verb class and base	Past stem	Present stem
1. *kʔeya* 'to be thirsty'	*kʔeya-*	*kʔeya-*
2. *kʔeya* 'to imitate'	*kʔeya-*	*kʔey-*
3a. *yuʔyaˑw* 'to become aware'	*yuʔyaˑ-*	*yuʔyaˑw-*
b. *ʔiy* 'to come'	*ʔi-*	*ʔiy-*
c. *ʔaˑn* 'to go'	*ʔaˑ-*	*ʔaˑn-*
4a. *laʔhi* 'to fly'	*laʔhi-,laʔh-*(pv)	*laʔhi-*
b. *šema* 'to call'	*šema-,šem-*(pv)	*šema-*
5. *tena-ʔu* 'to sing'	*tenaˑ-,ten-*(pv)	*tenaʔu-*
6a. *kʔaɬi* 'to become hot'	*kʔaɬ-*	*kʔaɬi-*
b. *šema-naʔma* 'not to call'	*šemanam-*	*šemanaʔma-*
c. *šema-naˑwa* 'to call' (plural subject)	*šemanap-*	*šemanaˑwa-, šemanaˑw-*(pv)
7. *ʔikʷa* 'to say'	*ʔikʷa-,ʔikʷ-*(pv)	*ʔikʷa-*
8a. *ten-eˑ* 'to be singing'	*teneˑ-,tene-*(pcc)	*teneˑ-,tene-*(pcc)
b. *ʔito-y* 'to be eating'	*ʔitoy-,ʔito-*(pcc)	*ʔitoy-,ʔito-*(pcc)
9a. *tena* 'to be music'	*tena-,ten-*(pv)	*tena-,ten-*(pʔv)
b. *yaɬa* 'to ask'	*yaɬa-,yaɬ-*(pv)	*yaɬa-,yaɬ-*(pʔv)
c. *ʔuli* 'to be inside'	*ʔuli-,ʔul-*(pv)	*ʔuli-,ʔul-*(pʔv), *ʔull-*(pv)
10a. *ʔiči* 'to be lazy'	*ʔiči-*	- - - - - -
b. *ɬupcʔi* 'to be yellow'	*ɬupcʔi-*	- - - - - -

Abbreviations: (pv) prevocalic, (pcc) pre–consonant-cluster, (pʔv) preglottal.

morpheme, as *tena* (class 9a) 'to be music'. The secondary base contains two or more morphemes, as *tena-ʔu* (class 5) 'to sing', composed of the causative *-ʔu*, a derivational suffix that forms class 5 verbs, added to the past stem of *tena*.

Some of the classes or subclasses have phonologically reduced forms in addition to their full forms. In classes with only a single present or past stem, the assignment of suffixes to stems is morphologically determined: a given suffix allomorph, or alternant, is assigned either to the past stem or to the present stem. Thus, the future suffix, which is always added to the present stem, has several allomorphs distributed among the various classes: the future form assigned to class 2 verbs, for example, is *-ʔanna* (*kʔey-ʔanna* 'he will imitate it') while the allomorph for class 6a verbs is *-nna* (*kʔaɬi-nna* 'it will get hot').

For classes with more than one present or past stem, the full forms are given first in table 1 and the phonologically reduced forms follow. Three types of phonologically determined stems are to be distinguished: the prevocalic form is employed before suffixes with an initial vowel, the preglottal before those beginning with a glottal stop followed by a vowel, and the pre–consonant-cluster before those beginning with two consonants, neither of which is a glottal stop. The full form associated with these types is then used before suffixes that manifest other phonological characteristics: if the stem has a prevocalic form, the full form adds all suffixes not beginning in a vowel, zero suffixes (-Ø) as well as those beginning in a consonant; if the stem has a pre–consonant-cluster form, the full form takes zero suffixes and suffixes beginning either in a vowel, a

single consonant, or two consonants if one of the two is ʔ. A few examples of words with *ʔotta* (class 9b) 'to be sharp' will help to clarify the distribution of suffix allomorphs among stems.

ʔotta-ʔka 'it was sharp': full form of the past stem; *-ʔka*, the past tense allomorph assigned to class 9.

ʔott-ʔappa 'when it was sharp': preglottal present stem; *-ʔappa*, a subordinating allomorph for classes 1, 2, and 9.

ʔotta-kkʔa-kka 'he sharpened it': full form of the past stem; *-kkʔa*, causative allomorph which is assigned to classes 7-9 and, being a derivational suffix, forms a new base, a verb of class 7; *-kka*, past tense allomorph for classes 7 and 8.

The two criteria for differentiating verbs into classes are the present versus past stem treatment and the selection of suffix allomorphs. These morphological criteria are illustrated in the following comments on some of the classes:

Class 1. Both the past and present stems retain the final vowel of the base. Only class 1 verbs use the unique allomorph *-ʔan* of the modificative subordinate (7.1.8.).

Class 2. The final base vowel is zeroed in the present stem. As the examples of table 1 indicate, homophonous verbs of classes 1 and 2 have the same past stems but different present stems. If the allomorphs suffixed to the past stem are also identical, homophonous words will result, as *kʔeya-ka* 'he was thirsty' or 'he imitated it'. But words formed from the present stem keep the two verbs distinct, even though the suffix allomorphs are the same: *kʔeya-ʔa* 'he is thirsty' but *kʔey-ʔa* 'he is imitating it'.

Class 3. Verbs of this class and of 8b are the only ones whose base ends in a consonant. The final consonant is deleted in the past stem of class 3 verbs but retained in verbs of class 8b. A number of suffixes have unique allomorphs for class 3: the present tense (7.2.4.) is formed with -a for 3a and 3b (yuʔyaˑw-a 'he is becoming aware') but with -eʔ for 3c (ʔaˑn-eʔ 'he is going'); only 3b adds the repetitive allomorph -ttela (8.2.1.).

Class 10. Verbs of this class are the only ones that cannot be inflected directly; they must first undergo derivational processes, and all their suffix derivations are assigned to the past stem. The class 10a base may be reduplicated (10.1.), or its past stem may add the punctiliar -ʔʔa (8.1.1.). Neither of these derivations is available to class 10b verbs, which select other derivational suffixes such as the causative -kʔa (8.3.) and the static -nna (8.4.1.).

6.2. TRANSITIVITY

In addition to class assignment, another covert category of Zuni is that of transitivity (Stout 1972). Verb bases are inherently transitive or intransitive: ʔaššuʔwa 'to speak to' is transitive; pen 'to speak' is intransitive. Transitivity status is indicated morphologically by the behavior of the verb in selecting affixes to denote plurality of subject and object. For the transitive verb, a suffix (8.5.) marks the subject plural; a prefix (9.1.1., 9.5.2.) does the double duty of marking the object plural of the transitive and the subject plural of the intransitive, which, of course, cannot take an object.

Verbs may be secondarily transitivized or intransitivized. But the processes that change the transitivity status of verbs are not pure transitivizers or intransitivizers; they carry other functions as well. The indirective prefix (9.3.) transitivizes an intransitive verb: kʔeccana 'to be happy' is intransitive, and a prefix would therefore indicate its plural subject; ʔan-kʔeccana 'to be happy with, to love' contains the indirective and is transitive, and its plural subject would now be marked by a suffix. But the indirective is also added to a transitive verb, and here it redirects the event to a different object or a second object: yała 'to ask' is a transitive whose object is that which is being asked ('to ask about it'); with the indirective prefix, ʔay-yała deflects the event to another object, the person being asked ('to ask him, her, them'). Similarly, any of the causative suffixes (8.2.3., 8.2.4., 8.3.) transitivize an intransitive and redirect the event of a transitive verb, as in toye 'to plant (e.g., the corn)', toye-kkʔa 'to cause (e.g., the man) to plant (e.g., the corn)'. In contrast, the static (8.4.1.) may be suffixed to a transitive to form an intransitive: ʔito 'to eat' is a transitive, but with the static suffix ʔito-na 'to be eaten, to have a spot eaten out' is an intransitive. The static may also be added to an intransitive verb, and in this case it converts the event to a state, with the verb remaining intransitive: ʔoʔła 'to become fat', ʔoʔła-na 'to be fat'.

7. VERB INFLECTIONS

Every inflected word ends in a single final suffix that marks the word class to which it belongs (4.2.). The final suffixes that inflect the verb fall into three functional categories—subordination, tense and tense-mode, and mode. The subcategories of subordination are: resultative (7.1.1.), adverbial (7.1.2.), adjunctive (7.1.3.), contemporaneous (7.1.4.), same subject (7.1.5.), different subject (7.1.6.), past agentive (7.1.7.), and modifactive (7.1.8.). The subcategories of tense and tense-mode are: past (7.2.1.), negative future tense or negative nonpast conditional (7.2.2.), negative past conditional (7.2.3.), present or imperative (7.2.4.), future tense or nonpast conditional (7.2.5.), and past conditional (7.2.6.). The varieties of mode are permissive (7.3.1.) and hortatory (7.3.2.). Each suffix treated here is identified in the verb system by indicating its meaning, its allomorphs (see also 3.2.4. and 3.2.5.), the assignment of each allomorph to the verb classes with which it is used, and the stem type—past or present—to which it is attached.

7.1. SUBORDINATION

Half the inflectional suffixes of the verb belong to the subordinating category. Most of these express various relationships to the following verb. In a sentence with several clauses, the verb in each clause bears a relation to the verb next following, the last of which is the main verb. The resultative suffix indicates the complementive goal of the main verb, sometimes translated by 'in order to, for the purpose of'. The adverbial subordinate performs the function of modifying the main verb. An overlapping function is fulfilled by the adjunctive, which may modify either a verb or a noun. The contemporaneous subordinate indicates an event occurring at the same time as that of the main verb. Two suffixes define the relationship between the subject of the subordinate verb and that of the following verb: one denotes that the two verbs have the same subject, the other that their subjects are different. Finally, two of the suffixes are primarily agentives: one indicates a past agentive; the other—the modifactive subordinate—precedes either the agentive particle ʔona or the verb that it modifies.

7.1.1. RESULTATIVE

-kan (with classes 1-6), -kkan (with 7-8), -ʔkan (with 9) and the past stem.

ho? ʔišema-kan ʔaˑne (I call.them-resultative will.go) 'I'll go to call them': ʔišema (4b) 'to call them'.

ʔayna-kkan ʔika (kill-resultative came) 'he came to kill it': ʔayna (7) 'to kill'.

7.1.2. ADVERBIAL

-nišʔiʔ (with classes 1-6), -nnišʔiʔ (with 7-9) and the past stem.

tešlan-niššiʔ peka (afraid-adverbial spoke) 'he spoke fearfully': *tešlana* (6a) 'to be afraid'.

cʔumme-nniššiʔ ʔa·łaʔu (tight-adverbial draw.apart) 'draw it apart tightly': *cʔumme* (9b) 'to be tight, to be strong'.

7.1.3. ADJUNCTIVE
-n (with classes 1-8), *-ʔ* (with 9) and the past stem.

yatonil hoł suski lesne-n ʔallukka (daily perhaps coyote do.this-adjunctive moved.about) 'all day long, it seems, Coyote went about doing this': *lesne·* (8a) 'to be doing this'.

tom ʔuččun sossona-ʔ coʔya (your shirt brown-adjunctive is.pretty) 'your brown shirt is pretty': *sossona* (9b) 'to be brown'.

7.1.4. CONTEMPORANEOUS
-(V)· (with classes 1-2, 4-9), *-a·* (with 3) and the present stem.

lesn hoł ʔimat ʔa·či yam tuna· ʔiłuwaškʔa·· ʔimoʔka (thus perhaps seemingly they.two their eyes make.them.run-contemporaneous sat) 'the two of them, it seems, sat there making their eyes run about in that way': *ʔiłuwaškʔa* (7) 'to cause them to run'.

ʔa·n-a· čuneka (go-contemporaneous stopped) 'he stopped going': *ʔa·n* (3c) 'to go'.

7.1.5. SAME SUBJECT
-nan (with classes 1-6a, 7-8) and the past stem, *-n* (with 6b-6c, 9) and the present stem.

pilak-nan kʷʔalaši pow ʔułłakʷin ʔa·ka (stand-same.subject crow sitting near.place went) 'getting up, he went near the place where Crow was sitting': *pilaku* (6a) 'to stand up from a lying position'.

hasuski moʔl ʔa·či ʔahna-n yam tunapka (coyote.weed berry they.two taken-same.subject his had.eyes) 'having taken the two coyote-weed berries, he used them for eyes': *ʔahna* (9a) 'to have taken'.

7.1.6. DIFFERENT SUBJECT
-ʔappa (with classes 1-2, 9), *-appa* (with 3), *-ppa* (with 4-8) and the present stem. In most of its occurrences this suffix loses its final *-pa* through reduction (see 3.3.2.), but the full form appears in prayers.

ʔiyuteʔčinaša· pow ʔułła-ʔap suski ʔokʷika (resting sitting near-different.subject coyote awoke) 'while he (Crow) was sitting near it, Coyote awoke': *ʔułła* (9a) 'to be near'.

toʔ ye·lana· kʷayikʔa-ppa... (you standing bring.out-different.subject...) 'when you bring yourself out...': *kʷayikʔa* (7) 'to cause to emerge'. This example is from a Zuni prayer to Father Sun.

7.1.7. PAST AGENTIVE
-kowaʔ (with classes 1-6), *-kkowaʔ* (with 7-8), *-ʔkowaʔ* (with 9) and the past stem. This suffix refers to one who or that which was the agent of the event or, with transitive verbs, either the agent or receiver of the event.

ʔutte-kowaʔ (bite-past.agentive) 'the one who bit it, that which was bitten': *ʔutte* (4b) 'to bite'.

ʔimat suski tanaya pałto-ʔkowaʔ łat ʔallukka (seemingly coyote forest boundary-past.agentive hunting went.about) 'it seems that Coyote went about hunting along the edge of the forest': *pałto* (9a) 'to be a boundary, to have an edge'.

7.1.8. MODIFICATIVE
-ʔan (with class 1), *-an* (with 3a-3b), *-n* (with 4-8), *-Ø* (with 2, 3c, 9) and the present stem.

čim hoł yam ʔallaše·-n ʔona yuteʔčikʔap topa kʷayip ta· s ʔuhs ʔona ʔallašanna (then perhaps his chase-modificative agentive causing.to.be.tired other coming.out again then that agentive would.chase) 'after he had tired out the one he was chasing, just as another one came out, he would chase that one': *ʔallaše·* (8a) 'to be chasing repeatedly'.

ʔela-Ø yałtoʔka (stand-modificative was.on.top) 'he was standing on top': *ʔela* (9a) 'to be standing'.

7.2. TENSE AND TENSE-MODE
Of the six suffixes in the category of tense and tense-mode, only the past inflection expresses a pure tense. The remaining elements refer to a mixture of temporal and modal concepts, such as the suffix denoting the present tense in some contexts and the imperative mode in others, or the suffix indicating a past tense in the conditional mode. The tenses expressed are past, present, and future; however, the future contrasts with a nonpast conditional. The modal references are the imperative, conditional, and negative.

7.2.1. PAST
-ka (with classes 1-6), *-kka* (with 7-8), *-ʔka* (with 9) and the past stem.

sutekʷkʷante ta·s hinik yam tenan ʔokkʔa-kka (stupid.coyote again maybe his song lost-past) 'again, it seems, stupid Coyote lost his song': *ʔokkʔa* (7) 'to lose'.

kʷʔalaši pow ʔułłakʷin teʔčinan ʔaššuʔwa-ʔka (crow sitting near.place arriving speak.to-past) 'arriving near the place where Crow was sitting, he (Coyote) spoke to him': *ʔaššuʔwa* (9b) 'to speak to'.

7.2.2. NEGATIVE FUTURE TENSE OR NEGATIVE NONPAST CONDITIONAL
-šukʷa (with classes 1-6), *-ššukʷa* (with 7-8), *-ʔšukʷa* (with 9) and the past stem. This suffix refers either to a negative mode in the future tense or to a negative conditional mode in the nonpast (present or future) tense.

kʷaʔ ʔitonap-šukʷa (not they.eat-negative.future) 'they will not eat it': *ʔitona·wa* (6c) 'to eat' (plural subject).

kʷaʔ muʔleʔ kʔokši-ʔšukʷa (not bread good-negative.nonpast.conditional) 'the bread would not be good (e.g., unless she baked it herself)': *kʔokši* (9b) 'to be good'.

7.2.3. NEGATIVE PAST CONDITIONAL

This function is performed by a composite suffix, made up of the allomorphs of the preceding suffix (7.22.) plus -ʔka, one of the past tense allomorphs. The combination, like this -šukʷa suffix, is added to the past stem. This composite form and the past conditional (7.26.) are the only inflectional suffix combinations in Zuni.

kʷaʔ tom hoʔ ʔitokʔa-ššukʷaʔka (not you I feed-negative.past.conditional) 'I would not have fed you (e.g., if I hadn't had plenty of food)': *ʔitokʔa* (7) 'to cause to eat, to feed'.

kʷaʔ piya-ʔšukʷaʔka (not be.hanging-negative.past.conditional) 'he would not have been hanged (e.g., if he hadn't tried to escape)': *piya* (9a) 'to be hanging'.

7.2.4. PRESENT OR IMPERATIVE

-ʔa (with classes 1, 2, 8), -a (with 3a-3b), -eʔ (with 3c, 6c), -Ø (with 4-6b, 7, 9b), -ye (with 9a), -e (with 9c) and the present stem.

suski s les kʷakka ʔama hom ʔan tuna· ʔiłuwahkʔa-Ø (coyote then this said show.me my of eyes make.them.run-imperative) 'then Coyote said, "Show me! Make my eyes run about!": *ʔiłuwahkʔa* (7) 'to cause to run'.

koʔnaʔ ton tewanan ʔa·teya-ye (how you day be-present) 'how are you these days?' (a formal greeting formula): *ʔa·teya* (9a) 'to be'.

7.2.5. FUTURE TENSE OR NONPAST CONDITIONAL

-ʔanna (with classes 1-2), -anna (with 3a-3b), -nna (with 4-6b, 7-8), -uwa (with 3c), -a (with 6c), -kʔanna (with 9) and the present stem.

we-ʔanna (sick-nonpast.conditional) 'he would be sick (if he hadn't taken the medicine)': *we* (1) 'to become sick'.

kʔakʷʔinna· tutunan hon penakʔam ʔa·peyep čim s hon ʔa·teʔčina-kʔanna (coffee drinking we nonsense talking now then we have.reached-future) 'if we continue drinking coffee and talking nonsense, then we will have reached the end': *ʔa·teʔčina* (9a) 'to have reached.' This is one of the popular sayings.

7.2.6. PAST CONDITIONAL

Like the negative past conditional (7.2.3.), the past conditional suffix is a composite element, composed of the future suffix plus -nka. It is added to the present stem.

čun-ʔannanka (quit-past.conditional) 'he should have quit': *čune* (2) 'to quit, to stop'.

hon ʔa·n-uwanka (we go-past.conditional) 'we were supposed to have gone': *ʔa·n* (3c) 'to go'.

7.3. MODE

Only two suffixes referring purely to mode are found among the inflectional elements. The permissive expresses a polite command when the subject is a second person; with a first- or third-person subject it makes a request or petition. Whereas a subject noun or pronoun may occur in the sentence containing a permissive verb, no overt subject accompanies the verb with the hortatory element. This suffix has the force of either a strong command to the person addressed or a request that includes the speaker, the request often translated as 'let's do so-and-so'.

7.3.1. PERMISSIVE

-tu (with classes 1-6), -ttu (with 7-8), -ʔtu (with 9) and the past stem.

tewunaʔ ʔoneyał hoʔnaʔ s ton leʔna ʔa·wona· ya·kʔanap-tu (thus pollen.road us then you this.way safely roads finish-permissive) 'please help us, you spirits, to reach the end of the sacred road safely' (from a Zuni prayer): *ya·kʔana·wa* (6c) 'to finish'.

hoʔ ʔayna-ttu (I kill-permissive) 'let me kill it': *ʔayna* (7) 'to kill'.

7.3.2. HORTATORY

-še (with classes 1-6), -šše (with 7-8), -ʔše (with 9) and the past stem.

tena·-še (sing-hortatory) 'let's sing': *tenaʔu* (5) 'to sing'.

šoli-ʔše (play.cards-hortatory) 'let's play cards': *šoli* (9a) 'to play the stick game, to play cards'. The culturally older meaning emerges from the analysis of this verb: *šo* 'arrow, stick, straw', *-li* '(to be) object in a shallow container'.

8. VERB DERIVATIONS: SUFFIXES

The derivations of the verb form a structurally and semantically loose system. Whereas all inflections are indicated by suffixes assigned to the final position of the word, the derivations are actualized by a variety of formal processes. Most derivational elements are suffixes, arranged in six positional slots preceding the final inflectional suffixes. The few prefixes fill five positional slots preceding the stem. Other derivations, limited in scope, change the shape of the base: two reduplicatives express voice-aspect functions, and some dozen suppletives (10.2.) duplicate the function of one of the prefixes in referring to subject and object number.

Only one category of meaning, that of mode, is found among both inflectional and derivational processes. The negative, included in the mixed tense-mode meaning of two inflectional suffixes (7.2.2., 7.2.3.), is also expressed by two derivational suffixes. However, other semantic functions are uniquely derivational. Within each of the categories of meaning, the following derivations occur:

Mode
   negative (8.1.2., 8.6.),
   perceptive (8.1.4.)
   indeterminate (9.2.)
Number
   plural subject of transitive verbs (8.5.)
   plural subject of intransitive or plural object
     of transitive verbs (9.1.1., 9.5.2., 10.2.)

Voice
   causative (8.3.)
   indirective (9.3.)
   reflective (9.4.)
   reciprocal (9.51.)
Aspect
   punctiliar (8.1.1.)
   repetitive (8.2.1.)
   inchoative or inceptive (8.2.2., 9.1.2.)
   static (8.4.1.)
   continuative (8.4.2.)
Mixed
   conversive causative punctiliar (9.2.3.)
   conversive causative repetitive (8.2.4.)
   mediopassive repetitive (10.1.1.)
   mediopassive semelfactive (10.1.2.)
Special
   collectives (8.1.3.)
   terrestrial (9.13.).

8.0.1.

The first two of the criteria employed in describing inflectional suffixes apply equally well to the verb-forming derivational suffixes, which may be identified, in part, by the meaning of the morpheme and its allomorphic forms. Whereas the inflectional elements are added only to verbs, the derivational suffixes may be attached to particles or nouns as well as to verbs. As further criteria, then, the description of derivational elements must include: the assignment of each allomorph to its appropriate word class—particle, noun, or verb; and, if added to a verb, the stem type (past or present) to which it is suffixed. Most derivational suffixes are added to verbs and all suffixes but one—the negative (8.1.2.)—are assigned to the past stem. Finally, in contrast to the inflections, the derivational suffixes do not end the word unit but, rather, add another layer of verb formation to the underlying stem. This feature requires an additional criterion for describing derivational suffixes, the identification of the verb class formed by the suffix.

The derivational suffixes are described below in the order of positional slots, beginning with the innermost, the position closest to the basic stem.

8.1.

Of the derivational suffixes, those aligned in the first position are the most numerous and the most varied in function. Two first- position suffixes are added to verb stems.

8.1.1. PUNCTILIAR

-ʔʔa (with class 10a) and the past stem forms class 10b verbs. This derivational element is uniquely restricted in its formal operations: it is assigned to only one verb subclass; it must be followed by another derivational suffix before the verb can be inflected.

čiti-ʔʔa-kʔa-n ʔaˑka (drag-punctiliar-causative-adjunctive went) 'it (the wagon) went along, causing him to make a dragging sound': čiti (10a) 'to make a dragging sound'.

8.1.2. NEGATIVE

-ʔamme (with class 9), -amme (with 6c) and the present stem, forms class 9b. Another set of negative allomorphs (8.6.) is distributed among the remaining verb classes.

kʷaʔ šopč-ʔamme-Ø (not naughty-negative-imperative) 'don't be naughty!': šopči (9b) 'to be naughty, mischievous'.

8.1.3.

Ten suffixes allocated to the first position comprise a homogeneous set with similar formal and semantic features. In their formal properties, they are added to nouns or particles, not to verbs; they form class 9 verbs or class 1 nouns, two word classes that are frequently linked in the Zuni lexicon (see 4.3.). Semantically, these suffixes refer to various types of collectivities or spatial arrangements. The suffixes and some examples are:
   -li '(to be) objects in a shallow container'
   -ppo '(to be) objects in a deep container'
   -pi 'to remove objects from a deep container', the only suffix of this set which forms verbs of class 4a rather than class 9 verbs or class 1 nouns
   -la '(to be) objects growing together on the ground'
   -tta '(to be) a growing collectivity'
   -ya '(to be) a growing mass'
   -(V)ˑti '(to be) objects in a pile'
   -ɬi '(to be) objects in a pile on top, (to be) the place where objects are piled'
   -na '(to be) objects on the surface'
   -lo '(to be) objects that have been buried'
maʔš ʔa-li-ʔka (well? stone-shallow.container-past) 'well, were there stones in it (e.g., the dish)?': ʔa (noun class 1a) 'stone'. This is a Zuni pun. The phrase, common in conversation, is normally understood as containing ʔali (verb class 9a) 'to be nice' and as meaning 'was it nice?' To this, the puning answer is ʔeɬa soliʔka 'no, there was sand in it'.

ta-tta-nne (wood-growing.collectivity-singular) 'tree': ta (noun class 2) 'wood'.

8.1.4. PERCEPTIVE

-ma (with particles) forms verbs of class 2. It is suffixed as a first-position element to a few exclamative particles to denote the perception or feeling associated with the meaning of the stem, as in ʔatu-ma 'to fear the physical pain of' (attributed only to women), containing ʔatu exclamative expressing emphasis (used only by women).

8.2.

The second position is devoted to suffixes of aspect. All are appended to the past stem of verbs. Two of the four suffixes in this positional slot contain, in addition to their aspectual force, a 'conversive' notion, that is, a meaning that is the converse or opposite of the meaning signified by the stem: for example, the conversive of 'to be closed' is 'to be open'.

8.2.1. REPETITIVE

Several formal anomalies characterize the repetitive. It occurs in six forms that resemble no allomorphic pattern found elsewhere in Zuni. It is unproductive, each of the forms being selectively affiliated with only a few verbs. The allomorphs form verbs of three different classes. Two of the allomorphs, -čo and -čela, although beginning in a consonant, are attached to the prevocalic past stem (of class 4 verbs). The forms of the repetitive are: -čo (with classes 4 and 6a) and -ččo (with 4b and 9a), which form class 4b verbs; -ela (with 4), -čela (with 4), and -ttela (with 3b and 4a), which form class 6a verbs; -šle (with 4b), which forms class 7 verbs.

yanhak-čo-ka 'he kept breathing': *yanhaku* (6a) 'to breathe'.

8.2.2. INCHOATIVE OR INCEPTIVE

-ti (with 1-2, 9, 10b) forms class 4a verbs.

s les suski ʔanikʷakka ʔaˑʔ s hoʔ ʔanikʷa-ti-ka (then this coyote said.to well! already I know-inchoative-past) 'then Coyote said to him, "Well! I've already learned it"': *ʔanikʷa* (9b) 'to know'.

8.2.3. CONVERSIVE CAUSATIVE PUNCTILIAR

-ha (with class 9) forms class 6a verbs. The semantic force of this suffix is 'to cause in a punctiliar (single) action the opposite of the action indicated by the stem': for instance, *yakna* (9a) 'grasp, hold back, receive', *yakna-ha* (6a) 'release, let go.'

ʔan tunaˑ ʔaˑči leʔ hoł y-eˑla-h-ka (his eyes they.two this perhaps reflexive-stand-conversive.causative.punctiliar-past) 'at this, it seems, his two eyes ran off': *ʔela* (9a) 'to be standing (sg. subj.)', with reflexive prefix *y-* (9.4.).

8.2.4. CONVERSIVE CAUSATIVE REPETITIVE

-ša (with class 9) forms class 6a verbs.

lesn hoł ʔimat ʔaˑči yam tunaˑ ʔi-łuwa-š-kʔa-ˑʔimoʔka (thus perhaps seemingly they.two their eyes reflexive-stand-conversive.causative.repetitive-causative-contemporaneous sat) 'thus, it seems, the two sat there making their eyes run around and around': *łuwa* (9a) 'to be standing (pl. subj.)'.

8.3. CAUSATIVE

The third position is assigned solely to causative morphemes suffixed to the past stem. The causatives appear in two forms, each with its allomorphs: -kʔa (with classes 1-6a, 10b) and -kkʔa (with 7, 9) form class 7 verbs; overlapping this distribution is -u (with 9), which forms class 4a, and -ʔu (with 9), which forms the unique class 5, whose only members are verbs derived by this causative element.

hoʔnaʔ toʔ ʔuwe łan ʔaˑwan teya-ʔu-Ø (us you injury large to be-causative-present) 'you are doing us a great injury' (a conventional phrase used in mourning): *teya* (9a) 'to be'.

8.4.

In the fourth position, two aspect suffixes—the static and the continuative—are added to the past stem.

8.4.1. STATIC

-na (with classes 1-7) and -nna (with 10b) form class 9 verbs or class 1 nouns.

tom hoʔ tewusuʔ te-kʔoha-nna-n ʔanšema (you I prayer terrestrial-light-static-singular ask) 'I ask you in prayer for life': *kʔoha* (10b) 'to be or become light in color'.

8.4.2. CONTINUATIVE

-yeˑ (with monosyllabic verbs of class 3c) and -eˑ (with other verbs ending in e or a) form class 8a; -y (with other verbs ending in i, o, or u) forms class 8b. Membership in class 8 is confined to verbs that have undergone this continuative derivation.

yam hasuski moweʔ ʔi-tun-e-kkow ʔakka laˑkʔ suski ʔaˑtunaˑ łupcʔinna (his coyote.weed berries reflexive have.eyes-continuative-past.agentive because today coyote eyes yellow) 'because he put coyote-weed berries where his eyes were, coyotes today have yellow eyes': *tuna* (9a) 'to have eyes', (noun class 1a) 'eye'.

8.5.

Only one morpheme is suffixed to the past stem in the fifth positional slot—the plural subject of transitive verbs. -naˑwa (with classes 1-6, 7-8) and -(V)ˑwa (with 9) form verbs of class 6c, composed solely of these pluralized verbs; -pa (with 9) forms class 6a verbs.

kʔošo-y-naˑw-eʔ (wash-continuative-plural.subject-present) 'they are washing it': *kʔošo* (4b) 'to wash'.

8.6.

The sixth and final derivational position contains one morpheme added to the past stem—the negative. -naʔma (with classes 1-6a, 7-8) forms verbs of the unique class 6b, confined to verbs with this negative suffix. Another negative suffix (8.1.2.) is used with classes 6c and 9.

kop leyʔap kʷaʔ homʔan toʔ tena-ˑ-naʔma-Ø (what happening not for.me you music-causative-negative-present) 'what's the matter that you aren't singing for me': *tena* (9a) 'to be music', (noun class 1a) 'song'.

9. VERB DERIVATIONS: PREFIXES

Like the derivational suffixes, the prefixes can be described in part by the meaning of the morpheme and its allomorphic forms. Unlike the suffixes, the prefixes are not distributed in accordance with word classes and stem types; nor do the prefixes, being preposed, alter the word-class or stem-type membership of the verbs to which they are attached. But for some prefixes the distribution of allomorphs is based upon the phonological characteristics of the initial phoneme in the following verb stem. Therefore, the descriptive criteria must include the relevant phonological features of the stem that govern the distribution of the prefix forms.

The prefixing derivations are treated in the order of their positions, starting with the first position adjacent to the stem and ending with the fifth position farthest from the stem.

9.1.

Three prefixes occupy the first positional slot.

9.1.1.

Plural subject of intransitive or plural object of transitive verbs. *tet-* (before *t*), *t-* (before the zeroed *ʔ*, see 3.2.2.), *te-* (before other consonants).

tet-tuna-ti-Ø (plural.subject-have.eyes-inchoative-imperative) 'open your (plural) eyes': *tuna* (9a) 'to have eyes'.

9.1.2. INCHOATIVE OR INCEPTIVE

y- (before the zeroed *ʔ*), *ʔi-* (before other consonants).

y-aʔa-ʔka (inchoative-be.a.hole-past) 'a hole developed', a figurative expression meaning 'he (she) became jealous': *ʔaʔa* (9a) 'to be a hole in an object'.

Most verbs add either this prefix or the suffix *-ti* (8.2.2.) for the inchoative or inceptive function. A few class 9a verbs require both affixes, as *ʔi-poča-ti* 'to become bad': *poča* (9b) 'to be bad'. This prefix-suffix combination is the only case in Zuni of a required cooccurrence of discontinuous morphemes.

9.1.3. TERRESTRIAL

te-, with no allomorphs, has reference to natural phenomena. It frequently denotes 'ground, earth, soil', as in *te-kʔina* 'the ground is wet': *kʔina* (9b) 'to be wet'. Verbs meaning 'to be hot' or 'to be cold' become, with *te-*, references to the weather.

9.2.

Assigned to the second position is a single prefix, the indeterminate. *yu-* occurs without allomorphs. Most commonly, it has the semantic force of suggesting an approximation, as in *yu-cʔikʔo* 'to be slightly bent', from *cʔikʔo* (9a) 'to be bent'. Sometimes it gives a specialized meaning to the stem:

yu-ʔassela 'to be envious', from *ʔassela* (9a) 'to be askew, to be crooked'.

čim hoł yam ʔallašeˑn ʔona yu-teʔči-kʔa-p... (then perhaps his one.he.was.chasing agentive indeterminate-arrive-causative-different.subject.subordinate...) 'then, it seems, just as he was tiring the one that he was chasing...': *yu-teʔči* 'to be tired', from *teʔči* (4a) 'to arrive'

9.3.

The third positional slot is filled by one prefix, the indirective. *ʔah-* (before *h*), *ʔal-* (before *l*), *ʔam-* (before *m*

or *p*), *ʔaw-* (before *w*), *ʔan-* (before all other consonants). This prefix either transitivizes an intransitive verb or, with a transitive verb, deflects the event to another object (6.2.).

kʔum čapin ʔal-laʔhi-nan yam ʔuttekow ʔakka laˑkʔ suski łepon kʷʔinnan taˑ hokti kʷʔinna (log burned indirective-jump-same.subject.subordinate his one.who.bit because today coyote snout black and tail black) 'because he jumped at the charred log and bit it, Coyote today has a black snout and a black tail': *laʔhi* (4a) 'to jump' (intransitive).

9.4.

The fourth-position prefix is the reflexive, *y-* (before the zeroed *ʔ*), *ʔi-* (before other consonants).

y-emma-kʔa-nap-ka (reflexive-increase-causative-plural.subject-past) 'they caused themselves to increase', an idiom meaning 'they became conceited': *ʔemma* (2) 'to increase'.

9.5.

The fifth and last position is occupied by two prefixes.

9.5.1. RECIPROCAL

ʔiˑw- (before the zeroed *ʔ* when it is followed by *i*), *ʔiˑy-* (before the zeroed *ʔ* when followed by other vowels), and *ʔiˑ-* (before other consonants).

ʔiˑy-an-šema-nap-ka (reciprocal-indirective-ask-plural.subject-past) 'they asked each other': *šema* (4b) 'to ask'.

9.5.2.

Plural subject of intransitive or plural object of transitive verbs. This function is performed by several sets of allomorphs. The great majority of verbs add *ʔaˑw-* (before the zeroed *ʔ*) and *ʔaˑ-* (before other consonants), also employed for the plural of some particles (13.2.3.). A few verbs take *y-* (before the zeroed *ʔ*) and *ʔi-* (before other consonants). The form *ʔukʷ-* has been found with only two verbs, *kʷato* 'to enter' and *kʷayi* 'to emerge'.

ʔaˑw-i-piyaˑ-nan ʔiˑmuka (plural.object-reflexive-hold.by.the.hand-causative-same.subject.subordinate sat) 'after shaking hands with them, he sat down': *piya* (9a) 'to hold by the hand'.

10. VERB DERIVATIONS: REDUPLICATION AND SUPPLETION

10.1.

Reduplication is weakly represented in Zuni; it is applied only to two-syllable verbs of class 10a. These verbs may undergo two reduplicative processes, both resulting in class 1 verbs. Semantically, the reduplications are used with verbs referring to various kinds of noises.

10.1.1. MEDIOPASSIVE REPETITIVE

The final reduplication of the first two phonemes, which may be symbolized by the formula 12312 derived from a 1234 base, expresses the notion of a repeated event that does not have an active agent. In the base formula, 1 and 3 refer to single Cs or C^{ʔ} clusters; 2 and 4 indicate Vs.

towto-ʔa (repeated.rumbling-present) 'there are pounding noises': *towo* (10a) 'to make a rumbling sound'.

10.1.2. MEDIOPASSIVE SEMELFACTIVE
The final reduplication of the last two phonemes (123434 from 1234) refers to an event with patterned or continuous repetitions.

hecʔucʔu-kʔa-Ø (patterned.pressing-causative-imperative) 'knead it, rub it': *hecʔu* (10a) 'to press down, to squeeze'.

10.2.
In their lexical meaning a few pairs of verbs include a reference to number, paralleling the meaning of the derivational prefixes that indicate the plural subject of intransitive or plural object of transitive verbs (9.1.1., 9.5.2.). The following are some examples of these verb pairs linked by suppletion: 'to be standing'—*ʔela* (sg. subj.), *łuwa* (pl. subj.), 'to be in a sitting position'—*ʔimo* (sg. subj.), *tina* (pl. subj.), 'to take'—*ʔahha* (sg. obj.), *wo·tiha* (pl. obj.), and 'to hold'—*łeya* (sg. obj.), *woppona* (pl. obj.).

11. THE NOUN
The structural system of the noun is considerably simpler than that of the verb. The noun adds only two inflectional suffixes, the singular and the plural. Its derivations include five suffixes, all belonging to a single conceptual category, and the process of compounding.

11.1. NOUN CLASSES
The classes of the noun, with their inflected forms, are listed in table 2. Of all the noun classes, class 1 is the most numerous and the most productive. A sampling of dictionary entries revealed that over 90 percent of the noun bases belong to class 1; furthermore, all the derivations that form nouns as well as verbs produce class 1a nouns (8.1.3.). Class 1b is a fairly large but closed set; it contains only noun bases, with no derivational processes creating new members. The two subclasses of 1 are phonologically selected: 1a is made up of polysyllables, 1b of monosyllables. Class 2 is a closed set, limited to a handful of monosyllabic bases. Class 3 nouns are polysyllables whose final vowel is deleted before the singular suffix: 3a is composed entirely of nouns formed by -*pa* 'objects in a deep container' or -*la* 'objects in a shallow container'; 3b and 3c are small closed sets, the former containing nouns ending in -*ma*, the latter those ending in -*ha* or -*ča*.

A few nouns of class 1, referring to masses or abstracts, occur in the plural only: *kʔaweʔ* 'water', *cema·weʔ* 'thought(s)'.

Table 2. Noun Classes and Inflections

Noun class and base		Singular stem and suffix	Plural stem and suffix
1a.	*pasi* 'sleeve'	*pasi-nne*	*pasi-·weʔ*
b.	*sa* 'dish'	*sa-ʔleʔ*	*sa-weʔ*
2.	*sa* 'bone'	*sa-mmeʔ*	*sa-weʔ*
3a.	*lupa* 'deep container of ashes'	*lup-ʔe*	*lupa-·weʔ*
b.	*noma* 'insect, scatterbrain'	*nom-meʔ*	*noma-·weʔ*
c.	*wiha* 'infant'	*wiha-Ø*	*wihe-weʔ*

SOURCE: Walker 1966; Lynn Nichols (communication to editors 1996).

11.2. NOUN INFLECTIONS
The inflectional suffixes for singular and plural appear in full forms and short forms.

11.2.1.
Singular (full form). -*nne* (with class 1a), -*ʔleʔ* (with 1b), -*mmeʔ* (with 2), -*ʔe* (with 3a), -*meʔ* (with 3b), -*Ø* (with 3c).

he-ʔl ʔitiw ʔona (coin-singular middle agentive) 'a half dollar': *he* (1b) 'coin, metal'.

11.2.2.
Plural (full form). -*weʔ* (with monosyllabic nouns), -·*weʔ* (with polysyllabic nouns).

šiwaya-·weʔ 'steam, automobiles': *šiwaya* (1a) 'automobile'.

11.2.3.
A short form of singular or plural inflection is used with a CV or CCV term occurring as a first-position stem in a close-knit syntactic construction. (Syntactic constructions are to be distinguished from compounds; see 5.5.) The head term may be either a monosyllabic noun or a monosyllable abbreviated from a longer noun or particle.

When the head term is singular, the suffix is -*ʔ* in a construction that is singular, -*Ø* in a plural construction.

he-ʔ cʔummenne (metal-singular resilient) 'a gun spring'; *he-Ø cʔumme·weʔ* 'gun springs': *he* (1b) 'metal, coin'.

li-ʔ šilowanne (money-singular red) 'a penny': *li-Ø šilowa·weʔ* 'pennies': *li-* abbreviated from *liya·li* (particle) 'unit of money' (from Spanish *real*).

When the head term is plural, the suffix is -(V)· in constructions that are either singular or plural.

mo-· čikʷa (spherical.object-plural sweet) 'peach, peaches': *mo* (1b) 'spherical object'.

A few examples have been found without abbreviation of the head term, as *ʔakʷʔa-· kʔakʷenne* (medicine-plural house) 'hospital': *ʔakʷʔa* (1a) 'medicine'.

11.3. NOUN DERIVATIONS
Suffixation and compounding are the derivational processes by which nouns may be formed.

497

11.3.1.

To derive a noun phrase from a syntactic construction, the full inflectional suffixes are added to the last term of the construction, in much the same manner as the English possessive in *the Queen of England's visit* is suffixed to the last term of the construction though it logically belongs to the first term. In Zuni, furthermore, the suffix is added to the last term whether it is a verb or noun stem. In *heˀ cˀummenne* (example in 11.2.3.), the stem of the second term is a verb: *cˀumme* (verb class 9a) 'to be resilient, to be strong'. However, the total construction is treated as a derived noun, taking its own inflection and functioning as a substantive in the larger syntactic context of the sentence.

11.3.2.

Noun-forming derivational suffixes may be added to particles or nouns but not to verbs. The five suffixes of this type fit into one positional slot preceding the inflectional element. They denote various kinds of collective or spatial groupings—a semantic category encountered among verb-forming derivations (8.1.3.). The suffixes are:

-limo 'dispersed objects', forms class 1a

-ɫpo 'objects in an arrangement' (e.g., a stack, a bundle), forms 1a

-paɫa 'wrapped objects', forms 1a

-la 'objects in a shallow container', forms 3a

-pa 'objects in a deep container', forms 3a.

Some examples are:

ˀate-limo-nne-ˀši (blood-dispersed-singular-interrogative) '(is it) spattered with blood?' *ˀate* (particle) 'blood'.

kˀa-p-ˀe powaye (liquid-deep.container-singular rests.on.a.surface) 'the bottle of liquid is on (e.g., the table)': *kˀa* (1b) 'liquid'.

11.3.3.

The compounding of stems is another technique for creating nouns. Noun compounds manifest one of the formal characteristics of constructional derivations (11.2.3.): in both cases the first-position stem appears in a CV or CCV structure, either a primary or an abbreviated monosyllable. However, in a noun compound the first-position element does not undergo inflection, as it does in a construction. Furthermore, the compound is phonologically identified as a unit word because it contains only one heavy stress (1.0.); in the construction, each component takes a heavy stress.

Noun compounds are formed from a combination of noun plus noun or noun plus verb. These compounds, being nouns, are inflected for number.

makuččinne 'bluejeans': *ma* (1b noun) 'salt', referring here to salt stains; *kučči* (1a noun) 'pants'.

weɫeyakʷkʷiˑweˀ 'anklets of porcupine quills': *we* (2 noun) 'mammal with paws'; *ɫeyakʷkʷi* (1a noun) 'turtle-shell ornament worn around calf of leg'.

nočapiˑweˀ 'coffee': *no* (1b noun) 'bean'; *čapi* (4a verb) 'to burn'.

12. THE PERSONAL PRONOUN

Table 3 presents the paradigm of personal pronouns. Where the subject and possessive pronouns undergo unique types of reduction, the reduced utterance-medial forms as well as the full utterance-final forms are listed; object pronouns do not occur finally and, consequently, are not differentiated for utterance position. Predictable reductions are not indicated in the table (see 3.3.-3.3.2.).

Within the sentence, pronouns vary in position relative to other words, except that they precede verbs, which must appear in final position (16.4.). When functioning as subjects or objects, the subject pronoun generally precedes the object.

ˀaˑč hoˀn ˀayyučiˀatika (they.two us were.amazed.at) 'the two of them were amazed at us'.

A possessive pronoun most frequently precedes the term that it modifies, as in *hom tunaˑwe* 'my eyes'. But these are merely preferred sequences. Zuni texts contain examples of other pronoun positions, which probably carry implications of emphasis or other stylistic features.

tom ˀan hoˀ tunaˑ ˀitonna (your of I eyes will.eat) 'I will eat your eyes'.

tom hoˀ ˀuttenna (you I will.bite) 'I will bite you'.

12.1. PERSON

The paradigm distinguishes three persons. Although the constituent morphemes of the total paradigm cannot be clearly identified, the underlying bases appears to be **hoˑ* first person, **toˑ* second person, and **ˀaˑ* third person. The third person is somewhat anomalous: it lacks a subject pronoun in the singular and plural, the third-person reference being indicated in context by the

Table 3. Personal Pronouns

| | Subject | | Object | Possessive | |
	Medial	Final		Medial	Final
Singular					
First person	*hoˀ*	*hoˑˀo*	*hom*	*hom*	*homma*
Second person	*toˀ*	*toˑˀo*	*tom*	*tom*	*tomma*
Third person	—	—	*ˀan*	*ˀan*	*ˀaˑni*
Dual					
First person	*hon*	*hoˀno*	*hoˀnaˀ*		*hoˀnaˀ*
Second person	*ton*	*toˀno*	*toˀnaˀ*		*toˀnaˀ*
Third person	*ˀaˑči*		*ˀaˑčiyaˀ*		*ˀaˑčiyaˀ*
Plural					
First person	*hon*	*hoˀno*	*hoˀnaˀ*		*hoˀnˀaˑwan*
Second person	*ton*	*toˀno*	*toˀnaˀ*		*toˀnˀaˑwan*
Third person	—	—	*ˀaˑwan*		*ˀaˑwan*

absence of a pronoun. Although third-person object pronouns are available, they are, in fact, normally omitted and used only for emphasis.

12.2. NUMBER AND CASE

The paradigm differentiates three numbers: singular, dual, and plural. But this maximal pattern is not carried through the paradigm consistently: dual and plural forms overlap for first- and second-person subjects and objects. The paradigm also discriminates three cases: subject, object, and possessive. But, again, object and possessive forms overlap for all persons in the singular and dual, and for the third person in the plural as well.

13. THE PARTICLE

13.1. FUNCTIONS

Particles—the uninflected class of words—constitute an important part of the Zuni lexicon and grammar. Roughly one-third of the forms listed in the Zuni dictionary (Newman 1958) are particles, and they cover a wide range of syntactic and semantic functions. They duplicate the syntactic function of nouns in being employed as substantives, that is, as subjects or objects of a verb. In some of the semantic categories of entity references, particles are distinct from nouns: particles, for example, include all kinship terms (*citta* 'mother', *papa* 'older brother'), reference to animals and human beings (*suski* 'coyote', *šiwani* 'rain priest'), and indefinites (*čuwa* 'someone', *ko?* 'something intangible'); nouns denote all body parts (*?asinne* 'hand', *lašokti-nne* 'ear') and items of clothing (*po?ya-nne* 'hat', *?učču-nne* 'shirt'). In some categories particles and nouns overlap: thus *?ašek?a* 'pine tree' and *?iši?naka* 'inner bark' are particles, but *homata-nne* 'juniper tree' and *c?ikʷkʷa-nne* 'bark, skin' are nouns.

Particles also function syntactically as modifiers (*hoḷi* 'perhaps', *k?ayu* 'fresh, fresh object'). This function they share with two types of inflected verbs 7.1.2., 7.1.3.) and with some nouns that refer to reified qualities (*wakʷ?ali-nne* 'limp object, fluffy object'). A few particles play the role of relators (*?akka* 'with, in', *?i·yama* 'up'), a function also performed by some enclitics (14.1.-14.3.). However, only particles serve as conjunctions (*si* 'and, then', *hapiš* 'or') and as exclamatives (*hi·ya* exclamative of surprise used only by women, *he·* exclamative of surprise used only by men).

13.2. PARTICLE DERIVATION

Particles are not only primary bases but also secondary forms derived by suffixation, prefixation, and compounding.

13.2.1.

Most of the 11 particle-forming suffixes are unproductive, being attached to stems of a restricted semantic type and having a narrow range of meaning or usage. Six of these suffixes are added only to particles.

13.2.1.1. CEREMONIAL

-mo is suffixed to particles denoting some kinship and ceremonial relationships; it forms words that are recited in reciprocal series by the two participants in the smoking ritual of the winter solstice ceremony. Thus, in the initial exchange, the first participant says *tačču-mo* (*tačču* 'father'), and the other responds with *tale-mo* (*tale* 'woman's brother's son, woman's clan brother'); in a later exchange, the first pronounces *nana-mo* (*nana* 'grandfather, grandson'), and the other answers with *tošle-mo* (*tošle* 'a ceremonial relationship').

13.2.1.2. ALTERNATIVE

-(V)· is added to the first of a pair of kinship terms. It denotes an alternative, like *hapiš* 'or' but appears to carry a humorous connotation. In one folktale, for example, Coyote keeps forgetting the song that he is trying to learn from Woodpecker. In telling himself that he will ask Woodpecker to sing the song again, Coyote refers to him as *papa·· suw hoḷ* (older.brother- or younger.brother perhaps). This implies that Coyote is uncertain whether to address Woodpecker as 'older brother', which would be respectful but self-demeaning, or as 'younger brother', which would give Coyote a superior kinship position but might insult Woodpecker.

13.2.1.3. FAMILIAR

-mme is attached to the abbreviated CV or CCV form primarily of kinship terms: thus, *ho-mme* (*hotta* 'grandmother, granddaughter') is used as a familiar term of address by a younger person to an old lady or by an older man to a young woman.

13.2.1.4. INTERROGATIONAL

-pi, *-ppi*, or *-?pi* is suffixed to indefinites to form interrogatives: *ko?-pi* or *ko-ppi* 'what? how?' (*ko?* 'something intangible'); *ko·wi-?pi* 'how much?' (*ko·wi* 'few').

13.2.1.5. SIMILITIVE

-na? is appended to the name of a tribe or other group to denote behavior characteristic of the group, as *šiwina?* 'in the Zuni manner' (*šiwi* 'Zuni').

13.2.1.6. VERNACULAR

-?ma is used with tribal or group names to refer to the language of the group, as *meliqa-?ma* 'English' (*meliqa* 'Anglo').

13.2.2.

Five of the particle-forming suffixes are added to verbs and, in some instances, to particles as well.

13.2.2.1. MULTIPLICATIVE

-*k?an*, limited to quantifying verbs and numeral particles, conveys the notion of 'so many times': *?emma-k?an* 'many times' (*?emma*, class 2 verb, 'to increase'); *topalekk?a-k?an* 'six times' (*topalekk?a*, particle, 'six').

13.2.2.2. PERSONAL

-*k?i* forms a few person references from verbs and particles, and it is also found with some unanalyzable particles denoting persons: *łašši-k?i* 'oldest male of household, husband' (*łašši*, class 2 verb, 'to become old'); *?okacci-k?i* 'wife', a somewhat derogatory term often translated as 'the old woman' (*?oka*, particle, 'female', but -*cci* is unidentifiable).

13.2.2.3. VALUED OBJECT

-*k*ʷ*a?*, found with class 10b verbs of color, refers to ceremonial or otherwise valued objects, as *łi??a-k*ʷ*a?* 'turquoise stone, blue corn' (*łi??a* 'to be blue, green').

13.2.2.4. INSTRUMENTAL

-*ka*, used primarily with class 9 verbs, denotes an instrument, as *?ačiya· ?otta-ka* 'knife sharpener' (*?ačiya·* 'knives', *?otta*, class 9b verb, 'to be sharp').

13.2.2.5. MEMBERSHIP

-(V)·*k*ʷ*e* is suffixed to verbs or particles to refer to a person or the people of a group: *pa-lokk?a-·k*ʷ*e* 'Ramah Navajo' (*pa-* abbreviated from *paču*, particle, 'Navajo', *lokk?a*, class 10b verb, 'to be gray'); *tehha·na-·k*ʷ*e* 'outlaws' (*tehha·na*, particle, from Spanish *tejano* 'Texan').

13.2.3.

The only prefix among particle derivations is the plural. *?a·w-* (before the zeroed *?*) and *?a·* (before other consonants) is used only with particles denoting persons: *?a·w-occi?* 'males' (*?occi?* 'male'); *?a·-šiwi* 'Zunis' (*šiwi* 'Zuni'). (See 9.5.2. for the verb prefix with the identical form and a similar function.)

13.2.4.

Like noun compounds (11.3.3.), particle compounds are composed of a first-position CV or CCV stem. But a wider range of word-class types may enter into particle compounds: the first-position element may be either a noun or a particle; the noun can combine only with a verb, but the particle may combine with a verb, noun, or another particle. Examples are: *ha-k?oha* 'white sage' (*ha*, class 1b noun, 'weed', *k?oha*, class 10b verb, 'to be white'); *me-?oše* 'tramp' (*me-* abbreviated from *meliqa*, particle, 'Anglo', *?oše*, class 1 verb, 'to be hungry'), *su-tek*ʷ*k*ʷ*ante* 'stupid Coyote', an epithet used in folktales (*su-* abbreviated from *suski*, particle, 'coyote', *tek*ʷ*k*ʷ*ante*, class 1a noun, 'stupid person'); *ho-tonaši* 'Old Lady Badger', a nickname applied to a woman anthropologist who studied the Zuni (*ho-* abbreviated from *hotta*, particle, 'grandmother, granddaughter', *tonaši*, particle, 'badger').

14. ENCLITICS

Enclitics are dependent morphemes attached to the end of complete words. As compared to suffixes, they are more loosely bound to their word nuclei: when added to inflected words, they are tacked on after the inflectional suffixes; most of them may be added freely to words of any class. However, their dependent status is manifested by their allomorphs, which, like suffix allomorphs, are conditioned by the forms that they follow. And like suffixes, enclitics cannot occur in isolation.

The five enclitics do not form a coherent semantic set. Three refer to location or direction, one is an interrogative, and one expresses a modal notion.

14.1. LOCATIVE

-*an* (after *w*) and -*?an* (elsewhere) is variously translated as 'in, at, on, by'.

homatt-?an ?el-?an tełu?w-an ?iču·nan s ?ałka (juniper-at standing-at shade-in lying then slept) 'lying in the shade where the juniper was standing, he then fell asleep': *homatta* (class 1a noun) 'juniper', *?ela* (class 9a verb) 'to be standing' *tełu?wa* (class 1a noun) 'shade, shadow'.

14.2. INESSIVE

-*annan* (after *w*) and -*?annan* (elsewhere) carries the meaning of 'in, into'.

?o-w-annan k?ol ?iyya?sek?a (flour-plural-into chili mix) 'mix the chili into the flour': *?o* (class 1b noun) 'flour'.

14.3. ALLATIVE

-*k*ʷ*in* denotes 'motion to, toward'.

*?ik*ʷ*?ałt suski powa-k*ʷ*in ?a·č ?ika* (back coyote resting-to they.two came) 'the two came to the place where Coyote was resting'; *powa* (class 9a verb) 'to be resting on the ground'.

14.4. INTERROGATIVE

-*?ši* (after a vowel) and -*ši* (after a consonant).

to?-š ?aššu?wa?ka (you-interrogative spoke.to) 'did you speak to him?': *to?* (pronoun) 'you (singular)'.

?anate-?ši (Indian.tobacco-interrogative) '(is it) Indian tobacco?': *?anate* (particle) 'Indian tobacco'.

14.5. ADVERSATIVE

-*?te* (after a vowel) and -*te* (after a consonant) is translated as 'even though, in spite of'.

tem łito-?t ?a·wika (still rain-even.though came) 'even though it was still raining, they came': *łito* (class 9a verb) 'to rain'.

THE SYSTEM OF UTTERANCES

15. UTTERANCE TYPES

15.1. THE NONPREDICATIVE UTTERANCE

Utterances may lack any explicit predicating elements such as verbs. An affirmative or negative particle (*ʔe* 'yes', *ʔetła* 'no') forms an acceptable utterance, as do any of the exclamative particles. Words may be linked without a verb copula, as in *lukno hom ʔiˑyanikinaˑweʔ* (these my relatives) 'these are my relatives'. Response fragments, which omit the predicating verb of a preceding question, are normal in casual speech: *ʔan kʔakʷʔa* 'at his house' may be the reply to 'where did you stay last night?' Formulaic and slang speech abounds in utterances without predicators. A formula used by women in mourning is *hanaˑ ʔiče hoʔnʔaˑwan (taččᵘ)* (Oh dear our [father]), 'Oh, our dear (father)!' Among slang expressions, a children's taunt current a number of years ago was *piš noʔli* 'fish nose', the allusion here being to the White man's image of the fish-nosed Indian portrayed on the buffalo nickel, when it was still in circulation, and on the calendar pictures.

15.2. THE SENTENCE

The sentence is the most frequent utterance type encountered in any of the styles—folktales, prayers, and casual speech. The minimal sentence contains a single word, a verb expressing a predication, the number of the subject, and, if the verb is transitive, the number of the object as well. When no substantive appears in the sentence, the third person is understood to be the subject or object: *šemaka* '(he) called (him)'; *ʔi-šemaka* '(he) called (them)', with plural object (9.5.2.); *šema-nap-ka* '(they) called (him)', with plural subject (8.5.); *ʔi-šema-nap-ka* '(they) called (them)'.

15.3. SUBSTANTIVE AND PREDICATE

The terms 'noun' and 'verb' have been reserved for application to Zuni word classes. To avoid confusion, "substantive" is employed instead of "noun" to denote the syntactic unit that functions as a subject or object in the sentence; the Zuni substantive may be a noun, a pronoun, a particle, or a phrase containing words of any of these classes. Likewise, the term "predicate" is used instead of "verb" to refer to the syntactic unit that predicates the event in which the subject is involved; in Zuni the predicate always contains a verb, but it may be expanded to include words of other classes.

16. SENTENCE TYPES AND COMPONENTS

16.1. SIMPLE AND COMPLEX SENTENCES

There are two types of sentence—simple and complex. The simple sentence is made up of a single independent predication, the predication being a word or sequence of words containing a predicate. The complex sentence is composed of one or more dependent predications and one independent predication.

The only necessary and sufficient component of the sentence is the independent predication, which may contain only the predicating verb or, in addition, substantives functioning as subjects or objects. Either of these basic syntactic structures, predicate or substantive, may appear in the minimal form of a single word or in the expanded form of a phrase, containing complements, modifiers, or coordinate constructions.

16.2. THE PREDICATE

The minimal predicate consists of a single verb functioning either as an independent or a dependent predication. The independent predication may constitute a sentence by itself (15.2.) or form part of a complex sentence; its verb is marked inflectionally by a suffix of tense-mode (7.2.) or mode (7.3.). The dependent predication is the satellite portion of a complex sentence; its verb is inflected by one of the subordinating suffixes (7.1.): *kʔał-nan ʔitocippoʔka* (become.hot-same.subject.subordinate curled.up) 'after getting hot, it curled up'. The predicate may be expanded through complementation, modification, or coordination.

16.2.1.
The predicate may be expanded by complementation of the governing verb. Some of the subordinating suffixes form verbs that function as complements.

hoʔ łata-ʔkan ʔaˑka (I hunt-resultative.subordinate [7.1.1.] went) 'I went to hunt'.

hoʔ tenaˑ-n hakkʔakka (I sing-adjunctive.subordinate [7.1.3.] requested) 'I requested him to sing'.

The syntactic role of complements is also assumed by nouns, pronouns, or particles as objects of the predicating verb.

ta-mm ʔipeʔkunan... (wood-singular tripping.over...) 'tripping over a piece of wood...'. The object of this dependent predication is the noun *ta* (class 2) 'wood'.

16.2.2.
Modifiers offer another means of expansion of the predicate. This adverbial function is expressed by a variety of particles, such as *siš* 'very, very much', *čimi* 'recently, now', *hanaʔte* 'immediately'. Several subordinating suffixes produce verbs that also function as predicate modifiers.

tettun-Ø ʔaˑwallukka (watch-modificative.subordinate [7.1.8.] went.about) 'they went about watching'.

tene-n čuneka (sing-adjunctive.subordinate stopped) 'he stopped singing'. For other suffixes forming predicate modifiers, see 7.1.2. and 7.1.4.

16.2.3.
Coordination of predicates occurs only with the dependent type, whose verbs are inflected by subordinating suffixes. The degree of elaboration in the use of this

syntactic device is one of the identifying features of style level. Complex sentences with a single dependent predication are common in casual speech. Sentences with two and, more rarely, three dependent predicates are found in folktales. A characteristic of prayer style is the use of strings of lengthy dependent predications linked in coordination.

(1) *lukka yatonne hoʔnʔaˑwan yatokka taččə yam tełaššinakʷi toʔ yeˑlanaˑ kʷayikʔappa*, (2) *yam ʔak ʔaˑkʔahkʷi yaˑn ʔaˑtey ʔona tom hoʔ halawtinan łeyaʔuppa*, (3) *yam ʔanikʷanan ʔakka homʔan halawtinan ʔahn ʔułłaˑnan....* (1) 'On this day you, our Father Sun, bringing yourself out rising from your sacred dwelling place, (2) my offering you our sacred cornmeal from those of us who have been here a lifetime, (3) with your power receiving from me the sacred cornmeal...'. Predicates (1) and (2) end with different-subject subordinates (7.1.6.); predicate (3), with a same-subject subordinate (7.1.5.).

16.3. THE SUBSTANTIVE

The minimal substantive is a single noun, pronoun, or particle that functions as the subject or object of a predicating verb; the object, being a complement of the verb, is part of the predicate (16.2.1.). Substantives, like predicates, are expanded by complementation, modification, or coordination.

16.3.1.

In substantive expansion by complementation, a particle, pronoun, or noun may function as the object complement of a verb or the complement of a particle.

hom ʔill-Ø ʔona ʔaššuʔwapka (me have-modification. subordinate agentive spoke.to) 'they spoke to the one having me', that is, 'they spoke to my spouse'. The expanded substantive complementing the verb is *hom ʔill ʔona*; the pronoun *hom* is the complement of the subordinate verb *ʔill*, which modifies the particle *ʔona*.

susk ʔan ʔaʔu (coyote for put.it.down) 'put it down for Coyote'. The expanded substantive complementing the verb is *susk ʔan*, in which *susk* is a particle complement of the particle *ʔan*.

16.3.2.

Substantive expansion is most frequently achieved through the use of modifiers, a function performed by any of the word-class types—verbs, nouns, particles, or pronouns. A subordinate verb formed with the modificative suffix is illustrated by *ʔill* in the example above (16.3.1.), and subordinates with the adjunctive (7.1.3.) or past agentive (7.1.7.) suffixes also function as modifiers in expanded substantives. The following are examples of noun, particle, and pronoun modifiers.

heˑ piʔleʔ (metals string) 'wire'. In this expanded substantive the noun *heˑ*, (plural of *he* (class 1b), modifies the noun *piʔleʔ*, singular of *pi* (class 1b).

hasuski moʔl ʔaˑči ʔahnan... (coyote.weed berry they.two getting) 'after getting the two coyote-weed berries'. The expanded substantive is *hasuski moʔl ʔaˑči*, in which both the particle *hasuski* and the pronoun *ʔaˑči* modify the noun *moʔl*, singular of *mo* (class 1b).

16.3.3.

As another syntactic device for expanding substantives, coordination is employed to link nouns, particles, or pronouns.

kʔola taˑp ʔoweʔ ʔahka (chili and flour bought) 'he bought chili and flour'. The particle *kʔola* and the noun *ʔoweʔ*, plural of *ʔo* (class 1b), are coordinated by the particle *taˑp*.

toʔ hapiš hoˑʔo 'you and I'. The pronouns *toʔ* and *hoˑʔo* are linked by the particle *hapiš*.

Some of the numbers above '10' are expanded substantives formed by coordinated particles: *haʔikʔan ʔastemła taˑp haʔin* (three.times 10 and three) '33'.

16.4. ORDER OF COMPONENTS

In complex sentences the independent predication always occurs finally. Within predications, whether dependent or independent, the verb is always terminal. In expanded predicates or substantives, the complement always precedes its governing term.

No other components of the sentence manifest an invariable order, but some preferential sequences can be discerned. Generally, particles modifying the predicate, such as *taˑ* 'again' or *čiš* 'if', appear first in the sentence. Among substantives the subject tends to precede the object. The fixed and preferred sequences are illustrated in the following sentence.

taˑčiš tam tununu susk ʔankʔohakʔanan s les kʷakka (meanwhile wood rumbler coyote perceiving then this said) 'meanwhile, when Woodpecker perceived Coyote, he said this'.

16.5. CONCORD

Concord, or agreement, operates in sentences containing negatives and in those involving subject or object number.

16.5.1.

A negative particle always accompanies a predication in which the verb contains one of the negative suffixes (7.2.2., 7.2.3., 8.1.2., 8.6.). The particle *ʔełła* is employed with imperative or permissive forms of negativized verbs, *kʷaʔ* with other forms of negativized verbs.

ʔełł kʔi-kʔa-naʔma-Ø (not wet-causative-negative-imperative) 'don't get it wet'.

kʷaʔ toʔ ʔoše-šukʷa (not you hungry-negative.future) 'you won't be hungry'.

16.5.2.

Number concord applies only when the subject or object is a substantive inflected for number—a noun or pronoun, not a particle. A subject or object in the singular agrees with the predicate verb, which signals its singular number by the absence of a plural subject or object affix. For the plural, the subject or object takes the plural inflection, and plurality is again marked in the verb by the presence of a plural subject or object affix.

yam ča-ʔleʔ hoʔ ʔotenna (my child-singular I will.make. dance) 'I will make my child dance'.

yam ča-weʔ hoʔ ʔaˑw-otenna (my child-plural I plural.object-will.make.dance) 'I will make my children dance'.

hon ʔaˑw-oteˑ-nap-ka (we plural.object-make.dance-plural.subject-past) 'we made them dance'.

The only distinctively marked dual form is the third-person pronoun (table 3). For first- and second-person pronouns, the dual is indicated by the undifferentiated dual-plural form in conjunction with a singular (non-plural) verb; the plural is denoted by the same pronominal form with a plural verb.

hoʔn ʔunaye (us sees) 'he sees us (dual)'.

hoʔn ʔaˑw-unaye (us plural.object-sees) 'he sees us (plural)'.

17. Selected Vocabulary

In the following vocabulary the Zuni forms are identified by abbreviations referring to word class: intransitive verb (iv), transitive verb (tv), noun (n), and particle (p). The inflectional classes of the verb and noun bases are indicated by numbers, for which tables 1 and 2 may be consulted. Pronouns, not included in the vocabulary, are listed in table 3. Entries having Zuni phrase equivalents are provided with word-by-word translations.

affinal relatives, man's *taˑlaˑkʷin* (p)

affinal relatives, woman's *ʔulaˑkʷin* (p)

all (human) *leˑwi* (p)

all (nonhuman) *temłan* (p)

and *taˑp* (p)

animal *wo* (n 1b)

arrow *šo* (n 1b)

arrowhead *timuˑši* (p)

ashes *lu* (n 1b)

aunt   See father's sister, mother's older sister, mother's younger sister

back *massi* (n 1a)

backbone *sappokała* (n 1a)

bad, be *poča* (iv 9b)

badger *tonaši* (p)

bark *cʔikʷkʷa* (n 1a)

bear *ʔanše* (p)

because *ʔakka* (p)

bee *ʔohhaˑpa* (p)

belly *kʔoppʔan* (p)

bewitch *ʔanʔaše* (tv 9b)

big, become *ła* (iv 1)

bird *woʔ cʔana* (n 1a) 'animal small'

bite *ʔutte* (tv 4b)

black, be *kʷʔi* (iv 10b)

blood *ʔate* (p)

blow *puʔʔa* (tv 4b)

bobcat *tepi* (p)

bone *sa* (n 2)

bow *piʔ ła* (n 1a) 'string across'

brains *ʔohe* (n 1a)

breathe *yanhaku* (iv 6a)

brother   See brother, man's younger; brother, older; sibling, woman's younger

brother, ceremonial *kihe* (p)

brother, man's younger *suwe* (p)

brother, older *papa* (p)

brother's daughter, woman's *ʔeyye* (p)

burn *čapi* (iv 4a)

buttocks *puʔci* (n 1a)

cactus, cholla *šuneppa* (p)

cactus, Joshua *kʔoˑši* (p)

cheek *poheči* (n 1a)

chest *poʔhata* (n 1a)

child *ča* (n 1b)

chipmunk *wahcʔucʔuka* (p)

clay *heii* (n 1a)

cloudy, be *lona* (iv 9a)

clowns (Mudheads) *koyemši* (p)

cold, become *cʔe* (iv 10b)

come *ʔiy* (iv 3b)

corn *ʔaˑtowa* (p)

corn, blue *łiʔʔakʷaʔ* (p)

corn, multicolored *kʔučučukʷin* (p)

corn, white *kʔohakʷaʔ* (p)

corn, yellow *łupcʔikʷaʔ* (p)

corn ear *mi* (n 1b)

corn husk *še* (n 1b)

corn kernel *ču* (n 1b)

cornmeal *sakʔo* (n 1a)

cornmeal, sacred *halawtina* (n 1a)

corn plant *šetta* (n 1a)

cottonwood *pola* (p)

count *yale* (tv 7)

coyote *suski* (p)

crane *kʔoˑlokta* (p)

crow *kʷʔalaši* (p)

cut *ʔapcʔi* (tv 4b)

dance *ʔota* (tv 9a)

dance leader *čiłči* (p)

daughter-in-law *ʔulani* (p)

day *yato* (n 1a)

die *ʔaše* (iv 4a)

dig *ʔakʔoʔu* (tv 5)

dirty *ʔančiʔmowa* (p)

dog *waccita* (p)

drink *tutu* (tv 4b)

dry, become *kʔusa* (iv 6a)

duck *ʔeya* (p)

dust *so* (n 1b)

eagle *kʔakʔali* (p)

ear *lašokti* (n 1a)

earth *ʔawiteli* (n 1a)

eat *ʔito* (tv 4b)

eight *haʔelekkʔa* (p)

elbow *mokči* (n 1a)

eleven *ʔastemła taˑp topinte* (p) 'ten and one'

eye *tuna* (n 1a)

face *noponni* (n 1a)

fall *lani* (iv 4a)

far, be *hołomaši* (iv 9b)

fat *ʔišana* (n 1a)

father *taččʷu* (p)

father's mother *wowo* (p)

father's sister *kuku* (p)

fear *ʔattana* (tv 6a)

feather *la* (n 1b)

female *ʔoka* (p)

few *koˑwi* (p)

fir *kʔałacʔilo* (p)

fire *ʔakli* (n 1a)

fish *kʔaššita* (p)

five *ʔapten* (p)

float *kʔaya* (tv 9a)

flower *ʔuteya* (n 1a)

fly *laʔhi* (iv 4a)

foggy, be *šipololo* (iv 9a)

foot *wekʷi* (n 1a)

forehead *haki* (p)

four *ʔaˑwiten* (p)

friend *kuwaye* (p)

frozen, become *łemm yo* (iv 1) 'board made'

give *ʔucʔi* (tv 6a)

good, be *kʔokši* (iv 9b)

gopher *yeyye* (p)

governor *taˑ puˑpu* (p) 'cane initiated'

grandfather, grandson *nana* (p)

grandmother, granddaughter *hotta* (p)

grass *pe* (n 1b)

green, be *łiʔʔa* (iv 10b)

guts *kʔo* (n 1b)

hair of body *ci* (n 1b)

hair of head *taya* (n 1a)

hand *ʔasi* (n 1a)

head *ʔošokʷkʷi* (n 1a)

hear *hatiyaˑw* (iv 3a)

heart *ʔikʔeˑna* (n 1a)

heavy, be *yukti* (iv 9b)

here *liˑła* (p)

hit *yaktoha* (tv 6a)

hold (singular object) *łeya* (tv 9a)

hold (plural object) *woppona*

horse *tuˑši* (p)

hot, become *kʔałi* (iv 6a)

how *koʔpi* (p)

humming bird *cʔuyya* (p)

hunt *łata* (tv 9a)

husband *ʔoyemši* (p)

ice *łem kʔaya* (n 1a) 'board liquid'

if *čiš* (p)

in *ʔakka* (p)

jaw *łeweči* (n 1a)

juniper *ʔayyikʔo* (p)

kachina *kokko* (p)

kill *ʔayna* (tv 7)

kiva *kiwihci* (n 1a)

knee *ʔošši* (n 1a)

know *ʔanikʷa* (iv 9b)

lake *kʔana* (n 1a)

laugh *šikʷi* (iv 9a)

leaf *haʔ yači* (n 1a) 'weed branch'

504

left side *wešikkʔa* (p)

leg *sakʷi* (n 1a)

lie *ʔa* (iv 9c)

lip *ʔišši* (n 1a)

live in a place *teya* (iv 9a)

liver *hakʷkʷali* (n 1a)

lizard *mišo* (p)

long, become *taša* (iv 1)

louse, body *me* (n 1b)

louse, rabbit *piłašo* (p)

male *ʔocciʔ* (p)

many *ʔemma* (p)

meat *ši* (n 1b)

medicine *ʔakʷʔa* (n 1a)

mother *citta* (p)

mother's brother *kaka* (p)

mother's older sister *hašši* (p)

mother's younger sister *cilu* (p)

mountain *yala* (n 1a)

mouth *ʔawati* (n 1a)

name *šiʔi* (n 1a)

near *lotte* (p)

neck *kʔisi* (n 1a)

night, become *tehłi* (iv 1)

nine *tenalekkʔa* (p)

nose *noʔli* (n 1a)

not *kʷaʔ* (p)

oak *taʔwi* (p)

old, become *łašši* (iv 2)

one *topinte* (p)

other one *topa* (p)

owl, horned *muhukʷi* (p)

person, be a *hoʔʔi* (iv 9b)

pierce *piłkʷe* (tv 4b)

pine *ʔašekʔa* (p)

plant *toye* (tv 7)

play *ʔikʔoša* (tv 6a)

prairie dog *kʔuši* (p)

priest, rain *šiwani* (p)

pull *ʔanahha* (tv 6a)

push *ʔulate* (tv 4b)

rabbit, cottontail *ʔokšikʔo* (p)

rabbit (jackrabbit) *pokʔa* (p)

rabbit (small jackrabbit) *šapahokʔo* (p)

rabbit stick *łeya* (n 1a)

rain *łito* (iv 9a)

rattlesnake *čittola* (p)

rectum *šowali* (n 1a)

red, be *šilowa* (iv 9b)

rib *šotto* (n 1a)

right, do it *lesnu* (iv 4b)

right side *ʔitokʷkʷa* (p)

river *kʔawina* (n 1a)

road *ʔona* (n 1a)

roadrunner *poyyi* (p)

root *łakʷimo* (n 1a)

rope *toʔni* (n 1a)

rotten, be *teči* (iv 9b)

rub *čišša* (tv 6a)

sage, purple *ʔaˑku* (p)

sage, white *ha kʔoha* (p) 'weed white'

salt, granulated *maˑ kʔose* (p) 'rock-salt salty'

sand *so* (n 1b)

say *ʔikʷa* (iv 7)

scorpion *šola* (p)

scratch *sikłi* (tv 4b)

see *ʔankʔohakʔa* (tv 7)

seeds *toˑšo* (n 1a)

seven *kʷilelekkʔa* (p)

sewed, be *pikła* (tv 9a)

sharp, be *ʔotta* (iv 9b)

sheep *kaneˑlu* (p) (< Spanish 'carnero')

short, be *koni* (iv 9b)

sibling, woman's younger *hanni* (p)

sing *tenaʔu* (tv 5)

sister See sibling, woman's younger; sister, man's younger; sister, older

sister, man's clan *ʔokana* (n 1a)

sister, man's younger *ʔikina* (p)

sister, older *kawu* (p)

sister's child, man's *kʔasse* (p)

sitting position, be in a (singular subject) *ʔimo* (iv 9c)

sitting position, be in a (plural subject) *tina* (iv 9a)

six *topalekkʔa* (p)

skin *cʔikʷkʷa* (n 1a)

skunk *supikʔo* (p)

sky *ʔaʔ poʔya* (n 1a) 'mica covering'

505

sleep (singular subject) *ʔala* (iv 6a)
sleep (pl. subj.) * yaˑtela* (iv 6a)
small, become *cʔa* (iv 1)
smell *musmu* (tv 4b)
smell, have a *teči* (iv 9b)
smoke *łikʔaya* (n 1a)
smooth, be *kʔałło* (iv 9b)
snake *ʔayasoʔa* (p)
snow *ʔupinna* (iv 9a)
spider *tohsito* (p)
spirit *hapa* (p)
spit *ʔičukkʔoti* (iv 4a)
spleen *pali* (n 1a)
split *ʔiˑšokʷiha* (tv 6a)
squeeze *hecʔu* (iv 10a)
squirrel, gray *yaši* (p)
squirrel, rock *ʔohči* (p)
standing, be (sg. subj.) *ʔela* (iv 9a)
standing, be (pl. subj.) *łuwa* (iv 9a)
star *moʔ yaču* (n 1a) 'spherical moon'
stepmother *ʔiniha* (p)
stick *ła* (n 2)
stomach *cu* (n 1b)
stone *ʔa* (n 1b)
straight, be *moła* (iv 9b)
suck *cici* (tv 4b)
sun *yatokka* (p)
swell *šole* (iv 1)
tail, animal *hokti* (n 1a)
tail, bird *kʔate* (n 1a)
ten *ʔastemłan* (p)
that *ʔuhsi* (p)
there (far from speaker) *lakʷkʷa* (p)
there (near person spoken to) *ʔiste* (p)
thick, be *yahoni* (iv 9b)
thigh *ʔoyyi* (n 1a)
thin, be *pisse* (iv 9b)
think *ceʔma* (tv 7)

this *lukka* (p)
three *haʔin* (p)
throw *ʔipaku* (tv 4b)
tied together, be *ʔihto* (iv 9a)
toe *tukni* (n 1a)
tongue *honni* (n 1a)
tooth *ʔoʔna* (n 1a)
transvestite, be a *łahmana* (tv 9a)
tree *tatta* (n 1a)
turkey *tona* (p)
turn it in the direction of *tunaʔu* (tv 5)
two *kʷilin* (p)
uncle   See mother's brother
vomit *yakʔo* (tv 4b)
wash *kʔošo* (tv 4b)
water *kʔa* (n 1b)
wet, become *kʔi* (iv 1)
what (intangible) *koʔpi* (p)
what (tangible) *kʷaʔpi* (p)
when *kaˑkʔipi* (p)
where *hoppi* (p)
white, be *kʔoha* (iv 10b)
who *čuwapi* (p)
wide, be *kʔapa* (iv 9b)
widow, widower *hammiši* (p)
wife *ʔoˑye* (p)
willow *pila* (p)
wind *pinna* (n 1a)
wing *ʔepisse* (n 1a)
wipe *kʔuskʔa* (tv 7)
witch *hałikʷi* (p)
with *ʔakka* (p)
worm *wi* (n 1b)
year *tepikʷayina* (n 1a)
yellow, be *łupcʔi* (iv 10b)
Zuni *šiwi* (p)

Sketch of Eastern Pomo, a Pomoan Language

SALLY McLENDON

Seven distinct languages were spoken in northern California by Indian peoples now referred to as Pomo. The speakers of these seven languages did not constitute a single tribe, as is often assumed, but lived in over 70 separate, politically independent, towns, in each of which a slightly different dialect of one of the seven languages was spoken (Gifford and Kroeber 1939:117, 119; vol. 8:274-288). The Pomoan language called

Eastern Pomo was the primary language of five towns distributed around the western half of Clear Lake about 100 miles north of what is now San Francisco. One, possibly two, other towns seem to have spoken both Eastern Pomo and Northern Pomo (vol. 8:274, 276, 286).

Before contact with Euro-Americans, speakers of these seven languages did not share a single name to

507

refer to each language, or to its speakers. Rather, each language had a word for speech or language, and the speech of neighboring towns was referred to as that town's language, or as the language of the people in a given cardinal direction (such as the north or west). Thus, for speakers of the language now called Eastern Pomo, the term *ka·Nú* meant 'language', 'speech', and 'word'. The language now called Southeastern Pomo, as spoken in the community known as 'Sulphur Bank' (to the east of the Eastern Pomo speech area), was called *xáwi·na·bax ka·Nú* 'those on top of the water's language'. The distinct language of the peoples in the several towns to the northwest (now called Northern Pomo) was called *ku·húlabax ka·Nú* 'northerner's language'. None of these groups referred to themselves by these terms.

Following the underlying principle of this native naming practice, Barrett (1908) established English names for the seven languages by adding a directional modifier to the word "Pomo," creating the language names—Northern Pomo, Central Pomo, Southern Pomo, Southwestern Pomo (Kashaya), Eastern Pomo, Southeastern Pomo, and Northeastern Pomo. These were used in 1995 by scholars but rarely by the native peoples themselves. The extension of the term "Pomo" (which derives from the Northern Pomo name of a town in Potter Valley, *pʰo·mo·*, merged with a form added to place-names in Northern Pomo to designate the people of a place, *-pʰóʔmaʔ*) to refer to the whole family of languages had first been suggested by Stephen Powers in 1877 (vol. 8:274).

Unfortunately, even professional anthropologists and linguists have been confused by this nomenclature, particularly since Barrett referred to these seven quite different languages as "dialects." Such usage has been understood to mean that speakers of one of these languages could understand speakers of another of these languages, as midwestern speakers of English can usually understand speakers of English in Boston. This is, in fact, not true. Speakers of any of these seven languages cannot understand speakers of any of the other languages, without actually learning them through an extended period of study and practice.

This area of northern California was linguistically extremely diverse at the time of initial contact with non-Indian peoples. Speakers of Eastern Pomo were bordered by speakers of four unrelated languages, now known by the names Yuki, Patwin, Lake Miwok, and Wappo, in addition to speakers of three other Pomoan languages. Gifford's (1926) census of one of the five Eastern-Pomo-speaking towns, *ší·kom*, in 1919 showed that in the mid-nineteenth century, somewhat over 10 percent of the spouses in this town were married in from neighboring communities where one of these other languages was spoken. Thus, one or more languages other than Eastern Pomo are likely to have been spoken in the five towns in which Eastern Pomo was the dominant language.

After serious settlement of the Clear Lake basin by Americans began in the early 1850s, the native residents of these five towns were forced to share with, and subsequently to cede to the settlers, their traditional territories and to abandon the traditional sites in which their towns had been located. In 1878 the former residents of several Eastern-Pomo-speaking towns banded together with two communities on the northern side of the lake where both Northern Pomo and Eastern Pomo seem to have been spoken to buy back 90 acres of their land north of the modern town of Upper Lake. They established an important community, called *xa·bé-ma·ìòlel*, in which both Eastern Pomo and Northern Pomo were spoken.

On the southern side of the lake, the Roman Catholic Saint Turibus Mission had been founded in 1867. Many members of the two Eastern-Pomo-speaking towns in Big Valley on the south side of the lake, *xa·bé-na·pʰò* 'rock-town' and *qu·Lá-na·pʰò* 'water lily-town', moved in 1870 to 160 acres bought by the church near where their towns had been traditionally located. Other former residents of these two towns subsequently joined *xa·bé-ma·ìòlel*, moved to the federal reservation 100 miles north in Round Valley, or individually bought small parcels of land in neighboring Scotts Valley. Another group from the town of *ší·kom* 'blanket standing (?)' rented land in the East Lake area.

In 1911 and 1912 land for government reservations was purchased next to *xa·bé-ma·ìòlel*, the self-owned community north of Upper Lake (the Upper Lake Rancheria), as well as on Robinson Creek (the Robinson Rancheria), in Scotts Valley (the Sugarbowl Rancheria), and in Big Valley (the Big Valley Rancheria, also called the Mission). Many of the former residents of *xa·bé-ma·ìòlel* moved to these new reservations, as did those living at the Saint Turibus Mission, or in Scotts Valley, or at East Lake. Eastern Pomo and to some extent Northern Pomo continued to be spoken in these new communities for most of the twentieth century.

Each of the original five towns apparently spoke a recognizably distinct variety of Eastern Pomo, but the forced relocation of these towns, their mergers, splits, and remergers over the past 150 years make it difficult to identify precisely what the differences were. In 1959 speakers agreed that the speech of Upper Lake (presumably *xa·bé-ma·ìòlel* and the later reservation adjacent to it) differed slightly from that of Big Valley (presumably the Saint Turibus Mission and the reservation established there) in pronunciation and vocabulary. For example, several speakers agreed that Big Valley called men's trousers *ša· kó· kàwuhu·*, literally 'leg-go inside', while Upper Lake called them *pántaluʔ* or *pántaloʔ* (from Spanish *pantalones*).

By 1959, although a few elderly people preferred to speak only Eastern Pomo, most speakers were bilingual in Eastern Pomo and English. Many if not most younger adults spoke only English, and there were no child speakers of the language. However, grandparents traditionally had a large role in the care of their grandchildren, and thus many adults who spoke only English in 1993 probably had some passive knowledge of Eastern Pomo. In 1993, the remaining speakers of Eastern Pomo were residents, former residents, or descendants of former residents, of the four rancherias (or reservations) in this area. Some speakers lived as far away as Chico, California.

1. SOURCES

The Eastern Pomo language has been studied in some detail by Kroeber (1911), de Angulo (1927, 1930-1935, 1930-1935a, 1935), de Angulo and Freeland (1928, 1930-1935), Halpern (1939-1940, 1953, 1964), McLendon (1959-1990, 1964, 1969, 1973, 1975, 1976, 1977, 1977a, 1978, 1978a, 1979, 1980, 1982), and Boggs, Augustine, and McLendon (1985) (fig. 1). Word lists of varying lengths and phonetic accuracy have been collected by travelers, scholars, and anthropologists since 1851 (Gibbs 1853; Bartlett 1852) (fig. 2).

This sketch derives from analysis of extended samples of the language collected from eight fluent speakers of Eastern Pomo during multiple periods of fieldwork (McLendon 1959-1990).

These speakers are: Agnes Fisher Bateman (AB) (b. 1895, d. 1968), identified as from šíʿkom (a town described by Gifford 1926 as dispersed in 1871). Wife of Leonard Bateman and sister-in-law of Maude Bateman Boggs.

Leonard Bateman (LB) (fig. 3), from xaʿbé-maʿìòlel. Husband of Agnes Bateman, younger half-brother of Maude Bateman Boggs, cousin on his mother's side of Lincoln Dennison (terminological father's father), former brother-in-law of William Graves, and cousin of Ralph Holder.

Maude Bateman Boggs (MB) (fig. 4), born at ḱóba·ṭà·ṗ, raised at Upper Lake. Former sister-in-law of William Graves, sister-in-law of Agnes Fisher Bateman.

Frances Posh Dennison (FD), (b. 1892, d. 1963). Born at the Old Mission Rancheria, resident of the Big Valley rancheria. Wife of Lincoln Dennison and cousin (terminological mother's younger sister) of William Graves.

Lincoln Dennison (LD), born and raised at xaʿbé-maʿìòlel. Husband of Frances Dennison and cousin (terminological father's father) of Leonard Bateman.

Mike Gomez (MG) (b. 1884). Born and raised at the Old Mission Rancheria and educated at the Carlisle Indian School.

William Graves (BG) (fig. 5). Born at daʿlá-da·nò in Big Valley and raised at the Old Mission Rancheria.

Phoebe Hearst Mus. of Anthr., Berkeley, Calif.: 18497.

Fig. 1. William Ralganal Benson (b. 1862, d. 1937). The first Eastern Pomo speaker to work extensively with a linguist, Benson aided in preparing the first grammar and dictionary and recorded several myths (de Angulo 1927, 1935, 1935a, 1935c; de Angulo and Freeland 1928). He co-authored the Pomo creation myth (de Angulo and Benson 1932) and published an account of the Clear Lake massacre of 1849 based on oral history (Benson 1932). Also a gifted artist, he may have made the feathered basket he holds. Photograph by Roger Sturtevant, Berkeley, Calif., about 1931.

Former brother-in-law of Leonard Bateman and Maude Bateman Boggs, and cousin (terminological nephew) of Frances Dennison.

Ralph Holder (RH) (fig. 6). Reared in Scotts Valley and at xaʿbé-maʿìòlel.

2. THE SOUNDS OF EASTERN POMO

Eastern Pomo has 38 consonants, five vowels, two degrees of length, three degrees of stress, and four types of junctures (table 1). Vowels can be either short or long, as can consonants when they occur in the middle of words.

Eastern Pomo thus has many more consonant sounds than English, but somewhat fewer vowels. In order to write Eastern Pomo accurately, so that each written symbol stands for one Eastern Pomo sound, more consonant letters are needed than are in the English alphabet. The existing English consonant symbols have therefore been adapted to the needs of Eastern Pomo, as described below.

Table 1. Phonemes

Consonants								
Voiceless unaspirated stops	*p*	*t*	*ţ*	*c*	*č*	*k*	*q*	
Voiceless aspirated stops	*pʰ*	*tʰ*	*ţʰ*	*cʰ*	*čʰ*	*kʰ*		
Voiceless glottalized stops	*ṗ*	*ṭ*	*ţ̣*	*ċ*	*č̣*	*ḱ*	*q̇*	*ʔ*
Voiced stops	*b*		*d*					
Voiceless fricatives		*s*			*š*	*x*		*h*
Flap			*r*					
Sonorants								
Voiceless nasals	*M*		*N*					
Voiced nasals	*m*		*n*					
Voiceless lateral			*L*					
Voiced lateral			*l*					
Voiceless semivowels	*W*				*Y*			
Voiced semivowels	*w*				*y*			
Vowels								
High	*i*	*u*						
Mid	*e*	*o*						
Low		*a*						

Length

Stress

Primary	Secondary	Weak (unmarked)

Junctures

Glottal catch juncture	'
Word space juncture	(indicated by space)
Comma juncture	,
Period juncture	.

2.1. CONSONANTS: STOPS

An important class of consonants in Eastern Pomo, called 'stops', is made by stopping the breath at one of six places in the mouth: the lips (like English *p*, *b*); the upper teeth (like French *t*, *d*); the alveolar ridge of gum just above and behind the upper teeth (like English *t*, *d*); the (hard) palate (similar to English *ch*); the velum or soft palate (like English *k*); and the back of the velum, between the velum and uvular (similar to the Parisian French *r*). A seventh stop is produced by stopping the breath at the glottis (or vocal cords) in the throat (table 1).*

2.1.1. VOICELESS STOPS

The majority of stops in Eastern Pomo are voiceless (like the English stops *p*, *t*, *k*). They are produced with the vocal cords pulled apart, so they do not vibrate as the air goes through. Eastern Pomo speakers distinguish three main types of voiceless stops at the first five of the seven places in the mouth and throat where stops are made (all except the back of the velum and the glottis).

One kind of voiceless stop is pronounced with a slight puff of air as the stoppage is released, similar to the pronunciation of English *p*, *t*, *k* at the beginning of words. This puff of air, which is technically called aspiration, is represented by a small raised h (ʰ) after a consonant letter. Thus Eastern Pomo *tʰ* should be pronounced like English *t* in

    tʰaˑʔáˑ 'sand'

while Eastern Pomo *pʰ*, *čʰ*, and *kʰ* should be pronounced like English *p*, *ch*, and *k* in words like:

    pʰúy 'fat'
    čʰíˑn 'how'
    kʰól 'small white worm'

A second type of voiceless stop is pronounced without a following puff of air or aspiration, similar to the pronunciation of *p*, *t*, and *k* in French or Spanish. These are unaspirated and written without the raised ʰ.[†] Thus

---

*Those Eastern Pomo stop sounds made by touching the upper teeth are represented by *t*, while those made by touching the alveolar ridge are represented by *ţ*.

Those made by stopping the air at the back of the velum are represented by *q*. Those made by stopping the breath at the palate are represented by *č*. The voiceless stop made by stopping the breath at the vocal cords (as in the English negative expression *uh-uh*) is written *ʔ*.

The letter *c* represents a group of sounds, called affricates, produced by stopping the breath at the upper teeth, then forcing it through a constricted passage between the alveolar ridge and the palate, similar in articulation to the final sound represented by *ts* in English *hats*.

[†]This means that the Eastern Pomo sound most like an English *t* is written *tʰ* as in *tʰór* 'rotten' while the Eastern Pomo sound written *t* is not pronounced like English t but like French and Spanish t, as in *túl* 'tag (a game)'. Similarly, the Eastern Pomo sounds most like English p and k are written *pʰ* and *kʰ*.

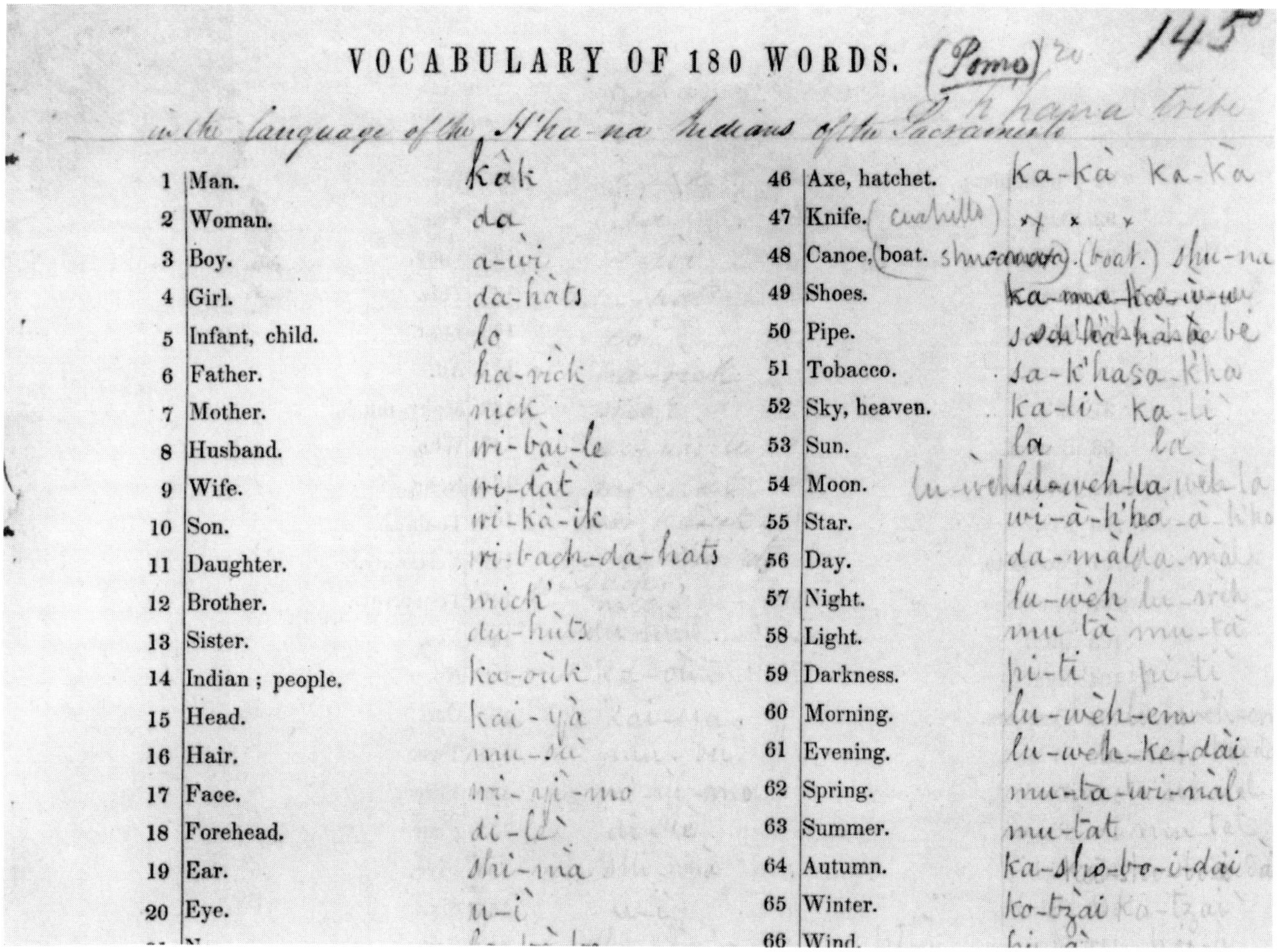

in the language of the H'ha-na Indians of the Sacramento [Tehama tribe]

#			#		
1	Man.	kâk	46	Axe, hatchet.	ka-kà ka-kà
2	Woman.	da	47	Knife. (cuchillo)	x x x x
3	Boy.	a-wi	48	Canoe. (boat. shu-na) (boat.)	shu-na
4	Girl.	da-hâts	49	Shoes.	ka-mu-koo-iu-wi
5	Infant, child.	lo	50	Pipe.	…be
6	Father.	ha-nick	51	Tobacco.	sa-k'hasa-k'ha
7	Mother.	nick	52	Sky, heaven.	ka-li ka-li
8	Husband.	wi-bai-le	53	Sun.	la la
9	Wife.	wi-dât	54	Moon.	lu-weh-la-weh-la-weh-la
10	Son.	wi-kâ-ile	55	Star.	wi-à-li'ho à
11	Daughter.	wi-bach-da-hâts	56	Day.	da-mal-ja-mà
12	Brother.	mich	57	Night.	lu-weh lu-weh
13	Sister.	da-hûts	58	Light.	mu-tà mu-tà
14	Indian ; people.	ka-ouk	59	Darkness.	pi-ti pi-ti
15	Head.	kai-yà	60	Morning.	lu-weh-em
16	Hair.	mu-sie	61	Evening.	lu-weh-ke-dai
17	Face.	wi-aji-mo	62	Spring.	mu-ta-wi-nal
18	Forehead.	di-lè	63	Summer.	mu-tat
19	Ear.	shi-ina	64	Autumn.	ka-sho-bo-i-dai
20	Eye.	u-i	65	Winter.	ko-tzai ko-tzai
			66	Wind.	

Smithsonian, NAA:ms. 1627.

Fig. 2. Vocabulary of Eastern Pomo collected in 1852 by John R. Bartlett, then U.S. Boundary Commissioner in San Diego, from the servant of a U.S. Army officer, probably the same "Indian who accompanied the [Roderick McKee] expedition as a servant of Dr. J.S. Griffin," who provided the first recorded vocabulary of the language to George Gibbs at Clear Lake in 1851 (Powell 1877:492, 504-508). Bartlett wrote the name for the language as H'ha-na (xá-Na 'on the water'), a name used to refer collectively to speakers of Eastern Pomo (Ralph Holder, personal communication 1976).

Eastern Pomo *t* should be pronounced like French or Spanish *t* in

>*tu·nú* 'mouse'

while Eastern Pomo *p, č, k* should be pronounced like Spanish *p, ch, k* in words like:

>*púl* 'straight'
>*čí·waʔ* 'goat' (from Spanish *chiva*)
>*kóy* 'sore'.

Unaspirated voiceless stops never occur as the final sound in a word.

The difference between aspirated voiceless stops, like *pʰ*, and unaspirated voiceless stops, like *p*, is an important one. Minimal and near-minimal pairs of words with very different meanings are distinguished by this difference. Compare

>*pʰó·l* 'magnesite bead' to *púl* 'straight, true'
>*pʰá* 'feces' to *pá·kaʔ* 'cow'
>*tʰów* 'now' to *tó·toʔ* 'blanket'

>*tʰé* 'fine eagle down' to *té·* 'weak, yielding'
>*tʰów* 'rafter, dipnet handle' to *tóykʰ* 'something that can't be helped'
>*čʰé* 'where' to *mi·čé* 'mortar basket'
>*kʰá* 'spider' to *ká* 'house'.

The third kind of voiceless stop is produced by stopping the breath at the vocal cords (or glottis) as well as in the mouth, and then releasing both, producing a popped sound. These sounds are called glottalized (or ejective) and are represented by a small raised comma above the consonant: *ṗ, ṫ, ƚ, č̓, k̓*. Such sounds are not used in European languages (although speakers in English sometimes use them for emphasis at the ends of words) but are widespread in the native languages of western North America. They contrast with both the aspirated and unaspirated sounds to distinguish meaning, as in:

511

Phoebe Hearst Mus. of Anthr., Berkeley, Calif.:15-20259.

Fig. 3. Leonard Bateman (b. 1893, d. 1968). He was born at *xa·bé-ma·ìòlel* to a father of the *xa·bé-na·pʰò* tribe from Big Valley and a mother of the *xówalekʰ* from Upper Lake. A reflective and precise speaker of Eastern Pomo, his insights into the grammar and semantic systems of the language have profoundly shaped this chapter. Like many Eastern Pomo men, he made clamshell beads late in life; here he poses with a pump drill and several strings of finished beads. Photograph by Josepha Haveman, Lakeport, Calif., 1960.

ṗa·lá·	'slug'
pʰa·lá·	'the one who goes last, in the rear'
pá·laʔ	'shovel' (from Spanish *pala*)
ƚú·l	'minnows'
tʰów	'now'
túl	'the game of tag'
ƚúnƚun	'ant'
ʈónʈon	'blowfly'
ʈʰów	'rafter, handle'
ka·ʈúl	'thin'
čé·	'mushroom'
čá·s	'Western winter wren'
čʰáy	'fish species (*Lavinia exilcauda chi*)'
mi·čé	'mortar basket'
ḱó	'egg, belly'
kʰól	'worm'
kóy	'sore'
ḱu·húm	'sedge rhizome, used for baskets'
ku·húm	'Eat!'

2.1.2. POSTVELAR VOICELESS STOPS

Only two types of stops are distinguished at the sixth, postvelar position: a voiceless glottalized stop, written *q̇*, and a voiceless plain stop, written *q*. The sound *q* is pronounced as an affricate [qˣ] before the vowel *a*, with a fricative release similar to the *r* of French speakers of Paris in pronouncing words like *crie* or *crac*. These two stops, while similar in pronunciation, distinguish important differences in meanings in words as shown by the minimal pair:

kʰi·qál	'to wipe window with squeegee'
kʰi·q̇ál	'to finish marking with a long flexible object, such as writing a letter'.

Like the other unaspirated voiceless stops (*p*, *t*, *ƚ*, *č*, *k*), *q* never occurs as the final sound in a word.

Both *q* and *q̇* are lenis (or 'relaxed') in their articulation. Both are rare before the front vowels *i* or *e*. There is one example of *q* before *i* and *e*:

qe·qí	'otter'.

There are no examples of the stop *q̇* before the vowel *e*, and only two examples before the vowel *i*:

q̇i·sú·l	'tall grass species (perhaps foxtail)'
q̇i·dákq̇i·dakʰ	'red'.

Phoebe Hearst Mus. of Anthr., Berkeley, Calif.:15-20255.

Fig. 4. Maude Bateman Boggs (b. 1888). She had the same father as Leonard Bateman, while her mother was from *ka·yáw* in Bachelor Valley, where both Northern and Eastern Pomo were spoken. She was one of the finest basketmakers of the mid-twentieth century and particularly knowledgable about the vocabulary and semantics of basketmaking as well as of traditional fish processing and food gathering and processing. She here holds a recently begun one-rod coiled basket. Photograph by Josepha Haveman, Robinson Rancheria, Calif., 1960.

Fig. 5. William Graves (b. 1872 or 1876, d. 1961), a doctor and renowned singer. He was born at *da·lá-da·nò* in Big Valley to a mother from the *qu·Lá-na·pʰò* tribe; although his father was White he grew up in an essentially monolingual community. Raised at the Old Mission Rancheria, he attended the St. Turibus Mission school as well as the Roman Catholic school at the San Rafael Mission. In addition to Eastern Pomo, English, and some Latin and Spanish, he spoke Northern Pomo. He was an innovative and creative speaker who tried to accommodate his extensive knowledge of the traditional culture and language to the many changes he witnessed. Photograph by Robert Bollini at Crabtree Springs, Calif., 1960.

The postvelar stops are quite distinct from the velar stops with which they have often been confused in earlier recordings of Eastern Pomo. Compare:

qóy	'swan'
q̇óy	'nape of the neck'
kóy	'sore'
k̇ó·y	'in the stomach'.

2.1.3. THE GLOTTAL STOP

The breath can also be stopped by completely closing the vocal cords. This produces a glottal stop (ʔ), the sound in the middle of the English negative expression *uh-uh*. An Eastern Pomo example is:

    ma·ʔáy 'food'.

2.1.4. VOICED STOPS

Two stops are voiced (like the English stops *b* and *d*), that is, produced with the vocal cords so close together that they vibrate as the breath is forced between them. These are the labial voiced stop *b* and the alveolar voiced stop *d*. Examples are:

bá	'that'
dá	'woman'.

The voiced stops are consistently voiced. Voiceless aspirated and glottalized stops are consistently voiceless. Voiceless unaspirated stops that contrast with voiced stops at the labial and alveolar places of articulation (*p* and *ṭ*) are also consistently voiceless. Voiceless unaspirated stops that do not contrast with voiced stops (*t*, *č*, *k*) may occasionally be somewhat voiced. This may be an innovation produced by bilingualism in which English is the second language.

2.1.5. VOICELESS AFFRICATES

Three sounds very similar to the voiceless stops begin by stopping the breath at the upper teeth and then releasing it through a narrowed passage at the beginning of the palate so that friction is produced. These are called affricates and written with the letter *c*. One is aspirated and written *cʰ*. It sounds rather like English *ts* in the word *hats* as in:

    cʰá·kaya '(one) runs away'.

A second is unaspirated and written *c*. It sounds like English *ts* pronounced with a French accent. An example is:

    cá·r 'clean'.

The third is glottalized and written *ċ*. An example is:

    ċálk̇a '(one) refuses, says no'.

All three are voiceless.

These three affricates are classed with the voiceless stops despite their phonetic difference because: they pattern like voiceless stops, occurring aspirated, unaspirated, and glottalized; phonetically two of the

Fig. 6. Ralph Holder (b. 1900 or 1906, d. 1992). Born at *síwaxal* to a mother from *qu·Lá-na·pʰò* in Big Valley and a father from *yi·má·* in Scotts Valley, he was brought up by his terminological grandfather Jim Bateman, from Big Valley. Precise and careful, Holder provided knowledge and insights regarding Eastern Pomo grammar and semantics that have greatly informed this chapter. Photograph by Julia Tucker, Upper Lake Rancheria, May 1973.

SKETCH OF EASTERN POMO, A POMOAN LANGUAGE

voiceless stop series (the palatal and the postvelar) have affricated pronunciations under certain conditions; and the unaspirated affricate *c* acts like the unaspirated voiceless stops in not occurring as the final sound in a word.

2.2. CONSONANTS: FRICATIVES

Another class of sounds, called fricatives, is made by forcing the breath through such a narrowed opening that friction is produced, as in the English sounds *s* or *f*. In Eastern Pomo, fricative sounds are produced by narrowing the passage through which the breath passes in one of four places: the upper teeth (written *s*, like English *s*), the (hard) palate (written *š*, like English *sh*), the (soft) palate or velum (written *x*, like German *ch*), and the glottis (written *h*, like English *h*). Examples are:

só	'clover'
šó·	'east'
xó	'fire'
hóyya?	'handsome, desirable'.

The fricatives, *s*, *š*, *x* are all pronounced longer (more dragged out) when final in a word.

2.3. CONSONANTS: SONORANTS

The last class of consonants, called sonorants, includes the nasals (like English *m*, *n*), the lateral (like English *l*), and the semivowels (like English *y* and *w*). Sonorants can be either voiced (as in English) or voiceless. The voiceless sonorants, which sound like a "breathy" or whispered version of the voiced sonorants are written *M*, *N*, *L*, *Y*, *W*. Some speakers of English use the voiceless sonorant [W] in the word *which* (when pronounced differently from *witch*), and most English speakers use the voiceless sonorant [Y] in the English words *hue* and *huge* (contrasting with *y* in *you*).

The difference between voiced and voiceless sonorants is important. There are many minimal pairs of words with very different meanings that are distinguished only by this difference. Compare:

Má·	'land (as opposed to water)'
má·	'you pl. (agent)'
Mí	'truth'
mí	'you sg. (patient)'
Nákʰ	'fish eggs'
nál	'backwards'
Ní·	'to say, sing'
níx	'to spread out one thing'
Líy	'army worm'
líkʰ	'long object to be vertical'
Lá·l	'goose'
lá·l	'month'
Wá·	'at the door'
wá·	'we (agent)'
Wíl	'abalone'
wí	'me (patient)'
Yá	'wind', 'bone'
yá·ya?	'untrue, a lie'
Yúl	'snow'
yú·l	'little while ago'.

2.4. THE CONSONANT *r*

The consonant *r* is pronounced word-initially as a retroflex continuant, medially as a flap or (before a stressed vowel) a retroflex continuant, and finally as a trill.

2.5. CONSONANT DISTRIBUTION

All consonant phonemes may occur initially in a word, as well as syllable-initially, although *r* occurs in word-initial position in only three words, two borrowed from Spanish. Voiceless unaspirated stops (*p*, *t*, *ţ*, *č*, *k*, *q*), the voiceless unaspirated affricate (*c*), voiced stops (*b*, *d*), the fricative *h*, and the voiceless sonorants (*M*, *N*, *L*, *W*, *Y*) never occur in syllable-final and therefore word-final position. Voiceless aspirated stops rarely occur syllable-initially following the last primary or secondary stress in a word.

Consonant clusters, sequences of two or more consonants within the same syllable, do not occur initially in a syllable, only finally in a syllable. The longest permissible consonant sequence within a syllable consists of two consonants plus length (·), as in:

ba·pʰórkʰ·hi	'shake something off the top of something' (such as a tree).

Two-consonant syllable-final clusters always have a voiced sonorant (*m*, *n*, *l*, *w*, *y*) or *r* as the first sound and *kʰ*, *ḱ*, or *?* as the second.

Across a syllable boundary the longest possible sequence consists of two consonants plus length, plus *h* or *l*, as in the example above. Sequences of like consonants always occur across syllable boundaries; sequences of consonant plus length occur within a syllable.

2.6. VOWELS

There are five vowels in Eastern Pomo, written *i*, *e*, *a*, *u*, *o*.

mí	'you sg. (patient)'
mé	'this'
má	'you sg. (agent)'
mó	'hole'
ku·mú	'all'

All five vowels can occur both short (or "quick") or long (that is, "dragged out"). Long or dragged out vowels are written with a raised dot after the vowel letter: *i·*, *e·*, *a·*, *u·*, *o·*.

The difference between long and short vowels distinguishes significant differences in meanings as illustrated by the following minimal pairs:

ší	'name'	versus *ší·*	'a gift of value (at funerals or weddings)'
di·lé	'forehead'	versus *di·lé·*	'middle'
ká	'house'	versus *ká·*	'one person to sit'
kóy	'sore'	versus *kó·y*	'to grow'
kʰúy	'not'	versus *kʰú·y*	'another'

2.7. STRESS

Three degrees of stress (or relative loudness) must be recognized: primary (´), secondary (ˋ), and weak (unmarked). Every word has one syllable that is louder than all the others and thus carries primary stress. The primary-stressed syllable will usually be either the first or the second syllable in the word.

The other syllables in that word will have either weak or secondary stress. Weak stress actually involves a sort of two-beat meter of alternating lighter and more heavily stressed syllables (da dá da dá). The weakest or lightest degree of stress occurs on a syllable immediately following a primarily or secondarily stressed syllable and every alternate subsequent syllable. Every second syllable after a primarily stressed syllable is slightly louder than an unstressed syllable immediately preceding or following it.

All roots carry primary stress. Most roots occur prefixed with a one-syllable instrumental prefix (CV·-); hence, a large proportion of the words in Eastern Pomo begin with a two-syllable sequence of the sort: CV·CV́.... However, roots cannot be identified in a large number of polysyllabic words, making it impossible to predict consistently the location of primary stress in terms of a particular type of morpheme. Although primary stress does occur on the second syllable of many such words, there are many other words in which it occurs on the first syllable, such as *dú·šux* 'quiet', *tʰíya* 'big, plural', *ǩáli* 'one', *lé·ma* 'five', *čá·mal* 'fly', *hí·baya* 'men', *ké·xa* 'father's younger brother, vocative', as well as inflected verb forms such as *dó·lakibaʔ* 'let's pound acorns!' Thus stress must be written.

Secondary stress primarily results from compounding. When two or more words, each containing a primary stress, are combined, all but one primary stress will be reduced to secondary stress. Thus the words *da·lá* 'flat, pan-shaped basket' and *da·nó* 'hill, mountain' when combined to form a place-name are pronounced *da·lá-da·nò*. (Compounds are written with hyphens.)

There are also a number of suffixes that contain a secondarily stressed syllable, irrespective of the pattern of alternating lighter and more heavily stressed syllables characteristic of the syllables following the primarily stressed syllable. This stress must be considered part of the suffix and marked. Suffixes that contain such an inherent secondary stress include: *-ki·mà* 'plural habitual', *-baʔè* 'subjunctive mode', *-bàya* 'sentence connective', and *-i·Nàʔ* 'intentive'.

3. GRAMMAR: MORPHOLOGY

3.1. INTRODUCTION

Eastern Pomo is an agglutinative language with a rich and complex morphology. Most words consist of smaller pieces called "morphemes" (short sequences of sounds, each with its own meaning), combined into sequences that can be quite long and complex. For example, the single Eastern Pomo word:

dó·lakibaʔ 'let's pound acorns'

is composed of four morphemes, none of which can be used alone. All are "bound" morphemes, which must be combined with other morphemes in order to be said and understood. These are:

dó- + *-·l-* + *-aki-* + *-baʔ*
pound.acorns.with.pestle   CONT   PL.AG   JUSSIVE

The Eastern Pomo word:

dó·lim 'Continue pounding acorns'
(addressed to a single person who has stopped pounding)

combines two of the same morphemes plus a third, different morpheme, the singular imperative suffix *-im*:

dó- + *-·l-* + *-im*
pound.acorns.with.pestle + CONT + SG.IMP

In the words above, the morphemes *dó-* + *-·l-* form a stem—a sequence of morphemes that act together as a unit, to which other suffixes are added. Stems are the basic morphological (and semantic) unit in Eastern Pomo.

3.2. STEMS

Stems are of two types: analyzable and unanalyzable. Analyzable stems must contain a root morpheme of the shape CV́(·) (such as *dó-*). Roots may be preceeded by an instrumental prefix‡, with the shape CV·- (3.3.), and may be followed by a member of one or two classes of manner suffixes, with the shape -C, -·, -CC, or -·C (such as the continuative -·l) (3.4.).

The stem *du·dí-* 'push with the hands', for example, consists of the instrumental prefix *du·-* 'with or affecting the fingertips' and the root *-dí-* 'place or maintain in a specific, appropriate position'. With the continuative manner suffix *-·l* added, as in *du·dí·l*, it means 'to push along continuously with the hands'.

Roots typically refer to various types of motions, actions, processes, or states. For example, the root *-dá-* refers to a range of activities that can be summarized as 'to force open, expose, generally by interrupting the enclosing surface'. Combined with the instrumental prefix *du·-* 'with the fingers', it forms the stem *du·dá-kʰ* 'to split something open with the fingers, such as a

---

‡The term instrumental prefix has been preserved here because it has become traditional to use in descriptions of Pomoan languages. In fact, no prefix refers uniquely to instrument. Prefixes can refer to the undergoer of the action, or the type or manner of action, in addition to the instrument of the action.

nutshell'. The same root combined with the instrumental prefix *mu·-* 'from internal pressures, from the inside out' forms the stem *mu·dá-kʰ* 'to split open from internal pressures, like an overripe melon'. The root *-q̇á-* refers to a range of activities that involve 'applying pressure'. Combined with the instrumental prefix *du·-* it forms the stem *du·q̇a-kʰ* 'to tighten, close off (as a water faucet, with the fingers)'. The same root combined with the prefix *mu·-* forms the stem *mu·q̇á-kʰ* 'to be knocked unconscious or dead'. These stems contain the punctual suffix *kʰ* (4.13.5.).

The bare root specifies a neutral flow or continuum of some activity or state, generally without either beginning or end, cause or, necessarily, result. The addition of an instrumental prefix specifies the instrument, means, medium, or experiencer of this flow. Compare the effect of different prefixes with the root *-ṭí-* 'motion with propulsive force that extends or spreads' plus the manner suffix *-r-* 'disseminative':

ma·-ṭʰí-r-kʰ	'to spread out with foot' *ma·-* 'with or affecting the foot'
mu·-ṭʰí-r-kʰ	'something that springs out of itself to spread out' *mu·-* 'from internal energy or motivation, from the inside out'
mi·-ṭʰí-r-kʰ	'to spread out with tip of foot' *mi·-* 'with the initial segment, point, end, such as the tip of the foot'
du·-ṭʰí-r-kʰ	'to spread out with the fingers' *du·-* 'with or affecting the fingers'
di·-ṭʰí-r-kʰ	'to spread out by dropping (as when a sack of acorns is dropped from a height of 3 or 4 feet, it splits, and the acorns spread out on the floor)' *di·-* 'by natural or unseen forces, such as gravity'
ša·-ṭʰí-r-kʰ	'to spread out with a stick' *ša·-* 'with a long object, particularly its point'
šu·-ṭʰí-r-kʰ	'to spread out something like a cloth' *šu·-* 'involving simultaneous pull in two opposite directions'

The addition of a member of one or both of the two classes of manner suffixes adds a more narrowed, focused point of view, highlighting aspects of the activity or state: does it continue, is it intermittent, is it focused or disseminated, does it have permanence or duration? For example, when the root *-dá-* 'to force open, expose...' is suffixed with the durative manner suffix *-l* it takes on the additional meaning of forcing open to the point of destroying the object receiving the action. Thus, while *du·-dá-kʰ* means 'to split open with the fingernails, or to split a finger', *du·-dá-l* means 'to

tickle to death' while *mu·-dá-l* means 'dead.' Compare the effect of combining a stem consisting of the prefix *ma-* 'with or affecting the foot' plus the root *-ṭí-* 'motion with propulsive force that extends or spreads' with the following manner suffixes:

ma·-ṭʰí-r-kʰ	'to spread out with foot'
with *-r-*	'disseminative,' which characterizes activity as being in rings, concentric circles, and consisting of repeated short rounded motions.
ma·-ṭʰí-n-kʰ	'to press, massage with the foot' (by walking on the back, as grandchildren did for grandparents)
with *-n-*	'with/from pressure inward', which generally penetrates or is encompassed.
ma·-ṭʰí-k̇	'to push, roll, something along with foot'
with *-k̇-*	'with/from a short segment of reciprocating motion or energy, especially oscillating, which is inherently repetitive in nature'

The Eastern Pomo analyzable stem thus characterizes behavior, experience, natural phenomena, and material culture in terms of forces and energies for which it specifies parameters such as type, source, direction, manner, duration, extent, and effect, implying a rather systematic and abstract analysis of the universe in terms not at variance with the principles of classical physics. Therefore, an analyzable stem may, and frequently does, apply to a number of situations that, from the point of view of a speaker of English, are quite distinct and not associated. For example, the stem

si·-qá-l
with/in.liquid.medium-transform-DUR

can mean both 'pure, cleaned off, all of one kind, homogeneous', and 'to lick something like ice cream off fingers'. The stem

pʰa·-q̇á-į̇(-ki-·)
from.kinetic.energy-apply.pressure-
INTENSIFIER-SEMEL-STAT

can mean both 'to pry/force abalones loose from rocks with an iron bar' and 'for high, flood water to come down a creek and wash something, such as a house or other property, away'.

At the same time, a single act or event is often susceptible to description by more than one stem, depending upon which of several aspects of the event attention is being focused on. These stems may then appear to be synonymous from the point of view of their English translation. Such a situation most frequently arises in stems that differ primarily by virtue of their prefixes. For example, the stems *ša·-nú·-l-kʰ* and *pʰa·-nú·-l-kʰ* could both be used to describe the act of half poking a snake to death. The use of the stem *ša·nú·lkʰ* would

the first three sentences from a *ma·rú·* are given below. Reference is made to two protagonists, Coyote Old Man and the unnamed fishermen whose fish dam he robs. The particle *kʰi* is used to refer to either of them, sometimes in the same sentence, but the switch referencing suffixes, the pattern of concord of *kʰi* with plural agent suffixes when referring to the fishermen, but not when referring to Coyote Old Man, and the judicious disambiguating use of the third-person masculine singular patient form of the pronoun, *mí·pal*, to refer to Coyote Old Man, keep the reference always clear. For ease in following the anaphora all references to Coyote Old Man are bracketed underneath, while all references to the fishermen are bracketed above:

1) ⌊*ku·nú·la-bù·ċike=xa*⌋ *ká·le,*
Coyote-Old.Man=HRSY sit/dwell(SG)-HRSY
yó-qa·q̇ò·-y, *nó-na·pʰò·-ti-yay.*
south-valley-LOC ash-village-(?)-LOC
'Coyote-Old=Man was staying at home in Big Valley, at *nó-na·pʰòti* (an ancient village site on Kelsey Creek)'

2) *ba=xa* ⌊*kʰi*⌋ . . . *híčʰ* ⌊*kʰi*⌋ *da·lám-akì·* *ku·ḷá-y=xa* ⌊*kʰi*⌋ *pʰu·dé·le*
that=HRSY 3d.person(AG) Clear.Lake.splittail 3d.person(AG) dam-PL.AG-STAT find-COREF (action of verb suffixed precedes in time that of main verb)=HRSY 3d.person(AG) steal-HRSY
'He found (that) they had damned for Clear Lake splittail (*Pogonichthys cisoides*), and he stole (that, i.e., the fish).'

3) *ba mí·n ye·hél-qan,* . . . ⌈*kʰi*⌉ *ba* ⌈*mí·p-al Yépʰ-ki·yakì·*⌉*y,*
                                                                      s-ref   coref
. . . ⌈*kʰi*⌉⌊*mí·p-al*⌋ *kó·q̇-a·kì·,* *ba·ṭʰí-yay.*
that like.that (previously mentioned in some general way) do-SR (action of verb suffixed precedes in time that of main verb), . . . 3d. person (AG) that he-PAT watch-SEMEL-PL.AG-COREF (action of verb suffixed precedes in time that of main verb), . . . 3d.person (AG) he-PAT shot-PL.AG-STATIVE, arrow-with.
'He (Coyote Old Man) had been doing like that, and they watched that for him, and shot him with an arrow.'

In addition, the consistent reference to the fishermen only with *kʰi* signals their lack of prominence in the discourse. The contrastive use of *mí·pal* in Sentence 3 to refer to Coyote Old Man when the fishermen (always referred to by the unprominent *kʰi*) are the agents of his shooting—ordinarily the prominent role in a sentence—assures Coyote Old Man consistent prominence in this portion of the discourse.

5. SELECTED VOCABULARY

above *káyuwa*
acorn *bu·dú*
acorn, black oak *li·šúy*
acorn, Douglas oak *wi·yú*
acorn, live oak *sé-bu·dù*
acorn, mush oak *ċi·pʰá*
acorn, poison oak *Máriyap̌*
acorn, white oak *q̇a·kʰúl*
acorn bread *só·y*
acorn bread, baked with baking powder dirt *xa·ró·*
acorn meal *wi·ṭʰá*
acorn meal, soaked *si·kʰúċ*
acorn mush *tʰo·ʔó·*
acorn soup *tʰo·ʔó·*
agreed, O.K. *ʔó·*
angelica *ba·k̇ó·*
animal *qa·qó·bax-ʔà·m* lit. 'thing of the wild'
ankle *qa·lá·*
ant *ṭúnṭun*
antler *ku·láw*
antler, horn *ʔá·*
apples *ba·šá*
arm *ċu·wá·*
armpit *da·má ~ da·má-mò·*
arrow *ba·ṭʰíy*
ash *q̇á·lap̌*
ash, white, on embers *xó-pʰu·lù·š*
ashes *nó*
ass *ṭá·*
asthma *ma·Yék̇*
automobile *xóy-ki·wà·l ~ kárentaʔ* (< Sp. *carreta* 'wagon')
autumn *si·ṭál-pʰu·bèx* lit. 'leaves blow down'
ax *há·čiʔ* (< Sp. *hacha*)
baby *k̇ú·s*
back *k̇i·dí*
bad *nís* (sg.) *nísa* (pl.)
to bake *ma·lú·*
bark (of tree) *xa·wál*
basket *šá·ri*
basket, parching, close-twined *da·lá*
basket, pounding *mi·čé*
basket, round twined, with sides *cʰi·ká-šà·ri*

541

basket, sifting spaced-twined *ša·láp̓*

basket, l-stick *c̓á·y šá·ri*

basket, 3-stick *xày-xó·mk̓a si·ṭól*

  See also cradlebasket, pack basket

basket root, black *c̓i·wíš*

basket root, white *k̓u·húm*

bass, larger *di·ṭʰá*

bass, small *ṭóx*

to baste *bi·qálkʰ*

bat (animal) *xa·tá·talaq̓*

bead, magnesite *pʰó·l*

bead of Washington clamshell *šáṭa·ne*

beak *xác̓i·da*

beans *hí·Wol ʔ*

bear *bu·ráqal*

bear, black *ši·yó·-bu·ràqal*

beard *xácʰucʰu*

to beat *du·ṭʰál-du·bàkʰ*

beaver *ṭʰi·Nór* (archaic)

bee *ka·ló*

beets *qo·máš*

belly *k̓ó*

below *yówwa*

belt, feather *kʰi·bú·qal*

to bend over and pick up from the ground objects
  (such as nuts, acorns, fallen pears or apples and
  wood) and put them in a container *da·k̓óy*

big *ba·ṭʰín* (sg.) *ṭʰíya* (pl.)

bird *c̓i·yá*

to give birth *k̓ú·s qa·wí*

to bite *qa·né·*

bitter, strong, peppery *bi·k̓ów*

black *mu·šáq̓*

blackberry *c̓íc̓ikʰòp̓*

blackbird *c̓ú·Li*

blackfish *ša·xál*

blanket, plain wool *tó·to ʔ*

blanket, rabbitskin *ší·c̓*

to blister *c̓i·pólkʰ*

blood *ba·láy*

to bloom *šo·bóy*

to blow (with the mouth) *pʰu·šú·l*

to blow (of wind) *Yá·*

542 blue *c̓a·kʰéc̓a·kʰèkʰ*

bluejay *c̓á·y*

body *ši·bá*

to boil *xó-kʰà·* See to contain

bone *Yá*

bone, fish *šá ṭa·né*

bow *šu·Múy ~ híntil ʔ-šu·Mùy*

boy *qa·wí·* (sg.) *qa·wíkʰ* (pl.)

brains *ṭó*

branch *yi·bú*

bread *só·y*

bread, acorn *xa·ró·, só·y*

to break off from twisting *c̓á·*

to break off by jerking *šu·q̓áṭki·*

breast, breast milk *si·dó·*

to breathe *pʰu·šé·nk̓*

to bring *kúrdi·* (sg.) *kúrbi·di·* (pl.)

to bring long object along *k̓é·l*

to bring along, to hunt *du·dúl*

brother See elder, younger brother

brother-in-law, husband's brother (own) *ma·qár*
  (other's) *-qár*

brother-in-law, sister's husband (own) *kó·ṭ* (other's)
  -ko·ṭ

brother-in-law, wife's brother (own) *ma·há·*
  (other's) *-há·*

brother's daughter, son (called the same as daughter,
  son)

buckeye *ba·šá*

bull *tó·ro ʔ* (< Sp. *toro*)

bullet *wá·la ʔ* (< Sp. *bala*)

to burn (animate subject) *ša·ṭó·* (sg.), *ša·lóṭma·* (pl.)
  pʰa·békʰ

  (inanimate subject) *ma·Lákʰ*

butterfly *xášày ʔšay*

buttocks *si·lí*

button *bóton ʔ* (< Sp. *botón*)

to buy *ba·qákʰ*

buzzard *ku·kʰí*

Cache Creek people *náwikʰ-kà·wkʰ ~ šó·bax-kà·wkʰ*

calf (of leg) *qa·líc̓*

carrot *ši·bú*

to carry in arms *pʰí·l* (sg.) *pʰí·pʰi·k̓* (pl. distributive)

to carry on back *kʰi·dí·l* (sg.) *kʰi·bé·l* (pl.)

cat *pú·s*

to catch, to copulate *da·k̓ó·*

caterpillar *xóši·ċ*

center pole in dance house *ša·bé·*

cents *xa·bé* See rock

cheeks *ba·lú*

cheer up *Yémaḱon*
  See sympathetic

chest *ye·ʔél*

chest, upper *ku·nú*

chicken *ká·ye·naʔ* (< Sp. *gallina* 'hen')

chief, female *dáxalikʰ*

chief, male *ká·xalikʰ*

child *qa·wí*

chin *q̇a·wás*

clam *xa·lá*

clam, Coast Washington *la·q̇ó*

claw *ríkʰ*

clean *cá·r*

clearing, bare place *kà·y-táš*

close by *kúra*

cloud *xa·bó*

clover *só* See also grass

coat *kápotaʔ* (< Sp. *capote* 'cloak')

cocoon, cocoon rattle *wa·yóy*

to coil (baskets) *kʰi·bú*

cold *qa·cʰíl*

to come here *kúruhu·* (sg.) *kúrpʰi·lì·* (pl.)

to contain a mass, quantity or number in the most
  appropriate container/enclosure for the given
  material, i.e., food in dish, sheep in corral, coffee
  in cup *kʰá·*

cool *ḱíw*

to copulate *ma·ʔá·* (polite form) *da·kʰó·*

corpse *ká·wkʰ mu·dál*

cottontail *ma·kʰíw*

cottonwood tree *q̇áša·lap̣*

to count/teach *du·yí·*

country, land, ground *ká·y*

cow *pá·kaʔ* (< Sp. *vaca*)

cowboy *pá·kaʔ-qa·wì·* ~ *káwayeruʔ* (< Sp.
  caballero)

coyote *ku·nú·la*

cradlebasket *xáy-ḱa·ṭòLi*

crane *ma·kʰó*

to crawl *da·póda·po·l*

crazy *kʰékʰeʔ*

creek, river *bi·dáme*

cricket *bi·córbi·còr*

crow *ʔáwʔaw*

crown (of head) *ki·nál*

to cry *ma·xár*

to cut *ka·dákʰ* (with knife)

to dance *xé-ḱi·yá·l*

dance house *Márakʰ*

it's dark *pʰi·tí*

daughter *qa·wé·liḷ* vocative: *níḱa* my daughter
  wax *dáxaċ*

daughter-in-law (own) *šówMiċ* (others) *-ʔóḷ*

day *dámal*

dead/to die *mu·dál*

deer *bi·šé*

deer (old word) *lu·q̇áwʔqaw*

delicious, sweet, good *ċi·qóm, cʰi·kʰécʰi·kʰè*

devil *xó-kà·wkʰ*

to die/dead *mu·dál*

difficult, hard *da·q̇ér*

digging stick *wa·šú-xày*

to dip (water) *xá ša·má·*

dirt *ḷá*

dirty *ċá·ċ* (sg.) *ċá·ċa* (pl.)

dishes *šá·ri* lit. 'basket'

doctor *ma·tú·* ~ *q̇o·ʔó-ḱi·yà·l-kà·wkʰ* lit. 'poison-
  doing man'

doe *mátʰi*

dog *háyu*

donkey *bú·ruʔ* (< Sp. *burro*)

dove *ma·yú·*

down *yów*

downstream *bi·dáw*

dream *xa·dúm*

dried cooked fish *q̇ú·l*

to drink *q̇ó·*

to drip (water) *xá di·tíḱ*

drunk *húracoʔ*

dry *ḱa·lól* (sg.) *ḱa·lóla* (pl.)

duck *q̇a·yá·n*

duck, tule *di·kúbu·hù*

eagle *šáy*

ear *ši·má·*

east *šó;* toward east *šó·l*

543

to eat *ku·hú* (by chewing) *qa·wá·l*

eel *ba·wól*

egg *ḱó*

eight *xókadò·l*

eighteen *ná·xòkadò·l ~ hádaqalna·xòkadò·l*

eighty *dó·laxày*

elbow *q̇u·sá*

elderberry *di·káydi·kày*

elderberry tree *qa·lúl*

elder brother (own) *méx* (other's) *-méx*

elder sister (own) *dé·x* (other's) *-de·x*

eleven *ná·ḱàli ~ hádaqalna·ḱàli*

elk *bo·ʔó ~ bo·ʔó-bi·šè*

empty/naked *yá·Mi*

enemy *xa·ká-na·pʰò*

during the evening/night *du·wéNa*

eye *ʔúy*

eyebrow *ʔúy ḱu·wí*

eyelash *ʔúy či·Mé*

face *ʔúyimo·*

falcon *ɫá·ɫa·*

far, at a distance *líla*

fart *pʰér*

fat *pʰúy*

father (own) *háriḱ* (other's) *-me·ʔé*

father-in-law (own) *ma·šá·* (other's) *-šá·*

father's father (own) *má·ɫile* (other's) *-bá·ɫile*

father's mother (own) *má·ċ* (other's) *-má·*

father's older brother (own) *má·ɫile* (other's) *-bá·ɫile*

father's younger brother (own) *kéx* (other's) *-kéx*

father's sister (own) *wé·x* (other's) *-wé·x*

fawn *nu·Wákʰ*

fear *kʰúlmanḱe* (I'm afraid)

feast *ma·ʔáy di·qà·kʰ*

feather *yi·ʔí*

feces *pʰá*

fifteen *xó·mḱamàr ~ hádaqalna·lè·ma*

one to fight *kʰíl ʔwa·*

filled *qa·bó*

finger *bi·Yà-ċú·xay*

fingernail *ríkʰ*

to finish, accomplish *ṭé·lqa, du·q̇ál*

544 to finish basket *q̇ás*

to finish (doing something) instrumental prefix
  + *-q̇ál*

fire *xó*

fish *šá* dried cooked *qú·l*

fish bone *šá-ɫa·nè*

fish worm *bi·lá*

five *lé·ma*

flea *be·rémal*

flicker (bird) *líkʰlikʰ*

flint, obsidian *xa·ká*

to flow (water) *xá ka·Núm*

flower *šu·bá·kʰ*

fly *ċá·ma·l*

to fly *pʰu·dí·l* (sg.) *pʰu·bé·l* (pl.)

foam *ša·ɫó*

fog *xa·bá*

food *ma·ʔáy*

foot *xa·má·*

forearm *bóṭʰqo*

forehead *di·lé*

to forget *di·qó·x*

fork *ša·čékʰ-xa·lè* lit. 'spearing-thing'

forty *xóčaxày*

four *dó·l*

fourteen *ná·dò·l, hádaqalna·dò·l*

fox *qa·q̇áw*

Friday *ki·híkʰ-lè·ma*

friend *wíNawa*

frog *mi·céqaray*

frost *yi·máw*

fruit *ma·ʔáy-ši·wèya*

full *ṗíɫ ~ qu·láš*

fur *či·Mé*

gall *bi·šéḱ*

to gamble *qá-di·mà·* (*di·má·* to hold with one hand)

to gather (pick off plant) *du·xá*

to gather (off ground) *da·ḱóy*

genitals, male or female *kʰa·wó*

ghost, spirit *q̇a·lúy-kà·wkʰ*

girl *dáxaċ* (sg.) *q̇a·rá·ya-qa·wìkʰ* (pl.); young lady *dáyawal* (sg.) *má·yawala* (pl.)

to give *si·xá·, di·qá* (one thing), *bi·díx* (more than one thing)

to give on more than one occasion *si·láx*

to give birth *ƙú·s qa·wí·*

to go *wá-du·kì·* (sg.) *di·kʰá·* (pl.)

to go away *cʰá·wuhu·* (sg.) *cʰá·pʰi·lì·* (pl.)

goat *čí·waʔ* (< Sp. *chiva*)

gold *ʔó·roʔ* (< Sp. *oro*)

good *ǫo·díy* (sg.) *ǫo·díya* (pl.) *či·qóm,*
  cʰi·kʰécʰi·kʰè

goose *Lá·l*

gopher *lámi*

grain *mu·ká*

granddaughter *wax dáxac̣* (or, grandmother term
  used by grandmother as self-reciprocal in address)

grandfather See father's father and mother's father

grandmother
  See mother's mother and father's mother

grandson *wax qa·wí·* (or, grandfather term used by
  grandfather as a self-reciprocal in address)

grapes *há·y*

grass *qa·čá* (also hay) ~ *ċa·kʰíl* ~ *ċa·pʰíl* (also clover
  species)

grasshopper *ša·qó*

gray *nó·ṭʰ* ~ *nónokʰ*

green *ċa·báċa·bàkʰ*

green brush *ló·ṭ*

to grind *dókʰ*

ground, land, country *ká·y*

grouse? *ku·búnku·bùn*

gum *xa·Wé·*

gun, bow *šu·Múy*

guts *tíripʰa* (< Sp. *tripa*)

hair *mu·sú*

hand *bi·Yá*

to hang down *kʰílqa·* (sg.) *pʰu·sáyƙ* (pl. distributive)

hard, difficult *da·qér*

to hate *ma·ʔáš*

hawk, chicken *či·yà-ma·néma·nè*

hawk, fish *ƙi·yá·*

hawk, small valley *ʔílʔil*

hawk, sparrow *ša·qáx-ba·bi·Yà*

hay, grass *qa·čá*

he *mí·p̣* him *mí·pal,* his *mí·pibax,* for him *mí·piba,* to
  him *mí·piNal,* with him *mí·piMaƙ*

head *kʰa·yá*

to hear *šó·kʰ*

heart *sa·má·y*

heavy *xa·líkʰ* (sg.) *xa·líka* (pl.)

hen *ká·ye·naʔ dá* (< Sp. *gallina* + *dá* 'female')

heron, green ("shypoke") *na·Wá*

hide (of animal) *ƙa·dác̣*

to hide (conceal) *da·qóm*

hill, mountain *da·nó*

hip *mo·ʔów*

to hit (with fist) *pʰa·sáxki·*

to hit (with object) *di·kʰó·*

hole *mó*

hoof, foot *xa·má·*

Hopland People *šóqo·wabax-kà·wkʰ*

horn, antler *ʔá*

horse *káwaʔ* ~ *káwayuʔ* (< Sp. *caballo*)

hot *xó*

house *ká*

how/what *cʰín*

how much *cʰíNakʰ*

hundred *ƙáli-sèntoʔ* (< *ƙáli* 'one' + Sp. *ciento*)

hungry *ma·ʔáy ma·rá·* (lit. 'food want')

to hunt *bo·ʔó·, du·dúl*

husband *báyle*

I *há·* me *wí* my *wax* for me *wíba* to me *wíNal*
  with me *wíMaƙ*

Indian *híntilʔ* (< Sp. *gentil* 'pagan')

iron (metal) *xa·ká*

iron (for ironing) *ʔà·m-ku·béx-xa·lè*

jaw *ǫa·wás*

to jump *káp̣ki·*

juniper berries *si·pʰú·*

key *yá·waʔ* (< Sp. *llave*)

kidney *xu·Lúmay*

to kill *šá·ƙ*

to kiss *si·p̣ú·l*

knee *ǫu·túl*

knife *kúčiyaʔ* (< Sp. *cuchillo*)

knife, pocket *náwahaʔ* (< Sp. *navaja*)

knoll *bu·tú*

to know *me·ʔél*

young lady See girl

lake, water *xá*

land, ground, country *ká·y*

to laugh *kʰu·wáy*

leaf *si·ṭál*

545

to leave *wá-du·kì·*

left (hand) *tʰa·Wíl*

leg *ša·kó*

leg, lower, front of *ke·ré·*

leg bone, upper *qó·m*

to lick *si·tál*

to lie (tell falsehood) *ba·šáḷ*

to lie down *mér* (sg.) *pʰi·ṭám* (pl.)

lightning *lóċ*

lips, mouth *xáċi·da*

little *kúč̣* (sg.) *kúča* (pl.)

liver *kʰa·Lál*

lizard *xá·tu·Nùtal*

lizard, mountain *xáyqu·Mùy*

long/tall *ba·kíl* (sg.) *qóla* (pl.)

long object to be perpendicular to a plane of reference *kókʰ*

loon *q̇ó·q̇*

louse, body *pʰe·réš*

louse, head *kí·*

lungs (?) *šó·ł*

maggot *ḷónḷon*

mallard *ċa·pʰú* (archaic)

man *ká·kʰ* (sg.) *hí·baya* (pl.)

  See also old man, young man

manzanita berry *ba·qáy*

manzanita tree *qa·yé·*

matches *xó-du·k̇èr-xa·lè*

meadow, valley *qa·qó*

mean *ku·nú·la*

measles *ḷa·pʰó* See smallpox

meat *bi·šé* lit. 'deer'

medicine *wéno?* (< Sp. *bueno?*)

to meet unexpectedly *di·tá·l*

menses *qálayòx ~ qál ~ qáli*

Mexican, Spaniard *pányor?* (< Sp. *español*)

Middletown People *ku·núla-qa·q̇òybax-kà·wkʰ*

milk (of cows) *lé·če?* (< Sp. *leche*) (breast) *si·dó·*

Mission People *quLá-na·pʰò-kà·wkʰ* lit. 'water lily-village-people'

mole *ḷí·didiw*

Monday *qa·lí·mi·dìkʰ*

money *pé·so?* (< Sp. *peso*)

546 moon *du·wé-là·*

morning, in the *du·wé·NaMi*

mortar *ku·ší·-xa·bè*

mosquito *du·lá?du·làw*

moss, tree *xa·lé· si·bú*

mother (own) *ník̇* (other's) -*tʰé*

mother-in-law (own) *ma·šá·* (others) -*šá·*

mother's brother (own) *cʰéċ* (others) -*cʰé·*

mother's father (own) *káċ* (others) -*ká·*

mother's mother (own) *qá·ċ* (others) -*qá·*

mother's older sister (own) *ḷʰú·ċ* (other's) -*ḷʰú·ċ*

mother's younger sister (own) *šéx* (other's) -*šéx*

mountain *da·nó*

mountain balm *ḷék̇-xa·lè*

mountain quail *k̇o·hóy*

mountain lion *wi·q̇á*

mountain mahogany *wa·šú*

mourning *da·qóy*

mouse *tu·nú*

mouse (bigger than house rat) *mó·ṭodòḷ*

mouth *xáċi·da*

mud *bó·r*

mule *múla?* (< Sp. *mula*)

mushroom *ċé·*

naked/empty *yá·Mi*

name *ší*

navel/umbilical cord *qó*

near *tʰi·bál*

neck, back *q̇óy*

neck, front *mi·Yá·*

needle *?áwoho?* (< Sp. *aguja*)

newt *wa·yá·x*

new *ši·wéy*

night, last *du·wé*; during the night, during the evening *du·wéNa*

nine *hádaqalšòm ~ hádaqalna·šòm*

nineteen *na·šòm ~ hádaqalna·šòm*

nipple *si·dó·-kʰa·yà*

no *kʰúyi* (don't want to)

  kʰúya (don't have)

  kʰúy (not)

north *ku·húla*; toward north *ku·húl*

people from the north (Mendocino County) *ku·húlabax-kà·wkʰ*

nose *lábo·bo*

oak, type of *lu·ḱé*

oak, poison *Máriyàṗ*

oak tree, white *qá·bayaṗ ~ qá·balaṗ*

oak tree, young *ba·ćóm*

obsidian, flint *xa·ká*

occiput *ća·dó·*

O.K., agreed *ʔó·*

old *bú·ćike*

old (worn) *q̇a·ṭá·*

old man *bú·ćike* (sg.) *búćiya* (pl.)

old woman *dáqara* (sg.) *má·qa·tʰora* (pl.)

one *ḱáli*

onions *xa·bá·y*

oriole *ća·káća·kàw*

otter *qi·qí*

owl, barn *ši·mà·kʰodókʰodòw*

owl, hoot *ma·cíkirì*

owl, screech *ma·sí·ɬ*

pack basket, close weave *bu·kú*

pack basket, open weave *ćó·y*

pancreas ? *ma·ṭé·*

paper *pá·pelʔ* (< Sp. *papel*)

pay *ma·nákʰ*

pears (upper lake dialect) *ši·dú, ši·dúḱ*; (mission dialect) *pʰi·čʰúṭʰudù*

penis *ma·ṭó·*

people, person *ká·wkʰ*

pepperwood nut *be·hé*

pepperwood nut with skin *há·li*

pepperwood tree *be·héṗ*

peppery, bitter, strong *bi·ḱów*

person, people *ká·wkʰ*

pestle *da·q̇ón*

to pierce (with gig) *pʰa·kʰó·*

pig *ḱó·če ʔ* (< Sp. *cocho*)

pigeon *ṭa·bá·ṭa·bàw*

pillow *kʰi·yéṗ*

pine, digger *ḱó·ṭʰi-xa·lè·*

pine, sugar *ḱe·ré·saṗ*

pine, yellow *xa·Wé·-xa·lè·*

pinole *yu·húy*

pocket *wó·lsaʔ*

poison *q̇o·ʔó*

potato *bú·*

potato, sweet *bú·-dù·lseʔ*

pond *xa ḱa·šó*

prisoner *pélesukʰ*

property, belongings of value *ća·bóɬ*

pubic hair, female's *bi·dá či·Mé*

pubic hair, male's *ʔáy či·Mé*

to push one stick with another *ša·yá·wkʰ*

quail *ša·qá·x* See also mountain quail

rabbit *mó·Ya*

raccoon *xa·Lús*

rafter *ṭʰów*

rain *kʰi·ké·*

rattlesnake *xá·s*

razor *di·q̇á·r-xa·lè*

real, true, genuine *pʰúḱ*

rectum *ṭá·-mò*

red *q̇edáq̇edàkʰ*

rib *mi·sá·kʰ*

rice *qa·ćíLi*

rifle *bi·šé šu·Múy*

right (correct) *q̇o·díy*

right (hand) *qákʰ*

ring *bi·YáNa-kʰíl* lit. 'suspended on the hand'

ripe *ćíkʰ*

river, creek *bi·dáme*

road (path) *dáday*

to roast *ma·ɬólqa*

robin *ći·ṭówṭow*

rock *xa·bé*

rooster *ḱá·ye·naʔ ḱá·kʰ* (< Sp. *gallina* 'hen' + *ḱá·kʰ* 'man')

root *cʰícʰ*

rope *číkoteʔ*

Round Valley People *ma·šá-xàybax-kà·wkʰ*

to run *kákʰ* (sg.) *ka·díkʰ* (pl.)

sack *hó·laʔ ~ kóstalaʔ ~ ma·šá-ho·laʔ*

saddle *sí·yaʔ* (< Sp. *silla*)

saliva *léx ~ qa·ćó·l*

salmon *du·kínaša*

salt *kʰe·ʔé*

sand *ṭʰa·ʔá*

Saturday *sá·waluʔ* (< Sp. *sábado*)

scissors *téheraʔ* (< Sp. *tijeras*)

to scorch (as of food) *pʰa·Wáṭʰ*

scorpion q̓átawìs

to scrape (roots, hides) di·q̓á·r

to scrape, scratch di·q̓á·ski·

to scratch (with claws, like dog) qa·békʰ

seagull ċi·k̓ómal

sea lion pʰi·yún

to see ká·r

  to look hé·ċ

seed qá·soy

to sell ʔélše

semen pʰu·ɫá·ʔwa ~ ʔáyi ṭʰór

seven kʰúlaxòčʰ

seventeen ná·kʰulaxòcʰ ~ hádaqalna·kʰùlaxočʰ

to sew bi·k̓íčʰki

she mi·ɫ her mí·ral hers mí·ribax for her
  mí·riba to her mí·riNal with her mí·riMak̓

sheep wá·re·kaʔ (< Sp. borrega 'lamb')

shirt kámisaʔ (< Sp. camisa)

shoes sápatoʔ (< Sp. zapato)

to shoot šóm (once) šómkʰ (repeatedly) kó·x
  (shoot and hit)

shore Má·

short buʔúč̓ (sg.) buʔúč̓a (pl.) ~
  bi·q̓úɫ (sg.) biq̓úɫa (pl.) ~
  bi·ṗóɫ (sg.) bi·ṗóɫa (pl.) ~
  bu·húš (sg.) bu·húša (pl.)

shoulder ċu·q̓ál

to shout si·q̓á·lkʰ

sick q̓a·lál

sinew yi·má

to sing xè-Ní· (sg.) xè-ló·ma (pl.)

sister See elder, younger sister

sister-in-law, brother's wife (own) míy (other's)
  -míy

sister-in-law, husband's sister (own) ma·qár
  (other's) -qár

sister-in-law, wife's sister (own) ma·há· (other's)
  -há·

sister's daughter, sister's son (own) ɫáx (other's)
  -ɫáx

to sit ká· (sg.) na·pʰó· (pl.)

six ċá·di

sixteen ná·ċa·di ~ hádaqalna·ċà·di

sixty xó·mk̓axày

skin ċi·dá

skunk nu·pʰér

sky qa·lí

to sleep si·má· mér (sg.) si·má· ku·ɫé·m (pl.)

sling bi·šék̓

small, tiny bu·húš
  See also short

smallpox bi·qóbi·qòw (also measles ?)

to smell mi·šé· (sg.) mi·múkʰ (pl.)

to smoke (tobacco) ṗókʰ

smooth ku·lé·ški· (smoothed)

snake qa·lúɫu·dùkʰ

snake, gopher xà·boʔóyal

snake, king xé·du·nà·r

snake, whip qa·líqàlʔqal

to sneeze ʔéčki

snot lés

snow Yúl

soap háwonʔ (< Sp. jabón)

soaproot ʔaṗ

soldier só·ltaweʔ (< Sp. soldades)

son qa·wé·liṗ
  vocative: hárik̓a
  my son wax qa·wí·

son-in-law (own) di·mó·ɫ (other's) -kéy

sour mó·ċ

south yó·; toward south yó·l

Spaniard, Mexican pányor (< Sp. español)

spider kʰá

spine k̓i·dí-Yà

to split pʰi·dákʰ (once)
  pʰi·bá·kʰ (repeatedly)

spoon kúčaraʔ (< Sp. cuchara)

spring (season) kà·y-xówakàx

spring (of water) xá·-qa·pʰà

squirrel qu·már

squirrel, small ground mu·líy

squirrel, tree sa·xálalày

to stand See long object to be perpendicular to a
  plane of reference

star ʔúyaxo

to steal pʰu·dí·

Stellar's jay sa·wálʔwal

to step cʰáṗki·

stick, digging wa·šú-xày

to stick and hold *ša·dím*

to stink *bá· nís mi·šé·nk̓e* 'that smells bad'

stomach *yu·xá*

store *té·nta?* (< Sp. *tienda*)

straight, true (of words) *pul*

strong, bitter, peppery *bi·k̓ów*

to suck *t̓ó·*

to suck out *si·dík^h*

to suck up *si·yá·w*

suckerfish *ša·mól*

sugar *sú·kara ~ k̓e·ré·sap̓* (*sú·kara?* < Sp. *azúcar*)

Sulphur Bank People *xáwi·nà·bax-kà·wk^h*

summer *mu·ta·winal*

sun *lá·*

Sunday *dóminko?* (< Sp. *domingo*)

swallow *t̓i·nít̓al*

swan *qóy*

sweat *mu·k^hé*

sweathouse *Márak^h*

sweet, delicious, good *c̓i·qóm ~ c^hi·k^héc^hi·k^he*

sweet substance *?ílibay*

to swell (up) *ma·bó·*

to swim *xá· qá·*

be sympathetic, in harmony, cheer up (said to those close to one when leaving on a long trip, to surviving relatives after a death) *Yémak̓on*

table *láme·sa?* (< Sp. *la mesa*)

tadpole *xa·bàkótolò*

tail *yi·bá*

to talk *ka·Nú·l*

tall/long *ba·kíl* (sg.) *qóla* (pl.)

to teach/count *du·yí*

tears *yu·xá*

teeth *ya·?ó*

to tell *t̓é·t̓ik^h*

ten *t̓ék̓ ~ hádaqal*

testicles *ya·qól*

thank you *?e·?e·?e·*

that *bá*

they *bé·k^h*, them *bé·kal*, their *bé·kibax*, to them *bé·kiNal*

thick *ca·náy* (sg.) *ca·náya* (pl.)

thigh, inside of leg *t̓^ha·Lá*

thigh, top of leg *ba·bú*

thin *pé·t^h* (sg.) *pé·t^ha* (pl.)

to think *di·nédi·nèlqa*

thirsty *xá ma·rá* lit. 'water want'

thirteen *hádaqalna·xò·mk̓a ~ ná·xo·mk̓a*

thirty *ná·hàdaqal*

this *mé*

thorn *t̓ír*

three *xó·mk̓a*

throat *mi·Yá·*

to throw round object (once) *di·?ól*, (repeatedly) *bi·nék^h* (distributive)

thunder *Líaka·k^h* (archaic), *qa·lìmaṭáw?ṭaw*, *qa·lìmaṭów?ṭow*

Thursday *ki·hík^h-dò·l*

tick *ṭa·lá*

toad *k̓a·wów*

tobacco *sa·xá*

toes *xa·mà·-qa·wík^h*

tongue *bál*

on top *wi·ná*

tree *xa·lé*

trousers *ša·k^hò-káwuhu·, pántalo?, pántalu?* (< Sp. *pantalón*)

trout *ma·láx*

Tuesday *ki·hík^h-xòč^h*

tuberculosis *tóse* (< Sp. *tos* 'cough')

tule, flat *há·l*

tule root, shoot *t̓^hi·bé·-ya·?ò* (young *ba·kó·*)

tule, round *ba·kó·*

tule, three-corner *qu·šál*

turkey *bóholote?* (< Sp. *guajolote*)

twelve *ná·xòč^h, hádaqalna·xoč^h*

twenty *xáydi·lè·ma*

to twine (baskets) *k̓í·š*

two *xóč^h*

Ukiah, Pinoletown People *bó·bax-kà·wk^h*

umbilical cord/navel *qó*

up *káyu*

uphill *qa·líl*

Upper Lake People *xá-k^hayàwbax-kà·wk^h*

upstream *da·nól*

urine *c^ho·?óy, č^ho·?óy*

vagina *bi·dá*

valley, meadow *qa·qó*

549

vertebrae *ḱi·dí-di·ḱùʈ^h*

visit *pášalʔ* (< Sp. *pasar*)

wagon *kárentaʔ* (< Sp. *carreta*)

to walk *wá·l*

to wash *da·só·l*

wasp *tʰa·rá*

water *xá*

we *wá·*, us *wa·l*, for us *wáyba*, ours *wáybax*, to us
  wáyNal, with us *wáyMaḱ*

weasel *ċi·lí·ċi·lìw*

to weave (baskets): to twine *ḱí·š*

  to coil *kʰi·bú·*

Wednesday *ki·híkʰ-xòmḱa*

week *sémanoʔ* (< Sp. *semana*)

west *bó·*; toward west *bó·l*

wet *xákʰ* (sg.) *xáka* (pl.)

what or how *čʰíʼn*

what? (I didn't hear) *háy*

wheat *tílikoʔ* (< Sp. *trigo*)

wheel *da·ḱó·*

when *čʰíʼnay*

where *čʰéʼ*

where from *čʰéʼwa*

where to *čʰéʼmal*

whiskey *xá-bi·ḱòw* lit. 'bitter/strong-water'

whistle, of bone *li·bú·*

white *pʰiʼłáw*

white man *ma·sáʼn*

who *ki·yáʼ*

whooping cough *qó·ḱ*

why *čʰíʼnʔìsa*

wide *ba·tʰína·ma, ba·tʰéna·ma*

wife *daḷ*

wildcat *da·lóm*

wilderness, area outside human communities, which

should only be entered with appropriate rituals of
preparation *qa·qó·*

willow *ba·kʰú·*

willow, basket *ċu·báha*

willow, black *ma·lúmma·lòw*

wind *Yá* (weather term)

windpipe *kʰa·ró*

wing *šál*

winter *xu·ċáy*

to wipe *da·qál*

wolf *cʰi·Méw*

woman *dá* (sg.) *ġa·rá·ya* (pl.)

  See also old woman, young lady

woodpecker *ġa·rá·čʰ*

woodpecker, big *ba·káka*

woodrat *čʰi·Níčʰ*

work *ki·híkʰ, tá·Walʔ* (< Sp. *trabajar*)

worm *kʰól*

  fish worm *bi·lá*

wrist *qa·ġón*

yawn *ḱá·š*

year *xu·ċáy* lit. 'winter'

yellow *qu·šíli-ši·bà* lit. 'lark body'

yellowhammer *ḷi·yál*

yellowjacket *tʰa·rá*

yes *ʔíʼ*

you (sg.) *máʼ*, object *míʼ*, yours *míʼbax*, to you *míʼNal*,
  with you *míʼMaḱ*, for you *míʼba*

you (pl.) *máʼ*, object *má·l*, yours *máybax*, to you
  máyNal, with you *máyMaḱ*, for you *máyba*

young *kúč* (sg.) *kúča* (pl.)

young lady *dáyawal* (sg.) *má·yawala* (pl.)

young man *šéʼla*

younger brother *dúʼxaċ*

younger sister *dúʼxaċ*

550

Sketch of Seneca, an Iroquoian Language

WALLACE L. CHAFE

1. INTRODUCTION

The Seneca language in 1993 was spoken by fewer than 200 people on the Tonawanda, Cattaraugus, and Allegany reservations in western New York State. Related languages include Cayuga, Onondaga, Oneida, Mohawk, and Tuscarora, as well as other languages that are extinct (Mithun 1979; vol. 15: 334-343). These languages form the Northern Iroquoian branch of the Iroquoian language family, whose Southern branch includes only the Cherokee language. In general structure the Northern Iroquoian languages are all quite similar, although in certain respects Seneca has undergone more radical changes than the others.

Seneca is noteworthy as the language of the early nineteenth-century prophet Handsome Lake, who was a Seneca chief (Wallace 1970; vol. 15: 442-448). There is almost no written record of the language before the nineteenth century, when the missionary Asher Wright and his Seneca collaborator William Jones devised a workable orthography that was used for religious and other publications. Lewis Henry Morgan's (1851) classic ethnography of the Iroquois includes a chapter on the language, as well as numerous items of culturally important vocabulary. Modern publications include the morphological description and dictionary in Chafe (1967), as well as the religious texts in Chafe (1961). Chafe (1963) is a short practical guide to Seneca orthography, morphology, and culturally significant vocabulary.

Numerous speakers of Seneca contributed their knowledge to this chapter. Especially helpful at various times were Solon Jones (fig. 1), Edward Curry (fig. 2), Albert and Geneva Jones, Tessie Snow, Corbett Sundown (fig. 3), Betsy Carpenter, Miriam Lee, Marie Biscup, Myrtle Peterson, Alberta Austin (fig. 4), and Lena Snow (fig. 5).

Seneca is a good example of a polysynthetic language whose words exhibit considerable fusion at morpheme boundaries. It maximizes the use of verbs, not only to express events and states (for a state, the correspondence is often to an English adjective), but also sometimes to express ideas of things (where English would employ a noun). Within Seneca verbs, inflectional and derivational elements appear as both prefixes and suffixes, and noun incorporation is common. A large array of pronominal prefixes distinguishes the roles of agent and patient rather than subject and object. Word order is determined by discourse function. New events and states are typically introduced before their participants have been identified, and in general the language follows a pattern by which more newsworthy information is stated earlier than less newsworthy.

2. PHONOLOGY

Seneca has undergone a great deal of phonological change that in some cases radically obscured the structure of the morphology. However, it is possible to reconstruct, both internally and through comparison with related languages, earlier stages of the language at which the morphological structure was more transparent.

As an example, the words *oʔgiʔ* 'I said' and *waęʔ* 'he said' have nothing in common except the final *ʔ*.

Fig. 1. Solon Jones (*gadžísdǫdyeʔ* 'Flying Spark') (b. 1890, d. 1960), an orator, ceremonial expert, leader in the Longhouse religion, linguistic and ethnographic consultant, and lacrosse player. He was a linguistic consultant to Chafe during 1956 and 1957. Photograph by William C. Sturtevant, Newtown Longhouse, Cattaraugus Reservation, N.Y., May 1957.

However, at an earlier recontructed stage, both words belonged to a more obviously structured paradigm: *waʔ-k-i-ʔ 'I said' and *waʔ-ha-i-ʔ 'he said'. Both words contained the factual prefix *waʔ-, followed by either the first-person agent prefix *k- or the masculine agent prefix *ha-, the verb root *-i- 'say', and the punctual aspect suffix *-ʔ. (Other Northern Iroquoian languages derive analogous words from a verb root *-ihrę- 'say' that occurs with the punctual aspect. Seneca shows no trace of the *-hrę- extension.) Subsequently, *waʔki became oʔgiʔ through a change of waʔ to oʔ before a consonant, plus the development of an earlier voice onset time that changed the originally voiceless k to a voiced g. The reconstructed *waʔhaiʔ became waęʔ through a sequence of changes, the first two of which took place before the stage of Proto–Northern Iroquoian: a loss of ʔ before h (restricted to certain morphological environments) and a coalescense of ai into ę (also morphologically restricted). These two changes yielded *wahęʔ, from which Seneca lost the intervocalic h, leading to the present waęʔ.

Because of this often extreme discrepancy between the current shape of words and their analysis into morphemes, Seneca words will be cited here in two forms: first their current pronunciation and then, in parentheses, a reconstruction of an earlier stage at which morphemes could be more easily segmented; for example, waęʔ (*waʔ-ha-i-ʔ) 'he said'. Hyphens will be used to show the morphemic segmentation when it is relevant

to the discussion. The parenthesized reconstructed forms do not represent a single coherent stage in the prehistory of Seneca. Some of them belong to the stage of Proto–Northern Iroquoian, but others to either earlier or later stages of Seneca prehistory (Chafe 1959). Their purpose is to serve as guides to an understanding of the present shape of Seneca words, many of which can be explained only in their historical context. Some of these reconstructions will take advantage of knowledge gained from comparisons with other Iroquoian languages, where internal reconstruction within Seneca alone would leave significant questions unanswered.

2.1. CONSONANTS

Linguists usually write the Northern Iroquoian languages with a small set of symbols for consonant phonemes. These symbols are shown in table 1. According to this way of writing, Seneca, having lost the r, would have only eight consonants, some of which have several phonetic realizations, or allophones. Certain of these consonants also cluster to form affricates that behave in certain respects like unitary consonants. It is quite possible to write Seneca consonants with only these eight symbols; however, such an orthography obscures the manner in which the language is actually pronounced and is much disfavored by Seneca speakers.

Table 2 shows the set of consonants that Seneca speakers regard as distinct from one another, as evidenced by their desire to distinguish them in writing in some fashion. These are the consonants and spellings that will be used here in the initial citations of words. Some are written with sequences of two or three letters, but all can be regarded as unitary consonants. It should be noted that the alveopalatal consonants are simply conditioned ("palatalized") variants of the alveolar consonants before i or y. In Chafe (1963) and (1967), as well as in the citations of Seneca words (in vol. 15), d, g, and š (being predictable variants) were written t, k, and s respectively, while the affricates tsh and tšh were both written ts, and dz and dž were both written j. In Chafe (1983) and in Seneca bilingual education programs š is written š̌, thy is written tšy, both dž and dy are written j, and ʔ is written with an apostrophe.

The obstruents form a distinct class as opposed to the resonants. Within the obstruent class there is an important distinction between the two laryngeal obstruents

Fig. 2. Edward Curry (shǫ·wǫ́ʔǫh) (b. 1890, d. 1975), carving a False Face mask. He was a preacher and upholder of the Seneca ceremonial tradition in the Coldspring Longhouse on the Allegany Reservation, N.Y. He was a linguistic consultant to Chafe during 1957 and 1958. Photograph by William C. Sturtevant, 1957.

Table 1. Northern Iroquoian Consonants as Traditionally Written by Linguists

	Alveolar	Palatal	Velar	Laryngeal
Obstruents				
stops	t		k	ʔ
fricatives	s			h
Resonants	n, r	y	w	

Table 2. Phonetically Distinct Seneca Consonants

	Alveolar	Alveopalatal	Palatal	Velar	Laryngeal
Obstruents					
stops					
plain	*t*			*k*	*ʔ*
voiceless-aspirated	*th*			*kh*	
voiced	*d*			*g*	
affricates					
voiceless-aspirated	*tsh*	*tšh*	*thy*		
voiced	*dz*	*dž*	*dy*		
fricatives					
aspirated	*sh*				
unaspirated	*s*	*š*			*h*
Resonants	*n*		*y*	*w*	

Fig. 3. Chief Corbett Sundown (*shogę́ʔdzo·wa·ʔ* 'Big Forehead', a Seneca chief's title) (b. 1909, d. 1992), a political leader, orator, ceremonial expert, and leader in the Tonawanda Longhouse. He was a linguistic consultant to Chafe during 1959 and on occasion thereafter. Photographed at the Tonawanda Reservation, N.Y., on Field Day, 1959.

(*ʔ* and *h*) and the other, oral obstruents. Seneca has no labial consonants. There are occasional nicknames that contain labial consonants (*góʔbit, dagam*), as do certain items of expressive vocabulary (*phloʔts* 'plop', *blæts* 'sound of fat legs slapping together'; Mithun 1982), but aside from such exceptional usages Seneca speakers do not close their lips while talking. The resonants *n*, *y*, and *w* need no special comment. All the Northern Iroquoian languages except Seneca and Onondaga have an additional, fourth resonant that is pronounced either *r* or *l*. Although this consonant was lost in Seneca, it left many traces of its former presence.

The six affricates in table 2 are of interest both phonetically and historically. The voiceless-aspirated versus voiced distinction parallels that in the oral stops, as can be seen in the contrast between the initial alveolar affricates in *tshaʔde·waʔ* 'it's the same size' and *dza·dak* 'seven'. As mentioned above, the alveopalatal affricates are versions of the alveolar affricates that occur when there is a following *i* or *y*: *tšhigéksaʔáah* 'when I was a small child', *džiˑyæh* 'dog'. The palatal affricates result from a fricativization of *y* when it immediately follows *th* or *d*: *hothyo·wiˑh* 'he has told about it', *idye·t* 'she's standing there'. The *y* segment of these affricates is realized as a voiceless or voiced palatal fricative (distinct from the voiceless and voiced alveopalatal fricatives written *š* and *ž*). In the International Phonetic Alphabet the *y* in *dy* would be written [j], while the *hy* in *thy* would be written [ç]. In contrast, the *š* of *tšh* would be written [ʃ], and the *ž* of *dž* would be written [ʒ].

Parallel to the stops and affricates, *sh* (an aspirated *s*) often results from a true sequence of *s* + *h*: *ęsha·yoʔ* (*ʔę-s-ha-yǫ-ʔ*) 'he will come back'. Between vowels *s* has a noticeably lenis pronunciation but is not a fully voiced [z]: *gya·sǫh* 'my name is'. The alveopalatal *š* results from the palatalization of *s* before *y*: *šya·sǫh* 'your name is', but *s* is not palatalized before *i*: *gahsíʔdaʔgeh* 'my foot'.

Some of these consonants are limited with respect to their distribution within syllables. The plain stops *t* and *k* occur only in syllable-final position, where they are released before an immediately following consonant but unreleased before a pause. In contrast, the voiceless-aspirated and voiced stops occur only in syllable-initial position. All the affricates occur only in syllable-initial position, as is true of *sh* and *š*. In most but not all of their occurrences, the two laryngeal consonants *ʔ* and *h* are ambisyllabic, serving both to close the preceding syllable and to open the following. Further remarks on syllable structure and its historical implications are included in 2.5.2.3.

2.2. VOWELS

Table 3 shows the set of vowels as they will be written here. In Chafe (1963) and (1967) *ę* and *ǫ* are written *ɛ* and *ɔ* respectively. In Chafe (1963) *æ* is written *ä*. In Chafe (1983) and in Seneca bilingual education programs *æ*, *ę*, and *ǫ* are written *ä*, *ë*, and *ö* respectively. Not counting the high back *u*, there are five oral vowels and two nasalized vowels. The nasalized vowels have a lower pronunciation than the *e* and *o*, to which they bear no synchronic or diachronic relation. Among the Northern Iroquoian languages, the vowel *æ* is shared by Seneca only with Onondaga and results in most cases from an earlier sequence *ra* (2.4.3.). In a few cases, it seems to have resulted from a coalescense of the sequence *ae*. The very common highlighting particle *næ·h*, for example, is evidently derived from *naeh*, a pronunciation that was sometimes heard in the 1960s.

The high back vowel *u* is an instance of sound symbolism. A word containing the verb root *-aʔaha-* 'small' may occur with every *a* changed to *u* to yield the meaning 'tiny': *niyágaʔáah* (*ni-yak-aʔaha-h*) 'she's small' thus becomes *niyúguʔúuh* 'she's tiny'. This vowel occurs only in words that express tininess.

Vowels may be either accented (highly pitched) or unaccented. Accented vowels are shown with an acute accent mark (for example *á*). Vowels may also be short (*a*), long (*a·*), or overlong (*a·a*). Details of accenting and lengthening are discussed in 2.5.

2.3. RECONSTRUCTED CHANGES IN CONSONANTS

The most important of the changes that led to the present shape of Seneca words are described in the paragraphs that follow. In some cases the order in which these changes took place was crucial to the present result. While no complete account of their ordering will be given here, it will be mentioned in cases where it has special relevance (see Chafe and Foster 1981).

2.3.1. CHANGES IN THE CLUSTERS *kn AND *tn

Seneca introduced an *h* into the cluster *kn*. Thus *knóhweʔs* became *khnǫeʔs* 'I like it' (where the *kh*

Fig. 4. Alberta Austin (b. 1930, d. 1994), well-known as a language teacher, linguist, and leader of a revival of the Seneca hymn singing tradition on the Cattaraugus Reservation, N.Y. She worked closely with Chafe on linguistic work from 1990 until her death. Photographed about 1990.

was subsequently reinterpreted as a unitary consonant). The same development evidently took place in the cluster *tn*, which first became *thn*, but subsequently the *t* was lost. Thus *tetninóhweʔs* became first *tethninóhweʔs* but then finally *dehnínǫeʔs* 'we (dual inclusive) like it'.

2.3.2. LOSS OF *t AND *k IN OBSTRUENT CLUSTERS

The two oral stops *t* and *k* were lost before a word-final *s*: *hatórats* became *hado·wæ·s* 'he hunts' (see 2.5.2.4. for the length in the final syllable). They were also lost before an *s* that was followed by an obstruent: *ótskraʔ* became *osgæʔ* 'saliva'. They were also lost word-finally when directly preceded by an oral obstruent: *waʔktókęst* became *oʔkdo·gęs* 'I straightened it'.

2.3.3. NASALIZATION OF *t

When *t* occurred word-finally after a nasalized vowel, because it was unreleased it was reinterpreted as *n*; thus, *kakę·t* became *gagę·n* 'white'.

Table 3. Seneca Vowels

| | Oral vowels | | Nasal vowels | |
	front	back	front	back
high	*i*	(*u*)		
mid	*e*	*o*	*ę*	*ǫ*
low	*æ*	*a*		

Fig. 5. Lena (Sibbie) Snow (*gawęniyóʔah* 'Little Good Word') (b. 1878, d. 1970), Seneca Turtle clan mother and folklore expert. She was a linguistic consultant to Chafe during 1957 and 1958. Photograph by William C. Sturtevant outside the Coldspring Longhouse, Allegany Reservation, N.Y., 1958.

2.3.4. LOSS OF *h

*h was lost between vowels: *hohístǫh became *hóísdǫh* 'he has shoved it'. It was also lost between a vowel and two obstruents, as well as between a vowel and a single word-final obstruent: *haʔswáhthaʔ became *haʔswáthaʔ* 'he's putting out the fire', *sáʔswaht became *saʔswat* 'put out the fire!' *h was also lost between a vowel and a resonant, but in that case there was compensatory lengthening of the vowel: *hahwatsíˑraʔ became *haˑwadžiˑyæʔ* 'his family'. Seneca now shows numerous instances of h between vowels, but all of them are cases in which there was once a resonant before the h that protected it from loss. Later the resonant itself was lost (2.3.5.). For example, *hǫnheʔ became *hǫheʔ* 'he's alive', and *hathárhaʔ became *hathaˑhaʔ* 'he talks, speaker'. Word-final *h was lost before another word within the same intonation unit (4.1.): *aˑ ne gyéˑ wáˑthyonyáˑnǫ́ʔ* 'ah one of them told about it', where the first three words in isolation would be *aˑh neh gyeˑh* (4.3.).

2.3.5. LOSS OF RESONANTS BEFORE LARYNGEALS

A resonant was lost before a laryngeal obstruent: see the preceding examples, and *hęnǫ́hsahaʔ* (*hęnahsáwhaʔ*) 'they begin'.

2.3.6. CHANGES IN *r

Before it was lost altogether, the resonant *r changed into one or another of the other resonants in certain environments. For example, *r became n before *y:

*waʔhakáryaʔk became *waˑganyaʔk* 'he broke off the story'. It became w between a long *o or *ǫ and an oral vowel: *hatóˑrats became *hadoˑwæˑs* 'he hunts'. It became y between a long *i and an oral vowel: *owíˑraʔ became *owiˑyæʔ* 'offspring'. It also became y between an oral obstruent and either *o or *ǫ: *waʔkrǫtóˑtęʔ became *oʔgyǫdoˑdęʔ* 'I set up a post'. In all other environments *r was lost, but not without affecting adjacent vowels in ways to be described in 2.4.3.

2.3.7. LOSS OF *y AND *w

In general, *y at the beginning of a pronominal prefix (3.1.1.2.) was lost after *ʔ and word-initially. Thus, the neuter patient prefix *yo- became o- after the factual prefix *waʔ- in *waʔoˑhęʔt* (*waʔyónhęʔt*) 'the next day', as well as in *otgiʔ* (*yotkiʔ*) 'it's dirty'. However, the y of the feminine agent prefix ye- was resistant to loss (or was analogically restored) in word-initial position: *yedaˑkheʔ* 'she's running'. There was a much more limited loss of *w, restricted to the first person patient prefix *wak(e)- in word-initial position (see examples in 2.3.8.). In addition the cluster *hw was lost intervocalically, in the same manner as intervocalic *h alone (2.3.4.): *knǫ́hweʔs became *khnǫeʔs*.

2.3.8. ALTERNATIONS OF y AND w WITH i AND o

Reflecting an alternation common to the Northern Iroquoian languages, a number of verb roots that end in y or w before a vowel end in i or o instead before the punctual aspect suffix ʔ or the imperative suffix -h: *agáhdędyǫˑh* (*wak-ahtęty-ǫˑh*) 'I'm going' but *oʔgáhdęˑdiʔ* (*waʔ-k-ahtęti-ʔ*) 'I went', *ageˑgwęh* (*wake-kw-ęh*) 'I've picked it' but *oʔgeˑgoʔ* (*waʔ-ke-ko-ʔ*) 'I picked it'.

2.3.9. CHANGE OF *waʔ TO oʔ

Word-initial *waʔ* before a consonant was replaced by *oʔ*: *waʔkiʔ became *oʔgiʔ* 'I said'.

2.3.10. PHONETIC CHANGES IN STOPS AND AFFRICATES

It may be useful to recapitulate the phonetic changes in stops and affricates that were mentioned in 2.1., since they are crucial to the orthography used here. These changes relate the consonant inventory in table 1 to that in table 2. First, the stops *t and *k and the affricate *ts became voiced before a vowel or resonant, so that they will be written d, g, and dz respectively. Second, *tsh and dz (< *ts) were palatalized before *i or *y, where they will be written tšh and dž. *s was palatalized before *y only, where it will be written š. Third, as part of the affricates thy and dy, y was fricativized, but no special symbol is used here to show that fricativization.

2.4. RECONSTRUCTED CHANGES IN VOWELS

2.4.1. SIMPLIFICATION OF TWO-VOWEL SEQUENCES

When a morpheme ending in a vowel was followed by a morpheme beginning in a vowel, the resulting two-vowel sequence was likely to be simplified in some way. This situation arose most often at the boundary between a pronominal prefix and a following stem. Hopkins (1987) suggests a strength hierarchy for Mohawk, according to which the stronger of two vowels remained and the other was deleted. A similar hierarchy applies to Seneca, where the vowels can be listed from strong to weak as ǫ-o-ę-e-i-a. Thus, for example, the addition of the pronominal prefix ho- 'masculine patient' to the stem -ahsę·h 'be fat' resulted in hohsę·h 'he's fat', and the addition of the same prefix to the stem -idáʔǫh 'be asleep' resulted in hodáʔǫh 'he's asleep'. In both cases the weaker vowels a and i were deleted in favor of the stronger o. Two identical vowels were simplified to a single vowel, as when ha- 'masculine agent' was added to -ado·wæ·s 'hunts' to produce hado·wæ·s 'he hunts'.

There are some restricted environments in which two vowels coalesced to produce a different vowel. For example, the sequence *ai yielded ę, as when ha- plus *-iʔtrǫʔ 'stay' combined to produce hęʔdyǫʔ 'he stays'. The feminine agent prefix ye- combined with a following a to produce yǫ-, as in yǫshe·das 'she counts, census taker', derived from the stem -ashe·tas.

The sequences *ęe and *ęo were replaced by e· and eo respectively: éʔyathyo·wiʔ (*ę-hey-at-hrory-ʔ) 'I will tell about him', eóyaʔdágehaʔ (*ę-ho-yaʔt-a-kenh-aʔ) 'it will help him'. This appears to be the only environment in which ę alternates with e.

Finally, when e is directly followed by another vowel, the e is lost in fast speech and the following vowel is lengthened; for example, eo is replaced by o·. Thus deonǫdawęnye·h (*te-hon-at-awęrye-·h) 'they are moving around' becomes do·nǫdawęnye·h. This change also takes place across word boundaries, after loss of intervocalic h at the boundary: neh hatha·haʔ 'the speaker' becomes n a·tha·haʔ. If the e was accented, the accent is preserved on the resulting long vowel: néh hatha·haʔ becomes n á·tha·haʔ.

2.4.2. The change of *a(ʔ)wa to ǫ
In an unusual development common to all the Northern Iroquoian languages, the sequence a(ʔ)wa (with or without the ʔ) became ǫ: ǫge·gęʔ (*waʔ-wake-kę-ʔ) 'it saw me'.

2.4.3. The Effect of *r on Adjacent Vowels
The vowel æ is derived in most cases from an *a that was originally preceded by *r. In the sequence *ra, the a became æ and subsequently the r was lost: *oʔkraʔ became oʔgæʔ '(falling) snow'. If the *ra was preceded by a short unaccented *a, the original *ara sequence became a long æ·: *kahsíkwaraʔ became gahsigwæ·ʔ 'fork'. If the *a preceding the *r was either long or accented, the following æ returned to a after the loss of the *r: *kaká·raʔ became gaga·aʔ 'story', and *okáhraʔ became ogáaʔ 'eye'.

In the sequence *aro the *a became e, but only if it was short: *sekaró·tęh became segeodęh 'tell a story!' With a long a·, *hoká·rot became hoga·ot 'he's telling a story'. Similarly, in the sequence *arǫ a short *a became ę: *ohsíkwarǫt became ohsigwęǫn 'rattlesnake' (literally 'it has a fork protruding from it'), but with a long a· *hotihsikwá·rǫt became hodíhsigwa·ǫn 'they've attached a fork to it'.

2.4.4. Progressive Nasalization
The vowel *a became ǫ after *n: *ohnaʔ became o·nǫʔ 'oil'. *a also became ǫ after a nasalized vowel, as well as after a nasalized vowel plus *ʔ, *w, or *sw: *kahóʔwaʔ became ga·ǫwǫʔ 'boat'. In parallel fashion, æ became ę after a nasalized vowel: *hoʔnikóhraʔ became hoʔnígǫę 'his mind', but æ became ę after n only for some speakers: *onráhtaʔ became either onæhdaʔ or onęhdaʔ 'leaf'.

2.4.5. Prothetic i
Seneca verbs must contain more than one syllable. If a verb would otherwise consist of a single syllable, a prothetic initial syllable consisting only of the vowel i was added. For example, instead of a word *dye·t 'she's standing there', in which all the expected morphemes are represented, Seneca has idye·t. This prothetic vowel, which can be reconstructed for Proto–Northern Iroquoian, was presumably related to the need for a penultimate syllable that would accept the Proto–Northern Iroquoian penultimate accent (2.5.1.).

2.5. Word-Level Prosody
Prosody within a Seneca word is a matter of the accenting and lengthening of vowels. Accenting is realized as higher pitch on the accented vowel. Vowel lengthening has two degrees: two mora vowels, as in the last syllable of gáʔga·ʔ 'crow', indicated with a raised dot, and three mora vowels, as in the last syllable of gaga·aʔ 'story', written as two identical vowels with a raised dot between them. Three mora vowels occupy the same total amount of time as three mora sequences consisting of two different vowels, as in i·at 'he's standing', where the added length is again indicated with a raised dot between the two vowels, each vowel in this case occupying one and a half moras. (There is no difference in pronunciation between i·a and a sequence that would have arisen historically as ia·.)

Although they both occupy two moras, there is a difference in pronunciation between a fully accented long vowel, as in the first syllable of háʔdathęs 'he's thirsty', and a sequence that consists of an accented short vowel followed by an identical unaccented short vowel, as in ogáaʔ 'eye'. The former has high pitch throughout, while the latter has high pitch only on the first mora. In the latter case, two separate vowels will be written. Although it is thus possible to have a sequence of two adjacent vowels, the first of which is accented and the second not, the opposite sequence does not occur. That is, there are no sequences of two adjacent vowels in which the first is unaccented and the second accented. When such cases would have arisen historically, the accent was extended to the entire sequence. For example, *oríhwaʔ 'cause' might have been expected to yield Seneca *oíwaʔ, but the word is actually pronounced óíwaʔ with high pitch on both the first and second vowels. In summary, whereas a sequence like ói remained as such, a sequence like oí came to be pronounced óí.

2.5.1. ACCENTING

Whereas the accent in Proto–Northern Iroquoian (K. Michelson 1988) was on the penultimate syllable in a word (with allowance for certain epenthetic vowels that did not count as syllabic nuclei), Seneca shifted to a different, iambic pattern that was based on counting forward from the beginning of the word instead of backward from the end, placing an accent on certain even-numbered syllables. With the exception of final syllables as well as certain penultimate syllables that were treated in special ways (2.5.2.3.), Seneca came to accent the vowel of any even-numbered closed syllable, as well as the vowel of any even-numbered open syllable if it was immediately followed by a nonfinal closed syllable.

One of the interesting complexities of Seneca phonology is the fact that the distinction between closed and open syllables was differently defined at different times and in different environments. In the case of the iambic pattern just described, a closed syllable was one whose vowel was followed by (1) a laryngeal obstruent, (2) a cluster of any two or more obstruents, or (3) the clusters sn, sw, ny, and some but not all instances of st. Thus, for example, Seneca shifted the accent from the penultimate to the second syllable of honǫ́thǫ·deʔ 'they (masculine) hear it', where the second syllable was closed by the obstruent cluster th. It also shifted the accent to the second syllable of hadídakheʔ 'they (masculine) are running' because the vowel of the following, third syllable was closed by the obstruent cluster kh. This pattern allowed a word to have more than one accent: hadíksaʔshǫ́ʔǫh 'children' (where the second syllable was closed by ks and the fourth syllable by ʔ). But it also allowed a word to have no accent at all, if none of its syllables was closed in the relevant manner: hadiwęnodadyeʔs 'the Thunderers'.

2.5.2. VOWEL LENGTHENING

Vowel length in Seneca has five sources. First, it may result from the loss of h or r between identical vowels (2.3.4., 2.3.6.): *haháʔdathęhs became há·ʔdathęs 'he's thirsty'. Second, it may compensate for an h that was lost between a vowel and a resonant (2.3.4.): *ohnékanohs became o·neganos 'water'. Third, some

but not all the aspect suffix allomorphs that consist of a final -ʔ or -h have the effect of lengthening the preceding vowel. These allomorphs will be written in reconstructions as -·ʔ and -·h: niyóʔdę·h (*ni-y-oʔtę-·h) 'the way it is'. Fourth, in fast speech length may compensate for the loss of a preceding e (2.4.1.). Fifth, and most relevant to the present discussion, length is added to certain vowels in both the penultimate and final syllables of words, depending on the consonants that follow. This last-mentioned kind of lengthening is complex and must be described in terms of several stages and environments.

2.5.2.1. PROTO–NORTHERN IROQUOIAN LENGTH IN OPEN PENULTIMATE SYLLABLES

In Proto–Northern Iroquoian there was lengthening of a penultimate vowel in an open syllable. Since these penultimate vowels were also accented, the length can be viewed as an additional manifestation of the prominence of penultimate syllables. However, although all penultimate syllables were accented (with allowance for epenthetic vowels that did not count as syllabic nuclei), only the vowels in open syllables were lengthened; those in closed syllables were accented but short. In this case the definition of closed syllable was broader than that set forth in 2.5.1.: all consonant clusters served to close a syllable, as did a single ʔ or h, which was in effect ambisyllabic.

With this pattern of penultimate lengthening as a starting point, Seneca modified it in different ways depending on whether the penultimate syllable was odd or even (2.5.2.2. and 2.5.2.3.). In general, whereas Seneca replaced the penultimate accent of Proto–Northern Iroquoian with an entirely new iambic accent pattern (2.5.1.), it retained the penultimate length, as illustrated again by honǫ́thǫ·deʔ 'they (masculine) hear it' from *honathǫ́·teʔ. However, in odd penultimate syllables the length was sometimes lost (2.5.2.2.), while in even penultimate syllables it was extended to additional instances (2.5.2.3.).

2.5.2.2. LOSS OF LENGTH IN ODD PENULTIMATE SYLLABLES CONTAINING a

At the Proto–Northern Iroquoian stage there were certain instances of the vowel a that were not lengthened because of their epenthetic status. Seneca generalized this failure to lengthen to all instances of a in odd penultimate syllables (affecting also the æ and ǫ that were derived from a; 2.4.3., 2.4.4.). Thus, *waʔakwá·kęʔ became waʔagwagęʔ 'we (plural exclusive) saw it'; *aóshratǫh became áóshædǫh 'it's winter'. As an exception to this development, the a remained long if it was in an odd penultimate syllable that was also the first syllable in a word: ha·dǫh 'he says'. But as an exception to the exception, in an imperative verb a was not lengthened even in an initial syllable: šyadǫ·h 'write!'

2.5.2.3. Additional Lengthening in Even Penultimate Syllables

Whereas odd penultimate syllables in Seneca show fewer instances of lengthening than were present in Proto–Northern Iroquoian, in even penultimate syllables the instances of lengthening were multiplied. In effect, any vowel in an even penultimate syllable came to be long, but unaccented, unless it was immediately followed by a laryngeal obstruent (*ʔ* or *h*), or in some cases by *st* (now *sd*): *otékhaʔ* became *odeˑkhaʔ* 'it burns, fire', *hayẹthwas* became *hayẹˑthwas* 'he plants, planter', *onákta* became *onọˑkdaʔ* 'space'. There was no lengthening, and the even-syllable accent was preserved in *ogáʔọh* 'it tastes good' (because of the following *ʔ*) and in *oʔnísdaʔ* 'corn on the cob' (because of the following *st*). But there are other instances of *st* that show lengthening and no accent: *gadžiˑsdaʔ* 'ember'. (Probably the instances of *st* without the lengthening stem from an earlier *hst*.)

This change in Seneca can be viewed as a type of resyllabification that was limited to even penultimate syllables. Whereas at an earlier stage a syllable boundary was located between the consonants of a cluster, in an even penultimate syllable Seneca reinterpreted the entire cluster following the vowel as constituting the onset of the following syllable. The preceding vowel thus now belonged to an open syllable and was for that reason lengthened. For example, what was earlier *o.ték.haʔ* became *o.teˑ.khaʔ*, where the period indicates a syllable boundary. Possibly it was as a byproduct of this resyllabification that what had earlier been interpreted as the clusters *th* and *kh* were reinterpreted as unitary consonants: as voiceless-aspirated stops that now contrasted with their voiced counterparts. Thus, *oteˑkhaʔ* was reinterpreted as *odeˑkhaʔ*, with the onsets of the second and third syllables reinterpreted as voiced and as voiceless-aspirated stops respectively. In any case, Seneca speakers refuse to recognize the presence of a separate *h* following the stop in such a word.

2.5.2.4. Lengthening in Final Syllables

Seneca also lengthened vowels in certain word-final syllables. Essentially, this lengthening arose in a final syllable that ended in a single oral obstruent: *ityet* became *idyeˑt* 'she's standing there'. When lengthening is not found before a single oral obstruent in the language today, there was a final consonant cluster at the time this lengthening took place. Thus, *wákhraht* did not acquire length in *oʔkhæt* 'I passed by' because the final vowel was earlier followed by *ht* (2.3.4.). However, some clusters were simplified before the lengthening took place. Thus, *hẹnatóˑrats* 'they hunt' lost the *t* of the final cluster at an earlier stage (2.3.2.), so that at the time of the lengthening the final vowel was followed only by *s* and the word became *hẹnọdoˑwæˑs*.

Lengthening in monosyllabic particles cannot always be accounted for in the ways just described, and it is to some extent unpredictable, as is the accenting of such particles. Thus, *giˑh* 'or' has a long vowel, but *dih* 'change of topic' a short one. Although the accenting of particles is determined in part by discourse factors, certain particles like *nǽˑh* 'highlighting' appear to have an inherent accent, while others (like *giˑh* and *dih*) are inherently unaccented.

2.5.2.5. Shortening in Vowel Sequences

After *r* was lost between vowels, if either of the vowels was long it was shortened: *orẹˊnaʔ* became *oẹnọʔ* 'song'; however, there was no shortening if the vowel preceding the *r* was a long penultimate vowel: *kakáˑraʔ* became *gagaˑaʔ* 'story'. Evidently this shortening in vowel sequences preceded the loss of intervocalic *h*, since it did not apply to vowel sequences resulting from that loss: *waháˑyọʔ* became *waaˑyọʔ*, written *waˑayọʔ* 'he arrived'.

All three- or four-mora clusters of two vowels (including two identical vowels) were shortened to two moras when they were located before the penultimate syllable. Without this shortening, for example, *waʔharihwasterist* would have become *wáˑiˑwásdeˑis*, but it is in fact pronounced *wáíwásdeˑis* 'he noticed it'.

3. Morphology

With respect to their internal structure, the words of Iroquoian languages have traditionally been regarded by linguists as falling into three major classes: verbs, nouns, and particles. At the two extremes, verbs often have a fairly complex morphological structure while particles usually consist of one, or occasionally two morphemes; nouns are intermediate in complexity. This classification on the basis of internal structure is to some extent independent of the functioning of words in discourse. For example, verbs may function in ways that English speakers are accustomed to associating with verbs, adjectives, or nouns, while particles may function as conjunctions, adverbs, determiners, numerals, and in various other ways. Words that refer to people or things may, from a morphological point of view, be nouns, verbs, or particles (in the sense that they may consist of only a single morpheme).

3.1. Verb Morphology

Seneca verbs are comparable to English clauses. Each verb expresses a total event or state, including its core participants. For example, whereas English might express an event as 'he became a White man', a clause with five words, Seneca expresses the same event as *wáˑnyọʔọ́ʔheʔt* (*wa-ha-hnyọʔọ-ʔheʔ-t*), including in this one word the factuality of the event (*wa-*), the fact that it applied to a single male human being (*-ha-*), the state of being a White person (*-hnyọʔọ-*), the process of entering into that state (*-ʔheʔ-*), and the fact that this was a single, punctual event (*-t*).

559

3.1.1. THE MINIMAL VERB

Each Seneca verb contains at least three parts: (1) a verb stem that categorizes the event or state, (2) a pronominal prefix that refers to one or more of the core participants in the event or state, and (3) an aspect suffix that specifies the aspect of the event or state. A minimal verb stem will be called a verb root. Thus, the event verb *hatha·ha?* 'he talks' is built on the verb root *-tha-* (*-thar-*) 'talk', preceded by the pronominal prefix *ha-* 'masculine agent' and followed by the habitual aspect suffix *-ha?*. The state verb *otgi?* 'it's dirty' is built on the verb root *-tgi-* (*-tki-*) 'be dirty', preceded by the pronominal prefix *o-* (*yo-*) 'neuter patient' and followed by the stative aspect suffix *-?*.

3.1.1.1. THE ASPECTS

The choice of an aspect affects the structure of the rest of the verb. Minimal verbs expressing states that are not the result of events occur only with the stative aspect suffix. Minimal verbs expressing events occur with any of four aspect suffixes. These suffixes have been given various names in Iroquoian linguistic studies, but here they will be called habitual, stative, punctual, and imperative. (The habitual has also been called the serial or iterative; the stative has also been called the perfective or descriptive.) Each of these suffixes occurs in a variety of allomorphs, conditioned by the last morpheme of the verb stem to which it is attached. Furthermore, while there are only four formally distinguishable suffixes, several of them have more than one meaning, as determined either by the stem to which they are attached or by the context in which the verb occurs. Semantically, then, the number of aspectual options is greater than four.

3.1.1.1.1. The Habitual Aspect

The habitual aspect is in a sense the simplest to describe, since it has no special consequences for the structure of the rest of the verb. It occurs in the reconstructible shapes *-ha?*, *-h*, *-s*, *-ahs*, *-?s*, *-e?s*, *-hs*, *-ęhs*, *-ǫhs*, *-se?*, *-Ø*. With all verb stems this aspect may have a habitual or generic meaning, lacking reference to any particular event: *hayę·thwas* 'he plants, is a planter'. With some but not all verb stems it may alternatively express an imperfective meaning like that of the English progressive: in an appropriate context the same word *hayę·thwas* means 'he is planting'. Thus, for the verb stems that allow both meanings the habitual aspect is ambiguous in the same manner as what are called present-tense verbs in various European languages, as when German *er pflanzt* may have a generic meaning 'he plants' or may correspond to English 'he is planting'. On the other hand, *hadęnotha?*, with a different stem, can have only the generic meaning 'he sings' and not the meaning 'he is singing', which for that stem is expressed with the stative aspect.

3.1.1.1.2. The Stative Aspect

The stative aspect suffix has the reconstructible shapes *-?*, *-·?*, *-h*, *-·h*, *-ęh*, *-ǫh*, *-ǫ·h*, *-ih*, *-Ø*. Its uses are more complex than those of the habitual suffix. Its simplest use, and that to which its name is most directly appropriate, is found at the end of a verb that expresses a state: *gagaide?* 'it's on a slant', *wi·yo·h* 'it's nice'. The simultaneous presence of several objects or people that are in the same state can be indicated with a stative plural suffix whose form may be *-?s* or *-hs*: *wi·yo?s* 'things are nice', *hadigowa·nęs* (*hati-kowanę-hs*) 'they (masculine plural) are important'. It is possible that this stative plural suffix should be regarded as a special use of the habitual suffix described in 3.1.1.1.1.

When the stative aspect suffix occurs with a verb that expresses an event, it may have a meaning like that of the English perfect, conveying the current relevance of a past event: *hoyę·thǫh* (*ho-yęthw-ęh*) 'he has planted'. (Evidently the reconstructed sequence *wę* in this verb was replaced by *ǫ*. Furthermore, the masculine agent prefix *ha-* has been replaced with the masculine patient prefix *ho-*.) The perfect meaning is the only possible meaning for this suffix with this verb stem, but in contrast the stative form *hodę·no·t* (*ho-atręnot-Ø*) does not have the perfect meaning 'he has sung', but rather the imperfective meaning 'he is singing'.

The difference between planting and singing, and hence the different meanings conveyed by the stative aspect suffix with these two stems, evidently lodges in the fact that planting is regarded as consequential while singing is not. Planting is an event that produces a new state of affairs significantly different from the old state of affairs. Singing does not produce such a difference (Chafe 1980). Particularly revealing in this regard is the fact that Seneca has two verb stems meaning 'cut', *-ya?k-* and *-hren-*, the first meaning 'sever' and the second 'make an incision'. The first is regarded as consequential, so that *hoyá?gǫh* (*ho-ya?k-ǫh*) has the perfect meaning 'he has cut (severed) it'. The second is regarded as nonconsequential, so that *ho·enęh* (*ho-hren-ęh*) has the progressive meaning 'he is cutting (making an incision in) it'. In short, for consequential verbs the stative aspect suffix expresses a perfect meaning while the habitual aspect suffix may express either a habitual or an imperfective meaning. For nonconsequential verbs, on the other hand, the stative aspect suffix expresses an imperfective meaning (the perfect meaning is impossible), and the habitual aspect suffix expresses only a habitual meaning. This distribution of aspects and meanings is summarized in table 4, where the words in single quotes indicate meanings and the cells in the matrix are filled with the names of aspect suffixes.

An additional peculiarity of the stative aspect is the fact that with intransitive prefixes it requires the use of

Table 4. Semantics of the Habitual and Stative Aspects

	'generic'	'imperfective'	'perfect'
Consequential verbs	habitual	habitual	stative
Nonconsequential verbs	habitual	stative	(impossible)

a patient rather than an agent pronominal prefix, even when the referent of the prefix functions as an agent. It would seem that both someone who has done something and someone who is doing something are treated by the language as people who are affected by the event and are in that respect patients. This use of patient prefixes with the stative aspect has been thoroughly grammaticized, and no other choice is possible; however, it is restricted to intransitive prefixes. The transitive prefixes that combine an agent with a patient occur with this aspect in the same manner as with any other.

3.1.1.1.3. The Punctual Aspect

The punctual aspect suffix has the shapes *-ʔ, *-·ʔ, *-aʔ, *-ęʔ, *-t, *-k, *-Ø. It is for the most part used for an event that is construed as a single occurrence, not repeated or extended over a significant period of time. Its meaning, in other words, is that which might otherwise be called perfective. It differs from the habitual and stative aspects in requiring the presence of an additional, modal prefix preceding the pronominal prefix. Thus, a punctual verb must have at least four parts: the modal prefix, the pronominal prefix, the verb stem, and the punctual suffix. By far the most common form of the punctual suffix is *-ʔ, but the other forms are conditioned by certain verb stems. After a stem ending in ʔ the punctual is regularly *-t, except that after iʔ it is *-k.

3.1.1.1.4. The Modal Prefixes

There are three modal prefixes, whose original function appears to have been to express degrees of factuality. They can be termed the factual (the highest degree), future (an intermediate degree), and optative (the lowest degree).

The factual expresses the speaker's unquestioning knowledge that the event either took place in the past or is taking place simultaneously with the speech act: wááyęthoʔ (*waʔ-ha-yęthw-ʔ) most often means 'he planted it', but it could also mean that the speaker sees him planting it right now. The past use is the more common of the two. At the stage of Proto–Northern Iroquoian the form of the factual prefix was usually *waʔ-, with three principal exceptions: (1) the ʔ was lost before an h, where the prefix became simply wa- (as in the example just given); (2) the factual prefix had the form *e- rather than waʔ- before any inclusive or second-person pronominal prefix except before a second-person singular agent prefix, where it remained waʔ-: edwáyęthoʔ (*e-twa-yęthw-ʔ) 'we (inclusive plural) planted it'; (3) in certain combinations

with prepronominal prefixes (3.1.3.), the factual prefix was realized simply as *-a-. In addition to exhibiting the variants just mentioned, Seneca has more recently replaced *waʔ- with oʔ- before a consonant: oʔgyę·thoʔ (*waʔ-k-yęthw-ʔ) 'I planted it'.

The future prefix, whose form is *ę-, expresses the speaker's expectation that something will happen: éóyęthoʔ (*ę-ha-yęthw-ʔ) 'he will plant it'. The event is not yet a fact, but the speaker expects it to become a fact. The future is often used as an imperative: ęhšyę·thoʔ (*ę-hs-yęthw-ʔ) '(you will) plant it!' The ę of the future is replaced by e before e and o (2.4.1.).

The optative prefix expresses the speaker's opinion that something might or should happen, with no certainty that it will: á·yę·thoʔ (*aa-ha-yęthw-ʔ) 'he might plant it' or 'he should plant it'. It usually has the form aa-, realized as a long a· that counts as two syllables. In the environments where the factual prefix is e-, the form of the optative is ae-: aedwayę·thoʔ (*ae-twa-yęthw-ʔ) 'we (inclusive plural) should plant it'.

3.1.1.1.5. The Imperative Aspect

The imperative suffix is identical in shape to the punctual, except that wherever the punctual has ʔ the imperative has h. Although it might not be considered an aspect in the usual sense, the imperative occurs in the same position in the verb as the other aspect suffixes. Imperative verbs most commonly have a second person pronominal prefix: šyęthoh '(you singular) plant it!', swayę·thoh '(you plural) plant it!'; however, first and third person imperatives ("hortatives") are possible: gyęthoh 'let me plant it!', hayę·thoh 'let him plant it!'

Under certain restricted circumstances the imperative suffix may occur with one of the modal prefixes. For example, it occurs with the future prefix in prohibitions, where the verb is preceded by the particle sę·nǫh or hę·nǫh 'don't!': sę·nǫ́ ęhšyę·thoh 'don't plant it!' It may occur with the factual prefix in the presence of the cislocative or repetitive prefix (3.1.3.1.), and with the optative prefix in the negative future construction (3.1.3.5.).

3.1.1.2. THE PRONOMINAL PREFIXES

There are 60 formally distinct pronominal prefixes. They express the person, gender, number, and case of the core participants in an event or state. Persons include first, second, and third, but there is also an exclusive-inclusive distinction in the dual and plural. Gender is relevant only to third person, where there is a distinction among masculine, feminine, and neuter. Feminine has a double meaning: it may refer to a female person, but it may also refer to people in general, 'one'. Neuter generally includes nonhuman animates as well as inanimates, but pets are sometimes treated as human and thus as either masculine or feminine. Number includes singular, dual, and plural, but in some instances dual and plural are merged into one nonsingular category. Dual pronominal prefixes are usually accompanied by the dualic prepronominal prefix (3.1.3.3.). Case includes agent and patient, but the patient case is also used for a beneficiary whenever one is present. Since beneficiaries are nearly always human whereas patients are often nonhuman, it can be said that there is a preference for marking human participants whenever possible.

The distinction between agents and patients is semantically complex, and in some instances has been grammaticized in such a way that its semantic basis is no longer apparent. The performer of an action is almost always expressed with an agent prefix, whether the verb is transitive or intransitive: *oʔgyęn* (*waʔ-k-yęht-Ø*) 'I hit it', *oʔgyǫ́* (*waʔ-k-yǫ-ʔ*) 'I arrived', both with the first person agent prefix *k-*. Most experiencers, whether perceptual, epistemic, or attitudinal, are also marked as agents: the following all contain the same first-person agent prefix *k-* or *ke-*: *oʔge·gę́* (*waʔ-ke-kę-ʔ*) 'I saw it', *gyędeˑih* (*k-yęter-ih*) 'I know it', and *khnǫeʔs* (*k-nǫhweʔ-s*) 'I like it'. Agent prefixes are also used to mark participants in more or less permanent or inherent states: *khnęˑyeˑs* (*k-hnęyes-Ø*) 'I'm tall', and *geˑnyǫ́ʔǫh* (*ke-hnyǫʔǫ-h*) 'I'm a White man'.

A patient prefix is used for a participant that is affected by an action, as well as one that is perceived, known, liked, and so on. The following examples contain the first-person patient prefix *wak-* or *wake-*: *ǫgyęn* (*waʔ-wak-yęht-Ø*) 'it hit me', *ǫge·gę́* (*waʔ-wake-kę-ʔ*) 'it saw me', *agyędeˑih* (*wak-yęter-ih*) 'it knows me', and *akhnǫ́eʔs* (*wak-nǫhweʔ-s*) 'it likes me'. A participant who is affected by an intransitive change of state is also marked as a patient: *ǫgáhdaʔt* (*waʔ-wak-ahtaʔ-t*) 'I got full'. A patient prefix is also used for one who is in a state regarded as temporary, as opposed to the permanent states illustrated at the end of the last paragraph: *agáhsęˑh* (*wak-ahsęˑh*) 'I'm fat'. Finally, with an intransitive verb in the stative aspect a participant that is semantically an agent is marked as a patient (3.1.1.1.2.).

While the use of agent and patient prefixes is less predictable semantically in the Northern Iroquoian languages than in some others, in most instances it is possible to reconstruct the motivation for uses that seem aberrant. For example, it is not surprising that smiling, interpreted as a temporary state, would take a patient prefix: *agyǫ·diˑh* (*wak-yǫti-·h*) 'I'm smiling'. When someone is asked to smile, as in taking a picture, the patient marking is retained, even though the smiler in such a case might be thought to behave as an agent: *sayǫ·dih* (*sa-yǫti-h*) 'smile!' with the second-person patient prefix *sa-*. The verb stem *-aty-* 'throw' treats the thrower as a patient. For example, the word *hǫgaˑdiʔ* (*h-waʔ-wak-aty-ʔ*) 'I threw it' contains the first-person patient prefix *wak-* (see 3.1.3.2. for the

translocative prefix *h-*). Apparently this verb stem once meant 'be divested of', for which a patient prefix would be appropriate. Although there was a semantic shift to 'throw', the patient prefix was retained. Motivations for agent-patient roles in the Iroquoian languages are discussed in detail, and compared with usages in other languages, by Mithun (1991).

Table 5 shows the total array of pronominal prefixes, cited in reconstructed forms to which the changes discussed in 2.3. and 2.4. apply. For example, the first-person singular agent prefix cited as *k-* at the top of the first column is pronounced *g-* before a vowel or resonant. In most cases where two forms are given, that with a final vowel occurs before a stem beginning with a consonant, while that with a final consonant occurs before a vowel stem. In the first- and second-person singular prefixes, the form with a final *e* occurs only before a following *k* or *s*. The neuter singular agent *w-* occurs before a following *a*, *e*, or *ę*, while *y-* occurs before *o* or *ǫ*. The feminine singular patient *ko-* occurs word-initially. Other variants are largely, though not entirely, predictable from 2.3. and 2.4. See Chafe (1967:19-22) for more details.

3.1.1.2.1. The Simple Agent Prefixes

The prefixes listed in the leftmost column of table 5 are the simple agent prefixes. They are used under two circumstances. First, a simple agent prefix is used when there is only one core participant (i.e., the verb is intransitive) and that participant is an agent, as described above. A simple agent prefix is also used with a transitive verb when one of the core participants is a human agent and the other is a nonhuman patient. Throughout the pronominal prefix system, whenever a human participant is combined with a nonhuman participant the nonhuman participant fails to receive any overt representation.

Several facts about these simple agent prefixes are worth noting. First, it can be seen that these prefixes make the maximum distinctions of person (including the exclusive-inclusive distinction), number (singular, dual, and plural), and gender (masculine, feminine, and neuter). Second, although masculine, feminine, and neuter are distinguished in the singular, in the dual and plural there is a merger of feminine and neuter. Finally, in accordance with the principle mentioned at the end of the last paragraph, a neuter singular agent is marked only when it is the only core participant in an event or state. When a neuter singular agent is paired with a human participant, only the human participant is marked.

3.1.1.2.2. The Simple Patient Prefixes

The prefixes in the first row of table 5 are the simple patient prefixes. They are also used under two circumstances. First, a simple patient prefix is used when there is only one core participant (i.e., the verb is intransitive) and that participant is a patient, as

Table 5. The Pronominal Prefixes (Reconstructed Forms)

Agents \ Patients	No patient	First singular	First dual	First plural	Second singular	Second dual	Second plural	Masculine singular	Feminine singular	Masculine nonsingular	Feminine-neuter nonsingular	Neuter singular
No agent		*wak- *wake-	*yǫkni-	*yǫkwa-	*sa-	*sni-	*swa-	*ho-	*yako- *ko-	*hoti- *hon-	*yoti- *yon-	*yo-
First singular	*k- *ke-				*kǫ- *kǫy-			*he- *hey-	*khe- *khey-			
Exclusive dual	*yakni-					*kni-		*shakni-	*yakhi- *yakhiy-			
Exclusive plural	*yakwa-						*kwa-	*shakwa-				
Inclusive dual	*tni-							*shetni-	*yethi- *yethiy-			
Inclusive plural	*twa-							*shetwa-				
Second singular	*hs- *hse-	*sk-						*hehs- *hehse-	*she- *shey-			
Second dual	*sni-		*skni-					*shesni-	*yetshi- *yetshiy-			
Second plural	*swa-			*skwa-				*sheswa-				
Masculine singular	*ha-	*hak- *hake-	*shǫkni-	*shǫkwa-	*hya-	*shesni-	*sheswa-	*ho-	*shako-	*hakǫ- *hakǫy-		
Feminine singular	*ye-	*yǫk-			*yesa-				*yǫtat- *yǫtate-	*kǫwǫti- *kǫwęn-		
Masculine dual	*hni-	*hǫk- *hǫke-	*yǫkhi- *yǫkhiy-		*hǫsa-	*yetshi- *yetshiy-		*howǫ- *howǫy-	*shakoti- *shakon-	*howǫti- *howęn-		
Masculine plural	*hati- *hęn-											
Feminine-neuter dual	*kni-											
Feminine-neuter plural	*wati- *węn-											
Neuter singular	*ka- *w- *y-											*kǫwǫ- *kǫwǫy-

described above. Second, such a prefix is also used with a transitive verb when one of the core participants is a human patient and the other a nonhuman agent.

The following points are worth noting with regard to these patient prefixes. First, no exclusive-inclusive distinction is made for patients. Second, the second-person dual and plural patient prefixes are identical with the corresponding agent prefixes. Third, in the third person, in addition to a merger of feminine and neuter, there is also a merger of dual and plural into a nonsingular (two or more) category. Finally, as would be expected from the principle mentioned above, a neuter singular patient is marked only when no human participant is present.

3.1.1.2.3. The Transitive Prefixes

Most of table 5 is occupied by the so-called transitive prefixes: those that mark both an agent and a patient within the same prefix.

The upper left quadrant of table 5 shows combinations of first- and second-person agents and patients.

So far as the singular combinations are concerned, a first-person agent with a second-person patient is expressed as *kǫ(y)-, whereas a second-person agent with a first-person patient is more transparently expressed as *sk(e)-. Duality and plurality are not specifically applied to either the agent or the patient. Thus, *kni- and *skni- mean that the agent, the patient, or both are dual (but neither is plural), while *kwa- and *skwa- mean that the agent, the patient, or both are plural.

Maximum distinctions are made for first- and second-person agents and patients when they are combined with a masculine singular agent or patient. The system is skewed in favor of the masculine singular category; elsewhere there are various mergers of person, number, and gender. Feminine singular agent is preserved as a category with a first-person singular or second-person singular patient, but otherwise it is merged with all other third persons, regardless of number, except for masculine singular. Feminine singular patient is merged with all other third persons, except for masculine singular, in all combinations with first- and second-person agents.

The lower right portion of table 5, where one third person is combined with another third person, is the least coherent part of the system. When one masculine singular agent is combined with another masculine singular patient, the prefix is *ho-, which is otherwise the simple masculine singular patient prefix. *hǫwǫ(y)- is used when any other third-person agent, regardless of gender or number, is combined with a masculine singular patient. When one feminine singular agent is combined with another feminine singular patient, the prefix is *yǫtat(e)-, which consists of the feminine singular agent prefix followed by the reflexive morpheme (3.1.4.2.). In other words 'she ... her' is expressed in the same way as 'she ... herself'.

There is a unique prefix *shako- for a masculine singular agent with a feminine singular patient, and another prefix *hakǫ(y)- for a masculine singular agent with any third-person nonsingular patient. The more complex prefix *shakoti-/*shakon- combines any nonsingular third-person agent with a feminine singular patient. When a feminine singular agent is combined with any nonsingular third-person patient, the prefix is *kǫwǫti-/*kǫwęn-. The combination of any nonsingular third-person agent with any nonsingular third-person patient is expressed as *hǫwǫti-/*hǫwęn-.

The prefix *kǫwǫ(y)-, which is used when a neuter singular agent is combined with a neuter singular patient, is the only transitive combination in which a neuter singular participant receives an overt marking.

3.1.1.2.4. THE PREFIX dži-
There is one additional prefix, dži- (*tsi-), that occurs in place of a regular pronominal prefix in the names of some animals: džigóhsahsę? 'wildcat', literally 'fat face', džinǫ́hsanǫh 'cricket', literally 'it watches over the house'.

3.1.2. EXTENSIONS OF THE ASPECT SUFFIXES
There are four major ways in which the aspect suffixes may be extended. The suffixes discussed in this section have in common only the fact that they are added to aspect suffixes. Their functions, as well as their effects on the verb as a whole, are quite diverse. One of them involves the marking of past tense, another the expression of progression through time or space, the third allows a habitual or stative verb to occur with one of the modal prefixes, and the fourth presents two complementary options that express either the finality or the ease of an event or state.

3.1.2.1. PAST TENSE
A past tense morpheme may be added to either the habitual or the stative aspect suffix when pastness is particularly salient. Often it is appropriately translated 'used to happen' or, with the stative aspect, 'had happened'. It is never added to the punctual aspect, which is typically used for past events in any case.

The forms of the past tense suffix are complex. The aspect suffix preceding it drops a final ? if it had one but otherwise occurs in its word-final form, subject to the changes described in Section 2. One form of the past-tense morpheme is *-hk, replacing a word-final ?: ode·kha? 'it is burning' becomes ode·khak 'it was burning'; hogá?de? 'he has a lot of it' becomes hogá?dek 'he had a lot of it'. Sometimes, the vowel preceding a final ? is lengthened instead: agéhse? 'I'm riding on its back' becomes agéhse·? 'I was riding on its back'. The form of the past tense suffix is *-ahk after the habitual allomorph -h and the stative allomorph -Ø: ha·dǫh 'he says' becomes hadǫ́ǫk (*ha-atǫ-h-ahk) 'he used to say'; hoga·ot 'he's telling a story' becomes hogeodak (*ho-gar-ot-Ø-ahk) 'he was telling a story'. The form is -kwa? after habitual allomorphs ending in s: yokhas 'it drips' becomes yokhásgwa? 'it used to drip'. Finally, the form is *-nǫ? after stative allomorphs ending in h: hogwęh 'he has picked it' becomes hogwę́·nǫ? (*ho-kw-ęh-nǫ?) 'he had picked it'.

3.1.2.2. THE PROGRESSIVE
The suffix that has traditionally been called the progressive in Iroquoian linguistic studies does not entirely coincide in meaning with the English aspect of the same name. Its form is *-atye-. It is added to the stative aspect suffix and is followed by another aspect suffix of its own. With event verbs, the progressive indicates that the event is in progress: odíyo·ǫdye? (*yoti-yǫ-h-atye-?) 'they (nonmasculine) are (in the process of) arriving' (referring to birds in the spring); compare odi·yǫ·h 'they have arrived'. With state verbs it means that the state is in effect 'along' a particular

interval of time or space: *ganóhsakda·dye?* (*ka-nohs-akt-Ø-atye-?*) 'along next to the house'; compare *ganóhsa·k* 'next to the house'.

3.1.2.3. THE MODALIZER

As noted in 3.1.1.1.3., the punctual aspect requires the presence of one of the three modal prefixes (factual, future, or optative). Ordinarily the modal prefixes do not occur with the habitual and stative aspects; however, there is a modalizer suffix that can be added to the habitual and stative aspect suffixes for the specific purpose of allowing the modal prefixes to occur with them. This device is particularly useful in making it possible for a habitual or stative verb to acquire a meaning of futurity or possibility. With the habitual aspect the result is a verb that is likely to be translated 'will (future) or might (optative) keep happening'. With the stative aspect it is likely to be translated 'will or might continue to be (a certain way)'. (The modalizer has also been called the continuative.)

The habitual aspect suffix preceding the modalizer occurs in its word-final form, except that *-s* is replaced by *-hs-* and *-ha?* by *-h-*. After a habitual aspect suffix the form of the modalizer is *-ek* after *s* and *-ak* otherwise: *eswé?se·k* (*e-swa-e-?s-ek*) 'you (plural) will keep being around', *eyéthe?tha·k* (*e-ye-the?t-h-ak*) 'she will keep pounding corn'. After a stative aspect suffix the form of the modalizer is *-ak*, except that *-k* replaces the stative *-?*: *eyogwenyó·ok* (*e-yo-kweny-oh-ak*) 'it will continue to be possible', *egá?hasde·k* (*e-ka-?haste-k*) 'it will continue to be strong'.

3.1.2.4. THE EVENTUATIVE AND FACILITATIVE

These two morphemes are added just before the stative aspect suffix. The eventuative morpheme, whose shape is *-s-* or *-os?-*, indicates that an event or state occurs 'eventually' or 'finally'. It is followed by the stative allomorph *-oh*: *agáhsehdás?oh* (*wak-ahseht-a-s?-oh*) 'I've finally hidden it'; *onénos?oh* (*yo-neno-s?-oh*) 'it's finally warm'; *ogwényos?oh* (*yo-kweny-os?-oh*) 'it's finally been able to'. The facilitative morpheme, whose shape is *-sk-*, indicates that something happens easily or with facility. It is followed by the stative allomorph *-o·h*: *o·nísgo·h* (*yo-hni-sk-o·h*) 'it barks at every little thing'; *onó?nowésgo·h* (*yo-no?nowe-sk-o·h*) 'it melts easily'.

3.1.3. THE PREPRONOMINAL PREFIXES

Besides the obligatory pronominal prefixes and the modal prefixes that are obligatory with the punctual aspect, there are a number of optional prefixes with diverse functions. All of them precede the pronominal prefix, and for that reason they can be classed together as prepronominal prefixes. (Lounsbury 1953 includes the modal prefixes in this class as well.) Their form and position relative to the three modal prefixes varies from one combination to another, in a manner that is summarized for typical combinations in table 6.

3.1.3.1. THE CISLOCATIVE AND REPETITIVE PREFIXES

These two prefixes occupy the same position in the verb and are in complementary distribution, but their functions are rather different.

The most common shape of the cislocative prefix is *t-*, but it occurs as *ti-* before any inclusive or second-person pronominal prefix except a second-person singular agent, with which it combines to produce the affricate *tsh-*. Combinations of the cislocative with the factual appear as *ta-* initially, but as *-ota-* after any other prepronominal prefix. Combinations of the cislocative with the optative appear as *oota-* everywhere. In general, if the meaning of the verb involves movement the cislocative specifies that the movement is toward the place of speaking: *thodi·yo·h* (*t-hoti-yo-·h*) 'they have come in', based on *-yo-* 'arrive'. If the meaning of the verb does not involve movement, the cislocative indicates that the event or state takes place or is in effect at a specific location not far away. Often it is translatable as 'there': *idye·t* (*i-t-ye-t*) 'she's standing there'. Other uses of the cognate prefix in Oneida, with which Seneca largely agrees, are discussed in detail by Abbott (1981).

The most common shape of the repetitive prefix is *s-*, but it occurs as *t-* before a following *sh* (creating homonymy with the cislocative), and it combines with a following *y* to form the affricate *dz*. It is *dži-* (*tsi-*) before any inclusive or second-person pronominal prefix except a second-person singular agent. Combinations of the repetitive with the factual appear as *sa-* initially, but as *-osa-* after any other prepronominal prefix. Combinations of the repetitive with the optative appear as *oosa-* everywhere. In general, the repetitive expresses the fact that the event or state represents another occurrence of some repeated phenomenon. It is most often translatable as 'again', 'back', or 'other': *shada·khe?* (*s-ha-takhe-?*) 'he's running again', *tshogwa·wi·h* (*t-shokwa-awi-·h*) 'he has given it back to us'. It combines with the verb root *-t-* 'stand' to mean 'one': *sga·t* (*s-ka-t-Ø*) 'one', *sgaksá?da·t* (*s-ka-ksa?t-a-t-Ø*) 'one child'. It combines obligatorily with certain verb roots such as *-ati-* 'be on the other side', as in *swa·dih* (*s-w-ati-h*) 'it's on the other side'. It occurs frequently in personal names, as in *sganyodaiyo?* (*s-ka-nyotar-iyo-?*) 'Handsome Lake' (literally something like 'the beautiful lake one').

3.1.3.2. THE TRANSLOCATIVE PREFIX

Although the translocative prefix is semantically paired with the cislocative, it does not occur in the same position in the verb and is quite different in form and distribution. It does not cooccur with the partitive, coincident, and contrastive prefixes (3.1.3.4.). Its shape

Table 6. Combinations of Prepronominal Prefixes With and Without Modal Prefixes (Reconstructed Forms)

Prepronominal prefixes	Modal prefixes			
	With no modal prefix	With factual	With future	With optative
No prepronominal prefix		*waʔ-	*ę-	*aa-
Cislocative	*t-	*ta-	*ęt-	*ǫǫta-
Repetitive	*s-	*sa-	*ęs-	*ǫǫsa-
Translocative	*he-	*hwaʔ-	*hę-	*haa-
Dualic	*te-	*waʔt-	*tę-	*taa-
Translocative + repetitive	*hes-	*hǫsa-	*hęs-	*hǫǫsa-
Dualic + cislocative	*tet-	*tǫta-	*tęt-	*tǫǫta-
Dualic + repetitive	*tes-	*tǫsa-	*tęs-	*tǫǫsa-
Dualic + translocative	*haʔte-	*haʔt-	*haʔtę-	*haʔtaa-
Dualic + translocative + repetitive	*haʔtes-	*haʔtǫsa-	*haʔtęs-	*haʔtǫǫsa-
Partitive	*ni-	*nǫʔ-	*nę-	*nǫǫ-
Partitive + cislocative	*nit-	*nǫta-	*nęt-	*nǫǫta-
Partitive + repetitive	*nis-	*nǫsa-	*nęs-	*nǫǫsa-
Partitive + dualic	*nǫʔte-	*nǫʔt-	*nǫʔtę-	*nǫʔtaa-
Partitive + dualic + cislocative	*nǫʔtet-	*nǫʔtǫta-	*nǫʔtęt-	*nǫʔtǫǫta-
Partitive + dualic + repetitive	*nǫʔtes-	*nǫʔtǫsa-	*nǫʔtęs-	*nǫʔtǫǫsa-
Coincident	*tshi-	*tshaʔ-	*tshę-	*tshaa-
Contrastive	*thi-	*thaʔ-	*thę-	*thaa-
Coincident combinations	Replace the *n* of partitive combinations with *tsh*, and the *ǫʔ* with *aʔ*.			
Contrastive combinations	Replace the *n* of partitive combinations with *th*, and the *ǫʔ* with *aʔ*.			
Negative	*teʔ-	*taʔa-		
Negative + cislocative	*teʔt-	*taʔǫta-		
Negative + repetitive	*teʔs-	*taʔǫsa-	See 3.1.3.5.	
Negative + translocative	*theʔ-			
Negative + dualic	*taʔte-			

is usually *he- before a consonant and *h- before a vowel. *h- also occurs before the factual prefix allomorph *wa-, but most current speakers have replaced word-initial *hw* with *w*, with the result that the translocative has no overt representation when it occurs with this factual allomorph. It is infixed within the negative morpheme, occurring immediately after the *t, and it appears as *haʔ- before the dualic prefix. Semantically, the translocative functions roughly as the opposite of the cislocative. If the meaning of the verb involves movement, the translocative specifies that the movement is away from the speaker or some other reference point: *heoyagę́ʔǫh* (*he-ho-yakę̨ʔ-ǫh) 'he has gone away', based on the stem *-yakę-ʔ- 'go out'. If the meaning of the verb does not involve movement, the translocative indicates that the event or state takes place or is in effect at a location distant from the speaker or some other reference point: *haˑdinǫˑgeʔ* (*he-hati-nakre-ʔ) 'they live over there' (Abbott 1981).

3.1.3.3. THE DUALIC PREFIX

The dualic prefix is formally complex with respect to both its shape and its order of occurrence with relation to other prefixes. It has the shape *te- when it is immediately followed by a pronominal prefix, or by the cislocative or repetitive prefix. It precedes the future and optative prefixes, where it is simply *t-. It follows the factual prefix, where it usually occurs as *-t-, but as *-ti- before any inclusive or second-person pronominal prefix except a second-person singular agent. The dualic has a variety of functions. It is used with the verb root *-ake- in counting two objects: *degáksaʔdaˑgeˑh* (*te-ka-ksaʔt-ake-ˑh) 'two children'. It also usually accompanies a dual pronominal prefix: *oʔdyákhniˑgę̨ʔ* (*waʔ-t-yakni-kę-ʔ) 'we (dual exclusive) saw it'. It may involve some sort of multiplication of an action: *oʔthaˑyaʔk* (*waʔ-t-ha-yaʔk-Ø) 'he broke it in pieces'; compare, without the dualic, *waˑayaʔk* (*waʔ-ha-yaʔk-Ø) 'he broke it'. It is required by many verb stems whose meanings involve change: *degadenyǫs* (*te-ka-teny-ǫhs*) 'it changes', *deyǫgwadawęnye·h* (*te-yǫkwa-at-awęnye-·h*) 'we are moving about'. Since the cislocative and repetitive cannot cooccur, the dualic substitutes for the repetitive when the cislocative is also present: *dethókdǫ·h* (*te-t-ho-aktǫ-·h*) 'he has come back'.

3.1.3.4. THE PARTITIVE, COINCIDENT, AND CONTRASTIVE PREFIXES

Like the cislocative and repetitive prefixes, these three prefixes also occupy the same position within a verb and are in contrastive distribution, but they too have quite different functions.

The partitive prefix has the shape *ni*- before a consonant and *n*- before a vowel, except that *nǫ?*- (from *na?*-) occurs before the dualic prefix. In general, the partitive refers to a particular degree or kind of some variable quality and is often translatable as 'how' or 'how much'. Verb stems expressing quantity or size require the partitive: *niwęnǫdi·h* (*ni-węn-at-i-·h*) 'how many of them there are', *niwá?a·h* (*ni-w-a?aha-h*) 'it's small'. It is used with the verb root *-ake*- in counting three or more objects: *sę nigáksa?da·ge·h* (*ni-ka-ksa?t-ake-·h*) 'three children'. Certain other verbs, such as *-yer*- 'do', also require the partitive: *nigye·ha?* (*ni-k-yer-ha?*) 'I do it'.

The coincident prefix has the shape *tshi*- (*tshi*-) before a consonant and *tsh*- before a vowel, except that *tsha?*- occurs before the dualic prefix. It expresses temporal subordination, and it is often translatable as 'when', 'while', or 'since': *tshigéksa?áah* (*tshi-ke-ks-a?aha-h*) 'when I was a child', *tshigǫ·he?* (*tshi-k-ǫnhe-?*) 'since I've been alive'.

The contrastive prefix has the shape *thi*- before a consonant and *th*- before a vowel, except that *tha?*- occurs before the dualic prefix. In general, it indicates a conflict with normal expectations: *thidyǫ·he?* (*thi-twa-ǫnhe-?*) 'we (inclusive plural) are living abnormally', and *thiyǫgwe?da·de?* (*thi-y-ǫgwe?t-a-te?*) 'it's a different person'. (As in other Northern Iroquoian languages, the *w* of the plural pronominal prefixes is replaced by *y* before *o* and *ǫ*.) See 3.1.3.5. for a special use of the contrastive prefix in negations.

3.1.3.5. THE NEGATIVE PREFIX

The expression of negation in Seneca, while straightforward in some respects, is in other ways difficult to describe because of both variation among speakers and the fact that certain usages are rare or moribund. Its usual expression is with the negative prefix, whose basic shape is *te?*-, with *ta?*- occurring before the dualic, factual, and optative prefixes. When the *te?*- is directly followed by a vowel, speakers usually change the *e* to harmonize with that vowel. The negative precedes all other prefixes, except that the translocative *h* is infixed within it to produce the form

the?-. Examples are *de?wi·yo·h* (*te?-w-iyo-·h*) 'it's not good'; *da?agenǫhdǫ?* (*te?-wak-ęnǫhtǫ-?*) 'I don't know'; *dé·nǫ·ǫkha?* (*te?-hen-ahǫk-ha?*) 'they don't understand'; *de?khe·gęh* (*te?-khe-kę-h*) 'I don't see her'; with the dualic, *da?degade·nyǫs* (*ta?-te-ka-teny-ǫhs*) 'it doesn't change'; with the translocative, *the?ge·tha?* (*t-h-e?-k-e·ht-ha?*) 'I don't go there'.

Two unique morphological constructions are used to express past and future negations. Past negations contain the negative prefix as described above, followed at the end of the word by the stative aspect suffix minus any final laryngeal obstruent belonging to that suffix, followed in turn by the negative past suffix *-?*: *de?khe·gę·?* (*te?-khe-kę-·h-·?*) 'I didn't see her' (cf. the stative *khe·gę·h* [*khe-kę-·h*] 'I've seen her'); *dó·da?ǫ·?* (*te?-ho-ita?-ǫ-·?*) 'he didn't go to sleep' (cf. the stative *hodá?ǫh* [*ho-ita?-ǫh*] 'he's asleep').

Future negations do not make use of the negative prefix at all. Instead, the word begins with the contrastive and optative prefixes and ends with the imperative suffix: *thá·khe·gęh* (*th-aa-khe-kę-h*) 'I won't see her', and *thǫ·saye·yǫh* (*th-ǫǫ-s-a-ye-yǫ-h*) 'she won't get back'.

Cooccurrence of the negative prefix with any of the modal prefixes is very restricted. The most common combination pairs the negative with the factual prefix, yielding the idiomatic meaning 'can't': *da?aye·gę?* (*ta?-a-ye-kę-?*) 'she can't see it'. It is not unusual to find the negative and factual along with the cislocative or repetitive: *da?ǫdaye·yǫ?* (*ta?-ǫt-a-ye-yǫ?*) 'she can't come in', and *da?ǫsaye·yǫ?* (*ta?-ǫs-a-ye-yǫ-?*) 'she can't come back'. The negative may occasionally occur with the optative prefix, as in *da?a·yogwe·ni?* (*ta?-aa-yo-kweny-?*) 'it might not be possible', but such uses are rare and would usually be expressed periphrastically: *nǫ· tha·yogwe·nih* 'I guess it won't be possible' (*nǫ·h* 'I guess').

Aside from the uses just mentioned, principally that of the negative with the factual (with or without the cislocative or repetitive), the negative does not ordinarily occur with the modal prefixes. Since the negative does occur with the translocative, dualic, and factual prefixes in the combinations summarized in table 6, its distribution in Seneca is somewhat broader than that reported for Oneida (Lounsbury 1953: 37, 47), where it fails to occur at all with the translocative, dualic, or any of the modal prefixes.

3.1.4. DERIVED VERB STEMS

The verb stem may consist of a simple verb root, or it may result from various derivational processes that produce more complex verb stems. These processes include the addition of one or more derivational suffixes, the middle or reflexive prefix, or an incorporated noun stem.

567

3.1.4.1. DERIVATIONAL SUFFIXES

There are more than a dozen suffixes that can be added to a verb root to produce a derived stem whose meaning and function differs in some way from the meaning and function of the root alone. The combinations of roots with derivational suffixes are lexically restricted: not all suffixes occur with all roots, and the resulting meanings are often unpredictable. Successive layers of derivation may occur, and the order of presentation below roughly reflects increasing distance from the verb root when more than one suffix is present. In general, if the preceding morpheme ends with a consonant and the derivational suffix begins with a consonant, the vowel *a* is added to separate the two consonants; see the third syllable in *agóʔkdaʔǫh* (*wak-oʔkt-a-ʔǫh*) 'I've gotten to the end' (3.1.4.1.6.) and various other examples below.

3.1.4.1.1. The Directive Suffix

The directive suffix, whose shape is *-n-*, occurs with a small number of verb roots all of which end in *e*, and all of which involve some kind of motion. It indicates that the motion takes place in a certain direction, and it is always accompanied by either the cislocative or the translocative prefix: *heˑenǫs* (*he-h-e-n-ǫhs*) 'he goes there' (cf. *-e-* 'go'), *thodakheˑnǫˑh* (*t-ho-takhe-n-ǫˑh*) 'he has run this way' (cf. *-takhe-* 'run').

3.1.4.1.2. The Archaic Undoer Suffix

There is a suffix with the shape *-hs(y)-* whose meaning involves the undoing of whatever is expressed by the root alone: *oʔtgéʔnyowéhsiʔ* (*waʔ-t-k-ę-ʔny-owe-hsy-ʔ*) 'I uncovered my hands, took my gloves off' (cf. *-owe-* 'cover'). It occurs with fewer verb roots than the new undoer suffix, of similar meaning (3.1.4.1.8.).

3.1.4.1.3. The Archaic Causative Suffixes

Another suffix of very limited distribution is the causative *-hw-*. It occurs with a small number of verb roots denoting states to produce a causative action: *hayęˑthwas* (*ha-yęt-hw-as*) 'he plants' (cf. *-yę(t)-* 'be established in a place'), *hoʔwęˑthwęh* (*ho-aʔwęt-hw-ęh*) 'he has massacred them' (cf. *-aʔwęt-* 'be dead', said of a group of people).

There is another causative suffix of very limited distribution that has the shape *-t-*: *onésdoˑdǫh* (*yo-nesto-t-ǫh*) 'it has frozen it' (cf. *-nesto-* 'be frozen'), *wáˑdíáshęˑt* (*waʔ-hati-hashę-t-Ø*) 'they called a council' (cf. *-hashę-* 'hold a council').

3.1.4.1.4. The Archaic Inchoative Suffix

Of similarly limited distribution is an inchoative suffix that has the shape *-ʔ-* or *-ę̨ʔ-* before the stative aspect suffix *-ǫh*, but *-h-* or *-ęh-* before the habitual (*-s*) and punctual (*-Ø*) aspect suffixes. A verb in the punctual aspect is thus unusual in showing a final *h* when this suffix is present. It derives a change of state from a state: *osnówęʔǫh* (*yo-snor-ęʔ-ǫh*) 'it's gottten fast' (cf. *-osnor(e)-* 'be fast'), *waʔósnoˑwęh* (*waʔ-o-snor-ęh-Ø*) 'it got fast'.

3.1.4.1.5. The New Causative Suffix

A more productive causative suffix appears as either *-ʔt-* or *-ht-*, depending on the preceding morpheme: *gahdǫ́ʔthaʔ* (*k-ahtǫ-ʔt-haʔ*) 'I make it disappear' (cf. *-ahtǫ-* 'be lost'), and *agétgihtǫh* (*wake-tki-ht-ǫh*) 'I've gotten it dirty' (cf. *-tki-* 'be dirty').

3.1.4.1.6. The New Inchoative Suffix

A more productive inchoative suffix appears as *-ʔ-*, *-heʔ-*, or *-ʔheʔ-*, depending on the preceding morpheme, and conditions the stative allomorph *-ǫh*, the habitual *-s*, and the punctual *-t*: *agóʔkdaʔǫh* (*wak-oʔkt-a-ʔ-ǫh*) 'I've gotten to the end' (cf. *-oʔkt-* 'be at the end'), *oʔyǫˑsheʔt* (*waʔ-y-ǫs-he-ʔ-t*) 'it became long' (cf. *-ǫs-* 'be long'), and *wáˑnyǫʔǫ́ʔheʔt* (*waʔ-ha-hnyǫʔǫ-ʔheʔ-t*) 'he became a White man' (cf. *-hnyǫʔǫ-* 'be a White man').

3.1.4.1.7. The Inchoative-Instrumental Suffix

There is also a suffix with the shape *-st-* that has sometimes an inchoative, sometimes an instrumental meaning: *oʔgánǫʔnos* (*waʔ-ka-naʔno-st-Ø*) 'it got cold' (cf. *-naʔno-* 'be cold'), *óéʔhesthaʔ* (*yo-hęʔhe-st-haʔ*) 'stopping place' (cf. *-hęʔhe-* 'stop').

3.1.4.1.8. The New Undoer Suffix

There is a more productive suffix with the undoer meaning (cf. 3.1.4.1.2.) that usually has the shape *-kw-*, although after a few verb roots it appears as *-ǫkw-*: *sehodǫˑgoh* (*se-nho-tǫ-kw-h*) 'open the door!' (cf. *-tǫ-* 'close'). The archaic and new undoer suffixes may occur together to indicate a repetition of the undoing: *oʔtgéʔnyowéhsǫˑgoʔ* (*waʔ-t-k-ę-ʔny-owe-hs-ǫkw-ʔ*) 'I uncovered my hands' (cf. *-owe-* 'cover').

3.1.4.1.9. The Distributive Suffix

The distributive suffix has a variety of shapes, all of which contain the vowel *ǫ*: *-ǫ-*, *-nyǫ-*, *-hǫ-*, *-hsǫ-*, etc. It pluralizes the event or state: *oʔkhniyǫˑdǫ́ʔ* (*waʔ-k-niyǫt-ǫ-ʔ*) 'I hung up several things' (cf. *-niyǫt-* 'hang up'); *háíhsakhǫh* (*ha-ihsak-hǫ-h*) 'he's looking for several things, looking in various places, looking at various times' (cf. *-ihsak-* 'look for'; the root *-ihsak-* is unusual in not causing the coalescense of *ai* into *ę*); and *onǫ́ǫkdeˑnyǫʔ* (*yo-nǫhǫkte-nyǫ-ʔ*) 'it hurts here and there' (cf. *-nǫhǫkte-* 'hurt').

3.1.4.1.10. The Instrumental Suffix

The instrumental suffix has the shape *-hkw-*. The resulting word refers to something that is 'used for' the activity expressed by the verb root: *yeniyǫdáhgwaʔ* (*ye-niyǫt-a-hkw-haʔ*) 'people use it for hanging, hanger' (cf. *-niyǫt-* 'hang'), *oʔgóʔkdak* (*waʔ-k-oʔkt-a-hkw-Ø*) 'I used it to end with' (cf. *-oʔkt-* 'be at the end').

3.1.4.1.11. The Dative Suffix

The dative suffix also has a variety of shapes, with the special peculiarity that one shape is used before the habitual and stative aspect suffixes, another before the punctual and imperative suffixes. Shapes that occur before the habitual and stative include *-ni-*, *-ʔse-*, and *-hse-*. Shapes that occur before the punctual and imperative suffixes include *-ę-*, *-ʔs-*, and *-hahs-*. The dative adds a beneficiary to the core participants of the verb, which thus acquires the meaning of doing something for someone's benefit: *hakhyadǫ·niˑh* (*hak-hyatǫ-ni-·h* 'he has written it for me', *wáˑkhyadǫǫs* (*waʔ-hak-hyatǫ-has-Ø*) 'he wrote it for me'.

3.1.4.1.12. The Ambulative Suffix

The ambulative suffix has the form *-hne-*. It conveys the fact that an event takes place while the agent is walking: *hadǫ́·neʔ* (*ha-atǫ-hne-ʔ*) 'he says it while walking', *wá·gę·neʔ* (*waʔ-ha-kę-hne-ʔ*) 'he saw it as he walked', and *hanǫ́·kdáni·neʔs* (*ha-nǫhǫkt-a-ni-hne-ʔs*) 'he's sick but walking around'.

3.1.4.1.13. The Andative and Purposive Suffixes

The andative suffix has a variety of shapes, which have in common the presence of a laryngeal consonant: *-ʔn-*, *-ʔh-*, *-h-*, *-hs-*, etc. Its meaning involves going to another place and doing something: *hagáweʔheʔs* (*ha-kawe-ʔh-eʔs*) 'he goes rowing' (cf. *-kawe-* 'row'), and *wa·dowæ·thaʔ* (*waʔ-ha-atorat-h-aʔ*) 'he went hunting' (cf. *-atorat-* 'hunt').

The andative suffix may be followed by any of the usual four aspect suffixes, but it may also be followed by another suffix that occurs only in this environment. This purposive suffix has the shape *-eʔ* and expresses the fact that the 'going' of the andative is performed for a purpose: *wáíhsa·kheʔ* (*waʔ-ha-ihsak-h-eʔ*) 'he went to look for it'.

3.1.4.2. THE MIDDLE AND REFLEXIVE PREFIXES

The verb root may be preceded by either of two derivational prefixes, one of which appears to be a reduplicated form of the other. Both specify an event as one in which the same person both performs and is affected by what happens.

The middle prefix usually has the shape *-at-*, although it may appear as *-ate-*, *-atę-*, *-an-*, *-ę-*, *-ęn-*, or *-ęni-* depending on the following verb stem. It is a typical middle voice marker, producing a lexicalized stem whose meaning involves an event in which the agent is also the participant affected by the event. Typically it converts a transitive verb into an intransitive: *sadyę·h* (*s-at-yę-·h*) 'sit down' (cf. *-yę-* 'establish in a place'), and *oʔdwado·wę·ʔ* (*waʔ-t-w-at-owę-·ʔ*) 'it split' (cf. *-owę-* 'split (something)'). The resultant meaning is sometimes unpredictable from the meaning of the root alone: *odǫ·ni·h* (*yo-at-ǫni-·h*) 'it's growing' (cf. *-ǫni-* 'make').

The reflexive prefix is a reduplicated form of the middle prefix, with the shape *-atat-*, *-atate-*, etc. As with the middle, the agent is the affected participant, but the two roles are more distinctly separated and usually involve the agent doing something deliberately to himself or herself: *oʔgádatheˑʔ* (*waʔ-k-atat-hren-·ʔ*) 'I cut myself', and *oʔgadade·gęʔ* (*waʔ-k-atate-kę-ʔ*) 'I saw myself' (as in a mirror). The combination of the reflexive prefix with the dualic prefix is used to express a reciprocal meaning, where several agents act on one another: *oʔthęnǫdade·gęʔ* (*waʔ-t-hęn-atate-kę-ʔ*) 'they (masculine plural) saw each other'.

3.1.4.3. INCORPORATED NOUN ROOTS

Often a verb root is preceded by an incorporated noun root, yielding a derived stem in which the meaning of the verb root and the meaning of the noun root are combined into a single lexicalized event or state. Usually the referent of the noun root plays the role of patient in the event: *agidzagǫh* (*wak-its-a-k-ǫh*) 'I'm eating fish' (cf. *-its-* 'fish', *-k-* 'eat'), but other roles are possible: *oʔgéʔhnyayęn* (*waʔ-ke-ʔhny-a-yęht-Ø*) 'I hit it with a stick' (cf. *-ʔhny-* 'stick', *-yęht-* 'hit'). From these examples it can be seen that when the noun root ends in a consonant and the following verb root begins with a consonant, the vowel *a* (in rare cases *i*) is inserted to keep the two consonants apart. Not all verb roots allow incorporation, but on the other hand there are other verb roots that require it, incorporating an empty noun root when no other is present. For example, in *oʔgé·nyo·dęʔ* (*waʔ-ke-hny-ot-ęʔ*) 'I stood it upright' the *-hny-* functions as such an empty noun root; cf. *oʔgáʔęno·dęʔ* (*waʔ-k-aʔęn-ot-ęʔ*) 'I stood a post upright' where the incorporated noun root is *-aʔęn-* 'post'. Noun incorporation in the Northern Iroquoian languages is discussed at length by Woodbury (1975a, 1975) and Mithun (1984).

3.2. NOUN MORPHOLOGY

Like verbs, words that are morphologically nouns usually contain at least three parts: (1) a noun stem (usually just a minimal noun root) that categorizes the referent, (2) a pronominal prefix that either indicates a possessor of the referent or is arbitrarily assigned by the noun stem, and (3) a noun suffix that may have a locative function or may simply show that the word is a noun. Thus, the noun *gagáwihsaʔ* 'shovel' is built on the noun root *-kawihs-* 'shovel', preceded by the arbitrarily assigned neuter agent pronominal prefix *ka-* and followed by the simple noun suffix *-aʔ*. The possessed noun *hogáwihsaʔ* 'his shovel' begins with the masculine patient prefix *ho-*, showing the possessor 'his'. The noun *gáǫshæ̨gǫ·h* (*ka-hǫshr-a-kǫ·h*) 'in the box' ends with the internal locative suffix *-kǫ·h* 'in'.

569

3.2.1. Pronominal Prefixes with Nouns

Unpossessed nominal referents are expressed with either the neuter patient prefix *o- or the neuter agent prefix *ka-. Whereas the neuter patient form that occurs with verbs can be reconstructed as *yo-, with Seneca losing the y in word-initial position, the other Northern Iroquoian languages show that Proto–Northern Iroquoian lacked the y with nouns. Similarly, the *w- that represents a neuter agent before verb stems beginning with a, e, or ę (3.1.1.2.) is absent before noun stems. The earliest of these prefixes seems from comparative evidence to have been the patient *o-, with the agent *ka- tending to be attached to nouns that express more recently introduced referents; compare oni·ya? 'snow' with gagáwihsa? 'shovel'. It is often impossible to predict which prefix will be used for a given noun root.

Possession is usually marked with a patient prefix (hogáwihsa? 'his shovel', but body parts take agent prefixes hagǫ́da?geh (*ha-kǫt-a?-geh) 'his nose' (3.2.2.). It is sometimes said that the agent prefixes show inalienable possession while the patient prefixes show alienable possession, but the principal distinction is between body parts and referents of other kinds. Kinship terms, which might be thought to show inalienable possession, in fact follow a complex morphology of their own (Chafe 1963: 19-26).

Some frequently used nouns often occur without a pronominal prefix: odžísdǫdá?shæ? (*o-tsist-ǫt-a-?shr-a?) 'strawberry', literally 'embers on it', alternates with džísdǫdá?shæ?; onǫdowá?ga·? alternates with nǫdowá?ga·? 'Seneca', literally 'pertaining to the great hill' (3.3.1., 3.3.3.).

3.2.2. Noun Suffixes

There are three productive noun suffixes. The simple noun suffix *-a? is used when neither of the two locative suffixes described below is present. It carries no meaning other than that the word is a noun: gáóshæ? (*ka-hǫshr-a?) 'box'. The internal locative suffix, *-kǫ·h, is added directly to the noun stem and expresses location in or under something: gáóshægǫ·h (*ka-hǫshr-a-kǫ·h) 'in the box', ganǫ́hsagǫ·h (*ka-nǫhs-a-kǫ·h) 'under the house'. The external locative suffix is added to the simple noun suffix, as well as to words of other kinds when they are used nominally. It has the shape *-keh (after ? or s) or *-neh (otherwise) and expresses location at or on something: gáóshæ?geh (*ka-ǫshr-a?-keh) 'on the box', ganǫ́hsesgeh (*ka-nǫhs-es-keh) 'at the longhouse', ǫgwé·neh (*ǫkweh-neh) 'where people are'. External body parts are usually expressed with the external locative suffix, even when no locative meaning is involved: ke?nyá?geh (*ke-?ny-a?-keh) is the usual way to say 'my finger', though it literally means 'on my finger'.

3.2.3. Nominalized Verbs

There is a suffix *-shr- or *-?shr- that can be added to a verb stem to produce a derived noun stem, which can then be used in the same manner as an ordinary noun root. The resultant meaning is unpredictable, but it involves some kind of object or abstraction that is associated with the verbal meaning in some way: ga·yádǫshæ? (*ka-hyatǫ-shr-a?) 'paper, book' (built on the verb root *-hyatǫ- 'write'), and ga?hásde?shæ? (*ka-?haste-?shr-a?) 'strength, power' (built on the verb root *-?haste- 'be strong'). A nominalized verb stem can be incorporated within another verb in the same fashion as an incorporated noun root: o?khyádǫshǽ·ni·nǫ? (*wa?-k-hyatǫ-shr-a-hninǫ-?) 'I bought a book'.

3.2.4. The Suffix -? with Proper Names

Verbs that do not otherwise end in ? take the ending -? when they are used as the established names of people or places: sganyotaiyo? 'Handsome Lake' (cf. ganyotaiyo·h 'beautiful lake'), ohi·yo? 'Allegany Reservation' (cf. ohi·yo·h 'beautiful river').

3.3. Miscellaneous Suffixes

There are several suffixes that can be added to the ends of entire words, in some cases either verbs or nouns, with a variety of functions that are difficult to categorize as a class.

3.3.1. The Augmentative Suffix

The augmentative suffix, *-kowa·h, expresses bigness or importance: hadíyosgo·wa·h 'he's a great fighter' (cf. hadi·yos 'he fights, is a fighter'), džinǫ́hdáíǫ́?go·wa·h 'rat' (cf. džinǫ́hdaiǫ·? 'mouse', literally, 'it meddles', 3.2.4.).

3.3.2. The Diminutive Suffix

The diminutive suffix *-?ah or *-hah (with intervocalic h preserved) expresses approximation or cuteness: gagę·t?ah 'it's whitish' (cf. gagę·n 'it's white'), hoyǫ́dihah 'Smiley' (cf. hoyǫ·dih 'he smiles'). The commonly used first-person pronoun ni?ah appears to be composed of neh 'the', í·? 'I' (3.4.), and the diminutive suffix, comparable to the English expression 'little old me'.

3.3.3. The Characterizer Suffix

The characterizer suffix, *-kha·? or *-ka·?, conveys the meaning 'pertaining to' but often with an unpredictable, lexicalized result: ǫgwé?ǫwe·kha·? 'pertaining to Indians, the Seneca language' (cf. ǫgwé?ǫ·weh 'Indian', literally 'real person', 3.3.8.); onǫ́da?ge·ga·? 'Onondaga', literally 'pertaining to being at the hill' (cf. onǫ́da?geh 'at the hill').

3.3.4. The Populative Suffix

The populative suffix *-hronǫ? creates reference to a person or people associated with a place: ohíyo·onǫ?

'person or people of the Allegany Reservation' (cf. *ohi·yo̧ˀ* 'Allegany Reservation', 3.2.4.); *oˀsóægó·ono̧ˀ* 'person or people of Pinewoods' (an area of the Cattaraugus Reservation; cf. *oˀsóægo̧·h* 'Pinewoods', literally 'in the pines', *-ˀsohr-* 'pine').

3.3.5. THE DECESSIVE SUFFIX

The decessive suffix *-kého̧·ˀ* expresses reference to a former, no longer existing state: *geksáˀá·gȩ·o̧ˀ* 'I was once a small child' (cf. *geksáˀa·h* 'I am a small child'), and *haksótgȩ·o̧ˀ* 'my late grandfather' (cf. *hakso·t* 'my grandfather').

3.3.6. THE PLURALIZER SUFFIX

The pluralizer suffix, *-sho̧ˀ* or *-sho̧ˀo̧h*, provides a way of pluralizing a noun or verb, in the case of the verb with an additional nominalizing function: *geˀnyáˀsho̧ˀ* 'my fingers' (cf. *keˀnyáˀgeh* 'my finger'), and *howéshóˀo̧h* 'his belongings' (cf. *ho·wȩh* 'it belongs to him').

3.3.7. THE INTENSIFIER SUFFIX

The intensifier suffix *-htsih* serves to intensify the meaning of whatever precedes it: *we·ȩhdžih* 'very far' (cf. *we·ȩh* 'far'). It is evidently the last element in the word *ónȩhdžih* 'a long time ago' (cf. *o·nȩh* 'now, then'). It appears to be followed by the stative aspect suffix in *sathó̧dehdži·wȩh* 'you are listening carefully' (cf. *satho̧·deˀ* 'you are listening').

3.3.8. THE PROTOTYPE SUFFIX

The suffix *-ˀo̧weh* indicates that something is prototypical or genuine: *o̧gwéˀo̧·weh* 'Indian', literally 'genuine person'; *ahdáhgwaˀo̧·weh* 'moccasin', literally 'genuine shoe'; and *oyȩ́ˀgwaˀo̧·weh* 'Indian tobacco', literally 'genuine tobacco'.

3.3.9. THE ENCLITIC *=kwa·h

Although it does not occur as a separate word, *=kwa·h* can be added to a verb or particle without changing the assignment of length to an originally penultimate syllable. The syllable preceding it is always accented. It has the meaning 'toward': *dyone·nó̧ˀ=gwa·h* 'toward the south' (cf. *dyone·no̧ˀ* 'south, where it is warm'), *neˀhó=gwa·h* 'in that direction' (cf. *neˀhoh* 'there').

3.4. PARTICLE MORPHOLOGY

Although most particles consist of only a single morpheme, a few are analyzable into separately recurring parts. For example, the question word particles *so̧·h* 'who?', *dȩˀȩh* 'what?', *ga·weh* 'where?', *wȩ·do̧h* 'when?' can be followed by *-diˀgwah* to yield a meaning like English 'whoever': *só̧diˀgwah* 'whoever', *dȩˀédiˀgwah* 'whatever', *gawédiˀgwah* 'wherever', *wȩdódiˀgwah* 'whenever'. These same particles may also be preceded by the negative prefix: *deˀwȩ·do̧h* 'never', *deˀso̧·ga·ˀ* 'nobody' (cf. *so̧·ga·ˀ* 'somebody'). Some combinations are particular and idiomatic, as

when the prototype suffix *-ˀo̧weh* occurs after the particle *agwas* 'very' in *agwásˀo̧weh* 'very truly'. Some particle sequences have been lexicalized, so that *neh* 'the' and *í·ˀ* 'I, we', for example, have been fused into *ní·ˀ* 'I, we'. Similarly, *neh* and *o·nȩh* 'now, then' together produce *no·nȩh* 'when'.

4. DISCOURSE

In order to express the idea of an event or state, speakers of any language must categorize the event or state itself, for example, as an instance of *singing* or of *being small*. They must also give recognition in some way to the participants in the event or state, say, the person who performs the singing or the thing that is small. In English these two functions—categorizing the event or state itself and recognizing the participants in it—are assigned to separate words, as in *he sang* or *it's small*. In Seneca the two functions are combined within a single word, as in *wa·dȩno·dȩˀ* 'he sang' or *niwáˀa·h* 'it's small'. It follows that the structure of the English clause corrresponds to a considerable extent to the structure of the Seneca word. For that reason, among others, as the discussion is broadened to include language that goes beyond single words, it will be described in terms of the flow of discourse rather than in terms of syntactic structures as they are traditionally conceived.

Example 1 below, an excerpt from a Seneca speaker's reminiscences of his childhood, exemplifies several features of discourse patterning. The example has been edited slightly to remove disfluencies whose discussion would go beyond the scope of the discussion here. The following conventions are used in the transcription. Sequences of dots represent pauses of various lengths: five dots an unusually long pause (in this case more than seven seconds), four dots a pause of about one second, three dots a pause of about one-half second, and two dots a pause of less than one-tenth of a second. At the end of each line a comma shows a rising pitch while a period shows a falling one; a semicolon shows a falling pitch that does not fall as low as that shown by the period.

The example is divided into lines that represent intonation units (see 4.1.). Each line is presented in a format of six sublines. The first subline shows the actual pronunciation that was used by the speaker, including the shortening of vowels at the beginning of an intonation unit, the elision of certain segments and syllables, and the introduction of certain discourse-conditioned accents. The second subline shows the pronunciation that would be given to each word if it were spoken slowly in isolation. The third subline has between bars the reconstructed form of polymorphemic words, with hyphens separating morphemes; monomorphemic words have no representation on this line. The second and third sublines together mirror the paired representations that were used above in the description of Seneca morphology. The fourth subline labels each of the morphemes in a polymorphemic word with the abbreviations listed in table 7. The fifth subline gives an English translation for each word. Finally, the sixth subline gives a free English translation for the entire intonation unit.

(1) Storytelling

(a) ..... *Onę   kho   ae   neʔ   ne   tšhigéksaʔáˑh,*
      oʾnęh khoh aeʔ neˑʔ neh   tšhigéksaʔáah
                 |tshi-ke-ks-aʔaha-h|
                 COIN-1A-child-small-STAT
   then   too   again   assert   the   when I was a small child
   And then again, when I was a small child,

(b) .... *neʔ   gęs   ne   hodiyiˑis,*
    neˑʔ   gęˑs   neh   hodiyeˑis,
              |hoti-yeri-s|
              MpP-proper-HAB
   assert   habitually   the   they meet
   they always meet

(c) *né   hęǫwe   agwéʔdyǫʔ,*
  neh   heˑǫweh   agwéʔdyǫʔ
            |yakwa-iʔtrǫ-ʔ|
            EXPA-live-STAT
  the   where   we live
  where we lived,

(d) ... *né   hęnǫdęnoˑtháʔ;*
   neh   hęnǫdęnoˑthaʔ
       |hęn-at-ręn-ot-haʔ|
      MpA-MID-song-stand.up-HAB
  the   they sing
  the singers;

(e) .. *gyǫʔ   gęs   hęnǫdeyęˑsthaʔ.*
    gyǫʔǫh gęˑs   hęnǫdeyęˑsthaʔ
           |hęn-ate-yę-st-haʔ|
         MpA-MID-know-INCH/INST-HAB
  hearsay   habitually   they are learning
  they were always learning.

(f) ... *Daˑ   neʔ   gęs   né   haʔdeyó*
   daˑh   neˑʔ   gęs   neh   haʔdeˑyǫˑh
                |haʔ-te-y-ǫ-ˑh|
                TLOC-DU-NA-enumerate-STAT
  so   assert   habitually   the   many things
  So it was always (with) many things (that)

  donǫdíwagęˑnyǫʔh,
  doˑnǫdíˑwagęˑnyǫˑh
  |te-hon-at-rihw-a-kęny-ǫˑh|
  DU-MpP-MID-story-Ø-win-STAT
  they are outdoing one another's stories
  they were outdoing one another's stories,

(g) ... *haʔdeyǫ́*   *dęnǫdáthyónyáˑnǫh.*
    haʔdeˑyǫˑh   *dęˑnǫdáthyonyáˑnǫh*
    |haʔ-te-y-ǫ-ˑh| |te-hęn-at-hrory-a-hnǫ-h|
    TLOC-DU-NA-   DU-MpA-MID-tell-Ø-
    enumerate-STAT   DIST-HAB
    many things   they are telling each other
  they were telling each other many things.

4.1. INTONATION UNITS

The seven lines numbered 1a through 1g represent intonation units: minimal prosodic segments of connected speech. They are recognizable from a conjunction of prosodic cues, the most important of which are the terminal pitch contour at the end of each unit (shown with commas, semicolons, and periods) and a pattern of acceleration at the beginning of the unit followed by deceleration at the end. Words that would have long vowels in isolation ordinarily appear with short vowels near the beginning of an intonation unit (for example *neʔ* rather than *neˑʔ*), but with the expected long vowels near the end. Furthermore, final syllables of the form ʔVh (where V stands for any vowel) are often dropped near the beginning of an intonation unit, as exemplified in 1e: *gyǫʔ* rather than *gyǫʔǫh*. Many, but not all, intonation units are also separated by the pauses that are

Table 7. Abbrevations for Morphemes

Ø	Zero (semantically empty)
1A	First-person agent
1A/MP	First-person agent with masculine patient
1P	First-person patient
2A	Second-person agent
2A/pP	Second-person agent with nonsingular patient
COIN	Coincident
DIR	Directive
DIST	Distributive
DU	Dualic
EXPA	Exclusive plural agent
EXpP	Exclusive plural patient
FAC	Factual
FUT	Future
HAB	Habitual
INCH/INST	Inchoative-Instrumental
INST	Instrumental
MA	Masculine agent
MA/FP	Masculine agent with feminine patient
MID	Middle
MP	Masculine patient
MpA	Masculine plural agent
MpP	Masculine plural patient
NA	Neuter agent
NP	Neuter patient
PL	Pluralizer
PUN	Punctual
SNS	Simple noun suffix
STAT	Stative
TLOC	Translocative

shown with the sequence of dots. In this case the only boundary without a pause is that between 1b and 1c. The intonation units in this example range in length from two to six words. From larger samples it appears that the modal length of a Seneca intonation is only two words, as compared with four words in English; evidently the difference can be attributed to the fact that Seneca words include more information than English words.

Each intonation unit expresses the idea of an event, a state, or a referent (a person or thing), in rough English translation as follows:

(a) when I was a small child	(state)
(b) they met	(event)
(c) where we lived	(state)
(d) the singers	(referent)
(e) they are learning	(event)
(f) they were outdoing one another in storytelling	(event)
(g) they were telling many things	(event).

Each of these ideas is expressed with a content word that is morphologically a verb, regardless of whether the idea itself is that of an event, a state, or a referent. Events and states are always expressed in Seneca with verbs, but referents may be expressed morphologically in three different ways—with verb morphology: *hęnǫdęnoʾthaʾ* 'they sing, singers'; with noun morphology: *oęnǫʾ* 'song'; and as a single morpheme: *džiʾyæh* 'dog'.

Whereas these content words categorize the event, state, or referent, they are usually accompanied by one or more particles, whose functions are varied—linking one discourse segment with another: *khoh* 'and', *daʾh* 'so', *hęʾǫweh* 'where'; providing a temporal orientation: *oʾnęh* 'now', *aeʾ* 'again', *gęs* 'habitually'; expressing modality: *neˑʾ* 'assertion'; expressing evidentiality: *gyǫʾǫh* 'hearsay'; and signaling identifiability: *neh* 'the'.

The majority of intonation units contain only one content word, but 1f and 1g include both a verb expressing an event and the word *haʾdeˑyǫˑh*, which is morphologically a verb but refers to 'many things'. These two intonation units, each with two content words, suggest a word order in which the word expressing the event or state comes last: roughly, a verb-final language. In other cases, the reverse is true. For example, when the same speaker at another point told how his mother used to preserve fruits and vegetables to eat during the winter, he concluded by saying:

(2) ...	*dyotgǫ́n*	*ǫgwaˑyę́ʾ*		*gwisdę́ʾshǫʾǫh.*
	dyotgoˑn	*ǫgwaˑyęʾ*		*gwisdę́ʾshǫʾǫh*
	|ǫkwa-yę-ʾ|			|kwistęʾ-shǫʾǫh|
	EXPP-have-STAT			something-PL
always	we have			some things
	we always had some things (to eat).			

Here, the state of having precedes the things that were had. It is relevant to note that in the corresponding English clause 'we always <u>had</u> things' the verb had is accented, in contrast, for example, to 'we always had <u>strawberries</u>'. In that case it would have been the strawberries that were more "newsworthy" (Mithun 1992), as compared with the vaguely identified things in 2. Seneca places the more newsworthy element first. In 2 it is the having that is more newsworthy, and thus the having precedes the things: a "verb-first" strategy. In 1f and 1g, in contrast, it is the large number of stories, expressed in the word *haʾdeˑyǫˑh*, that is more newsworthy.

A somewhat more complex example is provided by 3:

(3) ...	*oˑnǫʾ*	*ní*	*gę́s*	*né*	*ǫgwátšhisdódahgǫ́h,*
	oˑnǫʾ	*níˑʾ*	*gęˑs*	*neh*	*ǫgwátšhisdódahgǫh*
	|o-hn-aʾ|				|ǫkwa-at-tsist-ot-a-hkw-ǫh|
	NP-oil-SNS				EXPP-MID-ember-stand-Ø-INST-STAT
	oil	we	habitually	the	we use it for lamps
	We always used <u>oil</u> for our lamps.				

Here, not only the newsworthiness of the oil but also the fact that it contrasted with (previously mentioned) electricity led to its placement at the very beginning of the intonation unit. It was then followed by three particles before the final verb that expressed the manner in which the oil was used. Just previously the speaker had said that his family did not use electricity for their lamps, and thus the idea expressed by the final verb was already accessible and was, therefore, less newsworthy information.

4.2. SENTENCES

Example 1 consists of two sentences, each of which ends with the falling pitch contour that signals sentence closure. The first sentence consists of intonation units 1a through 1e, the second of 1f and 1g. While there are many patterns that can be observed in Seneca sentences, these two sentences illustrate patterns that occur frequently.

The first sentence begins with a temporal orientation of a type that is formulaic in Seneca reminiscences: 'when I was a child'. The next intonation unit, 1b, presents the core of the sentence: 'they always met'. Intonation unit 1c elaborates on the meeting by specifying where it took place: 'where we lived'. It is typical that the participants in the meeting had not yet been identified; intonation unit 1d finally characterizes them as 'the singers'. This pattern of event followed sometime later by identification is the usual way of introducing new referents, in marked contrast to the English pattern that would normally identify the referent first: *there were these singers, who came to our house*, or the like. There is a falling pitch at the end of 1d, transcribed with the semicolon, but it does not fall as far as the pitch at the end of 1e where the sentence is finally concluded. Intonation unit 1e illustrates another typically Seneca rhetorical device. After the event was categorized in 1b as a meeting, the speaker elaborated on it in 1e by characterizing it as a meeting in which learning took place. In summary, the abstract pattern of 1a through 1e consists of: (a) a temporal orientation of the core event, (b) the core event itself, (c) the location of the core event, (d) an identification of the participants in the core event, and (e) an elaboration of the core event.

The second sentence, consisting of intonation units 1f and 1g, introduced another aspect of these meetings: the fact that the singers exchanged stories. Its two intonation units categorized the storytelling in different ways. First, 1f said that the storytellers were trying to outdo one another; then 1g said that they were 'telling many things'. Just as 1e provided a different slant on the meeting, 1g gave a different slant on the storytelling. The kind of repetition often referred to with the term "couplets," which is especially characteristic of Meso-American rhetorical style (for example, Bright 1990), is not an obvious stylistic feature of Seneca, but repetitions like those illustrated in 1e and 1g may be seen as a related way of organizing what is said.

4.3. Topics

Taken together, the two sentences of 1 express a coherent larger chunk of information, the purpose of which was to provide a framework that would allow the speaker to tell one of the stories he remembered from those long-ago meetings at his house. That story immediately followed 1g. The totality of 1a through 1g expressed a coherent discourse topic: the meetings and the storytelling that took place at them. Discourse topics are generally introduced by sequences of orienting particles like those at the beginning of 1a. They are also likely to be separated from what preceded by a longer pause than is found within a topic, in this case a pause of seven seconds.

The story that followed was introduced with:

(4) .....*a·* *ne gyé·* *wá·thyonyá·nǫ·ʔ*,
    a·h neh gye·h *wá·thyonyá·nǫ·ʔ*
    |waʔ-ha-at-hrory-a-hnǫ-·ʔ|
    FAC-MA-MID-tell-
    Ø-DIST-PUN
    ah   the   one of them   he told about
    Ah, one of them told about,

The exclamation *a·* often signals transitions of this kind. Whereas the topic transition pause of 1.68 seconds that preceded 4 was by no means as long as that preceding 1a, it was significantly longer than any of the topic-internal pauses in 1. The shorter pause at the beginning of 4 reflected a less drastic transition than that between 1 and what preceded it.

In short, new topics are introduced with particles or particle sequences that reflect various levels of transition strength, as *onę kho ae?* 'and then again' at major boundaries and *a·* 'ah' at lesser ones. Topics are also separated by unusually long pauses where there is a major change of orientation, as at the beginning of 1, or shorter but still substantial pauses where the reorientation is minor, as at the beginning of 4.

4.4. Identifiability

One of the most frequently used Seneca particles is *neh*, which overlaps in function with the English definite article and is for that reason translated 'the'. However, the uses of *neh* in 1 show that this translation is not always appropriate. Both Seneca *neh* and English *the* signal the speaker's judgment that a referent is identifiable to the listener, but the two languages differ considerably in how they employ this signal. For example, proper names are ordinarily used under circumstances in which their referents are identifiable, and Seneca often introduces them with *neh*, as in *né Paul* 'Paul'. Although many other languages agree with Seneca in this respect, English uses simply *Paul* rather than *the Paul*.

The singers are introduced with *neh* in 1d, signaling their identifiability as the participants in the event that was introduced in 1b. The Seneca way of putting things is roughly captured in the translation 'they met, ... the singers'. In such cases Seneca accents the definite article to signal a new categorization of a referent that has already been introduced. English would accent only the noun.

More curious from an English point of view is the practice of prefixing the definite article to expressions of events and states. The literal translations are: 'the when I was a child' (1a), 'the they met' (1b), and 'the where we lived' (1c).

In such cases the *neh* functions as a kind of nominalizer, converting the event or state into a reified idea with a temporal extension like that of a noun. Something of the flavor of these expressions may be captured with translations like 'my being a child', 'their meeting', and 'our living'. It is relevant that these ideas are generic, not ideas of particular events or states. This use of *neh* with events and states appears, in fact, to be restricted to those that are generic. Perhaps this usage has a functional origin in the fact that many generic events and states are known to both speaker and hearer and are, for that reason, intrinsically identifiable: for example, the knowledge that the speaker was once a child (1a), or that he lived somewhere (1c). The identifiability of such cases may then have been generalized to generic knowledge that was not shared, such as that of the meetings in 1b.

4.5. ANOTHER EXAMPLE

The following example provides an opportunity to review and extend some of the points that were made above, while at the same time exemplifying the use of quotations. This speaker was talking about some problems she was having with hunters who were trespassing on her land:

(5) Warning

(a) ... *Da   onę   n   á·ę́?*,
    da·h   o·nęh   neh   ae?
    so   then   the   again
    Then again,

(b) *wáéowí?*   *neh*,
    wáéo·wi?   neh
    |wa?-he-hrory-?|
    FAC-1A/MP-tell-PUN
    I told him   the one,
    I told him,

(c) ... *mm   dę?   aya·sǫ́·h.*
    mm   dę?ę   haya·sǫh
                  |ha-yas-ǫh|
                  MA-be.called-STAT
    mm   what   he is called
    mm what's his name?

(d) ... *Hodí·ǫn.*
    hodí·ǫn
    |ho-at-rihw-ǫt-Ø|
    MP-MID-thing-be.attached-STAT
    he is responsible
    he was responsible (for keeping order).

(e) ... *Ne?   ne   shagoye·nǫ·s.*
    ne·?   neh   shagoye·nǫ·s
                   |shako-yena-s|
                   MA/FP-grab-HAB
    assert the   he grabs people
    It was the policeman.

(f)   Mm. (said by interlocutor)

(g) ... *Da   onę   wáéowí?*   *o?gí·?*,
    da·h o·nęh wáéo·wi?   o?gi?
                |wa?-he-hrory-?| wa?-k -i -?|
                FAC-1A/MP-tell-   FAC-1A-say-
                    PUN   PUN
    so   then   I told him   I said
    So then I told him I said,

(h) *da né?   ne?hó   ęhsé·?*   *o?gi?*,
    da· ne·?   ne?hoh   ęhse·?   o?gi?
               |ę-hs-e-n-?| wa?-k-i-?|
               FUT-2A-   FAC-1A-say-
               go-DIR-   PUN
               PUN
    so assert there   you will go   I said
    "So you will go there," I said,

(i) ... *ęshéowí?*   *higę́·h*   *o?gi?*,
    ęshé·owi?   hi·gę·h   o?gi?
    |ę-she-hrory-?| wa?-k-i-?|
    FUT-2A/PP-tell-   FACT-1A-PUN
        PUN
    you will tell them   that   I said
    "you will tell them," I said,

(j) *agénǫhdǫ́?*   *nǽ·h*,
    agénǫhdǫ?   nǽ·h
    |wak-ęnǫhtǫ-?|
    1P-know-STAT
    I know   emphasis
    "I do know

(k) ... *na?ót   hadíyashǫ́?*   *o?gi?.*
    na?ot   hadíyashǫ?   o?gi?
             |hati-yas-hǫ-?| wa?-k-i-?|
             MPA-be.called-   FAC-1A-say-PUN
                 DIST-STAT
    what sort   they are called   I said.
    what their names are," I said.

Intonation unit 5a is a typical topic introduction, consisting of nothing but a sequence of particles similar to those that introduced the storytelling excerpt in 1a: 'so then again'. In 5b, 'I told him', the speaker introduced an event in which she was one of the participants, but whose other participant was only gradually identified in 5c through 5e: 'what's his name, he was responsible, it was the policeman'. The last word in 5b illustrates still another use of the particle *neh*: as a weak demonstrative, translatable as 'the one', that served as a placeholder for a referent that would subsequently be categorized more adequately. With that referent finally established and acknowledged by the listener in 5f, 5g repeated what was said in 5a and 5b: 'so then I told him I said'. The direct quotes in 5h and 5i, 'you will go there, you will tell them', illustrate the use of the future mode as an imperative (3.1.1.1.4.).

4.6. QUOTATIONS

Seneca quotations usually take the form of direct speech, as in 5h through 5k, which pretend to replicate the words the speaker actually used in talking to the policeman. However, the speaker was telling the policeman that he himself should say something to the hunters, and the embedded quotation in 5j and 5k illustrates indirect speech: '(tell them that) I do know what their names are'. The policeman would actually have said 'she knows your names'. The indirect quote reflects the point of view of the speaker's conversation with the policeman, not of the policeman's projected conversation with the hunters. This speaker is an especially effective storyteller, and her use of both direct and indirect speech is one of the major devices by which she creates involvement in the events she relates.

4.7. OTHER GENRES AND STYLES

The discussion in this section has been based on casual conversational language and the informal personal narratives that are frequently included in conversations. Seneca is also rich in other ways of speaking, particularly in genres of oral literature and the varied styles of language they employ. Conspicuous in this regard are more formal stories and legends, as well as various types of religious and political speeches. Examples are the Cosmology story (transcribed in Hewitt 1903:221-254), the *gáíwi·yo·h* or Good Message of Handsome Lake (translated in Parker 1913), the elaborate Condolence Council that is performed for the installation of a new chief (Fenton 1946; Woodbury 1992), and the ubiquitous *ganǫ́ǫnyǫk* or Thanksgiving Speech (Chafe 1961; Foster 1974). Each genre is distinguished by characteristic formulaic phrases, special ways of constructing sentences, unique manifestations of epistemology, and strikingly different prosodic patterns. Chafe (1993) outlines some of the major differences between several of these styles. Elegance in the use of language has always been a strong value of the Seneca, as for speakers of the other Northern Iroquoian languages.

5. SELECTED VOCABULARY

afraid, be *geshá·nis* 'I'm afraid of it'

alive, be *gǫhe?* 'I'm alive'

all *gagwe·gǫh*

Allegany Reservation *ohi·yo?*

and *khoh*

animal, pet, slave *ganǫ·sgwa?*

animal, domestic, farm *gashe·nę?*

animal, wild *ganyo·?*

arm *onę·sha?*

arrow *ga?nǫ?*

ashes, dust *o?géę?*

ax *ado·gę?*

back *oswé?nǫ?*

bad *wa·etgę?* 'it's bad'

bark (of tree) *o?wádžisda?*

basket *ga?áshæ?*

beans *osáe?da?*

bear *nyágwai?*

bear clan members *hodidzǫní?ga·?*

beaver clan members *hodígę?ge·ga·?*

because *sę?ęh*

belly *otgwísda?* or *oshé·wa?*

berry, fruit *odží·ya?*

big *gowa·nęh* 'it's big'

bird *dži?déę?ǫ·?*

bite *o?gi·k* 'I bit it'

black *dzę·sdá?ę·?* 'it's black'

blood *otgwęhsa?*

blow *o?géǫ?da·t* 'I blew'

blue *dži·nyóae?* 'it's blue'

boat *ga·ǫwǫ?*

bone *o?nę·ya?*

bow (weapon) *wa?ę·nǫ?*

bowl game *gadzę́?gekha·?*

boy *haksá?a·h*

break, cut in pieces *o?tgya?k* 'I broke it'

breast, milk *onǫ́?gwa?*

breathe *o?gadǫ·wi?* 'I breathed'

burn *ode·kha?* 'it's burning, fire'

buttocks *o·nǫ́?sha?*

buy *o?khni·nǫ?* 'I bought it'

cat *dago·dži?*

Cattaraugus Reservation *ga?dæ·gę́sgę·ǫ?*

chair *gadži·ga·ya?*

chicken *dagǽ·?ę·?*

child, offspring *owi·yæ?*

claw, fingernail *o?éhda?*

cloud *ohdží?gæ?*

cold *onǫ́?no·h* 'it's cold'

cold (of weather) *otho·we?*

come *o?gáhge·t* 'I came'

cook (a meal) *o?gékhǫ·ni?* 'I cooked'

corn *onę́ǫ?*

corn on the cob *o?nísda?*

count *o?gáshe·t* 'I counted'

cry *o?tgáhsętho?* 'I cried'

cut (make an incision) *o?khe·?* 'I cut it'

dance *o?tga·t* 'I danced'

daytime *ę·deh*

deer *neogę?*

deer clan members *hodí·nyǫgwaiyo?*

die *hawé·eyǫ·h* 'he has died'

dig *o?gó?gwa·t* 'I dug'

dirty *otgi?* 'it's dirty'

dog *dži·yæh*

door *gahóa?*

576

drink *oʔkhnégeæʔ* 'I drank'

drum dance *gonéoǫʔ*

dry *ohę·h* 'it's dry'

duck *so·wæk*

dull *deyóthyoʔkdáʔǫh* 'it's gotten dull'

dust, ashes *oʔgéę*

ear *óǫhdaʔ*

earth, the *yǫędzadeʔ*

eat *oʔge·k* 'I ate it'

egg *oʔhǫ́hsaʔ*

eight *degyǫʔ*

embers, coals *gadži·sdaʔ*

eye *gagáaʔ*

fall *dawáʔsęʔt* 'it fell'

false face mask *gagǫ́hsaʔ*

far *we·ęh*

fat, grease, lard, oil *o·nǫʔ*

father *haʔnih*

feather *óæ̨ʔdaʔ*

feather dance *osdówæʔgo·wa·h*

few *dohgaʔah*

fight *oʔgadi·yoʔ* 'I fought'

finger *oʔnyaʔ*

fire *ode·khaʔ* 'it's burning'

fish *gędzǫh*

five *wis*

float *odóʔgæhgǫh* 'it's floating'

flower *awę́ǫʔ*

fly *oʔtkdę̨ʔ* 'I flew'

fog *osha·daʔ*

foot *ohsíʔdaʔ*

four *ge·ih*

freeze *oʔgánesdos* 'it froze'

frog *sgoʔæk*

fruit, berry *odžíʔyaʔ*

full *ganǫ·hǫh* 'it's full'

girl *yeksáʔa·h*

give *oʔkhe·yǫʔ* 'I gave it to her, them'

go, travel *oʔgáhtę·diʔ* 'I went'

good *wi·yo·h* 'it's good'

Good Message *gáíwi·yo·h*

grass *ogéoʔdzaʔ*

green *ganæ̨hdaikhǫʔ* 'it's green'

guts *oksǫ·węʔ*

hair *ogéʔæʔ*

hand *osʔóhdaʔ*

Handsome Lake *(s)ganyodaiyoʔ*

hawk clan members *hodíswęʔgaiyoʔ*

head *onǫ́ʔę·ʔ*

hear *agáthǫ·deʔ* 'I hear it'

hear, understand, obey *oʔgá·ǫk* 'I understood it'

heart *awę́nyahsaʔ*

heavy *osdeʔ* 'it's heavy'

here *nękhoh*

heron clan members *honǫdáę́ʔǫ·ga·ʔ*

hill *onǫdadeʔ*

hit *oʔgyęn* 'I hit it'

hold *ikhaʔ* 'I'm holding it'

hoop and javelin game *gage·daʔ*

horn (of animal) *onǫ́ʔgæ·ʔ*

hot *oʔdáię·h* 'it's hot'

house *ganǫ́hso·t*

hunt *gado·wæ·s* 'I hunt'

husk face mask *gadžíhsaʔ*

I, we *íʔ* or *níʔ*

ice *owi·sæʔ*

if *dyę·gwah*

in *i·wa·t* 'it's in it'

kill *oʔgi·yoʔ* 'I killed it'

knee *áǫshaʔ*

know (a fact) *agénǫhdǫʔ* 'I know it'

know, be acquainted with *gyęde·ih* 'I know it'

lake *ganyodaeʔ*

laugh *oʔgésgatgwęʔ* 'I laughed'

law, the great law *gayáneshæ̨ʔgo·wa·h*

leaf *onæ̨hdaʔ*

left (side) *sgetgwa·dih* 'my left side'

leg *ohsi·nǫʔ*

lie down *oʔgádyashę̨ʔ* 'I lay down'

like *khnǫeʔs* 'I like it'

live, stay, be seated *giʔdyǫʔ* 'I live'

liver *othwę́hsaʔ*

long *i·yǫ·s* 'it's long'

longhouse *ganǫ́hse·s*

louse *džiʔnǫ·h*

man, male *hadži·nǫh*

577

many *we·soʔ*

maple *wahdaʔ*

meat *oʔwáaʔ*

milk, breast *onǫ́ʔgwaʔ*

moon *(sǫ́ékhaˑʔ) gǽ·hgwaˑʔ*

mother *noʔyęh*

mouth *gehsága·ęn* 'my mouth'

name *gahsę·nǫʔ*

named, be *haya·sǫh* 'he is named'

narrow *niwadagwęhdaʔáah* 'it's narrow'

near *dosgęh*

neck *o·nyáʔsaʔ*

new *wa·se·ʔ* 'it's new'

night *sǫ·eh*

nine *dyohdǫ·h*

no *hęʔęh*

nose *gegǫ́daʔgeh* 'my nose'

old (of a person) *hagę́hdžih* 'he's old'

old (of a thing) *waga·yǫh* 'it's old'

one *sga·t*

other *o·yaʔ*

owl *oʔo·waˑʔ*

peace, well-being *sgę·nǫʔ*

person *ǫ·gweh*

Personal Chant *adǫ·węʔ*

pierce *oʔtgáʔis* 'I pierced it'

pig *gisgwi·s*

plant *oʔgyę·thoʔ* 'I planted it'

play *agátga·nye·h* 'I'm playing'

potato *onǫ́nǫʔdaʔ*

pull *dagádyę·ęthoʔ* 'I pulled it'

push *oʔtgáhdzaęʔ* 'I pushed it'

rabbit *gwaʔyǫ·ʔ*

raccoon *dzoʔæ·gaʔ*

rain *osdęǫdyǫ·h* 'it's raining'

rattle *gasdǫ́węʔsæʔ*

red *gwę́hdæ·ʔęˑʔ* 'it's red'

ribs *oyǫ·sgwaʔ*

right (side) *gę·ǫsdǫh* 'my right side'

right, correct *tgaye·iʔ* 'it's right'

river *gęhǫ·deʔ*

road *o·adeʔ*

root *okdéæʔ*

rope *gáǫhgæ·ʔ*

rotten *otgę·h* 'it's rotten'

round *deyóthweʔnǫ·ni·h* 'it's round'

rub *oʔgæ·nyeʔ* 'I rubbed it'

run *kdakheʔ* 'I'm running'

salt *odžíkheʔdaʔ*

sand *oʔnéhsaʔ*

say *oʔgiʔ* 'I said'

scratch, scrape *oʔge·ge·t* 'I scratched it'

sea *ganyodeowanęh* 'large lake'

see *oʔge·gęʔ* 'I saw it'

seed *onǫ́hgwęǫʔ*

seven *dza·dak*

sew *oʔgéʔnikhǫʔ* 'I sewed it'

sharp *o·yóʔthi·yet* 'it's sharp'

shoot *oʔgíʔya·k* 'I shot'

short *niwákʔa·h* 'it's short'

sing *oʔgadęno·dęʔ* 'I sang'

sit *oʔga·dyęˑʔ* 'I sat down'

six *ye·iʔ*

skin, hide *oʔšyóhsaʔ*

skunk *se·nǫ·h*

sky *géǫ́yadeʔ*

sleep *hodáʔǫh* 'he's asleep'

small *niwáʔa·h* 'it's small'

smell *oʔgádeswat* 'I smelled it'

smoke *oyę́ʔgwæ·ʔ*

smooth *gahsǫ́·wi·yo·h* 'it's smooth'

snake *osháisdaʔ*

snipe clan members *hodíʔnehsi·yoʔ*

snow (falling) *oʔgæʔ*

snow (on the ground) *oni·yaʔ*

snow (verb) *oʔgyǫ·dyǫ·h* 'it's snowing'

snowsnake game *ga·wa·saʔ*

soil *óéhdaʔ*

some *gye·h*

song *oęnǫʔ*

speak *age·thaˑʔ* 'I'm speaking'

spit, saliva *osgæʔ*

split *oʔtgo·węʔ* 'I split it'

spouse *né·yoˑʔ*

squash *o·nyǫ́hsaʔ*

squeeze *oʔgáhdžiyó·æk* 'I squeezed it'

stab, pierce *oʔgáʔgat* 'I stabbed it'
stand *iˑgeˑt* 'I'm standing'
star *odžíhsǫʔdaʔ*
stick *gaʔwásdaʔ, gaʔnhyaʔ*
stone *gaʔsgwaˑaʔ*
straight *odagwáíhsǫˑh* 'it's straight'
strawberry *džisdǫdáʔshæʔ*
strength *gaʔhásdeshæʔ*
suck *oʔkhnǫ́ʔgeæʔ* 'I sucked'
sugar *owæˑnǫʔ*
sun *(ędeˑkhaˑʔ) gǽˑhgwaˑʔ*
swell *ohdę́ʔgwęh* 'it's swollen'
swim, bathe *gadaˑwęh* 'I swim'
table *adékhwáˑhgwaʔ*
tail *gęhgaˑaʔ*
taste good *ogáʔǫh* 'it tastes good'
ten *washęˑh*
Thanksgiving Speech *ganǫ́ǫnyǫk*
that, there *neʔhoh*
thick *gaˑdęˑs* 'it's thick'
thin *nigadagéʔǫh* 'it's thin'
think *gęnǫ́hdǫnyǫh* 'I'm thinking'
this *nę̇ˑgęˑh*
three *sęh*
throw *hǫgaˑdiʔ* 'I threw it'
tie *oʔkhnǫ́hsǫˑdęʔ* 'I tied it'
tobacco *oyéʔgwaʔ*
today *węˑníshædeʔ*
tomorrow *ęyoˑhę́ʔt*
Tonawanda Reservation *thaˑnǫwǫdeʔ*
tongue *óǽʔnǫhsaʔ*
tooth *onóʔdzaʔ*
town *ganǫdayęʔ*

tree (standing) *gǽˑit*
tree, log *gaˑǫdaʔ*
turn *oʔwáthwadaˑseʔ* 'it turned'
turtle *haʔnoˑwaˑh*
turtle clan members *hadínyahdęˑh*
two *dekhniˑh*
vomit *ǫgényaʔgoʔ* 'I vomited'
walk *oʔtgáthaˑk* 'I walked'
warm *oneˑnǫʔ* 'it's warm'
wash *oʔkhnówaeʔ* 'I washed it'
water *oˑneganos*
we, I *íˑʔ or níˑʔ*
wet *oænǫwęˑh* 'it's wet'
what? *dęʔęh*
when? *węˑdǫh*
where? *gaˑweh*
white *gagęˑn* 'it's white'
who? *sǫˑh*
wide *wadaˑgwęn* 'it's wide'
wind *owǽˑdeʔ*
wing *onǽgǫsdaʔ*
wipe *oʔgǽgǫeʔ* 'I wiped it'
wolf clan members *honǫ́thaˑyǫˑnih*
woman *yeǫh*
wood *oyęˑdaʔ*
woods *gahaˑdaʔ*
work *agyóˑʔdeʔ* 'I'm working'
write *oʔkhyaˑdǫʔ* 'I wrote'
year *yoshǽˑdeʔ*
yellow *džítgwǽˑʔęʔ* 'it's yellow'
yesterday *theˑdęʔ*
you *íˑs or níˑs*

Sketch of Wichita, a Caddoan Language

DAVID S. ROOD

In 1991, Wichita was spoken by about a dozen people in central and south-central Oklahoma, principally around Anadarko and Gracemont, but also including Lawton. Together with Pawnee and Arikara, it forms the North Caddoan branch of the Caddoan family, of which Caddo is the only other living representative. Information is also available about one other North Caddoan language, Kitsai, which is extinct.

In the 1990s there were no dialect variations remaining among the various Wichita speakers, although formerly Waco, Tawakoni, and Wichita proper were recognized as separate dialects. For a survey of early recorded information about Caddoan languages and a discussion of the genetic relationships among them, see Taylor (1963, 1963a).

All fluent speakers in 1994 were older than 60. There were no living monolinguals. In 1965, speakers who could use the language tended to do so at every opportunity; older people gathered for socializing or for business preferred to conduct conversations in Wichita if possible; grandparents who wished to communicate about grandchildren with the parents of the children used Wichita as a "code," even though the parent was usually unable to respond in Wichita. These occasions never produced exclusively Wichita utterances; English words and sentences were frequently intermingled (see Rood 1989a for some detailed examples). Consequently, most of the continuous text data in Rood (1976, 1977) are in the form of stories or conversations that were dictated or staged expressly for the author.

In 1994 the language was spoken rarely, even by those who were able to do so.

Most of the data on which this description is based were collected in the summer of 1965 and throughout the academic year 1966-1967. Rood (1976) was based entirely on these data. Rood's main assistant from 1964 until the early 1980s was Bertha Provost (fig. 1), but information has also come from George Bates, May Lamar Davis (fig. 2), Berdina Holder, Doris Lamar (fig. 2), Elton Lamar, Leta Lamar, Vivian McCurdy (fig. 3), Frank Miller, Houston Miller, Clara Moonlight, Faye Owings, Bertha Picard, Helen Wheeler Querdibitty, Martha Reeder, and Lorraine Ross. Most of the texts from which the examples used below were drawn appear in Rood (1977).

PHONOLOGY

1. SYLLABLE NUCLEI

1.1. VOWELS AND LENGTH

Wichita utterances utilize three phonemic vowels: /i, e, a/. Each of these occurs either short, long, or overlong, with varying frequencies. In addition, a sequence of short vowel plus /w/ plus short vowel will often be pronounced [oˑ] (like the *oo* of German *Boot*), so that one

Fig. 1. Bertha Ross Provost (*ka·santatiyeh* 'following with a scalp', nicknamed *tikammac* 'grinding corn') (b. ca. 1890, d. 1983), and her great-grandson Lester Poolaw, Jr. Beginning in 1964, Provost shared much with Rood about traditional life and many Wichita stories, which she had learned from her grandmother.

Provost spoke only Wichita until she was 9 years old and was taken by force to the Riverside School in Anadarko, Okla. While she was a teenager her parents arranged her marriage to James Ross, who died soon after the birth of their second child. She then married William Henry Provost, a Sioux, who was a preacher. She helped him in his Bible classes and church services, often serving as the Wichita interpreter. Photographed probably at the Wichita and Pawnee gathering in Pawnee, Okla., about 1975 (digitally retouched).

actually hears four vowels (i, e, a, o) when listening to Wichita.

In this chapter, a raised dot following a vowel indicates that the vowel is held about twice as long as an unmarked vowel; a colon means it is held from two and one-half to three times as long as the short vowel.

1.1.1.

/i/ is phonetically mid or high front and unrounded. It can thus sound like any of the vowels in English *beat*, *bit*, or *bait* (although German *Beet* is closer than English *bait*). Usually it is higher (more like *beat*) when short, especially after [r], and lower (more like *Beet*) when lengthened, so that one hears [i] and [e·] or [e:]; nevertheless, this is not consistent, and the vowel is best described as ranging from [e] to [i], with these and all the phones in between being in free variation. This vowel occurs about equally often short, long, and overlong.

1.1.2.

/e/ is phonetically low, front unrounded [æ] or [ɛ]. It can thus sound like the vowel of either *cat* or *pet*. It very rarely occurs short, except in the sequence /eʔe/; and it is by far the most frequent overlong vowel. This distribution, as well as the strange configuration of the vowel system in general and the parallelism of [o·] = |VwV|, lead one to suspect that /e/ could be treated as

the sequence |ayi| or |iya|. But since there is often no evidence to motivate the choice of one of these sequences over the other, for the present /e/ must be retained in both the surface and underlying phonological representations of some forms (section 4).

1.1.3.

/a/ is usually a low, back, unrounded vowel [ɑ]. It is thus similar to the English vowel of *cot~caught* in the speech of many western and southern Americans. Before or after /w/, it is sometimes rounded slightly, to sound like the vowel of *caught* in most English dialects that separate *cot* and *caught*. When short in unstressed syllables, it is often raised and centralized to [ʌ] (like the *u* of *but*). The low central [a] (the vowel of *father*) is rarely heard anywhere. /a·/ and /a:/ are always low, back, and unrounded. Both /a/ and /a·/ are common, but /a:/ occurs in very few words. Contrast, however, *ná·ʔih* 'his' with *ná:ʔih* 'his child', or *hárah* 'there (used when pointing)', *ha·rí·h* 'that one', and *ha:rih* 'there, in that place'.

1.1.4.

[o·] is normally the only length variant for this phone. One word, [hoʔos] 'soon', presents the only other occurrence of a back, rounded vowel, but it does not force the conclusion that the language has a phoneme /o/ or /u/. From various kinds of evidence, it can be deduced that this word should be represented as |hawʔas|, and all the occurrences of [o·] represented as sequences involving |w|. Garvin (1950) contains several transcriptions of words with short /u/, all of which actually represent /a/ in a backing and rounding environment (Rood 1975).

1.1.5.

/i/ and /a/ are voiceless in word-final position. The preceding consonant is always either /k/ or /ʔ/. In the examples below, an underlying final vowel may be written after other consonants, but it is not pronounced there. There are no examples of /e/ in this environment, so there are no examples of voiceless /e/. Voiceless vowels are always short and may carry secondary stress.

1.1.6.

There are no vowel clusters. Garvin (1950) does describe several of them, but reexamination and the addition of further data have revealed that each of his clusters is either /VyV/ or an erroneous treatment of /w/. Furthermore, his discovery of variable length in certain environments was not confirmed by Rood (1965-1969).

1.2. PITCH AND STRESS

Every vowel will have either a high pitch (tone) (which in word-final position is a falling pitch contour) or a low pitch accompanying it. The distribution of pitches is entirely unpredictable and phonemic; stress, which

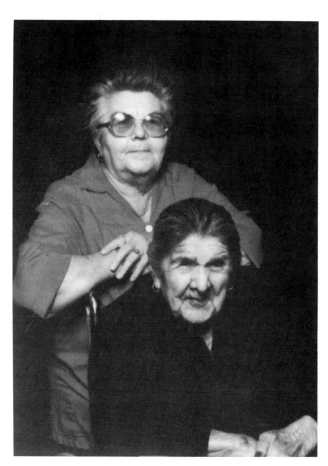

Fig. 2. Doris Jean Lamar (McLemore; b. 1927), standing, and her mother May Lamar (Davis; b. 1906). May grew up on her parents' allotment southeast of Gracemont Okla., and attended Riverside School in Anadarko and Haskell Institute in Kans. Doris was raised by her grandparents on the same allotment and grew up fluent in Wichita. For 30 years she worked as an educational aide at the boarding school. From about 1986 she was Rood's primary consultant. Both women were instrumental in producing a set of Wichita language lessons on tape. Photograph by Ron South, Chickasha, Okla., Aug. 1993.

occurs in three degrees (primary, secondary, and unstressed) can be predicted most of the time from the position of the pitches.

1.2.1.

The rules for stress prediction are complex, and unexplained counterexamples exist. For primary stress, a hierarchy of priorities exists: in a given word, all high-pitched syllables will have primary stress; if no high pitches occur in the word, long vowels receive primary stress; if neither high pitch nor a long vowel occurs in the word, the last voiced vowel has primary stress—except that in two-vowel words with only short, low-pitched vowels, neither vowel is more strongly stressed than the other.

1.2.2.

Once the primary stresses are established, secondary stress is assigned to alternate vowels (in either direction)

from the main stresses. A pattern of alternating stressed and unstressed syllables is thus developed, in which the stressed syllable can have either primary or secondary stress. If two primary stressed vowels occur in the same word and would seem to assign conflicting secondary stresses, the conflict is usually resolved by stopping at the place where the two overlap, allowing a sequence of two unstressed syllables if necessary.

1.2.3.

Examples are as follows. Bolding marks primary stress; underlining marks secondary stress; the acute accent marks high pitch.

(1) *nahe·hárih* 'creek' is stressed [na-he·-**há**-rih], following the rule that primary stress coincides with high pitch, and the rule that secondary stress occurs on alternate vowels from the pitch in either direction.

(2) *kinni·ca?ak?í·has?ih* 'alfalfa' (literally 'that which does not die out') is longer, but similar. The stresses are [kin-ni·-ca-?ak-**?í·**-has-?ih].

(3) *k?íta·kski·ya·k?a* 'millet' (literally 'coyote tail') demonstrates a secondary stress on a voiceless vowel; the pattern is [**k?í**-ta·ks-ki·-ya·k-?a].

(4) *tikasi·sk*ʷ 'he has a beard', stressed [ti-ka-**si·sk**ʷ], illustrates primary stress on a long vowel, plus secondary on alternate vowels from the primary.

(5) *niye·skic?i·s* 'baby' (literally 'unripe child') shows two primary stresses, one on each long vowel, and no secondary stresses: [ni-**ye·s**-kic-**?i·s**].

(6) *tika?acs* 'he is eating it' and *naka?acskih* 'the one who is eating it' illustrate words with short, low-pitched vowels and stress on the last vowel; note that the root, -ka?ac-, receives varying kinds of stress, depending on the shape of the rest of the word: [ti-ka-**?acs**; na-ka-?acs-**kih**].

(7) *árasi·cíte·riw* 'you finished it (put an edge or border on it)', stressed [**á**-ra-si·-**cí**-te·-riw], shows the suspension of the secondary stress assignment rule where conflict results. *ára-* would demand that -si·- be stressed, while -cí- would demand that the preceding -ra- be stressed; the result would be *[**á**-ra-si·-**cí**-...], which is not the actual form.

(8) counterexamples to the rules are of three types:

(a) Sometimes secondary stresses occur on adjacent syllables, without obvious reasons why. Note [**sá**·-ri-?i-ti-ka?a] 'Arapaho' as one instance.

(b) Secondary stresses sometimes occur on syllables adjacent to high pitches, as in [ka·-kin-na-**kʷhá·c**-?i-ki] 'apple' (literally, 'some things that are red').

Fig. 3. Vivian McCurdy (te·ska·hi·k²a 'corn woman') (b. 1925), who provided Rood information on Indian names. She was the enrollment clerk for the tribe in the late 1970s and early 1980s. Photograph by Emma I. Hansen, Anadarko, Okla., 1981.

(c) In some situations, the counting of alternate syllables seems to extend farther from one primary stress than from another, as in [kiya·kíriwa·c²árasarikita²ahí·riks] 'he brought the big (quantity of) meat up to the top (by making many trips)'. Here both syllables of -kita- 'top' receive secondary stress, the -ki- under the influence of -²á-, the -ta- under the influence of -hí-. According to the general patterns described above, only the -ta- should have been stressed.

In situations where secondary stresses occur in unexpected places, they are marked with a grave accent. Thus the example in 8c would be written kiya·kíriwa·c²árasarikità²ahí·riks.

Probably the resolution of some of these problems lies in ordering the stress-placement rules with vowel deletion rules (section 4.5.). Some vowels that must be

counted to determine stress placement are apt to have been deleted by later rules, thus destroying the obvious surface regularity. But this will not account for 8c, because kita is a single morpheme.

2. SYLLABLE MARGINS

Wichita uses no true labials, and no phonemic nasals, in its consonant system except for two verb roots |kammac| 'grind corn' and |camma·ci| 'hoe, cultivate'. The system has the following 10 members:

	labio-velar	alveolar	palatal	velar	glottal
stops	kʷ	t		k	²
affricate			c		
fricatives		s			h
approximants	w	r~n		y	

2.1.

The stops and affricate (/c/ = [ts]) are voiceless, unaspirated, and tense (similar to French voiceless stops). /s/ is alveolar, and varies freely from grooved to flat articulation (but usually one speaker prefers one articulation, the next the other). The phoneme written /r~n/ is an alveolar flap or tap ([ř], the single r of Spanish pero) which is nasalized when it occurs before other alveolars, when it is geminate, or when it is in initial position before vowels. In other words, the medial or final clusters beginning with this phoneme include [nc, nt, ns, nn, ř², řh]; initially, [n] and [řh] occur (and [ř] is voiceless here); intervocalically, [ř] is the allophone used. Both [ř] and /w/ (and the [w] component of /kʷ/) are voiceless in word-final position.

2.2.

Clusters of up to five consonants ([ncksk] in nahi²inckskih 'while sleeping' is the longest example) occur medially; up to four occur finally. These clusters are composed of alternating stop-continuant-stop-continuant sequences, or of series of continuants, or of both, where /c/ and /²/ function as either stop or continuant (Garvin 1950:182). In addition to [nn], the geminate clusters are /ss/ and /cc/ ([tsts]). Word initially, besides /rh/, the only clusters attested are /ks, th, k², ch, kʷh, kh, ckh, and kskh/. There is a contrast between initial vowel and initial /²/ plus vowel: /²i/- marks the third person of the negative indicative tense, while /i/- marks the equivalent form of the directive tense.

/y/ does not participate in any (surface) consonant clusters. It usually occurs between /i/ or /e/ and /a/, but rare instances of /iye/, /eye/, /aye/ and /aya/ exist. For examples, compare niye·s 'child', ka·si·²áre·ye²es²i 'the place is unknown', tà·yè·csà²as 'he is bringing fire', and ta·ya·rhára²as 'he is bringing wood'.

3. SYLLABLES

Every Wichita vowel is the nucleus of a syllable. In word-initial position only, the vowel may have from zero to four consonants preceding it: /a-kʷí-thah/

'above', /rhinc$^?$a/ 'trousers', /ckha·r$^?$a/ 'night', /kskha·r$^?$a/ 'joint where thigh attaches to hip'. In other positions in the word, at least one (and usually only one) consonant must precede the vowel in its syllable. Up to four consonants may follow the vowel in the syllable. In word-final position, all syllables end with either a consonant or a voiceless vowel.

Much of the description of syllable structure follows from the description of consonant clusters (section 2.2.). Despite the general canon of (C)(C)(C)(C)V(C)(C)(C)(C), the longest medial cluster found consists of only five consonants; so there must be some restrictions on the sequences of syllable types.

Phonetically, /c/ and /s/ are often syllabic between other consonants, but the conditions for this have not been determined.

4. UNDERLYING PHONOLOGY

Many Wichita morphemes have several pronunciations, depending on their contexts. For example, /ra·k/ 'non–third-person is plural' may also be /ra·r/, /ra·s/, /ha·k/, /ha·s/, /a·s/, /a·k/, or even /a·/, depending on the particular word in which it occurs. By establishing a single phonological shape, called the underlying shape, for the morpheme, and listing a few rules that describe how underlying sounds change in various environments, all these variations and many more can be explained. The underlying shape for 'non–third-person plural' is thus |ra·k|, identical in this case with one of the surface shapes.

The phonological system needed to account for all the morpheme variation differs somewhat from the surface structure system described above. The inventory of underlying phonological elements contains four vowels, |i, e, a, u| (and all but |u| occur both long and short); a pitch contrast; and 11 consonants: |k^w, t, k, $^?$, c, s, r, w, y, h| and |R|.

4.1.

At the most easily recoverable level, the underlying vowel system contains four members, |i, e, a| and |u|. A system of three members, |i, a, u|, is probably correct at a slightly deeper level (section 1.1.3. discusses an alternative analysis of |e|).

Underlying |u| is surface /i/ or /i·/ in all environments; but discovering which surface /i/s are to be taken as representatives of |u| is not simple, except in two environments.

It is apparent that a rule of the form

(9) i > a /_$^?$a

(read: |i| changes to /a/ in the environment before |$^?$a|) is needed to account for such variations as the following:

(10) |ti + ta·ras + $^?$ak + $^?$ariki| (indicative third person + horse + plural + stand) > tita·ras$^?$ak$^?$ariki 'the horses are standing'

(11) |ti + $^?$ak + $^?$ariki| (indicative third person + plural + stand) > ta$^?$ak$^?$ariki 'they are standing'

That is, third-person indicative tense marker |ti| appears as /ta-/ before the |$^?$a| of the plural marker.

Nevertheless, there are surface sequences of /i$^?$a/. The best account of these is to assume that the /i/ in this environment represents underlying |u|. Observe:

(12) |is + ru + $^?$ariki + iki| (imperative second-person + collective + stand + causative) > issi$^?$ari·ki 'set them down'

(13) |is + $^?$ariki + iki| (imperative second-person + stand + causative) > is$^?$ari·ki 'set it down'

(14) |ti + $^?$ariki + is| (indicative third person + stand + caustive imperfective) > ta$^?$ari·s 'he set it down'

The explanation of surface sequences of /i$^?$a/ despite the rule that |i| changes to /a/ before /$^?$a/ is thus accomplished by the establishment of an underlying |u|. The other environment where |u| solves a problem follows from the observation that a very general rule changes noninitial |t| to /c/ unless the |t| is followed by |u| or |a|. Hence the surface environment /-ti/ indicates an underlying |-tu|. Compare, for instance, 15-17. (In the examples, the term preverb refers to a separate part of some roots. Potentially, many morphemes may occur between the preverb and the rest of the root. Compare positions 5 and 10 in section 12.1.11.).

(15) |ta + t + i + i$^?$ahi| (indicative + first-person subject + preverb + hold) > taci·$^?$eh 'I am holding it'

(16) |ta + t + a· + uc + i + i$^?$ahi| (indicative + first-person subject + reflexive + possessive + preverb + hold) > tata·ci·$^?$eh 'I am holding my own'

(17) |ta + t + uc + i + i$^?$ahi| > tati·ci·$^?$eh 'I am holding his' (glosses of individual morphemes as in 15 and 16)

Note in these examples the first-person marking /c/ in 15, where it occurs before |i|, but /t/ in 16 and 17, where it occurs before |a| or |u| respectively. Note, too, that here |u| disappears after |a·| but becomes /i·/ in other environments.

4.2.

The difference between long and short vowels (for i and a at least) is distinctive in the underlying system as well as in the surface system. However, the overlong vowels are probably to be derived from sequences of long vowel plus consonant plus short vowel, where the consonant has been deleted. Internal evidence for this is scanty, but informal comparison with related languages reveals that Wichita frequently loses intervocalic |h| and |y| where other languages preserve them. Nevertheless, until further work can be completed, it is necessary to preserve the contrast between long and overlong to account for the differences in pairs of roots such as |ʔiˑsʔ| 'look at' versus |ʔiːs| 'see', or |reˑhi| 'put plural object lying' versus |reːhi| 'buy; choose; pick up'. It is highly probable that these pairs are related, one form somehow derived from the other; but the details are not presently recoverable.

4.3.

Many forms with high pitch on a vowel can be derived from an underlying form without the pitch, but with a more complex sequence of consonants than the surface structure presents. An obvious example is the word for 'house', |akhahrʔa|. If the second vowel of this word is the last voiced vowel in a surface structure word, it is long; hence the pronunciation in isolation is *akhaˑrʔa*. Elsewhere that vowel is short and high pitched, as in the compound *akhákhac* 'white house', underlying |akhahr + khac|. When the |-hrkh-| cluster is simplified, it leaves a high pitch behind on the vowel.

It therefore seems reasonable to assume that high pitch is a kind of compensation for (or marking of) an underlying consonant cluster simplification. Yet the residue of forms that cannot be treated this way is not negligible. Noun roots such as *téˑs* 'corn' and *kʔítaˑks* 'coyote' seem to have an inherent pitch on one of the root vowels; and neither internal reconstruction, nor morphophonemics, nor comparative evidence motivates an underlying form without pitch for such roots. It is therefore unavoidable that some vowels be marked for pitch in the underlying form.

4.4.

Underlying consonants include all those listed in the surface phonological description, plus |R|. The difference between |R| and |r| is that the latter coalesces with neighboring consonants to form clusters (e.g. |rs| > /ss/; |rt| > /c/; |rk| > /hk/; |rw| > /hkʷ/; |kr| > /rh/; etc.) while the former simply disappears in the same environments; both appear as [ř] between vowels or as [n] word-initially before a vowel.

4.5.

The process of going from underlying to surface forms involves three steps. First, certain vowels of the underlying forms are syncopated (deleted); second, the consonant clusters that result are simplified; finally, sounds are assimilated to their environments as illustrated in tables 1 and 2. An illustration of exactly how this process works is the word 'tree', literally, 'wood stands upright'. The underlying form is

(18) |ta + i + yaˑk + ri (ruʔ) + wi| (indicative + third-person subject + wood + collective + stand upright)

First, the |a| of |ta| and the |i| (or |u|) of |ri| are syncopated, although why these vowels are chosen instead of others is unexplained. Second, the intermediate form |tiyaˑkrwi| undergoes consonant cluster simplification, in which |krw| becomes /hkʷ/, and the vowel of 'wood'

Table 1. Cluster Simplification for Two-Consonant Clusters

Morpheme final	Morpheme initial |t|	|k|	|kʷ|	|ʔ|	|c|	|s|	|r|	|w|	|y|	|h|
|t|	ct	ck	ckʷ	cʔ	cc	c	c	ckʷ		ch
|k|	st	k	·kʷ	kʔ	·c	ks	rh	kʷ	h	kh
|ʔ|	t	k	kʷ	ʔ	c	s	r	w		
|c|	ct	ck	ckʷ	cʔ	cc	cs	c	ckʷ		{ch / cs}
|s|	st	sk	skʷ	sʔ	sc	ss	ss	skʷ	ss	{sh / ss}
|r|	c	hk	hkʷ	rʔ	nc	c	nn	hkʷ		rh
|h|	ˊt	ˊk	ˊkʷ	ˊʔ	ˊc	s	{ˊr / ·r}*	hw		ˊh
|y|	ˊt	ˊk		y			ˊr			·y

NOTES: */ˊr/ occurs when a voiced vowel follows in the word; /·r/ occurs otherwise.

A consonant on the left, followed by one on top, results in the surface structure consonants or cluster given at the appropriate intersection of the columns. A blank on the chart means no examples of the combination have occurred. There are no morphemes ending in /w/ or /kʷ/, so these phonemes are omitted from the vertical dimension of the chart. For |R| see section 4.4.

Table 2. Some Underlying Possibilities for Surface Consonants

Surface Structure	May represent underlying
kʷ	|kʷ|; |w|/ c, s, r, t_
t	|t|; |Rt|
k	|k|; |kk|; |Rk|
ʔ	|ʔ|
c	|c|; |t|; |cR|; |tr|; |rt|; |rs|
s	|s|; |r|; |sR|; |y|; |hs|; |k|/_t
w	|w|
r	|k|/_h; |R|; |r|
h	|h|; |y|/#_; |r|/r, s_; |r|/_k, kʷ

NOTE: To the right of the slashes are indicated special environments; thus |k|/_t means "underlying |k| before *t*", and |y|/#_ means "underlying |y| after word boundary."

receives a high pitch as part of this process. Finally, the word-final |i| is devoiced, and because it is not following /k/ or /ʔ/, it is lost; this leaves /kʷ/ in word-final position, where the [w] element is devoiced. The result is the surface structure form

(19) *tiyáˑhkʷ* 'tree'.

In the case of this word, numerous related forms with more and different morphemes enable the recovery of the |ta| and the |rV| with a very high degree of certainty. However, in many of the data the determination of the precise shapes of the underlying forms is difficult, if not impossible. It is therefore frequently the case that so-called underlying forms will be given below as if step one of the phonological realization process had already been accomplished. For example, 'tree' would most likely be cited as |ti + yaˑk + r + wi|, rather than as in 18.

4.6.

The consonant cluster simplification rules are given in table 1, for two-consonant clusters. Vowel rules not already mentioned are not included. Table 2 presents the consonant information from the point of view of the analyst seeking the underlying forms. These tables substitute here for the formal list of rules that would be needed in a complete grammar. See Rood (1975) for a more formal discussion of Wichita phonology.

GRAMMAR

5. CITATION OF FORMS

The examples used to illustrate Wichita grammar below will always be given in two forms. First, the surface phonemic form (an indication of pronunciation) will be presented, with the following modifications:

(a) [ř] and [n] will be distinguished, for mnemonic reasons, as *r* and *n*;

(b) [oˑ] will be written when the regular pronunciation of the form demands the contraction (the underlying form can be read from the second transcription);

(c) Vowels with irregular secondary stress will be written with a grave accent wherever the rules given in section 1.2.2. do not predict it correctly.

Second, a morpheme-by-morpheme analysis will be presented. Here each Wichita morpheme will be transcribed in its underlying (morphophonemic) form and translated. In this analysis, the plus sign (+) will be used to separate bound morphemes; the semicolon (;) will separate forms that are independent words in the surface structure. Occasionally, underlying forms will be written with *n* rather than *r* to distinguish two morphemes that would otherwise look identical. The most frequent example of that is *na* 'participle', which contrasts with *ra* 'indicative interrogative'. Moreover, although most morphemes, including verb roots, do not occur as separate words, hyphens will not be written, and vertical bars will not be used in these analyses.

6. ORGANIZATION OF THE DESCRIPTION

The theoretical approach taken here is that outlined in Chafe (1970).

6.1.

It is assumed that the simplest sentence in any language consists of a verb only. Other sentences, up to the most complex, are in effect expansions of the verb through the addition of nominal expressions, or through the addition of adverbial limitations or expansions of the basic meaning of the verb root. There are thus three categories of sentence-building elements: verbs, nouns, and modifiers.

Each of these categories is subdivided by various selectional restrictions inherent in the meaning of any given root: restrictions on the type of constructions in which the root can occur. For example, the English verb *talk* is selectionally restricted to occur with only human or anthropomorphized subjects, and normally does not take objects, while its semantically similar counterpart *say* must normally have an object that is in turn a sentence of some sort.

In addition, each of the classes of sentence-building elements has a set of possible inflectional units, which may optionally occur with it in any given sentence. These mark semantic variables such as tense, aspect, and number.

6.2.

The description of a language, therefore, proceeds most logically by first enumerating the selectional restrictions on verbs and then discussing verbal inflectional units. From there, it moves to similar discussion of nouns: first selectional, and then inflectional categories. Verbs are necessarily described first, for it is frequently the case that the choice of some verbal categories limits the choice of nominal categories in the sentence; but noun features never determine verb features. For full justification of this claim, see Chafe (1970:97ff.).

6.3.

The description will then move to explanation of how the enumerated elements and categories combine in the particular language under discussion, and what the phonological representations of the various categories might be.

6.4.

In such a description, the first stage (section 6.2.) is called the description of semantic structures, and the second (section 6.3.) is the description of the transformations that the semantic structures undergo in a particular language. This is followed by descriptions of linearization (statement of the sequences in which morphemes occur) and symbolization (the forms of the morphemes).

6.5.

No place was reserved for the modifier class of section 6.1. in the scheme outlined in sections 6.2.-3., because all those modifiers can ultimately be shown to be semantically either inflectional or verbal elements. However, proof of this is best left to discussion of linguistic theory, and for the purpose of describing a specific language and its structure, there will be many shortcuts. One section of this description will be devoted to various kinds of modifiers, without any attempt to take all of them back to their verbal origins.

Furthermore, there will be very few descriptions of those inflectional and selectional elements that have only covert effects on the surface structure, that is, that prevent rather than generate certain sentences or combinations of sentences. Instead, only those units that are reflected in specific Wichita morphemes will be enumerated. A major exception to this policy is the initial description of selectional restrictions on verbs, because these verb classes are so important for understanding the rest of the grammar.

6.6.

The outline of this description is as follows: section 7 is devoted to description of the semantic selectional and inflectional possibilities for verbs; section 8 accomplishes the same task for nouns. Section 9 describes modifiers of both nouns and verbs.

Section 10 is then devoted to the topic of derivation, or how roots that are selectionally of one class or type can be changed or modified to fit a different class.

In a formal grammar section 11 would begin the description of constructions and transformational rules needed to establish semantic structures for sentences and to convert these semantic structures into surface structures. Since such rules are largely superfluous in an informal description, section 11 describes Wichita surface structures, using word and morpheme order as the organizational criterion for the section. Section 11.1. describes the sequences of words in sentences and of morphemes in words; section 11.2. describes a selected set of surface structure constructions, such as subject and object number marking, and marking of possession. Readers who are accustomed to item-and-arrangement grammars will find section 11 the most familiar part of this sketch, while those who are interested in what is obligatory and optional in the expression of ideas in Wichita will be more enlightened by sections 7-10. The combination of these two approaches should give everyone an idea of how meanings are symbolized by speakers of Wichita. Considerations of Wichita structure from other theoretical perspectives can be found in Rood (1973, 1981, and 1989).

SEMANTIC STRUCTURE

7. THE VERB

7.1.

Wichita verbs are subdivided into at least four large classes on the basis of selectional restrictions. These classes are defined by the number and type of nominal expressions that occur with them. There are no surface morphemes to indicate the class to which a given verb belongs; nevertheless, syntactic restrictions on the construction possibilities indicate this information clearly.

7.1.1.

Typologically, Wichita has a kind of split-ergative case structure. Third-person number marking and noun incorporation distinguish ergative (subject of transitive verbs) from absolutive (everything else) in a rather pure fashion, as do all the noun phrases in Basque and many Australian languages. First and second person, in contrast, represent a split intransitive system, like that of Siouan languages: some intransitive verbs require for their subjects pronominal forms identical with the subject forms of transitive verbs, while other intransitive subjects match the object forms of transitive verbs.

Third-person pronominal forms exemplify a different version of the split-intransitive type. If any non–third-person pronoun is used, third person is unmarked (represented by Ø). Otherwise, the forms distinguish participants that are "in focus" from those that are "out of focus" (see 8.2.4.), but this contrast is suspended for those intransitive verbs that take transitive object pronouns for first and second persons. In these cases, only out-of-focus marking occurs.

Four category names from traditional grammar will be used here to label the relationships between nouns or pronouns and verbs. The names, and their semantic definitions, are as follows:

The agent is the person or thing which acts or controls the action. It is the single nominal with verbs like *go* and *dance*, and the active participant with verbs like *hit* or *eat*.

The patient is any nonactive or noncontrolling participant in an event. It is the only nominal found with a verb like *fall* or *be hungry*. (One is not actively hungry; one only suffers hunger.) With verbs like *hit* or *eat*, it is the suffering participant.

The subject is either the same as the agent, if there is one, or the only nominal in verb constructions that permit only one. Some subjects are therefore patients, while others are agents.

The object is the patient of a verb that has both an agent and a patient.

These four terms are used in two different ways in the following discussion (see table 3). If the terms are not qualified, the definitions just given will apply; in this case, the terms refer to the relationship between a predicate and its argument or arguments, that is, between a verb and the nouns or pronouns that occur with it.

But if the terms are used with "third person" and "non-third person," they are the names of particular morphemes. "Non–third-person subjects" are the forms that represent semantic agents, or the patients of Class 1 verbs (see next section); "non–third person objects" are the forms used for objects, and for the patients of class 2 verbs (see below). "Third-person agents" are the agents of transitive verbs, that is, the forms that would be in the ergative case in a straightforwardly ergative language. "Third-person patients" are everything else: subjects of intransitive verbs, and objects of transitive verbs.

In the examples here usually only "in focus" third persons are used, and the morpheme is glossed 'third-person subject'.

Table 3. Noun-Verb Relationships

Wichita Class	Verb Semantic type	Noun or Pronoun Semantic structure	Wichita third person number marking	Wichita non-third person	Wichita third person pronouns
1	active ('come', 'sing')	agent	patient	subject	+focus *or* -focus
	stative ('be dirty')	patient	patient	subject	+focus *or* -focus
2	stative ('be hungry')	patient	patient	object	-focus
	process ('fall')	patient	patient	object	-focus
3	transitive ('see')	agent and patient	agent and patient	subject and object	+focus *or* -focus subject; object unmarked[a]
4	process impersonal ('rain')	—	—	—	+focus
	stative impersonal ('be a creek')	—	—	—	+focus *or* -focus (see examples 50 and 51)

[a]If a non–third-person pronoun is present, third person is always represented by zero.

7.1.2.

The verb classes are as follows:

Class 1 includes action verbs, which have agents in the semantic structure. In the surface structure, first- and second-person pronouns are in the subjective case, while third-person forms may be either in or out of focus, and third-person number marking follows the rules for patient inflections. Examples are *u...ʔa* 'come', *hisha* 'go', *kira·h* 'sing', and *wa·waʔa* 'dine'. Many semantically stative verbs belong to this class in Wichita, too: verbs like *tac ʔi* 'be big', *he·c ʔi* 'be fat', *kʷha·c ʔi* 'be red', and *neʔestha·r ʔi* 'be dirty'.

Class 2 contains process verbs and those stative verbs not included in class 1. In the semantic structure, these verbs have only patients; in the surface structure, first- and second-person pronouns take their objective case forms, while third-person pronouns are always out of focus, and third-person number marking utilizes the forms for patient inflections. Examples are *u...weʔeha* 'fall', *ʔac* 'be cold', and *hiya·* 'be hungry'.

Class 3, transitive verbs, have both an agent and a patient in the semantic structure. Here the surface structure forms for first- and second-person pronouns are subjective for agents, and objective for patients. Third-person subjects may be either in or out of focus if both subject and object are third person; anything else (any third person with a first or second person in another role, or a third-person object) is unmarked. Third-person number forms are agent for subjects, patient for objects. Examples of such verbs include *ʔi:s* 'see', *kaʔac* 'eat', and *irasi* 'find'.

Class 4 contains only impersonal verbs. These verbs have no nominal in the semantic structure, and permit only third-person singular inflections in the surface structure. They include *a...hiriʔa* 'rain', *a...ʔi:ʔa* 'snow', *wa·wkʷic* 'heat lightning', *reʔerha* 'be a village or encampment', and *he·ha* 'be a creek' among many others. Most of these verbs take in-focus subjects, but at least one, *hanthiri* 'be daylight' requires an out-of-focus subject (see examples 50-51). Table 3 summarizes the facts about theoretical and Wichita verb classes and nominals.

7.1.3.

There may be a fifth class, beneficiary verbs, which have a beneficiary nominal in construction with them instead of or in addition to agents and patients. The only candidate for membership in this class and no other is the verb *uc...ʔi* 'be in a state' (used in expressions such as 'How are you?'); and even this is ambiguous, for the *uc* could be considered simply a preverb of this verb rather than the marker of a beneficiary, and the verb then placed in class 1. The analysis of other beneficiaries could take one of two directions: they could be considered subclasses of each of the classes already named, or they could be considered a fifth class, subdivided according to the criteria used to separate classes 1-4. The analysis that makes 'beneficiary' a selectional feature for verbs of classes 1-3 appears to be the more useful.

Class 1 verbs that require a beneficiary in addition to an agent include *uc...tate·tu* 'help'.

Class 2 verbs that require a beneficiary in addition to a patient are illustrated by *uR...ʔi* 'own, possess'.

Class 3 verbs that require a beneficiary in addition to an agent and a patient include *uc...ʔih* 'give (as a gift)'.

Verbs such as *(uc)...iʔahi* 'hold, keep' and many others permit an optional beneficiary, and the *uc* occurs only if such a beneficiary is expressed.

7.2.

The inflectional categories in Wichita verbs include mood, evidential, tense, and aspect. A slightly different version of sections 7.2.1.-7.2.4. appears in Rood (1975a).

7.2.1.

Mood has two members, subordinate and nonsubordinate or independent. The subordinate verbs occur only in sentences that also contain an independent verb.

7.2.2.

Evidential describes a statement by the speaker about the source of information: the quotative implies that the information was heard from someone else; the nonquotative means the speaker saw the event happen personally. This distinction occurs with (and is obligatory with) the aorist (past), the perfect, and the future tense forms; statements using other tenses are not marked obligatorily for evidential.

7.2.3.

Tense and aspect cooccur in a rather complex, overlapping set of categories, illustrated for independent verbs in figure 4.

7.2.3.1.

Figure 4 illustrates the tense and aspect structure as if it were a set of choices that Wichita speakers must make as they select the markers they will use for independent verbs in a given sentence. See figure 5 and section 7.2.3.2. for specific forms that illustrate the discussion.

First, speakers must decide whether to express a personal opinion about the statement, or simply to report the facts impersonally (note that this is not the evidential choice; that has to do with source of information, not opinion). If they elect to be impersonal, they must then determine whether or not time is important to their statement. Depending on this choice, they will continue along either the time or the -time branch of the tree.

If time does not matter, that is, if the -time branch is followed, speakers must nevertheless select an aspect; but they can elect to use an "unmarked" aspect if they wish. ("Unmarked" refers to the normal, ordinary state of affairs, the one that needs no special comment from the speaker.) If, however, they select a marked aspect, speakers have four choices here:

Perfective indicates that the act is completed and finished. If this aspect is chosen, evidence for the statement must also be given.

Intentive indicates that the subject plans or planned to carry out the act.

Habitual indicates that the act is habitual for the subject of the sentence ('he smokes', rather than 'he is smoking'.)

Durative indicates that the verb describes an activity that is coextensive with something else. English translations of this aspect usually contain phrases such as 'and all the time' or 'and at the same time' or 'meanwhile'.

The [-time] choice is analyzed as implying the absence of any time reference, rather than as present time, because this fits the facts more closely. The aspect clearly takes precedence in meaning over the time reference, and English translations vary in tense for individual forms. Perfective translates as English past; intentive usually translates as the "going to" future; habitual and durative regularly translate as present tense, with adverbs like 'always' or 'meanwhile' to support the aspectual interpretation. The unmarked timeless aspect is a simple indicative, sometimes translated as past, sometimes as present progressive.

Going back up the tree, if speakers decide that time is indeed important to their statements, they must choose between past and future time. Again, they choose either a marked or an unmarked aspect. With future time, the marked aspect will be either imperfective (indicating that there is no information about the state of the act with respect to completion) or habitual. With past time, they may choose either of these, or intentive. Moreover, bringing time into the picture obliges speakers to add something about their source of information, too. Observe that the durative aspect is not compatible with a time reference and that intentive cannot occur together with future time markers.

If, on the other side of the tree, the speakers first elect to offer personal opinions about the event together with their reports, they must then decide whether just to show surprise (by choosing the exclamatory tense marker), or whether to express an attitude about the subject of the verb. They may inflectionally state one of four such attitudes: that they are commanding the subject to do something; that they are wishing that the subject would do something; that they are stating an obligation or duty of the subject to do something; or that they are reporting some sort of plan on the subject's part.

Once they have chosen one of these opinions to offer, the rest of their choices are determined by the facts. If they are commanding, they can do it by giving instructions (directions, as in dictating a recipe or describing how something is made), or by giving direct orders. Instructions are implied if the directive tense markers are used; commands, if the imperative is chosen. If the imperative is used, it can be marked for future time (implying that the command need not be carried out right away), and if the future imperative is used, speakers can indicate whether the command is to

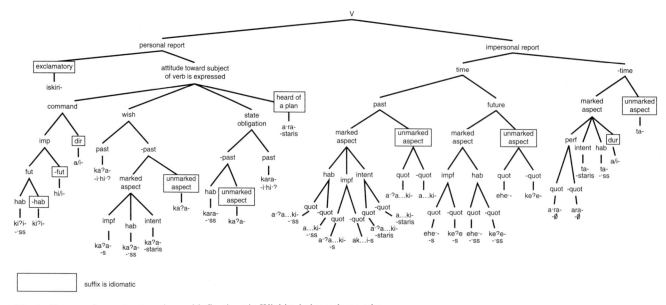

Fig. 4. Tense and aspect categories and inflections in Wichita independent verbs.

be followed once or habitually, by choosing or not choosing the habitual aspect.

When speakers decide to express a wish about the subject of the sentence or to state that the subject has a duty or obligation, they may again let time enter the picture if it is already too late. That is, they may inflect the verb for past if they are commenting on something that might have happened but in fact did not. The resulting English translation would be 'I wish she had' or 'he should have'.

Alternatively, they can assume that it is not too late and select either a marked or an unmarked aspect for the action. The only marked aspect for obligation or duty is habitual; for wishes, habitual, imperfective, and intentive are all possible.

7.2.3.2.

At the bottom of each branch of the tree in figure 4 is a prefix and a suffix for the completed verb form, the combination of which will express the sum of any meanings selected while passing through the tree. Each of these prefixes and suffixes can be given a mnemonic label, as has been done in the heads of the rows and columns of figure 5, where the possible combinations of (independent mood) prefixes and suffixes are given typical translations with the verb 'cook'.

Note that while both a prefix and a suffix must be used, and while the suffix labels are all aspectual in nature, not all the prefix labels are tenses. Note further that what has been called the unmarked aspect in the description of the semantics of the system is idiomatically sometimes imperfective, sometimes perfective,

depending on the prefix involved.

The |t| of the indicative morpheme changes to |r| for a question, and to |ʔ| for a negative statement, and the |a| of the aorist is dropped in questions.

7.2.3.3.

For the subordinate verbs, the choices are far fewer. Only two suffixes, perfective *h* and imperfective *skih*, are possible, and only five prefixes can occur:

|hi~i| 'conditional' (translated 'if' or 'when'). Note that this prefix is the same as that for imperative with independent verbs; only the mood marker distinguishes these forms.

|ha...ki| 'subjunctive'. This |ki| is the same as that of the aorist. The form is used where English would use 'would' or 'might' and often where English would use an infinitive, with or without *for* ('for him to go').

|na| 'general participle'. Translations are numerous, but all are nominalizations of sentences or temporally subordinate clauses, such as 'the one who...', '...ing', 'while ...ing', 'after ...ed', etc.

|ki| 'past participle'. This |ki| is also the same as the aorist and subjunctive |ki|. Translations are past tense forms of nominalized sentences. This form is the most frequently used one in personal names: *ki·cʔakʷakhariʔa·w* 'he who spoke to them' is an example.

|kara| 'debetative participle'. A subordinate sentence expressing the speaker's opinion that the subject of the sentence should or was supposed to do something. Translations usually include 'the time...was supposed to...' but can also be 'the one who was supposed to...'.

Fig. 5. Synopsis of tense aspect possibilities for a Wichita verb. Note that the actual prefixes and suffixes used with the verb, *ʔarasi* 'cook', do not correspond precisely with the underlying forms given at the row and column headings. The explanation lies in the morphophonemics of the verb for the prefixes and in the fact that this verb takes a causative suffix before aspect suffixes.

PREFIXES	SUFFIXES				
	perfective *(-∅)*	imperfective *(-s)*	intentive *(-staris)*	habitual *(-·ss)*	too late *(-i·hi·ʔ)*
aorist *a...ki-*	'She cooked it.' *ákaʔárasiki*	'She was cooking it.' *ákaʔarásis*	'She was going to cook it, but didn't.' *ákaʔarásistaris*	'She always used to cook it.' *ákaʔarásiki·ss*	_____
aorist quotative *a·ʔa...ki-*	'I heard that she cooked it.' *á·kaʔárasiki*	'I heard she was cooking it.' *á·kaʔarásis*	'I heard she was going to cook it.' *á·kaʔarásistaris*	'I heard she always used to cook it.' *á·kaʔarásiki·ss*	_____
future *ke·ʔe-*	'She will cook it.' *ke·ʔárasiki*	'She'll be cooking it.' *ke·ʔárasis*	_____	'It will be her job to cook it every time.' *ke·ʔárasiki·ss*	_____
future quotative *ehe·-*	'I heard she'll cook it.' *ehè·ʔárasiki*	'I heard she'll be cooking it.' *ehè·ʔárasis*	_____	'I heard it will be her job to cook it every time.' *ehè·ʔárasiki·ss*	_____
perfect *ara-*	'She's cooked it.' *araʔarásiki*	_____	_____	_____	_____
perfect quotative *a·ra-*	'I heard she's cooked it.' *á·raʔarásiki*	_____	'I heard she is going to cook it.' *á·raʔarásistaris*	_____	_____
indicative *ta/ti-*	_____	'She's cooking it; She's cooked it.' *taʔarásis*	'She's going to cook it.' *taʔarásistaris*	'She is always the one who cooks it.' *taʔarásiki·ss*	_____
exclamatory *iskiri-*	_____	'Look! She's cooking it!' *iskirá·rásis*	_____	_____	_____
durative *a/i-*	_____	'And all the time, she was cooking it.' *aʔarásis*	_____	_____	_____
directive *a/i-*	_____	'(And then) one cooks it.' *aʔarásis*	_____	_____	_____
imperative *hi/i-*	'Let her cook it.' *haʔarásiki*	_____	_____	_____	_____
future imperative *ki·ʔi-*	'And then you must let her cook it.' *ki·ʔarásiki*	_____	_____	'Let her always be the one to cook it.' *ki·ʔárasiki·ss*	_____
optative *ka·ʔa-*	'I wish she would cook it.' *ke·ʔeʔárasiki*	'I wish she would be cooking it.' *ke·ʔeʔárasis*	'I wish she'd plan to cook it.' *ke·ʔeʔárasistaris*	'I wish she'd always cook it.' *ke·ʔeʔárasiki·ss*	'I wish she had cooked it.' *ke·ʔeʔárasiki·hi·ʔ*
debetative *kara-*	_____	'She ought to cook it.' *kàraʔarásis*	_____	'She ought always to be the one to cook it.' *kàraʔarásiki·ss*	'She should have cooked it.' *karaʔárasiki·hi·ʔ*

591

7.2.4.

Other moods and aspects are expressed periphrastically in Wichita, much as they are in English. Ability, for instance, involves the use of a verb equivalent to 'to be able' or 'can':

(20) |hiʔincóꞏwisirʔi| 'be able'. (analysis uncertain except for *hiʔir* 'patient is animate'.)

(21) *cháh tachiʔincóꞏwisirʔi hatákicʔárasikih* 'I can still cook my own (food).' (*chah* 'still'; *ta* 'indicative' + *t* 'first-person subject' + *hiʔincóꞏwisirʔi* 'be able'; *ha...ki* 'subjunctive' + *t* 'first-person subject' + *a* 'reflexive' + *uc* 'dative' + *ʔarasi* 'cook' + *iki* 'causative' + *h* 'subordinate mood'.)

Similarly, possibility (English 'might') is expressed by the use of adverbs and the future:

(22) *eꞏkʷ hóʔos keʔetiꞏch* 'I might do it.' (*eꞏkʷ* 'maybe'; *hóʔos* 'soon'; *keʔe* 'future' + *t* 'first-person subject' + *uc* 'preverb' + *hi* 'do'.)

English *must* has varying translations, depending on which particular meaning it has in a given instance. When it implies a very firm but nevertheless polite imperative, Wichita uses the future imperative:

(23) *kiʔiskʷ* 'You must go.' (*kiʔi* 'future imperative' + *s* 'second-person subject' + *wa* 'go, perfective'.)

When *must* implies inevitability for the event, the adverb *teꞏʔ* 'anyway' is used. A typical sentence might be translated 'I'll have to do it anyway' or 'I must do it.' Another meaning of *must*, namely, that the sentence is the result of a deduction, will be translated with the adverb *wérah* 'maybe; probably; I guess':

(24) *kʔítaꞏks wérah hasʔaʔʔákicitàꞏheʔèh* 'Coyote must have had his knife with him'. (*kʔítaꞏks* 'Coyote'; *wérah* 'maybe; must'; *hasʔa* 'this is a story' + *aʔ* 'quotative' + *á* 'third-person subject and reflexive object' + *ki* 'aorist' + *uc* 'dative' + *i* 'extra vowel' (see section 12.1.10.)' + *taꞏha* 'knife' + *iʔahi* 'hold'.)

8. The Noun

8.1.

Nouns have selectional restrictions that are like the arbitrary gender-class assignments in, for example, Latin and German, in that they are inherent in the nouns and determine certain surface structure configurations of morphemes. However, in Wichita the assignment of these restrictions appears to correlate fairly consistently with physically observable facts about the object named by the noun.

The hierarchy of semantic selectional features in figure 6 summarizes the system. Each of the features named is of importance but, as in figure 4, the surface structure representation is of a whole branch of the tree, rather than of a single unit.

The first division of nouns is into those that can be counted and those that cannot. In general, this correlates with the possibility for plural marking: +count nouns can be marked for dual or plural; if not so marked, they are assumed to be singular. -Count nouns, on the other hand, cannot be pluralized.

8.1.1.

Those -count nouns that are also liquids are marked as such by a special morpheme, *kir*, that occurs in every sentence in which such a noun is a patient, such as in example 25:

(25) *taꞏtíꞏsaꞏskinnaʔas* 'He is bringing (liquid) medicine' (*ta* 'indicative' + *i* 'third-person subject' + *aꞏ* 'preverb' + *tiꞏsaꞏs* 'medicine' + *kir* 'liquid' + *ri* 'portative (changes motion verb to carry verb)' + *ʔa* 'come' + *s* 'imperfective'.)

8.1.2.

Those -count nouns that are not liquid are not otherwise marked in Wichita. This feature is labeled dry mass. Forms such as *yeꞏc* 'fire', *kirʔiꞏc* 'bread', and *kaꞏhiꞏc* 'salt' are included in this category.

(26) *tàꞏyèꞏcsàʔas* 'He is bringing fire.' (*ta* + *i* + *aꞏ* + *yeꞏc* 'fire' + *ri* + *ʔa* + *s*; unglossed morphemes as in 25.)

(27) *taꞏkáꞏhiꞏcsaʔas* 'He is bringing salt.' (Analysis as in 26, with *kaꞏhiꞏc* 'salt' in place of *yeꞏc*.)

8.1.3.

Wichita [+count] nouns are divided into those that are collectives and those that are not. The collective category includes most materials, such as wood; anything that normally comes in pieces, such as meat, corn, or flour; and any containers such as pots, bowls, or sacks when they are filled with pieces of something. However, it is not always clear to a speaker of English just why one noun should be in this category, while another fits into the dry mass classification. For example, salt is a noncountable dry mass, while flour, which is also powdery, is collective. Moreover, it is not always clear what the singular form of a collective will

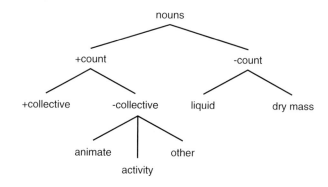

Fig. 6. Semantic selectional features that subclassify Wichita nouns.

mean. The singular of 'corn' means 'one ear of corn', while the singular of 'wood' means 'one piece of chopped wood'; and the singular of 'flour' is meaningless. Observe the behavior of the various nouns in 28-32, and the restrictions on referents that result from various verb markings in 33-36:

(28) *ta·rássara²as* 'He is bringing meat.' (This is the normal response when speakers are asked to translate the English sentence.) (*ta + i + a·* as in 25 + *²aras* 'meat' + *ra* 'collective' + *ri* + *²a + s* as in 25.)

(29) *ta·rássa²as* 'He is bringing (one piece of) meat.' (This is the semantically less probable form and is sometimes given reluctantly.) (The analysis is the same as 28, without *ra*.)

(30) *ta·ya·rhára²as* 'He is bringing wood.' (*ta + i + a· + ya·k* 'wood' + *ra* 'collective' + *ri* + *²a + s* as in 25.)

(31) *ta·ya·rhá²as* 'He is bringing one piece of chopped wood.' (This form is declared to "sound funny" by some speakers.) Analysis same as 30, but without *ra* 'collective'.)

(32) *ta·tí·sa·ssara²as* 'He is bringing medicine.' (Analysis same as 25, but with *ra* 'collective' in place of *kir* 'liquid'.)

(33) *is²ari·ki* 'Set it down' (refers to something countable, such as a chair). (*i* 'imperative' + *s* 'second-person subject' + *²arik* 'stand' + *iki* 'causative'.)

(34) *issi²ari·ki* 'Set it down' (refers to a sack or pot with something in it, or to wood, corn, etc.). (Same as 33, but with *ru* 'collective' before the portative.)

(35) *is²ak²ari·ki* 'Set it down' (refers to the plural of whatever was possible in 33). (Analysis same as 34, but here *²ak* 'noncollective plural' replaces *ru* 'collective'.)

(36) *issi²ak²ari·ki* 'Set them down' (refers to sacks, pots, or chairs). (Combines the *²ak* of 35 and the *ru* of 34 in a single form.)

It is easy to understand the distinction between 'collective' and plural through contrasting 34 with 35, but it is not clear why 36 should be equally applicable to both collective and noncollective nouns.

8.1.4.

Some of the noncollective nominals are also marked for other selectional restrictions. In particular, with some verbs, animate nouns (including first and second-person pronouns) require special treatment when they are patients in the sentence. Activities are also a separate category (see section 8.1.5.).

Whenever there is an animate patient or object of certain verbs such as *u...ra²a* 'bring' or *irasi* 'find', the morpheme |hi²ri| (/hir²/, /hi²r/, /hir²i/) also occurs with the verb. The use of this morpheme is not predictable by rule and must be specified for each verb in the language that requires it. Note that the regular translation of 'bring' with an animate patient is 'lead'.

(37) *tí·rass* 'He found it (inanimate).' (*ta* 'indicative' + *i* 'third-person subject' + *irasi* 'find' + *s* 'imperfective'.)

(38) *tihir²í·rass* 'he found it (animate).' (Analysis same as 37, with *hir²i* 'patient is animate' added before the root.)

(39) *ta·ra·²as* 'He is bringing it (inanimate, noncollective).' (*ta + i + a· + ri + ²a + s*, glosses as in 25.)

(40) *ta·hi²nna²as* 'He is leading it (bringing animate object).' (Analysis same as 39, with *hi²r* before the portative.)

(41) *he·hir²í·ras* 'Let him find you.' (*hi* 'imperative' + *a·* 'second-person object' + *hir²i* + *irasi* as in 38.)

(42) *tàkihìr²í·rass* 'He found me.' (Same as 38 except that *ki* 'first-person object' replaces *i* 'third-person subject'.)

8.1.5.

One other subcategory of nouns contains those that are names of activities. Naturally enough, most of these are nominalized verbs (section 10.3.). Like *hi²ri* 'patient is animate', the morpheme in question here, *wakhahr*, means 'patient is an activity'. It may occur without an overt noun, in which case it is often translated into English as 'way (of doing)' or 'what is going on'; or it may simply be an agreement feature in the verb, reflecting the active nature of the patient noun. Examples 43-46 demonstrate the use of this morpheme alone. Comparison of 43 with 44 shows that the activities are countable; 45 contrasted with 46 shows the change in meaning when *wakhahr* is left out. In 47, *wakhahr* agrees with an action noun but is left out when the noun is not an action.

(43) *né·²ah né·wakhárikih* 'devil' (literally, 'one who has bad ways'). (*né·²ah* 'bad'; *na* 'participle' + *uR* 'possessive' + *wakhahr* 'patient is an activity' + *²iki* 'be plural' + *h* 'subordinate mood'. Possession is discussed in 12.2.1.)

(44) *wi·c withího·h té·wakha·r²i* 'A man has a different way.' (*wi·c* 'man'; *witího·h* 'different'; *ta* 'indicative' + *i* 'third-person subject' + *uR* 'possessive' + *wakhahr* + *²i* 'be singular'.).

(45) *to·kha·r²í·ckh* 'It's the end (of an action).' (*ta* 'indicative' + *i* 'third-person subject' + *wakhahr* + *²í·ckha* 'be the end'.)

(46) *ti²í·ckh* 'It's the end (of something like a rope or ribbon)'. (Analysis same as 45, but here without *wakhahr*.)

(47) (a) *wickhé²es tikínni·ciri²í:hiris²i* 'It's a funny car'. (*wickhé²es* 'funny'; *ta* 'indicative' + *i* 'third-person subject' + *kínni·ciri²í:hiris* 'car' (see 72) + *²i* 'be'.)

593

(b) *wickhé?es to·kha·r?i na·?áskih* 'It's funny he came.' (*wickhé?es* 'funny'; *ta* 'indicative' + *i* 'third-person subject' + *wakhahr* + *?i* 'be'; *na* 'participle' + *a* 'preverb' + *?a* 'come' + *skih* 'subordinate imperfective'.)

8.1.6.
Countable nouns that are neither animate nor activities, such as chairs, apples, rocks, or body parts, do not require any semantic class agreement morphemes in the surface grammar of Wichita.

8.2.
The inflectional categories of nouns include case, number, person, focus, and definiteness.

8.2.1.
The important case categories in the semantic structure are agent, patient, and dative. These identify the nominal relationships with respect to verbs (section 7.1.). The surface reflections of these relationships are complex and differ from one type of nominal to another. See the sections on subject and object order (section 11.1.5.), person reference (section 11.1.11., nos. 4 and 6), possession (section 11.2.1.) and number marking (section 11.2.2.) for discussion of some of this complexity.

8.2.2.
Wichita nominals (if selectionally marked [+count]) can be inflected for singular, dual, or plural. In the case of collective nouns, plural is the normal condition, and dual probably never occurs; for other countable nouns, singular is the unmarked condition, and either dual or plural can occur with them. The surface details of number marking are described in section 11.2.2.

8.2.3.
Any animate Wichita noun can be inflected for person. The choices are first, second, inclusive, and third. The nonsingular first person is automatically exclusive, that is, it implies 'he or they and I', while the inclusive (which is always nonsingular) means 'you and I'. Non–third-person nouns with additional lexical information are of course rare, but examples include things such as first-person marking in 'chief' in an expression that is translated 'I, the chief,' and in 'women' in the phrase translated 'some of us older women'. The surface structure marks person in the verb (cf. section 11.1.11., nos. 4 and 6, and also example 77).

8.2.4.
Third-person nominals are marked in Wichita for position relative to the focus of attention. +Focus is the normal condition; -focus is used (a) when a subordinate character in a story is the subject of the verb; (b) to indicate that a named noun is patient rather than agent in a given sentence, or to mark the patient of a class 2 verb (see section 7.1.2.); and (c) to mark the agent of an active verb as indefinite or plural. The English equivalent to (b) with transitive verbs is often a passive construction; (c) is parallel to an impersonal or indefinite 'they' in some constructions, such as 'somebody forgot their coat' or 'they speak French in Algeria'. In this sketch, generally only examples of +focus marking are used, and the morpheme is referred to as 'third-person subject'.

8.2.5.
Third-person nouns in Wichita may be inflectionally marked definite; if they are not so marked, they are presumed to be indefinite. See section 11.2.3. for further discussion.

9. MODIFIERS
Modifiers really have no place in the description of the semantic structure of languages; they are ultimately all verbal or inflectional elements of some kind. Nevertheless, the picture of Wichita structure is considerably simplified if modifications of semantic structure are allowed, at least to the extent discussed below.

9.1.
Noun modifiers are best subdivided into three groups: quantifiers, demonstratives, and adjectives.

The quantifiers are much the same as in other languages. In the surface structure, they are either preposed or postposed to the noun they modify. Examples are *assé·hah* 'all', *ta·w?ic* 'few', and the numbers.

There are two demonstratives: *ti?ih* 'this' and *ha·rí·h* 'that'. They may occur with or without the definite inflection, and they may either precede or follow the noun they modify.

Surface structure adjectives are probably always stative verbs in the semantic structure; but in Wichita, a few descriptive adjectives such as 'big' and 'old' have surface forms different from the equivalent predicatives. It is almost as if the descriptive forms were inflections on noun stems, or the second elements of noun compounds, rather than adjectival modifiers:

(48) *akháriwa·c* or *akha·r?a niwa·c* 'big house'. (*akhahr* 'house'; *Riwa·c* 'big'. Final *-?a* is a noun suffix only used on certain roots when these are pronounced slowly or in isolation.)

(49) *akha·r?a tac ti·?i* or *tac ti·?i akha·r?a* 'The house is big.' (*tac* 'big'; *ta* 'indicative' + *i* 'third-person subject' + *i* 'extra vowel' (section 11.1.11., item 11) + *?i* 'be'.

In the examples, 48 shows the adjective 'big' (which is the word that the Wichita speaker will give first when asked to translate 'big', namely, *niwa·c*), while 49 shows the stative verb construction 'is big', *tac ti·?i*. Because of the lexical changes involved here, it is unlikely that either of these constructions can be derived from the other except at the semantic level; therefore, it seems best to recognize an adjective classification for morphemes such as *Riwa·c* 'big', *Rikic* 'little', *riya·s* 'old', and for the colors (such as *khac* 'white' and *kʷha·c* 'red'). These will be referred to as "true adjectives" below.

There are no Wichita constructions exclusively parallel to what are usually called relative clauses in other languages. For substitutes, see section 10.3.

9.2.

Verbal modifiers are traditionally separated into expressions of time, manner, and place. In Wichita, most time and manner modifications are formally subordinate sentences.

(50) *hi·hánthirih* 'tomorrow' (literally 'when it is day'.) (*hi·* 'conditional third-person out-of-focus subject' + *hanthiri* 'be daylight' + *h* 'subordinate mood'.)

(51) *ti?ikhánthiris?ih* 'yesterday' (literally 'this which was day.') (*ti?* 'this' + *i* 'out-of-focus subject' + *ki* 'aorist participle' *hanthiri* 'be daylight' + *s* 'imperfective' + *?i* 'stative' + *h* 'subordinate mood'.)

(52) *chih á·ki?í·rakháris?í·h* 'suddenly' (literally something like 'it was continuing in the state of happening.') (*chih* 'continues'; *a·* 'third-person subject quotative' + *ki* 'aorist' + *?í·rakhari* 'happen' + *s* 'imperfective' + *?i* 'be' or 'stative' + *h* 'subordinate'. Analysis is tentative.)

There is thus no need to regard these as anything but verbal constructions at any level. But a few time modifications, some manner modifications, and most place modifications are best treated as separate kinds of elements.

9.2.1.

The few particles that must be termed "time adverbs" are structurally proclitics some of the time, midway between words and prefixes. The rest of the time they are separate words, postposed to the verb they modify. They are accepted as separate words by speakers, but when they are preposed to the verb form, they condition a change in the phonology of the form through the insertion of an "extra" vowel after the preverb. Note what happens to 'I went' in example 53, depending on whether *hir?í·s* 'first' precedes or follows it.

(53) *hir?í·s taci·his* or *tachis hir?í·s* 'I went first.' (*hir?í·s* 'first'; *ta* 'indicative + *t* 'first-person subject' + *i* 'extra vowel' (in the first variant) + *hisha* 'go'.)

Some other morphemes that parallel the behavior of *hir?í·s* are *ti·?* 'at once', *has* 'permanently', *wah* 'already', *chah* 'still', and *chih* 'continues'.

9.2.2.

Instrumentals may be expressed in one of two ways: either they are independent nouns, in which case the suffix *Rá·hir?* identifies them; or they are body parts, in which case they are marked as instrumental by a characteristic location in the verb complex.

(54) *kirikir?i·sá·hir?* 'in Wichita (the language)'.

(55) *harhiwi·cá·hir? assi?ari·s* 'Put it aside in a bowl.' (*harhiwi·c* 'bowl' + *Rá·hir?* 'instrumental'; *a* 'directive tense' + *s* 'second-person subject' + *ru* 'collective' + *?ariki* 'stand' + *is* 'causative imperfective'. More literally, the form means 'using a bowl, cause it (collective) to stand'.)

(56) *tac?ickhité·shas* 'I peeked over the edge.' (*ta* 'indicative' + *t* 'first-person subject' + *?icka* 'face, instrumental' + *hita* 'edge' + *hishas* 'go past'. Literally, then, the form means 'using the face, I went over the edge'.)

9.2.3.

Another kind of adverbial, having the form of bound morphemes, occurs in two subtypes. One type has only one attested representative: *hí·riks* 'repeatedly', which occurs near the end of the verb form (section 11.1.11., no. 26).

The other type occurs toward the end of the first part of the verb (section 11.1.11., no. 15). Eight representatives have been identified: *Re·?í·R* 'first'; *i·se?í·R* 'for a while', *?ici* 'repeatedly', *?i·r?í·R* 'quickly', *?íyarhe·R* 'although', *?í·R* 'accidentally', *re·R* 'this is new information for you', and *i?i·R...hrih* 'this is a polite suggestion'. In the last example, the second element is the same as the verbal locative suffix.

9.2.4.

The independent particles that have adverbial functions include those like *akʷithah* 'above' and *ha·w?ic* 'below', which are locative, and those like *ísa?* 'thus, in this way', which are manner adverbials. Unlike the time particles described above, these do not change the phonology of the following verb, but like them, they may either precede or follow the forms with which they occur.

9.2.5.

Locative adverbs may be: demonstratives (*ti?rih* 'here', *harah* 'there', *hí·raka·h* 'way off'); nouns marked by the suffix *kiyah* (*?ika·kíyah* 'where the rock is'); verb particles marked by the suffix *hrih* (*niya·hkʷírih* 'where the tree is'); bound morphemes in the verb, situated just before the root (no. 22 of section 11.1.11.) (*kita* 'on top', etc.); or a combination of these.

(57) *?ika·kíyah tìkìte?ècaki* 'He is sitting on top of the rock.' (*?ika·* 'rock' + *kiyah* 'locative'; *ta* 'indicative' + *i* 'third-person subject' + *kita* 'top' + *?icaki* 'sit.')

(58) *niya·hkʷírih tìkìte?ècaki* 'He is sitting in the top of the tree.' (*na* 'particle' + *ya·k* 'wood' + *r* 595

'collective' + *wi* 'stand upright' + *hrih* 'locative'; remainder as in 57.)

There are between 20 and 30 morphemes like *kita*, and some of them can combine with each other. Additional examples include *hita* 'edge', *kata* 'on the side', *(i)wac* 'outside', *ha* 'in water', *ka* 'in a topless enclosure', and *ka·* 'in a completely enclosed space'. Combinations include things like *kataska* 'in an open area' + *ʔir* 'in a direction', giving *kataskeʔer* 'through the yard', or this plus *iwac* 'outside', giving *kataskeʔero·c* 'out the other way from the yard'.

9.3.

Modifiers of modifiers include principally intensifiers. There are several of these, one of which is the word *wickhé·h* 'very'; sometimes *kas* 'hard' is used in the same way. Alternatively, a bound morpheme in absolute initial position on the verb is used, as in examples 59 and 60:

(59) *kirikiyákihare·sʔi* 'They were deep in the water.' (*kiri* 'intensive' + *kiya* 'quotative' + *ki* 'aorist' + *ha* 'in water' + *re·hi* 'put plural object' + *s* 'imperfective' + *ʔi* 'stative'.)

(60) *kà·ʔà·ʔà·kóʔkhá·rʔa* 'Long ago it came to pass that...' (traditional opening for a story). (*kaʔ* 'intensive' + *a·ʔ* 'quotative' + *a·* 'third-person subject and preverb' + *ki* 'aorist' + *wakhahr* 'patient is an activity' + *ʔa* 'come'.)

9.4.

From the surface structure point of view, modifiers are thus of four types: particles, phrases, bound morphemes, and subordinate sentences. But these formal classes bear no resemblance to semantic classes; adjectives and adverbs are both represented by more than one type.

Particles can be true adjectives, such as *Riwa·c* 'big'; stative verbs such as *tac (ʔi)* '(be) big'; temporal proclitics, such as *has* 'permanently'; or intensives, such as *wickhé·h* 'very'.

Phrases can be locative adverbs or instrumental adverbs.

Bound morphemes can be true adjectives, as when *Riwa·c* 'big' is suffixed to a noun; adverbs such as *ʔi·R* 'by accident' or *hí·riks* 'repeatedly'; intensifiers such as *kiri*; or locative specifications such as *to·ra·* 'down in'.

Subordinate sentences can be adjectives, as when participles function similarly to English relative clauses (see section 10.3.); or adverbs such as example 50 'tomorrow'.

10. DERIVATION

There are two kinds of derivation important in Wichita; one alters some of the inherent features of nouns or verbs, and the other changes forms from one class to another.

10.1.

Verbs may be derived to fit a selectional class (section 7.1.) in which they do not basically belong.

10.1.1.

A stative verb may be changed into a process verb by use of one of the roots *ʔahrih* 'become' or *hi* 'do'; or it may be changed to a transitive verb by use of the root *ra·ʔi* 'make'. Note what happens to the stative root *kakic ʔi* 'be dry' when it becomes a process verb (examples 61-64) and to the stative root *tariwi·k ʔi* 'be round' when it becomes a transitive verb (examples 65 and 66):

(61) *tikakicʔáris* 'It is drying.' (*ta* 'indicative' + *i* 'third-person subject' + *kakic* 'dry' + *ʔahrih* 'become' + *s* 'imperfective'.)

(62) *tikakics* 'It is drying.' (*ta* + *i* + *kakic* + *hi* 'do' + *s*.)

(63) *tikakicahis* 'They are getting dry.' (*ta* + *i* + *kakic* + *ra* 'collective' + *hi* + *s*.)

(64) *á·rakakicsh* 'They got dry.' (*a·* 'quotative' + *ara* 'perfect third-person subject' + *kakic* + *ra* + *hi*.)

(65) *titáriwi·kʔi* 'It's round.' (*ta* + *i* + *tariwi·k* 'round' + *ʔi* 'be'.)

(66) *titariwi·rhirʔis* 'He is making them round.' (*ta* + *i* + *tariwi·k* + *ru* 'collective' + *ra·ʔi* 'make' + *s*.)

10.1.2.

Process (and some active) verbs are changed to transitive verbs through the use of the causative suffix *iki* 'perfective', *is* 'imperfective'. Frequently this coalesces with the root in unexpected ways. Thus *ʔariki* 'stand' becomes *ʔari·ki* 'cause to stand; put, perfective' and *ʔari·s* 'cause to stand, imperfective', while *ʔarasi* 'cook' becomes *ʔarasiki~ʔarasis* 'cook, causative (transitive)'. Example 67 is thus ambiguous, while 68 and 69 are clearly separate:

(67) *taʔarásis* 'It is cooking' or 'She is cooking it.' (*ta* 'indicative' + *i* 'third-person subject + *ʔarasi* 'cook' + either *s* 'imperfective' or *is* 'causative imperfective'.)

(68) *á·raʔarásiki* 'I heard she cooked it.' (*a·* 'quotative' + *ara* 'perfect third singular subject' + *ʔarasi* 'cook' + *iki* 'causative imperfective'.)

(69) *á·raʔaras* 'It cooked.' (Analysis same as 68, without -*iki*.)

10.1.3.

Additionally, active verbs of motion are derived to be transitive verbs of carrying by the use of *ri* 'portative': *u...ʔa* 'come' thus becomes *u...raʔa* 'bring'; *riya·s* 'go randomly' becomes *ririya·s* 'carry around; pace the floor with'; *hiʔiyas* 'cross water' becomes *rhiʔiyas* 'take across water'.

10.1.4.

Equally easily, many active or transitive verbs may be derived to express states. This is done by simply adding the verb *uc...ʔi* 'be in a certain state' to the completed form; the result is the meaning 'is in the state of' + the verb. Compare 70 and 71:

(70) *tackiraˑs* 'I am singing.' (*ta* 'indicative' + *t* 'first-person subject' + *kiraˑh* 'sing' + *s* 'imperfective'.)

(71) *tatiˑckiraˑsʔi* 'I like to sing; I am a singer.' (*ta* + *t* + *uc* 'preverb' + *kiraˑh* + *s* + *ʔi* 'be'.)

10.1.5.
Other verbs have irregular derivational mechanisms for changing to stative meaning. Motion verbs, for instance, such as 'come' and 'go', incorporate another root, such as *hiss* 'arrive there' or *wiss* 'arrive home' before the basic motion root to form stative stems. Process verbs tend to employ a simple perfective aspect inflection instead of derivational devices, so that 'It has fallen over' is equivalent to 'It is in the state of having fallen over; it's lying there'.

10.1.6.
Finally, there are phonologically unrelated roots whose meaning differs only in the selectional restrictions placed on them. Clearest are these: *waˑwaʔa* 'eat' is active, but intransitive (cf. English 'dine'), while *kaʔac* 'eat' is always transitive.

10.2.
Nouns are covertly derived to fit noninherent selectional classes. Recall *tíˑsaˑs* 'medicine' in examples 25 and 32 above, where the inherently collective root (of 32) is derived to represent a liquid root to fit example 25. In addition, of course, many animals become human in stories, with the consequence that 'human' morphological elements (such as *kiya* 'someone') may occur with them.

10.3.
By far the most common example of derivation is the device used to form nouns from verbs. This is simply the participle inflection described in section 7.2.3.3. By using participle markings, any verb or sentence can be nominalized, and the resulting construction can translate into English as a noun ('the eater'), a relative clause ('the one who is eating' or 'the thing she ate'), or a subordinate sentence with implications of preceding or simultaneous action ('after he ate', 'while she was eating', 'when he had eaten'). The Wichita for any of these translations would be *nakaʔacskih*.

This is also the principal device for accommodating new cultural items to the language. Note these forms:

(72) *kínniˑciriʔíːhirih* 'automobile' (literally, 'what goes without a harness'). *kíri* 'not' + *na* 'participle' + *uc* 'preverb' + *i* 'extra vowel (cf. 11.1.11., item 11) + *riʔiː* 'be harnessed'; remaining analysis uncertain, perhaps + *hir-* 'go' as in *hirʔaˑ* 'go and stop' + *hrih* 'locative'.)

(73) *kaˑkinnakʷháˑcʔikih* 'apple' (literally 'some things which are red'). (*kaˑ* 'indefinite pronoun' + *kiri* 'thing' (combination means 'something') + *na* 'participle' + *kʷhaˑc* 'red' + *ʔiki* 'be plural' + *h* 'subordinate mood'.)

(74) *náːsaˑkhíʔnnih* 'Sunday' (literally 'when it is his day'). (*na* 'participle' + *uR* 'possessive' + *saˑkhir* 'sun; day' + *ʔi* 'be' + *hrih* 'locative'.)

(75) *kíriwaréˑsaˑkhíʔnnih* 'Monday' (literally, 'when it is no longer his day'). (*kíri* 'not' + *wa* 'already' + *na* + *uR* + *i* 'extra vowel demanded by *kíri*' + *saˑkhir* + *ʔi* + *hrih* as in 74.)

For further examples, see the selected vocabulary, noting especially the names for other days of the week and terms for additional items borrowed from White culture.

SURFACE STRUCTURE

11. WORD AND MORPHEME ORDER
Wichita is a typical example of a polysynthetic language. Almost all the information in any simple sentence is expressed by means of bound morphemes in the verb complex; the only exceptions to this are: noun stems, specifically those functioning as agents of transitive verbs, but sometimes those in other functions as well; and specific modifying particles, mostly those described in section 9.2. This means, then, that most of the semantic units enumerated above show up as parts of the verb complex; whether they are semantically verb or noun units does not matter.

Nevertheless, one-word sentences are relatively rare. Any actual surface structure is apt to be complex, consisting of numerous subordinated sentences. A typical sentence from a story is the following:

(76) *wáˑcʔarʔa kiyaˑkíriwaˑcʔárasarikìtàʔahíˑrikss niyaˑhkʷírih.* 'The squirrel, by making many trips, carried the large quantity of meat up into the top of the tree, they say.' (*waˑcʔarʔa* 'squirrel'; *kiya* 'quotative' + *a...ki* 'aorist' + *a* 'preverb' + *Riwaˑc* 'big (quantity)' + *ʔaras* 'meat' + *Ra* 'collective' + *ri* 'portative' + *kita* 'top' + *ʔa* 'come' + *hiˑriks* 'repetitive' + *s* 'imperfective'; *na* 'participle' + *yaˑk* 'wood' + *r* 'collective' + *wi* 'be upright' + *hrih* 'locative'.)

Note that 'squirrel', the agent, occurs by itself, with no morphemes indicating number or anything else. The verb, in addition to the verbal units of 'quotative', 'aorist', 'repetitive', and 'imperfective', also contains morphemes that indicate that the agent is singular, the patient is collective, the direction of the action is to the top, and all the lexical information about the whole patient noun phrase, 'big quantity of meat'. The location is then further specified by another word, a locativized, nominalized verb that comes out in English as 'tree' but that is formally a subordinate sentence in Wichita. Note also:

(77) *ka·hi·k²a ho·h natíra·k^wakhà·r²ih* 'We women also had certain ways of doing things.' (*ka·hi·k²a* 'woman'; *hawah* 'also'; *na* 'participle' + *t* 'first-person subject' + *uR* 'possessive' + *ra·k* 'non–third-person is plural' + *wakhahr* 'patient is an activity' + *²i* 'be' + *h* 'subordinate mood'.)

Here again, the agent is a noun, expressed by a simple noun stem first in the sentence. The next element is a conjunctive particle, of which there are fewer than 10. Then comes the verb, in which all the other semantic information is incorporated: that the subject 'woman' is the first-person plural is shown by the *t* + *ra·k*; that the object is an activity is shown by the *wakhahr*. The purely verbal concepts of 'have' ('possessive' + 'be'), tense, and aspect are also part of the verb, but the point is that many of the semantically nominal units are expressed in the verb rather than in the noun.

Surface structure word classes can thus be seen to be three: nouns, verbs, and particles. Verbs are defined by their ability to take the affixes of figure 5, nouns by their ability to be incorporated, and particles by the absence of both of these properties. But since sentences often take over the functions of either nouns or particles, and since particles have many different functions, this classification of words gives little insight into the way Wichita sentences are constructed. For this, refer to the semantic structure descriptions above.

11.1.

The general outlines of the surface-structure ordering of sentence elements are as follows. The ordering of elements outside the verb ("independent words") is discussed before the verb complex itself. In general, the ordering is described as repeatedly coming from the center of the sentence. Thus if A B C is the first sequence described, and B is then ordered with D and E to the sequence D B E, the ultimate sequence will be A D B E C; in effect, D...E has pushed A and C farther "out" by its very presence.

11.1.1.

If two sentences are paired as hypothetical cause and effect (if..., then...), the "then" sentence comes first if it is a question; otherwise, either order is possible.

(78) *é·si·h karasi·chis kiyaháre·²íriyari·skih* 'What would you do if someone were to scare you?' (*é·* 'interrogative pronoun' + *si·h* 'event'; *kara* 'debetative tense' + *s* 'second-person subject' + *uc...hi* 'do' + *s* 'imperfective'; *kiya* 'someone' + *hi* 'conditional' + *a* 'second-person object' + *re·R* 'this is new information for you' + *²iriyari* 'go randomly' + *is*

'causative imperfective' + *kih* 'imperfective subordinate'.)

(79) *té·riya·h icihir²í·rasih* 'He better watch out if I find him!' (*té·riya·h* 'He better watch out!' (idiom, not further analyzable); *i* 'conditional' + *t* 'first-person subject' + *i* 'extra vowel' + *hir²i* 'patient is animate' + *irasi* 'find' + *h* 'subordinate perfective'.)

(80) *ti²i ísa² icak²ah hinnih ke²eci·cá·sto·ra·w* 'When I give this signal, we will all go down (into the canyon).' (*ti²i* 'this'; *ísa²* 'thus; in this manner'; *i* 'conditional' + *t* 'first-person subject' + *rak²a* 'say' + *h* 'subordinate mood'; *hinnih* 'and'; *ke²e* 'future' + *ciy* 'inclusive subject' + *uc* 'preverb' + *ra·k* 'non–third-person is plural' + *to·ra·* 'down into (a ditch or canyon)' + *wa* 'go, perfective'.)

11.1.2.

If a subordinate sentence describes a previous action, it will precede the main verb. This is a very common device for describing sequential actions in a story.

(81) *nahi²iyasisah nahité·tiskih kiyakí·ctawi·² hako·citih* 'After he had crossed the water and after he had gone out onto the bank, it was hard for him to get out from inside (where he had been sitting).' (*na* 'participle' + *hi²iyas* 'cross water' + *hisha* 'go, imperfective' + *h* 'subordinate'; *na* 'participle' + *hita* 'edge, bank' + *itu* 'exit' + *skih* 'imperfective subordinate'; *kiya* 'quotative' + *ki* 'aorist' + *uc...tawi·²* 'be difficult for'; *haki* 'subjunctive third-person subject' + *wac* 'outside' + *itu* 'exit' + *h* 'subordinate'.)

In this example, the first two clauses are translated with English 'after', which implies a time sequence for the events; the Wichita contains no equivalent word, but the relationship is clear from the sequence of the sentences themselves. The main verb is marked for tense, 'it was difficult', and another subordinate sentence, a 'for...to' clause, follows the main verb.

11.1.3.

Any sentence that functions as a modifier in the surface structure and that is not a participle (unless it fits the category of "prior action" described in section 11.1.2.) precedes the main verb. Examples are *á·ki²í·rakhann* 'suddenly', *chih á·ki²í·rakháris²i·²* 'all at once', *ciyaré·sirih* 'in plain sight', and *hi·hánthirih* 'tomorrow'.

11.1.4.

The only other kind of word that regularly occurs early in the surface sentence is a locative demonstrative; *ti²rih* 'here', *hí·raka·h* 'way over there', and *hárah* 'there' are the most common examples. Otherwise, the regular tendency in sentence construction is to place modifiers after whatever they modify. In example 81, the "for...to" clause modifies the main verb and follows it; in example 57, 'tree' modifies the main clause and follows it. Example 82 illustrates the principles of sections 11.1.3. and 11.1.4. together.

(82) *á·ki?í·rakhann a·ki?ickhité·s nare·he·hárih niya·rhi?i·rika·wírih.* 'Suddenly he peeked over the edge of the water where the tree leaned over it.' (*á·ki?í·rakhann* 'suddenly'; *a·ki* 'aorist third-person subject quotative' + *?icka* 'face, instrumental' + *hita* 'edge' + *hisha* 'go'; *na* 'participle' + *re·R* 'the' + *ha* 'water, locative' + *yiha* 'be a place' + *hrih* 'locative'; *na* 'participle' + *ya·k* 'wood' + *ri* 'collective' + *?i·rika·wi* 'lean over' + *hrih* 'locative'.)

In this example, a nonparticiple modifier is a sentence ('suddenly') preposed to the main verb; then two modifiers follow the main verb, both of which are participles, yet neither of which describes sequential activity prior to that of the main verb.

11.1.5.

The rules for ordering subject and object nouns with verbs depend on the surface structure form of the noun, and on the case relationship which is manifested by the noun.

If the noun is a participle (nominalized sentence) and is a patient, it will follow the verb. If there is a noun agent in the same sentence, it will precede the verb.

If the noun is one of a certain set of kinship terms (but not body parts), it must be possessed. But only if the syntax forbids the nouns from being incorporated (inserted in the main verb) does the actual verb 'have' show up in the surface structure. Compare the discussion of possession marking, section 11.2.1.

Other nouns that are patients may occur incorporated into the verb complex (see 'wood' in 'tree' in example 82, or 'meat' in example 76), or they may be preposed to the verb outside it. Then, if an agent occurs, it can either precede or follow this complex. This means that for sentences with unincorporated non-sentence patients, the order S-O-V or O-V-S is normal. Preposed agents were illustrated in 76 and 77, but both of these sentences showed incorporated patients. Other possibilities are as follows:

(83) *ka·hi·rá·í·c?a naré·r?ih ha·khas?a á·kikakack* 'The old woman cut the ropes.' (S-O-V). (*ka·hi·-* 'woman, combining form' + *ra·i·c* 'be old' + *?a* 'noun formative'; *na* 'third-person participle' + *re·R* 'the' + *?ih* 'be subordinate'; *ya·khas?a* 'rope'; *á·ki* 'third-person subject quotative aorist' + *kakack* 'cut plural object'.)

(84) *ka·hi·k?a kiyararé·r?ih wérah ni·?í·skih ti?i wi·c kíyararé·r?ih.* 'This man must have seen the woman.' (O-V-S). (*ka·hi·k?a* 'woman'; *kiya* 'subject is human' + *na* 'participle' + *re·R* 'the' + *?i* 'be' + *h* 'subordinate'; *wérah*

'maybe, must'; *na* 'participle' + *i...?i:s* 'see' + *kih* 'imperfective subordinate'; *ti?i* 'this'; *wi·c* 'man'; *kiyararé·r?ih* 'the' as analyzed earlier in the sentence.)

11.1.6.

If only one noun occurs in the sentence (with any except class 3 verbs), it will be the subject of the verb, whether it is semantically agent or patient. With class 3 verbs, it will be the object. In either case, the word order does not signal the case relationship: the noun may follow the verb (85), be incorporated in it (86), or precede it (87):

(85) *kà·?à·?à·kíhi·?iké·s?a né·rhir?a* 'Then the buffalo came down to the creek.' (*ka·?* 'this is a new topic' + *a·?* 'quotative' + *a...ki* 'aorist' + *a* 'preverb' + *hi·* 'ditch and creekbed' + *?ike·s* 'down into' + *?a* 'come'; *né·rhir?a* 'buffalo'.)

(86) *kiyaki·cíwa·cé·rhir?as?irhaw* 'There lay the big buffalo.' (*kiya* 'quotative' + *ki* 'aorist' + *uc...?irhawi* 'be lying' + *Riwa·c* 'big' + *né·rhir?as* 'buffalo, combining form'.)

(87) *né·rhir?a a·ki·we?eh* 'The buffalo fell over.' (*né·rhir?a* 'buffalo'; *a·ki* 'aorist third-person subject' + *u...we?eha* 'fall over'.)

11.1.7.

Dative objects may either precede or follow the verb, but they usually follow. If there is also a patient, it will either precede the verb or be incorporated. There are no examples of nonpronominal agent, patient, and dative all occurring with the same verb.

(88) *té·s tac?arhara?as ne?e·h* or *tac?asté·ssara?as ne?e·h* 'He is bringing corn to the chickens'. (*té·s* 'corn'; *ta* 'third-person subject indicative with preverb' + *uc* 'dative' *?ak* 'dative plural' + *ra* 'collective' + *ri* 'portative' + *?a* 'come' + *s* 'imperfective'; *ne?e·h* 'chicken'.)

11.1.8.

Adjectives modifying nouns are of three types, when word order is considered (section 9.1. and examples 48 and 49; Rood 1986). Those that are true adjectives will follow the noun they modify (see 48); of those that are stative verbs, construed with the verb 'be', some will precede the appropriate form of 'be' (see *icákis* in 89-91) while others will be incorporated in it (see *he·c* in 92 and 93). The noun will then precede (see 89 and 92), follow (see 90 and 93), or be incorporated into the resulting complex (if the adjective is not already incorporated) (see 91). 'The rock is pretty' can thus be expressed in three ways, while 'the horse is fat' has two translations (glosses are *icákis* 'pretty', *he·c* 'fat', *?ika·(?a)* 'rock', *kawá·rah* 'horse', *ti* 'indicative third singular subject', and *?i* 'be'):

(89) *?ika·?a icákis ti?i* 'The rock is pretty.'

(90) *icákis ti?i ?ika·?a* 'The rock is pretty.'

(91) *icákis tiʔikaˑʔi* 'The rock is pretty.'

(92) *kawáˑrah tiheˑcʔi* 'The horse is fat.'

(93) *tiheˑcʔi kawáˑrah* 'The horse is fat.'

(94) *kawáˑrah nahéˑcʔih icákis tiʔi* 'The fat horse is pretty.'

Example 94 shows the stative verb 'be fat' used as an adjective.

11.1.9.

When one noun modifies another, the order is modifier-modified (cf. 'Wichita' in the selected vocabulary for a possible exception). There are three uses for this construction:

(a) in forming noun compounds:

(95) *issiˑstaˑraˑc* 'needle' (*issiˑs* 'sinew' + *taˑraˑc* 'awl').

(96) *eˑckicʔa* 'milk' (*eˑcʔa* 'breast' + *kicʔa* 'liquid').

(b) in indicating the possessor of certain body parts:

(97) *néˑrhirʔaskáˑhkaksʔa* 'buffalo intestines' (*néˑrhirʔas* 'buffalo, combining form' + *káˑhkaksʔa* 'intestines').

(c) for appositive constructions:

(98) *niˑhaˑskʷaˑriks néˑrhirʔa* 'the old-man buffalo' (*niˑhaˑs* 'uncle' + *waˑriks* 'old'. This is not a name, but does refer to a specific, venerable buffalo in a story).

11.1.10.

Closest to the verb is the set of so-called proclitics (section 9.2.1.). These are semibound forms that may occur either immediately preceding or immediately following the verb complex, but that, if preceding, force a change in the phonology of the verb through the addition of an extra vowel at position 11 below (see section 11.1.11.). The order seems to be arbitrary when more than one of these proclitics occur together.

In addition to the time markers mentioned in section 9.2.1., this class includes *khíʔas* 'poor', which shows sympathy with the subject on the part of the speaker ('the poor thing'), and some of the preposed stative verbs (section 11.1.8.). Still phonologically in the proclitic class, but generally found only preposed to the verb and following the items just listed, are *kírih* 'negative, not' and *kiri* or *kaˑʔ* 'intensive', *kiya* 'someone', and *hasʔa*, which indicates that the word is part of a story. Frequently *kiya* and *hasʔa* coalesce to /kiyaˑsʔa/. If any of these items occur together, they do so in the order in which they are listed.

11.1.11.

Here is the order of elements within the verb itself:

1. |hi(ʔ)| (|iˑʔ| before aorist forms, |iˑk| before quotative aorists or perfects), indicating various things about the number of agents or patients (section 11.2.2.).

2. Quotative, either |kiya| or |aˑʔ| with the aorist, |aˑ| with the perfect. With the future, the quotative

coalesces with the future tense marker (position 3) to produce |eheˑ| 'future quotative'.

3. All tense/aspect prefixes except the aorist; the forms are given in figure 5, with additions as described in section 7.2.3.2. and 7.2.3.3. In the case of the subjunctive and the aorist, which are discontinuous, the first part of the morpheme occurs here.

4. Person of the subject or of the possessor of the subject. Morphemes are |t| 'first person' (often /c/ in actual forms, due to morphophonemic rules); |s| 'second person'; |i| or zero 'third person' (choice of form depends on the tense being used); |iˑ/ or /í/ or /íˑ/ (underlying |iy|) 'out-of-focus or indefinite person'; |ciy| 'inclusive person'. Note that the third-person and the indefinite person markers occur only when there is no object or when the object is also third person. In other words, they do not occur with any of the morphemes at position six except 'reflexive'.

5. The preverb of *ʔa* 'come', which seems to be |u| with first- and second-person subjects, but |a| with third-person and all object forms; or the morpheme |uR| 'possessive'.

6. Direct or dative object person markers, or marker for the person of a possessor when the possessed thing is the patient of the verb. Morphemes are |aˑ| 'reflexive', |ki| 'first person'; |a(ˑ)| 'second person'; zero 'third person'; |caˑki| 'inclusive'.

7. The aorist |ki| (section 7.2.3.3.).

8. If the object of the verb is something stated to be unknown, Wichita marks it by the use of a discontinuous morpheme, |a...réˑR|, the first part of which occurs here. The equivalent of the English sentence "I don't know what he is eating", for instance, is *taʔaréˑkaʔacs*, literally 'He is eating something unknown'.

9. The form |uc| 'dative'.

10. Regular preverb of the root, except 'come' or 'possessive' (see position 5, and section 11.2.).

11. The so-called "extra vowel" demanded by the proclitics or the tense exclamatory (section 11.1.10. and examples 53, 72, 75).

12. In negative sentences, the morpheme |yis| in this position marks the statement as definitely true.

13. The morpheme |raˑk|, which marks any or all non-third persons in the sentence as plural (section 11.2.2.).

14. The demonstrative |reˑR| 'the'.

15. One of the adverbial particles described in section 9.2.

16. The second part of |a...réˑR| 'unknown'.

17. |ʔak| 'dative or possessor is nonsingular'.

At this point, a patient noun or noun phrase can be incorporated. This is considered a syntactic rather than a morphological position, and the slot is not numbered for that reason.

18. The morpheme for 'collective' or 'patient is not

singular'. The shape of this varies from verb to verb, but the collective is usually |ru|, |ra|, or |r|.

19. The noncollective plural, usually |ʔak|. Instead of a morpheme here, some roots change form to mark plural. Examples include ʔarasi 'cook', plural waˑrasʔiˑrʔi; kaʔac 'eat', plural ʔa; and ki 'kill', plural ʔessa 'imperfective', and ʔeˑseˑʔ 'perfective'.

20. The morphemes required by the selectional features of the nouns: |hirʔi| 'patient is animate', |kir| 'patient is liquid', and |wakhahr| 'patient is an activity' (section 8.1.).

21. Either the portative (|ri|), which changes a verb of motion to one of carrying ('come' becomes 'bring', 'go' becomes 'take'), or a noun used instrumentally occurs here. Since these have never occurred together in the same word, the order that they might follow is still undetermined.

22. The locatives described in section 9.2.

23. |wa| 'dual' in a few verbs; see section 11.2.2.

24. The verb itself, which will include the root and derivational morphemes such as |ʔiri| 'while in a lying position', and |tata| 'while following'.

25. The distributive |(a)waˑ| is actually an infix, occurring just before the last consonant of the verb root. Compare examples 99 and 100:

(99) naˑckithah 'It is scattered in front of you.' (na 'participle' + uc 'preverb' + kitha 'be scattered' + h 'subordinate mood'.)

(100) naˑckitawaˑhah 'A lot of it is scattered all over.' (Same as 99, but with awaˑ 'distributive' infixed before the last consonant of the root.)

26. The morpheme for 'repeatedly', |hiˑriks|; see section 9.2.

27. The causative.

28. Any of the aspect suffixes listed across the top of figure 5, except 'too late'.

29. |ʔasʔ|, the second half of a discontinuous form meaning 'place' (section 11.2.4.) or any one of various derivational verb roots such as 'come', 'go', 'be', or 'be continual'. These verbs signify an activity or state simultaneous with the main verb. Many times these added roots then behave as if they were in position 24 and accept the affixes of positions 25-28 (especially 28) themselves.

30. Subordinate aspect markers, |h| 'perfective' or |skih| 'imperfective'.

31. The 'too late' aspect marker (cf. fig. 5).

32. |hrih| 'locative'.

These 32 positions for morphemes in the verb are absolutely rigid; there is no freedom of arrangement here at all, in contrast with the relative freedom described among independent elements in section 11.1.1.-11.1.10.

11.1.12.

The few morphemes that occur with nouns instead of in the verb are easily described. All the bound forms are suffixes, and include only kiyah 'locative', Raˑhirʔ 'instrumental', and (usually) for animate nouns s 'combining form'. The combining form is used in compounds of noun with noun (section 11.1.9.) or noun with true adjective (section 9.1.), and when the noun is incorporated in the verb.

A few nouns have irregularities in the combining forms. Those that end in /c/ or /s/ already in the citation form do not generally change in the combining form. Examples are waːkhac 'cow', kíkʔiˑs 'turtle', wiˑc 'man', niyeˑs 'child', and kʔítaːks 'coyote'. Those that end in suffixes other than ʔa in the citation form, such as |hrʔa| (akhahrʔa 'house', haˑhirahrʔa 'body of water', ksahrʔa 'bed') or |kʔa| (kaˑhiˑkʔa 'woman', tiˑkʔa 'pole') lose the suffix to derive the combining form (|akhá| 'house' or |kaˑhiˑ| 'woman', for example). In addition, kawáˑrah 'horse' has a suppletive combining form, taˑras. Although waːkhac 'cow' and kawáˑrah 'horse' are apparently loanwords, ultimately from Spanish, they seem to be fully integrated into Wichita structure except as just noted.

The free forms that modify nouns include only the demonstratives tiʔi 'this' and haˑríˑh 'that', and they may either precede or follow the noun. Other potential complexities in noun phrases—adjectives, possessives, the definite article—are always verb participles or subordinate sentences, so the result is treated as part of the syntax of complex sentences.

11.2.

Section 11.1. has presented the linear features of the surface structure of Wichita, outlining the order in which simple sentences are joined to form more complex structures and indicating in list form the morphemes and their order in simple sentences. More important than morpheme order are the details of surface structure expression of many of the semantic concepts outlined in the first part of this chapter. Six of these have been selected for detailed discussion: possession, number marking, the definite article, nonspecific pronouns, geographical terms, and indirect statements and questions.

11.2.1.

Surface structure marking of possession in Wichita is complex and varies according to whether the possessed entity is agent or patient, and again, according to whether the patient is marked as a surface structure subject or object.

The verb 'have, possess' in Wichita is uR...ʔi, a combination of the preverb 'possessive' and the root 'be'. Possession of a noun can be expressed by incorporating that noun in this verb and indicating the person of the possessor by the subject pronoun; the complex then receives participle markings, and the result is a noun.

(101) natíˑʔakʔih 'my wife'. (na 'participle' + t 'first-person subject' + uR 'possessive' + ʔak

601

'wife' + *ʔi* 'be' + *h* 'subordinate'.)

(101) *niyeˑs natîˑkih* 'my children'. (*niyeˑs* 'child'; *na* 'participle' + *t* 'first-person subject' + *uR* 'possessive' + *ʔiki* 'be plural' + *h* 'subordinate mood'.)

In example 102, the morphological construction is the same as in 101, but in 101 the noun is incorporated, in 102 it is not. Note that number is marked as if the surface structure noun were the subject of 'be', rather than the object of 'have', even though the pronoun indicating the possessor is also a subject in form.

Constructions such as 101 or 102 must be used if the possessed entity is the agent of a transitive verb. They may optionally be used for any other possessed nouns, too. However, if the possessed noun is the agent of an intransitive (active) verb, or a patient, it may be incorporated in the main verb instead of being marked by 'have'. In this case, the fact of possession is shown by the use of *uR* or *uc* at positions 5 or 9, respectively, of the verb. The person of the possessor will be marked by the subjective pronoun (position 4) if the possessed entity is the subject of the verb, but by the objective (or reflexive) pronoun (position 6) if the possessed entity is the surface object of the verb. The distinction between *uR* and *uc* is that the former is used with subjective pronouns, the latter with objective ones.

(103) *tatiˑcʔiˑs* 'I saw his.' (*ta* 'indicative' + *t* 'first-person subject' + *uc* 'dative' + *ʔiˑs* 'see'.)

In 103, the possessed entity is the surface object of the verb; the objective third-person pronoun is zero, but the fact that an objective rather than a subjective pronoun represents the possessor is indicated by the choice of *uc* rather than *uR*. Further examples include 104 and 105:

(104) *takiˑcʔiˑs* 'He saw mine.' (Same as 103, but with *ki* 'first-person object' instead of *t*.)

(105) *takiˑctaˑheʔeh* 'He is holding my knife.' (*ta* 'indicative' + *ki* 'first-person object' + *uc* 'dative' + *taˑha* 'knife' + *iʔahi* 'hold'.)

In 104, the possessed entity is object, as shown by the choice of *ki* to mark the person of the possessor. Example 105 shows the same relationships, but a possessed noun 'knife' appears in the construction as well.

Now compare 106, an active intransitive verb that has a surface subject and no object, with 107, a stative verb that has a surface structure object (and no subject):

(106) *tatíˑtàˑrashìs* 'My horse went.' (*ta* 'indicative' + *t* 'first-person subject' + *uR* 'possessive' + *taˑras* 'horse, combining form' + *hisha* 'go'.)

(107) *taˑkickʷitaʔas* 'Mine is boiling.' (*ta* 'indicative' + *a* 'preverb' + *ki* 'first-person object' + *uc* 'dative' + *wita* 'boil' + *ʔa* 'come' + *s* 'imperfective'.)

These two examples show clearly the difference between surface structure subject role for the possessed noun and surface structure object role for the same form, since in 106 the possessor is marked by the subject case

morpheme, while in 107 the object morpheme is used.

To summarize, possessed agents of transitive verbs are marked by subordinate sentences indicating possession. Possessed subjects of intransitive verbs are marked by using the subject pronoun indicating person of possessor, plus the morpheme *uR*, and incorporating the noun in the verb (106). Possessed patients (104, 105, 107) are marked by using the object case form of the pronoun showing the person of possessor, the morpheme *uc*, and then incorporating the noun.

11.2.2.

Number marking in the surface structure is not nearly as neat and simple as the description in the semantic structure would indicate. The assertion that all countable, noncollective nouns can be marked semantically singular, dual, or plural, section 8.2.2., seems to be true, But the surface structure forms are frequently ambiguous in a number of ways.

First, third-person nominals must be distinguished from those that are not third person. Second, surface agents must be distinguished from patients among the third-person forms, and surface subjects from objects among the non–third-person forms. Figure 7 gives an idea of this hierarchy.

Each of these four categories is marked for number differently, making a possible total of 12 markers for verbs with one nominal, or 24 for those with two. In fact, there are only six morphemes or combinations of morphemes (including zero) available to distinguish these 24 categories, so some ambiguity is inevitable. In this discussion, plural will mean 'more than two', and nonsingular will mean 'two or more'. Moreover, the discussion will frequently refer to the morpheme *ʔak*, which includes all the idiosyncratic number-marking devices mentioned at positions 18 and 19 of section 11.1.11.

A surface structure object in the non–third-person category can be clearly marked as singular, dual, or plural. The morpheme *raˑk* (position 13) marks plurality; a combination of *hi* (position 1) and *ʔak* (position 19) marks this object as dual. Singular is marked by zero. When the non–third-person object is marked for either dual or plural, it is impossible to indicate number for the subject or agent; consequently, the number of this entity is completely ambiguous. However, if the object is marked singular (by using zero), some indications of the subject number can be made. If that subject is also non–third-person, it can be marked singular (by zero) or nonsingular (by *hi* of position 1).

If both agent and patient are third person, a few intransitive verbs permit the same distinctions for patients as are possible for non-third objects: singular, dual, and plural. These verbs (such as 'come' and 'sit', and very few others) allow the morpheme *wa* to occur at position 23 to mark 'dual patient'. In all other cases, a position 18 or 19 morpheme such as *ʔak* means 'patient is plural'.

In the absence of *ʔak* or *wa*, a third-person agent may be marked nonsingular by the use of *hi* (position 1), or singular by the use of zero. But if position 18 or 19 is filled, there is no way to mark agent number: whether *hi* occurs or not, the number of the subject remains completely ambiguous. The result is the strange situation of extremely few morphemes to mark number, and yet free variation with no change in meaning between two of the possibilities. With nonsingular patients, the agent may be clearly marked singular by the absence of *hi*; but *hi* may also occur even if the agent is singular.

For verbs where both agent and patient are third person, then, patients are regularly marked singular or nonsingular, and if the patient is singular, agents may also be differentiated into singular or nonsingular. But if a patient is nonsingular, the agent is either shown to be singular or is unmarked for number.

What happens if the classes outlined in figure 7 are mixed and have subjects and objects that do not match in person class? Two possibilities exist.

If the patient is third person and the subject is non–third-person, that subject may be marked singular (by zero), nonsingular (by *hi*), or plural (by *raˑk*). Thus a dual subject will necessarily be marked by *hi*, but plural subjects may also be so marked. The patient may continue to be marked as described above.

When the roles are reversed, and the agent is third person while the object is non-third, the situation is similar to that for non-third to non-third: if the object is either dual or plural, it will be marked as already described, by *hi...ʔak* or *raˑk*, respectively, and subject number will be ambiguous. But if the object is singular, the subject can

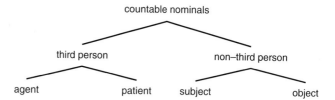

Fig. 7. Syntactic-role categories of third-person and non–third-person nominals.

be marked singular (by zero), or nonsingular (by *hi*).

Another way to examine this would be from the point of view of the hearer. Which combinations of number morphemes occur, and what do they mean? Partial glosses are as follows:

|hi| 'subject is nonsingular' (but cf. *hi...ʔak*)

|ʔak| 'third-person patient is nonsingular'

|raˑk| 'non–third-person is plural'. If both the subject and object are non-third person, reference is to the object only.

|hi...ʔak| 'non–third-person object is dual. If the form has no non–third-person object, the meaning is the same as for *ʔak* alone.

|raˑkʔak| 'combine meanings of *raˑk* and *ʔak*'

zero 'singular'

Note that *hi* never occurs with *raˑk*, and that when the object is non–third-person, *hi...ʔak* can refer only to that object—the usual reference of *hi* to the subject is suspended in this situation. See table 4 for a summary. In the table, the morphemes that can refer to the given combination of subject and object are represented, with

Table 4. Morphological Marking of Subject and Object Number Categories

	Object				
Subject	*Third-person singular*	*Third-person nonsingular*	*Non–third-person singular*	*Non–third-person dual*	*Non–third-person plural*
Third-person singular	Ø Ø	(Ø) (hi)...ʔak	Ø Ø	— hi...ʔak	— raˑk
Third-person nonsingular	hi Ø	— hi...ʔak	hi Ø	— hi...ʔak	— raˑk
Non–third-person singular	Ø Ø	(Ø) (hi)...ʔak	Ø Ø	— hi...ʔak	— raˑk
Non–third-person dual	hi Ø	— hi...ʔak	hi Ø	— hi...ʔak	— raˑk
Non–third-person plural	{raˑk / hi} Ø	{raˑk / hi} ʔak	hi Ø	— hi...ʔak	— raˑk

NOTE: The morpheme for subject number is given on the left of the column; that for the object number is on the right. For verbs with only one nominal, use the appropriate object (patient) marking. The dash indicates categories for which number cannot be marked and is therefore ambiguous.

603

the form referring to the subject on the left, the one referring to the object on the right. Parentheses mean the morpheme may or may not be present, but there is no necessary change of meaning when it is missing. The possibility of dual patients that are also third person (marked by *wa*) is ignored.

11.2.3.

The use of the definite article in Wichita is rather different from that of English. It appears that the form in Wichita means exclusively 'the one to which we have already referred' and is thus normally used only in a narrative or in connected conversation.

The morpheme is |ré·R| or |re·ʔeh|, plural |ri·ʔih|, and may occur in a number of positions: suffixed to the noun, incorporated in the verb 'be' and treated as a participial modifier of the noun, or as a bound form in the verb at position 14. Examples 108 and 109 show the difference in meaning between presence and absence of the form; examples 110-114 show variations in place of occurrence.

(108) *kʔíta·ks hinnih naré·ʔakʔih* 'The Coyote and his (the aforementioned, i.e., Coyote's) wife (*kʔíta·ks* 'coyote'; *hinnih* 'and'; *na* 'participle' + *uR* 'possessive' + *ré·R* 'the' + *ʔak* 'wife' + *ʔi* 'be' + *h* 'subordinate'.)

(109) *kʔíta·ks hinnih ná·kʔih* 'Coyote and his (the other's) wife'. (Analysis as in 108, except that *ré·R* is missing here.)

(110) *kʔíta·ks naré·r·ih ná·kʔih* '(The) wife of the (previously mentioned) coyote' (*kʔíta·ks* 'coyote'; *na* 'participle' + *ré·R* 'the' + *ʔi* 'be' + *h* 'subordinate mood'; 'wife' as in 109.)

(111) See example 84 for two more examples of *ré·R* in the participle of 'be'.

(112) *wi·céʔeh* 'the man' *wi·c* 'man' + *re·ʔeh* 'the'.

(113) *kʔíta·ks naré·ʔakʔih* 'The coyote's wife'. (Same as 110, but with 'the' incorporated as part of the 'his wife' form. Compare 108.)

(114) *naré·ʔira·cíʔih neʔe:skih* 'when her (the previously mentioned one's) brother saw her,' (*na* 'participle' + *ré·R* + *ʔira·ci* 'brother of a woman' + *ʔi* 'be' + *h* 'subordinate mood'; *na* 'participle' + *ʔi:s* 'see' + *kih* 'imperfective subordinate'.)

11.2.4.

Indefinite, negative, and interrogative pronouns (who?, someone, no one, something, nothing) form a coherent and consistent subset of vocabulary items in Wichita. One set of prefixes can occur with another set of indefinite nouns to form multiple pronouns. The prefixes are |ha·s| 'indirect', |e·| 'interrogative', |ka·| 'indefinite', and |ká·| 'negative'. The nouns include |kirih| 'thing', |kiyah| 'person', |ckinc| 'amount', |sis| 'extent of time or space', |ka·h| or |si·h...ʔas?| 'place', and |si·h| 'event'. Combinations are translated as in the following examples:

(115) *ha·skiyah* 'who' (in indirect questions)

(116) *ka·kiyah* 'somebody'

(117) *ká·kiyah* 'nobody'

(118) *e·kiyah* 'who?'

(119) *e·ka·h* 'where?'

(120) *e·ckinc* 'how much?; how many?'

(121) *ka·ckinc* 'a certain number; so many; so much'

(122) *ka·sis* 'a certain distance; sometime'

(123) *e·si·h* 'how?; what event?'

(124) *ká·kirih* 'nothing'

11.2.5.

Wichita nouns that are names of geographical phenomena are regularly formed from the locative verb markers (section 9.2.) and the verb *yiha* 'be a place'. To translate the English nouns, the participle of the verb is formed, using the locative indicator, and the result may be treated as either a noun or, if the locative ending *hrih* is attached to the participle, a locative expression.

(125) *nahe·hárih* 'where the creek is' (*na* 'participle' + *ha* 'water, locative' + *yiha* 'be a place' + *hrih* 'locative'.)

(126) *nihí·ke·hah* 'ditch; ravine; canyon' (*na* + *iy* 'out-of-focus subject' (here implying plural) + *hi·ka·* 'down in' + *yiha* 'be a place'.)

(127) *nakatáske·hárih* 'where the prairie is' (*na* 'participle' + *kataska* 'open space' + *yiha* 'be a place' + *hrih* 'locative'.)

In actual usage in Wichita, these forms are clearly verbs and can take any of the verbal inflections that seem appropriate to the context. Hence sentences like 128:

(128) *tikité·h* 'There is a hill.' (*ti* 'third-person subject indicative' + *kita* 'top' + *yiha* 'be a place'.)

11.2.6.

English and other Indo-European languages have a special construction for sentences that are the objects of verbs of mental activity—verbs like 'think', 'ask', 'say', and 'wonder'. These are usually called indirect statements or questions. *I wonder who he is*, or *Ask him where he's been* can serve as examples. In Wichita this kind of construction is possible, but it is used only in formal, narrative style. Ordinarily, the Wichita sentences translating these examples would be direct, nonsubordinate statements, more like *I wonder, "Who is he?"* or *Ask him, "Where have you been?"*. The construction used in the narratives involves substituting a pronoun prefixed by *ha·s* (see section 11.2.4.) for the subject of the sentence, and then using the conditional tense for the verb.

(129) *kíriʔo·kʔas ha·skiyah híʔih* 'He did not say who it was.' (*kíri* 'negative' + *ʔi* 'third-person subject, present negative' + *wakʔa* 'say' + *s* 'imperfective'; *ha·s* 'indirect pronoun' + *kiyah* 'person'; *hi* 'conditional' + *iy* 'out-of-focus subject' + *ʔi* 'be' + *h* 'subordinate'.)

12. CONCLUSION

In the picture of Wichita structure that emerges from the preceding information certain generalities are apparent. The surface phonology, while somewhat unusual (since it utilizes three degrees of length, no phonemic nasals, and no phonemic labial consonants, as well as a vowel system with only height distinctions and no front-back dimension) is nonetheless quite simple: the number of phonemes is small and the complexity of structure limited.

The morphophonemic system, on the other hand, is extremely complex, involving numerous changes when sounds come together in words.

The semantic system includes a number of obligatory distinctions that are foreign to English and omits others that English requires. For example, evidential is sometimes obligatory, focus distinctions in third-person pronouns are important, and both dual number and the inclusive-exclusive distinction are regularly expressed. On the other hand, there is no gender distinction in the pronouns, morphemes corresponding closely to the English articles are missing, and there is no construction used exclusively for relative clauses. Moreover, some predicate adjectives are different from their semantically equivalent descriptive correlates.

Finally, Wichita surface grammar is characterized by heavy use of bound morphemes in the verb, sentence constructions that depend on word structure rather than word order, and a high frequency of subordinate sentence constructions where English uses phrases or even unanalyzable particles.

13. SELECTED VOCABULARY

The words in the following list are citation forms, transcribed phonemically, except that verbs are given as verb stems (with leading hyphens in this list only); they can be cited only by adding tense and person prefixes and an aspect suffix to them (filling positions 3, then 4 or 6, and 28, 30, or 31 as described in section 11.1.11.).

acorn   *hawa·c*

all   *assé·hah*

and   *hinnih*

  and then   *híriwa·h*

animals   *íyaris²a*   'those which walk around'

ankle   *aski·s²a*   'foot bone'

Apache (Arizona)   *ìssìk^wità²a*

Apache (Fort Sill)   *kinne·s*   Also used for the 'enemy' or the 'bad guys' in stories.

arbor   *akhátawa²a*   'hanging house'

arm   *wi·r²a*

  lower arm   *issa·c²a*

  upper arm   *wíke·s²a*

arrow   *nikwa·c²a*   Also used for 'bullet'.

ashes   *ickha·r²a*   Also 'dust, sand'. If differentiation is required, *niye·ckhárhi·kic²a* 'lye water' is used. Compare *ye·c* 'fire'.

back   *nikiri²a*

bad   *né·²ah*

bark (tree)   *tí·k²ac²iya·c²a*   'pole shell'

bead (for hand game)   *ké·ris;* for craftwork use *ki·s²a* 'bone' for large size, *niyá·khac*, lit. 'white thing', for smaller sizes

because   *hi·wé²ewakha·r²a*

belly   *ká·k^wi·c²a*

big   *tac* (stative verb);   *Riwa·c* (adjective)

bird   *ichiri*

bite   *-ta²a*

black   *ka·r²i·s; cawic²a* 'dark; black'

blood   *wa·ckic²a*   Cf. *kic²a* 'water; liquid'.

blow   *-wa·ri·c*

bone   *ki·s²a*

book   *khá·ki·s²a*   Also used for 'paper'. Originally 'a transparent membrane'.

bow   *ksi·c²a*   Also 'gun'.

bread   *kir²i·c²a*

breast   *e·c²a*

breathe   *-hisciya·s*

brother (of a man)   *-a·²i·rás*   (Verb root, meaning more nearly 'he is a brother of...')

brother (of a woman)   *ra·cí²*   (Always possessed).

buffalo   *né·rhir²a* (male);   *ta·rha* (female)

burn   *-hiri*

buttocks   *ni²is*

caddo   *té·sa²a*   'friendly ones'

chair   *há·kassk^wi*   'wood-feet stand upright'.

chief   *í·ri·²a*

child   *niye·s*   incorporated form *a·*

claw   *isk^wic²a*

clothing   *ak^wa·ha·r²a*

cloud   *ke²e·r²a*

come   *u~a...²a*

Comanche   *na·ta²á:h*

cook   *-²arasi*

corn   *té·s*

corn (coarsely ground)   *cáka·s²a*

corn cob   *kiyá·khir²a*

corn, ear of   *ni·²ac²a*

corn husk   *tasa·r²a*

corn (parched)   *ka·sas²a*

corn silk   *ni²a·wic²a*

corn stalk   *tac²a*

605

corn tassle   *nikiri·ʔa*

count   *-ʔakʔi·ri·ki*

coyote   *kʔíta·ks*

cut   *-tara; -kack*

dance   *ichas* (noun);   *-ichasi* (verb)

day   *hiráthiris·ʔa* or *hánthiris·ʔa*   Also use *sa·khirʔa* 'sun'

die   *-teʔes*   This is basically a taboo word, and as such is not used for people. *kíriwaʔi·ʔi* 'He is no longer (here)' translates 'He is dead'. For plants, use *-kakichi* 'dry up'.

dig up   *-hawati; -hirá·ra*

dirty   *neʔestha·r*

doctor   *ikíwira·ʔa*

dog   *kiciye·h; wáseʔekʔa*; combining form *weʔes*

drink   *-kikʔa*

dry   *kakic*

dull   *kʷi·c*

dust   *neʔeckha·rʔa*

eagle   *ko·s*

ear   *a·cʔa*

earth   *hira·rʔa*

   Mother Earth   *híraciya·káhíkʔih neʔerʔíriwah* 'Our mother who is lying down' is the addressee of prayers offered before eating.

eat   *-kaʔac* (singular object); *-ʔa* (plural object) (transitive); *-wa·waʔa* (intransitive)

egg   *nikʷi·kʔa*

eight   *kiyátaw*   Cf. *taw* 'three'

elm   *teʔe·c*

eye   *kirikʔa*

face   *ickaʔa*

fall (down)   *-a·c...rirakʷ*

   (over)   *-iweʔeha*

   (off)   *-taksi*

far   *tac tiʔi·wah*   *tac* 'big' + *tiʔi·wah* 'it extends'

fat   *he·c; kira·sʔa* 'grease, lard'

father   *tá·tah* (vocative); *ʔiʔassi* (possessed)

fear   *-u...wakhánniya·s* 'be afraid'; *-hisica·s* 'be frightened'

feather   *ni·sʔa*

few   *tawʔic*

fight   *-ʔica·ri*

finger   *iskʔicʔa*

fire   *ye·cʔa* (noun); *-keʔe* 'be fire' (verb); *icka* (locative); *chirʔa* 'flame'. (Initial |y| is pronounced /h/.)

fish   *ka·cʔa*

five   *iskʷi·c*

float   *-a~u...hicaʔa* 'float to surface'; *-hicaʔiriya·s* 'float around on the surface'. Cf. *hi* 'water', *ca* 'surface', *ʔa* 'come' and *ʔiriya·s* 'go randomly'.

flow   *-uc...kíris*, from *kir* 'water' + *hisha* 'go'.

flower   *a·wicʔa*

fog   *-ʔiskʷa·wi* (verb)

foam   *wa·hi·sʔa*

foot   *as·ʔa*

four   *tá·kʷic*

freeze   *-ra·hi*

Friday   *acs nasa·khaskhírih*   'When a good day is going by.'

fruit   No generic term

full   *táwa·wi*

gamble   *-a·c...ʔaris*

gambler   *wakháteʔ*

give   *-reʔehisha* (imperfective), *-raʔa·w* (perfective) 'hand over'; *-uc...ʔih* 'as a gift'

good   *acs*

grass   *hí·ya·kha·rʔa; hanc* 'hay; dry grass'

green   *kawʔac*

guts   *niya:cʔa*

hair   *tiya:cʔa*

hand   *iskʔa*

he   *ha·rí·h*   'that one'

head   *weʔekʔa; ickiʔsʔa* 'forehead; top of head'

hear   *-ʔa·ckhéʔe; -ʔa·ckhikeʔe*. Cf. *a·cʔa* 'ear'

heart   *sikicʔa*

heavy   *kikʔi·c*

here   *tiʔrih*

hip   *ka·ski·sʔa* 'leg bone'

hit   *-ti·kʷ* 'snap; tap; hit'; *ʔisi* 'hit; sock'

hold   *-iʔahi*

horn   *ʔarikʔa*

horse   *kawá·rah*   Combining form *ta·ras*. Probably a loan from Spanish *caballo*.

house   *akha·rʔa*

   grass house   *háncʔakha·rʔa*

how   *e·si·h*

hunt   *-r...kiya·shis*

husband   *kirʔa* (always possessed)

I   *nacʔih*

ice   *na·hicʔa*

if   No single word. Use conditional tense forms.

in *ka* 'in topless enclosure; *ka·* 'in completely enclosed space'; *kha* 'on the bottom inside'.

kill *-ki* (singular object); *-ʔessa* (plural object); *-riya·kʔaw* 'murder'; also, for animals, *-teʔesiki* 'cause to die'

Kitsai *kíche·s*

Kiowa *ká·hi·waʔ*

knee *ki·skʷasʔa*

knife *ta·haʔa*

know *-wickaʔa*; non–third-person pronouns demand *-Ricka·ʔa* (cf. say); *-ʔïkha·rʔi* (optional for plural subject); *-riyakha·rʔi* 'know how'

lake No special word. Use *ha·hira·rʔa* 'body of water'

laugh *-wakharikikʷ*

leaf *kíʔinca·cʔa*

left (side) *assa·hah*

leg *ka·sʔa* 'above knee'; *ʔiki·sʔa* 'below knee'

lie *-ʔirhawi* 'be in a lying position'

lie *wákhiʔa* 'untruth'; *-iwákhiya·s* 'tell a lie'

live *-ʔicaki* 'sit; dwell'

liver *karikʔa*

long *tac tá·ki* 'big' + 'be a size'

louse *wi·c* Homonymous with 'man'

lungs *hákari·s*

man *wi·c*

many *ʔiyarhah*

meat *ʔaras·ʔa*

Monday *kíriwaré·sa·khíʔnnih* 'when it is no longer his day' (See example 75)

moon *wá·h*

mother *éciye·h* (vocative); *-ka·hi·k-* 'woman' (possessed). Cf. 'earth'

mountains *-wa·-* in e.g. *nawa·reʔerhárih* 'where there are mountains' (verb only)

mouth *ha·kaʔa*

mucus *incʔa*

name *hissa·rʔa*

narrow *kʔi·s tikateʔe* 'the side is small'

navel *niwi·cʔa*

near *tharah*

neck *kiticʔa*

new *hoʔos;* also 'recent, soon'

night *ckha·rʔa*

nine *chíʔass kínti·ʔi* 'one is not'

nose *tisʔa*

not *kírih*

old *tackʷah*

one *chíʔass* Occasionally in sentences *ass* is used. *chiʔ* 'only'

other *witího·h* 'different'

paint *sis*

Pawnee *awá·hí·h*

penis *wacʔa*

person *iha·s*

play *-a·c...ʔicha* Cf. 'dance'. *-irikwi* 'play ball'..

pole *ti·kʔa*

potatoes *kakickhárik* 'thick and dry'

pull *-hawati* 'from ground'

pumpkin *kéʔess*

rabbit *kó·kis*

rain *-a...hiriʔa* (verb only)

red *kʷha·c*

rib *sacʔa*

right (true) *-wé·h* (verb root; also means 'yes')

right side *acskʷíkeʔe·s* 'good arm side'

river *nahe·hárih* 'where the water-place is'; cf. lake

road *hachirʔa* (noun); *-yac* 'be a road' (verb)

root *ʔaski·cʔa*

rope *ya·khasʔa* (Initial *y* is pronounced /h/.)

rotten *ke·cʔa* Also used for 'brown'

rub *-teʔeriyar* 'rub against'; *-kiri* 'rub on'

salt *ka·hi·c*

sand *ki·cha·rʔa*

Saturday *wa·khácsa·khirʔa* 'cow day'

say *-wakʔa* (non–third-person pronouns use *-Rakʔa*)

scalp *ʔicki·sʔa* 'top of head'; *e·ssa·rʔa* 'captured scalp'

see *-ʔi:s*

seed *hikaʔasʔa*; *niki·sʔa* 'seed for planting'

seven *kiyáhwic* Cf. 'two' and 'eight'

sew *-riya·tíri*

sharp *-riʔacʔi* 'of a blade'; *-ʔickhacʔi* 'of a point'

shoot *-ʔiyaca* 'an arrow'; *-ʔiya·c* 'a person'

   shoot at *-iwariki*

short *thara tihírʔak* 'close' + 'be a height'

sing *-kira·h*

sit *-ʔicaki*

six *kíyehes*

skin *kitha·rʔa*

607

sky   *askha·r²a*; *askhákasir*

sleep   *-hi²inck*

small   *k²i·s* (stative verb); *Rikic* (adjective)

smoke   *wí²i·k²a* 'tobacco; tobacco smoke'; *ick^we²e·k²a* 'fire smoke'

snake   *hi·c*

snow   *hira·²a* (noun); *-a·...²i·²a* (verb)

spit (out)   *-hawati*

star   *hí·k^wirik²a*; North Star *ka·hasá·rkih* 'it always stands still'; Big Dipper *kiyahwicí·²ih* 'The Seven'; Morning Star *hasé·yasira²ah* 'It brings'.

stick   *ya·k^ws²a* (Initial |y| is pronounced /h/.)

stone   *²ika·²a*

sun   *sa·khir²a*   Also used for 'day'.

Sunday   *ná·sa·khí²nnih*   'when it is his day' (See example 74)

tail   *ki·ya·k²a*

ten   *iskhiri²awá·s*

testicles   *nikwi·k²a*   'egg'

that   *ha·rí·h*

there   *harah*

thick   *tac ta·cikit*   'big' + 'it has thickness'

thin   *k²i·s ta·cikit*   'small' + 'it has thickness'

think   No separate word. Use 'know'.

this   *ti²i*

thou   *nas²ih*

three   *taw*

throw   *-riwihi*

Thursday   *ní·c²arhi²irhé·sishah* 'the day they go to stay overnight'

tie   *-thiyaki*

toe   *²ask²ic²a*

toenail   *²askwic²a*

tongue   *hac²a*

tooth   *a·k²a*

Tawakoni   *tawa·kháriw*

tree   *tiya·hkw*

Tuesday   *wicha kínné·sa·khí²innih* 'twice it's not his day'

turn   *-tar²a·ti*

twenty   *chí²ass ti·cíksi²i*; *wicha ki²iskhiri²awá·s²arih* 'two tens'

two   *wic*

urinate   *-a·has*

urine   *ka·hásskic²a*

608   vagina   *ta·c²a*

Waco   *wí·ko·²*

warm   *wari·c*

wash   *-u...hicaki*

water   *kic²a* (isolation form); *kir* (combining form); *ha, hi* (locative)

we   *hiracíyarih* 'dual inclusive'; *hirac²arih* 'dual exclusive; *nacíra·k²ih* 'plural inclusive'; *nacá·k²ih* 'plural exclusive'

Wednesday   *nackháti·kih* 'the middle day'

what?   *e·kirih*

when?   *e·sis*

where?   *e·si·h...²as²;* *e·ka·h*

white   *khac*

White man   *istá·hi²i*

who?   *e·kiyah*

Wichita   *kirikir²i·s,* is usually said to mean 'Raccoon-Eyed', referring to the custom of tattooing the face, especially around the eyes. If this analysis is correct, the grammar of this compound is unique: *kirik* 'eye' + *kir²i·s* 'raccoon' violates the regular pattern of combining noun roots in the order modifier-modified. A possible explanation is that **kir²i·skirik(²a)*, the expected form, would mean 'hole in a raccoon', because of the homonymy of *kirik* 'eye' and *-kirik-* 'hole in'. It is more likely that this is a compound of an obsolete word, *kirika* (found in Kitsai) meaning 'person', and *hir²i·s* 'first', meaning 'first people'. The most serious problem with this etymology is that the loss of initial *h-* from the second element of the compound is unusual.

wide   *tac tikáte²e*   'The side is big'.

wife   *-²ak-* (possessed only)

wind   *niwe²é·r²a*   Also used for 'air'.

wing   *wíkariya·k²a*

witch   *niyá·khis*

with   suffix *Rá·hir²* 'instrumental'; use 'and'.

wolf   *wáse²ekha·r²a*

woman   *ka·hi·k²a*

woods   *niya·khánn²írih* 'where there is much timber'

worm   *ke²e·c*

yellow   *narisis*

yes   *wé:h*

Sketch of Thompson, a Salishan Language

LAURENCE C. THOMPSON, M. TERRY THOMPSON, AND STEVEN M. EGESDAL

The Thompson Indians of southern British Columbia speak a northern Interior Salish language with mild dialectal differentiation (fig. 1). Thompson and Thompson based their work on study with distinguished and exceptionally knowledgeable speakers, beginning primary work in 1964 with Chief William Samson (b. 1901, d. about 1990) of Kanaka Bar. Egesdal worked from 1980 to 1983 with Hilda Austin (fig. 2) of Lytton. The Thompsons worked from 1975 to 1989 with Mabel Joe (fig. 3) of Lower Nicola, from 1979 to 1989 with Mary Coutlee (fig. 4) of Merritt, and from 1968 to 1991 collecting the most extensive material from Annie York (fig. 5) of Spuzzum. As a young woman York studied specialized topics in the language with the oldest and most knowledgeable speakers available in preparation for medical interpreting work, and she had experience with several dialects. She was the principal guide in the analytical work. Primarily Spuzzum (Lower Thompson) dialect is represented here.

1. SOURCES

Early treatments of the Thompson language are few: Gibbs (1877), Good (1878, 1879, 1880, 1880a), Boas (1899), and Hill-Tout (1900). The most extensive earlier recording was done by James Teit, who was married to a Thompson woman and reportedly knew the language well. His notes and publications (Teit 1900, 1930, and manuscripts in the American Philosophical Society Library, Philadelphia) transcribe many words. The phonetic structure of the language is especially difficult, and these early researchers did little analysis. Boas's and Teit's transcriptions are often unreliable for phonetic detail and difficult to interpret, even after considerable experience.

Other field researchers have collected language data used for this chapter: Bouchard (1973, 1974), Kinkade (1989-1993), Kuipers (1973), Mayes (1975-1979), Suttles (1951, 1962), and Turner (1973-1989). Besides

these materials and Thompson and Thompson (1962-1982), Egesdal (1980-1984), and M.T. Thompson (1985-1991), there are manuscripts containing linguistic data in the Canadian Museum of Civilization, Hull, Quebec; the National Anthropological Archives, Smithsonian Institution, Washington; and the American Philosophical Society Library, Boas Collection. The monographic description by Thompson and Thompson (1992) contains an extensive list of references to earlier work on the language. Additional published sources include Laforet, Turner, and York (1993) on traditional food categories and M.T.

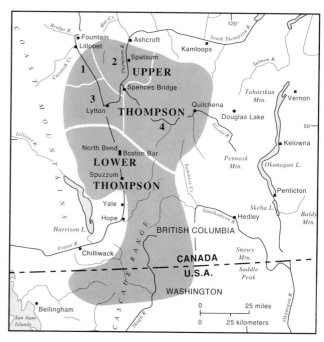

Fig. 1. Approximate precontact distribution of the Thompson language, though probably only the hunting range extended so far south. Upper Thompson dialects are: 1, Upper Fraser; 2. Spences Bridge; 3, Lytton; 4, Nicola (after Teit 1900).

Thompson and Egesdal (1993) and Egesdal and M.T. Thompson (1994) on analyses of legends. Thompson and Thompson (1996) is an exhaustive dictionary.

2. PHONOLOGY

2.1.

Consonants are charted in table 1. Some boxes extend over two categories; the consonant symbol is placed to reflect the primary articulation, with the empty spaces suggesting nondistinctive variants.

The first two obstruent categories contain stops (including affricates), which are forcefully articulated. The glottalized stops are ejectives. Plain stops and spirants tend to be heard as voiced in many voiced surroundings (spectrographic analysis has not shown actual voicing; Mayes 1979). Plain stops are unaspirated before vowels and resonants, but somewhat aspirated before a spirant, and regularly before another stop. In syllable-final position plain stops are strongly aspirated. In allegro speech, *p, t* are unreleased before their homorganic nasals *m, n*, respectively.

The resonants and spirants form a larger class of continuants. Of the resonants, *y, ẏ, w, ẇ* are semi-vowels; the rest are liquids. Resonants generally have syllabic status between two obstruents, between an obstruent and a pause, or between another resonant and an obstruent or pause. Perceiving laryngealization in resonants *ṁ, ṅ, l̇, ż*, etc., can be difficult, especially in allegro speech.

In table 1 the labials are regularly bilabial. The contrast between *p* and *ṗ* is particularly hard for the nonnative ear to discern (especially vis-à-vis postvelars *q* and *q̇*, which are easily distinguished). Dentals and laterals are articulated fundamentally with the tongue tip touching the back or roots of the upper teeth. *λ̇* is a glottalized dental stop with lateral affricative ejective release. *λ̇* is the only common dental ejective, as Proto-Salishan *ṫ and *λ̇ coalesced historically in Thompson. Glottalized dental *ṫ* accordingly is rare, limited to apparently borrowed or archaic words; it also occurs occasionally as a nondistinctive variant of *λ̇*. *t* is sporadically pronounced as an affricate [λ]. Lateral resonants *l, l̇* are relatively uncommon; historically Proto-Salishan *l, *l̇ > Th *y, ẏ*, and Th *l, l̇* are either borrowings or derive from Proto-Salishan *r, *ṙ (Kinkade and Thompson 1974). Glottalized *ṅ* (but not plain *n*) is assimilated to [ŋ̇] directly before a velar stop in the same syllable.

Among the postdentals, *ċ* is basically a glottalized postdental stop with sibilant affrication in its ejective release; it is palatalized frequently before a rounded uvular stop (e.g., *qʷ, q̇ʷ*). *z, ż* are alveolar slit spirants, resembling *z* in position, but *th* in English *breathe* in shaping. *z, ż* are articulated with some lateral opening, which can cause the nonnative ear to confuse them with *l, l̇*, respectively (and especially *ż* and *l̇*). *c, s* are alveolar, with hollowing of the tongue behind the tip; they

are not common, appearing primarily in special environments involving tongue-root retraction. *c̣* resembles the consonants in English *its*, *ṣ* the sibilant in *sauce*; both have a dark, hollow timbre, caused by a cupping of the tongue in back of the key point of articulation (but not retroflexed).

Among alveopalatals, spirant *s* is usually similar to the shibilants in English *shush*, and *c* is usually similar to the affricates in English *church* (or commonly those in *judge* when unaspirated). *y, ẏ* are palatal semi-vowels, very similar to *y* in English *yes, boy*.

Prevelar obstruents *k, k̇, x* are very front (almost palatal); *kʷ, k̇ʷ, xʷ* are rounded (labiovelar) and produced further back than their simple prevelar counterparts. Prevelars are noticeably backed in the neighborhood of a postvelar in the same word. Simple prevelars *k, k̇, x* seem to have a slight [ʲ] offglide in clusters and final position; *x* correspondingly often resembles the prevelar fricative [ç] in German *ich*. The prevelar resonants *γ, γ̇* are front velar spirants with very little friction; they are exceedingly rare and

Fig. 2. Hilda Austin (b. about 1912, d. 1994), with bulbs of yellow avalanche lily (*Erythronium grandiflorum*), which she collected in Botanie Valley, near Lytton, B.C. The bulbs were used in a "pudding" along with saskatoon berries, salmon eggs, deer fat, and roots. Austin, a talented storyteller, was Egesdal's linguistic consultant from 1980 to 1983. Photograph by Harriet Kuhnlein, Lytton, B.C., 1984.

Table 1. Consonants

	Labial	Dental	Lateral	Post-dental	Alveo-palatal	Simple (pre-)velar	Rounded (pre-)velar	Simple Post-velar	Rounded Post-velar	Laryngeal
Obstruents										
Stops, glottalized ejective	ṗ	ṫ	λ̓		ċ	k̓	k̓ʷ	q̓	q̓ʷ	
Stops, plain	p	t		ç	c	k	kʷ	q	qʷ	ʔ
Spirants			ɬ	ṣ	s	x	xʷ	x̣	x̣ʷ	h
Resonants										
Plain	m	n	l	z	y	γ	w	ʕ	ʕʷ	
Laryngealized	ṁ	ṅ	l̓	z̓	ẏ	γ̓	ẇ	ʕ̓	ʕ̓ʷ	

apparently are being replaced with *y, ẏ*. Older speakers (born before 1915) have *γ, γ̓*, where younger speakers (born after 1915) tend to have *y, ẏ*, especially in postvocalic position following [i], such as *niγpíkn̓* versus *niypíkn* 'noon.' Both groups have *γ* in words such as *syép* 'tree' or *smγéẇ* 'lynx.' Rounded prevelars *kʷ, k̓ʷ, xʷ* are produced at roughly the position of English [k] in *cool*. The resonants of this rounded prevelar set are simply the semivowels *w, ẇ*.

Simple postvelar obstruents *q, q̓, x̣* vary from very back (uvular) articulation to positions close to that of English [k] in *cool*. They are quite clearly distinguished from prevelars *k, k̓, x*, which themselves are rather far front. Rounded postvelars *qʷ, q̓ʷ, x̣ʷ* are most easily confused with their rounded prevelar counterparts *kʷ, k̓ʷ, xʷ*. While *qʷ, q̓ʷ, x̣ʷ* are sometimes clearly uvular, they are most often produced farther front, often very close to the place of articulation for the rounded prevelars *kʷ, k̓ʷ, xʷ*. The Nicola Valley dialect shows wider spacing (and thus less perceptual ambiguity) between the rounded prevelars and postvelars. Postvelar resonants *ʕ, ʕʷ, ʕ̓, ʕ̓ʷ*, are basically pharyngeals, produced by retraction of the tongue root and general narrowing of the pharynx. The plain pharyngeals *ʕ, ʕʷ* commonly have some uvular friction or occasionally a uvular trill, and occasionally some suggestion of creaky glottal production. The laryngealized counterparts *ʕ̓, ʕ̓ʷ*, usually involve a full glottal stop.

The laryngeal glottal stop *ʔ* is very common; laryngeal spirant *h* is relatively infrequent. *h* is sometimes difficult to distinguish from prevelar spirant *x*; *h* and postvelar spirant *x̣* vary freely in certain words.

2.2.

Vowels are shown in figure 6. The primary vowels are *i, u, e, ə*; the others are retracted counterparts, which are less common and to some extent automatic variants of primary vowels.

i, fundamentally similar to *i* in English *machine,* has variants resembling *é* in French *été* after postvelars, and *e* in English *jet* before postvelars. After a postvelar it frequently has a brief central onglide. *į* is similar to French *é*, but centralized and accompanied by lowering of the back of the tongue; it is rare.

u, basically similar to *u* in English *prune*, sounds like the vowel in *foot* in closed syllables before rounded prevelars, like *o* in French *mot* by postvelars and sometimes in other positions. After an unrounded velar it has a noticeable central onglide. *o* is low back rounded, resembling *o* in French *bonne* (and similar to the vowel of American English *law*).

e has a norm similar to the vowel in French *belle*, but it is higher before *y, ẏ*, and otherwise often lower (like the vowel in English *cat*), especially near retracted consonants. *a* ranges in the low central to back area, rather like *a* in American English *father, farm* and unrounded pronunciations of *o* in *hot, sob*.

ə (schwa) is lax; it varies from a rather low back unrounded vowel like that of most American pronunciations of *but, luck* adjacent to retracted consonants, to a lower high central unrounded vowel resembling the unstressed vowel in many American pronunciations of *roses*. It has rather high variants, fronted before palatals, backed and somewhat rounded adjacent to rounded velars. *ạ* is similar to the vowel of American *but, luck*, but lower and farther back.

The lax vowels *ə, ạ* oppose all the other vowels, which are tense. Certain vowels are homorganic (produced with roughly the same position of the vocal organs) to consonants: *i* to *y, u* to *w, a* to *ʕ, o* to *ʕʷ*; similarly, *e* acts morphophonemically as homorganic to *ʔ, h*.

2.3.

Intonational elements have not been extensively studied. The stresses marked are primary (´) and secondary (`). Unstressed syllables are unmarked except

Fig. 3. Mabel Joe (*lúsləstkʷu*; b. 1917) holding a mat made of common reed grasses (*Phragmites communis*) collected from Nicola Lake. It was used traditionally for drying berries. Well known for teaching both language and culture in the local schools, Joe worked with Sharon Mayes, and with M.T. Thompson to transcribe and translate texts. Photograph by Nancy Turner, Lower Nicola, B.C., 1985.

the grammatical system shows that such words are made up of strings of meaningful subparts, morphemes, many of which have vowels when they fall under stress. But each word has just a single main stress, and vowels mostly drop out of the unstressed morphemes. There are also some adaptations of consonants that come together.

The shape of a word with all its morphemes in full is an underlying form, cited between vertical bars, the morphemes separated by hyphens (-), double hyphens (=), root signs (√), brackets [ ], or the reduplication symbol (•): |√cúɫ=aqs-xi-t-exʷ|. The word as it is pronounced is a surface form, cited in italics (either with or without morpheme boundaries marked): /cúɫ=qs-x-t-xʷ/. Underlying forms are given where they seem necessary to clarify the discussion. Derivation of surface forms often involves several developments in a particular order, so that intermediate shapes of words can be recognized; sometimes it will help to cite several of these successive stages between vertical bars, the order of changes shown by greater-than signs,

Fig. 4. Mary Coutlee (*cəncənpínek*; b. about 1915) collecting the leaves and seed stalks of "wild celery" (*Lomatium nudicaule*). The leaves are used as a green vegetable, both raw and cooked, and the seeds as a flavoring for stews, soups, and tea. Coutlee studied at the University of Victoria, learning the phonetic system of writing her language and is well known for teaching language and culture in local schools. Photograph by Nancy Turner, Botanie Valley, B.C., 1980.

in underlying forms (˘). The distinct phrase-end intonations are: nonterminal (,)—ending below mid range without dramatic rise or fall, nonfinal sentence portion; general (.)—mid-high with last primary stress, abrupt drop to low, usual sentence end (including factual questions); soliciting (?)—mid-high with last primary stress, light rise, request for confirmation; and inconclusive(—)—abrupt rise from low mid on final syllable, indicating incompleteness, doubt, disinterest. Two marked individual segment intonations are distinguished: special emphasis (*aá*)—lilting rise in middle of stressed vowel, for emphasis, insistence; and rhetorical segment lengthening (*á···*)—extra-long segment (usually vowel) with high pitch, for colorful emphasis and discourse marking in narrative.

2.4. WORD FORMATION

The language displays long consonant clusters. As many as six successive obstruents have been observed in the same word without intervening vowels; for example, *cúɫqsxtxʷ* 'you point a gun at him'. Study of

612

meaning 'becomes': |√cúɫ=aqs-xi-t-exʷ| > |cúɫqsxitexʷ| > |cúɫqsxitxʷ| /cúɫ=qs-x-t-xʷ. (The intermediate steps show no separation between morphemes, and the number of steps may not be exhaustive.)

The following symbols and abbreviations are used in this sketch:

[...]	(brackets)	infix
|...|	(vertical bars)	underlying representation
/...	(slash)	what follows is the stem (surface form) of the lexical root
√...	(root sign)	root in underlying form
-	(hyphen)	non-reduplicating affix: ...- prefix, -... suffix
=	(double hyphen)	lexical suffix
•	(bullet)	reduplicating affix: ...•(/stem) prefix, (/stem)•... suffix, [•...] infix
--	(two hyphens)	regenerated form
-=	(hyphen and double hyphen)	regenerated form with lexical suffix
V···	(3 raised dots after vowel)	rhetorical lengthening of vowel
[']	(raised comma inside brackets)	(in underlying forms) glottalization of immediately preceding resonant
( )	(parentheses)	optional material
:	(colon within a word)	marking end of intransitive theme before transitive increment or possessive ending
C	(capital c)	any consonant
V	(capital v)	any vowel

The term root refers to the underlying phonetic form of a lexical morpheme without affixation, including reduplication, or morphophonemic changes caused by affixation. It is preceded by the root sign (√). The term stem is used to mean the surface form, which may be affected by any or all of the above. It is preceded by a slash (/), used as a stem marker. Some roots have only one surface stem, and it is identical to the underlying form of the root. This has sometimes been referred to as the "root stem." Here it is called the underlying stem. Many roots have several surface representations (stems), depending on the stress pattern introduced by morphophonemic changes. For example, |√cəw| 'do, make, work' (root), with stems /c[ʔ]uw-, /cəw- (underlying stem), cə•/cuʔ-, cə•/cw̓-, /cu-, /cuw-, /cw.

Simple words contain only a single morpheme, which is a root: /kʷəɫ [liquid] runs, spills'. Complex words contain one or more other morphemes, affixes, as well as the basic morpheme (the root): ʔes/kʷəɫ 'it is

Fig. 5. Annie York (zíx̣tkʷu; b. 1904, d. 1991), collecting saskatoon berries or serviceberries (*Amelanchier alnifolia*), the most important fruit for the Thompson people. York was the principal linguistic consultant of the Thompsons from 1968 to 1991. She learned to speak numerous dialects, translating for elderly Christian Indians and their doctors. Her knowledge of the culture, customs, history, genealogy, and ethnobotany of the region was renowned. Photograph by Robert D. Turner, Spuzzum, B.C., 1980.

spilled' (ʔes- 'stative aspect', a prefix), /kʷəɫ-t-és 'he pours it out' (-t 'transitive', -és 'third-person subject', suffixes). A stem is also a root expanded by compounding (with another root), adding grammatical affixes (e.g., inchoative, proportional) or lexical suffixes, or by adding certain presumably vestigial elements. When a word has several affixes they are not added all at once, but in successive layers of derivation, so that various stems can be recognized to which affixes are added. For example, in /cúɫ=qs-x-t-xʷ 'you point a gun at him':

|√cúɫ| 'point, direct'
|√cúɫ=aqs| 'point a gun' (=aqs 'nose, point, end', a lexical suffix [3.1.1.])
|√cúɫ=aqs-xi-t| 'point a gun at someone' (indirective |-xi|, which shows the action is directed toward another person, and |-t| 'transitive')
|√cúɫ=aqs-xi-t-exʷ| 'you point a gun at him'(|-exʷ| 'you [2d sg.subject]').

Some stems have infixes (enclosed in brackets in both underlying and surface forms): e.g., /qʷéc 'it is warm', |√qʷe[ʔˇ]c| /qʷ[ʔ]éc 'it gets warm', |√qʷe[ʔˇ]c=cin| /qʷe[ʔˇ]c=cín 'weather gets warm' (|[ʔˇ]| 'inchoative').

Words of different kinds are affected differently in derivation. Particles (3.1.2.) sometimes have their own stress, sometimes are unstressed; unstressed particles are either proclitic, belonging to the breath group of the following stressed word, or enclitic, similarly attached to the stressed word they come after. Major words (3.1.4.) are either transitive or intransitive

(3.3.); transitive words have a transitive increment at the end—a sequence of several morphemes added to a basic stem, the intransitive theme. In /cúɫ=qs-x-t-xʷ/ the intransitive theme |√cúɫ=aqs-| 'point nose (or front end)' and the transitive increment |-xi-t-exʷ| 'you act on some object with reference to a particular person' can be recognized. Intransitive themes often appear as intransitive words by themselves: /cúɫ/ 'he points out (a particular thing)', /cúɫ=qs/ 'he points a gun'.

The changes in morphemes within most words follow principles of internal combination; they are somewhat different in intransitive themes and in transitive increments. In talking, a person says several words together before he takes a breath; where words come together in such a breath group, morphemes are adapted in external combination; some changes are different from those in internal combination. Some words are extended by special principles from regularly derived stems; these are secondary formations, and the adaptations involved are like those of external combination. In underlying forms suffixes added in secondary formations are separated from stems by two hyphens (--) or a hyphen and a double hyphen in case of a lexical suffix (-=). (See also 2.5.)

2.5. STRESS PATTERNS

The main stress of a word is determined by the nature of the elements that make it up. Each morpheme has inherent stress characteristics, and there are regular rules for dominance. Prefixes are unstressed and do not affect the position of main stress. Infixes are specialized and best discussed with their particular formations. Main stress falls either on the root or on one of the suffixes of a word. Some roots and suffixes are strong: they have underlying primary stress (written with the acute accent in underlying forms). Other roots are weak.

In underlying stems a stem stands alone or last. In those involving a strong root, main stress falls on the syllable with underlying stress: |√tékɫ| /tékɫ/ 'it rains', |√xʷesít| /xʷesít/ 'she walks'. Where the root is weak, main stress falls on the latest unstressed vowel before the root's last consonant: |ʔes√səq| /ʔes/sáq/ 'split', |ʔes√k̓ʷeʔ| /ʔes/k̓ʷéʔ/ 'chewed', and |√sələk| /slák/ 'it turns'.

Some underlying vowels have secondary stress (marked with the grave accent in the underlying forms); they do not disappear as most other vowels do when unstressed. Such syllables occasionally retain the secondary stress in surface forms but usually are like other unstressed syllables. On the other hand, main word stress falls on a vowel with underlying secondary stress only if there is no other stressable vowel: |√k̓ʷinèx| /k̓ʷínex/ 'how many (are there)?', |√seyè| /séye/ '(there are) two', and |ɫuč•√ɫuč-t| /ɫuč•/ɫúč-t/ 'bushy'.

Suffixes are also of various shapes and several different underlying stress characteristics, which emerge as they combine with stems. A suffix captures stress from a stem when it is equal or greater in strength. Thus a strong suffix will take stress from either a weak or strong root: |-mémn| 'desiderative', |√cəw-mémn| /cu-mémn/ 'want to work', and |√tékɫ-mémn| /tekɫ-mémn/ 'trying to rain'. A nonstrong suffix will take stress from a weak root, but not from a strong root: |=qin| 'head, top', |√wuxʷt=qin| /wuxʷt=qín/ 'snow on top (of mountains)', and |ʔes√q̓áż=qin| /ʔes/q̓áż-qn/ 'slanted on top (roof of shelter)'.

However, there are differences among nonstrong suffixes with respect to further derivation. There are a few that capture stress from a weak stem, forming

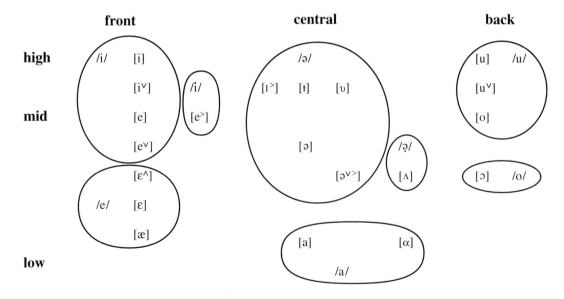

front   central   back

high /i/ [i]   /ə/   [u] /u/
      [iˇ]   /i/   [ɪ>] [ɫ] [ʊ]   [uˇ]
      [e]   [e>]   [o]
mid   [eˇ]   [ə]   /ə̣/
      [ɛ^]   [əˇ>] [ʌ] [ɔ] /o/
/e/ [ɛ]
      [æ]
                    [a]   [α]
low   /a/

614   Fig. 6. Primary vowels and retracted counterparts.

again a weak stem that will lose stress in further derivation; these are weak suffixes and are marked with |˘| in underlying forms; for example, |=xə̌n| 'foot, leg' captures stress from a weak root |√kəɬ| 'detach' in |ʔes√kəɬ=xə̌n| ʔes/kəɬ=xén 'have shoe(s) off' but loses it again to following |-ə̌me| 'middle voice' (also a weak suffix) in |√kəɬ=xə̌n-ə̌me| /kəɬ=xn-ə́m 'take shoe(s) off'.

Other suffixes (left unmarked in underlying forms) are ambivalent; they do not capture stress from a strong stem (e.g., |=qin| in ʔes/q̇áž=qn above), but when they do take stress, they create a stem that is strong in further derivation: |√kəɬ=qin:-t-es| > |kəɬqíntes| /kəɬ=qín-s 'she takes the top off it'.

Remaining suffixes either lack a vowel or have underlying secondary stress; they never take main word stress: |-t| 'immediate', |√péw-t| /péw-t 'swollen (just swelled up)', |√sə̌k-t| /sə́k-t 'got hit [by falling branch]'; |-è| 'imperative', |√x̌ʷəs-t-è| /x̌ʷə́s-t-e 'go home!', |√x̌ʷesít-è| /x̌ʷesít-e 'walk!'.

The addition of a strong suffix actually involves a new layer of derivation; a previously derived main stress in the stem is shifted to secondary: |√wík:-t-es| /wík-c 'she sees it', |√wík:-t-ə̌yxs| > |wìktíyxs| /wik-t-íyxs 'they see it', |√kəɬ=qin:-t-ə̌yxs| > |kəɬqíntə̌yxs| > |kəɬqìntíyxs| /kəɬ=qin-t-íyxs 'they take the top off it'.

Some strong suffixes have two syllables, both with underlying primary stress (e.g., |-éwíɬ| 'canoe, conveyance'). Following a weak stem main stress falls on the first syllable of the suffix and the second suffix syllable loses stress: |s√q̇ʷut=éwíɬ| > |sq̇ʷutéwiɬ| s/q̇ʷət=éwɬ '(other) side of the canoe'. But after a strong stem, main stress falls on the suffix's second syllable, and the first syllable shifts to secondary: |√zéx=éwíɬ| > |zèxèwíɬ| /zex=ewíɬ 'long canoe'.

After main stress is assigned certain changes take place in the segmented sequence. One prominent change is laryngeal movement. In the syllable directly before main stress a laryngeal (regardless of its underlying position) either precedes or follows the vowel, depending on the configuration of the syllable. If there is a single consonant or a cluster beginning in an obstruent intervening between the stressed vowel and the laryngeal, then the laryngeal precedes that consonant or cluster directly. In other words, the laryngeal ends the preceding syllable, and the single consonant or cluster begins the stressed syllable: |√mək̇ʷʔu:-t-es| > |mək̇ʷutés| > |mək̇ʷuʔtés| /mk̇ʷuʔ-t-és 'she wraps it', |√cəh:-t-es| > |cehtés| /ce-t-és 'he fixes it.' If there is no intervening consonant before the stressed vowel, or if there intervenes a cluster beginning in a resonant, then the laryngeal precedes the vowel of the first pretonic syllable. In other words, the laryngeal follows directly after the consonant (or cluster) that begins the syllable preceding the stressed one: |√mək̇ʷʔu=eṅih:-n-t-es| > |mək̇ʷuéṅihntés| /mək̇ʷʔ=éṅi-n-s 'she wraps, covers it up', |√cəh-ə̌me| > |cəhə́me| > |cheə́me| /ch-ém 'she puts

(things) away'.

Secondary formations (2.4.) are based on primary stems, which already have a main stress determined in the regular manner. The location of some affixes depends on the position of that main stress: |√čəʔ=eyèp| /č̇ʔ=éyep 'mat', with diminutive (6.7.1.) |√čəʔ=é[•ʔe]yèp| /č̇ʔ=é[•ʔ]yep 'little mat'; |k̇ʷáx̌ʷe 'box,' /k̇ʷá[•k̇ʷ]x̌ʷe 'little box'; /n/tɬ=úymx̌ʷ 'it strings out over the ground,' n-təɬ•/tɬ=ú[•ɬ]yṁx̌ʷ 'twinflower (Linnaea borealis)'. In secondary suffixation stress shifts to the first stressable suffix after the primary stem; the effect is the same as in the addition of a strong suffix to a strong stem. (A weak or ambivalent suffix in that position is thus treated as strong.) Further suffixes are treated as in primary formations. |nə√q̇íx̌=cin:--n-t-sut| n/q̇ix̌=cn--n-cút 'he locks himself in', |nə√x̌ʷél-əyx=eṅih:-n-t-ey-es| n/x̌ʷel-ix-=éṅi-n-t-i-s 'he flies over us' (n/x̌ʷél-ix 'he flies', |=eṅih| 'ear; position over, on top').

Unstressed portions of words are pretonic, before main stress; and posttonic, after main stress.

2.6. Retention of Unstressed Vowels
In unstressed syllables most underlying vowels disappear entirely; however, in special circumstances both tense and lax vowels are retained, and some tense vowels survive reduced to ə. In more rapid speech there is a tendency to reduce more and more of the surviving unstressed tense vowels to ə; these reductions are beyond the more careful speech reflected in transcription here. Certain configurations protect vowels from loss.

2.6.1.
Surviving tense vowels retain coloring when they: (1) have underlying stress: |√wík:-t-ə̌yxs| > |wìktíyxs| /wik-t-íyxs 'they see him', |k̇ʷinèx=eɬči ʔ| /k̇ʷənex=éɬči ʔ 'how many carcasses?'; (2) fall at end of a word: |√ʔíq̇ʷ=cin-ə̌me| /ʔíq̇ʷ=cn-me 'he shaves'; or (3) precede a laryngeal: |√ci[ʔˉ]ʕʷ-ə̌me| /ci[ʔ]ʕʷ-ə́m 'make (something) bleed', |√tə́ɬeʔ| /tə̇ɬeʔ 'tongue'.

2.6.2.
Otherwise surviving tense vowels are reduced to ə: (1) optionally in a pretonic syllable after a laryngeal: |ʔiƛ̌•√ʔíƛ̌-ə̌me| ʔiƛ̌•/ʔíƛ̌-m ~ ʔəƛ̌•/ʔíƛ̌-m 'they sing'; (2) optionally in a nonreduplicative final syllable before an obstruent: |√ʔúpən=ekst| /ʔúpn=ekst ~ /ʔúpn=əkst 'ten'; and (3) obligatorily in other cases: |s√q̇ʷut=éwíɬ| s/q̇ʷət=éwɬ '(other) side of the canoe', |wik•√wík:-t-ex̌ʷ| wek•/wík-t-x̌ʷ 'you see them', |√mús•mus| /mús•məs 'four people'.

In the case of optional reductions, words are hereafter transcribed with the unreduced vowels.

2.6.3.
Vowels with underlying stress remain except directly before the main-stressed vowel (|√seyè=use ʔ| >

|seyèúse'| /siy=úse'/ 'two berries') or posttonically in a dissyllabic strong suffix (|k̓ʷinèx=éwíɬ| > |k̓ʷinèxéwiɬ| /k̓ʷənex=éwɬ/ 'how many canoes?'): |ɬuʔè| ɬúʔe 'there (remote)', |√wík:-t-ə́yxs| > | wìktíyxs| /wik-t-íyxs/ 'they see him', |√pílə̀x:-n-t-es| /pílə̀x-e-s/ 'she informs him', |√seyè| > |séyè| /séye/ 'two'.

2.6.4.

Other pretonic vowels remain when they are protected: (1) after a liquid in a nonreduplicative prefix: |nə√ɬém̓-əyx| n(ə)/ɬém̓-ix 'he gets in'; (2) before a cluster beginning in a resonant: |√ƛ̓əq̓əm:-t-es| /ƛ̓ə́q̓əm-t-és/ 'he preaches to them', |√q̓ʔem:-s-t-es| /q̓ʔem-s-t-és/ 'she nurses [baby] at breast'; (3) in a prefix or stem's first syllable before any cluster: |sək•√sək-ə́p-s-t-es| sək•sək-p-s-t-és 'she causes them to get clubbed'; (4) as underlying tense vowels in any other type of syllable: |√k̓ʷinèx-eɬci'| > |k̓ʷinèxéɬci'| /k̓ʷənex=éɬci'/ 'how many carcasses?', |s√q̓ʷut-éwíɬ| > |sq̓ʷutéwiɬ| s/q̓ʷət=éwɬ '(other) side of the canoe'.

2.6.5.

Other posttonic vowels remain when they are protected: (1) before a laryngeal: |√k̓ʷáxʷeh| /k̓ʷáxʷe/ 'box' (|h| lost, 2.7., [19]); (2) in an intransitive theme after a cluster and before a glottalized liquid: |√ʔú[•ʔu]pən-'=ekst| > |ʔúʔpənekst| /ʔú[•ʔ]pə̇n=kst ~ /ʔú[•ʔ]pn̓=kst 'ten animals'; (3) in the last syllable of an intransitive word after a cluster and before any liquid: |nə√x̣ʷəl=us-tən| n(ə)/x̣ʷl=ús-t(ə)n 'grindstone, file'; (4) in an intransitive theme after any consonant or a retained unstressed vowel: |√ʔupən=ekst| /ʔúpn=ekst 'ten', |√ʔú'è-ə̌me| > |ʔú'ème| /ʔú'e-me 'she sings a lullaby', |s√ƛ̓ékye| s/ƛ̓ékye 'lunch'; (5) in the last syllable of a transitive increment after a cluster ending in a resonant: |√wík:-t-uym-es| /wík-t-im-es 'he sees you people'; (6) in a reduplicative affix after a cluster, or between identical obstruents unless a tense vowel follows: |√mús•mus| /mús•məs 'four people', |√túp•ŭp| /túp•əp 'it has been smashed'; but |ʔes-tə√k̓íx̣•ix̣-è| ʔes-t/k̓íx̣•x̣-e 'it is fried right away'.

2.7.

Sounds in combination develop according to a complicated set of rules affecting the derivation of words in a particular order, as given below. Unless otherwise indicated, rules apply in both internal and external combination. For the most part proclitic particles develop like prefixes, enclitic particles like suffixes.

(1) A secondary-stressed vowel is lost directly before the main-stressed vowel: |√seyè=use'| > |seyèúse'| /siy=úse' 'two berries.'

(2) (a) Pretonic unprotected |ə| is lost from successive syllables moving back from the main stress: |√səlak-ə́p:-s-t-es| > |sələkəpstés| > |sələkpstés| /səlk-p-s-t-és 'she gets it turned', |√ƛ̓əq̓əm:-t-es| > |ƛ̓əq̓əmtés| /ƛ̓ə́q̓əm-t-és 'he preaches to them'. (b) Pretonic tense

vowels adjacent to laryngeals or pharyngeals are treated like ə: |√ʕac-ə̌p:-s-t-es| > |ʕacəpstés| /ʕac-p-s-t-és 'he gets it snared' and |ʕac•√ʕac-ə̌p| > |ʕac͓ʕacə́p| ʕac•/ʕc-ə́p 'they get ensnared'.

(3) |ə| of |ə̌me| 'middle voice' (5.4.) is lost after a posttonic open syllable if the intervening consonant is a resonant (|√ʔíq̓ʷ=cin-ə̌me| > |ʔíq̓ʷcinme| /ʔíq̓ʷ=cn-me 'he shaves') or laryngeal (|√ʔécx̣eʔ-ə̌me| > |ʔécx̣eʔ-me 'he is power-questing'), or if there is no intervening consonant (√ʔuʔè-ə̌me| /ʔúʔe-me 'she sings a lullaby').

(4) Posttonic resonants are glottalized by glottalizing roots: |√ɬúkʷʔ:-n-t-es| > |ɬúkʷn̓tes| /ɬúkʷ-n̓-s 'he bails it out.'

(5) Unprotected vowels are lost from successive syllables of intransitive themes after the main stress: |√ƛ̓á[•ƛ̓a]q̓-əm[']-ekst| > |ƛ̓áƛ̓q̓əm̓ekst| /ƛ̓á[•ƛ̓]q̓-(ə)m̓=kst 'six animals' and |√ƛ̓áq̓•ƛ̓aq̓-əm[']=ekst| > |ƛ̓áq̓ƛ̓aq̓m̓ekst| /ƛ̓áq̓•ƛ̓aq̓-m̓=ekst 'six people.'

(6) Unprotected vowels are lost from the final syllable of transitive endings: |√máʕ:-xi-t-sem-es| > |máʕxitsems| (ultimately /máʕ-x-cm-s) 'he breaks something of mine'; compare |√wík:-t-uym-es| > |wíktuymes| /wík-t-im-es 'he sees you people', with protected vowel.

(7) |t| is lost from transitive increments after |n, n̓| before |n, s, xʷ| in syllable-final clusters: |√ʔúʔè:-n-t-en| > |ʔúʔentn| > |ʔúʔenn| (ultimately /ʔúʔe-n-e) 'I sing him a lullaby', |√ʔúʔè:-n-t-exʷ| > |ʔúʔentxʷ| /ʔúʔe-n-xʷ 'you sing him a lullaby', |ɬúkʷʔ:-n-t-es| > |ɬúkʷn̓ts| /ɬúkʷ-n̓-s 'he bails it out'.

(8) Within transitive increments |ts| becomes c: |√wík:-t-es| > |wíkts| /wík-c 'he sees her', |√wík:-t-sem-es| > |wíktsems| > |wíkcems| (ultimately /wík-cm-s) 'he sees me'. Loss of |t| from syllable-final clusters (rule [7]) accounts for the different treatment of |-sut| 'reflexive' (5.3.) under different stress conditions: |√cəkʷ:-n-t-sut| > |cəkʷntsút| > |cək̓ncút| (ultimately /cəkʷ-e-cút) 'he pulls himself up', |√cék:-n-t-sut| > |cékntst| > |céknst| (ultimately /cék-e-st) 'he cools himself'.

(9) Other unstressed vowels are lost from transitive increments: |√máʕ:-xi-t-sem-es| > |máʕxitsems| > |máʕxicems| /máʕ-x-cm-s 'he breaks something of mine'.

(10) Where |-cs| develops at the end of a transitive increment, |-s| is lost: |√wík:-t-si-es| > |wíktsis| > |wíkcis| > |wíkcs| /wík-c 'he sees you'.

(11) After a retracting root, an immediately following stressed vowel (except |i|) is retracted and c or s in that syllable is optionally converted to ç or ṣ: |nə√k̓əɬ=us:-n-t-es| > |nək̓ɬ̣ósns| n/k̓ɬ-ós-e-s 'he smears the window', |√k̓əl-ə̌me /k̓l-ə̌m 'she cuts', |nə√k̓əl=us-ə̌me| > |nək̓lósm| n/k̓l=ós-m 'she cuts out a pattern'.

(12) Contrast between |ə| and tense vowels is neutralized in several positions: (a) Before a pharyngeal, laryngeal, or semivowel, |ə| is converted to a homorganic

vowel: |ʔes√yəʕʷ| ʔes/yóʕʷ 'hidden', |√ẏəh| > |ẏéh| /ẏé 'good', |√zəy-t| /zíy=t '[liquid] flows', |ʔes√cəw| ʔes/cúw 'done'; (b) Before a rounded obstruent in a closed syllable (that is, ending in a consonant), |ə| is converted to u when stressed or preceded by a rounded consonant: |ʔes√cək̇ʷ| ʔes/cúk̇ʷ 'pulled', |√ṗíxʷ•ïxʷ| > ṗíxʷəxʷ /ṗíxʷ•ux̌ʷ 'unraveled'.

(13) Vowels are assimilated in certain stressed or closed syllables: (a) |ə́| (stressed) is converted to á before a simple postvelar: |ʔes√səq| ʔes/sáq 'split'; (b) |u|, whether underlying or developing from |ə| in rule [12], is converted to o in a closed syllable before a rounded postvelar: |√zúqʷ| /zóqʷ 'dead', |ʔes√ɬəqʷ| > |ʔesɬúqʷ| ʔes/ɬóqʷ 'seated astride [horse]', |√ṗíq̇ʷ•ïq̇ʷ| > |ṗíq̇ʷəq̇ʷ| > |ṗíq̇ʷuq̇ʷ| /ṗíq̇ʷ•oq̇ʷ 'crumbled'; (c) In internal combination, |ú| (stressed) is lowered to ó before z: |s√k̇ʷúz| s/k̇ʷóz 'aunt' (compare s/k̇ʷú[•k̇ʷ]ż 'auntie'); but in a secondary derivative, it remains unchanged: |√zuʔ[•zu([ʔ])]qʷ| /zú[•ż]qʷ '[small animal is] dead'; (d) |e| is converted to a: 1) before |z, ż| (|√ƛ̓eʔe[że]k| /ƛ̓áʔ[ze]k 'they arrive; cf. /ƛ̓ʔék 'he arrives'), 2) between postvelars (√qé[•qe]ck /qá[•q]ck 'elder brother (dimin.); cf. /qéck 'elder brother'), 3) between rounded obstruents (|nə√k̇ʷé[•k̇ʷe]ṅ-əme| n/k̇ʷá[•k̇ʷ]ṅ-ṁ 'he peeps, peeks'; cf. |√k̇ʷéṅ-n-t-es| /k̇ʷéṅ-e-s 'he looks at it'), 4) after postvelar continuants (|√x̌éc:n-t-es| /x̌ác-e-s 'he smokes (buckskin)', |nə√x̌e[ʔˀ]c=us| > |nəx̌eʔcús| n/x̌a[ʔ]c=ús 'he gets smoke in his eyes'; cf. |s√x̌e[ʔˀ]c| s/x̌[ʔ]éc 'smoke'; |√yəʕ-ele̓ʔ=x̌ən:-t-es| > |yʕéleʔxns| > |yʕáleʔxns| /yʕ-áleʔ=xe-s 'she drags him by the leg'; cf. |√cəh-ele̓ʔ=x̌ən:-t-es| > |chéleʔxns| /ch-éleʔ=xe-s 'she adjusts his (patient's) legs'), 5) optionally between labials and postvelars (|√péq:n-t-es| /páq-e-s ~ /péq-e-s 'she makes it pale'), 6) and in some less clearly understood environments anticipating retracted consonants at a distance (|√míceʔq-=eyeqʷ| > |miceʔqéyqʷ| /míceʔq-=áyqʷ 'sit on a log'; cf. |√x̌ʷesít-=eyeqʷ| /x̌ʷesit-=éyqʷ 'walk on a log' and |√míceʔq-=eẃs| /míceʔq-=éẃs 'sit on a horse').

(14) |t| is lost from most clusters: (a) Everywhere before another |t|: |nə√xʷesít-tən| n/xʷesí-tn 'conveyance', |√súxʷ:èst-t-exʷ| /sóx̌ʷes-t-xʷ 'you bring it down [from the mountain]', |nə√wís-t tək s√q̇ʷìn-t-sút| n/wís tək s/q̇ʷin-cút 'elevated language'; (b) In internal combination from posttonic syllables of intransitive themes after any consonant before a following stop: |s√cíq:etkəw| > |scíqtkw| s/cíq=k̇ʷu 'well [for water]', |nə√páʕʷ=etkəw| > |npáʕʷtkw| n/páʕʷ=k̇ʷu 'water is frozen'. (But |t| is usually retained at the end of an intransitive theme: |√púyt:s-t-exʷ| /púyt-s-t-xʷ 'you put him to bed').

(15) |n| is lost: (a) between |ʔ| or postconsonantal |m| and following |s, t|: |√ʔúqʷeʔ:-n-t-es| > |ʔúqʷeʔnts| > |ʔúqʷeʔns| ʔúqʷeʔ-s 'he drinks it', |ʔúqʷeʔ:-n-t-ep| > |ʔúqʷeʔntp| /ʔúqʷeʔ-t-p 'you people drink it',

|√pún:-min-t-es| > |púnmints| > |púnmins| > | púnmns| /pún-m-s 'he finds it', |√pún:-min-t-ep| > |púnmintp| > |púnmtp| /pún-m-t-p 'you people find it'; (b) After a stressed vowel before |x|: |√cʔexʷ:-min-xi-t-exʷ| /ceʔxʷ-mí-x-t-xʷ 'you congratulate him'.

(16) Simple velars are rounded when next to a rounded velar in the same syllable: |√néẃ:-xi-t-ey-es| > |néẃxyts| /néẃ-x-t-i-s 'the wind blows our [paper]', |s√kéẃ•kew| > |skéwkw| > |skéwk̇ʷw| s/kéw•k̇ʷu 'husband's sisters', |ʔes√k̇ʷák̇ʷ:-xi-s-t-exʷ| > |ʔesk̇ʷák̇ʷxtxʷ| ʔes/k̇ʷák̇ʷ-xʷ-s-t-xʷ 'you carry [something of] his'. (Simple velars are unaffected before a prevocalic rounded velar: |√k̇əwét:-n-t-es| > |k̇wétnts| /k̇wét-e-s 'she steps on it', |nə√k̇əxʷ-əme| n/k̇x̌ʷ-ám ' gouge out'.)

(17) Resonants become syllabic, and semivowels are replaced by homorganic vowels, |y, ẏ, w, ẇ| i, iʔ, u, uʔ (at word beginning, variation yə- ~ yi- ~ ʔi- is written simply y-; variation ẏə- ~ yiʔ- ~ ʔiʔ- is written ẏ-, etc.): (a) Between two consonants or a consonant and a word boundary: |s√yəʕʷ=etɬq| s/iʕʷ=álq 'secret [hidden] berry-patch', |√yəʕʷ-əyx| /yʕʷ-íyx 'he goes into hiding', |nə√ẏəh-eləws| n/iʔh-élus 'good-natured', |√ẏəh-éwíɬ| /ẏh-éwɬ 'good boat', |s√wméx| s/uméx 'life', |√wméx| /wméx 'alive'; (b) Between a consonant and a following vowel, with a brief syllabic phase followed by the regular consonantal value: |s√ƛ̓ék̇ye| s/ƛ̓ék̇(i)ye 'lunch', |núk̇ʷ•√núk̇ʷ-eʔ| > | nək̇ʷ(ṅ)núk̇ʷeʔ| nək̇ʷ(ə)•/núk̇ʷ-eʔ 'friends!'.

(18) Unglottalized syllabic nasals (developing in [17]) are vocalized to e before homorganic obstruents in internal combination: |√qéck-mp| /qéck-ep 'you people's older brother', |√sələk-n-t-es| > |səlkntés| /səlk-e-t-és 'he whirls her around', |√mén:-n-t-sem-es| > |ménntsems| > |ménncms| /mén-e-cm-s 'he shades me', |k̇ʷiw•√k̇ʷiw-əp-ele̓ʔ=x̌ən:-s-t-exʷ| > |k̇ʷəwk̇ʷəwpéleʔxnstxʷ| k̇ʷu•/k̇ʷu-p-éleʔ=xe-s-t-xʷ 'you cause him to slide', |√cənk̇ʷúst:-nɬ-óyxs| > |cənk̇ʷùstnɬíyxs| /cənk̇ʷust-eɬ-íyxs 'theirs'. Final syllabic |n| is also vocalized after another |n|: |√kíc:-n-t-en| > |kícntn| > |kícnn| /kíc-n-e 'I visit him'.

(19) |h| is lost except (a) before vowel: |ʔes√cəh| > |ʔescéh| ʔes/cé 'fixed', |√cəh:-t-es| > |cehtés| /ce-t-és 'he fixes it'; |√cəh=us:-n-t-es| > |chúsnts| /ch=ús-e-s 'she fixes the fire', (b) before a consonant after a stressed vowel where it reduplicates a preceding |h|: |√cəh[•əh]:-s-t-exʷ| > |chéhstexʷ| /ch[•éh]-s-t-xʷ 'you manage to fix it'.

(20) Except in reduplicative syllables, contrast is eliminated between syllabic resonants and resonants with an adjacent ə or homorganic vowel. Such transitional vowels are optionally retained or inserted. (In transcription here these vowels are written only when they parallel vowels retained between obstruents.) For example, (a) After a cluster-final plain resonant, before a final spirant other than s: |√k̇ʷést:-n-t-exʷ| >

|kʷéstntxʷ| > |kʷéstnxʷ| /kʷést-n-(ə)xʷ/ 'you name him';
(b) After any consonant before a resonant: |ʔes-nə√q̓íx̣=cin| > |ʔesnəq̓íx̣cən| ʔes-(ə)n(ə)/q̓íx̣=c(ə)n 'it is locked', |√né-xi-t-si-en| > |néxtsin| > |néxcn| /né-x-c-(ə)n/ 'I hand it to you', |√pún:-min-t-es| > |púnms| /pún-(ə)m-s/ 'he finds it', |√xʷák̓ʷ=uyəm̓xʷ| > |xʷák̓ʷyəm̓xʷ| > |xʷák̓ʷ(i)yəm̓xʷ| /xʷák̓ʷ=(i)y(ə)m̓x/ 'frosty ground', |√k̓əs-t-wə́ẏxʷ| /k̓əs-t-(u)wíʔx/ 'it gets bad, spoils'.

(21) In internal combination, a laryngeal is usually separated from a preceding obstruent by a brief ə: |s√ʔístk| s(ə)/ʔístk 'winter', |√cəh=us:-n-t-es| /c(ə)h=ús-e-s 'she fixes the fire'.

(22) Before an obstruent or single resonant, unstressed vowel-semivowel sequences are simplified to vocalized semivowels (as in 17); this change affects even a vowel with underlying secondary stress (although the vowel is occasionally retained in careful pronunciation): |nə√kéy:-s-t-wáxʷ| > |nəkèystwáxʷ| n/key-s-t-wáxʷ (careful), n/ki-s-t-wáxʷ 'they follow each other', |√ʔúʔè=eyt| > |ʔúʔeyt| /ʔúʔ=it 'she) sings lullaby to child', |√cəw-min| > |cuwmín| /cu-mín 'equipment'. (Before a resonant in a cluster the sequence is stable: |√cəw-nwéłn| /cuw-nwéłn 'she manages to get a job'. A sequence involving a glottalized semivowel is not affected before |ʔ|: s/kʷiẏ-ʔúy 'arrow [basic projectile]'.)

(23) A morpheme beginning in a vowel acquires initial h- directly after a vowel or pause: |√eʔwí| /heʔwí 'you're the one', |√ʔíq̓ʷ=cin-əme-è| > |ʔíq̓ʷ-cnmee| /ʔiq̓ʷ=c(ə)n-me-he 'shave!'

(24) Clusters of |ʔʔ| are simplified to single ʔ: |√sémeʔ-ʔúy| /seme-ʔúy 'Englishman (basic White person)'.

3. GRAMMATICAL ORGANIZATION

3.1. BASIC MEANINGFUL UNITS

The makeup of words already has been outlined (2.4.). Morphemes are of two types: lexical, designating entities, events, and concepts; and grammatical, indicating the reference and interrelationships of lexical morphemes and generally relating speech to situations, although they may include some lexical content as well.

3.1.1.
Lexical morphemes are mostly roots, the central components of longer words, conveying the greatest variety of meanings. Most of them can appear independently as simple (underived and uninflected) words, revealing that they are fundamentally intransitive in reference, indicating the nature of persons and things and the acts and states that describe or affect them: /ċyé |√c̓əẏéh| 'be a basket', /slə́k |√sələk| 'turn, whirl', /nés |√nés| 'go (to), set out (for a particular place)', /qʷnóxʷ |√qʷənúxʷ| 'be sick', /x̣áni |√x̣áṅih| 'be hurt, injured', /qʷéṅ |√qʷéṅ| 'be soaked through'.

However, there is also a large stock of lexical suffixes, which appear only attached to roots. They usually identify concrete entities (of nominal type, from the English point of view) and various extensions of them, sometimes very abstract ones: |=cin| 'mouth; lip, chin; speech, talking; eating; aperture, doorway, gate, entrance; edge, rim; bank, shore; palm, sole, joint'; |=éwíł| 'canoe, boat; conveyance of any sort; loading; container'.

3.1.2.
Grammatical morphemes include the affixes that serve as derivational and inflectional elements, added to roots and longer stems: for example, the prefix s- 'nominalizer' derives words referring to entities or concepts that are products or results of an action or situation; the suffix |-əyx| 'autonomous' makes inflected words referring to acts carried out independently under the subject's control (rather than where such control is lacking). There are also grammatical morphemes that are not parts of larger words but are independent elements in phrases, marking various syntactic functions; these are particles, such as ṅ 'interrogative', indicating that a sentence is a question. A few particles consist of grammatical affixes attached to grammatical bases; kn 'I' (intransitive subject marker) consists of a base |k| and the first person singular subject suffix |-en|.

3.1.3.
Reduplicative elements appear at several levels in word formation. Some processes are very common; several others are infrequent, and a number of them need further study. Many words appear only reduplicated; for example, k̓ʷəƛ̓•/k̓ʷíƛ̓p̓ 'flea', cəx̣ʷ•/cíx̣ʷ 'waterfall', səx̣•/sáx̣t 'rapids', səx̣•/sə́x̣-t 'he made a mistake'. Some roots appear only in reduplicative form; for example, |√cəy•cəy| /cíy•ci 'new' |√cəy•cəy=ełxʷ| /ci•cy=éłxʷ 'new house'.

Various reduplicative affixes are used (represented with cover symbols C, consonant; V, vowel). Prefixes regularly duplicate the first elements of their bases in order; infixes and suffixes duplicate the elements immediately preceding them. Several are regularly based on roots, yielding stems for inflection or derivation, such as |CVC•| 'augmentative' (5.6.2.): |cek•√cék| cək•/cék 'very cool'. On the other hand, the diminutive infix (6.7.1.) operates at the level of secondary derivation; it is based on full words and is positioned directly after the stressed vowel: |[•CV([ʔ])]|: s/pzú[•ż̓u]ʔ 'small bird' (s/pzúʔ 'animal, bird').

3.1.4.
Words are then the basic units of syntactic phrases; they are of two types. Major words are fundamentally predicative; they can serve as simple (one-word) sentences or clauses, or as the ultimate grammatical heads of sentences or clauses. Particles (3.1.2.) do not have such predicative functions but serve to modify phrases, clauses, and sentences in various ways.

3.2. PREDICATION

Thompson sentences consist of a predication, or a complex of several predications. The essential minimum of a predication is a predicate (7.1.), containing a transitive or intransitive word (3.3.). A predication also may involve one or more complements (7.2.) or adjuncts (7.3.), usually converted for this special use from underlying predicates.

Unless specially marked, predicates are in indicative mode. Imperative mode forms are created by adding imperative subject suffixes (5.5.) to intransitive and transitive stems. Any predicate can be cast in the conjunctive mode by use of the enclitic particle |w| (4.1.); such predicates are closely associated with another predicate (7.6.).

Aspectual and related notions are conveyed partly by affixes (5.1.), and partly by predicative particles (7.1.1., 7.1.3., 7.6.2.). Tense is not obligatorily marked; sentences translated here with the English present can usually equally well refer to the past or on occasion to the future. The interrelationships of predicates and their complements and adjuncts are clarified by particles (7.1., 7.3.).

3.3. TRANSITIVITY

While in given sentences it is possible to decide that one word is functioning in a nounlike fashion, another more like a verb, extensive study suggests that these categories refer more to elements in the English translations of sentences than to Thompson words in the original texts. (Thompson words are often glossed simply with English nouns, but they should always be understood as having potential predicative force; a fuller translation would be 'it is a...', 'they are...', 'there is/are...', etc.). There is a marked dichotomy between transitive and intransitive words, the former referring overtly to an active subject or agent and specifying or implying an object, the latter including all other major words, which frequently refer to a person or thing acting or being affected by an action without necessarily suggesting any second party. Unsuffixed roots are intransitive; there are also a number of suffixes that create complex intransitive themes. All transitives are marked by the suffix |-t| and are further inflected for person. Several special suffixes form complex transitive increments with |-t|, and most intransitive themes can be transitivized through one or more of these formations (5.2.).

3.4. CONTROL

Thompson predicates, both transitive and intransitive, show a pervasive bifurcation reflecting the degree of control an actor has over the action expressed in the predicative. That general notion of control is a basic logico-semantic distinction in the language. Control is not a simple binary division (plus or minus control), as

initially thought. Instead, control comprises a multivalent hierarchy of dominance. The relative force (mild versus strong) of control [ctl] can be represented by another binary feature, dominance [dom]. Morphemes (roots and affixes) may be unmarked for control mildly [-ctl -dom] or strongly [-ctl +dom], unmarked for control (neutral), or marked for control mildly [+ctl -dom] or strongly [+ctl +dom].

Noncontrol	Neutral		Control	
[-ctl]	[-ctl]	Unmarked for control	[+ctl]	[+ctl]
[+dom]	[-dom]		[-dom]	[+dom]

A large proportion of the roots in the language are marked [-ctl -dom]. A small but important number of roots are marked [+ctl +dom] (about 50 of some 2,000 roots currently identified). The strong control of those roots can be overridden by certain affixes that impart lessened control: /xʷesít/ [+ctl +dom] 'he walked', /xʷesit-nwéɬn/, 'he managed to walk' (non-control middle -nwéɬn [-ctl +dom]). The strongly marked for control root /xʷesít/ is overridden by the more strongly marked noncontrol affix -nwéɬn.

Basically, control marking is of two kinds: it may add the notion of some agent's control over an act not normally controlled, such as ʔes/péw 'it's swollen', where the root |√péw| is [-ctl -dom], versus /péw-ix 'it [toad] puffed up' where the autonomous suffix -ix (< |-əyx|) is marked [+ctl +dom]. The other is a more forceful notion indicating limitation or lack of control, as seen with the /xʷesit-nwéɬn example above.

Control intersects importantly with the other grammatical categories of the language (e.g., transitivity, aspect). The hierarchy of dominance and the combination of various roots, lexical suffixes, and affixes allows for numerous interesting permutations of control marking in predicatives. L. Thompson (1985) gives a full analysis of control in the language; Thompson and Thompson (1992:51-57) present additional exemplification and description of control. Van Eijk (1990) discusses the notion of control in neighboring Lillooet.

4. PRONOMINAL ELEMENTS

4.1. INTRANSITIVE SUBJECTS

The most common pronominal elements are subject suffixes:

	singular		plural
first person	|-en|		|-et|
second person	|-exʷ|		|-ep|
third person		|-es|	

The third-person form refers to both singular and plural subjects. Intransitive pronominal enclitics are formed by adding the above subject suffixes to particle bases that distinguish indicative |k| and conjunctive |w| modes.

These suffixes are added to the particle base |w|, forming the conjunctive subject pronoun enclitics. They follow either predicative words themselves or 619 elements just before them (in the following examples, *ʔił* 'and then'):

...*ʔił n/łém̉-ix wn* / ... *ʔił wn n/łém̉-ix* '...and I got in (a conveyance)'

...*ʔił /mén̉x-m uxʷ* / ... *ʔił uxʷ /mén̉x-m* '...and then you smoked'

...*ʔił n/xʔ-éʔ us* / ...*ʔił us n/xʔ-éʔ* '...and then he (or they) went up'

...*ʔił /nés ut* / ... *ʔił ut /nés* '...and then we went (there)'

...*ʔił /cʔés up* / ...*ʔił up /cʔés* '... and then you people came'

Third person *us* |w-es| often has impersonal reference:

n/wén•wn us '[when] morning comes',

...*ʔił us /tékł* '...and then it rained.'

Conjunctive phrases also appear independently with optative or imperative force: *n/łém̉-ix us* 'let him get in, may he get in!', /*cúk* *us* ... 'don't ...!' (lit. 'let it be finished...!'), /*ʔéx uxʷ teʔ* /*tékʷxʷeʔ* 'you be the Ruffed Grouse!' [/exist 2sg.sbj.conjunctive particular ruffed.grouse] (myth: Coyote transforms a person with that statement).

In indicative intransitive predicates the subject suffixes are attached instead to the base |k|, yielding the intransitive subject pronoun enclitics. In this set, the second-person singular has developed a fused form, and a third-person form is lacking.

	singular	plural
first person	*kn* |k-en|	*kt* |k-et|
second person	*kʷ* |k-exʷ|	*kp* |k-ep|
general third person		|∅|

n/łém̉-ix kn 'I get in (a conveyance)', /*ýé kʷ* 'you feel well',

/*mén̉x-m kt* 'we smoke', /*nés kp* 'you people go (there)'. Absent such markers, intransitive words refer to third-person subjects: *n/łém̉-ix* 'he gets in', /*mén̉x-m* 'they smoke'. Their exact reference can be clarified by demonstratives (7.1.2.) or by complements (7.2.) or adjuncts (7.3.).

4.2. Transitive Pronouns

Transitives are inflected for first- and second-person object as well as subject for all three persons. The pronominal suffixes follow |-t| 'transitive' in the order object-subject. The regular subject suffixes (4.1.) appear again; the endings are to some extent fused with transitive suffixes and there are some irregularities (these complications are discussed and examples of transitive forms are given in 5.2.).

4.2.1.

Objects are:

	singular	plural
first person	|-sem| ~ |-sey|	|-ey|
second person	|-si|	|-uym|
general third person		|∅|

The first-person singular |-sey| appears when the following suffix contains a labial. When an overt object suffix is lacking, a third-person object is understood.

The pronominal system suggests a split ergative structure. Handling of first- and second-person subjects—whether designating agents or patients—indicates a basic nominative-accusative type structure. Indicative predicates show transitive third-person object and intransitive third-person subject marked by zero (lack of any overt morpheme). The transitive subject is marked differently (with |-es|). That suggests an ergative structure for third-person indicative. (The conjunctive transitive third-person subject and intransitive third-person subject are marked with |-es|.) Two of the most common factors conditioning ergative-accusative splits are (1) syntactic level: subordinate clause case patterning may be accusative (conjunctive); and (2) person and number of logical subject: first- and second-person pronominals may pattern accusatively (Klaiman 1991:129).

4.2.2. Indefinite Subjects

There are transitives in which only the person or thing affected is indicated. These are called indefinite-subject forms (see also 7.2.1., 7.2.2.). The designation "passive" for the indefinite-subject forms would be misleading here: the focal person is marked formally as an object (among other reasons involving marking in the control system). The indefinite-subject forms shift focus from the transitive subject to the object. The indefinite-subject forms maintain topic reference in discourse. In traditional narratives, for instance, characters' identities are indicated by using regular subject forms when the focal character is the subject and someone else is the object, but indefinite-subject forms are used when the situation is reversed: /*cún-s* |√cún-t-∅-es| 'he [focal] told him (someone else)' when the focal character speaks to someone, but /*cún-t-m* |√cún-t-∅-em| 'someone told him [focal]' when someone speaks to the focal character. The indefinite subjects are marked with the object suffixes (third person by the absence of a suffix), but the final suffixes that follow do not form a cohesive pattern, and the analysis is not entirely clear. The suffix sequences are best simply listed:

	singular	plural
first person	|-sey-me|	|-ey-et|
second person	|-si-et|	|-uym-et|
third person		|-∅-em|

4.2.3. Detransitives

Finally, there are suffixes that reconvert transitive stems to intransitive: |-sut| 'reflexive' and |-wáxʷ| (for some speakers more often diminutive |-wé[•ẁ]xʷ|) 'reciprocal' refer to objects and require intransitive subject particles for first- or second-person subjects; |-ə́yxs| 'third-person plural' (only plural, while |-es| can refer to either singular or plural) indicates plural third persons acting on some other (third) person (singular or plural). |-ɔ́yxs| is grammatically instransitive because it cannot follow any overt object suffix. Forms with |-sut|, |-wáxʷ|, and |-ɔ́yxs| can be reconverted to transitive inflection to handle further relationships (5.3., 5.6.1.).

4.3.

Possessives are a mixed set of prefixes and suffixes bracketing the stem:

	singular	plural
first person	|nə-|	|-kt|
second person	|eʔ-|	|-mp|
third person		|-s|

Special morphophonemic rules affect some of these: |nə-| is omitted before the homonymous prefix |nə-| 'localizer' (6.3.1.); |eʔ-| loses the vowel following the direct complement particle |è| (7.2.1.); and |-s| is strengthened to -c after stems ending in s or ɬ.

In keeping with the predicative nature of full words, possessed words often have a verbal flavor in translation: *n/cítxʷ* 'my house', *n-s/yíq̓-m* 'I (am the one who) planted it', *n/kʷúm-mn* |nə-nə√kʷúm-min| 'my pocket', *heʔ-n/kʷúm-mn* 'your pocket', *heʔ-s/pú[•p]n̓* 'it is something you found', *ɬxʷe[ʔ]p-ít-kt* 'our clothes', *ɬk̓ʷáxʷe-mp* 'you people's box', *s/qác-ze-ep* (2.7., rule [18], vocalization of nasal) 'you people's father', *ɬkéyx-s* 'her arm/hand', *s/ƛ̓íʔ-s* 'he likes it', *s/c̓aqʔ=éwɬ-c* 'their canoe'. The specific third-person plural suffix |-ɔ́yxs| (4.2.3.) also appears as a possessive: *ɬxʷe[ʔ]p-it-íyxs* 'their clothes'.

4.4.

Independent pronouns are full predicative words. They furnish the strongest degree of emphasis for personal reference the system offers. In this set there is no general third-person form with both singular and plural reference; instead, there are separate words for third-person singular and plural. Derived from these pronouns are emphatic possessive words, also having predicative force, formed with |-nɬ| and possessive affixes. In the singular further derivatives with -əɬ are more common (reduplicative in type, reminiscent of limited control forms, 5.1.5.); only this extended form is used in the first-person plural. (Some special morphophonemic reductions are involved.)

/ncé-we 'I am the one'	/nce-nɬ(-əɬ) 'it is mine'
/(h)eʔwí 'you are the one'	/(h)eʔwí-nɬ(-əɬ) 'it is yours'
/cn-íɬ '(s)he is the one'	/cn-í-nɬ(-əɬ)-c 'it is his/hers'
/nmímɬ 'we are the ones'	/nmímɬ-əɬ-kt 'it is ours'
(/nmímeɬ, archaic)	
/pyépst 'you are the ones'	/pyépst-eɬ-ep 'it is you people's'
/can-kʷúst 'they are the ones'	/can-kʷust-eɬ-íyxs 'it is theirs'
	(/can-kʷúst-eɬ-c, archaic)

5. INFLECTION

5.1. BASIC INTRANSITIVES

5.1.1.

Stative aspect forms, marked by the prefix |ʔes-|, specify actions, accomplished facts, and states of affairs that have already come into effect at the main time of a sentence, and remain in effect at that time. |ʔes-| does not affect the control status (3.4.) of its stem. *ʔes-kəɬ•/kəɬ=xən* 'her shoes are off', *ʔes/cáq* 'it is parked, positioned (has been for sometime)', *ʔes-n/ɬém̓* 'it is already placed inside'. Statements of general or universal truths, characteristics, etc., are often cast in the stative: *ʔes/wə́l* 'it is open (country, not forested)', *ʔes/x̣íʔ* 'it is a sheer cliff'. It also provides the usual way to express possession: *ʔes/qáləx kn* 'I have a root-digger [stick]', *ʔes/cítxʷ* 'she has a house'.

5.1.2.

Immediate aspect is marked by the suffix |-t|, referring to (uncontrolled) actions and states that have just gone into effect; also more general states:

/sək-t kn 'I got hit (by branch I passed under)',
/qít-t kt 'we are awake (we just woke up)',
/wís-t kʷ 'you are in a high place',
/cék-t '(cooked food) has gotten cool',
/qém̓-t 'he got shot',
/cén̓-t kp 'you people got scratched (by briars)',
n/kʷéw-t kn 'I fell in the water'.

5.1.3.

Autonomous forms, marked by the control suffix |-əyx|, indicate an entity functioning independent of other entities, in control (3.4.): |√yəʕʷ| 'hide', */yʕʷ-íyx* 'he hides, goes into hiding', *ʔes/yʕʷ-íyx* 'he has gotten himself hidden, is in hiding'; |nə√ɬém̓| 'go into container', *n/ɬém̓-ix* 'he gets in (a conveyance), moves to a position so as to ride', *ʔes-n/ɬém̓-ix* 'he is riding, has gotten into a conveyance so as to ride'; |√ɬəʕʷ| 'bounce', */ɬʕʷ-íyx* 'he jumps'. Many terms referring to bodily posture and movement are cast in this form: */cíx̣ʷ-ix* 'lie down', */qʷc-íyx* 'move'. Some roots occur only with this suffix: */ɬéɬ-ix* 'stand', */q̓áz-ix* 'jump, run (away)', */tʕʷ-íyx* 'run'.

5.1.4.

Inchoative aspect conveys notions of (uncontrolled) developing action or changing state. The following examples include causative transitivizations (5.2.3.). The affix is a weak suffix |-ɔ́p| with weak roots: */sk-ɔ́p kn* 'I get hit (by falling branch)', */sək-p-s-t-és* 'she manages to club it', */səlk-ɔ́p* 'it gets turned (the wrong way)', */səlk-p-s-t-és* 'he gets it turned', */cw-ɔ́p* 'it gets made, done', */ɣn-ɔ́p kʷ* 'you are shivering'. With strong roots it infixes |[ʔˠ]| directly after the root vowel, forming a weak stem: */t[ʔˠ]ép* |√te[ʔˠ]p| 'it gets black', */te[ʔˠ]p-s-t-és* |te[ʔˠ]p:-s-t-es| 'she gets it black', */z[ʔˠ]úc̓* 621

|√zu[ʔˇ]c̓| 'it gets tight', /zu[ʔ]c̓-s-t-és |zu[ʔ]c̓:-s-t-es| 'he (unintentionally) makes it tighter'. It is curious that both inchoative allomorphs create weak stems; even the infix appropriate for strong roots is weak |[ʔˇ]|. This is regularly seen in causativization, exemplified above, which is especially common with inchoatives.

5.1.5.

Out-of-control is specified by a reduplicative affix that copies a stem's stressed vowel and immediately following consonant. It indicates a state or event is independent of any agent or influenced in only limited fashion by a particular agent, thus asserting explicitly the notion implicit in roots unmarked for control (3.4.). An agent involved acts accidentally or inefficiently or needs much time or special skill to accomplish the goal: /kíc•ǝc kt 'we have an unexpected visitor' (|√kíc•ic|; |√kíc| 'arrive (at someone's location)', /xʷús•ǝs |xʷús•ŭs| '(beer) is foaming', n/łém•m̓ |nǝ√łém•ĕm̓| 'something goes in bag unnoticed; (hitchhiker) finally gets a ride', /púy•i |√púy•ŭy| '(concave object) has been turned upside down'. With weak roots it functions like a weak suffix: /qʷc•ǝ́c |√qʷǝc•ɔ́c| 'it moves, trembles', /qʷǝ́c•c-s-t-éxʷ |√qʷǝc•ɔ́c:-s-t-exʷ| 'you manage to move it', /ch•éh-s-t-xʷ |√cǝh[•ɔ́h]-s-t-exʷ| 'you get it fixed'. It appears as an infix in a strong stem with more than a single consonant after the stressed vowel: mǝn̓•mén[•n̓]x 'he gets sick from smoking' (|√ménx| '(inhale) smoke'). (See also out-of-control secondary formations, 6.7.3.).

Often out-of-control forms suggest an agent other than the primary referent in control: /λ̓áq̓ʷ•oq̓ʷ kn 'it got nailed right in front of me (but I had no control over it)'. In a negative construction (7.5.3.) the combination indicates inability: tǝ•/tèʔ k s/púλ̓•ǝλ̓-m-s 'he can't get out'.

5.1.6.

Resultive aspect is marked by the suffix |-è|; it emphasizes the recent, often sudden, completion of an activity or change of state: ʔes/čáx̣-e |ʔes√čǝx̣-è| 'it is cleaned now', ʔes/łúq̓ʷ-e '(undergrowth) is cleared now' (|√łúq̓ʷ| 'bare'), ʔes/cáq-e '(car that was going very fast) came to a quick stop'. The resultive often cooccurs with the qualitative t- prefix (6.3.2.): ʔes-t/x̣ǝ́ł-e kn 'I feel refreshed, recuperated' (|√x̣ǝł| 'be active'), ʔes-t/mǝ́λ̓-e '(trees) are knocked down now'.

5.2.

Transitives all utilize |-t|, added directly to some roots; others are first extended by |-n| (some roots show both stems). No consistent semantic differences have been observed between the two formations, but it appears likely that at an earlier stage of the language |-n| created a control stem, which control roots (3.4.) did not need. Both types now form transitives implying control by the subject. There are also more specialized transitive stems, in which the position of |-n| is occupied by other transitive formative suffixes (5.2.3.-5.).

5.2.1.

Weak transitive stems afford the clearest view of endings, which are then stressed. Table 2 gives the paradigm of |√sǝk| 'hit with stick', which takes |-t| directly. /sǝk-t-éne 'I club him', is unexpected: -ne '1sg.sbj.-3obj.', invariable throughout the transitive system, is from the |-n-t| paradigm, where it developed regularly as an unstressed ending (5.2.2.). /sǝk-t-ém '1pl.sbj.-3.obj.' is apparently borrowed from the indefinite-subject form (third person). The second person indefinite-subject forms are also identical with the corresponding 1pl.sbj.-2obj. forms. But these are different syntactically. 2sg.sbj.-1pl.obj. and 2pl.sbj.-1pl.obj. forms are identical; formally /sǝk-t-éy-p 'you (sg. or pl.) club us' has 2pl.sbj. |-ep|.

Table 2. |-t| Inflection: Transitive Paradigm of |√sǝk| 'hit with stick'

Subjects	*1sg.*	*2sg.*	*Objects* *3d. person*	*1pl.*	*2pl.*
1sg.	— |—| /sǝk-cí-n |√sǝk-t-si-en|	/sǝk-t-éne |√sǝk-t-en(è)|	—|—|	/sǝk-t-úym-n |√sǝk-t-uym-en|
2sg.	/sǝk-cém-xʷ |√sǝk-t-sem-exʷ|	—|—|	/sǝk-t-éxʷ |√sǝk-t-exʷ|	/sǝk-t-éy-p (= 2pl.)	—|—|
3d. person	/sǝk-cém-s |√sǝk-t-sem-es|	/sǝk-cí-s |√sǝk-t-si-es|	/sǝk-t-és |√sǝk-t-es|	/sǝk-t-éy-s |√sǝk-t-ey-es|	/sǝk-t-úym-es |√sǝk-t-uym-es|
1pl.	—|—|	/sǝk-cí-t |√sǝk-t-si-et|	/sǝk-t-ém |√sǝk-t-em|	—|—|	/sǝk-t-úym-et |√sǝk-t-uym-et|
2pl.	/sǝk-céy-p |√sǝk-t-sey-ep|	—|—|	/sǝk-t-ép |√sǝk-t-ep|	/sǝk-t-éy-p |√sǝk-t-ey-ep|	—|—|
Indefinite	/sǝk-céy-me |√sǝk-t-sey-me|	/sǝk-cí-t |√sǝk-t-si-et|	/sǝk-t-ém |√sǝk-t-em|	/sǝk-t-éy-t |√sǝk-t-ey-et|	/sǝk-t-úym-et |√sǝk-t-uym-et|

Weak roots extended by |-n| differ only in stem, which ends in e (from |n|; 2.7., rule [18]): |√sələk:n-t-| 'turn around': /sälk-e-t-és 'she turns him', /sälk-e-cém-xʷ 'you turn me'.

A few weak roots permit neither |-t| nor |-n-t| inflection from the simple root; some of these form |-n-t| control transitives based on their inchoative (5.1.4.) stems: |√pəẏ| 'lose', |√pəẏ-ə̆p:-n-t-es| /piʔ-p-e-t-és 'he loses (animal that is following him) (intentionally)'; |√łəq| 'stick on flat surface', |√łəq-ə̆p:-n-t-es| /łəq-p-e-t-és 'she sticks it on (the wall)'.

5.2.2.
Strong transitive stems have unstressed endings, which then contract. Strong roots overwhelmingly take |-n-t| inflection, with |n| normally vocalized (2.7., rule [18]). Table 3 shows a typical paradigm. After a vocalic stem the connecting n is seen unvocalized: |√ʔúʔè:n-t-es| /ʔúʔe-n-s 'she sings him a lullaby'. Similarly, n appears after a protected vowel eliminated late in derivation (2.7., rule [20]): |√ʔínəwə:-n-t-| 'say what?': /ʔínw-n-s 'what does she tell him?', /ʔínw-n-cm-xʷ 'what do you tell me?' /ʔínw-n-t-im-et 'what do we tell you people?'. This inflection shows the regular origin of the '1sg.sbj.-3.obj.' ending -ne.

Rule (15) (2.7.) eliminates |n| from much of the paradigm of stems ending in |ʔ|: /ʔúqʷeʔ-n-e 'I drink it', /ʔúqʷeʔ-n-xʷ 'you drink it'; but /ʔúqʷeʔ-s 'he drinks it', /ʔúqʷeʔ-t-p 'you people drink it'.

Strong roots with simple |-t| inflection show less complex developments in the endings, but this paradigm has borrowed the '1sg.sbj.-3obj.' ending from the |-n-t| inflection: |wík:-t-| 'see': /wík(-t)-ne 'I see her' (-t- pronounced in Lytton, but absent in Spuzzum speech), /wík-t-xʷ 'you see her', /wík-cm-xʷ 'you see me', /wík-t-im-et 'we see you people', /wík-c-im-e

'someone sees me'. Morphophonemic developments (2.7., rules [6], [8-10]) result in homonymous forms for '3sbj.-3obj.' and '3sbj.-2sg.obj.': /wík-c |√wík:-t-es| 'he sees her', /wík-c |√wík:-t-si-es| 'he sees you' (cf. /sək-t-és 'he clubs her', /sək-cí-s 'he clubs you').

5.2.3. CAUSATIVE
The formative |-s| creates causative stems from most roots; it does not change the control status (3.4.) of the stem to which it is added. With most roots, then, it forms transitives implying that the action or state results from the activity of some agent who is not in full control, covering on the one hand accidental, unintentional, and haphazard or excessive acts, and on the other, feats that are difficult to perform or that require great skill or a long time.

For many roots there are parallel paradigms, affording contrast between |-s-t| noncontrol transitives and |-t| or |-n-t| control transitives: /cəm-t-és |√cəm:-t-es| 'she burns (bread to soak for therapeutic tea)', /cəm-s-t-és |cəm:-s-t-es| 'she (forgets what she's cooking and) burns it'; /wís-n-xʷ |√wís:-n-t-exʷ| 'you make it higher (than it was)', /wís-s-t-xʷ |√wís:-s-t-exʷ| 'you make it too high'. Semantic contrasts are not always so great, and often the different nuance is difficult to translate: /wík-t-xʷ |√wík:-t-exʷ| 'you see it', /wík-s-t-xʷ |√wík:-s-t-exʷ| 'you see it, catch a glimpse of it'.

|-s-t| transitivizes many more complex stems; among those discussed so far, autonomous (5.1.3.), inchoative (5.1.4.), and out-of-control (5.1.5.) stems are common: /yʕʷ-íyx-s-t-xʷ 'you help him hide', /sək-p-s-t-és 'she causes him to get clubbed; hits him accidentally (with her cane)', /kíc•əc-s-t-xʷ 'you manage to get him there (to the hospital)'. With stative (5.1.1.) stems there is a special semantic result: ongoing or habitual action is often meant (note contrasting glosses in the following examples): ʔes/kíc-s-ne 'I've

Table 3. |-n-t| Inflection: Transitive Paradigm of |√kíc| 'arrive at location of'

Subjects	Objects				
	1sg.	*2sg.*	*3d. person*	*1pl.*	*2pl.*
1sg.	—	/kíc-e-c-n	/kíc-n-e	—	/kíc-e-t-im-n
	|—	|√kíc-n-t-si-en|	|√kíc-n-t-en|	|—	|√kíc-n-t-uym-en|
2sg.	/kíc-e-cm-xʷ	—	/kíc-n-xʷ	/kíc-e-t-i-p	—
	|√kíc-n-t-sem-exʷ|	|—	|√kíc-n-t-exʷ|	(= 2pl.)	|—
3d. person	/kíc-e-cm-s	/kíc-e-c	/kíc-e-s	/kíc-e-t-i-s	/kíc-e-t-im-es
	|√kíc-n-t-sem-es|	|√kíc-n-t-si-es|	|√kíc-n-t-es|	|√kíc-n-t-ey-es|	|√kíc-n-t-uym-es|
1pl.	—	/kíc-e-c-t	/kíc-e-t-m	—	/kíc-e-t-im-et
	|—	/√kíc-n-t-si-et|	|√kíc-n-t-em|	|—	|√kíc-n-t-uym-et|
2pl.	/kíc-e-ci-p	—	/kíc-e-t-p	/kíc-e-t-i-p	—
	|√kíc-n-t-sey-ep|	|—	|√kíc-n-t-ep|	|√kíc-n-t-ey-ep|	|—
Indefinite	/kíc-e-ci-me	/kíc-e-c-t	/kíc-e-t-m	/kíc-e-t-i-t	/kíc-e-t-im-et
	|√kíc-n-t-sey-me|	|√kíc-n-t-si-et|	|√kíc-n-t-em|	|√kíc-n-t-ey-et|	|√kíc-n-t-uym-et|

623

been there all the time; I often go there', *ʔes/kíc-s-cm-s* 'he always comes to me (for things he needs); he's coming to see me', *ʔes/síq-s-c* 'he already has it (firewood) all split; he's splitting it'.

5.2.4. INDIRECTIVE

With basic transitive inflection most roots refer to persons or things as the direct objects of their action: */sǝk-t-éne* 'I club him/her' or 'I club it (an animal)' or 'I hit it (some object) with a stick'; */wík-t-xʷ* 'you see him/her/it (person, animal, or thing)'. The formative |-xi| 'indirective' forms stems (marked for control) that focus on some person or thing as the entity affected or interested in the transaction, and that redirect the action toward a goal related to this entity: */wík-x-c-n* |√wík:-xi-t-si-en| 'I see what you have', */čǝq̓ʷ-xí-c* |√čǝq̓ʷ:-xi-t-es| 'he writes (a letter) to her', */máʕ-x-t-im-es* |√máʕ:-xi-t-uym-es| 'he breaks something belonging to you people'. Although persons are most commonly the interested entities, other types are also found: */q̓ʷuʔ-xí-t-ne* 'I set a trap for it (a particular animal)', */n/čǝq̓=ús-x-c* |nǝ√čǝq̓=us:-xi-t-es| 'they add something to the contributions for a feast' (with figurative specialization: |√čǝq̓| 'throw and hit', |nǝ-...=us| 'eye').

Thompson indirectives operate exactly contrary to the usual English pattern involving two objects, where an interested party is introduced as an indirect object and the goal of the action remains the direct object. Thompson also has some simple roots that function as indirectives, for example, |√n̓ǝ| 'give': */n̓-t-éne* 'I give it to him'. One root has been reinterpreted as including the indirective *-xi* suffix: */né-x-t-xʷ* 'you hand it to him' (more literally 'you make him recipient of it'), but augmentative *nǝx•/né-x-t-xʷ* 'give someone little things'.

5.2.5. RELATIONAL

Noncontrol transitives denoting relations of action and states to objects are formed on stems extended by |-min|: */tˤʷ-íyx-m-ne* 'I jump for it' (|√tǝˤʷ| 'bounce' |√tǝˤʷ-ǝyx| 'jump'). Derived stems are often more abstract in reference than the underlying roots: */tǝk̓ʷ-mín-ne* |√tǝk̓ʷ:-min-t-en(è)| 'I remember him' (|√tǝk̓ʷ| 'hook'). The formation provides transitives for many stems not otherwise transitivized: */pún-mn-xʷ* 'you find it', */pún-m-t-im-et* |√pún:-min-t-uym-et| 'we find you people' (|-n-| lost, 2.7., rule [15]); */č[ʔ]oz-mín-ti-s* |√čo[ʔˇ]z:-min-tey-es| 'it gets dark on us' (|√čo[ʔˇ]z| 'get dark').

Relational derivatives sometimes contrast with simple transitives: */nóxʷ-m-s* |√núxʷ:-min-t-es| '(an animal) runs up to him' (|√núxʷ| 'progress on four or more legs'); compare */nóxʷ-e-s* |√núxʷ:-n-t-es| 'it crawls over it (many-legged insect crawling over a rock)'.

Relational stems can also be followed by the indirective (5.2.4.): */ceʔxʷ-mí-x-t-xʷ* |√ceʔxʷ:-min-xi-t-exʷ| 'you appreciate what he has done; you congratulate him' (|n| lost, 2.7., rule [15]).

5.2.6.

Conjunctive transitives are created simply by adding the third-person conjunctive enclitic |-w-es|. Thus transitives in the conjunctive mode are grammatically impersonal: */wík(-t)-ne ws* '(if) I see him' [/see(-transitive)-1sg.sbj. 1sg.sbj.conjunctive], *ʔił /cǝq-t-és us* 'and then he put it there' [and.then /put-transitive-3.sbj. 3.sbj.conjunctive].

5.3.

Reflexive and reciprocal forms introduce logically transitive objects but are grammatically intransitive, requiring intransitive subject particles (4.2.3.). |-sut| 'reflexive' and |-wáxʷ| 'reciprocal' follow |-t| 'transitive' directly:

/mén-e-st kn |√mén:-n-t-sut k-en| 'I get myself into the shade', */qǝs-cút* |√qǝs:-t-sut| 'he scratches himself',
/kʷukʷ-s-cút kt |kʷǝkʷ:-s-t-sut k-et| 'we are grateful, thankful' (lit. 'we make ourselves grateful'),
/sǝlk-e-cút |√sǝlǝk:-n-t-sut| 'she turns (herself) around';
/λ̓ǝqʷ-e-t-wáxʷ |√λ̓ǝqʷ:-n-t-wáxʷ| 'they fight (slap, beat each other)',
/pzen-t-wáxʷ kp |pǝzén:-t-wáxʷ k-ep| 'you people meet (coming from opposite directions)'.

As in many languages, reflexives often have extended or idiomatic meanings: */xeʔ-s-cút* |√xeʔ:-s-t-sut| 'she is haughty' (|√xeʔ| 'rise'), */cuw-e-cút* 'he goes questing for spirit power' (|√cǝw| 'do, make').

Where there are alternate stems from weak roots with |-t| and |-n-t| inflection, |-sut| and |-wáxʷ| are consistently added to the |-n-t| stem: */qʷi-t-és ~ /qʷiy-e-t-és* |√qʷǝy:(-n)-t-es| 'he coats it with a powdery substance', */qʷiy-e-cút* 'he gets coated (with dust)'; */xǝc-t-éne ~ /xǝc-e-t-éne* |√xǝc:(-n)-t-en(è)| 'I bet him (about something)', */xǝc-e-t-wáxʷ* 'they bet with each other'.

Reflexives can be retransitivized via the causative, the indirective, or relational: */yem--cút-s-t-xʷ* 'you bring him to be treated with affection,' */qʷin-cút-x-cm-s* 'he speaks for me (for my purposes),' */qʷin-cút-m-nxʷ* 'you talk about her.'

Reciprocals can be reconverted to transitive via the causative: |λ̓ǝqʷ-e-t-wáxʷ-s-ne| 'I fight with him', */xǝc-e-t-wáxʷ-s-t-xʷ* 'you bet with him'.

5.4.

Middle voice is marked by |-ǝ́me|. It refers to activities and states in which the subject is involved, perhaps is initiator, acting in particular with self-interest and full or considerable control, thus affording intransitive control oppositions parallel to the transitive ones (cf. 5.2.3.). Grammatically intransitive, they nevertheless often convey transitive meanings: */sk-ǝ́m* |√sǝk-ǝ́me| 'he clubs (someone or something)', */cw-ǝ́m* 'they work' (|√cǝw| 'do, make'), */séxʷ-m* 'he bathes', */ʔúʔe-me* |√ʔúʔè-ǝ́me| 'she sings a lullaby'. Middles frequently convey specialized meanings: /cíx̣ʷ-m/ 'he buys a wife' (reference to laying out goods for bride price: |√cíx̣ʷ| 'lay'). They are frequently causativized: /cuw-m-s-t-éx̣ʷ| |√cəw-ə́me:-s-t-exʷ| 'you make him work'; /séx̣ʷ-m-s-c| |√séx̣ʷ-ə́me-s-t-es| 'he makes him bathe'.

5.5.

Imperatives are formed on both intransitive and transitive stems (after object suffixes) by addition of |-è|, pluralized by immediately preceding |-wz|: /x̣ʷə́st-e 'go home!', /x̣ʷə́st-uz-e 'go home, you people!', n/té̇m-ix-e 'get in!', n/té̇m-ix-uz-e 'get in, you people!', /wík-cm-e |√wík:-t-sem-è| 'see me!', /wík-t-y-uz-e |√wík:-t-ey-wz-è| 'see us, you people!', /ník̇-e-t-e 'cut it!', /səlk-e-t-éy-e 'turn us around!'. With weak transitive stems -ét appears before imperative endings (perhaps originally a diminutive [6.7.1.] but now the only form for such stems): /sək-t-ét-è |√sək:-t(-ét)-è| 'club him!', /səlk-e-t-ét-uz-e |sələk:-n-t(-et)-wz-è| 'you people turn him around!'

Before imperative endings an element -x- is often found suffixed to various kinds of intransitive stems; it is especially common with middles: /séẏsi̇ʔ-x-e |√séẏ•seẏ-x-è| 'go and play!', /qeʔm-éyt-x-e |√qeʔem= eyt-x-è| 'nurse your baby!' (|=eyt| 'person, child'), /x̣ʎ̇-ə́m-x̣ʷ-uz-e |√x̣ə̇ʎ̇-ə́me-x-wz-è| 'chew, you people!', kəł•/kəł=xn-ə́m-x-e |kəł•√kəł=x̣ə̇n-ə́me-x-è| 'take off your shoes!' Forms with and without -x- have been recorded without semantic contrast: /cw-ə́m-x-e ~ /cw-ə́m-e 'work!'

A few roots show a special imperative singular: /nés-wė 'go!', /cʔés-wė 'come!', /wʔéx̣ʷ-wė 'remain (as you are), keep well!', /ʎ̇ʔék-wė 'arrive (safely, wherever you're going)!', (the last two commonly used as goodbye formulas). The corresponding plurals are regular: /nés-uz-e, /cʔés-uz-e, /wʔéx̣ʷ-uz-e, /ʎ̇ʔék̇ʷ-uz-e.

5.6. PLURALIZATION AND OTHER AUGMENTATIVE NOTIONS

Number is an obligatory opposition in first and second persons (except where second person uses the plural inflection for both singular and plural reference, 5.2.1.). But most simple third-person forms are ambiguous as to number. There are various ways of insisting on plural reference; some of these convey other ideas as well.

5.6.1.

Third-person plural |-ə́yxs| (4.2.3.) serves in both possessive (4.3.) and transitive (5.2.) paradigms. In the transitive it indicates third plural subject acting on a third singular or plural object: /sək-t-íyxs 'they club him/them', /nik̇-e-t-íyxs |√ník̇:-n-t-ə́yxs| 'they cut it/them', /łək̇ʷ-min-t-íyxs 'they recall it/them'. Grammatically intransitive, permitting no overt object pronouns (4.2.3.), it can be retransitivized by suffixing

|-n-t| to bring in other subjects and objects; here |-ə́yxs| refers to subjects or objects, depending on the other elements:

/sək-t-íyxs-n-e |√sək:-t-ə́yxs:-n-t-en| 'I club them',
/wik-t-íyxs-es |√wík:-t-ə́yxs:-n-t-es| 'she sees them',
/pun-m-t-íyxs-e-t-p |√pún:-min-t-ə́yxs:-n-t-ep| 'you people find them',
/k̇ʷeł-e-t-íyxs-e-t-i-s |√k̇ʷéł:-n-t-ə́yxs:-n-t-ey-es| 'they ask us to go with them',
/wik-t-íyxs-e-cm-s |√wík:-t-ə́yxs:-n-t-sem-es| 'they see me',
/wik-t-íyxs-e-t-m |√wík:-t-ə́yxs:-n-t-em| 'they are seen'.

5.6.2.

Augmentatives are formed with |CVC•|, commonly referring to several persons or things (intransitive subjects, transitive objects) as a group, but sometimes suggesting distribution over space or time: n-qi•/qáy-ix kt |nə-qáy•√qáy-əyx k-et| 'we all swim', s-qʷəm•/qʷə́m 'mountains', cėʔ•/č[ʔ]éł |čėʔ•√če[ʔˇ]ł| (5.1.4.) 'they get cold', wək•/wík-t-x̣ʷ 'you see them', ʎəṁ•/ʎə̇m-ép-e-s 'he chops all (the trees) down', ʔes-qəʎ̇•/qíʎ̇ 'he has lots of scars', qʷiʔ•/qʷúẏ 'there are clouds, it is cloudy, qʷuʔ•/qʷuʔ=úyṁx̣ʷ 'swamp (water here and there on the ground)', ʔes-cu•/cúw '(houses) built here and there', x̣ʷəl•/x̣ʷél=qs '(board in floor) pops up (whenever someone steps on one end)'. It can indicate repetitions of an act: səẏ•/səy-t-és '(Indian doctor) blows repeatedly on (patient, treating him)'. Or it may represent extensiveness or intensification of an activity or state, or large size: ʎəqʷ•/ʎəqʷʔ-úm kʷ 'you do a lot of sewing', wəs•/wís-t 'very high; they are up high', cȯʔ•/č[ʔ]óz |cȯʔ•√čo[ʔˇ]z| 'very dark', təx̣ʷ•/tóx̣ʷ-t 'quite correct; very straight, exact', tən•/tón-t 'pulled too hard, stretched', x̣ʷəm•/x̣ʷém-t 'he is very lonely; they are lonely', ʔes-ʔexʷ•/ʔéxʷ-t 'big landslide, avalanche; landslides all over', ʔes-t-pəł•/pə́ł-e 'brimming full'. With some intransitives logical parts or localities are referred to: ʔes-kəł•/kəł=x̣ən 'she has her shoes off (both feet)' (|kəł| 'detach', |=x̣ən| 'foot , leg').

Some words, already reduplicative, nevertheless form augmentatives: k̇ʷəʎ̇•k̇ʷəʎ̇•/k̇ʷíʎ̇p 'fleas' (k̇ʷəʎ̇•/k̇ʷíʎ̇p 'flea'), s-hiʔ•/hiʔhí̇ʔ 'male in-laws of ascending generations' (s/hiʔhí̇ʔ 'father-in-law').

Some augmentatives, especially those denoting states and qualities, are more common than the corresponding simplexes. Some words occur only in the augmentative: s-ki•/kíyėʔ 'ancestors, predecessors' (cf. s/kíyėʔ 'front'). Some do not form augmentatives at all; like most unaugmented words, they can have either singular or plural reference: n-kʷə•/kʷúsṅ 'star(s)'.

In a few augmentatives stress falls on the first syllable: s-kéw•/kʷu |s-kew•√kéw| 'woman's sisters-in-law, female cousins by marriage'. A few words have irregular augmentatives: cə•/cítx̣ʷ 'houses'.

625

5.6.3.

Plural infixes |[ʔy], [zʔe], [če]| form a few special plu-
rals: /ɫcé[ʔi]ck \√ɫcé[ʔy]ck| 'female in-laws of ascend-
ing generations (/ɫcéck 'mother-in-law'); /cʔé[ʔi]s 'they
come' (/cʔés 'she comes'; note also /cʔé[ʔi]-t 'we
come'), /né[ʔi]s 'they go' (/nés 'he goes', /né[ʔi]-t 'we
go'), /cú[ʔi]t \√cú[ʔy]t| 'they say' (/cút 'she says',
/cú[ʔi]t kt 'we say'); s/ čá[že]xt 'man's brothers-in-law,
male cousins by marriage' (sg. s/čéxt), /ƛ̓ʔá[že]k 'they
arrive'(/ƛ̓ʔék 'he arrives'); /wʔé[če]x ~ /wʔé[čə]x 'they
are located over there' (/wʔéx 'be located').

5.6.4. ABLAUT PLURAL ROOTS

A number of weak roots with |ə| have strong counter-
parts with a tense vowel (most commonly |í|) and plural
reference. With such roots augmentatives are freely
formed from both stems; with singular roots these suggest a few referents, with plural roots many (again
intransitive subjects, transitive objects). The following
list is not exhaustive:

Gloss	Singular	Plural
'pull out'	|√cəkʷ|	|√cíkʷ|
'tear'	|√cəˤ|	|√cíˤ|
'crack, check'	|√ƛ̄əq̓ʷ|	|√ƛ̄íq̓ʷ|
'knock off [berries into basket]'	|√səp|	|√síp|
'split'	|√səq|	|√síq|
'cut'	|√k̄əl|	|√k̄íl|
'hit with stick'	|√sək|	|√sék|
'splash'	|√yəqʷ|	|√yúqʷ|

5.6.5. SUPPLETIVE PLURAL STEMS

A number of other roots have as plural counterparts
unrelated (or nonsystematically related) stems. The following list is not exhaustive:

Gloss	Singular	Plural
'lay'	|√cút|	|√cíxʷ|; |nə√míx̣ʷ|
'sit'	|√míceʔq|	|√ɫáq|
'give'	|√nə|; |√m̓əṅ|	|nə√míʔ|
'die'	|√zúqʷ|	|√xʷáy|
'fall, drop'	|√kʷís|	|√zeƛ̓|
'weep'	|√wíyx|	|√k̄ʷíq̓|

5.7. MODAL EXTENSIONS

Several strong suffixes form stems with modal overtones.

5.7.1.

Noncontrol middle |-nwéɫn| emphasizes lack of control
(cf. 3.4., 5.1.5.): /zoqʷ-nwéɫn '(plant) is deadly poiso-
nous' (|√zúqʷ| 'die'), /q̓ay̓-nwéɫn 'he manages to shoot
(a deer)', /x̣ək-p-nwéɫn kt 'we finally understand; we
accidentally find out' (|√x̣ək| 'know', |-ə̌p| 'inchoat-
ive'). For transitive inflection the stem is converted
to -nwéṅ-, and |-t| is added directly: /q̓ay̓-nwéṅ-s
|√q̓ay̓-nwéṅ-t-es| 'she shoots him (accidentally)',
wəs•/wis-t-nwéṅ-t-m 'we finally manage to get (boards
for scaffold) high enough'.

5.7.2.

Desiderative |-mémn| expresses wishes and tendencies:
/q̓ax-mémn 'he wants to borrow something', /ˤʷoy̓t-
mémn kn 'I am sleepy' (/ˤʷóy̓t 'sleep'), /tekɫ-mémn 'it
looks like rain'. It sometimes conveys the notion
'almost': /q̓ʷeč-t-mémn 'almost full'. Control transi-
tives are created by adding |-t| directly to this stem
(with expected morphophonemic developments, 2.7.,
rules [7], [17-18]): /sək-méme-s \√sək-mémn:-t-es| 'she
feels like clubbing him'. However, the surface stem
used with third person /sək-méme- (n > e/ _t) is
extended analogically to position before first and second singular subjects: /sək-méme-ne 'I feel like clubbing him', /sək-méme-n-xʷ 'you feel like clubbing him'.

5.7.3.

Developmental |-wíʔx| covers increase, intensification,
change, and unexpected continuation of states and
actions: /qəɫmin-wíʔx 'he gets old(er); it wears out',
ʔes/citxʷ-wíʔx kp 'you people finally got a house'
(ʔes/cítxʷ kp 'you people have a house'), /wmex-wíʔx
'she's still living (I thought she had died)'. Transitives
are formed with |-s| 'causative': n/k̓s=eṅk-wíʔx-s-t-xʷ
'you make him angry' (|nə√k̓əs=eneʔk| lit. 'bad belly').

5.7.4.

Habitual |-úɫ| suggests preference, predilection, charac-
teristic behavior (intransitive only, but can be followed
by developmental; 5.7.3.): /ƛ̓z-úɫ 'she's a lazy person'
(/ƛ̓áz 'she's lazy (right now)'), /ƛ̓z-uɫ-wíʔx 'she's
getting lazy'. Stems commonly have augmentative
reduplication (5.6.2.): məɫ•/miɫt-úɫ 'she's fond of visiting', p̓uʔ•/p̓uʔ-m-úɫ 'perpetual flatulator (Skunk's
nickname)'.

5.7.5.

Translocational |-úləwɫ| indicates a trip of some length,
either walking or by some conveyance, for a specific
purpose: /ʔuqʷeʔ-úluɫ kt 'we go out for a drink'
(|√ʔúqʷeʔ| 'drink'), /sey̓•siʔ-úluɫ 'they go (to town) to
have a good time' (|√séy̓•sey̓| '(pl.) play, do things for
pleasure').

6. DERIVATION

More complex words are derived in several ways.

6.1. EXPANDED STEMS

6.1.1.

Compound stems are occasionally formed, involving
more than the usual single root: n/cəq/xʷéɫ-ne
|nə√cəq√xəẃéɫ:-n-t-en| 'I put it right on the road'
(|√cəq| 'set', |√xəẃéɫ| 'trail road'), n/čək/súp̓ kn 'I am
out of breath' (cf. /čək-s-t-éne 'I use it all up', /súp̓-m
kn 'I breathe'). In some cases the second element is
clearly an (otherwise) independent word rather than
just a root: /xəƛ̓-s/qáxaʔ kn 'I look after my horse' (cf.
/xəƛ̓-t-éne 'I take care of it', s/qáxaʔ 'dog; horse', with
s- 'nominalizer', 6.5.).

There is also a compounding element |-ɬ-|, which joins stems: /təm-ɬ/mʔ-ém/ 'he is unmarried' (|√tem| 'lack', |√məʔ-em| 'wife'); /təm-ɬ-n/λ́p=íče?/ 'he has no shirt on' (where the final element is an independent word |nə√λ̀əp=iče?| 'shirt'). It serves in particular to make compound numbers (with shortening of first elements, 8.1.): /mu-ɬ/ʔúpn=ekst |√mu(s)-ɬ√ʔúpən=ekst| 'forty (lit. four tens)'.

Some compound stems contain a first root that does not occur independently, although it may be quite productive; e.g., n/k̓əɬ- 'sharing, accompanying, co-' in n/k̓əɬ/kʷést 'has the same name' (|√kʷést| 'name'), n/k̓əɬ-we•/wíyx 'comourner; relative by marriage after death of linking relative (we•/wíyx 'weep'), n/k̓əɬ-n/qáy-ix 'swimming companion' (|nə√qáy-əyx| 'swim'). The first element in the common word /λu?-s/qáyx (Spuzzum /λ̀i?-s/qáyx) 'person', s/qáyx 'man' may be a similar bound root.

6.1.2.
Root extensions are poorly understood. A number of roots have shorter and longer forms, but the extensions are not productive, and semantic differences are elusive or inconsistent: |√səl| 'turn, spin', |√sələk| 'turn'; |√wəl| 'open, clear way through', |√wəluqʷ| 'clear way through'.

6.1.3.
Lexical suffixes (3.1.1.) extend roots and inchoative stems (5.1.4.), adding precision of reference and a variety of nuances—sometimes very subtle and highly specialized ones: /q́íx=yṁxʷ |√q́ix=uyəṁxʷ| 'hard ground' (|√q́ix| 'strong, firm', |=uyəṁxʷ| 'earth, land, place; (earth) oven'), n/xəṁ-p-=úyṁxʷ |nə√xəṁ-əp=uyəṁxʷ| 'dry area' (/xm-áp 'dry up'), n/cən-p-=úyṁxʷ '(passing train) echoes with a heavy sound' (/cn-áp 'echo'), /kʷa[?]ĺ=úyṁxʷ 'grass turns green' (/kʷ[?]ál 'turn green'), n/q́ʷy=úyṁxʷ-m 'she bakes in the earth oven' (|√q́ʷəy| 'cook', |-ə̆me| 'middle'), n/q́əst=úyṁxʷ-m 'she bakes bread in an iron pot in the ashes' (/q́əst-ám 'Indian vegetables steam-baked in a pit'), n/čáp=yṁxʷ 'sour-dough; yeast bread' (|√čáp| 'sour').

Parallel to complex words involving lexical suffixes speakers also use simpler predicates, adding detail by means of complements and adjuncts (7.2., 7.3.), which provide more specific identification of entities involved: /caˤ-p=íče? kʷ 'your clothing (dress or shirt) is torn', /cˤ-áp e ?-n/λ́p=íče? 'your shirt is torn'. The tendency to favor these syntactic constructions over the morphological ones with lexical suffixes is one of the characteristics of current usage.

Because of the wide range of extended meanings of both suffixes and roots, and frequent further metaphorical extensions, it is often impossible to predict the reference of a particular word from its components (/yˤʷ=ékst-m 'murder in secret' ['/hide=hand-middle.voice'], /caq=cín 'level area on edge of river' ['/put=mouth']), and sometimes difficult to recognize the semantic connection (n/cq=ús-m 'cook by boiling' ['localizer/put.face.eye.sun.fire-middle.voice'], where |=us| presumably refers to fire; /pi?=ép=uʔs=qn-me 'be greedy, push oneself ahead of everyone else' ['/one=bottom= top.surface=head-middle.voice'], apparently involving |√peyè?| 'one' and |=ep=eẇes=qin| 'back of crown of head').

Lexical suffixes frequently cluster in derivatives, furnishing yet further nuances and detailed references. Some combinations seem clearly to be compounded, specific reference followed by more general coverage: s/kiye?=qín=kst 'thumb', s/kiye?=qín=xn 'big toe', /xʷəl=qín=ks-tn 'nail file' (|√kiyè?| 'be ahead, in front, principal, eldest', |√xʷəl| 'grind, file', |=ekst| 'hand', |=xṅ| 'foot', |[']| 'specializing extension', 6.2.1., |=qiṅ=ekst| 'finger', |=qiṅ=xṅ| 'toe'); n/k̓m=énk=xn 'sole of foot', n/qs=énk=xn-me 'she tickles the sole of his foot' (|√k̓əm| 'focal area', |√qəs| 'tickle; scratch an itch', |=enek| 'belly, under side', (|=enek=xṅ| 'bottom of foot', |nə-| 'localized', |-ə̆me| 'middle').

Middle forms from stems extended by lexical suffixes are common, as some of the preceding examples show. The corresponding transitives are formed with simple |-t| inflection if the stem ends in |n, ṅ|, otherwise with |-n-t|: /sk=ép=qe-s |√sək=ep=qin:-t-es| 'she clubs him on (back of) head' (|=ep| 'bottom, rear', |=qin| 'head'), /ch=ékṅ-s |√cəh=ekəṅ:-t-es| 'she fixes his pack' (|√cəh| 'fix, adjust', |=ekəṅ| 'pack, bundle'); /ch=ús-e-s |cəh=us:-n-t-es| 'she fixes the fire' (|=us| 'face, eye, sun, fire').

Causative (5.2.3.), indirective (5.2.4.), and relational (5.2.5.) inflections are also common: /sk=ép=qe-s-c |√sək=ep=qin:-s-t-es| 'he (accidentally) hits on (back of) head (with pole), fells tree on him'; /cút=qs-x-t-xʷ |√cút=aqs:-xi-t-ex| 'you point gun at him' (|√cúɬ| 'point, direct', |=aqs| 'nose, point, end, weapon'); /kɬ=ékst-m-ne |√kəɬ=ekst:-min-t-en| 'I let go of it' (|√kəɬ| 'detach', |=ekst| 'hand').

6.2. SPECIALIZED STEMS

6.2.1.
Specializing extension |[']| appears to be the affix in a poorly understood process by which (usually posttonic) resonants take on glottalization in sporadic derivatives. The words reflect extensions of various sorts: /q́u?=qíṅ '(tree) stump' (|√q̀əẇ| 'break in two', |=qin| 'head, top'), cf. s/ɬəč=qín '(traditional) hairdo with top knot' (|√ɬəč| 'twist in several directions').

6.2.2.
Proportional |-íýCe?| (position, size, shape, etc., with relation to something else) derives a few stems, mostly followed by |-t| 'immediate' (5.1.2.); the roots are also poorly attested: /tx•í?xe?-t 'narrow piece', /ɬq̀•í?qe?-t 'short', /k̓ʷm•í?me? 'small'. /k̓í[•?k̓e?]t

'near' is similar in form but is relatable to a root |√kít| 'approach' (cf. *n/kít-ne* |nə√kít:-n-t-ene| 'I catch up with him'); it suggests this affix is a suffix with weak stems, but an infix replacing the stressed vowel in strong ones.

6.2.3.

Affective |Ce•| (often with specializing extension |[']|, 6.2.1.) derives stylistic variants connoting special attitudes ranging from familiarity, perhaps with overtones of nostalgia, to extreme specialization. The vowel of the |Ce•| prefix is most often reduced to |ə| in regular fashion, but some forms show *ə* varying with *e* and others consistently show *e*. The formation is unproductive (reflecting an old diminutive pattern), but provides many examples:

n-q̇ə•/q̇ə́ċ |nə-q̇e•√q̇əċ| 'woven part of snowshoes' (|√q̇əċ| 'weave'),

ʔes-cə•/cú ʔ |ʔes-ce•√cəw[']| 'it has a pattern' (|√cəw| 'do, make'),

s-pə•/plánt |s-pe•√pəlánt| 'skunk' (simplex *s/plánt* is rare),

kə•/kíc-ṅ-cm-s |ke•√kíc:-n[']t-sem-es| 'he haunts me' (cf. */kíc-e-cm-s* 'he comes to visit me').

6.3.1.

Localizer |nə-| signals localization or a more abstract specialization, as opposed to vaguer or more usual references of unmarked forms: *n/cíq-m* 'he digs a hole', */cíq-m* 'he digs (more generally)'; *n/ƛepeʔ=xə́n* |nə√ƛepeʔ=xə̌n| 'marrow in the leg bone', *s/ƛepéʔ* 'marrow'; *n/cúɬ-mn* 'compass' (|√cúɬ| 'indicate', |-min| 'means', 6.4.1.), */cúl-mn* 'index finger'. It often refers to inside or inner position: *n/pək̇ʷ-t-éne* 'I dump it in', */pək̇ʷ-t-éne* 'I dump it out'; *n/iʔh=ékst* 'right arm', *s/iʔh=ékst* 'right hand' (|√ẏəh| 'good', |=ekst| 'hand, lower arm', *s-* 'nominalizer', 6.5.). It sometimes conveys a partitive idea: *n/cék-m* 'she cools off part of it (something she is cooking, so as to taste it)', */cék-m* 'she cools it off (all of it)'. Some roots always have |nə-|: |nə√ɬéṁ| 'go inside'. With some lexical suffixes |nə-| signals a common shift in meaning: e.g., |=us| without the prefix often refers to 'face, surface', but with |nə-| rather to 'eye(s), seeing, window': */ćq̇=ús-e-s* |√čəq̇=us:-n-t-es| 'she hits him in face', *n/ćq̇=ús-e-s* 'she hits him in eye; hits his window', */pt=ús-tn* 'veil', *n/pt=ús-tn* 'window shade'. Some lexical suffixes regularly require |nə-|: e.g., |nə-...=eṅih| 'ear, side of head, side of something'; compare */ɬik̇ʷ=áqs* |√ɬəyək̇ʷ=aqs| 'bump one's nose', *n/ɬik̇ʷ=éṅi* 'bump side of one's head'.

6.3.2

Qualitative |tə-| is far less common. It suggests a quality, characteristic, or state; it is usually accompanied by the stative prefix (5.1.1.) and often by the resultative suffix (5.1.6.): *ʔes-t/píq* 'white', *ʔes-t/kʷə́z•kʷəz-t* 'smooth', *ʔes-t/xə́ɬ-e* 'he feels better', *ʔes-t/xəɬ-e-s-t-és* 'it makes him feel better'.

6.4.

Formative suffixes create various extended stems. Transitive formatives are discussed in 5.2.3.-5. There are also formatives making intransitive themes that function primarily as independent words.

6.4.1.

Instrumentals are found with two suffixes; some generalizations can be made covering most derivatives. Those with |-min| 'means' refer to implements, materials, or places for temporary or casual use; no control (3.4.) is specified, and connotation is often passive and concrete. Those with |-tən| 'way' refer to apparatus, tools, or areas for specific, more permanent use; control is implied, and connotation is usually active, often abstract. *n/xʷəl-mín* 'washboard' (|√xʷəl| 'grind'), *s/xʷəl-mín* 'sawdust, filings', */xʷəl=qín=ks-tn* |√xʷəl=qin[']=ekst-tən| 'nail file' (|=qin[']=ekst| 'finger'), *n/xʷl-ús-tn* 'file, grindstone' (|=us| 'face, edge'); *n/q̇ʷíċ-mn* 'washtub' (|√q̇ʷíċ| 'launder'), */q̇ʷíċ=če ʔ-tn* 'laundry soap' (|=iče ʔ| 'skin, clothes'); *n/zús-mn* 'jail' (|√zús| 'restrain'), */zús=ks-tn* |√zús=ekst-tən| 'handcuffs'; */cumín* 'equipment' (|√cəw| 'do, make, work'), *s/cu-tə́n* 'custom, way of doing things'. They sometimes occur together: *n/q̇ʷi-mín-tn* 'oven (in stove)' (|√q̇ʷəy| 'cook'), */q̇iʔ-mín* '(temporary) camp' (|/q̇íy-m| 'camp overnight'), */q̇iʔ-mín-tṅ* 'regular (customary) campground'. Some words seem to be frozen derivatives with |-min|: */qətmín* 'he is old'.

6.4.2.

Deictic formatives create a closed class of demonstratives. The resemblances of the words to one another and of the stems to various other elements can hardly be accidental, but semantic relationships are tenuous and unsystematic; the forms are best simply listed with their apparent relatives in table 4.

The A forms share *-ʔe*; the final vowel is optional except in *ɬúʔe*; the first five words share a longer sequence *-éʔ(e)*. The B forms seem to be emphatic words related to their first-column counterparts. (The negative */téʔ(e)* [7.5.3.] is similar in form, but quite different in meaning and use.) Some other deictic words also end in *-e*, which may be the same formative: *ʔéy-e* 'here' (note also *ʔéy-ɬ* 'now'), */ćíy-e* 'like this, the same way' (see also 6.4.3.).

6.4.3.

General formatives are various and are not well understood at present. A few samples are cited here. Some suffixes are widespread but derivatives seem to have no unifying meaning or function, and the stems are often not otherwise identifiable: e.g., *-e ʔ* in *s/pún-e ʔ* 'dead animal found and appropriated (by scavenger)' (|√pún| 'find'); *-í ʔ* in *s/kʷl-í ʔ* 'copper' (Lytton) (cf. |√kʷəl| 'green').

Other words that may include a formative are: */q̇álze ʔ* 'take sweatbath', */ʔéyćqe ʔ* 'outside', *s/xʷə́se ʔ*

Table 4. Demonstratives

A Forms	B Forms	Basic Stem
xéʔ(e) 'this, here (nearby); just referred to'	xʔé 'this, here (opposed to another)'	|xəl| 'particularizing' (7.3.1.)
néʔ(e) 'that (particular one), there; (established in context) as you already know'	nʔé 'right there'	|nəl| 'in, at, on' (7.3.2.)
wéʔ(e) 'that, there (to be established), wherever it may be'		|wəl| 'to(ward)' (7.3.2.)
téʔ(e) 'main interest, beyond, next, last, further, other'	tʔé 'about to be set forth'	|tel| 'oblique' (7.2.2.)
kéʔ(e) 'which? whatever, whichever, any; is it that...?' c-kéʔ(e) (emphatic)		|kəl| 'unrealized' (7.3.1.)
cíʔ(e) 'that, there (yonder); the other'		|c-| 'emphatic' (with a few stems)
ƛúʔe 'that, there (remote)'	ƛʔe 'that, there' (emphatic)	|ƛəl| 'established in past' (7.3.1.)
ƛə́ńe 'that (particular one)' (established unseen)		
kʷúkʷ 'not visible, spoken of' (unseen)		

'flowering currant', /káze? 'tell falsehood, lie', /q̓ʷúneʔ 'fermented salmon roe', /sí[•s]qeʔ 'uncle' (cf. |√síq| 'split [pl.]'), and presumably (with vowel assimilated, 2.7., rule [13]) s/qáxaʔ 'dog; horse', /qʷtíxaʔ 'louse'; -e in /máċe 'fly (insect)', s/núye 'beaver; money', /k̓ʷáxʷe 'box', /níwe 'spouse' (affectionate), /ƛék̓ye 'make lunch' (see also 6.4.2.); -iʔ in s/ċqíʔ 'piece of wood'.

Several kin terms (8.2.) share -zeʔ; of these s/kíx-zeʔ 'mother' seems based on /kíx 'elder sister', s/qác-zeʔ 'father' on /qéck 'elder brother', s/páp-zeʔ 'grandfather' on /pép (vocative [7.9.] for 'grandfather' or 'father').

6.5.

Nominalizer |s-| is prefixed to a great variety of stems, including most other full words; it precedes the stative (5.1.1.) and qualifying (6.3.) prefixes, but possessive prefixes precede it. It is convenient to call the derivatives nominals, but they should not be confused with nouns in a language like English; like other major words they are predicative (3.1.4., 3.3.). Kuipers (1968) and Kinkade (1983) discuss the absence of a compelling noun-verb dichotomy and the status of nominals in some other Salishan languages. Nominals refer to actions, situations, states, entities viewed as wholes or as facts, or as products, leftovers, or results. They are opposed to nonnominals (without |s-|), which

denote actions and states in progress; active entities; or situations viewed as dynamic, developmental in the past or generally. Note the following one-word sentences based on the root |√zík| 'fall;"

/zík-t. '(A tree) fell over, has just fallen.' (Also: "He fell over, fainted.") (immediate, 5.1.2.)

ʔes/zík. '(A tree has been uprooted and) has fallen; is falling.' (stative, 5.1.1.)

/zík-e-s. 'He felled it.' (transitive, 5.2.2.)

s/zík. "It is a log (tree that has fallen).' (nominal)

Both intransitives and transitives can be nominalized: /ċéw̓=s-tn 'soap, way to wash face' |√ċéw̓| 'wash', |=us| 'face', |-tən| 'way'), s/ċéw̓=s-tn 'water someone has washed face with' ('leftover from way to wash face'); /wík-ne 'I see him', /ʔe xéʔe /séye-s e s/wík-ne 'that is the second time I saw him' (/ʔe xéʔe 'that is the one', 6.4.2., 7.5.1.; /séye-s 'two of them', with -s third-person possessive, 4.3.; e direct complement particle, 7.2.1.).

6.6.

Postterminal suffixes can be added to most intransitive stems.

6.6.1.

Redefinition suffixes signal reinstatement of more fundamental meanings. |-ʔúy| 'basic, ordinary, plain, real, genuine', as in s/muɬec-ʔúy 'woman without profession', s/xeńx-ʔúy 'granite' ('plain rock'), /cw-əm-ʔúy 'work for room and board (no pay)', /q̓ʷu(ʔ)-ʔúy 'Fraser River' ('basic water'), often serves to reestablish the original meaning of simple words that have been transferred in reference to recently introduced items: s/kʷi(ʔ)-ʔúy 'arrow' (s/kʷíʔ 'bullet; lead ball; lead').

Less productive, but somewhat similar in meaning is |-ʔútye| 'simple, rustic, crude': /cw-əm-ʔútye 'work with hands; simple laborer', s/p̓em-ʔútye 'open fireplace' |√p̓ém| 'make fire', s/p̓ém '(cooking or camp) fire'), /citxʷ-ʔútye 'simple slab house'.

6.6.2.

Intensifying suffixes cover increase in scope or extent. |-ṁíx| 'definitive' indicates completion; an expert, extreme, or full application; the essence of something: /ʕʷoy̓t-ṁíx 'not recovering from anesthesia; sleeping late in the morning' (/ʕʷóy̓t 'sleep'), ʔes/caq-ṁíx '(car) is stalled (right on the road)' (|√cəq| 'put, place'), ʔes/ƛ̓q̓ʷuʔ-ṁíx '(clothes) are ready-made' |√ƛ̓əq̓ʷuʔ| 'sew'), /qi[ʔ]xʷ-mín-st-ṁíx 'perennial bachelor' (|√qay[ʔˇ]xʷ- min[']-t-sut-ṁíx| 'bachelor').

More specialized is |-núxʷ| 'persevering, surviving': n/xʷiʔt-núxʷ 'survive through to spring' (n/xʷúy̓t 'leave winter house for warm season; spring'), /ʕap-núxʷ 'make it through the day' (/ʕáp 'be twilight, evening'), /yəx-p-núxʷ 'come back to one's senses' (|√yəx-ə̆p| 'become wise, sane').

6.7.

Secondary formations are based on primary words. Certain processes are applied to stems after stress assignment (2.5.). In other cases affixes usually functioning in primary formations are added to full primary stems (see. 2.5.).

6.7.1.

Diminutives are freely created with the infix |[•CV([']])| (often with specializing extension |[']|, 6.2.1.). The basic meaning is small size or amount but there are many extended meanings, as commonly with diminutives in other languages: affection, endearment, modesty, and various specializations.

/ʕʷó[•ʕʷ]iʔt |√ʕʷó[•ʕʷo[']]ẏt| 'take a nap' (/ʕʷóyt 'sleep'),

s/x̣á[•x̣]iʔwi |s√x̣á[•x̣a[']]ẏwi| 'dear husband' (s/x̣áẏwi 'husband'),

/ɫaʔx̣•á[•x̣]ńs |√ɫaʔx̣•á[x̣a[']]ns| '(baby or animal) eats' (/ɫaʔx̣•áns '(grown person) eats'),

s-mi•/mé[•m̓]iʔx |s-məy•√me[•me[']]yx| 'worms' (s-mi•/méyx 'snakes'),

s/pzú[•ż]uʔ |s√pzú[•z[']]uʔ| '(small) bird' (s/pzúʔ 'animal'),

/kʷm[•í[•m̓]iʔm̓]eʔ 'tiny' (/kʷm[•íʔm]eʔ 'small'),

/ċé[•ċ]kʷ-m̓ |√ċé[•ċe[']]kʷ-əm| 'shine a light to attract fish to spear' (/ċékʷ-m 'shine a light'),

s-nuʔ•/né[•n]uʔ-t |s-néw•√né[•ne]w̓-t| 'little breeze blowing' (s-nuʔ•/néw̓-t 'wind blowing' [augmentative, suggesting repetition]).

Diminutives frequently occur based on augmentatives (5.6.2.) without a diminutive based on the corresponding simplex. Thus there are numerous defective sets like the following: /qʷɫi-n=éɫmx 'birchbark basket' (/qʷɫi-n 'birch'), qʷəɫ•/qʷɫi-n=éɫmx 'birchbark baskets', qʷəɫ•/qʷɫi-n=é[•n]ɫm̓x 'small birchbark baskets'.

6.7.2.

Repetitives are based only on augmentative stems (5.6.2.): |[eʔ]| (often with specializing extension |[']|, 6.2.1.) is infixed directly before the consonant beginning the stressed syllable. Derivatives refer to repetition of the same act or state over and over, often with vacillation, off and on, now one way, now another, etc.: n-wəz•[eʔ]/wáż-s-m̓ 'sun shows itself intermittently, now comes from behind a cloud, now goes under a cloud again' (|√wáz| 'show, appear', |=us| 'face, eye, sun, fire', |-m̓e| 'middle voice'), sən•[eʔ]/séń-t '(drunk person) staggers, keeps falling' (|√sén| 'fall over', |-t| 'immediate'), suʔ•[eʔ]/síẃ-ix 'he weaves off and on the road' (/síw-ix 'he turns off the road').

6.7.3.

Secondary inflection is especially common with the reflexive (5.3.): n/q̓íx̣•cn—n-cút |nə√q̓íx̣-cin—n-t-sut| 'he locks himself in' (cf. n/q̓íx̣•ce-s |nə√q̓íx̣-cin-t-es| 'he locks it'; |√q̓íx̣| 'secure', |=cin| 'mouth, aperture, door'). Simple transitives always take |-n-t|, regardless

of the class or final consonant of the primary stem: /wik—n-cút |√wík—n-t-sut| 'she sees herself' (cf. /wík-c |√wík-t-es| 'she sees him') (note also preceding example). With infixes, stress is determined by the primary form: ʔes-t/wə́l•l-e '(brush) has finally gotten cleared out now' (ʔes-t/wə́l-e |ʔes-tə√wəl-è| '(brush) is cleared out now'). Once created, secondary stems can be further inflected like primary stems: n/c=ét[•ət]kʷu-s-t-x̣ʷ 'you manage to place it in the water' (causativization [5.2.3.] of secondary out-of-control stem n/c=ét[•ət]kʷu, based on primary derivative n/c=étkʷu |nə√cə=etkəw| 'put in water'; |√cə| 'lay long obj.').

6.7.4.

Secondary lexical extension is common. A lexical suffix is added to an intransitive word already derived in the usual fashion. Meanings are usually extended or abstract. Recent coinages in the language frequently take this shape. /k̓ʷax̣ʷeh-=éwɫ |√k̓ʷáx̣ʷeh-=éwíɫ| '(railroad) boxcar', ʔes/ċəqʔ=ewɫ-=x̣ón kn |ʔes√ċəqəʔ=éwíɫ-=x̣ən k-en| 'I go by boat' (|=x̣ən| 'foot, leg, walk, go') (cf. ʔes/ċəqʔ=éwɫ kn 'I have a boat'), /zus-m-=éwɫ |√zús-əme-=éwíɫ| 'police car' (cf. /zús-m 'policeman', lit. 'he restrains [people]'). Secondary stems can then be further derived or inflected like primary stems: n/x̣ʷel-ix-=éni-n-t-i-s |nə√x̣ʷél-əyx-=eńih:-n-t-ey-es| 'he flies over us' (n/x̣ʷél-ix 'he flies', |=eńih| 'ear; position over, on top').

7. SYNTAX

The backbone of sentence structure is the predicate, the only obligatory element of minimum clauses. In more complicated clauses the predicate is the head element, with modifying complements or adjuncts, or both. Particles clarify details of relationship.

7.1.

Predicates vary from single major words to phrases involving several particles and certain other words. They normally appear first in their clauses.

7.1.1.

Predicative particles include the intransitive subject pronoun enclitics (4.1.), normally in first position after the predicate in the clitic string, followed by elements of evidential, modal, or aspectual force. Table 5 gives them in surface form (underlying forms are often unclear), showing their relative order (see also examples in 7.1.4.).

The following sentences exemplify the order of the predicative particles: ʔes-kəɫ•/kəɫ=x̣ón kʷ ń 'are you barefoot?', ʔes-kəɫ•/kəɫ=x̣ón kʷ nke '(I) guess you are barefoot', ʔes-kəɫ•/kəɫ=x̣ón kʷ ń ƛ̓əɫ 'do you already have your shoes off?', ʔes-kəɫ•/kəɫ=x̣ón kʷ ń ƛ̓əm̓ 'have you had your shoes off for some time already?', ʔes/xeƛ̓=ewíɫ nke ƛ̓əɫ '(I) guess the truck's already unloaded'; /míɫt kʷ ekʷu ƛu? 'they say you're just visiting'; /x̣ʷm-óp

Table 5. Order of Predicative Particles after Predicate Head

	Enclitic			Nonenclitic		
Intransitive Pronouns	Evidentials	Modal		Aspectuals	Emphatic	
kn, kʷ, etc.	n̓ 'interrogative'	we 'dubitative, in vain'		ƛ̓ət 'readied, contemporaneous'	ʔeł 'also, along with'	ƛ̓uʔ 'persistent'
wn, uxʷ, etc.	nke 'conjectural'	ƛ̓əp 'unusual'		ƛ̓əm̓ 'completed'	wiʔ 'indeed'	tuʔ 'emphatic'
	ekʷu 'reportive'	ske, seʔ 'presumptive, ought, should'		(u)y̓ ~ iʔ 'yet, still'	ceʔ 'ameliorative'	
	nukʷ 'perceptual'			mеł 'consequential'		

kʷ nukʷ 'I can see you're lonely'; /nés kʷ nke we 'I guess you went for no purpose', /séw-łn kn we ƛ̓ət 'I already inquired, but I doubt anything will come of it'; /nés kn ƛ̓ət 'I'm ready to go; I'm on my way'; /nés kʷ n̓ ƛ̓ət ƛ̓uʔ 'are you going, too?'; /téy-t kn iʔ 'I am still hungry'; /mél-ixʷ-uz-e məł 'you people had better rest'; /cʔés kʷ n̓ ƛ̓əm̓ ʔel ƛ̓uʔ 'did you come along, too, already?'; /séw-łn kn ƛ̓ət wiʔ 'I did indeed already ask'. The modal ske 'presumptive' usually takes the same position as the evidentials, but with an indicative intransitive pronoun it is replaced by seʔ, preceding the pronoun; neither particle combines with evidentials: /cu-t-é-xʷ ske ƛ̓əm 'you should have done it', ʔe /nés wn ske 'if I should go' (ʔe 'if', 7.6.2.), cu•cw-ə́m ske 'they ought to work'; /cw-ə́m seʔ kʷ 'you should work'.

7.1.2.

Deictic emphasis is furnished by demonstratives (6.4.2.), which follow any predicative particles (7.1.1.) and close simple predicates.

ʔes/xeƛ̓=ewíł nke ƛ̓ət xéʔe '(I) guess this truck's already unloaded',

ʔes/xeƛ̓=ewíł n̓ ƛ̓ət néʔe 'is it unloaded right there?',

/nés kʷ n̓ ƛ̓ət ƛ̓uʔ xéʔe 'are you ready to go, too?',

/q̓íy-m-e téʔe 'camp/stay overnight there!',

təxʷ•/tóxʷ-t-e ƛ̓uʔ wéʔe 'you'd better toe the mark!' said to someone who has a tendency to get into trouble (/tóxʷ-t 'straight').

Sequences of two demonstratives have been observed (see examples in 7.3.1.).

7.1.3.

Compound predicates contain, in addition to their major word (the predicate head), an auxiliary, which adds some modal or aspectual notion. A few words are limited to this function: |cúʔ| 'somewhat, in limited fashion', |wéƛ̓e| 'almost', |yəc̓úxʷ| 'just now, immediate past'. But the most common auxiliaries are major words adapted to this use with specialized meanings (in following glosses auxiliary meaning follows the semicolon): |xʷúy̓| 'go; future', |nés| 'go toward; incipient', |(w)ʔex| (often shortened) 'exist, be located, reside, stay; persistent, progressive, actual', |ƛ̓ʔek| 'continuative', |nə-wén̓| 'old; perfective'. They appear both before and after the predicate head, slightly more

emphatic when after; when first, they take the pronominal enclitics, and often other elements as well.

cúʔ kʷ n̓ ƛ̓ət /y̓e-wíʔx 'are you a little better now?', /c[ʔ]ék cùʔ 'it has gotten a little cooler';

wéƛ̓e kn n/zuqʷ=étkʷu ~ n/zuqʷ=étkʷu kn wéƛ̓e 'I nearly drowned' (|nə√zúqʷ-=etkəw| 'die in water');

yc̓óxʷ kn ƛ̓ət /séw-łn 'I just now inquired';

xʷúy̓ xeʔe /tékł-m-t-i-s 'we will get rained on',

xʷúy̓ kʷ n̓ /nés 'will you go?',

/mı̓łt-m-c-n xʷúy̓ 'I'm going to visit you';

nés kʷ n̓ /łáxi 'are you getting cold?';

(w)ʔéx kt /méw-e-me 'we are gossiping',

/t[ʔ]íkʷ ƛ̓uʔ uʔex 'it's still smoldering';

nwén̓ ƛ̓ət n-kʷəc•/kʷúce wéʔe 'they're already a good ways downriver there',

/cə́m-t ƛ̓əm̓ nwén̓ 'it's already burned';

ƛ̓ʔek /píx̣-m 'he kept on hunting'.

Combinations make for some delicate nuances of tense and aspect (for special word order in the following examples see 7.1.4.);

ƛ̓əm̓ xʷúy̓ kn /xʷást 'I was going to go home (but haven't gone yet)',

ƛ̓uʔ xʷúy̓ kn /xʷást 'I'm going to go home (about to be on my way)',

ƛ̓ət xʷúy̓ kn /xʷást 'I've made up my mind to go home'.

7.1.4.

Rearranged predicates have appearing before the predicate head nonenclitic particles that usually follow it (7.1.1.); they seem to differ primarily in emphasis or style:

ƛ̓əm̓ /pe[ʔ]xʷ-mín-t-m (ƛ̓əm̓) 'we got tired of it',

ƛ̓əm̓ /pe[ʔ]xʷ-mín-t-m ƛ̓ət ~ ƛ̓ət /pe[ʔ]xʷ-mín-t-m ƛ̓əm̓ 'suddenly we got tired of it.'

Rearrangement permits use of two particles of the same position class (and repetition of the same particle, as in the first example); it also increases flexibility with auxiliaries (7.1.3.).

7.2.

Complements, specifying third-person entities directly connected to predicates, are introduced by proclitic particles distinguishing relationships to their predicates

631

and to the general context. The heads of such complements are predicative words subordinated to their predicates by position and their introductory particles.

Certain entities associated with predicates are implicit. First- and second-person entities are marked in the predicate itself (section 4) and in context always refer to specific persons. However, third-person entities are often indicated only by absence of a first- or second-person marker; in any case their reference is not fully specified and may be unclear in the context. It is these third-person entities that are specified by complements, along with certain other logically related entities.

7.2.1.

Direct complements, introduced by |è|, specify the entities implicit in predicates. With intransitives and indefinite subjects these are subjects:

/q̇ʷc-ác e /tmíxʷ 'it's an earthquake' ['it.moves-uncontrolled direct earth'],

/níḱ-e-t-m e n/ʕʷyán-s 'he had an abdominal operation' ['it-is-cut direct his-belly'].

With a third-person possessed form, the possessor is specified: n/kʷuḱʷ-tán-s e /séytkn=mx 'it is the people's blessing' ['their-blessing direct people']. With transitives, complements specify primarily objects: /q̇áy-e-s e s/núḱʷeʔ-s 'he shot his friend' ['he-shoots-him direct his-friend']. But where first- or second-person objects are marked, complements specify subjects: n/kʷán-cém-s e /q̇ʷúʔ 'the water poisoned me' ['it-poisons-me direct water']. (See also 7.2.3.)

7.2.2.

Oblique complements, introduced by |te|, specify logically related entities that the predicate does not mark. This includes logical objects with simple intransitives (/pút kn xèʔe tə /tíy 'I've had enough tea' ['suffice I nearby oblique tea']) and with middles (/q̇ʷy/éw̓-m kt tə s-pəq•/páq 'we're picking Saskatoon berries' ['pick-harvest-food we oblique juicy-variety-Saskatoon-berries']). With various predicates they can refer to means, substances, and instruments:

/q̇ʷéc-ne tə s/łaʔx=áns 'I filled him up with food' ['I-fill-him oblique food'],

n/tγ-ús-m tə /q̇ʷúʔ 'they're sprinkling water over (the baked fish)' ['sprinkle-surface oblique water'],

/ƛ̓ə́ł-t kn tə /c̓iƛ̓ 'I got stuck up with pitch' ['sticky I oblique pitch'],

n/c̓éw̓=łc̓iʔ-t-m tə /ṣúp 'he's getting an enema' ['he-is-washed-inside oblique soap'],

n/q̇ʷec̓=ewíł tə s/cək-mín 'the (railroad) car is full of wood-chips' ['full-conveyance oblique wood-chips'].

They can specify the reference of incorporated lexical suffixes: /pu[•p]n̓=éwł tə s/c̓əqʔ=éwł 'he found a boat' ['he-finds-conveyance oblique boat'].

For indefinite-subject forms, agents with third-person patients are handled in this way: /q̇áy-e-t-m tə s/núḱʷeʔ-s 'he was shot by his friend' ['he-is-shot oblique his-friend']. However, with other indefinite-subject forms no agent can be specified (4.2.2.): /tékł-m-t-i-t 'we got rained on', /kən-céy-me 'someone helped me'.

7.2.3.

Complements with indirectives (5.2.4.) differentiate formally between interested entity (direct complement) and effective goal of the action (oblique): /n̓-t-éne he n/sínci 'I gave it to my brother', /n̓-t-éne tə /q̇ʷú 'I gave him some water'; /ne-t-éne tə s/kʷést 'I named him, gave him a name' ['I-name-him oblique name']; /q̇ʷúʔ-x-cm-e tə n-s/yíq̇-m 'water my garden for me!' ['water-for-me oblique my-garden']; /máʕ-x-cm-s tə n-s/zélt 'she broke my dish on me' ['she-breaks-for-me oblique my-dish'].

7.2.4.

Multiple complements are quite common, combining the various uses outlined above. Direct complements generally precede oblique, but either order is acceptable; clause-final position lends slight emphasis. /łaʔx=áns e n/cé[•ce]ʔ tə s/q̇ʷíy-t 'my younger sister ate some berries' ['she-eats direct my-younger-sister oblique fruit'], n/me[ʔ]n=ús-m tə s/q̇ʷúy•iʔ e s/kʷáḱʷes 'a cloud covered the sun' ['it-gets-eye-shaded oblique uncontrolled-clouding direct sun'].

Sentences with both subject and object specified as complements to a single transitive predicate are occasionally used. The order with the subject specifier first is preferable, although the object specifier can also come first; subject and object are thus recognized by context rather than by formal means: /né-x-c e /ƛ̓iʔ-s/qáyxʷ e s/kʷáze?-s tə s/kʷi(ʔ)-ʔúy (Spuzzum) 'the man gave his son a bow and arrow' ['he-gives-to-him direct person direct his-offspring oblique (bow-and-)arrow']; compare, with the same gloss, /néx-c e s/kʷáze?-s e /ƛ̓iʔ-s/qáyxʷ tə s/kʷi(ʔ)-ʔúy (Spuzzum). More commonly, the subject is understood in the context (either specified in a preceding sentence or simply clear in the situation) and the transitive sentence specifies only the object. Occasionally the transitive subject or object is specified in an adjunct (7.3.). In a few cases a transitive subject appears as an emphatic complement (7.2.6.).

7.2.5.

More complex uses of complements reveal various hierarchical relationships and serve to point up the fact that complements have underlying predicates as heads. In /pút e s/n̓-t-éne tə s/łaʔx=áns 'I gave him enough to eat' ['suffice direct what-I-give-him oblique food'], the intransitive predicate /pút has a direct complement specifying its subject ('what I give him') and an oblique complement ('as food, in the way of food'); s/n̓-t-éne is a nominalized transitive (6.5.). /ỷe-mín-ne tə s-n/iʔh=élus-c 'I like him because he's good-natured'

['I-good-relational-to-him oblique his-being-good-natured'] has an oblique complement specifying a reason; it has the underlying predicate *n/i?h-élus* 'he is good-natured'.

7.2.6.

Emphatic complements are transposed to the position directly before the predicate; the introductory particle is dropped. Such sentences are not common. Most often the transposed complement is a subject: *n/cə́[•ce]? /ła?x=áns tə s/q̓ʷíy-t* 'my younger sister ate some berries' ['my-younger-sister she-eats oblique fruit']' */λ̓i?-s/qáyxʷ /né-x-c e s/kʷə́ze?-s tə s/kʷi(?)-?úy* (Spuzzum) 'the man gave his son a bow and arrow' ['person he-gives-to-him direct his-offspring oblique (bow-and-) arrow'].

7.3.

Adjuncts are other predicate modifiers. They either refer to implied predicate references in more special (largely unpredictable) ways or introduce details beyond those suggested by the predicate forms.

7.3.1.

Simple adjuncts specify referents related to the predicate and indicate their temporal or aspectual relation to it. They are introduced by proclitic specializing particles. Generally the grammatical relationships involved are recognized contextually.

|łə| 'established in past' (entities or situations no longer in evidence or absent from immediate situation): */pi?-p-s-t-éne ł n/q̓wís=qn* 'I lost my axe (and haven't found it)' ['I-lose-it established-past my-axe'] (cf. */pi?-p-s-t-éne he n/q̓wís-qn* 'I lost my axe (but later found it again)', with direct complement); */?e s/yém-e-t-m ekʷu ł qəł/qəłmín* 'the old people (in the story) welcomed him, they say' ['introductory he-is-welcomed reportive established-past they-are-old'].

|kə| 'unrealized' (to be established in future; unknown, unreal, or contrary to fact; sometimes indefinite): */k̓[•i?k̓e?]t k s-n/ˤʷłóqʷ-s* 'it's close to boiling' ['near unrealized its-boiling'] (cf. */k̓[•i[•k̓i]?k̓e?]t e s/xʷesít-kt* 'let's just have a little walk' ['near-diminutive direct our-walking']; */?ə́sxe-s-cm-s k s/té? us nke* 'something or other made me sneeze' ['it-makes-me-sneeze unrealized what? conjunctive conjectural'] (adjunct is itself a conjunctive predicate, 7.6.1.); *tə•/té? k ?es/té?-s* 'they didn't have anything' ['there-is-not unrealized their-having-what?']; */cúkʷ us k e?-s/?íλ̓-m* 'don't sing!' ['finish conjunctive unrealized your-singing'].

|tək| 'descriptive' introduces adjuncts particularizing the entities being described or identified by their predicates: */yé kʷ tək /λ̓i?-s/qáyxʷ* (Spuzzum) 'you are a good person' ['good you descriptive person'], */λ̓íxʷeł xe? té? tək /čyé* 'it's a different basket' ['different nearby particular descriptive basket'], *qəł•/qəłmí···n ekʷu né?e tək sə•/séye /w?éx* 'there were two very old

people there, they say' ['they-are(-very)-old reportive established-in-context descriptive two-people be'].

|peł| 'inherent' introduces adjuncts particularizing entities related to their predicates in terms of origin, purpose, or proper function: *č/e xé? ł n-s/kíx-ze? pəł s/k̓ʷúxʷ* 'this basket was made by my mother' ['it-is (-emphatic) nearby established-past my-mother inherent product-of-basket-weaving'], */séme? xè? pəł pəl•/pí[•p]ləx-m* 'this is White people's news' ['White-person nearby inherent giving-news (-diminutive-augmentative)'].

|əł| 'collective' identifies with special emphasis a group of entities or unit expected to be together; it is very rare: */kʷén-t-m ekʷu xe?e ł əł /kíx-s* 'her older sisters took hold of her' ['they-grasp-her reportive nearby established-past collective her-older-sister']; *λ̓əł n/łé···m̓-ix ekʷu xe?e ł s/cm-é[•m̓]i?t ł əł /q̓ʷí[•q̓ʷ]λ̓•q̓ʷəλ̓-t* 'right away the children came in, those Smiling Ones (mythical four bear brothers who were transformers)' ['contemporaneous they-enter reportive nearby established-past children established-past collective smile-diminutive-characteristic-immediate'].

Occasionally a specializing particle combines with a complement particle. |kə| follows |è| or |te|: */xʷ?-ít tè?e he k n-s-zi?•/zá[•z]i?-tn̓* 'I do lots of little things here and there' ['many particular direct unrealized my-little-activities(-diminutive-augmentative)']; *n/łém̓=siṗ-e-cm-e tə k /súyp-m* 'bring me in some wood!' ['put-in-wood-for-me! oblique unrealized firewood'], */ła?x=áns kn ekʷu tə k s/q̓ʷíy-t* 'they tell me I ate some kind of berries [I don't remember]' ['eat I reportive oblique unrealized fruit']. (|tək| 'descriptive' probably developed from this latter combination, but is now used in circumstances where the functions of |te| and |kə| do not fit.) |łə| also follows |te| (rarely), but precedes |è|: */?uqʷe?-nwé-x-cm-s t ł n/tíy* 'she drank my tea' ['she-drinks-it-on-me(-out-of-control) oblique established-past my-tea']; *s/wét k /?úpi-t-m us e s/q̓ʷíy-t* 'who ate those berries?' ['who unrealized it-is-eaten-up conjunctive established-past direct fruit'] (first subordinated predicate is conjunctive, 7.6.1.).

|xə| 'particularizing' is relatively uncommon for some speakers, and it is elusive in meaning and function. It lends to predications an obscure kind of emphasis: *č/e xé?e he /qʷəz-t-és e x /q̓á[•q̓]ẏ-m̓* 'this [bow and arrow] is what's used for hunting' ['it-is(-emphatic) nearby direct they-use-it direct particularizing they-hunt(-diminutive)']. It can follow either |kə| or |łə|: *tə•/tè? kə x s/wík-t-m* 'we never saw him' ['there-is-not unrealized co-referential we-see-him'] (negative predicate reinforced to 'never'), */təq-t-és nke xe? te? kə x /zúm-t* 'a menstruating woman must have touched it' ['she-touches-it conjectural nearby particular unrealized particularizing she-menstruates'] (an unfortunate violation of taboo), *č/e xé?e ł əx e?-n/k̓əł/qláq̓* 'that's

the fellow you used to quarrel with' ['it-is(-emphatic) nearby established-past particularizing your-co-quarreler'].

Simple adjuncts with |ɫə| also cover temporal and instrumental notions: /wík-t-m e s/péʔec ɫ s-n/wén•wn 'we saw a bear this morning' ['we-see-it direct black-bear established-past morning'], /poˤʷ-t-és ekʷu n ɫ e s/ʔúɫxʷ ɫ /túɫkist-s 'he pounded on the inside with his stone hammer' ['he-pounds-it reportive at established-past direct the-inside established-past his-stone-hammer'] (for prepositional phrase see 7.3.2.).

7.3.2.
Prepositional phrases are adjuncts introduced by prepositions, proclitics followed by either |è| 'direct' (7.2.1.) or a specializing particle (7.3.1.) or both. They cover primarily locational and directional notions. The most important prepositions are |nə| 'at, to, in(to), on(to), with' (precise location or direction), |wə| 'to, toward' (direction or general location), |təw| 'from' (vantage point), and |təẃ| 'from' (origin), the last two apparently etymologically related. They also often appear with simply a demonstrative (6.4.2.).

/xzúm n ɫ e s/ʔúɫxʷ, /ḱʷm•íʔme? tu ɫ e /ʔéyċqe? he n/ḱʷén̓-tn-s '(the house) is big inside, (but) looks small from outside' ['big at established-past direct inside, small from established-past direct outside direct its-way-of-looking'].

/ʔe /míʔ-t kʷ tuʔ xéʔe 'you'll get infected from that fellow' ['future get-infected you origin nearby'].

/wʔéx kʷ u cíʔe w ɫ /cətxʷ-=ut-=úymxʷ 'you've been over there in Okanagan country' ['stay you toward yonder toward established-past Okanagan-land'];

/wʔéx kn n ʔéye 'I'm here' ['stay I at here'].

/kəɫ-t-é-t-e tuʔ k /ċy̓é 'take it out of some basket or other!' ['detach-it! origin unrealized basket'].

7.3.3. ADVERBS
In addition to full predicative words and phrases used as adjuncts, there are a few single words that appear only in this capacity. Two common adverbs are xʷúy̓ceʔ 'again' and cə-s-ʔéy-ɫ 'now': tə•/té? k s/púλ•əλ-m-s tuʔ xeʔe xʷúy̓ce? 'once again he couldn't get out of it' ['there-is-not unrealized his-managing-to-go-out origin nearby again']; /néxʷ-m tək /ċlóxʷ tək /síλɋt cə-s-ʔéy-ɫ 'it's a really hot day today' ['exceed descriptive hot descriptive day now'].

7.3.4.
Order of adjuncts and complements is flexible, allowing for placing an element in mildly emphatic final position (see also 7.2.4., 7.2.6.): /xʷ?-í[•?]t tək s/míyc e s/ɋá[•ɋ]iʔ-s '(they) got a good many deer (when they went) hunting' ['many(-diminutive) descriptive deer-as-game direct their-product-of-shooting']; cf. (with same gloss) /xʷ?-í[•?]t e s/ɋá[•ɋ]iʔ-s tək s/míyc.

7.4.
Attributive phrases have a head with a preceding modifier. They are used in place of single words acting as heads of predicates, adjuncts, or complements.

Descriptive phrases of this type are derived without formal change from predications with adjuncts introduced by |tək| 'descriptive' or |pəɫ| 'inherent' (7.3.1.): /y̓e tək /λuʔ-s/qáyxʷ 'a good person' (based on the predication meaning 'good is the person'), s/ċóɋ̓ tək s/ċaqʔ=éwɫ 'a paper boat' (based on the predication meaning '(of) paper is the boat'), /cu-t-és e /λə́x-t tək /mə́ċe 'honey bee' ['it-makes-it direct sweet descriptive stinging-hymenopter'] (based on the predication meaning 'the bee that makes honey' or, more literally, 'it makes sweet that bee'); s/λúleʔ pəɫ /λémn 'deer hair' (based on the predication meaning 'from the deer is the hair'), s/qáyxʷ pəɫ /qemút 'man's hat' (based on the predicate meaning 'for a man is the hat'), s/ċaqʔ=èwɫ-ʔúy pəɫ s/ċaqʔ=ékst 'canoe paddle' (based on the predicate meaning 'for the aboriginal canoe is the paddle').

The construction with |tək| is very common, and in many cases an underlying predication is unlikely: /néxʷm tək /y̓é 'it's very good' ['exceed descriptive good'], /péyeʔ tək /síλ-ɋt 'one day' ['one descriptive day'].

A simpler (and far less common) type is not marked in any overt way: s/kʷə́zeʔ-s s/múlec 'his daughter' ['his-offspring woman'].

7.5. LIMITED PREDICATIVES
There are a number of common words that appear in predicate head position but form predications primarily with other words.

7.5.1.
Introductory predicatives create predicates with demonstratives (6.4.2.), various adjuncts (7.3.), and nominals (6.5.): |√ʔé| 'there is, it is (that)..., that is...' has an emphatic counterpart ċ/é (derived with this special result with |c-| 'emphatic').

/ʔe λuʔ xeʔ•xéʔe k s/qʷc-íyxs 'they'll soon be gone' ['there-is persistent nearby(-augmentative) unrealized their-moving'];

ċ/e n̓ xéʔe k e?-n/tíy-tn 'is that your teapot?' ['it-is(-emphatic) interrogative nearby unrealized your-way-for-tea'];

/ʔé tuʔ xéʔe s/púλ-m-s 'it was out of there (where he just was) that he went' ['it-is origin nearby his-going-out'];

/ʔe s/uʔéx-s 'that's where he was'.

7.5.2.
Interrogative-indefinites appear as predicates in questions. For example, |keʔ(è)| 'which?, is it (that...?)', with its emphatic counterpart |c-keʔ(è)| (6.4.2.), |s√té?| 'what?', |s√wét| 'who?', and |√ʔkén-ə̆me| 'what's the matter?; why?'

ké⁷e k e⁷-s/xʷúy̓ /nés? 'will you go?' ['is-it-that? unrealized your-going depart'].

c-ké⁷e k s/xʷúy̓-ep /qʷc-íyx 'are you people about to leave?' ['is-it-that(-emphatic)? unrealized you-people's-going move'].

s/te⁷ k e⁷-s/cúw 'what are you doing?' ['what? unrealized your-doing'].

s/wét us nke xè⁷e pəł /c̓ỳè '(I) wonder whose basket this can be' ['who? conjunctive conjectural nearby inherent basket'].

/kén-m kn 'what did I do wrong?'.

/kén-m kʷ ƛ̓u⁷ /cu⁷-t-éxʷ 'why did you hit him?' ['why? you persistent you-punch-him'].

s/té⁷ compounds with a restricted element */pi⁷-* 'time when' to give */pi⁷-s/té⁷* 'when?': */pi⁷-s/té⁷ e xʷúy̓ up /c⁷és* 'when will you people come?' ['when? direct go you-people-conjunctive come'].

The indefinite meaning of these words emerges in combination with negatives (7.5.3.) and a few other words (e.g., */ték-m* 'all' in 7.5.4.).

7.5.3.
Negatives are |√te⁷| 'there is not' (forceful), its affective (6.2.3.) derivative |te•√té⁷| (more common), and |√tem| 'lack'.

The first two are usually followed by a nominalized adjunct introduced by |kə| 'unrealized' (7.3.1.); transitives remain unchanged, but intransitives are converted to possessive inflection (4.3.): *tə•/tè⁷ k s/cu-t-éne* 'I didn't do it' (*/cu-t-éne* 'I did it'), *tə•/tè⁷ k n-s/łáxi* 'I'm not cold' ['there-is-not unrealized my-being-cold'] (*/łáxi kn* 'I'm cold'), *tə•/té⁷ k n-s-⁷es/x̣áy̓wi* 'I (woman) am not married' (*⁷es/x̣áy̓wi kn*, lit. 'I have a husband'). There is also a less common construction converting intransitives to conjunctive (3.2.) in an adjunct introduced by |tək|: *tə•/té⁷ tək /x̣íy-m wn* 'I can't do anything about it' (*/x̣íy-m kn* 'I'm acting (in a particular way) for a reason/purpose'). Longer negative sentences typically show the same sort of continuing strings of adjuncts; transitives serving as adjuncts are sometimes possessed: *tə•/tè⁷ xe⁷e k e⁷-s/wík-t-xʷ tək /séytkn=mx ⁷es/cítxʷ wé⁷e* 'you can't see the people that own those houses there' ['there-is-not nearby unrealized your-what-you-see descriptive people direct they-have-house(s) particular-context']. These negatives appear with a suffix *-e* as single-word negative replies: */té⁷e* or *tə•/té⁷e* 'no!'

|√tem| is less common; it also can take possessed adjuncts introduced by |kə|: */tèm ekʷu té⁷ k e s/té⁷-s e /séytkn=mx* 'they say the people didn't have anything' ['lack reportive particular unrealized their-having-what? direct people'] (note semantic effect on *s/té⁷* 'what?'). In the conjunctive it yields a negative imperative (prohibitive): */tém us tè⁷e k e⁷-s-⁷es/kəł=xə́n* 'don't go barefoot!' ['lack conjunctive particular unrealized your-being-detached(-of)-foot']. A common

formula involves |√tem| nominalized in construction with |s√té⁷| 'what?': *s/tém e s/tè⁷ k s-k̓u•/k̓w-ét-ne* 'I won't step on it' ['lack direct what? unrealized what-I-step-on']. It also has causative inflection (5.2.3.) (*/təm-s-t-és* 'he doesn't believe it') and forms derivatives with certain lexical suffixes: */təm=éłus* 'there's a shortage of fish', */təm=éłci* 'there's no game (no carcasses at all)', */təm=éłzi⁷x* 'there are no berry bushes', */təm=éłq* 'there are no berries (on the bushes)', *n/təm=ə́ltn* 'there are no berries in the basket', */təm=úym̓xʷ* 'it's a lonely place'.

The root |√cúkʷ| 'finish' with the conjunctive provides negative imperatives. What is prohibited appears as an adjunct treated like those after *(tə•)/té⁷* and */tém*: */cúkʷ us k s/k̓ít-ix-m-cm-xʷ* 'don't come near me!' ['finish conjunctive unrealized you-approach-me'], */cúkʷ us k e⁷-s-yu⁷•/yu⁷s=xə́n* 'don't trip!' ['...your-trip-foot'].

7.5.4.
Intensifiers are very common but do not form independent predicates by themselves.

/néxʷ-m 'exceed' takes an adjunct introduced by |tək| (7.3.1.): */néxʷ-m tək /c̓əq̓-t-mìn-t-wáxʷ* 'they hit each other hard head on' ['exceed descriptive strike-against-each-other']. Such phrases then often serve as predicates for longer clauses: */néxʷ-m tək /c̓łóxʷ tək /síƛ̓-q̓t cə-s-⁷éy-ł* 'it's a very hot day today' ['exceed descriptive hot descriptive day now']. The simple stem */néxʷ* 'excessive' is less frequent; it takes a direct complement that is nominalized and possessed: */néxʷ e s/néx•əx-s* 'it's a big (dangerous) wave' ['excessive direct its-uncontrolled-billowing'].

/tékm 'all' participates in varied constructions: */tékm tək /máˤ=xe-tn* 'every month' ['all descriptive moon'], */tékm te⁷ e s/té⁷-s e qʷəc•/qʷc-íyx us tək s/kí⁷[•ki⁷]x pəł /cu-mín* 'everything runs by electricity' ['all particular direct its-what? direct they-move conjunctive descriptive thunder inherent means-of-doing'] (note semantic effect with *s/té⁷* 'what?'), */nés ƛ̓əm̓ /tékm ut* 'we all went' ['depart completed all we-conjunctive'].

7.5.5.
Numbers (system in 8.) also belong in this category; */təm-ł/pé[•p]ye⁷ tək /séytkn=mx n ⁷éy-e* 'there are nine people here' ['nine-persons descriptive people at here'], */qʷin-cút kn u⁷èx /pé[•p]ye⁷ wn* 'I'm talking to myself' ['talk I actual one-person I-conjunctive'].

7.6. CLAUSE PATTERNS
Each predicate with its satellite complements and adjuncts constitutes a clause. Since the major words that serve as heads of complements and adjuncts are themselves fundamentally predicative, these satellite elements actually contain subordinated predicates. However, it is useful to distinguish these simpler structures from more complex ones in which longer sequences are subordinated.

635

7.6.1. SUBORDINATING PATTERNS

Complements and adjuncts are subordinated to their predicates. Sometimes the subordination is marked only by the introductory particle: /s/pé²ec e /wík-ne 'it was a bear I saw' ['black-bear direct I-see-it']. More often the first predicative element of a complement or adjunct is nominalized: /ỳé te s/ník̓-e-s 'it's a good thing that he cut (the undergrowth back)' ['good oblique what-he-cuts']. /wík-ne ł s-n/wén•wn 'I saw him this morning' ['I-see-him established-past morning']. Some longer complements and adjuncts are themselves clauses of this sort: /pút e s/n̓-t-éne tə s/ła²x̣=áns 'I gave him enough to eat' ['suffice direct what-I-give-him oblique food'] (subordinated clause is /n̓-t-éne tə s/ła²x̣=áns 'I gave him food' with the head word nominalized; s/ła²x̣=áns is nominalized from /ła²x̣=áns 'eat'). (Note also examples in 7.5.2.)

Possessed (4.3.) satellites are also common: ²es-t/k̓ʷə́s-e he n-s/λ̓²ék 'just before dark I managed to get home' ['suddenly-getting-dark direct my-arriving'], n/xa[²]k̓ʷúym̓xʷ e n-s/k̓ʷén̓=łq 'my garden is getting dry' ['becomes-dry-earth direct my-watching-things-to-harvest'].

Other complements and adjuncts are marked by the conjunctive, which implies a closer relationship to the predicate: /séw-e-cm-s e wn /²ínu-t 'he asked me what I said' ['he-asks-me direct I-conjunctive say-what?'], n/k̓s=én̓k k̓ʷ ł /wík-c-n us 'when I saw you, you were cranky' ['angry you established-past I-see-you conjunctive'].

On the other hand, nominalized and possessed elements are not limited to satellite phrases: s/né-x-t-m tu² e s/k̓ʷú[•k̓ʷ]pi²-s 'it was given to him by his chief ['product-of-being-handed-to-him origin direct his-chief'], n-s/pú[•p]n̓ xe²e tək s/ċəq²=éwł 'I found that boat' ['my-finding(-diminutive) nearby descriptive boat'].

7.6.2.

Clause particles introduce many clauses. Some of these require a particular type of structure.

|weλ̓| 'that's why': téye, /xʷm-ə́p k̓ʷ nke wə́λ̓ u²ex k̓ʷ te²e /x̣íy-m 'say, you must be lonely, that's why you're acting that way' ['say!, get-lonely you conjectural that's-why actual you particular act-for-a-reason'].

|²e| 'advance notice, future; if, perhaps': ²e /wík-cn tək s/pi²h=éwt 'I'll see you tomorrow' ['future I-see-you descriptive one-day-removed'], ²e /tékł λ̓u² /²e k s/tém e s/té² k n-s/nés 'if it rains, I won't go at all' ['future rain so it-is unrealized lacking direct what? unrealized my-going'], ²e /x̣ʷóx̣ʷ-t-m̓-n-xʷ us λ̓u² /²e k s/pílex-cm-xʷ 'if you like it, tell me' ['future you-like-it conjunctive so it-is unrealized what-you-tell-me'].

|²ey-ł| (|²ił| Spuzzum) 'before; (and) then' requires the conjunctive wherever it appears. ²ił /k̓ʷen=ks-e-t-íyxs us, ²ił /k̓ʷíq̓-t us ł qəł•/qəł-mìn 'they shook hands

with him, and (then) they wept, those old people' ['then they-grasp-him-by-the-hand conjunctive, then they-weep conjunctive established-past they-are-old']. ²ił /cun-t-íyxs us /húm̓eł cə-s-²éy-ł 'and then they said to him "Goodbye, now"' ['then they-say-to-him conjunctive goodbye now'].

|λ̓u²| 'until; so (that)' is probably |λ̓u²| 'persistent' (7.1.1.) extended to clause particle function; transitional usage is seen in clauses like /ˢəlxʷ-e-t-és λ̓u² /cq-ə́p '(the trains) disturbed us with their noise all night' ['make-noise-on-us until daybreak']. It introduces a result or later circumstance, and it may be followed directly by a predicate: λ̓u² /kíc-x u ł e /má²=xe-tn 'until he reached the moon' ['until arrive-at destination toward established-past direct moon']. It is extremely common with predicates constructed with ²é 'it is' (7.5.1.) (combination pronounced λ̓u²e, 2.7., rule [25], but here written λ̓u² /²e for clarity) and a nominalized, often possessed, element. qʷi²•/qʷúy̓ λ̓u² /²e n-s/tém e s/te² k s/wík-ne he n-s-q̓a•/q̓níxʷeċk̓ '(when) it's cloudy, then I don't see my shadow at all' ['cloudy so it-is my-lacking direct what? unrealized what-I-see direct my-shadow']. /púλ̓-m tu² xé²e λ̓u² /²e s/wík-c e /k̓ʷm•í[•m]i²m̓e² tə s/²ístk-n λ̓u² /²e s/kíc-e-s 'when he got out of there, he saw a tiny little winter-house and went over to it' ['he-goes-out origin nearby so it-is what-he-sees direct small(-diminutive) oblique winter-house so it-is what-he-visits'].

Such clauses often begin sentences; the meaning is 'so then, next, and so, and then...': λ̓u² /²e tu² xè²e he s/púλ̓-m λ̓u² /²e s/kíc-e-s ł /péye² ł /cítxʷ 'so then he went out of there and went to another house' ['so it-is origin nearby direct going-out so it-is what-he-visits established-past one(-other) established-past house'].

7.7. COORDINATION

The particle ²eł 'and, but' (presumably the same as the predicative particle, 7.1.1.) operates at both phrase and clause level joining similar elements: /séye ²eł /séye, /²e s/mús-c 'two and two are four' ['two and two, it-is its-being-four'], si²•/séy̓•si² ²eł ²e•²e•/²úy-m̓ 'they're playing and laughing', ²es-q̓ə́λ•/q̓íλ=se² e s/²íxʷł ²eł /i²h=úse² e s/²íxʷł 'some berries are scarred but some are very good' ['there-are-scarred-berries direct some and good-berries direct some'].

The opposition of subordination and coordination is less sharply drawn in Thompson than, for example, in English. Actually, independent clauses of the types recognized in 7.6. could be considered coordinate with other clauses when they are juxtaposed in the same sentence, although in many cases English translations suggest a dependent status.

7.8.

Sentences are sequences bounded by terminal intonations (2.3.) or silence. The major sentence contains a clause or a series of clauses. Most examples given in the discussion on syntax above (7. et seq.) are major sentences, but intonation punctuation has been omitted for simpler serial presentation. Minor sentences are of two types—fragments and expletives (7.9.). Fragments are simply portions of clauses left incomplete because the context is adequate for understanding: *n ł e /ƙ*ʷ*áx*ʷ*e* 'in the box' (e.g., in answer to a query about the location of an object), *ł n-s/kíx-ze*ʔ 'my mother' (e.g., affirming who made a particular basket).

Major sentences are extremely varied. Because of the many possibilities for combination of clause elements a rigorous classification of types remains to be accomplished.

7.9.
Expletives are words occurring independently as the whole of minor sentences; they also appear as parts of longer sentences but are not integrated into the structure. Among these are the affirmation ʔí 'yes' (Spuzzum), ʔéy (Lytton); exclamations like ʔu (anticipation), téy(e) (calling attention), x*ʷ*st, x*ʷ*st, x*ʷ*st (expression of affection, used by old people); and a rich system of sound-imitative expressions, like *cáł* (sound of hot toasted dried salmon dipped in cool liquid), *cəxcəxáx̣* (chuffing of steam locomotive), *sətáx̣, sətáx̣, sətáx̣* (noise made by stiff cloth of woman's skirt rubbing as she walks).

Vocatives also belong here. They are common at the beginning or end of longer sentences, and also on occasion are inserted between regular sentence elements, usually set off from the rest of the utterance by nonterminal intonation (2.3.). Various words inflected for first-person possessive (4.3.) are used as vocatives: *n/kẓ̇é* (addressing unrelated older woman) ['my-grandmother'], *n-s/páp-ze*ʔ (for unrelated older man) ['my-grandfather']; but these two are not used to address real grandparents, for which there are special vocative forms: /yéy 'grandma!', /pép (for grandfather or father). Many special vocatives are related to corresponding nonvocative words: /sín (for younger brother; regular /sínci*ʔ*), /cə́•c (for younger sister; /cə́[•ce]*ʔ*), /kík (for mother; /s/kíx-ze*ʔ*), /ƙ*ʷ*úy (for aunt; /s/ƙ*ʷ*óz). A number of nominals (6.5.) have vocatives without *s-*: /núƙ*ʷ*e*ʔ* 'friend!' (s/núƙ*ʷ*e*ʔ*), /m*ʔ*-ém 'wife!' (s/m*ʔ*-ém).

8. SELECTED VOCABULARY
Underlying forms are given in some confusing cases, regularly for lexical suffixes. Transitives are in 3sbj.-3obj.form. Words having inherent plural reference are marked (pl.). Occasionally literal glosses are supplied within quotation marks. For pronouns, see 4.; for demonstratives, see 6.4.2.

above, high   *(n)/wís-t*

afraid, fear   /páq*ʷ*u*ʔ*

afraid, fear   /páq*ʷ*u*ʔ*-s-c   (frighten)

alive, live   /wméx

all   /tékm

and   ʔeł

and then...   ʔił

animal, large bird   s/pzú*ʔ*

arm (lower), hand |=ekst| (6.3.1.), /kéyx

arm (upper), shoulder |=exən|, s/q̓*ʷ*m=áx̣n

arrow   s/k*ʷ*i(*ʔ*)-*ʔ*úy   (cf. bow and arrow)

ashes   n/súy̓p-tṅ

at, in, on   n (7.3.2.)

aunt, great-aunt   s/ƙ*ʷ*óz

autumn   /łwéy̓st

back |=ikəṅ|, n/ƙm=íkṅ   (lengthwise)

back   n/łéwt   (laterally)

bad   /ƙə́s-t

bad   /ƙə́s-t ~ /ƙə̣́s-t   (evil; ill-tempered)

bank, edge of river   s/ƙəm=cín

bark of tree   /ṗe*ʔ*yén   (rough, heavy)

bark of tree   s-x*ʷ*əz•/x*ʷ*ə́z   (fine, prickly)

bark, inner red cedar   /sísek̓*ʷ*

basket, looseweave |=ełəmx|, /cy̓é   (general)

basket, water-carrying   s/q̓wáqeł

basket, large berry   s/ṗéṅeq

basket, small picking   /nẁéṁ-tṅ

beach   s-q̓a•/q̓ape*ʔ*=cín   (sandy)

beach   /λ́éx*ʷ*-t   (gravel)

belly |=ene(*ʔ*)k|, n/ʕ*ʷ*yə́n   (inside)

belly   n/pt=éṅk-tn   (abdomen, entrails)

below   n/λ̓p-éṅk   (under)

below   ʔes/lə̣́s   (low, from above)

berry, fruit |=use*ʔ*|, s/q̓*ʷ*íy-t   (general)

berry   s/ketúx*ʷ*   (blackberry)

berry   /mə́cək*ʷ*   (blackcap)

berry   s/cáq*ʷ*-m   (serviceberry, saskatoon berry)

berry   s-pəq•/páq   (serviceberry: juicy variety)

berry   s/i*ʔ*h=úse*ʔ*   (serviceberry: dry variety)

berry   s/x*ʷ*ús-m   (soapberry)

berry   s/łə́k-ṁ   (thimbleberry)

big   /x̣zúm

bird   s/pzú[•ẓ̇u]*ʔ*   (small)

bird   See animal

bite   /qəl-t-és

black   ʔes/tə́p•təp-t

blanket   /síċm

blanket made of mountain goat hair   *s/ná?z*

bleed   */c[?]íˤʷ*

blood   */petə́le?*

blow   */sɣ-ə́m*   (of shaman)

blow   */néẃ-t*   (of wind)

blow   */púxʷ-m*   (with mouth)

bone, small   *s/c̓ém̓*

bone, large   *q̓ʷə•/q̓ʷú?ł*

bow and arrow   */ckʷ=iṅek-?úy*

breast, milk   *s/q?ém*   (cf. suck)

breath   */súp̓*

breathe   */súp̓-m*

brother   See sibling

brother-in-law   See in-law

burn   */ˤʷi(y-e)-t-és*   (set fire, burn up)

burn   */k̓ʷəs-t-és*   (singe)

burn   */cəm-t-és*   (burn black)

burn   */p̓áˤ-t*   (flesh burns)

canoe |=éwíł|, *s/c̓əq?=éwł*

cedar (tree)   */kʷát=łp*

child   *s/k̓ʷú[•k̓ʷ]m=i?t*   (youngster)

child (son, daughter)   *s/kʷə́ze?*

children   *s/cm=éyt*   (pl.)

claw (animal's)   *s/kiye?=qín̓=xn*

clothing |=eł̓qs|, |=ic̓e?| (wrapping)

clothing   */xʷe[?]p-ít*   (thing made of cloth)

cloud   *s/qʷúy̓•i?*

cold   */c̓ə́ł-t*   (weather)

cold   */ł̓áxi*   (feel cold)

come   */c?és*

come   */ƛ̓?ék*   (arrive)

cook   */q̓ʷy-ə́m*

cook   *n/cu=cin--n-cút*   (do the cooking)

cooking pit, earth oven   *n/q̓əs=tə́m-tn*

count   */xzén-m*   (cf. big)

cousin   See sibling

coyote   *s-n/k̓y̓ép*

cradle basket   *n/qʷłí=y(t)-tn*

cradle basket, with baby in it   */qʷł=it-=éyt*

cry, weep   *we•/wíyx*

cry, weep   */k̓ʷíq̓-t*   (pl.)

cut   */k̓əl-t-és, /ník̓-e-s*

cut   */k̓íl-e-s*   (pl.)

638   cut in pieces   */c̓íẃ-e-s*

cut   */k̓ətxʷ-e-t-és*   (sever)

dance   */q̓ʷi?-cút*

daughter   See child

daughter-in-law or nephew's wife   */sépn*

day |=esq̓t|, */síƛ̓=q̓t*

deer   *s/ƛúle?*

deer (as game; meat)   *s/míyc*

die   */zóqʷ* |√zúqʷ|

die   */xʷáy-t*   (pl.)

different   */ƛíxʷeł*

dig (a hole)   *(n)/cíq-m*

dig (cedar roots)   */k̓ʷáw-e-me*

dig (roots for food)   */km̓-ə́m*

dig up   */ƛ̓q-ə́m*

dirty   *k̓əƛ•/k̓éƛ-t*

dive   *n/k̓em-úy̓=qn-me*

dog   *s/qáxa?*; usually diminutive *s/qá[•q]xa?*

dog   */ł̓ə́c̓=ł̓qn*   (wool-bearing dog)

downstream   *n/kʷúce*   (direction; cf. */kʷúce* 'go down toward water; toward fire in house')

downstream   */wúq̓ʷəl*   (by water)

downstream   */wtémtk*   (location)

drink   */?úqʷe?, /?úqʷe?-s*   (transitive)

dry   */k̓éx-t*

dry   */?es/xə́m̓*   (dehydrated)

dry   */sə́m̓-t*   (dripped dry, drained)

dry   *n/sˤ-ə́p*   (evaporated)

dull (of blade edge)   *n-mək̓ʷ•/mak̓ʷ=ús*

dust   *s/py̓úkʷ*

ear |=eṅih|, */ƛén̓i*

earth, ground |=uyəm̓xʷ|, */tmíxʷ*

eat   */ła?x=áns, /?úpi-s, |√?úpəy:-t-es|*   (transitive)

egg (of bird)   *?e•/?=úse?*

elk   *s/txéc̓*

eye |=us| 'eye, face, fire, sun' (6.3.1.), *n/k̓ʷƛ=ús-tn*

face |=us|, *s/k̓ʷƛ̓=ús*

fall   */kʷís*

fall   */záƛ̓-t*   (pl.)

fall (from standing position)   */zík-t*

fall (into water)   *n/kʷéw-t*

fall (suddenly)   */sén-t*

far   *kə•/kéẃ*

fat   *s/q̓ʷúc*   (animal fat)

fat   *s/ƛúy̓=sk̓ʷy̓e*   (fish oil)

fat /qʷtéɬ (grease)

father s/qác-zeʔ

father-in-law or spouse's uncle s/hiʔhíʔ

feather s/ƛ̓í[•ƛ̓]uʔ

feather /ƛ̓émn 'feathers, fur'

few təˑ/tèʔ k s/xʷʔ-ít (not many)

fight /ƛ̓əqʷ-e-t-wáxʷ (beat one another)

fire (controlled) |=us|, s/pém(-s)

fire (uncontrolled) s/ʕʷy-ə́p

fish |=eɬəws|, s/wéw̓ɬ (other than salmon; cf. salmon)

float /kʷéw-t

float /p̓[ʔ]ékʷ (come to surface)

flow /zíy-t (running)

flow /lxʷ-ə́p (fast)

flow /k̓ʷə́ɬ (pouring)

flower, blossom s/p̓áq̓-m

fly(ing) n/xʷél-ix

fog s/p̓úƛ̓-t

food |=ciɬn| (cf. eat)

foot See leg

forest, woods /zs̩=éwt

freeze: frozen (n)/páʕʷ-t, /ʔúxʷ-t

freeze /c̓əɬ-núxʷ (freeze to death)

freeze /xʷák̓ʷ-t (hard frost)

full /q̓ʷéc̓-t

fur See feather, leaf

give /ń-t-és

give n/míʔ-e-s (pl.)

give /né-x-c |√né(h)-xi-t-es| (hand over)

give away /xʷíc̓-m-s |√xʷíc̓:-min-t-es|

go /xʷúy (set out)

go /nés (depart, go to a destination)

go /qʷc-íyx (move, start out)

go /xʷə́s-t (go home)

good /y̓é |√y̓əh|

grandchild /ʔímc

grandfather (occasionally great-uncle) s/páp-zeʔ

grandmother (occasionally great-aunt) /kʒ́é

grass, hay s/yíq̓-m

great-aunt See grandmother, aunt

great-uncle See grandfather, uncle

green, yellow /kʷ[ʔ]áɬ (grass green)

green, yellow ʔes-tə/kʷɬ-ít (pale green or yellow)

green, yellow ʔes/kʷl-óʔ (dark yellow-green)

guts s/c̓m=énk

hair s/k̓ép=qn (Spuzzum /qéw-tn)

hand See arm

head |=qin|, /q̓ʷúm=qn

hear /qeʔním-e-s

heart s/xʷák̓ʷ•ukʷ

heavy /xm=énk

here ʔéy-e

hit /cuʔ-t-és (with fist)

hit /c̓əq̓-t-és (with projectile)

hit /sək-t-és (with stick, etc.)

hit /qém̓-e-s (hit target)

hit /túp-e-s (collide with)

horn, antler s/qʷáy̓=exkn

hot /c̓lóx̣ʷ |√c̓əlúx̣ʷ|

house |=eɬxʷ|, /cítxʷ

house s/ʔístk-n (winter house)

how? c̓/kéń-m

hunt (for game) /píx̣-m̓

hunt /q̓á[•q̓]ẏ-m̓ (shooting)

husband s/x̣áy̓wi

ice n/páʕʷ

if ʔe (7.6.2.)

in (see 'at', 6.3.1.)

in (n)/ʔúɬxʷ (enter)

in-law after death of linking relative n/k̓əɬ-we•/wí yx ('co-mourner') (conversational) n/qʷíc̓-tn (technical)

 in-law: man's male in-law of same generation (brother-in-law, wife's male cousin, cousin's husband) s/c̓éxt

 in-law: woman's female in-law of same generation (sister-in-law, husband's female cousin, cousin's wife) s/kéw

 in-law: spouse's relatives wən•/wíneʔxʷ

 in-law: spouse's in-law n/k̓əɬ/x̣iʔtném ('co-visitor to spouse's family')

 in-law of opposite sex in same generation (man's sister-in-law, wife's female cousin, cousin's wife; woman's brother-in-law, husband's male cousin, cousin's husband) s/ʔ=éstm

in-law of sibling or child s/xʷnémt

kill /púys-c |√púys-t-es|

kill /ƛ̓íqʷ-e-s (pl.)

kinnikinnick /ʔéyk (berries)

kinnikinnick /ʔik=éɬp (plant)

639

knee |=eẃès=xə̆n|, s/ḱm=éẃes=xn

know /x̣ək-s-t-és, /yəx̣-m-s-t-és

lake /péłus=kʷu

laugh ʔe•/ʔúy-ṁ

leaf |=eytxʷ| 'foliage, fur, plumage', /pcə́kł

left n/c̓ək̓ʷʔ=ékst (left arm)

leg |=eyəws|, |(-ele)=xə̆n| (leg, foot), s/q̓ʷáx̣t (id.)

lie down /cút-ix

lie down to sleep /cíx̣ʷ-ix, n/míx̣ʷ-ix (id., pl.)

lie down; lying (position) /púyt, ʔes/cút, ʔes/cíx̣ʷ

lightweight xʷukʷʷ•/xʷákʷ

liver n/x̣c̓éc̓-mn

long /zéx-t

louse /qʷtíx̣aʔ

man, male s/qáyx̣ʷ

many, much /xʷʔ-ít

meat |=ełc̓iʔ| (carcass), s/míyc cf. deer

moon, month /máˤ=xe-tn

mother s/kíx-zeʔ

mother-in-law or spouse's aunt (female in-law of
   ascending generation) /łcéck

mountain s/q̓ʷə́m

mouth |=cin|, /cú=cn, s/plíw=cn

name s/kʷést, /kʷést-e-s (name someone)

name /ʔúm-e-s (give name to)

name /ne-t-és (pronounce name)

narrow /tx•íʔxeʔ-t, /wn•íʔneʔ-t

narrow /q̓mə́ƛ̓ (tapering)

narrow ʔes/x̣ə́k̓ (tall and thin)

narrow /ʔúc̓-t (small around)

near /k̓[•íʔk̓eʔ]t

near ʔes/łéʔ (close by)

neck n/qʷz=áps-tn

nephew s/qʷséʔ

new /cíy•ci

niece s/ƛ̓əmk=éyt

night (s)/ˤáp (dusk)

night /sítist (dark)

no (tə•)/téʔe (no)

not (tə•)/téʔ (there is not)

not /tém 'lack' (7.5.3.)

nose |=aqs|, s/ṗs-áqs

numbers (basic numerals)

640   1 /péyeʔ

2 /séye

3 /keʔłés

4 /mús

5 /cíy=kst

6 /ƛ̓áq̓-m=ekst

7 /cúł=keʔ

8 /piʔúps

9 /təm-ł/péyeʔ

10 /ʔúpn=ekst

11 /ʔúpn=ekst ʔeł /péyeʔ

12 /ʔùpn=ekst ʔeł /séye, etc. (see coordinate
      phrases, 7.7.)

20 /si-ł/ʔúpn=ekst

21 /si-ł/ʔúpn=ekst ʔeł /péyeʔ, etc.

30 /keʔł/ʔúpn=ekst

40 /mu-ł/ʔúpn=ekst

50 /ci=k-ł/ʔúpn=ekst

60 /ƛ̓aq̓m=ek-ł/ʔúpn=ekst

70 /cuł=keʔ-ł/ʔúpn=ekst

80 /piʔup-ł/ʔúpn=ekst

90 /təm-ł/peyeʔ-ł/ʔúpn=ekst   (see compounds,
     6.1.1.)

100 /x̣əc-p=qí[•q]ṅ=kst

how many? /k̓ʷínex

numbers (persons)

1 /pé[•p]yeʔ

2 sə•/séye

3 kə•/keʔłés

4 /mús•məs

5 /cíy•ci=kst

6 /ƛ̓áq̓•ƛ̓əq̓-m=ekst

7 /cúł•cuł=keʔ

8 /piʔú[•ʔ]ps

9 /təm-ł/pé[•p]yeʔ

10 /ʔúp[•əp]n=ekst

how many (people)? /k̓ʷín[•k̓ʷn]ex

numbers (animals)

1 /pi•ʔéyeʔ

2 /sé[•s]ẏe

3 /keʔ[•k]łé[•ł]s

4. /mú[•ṁ]s

5 /cə́[•c]iʔ=kst

6 /ƛ̓á[•ƛ̓]q̓-ṁ=kst

7 /cú[•c]ł=keʔ

8 /piʔú[•ʔ]ps

9 /təm-ł/pi•ʔéyeʔ

10 /ʔú[•ʔ]pṅ=kst

how many (animals)? /k̓ʷí[•k̓ʷ]ṅex

numbers (counting)   Many other classes of things are counted with special derivatives through 10: e.g., berries, round objects, dollars: /piʔ=úseʔ, /siy=úseʔ, /keʔł=úseʔ, /mus-=úseʔ, /ci=ks=úseʔ, /ƛ̓aq̓-m=eks-=úseʔ, /cuł=keʔ-=úseʔ, /piʔups=úseʔ, /təm-ł/pi-=úseʔ, /ʔupn=eks-=úseʔ, /k̓ʷənex=úseʔ; blankets: /piʔ=íčeʔ, /siy=íčeʔ, etc.; outer garments: n/piʔ=éłqs, n/siy=éłqs, etc. (note n- prefix); fruit bushes and trees: /piʔ=éłziʔx, etc.; roots: /piʔ=úpeʔ, etc.; berries or roots by basketful: /piʔ=éłčzeʔ, etc.; fish caught: /piʔ=éłus, etc.; days: piʔ=ésq̓t, etc.

ocean, sea   /qʷuʔ-ṁíx   (also lower Fraser River; cf. water)

old   /qəłmín   (aged person)

old   n/wéṅ   (old thing, perhaps still in good condition)

path   See road

person, human being, Indian |=eyt|, /ƛ̓uʔ-s/qáyxʷ (Spuzzum /ƛ̓iʔ-s/qáyxʷ) (cf. man)

person, human, Indian |=eməx|, /séytkn=mx (pl.: 'people')

play   /séy̓•siʔ

prairie   s/péy-m

pull   /cəkʷ-t-és

pull   /cíkʷ-e-s   (pl.)

pull   /yaʕ-t-és   (drag)

pull out   /čáq-e-s

push   (n)/k̓ʷúp-e-s

push   /čək̓ʷ-t-és   (propel)

rain   s/tékł

rain   /tékł 'it rains'

red   ʔes/cíqʷ

right   n/iʔh=ékst   (right arm) (cf. good)

river   /qʷúʔ 'water'

road, trail, path |=xəwəy|, |=eẃs| (middle of), /xẃéł

roast or barbecue fish beside fire   /ƛ̓áq=seʔ-me

rock, stone |=ey̓st|, s/xéṅx

root |=upeʔ| 'root; tail', /k̓ʷmiʔxʷ=ép

root   /k̓ʷəṁy̓éxʷ   (cedar root, for basket making)

root   s/k̓éṁec   (dog-tooth [snow] lily root, for food)

rope |=eyek̓|, /x̣ʷíʔlm

rotten (spoiled)   /n[ʔ]áq̓

rotten (of wood)   /k̓ʷóqʷṅ

round   ʔes/q̓móx̣ʷ   (spherical)

round   ʔes/q̓yáq̓   (circular)

rub   /zəƛ̓-t-és

rub   /x̣ət-t-és   (against rough surface, grind)

rub between hands   /zéc-e-s

run   /tʕʷ-íyx

salmon   s/qy=éytn

salmon   /k̓ʷy̓íʔe   (Chinook, spring, king)

salmon   /k̓ʷúlu̓ʔxʷ   (chum, dog)

salmon   s/x̣áy=qs   (coho, silver)

salmon   /héniʔ   (pink, humpback)

salmon   s/x̣ʷáʔes   (sockeye, red, blueback)

salt   /čál-t

sand   s-q̓a•/q̓ápeʔ

say   /cú-t

say   /cún-s   (instruct)

say   /píləx-e-s   (inform)

say   /qʷin-cút   (talk)

say   /qʷin-t-és   (talk to)

say what?   /ʔínw-n-s

scratch   /ʔíx-e-s

scratch   /céṅ-e-s   (breaking skin)

scratch   /qəs-t-és   (to relieve itching)

scratch   /čyóʕʷ-e-s ~ /čiʕʷ-e-t-és   (claw)

see   /wík-c |√wík:-t-es|

see   /k̓ʷén-e-s   (look at)

seed   s/k̓əx=qín-tn

sew   /ƛ̓q̓ʷuʔ-t-és

sharp   n-x̣ʷəz•/x̣ʷz=ús   (of blade edge)

sharp   ʔes-čəm•/čm=áqs   (of point)

shoot   /q̓áy̓-e-s   (cf. hunt)

shoot   /łá[•ł]neč   (target shooting)

short   /łq̓•íʔq̓eʔ-t

sibling: elder brother or male cousin   /qéck

sibling: elder sister or female cousin   /kíx

sibling: younger brother or male cousin   /sínciʔ

sibling: younger sister or female cousin   /cá[•ce]ʔ (reference of sibling terms varies when applied to cousins: in Spuzzum a cousin is reckoned as older if his parent is older than ego's parent through whom they are related, regardless of actual chronological age; from Boston Bar upriver only chronological age relative to ego is pertinent. In all dialects s/q̓ʷó[•q̓ʷ]-zeʔ refers only to persons younger than ego.)

641

sibling: younger sibling   *s/q̓ʷó[•q̓ʷ]/-ze?*

sing   */?íƛ-m*

sister   See sibling

sister-in-law   See in-law

sit   */míce?q*

sit   */łáq-ix*   (pl.)

skin, pelt, hide   */sipéc̓*

skin, pelt, hide   *s/xil=éc̓*   (tanned buckskin)

sky   *s/ƛ̓íqt*

sleep   */ʕʷóy̓t*

small   */k̓ʷm•í?me?*

smell   */súm̓-e-s*

smell   */xʷ?úxʷ*   (give off odor)

smoke (of fire)   *s/x̣[?]éc*

smooth   *?es-t/k̓ʷóz•k̓ʷəz-t*   (polished)

smooth   *?es-t/k̓ʷóm•k̓ʷəm-t*   (flat, level)

smooth   */c̓x̣ʷ-ə́p*   (eroded by water)

smooth   *k̓ʷu•/k̓ʷíw*   (slippery)

snake   *s/méyx*

snow   *s/wúxʷt*

snow   */wúxʷt*   'it snows'

some (certain ones)   *s/?íxʷł*

son   See child

son-in-law or niece's husband   *s/cutéł*

spear   */łu?=mín*

spear   */mníp*   (fishing)

spit (expectorate)   */ptíx̣ʷ-m*

spit on   */ptíx̣ʷ-e-s*

spit out   */ptíx̣ʷ-m-s |√ptíx̣ʷ:-min-t-es| or /łáx̣ʷ-m-s |√łáx̣ʷ:-min-t-es|*

split   */sə̣q-t-és*

split   */sə̣q̓-t-és*   (crack)

spring (of water)   */ptúkʷ*

springtime   */təm̓łík, n/xʷúy̓t*

squeeze   */y̓ép-e-s*

squeeze   */c̓ip-e-t-és*   (pinch)

squeeze   */píc̓-e-s*   (press)

squeeze   */pi?-t-és*   (wring)

stab, pierce   */łu?-t-és*

stab, pierce   */x̣ə́p-t-és*   (pin, prick, sting)

stand(ing)   *?es/téł-ix*   (of person)

stand(ing)   *?es/c̓y-ə́p*   (of object)

stand(ing)   *?es/ɣép*   (sticking straight up out of ground)

star   *n-kʷə•/kʷúsn̓*

step on   */k̓w-é-t-e-s*

stick (of wood)   *|=eyèqʷ|*   (tree, wood, table, line), *s/x̣íc*

stick   */qálex̣*   (digging stick)

suck   */c̓úm̓-e-s*

suck   */q?ém*   (baby nurses)

summer   *s-n/q̓ʷy=énk*

sun   *|=us|, s/k̓ʷák̓ʷes*

sweat   */q̓ál=ze?*   (take sweatbath)

sweathouse   *n/q̓ál=ze?-tn*

sweating   */qʷáz•z*

swell up   */péw-t*

swell up   */px̣ʷ-ə́p*   (inflate, puff up)

swim   *n/qáy-ix*

swim   *n/x̣áy-ix*   (of fish)

tail   *|=upe?|, /s=úpe?*   (of animal, bird)

tail   *s/?-éle?=xn*   (of fish)

take, take hold   */kʷén-s |√kʷén:-t-es|, /kʷné-m*

there   *cí?e*   (not far)

there   *łú?e*   (remote)

there   *ł?é*   (over there)

thick   */pł ə́ł-t*

thick   */zúy-t*   (stout)

thick   */k̓q-ə́p*   (of liquid)

thin   */px̣•í?x̣a?-t*   (of layer) (cf. narrow)

think   */pt=ínus-m |√pt=ínəws:-min-t-es|*   (think about)

think   */łək̓ʷ-mín-s*   (remember)

throw   */c̓ə́q̓-mín-s*

throw down   */q̓(a)mín-s*   (cf. hit)

tie   */ʕac-t-és*

tie   */zús-e-s*   (restrain)

tongue   */tə̣́ł-e?*

tooth   *|=énís|*   'tooth, board, plank', */x̣yéxʷ*

trail   See road

tree   *|=eyeqʷ|, s/ɣép*   (cf. 'stand'), *|=ełp|*   (plant)

turn   */p̓iq̓=éytxʷ-e-s*   (leaf or page)

turn   */síw-ix*   (off road)

turn   */mén-ix*   (away from)

turn   */púy-e-s*   (upside down, of concave object)

turn around   */sə́lk-e-t-és*

turn over   */siq̓-e-t-és*

uncle, great-uncle   */sí[•s]qe?*

642

upstream   *n/kʷúme*   (direction: cf. /kʷúme 'go up away from water; from fire in house')

upstream   /ƛ̓áx̣-ix   (go by water)

upstream   *n/kʷú[•kʷ]ṁe*   (location)

vomit   /wéƛ̓k̓

vomit it out   /xʷúc̓-e-s

walk   /xʷesít

warm   *qəm•/qə́m-t*

warm   /qʷéc   (feel warm)

wash   /c̓éw̓-e-s

wash   /séxʷ-m   (bathe)

wash   /q̓ʷíc̓-e-s   (launder)

water |=etkəw|, /qʷú?

wet   /c̓[?]áq̓ʷ

wet   /ɬ[?]áƛ̓   (from spatter)

wet   /s[?]éw   (from undergrowth)

wet   /qʷ[?]éṅ   (soaked)

what?   *s/té?*   (cf. say)

when?   /pi?-s/té?

where?   *n /héṅ, w /héṅ*

white   *?es-t/píq*

who?   *s/wét*

why?   /kén-m   (7.5.2.)

wide   /ɬáq̓-t

wife   *s/m?-ém*

wind (blowing)   *s/néw̓-t*

wing   *s/c̓k=áx̣n*

winter   *s/?ístk*

wipe   /?ép̓-e-s

with   *ki?•/kéy̓-x*   (accompanying)

with   *n/k̓əɬ-*   (companion), (6.1.1.)

with   *?es-n/xí?*   (included, involved)

woman, female   *s/múɬec*

work   /cw-ə́m   (|√cəw| 'do, make')

worm   /?íx̣ic   (wood worm)

worm   *s-up•/up-l=í[•ɬ]ec̓e?*   (caterpillar)

worm   *wəp•wəp-l=í[•ɬ][•y]ek̓*   (id.)

worms   *s-mi?•/mé[•ṁ]i?x*   (diminutive augmentative of 'snake'; no sg., 6.7.1.)

year |=(sz)enxʷ|, /zəɬ-p=szénxʷ

year   *s/wúxʷ-t*   'snow'

yellow   See green

Sketch of Coahuilteco, a Language Isolate of Texas

RUDOLPH C. TROIKE

Coahuilteco was one of a number of languages formerly spoken in the area of south Texas and northeastern Mexico; so far as is known, all had become extinct by the middle of the twentieth century. The principal source of information on Coahuilteco is a bilingual confessor's manual putatively written by Bartolomé García, a Spanish Franciscan missionary at Mission San Francisco de la Espada in San Antonio (Texas) (fig. 1), and published in Mexico City in 1760. The title is *Manual para Administrar los Santos Sacramentos de Penitencia, Eucharistia, Extrema-Uncion, y Matrimonio: Dar Gracias despues de Comulgar, y Ayudar a Bien Morir: A los Indios de las Naciones: Pajalates, Orejones, Pacaos, Pacóas, Tilijayas, Alasapas, Pausanes, y otras muchas diferentes, que se hallan en las Missiones del Rio de San Antonio, y Rio Grande, pertenecientes â el Colegio de la Santissima Cruz de la Ciudad de Queretaro, como son: Los Pacuâches, Mescâles, Pampôpas, Tâcames, Chayopînes, Venados, Pamâques, y toda la Juventud de Pihuiques, Borrados, Sanipaos, y Manos de Perro* (vol. 10:349) (fig. 2), 'Manual for the Administration of the Holy Sacraments of Penitence, Eucharist, Extreme Unction, and Matrimony: Giving Thanks after Communion and Helping to Die Well: To the Indians of the Nations: Pajalates, Orejones, Pacaos, Pacóas, Tilijayas, Alasapas, Pausanes, and many other different ones, which are found in the Missions of the San Antonio River and the Rio Grande, belonging to the College of the Holiest Cross of the City of Queretaro, such as: the Pacuâches, Mescâles, Pampôpas, Tâcames, Chayopînes, Venados, Pamâques,

and all the youth of the Pihuiques, Borrados, Sanipaos, and Manos de Perro'. (García uses the circumflex over a vowel "â", as well as an acute accent "á", to indicate a long vowel. In citing forms from the *Manual* containing either of these marks, the circumflex will be used to transcribe García's orthography.)

An earlier, linguistically somewhat more primitive version exists in an undated manuscript entitled *Confesonario de Indios* discovered in 1962 (Del Hoyo 1965; Troike 1967a); its existence indicates that the published version was perhaps the product of several decades of work in the missions. The only other significant source of data is a companion manuscript to the *Confesonario* discovered along with it, bearing on the first page the title *Cuadernillo de lengua de. . .Pajalates de la Mision. . .Padre Pres[iden]te Fr. Gabriel [de]. . . Vergara* (the dots here represent gaps caused by the page's having been trimmed). Vergara was president of the San Antonio missions from 1725 until perhaps 1737 (Canedo 1968). This *Cuadernillo* contains word lists and verb paradigms from a variety of the language essentially identical to that of the *Manual*. It may have been intended as a grammatical and lexical questionnaire that interpreters were to fill out with forms from the Indian language as an aid in their work. The *Cuadernillo* was perhaps also connected with an *Arte* (grammar) of Coahuilteco referred to in the foreword to the *Manual*, but this is uncertain.

On the basis of the appearance of Vergara's name in the title of the *Cuadernillo*, Del Hoyo (1965) ascribes the work to him and questions García's authorship of the *Manual*. However, the notebook had been flipped

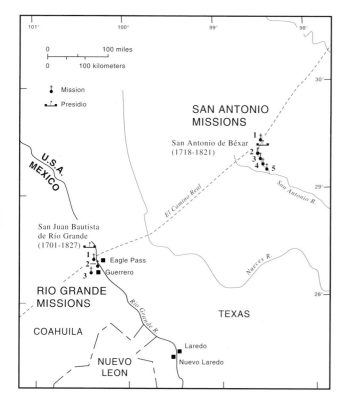

Fig. 1. Location of Spanish missions and associated presidios at San Antonio, Texas, and Guerrero, Coahuila, where Coahuilteco and other languages were spoken. San Antonio missions, with dates of establishment and abandonment: 1, San Antonio de Valero (1718-1793); 2, Nuestra Señora de la Purísima Concepción de Acuña (1731-1824); 3, San José y San Miguel de Aguayo (1720-1824); 4, San Juan Capistrano (1731-1824); 5, San Francisco de la Espada (1731-1824). Rio Grande missions, with dates of establishment and abandonment: 1, San Bernardo (1702-1829); 2, San Francisco Solano (1700-1716), removed to San Antonio and named San Antonio de Valero in 1718; 3, San Juan Bautista (1700-1829).

over to make a new title, which makes no mention of Vergara, and it carries a date read as 1732 by Del Hoyo and 1738 by Troike (1978). If the correct date is 1738, Vergara would no longer have been president of the missions, providing a rationale for beginning a new title page. The very tentative field-note–like nature of the entries in the *Cuadernillo*, compared with the quite well worked out translations of the *Confesonario*, argues for a definitely later date for the *Confesonario*. That they both predate the *Manual* is strongly suggested by their common lack of refinement in the representation of Coahuilteco sounds in comparison with the *Manual*.

Fr. Joseph Guadalupe Prado, a former missionary at Mission San Juan Capistrano who personally knew García's work, in a foreword to the *Manual* attests to García's authorship and his competence in the language (which Prado also knew), even to preaching sermons in it "con aprobacion de los Interpretes mas limados" ('with the approbation of the most polished interpreters') (in García 1760:[iv]). Elsewhere in the

forematter (p. xii), it is noted that García served in the Texas missions more than 12 years.

Little is known of García except that he was stated to have been at Mission Nuestra Señora de la Candelaria in 1750, where he was reported as being the oldest missionary there, and at Mission San Francisco de la Espada by 1756. If the figure of 12 years for García's service is correct, then he could not have composed the *Cuadernillo*, whether it is dated 1732 or 1738. On the other hand—particularly considering the remark regarding García's age—there could easily have been sufficient time for him to have authored the *Confesonario*. At the very least, in the *Manual* he may have edited and improved upon the efforts of earlier workers in the missions, particularly in the phonological accuracy of the orthography.

DE LA PENITENCIA.	3
Comulgaſte la Quareſma paſſada?	Quareſma app'ânmâm tupâyó mameyá comulgar am é?
Eres caſado?	Pil' mamêyatâyagûyam é?
Eres caſada?	Pil' mamêyâc'âu am é?
Has penſado todos tus pecados?	Taguajâyo, ſajpâm pinapſâ jamî (*vel* pin japſac'âuj) tuchêm mameinâcacó yam é?
Dime todos los pecados que has hecho: no me engañes: ſi me engañas, y ſi no me dices todos los pecados, te confeſſarâs mal, y te llevarâ el Demonio á el Inſierno: no me tengas miedo: no me tengas verguenza.	Taguajâyo, ſajpâm pinapſâ (*vel* pin apſac'âuj) japôi tuchêm taj um: tâjaſhîpt'am ajâm:tiashîpt'amêj, mi taguajâyo, ſajpâm pinapſâ (*vel* pin apſac'âuj) tuchêm tiaûm ajâm aguajtâ', ſajpamê japamâlcûita ſnajó', co tamôj ta t'oajâm tucuêt mac chô ſanpó: tiatâlam ajâm câm: tiajuâncam ajâm câm.
Le eſcondiſte à el Padre algun pecado grande en las otras Confeſſiones?	Japamâlcûita pil' atâ tuchîyó, ſajpâm pinapſâ (*vel* pin apſac'câuj) apnân mâ, cutâtze (*vel* totâtze)tupôm mameijuâlajêj am é? (*vel* mameyâpjâqej am é?)
Què coſa le callaſte á el	T'âjat (*vel* jat) pin ap- Pa-

SI Lib., García 1750:3

Fig. 2. A page from García's 1760 manual for the administration of church sacraments to the missionized Coahuilteco-speaking Indians in the San Antonio and Rio Grande missions (see vol. 10:349 for the title page and a page illustrating kinship terms). The sentences on this page illustrate the variety of personal prefixes used on the verb in past tense, imperative, conditional, future tense, and optative expressions, as well as the unique subject-person–marking on object phases. The borrowed Spanish verb *comulgar* 'receive communion' is used in the first question. Male and female terms for 'to marry' are distinguished in the second and third questions. Questions are marked by the question particle ⟨é⟩. The faint pencil marks on this copy were made by John R. Swanton while compiling his lexicon (Swanton 1940:10-54).

Apart from these materials, the only information on the languages formerly spoken in the San Antonio missions is limited to occasional words, names of individuals, or tertiary comments given in explorers' accounts or mission records (fig. 3). The description in this sketch is based almost entirely on the *Manual*; where other sources have been drawn upon, this fact has been noted.

García's *Manual* contains 88 numbered pages of text printed in parallel columns of Spanish and Coahuilteco (except for five pages that are wholly or partly in Latin) intended to provide instruction for the Indians in the sacraments of the Roman Catholic church. The contents of the book are as follows: 14 pages of forematter by Prado, García, and others (unnumbered; here they are assigned Roman numerals, beginning with the title page); the sacrament of penitence (pp. 1-31); the numeral system, a short vocabulary, and a few grammatical notes (31-34); the catechism (34-44); the sacrament of the Eucharist (45-55); the sacrament of extreme unction (56-64); the confession of faith of the dying (64-75); the sacrament of matrimony, which includes an extensive catalogue of kinship terms (76-87); and a correction of an earlier passage (88).

The text consists primarily of short sentences or paragraphs. These include questions, statements, and commands, with questions predominating. In only a few instances does a paragraph attain any considerable length. The total number of morphs in the text is estimated at about 20,000. The short and often repetitious nature of the sentences in many cases facilitates analysis, but at the same time the limitations of the text sometimes make it impossible to determine the composition of certain unique constructions or to discern the semantic significance or contextual conditioning of particular functional elements. The (fortunately infrequent) occurrence of typographical errors and the occasional mixture of San Antonio and Rio Grande dialect forms also at times pose problems for analysis.

IDENTIFICATION OF SPEAKERS AND VARIETIES

As the title page indicates, García's *Manual* was written for use in the Queretaran missions on the San Antonio River and the Rio Grande, where many small bands had been gathered by the middle of the eighteenth century. Although this title page lists the groups for which the *Manual* was intended, it remains uncertain to which specific band or bands the language of the *Manual* may be attributed, exactly where it was spoken, and how many other languages may have existed in the area. The name Coahuilteco for the language dates from 1864 when it was coined by the Mexican geographer Orozco y Berra (1864:63) from the name of the state (earlier province) of Coahuila, Mexico.

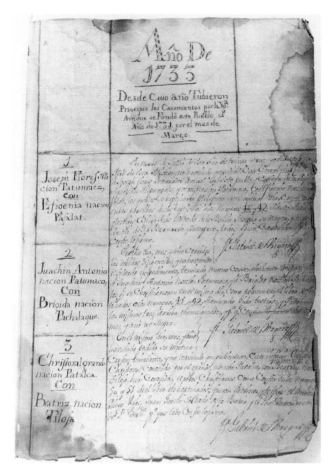

Catholic Arch. at San Antonio, Tex.

Fig. 3. First page of the 1733 marriage records of Mission Nuestra Señora de la Purísima Concepción de Acuna, in present-day San Antonio, Tex. The three couples whose marriages are recorded on this page came from 5 different bands, the Pajalat and Tilijae ("Tiloja"), who are named on García's title page, and the Patumaco, Pastaloca ("Pachalaque"), and Pitalac ("Patalca"), who were apparently also Coahuilteco-speaking. See list of Coahuilteco speakers by group (vol. 10:349).

Although he suggested "Tejano" as an alternative (also used by Pimentel 1865), this has not been followed by later writers, despite the fact that many of the bands speaking the language seem to have been native to Texas and to have ranged into Coahuila only secondarily (probably because the name Texas, or Tejas, was originally used to refer to the unrelated Caddo; the name is derived from Caddo *teša* 'friend', plus the Spanish plural *-s*).

In one of the earliest accounts from the area, Fr. Damian Massanet in 1691, after having traveled from the mission of San Salvador near Caldera, Coahuila, to a spot north of San Antonio, stated, "I may note that from the mission to this place there is still one language. . . . From this place to the Tejas [in East Texas] there are other languages" (Bolton 1910:422). In his foreword to the *Manual*, Prado, who worked among the missions of Texas and Coahuila for 22 years, declared that except for one mission, "todas las demàs desde nuestra Señora de los Dolores, que fue la primera hasta San Juan Capistrano la ultima, se fundaron con Indios, cuyo proprio lenguaje era el mismo, que en este Manual se contiene" ('all the rest from Nuestra Señora de los Dolores, which was the first, to San Juan Capistrano the last, were founded with Indians whose own language was the same as is contained in this *Manual*') (p. vi). Elsewhere he stated that Coahuilteco was "la Lengua mas comun à todas las conversiones Franciscanas, que se plantaron desde la Mission llamada la Candela hasta las que bordan las amenas margenes de el Rio de San Antonio, extremos distantes mas de cien leguas uno de otro" (p. v) ('the language that is most common to all the Franciscan conversions that have been planted from the mission named La Candela [in Coahuila] to those that border the banks of the San Antonio River, extremes more than 100 leagues distant from one another').

This testimony by persons directly familiar with the situation, as well as the testimony of the title page of the *Manual* itself, appears to be contradicted or at best modified by linguistic evidence from other sources. The Borrados and Alasapas, who are mentioned on the title page, lived in the area of central Nuevo Leon eastward into Tamaulipas (the Borrados were classified by Orozco y Berra as Tamaulipeco), though the Borrados are also reported in the vicinity of Laredo in 1758. Eugenio del Hoyo (1960) has published a list of translated Borrado place-names taken from documents in the Monterrey, Nuevo Leon, archives, which though difficult to analyze conclusively, appear to indicate that while there are a few lexical resemblances with other languages in the area, Borrado is a distinctly different language from Coahuilteco. The following examples illustrate some of the few similarities that can be found:*

	Borrado	*Others*
'mescal bean' (frijolillo)	"minaguapa"	*sami·n* (Coahuilteco)
'plural suffix'	"-que" [ke]	*-ke* (Coahuilteco—rare)
'water'	"guar(a)" [war]	*wan* (Pajalate)
'javelina' (hog)	"(a)moqua" [mokʷa]	(ex)mu´k (Comecrudo); esmo´k (Cotoname)
'dog'	"carama"	kla´m (Comecrudo)

*In this sketch, the following conventions will be used in citing forms. Double quotation marks will be used to indicate forms cited in their original orthography (whether from García or another source). Italic indicates phonemically transcribed forms when these are cited in the text. Spanish loanwords are spelled and capitalized as in Spanish. Brackets enclose phonetic transcriptions or occasionally indicate editorial insertion of missing elements.

In what little can be gleaned of a structural nature from these place-names, there is not much evident similarity to the language of the *Manual*.

Some words recorded in the books of one of the missions, San Francisco Solano, apparently during the time that it was located on the Rio Grande below Eagle Pass between 1703 and 1708 (Swanton 1940:5, 54), show extraordinarily little resemblance to Coahuilteco or anything else. Unfortunately, the specific group from which the words were obtained is not known, but the mission served the Xarame, Payuguan, Papanac, and Siaguan, none of whom is mentioned on the title page of the *Manual*.

Additionally, the much more extensive vocabularies collected by Jean L. Berlandier in 1829 and Albert S. Gatschet in 1886 near and along the Rio Grande from speakers of Comecrudo and Cotoname (also variously identified as Carrizo or Garza) not only reveal differences between them so great as to indicate that these two languages may be unrelated but also show equally profound differences from the language of García's *Manual* (Swanton 1940; see Goddard 1979 for further comparison and discussion).

The apparent contradiction between these assertions by people personally familiar with the situation on the one hand, and the actual linguistic data available from various groups in the area on the other, may be resolved by a further examination of some of the comments in the forematter to the *Manual*. Prado's statement quoted above—that all the missions were founded with Indians who spoke the language recorded in the *Manual*—suggests the Spanish practice, followed throughout northern Mexico, of settling Tlaxcalans as an initial nucleus to help "civilize" and Christianize the Indians who were brought in (this particular practice probably accounts for some of the Nahuatl loanwords in the *Manual*, discussed in Troike 1961). Prado says this was done in all the missions except one, though he does not name it; it may have been San Francisco Solano, from which Xarame Indians were taken to form the nucleus when it was refounded as Mission San Antonio de Valero (later known as the Alamo).

Prado (in García 1760:vi) goes on to say that when the earlier practice of ensuring that the missionized Indians always outnumbered the neophytes broke down, and Indians of the most diverse languages ("diversissimas lenguas") were brought in to the missions, the *Manual* became of very general use, because "la gente nueva â breve tiempo la entiende, ô habla, y los muchachos, que son la porcion de nuestra mayor esperanza, al año ya, como dicen, cortan el pelo en el dicho Idioma" ('the new people [entering a mission] in a short time understand it [Coahuilteco] or speak it, and the children, who are the part with our greatest hopes, by the end of a year cut their hair in this language, as they say'). This would appear to indicate that the

647

missionaries had made a lingua franca of Coahuilteco, at least in the missions. Prado's statement would also seem to explain why García mentioned in the title page that the *Manual* was intended for "all the *youth* of the Pihuiques, Borrados, Sanipaos, and Manos de Perro," implying that the older members of these bands did not speak the language. Whether Coahuilteco had currency as a lingua franca outside the missions, either before or after the efforts of the missionaries to promote it, is unknown.

As noted above, the exact groups to which Coahuilteco is to be attributed is uncertain. The Pajalates are clearly one—an inference that might have been made from the fact that they are the first-named group on the title page of the *Manual* and that they were among the groups in García's mission (San Francisco de la Espada). However, the question was settled conclusively by Del Hoyo's (1965) discovery of the *Cuadernillo de [la] lengua de [los] Pajalates*, an interpreter's guide developed for use in the Mission Nuestra Señora de la Purísima Concepción de Acuña, which shows such close similarity to the language of the *Manual* that there can be no doubt the two texts represent the same language. Of 32 lexical items common to both, all but one are either identical or virtually so.

	Cuadernillo	*Manual*
'carry'	-xʷačo·	-čo·
'earth'	tapakʷe	tap (pa) akʷe·
'forget'	-xaman	-xa·mam
'I'	čen, čen	cin
'very good'	šapanpan	šap̓a·n pam

(See Troike 1967a for additional comparisons.) Some of the divergences may be attributed to dialectal differences in the sources of the two documents, but most are due simply to refinements in the analysis and transcription of the language, perhaps by García (note that some of the same transcriptional differences are found between the *Manual* and the *Confesonario*: for further discussion of these, see section 1).

The *Manual* itself provides evidence for other dialects of Coahuilteco. Prado, in his foreword (p. xii), states that his "Indios Capistranos" used "chy" *či* (plural demonstrative stem) in place of the "chê" *če·* found in the *Manual*, and "y" for *e·* (the interrogative particle). Unfortunately, he did not identify which band he was referring to, if any in particular (there were also Pajalates at Capistrano), and these are the only specific differences he mentions.

However, he suggests that there were greater differences between the dialect of the *Manual* and that of the Indians of the Rio Grande (it is not clear to whom he refers here, whether the Xarames who were brought from San Francisco Solano, although they are not mentioned on the title page of the *Manual*, or some groups

still in missions on the Rio Grande). He notes that the kinship terms are "quite different" (*bien diversos*), and gives in addition some illustrative phonological differences (p. xiii):

San Antonio	*Rio Grande*
"sananô"	"sanân"
"so"	"sê"
"cuê"	"co"

There are "many other differences of this tenor," and he admonishes the missionary working with a particular group, using the *Manual* and his *Arte*, to find out what the differences are and to learn them. His discussion contains an interesting disquisition on the problems of translation and their implications for language policy in the missions. García himself, in his own prologue (p. xvi), explains that he has indicated in parentheses in the *Manual*, and with the Latin particle *vel*, "que las palabras de aquel parenthesis pertenecen â las Missiones de el Rio Grande, ô â otra Mission en particular" 'that the words within the parentheses belong to the Rio Grande missions, or to some other particular mission'. Since he nowhere identifies whether the alternative forms are Rio Grande dialect or other, where there is occasion to cite them they will be marked as RG, in contrast to SA (for San Antonio).

While the comparison of the *Cuadernillo* and García's *Manual* (or the *Confesonario*, for that matter) leads to the conclusion that the language of the *Manual* is to be identified with the Pajalates (presumably those of Mission San Francisco de la Espada), it is clear that several closely related dialects existed, though it is not known to which bands they may have been native (see Goddard 1979 for further discussion and comparisons). In addition, the missionaries were evidently promoting the use of the language as a lingua franca in the missions. Therefore, it seems preferable to follow the established practice of Swanton (1940) and others in employing the name Coahuilteco for the language, since it is neutral with respect to any particular variety or group and permits reference to any given variety by a designation clearly indicating it as such.

No date can be fixed for the extinction of Coahuilteco or other languages spoken by groups in the San Antonio missions (except Tonkawa and Karankawa). The missions were secularized in 1793-1794, and there are very few sources of linguistic information after that. Apache and Comanche pressure drove many of the Coahuiltecan groups to the coast, where they took refuge among and mingled with the Karankawa and other South Texas groups. Others, having been thoroughly acculturated, simply became an indistinguishable part of the local Spanish-Mexican population and disappeared as separate entities.

WIDER RELATIONSHIPS

The wider relationships of Coahuilteco, after nearly a century of study, remain highly uncertain. Powell (1891:68), following the usage of Orozco y Berra (1864), classified the Coahuilteco of García's *Manual* together with Comecrudo and Cotoname, as members of the Coahuiltecan family. Gatschet (1891:33, 38) applied the name Paikawa (or Paíkawan or Pakawá) to this same group of languages, a usage followed by Boas (1911:83) and Thomas (1911:38).

John R. Swanton in 1915 proposed a Coahuiltecan family consisting of two divisions, one containing Cotoname and Tonkawa, the other including Coahuilteco proper, Comecrudo, and Karankawa, although he also noted resemblances between Karankawa and Atakapan. Five years later, Sapir (1920), building on the data published by Swanton, proposed a wider relationship between Coahuiltecan and the Hokan stock in California. Finally, in Sapir's (1929) classification, Coahuiltecan became the link between Hokan and the remaining non-Algonquian languages of eastern North America in his great Hokan-Siouan phylum.

Swanton (1940) revised his earlier classification and excluded Tonkawa from the Coahuiltecan family, a conclusion confirmed by the work of Haas (1959), Bright (1956), and Troike (1967). Since Haas (1958a) has brought the validity of the entire Hokan-Siouan hypothesis into question, the linguistic position of Coahuilteco and the languages of south Texas and northeast Mexico is returned very much to where Powell left it, with the need remaining to examine the internal relations of these languages in detail as a prerequisite to reconsidering their wider relationships.

The degree of diversity among the languages of this area is so great that, as Swanton (1940:144) observed, "one would hardly be assured that any two of them belonged to the same stock." In this regard, it is interesting to note that Bright's (1956) study tended to substantiate the Hokan-Coahuiltecan relationship to a greater degree that it did the "Coahuiltecan" grouping itself. Although Swanton was inclined to the belief that all these languages were ultimately members of a single stock, his assessment of the classificatory picture remains almost startlingly valid in spite of new material from several languages (Swanton 1940:144):

> In view of the marked divergencies exhibited by the three supposedly "Coahuiltecan" dialects, their almost equally close connection with the supposedly independent Karankawan, and the further divergence shown by the San Francisco Solano vocabulary, I am of the opinion that the present classification of the tongues of this region into Coahuiltecan, Karankawan, Tamaulipecan—and probably also Olivean and Janambrian—families is wholly artificial, and that we do not know how many stocks there were.

A thorough review by Goddard (1979) of the available data on the languages of the area has served to underscore this statement and to reemphasize the fact that the Gulf coastal area of Texas and northern Mexico was probably linguistically the most complex in all of North America. Since the degree of linguistic diversity in an area usually corresponds to the length of settlement, this fact suggests great antiquity for the in situ differentiation of groups in this area. Ethnologically, the northwestern Gulf coast was occupied by some of the simplest hunting and gathering cultures on the continent. Swanton (1940) referred to it as the "cultural sink," and Kroeber (1939) considered it the only culture area in North America without a climax. Newcomb (1956), following a suggestion by Alex D. Krieger, proposed the name "Western Gulf culture area" for this area of hunting and gathering groups. Borrowing from earlier linguistic classifications, the ethnological literature generally uses the term "Coahuiltecan" for most of the bands in the area. The culture of these groups has been described by Ruecking (1953, 1954, 1954a, 1955), Troike (1961, 1962), Campbell (in vol. 10:343-358), and Salinas (1990).

Any attempt to describe the language of García's *Manual* cannot fail to acknowledge its debt to Swanton, whose numerous contributions to American Indian linguistics, while rarely noted, far outweigh those of many specialists in the field. His work on Coahuilteco, though presented modestly in the form of a vocabulary (Swanton 1940), necessarily involved a careful linguistic analysis of García's text, not only lexically but also grammatically and phonologically. If further analysis has added to his findings and occasionally corrected them in places (for example, Troike 1963), this is only to be expected, but it does not detract from the recognition of his pioneering achievement, nor from the fact that any future work on the language must build on the foundations that he laid.

1. PHONOLOGY

A linguistic analysis based on a written text of an extinct language—essentially a closed corpus—has both similarities to and differences from an analysis carried out with access to living speakers. The procedural problems become even more complex when the text is from an earlier period. An analysis such as this one is in some respects most difficult in the phonology, which must be inferred from the use of Spanish orthographic patterns together with a knowledge of sound changes and regional variations in Spanish, and from observations of orthographic patterns in the Coahuilteco text. In short, the analysis must apply the traditional procedures of philology, whose application to the study of American Indian languages is conveniently surveyed by Goddard (1973). The task is aided by the fact that García has furnished some valuable articulatory phonetic information in his introduction. Essentially, García made his own intuitive phonemic analysis and put it to use; the modern analyst can only examine his usage and draw inferences from it.

The fact that García carefully distinguishes types of sounds that are not found in Spanish or that are only allophonic in Spanish gives considerable confidence in his analysis, as does his remarkably consistent spelling. The excellence of his work should be noted particularly by those linguists who are inclined to dismiss any work done before the middle of the twentieth century. There is, of course, no way to recover phonological distinctions he may have missed, but an examination of the sound systems of surrounding languages suggests that it is unlikely that this is a serious problem. As to the question of psycholinguistic reality, it has been noted earlier that García was reputed to have had considerable fluency in the language.

It is regrettable that the location of García's original manuscript is unknown, so that the printed text must be relied upon. However, the accuracy of the *Manual* may be inferred from its internal consistency and from its close fidelity, apart from orthographical differences, to the manuscript of the *Confesonario*. In the course of analysis, several copies of the published work were examined to reduce errors from occasional poor printing impressions and to check for possible changes between printings, though none was found.

Error in the text (i.e., deviation from an accurate representation of the language) may be ascribed to three sources: faults of García's perception and usage, errors in the manuscript, and errors on the part of the typesetter. Evidently the printed text was not proofread by García until it was largely complete, as indicated by the fact that on the last two pages (87-88), he inserted a major correction of a paragraph from page 20. However, there are no corrections of minor orthographical variations elsewhere in the text. At times the correct form can be determined by comparison with other occurrences in the text, or from the meaning, but in some instances no certain determination can be made. Editorial emendations are indicated herein by placing an omitted letter in brackets, for example, *wa[k]-čo·-no·* (64:15; references are to page and line in the text).

It is not possible, owing to limitations of the text, to find minimal pairs or even minimal contrasts for all phonemes. Nevertheless, most are sufficiently well attested that traditional methods of phonemic analysis are applicable, though it is necessary to rely on textual consistency rather than informant reaction to validate a particular hypothesis of phonemic distinctiveness.

1.1. CONSONANTS

Coahuilteco has 24 consonants, with some uncertain evidence for another, θ. These are as shown in table 1.

Table 1. Coahuilteco Consonants

Present Sketch	Troike (1959, 1963)	Swanton (1940)
p	p	p
ṗ	p'	p'
t	t	t
ṭ	t'	t'
c	¢	tz
ċ	¢'	tz'
č	č	tc
č̇	č'	tc'
k	k	k
ḱ	k'	k'
kʷ	kʷ	kuV
ḱʷ	kʷ'	k'uV
θ	θ	k
s	s	s
š	š	c
x	x	x
xʷ	xʷ	xuV
h	h	h
l	l	l
ḷ	l'	l'
w	w	Vu ; guV
y	y	Vi
m	m	m
n	n	n

NOTE: V = any vowel.

There are two series of stops, a plain and a glottalized, both of which are voiceless. In addition, there is one fricative series, which is both voiceless and unglottalized, two laterals, two resonants, and two nasals.

García, in his introduction, makes no reference to the symbols "p", "t", "s", "l", "m", "n", "y", "j" (= x), "ch" (= č), or to the graphic sequences "gu" or "hu" (for w), so that it may be assumed their phonetic correspondences were roughly the same as in Spanish. The stops *p, t, k* were therefore probably voiceless and unaspirated (much as in English s*p*ill, s*t*ill, s*k*ill), the *t* being dental as in Spanish (see *ṭ* below).

García's orthography is remarkable for carefully distinguishing a series of glottalized stops and affricates, which he marks with an apostrophe following the consonant letter, a practice interestingly prefiguring that used in many twentieth-century linguistic transcriptions. (A tilde is occasionally used over "t" and "ch" in the *Cuadernillo*, perhaps also to indicate glottalization, but this cannot be confirmed since none of the forms in which it occurs is found in García.) His articulatory descriptions of these sounds are sufficiently detailed to permit their identification as glottalized. Of *ṗ, ṭ, ḱ*, he observes that "se han de pronunciar con alguna fuerza" ('they must be pronounced with some force') (p. xv). The *ṗ* is formed "golpeando con fuerza los labios" ('by striking the lips together with force'); the *ṭ* is a sharp, sudden sound (*tronido*), which is formed "hiriendo con fuerza la lengua en los dientes" ('by striking the tongue against the teeth with force'); and the *ḱ* is a certain click (*chasquido*), which is formed "en el nacimiento de la lengua" ('at the base of the tongue').

In the only morpheme combination in the text in which two glottalized stops happen to occur together, the first consonant loses its glottalization, so that *šip̉* appears as *šip* before *ṫ*: *pin piɫapšip̉* 'lies' (25:4) *tapašip̉am* 'he deceives me' (54:10-11).

Two affricates are distinguished by García, a dental *c* [ts] and a palatal, *č* [tš]. The palatal is written "ch," as in Spanish, while the dental is written "tz," and is pronounced "como en el Idioma Mexicano," ('as in Nahuatl') (p. xv). *č* occurs both before and after vowels but is not found word-finally in the text. *c* and *č* could be analyzed alternatively as clusters of *ts* and *tš*, respectively, but in general they pattern as single stops. Apart from these, the only other initial consonant cluster is the relatively rare sequence *tx* (in *txa·m* 'to live'), perhaps itself to be taken as still a third affricate. *c* occurs in word-final position, where there is no contrast with any other stop-fricative cluster. By chance, there are no sequences of *t* and *s* or *š*, except across clause boundaries, to contrast with these affricates; this circumstance results from the small number of morphemes in the text beginning with *s* or *š* or ending in *t*, and from the restrictions on their respective distributions.

The glottalized affricates *ċ* and *č̉*, spelled "t'z" (or "tz'") and "ch'", are of somewhat doubtful status, since García does not mention them in discussing the glottalized stops, and every form containing them also occurs elsewhere without the apostrophe. However, if *c* and *č* are considered to pattern with the stops, then *ċ* and *č̉* fill symmetrical positions in the pattern. Furthermore, it seems unlikely that either García or the typesetter would repeat an apostrophe in a form several times by accident, especially when this does not occur with other letters. On balance, the evidence is stronger in favor of recognizing them, but their status must be considered tentative. In any event, they are of extremely low frequency.

The labiovelar stop *kʷ* and its glottalized congener *ḱʷ* (always spelled "cu" and "c'u", respectively) clearly function as unit phonemes in Coahuilteco, since they contrast both with the sequence *kw* and with *ku*:

"mamicguâtz" *mamikwa·ċ* 'you beat them' (12:29) (*mamik-* 'you-them' + *wa·ċ* 'beat')
"mamîcc'uap'" *mami·kḱʷap̉* 'he kissed you' (22:13) (*mami·k-* 'he-you' + *ḱʷap̉* 'kiss')
"apamâlcûita" *apama·lku·yta* 'confessions' (6:11) (*a-* '3d person subj.' + *pa-* 'subordinating particle' + *ma·lku·yta* 'confess'; used as a nominal)

In addition, in García's orthography, "u" before a vowel is preceded only by "c"/"c'", "g", or "j" (with two exceptions, "h" and "n"), the combination in each case assumed to represent a unit phoneme (except in the context just cited, "cûi", where a long "û" is interpreted

as representing a full vowel, and the "i" following it, as a glide *y*).

The voiceless interdental fricative *θ* is postulated only tentatively as a phoneme in Coahuilteco on the basis of the sequence "ci" (which in Castilian would represent [θi]), which occurs only in several kinship terms: "jacîs" 'your mother's mother' (*xa-* 'your'), "jamacîs" 'your mother's sister', and "jamâcitan" 'your father's older sister'. Swanton (1940:17, 25) interprets the "c" in these forms as *k*, though García usually spells *k* with a "q" before front vowels. The spelling "z" in "aj juîzcuan" 'little pieces' (*ax-* '3d person pl.' + *xʷi·θkʷan* or *xʷi·ckʷan* 'be small'?) could also possibly represent *θ*, but it is probably a misprint for "tz" (as it clearly is in other contexts; it may also be a carryover from the *Confesonario*, in which "z" is generally used where "tz" appears in the *Manual*).

The *š*, which is not a Spanish phoneme, is recognized as phonemically distinct by García, who spells it "sh" and likens it to the pronunciation of "x" in Latin. More precisely, he describes the articulation as "encorbando, y encogiendo la punta de la lengua, para que no suene como s sola" ('curving and contracting the tip of the tongue, so that it does not sound like s alone') (p. xv). From this description it could be inferred that the sound was an alveopalatal fricative and that it was probably somewhat retroflexed. In final position *š* occurs only following *y*, where it appears to be in complementary distribution with *x*. This may be due simply to the small number of words containing *š* or may reflect constraints on phonological sequences ("neutralization") resulting from assimilation.

The orthographic sequence "ju" preceding a vowel letter is interpreted as a unit labiovelar phoneme *xʷ*, paralleling *kʷ*. It is not clear whether the sequence "Vuj" (V stands for any vowel) in word-final position represents *Vʷx*, with anticipatory labialization or metathesis of the labial and the fricative, or is merely an orthographic convention representing *Vxʷ*. The following comparisons suggest that *xʷ* is the correct analysis:

"ohâuj" : "ohâujuê" (*o* '3d person subj.' + *hawxʷ* 'be named' + *e·* 'question particle')
"sâuj" : "sâujuam" (*sa·wxʷ* 'verb postposition' + *am* 'past tense')
"mâuj" : "majuajûyo" (*ma·wx* 'hand'; *maxʷaxu·yo* 'five')

This conclusion is greatly strengthened by the spelling found in the Pajalate *Cuadernillo*, "najeju" 'my body', presumably *naxexʷ* or *nahexʷ* (*na-* 'my'), compared to the spelling of the same word in García, "nahâuj"; similarly, "sâuj" is spelled "saju" in the *Cuadernillo*. Although in transcribing García's forms phonemically in this sketch, the conservative position has been taken to follow spelling as the guide, so that "nahâuj" is written *naha·wx*, it should be kept in mind that this might be alternatively, and probably more correctly, transcribed as *naha·xʷ*.

651

The resonants, or glides, *w* and *y*, involve some problems of orthographic interpretation. In general, "gu" and "hu" before vowel letters and "u" after vowel letters are assumed to represent *w*. This interpretation differs from that of Swanton (1940:10), who considered that "gu" represented [w] before "o" and "a", but [g] before "e" and "i", as it does in the Spanish text. Even more problematic are the sequences in words such as "tâgu" 'woman' and "jagû" 'man'. It is possible that a [g] had developed as a positional variant of *w*, but the absence of any other voiced stops in the phonemic system of Coahuilteco makes it doubtful that a phonemic *g* should be proposed on such an equivocal basis.

García (p. xv) carefully distinguishes between his use of "y" and "i": "La y Griega hiere â la vocal que se le sigue. La i Latina no hiere â otra vocal; y pongo esta diferencia, para que se acierte la pronunciacion" ('the Greek y forms a syllable with the vowel that follows it. The Latin i does not form a syllable with another vowel; and I make this difference so that the correct pronunciation will be achieved'). This is one of the major orthographic advances of the *Manual* over the *Confesonario*, in which "i" was used in both functions. The use of "Vi" before a vowel, as in "maiûm" 'you say' (*may* 'you' + *u·m* 'say'), is assumed to indicate a syllable division, and probably a glottal stop [ʔ], between the "Vi" and the following vowel (cf. the frequent use of space before the same orthographically vowel-initial stems, discussed below). The "y" is never used unless a vowel follows.

García (p. xv) states that "h by itself, with a vowel or between two vowels, denotes that some nations pronounce it, articulating it like j, and others do not pronounce it except in such an obscure way (*tan confusamente*) that it is scarcely perceived." It is indicative of García's ability and perceptiveness that he was able to recognize this rather fine phonetic distinction, which was not present in his own Spanish. His remarks further suggest that he may have been employing it as a "diaphonemic" symbol, which merged phonetically with *x* in some dialects but in others was distinct. Perhaps because of this, or because of a carryover from an earlier version such as the *Confesonario*, which did not distinguish them, the text shows occasional substitution of "h" for "j" in spelling and vice versa.

There is some question as to whether [h] should be considered a phoneme, but the decision depends largely on theoretical considerations. A superficial minimal contrast among [h], [x], and [ʔ] can easily be shown, as in the following:

"japahâm" 'you eat' (*xa* 'you' + *p* 'subordinating prefix' + *a* 'induced prefix' + *ha·m* 'eat')

"japajâm apsâ" 'your soul' (*xa* 'you' + *p* 'subordinating prefix' + *a* 'induced prefix' + *xa·m* 'remember'; *a* '3d person' + *p* 'subordinating prefix' + *sa·* 'to be')

"japaâm c'auj" 'you do damage' (*xa* 'you' + *p* 'subordinating prefix' + *a* 'induced prefix' + *ʔa·m* 'to do'; *k̓awx* 'bad')

By structuralist canons, this would be sufficient to establish the status of *h* as a phoneme.

However, "h" postvocalically (with one questionable exception, it is always morpheme-initial) regularly alternates with zero postconsonantally:

"apahôi" 'he does' (*a* '3d person' + *p* 'subordinating prefix' + *a* 'induced prefix' + *ho·y* 'to do')

"apôi" 'he does' (*a* '3d person' + *p* 'subordinating prefix' + *o·y̓* 'to do'

The occurrence of [h] is thus predictable, raising the issue of whether it should be considered a phoneme. If it is taken as phonemic, its absence may be accounted for by including a morphophonemic deletion rule

$$h \rightarrow \emptyset / C\_V$$

in the phonology and setting up underlying forms accordingly.

The arguments concerning treating the glottal stop as a phoneme in Coahuilteco are closely interrelated with those for the treatment of [h]. García does not explicitly discuss this sound, but his orthographic usage suggests that he recognized its presence. With certain orthographically vowel-initial stems, he frequently leaves a space between the stem and the prefix, for example,

"nac âj" 'I give you' (*na* 'I' + *k* 'you' + [ʔa·x] 'give')

"japa âm" 'you do' (*xa* 'you' + *p* 'subordinating prefix' + *a* 'a-prefix' + [ʔa·m] 'do')

"taj ûm" 'you tell me' (*ta* 'me' + *x* 'you' + [ʔu·m] 'tell').

In addition, as noted above, García uses "y" when the sound forms a syllable with a following vowel and "i" where this does not occur. Thus he writes "mamaiâj" 'you give him' and "mamaiûm" 'you tell him' (cf. "mameyayâm" 'you were angry with him'; "-(a)-yâm" 'be angry'). If [h] were not treated as an underlying phoneme, but were inserted by rule, then these forms would have to be assumed to begin with ʔ in their underlying forms. Conversely, if *h* is assumed to be (morpho)phonemically underlying, phonetic [ʔ] may be predicted by a rule that introduces it before all vowel-initial stem morphemes. This last solution is the one that will be adopted in this chapter.

Positing [ʔ] in these environments creates an apparent contrast between glottalized stops and sequences of stop plus glottal stop, but the former occur within a single syllable whereas the latter are in separate syllables; cf. "nac'âi" [na.k̓a·y] 'I touch' (*na* 'I') and "nac âj" [nak.ʔa·x] 'I give you' (*na* 'I' + *k* 'you'.) Orthographic sequences of identical vowels are also assumed to have a [ʔ] between them: "ââ" 'yes', "jaâpjâisht'an" 'your older sister's daughter' (woman speaking) (*xa* 'your').

There are two laterals in Coahuilteco, one alveolar *l* presumably similar to that in Spanish, and a second, which García identifies orthographically with the glottalized stops by representing it as "l'", and like them says must be pronounced with some force. He (p. xv) describes the articulation of the *ỉ* as being "tocando con la punta de la lengua los dientes de arriba, y asomandola un tanto quanto" ('by touching the upper teeth with the tip of the tongue, and showing it a little'). This indicates that the sound was dental, and perhaps somewhat interdental, in articulation. Such a dental-alveolar contrast in laterals is rare but is found, for example, in Araucanian (Suarez 1959). *l* is stem-initial and final, but never word-initial, whereas *ỉ* occurs only postvocalically: *ỉil* 'day', *piỉ* 'one'. In the *Confesonario*, *ỉ* is sometimes represented as "lh", suggesting a voiceless articulation, an analysis also implied by García's statement that it is pronounced with force.

The nasals /m/ and /n/ are the second and seventh most frequent phonemes in the language, together comprising 15 percent of the text. They occur in all positions.

1.2. VOWELS

Coahuilteco has a system of 10 vowel phonemes with long and short contrasts in each of five articulatory positions. These are shown in table 2.

Since the orthographic representation of the vowels in Coahuilteco is the same as that in Spanish, it may be assumed that their phonetic character is similar. There are two front vowel positions, a high *i*, *i·*, and a mid *e*, *e·*; two back vowel positions, a high *u*, *u·* and a mid *o*, *o·*; and one low, presumably central, vowel position *a*, *a·*. There are a few morphemes that show orthographic variation between "o" and "u", suggesting that this distinction may not have been altogether firm, or that there may have been conditioning or dialectal factors that are not identified or identifiable. There are no positional restrictions on the occurrence of any of the vowels.

Long vowels are marked in the text by acute or circumflex accents. García specifically notes (xiv) that they are pronounced long and indicates that the two sets of accent marks are interchangeable, as his usage in the text also indicates: "T'âjat apchîyocâ?" 'How many times' (8:4-5); "T'ájat apchíyocá?" (34:4). (The accent marks in the Spanish text are usually of the grave type, presumably to make a contrast, e.g., *perdonarà*.)

No perfectly minimal pairs are available to demonstrate a contrast in length, but the following examples are illustrative: "jagû" *xawu·* 'man'; "tâgu" *ta·wu*

'woman'; *talo·m* 'fire', *ta·lam* 'fear'. Length is a concomitant feature of stress in Spanish (Navarro Tomás 1953:200-202); and in Spanish words used in the Coahuilteco text, the length mark is placed on the vowel corresponding to the stressed vowel in Spanish.

However, there are several problems with defining length as a distinctive feature. The first is that García is not consistent in marking length, though he is more consistent on certain morphemes than on others, and on stems more than affixes. The second is that a "rhythmic length" sometimes occurs on alternating syllables (usually of the minimum form CV) preceding a long stem vowel:

ak-čo· san	"he will carry them" (39:8)
a·k-saxo·p san	"something separates them" (85:24)
aha·wx tupamo·	"the body only" (40:2)
aha·wx tupa·mopa·	"the body only" (40:4)
mak-pa-ču·	"he carries you" (54:16-17)
ma·k-pa-ka·wa	"she loves you" (68:20-21)

The rhythmic length is marked rather inconsistently, so that it is not possible to determine precisely the constraints on its application.

1.3. INTONATION

García makes no mention of intonation in the language. Since it is not represented in the orthography, nothing more can be concluded about it than that it perhaps did not differ sufficiently from Spanish to attract any special attention, or that in the absence of a traditional framework for describing intonation, it did not draw any particular comment.

1.4. SYLLABLE STRUCTURE

Syllable structure is predominantly CV(·)(S)(C), that is, a single consonant followed by a short or long vowel, optionally followed by a semivowel *y* or *w* and/or a single consonant. A semivowel may follow a long vowel, as in "apahôuj" *apaho·wx* 'she lost' (although this may be interpreted alternatively as *apaho·xʷ*), *-ša·yš* 'be bad'. All vowel-initial syllables may be considered phonetically to begin with a glottal stop; alternatively the initial consonant may be considered phonemically optional in the formula.

The few recorded examples of consonant clusters in syllable initial positions, *klo·*, *sno·*, and *mantpam* 'truth', are probably to be regarded as resulting from reduced forms of *kalo·* 'dubitative', *san* 'future' + *o·* 'aux.', and *man* 'true' + *tupa·m* 'demonstrative', respectively. The only cluster that cannot be accounted for is *tx*, which may be, as mentioned earlier, a distinct affricate. Vowels occasionally cluster, as in *a·nua* 'moon', *atiu·tan* 'little', and *apama·o*, 'he ascends', though these could be considered as falling in separate syllables or as being separated by a glottal stop.

Based on a 10 percent sample of the text (every tenth page of text, containing 3,158 phonemes), an estimate **653**

Table 2. Vowel Phonemes of Coahuilteco

i	*i·*			*u*	*u·*
e	*e·*			*o*	*o·*
		a	*a·*		

of phoneme frequencies in Coahuilteco was made. The phoneme *a* alone comprised 26.5 percent of the sample, while *m* and *p* occupied 10 percent and 8.7 percent of the text, respectively. Together with *x* at 6.2 percent, these four phonemes comprise over half the text (51.4%). *t, o, n, e, i, u*, ranging from 5.6 percent to 3.5 percent, make up another 30 percent, and *y, k, s*, and *w* another 10 percent, so that 14 phonemes account for over 90 percent of the text, and 14 phonemes (or 16, depending on the analysis), the remaining 10 percent. Three, *c̣, č*, and *k̓ʷ*, did not occur in the sample. Long vowels were not computed here separately from short vowels.

2. VERBS

Coahuilteco might be characterized as a prefixing language, since verbal subjects and objects and noun possessors are marked by prefixes. However, plurality is often indicated by an infix, while suffixes are used on demonstratives to mark agreement of object noun phrases with the verbal subject, and tense and negation are indicated by enclitics and other postverbal elements. Morphological complexes on the whole are relatively short, and there is little morphophonemic variation.

2.1. VERB STEMS

Verb stems may be divided into two classes, *a*- stems and zero-stems, on the basis of the presence or absence of a classificatory prefix *a*- before the stem when the preceding personal prefix ends in a consonant. A number of stems cannot be classified, since they do not occur in this environment. About 25 verbs have been classified as *a*-stems, while almost twice as many zero-stems have been identified. Since other circumstances can give rise to the presence of an *a*- preceding the stem, not all the putative *a*-stems are certain, inasmuch as over one-third of them occur only once in the relevant context. No particular meaning can be ascribed to this prefix, or to the group of verbs it distinguishes, which includes *ka·wa* 'to want', *komulgar* (Sp.) 'to receive communion', *xle·* 'to say', *pi·lam* 'to live', *šipłam* 'to deceive'. Examples are: *mamey-na·kako· yam e·* 'have you thought?' (zero-stem) and *mamey-a·komulgar am e·* 'did you commune?' (*a*-stem); *a-p-kʷa·ncam* 'he died' (San Antonio) (zero-stem), and *a-p-a-xu·m* 'he died' (Rio Grande) (*a*-stem).

Verb stems may be simple, as *kʷa·n* 'go', or complex, as *kʷa·ncam* 'die' (cf. *xle·* 'say', *xle·cam* 'adore'; *xa·m* 'remember', *xa·mcam* 'wish'). Only a very few second-order elements such as *cam* are found, which are perhaps old derivational affixes or independent morphemes that have become encliticized (as *-ful* in English *spoonful*). Other examples include *ši·pe·* 'lie', *šipłam* 'deceive'; *ho·wx* 'lose' (?), *ho·wxłam* 'throw'; *šapa·n* 'be good', *ša·pa·wano·* 'cleanse' (pl.) (*-wa-*, plural infix). The small number of examples suggests

that the use of these elements was not part of a productive process and that even their segmentation might not be meaningful from a synchronic point of view.

Phrasal combinations involve a verb and a following independent element that (at least from a translational viewpoint) can be considered as forming a semantic unit with the verb, for example, *ča·lawx* 'give birth', *čalawx k̓a·wx* 'miscarry'; *ko· k̓a·wx* 'injure'; *a·m k̓a·wx* 'do evil'.

2.2. PLURALIZATION AND INDUCED *a*-PREFIX

Stems may be inflected for the plural by infixation, by partial suppletion, or by a combination of both (only the locative stem *sa·* has a completely suppletive plural, *če*). The plural reference may be to either the subject of the verb: *ma·mix-a·c-o* 'you-all know', *takpa-x-a·c-o wako· tuče·n* 'which they taught me'; or the object: *akpah-a·k-oxłam* 'he throws them'. Plurality need not be marked (?) in the verb stem: *tak-xo· wako· tuče·m* 'which it teaches us'. The plural infixes are *-ak-* (which is the most common), *-ac-, -ka-, -ke-, -ok-*, and *-wa-* (or *-aw-*). With one exception, each infix is consistently used with the same verb stems.

Plural stems containing these infixes are listed below; the singular stem is given first only where it is known to differ from the plural minus the infix (in some instances the singular is unattested). Variation in vowel length is due to "rhythmic lengthening" or occasionally to uncorrected scribal inconsistency.

ak: *kʷ-ak-a·ncam* 'die', *i̇-ak-a·i̇* 'hurt', *xox-ak-o·ymo* 'join, combine', *ho·wxłam/h-ak-o·xłam* 'throw', *š-ak-ayš* 'be bad', *x-ak-a·y* 'end', *(a)p-ak-a·m* 'have children' (?), *n-ak-an* 'be great', *šap̓-ak-an* 'be good', *n-a·k-ako·* 'think', *k̓m-a·k-o·x(sa·wx)* 'kneel', *č-ak-ey* 'hear'.

ac: *h-a·c-awxʷ* 'be called', *x-a·c-o* 'know', *ami·/am-a·c-a* 'have', *xle·/l-a·c-e* 'speak', *xum-ac* 'die' (RG dialect), *k-a·c-owo* 'pay for'; *k̓a·w/xek̓-a·c-awamke·* 'marry' (for a man), *xk̓-a·c-a·wxłam* 'dream', *k̓tay/k̓t-ac-e·y* 'pray'.

ka: *kʷa·cum/kʷa·c-ka-m* 'ask for', *tixamko·/łe·x-ka-mko·* 'burn'.

ke: *p̓a-ke-nmam* 'pass time', *k̓a·w/xek̓a·cawam-ke·* 'marry', *tu·/xta·yam-ke·* 'be related'. Note that in the last two, an additional discontinuous plural element *x(e) . . . am* may be isolated.

ok: *tpa·y-ok-a·m* 'live'.

wa: *spa·-wa-mo·* 'believe', *ša·p̓a-wa-no·* 'cleanse', *u·m/a-wa·-m* 'tell', *hoy/ha-wa-·y* 'do', *k̓o·xta-wa·-y* 'hit oneself repeatedly', compare *ta-wa·-y* '(our) mother'. Note that in all these examples, the infix could as well be analyzed as *-aw-*.

The verb *pi·* 'copulate' is unique in the text in having three plurals, *pi·ya* (with men as object), *pa·ymo* (with women or animals as object), and *xpi·w čik* (for repeated occurrences). These are the only morphological distinctions made between male and female referents in the text (if this is indeed the feature of the action being distinguished: it could instead be an agent-patient distinction) and the only example of a separate iterative verb form; *čik* is a pluralizing particle.

As indicated earlier, in certain environments an *a*-prefix may be induced on the stem if it is not already an *a*- stem. The most common environment is preceding the negative enclitic *(y)axa·m* 'not':

taxu·m 'you have told me' (25:18-21) (*ta* 'me' + *x* 'you' + *u·m* 'tell (sg.)')

taxau·m axa·m 'you have not told me' (26:14-17) (*ta* + *x* + *a* 'induced prefix' + *u·m*)

apo·y 'he did' (85:2) (*a* 'he' + *p* 'subordinating prefix' + *(h)o·y* 'do (sg.)')

apaho·y axa·m 'he did not do' (84:24) (*a* + *p* + *a* 'induced prefix' + *ho·y*)

2.3. PERSON INFLECTION

Verbs are inflected for subject and object by personal prefixes, which distinguish three persons and two numbers, though not all distinctions are made in all combinations. Prefixes also differ according to tense and mood, syntactic status (dependent, or independent) of the clause, particular combinations of subject and object persons, different verb stems, and dialect.

Prefix Set 1. The prefixes used for the subject of intransitive verbs in present tense, main-clause statements are given in table 3. The first person prefix *n*- is used before vowels, for example, *nowxča·lak axa·m* 'I did not steal' (33:6); *na*- occurs elsewhere. The same is true for *x*- versus *xa*-.

The reason for the variation in *o*- and *u*- for third person is not known, but the alternation is found in several other morphemes (e.g., *-tu·*, *to·* 'relative'). There is a certain complementarity in their occurrence with respect to particular verb stems, but this is not enough to account for the difference. The *w*- is simply the consonantal variant found before *a*-stems, or before an induced (negative) *a*-. Compare *u-kʷa·ncam* (RG *w-a-xu·m*) 'it dies' (40:4-5); *o-hawa·y* 'he was made' (37:23-24), *w-a·-hawa·y axa·m* 'they did not make'. This same set of intransitive subject prefixes is used in transitive constructions when the object is third-person singular, since it is unmarked (is zero).

First-person plural is regularly *najo*- (RG *naye*-), but *naw*- or *nawe*- appears several times in the Pajalate *Cuadernillo* before *a*-stems. The postverbal plural element *čik* is found only a few times in the text, and in several uses, but one of these is to indicate the plural second-person subject. The second-person prefix *xa*- is also used alone, often with either a plural verb stem or other indicator of plurality elsewhere in the context. The third-person plural prefix *ox*- is used only rarely, and elsewhere the singular prefix *u-/w*- is used with some other indication of plurality.

Prefix Set 2. The prefix combinations used for subjects and objects of transitive verbs in present tense, main clause statements are given in table 4. The subject prefixes used with the third-person singular object, which is zero, are the same as the intransitive prefixes (Set 1). The third singular subject is also unmarked with a first-person object. The combination of first-person subject with either second-person object or third-person plural object is the same, *nak*-. Similarly, the combination for third-person singular or plural subject with second-person (singular or plural) object is the same as that for second-person singular subject with third-person plural object, *mak*-. The alternation *uk-/wak*- is not explainable, since it is not motivated by the same conditions that produce the *u-/wa*- variation. In one instance of a second-person plural object, the particle *cam* occurs following the stem (cf. the use of *čik* to mark second-person plural subject, section 2.4.).

The basic principles exhibited in these combinations are (1) that the first person takes precedence over second and third persons, whether it is subject (*nak*-) or object (*tax*-, *ta*-, *tak*-), and (2) that the distinction between second-person singular and third-person plural is neutralized in object function, producing ambiguous prefix complexes (*nak*-, *mak*-). Some prefixes of this set (*x-/xa*-, *tax*-) are also used in imperative constructions (see Prefix Set 7).

Prefix Set 3. Subjects or subjects and objects of intransitive or transitive verbs in past tense main clause questions are given in table 5.

Past tense truth value (yes/no) questions are usually marked by a verbal enclitic *-(y)a·m* plus the interrogative particle *e·*. Since, given the nature of the text, there

Table 3. Prefix Set 1: Present Tense Main Clause Statement Intransitive Subject Prefixes

Sg.	1	*n-/na-*
	2	*x-/xa-*
	3	*o-/u-/w-*
Pl.	1	*naxo-* (Rio Grande *naye-*)
		(Pajalate *naxo-/naw-*)
	2	*xa- . . . (cik)*
	3	*ox-, u-/w-*

Table 4. Prefix Set 2: Present/Past Main Clause Statement Transitive Subject-Object Prefixes

Obj. Subj.	Sg. 1	2	3	Pl. 1	2	3
Sg. 1	—	*nak-*	*na-*	—	*nak-...cam*	*nak-*
2	*tax-*	—	*xa-*	?	—	*mak-*
3	*ta-*	*mak-*	*u-/wa-*	*tak-*	*mak-*	*uk-/wak-*
Pl. 3	?	*mak-*	*ox-, u-/wa-*	?	?	?

NOTE: Unattested combinations are indicated by question marks.   *655*

Table 5. Prefix Set 3: Past Tense Main Clause Question Subject and Subject-Object Prefixes

Obj. Subj.	None or 3 sg.	Sg. 2	Pl. 3
2sg.	*mamay-,* *mamey-*	—	*mamik-*
3sg. or pl.	*mi-/* *miw-*	*mamik-*	?

are no first-person questions, and since many third-person questions employ a different structure, the number of prefix combinations in this set is quite limited. There is no determinable difference between the prefixes *mamay-* and *mamey-*, which are used interchangeably, with *mamay-* being twice as frequent as *mamey-*:

   mamayna·koyam e·? 'Have you thought?' (7:15) (*mamay* 'you' + *na·ko* 'think' + *(y)am* 'past' + *e·* 'Q')
   mame·yna·koyam e·? 'Have you thought?' (9:7)
The third-person prefix *miw-* is used before *a*-stems and in the Rio Grande dialect:
   miwaxu·mkalo· yam e·? (RG) 'Did he perhaps die?' (39:20-21) (*miw* 'he' + *a* 'a-prefix' + *xu·m* 'die' + *kalo·* 'dubitative' + *yam* 'past' + *e·* 'Q')
As with *mak-*, *mamik-* is used for both combinations of second- and third-person subject and object:
   mamikma·s am e·? 'Did they see you?' (21:7-8) (*ma·s* 'see')
   mamikčapko yam e·? 'Did you kill them?' (14:28-29) (*čapko* 'kill')
   Cf.: *makma·s* 'They saw you.' (24:1-2)
      makmo· 'You bewitched them.' (8:16-17)
Apart from the use of *mamik-* to mark third-person plural object, no distinction is made in this prefix set between singular and plural.

Prefix Set 4. Future-conditional prefixes are given in table 6. The prefixes in this set have two distinct environmental ranges: in main clauses with a following future particle *kam*; and in if-clauses or contexts rendered in Spanish by subjunctives. Again, the same prefixes are used where no object is present or where the object is third-person singular. In most of these prefixes an *-i-* is found, contrasting with an *-a-* or no vowel in other prefix sets.

The only occurrences of a first-person singular subject are before negated verbs with induced *a-*, so that *niw-*

Table 6. Prefix Set 4: Future-Conditional (Irrealis) Prefixes

Obj. Subj.		Ø or 3	1	2
Sg.	1	*niw-*	—	*nik-*
	2	*may-/mi-*	*ti-*	—
	3	*i-/iw-*	*tiw-*	*mik-*
Pl.	1	*naye/nayw-*	—	?
	2	?	*tami-*	—

might be the allomorph just used before the *a-* (with perhaps *ni-* used elsewhere). In the second-person prefixes, with a couple of exceptions, *mi-* is used before *a-*, and *may-* is used directly before zero-stems. Third-person *i-* is found before zero-stems, and *iw-* before *a-*. First-person plural prefix *naye-* is used before zero-stems and *nayw-* before *a-*. A second-person singular prefix *mati-* (not shown in table 6) occurs twice in the text, but no special meaning can be assigned to it.

Prefix Set 5. Prefixes used with transitive and intransitive verbs in subordinated constructions are given in table 7. In most subordinate constructions, including nominalizations, a prefix *p-* (or *pa-*, if sequence conditions require it) occurs between the personal prefixes and the verb. Almost all the prefixes given in table 7 are also found in other contexts, but they form a set in that only these may be used before *p-/pa-*; compare *u-kʷaka·ncam* 'they died' and *a-pa-kʷaka·ncam* '(when) they died'. Since the line between subordinated verb constructions and nominalizations is very thin (cf. English *painting* in *He fell while painting the house* and *I admired his painting of the house*), it is not surprising that the same prefixes (the intransitive series) should be used both with subordinated verbs and with nouns.

It is not always clear what conditions govern the use of *p-/pa-*, since parallel sentences in Spanish may be translated by different constructions, some of which seem to require *p-/pa-* and hence these personal prefixes, while other constructions may or may not contain the subordinating prefix, and if they do not, may (or in some instances, as with third-person intransitive subject, must) use other prefixes, for example,

   nakaxʷa·kam taxta·wex sanino· (53:10-16)
   nakaxʷa·kam taxpata·wex san pa·n (55:2-8)
both translating 'I ask you, that you help me' (*na* 'I' + *k* 'you' + *a* 'induced prefix' + *xwa·kam* 'ask'; *ta* 'me' + *x* 'you' + *ta·wex* 'help'; *san* 'subordinate future particle' + *ino·* 'first person auxiliary' or *pa·* 'relator' + *n* 'first person'). Similarly,

   nakʷa·m, taxkʷa·cum sanaxo·mino· (67:10-17)
   nakʷa·m, ta·xpakʷa·cum san pa·n (51:1-11)
translate 'I hope that you will pardon me' (*na* 'I' +

Table 7. Prefix Set 5: Subordinate Clause Subject and Subject-Object Prefixes

Obj. Subj.		Ø or 3	1	2	3-Pl.
Sg.	1	*n-/na-*	—	*nak-*	?
	2	*x-/xa-*	*tax-*	—	?
	3	*a-; am-*	*ta-*	*mak-*	*ak-; uk-/wak-*
Pl.	1	*naxo-/naye-* (Rio Grande)	—	?	?
	2	?	?	—	?
	3	*ax-*	*tak-*	?	?

NOTE: Also used with deverbal forms.

$k^wa\cdot m$ 'hope'; ta 'me' + x 'you' + $k^wa\cdot cum$ 'pardon'; *san* 'future particle' + *axo·* 'second-person auxiliary' + *mino·* 'conjunction' or *pa·* 'relator' + *n* 'first person'; *san* is a future particle used in subordinated constructions, corresponding in part to *kam* in main clauses). Compare also:

> *naye·hawa·y kam* 'We will do' (44:12) (*naye·* 'we' + *ha-wa·-y* 'do-plural'; *kam* 'future')
>
> *na·xopa·hawa·y axa·m san tan* 'that we will not do' (43:21-22) (*na·xo* 'we' + *pa·* 'subordinating prefix' + *ha-wa·-y* 'do-plural'; *axa·m* 'not'; *san* 'future particle'; *ta* 'relator' (possible error for *pa*) + *n* 'first person').

Although *san pan* and related forms (*san pam, san ma·*) found in subordinate clauses always require *p-/pa-* on the subordinated verb, the prefix occurs only sporadically with *san po·*, which in addition to its use in subordinate clauses, is used in main clauses instead of *kam* to express the third-person future.

The *p-/pa-* prefix is required in past tense statements ending in *po·m*, despite the fact that these are usually in main clauses; *po·m* is used only after verbs with third-person subjects, always marked by subordinate-possessive third-person prefix *a-*: *Dios tupo· tawaxayo k^we·x apo·y po·m* 'God made everything'. (35:1-2) ('God demonstrative all locative + 3d-person-suffix 3d-person-prefix + p + do/make auxiliary')

The third-person singular prefix *am-* occurs several times in the text, but no distinction in meaning or usage between it and *a-* can be found.

There is also some indication in the text of a distinction between third-person plural object prefixes used in future and nonfuture contexts, though the difference could also be attributed to the auxiliaries used.

> *wa[k]-čo·-no·* 'that he carried them' (64:15)
> *ak-čo· san po·* 'that he will carry them' (66:7)
> *uk-a·ko·x̣iam-ino·* 'that he throws them' (65:3)
> *ak-pa-hako·x̣iam san po·* 'that he will throw them' (66:11)

The last two examples are also found on 39:8-9 and 39:14-15. A similar distinction is given in 41:9-13, though with different auxiliaries or other postverbal elements:

> *ioaxa·m tuk^we·x uka·ko·x̣iam ate·, tamo·x tuče· pitupa·moyo· akpaie·xkamko· sa·l . . . santupa·yok^we·x.* 'To the Inferno He throws them, so that . . . the Demons will always be burning them.' (hell the + in + 3d he + them + throws-pl. postverb, Devil the + plural + subject always they + them + burn will . . . so-that.)

Prefix Set 6. There is a poorly attested set of prefixes that may be reflexive in significance (see table 8).

The interpretation of these prefixes is somewhat uncertain. The first two are found in García only five times altogether: *xi-* occurs only twice, both times with the stem *-ka·wa*, which in other constructions means 'to want' or 'to love' (parallel to Spanish *querer*); the first-

Table 8. Prefix Set 6: Reflexive Prefixes

Sg.	1	*ni-*
	2	*xi-*
	3	*wi-* (Pajalate)
Pl.	1	*naxoy-* (Pajalate) (= *nax^wi-* ?)
	2	*mi-* (Pajalate)
	3	*wi-* (Pajalate)

person prefix is used once in the same construction, and twice with a verb meaning 'to hold'.

> *cin nika·wa sa·wx pam* 'I am very content.' (54:28)
> *xika·wa sa·wx* 'Be happy!' (53:3, 63:3-4)

A complete set of person prefixes is found on page 6 of the *Cuadernillo* (Del Hoyo (1965:32) with the verb 'wet oneself' (Spanish *mojarse*), *-xamašax^w*. The occurrence of *šax^w* presumably corresponds to *sa·wx* (or *sa·x^w*) in García, which is probably a reflexive auxiliary (see 2.4.).

Prefix Set 7. In imperative constructions, the second-person prefix *x-/xa-* is frequently used, either alone or together with the first-person object, as *tax-*. A special imperative prefix, *max-*, is also sometimes used, though García indicates that it may vary dialectally with simple *xa-*. In the last example, *ta-* may also be used preceding *max-*. No distinction is made between singular and plural.

> *x-otakcin* 'Walk with care!' (28:3)
> *Yo Pecador xa-mesti·a* 'Pray the Yo Pecador!' (1:3)
> *tax-ta·wex* 'Help me!' (72:16)
> *max-ma·s* 'Look!' (RG: *xa-ma·s*) (46:1)
> *max-na·kako·* 'Think!' (56:4)
> *tamax-čo·x* 'Bring it to me!' (8:29, 9:1)

Some indication of the uses of different prefixes with a single stem may be gained from table 9, which presents a partial paradigm of *-k^wa·ncam* 'to die', a zero-stem, and the corresponding Rio Grande dialect term *-xu·m*, an *a*-stem. Except where indicated, all forms are third person.

2.4. VERB PHRASES

Postverbal elements, or verb phrase constituents, serve a variety of functions, some of which have already been mentioned, such as the plural *čik*, the negative *(y)axa·m*, and the future *kam*. Most are written by García as separate words, but some, like *(y)axa·m*, show evidence of phonological (and occasional graphic) encliticization to preceding elements. By relative-order analysis, eight positions following the verb can be established. However, it is rare to find more than three filled at one time, and the full possibility is never realized. The positions are numbered outward from the verb (table 10). Position 1:

> *wako·* causative or transitivizer; *-xo·* 'to know'; *-xo· wako·* 'to teach'.
> *sa·wx^w* meaning uncertain, perhaps completive or

Table 9. Intransitive Verb Subject Prefixes, Partial Paradigm

	San Antonio dialect (Ø-stem)	Rio Grande dialect (a-stem)	
Main Clause:			
Statement:			
Present:	*uk"a·ncam*	*waxu·m*	'he dies', 'is dying'
Past (pos.):	*apk"a·ncam pom*	*apaxu·m pom*	'he died'
(neg.):	*apak"a·ncam awa·m pom*	*apaxu·m axa·m pom*	'he did not die'
Question:			
Yes/no (past):	*mik"a·ncam e·*	*miwaxu·m e·*	'did he die?'
Information:	*uk"a·ncam e·*	*waxu·m e·*	'(how) did he die?'
Dependent Clause:			
1)	*napak"a·ncam*	*napaxu·m*	'(that) I die'
2)	*xapak"a·ncam*	*xapaxu·m*	'(that) you die'
3)	*apak"a·ncam*	*apaxu·m*	'(that) he dies'
Conditional:			
1)	*niwak"a·ncam axa·m* (neg.)	*niwaxu·m axa·m*	'(if) I do not die'
2)	*mayk"a·ncam*	*miaxu·m*	'(if) you die'
3)	*ik"a·ncam*	*iwaxu·m*	'(if) he dies'

Table 10. Post-Verbal Elements: Relative Order

1	2	3	4	5	6	7	8
wak·	*čik*	*atapa·mo·*	*(y)axa·m*	*kalo·*	*(y)am*	(various auxiliaries:	*e·*
sa·wx"	*cam*				*pom*	*(i)no·*	
sal	*pam*				*kam*	*(a)xo·*	
wa·x	*cax in*				*san*		
ex	*canam (in)*						
k̓awx(?)	*(h)in*						

reflexive; *-ma·o sawx* 'ascend'; *-k̓mako·x sawx* 'to kneel'.

sal perhaps durative or imperfective marker; *cin pitupa·moyo· na·kpaka·wa sal santupa·yo·* 'so that I may always be loving you' (69:17-19).

wa·x pretensive; *mamayaxpi·w wa·x čik am e·?* 'Have you pretended to copulate?' (23:11-12)

ex meaning undetermined.

k̓awx 'bad'; as discussed earlier, this may properly be part of the verb stem (or theme), as in *-a·m k̓awx* 'injure'; *-ča·la·wx k̓awx* 'miscarry'.

Position 2:

čik second-person plural subject indicator in some contexts; also occurs with *-xpi·w* 'copulate repeatedly' and *-paxti·* 'companion'.

cam second-person plural object indicator in some contexts.

pam intensifier; *cin nika·wa sa·wx pam* 'I am very glad' (54:28).

cax in iterative, reversive; *-ma·lku·yta cax in* 'confess again'.

cana·m (in) reversive; *-tpa·yam cana·m in* 'return to life'; *-a·x cana·m* 'give back'. *(h)in* may also occur separately.

(h)in 'also', 'again'; *xaspa·mo hin e·?* 'Do you

believe also?'; *niwaho·y in axa·m ka·m* 'I will not do it again'.

Position 3:

(a)ta·pamo· desiderative; the *a-* occurs following a consonant. *xak̓a·w ata·pamo· e·?* 'Do you wish to marry?'

Position 4:

(y)axa·m negative; the *y-* occurs following a vowel.

Position 5:

k(a)lo· dubitative; the *-a-* is sometimes dropped when *kalo·* follows a stem or other element ending in a vowel. *ap[?]u·m kalo· sanpo·* 'perhaps he will tell'; *mana·m maysa· klo* 'if you become well'.

Position 6 (Tense)

(y)am past tense marker used only in main clause questions (primarily truth-value questions), almost always followed by interrogative particle *e·*; the *y-* occurs following a vowel.

pom past tense marker used only in main clause statements with third-person subjects; always requires subordinating prefix *p-/pa-*.

kam future particle used in main clause statements and questions.

san future particle used in subordinated constructions, including main clauses ending in an auxiliary.

658

Position 7:

> *(i)no·, (a)xo·,* etc. various auxiliaries built on a copulative stem -*o·* with personal prefixes (*in-* in first person, *ax-* second person); compare the similar structure of conjunctions. In certain constructions or with certain persons, the auxiliary may be used and the main verb (of the Spanish sentence) cast in a subordinated form.

Position 8:

> *e·* interrogative particle, normally occurring at the end of a question.

Additional elements:

The following postverbal elements cannot be fitted into the positional structure outlined above, either because they occur too infrequently or not in combination with other elements.

> *čon, čo* This may represent a secondary verb stem (compare -*čo·* 'carry') used to indicate translocative action, that is, motion away. Altogether they are found only three times in the text: *nakpama·s čo* 'I go to see you'.

> *(a)te·* The *a-* occurs following a consonant. No consistent meaning can be assigned to this element, though it probably has some aspectual or tense significance: *mama·yma·s ate· e·* 'Did you observe (the Mass)?'

3. NOUNS

Nouns, like verbs, may be pluralized by the use of infixes (in fact, by the same ones), though plurality is usually shown instead by the form of the demonstrative following the noun. Nouns for which plural forms are recorded are given below:

> *pa·m* 'son, child'   *ap-ak-am* 'children'
> *ta·y* 'mother'   *t-aw-a·y* 'mother' (of several)
> *pin* 'thing'   *pinwak* 'things'

A plural form of the subordinating prefix, *pi*, is used with some forms:

> *na·xo-pi·-tawa·y* 'our mother' (87:5)
> *naxo-pi-ma·ma* 'out father' (46:1-2)
> *pilta a-pi-k̓a·w* 'married ones' (16:6).

pi is also used in a regular subordinated verb construction: *mak-pi-ka·wa* '(as) they love you' (68:23).

Some nouns in the Spanish text are rendered directly by subordinated verb forms, for example, *apia·ɬ* 'sorrow' (pl. *apaɬaka·ɬ* 'sorrows'); *xapaka·wa sa·wx* 'your desire' (*sa·wx* 'reflexive'); *napatpa·yam sa·wx* 'my soul' (RG) (*tpa·yam* 'live'); *xapak̫a·xo* 'you are a shaman'.

At times an entire subordinated verbal phrase is used to translate a Spanish noun:

> *napaxa·m apsa·* 'my soul' (*xa·m* 'remember'; *sa·* 'be, exist')

> *saxpa·m pinapsa· nami·* 'my sin' (*saxpa·m* 'bad', *pin* 'thing')

> *pin napsak̓a·wx* 'my sin' (RG) (*k̓a·wx* 'bad')

3.1. INFLECTION

Nouns in Coahuilteco, as in many other American Indian languages, may be classified into inalienably possessed and alienably possessed. The former always occur with possessive (genitive) prefixes, while the latter may take these prefixes or may occur as uninflected free forms. However, the distinction is not certain, since it necessarily depends on the accidents of textual occurrence: there is no way to test whether a form could occur other than as it appears in the text. The possessive prefixes are used also with nominalized verb forms, which are marked by the subordinating prefix *p-/pa-*. The possessive prefixes are shown in table 11.

Inalienably possessed nouns include -*k̓a·w* 'husband', -*ha·wh* 'meat, body', -*paxti* 'companion', -*k̫a·w* 'womb', -*ha·c* 'blood' (RG -*k̫as*), -*(a)xasa·l* 'heart', -*co·c* 'chest', -*ta·m* 'breast', and various kinship terms. These follow the usual categories of body-part and kinship terms. Alienably possessed (for the most part totally uninflected) nouns include *a·nwa* (or *a·nua*) 'moon', *kuta·ce* 'priest', *paxe·* 'peyote', *txe·* 'dance', *atu·lam* 'year', and *taklaxpo·* 'owl'.

Some Coahuilteco nouns admit both affixal and periphrastic inflection, but it is not determinable whether this possibility extends to all possessed nouns, or is restricted to only a few. One word for 'father', *ma·ma*, occurs both with prefixes (23 times) and with independent possessive pronouns (21 times):

> *xama·ma* 'your father' (77:10)
> *ma·ma nami·* 'my father' (53:26).

Compare the following two lines from the same paragraph (67:6-7):

> *xami·n Dios nami· axo·mexo·* 'because you are my God' (you God my are+because)

> *xami·n naka·xana·y axo·mexo·* 'because you are my father'. (The prefix *nak-*, if correct, seems to imply a second person object relationship, i.e., I+you+father.)

As has been noted, possessive prefixes are used in nominalized verb constructions:

> *xamalku·yta xo· e·?* 'Have you confessed?' (9:15) (you+confess 2d-aux. Q)

> *xapama·lku·yta tuči·yo* 'in your confessions' (5:1-2) (your+*pa*+confess this+pl.+by).

In addition, noun stems are sometimes used with verbal inflections, even in contexts that translate

Table 11. Possessive Noun Prefixes

Sg.	1	*n-/na-*
	2	*x-/xa-*
	3	*a-*
Pl.	1	*naxo-*
	2	*x-/xa-*
	3	*ax-*

as nouns in Spanish (cf. *naka·xana·y* above), indicating that the line between noun and verb in Coahuilteco is not altogether sharply defined. Notable is the verbal inflection attached to the Spanish (perhaps via Nahuatl) loanward *timi·ko* (Sp. *Domingo*) 'Sunday' (see Troike 1961): *Apatimi·ko . . . tuče·m* '(On) Sundays' (10:1-3) (3d-person prefix+subordinating prefix+Sunday . . . this+pl.+2d-person suffix). Other examples follow.

> *xak*ʷ*a·n po e·?* 'Is he your mother's father?' (77:17) (your+mother's.father is Q)
>
> *xapak*ʷ*a·n wako· po e·?* 'Is he your wife's father?' (79:13) (you+*pa*+mother's.father causative is Q)
>
> *xapa·m* 'your son' (70:18) (your+child/son)
>
> *maka·pakam* 'your children' (12:10) (you-them/they-you+child-pl.)
>
> *ta·y nami·* 'my mother' (72:21) (mother my(= I+ have)); used vocatively
>
> *xami·n nakpata·y ano·* 'you are my mother' (72:14-15) (you I+you+*pa*+mother auxiliary; the *-k-* should perhaps be *-x-*; see discussion below, but also cf. *naka·xana·y* above)
>
> *na·xopi·tawa·y* 'our mother' (87:5) (our+*pi*+mother-pl.; *pi* is plural of *pa*)
>
> *ma·ma nami·* 'my father' (53:26) (father my)
>
> *napama·ma* 'my father' (54:1-2) (I/my+*pa*+father)

In at least one instance, assuming the form is correct, there is probable evidence of a possessive noun prefix preceding a verbal subject prefix: *na-x-paxti· čik san pa·n* 'be my companion' (72:16), in which the first person *na-* precedes the imperative prefix *x-*. (Since both *na-* and *x-* may be subject prefixes, however, alternative analyses are possible.)

3.2. DERIVATION

There are no regular derivational processes operative in Coahuilteco whereby one part of speech is systematically derived from another. A few stems, such as *k̓a·w* 'husband/to marry', *pi·lam* 'to live/people', and *ta·yawu·* 'wife/to marry' are used both nominally and verbally, but this is rare. The usual pattern is to use subordinated verb stems in noun positions:

> *maytxam kam* 'you will inhabit' (18:12) (you+dwell future)
>
> *xapatxam* 'your house' (17:8) (your+*pa*+dwell).

However, there are a small number of stems that show similarities suggesting possible derivational relationships, though no regularities can be found. In some instances, similarities may be no more than fortuitous.

*k̓*ʷ*a·x* 'womb'	*paxti·* 'companion'
*k̓*ʷ*a·na* 'be born'	*axte·* 'two'
pi·lam 'people/to live'	*ło·axa·m* 'hell'
pi· 'have sexual intercourse'	*ło·cam* 'descend'

awaya·m 'bird'   *mantpa·m* 'truth'
awa·yo 'cry'   *mana·m* 'well'

In several instances, a combination of a subordinated third-person verb form with an element *pil* (probably the same as *pil* 'one, something') translates an abstract noun in Spanish:

> *pilapa·mesti·a* 'doctrine' (*mesti·a* 'pray')
>
> *pila·paxle·* 'words' (*xle·* 'speak')
>
> *(pin) pilapši·p̓* 'a lie' (also *piłapši·p̓*) (cf. *pilta apik̓a·w* 'married ones'; *k̓a·w* 'marry').

3.3. PRONOUNS

Independent personal pronouns in Coahuilteco are, with one exception, built on the verbal stem *-ami·* 'to have'. The exception is the first-person form *cin* 'I'. There are only two series, the possessive and the subjective. The possessive series is formed by adding a possessive prefix to the stem; the subjective forms appear to be derived from the possessive by the addition of a suffix *-n*. Attested forms are shown in table 12. It should be noted that two different plural forms of the stem are used for the first- and second-person plural pronouns.

3.4. NOUN MODIFIERS

Noun modifiers or adjectives do not constitute a formal morphological class in Coahuilteco, but it is useful to group together for discussion those elements that may be said to modify nouns.

A number of these are subordinated verb forms with a third-person prefix *a-*. Although presumably the stems might also occur as predicates in main clauses, in fact they rarely do. Some examples follow:

> *apna·n* 'great'
>
> *apxo·hoimo·* 'together'
>
> *(pi·lam) wa·n ta· apexa·ma* 'Christian (people)' ([people] water that 3d.pers.+*pi*+wet ?)
>
> *apa·xw* 'many' (RG *oxa·wx*)
>
> *apša·yš* (pl. *apšaka·yš*) 'bad'
>
> *apšap̓a·n* (pl. *apšap̓a·kan*) 'good'
>
> *apca·y* 'old'
>
> *app̓a·nman* (pl. *app̓a·kenmam*) 'past'.

Four of the foregoing are used predicatively: *xa·xoxako·imo čik sanino·* 'that you-all combine (all of your sins)' (85:12-13), *waxa·wx*ʷ*axa·m* 'they are not many' (34:5), *ła·xat a·nua apči·ka mip̓a·kenmam e·?* 'How many moons have passed?' (13:23-24), *Dios*

Table 12. Independent Personal Pronouns

		Possessive	Subjective
Sg.	1	*nami·*	*cin*; *če·n, če·n* (Pajalate)
	2	*xami·*	*xami·n*; *xamen* (Pajalate)
	3	*ami·*	*tupo* (Pajalate, demonstrative)
Pl.	1	*na·xoama·ca*	*cakan* (Pajalate)
	2	?	*xama·kan*; *mamakon* (Pajalate)
	3	?	?

tupo·m apša·p̓a·n pam po·mino·m 'because God is very good' (30:5-6). In this last example, the subordinating prefix is used because of the following copulative element *po·*. (The *-m* on *tupo·m* is presumably an error.)

In addition, there are a small number of uninflected forms that are used as noun modifiers: *šan* 'little' (child), *ata* 'every', *axco·* 'other', *oxči·xu* 'few'; however, the last might be analyzed as containing a third-person plural prefix, *ox-*.

A few descriptive stems are found in predicative use that do not occur in noun phrases, such as *ca·* 'ill': *mameya·ca·kaloyam e·?* 'Were you perhaps ill?' (10:11). This, together with the examples above, serves to illustrate the fact that, as in many languages, adjectives in Coahuilteco are fundamentally a type of verb.

The intensifier *pam*, discussed earlier as part of the verb phrase, is also frequently used in noun modifier constructions, following the modifier (which is a subordinated verbal form):

talo·m apna·n pam '(the) very great fire' (28:28)
apa·wx pam 'very much' (33:11).

3.5. DEMONSTRATIVE-RELATORS

Demonstrative-relators constitute unquestionably the most distinctive aspect of Coahuilteco grammar, playing a major role in the apparently unique Coahuilteco system of subject-object concord (Troike 1981). They occur at the ends of noun phrases and serve to signal matters such as the function of the noun phrase in the sentence (subject or object), relative proximity, plurality, and location (cf. English demonstratives and related forms such as *this-that*, *that-those*, *here-there*), and the human or nonhuman gender of the noun with which they occur (cf. English *who* versus *which*).

The internal structure of demonstrative-relators is complex, consisting basically of a stative or copulative verbal stem, a deictic prefix, and a personal suffix showing agreement with the subject of the verb. Certain other poststem elements may occur, including a second stem. Both the prefix and the stem appear to be at least to some extent optional. A chart of all possible elements, showing their relative order, is given in table 13. The stems may also be used alone as copulas, or they may be used with intransitive verb prefixes in a copulative function.

The use of the same forms as demonstrative stems and as copulas may perhaps be understood in terms of the proposal that noun phrases represent the underlying predicates of embedded copular or existential sentences (i.e., a phrase such as *the man* may represent an underlying predication 'There is one who is a man').

García, in a grammatical note (pp. 33-34), gives a series of examples contrasting *če·* as a plural nonhuman copula and *pa·* as a plural human copula (33:21-22):

apa·wx če· 'They are many' (*a* 'third person' + *p* 'subordinator' + *a·wx* 'many'; *če·* 'be')
apa·wx pa· 'They are many (people)'.

As Swanton (1940:49) has observed, García is inconsistent in his use of these stems. Both, for example, are used with *pi·lam* 'people':

pi·lam wa·n ta· apexa·ma ače·x (42:3-4) (people Christian the)
pi·lam wa·n ta· apexa·ma tupa·t (42:10-11) (people Christian the).

Most forms used with *če·* (which has a bound allomorph *či·-* used before *-yo* or *če·*) are nonhuman, but a few human terms occur, including 'man', 'woman', and 'priest'. In addition, *paxe·* 'peyote', *ahe·wh* 'meat', and *sami·n* 'mescal bean' are apparently singular, although they may be used in a collective sense. García's use of *pa·* is at greater variance from his

Table 13. Demonstrative-Relator Structure

1 Deictic-2	2 Deictic-1	3 Stem-1	4	5	6	7 Stem-2	8 Suffix
	a- 'proximate'	*po·* 'human (sg.)'	*-ha-* 'as'	*-mo-* 'only'	*-yo-* 'with, by'	*po·*	*-Ø* 'subj.'
pi- 'emphatic distance'	*tu-, to* 'neutral'	*pa·* 'human (pl.)'	*-xa-* (?)	*-ka-* 'interrogative'		*pa·*	*-n* '1st obj.'
	ta- 'distant'	*če·, či·-* 'nonhuman (pl.)'				*če·, či·-*	*-m* '2d obj.'
		kʷe·, kʷi·-, *kʷa-* 'locative'				*kʷe·*	*-t* '3d obj.'
							-x '3d obj.'
ani- (Rio Grande *anu-*) 'interrogative'							*-yo* 'instrumental' (with, by)

statement, as the majority of forms used with one combination, *tupa·*, are singular, and a few are nonhuman ('thing', 'Mass', 'sin').

Singular human noun phrases are indicated by *po·*, which also occurs after 'people' and 'church'. It is also frequently used alone as a copula.

The stem *kʷe·* (with allomorphs *kʷi·*- before *-yo* or itself and *kʷa*- before *-ha*- or *-xa*-) has a locative significance, either of place or time:

Cruz tukʷe·t 'on the Cross'

tap pa akʷe· apaxa·y tukʷe·t 'when this world ends' (world this it-ends when).

Here *akʷe·* renders 'this' since earth is a location, and *tukʷe·t* renders 'on the' following the noun but 'when' following the verb, that is, it may serve as either a noun phrase relator (combining the functions of article and preposition) or clause relator (as a relative adverbial conjunction equivalent to 'at the time that').

The deictic prefixes distinguish four degrees of distance, with *a*- indicating proximity, *tu*- evidently a neutral distance (with an allomorph *to* when no stem follows it), *ta*- a definite distance, and *pi*- prefixed before either *tu*- or *ta*-, an emphatic distance. (These may perhaps be compared to Spanish *aquí, acá, allí, allá*, though they are probably more like English *this, the, that, that yonder*). The interrogative prefix *ani*- (RG *anu*-) yields forms such as *anikʷe·t* 'from where?' and *anipo·ka·* 'which (person)?'

The element *-ha*- following the stem generally corresponds to the conjunction *como* 'as' in Spanish, but at other times its significance is not clear. It is perhaps related to, or at least at times confused with, the element *-xa*-, which frequently occurs in question words and such combinations as *tukʷaxa·m* 'when'. The element *-mo(-)* has the significance 'only', as in *aha·wx tupamo·* 'the body only' (40:2); it is also apparently found in *xa·nmo·* 'alone'. The morpheme *-ka*- evidently has an interrogative significance, as it is widely used in question words, such as *ɫaxaka·t* 'why?'

The morpheme *-yo*, which can occur either preceding or following the second stem position (as well as directly following a noun) has a comitative or instrumental significance, for example, *ta·wu pitapo·yo·* 'with that woman', *santupa·yo* 'in order that'. At times, the combination of various morphemes may produce an idiosyncratic result, as in *pitupa·moyo·(kʷe·x)* 'always', which is used as an independent adverbial, or *pitupa·yokʷe·n* 'for that reason'.

In most instances, the second stem is a reduplication of the first, as in *akʷi·kʷe·x* 'here in this (world)', *tupa·hamopa·n* 'as', but other stems may occur as in *tupa·yokʷe·* 'with all'. However, it is not at all clear how constructions containing a second stem differ from those containing only a first stem, since García uses them in what otherwise seem parallel contexts.

The personal suffixes occurring on the end of

demonstratives are of considerable syntactic importance (the instrumental suffix *-yo* is mutually exclusive with the personal suffixes in this position). If no suffix is used, the noun phrase involved is the subject of the verb. If the noun phrase is an object of the verb, either oblique or direct, the demonstrative carries a personal suffix corresponding to the subject of the verb: *-n* first person; *-m* second person; *-t* or *-x* third person.

Dios tupo· makpakʷa·cum 'God may pardon you' (6:20-21)

Dios tupo·n naxoxɫe·wal wako· 'We annoyed God' (43:16-17)

Dios tupo·m xaka·wa xo e·? 'Do you love God' (7:1-3)

Dios tupo·t apak̓tace·y '(all) pray to God' (63:28-29)

In several instances the person agreement on the demonstrative disambiguates an otherwise ambiguous verbal prefix:

ɫa·xat apsaka· makma·s e·? 'How many saw you?' (24:1-2)

ɫa·xat apsaka·m makmo· e·? 'How many did you bewitch?' (8:16-17)

xawu· piɫ ɫan xata·m tače·t mamikk̓ay am e·? 'Has some man touched your breasts?' (22:14-16) (man one some your+breast those he-you+touch past Q)

pin penitenciaka·t, kuta·ce tupo· mamik[ʔ]ax e·? 'What penitence did the priest give you? (2:23-25) (thing penitence-what, priest the he-you + give Q)

kuta·ce tuče·m, mami·kaxa·maya· sawxʷam e·? 'Have you made fun of the priests?' (12:1-3) (priest the+pl. you-them+made.fun.of reflexive + past Q).

Both *-t* and *-x* are used to mark the objects of third-person subject verbs, and though there is a strong tendency (75 percent) for *-x* to occur preceding *u-/o-/wa*- and for *-t* to occur elsewhere, there is enough variation to suggest either that García himself was not entirely sure of the distinction, or that he was not always consistent in maintaining it. It is further possible that some dialect differences may have been involved.

In some constructions, the particle *ma·* (or *ma*) is used instead of a demonstrative to mark the object of a second-person subject verb, and *ta·* to mark the object of a third-person subject verb.

pin apšaka·yš ma·, mamikka· kalo· yam e·? 'Have you said bad things?' (11:22-24) (thing bad object.of.2d,you-them+say perhaps past Q)

pinwak apšaka·yš ta·, apa·lace· 'They say bad things' (13:1-3) (thing+pl. bad object.of.3d they+say-pl.)

3.6. NOUN PHRASES

The noun phrase (NP) in Coahuilteco has roughly the reverse structure of that in English: the head noun generally occurs first, followed by any modifiers, while the demonstrative is the last element in the construction and forms an immediate constituent with the noun. This may be summarized as follows:

NP = Noun + (Modifiers) + Demonstrative

An example is:

pi·lam apšapa·n tupa·t 'good people' (66:4-5) (people good the).

The only common exception to this order is *tawaxa·yo* 'all', which usually precedes the noun (cf. the position of *all* in English outside the rest of the noun phrase).

tawaxa·yo pi·lam wa·n ta· apexa·ma tupa·t 'all Christian people' (42:10-11) (all people Christian the)

As noted previously, possessive (genitive) pronouns also follow the noun they modify:

saxpa·m pinapsa· xami· tuče·m 'your sins' (3:7-9) (sin [=bad thing+3d+p+is] your the-pl.)

A possessive (or genitive) relation between two nouns is indicated by juxtaposing them without any special morphological marking:

Missa Hostia 'the Host of the Mass' (42:21-22)

Dios ata·y 'Mother of God' (37:21)

pi·lam apšapa·n, apaxa·m apsa· 'souls of the good people' (38:17-18) (people good, souls [= they + *pa* + remember they + *p* + are])

Relative clauses, like the single-word noun modifiers that may be derived from them, generally follow the noun they modify. There is no separate relative pronoun.

pi·nwakta·, kuta·ce tupo· makpata·nko tuče·m '(Did you do) the things the priest commanded you?' (2:18-21) (thing+pl.+object.of.3d, priest the+sg.+subject he-you+*pa*+command the+pl.+object.of.2d)

tawaxa·yo pi·lam makpaxie·wal wako· tuče·m '(You must pardon) all the people who angered you' (50:17-18) (all people they-you+*pa*+anger causative the+pl.+object.of.2d)

api̇aka·l, Jesu-Christo tupo· apak^wa·xa·y tuče·n '(I give you) the pains Jesus Christ suffered' (54:4-5) (3d+*p*+pain-pl., Jesus-Christ the+sg.+subjective he-*pa*-suffer the+pl.+obj.of.1st)

4. CONJUNCTIONS

Conjunctions in Coahuilteco are of two types. The unmodifiable particle *ko* 'and' is regularly used for joining noun phrases. It is frequently used for joining clauses as well, though other forms are also employed for that purpose, for example,

xu·yopama·wx axte·, ko pi̇l '11' (10 and 1).

Besides *ko*, Coahuilteco has a number of morphologically complex conjunctions built on the stems *ma-*, *me-*, and *mi-*. Inasmuch as the differences in these are not clear, they can only be listed for the present. Some forms, as will be noted, are distinguished by the occurrence of the personal suffixes *-n*, *-m*, *-x* on them, since they usually occur at the end of a clause and are marked to agree with the subject of the governing verb.

mak 'or'
mat 'and'
matpo·, matxo· 'but'
mex, mem, men 'and'
mexo·, mexta· 'and'
mi, mipo· 'and'
mim, min 'so'
mitxo· 'because'
mino· 'because'
mino·m, mino·x, mino·n 'and, so'

Examples are:

me·xta· Personas axtikpi·l̇ tupa· 'and the three Persons' (are one God);

mino·x poxoyok^we·x Virgen pax uha·wx 'and thus she is called Virgin';

mat, kuta·ce apna·n pa·m Sumo Pontifice pa apo· 'And, the very big Supreme Pontiff' (always commands all the Christian people well);

mem xapakomulga·r 'and (so that) you have communion'.

5. INTERROGATIVES

Interrogatives in Coahuilteco, as in most languages, are of two types. Truth-value questions—those that may be answered by 'yes' or 'no'—are marked by the interrogative particle *e·*, which is usually placed at the end of the sentence. Information questions—those in English asked by words such as *what, who, where*—are formed by a number of morphologically complex words or combinations distinguished primarily by the fact that they contain the morpheme *-ka*.

anipo·ka· 'which?'
anik^we·kat 'in where?'
i̇a·xaka·t 'why?'
pi̇lka 'who?'
i̇a·xat apči·ka 'how many?'
i̇a·xat apči·yoka 'how many times?'
i̇a·xat apsaka 'how many (people, things)?'
pin penitenciaka·t 'what penitence?'

6. SENTENCE STRUCTURE AND TYPOLOGY

The basic order of constituents in the Coahuilteco sentence is subject-object-verb (SOV):

cin Anillo apa·n naka·x 'I give you the ring' (87:1-2) (I ring this+first I-you+give)

Dios tupo· xa·papi·lam sa·wx tapa·t maktalo· sanpo· 'God will take away your life' (19:15-17) (God the you+*pa*+live reflexive the+third he-you+take future+3d-aux.)

The order is occasionally varied, usually for particular reasons, but in general the SOV order is consistently maintained. Given the considerable differences between Spanish and Coahuilteco syntax, there is perhaps no more impressive evidence of García's care in translation and his control of the language than the fact that there is little evidence of Spanish influence in the word order in the Coahuilteco text.

One reason for a variation in order is illustrated in an example cited earlier:

pin penitenciaka·t, kuta·ce tupo· mamik[ʔ]ax e·?
'What penitence did the priest give you?' (2:23-25)

As in English, a sentence constituent that is the focus of a question is often moved to the beginning of the sentence. In this example, perhaps because of the order-shift, García set the constituent off with a comma, which might indicate that there was an intonational break at that point.

When the object of a sentence is a long clause, it may either precede or follow the verb. Whether the object occurs to the left or the right appears to depend on the main clause verb itself. With *ka·wa* 'want, love', *xa·mcam* 'desire', *xa·tam* 'be unable', and *na·ko* 'think', the clause precedes; with other verbs (including *kʷa·m* 'hope', *xo·* 'know', *spa·mo* 'believe', *ta·nko* 'order', *tu·m* 'promise', *u·m* 'tell, advise'), the clause follows:

pa·ya·makʷe·t xapa·mi sanpa·m xaka·wa e·? 'Do you wish that he now be yours?' (86:9-10) (now+this you-(him)+pa+have future+copula+object.of.2d you+want Q)

ma·mayxo· kloya·m, na·mo ata·yawu· mikʷa·ncam ma e·? 'Do you know if his wife already died?' (83:18-20) (you+know perhaps+past, now his+wife she+die object.of.2d Q)

In general, with the second group of verbs, the object clause is much longer, so that the shift of the clause to follow the verb is perhaps largely a device to avoid front-heaviness in the sentence. However, it may also have served to reduce the potential cognitive processing problems created by center-embedding or 'nesting' of relative clauses, since Coahuilteco was one of the few languages of the world whose SOV structure permitted three levels of embedding. In this example, the main-clause complement object clause is shifted from the position marked <O> to avoid a fourth level:

[*xami·n*] <O> *xaspa·mo e·*, [you] <O> you + believe Q,
<*Dios tupo·* <God the
(*pi·lam* (people
{*pinwak ta·* {things
<*Dios piḻta apata·nko*> <God something he+pa+commands>
tuče·t} the-pl.+object.of.3d}
apawa·y tupa·t) they+pa+do-pl. the-pl.+object.of.3d)
akpaču· san apa·m>? he-them + pa + raise future that + object.of.2d>?

"Do you believe that God will raise up the people who do the things that God commands?" The structure of the complement clause is: $<S_1 (S_2 \{O_2 <S_3O_3V_3>\} V_2) V_1>$, where each subject (S) goes with the verb (V) having the same subscript, and the clauses (. . .) and {. . .} are the objects of the immediately following verbs.

The following list follows the Swadesh 200-word list (Hymes 1960) in order, omitting those items not found in the available sources. The designation (H) is used to identify an item taken from Del Hoyo (1965; for a complete list of words in that source see Troike 1967a). The abbreviations w.s. and m.s. with kin terms indicate 'woman speaking' and 'man speaking', respectively. Forms spelled by García with "g" that are transcribed with *w* are indicated by placing García's form in parentheses. Bound stems, usually verbs, are preceded by a hyphen.

1. all *tawaxa·yo*
2. and *ko*
3. animal *pinwaka·y*
7. bad *ḱawx, saxpa·m, -ša·yš*
9. because *mitxo·, mino·*
11. big *-na·n*
12. bird *awaya·m*
15. blood *-ha·c* (RG *-kʷa·s*)
19. burn (tr.) *-ṭi·xamko·, -(a)kayo* (H)
20. child *pa·m*
23. come *-ka·ḷ* (?; also 'go')
25. cut *-(a)ḱape* (H)
26. day *ṭil*
27. die *-kʷa·ncam* (RG *-xu·m*)
30. dog *kačo·wa* (H)
31. drink *-ko·wxʷ*
36. earth *ta·p (pa)*
37. eat *-ha·m*
43. father *-xana·y; (-)ma·ma* m.s.; *-ṭa·nawe·* ("*-t'ânagê*") w.s.
44. fear *ta·lam*
48. fire *talo·m*
50. five *xu·yopama·wx* (RG *ma·xʷaxu·yo*)
57. four *puwa·nċan*
60. give *-a·x*
61. good *-šapa·n; mana·m (ča·n); mapa* (H)
66. hand *-ma·wx*
69. hear *-čake·y* (pl.; sg. *-če·y* (?))
70. heart *-axasa·l*
72. here *akʷe·*
73. hit *-wa·c*
74. hold/take *-xʷa·c* (hold); *-ču·/-čo·* (take)
77. husband *-ḱa·w*
78. I *cin; čen, čen* (H)
80. if *awaxta; -e·x*

664

81. in -kʷeˑ (locative demonstrative stem; cf. 'here')

82. kill -čap; -(a)ĉan (H)

83. know -xoˑ

84. laugh -xaˑmayaˑ (laugh at, make fun of)

90. live -piˑlam (also 'people'); -txaˑm (dwell)

94. man/male xawuˑ ("jagû")

95. many -aˑwx (a subordinated verb stem)

96. meat ahaˑwh

97. mother -leˑyš (w.s.) (RG -cawaˑw); -taˑy

100. name -aˑwxʷ

102. near pawlikako (H)

105. night čum (RG takoˑm)

107. not (y)axaˑm

108. old -caˑy

109. one pił

110. other axcoˑ; hin

111. person piˑlam (people)

119. river wan akkan (H)

124. rub -ḱaˑy (touch, fondle, caress)

127. say -xleˑ; -kaˑ (-uˑm tell)

129. sea wan apanan (H; apnaˑn big)

130. see -maˑs; -maš (H)

138. sky uxʷaˑł

139. sleep -camoˑxʷ

140. small šan (child)

161. that ta-, pita- (demonstrative prefixes)

162. there takʷeˑ, pitakʷe

166. think -naˑko

167. this a- (demonstrative prefix)

168. thou xamiˑn

169. three axtikpił (two and one)

170. throw -hoˑwhłam

174. tree puman paxawčeˑ . . . m (H)

176. two axteˑ

181. water wan (see 'sea')

182. we čakan (H)

183. wet -xama (H)

184. what łaˑxaka (RG xaˑka); -ka

186. where anikʷeˑkat (RG anukʷeˑkat)

188. who piłka

190. wife taˑyawuˑ ("tâyagû")

194. with aˑwxyo; -yo

195. woman taˑwu ("tâgu")

198. ye xamaˑkan

199. year axakoˑ (RG atuˑlam)

665

Sketch of Sahaptin, a Sahaptian Language

BRUCE RIGSBY AND NOEL RUDE

1. Phonology
2. Grammatical Processes
3. Inflectional Syntax

4. Nominals
5. Verbs
6. Selected Vocabulary—Umatilla Sahaptin

Sahaptin is a native language of the Southern Plateau area that was spoken by several hundred Indian people in Washington and Oregon in the 1980s (fig. 1). It and its sister language, Nez Perce, make up the Sahaptian language family (table 1), which belongs to the great Penutian stock that is widely distributed throughout the California, Plateau, and Northwest Coast culture areas.

This sketch is based primarily upon the Umatilla Sahaptin dialect, which was spoken during late aboriginal times along the Columbia River, centering in two winter villages, *ímatalam* at the mouth of the Umatilla River and *náwawi* near present-day Alderdale, Washington, but it makes comparative remarks upon other dialects in appropriate places. In general, the Sahaptin dialects show syntactic uniformity, diverging mainly in lexicon and low-level phonology.

This chapter is dedicated to the Sahaptin-speaking people who, as teachers and friends of the authors, were sources of the data. Rigsby especially acknowledges *támskutalil*, Vera Spokane Jones (Umatilla) (fig. 2); and *wiyáwiikt*, Alex Saluskin (Yakima) (fig. 3). Rude especially acknowledges *ayatúkyaʔikt*, Carrie Sampson (Walla Walla), *tmáys*, Louise Beavert Lloyd (Wana); and *twípaytit*, Joseph Thompson (Walla Walla). Other friends who taught Rigsby Umatilla are Alice Barnhart, Susie Joe, Charles McKay, Walter Pond, and Inez Spino Reves; McKay and Reves also helped Rude. Friends and speakers of other dialects who helped us include: *wiyukšenéet*, Tom Andrews (Palouse); Cecelia Bearchum (Walla Walla); Virginia Beavert (Yakima), Verbena Greene (Warm Springs), Mary Jim (Walla Walla); *líkslaway*, Rose Lucy Yettona John (Wana) (fig. 4); Mary Dick John (Yakima); Elizabeth Jones (Walla Walla); Agnes Billy Mark (Rock Creek); George Nanamkin (Pshwanwapam); Ellen Saluskin (Yakima); Ada Sooksoit (Warm Springs) (fig. 5); Sam Sturgis (Walla Walla); Linton Winishut (Warm Springs); and Virginia Wyena (Wanapam). For them, here is a worship song of the Walla Walla prophetess *xúnway*:

> *waptáy=akut iláqayx̣išamš*
> *čáw=na kʷaaná átuukša,*
> *čúux̣a=pam wáta,*
> *čúux̣a=pam wáta...*

They say there's a small light shining
  that we don't see,
Be prepared,
Be prepared...

1. PHONOLOGY

This sketch employs a technical alphabet based upon common Americanist usage, but it and its conventions bear a close relationship to the different practical orthographies in use on the Umatilla, Warm Springs, and Yakima reservations (see table 2). Its autonomous phonemic level of representation indicates the distinctive surface phonetic contrasts.

The main orthographic conventions are that initial glottal stop before a vowel is not written and initial unstressed /ʔi-/ is not written before /m n l/ plus a consonant, for example, *nčí* 'big, large', but *ím* 'mouth'. This orthographic convention is used since initial /ʔ/ and /ʔi/ are predictable phonologically and do not cause glottalization in a preceding consonant. The space indicates word boundary, while the comma indicates a sentence-internal clause bound-

Table 1. Sahaptin Languages and Dialects

		Proto-Sahaptian	
	Sahaptin		Nez Perce
Northern Sahaptin		Southern Sahaptin	
Northwest	Northeast	(Columbia River)	
Klikitat	Palouse	Celilo	
Pshwanwapam	Walla Walla	John Day	
Taitnapam	Wanapam	Umatilla	
Yakima	Lower Snake	Rock Creek	
		Warm Springs	

ary, and (where relevant) the period ends sentences.

In alphabetical order, the Sahaptin phonemes are as follows.

1. /a/ A short low unrounded central vowel usually ranging from [ɑ] to [ʌ], although it may front to [a] or [ε] preceding or following /y/. Its normal variant sounds much like the vowel in English 'pup' and is always distinguished from the shorter /ɨ/.

2. /aa/ A long low unrounded vowel that never raises to mid height, ranging from [ɑ·] to [a·]. In the Northwest Sahaptin dialects, it may shorten and front when not stressed but always retains its tenser quality.

3. /c/ A plain voiceless dental rill affricate much like the cluster that ends English 'bats'. A unitary segment, it contrasts with the cluster /ts/, for example, *icímayca* 'He fed it', and *icímaytsa* 'He's feeding it'.

4. /c̓/ A glottalized dental rill affricate. Glottalized obstruents are realized with egressive glottalic pressure, as ejectives, with the degrees of "popping" dependent on dialect and speaker, as well as speech situation.

5. /č/ A plain voiceless alveopalatal surface affricate like the sound that begins English 'cheap'. It contrasts with the cluster /tš/: *míš iwíšayča* 'What happened?' and *míš iwíšaytša* 'What's happening?'

6. /č̓/ A glottalized alveopalatal surface affricate.

7. /h/ A voiceless laryngeal glide with no supralaryngeal friction, it is like the sound that begins English 'hat'.

8. /i/ A short high front unrounded vowel ranging from [ɪ] to [i], often similar to the vowel in English 'key', but shorter in duration and with no palatal offglide. It lowers to the [e] position near the uvulars /q q̓ x̣/.

9. /ii/ A long high front unrounded vowel that always has a tense quality. It has a schwa-like offglide before the uvulars and it lowers to the [e] position following them. It is similar to the vowel in English 'key' but longer and with no palatal offglide.

10. /ɨ/ A high central unrounded vowel that generally ranges about [ɨ]. It is invariably shorter in duration than the other short vowels.

11. /k/ A plain voiceless velar stop like the sound that begins English 'cup' except when followed by the high front vowels /i ii/ and the palatal glide /y/. It then fronts to the palatal [k] position like the sound that begins English 'key'.

12. /kʷ/ A plain voiceless labiovelar stop similar to the sound that begins English 'quick'. There is a phonetic contrast between the unitary /kʷ/, as in *x̣ax̣áykʷi* 'one who has money', and the sequence /kw/ in some complex forms, such as the reduplicated *walákwalak* 'butterfly', but generally the sequence /kw/ across a morpheme boundary realizes as simple phonetic [kʷ], as in *inákʷinana* 'He carried it'.

13. /k̓/ A glottalized velar stop that fronts to palatal position like its plain /k/ counterpart.

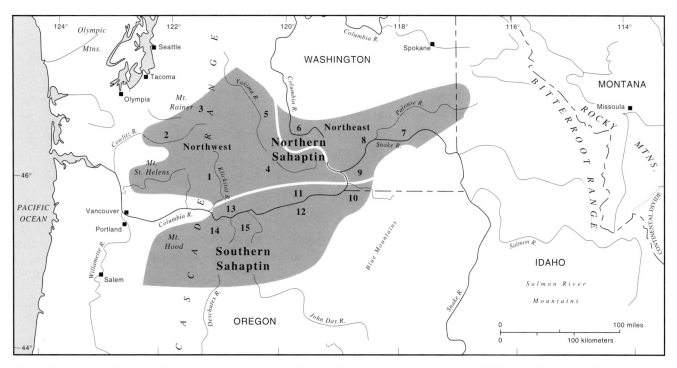

Fig. 1. Distribution of Sahaptin dialects and dialect clusters. Northern Sahaptin (Northwest cluster): 1, Klikitat; 2, Taitnapam (Upper Cowlitz); 3, Upper Nisqually (Mishalpam); 4, Yakima; 5, Pshwanwapam; (Northeast cluster): 6, Wanapam; 7, Palouse; 8, Lower Snake (Chamnapam, Wauyukma, and Naxiyampam); 9, Walla Walla (Waluulapam); Southern Sahaptin (Columbia River cluster): 10, Umatilla; 11, Rock Creek; 12, John Day; 13, Celilo (Wayampam); 14, Tenino; 15, Tygh Valley (Johnson 1993; Coe, Snow, and Benson 1986).

Fig. 2. Vera Spokane Jones (b. 1889, d. 1966) and her great-niece Cheryl Conner. Vera Jones was a linguistic consultant to Theodore Stern as well as Bruce Rigsby. She is proudly displaying a beaded buckskin dress, twined bags filled with roots, and commercial cooking ware, which were gifts from her trading partner. Trading partnerships, set up between unrelated individuals, included gift exchange and reciprocal feasting (Stern 1993:29-31). Photograph (digitally sharpened) by Theodore Stern, Umatilla Reservation, Ore., 1957.

Table 2. Key to Sahaptin Orthographies

Present technical alphabet	Yakima practical alphabet	Warm Springs official alphabet	Jacobs's (1931, 1934-1937) technical alphabet
a	a	a	a
aa	aa	aa	a·, ω·
c	ts	c	ts
c̓	ts'	c'	t́s
č	ch	č	tc
č̓	ch'	č'	t́c
h	h	h	h
i	i	i	i
ii	ii	ii	i·, ei, ε·
ɨ	ɨ	omitted	ə
k	k	k	k, ɢ
kʷ	kw	kw	kw, ɢw
k̓	k'	k'	ḱ
k̓ʷ	kw'	kw'	ḱw
l	l	l	l
ł	ł	ł	ł
λ	tł	tł	tł
λ̓	tł'	tł'	t́ł
m	m	m	m
n	n	n	n
p	p	p	p, в
p̓	p'	p'	ṗ
q	k̲	q	q
qʷ	k̲w	qw	qw
q̓	k̲'	q'	q̇
q̓ʷ	k̲w'	qw'	q̇w
s	s	s	s
š	sh	š	c
t	t	t	t, ᴅ
t̓	t'	t'	t́, t́θ
u	u	u	u
uu	uu	uu	u·, ω·
w	w	w, u*	w, u*
x	x	x̂	x
x̲	x̲	x	x̲
xʷ	xw	x̂w	xw
x̲ʷ	x̲w	xw	x̲w
y	y	y, i*	y, i*
ʔ	'	'	'

* As final members of dipthongs.

14. /k̓ʷ/ A glottalized labiovelar stop.
15. /l/ A voiced lateral vocoid much like the sound that begins English 'loon', never like that which ends 'pull'.
16. /ł/ A voiceless lateral spirant like Welsh *ll*. This sound is pronounced by placing the tongue tip just behind the dental margin and permitting the airstream to flow outward over either or both sides of the tongue.
17. /λ/ A voiceless lateral affricate. This infrequent sound begins like the plain /t/ and ends like /ł/. It contrasts with the cluster /tł/ (which always occurs across a morpheme boundary), as in *k̓pitłimá* 'a piece of beadwork', and with /tl/, as in *tlípa* 'fox'.
18. /λ̓/ A glottalized lateral affricate. This ejective, with its audible pop, is more common in occurrence than the nonglottalized /λ/.
19. /m/ A voiced bilabial nasal like the sound that begins English 'moon'.

20. /n/ A voiced dental nasal much like the sound that begins English 'noon', but the tongue tip is placed more forward to just behind the dental margin.
21. /p/ A plain voiceless bilabial stop like the sound that begins English 'pop'.

668

22. /p̓/ A glottalized bilabial stop. In the Rock Creek dialect, it is regularly an affricate [p̓ɸ].

23. /q/ A plain voiceless uvular stop similar to the sound that begins English 'cop', but pronounced farther back in the mouth.

24. /qʷ/ A plain voiceless labio-uvular stop similar to the sound that begins English 'quote', but pronounced farther back in the mouth.

25. /q̓/ A glottalized uvular stop.

26. /q̓ʷ/ A glottalized labio-uvular stop.

27. /s/ A voiceless dental rill spirant like the sound that begins English 'seat'.

28. /š/ A voiceless alveopalatal surface spirant like the sound that begins English 'sheet', but with no lip protrusion.

29. /t/ A plain voiceless dental stop much like the sound that begins English 'top', but the tongue tip makes closure just behind the dental margin.

30. /t̓/ Most Sahaptin speakers pronounce this sound as a glottalized slit affricate [θ̓], but some Warm Springs Reservation speakers regularly employ a glottalized

Fig. 4. Rose Lucy Yettona John (b. 1912). A fluent speaker with extensive cultural knowledge, she worked with Rude in the late 1980s, aiding him in both direct elicitations and textural translations. Photographed at her home near Granger, Wash., mid-1980s.

Fig. 3. Alex Saluskin, secretary of the Yakima Indian Council in 1955. He worked with Rigsby from 1964 to about 1970, helping to develop the Yakima practical alphabet, and dictated to him lexical and grammatical materials including chiefs' and other personal names, place-names as well as historical texts. Photograph by John W. Thompson, 1955.

dental stop [t̓] instead. Jacobs (1931:106-107) indicates that the stop variant was the norm over most of the Sahaptin-speaking community in the 1920s.

31. /u/ A short high back rounded vowel that ranges about [u], although it lowers to [o] position near the uvulars. Its phonetic norm is similar to the vowel in English 'boot', but shorter and with no labial offglide.

32. /uu/ A long high back rounded vowel. Although its phonetic norm is [u·], it drops to the [o] position near the uvulars. It is usually similar to the vowel in English 'loon', but longer and with no offglide.

33. /w/ A voiced labial glide like the sound that begins English 'wet'.

Fig. 5. Playing a stick game. seated, left to right, Ramona Starr with decorated drum; unidentified boy; Wilson Wewa, Jr., gesturing; Ada Sooksoit with undecorated drum; Adeline Miller; unidentified man with drum that reads "Yakima Tribe"; and Maggie Wewa. Photograph by Cynthia D. Stowell, at the Pi-Ume-Sha powwow, Warm Springs Indian Reservation, 1980.

34. /x/ A voiceless velar spirant like *ch* in Scottish *loch* or German *Bach*. This infrequent sound is pronounced with tongue and mouth in the same position as for /k/, but the airstream is not completely blocked, so that a smooth-sounding spirant is produced.

35. /x̱/ A voiceless uvular spirant. This frequent sound is pronounced with tongue and mouth in the same position as for /q/, but the airstream is not stopped, so that a rough-sounding fortis spirant, or even trill, is produced.

36. /xʷ/ A voiceless labiovelar spirant. This very infrequent sound is pronounced like /x/, but with the lips simultaneously rounded.

37. /x̱ʷ/ A voiceless labio-uvular spirant. This fairly frequent sound is pronounced like /x̱/, but with the lips simultaneously rounded.

38. /y/ A voiced palatal glide like the sound that begins English 'yet'.

39. /ʔ/ This glottal stop is the sound represented by the comma in the English interjection 'oh, oh'. Many Sahaptin speakers pronounce it at the beginning of words that otherwise appear to have an initial vowel. However, since initial glottal stops are not written in this orthography, they appear almost exclusively in intervocalic position.

Sahaptin has a typical Pacific Northwest phonemic inventory with a large set of obstruents: stops and affricates are distinguished in nine positions of articulation, spirants in seven. The contrast for stops and affricates is between a plain voiceless series and a glottalized one. Unlike its sister Nez Perce language and the neighboring Interior Salish languages, Sahaptin has a full set of three organic lateral obstruents, /ɬ λ λ̓/. The dorsal obstruents contrast by velar and uvular articulation, a pan-Pacific Northwest trait, and are further distinguished as labialized and plain. There is but a single plain sonorant series, although comparative evidence from Nez Perce indicates the presence of a glottalized sonorant series in the parent Proto-Sahaptian language (which are evidently always derivative of a sonorant plus glottal stop). Several Sahaptin forms, such as *ká?wit* 'root feast, first-fruits feast' and

670

hawí?liš 'brave, mean' (note Yakima *hawíliš*, Warm Springs *háwliš*) actually exhibit phonetic intervocalic [ẘ] and [l̥], but they are exceptional. Glottalized sonorants are found in Upper Nez Perce and in the adjacent Interior Salishan languages, and they were likely a feature of the nearby extinct Cayuse and Molala languages.

Disregarding the extra short /ɨ/ vowel, the phonetic contrasts are characteristic of a three-vowel system (with distinctive length) (table 3). In the modern Warm Springs Reservation dialects, what appears as stressed /i/ before a spirant in other dialects is truncated and one finds instead a true stressed voiceless spirant; for example, Warm Springs *tpš* 'face' and *tčš* 'hip' correspond to Umatilla *tpíš* and *tčíš*, respectively. Except for certain Warm Springs examples in the pronominal paradigms at the end of section 4, there are no stressed syllabic resonants indicated in this orthography. There is as yet no detailed description of syllable structure in Sahaptin.

The relations between the seven-vowel phonemes of the present autonomous phonemic analysis and the vowels that a deeper phonological analysis (for example, Rigsby and Silverstein 1969) establishes are complex and are not treated here.

Long vowels may be organic (primary) within morpheme boundaries, and they may develop secondarily from sequences of identical short vowels across a morpheme boundary. All long vowels are written as clusters of identical short vowels to maintain orthographic consistency and to show the transparency of secondary long vowels. Vowels of different quality do not cluster. Permitted diphthongs are /ay aay aw aaw iw iiw uy uuy/.

The overall articulatory set is relatively fortis as compared with Nez Perce. The plain stops and affricates are usually voiceless, although lightly voiced labial and dental stops are sometimes heard in the more western dialects. The plain stops and affricates always have aspirate release in final position and are generally lightly aspirated in other positions. The uvular and labio-uvular stops never occur in final position, nor do any of the glottalized stops and affricates (save in the Yakima and Warm Springs *tṗáanaq* 'canvas waterbag' and the sound-symbolic *huq̇húq̇* 'pig, hog'). On the whole, the glottalized obstruents are strongly articulated and easily heard as compared with the more lenis pronunciation of cognates among the Nez-Perce-speaking Cayuse around Pendleton, Oregon.

The clustering of consonants shows few restrictions and is common (table 4). All words begin with at least one consonant (recall that vowel-initials in this orthography actually have initial /?-/). Initial clusters of up to three members are permitted, medials of up to five members, and finals of up to four; *pɬxú* 'fresh', *pápatkʷalšíxša* 'they're getting married', and *látxtx*

Table 3. Sahaptin Vowels

	front	central	back
high	i, ii	ɨ	u, uu
low		a, aa	

Table 4. Sahaptin Consonants

	bilabial	dental	dental continuant	lateral	alveopalatal	velar	labiovelar	uvular	labio-uvular	laryngeals
Stops and affricates	p	t	c	ƛ	č	k	kʷ	q	qʷ	?
Glottalized stops and affricates	ṗ	t̓	c̓	ƛ̓	č̓	k̓	k̓ʷ	q̇	q̇ʷ	
Spirants and continuants			s	ɬ	š	x	xʷ	x̣	x̣ʷ	h
Nasals	m	n								
Lateral				l						
Glides	w		y							

'ashes'. Clusters of glottalized or labialized obstruents are not permitted. Where one might expect them to develop from reduplication, one instead observes their plain counterparts, *kk̓ʷáal* 'long ones'. Clusters of identical rearticulated consonants are also found: *ppl;áš* 'white ones', *ttáx̣š* 'willow tree', *ččú* 'quiet', *kkáasu* 'serviceberry bush', *qqápni* 'silly', *miɬɬákšaaš* 'I'm drowsy', and *isíllapša* 'he's dizzy'.

The laryngeals /h ?/ are usually found in initial position, less frequently in intervocalic position. The unique cluster /hw/ occurs in two onomatopoeic verb themes, *ihwíitša* 'he's whistling', and *iwahwákša* 'he (a dog) is barking', in the Columbia River dialects.

Primary stress, which is distinctive and is indicated by the acute accent, occurs on one syllable of every word. Examples of stress contrast are: *ámapa* 'husband' (objective case) and *amápa* 'island' (locative case); *páq̇inušana* 'he saw him' and *paq̇ínušana* 'they saw (him)'. Nondistinctive secondary and lesser stresses occur phonetically but are conditioned by phonetic and syntactic environments not discussed here.

Alternation in the phonetic shapes of morphemes is common and most often involves vocalic alternations arising from processes of ablaut, epenthesis, and truncation that may be phonologically or morphologically conditioned. Succeeding sections provide some allomorphic description by listing the alternants of stem and affixal morphemes.

The common consonantal alternations result from two processes. The velar stops /k k̓/ may palatalize to /č č̓/, and the affricates /c č/ simplify to /t/ before /s š/, respectively, for example, /c/ + /š/ becomes /t/ + /š/.   671

The alternations are treated here by listing alternants in appropriate sections (for fuller discussion, see Rigsby and Silverstein 1969:51).

Other consonantal alternations function in an elaborate system of consonantal symbolism that is variously productive or moribund in the several Sahaptin dialects. They give rise to at least the following ablaut sets:

c ~ č ~ ƛ	k ~ q	n ~ l
c̣ ~ č̣ ~ ƛ̣	k̓ ~ q̓	m ~ w
s ~ š ~ ł	x ~ x̣	

Some examples are:

pƛák, pccák 'bitter, pepper' (cf., *pƛáx̣* 'medicine' and *p̓ísx* 'sour')

kúčk 'a smaller piece', *kúƛk* 'a piece, chunk'

aasá 'nail, claw', *aałá* 'a bigger nail, claw'

qúqł 'hip joint', *q̣úx̣ł* 'knee', *k̓uxsk̓úxs* 'ankle (Warm Springs only)

miyánaš 'child', *miyálas* 'small baby'

tamalám 'gravel' (Umatilla), *tamaláw* 'gravel' (Yakima).

Other examples are found in Jacobs (1931:113-114). The similar Nez Perce symbolisms are treated in Aoki (1970:43-44) and those of the contiguous Wishram Chinookan in Sapir (1911:638-645).

Another common phonological process involves the optional, but usual, regressive assimilation of stressed vowels in verb prefixes such as *pá-* 'inverse', *piná-* 'sg. reflexive', and *ká-* 'with head, mouth, teeth, while eating' across a glottal stop to the following vowel. Some examples are:

pá'ilax̣yawiša. ~ píilax̣yawiša. 'He's drying it.'

piná'iƛiyawiya. ~ piníiƛiyawiya. 'He killed himself.'

iká'ilawiša. ~ ikíilawiša. 'He's tasting it.'

And in the Northeast Sahaptin dialects, /awa/ regularly reduces to /uu/, so that the following sort of correspondence is found:

Northeast Sahaptin	Other Sahaptin
púu	pawá '(they) are'
puučá	pawačá '(they) were'
úu	áwa '(he) has, (it) is'
úuča	áwača '(he) had, (it) was'

The word *páway* 'woman's brother's daughter' (vocative) is an exception.

2. GRAMMATICAL PROCESSES

Sahaptin is synthetic to mildly polysynthetic in morphological structure. Verbs often display polysynthesis, as seen in the sentence *i-šapá-tuti-yay-šan-a=aš níit* 'He was putting up my tent for me'. The constituent morphemes of the initial verb are:

i- '3d-person nominative subject' pronominal prefix

šapá- 'general causative' prefix

tuti- 'stand, be standing', an intransitive verb stem

-yay- 'benefactive' suffix

-šan 'imperfective aspect' suffix

-a 'past tense' suffix

=aš '1st-person singular' pronominal enclitic.

In technique of synthesis, Sahaptin is for the most part agglutinative, but it tends to be inflective in its pronoun paradigms and does employ some symbolism in its derivational morphology, for example, the process of vocalic ablaut that derives the adjective *čmáak^w* 'dirty, really black' from the simple adjective *čmúk* 'black'.

The grammatical processes used are affixation, clisis, reduplication, ablaut, compounding, suppletion, and order. Of them, affixation, specifically suffixation, is exploited to the greatest extent.

Clisis differs from affixation in that in the former attachment is to the first word in a clause, whereas in the latter it is to a word. Although clitics are always pronounced as part of the word to which they are attached, they are set apart from it by the = boundary in this orthography. Consider (see table 5):

watím=naš	*tk^wáynp-šan-a*	*yáamaš-yaw.*
yesterday=1SG	hunt-IMPV-PST	mule.deer-DAT
tk^wáynp-šan-a=aš	*yáamaš-yaw*	*watím.*
yáamaš-yaw=š	*tk^wáynp-šan-a*	*watím.*
(or *yáamaš-yaw=naš*)		

'Yesterday I was hunting for mule deer.'

In these examples, the '1 sg.' pronominal enclitic (in its various shapes *=naš ~ =aš ~ =š*) is attached to an adverb of time, *watím* 'yesterday', to a verb, *tk^wáynpšana* 'was hunting', and to a dative noun phrase, *yáamašyaw* 'for mule deer'.

Reduplication is common. Initial partial reduplication is exemplified in the formation of the plural adjective *ppláš* 'white ones' from the singular *pláš* 'white (one)'. Full reduplication with diminutive symbolism is seen in the noun *k̓usik̓úsi* 'dog', derived from *k̓úsi* 'horse', and in the adverb of time *maysx̣máysx̣* 'every day', derived from *máysx̣* 'tomorrow'. Many words occur only in full reduplicated form, for instance, *walákwalak* 'butterfly', *x̣úlx̣ul* 'troutlike fish' (generic), and *p̓ípi* 'guts, intestines'. Internal reduplication is found in a few forms like *pccák* 'bitter, pepper' and *x̣ttú* 'strong' (Yakima), which may have intensified meaning and should be compared to the simple forms *pƛák* 'bitter, pepper' and *x̣tú* 'strong' (Yakima).

Ablaut is the interchanging of vowels or consonants in the derivation of related forms. Vocalic ablaut is an old, no longer freely productive grammatical process in Sahaptin. In most cases, it functions to derive stative adjectives from verb stems, as in *ƛáax̣^w* 'all, everyone, everything' from *-ƛx̣^w-* (cf., *ikáƛx̣^wa* 'He ate it all up'). Consonantal ablaut, illustrated in the derivation of the noun *k̓úti* 'animal pal, pet' from *k̓úsi* 'horse', symbolically marks various affective categories.

Compounding is not so common in Sahaptin as in Nez Perce. It is exemplified in the nouns *wix̣ánči* 'big toe' and *pápinči* 'thumb', which should be compared to

Table 5. Abbreviations

1	First person
2	Second person
3	Third person
ABL	Ablative
ABS	Absolutive
AG	Agentive
ALL	Allative
BEN	Benefactive
CAUS	Causative
COM	Comitative
COND	Conditional
CSL	Cislocative
DAT	Dative
DIR	Directive object
DIS	Distributive
ERG	Ergative
EXC	Exclusive
FUT	Future
GEN	Genitive
GER	Gerund(ive)
HAB	Habitual
HORT	Hortative
IMP	Imperative
IMPV	Imperfective
INC	Inclusive
INCR	Stem increment
INSTR	Instrumental
INV	Inverse
LOC	Locative
NOM	Nominative, Nominalizer
NEG	Negative
O	Object Nominal
OBJ	Object(ive)
OBV	Obviative
PL	Plural
PPF	Present Perfect
PRIV	Privative
PROB	Probability
PST	Past
Q	Question
QUAN	Quantity
QUOT	Quotative
REC	Reciprocal
REF	Reflexive
REL	Relative
S	Subject Nominal
SG	Singular
STAT	Stative
SUBJ	Subject
TOP	Topic
TRL	Translocative
TRNS	Transitivizer
V	Verb

the adjective-plus-noun-head phrases *nčí wiX̱á* 'big foot' and *nčí ipáp* 'big hand'.

Suppletion is the replacement of some form by a phonetically dissimilar form in part of its paradigm. Clear cases are seen in the forms for 'boy' and 'girl'

	singular	dual	plural
Umatilla			
'boy'	*áswan*	*kátkaatin*	*kátkaatma*
'girl'	*p̓ínic,*	*p̓ilíin*	*p̓ilíma*
	p̓íic		
Walla Walla			
'boy'	*taX̱núčimt*	*amíisin*	*amíisma*
'girl'	*túuX̱anat*	*áp̓iliin*	*áp̓ilima*
Yakima			
'boy'	*áswan*	*amíisin*	*amíisma*
'girl'	*p̓íniks*	*p̓ilíyin*	*p̓ilíma*

Other examples are found among the kinship terms, but suppletion is definitely uncommon.

Word order as a grammatical process is of little syntactic importance. This even includes certain aspects of phrase order; for example, the words in a noun phrase sometimes occur discontinuously within a sentence. The extensive case-marking, cross-reference, and concord in the nominals and verbs of sentences provide such adequate indication of basic syntactic relations that word order is left quite free to perform its discourse-pragmatic function.

3. INFLECTIONAL SYNTAX

Sahaptin is a free-word-order language with extensive morphosyntactic development. It has both head and dependency-marking characteristics but perhaps leans a little more toward the dependency-marking side of the typology.

Among the more prominent characteristics of its inflectional syntax, Sahaptin exhibits a rich case-marking system that recalls modern Finnish or Turkish. Nominal suffixes (case endings) mark five relational cases—unmarked, inverse ergative, obviative ergative, objective, and genitive (or possessive)—and six adverbial cases—instrumental, locative, dative, benefactive, allative, and ablative (see table 6 for the forms with sample declensions of nonhuman and human nouns). The syntactic terrain turns unfamiliar as one looks to the related system of pronominal cross-reference that operates in Sahaptin sentences. To exemplify these and related concepts, consider first the following intransitive and transitive sentences:

(1) *iwínš   i-wínan-a.*
    man   3NOM-go-PST
    'The man went.'

(2) *iwínš   i-q̓ínun-a   yáamaš-na.*
    man   3NOM-see-PST mule.deer-OBJ
    'The man saw a/the mule deer.'

Note that in both sentences the verbal prefix *i-* agrees with the third-person subject. The objective noun in the

Table 6. Noun Case Endings

	Nonhuman	Human		
		Singular	Dual	Plural
Unmarked	Ø (ḱúsi 'horse')	Ø (iwínš 'man')	-in (awínšin)	-ma (awínšma)
Inverse ergative	-nim (ḱúsinim)	-nim (iwínšnim)	(no dual or plural forms)	
Obviative ergative	-in (ḱúsiyin)	-in (iwínšin)	(no dual or plural forms)	
Objective	-na (ḱúsina)	-na (iwínšna)	-inaman (awínšinaman)	-maaman (awínšmaaman)
Comitative	-in (ḱúsiyin)	-in (iwínšin)	(no dual or plural forms)	
Genitive	-(n)mí (ḱusinmí)	-(n)mí (iwinšmí)	-inamí (awínšinaman)	-maaní (awinšmaamí)
Benefactive	-ay (ḱúsiyay)	-(n)míyay (iwinšmíyay)	-inamíyay (awínšinamíyay)	-maamíyay (awinšmaamíyay)
Dative	-yaw (ḱúsiyaw)	-(n)míyaw (iwinšmíyaw)	-inamíyaw (awínšinamíyaw)	-maamíyaw (awinšmaamíyaw)
Allative	-kan (ḱúsikan)	-(n)míkan (iwinšmíkan)	-inamíkan (awínšinamíkan)	-maamíkan (awinšmaamíkan)
Ablative	-kni (ḱúsikni)	-(n)míkni (iwinšmíkni)	-inamíkni (awínšinamíkni)	-maamíkni (awinšmaamíkni)
Instrumental	-ki (ḱúsiki)	-(n)míki (iwinšmíki)	-inamíki (awínšinamíki)	-maamíki (awinšmaamíki)
Locative	-pa (ḱúsipa)	-(n)mípa (iwinšmípa)	-inamípa (awínšinamípa)	-maamípa (awinšmaamípa)

transitive clause (example 2) is case-marked with the suffix -na, whereas in neither clause is the subject noun 'man' case-marked. Now consider the following ditransitive sentence:

(3) xʷísaat-nim=naš   i-ní-ya   ináy ḱúsi.
    old.man-INV.ERG=1SG 3NOM-give-PST me horse
    'The old man gave me a horse.'

The root morphemes and their relators are:

1. xʷísaat 'old man' is a third-person singular human noun and subject in a transitive clause, which in this sentence requires ergative case-marking. When the object of the verb is a speech-act participant (here first person), the subject noun is case-marked with the inverse ergative suffix -nim.

2. =naš denotes first-person singular. Since the primary object is a speech-act participant, it is obligatorily coded by a second-position enclitic.

3. ni 'give' is a ditransitive verb inflected for the past perfective indicative by the suffix -a (which takes the form -ya after the vowel i). The prefix i- expresses obligatory agreement with all third-person subject nouns case-marked with -nim.

4. ináy 'me' is a first person singular independent personal pronoun. Its occurrence is not obligatory. It serves an emphatic or contrastive function.

5. ḱúsi 'horse' is a third-person singular nonhuman noun and the secondary object of the verb. It occurs in the unmarked case.

It is a fact of Sahaptin grammar that when the goal in a ditransitive clause (corresponding to the indirect object in an equivalent English clause) is human, it is the primary object. For rare exceptions and further examples, see Rude (1992).

Concord, as distinguished from government, refers to the agreement in number- and case-marking that holds between the head of a noun phrase and its several nominal adjuncts, as seen in the examples:

(4) ín=aš á-ḱinu-ša   payúwii-na   ṭmáma-an.
    I-1SG 3ABS-see-IMPV sick-OBJ   old.woman-OBJ
    'I see the sick old woman.'

(5) kú kʷná pa-winanúu-xan-a láxʷayx-pa čúuš-pa.
    and there 3PL.NOM-swim-   hot-LOC   water-
        HAB-PST   LOC
    'And there they would bathe in the hot water.'

Pronominal cross-reference is exemplified in example (3) above, whereby the verb is indexed for the person and number of its subject by a pronominal prefix (i-), and the first word of the sentence has attached to it an enclitic (=naš) that indicates that a first-person singular argument is a subject or primary object.

Cross-reference by the appropriate enclitic-prefix combinations is a feature of all grammatical Sahaptin sentences. It introduces redundancy and so makes possible the elliptical pronominalizations that characterize most occurring Sahaptin sentences. In most cases, the cross-referencing enclitics provide unambiguous indication of the subject and object of the sentence. Thus, in sentence (6), the third-person singular nonhuman patient object ḱúsi 'horse' has been elliptically pronominalized by deletion; (7) occurs without the emphatic first-person singular object pronoun ináy 'me'; in (8), the third-person singular human pronoun occurs instead of the inverse ergative subject noun xʷísaat 'old man'; and in (9), there are no nouns or independent pronouns.

(6) xʷísaat-nim=naš i-ní-ya ináy 'The old man gave it to me.'

(7) xʷísaat-nim=naš i-ní-ya 'The old man gave it to me.'

(8) p-nim=naš   i-ní-ya
    3SG-INV.ERG-1SG 3NOM-give-PST
    'He gave it to me.'

(9) *i-ní-ya=aš*
　　3NOM-give-PST=1SG
　　'He gave it to me.'

The freedom of word order in Sahaptin is surely not unrelated to the extensive case-marking and pronominal cross-reference. Thus, the words of sentence (3) may be "scrambled" as in:

(10) *iníya=aš x̌ʷísaatnim ináy k̓úsi,*
(11) *ináy=aš x̌ʷísaatnim iníya k̓úsi,*
(12) *k̓úsi=š* (or *k̓úsi=naš*) *x̌ʷísaatnim iníya ináy,* and

other reordered versions, providing that the first person singular enclitic (in one or another alternant) is attached to the first word of the sentence.

In one sense, the sentences (3), (10), (11), and (12) have the same meaning, yet they are not all equally appropriate to any situation of discourse, for they differ in that each has a different topic. First position (the word order slot defined by the second-position enclitics) highlights or topicalizes. Sentence (3) has the topic *x̌ʷísaat* 'old man', (10) has *iníya* 'gave' highlighted, (11) has *ináy* 'me', and (12) *k̓úsi* 'horse'. Thus sentence (12) might be an appropriate reply to the question *tún=am iníya* 'What did he give you?', although *k̓úsi=š* (or *k̓úsi=naš*) *iníya* 'A horse (it was that) he gave me' would sound less stilted. Topicalization remains a little understood facet of Sahaptin grammar that most speakers find difficult to explain, although they have no trouble in deciding whether a sentence is appropriate to some particular situation of discourse.

There are seven pronominal enclitics:

1. *=naš ~ =aš ~ =š* 'first-person singular'
2. *=na* (*=nan* in Northwest Sahaptin) 'first-person plural inc(lusive)'
3. *=nataš ~ =ataš ~ =taš* 'first-person plural exc(lusive)'
4. *=nam ~ =am ~ =m* 'second-person singular'

In Umatilla, the long *=naš*, *=nataš*, and *=nam* forms occur following final consonants (except *n*-finals); the *=aš*, *=ataš*, and *=am* forms after *n*-finals; *=aš*, *=ataš*, and *=nam* after *a*-finals; and the short *=š*, *=taš*, and *=m* forms after *i*- and *u*-finals. The Northwest Sahaptin dialects use the *=am* 'second singular' alternant after *a*-finals; thus Yakima *wínaša=am* 'you're going' corresponds to Umatilla *wínaša=nam*. However, the long and short forms may alternate even in a single speaker's speech. Phonetic rhythm and a tendency to reduce allomorphy by suppressing the short enclitic forms and using the longer, more highly characterized alternants may be significant considerations.

5. *=pam* 'second-person plural'
6. *=maš* 'second-person object with first-person subject (both singular)'
7. *=mataš* 'second-person object with first-person subject (one or both plural)'

The eight common pronominal verb prefixes are:

1. *i-* 'third-person nominative'
This prefix is optional before vowel-initial (actually ʔV-initial) themes and is preferably omitted in that position: *tmáma iʔáša ~ tmáma áša* 'The old woman entered, went in.'

2. *pa-* 'third-person plural nominative'
Older people occasionally use *ipa-*, which indicates that *i-* was originally just a third-person subjective prefix and *pa-* its pluralizer (which is still the function of the cognate Nez Perce morpheme *pe-*).

3. *á- ~ áw-* 'third-person absolutive'
áw- occurs before vowel-initial themes, *á-* elsewhere. In Umatilla, this pronominal marks subjects in intransitive clauses when they are possessors, and objects in transitive clauses when the subject is first or second person. In the Northwest dialects preserved in Jacobs (1929, 1934-1937), the function is broader, with any third-person subject of an intransitive verb or object of a transitive verb being coded optionally by this pronominal.

4. *pá-* 'inverse'

5. *patá- ~ patáw-* 'third-person plural subject with third-person object'
The equivalent prefix in the Northeast Sahaptin dialects is *paʔá-*, a sequence of 2 and 3 above. In the Northwest Sahaptin dialects, the same subject/object configuration is marked by a unique second position enclitic *=pat* and the *á- ~ áw-* prefix. Thus the Umatilla *patá- ~ patáw-* prefix has resulted from the fusing of the older enclitic *=pat* and the *á- ~ áw-* prefix into a new unitary prefix. *patáw-* occurs before vowel-initial themes, *patá-* elsewhere.

6. *piná-* 'singular reflexive'

7. *pamá-* 'plural reflexive'
The Northwest Sahaptin dialects use *pimá-* as the plural reflexive prefix.

The common Sahaptin reflexive construction requires that the verb be inflected by the appropriate reflexive prefix if the subject and object arguments are coreferential.

8. *pápa-* 'reciprocal'
Older speakers sometimes use *ipápa-*, which begins with the old third-person subjective element.

There are three major classes of sentence structures, viewed in terms of case-marking on nominals (if overtly present) and the associated cross-referencing by the pronominal enclitics and verb prefixes. The first class includes simple intransitives (those with unpossessed subjects), simple copulas, reflexives, and reciprocals. Table 7 presents their several enclitic-prefix combinations. The second major class comprises the transitive structures in their varied subject-object configurations. Table 8 treats their enclitic-prefix combinations. The third class composes the genitive copulas and the intransitives with possessed subjects. Table 9 details their enclitic-prefix combinations; note that only third-person nominals may be possessed.

Table 7. Agreement in Intransitive Clauses

Subject Nominal	Enclitic	Verb Prefix	Case-marking on Subject Nominal
1 sg.	=naš	—	—
1 pl. inc.	=na	—	—
1 pl. exc.	=nataš	—	—
2 sg.	=nam	—	—
2 pl.	=pam	—	—
3 sg.	—	i-	—
3 pl.	—	pa-	—
Reflexives			
1 sg.	=naš	piná-	—
1 pl. inc.	=na	pamá-	—
1 pl. exc.	=nataš	pamá-	—
2 sg.	=nam	piná-	—
2 pl.	=pam	pamá-	—
3 sg.	—	piná-	—
3 pl.	—	pamá-	—
Reciprocals			
1 pl. inc.	=na	pápa-	—
1 pl. exc.	=nataš	pápa-	—
2 pl.	=pam	pápa-	—
3 pl.	—	pápa-	—

Table 8. Agreement in Transitive Clauses

Subject Nominal	Object Nominal	Enclitic	Verb Prefix	Noun case-marking Subject	Object
1 sg.	2 sg.	=maš	—	—	obj. sg.
1 sg.	2 pl.	=mataš	—	—	obj. pl.
1 pl. exc.	2 sg.	=mataš	—	—	obj. sg.
1 pl. exc.	2 pl.	=mataš	—	—	obj. pl.
1 sg.	3 sg.	=naš	á-	—	obj. sg.
1 sg.	3 pl.	=naš	á-	—	obj. pl.
1 pl. inc.	3 sg.	=na	á-	—	obj. sg.
1 pl. inc.	3 pl.	=na	á-	—	obj. pl.
1 pl. exc.	3 sg.	=nataš	á-	—	obj. sg.
1 pl. exc.	3 pl.	=nataš	á-	—	obj. pl.
2 sg.	1 sg.	=nam	pá-	—	obj. sg.
2 sg.	1 pl.	=nam	—	—	obj. pl.
2 pl.	1 sg.	=pam	—	—	obj. sg.
2 pl.	1 pl.	=pam	—	—	obj. pl.
2 sg.	3 sg.	=nam	á-	—	obj. sg.
2 sg.	3 pl.	=nam	á-	—	obj. pl.
2 pl.	3 sg.	=pam	á-	—	obj. sg.
2 pl.	3 pl.	=pam	á-	—	obj. pl.
3 sg.	1 sg.	=naš	i-	inv. erg.	obj. sg.
3 sg.	1 pl. inc.	=na	i-	inv. erg.	obj. pl.
3 sg.	1 pl. exc.	=nataš	i-	inv. erg.	obj. pl.
3 pl.	1 sg.	=naš	pa-	—	obj. sg.
3 pl	1 pl. inc.	=na	pa-	—	obj. pl.
3 pl.	1 pl. exc.	=nataš	pa-	—	obj. pl.
3 sg.	2 sg.	=nam	i-	inv. erg.	obj. sg.
3 sg.	2 pl.	=pam	i-	inv. erg.	obj. pl.
3 pl.	2 sg.	=nam	pa-	—	obj. sg.
3 pl.	2 pl.	=pam	pa-	—	obj. pl.
3 sg. top.	3 sg.	—	i-	—	obj. sg.
3 sg.	3 sg. top.	—	pá-	obj. erg.	obj. sg.
3 sg.	3 pl.	—	i-	—	obj. pl.
3 pl. top.	3 sg.	—	pa-	—	obj. sg.
3 pl.	3 sg. top.	—	patá-	—	obj. sg.
3 pl.	3 pl.	—	pa-	—	obj. pl.

The interaction of the enclitics and verb prefixes is most complex in transitive clauses with nonidentical third-person subjects and objects, or first or second-person subjects and third-person objects, because there are several grammatical configurations possible: some (Types B and C below) are not included in table 8 to avoid further complexity. The use of the objective case endings is also involved. Briefly, there are three patterns observed in these transitive structures that may be schematized as follows:

(13) Type A.   *iwínš+in*   *pá+tuхnana yáamaš+na.*
    man+OBV.ERG 3INV+shot   mule.deer+OBJ
    'The man shot a mule deer.'

(14) Type A´. *ín=aš   á+tuхnana   yáamaš+na.*
    I=1SG   3ABS+shot   mule.deer+OBJ
    'I shot a mule deer.'

(15) Type B.   *iwínš i+tuхnána   yáamaš+na.*
    man   3NOM+shot   mule.deer+OBJ
    'The man shot a mule deer.'

(16) Type B´. *ín=aš   tuхnána   yáamaš+na.*
    I=1SG   shot   mule.deer+OBJ
    'I shot a mule deer.'

(17) Type C.   *iwínš i+tuхnána   yáamaš.*
    man   3NOM-shot   mule.deer
    'The man shot a mule deer.'

(18) Type C´. *ín=aš   tuхnána   yáamaš.*
    I=1SG   shot   mule.deer
    'I shot a mule deer.'

Table 9. Agreement in Intransitive Clauses with Genitive Subjects

Genitive	Enclitic	Verbal prefix	Noun Case-marking
1 sg.	=naš	—	genitive
1 pl. inc.	=na	—	genitive
1 pl. exc.	=nataš	—	genitive
2 sg.	=maš	—	genitive
2 pl.	=mataš	—	genitive
3 sg.	—	á-	genitive sg.
3 pl.	—	á-	genitive pl.

All sentences may have their constituent words scrambled, provided that the enclitic is in sentence-second position. Type C constructions, though structurally ambiguous, are nevertheless intelligible in context (otherwise Type A or B occurs).

Speaker intuitions are generally reported as preferring, or judging "best," the Type A construction. However, in all recorded texts, all three construction types regularly occur. Jacobs (1931:143) suggested that they contrasted as definite versus indefinite subject, and Rigsby once suspected that they might contrast as definite versus indefinite object. However, Rude's (1994) research and further data have shown the contrast to be one of topic continuity. In all the texts, the subject is topic in the Type B and C constructions, and the object is topic in the Type A construction. In the Type A construction, the object is coreferential with the subject in a preceding clause when that subject occurs in a Type B or C construction, and it is coreferential with the object when that object is coded in a Type A construction. And conversely, the subject in a Type B or C construction is coreferential with the object in a preceding Type A construction. Nearly every exception can be accounted for by intervening clauses of direct discourse and discontinuities evoked by first- and second-person arguments. Thus Types B and C can be classified as direct constructions, and Type A as an inverse. As an example of their functional contrast, compare the direct (the second clause) in (19) with the inverse (the second clause) in (20).

(19) *iwínš i-q̓ínun-a   wapaanłá-n ku k̓waaná*
man 3NOM-see-PST grizzly-OBJ and that.OBJ
i-ʔíłiyawi-ya.
3NOM-kill-PST
'The man saw a grizzly and he killed it'.

(20) *iwínš i-q̓ínun-a   wapaanłá-n ku*
man 3NOM-see-PST grizzly-OBJ and
pá-ʔíłiyawi-ya.
3INV-kill-PST
'The man saw a grizzly and it killed him.'

The ergative case has two forms:

The inverse ergative case ending *-nim* (*-im* after *n*-finals) marks the third-person singular subject of a transitive verb with a first- or second-person object and always co-occurs with the *i-* '3 sg. sbj.' verb prefix. Examples are:

(21) *łmáma-nim=š   i-ní-ya   ína*
old.woman-INV.ERG=1SG 3NOM-give-PST me
k̓pitłimá.
piece.of.beadwork
'The old woman gave me a piece of beadwork.'

(22) *iwínš-nim=nam. i-q̓ínu-ša.*
man-INV.ERG=1SG 3NOM-see-IMPV
'The man sees you.'

The obviative ergative case ending *-in* (allomorphs *-win ~ yn ~ -n*) marks the third-person singular subject of a transitive verb with a noncoreferential third-

person singular object. The obviative ergative is homophonous with the comitative and dual number suffix (except that the obviative ergative never suffixes to the plural form of a noun). It is probable that the dual/comitative suffix, which has a Nez Perce cognate (Aoki 1970:78), is the source of the Sahaptin obviative ergative. As obviative ergative, it always co-occurs with the *pá-* 'inverse' pronominal verb prefix and the *-na* (*-a ~ -an*) 'obj. sg.' case ending on the object nominal, if one is present. The *-win* alternant occurs after *u*-finals, *-yn* after *a*- finals, and *-n* after *y*-finals. Examples are:

(23) *x̣ʷísaat-in   pá-tuyayč-a   áswani-na.*
old.man-OBV.ERG INV-lecture-PST boy-OBJ.SG
'The old man lectured the boy.'

(24) *hulí-in   pá-wilapx̣ʷ-ša   łátx̣-na.*
wind-OBV.ERG INV-blow.up-IMPV dust-OBJ.SG
'The wind is blowing up the dust.'

All other subjects and predicate nominatives are unmarked for case.

The objective case has singular and plural forms. The objective singular is generally *-na* (*-nan* in Northwest Sahaptin), but *-a* after *n*-finals and *-an* after *a*-finals, while the objective plural is always *-aman*. The objective case-endings are used optionally to mark the object of a unitransitive verb and obligatorily to mark the primary object of a ditransitive. In unitransitive clauses object-marking is generally obligatory when the object is human. Some examples are:

(25) *ín=aš á-q̓inu-ša   awínš-in-aman.*
I=1SG 3ABS-see-IMPV men-DUAL-OBJ.PL
'I see the two men.'

(26) *čáw=nam paamaná á-yk-ša.*
NEG=2SG them.OBJ 3ABS-hear-IMPV
'Don't you hear them?'

(27) *kú-taš   awkú k̓ʷná á-waqitin-x̣an-a*
and=1PL.EXC then there 3ABS-look.for-HAB.PST
wawúkya-ma-aman.
bull.elk-PL-OBJ.PL
'And then there we would look for bull elk.'

(28) *x̣ʷísaat-in   paanáy pá-ni-ya   kúsi.*
old.man-OBV.ERG 3SG.OBJ INV-give-PST horse
'The old man gave him a horse.'

A special objective singular case-ending *-pa* is used with a small subclass of the kinship terms to indicate a possessor coreferential with the subject. An example is:

(29) *i-q̓ínun-a   ášaa-pa.*
3NOM-see-PST wife-OBJ
'He saw his wife.'

The genitive case also has singular and plural forms (genitive-marking in kin terms differs somewhat and is not treated here). In Umatilla, the genitive singular is generally *-nmí* after vowel-finals and *-mí* after consonant-finals, but nouns in final *-am* drop the *-m*, compensatorily lengthen the *a*-vowel, and add the *-mí* ending. Other dialects may differ slightly in the

677

distributions of -nmí and -mí. The genitive plural is always -amí. The genitive case has wide application, for example, a genitive of substance. It also marks the subjective nominals of gerundive nominalizations (see example 35). Examples are:

(30) tilaaki-nmí   miyánaš
     woman-GEN.SG child
     'the woman's child'

(31) tilaaki-ma-amí   miyánaš-ma
     woman-PL-GEN.PL child-PL
     'the women's children'

(32) wišxaa-mí   sínwi-t
     Wishram-GEN.SG speak-GER.NOM
     'the Wishram language' (cf. wíšxam 'Wishram')

(33) xʷisaat-mí   á-wa.
     old.man-GEN.SG 3ABS-be
     'It's the old man's.'

(34) áw   awkú spilyáy i-kkaanáywi-m-a
     now   then Coyote 3NOM-be.busy-CSL-PST
     aní-m-a   táqmaał ilkʷas-mí.
     make-CSL-PST hat   wood-GEN.SG
     'Now then Coyote busied himself making a hat out of wood.'

(35) xʷisaat-mí   á-wa   tuxúna-t.
     old.man-GEN.SG 3ABS-be shoot-GER.NOM
     'It was shot by the old man' literally 'It is the old man's shooting.'

The genitive case-endings are also used as catalytic or linking elements in forming the adverbial or oblique case-forms of human nouns and personal pronouns (see examples 41, 45, 51, 52, 65, 68).

The comitative (or associative) case is identical in form to the obviative ergative. Its syntactic context differs; whereas the obviative ergative always co-occurs with the inverse pronominal prefix pá-, the comitative requires plural agreement, either via verbal prefix or second position enclitic. Examples of the comitative are:

(36) kú kúuš-xi   tiláyma tílaaki-in
     and thus-same Tilayma woman-COM
     pa-wína-xan-a.
     3PL.NOM-go-HAB.PST
     'And so too Tilayma used to go with his wife.'

(37) yawtí=taš   wač-á ín-xay-n.
     companion-1PL.EXC be-PST my-friend-COM
     'We were companions, my friend and me.'

The instrumental case ending is generally -ki, although there are some marginal constructions in -kíl ~ -kín. It marks the instrument nominals and other related notions, for example, with human nominals, it best translates as 'about'. Examples are:

(38) á-tuxnan-a=aš   yáamaš-na
     3ABS-shoot-PST=1SG mule.deer-OBJ
     čin-ki   twínpaš-ki.
     this-INSTR gun-INSTR
     'I shot a mule deer with this gun.'

(39) wixa-kíl
     foot-INSTR
     'on foot, by foot'

(40) pa-nawát-ki
     DIS-belly-INSTR
     'belly to belly'

(41) šuyápu-ma   awínš-ma kʷáalisim
     Whiteman-PL men-PL   always
     pa-sínwi-ša   tilaaki-ma-amí-ki.
     3PL.NOM-talk-IMPV woman-PL-GEN.PL-INSTR
     'Whitemen are always talking about women.'

(42) á-šapatwana=aš wíwnu-na
     3ABS-mix=1SG   huckleberry-OBJ.SG
     pakukí-ki.
     salmon.flour-INSTR
     'I mixed huckleberries with salmon flour.'

(43) ín=aš á-tuxnan-a   yáamaš-na
     I-1SG 3ABS-shoot-PST mule.deer-OBJ.SG
     anáwi-t-ki.
     be.hungry-GER.NOM-INSTR
     'I shot a mule deer out of hunger, because of hunger.'

The locative case ending is generally -pa. It commonly indicates position 'in', 'at', or 'near' some nominal referent. With some verbs, it indicates motion 'into' or 'onto', and it also marks a number of not easily labeled relational notions, for example, with gerundive nominalizations, it translates as 'while, during'. Examples are:

(44) łmáma   i-túti-ša   míti čná
     old.woman 3NOM-stand-IMPV inside this.LOC
     níit-pa.
     house-LOC
     'The old woman is standing inside this house.'

(45) awinš-ma-amí-pa
     men-PL-GEN.PL-LOC
     'among the men, at the men's place'

(46) kú ċawín áš-a   níit-pa.
     and anyway enter-PST house-LOC
     'And she entered the house anyway.'*

(47) níix i-wá   qínu-pa.
     good 3NOM-be see-LOC
     'She's good-looking, nice to look at.'

(48) i-walptáyk-šan-a   xní-t-pa.
     3NOM-sing-IMPV-PST dig.roots-GER.NOM-LOC
     'She was singing while digging roots.'

The two directional cases in Sahaptin can be distinguished by labeling the case marked with -yaw the dative (Millstein 1990). It differs from the allative in that its basic meaning implies motion 'to' (as opposed to motion 'toward') a nominal goal. It also marks the

*In this sketch, Sahaptin third-person singular pronouns referring to people are translated at random as either 'he' ('him,' 'his') or 'she' ('her') when there is no determining context; either translation is correct.

goal in a ditransitive clause if the patient is human. It also suffixes to gerundive nominalizations.

(49) wána-(ya)w
river-DAT
'to the river'

(50) túx̣-šan-a=aš   níit-yaw.
return-IMPV-PST=1SG house-DAT
'I was returning to the house.'

(51) ináy=naš pa-táyman-a   iwinš-mí-yaw
me=1SG   3PL.NOM-sell-PST man-GEN.SG-DAT
'They sold me to the man.'

(52) i-šapá-wawyan-a=aš   wawyała-nmí-yaw
3NOM-CAUS-whip-PST=1SG whipman-GEN.SG-DAT
'He had the whipman whip me.'

(53) tamłámaywi-ša=aš   láwyala-t-yaw.
be.ignorant-IMPV=1SG fish.with.net-GER.NOM-DAT
'I don't know how to fish with a net,'

(53a) ałúk   i-wač-á   tux̣úna-t
difficult 3NOM-be-PST shoot-GEN.NOM
yáamaš-na   wáyix̣ti-t-yaw.
mule.deer-OBJ.SG run-GER.NOM-DAT
'It was difficult to shoot a running deer.'

The allative case is marked by -kan, or -čan in a few isolated forms where the palatalization is historic (Rigsby and Silverstein 1969:49-51). It has the meaning 'toward'. Some examples:

(54) yipáx̣ši-kan
downriver-ALL
'downriverward'

(56) míti-čan
down-ALL
'downward'

(57) pa-winá-ta   x̣máaš-kan.
3PL.NOM-go-FUT camas-ALL
'They'll go after camas, to the camas-place.'

There is also a peripheral caselike ending -laykan that appears to be built upon the -kan allative, although it is not strictly allative in meaning, as in čúuš-laykan 'along the river, by the water', watám-laykan 'by the lake', and ptín-laykan 'near the brush, bushes'.

The ablative case has a productive ending in -kni (-knik in Northwest Sahaptin), but a small set of nominals select an alternant in -čni (as with the allative -kan ~ -čan, the palatalization of the ablative -kni to -čni provides evidence for an earlier vocalic harmony). The ablative marks ablative and abessive senses and is also used to form the superlative of adjectives. Examples are:

(58) yipáx̣ši-kni
downriver-ABL
'from downriver'

(59) míti-čni   i-panáyti-m-a
below-ABL 3NOM-go.up-CSL-PST
'He came up from below.'

(60) i-ƛúp-waaničanwi-ya   ƙúsi-kni.
3NOM-jump-down-PST   horse-ABL
'He jumped down off the horse.'

(61) watx̣án=am   á- q̇inu-šan-a
interrogative=2SG 3ABS-see-IMPV-PST
ttmáy-ma-aman   wayám-kni.
maiden-PL-OBJ-PL Celilo-ABL
'Did you see the young women from Celilo?'

(62) nčí-kni
big-ABL
'the biggest (one)'

The benefactive case is marked by -ay (-yay after i). It typically marks nonhumans, nominal adjuncts of intransitive verbs, or benefactives in complex constructions. Some examples are:

(63) ku či i-wá   áčaš-ay tawtnúk.
and this 3NOM-be eye-BEN medicine
'And this medicine is for the eye.'

(64) aní-ya=aš   ƙúsi-yay   tawtnúk.
make-PST=1SG horse-BEN medicine
'I made the medicine for the horse.'

(65) pá-šapa-ʔani-ya   x̣apiłmí miyanaš-mí-yay.
INV-CAUS-make-PST knife   child-GEN.SG-BEN
'He had him make a knife for the child.'

Oblique human objects are typically treated as applicative objects. The nominal is case-marked the same as other objects, but the semantic case role is coded by verbal suffix (for a study of the historical development of the Sahaptian applicatives, see Rude 1991a). The directive suffixes -awa to the verb (-awan before a vowel; -yawa after i; -úu ~ -yúu in Northeast and Northwest Sahaptin). The following sentences illustrate. The last one illustrates the alternative of marking with the oblique dative case, which deemphasizes the human goal. Note that its status there as oblique requires the absence of the second position =naš 'me' (which is obligatory in example 67).

(66) iwínš-in   tílaaki-na
man-OBV.ERG woman-OBJ.SG
pá-wyanawi-yawan-a.
INV-arrive-DIR-PST
'The man came to the woman (the woman's place).'

(67) iwínš-nim=naš   i-wyánawi-yawan-a.
man-INV.ERG-1SG 3NOM-arrive-DIR-PST
'The man came to me (my place).'

(68) iwínš i-wyánawi-ya   in-mí-yaw.
man 3NOM-arrive-PST I-GEN.SG-DAT
'The man came to me (my place).'

Benefactive objects and possessors of the object are marked by the same verbal suffix. In Columbia River Sahaptin, the usual suffix is -ay (-yay after i). A second form -ani occurs in some dialects. Rigsby's main Yakima informant used both. Evidently, Jacobs's (1931:200-201) Taitnapam and Lower Snake informants also used both but with some indication in Lower Snake that the two realized different semantic categories, -ay marking objectivized possessors and -ani objectivized benefactives. In all extant dialects, 679 the occurrence of one or the other alternant is morphologically conditioned, and they are in complementary distribution. Rude's principal Walla Walla consultant, for example, uses *-ay* before consonants, and *-ani* before vowels. The Nez Perce dialects also differ in their use of one or the other of the cognate benefactive morphemes (Aoki 1970:7). The following sentences illustrate the treatment of benefactive and genitive objects. The last illustrates the alternative construction in which both possessor nominal and possessed nominal receive objective case-marking (concord in case-marking). In the latter, the possessed nominal is highlighted, and in the former the possessor.

(69) *in-mí   iwínš i-wátša-ay-xan-a*
     I-GEN.SG man   3NOM-beat.the.sticks-BEN-HAB-PST
     twáti-na.
     shaman-OBJ.SG
     'My husband used to beat the sticks for the shaman.'

(70) *q̓ínw-ay-šan-a꞊maš   imanáy   k̓úsi.*
     see-GEN-IMPV-PST꞊1SG   you.SG.OBJ   horse
     'I saw your horse.'

(71) *á-q̓inu-šan-a꞊aš   iminanáy*
     3ABS-see-IMPV-PST-1SG   you.SG.GEN.OBJ
     k̓úsi-na.
     horse-OBJ.SG
     'I saw your horse.'

Comitative objects are indicated by the applicative *-twa* suffixed to the verb (*-twi* in Northwest Sahaptin). The following are examples. The comitative noun case in the last example appears to downplay the status of 'with him'.

(72) *paʔáw-itamaši-twa-šan-a.*
     3PL.NOM+3OBJ-sweat-COM-IMPV-PST
     'They were sweating with him.' (Walla Walla)

(73) *pá-wyanawi-twan-a iwínš-na.*
     INV-arrive-COM-PST   man-OBJ.SG
     'He came with the man.'

(74) *pa-wyánawi-ya   iwínš-in.*
     3PL.NOM-arrive-PST man-COM
     'He came with the man.'

4. NOMINALS

Sahaptin nominals include noun, adjective, and pronoun subclasses (relative clauses and nominalized constructions are not treated here). Number and case are the major nominal inflectional categories. All nominals inflect for number in the syntactic cases, but only personal nominals inflect for number in the adverbial cases. There are three surface number categories: the singular is used for singular, generic, collective plural (such as a set of horses considered as a unitary group), and mass nominals; the dual is commonly used only for human nominals; and the plural is used for distributive plurals (e.g., a set of horses regarded as individuals distributed in space and/or time).

The singular is not marked for noun or adjective: *tílaaki* 'woman', *lámt* 'blue (one)'.

The dual suffix is *-in* (with allomorphs *-win* after *u*-finals, *-yn* after *a*-finals, and *-n* after *y*-finals), for example, *tílaaki-in* 'two women'.

The plural is indicated by a variety of means, the main one being the suffixation of *-ma*, such as *tílaaki-ma* 'women'. A second common plural formation is by reduplication, either full or partial, for example, *pšwá* 'stone, rock', *pšwápšwa* 'stones, rocks', *níix* 'good (one)', *aníxanix* 'good (ones)', *nčí* 'big (one)', *nčínči* 'big (ones)', *čmúk* 'black (one)', and *ččmúk* 'black (ones).' Reduplication and the *-ma* suffix co-occur in adjectives attributive to a (perhaps unexpressed) human noun, for example, *nčínči-ma* 'the old people, ancestors' and *milámlama* 'bad persons'. Noun and adjective plural formations are morphologically conditioned for the most part and show variation even among speakers of the same dialect.

A few Umatilla nouns show other, irregular, patterns of pluralization that may have been more widely used in the past. The first is a prefix *a-* that some speakers use to form the dual and plural of 'man'. Thus one encounters *iwínš* 'man', both *a-wínš-in* and *iwínš-in* 'two men', and *a-wínš* and *a-wínš-ma* 'men'. The pluralizing element *a-* is evidently cognate with the Nez Perce reduplicative *he-*, which occurs before the phonetic sequence /ʔi/: Nez Perce *titáʔc* 'good (ones)' (*taʔc* 'good') versus *heʔískit* 'trails' (*ʔískit* 'trail'). See Aoki (1970:42). Sahaptin *iwínš* 'man' is actually /ʔiwínš/, and thus *awínš* would represent an earlier *heʔ(i)wínš. A second marginal pluralizing suffix is *-tu*, as in *łmáma* 'old woman', *łmama-tú-win* 'two old women', and *łmama-tú* and *łmama-tú-ma* 'old women'.

Another restricted plural (or distributive) prefix is the *pa-* that pluralizes forms such as *tún* 'what' (indefinite-interrogative pronoun), *mún* 'when' (indefinite-interrogative time pronoun), *miná* 'where' (indefinite-interrogative locative pronoun), *máan* 'where, whither' (indefinite-interrogative allative pronoun), and *lísxam* 'once, one time' (derived with metathesis from *náxš* 'one' and *-am* 'time or times'). The plurals of these forms, respectively, are *pa-tún* 'sorts of things', *pa-mún* 'sometimes', *pa-mná* 'in places', *pa-máan* 'to places', and *pa-lísxam* 'seldom, rarely'. *pa-* also marks the distributive of objects, as seen in:

(1) *á-ny-a꞊aš   pa-niníipt* (or *pa-níipt*)
    3ABS-give-PST꞊1SG   DIS-two
    k̓úsi-yin   napwinanák.
    horse-DU   both.OBJ
    'I gave two horses each to both of them.' (Yakima)

(2) *pa-wxá-ki*
    DIS-foot-INSTR
    'foot to foot'

It is no doubt related historically to the homophonous *pa-* '3d-person plural nominative' verb prefix that now functions in the cross-reference system.

Gerundive nominalizations commonly pluralize with the *wí-* 'distributive of action' verb prefix: *waníct* 'name', *wí-wanict* 'names'.

Sahaptin nouns may be either simple or derived. The surface morphology of derived nouns includes deverbative and purely nominal constructions. Some of the more common derivational suffixes are the following:

1. *-łá* 'agentive'

This suffix derives nouns of agency from verbs. Transitive agentives often display a prefixed *pa-* (with secondary stress not marked here) that is simply the *pá-* 'inverse' prefix of the cross-reference system.

(3) *na-wina-łá*
    while.engaged.in.verbal.activity-go-AGT
    'thunder'

(3a) *pa-tkʷata-łá*
    INV-eat-AGT
    'cannibal'

An older alternant *-łam* occurs in *paxʷí-łam* (steal-AGT) 'thief'. In the Columbia River dialects, the *-łá* agentive may be suffixed to place nouns to designate a person from that place: *imatalam-łá* 'a Umatilla Indian' (cf, *ímatalam* 'name of winter village located at the mouth of the Umatilla River').

2. *-áł* 'negative agentive'

This suffix derives nouns of negative agency from verbs.

(4) *tkʷatan-áł*
    eat-NEG.AGT
    'one who hasn't eaten'

(5) *i-wá   wanp-áł.*
    3NOM-be sing.one's.spirit.power.song-NEG.AGT
    'He doesn't, can't sing spirit-power songs.'

3. *-t* 'gerundive nominalizer'

This productive suffix forms deverbative gerunds, many of which have primary specialized lexical meanings.

(6) *tkʷáta-t*
    eat-GER.NOM
    'food'

(7) *pá-ʔ i-nixʷa-t*
    INV-TRNS-be.good-GER.NOM
    'treaty'

(8) *wapáwa-t,   piná-wapawa-t*
    dress.up-GER.NOM SG.REF-dress.up-GER.NOM
    'Indian apparel, costume'

4. *-nút* 'privative' or '...-less'

Privative nominals ordinarily do not inflect for case and number but are used as independent predicative complements in expressions of nonpossession; however, as proper names they do take regular inflection.

(9) *i-wá   xaxaykʷ-nút.*
    3NOM-be metal/money-PRIV
    'He's broke, has no money.'

(10) *winanpš-nút*
    weapon-PRIV
    'Without-a-weapon' (a Umatilla chief's name. *winánpš* is a medio-passive noun derived from the complex verb theme *winá-np-* 'go get, take', which consists of an adverbial prefix *winá-* 'quickly' and stem *np-* 'take, seize'.)

5. *-pamá* 'pertaining to'

This suffix derives nouns with related meanings from other nouns and ablative noun phrases. Nouns so formed do not inflect for number and not ordinarily for case. *-pamá* also functions in caselike manner to mark underlying subordinated clauses of cause, several time-adverbial notions, and the notion 'about' in the informational sense.

(11) *miti-čni-pamá*
    down.under-ABL-pertaining.to
    'underclothing'

(12) *šaláwi-ša=aš   tuti-t-pamá.*
    be.tired-IMPV=1SG   stand-GER.NOM-pertaining.to
    'I'm tired from (as a result of) standing.'

(13) *kʷlawitit-pamá=aš   anáwi-ša.*
    evening-pertaining.to=1SG be.hungry-IMPV
    'I've been hungry since evening.'

(14) *watim-pamá-pa*
    yesterday-pertaining.to-LOC
    'the day before yesterday' (time-adverbial locative phrase)

(15) *čí=š   áw kú-ł   timnanáxin ánča*
    this-1SG now that-QUAN recount   again
    nusux-pamá   i-laxyawi-t-pamá.
    salmon-pertaining.to   TRNS-dry-GER.NOM-
                pertaining.to
    'This is all that I've recounted again now about drying salmon.'

Sahaptin adjectives are nominal in character; they may stand alone with no overt noun-head and they inflect for number and case, but they may be distinguished from nouns by weak syntactic criteria, namely by their usual occurrence preceding the noun-head and their agreement with it in number and case.

Adjectives may be simple or derived in morphological structure. The most common derived adjectives are deverbative stative constructions, formed by the suffix *-i* (with stressed alternant *-í*). Statives are formed freely from transitive and also intransitive verbs. Statives may also be derived from nouns; such forms may best be translated as 'one who has ...' and they recall the English past participial formations such as 'bejeweled' and 'beforested'.

(16) *lún-i*
    burn/be.alight-STAT
    'burnt (up)'

(17) *tútn-i*
    grind-STAT
    'ground (up), flour'

681

(18) *táaẋ-i*
    spirit.power-STAT
    'one who has spirit-power'

(19) *miyánaš-i*
    child-STAT
    'one who has children'

There are also several moribund adjectival constructions. *-á* derives adjectives from a few adverbs of time and place: *miimá* 'old' from *míimi* 'long ago', *ẋʷaamá* 'golden eagle' (literally 'the high above [one]') from *ẋʷáami* 'high above'. Historically, the *-á* reflects earlier *-má*, found also in *-pamá* 'pertaining to'. A few relict forms, such as, *átiš* 'ripe, cooked' and *wáq̇iš* 'alive', attest an old adjectival formative *-ʔiš* that remains common in Nez Perce. And other forms exhibit a moribund stative formation by vocalic ablaut (section 2).

The independent personal pronouns are distinguished for person, number, and case (tables 10-13). The first person inclusive-exclusive distinction is marked by the pronominal enclitic. Sex gender is not an overt syntactic category; thus the third-person singular pronoun may translate as 'he' or 'she'. However, typically, the third-person pronouns only anaphorically replace or deictically refer to human or personified nouns. The independent pronouns are commonly omitted in normal discourse and narration, unless they are topicalized, emphatic, or used to avoid ambiguity.

The basic paradigms are the subject, object, and genitive. The obviative ergative is always the same in form as the unmarked third-person dual, as is the comitative. The oblique or adverbial case suffixes are added to the genitive forms. The two forms of the oblique case suffixes are called here for convenience "plain" and "emphatic." An example of the former is *inmí-yay* 'for me', one with the latter *pinmi-láyk̇ay* 'for him or her.' The former marks mainly first person, the latter second and third person. Competing forms are generally available, especially in the third person. The Sahaptin dialects exhibit great diversity and independent restructuring by analogic processes in their independent pronoun paradigms.

The demonstrative pronouns (tables 14-16) are distinguished primarily by location near speaker, location removed from speaker, and location farther removed from speaker. They are marked for case, and in the syntactic cases, they inflect for singular and plural number, but they do not inflect for number in the adverbial cases. The demonstrative *yúk* 'that (one) over there, yonder' has a defective paradigm with no adverbial case-forms.

The demonstratives usually precede the noun-head, agreeing with it in number and case. They may stand independently and thus function as adverbs of place in the locative, dative, allative, and ablative cases. Personal forms for all oblique cases (including benefactive) are generally available in the singular, dual,

Table 10. Personal Pronouns: Subject Forms

	Singular	Dual	Plural
Umatilla			
1	*ín*	*napiiní, nápiin*	*náma*
2	*ím*	*imiiní*	*imáy*
3	*pín*	*piiní*	*pmáy*
3OBV.ERG	*piiní*		
3INV.ERG	*pním*		
Warm Springs			
1	*íni*	*napiní*	*naamáy*
2	*ími*	*iminí*	*imáy*
3	*pńni, mńni*	*piní*	*pmáy*
3OBV.ERG	*piní*		
3INV.ERG	*pńnm*		
Walla Walla			
1	*ín*	*nápin, napiiní*	*náma*
2	*ím*	*imiiní*	*imá, íma*
3	*pín*	*piiní*	*pmá*
3OVB.ERG	*piiní*		
3INV.ERG	*pním*		
Yakima			
1	*ínk*	*napiník*	*namák*
2	*ímk*	*iminík*	*imák*
3	*pínk*	*piiník*	*pmák*
3OBV.ERG	*piiník*		
3INV.ERG	*pnímk*		

and plural. Like the personal pronouns, they are built upon the genitive, and come in both "plain'' and "emphatic" forms.

The *čí* and *kʷ-* demonstratives also have minor paradigms of forms indicating quantity, length, manner, and direction (table 17).

A related form, *čiškín*, an instrumental phrase, has the special meaning 'in the Sahaptin language'. *kúma tanánma pasínwiẋa čiškín* 'Those Indians speak the Sahaptin language.'

Another complex demonstrative form, *kʷapín* 'that one aforementioned' in Columbia River and Northeast Sahaptin and *kʷpínk* in Northwest Sahaptin, is common in connected discourse. It may be attributive to a subject or object noun or may stand alone, but it does not inflect for number or case. It refers to an argument from a clause preceding the previous clause. Similarly, the absolute nominative *kʷay* 'that (one)' may be attributive to an absolute or objective head without further inflection.

The indefinite-interrogative pronouns are *šín* 'who', which refers to humans, and *tún* 'what', which refers to nonhumans (see table 18). They inflect for singular, dual, and plural number and for case, but many of the forms

Table 11. Personal Pronouns: Object Forms

	Singular	Dual	Plural
Umatilla			
1	ináy, ína	napiinamanáy	naamanáy, náaman
2	imanáy	imiinamanáy	imaamanáy
3	paanáy	piinamanáy	paamanáy
Warm Springs			
1	ináy	napinamáy	naamanáy
2	imanáy	iminamáy	imaamanáy
3	panáy	pinamáy	paamáy
Walla Walla			
1	ína	nápiinaman	náaman
2	imaaná	imiinamaná	imaamaná
3	paaná	piinamaná	paamaná
Yakima			
1	inák	napinanák	niimanák
2	imanák	iminanák	imamanák
3	pinák	pinanák	pimanák

Table 12. Personal Pronouns: Genitive Forms

	Singular	Dual	Plural
Umatilla			
1	inmí	napiinamí	naamí
2	imín	imiinamí	imaamín
3	pinmín	piinamí, piinamín	paamín
Warm Springs			
1	inmí	napinamí	naamí
2	imín	iminamín	imaamín
3	pnmín	pinamín	paamín
Walla Walla			
1	inmí	napiinamí	naamí
2	imín	imiinamín	imaamín
3	pinmín	piinamí	paamín
Yakima			
1	inmí	napinanmí	niimí
2	imínk	iminanmínk	imaamínk
3	pinmínk	pinanmínk	piimínk

are rarely seen in texts, and not all are given here (both pronouns have oblique personal forms derived from the genitive with "plain" and "emphatic" case suffixes).

The indefinite-interrogatives are used syntactically in interrogative constructions (with the questioned constituent attracted into sentence-initial position), in negative constructions, and in some affirmative constructions, for example, with the proclitic k^wa- 'I wonder', 'I suppose', 'I guess', etc. Examples are:

Table 13. Personal Pronouns: Oblique Suffixes

Note: Added to the genitive form of the appropriate person and number.

	Plain	Emphatic
Benfactive	-ay	-láyḱay
Dative	-yaw	-yawáy (Northwest -yúuk)
Allative	-kan	-kaní (Northwest -kaník)
Ablative	-kni (Northwest -knik)	-knín (Northwest -knínk)
Locative	-pa	-páyn (Northwest -páynk)
Instrumental	-ki	-kín (Northwest -kínk)

Table 14. čí 'this (one)' Paradigms

	Singular	Dual	Plural
Umatilla			
Absolute	čí	čiiní	číma
Ergative			
Obviative	čiiní		
Inverse	čínim		
Objective	čaaná	číinaman	čáaman
Genitive	činmí	čiinamí	čaamí
Instrumental	čínki, čínči		
Locative	čná 'here'		
Dative	íčin 'hither'		
Allative	čáan, čaaní		
Ablative	číni		
Warm Springs			
Absolute	čí	činí	čmá
Ergative			
Obviative	činí		
Inverse	čńnm		
Objective	čaaná	činamanáy	čaamanáy
Genitive	čnmí	činamín	čaamín
Instrumental	čńčin		
Locative	čná 'here'		
Dative	íčn 'hither'		
Allative	čáan, čaaní		
Ablative	čńni		
Yakima			
Absolute	íči	číin, číyin	číma, íčma
Ergative			
Obviative	číyin		
Inverse	čínim		
Objective	íčinak	číinaman	číimaman, íčiman
Genitive	čínmí	čiinamínk	čiimínk, čiimí
Instrumental	čínki		
Locative	íčnak 'here'		
Dative	íčin 'hither'		
Allative	íčiini		
Ablative	čínik		

683

Table 15. *ǩʷáy, kʷ-* 'that (one)' Paradigms

	Singular	Dual	Plural
Umatilla			
Absolute	*ǩʷáy*	*kʷiiní*	*kúma*
Ergative			
Obviative	*kʷiiní*		
Inverse	*kʷínim*		
Objective	*kʷaaná*	*kʷiinamanáy*	*kʷaamanáy*
Genitive	*kʷínmí*	*kʷiinamí*	*kʷaamí, kʷaamín*
Instrumental	*kʷínki*		
Locative	*kʷná* 'here'		
Dative	*íkʷin* 'hither'		
Allative	*kʷáan, kʷaaní*		
Ablative	*kʷíni*		
Warm Springs			
Absolute	*ǩʷáy, áy*	*kʷiní*	*kúma*
Ergative			
Obviative	*kʷiní*		
Inverse	*kʷńm*		
Objective	*kʷaaná*	*kʷinamanáy*	*kʷaamanáy*
Genitive	*kʷnmín*	*kʷinamín*	*kʷaamín*
Instrumental	*kʷńkʷi, kʷnkín*		
Locative	*kʷná* 'here'		
Dative	*íkʷn* 'hither'		
Allative	*kʷáan, kʷaaní*		
Ablative	*kʷńni*		
Yakima			
Absolute	*íǩʷak*	*kʷíin, kʷíyin*	*kʷúma, kʷmák*
Ergative			
Obviative	*kʷíin, kʷíyin*		
Inverse	*kʷínim*		
Objective	*íkʷinak*	*kʷíinaman*	*kúman*
Genitive	*kʷínmí*	*kʷiinamínk*	*kumínk*
Instrumental	*kʷínki*		
Locative	*íkʷnak* 'here'		
Dative	*íkʷin* 'hither'		
Allative	*íkuunik*		
Ablative	*kʷínik*		

(20) *šín i-túti-ša kʷná.*
    who 3NOM-stand-IMPV there
    'Who's standing there?'

(21) *tumín=maš wá táymu.*
    what.GEN-2OBJ/1SUBJ be news
    'What news do you have? (literally 'Of what do you have news?')

(22) *čáw=taš tún wač-á 'stove'-tún.*
    NEG-1PL.EXC what be-PST stove-what
    'We didn't have a stove.'

Table 16. *yúk* 'that (one) over there, yonder' Paradigms

	Singular	Plural
Umatilla		
Unmarked	*yúk*	*yúkma*
Objective	*yukʷaaná*	*yúkʷaaman*
Genitive	*yukunmí*	. . .

Table 17. Secondary Paradigms

Proximate		Distal	
. . .		*kúɫ*	'that much'
čáal	'this long, tall'	*kʷáal*	'that long, tall'
číš	'in this manner'	*kúuš*	'in that manner, thus, so'
čáy	'in this direction'	*kʷáy*	'in that direction'
čáan	'in this direction'	*kʷáan*	'in that direction'
čayní	'in this way, direction'	*kʷayní*	'in that way, direction'
čayníki	'in this manner'	*kʷayníki*	'in that manner'
čnín	'on this side'	*kʷnín*	'on that side'

(23) *čáw šín i-wyánawi-ya.*
    NEG who 3NOM-arrive-PST
    'No one came.'

(24) *čáw=naš túna á-ǩinun-a.*
    NEG=1SG what.OBJ 3ABS-see-PST
    'I didn't see anything.'

(25) *ín=aš á-ǩinu-šan-a kʷa-túna*
    I-1SG 3ABS-see-IMPV-PST wonder-what.OBJ
    ptín-pa.
    bushes-LOC
    'I saw something in the bushes, I think.'

Note the function of forms such as *túway* 'for what purpose' and *túnwašat* 'why'. As well, the filler word that speakers use when they cannot recall a word is built upon the *tú*-stem. Its unmarked form is *túwašin*, and its genitive is *tuwašinmí*; other case-forms have not been recorded. It may also be used verbally, *awkú kʷínki itúwašnima* 'And then he did whatchamacallit with that thing'. There is also a related minor indefinite-interrogative paradigm built upon *m-* 'indefinite-interrogative of place, quantity, length, manner, time, etc.' Younger speakers of all dialects tend to use *míš* as a general interrogative marker in sentence-initial position. In Umatilla, older speakers use *watχán* as the general interrogative marker; older Yakima speakers use *wáat*. The paradigm is presented in table 19.

A small number of nouns and adjectives may also function syntactically as pronouns. They are: *ƛáaχʷ* 'everyone, all', *ttúuš* 'some', *mílaa* 'few', *χlák* 'much, many', and *palaláy* 'a lot, many'. All but *palaláy* may inflect for the *-ma* plural.

The adverbs constitute a relatively small class, perhaps because many adverbial notions are expressed by

Table 18. Umatilla Indefinite-Interrogative Paradigm

	Singular	*Dual*	*Plural*
šín 'who'			
Absolute	*šín*	*šíin*	*šíman*
Ergative			
Obviative	*šíin*		
Inverse	*šínim*		
Objective	*šína*	*šíinaman*	*šáaman*
Genitive	*šimín*	*šiinamí*	*šaamín*
tún 'what'			
Absolute	*tún*	*túwin*	*túman*
Ergative			
Obviative	*túwin*		
Inverse	*túnim*		
Objective	*túna*	*túwinaman*	*túmaaman*
Genitive	*tumín*	*tuwinamí*	*tumaamín*
Benefactive	*túway, táay*		
Instrumental	*túkin*		
Dative	*túyaw*		
Allative	*túkan*		
Locative	*túpan*		

the adverbial case-system, the various demonstrative and indefinite-interrogative pronominal forms, and verb-thematic derivational affixes. Some adverbs of time are: *míimi* 'long ago; already'; *ƛíks* 'soon, by-and-by'; *áx̣ʷay* 'still, yet, later'; *kʷáalisim* 'always, often'; *táaminwa* 'always, forever'; *pakúuk* 'sometimes', *saʔát* 'for a (little) while'; *palísx̣am* 'seldom, rarely'; and *čawmún* 'never'.

Some adverbs of manner are: *kítu, ktúktu* 'quickly, fast'; *ƛwáy* 'slowly'; *húuy* 'in vain, be unable to'; *háw, hawháw* 'weakly, with no strength'; *qawqáw* 'separately'; and *q̇ʷíit* 'plainly'.

Modal adverbs are *páyš* 'maybe, possibly', and *láʔak* 'perhaps'. In most dialects, *páyš* also functions for 'if'. *čalawí*, used for 'if' in the more easterly dialects (including Umatilla), is evidently a borrowing from Nez Perce.

Table 19. Other Umatilla Indefinite-Interrogatives

miná, mán	'where' (locative)
máan	'where; whither' (allative)
míni	'from where, whence' (ablative)
míl	'how much'
míš	'how, in what manner'
mayní, mayníki	'how, in what manner'
máal	'how long'
mún	'when'

5. VERBS

Of the parts of speech, the Sahaptin verb has the most complex morphology. Three major positions may be recognized in its internal structure: 1, the pronominal prefix; 2, the theme; and 3, the auxiliary suffix complex. Position 1 may or may not be occupied, depending upon aspects of sentence structure external to the verb, for example, the pronominal prefixes cross-reference the clause for third-person subject (and object) arguments.

A verb theme, which may be of simple or complex constituency, always occupies position 2. The derivational morphology of complex themes involves a large inventory of affixal and stem morphemes and the processes by which they combine. Verb derivational affixes, mainly prefixes, do not comprise a semantically or syntactically unified set, apart from their occurrence within the surface thematic complex. Theme-derivational processes are typically restricted in productivity as compared to the inflectional processes of the auxiliary suffix complex.

Derivational processes are of several types—*wí-* 'distributive of action' and *reduplication of part or all of theme* 'iterative of action'.

(1) awkú kʷná ƛaax̣ʷ-tún
    then there all-what
    pa-wí-winp-in-x̣an-a tkʷátat.
    3NOM-DIS-buy-INCR-HAB-PST food
    'Then there they (the several women of a group) would buy all sorts of food.'

(2) aw=taš-kú kʷná ƛaax̣ʷ-tún
    now=1PL.EXC-and there all-what
    wí-šapša-x̣an-a.
    DIS-load-HAB-PST
    'And then there we would load everything (on the wagons).'

(3) i-ƛúp-ƛup-ša.
    3NOM-jump-jump-IMPV
    'He keeps on jumping up and down.'

(4) i-pá-qux̣-qux̣-ša.
    3NOM-with.hand-knock-knock-IMPV
    'He keeps on knocking (on the door).'

Included are processes of incorporating and the affixation of adverbial notions: *qá-* 'suddenly, spontaneously'; *máy-* 'in the morning'; *twá-* 'with the edge of a long object'; and *tísim-* 'while sitting'.

(5) ín=aš á-qa-q̇inun-a.
    I=1SG 3ABS-suddenly-see-PST
    'I caught sight of him all of a sudden.'

(6) i-máy-wiyanawi-ya .
    3NOM-morning-arrive-PST
    'He arrived in the morning.'

(7) i-twá-tima-šan-a
    3NOM-with.long.implement-mark-IMPV-PST
    tiičám-na.
    ground-OBJ.SG
    'He was drawing on the ground with a stick.'

(8) ín=aš tísim-tk^wata-ša.
    I=1SG while.sitting-eat-IMPV
    'I'm eating while sitting.'

Yet others, such as šapá- ~ sapá- ~ šáp- ~ sáp- 'general causative' and čá- 'restricted causative', function to derive complex verbs.

(9) ín=aš á-šapa-tk^watan-a núsux̣.
    I=1SG 3ABS-CAUS-eat-PST salmon
    'I made him eat salmon.'

(10) i-šapá-x̣alp-a.
    3NOM-CAUS-be.open-PST
    'He made it open up.'

(11) čá-x̣alp-in-k áčas.
    CAUS-be.open-INCR-IMP eye
    'Open up your (own) eyes!'

(12) ílk^as-na i-čá-k̓ila-k-a.
    wood-OBJ.SG 3NOM-CAUS-be.bent-
                stem.formant-PST
    'He bent the stick (with his own hands).'

There are also themes of complex morphological structure that are apparently lexicalized as idioms. For example, both wiyá-y̓ču- 'be frightened' and wiyá-nawi- 'arrive, come' contain an adverbial prefix wiyá- 'while going along', but their stems do not occur elsewhere and do not have localizable meaning.

The auxiliary suffix complex (table 20) of position 3 comprises a quite regular inflectional system that marks verbs for such categories as mood, aspect, directionality, and tense. The various combinations of morphemes are presented in diagram form in table 21.

There are three moods: indicative, conditional, and imperative. The indicative is the unmarked mood. It has the greatest number of functions and is most frequent in occurrence. It is used for statements, questions, polite hortative imperatives, and other sentence types.

The aspectual suffixes (of the indicative mood) take first position next to the verb theme. There is no perfective, the simple past tense serving this function. The imperfective suffix -ša ~ -šan indicates action in process and state or quality being manifested. The habitual or customary suffix -x̣a ~ -x̣an indicates the usual or customary character of an activity. Aspectual changes may sometimes best be translated by different English verbs. Note that the aspect markers are underlyingly /-šan/ and /-x̣an/: the /n/ surfaces in two different environments, before a vowel (the past -a), and before the translocative -či(č) in the Northeast dialects.

(13) i-wína.
    3NOM-go
    'He has just gone.' (present perfect)

(14) i-winán-a.
    3NOM-go-PST
    'He went.' (simple past = perfective)

Table 20. Auxiliary Suffix Combinations

	No Directional	Cislocative	Translocative Northwest and Columbia River Sahaptin	Northeast Sahaptin
Plain				
Perfect	-Ø, -in, -š[a]	-imš	-kikš	-čiš
Past	-a[a]	-ima	-kika	-čiča
Future	-ta	-imta	-kikta	-čita
Imperfect				
Present	-ša	-šamš	-šaykš	-šančiš
Past	-šana	-šama	-šayka	-šančiča
Future	-šata	-šamta	-šaykta	-šančita
Habitual				
Present	-x̣a	-x̣amš	-x̣aykš	-x̣ančiš
Past	-x̣ana	-x̣ama	-x̣ayka	-x̣ančiča
Future	-x̣ata	-x̣amta	-x̣aykta	-x̣ančita
Conditional				
	-tax̣na	-imtax̣na		
Imperatives				
Singular -k	-im			
Plural -tk	-imtk			
Warm Springs plurals				
-ti	-imti			

[a]In certain phonetic environments in at least some dialects of Northwest and Northeast Sahaptin, -a has been generalized as the present perfect, and -na as the past.

(15) i-wína-šan-čič-a.
    3NOM-go-IMPV-TRL-PST
    'He was going on.' (Walla Walla)

(16) i-wyánawi-š=tya.
    3NOM-arrive-PPF=instead
    'He has arrived instead.'

(17) wá-š=naš čímti twínpaš.
    be-PPF=1SG new gun
    'I have a new gun.'

(18) i-q̓inún-a.
    3NOM-see-PST
    'He caught sight of it.'

(19) i-q̓ínu-šan-a
    3NOM-see-IMPV-PST
    'He saw it.'

(20) i-šuk^án-a.
    3NOM-know-PST
    'He found it out, learned it.'

(21) i-šúk^a-šan-a.
    3NOM-know-IMPV-PST
    'He knew it.'

The present perfect is typically unmarked. It suggests present relevance and is generally translatable by the English present perfect (with 'have' or 'have just'). Comparative data from Nez Perce suggests that the bare verb stem originally served this function. In Columbia River Sahaptin, this is true of vowel stems, but consonant stems suffix -in in the present perfect. Most vowel stem verbs in first position before an

Table 21. Some Auxiliary Inflections of *wína-* 'go'

i-	wína	-Ø		-Ø.	'He has (just) gone.' (present perfect)
i-	winán	-Ø		-a.	'He went.' (past perfective)
i-	winá	-Ø	-m	-a.	'He came.'
i-	wína	-Ø	-kik	-a.	'He went away.'
i-	wína	-šan		-a.	'He was going.' (past imperfective)
i-	wína	-ša	-m	-a.	'He was coming.'
i-	wína	-xan		-a.	'He used to go.' (past habitual)
i-	wína	-xa	-m	-a.	'He used to come.'
i-	winá	-Ø	-m	-š.	'He has just come, is coming.' (present perfective)
i-	wína	-Ø	-kik	-š.	'He has just gone away, is going away.'
i-	wína	-ša		-Ø.	'He is going.' (present imperfective)
i-	wína	-ša	-m	-š.	'He is coming.'
i-	wína	-xa		-Ø.	'He goes.' (present habitual)
i-	wína	-xa	-m	-š.	'He comes.'
i-	winá	-Ø		-ta.	'He will go.' (future perfective)
i-	winá	-Ø	-m	-ta.	'He will come.'
i-	wína	-Ø	-kik	-ta.	'He will go away.'
i-	wína	-ša		-ta.	'He will be going.' (future imperfective)
i-	wína	-ša	-m	-ta.	'He will be coming.'
i-	wína	-xa		-ta.	'He will go.' (future habitual)
i-	wína	-xa	-m	-ta.	'He will come.'
i-	wína			-taxna.	'He would have gone, would go.' (conditional)
i-	wína		-m	-taxna.	'He would have come, would come.'
	wína			-k.	'Go.' (imperative singular)
	wína		-m	-Ø.	'Come!'
	wína			-tk.	'Go!' (imperative plural)
	wína		-m	-tk.	'Come!'

NOTE: Five positions are indicated here: 1, the third-person pronominal prefix *i-*; 2, the verb stem; 3, the aspectual suffixes; 4, the directionals; and 5, the tenses of the indicative mood and the conditional and imperative suffixes.

enclitic suffix *-š* in the present perfect. In much of Northwest and Northeast Sahaptin, *-a* has been reanalyzed as the present perfect, and *-na* as the past marker. The present perfect is unmarked but has an *-š* alternant that co-occurs with the directionals. In Columbia River Sahaptin, verb themes fall into two morphological classes, those with underlying final /n/ and those without. This final /n/ deletes in some environments, and variously in the dialects has been analogically spread into other environments for all verbs (as 'theme increment'). *i*-finals suffix *-ya* for the past. The future is always *-ta*. In the Northeast dialects, the *-xa* habitual (with *-Ø* present tense) has a short alternant in *-x*. The conditional mood suffix

is *-taxna* in Umatilla; *-taxnay* in Yakima; these two and a third form *-taxni* are variously found among the other dialects. In texts, the conditional precludes any other morpheme within the auxiliary suffix complex. However, most speakers in the 1980s judged grammatical its co-occurrence with the aspects and directionals as if it patterned with the tenses.

The imperative mood has endings for both singular and plural subjects. The imperative singular is usually *-k*, but *-Ø* after the cislocative. The imperative plural is always *-tk*, except that in the Warm Springs Reservation dialects it is *-ti*. The imperative never co-occurs with the translocative directional. That the "subject" in imperatives is second person is evident in that the 'inverse' marker *pá-* may occur with them; for instance, *pá-ni-m* 'Give it to me!' is cross-referenced by *pá-* (transitive action from 2d-person subject to 1st-person object). In true imperatives, the pronominal prefixes function much as they do in indicatives and conditionals. The position 2 pronominals are optional in true imperative constructions. It should also be noted that the longer true imperative constructions are paralleled by first, second, and third-person polite hortative imperatives that are always in the indicative. The last are formed with the subordinator *ana* (with allomorph *a*) in position 1 and bear a close resemblance to relative clauses in overt syntactic characteristics.

Motion verbs (and a few others) may be optionally marked for directionality. The cislocative suffix *-im* indicates motion or activity toward or with respect to the speaker, while the translocative *-kik* (*-čič* in Northeast Sahaptin) indicates motion away from the speaker. The cislocative is the unmarked member of the directionality opposition. This is consistent with several sorts of facts. First, the translocative is not so easily elicited in all parts of the verbal paradigm for all dialects. It is less common in discourse and in some cases might be better considered to be a restricted derivational suffix. Second, its phonetic shape and phonological peculiarities, along with the existence of an older and usually fossilized Sahaptian translocative **-en*, lead one to suspect that it is a later development borrowed from Nez Perce, which has the same morpheme realizing the same inflectional category. The cislocative *-im*, on the other hand, is an old Sahaptian morpheme and category. It is found in both daughter languages and is frequent in speech. Some evidence for its age is found in the themes *xní-* 'dig (roots)' and *xní-m-* 'dig a hole'. The first is a simple transitive root. The second is a complex intransitive form in which the cislocative functions as a derivational suffix. The resulting theme may be inflectionally marked by the renewed cislocative in the auxiliary (Rude 1991).

687

(22) *a=š   ín nák-winan-a, kú=nam tkʷatá-ta.*
    HORT=1SG I carry-go-PST and=2SG eat-FUT
    'Let me bring it, so you can eat.' (polite hortative)

(23) *a=na   tkʷatá-ta.*
    HORT=1PL.INC eat-FUT
    'Let's eat.' (polite hortative)

(24) *a=mataš   tkʷatá-ta-tk.*
    HORT=2OBJ.PL.2SUBJ eat-go.to-IMP.PL
    'Go eat!' (true imperative plural)

(25) *a=nam   tkʷatá-ta.*
    HORT=2SG eat-FUT
    'Eat!' (polite hortative)

(26) *a=pam   tkʷatá-ta.*
    HORT=2PL eat-FUT
    'Eat!' (polite hortative plural)

(27) *mán=maš   wá yáamaš*
    where=2OBJ/1SUBJ be mule.deer
    a=nam ƙwáy tuxnán-a.
    REL=2SG that shoot-PST
    'Where is the mule deer that you shot?' (relative clause)

(28) *ín=aš á-ɋinu-šan-a   kʷaaná iwínš-na*
    I=1SG 3ABS-see-IMPV-PST that.OBJ man-OBJ.SG
    ana-pín i-ɋásu-yayč-a.
    REL-3SG 3NOM-on.horse-cross-PST
    'I saw that man who rode across.' (relative clause)

Two verbs merit special attention. They are *wá* and *wíšayč-* (*wíšayk-* in Northeast Sahaptin, *txána-* in Warm Springs and Northwest Sahaptin), which are opposed as the perfective and inceptive, respectively, of 'be'. With only an underlying subject, *wá* means 'be' in the existential sense, while *wíšayč-* means 'happen, occur'. With a subject and predicate nominative as arguments, *wá* serves as the copula, and its suppletive partner means 'become'. In the indicative mood, *wá* inflects only for tense (it has a special past tense alternant *wač-*); it never takes the imperfective or habitual aspect suffixes. *wá* also inflects for the conditional mood, but not the imperative. *wá* may also be marked for the cislocative directional category and is then best translated as 'come'. On the other hand, *wíšayč-*, with the meanings 'happen, occur' and 'become', inflects only for the past and future perfective and the present imperfective in the indicative mood. It may also inflect for the conditional and the imperative moods. It has the sense 'used to be' in the past habitual aspect, and in the past, present, and future· imperfective and habitual aspects, it means 'stay, remain for a while'. *wač* is analyzed as an allomorph of the *wá*, as opposed to *-čá* being a special allomorph of the past tense that suffixes only to *wá*. There is no deciding factor in Sahaptin. But there is in Nez Perce. There *wek* is an allomorph of the copula *we*, which surfaces in both the past and future: *wéek-e* 'was' and *wek-ú?* 'will be'.

(29) *níit-pa   i-wá.*
    house-LOC 3NOM-be
    'He's in the house.'

(30) *míš i-wíšayč-a.*
    Q 3NOM-occur-PST
    'What happened?'

(31) *miyúux i-wač-á   nakákas.*
    chief 3NOM-be-PST my.maternal.uncle
    'My maternal uncle was a chief.'

(32) *xlák=nataš   wač-á ƙúsi.*
    many=1PL.EXC be-PST horse
    'We had many horses.'

(33) *čáa-pa-ƙa   i-wá-m-š   tanán.*
    near.by-LOC-too 3NOM-be-CSL-PPF person/Indian
    'The people are coming soon too.'

(34) *kú čáw=š ín páx-ša,*
    and NEG=1SG I remember-IMPV
    šimín ƙʷapín   tílaaki
    who.GEN aforementioned woman
    á-wšayč-a.
    3ABS-become-PST
    'And I don't remember whose that woman became.'

(35) *áł   i-wíšayč-xan-a.*
    generous 3NOM-be-HAB-PST
    'He used to be generous.'

(36) *čalawí=š wa-táxna xaxáykʷ,*
    if=1SG be-COND money
    kú=taš taymałáwas-yaw wína-taxna
    and=1PL.EXC store-DAT go-COND
    'If I had some money, we would go to the store.'

(37) *pa-kúuk áw xlák tanán*
    DIS-then now many Indians
    kʷná naamí-pa pa-wsáyč-in-xan-a.
    there our-LOC 3PL.NOM-stay-INCR-HAB-PST
    'And then sometimes many Indians would stay there at our place.'

When the verb is in position 1 in a clause, the position 2 enclitics become part of its morphology. The position 2 enclitics are of four positional subclasses *=tya* 'instead, rather'; *=xa* 'probably, must be'; the pronominal enclitics; and *=ta* 'doubt, reserve'. Two additional position 2 enclitics, *=tx* and *=at*, both 'skeptical query', are apparently restricted to the Northwest dialects. The modal *=akut* 'quotative' or 'hearsay' evidence seems not to co-occur with the other enclitics. Further examples are cited in Jacobs (1931:128-134).

(38) *i-wyánawi-ta=akut.*
    3NOM-arrive-FUT-QUOT
    'He'll come, they say.'

(39) *payúwi-ša=xa-aš.*
    be.sick-IMPV-PROB-1SG
    'I must be sick.'

(40) *šúkʷ-ša=tya=š.*
    know-IMPV-=instead/rather=1SG
    'But I know.'

6. Selected Vocabulary—Umatilla Sahaptin

afternoon *páčway*

alive *wáq̇iš* or *waq̇íšwi*

all, everyone, everything *ƚáax̣ʷ*

and *kú*

ankle *k̇uxsk̇úxs*

ashes *látx̣tx̣* or *lák̇im*

antelope *wáwataw*

back, spine *k̇úpaš*

bad *milá*

badger *šíki*

bald eagle *k̇ámamul*

bark (of tree) *psá*

(to) bark *wahwák-*

beaver *wišpúš*

belly *nawát*

big, large *nčí*

(to) bite *čánp-*

bitter, pepper *pƛák*

bitterroot *pyax̣í*

black *čmúk*

black bear *yáka*

blacktail deer *ƛálk*

blood *tilíwal*

cloud *páščt* or *šwáƚaš*

cold (of water) *k̇pís*

cold (of weather) *k̇sít*

(to) come, arrive *wiyánawi-*

cottontail rabbit *áykʷs*

cottonwood tree *x̣ápx̣ap*

(to) count, read *ititáma-*

couse root *x̣áwš*

coyote *spílya*

Coyote (in legends) *Spilyáy*

creature, bird, animal *kákya*

crow *áʔa*

(to) cut *šáx̣ƛk-*

day *ƚk̇ʷí* or *ƚk̇ʷít*

deer and elk (generic) *iwínat*

(to) die *ƛiyáwi-*

(to) dig a hole *x̣ním-*

(to) dig (roots) *x̣ní-*

diggingstick *kápin*

dipnet *twaluuƚáwas*

dirt, dust *ƚáƚx̣*

dirty *tatíi*

dog *k̇usik̇úsi*

(to) drink *čúun-*

dry *x̣yáw*

duck (generic), mallard duck *x̣átx̣at*

dull *pkʷáaš*

ear *mišyú*

earth, land, country *tiičám*

(to) eat *tkʷáta-*

eel, lamprey *k̇súyas*

egg *tamám*

elbow *k̇ášinu*

elk calf, calf, colt *q̇ayík* or *q̇áyq̇ay*

elk cow *tašímka*

empty *táalx̣*

evening *kʷláawit*

eye *áčaš*

face *tpíš*

(to) fall down *qátamčanwi-*

fast, quickly *kítu* or *ktúktu*

fast, swift *qaʔáw*

fat, grease *yápaš*

fawn *múps*

(to) fear, be afraid of (something) *skáw-*

feather *wáptas*

few *milá*

(to) fight *tíwi-*

(to) find *iyáx̣in-*

fire *ílkʷš* or *ílukš*

fish (generic) *waykáanaš*

(to) fish with net *láwyala-*

(to) fish with pole *wačílak-*

fish spear *aytanú* or *ptiyaƚawas*

fish weir *nax̣anáš*

(to) float *yáwayna-*

(to) flow *wána-*

flower *latít* or *latíš*

(to) fly *wáyna-*

fog *pásċat*

foot, leg *wix̣á*

(to) forget *láak-*

fox *tlípa*

(to) freeze (intransitive) *šíšaa-* or *taawáyi-*

frog *aluq̓wát*

fruit, berries *tmaanít*

full *kkím*

girl *p̓tínic* or *p̓tíic*

(to) give *ní-*

(to) go *wína-*

(to) go in, enter *áš-*

(to) go out *át-*

golden eagle *x̣ʷaamá* or *wáptas*

good *níix̣*

goose (generic), Canada goose *ákak*

grass *číick̓* or *číck̓*

green *x̣áx̣uš*

grizzly bear *wapaanɫá*

gun *twínpaš*

guts, intestines *p̓íp̓i*

hair *tútanik*

hand, arm *ipáp*

head *ɫamtáx̣*

(to) hear *yíkin-*

heart *timná*

heavy *qú*

hill *p̓uštáy*

(to) hit with hand or fist *pápƛ̓k-*

horn *yúkʷaas* or *yúkaas*

horned owl *miimánu*

horse *k̓úsi*

hot *láx̣ʷayx̣* or *láx̣ʷiix̣*

house *níit*

huckleberry *wíwnu*

(to) be hungry *anáwi-*

(to) hunt (large game) *tkʷáynp-*

ice *taawáy*

if *c̓alawí*

Indian carrot *sawítk*

Indian doctor, shaman *twáti*

Indian potato *anipáš*

jackrabbit *wilalík*

(to) jump *ƛúpin-*

(to) kick *tunáp̓ɫa-*

kidney *ak̓páyʔak̓pay*

(to) kill *íƛiyawi-*

knee *q̓úx̣ɫ*

690 knife *x̣apiɫmí*

(to) know *šúkʷa-*

lake *watám*

(to) laugh *tíya-*

leaf *ápaɫapɫ*

leftside *wáqacalkni*

(to) lie down *pináwx̣in-* or *pinálaw-*

lightweight *qaʔáaw*

(to) live, dwell *táwya-* or *táwyanayk-*

liver *siɫáx̣s*

long *k̓ʷáalk*

louse *apín* or *apílapil*

magpie *ác̓ay*

(to) make *aní-*

man *iwínš*

meat, flesh *nukút*

mink *ptyáw*

moon, month *álx̣ayx̣*

morning *máycqi*

mortar *k̓pk̓púɫ* or *k̓púɫ*

mountain goat *wáaw*

mountain sheep *tnúun*

mountain, peak *pátu*

mountains, upland wooded country *pítx̣anu*

mouse *lákas*

mouth *ím*

much, many *x̣lák*

mud *miƛiƛk*

mule deer (generic), mule deer doe *yáamaš*

mule deer buck *yukʷaasíns* or *yukaasíns*

mule deer spike buck *áswan* (= 'boy')

muskrat *ptís*

name *waníčt*

narrow *yuktyúkt*

near, close *c̓áa*

neck *tánwat*

new *čímti*

night *sc̓át*

no, not *čáw*

nose *níšnu* or *núšnu*

numbers

	Nonhuman	Human
1	*náx̣s*	
2	*nápt*	*nápu*
3	*mítaat*	*mítaw*

4 *pínapt*   *pínapu*

5 *páx̣at*   *páx̣naw*

6 *uyláxs*

7 *uynápt*

8 *uymátat*

9 *k̓úyc*

10 *pútimt*   *pútmu*

11 *pútimt kú náx̣š*

12 *pútimt kú nápt*

13 *pútimt kú mítaat*

14 *pútimt kú pínapt*

15 *pútimt kú páx̣at*

16 *pútimt kú uyláxs*

17 *pútimt kú uynápt*

18 *pútimt kú uymátat*

19 *pútimt kú k̓úyc*

20 *náaptit*

30 *matáaptit*

40 *pináaptit*

50 *páx̣aptit*

60 *uylxsáaptit*

70 *uynáaptit*

80 *uymitáaptit*

90 *k̓uycáaptit*

100 *putáaptit*

1,000 *táwsin* (loan from English)

ocean *atáčuuš*

old man *x̣ʷísaat*

old woman *ɬmáma*

otter *nukšay*

person, Indian *tanán*

pestle *pnáy*

pine tree *tápaš*

pine moss *k̓únč*

(to) place, put away *níč-*

(to) play *ɬq̓íwi-*

porcupine *šíšaaš*

(to) pull *čaku-* (*čákʷi-* in past) or *čáwayna-*

(to) push *šapáwayna-*

rain *ɬúx̣ɬux̣* or *ɬúx̣ɬux̣it*

rattlesnake *wáx̣puš*

raven *x̣úx̣ux̣*

raw, unripe *x̣ápiɬ*

red *lučá*

(to) remember *p̓íx̣in-*

rightside *niwítkni*

ripe, cooked *áɬiš*

river *wána* or *wánat*

road, trail, path *iščít*

robin *wíɬpakpak*

root *míċay*

rope *q̓ímx̣*

rotten *šišú* or *šišúni*

round, circular *ċíil*

round, spherical *k̓píit*

(to) rub *wáwšapnič-*

(to) run *wáyix̣ti-*

salmon (generic), Chinook salmon *núsux̣*

salt *katwaɬáwas* or *súul* (loan from English)

sand *sayáykʷ*

(to) say *náwa-* (*náwač-* in past)

(to) scratch *áya-*

(to) see *q̓ínun-*

seed *timná* (= 'heart')

(to) sew *wísx̣-*

sharp *čím*

short *k̓aywá*

shoulder *q̓ámkas*

silver salmon *súnx̣*

(to) sing *walptáyk-*

(to) sing (one's own spirit-power song) *wánp-*

(to) sit *áyč-* (*áy-* in imperfect)

skin, hide *apíx̣*

skunk *tiskáy*

sky *aykát* or *hawláak*

(to) sleep *nčún-*

slow *ɬwáy*

small, little *kiskís*

(to) smell (something) *nukši-*

(to) smell, stink *tíwa-*

smoke *láq̓uušt* or *láčkukt*

smooth *lulúu* or *tpíin*

snake *pyúš*

snow *púuy*

some *ttúuš*

sour *p̓ísx* or *p̓ísxni*

sparrowhawk *wapinyawaɬá*

(to) speak, talk *sínwi-*

(to) spit *káλin-*

(to) stab, pierce *pítya-*

(to) stand, be standing *túti-*

star *x̣aslú*

steelhead trout *šušáynš*

stomach; tripe *áq̇paaš*

stone, rock *pšwá*

straight *tk̓ʷíik̓ʷ* or *tk̓ʷíik̓*

strong *q̇ʷłtíp*

sturgeon *wílaps*

(to) suck *wac̓úp-*

summer *šátmiki*

sun *án*

swan *wišanałá*

sweet *c̓í*

(to) swell, be swollen *tít-*

(to) swim, bathe *winanúun-*

tail *wáłwas*

(to) take, get, buy *wínp-*

thick *łnú*

thin *awíix*

(to) think *px̣ʷín-* or *timnápx̣ʷin-*

throat *núq̇ʷaaš*

(to) throw *wix̣ín-*

(to) tie *káštk-*

tobacco *táwax̣*

tomorrow *máysx̣*

tongue *miłáaš*

tooth *k̓štín*

tree *ptáat* or *pátat*

troutlike fish (generic) *x̣úlx̣ul*

true, correct *kʷyáam*

turtle *alašík*

village *táwyanayt* or *tawyanikáwas*

(to) vomit *čipši-*

(to) wake up *táx̣ši-*

(to) walk along *tk̓ʷanáyti-*

warm *c̓múy*

(to) wash (clothes) *wápik-*

water *čúuš*

weak *šaláw*

wet *yáλpit*

what *tún*

when *mún*

where (at) *miná*

where (to) *máan*

whiskers, beard *šúu*

(to) whistle *hwíitin-*

white (of animals, people, stone, etc.) *qúyx̣*

white (of cloth, etc.) *pláš*

whitefish *símay*

white salmon, dog salmon *miłúla*

White person, 'Whiteman' *šuyápu*

who *šín*

wide *λináw*

willow tree *ttíx̣š*

wind *hulí* or *hulít*

wing *alíx̣alix̣*

winter *ánim*

wolf *x̣áliš*

woman *tílaaki*

wood, stick *ílkʷas* or *ílukas*

wood rat *wiší*

worm, maggot *sáysay*

year *anwíčt*

yellow *maqíš*

yes *íi*

yesterday *watím*

young man *ináw*

young woman, maiden *tmáy*

Sketch of Shoshone, a Uto-Aztecan Language

WICK R. MILLER

Shoshone belongs to the Central Numic branch of Uto-Aztecan, a branch that includes two other languages, Panamint, located in the Death Valley region of California and Nevada, and Comanche, located in the southern Plains. Shoshone was spoken across the largest area of the three languages, stretching from southwestern Nevada to southwestern Wyoming. Its speakers probably never numbered more than a few thousand.

In the 1990s, the Shoshone, located on several reservations and colonies in their original territory, preserved much of their original dialect diversity. The language was still widely spoken. Most children understood it to some degree, though in only a few households were the children still learning to speak it.

1. SOURCES

This sketch is based primarily on the speech of Maude Moon (fig. 1) and Lillie Pete. Many of the illustrative sentences are from stories told by Moon, who was from the Gosiute area near the Utah-Nevada border. Pete (b. 1917, d. 1984) was born at Ruby Valley, Nevada, but moved to Gosiute when a small child. She assisted in the recording of the stories from Moon and provided additional phonological and grammatical examples. A few example sentences are taken from other speakers who are from the Gosiute area or nearby; these sentences have been changed, where necessary, to conform to Pete's dialect.

Moon spoke a dialect that dropped initial /h/. Pete spoke a dialect that preserves it, and with her help the /h/ has been added in Moon's examples. Other

Fig. 1. Maude Moon (b. 1888, d. 1974), a Gosiute storyteller. From her uncle she received the Shoshone name *Pattun*, which was the name of a deadfall trap used for killing small mammals such as prairie dogs and chipmunks (Miller 1972:91-93). Moon began working with Wick Miller in 1965 and was his primary consultant. She told him about 40-50 mythological stories, as well as 40-50 ethnographic and historical accounts (Miller 1972:23). Photographer and date not recorded.

differences in Moon's speech, which are few, have been retained.

2. PHONOLOGY

There are four types of phonological elements—consonants, vowels, glottals, and final features (table 1). The final features are related to the consonantal and glottal elements. They are underlying abstract elements that are found in syllable-final position and are responsible for the consonantal processes that are typical of the Numic languages (2.1.); they are normally lost before vowels, glottals, certain consonants, and in final position. The syllable consists of a consonant or glottal plus one or two vowels. Initial syllables and, under certain restricted conditions, noninitial syllables of the word may start directly with a vowel. The syllable may be optionally closed by a final feature, or, under certain restricted conditions (2.2.), a glottal, but never a consonant.

2.1. CONSONANTAL PROCESSES AND FINAL FEATURES

The stops and nasals undergo certain changes when they come to stand in medial position, changes that take place in medial (morpheme, word, or sentence medial) position.

In the initial position, the stops are voiceless, unaspirated and usually lenis. In medial position they become spirantized, nasalized, geminated, or aspirated, the choice depending upon the nature of the final phonological element of the preceding syllable.

The processes are illustrated below for /p/ in *pia* 'mother' and *-pai* 'to have':

spirantized [β]: *ni pia* [ni βia] 'my mother', *co·pai* [tθo·βai] 'to have a great grandparent', *niwipai* [niwiβai] 'to have an Indian', *haipai* [haiβai] 'to have an uncle'.

nasalized [mb]: *in pia* [im bia] 'your mother', *co·mpai* [tθo·mbai] 'to have beads', *niwimpai* [niwimbai] 'to have liver'.

geminated [pp]: *tipappai* [tiβappai] 'to have pine nuts', *tuappai* [tuappai] 'to have a son'.

aspirated [φ]: *haihpai* [haiφai] 'to have a crow', *puihpai* [puiφai] 'to have an eye'.

The spirantized form is the one the stop takes when the preceding syllable simply ends with a vowel. In all other cases, the vowel is followed by a final feature. Nasalizing syllables end with an /n/, which assimilates to the position of articulation of the following stop. Geminating syllables end with a geminating element, written as /″/. The geminating final feature has no phonetic value of its own, but rather its presence is felt by its effect on the stop, which retains its stopped, fortis and voiceless character, and normally it is geminated,

Table 1. Phonological Elements

	Labial	Alveolar	Alveolar	Velar	Labiovelar
Consonants					
stops	*p*	*t*	*c*	*k*	*kʷ*
nasals	*m*	*n*			
sibilant			*s*		
semivowels	*w*		*y*		
Vowels					
i *i* *u*					
e *o*					
a /·/ (length)					
Glottals					
h and *ʔ*					
Final features					
nasalizing (*n*), geminating (″), and aspirating (*h*)					

NOTE: Accents written on the final vowel of verbs are diacritics distinguishing formal classes (2.1., end). The accents written in 2.4. mark nondistinctive stress. Capitalization follows English usage.

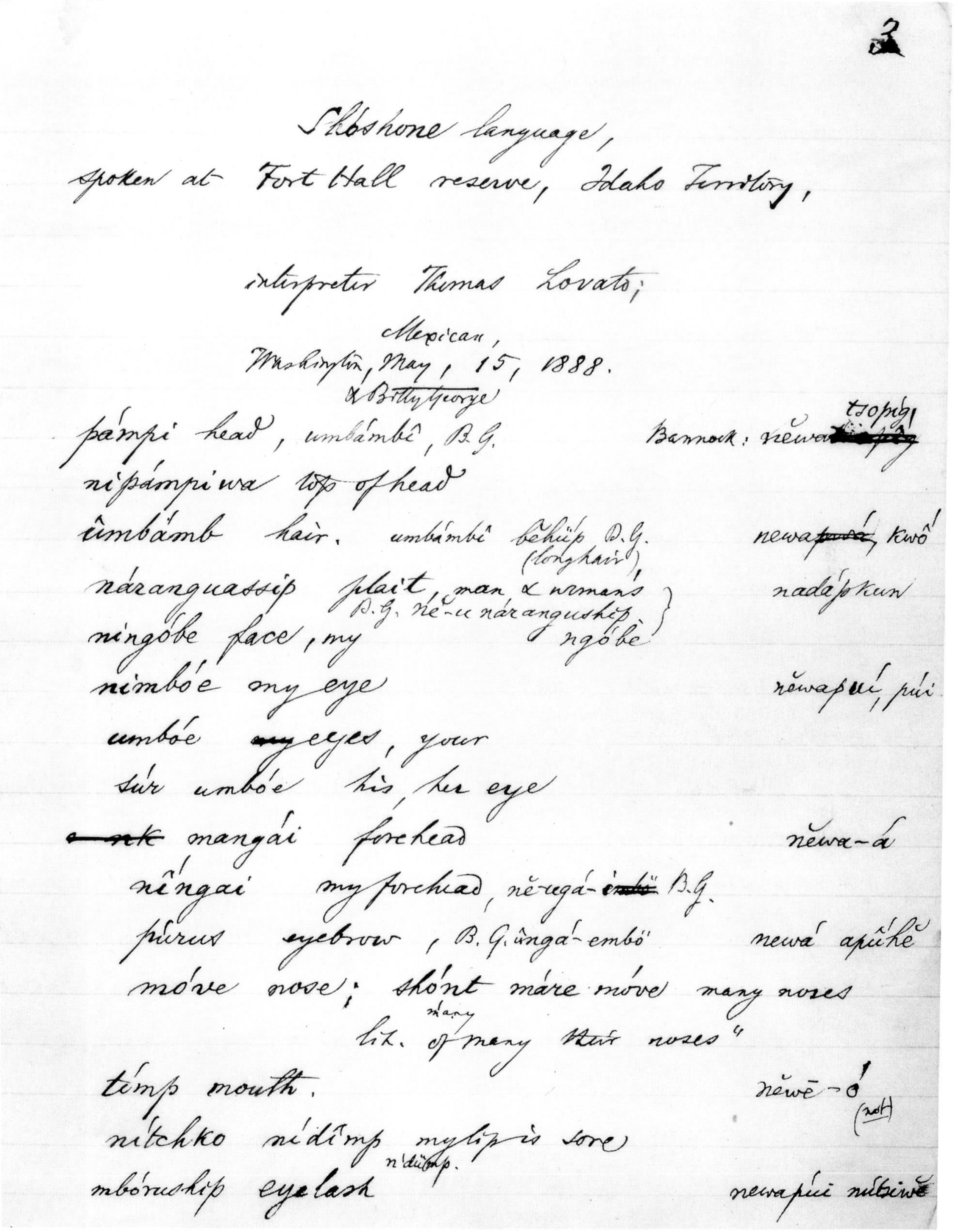
Shoshone language,
spoken at Fort Hall reserve, Idaho Territory,

interpreter Thomas Lovato; Mexican,
Washington, May, 15, 1888.
& Billy George

pámpi head, umbámbi, B.G. — Bannock: něwa tsopig
nipámpiwa top of head
ûmbámb hair. umbámbi behüp B.G. (long hair) — newa kwó
náranguassip plait, man & woman's B.G. né-u náranguship — nadápkun
ningóbe face, my — ngóbe
nimbó'e my eye — něwapui, púi
umbóe eyes, your
sur umbó'e his, her eye
mangái forehead — něwa-á
něngai my forehead, něugá- B.G.
púrus eyebrow, B.G. ünga-embö — newá apúhe
móve nose; shónt máre móve many noses
lit. "of many their noses"
tímp mouth. — něwē-o (not)
nitchko nídímp my lip is sore — n'dümp.
mbóruship eyelash — newapüi nübiwe

Fig. 2. Vocabularies of Northern Shoshone (left column) and the Bannock dialect of Northern Paiute (right column) collected from Thomas Lavatta (b. 1824, d. 1896), of Spanish or French descent, who lived at the Fort Hall Reservation, Idaho Terr., for many years. Albert S. Gatschet recorded the vocabulary in Washington, D.C., May 15, 1888, and later added words obtained from Billy George (Boise Valley Shoshone; b. 1854, d. 1945).

For another Shoshone vocabulary see vol. 11:101.

or lengthened, as well. Aspirating syllables end with /h/, which coalesces with the following stop to produce a voiceless fricative. The underlying form of the elements that initiated these changes in the preceding examples are, then:

niʉ 'my' (spirantizing)
co· 'great grandparent' (spirantizing)
niwɨ 'Indian' (spirantizing)
hai 'uncle' (spirantizing)
in 'your' (nasalizing)
co·n 'beads' (nasalizing)
niwin 'liver' (nasalizing)
tipa″ 'pine nuts' (geminating)
tua″ 'son' (geminating)
haih 'crow' (aspirating)
puih 'eye' (aspirating).

(Nasalization is written /n/ when it is word-final, but within a word as /m/ before /p/, but /n/ before other stops. Gemination is written as /″/ in word-final position, but by doubling the stop when it is in word medial position.)

The phonetic and phonemic form of the stops is given in table 2. The phonetic doublets for /t/ and /c/ are conditioned by the preceding vowel (see 2.5.).

The nasal consonants also undergo these processes. Illustrations are given for /m/ in mo²o 'hand', -ma 'with' (instrumental), and -ma²in 'with' (accompaniment):

spirantized [w̃]: nɨ mo²o [nɨ w̃o²o] 'my hand'; *co·ma²in* [tθo·w̃a²i] 'with the great grandparent'; *niwima²in* [niwɨw̃a²i] 'with the Indian'.

nasalized [mm]: *in mo²o* [im mo²o] 'your hand'; *co·mma* [tθo·mma] 'with the beads'.

geminated [mm]: *tipamma* [tiβamma] 'with the pine nuts'; *tuamma²in* [tuamma²i] 'with the son'.

aspirated [hw̃]: *haihma²in* [haihw̃a²i] 'with the crow'; *puihma* [puihw̃a] 'with the eye'.

The phonetic and phonemic form of the nasals is given in table 2. There is no distinction between the nasalized and geminated forms. The spirantized and aspirated form of the labial is a nasalized semivowel in all cases, but the dental nasal is a nasalized semivowel only when it follows a front vowel.

The fate of the final features in other environments must be discussed separately for each of the features. Before s, w, y, h, vowels, and in final position, the geminating feature /″/ drops without a trace. The final /n/ is retained when the objective suffix -a is added, such as co·na 'beads (objective)', but is dropped in all other cases when a vowel follows, or when final or followed by s, w, y, or h: *in ata* [ɨ ara] 'your uncle', *in wika* [ɨ wiɣa] 'your blanket', *co·n* [tθo·] 'beads'. Sometimes the final /n/ is reflected in a nasalized vowel: [tθo̜·, tθo̜·] 'beads'. Final /h/ will devoice the vowel it follows, provided that the vowel is short and unclustered, and that it is not in the first syllable of the word or root: *sappih* [sappɨ̥] 'stomach', *sappiha* [sappɨ̥ha], objective form (suffix -a), *sappihman* [sappɨ̥hma] 'on the stomach' (suffix -man), *sappihkuppan* [sappɨ̥xuppa] 'inside the stomach' (suffix -kuppa). A final /h/ is never realized as such when followed by s, w, y, or h, or when followed by a vowel other than the objective suffix -a, though its presence is often felt because of the devoicing of the vowel. However, it should be noted that clusters of hw, hy, and hs do occur in morpheme-medial position (see 2.2.).

There are several suffixes that begin with a final feature plus consonant. For example:

-nki, causative (6.4.)
-ppih, perfect (4.1.)
-ppinni, frequentive (4.1.)
-kkʷan, momentaneous (4.1.)
-mma·, 'finished doing...' (4.3.)
-cci, diminutive (11.3.)
-mpih, absolutive (11.2.).

When added to stems that end in a final feature, one of the features, usually the first one, is lost: *piyicci* 'little duck', *ponaicci* 'little mouse' (*piyin* and *ponaih* + *-cci*). Less often the second feature is lost: *ciampih* 'hips' (*cian* + *ppih*).

Table 2. Consonantal Processes

	Phonemic (initial position)	Spirantized phonetic	phonemic	Nasalized phonetic	phonemic	Geminated phonetic	phonemic	Aspirated phonetic	phonemic
STOPS	*p*	β	*p*	mb	*mp*	pp	*pp*	ɸ	*hp*
	t	r, ð	*t*	nd, n̪d	*nt*	tt, ţ̣t	*tt*	R, θ	*ht*
	c	ð, ž	*c*	ndθ, ñdʒ	*nc*	ttθ, čč	*cc*	θ, š	*hc*
	k	ɣ	*k*	ŋg	*nk*	kk	*kk*	x	*hk*
	kʷ	ɣʷ	*kʷ*	ŋgʷ	*nkʷ*	kkʷ	*kkʷ*	xʷ	*hkʷ*
NASALS	*m*	w̃	*m*	mm	*mm*	mm	*mm*	hw̃	*hm*
	n	n, ỹ	*n*	nn	*nn*	nn	*nn*	hn, hỹ	*hn*

NOTE: [r] and [R] are voiced and voiceless flaps.

Verb stems have been reshaped so that they end uniformly with a vowel and are not followed by a final feature. However, the verb in Panamint and some of the southern Shoshone dialects show traces; and the Gosiute dialect sometimes shows irregular traces of verb stems with final /n/.

There is a small set of verbal suffixes that alternate between geminated and aspirated:

-kkʷa/-hkʷa momentaneous (4.1.)
-kka/-hka resultative (4.1.)
-kkantin/-hkantin stative (4.1.)
-ppinni/-hpinni frequentive (4.1.)
-ttai/-htai 'finally' (4.3.)
-ttiki/-htiki 'start to' (4.4.).

(Henceforth such suffixes will be written -h/kkʷa, h/ppinni, etc.) Some verbs take the geminated suffixes (hipi-ppinni 'sipping'), whereas others take the aspirated suffixes (tikka-hpinni 'nibbling'). Verbs that take the geminated suffixes will be indicated by an acute accent: hipí 'drink', kammá 'taste'; and those taking the aspirated variants by a grave accent: tikkà 'eat', hotà 'dig', hannì 'do, fix'.

2.2. GLOTTALS

Both /h/ and /ʔ/ are found in morpheme-medial position, but only /h/ is found in morpheme-initial position. Glottals are prone to loss, especially in the Gosiute dialect. The vowels flanking a lost medial glottal sometimes combine to form a single syllable with a long vowel or a vowel cluster (2.3.), as si·pin 'willow', no·pin 'hill', and mia 'go' (from sihipin, noʔopin, and miʔa). Other times the two syllables are kept distinct, as siipin, noopin, and tioi 'disease' (from tiʔoi). A morpheme-medial syllable beginning with a vowel is always from this source.

Clusters of glottals plus nasal or semivowel are found within morphemes. So far these combinations of glottal plus consonant have been found: hm, hn, hw, hy, and ʔn.

tahmani 'spring time'
kahni 'house'
kuhwa 'husband'
muhyun 'door'
poʔnaih 'mouse'.

The /hn/ is very common, the /hm/ less so; all the rest are rare. Most examples of /hw/ and /hy/ are variants of /hm/ and /hn/. Some additional clusters are found in lexical items not found at Gosiute, for instance, /ʔw/ in waʔwati 'mosquito'; and some lexical items found with the glottal in other dialects are missing the glottal (especially the glottal stop) at Gosiute, for instance, kʷina· 'eagle', but in other dialects kʷiʔna·.

The cluster /hs/ is written in perhaps half a dozen words, for example, nattahsun 'medicine', kuttuhsippih 'ashes', kuppihsippih 'sweet cicely'. Phonetically the /hs/ is no different from any other medial /s/, but the

vowel before it is voiceless, a fact that can be accounted for only by assuming a following /h/ (2.3.).

2.3. VOWELS

A syllable contains a single vowel, either long or short, or a vowel cluster. The most common clusters contain two short vowels, a nonfront vowel plus /i/ (ai, oi, ui, ɨi) or a nonlow vowel plus /a/ (ia, ea, oa, ua ia). There is a close relation between /ai/ and /e/; some words have only /e/, as kʷesi 'tail', others only /ai/, as naipin 'girl', and still others vary, either dialectally or individually, as maison, meson 'cricket'. The relation between /ai/ and /e/ leads to some anomalies. The sequences /a·i/ (the only case of a long vowel in a cluster) and /e·/, both rare, almost always interchange: ha·iwi, he·wi 'dove'. The cluster /ai/ can follow any vowel but /i/ and /u/, giving a cluster of three vowels; the last two vowels are sometimes reduced to /e/, as in tiaippitin, tieppitin 'baby'; such sequences are not common.

A syllable that begins directly with a vowel is common in word-initial position but uncommon in medial position. Such medial syllables are the result of the loss of a glottal (see 2.2.) or the juxtaposition of two morphemes, one ending with a vowel, the other starting with a vowel: taihpui 'to fall asleep on one's feet' (ta- 'with the feet', ippui 'to sleep'); paohma· 'water baby' (pa·, pa- 'water', ohma· 'baby'); pahaa 'aunt' (objective)' (-a, objective suffix). An inorganic glottal stop is sometimes placed before a word-initial vowel, and occasionally also before a morpheme-initial vowel that is not in word-initial position.

There are two types of voiceless vowels, organic and inorganic. The inorganic ones, optional variants of short unclustered voiced vowels, are found in final position (with or without a following final feature): hucci [huttθi, huttθI] 'grandmother', punku [puŋgu, puŋkU] 'horse', siki [siɣi, sixI] 'leaf', kammu [kammu, kammU] 'jackrabbit', akkin [akkɨ, akkɨ] 'sunflower seed', moʔo [moʔo, moʔO] 'hand', tipa" [tiβa, tiɸA] 'pine nut'. A voiced obstruent (e.g. [g], [ɣ] is always devoiced before a voiceless vowel while a sonorant (e.g. [mm]) is optionally devoiced or murmured.

Organically voiceless vowels are always voiceless. They are found in all syllable positions except word initial. They are short, unclustered, in noninitial syllables and are followed by /h/: haincih [haiñčɨ] 'friend; sokkoppih [soɣoppɨ] 'land; sokoppiha [soɣoppɨha] 'land (objective form)'; sokoppihkuppan [soɣoppɨxuppa] 'inside the land'; haincihni· [haiñčɨni·] 'friends'; nattahsun [nattAsu] 'medicine'.

Final voiced vowels are usually followed by a glottal stop plus voiceless echo vowel: tukku [tukkuʔU] 'meat', tokoa [toɣoaʔA] 'rattlesnake', akkin [akkɨʔɨ] 'sunflower seed', hai [haiʔI] 'uncle'.

2.4. STRESS

Almost all of the Numic languages have an alternating stress pattern. It is absent in Kawaiisu, present only in attenuated form in Comanche, but it is strongly represented in all the other languages. Very roughly, every other mora is stressed, with long vowels and clusters counting as two moras, short vowels as one. The stressed mora is sometimes the even mora (in Southern Paiute), sometimes the odd mora (Shoshone); sometimes counting starts at the beginning (Shoshone), sometimes at the end (Mono). Shoshone exhibits a very clear alternating stress pattern, but there is considerable free variation. (The examples in this section are given in their phonemic form, with only stress and voiceless vowels indicated phonetically.)

The basic pattern is to stress every odd mora, with counting starting at the beginning of the word, and with the stress of the initial syllable usually a little stronger than in following syllables: CV́CVCV̀CVCV̀CV.... Clusters of a vowel plus /a/ always count as two moras, long vowels usually count as two, clusters with /i/ as second member usually count as one, and single short vowels always count as one. If the stress lands on the second mora of a long vowel, it shifts to the first, but a stress on /a/ in a vowel cluster does not shift. If the second syllable of a word is long, the first stress usually shifts to that syllable, and mora counting begins at that point: *kóttò·hkʷa, kottó·hkʷà* 'made a fire'. A final syllable is often stressed (provided it is not devoiced; see 2.3.): *nɨmmimàntin, nɨmmimàntɨn* 'one of us'. In two-syllable words, it always takes place if the medial consonant is a geminated or nasalized stop; and the stress is equal on both syllables: *áppɨ* 'father'; *kɨnká* 'onion'; *pɨ́ta, pɨtá* 'arm'.

Verbs seem to start their mora counting almost as often on the second mora as on the first: *hɨ́pikkʷà, hɨpɨ́kkʷa* 'drank'. This is especially common for the durative form of verbs, which is typically two syllables long with a geminated stop in medial position: *kattɨ* 'sitting'. If a stress, because of the shift to a noninitial syllable, comes to land on a vowel that normally would be devoiced because of a following /h/, the stress blocks the devoicing: *tɨ́kkAhkʷà, tikkáhkʷà* 'ate'.

2.5. OTHER PHONETIC ADJUSTMENTS: VARIA

The alveolars /c/ and /s/ are palatalized after the front vowels /i/ and /e/: *teci* [teži] 'brother-in-law', *haincih* [haiñčɨ] 'friend', *huiccu·* [huičču·] 'small bird', *pisappin* [piššappi] 'ocher'. Elsewhere /c/ is interdental, and /s/ is alveolar, sometimes slightly retroflex: *paci* [paði] 'older sister', *hucci* [huttθi] 'grandmother', *wanci* [wandði] 'antelope buck', *cuku* [tθuɣu] 'old man', *sosoni* [sossoni, ṣoṣṣoni] 'Shoshone'. Intervocalic /s/ is always geminated and fortis.

The /t/ is interdental after front vowels: *sitin* [siðɨ] 'this', *hitto·n* [hit̠o·] 'meadowlark', *taintin* [tainḏɨ]

'hole', *haihtukkan* [haiθukka] 'under the crow'. In all other environments it is alveolar: *sutin* [surɨ] 'that', *kintun* [kindu] 'yesterday', *tappottan* [tappotta] 'ankle bone', *tikkahtiki* [tikkARiki] 'start to eat'.

The spirantized and aspirated forms of /c/ and /t/ overlap. The [ð] is from /t/ after a front vowel, and /c/ after nonfront vowel, and similarly [θ] can reflect /ht/ or /hc/. Thus the phonemic form of [huðiðo·] is /hucito·n/ 'shin'.

A velar is somewhat more backed when next to /a/ and /o/, and more fronted when next to /i/ and /e/. The effect is from either the preceding or following vowel, but the following vowel seems to have the most effect. The Shoshone /k/ is somewhat more backed than its English equivalent.

3. THE SENTENCE AND ITS PARTS

3.1. PARTS OF SPEECH AND WORD ORDER

The parts of speech are verb, noun, pronoun, demonstrative, adjective, quantifier, numeral, adverb, and particle. The parts of the sentence are predicate, nominal, adverbial, and particle.

The sentence consists of at least a predicate, usually with one or more nominals. The most typical predicate is the verb (4.-9.). The verb enters into a variety of formations, the most important being associated with the aspect system (4.0.) Other parts of speech can also function as predicates, namely the noun and adverb (10.), adjective (14.), numeral (15.), and quantifier (16.); when they so function they often enter into some of the formations associated with the verbal system.

The nominal normally contains either a noun (11.) or a pronoun (12.). The noun may be modified by a demonstrative (13.), adjective (14.), numeral (15.), or quantifier (16.). The nominal is inflected for case and number (11.1.), and it can function as the subject, (direct) object, or indirect object of the sentence.

A sentence may be augmented by adverbials (20.) and particles (21.). Postpositions can convert a nominal into an adverbial (19.).

A predicate that has no underlying nominal associated with it is impersonal. A predicate with a single underlying nominal is intransitive, and one with two or more is transitive. The single nominal is the subject, and the additional nominals are the (direct) object and indirect object. The subject is in the subjective case, the objects in the objective case. Examples:

Ɨtiinna.
'It's hot (the weather).' (impersonal)

Kahnikuppan kunappai.
(house-inside wood-have; impersonal)
There is firewood in the house.'

698

MILLER

Sutin niwi winni tiasin.
(that person stand also; intransitive)
'That person stood up too.'

Ati·n niwini·n u wisuatikinnu.
(those people him missed; transitive)
'The people missed him.'

Ikka pihya· pimmin timpetta pekkanuhkʷa.
(this sweet their mouth kills; transitive)
'The sweetness kills their mouth.'

Ni sati·a cuhnippiha uttuhkʷa (or *Ni cuhnippiha sati·a uttuhkʷa*).
(I dog bone gave or I bone dog gave; transitive)
'I gave the bone to the ·dog.'

The order of elements is usually subject-predicate for intransitive, subject-object-predicate for transitive sentences. The direct and indirect objects may come in either order in respect to each other. Adverbial position is less rigid, but normally it is after the subject, with a temporal adverbial coming before a locative adverbial. Examples:

Sutin wihnu niwini·n umakan pitikʷa.
(that then people to-him arrived; *wihnu* is a particle, not adverb, see 21.0.)
'Then the people got to him.'

Niwi sakkuhtin peccikkinna.
(person there making-a-fuss)
'The person was making a fuss there.'

Ni kintun sokotihiya ke puninna.
(I yesterday deer not see)
'I didn't see a deer yesterday.'

Sutin supeni umakantun mianu.
(he then to-him went)
'He went to him then.'

The subject is frequently omitted:

Pinnan kopetta toccimma.
(his face wiped)
'He wiped his own face.'

Pin kahnikattun nukki.
(her to-house ran)*
'She ran to her own house.'

The omitted subject is usually best translated into English by a third-person pronoun, but sometimes contexts show that the omitted subject is a first or second person. Less commonly the object is omitted.

*In this sketch, Shoshone third-person singular pronouns referring to people are translated at random as either 'he' ('him', 'his') or 'she' ('her') when there is no determining context; either translation is correct.

Sometimes a word or phrase is brought to the first of the sentence to focus attention on it. Other times an element is put at the end of a sentence, almost as an afterthought.

3.2. NEGATIVE SENTENCES
A sentence is made negative by placing *ke* after the subject and before the predicate:

Uti·n ka·hiawoppih ke pitikʷanna.
(their rat-trapper not come)
'Their rat trapper did not come back.'

Ke puninna.
(not see)
'He didn't see anything.'

Utin tenkʷappi ke umakattun tekkʷanna.
(that man not to-him talk)
'The man wouldn't talk to him.'

Pinnan hainciha ke pekkawaihtin.
(his friend-obj. not kill)
'He won't kill his friend.'

Ke ma tikkati!
(not it eat)
'Don't eat it!'

3.3. INTERROGATIVE AND INDEFINITE SENTENCES
The enclitic particle /ha/ is used to make yes-no questions and to make indefinite sentences. It usually is placed after the first word of the sentence:

Sutin ha tennappi kimmatuih?
(that *ha* man come-will)
'Is that man coming?'

Takkawi·yu ha?
(snowing *ha*)
'Is it snowing?'

Ke ha akkʷa yakai.
(not *ha* unexpected cry)
'He started to cry unexpectedly.'

If placed at the end of the sentence, a shift of emphasis results:

In pohanaihkʷa ha?
'He doctored you, huh?'

Interrogative word questions are formed by placing an interrogative-indefinite word (17.) in sentence-initial position. The same words are used for indefinite word sentences, but the word then comes in its usual position in the sentence:

Hakke in puikka?
(who you see)
'Who did you see?'

Ni kian hakke puikka.
(I perhaps someone saw)
'I saw someone.'

4. THE ASPECT SYSTEM

Four classes of elements comprise the aspect system, which, when they cooccur, are in this order: secondary verb (4.4.); directional suffixes (4.2.); prefinal aspect suffixes (4.3.); and aspect suffixes, proper (4.1.). Normally, elements from the same class cannot cooccur.

The semantic domains covered by each class overlap. Secondary verbs typically indicate location, movement, and aspect notions. Directional suffixes indicate movement and less often aspect notions. Prefinal aspect suffixes indicate aspect notions. Aspect suffixes indicate aspect and less often tense notions. Most verbs must take one or another of these elements except when functioning as an imperative. If a prefinal aspect suffix is used, it must be followed by an aspect suffix, but an aspect suffix is not always required if a secondary verb or directional suffix is used.

The aspect system does not present neat paradigms. No single verb is found with all the aspect suffixes. Some aspect suffixes seem to have somewhat different meanings when used with different verbs, or when in different combinations with other elements of the aspect system, particularly when used with the prefinal aspect suffixes.

4.1. ASPECT SUFFIXES

The suffixes are:

-tin, generic. Also used for continuous activity, and, in some semantic contexts, interchangeable with the progressive.

-ppih, perfect.

-h/kkantin, stative.

-yu (*-yun* in some dialects), progressive.

-h/ppinni, frequentive. Used for intermittent activity, and in other dialects repetitive activity.

-nuh, *-nnuh*, completive. Usually past activity, with the implication usually that the activity took place over a period of time.

-h/kkʷan (sometimes *-h/kkun*), momentaneous. Usually past activity and contrasts with the completive by being of relatively short duration of time.

-tuʔih (varying with *-tuih*, *-toʔih*, *-toih*), future.

-nuhi, *-nnuhi*, expective. For future activity in which there is some uncertainty about its fulfillment.

-na, *-nna*, resultative.

-h/kka, resultative.

germinating the medial consonant, durative.

A few examples:

Ɨkicci niwɨ ke u puitin.
(nowadays people not him see-*tin*)
'People don't see him nowadays.'

Sutin yampa hotappih.
(she carrots dig-*ppih*)
'She already dug, had dug carrots.'

Ni tukkui tikkahkantin.
(I meat-obj. eat-*kantin*)
'I am full of meat.'

Ukka okaipitta sutin hanniyu.
(that-obj. cactus-obj. he gather-*yu*)
'He was gathering cactus.'

Ni koppe hipippinni.
(I coffee-obj. drink-*pinni*)
'I am drinking (sipping) coffee.'

Pia kotto·nuh.
(big make-fire-*nuh*)
'He made a big fire.'

Sutin ukuppan yaihkʷan.
(he inside enter-*h/kkʷan*)
'He went inside.'

Umakantun ni miʔatoih.
(to-him I go-*tuʔih*)
'I will go to him.'

Nu·n mekkuh sutin tennappi ni pekkanuhi.
(should let that man me kill-*nuhi*)
'Let that man kill me.'

Ukkuhtin waihyanna.
(there burn-*na*)
'A fire was burning there.'

Nakica ha kian eanna ke ni puikka.
(hope Q-particle maybe here not me see-*h/kka*)
'I hope he's not around here to see me.'

Many of the suffixes have multiple uses. The generic suffix is used to form participles and relatives (22.1.) and negative imperatives (7.), and it is at least historically to be related to the Set 2 postpositions (19.1.). The stative suffix is also used in participles and relatives (22.1.), as a possessive predicator (10.4.), and as a noun suffix (11.3.). A number of aspect suffixes are used in switch reference subordination: *-ppin*, *-h/kkʷan*, *-tuʔih*, *-na*, and *-h/kka(n)* (22.2., 22.3., 22.4.) The perfective suffix is used as an absolutive suffix (11.2.) and to form nouns from verbs (11.3.).

A dozen or more verbs form a durative by geminating the medial consonant of the root:

Hu·ppakanaihkantin toyakuppan nimmi.
(arrow-make-having mountains-in wander-durative; *nimɨ* 'to wander')
'Having made bows and arrows, he was wandering in the mountains.'

Sutin tiasin ettun poʔai happi.
(that also there road lie-durative; *hapí* 'to lie')
'There was also a road there to it.'

These forms do not allow any further suffixing. A second type of durative is formed by geminating the initial consonant of a directional suffix:

U no·kkintin.
(nó· 'carry on back', -kin 'thither', -tin generic)
'He kept on carrying it on his back, coming this way.'

Compare *U no·kintin.* 'He carried it on his back, coming this way.'

Verbs with no durative form that have a locative goal can be used without an aspect suffix:

Sikkihtun niwi umakantun to?i.
(here person him-toward emerge)
'A person came out to meet him here.'

Sittun panki wekippun takkiki.
(there up oblique walk)
'He went up on the oblique.'

The perfect and stative can combine to indicate remote past, thus violating the general rule that aspect suffixes do not cooccur. The form is *-ppih-kantin,* sometimes reduced to *-ppihantin:*

U paikkappih(k)antin.
He killed it, a long time ago.

4.2. DIRECTIONAL SUFFIXES
The suffixes are:
- *-kin,* hither
- *-kʷan,* thither
- *-kʷai,* random movement
- *-ni?i,* movement away and back again.

Some examples:

Sikkihtun to?ihkin.
(here-toward emerge-hither)
'He came out here toward him'

Sukkuh pitikʷan.
(there arrive-thither)
'They got there.'

Tukkun piapih sukkuh to·winikʷainna, ittun nimikʷainna.
(sheep's female there graze-around-na, through-here walking-around-na)
'A ewe was grazing there, and she was walking around here.'

Toyamantun miakʷaccih pie sokotihiya no·ni·.
(mountain-toward go-when already deer carry-away-and-back)
'Every time he went into the mountains, he carried back a deer.'

An aspect suffix is optional after a directional suffix. Not all combinations of suffixes occur, and some combinations are semantically irregular. For example, the resultative *-na* indicates present time or progressive action when after a directional suffix, and the directional *-kin* often has a repetitive meaning when followed by an aspect suffix:

Tikkakkinna antapasin, pinni tawittiakaku.
(eat-durative-*kin-na* no-attention, him passive-grease-rub-while)
'He kept eating, paying no attention, while he was being rubbed with grease.'

Tinkenumman u cawininkikkiyu.
(cliff-on him by-hand-stand-cause-durative-*ki-yu*)
'He kept making him stand on the very edge of the cliff.'

4.3. PREFINAL ASPECT SUFFIXES
A prefinal aspect suffix must be followed by an aspect suffix, proper, and sometimes the combination is semantically irregular:

- *-mmin,* 'had been, used to be ...-ing', used especially with the aspect suffixes *-tin, -tu?ih,* and *-na.*
- *-?i,* 'keeps on, kept on ...-ing', used especially with *-tin* and *-yu.*
- *-hVn* 'to finally and completely do it', used especially with *-tin, -yu,* and *-tu?ih* (V, a chameleon vowel that harmonizes with the preceding vowel). When used with future *-tu?ih,* it indicates remote or dubious future.
- *-mmà·,* 'finished', used with most aspect suffixes.
- *-h/ttaì,* 'for the last time, for good', used especially with *-ppih, -nuh, -h/kkʷan, -tu?ih,* and *-h/kka.*
- *-waih* 'unable to', restricted almost entirely to negative sentences, with *-tin* and *-yu.* The /h/ remains when *-yu* is added.

Some examples:

Usin wihnu tikkamminna.
(that then eat-*mminna*)
'From then on he had been eating (had plenty to eat).'

Kati?iyu.
(sit-*?iyu*)
'He kept on sitting.'

Pitihinkʷa.
(arrive-*hVnkʷa*)
'He finally got there.'

Ni tikkamma·hkʷa.
(I eat-*mma·hkʷa*)
'I finished eating.'

Tawih ma catto?ihtaintuih.
(we him hand-extract-*h/ttaintui*)
'Let's get him out of here (take him out for good).'

Ke hakattun kuhnewaihyu.
(not some-place run-*waihyu*)
'He couldn't run anywhere.'

Isin ke ma piawaihtin.
(this not him leave-*waihtin*)
'He isn't going to (is unable to) leave him alone.'

701

4.4. Secondary Verbs

There is a small group of verbs that can be added to other verbs to form loose compounds. When used in this way they are called secondary verbs. The meaning is sometimes specialized, and there is a tendency for it to become merely a formal element. An aspect suffix may follow, but there are restrictions on the resulting combinations. The secondary verbs are listed below, giving first form and meaning when functioning as secondary verbs, followed by form and meaning when functioning as main verbs:

-*hapi*, 'in a prone position' (*hapí* 'to lie', sg. subj.)
-*katɨ*, 'in an upright position' (*katɨ́* 'to sit', sg. subj.)
-*wini*, 'in a vertical position' (*wini* 'to stand', sg. subj.)
-*mmia*, 'becoming, getting; while moving, go in order to' (*miʔa* 'to go', sg. subj.)
-*nukki*, 'while moving, go in order to (faster motion)' (*nukkɨ* 'to run', sg. subj.)
-*no·*, 'while moving' (*nó·* 'to carry on the back')
-*nimi*, 'while wandering' (*nimɨ* 'to roam, wander, live', sg. subj.)
-*mpiti*, 'finished, completed' (*pitɨ* 'to arrive', sg. subj.)
-*h/ttiki*, 'start to' (*tikí* 'to put, place', sg. obj.)

Some examples:

Tukkun piapɨh sukkuh to·winikᵂainna.
(sheep's female there graze-stand-*kᵂainna*)
'The ewe stood there grazing.'

Umakantun miatɨhin wimmihammia.
(to-him going, tired-*mia*)
'Going to him, he got weaker.'

Tikkano·tin.
'He ate while riding or walking.'

Tikkahtiki.
'He started to eat.'

5. Instrumental Prefixes

The instrumental prefixes are typically used with instrumental verbs, a class of verbs that normally must occur with one of these prefixes. While some of the prefixes can only be used transitively, functioning as the instrument of the action, others can be used transitively or intransitively, in the later case functioning as an incorporated object. Thus with *ta″*- 'with the feet' and the instrumental verb -*nuà* 'to move':

Ni u tannuahkᵂa.
(I it foot-push-*hkᵂa*)
'I pushed it with my foot.'

Ni tannuahkᵂa.
'I pushed my foot.'

The prefixes are:

wi″-, with a long instrument; generalized, all purpose instrumental prefix (trans.); with the whole body (trans. and intrans.)
ci″-, with a sharp point (trans. only)
ca″-, with the hand, grasping (trans. only)
to″-, with the hand or fist, motion away from the body (trans. only)
ma-, with the hand, not grasping (trans. and intrans.)
ki″-, with the teeth or mouth (trans. only?)
ta″-, with the feet (trans. and intrans.)
mu-, with the nose; with the front (e.g. of a car) (trans. and instrans.)
pi″-, with the buttocks; with the back (e.g. of a car) (trans. and intrans.)
ku″-, by heat (intrans. only)
si″-, by cold (intrans. only)

The last two prefixes are not, strictly speaking, instrumental prefixes, since they indicate manner of action, but they are characteristically used with instrumental verbs.

Additional nonproductive prefixes that occur only with certain verbs are:

ta″-, with a rock (trans. only)
si″-, with the foot, violent motion (usually forward motion) (trans. only)
tammin-, with the knee; with the foot with backward motion (trans. and intrans.)
ku-, with the head (trans. and intrans.)
co-, with the head (trans. and intrans.)
ki·-, with the elbow (trans. and intrans.)

Some examples:

Ni u wikkaʔahkᵂan.
(I it *wi″*-cut)
'I cut it (e.g., with an ax).'

Ni wi·mma tukkui cikkaʔahkᵂa.
(I knife-with meat-obj. *ci″*-cut)
'I cut the meat with a knife.'

Ni kunika.
(I head-placed)
'I put the cap on.'

Hu·ppin kukkipahkᵂa.
(stick fire-broke)
'The stick broke by burning.'

Pin puihkatti toccimma yakaitin.
(his eye-at fist-scrape crying)
'He wiped his eyes, crying.'

The instrumental verbs form a fairly well-defined semantic class, namely those of hitting, breaking, cutting, and surface contact. They often have special forms for plural object. Except for a particular kind of passivization (6.1.), they must occur with an instrumental prefix. Some examples (listing the plural object form in parentheses, for those verbs that have it):

-ka?à (-kità), 'to cut flexible object(s)'
-kipà (-kipi·tà), 'to cut brittle object(s)'
-suné, 'to rub, scratch'
-kumpà (-tokì), to kill, beat'
-tamà (-tami·), 'to tie'
-sunkà·, 'to feel'
-ka?ì (-ponkà), 'to push'
-kiccì (-kiccai), 'to trample, mash'
-winoì, 'to shake a body part' (intr. only)
-yu·nkì, 'to stir something hot; to be dexterous'.

The prefixes can also be used with transitive verbs that do not require an instrumental prefix: yá· 'to carry', cayà· 'to carry in the hands', kiyà· 'to carry in the mouth'. An instrumental prefix on an intransitive verb makes the verb transitive, and typically co-occurs with the causative suffix -nkì: winí 'to stand', cawininkì 'to stand (him) up by means of the hands'.

The prefixes ni·"- 'by voice' and sun- 'by mind' (the second not a productive prefix) are instrumental prefixes in some Numic languages, but not in Shoshone, because they are not characteristically found with the same stems that take instrumental prefixes. Examples:

niyakai 'to make him cry by what one says' (yakaí 'cry')

ca·n nisua 'talk happily' (ca·n 'good', and suá 'think')

nikkumpà 'to have an argument, kill with words' (-kumpà 'to kill, beat')

sumpa·tù 'to learn something, to know somebody or something' (-pa·tu does not occur alone)

nasuntamà 'to remember, think about' (na- passive, -tamà 'to tie')

6. VOICE

6.1. PASSIVE
The passive is formed by prefixing na- to the verb. The logical subject is unexpressed, and the logical object is put in the subjective case. Examples:

Sutin napuihka.
(puí 'to see')
'You can see him, he is making himself seen.'
Tennappi naku·ppih.
(cp. Ne tennappia ku·kk"a. 'I buried the man.')
'The man is buried.'

Pa· nahipitin.
(hipí- 'to drink')
'The water is fit to drink'

The instrumental verbs (5.) have two passive formations. The first is a resultative and uses the bare stem with no prefix. The second prefixes ni·"- to the stem and seems to have the same meanings as the na-passive:

Hu·ppin ka?ahk"a. 'The stick broke, is broken.'
Hu·ppin ni·kka?atin. 'The wood can be broken or chopped.'
The na- passive can also be used with instrumental verbs, but then it is added to the verb containing the instrumental prefix:
Hu·ppin nacakka?ahk"a.
(stick na-hand-break-hk"a)
'The stick was broken by hand.'

6.2. REFLEXIVE AND RECIPROCAL
The reflexive and reciprocal are formed with the passive prefix na- with the subject of the reflexive optionally being marked by the suffix -sin 'own, self'. The reflexive pronoun (12.) may be used for third-person subjects; it is in initial position for the reflexive, but noninitial (usually second) position for the reciprocal. Some examples:

Ni napuihka.
(I na-see-aspect; also 'I am seen')
'I'm looking at myself.'

Tawih (or tawisin) nanankahka.
(we-[sin] na-hear-aspect)
'We (dual) hear ourselves.'

Pimmin (or pimmisin) nawasikk"a.
(they-refl.-[sin] na-kill-aspect)
'They (pl.) killed themselves.'

Tawih nanankahka.
(we-dual na-hear-aspect)
'We (dual) hear each other.'

Nawasikk"a piwih.
(na-kill-aspect they-dual-refl.)
'They (dual) killed each other.'

6.3. INDEFINITE SUBJECT AND OBJECT
The subject of a subordinate clause, unlike that of an independent clause, cannot be omitted (see 22.) However, it can be replaced by an indefinite subject prefix tan-, which produces, in effect, a passive:

Tikkakkinna antapisin, pinni tawittiakaku.
(eat-kkinna no-mind, him tan-grease-subord.-suffix)
'He kept eating paying no attention, while he was being greased.'

Sutin tampekkai tu·kk"asun.
(that tan-kill-subord.-suffix soldier)
'The one killed was a soldier.'

Ni hu·ppitta taweyanti himakk"a.
(I wood-obj. tan-burn-participle-obj. carried)
'I carried the wood for burning.'

The indefinite object prefix ti- is used with certain transitive verbs:
Ni tipekkannuh. 'I killed something.'
Ni tikoicoinnuh. 'I washed something.'
Ni tinittoinnuh. 'I sang something.'

703

6.4. CAUSATIVE, BENEFACTIVE, AND SENTENTIAL OBJECT COMPLEMENT

The causative and benefactive are both formed by the suffix *-nkì*. The one who is caused to do something, and the one who benefits are placed in the object case. In both cases there may be a direct object (also in the object case) if the underlying verb is transitive; the two objects may come in either order. Examples:

Tinkenumman u cawininkikkiyu.
(cliff-edge him hand-stand-*nki-kkiyu*)
'He kept making him stand on the very edge of the cliff.'

Ni nattahsuna naipiccia hipinkinna.
(I medicine-obj. girl-obj. drink-*nki-na*)
'I made the girl drink the medicine.'
Or: *Ne naipiccia nattahsuna hipinkinna.*

Tiasin ni hainciha sa·nki.
(again my friend-obj. boil-meat-*nki*)
'Boil some more meat for my friend.'

This suffix is also used for a sentential object complement:

Ma tikkatoiha ca·n suankinna.
(him eat-will-obj. good want-*nki-na*)
'(I) want him to eat.'

Cp. *Ni tikkasuahka.*
(I eat-want-*hka*)
'I want to eat.'

7. IMPERATIVE

The imperative verb usually has no aspect suffix, though it may have directional and other suffixes of the aspect system. Unlike many other Uto-Aztecan languages, the object of a transitive imperative is in the object rather than the subject case:

Ma tikka!
(it-obj. eat)
'Eat it!'

Pai hipi!
(water-obj. drink)
'Drink the water!'

The second-person subject pronoun is normally omitted, but it may be retained for emphasis:

Innin ma tikka! 'You eat it!'

Unlike finite verbs, subject number is obligatorily marked by means of the reflexive pronouns (12.), *piwih* (dual), *pimmin* (pl.); the singular is unmarked:

Yikʷi piwih!
'Sit down (dual)!'

Ma tikka pimmin!
'Eat (pl.) it!'

Negative imperatives take the generic aspect suffix *-tin* (4.1.):

Ke u tikkatin!
'Don't eat it!'

Ke katitin!
'Don't sit down!'

Ke sunni mati· yikʷitin, esin tahan haincihni·n.
(not thus them do-*tin*, that our friend-pl.)
'Don't do that to them, because they are our friends.'

The suffix *-mma*, added to a verb that has an aspect suffix, is used sometimes as a hortative:

Ni u puikkamma.
(I it see-aspect-*mma*)
'Let me see it.'

Hipikkumma.
(drink-aspect-*mma*)
'He must have drunk.'

8. VERB NUMBER

Third-person subject nonsingular number is optionally marked by the reflexive pronouns (12.), *piwih* (dual) and *pimmin* (pl.). These pronouns are also used for nonsingular second-person subject of imperatives (7.), but in this case the marking is obligatory. The pronouns normally come directly after the verb, but if a direct object or adverbial element is present that comes before the verb, the pronoun can be placed between that element and the verb:

Sekkitin pimmin kiyapitin.
(there they emerge)
'They came out of there.'

Mimiakun piwih.
(go they)
'The two of them left.'

Tennappini·n sukka tikkayu pimmin.
(man-pl. that-obj. eat they)
'The men ate that.'

Tennappini·n sukka pimmin tikkayu.
'The men ate that.'
Tennappini·n tikkayu· pimmin.
'The men ate.'
(But not *Tennappini·n pimmin tikkayu.*)

About 25 or so common verbs have special dual and plural forms. The number agrees with the subject for intransitive verbs, object for transitive verbs. The forms are sometimes suppletive, other times irregularly related. In most cases, the dual is a reduplicated form of either the singular or plural form, and in a few cases the singular and plural forms are the same with only the reduplicated dual being different. In the following examples, the listing is singular, dual, plural (along with alternate forms, where they exist):

hapí, kopí (kʷapí), kopikkan (kʷapikkan) 'to lie'
(plural *kokkopi* when the subject is inanimate)

*katí, yik*ʷ*í, yik*ʷ*ikkan* 'to sit'

winí, tacakkihkan, topoihkan 'to stand'

kimma, kikimma, kimmà 'to come'

mia, mimia, miá 'to go'

nimì, ninimì (yiyinkà), yinkà 'to wander, roam, survive, live'

pití, pippitì, pití 'to arrive'

ippiì, ikkoì, ikkoì 'to sleep'

*tek*ʷ*á, niwinì, niwinì* 'to talk'

pekkà, wasí, wasí 'to kill' (trans.)

yá·, himá, himá 'to carry' (trans.).

9. VERB REDUPLICATION

Reduplication is a productive process in most Uto-Aztecan languages, but not in Shoshone. It shows up sporadically for repeated activity:

Umantun sisi·winni.
(on-him redp-urinate-secondary verb; *sì·* 'to urinate')
'He urinated repeatedly on him.'

Oʔokaiyu.
(redp-flow-aspect; *okaí* 'to flow')
'It's flowing everywhere.'

10. NOMINAL AND ADVERBIAL PREDICATES

10.1. PREDICATE NOMINATIVE

The predicate nominative is formed by using a nominal, with no additional modification, as the predicate:

*Tenk*ʷ*appi ni haincih.*
(man my friend)
'The man is my friend.'

Sutin naipicci.
(that girl)
'It's a girl.'

A special type of predicate nominative is formed by using the demonstrative stem *-sin* with any of the proximal prefixes, except the definite ones in *s-* (13.). This demonstrative, which is used only in this construction, is the subject. It translates 'It/this/that...' when used with a nominal, and 'It/this/that is a fact that...' when used with a sentence functioning as a noun:

Usin tukummuhyun.
(that sky-door)
'It was the sky-door.'

*Usin caʔu tenk*ʷ*appi ni wikkumpahkantuʔih.*
(that certainly man me kill-will)
'It's for sure that the man will kill me.'

10.2. PREDICATE ADVERB

A locative adverb can be predicated by one of the three locative verbs: *hapí* 'lie', *katí* 'sit', and *winí* 'stand. The verb form must agree in number with the subject (8.). Examples:

Piatoya sakkah katti.
(Big-Mountain there-sit-durative)
'The Deep Creek Mountains are there.'

Toyapin sakkah happi.
(mountain there lie-durative)
'The mountains are there (of long, low-lying mountains).'

Sutin a·pesin kian sakkan Ciumpittan mahoi poʔai hapippih.
(that long-ago maybe that's Salt-Flat's around road lie-perfect)
'Long ago there was a road that went around the Salt Flats.'

It is possible to leave out the verb, in which case the position of the subject is left indefinite:

Ewaihtin sinnapin sukkuh.
(like-this aspen there)
'There were aspen trees there like this.'

10.3. "BECOME" WITH NOUNS AND ADVERBS

The verb *nahá-, ná-* is used with nouns, temporal adverbs, and locative adverbs:

*Mican pia na·kk*ʷ*a.*
(lamb's mother *na·*-aspect)
'She turned into a ewe.'

Tommo nahanuh.
(winter *naha*-aspect)
'Winter came.'

Sutin niwi sukkuh na·tin.
(that person there *na·*-aspect)
'There was a person there.'

A locative adverb with *na(h)á* indicates that the subject continues to be in place, whereas this notion is left unspecified in a predicate adverb (10.2.).

10.4. "MAKE," "HAVE," AND "EXIST" WITH NOUNS

The suffixes *-naì-, -pai,* and *-kantin* share a number of syntactic properties. While *-naì-* is used with the full set of verb suffixes, and must be followed by an aspect or other verb suffix, *-pai* can be used alone or with a limited array of suffixes. But *-kantin* cannot take any verb suffixes; it is an aspect suffix functioning as a predicate maker.

The suffix *-naì-* means 'to make', and the other two are used for possession: *-pai* for more permanent possession, more readily available and accessible; *-kantin* for less permanent possession, often with the notion that the possessor is characterized by what he possesses:

Ni kahninaiyu.
(I house-make-aspect)
'I'm making a house.'

Ke hakkaha tiʔoipai.
(not some sickness-have)
'He didn't have any more sickness.'

Sutin wihnu kʷiˑkkantin tiasin.
(that then wife-have also)
'He has a wife, too.'

Ni kahnipai.
'I have (own) a house.'

Ni kahnikantin.
'I have (rent) a house.'

The verbs with these suffixes may take nouns, adjective, or numeral objects, which are put in the object case:

Ni timpitta kahninaiyu.
(I rock-obj. house-make-aspect)
'I'm making a house out of rocks.'
Contrast: *Ni timpin kahninaiyu.* 'I'm making a rock house.'

Ni sukka kahninaiyu.
(I him-obj. house-make-aspect)
'I'm making a house for him.'

Ni sukka timpitta kahninaiyu
(or *Ni timpitta sukka kahninaiyu*).
'I'm making a house out of rocks for him.'

Isapaippih sukka ponaiha taipai.
(Coyote that-obj. Mouse-obj. brother-have)
'Coyote has Mouse for a younger brother.'

Hinnan pihi pohakanti timapeappihpai.
(some-obj. pelt-obj. doctor-obj. payment-have)
'They pay the doctor with some kind of a pelt.'

Ni wahatti kahnikantin.
(I two-obj. house-have).
'I have two houses.'

When used impersonally, that is without a subject, *-pai* means 'there is, it exists':

Kahnikuppa kunappai.
(house-inside wood-*pai*)
'There is firewood in the house.'

Hinna kian tiasin pakawisumpai.
(some must also arrow-string-*pai*)
'There was also some kind of bow string.'

10.5. OTHER PREDICATE MARKERS: *-TÚ* AND *-PƗKKÀ*

The suffix *-tú* 'to get, acquire an affinal relative' is used most commonly with *kʷihi″* 'wife' (*kʷihittú* 'to get married, of a man') and *kuhma* 'husband' (*kuhmatú* 'to get married, of a woman'), but it can be used with other affinal kin terms, for example, *monantú* 'to acquire a son-in-law'. The resulting predicate can be used with at least some of the aspect and other verbal suffixes.

The element *-pɨkkà* (perhaps related to the verb *pekkà* 'to kill') 'to be afflicted by' is used with only certain nouns. The forms do not take part in the full range of the tense aspect system. The element *-tiaì*

(*-kokoì, -koì* for dual and plural subject; see 8.), which is also the verb meaning 'to die', is used with the same nouns to indicate a more extreme state that *-pɨkkà*; it is almost always used with *-kantin* (aspect suffix, 4.1.; or alternatively possessive suffix 10.4.). Some nouns occur only with these elements, as *tiˑya-*:

Tipici tiˑyapikka. 'He was really scared.'

Others can occur alone, as *ohni-ppih* 'a cold', *ohnipikkà* 'to have a cold.' Some additional examples are:

pahopikkà 'to be hungry'
takupikkà 'to be thirsty'
tiwoipikkà 'to be sick' (*tiwoi* 'sickness')
tuhupikkà 'to be mad'
matuhupikkà 'to get an erection'
yokopikkà 'to act smart or stubborn' (*yokó* 'to copulate')
yuhupikkà 'to be fat' (*yuhu* 'fat')
noapikkà 'to be pregnant'.

11. NOUNS AND NOMINALS

A nominal consists of a head noun, with or without modifiers, or a pronoun (12.) In a nominal with one or more modifiers, the noun may be omitted, in which case the modifiers become noun substitutes. The modifier is a demonstrative (13.), adjective (14.), numeral (15.), or quantifier (16.). Most of the modifiers can also function as predicates, and when doing so have a number of verblike qualities. The relative order of modifiers is demonstrative + numeral + adjective + noun, or less commonly, with the adjective following the noun and the demonstrative and number in the same position. The quantifier, like the adjective, normally precedes the noun, but it may come after it. The position of the quantifier in relation to other modifiers is not clear, perhaps because quantifiers do not constitute a homogenous class. The modifiers must agree in case and number with the head noun. Some examples:

Sutin niwi sukkuh naˑtin.
(that person there was)
'There was a person there.'

Me sutin u suankinna.
(QUOT that her think)
'He thought about her.'

Sutin simmin tuˑmpihtin punku nukkimia.
(that one black horse running)
'That one black horse is running.'

Ni ukka simmia punkui puikka.
(I that-OBJ one-OBJ horse-OBJ see)
'I see that one horse.')

Itin tian kimmeniˑn tenkʷaniˑn nutaˑ.
(he also different-PL man-PL ran)
'He and the other men ran.'

A noun may also be modified by a possessive nominal, which comes just before the noun it modifies. In many Uto-Aztecan languages the possessed or modified noun is marked as such, but in Shoshone only the possessor is marked (11.1.):

Sukkan taintinan kammuhyumma pitik"a.
(that-POSS hole's door-at arrived)
'He got to the door of the cave.'

Etin un nampih ca·n napuni tiasin.
(this his shoe good looked also)
'These shoes of his looked nice too.'

11.1. NOUN INFLECTION: NUMBER AND CASE

The noun is inflected for three numbers—singular, dual, and plural—and three cases—subjective, objective, and possessive. The subjective singular is unmarked. The most typical function of the objective case is to mark the object of a transitive verb (3.1.), but it has other functions as well (see 22.2., 3.1., 10.4.). The most typical function of the possessive case is to mark the possessor in a possessor-possessed relationship (11.), but it has other functions as well (see 22.3., 19.3.).

The singular objective suffix, along with the related singular possessive suffix, has four forms, which can in part be predicted by the phonological shape of the noun (specifically, by the final vowel or final feature). Where it cannot be so predicted there is considerable dialect variation. The four forms are:

	Objective	Possessive
(1)	-tta	-ttan, -n
(2)	-a	-an
(3)	-Ø	-n
(4)	-i	-n, -an

The variants in (1) and (4) of the possessive are largely predictable. The first set is used with all nouns ending in the absolutive suffix -pin (11.2.), plus a few other nouns: *anin* 'ant', *wi·n* 'knife', and *kope* 'face'. The final -n is dropped before -tta, -ttan (2.1.): *toya-pin, toya-pi-tta* 'mountain'. The second set is used with nouns that end with /-n/ (excluding those that take the first set) and /-h/: *a·n, a·na* 'horn'; *pattun, pattuna* 'deadfall trap'; *haincih, hainciha* 'friend'; *nasa·ppih, nasa·ppiha* 'something boiled'. The third type, in which there is no change in the objective, is found with a number of nouns, all ending in -i or -e, and thus could be viewed as a special form of the fourth type, in which the -i objective is swallowed up by the preceding vowel: *eti, eti* (*etitta* in some dialects) 'gun'; *pehe, pehe* 'seeds'; *tape, tape* 'sun'; *kahni, kahni* 'house'; *timpe, timpe* (*timpetta* in some dialects) 'mouth'. The second and fourth types are used in all other cases, though -a is seldom used in the Gosiute dialect with nouns that end with -a. There is a certain amount of individual and considerable amount of dialect variation between -a and -i: *wa?ippi, wa?ippia* 'woman'; *punku, punkua* 'horse'; *taipo, taipoa* 'White

man'; *tieppiticci, tieppiticcia* 'baby'; *hupa, hupai* 'soup'; *tukku, tukkui* 'mountain sheep'; *wa·ko, wa·koi* 'frog'. When -i is added to /a/ it usually becomes /e/: *pia, piai* or *pie* 'mother'; *tipa", tipai* or *tipe* 'pine nuts'. A long vowel is usually shortened before -a or -i: *pa·, pa·i* or *pai* 'water'; *co·, co·a* or *coa* 'great grandparent'. Notice that /a·-i/ never becomes /e·/ or /e/. The -i often replaces a short vowel after a glottal stop and almost always replaces a short /i/: *mo?o, mo?oi* or *mo?i* 'hand'; *niwi, niwi* 'Indian, person'.

The nonsingular case endings are:

	Subjective	Objective	Possessive
Dual	-niwih	-nihi	-nihin
Plural	-ni·n	-ni·	-ni·n

There are a few human nouns that form their dual and plural stem by reduplication or suppletion:

tieppitin, titieppitin 'baby'
tua", tutua 'boy, child, son'
naipin, naiyin- 'girl'
tuicci, tuiccia- 'young man'
tuini, pi·a- 'boy'
hipico·, hihippiccia- 'old woman'
cuku, cuccukkuccia- 'old man'.

The first two forms may occur with or without a number suffix, but if they are unsuffixed, they are taken to be plural. The remaining nouns must have a number suffix added.

Number is obligatory for human nouns, optional of nonhuman animate nouns, and is used with inanimate nouns only to personify them. Number is indirectly indicated for inanimate nouns when they are used with a verb that suppletively indicates number (8.).

A noun, uninflected for number and case, can be used as an object, to indicate an indefinite numberless entity:

Innin wica tapun tikka.
(you should rabbit eat)
'You should eat cottontail rabbit.'
Contrast:

Innin wica tapuna tikka.
(you should rabbit-obj. eat)
'You should eat a (one) cottontail rabbit.'

11.2. ABSOLUTIVE SUFFIXES

Many nouns end with a suffix that has little or only vague meaning. Often a noun is also found both with and without the suffix, or with a different suffix, with or without a change in meaning. the suffixes are (with the objective form in parentheses):

-pin (-pitta)
-ppih (-ppiha) (-pih, -piha after -n)
-ppi (-ppia)
-ccih (-cciha)
-piccih, -piccih (-picciha, -picciha)
-mpih (-mpiha).

707

The *-pin* and *-ppih* are the most common, and also the vaguest in meaning. The *-pin* is especially common with natural phenomena and plants. The *-ppih*, derived from the perfect participle (22.3.) and perfect aspect suffix (4.1.), is sometimes used to form nouns from verb roots. Other times it is added to noun roots; it is especially common with body parts and is common, though somewhat less so, with natural phenomena and plants. The *-ppi* is found with only a few human nouns, often frozen to the stem. The *-ccih* is used almost entirely with animals, mostly small ones, and bugs. It is probably related to the diminutive suffix (11.3.). The *-piccih* (varying with *-piccih*) is found primarily with animate nouns, often fearsome beings. The *-mpih*, limited to four stems, is used to distinguish the berry or fruit from the plant. Examples:

takka-pin 'snow'
toya-pin 'mountain'
om-pin 'scree'
sinna-pin 'aspen'
tuttu·m-pin 'Mormon tea'
wasip-pin 'game animal' (cp. *wasí* 'to kill plural objects')
yuhu-pin 'grease' (cp. *yuhu* 'fat')
sia-pin 'feather'
si·ppih 'urine' (cp. *sí·* 'to urinate')
tikka-ppih 'food; bread' (cp. *tikkà* 'to eat')
sa-ppih 'belly'
ciam-pih 'hips'
soko-ppih 'earth' (*soko-pin* in some dialects)
kukuca-ppih 'birch tree'
nam-pih 'shoes'
pika-ppih 'buckskin'
tenna-ppi, tenkʷa-ppi 'man' (also *tenna, tenkʷa*)
tie-ppi 'baby' (cp. *tiaih* 'little')
atanku-ccih 'red ant'
posia-ccih 'louse'
nininkiwippu-ccih 'scorpion'
moki-ccih 'bag'
ponia-ccih 'skunk'
hono-piccih 'bat'
coʔa-piccih 'giant' (cp. *coʔa-ppih* 'ghost')
anta-piccih 'stranger, enemy' (cp. *anta* 'different')
tia-mpih 'serviceberry' (cp. *tia-pin* 'serviceberry plant')
to·na-mpih 'chokecherry' (cp. *to·nkisa-ppih* 'chokecherry tree').

In certain constructions, the absolute suffix is dropped, but the particulars vary for the different suffixes. The dropping is most frequent for *-pin* and *-ppih*:

sokotukkan, or *sokopintukkan* 'under the ground' (*sokopin* 'ground')
tukuwian 'sky penis' (Coyote's second penis, *tukumpin* 'sky')
Piatoya 'Deep Creek Mountains', lit. 'Big

Mountain' (cp. *pia toyapin* 'big mountain', when not a place-name)
sihi yikʷi 'to gather willow' (*sihipin* 'willow')
sokotihiya '(earth) deer' (*sokoppih* 'earth')
monampai 'to have a son-in-law' (*monappi* 'son-in-law').

In many Uto-Aztecan languages, the absolute suffix is dropped when the noun is possessed, but not in Shoshone.

11.3. OTHER NOUN SUFFIXES

These suffixes are (with the objective form in parentheses):

-cci (*-ccia*) diminutive
-kantin (*-kanti*) 'one having...' (also stative aspect suffix, 4.1. and participle, 22.1.)
-woppih (*-woppiha*) agentive
-nompih (*-nompiha*) 'something used for ...-ing'.

The first two suffixes are added to nouns; the last usually derive nouns from verbs. Some examples:

kahnicci 'little house'
appicci 'dear father'
pohakantin 'doctor, shaman'; *poha* 'supernatural power'
ni·ccappakikkankanti 'the one who was tied'; *ni·"-* passive prefix, *ca"-* 'by hand'; *-pakì* 'stuck'; *-kka* aspect suffix
nikkawoppih 'dancer'; *nikkà* 'to dance'
yuhuwoppih 'the fattest one'; *yuhu* 'fat'
puinompih 'binoculars'; *puí* 'to see'
yicinompih 'airplane'; *yicí* 'to fly'.

12. PRONOUNS

The pronoun is inflected for person (first, second, third, and third reflexive), number (singular, dual, plural; cp. 11.1.), and case (subjective, objective, possessive; cp. 3.1., 11.1.). Forms are listed in table 3. The third person distinguishes between near or in sight (*ma, man*) and far or out of sight (*u, un*); all other alternates in the table represent free or dialectic variation. There are no third-person subjective forms; the demonstratives answer to this function (13.). The third-person forms have a single set that is used for all three numbers (they are listed as singular for convenience). The nonsingular first persons distinguish inclusive and exclusive.

The reflexive possessive is used when the possessor is the same as the subject, the regular third person when it is different:

Pin kahnikattun nukki.
(her-REFL house-to ran)
'She ran to her (own) house.'

Sutin supeni un kahnikuppan yainnu.
(that then his house-inside entered)
'Then he went into his (the other person's) house.'

The reflexive objective is used when subject and object partially include each other:

Table 3. Pronouns

	Subjective	*Objective*	*Possessive*
Singular			
1st	*ni*	*nia, nie, ni*	*nian, ni*
2d	*innin, in*	*immi, in*	*in, immin*
3d	---	*u, ma*	*un, man*
3d refl.	*pinni(n?), pin*	*pinni*	*pinnan, pin*
Dual			
1st incl.	*tawih*	*tahi*	*tahan*
1st excl.	*niwih*	*nihi*	*nihin*
2d	*miwih*	*mihi*	*mihin*
3d refl.	*piwih*	*pihi*	*pihin*
Plural			
1st incl.	*tammin*	*tammi*	*tammin*
1st excl.	*nimmin*	*nimmi*	*nimmin*
2d	*mimmin*	*mimmi*	*mimmin*
3d refl.	*pimmin*	*pimmi*	*pimmin*

Table 4. Pronoun Base for Postpositions

	Regular	*With -tun*
Singular		
1st	*ni*	*ni"*
2d	*in*	*i"*
3d eius	*u, ma*	*u", ma"*
3d refl.	*pin*	?
Dual		
1st incl.	*taha*	*taha*
1st excl.	*nihi*	*nihi*
2d	*mihi*	*mihi*
3d refl.	?	?
Plural		
1st incl.	*tammi*	*timmi·*
1st excl.	*nimmi*	*nimmi·*
2d	*mimmi*	*mimmi·*
3d refl.	?	?

> *Sutin taka un kʷihi sekka hinnan pehe, yampe, sekka pimmi hanninkinna.*
> (that just his wife these somethings seeds, carrots, these them-REFL fixing; reflexive indirect object since 'wife' is included as part of 'them')
> 'Just his wife was fixing seeds, carrots, those things for them (for the family).'

The objective and possessive are also used in certain subordinate clauses that put the subject into the objective or possessive case (22.2., 22.3.). The third-person subjective pronouns are used essentially as number markers for verbs (7., 8.), for the reflexive and reciprocal (6.2.), and certain subordinate clauses (22.4.).

There are two series of pronouns (table 4), that are used with postpositions (19.). The second series is used with *-tun* 'at', the first with all others. A reflexive subject (noun or pronoun) may optionally be marked by *-sin* 'own' (see 6.2.).

Monosyllabic pronouns are enclitics that normally carry no stress and are phonetically prefixed to the following word (2.4.). When emphasized, they can stand alone, and carry stress, in which case the vowel is lengthened if it is short and unclustered.

13. DEMONSTRATIVES AND PROXIMAL PREFIXES

A demonstrative consists of two parts, a proximal prefix and demonstrative stem. The proximal prefixes are closely affiliated with the third-person pronouns (12.); historically they are nothing more than an elaborated set of pronouns. Most prefixes come in pairs, one with and one without an initial *s-*. The *s-* forms are more definite and are used for something previously mentioned. Each pair shows relative distance, primarily spacial distance, but also temporal and psychological

distance. The following examples illustrate the prefixes with the singular subjective demonstrative stem *-tin*:

> *si-, i-* near (*sitin* 'this')
> *se-, e-* not quite so near (*setin* 'this')
> *sa- a-* far, but in sight (*satin* 'that')
> *su-, u-* not in sight, usually far (*sutin* 'that')
> *ma-* makes no distinction, so that it covers all the above (*matin* 'this, that').

The force of the demonstrative is not so strong as in English, and it is often best translated by the definite article 'the'. When used without a noun, that is, as a noun substitute, it is best translated by a third-person pronoun; the subject form semantically takes the place of the missing third-person pronoun.

The number and case forms of the demonstrative stems are illustrated with the prefix *u-*:

	Subjective	Objective	Possessive
Singular	*utin*	*ukka*	*ukkan*
Dual	*utiwih*	*utihi*	*utihin*
Plural	*uti·n*	*uti·*	*uti·n*

The proximal prefixes occur with a number of other stems, especially adverbs (illustrated with the prefix *si-*):

> *si-wittin* 'this special kind of' (stem also *-ittin*, *-waittin*; inflected for case and number, with forms similar to the demonstrative stem)
> *si-kkih* 'here' (locative substitute; stem *-kkuh*, with the stem vowel often harmonizing with the prefix vowel; see 19.1.)
> *si-pe* 'then, here, about this time' (temporal and locative substitute); also *si-pettin*, *si-petti* (see 20.).
> *si-paka* 'this big'; also *si-paka·nten*, *si-peka*, *si-peka·ntin*, *si-peppaka·nti*.

si-nni(h) 'thus, like this, (look) like this' (see 20.).

si-waih 'this way, (seem) like this'; also *si-waihtin, si-waihti* (see 20.).

si-ahpe· 'about this much, about this time'

si-hoi 'around here, around this'

si-pinai 'behind this'

i-sin 'this is, it is' (not used with *s-*; see 10.1.).

14. ADJECTIVES

Adjectives can function as predicates or noun modifiers. When functioning as modifiers, they normally agree in case and number with the noun:

Punku piayu.
(horse big-*yu*)
'The horse is big.'

*Tuinippi k*ʷ*aimpih.*
(boy lazy)
'The boy is lazy.'

Piantin punku happi.
(big-*tin* horse lie)
'The big horse is lying down.'

Ni pianti punkui puikka.
(I big-*tin*-OBJ horse-OBJ see)
'I see the big horse.'

*Ni k*ʷ*aimpiha tuinippia puikka.*
(I lazy-OBJ boy-OBJ see).
'I see the lazy boy.'

There are two kinds of adjectives, those closely related to verbs (verbal adjectives), and those closely related to nouns (nominal adjectives). Verbal adjectives take a limited set of aspect suffixes when functioning as a predicate, and either take the suffix *-tin*, or, less commonly, *-kantin* (participial or aspect suffixes, see 22.1., 4.1.) when functioning as modifiers; the object forms are *-ti* and *-kanti*. The nominal adjectives are less common; they usually have the suffix *-ppih* (see 4.1., 11.2.). They do not take aspect suffixes.

Verbal adjectives may be derived from nouns by *-kè* (less commonly *-ya·*) 'it is ...-y', and *-toì* 'getting ...-y':

onakeyu 'it is salty'

onatoiyu 'it is getting salty'.

15. NUMERALS

All the numbers, except 'one', are essentially relative clauses with the participial suffix *-tin*, subjective; *-ti*, objective (or optionally *-ti·n, -ti·*, the plural form; *-tiwi, tihi*, dual forms, are used with 'two'). A special form ending with *-n* (undoubtedly from the possessive *-n*; see 11.1.) is used with time words in the singular and is listed second in the following list:

simmi (*simmia*, obj.), *siwin* 'one'

wahattiwi (*wa·ttiwi*), *wahan* 'two'

paittin, pahain 'three'

wacciwihtin, wacciwin 'four'

manekihtin, manekin 'five'

na·hpaihtin, na·hpain 'six'

ta·ccuihtin, ta·cuin 'seven'

wosiwihtin, osawin 'eight'

si·wimmihantin, si·wimihan 'nine' ('having one missing')

si·ma·htin, si·man '10'.

Some examples:

Wahattiwi niwiniwih suttun nunukkikinna.
(Two humans there riding)
'Two humans were riding by (on horseback) there.'

Nape wa·ttihi tutuakantin.
(each two-obj. children-have)
'They each had two children.'

Na·hpain tommohkantin.
(six year/winter-having)
'He is six years old.'

Na·hpain tape na·ppih un pitippih.
(six day became his coming)
'He came six days ago.'

The numbers above one are used predicatively with the aspect suffixes *-tin* (*-tiwi* with 'two') and *-yu*:

*Punku na·hpaiyu, taka ke tokain tenk*ʷ*ani·n.*
(horses six-*yu*, just/but not enough men)
'There are six horses, but not enough riders.'

16. QUANTIFIERS

The quantifiers do not form a uniform class. Some examples (with the objective forms in parentheses):

so·n, so·ntin (*so·nti*) 'many'

kimme (*kimmea*) 'different'

tukkumpe 'many' (same meaning as *so·ntin*?)

antappuntin (*-ti*) 'different' (*anta* 'alone')

oyoyintin (*oyoko*) 'all of'

sisimmi (*sisimmia*) 'one by one'.

The quantifier agrees in number and case with the noun it modifies. Most modifiers can also be predicated by the aspect suffixes *-tin* and *-yu*:

*Kimmeni·n tenk*ʷ*ani·n nuta·.*
(different-plural man-plural run-plural)
'The different men ran.'

Simmi punku antappuyu.
(one horse different-aspect)
'One horse is different.'

Punku so·ntin.
(horse many-aspect)
'There were many horses.'

17. INTERROGATIVE-INDEFINITE WORDS

These words are used in interrogative and indefinite sentences (3.3.). The forms are:

hakatin, someone; who? (animate)

hi·n, something; what? (inanimate)

710

hi·ttin, some (number); how many?

hakkah, some place; where?

himpe or *hakape*, some time; when?

hakani, some way; how?

hi(·)mpaka, some size; how big (long, tall, etc.)?

hakai, something; what? (of a noise or of something said).

Hakatin and *hi·n* are inflected for number and case:

	Subject	Object	Possessive
Singular	*hakatin*	*hakke*	*hakkan*
Dual	*hakatiwih*	*hakatihi*	*hakatihin*
Plural	*hakati·n*	*hakati·*	*hakati·n*

	Subject	Object	Possessive
Singular	*hi·n*, or *hinni*	*hinna*	*hinnan*, or *hinnin*
Dual	*hinniniwih*	*hi·nihi*	*hinnan*, or *hinnin*
Plural	*hi·nni·n*	*hi·ni·*	*hinnan*, or *hinnin*

The locative *hakkah* has six forms that correspond to the locative forms found for locative postpositions and locative substitutes (19.1.): *hakkah* (Set 1), *hakkahtin* (Set 2), *hakattun* (Set 3), *hakkahtun* (Set 4), *hakkahti* (Set 5), *hakkahku* (Set 6).

Additional forms are composed by combining these words with other elements:

hi·mpaka manak^wa, some distance; how far?

hakaittin, some kind; what kind? (*hakaitti*, obj.)

hakani na·kk^wa, something happened; what happened?

All the predicate forms (as in the last example) are made up through composition with forms of *hi·n* or *hakani*.

18. COMPOUNDING

Compounding is not an uncommon process. Most compounds have a noun as first element, and a noun or verb as second, with the resulting form normally belonging to the same part of speech as the second element. A noun in first position normally does not occur with the absolutive suffix (see 11.2.). Some examples are:

hu·eti 'bow': *hu·"-pin* 'stick', *eti* 'gun'

tukummuhyun 'sky door': *tukum-pin* 'sky', *muhyun* 'door'

ka·hiawoppih 'rat trapper': *ka·* 'rat', *hia* 'to trap', *-woppih* '-er'.

Some nouns have special first-position compound forms, such as *ka"-* for *kahni* 'house', *pa-* and *pan-* for *pa·* 'water', *ta-* and *ta·-* for *tape* 'sun' (in compounds, often meaning 'day, morning'), and others. Some examples:

kammuhyun '(house) door': *muhyun* 'door'

kakki· 'corner of a house': *ki·ppih* 'elbow'

kattaintin 'village, cluster of houses': *taintin* 'hole'

pahapí 'to swim': *hapí* 'to lie down'

panti?i 'killdeer': *ti?i* 'friend'

ta·yotì 'to get up in the morning (pl. subject)': *yotí* 'to get up (pl. subject)'.

A number of elements in Shoshone probably reflect older layers of compounding that have come to have special grammatical significance, namely the instrumental prefixes (5.), and many elements in the aspect system, in particular the secondary verbs (4.4.).

19. POSTPOSITIONS

Postpositions are suffixed to nominals, resulting, usually, in an adverbial. Most are added directly to the nominal (19.1., 19.2.), but a few must be first added to a pronoun, which is then used with the nominal (19.3.).

19.1. LOCATIVE POSTPOSITIONS AND LOCATIVE SUBSTITUTES

The most common postpositions are:

-pan 'on (top of)': *tankappihpan* 'on (his) knees'

-tukkan 'under': *sinnatukkan* 'under the aspen'

-kuppan 'inside': *kahnikuppan* 'inside the house'

-kapan, or *-kupan* 'between, among': *sohokapan* 'among the cottonwood trees'

-ka", *-kah*, or *-kan* 'at': *kahnika"* 'at the house'

-man 'on (the side of)': *toyaman* 'on the mountain'.

These postpositions, along with the locative substitute *-kkuh* (e.g., *su·kkuh* 'there'; see 13.), occur in sets of six (table 5). Set 1 is the basic root, with the other five consisting of the basic root plus a suffix. The forms follow a regular pattern except for some in set 3.

Set 1 is used with verbs of location, position, or rest. Set 2 shows general diffuse location. Set 3 indicates motion 'to' or 'through'. Set 4 indicates motion, also, but defines the end point, 'to, at'. Set 5 shows the starting point of motion, 'from'. Set 6 usually indicates the notion 'from there' or 'right there'. Sets 1-4 are used

Table 5. Locative Postpositions

	'on top'	'under'	'inside'	'among'	'at'	'on'	'there'
Set 1	*-pan*	*-tukkan*	*-kappan*	*-kapan*	*-ka"*	*-man*	*su·kkuh, -kkuhu*
Set 2	*-pantin*	*-tukkantin*	*-kuppantin*	*-kapantin*	*-kattin*	*-mantin*	*su·kkuhtin*
Set 3	*-pai*	*-tukkai*	*-kuppai*	*-kapai*	*-kai*	*-mannai*	*su·ttun*
Set 4	*-pantun*	*-tukkantun*	*-kuppantun*	*-kapantun*	*-kattun*	*-mantun*	*su·kkuhtun*
Set 5	*-panti*	*-tukkanti*	*-kuppanti*	*-kapanti*	*-katti*	*-manti*	*su·kkuhti*
Set 6	*-panku*	*-tukkanku*	*-kuppanku*	*-kapanku*	*-kakku*	*-manku*	*su·kkuhku*

primarily with intransitive verbs, set 6 primarily with transitive, and set 5 with both. Some examples:

Sekkih sinnatukkan seti sokotihiya.
(here aspen-under this deer, set 1)
'Deer were here under the aspen.'

Sukkuhtin kʷi·keyu.
(there smoke-was, set 2)
'There was smoke (around) there.'

Sittun panki wekippun tattiki.
(here up oblique walked, set 3)
'He went up on the oblique.'

Sutin wihnu toyamantun mianuh, niwɨ.
(that then mountain-on went, person, set 4)
'The person went to the mountains.'

Kuhuyapitikʷa ukkuhti.
(peer there, set 5)
'He looked out there.'

Pin puihkatti toccimma yakaitin.
(his eyes-at wiped crying, set 5)
'He wiped his eyes, while crying.'

Kiti sukkuhku ponaiha pekkahkʷa.
(cat there mouse-obj. killed, set 6)
'The cat killed the mouse (from) there.'

The set 3 locative substitute *-ttun* is sometimes used as the base to make hybrid forms:

Kiti suttunti kahnikatti ponaiha wekkiyu.
(cat there house-at mouse-obj. look-for, *su-ttunti*, 3 +
    5)
'The cat was looking around the house for the mouse.'

Some additional locative postpositions do not fit into the regular sets:
-*makan* (sometimes -*maka″*) 'to, toward (animate noun, only)'
-*tipihan* 'middle'
-*tipana(h)* 'at this side of'
-*kima(h)* 'at the edge of'.

19.2. Nonlocative Postpositions
-*tun* 'in respect to, at'
-*makantun* (or -*makattun*), -*makanti* (or -*makatti*), ablative or indirect relationship
-*pan* 'by (means of)'
-*man* 'with, by means of'
-*main*, -*ma'in*, -*ma'ain* (-*maihku*, -*ma'ihku*, -*ma'aihku*, objective) 'with, accompanying; and' (see 23.)
-*mantin* (-*manti*, objective), partitive 'a piece of, a few'

Some of these are locative postpositions used non-locatively. The postpositions -*tun* and -*makantun* are used only with animate nouns; -*tun* is used with a special pronoun base (see 12.). Examples:

Wa'ippitun tuhupikka.
(woman-at mad-got)
'He got mad at the woman.'

Utin tenkʷappi ke umakattun tekkʷanna.
(that man not him-to talk)
'That man wouldn't talk to him.'

Sutin atamohpan kimmayu.
(that car-by come)
'He came by car.'

Ɨtiinna umakattin.
(hot him-to)
'It was hot to him.'

Tukkumantin pisippih.
(meat-some rotten)
'Some of the meat is rotten.'

Ni tukkumanti tikkayu.
(I meat-some-obj. eating)
'I'm eating some of the meat.'

Ni hu·mman u wikkumpahka.
(I stick-with him clobbered)
'I clobbered him with a stick.'

Sepe tina· un mo'oman u cappitiikkiyu.
(then down his hand-with him held)
'He held him down by his hands.'

Setin tukku un tutuamaisin.
(that sheep their babies-with-own)
'There were sheep with their own babies.'

19.3. Postposition with Pronoun Copy
Certain postpositions are never added directly to the noun, but instead they are added to the third-person pronoun *ma* or *u*, and that combination is, in turn, placed after the noun in the possessive case. If the noun is omitted, certain of the postpositions require that it be replaced by a possessive pronoun. Some of the postpositions requiring a pronoun copy are:
ma·nankʷa 'on the other side' (from *ma-anankʷa*)
ma-manai 'in front of'
ma-hoi 'around'.
Example:

Sutin apesin kia, sakkan Ciumpittan mahoi po'ai hapippih.
(that long-ago must, that-poss. Salt-Flat's it-around road lie)
'Long ago, there was a road that went around the Salt Flats.'

20. Adverbials
In addition to the adverbials that are formed with postpositions (19.), there are a number of single-morpheme adverbs, such as *panki* 'up', *wekippun* 'oblique', *apiisai* 'later on', *ikicci* 'nowadays, at this time', *tommo* '(in) winter', *simmai* 'talking thus, said like this', *siwi·sin* 'all over':

Sittun panki wekippun tattiki.
(here up oblique walk)
'He went up on the oblique.'

Apiisai tayiikinku kukkeyu kunai hanniyu.
(later sun-set getting-wood firewood-obj. gather)
'Later when the sun was going down he went to gather firewood.'

Ikicci niwi ke u puitin.
(nowadays people not him see)
'People don't see him nowadays.'

There are several adverbial proforms that take the proximal prefixes (13.). The two most important are the locative *-kkuh* (19.1.), and *-pai* (*-pe*), which is basically a temporal proform, but it can also be used metaphorically for space:

Miʔakkinna, supe toʔinnu.
(going, then entered)
'He kept going, and then entered.'

Mape maccuhu winni.
(then/there exactly standing)
'It is standing right there.'

Adverbs can be formed from nouns with the suffixes *-waih* and *-ni"* 'like'. The difference in meaning or function of the two is not clear. Some examples:

Akkuhtin u nacammuhyun tacciumpinni" napuni.
(there it door star-like passive-see)
'There at the door it looks like a star.'

Nanah inni u ca·n yikʷinna wanappihwaih.
(just thus it good do clothlike)
'He did this to it well, as if it was cloth.'

Nanah kian nu·n tiaiwaih ni·sunkanna.
(just maybe perhaps die-like passive-feel; here *-waih* is added to a verb)
'He kept feeling as if he had died.'

The proximal prefixes (13.) can be used with these suffixes to make manner adverbial proforms: *sunni"*, *inni"*, *uwaih*, *mawaih*, etc. 'thus, in that (this) way'.

21. PARTICLES

Particles can be neither inflected nor queried. They are sometimes compounded with each other, sometimes followed by a suffix. Grammatically, they perform a variety of functions.

The modal particles make up the largest and most commonly occurring group. Some of the more common ones are:

ha question particle (see 3.3.)
wica 'should'
kian 'maybe, perhaps, must have'
nu·n, no·n 'perhaps, must (be), let, allow'
taka 'just, only, but'
tuku, tukuh 'just, only, must'
wihnu 'then'.

The modal usually comes after the first word of the sentence:

Innin wica ikka ni hainciha maka.
(you should this-obj. my friend-obj. feed)
'You should feed my friend.'

Hakani kian nu·n mi·ppih.
(someway maybe perhaps did)
'He must have done something.'

Isin tukuh un kahni.
(this must his house)
'This must be his house.'

Some of the other particles are:
ke 'not (see 3.2.)
me quotative particle
nanah 'just, only, any old way'
pie, piesin 'already'
tian 'again'
tiasin 'more, also'
tipici, tipican 'very'
timma-sin exclamative particle.
A few examples:

Me sutin u suankinna.
(quotative he her thought-about)
'He thought about her.'

Isin ke ma piawaihtin, me sutin.
(this not him leave-alone, quotative that)
'"He isn't going to leave him alone," he said.'

Nanah uman cittikiccih, u kʷitti.
(just on-it put, it shot)
'He just put (his arrow) on it and shot it.'

Sutin wihnu kʷi·kkantin tiasin.
(he then wife-have also)
'He also had a wife.'

Two elements, *-sin* 'only, own' and *-ca* '(that) very one' are similar to independent particles, except that they are suffixed forms. The *-sin*, which is probably a reduced form of *simmi* one', is often suffixed to other particles and frequently adds no additional meaning. It is also added to verbs and nouns and forms the reflexive with pronouns (12.). The suffix *-ca* is most commonly added to nouns or demonstratives:

Setin tukku un tutuamaisin.
(this sheep their babies-with-own)
'There were sheep with their own babies.'

Sutinca sukkan kaku
(that-very-one his grandmother)
'that very one's grandmother'

Nica hipitui.
(I-very-one drink-will)
'Let me drink.'

713

22. SUBORDINATION

In subordinate clauses, Shoshone, like most Uto-Aztecan languages, makes a fundamental distinction between identical reference (22.1.) and switch reference (22.2., 22.3.). In identical reference, the subject of the subordinate clause is coreferential with (identical with) the subject of the main clause (for adverbial clauses) or with the head noun in the main clause (for relative clauses). In switch reference, the subject is not coreferential (though it may overlap and be partially coreferential). Thus clauses that are treated as being similar in English (such as relative clauses or temporal clauses) are treated in two distinct ways in Shoshone. Examples of English sentences that would be translated with identical-reference clauses in Shoshone are (the subordinate clause is underlined):

The woman that was crying arrived. The crying woman arrived.

I saw a jackrabbit as I was walking along.

Sentences that translate switch reference include:

The woman that I saw ran away.

I saw her as she was digging carrots.

The subject of the identical-reference clause and the main clause is expressed just once, usually in whichever clause comes first (which is most apt to be the subordinate clause):

Ni miatin, kammui puikka.
(I walk-*tin*, rabbit-obj. see-aspect; *-tin* is the subordinate suffix)
'As I was walking along, I saw a jackrabbit.'

The subject of a switch-reference clause, on the other hand, must be expressed, and unlike a main clause subject, it can never be omitted (3.1.; but it can be replaced by the indefinite subject prefix *tan-*, see 6.3.). The subordination normally involves a change in case, with the subject being placed in either the object case (objective clause, 22.2.), or the possessive case (possessive clause, 22.3.). An example of an objective clause:

Ikkihti u yampa hotaku, u kupa.
(here her[objective] carrots dig-*ku*, her grabbed; *-ku* is the subordinate suffix)
'While she was digging carrots, he grabbed her.'

The objective pronoun *u* is the subject of the clause. Contrast this with:

Sutin tukuh pinna yampa hotatin.
(she just last-one carrots dig-aspect)
'She was digging carrots.'

Here *sutin*, a subjective demonstrative, is the subject of a main clause.

Subordination is accomplished by suffixation. The subordinate suffix takes the place of the aspect suffix, though other features of the aspect system, such as secondary verbs, directional suffixes, and prefinal aspect suffixes may be present (see 4.). The subordinate suffixes usually contain aspectual and temporal notions. Indeed, in many cases, the subordinate suffixes are really aspect suffixes doing double duty; but they normally cover a larger semantic range, since a smaller number of subordinate suffixes cover the same semantic territory as a larger number of aspect suffixes.

22.1. IDENTICAL REFERENCE CLAUSES

Three kinds of clauses belong here—participial, relative, and temporal. The participial and relative clauses are formed with the same verb suffixes, namely *-tin* (generic) 'while, as (at the same time)' and *-h/kkantin* (stative) 'when (after)', both of which are aspect suffixes (4.1.). The case and number forms for *-tin* are:

	Subjective	Objective	Possessive
Singular	*-tin*	*-ti* (or *-tina*)	*-tin* (or *-tinan*)
Dual	*-tiwih*	*-tihi*	(unattested)
Plural	*-ti·n*	*-ti·*	(unattested)

Parallel forms are found for *-kantin*.

The participial and relative clauses are often expressed in identical fashion:

Waʔippi yakaitin pitinu.
(woman cry-*tin* arrive)
'The crying woman arrived; the woman who was crying arrived.'

Both forms must agree in case with the head noun, but only the relative clause agrees in number. Thus the distinction between the two is seen in these examples with the dual stem *nawoi* 'cry':

Waʔippiniwih nawointiwih pippitinu.
(woman-dual cry-*tiwih* arrived)
'The two women who were crying arrived.'

Waʔippiniwih nawointin pippitinu.
(woman-dual cry-*tin* arrived)
'The two crying women arrived.'

Additional examples are:

U tihaniten, u no·kkʷa.
(it skin-*tin*, it packed)
'Skinning it, he packed it (home).'

Hu·ppakanaitin, toyaman katitin.
(arrows-make-*tin*, mountains-on sit)
'He is sitting in the mountains making arrows.'

Hu·ppakanaihkantin, toyakuppan nimmi.
(arrows-make-*kantin* mountain-inside wander)
'Having made arrows, he was wandering in the mountains.'

Ukkuhti wihnu ni·wenihkanti tukkui yuhui ya·.
(there-to then hanging-*kanti* sheep-obj. fat-obj. carry)
'He went and got his sheep fat, which was hanging up.'

Tennappian kintun pitippihkantinan sati· ni kiccia.
(man-poss. yesterday came-*ppih-kantinan* dog me bit)
'The dog of the man who came yesterday bit me.'
Or: *Tennappian sati· kintun pitippihkantin ni kiccia.*

Contrary to the general rule, the participial -*kantin* suffix can, when forming the relative clause, be added to the suffixes that are used to form switch reference possessive clauses, thus allowing for a greater expression of aspectual notions:

Utin tennappi kimmatuihkantin ni papi.
(that man come-*tuih-kantin* my brother)
'The man who will come is my brother.'

Ni tennappia tikkaihkanti puikka.
(I man-obj. eat-*ih-kanti* see)
'I see the man who has already eaten.'

Tennappi ni pihi uttuppihkantin pitinu.
(man me hide gave-*ppih-kantin* came)
'The man who gave me the hide came.'

The generic has another form, -*tihin*, which is used when the activity is continued for a period of time, or took place a long time ago.

The temporal clauses are marked by the suffixes -*si(h)*, or -*cci(h)*, with the difference between the two suffixes not known. The forms -*sihi* and -*ccihi* are used when the action is further in the past or is continued for a period of time (parallel to -*tin*, -*tihin*, above). The action of the subordinated verb takes place prior to the main verb, with the meaning 'First....., (then .....)':

Ni puikkʷaccih, miakʷa.
(I look-aspect-*ccih*, go-aspect)
'Looking, I left; First I looked, then I left.'

Often it is used in situations that would be expressed in English by a temporal or serial 'and'. The subordinate clause normally comes first. Some more examples:

U ima· tian un kʷihi yicinusi, sekka wittuhue tikicci, pai ukuppantun hanniccih, sa·kʷaina.
(it[pot] morning next his wife get-up-*si*, that-obj. pot-obj. set-*cci*, water-obj. it-inside place-*ccih*, boil-meat)
'The next morning his wife got up, set the pot (on the fire), put water in it, and boiled meat.'

Yicinusi miakkimminna, nacitto·hkantin.
(get-up-*si* walking, use-căne-*kantin*)
'Getting up, he went on, using his cane.'
(Note use of -*si* for prior action, the participial -*kantin* for contemporary action)

Ni miakʷa, tuhupikkacci.
(I left, mad-got-*cci*)
'I left because I was mad.'

U pekkakʷaccihi, mianu.
(it kill-*ccihi*, went)
'Going over to kill it, he went; he went over in order to kill it.'

22.2. SWITCH REFERENCE: OBJECTIVE CLAUSES

The objective clause (in which the subject of the subordinate clause is in the objective case) is used for adverbial clauses and postposition clauses. For the adverbial clauses, there are two suffixes, -*h/kkan* 'when (after)', and -*ku* 'while, as (at same time)'. The combination -*h/kkan-ku* is similar in meaning to -*ku* alone; perhaps it indicates that the activity continues for a longer period of time. The -*ku* and -*h/kkan-ku* sometimes function in a locative sense, but all three more commonly function in a temporal sense. Some examples:

Ukka ke sunni mimmi nahaku, mimmi wasittaikkʷantuih.
(that-obj. not thus you-obj. do-*ku*, you-obj. kill-will)
'If you don't do that, you will all be killed.'

Pinnankʷa, wihnu ukke taka pacaya· miannuhka, sotin pia kuiccun tennappi niwi na·tin u peccikkʷa.
(next then that-obj. alone water-hand-carry go-*hka*, that big cattle [buffalo] man human being her fetch-aspect)
'The next time she went there alone for water, the buffalo in the form of a human man took her away.'

Heyah sukkuh u naihka to²impitikʷa.
(right there she be-*hka* emerge-arrive-aspect)
'He came out where she was.'

Tape napuihkanku, tikoicoi.
(sun-obj. show-*hkan-ku*, wash)
'Do (your) washing while the sun is still showing.'

Ni tuhupikka, ni punkui u titikkahukka.
(I mad-got, my horse-obj. him steal-*kka*)
'I was mad because he stole my horse.'

If a third-person object of the subordinate clause is coreferential (identical) with the subject of the main clause then the objective form of a reflexive pronoun is used (*pinni, pihi, pimmi*, singular, dual, plural; see 12.):

Ca·n ni·sunkanna, pinni u wicciakamma·hka.
(good feel, him-refl. [man] him [dwarf] grease-rub-finish-*hka*)
'He [the man] felt good, when he [the dwarf] finished greasing him.'

A reflexive pronoun is also used when the subjects of both clauses are coreferential; but in this case, the subjects must overlap (be partially coreferential, differing in number), because if they were exactly identical the clause would not be a switch reference clause:

715

Sutin pihi pacaya· mimiaku, simmi sutin wa?ippi yikkʷi:
(that them-refl. [dual] water-hand-carry go-dual-*ku*, one that woman say; repeated *sutin* refers in both cases to 'that one woman'.)
'As they (dual) were getting water, one of the women said:'

Pimmi nuta·kka, sati· tenkʷappini· puikka.
(them-refl. [dog and men] run-plural-*kka*, dog man-pl.-obj. look-aspect)
'As they [the dog and the men] drove away, the dog looked at the men.'

The objective clause is also used with the postposition *-pa·ntun* 'by means of' (with the examples at hand, meaning 'for that reason'); likely other postpositions can be used, but only this one has been recorded. The subject is in the objective case, and then the postposition is suffixed to a verb that has been nominalized by the perfect suffix *-ppih* (see 4.1., 11.2.):

Utimpin pin kʷihi u kopappihpa·ntun, simme u suankippih.
(that-very-one his wife-obj. him hug-*ppih-pa·ntun*, say him cast-spell)
'Because he grabbed his wife, he put a spell on him.'

Sutin nittun tuhupikka, nia ontimpai hipippihpa·ntun.
(she me-at mad-got, me whisky-obj. drunk-*ppih-pa·ntun*)
'She got mad at me on account of my drinking whiskey.'

Cp. *Sutin nittun tuhupikka, nia ontimpai hipiku.*
(she me-at mad-got, me whiskey-obj. drink-*ku*)
'She got mad at me because I drank whiskey.'

22.3. SWITCH REFERENCE: POSSESSIVE CLAUSES

The possessive clause (in which the subject of the subordinate clause is in the possessive case) is used for relative clauses and possessive absolutes. The subordinate suffixes (with the objective forms in parentheses) are:

-na (no change) present
-h/kkan (*-h/kkai*) stative?
-h/kkʷan (*-h/kkʷai*) momentaneous
-ppih (*-ppiha*) perfect
-tu?ih (*-tu?iha*) future
-ih, -i (*-iha*) unmarked

All but the last suffix are also aspect suffixes (4.1.).

The relative clause usually follows the head noun, and it must agree with it in case and number:

Isin wosa nian no·ih.
(*i-sin* basket my carry-*ih*; see 10.1. for *i-sin*)
'This is the basket that I carried.'

Satin wa?ippi yakaitin ke tukkui pinni un makaiha tikkatin.
(that woman crying not meat-obj. her [obj.] his give-*ih-a* eat-aspect)
'That crying woman would not eat the meat that he gave her.'

The head noun can be deleted, leaving the relative clause as a noun substitute:

Isin nian no·ih.
'This is what I carried.'

Satin wa?ippi yakaitin ke pinni un makaiha tikkatin.
'That crying woman would not eat what he gave her.'

The relative clause can be moved out of its usual position and be separated from the head noun:

Ni sippiha puikka un pekkappiha.
(I sheep-obj. see his kill-*ppih-a*)
'I see the sheep that he killed.'

Un pekkappiha ni sippiha puikka.
'I see the sheep that he killed.'

If the head noun is deleted, and the relative clause moved, a pronoun is usually left behind to mark the place once occupied by the noun:

Ni (u) puikka un pekkappiha.
'I saw what he killed.'

The possessive absolute is a possessive clause that stands in an adverbial relation to the main clause:

Un kammu tikai miappih taka, ke pitinna.
(his jackrabbit hunt go-*ppih* just, not arrive-aspect)
'He went jackrabbit hunting but hasn't returned'
(or 'Having gone jackrabbit hunting, he hasn't returned').

22.4. ADVERBIAL RELATIVES IN PIN-

Adverbial relatives are a special type that stand in an oblique relation to the head noun. The clause, which may be either identical or switch reference, is introduced by a compound marker that consists of the third-person reflexive pronoun *pin-* (12.) plus an adverbial element. The adverbial element is most commonly a postposition, yielding, for example:

pimpan, where, on top of which
pinkahtun, where, to which, through which
pimman, by means of which (instrumental)
pimpan, by means of which (manner)
pimmanku, why

The second element can also be related to elements found in indefinites or adverbial substitutes:

pinkah, where (*sukkuh*, there; *hakkah*, some place; 19.1., 17.)

pimpe, when (*supe*, then; *himpe*, some time; 13., 17.)

pinnippun, in which direction (*supun*, that direction; *hakappun*, in some direction; 13.; 17.)

The subordinate suffixes used with possessive clauses (22.3.) are also used with the *pin-* clauses, both the identical and switch-reference *pin-* clauses; the clause must agree in number and gender with the head noun. The *pin-* element normally comes after the head noun, but it may come before:

Ni atamoha pimpan ni nukkituiha pitinkihka.
(I car-obj. *pin*-by I drive-*tuih*-obj. fix)
'I'm fixing the car that I'm going to drive (by means of which I'm going to drive).'

Ni huᐧppitta pintukkan un yaihkʷaiha sumpaᐧtuhka.
(I log-obj. *pin*-under his enter-*hkʷaih*-obj. know)
'I know which log he went under.'

Sutin nian pimpe tapeni pitippiha sumpaᐧtuhkantin.
(he my *pin*-then day-obj. arrive-*ppih*-obj. knows)
'He knows the day I came.'

Unlike other identical-reference clauses, the subject may be expressed in both the main and subordinate clause. However, the subject in the subordinate clauses can be omitted, provided that the *pin-* element is also omitted:

Ni atamoha nukkituiha pitinkihka. 'I'm fixing the car to run.'

The head noun of a *pin-* adverbial clause is usually omitted; the subject of the clause can come before or after the *pin-* element:

Sutin nian pimpe pitippiha sumpaᐧtuhkantin. 'He knows when I came.'

Sutin pimpe nian pitippiha sumpaᐧtuhkantin. 'He knows when I came.'

If the head noun is the subject of a main clause, and object of a relative clause, it may be placed in the objective; however, the relative clause stays in the subjective. If it is a *pin-* relative, it must be placed in the objective. Compare these three sentences:

Kaᐧpottoń sukkuh nacattikihka.
(rat-sticks there placed)
'The rat-trapping gear was sitting there.'

Kaᐧpotton (or *Kaᐧpottona*) *un cayaᐧppih sukkuh nacattikihka.*
(rat-sticks [or rat-sticks-obj.] his carry-*ppih* there placed)
'The rat-trapping gear that he carried was sitting there.'

Kaᐧpottona pinkuppa un cayaᐧppih sukkuh nacattikihka.
'The rat-trapping gear that he had carried inside was sitting there.'

23. COORDINATION

Nouns may be linked by the postposition *-main*, *-maʔain* (*-maihku*, *-maʔaihku*, obj.; see 19.2.), "with":

Ni taimain tikkayu.
(I brother-*main* eating)
'My brother and I are eating.'

Ni kammui cippihmaihku wasinnu.
(I rabbit-obj. prairie-dog-*maihku* kill [pl.])
'I killed the jackrabbit and prairie dog.'

'Or' linkage of clauses and phrases is accomplished by the compound particle *nuᐧntian* or *noᐧntian*, literally 'maybe-again':

Nuᐧnkia noᐧntian Cokopaᐧkattun noᐧntian Kʷinaᐧpaᐧkattun.
(perhaps either rough-water-toward or eagle-water-toward)
'He (went) to either Rough Springs or Eagle Springs.'

Ni wose nuᐧntian occe suwainna.
(I burden-basket-obj. maybe-again water-jug-obj. want)
'I want a burden basket or a water jug.'

'But instead' conjoining can be accomplished by use of the modal particle *taka* 'just, but':

Nimmin accuh ke kaᐧ hiatin, tukkui taka noᐧniᐧmmintihin, sokotihiya noᐧniᐧmmintihin, sukka tikkatin.
(we instead not rats trap, sheep-obj. but carrying-back, deer carrying-back, that eat)
'We don't trap rats, but instead getting sheep, deer, that's what we eat.'

The modal particle *wihnu* 'then' can also be used for 'but' linking:

Sutin tukkui tikkasuantin, ni wihnu oyoko u tikkahkʷa.
(he meat-obj. eat-wanted, I but all it eaten)
'He wanted to eat the meat, but I had eaten it all up.'

Sentences that are temporally related and conjoined in English by *and* are usually connected by the subordinate suffixes *-sih*, *-ccih* (provided the subjects are the same, see 22.1.). A looser relationship, one that need not be temporal, is indicated by starting a sentence with the demonstrative and modal particle *suten wihnu...*, literally 'that then'. An example:

Kahnikantin timmasin. Sutin wihnu kʷiᐧkkantin tiasin.
(house-have exclamative. he then wife-have also)
'He had a house. He had a wife, also.'

24. Selected Vocabulary

afraid *ti²iyapikkà*

all *oyo·n*

animal See game animal

antelope *kʷahatin* (*kʷahatina*, obj.)

arm *pita* (*pitai*, obj.)

arrive *pití, pippitì, pití* (sg., dual, pl. subj.)

arrow *pakan* (*pakana*, obj.)

ashes *kusippih* or *kuttuhsippih* (*-ppiha*, obj.)

aspen tree *sinkapin* or *sinnapin* (*-pitta*, obj.)

autumn *yipani*

baby *tieppitin* (*-tina*, obj.; *titieppitin*, dual and pl.)

back of body: *kʷehempih* (*-piha*, obj.)

bad (lit. 'not good') *keca·n, kica·n*

bark (see skin)

bear *wi·ta* (*wi·tai*, obj.)

belly *sa·ppih* (*-ppiha*, obj.)

belly button *siku* (*sikui*, obj.)

big *pia*

bird *kʷina·* (*kʷina·i*, obj.; big bird and eagle); *huiccu·* (*huiccu·a*, obj.; small bird)

bite *kicci²à*

black *tu·n*, or *tu·"*

blanket *wika* (*wika*, obj.); rabbit skin blanket *kammuwika*

blood *pi·ppin* (*-pitta*, obj.)

bone *cuhni* (*cuhnia*, obj.)

bow and arrow (lit. 'wooden gun') *hu·eti* (*-eti*, obj.)

boy *tuini* (*tuinii*, obj.; *pi·a*, dual, pl. stem)

breast *pici* (*picia*, obj.)

brother, older *papi* (*papia*, obj.); younger brother *tami* (*tamia*, obj.)

brown *ontin*

buffalo (lit. 'big cow') *pia kuiccun* (*kuiccuna*, obj.)

burn (intr.) *waihyá*

cactus (prickly pear) *wokaipin* (*-pitta*, obj.)

carry *yá·, himá* (sg., pl. obj.)

carry in the arms *kopá*

carry on the back *nó·*

cedar (juniper) tree *wa·ppin* or *samapin* (*-pitta*, obj.)

chief *tekʷahni* (*tekʷahnia*, obj.)

child *tua"* (*tuai*, obj.; *tutua*, dual, pl.)

claw *masiton* (also fingernail); *tasiton* (also toenail) (*-sitona*, obj.)

close, shut *-timà, -timì* (sg., pl. obj.)

cloud *pakinappih* (*-ppiha*, obj.)

cold *iicii*

come *kimma, kikimma, kimmà* (sg., dual, pl. subj.)

copulate *yokó*

cottonwood tree, or tree *sohopin* (*-pitta*, obj.)

coyote *icappi* (*icappia*, obj.); Coyote, the mythological creature: *Isapaippih* (*-ppiha*, obj.; from *isampih* 'a lie')

cry *yakaí, namoì, namoì* (sg., dual, pl. subj.)

cut flexible things *-ka²à, -kità,* sg., pl. obj.; cut brittle things; *-kipà, -kipi·tà,* sg., pl. obj.

dance *nikkà*

daughter *peti* (*peti*, obj.)

day *tapeni*

deer *tihiyan* or *sokotihiyan* (*tihiyana*, obj.; *soko-* is 'earth')

die *tiaì, kokoì, koì* (sg., dual, pl. subj.)

dig *hotà*

dirty *tuccappih*

dog *sati·* (*sati·a*, obj.)

down *tinna·*

dry *pasa*

dust *hukkun* (*hukkuna*, obj.)

ear *nenkih* (*nenkiha*, obj.)

earth *sokoppih* (*-ppiha*, obj.)

eat *tikkà*

egg *noyo* (*noyoi*, obj.)

eight *wosiwihtin* (*-tin*, obj.)

enter *yaí, yuyuà, wekú* (sg., dual, pl. subj.)

excrement *kʷitappih* (*-ppiha*, obj.)

eye *puih* (*puiha*, obj.)

fall over *annì, a²annì, anni·tì* or *hamià* (sg., dual, pl. subj.)

father *appi* (*appia*, obj.)

feather *siapin* (*-pitta*, obj.)

fire, to make a *kottò·*

fish *penkʷi* (*penkʷia*, obj.)

five *manekihtin* (*-tin*, obj.)

flesh, meat; mountain sheep *tukku* (*tukkui*, obj.)

fly; get up, rise *yicí, yiyicì* or *yoyotì, yotí* (sg., dual, pl. subj.)

foot *nampe* (*nampe* or *nampetta*, obj.)

four *wacciwihtin* (*-tin*, obj.)

full *tippai*

game animal (lit. 'that which is killed') *wasippin* (*-pitta*, obj.)

girl, young woman *naipin* (*-pitta*, obj.; *naiyin-*, dual, pl. stem)

give *uttù*

go, walk *mia, mimia, miá* (sg., dual, pl. subj.)

grass *puippih* (*-ppiha*, obj.)

grease *yuhupin* (*-pitta*, obj.)

green, blue *pui*

hair (see head)

hand *moʔo* (*moʔoi* or *moʔi*, obj.)

hard *kitta·*

head, hair *pampi* (*pampia* or *pampitta*, obj.)

hear *nankà*

heart *pihyin* (*pihyina*, obj.)

heavy *pittin*

hill *noʔopin* (*-pitta*, obj.)

hit *-tikʷà, paì* (sg., pl. obj.)

hold in the hands *caì*

hole *taintin* (*taintina*, obj.)

horn *a·n* (*a·na*, obj.)

horse; pet *punku* (*punkua*, obj.)

hot *itiì*

house *kahni* (*kahni*, obj.)

husband *kuhma* (*kuhmaa*, obj.)

ice *pa·kkappih* (*-ppiha*, obj.)

Indian, person: *niwi* (*niwi*, obj.)

jackrabbit *kammu* (*kammui*, obj.)

kill *pekkà, wasí, wasí* (sg., dual, pl. obj.)

knee *tankappih* or *tannappih* (*-ppiha*, obj.)

know *sumpa·tù* or *sumpanaì*

leaf *siki* (*siki*, obj.)

left (side); *kʷi·*

leg (lower) *o·n* (*o·na*, obj.); leg or thigh *tohopin* (*-pitta*, obj.)

lie *hapí, kopí* or *kʷapí, kopikkan* or *kʷapikkan* (sg., dual, pl. subj.); *kokkopi* (inanimate pl. subj.)

live, survive, wander *nimì, ninimì* or *yiyinkà, yinkà* (sg., dual, pl. subj.)

liver *nimin* (*nimina*, obj.)

long, tall *kipata*

louse *posiaccih* (*-cciha*, obj.)

man *tenkʷa* or *tenna* (*tenkʷai, tennai*, obj.); old man

cuku (cukua, obj.; cuccukkuccia-, dual, pl. stem); young man *tuicci* (*tuiccia*, obj.; *tuiccia-*, dual, pl. stem)

many *so·n, so·ntin* (*-ti*, obj.); *tukkumpe*

meat (see flesh)

milk *pica* (*picai*, obj.)

moon *mia* (*miai*, obj.)

mother *pia* (*piai*, obj.)

mountain *toyapin* (*-pitta*, obj.)

mountain sheep (see flesh)

mouth *timpe* (*timpe* or *timpetta*, obj.)

name *niha, nihya,* or *nanihai* (*nih(y)ai*, obj.)

neck *toyompih* (*-piha*, obj.); *kuta* (*kutai*, obj.)

new, young *iki*

night *tukani*

nine (lit. 'having one missing') *si·wimmihantin* (*-ti*, obj.)

nose *mupin* (*-pitta*, obj.)

old *piettimpih*

one *simmi* (*simmia*, obj.)

open *-tihpá, -tipaì* (dual, pl. obj.)

path *poʔai* (*poʔaia*, obj.)

penis *wian* (*wiana*, obj.)

person (see Indian)

pine nut (pinyon nut) *tipa″* (*tipai*, obj.)

pine nut tree (pinyon tree) *eko wa·ppin* or *tipa″ wa·ppin* (*-pitta*, obj.)

pine tree (*Pseudotsuga douglasii*) *wonkopin* (*-pitta*, obj.)

puke *wittoʔaì*

push *-kaʔì, -ponkà* (sg., pl. obj.)

rabbit net *wana* (*wanai*, obj.)

rain *imà* or *paimà*

red *enka*

right (side) *titunankʷa*

rise (see fly)

root *titina* (*titinai*, obj.)

rope *timukkun* (*timukkuna*, obj.)

round, spherical *pono*; round, circular *puinu*

run *nukkì, nunukkì, nutà·* (sg., dual, pl. subj.)

sage (*Artemisia tridentata*) *pohopin* (*-pitta*, obj.)

saliva *hiccippih* (*-ppiha*, obj.)

salt *onapin* (*-pitta*, obj.)

sand *pasiwampin* (*-pitta*, obj.)

say   *ni·kʷi*

see   *puí*

seed   *pehe* (*pehe*, obj.)

seven   *ta·ccuihtin* (*-ti*, obj.)

shaman   *pohokantin* (*-kanti*, obj.)

shoe   *nampih* (*-piha*, obj.)

sing   *nittoì*

sister, older   *paci* (*pacia*, obj.); younger sister *nammi* (*nammia*, obj.)

sit   *katí, yikʷí, yikʷikkan* (sg., dual, pl. subj.)

six   *na·hpaihtin* (*-ti*, obj.)

skin, bark   *poʔan* (*poʔana*, obj.)

sky   *tukumpi* (*-pitta*, obj.)

sleep   *ippiì, ikkoì, ikkoì* (sg., dual, pl. subj.)

small   *tiaih*

smell (tr.)   *kʷanà*; (intr.)   *ikwí*

smoke   *kʷi·ppih* (*-ppiha*, obj.)

snake or rattlesnake   *tokoa* (*tokoai*, obj.); bull snake *kokon* (*kokona*, obj.)

snow   *takkapin* (*-pitta*, obj.)

son   *tua″* (*tuai*, obj.; *tutua*, dual, pl.)

song   *hupia* (*hupiai*, obj.)

springtime   *tahmani*

stand   *winí, tacakkihkan, topoihkan* (sg., dual, pl. subj.)

star   *taciʔimpin* (*-pitta*, obj.)

stone   *timpin* (*-pitta*, obj.)

suck   *picí*

summer   *taca*

sun   *tape* (*tape*, obj.)

supernatural power   *poha* (*pohai*, obj.)

swell   *pekʷí*

swim   *pahapí*

tail   *kʷesi* (*kʷesia*, obj.)

talk   *tekʷá, niwinì, niwinì* (sg., dual, pl. subj.)

tall (see long)

taste (tr.)   *timmaì*; (intr.)   *kaɾmà*

ten   *si·ma·htin* (*-tin*, obj.)

think   *suà*

three   *paittin* (*-ti*, obj.)

throw   *tawí, petí* (sg., dual obj.)

tie   *-tamà, -tamì·* (sg., pl. obj.)

tobacco, cigarette   *pahun* (*pahuna*, obj.)

tongue   *ekon* (*ekona*, obj.)

tooth   *taman* (*tamana*, obj.)

tree See cottonwood tree

two   *wa·ttiwi* (*-tihi*, obj.)

up   *paʔa, panai,* or *panki*

urine   *si·ppih* (*-ppiha*, obj.)

vagina   *taʔi* (*taʔia*, obj.)

wake up   *tipuì, titipuì, tipuì* (sg., dual, pl. subj.)

walk (see go)

wash   *koicoì*

water   *pa·* (*pa·i*, obj.)

wife   *kʷihi* (*kʷihi*, obj.)

wind   *niaippih* (*-ppiha*, obj.)

wing   *kasa* (*kasai*, obj.)

winter, year   *tommo*

white   *tosa*

White man   *taipo* (*taipoa*, obj.)

woman   *waʔippi* (*waʔippia*, obj.); old woman *hipico·* (*hipico·a*, obj.; *hihippiccia-*, dual, pl. stem); see also girl

worm   *woapin* (*-pitta*, obj.)

yellow   *oa″*

young See new

Sources

HERBERT J. LANDAR

With the founding in 1879 of the Bureau of Ethnology of the Smithsonian Institution, bibliographic research in American Indian linguistics, pioneered by Albert Gallatin (1836, 1848), flourished. Maj. John Wesley Powell, director of the new Bureau, assigned the task of bibliographic research to James C. Pilling, who produced a series of volumes for tribes north of Mexico (1885, 1887, 1887a, 1888, 1889, 1891, 1892, 1893, 1893a, 1894). Supplementary bibliographies have appeared for language families or geographical areas, for example, Pentland and Wolfart (1982) for Algonquian, Krauss (1979) and Krauss and McGary (1980) for Athapaskan and other languages of Alaska and Canada, Bright (1982) for languages of California, and Booker (1991) for languages of the Southeast. On classifications used as programs for research, see Landar (1976, 1977) and Campbell and Mithun (1979). For dissertations, see Singerman (1996).

In this list an attempt has been made to cite, if possible, a printed grammar, dictionary, and collection of texts for each native language of North America. Seldom can one find these three items in print within easy reach of an educated public, for whom it is not useful to mention manuscripts, including valuable but unpublished and not easily available doctoral dissertations and master's theses. A limit of three to five printed sources per entry has generally been imposed. Important works have been excluded by this limit, even with occasional stretching; but sometimes a bibliography or two is listed at the end of an entry, for more sources.

In the absence of a full treatment for a particular language available briefer sources are substituted. The abbreviation G. thus indicates a grammar, where available; but if there is none, it indicates a sketch, for example, or as little as a sentence or two with grammatical information. The abbreviation W., similarly, indicates words, a dictionary if possible, but sometimes even a single word. The abbreviation T. indicates a collection of texts, ideally, but it may indicate just a few sentences in a grammar. Shorter works of linguistic anthropologists have been favored, on a criterion of quality, over more extensive studies by others.

The language names used are those in the classification table ("Introduction," table 3, this vol.). Other names used by Swanton (1952) and Landar (1973, 1977), have been listed with cross-references. Many names of dialects are also listed, if they have been used to label linguistic material. A reader interested in the Bannock tribe, for example, will find an entry for Bannock. The reader will find another entry for the Northern Paiutes, even though a single language was used by both tribes (also called Paviotso and Northern Paiute). Similarly, even though a single language, Chiwere, was used by speakers of Otoe, Iowa, and Missouri, the reader can look up Missouri as an entity. In some cases the names used are those of the sources and may, perhaps, be unrecognized synonyms of others. Thus there is an entry for Ausaima, identified by Kroeber on almost no evidence as the language of a Costanoan tribe or band. Since there are published words called Ausaima, there is an entry. Names of language families or other higher level classificatory units are supplied, in general, after the main entry word.

Though brevity is a goal, utility has determined some listings. Localized Eskimoan groups are listed, whether tribes or not, given the variety of Eskimo names and the density of documentation. Thus the reader can find entries for places mentioned in anthropological literature, Ammassalik, for example, or Inglestat. Brevity, on the other hand, has forced exclusion of some items in a series of articles. Garvin, for example, has published many important articles on Kootenai, but only Garvin (1951, 1954) is listed.

Abenaki. See Caniba, Wawenock, Penobscot, and Western Abenaki.

Achumawi (Palaihnihan). Also called Pit River. *G., T.*: Angulo and Freeland (1930) is a study of the language, including lists of words and illustrative sentences, pp. 117-120. *W.*: Olmsted (1964) includes 205 sets with reconstructed forms, English to Achumawi and Atsugewi, pp. 36-48. Bauman, Miles, and Leaf (1979) is a topically arranged student dictionary. Olmsted (1977) has an analyzed text.

Acoma (Keresan). *G., T.*: Miller (1965) discusses grammar, pp. 7-186; texts, pp. 189-259 (Acoma and English on facing pages, pp. 200-259). *W.*: Miller and Davis (1963) have 441 cognate sets with 384 Proto-Keresan reconstructions, based mainly on data from Acoma, Santa Ana, and Santo Domingo. (Miller 1959a) has kin terms.

Adai. *W.*: This extinct language is represented by 25 forms recorded by Sibley around 1804, given with commentary by Taylor (1963a:114).

Agawam (Eastern Algonquian). Also called Agawam-Nipmuck-Pocumtuck, and Loup. *W.*: John Pynchon's names of 13 months from 1645 appear in S. Jacobs (1856) and H.A. Wright (1949:253). See Day (1967) for data and philological notes.

Aglurmiut (dialect of Central Alaskan Yupik). *W.*: Khromchenko (1973) has words collected in 1822. Miyaoka (1974) analyzes a similar early wordlist.

Agua Caliente. See Cupeño.

Ahousat (dialect of Nootka). *W.*: Hess (1990) has Flores Island Ahousat, Nitinaht, and Makah words for 1-20, and 30 to 100 by tens, pp. 418-429.

Aht. See Nootka.

Ahtna (Athapaskan). Also spelled Ahtena. *G.*: Kari (1979) describes verb theme categories, 230 pp. *W., G.*: Kari (1990) has grammar, pp. 3-59; Ahtna-English dictionary, about 6,000 entries including morphophonemic and morphological data, pp. 63-468; problem words from previous sources, pp. 469-472; English-Ahtna index, about 11,250 entries, pp. 475-625; appendices on loan words, directionals, numerals, thematic and derivational strings, morphophonemics, and sample verb paradigms, pp. 628-698. *T.*: Kari (1986) has 21 Upper Ahtna stories in interlinear format, pp. 13-215. *G.*: Krauss and Golla (vol. 6:69-72) have phonological data.

Aivilik (dialect of Eastern Canadian Inuit). Also called North Baffin-Aivilik. *W.*: Birket-Smith (1928:25) has four words of Aivilik and a discussion of dialect features. *G.*: Harper (1979) surveys suffixes of Cumberland Peninsula and North Baffin Island. *G., W., T.*: Webster and Zibell (1976) have phonemic analysis, p. 277, about 170 words and phrases in a comparative vocabulary, pp. 286-317, and 42 sentences in a comparative survey, pp. 318-325. *G.*: A. Spalding (1992) is a grammar of North Baffin dialects. Dorais (1976) compares Aivilik, represented by Igloolik, with Labrador, Tarramiut, Cape Dorset, South Baffin, and Itivimmiut phonologically and morphologically. Dorais (1986:23) compares the Aivilik phonemic inventory of the dialect at Repulse Bay, Southampton Island, and Chesterfield Inlet with other Eskimo inventories.

Aklavik. See North Alaskan Inupiaq.

Akokisa. See Atakapan.

Akulurak. See Kuskokwim (Central Alaskan Yupik) and R. Carriker et al. (1976:29, 31).

Akwa'ala. See Paipai.

Alabama (Muskogean). *G., W.*: Rand (1968) has phonological data and perhaps 150 words. Folsom-Dickerson (1965) has 87 plants, pp. 55-61, and 81 medicinal plants, pp. 63-76, with Alabama and Koasati names if known. Hardy and Montler (1988) discuss imperfective gemination; Montler and Hardy (1991) discuss verbal morphology of negation. *W.*: Sylestine, Hardy, and Montler (1993) is a dictionary.

Alachome. See Chome.

Alaska North Slope. See North Alaskan Inupiaq.

Alaskan Yupik (Eskimo). See Central Alaskan Yupik and Pacific Yupik.

Aleut. An ambiguous term that has been used for Central Alaskan Yupik of Bristol Bay, for Pacific Yupik (Alutiiq, Sugcestun Aleut) of the Pacific Gulf, and for Aleut, listed immediately below.

Aleut (Eskimo-Aleut). *Eastern Aleut. G.*: V. Henry (1879) and Geoghegan (1944) are based on data from Veniaminov. *W.*: Marsh and Laughlin (1956:58-76) have about 310 anatomical and physiological terms. *Western Aleut. G., W.*: Bergsland and Dirks (1978) have Atkan grammar and lexicon. *T., W.*: Bergsland (1959) has data on names, pp. 11-55, Atkan texts, pp. 56-104, and Attuan texts, pp. 104-128. Bergsland and Dirks (1990) have 87 stories from Jochelson, with Aleut texts and translations on facing pages. Bergsland (1994) is a comprehensive dictionary.

Algonquin (dialect of Eastern Ojibwa). Algonquin comprises the full-vowel dialects of Eastern Ojibwa. *G., W.*: Cuoq (1886, 1891-1892) has a dictionary and grammar from Oka, originally the Nipissing dialect. Henderson (1973) discusses verbs and syntax. McGregor (1987) is a dictionary from Maniwaki. Volume 6:59 maps phonological and morphological criteria that distinguish dialects that have been called Algonquin. (Note: In fig. 3, isoglosses 1, 2, and 14 should run south of Golden Lake, and in fig. 4, isogloss 2 should run north of Maniwaki.) *T.*: Mathevet (1892) is a missionary text of 495 pp. See Northern Algonquin, Old Algonquin, Ojibwa.

Alliklik. See Tataviam.

Alsea (Alsean). *G., T.*: Frachtenberg (1917b, 1920a) has texts with phonetic information and notes. *G.*: Volume 7:568 has phonemes from Melville Jacobs. E. Buckley (1988) discusses Alsea temporal boundaries. *W.*: Drucker (1939a) lists about 39 kin terms. For Jacobs's and Leo Frachtenberg's manuscript materials, see volume 7. Also see Yaquina.

Alutiiq. See Pacific Yupik.

Ammassalik. See East Greenlandic.

Anaktuvuk Pass. See North Alaskan Inupiaq.

Ansayme. See Ausaima.

Antoniano (Salinan). *W.*: Pinart and Heizer (1952:73-82) have words. *G., T., W.*: Mason (1918), using Sitjar (1861), has a Salinan grammar, pp. 7-58; perhaps 470 lines of interlinear text; and about 1,275 vocabulary items, pp. 120-154. *W.*: A few words from Jacobsen have been published, for example in Haas (1964), Silver (1964), and McLendon (1964). *G., W.*: Turner (1980) discusses Salinan phonemes. See Migueleño.

Anvik, Anvik-Shageluk. See Ingalik.

Apache. See Chiricahua, Cibecue, Jicarilla, Kiowa-Apache, Lipan, Mescalero, Mimbreño, Pinaleño, San Carlos, and White Mountain Apache.

Apalachee (Muskogean). *G.:* Kimball (1987) has a sketch. *W.:* Kimball (1988) has an Apalachee-English vocabulary with 136 main entries, pp. 390-397. Haas (1949) gives vocabulary in discussing Muskogean comparative grammar. *T.:* A letter of 1688 was published by Buckingham Smith (1860).

Apalachicola. See Hitchiti.

Applegate. See Galice-Applegate.

Aranama. *W.:* Two words from a speaker of Tonkawa are given by Swanton (1940:124) and Goddard (1979a:372-373).

Arapaho (Algonquian). *G., W., T.:* Kroeber (1916) has some words, pp. 75-76, grammar, pp. 83-123, and about 63 lines of text, pp. 123-130. Salzmann has described Arapaho giving grammar, texts and other data, especially since 1956; for his study of the verb, see Salzmann (1967). Salzmann (1983) is an English-Arapaho dictionary. *W.:* older vocabularies of Arapaho and Gros Ventre are in Hayden (1862:323-339, 344-345).

Arctic Coast–Victoria Island. See Copper.

Arctic Quebec (dialect of Eastern Canadian Inuit). *G.:* Dorais (1986:23) compares the phonemic inventory of this dialect (equivalent to Itivimmiut plus Tarramiut) with other Eskimo inventories.

Arikara (Caddoan). *G., W.:* Hayden (1862:351-363) has grammar and vocabulary. Taylor (1963:118) has 25 items in five lists (Catlin, Maximillian, Hayden, Curtis, and Taylor) with a discussion of Caddoan linguistics. *T.:* Gilmore (1929) covers the Book of Genesis in Arikara. *G., W., T.:* Parks, Beltran, and Waters (1979) is an introduction to the language, 443 pp. *W.:* Parks (1986) is a dictionary, 77 pp., with over 2,000 entries. *T.:* Taylor (1977) has an Arikara text. Parks (1991) has extensive texts with interlinear and free translations.

Arizona Tewa (Kiowa-Tanoan). Also called Hopi-Tewa and historically Tano. *G.:* Yegerlehner (1957) is a dissertation on phonology and morphology. Yegerlehner (1959a) presents person markers. *W., T.:* Yegerlehner (1958) has a text, p. 267, broken down into a column of 40 elements. Kroskrity and Healing (1978) have a text. *G., W.:* Yegerlehner (1959) describes phonemes.

Arviligjuaq. See Netsilik.

Asiatic Eskimo. See Central Siberian Yupik, Naukan, and Sirenikski.

Assiniboine (Dakotan). *G., T.:* Levin's grammar (1964) covers phonology, morphology, and syntax, pp. 4-112, with interlinear texts, pp. 113-245. Lowie has published some texts; see Lowie (1909) and Lowie and Lowie (1960). See E. Carriker et al. (1976:24).

Atakapan. *G., T., W.:* Swanton (1929a) covers phonology, morphology, and vocabulary, with 900 words and analysis of 160 morphemes; Swanton has about 32 lines of interlinear text with notes, pp. 146-149. Gatschet and Swanton (1932) cover Eastern Atakapa and Western Atakapa, including the Akokisa dialect, with interlinear texts, pp. 9-20 (Western Atakapa), an Atakapa-English dictionary, pp. 21-181 (including an English-Atakapa index of perhaps 2,200 entries, pp. 161-181).

Atfalati. See Kalapuyan.

Atikamekw. See Attikamek.

Atka. See Aleut.

Atna. See Shuswap, Carrier, or Ahtna.

Atsina. See Gros Ventre.

Atsugewi (Palaihnihan). Also called Pit River. *G., W.:* Olmsted presents phonology (1958) and morphology (1961); he offers comparative vocabulary, with sound laws (1956, 1957, 1959), relating Shasta, Achumawi, and Atsugewi. Olmsted (1958) has a bibliography. *T.:* Walters (1977) has an analyzed text in the Apwaruge dialect.

Attikamek. *G., W.:* Rhodes and Todd (vol. 6:55-56) use a few words and phonological data to delimit this dialect. Cooper (1945) has verb paradigms and perhaps 60 words passim. Béland (1978) is a grammar and wordlist. *T.:* Guéguen (1889) is a catechism with prayers and hymns; text on pp. 5-190.

Auburn. See Nisenan.

Ausaima (Costanoan). *W.:* Kroeber discovered two or three words of Ausaima in the Mutsun vocabulary of Arroyo de la Cuesta (1862:9).

Awaswas (dialect of Northern Costanoan). Also called Santa Cruz, San Lorenzo. *W.:* A.S. Taylor (1860-1863) has vocabulary. Mason (1916:470-472) has about 136 items. Beeler (1972) has about 24 words in a comparative vocabulary. Levy (1976:22-35) has about 100 words in a comparative vocabulary. Kroeber (1910:243-248) has about 122 items. Pinart and Heizer (1952:7-34) have two lists, List II with about 250 words and List III with about 195 words. *W., T.:* Henshaw and Heizer (1955:160-174, 185-186) have vocabulary, with 22 phrases on p. 185.

Ayticha (dialect of Kings River Yokuts). Also spelled Aiticha. Also called Kocheyali. *W., G.:* Kroeber (1907a:320-321) has perhaps 25 words. Driver (1937) has Kocheyali kinship terms, p. 145, and 55 nouns and 16 numerals of Kocheyali in a comparative vocabulary, pp. 146-153. Kroeber (1963:186-210) has Ayticha forms in a comparative vocabulary of 270 words in 21 Yokuts dialects or languages.

Babine (Athapaskan). Also called Northern Carrier (vol. 6:413), comprising the Hagwilgate (Bulkley River, Western Carrier) and Babine Lake dialects. *G.:* Story (1984) discusses Babine and Carrier phonology. *W.:* Krauss (1979) discusses the Bulkley

River (Hagwilgate) dialect and gives one word. *G.*: Krauss and Golla (vol. 6:83) have phonological data. They put the Babine language into the phonological perspective of all other Northern Athapaskan languages, pp. 69-72.

Baffin. There are two dialects of Eastern Canadian Inuit on Baffin Island, Aivilik (North Baffin-Aivilik) and South Baffin (Southeast Baffin–Cape Dorset). See Aivilik, Cape Dorset, Southeast Baffin.

Baker Lake. See Caribou.

Bankalachi (dialect of Tubatulabal). *W.*: Kroeber (1907:71-98) has about 52 forms. Driver (1937:146-153) has 46 nouns and 16 numerals in a comparative vocabulary.

Bannock (Numic). *W.*: Kroeber (1907:71-89) has about 27 items from the Ft. Hall Reservation. *G., W.*: Kroeber (1909) has grammatical notes and a comparative vocabulary of 42 items, English-Bannock-Shoshoni, pp. 276-277. *G.*: Liljeblad (1950) covers phonemes. See Northern Paiute.

Barbareño (Chumashan). *W.*: See Pinart and Heizer (1952:36-71) for a Santa Barbara or Siuxton Chumash vocabulary of Alphonse Pinart, taken from Island Chumash speakers. See Henshaw and Heizer (1955:94-147) for a long vocabulary. Kroeber (1910:265-267, 269) has about 124 lexical items and a note on pronouns. *G., W.*: Beeler (1976) is a grammatical sketch. *G., W., T.*: Caballería y Collell (1892) has some 165 words and names, some notes on grammar, and about 32 lines of religious texts, pp. 34-47. *T., W.*: Beeler (1978a) has a Barbareño-English lexicon, about 580 entries, pp. 171-190, and 32 lines of interlinear text, pp. 191-193; Beeler and Whistler (1980) have an analyzed text.

Barrow (dialect of North Alaskan Inupiaq). Also called Point Barrow. *G.*: Schultze (1889) has a grammar and vocabulary for northwestern Alaska. *W.*: Wells and Kelly (1890) have 711 words and 307 phrases from Point Barrow. Jenness (1929:170-179) has perhaps 200 words in a comparative vocabulary. Webster and Zibell (1976) have about 170 words and phrases in a comparative vocabulary of Alaskan and Canadian Eskimo dialects. *T.*: Jenness (1924) has perhaps 260 lines of interlinear text. See North Alaskan Inupiaq. See Pidgin Eskimo.

Bay Miwok (Eastern Miwok). Also called Saclan. *W.*: Beeler (1955, 1959) has data from Arroyo de la Cuesta. *G., W.*: Callaghan (1971:449-451) has about 78 words and suffixes, with phonemic analysis.

Bearlake (Athapaskan). *G., T.*: Rushforth and Gorbet (1989) have notes on relative clauses, with some morpheme-by-morpheme analysis of sentences. *W., T.*: Rushforth (1991) compares nine Bearlake and ten Mescalero Apache classificatory verb stems, p. 253, and analyzes five Bearlake sentences, pp. 255-256. Rice (1989:1335-1354) has interlinear texts. *W.*:

Rice (1987) has a few words. *G.*: Krauss and Golla (vol. 6:69-72, 79-80) have phonological data; Bearlake is used as a lingua franca at Fort Franklin and Fort Norman. See Slave.

Bear River (dialect of Mattole). *W.*: P.E. Goddard (1929) and Nomland (1938) have words.

Beaver (Athapaskan). *G.*: Krauss and Golla (vol. 6:69-72, 81) have phonological data. *W.*: Garrioch (1885) has Beaver-English and English-Beaver word lists. Hoijer (1956a) has 82 items; Hoijer (1963:21-23) has perhaps 35 items. *T.*: P.E. Goddard (1917) has texts with interlinear translation. *G., W..*: P.E. Goddard (1917a) analyzes phonology and morphology, with lists of words passim.

Bella Bella. See Heiltsuk-Oowekyala.

Bella Coola (Salishan). *G.*: Nater (1984) is a Bella Coola grammar, about 170 pp. Newman (1947, 1969, 1969a, 1971) covers phonology and morphology, and Newman (1977) cites pronouns. P.W. Davis and Saunders (1978) deal with the syntax of embedded predications. *G., W.*: Haeberlin and Thompson (1974) discuss suffixes (English index, pp. 234-235, about 140 items) and have perhaps 25 items in a comparative vocabulary of 13 dialects or languages (listed below *s.v.* Nanaimo). *W., T.*: In his two-volume ethnography, McIlwraith (1948) has a vocabulary of about 1,925 entries (2:573-630), kin terms (1:150-156), and interlinear song texts with notes (2:573-630). *T.*: P.W. Davis and Saunders (1980) have interlinear texts with morpheme-by-morpheme analysis.

Beothuk. *W., G.*: Gatschet (1885-1890) collected words in old vocabularies and identified 20 morphemes. Hewson (1968, 1971) used vocabulary, especially in 58 cognate sets, Beothuk and Proto-Algonquian, to show ties. Hewson (1978) collects all the extant vocabularies.

Bering Strait (Inupiaq). See Big Diomede, King Island, Shishmaref, Wales.

Big Diomede (dialect of Seward Peninsula Inupiaq). *G.*: Menovschikov (1980) covers grammar. See R. Carriker et al. (1976:22-23).

Bidai. Eight putative words, recalled by a White settler, were printed by Gatschet (1891:103).

Biloxi (Ohio Valley Siouan). *G., W., T.*: Dorsey and Swanton (1912:1-318) have interlinear texts, pp. 13-138, sentences, pp. 138-167, a Biloxi-English dictionary, pp. 169-296, and an English-Biloxi index of about 2,100 entries, pp. 297-318. Einaudi (1976) is a modern grammar; analysis of seven sentences, pp. 171-183. *W.*: Haas (1968) has about 56 words, pp. 78-80, as well as Ohio Valley Siouan reconstructions (Biloxi, Ofo, Tutelo, about 33 items, pp. 83-84).

Blackfoot (Algonquian). Also Blackfeet. *G.*: Uhlenbeck (1938) is a Southern Peigan grammar. Frantz (1991) is an introductory grammar. For generative grammar, see Frantz (1971, 1978). *W.*: Uhlenbeck and van Gulik (1930, 1934) is a Southern Peigan dictionary, English-Blackfoot, 261 pp., and Blackfoot-English, 380 pp. Frantz and Russell (1989) have a dictionary of stems, roots, and affixes. Taylor (1989) has names of plants, pp. 364-369. *T.*: Uhlenbeck (1911, 1912) offers two volumes of texts. See E. Carriker et al. (1976:28-30).

Blood. See Blackfoot.

Blue Lake (subdialect of Chilula in Hupa). *W., G.*: Loud (1918:234-235, 253-255, 259-265, 290-292) has place names, names of plants and trees, and other vocabulary, with some grammatical notes.

Bodega Miwok (dialect of Coast Miwok). *W.*: Callaghan (1970) is a dictionary. An early study is Barrett (1908a:68-80). *T.*: Englelhardt (1929:91) has a Lord's Prayer.

Boothia Peninsula. See Netsilik.

Bristol Bay (dialect of Central Alaskan Yupik). *W.*: Jacobson (1984) indicates which words are localized in this dialect area.

Buena Vista (Yokutsan). *W.*: Dixon and Kroeber (1919:56-61) have words. Dialects of Buena Vista are Tulamni and Hometwoli.

Bulkley River. See Babine.

Caddo (Caddoan). *W.*: Taylor (1963:115) has 25 items in five lists. Spier (1924a:261-263) has 31 kin terms. Gursky (1965a) has Caddo words in a comparative vocabulary. *G.*: Chafe (1976:55-82) is a grammatical sketch. *G., W.*: Chafe (1968) discusses phonology and has a few words. Chafe (1977) has texts.

Cahitan (Uto-Aztecan). *G.*: Basilio (1737, 1890) is a grammar of Cáhita, an early form of Mayo. *W.*: Collard and Collard (1962) have a dictionary of Mayo. See Yaqui.

Cahto (California Athapaskan). Also spelled Kato. *G., W.*: P.E. Goddard (1912) presents phonology, pp. 4-18, and morphology, pp. 19-85, with lists of items and about 68 nouns, pp. 17-18. *W.*: Essene (1942:85-88) has about 325 words, with Lassik counterparts. *T.*: P.E. Goddard (1909) offers poorly transcribed texts. *W.*: Hoijer (1956) has a lexicostatistical list of words; Hoijer (1963:9-13) has words in comparative context.

Cahuilla (Takic). *G.*: Seiler (1977) and Sauvel and Munro (1982) are grammars. *W.*: Seiler and Hioki (1979) is a dictionary. *G., W.*: Munro (1990) has words with Takic reconstructions and morphological analysis; cognates in 142 sets, pp. 237-249 (Serrano-Kitanemuk, Gabrielino-Fernandeño, and Cupan with Luiseño, Cahuilla, and Cupeño). *T.*: Seiler (1970:37-159) has Cahuilla texts with English on facing pages. See also Wánikik.

Calusa. *W.*: A handful of words from 1575 are in Escalante Fontaneda (1944). Swanton (1922) offers place names.

Camanche. See Northern Sierra Miwok.

Cambridge Bay. See Copper Eskimo.

Campo (dialect of Kumeyaay). *W.*: Law (1961) has words in a comparative Yuman vocabulary . *G., W.*: Wares (1968:41-42, 77-96) touches on phonology and has 501 items in a comparative vocabulary. See Kumeyaay.

Caniba (dialect of Eastern Abenaki). *W.*: Râle (1833) is a dictionary. O'Brien (1887) sketches the noun using data from Râle. *T.*: Trumbull (1873:23-28) has two versions of the Lord's Prayer.

Cape Dorset (dialect of Eastern Canadian Inuit). Also called Kinngarmiut, Southwest Baffin. *G.*: Dorais (1975) is a description. Dorais (1976) compares certain phonological features with those of five other dialects (see *s.v.* Aivilik). Dorais (1986:23) compares the phonemic inventory of this dialect with inventories of other Eskimo dialects. See South Baffin.

Cape Farewell. See West Greenlandic.

Cape Prince of Wales. See Seward Peninsula Inupiaq.

Cape York. See Thule.

Caribou (dialect of Western Canadian Inuit). Includes materials on the Upper Kazan and Baker Lake dialects. *G.*: A.E. Spalding (1960) has a grammar of a Hudson Bay variety. Webster and Zibell (1976:276, 286-325) have phonemic analysis, about 170 words and phrases, and 42 sentences. *W.*: Birket-Smith (1928:28, 30, 31, 33-62) has about 506 words of Upper Kazan River in topical groups, mostly on pp. 33-46. *T.*: Rasmussen (1930:79-114) has about 70 lines of text and about a dozen words passim, especially on pp. 79-87. *W., T.*: Rasmussen (1930a:11-13, 64-65, 120-160) has perhaps 90 lines of interlinear texts and perhaps 500 words, including place names. *G.*: Dorais (1986:23) compares the phonemic inventory of Caribou with inventories of other Eskimo dialects.

Carolina Algonquian (Eastern Algonquian). *W.*: Swanton (1934), Geary (1955), and Quinn (1970:273) have words. See Pamlico. See Goddard (vol. 15:74), Pentland and Wolfart (1982:326).

Carrier (Athapaskan). *G., W.*: Morice (1932) is a major study of nearly 1,400 pages of Central Carrier. *T.*: Morice (1891) is a catechism and prayer book of 144 pp. R. Walker (1979), Cook (1985), and Pike (1986) discuss phonology. *W.*: Hoijer (1956a) has a list of words, with lexicostatistical computations. *W.*: Antoine et al. (1974) is a Central Carrier dictionary. *G.*: Krauss and Golla (vol. 6:69-72, 83-84) put Carrier into phonological and historical perspective. The phonemes of Central Carrier and the Buckley River Dialect of Babine, with notes on other dialects, are in vol. 6:413.

Carrizo de Camargo. See Cotoname.

Carrizo de Mamulique. See Mamulique.

Cascades. See Wasco-Wishram.

Catalineño (Santa Catalina dialect of Gabrielino). See Gabrielino.

Catawba (Siouan-Catawba). *G.:* Gatschet (1900a) has the first grammatical sketch. Siebert (1945, 1945a) discusses Catawba in terms of Siouan morphology. *T., W.:* Matthews and Red Thunder Cloud (1967) have about 300 lines of text with translation and analysis, pp. 7-19, and an English-Catawba lexicon of about 102 items, pp. 20-40.

Cathlamet (Upper Chinook). Also called Skilloots, Qaniak, Wakaikam. *T.:* Boas (1901) has extensive texts. *G.:* Hymes (1955) is a basic source. Silverstein (vol. 7:553) lists the phonemes. *W.:* Hale (1846:570-629) has about 62 Wakaikam words.

Cayuga (Iroquoian). *G., W.:* Chafe and Foster (1981) have phonological and morphological data, with sound laws and words passim. Mithun and Henry (1982) is a teaching grammar. *W.:* Schoolcraft (1846:271-277) has a vocabulary of 320 words from Adam Elliot. *T.:* Foster (1974, 1980) and Mithun and Woodbury (1980:9-25, 123-133, 149-155) present texts. See Mithun (1984c).

Cayuse. *W.:* Hale (1846:561, 570-629) has data from Whitman, about 196 items. *G., W.:* Rigsby (1966:369-378) has two verbal paradigms and about 50 sets with Molala comparisons.

Ꞓegiha. See Dhegiha.

Central Alaskan Yupik (Eskimoan). Also called Yup'ik. *G., W.:* Reed et al. (1977) is a grammar of 330 pp. with exercises and vocabulary. See "Sketch of Central Alaskan Yupik, an Eskimoan Language," this vol. *W., G.:* Jacobson (1984) is a comprehensive dictionary, with valuable grammatical data; bases, pp. 41-419; postbases, pp. 429-602; endings, pp. 605-616; enclitics, pp. 619-624; English-Yupik index, over 4,725 forms, pp. 693-757. Jacobson indicates which words are localized in these dialect areas: Bristol Bay, Hooper Bay–Chevak, Kuskokwim, Lake Iliamna, Nelson Island, Norton Sound (further localized to Unaliq and Kotlik areas, on the northern and southern shores of Norton Sound respectively), Nunivak Island, Nushagak River, Upper Kuskokwim, and Yukon. See R. Carriker et al. (1976:23-31).

Central Carrier. See Carrier.

Central Coash Salish. See Clallam, Halkomelem, Nooksack, Northern Straits, Squamish.

Central Eskimo. See Eastern Canadian Inuit, Tarramiut, Labrador, South Baffin, Cape Dorset, Aivilik, Cumberland Sound.

Central Kalapuya. See Kalapuyan.

Central Numic. Also called Plateau Shoshonean. See Panamint, Shoshone.

Central Ojibwa (dialect of Central Southern Ojibwa). *G., W.:* Rhodes and Todd (vol. 6:57-58) cover phonology and use morphological criteria to delimit this dialect. See Ojibwa.

Central Pomo (Pomoan). *W.:* Barrett (1908:56-68) has about 282 forms. Webb (1971:37-45) has about 235 items in a comparative vocabulary. *G., W.:* Oswalt (1964b) compares Central Pomo and Kashaya phonology, morphology, and vocabulary, with reconstructions. McLendon (1973) has cognate sets for Central Pomo, Eastern Pomo, Northeastern Pomo, Northern Pomo, Southeastern Pomo, Southern Pomo, and Southwestern Pomo, pp. 65-95, and a dictionary of protoforms, pp. 96-110. *G.:* Mithun (1990) describes morphology, syntax, and semantics, with numerous illustrative sentences.

Central Salish. See Clallam, Comox, Halkomelem, Lushootseed, Nooksack, Northern Straits, Pentlatch, Seshelt, Squamish, Twana. See Thompson and Kinkade (vol. 7:36-38).

Central Siberian Yupik (Eskimoan). *G., W.:* De Reuse (1994a) has extensive data on morphology, syntax, and lexicon, with numerous sentences. *G.:* Jacobson (1990) is a grammar with lessons and exercises; de Reuse (1988, 1989) discusses autolexical morphology and internal reconstruction. *W.:* Jacobson, Badten, et al. (1987) is a dictionary, 410 pp. Rasmussen and Ostermann (1941:36-41) list about 103 items compared with words of Wales Eskimo. For Russian sources from Chaplino, see Chaplinski. See Jacobson (1990a).

Central Sierra Miwok (Eastern Miwok). *W.:* Broadbent and Callaghan (1960:307-316) have words in a comparative vocabulary of about 285 items. *G., T.:* Freeland and Broadbent (1960) have Central Sierra Miwok–English entries, pp. 1-24; English–Central Sierra Miwok, pp. 27-52; texts, pp. 55-71. Freeland (1951) is a grammar with notes on Northern and Southern Sierra Miwok and texts from all varieties of Sierra Miwok.

Central Southern Ojibwa. See Central Ojibwa, Ojibwa.

Central Tanana. See Lower Tanana.

Central Wintun. See Nomlaki.

Central Yana (dialect of Yana). *G., T.:* Sapir (1923b:265-277) has 27 lines of interlinear text with translation and copious grammatical notes. See Yana.

Chalon (Northern Costanoan). Also called Soledad. *W.:* Levy (1976:22-35) has about 100 words in a comparative vocabulary. Beeler (1961:194-197) has about 37 words in a comparative vocabulary. Pinart and Heizer (1952:7-34) have about 170 words collected in 1878. Callaghan (1990a) has words of Chalon from Harrington. *W., T.:* Henshaw and Heizer (1955:160-174, 183-184, 186) have vocabulary and phrases.

Chalostaca (subdialect of Lower San Joaquin in Far Northern Valley Yokuts). *W.:* Kroeber (1959b:7-14) has words from Pinart in a comparative vocabulary.

Chandalar (dialect of Western Kutchin). Also called Natsit-Kutchin. Osgood (1936:103) has eight color words. See Kutchin.

Chapai. See Cocopa.

Chaplinski (dialect of Central Siberian Yupik). Also called Chaplino. *G.*: Menovshchikov (1962-1967) is a grammar. *T.*: Rubtsova (1954) has texts. *W.*: Rubtsova (1971) is a dictionary with about 19,000 entries. See Central Siberian Yupik. See Krauss (1976:190-198).

Chasta Costa (dialect of Tututni). *G.*: Sapir (1914) covers phonology and morphology. *W.*: Hoijer (1963:9-13) has words in a comparative vocabulary. A Rogue River vocabulary from Harrington in Landar (1977a) may be Chasta Costa. See Tututni.

Chawchila (dialect of Northern Valley Yokuts). Also spelled Chauchila. *G., W.*: Kroeber (1907a:320-321, 358-359) has 16 words and grammatical comments. Newman (1944) has basic grammar with words in lists passim. Kroeber (1963:186-210) has Chawchila words in a comparative vocabulary of 270 items in 21 Yokuts dialects or languages. Beeler (1971) has grammatical analysis in a discussion of Nopchinchi Yokuts. See Yawelmani.

Chehalis. See Upper Chehalis, Lower Chehalis.

Chelan. See Wenatchi. See E. Carriker et al. (1976:34).

Chemainus. See Halkomelem.

Chemakum (Chimakuan). Also spelled Chimakum. *G.*: Boas (1892) has notes on the language. *G., W.*: Swadesh (1955) has over 850 items in a Chemakum-English list, with Quileute comparisons, and an analysis of suffixes, pp. 62-63. J.V. Powell (1975) discusses Proto-Chimakuan, and J.V. Powell (1993) has words in a comparative discussion. See Adler (1961:199).

Chemehuevi (dialect of Ute). *G., W., T.*: Press (1979) has grammar with fine discussion of syntax, pp. 1-139; Chemehuevi-English lexicon of about 1,000 entries, pp. 146-158; English-Chemehuevi, pp. 159-174. Munro (1978) discusses the quotative pattern. *G., W.*: Kroeber (1909a:256-261) has grammatical notes with about 50 supplementary words on pp. 260-261. *W.*: The earliest printed vocabulary is Whipple's, with 172 items, in U.S. Army, Corps of Engineers (1855:71-76).

Cherokee (Iroquoian). *G.*: Eastern Cherokee verb morphology is described by Walker (1975a). *G., W.*: Bradley and Smith (1976) have 27 lessons, and Cherokee-English and English-Cherokee vocabularies. Feeling (1975) is a dictionary with almost 2,000 Cherokee-English entries, pp. 1-190, an English-Cherokee index, pp. 190-234; and an extensive grammar by William Pulte and Durbin Feeling, pp. 235-355. Feeling (1994) and Van Tuyl and Feeling

(1994) provide an introduction to verbal inflections. *T.*: Mooney and Olbrechts (1932) have extensive texts.

Chesterfield Inlet. See Aivilik.

Chetco. See Tolowa.

Chevak (dialect of Central Alaskan Yupik). *G., T.*: Woodbury (1983) discusses the syntax of clauses; he has a short interlinear text, pp. 310-315. *T.*: Woodbury (1984) has stories, 88 pp., with a cassette. Jacobson (1984) indicates which words are from the Hooper Bay-Chevak dialect.

Cheyenne (Algonquian). *W.*: Petter (1915) is an English-Cheyenne dictionary of over 1,100 pp. Glenmore and Leman (1985) is a topically arranged dictionary. *T.*: Petter (1934) is a New Testament in Cheyenne, 660 pp. Leman (1980a, 1987) has collections of texts. *G.*: Petter (1952) and Leman (1980) are grammars.

Chickasaw (Muskogean). *W.*: Gatschet (1884-1888, 1:56, 96) describes lexical differences of Chickasaw compared with other Choctaw dialects. Munro and Willmond (1994) is a dictionary with grammatical notes. *G.*: Speck (1907b) compares pronouns in Creek, Hitchiti, Choctaw and Chickasaw, pp. 477-478, and he has other forms from these languages. Munro (1983) discusses the syntax of clauses.

Chiglit. See Siglit.

Chilcotin (Athapaskan). *W.*: Boas (1924:37-38) has about 28 words in a comparative vocabulary. Tolmie and Dawson (1884:74B-77B) have 162 words. Morice (1893:109) has a few place names, with a map. Morice (1907) has 11 words. *G., W.*: King (1978) has phonology and vocabulary. *G.*: Krauss and Golla (vol. 6:69-72, 83-84) have phonological data. Cook (1983) discusses phonology. See Krauss (1979:867-868, 898).

Chilliwack (Halkomelem). Also called Stalo. *G.*: Galloway (1993) has a full grammar. *G., W.*: Elmendorf and Suttles (1960:13-27) have about 716 items in a comparative vocabulary, with phonological notes. *G., W., T.*: Hill-Tout (1903) has a Chilliwack glossary and Kwantlen texts. Gibbs (1877:270-283) has words. Durieu (1891) has prayers in shorthand characters. See Halkomelem.

Chilula (dialect of Hupa). *W.*: P.E. Goddard (1914) maps Chilula territory and gives several dozen place names with their meanings. *G., T.*: P.E. Goddard (1914b) has about 990 lines of interlinear texts, with grammatical notes. See Blue Lake, Hupa.

Chimakum. See Chemakun.

Chimariko. *G., W., T.*: Dixon (1910) has a grammar, pp. 307-339, an interlinear text with notes, pp. 339-361, and vocabulary (English-Chimariko, about 700 entries, pp. 363-370; Chimariko-English, pp. 370-379; place names, pp. 379-380). *G.*: Sapir (1918) discusses the first person plural. *W.*: Landar (1974) has 33 words, mainly body parts, from Harrington. Bauman (1980a) has about 36 placenames, pp. 18-24, some with translations or etymologies, including data from Harrington.

Chinook (Lower Chinook). Also called Chinook proper, Shoalwater. *G., W., T.*: Boas (1894a) has 186 pp. of text. Boas (1904) has about 640 words, 600 morphemes, and two paradigms. Boas (1911a) sketches the morphology, and presents an interlinear text, pp. 666-669. See Shoalwater. Silverstein (vol. 7:553) lists the phonemes.

Chinook Jargon. *W.*: Early studies are Gibbs (1863) and Hale (1846:635-650, 1890). J.V. Powell (1990) adds about 315 words previously unrecorded or uniquely recorded. *G.*: Modern studies are Silverstein (1972a) and Thomason (1983). *T.*: Jacobs (1936) has texts. Harris (1985) has a letter of 1881 with interlinear translation, and a Chinook Jargon bibliography.

Chipewyan (Athapaskan). Also see Yellowknife. *G., W.*: Li (1932) has grammatical notes and about 780 entries in a list of stems. Petitot (1876) has a dictionary with a grammatical sketch and paradigms. *G.*: Li (1946) is a sketch, and Legoff (1889a) and P.E. Goddard (1912a) are early grammars. Krauss and Golla (vol. 6:69-72, 80-81) and Cook (1983a) have phonological data. Haas (1968a) has notes from Yellowknife (vol. 6:80). *T.*: Li (1964) and Li and Scollon (1976) have texts from Fort Chippewyan, and Goddard (1912) has interlinear texts from Cold Lake and Heart Lake.

Chiricahua Apache (Apachean Athapaskan). Chiricahua and Mescalero are dialects of one language. *G.*: Hoijer (1946a) is a sketch. *T.*: Hoijer (1938) has texts. *W.*: Hoijer (1956a) has 100 words; Hoijer (1938a) has some 90 items with sound laws. See Mescalero, Mimbreño.

Chitimacha. *G.*: Swadesh (1946a) is a sketch. *G., W.*: Swanton (1919) has structural and lexical comparisons of Chitimacha, Tunica, and Atakapa.

Chiwere. See Iowa-Otoe, Missouri.

Chochenyo (Northern Costanoan). Also spelled Chocheño. Also called San Jose, Juichun, East Bay. *W.*: Kroeber (1910:243-248) has about 97 items. Beeler (1961) has short vocabularies of Juichun and Niles dialects. Beeler (1972) has words from a vocabulary classed as Bay Costanoan. Levy (1976:22-35) has about 100 words in a comparative vocabulary. Okrand (1989) has a few words.

Chocouyem. See Marin Miwok.

Choctaw (Muskokean). *G.*: Byington (1870) is a grammar. Haas (1946:326) has verb forms in a discussion of comparative grammar. Nicklas (1975) describes morphophonemics. *W.*: Byington (1915) is a dictionary. *T.*: Wright and Byington (1848) is a New Testament of 818 pp.

Cholovomne. See Chulamni.

Chome (Coahuilteco). *W.*: Damián Mazanet recorded 18 place-names, some with translations, which Swanton (1940:55) ascribed to the Chomes, Alachomes, Pamais, Parchaques, Yoricas, and Mescaleros (Goddard 1979a:366-367).

Choynimni (dialect of Kings River Yokuts). Also spelled Choinimni. *G., W.*: Kroeber (1907a) has 16 words, pp. 320-321, and a note on grammar, p. 352. Kroeber (1963:186-210) has Choynimni vocabulary in a comparison of 270 items in 21 Yokuts dialects or languages. *W.*: Driver (1937:146-153) has 55 nouns and 16 numerals in a comparative vocabulary.

Choynok (dialect of Southern Valley Yokuts). Also spelled Choinok. *G., W.*: Newman (1944) has a grammatical description. Kroeber (1907) has 16 words, pp. 320-321, and a note on grammar, p. 352. Kroeber (1963:186-210) has Choynok vocabulary in a comparison of 270 items in 21 Yokutsan dialects or languages. See Yawelmani.

Chugach (dialect of Pacific Yupik). *G.*: Birket-Smith (1953:235-248) has a sketch. *W.*: Anderson (1784), Portlock (1789:254-255), Dixon (1789:241), and Seton-Karr (1887:244) have words from Prince William Sound. For later studies see Pacific Yupik.

Chugamite. See Kodiak.

Chukaymina (dialect of Kings River Yokuts). Also spelled Chukaimina. *G., W.*: Kroeber (1907a) has 16 words, pp. 320-321, and a note on grammar, p. 351. Kroeber (1963:186-210) has Chukaiymina vocabulary in a comparison of 270 items in 21 Yokuts dialects or langauges. *W.*: Driver (1937:146-153) has 56 nouns and 16 numerals in a comparative vocabulary.

Chukchansi (dialect of Northern Valley Yokuts). *W.*: Kroeber (1963:186-210) has Chukchansi vocabulary in a comparison of 270 items in 21 Yokuts dialects or languages. Golla (1963:60-66) has an English-Yokuts comparative vocabulary of 333 sets, mostly with words of Chukchansi, Yawelmani, and Yawdanchi. Whistler and Golla (1986:353-356) have words of various Yokuts languages in cognate sets. *G., W.*: Grammatical and lexical data are presented by Newman (1944). *T.*: Berman (1980) has texts. See Yawelmani.

Chulamni (dialect of Far Northern Valley Yokuts). Also called Cholovomne, Tcholovone. *W.*: Kroeber (1959b:7-14) has words in a comparative vocabulary of about 120 items, pp. 7-13, with a separate list of about 19 items on pp. 13-14. Merriam (1955:133-138) has Pinart's (1894) 1880 vocabulary. See Whistler and Golla (1986:320-321).

Chumash. See Barbareño, Cruzeño, Ineseño, Mupu, Obispeño, Purisimeño, Santa Rosa, Ventureño.

Chunut (dialect of Southern Valley Yokuts). *W., G.*: Kroeber (1907a) has 16 words, pp. 320-321, and a grammatical note, p. 362. *W.*: Driver (1937) has 25 nouns and 16 numerals in a comparative vocabulary, pp. 146-153, and words passim. Kroeber (1963:186-210) has Chunut vocabulary in a comparison of 270 items in 21 Yokuts dialects or languages.

Cibecue Apache (dialect of Western Apache). *W.*: Basso (1966:170-172) has 37 items in phonetic writing. Basso (1967) has perhaps two dozen words including body parts, in a discussion of linguistic acculturation. Basso (1970) has perhaps 30 words and phrases. See also San Carlos Apache, White Mountain Apache.

Clackamas (dialect of Upper Chinook). *T.*: Jacobs (1958-1959) has about 570 pp. of texts, with notes. See also Wasco-Wishram.

Clallam (Central Salish). *G.*: Thompson and Thompson (1971) describe phonology, morphology, and syntax, and Newman (1977) cites pronouns. See Suttles (vol. 7:453) for Clallam phonemes. See Thompson and Kinkade (vol. 7:37) for Clallam reflexes of nine protophonemes.

Clatskanie (Pacific Coast Athapaskan). A dialect of Kwalhioqua-Clatskanie. Also spelled Tlatskanai. *G., W.*: Hale (1846:535, 570-629) has just a few lines on grammar and about 235 words, of which 210 seem to be common to both Clatskanie and Kwalhioqua. Boas and Goddard (1924a) have a word list of 322 items. Krauss (1969) has unpublished and reconstituted forms. See Krauss (1979:870).

Clatsop (dialect of Lower Chinook). *W.*: Hale (1846:570-629) has about 16 items.

Clayoquot. See Nootka.

Coahuilteco. *G., W.*: "Sketch of Coahuilteco, a Language Isolate of Texas," this vol. Troike (1981) presents phonemes, and discusses topics in morphology and syntax. Swanton (1940:10-55) has a Coahuilteco-English vocabulary, pp. 10-48; vocabulary and grammatical forms, pp. 49-50; English-Coahuilteco index, pp. 50-54 (about 500 items). Troike (1967:81) has about 80 Pajalate items, in a discussion of typological similarities of Coahuilteco and Tonkawa. *T.*: García (1760) is a confessional of some 88 pp. See Goddard (1979a:363-367).

Coast Miwok. See Bodega Miwok, Marin Miwok.

Coast Tsimshian (Tsimshianic). Also called Tsimshian. *G.*: Boas (1911a) is a sketch with an analyzed text. Dunn (1979c) is a grammar. Dunn describes connectives (1979a), pronominal concord (1979b), and nonbasal suffixes (1983). *G., W.*: Dunn and Hays (1983) discuss phonology and dialectology. *G., T.*: Mulder (1994) is a grammar with analyzed texts. *W.*: Garfield (1939) has over 200 terms for clan and society, indexed on pp. 335-339. Dunn (1978) is a dictionary. *T.*: Boas (1902) has about 220 pages of texts. Boas and Tate (1912) have texts, pp. 70-253, with a Tsimshian-English glossary, about 2,000 items. See Gitksan, Southern Tsimshian.

Coast Yuki (Yukian). *W.*: Barrett (1908) has about 130 forms, pp. 68-80, and about five names, pp. 260-263. Elmendorf (1968:22-35) has words in comparative vocabularies. See Yuki.

Cochimí. *G., T., W.*: Mixco (1978) has analyzed texts, grammatical notes, and a comparative word list.

Cochiti (dialect of Rio Grande Keresan). *G.*: Fox (1959) has a grammatical sketch. *W., T.*: Dumarest and Parsons (1919) have ceremonial terms and some songs. *W.*: Curtis (1907-1930, 16:65-122) has vocabulary. The first printed vocabulary, perhaps, is the 22 words in Whipple, Ewbank, and Turner (1855:86-89).

Cocomaricopa. See Maricopa.

"Coconoon" (dialect of Valley Yokuts). *W.*: Kroeber (1959a:7-13) has words in a comparative vocabulary of about 120 items; the quality is too poor for exact classification.

Cocopa (Yuman). *G.*: Crawford (1966) is an unpublished dissertation. *W.*: Crawford (1970) discusses baby talk. Wares (1968:37-38, 77-96) has phonological notes and words in a comparative Yuman vocabulary of 501 sets, pp. 77-96. *T.*: Crawford (1983) has texts, with Cocopa and English translation on facing pages, pp. 12-565, and notes, pp. 567-602.

Coeur d'Alene (Interior Salish). *G.*: Reichard (1945a) has morphology and perhaps 400 stems and other vocabulary items, pp. 54-63. Kinkade (1981) compares singular and plural roots in several Salishan languages. Newman (1977) cites pronouns. *W.*: Reichard (1960, 1960a) has perhaps several hundred items in a comparative vocabulary, pp. 57-60. Kinkade and Sloat (1972:31-44) list 810 words in an Interior Salish comparative vocabulary. See E. Carriker et al. (1976:34); Landar (1980).

Columbian (Interior Salish). Also called Columbia, Moses-Columbian, and Columbia-Moses. *W., G.*: Kinkade and Sloat (1972:31-44) list 810 words in a comparative vocabulary. Kinkade (1967a) includes a few words relating to uvular-pharyngeal resonants. Kinkade (1982) discusses reduplication, with Spokane and Thompson comparisons. *W.*: Krueger (1967) has 275 words. Kinkade (1980) is a dictionary. Hale (1846:570-629) has about 200 words from Walker and Eells. *T.*: Kinkade (1978) is a coyote story. See E. Carriker et al. (1976:35) and Mattina (1989:90-91). See Wenatchee.

Columbia River Sahaptin. See Sahaptin, Tenino, Umatilla.

Colville. See Okanagan.

Colville River (Inupiaq). *T.*: Jenness (1924:6-18, 33-38) has about 400 lines of interlinear text.

Comanche (Central Numic). *G.*: Charney (1993) is a full grammar. *T., W.*: Canonge (1958) has texts, pp. 1-130, and a Comanche-English vocabulary, pp. 131-156. *G., W.*: Robinson and Armagost (1990) is a dictionary and grammar of 365 pp. Osborn and Smalley (1949) describe stems and word formation. Casagrande (1954) is the first of three articles which describe affixation and morphology. McLaughlin (1983) discusses mode and aspect.

Comecrudo (Comecrudan). Also called Carrizo and Mulato. *W., T.*: Swanton (1940:55-118) has perhaps 1,200 lexical items and about 38 lines of text. See Goddard (1979a:369-370, 385).

Comox (Central Salish). Dialects are Island Comox and Sliammon or Mainland Comox (Homalco, Klahoose, Sliammon). *G.*: Hagège (1981) has a grammar of Sliammon, reviewed by P.D. Kroeber (1989). Sapir (1915e) describes noun reduplication, in about 55 pp. J.H. Davis (1971) and Watanabe (1994) describe phonology. *G., W.*: Haeberlin (1918:169-170) describes reduplication; Haeberlin and Thompson (1974) discuss suffixes (English index, pp. 234-235, about 140 items) and have perhaps 25 items in a comparative vocabulary of 13 dialects or languages (listed below, *under* Nanaimo). Timmers (1978) has a stem-list. *G., W., T.*: P.D. Kroeber (1988) discusses inceptive reduplication, with illustrative sentences. Volume 7:441 has phonemes.

Conestoga (Iroquoian). *W.*: Hanna (1911, 1) has personal names. See Susquehannock.

Connecticut. Ambiguous term for some Eastern Algonquian dialects (see Agawam, Housatonic, Mohegan-Pequot, Montauk, Naugatuck, Quiripi).

Conoy. See Nanticoke-Conoy.

Coos. See Hanis.

Copper (Western Canadian Inuit). Also called Arctic Coast (and Victoria Island), and Coppermine. *W.*: Jenness (1928) has a comparative vocabulary of Western Canadian Inuit dialects. Lowe (1983) is a dictionary for Kangiryuarmiut (Prince Albert Sound). *W., T.*: Rasmussen (1932:289-345) has a vocabulary and words passim, about 1,200 items, representing the Kangiryuarmiut (Kangerjuarmiut) and the Umingmaktôrmiut. He has about 1,060 lines of folk songs and about 600 lines of tales (songs, pp. 113-118, 140-191, interlinear tales, pp. 194-264). *T.*: Possibly 55 lines of text are in Jenness (1924:70-89). Métayer (1973) has three volumes of texts from Coppermine. *G., W., T.*: Webster and Zibell (1976) have phonemic analysis with phonemes of Coppermine (Qurluqtuq) and Cambridge Bay (Iqaluktuuttiaq), pp. 275-276; about 170 words and phrases in a comparative vocabulary; and 42 sentences in a comparative survey, pp. 318-325. *G.*: Jenness (1944) has grammatical notes on Western Canadian Inuit dialects. Lowe (1985) is a grammar of Kangiryuarmiut. Dorais (1986:23) compares the phonemic inventory of Copper with the inventories of other Eskimo dialects.

Coquille (dialect of Tututni). *W.*: Hoijer (1960) has about 65 forms and stems. For words also see Hoijer (1963).

Coronation (dialect of Western Canadian Inuit). Also called Coronation Gulf. *W.*: Jenness (1929:170-179) has perhaps 200 words in a comparative vocabulary. For words passim also see Jenness (1928:3-134).

Costanoan. See Ausaima, Awaswas, Chalon, Chochenyo, Karkin, Mutsun, Niles, Ramaytush, Rumsen, Tamyen.

Cotoname. Also called Carrizo de Camargo. *W.*: Swanton (1940:118-121) has about 150 items. See Goddard (1979a:370, 385).

Coushatta. See Koasati.

Coweset. See Narragansett.

Cowichan. See Halkomelem.

Cowlitz (Tsamosan Salishan). Also spelled Kawelitsk. *W.*: Hale (1846:570-629) has perhaps 200 items of Kawelitsk. Gallatin (1848:119) reproduced about 60 words. Kinkade and Sloat (1972:31-44) have a few words. *G., W.*: Kinkade (1973) discusses the alveopalatal shift in Cowlitz.

Cowlitz, Upper. See Upper Cowlitz.

Cree (Algonquian). *G.*: Rhodes and Todd (vol. 6:55-56) list Cree varieties based on features of phonology and morphology. See Attikamek, East Cree, Eastern Swampy Cree, Montagnais, Naskapi, Plains Cree, Western Swampy Cree, Woods Cree. See "Sketch of Cree, An Algonquian Language," this vol.

Creek (Muskogean). Also called Muskogee. *G.*: An old grammar is Buckner and Herrod (1860:49-138). Haas (1940, 1946a:330, 1948) has modern grammatical data. *W.*: Loughridge and Hodge (1890) is a dictionary. *W., T.*: Gatschet (1884-1888, 1:237-251) is a migration legend; in the corrected edition (1884-1888, 2), the text is on pp. 8-25, with a glossary, pp. 74-130.

Crow (Missouri River Siouan). *G.*: Kaschube (1967) is a grammar. *G., T.*: Lowie (1941) has a grammatical sketch, pp. 1-37, and an analyzed text, pp. 38-139, with 885 sentences. *W.*: Medicine Horse (1987) is a dictionary. Lowie (1960a), has various vocabularies, over a span of about 450 pp. *T.*: Lowie (1960) has about 550 pages of texts. Kaschube (1978) has texts. See E. Carriker et al. (1976:25-28).

Crow Flats Kutchin (dialect of Kutchin). Also called Vuntakutchin. *W.*: Osgood (1936:98, 122-123) has names of months and clans. See also Kutchin.

Cruzeño (Chumashan). *W.*: Pinart and Heizer (1952:36-71) have a vocabulary of 1878. *W., G.*: Kroeber (1910:265-267) uses about 94 items from Timmeno via Taylor, in Powers (1877:561-565), and has a note on pronouns, p. 269. See Santa Rosa Island.

Cumberland Sound (dialect of Eastern Canadian Inuit). *W.*: Boas (1894b) has perhaps 1,150 entries in a vocabulary that has comparisons with words of Labrador and Greenland. *W., T.*: Boas (1901) includes interlinear texts, pp. 333-337, 340-349, and about 150 shaman's words compared with ordinary words, pp. 350-354. See Central Eskimo, Melville Peninsula, Netsilik, South Baffin.

Cupeño (Takic). *G., W., T.*: Hill and Nolasquez (1973) describe the First People, 198 pp. *W.*: Bright and Hill (1967) use lexical material and Hill and Hill (1968) have about 36 English glosses for a comparative vocabulary with reconstructions, pp. 240-241. Munro (1990) has words in a comparative vocabulary (see *s.v.* Cahuilla).

Cusabo. *W.*: Swanton (1922:20-23) has place names and personal names and a few words ascribed to this dubious entity.

Cux. See Nunivak.

Dakota. See Sioux.

Deering-Buckland (dialect of North Alaskan Inupiaq). *W.*: Webster and Zibell (1970) have words found especially in this subdialect of Malimiut, as part of an Inupiaq dictionary.

Delaware (Eastern Algonquian). Munsee is the language of the Ontario Delawares; Unami (Delaware proper), of the Oklahoma Delawares. *W.*: Brinton and Anthony (1889) edited a dictionary that includes words from Munsee and Unami. Goddard (1973a) has kinship terms. *G.*: C.F. Voegelin (1946a) is a Unami sketch. Goddard (1979b) describes Munsee and Unami verb morphology and compares other Algonquian languages. *T.*: C.F. Voegelin (1945a) has Unami texts. See Goddard (vol. 15:72-73), Pentland and Wolfart (1982:329-331). See Munsee.

Delaware Jargon (Pidgin Delaware). *G.*: Goddard (1996) surveys grammatical structure. *T.*: Campanius (1696) uses this jargon in his catechism. *W.*: Prince (1912:511-523) has 261 lexical items dated around 1684. Goddard (1995) discusses words.

Dena'ina. See Tanaina.

Dhegiha. See Kansa, Omaha, Osage, Ponca, and Quapaw.

Diegueño (Delta-California Yuman). Varieties are Tipai (La Huerta), Ipai (Mesa Grande), and Kumeyaay (Baron Long). *G.*: Langdon (1970) is a substantial study of the Mesa Grande dialect of Ipai. Gorbet (1976) describes the syntax of nominals. *W.*: Couro and Hutcheson (1973) is a dictionary of Mesa Grande. Wares (1968:39-40, 77-96) describes phonology; he has words in a comparative Yuman vocabulary of 501 sets, pp. 77-96. Hinton (1976, 1978), R.A. Jacobs (1976), and Langdon (1976a) have texts. See Ipai, Kumeyaay, Tipai.

Diomede. See Big Diomede, King Island, Seward Peninsula Inupiaq.

Dogrib (Athapaskan). *G.*: Krauss and Golla (vol. 6:69-72, 79-80) have phonological data. Davidson (1963) describes active verbs. *G., W.*: Howren (1979) presents Fort Rae phonology. *W.*: Hoijer (1963:24-26) has some words from William Davidson. *T.*: Petitot (1887:299-335) has some texts. See Slavey.

Dumna (dialect of Northern Valley Yokuts). *W., G.*: Kroeber (1907a:320-321, 353-354, 356-357) has about 60 words and grammatical notes. Kroeber (1963:186-210) has Dumna vocabulary in a comparison of 270 items in 21 Yokuts dialects or languages.

Duwamish. See Lushootseed.

East Bay. See Chochenyo.

East Cape. See Naukanski Yupik.

East Coast of Hudson Bay. See Itivimmiut.

East Cree (Montagnais-Naskapi). *G., W.*: Rhodes and Todd (vol. 6:55-56) use a few words and phonological data to delimit this dialect. Vaillancourt (1978, 1980) has lessons. *W.*: MacKenzie et al. (1988) is a dictionary in syllabics and roman transcription.

Eastern Abenaki. See Caniba, Wawenock, and Penobscot. See Goddard (vol. 15:71).

Eastern Aleut. See Aleut.

Eastern Canadian Inuit (Eskimoan). Sometimes called Central Eskimo, Inuktitut. The Baffin subgroup has two dialects, North Baffin-Aivilik (called Iglulingmiut earlier) and South Baffin (Southeast Baffin)–Kinngarmiut (Southwest Baffin, called Kinngaqmiut earlier). The Quebec-Labrador subgroup has three or four dialects, Arctic Quebec (Northern Arctic Quebec Tarramiut, called Taqramiut earlier), Itivimmiut (East Coast of Hudson Bay), Labrador, and perhaps Rigolet. See Fortescue, Jacobson, and Kaplan (1994:xiii), Dorais (1976, 1986). *G., W.*: Spalding (1960) has grammar and words for Central and Eastern Arctic. *W.*: Boas (1888:659-666) has a glossary. Schneider (1985) is a two-way dictionary for Northern Quebec, Labrador, and Eastern Arctic dialects.

Eastern Kutchin. See Kutchin.

Eastern Ojibwa. See Algonquin, Mississauga, Ojibwa.

Eastern Pomo (Pomoan). *W.*: Webb (1971:37-45) has about 230 items. See McLendon (1973) *under* Central Pomo. *G., T.*: McLendon (1975) has phonology, morphology, and text analysis. McLendon (1977a, 1978a) has analyzed texts. See "Sketch of Eastern Pomo, a Pomoan Language," this vol.

Eastern Shoshone (Numic). Also called Wind River Shoshone. *G., T.*: Shimkin (1949) covers grammar, pp. 175-180, a text, pp. 180-182, and a translation, pp. 182-188. *G., W.*: Shimkin (1949) has a morpheme list. Davis (1966) has a phonological note, p. 126, and about 185 lexical items, pp. 134-139. *W.*: Shimkin (1947) has about 86 proper names, pp. 251-252, about 105 names of plants, pp. 271-275, and about 83 names of animals, pp. 276-278.

Eastern Swampy Cree (Algonquian). *G., W.:* Ellis (1983) is a pedagogical grammar. Rhodes and Todd (vol. 6:55-56) use a few words and phonological data to delimit this dialect. Ellis (1961, 1971) describes verbal paradigms.

East Greenlandic (Eskimoan). *G., T.:* Thalbitzer (1921) offers phonology, pp. 117-126, morphology, pp. 127-154, and texts, pp. 155-564. *W.:* Rink's East Greenlandic material is presented in a comparative vocabulary of about 258 main entries in Rink and Thalbitzer (1911:213-223). Gessain, Dorais, and Enel (1982) have 1,473 words translated into West Greenlandic, French, English, and Danish. *T., W.:* Vibæk (1907) recorded data from the Southeast Greenland dialect.

Eel River. See Nongatl, Lassik, Sinkyone, and Wailaki.

Entimbich (dialect of Monache). Also called Endimbich. Kroeber (1907:165) thought his data might be Wobunuch dialect, but Driver (1937) also obtained a Monache vocabulary called Entimbich. See Mono.

Entimbich (subdialect of Choynimni in Kings River Yokuts). Kroeber (1907a) was told that Entimbich Yokuts was very similar to Choynimni but obtained no data.

Eskimo (Eskimo-Aleut). *W.:* Fortescue, Jacobson, and Kaplan (1994) is a comparative dictionary, with words from all Eskimoan languages. See Aglurmiut, Aivilik, Akulurak, Aleut, Arctic Quebec, Asiatic Eskimo, Baffin, Barrow (Point Barrow), Bering Strait, Big Diomede, Bristol Bay, Cape Dorset, Caribou, Central Alaskan Yupik, Central Siberian Yupik, Chaplinski, Chevak, Chugach, Colville River, Copper, Coronation, Cumberland Sound, Deering-Buckland, East Greenlandic, Eastern Canadian Inuit, Fort Chimo, Hikoligjuaq, Hooper Bay–Chevak, Iglulik, Inglestat, Inuit, Inuvik, Itivimmiut, Kangianirmiut, King Island, Kivalina, Kobuk River, Kotzebue, Kuskokwim, Labrador, Maguse River, Malimiut, Naukanski Yupik, Nelson Island, Netsilik, Noatak, Nome, North Alaskan Inupiaq, Norton Sound, Nunivak, Nushagak River, Pacific Yupik, Pidgin Eskimo, Point Hope, Polar Eskimo, Pond Inlet, Qawiaraq, Rankin Inlet, Rigolet, Selawik, Shishmaref, Siglit, Sirenikski, South Baffin, Tarramiut, Tuktoyaktuk, Unaliq, Unalakleet, Ungava, Upper Kuskokwim (dialect of Central Alaskan Yupik), Wales, West Greenlandic, Western Canadian Inuit, Yukon.

Eskimo Point. See Caribou.

Esselen. *G., W.:* Kroeber (1904:49-68) is a key source, with all the then known Esselen data. Shaul (1995) has additional information and analysis, vocabularies, the longest of which, Henshaw's, has 110 words. *T.:* Kroeber (1908b:21) has a new sentence. *W.:* Pinart and Heizer (1952:73-82) has Pinart's vocabu-

lary of 1878. *G., W.:* Beeler (1961:197) discusses possible Esselen loans in Karkin Costanoan, and analyzes a few Esselen forms. For an evaluation of sources, see Beeler (1977).

Etchemin (Eastern Algonquian). Also spelled Etechemin. *W.:* Lescarbot (1609:697-703) has the numerals 1-10. (The name Etchemin has sometimes been used for Maliseet and Passamaquoddy.) See Hoffman (1955), Goddard (1972, vol. 15:70-71).

Euchre Creek. See Tututni.

Eudeve (Uto-Aztecan). *G.:* Shaul (1991) is an overview of morphosyntax based on an early grammar (Pennington 1981).

Eyak (Athapaskan-Eyak). *T.:* Krauss (1970a) is a collection of analyzed texts, 912 pp. Krauss (1982) has texts (with an Eyak cassette). *W.:* Krauss (1970) is a dictionary, about 3,000 pp. *G.:* Li (1956) describes nouns. Krauss (1964) has phonology and forms passim in 69 cognate sets, pp. 125-127. Krauss (1965) is a sketch. Krauss (1968) discusses noun classification systems, with Eyak examples, pp. 194-200. Krauss (1969) has Eyak forms in a discussion of comparative Nadene verb morphology. Leer (1991) describes number as an Eyak category, pp. 165-166, and has Eyak syntax, pp. 181-185. Krauss and Leer (1981) have numerous comparisons of Eyak and Athapaskan forms in a discussion of sonorants, 210 pp. See Krauss and McGary (1980:203-220) and De Laguna (vol. 7:189-196).

Fernandeño (dialect of Gabrielino). *W.:* Kroeber (1907:71-89) has about 96 forms. *W., G.:* Kroeber (1909a:251-252) has about 30 additional forms and a discussion of grammar, pp. 252-253. *W.:* Engelhardt (1927:142-143) has about 180 names of rancherias. See Bright (1974). See Gabrielino.

Flathead. See Kalispel.

Fort Chimo (dialect of Eastern Canadian Inuit). *G., W.:* Webster and Zibell (1976) have phonemic analysis, p. 278, and about 170 words and phrases in a comparative vocabulary, pp. 286-317.

Fox (Algonquian). Also called Mesquakie. Fox and Sauk are very similar dialects of one language. *G., T.:* W. Jones (1911) is a sketch. *T.:* Michelson (1925) has several of the texts Michelson published. *G.:* For modern data see Voorhis (1971a), Dahlstrom (1986), and Goddard (1990). *W., G.:* Bloomfield's lexicon was edited by Goddard (1994), with verbal paradigms. See volume 15:584-585. See Sauk.

Frederick VI Coast. See East Greenlandic.

Frobisher Bay. See South Baffin.

Gabrielino (Takic). Also called Gabrieleño, Kij. *G., W., T.:* Reid (1885) has 60 words, place names, paradigms and two lines of a song. *G., W.:* A. Woodward (1944) has 150 words and two paradigmatic tables. Hale (1846:566-567, 570-629) has 129 words and some notes on grammar. Engelhardt

(1927a) has 133 place-names. Munro (1990) has words in 142 cognate sets, pp. 237-249. *T.*: Roberts (1933) has song texts with interlinear translation in the Gabrielino proper and Santa Catalina dialects. See Bright (1974). See Fernandeño.

Galice-Applegate (Oregon Athapaskan). Also called Galice. *G.*: Hoijer (1966a) is a sketch; also see Hoijer (1971, 1973). *W.*: Hoijer (1956) has 89 items; also see Hoijer (1963:9-13) and Landar (1977a). *T.*: Jacobs (1968) has about 75 lines of text with translation and extended content and style commentary.

Garza (Comecrudan). *W.*: For the source of 23 items see Goddard (1979a:371).

Gashowu (Yokutsan). Also spelled Koshoo. *G., W.*: Kroeber (1907a:320-321, 352-353) has 16 words and a grammatical note. Kroeber (1963:186-210) has Gashowu vocabulary in a comparison of 270 items in 21 Yokuts dialects or languages. Newman (1944:13-239) covers comparative Yokuts phonology, morphology, and syntax. *W.*: Gifford (1922:83-84) has about 52 kin terms. Merriam and Heizer (1967a:417) have two or three words of Koshoo.

Giamina (Uto-Aztecan). *W.*: Kroeber (1907:128) has 13 putative words and numerals 1 through 6 from a Yokuts speaker of Yawelmani and Palewyami. Kroeber (1909a:263-265) has words in a comparative vocabulary and further discussion. See vol. 8:5, vol. 10:122.

Gitksan (Tsimshianic). Nisgha and Gitksan make up the Nass-Gitksan branch of Tsimshian. *G., W.*: Sapir (1920b) has 29 kin-term entries, pp. 262-263, and grammatical commentary. Hoard (1978) has about 42 forms, pp. 113-115, with fine phonetic, phonemic, and morphophonemic analysis. Rigsby and Ingram (1990) discuss obstruent voicing and glottalic obstruents. Tarpent (1983) describes Nisgha plurals. *W.*: Hindle and Rigsby (1973) is an English-Gitksan dictionary of about 1,200 forms. Dall (1877:145-156) has a Nisgha vocabulary. Boas (1924) has Nisgha forms passim. *T.*: Boas (1911a) has a text; Ridley (1881) is a prayer book, 8 pp.

Gjoa Haven. See Netsilik.

Gosiute. See Western Shoshone.

Greenlandic (Eskimoan). See Polar Eskimo, East Greenlandic, West Greenlandic.

Gros Ventre. See Gros Ventre (Arapahoan in Algonquian) and Hidatsa (Siouan).

Gros Ventre (Arapahoan in Algonquian). Also called Atsina. *W.*: Taylor 1967 has a vocabulary compared with Arapaho. *G., W., T.*: Kroeber (1916:75-76, 131-137) has words including numerals and kin terms, grammatical remarks, and 27 lines of interlinear text. Salzmann (1969) includes phonological material and lexical items in his article on salvage phonology; his bibliography has manuscript as well as printed sources. For historical phonology of Arapaho and Atsina see Goddard (1974).

Guaicura. *G.*: Baegert (1773:175-194, 1952:94-104) has a sketch.

Guale. *W.*: Swanton (1922) discusses possible Guale names.

Guarijío (Uto-Aztecan). *G., W.*: J.B. Johnson and Weitlaner de Johnson (1947) have a vocabulary with notes on phonetics.

Gwich'in. See Kutchin.

Hagwilgate. See Babine.

Haida. *G., T.*: Swanton (1911b) describes morphology and has a short interlinear text. *T.*: Swanton (1905a) has about 448 pp. of Skidegate texts. Swanton (1908) has Masset texts, pp. 271-802, and stems, prefixes, and suffixes, pp. 803-812. *G., W.*: Lawrence (1977) has grammar, pp. 12-155; a Haida-English stem dictionary, about 2,600 items, pp. 158-408; and an English-Haida index, pp. 409-464. *G.*: Enrico (1983) discusses the relative clause. Enrico (1991) describes the lexical phonology of Masset. See Krauss (1979:838-842), Thompson and Kinkade (vol. 7:31).

Haisla (Wakashan). *W.*: Olson (1940:184-185) has Kitamaat (Kitimat) kin terms. Lincoln and Rath (1986) is a dictionary with phonology. See volume 7:306. See Kwakiutl.

Halchidhoma (dialect of Maricopa). *W.*: Gifford (1918:158) has eight clan names. See Maricopa.

Halkomelem (Central Salish). *G.*: Gerdts (1988) discusses object and absolutive in the Cowichan dialect. *G., W.*: Elmendorf and Suttles (1960:13-27) list about 716 items from the Cowichan, Musqueam, and Chilliwack dialects in a comparative vocabulary, and discuss phonological data. Elmendorf (1962a:86-87, 92-93) has perhaps 187 items in a comparative vocabulary. Hess (1977:410-412) has 40 words. Gerdts (1991) describes morphology and syntax of Cowichan verbs. *T.*: Gerdts (1984) analyzes 134 numbered sentences. Hukari, Peter, and White (1977) have an interlinear text. See volume 7:453. See also Chilliwack, Nanaimo.

Halyikwamai. See Kahwan.

Han (Athapaskan). *G.*: Krauss and Golla (vol. 6:69-72, 77) have phonological data. *W.*: Hoijer (1963:18-20) has 34 items from David Shinen. Osgood (1971) has terms passim and about 23 kin terms from Richard Slobodin, p. 44. See Krauss and McGary (1980:395-404) and Krauss (1979).

Hanis (Coosan). Also called Coos. The following works deal with Hanis and Miluk, the Coosan languages. *G., W.*: Sapir and Swadesh (1953:134-137) discuss data selected from 152 groups of cognates, with comparisons. *G.*: Frachtenberg (1922) is a grammar. Pierce (1971) discusses Hanis phonemes. *T.*: Frachtenberg (1913a) and Jacobs (1939, 1940) provide texts.

Hano. See Arizona Tewa.

Hare (Athapaskan). *G.*, *W.*: Petitiot (1876) has Hare data in a comparative grammar (pp. XLVII-LXXXV plus folded charts at the end) and a dictionary, pp. 1-367, with perhaps 13,000 lexical items. *W.*: Rice (1980) is a dictionary. DeLancey (1990) discusses meanings of enclitics. *G.*: Hoijer (1971) has grammar; Hoijer (1956a, 1963:24-26) has words; Hoijer (1966) has sound laws with comparative vocabulary, in a study of phonology. Rice (1977) is a grammar of the dialect of Fort Good Hope. Rice (1987) discusses tone. Krauss and Golla (vol. 6:79-80) have phonological data; they identify a Slavey-Hare language with four dialects, Slavey (or Slave), Bearlake, Mountain, and Hare.

Havasupai (dialect of Upland Yuman). *G.*: Seiden (1963) is a grammar. Kozlowski (1972) analyzes deep structures of sentences. *W.*: Wares (1968:77-96) has lexical items in a comparative Yuman vocabulary of 501 sets. *W.*, *T.*: Spier (1946) has vocabulary and text in comparative perspective. *T.*: Spier (1924) has perhaps 300 lines of interlinear text. Kozlowski (1976) has analyzed texts. Hinton (1984) analyzes song texts.

Heiltsuk-Oowekyala (Wakashan). Heiltsuk is spoken by the Haihais and Bella Bella, Oowekyala by the Oowekeeno. *Heiltsuk.* Also called Bella Bella. *W.*, *T.*: Boas (1924a) has suffixes in a comparative vocabulary. Boas (1928) has texts, pp. 2-171, and a comparative vocabulary for Bella Bella, Rivers Inlet, and Kwakiutl, pp. 173-291. *W.*: Olson (1955) has some words including kin terms. *G.*, *W.*: Lincoln and Rath (1980:6-16, 30-36) have phonology. Rath (1981) is a dictionary and grammar. *T.*: Storie and Gould (1973) have Bella Bella stories. *Oowekyala.* Also called Oowekeeno, Owikeno, Wikeno, Rivers Inlet. *W.*, *T.*: Curtis (1907-1930, 10) has about 280 words in a comparative vocabulary, pp. 329-337, and about 25 lines of songs, pp. 311-315. Boas (1928) has texts, pp. 156-171, and words in his Kwatiutl vocabulary, pp. 173-291. *W.*: Olson (1954:253-255) has kin terms. *G.*: Hilton (vol. 7:312) has phonology. *T.*: Hilton, Rath, and Windsor (1982) have texts. See Kwakiutl.

Hidatsa (Missouri River Siouan). *G.*: Matthews (1965) is a transformational grammar, reviewed by K. Hale (1967a). *G.*, *W.*: W. Matthews (1877) is a grammar and dictionary. Robinett (1955) studies stems and themes, in the third of a series of articles. *G.*, *T.*: Harris and Voegelin (1939) have texts. Parks, Jones, and Hollow (1978) have texts edited by Jones, pp. 53-77, and a note on pronunciation, p. 123. See Gros Ventre in E. Carricker et al. (1976:30).

Hikoligjuaq (dialect of Caribou). *W.*, *T.*: Rasmussen (1930:37-38, 67-78) has about 107 names and 250 lines of text. See Caribou.

Hill Patwin (dialect of Patwin). *W.*, *T.*: Barrett (1919) has about 558 lines of text passim and perhaps several hundred lexical items passim. Dixon and Kroeber (1919:56-61) have about 37 items. Shafer (1961) gives a vocabulary of 315 items, and comparisons with River Patwin.

Hitchiti (Muskogean). *G.*: Haas (1946:330) has verbs with comparisons. *G.*, *W.*: Swanton (1924:48, 65-75) has 20 words in a comparative vocabulary, and data on verbs, pronouns, and morphology in general. *T.*, *W.*: Gatschet (1884-1888, 2) has a text, pp. 20-25, and vocabulary, pp. 134-179. See Mikasuki.

Hodogida. See Mono.

Holikachuk (Athapaskan). Also called (Upper) Innoko. *G.*: Krauss and Golla (vol. 6 1981:69-72, 74) have phonological data. *W.*: Kari (1978) is a noun dictionary of about 1,600 items in topical format. *G.*, *W.*: Krauss and Leer (1981) discuss Tlingit sonorants in relation to Athapaskan and Eyak, with citation of Holikachuk forms passim. See Krauss (1979:852-853) and Krauss and McGary (1980:293-300).

Hometwoli. See Tulamni.

Hooper Bay–Chevak. See Chevak.

Hopi (Uto-Aztecan). *G.*, *W.*: Malotki (1983) devotes 677 pp. to phonology, morphology, syntax, and semantics, with focus on verbs; utterances are translated throughout, morpheme by morpheme. *W.*: C.F. Voegelin and F.M. Voegelin (1957) is a rich source of lexical data. Albert and Shaul (1985) is a dictionary, Hopi-English, about 4,600 entries, pp. 13-113; English-Hopi, about 3,600 entries, pp. 114-204. *T.*: C.F. Voegelin and F.M. Voegelin (1960) have about 40 lines of interlinear text, pp. 73-75. Malotki and Lomatuway'ma (1984) have Coyote tales with Hopi and English on facing pages, 343 pp. Malotki and Lomatuway'ma (1987), and Lomatuway'ma (1993) have additional texts. *G.*: C.F. Vogelin and F.M. Voegelin (1967) discuss passive transformations from non-transitive bases. Masayesva Jeanne (1982) has morphophonemics. See Seaman (1977) for an annotated bibliography. Whorf (1946) has a sketch.

Housatonic. See Mahican.

Hoyima (subdialect of Merced in Northern Valley Yokuts). *W.*: Kroeber (1907:359-360) has six words or sentences taken from Chawchila and Chukchansi informants.

Hualapai. See Walapai.

Huchnom (dialect of Yuki). *W.*: Barrett (1908:68-80, 256-260) has about 270 words and fifteen names. Gifford (1922:118-119) has about 48 kin terms. Elmendorf (1968:22-35) has words in comparative vocabularies. See Bright (1982:151-152). See Yuki.

Hudson Bay (Eskimo). See Aivilik, Caribou, Itivimmiut.

Huimen (Coast Miwok?). *W.*: Beeler (1961:194), referring to an unpublished manuscript vocabulary at the Bancroft Library, gives one word.

Hupa (California Athapaskan). *G.*: Woodward (1964) has phonology. *G., W.*: Golla (1964a) describes noun stems. *T.*: P.E. Goddard (1903) has nearly 300 pp. of poorly transcribed texts. Golla (1977a) has an analyzed text. *W.*: Hoijer (1956a) has words. See also Chilula. See "Sketch of Hupa, an Athapaskan Language," this vol.

Huron (Iroquoian). Also called Huron-Petun. *W.*: Sagard-Théodat (1632) is a dictionary. *G.*: Chaumonot's 17th-century grammar of Lorette Huron was translated by Wilkie (1920) and analyzed by Lagarde (1980). *T.*: Brébœuf (1630) is a Christian Doctrine. See Wyandot.

Icy Cape. See Kangianirmiut.

Iglulik (Eastern Canadian Inuit). *W.*: Birket-Smith (1928:23-46) has words of Iglulik and from Melville Peninsula in comparative vocabularies. *W., T.*: Rasmussen (1930a:11-99) has about 1,000 lines of interlinear texts, pp. 11-61, and perhaps over 600 lexical items, pp. 62-99. *G.*: Dorais (1978) is a sketch.

Iliamna. see Lake Iliamna.

Illinois (Algonquian). *G., W., T.*: Le Boullenger (1725) has Illinois words, verbal paradigms, and perhaps 8,000 lines of religious texts in a manuscript French-Illinois dictionary. *T.*: Allouez (in Neilson 1908) is an Illinois prayer book apparently actually written by Sébastien Râle. See volume 15:585; Miami.

Ineseño (Chumashan). *W.*: Pinart and Heizer (1952:36-71) have a vocabulary of 1878. *W., T.*: Henshaw and Heizer (1955:94-148) have vocabulary and about 31 lines of the acts of faith, hope, and charity. *G., W.*: Kroeber (1904:31-43) is a sketch, including numerals and kin terms. Applegate (1976) describes reduplication. *W., G., T.*: Kroeber (1910) has about 126 lexical items, pp. 265-267; a grammatical note on pronouns and tense, p. 269, and pater noster texts with notes, pp. 269-271.

Ingalik (Athapaskan). *W.*: Kari (1978) is a noun dictionary in topical format. Hoijer (1956:324-332, 1963:18-20) has words. *G.*: Krauss and Golla (vol. 6:69-74) have phonological data. *T.*: Kari (1981) has interlinear texts based on Chapman (1914). Kari (1987c) is a collection of texts by Deacon. See Krauss and McGary (1980:275-292) and Krauss (1979:851-852).

Inglestat (subdialect of Malimiut in North Alaskan Inupiaq). *W.*: Jenness (1928:3-134) has perhaps several dozen words, from the north shore of Norton Sound. See North Alaskan Inupiaq.

Inner Koyukon. See Koyukon.

Interior Salish. See Columbian (Wenatchee), Coeur d'Alene, Kalispel, Lillooet, Okanagan, Shuswap, Thompson.

Inuit. Also Innuit, Inuktitut. Term for Eskimo, or more usually for Inuit-Inupiaq. See Landar (1976), R. Carriker et al. (1976:22-23). See Eskimo.

Inuktitut. See Eastern Canadian Inuit, Western Canadian Inuit.

Inupiaq. See North Alaskan Inupiaq, Seward Peninsula Inupiaq.

Inuvik (dialect of North Alaskan Inupiaq). *W., T.*: Webster and Zibell (1976:286-317) have about 170 words from Mackenzie Delta migrants (vol. 5:56) in a comparative vocabulary, and 42 sentences, pp. 316-325.

Iowa-Otoe. Also called Chiwere. *G.*: Hamilton and Irvin (1848) is a grammar of some 155 pp. Whitman (1947a) is another study of grammar. *W.*: Whitman (1937), Curtis (1907-1930, 19:230-238), and Wolff (1950-1951) have words. *T.*: Merrill (1837) translates 32 pages of Bible history. Hamilton and Irvin (1850) is a catechism. Dorsey (1880-1881) is an analyzed myth.

Ipai (Diegueño). *G.*: Langdon (1971) has Ipai data.

Iqaluktuuttiaq. See Copper Eskimo.

Isleta (dialect of Southern Tiwa). *W.*: Curtis (1907-1930, 16:261, 266-274) has about 273 words. *G., T.*: Leap (1970) describes phonology, morphology, syntax, and semology. *G., W.*: Leap (1970a) covers Tiwa noun classes. Allen and Frantz (1986) discuss goal advancement. *T.*: Gatschet (1891b) discusses a text.

Ita. See Polar Eskimo.

Itivimmiut (dialect of Eastern Canadian Inuit). Also called East Coast of Hudson Bay. *G.*: Dorais (1976) compares Itivimmiut phonologically and morphologically with five other mutually intelligible dialects (see under Aivilik). Dorais (1986:23) compares the phonemic inventory of this dialect with inventories of other Eskimo dialects.

James Bay Cree. See Eastern Swampy Cree and East Cree.

Jemez (Kiowa-Tanoan). *W.*: Curtis (1926:251-252, 260-261, 266-274) has about 300 words. K. Hale (1962) has about 100 forms in a comparative vocabulary.

Jicarilla (Apachean Athabaskan). *T.*: P.E. Goddard (1911a) has about 180 pp. of interlinear texts. *G.*: Hoijer (1945) is the initial article of a series on the Apachean verb. *W.*: Hoijer (1956:324-332, 1956a) has vocabulary.

Juaneño (dialect of Luiseño). Also called Natela, San Juan Capistrano. *G., W., T.*: Boscana (1933) has 40 words, 5 lines of song text, phonetic notes, and tribal names. Harrington (1933) has 32 lines of text and perhaps 480 words. Kroeber (1909) has grammatical notes, pp. 247-249; perhaps 150 words, pp. 249-250; and perhaps 20 sentences, p. 250. *G., W.*: Hale (1846:567, 570-629) has grammatical notes and 100 words.

Juichun. See Chochenyo.

Kachemak Bay. See Tanaina.

Kahwan (dialect of Cocopa). *W.*: Kroeber (1943:26-30) has words called Kahwan in a comparative vocabulary. On Kahwan and Halyikwamai, extinct dialects of Cocopa, see volume 10:4, 8, 10.

Kaibab Paiute. See Southern Paiute.

Kalapuyan (Takelman). Kalapuyan has three languages, Tualatin-Yamhill or Northern Kalapuyan, Central Kalapuyan, and Yoncalla (Yonkalla) or Southern Kalapuyan. *G., W.*: Shipley (1969:228-230) has 69 cognate sets for Takelma and Kalapuyan. Berman (1990) presents phonology, with 223 cognate sets, pp. 46-59, for Yamhill, Tualatin (Atfalati), Central Kalapuyan (six dialects, including Santiam, Mary's River), and Yoncalla. Hale (1846:564-566, 570-629) has words. *T.*: Jacobs (1945) is a monograph of 394 pp., with texts in Tualatin-Yamhill (pp. 135-203) and Central Kalapuyan (pp. 204-369). The phonemes of Tualatin-Yamhill and Central Kalapuyan are given in volume 7:547; some notes on grammar in volume 7:41-42.

Kalispel (Interior Salish). Also called Spokane-Kalispel, of which Flathead is a dialect. *G., W., T.*: Vogt (1940) has a grammar, texts, and a dictionary. Vogt (1940a) compares Kalispel, Spokane, Colville and Coeur d'Alene. *G., W.*: Hale (1846:537-542, 570-629) has grammatical notes and vocabulary. Mengarini (1861) and Giorda et al. (1879) are grammars. Kinkade (1981) discusses Salishan singular and plural roots, including those of Kalispel and Flathead. Kinkade (1981a) describes particles of Spokane, Kalispel, Flathead, and other Interior Salish groups. Haeberlin and Thompson (1974) discuss suffixes (English index, pp. 234-235, about 140 items) and have perhaps 25 items in a comparative vocabulary of 13 dialects or languages (listed below, *under* Nanaimo). *W.*: Giorda et al. (1877-1879) is a dictionary. Kruger (1960, 1961, 1961a) has about 525 words of Flathead. Kuipers (1970) has 157 roots common to Kalispel, Coeur d'Alene, Shuswap, and Squamish, in 167 sets of an etymological dictionary, with occasional forms of Halkomelem and Okanagan. See Newman (1977) *under* Twana. See Mattina (1989:91-92). See Spokane.

Kangianirmiut (dialect of North Alaskan Inupiaq). Rasmussen and Ostermann (1941:13-28) list about 400 words recorded at Icy Cape.

Kangiryuarmuit. See Copper.

Kansa (Dhegiha Siouan). Also called Kaw. *W.*: Dorsey (1885:924-927; 1894a) has Kansa, Omaha, and Ponca words in comparative vocabularies.

Karankawa. *G., W.*: Gatschet (1891) surveys available data. Swanton (1940:124-133) arranged the known vocabulary, Karankawa-English, pp. 124-130, English-Karankawa, pp. 130-133, with perhaps 340 items in the English list. Landar (1968) published a vocabulary of 158 words from Rafael Chowell, noting Cariban and Hokan resemblances. For observations on Karankawa sources and data, see Elmendorf (1965a) and Goddard (1979a:367-369, 385).

Karkin (Northern Costanoan). *W.*: Beeler (1961:192, 194-197) has about 50 items, p. 192, some of which he uses in a comparative vocabulary. *W., G.*: Callaghan (1988) discusses Beeler's data. Okrand (1989) puts Karkin in comparative perspective and establishes a sound law. Callaghan (1990a) discusses Karkin words used in counting.

Karok. *G., W., T.*: Bright (1957) has a grammar with texts and a dictionary.

Kashaya (Pomoan). Also called Southwestern Pomo. *W.*: Barrett (1908:56-68) has about 270 words. Webb (1971:37-45) has some 235 words in a comparative vocabulary. *T.*: Oswalt (1964:36-337) has texts, an annotated bibliography, pp. 22-27, and a map with place names, pp. 340-341. *G., W.*: Oswalt (1964b) compares Kashaya and Central Pomo. McLendon (1973) compares the phonologies of seven Pomoan languages, including Kashaya, and has words in a comparative vocabulary. *G.*: Oswalt (1983) describes the syntax of clauses.

Kaska (Athapaskan). Also called Nahane, Nahani, Tahltan. *G.*: Cook (1972) discusses stress and related rules of Dease River Kaska, called Tahltan (vol. 6:82). *W.*: Hoijer (1963:21-23) has about 35 items. Hoijer (1971a) has a note on phonology. *G.*: Krauss and Golla (vol. 6:69-72, 82-83) identify four dialects of Kaska (Frances Lake, Upper Liard, Dease River, and Nelson or Tselona), and discuss phonology and historical developments.

Kawaiisu (Numic). *G., W., T.*: Zigmond (1991) has a grammar and dictionary with texts. *G., W.*: Booth (1979) discusses postpositions as verbs. Davis (1966:126, 134-139) has phonological data and about 187 cognate sets. Klein (1959:235-238) has about 105 items in a comparative vocabulary with Mono and Southern Paiute. The first vocabulary published, with about 118 forms, was Kroeber's (1907:71-89). *W.*: Zigmond (1981) has ethnobotanical vocabulary. *T.*: Klein (1988) discusses variants of a myth.

Kechayi (dialect of Northern Valley Yokuts). *W., G.*: Kroeber (1907:320-321, 353) has 16 words and, p. 353, a grammatical note. Kroeber (1963:186-210) has Kechayi vocabulary in a comparison of 270 items in 21 Yokuts dialects or languages.

Kenai. See Outer Inlet Tanaina.

Kettle Falls. See Kalispel.

Khometwoli. See Tulamni.

Kickapoo (Algonquian). *G., T., W.*: Voorhis (1974) has grammar with focus on nouns and verbs, 120 pp. *G.*: Voorhis (1977, 1983) describes stem derivation. *T., G.*: Jones (1915) is a collection of tales, with notes by Michelson on phonetics, pp. 119-123, and on grammar, pp. 124-127. *W.*: Voorhis (1988) is a dictionary, with affix list, pp. 145-157. See Fox.

Kij. See Gabrielino.

Kiksht (Upper Chinookan). See Clackamas, Wasco-Wishram.

Kiliwa (Yuman). *G., T.*: Mixco (1983) has analyzed texts and a grammatical sketch. *G.*: Langdon (1971) explores sound symbolism. *G., W.*: Wares (1968:46-48, 77-96) has phonology and words in a comparative vocabulary of 501 sets, pp. 77-96. *W.*: Kroeber (1943:26-30) has words.

King Island (dialect of Seward Peninsula Inupiaq). Also called Ukiuvangmiut. *W.*: Jenness (1928:3-134) has several dozen words passim. King Island is the default dialect for Seward Peninsula Inupiaq words in Fortescue, Jacobson, and Kaplan (1994). *T.*: Kaplan (1988) has King Island Inupiaq and English on facing pages, pp. 40-249. See Carriker, Carroll, and Larsen (1976:22-23). See Seward Peninsula Inupiaq.

Kings River Yokuts. See Ayticha, Choynimni, Chukaymina, and Michahay.

Kinngarmuit. See Cape Dorset.

Kiowa (Kiowa-Tanoan). *G.*: Watkins and McKenzie (1984) describe phonology, morphology, and syntax. Merrifield (1959, 1959a) describes verb prefixes and nouns. *W.*: Harrington (1928) is a dictionary of 259 pp. *T.*: Harrington (1946) has three texts. Watkins (1990) has some interlinear sentences in short anecdotal stories.

Kiowa Apache. Also called Na'isha. *G.*: Bittle (1963) has paradigmatic morphology. See Hoijer (1945a) and subsequent articles on Apachean. *W.*: Hoijer (1938) has perhaps 90 items, with sound laws, reviewed in Hoijer (1971a). Hoijer (1963:7-9) has words in comparative perspective. Huld (1978) has vocabulary with reconstructions, and evidence that Na'isha is not an Apachean language. *G.*: Huld (1985) discusses regressive apicalization. See volume 10:393-400.

Kitamaat. See Haisla.

Kitanemuk (Takic). Also spelled Gitanemuk. *G., W.*: Kroeber (1907:71-89) has about 120 items, and Kroeber (1909a:255-256) has a grammatical note. See Bright (1974), with data from Harrington. See Serrano.

Kitsai (Caddoan). *W.*: U.S. Army, Corps of Engineers (1885:65-69) has about 62 words. *G., W.*: Bucca and Lesser (1969) describe phonology and morphophonemics; 91 vocabulary items, pp. 15-16. Lesser (1977) has interlinear texts. See Chafe (1979).

Kittitas. See Pshwanwapam.

Kivalina (dialect of North Alaska Inupiaq). *W.*: Webster and Zibell (1970) have words found especially in this dialect, as part of an Inupiat dictionary.

Kizh. See Gabrielino.

Klamath (Plateau Penutian). *G., W., T.*: Barker has texts (1963), a dictionary (1963a), and a grammar (1964). Still useful is Gatschet (1890), with texts, vol. 1, pp. 16-197; grammar, vol. 1, pp. 200-711; and a dictionary, vol. 2, pp. 1-705.

Klatskanai. See Clatskanie.

Klatsop. See Clatsop.

Klemtu. See Southern Tsimshian.

Klikitat (dialect of Northwest Sahaptin). *W.*: Hale (1846:570-629) lists about 122 words of this dialect. *T.*: Jacobs (1929, 1934-1837, 1:3-101, 2:1-89) presents texts.

Knight's Ferry (subdialect of Lakisamni in Far Northern Valley Yokuts). *W.*: Gifford (1922:85) has a kin term. Kroeber (1959:7-14) has words in a comparative vocabulary of about 120 items, pp. 7-13, and about 35 words on p. 14.

Knistenaux. See Cree.

Koasati (Muskogean). *G., T., W.*: Swanton (1924:47-48, 65-67) has morphology, about 20 words, and 13 lines of interlinear text on pp. 47-48; his vocabulary with Koasati words passim, pp. 65-75, compares Koasati, Natchez, and Hitchiti. *W.*: Kimball (1994) is a dictionary. Folsom-Dickerson (1965) has perhaps 120 words (see Alabama). *G.*: Haas (1946a:327-329) has verb forms. Kimball (1983) describes verb pluralization. Kimball (1991) is a grammar of 640 pp.

Kobuk River (dialect of North Alaskan Inupiaq). *T.*: Zibell (1968) is a reader. *W., T.*: Webster and Zibell (1976) have about 195 words and phrases of Kobuk River in a comparative vocabulary, pp. 286-317, and 42 sentences in a comparative survey, pp. 318-325. See North Alaskan Inupiaq.

Kocheyali. See Ayticha.

Kodiak. See Pacific Yupik.

Kohuana. See Kahuan.

Koniag. See Pacific Yupik.

Konkow (Maiduan). Also called Northwestern Maidu. *G., W.*: Ultan (1971) discusses sound symbolism.

Konomihu (Shastan). *W.*: Dixon (1905:216, 1931) has a few words. Merriam and Heizer (1967:235-249) have 60 or 70 words. Silver (1980) has perhaps 60 words in a comparative vocabulary, pp. 248-251, and a list of 40 English words with data from Konomihu and Shasta, pp. 256-257; bibliography, pp. 262-263. See New River Shasta.

Kootenai. Also spelled Kutenai. *G.*: Canestrelli and Boas (1926) is a grammar in Latin. Garvin has published important studies, of which we mention: *G., W.*: Garvin (1951), word classes; *T.*: Garvin (1954), a colloquial text. A volume of texts of almost 400 pp. is Boas and Chamberlain (1918). See the bibliographies of Adler (1961:200-201) and E. Carriker et al. (1976:41-43).

Koshoo. See Gashowu.

Koskimo. See Kwakiutl.

Koso. See Panamint.

Kotlik. See Norton Sound (dialect of Central Alaskan Yupik).

Kotzebue (dialect of North Alaska Inupiaq). Also called Kotzebue Sound. *W.:* Webster and Zibell (1970) have words found especially in this dialect, as part of an Inupiaq dictionary. *T.:* Zibell (1968) is a reader. See Malimiut.

Koyeti (dialect of Southern Valley Yokuts). *W.:* Driver (1937:146-153) has 56 nouns and 15 numerals in a comparative vocabulary. Golla (1964) has a few words. *G., W.:* Gamble (1975) has phonological data and about 23 words from Harrington. See Whistler and Golla (1986).

Koyukon (Athapaskan). *W.:* Henry (1975) is a noun dictionary. *G.:* Landar (1967a) using data from Jetté describes verbs. Jetté (1909) is third and last of an unfinished series on grammar. Axelrod (1990) has Central Yukon phonemes, p. 180, with verb morphology and semantics. Krauss (1976:327-328) and Krauss and Golla (vol. 6:69-72, 74-75) have phonological data. *T.:* Jetté (1904) is a missionary text, 126 pp. Attla (1989) has myths with Koyukon and English on facing pages, pp. 20-405; Attla (1990) has a myth cycle with Koyukon and English in parallel columns on the page, 24 episodes, pp. 1-149. See Krauss (1979:853-855) and Krauss and McGary (1980:301-350).

Kulespelm. See Kalispel.

Kumeyaay (Southern Diegueño). Also called Kamia. *W.:* Merriam and Heizer (1967:253-356) have perhaps 25 words and place names. See Campo.

Kuskokwim (dialect of Central Alaskan Yupik). *W.:* Jacobson (1984) indicates which words are localized in this dialect area. (Not to be confused with Upper Kuskokwim Athapaskan.)

Kutcha-kutchin. See Kutchin.

Kutchin (Athapaskan). Also spelled Gwich'in. Eastern Kutchin is also called Loucheux and Tukudh. *G., W.:* Petitot (1876) has Eastern Kutchin data in a comparative grammar, pp. XLVII-LXXXV plus a folded chart of comparisons; his dictionary, pp. 1-367, has about 13,000 lexical items. *G:* Krauss and Golla (vol. 6:69-72, 77-78) have phonological data on Eastern Kutchin of Canada, and Western Kutchin of Alaska. *W.:* Ritter (1976b) has about 1,200 semantically grouped entries in the Eastern Kutchin of Fort McPherson. Peter (1979) is a Western Kutchin elementary dictionary. Osgood (1936a:116-120, 136-137) has Eastern and Western Kutchin kin terms. See Parr (1974:76-79), Krauss (1979:858), Krauss and McGary (1980:405-455). *T.:* Petitot (1887:9-85) has Eastern Kutchin texts. Peter (1981) describes life at Fort Yukon and Artic Village with Western Kutchin and English on facing pages, 147 pp. Fredson and Sapir (1982) have Western Kutchin texts recorded in 1923. See Tukudh.

Kwakiutl (Wakashan). Also called Kawkw'ala. *G.:* Boas (1947) is an excellent grammar. *W.:* Boas (1893) is a vocabulary of almost 50 pp. Grubb (1977) is a dictionary, English-Kwakiutl, pp. 36-256, Kwakiutl-English, pp. 157-255. *T., W.:* Boas and Hunt (1902-1905) have 532 pp. of texts, with a Kwakiutl-English stem list, about 1,000 entries, pp. 514-532. Boas (1909) has ethnographic texts and words, including month names from Koskimo, Mamalilikulla, Nakwoktak, and Nimpkish, p. 413. Boas (1910) is a volume of texts of some 495 pp.; Boas (1935-1943) has texts in two volumes, one with translations, the other with texts. *G., W.:* Lincoln and Rath (1980) is a phonology and root list for the Kwakiutlan (Northern Wakashan) languages (Haisla, Heiltsuk-Oowekyala, and Kwakiutl). *Koskimo. W.:* Curtis (1907-1930, 10:329-337) has about 280 words in a comparative vocabulary. *Tlatlasikwala. W.:* Curtis (1907-1930, 10:329-337) has about 280 words. See Adler (1961:207-209), Thompson (1976:378). See Haisla, Heiltsuk-Oowekyala.

Kwalhioqua (Pacific Coast Athapaskan). *G., W.:* Hale (1946:535, 570-629) has about 40 items of this dialect of Kwalhioqua-Clatskanie. Hale has about 210 other items which may have been common to Kwalhioqua and Clatskanie. He has just a few lines on grammar, p. 535. *W.:* Boas and Goddard (1924a) have forms from Hale, Teit, and Gibbs. Krauss (1969) gives unpublished and "reconstituted" forms. See Krauss (1979:870; vol. 7:530-532). See Clatskanie.

Kwedech. See Laurentian.

Labrador (dialect of Eastern Canadian Inuit). *G.:* Kleinschmidt (1851) and Bourquin (1891) are grammars. L.R. Smith describes nouns and verbs (1977), derivational postbases (1978), and word formation (1980). Dorais (1976) compares phonological and morphological features of Labrador with those of five other dialects (see Aivilik). Dorais (1986:23) compares the phonemic inventory of Labrador with the inventories of other Eskimo dialects. *W.:* Erdmann (1864) is an Eskimo-German dictionary of 360 pp. Rasmussen and Ostermann (1941:13-28) have about 390 words in a comparative vocabulary with East Greenlandic and Kangianirmiut. Jeddore (1976) is a dictionary. *T.:* Binney, Perrett, and Hutton (1931) is a 237 pp. *Book of Knowledge.* Erdmann (1869) has 529 pp. of Scripture. See Rigolet.

Laguna (Keresan). *W.:* Curtis (1907-1930, 16:241, 244-245, 253, 256-259, 266-274) has perhaps 300 words. Gatschet (1879:403-485) has a vocabulary. *G., W., T.:* Boas (1923) offers phonetics, pp. 171-172, a text, pp. 172-173, and grammatical notes, pp. 173-180. *T.:* Boas (1928b) has two volumes of texts.

Lake. See Okanagan.

Lake Iliamna (dialect of Central Alaskan Yupik). *W.*: Jacobson (1984) indicates which words are localized in this dialect area.

Lake Iliamna (dialect of Tanaina). Osgood (1937:12, 208-221) has about 300 words. See Tanaina.

Lake Miwok (Miwokan). *W.*: Callaghan (1965) is a dictionary, Lake Miwok–English, pp. 10-195, English–Lake Miwok, pp. 198-287. Broadbent and Callaghan (1960:307-316) have words in a comparative vocabulary of about 285 items. *T.*: Callaghan (1977, 1980) has analyzed texts.

Lakhota. See Teton *under* Sioux.

Lassik (dialect of Eel River). *W.*: Essene (1942) has 57 personal names and a vocabulary of about 280 words, mostly with Cahto counterparts. Gifford (1922:20-21) has about 62 kin terms. See Parr (1974:139-141).

Lathrop (subdialect of Lower San Joaquin in Far Northern Valley Yokuts). *W.*: Kroeber (1959b:7-13) has words in a comparative vocabulary of about 120 items.

Laurentian (Iroquoian). Also called Kwedech, Hochelaga, Stadaconan. *W.*: Cartier obtained numerals, body-part terms, and other vocabulary in the 1530s (Biggar 1924). Gallatin (1836:376) uses Cartier's data in calling Laurentian a variety of Mohawk. Hale (1885) compares Cartier's words with Wyandot. Mithun (1979, 1982a) and Lounsbury (vol. 15:335) discuss the apparent dialectal mixture in the words obtained by Cartier.

Lenape Trading Jargon. See Delaware Jargon.

Lillooet (Interior Salish). *W.*: Gibbs (1877:270-283) has words in a comparative vocabulary. Kinkade and Sloat (1972:31-44) have a few words. B. Hayden (1992) has some resource vocabulary in the Fraser River dialect. *G., W.*: Boas (1891) has a grammatical note, pp. 685-686, and words in a comparative vocabulary, pp. 692-715, called Stlatlumh. Haeberlin and Thompson (1974) discuss suffixes (English index, pp. 234-235, about 140 items) and have perhaps 25 items in a comparative vocabulary. *G.*: Van Eijk (1988) discusses phonology and morphology. See Newman (1977) *under* Twana. *T.*: Le Jeune (1890) is a card with 12 promises to Margaret Mary. See Mattina (1989:89).

Lipan (Apachean). Also called Llanero. *G.*: Hoijer (1945) includes Lipan in a general coverage of Apachean grammar. *W.*: Hoijer (1938, 1956a, 1956b, 1963:7-9, 1971) offers vocabulary in various contexts. *T.*: Hoijer (1975) is a text. See Parr (1974:206).

Lkungen. See Songhees.

Loucheux. In some contexts Loucheux is synonymous with Eastern Kutchin, referring to what Émile Petitot called Dindjié. See Kutchin, Tukudh.

Loup (Eastern Algonquian). *W.*: Day (1975) has words and phrases from Mathevet. See Agawam. Called Loup A in volume 15:71.

Loup B (Eastern Algonquian). *W.*: Magnon de Terlaye (1755) has a word-list, 14 pp., perhaps just a mixture of dialects. See volume 15:71-72.

Lower Chehalis (Tsamosan Salish) *W.*: Hale (1846:536, 570-629) has about 237 items and notes on grammar. *G.*: Information on phonemes is in vol. 7:503. See Upper Chehalis.

Lower Chinook. See Chinook, Clatsop, Shoalwater.

Lower Cowlitz. See Cowlitz.

Lower Fraser. See Nanaimo.

Lower Piman (Uto-Aztecan). *G.*: A seventeenth-century grammar has been published by Pennington (1979-1980, 2).

Lower San Joaquin. See Chalostaca, Lathrop.

Lower Tanana (Athapaskan). Also called Tanana, Minto, or Minto-Nenana. *G., W.*: Krauss and Golla (vol. 6:69-72, 75-76) have phonological data. Some words and comments can be found in Krauss (1965:18-28, 1969). *G., W., T.*: Kari (1991) is an exercise volume of 27 pp.; Kari covers phonology and new orthography, with a 60 minute tape, a text, and 68 placenames. *W.*: Krauss (1974) is a preliminary dictionary of nouns. Hoijer (1956b:324-332) has kin terms from Robert McKennan. Hoijer (1963:15-17) has vocabulary. Volume 6:562 has Lower Tanana phonemes. *T.*: Titus and Titus (1991) have a text on basketry, with English translations, 28 pp. See Tanacross, Upper Tanana.

Lower Umpqua (dialect of Siuslaw). *G., T.*: Frachtenberg (1922) is a sketch of morphology, with interlinear texts. *T., W.*: Frachtenberg (1914) has phonetics, pp. 5-6, texts, pp. 7-102, and a vocabulary, Lower Umpqua-English, pp. 107-128, English-Lower Umpqua, pp. 128-140. See Thompson and Kinkade (vol. 7:42). See Siuslaw.

Luiseño (Takic). *G., T.*: Sparkman, Kroeber, and Grace (1960) is a grammar, pp. 5-174, with texts, pp. 177-217. *G.*: Malécot (1963) is first of a series on the Pauma dialect. Hyde (1971) is a grammar. Steele (1990) describes syntax. *W.*: Bright (1968) is a dictionary. *T.*: Hyde and Elliott (1994) have analyzed texts.

Lummi (dialect of Northern Straits Salish). *G.*: Demers (1974) discusses alternating roots. *W.*: Gibbs (1863) has about 20 pp. of vocabulary. Curtis (1907-1930, 9:183-195) has perhaps 300 words; names of Lummi villages, p. 174. See Galloway (1988) *under* Nooksack. Thompson and Kinkade (vol. 7:37) have Lummi reflexes of nine protophonemes. See Songhees.

Lushootseed (Central Salish). Also called Puget. *G.*: Snyder (1968a) has phonology and morphology based on the Duwamish dialect. *T., W.*: Snyder (1968) has texts, place names, and a dictionary. *W., G., T.*: Hess (1976) is a dictionary, revised by Bates, Hess, and Hilbert (1994). *T.*: Hilbert (1985) has 33

Skagit stories in English translation, and one Lushootseed text in the appendix. *W.*: Hess (1977:410-412) has about 60 words of Northern Lushootseed (covering Snohomish [26 words separately identified], Sauk-Suiattle, and Skagit [about 35 words separately identified]), and about 90 words of Southern Lushootseed, mostly in a set of comparative vocabularies. See Newman (1977) *under* Twana. Suttles and Lane have a phonological note (vol. 7:485) and a list of tribes (vol 7:486). See Duwamish, Nisqually, Puyallup, Skykomish, Snohomish.

Mackenzie Coast. See Siglit.

Mackenzie Delta. See Inuvik.

Maguse River (Western Canadian Inuit). *G.*: Webster and Zibell (1976:277) have a phonemic analysis. See Caribou.

Mahican (Eastern Algonquian). Also called Mohegan and Stockbridge, but not the same as Mohegan (see Mohegan-Pequot). *G., T., W.*: Edwards (1788) has vocabulary, pp. 6-8, a text, pp. 9-10, and grammatical observations, pp. 10-17. *W., T.*: Jenks (1804) has words and a text. *G., T.*: Prince (1905) has 44 lines of text, pp. 76-77, with grammatical analysis, pp. 78-84. *W.*: Gallatin (1836:305-367) has words from Jefferson, Heckewelder, Edwards, and Jenks, in a comparative vocabulary of 180 words. Schmick (in Masthay 1991) is a dictionary, with a phonemic analysis by David H. Pentland. See vol. 15:72, Pentland and Wolfart (1982:310).

Maidu (Maiduan). Also called Northeastern Maidu and Mountain Maidu. *T., W.*: Shipley (1963) has texts, pp. 10-81, and a dictionary, Maidu-English, pp. 87-209, English-Maidu, pp. 211-261. *G., T.*: Shipley (1964) has grammar and, pp. 73-87, texts. *W.*: Shipley (1961:50-51) has a list of 112 items compared with Nisenan, with reconstructed forms. See Konkow and Nisenan.

Makah (Wakashan). *W.*: Swan (1868) has words passim and a vocabulary, pp. 93-106. *G.*: Volume 7:422 lists phonemes. Haas (1969) has Makah forms used to reconstruct pronominal suffixes of Proto-Nootkan. Jacobsen (1969, 1986a) has data. See Nitinaht.

Malimiut (dialect of North Alaskan Inupiaq). Also spelled Malemiut, Malimyute. Varieties are called Norton Sound and Kobuk or Kobuk River. *T.*: Webster and Zibell (1976:318-325) have 42 Kobuk River sentences in a comparative survey. *G.*: Dorais (1986:23) compares the Malimiut phonemic inventory with phonemic inventories of other Eskimo dialects. See Inglestat.

Maliseet (Eastern Algonquian). A dialect of Maliseet-Passamaquoddy. *G., T.*: Sherwood (1986) describes morphology. Teeter (1971) has a grammatical sketch with text analysis, pp. 236-249. *W.*: Hale (1834) has a vocabulary and discussion. Chamberlain (1899)

has a vocabulary in a volume of 94 pp. *T.*: Rand (1870) is the Gospel of St. John, a text of 111 pp. See Goddard (vol. 15:70), Pentland and Wolfart (1982:310-311). See also Passamaquoddy.

Mamalilikulla. See Kwakiutl.

Mamulique (Comecrudan). See Goddard (1979a:385).

Mandan (Siouan). *G., T.*: Kennard (1936) is a grammar with interlinear text, pp. 33-41. *G., W.*: From an earlier day is the grammar, pp. 435-439, and vocabulary, pp. 349-444, of Hayden (1862). *W.*: Another old vocabulary is Kipp (1853). *T.*: Park, Jones, and Hollow (1978) have texts edited by Hollow, pp. 81-117, and a note on pronunciation, p. 124.

Maniwaki (dialect of Eastern Ojibwa). See Algonquin.

Maratino. *W.*: Swanton (1940:122-124) has about 59 words.

Maricopa (River Yuman). *G., W.*: Wares (1968:35-36, 77-96) has phonological data and lexical items in a comparative Yuman vocabulary of 501 sets. *W.*: Kroeber (1943:26-30) has words; Frisch (1968) has about 20 names of food. *G., T.*: Gordon (1983) discusses the syntax of clauses. *T.*: Sunn and Harwell (1976) have a text. See Halchidhoma.

Marin Miwok (dialect of Coast Miwok). *W.*: Gallatin (1848:128) has 48 words of San Rafael from Hale. Barrett (1908:68-80, 307-314) has about 250 forms. About 242 words appear in a comparative Miwok vocabulary of some 282 glosses. *T.*: Kroeber (1911:318) has seven lines of interlinear text, based on two versions of the Lord's Prayer in Coast Miwok from Duflot de Mofras (1844, 2:391), who used the rubrics Chocouyem (Rio del Sacramento) and Joukiousmé (San Rafael).

Mary's River. See Kalapuyan.

Massachusett (Eastern Algonquian). A dialect, with subvarieties, of Massachusett-Narragansett. *G., W., T.*: Goddard and Bragdon (1988) is an edition of native manuscripts; text, translation, and notes, pp. 30-471; grammar, pp. 473-594; Massachusett-English word index, perhaps 4,000 entries, pp. 595-752. *T.*: Eliot (1663) is a Bible. Mayhew (1709) is a psalter. *W.*: Wood (1634:[99-103]) has a vocabulary from the North Shore. Trumbull (1903) is a dictionary of 376 pp., based on Eliot's Bible. Prince (1907) has a salvage vocabulary of 29 words from Mashpee, with comparisons. Goddard (1981b, 1990d) discusses phonology. Allen (1856:191) has words and phrases from early accounts of Plymouth, showing pidginization. See Croft (1948:262-263), Goddard (vol. 15:72), Pentland and Wolfart (1982:311). See Narragansett.

Masset. See Haida.

Mattole (California Athapaskan). *G., W., T.*: Li (1930) is the basic source for grammar, vocabulary, and sentences. *G.*: Hoijer (1971) describes morphology in the context of comparative grammar. *W.*: Hoijer

(1956a) has 99 words; Hoijer (1963:9-13) has words with sound laws. See Bear River.

Mayo (Athapaskan). See Northern Tutchone.

Mayo (Uto-Aztecan). See Cahitan, Yaqui.

McCloud River (Wintu). *W.*: Stone (1877) has words.

Melville Peninsula. See Iglulik.

Menominee (Algonquian). Also spelled Menomini. *G.*: Bloomfield (1962) is a grammar; for errata see Goddard, Hockett, and Teeter (1972). Hockett (1981, 1981a) discusses Proto-Algonquian phonology and morphophonemics, and Menomini sound laws. *W.*: Bloomfield (1975) is a dictionary with about 7,200 entries, pp. 1-289. *T.*: Bloomfield (1928a) has texts in a volume of 607 pp. See Goddard (vol. 15:584).

Merced (dialect of Northern Valley Yokuts). *W.*: Kroeber (1959b:7-13) has words in a comparative vocabulary of about 120 items.

Mescalero (Apachean Athapaskan). Mescalero and Chiricahua are dialects of one language. *G.*: Hoijer (1945) and elsewhere has sketched Apachean grammar, relying mainly on the Navajo model. Rushforth (1991) discusses classificatory verbs, pp. 253, 258-259, in comparisons with Bearlake. *T.*: Hoijer and Opler (1938) have texts. *W.*: Hoijer (1938a, 1956b:324-332, 1963:7-9) has vocabulary. See Opler (1983:419). See Chiricahua.

Mescalero (Coahuilteco). See Chome.

Mesquakie. See Fox.

Methow. See Okanagan.

Miami (Algonquian). *G.*: Costa (1994) is a grammar of Miami-Illinois based on earlier sources. *G., W.*: Volney (1804:429-439 [in French, Volney 1803:525-532]) has data on nouns, pronouns, and verbs, with numerals and kin terms; he has about 195 lexical items in semantic groups, and about 18 forms for three verbs. *C.F.*: Voegelin (1938-1940) has some 2,400 lexical items copied from Dunn. See vol. 15:585. See Illinois.

Michahay (dialect of Kings River Yokuts). Also spelled Michahai. *G., W.*: Kroeber (1907a:320-321, 351) has 16 words and a grammatical note. Kroeber (1963:186-210) has Michahai vocabulary in a comparison of·270 items in 21 Yokuts dialects or languages. The Michahay band also spoke the Wobonuch dialect of Monache.

Micmac (Eastern Algonquian). *G., W.*: Maillard (1864) is a grammar, 101 pp. Pacifique (1939, 1990) has a pedagogical grammar. Fidelholtz (1978) covers 13 stem types and rules for intransitive present indicative person endings. *T.*: Rand (1853) has Matthew in Micmac. Rand published over 1,600 pp. of Micmac texts in phonetic characters; his Matthew has 118 pp. *W.*: Rand (1888) and DeBlois and Metallic (1984) have dictionaries. See Goddard (vol. 15:70).

Migueleño (Salinan). *W., T.*: Mason (1912) has four lines of song text, p. 178; several dozen place names,

pp. 106-108; words for foods, plants, etc., pp. 117-123; counting and measures, pp. 132-136; and kin terms, pp. 169-172. *G., T., W.*: Mason (1918) covers Salinan grammar, pp. 7-58; he has perhaps 190 lines of interlinear text, pp. 104-120, and about 990 vocabulary items, pp. 120-154. *W.*: Gallatin (1848:125-126) has about 26 items from Hale. Engelhardt (1929:58-59) has about 130 names of racherias and Indians. *G., W.*: Kroeber (1904:43-47) has numerals 1-10 and a grammatical note. See Antoniano.

Mikasuki (dialect of Hitchiti) *G., W.*: West (1962, 1974) deals with phonology. *G.*: Boynton (1983) describes verbal grammatical categories.

Miluk. See Hanis.

Mimbreño (dialect of Chiricahua). *W.*: About 25 words were published by the U.S. Army, Corps of Engineers (1855:85).

Minto-Nenana. See Lower Tanana.

Mississauga (dialect of Eastern Ojibwa). *G.*: Chamberlain (1892) is a basic study, 84 pp. *T.*: Chamberlain (1889) has about 15 lines of interlinear text.

Missouri (dialect of Chiwere). *W.*: Morgan (1871:293-382) equated Otoe and Missouri kinship vocabulary, though some differences existed between these dialects of Chiwere (Dorsey 1886). See Iowa-Otoe.

Miwokan (Utian). Broadbent and Callaghan (1960) have a comparative vocabulary. See Bodega Miwok, Central Sierra Miwok, Lake Miwok, Marin Miwok, Northern Sierra Miwok, Plains Miwok, and Southern Sierra Miwok.

Mixwunutunne. Also called Mikwunutunne or Dootoodu. See Tututni.

Modoc (dialect of Klamath). *W.*: Ray (1963) has a few words. Voegelin (1946:96-98) rejects the contention of Angulo and Freeland that Klamath and Modoc differ only slightly, and he gives examples of differences. *T., W.*: Gatschet (1894) has about 18 lines of interlinear song text, pp. 27-28, and a glossary of about 64 entries, Modoc-English, pp. 29-31.

Mohave (River Yuman). Also spelled Mojave. *G., W.*: Ware (1968:31-34, 77-96) has phonological data and lexical items in a comparative Yuman vocabulary of 501 sets, pp. 77-78. Kroeber (1911a) has a discussion of phonetic elements, with two dozen words or so passim. *W.*: Kroeber (1917b:340-348) has about 60 kinship terms. Kroeber and Harrington (1914) have a list of 75 items as well as phonetic data. *G.*: Munro (1976) discusses syntax; she has an index of perhaps 40 syntactic, inflectional and derivational, morphemes, pp. 326-330. Munro (1976a) discusses modals. *T.*: Munro (1976b) and Judith Crawford (1976a) have texts. See Kendall (vol. 10:8-9).

Mohawk (Iroquoian). *G., W.*: Bonvillain (1973) is a sketch of grammar; kinship terms, pp. 151-162; 38 particles, pp. 239-240; 114 affixes, pp. 241-247. *741*

G. Michelson (1973) has a sketch of grammar, pp. 1-21; Mohawk-English particles and roots, perhaps 840 main entries, pp. 22-133; English-Mohawk index, about 1,300 entries, pp. 134-186. *T.*: K. Michelson (1980) has an interlinear text with notes. Mithun (1976a) has Mohawk stories.

Mohegan-Pequot (Eastern Algonquian). The name Mohegan has also been used for Mahican. *W.*: Cowan (1973a) has a Pequot vocabulary recorded by Ezra Stiles in 1762. Prince and Speck (1904) have a glossary. *T.*: Speck (1904) has a text. Trumbull (1873:34) has the Lord's Prayer recorded by Experience Mayhew. *T., W., G.*: Speck (1928a) has a Mohegan diary, pp. 228-251, personal names, pp. 280-281, and grammar, pp. 281-287. Some of these and other sources were collected by Levine and Bonvillain (1980:51-136). See Goddard (vol. 15:72), Pentland and Wolfart (1982:314-315). See Montauk.

Möhineyam. See Vanyume, Serrano.

Molala (Plateau Penutian). Also spelled Molale. *W.*: Hale (1846:561, 570-629) has about 190 words, of questionable quality. Curtis (1907-1930, 8:195-198) has about 85 words. *G., W.*: Rigsby (1966) has grammatical and lexical data, some not previously published. His Cayuse-Molala comparative vocabulary, pp. 374-378, has about 50 sets of forms.

Monache. See Mono.

Mono (Numic). Also called Monache or Monachi, Mono-Monache. *G.*: Lamb (1958a) is a basic source. *G., W.*: Klein (1959:235-238) has about 105 items in a comparative vocabulary with Kawaiisu and Southern Paiute, as well as sound laws. I. Davis (1966:126, 134-139) has phonological notes and about 185 lexical items. *W.*: Driver (1937:146-153) has about 55 nouns and 16 numerals of dialects called Waksachi, Entimbich, Wobonuch (or Woponuch), Hodogida, and Tuhukwadj in a comparative vocabulary. *Owens Valley Paiute*: *W.*: Kroeber (1907a:71-89) has Owens River or Inyo words. Driver (1937:146-153) has about 54 nouns and 16 numerals for Owens Valley Paiute of Big Pine and of Independence in his comparative vocabulary.

Montagnais (Algonquian). *G.*: Rhodes and Todd (vol. 6:55-56) use a few words and phonological data to delimit this dialect. Clarke (1982) is a sketch of North West River (Sheshatshit) Montagnais with phonology, pp. 3-18; grammatical categories, pp. 18-23; nominal paradigms, pp. 24-38; data on verbs, pp. 38-42; independent order verbal paradigms, pp. 83-124; sentence types, pp. 125-153; notes and references, pp. 154-168. P. Martin (1991) is a grammar. *G., W.*: Lemoine (1901) devotes 347 pp. to a dictionary and grammar. *W.*: Drapeau (1991) is a dictionary. *T.*: Kapesh (1976, 1979) has written two books in Montagnais. Clarke and MacKenzie (1995:49-50) list texts. See Naskapi, East Cree.

Montauk (dialect of Mohegan-Pequot). *W.*: J.L. Gardiner (1798, 1824:28; Levine and Bonvillain 1980:15-16) took about 70 words, some of which were published by Gallatin (1836). Mohegan, Pequot, and Montauk were dialects of one language (vol. 15:72). See Mohegan-Pequot.

Monterey. See Rumsen.

Moose Cree (dialect of Eastern Swampy Cree). *G., W.*: Rhodes and Todd (vol. 6:55-56) use a few words and phonological data to delimit this dialect. See Eastern Swampy Cree.

Moses-Columbian. See Columbian.

Mountain (Athapaskan). *G.*: Krauss and Golla (vol. 6:69-72, 79-80) have phonological data, and Rice provides the phonemes of the Fort Norman dialect (vol. 6:326).

Muckleshoot. See Lushootseed.

Multnomah. A dialect of Upper Chinookan. See Wasco-Wishram.

Munsee Delaware (Eastern Algonquian). Also spelled Minsi. *W.*: Gallatin (1836:370) has words from Heckewelder. About 100 words from Heckewelder were published by Horsford; see Heckewelder and Horsford (1887). Goddard (1982) has historical phonology with many words. *T.*: Flood (1847:2-157) is a prayer book with English and Munsee on facing pages. See Goddard (vol. 15:72-73), Pentland and Wolfart (1982:318). See Delaware.

Mupu (dialect of Ventureño Chumash). *W.*: Pinart and Heizer (1952:36-71) have a vocabulary of the dialect of Santa Paula (Mupu) and Camulos (Kamulus).

Muskogee. See Creek.

Musqueam (dialect of Halkomelem). *G., W.*: Suttles (vol. 7:453) has phonological data. Elmendorf and Suttles (1960:13-27) list about 716 items in a comparative vocabulary, and provide phonological data as well. Elmendorf (1962a:86-87, 92-93) has perhaps 187 items in a comparative vocabulary. See Newman (1977) *under* Twana, and Galloway (1984, 1988) *under* Nooksack. See Halkomelem.

Mutsun (Costanoan). Also called San Juan Bautista. *G.*: Arroyo de la Cuesta (1861) is a grammar. *W., T.*: Arroyo de la Cuesta (1862) is a dictionary of almost 2,900 words and phrases. *G., W.*: Mason (1916) is a reworking of Arroyo's material to provide a convenient grammar, with structural analysis, pp. 402-426; a classified list of stems (not exhaustive), pp. 427-469; and a postscript, pp. 470-472, with a Mutsun-like vocabulary of an old woman from San Lorenzo, 136 items. *W.*: Levy (1976) has about 100 words in a comparative vocabulary. Callaghan (1990a) has words from Harrington.

Na'isha. See Kiowa Apache.

Nabesna. See Tanacross, Upper Tanana.

Nahani. The term Nahani (Nahane) refers to 'hostile outsiders', not to a single tribe (vol. 6:451-453). It has been used for Kaska, Mountain, Slavey, Tagish, Tahltan, Teslin Inland Tlingit, Tsetsaut, Northern and Southern Tutchone, and other languages.

Nakwoktak. See Kwakiutl.

Nambe (dialect of Rio Grande Tewa). *W., T.*: Curtis (1907-1930, 17:61-82) has about 80 names of clans, societies, and gods passim; he has seven lines of text with interlinear translation, pp. 68, 69, 77. *W.*: Harrington (1916:63-66) has 12 names of months. See Rio Grande Tewa.

Nanaimo (dialect of Cowichan Halkomelem). Also called Snanaimuq. *G., T.*: Haeberlin (1918:168-169) has words illustrating reduplication. Boas (1891) has a note, pp. 680-683, and words in a comparative vocabulary, pp. 692-715. *G., W.*: Haeberlin and Thompson (1974) discuss suffixes (English index, pp. 234-235, about 140 items) and have perhaps 25 items in a comparative vocabulary of these dialects or languages: Bella Coola, Comox, Kalispel, Lillooet, Lkungen, Nanaimo, Okanagan, Pentlatch, Sechelt, Shuswap, Squamish, Thompson, Tillamook. See Halkomelem.

Nanticoke-Conoy (Eastern Algonquian). *W.*: William Vans Murray's 1792 Naticoke vocabulary from the Choptank River was published by Speck (1927), 610 words, with other sources. See Goddard (vol. 15:73) for other Nanticoke sources and Conoy sentences from Andrew White. See Pentland and Wolfart (1982:318-319).

Naolan. The only known data are in Weitlaner (1948).

Narragansett (dialect of Massachusett-Narragansett). *W., T.*: R. Williams (1643) has short vocabularies and sentences showing dialect mixture. *W.*: Simmons and Aubin (1975) discuss kinship. See Croft (1948:263), Goddard (vol. 15:72), Pentland and Wolfart (1982:319).

Naskapi (Cree-Montagnais). *G., W.*: Rhodes and Todd (vol. 6:55-56) use a few words and phonological data to delimit this dialect. *W.*: MacKenzie and Jancewicz (1994) is a dictionary of the Schefferville dialect. Speck (1935:237-424) has vocabulary, which was commented on by Michelson (1937). See Montagnais.

Nass-Gitksan. See Gitksan.

Natchez. *G., T., W.*: Swanton (1924) has 12 lines of interlinear text, p. 47, vocabulary and grammatical data passim, and about 450 lexical items in a demonstration of sound laws, pp. 65-75. *W.*: Brinton (1873) has a vocabulary recorded by Ann Eliza Worcester Robertson. Haas (1956) has words in a comparative vocabulary. *G. W.*: Swanton (1907) has morphology and vocabulary.

Natick. See Massachusett.

Natsilingmiut. See Netsilik.

Natsit-kutchin. See Chandalar.

Naugatuck (dialect of Quiripi-Unquachog). *W.*: The vocabulary Ezra Stiles recorded in 1787 is published in Levine and Bonvillain (1980:50). See Quiripi.

Naukanski Yupik (Eskimoan). Also called Naukan. *G., W., T.*: Menovshchikov (1975) has grammar, texts, and a dictionary. See Krauss (1976:189-190), vol. 5:52. See Wales.

Navajo (Apachean Athapaskan). Also spelled Navaho. *G., W.*: Young and Morgan (1987) cover grammar in a Navajo-English colloquial dictionary with perhaps 4,800 main entries, pp. 1-812b, and an English-Navajo index, perhaps 8,500 items, pp. 813-1069. Young and Morgan (1992) have about 1,135 roots, with data on morphology and syntax, 1,466 pp. *T., G.*: Sapir and Hoijer (1942) have texts, pp. 16-441, with notes, 442-543. Landar (1964) is a study of syntax with analyzed texts. *G.*: Sapir and Hoijer (1967) cover phonology and morphology. Schauber (1979) explains interrogatives. See Landar (1967) for an annotated bibliography of the verb and discussion of morphology, and Landar (1977b) for a review, inter alia, of Hoijer's Apachean publications.

Nawathinehena (Arapahoan). *W.*: Kroeber (1916:75-76) has about 64 items. Salzmann (1960:39-41) gives sound laws.

Nelson Island (dialect of Central Alaskan Yupik). *W.*: Jacobson (1984) indicates which words are localized in this dialect area.

Nespelem. See Sanpoil-Nespelem.

Nĕtcă´ut'in (dialect of Ulkatcho Carrier). *W.*: Boas (1924:37-38) has about 24 words in a comparative vocabulary.

Netela. See Juaneño.

Netsilik (dialect of Western Canadian Inuit). Also called Boothia Peninsula, Central Eskimo. Dialects are Natsilingmiut, Arviligjuaq, and Utkuhikhalingmiut (Utkusiksalingmiut). *W.*: Birket-Smith (1928:26-28, 33-62) has a few words of Netsilik, pp. 27-28, plus 16 words of Arviligjuaq, p. 27, and about 500 items in semantic groups, pp. 33-62, from Simpson Peninsula. *G., W.*: Webster and Zibell (1976:276, 286-311, 324-325) have a phonemic analysis of Natsilingmiut from Gjoa Haven and about 160 words and phrases of Utkuhikhalingmiut. Briggs (1968) has lexical data of Utkuhikhalingmiut. *G.*: Dorais (1986:23) compares the Netsilik phonemic inventory with the inventories of other Eskimo dialects. See Rasmussen (1931).

Newittee (of Horatio Hale). A Nootka vocabulary collected at Nahwitti among the Kwakiutl. See Nootka; "The Classification of the Native Languages of North America," this volume.

New River Shasta (Shastan). *W.*: Dixon (1905:216, 1931) has a few words. Merriam (1930; Merriam and Heizer 1967a:235-249) called Dixon's Konomihu a separate stock, New River Tlohomtahhoi, and offered about 70 words and phrases, pp. 285-287, taken from a sole survivor who ordinarily spoke Hupa and Chimariko. See volume 8:222-223. See Konomihu.

Nez Perce (Sahaptian). *W.*: Aoki (1962:177-182) has perhaps 275 words in a comparative vocabulary, with reconstructions. Aoki (1994) is a massive dictionary with English index. *G., T.*: Aoki (1970) is the basic modern grammar, with a short text. *T.*: Phinney (1934) has nearly 500 pp. of interlinear text, with free translations. Aoki (1979) and Aoki and Walker (1989) have texts. See E. Carriker et al. (1976:30-33).

Niantic (dialect of Mohegan-Pequot). *W.*: A vocabulary recorded among the Narragansetts in 1769 by Ezra Stiles (Cowan 1973) may be Niantic. See volume 15:72.

Nicola (Athapaskan). Also called Nicola-Similkameen. *W.*: Boas (1895a) has about 50 words. Boas (1924:36-38) has 30 items compared with Chilcotin and Ulkatcho Carrier. See Parr (1974:83-84) and Krauss and Golla (vol. 6:83).

Nicoleño. See San Nicolas.

Niles (dialect of Chochenyo). *W.*: Beeler (1961:193-197) has about 59 items from a Curtin manuscript.

Nimpkish. See Kwakiutl.

Nipissing. See Algonquin.

Nipmuck. See Loup, Agawam.

Nisenan (Maiduan). Also called Southern Maidu. *T., W.*: Uldall and Shipley (1966) have texts, pp. 16-187, and a dictionary, Nisenan-English, pp. 191-245, English-Nisenan, pp. 247-282. Richard Smith (1977) has an analyzed text. *W.*: Shipley (1961:50-51) has a list of 112 items with Nisenan and Maidu comparisons. *Auburn dialect. G., W.*: Paul (1967) describes phonemes and has, pp. 19-23, several hundred words. See Sekumne.

Nisgha, Niska, Nishga. See Gitksan.

Nisqually (dialect of Southern Lushootseed). Also spelled Nisqualli. *W.*: Gibbs (1877:285-361) is a dictionary. Tolmie and Dawson (1884:50B-61B) have vocabulary. Hale (1846:570-629) has about 156 words. See Lushootseed.

Nitinaht (Nootkan). Also spelled Nitinat. *G.*: Haas (1969), using Nitinaht and other data, reconstructs pronominal suffixes of Proto-Nootkan. Klokeid (1976, 1978) discusses enclitics, and has sentence analysis. B.F. Carlson and Thomas (1979) discuss verbal morphology and syntax; see bibliography, pp. 326-327. *G., T.*: Sapir (1924a) has about 80 lines of text, pp. 76-79, with grammatical analysis, pp. 81-102. Swadesh and Swadesh (1933) have about 92 lines of interlinear text, pp. 195-197. See Nootka.

Noatak (dialect of North Alaskan Inupiaq). *W.*: Webster and Zibell (1970) have words found especially in this dialect, as part of an Inupiaq dictionary.

Nome (dialect of Seward Peninsula Inupiaq). *W.*: Jenness (1924:49-53) has about 10 words. See Qawiaraq.

Nomlaki (Wintuan). *W.*: Dixon and Kroeber (1919:56-61) have about 69 items. Pitkin and Shipley (1958) have a few words. Broadbent and Pitkin (1964) have some words. See Wintu.

Nondalton. See Tanaina.

Nongatl (dialect of Eel River). *W.*: Hoijer (1963:9-13) has some words from a P.E. Goddard manuscript. Kroeber (1967:270) has 125 items from Goddard. See Parr (1974:142-143).

Nooksack (Central Salish). *G., W., T.*: Galloway (1984) has perhaps 540 phonetically transcribed words and 15 sentences in a discussion of phonology and morphophonemics, with about 35 Halkomelem comparisons. *W.*: Hess (1977:411, 414) has a few words. Galloway (1988) has about 50 words in a comparative vocabulary with 47 numbered sets, and a glossary, pp. 327-329, of Proto–Central Salish reconstructions, indexed, pp. 329-332. Comparisons include forms of Comox, Halkomelem (Cowichan, Musqueam, Chilliwack), Songhees, Lummi, Lushootseed, Pentlatch, Saanich, Samish, Sechelt, Sooke, Squamish, and Twana. See volume 7:453 for Nooksack phonology.

Nootka (Wakashan). *W.*: Gallatin (1848) has words from Hale called Newittee. *G.*: Haas (1969c) using Nootka and other data reconstructs pronominal suffixes of Proto-Nootka. *T., G., W.*: Sapir and Swadesh (1939) have tales with grammatical notes and lexical materials. Sapir and Swadesh (1955) is a continuation, without notes. *G.*: Swadesh (1939) describes Nootka internal syntax. *W.*: J.W. Powell (1991) is a topically arranged dictionary with words from 12 Nootka dialects and Nitinaht. See Thompson and Kinkade (vol. 6:39-40).

Nopchinchi (dialect of Northern Valley Yokuts). Also spelled Noptinte. *G., T., W.*: Beeler (1971) interprets data from Arroyo de la Cuesta. *W.*: Kroeber (1959b) has vocabulary.

North Alaskan Inupiaq (Eskimoan). Also spelled Inupiat. *G.*: Kaplan (1982) discusses Inupiaq morphophonemics. Dorais (1986:23) compares the North Slope phonemic inventory with other Eskimo inventories. *G., W.*: Webster and Zibell (1970) is a dictionary in part topically arranged, with morphological bases, pp. 1-124, suffixes, pp. 167-185, and an English index, pp. 186-211; it also contains words from Anaktuvuk Pass, Barrow, Point Hope, and Wainwright. Reviewed by Correll (1972). MacLean (1980) is an Inupiaq dictionary with an Inupiaq-English stem list, an Inupiaq-English postbase list, and an English-Inupiaq stem and postbase list. *T.*: Webster and Zibell (1976:318-325) have 42 sentences of North Alaska in a comparative survey. See Barrow, Deering-Buckland, Inglestat, Inuvik, Kangianirmiut, Kivalina, Kobuk River, Kotzebue, Malimiut, Noatak, Point Hope, Selawik, Unalakleet.

North Baffin. See Aivilik.

Northeastern Pomo (Pomoan). *W.*: Barrett (1908:56-68) has about 254 forms. Webb (1971:37-45) has about 231 items. McLendon (1964:128-137) has words from Halpern in a comparative vocabulary.

Northeast Maidu. See Maidu.

Northeast Sahaptin. See Sahaptin.

Northern Algonquin (Northern Ojibwa). Called Algonquin in volume 6:54, 56-59. *W.*: Gilstrap (1978) has words and sentences in a dialect survey. *G.*: Daviault et al. (1978) and Piggott (1978) review features and dialect differences. Pagotto (1980) discusses syntax.

Northern Carrier. See Babine.

Northern Lushootseed. See Lushootseed.

Northern Paiute (Numic). Also called Paviotso. *G.*: Snapp, Anderson, and Anderson (1982) is an elaborate grammar. *G., W.*: I. Davis (1966:134-139) touches phonology and has about 185 lexical items for Duck Valley (Owyhee, Nevada). *W.*: K. Hale (1959:114-115) has about 96 words. *G., T.*: Marsden (1923) lists affixes and has five texts, pp. 180-191, for Northern Paiute in Oregon. Natches (1923) has a Northern Paiute–English verb list, pp. 245-255, with about 200 main entries, and texts, pp. 256-259. See Bannock.

Northern Pomo (Pomoan). *W.*: Barrett (1908:56-68) has about 270 forms. Webb (1971:37-45) has about 235 items. *G., W.*: McLendon (1973) has grammatical data and, on pp. 65-95, cognate sets with forms from Northern Pomo and the other Pomoan languages.

Northern Shoshone (Numic). *W.*: Gallatin (1848:88, 90, 92, 94) has 179 words of "Snake" from Hale; Kroeber (1907a:111, 116) comments on their dialectal affiliation.

Northern Sierra Miwok (Eastern Miwok). Also called Sierra Miwok. *G., W.*: Callaghan (1987a) is a Northern Sierra Miwok dictionary, pp. 39-302, with an English–Northern Sierra Miwok index, pp. 305-402. *W.*: Barrett (1908a:362-367) has a Northeastern Sierra vocabulary. See Central Sierra Miwok.

Northern Straits (Central Salish). Dialects of this language were spoken by six tribes, Lummi, Saanich, Samish, Semiahmoo, Songhees, Sooke. See Suttles (vol. 7:453). See Songhees, Lummi, Saanich, Samish, Sooke.

Northern Tepehuan (Uto-Aztecan). Rinaldini (1743) has a brief grammar with vocabulary and religious texts. See volume 10:120, 306. See Tepehuan.

Northern Tutchone (Athapaskan). *G.*: Krauss and Golla (vol. 6:69-72, 77-78) have phonological data. *W.*: Ritter (1976), in a Mayo noun dictionary, has about 1,000 semantically grouped entries. Ritter, McGinty, and Edwards (1977), in a Selkirk noun dictionary, have about 1,800 semantically grouped entries. See Krauss (1976a:293, 1979). See Tutchone.

Northern Wintun. See Wintu.

Northern Yana (dialect of Yana). *T.*: Sapir has 13 interlinear texts in Sapir and Dixon (1910:129-208). *W.*: Sapir (1918a:154-160) has 48 numbered kinship entries. *W., G.*: Sapir (1922a:215-234) has about 800 verb stems, pp. 217-224; about 325 verb suffixes, pp. 224-230; and other morphological elements, pp. 230-234. *G., T.*: Sapir (1923b:277-282) has 13 lines of interlinear text with a translation and copious grammatical notes. See Yana.

North Slope. See North Alaskan Inupiaq.

Northwest Greenlandic. See Polar Eskimo.

Northwest Maidu. See Konkow.

North West River. See Montagnais.

Northwest Sahaptin. See Pshwanwapam, Upper Cowlitz, Yakima.

Northwest Sierra Miwok. See Plains Miwok.

Norton Sound (dialect of Central Alaskan Yupik). *W.*: Jacobson (1984) indicates which words are localized in this dialect area. He also marks vocabulary localized within this area as Norton Sound, northern shore (Unaliq), and North Sound, southern shore (Kotlik). See Malimiut.

Nottoway (Iroquoian). *W.*: Gallatin (1836:305-367) has words in a comparative vocabulary. Gallatin (1848:115) has 54 forms, reprinted from Gallatin (1836). Wilson (1885:92-94) uses numerals in a comparative vocabulary. *G., W.*: Rudes (1981a) has Nottoway vocabulary with Northern Iroquoian comparisons.

Nsietshawus. See Tillamook.

Ntlakyapamuk. See Thompson.

Nunivak (dialect of Central Alaskan Yupik). Also called Cux, Nunivak Island, and Nunivârmiut. *W.*: Rasmussen and Ostermann (1941:28-36) list about 270 items in a comparative vocabulary. Jenness (1928:3-134) has perhaps several dozen words passim. Jacobson (1984) indicates which words are localized in this dialect area.

Nushagak River (dialect of Central Alaskan Yupik). *W.*: Jacobson (1984) indicates which words are localized in this dialect area.

Nutunutu (dialect of Southern Valley Yokuts). *W., G.*: Kroeber (1907a:320-321, 360) has 16 words and a grammatical note. Kroeber (1963:186-210) has Nutunutu vocabulary in a comparison of 270 items in 21 Yokuts dialects or languages. *W.*: Driver (1937:146-153) has 56 nouns and 16 numerals in a comparative vocabulary.

Obispeño (Chumashan). *W., G.*: Kroeber (1910:265-267) uses about 37 items from Hale in Gallatin (1848:126); he adds grammatical notes, pp. 268-269. *W.*: Henshaw and Heizer (1955:94-147) have a vocabulary.

Occaneechi (Ohio Valley Siouan). *W.*: Goddard (1972) discusses John Fontaine's Saponi vocabulary of

1716, perhaps a lingua franca based on a Siouan language. See Tutelo.

Ofo (Ohio Valley Siouan). *W.*: Dorsey and Swanton (1912:319-340) have an English-Ofo index of about 825 entries for their Ofo-English dictionary, pp. 319-331.

Ojibwa (Southern Ojibwa). Some varieties are called Chippewa. *G., W.*: Rhodes and Todd (vol. 6:57-58) describe phonology and delimit dialects. Baraga (1878-1880) is an extensive early grammar and dictionary. Nichols and Nyholm (1995) is a dictionary of the Southwestern dialect of Central Southern Ojibwa, and Rhodes is one of vowel-dropping varieties of Eastern Ojibwa and Ottawa. *T.*: Jones (1917-1919) has texts. Nichols (1988) has an anthology of analyzed texts in several varieties, with glossaries. See also Algonquin, Ottawa, Severn Ojibwa.

Okanagan (Interior Salish). Also spelled Okanagon, Okanogan. Also called Okanagan-Colville or Colville-Okanagan. *G., W., T.*: Mattina (1987b) is a fine dictionary of the Colville dialect with many illustrative sentences, 354 pp. Mattina (1985) has a Colville text, partly with interlinear translation, pp. 69-300, and a glossary of morphemes, pp. 303-354. Newman (1977) has pronouns. *G.*: Hebert (1982) explores aspect and transitivity in Nicola Lake Okanagan. Mattina (1973) is a Colville grammar, 156 pp. *G., W.*: Kinkade (1967a) has vocabulary in a discussion of phonology. Haeberlin (1918:160-161) discusses reduplication. Haeberlin and Thompson (1974) discuss suffixes and have items in a comparative vocabulary (see details *under* Lillooet and Nanaimo). *W.*: Kinkade and Sloat (1972:31-44) have words in their comparative vocabulary. Vocabulary is provided by Hill-Tout (1911) and Boas (1891:687-688, 692-715). See E. Carriker et al. (1976:35-36), Mattina (1989:89-90). See Sanpoil-Nespelem.

Okwanuchu (Shastan). Perhaps a dialect of Shasta. *W.*: Dixon (1905:216) has seven words.

Old Algonquin (Southern Ojibwa). Hanzeli (1969:67-99, 103-121) analyzes phonology and morphology and has appendices with extracts from manuscript grammars.

Omaha (dialect of Omaha-Ponca in Dhegiha). *W., T.*: Fletcher and La Flesche (1911) describe the Omaha, 672 pp., with linguistics passim and names, pp. 52-57, prayers, pp. 119-130, names, pp. 145-194. *T.*: For letters, see Dorsey (1891); other Omaha and Ponca texts are in Dorsey (1890). Hamilton (1868) is a scriptural work, 30 pp.

Oneida (Iroquoian). *G., T.*: Lounsbury (1953) is an essential study of morphology, with analyzed texts. *W.*: Ricciardelli (1966) discusses kinship, with data from the Thames River Oneida (near Muncey, Ontario). Morgan (1851) has a vocabulary. Antone et al. (1981) is a topically arranged dictionary. *G., T.,*

W.: K. Michelson (1981a) has three stories by Georgina Nicholas, with 77 pp. of interlinear text, morphological analysis, and a glossary of particles. Mithun and Woodbury (1980:41-44, 67-76) have texts.

Onondaga (Iroquoian). *W.*: Beauchamp (1893) has 192 names of plants and animals, pp. 113-123. *T.*: Hewitt (1903:141-220, 1928:612-791) has two cosmological texts. *T.*: Mithun and Woodbury (1980:56-66, 134-142, 158-160) have interlinear texts with analysis. J.A. Gibson (1992) is a long ritual text with full analysis. *G., W.*: Shea (1860) is a 17th-century dictionary, pp. 9-103, with grammatical notes, pp. 3-8. Chafe (1970) is an essential source for grammar, with some words passim. Woodbury (1975) discusses noun incorporation.

Oowekyala. See Heiltsuk-Oowekyala, Kwakiutl.

Ópata (Uto-Aztecan). *G.*: J.B. Johnson and Weitlaner de Johnson (1954) have a report. Shaul (1990) describes inflectional morphology, with references to early descriptions.

Osage (Dhegiha Siouan). *G., W.*: Wolff (1952, 1952a, 1958) covers grammar and has some vocabulary. *W., T.*: La Flesche (1932) is a dictionary, perhaps 6,600 main entries, Osage-English, pp. 5-226; perhaps 6,000 main entries, English-Osage, pp. 229-358; and an appendix, pp. 359-406, which includes sentences and miscellaneous notes on rituals and divisions of time. *T.*: La Flesche (1925) has songs, p. 76 ff., and texts of rites, pp. 375-630.

Otoe. See Iowa-Otoe.

Ottawa (Southern Ojibwa). Also spelled Odawa. *G., W., T.*: Blackbird (1887) contains a grammar, religious texts, and words, phrases, and sentences, pp. 107-128. Bloomfield (1957) has a grammar, sentences and texts, and a wordlist. *G.*: Hanzeli (1969:67-99, 122-124) has missionary manuscript material, some from Louis André, ca. 1688. Rhodes and Todd (vol. 6:57-58) cover phonology and use morphological criteria to delimit this dialect. Piggott (1980) is a generative analysis of phonology, with a valuable bibliography, pp. 391-399. *T:* Baraga (1837) is a life of Jesus, 211 pp. Baraga (1855) has about 350 pp. of prayers, hymns, and a catechism. Bloomfield and Nichols (1991) have texts, with a glossary, from a western, full-vowel dialect. See Ojibwa.

Outer Inlet Tanaina (dialect of Tanaina). *W.*: Osgood (1937:12, 208-221) has about 300 words in a comparative vocabulary. Old material labeled Kenai or Kenaitsy with data from Davydov, Rezanov, and Lisianskii, was published by Kruzenshtern (1813). *T.*: Kari and Boraas (1991) have 147 texts by Peter Kalifornsky in Outer Inlet Tanaina and English on facing pages, 485 pp. See Townsend (vol. 6:623-640). See Tanaina.

Owens Valley Paiute. See Mono.

Owikeno. See Oowekyala *under* Heiltsuk-Oowekyala.

Paamiut. See West Greenlandic.

Pacific Coast Athapaskan. See Chasta Costa, Chilula, Clatskanie, Galice-Applegate, Hupa, Cahto, Kwalhioqua, Lassik, Mattole, Nongatl, Sinkyone, Tolowa, Tututni, Upper Umpqua, Wailaki, Whilkut.

Pacific Yupik (Eskimoan). Also called Aleut, Alutiiq, Sugcestun, Sugpiaq, Suk. *Koniag.* W.: In Appendix II, Sauer (1802:9-14) has about 170 words. Leer (1978) is a dictionary of Kodiak Alutiiq, and Leer (1977) a short dictionary of the Alaska Peninsula dialect. T.: Tabios and Leer (1972) have stories from English Bay and Port Graham collected by Derenty Tabios and Seraphin Maganack, 36 pp. See Chugach.

Paipai (Yuman). Also called Akwa'ala. W.: Kroeber (1943:26-30) has words. G.W.: Wares (1968) discusses phonology, pp. 43-45, and has lexical items in a comparative Yuman vocabulary of 501 sets, pp. 77-96. G.: Joël (1966) is a dissertation on phonology and morphology. T.: Joël (1976) has an analyzed text.

Paiute. See Mono, Northern Paiute, Southern Paiute.

Pajalate. See Coahuilteco.

Palewyami (Yokutsan). Also called Paleuyami, Poso Creek. G., W.: Kroeber (1907a:320-321, 347-350) has a few words and grammatical notes. Kroeber (1963:186-210) has Palewyami vocabulary in a comparison of 270 items in 21 Yokuts dialects or languages. W.: Driver (1937:146-153) has 51 nouns and 16 numerals in a comparative vocabulary. Dixon and Kroeber (1919:56-61) have Poso Creek vocabulary.

Palouse (dialect of Northeast Sahaptin). G.: Rigsby (1965:309) has a remark on vowels. See Sahaptin, Walla Walla.

Pamai. See Chome.

Pame (Otomanguean). G.: Gibson (1956) describes phonemics and morphophonemics; other sources are given by Bright (1967).

Pamlico (dialect of Carolina Algonquian). Also called Pampticough, Pampticoe. W.: Lawson's (1709:225-230) vocabulary of 40 words was used by Gallatin (1836:375) and Pollard (1894:14). See Goddard (vol. 15:74), Pentland and Wolfart (1982:326). See Carolina Algonquian.

Pamunkey. W.: Pollard (1894:1-19) has 17 words from Dalrymple (1858) of unknown affiliation.

Panamint (Numic). W.: Kroeber (1907a), Driver (1937:146-153) and Miller (1967) have words. G.: Dayley (1989) has a grammar.

Papago (Uto-Aztecan). A dialect of Upper Piman (Pima Alto), also called Tohono O'odham. W.: Saxton, Saxton, and Enos (1983) is a Papago and Pima dictionary. Mathiot (1973) is a dictionary of usage. G., W.: Dolores (1913) has about 300 simple verb stems, pp. 244-251, and about 850 verbs in all,

pp. 244-255. G., T.: Saxton (1982) is a rich grammar with an analyzed text, pp. 263-266. T.: Alvarez and Hale (1970) have a text, pp. 89-93, with translation, pp. 93-97. Bahr (1975:61-71) has a ritual text. See volume 10:118. See Pima.

Parchaque. See Chome.

Passamaquoddy (Eastern Algonquian). A dialect of Maliseet-Passamaquoddy. G., T.: Prince (1914) discusses morphology. W.: Lesourd (1984) is a dictionary, about 3,500 entries, pp. 1-112; English index, pp. 115-184. Barratt (1851:11-23) has words. T.: Prince (1909) has about 75 lines of interlinear text, pp. 629-633, with notes, pp. 634-650. Prince (1921) has texts, some of which are retranscribed and edited in Wabnaki Bilingual Education Program (1976, 1976a, 1976b, 1976c). See Maliseet.

Patwin (Wintuan). Also called Copeh, Southern Wintun, Southerly Wintun. G.: Whistler (1981) has about 50 pp. on Hill Patwin grammar. W.: Gibbs (1860) has a vocabulary. Barrett (1980:81-87, 290-297) has about 279 forms and 53 names. Dixon and Kroeber (1919:56-61) have about 41 items. Broadbent and Pitkin (1964) have words in a comparative vocabulary. McKern (1922) has perhaps 50 words passim. T.: Whistler (1977a, 1978a) has analyzed interlinear texts. See also Suisun, Hill Patwin, River Patwin.

Paviosto. See Bannock, Northern Paiute.

Pawnee (Northern Caddoan). G., W., T.: Parks (1976) describes Pawnee grammar; he analyzes an interlinear text, pp. 338-356. W.: Taylor (1963:117) has 25 items in four lists. *South Band Pawnee.* G. T.: Weltfish (1936) has a text. Weltfish (1937) has phonetic notes, pp. 1-3, and interlinear and parallel text, pp. 1-251. G., T., W.: Weltfish (1958:306-310) has a text (from 1937:154-160) with literary analysis and linguistics notes. Parks (1977) has interlinear texts. See Chafe (1976).

Payaya (dialect of Coahuilteco). W.: Swanton (1940:55) has one word.

Pecos (dialect of Jemez). W.: Hodge (1896) has clan names. Hewett (1904) has clan and personal names.

Peel River Kutchin. See Kutchin.

Pend d'Oreille. See Kalispel.

Penobscot (dialect of Eastern Abenaki). G.: Voorhis (1979) has grammatical notes based on texts from Frank Speck. G., T., W.: Prince (1910) has an interlinear text, pp. 185-187, and words and phrases, pp. 188-208. Siebert (1988) has phonology, vocabulary, and sentences. W.: Eckstorm (1941) has vocabulary. Speck and Lion (1918) have interlinear texts.

Pentlatch (Central Salish). W.: Boas (1891:692-715) has words in a comparative vocabulary. Haeberlin and Thompson (1974) discuss suffixes and have items in a comparative vocabulary (see details under Nanaimo). See Kennedy and Bouchard (vol. 7:441).

Peoria (dialect of Illinois). *W.*: Michelson (1920:303) has four Peoria verbs. Morgan (1871) has Peoria kin terms. See Goddard (vol. 15:585). See Illinois.

Pequot. See Mohegan-Pequot.

Piankashaw (dialect of Miami-Illinois). *W.*: Morgan (1871) has kin terms. See Miami, Illinois. See Goddard (vol. 15:585).

Picuris (Northern Tiwa). *G.*: F. Trager (1975) discusses Picuris and Taos morphology. Zaharlick (1975) describes noun classes, noun suffixation, and pronominal reference. *G., W., T.*: F. Trager (1971b) covers phonology, has perhaps 40 words, and has a two-line interlinear text, p. 33. Spanish loans are noted. *W.*: F. Trager (1971a) covers Spanish influence on the calendar. *T.*: Harrington and Roberts (1928:289-397, 426-447) present stories and songs.

Pidgin Delaware. See Delaware Jargon.

Pidgin Eskimo. *W., T.*: Stefánsson (1909) has about 152 words, with illustrative sentences, pp. 222-232. Wells and Kelly (1890) is a dictionary.

Piegan. See Blackfoot.

Pima (Uto-Aztecan). Pima and Papago are dialects of Upper Piman (also called Pima Alto). *G., W.*: Saxton, Saxton, and Enos (1983) is a Papago and Pima dictionary. Parsons (1930:448-449) has about 40 kin terms. Whipple has about 68 words from Gila River Pima in U.S. Army, Corps of Engineers (1855:94). *T.*: Russell (1908) has songs and speeches. Bahr (1975:34-59) has two ritual texts. See Miller (vol. 10:113-124). See Papago.

Pinaleño (dialect of Western Apache). *W.*: U.S. Army, Corps of Engineers (1855:81-83) has vocabulary. See San Carlos Apache.

Piro (Kiowa-Tanoan). *W., T.*: Bartlett and Hodge (1909) have the Lord's Prayer, seven lines, p. 429, and 180 words, pp. 431-433. *W., G.*: Harrington (1909) has a comparative vocabulary of 180 items, pp. 572-579, with Bartlett's Piro, Isleta del Sur (a variety of Isleta), Isleta, Taos, Jemez, and San Ildefonso; Harrington sketches Piro morphology, pp. 580-591. *W.*: Leap (1971) has six color words of Piro, Isleta, and San Ildefonso, p. 327.

Piskwaus. See Columbian.

Pit River. See Achumawi.

Pitch. See Wailaki.

Plains Cree (Algonquian). *G., W.*: Lacombe (1874) is a grammar and dictionary. *G.*: Wolfart (1973) and Ahenakew (1987) are grammars. *W.*: Faries (1938) is a dictionary. *T.*: Bloomfield (1930, 1934) and Ahenakew and Wolfart (1992) have texts. See volume 6:55-56. See "Sketch of Cree, an Algonquian Language," this vol.

Plains Miwok (Eastern Miwok). Also called Northwest Sierra Miwok. *W.*: Kroeber (1906a:660-661) has 32 words in a comparative vocabulary. Barrett (1908a:362-367) has about 134 forms. Broadbent and Callaghan (1960:307-316) have words in a comparative vocabulary of about 285 items. Callaghan (1984) is a dictionary, Plains Miwok-English, about 1,400 entries, pp. 15-226, 303-309; English-Plains Miwok, about 2,400 entries, pp. 231-300.

Plymouth. See Massachusett.

Point Hope (dialect of North Alaskan Inupiaq). *T.*: Jenness (1924:3-4, 32) has about 22 lines of interlinear text; a song, p. 67, and two words, p. 69. See North Alaskan Inupiaq.

Polar Eskimo (dialect of West Greenlandic). Also called Thule, Ita, Northwest Greenlandic, and Cape York. *W.*: Birket-Smith (1928:33-62) has words in a comparative vocabulary. *G., W.*: Holtved (1952) has remarks on the dialect.

Pomoan. See Central Pomo, Eastern Pomo, Kashaya (Southwestern Pomo), Northeastern Pomo, Northern Pomo, Southeastern Pomo, Southern Pomo.

Ponca (dialect of Omaha-Ponca in Dhegiha Siouan). *W.*: Dorsey (1885:924-927) has 204 words in a comparative vocabulary. *G., W.*: Howard (1965) has a phonological note, p. XI, and words passim, for example, numerals, pp. 72-73, month names, pp. 73-74, kin terms, p. 82, Ponca names for various tribes with meanings if known, pp. 133-135. *G.*: Boas (1907) reports on articles, particles, verbal elements and pronouns, basing his analysis on texts from Dorsey. *T.*: Dorsey (1890, 1891) has texts.

Pond Inlet (subdialect of North Baffin in Eastern Canadian Inuit). *W., T.*: Webster and Zibell (1976) have phonemic analysis, p. 278, and about 170 words and phrases in a comparative vocabulary, pp. 286-317.

Poso Creek. See Palewyami.

Potawatomi (Algonquian). *G., W., T.*: Hockett (1948a) has phonemics and some morphology; (1948b), derivation, personal prefixes, and nouns; (1948c), the verb complex; (1948d), particles and texts. *G.*: J.O. Morgan (1966) covers the transitive animate verb. See volume 15:584.

"Potoyensee" (unclassified dialect in Eastern Miwok). *W.*: Merriam and Heizer (1966:36) have 11 words.

Powhatan. See Virginia Algoquian.

Prince William Sound. See Chugach.

Pshwanwapam (dialect of Northwest Sahaptin). Also called Kittitas. *T.*: Jacobs (1934-1937, 1:213-219, 269-272, 2:185-190, 235-238) has texts.

Puget Sound Salish. See Lushootseed.

Purisimeño (Chumashan). *T., W.*: Pinart and Heizer (1952:36-72) is a vocabulary of 1878, with two lines of text, p. 72. *W.*: Henshaw and Heizer (1955:94-147) is another vocabulary.

Puyallup (dialect of Southern Lushootseed). *T., W.*: M.W. Smith (1940) has four lines of songs, p. 103, and perhaps 350 words passim, with 40 kin terms, pp. 173-176. See Lushootseed.

Qawiaraq (dialect of Seward Peninsula Inupiaq). *G.*: Dorais (1986:23) compares the phonemic inventory of the Qawiaraq dialect of the South shore of Seward Peninsula with inventories of other Eskimo dialects. See volume 5:56. See Nome.

Quapaw (Dhegiha Siouan). Also called Arkansas. *W.*: Gallatin (1848:117) has words. Morgan (1871:291-382) has kin terms. *G., W.*: Rankin (1988) has data, comparisons with Kansa and Omaha-Ponca, and a bibliography.

Quechan (River Yuman). Also called Yuman. *W.*: Wares (1968:77-96) has lexical items in a comparative vocabulary of 501 sets. *G.*: Halpern (1946) is a sketch. *G., W.*: Halpern (1946a) has phonemics with many words passim. *G.*: Halpern (1947, 1947a) describes verbs. The last three articles are parts one, four, and five of a six-part series. *T.*: Halpern (1976) and Emerson and Halpern (1978) have analyzed texts. See Kendall (vol. 10:4-12).

Queen Charlotte's Island. See Haida.

Quileute (Chimakuan). *T.*: Andrade (1931), with a phonetic key on pp. IX-X, has interlinear texts, pp. 1-23, and texts with Quileute and English on facing pages, pp. 24-211. *G.*: Andrade (1933:151-292) is a sketch. J.V. Powell (1975a, 1976) has grammar. *W.*: J.V. Powell and Woodruff (1976) is a dictionary. Swadesh (1955a:62-72) has perhaps 300 items, compared with Chemakum. J.V. Powell (1975) has comparisons. See Adler (1961:199-200), J.V. Powell (vol. 7:431).

Quinault (Tsamosan Salishan). *W.*: Hale (1846:570-629) gives about 237 Lower Chehalis items, identifying 12 additional forms as Quinault variants. Olson (1936) has words. Gunther (1945) has a few botanical words. *G., W.*: Haeberlin (1918:164) discusses reduplication. Volume 7:503, 516-517 has phonology and sources.

Quinigua. *W.*: Hoyo (1960:500-515) has a vocabulary of the Borrados with morphological analysis of some forms; several hundred transcriptions from archived manuscripts of Monterrey, 1596-1799, are presented.

Quiripi (Eastern Algonquian). Also called Quinnipiac. *T.*: Pierson (1658) is an interlinear catechism of 67 pp. from Branford; it was edited by Trumbull, who added an introduction (Pierson 1873). *W.*: Townsend (1900) has personal names. *W.*: J. Pike (1953) has placenames. Naugatuck, Quiripi, and Unquachog are dialects of one language (vol. 15:72). See Pentland and Wolfart (1982:328). See Naugatuck.

Qurluqtuq. See Copper.

Rae. See Dogrib.

Ramaytush (Northern Costanoan). Also called San Francisco. *W.*: Alcantara (1852:494-505) has a vocabulary. Beeler (1961:194-197) has about 16 words in a comparative vocabulary. Kroeber (1910:243-248) has about 88 words. Levy (1976:22-35) has about 100 words in a comparative vocabulary. See A. Brown (1973).

Rankin Inlet (dialect of Eastern Canadian Inuit). *G.*: Mallon (1974, 1976) has lessons. *G., W., T.*: Webster and Zibell (1976) have phonemic analysis, p. 277, about 170 words and phrases in a comparative vocabulary, pp. 286-317, and 42 sentences in a comparative survey, pp. 318-325.

Repulse Bay. See Aivilik.

Rigolet (dialect of Eastern Canadian Inuit). *G., W.*: Dorais (1976:23) compares the phonemic inventory of this Labrador dialect with other inventories of Eskimo dialects; he has a few Rigolet words, pp. 41-42. Dorais (1977) is a sketch. See Labrador.

Rio Grande Tewa (Kiowa-Tanoan). *W.*: K. Hale (1962) has some forms, partly from Dozier. *G., W.*: Harrington (1912a) has phonological data and kinship terms. Dozier (1953) describes verb structure. *T.*: Speirs and Speirs (1968) is a reader, 38 pp. See Nambe, San Ildefonso, San Juan, Santa Clara, Tesuque.

River Patwin. (dialect of Patwin). *W.*: Dixon and Kroeber (1919:56-61) have about 37 items. Shafer (1961) gives a vocabulary of 315 items of River Patwin, and comparisons with Hill Patwin. See Patwin.

Rivers Inlet. See Heiltsuk-Oowekyala.

Rogue River. See Chasta Costa.

Round Lake. See Severn Ojibwa.

Rumsen (Southern Costanoan). Also called Monterey and Carmel. *W., T.*: Henshaw and Heizer (1955) have a vocabulary, pp. 160-174, and phrases, pp. 175-183, with more vocabulary, p. 186. Pinart and Heizer (1952:7-35) have about 640 words and about 23 lines of untranslated text. *W.*: Broadbent (1957), Beeler (1961:194-197), and Callaghan (1962) are sources. Levy (1976:22-35) has about 100 words in a comparative vocabulary, pp. 22-35, and a linguistic bibliography, pp. 54-56.

Saanich (dialect of Northern Straits Salish). *W.*: Hess (1977:410) has about 35 words of Saanich, mostly in a set of comparative vocabularies, pp. 410-412. *G.*: Montler (1986) is a grammar, 262 pp., with focus on grammatical categories, parts of speech, affixes, and stem morphology. *G., W.*: Efrat (1978:255-257) has about 17 words in a discussion of glottalized resonants. See volume 7:453 for a phonological note and Thompson and Kinkade (vol. 7:36-37) for Saanich reflexes of nine protophonemes.

Saclan. See Bay Miwok.

Sahaptin (Sahaptian). *G., W.*: Rigsby (1965) has data on Nez Perce and Sahaptin vowel systems and dialect differences. Aoki (1962:177-182) has a comparative vocabulary for Northern Sahaptin, with reconstructions. *T.*: Jacobs (1934-1937) has Northwest Sahaptin texts. See "Sketch of Sahaptin, a Sahaptian

Language," this volume. See Klikitat, Pshwanwapam, Tenino, Upper Cowlitz, Umatilla, Yakima.

Sahewamish (Central Salish). See Lushootseed.

Saint Francis Abenaki. See Western Abenaki.

Saint John's. See Maliseet.

Saint Lawrence Iroquoian. See Laurentian.

Saint Lawrence Island Eskimo. See Central Siberian Yupik.

Salinan. See Atoniano, Migueleño.

Salish. See Kalispel.

Samish (dialect of Northern Straits Salish). *W.*: Gunther (1945) has a few botanical words. *G., W.*: Galloway (1990) has phonology, morphology, and a classified wordlist.

San Antonio. See Coahuilteco.

San Antonio (Salinan). See Antoniano.

San Buenaventura. See Ventureño.

San Carlos Apache (dialect of Western Apache). *G.*: Edgerton (1963) analyzes sentence structure. Durbin (1964) covers phonology and morphology. *W.*: Hill (1963) has over 100 items with White Mountain Apache comparisons. *T.*: P.E. Goddard (1919) has interlinear texts, pp. 147-182, and texts with San Carlos and English on facing pages, pp. 183-367. *G., T.*: Shayne (1982) discusses Navajo and San Carlos use of object pronouns in transitive and intransitive sentences. See also Cibecue, Pinaleño, White Mountain.

Sandia (dialect of Southern Tiwa). *G.*: Brandt (1970) covers phonology and morphology, 151 pp,; Brandt (1970a:48) describes phonemes. Allen and Frantz (1986) discuss goal advancement.

San Felipe (dialect of Rio Grande Keresan). *W.*: Parsons (1923b) has names of clans, villages, and societies. White (1932a) has names of places, clans, birds, colors, and gods.

San Fernando. See Fernandeño.

San Francisco. See Ramaytush.

San Ildefonso (dialect of Rio Grande Tewa). *W., T.*: Curtis (1907-1930, 17:200-203) has about 250 words. Curtis has about 58 San Ildefonso clan names, p. 40, about 30 names of deities and sacred places, pp. 43-46, and one line of text, with interlinear translation, p. 39. *G., W., T.*: Harrington (1912) has over 100 words passim, some analyzed morphologically; phonetics, pp. 245-246; and about 14 lines of song texts, pp. 262-264. Harrington (1916) has 12 names of months. See Rio Grande Tewa.

San Jose. See Chochenyo.

San Juan (dialect of Rio Grande Tewa). *G.*: Speirs (1974) describes classificatory verb stems. *W., T.*: Curtis (1907-1930, 17:4-30, 187-189) has perhaps 50 words passim, including names of months, clans, and kinsmen; he has three lines of text with interlinear translation, p. 14. Harrington (1916:63-66) has month names. See Rio Grande Tewa.

San Juan Bautista. See Mutsun.

San Juan Capistrano. See Juaneño.

San Lorenzo. See Awaswas.

San Luis Obispo. See Obispeño.

San Luis Rey. See Luiseño.

San Miguel. See Migueleño.

San Nicolas (Takic?). *W.*: Kroeber (1907:153) cites the four known words. *W., T.*: Hudson (1978, 1978a) has 24 lines of songs from Harrington's unpublished notes. See Kroeber (1925:633), Applegate (1974a), volume 10:122.

Sanpoil-Nespelem (dialect of Okanagan). *W. T.*: Ray (1933) has perhaps over 100 words passim in a monograph on the Sanpoil and Nespelem, with about 21 lines of text, pp. 179, 195, 204-205.

San Rafael. See Marin Miwok.

Santa Ana (dialect of Rio Grande Keresan) *G., W., T.*: I. Davis (1964) has grammar, pp. 59-154; interlinear texts with notes, pp. 155-164; and about 1,000 words or forms, pp. 165-182, with an English index, pp. 182-190. *W.*: Miller and Davis (1963:319-328) have about 440 items.

Santa Clara (Northern Costanoan). See Tamyen.

Santa Clara (dialect of Rio Grande Tewa). *G., W.*: Hoijer and Dozier (1949) cover phonology and have some words. *W.*: Harrington (1916:63-66) has names of 11 months. See Rio Grande Tewa.

Santa Cruz. See Awaswas.

Santa Cruz Island. See Cruzeño.

Santa Rosa Island (dialect of Cruzeño Chumashan). *W.*: Pinart and Heizer (1952:36-71) have a vocabulary of 1878. *W., T.*: Henshaw and Heizer (1955:94-148) have a vocabulary, pp. 94-147, and 11 lines of song text, p. 148. See Cruzeño.

Santa Ynez. See Ineseño.

Santee, Santee-Sisseton. See Sioux.

Santiam. See Kalapuyan.

Santo Domingo (dialect of Rio Grande Keresan). *W.*: Miller and Davis (1963:319-328) have about 441 items. Parsons (1923:485-494) has vocabulary of social organizations. Whipple in U.S. Army, Corps of Engineers (1855:86-89) has about 206 items poorly transcribed but useful. *W., T.*: White (1935) has a glossary and miscellaneous short vocabularies, as well as songs.

Saponi (Ohio Valley Siouan). *G., W.*: Hoffman (1964:217) analyzes words from Byrd. *W.*: Alexander (1971) has 46 words and phrases taken by John Fontaine from refugee Saponi Indians. See Occaneechi.

"Saratoga" (dialect of Far Northern Valley Yokuts). *W.*: Kroeber (1959:7-8) has numerals 1-5 in a comparative vocabulary.

Sarcee (Athapaskan). Also spelled Sarsi. *G.*: Cook (1984) is a substantial grammar which covers phonology, morphology and syntax, with focus on verbs. Krauss and Golla (vol. 6:69-72, 84-85) have data on phonology in historical context. *G., W.:* Li (1931) touches on grammar, pp. 3-15, and has a list of about 650 sets of verb stems, pp. 15-27. Hoijer and Joël (1963) have 256 numbered items, in a study of nouns. *T.:* P.E. Goddard (1915) has about 1,400 lines of text with Sarcee and English on facing pages.

Satsop. See Upper Chehalis.

Sauk (dialect of Sauk-Fox). *W.:* Gallatin (1836:305-367) has words from Keating. *W., T.:* Skinner (1923) has words and sentences passim and an interlinear text. See Fox.

Sauk-Suiattle. See Lushootseed.

Saulteaux (Southern Ojibwa). *G., W.:* Rhodes and Todd (vol. 6:57-58) cover phonology and use morphological criteria to delimit this dialect. *G.:* Dumouchel and Brachet (1942) is a grammar.

Schoodiac. See Passamaquoddy.

Sechelt (Central Salish). Also spelled Seshelt, Siciatl. *W.:* Timmer (1977, 1978a) has an English-Sechelt word list and a stem list. Boas (1891:692-715) has words of Sechelt in a comparative vocabulary. Hill-Tout (1904) has words passim in an ethnological report. *G., W.:* Haeberlin and Thompson (1974) discuss suffixes and have items in a comparative vocabulary (see details *under* Nanaimo). Beaumont (1973) discusses statives. *G., W., T.:* Beaumont (1985) is a study of the language with stories and sayings, 305 pp. See vol. 7:441 for phonemes.

Sekani (Athapaskan). *G.:* Krauss and Golla (vol. 6:69-72, 81-82) and vol. 6:433 have phonological data. Hargus (1988) has phonology. *W.:* Hoijer (1963:21-23) has perhaps 35 items from Jenness and Honigmann. Jenness (1931) has about four names. Morice (1907:721-722, 735) has about five words. *T.:* Wilkinson and Wilkinson (1969) is a reader, 39 pp.; Wilkinson and Wilkinson (1969a) is a Bible story book.

Sekumne (dialect of Nisenan). *W.:* Gallatin (1848:124-125) has about 57 words from James Dwight Dana.

Selawik (dialect of North Alaskan Inupiaq.) *W.:* Webster and Zibell (1970) have words found especially in this dialect, as part of an Inupiaq dictionary. See Kobuk River.

Selish. See Kalispel.

Semiahmoo. See Northern Straits Salish.

Seminole. As a language name, *Seminole* is ambiguous. The Seminoles in Florida speak Mikasuki and Creek, and those in Oklahoma speak Creek. See Creek, Mikasuki.

Seneca (Iroquoian). *G., T.:* Chafe (1961) has thanksgiving rituals with English and Seneca on facing pages, pp. 16-145, and grammatical analysis, pp. 146-299. *G., W.:* Chafe (1967) is a study of morphology and a dictionary. Chafe (1980) discusses consequential verbs in Seneca and Onondaga. *T.:* Mithun and Woodbury (1980:3-8, 45-55, 96-103, 110-122, 143-148) have texts. Hewitt (1903:221-254) has a cosmological text. See "Sketch of Seneca, An Iroquoian Language," this vol.

Seri. *G.:* Marlett (1988) describes syllable structure. *W.:* Moser and Moser (1961) have a dictionary.

Serrano (Takic). *G.:* Hill (1967) is a grammar. *W.:* Kroeber (1909a:253-256) has perhaps 160 words. Gifford (1918:178-186) has 14 clan names, pp. 179-180, and words passim. Miller (1967) has words in cognate sets. Munro (1990) discusses Serrano-Kitanemuk, using Takic cognates in 142 sets.

Seshelt. See Sechelt.

Severn Ojibwa (Northern Ojibwa). *G., W.:* J.H. Rogers (1964) covers phonology and morphology, with a word list. Rhodes and Todd (vol. 6) cover phonology, pp. 57-58, and use morphological criteria, p. 57, to delimit this dialect.

Seward Peninsula Inupiaq. See Big Diomede, King Island, Nome, Qawiaraq, and Wales.

Shasta (Shastan). *G., W.:* Silver (1964) has phonological notes and a comparative vocabulary mainly of Shasta and Karok, with sound laws. *W.:* Bright and Olmsted (1959) have a vocabulary of some 55 pp. Olmsted (1956, 1957, 1959) has words in a comparative vocabulary, with sound laws. *T.:* Silver and Wicks (1977) have an analyzed text.

Shawnee (Algonquian). *G.:* C.F. Voegelin (1936) has productive paradigms. Goddard (1967a:102, 106) has additional forms. Parks (1975) describes noun inflection. *G., W.:* W. Miller (1959b) has sound laws. C.F. Voegelin (1938-1940) lists stems. *T.:* Alford (1929) translated the four Gospels into Shawnee, 200 pp. See Goddard (vol. 15:585).

Sheshaht (dialect of Nootka). *W.:* Cope (1919:150-151) has 12 names of months from Sapir.

Shikaviyam (dialect of Panamint). *W.:* Kroeber (1907:71-89) has the first published vocabulary, with some 112 forms. See Panamint.

Shinnecock (Eastern Algonquian). A dialect of uncertain classification. *W.:* Gatschet (1889:390) and M.R. Harrington (1903:39) have data. See Goddard (vol. 15:72). See Unquachog.

Shishmaref (dialect of Bering Strait Inupiaq). *W.:* Webster and Zibell (1970) have words found especially in this dialect, as part of an Iñupiat dictionary.

Shoalwater (dialect of Lower Chinook). *W.:* Hymes (1964b:96) has two items. Ray (1938:38-42, 63-67) has about 18 village names, with corresponding Chehalis names, p. 42; and personal names, pp. 63-67. *T.:* Hymes (1983a) analyzes a text from Boas (1894a). See Chinook.

Shoshone. See "Sketch of Shoshone, a Uto-Aztecan Language," this vol. See Eastern Shoshone, Northern Shoshone, Western Shoshone.

Shuswap (Interior Salish). Also called Sequapmuq, Atna. *G., W., T.*: Kuipers (1974) has grammar, texts, and a dictionary. *G., W.*: Kuipers (1975) is an English-Shuswap word list, about 1,800 items. Hale (1846:535-542, 570-629) has Atna data. Boas (1891) has a grammatical note and words, pp. 683-685, and Sequapmuq words in a comparative vocabulary, pp. 692-715. Haeberlin and Thompson (1974) discuss suffixes and have items in a comparative vocabulary (see details *s.v.* Nanaimo). See Newman (1977) *under* Twana. See Mattina (1989:88-89).

Sia. See Zia.

Siberian Yupik. See Naukanski Yupik, Central Siberian Yupik, Sirenikski.

Sierra Miwok (Eastern Miwok). The term Sierra Miwok was used to include Plains Miwok by Barrett (1908a:362-367), who has a comparative vocabulary of 145 numbered items for Plains ("Northwestern Sierra"), Amador ("Northeastern Sierra" [Koni belongs here]), Tuolumne (Central Sierra), Mariposa (Southern Sierra), Bodega (Coast), Marin (Coast), and Lake. See Central Sierra Miwok, Northern Sierra Miwok, Southern Sierrra Miwok.

Siglit (dialect of Western Canadian Inuit). Also called Sigliq, Mackenzie Coast, Chiglit, Tchiglit. *G., W.*: Petitot (1876) has grammatical notes and a vocabulary, pp. 1-75. *W.*: Jenness (1929:170-179) has perhaps 200 words in a comparative vocabulary, Lowe (1984) is a dictionary of 305 pp. *T.*: Jenness (1924:30-31, 42-43, 59-60) has about 35 lines of interlinear text. *G.*: Dorais (1986:23) compares the phonemic inventory of this dialect with inventories of other Eskimo dialects. See Tuktoyaktuk.

Siletz (dialect of Tillamook). *G., W.*: Frachtenberg (1917b) has phonetic data and a vocabulary of about 74 items. See Tillamook.

Simpson Peninsula. See Netsilik.

Sinkyone (dialect of Eel River). *W.*: Gifford (1922:22-23) has about 53 kin terms.

Sioux (Mississippi Valley Siouan). Dialects include Santee-Sisseton (Dakota), Teton (Lakhota), and Yankton-Yanktonai. *Santee. G., T.*: Riggs and Dorsey (1893) devote 271 pp. to grammar, texts (pp. 81-152), and ethnography. *W.*: Riggs (1890) is a dictionary with 675 pp. for a Dakota-English list. *Teton. G., T.*: Boas and Swanton (1911) describe Santee and Teton morphology and have an interlinear Teton text, pp. 954-958. *G.:*. Buechel (1939) and Boas and Deloria (1941) are grammars. Shaw (1980) covers morphophonemics. *W.*: Buechel (1970, 1983) is a dictionary of about 21,600 Lakhota-English entries, pp. 54-660, 798-833, with an English-Lakhota index, pp. 661-797, 834-847. *Yankton. W.*: Williamson (1886) has Santee, Teton, and Yankton words. *T.*: Cook and Cook (1882) is a catechism. *G., W., T.*: Stark (1962) has phonology, some words, and text,

pp. 28-35. See Assiniboine, Stoney. See "Sketch of Lakhota, a Siouan Language," this volume.

Sirenikski (Eskimoan). Also called Sirenik. *G., W.*: Krauss (1976:188-189) has phonological data and four words, as well as bibliographic references. *G., W., T.*: Menovshchikov (1964) has about 100 pp. of grammar, 68 pp. of texts, 2,700 items in a Sirenikski-Russian dictionary, and a comparative vocabulary of about 400 items.

Siuslaw. *G., W.*: Hymes (1966a) has phonology and a few words. Zenk (vol. 7:572) lists phonemes. See Zenk (vol. 7:579), Thompson and Kinkade (vol. 7:42). See Lower Umpqua.

Skagit (dialect of Northern Lushootseed). Also called Lower Skagit. Upper Skagit is a different dialect, for which data are lacking. *W.*: Hess (1977:410-412) has about 35 words of Skagit, mostly in a set of Lushootseed comparative vocabularies. Gunther (1945) has a few botanical words. See Lushootseed.

Skidegate. See Haida.

Skokomish. See Twana.

Skykomish (dialect of Northern Lushootseed). *W.*: Gunther (1945) has a couple of botanical words. Tweddell (1974:517-518) cites testimony that Skykomish was in Northern Lushootseed, but no forms; Hess (1977:403-419) concluded that it was in Southern Lushootseed. See Lushootseed.

Slavey (Athapaskan). Also called Slave. Bearlake, Hare, Mountain, and Slavey have been considered four dialects of a single language called Slavey or Slavey-Hare. *G.*: Krauss and Golla (vol. 6:69-72, 79-80) have phonological data. *G., W., T.*: Rice (1989) is an important, richly-detailed grammar, 1,370 pp. Rice (1991) discusses intransitives and unaccusatives. *W.*: MacNeish (1960) has Slave, Hare, and Chipewyan kin terms. *T.*: Monus and Monus (1970) is a reader, 61 pp. Moore and Wheelock (1990) have traditional texts. Bompas (1891) is a liturgical work, 278 pp.

Sliammon (dialect of Comox). *W.*: Elmendorf (1962b) has numerals 1-10 in a comparative vocabulary. Kinkade (1973) has three words. *G.*: See Newman (1977) *under* Twana. See Comox.

Smith River. See Tolowa.

Snake. See Northern Paiute, Shoshone.

Snanaimuq. See Nanaimo.

Snohomish (dialect of Northern Lushootseed). *G., W.*: Haeberlin (1918:164-167) has words in a discussion of reduplication. Hess (1966) discusses chameleon morphology; Hess (1967) is a grammar. *W.*: Haeberlin and Gunther (1930:56-57) have 22 kin terms. *T.*: Boulet (1879) is a prayer book and catechism of 32 pages. See Lushootseed.

Snoqualmie (dialect of Southern Lushootseed). *W.*: Haeberlin and Gunther (1930) have words passim, including kin terms. See Lushootseed.

Solano. *W.:* Swanton (1915:34-35) has 21 words. Swanton (1940:54-55) has about 47 English-Solano items. See Goddard (1979a:371-372).

Songhees (dialect of Northern Straits Salish). Also called Lkungen, Songish, Straits. *G., W.:* Haeberlin (1918:167-168); Haeberlin and Thompson (1974) discuss suffixes (English index, pp. 234-235, about 140 items) and have perhaps 25 items in a comparative vocabulary (see Nanaimo); for Songhees, there are three items, pp. 232-233. *W.:* Boas and Haeberlin (1927) have a few words in a comparative vocabulary. Elmendorf (1962b:86-87, 92-93) has about 187 items in a comparative vocabulary. *G.:* See Newman (1977) *under* Twana. Suttles (vol. 7:453) has a Songhees phonemic inventory; Thompson and Kinkade (vol. 7:37) have Songhees reflexes of nine protophonemes.

Sooke (dialect of Northern Straits Salish). *G.:* Efrat (1969) is a grammar of non-particles. *G., W.:* Efrat (1978) has about 78 words illustrating glottalized resonants. Thompson and Kinkade (vol. 7:37) have Sooke reflexes of nine protophonemes. See Songhees.

Souriquois. See Micmac.

Southampton Island. See Aivilik.

South Baffin (dialect of Eastern Canadian Inuit). Also called Iqalungmiut. *G.:* Dorais (1975a) describes the language. Dorais (1976) compares certain phonological features with those of five other dialects (see *under* Aivilik). Dorais (1986:23) compares the phonemic inventories of South Baffin and other Eskimo dialects.

Southeastern Pomo (Pomoan). *G., T.:* Moshinsky (1974) is a grammar with phonology, pp. 5-37; grammatical categories and syntax, pp. 41-106; syntactic rules, pp. 107-124; and text analysis, pp. 125-141. *W.:* Barrett (1908:56-68) has about 275 forms. Webb (1971:37-45) has about 238 items. Grekoff (1964:69-72) has 32 cognate sets for Southeastern Pomo, Southern Pomo, and Kashaya. McLendon (1964:128-137) has words from Halpern in a comparative vocabulary. *G., W.:* McLendon (1973) has vocabulary with reconstructions and analysis of prefixes. See Central Pomo for details.

Southern Diegueño. See Diegueño, Kumeyaay.

Southern Lushootseed. See Lushootseed.

Southern Okanagan (dialect of Okanagan). *W.:* Kinkade (1967a) has some words. See Okanagan.

Southern Paiute (dialect of Ute). *G., W., T.:* Sapir (1930-1931) has grammar and, pp. 276-296, an interlinear text and notes; Kaibab interlinear texts, pp. 308-393, and texts with Kaibab Paiute and English on facing pages, pp. 394-483; Uintah Ute texts, pp. 484-514; and notes, pp. 515-535; pp. 537-730 is a Southern Paiute dictionary. *W.:* Klein (1959:235-

238) has about 105 items in a comparative vocabulary with Mono and Kawaiisu. *T.:* Bunte (1980) has an analyzed Kaibab text.

Southern Pomo (Pomoan). *W.:* Barrett 1908:56-68) has about 282 forms. Webb (1971:37-45) has about 233 items. Grekoff (1964:69-72) has 32 cognate sets. McLendon (1964:128-137) has words in a comparative vocabulary. *G., W.:* McLendon (1973) has vocabulary with reconstructions and analysis of prefixes. See Central Pomo for details.

Southern Sierra Miwok (Eastern Miwok). *G., T., W.:* Broadbent (1964) has grammar, pp. 11-139, texts, pp. 142-209, and a dictionary, pp. 220-355. *W.:* Broadbent and Callaghan (1960:307-316) have words in a comparative vocabulary of about 285 items. Barrett (1919), Merriam and Heizer (1966:125-126), and Kroeber (1906:606-661) have vocabularies of Yosemite; Kroeber (1906a) also has vocabularies of Angels Camp and Pohonichi. See Central Sierra Miwok.

Southern Tepehuan. See Tepehuan.

Southern Tiwa. See Isleta, Sandia.

Southern Tsimshian (Tsimshianic). Also called Klemtu. *G., W.:* Dunn (1979a) discusses connectives. Dunn (1979) has phonology and words in a comparative vocabulary of 67 items. See Coast Tsimshian.

Southern Tutchone. See Tutchone.

Southern West Greenlandic. See West Greenlandic.

Southern Wintun. See Patwin, Hill Patwin, River Patwin, Suisun.

Southern Yana. See Yana.

Southwest Baffin. See Cape Dorset.

Southwestern Pomo. See Kashaya.

Spokane (dialect of Kalispel). *G.:* B.F. Carlson (1972) is a grammar. B.F. Carlson and Thompson (1982) describe Spokane and Thompson markers of control and reduplicative indication of noncontrol of action. See Newman (1977) *under* Twana. *W.:* Kinkade and Sloat (1972:31-44) have a number of lexical items in an Interior Salish comparative vocabulary. Vogt (1940) has comparisons with Kalispel, Colville, and Coeur d'Alene. Kinkade (1967a) has words in phonetic transcription. *T.:* B.F. Carlson (1978) has an analyzed text. Walker and Eells (1842:2-16) have spelling and reading lessons. See Kalispel.

Squamish (Central Salish). *G., T., W.:* Kuipers (1967-1969) has grammar, pp. 21-215, texts, pp. 219-242, and a dictionary with perhaps 3,000 entries or more. *G., W.:* Haeberlin and Thompson (1974) discuss suffixes and have items in a comparative vocabulary (see details *under* Nanaimo). See Newman (1977) *under* Twana. See Suttles (vol. 7:453) for phonemic inventories of Squamish, Nooksack, Songhees, Saanich, Sooke, and Clallam.

Squaxon (dialect of Nisqually). *W.*: Eells (1881:298-299) has vocabulary. Gunther (1945) has perhaps a dozen botanical words. See Lushootseed.

Stadaconan. See Laurentian.

Stockbridge. See Mahican.

Stoney (Dakotan). *G., W.*: Cook (1995) has words and a consonant inventory. Taylor (1983) and Shaw (1985) have phonology and examples.

Straits Salish. See Clallam, Northern Straits.

Sugcestun. See Pacific Yupik.

Suisun (dialect of Southern Patwin). *W.*: Kroeber (1932:354-355) has words. Englehardt (1924:410-411) has names of rancherias of Mission Dolores, some of which may be Suisun. See Patwin.

Suquamish. See Lushootseed.

Upper Inlet Tanaina (dialect of Tanaina). *W.*: Osgood (1937:12, 208-221) has about 300 words. See Tanaina.

Susquehannock (Iroquoian). *W.*: Mithun (1981) has vocabulary from Campanius (1696) with Iroquoian comparisons, and subgroupings. See Conestoga.

Swinomish (dialect of Northern Lushootseed). *W.*: Gunther (1945) has a botanical word or so. See Lushootseed.

Tachi (dialect of Southern Valley Yokuts). *G.*: Britsch (1984) discusses conditionals and hypotheticals. *W., T.*: Kroeber (1907a) has 16 words, pp. 320-321, grammatical notes and words and phrases, pp. 361-362, and eight lines of interlinear text, pp. 374-375. Kroeber (1963:186-210) has Tachi vocabulary in a comparison of 270 items in 21 Yokuts dialects or languages, as well as on pp. 222-223. *W.*: Driver (1937) has 19 words and 16 numerals in a comparative vocabulary, pp. 146-153, and words passim; Golla (1964) has a few words.

Taensa. Swanton (1980b) discusses the language, for which linguistic data are lacking, and has a bibliography of earlier publications. Haumonté and Adam (1882) is a hoax, with invented data.

Tagish (Athapaskan). *W.*: Hoijer (1963:24-26) has data from Gordon Marsh. *G.*: Krauss and Golla (vol. 6:69-72, 82-83) have phonological data. Vol. 6:481 has a phonemic inventory based on data from Golla and Marsh. See Kaska.

Tahltan (Athapaskan). *G.*: Krauss and Golla (vol. 6:82) has phonological data. Volume 6:458 has a phonemic inventory. *G., W.*: Nater (1989) has about 125 words passim, in a discussion of phonology.

Tait. See Chilliwack.

Taitnapam. See Upper Cowlitz.

Takelma (Takelman). *G., W.*: Sapir (1907) touches phonology and has vocabulary. Sapir and Swadesh (1953:134-137) discuss material selected from 152 groups of cognates, with comparisons. *G., T.*: Sapir (1922) is a sketch of phonology and morphology, with an interlinear text. *T., W.*: Sapir (1909) has texts, with a stem vocabulary at the end. *W.*: Shipley (1969:228-230) has 69 cognate sets of Takelma and Kalapuya.

"Takin" (subdialect of Nopchinchi in Northern Yokuts). *W.*: Kroeber (1959b:7-13) has words in a comparative vocabulary of about 120 items.

"Talatūi" (dialect of Plains Miwok). *W.*: Gallatin (1848:123) has about 72 forms, presumably from the Cosumnes River.

Tamyen (Northern Costanoan). Also called Santa Clara. *W.*: Beeler (1961:194-197) has about 35 words in a comparative vocabulary. Henshaw and Heizer (1955:160-174, 185) have a vocabulary, and nine phrases, on p. 185. Kroeber (1910) has about 114 words, pp. 243-248, and some ten lines of text (a Lord's Prayer from Duflot de Mofras), pp. 255-256. Levy (1976:22-35) has about 100 words in a comparative vocabulary, part of a discussion of historical phonology and subgrouping. Okrand (1989) has a few words, in comparative perspective. See Chochenyo.

Tanacross (Athapaskan). Also called Nabesna. *G.*: Krauss and Golla (vol. 6:69-72, 76) have phonological data, and volume 6:562 has a phonemic inventory. *W.*: Hoijer (1963:15-17) has Tanacross data from David Shinen in phonetic transcription. Hoijer (1971a) has Tanacross consonantal sound laws but no lexical forms. *T.*: Paul and Scollon (1980) have texts. See Upper Tanana.

Tanaina (Athapaskan). Also called Dena'ina. *G.*: Kari (1975) discusses verbs. Krauss and Golla (vol. 6:69-73) and volume 6:623 have phonological data. *W.*: Kari (1977a) has over 4,000 semantically grouped entries, supplemented by a Tanaina-English index, for dialects of Inland Tanaina (Nondalton data from Tenenbaum), Iliamna, Outer Inlet (Kachemak Bay), and Upper Inlet (Tyonek, Susitna). P.R. Kari (1991) has perhaps 140 names of plants and other vocabulary, for dialects named above (map, p. 2); about 20 parts of spruce and birch trees, pp. 206-207; and about 30 loan words from Russian, pp. 193-194. *T.*: Tenenbaum (1976) has six Nondalton interlinear texts by Antone Evan and Alexie Evan, in the third of a series of four volumes. Tenenbaum and McGary (1984) have interlinear texts. See Krauss and McGary (1980:241-273) and Krauss (1979:850-851). See Lake Iliamna, Kenai, Upper Inlet Tanaina.

Tanana. See Lower Tanana, Upper Tanana, and Tanacross.

Tano. See Arizona Tewa.

Taos (Northern Tiwa). *T., W.*: Harrington (1910a) has an interlinear text, pp. 40-41, and a Taos-English vocabulary, pp. 42-48. *G.*: Trager (1946) is a sketch of Taos grammar. Trager (1948, 1954, 1960, 1961) has data on phonology, morphology, syntax, semiology, and paralanguage. Rosen (1980) discusses morphology and syntax.

Tarahumara (Uto-Aztecan). *G.*: Brámbila (1953) is a

grammar. *W.*: Thord-Gray (1955) and K.S. Hilton (1993) are dictionaries. *T.*: Burgess (1978) has an analyzed text.

Tarramiut (dialect of Eastern Canadian Inuit). Also called Tahagmiut, Taqramiut, (Northern) Arctic Quebec. *G.*: Dorais (1976) compares certain phonological and morphological features of Tarramiut with those of five other dialects (see under Aivilik). Dorais (1986:23) compares the phonemic inventory of this dialect with inventories of other Eskimoan dialects.

Tataviam (Takic?). *W.*: Bright (1975) has words from Harrington. See volume 10:122.

Tatlit-kutchin. See Kutchin.

Tawasa (Timucuan). *W.*: Swanton (1929) publishes the only known vocabulary and compares it with Timucua. See Timucua.

Tchiglit. See Siglit.

Tcholovone. See Chulamni.

Ten'a. See Ingalik, Koyukon.

Tenino (dialect of Columbia River Sahaptin). *W.*: Aoki (1966:362-366) has about 48 items, kin terms from Murdock (1958). Aoki (1975:193) has a few words in a discussion of East Plateau diffusion. Rigsby (1978) has an analyzed text. See Sahaptin.

Tenino (Salishan). See Upper Chehalis.

Tepehuan (Uto-Aztecan). *G.*: Willett (1991) is a grammar of the eastern variety of Southern Tepehuan. See volume 10:120, 306. See Northern Tepehuan, Tepecano.

Tesuque (dialect of Rio Grande Tewa). Also spelled Tusuque. *W.*: Schoolcraft (1851-1857, 3:446-459) has perhaps 300 words plus numerals from David V. Whiting. *T.*: Curtis (1907-1930, 17:77) has three lines of text with interlinear translation.

Tête de Boule. See Attikamek.

Teton. See Sioux.

Tewa. See Arizona Tewa, Rio Grande Tewa.

Thompson (Interior Salish). Also called Ntlakyapamuk. *G., W.*: Good (1880a) has grammatical data and vocabulary. Haeberlin and Thompson (1974) discuss suffixes and have items in a comparative vocabulary (see details *s.v.* Nanaimo). *G.*: B.F. Carlson and Thompson (1982) compare Thompson and Spokane markers of control and reduplicative indication of noncontrol of action. *T.*: Good (1879) is a missionary text. *W.*: Boas (1891:692-715) has words in a comparative vocabulary. Kinkade and Sloat (1972:31-44) have a few words. See Newman (1977) *under* Twana. See Mattina (1989:89). See "Sketch of Thompson, A Salishan Language," this volume.

Thule. See Polar Eskimo.

Tillamook (Salishan). *G., T., W.*: Edel (1939) is a sketch with word lists and an interlinear text, pp. 52-53. *G.*: Thompson and Thompson (1966) review phonology. *G., W.*: Lexical data with some grammat-

ical analysis are provided by Hale (1846:536-537, 570-629) with some 296 items; and by Reichard (1960:57-60) with perhaps several hundred items in a comparative vocabulary. Haeberlin and Thompson (1974) discuss suffixes and have items in a comparative vocabulary (see details *under* Nanaimo). See Newman (1977) *s.v.* Twana. See Adler (1961:207), Thompson and Kinkade (vol. 7:39), Seaburg and Miller (vol. 7:567).

Timucua (Timucuan). *G., W.*: Granberry (1993) is a grammar and dictionary. *G.*: Granberry (1990) is a sketch of verbs and syntax. *G., W., T.*: Pareja (1886) is a 1614 grammar, 163 pp.; four pages of biblical text; 57 tables of paradigms; and about 2,300 words. *W., T.*: Gatschet and La Grasserie (1889) have some 20 words and 23 pages of biblical narrative. La Grasserie (1890) has six pages of text and about 1,000 words. Milanich and Sturtevant (1972) reproduce texts. See Pilling (1885:286-288, 716-717), Croft (1948:267-268).

Tipai (Diegueño). Also called Mexican Diegueño. *G., W.*: Wares (1968:41-42, 77-96) has phonological and lexical data. Law (1961) has words in a comparative vocabulary.

Tlatlasikwala. See Kwakiutl.

Tlatskanai. See Clatskanie.

Tlingit (Nadene). *G., W.*: Story and Naish (1973) describe Central Tlingit verbs and grammar (especially in a sketch, pp. 345-392); the Tlingit-English section of their verb dictionary has about 750 stems with theme definitions, pp. 15-252; they also have an English-Tlingit index, pp. 265-342. Krauss and Leer (1981) discuss Tlingit sonorants in relation to Athapaskan and Eyak, with citation of many Tlingit forms passim. *W.*: Naish and Story (1976) is a noun dictionary. De Laguna (1972) has Yakutat vocabulary passim. Dauenhauer and Dauenhauer (1987, 1990) have texts. *G., T.*: F. Williams and E. Williams (1978) have Tongass texts, with phonological data from Leer. See Krauss (1979:844-845) for notes on Tongass and Heinyaa. See volume 7:31. Volume 6:469 has the phonemes of Inland Tlingit, and volume 7:203 those of Tlingit proper.

Tolkapaya (Yavapai). *G.*: Chung (1976) describes tense markers. Hardy and Gordon (1980) discuss adverbial and modal constructions. *T.*: Munro (1978) has an analyzed text. See Bright (1982:74-76, 136C), volume 10:5, 38-39. See Yavapai.

Tolowa (Oregon Athapaskan). Also called Chetco-Tolowa. *G., W.*: J.O. Bright (1964) describes Smith River phonology. Collins (1985) has stem morphology. Collins (1989) has about 70 words, illustrating morphophonemics. Bommelyn (1984) is a story of 354 pp. *W.*: Waterman (1924) has place names. Gifford (1922:15-17) has about 70 kin terms. *T.*: E.D. Jacobs (1968, 1977) has two texts in the Chetco dialect.

755

Toltichi (subdialect of Dumna in Northern Valley Yokuts). *G., W.*: Kroeber (1907a) has grammatical data, pp, 355-356, and about 51 words, pp. 356-357, from a Dumna speaker. *W.*: Pitkin and Shipley (1958) have some data in a comparative vocabulary.

Tonaxa (dialect of Kootenai). Also called Plains Kootenai. *W.*: Teit and Boas (1930) have 29 words which Teit rescued as different from corresponding words in Kootenai proper. See Kootenai.

Tonkawa. *G.*: Hoijer (1933) is a sketch, shortened and revised in (1946b). Hoijer (1949a) describes suffixes and particles. *W.*: Hoijer (1949) is a dictionary with over 900 themes, pp. 4-69, and over 200 affixes, pp. 70-74. *T.*: Hoijer (1972) has 27 narratives, each in phonemic form with following translation.

Tsamosan Salishan. See Thompson and Kinkade (vol. 7:38-39). See Cowlitz, Lower Chehalis, Quinault, Upper Chehalis.

Tsetsaut (Athapaskan). *W., T.*: Boas and Goddard (1924a) have about 1,500 items in an English-Tsetsaut list; they have about 46 lines of interlinear text, pp. 34-35. *G., W.*: Tharp (1972) has grammatical notes and lexical forms for subgrouping. Krauss and Golla (vol. 6:69-72, 83) have phonological data.

Tsimshian. See Coast Tsimshian.

Tualatin. See Kalapuyan.

Tubar (Uto-Aztecan). *G., W.*: Materials collected in 1893 were published by Lionnet (1978).

Tubatulabal (Uto-Aztecan). *G.*: C.F. Voegelin (1935) is a grammar. Heath (1981) discusses phonology. *T.*: C.F. Voegelin (1935a) is a collection of texts, pp. 192-241, with grammatical notes, pp. 242-246. *W.*: C.F. Voegelin (1958a) is a dictionary with about 900 items. Driver (1937:146-153) has 46 nouns and 9 numerals of Bankalachi (West of Kern River), as well as 46 nouns and 16 numerals of Tubatulabal (East of Kern River), in a comparative vocabulary.

Tuktoyaktuk (subdialect of Siglit in Western Canadian Inuit). *G., W., T.*: Webster and Zibell (1976) have 42 sentences of this Alaskan dialect brought by migrants to the Mackenzie delta (vol. 5:56), in a comparative survey, pp. 318-325; phonemic inventory with allophones, p. 275; about 170 words and phrases in a comparative vocabulary, pp. 286-317.

Tukudh (dialect of Eastern Kutchin). Also spelled Tukuthe, Takudh. *T.*: McDonald (1886:5-567) is a New Testament. *W.*: McDonald (1871) has a set of Tukudh kin terms. See Kutchin.

Tulamni (dialect of Buena Vista Yokuts). *G., W.*: For Tulamni, Kroeber (1907a) has 16 words, pp. 320-321, and grammatical and lexical data, p. 350. Kroeber (1963:186-210) has vocabularies of Tulamni and Hometwoli in a comparison of 270 items in 21 Yokuts dialects or languages.

756 **Tunica.** *G.*: Haas (1941a, 1946) has a grammar and sketch. *T.*: Haas (1950a) has texts. *W.*: Haas (1953) is a dictionary, Tunica-English, pp. 201-295, affix list, pp. 299-173, English-Tunica, pp. 307-332.

Tuolumne. See Central Sierra Miwok.

Tuscarora (Iroquoian). *G.*: Mithun (1976) is a grammar. Rudes and Crouse (1987) have grammatical and cultural data from Hewitt. *W.*: Gallatin (1836:305-367, 1848:115) has vocabulary. Chew (1846) has about 350 words. Rudes (1987a) has roots, stems, and particles in a substantial dictionary based on data from Hewitt. *T.*: Wallace and Reyburn (1951) have a migration legend.

Tuskegee (Muskogean). *W.*: Swanton (1922) has 10 words said to be Tuskegee, similar to Alabama.

Tutchone (Athapaskan). *G.*: Krauss and Golla (vol. 6:69-72, 78-79) have phonological data. Volume 6:493 has phonemes for Northern Tutchone and Southern Tutchone. *W.*: Hoijer (1963:15-17) has Southern Tutchone data from McClellan. See Northern Tutchone.

Tutelo (Ohio Valley Siouan). *G., W.*: Hale (1883b) has grammar, pp. 13-35, and a vocabulary with Dakota and Hidatsa comparisons, pp. 36-47. Sapir (1913) has a phonetic note, pp. 296-297, and 55 items from a Cayuga speaker, pp. 295-296. *W.*: Frachtenberg (1913) has vocabulary. Wolff (1950-1951) includes Tutelo words in a comparative context. See Occaneechi, Saponi.

Tututni (Oregon Athapaskan). *G.*: Golla (1976) is a sketch. *W.*: Landar (1977a) has a Mixwunutunne vocabulary. See Miller and Seaburg (vol. 7:580, 587-588). *W.*: Hoijer (1960, 1963:9-13) gives about 47 forms and stems for the Euchre Creek dialect in his study of Pacific Coast Athapaskan of 1960, and forms in a more general context in his study of Athapaskan languages of 1963.

Twana (Central Salish). *G.*: Drachman (1969) has phonological data. *W.*: Elmendorf (1962b:86-87, 92-93) has about 187 items in a comparative vocabulary. Hess (1977:410-412) has 45 words of Twana from Kinkade in a set of Lushootseed comparative vocabularies. Newman (1977:304) has reconstructed five independent pronouns, cited in Twana and other Salishan languages (Bella Coola, Clallam, Coeur d'Alene, Colville, Kalispel, Lillooet, Musqueam, Lushootseed, Northern and Southern Shuswap, Okanagan, Sliammon, Songhees, Spokane, Squamish, Thompson, Tillamook, Upper Chehalis). See Galloway (1988) *under* Nooksack. *W., T.*: Eells (1877) has numerals and divisions of time, pp. 86-88, and 211 words, pp. 93-98, as well as songs. *W*: .Eells (1985:16) has words. Boas (1891) has words in a comparative vocabulary. *T.*: Elmendorf (1961) has texts. See Suttles and Lane (vol. 7:485) for a note on Twana phonology.

Tygh Valley. See Sahaptin.

Ugalákmūt. Also Ugaljachmutzi, Ugaléntsi, Ugalentz. See Eyak or Chugach.

Ukiuvangmiut See King Island, Seward Peninsula Inupiaq.

Umatilla (dialect of Columbia River Sahaptin). *W.*: Rigsby (1965a:307) has 25 items with Proto-Sahaptian reconstructions. Aoki (1966:362-366) has about 48 sets of items, with four items per set, from Rigsby. Aoki (1975:193) has four words in a discussion of East Plateau diffusion. See Sahaptin.

Umingmaktôrmiut. See Copper Eskimo.

Umpqua. See Upper Umpqua (Athapaskan) and Lower Umpqua (Siuslaw).

Unalachtigo (dialect of Unami). One possible word is identified by Goddard (1995:145). See Delaware, Pidgin Delaware.

Unalakleet (dialect of Central Alaskan Yupik). See Unaliq.

Unalakleet (dialect of North Alaskan Inupiaq). *W.*: Webster and Zibell (1970) have words found especially in this dialect, as part of an Inupiaq dictionary.

Unaliq (dialect of Central Alaskan Yupik). Swadesh (1952b), in the fifth of a series of articles on Unaliq and Proto Eskimo, has perhaps 750 Unaliq-English entries, each with comparisons, giving cognates in languages and dialects called Siberia, Nunivak, Kuskokwim, Wales, Barrow, Mackenzie, and Greenland. Rasmussen and Ostermann (1941:28-36) list about 270 words for the dialect around Norton Sound and others. Unaliq refers narrowly to the northern Norton Sound dialect; see Jacobson (1984:394). See Malimiut.

Unami Delaware. See Delaware.

Ungava (dialect of Eastern Canadian Inuit). Also called Ungava Bay. *G.*: Schneider (1967) is a grammar of Ungava or Eastern Canadian Inuit found on Baffin Island, in northern Quebec, and on the Labrador coast. *W.*: Schneider (1970) is an Ungava-French dictionary of about 27,000 entries. Schneider (1970a) is a French-Ungava dictionary of about 4,200 main entries. Dorais (1971) discusses the semantics of localizers.

Unquachog (dialect of Quiripi-Unquachog). *W.*: Jefferson's 1791 vocabulary is in Boyd (1982, 20:467-470). See Quiripi.

Upernavik. See West Greenlandic.

Upper Chehalis (Tsamosan Salishan). Dialects are Oakville Chehalis, Satsop, and Tenino Chehalis. *G., T.*: Boas (1935a) has an interlinear text, pp. 103-104, with detailed grammatical notes. *G., W.*: Kinkade (1963) covers phonology and morphology. *W.*: Kinkade (1991a) is a dictionary, 378 pp. Hess (1977:410-412) has 15 words from Kinkade in a set of Lushootseed comparative vocabularies. *G.*: See Newman (1977) *under* Twana. *T.*: Kinkade (1983a, 1984, 1987) has texts. See Hajda (vol. 7:503, 516-517).

Upper Chinook. See Cathlamet, Clackamas, Wasco-Wishram.

Upper Cowlitz (dialect of Northwest Sahaptin). Also called Taitnapam. *W.*: Aoki (1962:177-182) has Upper Cowlitz words in a comparative vocabulary of about 269 sets, with Nez Perce and Proto Sahaptian reconstructions. Aoki (1966:362-366) has about 48 sets of kin terms, four items per set, from Jacobs. *T.*: Jacobs (1934-1937, 1:102-124, 168-212, 223-246, 252-268, 2:90-110, 149-184, 193-211, 217-234) has texts.

Upper Inlet Tanaina (Athapaskan). *W.*: Osgood (1937:12, 208-221) has about 300 words. See Tanaina.

Upper Kuskokwim (Athapaskan). Called Kolchan in volume 6. *G.*: Krauss and Golla (vol. 6:69-72, 75) have phonological data. *W.*: Collins and Collins (1966) and Collins and Petruska (1979) are short dictionaries.

Upper Kuskokwim (dialect of Central Alaskan Yupik). *W.*: Jacobson (1984) indicates with this label words localized around Aniak. See Kuskokwim, Central Alaskan Yupik.

Upper Piman. See Papago, Pima.

Upper Tanana (Athapaskan). Called Nabesna by Osgood (1936). *G., W.*: Milanowski (1962) describes the sound system. Minoura (1994) compares the phonology of five dialects. Volume 6:69-72, 76-77 describes phonology, and volume 6:562 describes Tetlin phonemes and has a note on the Northway dialect. *W.*: Milanowski and John (1979) is a short dictionary.

Upper Umpqua (Oregon Athapaskan). Also called Umpqua. *G., W.*: Hale (1846:535, 570-629) has a minor note on grammar, p. 535, and about 240 words. *W.*: Gallatin (1848:105) has about 57 forms from Hale. Hoijer (1963:9-13) has words from Melville and Elizabeth Jacobs.

Ute (dialect of Ute). *G., W., T.*: Kroeber (1908c) is a sketch of Uintah Ute, with an interlinear text of about 44 lines, pp. 84-86. *G., W.*: Chamberlin (1909) has about 100 plant names, with analysis of roots and suffixes. Davis (1966:126, 134-139) has a phonological note and about 185 words of Cortez Ute. K. Hale (1959:115) has about 99 words. *G.*: Givón (1980) is a grammar. *W.*: Givón (1979) is a preliminary dictionary. *T.*: Sapir (1930-1931, pt. 2) has Uintah Ute texts. See Miller vol. 11:98-100. See Chemehuevi, Southern Paiute.

Utkuhikhalingmiut. See Netsilik.

Vanyume (dialect of Serrano). *W.*: Kroeber (1907c:71-89, 93-96) has words. Kroeber (1909) has a note on the plural. See vol. 10:122.

Ventureño (Chumashan). *W.*: Pinart and Heizer (1952:36-71) have a vocabulary collected in 1878. *W., T.*: Henshaw (in Heizer 1955:94-148; 187-193) has a vocabulary and texts. *G., W., T.:* Kroeber (1910:265-267) has about 81 words and a note on pronouns; he has a few lines of song text, p. 271. *T.:* Beeler (1967) has José Señán's confession book, 83 pp. *W.:* Englehardt (1933:207-209) has about 240 names of places of the San Luis Obispo district taken from mission registers. See Mupu.

Virginia Algonquian (Eastern Algonquian). *W.:* Geary (1953) has over 800 glosses from Strachey. *G., W.:* Siebert (1975) has historical phonology. See Croft (1948:262), Goddard (vol. 15:73-74), Pentland and Wolfart (1982:327-328).

Vuntakutchin. See Crow Flats Kutchin.

Waco (dialect of Wichita). *W.:* Whipple has about 138 words in U.S. Army, Corps of Engineers (1855:65-69). Taylor (1963:116) has data from Whipple and data from Marcy, dated 1852, which may also be Waco.

Wailaki (dialect of Eel River). *W.:* Hoijer (1963:9-13) has words from P.E. Goddard (1923). Gifford (1922:23-25) has about 60 kin terms. P.E. Goddard (1923) has about 86 place names on a map, as well as names of bands. P.E. Goddard (1924) has 29 place names on three maps, also listed on p. 225. *T.:* P.E. Goddard (1921) has 36 texts. Seaburg (1977, 1977a) has analyzed texts. Wailaki is a dialect of Eel River, along with Nongatl, Lassik, and Sinkyone.

Wainwright. See North Alaskan Inupiaq.

Wakaikam. See Cathlamet.

Wakichi (subdialect of Merced in Northern Valley Yokuts). *W.:* Kroeber (1907a:360) has five words from a Dumna consultant.

Waksachi. See Mono.

Walapai (dialect of Upland Yuman). Also spelled Hualapai. *G., W.:* Watahomigie, Bender, and Yamamoto (1982) have lessons in grammar, with vocabulary grouped topically, Walapai-English, pp. 477-527, English-Walapai, pp. 528-575. Redden (1966, 1966a) has phonology and morphology. Wares (1968:27-30, 77-96) has a phonological note and words in a comparative vocabulary. *G., T.:* Winter (1966) and Winter and Butcher (1976) have texts. See Havasupai.

Wales (dialect of Seward Peninsula Inupiaq). Also called Wales-Diomede or Bering Strait. *G.:* Jenness (1927) has phonology. *W.:* Rasmussen and Ostermann (1941:36-46) have about 360 words of Cape Prince of Wales in a comparative vocabulary with East Cape (Naukanski). *W., T.:* Jenness (1924:45-47, 56-64, 69) has about 26 lines of text and about 9 words passim. Jenness (1929:170-179) has a comparative vocabulary for Wales, Barrow, Mackenzie, Coronation, and West Greenland, with about 210 glosses. See Krauss (1979:825).

Walla Walla (Northeast Sahaptin). *W.:* Hale (1846: 570-629) has a vocabulary. See Sahaptin.

Wampanoag. See Massachusett.

758 **Wánikik** (dialect of Cahuilla). *G.:* Hill and Hill

(1968:238-239) discuss stress patterns. *G., W.:* Seiler (1967) has data.

Wappo (Yukian). *W.:* Sawyer (1965) is an English-Wappo vocabulary, 128 pp., with etymological notes passim. Elmendorf (1968:22-35) has words in comparative vocabularies. *T.:* Radin (1924) has about 143 pp. of texts. Sawyer and Somersal (1977) have an analyzed text. *G.:* Radin (1929) is a grammar, 194 pp. C.N. Li and Thompson (1976) cover the syntax of clauses. C.N. Li, Thompson, and Sawyer (1977) cover clause types, subject markers, and cases.

Wasco-Wishram (Upper Chinook). *G.:* Sapir (1907a, 1911) and Hymes (1975) have grammatical data. *G., W.:* Hale (1846:562-564, 570-629) has grammatical notes and vocabulary of "Watlala." *W.:* Spier and Sapir (1930:262-266) have kin terms. *T.:* Sapir (1909a) has texts. Hymes (1980a) has a superbly analyzed text.

Washoe. *G., T.:* Jacobsen (1964) is a grammar. Winter (1970) discusses reduplication. *W.:* Jacobsen (1958:197-204) has about 116 items in a comparative vocabulary with Karok. Jacobsen (1978) discusses Washo internal diversity. *T.:* Dangberg (1927) and Lowie and Lowie (1963) have texts.

Watlala. See Wasco-Wishram.

Wawenock (dialect of Eastern Abenaki). Also spelled Wawenoc. *T.:* Speck (1928) has myths from Bécancour, Quebec, perhaps not from the coastal Wawenock dialect.

Wauyukma (dialect of Northeast Sahaptin). *W.:* Aoki (1962).

Wea (dialect of Miami-Illinois). *W.:* Stanley (1852) has personal names. Morgan (1871:291-382) has Wea kin terms. *T., W.:* Anonymous (1837) has spelling lessons, a long vocabulary, and hymns, 48 pp.; Costa (1993) uses this for phonemic analysis. See Miami, Illinois.

Wechihit (dialect of Southern Valley Yokuts). Also spelled Wechikhit. *G., W.:* Kroeber (1907a:320-321, 360) has 16 words and a grammatical note. Kroeber (1963:186-210) has Wechihit vocabulary in a comparison of 270 items in 21 Yokuts dialects or languages.

Wenatchee. See Columbian.

Western Abenaki (Eastern Algonquian). Also called Saint Francis Abenaki. *G.:* Prince (1901) is a sketch. *W.:* Day (1959, 1961a) has vocabulary. *G., W.:* Day (1964) has data on phonology and vocabulary; Day (1994-1995) is a full dictionary. *T.:* Speck (1945a) has a text. See Day (1961), Goddard (vol. 15:70-77), Pentland and Wolfart (1982:298).

Western Apache. See Cibecue Apache, San Carlos Apache, White Mountain Apache.

Western Canadian Inuit. Western Canadian Inuit has the dialects Siglit, Caribou, Netsilik, and Copper.

Western Carrier. See Babine.

Western Kutchin. See Kutchin.

Western Shoshone (Numic). *W., T.*: Miller (1972) is a dictionary with text. *G.*: Crapo (1970) studies tolerance of variation by speakers of Duckwater Shoshone. McLaughlin (1989) discusses the phonetics of the Gosiute dialect. *W.*: K. Hale (1959:115-116) has about 94 words. Miller, Tanner, and Foley (1971) have lexicostatistic data. See Shoshone.

Western Swampy Cree (Cree). *G., W.*: Rhodes and Todd (vol. 6:55-58) use a few words and phonological data to delimit this dialect.

West Greenlandic (Eskimoan). *G.*: Kleinschmidt (1851) is a pioneering grammar. Bergsland (1956) is a structural description. Mey (1968, 1971) discusses 'to be' and reflexives. Rischel (1974, 1975) has generative morphophonemics in dialect geographical perspective. *W.*: Schultz-Lorentzen (1927) is a Greenlandic-English dictionary. *W., T.*: R. Petersen (1976) is a dictionary entirely in Greenlandic, useful as a text as well as a dictionary. *T.*: South Greenland (1911) inaugurates a series of monolingual texts of Proceedings of the Provincial Council of South Greenland (Danish translations were added from 1941). See Krauss (1976:221-226, 1979:832-836).

Whilkut (dialect of Hupa). *W.*: Gifford (1922:19) has kin terms. See Chilula, Hupa.

White Mountain Apache (dialect of Western Apache), *G., W.*: Greenfeld (1971) discusses names of playing cards. Greenfeld (1978) has phonology, with words passim. *W.*: Perry (1972) is a dictionary. Hill (1963) compares White Mountain and San Carlos Apache words. *T.*: P.E. Goddard (1920a) has interlinear texts, pp. 375-386, and texts with English and White Mountain Apache on facing pages, pp. 387-527. See also Cibecue, San Carlos Apache.

Wichita (Caddoan). *G., W.*: Rood (1976) is a sketch with morphemes indexed by Jean O. Charney: Wichita-English, about 645 entries, pp. 277-292; English-Wichita, pp. 293-305. Rood (1975a) covers inflectional categories. Garvin (1950) describes phonemes. *T.*: Rood (1977) has texts. See "Sketch of Wichita, A Caddoan Language," this vol.

"Wihinasht" (dialect of Northern Paiute). *W.*: Hale (1846:570-629) has about 200 words, some 56 of which were used by Gallatin (1848:121).

Wikchamni (dialect of Tule-Kaweah Yokuts). Also spelled Wükchamni. *G., W.*: Kroeber (1907a:320-321, 351) has 16 words and a grammatical note. Kroeber (1963:186-210, 223-224) has vocabulary, mainly in a comparison of 270 items in 21 Yokuts dialects or languages. Newman (1944:13-239) has grammatical and lexical data. *W.*: Merriam and Heizer (1967:410-411) have about 12 words, mostly names of neighboring tribes and languages. Driver (1937:146-153) has 50 nouns and 16 numerals in a comparative vocabulary. *G., W., T.*: Gamble (1978)

is a grammar with words passim and an interlinear text with notes, pp. 132-143.

Wikeno. See Heiltsuk-Oowekyala.

Wind River. See Eastern Shoshone.

Winnebago (Mississippi Valley Siouan). *G.*: Lipkind (1945) is a grammar, 68 pp. Susman (1943) discusses the accentual system. K. Hale and White Eagle (1980) is a generative account of phonology. *W., T.*: Radin (1923) has vocabulary passim, including clan names and kin terms, and a text of the war bundle ritual, with Winnebago and English on facing pages, pp. 446-529. Radin (1949) has texts.

Wintu (Wintuan). *G., W.*: Dixon and Kroeber (1919:56-61, 93, 96) have about 79 words and some grammatical data. *G., T.*: Pitkin (1984) has phonology, morphophonemics, and parts of speech, and an analyzed text with notes, pp. 268-283. *W.*: Pitkin (1985) is a substantial Wintu-English dictionary with an English-Wintu index. Broadbent and Pitkin (1964) have Wintu, Nomlaki, and Patwin forms compared with Miwokan forms; they have "Proto-Miwok-Wintun" reconstructions and sound laws. *T.*: Pitkin (1977, 1978) and Schlichter (1978) have texts. Demetrocopoulou (1935) has songs. See Nomlaki.

Wishram. See Wasco-Wishram.

Wiyot (Algic). *G., W.*: Teeter (1964) deals with phonology; he has words in a comparative vocabulary, with sound laws. *G., T.*: Teeter (1964a) has grammar with phonology and some analyzed texts, pp. 12-125; texts with Wiyot and English on facing pages, pp. 128-251. *G., T., W.*: Reichard (1925) covers Wiyot grammar, with texts and a dictionary of some 7,250 items. Teeter and Nichols (1993, 1993a) have interlinear texts and concordance. See Adler (1961:201-202).

Wobonuch (dialect of Monache). Also spelled Woponuch. *W.*: Kroeber (1907:71-89) has about 106 forms. Driver (1937:146-153) has 56 words and 16 numerals. See Mono.

Woccon (Catawban). Also called Waccoa. *W.*: Lawson (1709:225-230) has about 110 words compared with Tuscarora and Pamlico. For Schoolcraft's added Catawba comparisons, see Lawson and Schoolcraft (1855). The Woccon vocabulary is available also in Lawson (1937). *G., W.*: Carter (1980) compares Woccon and Catawba forms in 34 numbered sets, pp. 172-174, and Woccon and other Siouan words in 17 sets, pp. 176-177.

Wo'lasi (dialect of Southern Valley Yokuts). Also spelled Wowlas. *G., W.*: Kroeber (1907a:320-321, 363) has 16 words and a grammatical note. Kroeber (1963:186-210) has Wo'lasi vocabulary in a comparison of 270 items in 21 Yokuts dialects or languages.

Woods Cree (Cree). *G., W.*: Rhodes and Todd (vol. 6:55-56) use a few words and phonological data to delimit this dialect. *T.*: Ahenakew and Wolfart (1992:39-57, 356-361) have a text and notes.

Wükchami. See Wikchamni.

Wyandot (dialect of Huron). The Wyandot include merged Huron and Tionontati refugees. *G.*: Barbeau (1915) describes pronominal prefixes and phonology. *W.*: Hale (1885) compares Wyandot words with words of Cartier's Hochelaga. Gallatin (1836:305-367) has words from Johnston, Barton, and the War Department. William Walker (1852) has 75 numerals. *T.*: Barbeau (1960) has texts, 338 pp. Lounsbury (vol. 15:334-343) separates Huron data of Sagard-Theodat, 1623-1624, from that of Chaumonot, 1670, in Wilkie (1920) and Potier, 1745-1751, in Potier (1920, 1920a). See Huron.

Yachikumne (dialect of Far Northern Valley Yokuts). Also spelled Yachikamni. *W.*: Gifford (1922:85) has three kin terms. See Chulamni.

Yahi (dialect of Yana). *W.*: Sapir (1918:161-167) has 47 kin terms from Ishi. *G., T.*: Sapir (1923b:282-294) has 24 lines of interlinear text, with a translation and copious notes. See Yana.

Yakima (dialect of Northwest Sahaptin). *T.*: St. Onge (1872) has prayers, hymns and a catechism, 106 pp. Jacobs (1934-1937, 1:126-167, 247-251, 2:111-148, 212-216) has texts. *G., W.*: Pandosy (1862) is a grammar and dictionary, about 50 pp. See Aoki (1962).

Yamhill. See Kalapuyan.

Yana. *W.*: Sapir and Swadesh (1960) is a dictionary. See Central Yana, Northern Yana, Southern Yana, Yahi.

Yankton-Yanktonai. See Sioux.

Yaqui (Uto-Aztecan). Dialects of Cahitan are Yaqui and Mayo. *G., W., T.*: Jean B. Johnson (1962) has a grammar with texts and a vocabulary. *G.*: Lindenfeld (1973) presents syntax. Escalante (1990) discusses passives. *W.*: K. Hale (1959:118-119) has 100 words. *G., T.*: Mason (1923) is a sketch with about 10 lines of interlinear texts with analysis, pp. 209-212. Crumrine (1961) has phonological data, pp. 3-10, a bibliography, p. 11, and interlinear texts with analysis, pp. 13-43. See Cahitan.

Yaquina (Alsean). *W.*: Hale (1846:570-629) has about 133 items. For James Owen Dorsey's manuscript materials, see vol. 7:671.

Yatasi (Caddoan). Gatschet (1884:31-39) collected a vocabulary, which has not been analyzed.

Yavapai (Upland Yuman). Dialects are Yavepe (Northeastern Yavapai), Tolkapaya (Western Yavapai), and Kewevkapaya (Southeastern Yavapai (vol. 10:5-7, 38-39). *G., W.*: Kendall (1976) discusses important issues in Yavapai syntax; she has an index of 83 grammatical morphemes, pp. 243-247. *W.*: Wares (1968:77-96) has lexical items in a comparative vocabulary of 501 sets. Kroeber (1943:26-30) has vocabulary, as does Law (1961).

Kendall and Sloane (1976) and Kendall (1978) have texts. See Tolkapaya.

Yawdanchi (dialect of Tule-Kaweah Yokuts). *W.*: Dixon and Kroeber (1919:56-61) have words. Driver (1937:146-153) has words in a comparative vocabulary. Kroeber (1963:186-210) has Yawdanchi vocabulary in a comparison of 270 items in 21 Yokuts dialects or languages. Golla (1964) has vocabulary with comparisons. *G., W., T.*: Kroeber (1907a) has grammar, pp. 173-233, words especially on pp. 234-254, and interlinear texts, pp. 255-277.

Yawelmani (dialect of Southern Valley Yokuts). *W.*: Kroeber (1963:186-210) has Yawelmani vocabulary in a comparison of 270 items in 21 Yokuts dialects or languages. *G., W., T.*: Newman (1944) has grammatical data on Yawelmani, as well as Chawchila, Choynimni, Chukchansi, and Wikchamni, words partly in comparative vocabularies, and an analyzed interlinear text of about 41 lines, pp. 240-247. *G.*: Newman (1946) is a sketch. Newman (1966) describes word classes. Kuroda (1967) reinterprets phonology.

Yellowknife (dialect of Chipewyan), A Chipewyan dialect that became extinct before 1913 (vol. 6:80). *W.*: Hoijer (1956:324-332) has a few kin terms from Morgan (1871:293-382, line 66).

Ynezeño. See Ineseño.

Yokutsan. *G.*: Gamble (1975) discusses consonant symbolism. Gamble (1988) reconstructs pronouns. See Ayticha, Buena Vista, Chalostaca, Chawchila, Choynimni, Choynok, Chukaymina, Chukchansi, Chulamni, Chunut, Coconoon, Dumna, Entimbich, Gashowu, Hoyima, Kechayi, Knight's Ferry, Koyeti, Lathrop, Merced Falls, Michahay, Nopchinchi, Nutunutu, Palewyami, Saratoga, Tachi, Takin, Toltichi, Tulamni, Wakichi, Wechihit, Wikchamni, Wo'lasi, Yachikumne, Yawdanchi, Yawelmani.

Yoncalla. See Kalapuyan.

Yorica. See Chome.

Yosemite. See Southern Sierra Miwok.

Yuchi. *G.*: Wolff (1948) analyzes phonemes and morphemes. Wagner (1933) offers a sketch. Ballard (1975, 1978) discusses the pronominal system. Crawford (1973) has phonology. *T.*: Wagner (1931) is a collection of tales. Wolff (1951) has an analyzed text. Crawford (1979) reviews modern Yuchi research.

Yuki (Yukian). *W.*: Barrett (1908:68-80, 250-256) has about 271 words and 30 names. Elmendorf (1968:22-35) has several hundred words in comparative vocabularies. *W., G.*: Kroeber (1959a) discusses possible Athapaskan grammatical loans (tones, monosyllabic morphemes, multiple forms for verb stems). See Coast Yuki and Huchnom.

Yukon (dialect of Central Alaskan Yupik). *W.*: Jacobson (1984) indicates which words are localized in this dialect area. See Central Alaskan Yupik.

Yuma. See Quechan.

Yupik. See Central Alaskan Yupik, Pacific Yupik, Naukanski Yupik, Sirenikski, Central Siberian Yupik.

Yurok (Algic). *G., W., T.*: Robins (1958) has grammar, pp. 1-152, texts, pp. 155-183, and vocabulary, Yurok-English, pp. 189-272, English-Yurok, pp. 273-300. *G.*: Robins (1966) describes word classes. Berman (1972) describes subordinate clauses. *W.*: Teeter (1964:194-197) has about 85 Yurok and Wiyot lexical comparisons. Waterman (1920) has perhaps 1,200 place names and other words, pp. 187-273, with an alphabetical index of places, pp. 273-283. Berman (1982a) supplements words in Robins (1958).

Zia. (dialect of Rio Grande Keresan). *W.*: Stevenson (1894) has words.

Zuni. Also spelled Zuñi. *G.*: Newman (1965) is a grammar. Newman (1968) discusses equivalents of *to be*. Walker (1983) discusses personal pronouns. *W.*: Newman (1958) is a dictionary with perhaps 1,000 stems, Zuni-English, pp. 7-49, English-Zuni, pp. 50-108; and perhaps 140 affixes, pp. 109-117. *T.*: Bunzel (1932, 1932b, 1933) has texts. Tedlock (1978) has an interlinear text. See "Sketch of Zuni, a Language Isolate of New Mexico," this vol.

Contributors

This list gives the academic affiliations of authors at the time this volume went to press. The dates following the entries indicate when each manuscript was (1) first received in the General Editor's office; (2) accepted by the General Editor's office; and (3) sent to the author (or, if deceased, a substitute) for final approval after revisions and editorial work.

AFABLE, PATRICIA O., Handbook of North American Indians, Smithsonian Institution, Washington, D.C. Place-Names: 4/24/74; 12/8/95; 2/16/96.

BEELER, MADISON S. (deceased), Department of Linguistics, University of California, Berkeley. Place-Names: 4/24/74; 12/8/95; 2/16/96.

CALLAGHAN, CATHERINE A. (emerita), Department of Linguistics, Ohio State University, Columbus. Borrowing: 12/15/74; 2/3/94; 8/14/95.

CHAFE, WALLACE L. (emeritus), Department of Linguistics, University of California, Santa Barbara. Sketch of Seneca, an Iroquoian Language: 11/6/92; 5/21/93; 2/14/95.

EGESDAL, STEVEN M., Department of Linguistics, University of Hawaii at Manoa, Honolulu. Sketch of Thompson, a Salishan Language: 3/13/73; 8/20/93; 3/27/95.

FOSTER, MICHAEL K. (emeritus), Canadian Ethnology Service, Canadian Museum of Civilization, Hull, Quebec. Language and the Culture History of North America: 12/10/92; 8/17/93; 1/18/96.

FRENCH, DAVID H. (deceased), Department of Anthropology, Reed College, Portland, Oregon. Personal Names: 6/3/74; 2/3/94; 12/04/95.

FRENCH, KATHRINE S. (adjunct faculty), Department of Anthropology, Reed College, Portland, Oregon. Personal Names: 6/3/74; 2/3/94; 12/04/95.

GAMBLE, GEOFFREY, Office of the Provost, Washington State University, Pullman. Borrowing: 12/15/74; 2/3/94; 8/14/95.

GOLLA, VICTOR, Department of Ethnic Studies, Humboldt State University, Arcata, California. Sketch of Hupa, an Athapaskan Language: 5/25/73; 2/28/94; 1/26/95.

GODDARD, IVES, Department of Anthropology, Smithsonian Institution, Washington, D.C. Introduction: 4/5/95; 7/27/95; 3/11/96. The Description of the Native Languages of North America Before Boas: 12/7/94; 3/21/95; 12/05/95. The Classification of the Native Languages of North America: 6/23/94; 3/31/95; 3/1/96.

KINKADE, M. DALE, Department of Linguistics, University of British Columbia, Vancouver. Discourse: 9/8/92; 11/16/93; 9/14/95.

LANDAR, HERBERT J. (emeritus), Department of English, California State University, Los Angeles. Sources: 9/15/72; 2/3/94; 6/5/96.

MATTINA, ANTHONY, Linguistics Program, University of Montana, Missoula. Discourse: 9/8/92; 11/16/93; 9/14/95.

McLENDON, SALLY, Department of Anthropology, Hunter College and the Graduate Center, City University of New York, New York. Sketch of Eastern Pomo, a Pomoan Language: 2/17/77; 12/8/94; 6/15/95.

MILLER, WICK R. (deceased), Department of Anthropology, University of Utah, Salt Lake City. The Ethnography of Speaking: 8/11/74; 2/28/94; 10/23/95. Sketch of Shoshone, a Uto-Aztecan Language: 9/8/75; 2/3/94; 1/13/95.

MITHUN, MARIANNE, Department of Linguistics, University of California, Santa Barbara. Overview of General Characteristics: 6/4/92; 7/29/93; 6/8/95. The Description of the Native Languages of North America: Boas and After: 6/21/94; 3/23/95; 8/29/95.

MIYAOKA, OSAHITO, Department of Linguistics, Faculty of Letters, Kyoto University, Japan. Sketch of Central Alaskan Yupik, an Eskimoan Language: 5/3/72; 6/7/93; 4/4/95.

NEWMAN, STANLEY (deceased), Department of Anthropology, University of New Mexico, Albuquerque. Sketch of the Zuni Language: 7/10/72; 3/20/74; 3/25/96.

RIGSBY, BRUCE, Department of Anthropology and Sociology, University of Queensland, Saint Lucia, Australia. Sketch of Sahaptin, a Sahaptian Language: 6/19/74; 1/6/94; 4/11/95.

ROOD, DAVID S., Department of Linguistics, University of Colorado, Boulder. Sketch of Lakhota, a Siouan Language: 8/1/75; 2/28/94; 4/11/95. Sketch of Wichita, a Caddoan Language: 5/9//72; 12/28/94; 6/5/95.

RUDE, NOEL, Departamento de Letras y Lingüística, Universidad de Sonora, Hermosillo, Mexico. Sketch of Sahaptin, a Sahaptian Language: 6/19/74; 1/6/94; 4/11/95.

SILVERSTEIN, MICHAEL, Department of Anthropology, University of Chicago, Illinois. Dynamics of Linguistic Contact : 8/15/73; 4/14/95; 1/25/96.

TAYLOR, ALLAN R. (emeritus), Department of Linguistics, University of Colorado, Boulder. Nonspeech Communication Systems: 6/26/72; 2/3/94; 12/13/95. Sketch of Lakhota, a Siouan Language: 8/1/75; 2/28/94; 4/11/95.

THOMPSON, LAURENCE C. (emeritus), Department of Linguistics, University of Hawaii, Honolulu. Sketch of Thompson, a Salishan Language: 3/13/73; 8/20/93; 3/27/95.

THOMPSON, M. TERRY, Department of Linguistics, University of Hawaii, Honolulu. Sketch of Thompson, a Salishan Language: 3/13/73; 8/20/93; 3/27/95.

TROIKE, RUDOLPH C., Department of English, University of Arizona, Tucson. Sketch of Coahuilteco, a Language Isolate of Texas: 8/17/73; 8/16/93; 4/6/95.

WALKER, WILLARD B. (emeritus), Department of Anthropology, Wesleyan University, Middletown, Connecticut. Native Writing Systems: 9/16/74; 2/3/94; 12/14/95.

WOLFART, H.C., Department of Linguistics, University of Manitoba, Winnipeg. Sketch of Cree, an Algonquian Language: 8/26/75; 4/12/95; 10/13/95.

Bibliography

This list includes all references cited in the volume, arranged in alphabetical order according to the names of the authors as they appear in the citations in the text. Multiple works by the same author are arranged chronologically; second and subsequent titles by the same author in the same year are differentiated by letters added to the dates. Where more than one author with the same surname is cited, one has been arbitrarily selected for text citation by surname alone throughout the volume, while the others are always cited with added initials; the combination of surname with date in text citations should avoid confusion. Where a publication date is different from the series date (as in some annual reports and the like), the former is used. Dates, authors, and titles that do not appear on the original works are enclosed by brackets. For manuscripts, dates refer to time of composition. For publications reprinted or first published many years after original composition, a bracketed date after the title refers to the time of composition or the date of original publication.

ARCIA = Commissioner of Indian Affairs
1849- Annual Reports of the Commissioner of Indian Affairs to the Secretary of the Interior. Washington: Government Printing Office. (Reprinted: AMS Press, New York, 1976-1977.)

Abbott, Clifford
1981 Here and There in Oneida. *International Journal of American Linguistics* 47(1):50-57.

1984 Two Feminine Genders in Oneida. *Anthropological Linguistics* 26(2):125-137. Bloomington.

Aberle, David F.
1974 Historical Reconstruction and Its Explanatory Role in Comparative Ethnology; a Study in Method. Pp. 63-79 in Comparative Studies by Harold E. Driver and Essays in His Honor. Joseph G. Jorgensen, ed. New Haven, Conn.: HRAF Press.

1984 The Language Family as a Field for Historical Reconstruction. *Journal of Anthropological Research* 40(1):129-136.

Adair, James
1775 The History of the American Indians. Particularly Those Nations Adjoining the Mississippi, East and West Florida, Georgia, South and North Carolina, and Virginia. London: Printed for Edward and Charles Dilly. (Reprinted as: Adair's History of the American Indians. Samuel C. Williams, ed. Watauga Press, Johnson City, Tenn., 1930.)

1930 Adair's History of the American Indians [1775]. Edited under the auspices of the National Society of the Colonial Dames of America, in Tennessee, by Samuel Cole Williams, LL.D. Johnson City, Tenn.: The Watauga Press. (Reprinted: Argonaut Press, New York, 1966; Promontory Press, New York, 1986.)

Adams, John W.
1973 The Gitksan Potlatch: Population Flux, Resource Ownership and Reciprocity. Toronto and Montreal: Holt, Rinehart and Winston of Canada.

Adams, William Y., Dennis P. Van Gerven, and Richard S. Levy
1978 The Retreat from Migrationism. Pp. 483-532 in Annual Review of Anthropology. Bernard J. Siegel, ed. Palo Alto, Calif.: Annual Reviews Inc.

Adamson, Thelma, ed. and coll.
1934 Folk-tales of the Coast Salish. *Memoirs of the American Folk-Lore Society* 27. New York. (Reprinted: Kraus Reprint, New York, 1969.)

Adelung, Johann C., and Johann S. Vater
1806-1817 Mithridates oder allgemeine Sprachenkunde mit dem Vater Unser als Sprachprobe in bey nahe fünf hundert Sprachen und Mundarten. 4 vols. (vol. 3 in 3 pts.). Berlin: Vossischen Buchhandlung.

Adler, Fred W.
1961 A Bibliographical Checklist of Chimakuan, Kutenai, Ritwan, Salishan, and Wakashan Linguistics. *International Journal of American Linguistics* 27(3):198-210.

Agar, Michael
1974 Ethnography and Cognition. Minneapolis: Burgess Publishing Company.

Aginsky, Burt W.
1943 Central Sierra. Culture Element Distributions 24. *University of California Anthropological Records* 8(4):393-468. Berkeley.

Ahenakew, Freda
1987 Cree Language Structures: A Cree Approach. Winnipeg, Man.: Pemmican Publications.

1989 Kiskinahamawâkan-âcimowinisa / Student Stories. Written by Cree-speaking Students. Ed., trans., and with a Glossary by Freda Ahenakew. 2d ed., rev. *Algonquian and Iroquoian Linguistics, Memoir* 2. Winnipeg.

Ahenakew, Freda, and H. Christoph Wolfart
1983 Productive Reduplication in Plains Cree. Pp. 369-377 in Actes du Quatorzième Congrès des Algonquinistes. William Cowan, ed. Ottawa: Carleton University.

_____, eds. and trans.
1991 John Beaverbone's Story As Retold by Joseph Tootoosis. Pp. 1-12 in Linguistic Studies Presented to John L. Finlay. H.C. Wolfart, ed. *Algonquian and Iroquoian Linguistics, Memoir* 8. Winnipeg.

_____, eds. and trans.
1992 Kôhkominawak Otâcimowiniwâwa / Our Grandmothers' Lives, as Told in Their Own Words. Told by Glecia Bear et al. Saskatoon, Sask.: Fifth House Publishers.

Ainslie, George
1876 Notes on the Grammar of the Nez Percés Language. *Bulletin of the U.S. Geological and Geographical Survey of the Territories* 2(3):217-277. Washington.

[1876a] Catechism for Young Children, Translated into the Nez Perces Language. Philadelphia: Presbyterian Board of Education.

Albert, Roy, and David Leedom Shaul, comps.
1985   A Concise Hopi and English Lexicon. Philadelphia: J. Benjamins.

Albright, Robert W.
1958   The International Phonetic Alphabet: Its Backgrounds and Development. *Indiana University Research Center in Anthropology, Folklore, and Linguistics Publication* 7. (*International Journal of American Linguistics* 24(1), Pt. 3). Bloomington.

Alcantara, Pedro
1852   Costanos Vocabulary. Pp. 494-505 in Vol. 2 of Historical and Statistical Information Respecting the History, Condition and Prospects of the Indian Tribes of the United States. H.R. Schoolcraft, ed. 6 vols. Philadelphia: Lippincott, Grambo.

Alexander, Edward P.
1971   An Indian Vocabulary from Fort Christanna, 1716. *Virginia Magazine of History and Biography* 79(3):303-313. Richmond.

Alford, Dan K., and Wayne E. Leman, comps.
1976   English-Cheyenne Student Dictionary. Lame Deer, Mont.: Research Department of the Northern Cheyenne Bilingual Education Program.

Alford, Richard D.
1988   Naming and Identity: A Cross-Cultural Study of Personal Naming Practices. New Haven, Conn.: HRAF Press.

Alford, Thomas Wildcat
1929   The Gospel of Our Lord and Saviour Jesus Christ according to Matthew; Translated into the Shawnee Indian Language... Being the Version Set Forth A.D. 1611, compared with the most Ancient Authorities and Revised A.D. 1881. Xenia, Ohio: Dr. W.A. Galloway / The Aldine Publishing Company. (Cover title: The Four Gospels Of Our Lord Jesus Christ In Shawnee Indian Language.)

Algeo, John
1973   On Defining the Proper Name. *University of Florida. Humanities Monograph* 41. Gainesville.

Allen, Barbara Jane, and Donald G. Frantz
1986   Goal Advancement in Southern Tiwa. *International Journal of American Linguistics* 52(4):388-403.

Allen, Louis
1931   Siouan and Iroquoian. *International Journal of American Linguistics* 6(3-4):185-193.

Allen, William
1856   Wunnissoo, or The Vale of Hoosatunnuk, a Poem, with Notes. Boston: J.P. Jewett.

Allouez, Claude Jean *see* Neilson, J.L. Hubert

Alvarez, Albert
1965   Some Papago Puns. *International Journal of American Linguistics* 31(1):106-107.

Alvarez, Albert, and Kenneth L. Hale
1970   Toward a Manual of Papago Grammar: Some Phonological Terms. *International Journal of American Linguistics* 36(2):83-97.

American Association for the Advancement of Science
1892   [Section H: Anthropology. Bibliographic Notes.] Pp. 374-376 in *Proceedings of the 40th Meeting of the American Association for the Advancement of Science, Held at Washington, D.C., August, 1891*. Salem, Mass.: Published by the Permanent Secretary.

American Bible Society
1860   [The Cherokee New Testament. 1st ed. Title and text in Cherokee syllabic characters.] New York: American Bible Society. (Several reprints, incl.: 1957, 1980.)

Anastasio, Angelo
1972   The Southern Plateau: An Ecological Analysis of Intergroup Relations. *Northwest Anthropological Research Notes* 6(2):109-229. Moscow, Idaho.

Anderson, Benedict R. O'G.
1991   Imagined Communities: Reflections on the Origin and Spread of Nationalism. 2d ed., rev. and extended. London and New York: Verso.

Anderson, Douglas D.
1968   A Stone Age Campsite at the Gateway to America. *Scientific American* 218(6):24-33.

————
1970   Akmak: An Early Archeolgical Assemblage from Onion Portage, Northwest Alaska. *Acta Arctica* 16. Copenhagen.

————
1970a   Microblade Traditions in Northwestern Alaska. *Arctic Anthropology* 7(2):2-16.

Anderson, Johann
1746   Herrn Johann Anderson, I.V.D. und weyland ersten Bürgermeisters der freyen Kayserlichen Reichstadt Hamburg, Nachrichten von Island, Grönland und der Strasse Davis, zum wahren Nutze der Wissenschaften und der Handlung. Hamburg: Georg Christian Grund.

Anderson, William
1784   Vocabulary of the Language of Prince William's Sound. Pp. 375-376 in Voyages to the Pacific Ocean, by J. Cook and J. King. Vol. 2. London.

Andrade, Manuel J.
1931   Quileute Texts. *Columbia University Contributions to Anthropology* 12. New York. (Reprinted: AMS Press, New York, 1969.)

————
1933   Quileute. [Extract] Pp. 151-292 in Pt. 3 of Handbook of American Indian Languages. Franz Boas, ed. New York: Columbia University Press.

André, Anne *see* Kapesh, An Antane

Andrews, H.A., et al.
1943   Bibliography of Franz Boas. *Memoirs of the American Anthropological Association* 61. Menasha, Wis.

Andrews, William, Henry Barclay, and John Ogilvie
1769   The Order for Morning and Evening Prayer, and Administration of Sacraments, and Some Other Offices of the Church. New York: W. Weyman and Hugh Gaine.

Angulo, Jaime de
1927   Textes en langue "Pomo" (Californie). *Journal de la Société des Américanistes de Paris*, n.s. 19:129-144.

1930-1935 Pomo Semasiology. (Manuscript [Freeman No. 3014/30 (H5.2)] in American Philosophical Society Library, Philadelphia.)

1930-1935a The Reminiscences of a Pomo Chief: The Auto-biography of William Ralganal Benson. (Manuscript [Freeman No. 3015/30(H5.3)] in American Philosophical Society Library, Philadelphia.)

1935   Pomo Creation Myth. *Journal of American Folk-Lore* 48(189):203-262.

Angulo, Jaime de, and Lucy S. Freeland
1928   Miwok and Pomo Myths. *Journal of American Folk-Lore* 41(160):232-252.

1930   The Achumawi Language. *International Journal of American Linguistics* 6(2):77-120.

1930-1935 The "Clear Lake" Dialect of the Pomo Language in North Central California. (Manuscript [Freeman No. 3016/30(H5.4)] in American Philosophical Society Library, Philadelphia.)

Angulo, Jaime de, and William Ralganal Benson
1932   The Creation Myth of the Pomo Indians. *Anthropos: Revue Internationale d'Ethnologie et de Linguistique* 27(1-2):261-274, (5-6):779-795. Wien.

Anonymous
1684   The Indian Interpreter. (Manuscript, Salem Town Records, Book B.64-68, in the State Archives of New Jersey, Trenton.)

1707   Another Tongue brought in, to Confess the Great Saviour of the World. Or, Some Communications of Christianity, Put into a Tongue used among the Iroquois Indians, in America. And, Put into the Hands of the English and the Dutch Traders: To accommodate the Great Intention of Communicating the Christian Religion, unto the Salvages, among whom they may find anything of this Language to be Intelligible. Boston: B. Green.

[1740]   [Untitled vocabulary of 400-500 entries, German-Creek, some English-Creek and Creek-German, in orthography largely based on Greek.] (Manuscript in unpaginated notebook, 169 pp., Box 3382 in Moravian Archives, Bethlehem, Pennsylvania. Microfilm: Moravian Mission Records, Reel 38, Research Publications, New Haven, Conn.)

1837   The Wea Primer. Wev mvs nv kv ne, to Teach the Wea Language. Cherokee Nation: Mission Press.

[1969]   [Drivers' Training Manual. Title and text in cursive Cherokee syllabic characters.] (Mimeographed copy in W. Walker's possession; and in Cherokee National Historical Society Archives, Tahlequah, Okla.)

1972   Choose Indian Junior Miss at Pageant. *Kainai News* June 1:3. Cardston, Alta.

1974   Digest of Northern Learning Materials. Compiled by the Alaska Native Language Center/CNER, University of Alaska, Fairbanks.

1986   Passamaquoddy-Maliseet Vowel Sounds. [Pleasant Point, Perry, Maine]: Passamaquoddy/Maliseet Bilingual Program.

1988   Passamaquoddy-Maliseet Dictionary. [Pleasant Point, Perry, Maine]: Passamaquoddy/Maliseet Bilingual Program.

1995   MacDonald Will Be Transferred to Missouri. *Navajo Times* Thursday, Sept. 21, 1995:1. Window Rock, Navajo Nation, Ariz.

Antane Kapesh, An *see* Kapesh, An Antane

Antoine, Francesca, et al.
1974   Central Carrier Bilingual Dictionary. Fort Saint James, B.C.: Carrier Linguistic Committee.

Antone, Angela, et al.
1981   Tekalihwathé:tha'. [Oneida Teaching Dictionary.] London, Ont.: Centre for the Research and Teaching of Canadian Native Languages, The University of Western Ontario.

Aoki, Haruo
1962   Nez Perce and Northern Sahaptin: A Binary Comparison. *International Journal of American Linguistics* 28(3):172-182.

1963   On Sahaptian-Klamath Linguistic Affiliations. *International Journal of American Linguistics* 29(2):107-112.

1966   Nez Perce and Proto-Sahaptian Kinship Terms. *International Journal of American Linguistics* 32(4):357-368.

1970   Nez Perce Grammar. *University of California Publications in Linguistics* 62. Berkeley.

1971   A Note on Language Change. Pp. 1-9 in Studies in American Indian Languages. Jesse Sawyer, ed. *University of California Publications in Linguistics* 65. Berkeley.

1975   The East Plateau Linguistic Diffusion Area. *International Journal of American Linguistics* 41(3):183-199.

1979   Nez Perce Texts. *University of California Publications in Linguistics* 90. Berkeley.

1994   Nez Perce Dictionary. *University of California Publications in Linguistics* 122. Berkeley.

Aoki, Haruo, and Deward E. Walker, Jr.
1989   Nez Perce Oral Narratives. *University of California Publications in Linguistics* 104. Berkeley.

Applegate, Richard B.
1972   Ineseño Grammar. (Unpublished Ph.D. Dissertation in Linguistics, University of California, Berkeley.)

1974   Chumash Place Names. *The Journal of California Anthropology* 1(2):187-205. Banning, Calif.

1974a   An Index of Chumash Placenames. Pp. 19-46 in Papers on the Chumash. *San Luis Obispo County Archaeological Society Occasional Paper* 9. San Luis Obispo, Calif.

1976   Reduplication in Chumash. Pp. 271-284 in Hokan Studies: Papers from the First Conference on Hokan Languages Held in San Diego, California, April 23-25, 1970. Margaret Langdon and Shirley Silver, eds. (*Janua Linguarum. Series Practica* 181). The Hague: Mouton.

Arima, Eugene Y.
1976   Views on Land Expressed in Inuit Oral Traditions. Pp. 217-222 in Vol. 2 of Report: Inuit Land Use and Occupancy Project. Milton M. R. Freeman, ed. Ottawa: Department of Indian and Northern Affairs, Canada.

Arroyo de la Cuesta, Felipe
1821   Idiomas Californias, 1821. (Manuscript in the Bancroft Library, University of California, Berkeley.)

1861   Extracto de la gramatica Mutsun, ó de la lengua de los naturales de la Mision San Juan Bautista. Grammar of the Mutsun Language Spoken at the Mission of San Juan Bautista, Alta California. *Shea's Library of American Linguistics* 4. New York: Cramoisy Press.

1862   A Vocabulary or Phrase Book of the Mutsun Language of Alta California. *Shea's Library of American Linguistics* 8. New York: Cramoisy Press.

1878   Idiomas Californias, 1821. (Manuscript, copied from the original by E.T. Murray in 1878, with an Introduction by A.S. Gatschet; No. 385 in National Anthropological Archives, Smithsonian Institution, Washington.)

Ashlock, Joe L.
1930   Moses Was My Grandfather. *The Washington Farmer*, June 12 (Vol. 62, No. 24). Spokane.

Atimoyoo, Rose, et al.
1987   A Preliminary Check-list of Plains Cree Medical Terms. Freda Ahenakew, ed. Saskatoon: Saskatchewan Indian Languages Institute.

Attla, Catherine
1989   Bakk'aatʉgh Ts'ʉhʉniy: Stories We Live By: Traditional Koyukon Athabaskan Stories told by Catherine Attla. Transcribed by Eliza Jones. Translated by Eliza Jones and Chad Thompson. Nenana, Alaska: Yukon Koyukuk School District; Fairbanks: Alaska Native Language Center, University of Alaska.

1990   K'etetaalkkaanee, The One Who Paddled Among the People and Animals. The Story of an Ancient Traveler, told by Catherine Attla; transcribed and translated by Eliza Jones. Nenana, Alaska: Yukon Koyukuk School District; Fairbanks: Alaska Native Language Center, University of Alaska.

Aubery, Joseph
1715   Dictionnaire abnaquis-françois. (Manuscript in Musée d'Odanak, Pierreville, Quebec.)

1715a   Dictionnaire françois-abnaquis. (Manuscript in Musée d'Odanak, Pierreville, Quebec.)

Aubin, George F.
1978   Toward the Linguistic History of an Algonquian Dialect: Observations on the Wood Vocabulary. Pp. 127-137 in Papers of the Ninth Algonquian Conference. William Cowan, ed. Ottawa: Carleton University.

Aupaumut, Hendrick
1827   A Narrative of an Embassy to the Western Indians, from the Original Manuscript of Hendrick Aupaumut, with Prefatory Remarks by Dr. B.H. Coates. *Memoirs of the Historical Society of Pennsylvania* 2(1):61-131. Philadelphia.

1854   [History of the Muh-he-ka-ne-ok Indians, 1790.] Pp. 14-23 in Stockbridge, Past and Present; or, Records of an Old Mission Station, by Electa F. Jones. Springfield, Mass.: Samuel Bowles.

Axelrod, Melissa
1990   Incorporation in Koyukon Athapaskan. *International Journal of American Linguistics* 56(2):179-195.

Bad Heart Bull, Amos, and Helen H. Blish
1967   A Pictographic History of the Oglala Sioux. Lincoln: University of Nebraska Press.

Baegert, Johann Jakob
1773   Nachrichten von der Amerikanischen Halbinsel Californien: mit einen zweyfachen Anhang falscher Nachrichten. Mannheim: Churfürstl. Hof- und Academie-Buchdruckerey.

1952   Observations in Lower California. M.M. Brandenburg and Carl L. Baumann, trans. and eds. Berkeley: University of California Press.

Bahn, Paul
1991   Dating the First American. *New Scientist* (July 20):26-28.

Bahr, Donald M.
1975   Pima and Papago Ritual Oratory: A Study of Three Texts. O'odham Ha-ñíokculida: Mámce Ab Wáikk Háʼicu Amjeḍ. San Francisco: Indian Historian Press.

Bailey, Richard W.
1991   Images of English: A Cultural History of the Language. Ann Arbor: University of Michigan Press.

Bakker, Peter (Pieter Jan)
1989   "The Language of the Coast Tribes is Half-Basque": A Basque-American Indian Pidgin, 1540-1640. *Anthropological Linguistics* 31(3-4):117-147. Bloomington.

1992   "A Language of Our Own": The Genesis of Michif, The Mixed Cree-French Language of the Canadian Métis. (Unpublished Ph.D. Dissertation in Linguistics, University of Amsterdam, The Netherlands.)

1994 Michif, the Cree-French Mixed Language of the Métis Buffalo Hunters in Canada. Pp. 13-33 in Mixed Languages: 15 Case Studies in Language Intertwining. Peter Bakker and Maarten Mous, eds. (*Studies in Language and Language Use* 13). Amesterdam: IFOTT.

1994a Interethnic Communication in Canada, Alaska and Adjacent Areas. (To appear in: Atlas of Interethnic Communication in the Pacific. S.A. Wurm, ed.)

Balbi, Adrien
1826 Atlas ethnographique du globe, ou classification des peuples anciens et modernes d'après leurs langues, précédé d'un discours sur l'utilité et l'importance de l'étude des langues appliquée a plusieurs branches des connaissances humaines...avec environs sept cent vocabulaires des principaux idiomes connus et suivi du tableu physique, moral et politique de cinq parties du monde. 2 vols. Paris: Rey et Gravier.

Balikci, Asen
1963 Shamanistic Behavior Among the Netsilik Eskimos. *Southwestern Journal of Anthropology* 19(4):380-396.

1967 Female Infanticide on the Arctic Coast. *Man*, n.s. 2(4):615-625.

Ball, Phyllis, comp.
1984 Berard Haile Papers: Inventory, Boxes 1-39; in the University of Arizona Library, Special Collections. Tucson: University of Arizona Library.

Ballard, Arthur C.
1929 Mythology of Southern Puget Sound. *University of Washington Publications in Anthropology* 3(2):31-150. Seattle.

Ballard, William L.
1975 Aspects of Yuchi Morphonology. Pp. 153-187 in Studies in Southeastern Indian Languages. James M. Crawford, ed. Athens: University of Georgia Press.

1978 More on Yuchi Pronouns. *International Journal of American Linguistics* 44(2):103-112.

Bancroft, Hubert H.
1875-1876 The Native Races of the Pacific States of North America. 5 vols. New York: D. Appleton.

Baraga, Fridrik
1837 Jesus Obimadisiwin Ajonda Aking, Gwaiakossing Anamiewin Ejitwadjig, mi sa Catholique-Enamiadjig Gewabandangig. Paris: E.J. Bailly.

1850 A Theoretical and Practical Grammar of the Otchipwe Language, the Language Spoken by the Chippewa Indians: Which is Also Spoken by the Algonquin, Otawa, and Potawatami Indians, with Little Difference. For the Use of Missionaries, and Other Persons Living Among the Indians of the Above Named Tribes. Detroit: Jabez Fox.

1853 A Dictionary of the Otchipwe Language, Explained in English. This Language is Spoken by the Chippewa Indians, as Also by the Otawas, Potawatamis and Algonquins, with Little Difference. For the Use of Missionaries, and Other Persons Living Among the Above Mentioned Indians. Detroit: Jabez Fox.

1855 Katolik Otawa Anamie-Misinaigan. 5th ed. Cincinnati, Ohio: Joseph A. Hemann.

1878 A Theoretical and Practical Grammar of the Otchipwe Language for the use of Missionaries and Other Persons Living Among the Indians. Montreal: Beauchemin and Valois.

1878-1880 A Dictionary of the Otchipwe Language, Explained in English. New ed. 2 vols. Montreal: Beauchemin and Valois. (Reprinted: Ross and Haines, Minneapolis, 1966, 1973.)

Barbeau, C. Marius
1913 On Iroquoian Field-Work, 1912. Pp. 454-460 in *Canada. Department of Mines. Sessional Papers* 26. *Summary Report of the Geological Survey for the Calendar Year 1912.* Ottawa. [1914.]

1913a On Interior Salish Work, 1912. Pp. 461-463 in *Canada. Department of Mines. Sessional Papers* 26. *Summary Report of the Geological Survey for the Calendar Year 1912.* Ottawa. [1914.]

1915 Classification of Iroquoian Radicals with Subjective Pronominal Prefixes. *Canada. Department of Mines. Geological Survey Memoir* 46, *Anthropological Series* 7. Ottawa.

1929 Totem Poles of the Gitksan, Upper Skeena River, British Columbia. *Canada. Department of Mines. National Museum Bulletin* 61, *Anthropological Series* 12. Ottawa.

1949 How the Huron-Wyandot Language was Saved from Oblivion. *Proceedings of the American Philosophical Society* 93(3):226-232. Philadelphia.

1957 Trésor des anciens Jésuites. *Musée National du Canada Bulletin* 153, *Série anthropologique* 43. Ottawa.

1960 Huron-Wyandot Traditional Narratives in Translations and Native Texts. *National Museum of Canada Bulletin* 165, *Anthropological Series* 47. Ottawa.

1961 The Language of Canada in the Voyages of Jacques Cartier (1534-1538). Pp. 108-229 in Contributions to Anthropology, 1959. *National Museum of Canada Bulletin* 173, *Anthropological Series* 50. Ottawa.

Barber, Edwin A.
1876 Language and Utensils of the Modern Utes. *Bulletin of the U.S. Geological and Geographical Survey of the Territories* 2(1):71-76. Washington.

1877　　　Comparative Vocabulary of Utah Dialects. *Bulletin of the U.S. Geological and Geographical Survey of the Territories* 3(3):533-545. Washington.

Barbour, Philip L.

1967　　　Chicahominy Place Names in Captain John Smith's *True Relation. Names* 15(3):60-71.

1969　　　The Jamestown Voyages Under the First Charter, 1606-1609: Documents Relating to the Foundation of Jamestown. 2 vols. *Works of the Hakluyt Society,* 2d ser., nos. 136-137. Cambridge: Cambridge University Press for the Hakluyt Society.

1972　　　The Earliest Reconnaissance of the Chesapeake Bay Area: Captain John Smith's Map and Indian Vocabulary. Pt. 2. *Virginia Magazine of History and Biography* 80(1):21-51. Richmond.

1976　　　Ocanahowan and Recently Discovered Linguistic Fragments from Southern Virginia, C. 1650. Pp. 2-17 in Papers of the Seventh Algonquian Conference. William Cowan, ed. Ottawa: Carleton University.

1979　　　Variant English Spellings of Virginia and Maryland Place-Names Before 1620. Pp. 43-59 in Papers of the Tenth Algonquian Conference, 1978. William Cowan, ed. Ottawa: Carleton University.

Barker, M.A.R.

1963　　　Klamath Texts. *University of California Publications in Linguistics* 30. Berkeley.

1963a　　　Klamath Dictionary. *University of California Publications in Linguistics* 31. Berkeley.

1964　　　Klamath Grammar. *University of California Publications in Linguistics* 32. Berkeley. (Reprinted: Kraus Reprint, Millwood, N.Y., 1981.)

Barnes, R.B.

1982　　　Personal Names and Social Classification. Pp. [211]-226 in Semantic Anthropology. David Parkin, ed. *ASA Monograph* 22. London [etc.]: Academic Press.

Barnes, R.H.

1980　　　Hidatsa Personal Names: An Interpretation. *Plains Anthropologist* 25(90):311-331.

1984　　　Two Crows Denies It: A History of Controversy in Omaha Sociology. Lincoln and London: University of Nebraska Press.

Barnes, William C.

1960　　　Arizona Place Names. Rev. and enl. by Byrd H. Granger. Tucson: University of Arizona Press.

Barratt, Joseph

1851　　　The Indian of New England and the North-eastern Provinces: A Sketch of the Life of an Indian Hunter, Ancient Traditions Relating to the Etchemin Tribe, Their Modes of Life, Fishing, Hunting, &c.; With Vocabularies in the Indian and English. Middletown, Conn.: Charles H. Pelton. (Reprinted: Davies Book Co./Osiris Publications, Montreal, 1973.)

Barrett, Samuel A.

1908　　　The Ethno-geography of the Pomo and Neighboring Indians. *University of California Publications in American Archaeology and Ethnology* 6(1):1-332. Berkeley.

1908a　　　The Geography and Dialects of the Miwok Indians. *University of California Publications in American Archaeology and Ethnology* 6(2). Berkeley. (Reprinted: Kraus Reprint, New York, 1964.)

1911　　　The Dream Dance of the Chippewa and Menominee Indians of Northern Wisconsin. *Bulletin of the Public Museum of the City of Milwaukee* 1(2):251-406.

1919　　　Myths of the Southern Sierra Miwok *University of California Publications in American Archaeology and Ethnology* 16(1):1-28. Berkeley. (Reprinted: Kraus Reprint, New York, 1965.)

1919　　　The Wintun Hesi Ceremony. *University of California Publications in American Archaeology and Ethnology* 14(4):437-488. Berkeley. (Reprinted: Kraus Reprint, New York, 1965.)

Barringer, George M., Hubert J. Cloke, Emmett Curran, and Jon K. Reynolds

1976　　　The American Mission: Maryland Jesuits from Andrew White to John Carroll (An Exhibit in the Special Collections Division, Georgetown University Library, 27 September-29 November, 1976). Washington.

Bartholinus, Thomas

1675　　　Vocabula gróenlandica collecta á Casp. Bartholino, J.U.D. Pp. 71-77 in *Acta Medica & Philosophica Hafniensia* 2. Copenhagen.

Bartlett, John R.

1852　　　Vocabulary of 180 Words; in the Language of the H'hana Indians of the Sacramento. (Manuscript No. 1627 [pp. 145-146] in National Anthropological Archives, Smithsonian Institution, Washington. Published: Pp. 503-508 in Tribes of California, by Stephen Powers. *Contributions to North American Ethnology.* 3. Washington, 1877. Reprinted: AMS, New York, 1976.)

Bartlett, John R., and F.W. Hodge

1909　　　The Language of the Piro. Introduction by F.W. Hodge. *American Anthropologist,* n.s. 11(3):426-433.

Barton, Benjamin Smith

1797　　　New Views of the Origin of the Tribes and Nations of America. Philadelphia: John Bioren, for The Author. (Reprinted: University Microfilms, Ann Arbor, 1968.)

1798　　　New Views of the Origin of the Tribes and Nations of America. 2d ed. Philadelphia: John Bioren, for The Author. (Reprinted: Kraus Reprint, New York, 1976.)

Bartram, William

1792　　　Travels through North and South Carolina, Georgia, East and West Florida, the Cherokee Country, the Extensive Territories of the Muscogulges or Creek Confederacy, and the Country of the Choctaws; [etc.]. London: Reprinted for J. Johnson. (Reprinted in facsimile: University of Virginia Press, Charlottesville, 1980.) *769*

Basgall, Mark E.
1982   Archaeology and Linguistics: Pomoan Prehistory as Viewed from Northern Sonoma County, California. *Journal of California and Great Basin Anthropology* 4(2):3-22.

Basilio, Tommaso
1737   Arte de la lengua cahita conforme à las reglas de muchos peritos en ella. Compuesto por un padre de la Compañia de Jesus, missionero de mas de treinta años en la provincia de Cynaloa. Mexico City: Impr. de D.F.X. Sanchez.

———
1890   Arte de la lengua cahita, por un padre de la Compañia de Jesús. Contiene las reglas gramaticales y un vocabulario de dicho idioma, usado por los Yaquis y los Mayos en el estado de Sonora y por algunos indios del Rio del Fuerte en el de Sinaloa, y un catecismo de la doctrina cristiana en cahita y español por otro padre de la misma Compañia...Con una introducción, notas y un pequeño diccionario, Eustaquio Buelna, ed. Mexico City: Impr. del Gobierno federal.

Bass, Althea
1936   Cherokee Messenger. Norman: University of Oklahoma Press. (Reprinted in 1968.)

Basse, Bjarne, and Kirsten Jensen, eds.
1979   Eskimo Languages: Their Present-Day Conditions. Aarhus, Denmark: Arkona.

Basso, Keith H.
1966   The Gift of Changing Woman. Pp. 113-173 in *Bureau of American Ethnology Bulletin* 196. *Anthropological Papers* 76. Washington.

———
1967   Semantic Aspects of Linguistic Acculturation. *American Anthropologist*, n.s. 69(5):471-477.

———
1969   Western Apache Witchcraft. *Anthropological Papers of the University of Arizona* 15. Tucson.

———
1970   "To Give up on Words": Silence in Western Apache Culture. *Southwestern Journal of Anthropology* 26(3):213-230. (Reprinted: Pp. 80-98 in Western Apache Language and Culture: Essays in Linguistic Anthropology, by Keith H. Basso. University of Arizona Press, Tucson, 1990.)

———
1984   "Stalking with Stories": Names, Places, and Moral Narratives among the Western Apache. Pp. 19-55 in Text, Play, and Story: The Construction and Reconstruction of Self and Society. Edward M. Bruner, ed. *1983 Proceedings of The American Ethnological Society*. Washington. (Reprinted: Pp. 99-107 in Western Apache Language and Culture: Essays in Linguistic Anthropology, by Keith H. Basso. University of Arizona Press, Tucson, 1990.)

———
1984a   Western Apache Place-Name Hierarchies. Pp. 78-94 in Naming Systems. Elizabeth Tooker, ed. (*1980 Proceedings of the American Ethnological Society*.) Washington: AES.

———
1988   "Speaking with Names": Language and Landscape among the Western Apache. *Cultural Anthropology* 3(2):99-130. (Reprinted: Pp. 138-173 in Western Apache Language and Culture, by Keith H. Basso. University of Arizona Press, Tucson, 1990.)

Basso, Keith H., and Ned Anderson
1973   A Western Apache Writing System: The Symbols of Silas John. *Science* 180(4090/June 8):1013-1022.

Bateman, Richard M., et al.
1990   Speaking of Forked Tongues: The Feasibility of Reconciling Human Phylogeny and the History of Language. *Current Anthropology* 31(1):1-24.

———
1990a   On Human Phylogeny and Linguistic History: Reply to Comments. *Current Anthropology* 31(2):177-183.

Bates, Dawn, Thom Hess, and Vi Hilbert
1994   Lushootseed Dictionary. Dawn Bates, ed. Seattle and London: University of Washington Press.

Bauman, James J.
1980   A Guide to Issues in Indian Language Retention. Washington, D.C.: Center for Applied Linguistics.

———
1980a   Chimariko Placenames and the Boundaries of Chimariko Territory. Pp. 11-29 in American Indian and Indoeuropean Studies: Papers in Honor of Madison S. Beeler. Kathryn Klar, Margaret Langdon, and Shirley Silver, eds. *Trends in Linguistics, Studies and Monographs* 16. The Hague: Mouton.

Bauman, James J., with Ruby Miles and Ike Leaf, comps.
1979   Pit River Teaching Dictionary. Anchorage: National Bilingual Materials Development Center, Rural Education Affairs, University of Alaska.

Baumhoff, Martin A.
1958   California Athabascan Groups. *University of California Anthropological Records* 16(5):157-238. Berkeley.

Baumhoff, Martin A., and David L. Olmsted
1963   Palaihnihan: Radiocarbon Support for Glottochronology. *American Anthropologist* 65(2):278-284.

———
1964   Notes on Palaihnihan Culture History: Glottochronology and Archaeology. Pp. 1-12 in Studies in Californian Linguistics. William Bright, ed. *University of California Publications in Linguistics* 34. Berkeley and Los Angeles.

Bauxar, J. Joseph
1957   Yuchi Ethnoarchaeology. Parts I-V. *Ethnohistory* 4(3):279-301, (4):369-464.

Beaglehole, Ernest, and Pearl Beaglehole
1935   Hopi of the Second Mesa. *American Anthropological Association Memoir* 44. Menasha, Wis.

Beaglehole, John C., ed.
1967   The Journals of Captain James Cook on His Voyages of Discovery. 4 vols. and portfolio. Vol. 3: The Voyage of the *Resolution* and *Discovery*, 1776-1780. 2 pts. (*Hakluyt Society Extra Series* 36.) Cambridge: Cambridge University Press for the Hakluyt Society.

Beals, Ralph L.
1933   Ethnology of the Nisenan. *University of California Publications in American Archaeology and Ethnology* 31(6):335-414. Berkeley.

_____
1943   The Aboriginal Culture of the Cáhita Indians. *Ibero-Americana* 19. Berkeley.

_____
1945   The Contemporary Culture of the Cáhita Indians. *Bureau of American Ethnology Bulletin* 142. Washington.

Bean, Lowell John
1972   Mukat's People: The Cahuilla Indians of Southern California. Berkeley: University of California Press.

Bean, Susan S.
1980   Ethnology and the Study of Proper Names. *Anthropological Linguistics* 22(7):305-316.

Bear, Glecia *see* Nêhiyaw / Bear, Glecia

Beardsley, Richard K.
1954   Temporal and Areal Relationships in Central California Archaeology. *University of California Archaeological Survey Reports* 24, 25. Berkeley.

Beardy, L.
1988   Pisiskiwak Kâ-pîkiskwêcik / Talking Animals. Ed. and trans. [and with a Glossary] by H.C. Wolfart. *Algonquian and Iroquoian Linguistics, Memoir* 5. Winnipeg, Man.

Beattie, Judith H.
1985-1986 Indian Maps in the Hudson's Bay Company Archives: A Comparison of Five Area Maps Recorded by Peter Fidler, 1801-1802. *Archivaria* 21:166-175. Ottawa.

Beauchamp, William M.
1881   The Indian Prayer Book. *The Church Eclectic* 9(5):415-422. Utica, N.Y.

_____
1892   The Iroquois Trail, or Foot-prints of the Six Nations, in Customs, Traditions, and History. Fayetteville, N.Y.: Printed by H.C. Beauchamp, Recorder Office.

_____
1893   Indian Names in New York, with a Selection from Other States. Fayetteville, N.Y.: The Author.

_____
1907   Civil, Religious and Mourning Councils and Ceremonies of Adoption of the New York Indians. *New York State Museum, Bulletin* 113, *Archeology* 13. Albany. (Reprinted: The University of the State of New York, the State Education Department, Albany, 1975.)

_____
1907a   Aboriginal Place Names of New York. *New York State Museum, Bulletin* 108, *Archaeology* 12. Albany. (Reprinted: Grand River Books, Detroit, Mich., 1971.)

Beaumont, Ronald C.
1973   Sechelt Statives. *Canadian Journal of Linguistics* 18(2):102-112.

_____
1985   She Shashishalhem / The Sechelt Language: Language, Stories and Sayings of the Sechelt Indian People of British Columbia. Penticton, B.C.: Theytus Books.

Beck, Horace
1947   Algonquin Folklore from Maniwaki. *Journal of American Folk-Lore* 60(237):259-264.

Becker, Donald W.
1964   Indian Place Names in New Jersey. Cedar Grover, N.J.: Phillips-Campbell Publishing.

Bee, Robert L.
1963   Changes in Yuma Social Organization. *Ethnology* 2(2):207-227.

Beeler, Madison S.
1954   Sonoma, Carquinez, Umunhum, Colma: Some Disputed California Names. *Western Folklore* 13(4):268-277.

_____
1955   Saclan. *International Journal of American Linguistics* 21(3):201-209.

_____
1957   On Etymologizing Indian Place-Names. *Names* 5(4):236-240.

_____
1959   Saclan Once More. *International Journal of American Linguistics* 25(1):67-68.

_____
1961   Northern Costanoan. *International Journal of American Linguistics* 27(3):191-197.

_____
1966   Hueneme. *Names* 20(1):56-59.

_____
1967   The Ventureño Confesionario of José Sénan, O.F.M. *University of California Publications in Linguistics* 47. Berkeley.

_____
1971   Nopṭinṭe Yokuts. Pp. 11-76 in Studies in American Indian Languages. Jesse Sawyer, ed. *University of California Publications in Linguistics* 65. Berkeley.

_____
1972   An Extension of San Francisco Bay Costanoan? *International Journal of American Linguistics* 38(1):49-54.

_____
1976   Barbareño Chumash Grammar: A Farrago. Pp. 251-269 in Hokan Studies: Papers from the First Conference on Hokan Languages Held in San Diego, California, April 23-25, 1970. Margaret Langdon and Shirley Silver, eds. *Janua Linguarum, Series Practica* 181. The Hague and Paris: Mouton.

_____
1977   The Sources for Esselen: A Critical Review. Pp. 37-45 in *Proceedings of the Third Annual Meeting of the Berkeley Linguistic Society*. Berkeley.

_____
1978   Esselen. *The Journal of California Anthropology, Papers in Linguistics* 1:3-37. Banning, Calif.

_____
1978a   Barbareño Chumash Text and Lexicon. Pp. 171-193 in Linguistic and Literary Studies in Honor of Archibald A. Hill. Vol. 2: Descriptive Linguistics. Mohammad Ali Jazayery, Edgar C. Polomé, and Werner Winter, eds. *Trends in Linguistics, Studies and Monographs* 8. The Hague and New York: Mouton Publishers.

771

Beeler, Madison S., and Kenneth W. Whistler
1980   Coyote, Hawk, Raven and Skunk (Barbareño Chumash).
        Pp. 88-96 in Coyote Stories, II. Martha B. Kendall, ed.
        *International Journal of American Linguistics. Native
        American Texts Series, Monograph* 6. Chicago: The
        University of Chicago Press.

Béland, Jean-Pierre
1978   Atikamekw Morphology and Lexicon. (Ph.D. Dis-
        sertation in Linguistics, University of California,
        Berkeley.)

Belcourt, George Antoine
1839   Principes de la langue des sauvages appelés Sauteux.
        Quebéc: Fréchette.

Bell, Robert
1891   Meanings of Indian Geographical Names in the Country
        Around Sudbury. Pp. 91F-95F of Report on the Sudbury
        Mining District. *Annual Report for the Geological
        Survey of Canada*, n.s. 5, Pt. 1. Ottawa: S.E. Dawson.

Beltrami, J.C. "Giacomo Costantino"
1962   A Pilgrimage in America Leading to the Discovery of
        the Sources of the Mississippi and Bloody River; With a
        Description of the Whole Course of the Former, and of
        the Ohio. Chicago: Quadrangle Books. (First English
        ed.: Hunt and Clarke, London, 1828.)

Benavides, Alonso de
1916   The Memorial of Fray Alonso de Benavides, 1630. Mrs.
        Edward E. Ayer, trans. Frederick W. Hodge and Charles
        F. Lummis, eds. Chicago: Privately Printed. (Reprinted:
        Horn and Wallace, University of New Mexico Press,
        Albuquerque.)

_____
1945   Fray Alonso de Benavides' Revised Memorial of 1634,
        with Numerous Supplementary Documents Elaborately
        Annotated. Frederick W. Hodge, George P. Hammond,
        and Agapito Rey, eds. Albuquerque: The University of
        New Mexico Press.

Benedict, Ruth
1932   Configurations of Culture in North America. *American
        Anthropologist*, n.s. 34(1):1-27.

Bennett, Jo Anne, and John W. Berry
1989   The Meaning and Value of the Syllabic Script for Native
        People. Pp. 31-42 in Actes du Vingtième Congrès des
        Algonquinistes. William Cowan, ed. Ottawa: Carleton
        University.

Bennett, Wendell C., and Robert M. Zingg
1935   The Tarahumara: An Indian Tribe of Northern Mexico.
        *University of Chicago Publications in Anthropology:
        Ethnological Series*. Chicago: The University of
        Chicago Press.

Benson, William Ralganal
1932   The Stone and Kelsey "Massacre" on the Shores of Clear
        Lake in 1849: The Indian Viewpoint. Introduction by
        Max Radin. *California Historical Society Quarterly*
        11(3):266-272. San Francisco.

Berghaus, Heinrich
1852   Allgemeiner ethnographischer Atlas; oder Atlas der
        Völkerkunde. Gotha: Justus Perthes.

Bergsland, Knut
1956   A Grammatical Outline of the Eskimo Language of West
        Greenland. Oslo. (Mimeographed.)

_____
1958   Aleut and Proto-Eskimo. Pp. 624-631 in *Proceedings of
        the 32d International Congress of Americanists,
        Copenhagen, 1956*. Copenhagen: Munksgaard.

_____
1958a   Is Lexico-statistic Dating Valid? Pp. 654-657 in *Pro-
        ceedings of the 32d International Congress of Ameri-
        canists, Copenhagen, 1956*. Copenhagen: Munksgaard.

_____
1959   Aleut Dialects of Atka and Attu. *Transactions of the
        American Philosophical Society*, n.s. 49(3). Philadelphia.

_____
1959a   The Eskimo-Uralic Hypothesis. *Journal de la Société
        Finno-ougrienne* 61(2):1-29. Helsinki.

_____
1986   Comparative Eskimo-Aleut Phonology and Lexicon.
        Journal de la Société Finno-ougrienne 80:63-137.
        Helsinki.

_____
1989   Comparative Aspects of Aleut Syntax. *Journal de la
        Société Finno-ougrienne* 82:7-80. Helsinki.

_____
1994   Aleut Dictionary, *Unangam Tunudgusii*: An Unabridged
        Lexicon of the Aleutian, Pribilof, and Commander
        Islands Aleut Language. Fairbanks: University of
        Alaska, Alaska Native Language Center.

Bergsland, Knut, and Moses Dirks, comps.
1978   Introduction to Atkan Aleut Grammar and Lexicon.
        Anchorage: University of Alaska, National Bilingual
        Materials Development Center.

_____
1990   Unangam Ungiikangin Kayux Tunusangin. Unangam
        Uniikangis Ama Tunuzangis. Aleut Tales and Narra-
        tives, collected by Waldemar Jochelson. Fairbanks:
        Alaska Native Language Center.

Bergsland, Knut, and Hans Vogt
1962   On the Validity of Glottochronology. *Current Anthro-
        pology* 3(2):115-129, 148-153.

Berlandier, Jean Louis, and Rafael Chowell
1828-1829 [Vocabularies of Languages of South Texas and the
        Lower Rio Grande.] (Manuscript, Additional Manu-
        scripts No. 38720, British Library, London.)

Berlin, Brent
1972   Speculations on the Growth of Ethnobotanical Nomen-
        clature. *Language in Society* 1(1):51-86. Cambridge.

Berlin, Brent, Dennis E. Breedlove, and Peter H. Raven
1973   General Principles of Classification and Nomenclature
        in Folk Biology. *American Anthropologist* 75(1):214-
        242.

Berman, Howard
1972   Subordinate Clauses in Yurok: A Preliminary Report.
        Pp. 256-261 in The Chicago Which Hunt: Papers from
        the Relative Clause Festival. Chicago: The Chicago
        Linguistic Society.

772

1980   Two Chukchansi Coyote Stories. Pp. 56-70 in Coyote Stories II. Martha B. Kendall, ed. *International Journal of American Linguistics. Native American Texts Series, Monograph* 6. Chicago: The University of Chicago Press.

1981   [Review of] The Languages of Native America: Historical and Comparative Assessment, ed. by Lyle Campbell and Marianne Mithun, 1979. *International Journal of American Linguistics* 47(3):248-262.

1982   Two Phonological Innovations in Ritwan. *International Journal of American Linguistics* 48(4):412-420.

1982a   A Supplement to Robins's Yurok-English Lexicon. *International Journal of American Linguistics* 48(2): 197-222.

1983   Some California Penutian Morphological Elements. *International Journal of American Linguistics* 49(4): 400-412.

1984   Proto-Algonquian-Ritwan Verbal Roots. *International Journal of American Linguistics* 50(3):335-342.

1990   An Outline of Kalapuya Historical Phonology. *International Journal of American Linguistics* 56(1):27-59.

1990a   New Algonquian-Ritwan Cognate Sets. *International Journal of American Linguistics* 56(3):431-434.

1992   A Comment on the Yurok and Kalapuya Data in Greenberg's *Language in the Americas*. *International Journal of American Linguistics* 58(2):230-233.

Berman, Judith
1991   The Production of the Boas-Hunt Kwakw'ala Texts. (Paper presented at the 26th International Conference on Salish and Neighbouring Languages, Vancouver, B.C.)

1992   Oolachan-Woman's Robe: Fish, Blankets, Masks, and Meaning in Boas's Kwakw'ala Texts. Pp. 125-162 in On the Translation of Native American Literatures. Bryan Swann, ed. Washington: Smithsonian Institution Press.

1994   George Hunt and the Kwak'wala Texts. *Anthropological Linguistics* 36(4):483-514.

Bertelsen, Alfred
1918   Navnegivning i Grønland. [Personal Names in Greenland.] *Meddelelser om Grønland* 56:221-287. Copenhagen.

Berthelsen, Christian
1990   Greenlandic in Schools. Pp. 333-339 in Arctic Languages: An Awakening. Dirmid R.F. Collis, ed. Paris: Unesco.

1990a   Greenlandic Literature. Pp. 343-353, 363-364 in Arctic Languages: An Awakening. Dirmid R.F. Collis, ed. Paris: Unesco.

Berton, Francis
1878   Vocabulaire des indiens de la vallée de Napa et du Clear Lake en Californie [1851]. Geneva: F. Turrettini.

Bessell, Nicola E.
1992   Towards a Phonetic and Phonological Typology of Post-Velar Articulation. (Unpublished Ph.D. Dissertation in Linguistics, The University of British Columbia, Vancouver.)

Bettinger, Robert L., and Martin A. Baumhoff
1982   The Numic Spread: Great Basin Cultures in Competition. *American Antiquity* 47(3):485-503.

Beverley, Robert
1722   The History of Virginia, in Four Parts. 2d ed., rev. and enl. London: F. Fayram and J. Clarke, and T. Bickerton.

1947   The History and Present State of Virginia [1705]. Louis B. Wright, ed. Chapel Hill: University of North Carolina Press. (Reprinted: Dominion Books, Charlottesville, Va., 1968.)

Bevis, William
1974   American Indian Verse Translations. *College English* 35(6):693-703.

Bierhorst, John
1985   The Mythology of North America. New York: William Morrow.

Biggar, Henry P., ed.
1924   The Voyages of Jacques Cartier: Published from the Originals with Translations, Notes, and Appendices. *Publications of the Public Archives of Canada* 11. Ottawa.

Binford, Lewis R.
1967   An Ethnohistory of the Nottoway, Meherrin and Weanock Indians of Southeastern Virginia. *Ethnohistory* 14(3-4):104-218.

Binney, George
1931   The Eskimo Book of Knowledge... Rendered into the Labrador Dialect... . W.W. Perrett and S.K. Hutton, trans. London: Hudson's Bay Company.

Birch, Sampson, comp.
1835   Cahta Holisso, Cikosi aikhana. Shawanoe Baptist Mission, Indian Terr.: J. Meeker.

Birket-Smith, Kaj
1928   Five Hundred Eskimo Words. A Comparative Vocabulary from Greenland and Central Eskimo Dialects. *Report of the Fifth Thule Expedition 1921-24.* Vol. 3(3). Copenhagen: Gyldendalske.

1929   The Caribou Eskimos: Material and Social Life and Their Cultural Position. *Report of the Fifth Thule Expedition, 1921-1924*, Vol. 5(1-2). Copenhagen.

1953   The Chugach Eskimo. *Nationalmuseet. Nationalmuseets Skrifter, Etnografisk Række* 6. Copenhagen.

1959   The Eskimos. W.E. Calvert, trans. Revised by C. Daryll Forde. London: Methuen.

Birket-Smith, Kaj, and Frederica de Laguna
1938   The Eyak Indians of the Copper River Delta, Alaska. København: Levin & Munksgaard.

Bittle, William E.
1963 Kiowa-Apache. Pp. 76-101 in Studies in the Athapaskan Languages. Harry Hoijer, ed. *University of California Publications in Linguistics* 29. Berkeley.

Black, Lydia T.
1977 Ivan Pan'kov—An Architect of Aleut Literacy. *Arctic Anthropology* 14(1):94-107. Madison.

Black, Robert A.
1967 Hopi Grievance Chants: A Mechanism of Social Control. Pp. 54-67 in Studies in Southwestern Ethnolinguistics. Dell Hymes and William E. Bittle, eds. The Hague and Paris: Mouton.

Black, Samuel
1829 [Report by Chief Trader Samuel Black to the Governor and Committee of the Hudson's Bay Company, dated 'Willa Walla' 25 March 1829.] (Manuscript B.146/e/2, fo. 20(N3216) in Hudson's Bay Company Archives, Winnipeg, Man.)

Black-Rogers, Mary
1991 [Review of] Nichols, John D., ed., "Statement by the Indians": A Bilingual Petition of the Chippewas of Lake Superior, 1864 [and] An Ojibwe Text Anthology. *The American Indian Quarterly* 15(2):245-247. Berkeley.

Blackbird, Andrew J.
1887 History of the Ottawa and Chippewa Indians of Michigan; A Grammar of Their Language, and Personal and Family History of the Author. Ypsilanti, Mich.: The Ypsilantian Job Printing House. (Reprinted as: Complete Both Early and Late History of the Ottawa and Chippewa Indians of Michigan [etc.]. Babcock and Darling, Harbor Springs, Mich., 1897.)

Blackman, Margaret B.
1973 Totems to Tombstones: Culture Change as Viewed Through the Haida Mortuary Complex, 1877-1971. *Ethnology* 12(1):47-56.

Blain, Eleanor M.
1994 Emphatic *wiya* in Plains Cree. (Paper presented at the Twenty-sixth Algonquian Conference, Winnipeg.)

Blanchard, Ira D.
1834 Linapi'e Lrkvekun, Apwivuli Kavuni Vawinj Wato. Shawnee Mission, Indian Terr.: J. Meeker.

Blin-Lagarde, Pierrette
1972 Une étude historique dans les langues de la famille huronne-iroquoise. (Unpublished M.A. Thesis in Linguistics, McGill University, Montreal.)

Blomkvist, E.E.
1975 Istoriâ izucheniiâ v Rossii îazykov severoamerikanskikh indeĭtsev (iz arkhiva). [History of the Study of North American Indian Languages in Russia (from Archives)]. (Manuscript in Sbornik Muzee Antropologii i Etnografii, Inst. Etnografii, Russian Academy of Sciences, Moscow.)

Bloomfield, Leonard
1909 A Šemasiologic Differentation in Germanic Secondary Ablaut. (Ph.D. Dissertation in Linguistics, University of Chicago; Published in: *Modern Philology* (Oct., 1909):245-288; (Jan., 1910):345-382.)

1914 An Introduction to the Study of Language. New York: Henry Holt and Co.; London: G. Bell. (Reprinted: Joseph F. Kess, ed. John Benjamins, Amsterdam, 1983.)

1917 Tagalog Texts with Grammatical Analysis. 3 Pts. Urbana: University of Illinois. (Reprinted: Johnson Reprint Corp., New York, 1967.)

1917a Subject and Predicate. *Transactions and Proceedings of the American Philological Association [for] 1916*, vol. 47:13-22. Boston.

1925 On the Sound-System of Central Algonquian. *Language: Journal of the Linguistic Society of America* 1(4):130-156.

1925a Why a Linguistic Society? *Language: Journal of the Linguistic Society of America* 1(1):1-5.

1926 A Set of Postulates for the Science of Language. *Language: Journal of the Linguistic Society of America* 2(3):153-164. (Reprinted: *International Journal of American Linguistics* 15(4):195-202, 1949.)

1927 Literate and Illiterate Speech. *American Speech* 2(10):432-439. Baltimore. (Reprinted: Pp. 391-396 in Language in Culture and Society. Dell Hymes, ed. Harper and Row, New York, 1964; and Pp. 147-156 in A Leonard Bloomfield Anthology. Charles F. Hockett, ed. Indiana University Press, Bloomington, 1970.)

1928 The Plains Cree Language. Pp. 427-431 in Vol. 2 of *Atti del XXII Congresso Internazionale degli Americanisti. Roma, settembre 1926. [Proceedings of the 22d International Congress of Americanists]*. 2 vols. Rome.

1928a Menomini Texts. *Publications of The American Ethnological Society* 12. New York: G.E. Stechert. (Reprinted: AMS Press, New York, 1974.)

1930 Sacred Stories of the Sweet Grass Cree. *Canada. National Museum Bulletin* 60, *Anthropological Series* 11. Ottawa. (Reprinted: AMS Press, New York, 1976; Fifth House, Saskatoon, Sask., 1993.)

1933 Language. New York: Holt, Rinehart and Winston. (Reprinted, with a new Foreword by Charles F. Hockett: University of Chicago Press, Chicago, 1984.)

1934 Plains Cree Texts. *Publications of The American Ethnological Society* 16. New York: G.E. Stechert & Co. (Reprinted: AMS Press, New York, 1974.)

1939 Menomini Morphophonemics. Pp. 105-115 in Etudes phonologiques dediées à la mémoire de M. le Prince N.S. Trubetzkoy. *Travaux du Cercle Linguistique de Prague* 8. Prague. (Reprinted: Pp. 351-362 in A Leonard Bloomfield Anthology. Charles F. Hockett, ed. Indiana University Press, Bloomington, 1970.)

1946 Algonquian. Pp. 85-129 in Linguistic Structures of Native America. Harry Hoijer, ed. *Viking Fund Publications in Anthropology* 6. New York: Wenner Gren.

1957   Eastern Ojibwa: Grammatical Sketch, Texts and Word List. Charles F. Hockett, ed. Ann Arbor: University of Michigan Press.

1962   The Menomini Language. [Charles F. Hockett, ed.] New Haven, Conn.: Yale University Press.

1972   The Original Preface to Linguistic Structures of Native America. *International Journal of American Linguistics* 38(4):265-266.

1975   Menomini Lexicon. Charles F. Hockett, ed. *Milwaukee Public Museum Publications in Anthropology and History* 3. Milwaukee. (The spelling 'Menominee' appears on the cover.)

1984   Cree-English Lexicon. 2 vols. (*HRAFlex Books* NG4-001. *Language and Literature Series: Native American Linguistics* 2). New Haven, Conn.: Human Relations Area Files.

Bloomfield, Leonard, and John D. Nichols
1991   The Dog's Children: Anishinabe Texts Told by Angeline Williams. Ed. and trans. by Leonard Bloomfield. Newly ed. and with a Glossary by John D. Nichols. (*Publications of the Algonquian Text Society*). Winnipeg: The University of Manitoba Press.

Boas, Franz
1881   Beiträge zur Erkentniss der Farbe des Wassers. (Inaugural-Dissertation zu Erlangung der philosophischen Doctorwürde). Kiel: Schmidt und Klaunig.

1885   The Eskimo of Baffin Land. *Transactions of the Anthropological Society of Washington* 3:95-102. Washington.

1888   The Central Eskimo. Pp. 399-669 in *6th Annual Report of the Bureau of [American] Ethnology for 1884-1885.* Washington.

1889   On Alternating Sounds. *American Anthropologist*, o.s. 2(1):47-53.

1889a   [Letter to Henry W. Henshaw, October 20, 1889.] (Manuscript, Letters Received, in Bureau of American Ethnology Correspondence Files, National Anthropological Archives, Smithsonian Institution, Washington.)

1890   [Letter to Henry W. Henshaw, May 16, 1890.] (Manuscript, Letters Received, in Bureau of American Ethnology Correspondence Files, National Anthropological Archives, Smithsonian Institution, Washington.)

1890a   [Letter to Henry W. Henshaw, November 20, 1890.] (Manuscript, Letters Received, in Bureau of American Ethnology Correspondence Files, National Anthropological Archives, Smithsonian Institution, Washington.)

1890b   [Letter to Henry W. Henshaw, December 6, 1890.] (Manuscript, Letters Received, in Bureau of American Ethnology Correspondence Files, National Anthropological Archives, Smithsonian Institution, Washington.)

1891   Second General Report on the Indians of British Columbia. Pp. 562-715 in *60th Annual Report of the British Association for the Advancement of Science for 1890.* London.

1892   Notes on the Chemakum Language. *American Anthropologist*, o.s. 5(1):37-44.

1893   Vocabulary of the Kwakiutl Language. *Proceedings of the American Philosophical Society* 31(140):34-82. Philadelphia.

1894   Classification of the Languages of the North Pacific Coast. Pp. 339-346 in Memoirs of the International Congress of Anthropology. C. Staniland Wake, ed. Chicago: Schulte.

1894a   Chinook Texts. *Bureau of American Ethnology Bulletin* 20. Washington.

1894b   Der Eskimo-Dialekt des Cumberland-Sundes. *Mittheilungen der Anthropologischen Gesellschaft in Wien* 24:97-114. Vienna.

1895   Indianische Sagen von der Nord-pacifischen Küste Amerikas. Berlin: A. As[c]her. (Reprinted: Holos Verlag, Bonn, Germany, 1992.)

1895a   The Indians of British Columbia: Physical Characteristics of the Tribes of the North Pacific Coast, the Tinneh Tribe of Nicola Valley, the Ts'ᴇts'ā´ut, the Nîsk·a´, Linguistics of Nîsk·a´ and Ts'ᴇts'ā´ut , Vocabulary of the Tinneh Tribes of Canada. Pp. 523-592 in *65th Annual Report of the British Association for the Advancement of Science for 1894.* London.

1897   The Social Organization and the Secret Societies of the Kwakiutl Indians. Pp. 311-738 in *Report of the U.S. National Museum for 1895.* Washington. (Reprinted: Johnson Reprint, New York, 1970.)

1899   Linguistics: The Ntlakya´pamuǫ. Pp. 654-663 in *68th Report of the British Association for the Advancement of Science for 1898.* London.

1901   Kathlamet Texts. *Bureau of American Ethnology Bulletin* 26. Washington. (Reprinted: Scholarly Press, St. Clair Shores, Mich., 1977.)

1901-1907   The Eskimo of Baffin Land and Hudson Bay; from Notes Collected by Capt. George Comer, Capt. James S. Mutch and Rev. E.J. Peck. 2 vols. *Bulletin of the American Museum of Natural History* 15. New York. (Reprinted: AMS Press, New York, 1975.)

1902   Tsimshian Texts [Nass River Dialect]. *Bureau of American Ethnology Bulletin* 27. Washington. (Reprinted: Scholarly Press, St. Clair Shores, Mich., 1977; Native American Book Publishers, Brighton, Mich., 1990.)

1904   The Vocabulary of the Chinook Language. *American Anthropologist*, n.s. 6(1):118-147.

1905   The Jesup North Pacific Expedition. Pp. 91-100 in *Proceedings of the 13th International Congress of Americanists, Held in New York in 1902*. Easton, Penn.: Eschenbach Printing Co.

1907   Notes on the Ponka Grammar. (Extrait des Mémoires et Délibérations du XVe Congrès des Américanistes Tenu à Québec, du 10 au 15 Septembre 1906.) Québec: Dussault et Proulx.

1909   The Kwakiutl of Vancouver Island. *Publications of the Jesup North Pacific Expedition* 5(2):301-522; *Memoirs of the American Museum of Natural History* 8(2). New York. (Reprinted: AMS Press, New York, 1975.)

1910   Kwakiutl Tales. *Columbia University Contributions to Anthropology* 2. New York. (Reprinted: AMS Press, New York, 1969.)

1910a   Ethnological Problems in Canada. *Journal of the Royal Anthropological Institute of Great Britain and Ireland* 40:529-539. London. (Reprinted: Pp. 331-343 in Race, Language and Culture by Franz Boas. New York, Macmillan, 1940.)

1911   Introduction. Pp. 5-83 in Pt. 1 of Handbook of American Indian Languages. Franz Boas, ed. *Bureau of American Ethnology Bulletin* 40. Washington. (Reprinted as: Introduction to *Handbook of American Indian Languages*, with J.W. Powell's Indian Linguistic Families of America North of Mexico. Preston Holder, ed. University of Nebraska Press, Lincoln, 1966.)

1911a   Tsimshian. Pp. 283-422 in Pt. 1 of Handbook of American Indian Languages. *Bureau of American Ethnology Bulletin* 40. Washington.

1911b   Kwakiutl. Pp. 423-557 in Pt. 1 of Handbook of American Indian Languages. *Bureau of American Ethnology Bulletin* 40. Washington.

1911c   Chinook. Pp. 559-677 in Pt. 1 of Handbook of American Indian Languages. *Bureau of American Ethnology Bulletin* 40. Washington. (Pp. 673-677 is: Wishram Text, by Edward Sapir.)

———, ed.
1911-1941   Handbook of American Indian Languages. 4 Pts. Pts. 1-2, *Bureau of American Ethnology Bulletin* 40, Washington; Pt. 3, J.J. Augustin, Glückstadt and New York (also issued as extracts); Pt. 4, [only] Tunica, by Mary Haas, J.J. Augustin, New York, 1941.

1912   Tsimshian Texts (New Series). *Publications of the American Ethnological Society* 3:65-285. Leyden, The Netherlands.

1916   Tsimshian Mythology. Based on Texts Recorded by Henry W. Tate. Pp. 29-1037 in *31st Annual Report of the Bureau of American Ethnology for 1909-1910*. Washington.

1917   Introductory. *International Journal of American Linguistics* 1(1):1-8. (Reprinted: Pp. 199-210 in Race, Language and Culture, by Franz Boas. Macmillan, New York, 1940.)

1920   The Classification of American Languages. *American Anthropologist*, n.s. 22(4):367-376. (Reprinted: Pp. 211-218 in Race, Language and Culture, by Franz Boas. The Free Press, New York, 1940.)

1921   Ethnology of the Kwakiutl (Based on Data Collected by George Hunt). 2 Pts. Pp. 43-1481 in *35th Annual Report of the Bureau of American Ethnology for 1913-1914*. Washington.

1923   A Keresan Text. *International Journal of American Linguistics* 2(3-4):171-180.

1924   Vocabulary of an Athapascan Tribe of Nicola Valley, British Columbia. *International Journal of American Linguistics* 3(1):36-38.

1924a   A Revised List of Kwakiutl Suffixes. *International Journal of American Linguistics* 3(1):117-131.

1925   Contributions to the Ethnology of the Kwakiutl. *Columbia University Contributions to Anthropology* 3. New York.

1925a   Keresan Texts. 2 Pts. *Publications of the American Ethnological Society* 8. New York.

1926   Additional Notes on the Kutenai Language. [Appended to: Grammar of the Kutenai Language, by Pater Philippo Canestrelli.] *International Journal of American Linguistics* 4(1):85-104.

1928   Bella Bella Texts. *Columbia University Contributions to Anthropology* 5. New York. (Reprinted: AMS Press, New York, 1969.)

1928a   The Informants. Pp. 431-454 in Coiled Basketry in British Columbia and Surrounding Region, by Hermann K. Haeberlin, James A. Teit, and Helen H. Roberts. Pp. 119-484 in *41st Annual Report of the Bureau of American Ethnology for 1919-1924*. Washington.

1928b   Keresan Texts. 2 vols. *Publications of the American Ethnological Society* 8. New York.

1929   Classification of American Indian Languages. *Language: Journal of the Linguistic Society of America* 5(1):1-7. (Reprinted: Pp. 219-225 in Race, Language and Culture, by Franz Boas. Macmillan, New York, 1940.)

1929a   Metaphorical Expression in the Language of the Kwakiutl Indians. Pp. 147-153 in Verzameling van Opstellen door Oud-Leeringen en Bevriende Vakgenooten Opgedragen aan Mgr. Prof. Dr. Jos. Schrijen, 3 May 1929. Chartres, France. (Reprinted: Pp. 232-239 in Race, Language, and Culture, by Franz Boas. Macmillan, New York, 1940.)

1932   Bella Bella Tales. *Memoirs of the American Folk-Lore Society* 25. New York. (Reprinted: Kraus Reprint, Millwood, N.Y., 1973.)

1932a   Current Beliefs of the Kwakiutl Indians. *Journal of American Folk-Lore* 45(176):177-260.

1932b   Note on Some Recent Changes in the Kwakiutl Language. *International Journal of American Linguistics* 7(1-2):90-93.

1934   Geographical Names of the Kwakiutl Indians. *Columbia University Contributions to Anthropology* 20. New York.

1935   Kwakiutl Culture as Reflected in Mythology. *Memoirs of the American Folk-Lore Society* 28. New York.

1935a   A Chehalis Text. *International Journal of American Linguistics* 8(2):103-110.

1935-1943 Kwakiutl Tales. (New Series). 2 Pts. Part I: Translations; Part II: Texts. *Columbia University Contributions to Anthropology* 26(Pts. 1-2). New York. (Reprinted: AMS Press, New York, 1969.)

1938   Language. Pp. 124-145 in General Anthropology. Franz Boas, ed. Boston: D.C. Heath and Company.

1939   A Report of the Committee on Research in American Native Languages, 1927-1937. *American Council of Learned Societies. Bulletin* 29:105-115. Washington.

1947   Kwakiutl Grammar, with a Glossary of the Suffixes. Helene Boas Yampolsky and Zellig S. Harris, eds. *Transactions of the American Philosophical Society*, n.s. 37(3):201-378.-(Reprinted: AMS Press, New York, 1976.)

1966   Kwakiutl Ethnography. Helen Codere, ed. Chicago and London: The University of Chicago Press.

Boas, Franz, and Alexander F. Chamberlain
1918   Kutenai Tales. *Bureau of American Ethnology Bulletin* 59. Washington.

Boas, Franz, and Ella Deloria
1933   Notes on the Dakota, Teton Dialect. *International Journal of American Linguistics* 7(3-4):97-121.

1941   Dakota Grammar. *Memoirs of the National Academy of Sciences* 23(Pt. 2). Washington: U.S. Government Printing Office. (Reprinted: AMS, New York, 1976; Dakota Press, Sioux Falls, S.Dak., 1979.)

Boas, Franz, and Pliny E. Goddard
1924   Ts'ets'aut, an Athapascan Language from Portland Canal, British Columbia. *International Journal of American Linguistics* 3(1):1-35.

1924a   Vocabulary of an Athapascan Dialect of the State of Washington. *International Journal of American Linguistics* 3(1):39-45.

Boas, Franz, and Herman K. Haeberlin
1927   Sound Shifts in Salishan Dialects. *International Journal of American Linguistics* 4(2-4):117-136.

Boas, Franz, and George Hunt
1902-1905 Kwakiutl Texts. *Publications of the Jesup North Pacific Expedition* 3(1-3); *Memoirs of the American Museum of Natural History* 5(1-3). New York. (Reprinted: AMS Press, New York, 1975.)

1906   Kwakiutl Texts (Second Series). *Publications of the Jesup North Pacific Expedition* 10(1); *Memoirs of the American Museum of Natural History* 14(1). Leyden and New York. (Reprinted: AMS Press, New York, 1975.)

Boas, Franz, and John R. Swanton
1911   Siouan: Dakota (Teton and Santee Dialects) with Remarks on the Ponca and Winnebago. Pp. 875-965 in Pt. 1 of Handbook of American Indian Languages. *Bureau of American Ethnology Bulletin* 40. Washington. (Pp. 959-965 is: Winnebago Text, by Paul Radin.)

Boas, Franz, and Henry W. Tate
1912   Tsimshian Texts. Pp. 65-285 in *Publications of the American Ethnological Society* 3. Leyden, The Netherlands: E.J. Brill.

Boas, Franz, Pliny E. Goddard, Edward Sapir, and Alfred L. Kroeber
1916   Phonetic Transcription of Indian Languages: Report of Committee of American Anthropological Association. *Smithsonian Miscellaneous Collections* 66(6). Washington.

Bodine, John J.
1968   Taos Names: A Clue to Linguistic Acculturation. *Anthropological Linguistics* 10(5):23-27.

Boggs, Nathan (Sandy), Wilbur Augustine, and Sally McLendon
1985   Beginning Lessons in Eastern Pomo. Sacramento, Calif.: San Juan Unified School District Indian Bilingual Program - Title VII.

Bolen, Anne, and Louanna Furbee
1991   Plains Sign Language Gestures Accompanying the English Speech of Otoe-Missouria Indians. (Paper presented at the 11th Annual Siouan and Caddoan Linguistics Conference, Stillwater, Okla., Sept. 23, 1991.)

Bolton, Herbert E.
1910 Sana. Pp. 422-423 in Pt. 2 of Handbook of American Indians North of Mexico. Frederick W. Hodge, ed. 2 Pts. *Bureau of American Ethnology Bulletin* 30. Washington.

1914 Athanase de Mézières and the Louisiana-Texas Frontier, 1768-1780. 2 vols. Cleveland, Ohio: Arthur H. Clark.

1914a The Founding of the Missions on the San Gabriel River, 1745-1749. *Southwestern Historical Quarterly* 17(4): 323-378. Austin.

_____, ed.
1930 Anza's California Expeditions. 5 vols. Berkeley: University of California Press. (Reprinted: Russell and Russell, New York, 1966.)

Bommelyn, Loren, et al.
1984 The Tolowa Language. Arcata, Calif.: Center for Community Development, Humboldt State University.

Bompas, William C.
1891 Part of the Book of Common Prayer, and Administration of the Sacraments, and Other Rites and Ceremonies of the Church, According to the Use of the Church of England... Adapted to the Use of the Tenni Indians of Mackenzie River... . London.

Bonvillain, Nancy
1973 A Grammar of Akwesasne Mohawk. *National Museum of Man, Ethnology Division, Mercury Series* 8. Ottawa.

Booker, Karen M.
1991 Languages of the Aboriginal Southeast: An Annotated Bibliography. (*Native American Bibliography Series* 15). Metuchen, N.J.: The Scarecrow Press.

1993 More on the Development of Proto-Muskogean *kʷ. *International Journal of American Linguistics* 59(4)405-415.

Booker, Karen M., Charles M. Hudson, and Robert L. Rankin
1992 Place Name Identification and Multilingualism in the Sixteenth-Century Southeast. *Ethnohistory* 39(4):399-451.

Booth, Curtis G.
1979 Postpositions as Verbs in Kawaiisu. *International Journal of American Linguistics* 45(3):245-250.

Borden, Charles E.
1950 Preliminary Report on Archaeological Investigations in the Fraser Delta Region. *Anthropology in British Columbia* 1:13-27. Victoria.

1951 Facts and Problems of Northwest Coast Prehistory. *Anthropology in British Columbia* 2:35-52. Victoria.

1954 Some Aspects of Prehistoric Coastal Interior Relations in the Pacific Northwest. *Anthropology in British Columbia* 4:26-32. Victoria.

1954a Distribution, Culture and Origin of the Indigenous Population of British Columbia. Pp. 186-196 in *Transactions of the Seventh British Columbia Natural Resources Conference*. Victoria.

1970 New Evidence of Early Cultural Relations between Eurasia and Western North America. Pp. 331-337 in Vol. 3 of *Proceedings of the 8th International Congress of Anthropological and Ethnological Sciences. Tokyo, Sept. 8-9, 1968*. 3 vols. Tokyo: Science Council of Japan.

1975 Origins and Development of Early Northwest Coast Culture to about 3000 B.C. *Canada. National Museum of Man. Mercury Series. Archaeological Survey Papers* 45. Ottawa.

1979 Peopling and Early Cultures of the Pacific Northwest. *Science* 203(4384):963-971.

Boscana, Geronimo
1933 Chinigchinich (Chi-ñi´ch-ñich). A Revised and Annotated Version of Alfred Robinson's Translation of Father Geronimo Boscana's Historical Account of the Belief, Usages, Customs and Extravagencies of the Indians of This Mission of San Juan Capistrano Called the *Acagchemem* Tribe [1846]. P.T. Hanna, ed. Santa Ana, Calif.: Fine Arts Press.

Bossu, Jean-Bernard
1962 Travels in the Interior of North America, 1751-1752. Seymour Feiler, ed. and trans. Norman: University of Oklahoma Press.

Bouchard, Randy
1973 How To Write the Thompson Language. (Manuscript and accompanying tape recording of Mrs. Mamie Henry of Lytton, B.C., pronouncing exemplary material. In Bouchard's possession, British Columbia Indian Language Project, Victoria.)

1974 [Notes on Thompson Ethnobotany; commentary on Turner 1973-1974, and additions.] (Unpublished manuscript in Bouchard's possession.)

Bouchard, Randy, and Dorothy I.D. Kennedy
1979 Ethnography of the Franklin D. Roosevelt Lake Area. Victoria: British Columbia Indian Language Project.

1984 Indian History and Knowledge of the Lower Similkameen River - Palmer Lake Area. Victoria: British Columbia Indian Language Project.

Boulet, Jean Baptiste
1879 Prayer Book and Catechism in the Snohomish Language. Tulalip, Wash. Terr.: Tulalip Mission Press.

Bourke, John G.
1892 The Medicine-Men of the Apache. Pp. 443-603 in *9th Annual Report of the Bureau of [American] Ethnology for 1887-1888*. Washington.

Bourquin, Theodor
1891 Grammatik der Eskimo-Sprache, wie sie an der Labradorküste gesprochen wird. London: Moravian Mission Agency.

Bowden, Henry W., and James P. Ronda
1980 John Eliot's Indian Dialogues: A Study in Cultural Interaction [1671]. (*Contributions in American History* 88). Westport, Conn.: Greenwood Press. (Originally printed in 1671 by M. Johnson, Cambridge, Mass.)

Bowers, Alfred W.
1950   Mandan Social and Ceremonial Organization. Chicago: University of Chicago Press. (Reprinted: University of Idaho Press, Moscow, 1991.)

——   1965   Hidatsa Social and Ceremonial Organization. *Bureau of American Ethnology Bulletin* 194. Washington.

Boyd, Julian P., ed.
1982   Jefferson's Vocabulary of the Unquachog Indians [14 June 1791]. Pp. 467-470 in The Papers of Thomas Jefferson, Volume 20: 1 April to 4 August 1791. Julian P. Boyd, ed.; Ruth W. Lester, assist. ed. Princeton, N.J.: Princeton University Press.

Boynton, Sylvia S.
1983   Split Ergativity in Mikasuki. Pp. 360-366 in 1982 Mid-American Linguistics Conference Papers. Frances Ingemann, ed. Lawrence, Kans.: Department of Linguistics, University of Kansas.

Brackenridge, Henry M.
1814   Views of Louisiana; Together with a Journal of a Voyage up the Missouri River, in 1811. Pittsburgh: Cramer, Spear, and Eichbaum.

Bradbury, John
1817   Travels in the Interior of America in the Years 1809, 1810, and 1811. London: Sherwood, Neely, and Jones.

Bradley, Ruth H., and Betty S. Smith
1976   Beginning Cherokee. Norman: University of Oklahoma Press.

Brady, Erika
1985   The Box That Got the Flourishes: The Cylinder Phonograph in Folklore Fieldwork, 1890-1937. (Unpublished Ph.D. Dissertation in Folklore, Indiana University, Bloomington.)

——   , et al.
1984-   The Federal Cylinder Project: A Guide to Field Cylinder Collections in Federal Agencies. 5 vols. through 1990. Vol. 1: Introduction and Inventory. Erika Brady, Maria La Vigna, Dorothy Sara Lee, and Thomas Vennum, eds., 1984. Vol. 8: Early Anthologies. Dorothy Sara Lee, ed., 1984. Vol. 2: Northeastern Indian Catalog; Southeastern Indian Catalog. Judith A. Grey and Dorothy Sara Lee, eds., 1985. Vol. 3: Great Basin/Plateau Indian Catalog; Northwest Coast/Arctic Indian Catalog. Judith A. Gray, ed., 1988. Vol. 5: California Indian Catalog; Middle and South American Indian Catalog; Southwestern Indian Catalog—I. Judith A. Grey and Edwin J. Schupman, Jr., eds., 1990. Washington: American Folklife Center, Library of Congress.

Brámbila, David
1953   Gramática Rarámuri. Colaboración de José Vergara Bianchi. México: Editorial Buene Prensa.

Brandon, William, comp.
1971   The Magic World : American Indian Songs and Poems. New York: William Morrow. (Reprinted: Ohio University Press, Athens, 1991.)

Brandt, Elizabeth A.
1970   Sandia Pueblo, New Mexico: A Linguistic and Ethnolinguistic Investigation. (Unpublished Ph.D. Dissertation in Anthropology, Southern Methodist University, Dallas, Texas.)

——   1970a   On the Origins of Linguistic Stratification: The Sandia Case. *Anthropological Linguistics* 12(2):46-50.

——   1980   On Secrecy and the Control of Knowledge: Taos Pueblo. Pp. 123-146 in Secrecy: A Cross-Cultural Perspective. Stanton K. Tefft, ed. New York [and] London: Human Sciences Press.

——   1981   Native American Attitudes Toward Literacy and Recording in the Southwest. *Journal of the Linguistic Association of the Southwest* 4(2):185-195.

——   1988   Applied Linguistic Anthropology and American Indian Language Renewal. *Human Organization* 47(4):322-329.

Brant, Charles S.
1949   The Cultural Position of the Kiowa-Apache. *Southwestern Journal of Anthropology* 5(1):56-61.

——   1969   Jim Whitewolf: The Life of a Kiowa Apache Indian. New York: Dover Publications.

Braroe, Niels Winther
1975   Indian & White: Self-Image and Interaction in a Canadian Plains Community. Stanford, Calif.: Stanford University Press.

Brébœuf, Jean de
1630   Doctrine Chrestienne. Rouen: Richard l'Allemant.

Brenckle, Joseph J.
1975   Russian Influence on Native Alaskan Culture. *Slavic and East European Journal* 19(4):421-424.

Breschini, Gary S., and T. Haversat
1980   Preliminary Archaeological Report and Archaeological Management Recommendations for Ca-Mnt-170, on Pescadero Point, Monterey County, California. (Unpublished report in Breschini and Haversat's possession.)

Brice-Bennett, Carole, ed.
1977   Our Footprints are Everywhere: Inuit Land Use and Occupancy in Labrador. Nain: Labrador Inuit Association.

Briggs, Jean L.
1968   Utkuhikhalingmiut Eskimo Emotional Expression. Ottawa: Northern Science Research Group, Department of Indian Affairs and Northern Development.

Bright, Jane O.
1964   The Phonology of Smith River Athapaskan (Tolowa). *International Journal of American Linguistics* 30(2):101-107.

Bright, William
1954   Some Northern Hokan Relationships: A Preliminary Report. *University of California Publications in Linguistics* 10(1):63-67.

——   1955   A Bibliography of the Hokan-Coahuiltecan Languages. *International Journal of American Linguistics* 21(3):276-285.

779

1956 Glottochronologic Counts of Hokaltecan Material. *Language: Journal of the Linguistic Society of America* 32(1):42-48.

1957 The Karok Language. *University of California Publications in Linguistics* 13. Berkeley.

1958 Karok Names. *Names* 6(3):172-179.

1960 Animals of Acculturation in the California Indian Languages. *University of California Publications in Linguistics* 4(4):215-246. Berkeley.

1964 A Bibliography of the Publications of Harry Hoijer Through 1963. *International Journal of American Linguistics* 30(2):169-174.

1967 Inventory of Descriptive Materials. Pp. 9-62 in Handbook of Middle American Indians, Vol. 5: Linguistics. Norman A. McQuown, vol. ed., Robert Wauchope, gen. ed. Austin: University of Texas Press.

1968 A Luiseño Dictionary. *University of California Publications in Linguistics* 51. Berkeley.

1974 Three Extinct American Indian Languages of Southern California. Pp. 573-574 in American Philosophical Society Year Book. Philadelphia: American Philosophical Society.

1975 The Alliklik Mystery. *Journal of California Anthropology* 2(2):228-230. Riverside: Malki Museum Press.

1976 The First Hokan Conference: Conclusions. Pp. 361-363 in Hokan Studies. Margaret Langdon and Shirley Silver, eds. (*Janua Linguarum, Series Practica* 181). The Hague, Paris: Mouton.

————, ed.
1978 Coyote Stories. *International Journal of American Linguistics. Native American Text Series Monograph* 1. Chicago: The University of Chicago Press..

1979 A Karok Myth in "Measured Verse": The Translation of a Performance. *Journal of California and Great Basin Anthropology* 1(1):117-123. Banning, Calif. (Reprinted: Pp. 91-100 in American Indian Linguistics and Literature, by William Bright, Mouton, Berlin, 1984.)

1980 Coyote's Journey. *American Indian Culture and Research Journal* 4(1-2):21-48. Los Angeles. (Reprinted: Pp. 101-131 in American Indian Linguistics and Literaure, by William Bright, Mouton, Berlin, 1984.)

1982 Bibliography of the Languages of Native California, Including Closely Related Languages of Adjacent Areas. (*Native American Bibliography Series* 3). Metuchen, N.J.: Scarecrow Press.

1982a Poetic Structure in Oral Narrative. Pp. 171-184 in Spoken and Written Language: Exploring Orality and Literacy. Deborah Tannen, ed. (*Advances in Discourse Processes* 9). Norwood, N.J.: ABLEX. (Reprinted: Pp. 133-148 in American Indian Linguistics and Literature, by William Bright, Mouton, Berlin, 1984.)

1984 Place Name Dictionaries and American Indian Place Names. Pp. 63-75 in American Indian Linguistics and Literature, by William Bright. Berlin: Mouton.

1990 "With One Lip, With Two Lips": Parallelism in Nahuatl. *Language: Journal of the Linguistic Society of America* 66(3):437-452.

1990a The Collected Works of Edward Sapir, V: American Indian Languages [vol.] 1. Berlin and New York: Mouton de Gruyter.

1993 A Coyote Reader. Berkeley: University of California Press.

1993a Colorado Place Names. Boulder, Colo.: Johnson's Books.

Bright, William, and Jane Hill
1967 The Linguistic History of the Cupeño. Pp. 351-371 in Studies in Southwestern Ethnolinguistics. Dell H. Hymes and William Bittle, eds. The Hague and Paris: Mouton.

Bright, William, and David L. Olmsted
1959 A Shasta Vocabulary. *Kroeber Anthropological Society Papers* 20:1-55. Berkeley.

Brightman, Robert
1989 Tricksters and Ethnopoetics. *International Journal of American Linguistics* 55(2):179-203.

Bringas de Manzaneda y Encinas, Diego Miguel
1977 Friar Bringas Reports to the King: Methods of Indoctrination on the Frontier of New Spain, 1796-1797. Daniel S. Matson and Bernard L. Fontana, trans. and eds. Tucson: University of Arizona Press.

Brink, Jacob H. van den
1974 The Haida Indians: Cultural Change Mainly Between 1876-1970. (*Monographs and Theoretical Studies in Sociology and Anthropology in Honour of Nels Anderson. Publication* 8). Leiden: E.J. Brill.

Brinton, Daniel G.
1870 Contributions to a Grammar of the Muskokee Language. *Proceedings of the American Philosophical Society* 11(83):301-309. Philadelphia.

1873 On the Language of the Natchez. *Proceedings of the American Philosophical Society* 13(91):483-499. Philadelphia. (Reprnted: Kraus Reprint, New York, 1967.)

1882 The Maya Chronicles. *Brinton's Library of Aboriginal American Literature* 1. Philadelphia: D.G. Brinton. (Reprinted: AMS Press, New York, 1969.)

1883   Aboriginal American Authors and Their Productions; Especially Those in the Native Languages. A Chapter in the History of Literature. Philadelphia: D.G. Brinton. (Reprinted: Checagou Reprints, Chicago, 1970.)

1885   The Taensa Grammar and Dictionary: A Deception Exposed. *American Antiquarian and Oriental Journal* 7(2):108-113. Chicago.

1885a   The Taensa Grammar and Dictionary: Reply to M. Lucien Adam. *American Antiquarian and Oriental Journal* 7(5):275-276. Chicago.

1885b   The Lenâpé and Their Legends; with the Complete Text and Symbols of the Walam Olum, a New Translation, and an Inquiry into Its Authenticity. (*Brinton's Library of Aboriginal American Literature* 5). Philadelphia: D.G. Brinton. (Reprinted: AMS Press, New York 1969.)

1888   Linguistique américaine. *Revue de Linguistique et de Philologie Comparée* 21:54-56. Paris.

1890   Essays of an Americanist. Philadelphia: Porter and Coates.

1890a   [Letter to Henry W. Henshaw, June 10, 1890.] (Manuscript, Letters Received, in Bureau of American Ethnology Correspondence Files, National Anthropological Archives, Smithsonian Institution, Washington.)

1890b   [Letter to Henry W. Henshaw, August 1, 1890.] (Manuscript, Letters Received, in Bureau of American Ethnology Correspondence Files, National Anthropological Archives, Smithsonian Institution, Washington.)

1890c   [Letter to Henry W. Henshaw, August 5, 1890.] (Manuscript, Letters Received, in Bureau of American Ethnology Correspondence Files, National Anthropological Archives, Smithsonian Institution, Washington.)

1890d   [Letter to Henry W. Henshaw, August 15, 1890.] (Manuscript, Letters Received, in Bureau of American Ethnology Correspondence Files, National Anthropological Archives, Smithsonian Institution, Washington.)

1890e   [Letter to Henry W. Henshaw, November 7, 1890.] (Manuscript, Letters Received, in Bureau of American Ethnology Correspondence Files, National Anthropological Archives, Smithsonian Institution, Washington.)

1890f   [Letter to Henry W. Henshaw, November 15, 1890.] (Manuscript, Letters Received, in Bureau of American Ethnology Correspondence Files, National Anthropological Archives, Smithsonian Institution, Washington.)

1890g   [Letter to Henry W. Henshaw, December 6, 1890.] (Manuscript, Letters Received, in Bureau of American Ethnology Correspondence Files, National Anthropological Archives, Smithsonian Institution, Washington.)

1891   The American Race: A Linguistic Classification and Ethnographic Description of the Native Tribes of North and South America. New York: N.D.C. Hodges.

1891a   [Announcements of the publication of Brinton's *The American Race.*] *Science* 17(416):55, (420):112, (425):182.

1891b   Classification of American Languages. *Science* 17(421):121.

Brinton, Daniel G., and Albert S. Anthony, eds.
1889   A Lenâpé-English Dictionary, From an Anonymous MS., in the Archives of the Moravian Church at Bethlehem, Pa. Philadelphia: The Historical Society of Pennsylvania. (Main title page has 1888 imprint.) (Reprinted: University Microfilms International, Ann Arbor, Mich., 1977.)

British Association for the Advancement of Science
1974   Reprint of Report of the Committee for Investigating and Publishing Reports on the Physical Characters, Languages, and Industrial and Social Conditions of the North-Western Tribes of the Dominion of Canada, from the *Report of the Meeting of the British Association for the Advancement of Science....* Roderick Sprague and Deward E. Walker, Jr., eds. *Northwest Anthropological Research Notes* 8(1/2). Moscow, Idaho.

Britsch, Susan
1984   Conditionals and Hypotheticals in Tachi Yokuts. *Journal of California and Great Basin Anthropology* 4:45-63. Riverside, Calif.

Britsch-Devany, Susan
1988   The Collaborative Development of a Language Renewal Program for Preschoolers. *Human Organization* 47(4):297-302.

Broadbent, Sylvia M.
1957   Rumsen I: Methods of Reconstitution. *International Journal of American Linguistics* 23(4):275-280.

1964   The Southern Sierra Miwok Language. *University of California Publications in Linguistics* 38. Berkeley.

Broadbent, Sylvia M., and Catherine A. Callaghan
1960   Comparative Miwok: A Preliminary Survey. *International Journal of American Linguistics* 26(4):301-316.

1964   A Comparison of Miwok and Wintun. Pp. 19-45 in Studies in Californian Linguistics. William Bright, ed. *University of California Publications in Linguistics* 34. Berkeley and Los Angeles.

Broch, Harold Beyer
1974   A Note on the Hare Indian Color Terms Based on Brent Berlin and Paul Kay: Basic Color Terms. *Anthropological Linguistics* 16(5):192-196.

Brown, Alan K.
1973   San Francisco Bay Costanoan. *International Journal of American Linguistics* 39(3):184-189.

Brown, Cecil H.
1994   Lexical Acculturation in Native American Languages. *Current Anthropology* 35(2):95-117.

Brown, James A.
1983   What Kind of Economy Did the Oneota Have? Pp. 107-112 in Oneota Studies. Gaye Gibbon, ed. *University of Minnesota Publications in Anthropology* 1. Minneapolis.

Brown, Roger, and Albert Gilman
1958   The Pronouns of Power and Solidarity. Pp. 253-276 in Style in Language. Thomas A. Sebeok, ed. New York: Wiley and Sons. Cambridge, Mass.: Technology Press.

Brumble, H. David, III
1981   An Annotated Bibliography of American Indian and Eskimo Autobiographies. Lincoln: University of Nebraska Press.

————
1988   American Indian Autobiography. Berkeley: University of California Press.

Bruner, Edward M.
1956   Primary Group Experience and the Processes of Acculturation. *American Anthropologist* 58(4):605-623.

————
1961   Mandan. Pp. 187-277 in Perspectives in American Indian Culture Change. Edward H. Spicer, ed. Chicago: The University of Chicago Press.

Bruyas, Jacques
1863   Radices verborum iroquæorum. (*Shea's Library of American Linguistics* 10). New York: Cramoisy Press.

Bucca, Salvador, and Alexander Lesser
1969   Kitsai Phonology and Morphophonemics. *International Journal of American Linguistics* 35(1):7-19.

Buck, Mildred, and James Kari
1975   Ahtna Noun Dictionary. Fairbanks: University of Alaska, Alaska Native Language Center.

Buckley, Eugene
1988   Temporal Boundaries in Alsea. *Berkeley Linguistics Society* 14:10-22.

Buckley, Thomas
1984   Yurok Speech Registers and Ontology. *Language in Society* 13(4):467-488. Cambridge.

Buckner, H.F., and Goliah Herrod
1860   A Grammar of the Maskωke, or Creek Language, to Which are Prefixed Lessons in Spelling, Reading, and Defining. Marion, Ala.: The Domestic and Indian Mission Board of the Southern Baptist Convention.

Buechel, Eugene
1924   Wowapi Wakan Wicowoyake Yuptecelapi kin: Bible History in the Language of the Teton Sioux Indians. New York, [etc.]: Benziger Brothers.

————
1927   [Sursum corda]. Lakota Wocekiye na Olowan Wowapi: Sioux Indian Prayer and Hymn Book. St. Louis, Mo.: Central Bureau of the Catholic Central Verein of America.

————
1939   A Grammar of Lakota: The Language of the Teton Sioux Indians. (St. Francis, S.Dak., St. Francis Mission). St. Louis, Mo.: John S. Swift.

————
1970   A Dictionary of the Teton Dakota Sioux Language: Lakota-English, English-Lakota; with Considerations Given to Yankton and Santee [...]. Paul Manhart, ed. Pine Ridge, S.Dak.: Red Cloud Indian School, Inc., Holy Rosary Mission. (Reprinted in 1984.)

————
1983   A Dictionary of Teton Sioux; Lakota-English:English-Lakota; Lakota-Ieska: Ieska-Dakota... . Pine Ridge, S.Dak.: Red Cloud Indian School, Inc., Holy Rosary Mission.

Bugge, Aage
1952   The Native Greenlander - A Blending of Old and New. *Arctic* 5(1):45-53.

Bullchild, Percy
1985   The Sun Came Down. San Francisco: Harper and Row. (Reprinted in 1990.)

Bunte, Pamela A.
1980   The Birdpeople (Southern Paiute). Pp. 111-118 in Coyote Stories II. Martha B. Kendall, ed. *International Journal of American Linguistics. Native American Text Series. Monograph* 6. Chicago: University of Chicago Press.

Bunte, Pamela A., and Robert J. Franklin
1987   From the Sands to the Mountain: Change and Persistence in a Southern Paiute Community. Lincoln: University of Nebraska Press.

Bunzel, Ruth L.
1932   Zuñi Ritual Poetry. Pp. 611-835 in *47th Annual Report of the Bureau of American Ethnology for 1929-1930*. Washington.

————
1932a   Introduction to Zuñi Ceremonialism. Pp. 467-544 in *47th Annual Report of the Bureau of American Ethnology for 1929-1930*. Washington.

————
1932b   Zuñi Origin Myths. Pp. 545-609 in *47th Annual Report of the Bureau of American Ethnology for 1929-1930*. Washington.

————
1933   Zuni Texts. *Publications of the American Ethnological Society* 15. New York. (Reprinted: AMS Press, New York, 1974.)

————
1933-1938 Zuñi. Pp. 385-515 in Pt. 3 of Handbook of American Indian Languages. Franz Boas, ed. Glückstadt-Hamburg-New York: J.J. Augustin.

Burch, Ernest S., Jr.
1975   Eskimo Kinsmen: Changing Family Relationships in Northwest Alaska. *American Ethnological Society Monograph* 59. St. Paul, Minn.

————
1983   Peoples of the Arctic. Map. Washington: National Geographic Society.

————
1994   The Cultural and Natural Heritage of Northwest Alaska. Vol. V: The Iñupiaq Nations of Northwest Alaska. Kotzebue, Alaska: NANA Museum of the Arctic, and Anchorage: U.S. National Park Service, Alaska Region.

782

Bureau of Indian Affairs
1991   Indian Service Population and Labor Force Estimates/ Local Estimates of Resident Indian Population and Labor Force Estimates, January 1991. Washington: U.S. Department of the Interior, Bureau of Indian Affairs.

Burgess, Don
1978   Rabbit Steals Coyote's Bladder (Western Tarahumara). Pp. 178-183 in Coyote Stories. William Bright, ed. *International Journal of American Linguistics. Native American Texts Series Monograph* 1. Chicago: The University of Chicago Press.

Buschmann, Johann Carl Eduard
1855   Verwandschaft der Kinai-Idiome des russischen Nordamerika's mit dem grossen athapaskischen Sprachstamme. Pp. 231-236 in *Bericht über die zur Bekanntmachung geeigneten Verhandlungen der Königlichen Preussischen Akademie der Wissenshaften zu Berlin, 1854.* Berlin.

1856   Der athapaskische Sprachstamm. Pp. 149-319 in Philologische und historische Abhandlungen. *Abhandlungen der Königlichen Akademie der Wissenschaften zu Berlin, 1855.* Berlin.

1857   Die Pima-Sprache und die Sprache der Koloschen. Pp. 321-432 in Philologische und historische Abhandlungen, *Abhandlungen der Königlichen Akademie der Wissenschaften zu Berlin, 1856.* Berlin.

1859   Die Spuren der aztekischen Sprache im nördlichen Mexico und höheren amerikanischen Norden. Zugleich eine Musterung der Völker und Sprachen des nördlichen Mexico's und der Westseite Nordamerika's von Guadalaxara an bis zum Eismeer. Pp. 1-819 in *Abhandlungen der Königlichen Akademie der Wissenschaften zu Berlin, 1854* (Zweiter Supp.-Band). Berlin.

Butler, Ruth L., comp.
1937   A Check List of Manuscripts in the Edward E. Ayer Collection. Chicago: The Newberry Library.

Buttrick, Daniel S., and David Brown
1819   Tsvlvki Sqclvclv, A Cheroke Spelling Book. Knoxville: F.S. Heiskell and H. Brown. ("D.S. Butrick" on title page.)

Byington, Cyrus A.
1870   Grammar of the Choctaw Language: Edited from the Original MSS. in the Library of the American Philosophical Society. Daniel G. Brinton, ed. Philadelphia: McCalla and Stavely. (Reprinted: Kraus Reprint, New York, 1967.)

1915   A Dictionary of the Choctaw Language. John R. Swanton and Henry S. Halbert, eds. *Bureau of American Ethnology Bulletin* 46. Washington.

Caballería y Collell, Juan
1892   History of the City of Santa Barbara, California. From its Discovery to Our Own Days. Edmund Burke, trans. Santa Barbara, Calif.: F. de P. Gutierrez. (Reprinted: Schauer Printing Studio, Santa Barbara, Calif., 1928.)

Cabot, Pedro, Francisco Dumetz, and Buenaventura Sitjar
1771-1830 [Salinan Grammatical Notes and Religious Translations]. (Manuscript, 45 leaves, with notes from Alexander Taylor, in Boston Athenaeum, Boston.)

Callaghan, Catherine A.
1958   California Penutian: History and Bibliography. *International Journal of American Linguistics* 24(3):189-194.

1962   Comparative Miwok-Mutsun with Notes on Rumsen. *International Journal of American Linguistics* 28(2):87-107.

1964   Phonemic Borrowing in Lake Miwok. Pp. 46-53 in Studies in Californian Linguistics. William Bright, ed. *University of California Publications in Linguistics* 34. Berkeley.

1965   Lake Miwok Dictionary. *University of California Publications in Linguistics* 39. Berkeley.

1967   Miwok-Costanoan as a Subfamily of Penutian. *International Journal of American Linguistics* 33(3):224-227.

1970   Bodega Miwok Dictionary. *University of California Publications in Linguistics* 60. Berkeley.

1971   Saclan: A Reexamination. *Anthropological Linguistics* 13(9):448-456.

1972   Proto-Miwok Phonology. *General Linguistics* 12(1):1-31.

1977   Coyote the Impostor (Lake Miwok). Pp. 10-16 in Northern California Texts. Victor Golla and Shirley Silver, eds. *International Journal of American Linguistics. Native American Text Series* 2(2). Chicago: University of Chicago Press.

1980   Coyote's Knee Rock (Lake Miwok). Pp. 81-87 in Coyote Stories II. Martha B. Kendall, ed. *International Journal of American Linguistics. Native American Texts Series Monograph* 6. Chicago: University of Chicago Press.

1982   The Homeland of the Proto-Miwok. (Unpublished typescript in Callaghan's possession.)

1984   Plains Miwok Dictionary. *University of California Publications in Linguistics* 105. Berkeley.

1987   Lake Miwok Naturalization of Borrowed Phonemes. Pp. 84-93 in A Festschrift for Ilse Lehiste. Brian D. Joseph and Arnold M. Zwicky, eds. *Ohio State University Working Papers in Linguistics* 35. Columbus.

1987a   Northern Sierra Miwok Dictionary. *University of California Publications in Linguistics* 110. Berkeley.

1988   Karkin Revisited. *International Journal of American Linguistics* 54(4):436-452.

1990   Comment on Bateman, et al. *Current Anthropology* 31(1):15-16.

1990a   Proto-Costanoan Numerals. *International Journal of American Linguistics* 56(1):121-133.

Callender, Charles
1962   Social Organization of the Central Algonkian Indians. *Milwaukee Public Museum Publications in Anthropology* 7. Milwaukee.

Campanius, Johannes
1696   Lutheri Catechismus: Öfwersatt på American-Virginiske Språket. [Luther's Catechism translated into the American Language.] Stockholm: Burchardi, J.J. Genath. (Reprinted: Ivar Haeggström, Almqvist and Wiksell, Stockholm and Uppsala, 1937. English trans. by Daniel Nystrom and E.W. Olson. Swedish American Tercentenary Association, New York, 1938.)

1937   Martin Luther's Little Catechism Translated into Algonquian Indian by Johannes Campanius. Facsimile of the Printed Edition, Stockholm 1696, with Some Notes by Isak Collijn. (*New Sweden Tercentenary Publications*). Stockholm and Uppsala: Ivar Haeggström, Almqvist and Wiksell.

1938   Luther's Catechism; Translated into the American-Virginian Language. English Version by Rev. Daniel Nystrom and E.W. Olson. New York: Swedish American Tercentenary Association.

Campbell, Lyle
1976   [Review of] Lexical Reconstruction: The Case of the Proto-Athapaskan Kinship System, by Isidore Dyen and David F. Aberle. *American Anthropologist* 78(2):454-455.

1979   Middle American Languages. Pp. 902-1000 in The Languages of Native America: Historical and Comparative Assessment. Lyle Campbell and Marianne Mithun, eds. Austin: University of Texas Press.

1988   [Review of] Language in the Americas, by J.H. Greenberg. *Language: Journal of the Linguistic Society of America* 64(3):591-615.

1991   On So-called Pan-Americanisms. *International Journal of American Linguistics* 57(3):394-397.

1995   The Classification of American Indian Languages and What It Means for the Peopling of the Americas. In Proceedings of the Conference on Language and Prehistory, Boulder, Colorado, March 1990. Allan R. Taylor, ed. Stanford, Calif.: Stanford University Press. (In press.)

Campbell, Lyle, and Ives Goddard
1990   Summary Report: American Indian Languages and Principles of Language Change. Pp. 17-32 in Linguistic Change and Reconstruction Methodology. (*Trends in Linguistics, Studies and Monographs* 45.) Philip Baldi, ed. Berlin and New York: Walter de Gruyter.

Campbell, Lyle, and Ronald W. Langacker
1978   Proto-Aztecan Vowels: Parts I, II, III. *International Journal of American Linguistics* 44(2):85-102, (3):197-210, (4):262-279.

Campbell, Lyle, and Marianne Mithun, eds.
1979   The Languages of Native America: Historical and Comparative Assessment. Austin: University of Texas Press.

1979a   Introduction: North American Indian Historical Linguistics in Current Perspective. Pp. 3-69 in The Languages of Native America: Historical and Comparative Assessment. Lyle Campbell and Marianne Mithun, eds. Austin: University of Texas Press.

Campbell, Lyle, and David Oltrogge
1980   Proto-Tol (Jicaque). *International Journal of American Linguistics* 46(3):205-223.

Canada. Board on Geographic Names
1928   Place-Names of Alberta. Ottawa: Department of the Interior.

1933   Place-Names of Manitoba. Ottawa: Department of the Interior.

Canada. Indian Affairs Branch
1970   Linguistic and Cultural Affiliations of Canadian Indian Bands. G.W. Neville, comp. and ed. Ottawa: Department of Indian Affairs and Northern Development, Indian Affairs Branch. (Revised ed.: Indian and Northern Affairs Canada, Ottawa, 1980.)

Canedo, Lino Gómez
1968   Primeras exploraciones y poblamiento de Texas, 1686-1694. *Noticias geográficas e historicas del Noreste de México* 3. *Publicaciones del Instituto Tecnológico y de Estudios Superiores de Monterrey Serie Historia* 6. Monterrey, Nuevo León. (Reprinted, 2d ed.: *Biblioteca Porrúa* 93, Editorial Porrúa, Mexico, 1988.)

Canestrelli, Philip
1891   Catechism of Christian Doctrine, Prepared and Enjoined by Order of the Third Plenary Council of Baltimore, Translated into Flat-head. Maryland: Woodstock College. (Reprinted: Gonzaga Cowles Rare Book Library, Spokane, Wash., 1908.)

1894   Linguae Ksanka (Kootenai) elementa grammaticae. Santa Clara, Calif.: N.H. Downing. (Some copies bound and reissued with the title *A Kootenai Grammar*, Oregon Province Archives, Gonzaga University, Spokane, Wash., 1959).

1926   Grammar of the Kutenai Language. Franz Boas, ed. *International Journal of American Linguistics* 4(1):1-84.

Cann, Rebecca
1995   Genetic Evidence from Mitochondrial DNA for the Peopling of the Americas. In Proceedings of the Conference on Language and Prehistory, Boulder, Colorado, March 1990. Allan R. Taylor, ed. Stanford, Calif.: Stanford University Press. (In press.)

Canonge, Elliott
1958   Comanche Texts. Norman: University of Oklahoma, Summer Institute of Linguistics.

Carlson, Barry F.
1972   A Salish Language of Eastern Washington. *University of Hawaii Working Papers in Linguistics* 4(4). Honolulu.

———
1978   Coyote and Gopher (Spokane). Pp. 3-14 in Coyote Stories. William Bright, ed. *International Journal of American Linguistics. Native American Texts Series Monograph* 1. Chicago: The University of Chicago Press.

Carlson, Barry F., and Pauline Flett, comps.
1989   Spokane Dictionary. *University of Montana Occasional Papers in Linguistics* 6. Missoula.

Carlson, Barry F., and John Thomas
1979   The Nitinaht Inferential. *Anthropological Linguistics* 21(7):317-327.

Carlson, Barry F., and Laurence C. Thompson
1982   Out of Control in Two (Maybe More) Salish Languages. *Anthropological Linguistics* 24(1):51-65.

Carlson, Roy L.
1979   The Early Period of the Central Coast of British Columbia. *Canadian Journal of Archeology* 3:211-228.

———
1983   The Far West. Pp. 73-96 in Early Man in the New World. Richard Shutler, Jr., ed. Beverly Hills, Calif. [etc.]: Sage Publications.

Carrier Linguistic Committee
1974   Central Carrier Country, British Columbia, Canada. Fort Saint James, B.C.: Summer Institute of Linguistics.

Carrière, Gaston
1951   Contribution des Oblats de Marie Immaculée de langue francaise aux études de linguistique et d'ethnologie du nord canadien. *Culture* 12:213-226.

———
1970   Catalogue des manuscrits en langues indiennes conservés aux archives oblates, Ottawa. *Anthropologica* 12(2):151-179.

———
1972   Contributions des missionaires a la sauvegarde de la culture indienne. *Etudes Oblates* July-September:165-204.

———
1972a   Adrien-Gabriel Morice, O.M.I. (1859-1938): Essai de bibliographie. *Revue de l'Université d'Ottawa* 42:325-341. Ottawa.

Carriker, Eleanor, Robert C. Carriker, Clifford A. Carroll, and W.L. Larsen
1976   Guide to the Microfilm Edition of the Oregon Province Archives of the Society of Jesus Indian Language Collection: The Pacific Northwest Tribes. Spokane, Wash.: Gonzaga University.

Carriker, Robert C., Clifford A. Carroll, and W.L. Larsen.
1976   Guide to the Microfilm Edition of the Oregon Province Archives of the Society of Jesus Indian Language Collection: The Alaska Native Languages. Spokane, Wash.: Gonzaga University.

Carter, Richard T.
1974   Teton Dakota Phonology. *University of Manitoba Anthropology Papers* 10. Winnipeg.

———
1980   The Woccon Language of North Carolina: Its Genetic Affiliations and Historical Significance. *International Journal of American Linguistics* 46(3):170-182.

Cartier, Jacques
1545   Brief Recit, et Succincte Narration, de la Navigation Faïcte es Ysles de Canada, Hochelage et Sagenay et Autres, Avec Particulieres Meurs, Langaige & Cerimonies des Habitans d'Icelles: Fort Delectable Voir. (Reprinted: *Massachusetts Historical Society. American Series* 121. Boston, 1924.)

Carver, Jonathan
1778   Travels Through the Interior Parts of North America, in the Years 1766, 1767, and 1768. London: The Author.

Casagrande, Joseph B.
1948   Comanche Baby Language. *International Journal of American Linguistics* 14(1):11-14. (Reprinted: Pp. 245-248 in Language in Culture and Society. Dell Himes, ed. Harper and Row, New York, 1964.)

———
1954   Comanche Linguistic Acculturation I. *International Journal of American Linguistics* 20(2):140-151.

———
1954-1955 Comanche Linguistic Acculturation I, II, III. *International Journal of American Linguistics* 20(2):140-151, (3):217-237; 21(1):8-25.

Cass, Lewis
1821   Inquiries, Respecting the History, Traditions, Languages, Manners, Customs, Religion, &c. of the Indians, Living Within the United States. Detroit: Sheldon and Reed. (Reprinted in 1823.)

———
1821a   Additional Inquiries Respecting the Indian Languages. [Detroit: Sheldon and Reed.]

———
1823   Inquiries Respecting the History, Traditions, Languages, Manners, Customs, Religion, etc. of the Indians, Living Within the United States. 2d. ed. Detroit: Sheldon and Reed.

———
1826   Remarks on the Condition, Character, and Languages of the North American Indians. *North American Review* 22(1):1-70. Boston.

Cassidy, Frederic G.
1947   The Place-Names of Dane County, Wisconsin. Foreword by Robert L. Ramsay. *Publication of the American Dialect Society* 7. Greensboro, N.C.

Cataldo, Joseph Mary
1914   Jesus-Christ-nim kinne uetas-pa kut ka-kala time-nin i-ues pilep-eza-pa taz-pa tamtai-pa numipu-timt-ki (The Life of Jesus Christ from the Four Gospels, in the Nez Perces Language.) Portland, Oreg.: Schwab Printing.

———
1915   Jesus-Christ-nim kinne uetas-pa kut ka-kala time-nin i-ues pilep-eza-pa taz-pa tamtai-pa numipu-timt-ki (The Life of Jesus Christ from the Four Gospels, in the Nez Perces Language.) Portland, Oreg.: Schwab Printing.

Catholic Church Records of the Pacific Northwest
1972   Vancouver, Volumes I and II, and Stellamaris Mission. Mikell DeLores Wormell Warner, trans. Harriet Duncan Munnick, ed. St. Paul, Oreg.: French Prairie Press.

Caulfield, Richard, Walter J. Peter, and Clarence Alexander, comps.
1983   Gwich'in Athabaskan Place Names of the Upper Yukon-Porcupine Region, Alaska: A Preliminary Report. Katherine Peter, trans. *Alaska Fish and Game, Subsistence Division, Technical Paper* 83. Juneau.

Cavalli-Sforza, Luigi Luca, Alberto Piazza, Paolo Menozzi, and Joanna Mountain
1988   Reconstruction of Human Evolution: Bringing Together Genetic, Archaeological, and Linguistic Data. *Proceedings of the National Academy of Science of the United Sates of America* 85(16):6002-6006. Washington.

Chafe, Wallace L.
1959   Internal Reconstruction in Seneca. *Language: Journal of the Linguistic Society of America* 35(3):477-495.

1960   Seneca Morphology I: Introduction. *International Journal of American Linguistics* 26(1):11-22.

1961   Seneca Thanksgiving Rituals. *Bureau of American Ethnology Bulletin* 183. Washington.

1962   Estimates Regarding the Present Speakers of North American Indian Languages. *International Journal of American Linguistics* 28(3):162-171.

1962a   [Review of] The Language of Canada in the Voyages of Jacques Cartier (1534-1538), by Marius Barbeau [1961]. *American Anthropologist*, n.s. 64(3):679-681.

1963   Handbook of the Seneca Language. *New York State Museum and Science Service Bulletin* 388. Albany.

1964   Another Look at Siouan and Iroquoian. *American Anthropologist*, n.s. 66(4, Pt. 1):852-862.

1964a   Linguistic Evidence for the Relative Age of Iroquois Religious Practices. *Southwestern Journal of Anthropology* 20(3):278-285.

1965   Corrected Estimates Regarding Speakers of Indian Languages. *International Journal of American Linguistics* 31(4):345-346.

1967   Seneca Morphology and Dictionary. *Smithsonian Contributions to Anthropology* 4. Washington.

1968   The Ordering of Phonological Rules. *International Journal of American Linguistics* 34(2):115-136.

1970   A Semantically Based Sketch of Onondaga. *Indiana University Publications in Anthropology and Linguistics Memoir* 25. Bloomington.

1970   Meaning and the Structure of Language. Chicago: University of Chicago Press. (Reprinted in 1975.)

1973   Siouan, Iroquoian, and Caddoan. Pp. 1164-1209 in Current Trends in Linguistics, Vol. 10: Linguistics in North America (Pt. 2). Thomas A. Sebeok, ed. The Hague [and] Paris: Mouton.

1973a   The Northern Iroquoian Languages. (Unpublished typescript in Chafe's possession.)

1976   The Caddoan, Iroquoian, and Siouan Languages. *Trends in Linguistics. State-of-the-Art Reports* 3. W. Winter, ed. The Hague - Paris: Mouton.

1977   Caddo Texts. Pp. 27-43 in Caddoan Texts. Douglas R. Parks, ed. *International Journal of American Linguistics. Native American Texts Series* 2(1). Chicago: The University of Chicago Press.

1977a   The Evolution of Third Person Verb Agreement in Iroquoian Languages. Pp. 493-524 in Mechanism of Syntactic Change. Charles N. Li, ed. Austin: University of Texas Press.

1979   Caddoan. Pp. 213-235 in The Languages of Native America: Historical and Comparative Assessment. Lyle Campbell and Marianne Mithun, eds. Austin: University of Texas Press.

1980   Consequential Verbs in the Northern Iroquoian Languages and Elsewhere. Pp. 43-49 in American Indian and Indoeuropean Studies: Papers in Honor of Madison S. Beeler. Kathryn Klar, Margaret Langdon, and Shirley Silver, eds. The Hague: Mouton.

1983   Seneca Language Dictionary: Onödowa̱´ga:´ Gawë:nö´ Oiwa´shö´öh / Words of the Seneca Language. Salamanca, N.Y.: Seneca Bilingual Education Program, Salamanca City Central School District.

1987   [Comment on] Language in the Americas, by Joseph H. Greenberg. *Current Anthropology* 28(5):652-653.

1992   Uses of the Defocusing Pronomial Prefixes in Caddo. *Anthropological Linguistics* 32(1-2):57-68.

1993   Seneca Speaking Styles and the Location of Authority. Pp. 72-87 in Responsibility and Evidence in Oral Discourse. Jane H. Hill and Judith T. Irvine, eds. (*Studies in the Social and Cultural Foundations of Language* 15). Cambridge: Cambridge University Press.

Chafe, Wallace L., and Michael K. Foster
1981   Prehistoric Divergences and Recontacts Between Cayuga, Seneca, and the Other Northern Iroquoian Languages. *International Journal of American Linguistics* 47(2):121-142.

786

Chamberlain, Alexander F.
1889   Tales of the Mississaguas. *Journal of American Folk-Lore* 2(5):141-147.

1890   Notes on Indian Child-Language. *American Anthropologist*, o.s. 3(3):237-241.

1891   Words of Algonkian Origin. *Science*, o.s. 18(457):260-261.

1892   The Language of the Mississaga Indians of Skŭgog: A Contribution to the Linguistics of the Algonkian Tribes of Canada. Philadelphia: MacCalla & Co.

1896   Kootenay Indian Personal Names. Pp. 260-261 in *Proceedings for the 44th Meeting, 1895, of the American Association for the Advancement of Science.* Salem, Mass.

1899   American Indian Names of White Men and Women. *Journal of American Folk-Lore* 12(44):24-31.

1907   Chinook Jargon. Pp. 274-275 in Pt. 1 of Handbook of American Indians North of Mexico. Frederick W. Hodge, ed. *Bureau of American Ethnology Bulletin* 30. Washington.

1910   Nith-songs. P. 77 in Pt. 2 of Handbook of American Indians North of Mexico. Frederick W. Hodge, ed. *Bureau of American Ethnology Bulletin* 30. Washington.

Chamberlain, Montague
1899   Maliseet Vocabulary, by Montague Chamberlain, with an Introduction by William F. Ganong. Cambridge, Mass.

Chamberlin, Ralph V.
1909   Some Plant Names of the Ute Indians. *American Anthropologist*, n.s. 11(1):27-40.

1913   Place and Personal Names of the Gosiute Indians of Utah. *Proceedings of the American Philosophical Society* 52(208):1-20. Philadelphia.

Champlain, Samuel de
1632   Les voyages de la Nouvelle France occidentale, dicte Canada, faits par le Sr. de Champlain Xainctongeois, Capitaine pour le Roy en la Marine du Ponant, & toutes les descouvertes qu'il a faites en ce païs depuis l'an 1603, iusques en l'an 1629. Paris: Claude Collet.

Chapman, John W.
1914   Ten'a Texts and Tales from Anvik. *Publications of the American Ethnological Society* 6:1-230. Washington.

Chaput, Donald
1966   From Indian to French: A Female Name Curiosity. *Names* 14(2):143-149.

Charles, Lucile H.
1951   Drama in First-naming Ceremonies. *Journal of American Folk-Lore* 64(251):11-35.

Charlevoix, Pierre François Xavier de
1744   Histoire et description generals de la Nouvelle France, avec le Journal historique d'un voyage fait par ordre du Roi dans l'Amérique Septentrionnale. 6 vols. Paris: Nyon fils.

Charney, Jean Ormsbee
1993   A Grammar of Comanche. (*Studies in the Anthropology of North American Indians.*) Lincoln and London: University of Nebraska Press.

Chase, A.W.
1869   Siletz, or "Lo" Reconstructed. *Overland Monthly* 2(5): 424-434.

Chaumonot, Pierre-Joseph-Marie
1920   Grammar of the Huron Language...by a Missionary.... John Wilkie, trans., Alexander Fraser, ed. Pp. 725-777 in *Fifteenth Report of the Bureau of Archives for the Province of Ontario.* Toronto. (Earlier published in *Transactions of the Literary and Historical Society of Quebec* 2:94-198, 1831.)

Chew, William
1846   Vocabulary of the Tuscarora, from William Chew, Written Out and Transmitted by the Rev. Gilbert Rockwood. Pp. 251-258 in Report of Mr. Schoolcraft to the Secretary of State. *New York State. Senate Document* 24(Jan. 22, 1846). Albany.

Chiltoskey, Mary Ulmer
1972   Cherokee Words with Pictures. Cherokee, N.C.: M. Ulmer and G.B. Chiltoskey; [also] Sylva, N.C.: Herald Publishing Co.; Asheville, N.C.: Gilbert Printing Co.

Chittenden, Hiram M., and Alfred T. Richardson, eds.
1905   Life, Letters and Travels of Father Pierre-Jean de Smet, S.J. 1801-1873. 4 vols. New York: Francis P. Harper. (Reprinted: Kraus Reprint Corporation, New York, 1969.)

Chung, Sandra
1974   Remarks on Pablo Tac's *La Lingua degli Indi Luiseños.* *International Journal of American Linguistics* 40(4): 292-307.

1976   Compound Tense Markers in Tolkapaya. Pp. 119-128 in Proceedings of the First Yuman Languages Workshop Held at the University of California, San Diego, June 16-21, 1975. James E. Redden, ed. *Southern Illinois University Museum Studies, Research Record* 7. Carbondale.

Ciccarello, Edmund L., chief ed.
1984   Navajo Children's Literature, Volume I. Albuquerque, N.M.: Native American Materials Development Center.

Claesse, Lawrence
1715   The Morning and Evening Prayer, The Litany, Church Catechism, Family Prayers, and Several Chapters of the Old and New-Testament, Translated into the *Mahaque Indian* Language [etc.]. New York: Printed by William Bradford.

Clark, Donald W.
1979   Ocean Bay: An Early North Pacific Maritime Culture. *Canada. National Museum of Man. Mercury Series. Archaeological Survey Paper* 86. Ottawa.

1982   From Just Beyond the Southern Fringe: A Comparison of Norton Culture and the Contemporary Kachemak Tradition of Kodiak Island. *Arctic Anthropology* 19(2):123-132.

Clark, Ella E.
1953   Indian Legends of the Pacific Northwest. Berkeley: University of California Press. (Reprinted in 1958 and 1966.)

Clark, Thomas L.
1978   A Semantic Class in the Great Basin. *Names* 26(1): 48-57.

Clark, William P.
1885   The Indian Sign Language, with Brief Explanatory Notes [etc.]. Philadelphia: L.R. Hamersly and Company. (Reprinted: University of Nebraska Press, Lincoln, 1982.)

Clarke, Sandra
1982   North-West River (Sheshātshīt) Montagnais: A Grammatical Sketch. *Canada. National Museum of Man. Mercury Series. Ethnology Service Paper* 80. Ottawa.

Clarke, Sandra, and Marguerite MacKenzie, comps.
1995   Cree / Montagnais / Naskapi Reference Bibliography. *Algonquian and Iroquoian Linguistics* 20(4):39-56. Winnipeg, Man.

Clarke, Sandra, Marguerite MacKenzie, and Deborah James
1993   Preverb Usage in Cree/Montagnais/Naskapi. Pp. 32-45 in Papers of the Twenty-fourth Algonquian Conference. William Cowan, ed. Ottawa: Carleton University.

Claus, Daniel
1780   The Order for Morning and Evening Prayer and Administration of the Sacraments, and Some Other Offices of the Church of England. Quebec: William Brown.

1781   A Primer for the Use of the Mohawk Children To Acquire the Spelling and Reading of Their Own: As Well as To Get Acquainted With the English Tongue, Which for That Purpose Is Put on the Opposite Page. Montreal: Printed at Fleury Mesplets. (Reprinted: C. Buckton, London, 1786.)

1787   The Book of Common Prayer and Administration of the Sacraments, and Other Rites and Ceremonies of the Church...; The Gospel According to St. Mark Translated into the Mohawk Language by Captn. Joseph Brant. London: C. Buckton.

Clements, William M.
1990   Schoolcraft as Textmaker. *Journal of American Folklore* 103(408):177-192.

1992   "Tokens of Literary Faculty": Native American Literature and Euroamerican Translation in the Early Nineteenth Century. Pp. 33-50 in On the Translation of Native American Literatures. Brian Swann, ed. Washington: Smithsonian Institution Press.

Clements, William M., and Frances M. Malpezzi, comps.
1984   Native American Folklore, 1879-1979: An Annotated Bibliography. Athens, Ohio: Swallow Press.

Clifton, James A.
1977   The Prairie People: Continuity and Change in Potawatomi Indian Culture, 1665-1965. Lawrence: The Regents Press of Kansas.

Codere, Helen
1950   Fighting with Property. *Monograph of the American Ethnological Society* 18. New York.

1961   Kwakiutl. Pp. 431-516 in Perspectives in American Indian Culture Change. Edward H. Spicer, ed. Chicago: The University of Chicago Press.

Coe, Michael, Dean Snow, and Elizabeth Benson
1986   Atlas of Ancient America. New York: Facts On File.

Coleman, Michael C.
1993   American Indian Children at School, 1850-1930. Jackson, Miss.: University Press of Mississippi.

Collard, Howard, and Elisabeth Scott Collard
1962   Castellano-mayo, mayo-castellano. México: Instituto Lingüístico de Verano.

Collins, Henry B., Jr.
1951   The Origin and Antiquity of the Eskimo. Pp. 423-467 in *Annual Report of the Smithsonian Institution for 1950.* Washington.

1954   Comment [on Swadesh (1954)]. *American Anthropologist*, n.s. 56(3):364-372.

1960   Comment on: The Archaeology of Bering Strait, by J.L. Giddings. *Current Anthropology* 1(2):131-136.

1962   Bering Strait to Greenland. Pp. 125-139 in Prehistoric Cultural Relations Between the Arctic and Temperate Zones of North America. J.M. Campbell, ed. *Arctic Institute of North America Technical Paper* 11. Montreal.

1964   The Arctic and Subarctic. Pp. 85-114 in Prehistoric Man in the New World. Jesse D. Jennings and Edward Norbeck, eds. Chicago and London: University of Chicago Press.

Collins, James
1985   Pronouns, Markedness, and Stem Change in Tolowa. *International Journal of American Linguistics* 51(4):368-372.

1989   Nasalization, Lengthening, and Phonological Rhyme in Tolowa. *International Journal of American Linguistics* 55(3):326-340.

Collins, June McCormick
1966   Naming, Continuity, and Social Inheritance Among the Coast Salish of Western Washington. *Papers of Michigan Academy of Science, Arts, and Letters* 51:425-436. Ann Arbor.

1974   Valley of the Spirits: The Upper Skagit Indians of Western Washington. Seattle: University of Washington Press.

Collins, Raymond, and Sally Jo Collins
1966   Upper Kuskokwim Athapaskan Dictionary. Fairbanks: Summer Institute of Linguistics.

Collins, Raymond, and Betty Petruska, comps.
1979   Dinak'i (Our Words): Upper Kuskokwim Athabaskan Junior Dictionary. Anchorage: University of Alaska, National Bilingual Materials Development Center.

Colson, Elizabeth
1953   The Makah Indians: A Study of an Indian Tribe in Modern American Society. Minneapolis: University of Minnesota Press. (Reprinted: Greenwood Press, Westport, Conn., 1974.)

Conklin, Harold C.
1959   Linguistic Play in its Cultural Context. *Language* 35(4):631-636. (Reprinted: Pp. 295-300 in Language in Culture and Society. Dell Hymes, ed. Harper and Row, New York, 1964.)

————
1962   Lexicographical Treatment of Folk Taxonomies. *International Journal of American Linguistics* 28(2, Pt. 4):119-141.

Cook, Emily S.
1905   What's in a Name? Pp. 423-424 in *Annual Reports of the Department of the Interior for the Fiscal Year Ended June 30, 1904.* Indian Affairs, Pt. I: Report of the Commissioner, and Appendixes. Washington.

Cook, Eung-Do
1972   Stress and Related Rules in Tahltan. *International Journal of American Linguistics* 38(4):231-233.

————
1983   Chilcotin Flattening. *Canadian Journal of Linguistics* 28(2):123-132.

————
1983a   Chipewyan Vowels. *International Journal of American Linguistics* 49(4):413-427.

————
1984   A Sarcee Grammar. Vancouver: University of British Columbia Press.

————
1985   Carrier Nasals. *International Journal of American Linguistics* 51(4):377-379.

————
1991   Lexical Derivation and Stress in Cree. Pp. 21-29 in Papers of the Twenty-second Algonquian Conference. William Cowan, ed. Ottawa: Carleton University.

————
1995   Is There Any Convergence in Language Death? Evidence from Chipewyan and Stoney. *Journal of Linguistic Anthropology* 5(2):217-231.

Cook, Eung-Do, and Keren D. Rice, eds.
1989   Athapaskan Linguistics: Current Perspectives on a Language Family. *Trends in Linguistics. State-of-the-Art Reports* 15. Berlin [and] New York: Mouton de Gruyter.

Cook, James, and James King
1784   A Voyage to the Pacific Ocean, Undertaken by the Command of His Majesty, for Making Discoveries in the Northern Hemisphere. 3 vols. (Vol. 3 by James King). London: Printed by W. and A. Strahan for G. Nicol and T. Cadell.

Cook, Joseph Witherspoon, and Charles Smith Cook
1882   Calvary Wiwicawangapi Kin, qa Wokiksuye Anpetu Kin Koya. Niobrara: Niobrara Mission.

Cooke, Charles A.
1952   Iroquois Personal Names—Their Classification. *Proceedings of the American Philosophical Society* 96(4):427-438. Philadelphia.

Cooper, John M.
1945   Tête-de-Boule Cree. *International Journal of American Linguistics* 11(1):36-44.

Cooter, David
1989   L'Apparat françois-montagnais du Père Laure. Pp. 79-85 in Actes du Vingtième Congrès des Algonquinistes. William Cowan, ed. Ottawa: Carleton University.

Cope, Leona
1919   Calendars of the Indians North of Mexico. *University of California Publications in American Archaeology and Ethnology* 16(4):119-176. Berkeley. (Reprinted: Kraus Reprint Corp., New York, 1965.)

Corlies, William H.R., and Tillie Paul
1885   Gospel Hymns with the Lord's Prayer Translated into the Klinkit Indian Language of Alaska. Philadelphia: William Syckelmoore.

Correll, Thomas C.
1972   [Review of] Iñupiat Eskimo Dictionary (1970) by D.H. Webster and W. Zibell. *International Journal of American Linguistics* 38(1):76-77.

————
1976   Language and Location in Traditional Inuit Societies. Pp. 173-180 in Vol. 2 of Report: Inuit Land Use and Occupancy Project. Milton M. R. Freeman, ed. Ottawa: Department of Indian and Northern Affairs, Canada.

Cortina-Borja, Mario, and Leopoldo Valiñas C.
1989   Some Remarks on Uto-Aztecan Classification. *International Journal of American Linguistics* 55(2):214-239.

Costa, David J.
1993   The Mission Press Wea Primer of 1837. Pp. 46-63 in Papers of the Twenty-fourth Algonquian Conference. William Cowan, ed. Ottawa: Carleton University.

————
1994   The Miami-Illinois Language. (Ph.D. Dissertation in Linguistics, University of California, Berkeley.)

Costello, Joseph A.
1895   The Siwash, Their Life Legends and Tales: Puget Sound and Pacific Northwest. Seattle: The Calvert Company. (Reprinted: Ye Galleon Press, Fairfield, Wash., 1986.)

Coté, Margaret R., Solomon Ratt, and Terry J. Klokeid
1987   Conditional Sentences in Cree and Saulteaux. Pp. 49-57 in Papers of the Eighteenth Algonquian Conference. William Cowan, ed. Ottawa: Carleton University.

Cotton, Josiah
1829   Vocabulary of the Massachusetts (or Natick) Indian Language. [John Pickering, ed.] Cambridge, Mass.: E.W. Metcalfe.

1830   Vocabulary of the Massachusetts (or Natick) Indian Language. [John Pickering, ed.] *Massachusetts Historical Society Collections*, 3rd. ser. 2:147-257. Cambridge, Mass.

Coues, Elliot, ed.
1897   New Light on the Early History of the Northwest. The Manuscript Journal of Alexander Henry, Fur Trader of the Northwest Company, and of David Thompson... 1799-1814.... 3 vols. New York: Francis P. Harper. (Reprinted: Ross and Haines, Minneapolis, 1965.)

1900   On the Trail of a Spanish Pioneer: The Diary and Itinerary of Francisco Garcés in His Travels through Sonora, Arizona, and California, 1775-1776. 2 vols. New York: Francis P. Harper.

Couro, Ted, and Christina Hutcheson
1973   Dictionary of Mesa Grande Diegueño: 'Iipay Aa - English, English - 'Iipay Aa. With Introduction and Notes by Margaret Langdon. Banning, Calif.: Malki Museum Press.

Cowan, William
1973   Narragansett 126 Years After. *International Journal of American Linguistics* 39(1):7-13.

1973a   Pequot from Stiles to Speck. *International Journal of American Linguistics* 39(3):164-172.

1983   Montagnais in the 17th Century. *Anthropological Linguistics* 25(4):404-410. Bloomington.

1984   John Eliot's Indian Grammar. Pp. 293-300 in Matériaux pour une histoire des théories linguistiques. Sylvain Auroux et. al., eds. (*Travaux et Recherches, Université Lille III.*) Lille.

1984   [Review of] North-West River (Sheshatshit) Montagnais: A Grammatical Sketch, by Sandra Clarke (1982). *International Journal of American Linguistics* 50(2):247-249.

1991   Philological Spadework in the *Jesuit Relations*: A Letter in Algonquin. Pp. 48-57 in Papers of the Twenty-Second Algonquian Conference. William Cowan, ed. Ottawa: Carleton University.

Cowan, William, Michael K. Foster, and Konrad Koerner, eds.
1986   New Perspectives in Language, Culture, and Personality: Proceedings of the Edward Sapir Centenary Conference. (Ottawa, 1-3 October 1984). Amsterdam/Philadelphia: John Benjamins.

Cox, Ross
1957   The Columbia River; or, Scenes and Adventures During a Residence of Six Years on the Western Side of the Rocky Mountains Among the Various Tribes of Indians Hitherto Unknown; Together with "A Journey Across the American Continent" [1831]. Edgar I. Stewart and Jane R. Stewart, eds. Norman: University of Oklahoma Press.

Cranz, David
1765   Historie von Grönland, enthaltend die Beschreibung des Landes und der Einwohner, und insbesondere die Geschichte der dortigen Mission der Evangelischen Brüder zu Neu-Herrnhut und Lichtenfels. Barby, Germany: H.D. Ebers.

1767   The History of Greenland: Containing a Description of the Country, and Its Inhabitants. Translated from the High-Dutch. 2 vols. London: Brethren's Society.

Crapo, Richley H.
1970   The Social Dynamics of Language Replacement and Linguistic Acculturation among the Duckwater Reservation Shoshone of Nevada. (Unpublished Ph.D. Dissertation in Anthropology, University of Utah, Salt Lake City.)

Crawford, James M.
1966   The Cocopa Language. (Unpublished Ph.D. Dissertation in Linguistics, University of California, Berkeley, Calif.)

1970   Cocopa Baby Talk. *International Journal of American Linguistics* 36(1):9-13.

1972   The Mobilian Trade Jargon. (Paper presented at the 8th Annual Meeting of the Southern Anthropological Society, Columbia, Mo., February, 1972; copy in Michael Silverstein's possession.)

1973   Yuchi Phonology. *International Journal of American Linguistics* 39(3):173-179.

1975   Studies in Southeastern Indian Languages. Athens: The University of Georgia Press.

1975a   Southeastern Indian Languaes. Pp. 1-120 in Studies in Southeastern Indian Languages. James M. Crawford, ed. Athens: The University of Georgia Press.

1976   A Comparison of Chimariko and Yuman. Pp. 177-192 in Hokan Studies. Margaret Langdon and Shirley Silver, eds. (*Janua Linguarum, Series Practica* 181). The Hague: Mouton.

1978   The Mobilian Trade Language. Knoxville: University of Tennessee Press.

1978a   More on Cocopa Baby Talk. *International Journal of American Linguistics* 44(1):17-23.

1979   Timucua and Yuchi: Two Language Isolates of the Southeast. Pp. 327-354 in The Languages of Native America: Historical and Comparative Assessment. Lyle Campbell and Marianne Mithun, eds. Austin: University of Texas Press.

1981   [Review of] The Natchez: Annotated Translations from Antoine Simon le Page du Pratz's Histoire de la Louisiane and a Short English-Natchez Dictionary, by Charles D. Van Tuyl, with Ethnographic Footnotes, Natchez Transcription, Sound System, Kinship Terminology and Kinship System, by Willard Walker. *Plains Anthropologist* 26(93):255-257. Lincoln, Neb.

1983   Cocopa Texts. *University of California Publications in Linguistics* 100. Berkeley.

1988   On the Relationship of Timucua to Muskogean. Pp. 157-164 in In Honor of Mary Haas: From the Haas Festival Conference on Native American Linguistics. William Shipley, ed. Berlin: Mouton de Gruyter.

Crawford, John C.
1983   Speaking Michif in Four Metis Communities. *Canadian Journal of Native Studies* 3(1):47-55.

Crawford, Judith
1976   Seri and Yuman. Pp. 305-324 in Hokan Studies. Margaret Langdon and Shirley Silver, eds. (*Janua Linguarum, Series Practica* 181). The Hague: Mouton.

1976a   Seven Mohave Texts. Pp. 31-42 in Yuman Texts. Margaret Langdon, ed. *International Journal of American Linguistics, Native American Texts Series* 1(3). Chicago: University of Chicago Press.

Cressman, Luther S., et al.
1960   Cultural Sequences at The Dalles. *Transactions of the American Philosophical Society*, n.s. 50(10). Philadelphia.

1977   Prehistory of the Far East: Homes of Vanished Peoples. Salt Lake City: University of Utah.

Crissey, Forrest
1906   Renaming the Indians. *The World To-day: A Monthly Record of Human Progress* 10(1):84-90.

Critchley, Macdonald
1939   The Language of Gesture. London: E. Arnold. (Reprinted: Norwood Editions, Norwood, Penn., 1977.)

Croft, Kenneth
1948   A Guide to Source Material on Extinct North American Indian Languages. *International Journal of American Linguistics* 14(4):260-268.

Crowell, Edith E.
1949   A Preliminary Report on Kiowa Structure. *International Journal of American Linguistics* 15(3):163-167.

Cruikshank, Julie
1991   Reading Voices, Dän Dhá Ts'edenintth'é: Oral and Written Interpretations of the Yukon's Past. Vancouver and Toronto: Douglas and McIntyre.

Cruikshank, Julie, with Angela Sidney, Kitty Smith, and Annie Ned
1990   Life Lived Like a Story: Live Stories of Three Yukon Native Elders. Lincoln: University of Nebraska Press.

Crum, Beverly
1980   Newe Hupia—Shoshoni Poetry Songs. *Journal of California and Great Basin Anthropology, Papers in Linguistics* 2(1):3-23. Banning, Calif.

Crum, Beverly, and John Dayley
1993   Western Shoshoni Grammar. *Boise State University. Occasional Papers and Monographs in Cultural Anthropology and Linguistics* 1. Bosie, Idaho.

Crumrine, Lynne S.
1961   The Phonology of Arizona Yaqui with Texts. *Anthropological Papers of the University of Arizona* 5. Tucson.

1968   An Ethnography of Mayo Speaking. *Anthropological Linguistics* 10(2):19-31. Bloomington.

Cumming, William P., S.E. Hillier, D.B. Quinn, and G. Williams
1974   The Exploration of North America, 1630-1776. New York: G.P. Putnam and Sons.

Cuoq, Jean-André
1864   Jugement erroné de M. Ernest Renan sur les langues sauvages. Montreal: Typographie d'Eusèbe Senécal.

1866   Études philologiques sur quelques langues sauvages de l'Amérique. Montreal: Dawson Brothers.

1869   Jugement erroné de M. Ernest Renan sur les langues sauvages par l'auteur des Études philologiques. 2. éd. entièrement refondue. Montreal: Dawson Brothers / J.B. Rolland et fils. (Cover title has 1870 imprint.)

1872   Cantique en langue algonquine. Paris: Jouaust.

1882   Lexique de la langue iroquoise avec notes et appendices. Montreal: J. Chapleau.

1886   Lexique de la langue algonquine. Montreal: J. Chapleau.

1891-1893 Grammaire de la langue algonquine. *Proceedings and Transactions of the Royal Society of Canada for 1891-1893*: 9(1):85-114; 10(1):41-119. Ottawa.

1894   Anotc kekon [Miscellany]. *Société royale du Canada, Mémoires* 11(1):137-179. Ottawa.

Curtin, Jeremiah
1888   [Letter to H.W. Henshaw, February 7, 1888.] (Manuscript No. 300-b, National Anthropological Archives, Smithsonian Institution, Washington.)

Curtis, Edward S.
1907-1930 The North American Indian: Being a Series of Volumes Picturing and Describing the Indians of the United States, the Dominion of Canada, and Alaska. Frederick W. Hodge, ed. 20 vols. Norwood, Mass.: Plimpton Press. (Reprinted: Johnson Reprint, New York, 1970.)

Cushing, Frank H., coll. and trans.
1901   Zuñi Folk Tales. New York: G.P. Putnam's Sons. (Reprinted: A.A. Knopf, New York, 1931.)

1920   Zuñi Breadstuff. *Museum of the American Indian, Heye Foundation. Indian Notes and Monographs* 8. New York. (Reprinted in 1974.)

Cushman, Horatio B.
1899   History of the Choctaw, Chicasaw, and Natchez Indians. Angie Debo, ed. Greenville, Tex.: Headlight Printing House.

Custer, George Armstrong
1876   My Life on the Plains; Or, Personal Experiences with Indians. New York: Sheldon and Company. (Reprinted: University of Nebraska Press, Lincoln, 1952; University of Oklahoma Press, Norman, 1962, 1976.)

Cutler, Charles L.
1994   O Brave New Words! Native American Loanwords in Current English. Norman: University of Oklahoma Press.

Dahlstrom, Amy L.
1982   A Functional Analysis of Switch-Reference in Lakhota Discourse. Pp. 72-81 in *Papers from the Eighteenth Regional Meeting [of the] Chicago Linguistic Society. April 15-16, 1982.* Kevin Tuite, Robinson Schneider, and Robert Chametzky, eds. Chicago.

1986   Discontinuous Constituents in Fox. Pp. 53-73 in Native American Languages and Grammatical Typology. Paul D. Kroeber and Robert E. Moore, eds. Bloomington: Indiana University Linguistics Club.

1989   Morphological Change in Plains Cree Verb Inflexion. *Folia Historica Linguistica* IX(2):59-71.

1991   Plains Cree Morphosyntax. (*Outstanding Dissertations in Linguistics*). New York: Garland. (Original: Ph.D. Dissertation in Linguistics, University of California, Berkeley, 1986.)

Dall, William H.
1870   On the Distribution of the Native Tribes of Alaska and the Adjacent Territory. Pp. 263-273 in *Proceedings of the American Association for the Advancement of Science for 1869.* Cambridge, Mass.

1870a   Alaska and Its Resources. Boston: Lee and Shepard. (Reprinted: Arno Press, New York, 1970.)

1877   Tribes of the Extreme Northwest. Pp. 1-156 in Vol. 1 of *Contributions to North American Ethnology.* John Wesley Powell, ed. Washington: U.S. Geographical and Geological Survey of the Rocky Mountain Region.

Dalrymple, Edwin A.
1858   [King William County Pamunkey Vocabulary]. *Historical Magazine and Notes and Queries Concerning the Antiquities, History and Biography of America, 1st ser.* 2:182. New York.

Damas, David
1972   The Structure of Central Eskimo Associations. Pp. 40-55 in *Proceedings of the 1971 Annual Spring Meeting of the American Ethnological Society (Supplement).* Seattle.

Dangberg, Grace M.
1927   Washo Texts. *University of California Publications in American Archaeology and Ethnology* 22(3):391-443. Berkeley. (Reprinted: Kraus Reprint Corp., New York, 1965.)

Daniels, Billy, Jr., and Mary Daniels
1975   Neshnabe Nebye'gen: Writing Potawatomi / Book One: Vowels. John Nichols, ed. Milwaukee: University of Wisconsin, Milwaukee, for Great Lakes Inter-Tribal Council, Inc.

1975a   Potawatomi Traditional Writing. John Nichols, ed. Milwaukee: University of Wisconsin, Milwaukee, for Great Lakes Inter-Tribal Council, Inc.

Daniels, Robert E.
1970   Cultural Identities Among the Oglaia Sioux. Pp. 198-245 in The Modern Sioux: Social Systems and Reservation Culture. Ethel Nurge, ed. Lincoln: University of Nebraska Press.

Darnell, Regna D.
1969   The Development of American Anthropology, 1879 to 1920: From the Bureau of American Ethnology to Franz Boas. (Unpublished Ph.D. Dissertation in Anthropology, University of Pennsylvania, Philadelphia.)

1970   The Kaska Aesthetic of Speech Use. *Western Canadian Journal of Anthropology* 2(1):130-139. Edmonton, Alta.

1971   The Powell Classification of American Indian Languages. *Papers in Linguistics* 4(1):70-110. Alberta.

1971a   The Bilingual Speech Community: A Cree Example. Pp. 155-172 in Linguistic Diversity in Canadian Society. Regna Darnell, ed. Edmonton, Alta., and Champaign, Ill.: Linguistic Research, Inc.

1973   Cree-English Bilingualism in Northern Alberta. (Paper presented at the 9th International Congress of Anthropological and Ethnological Sciences, Chicago, 1973.)

1974   Correlates of Cree Narrative Performance. Pp. 315-336 in Explorations in the Ethnography of Speaking. Richard Bauman and Joel Sherzer, eds. London and New York: Cambridge University Press.

1988   Daniel Garrison Brinton: The "Fearless Critic" of Philadelphia. *University of Pennsylvania Publications in Anthropology* 3. Philadelphia.

1990   Edward Sapir: Linguist, Anthropologist, Humanist. Berkeley: University of California Press.

Dauenhauer, Nora M., and Richard Dauenhauer, eds.
1987   Haa Shuká, Our Ancestors: Tlingit Oral Narratives. (*Classics of Tlingit Oral Literature* 1). Seattle: University of Washington Press; Juneau: Sealaska Heritage Foundation.

1990   Haa Tuwunáagu Yís, For Healing Our Spirit: Tlingit Oratory. (*Classics of Tlingit Oral Literature* 2). Seattle: University of Washington Press; Juneau: Sealaska Heritage Foundation.

1994   Haa Kusteeyí, Our Culture: Tlingit Life Stories. (*Classics of Tlingit Oral Literature* 3). Seattle: University of Washington Press; Juneau: Sealaska Heritage Foundation.

Daviault, Diane
1987   Un aperçu de la morphologie verbale dans la grammaire du Père Nicolas. Pp. 69-94 in Papers of the Eighteenth Algonquian Conference. William Cowan, ed. Ottawa: Carleton University.

1988   Aspects of the Historical Evolution of Obviative Marking in Ojibwa. Pp. 17-29 in Papers of the Nineteenth Algonquian Conference. William Cowan, ed. Ottawa: Carleton University.

Daviault, Diane, M. Dufresne, S. Girouard, J.D. Kaye, and P. Legault
1978   L'algonquin du nord. Pp. 55-60 in Papers of the Ninth Algonquian Conference. William Cowan, ed. Ottawa: Carleton University.

Davidson, George
1901   Explanation of an Indian Map of the Rivers, Lakes, Trails, and Mountains from the Chilkaht to the Yukon Drawn by the Chilkaht Chief, Kohklux, in 1869. *Mazama* 2(2):75-82. Portland, Ore.

Davidson, William
1963   A Preliminary Analysis of Active Verbs in Dogrib. Pp. 48-55 in Studies in the Athapaskan Languages. Harry Hoijer, ed. *University of California Publications in Linguistics* 29. Berkeley.

Davis, Irvine
1959   Linguistic Clues to Northern Rio Grande Prehistory. *El Palacio* 66(3):73-84.

1964   The Language of Santa Ana Pueblo. Pp. 53-190 in *Bureau of American Ethnology Bulletin* 191. Anthropological Papers 69. Washington.

1966   Numic Consonantal Correspondences. *International Journal of American Linguistics* 32(2):124-140.

1974   Keresan-Caddoan Comparisons. *International Journal of American Linguistics* 40(3):265-267.

1979   The Kiowa-Tanoan, Keresan, and Zuni Languages. Pp. 390-443 in The Languages of Native America: Historical and Comparative Assessment. Lyle Campbell and Marianne Mithun, eds. Austin: University of Texas Press.

1989   A New Look at Aztec-Tanoan. Pp. 365-380 in General and Amerindian Ethnolinguistics: In Remembrance of Stanley Newman. Mary Ritchie Key and Henry M. Hoenigswald, eds. Berlin and New York: Mouton de Gruyter.

Davis, John H.
1971   Notes on Mainland Comox Phonology. Pp. 12-30 in *Sacramento Anthropological Society Papers* 11. Sacramento.

Davis, Philip W., and Ross Saunders
1978   Bella Coola Syntax. Pp. 37-65 in Linguistic Studies of Native Canada. Eung-Do Cook and Jonathan Kaye, eds. Vancouver: University of British Columbia Press.

1980   Bella Coola Texts. *British Columbia Provincial Museum Heritage Record* 10. Victoria.

Davis, W.M.
1915   Biographical Memoir of John Wesley Powell, 1834-1902. Pp. 8-83 in Vol. 8 of National Academy of Sciences Biographical Memoirs. Washington: National Academy of Sciences.

Davydov, Gavriil Ivanovich
1810-1812 Dvukratnoe puteshestvīe v Ameriku morskikh ofiserov Khvostova i Davydova, pisannoe sim posliednim (A Double Voyage to America by the Naval Officers Khvostov and Davydov, Written by the Latter). 2 vols. St. Petersburg: Morskaīa Tipografiīa.

1977   Two Voyages to Russian America, 1802-1807 [1810-1812]. Richard A. Pierce, ed. Colin Bearne, trans. *Materials for the Study of Alaska History* 10:235-249. Kingston, Ont.: Limestone Press.

Dawson, George M.
1888   Notes and Observations on the Kwakiool People of the Northern Part of Vancouver Island and Adjacent Coasts, Made in the Summer of 1885. *Proceedings and Transactions of the Royal Society of Canada for 1887* 5(2):63-98. Montreal.

1888a   Report on an Exploration in the Yukon District, N.W.T. and Adjacent Portions of British Columbia, 1887. *Canadian Geological Survey Report* 3, Pt. B. Montreal: Dawson Bros.

1889   Short Vocabulary of the Tahl-tan. *Geological and Natural History Survey of Canada, Annual Report*, n.s. 3(Pt. 1), Report B, Appendix 2. Montreal.

Day, Gordon M.
1959   Note on St. Francis Nomenclature. *International Journal of American Linguistics* 25(4):272-273.

1961   A Bibliography of the Saint Francis Dialect. *International Journal of American Linguistics* 27(1):80-85.

1961a   The Name Contoocook. *International Journal of American Linguistics* 27(2):168-171.

1964   A St. Francis Abenaki Vocabulary. *International Journal of American Linguistics* 30(4):371-392.

1967   An Agawam Fragment. *International Journal of American Linguistics* 33(3):244-247.

1975   The *Mots loups* of Father Mathevet. *Canada. National Museum of Man. Publications in Ethnology* 8. Ottawa.

1975a   Early Merrimack Toponymy. Pp. 372-389 in Papers of the Sixth Algonquian Conference. William Cowan, ed. Ottawa: Carleton University.

1977   Indian Place-Names as Ethnohistoric Data. Pp. 26-31 in Actes du Huitième Congrès des Algonquinistes. William Cowan, ed. Ottawa: Carleton University.

1981   Abenaki Place-Names in the Champlain Valley. *International Journal of American Linguistics* 47(2):143-171.

1994-1995 Western Abenaki Dictionary. Volume 1: Abenaki-English. Volume 2: English-Abenaki. *Canada. Museum of Civilization. Mercury Series. Ethnology Service Papers* 128-129. Hull, Que.

Dayley, John P.
1989   Tümpisa (Panamint) Shoshone Grammar. *University of California Publications in Linguistics* 115. Berkeley.

d'Azevedo, Warren L.
1956   Washo Place Names. (Manuscript, in Department of Anthropology, University of Nevada, Reno.)

1963   The Washo Indians of California and Nevada. *University of Utah Anthropological Papers* 67. Salt Lake City.

de Angulo, Jaime *see* Angulo, Jaime de

DeBlois, Albert D.
1991   Micmac Texts. *Canadian Museum of Civilization. Ethnology Service. Mercury Series Paper* 117. Hull, Quebec.

DeBlois, Albert D., and Alphonse Metallic
1984   Micmac Lexicon. *Canada. National Museum of Man. Mercury Series. Ethnology Service Paper* 91. Ottawa.

Dedrick, John M.
1977   Spanish Influence on Yaqui Grammar? *International Journal of American Linguistics* 43(2):144-149.

Dejean, Auguste
1830   Anichinabek Amisinahikaniwa, Kicheanameatchik, Catonik, Otawak Wakanakessi. Detroit: Geo. L. Whitney.

De Laet, Joannes *see* Laet, Johannes de

de Laguna, Frederica
1952   Some Dynamic Forces in Tlingit Society. *Southwestern Journal of Anthropology* 8(1):1-12.

1954   Tlingit Ideas About the Individual. *Southwestern Journal of Anthropology* 10(2):172-191.

1972   Under Mount Saint Elias: The History and Culture of the Yakutat Tlingit. 3 Pts. *Smithsonian Contributions to Anthropology* 7. Washington.

1972   Under Mount Saint Elias: The History and Culture of the Yakutat Tlingit. 3 Pts. *Smithsonian Contributions to Anthropology* 7. Washington.

1986   [Interview in] Reminiscences About Edward Sapir. Edward M. Fenton et al., participants. Pp. 371-403 in New Perspectives in Language, Culture, and Personality. *Proceedings of the Edward Sapir Centenary Conference, Ottawa, 1-3 October, 1984.* William Cowan, Michael K. Foster, and Konrad Koerner, eds. Amsterdam: John Benjamins.

DeLancey, Scott
1987   Klamath and Wintu Pronouns. *International Journal of American Linguistics* 53(4):461-464.

1988   Klamath Stem Structure in Genetic and Areal Perspective. In Papers from the 1988 Hokan-Penutian Workshop. Scott DeLancey, ed. Eugene: University of Oregon, Department of Linguistics.

1990   Notes on Evidentiality in Hare. *International Journal of American Linguistics* 56(1):152-158.

1992   Klamath and Sahaptian Numerals. *International Journal of American Linguistics* 58(2):235-239.

DeLancey, Scott, Carol Genetti, and Noel Rude
1988   Some Sahaptian-Klamath-Tsimshianic Lexical Sets. Pp. 195-224 in In Honor of Mary Haas: From the Haas Festival Conference on Native American Linguistics. William Shipley, ed. Berlin, New York, and Amsterdam: Mouton de Gruyter.

Deland, Charles E.
1908   The Aborigines of South Dakota Part II: The Mandan Indians. *South Dakota Historical Collections* 4. Pierre.

del Hoyo, Eugenio
1960   Vocablos de la Lengua Quinigua de los Indios Borrados del Noreste de México. *Sobretiro de Humanitas* 1(1):489-515. Monterrey, México: Universidad de Nuevo León.

_____, ed.
1965   El Cuadernillo de la Lengua de los Indios Pajalates (1732) por Fray Gabriel de Vergara, y El Confesonario de Indios en Lengua Coahuilteca. *Publicaciones del Instituto Tecnológico y de Estudios Superiores de Monterrey, Serie Historia* 3. Monterrey, México.

Deloria, Ella C.
1932   Dakota Texts. *Publications of the American Ethnological Society* 14. (Reprinted: AMS Press, New York, 1974; University of South Dakota Press, Freeman, S.D., 1992.)

DeMallie, Raymond J.
1976   Carver's Dakota Dictionary. Pp. 210-221 in The Journals of Jonathan Carver and Related Documents, 1766-1770. John Parker, ed. St. Paul: Minnesota Historical Society Press.

1978 George Bushotter: The First Lakota Ethnographer, Teton Sioux, 1864-1892. Pp. 91-102 in American Indian Intellectuals. Margot Liberty, ed. *1976 Proceedings of the American Ethnological Society*. St. Paul, Minn.: West Publishing Co.

Demers, Modeste, F.N. Blanchet, and L.N. St. Onge
1871 Chinook Dictionary, Catechism, Prayers, and Hymns. Montreal: [Quebec Mission].

Demers, Richard A.
1974 Alternating Roots in Lummi. *International Journal of American Linguistics* 40(1):15-21.

Demetracopoulou, Dorothy
1935 Wintu Songs. *Anthropos* 30:483-494.

Denig, Edwin Thompson
1930 Indian Tribes of the Upper Missouri. J.N.B. Hewitt, ed. Pp. 375-628 in *46th Annual Report of the Bureau of American Ethnology for 1928-1929*. Washington.

Denny, J. Peter
1991 Three Problems in the Archeology of Eastern Algonquian. *Algonquian and Iroquoian Linguistics* 16(1):5-6.

1991a The Algonquian Migration from Plateau to Midwest: Linguistics and Archaeology. Pp. 103-124 in Papers of the Twenty-Second Algonquian Conference. William Cowan, ed. Ottawa: Carleton University.

Densmore, Frances
1918 Teton Sioux Music. *Bureau of American Ethnology Bulletin* 61. Washington. (Reprinted: Da Capo Press, New York, 1972; University of Nebraska Press, Lincoln, 1992.)

1929 Chippewa Customs. *Bureau of American Ethnology Bulletin* 86. Washington. (Reprinted: Johnson Reprint, New York, 1970.)

de Reuse, Willem J.
1987 One Hundred Years of Lakota Linguistics (1887-1987). *Kansas Working Papers in Linguistics* 12:13-42. Lawrence.

1988 The Morphology/Semantics Interface: An Autolexical Treatment of Eskimo Verbal Affix Order. Pp. 112-125 in CLS 24: Papers from the 24th Annual Regional Meeting of the Chicago Linguistic Society. Part One: The General Session. Lynn MacLeod, Gary Larson, and Diane Brentari, eds. Chicago: Chicago Linguistics Society, University of Chicago.

1989 Morphological Change and Internal Reconstruction in Eskimo. Pp. 56-67 in CLS 25: Papers from the 25th Annual Regional Meeting of the Chicago Linguistics Society. Pt. 1. Caroline Wiltshire, Randolph Graczyk, and Bradley Music, eds. Chicago: Chicago Linguistics Society, University of Chicago.

1990 A Supplementary Bibliography of Lakota Language and Linguistics (1887-1990). *Kansas Working Papers in Linguistics* 15(2):146-165. Lawrence.

1994 Noun Incorporation in Lakota (Siouan). *International Journal of American Linguistics* 60(3):199-260.

1994a Siberian Yupik Eskimo: The Language and Its Contacts with Chukchi. Salt Lake City: University of Utah Press.

de Smet, Pierre Jean *see* Smet, Pierre Jean de

De Smet, Pierre Jean *see* Smet, Pierre Jean de

Devereux, George
1949 Mohave Voice and Speech Mannerisms. *Word* 5(3):268-272. (Reprinted: Pp. 267-271 in Language in Culture and Society. Dell Hymes, ed. Harper and Row, New York, 1964.)

1951 Mohave Indian Verbal and Motor Profanity. Pp. 99-127 in Psychoanalysis and the Social Sciences. Géza Róheim, ed. New York: International University Press.

De Voto, Bernard, ed.
1953 The Journals of Lewis and Clark. Boston: Houghton Mifflin. (Reprinted: Franklin Library, Franklin Center, Penn, 1982.)

Dick, Russel, Ed Williams, and Arie Poldervaart
1991 Yerington Paiute Grammar. Dallas: Summer Institute of Linguistics.

Diebold, A. Richard, Jr.
1960 Determining the Centers of Dispersal of Language Groups. *International Journal of American Linguistics* 26(1):1-10.

Dijk, Teun A. van, ed.
1985 Handbook of Discourse Analysis. 4 vols. London [and] Orlando, Fla.: Academic Press.

Dinneen, Francis P.
1990 A 17th-Century Account of Mohawk. *Historiographia Linguistica* 17(1-2):67-85. Amsterdam.

Dixon, George
1789 A Voyage Round the World. London: George Goulding. (Reprinted: N. Israel, Amsterdam [and] Da Capo Press, New York, 1968.)

Dixon, Roland B.
1905 The Shasta-Achomawi: A New Linguistic Stock, with Four New Dialects. *American Anthropologist*, n.s. 7(2):213-217.

1905a The Northern Maidu. *American Museum of Natural History Bulletin* 17(3):119-346.

1910 The Chimariko Indians and Language. *University of California Publications in American Archaeology and Ethnology* 5(5):293-380. Berkeley.

1912 Maidu Texts. *Publications of the American Ethnological Society* 4. Leyden, The Netherlands: E.J. Brill. (Reprinted: AMS Press, New York, 1974.)

1931 Dr. Merriam's "Tló-hom-tah´-hoi." *American Anthropologist*, n.s. 33(2):264-267.

Dixon, Roland B., and Alfred L. Kroeber
1903   The Native Languages of California. *American Anthropologist*, n.s. 5(1):1-26.

1912   Relationship of the Indian Languages of California. *American Anthropologist*, n.s. 14(4):691-692. (Reprinted in: *Science*, n.s. 37(945):225, 1913.)

1913   New Linguistic Families in California. *American Anthropologist* 15(4):647-655.

1919   Linguistic Families of California. *University of California Publications in American Archaeology and Ethnology* 16(3):47-118. Berkeley.

Dobbs, Arthur
1744   An Account of the Countries Adjoining to Hudson's Bay, in the North-west Part of America.... London: J. Robinson.

Dockstader, Fredrick J.
1953   Spanish Loanwords in Hopi: A Preliminary Checklist. *International Journal of American Linguistics* 21(2):157-159.

Dodge, Richard Irving
1882   Our Wild Indians: Thirty-Three Years' Personal Experience among the Red Men of the Great West, [etc.]. Hartford, Conn.: A.D. Worthington; Chicago: A.G. Nettleton, [etc.]. (Reprinted: Archer House, New York, 1959; Corner House Pub., Williamstown, Mass., 1978.)

Dolores, Juan
1913   Papago Verb Stems. *University of California Publications in American Archaeology and Ethnology* 10(5):241-263. Berkeley.

1923   Papago Nominal Stems. J. Alden Mason, ed. *University of California Publications in American Archaeology and Ethnology* 20(1):19-31. Berkeley.

1936   Papago Nicknames. J. Alden Mason, ed. Pp. 45-47 in Essays in Anthropology Presented to A.L. Kroeber in Celebration of His Sixtieth Birthday, June 11, 1936. Robert H. Lowie, ed. Berkeley: University of California Press.

Domínguez, Francisco Atanasio
1956   The Missions of New Mexico, 1776; A Description by Fray Francisco Atanasio Domínguez, with Other Contemporary Documents. Eleanor B. Adams and Fray Angelico Chavez, trans. Albuquerque: University of New Mexico Press.

Donehoo, George P.
1928   A History of the Indian Villages and Place Names in Pennsylvania. Harrisburg, Pa.: The Telegraph Press.

Donnellan, Keith S.
1970   Proper Names and Identifying Descriptions. *Synthese* 21(3-4):335-358. Dordrecht, Holland. (Reprinted: Pp. 356-379 in Semantics of Natural Language. Donald Davidson and Gilbert Harman, eds. 2d ed. D. Reidel, Dordrecht, 1972.)

Donskoy, Vladimir
1895   Molitvy na Koloshenskom Narechii. [Prayers in the Tlingit Dialect.] New York: Tipografiya Gr. Weinstein.

Dorais, Louis-Jacques
1971   Some Notes on the Semantics of Eastern Eskimo Localizers. *Anthropological Linguistics* 13(3):91-95.

1975   Kinngaqmiut uqausingit: The Inuit Language in Cape Dorset, N.W.T. Québec: Université Laval, Association Inuksiutiit Katimajiit.

1975a   Iqalungmiut uqausingit: Southeast Baffin Inuit Language. Québec: Université Laval, Association Inuksiutiit Katimajiit.

1976   Some Phonological Characteristics of Eastern Canadian Inuit. *Anthropological Linguistics* 18(8):387-392.

1977   Le Parler Inuit de Rigolet (Labrador). *Études/Inuit/Studies* 1(2):113-117.

1978   Iglulingmiut uqausingit/The Inuit Language of Igloolik/Le Parler Inuit d'Igloolik. Quebec: Association Inuksiutiit Katimajiit.

1986   Inuktitut Surface Phonology: A Trans-Dialectal Survey. *International Journal of American Linguistics* 52(1):20-53.

1990   The Canadian Inuit and Their Language. Pp. 185-289 in Arctic Languages: An Awakening. Dirmid R.F. Collis, ed. Paris: UNESCO.

1993   From Magic Words to Word Processing: A History of the Inuit Language. Iqaluit, Alaska: Arctic College (Nunatta Campus).

Dorian, Nancy C.
1993   A Response to Ladefoged's Other View of Endangered Languages. *Language: Journal of the Linguistic Society of America* 69(3):575-579.

Dorsey, George A., and James R. Murie
1940   Notes on Skidi Pawnee Society. Prepared for publication by Alexander Spoehr. *Field Museum of Natural History Anthropological Series* 27(2):67-119. Chicago.

Dorsey, James Owen
1880-1881 The Rabbit and the Grasshopper: An Otoe Myth. *American Antiquarian and Oriental Journal* 3(1):24-27. Chicago.

1884   Omaha Sociology. Pp. 205-370 in *3d Annual Report of the Bureau of [American] Ethnology for 1881-'82*. Washington.

1885   On the Comparative Phonology of Four Siouan Languages. Pp. 919-929 in *Smithsonian Institution Annual Report for 1883*. Washington.

1886   Indian Personal Names. *Proceedings of the American Association for the Advancement of Science* 34:393-399. Salem, Mass.

1889 [Letter to H.W. Henshaw, February 20, 1889.] (Manuscript No. 4800/401, National Anthropological Archives, Smithsonian Institution, Washington.)

1890 The Ȼegiha Language. *Contributions to North American Ethnology* 6. Washington: U.S. Geographical and Geological Survey of the Rocky Mountain Region.

1890a Indian Personal Names. *American Anthropologist*, o.s. 3(3):263-268.

1891 Omaha and Ponka Letters. *Bureau of American Ethnology Bulletin* 11. Washington.

1894 A Study of Siouan Cults. Pp. 352-544 in *11th Annual Report of the Bureau of [American] Ethnology for 1889-'90*. Washington.

1894a The Biloxi Indians of Louisiana. Pp. 267-287 in *Proceedings of the American Association for the Advancement of Science, 42d Meeting, Madison, Wisconsin, August, 1893*. Salem, Mass.

Dorsey, James Owen, and John R. Swanton
1912 A Dictionary of the Biloxi and Ofo Languages, Accompanied with Thirty-one Biloxi Texts and Numerous Biloxi Phrases. *Bureau of American Ethnology Bulletin* 47. Washington. (Reprinted in 1916.)

Douaud, Patrick C.
1985 An Ethnolinguistic Profile of the Canadian Metis. *Canada. National Museum of Man. Mercury Series. Ethnology Service Paper* 99. Ottawa.

Doublehead, Hiner, and Wesley Procter, eds.
1965 [Cherokee Newsletter; in Cherokee syllabic characters and English.] Chicago: Carnegie Corporation Cross-Cultural Education Project of the University of Chicago.

Douglas-Lithgow, Robert A.
1909 Dictionary of American-Indian Place and Proper Names in New England; with Many Interpretations, etc. Salem, Mass.: Salem Press.

Downs, James F.
1966 The Two Worlds of the Washo, an Indian Tribe of California and Nevada. New York: Holt, Rinehart and Winston.

Dozier, Edward P.
1953 Tewa, II: Verb Structure. *International Journal of American Linguistics* 19(2):118-127.

1954 The Hopi-Tewa of Arizona. *University of California Publications in American Archaeology and Ethnology* 44(3):259-376. Berkeley.

1956 Two Examples of Linguistic Acculturation: The Yaqui of Sonora and Arizona and the Tewa of New Mexico. *Language: Journal of the Linguistic Society of America* 32(1):146-157. (Reprinted: Pp. 511-520 in Language in Culture and Society. Dell Hymes, ed. Harper and Row, New York, 1964.)

1961 Rio Grande Pueblos. Pp. 94-186 in Perspectives in American Culture Change. Edward H. Spicer, ed. Chicago: University of Chicago Press.

1970 The Pueblo Indians of North America. New York: Holt, Rinehart and Winston. (Reprinted: Waveland Press, Prospect Heights Ill., 1933.)

Drachman, Gaberell
1969 Twana Phonology. *Working Papers in Linguistics, Ohio State University* 5. Columbus.

Drapeau, Lynn
1991 Dictionnaire montagnais-français. Sillery, Qué.: Presses de l'Université du Québec.

1992 [Abstract of] Relexification and Code-Mixing in French-Montagnais: A Clue into the Origin of Méchif. (1992 Belcourt Lecture, University of Manitoba and St. Paul's College). *Algonquian and Iroquoian Linguistics* 17(4):46. Winnipeg.

Drechsel, Emanuel J.
1979 Mobilian Jargon: Linguistic, Sociocultural, and Historical Aspects of an American Indian Lingua Franca. (Unpublished Ph.D. Dissertation in Anthropology, University of Wisconsin, Madison.)

1983 Towards an Ethnohistory of Speaking: The Case of Mobilian Jargon, an American Indian Pidgin of the Lower Mississippi Valley. *Ethnohistory* 30(3):165-176. Lubbock, Tex.

1984 Structure and Function in Mobilian Jargon: Implications for the Pre-European Existence of an American Indian Pidgin. *Journal of Historical Linguistics and Philology* 1(2):141-185.

1985 Algonquian Loanwords in Mobilian Jargon. *International Journal of American Linguistics* 51(4):393-396.

1986 Speaking "Indian" in Louisiana. *Natural History* 95(9):4, 6, 8, 10, 12.

1987 On Determining the Role of Chickasaw in the History and Origin of Mobilian Jargon. *International Journal of American Linguistics* 53(1):21-29.

1993 Questions of Algonquian Loanwords in Mobilian Jargon and Iroquoian Speakers of Mobilian Jargon. *Algonquian and Iroquoian Linguistics* 18(1):5-9.

Driver, Harold E.
1936 Wappo Ethnography. *University of California Publications in American Archaeology and Ethnology* 36(3):179-220. Berkeley.

1937 Culture Element Distributions 6: Southern Sierra Nevada. *University of California Anthropological Records* 1(2):53-154. Berkeley.

1961 Indians of North America. Chicago and London: The University of Chicago Press.

1975 Culture Groups and Language Groups in Native North America. Pp. 99-111 in Linguisitcs and Anthropology: In Honor of C.F. Voegelin. Dale M. Kinkade, Kenneth L. Hale, and Oswald Werner, eds. Lisse: The Peter de Ridder Press.

Drucker, Philip
1937 Culture Element Distributions 5: Southern California. *University of California Anthropological Records* 1(1):1-52. Berkeley.

1937a The Tolowa and Their Southwest Oregon Kin. *University of California Publications in American Archaeology and Ethnology* 36(4):221-300. Berkeley.

1939 Rank, Wealth, and Kinship in Northwest Coast Society. *American Anthropolgist*, n.s. 41(1):55-65.

1939a Contributions to Alsea Ethnography. *University of California Publications in American Archaeology and Ethnology* 35(7):81-101. Berkeley. (Reprinted: Kraus, New York, 1965.)

1951 The Northern and Central Nootkan Tribes. *Bureau of American Ethnology Bulletin* 144. Washington.

1955 Indians of the Northwest Coast. New York and Toronto: McGraw-Hill Book Company. (Published for The American Museum of Natural History, *Anthropological Handbook* 10.) (Reprinted: Natural History Press, Garden City, N.Y., 1963.)

1955a Sources of Northeast Coast Culture. Pp. 59-81 in New Interpretations of Aboriginal American Culture History. Washington D.C.: Anthropological Society of Washington.

1958 The Native Brotherhoods: Modern Intertribal Organizations on the Northwest Coast. *Bureau of American Ethnology Bulletin* 168. Washington.

1965 Cultures of the North Pacific Coast. San Fancisco: Chandler Publishing Co.

Druke, Mary A.
1976 An Investigation of Sachemship Names Among the Iroquois Indians. (Paper for Proper Names Seminar, Department of Anthropology, University of Chicago; manuscript in Druke's possession.)

Drury, Clifford M.
1976 Nine Years with the Spokane Indians: The Diary, 1838-1848, of Elkanah Walker. Glendale, Calif.: Arthur H. Clark.

Du Bois, Cora A.
1932 Tolowa Notes. *American Anthropologist*, n.s. 34(2):248-262.

1935 Wintu Ethnography. *University of California Publications in American Archaeology and Ethnology* 36(1):1-148. Berkeley.

Dürr, Michael, Erich Kasten, and Egon Renner, eds.
1992 Franz Boas: Ethnologe, Anthropologe. Sprachwissenschaftler. Ein Wegbereiter der Modernen Wissenschaft vom Menschen. Berlin: Die Staatsbibliotek.

Duff, Wilson
1952 The Upper Stalo Indians of the Fraser Valley, British Columbia. *British Columbia Provincial Museum. Anthropology in British Columbia Memoir* 1. Victoria.

Duflot de Mofras, Eugène
1844 Exploration du territoire de l'Orégon, des Californies et de la Mer Vermeille, exécutée pendant les années 1840, 1841 et 1842. 2 vols. Paris: Arthus Bertrand.

Dufour, Rose
1975 Le phénomène du *sipiniq* chez les Inuit d'Iglulik. *Recherches Amérindiennes au Québec* 5(3):65-69.

Dumarest, Noël, and Elsie Clews Parsons, ed.
1919 Notes on Cochiti, New Mexico. *Memoirs of the American Anthropological Association* 6:137-236.

Dumond, Don E.
1965 On Eskaleutian Linguistics, Archaeology, and Prehistory. *American Anthropologist* 67(5):1231-1257.

1969 Toward a Prehistory of the Na-Dene with a General Comment on Population Movements Among Nomadic Hunters. *American Anthropologist* 71(5):857-863.

1975 Coastal Adaptation and Cultural Change in Alaskan Eskimo Prehistory. Pp. 167-180 in Prehistoric Maritime Adaptations of the Circumpolar Zone. William Fitzhugh, ed. The Hague, Paris: Mouton.

1977 The Eskimos and Aleuts. London: Thames and Hudson.

1987 A Reexamination of Eskimo-Aleut Prehistory. *American Anthropologist* 89(1):32-56.

1987a The Eskimos and Aleuts. Rev. ed. London: Thames and Hudson.

Dumouchel, Paul A., and Joseph Brachet
1942 Grammaire saulteuse. St. Boniface, Man.: Province Oblate du Manitoba.

Dunbar, John
1836 Lawyrawkʊlārits Pany Kwta. [Boston.]

Dundes, Alan
1964 The Morphology of North American Indian Folktales. *FF Communications* 81.3(195). Helsinki: Suomalainen Tiedeakatemia. (Reprinted in 1980.)

1964a A Choctaw Tongue-Twister and Two Examples of Creek Word Play. *International Journal of American Linguistics* 30(2):194-196.

1967 North American Indian Folklore Studies. *Journal de la Société des Américanistes* 56(1):53-79. Paris.

_____ , comp.
1976 Folklore Theses and Dissertations in the United States [1880-1968]. *Publications of the American Folklore Society. Bibliographical and Special Series* 27. Austin: University of Texas Press for the American Folklore Society.

Dunlap, Arthur R., and Clinton A. Weslager
1950 Indian Place-Names in Delaware. Wilmington: The Archaeological Society of Delaware.

Dunn, John A.
1978 A Practical Dictionary of the Coast Tsimshian Language. *National Museums of Canada. Mercury Series. Ethnology Service Paper* 42. Ottawa. (Reprinted, new one-vol. ed. with the Reference Grammar [1979c] under title: Sm'algyax: A Reference Dictionary and Grammar for the Coast Tsimshian Language. University of Washington Press and Sealaska Heritage Foundation, 1995.)

1979 Tsimshian Internal Relations Reconsidered: Southern Tsimshian. Pp. 62-82 in The Victoria Conference on Northwestern Languages (Nov. 4-5, 1976). Barbara S. Efrat, ed. Victoria: British Columbia Provincial Museum.

1979a Tsimshian Connectives. *International Journal of American Linguistics* 45(2):131-140.

1979b Pronominal Concord in Coast Tsimshian. *International Journal of American Linguistics* 45(3):224-231.

1979c A Reference Grammar for the Coast Tsimshian Language. *National Museums of Canada. Mercury Series. Ethnology Service Paper* 55. Ottawa. (Reprinted, new one-vol. ed. with the Reference Dictionary [1978] under title: Sm'algyax: A Reference Dictionary and Grammar for the Coast Tsimshian Language. University of Washington Press and Sealaska Heritage Foundation, 1995.)

1983 Coast Tsimshian Non-Basal Suffixes. *Anthropological Linguistics* 25(1):1-18.

Dunn, John A., and Rick A. Hays
1983 Tsimshian Uvular Syllables. *International Journal of American Linguistics* 49(1):46-63.

Dunning, Robert W.
1959 Social and Economic Change Among the Northern Ojibwa. Toronto: University of Toronto Press.

Duponceau, Peter S.
1838 Mémoire sur le système grammatical des langues de quelques nations indiennes de l'Amérique du Nord. Paris: A. Pihan de la Forest.

Duralde, Martin
1802 [Letter to William Dunbar Accompanying Vocabularies of Atakapa and Chitimacha, 24 April.] (Manuscript, American Philosophical Society Library, Philadelphia.) [Mss. Collection 185, items 12 and 13.]

Durbin, Marshall E.
1964 A Componential Analysis of the San Carlos Dialect of Western Apache: A Study Based on the Analysis of the Phonology, Morphophonics, and Morphemics. (Unpublished Ph.D. Dissertation, State University of New York, Buffalo, N.Y.)

Durieu, Paul
1891 Prayers in Stalo by Rt. Rev. Bishop Durieu. O.M.I. Stalo. Morning Prayers. [Kamloops, B.C.: St. Mary's Mission.]

Durlach, Theresa Mayer
1928 The Relationship Systems of the Tlingit, Haida and Tsimshian. *Publications of the American Ethnological Society* 11. New York.

Dusenberry, Verne
1962 The Montana Cree: A Study in Religious Persistence. Stockholm: Almqvist & Wiksell.

Dyen, Isidore
1956 Language Distribution and Migration Theory. *Language: Journal of the Linguistic Society of America* 32(4):611-626.

1962 The Lexicostatistically Determined Relationship of a Language Group. *International Journal of American Linguistics* 28(3):153-161.

1962a The Lexicostatistical Classification of the Malayopolynesian Languages. *Language: Journal of the Linguistic Society of America* 38(1):38-46.

1963 Lexicostatistically Determined Borrowing and Taboo. *Language: Journal of the Linguistic Society of America* 39(1):60-66.

1964 On the Validity of Comparative Lexicostatistics. Pp. 238-247 in Proceedings of the 9th International Congress of Linguists. Horace G. Lunt, ed. London, The Hague, Paris: Mouton.

1965 Lexicostatistics in Comparative Linguistics. *Lingua* 13(3):230-239. (Reprinted: Pp. 150-160 in Linguistic Subgrouping and Lexicostatistics, by Isidore Dyen. Mouton, The Hague, 1975.)

1975 Linguistic Subgrouping and Lexicostatistics. *Janua Linguarum Series Minor* 175. The Hague: Mouton.

Dyen, Isidore, and David F. Aberle
1974 Lexical Reconstruction: The Case of the Proto-Athapaskan Kinship System. London and New York: Cambridge University Press.

Dyk, Walter
1938 Son of Old Man Hat: A Navaho Autobiography. New York: Harcourt, Brace. (Reprinted: University of Nebraska Press, Lincoln, 1967.)

1947 A Navaho Autobiography. *Viking Fund Publications in Anthropology* 8. New York. (Reprinted: Johnson Reprint, N.Y., 1967.)

Eames, Wilberforce

1890 Bibliographic Notes on Eliot's Indian Bible and on His Other Translations and Works in the Indian Language of Massachusetts. [Separate from] *Bureau of [American] Ethnology Bulletin* 13. Washington.

Eastman, Charles A. (Ohiyesa)

1977 From the Deep Woods to Civilization: Chapters in the Autobiography of an Indian [1916]. Lincoln: University of Nebraska Press.

Eckstorm, Fannie H.

1941 Indian Place-names of the Penobscot Valley and the Maine Coast. *University of Maine Studies in History and Government*, 2d ser. 55; *The Maine Bulletin* 44(4). (Reprinted: University of Maine Press, Orono, 1960, 1978.)

Edel, May M.

1939 The Tillamook Language. *International Journal of American Linguistics* 10(1):1-57.

Edgerton, Fay E.

1963 The Tagmemic Analysis of Sentence Structure in Western Apache. Pp. 102-148 in Studies in the Athapaskan Languages. Harry Hoijer, ed. *University of California Publications in Linguistics* 29. Berkeley.

Edwards, Jane A.

1992 Transcription of Discourse. Pp. 367-371 in Vol. 1 of International Encyclopedia of Linguistics. [4 vols.] William Bright, ed. New York: Oxford University Press.

Edwards, Jonathan, Jr.

1788 Observations on the Language of the Muhhekaneew Indians; in Which the Extent of that Language in North America is Shown; its Genius is Grammatically Traced; Some of its Peculiarities, and Some Instances of Analogy Between that and the Hebrew are Pointed Out. New Haven: Josiah Meigs, Printer, for the Connecticut Society of Arts and Sciences.

Edwards, Mary

1954 Cree: an Intensive Language Course. Meadow Lake, Sask.: Northern Canada Evangelical Mission.

Eells, Myron

1877 The Twana Indians of the Skokomish Reservation in Washington Territory. *U.S. Geological and Geographical Survey of the Territories Bulletin* 2(1):57-114. Washington.

1880 [Correspondence in Regard to Twana, Clallam, and Chemakum Indians of Washington Territory.] *The American Antiquarian* 3(1):52-54. Chicago.

1881 The Twana Language of Washington Territory. *American Antiquarian and Oriental Journal* 3(4):296-303. Chicago.

1889 The Twana, Chemakum, and Klallam Indians of Washington Territory. Pp. 605-681 in *Annual Report of the Smithsonian Institution for the Year Ending June 30, 1887.* Washington.

1894 The Chinook Jargon. *American Anthropologist*, o.s. 7(3):300-312.

1985 The Indians of Puget Sound: The Notebooks of Myron Eells. George Pierre Castile, ed. Seattle: University of Washington Press; Walla Walla: Whitman College.

Efrat, Barbara Silverman

1969 A Grammar of Non-particles in Sooke, a Dialect of Straits Coast Salish. (Unpublished Ph.D. Dissertation in Linguistics, University of Pennsylvania, Philadelphia.)

1978 The Interpretation of Glottalized Resonants in Straits Salish. Pp. 251-257 in Linguistic and Literary Studies In Honor of Archibald A. Hill. Vol. 2: Descriptive Linguistics. Mohammad Ali Jazayery, Edgar C. Polomé, and Werner Winter, eds. *Trends in Linguistics, Studies and Monographs* 8. The Hague: Mouton Publishers.

Egede, Hans Poulsen

1729 Det gamle Grønlands nye perlustration; eller: en kort Beskrivelse om de gamle Nordske Colonets Begryndelse og Undergang i Grønland. Gronlands Situation. [The New Perlustration of Old Greenland, or a Short Description of the Founding and Destruction of the Old Norse Colony in Greenland. The Situation in Greenland.] Copenhagen: Hieronymus Christian Pauli.

1741 Det gamle Grønlands nye perlustration, eller Natural-historie, og beskrivelse over det gamle Grønlands situation, luft, temperament, og beskaffenhed [The New Perlustration or Natural History of Old Greenland, and Description of the Situation, Air, Temperament, and Character of Old Greenland]. Copenhagen: J.C. Groth.

Egede, Poul Hansen

1750 Dictionarium Grönlandico-Danico-Latinum, complectens primitiva cum suis derivatis, quibus interjectae sunt voces primariae è Kirendo Augekkutorum, adornatum a Paulo Egede. Copenhagen: G.F. Kisel. (Microfiche: Inter Dokumentation Co., Leiden, 1970.)

1760 Grammatica Grönlandica Danico-Latina. Copenhagen: G.F. Kisel.

Egesdal, Steven M.

1980-1983 [Fieldnotes on the Thompson Language.] (Unpublished manuscript in Egesdal's possession.)

1992 Stylized Characters' Speech in Thompson Salish Narrative. *University of Montana Occasional Papers in Linguistics* 9. Missoula.

Egesdal, Steven M., and M. Terry Thompson

1994 Hilda Austin's Telling of "Qʷíqʷʔλ'qʷəλ't: A Traditional Nłeʔképmx Legend". Pp. 313-331 in Coming to Light: Contemporary Translations of Native Literatures of North America. Brian Swann, ed. New York: Random House.

Eggan, Dorothy

1943 The General Problem of Hopi Adjustment. *American Anthropologist* 45(3):357-373.

Eggan, Fred

1950 Social Organization of the Western Pueblos. Chicago: The University of Chicago Press.

1952   The Ethnological Cultures and Their Archeological Backgrounds. Pp. 35-45 in Archeology of Eastern United States. James B. Griffin, ed. Chicago: University of Chicago Press.

1955   The Cheyenne and Arapaho Kinship System. Pp. 35-95 in Social Anthropology of North American Tribes. Fred Eggan, ed. 2d ed. Chicago: The University of Chicago Press.

1958   Glottochronology: A Preliminary Appraisal of the North American Data. Pp. 645-653 in *Proceedings of the 32d International Congress of Americanists, 1956.* Copenhagen: Munksgaard.

Ehrensperger, Edward C., ed.
1941   South Dakota Place-Names. 6 pts. Vermillion: University of South Dakota Department of English.

Ehret, Christopher
1976   Linguistic Evidence and Its Correlation with Archaeology. *World Archaeology* 8(1):5-18.

Eijk, Jan P. van
1988   Lillooet Forms for 'Pretending' and 'Acting Like'. *International Journal of American Linguistics* 54(1):106-110.

1990   Intransitivity, Transitivity, and Control in Lillooet Salish. Pp. 47-64 in Unity and Diversity: Papers Presented to Simon C. Dik on His 50th Birthday. Harm Pinkster and Inge Greene, eds. Dordrecht, Holland [and] Providence, R.I.: Foris Publications.

Eijk, Jan P. van, and Thom Hess
1986   Noun and Verb in Salish. *Lingua: International Review of General Linguistics* 69(4):319-331. Amsterdam.

Einaudi, Paula Ferris
1976   A Grammar of Biloxi. New York: Garland Publishing.

Eliot, John
1655   [The Book of Genesis, Translated into the Massachusetts Indian Language.] Cambridge, Mass.: Samuel Green.

1663   The Holy Bible: Containing the Old Testament and the New. Translated into the Indian Lanuguage... by John Eliot. Cambridge, Mass.: Samuel Green and Marmaduke Johnson.

1666   The Indian Grammar Begun; or, An Essay to Bring the Indian Language into Rules for the Help of Such as Desire to Learn the Same for the Furtherance of the Gospel Among Them. Cambridge, Mass.: Marmaduke Johnson. (Reprinted: *Old South Leaflets* 3(52), Boston, 1896.)

1669   The Indian Primer; or The Way of Training Up our Indian Youth in the Good Knowledge of God, in the Knowledge of the Scriptures and in an Ability to Reade. Cambridge, Mass. (Facsimile reprint: Edinburgh, 1880.)

1672   The Logick Primer: Some Logical Notions to Initiate the Indians in the Knowledge of the Rule of Reason. Cambridge, Mass.: Marmaduke Johnson. (Reprinted: Cleveland, 1904.)

1822   The Indian Grammar Begun: or, An Essay to Bring the Indian Language into Rules, for the Help of Such as Desire to Learn the Same, for the Furtherance of the Gospel Among Them [1666]. [John Pickering and Peter S. Du Ponceau, eds.] *Massachusetts Historical Society Collections*, 2d. ser. 9:223-312, i-liv. Boston.

1822a   A Grammar of the Massachusetts Indian Language. By John Eliot. A New Edition: With Notes and Observations, by Peter S. Du Ponceau, LL.D. and an Introduction and Supplementary Observations, by John Pickering. As Published in the Massachusetts Historical Collections. Boston: Phelps and Farnham.

Ellanna, Linda J., and Andrew Balluta
1992   *Nuvendaltin Quht'ana*: The People of Nondalton. Cartographic illus. by George K. Sherrod. Washington: Smithsonian Institution Press.

Elliott, A. Marshall
1886   Speech Mixture in French Canada. *Publications of the Modern Language Association of America* 2(2):158-186.

Elliott, Henry Wood
1886   Our Arctic Province: Alaska and the Seal Islands. New York: Charles Scribner's Sons.

Ellis, C. Douglas
1961   The So-called Interrogative Order in Cree. *International Journal of American Linguistics* 27(2):119-124.

1971   Cree Verb Paradigms. *International Journal of American Linguistics* 37(2):76-95.

1973   A Proposed Standard Roman Orthography for Cree. *The Western Canadian Journal of Anthropology* 3(4):1-37. Edmonton, Alta.

1983   Spoken Cree: West Coast of James Bay. John Wynne, Anne Scott, and Xavier Sutherland, informants. Rev. ed. Edmonton: Pica Pica Press of the University of Alberta. (First edition published by: Anglican Church of Canada, Dept. of Missions, Toronto, 1962.)

1989   "Now, Then, Still Another Story". Literature of the Western James Bay Cree: Content and Structure. Winnipeg, Man.: Voices of Rupert's Land.

_____ , ed.
1995   Âtalôhkâna Nêsta Tipâcimowina / Cree Legends and Narratives from the West Coast of James Bay. Told by Simeon Scott et al. Text and trans. (*Publications of the Algonquian Text Society / Collection de la Société d'édition de textes algonquiens*). Winnipeg: University of Manitoba Press.

Ellis, Florence Hawley
1952   Jemez Kiva Magic and Its Relation to Features of Prehistoric Kivas. *Southwestern Journal of Anthropology* 8(2):147-163.

1967   Where Did the Pueblo People Come From? *El Palacio* 74(3):35-43.

Elmendorf, William W.
1946   Twana Kinship Terminology. *Southwestern Journal of Anthropology* 2(4):420-432.

1951   Word Taboo and Lexical Change in Coast Salish. *International Journal of American Linguistics* 17(4):205-208.

1961   Skokomish and Other Coast Salish Tales. 3 Pts. *Washington State University. Research Studies* 29(1):1-37, (2):84-117, (3):119-150.

1962   Lexical Relation Models as a Possible Check on Lexicostatistic Inferences. *American Anthropologist*, n.s. 64(4):760-770.

1962a Lexical Innovation and Persistence in Four Salish Dialects. *International Journal of American Linguistics* 28(2):85-96.

1962b Relations of Oregon Salish as Evidenced in Numerical Stems. *Anthropological Linguistics* 4(2):1-16.

1963   Yukian-Siouan Lexical Similarities. *International Journal of American Linguistics* 29(4):300-309.

1964   Item and Set Comparison in Yuchi, Siouan, and Yukian. *International Journal of American Linguistics* 30(4):328-340.

1965   Linguistic and Geographic Relations in the Northern Plateau Area. *Southwestern Journal of Anthropology* 21(1):63-78.

1965a Some Problems in the Regrouping of Powell Units. *Canadian Journal of Linguistics* 10(2-3):93-104. (With discussion by Wallace Chafe, William Elmendorf, Mary Haas, Morris Swadesh, Harry Hoijer, and Carl Voegelin, pp. 104-107.)

1968   Lexical and Cultural Change in Yukian. *Anthropological Linguistics* 10(7):1-41. (Reprinted: Pp. 171-242 in A Retrospective of the Journal *Anthropological Linguistics*: Selected Papers, 1959-1985; *Anthropological Linguistics* 35(1-4), 1993 [1994].)

1969   Geographic Ordering, Subgrouping, and Olympic Salish. *International Journal of American Linguistics* 35(3):220-225.

1970   Word Tabu and Change Rates: Tests of a Hypothesis. Pp. 74-85 in Languages and Cultures of Western North America: Essays in Honor of Sven S. Liljeblad. Earl H. Swanson, Jr., ed. Pocatello: The Idaho State University Press.

1973   Lexical Determination of Subgrouping. Pp. 108-117 in Lexicostatistics in Genetic Linguistics: Proceedings of the Yale Conference, Yale University, April 3-4, 1971. Isidore Dyen, ed. Paris and The Hague: Mouton.

1981   Last Speakers and Language Change: Two Californian Cases. *Anthropological Linguistics* 23(1):36-49 .

1981a Features of Yukian Pronominal Structure. *Journal of California and Great Basin Anthropology, Papers in Linguistics* 3:3-16.

Elmendorf, William W., and Afred L. Kroeber
1960   The Structure of Twana Culture, with Comparative Notes on the Structure of Yurok Culture by A.L. Kroeber. *Washington State University. Research Studies, Monographic Supplement* 2. Pullman.

Elmendorf, William W., and Wayne Suttles
1960   Pattern and Change in Halkomelem Salish Dialects. *Anthropological Linguistics* 2(7):1-32.

Embleton, Sheila M.
1985   Lexicostatistics Applied to the Germanic, Romance, and Wakashan Families. *Word* 36(1):37-60.

1986   Statistics in Historical Linguistics. *Quantitative Linguistics* 30. Bochum: Studienverlag Dr. N. Brockmeyer.

Emerson, Lee, and Abraham M. Halpern
1978   Coyote and Quail (Yuma-Quechan). Pp. 124-136 in Coyote Stories. William Bright, ed. *International Journal of American Linguistics. Native American Texts Series Monograph* 1. Chicago: University of Chicago Press.

Emmons, George Thornton
1911   The Tahltan Indians. *University of Pennsylvania Museum. Anthropological Publications* 4(1). Philadelphia.

1991   The Tlingit Indians. Edited with additions by Frederica de Laguna and a Biography by Jean Low. Seattle: University of Washington Press. New York: American Museum of Natural History.

Engelhardt, Zephyrin
1908-1915 The Missions and Missionaries of California. 4 vols. San Francisco: James H. Barry Co.

1924   San Francisco or Mission Dolores. Chicago: Franciscan Herald Press.

1927   San Fernando Rey: The Mission of the Valley. Chicago: Franciscan Herald Press.

1927a San Gabriel Mission and the Beginnings of Los Angeles. San Gabriel, Calif.: Mission San Gabriel.

1929   San Miguel, Arcangel: The Mission on the Highway. Santa Barbara, Calif.: Mission Santa Barbara.

1933   Mission San Luis Obispo in the Valley of the Bears. Santa Barbara, Calif.: Mission Santa Barbara.

Enrico, John
1983   Tense in the Haida Relative Clause. *International Journal of American Linguistics* 49(2):134-166.

1989   The Haida Language. Pp. 223-247 in The Outer Shores. Geoffrey G.E. Scudder and Nicholas Gessler, eds. Queen Charlotte Islands: Museum Press.

1991   The Lexical Phonology of Masset Haida. *Alaska Native Language Center Research Papers* 8. Fairbanks: Alaska Native Language Center.

Erdmann, Friedrich
1864   Eskimoisches Wörterbuch, Gesammelt von den Missionaren in Labrador. 2 vols. Budissin.

1869   Testamentetotak; Josuab Aglanginit, Esterib Aglangit Tikkilugit. [Old Testament; from the Book of Joshua to the Book of Esther.] Stolpen: G. Winterib Nênerlauktangit.

Erdoes, Richard,
1984   American Indian Myths and Legends. (*Pantheon Fairy Tale & Folklore Library*). New York: Pantheon Books.

Erickson, Vincent
1981   Quatre cas d'adoption et de changement de nom chez les Malécites de la réserve de Tobique (Nouveau-Brunswick), au XIXe siècle. *Recherches Amérindiennes au Québec* 11(3):221-230.

Escalante Fontaneda, Hernando d'
1944   Memoir of Do. d'Escalante Fontaneda Respecting Florida, Written in Spain About the Year 1575. Trans. from the Spanish with Notes by Buckingham Smith (Washington, 1854). David O. True, ed. *University of Miami and the Historical Association of Southern Florida Miscellaneous Publications* 1. Miami.

Escalante, Fernando
1990   Setting the Record Straight on Yaqui Passives. *International Journal of American Linguistics* 56(2): 289-292.

Espinosa y Tello, José
1802   Relación del viage hecho por las goletas Sutil y Mexicana. Madrid: Imprenta Real. (Reprinted: Chimalistac, Mexico City, 1958.)

Espinosa, Aurelio M.
1940   First Expedition of Vargas into New Mexico, 1692. Albuquerque: University of New Mexico Press.

Essene, Frank
1942   Round Valley. Culture Element Distributions, XXI. *University of California Anthropological Records* 8(1):1-97. Berkeley.

Euler, Robert C.
1964   Southern Paiute Archaeology. *American Antiquity* 29(3):379-381.

Evans, G. Edward,
1979   Bibliography of Language Arts Materials for Native North Americans: Bilingual, English as a Second Language and Native Languages Materials, 1975-1976; With Supplemental Entries for 1965-1974. Los Angeles: University of California, American Indian Studies Center.

Evans, James
1837   The Speller and Interpreter, in Indian and English, for the Use of the Mission Schools, and Such as May Desire to Obtain a Knowledge of the Ojibway Tongue. New-York: D. Fanshaw.

Ewers, John C.
1955   The Horse in Blackfoot Indian Culture, with Comparative Material from Other Western Tribes. *Bureau of American Ethnology Bulletin* 159. Washington.

Ezell, Paul H.
1961   The Hispanic Acculturation of Gila River Pimas. *American Anthropologist*, n.s. 65(5, Pt. 2); *American Anthropological Association Memoir* 90. Menasha, Wis.

Fabricius, Otto
1791   Forsøg til en forbedret Grønlandsk Grammatica. [Essay at an Improved Greenlandic Grammar.] Copenhagen: C.F. Schubart for Kongelige Vaysenhuses Bogtrykkerie.

1801   Forsøg til en forbedret Grønlandsk Grammatica. [Essay at an Improved Greenlandic Grammar.] 2 vols. Copenhagen: C.F. Schubart.

1804   Den Grønlandske Ordbog, forbedret og forøget. [The Greenlandic Dictionary, Improved and Expanded.] Copenhagen: C.F. Schubart.

Fabvre, Bonaventure
1970   Racines montagnaises. Transcribed by Lorenzo Angers and Gerard McNulty. Quebec: Presses de l'Université Laval.

Fairbanks, Charles H.
1974   Ethnohistorical Report on the Florida Indians. Pp. 9-303 in Florida Indians III: American Indian Ethnohistory, Southern and Southeastern Indians. New York: Garland Publishing.

Fant, Louie J., Jr.
1964   Say It With Hands. Washington, D.C.: Gallaudet College Press. (Reprinted: National Association of the Deaf, Silver Spring, Maryland, 1971.)

Faries, Richard, ed.
1938   A Dictionary of the Cree Language; as Spoken by the Indians in the Provinces of Quebec, Ontario, Manitoba, Saskatchewan and Alberta. Based upon the Foundation Laid by E.A. Watkins; Revised, Enriched, and Brought Up-to-Date by J.A. Mackay... [et al.]. Toronto: Published under the Direction of the General Synod of the Church of England in Canada. (Reprinted: Anglican Book Centre, Toronto, 1986.)

Farnell, Brenda M.
1990   Plains Indian Sign-Talk: Action and Discourse Among the Nakota (Assiniboine) People of Montana. (Ph.D. Dissertation in Anthropology, Indiana University, Bloomington. Rev. and publ. under title: Do You See What I Mean? Plains Indian Sign Talk and the Embodiment of Action. University of Texas Press, Austin, 1995.)

1994   Ethnographics and the Moving Body. *Man: Journal of the Royal Anthropological Institute* 29(4):929-974.

1995   Do You See What I Mean? Plains Indian Sign Talk and the Embodiment of Action. Austin: University of Texas Press.

_____, ed.

1995a Action Sign Systems in Cultural Context: The Visible and the Invisible in Movement and Dance. Metuchen, N.J.: Scarecrow Press.

Farrand, Livingston

1907 Chimakuan Family. P. 269 in Pt. 1 of Handbook of American Indians North of Mexico. Frederick W. Hodge, ed. 2 vols. *Bureau of American Ethnology Bulletin* 30. Washington. (Reprinted: Rowman and Littlefield, New York, 1971.)

Fee, Chester A.

1941 Oregon's Historical Esperanto: The Chinook Jargon. *Quarterly of the Oregon Historical Society* 42(2):176-185. Portland.

Feeling, Durbin D.

1975 Cherokee-English Dictionary. William Pulte, ed. Tahlequah, Okla.: Cherokee Nation of Oklahoma.

1994 A Structured Approach to Learning the Basic Inflections of the Cherokee Verb. Foreword by Wilma P. Mankiller. Muskogee, Okla.: Indian University Press.

Fenton, William N.

1936 An Outline of Seneca Ceremonies at Coldspring Longhouse. *Yale University Publications in Anthropology* 9. New Haven, Conn. (Reprinted in 1970.)

1940 Problems Arising from the Historic Northeastern Position of the Iroquois. Pp. 159-252 in Essays in Historical Anthropology of North America. *Smithsonian Miscellaneous Collections* 100. Washington.

1946 An Iroquoian Condolence Council for Installing Cayuga Chiefs in 1945. *Journal of the Washington Academy of Sciences* 36(4):110-127.

1956 Toward the Gradual Civilization of the Indian Natives: The Missionary and Linguistic Work of Asher Wright (1803-1875) among the Senecas of Western New York. *Proceedings of the American Philosophical Society* 100(6):567-581. Philadelphia.

1965 The Iroquois Confederacy in the Twentieth Century: A Case Study of the Theory of Lewis H. Morgan in "Ancient Society." *Ethnology* 4(3):251-265.

Feraca, Stephen E., ed.

1994 The Wounded Bear Winter Count, 1815-1816, 1896-1897; with Notations in Lakota. Kendall Park, N.J.: Lakota Books.

Fidelholtz, James L.

1978 Micmac Intransitive Verb Morphology. Pp. 67-87 in Linguistic Studies of Native Canada. Eung-Do Cook and Jonathan Kaye, eds. Vancouver: University of British Columbia Press.

Fiedel, Stuart J.

1987 Algonquian Origins: A Problem in Archaeological-Linguistic Correlation. *Archaeology of Eastern North America* 15(1):1-11.

1990 Middle Woodlands Algonquian Expansion: A Refined Model. *North American Archaeologist* 11(3):209-230.

1991 Correlating Archaeology and Linguistics: The Algonquian Case. *Man in the Northeast* 41:9-32.

Fienup-Riordan, Ann

1983 The Nelson Island Eskimo: Social Structure and Ritual Distribution. Anchorage: Alaska Pacific University Press.

Fiero, Charles

1985 Style Manual for Syllabics; with Introduction by Mary Mitchell. Pp. 95-104 in Promoting Native Writing Systems in Canada, Barbara Burnaby, ed. Toronto: OISE Press/The Ontario Institute for Studies in Education.

Firth, Raymond

1956 Elements of Social Organization. 2d ed. London: Watts & Co.

Firth, William G., comp.

1991 Gwich'in Language Dictionary / Gwich'in Ginjìk Dìnehtł'eh. 1st ed. [No place]: Department of Culture and Communications, Government of the Northwest Territories.

Fishman, Joshua A.

1991 Reversing Language Shift: Theoretical and Empirical Foundations of Assistance the Threatened Languages. *Multilingual Matters* 76. Clevedon, England: Multilingual Matters, Ltd.

Fishman, Joshua A., Michael H. Gertner, Esther G. Lowy, and William G. Milan

1985 The Rise and Fall of the Ethnic Revival: Perspectives on Language and Ethnicity. *Contributions to the Sociology of Language* 37. Berlin: Mouton.

Fladmark, Knut R.

1975 A Paleoecological Model for Northwest Coast Prehistory. *Canada. National Museum of Man. Mercury Series. Archaeological Survey Papers* 43. Ottawa.

1978 The Feasibility of the Northwest Coast as a Migration Route for Early Man. Pp. 119-128 in Early Man in America from a Circum-Pacific Perspective. Alan L. Bryan, ed. *Occasional Papers of the Department of Anthropology, University of Alberta* 1. Edmonton.

1979 Routes: Alternative Migration Corridors for Early Man in North America. *American Antiquity* 44(1):55-69.

1983 Times and Places: Environmental Correlates of Mid-to-Late Wisconsinan Human Population Expansion in North America. Pp. 13-41 in Early Man in the New World. Richard Shutler, Jr., ed. Beverly Hills, Calif.: Sage Publications.

1986 Getting One's Berings. *Natural History* 95(11):8-19.

1990 Possible Early Human Occupation of the Queen Charlotte Islands, British Columbia. *Canadian Journal of Archaeology* 14:183-197.

Flanigan, Beverly Olson
1984   American Indian English in Early Historical Documents: Evidence for Pidgin Transmission in the New World. (Manuscript in Flanigan's possession.)

Flannery, Regina
1946   Men's and Women's Speech in Gros Ventre. *International Journal of American Linguistics* 12(3):133-135.

———
1953   The Gros Ventres of Montana: Part I, Social Life. *The Catholic University of America, Anthropological Series* 15. Washington.

Fletcher, Alice C.
1890   A Phonetic Alphabet Used by the Winnebago Tribe of Indians. *Journal of American Folk-Lore* 3(11):299-301.

———
1890a   The Phonetic Alphabet of the Winnebago Indians. Pp. 354-357 in *Proceedings of the American Association for the Advancement of Science, 38th Meeting, held at Toronto, Ont., August 1889.* Salem, Mass.

———
1891   The Nez Perce Country. (Paper read before the American Association for the Advancement of Science 40th Meeting, August 1891, Washington. Manuscript No. 4558.59 in Fletcher-La Flesche Papers, National Anthropological Archives, Smithsonian Institution, Washington.)

———
1899   A Pawnee Ritual Used When Changing a Man's Name. *American Anthropologist*, n.s. 1(1):82-97.

———
1904   The Hako: A Pawnee Ceremony. Assisted by James R. Murie; Music transcribed by Edwin S. Terry. Pp. 3-372 in Pt. 2 of *22d Annual Report of the Bureau of American Ethnology for 1900-1901.* Washington.

———
1905   Indian Names. Pp. 424-426 in *Annual Reports of the Department of the Interior for the Fiscal Year Ended June 30, 1904.* Indian Affairs, Pt. I: Report of the Commissioner, and Appendixes. Washington.

Fletcher, Alice C., and Francis La Flesche
1911   The Omaha Tribe. Pp. 17-654 in *27th Annual Report of the Bureau of American Ethnology for 1905-1906.* Washington.

Fleurieu, Charles Pierre Claret de
1801   Voyage autour du monde pendant les années 1790, 1791, et 1792. 2 vols. Paris: Imprimerie de la République.

Flexner, Stuart Berg, ed. in chief
1987   The Random House Dictionary of the English Language. Second Edition. Unabridged. New York: Random House.

Flint, Maurice S., ed.
1954   Revised Eskimo Grammar. Toronto: [no publisher.]

Flood, Richard, trans.
1847   Morning and Evening Prayers, the Administration of the Sacraments, and Other Rites and Ceremonies of the Church. According to the Use of The United Church of England and Ireland. [English and Munsee.] London: Printed by William Watts for the Society for Promoting Christian Knowledge. (1886 reprint attributed to J.B. Wampum and H.C. Hogg.)

Florez Leyra, Alfonso
1992   Testamento [January 1, 1989]. Pp. 74-84 in Don Alfonso Florez Leyra's 'Testamento': Holograph, Transcription, and Translation; by Larry Evers and Felipe S. Molina. *Journal of the Southwest* 34(1). Tucson.

Fogelson, Raymond D.
1978   Major John Norton as Ethno-ethnologist. *Journal of Cherokee Studies* 3(4):250-255.

Foley, John M.
1986   Tradition and the Collective Talent: Oral Epic, Textual Meaning, and Receptionalist Theory. *Cultural Anthropology* 1(2):203-222.

Folsom-Dickerson, William E.S.
1965   The White Path. San Antonio, Tex.: Naylor.

Ford, Richard I., Albert H. Schroeder, and Stewart L. Peckham
1972   Three Perspectives on Puebloan Prehistory. Pp. 19-39 in New Perspectives on the Pueblos. Alfonso Ortiz, ed. Albuquerque: University of New Mexico Press.

Forde, C. Daryll
1931   Ethnography of the Yuma Indians. *University of California Publications in American Archaeology and Ethnology* 28(4):83-278. Berkeley.

Fortes, M. Meyer
1955   Names Among the Tallensi of the Gold Coast. Pp. 337-349 in Afrikanistische Studien. J. Lukas, ed. Berlin: Akademie-Verlag.

Fortescue, Michael D.
1980   Affix Ordering in West Greenlandic Derivational Processes. *International Journal of American Linguistics* 46(4):259-278.

———
1981   Endoactive-exoactive Markers in Eskimo-Aleut, Tungus and Japanese—An Investigation into Common Origins. Pp. 5-42 in The Language of the Inuit: Historical, Phonological and Grammatical Issues. Louis-Jacques Dorais, ed. *Études/Inuit/Studies* 5(Supplementary Issue).

———
1990   From the Writings of the Greenlanders / Kalaallit atuakkiaannit. [Fairbanks]: University of Alaska Press.

Fortescue, Michael D., Steven A. Jacobson, and Lawrence D. Kaplan
1994   Comparative Eskimo Dictionary; with Aleut Cognates. *University of Alaska. Alaska Native Language Center Research Paper* 9. Fairbanks.

Foster, George M.
1944   A Summary of Yuki Culture. *University of California Anthropological Records* 5(3):155-244. Berkeley.

Foster, Michael K.
1971   Sociolinguistic Profile of the Longhouse Iroquois at Six Nations Reserve, Canada. (Manuscript in Foster's possession.)

1974 From the Earth to Beyond the Sky: An Ethnographic Approach to Four Longhouse Iroquois Speech Events. (Ph.D. Dissertation in Anthropology, University of Pennsylvania, Philadelphia. Published: *Canada. National Museum of Man. Mercury Series. Ethnology Service Paper* 20. Ottawa, 1974.)

1974a When Words Became Deeds: An Analysis of Three Iroquois Longhouse Speech Events. Pp. 354-367 in Explorations in the Ethnography of Speaking. Richard Bauman and Joel Sherzer, eds. London and New York: Cambridge University Press. (Reprinted, 2d ed., 1989.)

1980 The Cayuga Kanóhonyok (Thanksgiving Address). Pp. 9-25 in Northern Iroquoian Texts. Marianne Mithun and Hanni Woodbury, eds. *International Journal of American Linguistics. Native American Texts Series, Monograph* 4. Chicago: The University of Chicago Press.

1987 Linguistic Aspects of the In Situ Hypothesis of Iroquoian Origins. (Paper presented at the 1987 Conference on Iroquoian Research, Rensselaerville, New York.)

1988 The Impact of Sapir's Six-Phylum Scheme on Speculation about North American Indian Culture History: A Bibliographic Essay. *Anthropological Linguistics* 30(1):37-67.

Fowler, Catherine S.
1972 Some Ecological Clues to Proto-Numic Homelands. Pp. 105-121 in Great Basin Cultural Ecology: A Symposium. Don D. Fowler, ed. *University of Nevada, Desert Research Institute Publications in the Social Sciences* 8. Reno.

1983 Some Lexical Clues to Uto-Aztecan Prehistory. *International Journal of American Linguistics* 49(3):224-257.

Fowler, Don D., and Catherine S. Fowler, eds.
1971 Anthropology of the Numa: John Wesley Powell's Manuscripts on the Numic Peoples of Western North America, 1868-1880. *Smithsonian Contributions to Anthropology* 14. Washington.

Fox, J. Robin
1959 A Note on Cochiti Linguistics. Pp. 557-572 in Cochití, a New Mexico Pueblo, Past and Present. Charles H. Lange, ed. Austin: University of Texas Press. (Reprinted: University of New Mexico Press, Albuquerque, 1990.)

1968 Multilingualism in Two Communities. *Man*, n.s. 3(3):456-464.

Frachtenberg, Leo J.
1913 Contributions to a Tutelo Vocabulary. *American Anthropologist*, n.s. 15(3):477-479.

1913a Coos Texts. *Columbia University Contributions to Anthropology* 1. New York. (Reprinted: AMS Press, New York, 1969.)

1914 Lower Umpqua Texts and Notes on the Kusan Dialects. *Columbia University Contributions to Anthropology* 4. New York.

1917 Siuslawan (Lower Umpqua). [Extract] Pp. 431-629 in Pt. 2 of Handbook of American Indian Languages. Franz Boas, ed. *Bureau of American Ethnology Bulletin* 40. Washington.

1917a Myths of the Alsea Indians of Northwestern Oregon. *International Journal of American Linguistics* 1(1):64-75.

1917b A Siletz Vocabulary. *International Journal of American Linguistics* 1(1):45-46.

1918 Comparative Studies in Takelman, Kalapuyan and Chinookan Lexicography: A Preliminary Paper. *International Journal of American Linguistics* 1(2):175-182.

1920 Abnormal Types of Speech in Quileute. *International Journal of American Linguistics* 1(4):295-299.

1920a Alsea Texts and Myths. *Bureau of American Ethnology Bulletin* 67. Washington.

1922 Coos. *Bureau of American Ethnology Bulletin* 40(Pt. 2):297-429. Washington.

1922a Siuslawan (Lower Umpqua). *Bureau of American Ethnology Bulletin* 40(Pt. 2):431-629. Washington.

Franchère, Gabriel
1820 Relation d'un voyage à la Côte du Nord-ouest de l'Amérique septentrionale, dans les années 1810, 11, 12, 13, et 14. Montreal: C.B. Pasteur.

Franciscan Fathers
1910 An Ethnologic Dictionary of the Navaho Language. St. Michaels, Ariz.: The Franciscan Fathers. (Reprinted: Max Breslauer, Leipzig, 1929.)

Franquelin, Jean-Baptiste Louis
1684 Carte de la Louisiane ou des voyages du Sr. de la Salle et des pays qu'il a découverts depuis la Nouvelle France jusqu'au Golfe Mexique, les années 1679, 80, 81 & 82. Paris. (Facsimile in Vol. 63, frontispiece, of JR, Reuben G. Thwaites, ed., Cleveland, 1900.)

Frantz, Donald G.
1971 Toward a Generative Grammar of Blackfoot. *Summer Institute of Linguistics Publications in Linguistics and Related Fields* 34. Santa Ana: Summer Institute of Linguistics.

1972 Cheyenne Distinctive Features and Phonological Rules. *International Journal of American Linguistics* 38(1):6-13.

806

1978 Copying from Complements in Blackfoot. Pp. 89-109 in Linguistic Studies of Native Canada. Eung-Do Cook and Jonathan D. Kaye, eds. Lisse, The Netherlands: Peter de Ridder Press; Vancouver: University of British Columbia Press.

1991 Blackfoot Grammar. Toronto: University of Toronto Press.

Frantz, Donald G., and Norma J. Russell
1989 Blackfoot Dictionary of Stems, Roots, and Affixes. Toronto: University of Toronto Press. (New ed., 1995.)

Frederick, Peter J., comp.
1989-1993 Native American Autobiographies (and Autobiographical/Biographical Criticism). (Unpublished manuscript in Frederick's possession; copy in Handbook bibliographic files.)

Fredrickson, David A.
1974 Cultural Diversity in Early Central California: A View from the North Coast Ranges. Journal of California Anthropology 1(1):41-53.

1984 The North Coastal Region. Pp. 471-527 in California Archaeology. Michael J. Moratto, ed. New York, [etc.]: Academic Press.

Fredson, John, and Edward Sapir
1982 John Fredson Edward Sapir Hàa Googwandak: Stories Told by John Fredson to Edward Sapir. Retranscribed by Katherine Peter; edited and translated by Jane McGary; [etc.]. Fairbanks: Alaska Native Language Center.

Freeland, Lucy S.
1930 The Relationship of Mixe to the Penutian Family. International Journal of American Linguistics 6(1):28-33.

1951 Language of the Sierra Miwok. Indiana University Publications in Anthropology and Linguistics Memoir 6. Supplement to International Journal of American Linguistics 17(1). Baltimore, Md.

Freeland, Lucy S., and Sylvia M. Broadbent
1960 Central Sierra Miwok Dictionary With Texts. University of California Publications in Linguistics 23. Berkeley.

Freeman, John F., comp.
1966 A Guide to Manuscripts Relating to the American Indian in the Library of The American Philosophical Society. Murphy D. Smith, ed. consult. Memoirs of the American Philosophical Society 65. Philadelphia.

Freeman, Milton M.R., ed.
1976 Report: Inuit Land Use and Occupancy Project. 3 vols. Ottawa: Department of Indian and Northern Affairs.

Frege, Gottlob
1952 On Concept and Object. P.T. Geach, trans. Pp. 42-55 in Translations from the Philosophical Writings of Gottlob Frege. Peter Geach and Max Black, eds. Oxford: Basil Blackwell.

1952a On Sense and Reference. Max Black, trans. Pp. 56-78 in Translations from the Philosophical Writings of Gottlob Frege. Peter Geach and Max Black, eds. Oxford: Basil Blackwell.

Frémont, John Charles
1845 Report of the Exploring Expedition to the Rocky Mountains in the Year 1842, and to Oregon and North California in the Years 1843-'44. Washington: Gales and Seaton. (Reprinted: Smithsonian Institution Press, Washington, 1988.)

French, Benjamin Franklin, ed.
1850 Historical Collections of Louisiana. Part II. 2d ed. Philadelphia: Daniels and Smith.

French, David H.
1958 Cultural Matrices of Chinookan Non-Casual Language. International Journal of American Linguistics 24(4):258-263.

French, David H., and Kathrine S. French
1949-1992 [Ethnographic and Linguistic Notes from Fieldwork among Sahaptin-speaking Residents on the Warm Springs Reservation, Oregon.] (Manuscripts in David and Kathrine French's possession.)

1950-1992 [Ethnographic and Linguistic Notes from Fieldwork among Wasco, Wishram, and Cascades Residents at Warm Springs, Oreg., Yakima, Wash., and along the Columbia River.] (Manuscripts in David and Kathrine French's possession.)

French, Kathrine S.
1955 Culture Segments and Variation in Contemporary Social Ceremonialism on the Warm Springs Reservation, Oregon. (Unpublished Ph.D. Dissertation in Anthropology, Columbia University, New York City.)

Friedrich, Paul
1970 Proto-Indo-European Trees: The Arboreal System of a Prehistoric People. Chicago and London: The University of Chicago Press.

Friedrichs, Michael
1994 Tecumseh's Forty-one Names in the English Language: Some Remarks about their Genesis. European Review of Native American Studies 8(2):7-10. Vienna, Austria.

Frisch, Jack A.
1968 Maricopa Foods: A Native Taxonomic System. International Journal of American Linguistics 34(1):16-20.

Fulford, George
1989 A Structural Analysis of Mide Song Scrolls. Pp. 132-153 in Actes du Vingtième Congrès des Algonquinistes. William Cowan, ed. Ottawa: Carleton University.

Gabelentz, Hans Georg Conor von der
1852 Kurze Grammatik der tscherokesischen Sprache. Zeitschrift für die Wissenschaft der Sprache, Pt. 3:257-300. Greisswald.

Gagné, Raymond C.
1961 Tentative Standard Orthography for Candian Eskimos. 1st ed. Ottawa: Department of Northern Affairs and Natural Resources, Welfare Division. (3d ed., rev., 1965.)

Gagnon, François-Marc
1979 L'expérience ethnographique de Louis Nicolas. Recherches amérindiennes au Québec 8(4):281-295. Montreal.

Gaines, Ruth
1929 A Montagnais Prayer-Book and a Mohawk Primer. Museum of the American Indian, Heye Foundation. Indian Notes 6(2):138-147. New York.

Gallatin, Albert

1836   A Synopsis of the Indian Tribes Within the United States East of the Rocky Mountains, and in the British and Russian Possessions in North America. Pp. 1-422 in Archaeologia Americana: *Transactions and Collections of the American Antiquarian Society* 2. Cambridge.

———

1848   Hale's Indians of North-West America, and Vocabularies of North America: With an Introduction. Pp. xxiii-clxxxviii, 1-130 in *Transactions of the American Ethnological Society* 2. New York.

Galloway, Brent D.

1984   A Look at Nooksack Phonology. *Anthropological Linguistics* 26(1):13-41.

———

1988   Some Proto-Central Salish Sound Correspondences. Pp. 293-344 in In Honor of Mary Haas: From the Haas Festival Conference on Native American Linguistics. William Shipley, ed. Berlin: Mouton de Gruyter.

———

1988a   The Upriver Halkomelem Language Program at Coqualeetza. *Human Organization* 47(4):291-297.

———

1990   A Phonology, Morphology, and Classified Word List for the Samish Dialect of Straits Salish. Hull, Que.: Canadian Museum of Civilization.

———

1993   A Grammar of Upriver Halkomelem. *University of California Publications in Linguistics* 96. Berkeley.

Galloway, Brent D., and Allan Richardson

1983   Nooksack Place Names: An Ethnohistorical and Linguistic Approach. Pp. 133-196 in *Working Papers of the 18th International Conference on Salishan Languages.* Seattle: University of Washington.

Galois, Robert

1994   Kwakwa̱ka̱'wakw Settlements, 1775-1920: A Geographical Analysis and Gazetteer. With Contributions by Jay Powell and Gloria Cranmer Webster (on Behalf of the U'mista Cultural Centre, Alert Bay, British Columbia.) Vancouver: UBC Press; Seattle: University of Washington Press.

Gamble, Geoffrey

1975   Consonant Symbolism in Yokuts. *International Journal of American Linguistics* 41(4):306-309.

———

1978   Wikchamni Grammar. *University of California Publications in Linguistics* 89. Berkeley: University of California Press.

———

1988   Reconstructed Yokuts Pronouns. *Diachronica* 5(1-2):59-71. Hildesheim, Germany.

Gamkrelidze, Thomas V., and V.V. Ivanov

1990   The Early History of Indo-European Languages. *Scientific American* (March):110-116.

Gannet, Henry

1902   The Origin of Certain Place Names in the State of Mississippi. *Publications of the Mississippi Historical Society* 6:339-349. Jackson.

———

1905   American Names. *Geological Survey Bulletin* 258. Washington: Government Printing Office. (Reprinted: Public Affairs Press, Washington, 1947.)

Ganong, William F.

1896   A Monograph of the Place-Nomenclature of the Province of New Brunswick. Pp. 175-289 in *Proceedings and Transactions of the Royal Society of Canada for 1896,* ser. 2, vol. 2, sec. 2. Ottawa. (Reprinted: John Durie and Son, Ottawa, 1896.)

———, ed. and trans.

1910   New Relation of Gaspesia, with the Customs and Religion of the Gaspesian Indians, by Father Christien Le Clercq. Toronto: The Champlain Society. (Reprinted: Greenwood Press, New York, 1968.)

———

1912-1916 An Organization of the Place-Nomenclature of the Maritime Provinces of Canada. *Proceedings and Transactions of the Royal Society of Canada,* ser. 3, vol. 5, sec. 2:179-193; vol. 6, sec. 2:179-199; vol. 7, sec. 2:81-106; vol. 8, sec. 2:259-293; vol. 9, sec. 2:375-448. Ottawa.

———

1930   Crucial Maps in the Early Cartography and Place-Name Nomenclature of the Atlantic Coast of Canada, II. Pp. 135-187 in sec. 2, *Transactions of the Royal Society of Canada for 1930.* Ottawa.

———

1964   Crucial Maps in the Early Cartography and Place-Name Nomenclature of the Atlantic Coast of Canada. Introduction, commentary, and map notes by Theodore E. Layng. (*Royal Society of Canada Special Publication* 7.) Toronto: Toronto University Press.

García, Bartolomé "Bartholome Garcia"

1760   Manual para administrar los Santos Sacramentos de Penitencia, Eucharistia, Extrema-Uncion, y Matrimonio: Dar Gracias Despues de Comulgar, y Ayudar a Bien Morir A los Indios de las Naciones: Pajalates, Orejones, Pacaos, Pacóas, Tilijayas, Alasapas, Pausanes, y otras muchas diferentes, que se hallan en las Missiones del Rio de San Antonio, y Rio Grande, pertenecientes â el Colegio de la Santissima Cruz de la Ciudad de Queretaro, como son: Los Pacuâches, Mescâles, Pampôpas, Tâcames, Chayopînes, Venados, Pamâques, y toda la Juventud de Pihuiques, Borrados, Sanipaos, y Manos de Perro. [Mexico City]: Imprenta de los Herederos de Doña Maria de Rivera.

Gardiner, Alan

1954   The Theory of Proper Names. A Controversial Essay. 2d ed. London: Oxford University Press.

Gardiner, John Lyon

1798   A Vocabulary of the Indian Language Spoken by the Montauk Tribe. (Copy, Manuscript No. 22 in National Anthropological Archives, Smithsonian Institution, Washington.)

———

1824   Montauk Vocabulary, Taken Down from the Lips of a Montauk Chief. P. 28 in A Sketch of the First Settlement of the Several Towns on Long-Island, by Silas Wood. Brooklyn, N.Y.: Alden Spooner.

Garfield, Viola E.

1939   Tsimshian Clan and Society. *University of Washington Publications in Anthropology* 7(3):167-340. Seattle.

1953   Contemporary Problems of Folklore Collecting and Study. *Anthropological Papers of the University of Alaska* 1(2):25-36. College.

Garrioch, Alfred C.
1885   A Vocabulary of the Beaver Indian Language Consisting of Part I, Beaver-English, Part II, English-Beaver-Cree. London: Society for Promoting Christian Knowledge.

Garvin, Paul L.
1947   Christian Names in Kutenai. *International Journal of American Linguistics* 13(2):69-77.

1950   Wichita I: Phonemics. *International Journal of American Linguistics* 16(4):179-184.

1951   Kutenai IV: Word Classes. *International Journal of American Linguistics* 17(2):84-97.

1954   Colloquial Kutenai Text: Conversation II. *International Journal of American Linguistics* 20(4):316-334.

Garvin, Paul L., and Madeleine Mathiot
1960   The Urbanization of the Guaraní Language: A Problem in Language and Culture. Pp. 783-790 in Men and Cultures. Anthony F.C. Wallace, ed. (*Selected Papers of the Fifth International Congress of Anthropological and Ethnological Sciences, Philadelphia, Sept. 1-9, 1956.*) Philadelphia: University of Pennsylvania Press.

Gasque, Thomas J., and John Van Balen
1989   Early Maps of Dakota: Their Use in Placename Research. *Names* 37(2):165-182.

Gatschet, Albert S.
1875   Report on the Pueblo Languages of New Mexico, and of the Moquis in Arizona; Their Affinity to Each Other and to the Languages of the Other Indian Tribes. Pp. 180-187 in the *[Sixth] Annual Report upon the Geographical Explorations and Surveys West of the One Hundredth Meridian, 1875* by George M. Wheeler. (Appendix LL of the Annual Report of the Chief of Engineers for 1875). Washington: Government Printing Office.

1876   Analytic Report upon Indian Dialects.... Extract from Appendix JJ to *Annual Report of the Chief of Engineers for 1876* by Lt. George M. Wheeler, Vol. 3:550-563. *U.S. Geographical Surveys of the One Hundredth Meridian.* Washington: Government Printing Office.

1876a   Zwölf Sprachen aus dem Südwesten Nordamerikas (Pueblos- und Apache-Mundarten; Tonto, Tonkawa, Digger, Utah). Weimar: Hermann Böhlau. (Reprinted: Humanities Press, New York, 1970.)

1877   Indian Languages of the Pacific States and Territories. *Magazine of American History with Notes and Queries* 1(3):145-171. New York.

1877a   Die Sprache der Tonkawas. *Zeitschrift für Ethnologie* 9:64-73. Berlin: Berliner Gesellschaft für Anthropologie, Ethnologie und Urgeschichte.

1877b   Volk und Sprache der Timucua. *Zeitschrift für Ethnologie* 9:245-260. Berlin: Berliner Gesellschaft für Anthropologie, Ethnologie und Urgeschichte.

1877-1892   Der Yuma-Sprachstamm nach den neuesten handschriftlichen Quellen [I-IV]. *Zeitschrift für Ethnologie* 9:341-350, 365-418[I]; 15:123-147[II]; 18:97-122[III]; 24:1-18[IV]. Berlin: Berliner Gesellschaft für Anthropologie, Ethnologie und Urgeschichte.

1878   [Introduction to Idiomas Californias, 1821, by Felipe Arroyo de la Cuesta.] (In Manuscript No. 385, National Anthropological Archives, Smithsonian Institution, Washington.)

1879   Classification into Seven Linguistic Stocks of Western Indian Dialects Contained in Forty Vocabularies. Pp. 403-485 in Vol. 7 of *Report Upon United States Geographical Surveys West of the 100th Meridian, in Charge of 1st Lt. George M. Wheeler.* Washington: Government Printing Office.

1879a   Linguistic Notes. *American Antiquarian and Oriental Journal* 1(4):267-269. Chicago.

1879b   Linguistic Notes. *American Antiquarian and Oriental Journal* 2(1):76-79. Chicago.

1879c   Volk und Sprache der Máklaks im südwestlichen Oregon. *Globus: Illustrirte Zeitschrift für Länder- und Völkerkunde* 35:167-171. Braunschweig.

1882   Indian Languages of the Pacific States and Territories and of the Pueblos of New Mexico. *The Magazine of American History with Notes and Queries* 8:254-263. New York.

1882a   Quelques noms géographiques du sud-est des Etats-Unis d'Amerique. *Revue de Linguistique et de Philologie Comparée* 15:293-299. Paris.

1884   [Yatasi Notes, in Caddo Notebook, 1882-1888]. (Manuscript No. 2017, National Anthropological Archives, Smithsonian Institution, Washington.)

1884a   [Tonkawa Fieldnotes, collected at Fort Griffen, Texas.] (Manuscript No. 1008, National Anthropological Archives, Smithsonian Institution, Washington.)

1884-1888   A Migration Legend of the Creek Indians, with a Linguistic, Historic and Ethnographic Introduction. 2 vols. [Vol. 1 issued as *Brinton's Library of Aboriginal American Literature* 4; Vol. 2 titled: A Migration Legend of the Creek Indians, Texts and Glossaries in Creek and Hitchiti with a Linguistic, Historic, and Ethnographic Introduction and Commentary.] Philadelphia: D.G. Brinton; St. Louis, Mo.: Printed for the Author by R.P. Studley. (Reprinted, 2 vols. in 1: Kraus Reprint, New York, 1969.)

1885-1890 The Beothuk Indians. *Proceedings of the American Philosophical Society* 2(120):408-424, 23(123):411-432, 28(132):1-16. Philadelphia.

1886 On the Affinity of the Cheroki to the Iroquois Dialects. Pp. xl-xlv in Proceedings of the Seventeenth Annual Session, New Haven, 1885. *Transactions of the American Philological Association [for] 1885*, vol. 16. Cambridge, Mass.

1886a Die Karankawa Indianer. *Globus: Illustrirte Zeitschrift für Länder- und Völkerkunde* 49:123-125. Braunschweig.

1886b The Beothuk Indians [II]. *Proceedings of the American Philosophical Society* 23(i23):411-432. Philadelphia.

1886c [Letter to John W. Powell, July 31, 1886.] (Manuscript, Letters Received, in Bureau of American Ethnology Correspondence Files, National Anthropological Archives, Smithsonian Institution, Washington.)

1887 Ethnologic Results Obtained Upon an Expedition in the South-West of the United States. Two Ethnographic Maps: Linguistic Families of the Gulf States. *Science* 9(221):411-414.

1887a [Bidai, Language of Eastern Texas: Extract from a Letter from Rufus Grimes, November 15, 1887.] (Manuscript No. 1286, National Anthropological Archives, Smithsonian Institution, Washington.)

1888 The Mutsun Linguistic Family of Middle California: A Comparative Table of Affinities Drawn from its Numerous Dialects. [January, 1888, with two large tables.] (Manuscript No. 300-a, National Anthropological Archives, Smithsonian Institution, Washington.)

1888a Réplique à M.D.G. Brinton au sujet de son article *Linguistique americaine. Revue de Linguistique et de Philologie Comparée* 21:199-208. Paris.

1888b People and Language of the Adai of Louisiana. (Manuscript No. 254, National Anthropological Archives, Smithsonian Institution, Washington.)

1889 Linguistic and Ethnographic Notes. *American Antiquarian* XI(6):389-392 [398]. Chicago.

1890 The Klamath Indians of Southwestern Oregon. 2 Pts. *Contributions to North American Ethnology* 2. Washington: U.S. Geographical and Geological Survey of the Rocky Mountain Region.

1891 The Karankawa Indians, the Coast People of Texas. *Archaeological and Ethnological Papers of the Peabody Museum, Harvard University* 1(2):65-167. Cambridge.

1891a Two Indian Documents (I. Migration of the Witchita Indians. II. Removal of the Taensa Indians). *American Antiquarian and Oriental Journal* 13(4):249-254. Chicago.

1891b A Mythic Tale of the Isleta Indians. *Proceedings of the American Philosophical Society* 29:208-218.

1894 Songs of the Modoc Indians. *American Anthropologist*, n.s. 7(1):26-31.

1897 All Around the Bay of Passamaquoddy. *National Geographic Magazine* 8(1):16-24. Washington.

1900 The Waikuru, Seri, and Yuma Languages. *Science* 12(302):556-558.

1900a Grammatic Sketch of the Catawba Language. *American Anthropologist*, n.s. 2(3):527-549.

1901 Towns and Villages of the Creek Confederacy in the XVIII and XIX Centuries. *Publications of the Alabama Historical Society, Miscellaneous Collections* 1:386-415. Montgomery.

1902 Onomatology of the Catawba River Basin. *American Anthropologist*, n.s. 4(1):52-56.

Gatschet, Albert S., and Raoul de La Grasserie
1889 Textes Timucua. *Revue de Linguistique et de Philologie Comparée* 22:320-346.

Gatschet, Albert S., and John R. Swanton
1932 A Dictionary of the Atakapa Language, Accompanied by Text Material. *Bureau of American Ethnology Bulletin* 108. Washington. (Reprinted: Scholarly Press, St. Claire Shores, Mich., 1974.)

Gatschet, Albert S., Leo J. Frachtenberg, and Melville Jacobs
1945 Kalapuya Texts. Pt. 3: Kalapuya Texts. *University of Washington Publications in Anthropology* 11(3):143-369. Seattle.

Gayton, Anna H.
1935 Areal Affiliations of California Folktales. *American Anthropologist*, n.s. 37(4):582-599.

1945 Yokuts and Western Mono Social Organization. *American Anthropologist*, n.s. 47(3):409-426.

1948 Yokuts and Western Mono Ethnography. Pt. 1: Tulare Lake, Southern Valley, and Central Foothill Yokuts. *University of California Anthropological Records* 10(1). Berkeley and Los Angeles.

Gayton, Anna H., and Stanley S. Newman
1940 Yokuts and Western Mono Myths. *University of California Anthropological Records* 5(1):1-109. Berkeley. (Reprinted in part: Pp. 372-381 in Language in Culture and Society. Dell Hymes, ed. Harper and Row, New York, 1964.)

Geary, James A.
1943   The Proto-Algonquian Form for 'I-Thee'. *Language: Journal of the Linguistic Society of America* 19(2):147-151.

1953   Strachey's Vocabulary of Indian Words Used in Virginia, 1612. Pp. 208-214 in The Historie of Travell into Virginia Britania (1612). Louis B. Wright and Virginia Freund, eds. *Works Issued by the Hakluyt Society*, ser. 2, 103. London. (Reprinted: Kraus Reprint, New York, 1967.)

1955   List of Indian Words Found in the Documents, with Notes on Their Meaning. Pp. 884-900 in Vol. 2 of the Roanoke Voyages, 1584-1590; Documents to Illustrate the English Voyages to North America Under the Patent Granted to Walter Raleigh in 1584. David B. Quinn, ed. 2 vols. London: Cambridge University Press for the Hakluyt Society.

Gennep, Arnold van
1960   The Rites of Passage. Monika B. Vizedom and Gabrielle L. Caffee, trans. Chicago: The University of Chicago Press.

Gentry, Howard Scott
1963   The Warihio Indians of Sonora-Chihuahua: An Ethnographic Survey. *Anthropological Papers* 65, *Bureau of American Ethnology Bulletin* 186:61-144. Washington.

Geoghegan, Richard H.
1944   The Aleut Language: The Elements of Aleut Grammar with a Dictionary in Two Parts Containing Basic Vocabularies of Aleut and English. Fredericka I. Martin, ed. Washington: U.S. Department of the Interior.

George, M.C.
1914   Address Delivered at Dedication of Grand Ronde Military Block House at Dayton City Park, Oregon, Aug. 23, 1912. *Oregon Historical Society Quarterly* 15(1):64-70.

Gerdts, Donna B.
1984   A Relational Analysis of Halkomelem Causals. Pp. 169-204 of Syntax and Semantics. Vol. 16: The Syntax of Native American Languages. Eung-Do Cook and Donna B. Gerdts, eds. New York: Academic Press.

1988   Object and Absolutive in Halkomelem Salish. New York and London: Garland Publishing.

1991   Unaccusative Mismatches in Halkomelem Salish. *International Journal of American Linguistics* 57(2):230-250.

Gessain, Robert
1967   Makout, mon frère, fils de mon fils. *Sciences* 49-50:35-41.

1980   Nom et réincarnation chez les Ammassalimiut. *Boréalis* 15-16.

Gessain, Robert, Louis-Jacques Dorais, and C. Enel
1982   Vocabulaire du Groenlandais de l'est: 1473 Mots de la Langue Ammassalimmiut avec leur traduction en Groenlandais de l'Ouest, Français, Anglais et Danois. Paris: Centre de Recherches Anthropologiques, Musée de l'Homme.

Gibbon, Guy E.
1983   Oneota Origins Revisited. Pp. 85-89 in Oneota Studies. Guy E. Gibbon, ed. *University of Minnesota Publications in Anthropology* 1. Minneapolis.

Gibbs, George
1853   Vocabularies of Indian Languages in Northwest California. Pp. 428-445 in Vol. 3 of Historical and Statistical Information Respecting the History, Condition and Prospects of the Indian Tribes of the United States. Henry Rowe Schoolcraft, ed. Philadelphia: Lippincott, Grambo. (Reprinted: University of California Archaeological Research Facility, Berkeley, 1972.)

1855   Report....to Captain Mc'Clellan on the Indian Tribes of the Territory of Washington. Pp. 402-434 in Report of Explorations for a Route....from St. Paul to Puget Sound, by I.I. Stevens. In Vol. 1 of Reports of Explorations and Surveys....from the Mississippi River to the Pacific Ocean....1853-4 [etc.]. *33d Congress, 2d Sess. Senate Executive Document No. 78.* (Serial No. 758). Washington: Beverly Tucker, Printer. (Reprinted: Ye Galleon Press, Fairfield, Wash., 1972.)

1860   [Copeh Vocabulary (Southern Wintun).] Pp. 428-434 in Vol. 3 of Historical and Statistical Information Respecting the History, Condition and Prospects of the Indian Tribes of the United States. Henry Rowe Schoolcraft, ed. Philadelphia: Lippincott, Grambo. (Reprinted: University of California Archaeological Research Facility, Berkeley, 1972.)

1861   Instructions for Research Relating to the Ethnology and Philology of America. Washington: Smithsonian Institution.

1863   A Dictionary of the Chinook Jargon, or, Trade Language of Oregon. *Smithsonian Miscellaneous Collections* 7(1), *Publication* 161. Washington. (Issue also as: *Shea's Library of American Linguistics* 12. New York. Reprinted: AMS Press, New York, 1970.)

1863a   Instructions for Research Relative to the Ethnology and Philology of America. *Smithsonian Miscellaneous Collections* 160:i-iv, 1-34. Washington: Smithsonian Institution.

1863b   Alphabetical Vocabularies of the Clallam and Lummi. (*Shea's Library of American Linguistics* 11). New York: Cramoisy Press.

1865   Instructions Relative to the Ethnology and Philology of America. Appendix A: Physical Character of the Indian Races; Appendix B: Numeral Systems. *Smithsonian Miscellaneous Collections* 160:35-51. Washington: Smithsonian Institution.

1877   Tribes of Western Washington and Northwestern Oregon. Pp. 157-361 in *Contributions to North American Ethnology* 1. Washington: U.S. Geographical and Geological Survery of the Rocky Mountain Region.

1877a   Vocabulary of the Nikutemukh. Pp. 248-264 in *Contributions to North American Ethnology* 1. Washington: U.S. Geographical and Geological Survey of the Rocky Mountain Region.

Gibson, Ann J., and John H. Rowe, comps.
1961   A Bibliography of the Publications of Alfred Louis Kroeber. *American Anthropologist*, n.s. 63(5):1060-1087.

Gibson, John A.
1992   Concerning the League: The Iroquois Tradition as Dictated in Onondaga by John Arthur Gibson. Newly Elicited, Edited and Translated by Hanni Woodbury in Collaboration with Reg Henry and Harry Webster on the Basis of A.A. Goldenweiser's Manuscript. *Algonquian and Iroquoian Linguistics, Memoir* 9. Winnipeg, Man.

Gibson, Lorna F.
1956   Pame (Otomi) Phonemics and Morphophonemics. *International Journal of American Linguistics* 22(4):242-265.

Gibson, Robert O.
1985   Ethnogeography of the Northern Salinan. Pp. 152-221 in Excavations at Mission San Antonio, 1976-1978. R.L. Hoover and J.G. Costello, eds. *University of California. Institute of Archaeology Monograph* 26. Los Angeles.

Gifford, Edward W.
1916   Miwok Moieties. *University of California Publications in American Archaeology and Ethnology* 12(4):139-194. Berkeley.

1918   Clans and Moieties in Southern California. *University of California Publications in American Archaeology and Ethnology* 14(2):155-219. Berkeley.

1922   Californian Kinship Terminologies. *University of California Publications in American Archaeology and Ethnology* 18(1):1-285. Berkeley.

1926   Clear Lake Pomo Society. *University of California Publications in American Archaeology and Ethnology* 18(2):287-390. Berkeley.

1926a   California Anthropometry. *University of California Publications in American Archaeology and Ethnology* 22(2):217-390. Berkeley.

1931   The Kamia of Imperial Valley. *Bureau of American Ethnology Bulletin* 97. Washington.

1932   The Northfork Mono. *University of California Publications in American Archaeology and Ethnology* 31(2):15-65. Berkeley.

1933   The Cocopa. *University of California Publications in American Archaeology and Ethnology* 31(5):257-334. Berkeley.

1936   Northeastern and Western Yavapai. *University of California Publications in American Archaeology and Ethnology* 34(4):247-354. Berkeley.

Gifford, Edward W., and Alfred L. Kroeber
1939   Pomo. Culture Element Distributions, IV. *University of California Publications in American Archaeology and Ethnology* 37(4):117-254. Berkeley. (Reprinted: Kraus Reprint, New York, 1965.)

Gifford, Eli
1995   The Many Speeches of Chief Seathl: The Manipulation of the Record for Religious, Political, and Environmental Causes. *Sonoma State University. Occasional Papers on Native American Studies* 1. Rohnert Park, Calif.

Gilbert, William H., Jr.
1943   The Eastern Cherokees. *Anthropological Papers* 23, *Bureau of American Ethnology Bulletin* 133:169-414. Washington.

1955   Eastern Cherokee Social Organization. Pp. 285-338 in Social Anthropology of North American Tribes. Fred Eggan, ed. 2d ed. Chicago: University of Chicago Press.

Gilfillan, Joseph A.
1887   Minnesota Geographical Names Derived from the Chippewa Language. Pp. 451-477 in *The 15th Annual Report of the Geological and Natural History Survey of Minnesota, 1886*. St. Paul.

Gill, Charles
1886   Notes sur de vieux manuscrits abénakis. Montreal: Eusèbe Senécal & fils.

Gille, Johannes
1939   Zur Lexicologie des Alt-Algonkin. *Zeitschrift für Ethnologie* 71:71-86. Berlin: Berliner Gesellschaft für Anthropologie, Ethnologie und Urgeschichte.

Gillis, Frank J.
1984   The Incunabula of Instantaneous Ethnomusicological Sound Recordings, 1890-1910: A Preliminary List. Pp. 322-355 in Problems and Solutions: Occasional Essays in Musicology Presented to Alice M. Moyle. Jamie C. Kassler and Jill Stubington, eds. Sydney, NSW: Hale and Iremonger.

Gilmore, Melvin R.
1929   The Arikara Book of Genesis. *Papers of the Michigan Academy of Science, Arts and Letters* 12:95-120.

Gilstrap, Roger
1978   Algonquin Dialect Relationships in Northwestern Quebec. *Canada. National Museum of Man, Mercury Series. Ethnology Service Paper* 44. Ottawa.

Giorda, Joseph, Joseph Bandini, Joseph Guidi, Gregory Mengarini, and Leopold Van Gorp
1877-1879 A Dictionary of the Kalispel or Flat-head Indian Language. Compiled by the Missionaries of the Society of Jesus. Pt. I: Kalispel-English; Pt. II: English-Kalispel. Montana: St. Ignatius Print.

1879   Appendix to the Kalispel-English Dictionary, Compiled by the Missionaries of the Society of Jesus. Montana: St. Ignatius Print.

Givón, Talmy, comp.
1979   Ute Dictionary. Preliminary Edition. Ignacio, Colo.: Ute Press, The Southern Ute Tribe.

_____ , ed.
1980   Ute Reference Grammar. Ignacio, Colo.: Ute Press, The Southern Ute Tribe.

Glenmore, Josephine Stands In Timber, and Wayne Leman
1984   Cheyenne Topical Dictionary. Busby, Mont.: Cheyenne Translation Project.

1985   Cheyenne Topical Dictionary. Rev. ed. Busby, Mont.: Cheyenne Translation Project.

Glenn, James R.
1992   Guide to the National Anthropological Archives, Smithsonian Institution. Washington: National Anthropological Archives.

Goddard, Ives
1965   The Eastern Algonquian Intrusive Nasal. *International Journal of American Linguistics* 31(3):206-220.

1967   Notes on the Genetic Classification of the Algonquian Languages. Pp. 7-12 in Contributions to Anthropology: Linguistics, I (Algonquian). *Anthropological Series* 78, *National Museum of Canada Bulletin* 214. Ottawa.

1967a   The Algonquian Independent Indicative. Pp. 66-106 in Contributions to Anthropology: Linguistics I (Algonquian). *Anthropological Series* 78, *National Museum of Canada Bulletin* 214. Ottawa.

1971   The Ethnohistorical Implications of Early Delaware Linguistic Materials. *Man in the Northeast* 1:14-26. Rindge, N.H.

1972   [Brief Mention of] An Indian Vocabulary from Fort Christanna, 1716, by Edward P. Alexander. *International Journal of American Linguistics* 38(3):220.

1972a   Historical and Philological Evidence Regarding the Identification of the Mascouten. *Ethnohistory* 19(2): 123-134.

1972b   Three New Algonquian Languages. *Algonquian Linguistics Newsletter* 1(2-3):5-6.

1973   Philological Approaches to the Study of North American Indian Languages: Documents and Documentation. Pp. 727-745 in Current Trends in Linguistics, Vol. 10: Linguistics in North America (Pt. 1). Thomas A. Sebeok, ed. The Hague: Mouton.

1973a   Delaware Kinship Terminology. *Studies in Linguistics* 23:39-56.

1974   An Outline of the Historical Phonology of Arapaho and Atsina. *International Journal of American Linguistics* 40(2):102-116.

1974a   Remarks on the Algonquian Independent Indicative. *International Journal of American Linguistics* 40(4):317-327.

1974b   Dutch Loanwords in Delaware. Pp. 153-160 in A Delaware Indian Symposium. Herbert C. Kraft, ed. (*Anthropological Series* 4). Harrisburg: The Pennsylvania Historical and Museum Commission.

1975   Algonquian, Wiyot, and Yurok: Proving a Distant Genetic Relationship. Pp. 249-262 in Linguistics and Anthropology: In Honor of C.F. Voegelin. M. Dale Kinkade, Kenneth L. Hale, and Oswald Werner, eds. Lisse: Peter de Ridder Press. (Separately issued as: *PdR Press Publications in the Methodology of Comparative Linguistics* 1. Peter de Ridder Press, Lisse, 1975.)

1977   Some Early Examples of American Indian Pidgin English from New England. *International Journal of American Linguistics* 43(1):37-41.

1977a   [Review of] Indian Names in Connecticut, by James Hammond Trumbull (Archon Books, Hamden, Conn., 1974). *International Journal of American Linguistics* 43(2):157-159.

1978   A Further Note on Pidgin English. *International Journal of American Linguistics* 44(1):73.

1979   Comparative Algonquian. Pp. 70-132 in The Languages of Native America: Historical and Comparative Assessment. Lyle Campbell and Marianne Mithun, eds. Austin: University of Texas Press.

1979a   The Languages of South Texas and the Lower Rio Grande. Pp. 355-389 in The Languages of Native America: Historical and Comparative Assessment. Lyle Campbell and Marianne Mithun, eds. Austin: University of Texas Press.

1979b   Delaware Verbal Morphology: A Descriptive and Comparative Study. (*Outstanding Dissertations in Linguistics*). New York and London: Garland.

1979c   The Evidence for Eastern Algonquian as a Genetic Subgroup. *Algonquian Linguistics* 5(2):19-22.

1980   Eastern Algonquian as a Genetic Subgroup. Pp. 143-158 in Papers of the Eleventh Algonquian Conference. William Cowan, ed. Ottawa: Carleton University.

1981   [Review of] A Key into the Language of America. Edited with a Critical Introduction, Notes, and Commentary by John J. Teunissen and Evelyn J. Hinz. Detroit: Wayne State University Press, 1973. *International Journal of American Linguistics* 47(4):344-355.

1981a   Against the Linguistic Evidence Claimed for Some Algonquian Dialectal Relationships. *Anthropological Linguistics* 23(7):271-297.

1981b Massachusett Phonology: A Preliminary Look. Pp. 57-105 in Papers of the Twelfth Algonquian Conference. William Cowan, ed. Ottawa: Carleton University.

1982 The Historical Phonology of Munsee. *International Journal of American Linguistics* 48(1):16-48.

1983 The Eastern Algonquian Subordinative Mode and the Importance of Morphology. *International Journal of American Linguistics* 49(4):351-387.

1984 The Obviative in Fox Narrative Discourse. Pp. 273-286 in Papers of the Fifteenth Algonquian Conference, 1983. William Cowan, ed. Ottawa: Carleton University.

1984a The Study of Native North American Ethnonymy. Pp. 95-107 in Naming Systems. Elizabeth Tooker, ed. (*1980 Proceedings of the American Ethnological Society.*) Washington: AES.

1986 Sapir's Comparative Method. Pp. 191-214 in New Perspectives in Language, Culture, and Personality: Proceedings of the Edward Sapir Centenary Conference (Ottawa, 1-3 October 1984). William Cowan, Michael K. Foster, and Konrad Koerner, eds. Amsterdam and Philadelphia: John Benjamins.

1987 Leonard Bloomfield's Descriptive and Comparative Studies of Algonquian. Pp. 179-217 in Leonard Bloomfield: Essays on his Life and Work. Robert A. Hall, Jr. and Konrad Koerner, eds. (*Studies in the History of the Language Science* 47). Amsterdam and Philadelphia: John Benjamins.

1987a [Comment on] Language in the Americas, by Joseph H. Greenberg. *Current Anthropology* 28(5):656-657.

1988 Stylistic Dialects in Fox Linguistic Change. Pp. 193-209 in Historical Dialectology: Regional and Social. Jacek Fisiak, ed. (*Trends in Linguistics. Studies and Monographs* 37). Berlin; New York [etc.]: Mouton de Gruyter.

1990 Aspects of the Topic Structure of Fox Narratives: Proximate Shifts and the Use of Overt and Inflectional NPs. *International Journal of American Linguistics* 56(3):317-340.

1990a Some Literary Devices in the Writings of Alfred Kiyana. Pp. 159-171 in Papers of the Twenty-first Algonquian Conference, 1989. William Cowan, ed. Ottawa: Carleton University.

1990b [Review of] Language in the Americas, by Joseph H. Greenberg. *Linguistics* 28(3):556-558.

1990c Algonquian Linguistic Change and Reconstruction. Pp. 99-114 in Linguistic Change and Reconstruction Methodology. Philip Baldi, ed. (*Trends in Linguistics, Studies and Monographs* 45). Berlin and New York: Mouton de Gruyter.

1990d Unhistorical Features in Massachusett Orthography. Pp. 227-244 in Historical Linguistics and Philology. Jacek Fisiak, ed. (*Trends in Linguistics. Studies and Monographs* 46.) Berlin [and] New York: Mouton de Gruyter.

1991 Oklahoma Delaware Personal Names. *Man in the Northeast* 41(Spring):1-7.

1993 Songs in Fox (Mesquakie) Texts: Linguistics and Philology. Pp. 212-239 in Papers of the Twenty-fourth Algonquian Conference. William Cowan, ed. Ottawa: Carleton University.

1994 The West-to-East Cline in Algonquian Dialectology. Pp. 187-211 in Actes du Vingt-cinquième Congrès des Algonquinistes. William Cowan, ed. Ottawa: Carleton University.

1994a Leonard Bloomfield's Fox Lexicon: Critical Edition. *Algonquian and Iroquoian Linguistics, Memoir* 12. Winnipeg.

1995 The Delaware Jargon. Pp. 137-149 in New Sweden in America. Carol E. Hoffecker, Richard Waldron, Lorraine E. Williams, and Barbara E. Benson, eds. Newark: University of Delaware Press; London: Associated University Presses.

1996 Pidgin Delaware. In: Contact Languages: A Wider Perspective. Sarah G. Thomason, ed. Amsterdam: Benjamins. (In press.)

Goddard, Ives, and Kathleen J. Bragdon
1988 Native Writings in Massachusett. 2 vols. *Memoirs of the American Philosophical Society* 185. Philadelphia.

Goddard, Ives, and Lyle Campbell
1994 The History and Classification of American Indian Languages: What are the Implications for the Peopling of the Americas? Pp. 189-207 in Method and Theory for Investigating the Peopling of the Americas. Robson Bonnichsen and D. Gentry Steele, eds. (*Peopling of the Americas Publications*). Corvallis: Oregon State University Center for the Study of the First Americans.

Goddard, Ives, Charles F. Hockett, and Karl V. Teeter
1972 Some Errata in Bloomfield's Menomini. *International Journal of American Linguistics* 38(1):1-5.

Goddard, Pliny E.
1903 Life and Culture of the Hupa. *University of California Publications in American Archaeology and Ethnology* 1(1):1-88. Berkeley.

1904 Hupa Texts. *University of California Publications in American Archaeology and Ethnology* 1(2). Berkeley. (Reprinted: Kraus Reprint, New York, 1964.)

1905   Morphology of the Hupa Language. *University of California Publications in American Archaeology and Ethnology* 3. Berkeley.

1906   Lassik Tales. *Journal of American Folk-Lore* 19(73):133-140.

1907   The Phonology of the Hupa Language. Pt. 1: The Individual Sounds. *University of California Publications in American Archaeology and Ethnology* 5(1):1-19. Berkeley.

1909   Kato Texts. *University of California Publications in American Archaeology and Ethnology* 5(1):65-238. Berkeley.

1911   Athapascan (Hupa). Pp. 85-158 in Handbook of American Indian Languages. Franz Boas, ed. (Pt. 1) *Bureau of American Ethnology Bulletin* 40. Washington.

1911a   Jicarilla Apache Texts. *Anthropological Papers of the American Museum of Natural History* 8:1-276. New York.

1912   Texts and Analysis of Cold Lake Dialect, Chipewyan. *Anthropological Papers of the American Museum of Natural History* 10(1):1-65. New York.

1912a   Analysis of Cold Lake Dialect, Chipewyan. *Anthropological Papers of the American Museum of Natural History* 10(2):67-170. New York.

1912b   Elements of the Kato Language. *University of California Publications in American Archaeology and Ethnology* 11(1):1-176, plates 1-45. Berkeley. (Reprinted: Kraus Reprint Co., New York, 1965.)

1914   Notes on the Chilula Indians of Northwestern California. *University of California Publications in American Archaeology and Ethnology* 10(6):265-288. Berkeley.

1914a   The Present Condition of our Knowledge of North American Languages. *American Anthropologist,* n.s. 16(4):555-601.

1914b   Chilula Texts. *University of California Publications in American Archaeology and Ethnology* 10(7):289-379. Berkeley. (Reprinted: Kraus Reprint Co., New York, 1964.)

1915   Sarsi Texts. *University of California Publications in American Archaeology and Ethnology* 11(3):189-277. Berkeley.

1917   Beaver Texts. *Anthropological Papers of the American Museum of Natural History* 10(5):295-397. New York.

1917a   Beaver Dialect. *Anthropological Papers of the American Museum of Natural History* 10(5):399-546. New York.

1919   San Carlos Apache Texts. *Anthropological Papers of the American Museum of Natural History* 24(3):141-367. New York.

1920   Has Tlingit a Genetic Relation to Athapascan? *International Journal of American Linguistics* 1(4):266-279.

1920a   White Mountain Apache Texts. *Anthropological Papers of the American Museum of Natural History* 24(4):369-527. New York.

1921   Wailaki Texts. *International Journal of American Linguistics* 2(3-4):77-135.

1923   The Habitat of the Wailaki. *University of California Publications in American Archaeology and Ethnology* 20(6):93-109. Berkeley.

1924   Habitat of the Pitch Indians, a Wailaki Division. *University of California Publications in American Archaeology and Ethnology* 17(4):217-225. Berkeley.

1929   The Bear River Dialect of Athapascan. *University of California Publications in American Archaeology and Ethnology* 24(5):291-324. Berkeley.

Goff, John H.
1975   Placenames of Georgia: Essays of John H. Goff. Francis Lee Utley and Marion R. Hemperley, eds. Athens: University of Georgia Press.

Goldenweiser, Alexander A.
1912   On Iroquois Work, 1911. Pp. 386-387 in *Summary Report of Geological Survey Branch of the Canadian Department of Mines for the Calendar Year 1911.* Ottawa.

1914   On Iroquois Work, 1912. Pp. 464-475 in *Summary Report of Geological Survey Branch of the Canadian Department of Mines for the Calendar Year 1912.* Ottawa.

1914a   On Iroquois Work, 1913-1914. Pp. 365-372 in *Summary Report of Geological Survey Branch of the Canadian Department of Mines for the Calendar Year 1913.* Ottawa.

Goldfrank, Esther Schiff
1927   The Social and Ceremonial Organization of Cochiti. *American Anthropological Association Memoir* 33. Menasha, Wis.

Goldman, Irving
1940   The Alkatcho Carrier of British Columbia. Pp. 333-386 in Acculturation in Seven American Indian Tribes. Ralph Linton, ed. New York: D: Appleton-Century.

1975   The Mouth of Heaven: An Introduction to Kwakiutl Religious Thought. New York: John Wiley & Sons.   *815*

Goldschmidt, Walter
1951   Nomlaki Ethnography. *University of California Publications in American Archaeology and Ethnology* 42(4):303-443. Berkeley.

Golla, Victor
1964   Comparative Yokuts Phonology. *University of California Publications in Linguistics* 34(1):54-66. Berkeley.

1964a   An Etymological Study of Hupa Noun Stems. *International Journal of American Linguistics* 30(2):108-117.

1970   Hupa Grammar. (Unpublished Ph.D. Dissertation in Linguistics, University of California, Berkeley.)

1973   Northwest California Renaissance: The Hupa Language Teaching Program. (Paper presented at the Annual Meeting of the American Anthropological Association, New Orleans, November 1973.)

1976   Tututni (Oregon Athapaskan). *International Journal of American Linguistics* 42(3):217-227.

1977   A Note on Hupa Verb Stems. *International Journal of American Linguistics* 43(4):355-358.

1977a   Coyote and Frog (Hupa). Pp. 17-25 in Northern California Texts. Victor Golla and Shirley Silver, eds. *International Journal of American Linguistics. Native American Texts Series* 2(2). Chicago: The University of Chicago Press.

1984   The Sapir-Kroeber Correspondence: Letters between Edward Sapir and A.L. Kroeber. *University of California Survey of California and Other Indian Languages, Report* 6. Berkeley.

1985   A Short Practical Grammar of Hupa. 1st ed. Hoopa, Calif.: Hoopa Valley Tribe, Hupa Language Program.

1986   Sapir, Kroeber, and North American Indian Linguistic Classification. Pp. 17-38 in New Perspectives in Language, Culture, and Personality. *Proceedings of the Edward Sapir Centenary Conference, Ottawa, 1-3 October 1984.* William Cowan, Michael K. Foster, and Konrad Koerner, eds. Amsterdam and Philadelphia: John Benjamins.

1987   Athabaskan Languages of S.W. Oregon and N.W. California. (Paper read at the 1987 Athabaskan Conference, Victoria, B.C., August 10, 1987; in Golla's possession.)

1988   [Review of] Language in the Americas, by Joseph H. Greenberg. *American Anthropologist* 90(2):434-435.

1991   The Collected Works of Edward Sapir, VI: American Indian Languages [vol.] 2. Berlin [and] New York: Mouton de Gruyter.

1992   A Bit of History. *The Society for the Study of the Indigenous Languages of the Americas Newsletter* 11(2):10-11.

Good, John Booth
1878   The Morning and Evening Prayer, and Litany, with Prayers and Thanksgivings, Translated into the Neklakapamuk Tongue, for the Use of the Indians of the St. Paul's Mission, Lytton, British Columbia. Victoria, B.C.: St. Paul's Mission Press.

1879   The Office for Public Baptism and the Order of Confirmation, with Select Hymns and Prayers Translated into the Neklakapamuk or Thompson Tongue for the Use of the Indians of the St. Paul's Mission, Lytton, British Columbia. Victoria, B.C.: St. Paul's Mission Press.

1880   Offices for the Solemnizat[i]on of Matrimony, the Visitation of the Sick, and the Burial of the Dead. Translated into the Nitlakapamuk or Thompson Indian Tongue. Victoria, B.C.: St. Paul's Mission Press.

1880a   A Vocabulary and Outlines of Grammar of the Nitlakapamuk or Thompson Tongue. Victoria, B.C.: St. Paul's Mission Press.

Goodchild, Peter, ed.
1991   Raven Tales: Traditional Stories of Native Peoples. Chicago: Chicago Review Press.

Goodenough, Ward H.
1965   Personal Names and Modes of Address in Two Oceanic Societies. Pp. 265-276 in Context and Meaning in Cultural Anthropology. Melford E. Spiro, ed. New York: The Free Press.

Goodwin, Grenville
1937   The Characteristics and Function of Clan in a Southern Athapascan Culture. *American Anthropologist*, n.s. 39(3):394-407.

1938   White Mountain Apache Religion. *American Anthropologist*, n.s. 40(1):24-37.

1942   The Social Organization of the Western Apache. Chicago: The University of Chicago Press.

Goodwin, Grenville, and Charles Kaut
1954   A Native Religious Movement Among the White Mountain and Cibecue Apache. *Southwestern Journal of Anthropology* 10(4):385-404.

Gorbet, Larry P.
1973   How To Tell a Head When You See One: Disambiguation in Diegueño Relative Clauses. *Linguistic Notes from La Jolla* 5:63-82. San Diego: University of California, Department of Linguistics.

1976   A Grammar of Diegueño Nominals. New York and London: Garland Publishing.

Gordon, Jeffrey J.
1984   Onondaga Iroquois Place-Names: An Approach to Historical and Contempory Indian Landscape Perception. *Names* 32(3):218-233.

Gordon, Lynn
1983   Switch-Reference, Clause Order, and Interclausal Relationships in Maricopa. Pp. 83-104 in Switch-Reference and Universal Grammar. John Haiman and Pamela Munro, eds. (*Typological Studies in Language* 2). Amsterdam / Philadephia: John Benjamins.

Goss, James A.
1965   Ute Linguistics and Anasazi Abandonment of the Four Corners Area. Pp. 73-81 in Contributions to the Wetherill Mesa Archaeological Project. H. Douglas Osborne, comp. *Memoirs of the Society for American Archaeology* 19. Salt Lake City.

1967   Ute Language, Kin, Myth, and Nature: A Demonstration of a Multi-Dimensional Folk Taxonomy. *Anthropological Linguistics* 9(9):1-11.

1968   Culture-Historical Inference from Utaztecan Linguistic Evidence. Pp. 1-42 in Utaztecan Prehistory. Earl H. Swanson, ed. *Occasional Papers of the Idaho State University Museum* 22. Pocatello.

1973   Ute Naming: A Predictive Model. (Paper presented at the 72d Annual Meeting of the American Anthropological Association, New Orleans.)

1974   Gumming to Glory: A Ute Sociolinguistic Note. (Paper presented at the Northwest Anthropological Conference, Corvallis, Oreg., March 1974.)

1977   Linguistic Tools for the Great Basin Prehistorian. Pp. 49-70 in Models and Great Basin Prehistory: A Symposium. Don D. Fowler, ed. *Desert Research Institute Publications in the Social Sciences* 12. Reno and Las Vegas, Nev.

Granberry, Julian
1956   Timucua I: Prosodics and Phonemics of the Mocama Dialect. *International Journal of American Linguistics* 22(1):97-105.

1990   A Grammatical Sketch of Timucua. *International Journal of American Linguistics* 56(1):60-101.

1993·   A Grammar and Dictionary of the Timucua Language. 3d ed. Tuscaloosa: University of Alabama Press.

Granger, Byrd Howell
1961   Naming: In Customs, Beliefs, and Folk Tales. *Western Folklore* 20(1):27-37.

Green, Eugene, and Celia Millward
1971   Generic Terms for Water and Waterways in Algonquian Place Names. *Anthropological Linguistics* 13(1):33-52.

Greenberg, Joseph H.
1960   General Classification of Central and South American Languages. Pp. 791-794 in Men and Cultures, Selected Papers of the Fifth International Congress of Anthropological and Ethnological Sciences. Philadelphia, Sept. 1-9, 1956. Anthony F.C. Wallace, ed. Philadelphia: University of Pennsylvania Press.

1979   The Classification of American Indian Languages. Pp. 7-22 in Papers of the 1978 Mid-America Linguistics Conference at Oklahoma. Ralph E. Cooley, Marvin R. Barnes, and John A. Dunn, eds. Norman: University of Oklahoma Press.

1987   Language in the Americas. Stanford, Calif.: Stanford University Press.

1989   Classification of American Indian Languages: A Reply to Campbell. *Language: Journal of the Linguistic Society of America* 65(1):107-114.

1993   Observations Concerning Ringe's *Calculating the Factor of Chance in Language Comparison. Proceedings of the American Philosophical Society* 137(1):79-90. Philadelphia.

Greenberg, Joseph H., and Morris Swadesh
1953   Jicaque as a Hokan Language. *International Journal of American Linguistics* 19(3):216-222.

1985   Convergence of Evidence for the Peopling of the Americas. *Collegium Anthropologicum* 9(1):33-42.

1986   The Settlement of the Americas: A Comparison of the Linguistic, Dental, and Genetic Evidence. *Current Anthropology* 27(5):477-497.

Greene, Candace S., ed.
1993   Saynday Was Coming Along.... Washington, D.C.: Smithsonian Institution Traveling Exhibition.

Greenfeld, Philip J.
1971   Playing Card Names in Western Apache. *International Journal of American Linguistics* 37(3):195-196.

1978   Some Special Phonological Characteristics of the White Mountain Dialect of Apachean. *Anthropological Linguistics* 20(4):150-157.

Greenlee, Robert F.
1944   Medicine and Curing Practices of the Modern Florida Seminoles. *American Anthropologist* 46(3):317-328.

Gregg, Josiah
1844   Commerce of the Prairies; or, The Journal of a Santa Fé Trader, During Eight Expeditions Across the Great Western Prairies, and a Residence of Nearly Nine Years in Northern Mexico. 2 vols. New York: H.G. Langley. (Reprinted: University of Oklahoma Press, Norman, 1954.)

Grekoff, George V.
1964   A Note on Comparative Pomo. Pp. 67-72 in Studies in Californian Linguistics. William Bright, ed. *University of California Publications in Linguistics* 34. Berkeley and Los Angeles.

Griffin, James B.
1937   The Archaeological Remains of the Chiwere Sioux. *American Antiquity* 2(3):180-181.

1942   On the Historic Location of the Tutelo and the Moheton in the Ohio Valley. *American Anthropologist*, n.s. 44(2):275-280.

1943   The Fort Ancient Aspect: Its Cultural and Chronological Position in Mississippi Valley Archaeology. Ann Arbor: University of Michigan Press (Reprinted: *University of Michigan Museum of Anthropology Anthropological Papers* 28, Ann Arbor, 1966.)

1944   The Iroquois in American Prehistory. *Papers of the Michigan Academy of Science, Arts, and Letters* 29:357-374. Ann Arbor.

1960   A Hypothesis for the Prehistory of the Winnebago. Pp. 809-865 in Culture in History: Essays in Honor of Paul Radin. Stanley Diamond, ed. New York: Columbia University Press.

1964   The Northeast Woodlands Area. Pp. 223-258 in Prehistoric Man in the New World. Jesse D. Jennings and Edwards Norbeck, eds. Chicago and London: University of Chicago Press.

Grimes, Barbara F.
1992   Ethnologue: Languages of the World. 12th ed. Richard S. Pittman and Joseph E. Grimes, eds. Dallas, Tex.: Summer Institute of Linguistics.

Grimm, Thaddeus C.
1985   Time-Depth Analysis of Fifteen Siouan Languages. *Siouan and Caddoan Linguistics* (June):12-27.

1987   A Comparison of Catawba with Biloxi, Mandan and Dakota. *International Journal of American Linguistics* 53(2):175-182.

Grinnell, George Bird
1893   Pawnee Hero Stories and Folk Tales. New York: Charles Scribner and Sons.

1906   Cheyenne Stream Names. *American Anthropologist*, n.s. 8(1):15-22.

1913   Some Indian Stream Names. *American Anthropologist*, n.s. 15(2):327-331.

1923   The Cheyenne Indians: Their History and Ways of Life. 2 vols. New Haven, Conn.: Yale University Press.

Grønlands Landsråds Forhandlinger. Efterårssamling
1972   Beretning til Landsrådet fra Landsrådets Sprog- og retningsudvalg [Report to the Provincial Council from the Provincial Council Committee on Language and Orthography]. Godthåb, [Greenland].

Gross, Feliks
1951   Language and Value Changes among the Arapaho. *International Journal of American Linguistics* 17(1):10-17.

Grubb, David McC.
1977   A Practical Writing System and Short Dictionary of Kwakw'ala (Kwakiutl). *Canada. National Museum of Man. Mercury Series. Ethnology Service Paper* 34. Ottawa.

Gruber, Jacob W.
1967   Horatio Hale and the Development of American Anthropology. *Proceedings of the American Philosophical Society* 111:5-37. Philadelphia.

Gruhn, Ruth
1988   Linguistic Evidence in Support of the Coastal Route of Earliest Entry into the New World. *Man*, n.s. 23(1):77-100.

1994   The Pacific Coastal Route of Initial Entry: An Overview. Pp. 249-256 in Method and Theory for Investigating the Peopling of the Americas. Robson Bonnichsen and D. Gentry Steele, eds. Corvallis, Ore.: Oregon State University.

1995   The Pacific Coastal Route: An Alternative Model of the Initial Peopling of the Americas. In Proceedings of the Conference on Language and Prehistory, Boulder, Colorado, March 1990. Allan R. Tayor, ed. Stanford, Calif.: Stanford University Press. (In press.)

Gubser, Nicholas J.
1965   The Nunamiut Eskimos: Hunters of Caribou. New Haven, Conn.: Yale University Press.

Gudde, Erwin G.
1960   California Place Names: The Origin and Etymology of Current Geographical Names. Berkeley: University of California Press.

1969   California Place Names: The Origin and Etymology of Current Geographical Names. Berkeley: University of California Press.

Gudgel-Holmes, Dianne, comp. and ed.
1991   Native Place Names of the Kantishna Drainage, Alaska: Kantishna Oral History Project. Anchorage: U. S. Department of the Interior, National Park Service, Alaska Region.

Guéguen, Jean-Pierre
1889   Niirawe Aiamie Masinaigan, ou, Recueil de Prières, Catéchisme, Chemin de la Croix et Cantiques. Montréal: Beauchemin et Fils.

Guemple, D. Lee
1965   Saunik: Name Sharing as a Factor Governing Eskimo Kinship Terms. *Ethnology* 4(3):323-335.

1972   Introduction. Pp. 1-8 in *Proceedings of the 1971 Annual Spring Meeting of the American Ethnological Society (Supplement)*. Seattle.

1972a   Kinship and Alliance in Belcher Island Eskimo Society. Pp. 56-78 in *Proceedings of the 1971 Annual Spring Meeting of the American Ethnological Society (Supplement)*. Seattle.

Gulick, Charlotte V.
1961   The Name Book: A Dictionary of American Indian Words from Which Girls Can Derive Their Camp Fire Names. New York: Camp Fire Girls, Division of Program Services.

Gulick, John
1958   Language and Passive Resistance among the Eastern Cherokees. *Ethnohistory* 5(1):60-81. Bloomington.

Gumperz, John J.
1962   Types of Linguistic Communities. *Anthropological Linguistics* 4(1):28-40. Bloomington. (Reprinted: Pp. 460-472 in Readings in the Sociology of Language. Joshua A. Fishman, ed. The Hague and Paris: Mouton.)

Gunnerson, Dolores A.
1956   The Southern Athabascans: Their Arrival in the Southwest. *El Palacio* 63(11-12):346-365.

1972   Man and Bison on the Plains in the Protohistic Period. *Plains Anthropologist* 17(55):1-10.

Gunnerson, James H.
1962   Plateau Shoshonean Prehistory: A Suggested Reconstruction. *American Antiquity* 28(1):41-45.

Gunnerson, James H., and Dolores A. Gunnerson
1971   Apachean Culture: A Study in Unity and Diversity. Pp. 7-27 in Apachean Culture History and Ethnology. Keith H. Basso and Morris E. Opler, eds. *Anthropological Papers of the University of Arizona* 21. Tucson.

Gunther, Erna
1927   Klallam Ethnography. *University of Washington Publications in Anthropology* 1(5):171-314. Seattle.

1945   Ethnobotany of Western Washington. *University of Washington Publications in Anthropology* 10(1):1-62. Seattle.

Gursky, Karl-Heinz
1964   The Linguistic Position of the Quinigua Indians. *International Journal of American Linguistics* 30(4):325-327.

1965   Zur Frage der historischen Stellung der Yuki-Sprachfamilie. *Abhandlungen der Völkerkundlichen Arbeitsgemeinschaft* 8:1-25. Nortorf, Germany.

1965a   Lexical Similarities Between Caddoan and Algonkian-Gulf. *Anthropological Linguistics* 7(4):104-109.

1966   Der augenblickliche Stand der Erforschung der nordamerikanischen Sprachen. *Anthropos* 61(3-6):401-454. Freiburg.

1966a   On the Historical Position of Waikuri. *International Journal of American Linguistics* 32(1):41-45.

1974   Der Hoka-Sprachstamm: eine Bestandsaufnahme des lexikalischen Beweismaterials. *Orbis* 23(1):170-215. Louvain.

Haas, Mary R.
1940   Ablaut and its Function in Muskogee. *Language: Journal of the Linguistic Society of America* 16(2):141-150.

1941   The Classification of the Muskogean Languages. Pp. 41-56 in Language, Culture, and Personality: Essays in Memory of Edward Sapir. Leslie Spier, A. Irving Hallowell, and Stanley S. Newman, eds. Menasha, Wis.: Sapir Memorial Publication Fund. (Reprinted: Greenwood Press, Westport, Conn., 1983.)

1941a   Tunica. Extract from Handbook of American Indian Languages, Pt. 4:1-143. New York: J.J. Augustin.

1944   Men's and Women's Speech in Koasati. *Language: Journal of the Linguistic Society of America* 20(3):142-149. (Reprinted: Pp. 228-232 in Language in Culture and Society. Dell Hymes, ed. Harper and Row, New York, 1964.)

1945   Dialects of the Muskogee Language. *International Journal of American Linguistics* 11(2):69-74.

1946   A Grammatical Sketch of Tunica. Pp. 337-366 in Linguistic Structures of Native America. Harry Hoijer, ed. *Viking Fund Publications in Anthropology* 6. New York. (Reprinted: Johnson Reprint Co., New York, 1963.)

1946a   A Proto-Muskogean Paradigm. *Language: Journal of the Linguistic Society of America* 22(4):326-332.

1947   The Development of Proto-Muskogean *k^w. *International Journal of American Linguistics* 13(3):135-137.

1948   Classificatory Verbs in Muskogee. *International Journal of American Linguistics* 14(4):244-246.

1949   The Position of Apalachee in the Muskogean Family. *International Journal of American Linguistics* 15(2):121-127.

1950   On the Historical Development of Certain Vowels in Creek. *International Journal of American Linguistics* 16(3):122-125.

1950a   Tunica Texts. *University of California Publications in Linguistics* 6:1-174. Berkeley.

1951   The Proto-Gulf Word for *Water* (with Notes on Siouan-Yuchi). *International Journal of American Linguistics* 17(2):71-79.

1951a   Interlingual Word Taboos. *American Anthropologist*, n.s. 55(3):338-344. (Reprinted: Pp.489-493 in Language in Culture and Society. Dell Hymes, ed. Harper and Row, New York, 1964.)

1952 The Proto-Gulf Word for *Land* (with a Note on Proto-Siouan). *International Journal of American Linguistics* 18(4);238-240.

1953 Tunica Dictionary. *University of California Publications in Linguistics* 6. Berkeley.

1954 The Proto-Hokan-Coahuiltecan Word for 'Water'. Pp. 57-62 in Papers from the Symposium on American Indian Linguistics Held at Berkeley July 7, 1951. C. D. Chrétien, et al., eds. *University of California Publications in Linguistics* 10. Berkeley and Los Angeles.

1956 Natchez and the Muskogean Languages. *Language: Journal of the Linguistic Society of America* 32(1):61-72.

1957 Thai Word-Games. *Journal of American Folklore* 70(276):173-175. (Reprinted: Pp. 301-303 in Language in Culture and Society. Dell Hymes, ed. Harper and Row, New York, 1964.)

1958 Algonkian-Ritwan: The End of a Controversy. *International Journal of American Linguistics* 24(3):159-173.

1958a A New Linguistic Relationship in North America: Algonkian and the Gulf Languages. *Southwestern Journal of Anthropology* 14(3):231-264.

1959 Tonkawa and Algonkian. *Anthropological Linguistics* 1(2):1-6.

1960 Some Genetic Affiliations of Algonkian. Pp. 977-992 in Culture in History: Essays in Honor of Paul Radin. Stanley Diamond, ed. New York: Columbia University Press. (Reprinted: Octagon Books, New York, 1981.)

1961 Comment on Floyd G. Lounsbury's "Iroquois-Cherokee Linguistic Relations." Pp. 21-23 in Symposium on Cherokee and Iroquois Culture. William N. Fenton and John Gulick, eds. *Bureau of American Ethnology Bulletin* 180. Washington.

1963 Shasta and Proto-Hokan. *Language: Journal of the Linguistic Society of America* 39(1):40-59.

1964 Athapaskan, Tlingit, Yuchi, and Siouan. Pp. 495-500 in Vol. 2 of *XXXV Congreso Internacional de Americanistas, México, 1962: Actas y Memorias*. 3 vols. Mexico City.

1964a California Hokan. Pp. 73-87 in Studies in Californian Linguistics. William Bright, ed. *University of California Publications in Linguistics* 34. Berkeley and Los Angeles.

1965 Is Kutenai Related to Algonquian? *Canadian Journal of Linguistics* 10:77-92. Toronto.

1966 Wiyot-Yurok-Algonkian and Problems of Comparative Algonkian. *International Journal of American Linguistics* 32(2):101-107.

1967 On the Relations of Tonkawa. Pp. 310-320 in Studies in Southwestern Ethnolinguistics: Meaning and History in the Languages of the American Southwest. Dell Hymes and William E. Bittle, eds. (*Studies in General Anthropology*). The Hague: Mouton.

1968 The Last Words of Biloxi. *International Journal of American Linguistics* 34(2):77-84.

1968a Notes on a Chipewyan Dialect. *International Journal of American Linguistics* 34(3):165-175.

1969 The Prehistory of Languages. (*Janua Linguarum. Series Minor* 57). The Hague: Mouton.

1969a Grammar or Lexicon? The American Indian Side of the Question from Duponceau to Powell. *International Journal of American Linguistics* 35(3):239-255. (Reprinted under the title: The Problem of Classifying American Indian Languages: From Duponceau to Powell. Pp. 130-163 in Language, Culture, and History: Essays by Mary R. Haas. Anwar S. Dil, ed. Stanford University Press, Stanford, 1978.)

1969b Swanton and the Biloxi and Ofo Dictionaries. *International Journal of American Linguistics* 36(4):286-290.

1969c Internal Reconstruction of the Nootka-Nitinat Pronominal Suffixes. *International Journal of American Linguistics* 35(2):108-124.

1970 Consonant Symbolism in Northwestern California: A Problem in Diffusion. Pp. 86-96 in Languages and Cultures of Western North America: Essays in Honor of Sven S. Liljeblad. Earl H. Swanson, Jr., ed. Pocatello: The Idaho State University Press.

1972 The Expression of the Diminutive. Pp. 148-152 in Studies in Linguistics in Honor of George L. Trager. M. Estellie Smith, ed. The Hague and Paris: Mouton.

1973 The Southeast. Pp. 1210-1249 in Current Trends in Linguistics, Vol. 10: Linguistics in North America (Pt. 2). Thomas A. Sebeok, ed. The Hague and Paris: Mouton.

1975 What is Mobilian? Pp. 257-263 in Studies in Southeastern Indian Languages. J.M. Crawford, ed. Athens: University of Georgia Press.

1976 American Indian Linguistic Prehistory. Pp. 23-58 in Vol. 1 of Native Languages of the Americas. Thomas A. Sebeok, ed. 2 vols. New York and London: Plenum Press.

1976a   Boas, Sapir, and Bloomfield. Pp. 59-69 in American Indian Languages and American Linguistics: Papers of the Second Golden Anniversary Symposium of the Linguistic Society of America, Held at the University of California, Berkeley on November 8 and 9, 1974. Wallace L. Chafe, ed. Lisse, Belgium: The Peter de Ridder Press.

1978   Language, Culture, and History. Anwar S. Dil, comp. Stanford, Calif.: Stanford University Press.

1979   Southeastern Languages. Pp. 299-326 in The Languages of Native America: Historical and Comparative Assessment. Lyle Campbell and Marianne Mithun, eds. Austin: University of Texas Press.

Haberland, Wolfgang
1986   Ich, Dakota. Pine Ridge Reservation 1909: Photographien von Frederick Weygold. Berlin: Dietrich Reimer.

Hadley, Lewis F.
1893   Indian Sign Talk; Being a Book of Proofs of the Matter Printed on Equivalent Cards Designed for Teaching Sign Language, by In-go-nom-pa-shi (pseud.). Chicago: Baker and Company.

Haeberlin, Herman K.
1918   Types of Reduplication in the Salish Dialects. International Journal of American Linguistics 1(2):154-174.

1921   Notes on the Composition of the Verbal Complex in Haida. International Journal of American Linguistics 2(3-4):159-162.

Haeberlin, Herman K., and Erna Gunther
1930   The Indians of Puget Sound. University of Washington Publications in Anthropology 4(1):1-84. Seattle.

Haeberlin, Herman K., and M. Terry Thompson, ed.
1974   Distribution of the Salish Substantival (Lexical) Suffixes. Anthropological Linguistics 16(6):219-350.

Hagège, Claude
1981   Le comox lhaamen de Colombie Britannique: présentation d'une langue amérindienne. Amerindia: revue d'ethnolinguistique amérindienne, numéro spécial 2. Paris.

Haile, Berard
1938   Origin Legend of the Navaho Enemy Way: Text and Translation. Yale University Publications in Anthropology 17. New Haven, Conn.

Haile, Berard, and Maud Oakes, comps. and trans.
1957   Beautyway: A Navaho Ceremonial. Leland C. Wyman, ed. (Bollingen Series 53.) New York: Pantheon Books.

Haiman, John, and Pamela Munro, eds.
1983   Switch-Reference and Universal Grammar: Proceedings of a Symposium on Switch Reference and Universal Grammar, Winnipeg, May 1981. (Typological Studies in Language 2). Amsterdam / Philadelphia: John Benjamins.

Hakluyt, Richard
1589   The Principall Navigations, Voiages and Discoveries of the English Nation, Made by Sea or over Land, to the Most Remote and Farthest Distant Quarters of the Earth at any Time within the Compasse of these 1500 Years. London: George Bishop, Ralph Newberie, and Christopher Barker.

1599-1600 The Principal Navigations, Voyages, Traffiqves and Discoveries of the English Nation, Made by Sea or Ouer-land, to the Remote and Farthest Distant Quarters of the Earth, at any Time within the Compasse of these 1600 Years. London: George Bishop, Ralph Newberie, and Robert Barker.

1965   The Principall Navigations, Voiages and Discoveries of the English Nation by Richard Hakluyt, Imprinted at London, 1589. A Photo-Lithographic Facsimile with an Introduction by David Beers Quinn and Raleigh Ashlin Skelton and with a New Index by Alison Quinn. Cambridge: Cambridge University Press for the Hakluyt Society and the Peabody Museum of Salem.

Halbert, Henry S.
1898-1899 Choctaw Indian Names in Alabama and Mississippi. Transactions of the Alabama Historical Society 3:64-77. Tuscaloosa.

1900   Choctaw Crossing Places on the Tombigbee. Publications of the Alabama Historical Society 1:430-431. Montgomery.

1900a   Danville's Map of East Mississippi. Publications of the Mississippi Historical Society 3:367-371. Jackson.

1902   Bernard Romans Map of 1772. Publications of the Mississippi Historical Society 6:415-439. Jackson.

Hale, Horatio
1834   Remarks on the Language of the St. John's or Wlastukweek Indians, with a Penobscot Vocabulary. Boston: [Horatio Hale].

1846   Ethnography and Philology. Vol. 6 of United States Exploring Expedition During the Years 1838, 1839, 1840, 1841, 1842, Under the Command of Charles Wilkes, U.S.N. Philadelphia: Lea and Blanchard. (Reprinted: Gregg Press, Ridgewood, N.J., 1968.)

1883   The Iroquois Book of Rites. (Brinton's Library of Aboriginal American Literature 2). Philadelphia: D.G. Brinton. (Reprinted: University of Toronto Press, 1963; AMS Press, New York, 1969.)

1883a   Indian Migrations, as Evidenced by Language. Part I: The Huron-Cherokee Stock. The American Antiquarian and Oriental Journal 5(1):18-28.

1883b   The Tutelo Tribe and Language. Proceedings of the American Philosophical Society 21(114):1-47. Philadelphia.

1885   A Comparative Vocabulary of Words in the "Language of Hochelaga and Canada" as Given by Cartier, and the Corresponding Words in the Language of the Wyandot... . Pp. 79-80 in The Huron-Iroquois of Canada, by D. Wilson. *Royal Society of Canada Proceedings and Transactions for 1884. Transactions* 2 (Pt. 2). Montreal.

1890   An International Idiom: A Manual of the Oregon Trade Language, or "Chinook Jargon". London: Whittaker and Co.

1891   Remarks on the Ethnology of British Columbia: Introductory to the Second General Report of Dr. Franz Boas on the Indians of that Province. Pp. 553-562 in Sixth Report on the North-Western Tribes of Canada (with Map). *60th Report of the British Association for the Advancement of Science for 1890.* London.

Hale, Kenneth L.
1958   Internal Diversity in Uto-Aztecan: I. *International Journal of American Linguistics* 24(2):101-107.

1959   Internal Diversity in Uto-Aztecan: II. *International Journal of American Linguistics* 25(2):114-121.

1959a   A Papago Grammar. (Unpublished Ph.D. Dissertation in Linguistics, Indiana University, Bloomington.)

1962   Jemez and Kiowa Correspondences in Reference to Kiowa-Tanoan. *International Journal of American Linguistics* 28(1):1-5.

1964   The Sub-grouping of Uto-Aztecan Languages: Lexical Evidence for Sonoran. Pp. 511-517 in Vol. 2 of *XXXV Congreso Internacional de Americanistas, Mexico, 1962: Actas y Memorias.* 3 vols. Mexico.

1967   Toward a Reconstruction of Kiowa-Tanoan Phonology. *International Journal of American Linguistics* 33(2):112-120.

1967a   [Review of] Hidatsa Syntax, by G.H. Matthews (1965). *International Journal of American Linguistics* 33(4):328-341.

Hale, Kenneth L., and Josie White Eagle
1980   A Preliminary Metrical Account of Winnebago Accent. *International Journal of American Linguistics* 46(2): 117-132.

Hale, Kenneth L., Michael Krauss, Lucille J. Watahomigie, Akira Y. Yamamoto, Colette Craig, La Verne Masayesva Jeanne, and Nora C. England
1992   Endangered Languages. *Language: Journal of the Linguistic Society of America* 68(1):1-42.

Hall, Alfred J.
1889   A Grammar of the Kwagiutl Language. *Transactions of the Royal Society of Canada for 1888,* 6(2):59-105. Montreal: Dawson Brothers.

Hall, Robert A., Jr.
1990   A Life for Language: A Biographical Memoir Leonard Bloomfield. (*Studies in the History of t Language Sciences* 55). Amsterdam and Philadelphi John Benjamins.

Hall, Robert A., Jr., and Konrad Koerner, eds.
1987   Leonard Bloomfield: Essays on His Life and Wor (*Studies in the History of the Language Sciences* 4 Amsterdam and Philadelphia: John Benjamins.

Hallowell, A. Irving
1955   Culture and Experience. Philadelphia: University Pennsylvania Press.

1960   Ojibwa Ontology, Behavior, and World View. Pp. 19- in Culture in History: Essays in Honor of Paul Rad Stanley Diamond, ed. New York: Columbia Universi Press for Brandeis University.

1963   American Indians, White and Black: The Phenomen of Transculturalization. *Current Anthropology* 4(5):5 531.

Hally, David J., ed.
1994   Ocmulgee Archaeology, 1936-1986. Athens: Universi of Georgia Press.

Halpern, Abraham M.
1939-1940 Memorandum on the Survey of Pomo Languages. (Ma uscript [Freeman No. 3017(150)] in American Philos phical Society Library, Philadelphia.)

1942   Yuma Kinship Terms. *American Anthropologist,* n 44(3):425-441.

1946   Yuma. Pp. 249-288 in Linguistic Structures of Nati America. Harry Hoijer, ed. *Viking Fund Publications Anthropology* 6. New York.

1946a   Yuma I: Phonemics. *International Journal of Americ Linguistics* 12(1):25-33.

1947   Yuma IV: Verb Themes. *International Journal American Linguistics* 13(1):18-30.

1947a   Yuma V: Conjugation of the Verb Theme. *Internation Journal of American Linguistics* 13(2):92-107.

1953   A Dualism in Pomo Cosmology. *Kroeber Anthr pological Society Papers* 8, 9.

1964   A Report on a Survey of Pomo Languages. Pp. 88-93 Studies in Californian Linguistics. William Bright, e *University of California Publications in Linguistics* 3 Berkeley and Los Angeles.

1976   Kukumat Became Sick—A Yuma Text. Pp. 5-25 Yuman Texts. Margaret Langdon, ed. *Internation Journal of American Linguistics, Native American Te Series Monograph* 1(3). Chicago: University of Chica Press.

Hamilton, William
1868   Translations into the Omaha Language, with Portions of Scripture; also, A Few Hymns. New York: Edward O. Jenkins.

1885   Indian Names and Their Meaning. *Nebraska State Historical Society Transactions and Reports* 1:73-75. Lincoln, Nebr.

Hamilton, William, and Samuel McCleary Irvin
1848   An Ioway Grammar, Illustrating the Principles of the Language Used by the Ioway, Otoe, and Missouri Indians. [Wolf Creek, Nebr.]: Ioway and Sac Mission Press.

1850   We-wv-hæ-kju. [Some Questions.] [Wolf Creek, Nebr.: Ioway and Sac Mission Press (With their: Original Hymns in the Ioway Language. Indian Terr., Ioway and Sac Mission Press, 1843.)]

Hammerich, Louis L.
1936   Personalendungen und Verbalsystem im Eskimoischen. *Det Kgl. Danske Videnskabernes Selskab. Historiske-filologiske Meddelelser* 23(2). Copenhagen: Levin and Munksgaard.

1953   Russian Loan Words in Alaska. Pp. 114-126 in *Proceedings of the 30th International Congress of Americanists, held at Cambridge, 18-23 August 1952.* London: Royal Anthropological Institute.

1954   The Russian Stratum in Alaskan Eskimo. *Slavic Word* 3:401-428. [A Slavic supplement to *Word* 10(4).] New York.

1958   The Western Eskimo Dialects. Pp. 632-639 in *Proceedings of the 32d International Congress of Americanists, Copenhagen, 8-14 August 1956.* Copenhagen: Munksgaard.

1958a   The Origin of the Eskimo. Pp. 640-644 in *Proceedings of the 32d International Congress of Americanists.* Copenhagen: Munksgaard.

1960   Some Linguistic Problems of the Arctic. *Acta Arctica* 12:83-89.

1976   The Eskimo Language. Pp. 43-80 in Papers on Eskimo and Aleut Linguistics. Eric Hamp, ed. Chicago: Chicago Linguistic Society.

Hamp, Eric P.
1956   [Review of Theory of Names, by Ernst Pulgram.] *Romance Philology* 9:346-350.

1959   Proper Names in Scottish Gaelic. *Names* 7(1):57-59.

1975   On Zuni-Penutian Consonants. *International Journal of American Linguistics* 41(4):310-312.

1976   On Eskimo-Aleut and Luoravetlan. Pp. 81-92 in Papers in Eskimo and Aleut Linguistics. Eric P. Hamp, ed. Chicago: Chicago Linguistic Society.

_____ , ed.
1976a   Papers on Eskimo and Aleut Linguistics. Chicago: Chicago Linguistic Society.

Hanna, Charles A.
1911   The Wilderness Trail; or, the Ventures and Adventures of the Pennsylvania Traders on the Allegheny Path, etc. 2 vols. New York: G.P. Putnam's Sons. (Reprinted: AMS Press, New York, 1972.)

Hanzeli, Victor E.
1969   Missionary Linguistics in New France: A Study of Seventeenth- and Eighteenth-Century Descriptions of American Indian Languages. (*Janua Linguarum (Series Maior)* 29). The Hague: Mouton.

Hardy, Heather K., and Lynn Gordon
1980   Types of Adverbial and Modal Constructions in Tolkapaya. *International Journal of American Linguistics* 46(3):183-196.

1988   Imperfective Gemination in Alabama. *International Journal of American Linguistics* 54(4):399-415.

Hargus, Sharon
1988   The lexical phonology of Sekani. New York: Garland.

Harper, Ken
1979   Suffixes of the Eskimo Dialects of Cumberland Peninsula and North Baffin Island. *Canada. National Museum of Man. Mercury Series. Ethnology Service Paper* 54. Ottawa.

1985   The Early Development of Inuktitut Syllabic Orthography. *Études/Inuit/Studies* 9(1):141-162. Québec.

Harrington, John Peabody
1909   Notes on the Piro Language. *American Anthropologist*, n.s. 11(4):563-594.

1910   On Phonetic and Lexic Resemblances between Kiowan and Tanoan. *American Anthropologist*, n.s. 12(1):119-123. (Issued also in *Papers of the School of American Archaeology* 12. Santa Fe, N.M., 1910.)

1910a   An Introductory Paper on the Tiwa Language Dialect of Taos, New Mexico. *American Anthropologist*, n.s. 12(1):11-48.

1910b   A Brief Description of the Tewa Language. *American Anthropologist*, n.s. 12(4):497-504.

1912   The Tewa Indian Game of "Cañute". *American Anthropologist*, n.s. 14(2):243-286.

1912a   Tewa Relationship Terms. *American Anthropologist*, n.s. 14(3):472-498.

1913   [Note on Chumashan and Yuman Relationship.] *American Anthropologist*, n.s. 15(6):716.

1916   The Ethnogeography of the Tewa Indians. Pp. 29-618 in *29th Annual Report of the Bureau of American Ethnology for 1907-1908*. Washington.

1917   [Note on Chumashan and Washoe Relationship.] *American Anthropologist*, n.s. 19(1):154.

1920   Old Indian Geographical Names Around Santa Fe, New Mexico. *American Anthropologist*, n.s. 22(2):341-359.

1928   Vocabulary of the Kiowa Language. *Bureau of American Ethnology Bulletin* 84. Washington.

1932   Tobacco Among the Karuk Indians of California. *Bureau of American Ethnology Bulletin* 94. Washington.

1933   Annotations. Pp. 91-246 in Chinigchinich (Chi-ñi´ch-ñich). A Revised and Annotated Version of Alfred Robinson's Translation of Father Geronimo Boscana's Historical Account of the Belief, Usages, Customs and Extravagencies of the Indians of This Mission of San Juan Capistrano Called the *Acagchemem* Tribe [1846]. P.T. Hanna, ed. Santa Ana, Calif.: Fine Arts Press.

1938   The American Indian Sign Language [Pt. 2]. *Indians at Work* 5(11):28-32. Washington. (Reprinted: Pp. 117-121 in Vol. 2 of Aboriginal Sign Languages of the Americas and Australia. 2 vols. D. Jean Umiker-Sebeok and Thomas A. Sebeok, eds. Plenum Press, New York and London, 1978.)

1944   The Origin of Our State Names. *Journal of the Washington Academy of Sciences* 34:244-259.

1946   Three Kiowa Texts. *International Journal of American Linguistics* 12(4):237-242.

1955   The Original Strachey Vocabulary of the Virginia Indian Language. *Anthropological Papers* 46; *Bureau of American Ethnology Bulletin* 157:189-202. Washington.

1974   Sibilants in Ventureño. *International Journal of American Linguistics* 40(1):1-9.

Harrington, John Peabody, and Helen H. Roberts
1928   Picurís Children's Stories with Texts and Songs. *Bureau of American Ethnology Annual Report* 43. Washington.

Harrington, Mark R.
1903   Shinnecock Notes. *Journal of American Folk-Lore* 16(60):37-39.

1913   A Preliminary Sketch of Lenape Culture. *American Anthropologist*, n.s. 15(2):208-235.

Harriot, Thomas
1588   A Briefe and True Report of the New Found Land of Virginia. London. (Reprinted: Pp. 317-387 in Vol. 1 of The Roanoke Voyages, 1584-1590. 2 vols. David B. Quinn, ed. Cambridge University Press for the Hakluyt Society, London, 1955.)

1972   A Briefe and True Report of the New Found Land of Virginia. The Complete 1590 Edition with the 28 Engravings by Theodor de Bry After the Drawings of John White and Other Illustrations, with a New Introduction by Paul Hulton. New York: Dover.

Harris, Barbara P.
1985   Klahowiam Mr Smis: Context of Culture as a Factor in the Interpretation of a Chinook Jargon Text. *Anthropological Linguistics* 27(3):303-317.

Harris, Zellig S.
1944   Yokuts Structure and Newman's Grammar. *International Journal of American Linguistics* 10(4):196-211.

Harris, Zellig S., and Charles F. Voegelin
1939   Hidatsa Texts: With Grammatical Notes and Phonograph Transcriptions. Pp. 173-239 in *Indiana Historical Society, Prehistoric Research Series* 1. Indianapolis.

Harrison, Charles
1895   Haida Grammar. Alex. F. Chamberlain, ed. *Transactions of the Royal Society of Canada for 1895-1896*, 2d. ser., vol. 1(2):123-226. Montreal.

Hartley, Alan H.
1980   The Expansion of Ojibway and French Place-Names into the Lake Superior Region in the Seventeenth Century. *Names* 28(1):43-68.

1981   Preliminary Observations on Ojibwa Place-Names. Pp. 31-39 in Papers of the Twelfth Algonquian Conference. William Cowan, ed. Ottawa: Carleton University.

Harvey, Byron, III
1963   Masks at a Maskless Pueblo: The Laguna Colony Kachina Organization at Isleta. *Ethnology* 2(4):478-489.

Harvey, Gina
1974   Dormitory English. Pp. 283-293 in Southwestern Areal Linguistics. Garland D. Bills, ed. San Diego, Calif.: Institute for Cultural Pluralism, San Diego State University.

Haugen, Einar I.
1966   Language Conflict and Language Planning: The Case of Modern Norwegian. Cambridge, Mass.: Harvard University Press.

Haumonté, Jean Dominique, J. Parisot, and Lucien Adam
1882   Grammaire et vocabulaire de la langue Taensa avec textes traduits et commentés. *Bibliothèque Linguistique Américaine* 9. Paris: Maisonneuve et Cie. (Reprinted: Kraus Reprint, Nendeln, 1968.)

Hawkes, Ernest W.
1916   The Labrador Eskimo. *Canada. Department of Mines. Geological Survey, Memoir* 91, *Anthropological Series* 14. Ottawa.

Hayden, Brian, ed.
1992   A Complex Culture of the British Columbia Plateau: Traditional *Stl'átl'imx* Resource Use. Vancouver: UBC Press.

Hayden, Ferdinand Vandeveer
1862   Contributions to the Ethnography and Philology of the Indian Tribes of the Missouri Valley. *Transactions of the American Philosophical Society* 12, n.s., pt. 2:231-461. Philadelphia: C. Sherman and Son.

1869 Brief Notes on the Pawnee, Winnebago, and Omaha Languages. *Proceedings of the American Philosophical Society for 1868*, 10:389-421. Philadelphia.

Headley, Robert K., Jr.
1971 The Origin and Distribution of the Siouan-Speaking Tribes. (Unpublished M.A. Thesis in Anthropology, Catholic University of America, Washington, D.C.)

Hearne, Samuel
1795 A Journey from Prince of Wales's Fort in Hudson's Bay to the Northern Ocean ... in the Years 1769, 1770, 1771, & 1772. London: A. Strahan and T. Cadell. (Reprinted: Tuttle, Rutland, Vt. 1971.)

———
1968 A Journey From Prince of Wales's Fort in Hudson's Bay to the Northern Ocean [1795]. Amsterdam: N. Israel; New York: Da Capo Press.

Heath, Jeffrey
1977 Uto-Aztecan Morphophonemics. *International Journal of American Linguistics* 43(1):27-36.

———
1978 Uto-Aztecan *na-Class Verbs. *International Journal of American Linguistics* 44(3):211-222.

———
1981 Tübatulabal Phonology. Pp. 188-217 in *Harvard Studies in Phonology* 2. George N. Clements, ed. Bloomington: Indiana University Linguistics Club.

———
1985 Proto-Northern Uto-Aztecan Principles. *International Journal of American Linguistics* 51(4):441-443.

Hébert, Léo-Paul
1979 La Brosse, Jean-Baptiste de. Pp. 423-425 in Vol. 4 (1771 to 1800) of Dictionary of Canadian Biography. Toronto: University of Toronto Press.

Hebert, Yvonne M.
1982 Aspect and Transitivity in (Nicola Lake) Okanagan. Pp. 195-215 in Syntax and Semantics. Vol. 15: Studies in Transitivity. Paul J. Hopper and Sandra A. Thompson, eds. New York: Academic Press.

Heckewelder, John Gottlieb E.
1819 An Account of the History, Manners, and Customs, of the Indian Nations, Who Once Inhabited Pennsylvania and the Neighboring States. *American Philosophical Society, Transactions of the Historical and Literary Committee* 1. Philadephia.

———
1834 Names Which the Lenni Lenapes or Delaware Indians, Who Once Inhabited this Country, Had Given to Rivers, Streams, Places &x., &c., Within the Now States of Pennsylvania, New Jersey, Maryland, and Virginia. *Transactions of the American Philosophical Society* 4:351-396. Philadelphia.

———
1876 History, Manners, and Customs of the Indian Nations Who Once Inhabited Pennsylvania and the Neighbouring States. [1819]. New and rev. ed. with an Introduction and Notes by William C. Reichel. *Memoirs of the Historical Society of Philadelphia* 12. Philadelphia.

———
1958 Thirty Thousand Miles with John Heckewelder. Paul A.W. Wallace, ed. Pittsburgh, Penn.: University of Pittsburgh Press.

Heckewelder, John Gottlieb E., and Peter S. Duponceau
1819 A Correspondence Between the Rev. John Heckewelder, of Bethlehem, and Peter S. Duponceau, Esq., Corresponding Secretary of the Historical and Literary Committee of the American Philosophical Society, Respecting the Languages of the American Indians. *Transactions of the Committee of History, Moral Science and General Literature of the American Philosophical Society* 1:351-448. Philadelphia.

Heckewelder, John Gottlieb E., and E.N. Horsford, ed.
1887 Comparative Vocabulary of Algonquin Dialects. From Heckewelder's Manuscripts in the Collections of the American Philosophical Society, Philadelphia. Cambridge, Mass.: John Wilson and Son, University Press.

Heepe, M., ed.
1928 Lautzeichen und ihre Anwendung in verschiedenen Sprachgebieten. Berlin: Reichsdruckerei.

Heidenreich, Conrad E.
1988 An Analysis of the 17-th Century Map "Novvelle France". *Cartographica* 25(3):67-111. Toronto.

Heine, Bernd, and Mechthild Reh
1984 Grammaticalization and Reanalysis in African Languages. Hamburg: Helmut Buske.

Heine, Bernd, Ulrike Claude, and Friederike Hünnemeyer
1991 Grammaticalization: A Conceptual Framework. Chicago: The University of Chicago Press.

Heinrich, Albert C.
1960 Structural Features of Northwestern Alaskan Eskimo Kinship. *Southwestern Journal of Anthropology* 16(1):110-126.

———
1963 Personal Names, Social Structure, and Functional Integration. *Montana State University. Department of Sociology, Anthropology and Social Welfare. Anthropology and Sociology Papers* 27. Missoula.

———
1969 Social Integration and Personal Names in an Eskimo Group. *Journal of Karnatak University—Social Sciences* 5(April):1-14. Dharwar, India.

———
1971 Some Borrowing from German into Eskimo. *Anthropological Linguistics* 13(3):96-99.

Heizer, Robert F.
1947 Francis Drake and the California Indians, 1579. *University of California Publications in American Archaeology and Ethnology* 42:251-302. Berkeley.

———, ed.
1952 California Indian Linguistic Records: The Mission Indian Vocabularies of Alphonse Pinart. *University of California Anthropological Records* 15(1):1-84. Berkeley.

———, ed.
1955 California Indian Linguistic Records: The Mission Indian Vocabularies of H.W. Henshaw. *University of California Anthropological Records* 15(2):85-202. Berkeley.

1966   Languages, Territories, and Names of California Indian Tribes. Berkeley and Los Angeles: University of California Press.

_____ , ed.
1967   C. Hart Merriam's Ethnographic Notes on California Indian Tribes III: Ethnological Notes on Central California Indian Tribes. *Reports of the University of California Archaeological Survey* 68(3):371-403. Berkeley.

1974   Elizabethan California. Ramona, Calif.: Ballena Press.

1975   Chumash Place Name Lists: Compilations by A.L. Kroeber, C. Hart Merriam, and H.W. Henshaw. Berkeley: University of California, Archaeological Research Facility.

Heizer, Robert F., and William W. Elmendorf
1942   Francis Drake's California Anchorage in the Light of the Indian Language Spoken There. *Pacific Historical Review* 11:213-217.

Henderson, T.S.T.
1973   Verbal Modes in Algonkin. *Studies in Linguistics* 23:57-62. Dekalb, Ill.

Henkelman, James W., and Kurt H. Vitt
1985   Harmonious To Dwell: The History of the Alaska Moravian Church 1885-1985. Bethel, Alaska: The Moravian Seminary and Archives.

Hennigh, Lawrence
1972   You Have to Be a Good Lawyer to Be an Eskimo. Pp. 89-109 in *Proceedings of the 1971 Annual Spring Meeting of the American Ethnological Society (Supplement)*. Seattle and London.

Henry, Alexander
1988   The Journal of Alexander Henry the Younger, 1799-1814. Barry M. Gough, ed. 2 vols. (*Publications of the Champlain Society* 56). Toronto: Champlain Society.

Henry, David
1975   Dinaak'a—Our Language. Anchorage: Alaska Native Language Center.

Henry, David, and Kay Henry
1965   Koyukon Classificatory Verbs. *Anthropological Linguistics* 7(4, Pt. 2):110-116.

1969   Koyukon Locationals. *Anthropological Linguistics* 11(4):136-142.

1969a   Hadohzil-eeyah. We Are Reading. Fairbanks: Summer Institute of Linguistics.

Henry, Victor
1879   Esquisse d'une Grammaire Raisonnée de la Langue Aléoute d'après la Grammaire et le Vocabulaire de Ivan Veniaminov. Paris: Maisonneuve.

Henshaw, Henry W.
1888   [Report on] Linguistic Map. *American Anthropologist*, o.s. 1(4):293-294.

1890   A New Linguistic Family in California. *American Anthropologist*, o.s. 3(1):45-49.

1955   *see* Heizer, Robert F. 1955

Henshaw, Henry W., and Leo Frachtenberg
1910   Shahaptian Family. Pp. 519-520 in Pt. 2 of Handbook of American Indians North of Mexico. Frederick W. Hodge, ed. *Bureau of American Ethnology Bulletin* 30. Washington.

Hertzberg, Hazel W.
1971   The Search for American Indian Identity: Modern Pan-Indian Movements. Syracuse, N.Y.: Syracuse University Press.

Hervás y Panduro, Lorenzo
1800-1805 Catálogo de la lenguas de las naciones conocidas, y numeracion, division, y clases de estas segun la diversidad de sus idiomas y dialectos. 6 vols. Madrid: La Imprenta de la Administración del Real Arbitrio de Beneficencia.

Herzog, George
1941   Culture Change and Language: Shifts in the Pima Vocabulary. Pp. 66-74 in Language, Culture, and Personality: Essays in Memory of Edward Sapir. Leslie Spier, A. Irving Hallowell, and Stanley S. Newman, eds. Menasha, Wis.: Sapir Memorial Publication Fund. (Reprinted: Greenwood Press, Westport, Conn. 1983.)

Herzog, George, Stanley S. Newman, Edward Sapir, Mary Haas Swadesh, Morris Swadesh, and Charles F. Voegelin
1934   Some Orthographic Recommendations; Arising Out of Discussions by a Group of Six Americanist Linguists. *American Anthropologist*, n.s. 36(4):629-631.

Hess, Thom.
1966   Snohomish Chameleon Morphology. *International Journal of American Linguistics* 32(4):350-356.

1967   Snohomish Grammatical Structure. (Unpublished Ph.D. Dissertation in Linguistics, University of Washington, Seattle.)

1976   Dictionary of Puget Salish. Seattle and London: University of Washington Press.

1977   Lushootseed Dialects. *Anthropological Linguistics* 19(9):403-419.

1990   A Note on Nitinaht Numerals. *International Journal of American Linguistics* 56(3):427-431.

Hewett, Edgar L.
1904   Studies on the Extinct Pueblo of Pecos. *American Anthropologist*, n.s. 6(4):426-439.

Hewitt, J.N.B.
1887   The Cheroki an Iroquoian Language. A Critical Study and Comparison of Etymologies, Words, Sentence-words, Phrase-forms and Conjugations Common to the Cherokian and Iroquoian Tongues To Establish Their Common Origin. (Manuscript No. 447 in National Anthropological Archives, Smithsonian Institution, Washington.)

1891   [Manuscript Annotations on Map of Linguistic Stocks of American Indians North of Mexico, by J. W. Powell.] (Manuscript [map] No. 3869, National Anthropological Archives, Smithsonian Institution, Washington.)

1894   On the Evidence of Linguistic Relationship Between the Shahaptian and the Waiilatpuan Groups of Tongues. (Manuscript No. 679, National Anthropological Archives, Smithsonian Institution, Washington.)

1898   Comparative Lexicology. Pp. 299-344 in The Seri Indians, by W J McGee. *17th Annual Report of the Bureau of American Ethnology for 1895-1896.* Washington.

1903   Iroquoian Cosmology, First Part. Pp. 127-339 in *21st Annual Report of the Bureau of American Ethnology for 1899-1900.* Washington.

1910   Wathatotarho. Pp. 921-922 in Pt. 2 of Handbook of American Indians North of Mexico. Frederick W. Hodge, ed. *Bureau of American Ethnology Bulletin* 30. Washington.

1928   Iroquoian Cosmology, Second Part. Pp. 449-819 in *43d Annual Report of the Bureau of American Ethnology for 1925-1926.* Washington.

1939   Notes on the Creek Indians. John R. Swanton, ed. Pp. 119-159 in *Anthropological Papers* 10, *Bureau of American Ethnology Bulletin* 123. Washington.

Hewitt, J.N.B., and William N. Fenton
1945   Some Mnemonic Pictographs Relating to the Iroquois Condolescence Council. *Journal of the Washington Academy of Sciences* 35(10):301-315. Menasha, Wis.

Hewson, John
1968   Beothuk and Algonkian: Evidence Old and New. *International Journal of American Linguistics* 34(2):85-93.

1971   Beothuk Consonant Correspondences. *International Journal of American Linguistics* 37(4):244-249.

1972   Errata in Bloomfield's Algonquian Sketch. *International Journal of American Linguistics* 38(1):77.

1978   Beothuk Vocabularies: A Comparative Study. *Technical Papers of the Newfoundland Museum* 2. St. John's.

1981-1982 The Name *Presentic* and Other Ancient Micmac Toponyms. *The Newfoundland Quarterly* 76(4):11-14. St. John's.

1994   An 18th-Century Missionary Grammarian: Micmac Studies of Father Maillard. *Historiographia Linguistica* 21(1-2):65-76. Amsterdam.

Hewson, John, and Bernard Francis 1990 *see* Pacifique, [père] 1990

Hickerson, Harold
1967   A Note of Inquiry on Hockett's Reconstruction of PCA. *American Anthropologist* 69(3-4):362-363.

Hickerson, Harold, Glen D. Turner, and Nancy P. Hickerson
1952   Testing Procedures for Estimating Transfer of Information among Iroquois Dialects and Languages. *International Journal of American Linguistics* 18(1):1-8.

Hickerson, Nancy P.
1959   An Acoustic Analysis of Shawnee: IV. *International Journal of American Linguistics* 25(2):97-104.

Hilbert, Vi
1985   Haboo: Native American Stories from Puget Sound. Seattle: University of Washington Press.

1991   When Chief Seattle (Siʔał) Spoke. Pp. 259-266 in A Time of Gathering: Native Heritage in Washington State. Robin K. Wright, ed. Seattle: Burke Museum [and] University of Washington Press.

Hilger, M. Inez
1944   Ceremonia Para Dar Nombre a un Niño Indio Chippewa. *América Indígena* 4(3):237-242.

1946   Notes on Cheyenne Child Life. *American Anthropologist*, n.s. 48(1):60-69.

1951   Chippewa Child Life and Its Cultural Background. *Bureau of American Ethnology Bulletin* 146. Washington.

1952   Arapaho Child Life and Its Cultural Background. *Bureau of American Ethnology Bulletin* 148. Washington.

Hill, Archibald A.
1952   A Note on Primitive Languages. *International Journal of American Linguistics* 18(4):172-177. (Reprinted in part: Pp. 86-88 in Language in Culture and Society. Dell Hymes, ed. Harper and Row, New York, 1964.)

Hill, Faith
1963   Some Comparisons Between the San Carlos and White Mountain Dialects of Western Apache. Pp. 149-154 in Studies in the Athapaskan Languages. Harry Hoijer, ed. *University of California Publications in Linguistics* 29. Berkeley.

Hill, Jane H., and Kenneth C. Hill
1968   Stress in the Cupan (Uto-Aztecan) Languages. *International Journal of American Linguistics* 34(4):233-241.

Hill, Jane H., and Rocinda Nolasquez
1973   Mulu'wetam: The First People. Banning, Calif.: Malki Museum Press.

Hill, Kenneth C.
1967   A Grammar of the Serrano Language. (Unpublished Ph.D. Dissertation in Linguistics, University of California, Los Angeles.)

Hill, W.W.
1936   Navaho Warfare. *Yale University Publications in Anthropology* 5. New Haven, Conn.

1943   Navaho Humor. Pp. 3-28 in *General Series in Anthropology* 9. Menasha, Wis.

Hill-Tout, Charles
1900   Notes on the N'tlaka´pamuq of British Columbia, a Branch of the Great Salish Stock of North America. Pp. 500-584 in *69th Report of the British Association for the Advancement of Science for 1899*. London.

1903   Ethnological Studies of the Mainland Halkome´lem, a Division of the Salish of British Columbia. Pp. 355-449 in *72d Report of the British Association for the Advancement of Science for 1902*. London.

1904   Report on the Ethnology of the Siciatl of British Columbia, A Coast Division of the Salish Stock. *Journal of the Anthropological Institute of Great Britain and Ireland* 34:34, 36-91.

1905   Some Features of the Language and Culture of the Salish. *American Anthropologist*, n.s. 7(4):674-687.

1907   British North America. 1: The Far West, the Home of the Salish and Dene. (*The Native Races of the British Empire*). London: Archibald Constable.

1907a   Report on the Ethnology of the South-Eastern Tribes of Vancouver Island, British Columbia. *Journal of the Royal Anthropological Institute* 37(July-Dec.):306-374.

1911   Report on the Ethnology of the Okanák·en of British Columbia, an Interior Division of the Salish Stock. *Journal of the Anthropological Institute of Great Britain and Ireland* 41:130, 137-144.

Hilton, K. Simón
1993   Diccionario tarahumara de Samachique, Chihuahua, México. Ed. especial corr. y actual. Tucson, Ariz.: Instituto Lingüístico de Verano.

Hilton, Susanne F., John C. Rath, and Evelyn W. Windsor, eds.
1982   Oowekeeno Oral Traditions as Told by the Late Chief Simon Walkus, Sr. *Canada. National Museum of Man. Mercury Series. Ethnology Service Papers* 84. Ottawa.

Hindle, Lonnie, and Bruce Rigsby
1973   A Short Practical Dictionary of the Gitksan Language. *Northwest Anthropological Research Notes* 7(1). Moscow, Idaho.

Hinsley, Curtis M.
1981   Savages and Scientists: The Smithsonian Institution and the Development of American Anthropology, 1846-1910. Washington: Smithsonian Institution Press. (Reprinted as: The Smithsonian and the American Indian: Making of a Moral Anthropology in Victorian America. Smithsonian Institution Press, Washington, 1994.)

Hinton, Leanne
1976   The Tar Baby Story (Diegueño). Pp. 101-106 in Yuman Texts. Margaret Langdon, ed. *International Journal of American Linguistics. Native American Texts Series* 1(3). Chicago: The University of Chicago Press.

1978   Coyote Baptizes the Chickens (La Huerta Diegueño). Pp. 117-120 in Coyote Stories. William Bright, ed. *International Journal of American Linguistics. Native American Texts Series Monograph* 1. Chicago: The University of Chicago Press.

1984   Havasupai Songs: A Linguistic Perspective. (*Ars Linguistica* 6). Tübingen, Germany: Gunter Narr.

1991   Takic and Yuman: A Study in Phonological Convergence. *International Journal of American Linguistics* 57(2):133-157.

1994   Flutes of Fire: Essays on California Indian Languages. Berkeley: Heyday Books.

Hinton, Leanne, and Yolanda Montijo
1994   In Our Own Words: How Much Is Really Left of California's Native Languages? *News from Native California* 7(4):4-9. Berkeley.

Hinton, Leanne, and Lucille J. Watahomigie, eds.
1984   Spirit Mountain: An Anthology of Yuman Story and Song. (*Sun Tracks: An American Indian Literary Series* 10). Tucson: University of Arizona Press.

Hinz, John
1944   Grammar and Vocabulary of the Eskimo Language as Spoken by the Kuskokwim and the Southwest Coast Eskimos of Alaska. Bethlehem, Pa.: Society for Propagating the Gospel.

Hitchcock, Ethan A.
1930   A Traveler in Indian Territory: The Journal of Ethan Allen Hitchcock, Late Major-General in the United States Army. Grant Foreman, ed. Cedar Rapids, Iowa: The Torch Press.

Hoard, James E.
1978   Obstruent Voicing in Gitksan: Some Implications for Distinctive Feature Theory. Pp. 111-119 in Linguistic Studies of Native Canada. Eung-Do Cook and Jonathan D. Kaye, eds. Lisse: Peter de Ridder Press Vancouver: University of British Columbia Press.

Hockett, Charles F.
1939   The Potawatomi Language. (Ph.D. Dissertation in Linguistics, Yale University, New Haven, Conn.)

1948   Implications of Bloomfield's Algonquian Studies. *Language* 24(1):117-131. (Reprinted in revised form: Pp. 599-609 in Language in Culture and Society. Dell Hymes, ed. New York: Harper and Row, 1964.)

1948a   Potawatomi I: Phonemics, Morphophonemics, and Morphological Survey. *International Journal of American Linguistics* 14(1):1-10.

1948b   Potawatomi II: Derivation, Personal Prefixes, and Nouns. *International Journal of American Linguistics* 14(2):63-73.

1948c   Potawatomi III: The Verb Complex. *International Journal of American Linguistics* 14(3):139-149.

1948d   Potawatomi IV: Particles and Sample Texts. *International Journal of American Linguistics* 14(4):213-225.

1956   Idiom Formation. Pp. 222-229 in For Roman Jakobson: Essays on the Occasion of His Sixtieth Birthday, 11 October 1956. Morris Halle et al., comps. The Hague: Mouton.

1957   Central Algonquian Vocabulary: Stems in /k-/. *International Journal of American Linguistics* 23(4):247-268.

1958   A Course in Modern Linguistics. New York: The Macmillan Company.

1964   The Proto Central Algonquian Kinship System. Pp. 239-257 in Explorations in Cultural Anthropology: Essays in Honor of George P. Murdock. Ward H. Goodenough, ed. New York: McGraw-Hill.

1966   What Algonquian Is Really Like. *International Journal of American Linguistics* 32(1):59-73.

1966a   The Problem of Universals in Language. Pp. 1-29 in Universals of Language. Joseph H. Greenberg, ed. Cambridge: The M.I.T. Press.

_____, ed.
1970   A Leonard Bloomfield Anthology. Bloomington: Indiana University Press. (Abridged ed.: University of Chicago Press, Chicago, 1987.)

1977   [Review of] Lexical Reconstruction: The Case of the Proto-Athapaskan Kinship System, by Isidore Dyen and David F. Aberle. *Current Anthropology* 18(1):84-91.

1981   The Phonological History of Menominee. *Anthropological Linguistics* 23(2):51-87.

1981a   Errata in "The Phonological History of Menominee." *Anthropological Linguistics* 23(7):326.

Hockett, Charles F., and Robert A. Hall, Jr.
1987   A New Leonard Bloomfield Bibliography. Pp. 221-233 in Leonard Bloomfield: Essays on His Life and Work. Robert A. Hall, Jr., and Konrad Koerner, eds. (*Studies in the History of the Language Sciences* 47). Amsterdam and Philadelphia: John Benjamins.

Hodge, Frederick W.
1896   Pueblo Indian Clans. *American Anthropologist*, o.s. 9(10):345-352.

1907   Advance Report on the Nomenclature of Indian Linguistic Families. (Report Presented to the Joint Meeting of the American Anthropological Association, Section H of the American Association for the Advancement of Science, and the American Folk-Lore Society at the University of Chicago from December 30, 1907 to January 2, 1908). (Copy in the F. W. Hodge Collection, Southwest Museum, Los Angeles.)

_____, ed.
1907-1910 Handbook of American Indians North of Mexico. 2 Pts. *Bureau of American Ethnology Bulletin* 30. Washington. (Reprinted: Rowman and Littlefield, New York, 1971.)

1921   Report of the Ethnologist-in-Charge. Pp. 7-37 in *35th Annual Report of the Bureau of American Ethnology for 1913-1914*. Washington.

Hodge, Frederick W., and C. Hart Merriam
1931   Henry Weatherbee Henshaw. *American Anthropologist*, n.s. 33(1):98-105.

Hoffman, Bernard G.
1955   Souriquois, Etechemin, and Kwĕdĕch — A Lost Chapter in American Ethnography. *Ethnohistory* 2(1):65-87.

1959   Iroquois Linguistic Classification from Historical Materials. *Ethnohistory* 6(2):160-185.

1961   Cabot to Cartier: Sources for a Historical Ethnography of Northeastern North America, 1497-1550. Toronto: University of Toronto Press.

1964   Observations on Certain Ancient Tribes of the Northern Appalachian Province. Pp. 191-245 in *Bureau of American Ethnology Bulletin* 191. *Anthropological Papers* 70. Washington.

Hofsinde, Robert (Grey-Wolf, pseud.)
1956   Indian Sign Language. New York: The Morrow Company.

Hoijer, Harry
1933   Tonkawa, an Indian Language of Texas. Pp. 1-148 in Pt. 3 of Handbook of American Indian Languages. Franz Boas, ed. New York: Columbia University Press.

1938   The Southern Athapaskan Languages. *American Anthropologist*, n.s. 40(1):75-87.

1941   Methods in the Classification of American Indian Languages. Pp. 3-14 in Language, Culture, and Personality: Essays in Memory of Edward Sapir. Leslie Spier, A. Irving Hallowell, and Stanley S. Newman, eds. Menasha, Wis.: Sapir Memorial Publication Fund. (Reprinted: Greenwood Press, Westport, Conn. 1983.)

1945   The Apachean Verb, Part I: Verb Structure and Pronominal Prefixes. *International Journal of American Linguistics* 11(4):193-203.

_____, ed.
1946   Linguistic Structures of Native America. (Editor's Introduction, pp. 9-29). *Viking Fund Publications in Anthropology* 6. New York: Wenner-Gren Foundation for Anthropological Research. (Reprinted: Johnson Reprint, New York, 1963, 1971.)

1946a   Chiricahua Apache. Pp. 55-84 in Linguistic Structures of Native America. Harry Hoijer, ed. *Viking Fund Publications in Anthropology* 6. New York.

1946b   Tonkawa. Pp. 289-311 in Linguistic Structures of Native America. Harry Hoijer, ed. *Viking Fund Publications in Anthropology* 6. New York.

1949   An Analytical Dictionary of the Tonkawa Language. *University of California Publications in Linguistics* 5. Berkeley.

1949a   Tonkawa Syntactic Suffixes and Anaphoric Particles. *Southwestern Journal of Anthropology* 4(1):37-55. Albuquerque.

1954   Some Problems of American Indian Linguistic Research. Pp. 3-12 in Papers from the Symposium on American Indian Linguistics Held at Berkeley, July 7, 1951. C.D. Chrétien, et al., eds. *University of California Publications in Linguistics* 10. Berkeley.

1956   Lexicostatistics: A Critique. *Language: Journal of the Linguistic Society of America* 32(1):49-60.

1956a   The Chronology of the Athapaskan Languages. *International Journal of American Linguistics* 22(4):219-232.

1956b   Athapaskan Kinship Systems. *American Anthropologist*, n.s. 58(2):309-333.

1958   Comment [on Voegelin (1958)]. Pp. 58-59 in Migrations in New World Culture History. Raymond H. Thompson, ed. *University of Arizona Social Science Bulletin* 27. Tucson: University of Arizona Press.

1960   Athapaskan Languages of the Pacific Coast. Pp. 960-976 in Culture in History: Essays in Honor of Paul Radin. Stanley Diamond, ed. New York: Columbia University Press.

1962   Linguistic Sub-grouping by Glottochronology and by the Comparative Method: The Athapaskan Languages. *Lingua: International Review of General Linguistics* 11:192-198. Amsterdam.

1963   The Athapaskan Languages. Pp. 1-29 in Studies in the Athapaskan Languages. Harry Hoijer, ed. *University of California Publications in Linguistics* 29. Berkeley.

1966   Hare Phonology: An Historical Study. *Language: Journal of the Linguistic Society of America* 42(2):499-507.

1966a   Galice Athapaskan: A Grammatical Sketch. *International Journal of American Linguistics* 32(4):320-327.

1971   Athapaskan Morphology. Pp. 113-147 in Studies in American Indian Languages. Jesse Sawyer, ed. *University of California Publications in Linguistics* 65. Berkeley.

1971a   The Position of the Apachean Languages in the Athapaskan Stock. Pp. 3-6 in Apachean Culture History and Ethnology. Keith H. Basso and Morris E. Opler, eds. *Anthropological Papers of the University of Arizona* 21. Tucson.

1972   Tonkawa Texts. *University of California Publications in Linguistics* 73. Berkeley.

1973   Galice Noun and Verb Stems. *Linguistics: An International Review* 104:49-73.

1974   A Navajo Lexicon. *University of California Publications in Linguistics* 78. Berkeley.

1975   The History and Creation of the Lipan, as Told by Augustina Zuazua. *Linguistics: An International Review* 161:5-37.

Hoijer, Harry, and Edward P. Dozier
1949   The Phonemes of Tewa, Santa Clara Dialect. *International Journal of American Linguistics* 15(3):139-144.

Hoijer, Harry, and Janet Joël
1963   Sarsi Nouns. Pp. 62-75 in Studies in the Athapaskan Languages. Harry Hoijer, ed. *University of California Publications in Linguistics* 29. Berkeley.

Hoijer, Harry, and Morris E. Opler
1938   Chiricahua and Mescalero Apache Texts. Chicago: University of Chicago Press. (Reprinted: AMS Press, New York, 1980.)

Hollow, Robert C.
1970   A Mandan Dictionary. (Unpublished Ph.D. Dissertation in Linguistics, University of California, Berkeley.)

Hollow, Robert C., and Douglas R. Parks
1980   Studies in Plains Linguistics: A Review. Pp. 68-97 in Anthropology on the Great Plains. W. Raymond Wood and Margot Liberty, eds. Lincoln: University of Nebraska Press.

Holm, Thomas Campanius
1834   A Short Description of the Province of New Sweden. Now Called by the English, Pennsylvania, in America. Compiled from the Relations and Writings of Persons Worthy of Credit, and Adorned with Maps and Plates. Peter S. DuPonceau, ed. Philadelphia: M'Carty and Davis.

Holmberg, Heinrich Johan von
1856   Ethnographische Skizzen über die Völker des russischen Amerika. 2 vols. Helsinki: H.C. Friis. (Reprinted as *Holmberg's Ethnographic Sketches.* Marvin W. Falk, ed.; Fritz Jaensch, trans. Fairbanks: University of Alaska Press, 1985.)

Holmer, Nils M.
1948   Indian Place Names in North America. (*Essays and Studies on American Language and Literature* 7). S.B. Liljegren, ed. Upsala: The American Institute in the University of Upsala. (Reprinted: Kraus Reprint, Nendeln, Liechtenstein, 1973.)

1967   The Native Place Names of Arctic America I. *Names* 15(3):182-196.

1969   The Native Place Names of Arctic America II. *Names* 17(2):138-158.

Holmes, Abiel
1804   Memoir of the Moheagan Indians. *Collections of the Massachusetts Historical Society* [1st ser.] 9:75-99. Boston. (Published separately with title: A Memoir of the Moheagan Indians. Written in the year M.DCC.IV. Boston, 1804.)

Holmes, William H.
1886   Ancient Pottery of the Mississippi Valley. Pp. 361-436 in *4th Anual Report of the Bureau of [American] Ethnology for 1882-'83*. Washington.

Holtved, Erik
1952   Remarks on the Polar Eskimo Dialect. *International Journal of American Linguistics* 18(1):20-24.

Holway, Hope
1959   Ann Eliza Worcester Robertson as a Linguist. *The Chronicles of Oklahoma* 37(1):35-44, 108-122.

Honigmann, John J.
1949   Culture and Ethos of Kaska Society. *Yale University Publications in Anthropology* 40. New Haven, Conn.

1954   The Kaska Indians: An Ethnographic Reconstruction. *Yale University Publications in Anthropology* 51. New Haven, Conn.

1956   The Attawapiskat Swampy Cree. *Anthropological Papers of the University of Alaska* 5(1):23-82. College.

Honigmann, John J., and Irma Honigmann
1970   Arctic Townsmen: Ethnic Backgrounds and Modernization. Ottawa: Canadian Research Centre for Anthropology, Saint Paul University.

Hooper, Lucile
1920   The Cahuilla Indians. *University of California Publications in American Archaeology and Ethnology* 16(6):315-380. Berkeley.

Hopkins, Alice W.
1987   Vowel Dominance in Mohawk. *International Journal of American Linguistics* 53(4):445-459.

Hopkins, Nicholas A.
1965   Great Basin Prehistory and Uto-Aztecan. *American Antiquity* 31(1):48-60.

Hopkins, Sarah Winnemucca
1883   Life Among the Paiutes: Their Wrongs and Claims. Mrs. Horace Mann, ed. Boston: Cupples, Upham; New York: G.P. Putnam's Sons. (Reprinted: Chalfant Press, Bishop, Calif., 1969; University of Nevada Press, Reno, 1994.)

Hopper, Paul J., and Elizabeth C. Traugott
1993   Grammaticalization. (*Cambridge Textbooks in Linguistics*). Cambridge, England, and New York: Cambridge University Press.

Horden, John
1881   A Grammar of the Cree Language, as Spoken by the Cree Indians of North America. London: Society for Promoting Christian Knowledge.

Horsford, Eben N.
1886   The Indian Names of Boston and Their Meaning. Cambridge: The University Press.

Hoskins, John B.
1941   The Narrative of a Voyage to the North West Coast of America and China on Trade and Discoveries by John Hoskins Performed in the Ship *Columbia Rediviva*, 1790, 1791, 1792, and 1793. Pp. 161-289 in Voyages of the "Columbia" to the Northwest Coast, 1787-1790 and 1790-1793. F.W. Howay, ed. *Massachusetts Historical Society Collections* 79. Boston. (Reprinted: Da Capo Press, New York, 1969.)

Howard, James H.
1965   The Ponca Tribe. *Bureau of American Ethnology Bulletin* 195. Washington.

1972   Notes on the Ethnogeography of the Yankton Dakota. *Plains Anthropologist* 17(58, pt. 1):281-307. Lincoln, Neb.

Howard, Philip G.
1963   A Preliminary Presentation of Slave Phonemes. Pp. 42-47 in Studies in the Athapaskan Languages. Harry Hoijer, ed. *University of California Publications in Linguistics* 29. Berkeley.

Howay, Frederic W.
1942   The Origin of the Chinook Jargon. *British Columbia Historical Quarterly* 6(4):225-250. Victoria.

1943   Origin of the Chinook Jargon on the North West Coast. *Oregon Historical Society Quarterly* 44(1):27-55.

Howren, Robert
1979   The Phonology of Rae Dogrib. Pp. 7-40 in Contributions to Canadian Linguistics. *National Museum of Man. Mercury Series. Canadian Ethnology Service Paper* 50. Ottawa.

Howse, Joseph
1844   A Grammar of the Cree Language; With Which Is Combined an Analysis of the Chippeway Dialect. London: J.G.F. and J. Rivington. (Reprinted: Trübner, London, 1865.)

Hoyo, Eugenio del
1960   Vocablos de la Lengua Quinigua de los Indios Borrados del Noreste de Mexico. *Humanitas* 1(1):489-515. Mexico.

1965   El cuadernillo de la lengua de los indios Pajalates (1732) por Fray Gabriel de Vergara, y El confesionario de indios en lengua coahuilteca. [With a biographical note on Fray Gabriel de Vergara by Lino Gómez Canedo]. *Publicaciones del Instituto Tecnológico y de Estudios Superiores de Monterrey (Serie Historia)* 3. Monterrey, Nuevo León, Mexico.

Hrdlička, Aleš
1904   Notes on the Indians of Sonora, Mexico. *American Anthropologist*, n.s. 6(1):51-89.

831

1945 The Aleutian and Commander Islands and Their Inhabitants. Philadelphia: The Wistar Institute of Anatomy and Biology.

Hubbard, Lucius
1884 Some Indian Place-Names in Northern Maine, with Explanations Derived from the Indians and a Cross-Index. Boston: James R. Osgood & Co.

Huden, John C.
1957 Indian Place Names in Vermont. Burlington, Vt.: The Author.

1962 Indian Place Names of New England. *Contributions from the Museum of the American Indian, Heye Foundation* 18. New York: Museum of the American Indian.

Hudson, Charles
1990 The Juan Pardo Expeditions: Explorations of the Carolinas and Tennessee, 1566-1568. Washington and London: Smithsonian Institution Press.

Hudson, Charles, and Carmen Chaves Tesser, eds.
1994 The Forgotten Centuries: Indians and Europeans in the American South, 1521-1704. Athens: University of Georgia Press.

Hudson, Charles, Chester B. DePratter, and Marvin T. Smith
1989 Hernando de Soto's Expedition Through the Southern United States. Pp. 77-149 in First Encounters: Spanish Exploration in the Caribbean and the United States, 1492-1570. Jerald T. Milanich and Susan Milbraith, eds. Gainesville, Fla: University of Florida Press and Florida Museum of Natural History.

Hudson, Travis
1977 Patterns of Chumash Names. *The Journal of California Anthropology* 4(2):259-272. Banning.

1978 Some J.P. Harrington Notes on the "Lone Woman" of San Nicolas Island. *Masterkey* 52(1):23-28.

1978a An Additional Harrington Note on the "Lone Woman" of San Nicolas. *Masterkey* 52(4):151-154.

Hughes, Charles C.
1958 An Eskimo Deviant from the "Eskimo" Type of Social Organization. *American Anthropologist* 60(6):1140-1147.

1960 An Eskimo Village in the Modern World. With the collaboration of Jane M. Hughes. Ithaca, N.Y.: Cornell University Press.

Hughes, Richard E.
1992 California Archaeology and Linguistic Prehistory. *Journal of Anthropological Research* 48(4):317-338.

Hukari, Thomas E., Ruby Peter, and Ellen White
1977 Halkomelem. Pp. 33-68 in Northwest Coast Texts. Barry F. Carlson, ed. *International Journal of American Linguistics. Native American Texts Series* 2(2). Chicago: The University of Chicago Press.

Huld, Martin
1978 Athapaskan Bears. *International Journal of American Linguistics* 49(2):186-195.

1985 Regressive Apicalization in Na'isha. *International Journal of American Linguistics* 51(4):461-463.

Hultkrantz, Åke
1953 Conceptions of the Soul Among North American Indians: A Study in Religious Ethnology. *The Ethnographical Museum of Sweden (Statens Etnografiska Museum) Monograph Series Publication* 1. Stockholm.

Hulton, Paul, and David Beers Quinn
1964 The American Drawings of John White, 1577-1590, with Drawings of European and Oriental Subjects. I: A Catalogue Raisonné and a Study of the Artist. With Contributions from W.C. Sturtevant, C.E. Raven, R.A. Skelton, and Louis B. Wright. London and Chapel Hill: The Trustees of the British Museum and the University of North Carolina Press.

Humfreville, J. Lee
1903 Twenty Years Among Our Hostile Indians. 2d ed. rev. and enl. New York: Hunter and Co.

Hunn, Eugene S.
1991 Native Place Names on the Columbia Plateau. Pp. 170-177 in A Time of Gathering: Native Heritage in Washington State. Robin K. Wright, ed. Seattle and London: Burke Museum and University of Washington Press.

1994 Place-Names, Population Density, and the Magic Number 500. *Current Anthropology* 35(1):81-85.

Hunn, Eugene S., with James Selam and Family
1990 Nch'i-Wána, "The Big River": Mid-Columbia Indians and Their Land. Seattle and London: University of Washington Press.

Hunter, Helen E.
1943 Record of Field Work by Frances Densmore for the Bureau of American Ethnology, 1907-1941, on Music and Customs of the American Indians, with Biography and Personal Memoranda. (Typescript filed with Manuscript No. 4250, Box 2, Folder 25, National Anthropological Archives, Smithsonian Institution, Washington.)

Hunter, James
1875 A Lecture on the Grammatical Construction of the Cree Language [1862]. London: Printed for the Society for Promoting Christian Knowledge.

Huntsman, Jeffrey F.
1983 Traditional Native American Literature: The Translation Dilemma. Pp. 87-97 in Smoothing the Ground: Essays on Native American Oral Literature. Brian Swann, ed. Berkeley: University of California Press.

Hurley, William M.
1968 The Kickapoo Whistle System: A Speech Surrogate. *Plains Anthropologist* 13(41):242-247.

Hyde, George E.
1937 Red Cloud's Folk: A History of the Oglala Sioux. Norman: University of Oklahoma Press. (Reprinted in 1957, 1967, 1976.)

Hyde, Villiana Calac
1971 An Introduction to the Luiseño Language. R.W. Langacker, ed. Banning, Calif.: Malki Museum Press.

Hyde, Villiana Calac, and Eric Elliott
1994   Yumáyk Yumáyk: Long Ago. *University of California Publications in Linguistics* 125. Berkeley.

Hyer, Joseph K., and William S. Starring, comps.
1866   Lahcotah. Dictionary of the Sioux Language. (Compiled with the aid of Charles Guerreu, Indian Interpreter.) Fort Laramie, Dakota [Terr.]: [The Authors]. (Facsimile ed.: Yale University Press, New Haven, Conn., 1968.)

Hymes, Dell H.
1955   The Language of the Kathlamet Chinook. (Ph.D. Dissertation in Linguistics, Indiana University, Bloomington. Photocopy: University Microfilms, Ann Arbor, Mich. 1975.)

1955a   Positional Analysis of Categories: A Frame for Reconstruction. *Word* 11(1):10-23.

1956   Na-Déné and Positional Analysis of Categories. *American Anthropologist* 58(4):624-638.

1957   A Note on Athapaskan Glottochronology. *International Journal of American Linguistics* 23(4):291-297.

1958   Linguistic Features Peculiar to Chinookan Myths. *International Journal of American Linguistics* 24(4):253-257.

1960   Lexicostatistics So Far. *Current Anthropology* 1(1):3-34, 41-44.

1961   Functions of Speech: An Evolutionary Approach. Pp. 55-83 in Anthropology and Education. Frederick C. Gruber, ed. Philadelphia: University of Pennsylvania Press.

1962   The Ethnography of Speaking. Pp. 13-53 in Anthropology and Human Behavior. Thomas Gladwin and William C. Sturtevant, eds. Washington, D.C.: Anthropological Society of Washington.

1962a   [Comment on Bergsland and Vogt (1962).] *Current Anthropology* 3(2):136-141.

1964   The Problem of Penutian. Pp. 453-456 in Vol. 2 of *XXXV Congreso Internacional de Americanistas, Mexico, 1962: Actas y Memorias*. 3 vols. Mexico.

1964a   Evidence for Penutian in Lexical Sets with Initial *c- and *s-. *International Journal of American Linguistics* 30(3):213-242.

1964b   'Hail' and 'Bead': Two Penutian Etymologies. Pp. 94-98 in Studies in Californian Linguistics. William Bright, ed. *University of California Publications in Linquistics* 34. Berkeley and Los Angeles.

1964c   Language in Culture and Society: A Reader in Linguistics and Anthropology. New York, Evanston, and London: Harper and Row.

1966   Two Types of Linguistic Relativity. With Examples from Amerindian Ethnography. Pp. 114-167 in Sociolinguistics: Proceedings of the UCLA Sociolinguistics Conference, 1964. William Bright, ed. The Hague and Paris: Mouton.

1966a   Some Points of Siuslaw Phonology. *International Journal of American Linguistics* 32(4):328-342.

1972   Models of the Interaction of Language and Social Life. Pp. 35-71 in Directions in Sociolinguistics: The Ethnography of Speaking. John Gumperz and Dell Hymes, eds. New York: Holt, Rinehart and Winston.

1974   Foundations in Sociolinguistics: An Ethnographic Approach. Philadelphia: University of Pennsylvania Press.

1974a   Speech and Language: On the Origins and Foundations of Inequality Among Speakers. Pp. 45-71 in Language as a Human Problem. Morton Bloomfield and Einar Haugen, eds. New York: W. W. Norton.

1975   Breakthrough into Performance. Pp. 11-74 in Folklore: Performance and Communication. Dan Ben-Amos and Kenneth S. Goldstein, eds. The Hague: Mouton. (Reprinted: Pp. 79-141 in "In Vain I Tried to Tell You": Essays in Native American Ethnopoetics, by Dell H. Hymes, University of Pennsylvania Press, Philadelphia, 1981.)

1976   Louis Simpson's "The Deserted Boy." *Poetics* 5(2):119-155. (Reprinted: Pp. 142-183 in "In Vain I Tried to Tell You": Essays in Native American Ethnopoetics, by Dell H. Hymes, University of Pennsylvania Press, Philadelphia, 1981.)

1979   How to Talk Like a Bear in Takelma. *International Journal of American Linguistics* 45(2):101-106. (Reprinted: Pp.65-76 in "In Vain I Tried to Tell You": Essays in Native American Ethnopoetics, by Dell H. Hymes, University of Pennsylvania Press, Philadelphia, 1981.)

1980   Commentary. Pp. 389-423 in Theoretical Orientations in Creole Studies. Albert Valdman and Arnold Highfield, eds. New York: Academic Press.

1980a   Verse Analysis of a Wasco Text: Hiram Smith's "At'unaqa". *International Journal of American Linguistics* 46(2):65-77.

1981   "In Vain I Tried to Tell You": Essays in Native American Ethnopoetics. *Studies in Native American Literature* 1. Philadelphia: University of Pennsylvania Press.

1983   Essays in the History of Linguistic Anthropology. (*Amsterdam Studies in the Theory and History of Linguistic Science* III. *Studies in the History of Linguistics* 25). Amsterdam and Philadelphia: John Benjamins.

1983a   Poetic Structure of a Chinook Text. Pp. 507-525 in Essays in Honor of Charles F. Hockett. Frederick B. Agard, Gerald Kelley, Adam Makkai, and Valerie Becker Makkai, eds. Leiden, The Netherlands: E.J. Brill.

1987   Tonkawa Poetics: John Rush Buffalo's "Coyote and Eagle's Daughter". Pp. 17-61 in Native American Discourse: Poetics and Rhetoric. Joel Sherzer and Anthony C. Woodbury, eds. *Cambridge Studies in Oral and Literate Culture* 13. Cambridge.

1992   Use All There Is to Use. Pp 83-124 in On the Translation of Native American Literatures. Brian Swann, ed. Washington: Smithsonian Institution Press

Hymes, Dell H., and Harold E. Driver
1958   Concerning the Proto-Athapaskan Kinship System. *American Anthropologist* 60(1):152-155.

Hymes, Dell H., and John G. Fought
1981   American Structuralism. (*Janua Linguarum. Series Major* 102). The Hague and New York: Mouton.

Hymes, Dell H., and Henry Zenk
1987   Narrative Structure in Chinook Jargon. Pp. 445-465 in Pidgin and Creole Languages: Essays in Memory of John E. Reinecke. G.G. Gilbert, ed. Honolulu: University of Hawaii Press.

Hymes, Virginia
1987   Warm Springs Sahaptin Narrative Analysis. Pp. 62-102 in Native American Discourse: Poetics and Rhetoric. Joel Sherzer and Anthony C. Woodbury, eds. *Cambridge Studies in Oral and Literate Culture* 13. Cambridge.

Inglis, Richard, and George MacDonald
1975   5,000 Years of History on the West Coast. *Canadian Geographical Journal* 91(6):32-37.

International Phonetic Association
1949   The Principles of the International Phonetic Association, Being a Description of the International Phonetic Alphabet and the Manner of Using It. London: Department of Phonetics, University College. (Reprinted in 1967.)

1989   Report on the 1989 Kiel Convention. *Journal of the International Phonetic Association* 19(2):67-80. London.

Irving, William N.
1962   A Provisional Comparison of Some Alaskan and Asian Stone Industries. Pp. 55-68 in Prehistoric Culture Relations Between the Arctic and Temperate Zones of North America. J.M. Campbell, ed. *Arctic Institute of North America Technical Paper* 11. Montreal.

1969-1970 The Arctic Small Tool Tradition. Pp. 340-342 in Vol. 3 of *Proceedings of the International Congress of Anthropological and Ethnological Sciences, 1968.* 3 vols. Tokyo.

Isham, James
1949   James Isham's Observations on Hudsons Bay, 1743, and Notes and Observations on a Book Entitled *A Voyage to Hudsons Bay in the Dobbs Galley,* 1749. E.E. Rich, ed., assisted by A.M. Johnson. (*Publications of the Champlain Society, Hudson's Bay Company Series* 12). Toronto: The Champlain Society.

JR = Thwaites, Reuben G., ed.
1896-1901 The Jesuit Relations and Allied Documents: Travels and Explorations of the Jesuit Missionaries in New France, 1610-1791; The Original French, Latin, and Italian Texts, with English Translations and Notes. 73 vols. Cleveland: Burrows Brothers. (Reprinted: Pageant, New York, 1959.)

Jackson, Barbara D.
1980   A Peyote Community in Northern Minnesota. Pp. 127-193 in Anishinabe: 6 Studies of Modern Chippewa. J. Anthony Paredes, ed. Tallahassee: University Presses of Florida.

Jackson, Donald D., ed.
1962   Letters of the Lewis and Clark Expedition with Related Documents, 1783-1854. Urbana, Ill.: University of Illinois Press. (2d ed., with additional documents and notes, 1978.)

_____ , ed.
1966   The Journals of Zebulon Montgomery Pike, with Letters and Related Documents. 2 vols. Norman, Okla.: University of Oklahoma Press.

_____ , ed.
1978   Letters of the Lewis and Clark Expedition, with Related Documents, 1783-1854. 2d. ed., with additional documents and notes. 2 vols. Chicago: University of Illinois Press.

Jackson, Thomas L.
1989   Reconstructing Migrations in California Prehistory. *American Indian Quarterly* 13(4):359-368.

Jacobs, Elizabeth D.
1959   Nehalem Tillamook Tales. Melville Jacobs, ed. *University of Oregon Monographs. Studies in Anthropology* 5. Eugene. (Reprinted in 1990.)

1968   A Chetco Athabaskan Myth Text from Southwestern Oregon. *International Journal of American Linguistics* 34(3):192-193.

1977   A Chetco Athapaskan Text and Translation. *International Journal of American Linguistics* 43(4):269-273.

Jacobs, Melville
1929   Northwest Sahaptin Texts, 1. *University of Washington Publications in Anthropology* 2(6). Seattle.

1931   A Sketch of Northern Sahaptin Grammar. *University of Washington Publications in Anthropology* 4(2). Seattle.

1932   Notes on the Structure of the Chinook Jargon. *Language: Journal of the Linguistic Society of America* 8(1):27-50.

1934-1937 Northwest Sahaptin Texts. 2 Pts. Pt. 1: English; Pt. 2: Sahaptin. *Columbia University Contributions to Anthropology* 19. New York.

1936 Texts in Chinook Jargon. *University of Washington Publications in Anthropology* 7(1):1-27. Seattle.

1937 Historic Perspectives in Indian Languages of Oregon and Washington. *Pacific Northwest Quarterly* 28(1):55-74. Seattle.

1939 Coos Narrative and Ethnologic Texts. *University of Washington Publications in Anthropology* 8(1):1-126. Seattle.

1940 Coos Myth Texts. *University of Washington Publications in Anthropology* 8(2):127-260. Seattle.

1945 Kalapuya Texts. (Pt. 1: Santiam Kalapuya Ethnologic Texts, by M. Jacobs. Pt. 2: Santiam Kalapuya Myth Texts, by M. Jacobs. Pt. 3: Kalapuya Texts, by A.S. Gatschet, L.J. Frachtenberg, and M. Jacobs.) *University of Washington Publications in Anthropology* 11. Seattle.

1954 The Areal Spread of Sound Features in the Languages North of California. Pp. 46-56 in Papers from the Symposium on American Indian Linguistics, Held at Berkeley, July 7, 1951. *University of California Publications in Linguistics* 10. Berkeley.

1958-1959 Clackamas Chinook Texts. 2 Pts. *Indiana University Research Center in Anthropology, Folklore, and Linguistics Publications* 8, 11; *International Journal of American Linguistics* 24(2, Pt. 2), 25(2, Pt. 2).

1959 The Content and Style of an Oral Literature: Clackamas Chinook Myths and Tales. *Viking Fund Publications in Anthropology* 26. New York.

1960 The People Are Coming Soon: Analyses of Clackamas Chinook Myths and Tales. Seattle: University of Washington Press.

1964 Pattern in Cultural Anthropology. Homewood, Ill.: The Dorsey Press.

1968 An Historical Event Text from a Galice Athabaskan in Southwestern Oregon. *International Journal of American Linguistics* 34(3):183-191.

Jacobs, Roderick A.
1976 Hattepaa Hellyaaw—Coyote and Rabbit [The Rabbit and the Coyote (Diegueño)]. Pp. 107-112 in Yuman Texts. Margaret Langdon, ed. *International Journal of American Linguistics. Native American Texts Series* 1(3). Chicago: The University of Chicago Press.

Jacobs, Sarah "S.J. of N."
1856 Indian Names of the Months. *New England Historical and Genealogical Register* 10(2):166.

Jacobsen, William H., Jr.
1958 Washo and Karok: An Approach to Comparative Hokan. *International Journal of American Linguistics* 24(3):195-212.

1961 Switch-reference: A Hokan-Coahuiltecan Syntactic Device. (Paper presented at the Twenty-sixth Annual Meeting of the Linguistic Society of America.)

1964 A Grammar of the Washo Language. (Unpublished Ph.D. Dissertation in Linguistics, University of California, Berkeley.)

1966 Washo Linguistic Studies. Pp. 113-136 in The Current Status of Anthropological Research in the Great Basin: 1964. Warren L. d'Azevedo, et al., eds. *Desert Research Institute, Technical Report Series S-H, Social Sciences and Humanities Publication* 1. Reno, Nev.

1966a Comments on Linguistics. Pp. 259-264 in The Current Status of Anthropological Research in the Great Basin: 1964. Warren L. d'Azevedo, et al., eds. *Desert Research Institute, Technical Report Series S-H, Social Sciences and Humanities Publication* 1. Reno, Nev.

1967 Switch-reference in Hokan-Coahuiltecan. Pp. 238-263 in Studies in Southwestern Ethnoliguistics: Meaning and History in the Languages of the American Southwest. Dell H. Hymes and William E. Bittle, eds. The Hague: Mouton.

1968 Comment on James A. Goss's "Culture-Historical Inference from Utaztecan Linguistic Evidence." Pp. 43-52 in Utaztecan Prehistory. Earl H. Swanson, ed. *Occasional Papers of the Idaho State University Museum* 22. Pocatello, Idaho.

1969 Origin of the Nootka Pharyngeals. *International Journal of American Linguistics* 35(2):125-153.

1976 Observations on the Yana Stop Series in Relationship to Problems of Comparative Hokan Phonology. Pp. 203-236 in Hokan Studies. Margaret Langdon and Shirley Silver, eds. *Janua Linguarum, Series Practica* 181. The Hague, Paris: Mouton.

1976a Wakashan. (Paper presented at the Northwest Coast Studies Conference; in Jacobsen's possession.)

1978 Washo Internal Diversity and External Relations. Pp. 115-147 in Selected Papers from the 14th Great Basin Anthropological Conference. Donald R. Tuohy, ed. *Ballena Press Publications in Archaeology, Ethnology and History* 11. Socorro, New Mexico.

1979   Hokan Inter-Branch Comparisons. Pp. 545-591 in The Languages of Native America: Historical and Comparative Assessment. Lyle Campbell and Marianne Mithun, eds. Austin and London: University of Texas Press.

1979a   Wakashan Comparative Studies. Pp. 766-791 in The Languages of Native America: Historical and Comparative Assessment. Lyle Campbell and Marianne Mithun, eds. Austin and London: University of Texas Press.

1979b   Chimakuan Comparative Studies. Pp. 792-802 in The Languages of Native America: Historical and Comparative Assessment. Lyle Campbell and Marianne Mithun, eds. Austin and London: University of Texas Press.

1979c   Noun and Verb in Nootkan. Pp. 83-155 in The Victoria Conference on Northwestern Languages, Victoria, B.C. November 4-5, 1976. Barbara S. Efrat, ed. *British Columbia Provincial Museum. Heritage Record* 4. Victoria.

1980   Inclusive/Exclusive: A Diffused Pronomial Category in Native Western North America. Pp. 204-227 in Papers from the Parasession on Pronouns and Anaphora, Chicago Linguistic Society, April 18-19, 1980. Jody Kreiman and Almerindo E. Ojeda, eds. Chicago: Chicago Linguistic Society.

1983   Typological and Genetic Notes on Switch-Reference Systems in North American Indian Languages. Pp. 151-183 in Switch-Reference and Universal Grammar, Winnipeg, May 1981. John Haiman and Pamela Munro, eds. (*Typological Studies in Language* 2). Amsterdam / Philadelphia: J. Benjamins.

1986   Washo Linguistic Prehistory. Pp. 33-58 in Papers from the 1983, 1984, and 1985 Hokan-Penutian Languages Conferences. *Occasional Papers on Linguistics* 13. Carbondale: Department of Linguistics, Illinois University.

1986a   The Heterogeneity of Evidentials in Makah. Pp. 3-28 in Evidentiality: The Linguistic Coding of Epistemology. Wallace Chafe and Johanna Nichols, eds. Norwood, N.J.: Ablex.

1986b   Washo Linguistic Studies. Pp. 113-136 in The Current Status of Anthropological Research in the Great Basin: 1964. Warren L. d'Azevedo et al., eds. *University of Nevada, Desert Research Institute Social Sciences and Humanities Publications* 1. Reno.

1988   A Look at Greenberg's Almosan-Keresiouan Hypothesis. (Paper presented at the 23d International Conference on Salish and Neighboring Languages, Eugene, Oreg.)

1988a   Greenberg on Hokan. (Paper presented at the 1988 Hokan-Penutian Workshop, Eugene, Oreg.)

1989   On Objective Techniques for Relating Languages and the Haida-Na-Dene Hypothesis. (Typescript in Jacobsen's possession.)

1989a   The Pacific Orientation of Western North American Languages. (Paper presented at the Circum-Pacific Prehistory Conference, Seattle, Wash., August 1989.)

1993   Another Look at Sapir's Evidence for Inclusion of Haida in Na-Dene. (Manuscript in Linguistic Society of America Archives.)

1995   Towards a Uniform Evaluation of Proposed Genetic Relationships: Greenberg's North American Amerind. In Proceedings of the Conference on Language and Prehistory, Boulder, Colorado, March 1990. Allan R. Talyor, ed. Stanford, Calif.: Stanford University Press. (In press.)

Jacobson, Anna W.
1990   Elnguq. Fairbanks: Alaska Native Language Center.

Jacobson, Steven A.
1984   Yup'ik Eskimo Dictionary. Fairbanks: Alaska Native Language Center.

1990   A Practical Grammar of the St. Lawrence Island / Siberian Yupik Eskimo Language. Fairbanks: Alaska Native Language Center.

1990a   Comparison of Central Alaskan Yup'ik Eskimo and Central Siberian Yupik Eskimo. *International Journal of American Linguistics* 56(2):264-286.

1995   A Practical Grammar of the Central Alaskan Yup'ik Eskimo Language; with Yup'ik Readings by Anna W. Jacobson. Fairbanks: Alaska Native Language and Program, University of Alaska.

Jacobson, Steven A., et al.
1987   A Dictionary of the St. Lawrence Island / Siberian Yupik Eskimo Language. 2d preliminary ed. Fairbanks: Alaska Native Language Center.

Jakobson, Roman
1971   Shifters, Verbal Categories, and the Russian Verb. Pp. 130-147 in Selected Writings, Vol. II: Word and Language. The Hague and Paris: Mouton.

James, Deborah
1982   Past Tense, Imperfective Aspect and Irreality in Cree. Pp. 143-160 in Papers of the Thirteenth Algonquian Conference. William Cowan, ed. Ottawa: Carleton University.

1984   Raising to Subject in Cree: A Problem For Subjacency? Pp. 205-214 in the Syntax of Native American Languages. Eung-Do Cook and D.B. Gerds, eds. (*Syntax and Semantics* 16). New York: Academic Press.

1986   Foreground and Background in Moose Cree Narratives. Pp. 155-174 in Actes du Dix-septième Congrès des Algonquinistes. William Cowan, ed. Ottawa: Carleton University.

1991   Preverbs and the Function of Clauses in Moose Cree. Winnipeg, Man.: Voices of Rupert's Land.

1991a   Preterit Forms in Moose Cree as Markers of Tense, Aspect, and Modality. *International Journal of American Linguistics* 57(3):281-297.

James, Edwin
1823   Account of an Expedition from Pittsburgh to the Rocky Mountains, Performed in the Years 1819 and '20; by Order of the Hon. J.C. Calhoun, Sec'y of War: Under the Command of Major Stephen H. Long. 2 vols., with an Atlas. Philadelphia: H.C. Carey and I. Lea.

Jameson, J. Franklin, ed.
1909   Narratives of New Netherland, 1609-1664. (*Original Narratives of Early American History*). New York: Charles Scribner's Sons. Reprinted: Barnes and Noble, New York, 1959.)

Jeddore, Rose, ed.
1976   Labrador Inuit Uqausingit. Saint John's: Memorial University of Newfoundland and Labrador Inuit Committee.

Jenks, William
1804   Specimen of the Moheagan Language, Taken at Cambridge, February 28, 1804. In Memoir of the Moheagans by Abiel Holmes. *Massachusetts Historical Society Collections*, 1st ser., vol. 9:98-99.

Jenness, Diamond
1922   The Life of the Copper Eskimos. *Report of the Canadian Arctic Expedition 1913-1918. Southern Party—1913-1916*, Vol. 12 (Pt. A). Ottawa.

1924   Eskimo Folk-Lore. Myths and Traditions from Northern Alaska, the Mackenzie Delta and Coronation Gulf. *Report of the Canadian Arctic Expedition, 1913-18.* Vol. 13. Ottawa.

1927   Notes on the Phonology of the Eskimo Dialect of Cape Prince of Wales, Alaska. *International Journal of American Linguistics* 4(2-4):168-180.

1928   Eskimo Language and Technology. Part A: Comparative Vocabulary of the Western Eskimo Dialects. *Report of the Canadian Arctic Expedition, 1913-18.* Vol. 15. Ottawa.

1929   Notes on the Phonology of the Eskimo Dialect of Cape Prince of Wales, Alaska. *International Journal of American Linguistics* 4(2-4):168-180.

1931   The Sekani Indians of British Columbia. *Proceedings and Transactions of the Royal Society of Canada*, 3rd ser. 25(2):21-35. Ottawa.

1932   The Indians of Canada. *Anthropological Series* 15, *National Museum of Canada Bulletin* 65. Ottawa. (Reprinted in 1934.)

1937   The Sekani Indians of British Columbia. *National Museum of Canada Bulletin* 84, *Anthropological Series* 20. Ottawa.

1938   The Sarcee Indians of Alberta. *National Museum of Canada Bulletin* 90, *Anthropological Series* 23. Ottawa.

1943   The Carrier Indians of the Bulkley River: Their Social and Religious Life. *Anthropological Papers* 25, *Bureau of American Ethnology Bulletin* 133. Washington.

1944   Grammatical Notes on Some Western Eskimo Dialects. *Report of the Canadian Arctic Expedition, 1913-18.* Vol. 15(B). Ottawa.

Jennings, Jesse D.
1964   The Desert West. Pp. 149-174 in Prehistoric Man in the New World. Jesse D. Jennings and Edward Norbeck, eds. Chicago: University of Chicago Press.

1974   Prehistory of North America. 2d ed. New York: McGraw-Hill.

Jennings, Jesse D., and Edward Norbeck
1955   Great Basin Prehistory: A Review. *American Antiquity* 21(1):1-11.

Jett, Stephen C.
1970   An Analysis of Navajo Place-Names. *Names* 18(3):175-184.

1977   Comment on Goss' "Linguistic Tools for the Great Basin Prehistorian." Pp. 71-78 in Models and Great Basin Prehistory: A Symposium. Don D. Fowler, ed. *Desert Research Institute Publications in the Social Sciences* 12. Reno and Las Vegas.

Jetté, Jules
1904   Yoyit Rokanaga. Nulator Roka Do-Daletloye. Winnipeg: Free Press.

1909   On the Language of the Ten'a (iii). *Man* 9:21-25.

Jette, Julius
1991   [Letter to Ralph P. Mackie, Superintendent of Mount McKinley National Park, February 18, 1926.] Pp. 135-144 in Native Place Names of the Kantishna Drainage, Alaska: Kantishna Oral History Project. Dianne Gudgel-Holmes, ed. Anchorage: U.S. Department of the Interior, National Park Service, Alaska Region.

Joël, Judith
1964   Classification of the Yuman Languages. Pp. 99-105 in Studies in Californian Linguistics. William Bright, ed. *University of California Publications in Linguistics* 34. Berkeley.

1966   Paipai Phonology and Morphology. (Unpublished Ph.D. Dissertation in Linguistics, University of California, Los Angeles.)

1976   The Earthquake of '57: A Paipai Text. Pp. 84-91 in Yuman Texts. Margaret Langdon, ed. *International Journal of American Linguistics, Native American Texts Series, Monograph* 1(3). Chicago: University of Chicago Press.

1978   The Yuman Word for 'Bean' as a Clue to Prehistory. *Journal of California Anthropology, Papers in Linguistics* 1:77-92.

Joffe, Nathalie F.
1940   The Fox of Iowa. Pp. 259-332 in Acculturation in Seven American Indian Tribes. Ralph Linton, ed. New York: D. Appleton-Century.

Johnson, Frederick
1940   The Linguistic Map of Mexico and Central America. Pp. 88-114 in The Maya and Their Neighbors. Clarence L. Hay, et al., eds. New York: Appleton-Century.

1943   Notes on Micmac Shamanism. *Primitive Man* 16(3-4):53-80. Washington.

Johnson, Jean B.
1950   The Opata: An Inland Tribe of Sonora. *University of New Mexico Publications in Anthropology* 6. Albuquerque.

1962   El idioma Yaqui. *Instituto Nacional de Antropología e Historia, Depto. de Investigaciones Antropológicas, Publicaciones* 10. México.

Johnson, Jean B., and Irmgard Weitlaner de Johnson
1947   Un vocabulario Varohío. *Revista Mexicana de Estudios Antropológicos* 9:27-45. Mexico.

1954   Opata: Dialect of Tonichi, Sonora. Pp. 390-397 in Vocabularies for Languages of the Uto-Aztecan Family. Harold H. Key, coll. *Microfilm Collection of Manuscripts on Middle American Cultural Anthropology* 38. Chicago: University of Chicago Library.

Johnson, Michael G.
1993   The Native Tribes of North America: A Concise Encyclopedia. London: Windrow and Greene.

Johnson, Samuel V.
1978   Chinook Jargon: A Computer Assisted Analysis of Variation in an American Indian Pidgin. (Unpublished Ph.D. Dissertation in Anthropology, University of Kansas, Lawrence.)

Johnston, John
1849   Vocabularies of the Shawanoese and Wyandott Languages, etc. Pp. 590-594 in Historical Collections of Ohio; Containing a Collection of the Most Interesting Facts, Traditions, Biographical Sketches, Anecdotes, etc. Relating to its General and Local History: With Descriptions of its Counties, Principal Towns and Villages. Cincinnati: Bradley and Anthony.

Jones, Charles C., Jr.
1868   Historical Sketch of Tomo-chi-chi, Mico of the Yamacraws. Albany: Joel Munsell. (Reprinted: Kraus Reprint, Milwood, N.Y., 1975.)

Jones, Electa F.
1854   Stockbridge, Past and Present; or, Records of an Old Mission Station. Springfield, Mass.: Sam. Bowles.

Jones, Eliza
1986   Koyukon Ethnogeography. *Alaska Historical Commission Studies in History* 171. Fairbanks: University of Alaska. Alaska Native Language Center.

Jones, Eliza, and Melissa Axelrod, eds.
1983   Sitsiy Yugh Noholnik Ts'in': As My Grandfather Told It, by Catherine Attla. Fairbanks: Alaska Native Language Center.

Jones, George Fenwick, ed.
1966   Henry Newman's Salzburger Letterbooks. *Wormsloe Foundation Publications* 8. Athens, Ga.: University of Georgia Press.

Jones, Gwyn
1964   The Norse Atlantic Saga: Being the Norse Voyages of Discovery and Settlement to Iceland, Greenland, and America. London: Oxford University Press.

Jones, John
1858-1859 Across the Plains: My Trip from Faribault. Minn., to Oregon, Via Saskatchewan Route, British America. (Manuscript No. 2243 in the Everett D. Graff Collection of Western Americana, The Newberry Library, Chicago.)

Jones, John, and Peter Jones
1831   The Gospel According to St. John, Translated into the Chippeway Tongue. London: The British and Foreign Bible Society.

Jones, Linda K., and Ned R. Coleman
1979   Towards a Discourse Perspective of Modes and Tenses in Kickapoo Narratives. Pp. 69-95 in Discourse Studies in Mesoamerican Languages. Volume 1: Discussion. Linda K. Jones, ed. Robert E. Longacre, proj. dir. *Summer Institute of Linguistics. Publications in Linguistics* 58(1). Dallas: The Summer Institute of Linguistics and The University of Texas at Arlington.

Jones, Livingston French
1914   A Study of the Thlingets of Alaska. New York: Fleming H. Revell. (Reprinted: Johnson Reprint, New York, 1970.)

Jones, Peter
1836   Nʋgʋmouinʋn genʋnʋgʋmouat igiu anishinabeg anʋmiajig. Boston: Crocker and Brewster for the American Board of Commissioners for Foreign Missions.

Jones, William
1904   Some Principles of Algonquian Word-formation. (Ph.D. Dissertation [in Anthropology], Columbia University, New York. Published in: *American Anthropologist*, n.s. 6(3):369-411, 1904.)

1906   An Algonquian Syllabary. Pp. 88-93 in Boas Anniversary Volume: Anthropological Papers Written in Honor of Franz Boas. Berthold Lanfer, ed. New York: G.E. Stechert.

1907   Fox Texts. *Publications of the American Ethnological Society* 1. Leyden. (Reprinted: AMS Press, New York, 1974.)

1911   Algonquian (Fox). Revised by Truman Michelson. Pp. 735-873 in Pt. 1 of Handbook of American Indian Languages. Franz Boas, ed. *Bureau of American Ethnology Bulletin* 40. Washington.

1915　Kickapoo Tales. Truman Michelson, trans. *Publications of the American Ethnological Society* 9. Leyden. (Reprinted: AMS Press, New York, 1974.)

1917-1919 Ojibwa Texts. Truman Michelson, ed. 2 Pts. *Publications of the American Ethnological Society* 7. Leyden, The Netherlands. (Reprinted: AMS Press, New York, 1974.)

1939　Ethnography of the Fox Indians. Margaret W. Fisher, ed. *Bureau of American Ethnology Bulletin* 125. Washington.

Jorgensen, Joseph G.
1969　Salish Language and Culture: A Statistical Analysis in Internal Relationships, History, and Evolution. *Indiana University Publications, Language Science Monographs* 3. C.F. Voegelin, ed. Bloomington: Indiana University.

Joseph, Alice, Rosamond B. Spicer, and Jane Chesky
1949　The Desert People: A Study of the Papago Indians. (*Indian Education Research Series* 4). Chicago: University of Chicago Press.

Justeson, John S., and Laurence D. Stephens
1993　The Evolution of Syllabaries from Alphabets: Transmission, Language Contrast, and Script Typology. *Die Sprache: Zeitschrift für Sprachwissenschaft, 1991-1993*, vol. 35(1):2-46. Wien.

Kaiser, Rudolf
1987　Chief Seattle's Speech(es): American Origins and European Reception. Pp. 497-536 in Recovering the Word: Essays on Native American Literature. Brian Swann and Arnold Krupat, eds. Berkeley: University of Californa Press.

Kalifornsky, Peter
1977　Kahtnuht'ana Qenaga: The Kenai People's Language. Jim Kari, ed. Fairbanks: University of Alaska, Alaska Native Language Center.

1991　A Dena'ina Legacy, K'tl'egh'i Sukdu: The Collected Writings of Peter Kalifornsky. James Kari and Alan Boraas, eds. Fairbanks: University of Alaska, Alaska Native Language Center.

Kalmár, Ivan
1979　Case and Context in Inuktitut (Eskimo). *National Museums of Canada. Mercury Series. Ethnology Service Papers* 49. Ottawa.

Kapesh, An Antane
1976　Eukuan Nin Matshimanitu Innu-iskueu / Je suis une maudite sauvagesse. José Mailhot, trans. Montréal: Editions Leméac. (Reprinted: Des Femmes, Paris, 1982.)

1979　Tante Nana Etutamin Nitassi / Qu'as-tu fait de mon pais? Les Traductions montagnaises Sept-Iles & José Mailhot, trans. Montréal: Les Editions impossibles.

Kaplan, Lawrence D.
1981　Phonological Issues in North Alaskan Iñupiaq. *Alaska Native Language Center Research Papers* 6. Fairbanks.

1982　Consonant Alternation in Iñupiaq Eskimo. *International Journal of American Linguistics* 48(4):385-393.

_____, ed.
1988　Ugiuvangmiut Quliapyuit / King Island Tales: Eskimo History and Legends from Bering Strait. Fairbanks: King Island Native Community and University of Alaska Native Language Center.

Kappler, Charles J., ed. and comp.
1904-1941 Indian Affairs: Laws and Treaties. 5 vols. Washington: U.S. Government Printing Office. (Reprinted: AMS Press, New York, 1971.)

Kari, James
1975　The Disjunct Boundary in the Navajo and Tanaina Verb Prefix Complexes. *International Journal of American Linguistics* 41(4):330-345.

1977　Linguistic Diffusion between Tanaina and Ahtna. *International Journal of American Linguistics* 43(4): 274-288.

1977a　Dena'ina Noun Dictionary. Fairbanks: Alaska Native Language Center.

1978　Deg Xinag. Ingalik Noun Dictionary (Preliminary). Fairbanks: Alaska Native Language Center.

1978a　Holikachuk Noun Dictionary (Preliminary). Fairbanks: Alaska Native Language Center; Juneau: Bureau of Indian Affairs Education Program.

1979　Athabaskan Verb Theme Categories: Ahtna. *Alaska Native Language Center Research Papers* 2. Fairbanks.

1981　Athabaskan Stories From Anvik: Rev. John W. Chapman's "Ten'a Texts and Tales." Fairbanks: Alaska Native Language Center.

1983　Ahtna Place Names Lists. Preliminary edition. Compiled by James Kari and Mildred Buck. Fairbanks: Copper River Native Association and Univesity of Alaska, Alaska Native Language Center.

1985　A Note on Athapaskan Directionals. *International Journal of American Linguistics* 51(4):471-473.

_____, transcr. and ed.
1986　Tatl'ahwt'aenn Nenn': The Headwaters People's Country. Narratives of the Upper Ahtna Athabaskans. Fairbanks: Alaska Native Language Center.

1987　Dena'ina Place Names and Territorial Knowledge. Pp. 29-33 in Shem Pete's Alaska: The Territory of the Upper Cook Inlet Dena'ina. James Kari and James A. Fall, comps and eds. Fairbanks: University of Alaska, Alaska Native Language Center and the CIRI Foundation.

1987a　The Athabaskan Names for Mount McKinley. P. 149 in Shem Pete's Alaska: The Territory of the Upper Cook Inlet Dena'ina. James Kari and James A. Fall, comps. and eds. Fairbanks: University of Alaska, Alaska Native Language Center and the CIRI Foundation.

1987b   The Wrangell Map of 1839. Pp. 34-35 in Shem Pete's Alaska: The Territory of the Upper Cook Inlet Dena'ina. James Kari and James A. Fall, comps. and eds. Fairbanks: University of Alaska, Alaska Native Language Center and the Ciri Foundation.

1987c   Engithidong Xugixudhoy: Their Stories of Long Ago, told by Belle Deacon. Fairbanks: Alaska Native Language Center.

1988   Some Linguistic Insights into Dena'ina Prehistory. Pp. 319-338 in The Late Prehistoric Development of Alaska's Native People. R.D. Shaw, R.K. Harritt, and D.E. Dumond, eds. *Aurora: Alaska Anthropological Association Monograph Series* 4. Anchorage.

1989   Some Principles of Alaska Athabaskan Toponymic Knowledge. Pp. 129-149 in General and Amerindian Ethnolinguistics: In Remembrance of Stanley Newman. Mary R. Key and Henry M. Koenigswald, eds. Berlin: Mouton de Gruyter.

1989a   Some Linguistic Insights into Dena'ina Prehistory. Pp. 533-574 in Athapaskan Linguistics: Current Perspectives on a Language Family. Eung-Do Cook and Keren D. Rice, eds. Berlin: Mouton de Gruyter.

1990   Ahtna Athabaskan Dictionary. Fairbanks: Alaska Native Language Center.

1991   Lower Tanana Athabaskan Listening and Writing Exercises. Fairbanks: Alaska Native Language Center.

1994   Local vs. Regional Place Naming Conventions in Alaska Athabaskan Languages. *Proceedings of the Twenty-Third Western Conference on Linguistics* 6. Sharon Hargus, Gerald R. McMenamin, and Vida Samiian, eds. Fresno: California State University, Department of Linguistics.

Kari, James, and Alan Boraas, eds. 1991 *see* Kalifornsky, Peter 1991

Kari, James, and James A. Fall, comps. and eds.
1987   Shem Pete's Alaska: The Territory of the Upper Cook Inlet Dena'ina. Fairbanks: Alaska Native Language Center, University of Alaska and the CIRI Foundation.

Kari, James, and Priscilla R. Kari
1982   Dena'ina Elnena: Tanaina Country. Jane McGary, ed. Fairbanks: University of Alaska, Alaska Native Language Center.

Kari, James, and Bernard Spolsky
1973   Trends in the Study of Athapaskan Language Maintenance and Bilingualism. *Navajo Reading Study Progress Report* 21. Albuquerque: University of New Mexico.

Kari, Priscilla R.
1983   Land Use and Economy of Lime Village. *Alaska Fish and Game. Subsistence Division. Technical Paper* 80. Juneau.

1991   Tanaina Plantlore. Dena'ina K'et'una: An Ethnobotany of the Dena'ina Indians of Southcentral Alaska. 3rd ed., revised. Fairbanks: Alaska Native Language Center with Alaska Natural History Association and National Park Service.

Kaschube, Dorothea V.
1967   Structural Elements of the Language of the Crow Indians of Montana. *University of Colorado Studies. Series in Anthropology* 14. Boulder.

_____, ed.
1978   Crow Texts. *International Journal of American Linguistics. Native American Texts Series Monograph* 2. Chicago: The University of Chicago Press; Ann Arbor, Mich.: University Microfilms International.

Kauder, Christian
1866   Buch das gut, enthaltend des Katechismus, Betrachtung, Gesang. Wien: Die kaiserliche wie auch königliche Buchdruckerei [etc.].

Kaufman, Terrence S.
1971   A Report on Chinook Jargon. Pp. 275-278 in Pidginization and Creolization of Languages. Dell Hymes, ed. (*Proceedings of a Conference Held at the University of the West Indies, Mona, Jamaica, April 1968.*) Cambridge: Cambridge University Press.

1974   Meso-American Indian Languages. Pp. 956-963 in Vol. 11 of *Encyclopaedia Britannica*, 15th ed. Chicago. (Reprinted: Pp. 785-792 in Vol. 22 of *Encyclopaedia Britannica*, 15th ed. Chicago, 1985.)

1974a   Idiomas de Mesoamérica. Guatemala: Editorial José de Pineda Ibarra.

1989   Long-range and Mid-range Comparison: The Cases of Otomangue and Hokan. (Paper presented at the Summer Meeting of the Society for the Study of Indigenous Languages of the Americas, Tucson, Ariz., July 2, 1989.)

1989a   Some Hypotheses Regarding Proto-Hokan Grammar. (Paper presented at the Summer Meeting of the Society for the Study of Indigenous Languages of the Americas, Hokan-Penutian Workshop, Tucson, Ariz., July 4-5, 1989.)

Kaye, Jonathan D., Glyne L. Piggott, and Ken Tokaichi, eds.
1971   Odawa Language Project: First Report. *University of Toronto. Department of Anthropology. Centre for Linguistic Studies. Linguistic Series* 1. Toronto. (Reprinted, 2d ed., 1973.)

Keane, A.H.
1878   Ethnography and Philology of America. Pp. 443-561 (Appendix) in Central America, the West Indies, and South America. Henry W. Bates, ed. (*Stanford's Compendium of Geography and Travel*). London: Edward Stanford.

Keeling, Richard
1991   A Guide to Early Field Recordings (1900-1949) at the Lowie Museum of Anthropology. *University of California Publications: Catalogs and Bibliographies* 6. Berkeley.

Keen, John H.
1906   A Grammar of the Haida Language. London: Society for Promoting Christian Knowledge.

Kegg, Maude
1991   Portage Lake: Memories of an Ojibwe Childhood. John D. Nichols, ed. Edmonton: University of Alberta Press.

Kelley, Klara B., and Harris Francis
1994   Navajo Sacred Places. Bloomington and Indianapolis: Indiana University Press.

Kelley, William A., and Frances H. Willard
1906   Grammar and Vocabulary of the Hlingit Language of Southeastern Alaska. Pp. 715-766 in *U.S. Bureau of Education Report of the Commissioner of Education for 1904*. Washington: Government Printing Office. (Reprinted: Shorey Book Co., Seattle, 1971, 1974.)

Kelly, Isabel T.
1932   Ethnography of the Surprise Valley Paiute. *University of California Publications in American Archaeology and Ethnology* 31(3):67-210. Berkeley.

1964   Southern Paiute Ethnography. *University of Utah Anthropological Papers* 69. Salt Lake City.

Kelly, Williams H.
1942   Cocopa Gentes. *American Anthropologist* 44(1):675-691.

1949   Cocopa Attitudes and Practices with Respect to Death and Mourning. *Southwestern Journal of Anthropology* 5(2):151-164.

Kendall, Daythal, comp.
1982   A Supplement to *A Guide to Manuscripts Relating to the American Indian in the Library of the American Philosophical Society*. *Memoirs of the American Philosophical Society* 65(supplement). Philadelphia.

Kendall, Martha B.
1976   Selected Problems in Yavapai Syntax: The Verde Valley Dialect. New York: Garland Publishing.

1978   Five Coyote Anecdotes (Yavpe). Pp. 155-161 in Coyote Stories. William Bright, ed. *International Journal of American Linguistics. Native American Texts Series Monograph* 1. Chicago: The University of Chicago Press.

1980   Exegesis and Translation: Northern Yuman Names as Texts. *Journal of Anthropological Research* 36(3):261-273.

Kendall, Martha B., and Emily-Sue Sloane
1976   Skara Kʔaˑmca: The Lofty Wanderer (Yavapai). Pp. 68-83 in Yuman Texts. Margaret Langdon, ed. *International Journal of American Linguistics. Native American Texts Series* 1(3). Chicago: The University of Chicago Press.

Kennard, Edward A.
1936   Mandan Grammar. *International Journal of American Linguistics* 9(1):1-43.

1963   Linguistic Acculturation in Hopi. *International Journal of American Linguistics* 29(1):36-41.

Kennedy, Dorothy I.D., and Randy Bouchard
1992   *Stl'átl'imx* (Fraser River Lilloet) Fishing. Pp. 266-352 in A Complex Culture of the British Columbia Plateau: Traditional *Stl'átl'imx* Resource Use. Brian Hayden, ed. Vancouver: UBC Press.

Kenny, Hamill
1956   Algonquian Names. *Names* 4(1):54-58.

1961   The Origin and Meaning of the Indian Place Names of Maryland. Baltimore: Waverly Press.

1976   Place-Names and Dialects: Algonquian. *Names* 24(2):86-100.

Kenyon, Susan M.
1977   Traditional Trends in Modern Nootka Ceremonies. *Arctic Anthropology* 14(1):25-38.

Khromchenko, Vasilii Stepanovich
1973   V.S. Khromchenko's Coastal Explorations in Southwestern Alaska, 1822. James W. VanStone, ed. *Fieldiana: Anthropology* 64. Chicago.

Kilpatrick, Anna G., and Jack F. Kilpatrick, eds.
1966   Chronicles of Wolftown: Social Documents of the North Carolina Cherokees, 1850-1862. *Bureau of American Ethnology Bulletin* 196, *Anthropological Papers* 75. Washington.

Kilpatrick, Jack F., and Anna G. Kilpatrick, eds.
1968   New Echota Letters: Contributions of Samuel A. Worcester to the Cherokee Phoenix. Dallas, Tex.: Southern Methodist University Press.

Kimball, Geoffrey D.
1983   Verb Pluralization in Koasati. Pp. 401-411 in 1982 Mid-America Linguistics Conference Papers. Frances Ingemann, ed. Lawrence: Department of Linguistics, University of Kansas.

1987   A Grammatical Sketch of Apalachee. *International Journal of American Linguistics* 53(2):136-174.

1988   An Apalachee Vocabulary. *International Journal of American Linguistics* 54(4):387-398.

1989   Another Proposal for Subgrouping the Muskógean Languages. (Paper presented at the Summer Meeting of the Society for the Study of Indigenous Languages of the Americas, Tucson, Ariz., July 1, 1989.)

1989a   Peregrine Falcon and Great Horned Owl: Ego and Shadow in a Koasati Tale. *Southwest Journal of Linguistics* 9(1):45-74. El Paso, Tex.

1991   Koasati Grammar. (*Studies in the Anthropology of North American Indians*). Lincoln: Univeristy of Nebraska Press.

1992   A Critique of Muskogean, "Gulf," and Yukian Material in *Language in the Americas. International Journal of American Linguistics* 58(4):447-501.

1994   Koasati Dictionary. (*Studies in the Anthropology of North American Indians.*) Lincoln and London: University of Nebraska Press.

King, A. Richard
1967   The School at Mopass: A Problem of Identity. New York: Holt, Rinehart and Winston.

King, Duane H.
1975   A Grammar and Dictionary of the Cherokee Language. (Unpublished Ph.D. Dissertation in Linguistics, University of Georgia, Athens, Ga.)

1977   Who Really Discovered the Cherokee-Iroquois Linguistic Relationship. *Journal of Cherokee Studies* 2(4):401-404. Cherokee, N.C.

King, Quindel
1978   Chilcotin Phonology and Vocabulary. Pp. 41-66 in Contributions to Canadian Linguistics. Eung-Do Cook and Jonathan D. Kaye, eds. *National Museum of Man, Mercury Series* 50. Ottawa.

Kinietz, W. Vernon
1939   Birch Bark Records Among the Chippewa. *Proceedings of the Indiana Academy of Science* 49:38-40. Fort Wayne, Ind.

1946   Delaware Culture Chronology. *Indiana Historical Society Prehistory Research Series* 3(1). Indianapolis.

1947   Chippewa Village: The Story of Katikitegon. *Cranbrook Institute of Science Bulletin* 25. Bloomfield Hills, Mich.

Kinkade, M. Dale
1963   Phonology and Morphology of Upper Chehalis. (Ph.D. Dissertation in Linguistics, Indiana University, Bloomington. Published in 4 Pts.: *International Journal of American Linguistics* 29(3):181-195, (4):345-356; 30(1):32-61, (3):251-260, 1963-1964.)

1967   On the Identification of the Methows (Salsh). *International Journal of American Linguistics* 33(3):193-197.

1967a   Uvular-Pharyngeal Resonants in Interior Salish. *International Journal of American Linguistics* 33(3): 228-234.

1973   The Alveopalatal Shift in Cowlitz Salish. *International Journal of American Linguistics* 39(4):224-231.

1975   The Lexical Domain of Anatomy in Columbian Salish. Pp. 423-443 in Linguistics and Anthropology: In Honor of C.F. Voegelin. M. Dale Kinkade, Kenneth L. Hale, and Oswald Werner, eds. Lisse, The Netherlands: Peter de Ridder Press. (Separately printed: *Publications on Salish Languages* 1. Lisse, The Netherlands: Peter de Ridder Press, 1975.)

1978   "Coyote and Rock" (Columbian Salish). Pp. 15-20 in Coyote Stories. William Bright, ed. *International Journal of American Linguistics. Native American Texts Series Monograph* 1. Chicago: University of Chicago Press.

1980   Dictionary of the Moses-Columbia Language. Nespelem, Wash.: Colville Confederated Tribes.

1981   Singular vs. Plural Roots in Salish. *Anthropological Linguistics* 23(6):262-269.

1981a   Interior Salishan Particles. *Anthropological Linguistics* 23(8):327-343.

1982   Columbian (Salish) C2-Reduplication. *Anthropological Linguistics* 24(1):66-72.

1983   Salish Evidence Against the Universality of 'Noun' and 'Verb'. *Lingua* 60(1):25-39. Amsterdam.

1983a   "Daughters of Fire": Narrative Verse Analysis of an Upper Chehalis Folktale. Pp. 267-278 in North American Indians: Humanistic Perspectives. James S. Thayer. ed. *University of Oklahoma. Department of Anthropology. Papers in Anthropology* 24(2). Norman.

1984   "Bear and Bee": Narrative Verse Analysis of an Upper Chehalis Folktale. Pp. 246-261 in 1983 Mid-America Linguistics Conference Papers. David S. Rood, ed. Boulder: University of Colorado, Department of Linguistics.

1987   Bluejay and His Sister. Pp. 255-296 in Recovering the Word: Essays on Native American Literature. Brian Swann and Arnold Krupat, eds. Berkeley: University of California Press.

1989   Comparative Linguistic Evidence about Salish Prehistory. (Paper presented at the Conference on American Indian Languages, American Anthropological Association, Washington, D.C., Nov. 1989.)

1989-1993 [Fieldnotes on the Thompson Language.] (Unpublished manuscript in Kinkade's possession.)

1990   Sorting Out Third Persons in Salishan Discourse. *International Journal of American Linguistics* 56(3):341-360.

1991   The Decline of Native Languages in Canada. Pp. 157-176 in Endangered Languages. Robert H. Robins and Eugenius M. Uhlenbeck, eds. Oxford/New York: BERG; distributed [...] by St Martin's Press, New York.

1991a   Upper Chehalis Dictionary. *University of Montana Occasional Papers in Linguistics* 7. Missoula.

842

1992   Translating Pentlatch. Pp. 163-175 in On the Translation of Native American Literatures. Brian Swann, ed.. Washington: Smithsonian Institution Press.

Kinkade, M. Dale, and J.V. Powell
1976   Language and the Prehistory of North America. *World Archaeology* 8(1):83-100.

Kinkade, M. Dale, and Clarence Sloat
1972   Proto-Eastern Interior Salish Vowels. *International Journal of American Linguistics* 38(1):26-48.

Kinkade, M. Dale, and Laurence C. Thompson
1974   Proto-Salish *r. *International Journal of American Linguistics* 40(1):22-28.

Kinkade, M. Dale, et al.
1987   New Caledonia and Columbia. Map. Plate 66 in Historical Atlas of Canada. Vol. 1. R. Cole Harris, ed., and Geoffrey J. Matthews, cart. Toronto: University of Toronto Press.

Kipp, James
1853   Vocabulary of the Mandan. Pp. 255-256, 446-459 in Vol. 3 of Historical and Statistical Information, Respecting the History, Condition and Prospects of the Indian Tribes of the United States. H.R. Schoolcraft, ed. Philadelphia: Lippincott, Grambo.

Kirkby, William West
1881   The New Testament; Translated into the Chipewyan Language by [...]. London: Printed for the British and Foreign Bible Society.

Kittredge, George Lyman
1904   The Old Farmer and His Almanack: Being Some Observations on Life and Manners in New England... . Boston: William Ware and Company.

Klaiman, M.H.
1991   Grammatical Voice. (*Cambridge Studies in Linguistics* 59). Cambridge: Cambridge University Press.

Klar, Kathryn
1977   Topics in Historical Chumash Grammar. (Unpublished Ph.D. Dissertation in Linguistics, University of California, Berkeley.)

Klein, Sheldon
1959   Comparative Mono-Kawaiisu. *International Journal of American Linguistics* 25(4):233-238.

1988   Narrative Style in Variants of a Kawaiisu Myth Text. Pp. 467-482 in In Honor of Mary Haas: From the Haas Festival Conference on Native American Linguistics. Berlin: Mouton de Gruyter.

Kleinschmidt, Samuel Petrus
1851   Grammatik der grönlandischen Sprache mit theilweisem Einschluss des Labradordialects. Berlin: G. Reimer. (Reprinted as: Grammatik der grönlandischen Sprache mit teilweisem Einschluss des Labradordialects. Georg Olms Verlagsbuchhandlung, Hildesheim, Germany, 1968.)

1871   Den Grønlandske Ordbog. [The Greenlandic Dictionary]. H.F. Jørgensen, ed. Copenhagen: Louis Klein.

1964   Kleinschmidts Briefe an Theodor Bourquin. Erik Holtved, ed. *Meddelelser om Grønland* 140(3). Copenhagen: C.A. Reitzels Forlag.

Klingberg, Frank J., ed.
1956   The Carolina Chronicle of Dr. Francis le Jau, 1706-1717. Berkeley: University of California Press. (Reprinted: Kraus Reprint, Millwood, N.Y., 1980.)

Klokeid, Terry J.
1969   Notes on the Comparison of Wakashan and Salish. *University of Hawaii Working Papers in Linguistics* 1:1-19. Honolulu.

1976   Encliticization in Nitinaht. Pp. 211-246 in Working Papers for the XIth International Conference on Salish Languages. Seattle: University of Washington.

1978   Surface Structure Constraints and Nitinaht Enclitics. Pp. 157-176 in Linguistic Studies of Native Canada. Eung-Do Cook and Jonathan D. Kaye, eds. Lisse, The Netherlands: Peter de Ridder Press; Vancouver, B.C.: University of British Columbia Press.

Kluckhohn, Clyde
1962   Navaho Witchcraft [1944]. Boston: Bacon Press.

Kluckhohn, Clyde, and Dorothea C. Leighton
1946   The Navaho. Cambridge, Mass.: Harvard University Press.

1962   The Navaho. Rev. ed. Garden City, N.Y.: Doubleday.

Kniffen, Fred B.
1928   Achomawi Geography. *University of California Publications in American Archaeology and Ethnology* 23(5):297-332. Berkeley.

1939   Pomo Geography. *University of California Publications in American Archaeology and Ethnology* 36(6):353-400. Berkeley.

Knipe, Christopher
1868   Some Account of the Takaht Language, as Spoken by Several Tribes on the Western Coast of Vancouver Island. London: Hatchard.

Koerner, Konrad, ed.
1984   Edward Sapir: Appraisals of His Life and Work. (*Studies in the History of the Language Sciences* 36). Amsterdam and Philadelphia: John Benjamins.

Kohl, Johann G.
1956   Kitchi-Gami. Wanderings Round Lake Superior [1860]. Minneapolis: Ross and Haines.

Koontz, John E.
1983   Siouan Syncopating *r-Stems. *Na'páo: A Saskatchewan Anthropology Journal* 13:11-23. Saskatoon, Sask.

Kowta, Makato
1969   The Sayles Complex: A Late Milling Stone Assemblage from Cajon Pass and the Ecological Implications of Its Scraper Planes. *University of California Publications in Anthropology* 6. Berkeley and Los Angeles.

843

Kozlowski, Edwin L.
1972   Havasupai Simple Sentences. (Unpublished Ph.D. Dissertation in Linguistics, Indiana University, Bloomington.)

——— 1976   Three Havasupai Tales. Pp. 51-60 in Yuman Texts. Margaret Langdon, ed. *International Journal of American Linguistics, Native American Texts Series Monograph* 1(3). Chicago: University of Chicago Press.

Kraus, Bertram S.
1944   Acculturation: A New Approach to the Iroquoian Problem. *American Antiquity* 9(3):302-318.

Krause, Aurel
1885   Die Tlingit-Indianer: Ergebnisse einer Reise nach der Nordwestküste von America...in den Jahren 1880-1881. Jena, Germany: Hermann Costenoble.

——— 1956   The Tlingit Indians: Results of a Trip to the Northwest Coast of America and the Bering Straits. Erna Gunther, trans. (*Monographs of the American Ethnological Society* 26). Seattle: University of Washington Press.

Krauss, Michael E.
1964   Proto-Athapaskan-Eyak and the Problem of Na-Dene, I: The Phonology. *International Journal of American Linguistics* 30(2):118-131.

——— 1965   Proto-Athapaskan-Eyak and the Problem of Na-Dene, II: Morphology. *International Journal of American Linguistics* 31(1):18-28.

——— 1965a   Eyak: A Preliminary Report. *Canadian Journal of Linguistics* 10(2-3):167-187.

——— 1968   Noun-Classification Systems in Athapaskan, Eyak, Tlingit and Haida Verbs. *International Journal of American Linguistics* 34(3):194-203.

——— 1969   On the Classification in the Athapascan, Eyak, and the Tlingit Verb. *Indiana University Publications in Anthropology and Linguistics Memoir* 24. *International Journal of American Linguistics* 35(4, Pt. 2):49-83.

——— 1970   Eyak Dictionary. Cambridge, Mass.: MIT Microform Laboratory.

——— 1970a   Eyak Texts. Cambridge, Mass.: MIT Microphoto Laboratory.

——— 1973   Eskimo-Aleut. Pp. 796-902 in Current Trends in Linguistics, Vol. 10: Linguistics in North America (Pt. 2). Thomas A. Sebeok, ed. The Hague: Mouton.

——— 1973a   Na-Dene. Pp. 903-978 in Current Trends in Linguistics, Vol. 10: Linguistics in North America (Pt. 2). Thomas A. Sebeok, ed. The Hague: Mouton.

——— 1974   Minto-Nenana Athabaskan Noun Dictionary. Fairbanks: Alaska Native Language Center.

——— 1976   Eskimo-Aleut. Pp. 175-281 in Vol. 1 of Native Languages of the Americas. Thomas A. Sebeok, ed. 2 vols. New York and London: Plenum Press.

——— 1976a   Na-Dene. Pp. 283-358 in Vol. 1 of Native Languages of the Americas. Thomas A. Sebeok, ed. 2 vols. New York and London: Plenum Press.

——— 1979   Na-Dene and Eskimo-Aleut. Pp. 803-901 in The Languages of Native America: Historical and Comparative Assessment. Lyle Campbell and Marianne Mithun, eds. Austin and London: University of Texas Press.

——— 1980   Alaska Native Languages: Past, Present, and Future. *Alaska Native Language Center Research Papers* 4. Fairbanks.

——— 1982   In Honor of Eyak: The Art of Anna Nelson Harry. Fairbanks: Alaska Native Language Center.

——— 1982a   Native Peoples and Languages of Alaska. Map. Fairbanks: University of Alaska, Native Language Center. (Revision of 1975 map with same name.)

——— 1985   Yupik Eskimo Prosodic Systems: Descriptive and Comparative Studies. *Alaska Native Language Center Research Papers* 7. Fairbanks.

——— 1986   Edward Sapir and Athabaskan Linguistics. Pp. 147-190 in New Perspectives in Language, Culture, and Personality (*Proceedings of the Edward Sapir Centenary Conference, Ottawa, 1-3 October 1984*). William Cowan, Michael K. Foster, and Konrad Koerner, eds. Amsterdam: John Benjamins.

——— 1988   Many Tongues—Ancient Tales. Pp. 145-150 in Crossroads of Continents. William W. Fitzhugh and Aron Crowell, eds. Washington: Smithsonian Institution.

——— 1991   Number and Viability of Native American Languages by State and Province. (Typescript, 2 pages, to accompany the presidential address to the Society for the Study of the Indigenous Languages of the Americas, American Anthropological Association Annual Meeting, Nov., 1991, Chicago.)

Krauss, Michael E., and Jeff Leer
1981   Athabaskan, Eyak, and Tlingit Sonorants. *Alaska Native Language Center Research Papers* 5. Fairbanks.

Krauss, Michael E., and Mary Jane McGary
1980   Alaska Native Languages: A Bibliographical Catalogue, Part One: Indian Languages. *Alaska Native Language Center Research Papers* 3. Fairbanks.

Kripke, Saul A.
1972   Naming and Necessity. Pp. 253-355 in Semantics of Natural Languages. Donald Davidson and Gilbert Harman, eds. 2d ed. Dordrecht and Boston: D. Reidel Publishing.

844

Kroeber, Alfred L.

1902   A Preliminary Sketch of the Mohave Indians. *American Anthropologist,* n.s. 4(2):276-285.

1904   The Languages of the Coast of California South of San Francisco. *University of California Publications in American Archaeology and Ethnology* 2(2):29-80. Berkeley. (Reprinted: Kraus Reprints, New York, 1964.)

1905   Systematic Nomenclature in Ethnology. *American Anthropologist,* n.s. 7(4):579-593.

1906   Yokuts Names. *Journal of American Folk-Lore* 19(73): 142-143.

1906a   The Dialectic Divisions of the Moquelumnan Family in Relation to the Internal Differentiation of the Other Linguistic Families of California. *American Anthropologist,* n.s. 8(4):652-663.

1907   Shoshonean Dialects of California. *University of California Publications in American Archaeology and Ethnology* 4(3):65-165. Berkeley.

1907a   The Yokuts Language of South Central California. *University of California Publications in American Archaeology and Ethnology* 2(5):165-377. Berkeley.

1908   Ethnology of the Gros Ventre. *American Museum of Natural History Anthropological Papers* 1(4):139-281. New York.

1908a   Ethnography of the Cahuilla Indians. *University of California Publications in American Archaeology and Ethnology* 8(2):29-68. Berkeley.

1908b   A Mission Record of the California Indians. *University of California Publications in American Archaeology and Ethnology* 8(1):1-27. Berkeley.

1908c   Notes on the Ute Language. *American Anthropologist,* n.s. 10(1):74-87.

1909   The Bannock and Shoshoni Languages. *American Anthropologist,* n.s. 11(2):266-277.

1909a   Notes on Shoshonean Dialects of Southern California. *University of California Publications in American Archaeology and Ethnology* 8(5):235-269. Berkeley. (Reprinted: Kraus Reprints, New York, 1964.)

1910   The Chumash and Costanoan Languages. *University of California Publications in American Archaeology and Ethnology* 9:259-263. Berkeley.

1911   The Languages of the Coast of California North of San Francisco. *University of California Publications in American Archaeology and Ethnology* 9(3):273-435. Berkeley.

1911a   Phonetic Elements of the Mohave Language. *University of California Publications in American Archaeology and Ethnology* 10(3):45-96. Berkeley.

1913   The Determination of Linguistic Relationship. *Anthropos* 8:389-401. Salzburg.

1915   Serian, Tequistlatecan, and Hokan. *University of California Publications in American Archaeology and Ethnology* 11(4):279-290. Berkeley.

1915a   A New Shoshonean Tribe in California. *American Anthropologist,* n.s. 17(4):773-775.

1916   Arapaho Dialects. *University of California Publications in American Archaeology and Ethnology* 12(3):71-138. Berkeley.

1916a   California Place Names of Indian Origin. *University of California Publications in American Archaeology and Ethnology* 12(2):31-69. Berkeley.

1917   Zuñi Kin and Clan. *American Museum of Natural History Anthropological Papers* 18(2):39-204. New York.

1917a   The Tribes of the Pacific Coast of North America. Pp. 385-401 in *Proceedings of the 19th International Congress of Americanists, Washington, 15.*

1917b   California Kinship Systems. *University of California Publications in American Archaeology and Ethnology* 12(9):339-396. Berkeley.

1922   Elements of Culture in Native California. *University of California Publications in American Archaeology and Ethnology* 13(8):259-328. Berkeley.

1923   The History of Native Culture in California. *University of California Publications in American Archaeology and Ethnology* 20(8):123-142. Berkeley.

1925   Handbook of the Indians of California. *Bureau of American Ethnology Bulletin* 78. Washington. (Reprinted: California Book Company, Berkeley, 1953, 1970; Dover Publications, New York, 1976.)

1929   The Valley Nisenan. *University of California Publications in American Archaeology and Ethnology* 24(4):253-290. Berkeley

1932   The Patwin and Their Neighbors. *University of California Publications in American Archaeology and Ethnology* 29(4):253-423. Berkeley.

1934   Uto-Aztecan Languages of Mexico. *Ibero-Americana* 8:1-27. Berkeley.

1936   Karok Towns. *University of California Publications in American Archaeology and Ethnology* 35(4):29-38. Berkeley.

1937   Athabsacan Kin Term Systems. *American Anthropologist*, n.s. 39(4):602-608.

1939   Cultural and Natural Areas of Native North America. *University of California Publications in American Archaeology and Ethnology* 38:1-242. Berkeley. (Reprinted: University of California Press, Berkeley, 1963; Kraus Reprint, Millwood, N.Y., 1976.)

1943   The Classification of the Yuman Languages. *University of California Publications in Linguistics* 1(3):21-40. Berkeley.

1955   Linguistic Time Depth Results So Far and Their Meaning. *International Journal of American Linguistics* 21(2):91-104.

1958   Sign Language Inquiry. *International Journal of American Linguistics* 24(1):1-19. (Reprinted: Pp. 185-203 in Vol. 2 of Aboriginal Sign Languages of th Americas and Australia. 2 vols. D. Jean Umiker-Sebeok and Thomas A. Sebeok, eds. Plenum Press, New York and London, 1978.)

1959   Recent Ethnic Spreads. *University of California Publications in American Archaeology and Ethnology* 47(3):235-310. Berkeley.

1959a   Possible Athabascan Influence on Yuki. *International Journal of American Linguistics* 25(1):59.

1959b   Northern Yokuts. *Anthropological Linguistics* 1(8):1-19.

1960   Powell and Henshaw: An Episode in the History of Ethnolinguistics. *Anthropological Linguistics* 2(4):1-5.

1960a   Yurok Speech Usages. Pp. 993-999 in Culture in History: Essays in Honor of Paul Radin. Stanley Diamond, ed. New York: University of Columbia Press for Brandeis University.

1963   Yokuts Dialect Survey. *University of California Anthropological Records* 11(3):177-252.

1967   Goddard's California Athabascan Texts. *International Journal of American Linguistics* 33(4):269-275.

Kroeber, Alfred L., and George W. Grace
1960   The Sparkman Grammar of Luiseño. *University of California Publications in Linguistics* 16. Berkeley.

Kroeber, Alfred L., and John P. Harrington
1914   Phonetic Elements of the Diegueño Language. *University of California Publications in American Archaeology and Ethnology* 11(2):177-188.

Kroeber, Alfred L., et al.
1943   Franz Boas, 1858-1942. *Memoirs of the American Anthropological Association* 61. (Reprinted: Kraus Reprint, New York, 1969.)

Kroeber, Karl
1981   An Introduction to the Art of Traditional American Indian Narration. Pp. 1-24 in Traditional Literatures of the American Indian: Texts and Interpretations. Karl Kroeber, comp. and ed. Lincoln: University of Nebraska Press.

Kroeber, Paul D.
1988   Inceptive Reduplication in Comox and Interior Salishan. *International Journal of American Linguistics* 54(2):141-167.

1989   [Review of]: Le comox lhaamen de Colombie Britannique: Présentation d'une langue amérindienne. By Claude Hagège. Amerindia: Revue d'ethnolinguistique amérindienne, numéro special 2, 1981. *International Journal of American Linguistics* 55(1):106-115.

Kroeber, Theodora
1969   Ishi in Two Worlds: A Biography of the Last Wild Indian in North America. Berkeley: University of California Press. (Reprinted in 1976.)

Kronenfeld, David B., and Lynn L. Thomas
1983   Revised Lexicostatistical Classification of Salishan Languages. *American Anthropologist* 85(2):372-378.

Kroskrity, Paul V.
1981   Toward a Sociolinguistic History of the Tewa. (Paper presented at the School of American Research Advanced Seminar on the Tewa, Santa Fe, N.M.)

1983   On Male and Female Speech in the Pueblo Southwest. *International Journal of American Linguistics* 49(1):88-91.

1985   Growing with Stories: Line, Verse, and Genre in an Arizona Tewa Text. *Journal of Anthropological Research* 41(2):183-199.

1993   Language, History, and Identity: Ethnolinguistic Studies of the Arizona Tewa. Tucson and London: University of Arizona Press.

Kroskrity, Paul V., and Dewey Healing
1978   Coyote and Bullsnake (Arizona Tewa). Pp. 162-170 in Coyote Stories. William Bright, ed. *International Journal of American Linguistics. Native American Texts Series Monograph* 1. Chicago: The University of Chicago Press.

Krueger, John R.
1960   Miscellanea Selica I: A Flathead Supplement to Vogt's Salishan Studies. *Anthropological Linguistics* 2(7):33-38.

1961   Miscellanea Selica II: Some Kinship Terms of the Flathead Salish. *Anthropological Linguistics* 3(2):11-18.

1961a   Miscellanea Selica III: Flathead Animal Names and Anatomical Terms. *Anthropological Linguistics* 3(9):43-52.

1963   Two Early Grammars of Cherokee. *Anthropological Linguistics* 5(3):1-57.

1967   Miscellanea Selica IV: An Interim Moses' Columbia (Wenatchee) Salishan Vocabulary. *Anthropological Linguistics* 9(2):5-11.

Krupat, Arnold
1985   For Those Who Come After: A Study of American Indian Autobiography. Berkeley: University of California Press.

1992   On the Translation of Native American Song and Story: A Theorized History. Pp. 3-32 in On the Translation of Native American Literatures. Brian Swann, ed. Washington: Smithsonian Institution Press.

Kruse, Robert
1991   The Henry Rowe Schoolcraft Collection: A Catalogue of Books in Native American Languages in the Library of the Boston Athenæum. Foreword by Nathan C. Shiverick. Boston: The Boston Athenæum.

Krusenstern, Adam *see* Kruzenshtern, Ivan Fedorovich

Kruzenshtern, Ivan Fedorovich (Adam Johann-Anton von Krusenstern)
1813   Wörter-Sammlungen aus den Sprachen einiger Völker des östlichen Asiens und der Nordwest Küste von Amerika. St. Petersburg: Gedruckt in der Druckerey der Admiralität.

Kuhm, Herbert W.
1952   Indian Place-Names in Wisconsin. *Wisconsin Archeologist* 33(1-2):1-157. Milwaukee.

Kuipers, Aert H.
1967-1969 The Squamish Language: Grammar, Texts, Dictionary. 2 vols. *Janua Linguarum, Series Practica* 73(1-2). The Hague: Mouton.

1968   The Categories Verb-Noun and Transitive-Intransitive in English and Squamish. *Lingua: International Review of General Linguistics* 21:610-626. Amsterdam.

1970   Towards a Salish Etymological Dictionary. *Lingua: International Review of General Linguistics* 26(1):46-72. Amsterdam.

1973   [Thompson Word List.] (Unpublished manuscript in Kuipers's possession.)

1974   The Shuswap Language: Grammar, Texts, Dictionary. *Janua Linguarum, Series Practica* 225. The Hague: Mouton.

1975   A Classified English-Shuswap Word-List. *Publications on Salish Languages* 3. Lisse, The Netherlands: Peter de Ridder.

1978   On the Phonological Typology of Proto-Salish. Pp. 607-621 in vol. 4 of *Proceedings of the 42d International Congress of Americanists*. Paris.

1981   On Reconstructing the Proto-Salish Sound System. *International Journal of American Linguistics* 47(4):-323-335.

Kuroda, S.Y.
1967   Yawelmani Phonology. *Massachusetts Institute of Technology Research Monograph* 43. Cambridge, Mass.

Kuryłowicz, Jerzy
1966   La position linguistique du nom propre. Pp. 362-370 in Readings in Linguistics II. Eric P. Hamp, Fred W. Householder, and Robert Austerlitz, eds. Chicago and London: University of Chicago Press.

Kwatchka, Patricia B., ed.
1994   Perspectives on the Southeast: Linguistics, Archaeology, and Ethnohistory. *Southern Anthropological Society Proceedings* 27. Mary W. Helms, series ed. Athens: University of Georgia Press.

La Brosse, Jean-Baptiste de "Jan-Batist Nudenans"
1760   Radicum wabanakæarum sylva ... collecta ... a J.B. Nudenans anno 1760. (Manuscript in Musée d'Odanak, Pierreville, Quebec.) (Title from Gill 1886.)

1767   Nehiro-iriniui aiamihe Massinahigan, Shatshegutsh, Mitinekapitsh, Iskuamiskutsh, Netshekatsh, Misht', Assinitsh, Shekutimitsh, Ekuanatsh, Ashuabmushuanitsh, Piakuagamitsh, Gaie missi missi nehiro-iriniui Astshitsh ka tatjits, ka kueiasku aiamihatjits ka utshi. Uabistiguiatsh [Quebec]: Broun gaie Girmor. (Reprinted: C. Le François, Quebec, 1817; J.-B. Fréchette, Quebec, 1844.)

Lacombe, Albert
1874   Dictionnaire de la langue des Cris. Montréal: Beauchemin et Valois.

1874a   Grammaire de la langue des Cris. Montréal: Beauchemin et Valois.

1886   Prières, cantiques, catéchisme, etc., en langue crise. Montréal: Beauchemin et fils.

Ladefoged, Peter
1992   Another View of Endangered Languages. *Language: Journal of the Linguistic Society of America* 68(4):809-811.

Laet, Joannes de
1630   Beschrijvinghe van West-Indien. 2d ed. Leyden, The Netherlands: Elzevier.

1633   Novus orbis, seu, Descriptionis Indiæ occidentalis, libri XVIII; auctore Joanne de Laet Atwerp; novis tabulis geographicis et variis animantium, plantarum fructuumque iconibus illustrati. Lugd. Batav.: apud Elzevirios. (Half-title: Joannis de Laet Americae utriusque descriptio.)

847

1882   L'Histoire du Nouveau Monde ou Description des Indes Occidentales. Nouvelle France. Livre Second. Réimpression. Québec: Delisle.

1909   From the "New World," by Johan de Laet, 1625, 1630, 1633, 1640. Pp. 29-60 in Narratives of New Netherland, 1609-1664. (*Original Narratives of Early American History.*) New York: Barnes and Noble.

La Farge, Oliver
1959   Foreword. Pp. 7-9 in The Inland Whale: Nine Stories Retold from California Indian Legends by Theodora Kroeber. Bloomington: Indiana University Press. (Reprinted: University of California Press, Los Angeles, 1971.)

La Flesche, Francis
1921   The Osage Tribe: Rite of the Chiefs; Sayings of the Ancient Men. Pp. 37-604 in *36th Annual Report of the Bureau of American Ethnology for 1914-1915.* Washington.

1925   The Osage Tribe: The Rite of Vigil. Pp. 31-636 in *39th Annual Report of the Bureau of American Ethnology for 1917-1918.* Washington.

1928   The Osage Tribe: Two Versions of the Child-naming Rite. Pp. 23-164 in *43d Annual Report of the Bureau of American Ethnology for 1925-1926.* Washington.

1932   A Dictionary of the Osage Language. *Bureau of American Ethnology Bulletin* 109. Washington. (Reprinted: Native American Publishers, Brighton, Mich., 1990.)

Laforet, Andrea, Nancy J. Turner, and Annie York
1993   Traditional Foods of the Fraser Canyon Nɬeʔképmx. Pp. 191-213 in American Indian Linguistics and Ethnography in Honor of Laurence C. Thompson. Anthony Mattina and Timothy Montler, eds. *University of Montana Occasional Papers in Linguistics* 10. Missoula.

Lagarde, Pierrette L.
1980   Le verbe huron: étude morphologique d'après une description grammaticale de la seconde moitié du XVIIe siècle. Paris: Editions L'Harmattan.

La Grasserie, Raoul de
1890   Textes Analysés et Vocabulaire de la Langue Timucua. Pp. 403-437 in *Proceedings of the International Congress of Americanists, 7th Session, 1888.*

Lahontan, Louis-Armand de Lom d'Arce (Baron de)
1703   Nouveaux voyages de Mr. le Baron de Lahontan dans l'Amerique septentrionale. 2 vols. in 1. The Hague: Frères l'Honoré.

Lamb, Sydney M.
1958   Linguistic Prehistory in the Great Basin. *International Journal of American Linguistics* 24(2):95-100.

1958a   Mono Grammar. (Unpublished Ph.D. Dissertation in Linguistics, University of California, Berkeley.)

1959   Some Proposals for Linguistic Taxonomy. *Anthropological Linguistics* 1(2):33-49.

1964   The Classification of the Uto-Aztecan Languages: A Historical Survey. Pp. 106-125 in Studies in Californian Linguistics. William Bright, ed. *University of California Publications in Linguistics* 34. Berkeley.

1964a   Linguistic Diversification and Extinction in North America. Pp. 457-464 in Vol. 2 of *XXXV Congreso Internacional de Americanistas, Mexico, 1962: Actas y Memorias.* 3 vols. Mexico.

Lamb, W. Kaye, ed.
1942   Documents Relating to the Mystery of Mrs. Barkley's Diary. *British Columbia Historical Quarterly* 6(1):49-59.

1970   The Journals and Letters of Sir Alexander Mackenzie. *Hakluyt Society. [Works] Extra ser.* 41. Cambridge: Cambridge University Press.

Landar, Herbert
1964   Navaho Syntax. *Language Dissertation* 57. Supplement to *Language: Journal of the American Linguistic Society* 39(3, Pt. 2). Baltimore.

1967   Two Athapaskan Verbs of 'Being' (With Annotated Bibliography). Pp. 40-74 in The Verb 'Be' and Its Synonyms: Philosophical and Grammatical Studies 1. Classical Chinese, Athapaskan, Mundari. *Foundations of Language Supplementary Series* 1. John W.M. Verhaar, ed. Dordrecht: D. Reidel Publishing Co.

1967a   Ten'a Classificatory Verbs. *International Journal of American Linguistics* 33(4):263-268.

1968   The Karankawa Invasion of Texas. *International Journal of American Linguistics* 34(4):242-258.

1973   The Tribes and Languages of North America: A Checklist. Pp. 1253-1441 in Current Trends in Linguistics, Vol. 10: Linguistics in North America. Pt. 2. Thomas A. Sebeok, ed. The Hague and Paris: Mouton.

1974   Bibliographic Note: Chimariko. *International Journal of American Linguistics* 40(3):247-248.

1976   An Innuit Bibliography. Pp. 108-139 in Papers on Eskimo and Aleut Linguistics. Eric Hamp, ed. Chicago: Chicago Linguistic Society.

1976a   Checklist Annotations. *International Journal of American Linguistics* 42(4):379-382.

1977   North American Indian Languages. Pp. 207-400 in Vol. 2 of Native Languages of the Americas. Thomas A. Sebeok, ed. New York and London: Plenum Press.

1977a   Three Rogue River Athapaskan Vocabularies. *International Journal of American Linguistics* 43(4):289-301.

1977b   Harry Hoijer (1904-1976): An Annotated Bibliography. *International Journal of American Linguistics* 43(4): 339-354.

1980   American Indian Linguistic Contributions of Gladys A. Reichard: A Bibliography. *International Journal of American Linguistics* 46(1):37-40.

Landerholm, Carl, trans. and ed.
1956   Notices and Voyages of the Famed Quebec Mission to the Pacific Northwest.... Portland, Oreg.: Champoeg Press for the Oregon Historical Society.

Landes, Ruth
1937   Ojibwa Sociology. *Columbia University Contributions to Anthropology* 29. New York.

1938   The Ojibwa Woman. *Columbia University Contributions to Anthropology* 31. New York.

1970   The Prairie Potawatomi: Tradition and Ritual in the Twentieth Century. Madison: University of Wisconsin Press.

Langacker, Ronald W.
1970   The Vowels of Proto-Uto-Aztecan. *International Journal of American Linguistics* 36(3):169-180.

1977   The Syntax of Postpositions in Uto-Aztecan. *International Journal of American Linguistics* 43(1):11-26.

1977a   An Overview of Uto-Aztecan Grammar. (*Studies in Uto-Aztecan Grammar* 1, *Summer Institute of Linguistics Publications in Linguistics* 56). Arlington, Tex.: Summer Institute of Linguistics and the University of Texas at Arlington.

Langdon, Margaret
1970   A Grammar of Diegueño: The Mesa Grande Dialect. *University of California Publications in Linguistics* 66. Berkeley.

1971   Sound Symbolism in Yuman Languages. Pp. 149-173 in Studies in American Indian Languages. Jesse Sawyer, ed. *University of California Publications in Linguistics* 65. Berkeley.

1974   Comparative Hokan-Coahuiltecan Studies: A Survey and Appraisal. *Janua Linguarum, Series Critica* 4. The Hague and Paris: Mouton.

1976   The Proto-Yuman Vowel System. Pp. 129-149 in Hokan Studies: Papers from the First Conference on Hokan Languages. Margaret Langdon and Shirley Silver, eds. (*Janua Linguarum, Series Practica* 181). The Hague: Mouton.

1976a   The Story of Eagle's Nest — A Diegueño Text. Pp. 113-133 in Yuman Texts. Margaret Langdon, ed. *International Journal of American Linguistics*. Native American Texts Series 1(3). Chicago: The University of Chicago Press.

1979   Some Thoughts on Hokan with Particular Reference to Pomoan and Yuman. Pp. 592-649 in The Languages of Native America: Historical and Comparative Assessment. Lyle Campbell and Marianne Mithun, eds. Austin and London: University of Texas Press.

Langdon, Margaret, and Pamela Munro
1980   Yuman Numerals. Pp. 121-136 in American Indian and Indo-European Studies: Papers in Honor of Madison S. Beeler. Kathryn Klar, Margaret Langdon, and Shirley Silver, eds. The Hague and Paris: Mouton.

1984   California t/ṭ. *Journal of California and Great Basin Anthropology Papers in Linguistics* 4:139-165.

Lange, Charles H.
1953   The Role of Economics in Cochiti Pueblo Culture Change. *American Anthropologist*, n.s. 55(5, Pt. 1):674-694.

1959   Cochití: a New Mexico Pueblo, Past and Present. Austin: University of Texas Press. (Reprinted: University of New Mexico Press, Albuquerque, 1990.)

Langen, Toby C.S.
1986   Notes on Form in Some Northwest Coast Tales. (Paper presented at the 21st International Conference on Salish and Neighboring Languages, Seattle, Wash.)

1992   Translating Form in Classical American Indian Literature. Pp. 191-207 in On the Translation of Native American Literatures. Brian Swann, ed. Washington: Smithsonian Institution Press.

Lanning, C.M.
1882   A Grammar and Vocabulary of the Blackfoot Language, Being a Concise and Comprehensive Grammar for the Use of the Learner, to Which is Added an Exhaustive Vocabulary. Compiled from translations by Joseph Kipp and W.S. Gladston, Jr. Fort Benton, Mont.: The Author.

Lanning, John T.
1935   The Spanish Missions of Georgia. Chapel Hill: University of North Carolina Press.

Lantis, Margaret
1946   The Social Culture of the Nunivak Eskimo. *Transactions of the American Philosophical Society* 35(3):153-323. Philadelphia.

Lapérouse, Jean François de Galaup de
1797   Voyage de La Pérouse autour du monde. 4 vols. and atlas. M.L.A. Milet-Mureau, ed. Paris: Imprimerie de la République.

Larock, V.
1932   Essai sur la valeur sacrée et la valeur sociale des noms de personnes dans les sociétés inférieures. Paris: Librairie Ernest Leroux. (First published in: *Revue de l'Histoire des Religions* 101:27-67, 101-201, 1930.)

Laski, Vera
1958   Seeking Life. *Memoirs of the American Folklore Society* 50. Philadelphia.

Lasley, Mary (Bee-wah-thee-wah)
1902   Sac and Fox Tales. *Journal of American Folk-Lore* 15(58):170-178.

Latham, Robert G.
1846   Miscellaneous Contributions to the Ethnography of North America. *Proceedings of the Philological Society of London* 2:31-50.

1848   On the Languages of the Oregon Territory. *Journal of the Ethnological Society of London* 1:154-166.

1856   On the Languages of Northern, Western, and Central America. Pp. 57-115 in *Transactions of the Philological Society of London for 1856.*

1860   Opuscula: Essays Chiefly Philological and Ethnological. London: Williams and Norgate.

1862   Elements of Comparative Philology. London: Walton and Maberly.

Lathrap, Donald W., and Rudolph C. Troike
1988   Relationship Between Linguistic and Archaeological Data in the New World. Pp. 4-22 in Archaeology and Linguistics. A.M. Mester and C. McEwan, eds. *Journal of the Steward Anthropological Society for 1983-1984,* vol. 15(1-2). Urbana, Ill.

Latorre, Felipe A., and Delores L. Latorre
1976   The Mexican Kickapoo Indians. (*The Texas Pan American Series*). Austin and London: University of Texas Press.

Laudonnière, René Goulaine de
1853   L'Histoire notable de la Floride située ès Indes Occidentales, contenant les trois voyages faits en icelle par certains capitaines et pilotes françois. Paris: P. Jannet.

Laughlin, William S.
1952   The Aleut-Eskimo Community. *Anthropological Papers of the Universty of Alaska* 1(1):25-43. College Alaska.

1963   The Earliest Aleuts. *Anthropological Papers of the University of Alaska* 10(2):73-91.

1963a   Eskimos and Aleuts: Their Origins and Evolution; Physiological and Cultural Adaptation to Facilitate the Evolutionary Success of Eskimo-Aleut Stock. *Science* 142(3593):633-645.

1975   Aleuts: Ecosystem, Holocene History, and Siberian Origin. *Science* 189(4202):633-645.

1980   Aleuts: Survivors of the Bering Land Bridge. New York: Holt, Rinehart and Winston.

Laughlin, William S., and Jean S. Aigner
1975   Aleut Adaptation and Evolution. Pp. 181-201 in Prehistoric Maritime Adaptations of the Circumpolar Zone. W. Fitzhugh, ed. The Hague, Paris: Mouton.

Laughlin, William S., and Gordon H. Marsh
1951   A New View of the History of the Aleutians. *Arctic* 4(2):75-88.

Laure, Pierre Michel
1988   Apparat français-montagnais [1726]. *Collection Tekouerimat* 9. David E. Cooter, ed. Sillery: Presses de l'Université du Québec.

Laurencich-Minelli, Laura
1990   Cardinal Giuseppe Mezzofanti, Scholar of American Indian Languages: His Studies and his Manuscripts. *European Review of Native American Studies* 4(2):27-30. Vienna.

Laurent, Joseph (Sozap Lolô)
1884   New Familiar Abenakis and English Dialogues; the First Ever Published on the Grammatical System, by Jos. Laurent, Abenakis Chief. Quebec: L. Brousseau.

La Vérendrye, Pierre Gaultier de Varennes de
1927   Journals and Letters of Pierre Gaultier de Varennes de la Vérendrye and His Sons; with Correspondence between the Governors of Canada and the French Court, Touching the Search for the Western Sea. Edited with Introduction and Notes by Lawrence J. Burpee. Toronto: The Champlain Society. (Reprinted: Greenwood Press, New York, 1968.)

Law, Howard W.
1961   A Reconstructed Proto-Culture Derived from Some Yuman Vocabularies. *Anthropological Linguistics* 3(4):45-57.

Lawrence, Erma, comp.
1977   Haida Dictionary. [Fairbanks]: The Society for the Preservation of Haida Language and Literature and The Alaska Native Language Center, University of Alaska.

Lawson, Edwin D., comp.
1987   Personal Names and Naming: an Annotated Bibliography. Westport, Conn.: Greenwood Press.

Lawson, John
1709   A New Voyage to Carolina; Containing the Exact Description and Natural History of that Country, Together with the Present State Thereof and a Journal of a Thousand Miles Travelled Through Several Nations of Indians, Giving a Particular Account of their Customs, Manners, etc. London. (Reprinted as: The History of Carolina. Strother and Marcom, Raleigh, 1860. Also as: Lawson's History of North Carolina. Garrett and Massie, Richmond, 1937.)

1937   Lawson's History of North Carolina [1709]. Frances Latham Harriss, ed. Richmond, Va.: Garrett and Massie.

1967   A New Voyage to Carolina [1709]. Hugh T. Lefler, ed. Chapel Hill: University of North Carolina Press.

Lawson, John, and Henry R. Schoolcraft
1855   Comparisons of the Languages of the Ancient Pampticos of N. Carolina with the Algonquin Language; and of the Ancient Waccoa, of that State, and the Catawba, of S. Carolina. Pp. 552-558 of Vol. 5 of Historical and Statistical Information, Respecting the History, Condition and Prospects of the Indian Tribes of the United States. H.R. Schoolcraft, ed. Philadelphia: Lippincott, Grambo. (Reprinted: Schoolcraft's Indian Tribes, 6 vols., indexed by F.S. Nichols (1954), Paladin Press, New York, 1969; AMS Press, New York, 1979.)

Leach, Edmund
1976   Culture and Communication: The Logic by Which
        Symbols Are Connected. An Introduction to the Use of
        Structural Analysis in Social Anthropology. Cambridge
        and London: Cambridge University Press.

Leap, William L.
1970   The Language of Isleta, New Mexico. (Unpublished
        Ph.D. Dissertation in Anthropology, Southern
        Methodist University, Dallas, Texas.)

————
1970a   Tiwa Noun Class Semology: A Historical View. *Anthro-
        pological Linguistics* 12(2):38-45.

————
1971   Who Were the Piro? *Anthropological Linguistics*
        13(7):321-330.

————
1973   Language Pluralism in a Southwestern Pueblo: Some
        Comments on Isletan English. Pp. 275-293 in
        Bilingualism in the Southwest. Paul R. Turner, ed.
        Tucson: University of Arizona Press. (Reprinted, 2d ed.,
        rev., 1982.)

————
1974   Ethnics, Emics, and the New Ideology: The Identity
        Potential of Indian English. Pp. 51-62 in Social and
        Cultural Identity: Problems of Persistence and Change.
        Thomas K. Fitzgerald, ed. (*Southern Anthropological
        Society Proceedings* 8). Athens: Distributed by the
        University of Georgia Press.

————
1988   Applied Linguistics and American Indian Languages
        Renewal: Introductory Comments. *Human Organization*
        47(4):283-291.

————
1993   American Indian English. Salt Lake City: University of
        Utah Press.

Leavitt, Robert M., and David A. Francis, eds.
1986   Kolusuwakonol: Peskotomuhkati-Wolastoqewi naka
        Ikolisomani Latuwewakon. *Philip S. LeSourd's* English
        and Passamaquoddy-Maliseet Dictionary. Fredericton,
        N.B.: Micmac-Maliseet Institute, University of New
        Brunswick.

————
1990   Wapapi Akonutomakonol = The Wampum Records:
        Wabanaki Traditional Laws; as Recounted by Lewis
        Mitchell and Originally Published in 1897. Revised,
        edited and annotated with a new translation.
        Fredericton, N.B.: Micmac-Maliseet Institute, Uni-
        versity of New Brunswick.

Le Boulanger, Jean B. *see* Le Boullenger, Jean-Baptiste

Le Boullenger, Jean-Baptiste
[1725] [French-Illinois Dictionary.] (Manuscript in the John
        Carter Brown Library, Brown University, Providence,
        R.I.)

Le Clercq, Chrétien
1881   First Establishment of the Faith in New France [1691].
        John Gilmary Shea, trans. and ed. 2 vols. New York:
        John G. Shea.

————
1910   New Relation of Gaspesia; with the Customs and
        Religion of the Gaspesian Indians [1691]. William F.
        Ganong, trans. and ed. *Publications of the Champlain
        Society* 5. Toronto. (Reprinted: Greenwood Press, New
        York, 1968.)

Lee, Daniel, and J.H. Frost
1844   Ten Years in Oregon. New York: J. Collord.

Leechman, Douglas
1926   The Chinook Jargon. *American Speech* 1(10):531-534.

Leechman, Douglas, and Robert A. Hall, Jr.
1955   American Indian Pidgin English: Attestations and
        Grammatical Peculiarities. *American Speech* 30(3):163-
        172.

Leer, Jeff
1977   Short Dictionary of Alaska Peninsula Sugcestun.
        Fairbanks: Alaska Native Language Center.

————
1978   A Conversational Dictionary of Kodiak Alutiiq.
        Fairbanks: Alaska Native Language Center.

————
1979   Proto-Athabaskan Verb Stem Variation. *Alaska Native
        Language Research Paper* 1. Fairbanks.

————
1989   Directional Systems in Athapaskan and Na-Dene. Pp.
        575-622 in Athapaskan Linguistics: Current Per-
        spectives on a Language Family. Eung-Do Cook and
        Keren D. Rice, eds. Berlin: Mouton de Gruyter.

————
1990   Tlingit: A Portmanteau Language Family? Pp. 73-98 in
        Linguistic Change and Reconstruction Methodology.
        Philip Baldi, ed. (*Trends in Linguistics, Studies and
        Monographs* 45). Berlin and New York: Mouton de
        Gruyter.

————
1991   Evidence for a Northern Northwest Coast Language
        Area: Promiscuous Number Marking and Periphrastic
        Possessive Constructions in Haida, Eyak, and Aleut.
        International Journal of American Linguistics 57(2):
        158-193.

Lees, Robert B.
1953   The Basis of Glottochronology. *Language: Journal of
        the Linguistic Society of America* 29(2):113-127.

Lefebvre, Gilles R.
1957   A Draft Orthography for the Canadian Eskimo: Towards
        a Future Unification with Greenlandic. (*NCRC*-57-1).
        Ottawa: Northern Co-ordination and Research Centre,
        Department of Northern Affairs and National
        Resources. (Reprinted in 1958.)

Legendre, Géraldine, and David S. Rood
1992   On the Interaction of Grammar Components in Lakhóta:
        Evidence from Split Intransitivity. Pp. 380-394 in
        *Proceedings of the 18th Annual Meeting of the Berkeley
        Linguistics Society, February 14-17, 1992*. Laura A.
        Buszard-Welcher, Lionel Wee, and William Weigel,
        eds. Berkeley, Calif.: BLS.

Legler, Henry E.
1903   Origin and Meaning of Wisconsin Place Names, with Special Reference on Indian Nomenclature. *Transactions of the Wisconsin Academy of Sciences, Arts, and Letters* 14(1):16-39. Madison.

Legoff, Laurent
1889   Grammaire de la langue montagnaise. Montréal.

_____
1889a   Histoire de l'Ancien Testament Racontée aux Montagnais. Montréal.

_____
1926   Dictionnaire français-montagnaise. Lyon: Société Saint-Augustin, Desclée, de Brouwer.

Lehmann, Walter
1915   Über die Stellung und Verwandschaft der Subtiaba-Sprache. *Zeitschrift für Ethnologie* 47:1-34. Berlin.

_____
1920   Zentral-Amerika 1: Die Sprachen Zentral-Amerikas in ihren Beziehungen zueinander sowie zu Sud-Amerika und Mexiko. Berlin: D. Reimer.

Leibowitz, Arnold H.
1971   A History of Language Instruction in American Indian Schools: The Imposition of English by Government Policy. Pp. 1-6 in Bilingual Education for American Indians. *Indian Education, Curriculum Bulletin* 3. Washington, D.C.: Office of Education Programs, U.S. Bureau of Indian Affairs.

Leighton, Anna L.
1985   Wild Plant Use by the Woods Cree (Nihîthawak) of East-Central Saskatchewan. *Canada. National Museum of Man. Mercury Series. Ethnology Service Paper* 101. Ottawa.

_____
1993   Botanical Aspects of Cree-Montagnais-Naskapi Plant Names, Found in Written Sources. Pp. 253-261 in Papers of the Twenty-fourth Algonquian Conference. William Cowan, ed. Ottawa: Carleton University.

Leighton, Dorothea C., and Clyde Kluckhohn
1947   Children of the People: The Navaho Individual and His Development. Cambridge, Mass.: Harvard University Press. (Reprinted: Octagon Books, New York, 1969.)

Le Jeune, Jean-Marie Raphael
1886   Practical Chinook Vocabulary Comprising All and the Only Usual Words of that Wonderful Language... Kamloops, B.C.: St. Louis Mission.

_____
1890   Nelh te skoalwtz Jesu-Kri n Ste Marguerite Mali Alacok. Shoat koe lamhal a tn sptenosem. Dayton, Ohio: P.A. Kemper.

_____
1891-1905 Kamloops Wawa. Kamloops, B.C.: [St. Louis Mission.]

_____
1896-1897 Polyglot Manual. 11 Pts.: English Manual...; Chinook Manual...; Latin Manual...; Stalo Manual...; Thompson Manual...; Lillooet Manual...; Okanagan Manual...; Shushwap Manual...; Skwamish Manual...; Sheshel Manual...; Slayamen Manual.... Kamloops, B.C.: [St. Louis Mission.]

Le Jeune, Paul
1635   Relation de ce qui s'est passé en la Novelle France, en l'année 1635. Pp. 7-198 in Vol. 8 of The Jesuit Relations and Allied Documents: Travel and Explorations of the Jesuit Missionaries in New France, 1610-1791; the Original French, Latin, and Italian Texts, with English Translations and Notes. 73 vols. Cleveland: Burrows Brothers. (Reprinted: Pageant, New York, 1959.)

Leman, Wayne E.
1980   A Reference Grammar of the Cheyenne Language. 2 vols. *University of Northern Colorado Museum of Anthropology, Occasional Publications in Anthropology, Linguistic Series* 5. Greeley, Colorado.

_____
1980a   Cheyenne Texts: An Introduction to Cheyenne Literature, Told by Cheyennes. *University of Northern Colorado Museum of Anthropology, Occasional Publications in Anthropology, Linguistic Series* 6. Greeley, Colorado.

_____, ed.
1987   Náévåhóo'ȯhtséme / We Are Going Back Home: Cheyenne History and Stories Told by James Shoulderblade and Others. *Algonquian and Iroquoian Linguistics, Memoir* 4. Winnipeg, Man.

Lemert, Edwin H.
1952   Stuttering Among the North Pacific Coastal Indians. *Southwestern Journal of Anthropology* 8(4):429-441.

Lemoine, Georges
1901   Dictionnaire français-montagnais avec un vocabulaire montagnais-anglais, une courte liste de noms geographiques et une grammaire montagnaise. Boston: W.B. Cabot and P. Cabot.

_____
1912   Dictionnaire français-algonquin. Quebec, Montreal, and Mattawa: Oblate Fathers [Pp. 1-258 printed 1909 at Chicoutimi: G. Delisle, Bureaux du journal "Le Travailleur"; pp. 259-512 printed 1911 at Quebec: Imp. l'Action Sociale Ltée. Publication information on "Lettre d'approbation" separately inserted.]

Lenneberg, Eric H., and John M. Roberts
1956   The Language of Experience: A Study in Methodology. *Indiana University Publications in Anthropology and Linguistics, Memoir* 13, Supplement to *International Journal of American Linguistics* 22(2). Baltimore.

Le Page du Pratz, Antoine Simon
1758   Histoire de la Louisiane... . 3 vols. Paris: De Bure, l'aînè.

Lepsius, Richard
1855   Das allgemeine linguistische Alphabet: Grundsätze der Übertragung fremder Schriftsysteme und bisher noch ungeschriebener Sprachen in europäische Buchstaben. Berlin: W. Hertz.

_____
1863   Standard Alphabet for Reducing Unwritten Languages and Foreign Graphic Systems to a Uniform Orthography in European Letters. 2d ed. London: Williams and Norgate; Berlin: W. Hertz.

Lescarbot, Marc
1609   Histoire de la Nouvelle France,... . Paris: Jean Mil[l]ot.

1612 Histoire de la Nouvelle-France; suivie des Muses de la Nouvelle-France. 2d ed. 3 vols. Paris: Jean Millot. (Reprinted: Librairie Tross, Paris, 1866.)

1907-1914 The History of New France. 3 vols. Translated and with Notes and Appendices by W.L. Grant. Introduction by H.P. Biggar. *Publications of the Champlain Society* 1 (1907), 7 (1911), 11 (1914). Toronto: The Champlain Society. (Trans. of the 3d ed., Paris, 1618.)

LeSourd, Philip S. *see* Leavitt, Robert M., and David A. Francis, eds. 1986

Lesser, Alexander
1930 Some Aspects of Siouan Kinship. Pp. 563-571 in *Proceedings of the 23d International Congress of Americanists, New York, 1928.* New York.

1977 Kitsai Texts. Pp. 44-64 in Caddoan Texts. Douglas R. Parks, ed. *International Journal of American Linguistics. Native American Texts Series* 2(1). Chicago: The University of Chicago Press.

Lesser, Alexander, and Gene Weltfish
1932 Composition of the Caddoan Linguistic Stock. *Smithsonian Miscellaneous Collections* 87(6):1-15. Washington.

Lévi-Strauss, Claude
1966 The Savage Mind. Translated. London: Weidenfeld and Nicolson. (Original: La Pensée Sauvage, Paris, 1962).

Levin, Norman B.
1964 The Assiniboine Language. *Indiana University Research Center in Anthropology, Folklore, and Linguistics Publication* 32. *International Journal of American Linguistics* 30(3, Pt. 2).

Levine, Gaynell S., and Nancy Bonvillain, eds.
1980 Languages and Lore of the Long Island Indians. (*Suffolk County Archaeological Association. Readings in Long Island Archaeology and Ethnohistory* 4). Lexington, Mass.: Ginn Custom Publishing, for the Suffolk County Archaeological Association.

Levine, Robert D.
1979 Haida and Na-Dene: A New Look at the Evidence. *International Journal of American Linguistics* 45(2):157-170.

Levy, Richard S.
1976 Costanoan Internal Relationships. Berkeley: University of California, Department of Anthropology, Archaeological Research Facility.

1978 The Linguistic Prehistory of California: A Processual View. (Paper presented at the Annual Meeting of the Society of American Archaeology, Tucson, Ariz.)

1979 The Linguistic Prehistory of Central California: Historical Linguistics and Culture Process. (Paper in Levy's possession.)

Lewin, Roger
1988 Linguists Search for the Mother Tongue. *Science* 242(4882):1128-1129.

Lewis, Arthur
1904 The Life and Work of the Rev. E.J. Peck among the Eskimos. London: Hodder and Stoughton. New York: A.C. Armstrong and Son. (Reprinted, 3rd ed.: Hodder and Stoughton, London, 1908.)

Lewis, G. Malcolm
1980 Indian Maps. Pp. 9-23 in Old Trails and New Directions: Papers of the Third North American Fur Trade Conference. Carol M. Judd and Arthur J. Ray, eds. Toronto: University of Toronto Press.

1993 Metrics, Geometries, Signs, and Language: Sources of Cartographic Miscommunication Between Native and Euro-American Cultures in North America. *Cartographica* 30(1):98-106. Toronto.

Li, Charles N., and Sandra A. Thompson
1976 Strategies for Signaling Grammatical Relations in Wappo. Pp. 450-458 in Papers from the Twelfth Regional Meeting, Chicago Linguistic Society. Salikoko Mufwene, Carol A. Walker, and Sanford B. Steever, eds. Chicago: Chicago Linguistic Society, University of Chicago.

Li, Charles N., Sandra A. Thompson, and Jesse O. Sawyer
1977 Subject and Word Order in Wappo. *International Journal of American Linguistics* 43(2):85-100.

Li, Fang-Kuei
1930 Mattole, an Athabaskan Language. *University of Chicago Publications in Anthropology, Linguistic Series.* Chicago: University of Chicago Press.

1931 A Study of Sarcee Verb-Stems. *International Journal of American Linguistics* 6(1):3-27.

1933 List of Chipewyan Stems. *International Journal of American Linguistics* 7(3-4):122-151.

1946 Chipewyan. Pp. 398-423 in Linguistic Structures of Native America. Harry Hoijer, ed. *Viking Fund Publications in Anthropology* 6. New York.

1956 A Type of Noun Formation in Athabaskan and Eyak. *International Journal of American Linguistics* 22(1):45-48.

1964 A Chipewyan Ethnological Text. *International Journal of American Linguistics* 30(2):132-136.

Li, Fang-Kuei, and Ronald Scollon
1976 Chipewyan Texts. *Institute of History and Philology, Academica Sinica, Special Publications* 71. Taipei.

Liberty, Margot
1978 Francis La Flesche: The Osage Odyssey; Omaha, 1857-1932. Pp. 44-59 in American Indian Intellectuals. Margot Liberty, ed. *1976 Proceedings of the American Ethnological Society.* St. Paul, Minn.: West Pub. Co.

Liljeblad, Sven
1950 Bannack I: Phonemes. *International Journal of American Linguistics* 16(3):126-131.

Lillard, Jeremiah B., Robert F. Heizer, and Franklin Fenenga
1939   An Introduction to the Archaeology of Central California. *Sacramento Junior College, Department of Anthropology Bulletin* 2. Sacramento.

Lincoln, Neville J., and John C. Rath
1980   North Wakashan Comparative Root List. *Canada. National Museum of Man. Mercury Series. Ethnology Service Paper* 68. Ottawa.

————
1986   Phonology, Dictionary, and Listing of Roots and Lexical Derivates of the Haisla Language of Kitlope and Kitimaat, B.C. 2 vols. *Canada. Museum of Civilization. Mercury Series. Ethnology Service Papers* 103. Ottawa.

Lindenfeld, Jacqueline
1971   Semantic Categorization as a Deterrent to Grammatical Borrowing: A Yaqui Example. *International Journal of American Linguistics* 37(1):6-14.

————
1973   Yaqui Syntax. *University of California Publications in Linguistics* 76. Berkeley.

Linderman, Frank Bird
1930   American: The Life Story of a Great Indian; Plenty-Coups, Chief of the Crows. New York: The John Day Company.

Lindeström, Peter M.
1925   Geographia Americae with an Account of the Delaware Indians Based on Surveys and Notes Made in 1654-1656. Translated from the Original Manuscript with Notes, Introduction, and an Appendix of Indian Geographical Names with Their Meanings, by Amandus Johnson. Philadelphia: Swedish Colonial Society.

Linton, Ralph, ed.
1940   Acculturation in Seven American Indian Tribes. New York: D. Appleton-Century.

Lionnet, Andrés
1978   El Idioma tubar y los tubares, según documentos inéditos de C.S. Lumholtz y C.V. Hartman. Mexico City: Universidad Iberoamericana.

Lipkind, William
1945   Winnebago Grammar. New York: King's Crown Press.

Lisiânskiĭ, I͡Uriĭ Fedorovich
1812   Puteshestvīe vokrug svīeta v 1803, 4, 5, i 1806 godakh, po povelīeniŭ Ego Imperatorskago Velichestva Aleksandra Pervago, na korablīe *Nevīe* [A Voyage Around the World in the Years 1803-1806: Performed by Order of His Imperial Majesty Alexander the First, Emperor of Russia, in the Ship *Neva*]. 2 vols. St. Petersburg: Naval Printing Office.

Little, Elizabeth A.
1984   Indian Place Names on Nantucket Island. Pp. 345-362 in Papers of the Fifteenth Algonquian Conference. William Cowan, ed. Ottawa: Carleton University.

Littlefield, Daniel F., and Lonnie E. Underhill
1971   Renaming the American Indian: 1890-1913. *American Studies* 12(2):33-45.

Loeb, Edwin M.
1926   Pomo Folkways. *University of California Publications in American Archaeology and Ethnology* 19(2). Berkeley. (Reprinted: Kraus Reprint, New York, 1965.)

————
1932   The Western Kuksu Cult. *University of California Publications in American Archaeology and Ethnology* 33(1). Berkeley.

Loew, Oscar
1876   Notes Upon the Ethnology of Southern California and Adjacent Regions. Pp. 541-547 in *Annual Report of the U.S. War Department, Report of the Chief of Engineers for 1876*. Vol. 23, Appendix J.J., Part H. 14. Washington.

Lomatuway'ma, Michael
1993   Hopi Ruin Legends = Kiqtutuwutsi. Ekkehart Malotki, coll., trans., and ed. Lincoln: University of Nebraska Press for Northern Arizona University.

Lombardo, Natal
1702   Arte de la lengua teguima vulgarmente llamada ópata. Mexico: Miguel de Ribera.

Longacre, Robert E.
1957   Quality and Quantity in Cree Vowels. *Journal of the Canadian Linguistic Association* 3:66-70.

Longacre, Robert E., and René Millon
1961   Proto-Mixtecan and Proto-Amuzgo-Mixtecan Vocabularies: A Preliminary Cultural Analysis. *Anthropological Linguistics* 3(4):1-44.

Longfellow, Henry W.
1855   The Song of Hiawatha. Boston: Ticknor and Fields.

Lopatin, Ivan A.
1945   Social Life and Religion of the Indians in Kitimat, Birtish Columbia. *University of Southern California Social Science Series* 26. Los Angeles.

Loskiel, Georg Heinrich
1789   Geschichte der Mission der evangelischen Brüder unter den Indianern in Nordamerika. Leipzig: Paul Gotthelf Kummer.

Loud, Llewellyn L.
1918   Ethnogeography and Archaeology of the Wiyot Territory. *University of California Publications in American Archaeology and Ethnology* 14(3):221-436.

Loughridge, Robert M., and David M. Hodge
1890   English and Muskokee Dictionary Collected from Various Sources and Revised [and] Dictionary of the Muskokee or Creek Language in Creek and English. St. Louis: J.T. Smith. (Reprinted: Westminster Press, Philadelphia, 1914.)

Lounsbury, Floyd G.
1949   Iroquoian Morphology. (Ph.D. Dissertation in Linguistics, Yale University, New Haven, Conn. Published in 1953 as "Oneida Verb Morphology"; *Yale University Publications in Anthropology* 48. Reprinted: Human Relations Area Files Press, New Haven, 1976.)

————
1953   Oneida Verb Morphology. *Yale University Publications in Anthropology* 48. New Haven, Conn.

————
1960   Iroquois Place Names in the Champlain Valley. Pp. 23-66 in Report of the New York-Vermont Interstate Commission on the Lake Champlain Basin, 1960 (Legislative Document No. 9). Albany. (Reprinted: State University of New York, State Education Department, Albany, 1970.)

854

1961   Iroquois-Cherokee Linguistic Relations. Pp. 9-17 in Symposium on Cherokee and Iroquois Culture. *Bureau of American Ethnology Bulletin* 180. Washington.

1964   The Formal Analysis of Crow- and Omaha-Type Kinship Terminologies. Pp. 351-393 in Explorations in Cultural Anthropology: Essays in Honor of George P. Murdock. Ward H. Goodenough, ed. New York: McGraw-Hill.

1968   One Hundred Years of Anthropological Linguistics. Pp. 153-264 in One Hundred Years of Anthropology. J.O. Brew, ed. Cambridge, Mass.: Harvard University.

Lowe, Ronald
1983   Kangiryuarmiut uqauhingita numiktittidjutinit: Basic Kangiryuarmiut Eskimo Dictionary. Inuvik, N.W.Terr.: Committee for Original Peoples Entitlement.

1984   Siglit inuvialiut uqausiita kipuktirutait: Basic Siglit Inuvialuit Eskimo Dictionary. Inuvik, N.W.Terr.: Committee for Original Peoples Entitlement.

1985   Basic Kangiryuarmiut Eskimo Grammar. Inuvik, N.W.Terr.: Committee for Original Peoples Entitlement.

Lowie, Robert H.
1909   The Assiniboine. *American Museum of Natural History Anthropological Papers* 4(1):1-270. New York. (Reprinted: AMS Press, New York, 1975.)

1909a   The Northern Shoshone. *American Museum of Natural History Anthropological Papers* 2(2):165-306. New York.

1912   Social Life of the Crow Indians. *American Museum of Natural History Anthropological Papers* 9(2):179-248. New York.

1913   Military Societies of the Crow Indians. *American Museum of Natural History Anthropological Papers* 11(3):145-217. New York.

1914   Crow Rapid-Speech Puzzles. *Journal of American Folk-Lore* 27(106):330-331.

1917   Notes on the Social Organization and Customs of the Mandan, Hidatsa and Crow Indians. *American Museum of Natural History Anthropological Papers* 21(1):1-99. New York.

1924   Notes on Shoshonean Ethnography. *American Museum of Natural History Anthropological Papers* 20(3):185-314. New York.

1929   Hopi Kinship. *American Museum of Natural History Anthropological Papers* 30(7):361-388. New York.

1934   Some Moot Problems in Social Organization. *American Anthropologist*, n.s. 36(3):321-330.

1935   The Crow Indians. New York: Farrar and Rinehart. (Reprinted: Holt, Rinehart and Winston, New York, 1956; University of Nebraska Press, Lincoln, 1983.)

1939   Ethnographic Notes on the Washo. *University of California Publications in American Archaeology and Ethnology* 36(5):301-352. Berkeley.

1941   The Crow Language: Grammatical Sketch and Analyzed Text. *University of California Publications in American Archaeology and Ethnology* 39(1):1-142.

1959   Crow Curses. *Journal of American Folklore* 72(284): 105.

1960   Crow Texts. Berkeley: University of California Press.

1960a   Crow Word Lists: Crow-English and English-Crow Vocabularies. Berkeley: University of California Press.

Lowie, Robert H., and Louella Cole Lowie, ed.
1960   A Few Assiniboine Texts. *Anthropological Linguistics* 2(8):1-30.

1963   Washo Texts. *Anthropological Linguistics* 5(7):1-30.

Lowie, Robert H., Louella Cole Lowie, and Madge D. Richardson, comps.
1958   Bibliography of Robert H. Lowie. *American Anthropologist*, n.s. 60(2):362-375.

Luckenbach, Alvin H., Wayne E. Clark, and Richard S. Levy
1987   Rethinking Cultural Stability in Eastern North American Prehistory: Linguistic Evidence from Eastern Algonquian. *Journal of Middle Atlantic Archaeology* 3:1-33.

Lucy-Fossarieu, [Pierre Henri Richard] de
1881   Les langues indiennes de la Californie. Étude de philologie ethnographique. *Extrait du Compte rendu sténographique du Congrès international des sciences ethnographiques*, tenue à Paris du 15 au 17 juillet 1878. Paris: Imprimerie Nationale.

Luebke, Frederick C.
1987   Indian Maps: Their Place in the History of Plains Cartography. Pp. 63-80 in Mapping the North American Plains: Essays in the History of Cartography. Frederick C. Luebke, Frances W. Kaye, and Gary E. Moulton, eds. Norman: University of Oklahoma Press and Lincoln: Center for Great Plains Studies, University of Nebraska-Lincoln.

Lumholtz, Carl S.
1894   Tarahumari Life and Customs. *Scribner's Magazine* 16(3):296-311. New York.

1902   Unknown Mexico: A Record of Five Years' Exploration among the Tribes of the Western Sierra Madre; in the Tierra Caliente of Tepic and Jalisco; and among the Tarascos of Michoacan. 2 vols. New York: Charles Scribner's Sons. (Reprinted: Rio Grande Press, Glorieta, N.M., 1973.)

Luthin, Herbert W.
1991   Restoring the Voice in Yanan Traditional Narrative: Prosody, Performance and Presentational Form. 2 vols. (Unpublished Ph.D. Dissertation in Linguistcs, University of California, Berkeley.)

Lykins, Johnston
1834   Siwinowe eawekitake. Shawannoe Mission, Indian Terr.: J. Meeker.

_____
1837   Wafafe wagrysy. Shawannoe Mission, Indian Terr.: J.G. Pratt.

Lyons, John
1977   Semantics. Cambridge: Cambridge University Press.

McAllister, J. Gilbert
1955   Kiowa-Apache Social Organization. Pp. 97-169 in Social Anthropology of North American Tribes. Fred Eggan, ed. 2d ed. Chicago: University of Chicago Press.

McClellan, Catharine
1970   The Girl Who Married the Bear: A Masterpiece of Indian Oral Tradition. *Canada. National Museum of Man. Publications in Ethnology* 2. Ottawa.

_____
1953   The Inland Tlingit. Pp. 47-52 in Asia and North America: Transpacific Contacts. Marian W. Smith, comp. *Memoirs of the Society for American Archaeology* 9. Salt Lake City. (Reprinted: Kraus Reprint, Millwood, N.Y., 1974.)

_____
1954   The Interrelations of Social Structure with Northern Tlingit Ceremonalism. *Southwestern Journal of Anthropology* 10(1):75-96.

McCoy, Isaac
1840   History of Baptist Indian Missions; Embracing Remarks on the Former and Present Condition of the Aboriginal Tribes; Their Settlement within the Indian Territory, and Their Future Prospects. Washington: W.M. Morrison; New York: H. and S. Raynor.

MacDonald, George F.
1969   Preliminary Culture Sequences from the Coast Tsimshian Area, British Columbia. *Northwest Anthropological Research Notes* 3(2):240-254.

MacDonald, Peter, with Ted Schwarz
1993   The Last Warrior: Peter MacDonald and the Navajo Nation. New York: Orion Books.

McDonald, Robert
1871   [Terms of Relationship of the Tukuthe.] Pp. 293-382, line 68, in Systems of Consanguinity and Affinity of the Human Family, by L.H. Morgan. *Smithsonian Contributions to Knowledge* 17. Washington: Smithsonian Institution.

_____, trans.
1886   The New Testament of Our Lord and Saviour Jesus Christ. Translated into Takudh [...]. London: Printed for the British and Foreign Bible Society.

McGary, Jane, comp.
1979   Bibliography of Educational Publications for Alaska Native Languages. 2d ed. Rosslyn, Va.: National Clearinghouse for Bilingual Education; Juneau: Alaska State Department of Education, Bilingual-Bicultural Program.

McGhee, Robert
1976   Parsimony Isn't Everything: An Alternative View of Eskaleutian Linguistics and Prehistory. *Canadian Archaeological Association Bulletin* 8:62-81.

_____
1978   Canadian Arctic Prehistory. Toronto and New York: Van Nostrand, Reinhold.

_____
1988   A Scenario for Eskimo-Aleut Prehistory. Pp. 369-377 in The Late Prehistory Development of Alaska's Native People. Robert D. Shaw, Roger K. Harritt, and Don E. Dumond, eds. *Aurora: Alaska Anthropological Association Monograph Series* 4. Anchorage.

McGregor, Ernest
1987   Algonquin Lexicon. Maniwaki, Que.: River Desert Education Authority.

McIlwraith, Thomas F.
1948   The Bella Coola Indians. 2 vols. Toronto: University of Toronto Press.

McKennan, Robert A.
1959   The Upper Tanana Indians. *Yale University Publications in Anthropology* 55. New Haven.

Mackenzie, Alexander
1801   Voyages from Montreal, on the River St. Laurence, Through the Continent of North America, to the Frozen and Pacific Oceans, in the Years 1789 and 1793. London: T. Cadell and W. Davies.

_____
1970   The Journals and Letters of Sir Alexander Mackenzie. W. Kaye Lamb, ed. Cambridge: Cambridge University Press for the Hakluyt Society.

MacKenzie, Marguerite E.
1971   The Eastern (Mistassini) Cree Verb: Derivational Morphology. (Unpublished M.A. Thesis in Linguistics, McGill University, Montreal.)

_____
1980   Towards a Dialectology of Cree-Montagnais-Naskapi. (Ph.D. Dissertation in Linguistics, University of Toronto. Microfiche: Canadian Theses on Microfiche Service, National Library of Canada, Ottawa, 1982.)

MacKenzie, Marguerite E., and Bill Jancewicz
1994   Naskapi Lexicon / Lexique Naskapi. Vol. 1: Naskapi - English/French; Vol. 2: English - Naskapi; Vol. 3: French - Naskapi. Kawawachikamach, Que.: Naskapi Development Center.

MacKenzie, Marguerite, E., et al.
1988   Cree Lexicon: Eastern James Bay Dialects. [Chisasibi, Que.]: Cree School Board. (Imprint date, 1987.)

McKern, W.C.
1922   Functional Families of the Patwin. *University of California Publications in American Archaeology and Ethnology* 13(7):235-258.

McKinley, Robert
1971   Why Do Crow and Omaha Kinship Terminologies Exist? A Sociology of Knowledge Interpretation. *Man* 6(3):408-426.

McLaughlin, Daniel J.
1992   When Literacy Empowers: Navajo Language in Print. Albuquerque: University of New Mexico Press.

856

McLaughlin, John E.
1983 From Aspect to Tense, or, What's -*nuh* in Comanche. Pp. 412-426 in 1982 Mid-America Linguistics Conference Papers. Frances Ingemann, ed. Lawrence: Department of Linguistics, University of Kansas.

1989 A Note on the Change of Strident to Nonstrident in Gosiute Shoshoni. *International Journal of American Linguistics* 55(2):240-247.

MacLean, Edna Ahgeak
1980 Iñupiallu Tannillu Uqalunisa Illanich: Abridged Iñupiaq and English Dictionary. Fairbanks: Alaska Native Language Center.

McLendon, Sally
1959-1990 [Eastern Pomo Linguistic Fieldnotes.] (Notebooks in McLendon's possession.)

1964 Northern Hokan (b) and (c): A Comparison of Eastern Pomo and Yana. Pp. 126-144 in Studies in Californian Linguistics. William Bright, ed. *University of California Publications in Linguistics* 34. Berkeley.

1969 Spanish Words in Eastern Pomo. *Romance Philology* 23(1):39-53.

1973 Proto Pomo. *University of California Publications in Linguistics* 71. Berkeley.

1975 A Grammar of Eastern Pomo. *University of California Publications in Linguistics* 74. Berkeley.

1976 The Proto-Pomo Pronominal System. Pp. 29-54 in Hokan Studies: Papers from the First Conference on Hokan Languages. Margaret Langdon and Shirley Silver, eds. (*Janua Linguarum, Series Practica* 181). The Hague and Paris: Mouton.

1977 Cultural Presuppositions and Discourse Analysis: Patterns of Presupposition and Assertion of Information in Eastern Pomo and Russian Narrative. Pp. 153-189 in Linguistics and Anthropology. Muriel Saville-Troike, ed. *Georgetown University Round Table on Languages and Linguistics 1977*. Washington: Georgetown University Press.

1977a Bear Kills Her Own Daughter-in-Law, Deer (Eastern Pomo). Pp. 26-65 in Northern California Texts. Victor Golla and Shirley Silver, eds. *International Journal of American Linguistics. Native American Texts Series* 2(2). Chicago: The University of Chicago Press.

1978 Ergativity, Case, and Transitivity in Eastern Pomo. *International Journal of American Linguistics* 44(1):1-9.

1978a Coyote and the Ground Squirrels (Eastern Pomo). Pp. 87-111 in Coyote Stories. William Bright, ed. *International Journal of American Linguistics. Native American Texts Series Monograph* 1. Chicago: The University of Chicago Press.

1979 Clitics, Clauses, Closures and Discourse in Eastern Pomo. Pp. 637-646 in Proceedings of the Fifth Annual Meeting of the Berkeley Linguistic Society. Berkeley: BLS.

1980 How Languages Die: A Social History of Unstable Bilingualism Among the Eastern Pomo. Pp. 137-150 in American Indian and Indoeuropean Studies: Papers in Honor of Madison S. Beeler. Kathryn A. Klar, Margaret Langdon, and Shirley Silver, eds. (*Trends in Linguistics. Studies and Monographs* 16). The Hague: Mouton.

1982 Meaning, Rhetorical Structure, and Discourse Organization in Myth. Pp. 284-305 in Analyzing Discourse: Text and Talk. Deborah Tannen, ed. *Georgetown University Round Table on Languages and Linguistics 1981*. Washington.

MacMillan, Donald B.
1943 Eskimo Place Names and Aid to Conversation. *Hydrographic Office Miscellaneous Publication* 10,578. Washington: U.S. Navy Hydrographic Office.

McMurtrie, Douglas C.
1931 Early Printing in Michigan, with a Bibliography of the Issues of the Michigan Press, 1796-1850. Chicago: John Calhoun Club.

1933 The Shawnee Sun: The First Indian-language Periodical Published in the United States. *Kansas Historical Quarterly* 2(4):339-342. Topeka.

McMurtrie, Douglas C., and Albert H. Allen
1930 Jotham Meeker, Pioneer Printer of Kansas; with a Bibliography of the Known Issues of the Baptist Mission Press at Shawanoe, Stockbridge, and Ottawa, 1834-1854. Chicago: Eyncourt Press.

MacNeish, June Helm
1960 Kin Terms of Arctic Drainage Déné: Hare, Slavery, Chipewyan. *American Anthropologist*, n.s. 62(2):279-295.

MacNeish, Richard S.
1952 Iroquois Pottery Types: A Technique for the Study of Iroquois Prehistory. *Anthropological Series* 31, *National Museum of Canada Bulletin* 124. Ottawa.

McNickle, D'Arcy
1936 The Surrounded. New York: Dodd, Mead. (Reprinted: University of New Mexico Press, Albuquerque, 1978.)

Madsen, David B.
1975 Dating Paiute-Shoshoni Expansion in the Great Basin. *American Antiquity* 40(1):82-86.

Magnon de Terlaye, François-Auguste
[1755] Langue de[s] Loups. Follows p. 274 in [Dictionnaire Onontagué-Français]. (Manuscript in the Archives Indiennes, Notre-Dame de Montréal, Place d'Armes, Montréal, Québec.)

Mailhot, José
1985 Implementation of Mother-Tongue Literacy among the Montagnais: Myth or Reality? Pp. 17-26 in Promoting Native Writing Systems in Canada. Barbara Burnaby, ed. Toronto: OISE Press / The Ontario Institute for Studies in Education.

1992   Deux lettres montagnaises du XVIIIe siècle. *Recherches Amérindiennes au Québec* 22(1):3-16.

Maillard, Pierre-Antoine-Simon
1864   Grammar of the Mikmaque Language of Nova Scotia. Joseph-M. Bellenger, ed. (*Shea's Library of American Linguistics* 9). New York: Cramoisy Press.

Malaspina, Alessandro
1885   Viaje político-científico alrededor del mundo por las corbetas *Descubierta* y *Atrevida* al mando de los capitanes del navío D. Alejandro Malaspina y Don José de Bustamante y Guerra desde 1789 á 1794. Madrid: Impr. de la Viuda é Hijos de Abienzo.

Malécot, André
1963   Luiseño, A Structural Analysis I: Phonology. *International Journal of American Linguistics* 29(2):89-95.

Mallery, Garrick
1877   A Calendar of the Dakota Nation. Pp. 3-25 in Vol. 3 of *Bulletin of the United States Geological and Geographical Survey of the Territories.* F.V. Hayden, U.S. Geologist-in-Charge. Washington: U.S. Goverment Printing Office.

1880   A Collection of Gesture-Signs and Signals of the North American Indians with Some Comparisons. Washington: Government Printing Office. (Reprinted: Pp. 77-406 in Vol. 1 of Aboriginal Sign Languages of the Americas and Australia. 2 vols. D. Jean Umiker-Sebeok and Thomas A. Sebeok, eds. Plenum Press, New York and London, 1978.)

1881   Sign Language Among North American Indians Compared With That Among Other Peoples and Deaf-Mutes. Pp. 263-552 in *1st Annual Report of the Bureau of [American] Ethnology [for] 1879-'80.* Washington. (Reprinted, with articles by A.L. Kroeber and C.F. Voegelin in: *Approaches to Semiotics* 14. Mouton, The Hague, 1972.)

1886   Pictographs of the North American Indians: A Preliminary Paper. Pp. 3-256 in *4th Annual Report of the Bureau of [American] Ethnology [for] 1882-'83.* Washington.

1893   Picture-Writing of the American Indians. Pp. 3-822 in *10th Annual Report of the Bureau of [American] Ethnology [for] 1888-'89.* Washington. (Reprinted, 2 vols.: Dover Publications, New York, 1972.)

Mallon, Sidney T.
1974   Inuktitut: Phase One. (Rankin Inlet Version.) Yellowknife, N.W.Terr.: Dept. of Education, Northwest Territories, Inuktitut Learning Services.

1976   Inuktitut: Phase Two. (Rankin Inlet Version.) Yellowknife, N.W.Terr.: Dept. of Education, Northwest Territories, Inuktitut Learning Services.

Malotki, Ekkehart
1978   Hopitutuwutsi / Hopi Tales: A Bilingual Collection of Hopi Indian Stories. Flagstaff: Museum of Northern Arizona Press. (Reprinted: Sun Tracks and the University of Arizona Press, Tucson, 1983.)

1983   Hopi Time. (*Trends in Linguistics, Studies and Monographs* 20). Berlin, New York, and Amsterdam: Mouton Publishers.

Malotki, Ekkehart, and Michael Lomatuway'ma
1984   Hopi Coyote Tales / Istutuwutsi. *American Tribal Religions* 9. Lincoln: University of Nebraska Press.

1987   Stories of Maasaw, a Hopi God. *American Tribal Religions* 10. Lincoln: University of Nebraska Press.

Manaster Ramer, Alexis
1992   A Northern Uto-Aztecan Sound Law: **-c-* → *-y-.* *International Journal of American Linguistics* 58(3): 251-268.

Mandelbaum, David G.
1940   The Plains Cree. *American Museum of Natural History Anthropological Papers* 37(2):155-316. New York. (Reprinted: AMS Press, New York, 1979.)

———, ed.
1949   Selected Writings of Edward Sapir in Language, Culture and Personality. Berkeley: University of California Press. (Reprinted in 1963.)

Mandelbaum, May
1938   The Individual Life Cycle. Pp. 101-129 in the Sinkaietk or Southern Okanagon of Washington, by Walter Cline et al. Leslie Spier, ed. *General Series in Anthropology* 6, *Contributions from the Laboratory of Anthropology* 2. Menasha, Wis.

Marcy, Randolph B.
1853   Vocabularies of the Comanches and Witchitas...With Some General Remarks by Prof. W.W. Turner. Pp. 305-311 (Appendix H) in Exploration of the Red River of Louisiana in the Year 1852 by Randolph B. Marcy and George B. McClellan. In *U.S. Congress. Senate. 32d Cong., 2d sess. Senate Executive Doc. No. 54.* Washington: Robert Armstrong, Public Printer.

Margry, Pierre, ed.
1876-1886 Découvertes et établissements des Français dans l'ouest et dans le sud de l'Amérique septentrionale, 1614-1754: Mémoires et documents originaux. 6 vols. Paris: D. Jouaust.

Marlett, Stephen A.
1988   The Syllable Structure of Seri. *International Journal of American Linguistics* 54(3):245-278.

Marsden, W.L.
1923   The Northern Paiute Language of Oregon. *University of California Publications in American Archaeology and Ethnology* 20(11):175-191.

Marsh, Gordon H.
1954   A Comparative Survey of Eskimo-Aleut Religion. *Anthropological Papers of the University of Alaska* 3(1):21-36. College.

Marsh, Gordon H., and William S. Laughlin
1956   Human Anatomical Knowledge among the Aleutian Islanders. *Southwestern Journal of Anthropology* 12(1):38-78. Albuquerque.

Marsh, Gordon H., and Morris Swadesh
1951   Kleinschmidt Centennial V: Eskimo Aleut Correspondences. *International Journal of American Linguistics* 17(4):209-216.

858

Martijn, Charles A.
1991   Gepèg (Québec): un toponyme d'origine micmaque. *Recherches Amérindiennes au Québec* 21(3):51-64. Montreal.

Martin, Jack
1991   Lexical and Syntactic Aspects of Creek Causatives. *International Journal of American Linguistics* 57(2):194-229.

_____
1994   Modeling Language Contact in the Prehistory of the Southeastern United States. Pp. 14-24 in Perspectives on the Southeast: Linguistics, Archaeology, and Ethnohistory. Patricia B. Kwachka, ed. (*Southern Anthropology Society Proceedings* 27). Athens and London: The University of Georgia Press.

_____
1994a   Implications of Plural Reduplication, Infixation, and Subtraction for Muskogean Subgrouping. *Anthropological Linguistics* 36(1):27-55.

Martin, Jeanette P.
1975   A Survey of the Current Study and Teaching of North American Indian Languages in the United States and Canada. *CAL-ERIC/CLL Series on Languages and Linguistics* 17. Arlington, Va.: Center for Applied Linguistics.

Martin, Pierre
1991   Le montagnais: langue algonquienne du Québec. *Langues et Sociétés d'Amérique traditionelle* 3. Paris: Éditions Peeters.

Martin, Pierre, et al.
1978   La longueur des voyelles en Cris. *Review Canadienne de Linguistique* 23:84-106.

Masayesva Jeanne, LaVerne
1982   Some Phonological Rules of Hopi. *International Journal of American Linguistics* 48(3):245-270.

Mason, J. Alden
1912   The Ethnology of the Salinan Indians. *University of California Publications in American Archaeology and Ethnology* 10(4):97-240.

_____
1916   The Mutsun Dialect of Costanoan, Based on the Vocabulary of De la Cuesta. *University of California Publications in American Archaeology and Ethnology* 11(7):399-472. Berkeley. (Reprinted: Kraus Reprints, New York, 1965.)

_____
1917   Tepecano: A Piman Language of Western Mexico. *Annals of the New York Academy of Sciences* 25:309-416. New York.

_____
1918   The Language of the Salinan Indians. *University of California Publications in American Archaeology and Ethnology* 14(1):1-154. Berkeley. (Reprinted: Kraus Reprint, New York, 1965.)

_____
1918a   Tepecano Prayers. *International Journal of American Linguistics* 1(2):91-153.

_____
1923   A Preliminary Sketch of the Yaqui Language. Pp. 193-212 in Phoebe Apperson Hearst Memorial Volume on the Twentieth Anniversary of the Organization of the Department and Museum of Anthropology of the University of California, September 10, 1901. A.L. Kroeber, ed. Berkeley: University of California Press. (*University of California Publications in American Archaeology and Ethnology* 20.)

_____
1936   The Classification of the Sonoran Languages. Pp. 183-198 in Essays in Anthropology Presented to A.L. Kroeber in Celebration of His Sixtieth Birthday, June 11, 1936. Robert H. Lowie, ed. Berkeley: University of California Press.

_____
1940   The Native Languages of Middle America. Pp. 52-87 in The Maya and Their Neighbors. Clarence L. Hay, et al., eds. New York: D. Appleton-Century.

_____
1946   Notes on the Indians of the Great Slave Lake Area. *Yale University Publications in Anthropology* 34. New Haven, Conn.

Mason, Otis T.
1879   [Anthropological News: Caddo vocabulary list prepared by John Sibley in 1804]. *American Naturalist* 13(12): 787-790. Washington.

_____
1893   Summary of Progress in Anthropology in 1891. Pp. 433-502 in *Annual Report of the Board of the Regents of the Smithsonian Institution...to July 1891*. Washington: Government Printing Office.

_____
1893a   Progress of Anthropology in 1892. Pp. 465-481 in *Annual Report of the Board of the Regents of the Smithsonian Institution...to July 1892*. Washington: Government Printing Office.

Mason, William
1861   Kanachi kichi masinaikan, kayasi tistemint, mina oski tistemint [...]. [The Bible, Old Testament, and New Testament ... in Cree syllabic characters]. London: Printed for the British and Foreign Bible Society.

Massey, William C.
1949   Tribes and Languages of Baja California. *Southwestern Journal of Anthropology* 5(3):272-307. Albuquerque.

Masta, Henry Lorne
1932   Abenaki Indian Legends, Grammar and Place Names. Victoriaville, P.Q.: La Voix des boisfrancs.

Masthay, Carl
1980   Mahican-Language Hymns, Biblical Prose, and Vocabularies from Moravian Sources, with 11 Mohawk Hymns (Transcription and Translation). St. Louis, Mo.: The Author.

_____ , ed.
1991   Schmick's Mahican Dictionary. With a Mahican Historical Phonology by David H. Pentland. (*Memoirs of the American Philosophical Society* 197). Philadelphia.

859

Mather, Elsie P.
1985   Cauyarnariuq. [It is Time for Drumming.] Phyllis Morrow, ed. *Alaska Historical Commission Studies in History* 184. Bethel: Lower Kuskokwim School District, Bilingual/Bicultural Department.

Mathevet, Jean Claude
1892   Ka Titc Tebeniminang Jezos, Ondaje Aking. [Life of Christ.] 2d ed. Montréal.

Mathiot, Madeleine
1973   A Dictionary of Papago Usage. Bloomington: Indiana University Press.

Matson, Emerson N.
1968   Longhouse Legends. Camden, N.J.: Thomas Nelson and Sons.

————, comp.
1972   Legends of the Great Chiefs. Nashville, Tenn.: Thomas Nelson. (Reprinted, 2d ed.: Storypole Press, Tacoma, Wash., 1984.)

Matthews, G. Hubert
1958   Handbook of Siouan Languages. (Unpublished Ph.D. Dissertation in Linguistics, University of Pennsylvania, Philadelphia.)

1959   Proto-Siouan Kinship Terminology. *American Anthropologist* 61(2):252-278.

1965   Hidatsa Syntax. The Hague: Mouton.

1970   Some Notes on the Proto-Siouan Continuants. *International Journal of American Linguistics* 36(2):98-109.

1979   Glottochronology and the Separation of the Crow and Hidatsa. *Archaeology of Montana* 20(3):113-125.

Matthews, G. Hubert, and Red Thunder Cloud
1967   Catawba Texts. *International Journal of American Linguistics* 33(1):7-24.

Matthews, Washington
1873-1874 Grammar and Dictionary of the Language of the Hidatsa (Minnetarees, Grosventres of the Missouri). 2 vols. *Shea's Library of American Linguistics*, ser. 2(1-2). New York: Cramoisy Press.

1877   Ethnography and Philology of the Hidatsa Indians. *U.S. Geological and Geographical Survey, Miscellaneous Publications* 7. Washington: Government Printing Office.

1887   The Mountain Chant: A Navajo Ceremony. Pp. 379-467 in *5th Annual Report of the Bureau of American Ethnology for the Years 1883-1884*. Washington.

1888   Prayer of a Navajo Shaman. *American Anthropologist*, o.s. 1(2):149-170.

————, coll. and trans.
1897   Navaho Legends. *Memoirs of the American Folk-Lore Society* 5. Boston. (Reprinted: Kraus Reprint, New York, 1969.)

Mattina, Anthony
1970   Phonology of Alaskan Eskimo, Kuskokwim Dialect. *International Journal of American Linguistics* 36(1):38-45.

1973   Colville Grammatical Structure. *University of Hawaii Working Papers in Linguistics* 5(4). Honolulu.

1985   The Golden Woman: The Colville Narrative of Peter J. Seymour; Translated by Anthony Mattina and Madeline deSautel. Tucson: University of Arizona Press.

1987   North American Indian Mythography: Editing Texts for the Printed Page. Pp. 129-148 in Recovering the Word: Essays on Native American Literature. Brian Swann and Arnold Krupat, eds. Berkeley: University of California Press.

1987a   On the Comparison of Versions of Texts. (Paper presented at the 22d International Conference on Salish and Neighbouring Languages, Victoria, B.C.)

1987b   Colville-Okanagan Dictionary. *University of Montana Occasional Papers in Linguistics* 5. Missoula: Linguistics Laboratory, Department of Anthropology, University of Montana.

1989   Interior Salish Post-Vogt: A Report and Bibliography. *International Journal of American Linguistics* 55(1):85-94.

1994   Blue Jay and His Brother-in-Law Wolf. Pp. 332-345 in Coming to Light: Contemporary Translations of the Native Literatures of North America. Brian Swann, ed. New York: Random House.

Mattina, Anthony, and Timothy Montler, eds.
1993   American Indian Linguistics and Ethnography in Honor of Laurence C. Thompson. *University of Montana Occasional Papers in Linguistics* 10. Dallas: Summer Institute of Linguistics.

Maud, Ralph
1978   The Salish People: The Local Contribution of Charles Hill-Tout. 4 vols. Vancouver, B.C.: Talonbooks.

1982   A Guide to B.C. Indian Myth and Legend: A Short History of Myth-collecting and a Survey of Published Texts. Vancouver, B.C.: Talonbooks.

1993   The Porcupine Hunter and Other Stories: The Original Tsimshian Texts of Henry W. Tate. Newly Transcribed from the Original Manuscripts and Annotated (etc.). Vancouver, B.C.: Talonbooks.

Maurault, J.A.
1866   Histoire des abenakis depuis 1605 jusqu'à nos jours. Québec: Atelier Typographique de la "Gazette de Sorel."

Maximilian Alexander Philipp (Prinz zu Wied)
1839-1841 Reise in das innere Nord-America in den Jahren 1832 bis 1834. 2 vols. and atlas. Coblenz: J. Hoelscher.

1843   Travels in the Interior of North America [...] Translated from the German, by H. Evans Lloyd; to Accompany the Original Series of Eighty-one Elaborately-coloured Plates [...] London: Ackermann and Co. (Originally publ.: Reise in das innere Nord-America in den Jahren 1832 bis 1834. J. Hoelscher, Coblenz, 1839-1841. Engl. ed. reprinted in Vols. 22-25 of Early Western Travels, 1748-1846. Reuben G. Thwaites, ed. The Arthur H. Clark Co., Cleveland, Ohio, 1906.)

1906   Maximilian, Prince of Wied's, Travels in the Interior of North America, 1832-1834. Pts. 1, 2, and 3. Vol. 22 of Early Western Travels, 1748-1846. Reuben G. Thwaites, ed. Cleveland: Arthur H. Clark.

Mayes, Sharon
1975-1979 [Fieldnotes on the Thompson Language.] (Unpublished manuscripts in M. Terry Thompson's possession, University of Hawaii, Honolulu.)

1979   An Acoustic Analysis of Thompson Velar /k/ and Uvular /q/. *University of Hawaii Working Papers in Linguistics* 11(1):11-22. Honolulu.

Mayhew, Experience
1709   Massachuset Psalter. Boston: B. Green for the Honourable Company for the Propagation of the Gospel in New England.

1885   Letter of Experience Mayhew, 1722, on the Indian Language. *New England Historical and Genealogical Register* 39:10-17.

Mayhew, Lillian A.M.B.
1905   Report of Field Matron at Wadsworth, Nev. Pp. 247-248 in *Annual Reports of the Department of the Interior for the Fiscal Year Ended June 30, 1904*. Indian Affairs, Part I: Report of the Commissioner and Appendixes. Washington.

Mazzuchelli, Samuel
1833   Ocangra Aramee Wawa<u>k</u>a<u>k</u>ara (Or Winnebago Prayer Book). Detroit: Geo. L. Whitney.

Mead, Margaret
1932   The Changing Culture of An Indian Tribe. *Columbia University Contributions to Anthropology* 15. New York: Columbia University Press.

Medicine Horse, Mary Helen (Ishtaléeschia Báachiia Héeleetaalawe), comp.
1987   A Dictionary of Everyday Crow: Crow-English / English-Crow. Rev. ed. Preface by G.H. Matthews. Crow Agency, Mont.: Bilingual Materials Development Center.

Meillet, Antoine
1912   L'évolution des formes grammaticales. *Scientia: Rivista di scienza* 12(26). (Reprinted: Pp. 130-148 in Linguistique historique et linguistique générale, by A. Meillet. *Collection linguistique publiée par la Société de Linguistique de Paris* 8. Paris, 1921.)

Mekeel, Scudder
1935   Names. Pp. 128-129 in Walapai Ethnography. A.L. Kroeber, ed. *American Anthropological Association Memoir* 42. Menasha, Wis.

Meltzer, David J.
1989   Why Don't We Know When the First People Came to North America? *American Antiquity* 54(3):471-490.

Mengarini, Gregory
1861   A Selish or Flat-Head Grammar. (*Shea's Library of American Linguistics* 2). New York: Cramoisy Press.

Mennonite Indian Leaders Council
1982   Tsese-Ma'heone-Nemeotôtse: Cheyenne Spiritual Songs. Newton, Kans.: Faith and Life Press.

Menovshchikov, Georgiĭ Alekseevich
1962-1967 Grammatika iazyka aziatskikh ėskimosov. [Grammar of the Language of Asiatic Eskimos.] 2 vols. Leningrad: Izdatel´stvo "Nauka", Leningradskoe Otdelenie.

1964   IAzyk sirenikskikh ėskimosov: fonetika, ocherk morfologii, teksty i slovar´. [Language of the Sirenik Eskimos: Phonetics, Morphological Sketch, Texts, and Dictionary.] Moscow and Leningrad: Izdatel´stvo "Nauk."

1975   IAzyk naukanskikh ėskimosov: foneticheskoe vvedenie, ocherk morfologii, teksty, slovar´. [Language of the Naukan Eskimos: Introduction to Phonetics, Morphological Sketch, Texts, Dictionary.] Leningrad: Izdatel´stvo "Nauka."

1980   IAzyk ėskimosov Beringova proliva. [The Language of the Bering Strait Eskimos.] Leningrad: "Nauka" Leningradskoe Otdelenie.

Merlan, Francesca
1985   Split Intransitivity: Functional Opposition in Intransitive Inflection. Pp. 324-362 in Grammar Inside and Outside the Clause: Some Approaches to Theory from the Field. Johanna Nichols and Anthony C. Woodbury, eds. Cambridge: Cambridge University Press.

Merrell, James H.
1989   The Indians' New World: Catawba and Their Neighbors from European Contact Through the Era of Removal. Chapel Hill and London: University of North Carolina Press, for the Institute of Early American History and Culture, Williamsburg, Va.

Merriam, C. Hart
1904   Distribution of Indian Tribes in the Southern Sierra and Adjacent Parts of the San Joaquin Valley, California. *Science* 19(494):912-917.

1930   The New River Indians: Tló-hōm-tah´-hoi. *American Anthropologist*, n.s. 32(2):280-293.

1976   Indian Village and Camp Sites in Yosemite Valley (1917). Pp. 47-53 in A Collection of Ethnographical Articles on the California Indians. Robert F. Heizer, ed. Ramona, Calif.: Ballena Press.

Merriam, C. Hart, and Robert F. Heizer
1966   Ethnographic Notes on California Indian Tribes. *University of California Archaeological Survey Reports* 68(1):1-166. Berkeley.

1967   Ethnographic Notes on California Indian Tribes. II: Ethnological Notes on Northern and Southern California Indian Tribes. *University of California Archaeological Survey Reports* 68(2):167-256. Berkeley.

1967a   Ethnographic Notes on California Indian Tribes. III: Ethnological Notes on Central California Indian Tribes. *University of California Archaeological Survey Reports* 68(3):257-448. Berkeley.

1968   Village Names in Twelve California Mission Records. *University of California Archaeological Survey Reports* 4. Berkeley.

Merriam, C. Hart, et al., eds.
1955   Studies in California Indians. Ed. by the Staff of the Department of Anthropology of the University of California. Berkeley and Los Angeles: University of California Press.

Merrifield, William R.
1959   The Kiowa Verb Prefix. *International Journal of American Linguistics* 25(3):168-176.

1959a   Classification of Kiowa Nouns. *International Journal of American Linguistics* 25(4):269-271.

Merrill, Moses
1837   The History of Our Lord and Saviour Jesus Christ... by the Rev. Samuel Leiberkühn, M.A.; Translated into the Language of the Otoe, Ioway, and Missouri Tribes of Indians by Moses Merrill, Missionary of the Baptist Board of Foreign Missions; Assisted by Louis Dorion, Interpreter. Part I. Shawanoe Baptist Mission: J. Meeker, Printer.

Meserve, Walter T.
1956   English Works of Seventeenth-Century Indians. *American Quarterly* 8(3):264-276.

Métayer, Maurice
1973   Unipkat, Traditions esquimaudes de Coppermine. 3 vols. Québec: Université Laval.

Mey, Jacob
1968   On the Notion 'to be' in Eskimo. Pp. 1-34 in Vol. 2 of The Verb 'Be' and Its Synonyms: Philosophical and Grammatical Studies. J.W.M Verhaar, ed. *Foundations of Language Supplementary Series* 6. Dordrecht, The Netherlands: D. Reidel.

1971   Reflexives in Eskimo. *International Journal of American Linguistics* 37(1):1-5.

Michaëlius, Jonas
1909   Letter of Reverend Jonas Michaëlius, 1628. Pp. 117-133 in Narratives of New Netherland, 1609-1664. J. Franklin Jameson, ed. (*Original Narratives of Early American History* 2). New York: Barnes and Noble.

Michaels, David
1971   A Note on Some Exceptions in Zuni Phonology. *International Journal of American Linguistics* 37(3):189-192.

Michelson, Gunther
1973   A Thousand Words of Mohawk. *Canada. National Museum of Man. Mercury Series. Ethnology Service Paper* 5. Ottawa.

Michelson, Karin E.
1980   Mohawk Text: The Edge of the Forest Revisited. Pp. 26-40 in Northern Iroquoian Texts. Marianne Mithun and Hanni Woodbury, eds. *International Journal of American Linguistics. Native American Texts Series Monograph* 4. Chicago: The University of Chicago Press.

1981   A Philological Investigation into Seventeenth Century Mohawk. *International Journal of American Linguistics* 47(2):91-102.

_____, ed.
1981a   Three Stories in Oneida. Georgina Nicholas, Storyteller and Translator. *Canada. National Museum of Man. Mercury Series, Ethnology Service Paper* 73. Ottawa.

1988   A Comparative Study of Lake-Iroquoian Accent. Dordrecht [and] Boston: Kluwer Academic.

Michelson, Truman
1912   Preliminary Report on the Linguistic Classification of Algonquian Tribes. Pp. 221-290 in *28th Annual Report of the Bureau of American Ethnology for 1906-1907.* Washington.

1914   Two Alleged Algonquian Languages of California. *American Anthropologist*, n.s. 16(2):361-367.

1915   Rejoinder to Sapir. *American Anthropologist*, n.s. 17(1):194-198.

1920   Two Phonetic Shifts Occurring in Many Algonquian Languages. *International Journal of American Linguistics* 1(4):300-304.

1921   The Owl Sacred Pack of the Fox Indians. *Bureau of American Ethnology Bulletin* 72. Washington.

1925   The Mythical Origin of the White Buffalo Dance of the Fox Indians, Together with Texts on Four Minor Sacred Packs Appertaining to this Ceremony. Pp. 23-289 in *40th Annual Report of the Bureau of American Ethnology for 1918-1919.* Washington.

1925a   The Autobiography of a Fox Indian Woman. Pp. 291-349 in *40th Annual Report of the Bureau of American Ethnology for 1918-1919.* Washington.

1925b   Notes on the Fox Society Known as Those Who Worship the Little Spotted Buffalo. Pp. 497-539 in *40th Annual Report of the Bureau of American Ethnology for 1918-1919.* Washington.

1925c   The Traditional Origin of the Fox Society Known as "The Singing Around Rite". Pp. 541-658 in *40th Annual Report of the Bureau of American Ethnology for 1918-1919.* Washington.

1927 Fox Linguistic Notes. Pp. 403-408 in Festschrift Meinhof: Sprachwissenschaftliche und andere Studien. Hamburg: L. Friederichsen. Glückstadt und Hamburg: J.J. Augustin.

1927a Contributions to Fox Ethnology. *Bureau of American Ethnology Bulletin* 85. Washington.

1928 Notes on the Fox Indians. *Bureau of American Ethnology Bulletin* 87. Washington.

1929 Observations on the Thunder Dance of the Bear Gens of the Fox Indians. *Bureau of American Ethnology Bulletin* 89. Washington.

1930 Contributions to Fox Ethnology, II. *Bureau of American Ethnology Bulletin* 95. Washington.

1935 Phonetic Shifts in Algonquian Languages. *International Journal of American Linguistics* 8(3-4):131-171.

1937 Some Linguistic Features of Speck's "Naskapi". *American Anthropologist*, n.s. 39(2):370-372.

1939 Linguistic Classification of Cree and Montagnais-Naskapi Dialects. *Bureau of American Ethnology Bulletin* 123:67-84. Washington.

Milan, Frederick A.
1964 The Acculturation of the Contemporary Eskimo of Wainwright, Alaska. *Anthropological Papers of the University of Alaska* 11(2):1-97. College, Alaska.

Milanich, Jerald T., and William C. Sturtevant
1972 Francisco Pareja's 1613 Confessionario: A Documentary Source for Timucuan Ethnography. With trans. by Emilio F. Moran. Tallahassee: Florida Department of State, Division of Archives, History, and Records Management.

Milanowski, Paul G.
1962 Sound System of Upper Tanana Athapaskan: A Preliminary View. *Alaskan Science Conference* 12:7-10. College, Alaska: American Association for the Advancement of Science, Alaska Division.

1979 Nee'aaneegn': Upper Tanana (Tetlin) Junior Dictionary. Anchorage: University of Alaska, National Bilingual Materials Development Center.

Mill, John Stuart
1973 A System of Logic, Ratiocinative and Inductive, Being a Connected View of Principles of Evidence and the Methods of Scientific Investigation [1843]. J.M. Robson, ed. Introduction by R.F. McRae. 2 vols. Toronto: University of Toronto Press.

Miller, Amy Whitmore
1990 A Grammar of Jamul Diegueño. (Unpublished Dissertation in Linguistics, University of California, San Diego.)

Miller, Mary R.
1967 Attestations of American Indian Pidgin English in Fiction and Nonfiction. *American Speech* 42(2):142-147.

Miller, Nathan
1927 Some Aspects of the Name in Culture-history. *American Journal of Sociology* 32(4):585-600.

Miller, Wick R.
1956-1959 Linguistic and Ethnolinguistic Fieldwork among Acoma Indians Living in the San Francisco Bay Area. (Fieldnotes in Miller's possession.)

1959 A Note on Kiowa Linguistic Affiliations. *American Anthropologist* 61(1):102-105.

1959a Some Notes on Acoma Kinship Terminology. *Southwestern Journal of Anthropology* 15(2):179-184.

1959b An Outline of Shawnee Historical Phonology. *International Journal of American Linguistics* 25(1):16-21.

1964 The Shoshonean Languages of Uto-Aztecan. Pp. 145-148 in Studies in Californian Linguistics. William Bright, ed. *University of California Publications in Linguistics* 34. Berkeley.

1965 Acoma Grammar and Texts. *University of California Publications in Linguistics* 40. Berkeley.

1965-1993 Linguistic and Ethnolinguistic Fieldwork among the Shoshone of California, Nevada, Utah, Idaho, and Wyoming. (Fieldnotes in Miller's possession.)

1966 Anthropological Linguistics in the Great Basin. Pp. 75-112 in The Current Status of Anthropological Research in the Great Basin: 1964. Warren L. d'Azevedo et al., eds. *University of Nevada, Desert Research Institute Social Sciences and Humanities Publications* 1. Reno.

1967 Uto-Aztecan Cognate Sets. *University of California Publications in Linguistics* 48. Berkeley.

1970 Western Shoshoni Dialects. Pp. 17-36 in Languages and Cultures of Western North America: Essays in Honor of Sven S. Liljeblad. Earl H. Swanson, ed. Pocatello: The Idaho State University Press.

1971 The Death of a Language, or: Serendipity among the Shoshoni. *Anthropological Linguistics* 13(3):114-120.

1972 Newe Natekwinappeh: Shoshoni Stories and Dictionary. *University of Utah Anthropological Papers* 94. Salt Lake City.

1972a Obsolescing Languages: The Case of the Shoshoni. *Language in American Indian Education: a Newsletter of the Office of Education Programs, Bureau of Indian Affairs* (Winter):1-12. Salt Lake City: University of Utah for the Bureau of Indian Affairs.

1980   Speaking for Two: Respect Speech in the Guarijio of Northwest Mexico. Pp. 196-206 in *Proceedings of the Sixth Annual Meeting of the Berkeley Linguistics Society, 16-18 February 1980.* Bruce R. Caron et al., eds. Berkeley: BLS.

1983   A Note on Extinct Languages of Northwest Mexico of Supposed Uto-Aztecan Affiliation. *International Journal of American Linguistics* 49(3):328-347.

1984   The Classification of the Uto-Aztecan Languages Based on Lexical Evidence. *International Journal of American Linguistics* 50(1):1-24.

Miller, Wick R., and Irvine Davis
1963   Proto-Keresan Phonology. *International Journal of American Linguistics* 29(4):310-330.

1971   A Lexicostatistic Study of Shoshoni Dialects. *Anthropological Linguistics* 13(4):142-164.

Mills, L. Elaine, Ann J. Brickfield, and Louise G. Mills, eds.
1981-1991 The Papers of John Peabody Harrington in the Smithsonian Institution, 1907-1957. 9 vols. Millwood and White Plains, N.Y.: Kraus International Publications. (Vol. 10, in press, 1996.)

Millstein, Henry
1990   Warm Springs Sahaptin. (Unpublished manuscript in Culture and Heritage Department, Confederated Tribes of the Warm Springs Reservation, Warm Springs, Oreg.)

Miner, Kenneth L.
1974   John Eliot of Massachusetts and the Beginnings of American Linguistics. *Historiographia Linguistica* 1(2):169-183.

Minorua, Nobakatsu
1994   A Comparative Phonology of the Upper Tanana Athabaskan Dialects. Pp. 159-196 in Languages of the North Pacific Rim. Osahito Miyaoka, ed. *Hokkaido University Publications in Linguistics* 7. Sapporo, Japan.

Mithun, Marianne
1976   A Grammar of Tuscarora. New York: Garland Publishing.

1976a   Kanien'keha' Okara'shon:'a [Mohawk stories.] *New York State Museum Bulletin* 427. Albany.

1979   Iroquoian. Pp. 133-212 in The Languages of Native America: Historical and Comparative Assessment. Lyle Campbell and Marianne Mithun, eds. Austin: University of Texas Press.

1981   Stalking the Susquehannocks. *International Journal of American Linguistics* 47(1):1-26.

1982   The Synchronic and Diachronic Behavior of Plops, Squeaks, Croaks, Sighs, and Moans. *International Journal of American Linguistics* 48(1):49-58.

1982a   The Mystery of the Vanished Laurentians. Pp. 230-242 in Papers from the 5th International Congress on Historical Linguistics. Anders Ahlqvist, ed. *Amsterdam Studies in the Theory and History of Linguistic Science, Series IV, Current Issues in Linguistic Theory* 21. Amsterdam: John Benjamins.

1984   The Evolution of Noun Incorporation. *Language* 60(4):847-894.

1984a   Principles of Naming in Mohawk. Pp. 40-54 in Naming Systems. Elizabeth Tooker, ed. (*1980 Proceedings of the American Ethnological Society.*) Washington: AES.

1984b   The Proto-Iroquoians: Culture Reconstruction from Lexical Materials. Pp. 259-281 in Extending the Rafters: Interdisciplinary Approaches to Iroquoian Studies. Michael K. Foster, Jack Campisi, and Marianne Mithun, eds. Albany: State University of New York Press.

1984c   Levels of Linguistic Structure and the Rate of Change. Pp. 301-332 in Historical Syntax. Jacek Fisiak, ed. *Trends in Linguistics. Studies and Monographs* 23. Berlin: Mouton.

1985   Untangling the Huron and the Iroquois. *International Journal of American Linguistics* 51(4):504-507.

1989   The Incipient Obsolescence of Polysynthesis: Cayuga in Ontario and Oklahoma. Pp. 243-257 in Investigating Obsolescence: Studies in Language Contraction and Death. Nancy C. Dorian, ed. (*Studies in the Social and Cultural Foundations of Language* 7). Cambridge: Cambridge University Press.

1990   Third-Person Reference and the Function of Pronouns in Central Pomo Natural Speech. *International Journal of American Linguistics* 56(3):361-376.

1991   Active/Agentive Case Marking and Its Motivations. *Language* 60(3):510-546.

1992   Is Basic Word Order Universal? Pp. 15-61 in Pragmatics of Word Order Flexibility. (*Typological Studies in Language* 2.) Doris L. Payne, ed. Amsterdam/Philadelphia: John Benjamins.

1993   "Switch-reference": Clause Combining in Central Pomo. *International Journal of American Linguistics* 59(2):119-136.

1995   Morphological and Prosodic Forces Shaping Word Order. In Word Order in Discourse. Pamela Downing and Michael Noonan, eds. (*Typological Studies in Language* 30). Amsterdam [and] Philadelphia: John Benjamins.

1997   The Languages of Native North America. Cambridge: Cambridge University Press.

Mithun, Marianne, and Wallace L. Chafe
1979   Recapturing the Mohawk Language. Pp. 3-33 in Languages and Their Status. Timothy Shopen, ed. Cambridge, Mass.: Winthrop Publishers. (Reprinted: University of Pennsylvania Press, Philadelphia, 1987.)

Mithun, Marianne, and Reginald Henry
1982   Watęwayę́stanih: A Cayuga Teaching Grammar. Brantford, Ont.: Woodland Indian Cultural Education Centre.

Mithun, Marianne, and Hanni Woodbury, eds.
1980   Northern Iroquoian Texts. *International Journal of American Linguistics. Native American Texts Series Monograph* 4. Chicago: The University of Chicago Press.

Mixco, Mauricio J.
1978   Cochimí and Proto-Yuman: Lexical and Syntactic Evidence for a New Language Family in Lower California. *University of Utah Anthropological Papers* 101. Salt Lake City.

————
1983   Kiliwa Texts: "When I Have Donned My Crest of Stars". *University of Utah Anthropological Papers* 107. Salt Lake City.

Miyaoka, Osahito
1971   Syllable Modification and Quantity in Yuk Phonology. *International Journal of American Linguistics* 37(4): 219-226.

————
1974   An Eskimo Tribe Near "Mount Saint Elias (Alaska)." *Arctic Anthropology* 11(1):73-80.

————
1980   Alaska Native Languages in Transition. Pp. 169-203 in Alaska Native Culture and History. Yoshinobu Kotani and William B. Workan, eds. (*Senri Ethnological Studies* 4). Osaka, Japan: National Museum of Ethnology.

Miyaoka, Osahito, and Elsie P. Mather
1979   Yup'ik Eskimo Orthography. Rev. ed. Bethel, Alaska: Kuskokwim Community College, Yup'ik Language Center.

Mochon, Marion Johnson
1972   Language, History and Prehistory: Mississippian Lexico-Reconstruction. *American Antiquity* 37(4):478-503.

Momaday, N. Scott
1974   Native American Attitudes to the Environment. Pp. 79-85 in Seeing with a Native Eye: Essays on Native American Religion. W. Capps, ed. New York: Harper and Row.

————
1976   The Names: a Memoir. New York: Harper and Row. (Reprinted: University of Arizona Press, Tucson, 1987.)

Monteith, Carmeleta L.
1984   Literacy among the Cherokee in the Early Nineteenth Century. *Journal of Cherokee Studies* 9(2):56-75. Cherokee, N.C.

Montler, Timothy R.
1986   An Outline of the Morphology and Phonology of Saanich, North Straits Salish. *University of Montana. Occasional Papers in Linguistics* 4. Missoula.

Montler, Timothy R., and Heather K. Hardy
1991   The Phonology of Negation in Alabama. *International Journal of American Linguistics* 57(1):1-23.

Monus, Victor, and Anita Monus
1970   Dene Yatie (Slave Reader 1). Calgary, Alta.: Summer Institute of Linguistics.

Moodie, D. Wayne, and Barry Kaye
1977   The Ac Ko Mok Ki Map. *The Beaver: Magazine of the North* (Spring issue):4-15. Winnipeg.

Moodie, D. Wayne, A.J.W. Catchpole, and Kerry Abel
1992   Northern Athapaskan Oral Traditions and White River Volcano. *Ethnohistory* 39(2):148-171.

Mooney, James
1889   Evolution in Cherokee Personal Names. *American Anthropologist* 2(1):61-62.

————
1891   The Sacred Formulas of the Cherokee. Pp. 301-397 in *7th Annual Report of the Bureau of [American] Ethnology for 1885-1886.* Washington.

————
1892   Kiowa Name Changes. *American Anthropologist* 5(3): 272.

————
1894   The Siouan Tribes of the East. (With map.) *Bureau of American Ethnology Bulletin* 22. Washington.

————
1898   Calendar History of the Kiowa Indians. Pp. 129-445 in Pt. 1 of *17th Annual Report of the Bureau of American Ethnology for 1895-1896.* Washington.

————
1900   The Cherokee River Cult. *Journal of American Folk-Lore* 13(48):1-10.

————
1907   Arawakan Colony. P. 74 in Pt. 1 of Handbook of American Indians North of Mexico. Frederick W. Hodge, ed. *Bureau of American Ethnology Bulletin* 30. Washington.

————
1907a   Kiowa. Pp. 669-701 in Pt. 1 of Handbook of American Indians North of Mexico. Frederick W. Hodge, ed. 2 vols. *Bureau of American Ethnology Bulletin* 30. Washington.

————
1910   Wichita. Pp. 947-950 in Pt. 2 of Handbook of American Indians North of Mexico. Frederick W. Hodge, ed. 2 vols. *Bureau of American Ethnology Bulletin* 30. Washington.

Mooney, James, and Frans M. Olbrechts
1932   The Swimmer Manuscript: Cherokee Sacred Formulas and Medicinal Prescriptions. Revised, completed, and edited by Frans M. Olbrechts. *Bureau of the American Ethnology Bulletin* 99. Washington.

Moore, John H.
1984   Cheyenne Names and Cosmology. *American Ethnologist* 11(2):291-312.

Moore, Patrick
1993   Kaska Place Names. (Manuscript in Yukon Native Language Centre, Whitehorse, Yukon, and in Moore's possession.)

Moore, Patrick, and Angela Wheelock, eds.
1990   Wolverine Myths and Visions: Dene Traditions from Northern Alberta. (*Studies in the Anthropology of North American Indians*). Lincoln: University of Nebraska Press.

Moore, William F.
1930   Indian Place Names in Ontario. Toronto: Macmillan.

Moratto, Michael J.
1984   California Archaeology. New York, [etc.]: Academic Press.

Morgan, Dale L., and George P. Hammond
1963   A Guide to the Manuscript Collections. Berkeley: University of California Press for the Bancroft Library.

Morgan, James O.
1966   A Comparison of the Transitive Animate Verb in Eight Algonquian Languages. *Anthropological Linguistics* 8(5, 2):1-16.

Morgan, Lewis Henry
1851   League of the Ho-dé-no-sau-nee, or Iroquois. Rochester, N.Y.: Sage and Brother.

1870   Indian Migrations. *North American Review* 110:33-82. New York.

1871   Systems of Consaguinity and Affinity of the Human Family. *Smithsonian Contributions to Knowledge* 17. Washington. (Reprinted: Humanities Press, New York, 1966.)

1901   League of the Ho-dé-no-sau-nee or Iroquois [1851]. A new edition, with additional matter. Herbert M. Lloyd, ed. 2 vols. New York: Dodd, Mead. (Reprinted: Human Relations Area Files, New Haven, Conn., 1954; Burt Franklin, New York, 1966.)

Morice, Adrien-Gabriel
1889   The Western Dénés—Their Manners and Customs. *Proceedings of the Canadian Institute*, 3d ser. 7(1):109-174. Toronto.

1891   Le petit catéchisme à l'usage des sauvages Porteurs. Texte et traduction avec notes suivi des prières du matin et du soir. [Lake Stuart, B.C.]: Mission du Lac Stuart.

1893   Are the Carrier Sociology and Mythology Indigenous or Exotic? Pp. 109-126 in *Proceedings and Transactions of the Royal Society of Canada for the Year 1892*, ser. 1, sect. 2, vol. 10. Ottawa.

1907   The Unity of Spech among the Northern and the Southern Déné. *American Anthropologist*, n.s. 9(4):720-737.

1932   The Carrier Language (Déné Family): A Grammar and Dictionary Combined. 2 vols. *Bibliothèque linguistique Anthropos* 9-10. St.-Gabriel-Mödling, Austria: Verlag der Internationalen Zeitschrift "Anthropos".

1933   Carrier Onomatology. *American Anthropologist, n.s.* 35(4):632-658.

Morison, Mrs. O.
1889   Tsimshian Proverbs. *Journal of American Folk-Lore* 2(7):285-286.

Morris, William, ed.
1973   The American Heritage Dictionary of the English Language. Boston and New York: American Heritage and Houghton Mifflin.

Morse, Jedidiah
1822   A Report to the Secretary of War of the United States, on Indian Affairs; Comprising a Narrative of a Tour Performed in the Summer of 1820 [etc.]. New-Haven, Conn.: S. Converse.

Morvillo, Anthony
1891   Grammatica linguæ numipu. Desmet, Idaho: Indian Boys' Press.

1895   A Dictionary of the Numípu or Nez Perce Language by a Missionary of the Society of Jesus, in the Rocky Mountains. Pt. 1: English-Nez Perce. St. Ignatius, Mont.: St. Ignatius Mission.

Morvillo, Anthony, and Joseph Mary Cataldo
1888   Paradigma verbi activi lingua Numipu vulgo Nez Perce studio PP. Missionariorum S.J. in Montibus Saxosis. Desmet, Idaho Terr.

Moser, Edward, and Mary B. Moser, comps.
1961   [Vocabulario Seri]: Seri-Castellano, Castellano-Seri. *Serie de vocabularios indígenas Mariano Silva y Aceves* 5. México: Instituto Lingüístico de Verano en cooperación con la Direción General de Asuntos Indígenas de la Secretaría de Educación Pública.

Moshinsky, Julius B.
1974   A Grammar of Southeastern Pomo. *University of California Publications in Linguistics* 72. Berkeley.

1976   Historical Pomo Phonology. Pp. 55-76 in Hokan Studies: Papers from the First Conference on Hokan Languages. Margaret Langdon and Shirley Silver, eds. (*Janua Linguarum. Series Practica* 181). The Hague: Mouton.

Moulton, Gary E., ed.
1983-   The Journals of the Lewis and Clark Expedition. 10 vols. through 1996. (Sponsored by the Center for Great Plains Studies, University of Nebraska, Lincoln, and the American Philosophical Society, Philadelphia.) Lincoln: University of Nebraska Press.

Mourning Dove (Humis'huma)
1933   Coyote Stories. Caldwell, Idaho: Caxton Printers. (Reprinted, with Introd. and Notes by Jay Miller: University of Nebraska Press, Lincoln, 1990.)

Moziño Suárez de Figueroa, José Mariano
1913   Noticias de Nutka; Diccionario de la lengua de los nutkeses y Descripción del volcán de Tuxtla. Mexico City: Sociedad Mexicana de Geografía y Estadística.

1970   Noticias de Nutka: An Account of Nootka Sound in 1792. Iris Higbie Wilson, trans. and ed. Seattle: University of Washington Press.

Müller-Wille, Ludger, et al.
1987   Gazetteer of Inuit Place Names in Nunavik (Quebec, Canada). Inukjuak, Que.: Avataq Cultural Institute.

Mulder, Jean Gail
1988   Ergativity in Coast Salish Tsimshian (Sm'algyax). (Ph.D. Dissertation in Linguistics, University of California, Los Angeles. Published: *University of California Publications in Linguistics* 124. Berkeley, 1994.)

1994   Ergativity in Coast Tsimshian (Sm'algyax). *University of California Publications in Linguistics* 124. Berkeley.

Munro, Pamela
1976   Mojave Syntax. New York: Garland. (Originally issued as: Topics in Mojave Syntax. Ph.D. Dissertation in Linguistics, University of California, San Diego, 1974.)

1976a   Mojave Modals. Pp. 55-62 in *Proceedings of the 1st Yuman Languages Workshop*. James E. Redden, ed. Carbondale: Southern Illinois University.

1976b   Two Stories by Nellie Brown (Mojave). Pp. 43-50 in Yuman Texts. Margaret Langdon, ed. *International Journal of American Linguistics. Native American Texts Series* 1(3). Chicago: The University of Chicago Press.

1978   Chemehuevi 'Say' and the Uto-Aztecan Quotative Pattern. Pp. 149-171 in Slected Papers from the 14th Great Basin Anthropological Conference. Donald R. Tuohy, ed. Socoro, N.M.: Ballena Press.

1984   On the Western Muskogean Source for Mobilian. *International Journal of American Linguistics* 50(4):451-465.

1987   Introduction: Muskogean Studies at UCLA. Pp. 1-6 in Muskogean Linguistics. Pamela Munro ed. *UCLA Occasional Papers in Linguistics* 6. Los Angeles: Department of Linguistics, University of California.

1990   Stress and Vowel Length in Cupan Absolute Nouns. *International Journal of American Linguistics* 56(2):217-250.

1993   The Muskogean II Prefixes and Their Significance for Classification. *International Journal of American Linguistics* 59(4):374-404.

Munro, Pamela, and Lynn Gordon
1982   Syntactic Relations in Western Muskogean: A Typological Perspective. *Language: Journal of the Linguistic Society of America* 58(1):81-115.

Munro, Pamela, and Catherine Willmond
1994   Chickasaw: An Analytical Dictionary. Norman: University of Oklahoma Press.

Murdoch, John
1888   Dr. Rink's "Eskimo Tribes". [Review of: The Eskimo Tribes: Their Distribution and Characteristics, Especially in Regard to Language. With a Comparative Vocabulary and a Sketch-map. Copenhagen and London, 1887.] *American Anthropologist* [o.s.] 1(1):125-133.

Murdoch, John Stewart
1981   Syllabics: A Successful Educational Innovation. (Master's Thesis in Education, University of Manitoba, Winnipeg.)

Murdock, George Peter
1934   Kinship and Social Behavior Among the Haida. *American Anthropologist*, n.s. 36(3):355-385.

1936   Rank and Potlatch Among the Haida. *Yale University Publications in Anthropology* 13. New Haven.

1949   Social Structure. New York: Macmillan. (Reprinted: The Free Press, New York, 1965.)

1955   North American Social Organization. *Davidson Journal of Anthropology* 1(2):85-95.

1958   Social Organization of the Tenino. Pp. 308-310 in Vol. 1 of Miscellanea Paul Rivet Octogenario Dicata. [Thirty-first International Congress of Americanists, São Paolo, Brazil, 1954.] Mexico: Universidad Nacional Autónoma.

Murie, James R.
1981   Ceremonies of the Pawnee. Pt. 1: The Skiri. Pt. 2: The South Bands. Douglas R. Parks, ed. *Smithsonian Contributions to Anthropology* 27. Washington.

1989   Ceremonies of the Pawnee. Douglas R. Parks, ed. Lincoln: University of Nebraska Press, in cooperation with the American Indian Studies Research Institute, Indiana University. (First Published: *Smithsonian Contributions to Anthropology* 27, 1981.)

Murray, Janette K.
1974   Ella Deloria: A Biographical Sketch and Literary Analysis. (Unpublished Ph.D. Dissertation in Teacher Education, University of North Dakota, Grand Forks.)

Murray, Stephen O.
1994   Theory Groups and the Study of Language in North America; A Social History. (*Studies in the History of the Language Series* 69). Amsterdam and Philadelphia: John Benjamins.

Myer, W.E.
1928   Indian Trails of the Southeast. Pp. 727-857 in *42d Annual Report of the Bureau of American Ethnology for 1924-1925*. Washington.

Myers, Albert Cook, ed.
1937   William Penn: His Own Account of the Lenni Lenape or Delaware Indians, 1683. Moylan, Delaware County, Pa.: The Author.

1970   William Penn's Own Account of the Lenni Lenape or Delaware Indians. Rev. ed. Somerset, N.J.: Middle Atlantic Press.

Nabokov, Peter, ed.
1991   Native American Testimony: A Chronicle of Indian-White Relations from Prophecy to the Present, 1492-1992. New York: Viking Penguin.

Naish, Constance, and Gillian L. Story
1976   English-Tlingit Dictionary: Nouns. [Rev. ed.] [Sitka, Alaska]: Sheldon Jackson College.

Nansen, Fridtjof
1894   Eskimo Life. William Archer, trans. London: Longmanns, Green.

Natches, Gilbert
1923   Northern Paiute Verbs. *University of California Publications in American Archaeology and Ethnology* 20(14):243-259. Berkeley.

Nater, Hank F.
1984   The Bella Coola Language. *Canada. National Museum of Man. Mercury Series. Ethnology Service Paper* 92. Ottawa.

——
1989   Some Comments on the Phonology of Tahltan. *International Journal of American Linguistics* 55(1):25-42.

National Anthropological Archives
1975   Catalog to Manuscripts at the National Anthropological Archives, Department of Anthropology, National Museum of Natural History, Smithsonian Institution, Washington. 4 vols. Boston: G.K. Hall.

Navarro Tomás, Tomás
1953   Manual de pronunciación española. 4th ed. New York: Hafner. (Reprinted, 6th ed., in 1967.)

Navin, Frank
1943   [Micmac ideograms, copied from Christian Kauder's 1866 *Katechismus*; with an interlinear transcription of the Micmac words.] (Manuscript No. 4634, National Anthropological Archives, Smithsonian Institution, Washington, D.C.)

Nêhiyaw / Bear, Glecia
1991   Wanisinwak Iskwêsisak: Awâsisasinahikanis / Two Little Girls Lost in the Bush: A Cree Story for Children. Freda Ahenakew and H.C. Wolfart, eds. and trans. Saskatoon, Sask.: Fifth House Publishers.

Neilson, J.L. Hubert
1908   Facsimile of Père Marquette's Illinois Prayer Book: It's [sic] History by the Owner, Colonel J.L. Hubert Neilson. [Written by Sébastien Râle.] Quebec: Quebec Literary and Historical Society.

Nelles, Abraham, and John Hill
1842   The Book of Common Prayer, According to the Use of the Church of England, Translated into the Mohawk Language. Hamilton, Ont.: Ruthven's Book and Job Office.

Nelson, Edward W.
1899   The Eskimo About Bering Strait. Pp. 3-518 in Pt. 1 of *18th Annual Report of the Bureau of American Ethnology for 1896-1897*. Washington.

Nelson, William
1894   The Indians of New Jersey; Their Origin and Development, Manners and Customs, Religion and Government, with Notices of Some Indian Place Names. Paterson, N.J.: The Press Printing and Publishing Company.

Netsvetov, Iakov
[1835-1843] [Russian—Fox Island Aleut Dictionary]. (Manuscript in Alaska Russian Church Archives, Library of Congress, Washington.)

Newcomb, William W., Jr.
1956   A Reappraisal of the "Cultural Sink" of Texas. *Southwestern Journal of Anthropology* 12(2):145-153.

——
1956a   The Culture and Acculturation of the Delaware Indians. *University of Michigan Museum of Anthropology. Anthropological Papers* 10. Ann Arbor.

Newman, Stanley S.
1944   Yokuts Language of California. *Viking Fund Publications in Anthropology* 2. New York. (Reprinted: Johnson Reprint, New York, 1963.)

——
1946   The Yawelmani Dialect of Yokuts. Pp. 222-248 in Linguistic Structures of Native America. Harry Hoijer, ed. *Viking Fund Publications in Anthropology* 6. New York.

——
1947   Bella Coola I: Phonology. *International Journal of American Linguistics* 13(3):129-134.

——
1951   [Review of] Selected Writings of Edward Sapir in Language, Culture, and Personality, ed. by David G. Mandelbaum...1946. *International Journal of American Linguistics* 17(1):180-186.

——
1954   American Indian Linguistics in the Southwest. *American Anthropologist* 56(4):626-634.

——
1955   Vocabulary Levels: Zuñi Sacred and Slang Usage. *Southwestern Journal of Anthropology* 11(4):345-354. Albuquerque. (Reprinted: Pp. 397-403 in Language in Culture and Society. Dell Hymes, ed. Harper and Row, New York, 1964.)

——
1958   Zuni Dictionary. *Indiana University Research Center in Anthropology, Folklore, and Linguistics. Publication* 6. Bloomington.

——
1959   [Review of] Migrations in New World Culture History, ed. by Raymond H. Thompson. *Language: Journal of the Linguistic Society of America* 35(4):715-717.

——
1964   Comparison of Zuni and California Penutian. *International Journal of American Linguistics* 30(1):1-13.

——
1965   Zuni Grammar. *University of New Mexico Publications in Anthropology* 14. Albuquerque.

——
1966   Word Classes in Yokuts. *Lingua* 17(1-2):182-199.

——
1968   Zuni Equivalents of English 'to Be'. Pp. 60-70 in The Verb 'Be' and its Synonyms: Philosophical and Grammatical Studies (2). John W.M. Verhaar, ed. *Foundations of Language Supplementary Series* 6. Dordrecht: D. Reidel.

1969   Bella Coola Grammatical Processes and Form Classes. *International Journal of American Linguistics* 35(2): 175-179.

1969a   Bella Coola Paradigms. *International Journal of American Linguistics* 35(4):299-306.

1971   Bella Coola Reduplication. *International Journal of American Linguistics* 37(1):34-38.

1974   Linguistic Retention and Diffusion in Bella Coola. *Language in Society* 3(2):201-214.

1976   Salish and Bella Coola Prefixes. *International Journal of American Linguistics* 42(3):228-242.

1977   The Salish Independent Pronoun System. *International Journal of American Linguistics* 43(4):302-314.

1979   A History of the Salish Possessive and Subject Forms. *International Journal of American Linguistics* 45(3): 207-223.

1979a   The Salish Object Forms. *International Journal of American Linguistics* 45(4):299-308.

1980   Functional Changes in the Salish Pronominal System. *International Journal of American Linguistics* 46(3):155-167.

Niblack, Albert P.
1890   The Coast Indians of Southern Alaska and Northern British Columbia. Pp. 225-386 in *Report of the U.S. National Museum for 1888*. Washington.

Nichols, Frances S., comp.
1954   Index to Schoolcraft's "Indian Tribes of the United States." *Bureau of American Ethnology Bulletin* 152. Washington.

Nichols, Johanna
1971   Diminutive Consonant Symbolism in Western North America. *Language: Journal of the Linguistic Society of America* 47(4):826-848.

1990   Linguistic Diversity and the First Settlement of the New World. *Language: Journal of the Linguistic Society of America* 66(3):475-521.

1995   The Prehistory of Linguistic Diversity, 2: The Origin of New World Languages. In Proceedings of the Conference on Language and Prehistory, Boulder, Colorado, March 1990. Allan R. Taylor, ed. Stanford, Calif.: Stanford University Press. (In press.)

Nichols, John D.
1974   Notes on a Traditional Potawatomi Writing System. (Unpublished manuscript in Nichols's possession.)

1979   Pejorative Consonant Symbolism in Two Ojibwe Dialects. *Algonquian Linguistics* 4:42-43.

1984   The Composition Sequence of the First Cree Hymnal. Pp. 1-21 in Essays in Algonquian Bibliography in Honour of V.M. Dechene. H.C. Wolfart, ed. *Algonquian and Iroquoian Linguistics Memoir* 1. Winnipeg, Man.

_____, ed.
1988   An Ojibwe Text Anthology. (*Studies in the Interpretation of Canadian Native Languages and Cultures. Text Series* 2). London, Ont.: University of Western Ontario, Centre for Research and Teaching of Canadian Native Languages.

1991   "Chant to the Fire-fly": A Philological Problem in Ojibwe. Pp. 113-126 in Linguistic Studies Presented to John L. Finlay. H.C. Wolfart, ed. *Algonquian and Iroquoian Linguistics, Memoir* 8. Winnipeg, Man.

1996   The Cree Syllabary. Pp. 607-611 in The World's Writing Systems. Peter D. Daniels and William Bright, eds. New York [and] Oxford: Oxford University Press.

Nichols, John D., and Earl Nyholm
1995   A Concise Dictionary of Minnesota Ojibwe. Minneapolis: University of Minnesota Press.

Nichols, Michael J.P.
1981   Old California Uto-Aztecan. Pp. 5-41 in Survey Reports 1981. *Survey of California and Other Indians Languages* 1. Alice Schlichter, Wallace L. Chafe, and Leanne Hinton, eds. Berkeley: University of California.

Nicklas, Thurston Dale
1975   Choctaw Morphophonemics. Pp. 237-249 in Studies in Southeastern Indian Languages. James M. Crawford, ed. Athens: University of Georgia Press.

Nicodemus, Lawrence G.
1975   Snchitsu'umshts: the Coeur d'Alene Language. 2 vols. and 6 sound cassettes. Vol. 1: The Grammar. Coeur d'Alene-English Dictionary. Vol. 2: English-Coeur d'Alene Dictionary. Plummer, Idaho: Coeur d'Alene Tribal Council.

Nicolar, Joseph
1893   The Life and Traditions of the Red Man. Bangor, Maine: C.H. Glass. (Reprinted: Saint Annes Point Press, Fredericton, N.B., 1979.)

Nicollet, Joseph N.
1843   Report Intended to Illustrate a Map of the Hydrographical Basin of the Upper Mississippi River. Washington: Blair and Rives.

Niemczycki, Mary Ann Palmer
1984   The Origin and Development of the Seneca and Cayuga Tribes of New York State. *Rochester Museum and Science Center, Research Records* 17. Charles F. Hayes III, gen. ed. Rochester, N.Y.

Nomland, Gladys Ayer
1938   Bear River Ethnography. *University of California Anthropological Records* 2(2):91-126.

Nomland, Gladys Ayer, and Alfred L. Kroeber
1936   Wiyot Towns. *University of California Publications in American Archaeology and Ethnology* 35(5):39-48. Berkeley.

Norman, Howard A., coll. and trans.
1976   The Wishing Bone Cycle: Narrative Poems from the Swampy Cree Indians. New York: Stonehill Publishing Company.

1982   The Wishing Bone Cycle: Narrative Poems from the Swampy Cree Indians. Expanded ed. Santa Barbara, Calif.: Ross-Erikson.

Norton, John
1804   Nene Karighwiyoston Tsinihorighhoten Ne Saint John. (The Gospel According to Saint John). London: Phillips and Fardon for the British and Foreign Bible Society.

1970   The Journal of Major John Norton, 1816. Carl F. Klinck and James J. Talman, eds. Toronto: The Champlain Society.

Nuttall, Mark
1994   Names and Name-sharing in a Greenlandic Community. The Musk-Ox 40(final issue):66-69. Saskatoon, Sask.

Nyman, Elizabeth, and Jeff Leer
1993   Gágiwdułàt: Brought Forth to Reconfirm: The Legacy of a Taku River Tlingit Clan. Fairbanks and Whitehorse: Yukon Native Language Centre and Alaska Native Language Center.

Oberg, Kalervo
1934   Crime and Punishment in Tlingit Society. American Anthropologist, n.s. 36(2):145-156.

1973   The Social Economy of the Tlingit Indians. Monograph of the American Ethnological Society 55. Seattle: University of Washington Press.

O'Brien, Michael C.
1887   Grammatical Sketch of the Ancient Abnaki, Outlined in the Dictionary of Fr. Sebastian Râle, S.J. Part I.—The Abnaki Noun. Collections of the Maine Historical Society 9:259-294. Portland, Maine.

Ogg, Arden C.
1991   Connective Particles and Temporal Cohesion in Plains Cree Narrative. (M.A. Thesis in Linguistics, University of Manitoba, Winnipeg.)

O'Grady, R.T., I. Goddard, R.M. Bateman, W.A. DiMichele, V.A. Funk, W.J. Kress, R. Mooi, and P.F. Cannell
1989   Genes and Tongues. Science 243(4399):1651.

Okrand, Marc
1977   Mutsun Grammar. (Unpublished Ph.D. Dissertation in Linguistics, University of California, Berkeley.)

1989   More on Karkin and Costanoan. International Journal of American Linguistics 55(2):254-258.

Olearius, Adam
1656   Relation du voyage de Moscovie, Tartarie et Perse.... Paris: Gervais Clouzier.

1659   Relation du voyage d'Adam Olearius en Moscovie, Tartarie et Perse.... 2 vols. Paris: Jean du Puis.

Olmsted, David L.
1954   Achumawi-Atsugewi Non-Reciprocal Intelligibility. International Journal of American Linguistics 20(3): 181-184.

1956   Palaihnihan and Shasta, I: Labial Stops. Language: Journal of the Linguistic Society of America 32(1):73-77.

1957   Palaihnihan and Shasta, II: Apical Stops. Language: Journal of the Linguistic Society of America 33(2):136-138.

1958   Atsugewi Phonology. International Journal of American Linguistics 24(3):215-220.

1959   Palaihnihan and Shasta III: Dorsal Stops. Language: Journal of the Linguistic Society of America 35(4):637-644.

1961   Atsugewi Morphology I: Verb Inflection. International Journal of American Linguistics 27(2):91-113.

1964   A History of Palaihnihan Phonology. University of California Publications in Linguistics 35. Berkeley.

1966   Achumawi Dictionary. University of California Publications in Linguistics 45. Berkeley.

1977   Loon, Coyote and Fox (Ajumawi). Pp. 66-70 in Northern California Texts. Victor Golla and Shirley Silver, eds. International Journal of American Linguistics. Native American Texts Series 2(2). Chicago: The University of Chicago Press.

Olmsted, Earl P.
1991   Blackcoats among the Delawares: David Zeisberger on the Ohio Frontier. Kent, Ohio: Kent State University Press.

Olrik, Axel
1965   Epic Laws of Folk Narrative. Pp. 129-141 in The Study of Folklore. Alan Dundes, ed. Englewood Cliffs, N.J.: Prentice Hall.

Olson, Ronald L.
1933   Clan and Moiety in Native America. University of California Publications in American Archaeology and Ethnology 33(4):351-422. Berkeley.

1936   The Quinault Indians. University of Washington Publications in Anthropology 6(1):1-190. Seattle.

1940   The Social Organization of the Haisla of British Columbia. University of California Anthropological Records 2(5):169-200. Berkeley.

1954   Social Life of the Owikeno Kwakiutl. University of California Anthropological Records 14(3):213-260. Berkeley.

1955   Notes on the Bella Bella Kwakiutl. *University of California Anthropological Records* 14(5):319-348. Berkeley.

Oltrogge, David
1977   Proto Jicaque-Subtiaba-Tequistlateco: A Comparative Reconstruction. Pp. 1-52 in Two Studies in Middle American Comparative Linguistics, by David Oltrogge and Calvin R. Rensch. (*Summer Institute of Linguistics Publications in Linguistics* 55). Arlington, Tex.: Summer Institute of Linguistics and the University of Texas at Arlington.

O'Neil, Stephen, and Nancy H. Evans
1980   Notes on Historical Juaneño Villages and Geographical Features. *Journal of California and Great Basin Anthropology* 2(2):226-232. Banning, Calif.

Opler, Marvin K.
1940   The Southern Ute of Colorado. Pp. 119-203 in Acculturation in Seven American Indian Tribes. Ralph Linton, ed. New York: D. Appleton-Century.

Opler, Morris E.
1936   The Kinship Systems of the Southern Athabaskan-Speaking Tribes. *American Anthropologist* 38(4):620-633.

1941   An Apache Life-Way: The Economic, Social, and Religious Institutions of the Chiricahua Indians. Chicago: University of Chicago Press. (Reprinted in 1965.)

1945   The Lipan Apache Death Complex and Its Extensions. *Southwestern Journal of Anthropology* 1(1):122-141.

1946   Reaction to Death Among the Mescalero Apache. *Southwestern Journal of Anthropology* 2(4):454-467.

1952   The Creek "Town" and the Problem of Creek Indian Political Reorganization. Pp. 165-180 in Human Problems in Technological Change: A Casebook. Edward H. Spicer, ed. New York: Russell Sage Foundation.

1969   Apache Odyssey: A Journal Between Two Worlds. New York: Holt, Rinehart and Winston.

Opler, Morris E., and William E. Bittle
1961   The Death Practices and Eschatology of the Kiowa Apache. *Southwestern Journal of Anthropology* 17(4):383-394.

Opler, Morris E., and Harry Hoijer
1940   The Raid and War-Path Language of the Chiricahua Apache. *American Anthropologist* 42(4, Pt. 1):617-634.

Oquilluk, William A.
1973   People of Kauwerak: Legends of the Northern Eskimo. Anchorage: AMU Press. (Reprinted, 2d ed.: Alaska Pacific University Press, Anchorage, 1981.)

Oregon Historical Society
1956   Notices and Voyages of the Famed Quebec Mission to the Pacific Northwest: Being the Correspondence, Notices, etc., of Fathers Blanchet and Demers, Together with those of Fathers Bolduc and Langlois... Mission to the Engagés of the Hudson's Bay Company and the Pagan Natives, 1838 to 1847. Portland: Oregon Historical Society.

Ornstein, Jacob
1976   Sociolinguistic Constraints on Lexical Borrowing in Tarahumara: Explorations in 'Langue and Parole' and 'Existential Bilingualism'—an Approximation. *Anthropological Linguistics* 18(2):70-93.

Orozco y Berra, Manuel
1864   Geografía de las lenguas y carta etnográfica de México; precedidas de un ensayo de clasificación de las mismas lenguas y de apuntes para las inmigraciones de las tribus. México: J.M. Andrade y F. Escalante.

Ortega, José de
1732   Vocabulario en lengua castellana y cora. Mexico City. (Reprinted: *Boletín de la Sociedad Mexicana de Geografía y Estadística* 1a época, 8:561-605, Mexico City, 1890.)

Orth, Donald J.
1967   Dictionary of Alaska Place Names. *U.S. Department of the Interior Geological Survey Professional Paper* 567. Washington.

Ortiz, Alfonso
1969   The Tewa World: Space, Time, Being, and Becoming in a Pueblo Society. Chicago: The University of Chicago Press.

Osborn, Henry, and William A. Smalley
1949   Formulae for Comanche Stem and Word Formation. *International Journal of American Linguistics* 15(2):93-99.

Osgood, Cornelius
1936   The Distribution of the Northern Athapaskan Indians. *Yale University Publications in Anthropology* 7:3-23. New Haven, Conn.

1936a   Contributions to the Ethnography of the Kutchin. *Yale University Publications in Anthropology* 14. New Haven: Yale University Press.

1937   The Ethnography of the Tanaina. *Yale University Publications in Anthropology* 16. New Haven: Yale University Press.

1971   The Han Indians: A Compilation of Ethnographic and Historical Data on the Alaska-Yukon Boundary Area. *Yale University Publications in Anthropology* 74. New Haven: Department of Anthropology, Yale University.

Ossenberg, Nancy S.
1994   Origins and Affinities of the Native Peoples of Northwestern America: The Evidence of Cranial Nonmetric Traits. Pp. 79-115 in Method and Theory for Investigating the Peopling of the Americas. Robson Bonnichsen and D. Gentry Steele, eds. Corvallis, Ore.: Oregon State University.

871

Oswalt, Robert L.

1958   Russian Loan Words in Southwestern Pomo. *International Journal of American Linguistics* 24(3):245-247.

1964   Kashaya Texts. *University of California Publications in Linguistics* 36. Berkeley.

1964a   The Internal Relationships of the Pomo Family of Languages. Pp. 413-427 in Vol. 2 of *XXXV Congreso Internacional de Americanistas, Mexico, 1962: Actas y Memorias*. 3 vols. Mexico.

1964b   A Comparative Study of Two Pomo Languages. Pp. 149-162 in Studies in Californian Linguistics. William Bright, ed. *University of California Publications in Linguistics* 34. Berkeley.

1976   Comparative Verb Morphology of Pomo. Pp. 13-28 in Hokan Studies: Papers from the First Conference on Hokan Languages. Margaret Langdon and Shirley Silver, eds. (*Janua Linguarum, Series Practica* 181). The Hague: Mouton.

1976a   Baby Talk and the Genesis of Some Basic Pomo Words. *International Journal of American Linguistics* 42(1):1-13.

1978   An Exploration of the Affinity of Wappo and Some Hokan and Penutian Languages. Pp. 56-71 in Proceedings of the 1978 Hokan Languages Workshop. *Southern Illinios University Department of Linguistics, Occasional Papers* 5. Carbondale.

1983   Interclausal Reference in Kashaya. Pp. 267-290 in Switch Reference and Universal Grammar: Proceedings of a Symposium on Switch Reference and Universal Grammar, Winnipeg, May 1981. John Haiman and Pamelo Munro, eds. Amsterdam and Philadelphia: John Benjamins Publishing Co.

Oswalt, Wendell H.

1963   Mission of Change in Alaska: Eskimos and Moravians on the Kuskokwim. San Marino, Calif.: The Huntington Library.

1963a   Napaskiak: An Alaskan Eskimo Community. Tucson: University of Arizona Press.

1967   Alaskan Eskimos. San Francisco: Chandler Publishing Company.

1973   This Land Was Theirs: A Study of the North American Indian. 2d ed. New York: John Wiley & Sons.

Pacifique, [père]

1939   Leçons grammaticales théoriques et pratiques de la langue micmaque. Sainte-Anne de Restigouche, Qué.: Bureau du Messager Micmac.

1990   The Micmac Grammar of Father Pacifique. Translated and Retranscribed by John Hewson and Bernard Francis. *Algonquian and Iroquoian Linguistics, Memoir* 7. Winnipeg, Man.

Pagotto, Louise

1980   On Complementizer Adjuncts in the Rapid Lake Dialect of Algonquin. Pp. 231-246 in Papers of the Eleventh Algonquian Conference. William Cowan, ed.

Palmer, Gary B.

1988   The Language and Culture Approach in the Coeur d'Alene Language Preservation Project. *Human Organization* 47(4):307-317.

1990   'Where There are Muskrats': The Semantic Structure of Coeur d'Alene Place Names. *Anthropological Linguistics* 32(3-4):263-294.

Palmer, Katherine Van Wikle, coll.

1925   Honne, the Spirit of the Chehalis: The Indian Interpretation of the Origin of the People and Animals — as Narrated by George Saunders. Geneva, N.Y.: Press of W.F. Humphrey.

Pandosy, Marie-Charles

1862   Grammar and Dictionary of the Yakama Language. George Gibbs and John Gilmary Shea, trans. (*Shea's Library of American Linguistics* 6). New York: Cramoisy Press.

Papen, Robert A.

1987   Linguistic Variation in the French Component of Métif Grammar. Pp. 247-259 in Papers of the Eighteenth Algonquian Conference. William Cowan, ed. Ottawa: Carleton University.

Pareja, Francisco

1886   Arte de la lengua timuquana compuesto en 1614 por el P^e Francisco Pareja. Lucien Adam and Julian Vinson, eds. Paris: Maissonneuve Frères et Ch. Leclerc. (Reprinted: Arte y pronunciacion en lengua timuquana y castellana. Kraus Reprints, Nendeln, Lichtenstein, 1968.)

Park, Willard Z.

1934   Paviotso Shamanism. *American Anthropologist*, n.s. 36(1):98-113.

Parker, Arthur C.

1913   The Code of Handsome Lake, the Seneca Prophet. *New York State Museum Bulletin* 163. Albany.

1916   The Origin of the Iroquois as Suggested by Their Archaeology. *American Anthropologist*, n.s. 18(4):479-507.

1922   The Archaeological History of New York. 2 Pts. *New York State Museum Bulletin* 235-238. Albany.

1968   Parker on the Iroquois: Iroquois Uses of Maize and Other Food Plants; The Code of Handsome Lake, the Seneca Prophet; The Constitution of the Five Nations. [3 works in 1 vol.] Willian N. Fenton, ed. Syracuse: Syracuse University Press.

Parker, Samuel
1838   Journal of an Exploring Tour beyond the Rocky Mountains, under the Direction of the A.B.C.F.M. Performed in the years 1835, '36, and '37. (Reprinted in facsimile: Ross and Haines, Minneapolis, 1967.)

Parks, Douglas R.
1975   Shawnee Noun Inflection. Pp. 135-161 in Studies in Southeastern Indian Languages. James M. Crawford, ed. Athens: University of Georgia Press.

_____
1976   A Grammar of Pawnee. New York and London: Garland Publishing.

_____
1977   Pawnee Texts: Skiri and South Bands. Pp. 65-90 in Caddoan Texts. Douglas R. Parks, ed. *International Journal of American Linguistics. Native American Texts Series* 2(1). Chicago: The University of Chicago Press.

_____
1979   Bands and Villages of the Arikara and Pawnee. *Nebraska History* 60(2):214-239. Lincoln.

_____
1979a   Pawnee Personal Names: A Linguistic and Ethnographic Analysis. (Manuscript in Parks's possession.)

_____
1979b   The Northern Caddoan Languages: Their Subgrouping and Time Depths. *Nebraska History* 60(2):197-213. Lincoln.

_____
1980   A Comparison of Pawnee and Arikara Personal Names. (Manuscript in Parks's possession.)

_____
1986   An English-Arikara Student Dictionary. Roseglen, N.Dak.: White Shield School District.

_____
1989   Editor's Introduction. Pp. 1-28 in Ceremonies of the Pawnee. James R. Murie. Douglas R. Parks, ed. Lincoln: University of Nebraska Press, in cooperation with the American Indian Studies Research Institute, Indiana University.

_____
1990   Report on the Siouan Dialect Survey. (Paper presented at the American Anthropological Association Meeting, Washington.)

_____
1991   Traditional Narratives of the Arikara Indians. 4 vols. Vol. 1: Stories of Alfred Morsette: Interlinear Linguistic Texts; Vol. 2: Stories of Other Narrators: Interlinear Linguistic Texts; Vol. 3: Stories of Alfred Morsette: English Translations; Vol. 4: Stories of Other Narrators: English Translations. (*Studies in the Anthropology of North American Indians*). Lincoln: University of Nebraska Press.

Parks, Douglas R., and Raymond J. DeMallie
1992   Plains Indian Native Literatures. *Boundary 2* 19(3):105-147. Binghamton, N.Y.

Parks, Douglas R., and Waldo R. Wedel
1985   Pawnee Geography: Historical and Sacred. *Great Plains Quarterly* 5:143-176. Lincoln.

Parks, Douglas R., Janet Beltran, and Ella P. Waters
1979   An Introduction to the Arikara Language. Bismarck, N.Dak.: North Dakota Indian Languages Program, Mary College.

Parks, Douglas R., A. Wesley Jones, and Robert C. Hollow, eds.
1978   Earth Lodge Tales from the Upper Missouri: Traditional Stories of the Arikara, Hidatsa, and Mandan. Bismarck, N.Dak.: North Dakota Indian Languages Program, Mary College.

Parr, Richard T.
1974   A Bibliography of the Athapaskan Languages. *Canada. National Museum of Man. Mercury Series. Ethnology Division Paper* 14. Ottawa.

Parsons, Elsie Clews
1923   Laguna Genealogies. *American Museum of Natural History Anthropological Papers* 19(5):135-292. New York.

_____
1923a   Zuñi Names and Naming Practices. *Journal of American Folk-Lore* 36(140):171-176.

_____
1923b   Notes on San Felipe and Santo Domingo. *American Anthropologist*, n.s. 25(4):485-494.

_____
1925   The Pueblo of Jemez. Andover, Mass.: Published for the Department of Archaeology, Phillips Academy, by the Yale University Press.

_____
1926   Micmac Notes: St. Ann's Mission on Chapel Island, Bras d'Or Lakes, Cape Breton Island. *Journal of American Folk-Lore* 39(154):460-485.

_____
1927   Witchcraft Among the Pueblos: Indian or Spanish? *Man* 27:106-112, 125-128.

_____
1929   The Social Organization of the Tewa of New Mexico. *American Anthropological Association Memoir* 36. Menasha, Wis.

_____
1930   Notes on the Pima, 1926. *American Anthropologist*, n.s. 30(3):445-464.

_____
1932   Isleta, New Mexico. Pp. 193-466 in *47th Annual Report of the Bureau of American Ethnology for 1929-1930*. Washington.

_____
1936   Riddles and Metaphors among Indian Peoples. *Journal of American Folklore* 49(193):171-174.

_____
1937   Naming Practices in Arizona. *American Anthropologist*, n.s. 39(3)1:561-562.

_____
1939   Pueblo Indian Religion. 2 vols. Chicago: The University of Chicago Press.

_____
1941   Notes on the Caddo. *American Anthropological Association Memoir* 57. Menasha Wis.

Patterson, Trudi A.
1990   Theoretial Aspects of Dakota Morphology and Phonolo-
        gy. (Unpublished Ph.D. Dissertation in Linguistics,
        University of Illinois at Urbana-Champaign.)

1991   Phonological Nasality in Lakʰota. Pp. 551-563 in *1990
        Mid-America Conference Papers*. Frances Ingemann,
        ed. Lawrence: University of Kansas, Department of
        Linguistics.

Paul, Gaither, and Ronald Scollon
1980   Stories for My Grandchildren. Told by Gaither Paul.
        Ron Scollon, ed. Fairbanks: University of Alaska,
        Native Language Center.

Paul, Joan S.
1967   Phonemic Analysis of Auburn Nisenan: A Dialect of
        Maidu. *Anthropological Linguistics* 9(9):12-24.

Pearson, Bruce L.
1978   On the Indian Place Names of South Carolina. *Names*
        26(1):58-67.

Pease, Theodore C., and Ernestine Jenison, eds.
1940   Illinois on the Eve of the Seven Years' War, 1747-1755.
        (*French Series* 3). *Collections of the Illinois State
        Historical Library* 29. Springfield, Ill.

Peck, Edmund J.
1878   Portions of the Holy Scripture, for the Use of the
        Esquimaux on the Northern and Eastern Shores of
        Hudson's Bay. London: The Society for Promoting
        Christian Knowledge.

1883   Eskimo Grammar. Toronto: [no publisher.]

1925   A Dictionary of the Eskimo Language, Compiled from
        Erdman's Eskimo-German Edition, 1864. W.G. Walton,
        ed. Hamilton, Ont.: Church of the Ascension Thank-
        Offering Fund.

Pénicault, André *see* Pénigaut, André-Joseph

Pénigaut, André-Joseph
1953   Fleur de Lys and Calumet. Translated from French
        Manuscripts and Edited by Richebourg Gaillard
        McWilliams. Baton Rouge: Louisiana State University
        Press.

Penn, William
1912   Letter from William Penn to the Committee of the Free
        Society of Traders, 1683. Pp. 217-244 in Narratives of
        Early Pennsylvania, West New Jersey and Delaware,
        1630-1707. Albert C. Myers, ed. New York: Charles
        Scribners and Sons.

Penney, Grace Jackson
1953   Tales of the Cheyennes. Illustrations by Walter Richard
        West. Boston: Houghton Mifflin; Cambridge, Mass.:
        The Riverside Press.

Pennington, Campbell W., ed.
1979   The Pima Bajo of Central Sonora, Mexico, Vol. 2:
        Vocabulario en la Lengua Nevome. Salt Lake City:
        University of Utah Press. (Vol. I: The Material Culture,
        publ. in 1980.)

1981   Arte y vocabulario de la lengua dohema, heve, o eudeva.
        "Anónimo (Siglo XVII)." Mexico City: Universidad
        Nacional Autónoma de México.

Pentland, David H.
1975   Diminutive Consonant Symbolism in Algonquian. Pp.
        237-252 in Papers of the Sixth Algonquian Conference.
        William Cowan, ed. *Canada. National Museum of Man.
        Mercury Series. Ethnology Service Paper* 23. Ottawa.

1975a   Cartographic Concepts of the Northern Algonquians.
        Cartographica 12:149-160. Toronto.

1976   In Defence of Edward Umfreville. Pp. 62-104 in Papers
        of the Seventh Algonquian Conference. William Cowan,
        ed. Ottawa: Carleton University.

1977   Nêhiyawasinahikêwin: A Standard Orthography for the
        Cree Language. Regina: Saskatchewan Indian Federated
        College. (Rev. ed.: Department of Linguistics, Uni-
        versity of Calgary; various facsimile reprints.)

1978   A Historical Overview of Cree Dialects. Pp. 104-126 in
        Papers of the Ninth Algonquian Conference. William
        Cowan, ed. Ottawa: Carleton University.

1979   Algonquian Historical Phonology. (Unpublished Ph.D.
        Dissertation in Anthropology, University of Toronto,
        Ont.).

1979a   Does 'Eastern Algonquian' Really Exist? *Algonquian
        Linguistics* 4(4):36-41.

1991   Henry Kelsey's Christmas Message, 1696. Pp. 127-138
        in Linguistic Studies Presented to John L. Finlay. H.C.
        Wolfart, ed. *Algonquian and Iroquoian Linguistics,
        Memoir* 8. Winnipeg.

Pentland, David H., and H. Christoph Wolfart
1982   Bibliography of Algonquian Linguistics. Winnipeg:
        University of Manitoba Press.

Perdue, Theda
1994   The Sequoyah Syllabary and Cultural Revitalization. Pp.
        116-125 in Perspectives on the Southeast: Linguistics,
        Archaeology, and Ethnohistory. Patricia B. Kwachka,
        ed. (*Southern Anthropological Society Proceedings* 27).
        Athens and London: The University of Georgia Press.

Perry, Edgar, C.Z. Quintero, Sr., C.D. Davenport, and C.B. Perry,
comps.
1972   Western Apache Dictionary. Fort Apache, Ariz.: White
        Mountain Apache Tribe.

Perry, Richard J.
1983   Proto-Athapaskan Culture: The Use of Ethnographic
        Reconstruction. *American Ethnologist* 10(4):715-733.

Peter, Katherine
1979   Dinjii Zhuh Ginjik Nagwan Tr'iłtsąįį / Gwich'in Junior
        Dictionary. Anchorage: National Bilingual Materials
        Development Center, Rural Education Affairs,
        University of Alaska.

1981   Neets'ąįį Gwiindaii: Living in the Chandalar Country.
        Fairbanks: Alaska Native Language Center.

Peters, Bernard C.
1981   The Origin and Meaning of Place Names Along the
            Pictured Rocks National Seashore. *Michigan Academi-
            cian* 14(1):41-55. Ann Arbor.

1981a   The Origin of Some Stream Names Along Michigan's
            Lake Superior Shoreline. *Inland Seas* 37(1):6-12.
            Vermillion, Ohio.

1984   The Origin and Meaning of Chippewa Place Names
            Along the Lake Superior Shoreline Between Grand
            Island and Point Abbaye. *Names* 32(3):234-251.

1985   The Origin and Meaning of Chippewa and French Place
            Names Along the Shoreline of the Keweenaw Peninsula.
            Michigan Academician 17(2):195-211. Ann Arbor.

1986   The Origin and Meaning of Place Names Along the Lake
            Superior Shoreline Between Keweenaw Portage and
            Montreal River. *Michigan Academician* 18(3):411-429.
            Ann Arbor.

1994   The Origin and Meaning of Place Names Along
            Michigan's Lake Superior Shoreline Between Sault Ste.
            Marie and Grand Marais. *Michigan Academician*
            26(1):1-17. Ann Arbor.

Petersen, Jonathan
1968   Ordbogêraк. Rev. ed. København: Ministeriet for
            Grønland. (First ed.: Godthåb, 1951.)

Petersen, Karen Daniels
1971   Plains Indian Art from Fort Marion. Norman: University
            of Oklahoma Press.

Petersen, Robert
1976   ʃ: Kitâta кerкane atorneкarnera dialektinutdlo avdlanut
            atássuteкarnera / Kitaata qeqqani atorneqarnera dialekt-
            inullu allanut atassuteqarnera. [š: On the Variation and
            the Common Traits Among the Dialects]. København:
            Københavns Universitets Institut for Eskimologi.
            (Typescript.)

1990   The Greenlandic Language: Its Nature and Situation. Pp.
            293-308, 363-364 in Arctic Languages: An Awakening.
            Dirmid R.F. Collis, ed. Paris: Unesco.

Peterson, John H., Jr.
1985   A Choctaw Source Book. New York and London:
            Garland Publishing.

Petitot, Émile
1876   Dictionnaire de la langue dènè-dindjié: dialectes mon-
            tagnais ou chippéwayan, peaux de lièvre et loucheux.
            Paris: Ernest Leroux, éditeur, Libraire de la société
            Asiatique de Paris, &c.

1876a   Vocabulaire français-esquimaux: dialecte des tchiglit
            des bouches du Mackenzie et de l'Anderson.
            (*Bibliothèque de Linguistique et d'Ethnographie
            Américaines* 3). Paris: E. Leroux.

1887   Traditions Indiennes du Canada Nord-Ouest. Alençon:
            Renaut de Broise.

Petroff, Ivan *see* U.S. Census Office. 10th Census. 1884

Petter, Rodolphe C.
1907   Sketch of the Cheyenne Grammar. *Memoirs of the
            American Anthropological Association* 1(Pt. 6):443-
            478. Lancaster, Pa.

1915   English-Cheyenne Dictionary. Kettle Falls, Wash.:
            Valdo Petter.

1934   Zemona hoemao Maheonhoestomohestova zeenano
            ninitaehaman na nivostanevstomanehaman Jesus
            Maheonxostaanasz. [Bible. New Testament.] New
            York: American Bible Society.

1952   Cheyenne Grammar. Newton, Kans.: Mennonite Pub-
            lication Office.

Pettitt, George A.
1946   Primitive Education in North America. *University of
            California Publications in American Archaeology and
            Ethnology* 43(1):1-182. Berkeley.

Philips, Susan U.
1970   Acquisition of Rules for Appropriate Speech Usage. Pp.
            77-101 in Bilingualism and Language Contact. James E.
            Alatis, ed. (*Georgetown University Round Table on
            Languages and Linguistics 1970*). Washington, D.C.:
            Georgetown University Press.

1974   Warm Springs 'Indian Time': How the Regulation of
            Participation Affects the Progression of Events. Pp. 92-
            109 in Explorations in the Ethnography of Speaking.
            Richard Bauman and Joel Sherzer, eds. London and
            New York: Cambridge University Press. (Reprinted, 2d
            ed., 1989.)

1974a   The Role of the Listener in the Regulation of Talk: Some
            Sources of Cultural Variability. (Paper presented at the
            Annual Meeting of the American Anthropological
            Association, Mexico City, November, 1974.)

1975   Literacy as a Mode of Communication on the Warm
            Springs Indian Reservation. Pp. 367-382 in Vol. 2 of
            Foundations of Language Development: A Multi-
            disciplinary Approach. 2 vols. Eric H. Lenneberg and
            Elizabeth Lenneberg, eds. New York: Academic Press;
            Paris: The UNESCO Press.

1976   Some Sources of Cultural Variability in the Regulation
            of Talk. *Language in Society* 5(1):81-85.

1983   The Invisible Culture: Communication in Classroom and
            Community on the Warm Springs Indian Reservation.
            New York: Longman. (Reprinted: Waveland Press,
            Prospect Heights, Ill., 1993.)

Phillips, Emily M.
1930   Story of Chipmunk. *The Washington Farmer* August 14
            (Vol. 62, No. 7):(129) 9. Spokane, Wash.

875

Phillips, Philip, James A. Ford, and James B. Griffin
1951   Archaeological Survey in the Lower Mississippi Alluvial Valley, 1940-1947. *Papers of the Peabody Museum of American Archaeology and Ethnology, Harvard University* 25. Cambridge, Mass.

Phinney, Archie
1934   Nez Percé Texts. *Columbia University Contributions to Anthropology* 25. New York. (Reprinted: AMS Press, New York, 1969.)

Pickering, John
1820   An Essay on a Uniform Orthography for the Indian Languages of North America. Cambridge: University Press-Hilliard and Metcalf.

_____
[1830] A Grammar of the Cherokee Language. [Boston: Mission Press.]

Pico, Juan Esteban
1884   San Buenaventura or Mis-ka-ná-kan (Ventureño Chumash) Vocabulary, San Buenaventura, California, November 18, 1884. (Manuscript No. 293-a in National Anthropological Archives, Smithsonian Institution, Washington.)

_____
1888   [List of place names entitled "Lista de los nombres de las rancherias indigenas [conocidas] desde la Punta de Concepcion hasta Maligo," with notes by H.W. Henshaw.] (Manuscript, J.P. Harrington Papers, Box 544, Folder 3 [Microfilm Roll 95, Frames 0436-0438] in National Anthropological Archives, Smithsonian Institution, Washington.)

_____
1891   [Text entitled "Cuatro de Julio de 1890" in parallel columns in Ventureño Chumash and Spanish, 6 pages, accompanied by a letter to H.W. Henshaw in Spanish, 2 pages, April 21, 1891.] (Manuscript No. 3718 in National Anthropological Archives, Smithsonian Institution, Washington.)

Piddocke, Stuart
1965   The Potlatch System of the Southern Kwakiutl: A New Perspective. *Southwestern Journal of Anthropology* 21(3):244-264.

Pierce, Joe E.
1954   Crow vs. Hidatsa in Dialect Distance and in Glottochronology. *International Journal of American Linguistics* 20(2):134-136.

_____
1971   Hanis (Coos) Phonemics. *Linguistics: An International Review* 75:31-42.

Pierce, Richard A.
1990   Russian America: A Biographical Dictionary. Kingston, Ont.: The Limestone Press.

Pierson, Abraham [Abraham Peirson]
1658   Some Helps for the Indians Shewing Them How to Improve their Natural Reason, to Know the True God, and the True Christian Religion. Cambridge, Mass.: Samuel Green.

_____
1873   Some Helps for the Indians: A Catechism in the Language of the Quiripi Indians of New Haven Colony. Reprinted from the Original Edition, Cambridge, 1658. Introduction by J. Hammond Trumbull. (*Connecticut Historical Society Collections* 3). Hartford: M.H. Mallory.

Piggott, Glyne L.
1978   Algonquin and Other Ojibwa Dialects: A Preliminary Report. Pp. 160-187 in Papers of the Ninth Algonquian Conference. William Cowan, ed. Ottawa: Carleton University.

_____
1980   Aspects of Odawa Morphophonemics. New York: Garland Publishing. (Originally issued as: Ph.D. Dissertation in Linguistics, University of Toronto, 1974.)

Piggott, Glyne L., and Jonathan Kaye, eds.
1973   Odawa Language Project: Second Report. *Centre for Linguistic Studies, Linguistic Series* 1. Toronto.

Pike, Eunice V.
1986   Tone Contrasts in Central Carrier (Athapaskan). *International Journal of American Linguistics* 52(4):411-418.

Pike, Judith J.
1953   A Study of Place Names in Middletown, Connecticut. (Unpublished M.A. Thesis, Trinity College, Hartford, Conn.)

Pilling, James Constantine
1885   Proof-sheets of a Bibliography of the Languages of the North American Indians. *Bureau of [American] Ethnology Miscellaneous Publication* 2. Washington. (Reprinted: Central Book Co., Brooklyn, N.Y., 1966.)

_____
1887   Bibliography of the Eskimo Language. *Bureau of [American] Ethnology Bulletin* 1. Washington. (Reprinted as vol. 1, pt. 1 of 3 vols.: AMS Press, New York, 1973.)

_____
1887a   Bibliography of the Siouan Languages. *Bureau of [American] Ethnology Bulletin* 5. Washington. (Reprinted as vol. 1, pt. 2 of 3 vols.: AMS Press, New York, 1973.)

_____
1888   Bibliography of the Iroquoian Languages. *Bureau of [American] Ethnology Bulletin* 6. Washington. (Reprinted as vol. 1, pt. 3 of 3 vols.: AMS Press, New York, 1973.)

_____
1889   Bibliography of the Muskhogean Languages. *Bureau of [American] Ethnology Bulletin* 9. Washington. (Reprinted as vol. 1, pt. 4 of 3 vols.: AMS Press, New York, 1973.)

_____
1891   Bibliography of the Algonquian Languages. *Bureau of [American] Ethnology Bulletin* 13. Washington. (Reprinted as vol. 2, pt. 5 of 3 vols.: AMS Press, New York, 1973.)

1892   Bibliography of the Athapascan Languages. *Bureau of [American] Ethnology Bulletin* 14. Washington. (Reprinted as vol. 3, pt. 6 of 3 vols.: AMS Press, New York, 1973.)

1893   Bibliography of the Chinookan Languages (Including the Chinook Jargon). *Bureau of [American] Ethnology Bulletin* 15. Washington. (Reprinted as vol. 3, pt. 7 of 3 vols.: AMS Press, New York, 1973.)

1893a   Bibliography of the Salishan Languages. *Bureau of [American] Ethnology Bulletin* 16. Washington. (Reprinted as vol. 3, pt. 8 of 3 vols.: AMS Press, New York, 1973.)

1894   Bibliography of the Wakashan Languages. *Bureau of [American] Ethnology Bulletin* 19. Washington. (Reprinted as vol. 3, pt. 9 of 3 vols.: AMS Press, New York, 1973.)

Pimentel, Francisco
1862-1865   Cuadro Descriptivo y Comparativo de las Lenguas Indígenas de México. 2 vols. México: Imprenta de Andrade y Escalante.

Pinart, Alphonse Louis
1894   Études sur les Indiens Californiens. *Revue de Linguistique et de Philologie Comparée* 27:79-87.

Pinart, Alphonse Louis, and Robert F. Heizer *see* Heizer, Robert F., ed. 1952

Pinnow, Heinz-Jürgen
1964   Die nordamerikanischen Indianersprachen: ein Überblick über ihren Bau und ihre Besonderheiten. Wiesbaden: Harrassowitz.

1964a   On the Historical Position of Tlingit. *International Journal of American Linguistics* 30(2):155-168.

1968   Genetic Relationship vs. Borrowing in Na-Dene. [Translation.] *International Journal of American Linguistics* 34(3):204-211.

1977   Geschichte der Na-Dene-Forschung. *Indiana: Beiträge zur Völker- und Sprachenkunde, Archäologie und Anthropologie des indianischen Amerika*, supp. 5. Berlin.

1985   Sprachhistorische Untersuchung einiger Tiernamen in Haida. *Abhandlungen der Völkerkundlichen Arbeitsgemeinschaft* 39. Nortorf, Germany.

1985a   Das Haida als Na-Dene Sprache. Teil I, II, III, IV. *Abhandlungen der Völkerkundlichen Arbeitsgemeinschaft* 43, 44, 45, 46. Nortorf, Germany.

1986   Die Zahlwörter des Haida in Sprachvergleichender Sicht. *Abhandlungen der Völkerkundlichen Arbeitsgemeinschaft* 47. Nortorf, Germany.

1990   Die Na-Dene Sprachen in Lichte der Greenberg-Klassifikation. *Abhandlungen der Völkerkundlichen Arbeitsgemeinschaft* 64. Nortorf, Germany.

Pino, Pedro B.
1812   Exposición sucinta y sencilla de la provincia del Nuevo México. Cadiz.

Pitkin, Harvey
1977   Coyote and Bullhead (Wintu). Pp. 82-104 in Northern California Texts. Victor Golla and Shirley Silver, eds. *International Journal of American Linguistics. Native American Texts Series* 2(2). Chicago: University of Chicago Press.

1978   Squirrel and Acorn-Woman (Wintu). Pp. 32-44 in Coyote Stories. William Bright, ed. *International Journal of American Linguistics. Native American Texts Series Monograph* 1. Chicago: University of Chicago Press.

1984   Wintu Grammar. *University of California Publications in Linguistics* 94. Berkeley.

1985   Wintu Dictionary. *University of California Publications in Linguistics* 95. Berkeley.

Pitkin, Harvey, and William F. Shipley
1958   A Comparative Survey of California Penutian. *International Journal of American Linguistics* 24(3):174-188.

Platero, Linda S., chief ed.
1984   Navajo Children's Literature, Volume II. Albuquerque, N.M.: Native American Materials Development Center.

Pollard, John Garland
1894   The Pamunkey Indians of Virginia. *Bureau of American Ethnology Bulletin* 17. Washington.

Portlock, Nathaniel
1789   A Voyage Round the World; But More Particularly to the North-west Coast of America; Performed in 1785, 1786, 1787 and 1788 [etc.]. London: Printed for J. Stockdale and G. Goulding. (Reprinted: Da Capo Press, New York, 1968.)

Poser, William
1992   The Salinan and Yurumanguí Data in *Language in the Americas*. *International Journal of American Linguistics* 58(2):202-229.

1993   [Book Notice of] A Guide to the World's Languages, Vol. I: Classification. 2d. ed., by Merritt Ruhlen. *Language: Journal of the Linguistic Society of America* 69(1):220-222.

1993a   [Book Notice of] On Calculating the Factor of Chance in Language Comparison, by Donald A. Ringe, Jr. *Language: Journal of the Linguistic Society of America* 69(3):635-636.

Potier, Pierre
1920   Elementa grammaticae huronicae [1745]. Pp. 1-157 in *15th Report of the Bureau of Archives for the Province of Ontario for the Years 1918-1919*. Alexander Fraser, ed. Toronto: Clarkson W. James.

1920a Radices huronicae [1751]. Pp. 159-455 in *15th Report of the Bureau of Archives for the Province of Ontario for the Years 1918-1919.* Alexander Fraser, ed. Toronto: Clarkson W. James.

Powell, Donald M.
1961 A Preliminary Bibliography of the Published Writings of Berard Haile, O.F.M. *The Kiva* 26(4):44-47.

Powell, James V.
1975 Proto-Chimakuan: Materials for a Reconstruction. *University of Hawaii Working Papers in Linguistics* 7(2). Honolulu.

1975a Quileute Language: Book 1. La Push, Wash.: Quileute Tribe.

1976 Quileute Language: Book 2. La Push, Wash.: Quileute Tribe.

1990 Chinook Jargon Vocabularies and the Lexicographers. *International Journal of American Linguistics* 56(1): 134-151.

1991 Our World - Our Ways: T'aat'aaqsapa Cultural Dictionary. [British Columbia]: Nuuchahnulth Tribal Council.

1993 Chimakuan and Wakashan—the Case for Remote Common Origin: Another Look at Suggestive Sound Correspondences. Pp. 451-470 in American Indian Linguistics and Ethnography in Honor of Laurence C. Thompson. Anthony Mattina and Timothy Montler, eds. *University of Montana Occasional Papers in Linguistics* 10. Missoula.

Powell, James V., and Vickie Jensen
1976 Quileute: An Introduction to the Indians of La Push. Seattle: University of Washington Press.

Powell, James V., and Fred Woodruff, Sr.
1976 Quileute Dictionary. *Northwest Anthropological Research Notes. Memoirs 3.* Moscow, Idaho.

Powell, James V., William Penn, et al.
1972 Place Names of the Quileute Indians. *Pacific Northwest Quarterly* 63(3):105-112. Seattle.

Powell, John Wesley
1877 Introduction to the Study of Indian Languages, with Words, Phrases, and Sentences To Be Collected. Washington: Government Printing Office.

1877a Linguistics. Pp. 439-613 in Tribes of California, by Stephen Powers. *Contributions to North American Ethnology* 3. Washington: U.S. Geographical and Geological Survey of the Rocky Mountain Region. (Reprinted: AMS, New York, 1976.)

1878 The Nationality of the Pueblos. *The Rocky Mountain Presbyterian*, November 1878. Denver.

1880 Introduction to the Study of Indian Languages, with Words, Phrases, and Sentences To Be Collected; 2d ed., with Charts. Washington: Government Printing Office.

1880a Pueblo Indians. *American Naturalist* 14(8):603-605. Chicago.

1881 Wyandot Government: A Short Study of Tribal Society. Pp. 57-69 in *1st Annual Report of the Bureau of [American] Ethnology for 1879-1880.* Washington.

1887 Report of the Director. Pp. xvii-liii in *5th Annual Report of the Bureau of [American] Ethnology for 1883-1884.* Washington.

1888 Report of the Director. Pp. xxiii-lviii in *6th Annual Report of the Bureau of [American] Ethnology for 1884-1885.* Washington.

1891 Indian Linguistic Families of America North of Mexico. Pp. 1-142 in *7th Annual Report of the Bureau of [American] Ethnology for 1885-1886.* With map. Washington. (Reprinted with Franz Boas's Introduction to *Handbook of American Indian Languages.* Preston Holder, ed. University of Nebraska Press, Lincoln, 1966.)

1891a The Study of Indian Languages. *Science* 17(418):71-74.

1894 Map of Linguistic Stocks of American Indians Chiefly Within the Present Limits of the United States. [Facing] p. 36 in Report on Indians Taxed and Indians Not Taxed in the United States (Except Alaska) at the Eleventh Census: 1890. Washington: Government Printing Office. (Reprinted: Norman Ross Publishing, New York, 1994.)

1897 Report of the Director. Pp. xv-cxxi in *15th Annual Report of the Bureau of [American] Ethnology for 1893-1894.* Washington.

1906 [Map of] Linguistic Families of American Indians North of Mexico. [Revised by Members of the Staff of Bureau of American Ethnology.] *Bureau of American Ethnology Miscellaneous Publications* 7. Washington.

1915 [Map of] Linguistic Families of American Indians North of Mexico. Revised by Members of the Staff of the Bureau of American Ethnology. *Bureau of American Ethnology Miscellaneous Publications* 11. Washington.

Powell, Margaret S., and Stephen D. Powell
1990 Bibliography of Placename Literature, United States and Canada, 1980-1988. *Names* 38(1-2):49-141.

Powers, Stephen
1872 The Northern California Indians [I-VI]. *Overland Monthly* 8(4):325-333; 8(5):425-435; 8(6):530-539; 9(2):155-164; 9(4):305-313; 9(6):498-507. (Reprinted: AMS Press, New York, 1965.)

1873-1874 The California Indians [VII-XIII]. *Overland Monthly* 10(4):322-333; 10(6):535-545; 11(2):105-116; 12(1): 21-31; 12(5):412-424; 12(6):530-540; 13(6):542-550. (Reprinted: AMS Press, New York, 1965.)

1876 Vocabulary of the Washo Language. (Manuscripts No. 950-951 in National Anthropological Archives, Smithsonian Institution, Washington.)

1877 Tribes of California. *Contributions to North American Ethnology* 3. John Wesley Powell, ed. Washington: U.S. Geographical and Geological Survey of the Rocky Mountain Region. (Reprinted: with Introduction and Notes by Robert F. Heizer. University of California Press, Berkeley, 1976.)

Powers, William K.
1992 Translating the Untranslatable: The Place of the Vocable in Lakota Song. Pp. 293-310 in On the Translation of Native American Literatures. Brian Swann, ed. Washington: Smithsonian Institution Press.

Powers, William R., and John F. Hoffecker
1989 Late Pleistocene Settlement in the Nenana Valley, Central Alaska. *American Antiquity* 54(2):263-287.

Powicke, Frederick James
1931 Some Unpublished Correspondence of the Reverend Richard Baxter and the Reverend John Eliot, the Apostle of the American Indians, 1656-1682. Manchester, U.K.: Manchester University Press.

Press, Margaret L.
1979 Chemehuevi: A Grammar and Lexicon. *University of California Publications in Linguistics* 92. Berkeley.

Preston, Richard
1980 Reflections on Sapir's Anthropology in Canada. *Canadian Review of Sociology and Anthropology* 17(4):367-375.

Price, Richard, and Sally Price
1972 Saramaka Onomastics: An Afro-American Naming System. *Ethnology* 11(4):341-367.

Prince, J. Dyneley
1897 The Passamaquoddy Wampum Records. *Proceedings of the American Philosophical Society* 36(156):479-495. Philadelphia.

1899 Some Passamaquoddy Witchcraft Tales. *Proceedings of the American Philosophical Society* 38(160):181-189. Philadelphia.

1901 The Modern Dialect of the Canadian Abenakis. Pp. 343-362 in Miscellanea linguistica in onore di Graziadio Ascoli. Turin: E. Loescher.

1902 A Modern Delaware Tale. *Proceedings of the American Philosophical Society* 41(168):20-34. Philadelphia.

1905 A Tale in the Hudson River Indian Language. *American Anthropologist*, n.s. 7(1):74-84.

1907 Last Living Echoes of the Natick. *American Anthropologist*, n.s. 9(3):493-498.

1909 A Passamaquoddy Aviator. *American Anthropologist*, n.s. 11(4):628-650.

1910 The Penobscot Language of Maine. *American Anthropologist*, n.s. 12(1):183-208.

1912 An Ancient New Jersey Indian Jargon. *American Anthropologist*, n.s. 14(3):508-524.

1914 The Morphology of the Passamaquoddy Language of Maine. *Proceedings of the American Philosophical Society* 53:92-117. Philadelphia.

1921 Passamaquoddy Texts. *Publications of the American Ethnological Society* 10. Franz Boas, ed. New York: G.E. Stechert. (Reprinted: AMS Press, New York, 1974.)

Prince, J. Dyneley, and Frank G. Speck
1904 Glossary of the Mohegan-Pequot Language. *American Anthropologist*, n.s. 6(1):18-45.

Propp, Vladimir
1958 Morphology of the Folktale. Laurence Scott, trans. *Indiana University Research Center in Anthropology, Folklore, and Linguistics Publication* 10; *American Folklore Society Bibliographical and Special Series* 9. Bloomington. (2d ed., Louis A. Wagner, ed. University of Texas Press, Austin, 1968.)

Proudfit, S.V.
1888 [Minutes of the 130th Regular Meeting, Anthropological Society of Washington, January 3, 1888, with an Abstract of H. W. Henshaw's Paper on the Linguistic Map of North America.] (Manuscript No. 4821, Box 3, in National Anthropological Archives, Smithsonian Institution, Washington.)

Proulx, Paul
1980 The Linguistic Evidence on Algonquian Prehistory. *American Anthropologist*, n.s. 22(1):1-21.

1980a The Subordinative Order of Proto-Algonquian. *International Journal of American Linguistics* 46(4):289-300.

1982 The Linguistic Evidence on the Algonquian-Iroquoian Encounter. Pp. 189-211 in Approaches to Algonquian Archaeology. Margaret G. Hanna and Brian Kooyman, eds. Proceedings of the Thirteenth Annual Conference of the Archaeological Association of the University of Calgary. Calgary.

1984 Proto-Algic I: Phonological Sketch. *International Journal of American Linguistics* 50(2):165-207.

1984a Two Models of Algonquian Linguistic Prehistory: Diffusion Versus Genetic Subgrouping. *Anthropological Linguistics* 26(4):393-434.

879

1985   Proto-Algic II: Verbs. *International Journal of American Linguistics* 51(1):59-93.

1989   A Sketch of Blackfoot Historical Phonology. *International Journal of American Linguistics* 55(1):43-82.

Pullum, Geoffrey K., and William A. Ladusaw
1986   Phonetic Symbol Guide. Chicago and London: The University of Chicago Press.

Pulte, William
1975   The Position of Chickasaw in Western Muskogean. Pp. 251-256 in Studies in Southeastern Indian Languages. James M. Crawford, ed. Athens: The University of Georgia Press.

Pyrlaeus, Johann Christoph
1745   Onondagoische Wörterverzeichniss von Christopher Pyrlaeus. (Manuscript in Moravian Mission, Bethlehem, Pennsylvania.)

1745-1751 Affixa nominum et verborum linguæ macquaicæ cum vocabulario ejusdem linguæ. (Manuscript, 178 pp., in the Library of the Pennsylvania Historical Society, Philadelphia.)

1745-1751a Adjectiva nomina et pronomina linguæ macquaicæ cum non nullis de verbis, adverbis ac præpositionis ejusdem linguæ. (Manuscript, 105 pp., in the Library of the Pennsylvania Historical Society, Philadelphia.)

1745-1751b [The First, Second, and Third Chapters of Genesis, and First and Second Chapters of Matthew in the Mohawk Language.] (Manuscript, 18 pp., in the Library of the Pennsylvania Historical Society, Philadelphia.)

1745-1751c [Mohawk Vocables Obtained from the Oneida Chief Shikellimy.] (Manuscript, 6 pp., in the Library of the Pennsylvania Historical Society, Philadelphia.)

Quain, B.H.
1937   The Iroquois. Pp. 240-281 in Cooperation and Competition Among Primitive Peoples. Margaret Mead, ed. New York and London: McGraw-Hill.

Quine, Willard Van Orman
1960   Word and Object. New York and London: The Technology Press of the Massachusetts Institute of Technology and John Wiley & Sons.

Quinn, David B.
1955   The Roanoke Voyages, 1584-1590: Documents to Illustrate the English Voyages to North America Under the Patent Granted to Walter Raleigh in 1584. 2 vols. London: Cambridge University Press for The Hakluyt Society.

1970   Thomas Hariot and the Virginia Voyages of 1602. *The William and Mary Quarterly*, 3d. ser. 27(2):268-281. Williamsburg, Va.

Quinn, David B., and Alison M. Quinn, eds.
1983   The English New England Voyages, 1602-1608. (*Hakluyt Society Second Series* 161). London: The Hakluyt Society.

Quinney, John
1795   The Assembly's Catechism. Stockbridge, Mass.: Loring Andrews.

Quinney, John, and Henrick Aupaumut
1818   The Assembly's Shorter Catechism. [No place: no publisher.]

Radin, Paul
1910   The Clan Organization of the Winnebago. *American Anthropologist*, n.s. 12(2):209-219.

1915   Literary Aspects of North American Mythology. *Canada. Geological Survey Museum Bulletin* 16; *Anthropological Series* 6. Ottawa. (Reprinted: Norwood Editions, Norwood, Pa., 1973.)

1915a   The Social Organization of the Winnebago Indians, an Interpretation. *Canada. Department of Mines. Geological Survey, Museum Bulletin* 10, *Anthropological Series* 5:1-40. Ottawa.

1919   The Genetic Relationship of the North American Indian Languages. *University of California Publications in American Archaeology and Ethnology* 14(5):489-502. Berkeley.

1920   The Autobiography of a Winnebago Indian. *University of California Publications in American Archaeology and Ethnology* 16(7):381-473. Berkeley. (Reprinted: University of Nebraska Press, Lincoln, 1983.)

1923   The Winnebago Tribe. Pp. 35-550 in *37th Annual Report of the Bureau of American Ethnology for 1915-1916*. Washington.

1924   Wappo Texts: First Series. *California Publications in American Archaeology and Ethnology* 19(1):1-147.

1929   A Grammar of the Wappo Language. *University of California Publications in American Archaeology and Ethnology* 27(1):1-194.

1949   The Culture of the Winnebago: As Described by Themselves. *Special Publications of the Bollingen Foundation* 1. *Indiana University Publications in Anthropology and Linguistics, Memoir* 2. Baltimore.

1954-1956 The Evolution of an American Indian Prose Epic: A Study in Comparative Literature. 2 Pts. Basel, Switzerland: Ethnographical Museum.

1956   The Trickster: A Study in American Indian Mythology. New York: Bell.

Radloff, Leopold
1858   Über die Sprache der Ugalachmut. *Bulletin de la Classe Historico-Philologique de l'Académie Impériale des Sciences de St. Pétersbourg* 15:25-37, 49-63, 125-139; *Mélanges Russes* 3:468-524. St. Petersburg.

1874   Leopold Radloffs Wörterbuch der Kinai-Sprache. Anton Schiefner, ed. *Mémoires de l'Académie Impériale des Sciences de St. Petersbourg* 7th ser., vol. 21(8). St. Petersburg.

Rafinesque, Constantine S., ed.
1832-1833   Atlantic Journal, and Friend of Knowledge. 8 pts. Philadelphia.

Rainey, Froelich G.
1947   The Whale Hunters of Tigara. *American Museum of Natural History Anthropological Papers* 41(2):231-283. New York.

Râle, Sébastien "Sebastian Rasles"
1833   A Dictionary of the Abnaki Language, in North America, by Father Sebastian Rasles [1691-1722]; With an Introductory Memoir and Notes, by John Pickering, A.A.S. John Pickering, ed. *Memoirs of the American Academy of Arts and Sciences*, n.s. 1:370-574. Cambridge, Mass.

Ramsay, Robert L., Allen W. Read, and Esther G. Leech
1934   Introduction to a Survey of Missouri Place-Names. *University of Missouri Studies* 9(1). Columbia.

Rand, Earl
1968   The Structural Phonology of Alabaman, a Muskogean Language. *International Journal of American Linguistics* 34(2):94-103.

Rand, Silas T.
1853   The Gospel According to Saint Matthew, in the Micmac Language. Charlottetown, P.E.I.: British and Foreign Bible Society.

1870   The Gospel According to St. John in the Language of the Malliseet Indians of New Brunswick. London: British and Foreign Bible Society.

1875   A First Reading Book in the Micmac Language. Halifax: Nova Scotia Printing Co.

1888   Dictionary of the Language of the Micmac Indians, Who Reside in Nova Scotia, New Brunswick, Prince Edward Island, Cape Breton and Newfoundland. Halifax: Nova Scotia Printing Co. (Reprinted: Johnson Reprint, New York, 1972.)

1919   Micmac Place-Names in the Maritime Provinces and Gaspé Peninsula Recorded Between 1852 and 1890. Collected, arranged, and indexed by William P. Anderson. Ottawa: Geographic Board of Canada.

Randall, Betty U.
1949   The Cinderella Theme in Northwest Coast Folklore. Pp. 243-285 in Indians of the Urban Northwest. Marian W. Smith, ed. *Columbia University Contributions to Anthropology* 36. New York. (Reprinted: AMS Press, New York, 1969.)

Rankin, Robert L.
1979   Linguistic Evidence for the Earlier Location of the Ofo. (Paper presented at the Annual Meeting of the American Anthropological Association/Conference on American Indian Languages, Cincinnati, Ohio, 1 Dec., 1979.)

1981   [Review of] The Caddoan, Iroquoian, and Siouan Languages, by Wallace L. Chafe. *International Journal of American Linguistics* 47(2):172-186.

1985   Quapaw as a Historically Dhegiha Language: Grammar. (Paper presented at the Fifth Annual Siouan and Caddoan Languages Conference, Tulsa, Okla.)

1988   Quapaw: Genetic and Areal Affiliations. Pp. 629-650 in In Honor of Mary Haas: From the Haas Festival Conference on Native American Linguistics. William Shipley, ed. Berlin: Mouton de Gruyter.

1992   [Review of] Language in the Americas, by J.H. Greenberg. *International Journal of American Linguistics* 58(3):324-351.

1992a   Siouan Succotash: Using Cultigen Terminology to Try to Date Siouan Linguistic Splits. (Typescript in Rankin's possession.)

Ransom, Jay Ellis
1941   Aleut Semaphore Signals. *American Anthropologist* 43(3, Pt. 1):422-427.

1945   Writing as a Medium of Acculturation among the Aleut. *Southwestern Journal of Anthropology* 1(3):333-344.

1946   Aleut Linguistic Perspective. *Southwestern Journal of Anthropology* 2(1):48-55.

Rasmussen, Knud
1908   The People of the Polar North: A Record. Compiled from the Danish Originals. G. Herring, ed. London: Kegan Paul, Trench, Trübner.

1927   Across Arctic America: Narrative of the Fifth Thule Expedition. New York and London: G.P. Putnam's Sons.

1929   Intellectual Culture of the Iglulik Eskimos. *Report of the Fifth Thule Expedition 1921-24; The Danish Expedition to the Arctic North America in Charge of Knud Rasmussen, Ph.D.* 7(1). Copenhagen.

1930   Intellectual Culture of the Caribou Eskimos. *Report of the Fifth Thule Expedition 1921-24; The Danish Expedition to the Arctic North America in Charge of Knud Rasmussen, Ph.D.* 7(2). Copenhagen.

1930a   Iglulik and Caribou Eskimo Texts. *Report of the Fifth Thule Expedition 1921-24; The Danish Expedition to the Arctic North America in Charge of Knud Rasmussen, Ph.D.* 7(3). Copenhagen.

1931   The Netsilik Eskimos: Social Life and Spiritual Culture. *Report of the Fifth Thule Expedition 1921-24; The Danish Expedition to the Arctic North America in Charge of Knud Rasmussen, Ph.D.* 8(1-2). Copenhagen.

1932   Intellectual Culture of the Copper Eskimos. *Report of the Fifth Thule Expedition 1921-24; The Danish Expedition to the Arctic North America in Charge of Knud Rasmussen, Ph.D.*9. Copenhagen.

Rasmussen, Knud, comp., and H. Ostermann, ed.
1941   Alaskan Eskimo Words. *Report of the Fifth Thule Expedition 1921-24: The Danish Expedition to the Arctic North America in Charge of Knud Rasmussen, Ph.D.*, vol. 3(4). Copenhagen. (Reprinted: AMS Press, New York, 1976.)

Rath, John C.
1981   A Practical Heiltsuk-English Dictionary with a Gramatical Introduction. *Canada. National Museum of Man. Mercury Series. Ethnology Service Paper* 75. Ottawa.

Raven, Christopher
1984   Northeastern California. Pp. 431-469 in California Archaeology. Michael J. Moratto, ed. New York, [etc.]: Academic Press.

Ray, Dorothy Jean
1964   Nineteenth Century Settlement and Subsistence Patterns in Bering Strait. *Arctic Anthropology* 2(1):61-94. Madison, Wis.

1971   Eskimo Place Names in Bering Strait and Vicinity. *Names* 19(1):1-33.

1975   The Eskimos of Bering Strait, 1650-1898. Seattle: University of Washington Press.

Ray, Verne F.
1933   The Sanpoil and Nespelem: Salishan Peoples of Northeastern Washington. *University of Washington Publications in Anthropology* 5. Seattle. (Reprinted: AMS Press, New York, 1980.)

1938   Lower Chinook Enthographic Notes. *University of Washington Publications in Anthropology* 7(2):29-165. Seattle.

1963   Primitive Pragmatists: The Modoc Indians of Northern California. Seattle: University of Washington Press for American Ethnological Society. (Reprinted in 1973.)

Rayburn, J.A.
1967   Geographical Names of Amerindian Origin in Canada I. *Names* 15(3):203-215.

1969   Geographical Names of Amerindian Origin in Canada II. *Names* 17(2):149-158.

Read, Allen Walker
1941   The English of Indians (1705-1745). *American Speech* 16:72-74.

Read, William A.
1927   Louisiana Place-Names of Indian Origin. *Louisiana State University and Agricultural and Mechanical College, University Bulletin*, n.s. 19(2). Baton Rouge.

1934   Florida Place-Names of Indian Origin and Seminole Personal Names. Baton Rouge: Louisiana State University Press.

1934a   Bibliography of Library Sources for the Study of the Place-Names of Missouri. Pp. 39-59 in Introduction to a Survey of Missouri Place-Names, by Robert L. Ramsay, Allen W. Read, and Esther G. Leech. *The University of Missouri Studies* 9(1). Columbus.

1937   Indian Place-Names in Alabama. *Louisiana State University Studies* 29. Baton Rouge: Louisiana State University Press. (Revised and reprinted with foreword, appendix, and index by James B. McMillan. University of Alabama Press, University, 1984.)

1938   Ten Alabama Place-Names. *American Speech* 13(1):79-80. Boston.

1949   Indian Stream Names in Georgia. *International Journal of American Linguistics* 15(2):128-132.

1950   Indian Stream Names in Georgia II. *International Journal of American Linguistics* 16(4):203-207.

Reckord, Holly
1983   Where Raven Stood: Cultural Resources of the Ahtna Region. *Cooperative Park Studies Unit, Occasional Paper* 35. Fairbanks.

Redden, James E.
1966   Walapai I: Phonology. *International Journal of American Linguistics* 32(1):1-16.

1966a   Walapai II: Morphology. *International Journal of American Linguistics* 32(2):141-163.

Reed, Erik K.
1943   The Southern Tewa Pueblos in the Historic Period. *El Palacio* 50(11):254-264, (12):276-288.

1949   Sources of Upper Rio Grande Pueblo Culture and Population. *El Palacio* 56(6):163-184.

Reed, Irene, Osahito Miyaoka, Steven Jacobson, Paschal Afcan, and Michael Krauss
1977   Yup'ik Eskimo Grammar. Fairbanks: Alaska Native Language Center.

Reichard, Gladys A.
1921   Literary Types and Dissemination of Myths. *Journal of American Folk-Lore* 34(133):269-307.

1925   Wiyot Grammar and Texts. *University of California Publications in American Archaeology and Ethnology* 22(1):1-215.

1928   Social Life of the Navajo Indians, with Some Attention to Minor Ceremonies. *Columbia University Contributions to Anthropology* 7. New York.

1933-1938 Coeur d'Alene. Pp. 517-707 in Pt. 3 of Handbook of American Indian Languages. Franz Boas, ed. Glückstadt-Hamburg-New York: J.J. Augustin.

1944 Prayer: The Compulsive Word. (*Monographs of the American Ethnological Society* 7). New York: J.J. Augustin. (Reprinted: University of Washington Press, Seattle, 1966.)

1944a Individualism and Mythological Style. *Journal of American Folklore* 57(223):16-25.

1945 Linguistic Diversity among the Navaho Indians. *International Journal of American Linguistics* 11(3):156-168.

1945a Composition and Symbolism of Coeur d'Alene Verb-Stems. *International Journal of American Linguistics* 11(1):47-63.

1947 An Analysis of Coeur d'Alene Indian Myths. *Memoirs of the American Folklore Society* 41. Philadelphia.

1950 Navaho Religion: A Study of Symbolism. 2 vols. (*Bollingen Series* 18). New York: Pantheon Books. (Reprinted: Princeton University Press, Princeton, N.J., 1970 and 1990.)

1960 A Comparison of Five Salish Languages: VI. *International Journal of American Linguistics* 26(1):50-61.

1960a A Comparison of Five Salish Languages. Baltimore: Waverly Press.

Reid, Dianne
1991 Cree Language Commission. *Algonquian and Iroquoian Linguistics* 16(3):16-17. Winnipeg, Man.

Reid, Hugo
1885 Hugo Reid's Account of the Indians of Los Angeles Co., California, with Notes by W.J. Hoffman. *Essex Institute Bulletin* 17:1-33.

Reid, Robie L.
1942 The Chinook Jargon and British Columbia. *British Columbia Historical Quarterly* 6(1):1-11.

Reinholtz, Charlotte
1994 Discontinuous Constituents in Swampy Cree. (Paper presented at the Twenty-sixth Algonquian Conference, Winnipeg.)

Reinholtz, Charlotte, and Kevin Russell
1994 Quantified NPs in Pronominal Argument Languages: Evidence from Swampy Cree. (Paper presented at the 25th Annual Meeting of the North-East Linguistics Society. Amherst, Mass.)

Renker, Ann M., and Greig W. Arnold
1988 Exploring the Role of Education in Cultural Resource Management: The Makah Cultural and Research Center Example. *Human Organization* 47(4):302-307.

Rensch, Calvin R.
1977 Classification of the Otomanguean Languages and the Position of Tlapanec. Pp. 53-108 in Two Studies in Middle American Comparative Linguistics by David Oltrogge and Calvin R. Rensch. (*Summer Institute of Linguistics Publications in Linguistics* 55). Arlington, Texas: Summer Institute of Linguistics and the University of Texas at Arlington.

Renville, Joseph
1839 Extracts from Genesis and the Psalms, with the Third Chapter of Proverbs, and the Third Chapter of Daniel, in the Dacota Language. Thomas S. Williamson, ed. Cincinnati: Kendall and Henry for the American Board of Commissioners for Foreign Missions.

Reyburn, William D.
1954 Cherokee Verb Morphology III. *International Journal of American Linguistics* 20(1):44-64.

Rezanov, Nikolai Petrovich
[1805] Slovar' Unalashkinskago, Kad'iakskago, Kinaiskago, Koliuzhskago, Ugaliakmutskago i Chugatskago Yazykov [Dictionary of the Eastern Aleut, Koniag Pacific Eskimo, Tanaina, Tlingit, Eyak, and Chugach Pacific Eskimo Languages]. (Manuscript 118, 61 pp., Fond Adelunga, Academy of Sciences, St. Petersburg; Copy in the Alaska Native Language Center, University of Alaska, Fairbanks.)

Rhodes, Richard A.
1977 French Cree—A Case of Borrowing. Pp. 6-25 in Actes du Huitième Congrès des Algonquinistes. William Cowan, ed. Ottawa: Carleton University.

1979 Some Aspects of Ojibwa Discourse. Pp. 102-117 in *Papers of the Tenth Algonquian Conference, 1978*. William Cowan, ed. Ottawa: Carleton University.

1982 Algonquian Trade Languages. Pp. 1-10 in Papers of the Thirteenth Algonquian Conference. William Cowan, ed. Ottawa: Carleton University.

1985 Eastern Ojibwa-Chippewa-Ottawa Dictionary. *Trends in Linguistics. Documentation* 3. Berlin, New York, Amsterdam: Mouton.

1986 Métchif - A Second Look. Pp. 287-296 in Papers of the Seventeenth Algonquian Conference. W. Cowan, ed. Ottawa: Carleton University.

1990 On the Classification of Central Algonquian. (Typescript in Rhodes's possession.)

Ricciardelli, Catherine H.
1966 Kinship Systems of the Oneida Indians. (Unpublished Ph.D. Dissertation in Anthropology, University of Pennsylvania, Philadelphia.)

Rice, Julian
1992 Deer Woman and Elk Men: The Lakota Narratives of Ella Deloria. Albuquerque: University of New Mexico Press.

1992a Narrative Styles in *Dakota Texts*. Pp. 276-292 in On the Translation of Native American Literatures. Brian Swann, ed. Washington: Smithsonian Institution Press.

1993   Ella Deloria's Iron Hawk. Albuquerque: University of New Mexico Press.

Rice, Keren Dichter
1977   A Preliminary Grammar of Fort Good Hope Slave (Hare). Ottawa: Department of Indian Affairs and Northern Development.

1980   Hare Dictionary. Toronto: Northern Social Research Division, Department of Indian and Northern Affairs.

1987   Metrical Structure in a Tone Language: The Foot in Slave (Athapaskan). Pp. 239-252 in CLS 23: Papers from the 23rd Annual Regional Meeting of the Chicago Linguistic Society. Pt. 2. Parasession on Autosegmental and Metrical Phonology. Anna Bosch, Barbara Need, and Eric Schiller, eds. Chicago: Chicago Linguistic Society.

1989   A Grammar of Slave. *Mouton Grammar Library* 5. Berlin and New York: Mouton de Gruyter.

1991   Intransitives in Slave (Northern Athapaskan): Arguments for Unaccusatives. *International Journal of American Linguistics* 57(1):51-69.

Richardson, John
1851   Arctic Searching Expedition: A Journal of a Boat-Voyage through Rupert's Land and the Arctic Sea... 2 vols. London: Longman, Brown, Green, and Longmans.

Ridley, William
1881   A Selection of Prayers Translated From the Book of Common Prayer in the Giatikshan Language for Use at the Public Services. Victoria, B.C.

Riggs, Stephen R.
1852   Grammar and Dictionary of the Dakota Language. *Smithsonian Contributions to Knowledge* 4. Washington.

1890   A Dakota-English Dictionary. James Owen Dorsey, ed. *Contributions to North American Ethnology* 7. Washington: U.S. Geographical and Geological Survey of the Rocky Mountain Region.

1893   Dakota Grammar, Texts, and Ethnography. James Owen Dorsey, ed. *Contributions to North American Ethnology* 9. Washington: U.S. Geographical and Geological Survey of the Rocky Mountain Region.

Rigsby, Bruce J.
1965   Continuity and Change in Sahaptian Vowel Systems. *International Journal of American Linguistics* 31(4):306-322.

1965a   Linguistic Relations in the Southern Plateau. (Unpublished Ph.D. Dissertation in Anthropology, University of Oregon, Salem.)

1966   On Cayuse-Molala Relatability. *International Journal of American Linguistics* 32(4):369-378.

1969   The Waiilatpuan Problem: More on Cayuse-Molala Relatability. *Northwest Anthropological Research Notes* 3(1):68-146. Moscow, Idaho.

1970   A Note on Gitksan Speech-Play. *International Journal of American Linguistics* 36(3):212-215.

1972   [Review of] Nez Perce Grammar, by Haruo Aoki. *Language: Journal of the Linguistic Society of America* 48(3):737-742.

1978   Coyote and the Dogs (Sahaptin). Pp. 21-25 in Coyote Stories. William Bright, ed. *International Journal of American Linguistics. Native American Texts Series Monograph* 1. Chicago: The University of Chicago Press.

1981   Some Linguistic Insights into Recent Tsimshian Prehistory. (Typescript in Rigsby's possession.)

1989   A Later View of Gitksan Syntax. Pp. 245-260 in General and Amerindian Ethnolinguistics: In Remembrance of Stanley Newman. Mary Ritchie Key and Henry M. Hoenigswald, eds. Berlin and New York: Mouton de Gruyter.

Rigsby, Bruce J., and John Ingram
1990   Obstruent Voicing and Glottalic Obstruents in Gitksan. *International Journal of American Linguistics* 56(2): 251-263.

Rigsby, Bruce J., and James Kari
1987   Gitksan and Wet'suwet'en Linguistic Relations. (Report on File at the Office of the Gitksan Wet'suwet'en Hereditary Chiefs, Hazelton, B.C.)

Rigsby, Bruce J., and Michael Silverstein
1969   Nez Perce Vowels and Proto-Sahaptian Vowel Harmony. *Language: Journal of the Linguistic Society of America* 45(1):45-59.

Rinaldini, Benito
1743   Arte de la lengua Tepeguana, con vocabulario, confesionario y catechismo, en que se explican los mysterios de nuestra santa fè catholica, mandamientos de la Ley de Dios, y nuestra Santa Madre Iglesia. Mexico City: Viuda de J. de Hogal.

Ringe, Donald A., Jr.
1992   On Calculating the Factor of Chance in Language Comparison. *Transactions of the American Philosophical Society* 82, Pt. 1. Philadelphia.

1993   A Reply to Professor Greenberg. *Proceedings of the American Philosophical Society* 137(1):91-109. Philadelphia.

Rink, Hinrich J.
1877   Danish Greenland: Its People and Its Products. Robert Brown, ed. London: Henry S. King.

Rink, Hinrich J., and William Thalbitzer
1911   The East Greenland Dialect According to the Annotations Made by the Danish East Coast Expedition to Kleinschmidt's Greenlandic Dictionary by H. Rink. Rev. and ed. by William Thalbitzer. *Meddelelser om Grønland* 39(4):203-223. Copenhagen.

Rischel, Jørgen
1974   Topics in West Greenlandic Phonology: Regularities Underlying the Phonetic Appearance of Word forms in a Polysynthetic Language. Copenhagen: Akademisk Forlag.

1975   Asymmetric Vowel Harmony in Greenlandic Fringe Dialects. Pp. 1-48 in *9th Annual Report of the Institute of Phonetics, University of Copenhagen.* Copenhagen.

Ritchie, William A.
1961   Iroquois Archaeology and Settlement Patterns. Pp. 25-38 in Symposium on Cherokee and Iroquois Culture. William N. Fenton and John Gulick, eds. *Bureau of American Ethnology Bulletin* 180. Washington.

Ritter, John T.
1976   Mayo Indian Language Noun Dictionary. Whitehorse, Yukon Terr.: Government Department of Education.

1976a   Kutchin Place Names, Evidence of Aboriginal Land Use. *Dene Rights* 3:111-135. Yellowknife, N.W. Terr.

1976b   Gwich'in (Loucheux) Athapaskan Noun Dictionary, Fort McPherson Dialect. Whitehorse, Yukon Terr.: The Queen's Printer for the Yukon.

Ritter, John T., Tommy McGinty, and Johnson Edwards
1977   The Selkirk Indian Language Noun Dictionary (Northern Tutchone Athapaskan). Whitehorse, Yukon Terr.: Yukon Native Languages Project, Council for Yukon Indians.

Ritzenthaler, Robert E.
1945   The Acquisition of Surnames by the Chippewa Indians. *American Anthropologist*, n.s. 47(1):175-177.

1953   The Potawatomi Indians of Wisconsin. *Bulletin of the Public Museum of the City of Milwaukee* 19(3):105-174. Milwaukee.

Ritzenthaler, Robert E., and Frederick A. Peterson
1954   Courtship Whistling of the Mexican Kickapoo Indians. *American Anthropologist*, n.s. 56(6, Pt. 1):1088-1089.

1956   The Mexican Kickapoo Indians. *Milwaukee Public Museum Publications in Anthropology* 2. Milwaukee. (Reprinted: Greenwood Press, Westport, Conn., 1970.)

Rivers, Betty, and Terry L. Jones
1993   Walking Along Deer Trails: A Contribution to Salinan Ethnogeography Based on the Field Notes of John Peabody Harrington. *Journal of California and Great Basin Anthropology* 15(2):146-175. Banning, Calif.

Robbe, Pierre
1981   Les noms de personne chez les Ammassalimiut. *Études/Inuit/Studies* 5(1):45-82.

Roberts, Helen H.
1933   Form in Primitive Music. New York: Norton.

Roberts, Helen H., and Diamond Jenness
1925   Eskimo Songs: Songs of the Copper Eskimos. *Canadian Arctic Expedition, 1913-1918, Report* 14. Ottawa: F.A. Acland.

Robertson, Ann Eliza W., and Others
1887-1891 Pu pucase momet pu hesayecv Cesvs Klist en Testement Mucvsat. New York: American Bible Society.

Robinett, Florence M.
1954   Hidatsa Grammar. (Ph.D. Dissertation in Linguistics, Indiana University, Bloomington. Photocopy: University Microfilms International, Ann Arbor, Mich., 1980.)

1955   Hidatsa III: Stems and Themes. *International Journal of American Linguistics* 21(3):210-216.

Robins, Robert H.
1958   The Yurok Language: Grammar, Texts, Lexicon. *University of California Publications in Linguistics* 15. Berkeley.

1962   The Third Person Pronominal Prefix in Yurok. *International Journal of American Linguistics* 28(1):14-18.

1966   Word Classes in Yurok. *Lingua* 17(1-2):210-229.

1987   Duponceau and Early Nineteenth Century Linguistics. Pp. 435-446 in Papers in the History of Linguistics. (*Proceedings of the Third International Conference on the History of the Language Sciences, Princeton, 19-23 August 1984*). Hans Aarsleff, Louis G. Kelly, and Hans-Josef Niederehe, eds. Amsterdam and Philadelphia: John Benjamins.

Robins, Robert H., and Eugenius M. Uhlenbeck, eds.
1991   Endangered Languages. Published with the authority of the Permanent International Committee of Linguists (CIPL). Oxford/New York: Berg; St Martin's Press.

Robinson, Doane
1910   Young Man Afraid of His Horses. P. 1001 in Pt. 2 of Handbook of American Indians North of Mexico. Frederick W. Hodge, ed. *Bureau of American Ethnology Bulletin* 30. Washington. (Reprinted: Rowman and Littlefield, New York, 1971.)

Robinson, Harry
1989   Write in on Your Heart: The Epic World of an Okanagan Storyteller. Wendy Wickwire, ed. and comp. Vancouver, B.C.: Talonbooks/Theytus.

Robinson, Lila Wistrand, and James Armagost
1990   Comanche Dictionary and Grammar. *Summer Institute of Linguistics and the University of Texas at Arlington Publications in Linguistics* 92. Dallas: Summer Institute of Linguistics.

Robinson, Percy
1945   Some of Cartier's Place-Names, 1535-1536. *The Canadian Historical Review* 26(4):401-405. Toronto.

Roe, Michael, ed.
1967   The Journals and Letters of the Captain Charles Bishop on the North-West Coast of America, in the Pacific and in New South Wales, 1794-1799. (*Hakluyt Society Publications*, 2d ser., Vol. 131). Cambridge: Cambridge University Press.

Rogel, Juan
1861   Rogel's Account of the Florida Mission. *Historical Magazine*, 1st ser. 5:327-330.

Rogers, Edward S., and Jean H. Rogers
1963   The Individual in Mistassini Society from Birth to Death. Contributions to Anthropology 1960, Pt. II. *National Museum of Canada, Bulletin 190, Anthropological Series* 60:14-36. Ottawa.

Rogers, Edward S., and Mary Black Rogers
1978   Method for Reconstructing Patterns of Change: Surname Adoption by the Weagamow Ojibwa, 1870-1950. *Ethnohistory* 25(4):319-345.

Rogers, Jean H.
1960   Notes on Mistassini Phonemics and Morphology. *National Museum of Canada. Bulletin 167, Anthropological Series 48, Contributions to Anthropology [for] 1958*:90-113. Ottawa.

_____
1964   Survey of Round Lake Ojibwa Phonology and Morphology. *National Museum of Canada Bulletin. Contributions of Anthropology* 194:94-154. Ottawa.

Rogers, Richard A.
1985   Glacial Geography and Native North American Languages. *Quaternary Research* 23(1):130-137.

_____
1985a   Wisconsin Glaciation and the Dispersal of Native Ethnic Groups in North America. Pp. 105-113 in Woman, Poet, Scientist: Essays in New World Anthropology Honoring Dr. Emma Louise Davis. Thomas C. Blackburn, ed. *Ballena Press Anthropological Papers* 29. Los Altos, Calif.: Ballena Press/Great Basin Foundation.

_____
1986   Language, Human Subspeciation and Ice Age Barriers in Northern Siberia. *Canadian Journal of Anthropology* 5:11-22.

_____
1987   [Comment on] Language in the Americas, by Joseph H. Greenberg. *Current Anthropology* 28(5):662-663.

Rohner, Ronald P.
1967   The People of Gilford: A Contemporary Kwakiutl Village. *National Museum of Canada Bulletin* 225, *Anthropological Series* 83. Ottawa.

Romney, A. Kimball
1957   The Genetic Model and Uto-Aztecan Time Perspective. *Davidson Journal of Anthropology* 3(2):35-41.

Rood, David S.
1965-1969 [Linguistic Fieldnotes on Wichita.] (Unpublished manuscripts in Rood's possession.)

_____
1971   Wichita: An Unusual Phonology System. *Colorado University Research in Linguistics* 1:R1-R24. Boulder. (Mimeograph.)

_____
886   1971a   Agent and Object in Wichita. *Lingua* 28(1/2):100-107.

_____
1973   Aspects of Subordination in Lakhota and Wichita. Pp. 71-88 in You Take the High Node and I'll Take the Low Node: Papers from the Comparative Syntax Festival [...] 12 April 1973. Claudia Corum, T. Cedric Smith-Stark, and Ann Weiser, eds. Chicago: Chicago Linguistic Society.

_____
1973a   Swadesh's Keres-Caddo Comparison. *International Journal of American Linguistics* 39(3):189-190.

_____
1975   Implications of Wichita Phonology. *Language* 51(2):315-337.

_____
1975a   Wichita Verb Structure: Inflectional Categories. Pp. 121-134 in Studies in Southeastern Indian Languages. James M. Crawford, ed. Athens: University of Georgia Press.

_____
1976   Wichita Grammar. New York: Garland Publishing. (Originally issued as: Wichita Grammar: a Generative Semantic Sketch. Ph.D. Dissertation in Linguistics, University of California, Berkeley, 1969.)

_____
1977   Wichita Texts. Pp. 91-128 in Caddoan Texts, by Douglas R. Parks. *International Journal of American Linguistics. Native American Texts Series* 2(1). Chicago: The University of Chicago Press.

_____
1978   Siouan Linguistics: An Assessment. *Newsletter of Siouan and Caddoan Linguistics* (August):1-16.

_____
1979   Siouan. Pp. 236-298 in The Languages of Native America: Historical and Comparative Assessment. Lyle Campbell and Marianne Mithun, eds. Austin and London: University of Texas Press.

_____
1981   Wichita and Syntactic Structural Typology. Pp. 365-376 in 1980 Mid-American Linguistics Conference Papers. Michael M.T. Henderson, ed. Lawrence, Kans.: Department of Linguistics, University of Kansas.

_____
1986   "To Be" in Wichita. In Festschrift for Margaret Langdon. Leanne Hinton and Pamela Munro, eds. Berkeley: University of California Press. (In press.)

_____
1989   Wichita: Partially Configurational? (Paper presented at the Conference on Non-standard Case and Argument Structure, LSA Summer Institute, Tucson, July 6-8, 1989.)

_____
1989a   Code Switching in a Wichita Text. Pp. 101-113 in Papers from the Twenty-third Annual Mid-America Linguistics Conference, 1988. John A. Dunn, comp. Norman: Department of Modern Languages, Literatures, and Linguistics, University of Oklahoma.

Rooth, Anna B.
1957   The Creation Myths of the North American Indians. *Anthropos* 52(3-4):497-508. (Reprinted: Pp. 166-181 in Sacred Narrative: Readings in the Theory of Myth. Alan Dundes, ed. University of California Press, Berkeley, 1984.)

Rose, Suzanne M.
1981   Kyuquot Grammar. (Unpublished Ph.D. Dissertation in Linguistics, University of Victoria, Victoria, B.C.)

Rosen, Carol
1990   Rethinking Southern Tiwa: The Geometry of a Triple-Agreement Language. *Language: Journal of the Linguistic Society of America* 66(4):669-713.

Rosman, Abraham, and Paula G. Rubel
1971   Feasting with Mine Enemy: Rank and Exchange Among North-west Coast Societies. New York: Columbia University Press.

———
1972   The Potlatch: A Structural Analysis. *American Anthropologist* 74(3):658-671.

Ross, Alexander
1849   Adventures of the First Settlers on the Oregon or Columbia River: Being a Narrative of the Expedition Fitted Out by John Jacob Astor, to Establish the "Pacific Fur Company", with an Account of Some Indian Tribes on the Coast of the Pacific. London: Smith, Elder. (Reprinted: Citadel Press, New York, 1969.)

Ross, Bernard R., William L. Hardisty, and Strachan Jones
1872   Notes on the Tinneh or Chepewyan Indians of British and Russian America. Pp. 303-327 in *Annual Report of the Smithsonian Institution for the Year 1866.* Washington.

Ross, Philip E.
1991   Hard Words. *Scientific American* 264(4):138-147.

Roth, Christopher F.
1992   Towards an Early Social History of Chinook Jargon. (Unpublished M.A. Thesis in the Social Sciences, The University of Chicago.)

Rothenberg, Jerome
1992   "We Explain Nothing, We Believe Nothing": American Indian Poetry and the Problematics of Translation. Pp. 64-79 in On the Translation of Native American Literatures. Brian Swann, ed. Washington: Smithsonian Institution Press.

Rubt͡sova, Ekaterina Semenovna
1954   Materialy po i͡azyku i fol´kloru ėskimosov (Chaplinskiĭ dialekt). [Materials on the Language and Folklore of the Eskimos (Chaplino Dialect)]. Pt. 1. Moscow-Leningrad: Izdatel´stvo Akademii Nauk SSSR, Institut I͡Azykoznanii͡a.

———
1971   Ėskimossko-russkiĭ slovar´. [Eskimo-Russian Dictionary]. G.A. Menovshchikov, ed. Moscow: Izdatel´stvo "Sovetskai͡a Ent͡siklopedii͡a."

Rude, Noel
1987   Some Klamath-Sahaptian Grammatical Correspondences. *Kansas Working Papers in Linguistics* 12(1): 189-190. Lawrence.

———
1991   On the Origin of the Nez Perce Ergative NP Suffix. *International Journal of American Linguistics* 57(1):24-50.

———
1991a   Verbs to Promotional Suffixes in Sahaptian and Klamath. Pp. 185-199 in Approaches to Grammaticalization. Elizabeth Closs Traugott and Bernd Heine, eds. (*Typological Studies in Language* 19, Pt. 2). Amsterdam/Philadelphia: J. Benjamins.

———
1992   Dative Shifting in Sahaptin. *International Journal of American Linguistics* 58(3):316-320.

———
1994   Direct, Inverse and Passive in Northwest Sahaptin. Pp. 101-119 in Voice and Inversion. T. Givón, ed. (*Typological Studies in Language* 28). Amsterdam/Philadelphia: J. Benjamins.

Rudes, Blair A.
1974   Sound Changes Separating Siouan-Yuchi from Iroquois-Caddoan. *International Journal of American Linguistics* 40(2):117-119.

———
1976   Historical Phonology and the Development of the Tuscarosa Sound System. (Unpublished Ph.D. Dissertation in Linguistics, State University of New York at Buffalo, Buffalo.)

———
1981   Cowinchahawkon/Akawęč̓á·ka·ʔ: The Meherrin in the Nineteenth Century. *Algonquian and Iroquoian Linguistics* 6(3):32-34. Winnipeg.

———
1981a   A Sketch of the Nottoway Language from a Historical-Comparative Perspective. *International Journal of American Linguistics* 47(1):27-49.

———
1982   The Number Vocabulary of Proto-Macro-Siouan. (Paper presented at the 1982 American Anthropological Association Annual Meetings, Washington, D.C.)

———
1987   A Comparison of the Yuchi, Catawban, and Siouan Languages. (Paper presented at the Fourteenth Kentucky Foreign Language Conference in Lexington, Ky., 1987.)

———
1987a   Tuscarora Roots, Stems, and Particles: Towards a Dictionary of Tuscarora. *Algonquian and Iroquoian Linguistics, Memoir* 3. Winnipeg.

———
1995   Iroquoian Vowels. *Anthropological Linguistics* 37(1): 16-69.

Rudes, Blair A., and Dorothy Crouse
1987   The Tuscarora Legacy of J.N.B. Hewitt: Materials for the Study of Tuscarora Language and Culture. 2 vols. *Canadian Museum of Civilization. Mercury Series. Ethnology Service Paper* 108. Ottawa.

Ruecking, Frederick, Jr.
1953   The Economic System of the Coahuiltecan Indians of Southern Texas and Northern Mexico. *Texas Journal of Science* 5(4):480-497. San Marcos.

1954   Bands and Band-clusters of the Coahuiltecan Indians. *University of Texas. Student Papers in Anthropology* 1(2):1-24. Austin.

1954a   Ceremonies of the Coahuiltecan Indians of Northeastern Mexico. *Texas Journal of Science* 6(3):330-339. San Marcos.

1955   The Social Organization of the Coahuiltecan Indians of Southern Texas and Northeastern Mexico. *Texas Journal of Science* 7(4):357-388. Austin.

Ruggles, Richard I.
1991   A Country So Interesting: The Hudson's Bay Company and Two Centuries of Mapping, 1670-1870. Montreal and Kingston: McGill-Queen's University Press.

Ruhlen, Merritt
1987   Voices from the Past. *Natural History* 3(March):6-10.

1989   Phylogenetic Relations of Native American Languages. (Paper given at the Symposium on Prehistoric Mongoloid Dispersals, Sapporo, Japan, December 18-19, 1989.)

1991   A Guide to the World's Languages. Vol. 1: Classification (With a Postscript on Recent Developments). Stanford, Calif.: Stanford University Press. (First edition, 1987.)

Rundstrom, Robert A.
1991   Mapping, Postmodernism, Indigenous People and the Changing Direction of North American Cartography. *Cartographica* 28(2):1-12. Toronto.

1993   The Role of Ethics, Mapping, and the Meaning of Place in Relations Between Indians and Whites in the United States. *Cartographica* 30(1):21-28. Toronto.

Rushforth, Scott
1991   Uses of Bearlake and Mescalero (Athapaskan) Classificatory Verbs. *International Journal of American Linguistics* 57(2):251-266.

Rushforth, Scott, and Larry Gorbet
1989   Notes on Bearlake Athapaskan Relative Clauses. *International Journal of American Linguistics* 55(4):455-467.

Russell, Bertrand
1940   An Inquiry into Meaning and Truth. New York: W.W. Norton.

Russell, Frank
1908   The Pima Indians. Pp. 3-389 in *26th Annual Report of the Bureau of American Ethnology for 1904-1905.* Washington. (Reprinted with Introduction, Citation Sources, and Bibliography by Bernard L. Fontana. University of Arizona Press Tucson, 1975.)

Russell, Kevin
1991   Obviation as Discourse Structure in Swampy Cree *âcimowin.* Pp. 320-335 in Papers of the Twenty-second Algonquian Conference. William Cowan, ed. Ottawa: Carleton University.

1992   Palatalization and Epenthesis in Plains Cree. Pp. 269-284 in Proceedings of the 1992 Annual Conference of the Canadian Linguistic Association. C. Dyck, J. Gomescki, and T. William, eds. Toronto: Working Papers in Linguistics.

Rustige, Rona, coll.
1988   Tyendinaga Tales. Kingston, Ont.: McGill-Queen's University Press.

Ruttenber, E.M.
1906   Indian Geographical Names. *Proceedings of the New York State Historical Association* 6 (Supplement). Albany.

Rydjord, John
1968   Indian Place Names: Their Origin, Evolution, and Meanings, Collected in Kansas from the Siouan, Algonquian, Shoshonean, Caddoan, Iroquoian, and Other Tongues. Norman: University of Oklahoma Press.

Rye, William B., ed.
1851   The Discovery and Conquest of Terra Florida, by Don Ferdinando de Soto, and Six Hundred Spaniards, his Followers; written by a Gentleman of Elvas. Translated out of Portuguese by Richard Hakluyt [1611]. London: Printed for the Hakluyt Society.

Sagard-Théodat, Gabriel
1632   Dictionnaire de la langue huronne. Paris: Denys Moreau.

1865   Le grand voyage du pays des Hurons, situé en l'Amerique vers la Mer douce, ès derniers confins de la Nouvelle France dite Canada. Avec un Dictionnaire de la langue huronne. Paris: Librairie Tross.

St. Clair, Harry Hull, and Leo J. Frachtenberg
1909   Traditions of the Coos Indians of Oregon. *Journal of American Folk-Lore* 22(83):25-41.

St. Onge, Louis Napoléon
1872   Alphabet yakama contenant les prières, les cantiques et le catéchisme dans la même langue. Montréal: Imprimé à la Providence.

Saladin d'Anglure, Bernard
1970   Nom et parenté chez les Esquimaux Tarramiut de Nouveau-Québec (Canada). Pp. 1013-1039 in Vol. 2 of Échanges et communications: mélanges offerts à Claude Lévi-Strauss à l'occasion de son 60ème anniversaire. 2 vols. Jean Pouillon and Pierre Maranda, eds. The Hague and Paris: Mouton.

Salinas, Martín
1990   Indians of the Rio Grande Delta: Their Role in the History of Southern Texas and Northeastern Mexico. Austin: University of Texas Press.

Salmon, Vivian
1992   Thomas Harriot (1560-1621) and the English Origins of Algonkian Linguistics. *Historiographia Linguistica* 19(1):25-56. Amsterdam.

Salzmann, Zdeněk
1951   Contrastive Field Experience with Language and Values of the Arapaho. *International Journal of American Linguistics* 17(2):98-101.

1960   Two Brief Contributions Toward Arapaho Linguistic History. *Anthropological Linguistics* 2(7):39-48.

1967 Arapaho VII: Verb. *International Journal of American Linguistics* 33(3):209-223.

1969 Salvage Phonology of Gros Ventre (Atsina). *International Journal of American Linguistics* 35(4):307-314.

_____, comp.
1983 Dictionary of Contemporary Arapaho Usage. *Arapaho Language and Culture Instructional Materials Series* 4. William J. C'Hair, gen. ed. Wind River Reservation, Wyo.

Samarin, William J.
1986 Chinook Jargon and Pidgin Historiography. *Canadian Journal of Anthropology* 5(1):23-34. Toronto.

1988 Jargonization Before Chinook Jargon. *Northwest Anthopological Research Notes* 22(2):219-258.

1992 Arctic Origin and Domestic Development of Chinook Jargon. (Paper presented at the 9th International Tromsí Symposium on Language, Arctic Pidgins; Tromsí, Norway, 4-6 June 1992. Copy in Michael Silverstein's possession.)

Sampson, Martin J.
1938 The Swinomish Totem Pole; Tribal Legends. (Told to Rosalie Whitney.) Bellingham, Wash.: Union Printing Company.

Santa Ana, Benito Fernandez de
1961 Descripción de las misiones del Colegio de la Santa Cruz, en el Rio de San Antonio, año de 1740. Pp. 303-312 in Documentos para la historia eclesiástica y civil de la provincia de Texas o Nuevas Philipinas, 1720-1779. José Porrúa Turanzas, ed. *Colección chimalistac de libros y documentos acerca de la Nueva España* 12. Madrid.

Sapir, Edward
1907 Notes on the Takelma Indians of Southwestern Oregon. *American Anthropologist*, n.s. 9(2):251-275.

1907a Preliminary Report on the Language and Mythology of the Upper Chinook. *American Anthropologist*, n.s. 9(3):533-544.

1909 Takelma Texts. *University of Pennsylvania. University Museum. Anthropological Publications* 2(1):-267. Philadelphia.

1909a Wishram Texts; Together with Wasco Tales and Myths, collected by Jeremiah Curtin and edited by Edward Sapir. *Publications of the American Ethnological Society* 2. Leyden. (Reprinted: AMS Press, New York, 1974.)

1910 Yana Texts; Together with Yana Myths. Roland B. Dixon, coll. *University of California Publications in American Archaeology and Ethnology* 9(1):1-235. Berkeley.

1910a Song Recitative in Paiute Mythology. *Journal of American Folk-Lore* 23(90):455-472. (Reprinted in part: Pp. 463-467 in Selected Writings of Edward Sapir in Language, Culture and Personality. David G. Mandelbaum, ed. University of California Press, Berkeley and Los Angeles, 1949, 1963.)

1911 Diminutive and Augmentative Consonantism in Wishram. Pp. 638-645 in Pt. 1 of Handbook of American Indian Languages. Franz Boas, ed. *Bureau of American Ethnology Bulletin* 40. Washington.

1911a An Anthropological Survey of Canada. *Science* 34(884):789-793.

1912 Language and Environment. *American Anthropologist*, n.s. 14(2):226-242. (Reprinted: Pp. 89-103 in Selected Writings of Edward Sapir in Language, Culture and Personality. David G. Mandelbaum, ed. University of California Press, Berkeley and Los Angeles, 1949, 1963.)

1913 A Tutelo Vocabulary. *American Anthropologist*, n.s. 15(2):295-297.

1913a Wiyot and Yurok, Algonkin Languages of California. *American Anthropologist*, n.s. 15(4):617-646.

1913-1914 Southern Paiute and Nahuatl, a Study in Uto-Aztekan. 2 Pts. *Journal de la Société des Américanistes de Paris*, n.s. 10(2):379-425; 11(2):443-488. Paris. (Pt. 2 also publ. in: *American Anthropologist* 17(1):98-120, (2):306-328.)

1914 Notes on Chasta Costa Phonology and Morphology. *University of Pennsylvania. University Museum. Anthropological Publications* 2(2):271-340. Philadelphia.

1915 Algonkin Languages of California: A Reply. *American Anthropologist*, n.s. 17(1):188-194.

1915a Epilogue [to Sapir-Michelson Controversy]. *American Anthropologist*, n.s. 17(1):198.

1915b The Na-Dene Languages: A Preliminary Report. *American Anthropologist*, n.s. 17(4):534-558.

1915c Abnormal Types of Speech in Nootka. *Canada. Department of Mines. Geological Survey. Memoir* 62; *Anthropological Series* 5. Ottawa. (Reprinted: Pp. 179-196 in Selected Writings of Edward Sapir in Language, Culture and Personality. David G. Mandelbaum, ed. University of California Press, Berkeley and Los Angeles, 1949, 1963.)

1915d A Sketch of the Social Organization of the Nass River Indians. *Canada. Department of Mines. Geological Survey, Museum Bulletin* 19. *Anthropogical Series* 7. Ottawa.

1915e   Noun Reduplication in Comox, a Salish Language of Vancouver Island. *Canada. Department of Mines. Geological Survey, Memoir* 63. *Anthropological Series* 6. Ottawa.

1916   Time Perspective in Aboriginal American Culture: A Study in Method. *Canada. Department of Mines. Geological Survey, Memoir* 90, *Anthropogical Series* 13. Ottawa. (Reprinted: Pp. 389-462 in Selected Writings of Edward Sapir in Language, Culture and Personality. David G. Mandelbaum, ed. University of California Press, Berkeley and Los Angeles, 1949, 1963.)

1917   The Position of Yana in the Hokan Stock. *University of California Publications in American Archaeology and Ethnology* 13(1):1-34. Berkeley.

1917a   The Status of Washo. *American Anthropologist*, n.s. 19(3):449-450.

1917b   The Na-Dene Languages, A Preliminary Report. *American Anthropologist*, n.s. 17(3):534-558.

1918   Yana Terms of Relationship. *University of California Publications in American Archaeology and Ethnology* 13(4):153-173. Berkeley.

1920   The Hokan and Coahuiltecan Languages. *International Journal of American Linguistics* 1(4):280-290.

1920a   A Note on the First Person Plural in Chimariko. *International Journal of American Linguistics* 1(4):291-294.

1920b   Nass River Terms of Relationship. *American Anthropologist*, n.s. 22(3):261-271.

1921   A Supplementary Note on Salinan and Washo. *International Journal of American Linguistics* 2(1-2):68-72.

1921a   A Characteristic Penutian Form of Stem. *International Journal of American Linguistics* 2(1-2):58-67.

1921b   A Bird's-Eye View of American Languages North of Mexico. *Science*, n.s. 54(1400):408.

1921c   Language: An Introduction to the Study of Speech. New York: Harcourt, Brace. (Reprinted in 1949, 1957.)

1921-1923   The Phonetics of Haida. *International Journal of American Linguistics* 2(3-4):143-158.

1922   The Takelma Language of Southwestern Oregon. Pp. 1-296 in Pt. 2 of Handbook of American Indian Languages. Franz Boas, ed. *Bureau of American Ethnology Bulletin* 40. Washington.

1922a   The Fundamental Elements of Northern Yana. *University of California Publications in American Archaeology and Ethnology* 13(6):215-234. Berkeley.

1923   A Type of Athabaskan Relative. *International Journal of American Linguistics* 2(3-4):136-142.

1923a   The Algonkin Affinity of Yurok and Wiyot Kinship Terms. *Journal de la Société des Américanistes de Paris*, n.s. 15:36-74. Paris.

1923b   Text Analyses of Three Yana Dialects. Pp. 261-294 in Phoebe Apperson Hearst Memorial Volume on the Twentieth Anniversary of the Organization of the Department and Museum of Anthropology of the University of California, September 10, 1901. A.L. Kroeber, ed. *University of California Publications in American Archaeology and Ethnology* 20. Berkeley.

1924   Personal Names Among the Sarcee Indians. *American Anthropologist*, n.s. 26(1):108-119.

1924a   The Rival Whalers, A Nitinat Story. *International Journal of American Linguistics* 3(1):76-102.

1925   The Hokan Affinity of Subtiaba in Nicaragua. *American Anthropologist*, n.s. 27(3):402-435, (4):491-527.

1925a   Sound Patterns in Language. *Language: Journal of the Linguistic Society of America* 1(2):37-51.

1929   Central and North American Languages. Pp. 138-141 in Vol. 5 of Encyclopaedia Britannica. 14th ed. London and New York: Encyclopaedia Britannica Company. (Reprinted: Pp. 169-178 in Selected Writings of Edward Sapir in Language, Culture, and Personality. David G. Mandelbaum, ed., University of California Press, Berkeley and Los Angeles, 1949, 1963; also, Johnson Reprint Corporation, New York, 1968.)

1929a   Male and Female Forms of Speech in Yana. Pp. 79-85 in Donum Natalicium Schrijnen. St. W.J. Teeuwen, ed. Nijmegen-Utrecht: Uitgeverij Dekker & van de Vegt. (Reprinted: Pp. 335-341 in Vol. 5 of The Collected Works of Edward Sapir. William Bright, ed. Mouton de Gruyter, Berlin and New York, 1990.)

1929b   Nootka Baby Words. *International Journal of American Linguistics* 5(1):118-119.

1930-1931   The Southern Paiute Language. 3 Pts. Pt. 1: Southern Paiute, a Shoshonean Language. Pt. 2: Texts of the Kaibab Paiutes and Uintah Utes. Pt. 3: Southern Paiute Dictionary. *Proceedings of the American Academy of Arts and Sciences* 65(1):1-296, (2):297-535, (3):537-730.

1931   The Concept of Phonetic Law as Tested in Primitive Languages by Leonard Bloomfield. Pp. 297-306 in Methods in Social Science: A Casebook. Stuart A. Rice, ed. Chicago: University of Chicago Press. (Reprinted: Pp. 73-82 in Selected Writing of Edward Sapir in Language, Culture and Personality. David G. Mandelbaum, ed. University of California Press, Berkeley and Los Angeles, 1949, 1963; also, Johnson Reprint Corporation, New York, 1968.)

1932   Two Navaho Puns. *Language: Journal of the Linguistic Society of America* 8(3):217-219.

1933   The Psychological Reality of Phonemes. Pp. 46-60 in Selected Writings of Edward Sapir. David Mandelbaum, ed. Berkeley: University of California Press. (Reprinted from: La Réalité psychologique des phonèmes. *Journal de Psychologie Normale et Pathologique* 30:247-265, 1933.)

1936   Internal Linguistic Evidence Suggestive of the Northern Origin of the Navaho. *American Anthropologist*, n.s. 38(2):224-235. (Reprinted: Pp. 213-224 in Selected Writings of Edward Sapir in Language, Culture and Personality. David G. Mandelbaum, ed., University California Press, Berkeley and Los Angeles, 1949, 1963; also, Johnson Reprint Corporation, New York, 1968.)

1942   Navaho Texts; with Supplementary Texts by Harry Hoijer, ed. Iowa City: Linguistic Society of America, University of Iowa.

1949   Selected Writings of Edward Sapir in Language, Culture and Personality. David G. Mandelbaum, ed. Berkeley and Los Angeles: University of California Press. (Reprinted in 1963; also, Johnson Reprint Corporation, New York, 1968.)

1949a   Salish-Wakashan Comparisons. Pp. 171-173 in Indians of the Urban Northwest. Marian W. Smith, ed. *Columbia University Contributions to Anthropology* 36. New York.

1990   The Collected Works of Edward Sapir. Vol. 5: American Indian Languages 1. William Bright, ed. Berlin and New York: Mouton de Gruyter.

1990a   The Collected Works of Edward Sapir. Vol. 8: Takelma Texts and Grammar. Victor Golla, ed. New York and Berlin: Mouton de Gruyter.

Sapir, Edward, and Roland B. Dixon
1910   Yana Texts by Edward Sapir, Together with Yana Myths Collected by Roland B. Dixon. *University of California Publications in American Archaeology and Ethnology* 9(1):1-235.

Sapir, Edward, and Harry Hoijer
1942   Navaho Texts; by Edward Sapir. With Supplementary Texts by Harry Hoijer. Harry Hoijer, ed. Iowa City, Iowa: Linguistic Society of America.

1967   The Phonology and Morphology of the Navaho Language. *University of California Publications in Linguistics* 50. Berkeley.

Sapir, Edward, and Morris Swadesh
1939   Nootka Texts: Tales and Ethnological Narratives, with Grammatical Notes and Lexical Material. Philadelphia: University of Pennsylvania, Linguistic Society of America. (Reprinted: AMS Press, New York, 1978.)

1953   Coos-Takelma-Penutian Comparisons. *International Journal of American Linguistics* 19(2):132-137.

1955   Native Accounts of Nootka Ethnography. *Indiana University Research Center in Anthropology, Folklore, and Linguistics Publication* 1; *International Journal of American Linguistics* 21(4, pt. 2). (Reprinted: AMS Press, New York, 1978.)

1960   Yana Dictionary. Mary R. Haas, ed. *University of California Publications in Linguistics* 22. Berkeley.

Sard-Khom (Robert J. Jackson)
1906   The Story of the Sun: A Legend of the Chehalis Indians. *Washington Magazine* 1(3):178-186. Seattle, Wash.

Sauer, Martin
1802   An Account of a Geographical and Astronomical Expedition to the Northern Parts of Russia. London.

Saussure, Ferdinand de
1959   Course in General Linguistics. Charles Bally and Albert Sechehaye, eds. in collab. with Albert Reidlinger. Wade Baskin, trans. New York: Philosophical Library. (Original: Cours de linguistique générale. Paris, 1916.)

Sauvel, Katherine Siva, and Pamela Munro
1982   Chem'ivillu': Let's Speak Cahuilla. Banning and Los Angeles: Malki Museum Press and American Indian Studies Center, University of California, Los Angeles.

Sawyer, Jesse O., Jr.
1964   The Implications of Spanish /r/ and /rr/ in Wappo History. *Romance Philology* 18(2):165-177. Los Angeles.

1965   English-Wappo Vocabulary. *University of California Publications in Linguistics* 43. Berkeley.

1980   The Non-genetic Relationship of Wappo and Yuki. Pp. 209-219 in American Indian and Indoeuropean Studies: Papers in Honor of Madison S. Beeler. Kathryn Klar, Margaret Langdon, and Shirley Silver, eds. *Trends in Linguistics, Studies and Monographs* 16. The Hague: Mouton.

Sawyer, Jesse O., Jr., and Laura Fish Somersal
1977   Bear Woman and Her Children (Wappo). Pp. 105-113 in Northern California Texts. Victor Golla and Shirley Silver, eds. *International Journal of American Linguistics. Native American Texts Series* 2(2). Chicago: The University of Chicago Press.

Saxton, Dean
1982   Papago. Pp. 93-266 in Uto-Aztecan Grammatical Sketches. Ronald W. Langacker, ed. *Summer Institute of Linguistics, Publications in Linguistics* 56(3). Dallas: Summer Institute of Linguistics.

Saxton, Dean, and Lucille Saxton, comps.
1969   Dictionary: Papago & Pima to English, O'odham-Mil-gahn; English to Papago & Pima, Mil-gahn-O'odham. Tucson: University of Arizona Press. (Reprinted, 2d ed., rev. and expanded, 1983.)

Saxton, Dean, Lucille Saxton, and Susie Enos
1983   Dictionary: Papago/Pima-English, English-Papago/Pima: O'otham–Mil-gahn, Mil-gahn–O'otham. 2d ed. R.L. Cherry, ed. Tucson: University of Arizona Press.

Scancarelli, Janine
1992   Aspiration and Cherokee Orthographies. Pp. 135-152 in The Linguistics of Literacy. Pamela Downing, Susan D. Lima, and Michael Noonan, eds. (Typological Studies in Language 21). Philadelphia and Amsterdam: John Benjamins.

_____
1996   Cherokee Writing. Pp. 587-592 in The World's Writing Systems. Peter T. Daniels and William Bright, eds. New York [and] Oxford: Oxford University Press.

Schauber, Ellen
1979   The Syntax and Semantics of Questions in Navajo. New York and London: Garland Publishing.

Schenk, Sara M., and Edward W. Gifford
1952   Karok Ethnobotany. University of California Anthropological Records 13(6):377-392.

Schlichter, Alice
1978   Coyote and Badger (Wintu). Pp. 45-50 in Coyote Stories. William Bright, ed. International Journal of American Linguistics. Native American Texts Series Monograph 1. Chicago: University of Chicago Press.

Schmick, Johann Jacob see Masthay, Carl

Schmitt, Alfred
1951   Die Alaska-Schrift und ihre Schriftgeschichtliche Bedeutung. (Münstersche Forschungen 4). Marburg, [Germany]: Simons.

Schneider, Lucien
1967   Grammaire Esquimaude du Sous-Dialecte de l'Ungava. Québec: Ministère des Richesses Naturelles, Direction Générale du Nouveau-Québec.

_____
1970   Dictionnaire Esquimau-Français du Parler de l'Ungava et Contrées Limitrophes. Nouvelle édition augmentée. Travaux et Documents du Centre d'Études Nordiques 3. 2d ed. Québec: Les Presses de l'Université Laval.

_____
1970a   Dictionnaire Français-Esquimau du Parler de l'Ungava et Contrées Limitrophes. Travaux et Documents du Centre d'Études Nordiques 5. Québec: Les Presses de l'Université Laval.

_____
1985   Ulirnaisigutiit: An Inuktitut-English Dictionary of Northern Quebec, Labrador and Eastern Arctic Dialects (with an English-Inuktitut Index). Translated and transliterated by Dermot Roman F. Collis. Québec: Presses de l'Université Laval.

Schoenberg, Wilfred P.
1957   Jesuit Mission Presses in the Pacific Northwest: A History and Bibliography of Imprints, 1876-1899. Portland, Oreg.: Champoeg Press.

Schoolcraft, Henry Rowe
1845   Oneóta, or Characteristics of the Red Race of America. From Original Notes and Manuscripts. New York: Wiley and Putnam.

_____
1846   Report of Mr. Schoolcraft, to the Secretary of State, Transmitting the Census Returns in Relation to the Indians. [New York] Senate Document No. 24 (January 22, 1846). Albany.

_____
1847   Notes on the Iroquois; or Contributions to American History, Antiquities, and General Ethnology. Albany: Erastus H. Pease and Co.

_____
1851-1857 Historical and Statistical Information, Respecting the History, Condition and Prospects of the Indian Tribes of the United States; Collected and Prepared Under the Direction of the Bureau of Indian Affairs, Per Act of Congress of March 3d, 1847. 6 vols. Philadelphia: Lippincott, Grambo.

Schroeder, Albert H.
1963   Comment on Gunnerson's "Plateau Shoshonean Prehistory." American Antiquity 28(4):559-560.

Schuller, Rudolf, ed.
1925   La única gramática conocida de la lengua pame. Talleres Gráficos del Departamento Antropológico. Mexico City.

Schultz-Lorentzen, Christian W.
1927   Dictionary of the West Greenland Eskimo Language. Meddelelser om Grønland 69. Copenhagen. (Reprinted in 1967.)

_____
1945   A Grammar of the West Greenland Language. Annie I. Fausbøll, trans. Meddelelser om Grønland 129(3). Copenhagen.

Schultze, Augustus
1889   A Brief Grammar and Vocabulary of the Eskimo Language of North-western Alaska. Bethlehem, Pa.: Moravian Publishing Office.

_____
1894   Grammar and Vocabulary of the Eskimo Language of Northwestern Alaska, Kuskoquim District. Bethlehem, Pa.: Moravian Publishing Office.

Schwatka, Frederick
1899   In the Land of Cave and Cliff Dwellers. New ed. Boston: Educational Publishing.

Schweitzer, Marjorie M.
1985   Giving Them a Name: An Otoe-Missouria Ceremony. Moccasin Tracks (April):4-7.

Scott, Lalla
1966   Karnee: A Paiute Narrative. Annotated by Charles R. Craig. Reno: University of Nevada Press. (Reprinted in 1992.)

Scouler, John
1841   Observations on the Indigenous Tribes of the N.W. Coast of America. Journal of the Royal Geographical Society 11:215-251. London.

1905   Dr. John Scouler's Journal of a Voyage to N.W. America [1824]. F.G. Young, ed. *Oregon Historical Society Quarterly* 6(1):54-75, (2):159-205, (3):276-287.

Seaburg, William R.
1977   The Man Who Married a Grizzly Girl (Wailaki). Pp. 114-120 in Northern California Texts. Victor Golla and Shirley Silver, eds. *International Journal of American Linguistics. Native American Texts Series Monograph* 2(2). Chicago: The University of Chicago Press.

1977a   A Wailaki (Athapaskan) Text with Comparative Notes. *International Journal of American Linguistics* 43(4): 327-332.

1982   Guide to Pacific Northwest Native American Materials in the Melville Jacobs Collection and in Other Archival Collections in the University of Washington Libraries. *University of Washington Libraries Communications in Librarianship* 2. Seattle.

Sealock, Richard B., and Margaret S. Powell
1974   Place-Name Literature, United States and Canada, 1971-1974. *Names* 22(4):150-164.

1975   Place-Name Literature, United States and Canada, 1975. *Names* 23(4):296-299.

1979   Place-Name Literature, United States and Canada, 1979. *Names* 27(4):235-250.

Sealock, Richard B., and Pauline A. Seely
1948   Bibliography of Place-Name Literature—United States, Canada, Alaska, and Newfoundland. Chicago: American Library Association.

1967   Bibliography of Place-Name Literature—United States and Canada. 2d ed. Chicago: American Library Association.

Sealock, Richard B., Margaret M. Sealock, and Margaret S. Powell
1982   Bibliography of Place-Name Literature: United States and Canada. 3d ed. Chicago: American Library Association.

Seaman, P. David
1977   Hopi Linguistics: An Annotated Bibliography. *Anthropological Linguistics* 19(2):78-98.

Searle, John R.
1958   Proper Names. *Mind* 67:166-173.

1967   Proper Names and Discriptions. Pp. 487-491 in Vol. 6 of The Encyclopedia of Philosophy. Paul Edwards, ed. New York and London: The Macmillan Company and The Free Press.

1969   Speech Acts: An Essay in the Philosophy of Language. Cambridge: Cambridge University Press.

Sears, William H.
1964   The Southeastern United States. Pp. 259-287 in Prehistoric Man in the New World. Jesse D. Jennings and Edward Norbeck, eds. Chicago: University of Chicago Press.

Sebeok, Thomas A., ed.
1973   Linguistics in North America. *Current Trends in Linguistics* 10. 2 pts. The Hague and Paris: Mouton.

Seeber, Pauleena M.
1982   Eastern Algonquian Prehistory: Correlating Linguistics and Archaeology. Pp. 135-146 in Approaches to Algonquian Archaeology. Margaret G. Hanna and Brian Kooyman, eds. Calgary: University of Calgary Archaeological Association.

1986   Dialect Symbols in Aubery's Dictionary. Pp. 297-312 in Actes du Dix-Septième Congrès des Algonquinistes. William Cowan, ed. Ottawa: Carleton University.

Seely, Pauline A., and Richard B. Sealock
1955   Place-Name Literature, United States and Canada, 1952-1954. *Names* 3(2):102-116.

1958   Place-Name Literature, United States and Alaska, 1946-1951. *Names* 6(1):26-50.

1959   Place-Name Literature, United States, 1955-1959. *Names* 7(4):203-232.

1961   Place-Name Literature, Canada. *Names* 9(3):165-174.

1962   Place-Name Literature, United States, 1959-1961. *Names* 10(2):127-144.

1963   Place-Name Literature, United States and Canada, 1961-1962. *Names* 11(2):115-133.

1968   Place-Name Literature, United States, 1965-1967. *Names* 16(2):146-160.

1970   Place-Name Literature, United States, 1967-1969. *Names* 18(3):208-222.

1972   Place-Name Literature, United States and Canada, 1969-1971. *Names* 20(4):240-265.

Seiden, William
1963   Havasupai Phonology and Morphology. (Unpublished Ph.D. Dissertation in Linguistics, Indiana University, Bloomington.)

Seiler, Hansjakob
1967   Structure and Reconstruction in Some Uto-Aztecan Languages. *International Journal of American Linguistics* 33(2):135-147.

1970   Cahuilla Texts; With an Introduction. *Indiana University Language Science Monographs* 6. Bloomington.

1977   Cahuilla Grammar. Banning, Calif.: Malki Museum Press.

Seiler, Hansjakob, and Kojiri Hioki
1979   Cahuilla Dictionary. Banning, Calif.: Malki Museum Press.

Señan, José
1967   The Ventureño Confessionario of José Señan, O.F.M. [1815-1819]. Madison S. Beeler, ed. *University of California Publications in Linguistics* 47. Berkeley.

Service, Elman
1947   Recent Observations on Havasupai Land Tenure. *Southwestern Journal of Anthropology* 3(4):360-366.

Seton, Ernest Thompson
1918   Sign Talk: A Universal Signal Code, without Apparatus, for Use in the Army, Navy, Camping, Hunting, and Daily Life. The Gesture of the Cheyenne Indians [etc.]. Prepared with Assistance from General Hugh L. Scott, U.S.A. The French and German Equivalent Words Added by Lillian Delger Powers, M.D. Garden City, N.Y.: Doubleday, Page and Co.

Seton-Karr, Heywood W.
1887   Shores and Alps of Alaska. London: Law, Marston, Searle, and Rivington.

Shafer, Robert
1947   Penutian. *International Journal of American Linguistics* 13(4):205-219.

_____
1952   Notes on Penutian. *International Journal of American Linguistics* 18(4):211-216.

_____
1961   Tones in Wintun. *Anthropological Linguistics* 3(6):17-30.

Shaul, David L.
1985   Azteco-Tanoan ***-l/r-. *International Journal of American Linguistics* 51(4):584-586.

_____
1986   Linguistic Adaptation and the Great Basin. *American Antiquity* 51(2):415-416.

_____
1988   Esselen: Utian Onomastics. Pp. 693-704 in In Honor of Mary Haas: From the Haas Festival Conference on Native American Linguistics. William Shipley, ed. Berlin: Mouton de Gruyter.

_____
1990   Teguima (Opata) Inflectional Morphology. *International Journal of American Linguistics* 56(4):561-573.

_____
1991   Eudeve Morphosyntax: An Overview. *International Journal of American Linguistics* 57(1):70-107.

_____
1995   The Huelel (Esselen) Language. *International Journal of American Linguistics* 61(2):191-239.

Shaw, George C.
1909   The Chinook Jargon and How to Use It: A Complete and Exhaustive Lexicon of the Oldest Trade Language of the American Continent. Seattle: Rainier Printing Co.

Shaw, Patricia A.
1980   Theoretical Issues in Dakota Phonology and Morphology. (*Outstanding Dissertations in Linguistics*). New York: Garland.

_____
1985   Coexistent and Competing Stress Rules in Stoney (Dakota). *International Journal of American Linguistics* 51(1):1-18.

Shayne, Joanne
1982   Some Semantic Aspects of *Yi-* and *Bi-* in San Carlos Apache. Pp. 379-407 in Syntax and Semantics. Vol. 15: Studies in Transitivity. Paul J. Hopper and Sandra A. Thompson, eds. New York: Academic Press.

Shea, John Gilmary
1852   Discovery and Exploration of the Mississippi Vally: with the Original Narratives of Marquette, Allouez, Membré, Hennepin, and Anastase Douay. New York: J.S. Redfield.

_____, ed.
1860   A French-Onondaga Dictionary, from a Manuscript of the Seventeenth Century. (*Shea's Library of American Linguistics* 1). New York: Cramoisy Press.

Sherwood, David F.
1986   Maliseet-Passamaquoddy Verb Morphology. *National Museums of Canada. Mercury Series. Ethnology Service Paper* 105. Ottawa.

Sherzer, Joel
1970   Talking Backwards in Cuna: The Sociological Reality of Phonological Descriptions. *Southwestern Journal of Anthropology* 26(4):343-353.

_____
1973   Areal Linguistics in North America. Pp. 749-795 in Current Trends in Linguistics, Vol. 10: Linguistics in North America (Pt. 2). Thomas A. Sebeok, ed. The Hague and Paris: Mouton.

_____
1976   Areal Linguistics in North America. Pp. 121-173 in Vol. 1 of Native Languages of the Americas. Thomas A. Sebeok, ed. 2 vols. New York and London: Plenum Press.

_____
1976a   Play Languages: Implications for (Socio) Linguistics. Pp. 19-36 in Speech Play. Barbara Kirshenblatt-Gimblett, ed. Philadelphia: University of Pennsylvania Press.

Sherzer, Joel, and Richard Bauman
1972   Areal Studies and Culture History: Language as a Key to the Historical Study of Culture Contact. *Southwestern Journal of Anthropology* 28(2):131-152.

Shimkin, Demitri B.
1947   Wind River Shoshone Literary Forms: An Introduction. *Journal of Washington Academy of Sciences* 37(10):329-353. Washington. (Reprinted in part: Pp. 344-351 in Language in Culture and Society. Dell Hymes, ed. Harper and Row, New York, 1964.)

_____
1949   Shoshone I: Linguistic Sketch and Text; Shoshone II: Morphene List. *International Journal of American Linguistics* 15(3):175-188, (4):203-212.

Shimony, Annemarie Anrod
1961   Conservatism Among the Iroquois at the Six Nations Reserve. *Yale University Publications in Anthropology* 65. New Haven.

Shipley, William F.
1957   Some Yukian-Penutian Lexical Resemblances. *International Journal of American Linguistics* 23(4):268-274.

1961   Maidu and Nisenan: A Binary Survey. *International Journal of American Linguistics* 27(1):46-51.

1962   Spanish Elements in the Indigenous Languages of Central California. *Romance Philology* 16(1):1-21.

1963   Maidu Texts and Dictionary. *University of California Publications in Linguistics* 33. Berkeley.

1964   Maidu Grammar. *University of California Publications in Linguistics* 41. Berkeley.

1966   The Relation of Klamath to California Penutian. *Language: Journal of the Linguistic Sociaty of America* 42(2):489-498.

1969   Proto-Takelman. *International Journal of American Linguistics* 35(3):226-230.

1970   Proto-Kalapuyan. Pp. 97-106 in Languages and Cultures of Western North America: Essays in Honor of Sven S. Liljeblad. Earl H. Swanson, Jr., ed. Pocatello: Idaho State University Press.

1973   California. Pp. 1046-1078 in Current Trends in Linguistics, vol. 10: Linguistics in North America (Pt. 2). Thomas A. Sebeok, ed. The Hague and Paris: Mouton.

1976   California. Pp. 427-459 in Vol. 1 of Native Languages of the Americas. Thomas A. Sebeok, ed. 2 vols. New York and London: Plenum Press.

1980   Penutian among the Ruins: A Personal Assessment. Pp. 437-441 in *Proceedings of the Sixth Annual Meeting of the Berkeley Linguistics Society, 16-18 February, 1980.* Bruce R. Caron, Meredith A.B. Hoffmann, Marilyn Silva, et al., eds. Berkeley: BLS.

1988   Penutian among the Ruins: A Personal Assessment. Pp. 59-63 in Archaeology and Linguistics. A.M. Mester and C. McEwan, eds. *Journal of the Steward Anthropological Society for 1983-1984*, vol. 15(1-2). Urbana, Ill.

_____ , ed. and trans.
1991   The Maidu Indian Myths and Stories of Hánc'ibyjim. Berkeley, Calif.: Heyday Books.

Sibley, John
1832   Historical Sketches of the Several Indian Tribes in Louisiana, South of the Arkansas River, and between the Mississippi and River Grande. Pp. 721-725 in American State Papers: Documents, Legislative and Executive, of the Congress of the United States, Vol. IV [i.e. I.], Class II: Indian Affairs. Washington: Gales and Seaton.

Sidney, Angela
1980   Place Names of the Tagish Region, Southern Yukon. Whitehorse, Yukon: Council for Yukon Indians, Yukon Native Languages Project.

Siebert, Frank T., Jr.
1941   Certain Proto-Algonquian Consonant Clusters. *Language* 17(4):298-303.

1943   [Review of] Indian Place Names of the Penobscot Valley and the Maine Coast, by Fannie Hardy Eckstorm, 1941. *New England Quarterly* 16:503-507.

1945   Linguistic Classification of Catawba: Part I. *International Journal of American Linguistics* 11(2):100-104.

1945a   Linguistic Classification of Catawba: Part II. *International Journal of American Linguistics* 11(4):211-218.

1967   The Original Home of the Proto-Algonquian People. Pp. 13-47 in Contributions to Anthropology: Linguistics, I (Algonquian). *Anthropological Series* 78, *National Museum of Canada Bulletin* 214. Ottawa.

1975   Resurrecting Virginia Algonquian from the Dead: The Reconstituted and Historical Phonology of Powhatan. Pp. 285-453 in Studies in Southeastern Indian Languages. James M. Crawford, ed. Athens: University of Georgia Press.

1980   The Penobscot Dictionary Project: Preferences and Problems of Format, Presentation, and Entry. Pp. 113-127 in Papers of the Eleventh Algonquian Conference. William Cowan, ed. Ottawa: Carleton University.

1988   The Suprasegmental Phonemes of the Penobscot Dialect of Eastern Abenaki, an Eastern Algonquian Language. Pp. 715-763 in In Honor of Mary Haas: From the Haas Festival Conference on Native American Linguistics. William Shipley, ed. Berlin: Mouton de Gruyter.

Silko, Leslie M.
1981   Storyteller. New York: Seaver Books. (Reprinted in 1986.)

Silver, Shirley
1964   Shasta and Karok: A Binary Comparison. Pp. 170-181 in Studies in Californian Linguistics. William Bright, ed. *University of California Publications in Linguistics* 34. Berkeley.

1966   The Shasta Language. (Unpublished Ph.D. Dissertation in Linguistics, University of California, Berkeley.)

1980   Shasta and Konomihu. Pp. 245-263 in American Indian and Indoeuropean Studies. Kathryn A. Klar, et al., eds. (*Trends in Linguistics: Studies and Monographs* 16). The Hague: Mouton.

895

Silver, Shirley, and Wick R. Miller
1997   American Indian Languages in Cultural and Social Context. Tucson: University of Arizona Press.

Silver, Shirley, and Clara Wicks
1977   Coyote Steals the Fire (Shasta). Pp. 121-131 in Northern California Texts. Victor Golla and Shirley Silver, eds. *International Journal of American Linguistics. Native American Texts Series* 2(2). Chicago: The University of Chicago Press.

Silverstein, Michael
1966-1974 [Upper Chinookan Linguistic and Ethnographic Notes, from Fieldwork on the Yakima Reservation, Oregon, and Points on the Columbia River.] (Manuscripts in Silverstein's possession.)

1971   Whitney on Language: Selected Writings of William Dwight Whitney. Cambridge, Mass.: MIT Press.

1971a   Language Contact and the Problem of Convergent Generative Systems: Chinook Jargon. Pp. 191-192 in Pidginization and Creolization of Languages. Dell Hymes, ed. Cambridge: Cambridge University Press.

1972   Studies in Penutian, I. California, 1: The Structure of an Etymology. (Unpublished Ph.D. Dissertation in Linguistics, Harvard University, Cambridge, Mass.)

1972a   Chinook Jorgon: Language Contact and the Problem of Multi-Level Generative Systems. *Language: Journal of the Linguistic Society of America* 48(2):378-406, (3):596-625.

1974   Dialectal Developments in Chinookan Tense-Aspect Systems, An Areal-Historical Analysis. *International Journal of American Linguistics Memoir* 29 (=IJAL 40(4), pt. 2).

1975   On Two California Penutian Roots for 'Two'. *International Journal of American Linguistics* 41(4):369-380.

1979   Penutian: An Assessment. Pp. 650-691 in The Languages of Native America: Historical and Comparative Assessment. Lyle Campbell and Marianne Mithun, eds. Austin: University of Texas Press.

1984   The 'Value' of Objectual Language. (Paper presented at the 83d Annual Meeting of the American Anthropological Association, Denver, Colo.) (Manuscript in Silverstein's possession.)

Silvy, Antoine
1974   Dictionnaire montagnais-français (ca. 1678-1684). Lorenzo Angers, David E. Cooter, and Gérard E. McNulty, transcribers. Montreal: Les Presses de L'Université du Québec.

Simmons, William S.
1986   The Spirit of the New England Tribes: Indian History and Folklore, 1620-1984. Hanover, N.H.: University Press of New England.

Simmons, William S., and George F. Aubin
1975   Narragansett Kinship. *Man in the Northeast* 9:21-31.

Simons, Berthold
1989   Komplexe Sätze im Dakota (Sioux). (*Continuum* 6). Frankfurt am Main: Peter Lang.

Simpson, James H.
1850   Journal of a Military Reconnaissance from Santa Fe, New Mexico, to the Navajo Country... in 1849, by James Simpson, A.M., First Lieutenant Corps of Topographical Engineers. Pp. 56-139 in *31st Cong., 1st Sess. Senate Executive Doc. No. 64 (Serial No. 562)*. Washington: Government Printing Office.

1852   Journal of a Military Reconnaissance from Santa Fé, New Mexico, to the Navajo Country... in 1849. Philadelphia: Lippincott, Grambo.

1876   Explorations Across the Great Basin of the Territory of Utah for a Direct Wagon-Route from Camp Floyd to Genoa, in Carson Valley, in 1859, by Captain J. H. Simpson, Corps of Topographical Engineers. Washington: Government Printing Office.

1964   Navaho Expedition: Journal of a Military Reconnaissance from Santa Fe, New Mexico, to the Navaho Country Made in 1849. Frank McNitt, ed. Norman: University of Oklahoma Press.

Sims, Christine P., and Hilaire Valiquette
1990   More on Male and Female Speech in (Acoma and Laguna) Keresan. *International Journal of American Linguistics* 56(1):162-166.

Singerman, Robert
1996   Indigenous Languages of the Americas: A Bibliography of Dissertations and Theses. Lanham, Md.: Scarecrow Press.

Singh, Ram Raj Prasad
1966   Aboriginal Economic System of the Olympic Peninsula Indians, Western Washington. *Sacramento Anthropological Society Paper* 4. Sacramento.

Sioui, Anne-Marie
1979   Qui est l'auteur du Codex canadiensis? *Recherches amérindiennes au Québec* 8(4):271-279. Montreal.

Sitjar, Buenaventura
1771-1808 [Confessional in Antoniano Salinan.] (Manuscript in Special Collections, Georgetown University Library, Washington, D.C.)

1861   Vocabulario de la lengua de los naturales de la Misión de San Antonio, Alta California. (*Shea's Library of American Linguistics* 7). New York: Cramoisy Press.

Skinner, Alanson
1913   Social Life and Ceremonial Bundles of the Menomini. *American Museum of Natural History Anthropological Papers* 13(1):1-165. New York.

1915   Societies of the Iowa, Kansa, and Ponca Indians. *American Museum of Natural History Anthropological Papers* 11(9):679-801. New York.

1919   A Sketch of Eastern Dakota Ethnology. *American Anthropologist*, n.s. 21(2):164-174.

1919a   Some Menomini Indian Place Names in Wisconsin. *Wisconsin Archaeologist* 18(3):97-102. Milwaukee.

1921   Material Culture of the Menomini. *Museum of the American Indian, Heye Foundation, Indian Notes and Monographs* 20. New York.

1923   Observations on the Ethnology of the Sauk Indians. *Bulletin of the Public Museum of the City of Milwaukee* 5(1):1-58, (2):59-118, (3):119-180. Milwaukee.

1924   The Mascoutens or Prairie Potawatomi Indians. Pt. I, Social Life and Ceremonies. *Bulletin of the Public Museum of the City of Milwaukee* 6(1):1-262. Milwaukee.

1925   Observations on the Ethnology of the Sauk Indians. Pt. II: War Customs. *Bulletin of the Public Museum of the City of Milwaukee* 5(2):59-118. Milwaukee.

1926   Ethnology of the Ioway Indians. *Bulletin of the Public Museum of the City of Milwaukee* 5(4):181-354. Milwaukee.

Slickpoo, Allen P., Sr., and Deward E. Walker, Jr.
1973   Noon Nee-Me-Poo (We, The Nez Perces): Culture and History of the Nez Perces. Vol. 1. Lapwai: Nez Perce Tribe of Idaho.

Smet, Pierre-Jean de
1843   Letters and Sketches, with a Narrative of a Year's Residence Among the Indian Tribes of the Rocky Mountains. Philadelphia: M. Fithian. (Reprinted: Pp. 127-411 in Vol. 27 of Early Western Travels, 1748-1846. Reuben G. Thwaites, ed. Arthur H. Clark, Cleveland, Ohio, 1906.)

1844   Voyages aux montagnes Rocheuses, et une année de séjour chez les tribus indiennes du vaste territoire de l'Oregon. Malines: P.J. Hanicq.

1863   New Indian Sketches. New York: D.&J. Sadlier.

Šmitek, Zmago
1993   Baraga, Schoolcraft, and the Beginnings of American Ethnology. *European Review of Native American Studies* 7(2):39-41. Vienna.

Smith, Buckingham T.
1858   The Timuquana Language. *Historical Magazine*, 1st. ser. 2:1-3. New York.

1860   [Documents in the Spanish and two of the early tongues of Florida (Apalachian and Timuquan)]. [1688.] (Facsimile, 12 pp., ed. of 50 copies, in Manuscript Division, Library of Congress.)

1862   Grammar of the Pima or Névome, a Language of Sonora, from a Manuscript of the XVIII Century. (*Shea's Library of American Linguistics* 5). New York: Cramoisy Press.

Smith, Donald B.
1975   The Mississauga, Peter Jones, and the White Man: The Algonkians' Adjustment to the Europeans on the North Shore of Lake Ontario to 1860. (Unpublished Ph.D. Dissertation in History, The University of Toronto, Toronto, Ont.)

Smith, Elsdon C., comp.
1952   Personal Names: A Bibliography. New York: The New York Public Library. (Reprinted: Gale Research Compnay, Detroit, Mich., 1965.)

1953-1976   [Annual Bibliography of Personal Names, 1952-1975.] *Names* 1-24. [Titles, issue numbers, pages vary.]

Smith, Huron H.
1933   Ethnobotany of the Forest Potawatomi Indians. *Bulletin of the Public Museum of the City of Milwaukee* 7(1):1-230. Milwaukee, Wis.

Smith, Lawrence R.
1977   Some Grammatical Aspects of Labrador Inuttut (Eskimo): A Survey of the Inflectional Paradigms of Nouns and Verbs. *Canada. National Museum of Man. Mercury Series. Ethnology Service Paper* 37. Ottawa.

1978   A Survey of Derivational Postbases of Labrador Inuttut (Eskimo). *Canada. National Museum of Man. Mercury Series. Ethnology Service Paper* 45. Ottawa.

1980   Some Categories and Processes of Labrador Inuttut Word Formation. *International Journal of American Linguistics* 46(4):279-288.

Smith, Marian W.
1940   The Puyallup-Nisqually. *Columbia University Contributions to Anthropology* 32. New York. (Reprinted: AMS Press. New York, 1969.)

Smith, Marvin T.
1987   Archaeology of Aboriginal Culture Change in the Interior Southeast: Depopulation during the Early Historic Period. (*Ripley P. Bullen Monographs in Anthropology and History* 6). Gainesville: University of Florida Press and Florida State Museum.

Smith, Murphy D.
1983   Peter Stephen Duponceau and his Study of Languages: an Historical Account. *Proceedings of the American Philosophical Society* 127(3):143-179. Philadelphia.

Smith, Richard
1977   Bear and Deer Woman (Nisenan). Pp. 132-146 in Northern California Texts. Victor Golla and Shirley Silver, eds. *International Journal of American Linguistics. Native American Texts Series* 2(2). Chicago: The University of Chicago Press.

Smith, Watson, and John M. Roberts
1954   Zuni Law: A Field of Values. *Harvard University. Papers of the Peabody Museum of American Archaeology and Ethnology* 43(1); *Reports of the Rimrock Project. Values Series* 4. Cambridge, Mass. (Reprinted: Kraus Reprint, Millwood, N.Y., 1973.)

Smithson, Carma Lee
1959   The Havasupai Woman. *University of Utah Anthropological Papers* 38. Salt Lake City. (Reprinted: Johnson Reprint, New York, 1971.)

Smithsonian Institution. Bureau of [American] Ethnology
1885   Linguistic Families of the Indian Tribes North of Mexico, with Provisional List of the Principal Tribal Names and Synonyms. [Pt. 1: Henry W. Henshaw, comp.; pt. 2: James Mooney and Henry W. Henshaw, comps.] *Miscellaneous Publication* 3. Washington.

Smithsonian Institution. Bureau of American Ethnology
1926   Circular of Information Regarding Indian Popular Names. Washington: Smithsonian Institution, Bureau of American Ethnology.

Snapp, Allen,
1982   Northern Paiute. Pp. 1-92 in Studies in Uto-Aztecan Grammar, Vol. 3: Uto-Aztecan Grammatical Sketches. Ronald W. Langacker, ed. (*Publications in Linguistics* 56). Arlington, Tex.: Summer Institute of Linguistics and University of Texas.

Snow, Dean R.
1976   The Archaeological Implications of the Proto-Algonquian Urheimat. Pp. 340-346 in Papers of the Seventh Algonquian Conference, 1975. William Cowan, ed. Ottawa: Carleton University.

1976a   The Archaeology of North America. New York: The Viking Press.

1977   Archeology and Ethnohistory in Eastern New York. Pp. 107-112 in Current Perspectives in Northeastern Archeology. *Researches and Transactions of the New York State Archeological Association* 17(1):107-112.

1980   The Archeology of New England. New York: Academic Press.

1984   Iroquois Prehistory. Pp. 241-257 in Extending the Rafters: Interdisciplinary Approaches to Iroquoian Studies. Michael K. Foster, Jack Campisi, and Marianne Mithun, eds. Albany: State University of New York Press.

1995   Migration in Prehistory: The Northern Iroquoian Case. *American Antiquity* 60(1):59-79.

Snyder, Warren A.
1968   Southern Puget Sound Salish: Texts, Place Names and Dictionary. *Sacramento Anthropological Society Papers* 9. Sacramento, Calif.

1968a   Southern Puget Sound Salish: Phonology and Morphology. *Sacramento Anthropological Society Papers* 8. Sacramento, Calif.

Sølver, C.V.
1957   Eskimo Maps from Greenland. *Archaeology* 10(4):188-190. Cambridge.

Sørensen, Holger Steen
1958   Word-Classes in Modern English, with Special Reference to Proper Names. With an Introductory Theory of Grammar, Meaning, and Reference. Copenhagen: G.E.C. Gad Publisher.

1963   The Meaning of Proper Names with a Definiens Formula for Proper Names in Modern English. Copenhagen: G.E.C. Gad Publisher.

South Greenland
1911   Nalunaerutit. [Proceedings of the Provincial Council of South Greenland.] Gothab, Greenland.

Spalding, Alex E.
1960   A Grammar of the East and West Coasts of Hudson Bay. Ottawa: Northern Administration Branch, Department of Northern Affairs and National Resources.

1992   Inuktitut: A Grammar of North Baffin Dialects. 2 vols. Winnipeg, Man.: Wuerz. (Vol. 1 previously publ. as: Learning to Speak Inuktitut: A Grammar of North Baffin Dialects. Centre for Research and Teaching of Canadian Native Languages, University of Western Ontario, London, Canada, 1979.)

Spalding, Henry Harmon
1839   Nez-Perces First Book, Designed for Children and New Beginners. Clear Water, [Idaho]: Mission Press.

1840   Numipuain Shapahitamanash Timash: Primer in the Nez Percés Language. Lapwai, Idaho: Mission Press.

1871   Matthewnim Taaiskt: The Gospel According to Matthew Translated into the Nez Perces Language. New York: American Bible Society.

Sparkman, Philip S.
1905   Sketch of the Grammar of the Luiseño Language of California. *American Anthropologist*, n.s. 7(4):656-662.

Sparkman, Philip S., Alfred L. Kroeber, and George W. Grace
1960   The Sparkman Grammar of Luiseño. *University of California Anthropological Records* 13(1). Berkeley.

Speare, Jean E., ed.
1977   The Days of Augusta. Seattle, Wash.: Madrona Publishers.

Speck, Frank G.
1904   A Modern Mohegan-Pequot Text. *American Anthropologist*, n.s. 6(4):469-476.

1907   The Creek Indians of Taskigi Town. *American Anthropological Association Memoir* 2(2):99-164.

1907a   Some Outlines of Aboriginal Culture in the Southeastern States. *American Anthropologist*, n.s. 9(2):287-295.

1907b   Some Comparative Traits of the Muskogian Languages. *American Anthropologist*, n.s. 9(3):470-483.

1909   Ethnology of the Yuchi Indians. *University of Pennsylvania, University Museum. Anthropological Publications* 1(1). Philadelphia. (Reprinted: AMS Press, New York, 1980.)

1911 Ceremonial Songs of the Creek and Yuchi Indians. With Music Transcribed by Jacob D. Sapir. *University of Pennsylvania, University Museum. Anthropological Publications* 1(2):157-245. Philadelphia. (Reprinted in: Creek Source Book. William C. Sturtevant, ed. Garland Publishing, New York, 1987.)

1915 The Family Hunting Band as the Basis of Algonkian Social Organization. *American Anthropologist.* n.s. 17(2):289-305.

1915a Family Hunting Territories and Social Life of Various Algonkian Bands of the Ottawa Valley. *Canada. Department of Mines. Geological Survey, Memoir 70, Anthropological Series 8.* Ottawa.

1917 The Social Structure of the Northern Algonkian. *American Sociological Society Publication* 12:82-100. Chicago.

1917a Game Totems Among the Northeastern Algonkians. *American Anthropologist,* n.s. 19(1):9-18.

1923 Mistassini Hunting Territories in the Labrador Peninsula. *American Anthropologist,* n.s. 25(4):452-471.

1927 The Nanticoke and Conoy Indians with a Review of Linguistic Material from Manuscript and Living Sources: an Historical Study. *Papers of the Historical Society of Delaware,* n.s. 1. Wilmington.

1928 Native Tribes and Dialects of Connecticut: A Mohegan-Pequot Diary. Pp. 199-287 in *43d Annual Report of the Bureau of American Ethnology for 1925-1926.* Washington.

1935 Naskapi: Savage Hunters of the Labrador Peninsula. Norman: University of Oklahoma Press.

1945 The Iroquois: A Study in Cultural Evolution. *Cranbrook Institute of Science Bulletin* 23. Bloomfield Hills, Mich.

1945a Abnaki Text. *International Journal of American Linguistics* 11(1):45-46.

Speck, Frank G., and George Herzog
1942 The Tutelo Spirit Adoption Ceremony: Reclothing the Living in the Name of the Dead. [With] Transcriptions and Analysis of Tutelo Music [by] George Herzog. Harrisburg: Pennsylvania Historical Commission.

Speck, Frank G., and Newell Lion
1918 Penobscot Transformer Tales. Dictated by Newell Lion. *International Journal of American Linguistics* 1(3):187-244.

Speck, Frank G., and C.E. Schaeffer
1942 Catawba Kinship and Social Organization with a Resume of Tutelo Kinship Terms. *American Anthropologist,* n.s. 44(4, Pt.1):555-575.

Speirs, Anna
1974 Classificatory Verb Stems in Tewa. *Studies in Linguistics* 24:45-64.

Speirs, Randall, and Anna Speirs
1968 Tewa Reading Book. Espanola, N.M.: Summer Institute of Linguistics.

Spencer, Robert F.
1947 Spanish Loanwords in Keresan. *Southwestern Journal of Anthropology* 3(2):130-146.

1959 The North Alaskan Eskimo: A Study in Ethnology and Society. *Bureau of American Ethnology Bulletin* 171. Washington.

Spencer, Robert F., Jesse D. Jennings, et al.
1965 The Native Americans. New York: Harper and Row.

Spicer, Edward H.
1943 Linguistic Aspects of Yaqui Acculturation. *American Anthropologist,* n.s. 45(3):410-426.

1961 Yaqui. Pp. 7-93 in Perspectives in American Indian Culture Change. Edward H. Spicer, ed. Chicago: The University of Chicago Press.

1962 Cycles of Conquest: The Impact of Spain, Mexico, and the United States on the Indians of the Southwest, 1533-1960. Tucson: University of Arizona Press.

Spier, Leslie
1924 Havasupai (Yuman) Texts. *International Journal of American Linguistics* 3(1):109-116.

1924a Witchita and Caddo Relationship Terms. *American Anthropologist,* n.s. 26(2):258-263.

1928 Havasupai Ethnography. *American Museum of Natural History Anthropological Papers* 24(3). New York. (Reprinted: AMS Press, New York, 1979.)

1929 Problems Arising From the Cultural Position of the Havasupai. *American Anthropologist,* n.s. 31(2):213-222.

1930 Klamath Ethnography. *University of California Publications in American Archaeology and Ethnology* 30(1):1-338. Berkeley.

1933 Yuman Tribes of the Gila River. Chicago: The University of Chicago Press.

1936 Cultural Relations of the Gila River and Lower Colorado Tribes. *Yale University Publications in Anthropology* 3. New Haven. Conn.

1946 Comparative Vocabularies and Parallel Texts in Two Yuman Languages of Arizona. *University of New Mexico Publications in Anthropology* 2:144-150. Albuquerque.

899

——— 1953 Some Observations on Mohave Clans. *Southwestern Journal of Anthropology* 9(3):324-342.

Spier, Leslie, and Edward Sapir
1930 Wishram Ethnography. *University of Washington Publications in Anthropology* 3(3):151-300. Seattle.

Spinden, Herbert J.
1908 The Nez Percé Indians. *American Anthropological Association Memoir* 2(3):165-274.

Spink, John, and D.W. Moodie
1972 Eskimo Maps from the Canadian Eastern Arctic. *Cartographica Monograph* 5. Toronto: York University.

——— 1976 Inuit Maps from the Canadian Eastern Arctic. Pp. 39-46 in Vol. 2 of Report: Inuit Land Use and Occupancy Project. Milton M.R. Freeman, ed. Ottawa: Department of Indian and Northern Affairs.

Spoehr, Alexander
1941 Camp, Clan, and Kin Among the Cow Creek Seminole of Florida. *Field Museum of Natural History Anthropological Series* 33(1):3-27. Chicago.

——— 1942 Kinship System of the Seminole. *Field Museum of Natural History Anthropological Series* 33(5):31-113. Chicago.

Spolsky, Bernard, and P. Irvine
1982 Sociolinguistic Aspects of the Acceptance of Literacy in the Vernacular. Pp. 73-79 in Bilingualism and Language Contact: Spanish, English, and Native American Languages. Florence Baskin, Elizabeth Brandt, and Jacob Ornstein-Galicia, eds. New York: Teachers College Press.

Spradley, James P.
1969 Guests Never Leave Hungry: The Autobiography of James Sewid, a Kwakiutl Indian. New Haven, Conn.: Yale University Press.

Springer, James Warren, and Stanley R. Witkowski
1983 Siouan Historical Linguistics and Oneota Archaeology. Pp. 69-83 in Oneota Studies. Guy E. Gibbon, ed. *University of Minnesota Publications in Anthropology* 1. Minneapolis.

Spuhler, James N.
1979 Genetic Distances, Trees, and Maps of North America Indians. Pp. 135-183 in The First Americans: Origins, Affinities, and Adaptations. William S. Laughlin and Albert B. Harper, eds. (*Proceedings of the Wenner-Gren Foundation for Anthropological Research, Burg Wartenstein, 1976*). New York, Stuttgart: Gastav Fischer.

Stanley, J.M.
1852 Portraits of North American Indians. *Smithsonian Institution Miscellaneous Collections* 53. Washington.

Stark, Donald S.
1962 Boundary Markers in Dakota. *International Journal of American Linguistics* 28(1):19-35.

Stearns, Mary Lee
1977 The Reorganization of Ceremonial Relations in Haida Society. *Arctic Anthropology* 14(1):54-63.

Steele, Susan
1979 Uto-Aztecan: An Assessment for Historical and Comparative Linguistics. Pp. 444-544 in The Languages of Native America: Historical and Comparative Assessment. Lyle Campbell and Marianne Mithun, eds. Austin: University of Texas Press.

——— 1990 Agreement and Anti-Agreement: A Syntax of Luiseño. *Studies in Natural Language and Linguistic Theory* 17. Dordrecht: Kluwer.

Stefánsson, Vilhjálmur
1909 The Eskimo Trade Jargon of Herschel Island. *American Anthropologist*, n.s. 11(2):217-232.

——— 1913 My Life with the Eskimo. New York: Macmillan.

——— 1914 The Stefánsson-Anderson Arctic Expedition of the American Museum: Preliminary Ethnological Report. *American Museum of Natural History Anthropological Papers* 14(1):1-395. New York.

——— 1921 The Friendly Arctic: The Story of Five Years in Polar Regions. New York: Macmillan. (Reprinted, 2d ed., 1943.)

Stefánsson, Vilhjálmur, and Eloise McCaskill
1938 The Three Voyages of Martin Frobisher in Search of a Passage to Cathay and India by the North-West, A.D. 1576-8. From the Original 1578 text of George Best. 2 vols. London: The Argonaut Press.

Stephen, Alexander M.
1936 Hopi Journal of Alexander M. Stephen. Elise Clews Parsons, ed. 2 vols. *Columbia University Contributions to Anthropology* 23. New York.

Stern, Bernhard J.
1934 The Lummi Indians of Northwest Washington. *Columbia University Contributions to Anthropology* 17. New York.

Stern, Theodore
1966 The Klamath Tribe: A People and Their Reservation. Seattle and London: University of Washington Press.

——— 1993 Chiefs and Chief Traders: Indian Relations at Fort Nez Percés, 1818-1855. Corvallis: Oregon State University Press.

Stevens, Jedediah Dwight
1836 Sioux Spelling-Book, Designed for the Use of Native Learners. Boston: The Board of Commissioners for Foreign Missions.

Stevenson, Matilda Coxe
1894 The Sia. Pp. 3-157 in *11th Annual Report of the Bureau of [American] Ethnology for 1889-1890*. Washington.

——— 1904 The Zuñi Indians: Their Mythology, Esoteric Fraternities, and Ceremonies. *23d Annual Report of the Bureau of American Ethnology for 1901-1902*. Washington. (Reprinted: Rio Grande Press, Glorieta, N.M., 1970.)

1915   Ethnobotany of the Zuñi Indians. Pp. 31-102 in *13th Annual Report of the Bureau of American Ethnology for 1908-1909.* Washington.

Steward, Julian H.
1931   The Ceremonial Buffoon of the American Indian. *Papers of the Michigan Academy of Science, Arts, and Letters* 14. Ann Arbor.

1933   Ethnography of the Owens Valley Paiute. *University of California Publications in American Archaeology and Ethnology* 33(3):233-350. Berkeley.

1934   Two Paiute Autobiographies. *University of California Publications in American Archaeology and Ethnology* 33(5):423-438. Berkeley.

1938   Basin-Plateau Aboriginal Sociopolitical Groups. *Bureau of American Ethnology Bulletin* 120. Washington. (Reprinted: University of Utah Press, Salt Lake City, 1970.)

1943   Northern and Gosiute Shoshoni. Culture Element Distributions 23. *University of California Anthropological Records* 8(3):263-392. Berkeley.

Steward, Julian H., ed.
1946-1959 Handbook of South American Indians. 7 vols. *Bureau of American Ethnology Bulletin* 143. Washington. (Reprinted: Cooper Square Publishers, New York, 1963.)

1960   John Reed Swanton, February 19, 1893–May 2, 1958. Pp. 329-349 in *National Academy of Sciences. Biographical Memoirs* 14. Washington.

Stewart, George R.
1975   Names on the Globe. New York: Oxford University Press.

Stewart, Joseph L.
1960   The Problem of Stuttering in Certain North American Indian Societies. *The Journal of Speech and Hearing Disorders, Monograph Supplement* 6. Washington.

Stewart, Omer C.
1941   Northern Paiute. Culture Element Distributions 14. *University of California Anthropological Records* 4(3):361-446. Berkeley.

1942   Ute-Southern Paiute. Culture Element Distributions 18. *University of California Anthropological Records* 6(4):231-360. Berkeley.

1943   Notes on Pomo Ethnogeography. *University of California Publications in American Archaeology and Ethnology* 40(2):29-62. Berkeley.

1944   Washo-Northern Paiute Peyotism: A Study in Acculturation. *University of California Publications in American Archaeology and Ethnology* 40(3):63-142. Berkeley and Los Angeles.

Stiles, Ezra 1762 *see* Cowan, William 1973a

Stiles, Ezra
1787   [Vocabulary of Naugatuck.] (Manuscript of Words Obtained from Sarah Maweek, in Beinecke Library, Yale University, New Haven, Connecticut.)

Stirling, Matthew W.
1938   Three Pictographic Autobiographies of Sitting Bull. *Smithsonian Miscellaneous Collections* 97(5). Washington. (Reprinted in German under title: Sitting Bull, Drei piktographische Autobiographien. Verlag für Amerikanistik, Wyk auf Foehr, Germany, 1993.)

Stocking, George W., Jr.
1974   The Boas Plan for the Study of American Indian Languages. Pp. 454-484 in Studies in the History of Linguistics: Traditions and Paradigms. Dell Hymes, ed. Bloomington: Indiana University Press.

Stokes, Jeff
1985   Natural Resource Utilization of Four Upper Kuskokwim Communities. *Alaska Department of Game, Subsistence Division, Techical Paper* 86. Juneau.

Stone, Livingston
1877   Win-tūn´ of McCloud River. Albert S. Gatschet, ed. *Contributions to North American Ethnology* 3:519, 531-534. Washington.

Storie, Susanne, and Jennifer Gould, eds.
1973   Bella Bella Stories. Victoria, B.C.: British Columbia Advisory Committee.

Story, Dee Ann
1978   Some Comments on Anthropological Studies Concerning the Caddo. Pp. 46-68 in Texas Archaeology: Essays Honoring R. King Harris. Kurt House, ed. Dallas: Southern Methodist University Press. (Facsimile reprint: The Southern Caddo: An Anthology. H.F. Gregory, ed.; Garland Publishing, New York, 1986.)

Story, Gillian L.
1984   Babine and Carrier Phonology: An Historically Oriented Study. *Summer Institute of Linguistics Publications in Linguistics* 70. Dallas: Summer Institute of Linguistics and the University of Texas at Arlington.

Story, Gillian L., and Constance M. Naish, comps.
1973   Tlingit Verb Dictionary. Part 1: English-Tlingit; Part 2: Tlingit-English. College: University of Alaska, Alaska Native Language Center.

Stout, Carol C.
1972   Zuni Transitivity: A Generative Approach. (Unpublished Ph.D. Dissertation in Linguistics, University of New Mexico, Albuquerque.)

Strehlow, T.G.H.
1947   Aranda Traditions. Melbourne: Melbourne University Press. (Reprinted: Johnson Reprint, New York, 1968.)

Strong, William D.
1929   Aboriginal Society in Southern California. *University of California Publications in American Archaeology and Ethnology* 26:1-349. Berkeley.

Sturtevant, William C.
1948   Origin and History of Chinook Jargon. (Manuscript in Sturtevant's possession.)

1958   Siouan Languages in the East. *American Anthropologist,* n.s. 60(4):738-743.

1959   The Authorship of the Powell Classification. *International Journal of American Linguistics* 25(3):196-199.

1960   A Seminole Medicine Maker. Pp. 505-532 in In the Company of Man: Twenty Portraits by Anthropologists. Joseph B. Casagrande, ed. New York: Harper & Brothers.

1964   Studies in Ethnoscience. *American Anthropologist*, n.s. 66(3, Pt. 2):99-131.

1971   Creek into Seminole. Pp. 92-128 in North American Indians in Historical Perspective. Eleanor Burke Leacock and Nancy Oestreich Lurie, eds. New York: Random House.

1981   [Summary of a talk on the origins of Chinook Jargon.] *California-Oregon Languages Newsletter* 4(4):4. Washington, D.C.

1994   The Misconnection of Guale and Yamasee with Muskogean. *International Journal of American Linguistics* 60(2):139-148.

Suárez, Jorge A.
1959   The Phonemes of an Araucanian Dialect. *International Journal of American Linguistics* 25(3):177-181.

1979   Observaciones sobre la evolución fonológica del tlapaneco. *Anales de Antropología* 16:371-386. Mexico.

1980   [Review of] Two Studies in Middle American Comparative Linguistics by David Oltrogge and Calvin R. Rensch. *International Journal of American Linguistics* 46(1):56-60.

1983   La lengua tlapaneca de Malinaltepec. Mexico: Instituto Nacional Autónoma de México.

1986   Elementos gramaticales otomangues en tlapaneco. Pp. 267-284 in Language in Global Perspective: Papers in Honor of the 50th Anniversary of the Summer Institute of Linguistics, 1935-1985. Benjamin E. Elson, ed. Dallas, Tex.: Summer Institute of Linguistics.

Summer Institute of Linguistics
1992   Bibliography of the Summer Institute of Linguistics. Dallas, Tex.: Summer Institute of Linguistics.

Sunn, Nick, and Henry O. Harwell
1976   An Account of Maricopa Origins. Pp. 26-30 in Yuman Texts. Margaret Langdon, ed. *International Journal of American Linguistics*. Native American Texts Series 1(3). Chicago: The University of Chicago Press.

Susman, Amelia L.
1940   The Winnebago Syllabary. (Manuscript [Freeman *Guide* No. 3903] in the Library of the American Philosophical Society, Philadelphia.)

1941   Word Play in Winnebago. *Language: Journal of the Linguistic Society of America* 17(4):342-344.

1943   The Accentual System of Winnebago. (Unpublished Ph.D. Dissertation in Philosophy, Columbia University, New York.)

Suttles, Wayne
1951   [Fieldnotes on Thompson Kinship Terms and Miscellaneous Cultural Traits.] (Unpublished manuscript in Suttles's possession.)

1958   Private Knowledge, Morality, and Social Classes Among the Coast Salish. *American Anthropologist*, n.s. 60(3):497-507.

1962   [Fieldnotes on Thompson Kinship Terms.] (Unpublished manuscript in Suttles's possession.)

1987   The Recent Emergence of the Coast Salish—the Function of an Anthropological Myth [1975]. Pp. 256-264 in Coast Salish Essays, by Wayne Suttles. Vancouver, Seattle and London: Talonbooks/University of Washington Press.

1987a   Northwest Coast Linguistic History—a View from the Coast [1979]. Pp. 265-281 in Coast Salish Essays, by Wayne Suttles. Vancouver, Seattle and London: Talonbooks/University of Washington Press.

Suttles, Wayne, and William W. Elmendorf
1963   Linguistic Evidence for Salish Prehistory. Pp. 40-52 in Symposium on Language and Culture. Proceedings of the 1962 Annual Spring Meeting of the American Ethnological Society. Viola E. Garfield and Wallace L. Chafe, eds. Seattle: University of Washington.

Swadesh, Mary Haas, and Morris Swadesh
1933   A Visit to the Other World, a Nitinat Text (With Translation and Grammatical Analysis). *International Journal of American Linguistics* 7(3-4):195-208.

Swadesh, Morris
1933   Chitimacha Verbs of Derogatory or Abusive Connotation with Parallels from European Languages. *Language: Journal of the Linguistic Society of America* 9(2):192-201.

1939   Nootka Internal Syntax. *International Journal of American Linguistics* 9(2-4):77-102.

1941   Observations of Pattern Impact on the Phonetics of Bilinguals. Pp. 59-65 in Language, Culture, and Personality: Essays in Memory of Edward Sapir. L.A. Spier et al., eds. Menasha, Wis.: Sapir Memorial Publication Fund.

1946   South Greenlandic (Eskimo). Pp. 30-54 in Linguistic Structures of Native America. Harry Hoijer, ed. *Viking Fund Publications in Anthropology* 6. New York.

1946a   Chitimacha. Pp. 312-336 in Linguistic Structures of Native America. Harry Hoijer, ed. *Viking Fund Publications in Anthropology* 6. New York.

1948   Sociologic Notes on Obsolescent Languages. *International Journal of American Linguistics* 14(4):226-235.

1949   The Linguistic Approach to Salish Prehistory. Pp. 161-171 in Indians of the Urban Northwest. Marian W. Smith, ed. *Columbia University Contributions to Anthropology* 36. New York.

1950   Salish Internal Relationships. *International Journal of American Linguistics* 16(4):157-167.

1951   Diffusional Cumulation and Archaic Residue as Historical Explanations. *Southwestern Journal of Anthropology* 7(1):1-21. (Reprinted: Pp. 624-635 in Language in Culture and Society. Dell Hymes, ed., Harper and Row, New York, 1964.)

1951a   Kleinschmidt Centennial III: Unaaliq and Proto Eskimo. *International Journal of American Linguistics* 17(2):66-70.

1952   Lexico-statistic Dating of Prehistoric Ethnic Contacts; With Special Reference to North American Indians and Eskimos. *Proceedings of the American Philosophical Society* 96(4):452-463. Philadelphia.

1952a   Salish Phonologic Geography. *Language: Journal of the Linguistic Society of America* 28(2):232-248. (Reprinted: Pp. 293-312 in The Origin and Diversification of Language. Joel Sherzer, ed. Aldine, Chicago, 1971.)

1952b   Unaaliq and Proto Eskimo V: Comparative Vocabulary. *International Journal of American Linguistics* 18(4):241-256.

1953   Mosan I: A Problem of Remote Common Origin; Mosan II: Comparative Vocabulary. *International Journal of American Linguistics* 19(1):26-44, (3):223-236.

1953a   Salish-Wakashan Lexical Comparisons Noted by Boas. *International Journal of American Linguistics* 19(4):290-291.

1954   Time Depths of American Linguistic Groupings. (Comments by George I. Quimby, Henry B. Collins, Emil W. Haury, Gordon F. Ekholm, and Fred Eggan). *American Anthropologist* 56(3):361-377.

1954a   Perspectives and Problems of Amerindian Comparative Linguistics. *Word* 10(2-3):306-332. New York.

1954-1955   Algunas fechas glottocronológicas importantes para la prehistoria nahua. *Revista Mexicana de Estudios Antropológicos* 14(1):173-192.

1955   Towards Greater Accuracy in Lexicostatistic Dating. *International Journal of American Linguistics* 21(2):121-137.

1955a   Chemakum Lexicon Compared With Quileute. *International Journal of American Linguistics* 21(1):60-72.

1956   Problems of Long-range Comparison in Penutian. *Language: Journal of the Linguistic Society of America* 32(1):17-41.

1958   Some New Glottochronologic Dates for Amerindian Linguistic Groups. Pp. 671-674 in *Proceedings of the 32d International Congress of Americanists, Copenhagen, 1956.* Copenhagen: Munksgaard.

1959   The Mesh Principle in Comparative Linguistics. *Anthropological Linguistics* 1(2):7-14.

1959a   Linguistics as an Instrument of Prehistory. *Southwestern Journal of Anthropology* 15(1):20-35. (Reprinted in modified form: Pp. 574-585 in Language in Culture and Society. Dell Hymes, ed. Harper and Row, New York, 1964.)

1959b   Mapas de clasificación linguistica de México y las Américas. *Cuadernos del Instituto de Investigaciones Históricas de la Universidad Nacional Autónoma de México, Publicaciones* 5, serie 1, Serie Antropológica 8. México, D.F.

1962   Linguistic Relations across Bering Strait. *American Anthropologist,* n.s. 64(6):1262-1291.

1962a   Comment on Bergsland and Vogt [1962]. *Current Anthropology* 3(2):143-145.

1963   Nuevo ensayo de glotocronología Yutonahua. *Anales del Instituto Nacional de Antropología e Historia* 15(44):263-302. Mexico, D.F.

1964   Linguistic Overview. Pp. 527-556 in Prehistoric Man in the New World. Jesse D. Jennings and Edward Norbeck, eds. Chicago: Published for William Marsh Rice University by the University of Chicago Press.

1964a   Glottochronology. Pp. 289-290 in A Dictionary of the Social Sciences. Julius Gould and William L. Kolb, eds. Norwich: Tavistock Publications.

1965   Kalapuya and Takelma. *International Journal of American Linguistics* 31(3):237-240.

1967   Linguistic Classification in the Southwest. Pp. 281-309 in Studies in Southwestern Ethnolinguistics. Dell Hymes and William E. Bittle, eds. The Hague: Mouton.

1967a   Lexicostatistic Classification. Pp. 79-115 in Handbook of Middle American Indians, Vol. 5: Linguistics. Norman McQuown, vol. ed. Robert Wauchope, gen. ed. 16 vols., plus Supplements. Austin: University of Texas Press.

1971   The Origin and Diversification of Language. Joel Sherzer, ed. Chicago: Aldine.

Swan, James G.
1868   The Indians of Cape Flattery, at the Entrance to the Strait of Fuca, Washington Territory. *Smithsonian Contributions to Knowledge* 220. Washington.

Swann, Brian
1987   A Note on Translation, and Remarks on Collaboration. Pp. 247-254 in Recovering the Word: Essays on Native American Literature. Brian Swann and Arnold Krupat, eds. Berkeley: University of California Press.

_____, ed.
1992   On the Translation of Native American Literatures. Washington: Smithsonian Institution Press.

_____, ed.
1994   Coming to Light: Contemporary Translations of the Native Literatures of North America. New York: Random House.

Swann, Brian, and Arnold Krupat, eds.
1987   I Tell You Now: Autobiographical Essays by Native American Writers. Lincoln: University of Nebraska Press.

Swanton, John R.
1905   Contributions to the Ethnology of the Haida. *Jesup North Pacific Expedition* 5, *American Museum of Natural History Memoir* 8(1):1-300. Leiden and New York.

1905a   Haida Texts and Myths. Skidegate Dialect. *Bureau of American Ethnology Bulletin* 29. Washington.

1907   Ethnological Position of the Natchez Indians. *American Anthropologist*, n.s. 9(3):513-528.

1908   Social Condition, Beliefs, and Linguistic Relationship of the Tlingit Indians. Pp. 391-486 in *26th Annual Report of the Bureau of American Ethnology for 1904-1905*. Washington.

1908a   Haida Texts—Masset Dialect. *Publications of the Jesup North Pacific Expedition* 10(2), *Memoirs of the American Museum of Natural History* 14(2). Leiden, The Netherlands: E.J. Brill; New York: G.E. Stechert. (Reprinted: AMS Press, New York, 1975.)

1908b   The Language of the Taensa. *American Anthropologist*, n.s. 10(1):24-32.

1909   A New Siouan Dialect. Pp. 477-486 in Putnam Anniversary Volume: Anthropological Essays Presented to Frederic Ward Putnam in Honor of His Seventieth Birthday, April 16, 1909. New York: G.E. Stechert. (Reprinted: AMS Press, New York, 1976.)

1910   Names and Naming. Pp. 16-18 in Pt. 2 of Handbook of American Indians North of Mexico. Frederick W. Hodge, ed. *Bureau of American Ethnology Bulletin* 30. Washington.

1911   Indian Tribes of the Lower Mississippi Valley and Adjacent Coast of the Gulf of Mexico. *Bureau of American Ethnology Bulletin* 43. Washington.

1911a   Tlingit. Pp. 159-204 in Pt. 1 of Handbook of American Indian Languages. Franz Boas, ed. *Bureau of American Ethnology Bulletin* 40. Washington.

1911b   Haida. Pp. 205-282 in Pt. 1 of Handbook of American Indian Languages. Franz Boas, ed. *Bureau of American Ethnology Bulletin* 40. Washington.

1915   Linguistic Position of the Tribes of Southern Texas and Northeastern Mexico. *American Anthropologist*, n.s. 17(1):17-40.

1919   A Structural and Lexical Comparison of the Tunica, Chitimacha, and Atakapa Languages. *Bureau of American Ethnology Bulletin* 68. Washington.

1922   Early History of the Creek Indians and Their Neighbors. *Bureau of American Ethnology Bulletin* 73. Washington. (Reprinted: Johnson Reprint, New York, 1970.)

1923   New Light on the Early History of the Siouan Peoples. *Journal of the Washington Academy of Sciences* 13(3):33-43.

1924   The Muskhogean Connection of the Natchez Language. *International Journal of American Linquistics* 3(1):46-75.

1928   Social Organization and Social Usages of the Indians of the Creek Confederacy. Pp. 23-472 in *42d Annual Report of the Bureau of American Ethnology for 1924-1925*. Washington. (Reprinted: Johnson Reprint, New York, 1970.)

1928a   Religious Beliefs and Medical Practices of the Creek Indians. Pp. 473-672 in *42d Annual Report of the Bureau of American Ethnology for 1924-1925*. Washington.

1928b   Aboriginal Culture of the Southeast. Pp. 673-726 in *42d Annual Report of the Bureau of American Ethnology for 1924-1925*. Washington.

1928c   Social and Religious Beliefs and Usages of the Chickasaw Indians. Pp. 169-273 in *44th Annual Report of the Bureau of American Ethnology for 1926-1927*. Washington.

1929   The Tawasa Language. *American Anthropologist*, n.s. 31(3):435-453.

1929a   A Sketch of the Atakapa Language. *International Journal of American Linguistics* 5(2-4):121-149.

1931   Source Material for the Social and Ceremonial Life of the Choctaw Indians. *Bureau of American Ethnology Bulletin* 103. Washington. (Reprinted, with an Introduction by Virginia Pounds Brown: Birmingham Public Library Press, Birmingham, Ala., 1993.)

1934   Newly-discovered Powhatan Bird Names. *Journal of the Washington Academy of Sciences* 24(2):96-99. Washington.

1936   Early History of the Eastern Siouan Tribes. Pp. 371-381 in Essays in Anthropology Presented to A.L. Kroeber. Robert H. Lowie, ed. Berkeley: University of California Press.

1939   Final Report of the United States De Soto Expedition Commission. *76th Congress, 1st Session, House Document No.* 71. Washington: Government Printing Office. (Reprinted: *Classics in Smithsonian Anthropology*, Smithsonian Institution Press, Washington, 1985.)

1940   Linguistic Material from the Tribes of Southern Texas and Northeastern Mexico. *Bureau of American Ethnology Bulletin* 127. Washington.

1942   Source Material on the History and Ethnology of the Caddo Indians. *Bureau of American Ethnology Bulletin* 132. Washington.

1943   Siouan Tribes and the Ohio Valley. *American Anthropologist*, n.s. 45(1):49-66.

1946   The Indians of the Southeastern United States. *Bureau of American Ethnology Bulletin* 137. Washington. (Reprinted: *Classics in Smithsonian Anthropology* 2. Smithsonian Institution Press, Washington, 1979.)

1952   The Indian Tribes of North America. *Bureau of American Ethnology Bulletin* 145. Washington. (Several reprints, incl.: Smithsonian Institution Press, Washington, 1974, 1979, 1984; Scholarly Press, St. Clair Shores, Mich., 1976; Native American Book Publishers, Brighton, Mich., 1990.)

Swiggers, Pierre
1985   Munsee Borrowings from Dutch: Some Phonological Remarks. *International Journal of American Linguistics* 51(4):594-597.

Sylestine, Cora, Heather K. Hardy, and Timothy Montler
1993   Dictionary of the Alabama Language. Austin: University of Texas Press.

Szabo, Joyce M.
1989   Medicine Lodge Treaty Remembered. *American Indian Art Magazine* 14(4):52-59.

1994   Howling Wolf and the History of Ledger Art. Albuquerque: University of New Mexico Press.

Szathmary, Emőke J.E.
1978   Are the Biological Differences Between North American Indians and Eskimos Truly Profound? *Current Anthropology* 12(4):673-701.

1986   [Comment on Greenberg, Turner, and Zegura 1986]. *Current Anthropology* 27(5):490-491.

Tabeau, Pierre-Antoine
1939   Tabeau's Narrative of Loisel's Expedition to the Upper Missouri. Annie Heloise Abel, ed. Rose Abel Wright, trans. Norman: University of Oklahoma Press.

Tabios, Derenty, and Jeff Leer, eds.
1972   Sugcestun Unigkuat: Paluwigmiut Nanwalegmiut-hlu Quli'anguahlrit. Fairbanks: Center for Northern Educational Research, University of Alaska.

Tac, Pablo (Paulus)
1926   La lingua degli Indi Luiseños (Alta California) secondo gli appunti grammaticali inediti di un chierico indigeno conservati tra i manoscritti Mezzofanti nell'Archiginnasio di Bologna. [A cura di] Carlo Tagliavini. *Biblioteca de "L'Archiginnasio"*, ser. 2, No. 31. Bologna: Nicola Zanichelli.

Taché, Joseph-Charles
1884   Forestiers et voyageurs: moeurs et légendes canadiennes. Montréal: Cadieux et Derome. (Reprinted: Fides, Montréal, 1946, 1981.)

Tagliavini, Carlo 1926 *see* Tac, Pablo

Tagliavini, Carlo
1930   Frammento d'un dizionarietto Luiseño-Spagnuolo scritto da un indigeno. Pp. 905-917 in *Proceedings of the 23d International Congress of Americanists for 1928*. New York.

Talayesva, Don C.
1942   Sun Chief: The Autobiography of a Hopi Indian. Leo W. Simmons, ed. New Haven, Conn.: Yale University Press for the Institute of Human Relations.

Talmy, Leonard A.
1972   Semantic Structures in English and Atsugewi. (Unpublished Ph.D. Dissertation in Linguistics, University of California, Berkeley.)

Tanner, John
1830   A Narrative of the Captivity and Adventures of John Tanner During Thirty Years' Residence Among the Indians of the Interior of North America. Edwin James, ed. New York: G. and C. and H. Carvill. (Reprinted: Garland, New York, 1975.)

Tarpent, Marie-Lucie
1983   Morphophonemics of Nisgha Plural Formation: A Step Towards Proto-Tsimshian Reconstruction. Pp. 123-214 in Studies in Native American Languages II. *Kansas Working Papers in Linguistics* 8.

Tax, Sol
1955   The Social Organization of the Fox Indians. Pp. 241-282 in Social Anthropology of North American Tribes. Fred Eggan, ed. 2d ed. Chicago: University of Chicago Press.

905

Taylor, Alexander S.
1860-1863 California Notes: The Indianology of California. *The California Farmer and Journal of Useful Sciences* 13(3)-20(12). San Francisco.

Taylor, Allan R.
1960   Blackfoot Historical Phonology: A Preliminary Survey. (With One-Page Addendum Dated 1978). (Manuscript in Survey of California and Other Indian Languages, University of California at Berkeley.)

1962   Spanish 'manteca' in Alaska. *Romance Philology* 16(1):30-32.

1963   The Classification of the Caddoan Languages. *Proceedings of the American Philosophical Society* 107(1):51-59. Philadelphia.

1963a   Comparative Caddoan. *International Journal of American Linguistics* 29(2):113-131.

1967   Initial Change in Blackfoot. *Contributions to Anthropology* 1, *Linguistics* 1 (*Algonquian*), National Museum of Man Bulletin 214, *Anthropological Series* 78. Ottawa.

1974   Some Traits of the Dakota Language Revised: Lakhota Clause-final Enclitics. (Paper presented at the 73d Annual Meeting of the American Anthropological Association, Mexico City.)

1976   On Verbs of Motion in Siouan Languages. *International Journal of American Linguistics* 42(4):287-296.

1977   Arikara Text. Pp. 20-26 in Caddoan Texts, Douglas R. Parks, ed. *International Journal of American Linguistics. Native American Texts Series Monograph* 2(1). Chicago: University of Chicago Press.

1981   Indian Lingua Francas. Pp. 175-195 in Language in the USA. Charles A. Ferguson and Shirley B. Heath, eds. Cambridge: Cambridge University Press.

1983   Old Vocabularies and Linguistic Research: The Case of the Assiniboine. Pp. 31-44 in Proceedings of the Second Siouan Languages Conference, 1982. Mary C. Marino, ed. *Na'pāo: A Saskatchewan Anthropology Journal* 13(October/Special Issue). Saskatoon, Sask.

1989   Review Essay: Two Decades of Ethnobotany in the Northwest Plains. *International Journal of American Linguistics* 55(3):359-381.

1992   Language Obsolescence, Shift, and Death in Several Native American Communities. *International Journal of the Sociology of Language* 93. New York: Mouton de Gruyter.

Taylor, Herbert C., Jr., and Wilson Duff
1956   A Post-contact Southward Movement of the Kwakiutl. *Washington State College. Research Studies* 24(1):56-66. Pullman.

Taylor, Walter W.
1961   Archaeology and Language in Western North America. *American Antiquity* 27(1):71-81.

Tedlock, Dennis
1972   Finding the Center: Narrative Poetry of the Zuñi Indians. New York: Dial Press. (Reprinted: University of Nebraska Press, Lincoln, 1978.)

1978   Coyote and Junco. Pp. 171-177 in Coyote Stories. William Bright, ed. *International Journal of American Linguistics. Native American Texts Series, Monograph* 1. Chicago: The University of Chicago Press.

1983   On the Translation of Style in Oral Narrative. Pp. 57-77 in Smoothing the Ground: Essays on Native American Oral Literature. Brian Swann, ed. Berkeley: University of California Press.

Tedlock, Dennis, and Joseph Peynetsa, trans.
1972   A Prayer Over Dead Rabbits. *Alcheringa* 4:60-61. New York.

1978   Oratory in Three Languages. Sound recording attached to *Alcheringa* 4(1). New York.

Teeter, Karl V.
1964   The Wiyot Language. *University of California Publications in Linguistics* 37. Berkeley and Los Angeles.

1964a   Wiyot and Yurok: A Preliminary Study. Pp. 192-198 in Studies in Californian Linguistics. William Bright, ed. *University of California Publications in Linguistics* 34. Berkeley and Los Angeles. Press.

1964b   Algonquian Languages and Genetic Relationship. Pp. 1026-1033 in Proceedings of the 9th International Congress of Linguists. Horace G. Lunt, ed. London, The Hague, Paris: Mouton.

1965   The Algonquian Verb: Notes Toward a Reconsideration. *International Journal of American Linguistics* 31(2):221-225.

1967   Genetic Classification in Algonquian. Pp. 1-6 in Contributions to Anthropology: Linguistics I (Algonquian). *Anthropological Series* 78, *National Museum of Canada Bulletin* 214. Ottawa.

1971   The Main Features of Malecite-Passamaquoddy Grammar. Pp. 191-249 in Studies in American Indian Languages. Jesse Sawyer, ed. *University of California Publications in Linguistics* 65. Berkeley.

1973   Algonquian. Pp. 1143-1163 in Current Trends in Linguistics, Volume 10: Linguistics in North America (Pt. 2). Thomas A. Sebeok, ed. The Hague and Paris: Mouton.

1974   Some Algic Etymologies. *International Journal of American Linguistics* 40(3):197-201.

Teeter, Karl V., and John D. Nichols
1993   Wiyot Handbook I: Glossary and Concordance. *Algonquian and Iroquoian Linguistics, Memoir* 10. Winnipeg, Man.

1993a   Wiyot Handbook II: Interlinear Translation and English Index. *Algonquian and Iroquoian Linguistics, Memoir* 11. Winnipeg, Man.

Teit, James A.
1900   The Thompson Indians of British Columbia. Franz Boas, ed. *Memoirs of the American Museum of Natural History* 2, Anthropology 1(4); *Publications of the Jesup North Pacific Expedition* 1(4). New York. (Reprinted: AMS Press, New York, 1975.)

1928   The Middle Columbia Salish. *University of Washington Publications in Anthropology* 2(4):89-128. Seattle.

1930   Ethnobotany of the Thompson Indians. Elsie Viault Steedman, ed. Pp. 441-522 in *45th Annual Report of the Bureau of American Ethnology for 1927-1928.* (Reprinted: The Shorey Book Store, Seattle, Wash., 1973.)

1930a   The Salishan Tribes of the Western Plateaus. Franz Boas, ed. Pp. 23-396 in *45th Annual Report of the Bureau of American Ethnology for 1927-1928.* Washington. (Reprinted: Shorey Book Store, Seattle, Wash., 1973.)

1956   Field Notes on the Tahltan and Kaska Indians: 1912-1915. J.H. MacNeish, ed. *Anthropologica* 3:39-171. Ottawa.

Teit, James A., and Franz Boas
1930   Traditions and Information Regarding the Tona´xa. *American Anthropologist*, n.s. 32(4):625-632.

Tenenbaum, Joan M.
1976   Dena'ina Sukdu'a III. Dghiliq' Sukdu'a. Tanaina Stories III. Mountain Stories. Fairbanks: Alaska Native Language Center.

Tenenbaum, Joan M., and Mary Jane McGary
1984   Dena'ina Sukdu'a: Tanaina Stories by Antone Evan et al. Fairbanks: Alaska Native Language Center.

Tennant, Edward A., and Joseph N. Bitar, gen. eds.
1981   Yuut Qanemciit: Yupiit Cayaraita Qanrutkumallrit / Yupik Lore: Oral Traditions of an Eskimo People. Bethel, Alaska: Lower Kuskokwin School District.

Thalbitzer, William
1904   A Phonetical Study of the Eskimo Language. *Meddelelser om Grønland* 31. Copenhagen.

1904a   Eskimo Place-Names from North Greenland. Pp. 326-371 in A Phonetical Study of the Eskimo Language, Based on Observations Made on a Journey in North Greenland, 1900-1901. *Meddelelser om Grønland* 31. Copenhagen.

1913   Four Skræling Words from Markland (Newfoundland) in the Saga of Erik the Red (Eirikr rauði). Pp. 87-95 in Pt. 1 of *Proceedings of the 18th International Congress of Americanists for 1912.* London: Harrison and Sons.

1921   The Aleutian Language Compared with Greenlandic: A Manuscript by Rasmus Rask, Dating from 1820, Now in the Royal Library at Copenhagen. *International Journal of American Linguistics* 2(1-2):40-57.

1921a   The Ammassalik Eskimo. Languge and Folklore. *Meddelelser om Grønland* 40(3, Pt. 2):113-564. Copenhagen: Bianco Luno.

1954   Bibliografi, 1900-1953. *Meddelelser om Grønland* 140. Copenhagen.

Tharp, George W.
1972   The Position of the Tsetsaut Among Northern Athapaskans. *International Journal of American Linguistics* 38(1):14-25.

The Children of Kingfisher Indian Day School
1970   Our Cree Dictionary. By The Children of Kingfisher Indian Day School, Kingfisher Lake, via Central Patricia, Ontario, Canada; R.V.F. Ryan, Teacher. Toronto: Education Division, Indian Affairs Branch, Indian Affairs and Northern Development.

Thibault, Jean Baptiste
1866   Prières, cantiques, catéchisme, etc. en langue crise. Montréal: Louis Perrault.

Thibert, Arthur
1958   English-Eskimo / Dictionary / Eskimo-English. Rev. ed. Ottawa: Research Center for Amerindian Anthropology.

Thieme, Paul
1964   The Comparative Method for Reconstruction in Linguistics. Pp. 585-597 in Language in Culture and Society: A Reader in Linguistics and Anthropology. Dell Hymes, ed. New York: Harper and Row.

Thomas, Cyrus
1902   Provisional List of Linguistic Families, Languages, and Dialects of Mexico and Central America. *American Anthropologist*, n.s. 4(2):207-216.

1911   Indian Languages of Mexico and Central America, and Their Geographical Distribution. *Bureau of American Ethnology Bulletin* 44. Washington.

Thomas, Edward Harper
1927   The Chinook Jargon. *American Speech* 2(4):377-384.

1935   Chinook: A History and Dictionary of the Northwest Coast Trade Jargon. Portland, Oreg.: Metropolitan Press.

Thomas, Gabriel
1698   An Historical and Geographical Account of the Province and Country of Pensilvania; and West-New-Jersey in America. London: A. Baldwin. (Facsimile lithograph: Henry A. Brady, New York, 1848.)

Thomason, Sarah G.
1980   On Interpreting 'The Indian Interpreter.' *Language in Society* 9:167-193.

1980a   Morphological Stability, With and Without Language Contact. Pp. 359-372 in Historical Morphology. Jacek Fisiak, ed. The Hague: Mouton.

907

1983   Chinook Jargon in Areal and Historical Context. *Language: Journal of the Linguistic Society of America* 59(4):820-870.

Thomason, Sarah G., and Terrence Kaufman
1988   Language Contact, Creolization, and Genetic Linguistics. Berkeley: University of California Press.

Thompson, Chad
1990   K'etetaalkkaanee: An Analytical Companion Volume. Fairbanks: Alaska Native Language Center.

Thompson, David
1971   Travels in Western North America 1784-1812. Victor G. Hopwood, ed. Toronto: Macmillan of Canada.

Thompson, Laurence C.
1973   The Northwest. Pp. 979-1045 in Current Trends in Linguistics 10: Linguistics in North America (Pt. 2). Thomas A. Sebeok, ed. The Hague and Paris: Mouton.

1976   The Northwest. Pp. 359-425 in Vol. 1 of Native Languages of the Americas. Thomas A. Sebeok, ed. 2 vols. New York and London: Plenum Press.

1979   Salishan and the Northwest. Pp. 692-765 in The Languages of Native America: Historical and Comparative Assessment. Lyle Campbell and Marianne Mithun, eds. Austin: University of Texas Press.

1985   Control in Salish Grammar. Pp. 391-428 in Relational Typology. Frans Plank, ed. *Trends in Linguistics, Studies and Monographs* 28. The Hague: Mouton.

Thompson, Laurence C., and M. Terry Thompson
1962-1982 [Fieldnotes on the Thompson Language.] (Unpublished manuscripts in L.C. and M.T. Thompson's possession, University of Hawaii, Honolulu.)

1966   A Fresh Look at Tillamook Phonology. *International Journal of American Linguistics* 32(4):313-319.

1971   Clallam: A Preview. Pp. 251-294 in Studies in American Indian Languages. Jesse Sawyer, ed. *University of California Publications in Linguistics* 65. Berkeley.

1992   The Thompson Language. *University of Montana Occasional Papers in Linguistics* 8. Missoula.

1996   Thompson River Salish Dictionary. *University of Montana Occasional Papers in Linguistics* 12. Missoula.

Thompson, M. Terry
1985-1991 [Fieldnotes on the Thompson Language.] (Unpublished manuscript in M. Terry Thompson's possession.)

Thompson, M. Terry, and Steven M. Egesdal
1993   Annie York's Push-Back-Sides-of-His-Hair (nʔik'ʔik'n'incút): A Traditional Thompson River Salish Legend with Commentary. Pp. 279-302 in American Indian Linguistics and Ethnography in Honor of Laurence C. Thompson. Anthony Mattina and Timothy Montler, eds. *University of Montana Occasional Papers in Linguistics* 10. Missoula.

Thompson, Stith
1929   Tales of the North American Indians. Bloomington: Indiana University Press.

1946   The Folktale. New York: The Dryden Press.

1955-1958 Motif-index of Folk-literature. Rev. and enl. ed. 6 vols. Bloomington: Indiana University Press. (Originally published in 1932-1936.)

Thord-Gray, Ivor
1955   Tarahumara-English, English-Tarahumara Dictionary and an Introduction to Tarahumara Grammar. Coral Gables, Fla.: University of Miami Press.

Thornton, Harrison R.
1931   Among the Eskimos of Wales, Alaska. Baltimore: Johns Hopkins Press. (Reprinted: AMS Press, New York, 1976.)

Thurnwald, Richard, et al.
1927   Name, Namengebung. Pp. 432-448 in Reallexikon der Vorgeschichte unter Mitwirkung zahlreicher Fachgelehrter, Vol. 8. Max Ebert, ed. Berlin: Verlag Walter de Gruyter.

Thwaites, Reuben G., ed.
1904-1905 Original Journals of the Lewis and Clark Expedition 1804-1806... . 8 vols. New York: Dodd, Mead.

1904-1907 Early Western Travels, 1748-1846: A Series of Annotated Reprints of Some of the Best and Rarest Contemporary Volumes of Travel, Descriptive of the Aborigines and Social and Economic Conditions in the Middle and Far West, During the Period of Early American Settlement. 38 vols. Cleveland, Ohio: Arthur H. Clark.

1905   New Voyages to North-America by the Baron de Lahontan. 2 vols. Chicago: A.C. McClurg. (Orig. trans., London: H. Bonwicke et al., 1703.)

Timmers, Jan
1977   A Classified English-Sechelt Word-List. Lisse, The Netherlands: The Peter de Ridder Press.

1978   Comox Stem-List. Leiden, The Netherlands: [no publisher.]

1978a   Sechelt Stem-List. Leiden, The Netherlands: [no publisher.]

Tims, John W.
1889   Grammar and Dictionary of the Blackfoot Language in the Dominion of Canada, for the Use of Missionaries, Schoolteachers, and Others. London: Society for Promoting Christian Knowledge.

Titiev, Mischa
1946   Suggestions for the Further Study of Hopi. *International Journal of American Linguistics* 12(2):89-91.

Titus, Dorothy, and Matthew Titus
1991   This is the Way We Make Our Baskets: Dats'en Lo K'iyh Tth'ok Tr'eghonh. Fairbanks: Alaska Native Language Center.

Toelken, J. Barre
1969   The "Pretty Language" of Yellowman: Genre, Mode,
           and Texture in Navaho Coyote Narratives. *Genre*
           2(3):211-235. Chicago.

Tolmie, William Fraser, and George M. Dawson
1884   Comparative Vocabularies of the Indian Tribes of
           British Columbia, with a Map Illustrating Distribution.
           Montreal: Dawson Brothers.

Tom, Gertie
1988   Ekiyi: Gyò Cho Chú; My Country: Big Salmon River.
           With map. Whitehorse, Yukon Terr.: Yukon Native
           Language Centre.

Tomkins, William
1926   Universal Indian Sign Language of the Plains Indians of
           North America [etc.]. San Diego, Calif.: William
           Tomkins. (The 1931 [5th] ed. reprinted by Dover
           Publications, New York, 1969.)

Tooker, Elisabeth
1960   Three Aspects of Northern Iroquoian Culture Change.
           Pennsylvania Archaeologist 30(2):65-71.

1964   An Ethnography of the Huron Indians, 1615-1649.
           Bureau of American Ethnology Bulletin 190. Washington.

1970   Northern Iroquian Sociopolitical Organization. *American Anthropologist* 72(1):90-97.

1970a   The Iroquois Ceremonial of Midwinter. Syracuse:
           Syracuse University Press.

1971   Clans and Moieties in North America. *Current Anthropology* 12(3):357-376.

Tooker, William W.
1911   The Indian Place-Names on Long Island and Islands
           Adjacent, With Their Probable Significations.
           Alexander F. Chamberlain, ed. New York: John Jermain
           Memorial Library. (Reprinted: Ira J. Friedman, Port
           Washington, N.Y., 1962.)

Toomey, Thomas N.
1917   Proper Names from the Muskhogean Languages. *Hervas Laboratories of American Linguistics Bulletin* 3. St.
           Louis.

Townshend, Charles H.
1900   The Quinnipiack Indians and Their Reservation. New
           Haven, Conn.: Tuttle, Morehouse and Taylor.

Trager, Felicia Harben
1971   An Annotated Bibliography of the Publications and
           Writings of George L. Trager through 1970. *Southern
           Methodist University. Studies in Linguistics. Occasional
           Papers* 12. Dallas, Tex.

1971a   Some Aspects of "Time" at Picuris Pueblo (With an
           Addendum on the Nootka). *Anthropological Linguistics*
           13(7):331-338.

1971b   The Phonology of Picuris. *International Journal of
           American Linguistics* 37(1):29-33.

1975   Morphemic Change in Picuris: A Case of Culture
           Contact? *Studies in Linguistics* 25:89-93.

Trager, George L.
1939   The Days of the Week in the Language of Taos Pueblo,
           New Mexico. *Language: Journal of the Linguistic
           Society of America* 15(1):51-55.

1942   The Historical Phonology of the Tiwa Languages.
           Studies in Linguistics 1(5):1-10. New Haven, Conn.

1943   The Kinship and Status Terms of the Tiwa Languages.
           American Anthropologist, n.s. 45(4):557-571.

1944   Spanish and English Loanwords in Taos. *International
           Journal of American Linguistics* 10(4):144-158.

1945   [Review of] Map of North American Indian Languages;
           compiled and drawn by C.F. Voegelin and E.W.
           Voegelin. *International Journal of American Linguistics*
           11(3):186-189.

1946   An Outline of Taos Grammar. Pp. 184-221 in Linguistic
           Structures of Native America. Harry Hoijer, ed. *Viking
           Fund Publications in Anthropology* 6. New York.

1948   Taos I: A Language Revisited. *International Journal of
           American Linguistics* 14(3):155-160.

1951   Linguistic History and Ethnographic History in the
           Southwest. *Journal of the Washington Academy of
           Sciences* 41(11):341-343.

1954   Taos II: Pronominal Reference. *International Journal of
           American Linguistics* 20(3):173-180.

1960   Taos III: Paralanguage. *Anthropological Linguistics*
           2(2):24-30.

1961   Taos IV: Morphemics, Syntax, Semology in Nouns and
           in Pronominal Reference. *International Journal of
           American Linguistics* 27(3):211-222.

1967   The Tanoan Settlement of the Rio Grande Area: A Possible Chronology. Pp. 335-350 in Studies in
           Southwestern Ethnolinguistics: Meaning and History in
           the Languages of the American Southwest. Dell Hymes
           and William E. Bittle, eds. The Hague: Mouton.

Trager, George L., and Felicia E. Harben
1958   North American Indian Languages: Classification and
           Maps. *Studies in Linguistics, Occasional Papers* 5.
           Buffalo, N.Y.

1970   The Cardinal Directions at Taos and Picuris. *Anthropological Linguistics* 12(2):1-37.

1959   Kiowa and Tanoan. *American Anthropologist*, n.s.
           61(6):1078-1083.

Traveller Bird
1971   Tell Them They Lie: The Sequoyah Myth. Los Angeles: Westernlore Press.

Trigger, Bruce G.
1970   The Strategy of Iroquois Prehistory. *Ontario Archaeology* 14:3-48.

_____
1976   The Children of Aataentsic: A History of the Huron People to 1660. Kingston and Montreal: McGill-Queen's University Press.

Troike, Rudolph C.
1959   A Descriptive Phonology and Morphology of Coahuilteco. (Unpublished Ph.D. Dissertation in Linguistics, University of Texas, Austin.)

_____
1961   A Nahuatl Loan-word in Coahuilteco. *International Journal of American Linguistics* 27(2):172-175.

_____
1961a   Researches in Coahuiltecan Ethnography. *Bulletin of the Texas Archeological Society* 30(for 1959):301-309. Austin.

_____
1962   Notes on Coahuiltecan Ethnography. *Bulletin of the Texas Archeological Society* 32(for 1961):57-63. Austin.

_____
1963   A Contribution to Coahuilteco Lexicography. *International Journal of American Linguistics* 29(4):295-299.

_____
1967   A Structural Comparison of Tonkawa and Coahuilteco. Pp. 321-332 in Studies in Southwestern Ethnolinguistics. Dell H. Hymes and William E. Bittle, eds. The Hague: Mouton.

_____
1967a   [Review of: *El Cuadernillo de la Lengua de los Indios Pajalates y el Confesionario de Indios en Lengua Coahuilteca.* Eugenio del Hoyo, ed.] *International Journal of American Linguistics* 33(1):78-82.

_____
1976   The Linguistic Classification of Cochimi. Pp. 159-164 in Hokan Studies: Papers from the First Conference on Hokan Languages. Margaret Langdon and Shirley Silver, eds. (*Janua Linguarum, Series Practica* 181). The Hague: Mouton.

_____
1978   The Date and Authorship of the Pajalate (Coahuilteco) Cuadernillo. *International Journal of American Linguistics* 44(4):168-171.

_____
1981   Subject-Object Concord in Coahuilteco. *Language: Journal of the Linguistic Society of America* 57(3):658-673.

Trumbull, James Hammond
1870   On the Composition of Indian Geographical Names. *Connecticut Historical Society Collections* 2. Hartford.

_____
1873   Notes on Forty Versions of the Lord's Prayer in Algonkin Languages. *Transactions of the American Philological Association, 1872*: 113-218. Hartford.

_____
1881   Indian Names of Places etc., in and on the Borders of Connecticut: With Interpretations of Some of Them. Hartford: [For the Author]. (Reprinted: Archon Books, Hamden, 1974.)

_____
1903   Natick Dictionary. *Bureau of American Ethnology Bulletin* 25. Washington.

_____
1974   Indian Names in Connecticut. Hamden: Archon Books.

Tuck, James A.
1975   The Northeastern Maritime Continuum: 8000 Years of Cultural Development in the Far Northeast. *Arctic Anthropology* 12(2):139-147.

_____
1977   A Look at Laurentian. Pp. 31-40 in Current Perspectives in Northeastern Archaeology. R.E. Funk and C.F. Hayes, eds. *New York State Archaeological Association Researches and Transactions* 17.

Turner, Christy G., II
1983   Dental Evidence for the Peopling of the Americas. Pp. 147-157 in Early Man in the New World. Richard Shutler, Jr., ed. Beverly Hills, London, New Delhi: Sage Publications.

_____
1986   The First Americans: The Dental Evidence. *National Geographic Research* 2(1):37-46.

Turner, Katherine
1980   The Reconstituted Phonemes of Salinan. *Journal of California and Great Basin Anthropology, Papers in Linguistics* 2:53-92.

Turner, Ken
1987   Bringing It All Back Home: Joel Sherzer and the San Blas Kuna. *International Journal of American Linguistics* 53(1):86-102.

Turner, Lucien M.
1894   Ethnology of the Ungava District, Hudson Bay Territory. Pp. 159-350 in *11th Annual Report of the Bureau of [American] Ethnology for 1889-1890.* Washington.

Turner, Nancy J.
1973-1989 [Fieldnotes on Thompson Ethnobotany.] (Unpublished manuscript in Turner's possession.)

Turner, Nancy J., Laurence C. Thompson, M. Terry Thompson, and Annie Z. York
1990   Thompson Ethnobotany: Knowledge and Usage of Plants by the Thompson Indians of British Columbia. *Royal British Columbia Museum Memoir* 3. Victoria.

Turner, William W.
1852   The Apaches: A Paper Read Before the American Ethnological Society. *Literary World* 272(April 17, 1852):281-282.

Turney-High, Harry Holbert
1937   The Flathead Indians of Montana. *American Anthropological Association Memoir* 48. Menasha, Wis.

_____
1941   Ethnography of the Kutenai. *American Anthropological Association Memoir* 56. Menasha, Wis.

Turquetil, Arsène
1926 Notes sur les Esquimaux de Baie Hudson. Tribus, notes sur coutumes religieuses, genre de vie, chasse et pêche. *Anthropos* 21(3-4):419-434.

1929 The Religion of the Central Eskimo. *Primitive Man* 2:57-64. Washington, D.C.: Catholic Anthropological Conference.

Tuttle, Edward F.
1976 Borrowing Versus Semantic Shift: New World Nomenclature in European Languages. Pp. 595-611 in Vol. 2 of First Images of America: The Impact of the New World on the Old. Fredi Chiapelli, ed. Berkeley: University of California Press.

Tweddell, Colin E.
1974 A Historical and Ethnological Study of the Snohomish Indian People: A Report Specifically Covering Their Aboriginal and Continued Existence, and Their Effective Occupation of a Definable Territory. Pp. 475-694 in Coast Salish and Western Washington Indians, II. New York: Garland.

Tyhurst, Robert
1992 Traditional and Contemporary Land and Resource Use by *Ts'kw'ayláxw* and *Xáxli'p* Bands. Pp. 355-404 in A Complex Culture of the British Columbia Plateau: Traditional *Stl'átl'imx* Resource Use. Brian Hayden, ed. Vancouver: UBC Press.

Tyler, Stephen A.
1986 On Being Out of Words. *Cultural Anthropology* 1(2):131-137.

Tyrrell, Joseph B.
1887 Cree and Stoney Indian Names of Places Within the Area of the Accompanying Map. Pp. 172E-176E of Report on a Part of Northern Alberta, and Portions of Adjacent Districts of Assiniboia and Saskatchewan. *Annual Report for the Geological and Natural History Survey of Canada* , n.s. 2. Montreal: Dawson.

1898 Chippewyan Names of Places in the Country Here Reported On. Pp. 194F-195F of Report on the Doobaunt, Kazan, and Ferguson Rivers and the Northwest Coast of Hudson Bay. *Annual Report for the Geological Survey of Canada*, n.s. 9. Ottawa: S.E. Dawson.

1915 Algonquian Indian Names of Places in Northern Canada. *Transactions of the Royal Canadian Institute* 10(3):213-231. Toronto.

Tyzhnov, Il´ïa
1848 Aleutsko-kad´ïakskïï bukvar´ [Koniag Pacific Yupik Primer]. St. Petersburg: Synod Press.

Ubelaker, Douglas H., and Richard L. Jantz
1986 Biological History of the Aboriginal Population of North America. *Rassengeschichte der Menschheit* 11 (Amerika I: Nordamerika, Mexico). München: R. Oldenbourg.

Uhlenbeck, Christian C.
1911 Original Blackfoot Texts from the Southern Peigans, Blackfoot Reservation, Teton Country, Montana. With the Help of Joseph Tatsey, Collected and Published with an English Translation. *Verhandelingen der Koninklijke Akademien van Wetenschappen te Amsterdam, Afdeeling Letterkunde*, n.r. 12(1). Amsterdam: Johannes Müller.

1912 A New Series of Blackfoot Texts from the Southern Peigans, Blackfoot Reservation, Teton County, Montana, With the Help of Joseph Tatsey. *Verhandelingen der Koninklijke Akademie van Wetenschappen te Amsterdam, Afdeeling Letterkunde*, n.r. 13(1). Amsterdam, Johannes Müller. (Reprinted: AMS Press, New York, 1978.)

1938 A Concise Blackfoot Grammar, Based on Material from the Southern Peigans. *Verhandelingen der Koninklijke Akademie van Wetenschappen te Amsterdam, Afdeeling Letterkunde*, n.r. 41. Amsterdam. (Reprinted: AMS Press, New York, 1978.)

Uhlenbeck, Christian C., and R.H. van Gulik
1930 An English-Blackfoot Vocabulary, Based on Material from the Southern Peigans. *Verhandelingen der Koninklijke Akademie van Wetenschappen te Amsterdam, Afdeeling Letterkunde*, n.r. 29(4). Amsterdam. (Reprinted: AMS Press, New York, 1979.)

1934 A Blackfoot-English Vocabulary; Based on Material from the Southern Peigans. *Verhandelingen der Koninklijke Akademie van Wetenschappen te Amsterdam, Afdeeling Letterkunde*, n.r. 33(2). Amsterdam. (Reprinted: AMS Press, New York, 1984.)

Uldall, Hans Jorgen, and William F. Shipley
1966 Nisenan Texts and Dictionary. *University of California Publications in Linguistics* 46. Berkeley.

Ultan, Russel
1971 A Case of Sound Symbolism in Konkow. Pp. 295-301 in Studies in American Indian Languages. Jesse Sawyer, ed. *University of California Publications in Linguistics* 65. Berkeley.

Umfreville, Edward
1790 The Present State of Hudson's Bay; Containing a Full Description of that Settlement, and the Adjacent Country; and Likewise of the Fur Trade, with Hints for its Improvement, &c. London: Charles Stalker.

1954 The Present State of Hudson's Bay, Containing a Full Description of that Settlement and the Adjacent Country and Likewise of the Fur Trade, with Hints for its Improvement, etc. [1790]. W. Stewart Wallace, ed. Toronto: Ryerson Press.

Umiker-Sebeok, D. Jean, and Thomas A. Sebeok, eds.
1978 Aboriginal Sign Languages of the Americas and Australia. 2 vols. New York and London: Plenum Press.

Underhill, Lonnie E.
1968 Indian Name Translation. *American Speech* 43(2):114-126.

Underhill, Robert
1976 Noun Bases in Two Eskimo Dialects: A Study in Comparative Morphophonemics. Pp. 239-271 in Papers on Eskimo and Aleut Linguistics. Eric P. Hamp, ed. Chicago: Chicago Linguistic Society.

Underhill, Ruth M.
1939 Social Organization of the Papago Indians. *Columbia University Contributions to Anthropology* 30. New York (Reprinted: AMS Press, New York, 1969.)

1946   Papago Indian Religion. *Columbia University Contributions to Anthropology* 33. New York (Reprinted: AMS Press, New York, 1969.)

1953   Here Come the Navaho! Washington: U.S. Bureau of Indian Affairs, Branch of Education.

U.S. Army. Corps of Engineers
1855   Report Upon the Indian Tribeś, by Lieut. A.W. Whipple, Thomas Ewbank, Esq., and Prof. Wm. W. Turner. Washington: War Department.

U.S. Bureau of the Census. Department of Commerce, 13th Census
1915   Indian Population in the United States and Alaska, 1910. Washington: Government Printing Office.

U.S. Bureau of the Census. Department of the Interior, 11th Census
1894   Report on Indians Taxed and Indians Not Taxed in the United States (Except Alaska) at the Eleventh Census: 1890. Washington: Government Printing Office. (Reprinted: Norman Ross Publishing, New York, 1994.)

U.S. Census Office. 10th Census
1884   Report on the Population, Industries, and Resources of Alaska, by Ivan Petroff. 10th Census: 1880. Washington: Government Printing Office.

U.S. Department of War. Office of Indian Affairs
1826   [Circular Letter Requesting Information on Indian Languages.] Pt. I: Vocabulary; Pt. II: Verbal Forms and Select Sentences; Pt. III (1826): A Table of Indian Tribes of the United States, East of the Stony Mountains, Arranged According to Languages and Dialects, Furnished by Albert Gallatin. Washington. (Pt. III, Microfilm No. M234, Roll 429, Frames 727-730, National Archives, Washington.)

U.S. Office of Indian Affairs
1941   Place Names on the Papago, Gila Bend and San Xavier Indian Reservations. Sells, Ariz.: Sells Indian Agency.

Upham, Warren
1969   Minnesota Geographic Names: Their Origin and Historic Significance. Reprint. Edited with New Introduction by James T. Dunn. St. Paul: Minnesota Historical Society.

Vaillancourt, Louis-Philippe
1978   Cours de cris, premier degré. (*Collection Tekouerimat* 6). Montréal: Les Presses de l'Université du Quebéc.

1980   Cours de cris, deuxième degré. (*Collection Tekouerimat* 7). Montréal: Les Presses de l'Université du Quebéc.

Valiquette, Hilaire Paul
1990   A Study of a Lexicon of Laguna Keresan. 2 vols. (Unpublished Ph.D. Dissertation in Linguistics, University of New Mexico, Albuquerque.)

Valle, Francisco
1892   Quaḋerno de algunas reglas y apuntes sobre el idioma pame. Pp. 287-314 in Bibliografía española de lenguas indígenas de América. Conde de Viñaza, Madrid. (New edition: La única gramática conocida de la lengua pame. Rudolf Schuller, ed., Mexico City, 1925.)

Vancouver, George
1801   A Voyage of Discovery to the North Pacific Ocean, and Round the World.... New ed., with corrections, [etc.]. John Vancouver, ed. 6 vols. London: John Stockdale.

Vandall, Peter, and Joe Douquette
1987   Wâskahikaniwiyiniw-âcimowina / Stories of the House People. Freda Ahenakew, ed. and trans. (*Publications of the Algonquian Text Society / Collection de la Société d'édition de textes algonquiens*). Winnipeg: University of Manitoba Press.

Van den Bogaert, Harmen Meyndertsz
1988   A Journal into Mohawk and Oneida Country, 1634-1635: The Journal of Harmen Meyndertsz van den Bogaert. Charles T. Gehring and William A. Starna, eds. and trans., with Wordlist and Linguistic Notes by Gunther Michelson. Syracuse: Syracuse University Press.

van Dijk, Teun A. *see* Dijk, Teun A. van

van Eijk, Jan P. *see* Eijk, Jan P. van

van Gennep, Arnold *see* Gennep, Arnold van

VanStone, James W.
1962   Point Hope: An Eskimo Village in Transition. Seattle: University of Washington Press.

Van Tuyl, Charles D.
1979   The Natchez: Annotated Translations from Antoine Simon le Page du Pratz's Histoire de la Louisiane and a Short English-Natchez Dictionary, with Ethnographic Footnotes, Natchez Transcription, Sound System, Kinship Terminology, and Kinship System by Willard Walker. (*Oklahoma Historical Society Series in Anthropology* 4). Oklahoma City.

Van Tuyl, Charles D., and Durbin D. Feeling
1994   An Outline of Basic Verb Inflections of Oklahoma Cherokee. Muskogee, Okla.: Indian University Press.

Van Valin, Robert D., Jr.
1985   Case Marking and the Structure of the Lakhota Clause. Pp. 363-413 in Grammar Inside and Outside the Clause: Some Approaches to Theory from the Field. Johanna Nichols and Anthony C. Woodbury, eds. Cambridge and New York: Cambridge University Press.

1987   The Role of Government in the Grammar of Head-marking Languages. *International Journal of American Linguistics* 53(4):371-397.

Van Valkenburgh, Richard F.
1941   Diné Bikéyah. Lucy Wilcox Adams and John C. McPhee, eds. Window Rock, Ariz.: U.S. Department of the Interior Office of Indian Affairs, Navajo Service.

1974   Navajo Sacred Places. Clyde Kluckhohn, ed. Pp. 9-199 in Navajo Indians III. (*American Indian Ethnohistory Series: Indians of the Southwest.*) New York: Garland.

Van Valkenburgh, Richard F., and Scotty Begay
1938   Sacred Places and Shrines of the Navajo: Part I: The Sacred Mountains. *Museum of Northern Arizona Museum Notes* 2:29-34. Flagstaff.

Vaughan, J. Daniel
1984   Tsimshian Potlatch and Society: Examining a Structural Analysis. Pp. 58-68 in The Tsimshian and Their Neighbors of the North Pacific Coast. Jay Miller and Carol M. Eastman, eds. Seattle and London: University of Washington Press.

912

Veniaminov, Ivan Evĭeevich Popov

1840   Zapiski ob ostrovakh Unalashkinskago otdĭela. [Notes on the Islands of the Unalaska District.] Vols. 1 and 2. St. Petersburg: Russian-American Company. (English translation: The Limestone Press, Kingston, Ont., 1985.)

1840a   Zapiski ob Atkhinskikh Aleutakh i Koloshakh. Sostavlĭaŭshchĭe tretiŭ chast´ Zapisok ob Ostrovakh Unalashkinskago otdĭela [Notes on the Atka Aleuts and Tlingits. Constituting the Third Part of *Notes on the Islands of the Unalaska District*]. St. Petersburg: Russian-American Company.

1846   Zamĭechanĭía o koloshenskom i kad´íakskom íazykakh i otchasti o prochikh rossĭísko-amerikanskikh, s priso-vokuplenĭem rossĭísko-koloshenskago slovarĭa, soderzhashchago bolĭee 1000 slov, iz koikh na nĭekoto-ryĭa sdĭelany poĭasnenĭía [Remarks on the Tlingit and Koniag Languages, and Partly on Others of Russian-America, with the Addition of a Russian-Tlingit Vocabulary Containing More Than 1,000 Words, Some With Explanations]. St. Petersburg: Akademiia Nauk. (Typescript translation by R.H. Geoghegan in Alaska State Library, Juneau.)

1846a   Opyt grammatiki aleutsko-lis´evskago íazyka. [An Essay at a Grammar of the Fox Island Aleut Language.] 2 pts. St. Petersburg: Akademiia Nauk.

1984   Notes on the Islands of the Unalashka District. Lydia T. Black and R.H. Geoghegan, trans. Richard A. Pierce, ed. (*Alaska History* 27). Fairbanks, Alaska, and Kingston, Ont.: Elmer E. Rasmussen Library Translation Program, University of Alaska and Limestone Press.

Veniaminov, Ivan Evĭeevich Popov, and Iakov Netsvetov

1893   Nachatki khristĭanskago uchenĭía... na aleutsko-lis´evskĭí perevel [Rudiments of Christian Doctrine ... translated into the Fox Island Aleut Language]. St. Petersburg: Synod Press. (Originally publ. in 1840.)

Vennum, Thomas, Jr.

1980   A History of Ojibwa Song Form. *Selected Reports in Ethnomusicology* 3(2):42-75.

Verdery, Mark T.

1983   Indian Names of Major Rivers. *Names in South Carolina* 16:30-31. Columbia, S.C.

Verwyst, Chrysostom

1892   Geographical Names in Wisconsin, Minnesota, and Michigan, Having a Chippewa Origin. *Collections of the State Historical Society of Wisconsin* 12:390-398. Madison.

1916   A Glossary of Chippewa Indian Names of Rivers, Lakes, and Villages. *Acta et Dicta* 4:253-274. St. Paul, Minn.

Vetromile, Eugene

1866   The Abnakis and Their History; or Historical Notes on the Aborigines of Acadia. New York: James B. Kirker.

Vibæk, Poul

1907   Contributions to the Study of the Eskimo Language in Greenland. *Meddelelser om Grønland* 33. Copenhagen.

Vickers, Ovid

1983   Mississippi Choctaw Names and Naming: A Diachronic View. *Names* 31(2):117-122.

Villiers du Terrage, Marc de, and Paul Rivet

1919   Les indiens du Texas et les expéditions françaises de 1720 et 1721 à la 'Baie Saint-Bernard.' *Journal de la Société des Américanistes de Paris* 11(2):403-442.

1929   Deux vocabulaires inédits recueillis au Texas vers 1688. *Journal de la Société des Américanistes de Paris* 21(2):307-311.

Vinson, Julien

1886   La langue Taensa. *Revue de Linguistique et de Philologie Comparée* 19(2):147-169. Paris: Maisonneuve Frères et Ch. Leclerc.

Voegelin, Charles F.

1935   Tübatulabal Grammar. *University of California Publications in American Archaeology and Ethnology* 34(2):55-190. Berkeley.

1935a   Tübatulabal Texts. *University of California Publications in American Archaeology and Ethnology* 34(3):191-246. Berkeley.

1936   Productive Paradigms in Shawnee. Pp. 391-403 in Essays in Anthropology in Honor of Alfred Louis Kroeber. Robert H. Lowie, ed. Berkeley: University of California Press.

1938-1940 Shawnee Stems and the Jacob P. Dunn Miami Dictionary. *Indiana Historical Society Prehistory Research Series* 1:63-108, 135-167, 289-323, 345-406, 409-478. Indianapolis.

1939   Ofo-Biloxi Sound Correspondences. *Proceedings of the Indiana Academy of Science* 48:23-26.

1941   Proto-Algonquian Consonant Clusters in Delaware. *Language: Journal of the Linguistic Society of America* 17(2):143-147.

1941a   Historical Results of Crow-Hidatsa Comparisons, According to Three Methods. *Proceedings of the Indiana Academy of Science* 50:39-42.

1941b   Internal Relationships of Siouan Languages. *American Anthropologist*, n.s. 43(2, Pt.1):246-249.

1941c   North American Indian Languages Still Spoken and Their Genetic Relationships. Pp. 15-40 in Language, Culture, and Personality: Essays in Memory of Edward Sapir. Leslie Spier, A. Irving Hallowell, and Stanley S. Newman, eds. Menasha, Wis.: Sapir Memorial Publication Fund. (Reprinted: Greenwood Press, Westport, Conn., 1983.)

1942   Word Distortions in Delaware Big House and Walam Olum Songs. *Proceedings of the Indiana Academy of Science* 51:48-54. Indianapolis.

1944 Influence of Area in American Indian Linguistics. *Word* 1(1):54-58. (Reprinted: Pp. 638-641 in Language in Culture and Society. Dell Hymes, ed., Harper and Row, New York, 1964.)

1945 Relative Chronology of North American Linguistic Types. *American Anthropologist,* n.s. 47(2):232-234.

1945a Delaware Texts. *International Journal of American Linguistics* 11(2):105-119.

1946 Notes on Klamath-Modoc and Achumawi Dialects. *International Journal of American Linguistics* 12(2):96-101.

1946a Delaware, An Eastern Algonquian Language. Pp. 130-157 in Linguistic Structures of Native America. Harry Hoijer, ed. *Viking Fund Publications in Anthropology* 6. New York.

1952 The Boas Plan for the Presentation of American Indian Languages. *Proceedings of the American Philosophical Society* 96(4):439-451. Philadelphia.

1958 The Dispersal Factor in Migrations and Immigrations in New World Culture History. Raymond H. Thompson, ed. *University of Arizona Social Science Bulletin* 27. Tucson: University of Arizona Press.

1958a Working Dictionary of Tübatulabal. *International Journal of American Linguistics* 24(3):221-228.

1959 An Expanding Language, Hopi. *Plateau* 32(2):33-39. Flagstaff, Ariz.

1960 Casual and Noncasual Utterances within Unified Structure. Pp. 57-68 in Style in Language. Thomas A. Sebeok, ed. Cambridge, Mass.: M.I.T. Press.

1962 [Comment on] Bergsland and Vogt (1962). *Current Anthropology* 3(2):146-148.

Voegelin, Charles F., and Robert C. Euler
1957 Introduction to Hopi Chants. *Journal of American Folklore* 70(276):115-136.

Voegelin, Charles F., and Florence M. Robinett
1954 'Mother Language' in Hidatsa. *International Journal of American Linguistics* 20(1):65-70

Voegelin, Charles F., and Erminie W. Voegelin
1935 Shawnee Name Groups. *American Anthropologist,* n.s. 37(4):617-635.

1944 Map of North American Indian Languages. *American Ethnological Society Publication* 20. (Published by the American Ethnological Society and Indiana University). New York: J.J. Augustin.

1946 Linguistic Considerations of Northeastern North America. Pp. 178-194 in Man in Northeastern North America. Frederick Johnson, ed. *Papers of the Robert S. Peabody Foundation for Archaeology* 3. Andover, Mass.

Voegelin, Charles F., and Florence M. Voegelin
1957 Hopi Domains: A Lexical Approach to the Problem of Selection. *Indiana University Publications in Anthropology and Linguistics Memoir* 14. *International Journal of American Linguistics* 23(2, Pt. 2):1-82. Baltimore: Waverly Press.

1960 Selection in Hopi Ethics, Linguistics, and Translation. *Anthropological Linguistics* 2(2):48-78.

1964 Languages of the World: Native America Fascicle One. *Anthropological Linguistics* 6(6):1-149.

1965 Languages of the World: Native America Fascicle Two. *Anthropological Linguistics* 7(7):1-150.

1966 Map of North American Indian Languages. *American Ethnological Society. Revised Publication* 20. [New York]: Prepared and printed by Rand McNally.

1967 Passive Transformations from Non-Transitive Bases in Hopi. *International Journal of American Linguistics* 33(4):276-281.

1970 Cross-Cultural Typologies and Folk Taxonomies. Pp. 1132-1147 in Échanges et communications: mélanges offerts à Claude Lévi-Strauss à l'occasion de son 60ème anniversaire. Vol. 2 of Jean Pouillon and Pierre Maranda, eds. The Hague and Paris: Mouton.

1970a Hopi Names and No Names (with Reference to Households in Social Organization). Pp. 47-53 in Languages and Cultures of Western North America. Essays in Honor of Sven S. Liljeblad. Earl H. Swanson, Jr., ed. Pocatello: The Idaho State University Press.

1971 The Autonomy of Linguistics and the Dependence of Cognitive Culture. Pp. 303-317 in Studies in American Indian Lauguages. Jesse O. Sawyer, ed. Berkeley: University of California Press.

1977 Classification and Index of the World's Languages. New York: Elsevier.

Voegelin, Charles F., Florence M. Voegelin, and Kenneth L. Hale
1962 Typological and Comparative Grammar of Uto-Aztecan: I (Phonology). *Indiana University Publications in Anthropology and Linguistics, Memoir* 17. Bloomington.

Voegelin, Charles F., Florence M. Voegelin, and Noel W. Schutz, Jr.
1967 The Language Situation in Arizona as Part of the Southwestern Culture Area. Pp. 403-451 in Studies in Southwestern Ethnolinguistics. Dell Hymes and William E. Bittle, eds. The Hague and Paris: Mouton.

Voegelin, Erminie W.
1938   Tübatulabal Ethnography. *University of California Anthropological Records* 2(1):1-90. Berkeley.

——
1939   Orthography. Pp. xix-xxi in Shawnese Traditions: C.C. Trowbridge's Account. Vernon Kinietz and Erminie W. Voegelin, eds. *Occasional Contributions from the Museum of Anthropology of the University of Michigan* 9. Ann Arbor.

——
1942   Northeast California. Culture Element Distributions 20. *University of California Anthropological Records* 7(2):47-252. Berkeley.

Voevodskii, Stepan V.
1858   [Chugach Eskimo Vocabulary. "Near Mt. S. Elias." 60 words. 1858.] (Manuscript No. 334, Microfilm Reel No. 22 in National Anthropological Archives, Smithsonian Institution, Washington.)

Vogel, Virgil J.
1963   Indian Place Names in Illinois. *Illinois State Historical Society Pamphlet Series* 4. Springfield, Ill.

——
1983   Iowa Place Names of Indian Origin. Iowa City: University of Iowa Press.

——
1986   Indian Names in Michigan. Ann Arbor: Univerity of Michigan Press.

——
1991   Indian Names on Wisconsin's Map. Madison: The University of Wisconsin Press.

Vogt, Evon Z.
1961   Navaho. Pp. 278-336 in Perspectives in American Indian Culture Change. Edward H. Spicer, ed. Chicago: The University of Chicago Press.

Vogt, Hans K.
1940   The Kalispel Language; An Outline of the Grammar with Text, Translations and Dictionary. Oslo: Norske Videnskaps-akademi.

——
1940a   Salishan Studies: Comparative Notes on Kalispel, Spokan, Colville and Coeur d'Alene. *Skrifter utgitt av Det Norske Videnskaps-Akademi* II. Hist.-Filos. Klasse 2. Oslo.

Vollmar, Rainer
1981   Indianische Karten Nordamerikas: Beiträge zur historischen Kartographie vom 16. bis zum 19. Jahrhundert. Berlin: Dietrich Reimer.

Volney, Constantin François Chasseboeuf de
1803   Tableau du climat et du sol des États-Unis d'Amérique. 2 vols. (Miami Vocabulary, pp. 1-8 after p. 524 in Vol. 2.) Paris: Courcier et Dentu. (Reprinted: Hafner, New York, 1968.)

——
1804   A View of the Soil and Climate of the United States of America. Philadelphia: M. and J. Conrad, etc.

Voorhis, Paul H.
1971   Notes on Kickapoo Whistle Speech. *International Journal of American Linguistics* 37(4):238-243.

——
1971a   New Notes on the Mesquakie (Fox) Language. *International Journal of American Linguistics* 37(2):63-75.

——
1972   Mesquakie and Kickapoo Standard Orthography. (Manuscript in Voorhis's possession.)

——
1974   Introduction to the Kickapoo Language. *Indiana University Research Center for the Language Sciences. Language Science Monographs* 13. Bloomington.

——
1977   Notes on Kickapoo Derivation. *International Journal of American Linguistics* 43(1):42-55.

——
1978   Some Glottochronological Dates for Algonquian and Siouan Peoples. *Archaeo-Facts* 5(4):8-18.

——
1979   Grammatical Notes on the Penobscot Language from Frank Speck's Penobscot Transformer Tales. *University of Manitoba Anthropology Papers* 24. Winnipeg.

——
1983   Notes on the Kickapoo Medial Suffixes. *International Journal of American Linguistics* 49(1):77-86.

——
1988   Kickapoo Vocabulary. *Algonquian and Iroquoian Linguistics. Memoir* 6. Winnipeg. Man.

Voorhis, Paul H., et al.
1977   A Cree Phrase Book Based on the Dialects of Manitoba. Brandon, Man.: Department of Native Studies, Brandon University.

Voth, Henry R.
1905   Oraibi Natal Customs and Ceremonies. *Field Columbian Museum Publication* 97; *Anthropological Series* 6(2):47-61. Chicago.

——
1905a   Hopi Proper Names. *Field Columbian Museum Publication* 100; *Anthropological Series* 6(3):[63]-113. Chicago.

Vreeland, Herbert H.
1958   The Concept of Ethnic Groups as Related to Whole Societies. Pp. 81-88 in Anthropology and African Studies. William M. Austin, ed. (*Ninth Georgetown University Roundtable on Linguistics and Language Studies*). Washington: Georgetown University Press.

Wabnaki Bilingual Education Program
1973   Eli Posonutekhotimok [How baskets are made]. Indian Township, Maine: Wabnaki Bilingual Education Program, Title VII ESEA.

——
1976   Pestomuhkati Atkuhkakonol / Passamaquoddy Legends: Espons / Raccoon. Indian Township, Maine: Wabnaki Bilingual Education Program, ESEA Title VII.

——
1976a   Pestomuhkati Atkuhkakonol / Passamaquoddy Legends: Mikcic / Turtle. Indian Township, Maine: Wabnaki Bilingual Education Program, ESEA Title VII.

——
1976b   Pestomuhkati Atkuhkakonol / Passamaquoddy Legends: Koluskap Naka 'Siwiyi Oqim Wocawson / Koluskap and His Relatives Loon Wind. Indian Township, Maine: Wabnaki Bilingual Education Program, ESEA Title VII.

1976c   Pestomuhkati Atkuhkakonol / Passamaquoddy Legends: Pukcinsqehs / The Tree-Stump Woman; Kiwahqiyik / The Giants. Indian Township, Maine: Wabnaki Bilingual Education Program, ESEA Title VII.

Wachtmeister, Arvid
1956   Naming and Reincarnation Among the Eskimos. *Ethnos* 21(1-2):130-142.

Wagner, Günter
1931   Yuchi Tales. *Publications of The American Ethnological Society* 13. New York. (Reprinted: AMS Press, New York, 1974.)

1933   Yuchi. Extract from Handbook of American Indian Languages, Pt. 3:293-384. Franz Boas, ed. Glückstadt, Germay: J.J. Augustin; New York: Columbia University Press.

Walker, Alexander
1982   An Account of a Voyage to the North West Coast of America in 1785 & 1786. Robin Fisher and J.M. Bumsted, ed. Vancouver/Toronto: Douglas & McIntyre; Seattle: University of Washington Press.

Walker, Elkanah, and Cushing Eells
1842   Etshiit thlu sitskai thlu siais thlu sitskaisitlinish. Lapwai, Idaho: Oregon Mission Press.

Walker, Richard
1979   Central Carrier Phonemics. Pp. 93-107 in Contributions to Canadian Linguistics. D.W. Zimmerly, ed. *Canada. National Museum of Man. Mercury Series. Ethnology Service Paper* 50. Ottawa.

Walker, Willard
1966   Inflectional Class and Taxonomic Structure in Zuni. [With a note by Stanley Newman.] *International Journal of American Linguistics* 32(3):217-227.

1969   Notes on Native Writing Systems and The Design of Native Literacy Programs. *Anthropological Linguistics* 11(5):148-166. Bloomington.

1974   The Winnebago Syllabary and the Generative Model. *Anthropological Linguistics* 16(8):393-414. Bloomington.

1975   The Proto-Algonquians. Pp. 633-647 in Linguistics and Anthropology: In Honor of C.F. Voegelin. M. Dale Kinkade, Kenneth L. Hale, and Oswald Werner, eds. Lisse: The Peter de Ridder Press.

1975a   Cherokee. Pp. 189-236 in Studies in Southeastern Indian Languages. James M. Crawford, ed. Athens: University of Georgia Press.

1981   Native American Writing Systems. Pp. 145-174 in Language in the USA. Charles A. Ferguson and Shirley Brice Heath, eds. Cambridge and New York: Cambridge University Press.

1983   What Zuni Is Really Like. Pp. 551-562 in Essays in Honor of Charles F. Hockett. Frederick B. Agard, Gerald Kelley, Adam Makkai, and Valerie Becker Makkai, eds. Leiden: E.J. Brill.

1984   Literacy, Wampums, the *gúdebuk*, and How Indians in the Far Northeast Read. *Anthropological Linguistics* 26(1):42-52. Bloomington.

1984a   The Design of Native Literacy Programs and How Literacy Came to the Cherokees. *Anthropological Linguistics* 26(2):161-169. Bloomington.

1985   The Roles of Samuel A. Worcester and Elias Boudinot in the Emergence of a Printed Cherokee Syllabic Literature. *International Journal of American Linguistics* 51(4):610-612.

Walker, Willard, and James Sarbaugh
1993   The Early History of the Cherokee Syllabary. *Ethnohistory* 40(1):70-94.

Walker, William
1852   Numerals of the Wyandot. Pp. 218-220 in Vol. 2 of Historical and Statistical Information Respecting the History, Condition and Prospects of the Indian Tribes of the United States. H.R. Schoolcraft, ed. Philadelphia: Lippincott, Grambo.

Wallace, Anthony F.C.
1970   The Death and Rebirth of the Seneca. New York: Knopf. (Reprinted in 1973.)

Wallace, Anthony F.C., and William D. Reyburn
1951   Crossing the Ice. A Migration Legend of the Tuscarora Indians. *International Journal of American Linguistics* 17(1):42-47.

Wallace, John Robert
1954   Warm Springs Sahaptin Enculturation. (Unpublished B.A. Thesis in Anthropology and Psychology, Reed College, Portland, Oreg.)

Wallace, William J., and Edith S. Taylor
1950   Hupa Sorcery. *Southwestern Journal of Anthropology* 6(2):188-196.

Wallis, Wilson D., and Ruth Sawtell Wallis
1955   The Micmac Indians of Eastern Canada. Minneapolis: University of Minnesota Press.

Walls, Robert E., comp. and ed.
1987   Bibliography of Washington State Folklore and Folklife: Selected and Partially Annotated. Seattle: Washington State Folklife Council and the University of Washington Press.

Walters, Diane
1977   Coyote and Moon Woman (Apwarukeyi). Pp. 147-157 in Northern California Texts. Victor Golla and Shirley Silver, eds. *International Journal of American Linguistics. Native American Texts Series* 2(2). Chicago: The University of Chicago Press.

Wares, Alan C.
1968   A Comparative Study of Yuman Consonantism. (*Janua Linguarum. Series Practica* 57). The Hague and Paris: Mouton.

Warhus, Mark
1993   Cartographic Encounters: An Exhibition of Native American Maps from Central Mexico to the Arctic. *Mapline*, Special Number 7. Chicago.

Warkentin, John, and Richard I. Ruggles, eds.
1970   Manitoba Historical Atlas: A Selection of Facsimile Maps, Plans, and Sketches from 1612 to 1969. Winnipeg: Historical and Scientific Society of Manitoba.

Warren, Claude N.
1984   The Desert Region. Pp. 339-430 in California Archaeology. Michael J. Moratto, ed. New York, [etc.]: Academic Press.

Watahomigie, Lucille J., Jorine Bender, and Akira Y. Yamamoto
1982   Hualapai Reference Grammar. Los Angeles: American Indian Studies Center, University of California.

Watanabe, Honoré
1994   A Report on Sliammon (Mainland Comox) Phonology and Reduplication. Pp. 217-262 in Languages of the North Pacific Rim. Osahito Miyaoka, ed. *Hokkaido University Publications in Linguistics* 7. Sapporo, Japan.

Waterhouse, Viola G.
1976   Another Look at Chontal and Hokan. Pp. 325-343 in Hokan Studies: Papers from the First Conference on Hokan Languages. Margaret Langdon and Shirley Silver, eds. (*Janua Linguarum, Series Practica* 181). The Hague: Mouton.

Waterman, Thomas T.
1914   The Explanatory Element in the Folk-tales of the North American Indians. *Journal of American Folk-Lore* 27(103):1-54.

———
1920   Yurok Geography. *University of California Publications in American Archaeology and Ethnology* 16(5):177-314. Berkeley and Los Angeles.

———
1922   Tlingit Geographical Names for Extreme Southeast Alaska, with Historical and Other Notes. (Manuscript No. 2938, National Anthropological Archives, Smithsonian Institution, Washington.)

———
1924   The Village Sites in Tolowa and Neighboring Areas in Northwestern California. *Anthropological Linguistics* 27(4):528-543.

Watkins, Calvert
1971   Indo-European and the Indo-Europeans. Pp. 1496-1502 in The American Heritage Dictionary of the English Language. William Morris, ed. Boston, New York, Atlanta: American Heritage Publishing.

Watkins, Edward A.
1865   A Dictionary of the Cree Language, as Spoken by the Indians of the Hudson's Bay Company's Territories. Pt. 1: English-Cree; Pt. 2: Cree-English. London: Society for Promoting Christian Knowledge.

Watkins, Laurel J.
1978   On *w and *y in Kiowa-Tanoan. Pp. 477-484 in Proceedings of the Fourth Annual Meeting of the Berkeley Linguistics Society, February 18-20, 1978. Jeri J. Jaeger, Anthony C. Woodbury, et al., eds. Berkeley: BLS.

———
1984   A Grammar of Kiowa. (*Studies in the Anthropology of North American Indians*). Lincoln: University of Nebraska Press.

———
1990   Noun Phrase Versus Zero in Kiowa Discourse. *International Journal of American Linguistics* 56(3):410-426.

———
1993   The Discourse Functions of Kiowa Switch-reference. *International Journal of American Linguistics* 59(2):137-164.

Watkins, Laurel J., and Parker McKenzie
1984   A Grammar of Kiowa. *Studies in the Anthropology of North American Indians*. Lincoln and London: University of Nebraska Press.

Wauchope, Robert, gen. ed.
1964-1976 Handbook of Middle American Indians. 16 vols. plus Supplements (5 vols., 1981-1992). Austin: University of Texas Press.

Webb, Nancy M.
1971   A Statement of Some Phonological Correspondences Among the Pomo Languages. *Indiana University Publications in Anthropology and Linguistics Memoir* 26. *International Journal of American Linguistics* 37(3, Pt. 2). Baltimore: Waverly Press.

———
1972   Errata: A Statement of Some Phonological Correspondences Among the Pomo Languages, IUPAL Memoir 26 (IJAL 37.3 Part II, July 1971). *International Journal of American Linguistics* 38(1):77.

Webster, Donald H., and Wilfried Zibell
1970   Iñupiat Eskimo Dictionary. Fairbanks: University of Alaska and Summer Institute of Linguistics.

———
1976   Report of Canadian Eskimo Language Survey, 1968. Pp. 272-327 in Papers on Eskimo and Aleut Linguistics. Eric P. Hamp, ed. Chicago: Chicago Linguistic Society.

Wedel, Waldo
1964   The Great Plains. Pp. 193-220 in Prehistoric Man in the New World. Jesse D. Jennings and Edward Norbeck, eds. Chicago: University of Chicago Press.

Weeks, Thelma E.
1971   Child-naming Customs Among the Yakima Indians. *Names* 19(4):252-256.

Weinreich, Uriel
1953   Languages in Contact: Findings and Problems. *Publications of the Linguistic Circle of New York* 1. New York. (Reprinted: Mouton, The Hague, Paris, 1963-1968.)

———
1966   On the Semantic of Languages. Pp. 142-216 in Universals of Language, Report of a Conference Held at Dobbs Ferry, New York, April 13-15, 1961. Joseph H. Greenberg, ed. 2d ed. Cambridge: M.I.T. Press.

Weiss, Albert
1925   One Set of Postulates for a Behavioristic Psychology. *Psychological Review* 32(1):83-87. Lancaster, Penn., and Princeton, N.J.

Weitlander, Roberto J.
1948   Un idioma desconocido del Norte de México. Pp. 205-227 in *Actes du XXVIII Congrès International des Américanistes, Paris, 1947*. Paris: Société des Américanistes.

917

Weller, Susan C., and Charles H. Buchholtz
1986   When a Single Clustering Method Creates More than One Tree: a Reanalysis of the Salish Languages. *American Anthropologist* 88(3):667-674.

Wells, Roger, Jr., and John W. Kelly, comps.
1890   English-Eskimo and Eskimo-English Vocabularies. Preceded by Ethnographical Memoranda Concerning the Arctic Eskimos in Alaska and Siberia, by John W. Kelly. *U.S. Bureau of Education Circular of Information* 2; *Whole Number* 165. Washington: Government Printing Office.

Weltfish, Gene
1936   The Vision Story of Fox-Boy, a South Band Pawnee Text (With Translation and Grammatical Analysis). *International Journal of American Linguistics* 9(1):44-75.

_____
1937   Caddoan Texts: Pawnee, South Band Dialect. *American Ethnological Society Publication* 17. New York.

_____
1958   The Linguistic Study of Material Culture. *International Journal of American Linguistics* 24(4):301-311.

_____
1965   The Lost Universe. New York: Basic Books.

Wendorf, Fred
1954   A Reconstruction of Northern Rio Grande Prehistory. *American Anthropologist*, n.s. 56(2):200-227.

Wendorf, Fred, and Erik K. Reed
1955   An Alternative Reconstruction of Northern Rio Grande Prehistory. *El Palacio* 62(5-6):131-173.

Wenger, Patrick M.
1973   Numerical Taxonomy and Linguistic Classification: West Coast Languages as a Test Case. (Unpublished Ph.D. Dissertation in Anthropology, University of California, Davis.)

Werner, Oswald
1963   A Typological Comparison of Four Trader Navaho Speakers. (Unpublished Ph.D. Dissertation in Anthropology, Indiana University, Bloomington. University Microfilms International, Ann Arbor, Mich., no. 64-5507.)

Weslager, Clinton A.
1959   European Personal Names Given to the Eastern Indians. *Names* 7(1):54-56.

_____
1971   Name-giving Among the Delaware Indians. *Names* 19(4):268-283.

West, [John] David
1962   The Phonology of Mikasuki. *Studies in Linguistics* 16(3-4):77-91.

_____
1974   The Phonology of Mikasuki. *University of South Florida Language Quarterly* 12(3-4):2-8.

West, LaMont, Jr.
1960   The Sign Language, An Analysis. 2 vols. (Unpublished Ph.D. Dissertation in Anthropology, Indiana University, Bloomington. Xerographic reprint: University Microfilms International, Ann Arbor, Mich., 1977.)

Wheeler, Clinton J.
1982   An Inquiry into the Proto-Algonquian System of Social Classification and Marriage: A Possible System of Symmetric Prescriptive Alliance in a Lake Forest Archaic Culture During the Third Millennium B.C. *Journal of the Anthropological Society of Oxford* 13(2):165-174.

Wheeler, Everett P., II
1953   List of Labrador Eskimo Place Names. *National Museum of Canada Bulletin* 131, *Anthropological Series* 34:1-105. Ottawa.

Wheeler, George M.
1879   Linguistics. Pp. 424-485 (Appendix) in *Report Upon U.S. Geographical Surveys West of the One Hundredth Meridian, Archaeology* 7 (in Charge of Lt. George M. Wheeler). Washington: Government Printing Office.

Wheeler, John F. [printer] *see* Anonymous 1837

Whipple, Amiel Weeks
1941   A Pathfinder in the Southwest: The Itinerary of Lieutenant A.W. Whipple During his Explorations for a Railway Route from Fort Smith to Los Angeles in the Years 1853 & 1854. Grant Foreman, ed. Norman: University of Oklahoma Press.

Whipple, Amiel Weeks, Thomas Ewbank, and William W. Turner
1855   Report Upon the Indian Tribes. Pt. 3 of U.S. War Department Reports of Explorations and Surveys to Ascertain the Most Practical and Economical Route for a Railroad from the Mississippi River to the Pacific Ocean, Made in 1853-1854. *U.S. Congress. 33d Cong., 2d Sess., Senate Executive Doc. No. 78* (Serial No. 752). Washington.

Whistler, Kenneth W.
1977   Wintun Prehistory: An Interpretation Based on Linguistic Reconstruction of Plant and Animal Nomenclature. Pp. 157-174 in *Proceedings of the Third Annual Meeting of the Berkeley Linguistics Society, February 19-21*. Berkeley.

_____
1977a   Deer and Bear Children (Patwin). Pp. 158-178 in Northern California Texts. Victor Golla and Shirley Silver, eds. *International Journal of American Linguistics. Native American Text Series* 2(2). Chicago.

_____
1978   California Prehistory: A Crossdisciplinary Survey. (Typescript in Whistler's possession.)

_____
1978a   Mink, Bullethawk and Coyote (Patwin). Pp. 51-61 in Coyote Stories. William Bright, ed. *International Journal of American Linguistics, Native American Texts Series Monograph* 1. Chicago.

_____
1979   Linguistic Prehistory in the Northwest California Culture Area. Pp. 11-26 in A Study of Cultural Resources in Redwood National Park. Polly McW. Bickel, comp. Denver: U.S. National Park Service. (Unpublished report.)

_____
1981   Ablaut in Hill Patwin. Pp. 42-94 in *Survey of California and Other Indian Languages, Reports* 1. Berkeley: University of California, Department of Linguistics.

1983   Orthographic Conventions Used by Juan Estevan Pico in Writing Ventureño Chumash. (Manuscript, 1 p. of typewritten notes, March 20, 1983. In *Handbook* bibliographic files.)

1984   Linguistics and Archaeology. Pp. 107-136 in Cultural Resources Overview of the Southern Sierra Nevada. Bishop, Calif.: U.S. Forest Service.

1988   Pomo Prehistory: A Case for Archaeological Linguistics. Pp. 64-98 in Archaeology and Linguistics. A.M. Mester and C. McEwan, eds. *Journal of the Steward Anthropological Society for 1983-1984* 15(1-2). Urbana, Ill.

Whistler, Kenneth W., and Victor Golla
1986   Proto-Yokuts Reconsidered. *International Journal of American Linguistics* 52(4):317-358.

White, Andrew
[1640]   [Five Pages of Manuscript Translations of Religious Texts in English, Latin, and Conoy (Piscataway) in the Hand of Rev. Andrew White S.J. on the front Endpapers of a Copy of a 1610 *Manuale Sacerdotum* ("Douai: L. Kellam").] (In the Special Collections of the Georgetown University Library, Washington.)

White, Charles B.
1957   A Comparison of Theories on Southern Athapaskan Kinship Systems. *American Anthropologist*, n.s. 59(3):434-448.

White, James
1910   Place-Names in the Thousand Islands, St. Lawrence River. Ottawa: Government Printing Bureau.

White, John K.
1962   On the Revival of Printing in the Cherokee Language. *Current Anthropology* 3(5):511-514. Chicago.

White, Leslie A.
1932   The Acoma Indians. Pp. 17-192 in *47th Annual Report of the Bureau of American Ethnology for 1929-1930.* Washington.

1932a   The Pueblo of San Felipe. *American Anthropological Association Memoir* 38.

1935   The Pueblo of Santo Domingo, New Mexico. *American Anthropological Association Memoir* 43. (Reprinted: Kraus Reprint, Millwood, N.Y., 1974.)

1942   The Pueblo of Santa Ana, New Mexico. *American Anthropological Association Memoir* 60.

1943   New Material from Acoma. *Anthropological Papers* 32, *Bureau of American Ethnology Bulletin* 136:301-359. Washington.

1944   A Ceremonial Vocabulary among the Pueblos. *International Journal of American Linguistics* 10(4):161-167.

1962   The Pueblo of Sia, New Mexico. *Bureau of American Ethnology Bulletin* 184. Washington.

White, Raymond C.
1953   Two Surviving Luiseño Indian Ceremonies. *American Anthropologist*, n.s. 55(4):569-578.

Whitecalf, Sarah
1993   Kinêhiyâwiwininaw Nêhiyawêwin / The Cree language Is Our Identity: The La Ronge Lectures of Sarah Whitecalf. H.C. Wolfart and Freda Ahenakew, eds. and trans. (*Publications of the Algonquian Text Society / Collection de la Société d'édition de textes algonquiens*). Winnipeg: University of Manitoba Press.

Whiteley, Peter
1992   *Hopitutungwni:* "Hopi Names" as Literature. Pp. 208-227 in On the Translation of Native American Literatures. Brian Swann, ed. Washington and London: Smithsonian Institution Press.

Whitman, William
1937   The Oto. *Columbia University Contributions to Anthropology* 28. New York.

1940   The San Ildefonso of New Mexico. Pp. 390-460 in Acculturation in Seven American Indian Tribes. Ralph Linton, ed. New York: D. Appleton-Century.

1947   The Pueblo Indians of San Ildefonso: A Changing Culture. *Columbia University Contributions to Anthropology* 34. New York.

1947a   Descriptive Grammar of Ioway-Oto. *International Journal of American Linguistics* 13(4):233-248.

Whitney, William Dwight
1862   On Lepsius's Standard Alphabet. *Journal of the American Oriental Society* 7:299-332. New Haven.

Whorf, Benjamin Lee
1935   [Review of] Uto-Aztecan Languages of Mexico, by A.L. Kroeber. *American Anthropologist*, n.s. 37(2):343-345.

1935a   The Comparative Linguistics of Uto-Aztecan. *American Anthropologist*, n.s. 37(4):600-608.

1946   The Hopi Language, Toreva Dialect. Pp. 158-183 in Linguistic Structures of Native America. Harry Hoijer, ed. *Viking Fund Publications in Anthropology* 6. New York.

1956   Language, Thought, and Reality: Selected Writings of Benjamin L. Whorf. John B. Carroll, ed. Cambridge, Mass.: M.I.T.; New York: John Wiley. (Reprinted in 1964, 1991.)

Whorf, Benjamin Lee, and George L. Trager
1937   The Relationship of Uto-Aztecan and Tanoan. *American Anthropologist* 39(4):609-624.

Wied-Neuwied, Maximilian Alexander Philipp, prinz von   *see* Maximilian Alexander Philipp (Prinz zu Wied)

Wildhage, Wilhelm
1988   Die Winterzählungen der Oglala. Wyk auf Foehr, Germany: Verlag für Amerikanistik.

Wilkes, Charles
1845   Narrative of the United States Exploring Expedition, During the Years 1838, 1839, 1840, 1841, 1842. 5 vols. and Atlas. Philadelphia: Lea and Blanchard.

Wilkie, John
1920   Grammar of the Huron Language, by a Missionary of the Village of the Huron Indians at Lorette, near Quebec, Found Among the Papers of the Mission, and Translated from the Latin. Pp. 725-777 of *Fifteenth Report, Bureau of Archives for the Province of Ontario 1918-1919.* Toronto.

Wilkinson, David B., and Mildred Martin
1976   Nak'azdli Bughuni, 2: Workbook. Fort Saint James, B.C.: Carrier Linguistic Committee.

Wilkinson, David B., and Kay Wilkinson
1969   Sekani. Ware, B.C.: Summer Institute of Linguistics.

———
1969a   Sekani Bible Story Book. Fort Saint James, B.C.: Summer Institute of Linguistics.

Willett, Thomas L.
1991   A Reference Grammar of Southeastern Tepehuan. Dallas, Tex.: Summer Institute of Linguistics.

Willey, Gordon R.
1958   Archaeological Perspective on Algonkian-Gulf Linguistic Relationships. *Southwestern Journal of Anthropology* 14(3):265-272.

———
1966   North and Middle America. Vol. 1 of An Introduction to American Archaeology. 2 vols. Englewood Cliffs: Prentice Hall.

Williams, Eleazar
1813   Gaiatonsera ionteweienstakwa, ongwe onwe gawennontakon...A Spelling Book, in the Language of the Seven Iroquois Nations. Plattsburgh: F.C. Powell.

———
1853   The Book of Common Prayer, According to the Use of the Protestant Episcopal Church in the United States of America. New York: Protestant Episcopal Tract Society.

Williams, Frank, and Emma Williams
1978   Tongass Texts. Jeff Leer, ed. Fairbanks: Alaska Native Language Center.

Williams, Johnathan
1891   [Map Drawn of Nez Perce Country by Johnathan "Billy" Williams for Alice Cunningham Fletcher, June 10 and 11, 1891.] (Manuscript No. 4558.58 in Fletcher-La Flesche Papers, National Anthropological Archives, Smithsonian Institution, Washington.)

Williams, Marianne Mithun
1976   A Grammar of Tuscarora. New York: Garland Publishing.

Williams, Roger
1643   A Key into the Language of America: or, an Help to the Language of the Natives in that Part of America, Called New England. Together, with Briefe Observations of the Customes, Manners, and Worships &c of the Aforesaid Natives, in Peace and Warre, in Life and Death. On all Which are Added Spiritual Observations, General and Particular.... London: Gregory Dexter.

———
1866   A Key into the Language of America [1643]. J. Hammond Trumbull, ed. *Publications of the Narragansett Club*, 1st ser. 1(2):1-219. Providence.

———
1936   A Key into the Language of America [1643]. 5th ed. Providence: The Rhode Island and Providence Plantations Tercentenary Commission.

———
1973   A Key into the Language of America [1643]. John T. Teunissen and Evelyn J. Hinz, eds. Detroit: Wayne State University Press.

Williams, Samuel C.
1930   Adair's History of the American Indians. Johnson City, Tenn.: The National Society of Colonial Dames of America.

Williams, Stephen
1990   The Vacant Quarter and Other Late Events in the Lower Valley. Pp. 170-180 in Towns and Temples Along the Mississippi. David H. Dye and Cheryl Anne Cox. Tuscaloosa: University of Alabama Press.

Williamson, A.W.
1885   Minnesota Geographical Names Derived from the Dakota Language, with Some That are Obsolete. Pp. 104-112 in *13th Annual Report of the Geological and Natural History Survey of Minnesota, 1884.* St. Paul.

Williamson, John P.
1886   An English-Dakota School Dictionary. Waśicun qa Dakota Ieska Wowapi. Yankton Agency, Dakota Terr.: Iapi Oaye Press.

Wilmeth, Roscoe
1979   An Athabaskan Hypothesis. *Canadian Journal of Archaeology* 3:33-40.

Wilson, Alan
1995   Navajo Place Names: An Observer's Guide. Guildford, Conn.: Audio Forum.

Wilson, Alan, and Gene Dennison
1970   Laughter: The Navajo Way. Gallup: University of New Mexico, Gallup Branch.

Wilson, Daniel
1885   The Huron-Iroquois of Canada, a Typical Race of American Aborigines. *Royal Society of Canada, Proceedings and Transactions for 1884*, 2(2):55-106. Montréal.

Wilson, Iris H., trans. and ed.
1970   Noticias de Nutka: An Account of Nootka Sound in 1972. By José Mariano Moziño. Trans. and ed. by Iris Higbie Wilson. Foreword by Philip Drucker. (*American Ethnological Society, Monographs* 50). Seattle: University of Washington Press. (Original manuscript in Spanish, 1793; ed. by Alberto M. Carreño and pub. by Sociedad Mexicana de Geografía y Estadística, Mexico, 1913.)

Winget, Andrew, ed.
1994   Dictionary of Native American Literature. (*Garland Reference Library of the Humanities* 1815). New York: Garland.

Winship, George Parker
1896 The Coronado Expedition, 1540-1542. Pp. 329-637 in Pt. 1 of *14th Annual Report of the Bureau of American Ethnology [for] 1892-'93*. Washington. (Reprinted: Rio Grande Press, Chicago, 1964.)

Winter, Werner
1966 Yuman Languages II: Wolf's Son — A Walapai Text. *International Journal of American Linguistics* 32(1):17-40.

1967 The Identity of the Paipai (Akwaʔala). Pp. 372-378 in Studies in Southwestern Ethnolinguistics. Dell H. Hymes and William E. Bittle, eds. The Hague and Paris: Mouton.

1970 Reduplication in Washo: A Restatement. *International Journal of American Linguistics* 36(3):190-198.

Winter, Werner, and Christel Jarr Butcher
1976 Robber's Roost — a Walapai Tale. Pp. 61-67 in Yuman Texts. Margaret Langdon, ed. *International Journal of American Linguistics. Native American Texts Series* 1(3). Chicago: The University of Chicago Press.

Wissler, Clark
1911 The Social Life of the Blackfoot Indians. *American Museum of Natural History Anthropological Papers* 7(1):1-64. New York.

1922 The American Indian: An Introduction to the Anthropology of the New World. 2d ed. New York: Oxford University Press, American Branch.

Witherspoon, Gary
1970 A New Look at Navajo Social Organization. *American Anthropologist* 72(1):55-65.

Wolfart, H. Christoph
1971 Plains Cree Internal Syntax and the Problem of Noun-Incorporation. Pp. 511-518 in Vol. 3 of *Verhandlungen des XXXVIII. Internationalen Amerikanistenkongresses, Stuttgart-München, 12. bis 18. August 1968. [Proceedings of the 38th International Congress of Americanists]*. 3 vols. München: Klaus Renner Verlag.

1973 Plains Cree: a Grammatical Study. *Transactions of the American Philosophical Society*, n.s. 63(5). Philadelphia.

1973a Boundary Maintenance in Algonquian: A Linguistic Study of Island Lake, Manitoba. *American Anthropologist* 75(5):1305-1323.

1978 How Many Obviatives: Sense and Reference in a Cree Verb Paradigm. Pp. 255-272 in Linguistic Studies of Native Canada. Eung-Do Cook and J.D. Kaye, eds. Lisse: Peter de Ridder Press / Vancouver: University of British Columbia Press.

1980 Marked Terms for Marginal Kin. Pp. 283-293 in Papers of the Eleventh Algonquian Conference. William Cowan, ed. Ottawa: Carleton University.

1984 Notes on the Cree Texts in Petitot's *Traditions indiennes du Canada Nord-Ouest*. Pp. 47-78 in Essays in Algonquian Bibliography in Honour of V.M. Dechene. H. Christoph Wolfart, ed. *Algonquian and Iroquoian Linguistics, Memoir* 1. Winnipeg.

1988 The Beginnings of Algonquian Lexicography. *Proceedings of the American Philosophical Society* 132(1):119-127. Philadelphia.

1989 Prosodische Grenzsignale im Plains Cree. *Folia Linguistica* 23:327-334.

1989a Cree Midwifery: Linguistic and Literay Observations. Pp. 326-342 in Actes du Vingtième Congrès des Algonquinistes. William Cowan, ed. Ottawa: Carleton University.

1989b Lahontan's Bestseller (1703). *Historiographia Linguistica* 16:1-28. Amsterdam.

1991 Passives With and Without Agents. Pp. 171-190 in Linguistic Studies Presented to John L. Finlay. H.C. Wolfart, ed. *Algonquian and Iroquoian Linguistics, Memoir* 8. Winnipeg.

1992 Notes. Pp. 351-408 in Kôhkominawak Otâcimowiniwâwa / Our Grandmothers' Lives, as Told in Their Own Words. Freda Ahenakew and H.C. Wolfart, eds. Saskatoon, Sask.: Fifth House Publishers.

Wolfart, H. Christoph, ed. and trans. 1988 *see* Beardy, L.

Wolfart, H. Christoph, and Freda Ahenakew
1987 Notes on the Orthography and the Glossary. Pp. 113-126 in Wâskahikaniwiyiniw-âcimowina / Stories of the House People, Told by Peter Vandall and Joe Douquette. Freda Ahenakew, ed. and trans. (*Publications of the Algonquian Text Society / Collection de la Société d'édition de textes algonquiens*). Winnipeg: University of Manitoba Press.

1987a The Structure of Body-part Verbs as Illustrated in a Cree Medical Glossary. *Algonquian and Iroquoian Linguistics* 12:32-41. Winnipeg.

Wolfart, H. Christoph, and Janet F. Carroll
1981 Meet Cree: Guide to the Cree Language. New and completely rev. ed. Edmonton: University of Alberta Press / Lincoln and London: University of Nebraska Press. (Originally publ. under title: Meet Cree, A Practical Guide of the Cree Language. University of Alberta Press, Edmonton, 1973.)

Wolfart, H. Christoph, and David H. Pentland
1979 The "Bowrey" Dictionary and Henry Kelsey. Pp. 37-42 in Papers of the Tenth Algonquian Conference. William Cowan, ed. Ottawa: Carleton University.

Wolff, Hans
1948 Yuchi Phonemes and Morphemes, with Special Reference to Person Markers. *International Journal of American Linguistics* 14(4):240-243.

1950-1951   Comparative Siouan. 4 Pts. *International Journal of American Linguistics* 16(2):61-66, (3):113-121, (4):168-178; 17(4):197-204.

1951   Yuchi Text with Analysis. *International Journal of American Linguistics* 17(1):48-53.

1952   Osage I: Phonemes and Historical Phonology. *International Journal of American Linguistics* 18(1):63-68.

1952a   Osage II: Morphology. *International Journal of American Linguistics* 18(4):231-237.

1958   An Osage Graphemic Experiment. *International Journal of American Linguistics* 24(1):30-35.

Wood, W. Raymond, and Alan S. Downer
1977   Notes on the Crow-Hidatsa Schism. Pp. 83-100 in Trends in Middle Missouri Prehistory: A Festschrift Honoring the Contributions of Donald J. Lehmer. W.R. Wood, ed. *Plains Anthropologist Memoir* 13.

Wood, William
1634   New Englands Prospect. A true, lively and experimentall description of that part of America, commonly called New England: discovering the state of that Countrie, both as it stands to our new-come English Planters; and to the old Native Inhabitants. London: Tho. Cotes.

1865   Wood's New England's Prospect [1634]. *Publications of the Prince Society* 1. Boston. (Reprinted: Burt Franklin, New York, 1967.)

1977   New England's Prospect [1635]. Alden T. Vaughan, ed. (*The Commonwealth Series*: Winifred E.A. Bernhard, gen. ed). Amherst: University of Massachusetts Press.

Woodbury, Anthony C.
1983   Switch Reference, Syntactic Organization, and Rhetorical Structure in Central Yup'ik Eskimo. Pp. 291-315 in Switch Reference and Universal Grammar: Proceedings of a Symposium on Switch Reference and Universal Grammar, Winnipeg, May 1981. John Haiman and Pamela Munro, eds. Amsterdam; Philadelphia: John Benjamins Publishing Co.

1984   Cev'armiut Qanemciit Qulirait-llu: Eskimo Narratives and Tales from Chevak, Alaska; Told by Tom Imgalrea [et al.]. Leo Moses and Anthony C. Woodbury, trans. Fairbanks: University of Alaska, Alaska Native Language Center. (Reprinted in 1989.)

1985   The Functions of Rhetorical Structure: A Study of Central Alaskan Yupik Eskimo Discourse. *Language in Society* 14(2):153-190. Cambridge.

1987   Rhetorical Structure in a Central Alaskan Yupik Traditional Narrative. Pp. 176-239 in Native American Discourse: Poetics and Rhetoric. Joel Sherzer and Anthony C. Woodbury, eds. *Cambridge Studies in Oral and Literate Culture* 13. Cambridge.

Woodbury, Hanni J.
1975   Onondaga Noun Incorporation: Some Notes on the Interdependence of Syntax and Semantics. *International Journal of American Linguistics* 41(1):10-20.

1975a   Noun Incorporation in Onondaga. (Unpublished Ph.D. Dissertation in Anthropology, Yale University, New Haven, Conn.)

1980   Shohé:yis, Tall Corn. Pp. 56-66 in Northern Iroquoian Texts. Marianne Mithun and Hanni Woodbury, eds. *International Journal of American Linguistics*. *Native American Texts Series Monograph* 4. Chicago; The University of Chicago Press.

_____, ed. and trans.
1992   *See* Gibson, John A.

Woodward, Arthur
1944   Gabrielino Indian Language. *Masterkey* 18(5):145-150.

Woodward, Mary F.
1964   Hupa Phonemics. Pp. 199-216 in Studies in Californian Linguistics. William Bright, ed. *University of California Publications in Linguistics* 34. Berkeley.

Woodward, Thomas S.
1859   Woodward's Reminiscences of Creek, or Muscogee Indians, Contained in Letters to Friends in Georgia and Alabama,... . Montgomery, Ala.: Barrett and Wimbish.

Worcester, Samuel A.
1828   Cherokee Alphabet. *The Missionary Herald* 24(5):162-163. Boston.

1828a   Invention of the Cherokee Alphabet. *The Missionary Herald* 24(10):330-332. Boston.

Workman, William B.
1974   The Cultural Significance of a Volcanic Ash Which Fell in Upper Yukon Basin About 1400 Years Ago. Pp. 239-259 in International Conference on the Prehistory and Paleoecology of Western North America Arctic and Sub-Arctic, University of Calgary, 1972. Scott Raymond and Peter Schledermann, eds. Calgary: University of Calgary, Department of Archaeology.

1979   The Significance of Volcanism in the Prehistory of Subarctic Northwest North America. Pp. 339-371 in Volcanic Activity and Human Ecology. P.D. Sheets and D.K. Grayson, eds. New York: Academic Press.

Worth, Dean Stoddard
1960   Russian 'kniga', Southwestern Pomo 'kalikak'. *International Journal of American Linguistics* 26(1):62-66.

1963   Russian and Alaskan Eskimo. *International Journal of Slavic Linguistics and Poetics* 7:72-79.

Worth, John E.
1993   Prelude to Abandonment: The Interior Provinces of Early 17th-Century Georgia. *Early Georgia* 21(1):24-58. Athens, Ga.

1995   The Struggle for the Georgia Coast: An 18th-Century Spanish Retrospective on Guale and Mocama. *Anthropological Papers of the American Museum of Natural History* 75. New York.

Wrangell, Ferdinand Petrovich von
1839   Obitateli sĩevero-zapadnikh beregov Ameriki [Inhabitants of the Northwestern Shores of America]. *Syn Otechestva* 7(Sect. 3):51-82. St. Petersburg.

1839a   Statistische und ethnographische Nachrichten über die russischen Besitzungen an der Nordwestküste von Amerika. K.E. von Baer, ed. St. Petersburg: Buchdruckerei der Kaiserlichen Akademie der Wissenschaften.

1970   The Inhabitants of the Northwest Coast of America [1839]. James W. VanStone, trans. *Arctic Anthropology* 6(2):5-20. Madison.

1980   Russian America: Statistical and Ethnographic Information [1839]. Mary Sadouski, trans. (*Materials for the Study of Alaska History* 15). Kingston, Ont.: The Limestone Press.

Wright, Alfred, and Cyrus Byington
1825   A Spelling Book, Written in the Chahta Language with an English Translation. Cincinnati: Morgan, Lodge, and Fisher.

1848   The New Testament of Our Lord and Saviour Jesus Christ, Translated into the Choctaw Language. New York: American Bible Society.

Wright, Allen
1880   Chahta Leksikon: A Choctaw in English Definition. St. Louis: Presbyterian Publishing Company.

Wright, Asher
1836   Diuhsa´wahgwahgaya´doshäh [Beginning Book]. Boston: Crocker and Brewster.

1842   Go´wäṉa gwa´ihsat´hah yon de´yăs dah´gwah. A Spelling-book in the Seneca Language: with English Definitions. Buffalo-Creek Reservation, N.Y.: Mission Press.

1872   Hoi´wiyos´doshäh neh Chaga´oheedʋs, geeih´ niga´yados´hägee; kuh heniodiyăṉa wăh´syoh nago´iodʋk. The Four Gospels and the Acts of the Apostles, in the Seneca Language. New York: American Bible Society.

Wright, Gary A.
1978   The Shoshonean Migration Problem. *Plains Anthropologist* 23(80):133-137.

Wright, Harry A.
1949   [Agawam month names.] P. 253 in Vol. 1 of The Story of Western Massachusetts. 4 vols. New York: Lewis Historical Publishing Co.

Wright, James V.
1966   The Ontario Iroquois Tradition. *National Museum of Canada Bulletin* 210, *Anthropological Series* 75. Ottawa.

1972   Ontario Prehistory: An Eleven-thousand Year Archaeological Outline. Ottawa: National Museum of Man, Archaeological Survey of Canada.

1984   The Cultural Continuity of the Northern Iroquoian Speaking Peoples. Pp. 283-299 in Extending the Rafters: Interdisciplinary Approaches to Iroquoian Studies. Michael K. Foster, Jack Campisi, and Marianne Mithun, eds. Albany: State University of New York Press.

1987   Cultural Sequences, 4000-1000 BC. Map. Plate 7 in Historical Atlas of Canada. Vol. 1. R. Cole Harris, ed., and Geoffrey J. Matthews, cart. Toronto: University of Toronto Press.

1987a   Cultural Sequences, 1000 BC-AD 500. Map. Plate 8 in Historical Atlas of Canada. Vol. 1. R. Cole Harris, ed., and Geoffrey J. Matthews, cart. Toronto: University of Toronto Press.

1987b   Cultural Sequences, AD 500-European Contact. Map. Plate 9 in Historical Atlas of Canada. Vol. 1. R. Cole Harris, ed., and Geoffrey J. Matthews, cart. Toronto: University of Toronto Press.

Wright, James V., V.K. Prest, and J.-S. Vincent
1987   Cultural Sequences, 8000-4000 BC. Map. Plate 6 in Historical Atlas of Canada. Vol. 1. R. Cole Harris, ed., and Geoffrey J. Matthews, cart. Toronto: University of Toronto Press.

Wright, Louis B., and Virginia Freund, eds.
1953   The Historie of Travell into Virginia Britania (1612). London: Cambridge University Press for the Hakluyt Society.

Wright, Robert
1991   Quest for the Mother Tongue. *Atlantic Monthly* April:39-68.

Wright, Roy A.
1974   The People of the Panther—A Long Erie Tale. Pp. 47-118 in Papers in Linguistics from the 1972 Conference on Iroquoian Research. Michael K. Foster, ed. *Canada. National Museum of Man, Ethnology Division, Mercury Series Paper* 10. Ottawa.

1978   Wendat Sounds in European Letters: Evidence for Huron Dialect Groups in 17th Century French Travel Writers. *University of Ottawa Quarterly* 48(1-2):148-168.

1978a   The Relationship of Neutral (Atiwendaronk) to the Other Iroquoian Dialects. (Typescript in Wright's Possession.)

Wurm, S.A.
1977   [Review of] Lexical Reconstruction: The Case of the Proto-Athapaskan Kinship System, by Isidore Dyen and David F. Aberle. *Current Anthropology* 18(1):82-84.

Wurtzburg, Susan, and Lyle Campbell
1995   North American Indian Sign Language: Evidence of Its Existence Before European Contact. *International Journal of American Linguistics* 61(2):153-167.

Wycoco, Remedios S.
1951   The Types of North-American Indian Tales. (Unpublished Ph.D. Dissertation in Folklore, Indiana University, Bloomington.)

Wzokhilain, Peter Paul
1830   Wobanaki kimzowi awighigan. [Abenaki Primer.] Boston: Crocker and Brewster.

_____
1830a   Wawasi lagidamwoganek mdala chowagĭdamwoganal tabtagil, oṅkawodokodozwal wji pobatami kidwogan. [Holy laws ten commandments with explanations for Christian instruction.] Boston: Crocker and Brewster.

_____
1832   Kagakimzouiasis ueji Uo'banakiak adali kimo'gik aliuitzo'ki Za Plasua. [Cathechism of the Diocese of Quebec, in the Abenaki language, St. Francis dialect.] Basse-Ville, Qué.: Fréchette.

_____
1844   St. Mark. [Written in the Abenaki language.] Montréal: [no publisher.]

Yanan, Eileen
1971   Coyote and the Colville. Omak, Wash.: St. Mary's Mission.

Yava, Albert
1978   Big Falling Snow: A Tewa-Hopi Indian's Life and Times and the History and Traditions of His People. Harold Courlander, ed. New York: Crown Publishers. (Reprinted: University of New Mexico Press, Albuquerque, 1982, 1992.)

Yee, Mary
1956   [Barbareño Chumash Notebook.] (Manuscript in possession of her daughter Ernestine McGovran.)

Yegerlehner, John
1957   Phonology and Morphology of Hopi-Tewa. (Unpublished Ph.D. Dissertation [in Anthropology], Indiana University, Bloomington.)

_____
1958   Structure of Arizona Tewa Words, Spoken and Sung. International Journal of American Linguistics 24(4):264-267.

_____
1959   Arizona Tewa I: Phonemes. International Journal of American Linguistics 25(1):1-7.

_____
1959a   Arizona Tewa II: Person Markers. International Journal of American Linguistics 25(2):75-80.

Yoke, Jim
1934-1937 Upper Cowlitz Geographic Notes. Pp. 228-237 in Pt. 1 (English) and Pp. 198-204 in Pt. 2 (Sahaptin) of Northwest Sahaptin Texts, by Melville Jacobs. Columbia University Contributions to Anthropology 19. New York.

York, Annie, Richard Daly, and Chris Arnett
1993   They Write Their Dream on the Rock Forever: Rock Writings of the Stein River Valley of British Columbia. Vancouver, B.C.: Talonbooks.

Young, Robert W.
1977   Written Navajo: A Brief History. Pp. 459-470 in Advances 'in the Creation and Revision of Writing Systems. Joshua Fishman, ed. Thé Hague and Paris: Mouton.

Young, Robert W., and William Morgan
1943   The Navaho Language; The Elements of Navaho Grammar with a Dictionary in Two Parts Containing Basic Vocabularies of Navaho and English. Washington: United States Indian Service, Education Division. (Reprinted: Deseret Book Company, Salt Lake City, 1962.)

_____
1954   Navajo Historical Selections. Navajo Historical Series 3. Phoenix, Ariz.: Phoenix Indian School Print Shop for the Bureau of Indian Affairs.

_____
1980   The Navajo Language: A Grammar and Colloquial Dictionary. [2 pts.] Albuquerque: University of New Mexico Press.

_____
1987   The Navajo Language: A Grammar and Colloquial Dictionary. Rev. ed. Albuquerque: University of New Mexico Press.

_____
1992   Analytical Lexicon of Navajo. Albuquerque: University of New Mexico Press.

Yukon Native Language Center
1990   Kaska Literacy Training Materials, 1988-1990. Whitehorse, Yukon: Yukon Native Language Centre.

Zagoskin, Lavrentiĭ Alekseevich
1847-1848 Peshekhodnaĭa opis' chasti russkikh vladi̇̄eniĭ v Ameriki̇̄e [An Ambulatory Survey of Part of the Russian Possessions in America]. 2 vols. St. Petersburg: K. Kraĭĭa.

_____
1967   Lieutenant Zagoskin's Travels in Russian America, 1842-1844; The First Ethnographic and Geographic Investigations in the Yukon and Kuskokwim Valleys of Alaska. Henry N. Michael, ed. (Anthropology of the North: Translations from Russian Sources 7). Toronto: University of Toronto Press for the Arctic Institute of North America.

Zaharlick, Amy
1975   Pronominal Reference in Picuris. Studies in Linguistics 25:79-88.

Zárate Salmerón, Gerónimo de
1966   Relaciones. Alicia Ronstadt Milich, trans. Albuquerque: Horn and Wallace.

Zeisberger, David
1776   Essay of a Delaware-Indian and English Spelling Book, for the Use of the Schools of the Christian Indians on Muskingum River. Philadelphia: Henry Miller.

_____
1776a   Onondagaische grammatica. (Manuscript, with trans. by Peter S. Duponceau, 176 pp., in Pennsylvania Historical Society, Philadelphia.)

924

1806 Delaware Indian and English Spelling Book, for the Schools of the Mission of the United Brethren. Philadelphia: Mary Cist.

1821 The History of our Lord and Saviour Jesus Christ: Comprehending all that the Four Evangelists Have Recorded Concerning Him, by Samuel Lieberkuhn. Translated into the Delaware Indian Language. New York: Daniel Fanshaw.

1827 A Grammar of the Language of the Lenni Lenape or Delaware Indians. Peter S. Duponceau, ed. and trans. *Transactions of the American Philosophical Society*, n.s. 3:65-250. Philadelphia.

1887 Zeisberger's Indian Dictionary: English, German, Iroquois—the Onondaga and Algonquin—the Delaware. Printed from the Original Manuscript in Harvard College Library. Cambridge: John Wilson and Son.

1887a Vocabularies by Zeisberger [1750-1808]: From the Collection of Manuscripts Presented by Judge Lane to Harvard University. Nos. 1 and 2. Cambridge: John Wilson and Son.

1888 Essay of an Onondaga Grammar, or a Short Introduction to Learn the Onondaga *al.* Maqua Tongue. [John Ettwein, ed.] *Pennsylvania Magazine of History and Biography* 11:442-453; 12:65-75, 233-239, 325-340. Philadelphia.

1910 David Zeisberger's History of Northern American Indians / A History of the Indians. Archer B. Hulbert and William N. Schwarze, eds. *Ohio [State] Archaeological and Historical Quarterly* 19(1-2):1-189. Columbus. (Reprinted: A.W. McGraw, Columbus, Ohio, 1991.)

1912 The Diaries of Zeisberger Relating to the First Missions in the Ohio Basin [1767-1769]. (*The Moravian Records* 2). Archer B. Hulbert and William N. Schwarze, eds. *Ohio [State] Archaeological and Historical Quarterly* 21(1):1-125. Columbus.

Zenk, Henry
1984 Chinook Jargon and Native Cultural Persistence in the Grand Ronde Indian Community, 1856-1907: A Special Case of Creolization. (Unpublished Ph.D. Dissertation in Anthropology, University of Oregon, Eugene.)

Zepeda, Ofelia
1982 When It Rains: Papago and Pima Poetry / Mat hekid o ju:, 'O'odham Ha-cegitodag. *Sun Tracks: An American Indian Literary Series* 7. Tucson.

1983 A Papago Grammar. Tucson: University of Arizona Press.

Zepeda, Ofelia, and Jane H. Hill
1991 The Condition of Native American Languages in the United States. Pp. 135-155 in Endangered Languages. Robert H. Robins and Eugenius M. Uhlenbeck. Oxford/ New York: Berg; distributed [...] by St Martin's Press, New York.

Zibell, Wilfried
1968 Iñupiam uḳaɬhi (Eskimo Reader for the Kobuk River-Kotzebue Sound Area). Fairbanks: Summer Institute of Linguistics.

Zigmond, Maurice L.
1981 Kawaiisu Ethnobotany. Salt Lake City: University of Utah Press.

1991 Kawaiisu: A Grammar and Dictionary with Texts. Pamela Munro, ed. *University of California Publications in Linguistics* 119. Berkeley.

Zolbrod, Paul G.
1983 Poetry and Culture: The Navajo Example. Pp. 221-244 in Smoothing the Ground: Essays on Native American Oral Literature. Brian Swann, ed. Berkeley: University of California Press.

1992 Navajo Poetry in Print and in the Field: An Exercise in Text Retrieval. Pp. 242-256 in On the Translation of Native American Literatures. Brian Swann, ed. Washington: Smithsonian Institution Press.

Zumwalt, Rosemary Lévy
1992 Wealth and Rebellion: Elsie Clews Parsons, Anthropologist and Folklorist. Chicago: University of Illinois Press.

Index

Italic numbers indicate material in a figure; roman numbers, material in the text.

All variant names of groups are indexed, with the occurrences under synonymy discussing the equivalences. Variants of group names that differ from those cited only in their capitalization, hyphenation, or accentuation have generally been omitted; variants that differ only in the presence or absence of one (noninitial) letter or compound element have been collapsed into a single entry with that letter or element in parentheses.

The entry Indian words *indexes, by language, all words appearing in the standard orthographies and some others.*

A

Aagesen, Henrik: 63
Abbott, Clifford: 52, 61
abbreviations: 2, 721. Central Alaskan Yupik: 327. Cree: 392. Sahaptin: 673. Thompson: 613. Zuni: 489
Abenaki: 721
Abenaki, Eastern: 3, 4, 19, 20, 22, 47, 59, 60, 122, 731. pictography: 289
Abenaki, Saint Francis: 750
Abenaki, Western: 3, 4, 28, 47, 56, 60, 758. place-names: 190, 191, 193. writing systems: 161–162. *See also* Indian words
Abenakian: 4. place-names: 197
ablative; Sahaptin: 679
ablaut; Sahaptin: 672
absolute; Shoshone: 707–708
accent; Central Alaskan Yupik: 335–338. Seneca: 558. *See also* intonation; stress
Achumawi: 3, 239, 721. classification: 6, 294, 295. description: 47, 48, 54, 55, 59. phonology: 137, 138. place-names: 198. prehistory: 87. synonymy: 295
Ackomokki: 195, *196*
Ackroyd, Lynda: 62
Acolapissa: 124, 133
Acoma: 54, 61, 96, *218*, 226, 228, 239, 721. classification: 297, 298, 321. grammar: 154. naming: 204, 211. word classes: 139. *See also* Indian words
Acoma-Laguna: 3, 7. *See also* Keresan, Western
active theme; Hupa: 375–377
activities; Wichita nouns: 593–594
Adai: 3, 104, 722. classification: 8, 291, 299, 302, 305, 320, 320

Adair, John: 125, 126
Adaizan; classification: 300, 305. synonymy: 302
Adaize; synonymy: 291
Adams, William Y.: 131
Adamson, Thelma: 269
Adayes; synonymy: 291
Adelung, J.C.: 26, 290
Adena-Hopewell cultures: 103
adjectives; Eastern Pomo: 526. Sahaptin: 681–682. Seneca: 552. Shoshone: 710. Wichita: 594–595, 596, 599–600
adjuncts; Thompson: 633–634
Adolph, Victor: *241*
adverbial qualification: 152–153
adverbs; Hupa: 370, 372–373, 377. Lakhota: 451–453. Sahaptin: 684–685. Shoshone: 698, 705, 712–713, 716–717. Thompson: 634. Wichita: 595–596
Afcan, Paschal L.: 54, 326, *326*
affixes: 140–141, 153. Lakhota: 461–462. Sahaptin: 672. Zuni: 487. *See also* prefixes; suffixes
affricates: Coahuilteco: 651. Eastern Pomo: 513–514. phonetic alphabets: 12–13. Sahaptin: 670. Seneca: 556. Thompson: 610, 611. Wichita: 583. Zuni: 485
afterlife: 272
Agawam: 722
age: ethnography of speaking: 230. names and: 201
agent-patient system: 149, 533–534, 562–563
Aglurmiut: 722. classification: 317
Agua Caliente: 722
Aguilar, Jose: *218*
Ahenakew, Freda: 57
Ahmaogak, Roy: 180
Ahousat: 722
Aht: 722. synonymy: 294
Ahtna: 3, 25, 32, 62, 722. borrowing: 111, 116. Central: 5. classification: 5, 298. Lower: 5. place-names: 190, 191–192, 193, 195, 199. prehistory: 74. Western: 5. writing system: 177. *See also* Indian words
Ahyokeh: 163
Ainslie, George: 38
Ais; classification: 308
Aivilik: 4, 722
Akkadian: 228
Aklavik: 722
Akokisa: 722. classification: 8, 299, 308
Akulurak: 722
Akwa'ala: 722
Alabama: 3, 33, 61, 722. borrowing: 114. classification: 8, 291, 292, 299. linguistic contact: 124, 125, 126, 133. names: 211. *See also* Indian words
Alabama-Koasati: 109, 126. classification: 321
Alabama-Koasati-Apalachee; classification: 321

Alachome: 722
Alamo. *See* missions, San Antonio de Valero
Alasapas: 644, 647
Alaskan. *See* Yupik
Alaska Native Language Center: 54, 177, 180–181, 190, 198
Alaskan Yupik: 722
Alcalá Galiano, Dionisio: 26
Alcheringa: 257
Aleut: 3, 243, 722. borrowing: 111. classification: 4, 292, 301, 320. Commander Island: 63. Copper Island creole: 3. description: 25, 32, 37, *57*, 58, 63, 70. Eastern: 4, 32, 181, *289*, 292, 731. English: 135. glottochronology: 72. grammar: *183*. divergence times: 72. history: 184. names and naming: 209, 210, 211, 212, 215, 216. orthography: *183*. place-names: 185, *188*, 190, 192, 193, 198. Pribilof Island: 216. Russian: 135. semaphore: 288, *289*. synonymy: 302, 722. Western: 4, 32, 181. writing systems: 180, 181, *183*, 184. *See also* Indian words
Alexander, Sally: 246
Alford, Thomas Wildcat: 168
Algic; archeology: 98. classification: 4, 314, 316, 320. homeland: 97. prehistory: 70, 79, 85, 90, 97–100, 102, 110
Algonkian: 120. classification: 313. synonymy: 302
Algonkian-Gulf: 110
Algonkin; classification: 314. synonymy: 291
Algonkine; synonymy: 119
Algonkin-Lenape; synonymy: 291, 292
Algonkin-Ritwan; classification: 314
Algonkin-Wakashan: 79, 97–98. classification: 81, 313, 314, 316, 318
Algonquian: 19–23, 25, 27–30, 49, 50, 52, 55, 60, 97, 106, 107–108, 230, 237, 390–439, 721. borrowing: 111. classification: 4, 290–292, 292, 299, 302, 308, 311, 313, 316, 318, 320. discourse: 260, 264, 270. grammar: 142, 146, 150. homeland: 99–100. linguistic contact and: 121, 126, 129. literacy: 158. location: 319–320. naming: 210. phonology: 137. place-names: 190, 194, 195, 197, 199. prehistory: 98–100. writing system: 173–176. *See also* Indian words
Algonquian and Iroquoian Linguistics: 61, 391
Algonquian, Central; classification: 290, 291. names: 216
Algonquian, Eastern: 19, 66. classification: 4, 290, 291, 318, 320. linguistic contact: 122. place-names: 195. prehistory: 99, 100, 106. writing systems: 158–159
Algonquian, Great Lakes; names: 216. syllabary: 168–172. writing system: 168–169, 173.

Chinookan: 672. classification: 6, 230, 231, 237, 291, 294, 302, 311, 315, 319, 320. description: 27, 38, 39, 44, 47. discourse: 249, 262, 265, 266. grammar: 143, 149. homeland: 82. location: 83. names and naming: 208, 210, 214, 217. phonology: 137. prehistory: 70, 83, 88, 89. trade: 127

Chinook Jargon: 25, 27, 39, 44, 47, 51, 228, 728. borrowing: 116. linguistic contact and: 127–130. location: 128. translation: 258, 269. *See also* Indian words

Chinook, Lower: 3, 6, 39, 44, 47, 83, 129, 143, 214, 739. classification: 294. *See also* Indian words

Chinook, Upper: 6, 143, 269, 757. classification: 294

Chinook Wawa; synonymy: 127

Chipewyan: 3, 5, 23, 25, 36, 49, 58, 59, 62, 75, 242. linguistic contact: 118, 119, 120, 135. literacy: 177. names: 201. place-names: 199. writing systems: 176, 177, *177*

Chipmunk: 248

Chippewa: 168, 238. Bad River: *219*. names and naming: 203, 204, 214, 217, 220. pictography: *284*, 289. synonymy: 119. *See also* Ojibwa

Chippewa, Southwestern: names: 216, 217

Chiricahua: 3, 5, 36, 49, 728. names: 200, 201, 202, 211, 212. prehistory: 76, 77

Chitimacha: 3, 33, 47, 49, 236, 728. borrowing: 98, 109, 110. classification: 8, 291, 299, 302, 312, 313, 314, 316, 319, 320. linguistic contact: 124, 125

Chitimachan; classification: 300. synonymy: 302, 312

Chiwere: 3, 8, 61, 101, 102, 103, 728. classification: 322

Chochenyo: 3, 6, 728

Chocouyem: 728

Choctah: synonymy: 126

Chocta-Muskhog: synonymy: 291, 292

Choctaw: 3, 109, 125, *219*, 728. borrowing: 114. characteristics: 143. classification: 8, 292, 299, 322. description: 28, *30*, 32, 33, 61. linguistic contact: 125, 126, 135. location: 10. names: 201, 214. pidgin: 10, 228. place-names: 190, 192, 199. prehistory: 109, 110. synonymy: 124. writing systems: 168. *See also* Indian words

Choctaw-Muskhogee; synonymy: 292

Choctaw tribe: 228, 236, 237. history: 133

Chocuyem; synonymy: 296

Cholovomne: 728

Chome: 728

Chontal; classification: 313. synonymy: 314

Chontal de Oaxaca; synonymy: 311

Chowell, Rafael: 33–34

Choynimni: 6, 728

Choynok: 6, 728

Christianity: 158–159, *160,* 176, 217, 232, *234, 276–277,* 284, 285, *285, 581.* hymns: 252. *See also* missionaries

Chuck, Charley H.: *171*

Chuckchi: classification: 303

Chugach: 4, 32, 728. names: 213, 216

Chugamite: 728

Chukaymina: 6, 728

Chukchansi: 6, 54, 62, 728

Chukchi: classification: 318

Chukchi-Kamchatkan: *69*

Chukotan: synonymy: 71

Chukotko-Kamchatkan; classification: *69,* 71, 73, 318, 319

Chulamni: 728. synonymy: 6

Chumash: 728. classification: 311, 311, 313, 314, 320. Central: 320. names: 217. Northern: 320. synonymy: 302. *See also* Barbareño; Cruzeño; Ineseño; Island Chumash; Obispeño; Purisimeño; Ventureño

Chumashan: 39, 41, 84, 86, 93. classification: 7, 296, 297, 298, 301, 302, 311–311, 315, 319, 320. grammar: 147, 149, 153. phonology: 137. place-names: 195, 197. Spanish period: 134. synonymy: 311

Chunut: 6, 728–729

Church Missionary Society: 30, 32

Cibecue: 5, 729

cislocative; Seneca: 565

Clackamas. *See* Chinook

Claesse, Lawrence: 24

Clallam: 3, 6, 37, 52, 62, 729. classification: 293. names: 212. prehistory: 82

Clark, Darrellene: *218*

Clark, George Rogers: *284*

Clark, William: 26, 39, 118, *196,* 246, 275

Clarke, Sandra: 60

Classical period: 96

classification: 4–8, 67, 290–323. after Powell: 311–313. after Sapir: 314–323. Campbell and Mithun's: 320. Powell's: 299–308, *301, 304, 306, 307, 309, 310.* reductionist: 67. Sapir's: 67, *68,* 313–314. splitters': 67

classifiers; Hupa verbs: 369–370

Clatskanie: 3, 36, 729. classification: 5, 293

Clatsop: 38, 128, 729

Claus, Daniel: 24

clauses. 156–157. Eastern Pomo: 527–528, 533, 540. Sahaptin: 676. Shoshone: 703, 714–751. Thompson: 635–636

Clayoquot: 729

Clear Lake: 83

clicks; phonology: 137

clitics: 140. Sahaptin: 672. *See also* enclitics; proclitics

Coahuiltecan: 84–85, 649.

classification: 301, 308, 311, 313, 314, 315, 316, 319. synonymy: 302

Coahuilteco: 3, 25, 84–85, 644–665, 729. borrowing: 116. classification: 7, 301, 302, 314, 315, 316, 320. location: 644, 646–647. grammar: 155. phonology: 137. vocabulary: 664–665. word classes: 139. *See also* Indian words

Coast Miwok: 3, 6, 17, 40, 89, 296, 729

Coast Salish; classification: 321. discourse: 270. names and naming: 204, 209, 210, 212, 220

Coast Tsimshian: 3, 729. classification: 6, 322. description: 37, 44, 48, 57. discourse: 271. grammar: 149, 150. prehistory: 83. *See also* Indian words; Tsimshian

Coast Yuki: 729. classification: 7, 295, 323

Cochimí: 729. classification: 7, 297, 298, 300, 323. prehistory: 84, 86–87. synonymy: 305, 311, 311, 323

Cochimí-Yuman; synonymy: 303, 308

Cochiti: 7, 44, 61, 96, 225, 226, 729. names and naming: 202, 204, 217

Cockenoe: 135

Coco-Maricopas: 729. synonymy: 291

"Coconoon": 729

Cocopa: 3, 7, 54, 61, 118, 235, 729. names and naming: 206, 210, 212. phonology: 137. place-names: 198

Coeur d'Alene: 3, 6, 47, 57, 62, *219,* 729. place-names: 191, 192, 193, 198. *See also* Indian words

cognates; Keresan: 96. Salishan: 78

Cohoe, Benelda: *218*

coincident; Seneca: 567

Colbert, Robert: *219*

Coleman, Bailey: *241*

collective; Thompson: 633. Wichita: 593

Collins, Ray: 62

Collison, William Henry: 37

Collord, Thomas: 54

Columbian: 3, 6, 51, 62, 237, 729. discourse: 267–269, 273. Moses Band: *218,* 248. naming: 209

Columbus, Christopher: 17

Colville: 6, 52, 58, 62, *219,* 237, 729

Colville River: 729

Comanche: 3, *219,* 240–241, 242, 648, 693, 729–730. baby talk: 235, 239. classification: 7, 291, 299. description: 34, 59, 61, 94, 125. names: 215. phonology: 698. sign language: 275, *276,* 282. *See also* Indian words

Comecrudan: 84–85. classification: 7, 302, 316, 319

Comecrudo: 3, 34, 647, 649, 730. classification: 7, 301, 314, 316, 320

comitative: 152

commands; Eastern Pomo: 529–530, 532

Committee on Nomenclature of Indian Linguistic Families North of Mexico: 308

Eastern Pomo: 514. phonetic alphabets: 12–13
Frobisher, Martin: 18
Frobisher Bay: 732
Friendly Village: 25
Frost, J.H.: 38
Frost Island phase: 108
fur trade: 119–120, 127–128, 247, 391
Furbee, Louanna: 61
future; Coahuilteco: 656

G

Gabrielino: 3, 7, 46, 732–733
Gaffen, Mitch: *219*
Gagné, R.C.: 180
Galaup de Lapérouse, Jean François de: 25
Galice: 3, 5, 47, 51, 59, 364, 733
Gallatin, Albert: 26, 290, 291, 721
Galloway, Brent: 54, 61, 62
Gamble, Geoffrey: 54, 62
games; hand game: 224. Sahaptin: *670*
Gamez, Silvestre: 59
Garcés, Francisco: 118, 134, 297
García, Bartolomé: 25, 644, 645, *645*, 646, 648, 650, 651, 652, 653
Gardiner, Donna: 61
Gardiner, Dwight: 62
Garza: 3, 34. classification: 7, 316. synonymy: 647, 733
Gashowu: 3, 6, 733. classification: 323
gathering: *610, 612, 613*
Gatschet, Albert S.: 33, 34, 38, 39, 40, *208*, 292, 647, *695*
Gay Head Congregational Church: 159, *160*
Geary, James A.: 18
gender (grammatical): 142–144. Cree: 392, 393, 398–399. Seneca: 561, 564. Wichita: 605
gender (sex); men's and women's speech: 230. names: 200–201
General Central Yupik: 4, 326
genetic relationships: 60, 70
Geographical and Geological Survey of the Rocky Mountain Region: 298
George, Billy: *695*
George, Tillie: 58
Gerdts, Donna: 62
German: 130, 160, *162*
gerundials: 156
Giamina: 733
Gibbs, George: 37, 39, 198, 293, *511*
Gibson, James: 52
Gibson, Tony: *219*
Gill, De Lancey: *56*
Gingewanno: *284*
Gioloco; synonymy: 296
Giorda, Joseph: 37, 38, *39*
Gist, George: 162
Gitksan: 6, 37, 83, 237, 733, 743. borrowing: 83. classification: 322. names: 217
Givón, Talmy: 61
Gjoa Haven: 733
Gladston, W.S. Jr.: 30
Glenmore, Josephine Stands-in-Timber:

57
glides; Coahuilteco: 652. Lakhota: 443–444, 447
glottal stops; Coahuilteco: 650, 651, 652. Eastern Pomo: 513. phonetic alphabets: 14–15. Shoshone: 694, 697. Thompson: 610, 611. Zuni: 487
glottochronology: 65. Athapaskan-Eyak: 75–76, 76–77. Caddoan: 104. Chimakuan: 82. Eskimo-Aleut: 71–74. Hokan: 84–85. Iroquoian: 105. Penutian: 89, 90. Proto-Athapaskan: 75–76. Salishan: 78–79. Siouan-Catawba: 101–102. Uto-Aztecan: 91. Yokuts: 90. Yukian: 83
Goddard, Ives: 56, 60, 242
Goddard, Pliny Earle: 45, 59, 263, 312, 365
Goldenweiser, Alexander: 47
Golla, Victor: 54, 62, 263
Golovko, Evgeniy: 54, 63
Gomez, Mike: 509
Good, John Booth: 38
Goodstriker, Jim: *219*
Good Tracks, Jimm: 61
Goossen, Irvy: 62
Gordon, Lynn: 61
Gosiute: 198, 215, 733. phonology: 697
Gouge, Toby: *219*
Gouy, Edouard: 58
Grace, George: 59
Graczyk, Randolph: 61
grammar: 1–3, 142–155. Central Alaskan Yupik: 339–355. Coahuilteco: 654–663. Cree: 393–402. Eastern Pomo: 515–527. Hupa: 369–383. Lakhota: 449–450. Sahaptin: 672–673. Seneca: 552, 559–571. Shoshone: 697, 702–708. Thompson: 618–619. Wichita: 586–587, 605. Zuni: 484, 488–503
Grann, Niels: 63
Graves, William: 509, *513*
Gravier, Jacques: 21
Great Basin culture area; mythology: 269. songs: 233
Green, Verbena: 666
Greenberg, Joseph: 67, 317
Greenlandic: 21, 31, 54, 63, 733. discourse: 252. glottochronology: 72. names: 214. Northwest: 745. South: 49. writing systems: 178–179. *See also* East Greenlandic; West Greenlandic
Greenlandic Language Commission: 198
Gregg, Josiah: 294, 297
Griffin, J.S.: *511*
Gros Ventre: 3, 4, 235, 239, 242, 733. classification: 4, 291, 292. description: 23, 46, 54, 60. men's and women's speech: 230. names and naming: 206, 220. sign language: 276. synonymy: 291
Guaicura: 3, 26, 733. classification: 7,

68, 297, 298, 301, 303, 305, 311, 318
Guale: 17, 733
Guarijío: 3, 7, 230, 322, 733. Lowland: 7. names: 216. Upland: 7
Guerin, Arnold: 58
Guerreu, Charles: *42*
Guess, George: 31
Guichart de Kersident, Vincent-Fleuri: 22, 23
Guiloco; synonymy: 296
Guiluco; classification: 296. synonymy: 296
Gulf: 98, 102, 110. classification: 316
Gulf coast culture area: 649
Gun Shows: *218*
Gunther, Erna: 269
Gunther Pattern: 98
Gwich'in: 733
Gypsum period: 93

H

Ha'anahawunena; location: 9
Haas, Mary R.: 49, 53, 144–145, 152, 231, 316
habitual; Seneca: 560. Thompson: 626. Wichita: 589
Hadley, Wade: *233*
Haeberlin, Hermann: 47, 269
Haeltzukan; classification: 300, 303, 304
Hagwilgate: 733
Haida: 3, 5, 37, 44, 47, 230, 733. borrowing: 116. classification: 5, 60, 67, 291, 294, 302, 312, 313, 314, 317, 318, 319, 320. description: 25, 37, 48, 55, 58, 62. genetic relationships: 76. grammar: 149, 151, 153, 157. linguistic contact: 121, 157. names: 201, 202, 212, 214, 217. phonology: 137. prehistory: 70, 74, 107. writing systems: 177. *See also* Indian words
Haihais: 5
Haile, Berard: 49, 58
Hailtsa; synonymy: 294
Hair, Sam: *184*
Hairy Arm: *208*
Haisla: 3, 5, 58, 62, *241*, 733
Hakluyt, Richard: 18
Halchidhoma: 7, 733. history: 134
Hale, Horatio: 290, 293
Hale, Kenneth L.: 52, 61, 62
Halkomelem: 3, 54, 62, *241*, 733. classification: 6, 293. place-names: 198
Halkomelem, Upriver: 38. place-names: 192, 193. *See also* Chilliwack; Indian words
Hall, Alfred James: 37
Hall, Christopher: 18
Halpern, Abraham: 51
Halyikwamai: 7, 733
Hamilton, William: 35, 36
Hammerich, Louis L.: 54
Han: 3, 5, 54, 62, 733. writing systems: 176
Handsome Lake: 552
Hanis: 3, 6, 47, 51, 733–734. discourse:

935

938

939

Métis: 113, 133
Mexican Boundary Commission survey: 34
Mezzofanti, Giuseppe: 42
Miami: 3, 4, 26, 30, 99, 741. synonymy: 168
Michaëlius, Jonas: 123
Michahay: 6, 741
Michelson, Karin: 61
Michelson, Truman: 55, *250, 311*
Micmac: 3, 4, 238, 243, 741. borrowing: 122. description: 18, 19, 21, 22, 30, 46, 47, 52, 56, 57, 58, 60. discourse: 249, 253. linguistic contact: 122, 132. names and naming: 204, 215, 216. orthography: 285, *285.* pictography: 284, 285, *285.* place-names: 191, 194. 197. writing systems: 161–162. *See also* Indian words
Micmac Messenger, The: 161
microblade traditions: 77, 80
Middendorff, Vladimir: 37
middle voice; Thompson: 624–625
Midgette, Sally: 62
migration: 79–80. Asia to North America: 70, 72–73, 77. Hokan: 85. Kiowa: 96. Pai: 93. Penutian: 85, 88–89. Tiwa: 96
Migueleño: 7, 40, 41, 46, 741. synonymy: 296
Mikasuki: 8, 61, 109, 321, 741. *See also* Hitchiti
Mike, Cheryl: *219*
Miller, Adeline: *670*
Miller, Amy W.: 61, 151
Miller, Frank: 580
Miller, Houston: 580
Miller, Wick: 54, 61, *694*
millingstone cultures: 86, 87
Mills, Jimmy: *219*
Miluk: 3, 6, 47, 51, 269, 741
Mimbreño: 741
Miner, Kenneth: 173
Minnetaree: 118
Minoura, Nobukatsu: 62
Minto-Nenana: 5, 741
Mishalpam: 6. synonymy: *667*
missionaries: 22, 23, 27, 30, 32, 36, 38, 58–59, 116, 129, 163, 168, 176, 216, 245–246, 248, 365, 391, 552. Anglican: 37, 38, 176, *184.* Baptist: 28, 30, 32. Congregationalist: 19, 23, 28, 30, 31, 37. Dutch Reformed: 24. Episcopal: 30, 36. Franciscan: 18, 25, 41, 112, 178, 644, 645, *645,* 646. French: 162. Jesuit: 19, 20, 21, 23, 36, 37–38, *451.* Lutheran: 18, 21, 24, 25, 112, 245, 247. Mennonite: 59. Methodist: 28, 38, 135, 174. Moravian: 23, 24, 25, 28, 31–32, 58–59, 160, *162,* 179, *184,* 284. naming: 216–217. Oblates of Mary Immaculate: 32, 36, 38, 176, 180. Presbyterian: 28, 33, 35, 38. Protestant: 128. Puritan: 19. Recollect: 19, 21. Roman Catholic:

27, 28, 34, 37, 39, 58, 128, 132, 177, 216, 284, 285, *285.* Russian Orthodox: 32, 135, 181, 216. Spanish: 133, 134. Sulpician: 22, 27. *See also* missions
Mission Indians: 134
missions: Anglican: 37. Arizona: 42. Bethel: 181. California: 41, 42. Dakota: 35. French: 132. Holy Rosary: *451.* Illinois: 21. Ioway and Sac: 35. Jesuit: 132. La Soledad: 297. Moravian: 23, 32, 159. New Mexico: 42. Northern Canadian Evangelical: 177. Nuestra Señora de la Candelaria: 645. Nuestra Señora de la Purísima Concepción de Acuña: *645, 646,* 648. Nuestra Señora de los Dolores: 647. Otoe-Omaha Mission: 35. Saint Turibus: 508, *513.* Saint Francis: *451.* Saint Francis Xavier: *218.* San Antonio de Padua: 41, *41.* San Antonio de Valero: *645,* 647. San Bernardo: *645.* San Buenaventura: *41.* San Diego de Alcalá: 134. San Francisco de la Espada: 644, *645,* 648. San Francisco de Solano: 113, 296 *645,* 647, 648, 649. San José y San Miguel de Aguayo: *645.* San Juan Bautista: 41, 148, *645.* San Juan Capistrano: 645, *645,* 647, 750. San Rafael: 113, *513.* Spanish: 22, *39,* 41, *41,* 113, 134, 148, *218,* 275, 296, *451.* Texas: 275
Mississauga: 216, 741
Mississippian tradition: 103, 105, 110. Late: *274.* pottery: *274*
Mississippi Valley: 8
Missouri: *219,* 741. classification: 8, 322
Mistaken Chief, Dan (or Duane): *219*
Mistassini: names: 217. phonology: 137–138. *See also* Indian words
Mitchell, Lewis: 161–162, 251, *251*
Mitchif: 3, 4, 60, 113, 114. linguistic contact: 129, 132–133. writing systems: 173. *See also* Indian words
Mithun, Marianne: 52, 61, 237
Miwok: 62. borrowing: 112, 113, 114, 115. classification: 6, 296, 311, 320. discourse: 272. Eastern: 6, 115, 289. grammar: 145. linguistic contact: 134. Marin: 6, 740. names and naming: 210, 211. Northwest Sierra: 745. pictography: 289. prehistory: 85. Sierra: 89, 90, 93, 752. synonymy: 296, 302. Western: 6. *See also* Bay Miwok; Bodega Miwok; Central Sierra Miwok; Coast Miwok; Indian words; Lake Miwok; Miwokan; Northern Sierra Miwok; Plains Miwok; Southern Sierra Miwok
Miwokan: 41, 88, 90, 741. classification: 6, 296, 302, 302, 311. place-names: 197. synonymy: 311. *See also* Miwok
Miwok-Costanoan: 39. classification:

313, 314, 319. synonymy: 322. *See also* Utian
Mixco, Mauricio: 61
Mixe-Zoque: 314, 315
Mixe-Zoquean; classification: 314, 316
Mixwunutunne: 741
Miyaoka, Osahito: 54, 63, *326, 327*
Mobilian Jargon: 10, 61, 120, 124–127, 228. *See also* Indian words
modal extensions; Thompson: 626
modality: 154–155
modalizer; Seneca: 565
mode; Cree: 404–408. Hupa: 370. Seneca: 561. Zuni: 493
models: 51
modifiers; Coahuilteco: 660–661. Wichita: 586–587, 594–596
Modoc: 6, 741. classification: 311, 313, 314, 319, 320. discourse: 249. naming: 220. phonology: 137
Mogollon: 96
Mohave: 3, 46, 61, 231, 236, 238, 741. beliefs: 239. classification: 7, 311. names and naming: 203, 210, 212, 213. oratory: 231. swearing: 236.
Mohawk: 3, 227, 228, 240, 243, 552, 741–742. Caughnawaga: 30. classification: 8, 320. description: 21, 22, 23–24, *24,* 27, 30, 46, 48, 52, 55, 61. discourse: 249. grammar: 143. language shift: 241. names: 214. place-names: 189, 190, 191, 192, 193, 197. phonology: 137, 138. prehistory: 105. word classes: 138–139. writing systems: 162, *164. See also* Indian words
Mohegan: 3, 5, 47, 742
Möhineyam: 742
Moisie: 4
Molala: 3, 671, 742. classification: 6, 291, 294, 302, 313, 314, 315, 319, 320. description: 39, 47, 51. discourse: 269. prehistory: 82
Monache: 7, 54, 61, 230, 742
Moneton; classification: 322
Mono: 3, 7, 46, 94, 742. phonology: 698. place-names: 198. *See also* Monache; Owens Valley Paiute
Monqui: 3, 7. classification: 297
Monsoupelea; location: 9
Montagnais: 3, 4, 99, 391, 742. borrowing: 122. description: 20, 22, *22,* 28, 47, 48, 60, 61. discourse: 252, 270. linguistic contact: 119, 122, 133. place-names: 199. writing systems: 173–176, *175. See also* Indian words
Montagnais Jargon: 122
Montana Salish; synonymy: *234*
Montauk: 5, 742
Monterey: 742. synonymy: 6
Monterey Pattern culture: 89
Montler, Timothy: 52, 61, 62
Montour, Nelles: 160
mood; Central Alaskan Yupik: 335, 339–343. Eastern Pomo: 536. Sahaptin: 686. Wichita: 590, 592

Wenro: 105
Werner, Oswald: 131
West, Walter Richard: *274*
Western Abenaki. *See* Abenaki, Western
Western Apache. *See* Apache, Western
Western Canadian Inuit: 3, 4, 32, 758
Western Carrier: 758
Western Fluted Point tradition: 86
Western Gulf culture area: 649
Western Kutchin. *See* Kutchin
Western Pluvial Lakes tradition: 88
Western Shoshone: 7, 54, 198, 215,758–759
Western Swampy Cree: 3, 4, 34, 50, 176, *242,* 759. writing systems: 174, *175,* 176
West Greenlandic: 3, 4, 24, 54, 58, 63, 72, 178–179, 758, 759
Wewa, Maggie: *670*
Wewa, Wilson Jr.: *670*
Weygold, Frederick: *276*
Weyot; synonymy: 295
Wheeler, Benjamin Ide: 59
Wheeler, George M.: 27, 40, 298
Whilkut: 5, 364, 759
Whipple, Amiel Weeks: 27, 36, 40, 294
Whistler, Ken: 54, 62, *206*
whistle speech: 287–288
White: 195
White, Amari: *219*
White, Andrew: 18
White, John: 18
White Bear: *208*
White-bear: *206*
White buffalo: *206*
White Eagle: *208*
White Eagle, Charley: *218*
White Eagle, Josie: 57
White-hair: *206*
Whiteman, Kenneth: *219*
White Mountain Apache: 5, 759. naming: 209
White-plume: *206*
Whiteplume, James: *234*
Whiteshield: *208*
White Swan: 289
White-tail: *206*
Whitney, William Dwight: 17, 26
Whorf, Benjamin L.: 49
Wichita: 3, 580–608, 759. classification: 8, 291, 299, 319–320. description: 36, 54, 61, 102, 104. discourse: 257, 262. location: 580. grammar: 149. synonymy: 294. vocabulary: 605–608. word formation: 141. *See also* Indian words
wigwag: 288
"Wihinasht": 759
Wikchamni: 6, 54, 62, 759. phonology: 138 *See also* Indian words
Wikeno: 759
Wilkes, Charles: 36, 132, 134
Wilkinson, David: *179*
Willapa: 5
Willard, Francis H.: 37
956 Williams, Bobbie: *219*

Williams, Eleazer: 30
Williams, Nakoa: *219*
Williams, Robert: 61
Williams, Roger: 19, 245
Williams, Watson: 60
Willie, Mary Ann: 58, 62
Wilson, Alan: 62
Windmiller Pattern: 89
Wind River: 759
Windsor, Evelyn: 62
Wingenum: *284*
Winishut, Linton: 666
Winnebago: 3, 8, 102, 103, 237, 759. classification: 38, 22. description: 26, 34, 36, 47, 52, 57. discourse: 251, 270. naming: 206, 209, 210. phonology: 171. place-names: 197. prehistory: 100, 101. syllabary: 171. writing systems: 171. *See also* Indian words
Wintoon; synonymy: 295
Wintu: 3. 6, 197, 759. borrowing: 112, 115. classification: 295, 314. description: 46, 47, 51, 54, 62. discourse: 249. grammar: 152. names: 212. *See also* Indian words
Wintuan; classification: 6, 295, 298, 302, 311, 313, 319, 320. description: 39, 62. phonology: 137. prehistory: 82, 88, 89, 90
Wintun; classification: 295, 311, 313, 319. synonymy: 295, 298, 300
Wisconsin Native American Languages Project: *172*
Wishok; synonymy: 303
Wishokan; classification: 303
Wishosk; synonymy: 295, 302
Wishoskan; classification: 300. synonymy: 302, 311
Wishram: 6, 38, 47, 235, 239, 271, 273, 672, 758, 759. grammar: 143. names and naming: 202, 212, 213, 214, 215. *See also* Indian words
Witherspoon, Gary: 62
Witsuwit'en; synonymy: 5, 62
Wiyot: 3, 759. classification: 5, 295, 302, 311, 313, 314, 317, 318, 319. description: 39, 46, 47, 53. phonology: 137, 237. place-names: 197. prehistory: 97, 98
Wiyot-Yurok; classification: 313. *See also* Ritwan
Wobonuch: 7, 759
Woccon: 3, 25, 101, 103, 291, 292, 759. classification: 8, 301, 305, 322, 322
Wo'lasi: 6, 759
Wolfart, H. Christoph: 60
Womkon, Adelinda: 58, 63
Wood, William: 19
Woodbury, Anthony: 54, 63
Woodbury, Hanni: 52, 61
Woodcock, Joe: *234*
Woodland period: 99, 103, 105, 106, 108, 109
Woods Cree: 3, 4, 22–23, 28, 390, 759. names: 215. writing systems: 171, *175. See also* Indian words

Woodward, Mary: 365
Wookons; synonymy: 291
Worcester, Samuel A.: 31, 163
word classes; Eastern Pomo: 522–527. Zuni: 488
word format'on; Cree: 424–428, 429. Thompson: 612–614
word-level prosody; Seneca: 557–559
word modifiers; Hupa: 381
word order: 148. Eastern Pomo: 527, 536–537. Sahaptin: 673, 675. Seneca: 552. Shoshone: 698–699. Wichita: 597–601. Zuni: 502
words; kinds of: 138–140. meaningful pieces: 140–142. Thompson: 618. Zuni: 488–500
word sequence; Zuni: 487–488
word structure; Lakhota: 446–450. Zuni: 485–486
word taboos: 66, 71–72, 79, 236. names: 212–213, 236
Wrangell, Ferdinand Petrovich von: 32, 37, 195, 292
Wright, Alfred: 32
Wright, Allen: 33
Wright, Asher: 30, 162, 552
writing systems: 11, 158–184, *242.* ideographic: 181. pictographs: *208.* programs: *184.* Russian and: 181, 184, *183. See also* orthography
Wükchami: 760
Wyandot: 760. classification: 8, 292. description: 21, 23, 55. names and naming: 210, 216. pictography: *284,* 289
Wyena, Virginia: 666
Wyeth, Captain: 128
Wzôkhilain, Peter Paul. *See* Osunkhirhine, Pierre Paul

X
Xarame: 647, 648

Y
Yachikumne: 6, 760
Yahi: 7, 47, 760. names: 213
Yakima: 6, 38, *218,* 666, *667,* 671, 672, 675, 760. names: 215. pronouns: 683. sign language: *276.* verbs: 687
Yakima Indian Council: *669*
Yakima Tribe: *670*
Yakna-Chitto: 124
Yakona; synonymy: 302
Yakonan; classification: 295, 302, 308, 312, 314, 319. synonymy: 302, 311
Yakutat: 25
yama: 124
Yamamoto, Akira: 61, 243
Yamhill: 3, 6, 47, 59, 294, 760
Yana: 3, 760. classification: 7, 230, 295, 296, 300, 303, 311, 313, 314, 319, 320. description: 46, 47, 48. discourse: 249, 271. names: 201, 213. phonology: 137. prehistory: 84, 90
Yanan; classification: 300, 319, 320. synonymy: 300, 303, 311. *See also*

Yana

Yankton: 8, 34, 441. place-names: 195. *See also* Sioux

Yanktonai: 8, *223, 286,* 441. pictography: *286. See also* Sioux

Yaqui: 7, 134, 241, 760. borrowing: 111–112, 113. classification: 322. English and: 136. names and naming: 215, 216, 220. Spanish and: 133, 134. *See also* Indian words

Yaquina: 3, 760. classification: 8, 294, 301, 308

Yatasi: 3, 760. classification: 8, 299, 320

Yatchmeneff, Ivan Alexis: *57*

Yavapai: 7, 760. description: 54, 61. names: 202. prehistory: 86

Yawdanchi: 6, 760

Yawelmani: 6, 760. clauses: 156. *See also* Indian words

Yazoo: 125

Yazzi, Kevin: *218*

Yazzie, Ated Tsotsie: *232*

Yécora-Maycoba: 7

Yee, Mary: 147

Yellow Bear: *208*

Yellow Hawk: *208*

Yellowknife: 120, 760

Yellow Old Woman, T.: *219*

Yellow Serpent: 135

Yellow-wolf: *206*

Yepachi: 7

Ynezeño: 760

Yocut; synonymy: 296

Yokuts; classification: 311, 313, 314, 319, 320. synonymy: 296, 302. *See also* Indian words; Yokutsan

Yokutsan: 760. classification: 6, 227, 231, 235, 238,296, 302, 311, 313, 314, 319, 320, 323. description: 39, 41, 42, 46, 49, 51, 52, 62. names and naming: 200, 206, 212. phonology: 137. place-names: 195. prehistory: 82, 88, 90, 93. Spanish and: 134. *See also* Yokuts

Yoncalla: 3, 6, 47, 51, 760

Yorica: 760

York, Annie: 609, *613*

Yosemite: 760

Youchigant, Sesostrie: 263

Young, Robert: 57, 59, 62

Youngbird, Edmund: *241*

Young Man Afraid of His Horses: *215*

Yuchi: 3, 83, 102, 103, 107, *219,* 227, 760. classification: 8, 291, 299, 314, 316, 318, 319, 320. description: 25, 33, 55. grammar: 144, 149, 152. linguistic contact: 121. location: 9. naming: 206. phonology: 137. place-names: 195, 199. prehistory: 102, 105. *See also* Indian words

Yukaghir; classification: 303

Yuki: 3, 508, 760. classification: 7, *69,* 295, 314, 319, 323. description: 46, 54, 61, 87. grammar: 149. names and naming: 211, 220. phonology: 137. prehistory: 83, 84. synonymy: 295, 301. *See also* Coast Yuki

Yukian: 75, 87, 89, 102. classification: 7, 295, 300, 303, 316, 318, 320, 323. glottochronology: 83. homeland: 84. location: 83, 84, 85–86. Northern: 323. place-names: 195. prehistory: 83–84, 86, 93

Yukon: 326, 760

Yukon (Ingalik): 5

Yukon Native Language Center: 198

Yukon (Yupik): 326

Yuma: 760. classification: 311. synonymy: 137, 297, 298, 303. *See also* Quechan

Yuman; classification: 7, 233, 291, 294, 297, 298, 300, 303, 305, 308, 311, 313, 319, 320, 323. clauses: 156. description: 40, 61. grammar: 151. naming: 210, 220. Northern: 220. phonology: 137. place-names: 195, 198. prehistory: 84, 86–87, 91, 93, 94. reconstructed vocabulary: 86–87.

River: 323. synonymy: 301, 308, 311, 323. Upland: 3, 7, 86, 213

Yupik: 4, 761. classification: 70, 292, 320. grammar: 151. Russian and: 135. word classes: 139. *See also* Central Alaskan Yupik; Central Siberian Yupik; Pacific Yupik

Yurok: 3, 232, 236, 237, 238, 239,364, 761. classification: 5, 294, 295, 300, 311, 313, 314, 316, 318, 319. description: 39, 46, 47, 48, 55. names: 214. phonology: 137. place-names: 190, 191, 192, 193, 197. prehistory: 97, 98. *See also* Indian words

Yurumanguí; classification: 318

Z

Zachary, Jack: *219*

Zagoskin, Lavrentii Alekseevich: 36

Zaharlick, Amy: 61

Zárate Salmerón, Gerónimo de: 42

Zeisberger, David: 23, 24, 28, 245, 292

Zepeda, Ofelia: 57–58, 61

Zia: 7, 96, 761. names and naming: 204, 213

Zigmond, Maurice: 61

Zoque; classification: 315

Zuni: 3, 91, *218,* 224, 225, 226, 228, 229, 238, 483–506, 761. borrowing: 111, 112. classification: 7, 297, 298, 303, 313, 316, 318, 319, 320. description: 39, 40, 44, 46, 47, 49, 52. discourse: 249, 255, 257–258, 260. grammar: 155. location: 483. names and naming: 201, 202, 203, 211, 214, 215. phonology: 137. place-names: 198. prehistory: 91, 95, 96, 97, 141. vocabulary: 503–506. *See also* Indian words

Zuñi; classification: 314. synonymy: 297, 301

Zuñian; classification: 300. synonymy: 301

ISBN 0-16-048774-9

9 780160 487743

90000